SCOTT®

1989
Specialized Catalogue of United States Stamps

SIXTY-SEVENTH EDITION

CONFEDERATE STATES • CANAL ZONE • DANISH WEST INDIES
GUAM • HAWAII • UNITED NATIONS

UNITED STATES ADMINISTRATION:
Cuba • Puerto Rico • Philippines • Ryukyu Islands
Marshall Islands • Micronesia • Palau

PRESIDENT/PUBLISHER	**Wayne Lawrence**
VICE PRESIDENT	**Charles M. Pritchett**
EDITORIAL DIRECTOR	**Richard L. Sine**
EDITOR	**William W. Cummings**
ASSISTANT EDITOR	**William H. Hatton**
PRICING EDITOR	**Martin J. Frankevicz**
NEW ISSUES EDITOR	**Robin A. Denaro**
COMPUTER CONTROL COORDINATOR	**Elaine Cottrel**
EDITORIAL ASSISTANTS	**Joyce A. Cecil**
	Mary D. Sturwold
PRICING ANALYSTS	**David C. Akin**
	Roger L. Listwan
ART/PRODUCTION DIRECTOR	**Edward Heys**
PRODUCTION COORDINATOR	**Nancy S. Martin**
DIRECTOR OF MARKETING & SALES	**Stuart J. Morrissey**
ADVERTISING MANAGER	**David Lodge**

TABLE OF CONTENTS

Copyright Notice

Trademark Notice

Please Note

UNITED STATES
Commemorative Album Pages!

Your first investment will be a lasting investment with White Ace

When everything has to be perfect, choose a White Ace stamp album . . . just as generations of satisfied collectors have done.

Consider, for example, White Ace pages for U.S. commemoratives. Made of acid-free card stock, so they won't yellow or crease with use, they have colorful border illuminations to highlight your displays, and under each mounting frame is the story behind the stamp. Also, because the album is looseleaf style and published in sections, you have maximum flexibility when it comes to building your collection. What more can you expect? Annual supplements, of course; a large capacity binder with gold titling; matching border blank pages for covers and other items; and a dustcase that gives the ultimate in protection. If you're a typical philatelist, you seek top quality when purchasing stamps. If this desire for the best extends to your albums, then White Ace probably is the logical choice.

Colorful . . .
Historical . . .
Sectional!

White Ace

PLATE NUMBER COILS

1981-84

Transportation Issue

Scott 1905

Scott 1906

Scott 1907

Collect the Scott Way... with Scott's

PLATE NUMBER COIL ALBUMS

Featuring:

● Three albums. Spaces for all Plate Number Coils listed in the *Scott U.S. Specialized Catalogue*. Two albums for strips of three, both will accommodate strips of five. Brand new is the Scott Comprehensive Plate Number Coil Singles Album.

● The Plate Number Coil pages provide spaces for one example of each strip. The Comprehensive Album (binder included) and the Singles Album provide spaces for every plate number of every issue.

● Chemically neutralized paper protects your stamps for generations.

● Pages may be housed in a handsome sturdy binder.

● Yearly supplements available to keep your album up-to-date.

● Scott numbers with each space in the album.

INDEX

The capital letters in parentheses and below "Revenues" are used with the catalogue numbers to indicate the different classifications.

SS1   SS2   SS3

SS4   SS5   SS6

SS7   SS8   SS9

SPECIAL NOTICES

Listings

This Catalogue lists the various groups of United States stamps in specialized detail. The form of listing is similar to that used in Scott's Standard Postage Stamp Catalogue. Example:

United States

230   A71   1c   deep blue   22.50   30

The number (230) in the first column is the index or identification number. The letter-number combination (A71) indicates the design and refers to the illustration having this (A71) designation. Next comes the denomination (1c), followed by the color (deep blue). The prices are in two columns at the right, the first (22.50) being that of an uncanceled stamp, and the second (30) of a canceled one.

With stamps printed in two or more colors, the color given first is that of the frame or outer parts of the design, starting at the upper left corner. The colors that follow are those of the vignette or inner parts of the design. For stamps, paper color follows in italics.

When a stamp is printed in black on colored paper, the color of the paper alone is given in italics.

Pricing Limitations

Each price appearing in this catalogue represents an estimate by Scott Publishing Co. of the current value basis for a specimen of that single stamp multiple or cover, available for purchase by a collector in the retail stamp market, (or, where noted, set of stamps) with no flaws; all perforations intact; unfaded color; reasonable centering, i.e., no worse than the design not quite touching the perforations on some issues and much closer to perfect centering on more recent issues; and for unused stamps with the major part of the gum intact (early issues); lightly hinged until 1959; never hinged 1960 on (unless the stamp was issued without gum). Exceptional copies often bring higher prices. Because this catalogue is issued only once each year, it is impossible for it to reflect the price fluctuations that may occur over the short term. What should remain constant, however, is the relative price (value) of items over the long term.

These prices are not intended to reflect "wholesale" transactions, i.e., between dealers or a collector selling to a dealer. Many factors may affect the differential between an individual price shown in these pages and the actual price of a transaction: individual bargaining, the effect of dealer mark-up and profit margins, condition of the item in question, changes in popularity of the item, temporary change in supply of the item, local custom, unusual postal markings on a used example of the item, unexpected political situations within the country of issue, newly discovered philatelic or other information, or changes in the relative value of that nation's currency against the U.S. dollar.

As a point of philatelic economic fact, the lower the price for an item in this catalogue, the greater the percentage of that price which is attributed to dealer mark-up and profit margin. Thus, packets of 1,000 different stamps — all of which have a catalogue price of at least 5 cents — normally sell for considerably less than $50!

Scott Publishing Co. endeavors to obtain more than one judgment of the prices and to incorporate in its pricing the various price factors listed above. There can be no assurance, however, that all of the prices listed are accurate estimates of prices which would be paid in actual transactions. Some of the items listed have not been publicly traded recently. The pricing, therefore, is based on the editors' estimates of the probable prices which the stamp would command if it were offered individually for sale to a collector.

Users of this Catalogue should not enter into any transaction solely in reliance on the prices, valuations, or stamp availability information set forth in the Catalogue. Persons wishing to further establish the value of a particular stamp or other material may wish to consult with recognized stamp experts (collector or dealer) and review current information or recent developments which would affect stamp prices.

Scott Publishing Co. assumes no obligation to revise the prices during the distribution period of this Catalogue or to advise users of other factors, such as stamp availablity, political and economic conditions, or collecting preferences, all of which may have an immediate positive or negative impact on prices. The publisher endeavors to balance these factors with its general understanding of stamp pricing considerations to avoid unnecessary fluctuations in the prices included in this Catalogue.

It should be noted that persons contributing pricing information also may deal in stamps and/or may maintian substantial personal stamp collections. They may buy, sell, and deal in stamps for their own account and for the account of others and therefore may have both a direct and indirect interest in the price of the stamps. In some cases, the references to prices may reflect valuations of their personal holdings for stamps in which they deal for themselves and others.

Understanding Pricing Notations

The absence of a price does not necessarily indicate that the stamp is scarce or rare. In the United States listings, a dash in the price column means that the stamp is known in a stated form or variety, but that information is lacking or insufficient for pricing.

The minimum price of a stamp is fixed at 5 cents to cover a dealer's labor and service cost of purchasing that stamp at wholesale and preparing it for resale. As noted above, the sum of these list prices does not properly represent the "value" of a packet of unsorted or unmounted stamps sold in bulk which generally consists of only the lesser valued stamps.

Prices in the "unused" column are for stamps that have been hinged for United States items through 1960. Prices for unused stamps after that date are for unhinged examples. Where prices for a used example of a stamp is considerably higher than for the unused stamp, the price applies to a stamp showing a distinct contemporary postmark of origin.

Examination

Scott Publishing Co. cannot undertake to pass upon genuineness or conditon of stamps, to appraise or identify. For expertizing, the company refers collectors to the several committees which do this work. These include the American Philatelic Expertization Service, P.O. Box 8000, State College, PA 16803, Professional Stamp Expertizing 12651 So. Dixie Highway, Suite 326, Miami, FL 33156 and the Philatelic Foundation Expert Committee, 21 East 40th St., New York, N.Y. 10016.

Covers

Prices paid for stamps on original covers vary greatly in accordance with condition, appearance, cancellation or postmark and usage. Prices given are for the commonest form with stamps in fine condition "tied on" by the cancellation. A stamp is said to be "tied" to an envelope or card when the cancellation or postmark falls on both the stamp and envelope or card. Letters addressed to foreign countries showing unusual rates and transit markings are much in demand and othen bring large premiums.

Prices are for covers bearing a single copy of the stamp referred to used during the period when the stamp was on sale at post offices. If the postage rate was higher than the denomination of the stamp, then the stamp must represent the highest denomination possible to use in making up this rate. As a general rule the stamp must be "tied" to the cover. Exceptions include some of the early local adhesives for which canceling was not customary.

Prices for patriotic covers of the Civil War period (bearing pictorial designs of a patriotic nature) are for the commonest designs. Over 11,000 varieties of designs are known.

Cancellations

As a complete treatment of this subject is impossible in a catalogue of this limited size, only postal markings of meaning or of color are recorded, while those owing their origin to fancy are disregarded. The former were necessary for the proper functioning of the Postal Service; the latter were the results of the whim of some postal official. Many of these odd designs, however, command high prices dependent on their scarcity and clearness of impression.

Though there are many types of most of the cancellations that are listed, only one of each is illustrated. The prices quoted are for the commonest type of each.

Prices for cancellation varieties are for specimens off cover. If on cover, the distinctive cancellation must be on the stamp in order to merit catalogue valuation. However, postmarks that denote origin or a service (as distinct from canceling a stamp) merit catalogue valuation when on a cover apart from the stamp, provided the stamp is otherwise tied to the cover by a cancellation.

One type of "Paid" cancellation used in Boston, and pictured under Postal Markings — Examples, is common and prices are for types other than this.

INFORMATION FOR COLLECTORS

For the sake of clarity this section is separated into two main divisions, as follows:

1—A general index to philatelic terms (which immediately follows), and

2—An explanation of the terms themselves grouped under subjects in the following order:

    Plate
    Printing
    Paper
    Perforations
    Luminescence
    Postal Markings

The general index lists all terms with explanation or designates proper subject under which the explanation may be found.

Index of Information for Collectors

Bisect:

Diagonal   Horizontal   Vertical

Stamps cut in half so that each portion prepaid postage, used in emergencies where no stamps of the lower denomination were available. These may be diagonal, horizontal or vertical. Example: No. 2a. Listings are for bisects on full covers. Those on piece or part of a cover sell for considerably less.

Bureau Issues: U.S. stamps issued after the Bureau of Engraving and printing started printing U.S. stamps in 1894.

Bureau Prints: A term applied to precancellations applied by the Bureau of Engraving and Printing at Washington, D.C. See: Precancellations.

Commemorative Stamps: Special issues which commemorate some anniversary or event of local, national or international importance, or which honor some person. Usually such stamps are used for a limited period concurrently with the ordinary series. Examples: Nos. 230-245, 620-621, 946, 1266, C68, U218- U221, UC25, R733.

Cut Square: An envelope stamp cut rectangularly or square from the envelope.

Error: A stamp is called an error when it differs from the normal variety by some mistake or omission in the inscription, color, paper, impression, watermark or perforation.

First Day Cover: A philatelic term to designate the use of a certain stamp (on cover) on the first day of sale at a place officially designated for such sale or so postmarked.

Gum Breaker Ridges: Colorless marks across the backs of some rotary press stamps, impressed during manufacture to prevent curling. Many varieties of "gum breaks" exist.

Original Gum: A stamp is described as "O.G." if it has the original gum as applied when printed. Some are issued without gum, as

Nos. 730, 731, 735, 752, etc.; government reproductions, as Nos. 3 and 4, and official reprints.

Overprint . . . . See Printing

Pair Imperf. Between . . . . See Perforations
Pane . . . . See Plate
Part Perforate . . . . See Perforations
Paste-up . . . . See Plate
Paste-up Pair . . . . See Plate

Patriotic Covers: Envelopes of the Civil War, Spanish-American War, World War I and II periods showing patriotic designs or inscriptions.

Pelure Paper . . . . See Paper
Phosphor Tagged . . . . See Luminescence
Plate, 400-Subject . . . . See Plate
Plate Arrangement . . . . See Plate
Plate Flaws . . . . See Plate
Plates for Stamp Booklets . . . . See Plate
Plates for Coil Stamps . . . . See Plate
Plate Markings . . . . See Plate
Plate Numbers . . . . See Plate
Postal Markings, History of . . . . See Postal Markings
Postmarks . . . . See Postal Markings
Printing, Methods of . . . . See Printing
Printed on Both Sides . . . . See Printing
Proofs . . . . See Printing

Propaganda Covers: Envelopes carrying inscriptions pertaining to Cheaper Postage, Temperance, Anti-Slavery, etc.

Railroad Postmarks . . . . See Postal Markings
Receiving Mark . . . . See Postal Markings
Recut . . . . See Plate
Recutting . . . . See Plate
Re-engraved . . . . See Plate
Re-entry . . . . See Plate
Registry Markings . . . . See Plate Markings
Reissues . . . . See Printing
Relief . . . . See Plate
Reprints . . . . See Printing
Retouch . . . . See Plate
Rosette Crack . . . . See Printing
Rotary Press Printings . . . . See Printing
Rotary Press Double Paper . . . . See paper
Rough Perforation . . . . See Perforations
Rouletting . . . . See Perforation

Se-tenant: Joined together. Applies to pairs or larger multiples embracing stamps of different denomination, design, surcharge or overprint. Examples: Nos. 1421a and 1451a.

Sheet . . . . See Plate
Shifted Transfer . . . . See Plate
Ship Postmarks . . . . See Postal Markings
Short Transfer . . . . See Plate
Silk Paper . . . . See Paper

Specialization: Term usually applied to the study and collection of the stamps of any special issue or group as distinguished from collecting along general lines.

Special Printings . . . . See Printing
Split Grill . . . . See Paper

Stampless Covers: Prior to the issuance of United States Government adhesive postage stamps, and for some time thereafter, letters were mailed "collect" or postage was prepaid in cash. In such instances the covers often bear, in addition to the town postmark, a notation such as "Paid," "Paid 10," etc. The beginner is apt to confuse these stampless covers with the rare postmasters' provisionals issued prior to government stamps.

While many of these covers are inexpensive they are of historical value to collectors interested in the postal history and operations of the United States Post Office Department.

Stars . . . . See Plate markings
Stitch Watermark . . . . See Paper
Strip: A number of unsevered stamps forming a vertical or horizontal row.
Surface Printing . . . . See Printing
Surcharges . . . . See Printing

Tete beche: A French term applied to stamps printed upside down or sideways, in relation to one another. This is usually due to accidental insertion of one or more cliches in a stamp plate wrong way up, or by wrong transfers. Tete beche stamps must be collected in pairs; when separated the stamps show no peculiarity. Some issues are deliberately printed tete beche. See U.S. Nos. 1745-1948.

Tied On . . . . See Postal Markings
Transfer . . . . See Plate
Transfer Roll . . . . See Plate
Triple Transfer . . . . See Plate

Type: 1. The catalogue illustration of the stamp design. The Kennedy memorial stamp is type A678. 2. One of two or more forms of the design, differing in one or more details. The corner triangles of Nos. 248-252 are illustrated and listed in Types I, II and III.

Typeset . . . . See Printing
Typeset Stamps . . . . See Printing
Typography . . . . See Printing

Vertical Half . . . . See Bisect

Watermarks . . . . See Paper
Wet Printings . . . . See note after No. 1029
Wove Paper . . . . See Paper

Plate—Line Engraving (Intaglio)
The Process

Die

Transfer Roll

Plate

Die — Making the "die" is the initial operation. The "die is a small flat piece of soft steel on which the subject (design) is recess engraved in reverse. Dies are usually of a "single subject" type; but dies exist with "multiple subjects" of the same design, or different designs. After the engraving is completed, the "die" is hardened to withstand the stress of subsequent operations.

Transfer Roll — The next operation is the making of the "transfer roll" which, as its name implies, is the medium used to transfer the subject from the "die" to the "plate". A blank roll of soft steel, mounted on a mandrel, is placed under the bearers of a "transfer press", so as to allow it to roll freely on its axis. The hardened "die" is placed on the bed of the press and the face of the roll is brought to bear on the "die" under pressure. The bed is then rocked back and forth under increasing pressure until the soft steel of the roll is forced into every line of the "die". The resulting impression on the roll is known as a "relief" or a "relief transfer." Several "reliefs" are usually rocked in on each roll. After the required "reliefs" have been made, the roll is hardened.

Relief — A "relief" is the normal reproduction of the design on the "die" in reverse. A "defective relief", caused by a minute piece of foreign material lodging on the "die", may occur during the "rocking in" process, or from other causes. Imperfections in the steel of the transfer roll may also result in a breaking away of parts of the design; if the damaged relief is continued in use, it will transfer a repeating defect to the plate. Also, reliefs are sometimes deliberately altered. "Broken relief" and "altered relief" are terms used to designate these changed conditions.

Plate — A flat piece of soft steel replaces the "die" on the bed of the transfer press and one of the "reliefs" on the transfer roll is brought to bear on it. The position on the plate is determined by "position dots", which have been lightly marked on the plate in advance. After the position of the "relief" is determined, pressure is brought to bear and, by following the same method used in the making of the transfer roll, a "transfer" is entered, which reproduces in reverse every detail of the design of the "relief". As many "transfers" are entered on the plate as there are to be subjects.

After the required "transfers" have been entered, the position dots, layout dots and lines, scratches, etc., are generally burnished out; and any required "guide lines", "plate numbers" or other marginal markings are added. A proof impression is then taken and if "certified" (approved), the plate is machined for fitting to the press, hardened and sent to the plate vault until used.

Rotary press plates, after being certified, require additional machining. They are curved to fit the press cylinder and "gripper slots" are cut into the back of each plate to receive the "grippers", which hold the plate securely in the press, after which the plate is hardened.

The practice of chromium plating the steel plates began in 1927. It reduces wear and secures increased production, as the plates may be replated many times.

Transfer — An impression entered on the plate by the transfer roll. A "relief transfer" is also made when entering the design of the die on the transfer roll.

Double Transfer — A term used to describe the condition of a "transfer" on a plate that shows evidences of a duplication of all, or a portion of the design. It is usually the result of the changing of the registration between the "relief" and the "plate", during the rolling in of the original entry. It is sometimes necessary to remove the original "transfer" from a plate and enter the "relief" a second time, when the finished re-transfer shows indications of the original "transfer", due to incomplete erasure, the result is also a "double transfer".

Triple Transfer — Similar to a "double transfer" but showing evidences of a third entry or two duplications.

Re-entry — When executing a "re-entry", the transfer roll is reapplied to the plate at some time after it has been put to press. Thus, worn-out designs may be resharpened by carefully re-entering the transfer roll. If not very carefully entered, the registration will not be true and a "double transfer" will result. With the protective qualities of "chromium plating", it is no longer necessary to resharpen the plate. In fact, after a plate has been curved for the rotary press, it is impossible to make a re-entry.

Shifted Transfer (Shift) — In transferring, the metal displaced on the plate by the entry of the ridges, constituting the design on the transfer roll, is forced ahead of the roll, as well as pressed out at the sides.

The amount of displaced metal increases with the depth of the entry, but when the depth is increased evenly, the design will be uniformly entered. Most of the displaced metal is pressed ahead of the roll. If too much pressure is exerted on any "pass" (rocking), the impression of the previous partial entry may be floated (pushed) ahead of the roll and thus cause a duplication of the final design, appearing as an increased width of frame lines or a doubling of the lines.

The ridges of the displaced metal are flattened out by hammering or rolling the back of the plate along the space occupied by the subject margins.

Short Transfer — It sometimes happens that the transfer roll is not rocked its entire length in the entering of a transfer on a plate, with the result that the finished transfer fails to show the complete design. This is known as a "short transfer." Short transfers are known to have been made deliberately, as in the type III of the one-cent issue of 1851-1860, or accidentally, as in the ten-cent 1847, No. 2.

Re-engraved — A term used in connection with "line engraving". Either the die that has been used to make a plate or the plate itself may have its "temper" drawn (softened) and be re-cut. The resulting impressions from such re-engraved die or plate may differ very slightly from the original issue, and are known as "re-engraved".

Recut — A "recut" is line strengthening or altering by use of an engraving tool on unhardened plates.

Retouching — A "retouch" is line strengthening or altering by means of etching.

Plate—Arrangement

Arrangement — The first engraved plates used to produce United States postage stamps in 1847 contained 200 subjects. The number of subjects to a plate varied between 100 and 300 until the issue of 1890, when the 400-subject plate was first laid down. Since that time, this size of plate has been used for a majority of the regular postal issues. Exceptions to this practice exist and will be found listed under the headings of the various issues in the catalogue.

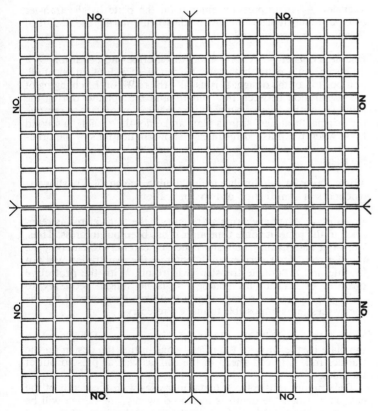

A typical 400-subject plate of 1922.

Plate Markings — The illustration above shows a typical 400-subject flat plate of the 1922 issue with markings as found on this type of plate. Other layouts and markings will be described further on in the text.

Sheet — In single color printings, the complete impression from a plate is termed a sheet. A sheet of multicolored stamps (two or more colors) may come from a single impression of a plate (many Giori-type press printings from 1957) or from as many impressions from separate plates as there are inks used for the particular stamp. Combination process printings may use both methods of multi-color production: Giori-type intaglio with offset lithography or with photogravure.

The Huck multicolor press (the "nine-color press") uses plates of different format (40, 80 or 72 subjects). The sheet it produces has 200 subjects for normal-size commemoratives or 400 subjects for ordinary-size stamps, similar to the regular products of other presses.

See note on the Combination Press following No. 1703.

Pane — A pane is the part of the original sheet that is issued for sale at post offices. A pane may be the same as an entire sheet where the plate is small, or it may be a half, or a quarter, or some other regular fraction of a sheet where the plate is large. The illustration shows the layout of a 400-subject sheet from a flat plate which for issuance would have been divided along the intersecting guide lines into four panes of 100.

Panes are classified in normal reading position according to their location on the printed sheet by being designated "U.L." (Upper left), "U.R." (Upper Right), "L.L." (Lower Left) and "L.R." (Lower Right). Where only two panes appear on a sheet, they are designated "R" (Right), "L" (Left) or "T" (Top), "B" (Bottom), depending on whether the sheet is divided vertically or horizontally.

To fix the location of a particular stamp on any pane, the pane is held with the subjects in the normal position and a position number is given to each stamp starting with the first stamp in the upper left corner and proceeding horizontally to the right, then starting on the second row at the left and across to the right, and so on to the last stamp in the lower right corner. (For a discussion on applying this system of designation to the product of the Huck multicolor press, see article "Position Description for Stamps Printed on the 9-color Huck Press," by George W. Brett, The United States Specialist, July, 1974, v. 45, p. 306.)

It is important to remember that in describing the location of a stamp on a sheet prior to 1894, the practice is to give the stamp position number first, then the pane position and finally the plate number: "1 R 22", as on No. 160. Beginning with the 1894 issue and on all later issues, the method used is to give the plate number first, then the position of the pane and finally the position number of the stamp: "16807 L.L. 48", as on No. 619; or "2138 L. 2", as on No. 323.

Plates For Stamp Booklets — These are illustrated and fully described under "Booklet Panes."

Booklets — These are stamps issued in small booklets for the convenience of users. Except for Nos. BK64 and BK65 (A.E.F.) they were sold by the post office at a 1¢ premium until 1962.

Booklet Panes — Small panes especially printed and cut to be sold in booklets. Panes are straight-edged on bottom and both sides, but perforated between the stamps.

Booklets, A.E.F. — Prepared principally for the use of the U.S. Army in France, during World War I. Issued in 1c and 2c denominations with 30 stamps to a pane (10 x 3), bound at right or left. As soon as Gen. John J. Pershing's organization reached France, soldiers' mail was sent free by the use of franked envelopes. Stamps were required during the war for the civilian personnel, also for registry mail, parcel post and other divisions of the postal service. See Nos. 498f, 499f, BK64, BK65.

Coil Stamps

Originally in 1908-09 coils were made in two sizes, 500 or 1,000 stamps, arranged endways or sideways and issued with or without perforations.

Stamps issued in rolls for use in affixing or vending machines were made first by private companies and later by the Bureau of Engraving and Printing. Originally it was customary for the Post Office Department to sell, to the private vending machine companies and others, imperforate sheets of stamps printed from the ordinary 400-subject flat plates. These sheets were then pasted together end-to-end or side-to-side by the purchaser and cut into rolls as desired, the perforations being applied to suit the requirements of the individual machines. Such "Private Perforations" are listed under "Vending and Affixing Machine Perforations." See Index.

Later the Bureau produced coils by the same method, also in sizes of 500 or 1,000 stamps, arranged endways or sideways and issued with or without perforations.

With the introduction of the Stickney rotary press, curved plates made for use on these presses were put into use at the Bureau, and the sale of imperforate sheets was discontinued. This marked the end of the "Private Perforations," Rotary press coils have been printed on a number of presses and have been made in sizes of 100, 500, 1,000 and 3,000 stamps.

Paste-up — Term used to describe the junction of two flat-plate printings joined by pasting the edge of one sheet onto the edge of another sheet to make coils. The two-stamp specimen to show this joining would be a "paste-up pair."

Line Pair — Pair of flat-plate-printed coil stamps with printed line between. This line is identical with the "Guide Line" in sheets. See "Plate Markings."

Joint Line — The edges of two curved plates do not meet exactly on the press, and the small space between them takes ink and prints a line. A pair of rotary-press-printed stamps with such a line between is called a "joint line pair."

Coils printed on the Multicolor Huck Press do not have constant lines. Occasionally accumulated ink will print partial lines in one or more colors. These are not listed in this catalogue. The "B" and "C" presses do not print joint lines at all.

Splice — Term used to describe the junction of two rotary-press printings joined by butting the ends of the continuous-printed web together and pasting a strip of perforated translucent paper on the back of the junction. The two-stamp specimen to show this would be a "spliced pair."

A splice might be made for repair of a single coil which broke, but was most often made to join two continuous-printed webs to make up a desired count. To facilitate counting, the two parts joined were usually broken at their joint lines and these lines placed together at the butt joint.

Hidden Plate Number — A plate number may be found entire on a coil made from flat plates, but is usually hidden by a part of the next sheet which had been lapped over it. These are valued the same as or slightly less than line pairs.

Plate Number — On a rotary-press coil the top or bottom part of a plate number may show. The number was entered on the plate so as to be cut off when the web was sliced into coils, and could be found only when the web was sliced off center.

Every rotary coil plate number was adjacent to a joint line, so both features could occur together in one strip. Logic would call for breaking the coil into strips so that the favored feature, either the line or the plate number, would be at mid-strip.

Beginning with No. 1891 the plate number is placed so that it will not be trimmed off. These are collected unused with the plate number stamp in the center of a strip of three or five stamps. The line, if any, will be at the right side of the plate number stamp. On the Cottrell Press the number occurs on every 24th stamp (see No. 2115); on the "B" press every 52nd stamp; and on the "C" Press every 48th stamp.

Coil Waste — Certain stamps issued in perforated sheets which were prepared from short lengths left over at the end of a run of printing stamps to be made into coils. Sometimes the salvaged sections were those which had been laid aside for mutilation because of some defect. As the paper had been moistened during printing, it sometimes stretched slightly, providing added printing surface at the end of a run. Sheets of 70, 100 and 170 have been seen. See Nos. 538-541, 544-546, 578-579, 594-595.

"**T**" — Appears on copies of No. 2115b printed on an experimental paper. The copy with plate number reads "T1."

Plate Markings

Guide Lines — Horizontal or vertical colored lines between the stamps, and extending wholly or partially across the sheet are "guide lines." They serve as guides for the operators of perforating machines, or to indicate the line of separation of the sheet into panes.

A block of stamps divided by any of the guide lines is known as a "Line" or "Guide Line Block", while the block of stamps from the exact center of the sheet, showing the crossed guide lines, is a "Center Line Block."

Gutters — Ordinarily when guide lines are used to divide the sheet into panes, the spaces between the panes are not greater than the space between any other of the stamps on the sheet. On some plates, however, a wide space or "Gutter" is left between the panes, and on such plates the "guide lines" usually do not appear.

Stamps showing this wide space running between are called "gutter pairs" or "gutter blocks," and a block of stamps from the exact center of the sheet showing the two wide spaces crossing is known as a "Center Gutter Block" or "Cross Gutter Block."

To qualify as a "gutter pair" or "gutter block" the stamps on both sides of the gutter must be intact, including perforation teeth.

Arrows — On issues between 1870 and 1894 guide lines were not usually used, but marginal arrow shaped markings, known as "arrows", were substituted, and served the same purpose as the guide lines. Since 1894, guide lines with arrows at both ends have been the standard practice on flat plate printings.

A marginal block of four stamps showing the "arrow" centered at one edge is called a "Margin Block with Arrow", but the number of stamps in the block need not necessarily be limited to four.

Registry Markings — Various shaped marks used as an aid in properly registering the frame and vignette impressions of bicolored stamps. In the catalogue listing, a "registry marking" is referred to as an "arrow marker".

Imprint — An oblong rectangular design containing the name of the producer of the stamps, appearing on the sheet margin adjoining the plate number.

A block of stamps with the sheet margin attached, bearing the "imprint," is known as an "Imprint Block." Imprints and plate numbers are usually collected in blocks of six, or of sufficient length to include the entire marking. In 1894-95 the fashion was to collect imprints in strips of three and these have been noted in the catalogue.

The imprint and plate number are found in eight types, illustrated after Nos. 245 and E3. Example: "T V" means Type V.

Plate Numbers — Serial numbers assigned to plates, appearing on one or more margins of the sheet or pane to identify the plate.

Flat Press Plate Numbers — are usually collected in a marginal block of six stamps with the plate number centered in the margin.

Rotary Press Plate Numbers — are collected in a corner margin block large enough to show the plate number(s) and its position along the margin. Most regular issues have a single plate number at the corner of the sheet, and for these a block of four suffices. During 1933-39 some plates had the number opposite the third stamp (up or down) from the corner of the sheet and for these the number is customarily collected in a corner block of no less than eight stamps. Multicolored stamps may have more than one plate number in the sheet margin and the "plate block" may then be expanded to suit the collector's desire.

The Catalogue listing includes enough stamps to include all numbers. Se-tenant issues will include all the designs in the plate number block. When a continuous design is involved (Nos. 1629-1631) the complete design will be included in the plate number block. The entire pane constitutes the plate number block for issues such as the State Birds and Flowers (Nos. 1953-2002).

Plate numbers take a further designation from the position on the sheet in which they appear, thus there would be U.L. (Upper Left), etc.

See note following No. 1703 for description of Combination Press markings.

Stars — "Stars" on the flat plates were used to indicate a change from the previous spacing of the stamps, and were used as a check on the assignment of the printed sheets to a perforating machine of the proper setting. Stars appear on certain rotary plates used for printing stamps for coils, appearing adjacent to the plate joint line and above stamp No. 1 on the 170-subject plates, and to the left of stamp No. 141 on the 150-subject plates.

"A" — See definition for flat plate "stars".

"C.S." and "C" — Indicate that the plate is made of "Chrome Steel".

"F" — Used to indicate the plate is ready for hardening. This appears only on flat plates and generally precedes the upper right plate number.

"EI" — Signifies "Electrolytic Iron" and is used to designate plates made by the electrolytic process.

"Top" — A marking on the top sheet margin of printings from both plates of certain bicolored issues and used to check printings for "inverts". Beginning with the 6c bicolored airmail issue of 1938, bicolored crosses also appear as an additional check.

"Coil Stamps" — Appearing on the side sheet margins to designate plates used in the production of endwise coils.

"S 20", "S 30", "S 40" — Marginal markings appearing on certain 150 and 170-subject rotary press plates to designate experimental variations in the depth and character of the frame line to overcome excess inking. "S 30" was adopted as the standard. Blocks showing these markings are designated as "Margin Block with S 20", etc., in the catalogue.

Initials — Initials in sheet margins were used to identify individuals in the Bureau who participated in the production or use of the plates.

Gutter Dashes — On the first 400-subject rotary plates, 3/16 inch horizontal dashes appear in the gutter between the 10th and 11th vertical rows of stamps. This arrangement was superseded by dashes 3/16 inch long at the extreme ends of the vertical and horizontal gutters, and ¼ inch cross at the central gutter intersection. This latter arrangement continued until replaced by the scanning marks on the Electric Eye plates. See Electric Eye.

Margin — The border outside the printed design of a stamp, or the similar border of a sheet of stamps. A block of stamps from the top, side or bottom of a sheet or pane to which is attached the margin is known as a "Margin Block". A block of stamps from the corner of a sheet with full margins attached to two adjoining sides is known as a "Corner Block".

Note — In the foregoing, it is indicated that a certain number of stamps make up an Arrow or Plate Number Block. Naturally any block of stamps, no matter how large or small, which had an arrow or a plate number on its margin would be designated by that name. But the usual practice is to collect flat Plate Numbers in margin blocks of 6, and Arrow Blocks in margin blocks of 4. Plate Number Blocks from rotary press printings are generally collected

in blocks of 4 as the plate number usually appears beside the stamp at any of the four corners of the sheet. Also, particularly in bicolored stamps, an Arrow Block is not separated from a Plate Number Block. Thus the two together form a block of 8 or 10 as the case might be.

Printing

Methods Used — The methods employed in producing United States stamps include all four basic forms of printing: "Engraved", "Photogravure", "Lithographed" and "Typographed".

Engraved (Recess or Intaglio-Engraved) — In this process the ink is received and held in lines depressed below the surface of the plate, and in printing from these plates the damp paper is forced down into the depressed lines and picks up the ink. In consequence the lines on the face of the stamps are slightly raised and when seen from the back of the stamp are slightly depressed. When the ornamental work is engraved by a machine, it is called "engine turned" or lathe work engraving. A good example of lathe work background is the 3c of 1861.

Engraved stamps were printed only with flat plates until 1915 when Rotary Press Printing was introduced. "Wet" and "Dry" printings are explained in the note after No. 1029. The Giori press, used to print certain U.S. stamps since 1957 (see No. 1094, the 4c Flag issue), applies two or three different colored ink simultaneously.

The Huck Multicolor press, put into service at the Bureau of Engraving and Printing in 1968, was first used to produce the 1968 Christmas stamp (No. 1363) and the 6c Flag coil (No. 1338A). Developed by the Bureau's technical staff and the firm of graphic arts engineers whose name it bears, the Huck Multicolor prints, phosphor tags, gums and perforates stamps in a continuous operation, doing the printing in as many as nine colors. Fed by paper from a roll, the Huck Multicolor uses many recess-engraved plates of smaller size than any used previously for U.S. stamp printing. Its product has certain characteristics which other U.S. stamps do not have. Post office panes of No. 1363, for example, show seven or eight plate numbers in the margins.

Photogravure — In this rapid process of reproduction, the design is usually photographed through an extremely fine screen lined in minute quadrille. This breaks up the reproduction into tiny dots. These dots are etched into the plate and the depressions thus formed hold the ink, which is lifted out by the paper when it is pressed against the plate.

For U.S. stamps, photogravure first appeared in 1967 with the Eakins 5c, No. 1335. The early photogravure stamps were printed in the plates of outside contractors until the Bureau obtained the multicolor Andreotti press in 1971. The earliest "Andreotti" stamp is No. 1426, the Missouri Statehood 8c. Color control bars, dashes or dots are printed on the margin of one pane in each "Andreotti" sheet of 200, 160 or 128. These are generally collected in blocks of 20 or 16 (two full rows of one pane) which include the full complement of plate numbers, Mr. Zip and the Zip and Mail Early slogans.

Details on the Combination Press follow No. 1703.

Lithography — A common and the cheapest process for printing stamps. In this method the design is drawn by hand or transferred from an original engraving to the surface of a lithographic stone or metal plate in greasy ink. The stone or plate is wet with an acid fluid, which causes it to repel the printing ink except on the greasy lines of the design. A fine lithographic print closely resembles an engraving, but the lines are not raised on the face or depressed on the back, and there is usually a duller appearance in the lithograph than in the engraving.

Offset Printing or Offset Lithography — is a modern development of the lithographic process. Anything that will print — type, woodcuts, photoengravings, plates engraved or etched in intaglio, halftone plates, linoleum blocks, lithographic stones or plates, photoggravure plates, rubber stamps, etc., may be used. Greasy ink is applied to the dampened plate or form and an impression made on a rubber blanket. Paper is immediately pressed against the blanket, which transfers the ink. Because of its greater flexibility, offset printing has largely displaced lithography. Since the processes and results obtained are similar, stamps printed by either of these two methods are designated "lithographed."

The first application was in printing Post Office seals, probably using stone printing bases. Offset lithography was used for the 1914 documentary revenues, Nos. R195-R216. Postage stamps followed in 1918-20 (Nos. 525-536) because of wartime ink, plate and manpower shortages in connection with the regular line-intaglio production.

The next use of offset lithography for postage stamps was in 1964 with the Homemakers 5c, No. 1253, in combination with line-intaglio. Many similar issues followed, including the Bicentennial souvenir sheets in 1976, Nos. 1686-1689, which were all offset-litho. The process serves best for soft backgrounds and tonal effects.

Typography — The exact reverse of engraved plate printing. In this process the parts of the design which are to show in color are left at the original level of the plate and the spaces between are cut away. The ink is applied to the raised lines on the plate and the pressure of printing forces these lines, more or less, into the paper, impressing the colored lines of the face of the stamp and slightly raising them on the back of the stamp. In practice a large number of electrotypes of the original are made and assembled together into a plate with the requisite number of designs for printing a sheet of stamps. Stamps printed by this process show great uniformity, and the process is cheaper than intaglio printing.

The first American stamp use of typography or letterpress under national authority was the 1846 "2" surcharge on the United States City Despatch Post 3c, Carrier stamp No. 6LB7. The next time was for the 1865 Newspaper and Periodical stamp issue which for security reasons combined the techniques of machine engraving, colorless embossing and typography, creating an unusual first.

Most U.S. stamp typography consists of overprints such as those for Canal Zone, the Molly Pitcher 2c, the Kansas-Nebraska controls, precancels and specimens.

Embossed (Relief) Printing — A method in which the design is sunk in the metal of the die and the printing is done against a yielding platen, such as leather or linoleum, which is forced up into the depression of the die, thus forming the design on the paper in relief. Embossing may be done without color, or with part color and part colorless, as the U.S. stamped envelopes.

Printing—Terms Used

Multicolored Stamps — Until 1957 when the Giori press was introduced, producing stamps in two or more colors with a single press run, bicolored stamps were printed on a flat bed press in two runs. Example: the Norse-American issue of 1925 (Nos. 620-621). In the flat press bicolors, if the sheet were fed to the press on the second run in reversed position, the part printed in the second color would be upside down, producing Inverted Centers, such as No. C3a. Many bicolored and multicolored stamps show varying degrees of poor alignment of the colors. Such varieties are not listed.

Bureau Prints — (Precancels) Stamps having cancellations applied before the stamps are sold to the public holding permits for their purchase. The cancellations are printed on the stamps during the process of manufacture by the Bureau of Engraving and Printing, and consist of the name of the city and state where the stamps are to be used, lines, or the class of mail. "City type" precancels have the cancellations printed on them before sale but the printing differs in type from the "Bureau Prints" and is done locally. See "postal markings."

Color Trials. — These are printings in various colors made to facilitate selection of color for the issued stamps.

Double Impression — A second impression of a stamp over the original impression. It should not be confused with a "double transfer" which is a plate imperfection and does not show a doubling of the entire design. A double impression shows every line clearly doubled. See: "Printed on Both Sides".

Essay — A design submitted in stamp form but not accepted in that form for issuance. Printings in various colors other than the issued stamp are known as "Color Trials". See: "Color Trials".

Inverted Center — A stamp with the center printed upside down in relation to the rest of the design. A stamp with the center printed upside down in relation to the rest of the design. A stamp may be described as having an "Inverted Center" even if the center is printed first. See: "Multicolored Stamps".

Flat Plate Printing — See: "Flat Press Printing".

Flat Press Printing — Stamp printed on the ordinary flat-bed press, as distinguished from rotary press printing. See: "Plate".

Overprint — Any word, inscription or device printed across the face of a stamp to alter its use or locality, or to serve a special purpose. An example of the last is No. 646, which is No. 634 overprinted "Molly Pitcher" as a memorial to the Revolutionary War heroine. See: "Surcharge".

Printed On Both Sides — Occasionally a sheet of stamps already printed will, through error, be turned over and passed through the press a second time, thus creating the rare "printed on both sides" variety. On one side the impression is almost always poor or incomplete. This is often confused with an offset which occurs when sheets of stamps are stacked while the ink is still wet. There is, however, an outstanding difference: the "printed on both sides" variety shows a positive design (all inscriptions reading correctly) on both sides of the paper. An "offset" shows a reverse impression on the back of the stamp, that is, all wording, etc., reading backwards. See: "Double Impression".

Proofs — Trial printings of a stamp made from the original die or the finished plate.

Reissues — An official printing of a stamp, or stamps, that had been discontinued. This term is usually applied to fresh printings of such stamps, which can be distinguished in some way from those of the original issue. While reissues are usually intended for regular usage, there are exceptions, as Nos. 40, etc., 102, etc., reissued during the Centennial Exposition for stamp collectors. See: "Reprints", "Special Printings".

Reprints — Impressions from the original plates, blocks or stones, from which the original stamps were printed, taken after the issuance of the stamps to post offices had ceased and their postal use had been voided. See: "Reissues", "Special Printings".

Reproductions — Stamps made from a new plate to imitate the original issue. See Nos. 3-4. See "Souvenir Cards" section of this Catalogue.

Rotary Press Printings — These are stamps which have been printed on a rotary type press from curved plates as compared to stamps printed from flat plates on a flat bed press. Rotary press stamps are longer or wider than the same stamps printed from flat plates. All rotary press printings through 1953, except coil waste end (such as No. 538), exist with horizontal "Gum Breaker Ridges" varying from 1 to 4 a stamp. See: "Plate".

Special Printings — Stamps of current design reissued, as during the Centennial Exposition of 1876. Examples: Nos. 167-177, 752-771. See "Reissues"; "Reprints".

Surcharge — An overprint which alters or restates the face value or denomination of the stamp to which it was applied (as No. K1, where U.S. stamps were surcharged for Offices in China). Many "surcharges" are typeset. See: "Overprint": "Typeset".

Typeset — Made from movable type.

Typeset Stamps — Printed from ordinary printer's type. Sometimes electrotype or stereotype plates are made, but as such stamps are usually printed only in small quantities for temporary use, movable type is often used for the purpose. This method of printing is apt to show lack of uniformity and broken type. See Hawaii, Nos. 1-4, 12-26.

Printing—Common Flaws

Cracked Plate — A term to describe stamps which show evidences that the plate, from which they were printed, was cracked.

Plate cracks come from various causes, each resulting in a different formation of the crack and its intensity. Cracks similar to the above illustration are quite common in the older issues and are largely due to too-quick immersion in the cooling bath when being tempered. These cracks are known as crystallization cracks. A jagged line running generally in one direction and most often in the gutter between stamps is due to the stress of the steel during the rolling in or transferring process.

In curved plates (rotary) there are two types of cracks. One is the bending or curving crack, which is quite marked and always runs in the direction in which the plate is curved.

The illustration shows the second type, which is the "Gripper Crack" and is caused by the cracking of the plate over the slots cut in the under side of the plate, which receive the "grippers" that fasten the plate to the press. These occur only on curved plates. They are to be found in the row of stamps adjoining the plate joint, and appear on the printed impression as light irregular colored lines, usually parallel to the plate joint line.

Rosette Crack — A cluster of fine cracks radiating from a central point in irregular lines. Usually caused by the plate receiving a blow.

Scratched Plate — Caused by foreign matter scratching the plate. These are usually too minor to mention. See: "Gouge".

Gouge. — Exceptionally heavy, usually short scratch. May be caused by a tool falling on the plate.

Surface Stains — Irregular circular marks resembling the outline of a pond on a map. Authorities differ as to the cause and they are too minor to list.

Paper

Paper consists of vegetable fibers, linen, cotton, straw, wood and certain grasses, which, after being pulped and bleached, are spread evenly and thinly, by hand or machinery first upon a wire cloth. The resultant film consolidates into a wet web of pulp, which being passed to felt cloths and through other processes becomes a sheet of paper. This is then finished and cut into sheets for printing. Any coloring is added to the pulp mixture before it is run on the wire cloths.

Paper falls broadly into two divisions: "wove" and "laid". The difference in the appearance is caused by the wire cloth upon which the pulp is first formed.

Wove — In "wove" paper the wire cloth is of an even and closely woven nature, producing a sheet of uniform texture throughout, showing no light or dark figures when held to the light.

Laid — If the wire cloth is formed of closely spaced parallel wires crossed at much wider intervals by cross wires, the resultant paper will show alternate light and dark lines, and is called "laid" paper. The distances apart and the thickness of the lines vary but on any one piece of paper they are all like.

Paper is also distinguished as thick or thin, hard or soft, and by its color, as bluish, yellowish, greenish, etc.

Pelure — Pelure paper is a very thin, semi-transparent paper, which may be either wove or laid.

Bluish — The 1909 bluish paper was made with 35 percent rag stock instead of all wood pulp. The bluish color goes through the paper, showing clearly on back and face.

Manila — Manila paper is a coarse paper formerly made of Manila hemp fiber. Since about 1890, so-called "Manila" paper has been manufactured entirely from wood fiber. It is used for cheaper grades of envelopes and newspaper wrappers. It is usually a natural light brown, and sometimes color is added, as in the United States "amber Manila" envelopes. It may be wove or laid.

Silk — Silk paper in philately is of two kinds: first, that in which one or more threads of silk, embedded in the substance of the paper, extend across the stamp. In the catalogues this style of paper is usually designated as "with silk threads". Many United States revenues are on paper which has short silk fibers strewn over it and impressed into it during manufacture. This is the second style and is called simply "silk paper".

Ribbed — Paper which shows fine parallel ridges on one or both sides of a stamp.

India — India paper is a soft, silky appearing wove paper, usually used for proof impressions.

Double Paper — Double paper, as patented by Charles F. Steel, consisted of two layers, a thin surface paper and a thicker backing paper. The paper was supposed to be an absolute safeguard against cleaning, for any attempt to remove the cancellation would result in the destruction of the upper layer. The Continental Bank Note Co. experimented with this paper in the course of printing Nos. 156-165.

China Clay Paper — See note above No. 331.

Fluorescent or Bright Paper — See Luminescence.

Rotary Press Double Paper

Rotary press printings are occasionally found printed on a double sheet of paper. The web of paper used on these presses must be continuous. Therefore any break in the process of manufacture must be lapped and pasted. This overlapping portion, when printed upon, is known as a "Double Paper" variety. Recently the lapped ends are joined with transparent adhesive tape.

In one instance known, two splices have been made, thus giving three thicknesses of paper. Double paper varieties were first listed because of their novelty and scarcity. These listings are now discontinued as all Rotary Press stamps may exist on double paper. Interest has lessened due to increasing finds.

Paper — Watermarks

Closely allied to the paper, as they are ususally formed in the process of manufacturing the paper. Watermarks of the United States consist of the letters "USPS" (No. 264, etc.); "USPOD" (No. UX1, etc.); seal of the U.S. (No. OX11, etc.) "USIR" (No. RF3, etc.), and are composed of double-lined and single-lined letters. They are formed of wire or cut from metal and soldered to the frame on which the pulp is caught or to a roll under which it is passed. The action of these is similar to the wires causing the "laid" lines, the designs making thin places in the paper which show by transmitting light. The best method to detect them is to lay the stamp face down on a tray with a black background and immerse in a commercial brand of watermark fluid, which brings up the watermark in dark lines against a lighter background. (Note: This method of detecting watermarks is dangerous for certain foreign stamps printed with inks that run when immersed. It is advisable to first test an inexpensive stamp from the same set.

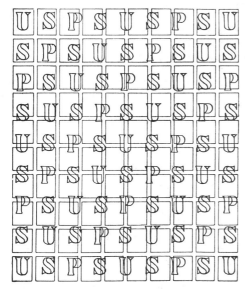

Wmk. 191
PERIOD OF USE
Postage: 1895-1910   Revenue: none

In the 1895-98 issues, the paper was used so that the watermark letters read horizontally (USPS) on some impressions and vertically on other impressions.

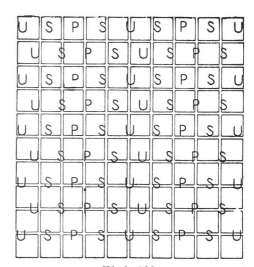

Wmk. 190
PERIOD OF USE
Postage: 1910-1916   Revenue: 1914

USIR
Wmk. 191R
PERIOD OF USE
Postage (unintentionally): 1895   Revenue: 1878 to 1958
   (271a, 272a), 1951 (832b)

Paper watermarked USPOD was used for Postal Cards from 1873 to 1875. For watermarks on stamped envelope paper, see Envelope Section.

Watermarks may be found normal, reversed, inverted, inverted reversed and sideways, as seen from the back of the stamp.

Stitch Watermark — A type of watermark consisting of a row of short parallel lines. This is caused by the stitches, which join the ends of the band on which the paper pulp is first formed. "Stitch watermarks" have been found on a great many issues and may exist on all.

Paper — Grills

Grill — The grill consists of small square pyramids in parallel rows impressed or embossed on the stamp, with the object to break the fibers of the paper so that the cancellation ink would soak in and make washing for re-use impossible. Grill impressions, when viewed from the face of the stamp may be either "points up" or "points down". Used on U.S. stamps No. 79-101, 112-122, 134-144, 156-165, 178-179.

Regular Grill   Continuous Marginal   Split Grill
                        Grill

Continuous Marginal Grill — Includes continuous rows of grill points impressed by the untrimmed parts of the ends of the grill rollers, noted as "end roller grill" on the 1870 and 1873 issues, and those grills which came from a continuous band lengthwise of the roller.

Split Grill — Describes a stamp showing portions of two or more grills, caused by a sheet being fed under the grill roller "off center".

Double (or Triple) Grill — A stamp showing two or more separate grill impressions. Not to be confused with a split grill, which shows two or four partial impressions from a single grill impression.

Rotary Grills — The grilled appearance occasionally found on rotary press printings is unintentionally produced by a knurled roller during the perforating process.

Grill-like impressions can be left on stamps dispensed from vending machines.

Perforations

Perforation — The chief style of separation of stamps, and the one which today is in almost universal use, is called "perforating". By this process the paper between the stamps is cut away in a line of holes, usually round, leaving little bridges of paper between the stamps to hold them together until they are to be separated. These little bridges are called the teeth of the perforation, and of course project from the stamp when it is torn from the pane. As the gauge of the perforation is often a guide to the date of issue of the stamp, it is necessary to measure them and describe them by a gauge number. Thus we say a stamp is perforated 12 or 10½. This does not mean that there are 12 or 10½ perforations on the side or end of the stamp, but that 12 or 10½ perforations can be counted in the space of two centimeters. This space has been arbitrarily adopted by collectors the world over as the length in which perforations shall be measured, and the number of perforations in two centimeters is called the gauge of that perforation. Thus a stamp perforated 12 would have perforations so spaced that twelve of them would measure two centimeters. United States stamps from 1861 to 1912 were perforated 12, and give readily obtainable material for testing the above rule.

Perforation Gauge — Gauge for measuring perforations as above.

Fine Perforation — Perforation with small holes and teeth close together.

Coarse Perforation — Perforation with large holes and teeth far apart, frequently irregularly spaced.

Rough Perforation — Holes not clean cut, but jagged.

Compound Perforation — Where perforations at the top and bottom differ from the perforations at the sides. In describing "compoud perforations" the gauge of the top is given first, then the sides. Some stamps are found where one side will differ from the other three, and in this case the reading will be the top first, then the right side, then the bottom and the left side last.

Double Perforations — Often found on early U.S. revenue stamps and occasionally on regular postage issues, double perforations are applied in error. They do not generally command a premium over catalogue prices of properly perforated stamps. These are not to be confused with a variety found on occasional rotary press printings where stamps adjacent to the center gutters will show the entire width of the gutter and a line of perforations on the far end of the gutter. These are caused by the sheet having been cut when off center and they are called "Gutter Snipes". They command a small premium.

Many double perforations were privately made to increase the value of the stamp. These are considered to be damaged stamps.

Electric Eye

An electronically controlled mechanical device acting as a guide in the operation of the perforating machine. Positive identification of stamps perforated by the "electric eye" process may be made by means of the distinctive marks in the gutters and margins of the full sheets on the printed web of paper. The original marks consisted of a series of heavy dashes dividing the vertical sheet gutter between the left and right panes (illustration "A"), together with a single line ("Margin Line," illustration "B"), in the right sheet margin at the end of the horizontal sheet gutter between the upper and lower panes. They were first used in 1933 on 400-subject plates for stamp No. 634, which was distributed to post offices in 1935 (special plates Nos. 21149-50; 21367-68). On these plates the plate numbers were placed opposite the ends of the third row of stamps from the top or bottom of the full sheet.

In later experiments the margin line was broken up into closely spaced thin vertical lines. Then it was again returned to its original form but somewhat narrower.

In 1939 the Bureau installed a new perforating machine which required a different layout to operate the centering mechanism. The vertical dashes remained the same but the margin line was removed from the right sheet margin and a corresponding line ("Gutter Bar," illustration "C"), was placed in the left sheet margin at the end of the horizontal sheet gutter. Additional horizontal lines ("Frame Bars," illustration "D"), were added in the left sheet margin opposite the top frame line of the adjacent stamp design of all horizontal rows except the upper horizontal row of each left pane, where the frame bar is omitted. The plate numbers were moved back to their normal positions adjoining the corner stamps. Plates for the two types of machines could not be interchanged.

Later in 1939 a "convertible" plate was employed. This consisted of a combination of the two previous layouts, the current one with the addition of a margin line (B) in its former position in the right sheet margin, thus making the perforation possible on either machine.

Originally laid out as 400-subject plates, electric eye plates were later used for 200-subject horizontal format and 200-subject vertical format (Commemorative, Special Delivery and Air Mail issues), 280-subject ("Famous Americans," "Edison" and "Carver" issues) and 180 and 360-subject plates (booklet panes of the "ordinary," "air mail," "postal savings" and "war savings" issues). At present, all rotary press plates receive the "electric eye" marks with the exception of the 150 and 170-subject plates used for the printing of coil stamps.

In laying out the plates for the 400-subject and 200-subject horizontal format issues, the marks retained the same relative positions to the stamp designs. This was changed, however, in entering the designs for the stamps on the 200-subject vertical format and 280-subject issues, in that the stamp designs were turned 90 degrees, that is, the designs were entered on the plates with the longer dimension horizontal. Although the electric eye marks were entered on the plates in the usual positions, on the printed sheets they appear as though shifted 90 degrees when the stamps are held in the customary upright position. Thus, a "horizontal" mark on a 400-subject or 200-subject horizontal format sheet would become a "vertical" mark on a 200-subject vertical format or 280-subject sheet. This situation has caused confusion among collectors and dealers in determining a definite description of the various marks. The designation of the position of the plate numbers also has not been uniform for the "turned" designs.

To solve this "confusion," the Bureau Issues Association adopted a standardized terminology of all the marks appearing on the "electric eye" sheets, "Dashes" (A), "Margin Line" (B), "Gutter Bar" (C) and "Frame Bars" (D), whereby each type of mark may be readily identified without referring to its plate number position. The "plate number" designation of the panes will continue to be established by holding the pane of stamps with the designs in an upright position; the corner of the pane on which the plate number appears will determine whether the pane is "upper left" (UL), "upper right" (UR), "lower left" (LL), or "lower right" (LR).

Scott Publishing Co. — will use these terms in its catalogues, wherever necessary.

Imperforate — Stamps without perforations, rouletting or other forms of separation.

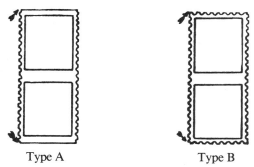

Type A   Type B

Part-Perforate — Stamps with perforations on the two opposite sides, the other two sides remaining imperforate.

Vertical Pair Imperforate Horizontally — (Type A, illustrated) This indicates that the pair is fully perforated vertically but is imperforate horizontally.

Horizontal Pair Imperforate Vertically — (Type A) This indicates that the pair is fully perforated horizontally but is imperforate vertically.

Vertical Pair Imperforate Between — (Type B, illustrated) This indicates that the vertical pair is fully perforated at the top, sides and bottom but is imperforate between the stamps.

Horizontal Pair Imperforate Between — (Type B) This indicates that the horizontal pair is fully perforated at the top, sides and bottom but is imperforate between the stamps.

Of the above types A and B, type A is the commoner. Examples: U.S. Revenue stamps, 1862, etc. An example of a vertical pair type B is No. 499c.

Block of four, Imperforate Within — Examples exist of blocks of four that are perforated on all four outside edges but lack both horizontal and vertical perforations within the block. See Smokey the Bear, No. 2096c, for an accidental example and Nos. RS173j and RS174j, where the internal perforations were intentionally omitted to create 4¢ "stamps" from four 1¢ stamps.

Rouletting — Short consecutive cuts in the paper to facilitate separation of the stamps, made with a toothed wheel or disc.

Luminescence

Kinds of Luminescence — Fluorescence and phosphorescence, two different luminescent qualities, are found in U.S. postage stamps and postal stationery. While all luminescent stamps glow when exposed to shortwave ultraviolet (UV) light, only those with phosphorescent properties display brief afterglow when the UV light source is turned off.

Fluorescent or 'Hi-bright' Papers — The Bureau of Engraving and Printing, accepting stamp paper without regard to fluorescent properties, unknowingly used a mix of infinitely varying amounts of fluorescent optical brighteners added during the papermaking process. In March, 1964, to preserve uniformity of product and as a safeguard for an emerging but still incomplete plan for nation-wide use of luminescent stamps, purchasing specifications were amended to limit the use of fluorescent paper brighteners. The amended specification permitted paper with some brightener content, but excluded brilliantly glowing papers known in trade jargon as "Hi-bright." Stamps printed on such papers emit a distinctive, intense whitish-violet glow when viewed with either long or short-wave UV. In following years stamps were produced on papers with lower levels of fluorescence permitted by amended specifications.

Tagged Stamps — The Post Office Department field-tested automated mail-handling equipment to face, cancel and sort mail at rates up to 30,000 pieces an hour, by sensing UV-light-activated afterglow from phosphorescent substances. For the first tests at Dayton, Ohio, started after Aug. 1, 1963, 8c carmine airmail stamps (No. C64a) were overprinted (tagged) with a so-called "nearly invisible" calcium-silicate compound which phosphoresces orange-red when exposed to shortwave UV. A facer-canceler, with modifications that included a rapidly cycling on-off UV light, activated the phosphor-tagged airmail stamps and extracted envelopes bearing them from the regular flow of mail.

While the airmail extraction test was still in progress, the entire printing of the City Mail Delivery commemorative (No. 1238) was ordered tagged with a yellow-green glowing zinc-orthosilicate comound intended for use with the automated recognition circuits to be tested with surface transported letter mail. After the first day ceremonies Oct. 26, 1963, at Washington, it was learned the stamps had been tagged to publicize the innovative tests by coupling tagging with stamps memorializing "100 years of postal progress" and to provide the first national distribution of tagged stamps for collectors. Between Oct. 28 and Nov. 2, to broaden the scope of the test in the Dayton area, the 4c and 5c denominations of the regular issue (Nos. 1036b, 1213b, 1213c and 1229a) were issued with the same green glowing compound applied in an experimental tagging format.

By June, 1964, testing had proven sufficiently effective for the Post Office Department to order all 8c airmail adhesive stamps phosphor-tagged for general distribution. By January, 1966, all airmail stamps regardless of denomination were ordered tagged. Meanwhile, from 1963 through 1965, limited quantities of the Christmas issues (Nos. 1240a, 1254a-1257a and 1276a) were tagged for use in the continuing test in the Dayton area.

On May 19, 1966, the use of phosphor-tagged stamps was expanded to the Cincinnati Postal Region which then included offices in Ohio, Kentucky and Indiana. During the last half of 1966, primarily to meet the postal needs of that region, phosphor-tagged issues were authorized to include additional denominations of regular issues, some postal stationery, and about 12 percent of each commemorative issue starting with the National Park Service 5c (No. 1314a) and continuing through the Mary Cassatt 5c (No. 1322a). After Jan. 1, 1967, most regular values through the 16c, all commemoratives, and additional items of postal stationery were ordered tagged.

However, adhesive stamps precanceled by the Bureau of Engraving and Printing were not tagged, except No. 1394, 1596, 1608 and 1610. Since there was no need to cancel mail with these stamps and since precancel permit holders post such mail already faced, postal officials by-passed facer-canceler operations and avoided the cost of tagging.

Phosphorescent overprints when newly issued are practically invisible in ordinary light, but after aging three to five years the tagging discolors and appears tawny or toasted. When viewed with UV there is little change in the hue of either orange-red or yellow-green emitted light. Even though observable discoloration exists, the presence or absence of tagging is best determined by examination with UV light.

Bar tagging, instead of the usual overall phosphorescent overprint, was used for some stamps starting with No. 1468, the Andreotti-printed Mail Order Business 8c.

Band tagging, a bar extending across two or more stamps, was first used for Nos. 1489-1498.

Most of the luminescent issues of 1967-70 exist with the luminescent coating unintentionally omitted. This group includes Nos. 1323-1338, 1339, 1342-1356, 1358, 1360, 1365-1370, 1372-1374. Earlier omissions of luminescence include Nos. 1238, 1278, 1281, 1298, 1305.

In some postal stationery, such as Nos. U551, UC40, UX48a and UX55, the luminescent element is in the ink with which the stamp design is printed.

The luminescent varieties of stamped envelopes Nos. U550 and UC37 were made by adding a vertical phosphorescent bar or panel at left of stamp. On No. UC42, this "glow-bar" passes through the tri-globe design.

Caution — Users of UV light should avoid prolonged exposure which can burn the eyes. Sunglasses or prescription eyeglasses, tinted or plain, screen the rays and provide protection.

Postal Markings

Postal markings are those marks placed by the post office of this or other countries on the stamp or cover or both, which indicate mailing place of a letter, date, rate, route, accounting between post offices, etc.

In addition to the basic town markings there are many varieties of supplemental markings. These include rate marks, route marks, obliterators, special dating markings usually found on advertised or dead letter covers, transportation markings (rail, steam, ship, airmail, etc), and services markings (advertised, forwarded, missent, second delivery, mail route, too late, charged, paid box, due, returned for postage, soldier's letter, held for postage, short paid, unpaid, not paid, paid, free, dead letter office, etc.)

In what is now the United States, these markings originated in the Colonial period when manuscript postal markings were first introduced under the Ordinance of Dec. 10, 1672, of New York which established an inland postal system between the colonies. A "Post Payd" is found on the first letter ever sent under this system, on Jan. 22, 1673. Manuscript postal markings continued in use right on through the pre-stamp period and can still be found on some letters in the present era.

Handstamp postal markings were introduced at New York in 1756 when a post office packet service was established between Falmouth, England, and New York. The marking was a two-line straightline reading NEW/YORK. Similar markings were later introduced at other towns such as ANNA/POLIS ((by 1766), CHARLES/TOWN (by 1770), PHILA/DELPHIA (by 1766), HART/FORD (by 1766), etc., while other offices received a single-line marking: BOSTON (by 1769), ALBANY (by 1773), PENSA-COLA (by 1772), SAVANNA (by 1765), BALTIMORE (by 1772), WMSBURG (by 1770).

Some of these early letters also bear a circular date stamp containing the month in abbreviated form as "IV" (June) or "IY" (July) and the date in a 14-17mm circle. Known from at least nine towns, these are called "Franklin marks," after Benjamin Franklin, then Deputy Postmaster General for the English Crown, or "American Bishopmarks" to distinguish them from the Bishopmark used in England, which has a center line.

During 1774-1775, an American "provisional" postal system was set up in opposition to that of the English Crown. Both manuscript and handstamp markings have been attributed to it by various students. This system was taken over by Congress on July 26,

1775, and the same markings were continued in use. The earliest reported Congressional marks are a manuscript "Camb Au 8" and a blue-green straightline "NEW*YORK*AU:24". Postal markings are known throughout the Revolution, including English occupation markings, and most are manuscript.

In the post-war Confederation period, handstamped circular markings were introduced at Charleston, S.C. (1778-1780), and later at New London, Conn. (1793). However, straightlines and manuscripts dominated until oval markings became widespread around 1800, with circles becoming the predominant marking shortly thereafter.

Handstamp rate markings are known as early as the pennyweight markings of Albany in 1789. They become more common in the 1830's, and almost standard by the "5" and "10" cent rate period which began July 1, 1845. This is also when envelopes began replacing folded lettersheets (before that date, envelopes were charged with an extra rate of postage). These "5", "10", and the succeeding "3", "6", "5", and "10" rates of 1851-56, were common on domestic mail until prepayment became compulsory on all but drop or local letters on April 1, 1855, and on foreign mail until about 1875.

Only 1.3% of all letters posted between 1847 and 1852 bore stamps. This proportion increased to 25% in 1852, 32% in 1853, 34% in 1854, 40% in 1855 and 64% in 1856. The attic searcher or collector who has never seen a prestamp or "stampless" cover obviously would be wrong to assume that one was a great rarity, although some are highly prized. Most, however, are more common than the stamps of the period.

While the government began issuing handstamps as early as 1799, and obliterators in 1847, many postmasters were required or permitted to purchase their own canceling devices or to use pen strokes. Pen cancellations continued to be common in the smaller offices into the 1880's. Because of collector prejudice against pen-canceled stamps, many have ended up being "cleaned." These are sold either as unused or with a different, faked cancellation to cover the evidence of cleaning. Ultraviolet light will usually reveal traces of the original pen marking.

From around 1850 until 1900 many postmasters used obliterators cut from wood or cork. Many bear fanciful designs such as bees, bears, chickens, locks, eagles, Masonic symbols, flags, numerals, etc. Some of the designs symbolized the town of origin. These are not listed in this catalogue as they owe their origin to the whim of some individual rather than a requirement of the postal regulations. Many command high prices and are eagerly sought by collectors. This has led to extensive forgery of such markings so that collectors are well advised to check them carefully.

Rapid machine cancellations were introduced at Boston in 1880-90 and later spread across the country. Each of the various canceling machine types had identifiable characteristics and collectors do form collections of them. One subspecialty is that of flag cancellations. While handstamp flag designs are known earlier, the first machine flag cancellation was that of Boston in November-December 1894.

Specialists have noted that different canceling inks are used at different times, depending partly on the type of canceling device used. Rubber handstamps, prohibited in 1893 although used for parcel post and precanceling after that date, require a different type of ink from the boxwood or type-metal cancelers of the classic period, while a still different ink is used for the steel devices of the machine cancels.

Registry of letters was first authorized in the Dutch colony of New Netherland on overseas mail. Records of valuable letters were kept by postmasters throughout the stampless period while an "R" marking was introduced at Philadelphia in 1845 for "recorded" mail. Cincinnati also had such a "recorded" system. The first appearance of the word "registered" appears on mail in November, 1847, in manuscript, and in handstamp in May, 1850. However, the official registration system for U.S. mail did not begin until July 1, 1855.

In recent years the handstamped and machine types of cancellations have been standardized by the Post Office Department and supplied to the various post offices.

Postmarks — Markings to indicate the office of origin, or manner of the postal conveyance. Generally speaking the postmark refers to the post office of origin, but sometimes there are also receiving postmarks of the post office of destination or of transit. Other post office markings include: Advertised, Forwarded, Mail Route, Missent, Paid, Not Paid, Second Delivery, Too Late, etc., etc. Postmarks often serve also to cancel postage stamps with or without additional obliterating cancels.

Cancellations — A cancellation is a postal marking which cancels the stamp, making its further use impossible. As used in the listings in this Catalogue, cancellations include both postmarks used as cancellations, and obliterations intended primarily to cancel (or "kill") the stamp.

Carrier Postmarks — These usually show the words "Carrier", "City Delivery" or "U.S. P.O. Dispatch". (See illustration under Cancellations.) They were applied to letters to indicate the delivery of mail by U.S. Government carriers. These markings should not be confused with those of Local Posts or other private mail services which used postmarks of their own. Free delivery of city mail by carriers was begun on July 1, 1863.

Free — Handstamp generally used on free, franked mail. Occasionally seen on early adhesives of the U.S. used as a canceling device.

Railroad Postmarks — Usually handstamps, used to postmark unpouched mail received by Route Agents of the Post Office Department traveling on trains on railway mail routes. The route name in an agent's postmark often was similar to the name of the railroad or included the terminals of the route. The earliest known use of the word "Railroad" as a postmark is 1838. Route Agents gradually became R.P.O. clerks and some continued to use their handstamps after the Route Agent service ceased June 30, 1882. The railroad postmarks of the 1850 period and later usually carried the name of the railroad.

A sub-group of railroad postmarks comprises those applied in the early days by railroad station agents, using the railroad's ticket dating handstamp as a postmark. Sometimes the station agent was also the postmaster.

In 1864, the Post Office Department equipped cars for the general distribution of mails between Chicago and Clinton, Iowa.

Modern railroad marks such as "R.P.O." (Railway Post Office) indicate transportation by railroad cars on designated routes and distribution of mail in transit. "R.M.S." (Railway Mail Service) is a mark indicating transportation by railroad, and includes Railway Post Office, Terminal Railway Post Office, Transfer Office, Closed Mail Service, Air Mail Field and Highway Post Office.

Effective Nov. 1, 1949, the Railway Mail Service (RMS) was merged with others of like nature under the new consolidated title, Postal Transportation Service (PTS).

The modern "Railway marks" are quite common and are not the types referred to under cancellations as listed in the catalogue.

Way Markings — Way letters are those received by a mailcarrier on his way between post offices and delivered at the first post office he reached. The postmaster ascertained where the carrier received them and charged, in his postbills, the postage from those places to destination. He wrote "Way" against those charges in his bills and also wrote or stamped "Way" upon each letter. If the letter were exempt from postage, it should have been marked "Free."

"Mail-carrier" in the foregoing paragraph refers to any carrier under contract to carry U.S. mails: a stage line, a horseback rider, or a steamboat or railroad that did not have a route agent on board. Only unpouched mail (not previously placed in a post of-

fice) was eligible for a Way fee of 1 cent. The postmaster paid this fee to the carrier, if demanded, for the carrier's extra work of bringing the letter individually to the post office. For a limited time at certain post offices, the Way fee was added to the regular postage. This explains the use of a numeral with "Way."

Packet Markings — Packet markings listed in this catalogue are those applied on a boat traveling on inland or coastal waterways. This group does not include mail to foreign countries that contains the words "British Packet," "American Packet," etc., or their abbreviations (Br. Pkt., etc.); these are U.S. foreign-mail exchange-office markings.

Listed packet markings are in two groups: (1) Waterways route-agent markings which denote service exactly the same as that of railroad route-agent markings except that the route agent traveled on a boat instead of a train. (2) Name-of-boat markings placed on the cover to advertise the boat or, as some believe, to expedite payment of Way and Steam fees at the post office where such letters entered the U.S. mails.

Occasionally waterways route-agent markings included the name of a boat, or "S.B.," "STEAMBOAT," "STEAM," or merely a route number. Such supplemental designations do not alter the character of the markings as route-agent markings.

19th Century U.S. Express Mail Postmarks — In pre-stamp days these represented either an extra-fast mail service or mail given into the care of an express-mail messenger who also carried out-of-mail express packages, permitted as a practical means of competing with package express companies that also carried mail in competition with U.S. mails. Several of these early postmarks were later used by U.S. mail route agents on the New York-Boston and New York-Albany runs, or by U.S. steamboat letter carriers on the coastal run between Boston and St. John, N.B.

Steamboat or Steam Markings — Except the circular markings reading "Maysville Ky. Steam" and "Terre Haute Stb." and the rectangular "Troy & New York Steam Boat," these markings contain only the word "STEAMBOAT" or "STEAM," with or without a rating numeral. They represent service exactly similar to that of Way markings, except that the carrier was an inland or coastal steamer that had no contract to carry U.S. mails. Such boats, however, were required by law to carry to the nearest post office any mail given them at landings. The boat owner was paid a 2-cent fee for each letter so delivered, except on Lake Erie where the fee was 1 cent. At some post offices in the early days the Steamboat fee was added to regular postage. In 1861 the 2-cent fee was again added to the postage, and in 1863 double postage was charged.

Ship Postmarks — Postal markings indicating arrival on a private ship (one not under contract to carry mails). This marking was applied to letters delivered by such ships to the post office at their port of entry as required by law, for which they received a fee and the letters were taxed with a specified fee for the service in place of the ordinary open postage.

The use of U.S. postage stamps on ship letters is unusual, except for letters from Hawaii, because the U.S. inland postage on ship letters from a foreign point did not need to be prepaid. "U.S. SHIP" is a special marking applied to mail posted on naval vessels, especially in the Civil War period.

Steamship Postmarks — These are akin to Ship postmarks but they appear to have been used mostly on mail from Caribbean or Pacific ports to New Orleans or Atlantic ports carried on steamships having a U.S. mail contract. An associated numeral usually designates the through rate from where the letter was received by the ship to its inland destination.

Receiving Mark — Impression placed on the back of envelopes by the receiving office to indicate name of office and date of arrival. Also known as "backstamp". Generally discontinued about 1913, but was employed for a time on airmail service until it was found the practice slowed up the service. Now used on Registry and Special Delivery mail.

Miscellaneous Route Markings — Wordings associated with the previously described markings include Bay Route, River Mail, Steamer, Mail Route, etc. Classification of the marking is ordinarily evident from usage, or it can be identified from publications on postal markings.

U.S. Foreign-Mail Exchange-Office Markings — These serve to meet the accounting requirements of the various mail treaties before the Universal Postal Union was established. The markings usually designate the exchange office or the carrier (British Packet, Bremen Packet, American Packet, etc.). Sometimes they are a restatement of the through rate, or a numeral designating the amount credited or debited to the foreign country as a means of allocating the respective parts of the total postage, according to conditions of route, method of transit, weight, etc.

Gridiron Cancellations — Commonest types of cancellations on early U.S. stamps. Consist of circles enclosing parallel lines. There are, however, many varieties of grid cancellations, especially the New York square grid.

Paid Markings — Generally consist of the word "PAID," sometimes within a frame, indicating regular postage prepaid by the sender of a letter. They are found as separate handstamps, within town or city postmarks, and as a part of obliterating cancels. In each case the "paid" marking may be used with or without an accompanying or combined rate numeral indication.

Precancels — Stamps having the cancellation applied before the article is presented for mailing. The purpose is to reduce handling and speed up the mails. A permit is required for use by the public except for special cases such as the experiments using Nos. 1384a,

1414-1418a, or 1552 for Christmas mail. Normally the precanceling is done with devices not used for ordinary postal service. Most precancellations consist of the city and state names between two lines or bars.

Precancels are divided into two groups: "locals" and "Bureaus." Locals are printed, usually from 100-subject plates, or handstamped at the office using the stamps by means of a 10 or 25-subject device having a rubber, metal or vinyl surface. Most locals are made with devices furnished by the Postal Service, but a number have been made with devices created in the city using them. Early locals include the printed "PAID" or "paid" on Nos. 7 and 9, the "CUMBERLAND, ME." on Nos. 24-26 and the Glen Allen, Va., stars.

Many styles of precancellation are known. Over 600,000 different precancels exist from more than 20,000 post offices in the United States.

The Bureaus, or Bureau Prints, are precancels printed by the Bureau of Engraving and Printing. They originated in 1916 when postal officals were seeking ways to reduce costs as well as increase the legibility of the overprint. They tried applying the precancellation at the Bureau during the production of the stamps which resulted in the "experimentals." These 16 denominations, including two dues, were issued for Augusta, Me. (1 value), Springfield, Mass. (14 values), and New Orleans (6 values) in quantities ranging from 4,000,000 down to 10,000. Electrotype plates mounted on a flat bed press were used to print the precancellations.

Regular production of Bureau Prints began on May 2, 1923, with No. 581 precanceled New York, N.Y. All regular Bureaus until 1954 were produced by the Stickney rotary press, whereby the stamps, immediately after printing, pass under the precanceling plates. Then the roll is gummed, perforated and cut into sheets or coils. Since 1954 a variety of printing methods have been used.

Tied On — A stamp is "tied on" when the cancellation (or postmark) extends from the stamp to the envelope.

POSTAL MARKINGS
Examples of Cancellations

Numerals
Prices are for rating marks such as those illustrated. Later types of numerals in grids, targets. etc. are common.

WAY

The Common Boston Paid Cancellation
(Prices are for types other than this)

PAID ALL

PAID

STEAMBOAT

SHIP STEAM

FREE

Steamship

Steamboat
(Route agent marking)

Packet Boat
(Name-of-boat marking)

Packet Boat
(Name-of-boat marking)

Packet Boat
(Name-of-boat marking)

Railroad
(Route agent marking)

U.S. Express Mail
(Route agent marking)

(In red on letter to Germany via Prussian Closed Mail, via British Packet. Credits 7 cent to Prussia.)

Carrier

Express Company

Canadian

Army Field Post

Town

Fort

Year dated

U.S. Postmark used in China

Vera Cruz, Mexico, 1914

Exposition Station.
Used while exposition is open.
Many styles

Exposition advertising.
Used before exposition opens.
Many styles.

U.S. Postmark used in Japan

New York City Foreign Mail

A group of design cancellations used during the period from 1871 to 1877 in New York City on outgoing foreign mail only. This group of handstamps totals about 200 different fancy stars, geometric designs, wheels, conventionalized flowers, etc., the majority within a circle 26-29mm. in diameter. Examples follow.

Patent Defacing Cancellations

When adhesive stamps came into general use, the Post Office Department made constant efforts to find a type of cancellation which would make the re-use of the stamp impossible. Many patents were granted to inventors and some of the cancellations (killers) came into more or less general use. Some of them appear in combination with the town postmarks.

About 125 different types are known on the stamp issues up to about 1887. Their principal use and greatest variety occur on Nos. 65, 147, 158, 183 and 184.

Generally speaking, Patent Cancellations fall into three groups:
1. Small pins or punches which pierce the paper or depress it sufficiently to break the fiber.
2. Sharp blades or other devices for cutting the paper.
3. Rotation of a portion of the canceller so that part of the paper is scraped away.

Four are illustrated below:

1. Dot punches through paper.   **2.** Blades cut the paper.

2. Small circle cuts the paper.   **3.** Scraped in the shaded circle.

Supplementary Mail

Supplementary Mail markings designate the special P.O. service of dispatching mail after the regular mail closed. Two kinds of supplementary mail were available:

1. Foreign mail. For New York the Postmaster General established in 1853 a fee of double the regular rate. This paid for getting the mail aboard ship after the regular mail closing and before sailing time. The service continued until 1939. Postmark types A, D, E, F and G were used.

In several other ports similar service was provided without special postmarks. Honolulu used a "Late Fee" handstamp.

2. Domestic mail. For Chicago the extra fee entitled a letter to catch the late East-bound train. Postmark types B and C were used. No foreign destination was implied.

Similar service without "Supplementary" in the postmark was apparently available in Philadelphia and possible elsewhere.

Type A   Type D   Type E

Type F
Combination Handstamp
(Also comes with numeral "1")
(Stamps with numeral cancel alone do not qualify
for Supplementary Mail cancel premiums.)

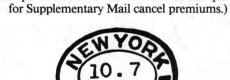

c
Type G
(also with other numerals)

Type B   Type C

World War I Soldiers' Letters

At the time the United States declared war against Germany on April 6, 1917, a postal regulation existed to the effect that letters could be sent without prepayment of postage by soldiers, sailors and marines to places in the United States when endorsed "Soldier's letter," etc., and countersigned by an officer, and only the single rate collected from the recipient (Sec. 406 P.L.R. May 4, 1914). Few of the enlisted men, however, took advantage of this privilege in sending letters while in the United States and practically all letters sent by soldiers from some 200 World War I military post offices (Fig. A) in the United States bear regular postage stamps.

Fig. A

Soon after the arrival of the first units of the American Expeditionary Force in France this regulation was modified to include letters which, although not endorsed, bore the postmark of the United States Army Postal Service (Postal Guide, August, 1917). The War Revenue Act of Congress of October 3, 1917 (section 1100), provided free postage for soldiers, sailors and marines assigned to duty overseas.

Therefore, letters from members of the A.E.F. sent before October, 1917, without postage stamps were properly charged with postage due, while those sent after that time went through post free.

This provision of free postage did not ordinarily apply to civilians permitted to accompany the army, such as welfare workers, Post Office Dept. representatives, war correspondents and others; neither did it apply to the registration fee on soldiers' letters nor to parcel post matter. It was necessary to pay such postage by means of postage stamps.

Fig. B   Fig. C

United States Army post offices, (Fig. B), known as A.P.O.'s were established in France, the earliest being that at St. Nazaire on July 10, 1917. The A.P.O.'s were at first operated by the Post Office Dept., but in May, 1918, Military Postal Express Service was established (Fig. C) and the army took over their operation. Later the name was changed to Postal Express Service (Fig. D).

Fig. D   Fig. E

Army post offices were given code numbers, and were at first numbered from No. 1 (St. Nazaire) to No. 18 (Saumur). In December, 1917, they were renumbered 701, 702, etc., and some 169 A.P.O.'s were established on the Western Front, including offices in Italy, Belgium, Netherlands, Luxembourg and Germany after the Armistice. Most of the A.P.O.'s were located at fixed places, but "mobile" post offices were assigned to divisions, army corps and armies and were moved from place to place. Many A.P.O.'s had stations or branches, some of which used postmarks with different code numbers from those assigned to the main office.

Until July, 1919, all A.E.F. mail was censored, and letters will be found with "company" censor marks (Fig. E) as well as "regimental" censor marks (Fig. F). Distinctive censor marks were used at the base censor's office in Paris (Fig. G).

Fig. F   Fig. G

An interesting variety of subsidiary markings will be found on soldiers' letters, typical being: ADDRESSEE RETURNED TO U.S.A., CANNOT BE FOUND, DECEASED - VERIFIED, NO RECORD, SOLDIER'S MAIL, and UNIT RETURNED TO U.S.

Many styles of stationery were used, mainly those furnished by welfare organizations. Only a few pictorial envelopes were used; but a considerable variety of patriotic and pictorial post cards may be obtained, in addition to officially printed form post cards.

Fig. H   Fig. I

A postal agency was in operation in Siberia from 1918 to 1920 and distinctive postmarks (Fig. H) and censor marks were used there. A few American soldiers were sent to North Russia, and postmarks used there were those of the British Expeditionary Force's North Russia postal service (Fig. I).

World War I postmarks have been classified by collectors, and the "American Classification System" prepared by the War Cover Club is in general use by collectors of these items.

World War II

Commencing in January, 1941, U.S. post offices were established in Newfoundland, Bermuda and other naval bases acquired as a result of the exchange of destroyers with Great Britain. The names of the bases were at first included in the postmark, later A.P.O. code numbers were adopted, in a similar manner to those used during World War I. Towards the middle of 1942 the A.P.O. numbers were cut out of the postmark so that nothing appears to indicate the A.P.O. at which a letter was mailed, although the already established practice was continued of the writer giving his A.P.O. number in the return address. Early in 1943, A.P.O. numbers were replaced in the postmarking stamps at many military post offices.

More than 1,000 different A.P.O. numbers were used. At least 90 types of postmarks exist, of which 45 are handstamped and 40 machine-struck.

The armed services, both at home and abroad, were given the franking privilege early in April, 1942, the frank consisting of the written word "Free" in the upper right corner of the envelope.

A wide variety of censor marks was used, differing radically in design from those used during World War I.

Bureau Precancels

AUGUSTA
MAINE

NEW
ORLEANS
LA.

SPRINGFIELD
MASS.

Experimentals

PERU
IND.

LANSING
MICH.

SAINT LOUIS
MO.

New Orleans
La.

San Francisco
Calif.

PORTLAND
ME.

LAKEWOOD
N.J.

KANSAS
CITY
MO.

POUGHKEEPSIE
N.Y.

LONG ISLAND
CITY, N.Y.

CORPUS
CHRISTI
TEXAS

ATLANTA
GEORGIA

ATLANTA
GA.

PEORIA
IL

CINCINNATI
OH

Blk. Rt.
CAR-RT
SORT

Bulk Rate

Nonprofit
Org.

Nonprofit
Org.

PRESORTED
FIRST-CLASS

ZIP+4

Local Precancels

QUINCY
ILLINOIS

FITCHBURG
MASS.

LOS ANGELES
CALIF.

Fergus Falls
Minn.

COVINGTON
KY.

REDWOOD CITY
CALIF.

BELMONT
CALIF.

ELGIN
ILLINOIS

Electroplates

Ashland
Wis.

PALMYRA
N. Y.

Northhampton
MASS.

DES PLAINES
ILL.

RICHMOND
VA.

BROOKFIELD
ILLINOIS

PAONIA
COLO.

GOSHEN
IND

TOWER CITY
N. DAK.

NEW BRUNSWICK
N. J.

ORLANDO,
FLA.

RICHTON PARK
ILL.

MULINO,
OREG.

PINE HILL
N.Y.

FARRELL,
PA

SACRAMENTO
CA

Handstamps

TERRITORIAL AND STATEHOOD DATES

	Territorial Date	**Statehood Date**	
Alabama	Aug. 15, 1817	Dec. 14, 1819	Territory by Act of March 3, 1817, effective Aug. 15, 1817.
Alaska	Oct. 18, 1867	Jan. 3, 1959	A District from Oct. 18, 1867, until it became an Organized Territory Aug. 24, 1912.
Arizona	Feb. 24, 1863	Feb. 14, 1912	This region was sometimes called Arizona before 1863 though still in the Territory of New Mexico.
Arkansas	July 5, 1819*	June 15, 1836	The Territory was larger than the State. The left-over area to the west after statehood had post offices which continued for some years to use an Arkansas abbreviation in the postmarks though really in the "Indian Country."
California		Sept. 9, 1850	Ceded by Mexico by the Guadalupe-Hidalgo Treaty, concluded Feb. 2, 1848 and proclaimed July 4, 1848. From then until statehood, California had first a military government until Dec. 20, 1849 and then a local civil government. It never had a territorial form of government.
Colorado	Feb. 28, 1861	Aug. 1, 1876	
Dakota	March 2, 1861	Nov. 2, 1889	Became two states — North and South Dakota.
Deseret	March 5, 1849		March 5,1849 Brigham Young created the unofficial territory of Deseret. In spite of the fact that Utah Territory was created Sept. 9, 1850, Deseret continued to exist unofficially in what is now Utah for several years, at least as late as 1862.
Frankland or Franklin			This unofficial state was formed in Aug. 1784 in the northeast corner of what is now Tennessee, and the government existed until 1788. In reality it was part of North Carolina.
Florida	March 30, 1822	March 3, 1845	
Hawaii	Aug. 12, 1898	Aug. 21, 1959	The territorial date given is that of the formal transfer to the United States, with Sanford B. Dole as first Governor.
Idaho	March 3, 1863	July 3, 1890	
Illinois	March 2, 1809*	Dec. 3, 1818	
Indiana	July 5, 1800*	Dec. 11, 1816	There was a residue of Indiana Territory which continued to exist under that name from Dec. 11, 1816 until Dec. 3, 1818 when it was attached to Michigan Territory.
Indian Territory		Nov. 16, 1907	In the region first called the "Indian Country," established June 30, 1834. Never had a territorial form of government. Finally, with Oklahoma Territory, became the State of Oklahoma, Nov. 16, 1907.
Iowa	July 4, 1838	Dec. 28, 1846	
Jefferson	Oct. 24, 1859		An unofficial territory from Oct. 24, 1859 to Feb. 28, 1861. In reality it included parts of Kansas, Nebraska, Utah and New Mexico Territories, about 30% being in each of the first three and 10% in New Mexico. The settled portion was mostly in Kansas Territory until Jan. 29, 1861 when the State of Kansas was formed from the eastern part of Kansas Territory. From this date the heart of "Jefferson" was in unorganized territory until Feb. 28, 1861, when it became the Territory of Colorado.
Kansas	May 30, 1854	Jan. 29, 1861	
Kentucky		June 1, 1792	Never a territory. Was part of Virginia until statehood.
District of Louisiana	Oct. 1, 1804		An enormous region — all of the Louisiana Purchase except the Territory of Orleans. Created by Act of March 26, 1804, effective Oct. 1, 1804 and attached for administrative purposes to the Territory of Indiana.
Territory of Louisiana	July 4, 1805		By Act of March 3, 1805, effective July 4, 1805, the District of Louisiana became the Territory of Louisiana.
District of Maine		March 16, 1820	What is now the State of Maine was before statehood called the District of Maine and belonged to Massachusettes.
Michigan	July 1, 1805	Jan. 26, 1837	

	Territorial Date	Statehood Date	
Minnesota	March 3, 1849	May 11, 1858	
Mississippi	May 7, 1798	Dec. 10, 1817	Territory by Act of April 7, 1798, effective May 7, 1798.
Missouri	Dec. 7, 1812	Aug. 10, 1821	The State was much smaller than the Territory. The area to the west and northwest of the State, which had been in the Territory, was commonly known as the "Missouri Country" until May 30, 1854 and certain of the post offices in this area show a Missouri abbreviation in the postmark.
Montana	May 26, 1864	Nov. 8, 1889	
Nebraska	May 30, 1854	March 1, 1867	
Nevada	March 2, 1861	Oct. 31, 1864	
New Mexico	Dec. 13, 1850	Jan. 6, 1912	
North Dakota		Nov. 2, 1889	Had been part of the Territory of Dakota.
Northwest Territory	July 13, 1787		Ceased to exist March 1, 1803 when Ohio became a state. The date given is in dispute, Nov. 29, 1802 often being accepted.
Ohio		March 1, 1803	Had been part of Northwest Territory until statehood.
Oklahoma	May 2, 1890	Nov. 16, 1907	The State was formed from Oklahoma Territory and Indian Territory.
Oregon	Aug. 14, 1848	Feb. 14, 1859	
Orelans	Oct. 1, 1804		A Territory by Act of March 26, 1804, effective Oct. 1, 1804. Became with certain boundary changes, the State of Louisiana, April 30, 1812.
South Dakota		Nov. 2, 1889	Had been part of Dakota Territory.
Southwest Territory			Became the State of Tennessee, with minor boundary changes, June 1, 1796.
Tennessee		June 1, 1796	Had been Southwest Territory before statehood.
Texas		Dec. 29, 1845	Had been an independent Republic before statehood.
Utah	Sept. 9, 1850	Jan. 4, 1896	
Vermont		March 4, 1791	Until statehood, had been a region claimed by both New York and New Hampshire.
Washington	March 2, 1853	Nov. 11, 1889	
West Virginia		June 20, 1863	Had been part of Virginia until statehood.
Wisconsin	July 4, 1836	May 29, 1848	The State was smaller than the Territory, and the left-over area continued to be called the Territory of Wisconsin until March 3, 1849.
Wyoming	July 29, 1868	July 10, 1890	

* The dates followed by an asterisk are one day later than those generally accepted. The reason is that the Act states, with Arkansas for example, "from and after July 4." While it was undoubtedly the intention of Congress to create Arkansas as a Territory on July 4, the United States Supreme Court decided that "from and after July 4," for instance, meant "July 5."

Territorial and statehood data compiled by Dr. Carroll Chase and Richard McP. Cabeen.

DOMESTIC LETTER RATES

Effective Date	Prepaid	Collect
1845, July 1		
Reduction from 6¢ to 25¢ range on single-sheet letters		
Under 300 miles, per ½ oz.	5¢	5¢
Over 300 miles, per ½ oz.	10¢	10¢
Drop letters	2¢	
1847-1848		
East, to or from Havana (Cuba) per ½ oz.	12½c	12½c
East, to or from Chagres (Panama) per ½ oz.	20c	20c
East, to or from Panama, across Isthmus, per ½ oz.	30c	30c
To or from Astoria (Ore.) or Pacific Coast, per ½ oz.	40c	40c
Along Pacific Coast, per ½ oz.	12½c	12½c
1847, July 1		
Unsealed circulars		
1 oz. or less	3c	
1851, July 1		
Elimination of rates of 1847-1848 listed above		
Up to 3,000 miles, per ½ oz.	3c	5c
Over 3,000 miles, per ½ oz.	6c	10c
Drop letters	1c	
Unsealed circulars		
1 oz. or less up to 500 miles	1c	
Over 500 miles to 1,500 miles	2c	
Over 1,500 miles to 2,500 miles	3c	
Over 2,500 miles to 3,500 miles	4c	
Over 3,500 miles	5c	
1852, September 30		
Unsealed circulars		
3 oz. or less anywhere in U.S.	1c	
Each additional ounce	1c	
(Double charge if collect)		
1855, April 1		
Prepayment made compulsory		
Not over 3,000 miles, per ½ oz.	3c	
Over 3,000 miles, per ½ oz.	10c	
Drop letters	1c	
1863, July 1		
Distance differential eliminated		
All parts of United States, per ½ oz.	3c	

Effective Date	Prepaid
1883, October 1	
Letter rate reduced one-third	
All parts of United States, per ½ oz.	2c
1885, July 1	
Weight increased to 1 oz.	
All parts of United States, per 1 oz.	2c
1896, October 1	
Rural Free Delivery started	
1917, November 2	
War emergency	
All parts of United States, per 1 oz.	3c
1919, July 1	
Restoration of pre-war rate	
All parts of United States, per 1 oz.	2c
1932, July 6	
Rise due to depression	
All parts of United States, per 1 oz.	3c
1958, August 1	
All parts of United States, per 1 oz.	4c
1963, January 7	
All parts of United States, per 1 oz.	5c
1968, January 7	
All parts of United States, per 1 oz.	6c
1971, May 16	
All parts of United States, per 1 oz.	8c
1974, March 2	
All parts of United States, per 1 oz.	10c
1975, December 31	
All parts of United States, 1st oz.	13c
1978, May 29	
All parts of United States, 1st oz.	15c
1981, March 22	
All parts of United States, 1st oz.	18c
1981, November 1	
All parts of United States, 1st oz.	20c
1985, February 17	
All parts of United States, 1st oz.	22c

ACKNOWLEDGEMENTS

The editors extend sincere thanks to all those who have helped, by giving their time and knowledge, in the annual task of revising *The Scott Specialized Catalogue* in line with the goal of a complete, accurate United States philatelic handbook.

No lists of aides can be complete, and several helpers prefer anonymity. The following individuals are chiefly those who have undertaken to assist on one or more specific areas.

Arthur L.F. Askins
Philip T. Bansner
Brian M. Bleckwenn
John R. Boker Jr.
Vernon E. Bressler
George W. Brett
Robert Dumaine
Falk Finkelburg
Morton P. Goldfarb
Brian M. Green

Calvet M. Hahn
John Hain
John B. Head
Bruce L. Hecht
Robert R. Hegland
Cordell Hoffer
Eric Jackson
Mrs. Alvin R. Kantor
Warren Kaplan

Lewis S. Kaufman
Thomas C. Kingsley
Victor B. Krievins
Joseph E. Landry Jr.
Steve Levine
Dana Linett
James T. McCusker
Walter J. Mader III
Robert L. Markovits

Adam Perkal
Stanley M. Piller
Gilbert N. Plass
Henrik Pollak
Peter A. Robertson
William N. Salomon
Henry B. Scheuer
Jacques C. Schiff, Jr.
Richard Schwartz

Rick Schwartz
Robert A. Siegel
Edward Siskin
Sherwood Springer
Samuel S. Smith
Berb Taub
Jerome S. Wagshal
William R. Weiss, Jr.
Al Zimmerman.

Among the organizations that have helped are:

American Air Mail Society
102 Arbor Road, Cinnaminson, NJ 08077

American First Day Cover Society
1611 Corrall Drive, Houston, TX 77090

American Philatelic Society
P.O. Box 8000, State College, PA 16803

American Revenue Association
Bruce Miller, Sec'y, 701 S. First Ave., Suite 332, Arcadia, CA 91006

Bureau Issues Association
P.O. Box 1047, Belleville, IL 62223

Canal Zone Study Group
Alfred R. Bew, Sec'y., 29 S. South Carolina Ave., Atlantic City, NJ 08401

Confederate Stamp Alliance
Brian M. Green, P.O. Box 1816, Kernersville, NC 27285

Essay-Proof Society
David E. McGuire, RD #4, Colonial Dr., Katonah, NY 10536

Philatelic Foundation
21 East 40th Street, New York, NY 10016

Precancel Stamp Society
12045 Hickory Hills Court, Oakton, VA 22124

Ryukyu Philatelic Specialist Society, Ltd.
Dr. A. L-F, Askins, P.O. Box 4092, Berkeley, CA 94704

United Postal Stationery Society
P.O. Box 48, Redlands, CA 92373

U.S. Philatelic Classics Society
Robert R. Hegland, P.O. Box 1011, Falls Church, VA 22041

U.S. Possessions Philatelic Society
Kenneth M. Koller, Sec'y., 217 Tyler Ave., Cuyahoga Falls, OH 44221

The editors also thank the United States Postal Service and the Bureau of Engraving and Printing.

POSTMASTERS GENERAL OF THE UNITED STATES

1775 Benjamin Franklin, July 26.
1776 Richard Bache, Nov. 7.
1782 Ebenezer Hazard, Jan. 28.
1789 Samuel Osgood, Sept. 26.
1791 Timothy Pickering, Aug. 12.
1795 Joseph Habersham, Feb. 25.
1801 Gideon Granger, Nov. 28.
1814 Return J. Meigs, Jr., Apr. 11.
1823 John McLean, July 1.
1829 William T. Barry, Apr. 6.
1835 Amos Kendall, May 1.
1840 John M. Niles, May 26.
1841 Francis Granger, Mar. 8.
1841 Charles A. Wickliffe, Oct. 13.
1845 Cave Johnson, Mar. 7.
1849 Jacob Collamer, Mar. 8.
1850 Nathan K. Hall, July 23.
1852 Samuel D. Hubbard, Sept. 14.
1853 James Campbell, Mar. 8.
1857 Aaron V. Brown, Mar. 7.
1859 Joseph Holt, Mar. 14.
1861 Horatio King, Feb. 12.
1861 Montgomery Blair, Mar. 9.
1864 William Dennison, Oct. 1.

1866 Alexander W. Randall, July 25.
1869 John A. J. Creswell, Mar. 6.
1874 Jas. W. Marshall, July 7.
1874 Marshall Jewell, Sept. 1.
1876 James N. Tyner, July 13.
1877 David McK. Key, Mar. 13.
1880 Horace Maynard, Aug. 25.
1881 Thomas L. James, Mar. 8.
1882 Timothy O. Howe, Jan. 5.
1883 Walter Q. Gresham, Apr. 11.
1884 Frank Hatton, Oct. 14.
1885 Wm. F. Vilas, Mar. 7.
1888 Don M. Dickinson, Jan. 17.
1889 John Wanamaker, Mar. 6.
1893 Wilson S. Bissell, Mar. 7.
1895 William L. Wilson, Apr. 4.
1897 James A. Gary, Mar. 6.
1898 Charles Emory Smith, Apr. 22.
1902 Henry C. Payne, Jan. 15.
1904 Robert J. Wynne, Oct. 10.
1905 Geo. B. Cortelyou, Mar. 7.
1907 Geo. von L. Meyer, Mar. 4.
1909 Frank H. Hitchcock, Mar. 6.
1913 Albert S. Burleson, Mar. 5.

1921 Will H. Hays, Mar. 5.
1922 Hubert Work, Mar. 4.
1923 Harry S. New, Mar. 4.
1929 Walter F. Brown, Mar. 6.
1933 James A. Farley, Mar. 4.
1940 Frank C. Walker, Sept. 11.
1945 Robert E. Hannegan, July 1.
1947 Jesse M. Donaldson, Dec. 16.
1953 Arthur E. Summerfield, Jan. 21.
1961 J. Edward Day, Jan. 21.
1963 John A. Gronouski, Sept. 30.
1965 Lawrence F. O'Brien, Nov. 3.
1968 W. Marvin Watson, Apr. 26.
1969 Winton M. Blount, Jan. 22.

U.S. POSTAL SERVICE
1971 Elmer T. Klassen, Dec. 7.
1975 Benjamin Bailar, Feb. 15.
1978 William F. Bolger, Mar. 1.
1985 Paul N. Carlin, Jan. 1.
1986 Albert V. Casey, Jan. 6.
1986 Preston R. Tisch, Aug. 17.
1988 Anthony M. Frank, Mar. 1.

IDENTIFIER OF DEFINITIVE ISSUES
Arranged by Type Numbers

ISSUES OF 1847-75

A1 Benjamin Franklin   **Reproduction**

5c On the originals the left side of the white shirt frill touches the oval on a level with the top of the "F" of "Five". On the reproductions it touches the oval about on a level with the top of the figure "5".

A2 George Washington   **Reproduction**

Original

Reproduction

10c On the originals line of coat (A) points to "T" of TEN and (B) it points between "T" and "S" of CENTS.

On the reproductions line of coat (A) points to right tip of "X" and line of coat (B) points to center of "S."

On the reproductions the eyes have a sleepy look, the line of the mouth is straighter, and in the curl of the hair near the left cheek is a strong black dot, while the originals have only a faint one.

Imperforate and Unwatermarked

Design Number		Scott Number
A1	5c red brown	1
A1	5c dark brown	1a
A1	5c orange brown	1b
A1	5c red orange	1c
A1	5c blue (reproduction)	948a
A3	5c red brown (reproduction)	3
A2	10c black	2
A2	10c brown orange (reproduction)	948b
A4	10c black (reproduction)	4

ISSUE OF 1851-75

A5 Franklin

A5

Type I Has a curved line outside the labels with "U. S. Postage" and "One Cent". The scrolls below the lower label are turned under, forming little balls. The scrolls and outer line at top are complete.

A6

Type Ia Same as I at bottom but top ornaments and outer line at top are partly cut away.

Type Ib Same as I but balls below the bottom label are not so clear. The plume-like scrolls at bottom are not complete.

A7

Type II The little balls of the bottom scrolls and the bottoms of the lower plume ornaments are missing. The side ornaments are complete.

A8

Type III The top and bottom curved lines outside the labels are broken in the middle. The side ornaments are complete.

Type IIIa Similar to III with the outer line broken at top or bottom but not both. Type IIIa from Plate IV generally shows signs of plate erasure between the horizontal rows. Those from Plate IE show only a slight break in the line at top or bottom.

A9 Type IV

A20 Type V

Type IV Similar to II, but with the curved lines outside the labels recut at top or bottom or both.

The seven types listed account for most of the varieties of recutting.

Type V Similar to type III of 1851-56 but with side ornaments partly cut away.

A5	1c blue, type I, imperf.	5
A5	1c blue, type Ib, imperf.	5A
A5	1c blue, type I, perf. 15	18
A5	1c bright blue, perf. 12	40
A6	1c blue, type Ia, imperf.	6
A6	1c blue, type Ia, perf. 15	19
A7	1c blue, type II, imperf.	7
A7	1c blue, type II, perf. 15	20
A8	1c blue, type III, imperf.	8
A8	1c blue, type IIIa, imperf.	8A
A8	1c blue, type III, perf. 15	21
A8	1c blue, type IIIa, perf. 15	22
A9	1c blue, type IV, imperf.	9
A9	1c blue, type IV, perf. 15	23
A20	1c blue, type V, perf. 15	24
A20	1c blue, type V, perf. 15, laid paper	24b

A10 Washington, Type I

A10 Type I *There is an outer frame line at top and bottom.*

A21 Type II *The outer line has been removed at top and bottom.*

Type IIa The side frame lines extend only to the top and bottom of the stamp design. All type IIa stamps are from plates X and XI (each exists in 3 states), and these plates produced only type IIa. The side frame lines were recut individually for each stamp, thus being broken between the stamps vertically.

A11 Jefferson, Type I *There are projections on all four sides.*

A22 Type II *The projections at top and bottom are partly cut away. Several minor types could be made according to the extent of cutting of the projections.*

Nos. 40-47 are reprints produced by the Continental Bank Note Co. for the Centennial Exposition of 1876. The stamps are on white paper without gum, perf. 12. They were not good for postal use. They also exist imperforate.

A10	3c orange brown, type I, imperf.	10
A10	3c dull red, type I, imperf.	11
A10	3c claret, type I, imperf.	11a
A10	3c rose, type I, perf. 15	25
A10	3c scarlet, perf. 12.	41
A21	3c dull red, type II, perf. 15	26
A21	3c dull red, type IIa, perf. 15	26a
A11	5c red brown, type I, imperf.	12
A11	5c brick red, type I, perf. 15	27
A11	5c red brown, type I, perf. 15	28
A11	5c Indian red, type I, perf. 15	28A
A11	5c brown, type I, perf. 15	29
A22	5c orange brown, type II, perf. 15	30
A22	5c brown, type II, perf. 15	30A
A22	5c orange brown, type II, perf. 12	42

A12 Washington, Type I   **A16** Washington

A12 Type I *The shells at the lower corners are practically complete. The outer line below the label is very nearly complete. The outer lines are broken above the middle of the top label and the "X" in each upper corner.*

A13 Type II *The design is complete at the top. The outer line at the bottom is broken in the middle. The shells are partly cut away.*

A14 Type III *The outer lines are broken above the top label and the "X" numerals. The outer line at the bottom and the shells are partly cut away as in Type II.*

A15 Type IV *The outer lines have been recut at top or bottom or both.*

A23 Type V *The side ornaments are slightly cut away. Usually only one pearl remains at each end of the lower label but some copies show two or three pearls at the right side. At the bottom, the outer line is complete and the shells nearly so. The outer lines at top are complete except over the right "X".*

A12	10c green, type I, imperf.	13
A12	10c green, type I, perf. 15	31
A12	10c blue green, perf. 12.	43
A13	10c green, type II, imperf.	14
A13	10c green, type II, perf. 15	32
A14	10c green, type III, imperf.	15
A14	10c green, type III, perf. 15	33
A15	10c green, type IV, imperf.	16
A15	10c green, type IV, perf. 15	34
A23	10c green, type V, perf. 15	35
A16	12c black, imperf.	17
A16	12c black, plate I, perf. 15	36

A16	12c black, plate III	36b
A16	12c greenish black, perf. 12	44

A17 Washington

A18 Franklin   **A19** Washington

A17	24c gray lilac, perf. 15	37
A17	24c gray, perf. 15	37a
A17	24c red lilac, perf. 15	37b
A17	24c gray lilac, imperf.	37c
A17	24c blackish violet, perf. 12	45
A18	30c orange, perf. 15	38
A18	30c orange, imperf.	38a
A18	30c yellow orange, perf. 12	46
A19	90c blue, perf. 15	39
A19	90c blue, imperf.	39a
A19	90c deep blue, perf. 12	47

ISSUES OF 1861-75

This series is divided into three groups known as "First Designs," "Second Designs" and "Grills." The first issue is printed on thin, semi-transparent paper; the paper used for the second and grilled issues is usually thicker and opaque.

A24a

A24 Franklin

A24 *A dash has been added under the tip of the ornament at right of the numeral in upper left corner.*

A24a	1c indigo, thin paper, perf. 12	55
A24	1c blue, perf. 12	63
A24	1c ultramarine, perf. 12	63a
A24	1c dark blue, perf. 12	63b
A24	1c blue, same, laid paper	63c
A24	1c blue, grill 11x14 mm	85A
A24	1c blue, grill 11x13 mm	86
A24	1c dull blue, same	86a
A24	1c blue, grill 9x13 mm	92
A24	1c pale blue, same.	92a
A24	1c blue, no grill, hard white paper	102

A25a

A25 Washington

A25 *Ornaments at corners have been enlarged and end in a small ball.*

A25a	3c brown rose, thin paper, see illustration A25a	56
A25	3c pink, see illustration A25	64
A25	3c pigeon blood pink, no grill, perf. 12	64a
A25	3c rose pink, same	64b
A25	3c lake, same	66
A25	3c scarlet, same	74
A25	3c rose, same	65
A25	3c rose, grilled all over	79
A25	3c rose, grill 18x15 mm	82
A25	3c rose, grill 13x16 mm	83
A25	3c rose, grill 12x14 mm	85
A25	3c rose, grill 11x14 mm	85C
A25	3c rose, grill 11x13 mm	88
A25	3c lake red, same	88a
A25	3c red, grill 9x13 mm	94
A25	3c rose, same	94a
A25	3c brown red, no grill, hard white paper	104

A26a

A26 Jefferson

A26 *A leaflet has been added to the foliated ornaments at each corner.*

A26a	5c brown, thin paper, see illustration A26a	57
A26	5c buff, see illustration A26	67
A26	5c brown yellow, no grill	67a
A26	5c olive yellow, no grill	67b

A26	5c red brown, no grill	75
A26	5c brown, no grill	76
A26	5c dark brown, no grill	76a
A26	5c brown, laid paper	76b
A26	5c brown, grilled all over	80
A26	5c dark brown, same	80a
A26	5c brown, grill 9x13 mm	95
A26	5c black brown, same	95a
A26	5c brown, no grill, hard white paper	105

A27a

A27 Washington

A27 *A heavy curved line has been cut below the stars and an outer line added to the ornaments above them.*

A27a	10c dark green, thin paper, see illustration A27a	58
A27a	Same used	62B
A27	10c yellow green, see illustration A27	68
A27	10c dark green, same	68a
A27	10c green, grill 11x14 mm	85D
A27	10c green, grill 11x13 mm	89
A27	10c yellow green, grill 9x13 mm	96
A27	10c dark green, same	96a
A27	10c green, no grill, hard white paper	106

A28a Washington   **A28** Washington

A28a	12c black, thin paper, see illustration A28a	59
A28	12c black, see illustration A28	69
A28	12c black, grill 11x14 mm	85E
A28	12c black, grill 11x13 mm	90
A28	12c black, grill 9x13 mm	97
A28	12c black, hard white paper, no grill	107

A29 Washington   **A30** Franklin

A29	24c dark violet, thin paper, no grill	60
A29	24c violet, same	70c
A29	24c grayish lilac, same	70d

A29	24c red lilac, no grill	70
A29	24c brown lilac, no grill	70a
A29	24c steel blue, no grill	70b
A29	24c lilac, no grill	78
A29	24c grayish lilac, no grill	78a
A29	24c gray, no grill	78b
A29	24c blackish violet, no grill	78c
A29	24c gray lilac, grill 9x13 mm	99
A29	24c deep violet, hard white paper, no grill	109
A30	30c red orange, thin paper, no grill	61
A30	30c orange, no grill	71
A30	30c orange, grilled all over	81
A30	30c orange, grill 9x13 mm	100
A30	30c brownish orange, hard white paper, no grill	110

A31a

A31 Washington

A31 *Parallel lines from an angle above the ribbon with "U.S. Postage"; between these lines a row of dashes has been added and a point of color to the apex of the lower line.*

A31a	90c dull blue, thin paper, see illustration A31a	62
A31a	90c dull blue, imperf., pair	62a
A31	90c blue, see illustration A31	72
A31	90c pale blue, same	72a
A31	90c dark blue, same	72b
A31	90c blue, grill 9x13 mm	101
A31	90c blue, hard white paper, no grill	111

ISSUES OF 1861-75

A32 Jackson   **A33** Lincoln

Perf. 12, Unwmkd.

A32	2c black, no grill	73
A32	2c black, laid paper	73d
A32	2c black, grill 12x14 mm	84
A32	2c black, grill 11x14 mm	85B
A32	2c black, grill 11x13 mm	87
A32	2c black, grill 9x13 mm	93
A32	2c black, hard white paper, no grill	103
A33	15c black, no grill	77
A33	15c black, grill 11x14 mm	85F
A33	15c black, grill 11x13 mm	91
A33	15c black, grill 9x13 mm	98
A33	15c black, hard white paper, no grill	108

ISSUES OF 1869-80

A34 Franklin

A34	1c buff, grill 9½x9 mm	112
A34	1c buff, no grill	112b
A34	1c buff, no grill, hard white paper	123
A34	1c buff, no grill, soft porous paper	133
A34	1c brown orange, same without gum	133a

A35 Pony Express   **A36** Baldwin 4-4-0 Locomotive, c. 1857

A35	2c brown, grill 9½x9 mm	113
A35	2c brown, no grill	113b
A35	2c brown, no grill, hard white paper	124
A36	3c ultramarine, grill 9½x9 mm	114
A36	3c ultramarine, no grill	114a
A36	3c blue, no grill, hard white paper	125

A37 Washington   **A38** Shield and Eagle

A39 S. S. Adriatic

A37	6c ultramarine, grill 9½x9 mm	115
A37	6c blue, no grill, hard white paper	126
A38	10c yellow, grill 9½x9 mm	116
A38	10c yellow, no grill, hard white paper	127
A39	12c green, grill 9½x9 mm	117
A39	12c green, no grill, hard white paper	128

A40 Landing of Columbus

A40 Type I *Picture unframed*

A40a Type II *Picture framed*

Type III same as Type I but without the fringe of brown shading lines around central vignette.

A40	15c brown & blue, type I, grill 9½x9 mm	118
A40	15c brown & blue, type I, no grill	118a
A40	15c brown & blue, type III, no grill, hard white paper	129
A40a	15c brown & blue, type II, grill 9½x9 mm	119

A41 The Declaration of Independence

A42 Shield, Eagle   **A43** Lincoln
and Flags

A41	24c green & violet, grill 9½x9 mm	120
A41	24c green & violet, no grill	120a
A41	24c green & violet, no grill, hard white paper	130
A42	30c blue & carmine, grill 9½x9 mm	121
A42	30c blue & carmine, no grill	121a
A42	30c blue & carmine, no grill, hard white paper	131
A43	90c carmine & black, grill 9½x9 mm	122
A43	90c carmine & black, no grill	122a
A43	90c carmine & black, no grill, hard white paper	132

ISSUES OF 1870-88

The secret mark shown in the detail of A45a is seldom found on the actual stamps. Stamps Nos. 146 and 157 are best identified by color which is red brown for No. 146 and brown for No. 157.

Note I: Special printings of 1880-83 — All denominations of this series were printed on special order from the Post Office Department during the period the stamps were current. The paper being the same as used on the then current issue, the special printings are extremely difficult to identify. The 2c brown, 7c scarlet vermilion, 12c blackish purple and 24c dark violet are easily distinguished by the soft porous paper as these denominations were never previously printed on soft paper. The other denominations can be distinguished by shades only, those of the special printings being slightly deeper and richer than the regular issue. The special printings except No. 211B were issued without gum. The only certain way to identify them is by comparison with stamps previously established as special printings.

A44 Franklin

A44

A44a With secret mark *In the pearl at the left of the numeral "1" there is a small dash.*

A44b Re-engraved *The vertical lines in the upper part of the stamp have been so deepened that the background often appears to be solid. Lines of shading have been added to the upper arabesques.*

A44	1c ultramarine, with grill	134
A44	1c ultramarine, no grill	145
A44a	1c ultramarine, white wove paper	156
A44a	1c ultramarine, with grill	156e
A44a	1c ultramarine, hard white paper, without gum	167
A44a	1c dark ultra, soft porous paper	182
A44a	1c dark ultra, soft porous paper, without gum (See note I)	192
A44b	1c gray blue	206

A45 Jackson

A45

45a *Under the scroll at the left of "U.S." there is a small diagonal line.*

A45	2c red brown, with grill	135
A45	2c red brown, no grill	146
A45a	2c brown, white wove paper	157
A45a	2c brown, with grill	157c
A45a	2c dark brown, hard white paper, without gum	168
A45a	2c black brown, soft porous paper, without gum	193
A45a	2c vermilion, yellowish paper	178
A45a	2c vermilion, imperf.	178a
A45a	2c vermilion, with grill	178c
A45a	2c vermilion, soft porous paper	183
A45a	2c carmine vermilion, hard white paper, without gum	180
A45a	2c scarlet vermilion, soft porous paper (See note I)	203

A46 Washington

A46

A46a With secret mark *The under part of the tail of the left ribbon is heavily shaded.*

A46b Re-engraved *The shading at the sides of the central oval appears only about one half the previous width. A short horizontal dash has been cut about 1 mm. below the "TS" of "CENTS".*

A47 Lincoln   A47

A47a With secret mark *The first four vertical lines of the shading in the lower part of the left ribbon have been strengthened.*

A47b Re-engraved. *6c on the original stamps four vertical lines can be counted from the edge of the panel to the outside of the stamp. On the re-engraved stamps there are but three lines in the same place.*

A48 Edwin McMasters   A49 Thomas Jefferson
Stanton

A48   **A48a** With secret mark *Two small semi-circles are drawn around the ends of the lines which outline the ball in the lower right hand corner.*

A49   **A49a** With secret mark *A small semi-circle in the scroll at the right end of the upper label.*

A49b Re-engraved *On the original stamps there are five vertical lines between the left side of the oval and the edge of the shield. There are only four lines on the re-engraved stamps. In the lower part of the re-engraved stamps the horizontal lines of the background have been strengthened.*

A50 Henry Clay   A50

A50a With secret mark *The balls of the figure "2" are crescent shaped.*

A51 Webster   A51

A51a With secret mark *In the lower part of the triangle in the upper left corner two lines have been made heavier forming a "V". This mark can be found on some of the Continental and American (1879) printings, but not all stamps show it.*

A52 General Winfield Scott

A53 Hamilton   A54 Perry

Secret marks were added to the dies of the 24c, 30c and 90c but new plates were not made from them. The various printings of these stamps can be distinguished only by the shades and paper.

A53	30c gray black, white wove paper, no grill	165
A53	30c greenish black, white wove paper	165a
A53	30c greenish black, with grill	165c
A53	30c greenish black, hard white paper, without gum	176
A53	30c greenish black, soft porous paper, without gum (See note I)	201
A53	30c orange brown	217
A54	90c carmine, with grill	144
A54	90c carmine, no grill	155
A54	90c carmine, soft porous paper	191
A54	90c rose carmine, white wove paper	166
A54	90c violet carmine, hard white paper, without gum	177
A54	90c dull carmine, soft porous paper, without gum (See note I)	202
A54	90c purple	218

ISSUES OF 1875-88

A55 Taylor

A56 Garfield

Perf. 12, Unwmkd.

A55	5c blue, yellowish wove paper, no grill	179
A55	5c blue, with grill	179c
A55	5c bright blue, hard, white wove paper, without gum	181
A55	5c blue, soft porous paper	185
A55	5c deep blue, soft porous paper, without gum (See note I)	204
A56	5c yellow brown	205
A56	5c gray brown, soft porous paper, without gum (See note I)	205C
A56	5c indigo	216

A57 Washington

A58 Jackson

A57	2c red brown	210
A57	2c pale red brown, soft porous paper, with gum (See note I)	211B
A57	2c green	213
A58	4c blue green	211
A58	4c deep blue green, soft porous paper, without gum (See note I)	211D
A58	4c carmine	215

A59 Franklin

A59	1c ultramarine	212

ISSUES OF 1890-93

A60 Franklin

A61 Washington

A62 Jackson

A63 Lincoln

A64 Grant

A66 William T. Sherman

A65 Garfield

A67 Daniel Webster

A68 Henry Clay

A69 Jefferson

A70 Perry

A60	1c dull blue	219
A61	2c lake	219D
A61	2c carmine	220
A62	3c purple	221
A63	4c dark brown	222
A64	5c chocolate	223
A65	6c brown red	224
A66	8c lilac	225
A67	10c green	226
A68	15c indigo	227
A69	30c black	228
A70	90c orange	229

ISSUES OF 1894 TO 1899

This series, the first to be printed by the Bureau of Engraving and Printing, closely resembles the 1890 series but is identified by the triangles which have been added to the upper corners of the designs.

The Catalogue divides this group into three separate series, the first of which was issued in 1894 and

is unwatermarked. In 1895 the paper used was watermarked with the double line letters USPS (United States Postal Service). The stamps show one complete letter of the watermark or parts of two or more letters.

This watermark appears on all United States stamps issued from 1895 until 1910.

In 1898 the colors of some of the denominations were changed, which created the third series noted in the Catalogue.

Other than the watermark, or lack of it, there are three types of the corner triangles used on the 2 cent stamps and two variations of designs are noted on the 10 cent and $1 denomination. In the following list all of these variations are illustrated and described immediately preceding the denominations on which they appear.

Wmkd. USPS (191) Horizontally

or USPS Vertically

(Actual size of letter)

A87 Franklin

A88 Washington

A89 Jackson

A90 Lincoln

A91 Grant

A92 Garfield

A93 Sherman

A94 Webster

A95 Clay

A96 Jefferson

A97 Perry

 A98 James Madison

 A99 John Marshall

A87	1c ultramarine, unwmkd.	246
A87	1c blue, unwmkd.	247
A87	1c blue, wmkd.	264
A87	1c deep green, wmkd.	279
A87	1c on 1c yellow green, "CUBA"	Cuba 221
A87	1c deep green, "GUAM"	Guam 1
A87	1c yellow green, "PHILIPPINES"	Phil. 213
A87	1c yellow green, "PORTO RICO"	P.R. 210
A87	1c yellow green, "PUERTO RICO"	P.R. 215

Type I (Triangle I) *The horizontal lines of the ground work run across the triangle and are of the same thickness within it as without.*

Type II (Triangle II) *The horizontal lines cross the triangle but are thinner within it than without.*

Type III (Triangle III) *The horizontal lines do not cross the double lines of the triangle. The lines within the triangle are thin, as in Type II. Two varieties of Type III are known, but the variations are minor.*

A88	2c pink, type I, unwmkd.	248
A88	2c carmine lake, type I, unwmkd.	249
A88	2c carmine, type I, unwmkd.	250
A88	2c carmine, type I, wmkd. USPS	265
A88	2c carmine, type II, unwmkd.	251
A88	2c carmine, type II, wmkd.	266
A88	2c carmine, type III, unwmkd.	252
A88	2c carmine, type III, wmkd.	267
A88	2c red, type III, wmkd.	279B
A88	2c rose carmine, type III, wmkd.	279c
A88	2c orange red, type III, wmkd.	279d
A88	2c booklet pane of 6, wmkd., single stamps with 1 or 2 straight edges	279e

A88	2c on 2c carmine, type III "CUBA"	Cuba 222
A88	2½c on 2c red, type III, "CUBA"	Cuba 223
A88	2c carmine, type III, "GUAM"	Guam 2
A88	2c orange red, type III, "PHILIPPINES"	Phil. 214
A88	2c carmine, type III, "PHILIPPINES"	Phil. 214a
A88	Same, booklet pane of 6	Phil. 214b
A88	2c carmine, type III, "PORTO RICO"	P.R. 211
A88	Same, "PUERTO RICO"	P.R. 216
A89	3c purple, unwmkd.	253
A89	3c purple, wmkd.	268
A89	3c on 3c purple, "CUBA"	Cuba 224
A89	3c purple, "GUAM"	Guam 3
A89	3c purple "PHILIPPINES"	Phil. 215
A90	4c dark brown, unwmkd.	254
A90	4c dark brown, wmkd.	269
A90	4c rose brown, wmkd.	280
A90	4c lilac brown, wmkd.	280a
A90	4c orange brown, wmkd.	280b
A90	4c lilac brown, "GUAM"	Guam 4
A90	4c orange brown, "PHILIPPINES"	Phil. 220
A91	5c chocolate, unwmkd.	255
A91	5c chocolate, wmkd.	270
A91	5c dark blue, wmkd.	281
A91	5c on 5c blue, "CUBA"	Cuba 225
A91	5c blue, "GUAM"	Guam 5
A91	5c blue, "PHILIPPINES"	Phil. 216
A91	5c blue, "PORTO RICO"	P.R. 212
A92	6c dull brown, unwmkd.	256
A92	6c dull brown, wmkd. USPS	271
A92	6c dull brown, wmkd. USIR	271a
A92	6c lake, wmkd. USPS	282
A92	6c purplish lake, wmkd.	282a
A92	6c lake, "GUAM"	Guam 6
A92	6c lake, "PHILIPPINES"	Phil. 221
A93	8c violet brown, unwmkd.	257
A93	8c violet brown, wmkd. USPS	272
A93	8c violet brown, wmkd. USIR	272a
A93	8c violet brown, "GUAM"	Guam 7
A93	8c violet brown, "PHILIPPINES"	Phil. 222
A93	8c violet brown, "PORTO RICO"	P.R. 213

Type I *The tips of the foliate ornaments do not impinge on the white curved line below "ten cents."*

Type II *The tips of the ornaments break the curved line below the "e" of "ten" and the "t" of "cents."*

A94	10c dark green, unwmkd.	258
A94	10c dark green, wmkd.	273
A94	10c brown, type I, wmkd.	282C
A94	10c orange brown, type II, wmkd.	283
A94	10c on 10c brown, type I, "CUBA"	Cuba 226
A94	Same, type II, "CUBA"	Cuba 226A
A94	10c brown, type I, "GUAM"	Guam 8
A94	10c brown, type II, "GUAM"	Guam 9
A94	10c brown, type I, "PHILIPPINES"	Phil. 217
A94	10c orange brown, type II, "PHILIPPINES"	Phil. 217A
A94	10c brown, type I, "PORTO RICO"	P.R. 214
A95	15c dark blue, unwmkd.	259
A95	15c dark blue, wmkd.	274

A95	15c olive green, wmkd.	284
A95	15c olive green, "GUAM"	Guam 10
A95	15c olive green, "PHILIPPINES"	Phil. 218
A95	15c light olive green, "PHILIPPINES"	Phil. 218a
A96	50c orange, unwmkd.	260
A96	50c orange, wmkd.	275
A96	50c orange, "GUAM"	Guam 11
A96	50c orange, "PHILIPPINES"	Phil. 219

A97 Type I *The circles enclosing "$1" are broken where they meet the curved line below "One Dollar."*

A97 Type II *The circles are complete.*

A97	$1 black, type I, unwmkd.	261
A97	$1 black, type I, wmkd.	276
A97	$1 black, type II, unwmkd.	261A
A97	$1 black, type II, wmkd.	276A
A97	$1 black, type I, "GUAM"	Guam 12
A97	$1 black, type II, "GUAM"	Guam 13
A97	$1 black, type I, "PHILIPPINES"	Phil. 223
A98	$2 bright blue, unwmkd.	262
A98	$2 bright blue, wmkd.	277
A98	$2 dark blue, wmkd.	277a
A98	$2 dark blue, "PHILIPPINES"	Phil. 224
A99	$5 dark green, unwmkd.	263
A99	$5 dark green, wmkd.	278
A99	$5 dark green, "PHILIPPINES"	Phil. 225

ISSUES OF 1902-17

 A115 Franklin

 A116 Washington

 A117 Jackson

 A118 Grant

 A119 Lincoln

 A120 Garfield

 A121 Martha Washington

 A122 Daniel Webster

A123 Benjamin Harrison   **A124** Henry Clay

A125 Jefferson   **A126** David G. Farragut

A127 Madison   **A128** Marshall

**Unless otherwise noted all stamps are
Perf. 12 and Wmkd. (191)**

Single stamps from booklet panes show 1 or 2 straight edges.

A115	1c blue green	300
A115	1c booklet pane of 6	300b
A115	1c blue green, imperf.	314
A115	1c blue green, perf. 12 horiz., pair	316
A115	1c blue green, perf. 12 vert., pair	318
A115	1c blue green, "CANAL ZONE PANAMA"	C.Z. 4
A115	1c blue green, "PHILIPPINES"	Phil. 226
A116	2c carmine	301
A116	2c booklet pane of 6	301c
A116	2c carmine, "PHILIPPINES"	Phil. 227
A116	2c carmine, same, booklet pane of 6	Phil. 227a
A117	3c bright violet	302
A117	3c bright violet, "PHILIPPINES"	Phil. 228
A118	4c brown	303
A118	4c brown, imperf.	314A
A118	4c brown, "PHILIPPINES"	Phil. 229
A118	4c orange brown, "PHILIPPINES"	Phil. 229a
A119	5c blue	304
A119	5c blue, imperf.	315
A119	5c blue, perf. 12 horiz. pair	317
A119	5c blue, "CANAL ZONE PANAMA"	C.Z. 6
A119	5c blue, "PHILIPPINES"	Phil. 230
A120	6c claret	305
A120	6c brownish lake, "PHILIPPINES"	Phil. 321
A121	8c violet black	306
A121	8c violet black, "CANAL ZONE PANAMA"	C.Z. 7
A121	8c violet black, "PHILIPPINES"	Phil. 232
A122	10c pale red brown	307
A122	10c pale red brown, "CANAL ZONE PANAMA"	C.Z. 8
A122	10c pale red brown, "PHILIPPINES"	Phil. 233
A122	10c red brown, "PHILIPPINES"	Phil. 233a
A123	13c purple black	308
A123	13c purple black, "PHILIPPINES"	Phil. 234
A124	15c olive green	309
A124	15c olive green, "PHILIPPINES"	Phil. 235
A125	50c orange	310

A125	50c orange, "PHILIPPINES"	Phil. 236
A126	$1 black	311
A126	$1 black, "PHILIPPINES"	Phil. 237
A127	$2 dark blue	312
A127	$2 dark blue, unwmkd., perf. 10	479
A127	$2 dark blue, "PHILIPPINES"	Phil. 238
A128	$5 dark green	313
A128	$5 light green, unwmkd., perf. 10	480
A128	$5 dark green, "PHILIPPINES"	Phil. 239

ISSUES OF 1903

A129 Washington

Die I

Die II

Specialists recognize over a hundred shades of this stamp in various hues of vermilion, red, carmine and lake. The Scott Catalogue lists only the most striking differences.

The Government coil stamp, No. 322 should not be confused with the scarlet vermilion coil of the International Vending Machine Co., which is perforated 12½ to 13.

A129	2c carmine, wmkd.	319
A129	2c lake, die I	319a
A129	2c carmine rose, die I	319b
A129	2c scarlet, die II	319c
A129	2c lake, die II	319f
A129	2c various shades, booklet pane of 6, die I	319g
	Same, die II	319h
A129	2c carmine, die II	319i
A129	2c carmine, imperf.	320
A129	2c lake, imperf.	320a
A129	2c scarlet, imperf.	320b
A129	2c carmine, perf. 12 horiz.	321
A129	2c carmine, perf. 12 vert.	322
A129	2c carmine, "CANAL ZONE PANAMA"	C.Z. 5
A129	2c scarlet, same	C.Z. 5a
A129	2c carmine, "PHILIPPINES"	Phil. 240
A129	2c carmine, same, booklet pane of 6	Phil. 240a

ISSUES OF 1908-09

This series introduces for the first time the single line watermark USPS. Only a small portion of several letters is often all that can be seen on a single stamp.

A138 Franklin   **A139** Washington

Wmk. 190

A138	1c green, perf. 12, double line wmk.	331
A138	1c green, perf. 12, single line wmk.	374
A138	1c green, perf. 12, bluish paper	357
A138	1c green, imperf., double line wmk.	343
A138	1c green, imperf., single line wmk.	383
A138	1c green, perf. 12 horiz., double line wmk.	348
A138	1c green, perf. 12 horiz., single line wmk.	385
A138	1c green, perf. 12 vert., double line wmk.	352
A138	1c green, perf. 12 vert., single line wmk.	387
A138	1c green, perf. 8½ horiz., single line wmk.	390
A138	1c green, perf. 8½ vert., single line wmk.	392
A139	2c carmine, perf. 12, double line wmk.	332
A139	2c carmine, perf. 12, single line wmk.	375
A139	2c carmine, perf. 12, bluish paper	358
A139	2c carmine, perf. 11, double line wmk.	519
A139	2c carmine, imperf., double line wmk.	344
A139	2c carmine, imperf., single line wmk.	384
A139	2c carmine, perf. 12 horiz., double line wmk.	349
A139	2c carmine, perf. 12 horiz., single line wmk.	386
A139	2c carmine, perf. 12 vert., double line wmk.	353
A139	2c carmine, perf. 12 vert., single line wmk.	388
A139	2c carmine, perf. 8½ horiz. single line wmk.	391
A139	2c carmine, perf. 8½ vert., single line wmk.	393

Single stamps from booklet panes show
1 or 2 straight edges.

A138	1c green, booklet pane of 6.	331a
A138	1c green, booklet pane of 6.	374a
A139	2c carmine, booklet pane of 6	332a
A139	2c carmine, booklet pane of 6	375a

ISSUES OF 1908-21

FLAT BED AND ROTARY PRESS STAMPS

The Rotary Press Stamps are printed from plates that are curved to fit around a cylinder. This curvature produces stamps that are slightly larger, either horizontally or vertically, than those printed from flat plates. Designs of stamps from flat plates measure about 18½-19 mm. wide by 22 mm. high. When the impressions are placed sidewise on the curved plates the designs are 19½-20 mm. wide; when they are placed vertically the designs are 22½ to 23 mm. high. A line of color (not a guide line) shows where the curved plates meet or join on the press.

Rotary Press Coil Stamps were printed from plates of 170 subjects for stamps coiled sidewise, and from plates of 150 subjects for stamps coiled endwise.

A140 Washington

TYPES OF TWO CENTS

TYPE I

TYPE Ia

Type Ia *The design characteristics are similar to type I except that all of the lines of the design are stronger.*

The toga button, toga rope and rope shading lines are heavy.

The latter characteristics are those of type II, which, however, occur only on impressions from rotary plates.

Used only on flat plates 10208 and 10209.

TYPE II

Type II *Shading lines in ribbons as on type I.*

The toga button, rope and rope shading lines are heavy.

The shading lines of the face at the lock of hair ends in a strong vertical curved line.

Used on rotary press printings only.

TYPE III

Type III *Two lines of shading in the curves of the ribbons.*

Other characteristics similar to type II.

Used on rotary press printings only.

TYPE IV

Type IV *Top line of the toga rope is broken.*

The shading lines in the toga button are so arranged that the curving of the first and last form "DID".

The line of color in the left "2" is very thin and usually broken. Used on offset printings only.

TYPE V

Type V *Top line of the toga is complete.*

There are five vertical shading lines in the toga button.

The line of color is the left "2" is very thin and usually broken.

The shading dots on the nose are as shown on the diagram.

Used on offset printings only.

TYPE Va

Type Va *Characteristics are the same as type V except in the shading dots of the nose. The third row*

of dots from the bottom has four dots instead of six. The overall height is ⅓ mm. shorter than type V.

Used on offset printings only.

TYPE VI

Type VI *General characteristics the same as type V except that the line of color in the left "2" is very heavy. Used on offset printings only.*

TYPE VII

Type VII *The line of color in the left "2" is invariably continuous, clearly defined and heavier than in type V or Va but not as heavy as type VI.*

An additional vertical row of dots has been added to the upper lip.

Numerous additional dots have been added to the hair on top of the head.

Used on offset printings only.

1c A138 Portrait of Franklin, value in words.
1c A140 Portrait of Washington, value in numerals.
2c A139 Portrait of Washington, value in words.
2c A140 Portrait of Washington, value in numerals.

A140	1c green, perf. 12, single line wmk. . .	**405**
A140	1c green, same, booklet pane of 6 . .	**405b**
A140	1c green, perf. 11, flat plate, unwmkd.	**498**
A140	1c green, same, booklet pane of 6 . . .	**498e**
A140	1c green, same, booklet pane of 30 . .	**498f**
A140	1c green, perf. 11, rotary press measuring 19mm.x22½mm., unwmkd.	**544**
A140	1c green, same, measuring 19½ to 20mmx22mm	**545**
A140	1c gray green, perf. 11, offset, unwmkd.	**525**
A140	1c dark green, same	**525a**
A140	1c gray green, perf. 12½	**536**
A140	1c green, perf. 11x10.	**538**
A140	1c green, perf. 10x11.	**542**
A140	1c green, perf. 10, single line wmk. . .	**424**
A140	1c green, same, perf. 12x10	**424a**
A140	1c green, same, perf. 10x12	**424b**
A140	1c green, same, booklet pane of 6 . .	**424d**
A140	1c green, perf. 10, flat plate, unwmkd.	**462**
A140	1c green, same, booklet pane of 6 . .	**462a**
A140	1c green, perf. 10, rotary press, unwmkd.	**543**
A140	1c green, imperf., single line wmk. . .	**408**
A140	1c green, imperf., unwmkd.	**481**
A140	1c green, imperf., offset	**531**
A140	1c green, perf. 10 horiz., flat plate, single line wmk.	**441**
A140	1c green, same, rotary press	**448**

A140 1c green, perf. 10 horiz., rotary press,
         unwmkd.......................... **486**
A140 1c green, perf. 10 vert., flat plate, single
         line wmk....................... **443**
A140 1c green, same, rotary press........ **452**
A140 1c green, perf. 10 vert., rotary press,
         unwmkd.......................... **490**
A140 1c green, perf. 8½ horiz. single
         line wmk....................... **410**
A140 1c green, perf. 8½ vert., same **412**
A140 2c carmine, perf. 12, type I, single line
         wmk............................. **406**
A140 2c carmine, same, booklet pane of 6 **406a**
A140 2c pale car. red, perf. 11, single line
         wmk., type I.................... **461**
A140 2c rose, perf. 11, flat plate, unwmkd.,
         type I.......................... **499**
A140 2c rose, same, booklet pane of 6 .... **499e**
A140 2c rose, same, booklet pane of 30 ... **499f**
A140 2c deep rose, perf. 11, unwmkd.,
         type Ia......................... **500**
A140 2c carmine rose, perf. 11, rotary press,
         unwmkd., type III............... **546**
A140 2c carmine, perf. 11, offset, unwmkd.,
         type IV **526**
A140 2c carmine, same, type V.......... **527**
A140 2c carmine, same, type Va......... **528**
A140 2c carmine, same, type VI **528A**
A140 2c carmine, same, type VII **528B**
A140 2c carmine rose, perf. 11x10, type II. **539**
A140 2c carmine rose, same, type III **540**
A140 2c rose red, perf. 10, single line wmk.,
         type I.......................... **425**
A140 2c rose red, perf. 10x12.......... **425c**
A140 2c rose red, perf. 12x10, single line
         wmk., type I.................... **425d**
A140 2c rose red, same, perf. 10, booklet
         pane of 6...................... **425e**
A140 2c carmine, perf. 10, unwmkd., type I **463**
A140 2c carmine, same, booklet pane of 6 **463a**
A140 2c carmine, imperf., flat plate, single
         line wmk., type I............... **409**
A140 2c carmine, imperf., rotary press,
         single line wmk., type I **459**
A140 2c carmine, imperf., flat plate,
         unwmkd., type I................. **482**
A140 2c deep rose, same, type Ia **482A**
A140 2c carmine rose, imperf., offset,
         unwmkd., type IV **532**
A140 2c carmine rose, same, type V **533**
A140 2c carmine, same, type Va......... **534**
A140 2c carmine, same, type VI **534A**
A140 2c carmine, same, type VII **534B**
A140 2c carmine rose, perf. 10 horiz., flat
         plate, single line wmk., type I **442**
A140 2c red, same, rotary press.......... **449**
A140 2c carmine, same, type III........ **450**
A140 2c carmine, perf. 10 horiz., rotary
         press unwmkd., type II **487**
A140 2c carmine, same, type III **488**
A140 2c carmine, perf. 10 vert., flat plate,
         single line wmk., type I **444**
A140 2c carmine rose, same, rotary press.. **453**
A140 2c red, same, type II **454**
A140 2c carmine, same, type III **455**
A140 2c carmine, perf. 10 vert., rotary press,
         unwmkd., type II **491**
A140 2c carmine, same, type III **492**
A140 2c carmine, perf. 8½ horiz., type I... **411**
A140 2c carmine, perf. 8½ vert., type I.... **413**
A140 3c deep violet, perf. 12, double line
         wmk., type I.................... **333**
A140 3c deep violet, perf. 12, single line
         wmk., type I.................... **376**
A140 3c deep violet, perf. 12, bluish paper,
         type I.......................... **359**
A140 3c light violet, perf. 11, unwmkd.,
         type I.......................... **501**

A140 3c light violet, same, booklet pane
         of 6 .... **501b**
A140 3c dark violet, perf. 11, unwmkd.,
         type II......................... **502**
A140 3c dark violet, same, booklet pane
         of 6 .... **502b**
A140 3c violet, perf. 11, offset, type III ... **529**
A140 3c purple, same, type IV **530**
A140 3c violet, perf. 11x10, type II...... **541**
A140 3c deep violet, perf. 10, single line
         wmk., type I **426**
A140 3c violet, perf. 10, unwmkd., type I.. **464**
A140 3c deep violet, imperf., double line
         wmk., type I.................... **345**
A140 3c violet, imperf., unwmkd., type I.. **483**

TYPES OF THREE CENTS

Type I *The top line of the toga rope is weak and the rope shading lines are thin. The 5th line from the left is missing. The line between the lips is thin.*

Type II *The top line of the toga rope is strong and the rope shading lines are heavy and complete.*
The line between the lips is heavy.
Used on both flat plate and rotary press printings.

Type III *The top line of the toga rope is strong but the 5th shading line is missing as in type I.*
Center shading line of the toga button consists of two dashes with a central dot.
The "P" and "O" of "POSTAGE" are separated by a line of color.
The frame line at the bottom of the vignette is complete.
Used on offset printings only.

Type IV *The shading lines of the toga rope are complete.*
The second and fourth shading lines in the toga button are broken in the middle and the third line is continuous with a dot in the center.
The "P" and "O" of "POSTAGE" are joined.
The frame line at the bottom of the vignette is broken.
Used on offset printings only.

A140 3c violet, same, type II **484**
A140 3c violet, imperf., offset, type IV ... **535**
A140 3c deep violet, perf. 12 vert., single
         line wmk., type I **389**
A140 3c violet, perf. 10 vert., flat plate,
         single line wmk., type I **445**
A140 3c violet, perf. 10 vert., rotary press,
         single line wmk., type I **456**
A140 3c violet, perf. 10 vert., rotary press,
         unwmkd., type I................ **493**
A140 3c violet, same, type II **494**
A140 3c violet, perf. 10 horiz., type I **489**
A140 3c deep violet, perf. 8½ vert., type I. **394**
A140 4c orange brown, perf. 12, double line
         wmk............................. **334**
A140 4c orange brown, perf. 12,
         bluish paper **360**
A140 4c brown, perf. 12, single line wmk. . **377**
A140 4c brown, perf. 11, unwmkd........ **503**
A140 4c brown, perf. 10, single line wmk. . **427**
A140 4c orange brown, perf. 10, unwmkd.. **465**
A140 4c orange brown, imperf........... **346**
A140 4c orange brown, perf. 12 horiz. **350**
A140 4c orange brown, perf. 12 vert. **354**
A140 4c brown, perf. 10 vert., flat plate,
         single line wmk. **446**
A140 4c brown, same, rotary press **457**
A140 4c orange brown, perf. 10 vert., rotary
         press, unwmkd. **495**
A140 4c brown, perf. 8½ vert., single line
         wmk............................. **395**
A140 5c blue, perf. 12, double line wmk. .. **335**
A140 5c blue, perf. 12 bluish paper....... **361**
A140 5c blue, perf. 12, single line wmk. ... **378**
A140 5c blue, perf. 11, unwmkd.......... **504**
A140 5c rose (error), same............. **505**
A140 5c carmine (error), perf. 10, unwmkd. **467**
A140 5c blue, perf. 10, single line wmk. ... **428**
A140 5c blue, perf. 12x10 .... **428a**
A140 5c blue, perf. 10, unwmkd.......... **466**
A140 5c blue, imperf................... **347**
A140 5c carmine (error), imperf......... **485**
A140 5c blue, perf. 12 horiz. **351**
A140 5c blue, perf. 12 vert. **355**
A140 5c blue, perf. 10 vert., flat plate,
         single line wmk................. **447**
A140 5c blue, same, rotary press **458**
A140 5c blue, perf. 10 vert., rotary press,
         unwmkd......................... **496**
A140 5c blue, perf. 8½ vert............. **396**
A140 6c red orange, perf. 12, double
         line wmk....................... **336**
A140 6c red orange, perf. 12, bluish paper . **362**

A140	6c red orange, perf. 12, single line wmk.	379
A140	6c red orange, perf. 11, unwmkd.	506
A140	6c red orange, perf. 10, single line wmk.	429
A140	6c red orange, perf. 10, unwmkd.	468
A140	7c black, perf. 12, single line wmk.	407
A140	7c black, perf. 11, unwmkd.	507
A140	7c black, perf. 10, single line wmk.	430
A140	7c black, perf. 10, unwmkd.	469
A140	8c olive green, perf. 12, double line wmk.	337
A140	8c olive green, perf. 12, bluish paper.	363
A140	8c olive green, perf. 12, single line wmk.	380
A140	10c yellow, perf. 12, double line wmk.	338
A140	10c yellow, perf. 12, bluish paper	364
A140	10c yellow, perf. 12, single line wmk.	381
A140	10c yellow, perf. 12 vert.	356
A140	13c blue green, perf. 12, double line wmk.	339
A140	13c blue green, perf. 12, bluish paper	365
A140	15c pale ultra, perf. 12, double line wmk.	340
A140	15c pale ultra, perf. 12, bluish paper	366
A140	15c pale ultra, perf. 12, single line wmk.	382
A140	50c violet	341
A140	$1 violet brown	342

ISSUES OF 1912-19

A148

A149 Franklin

Designs of 8c to $1 denominations differ only in figures of value.

A148	8c pale olive green, perf. 12, single line wmk.	414
A148	8c olive bister, perf. 11, unwmkd.	508
A148	8c pale olive grn., perf. 10, single line wmk.	431
A148	8c olive green, perf. 10, unwmkd.	470
A148	9c salmon red, perf. 12, single line wmk.	415
A148	9c salmon red, perf. 11, unwmkd.	509
A148	9c salmon red, perf. 10, single line wmk.	432
A148	9c salmon red, perf. 10, unwmkd.	471
A148	10c orange yellow, perf. 12, single line wmk.	416
A148	10c orange yellow, perf. 11, unwmkd.	510
A148	10c orange yellow, perf. 10, single line wmk.	433
A148	10c orange yellow, perf. 10, unwmkd.	472
A148	10c orange yellow, perf. 10 vert., same	497
A148	11c light green, perf. 11, unwmkd.	511
A148	11c dark green, perf. 10, single line wmk.	434
A148	11c dark green, perf. 10, unwmkd.	473
A148	12c claret brown, perf. 12, single line wmk.	417
A148	12c claret brown, perf. 11, unwmkd.	512
A148	12c brown carmine, same	512a
A148	12c claret brown, perf. 10, single line wmk.	435
A148	12c copper red, same	435a
A148	12c claret brown, perf. 10, unwmkd.	474
A148	13c apple green, perf. 11, unwmkd.	513
A148	15c gray, perf. 12, single line wmk.	418

A148	15c gray, perf. 11, unwmkd.	514
A148	15c gray, perf. 10, single line wmk.	437
A148	15c gray, perf. 10, unwmkd.	475
A148	20c ultramarine, perf. 12, single line wmk.	419
A148	20c light ultra., perf. 11, unwmkd.	515
A148	20c ultramarine, perf. 10, single line wmk.	438
A148	20c light ultra, perf. 10, unwmkd.	476
A148	30c orange red, perf. 12, single line wmk.	420
A148	30c orange red, perf. 11, unwmkd.	516
A148	30c orange red, perf. 10, single line wmk.	439
A148	30c orange red, perf. 10, unwmkd.	476A
A148	50c violet, perf. 12, single line wmk.	421
A148	50c violet, perf. 12, double line wmk.	422
A148	50c red violet, perf. 11, unwmkd.	517
A148	50c violet, perf. 10, single line wmk.	440
A148	50c light violet, perf. 10, unwmkd.	477
A148	$1 violet brown, perf. 12, double line wmk.	423
A148	$1 violet brown, perf. 11, unwmkd.	518
A148	$1 deep brown, same	518b
A148	$1 violet black, perf. 10, double line wmk.	460
A148	$1 violet black, perf. 10, unwmkd.	478

ISSUES OF 1918-20

Perf. 11 Unwmkd.

A149	$2 org. red & blk.	523
A149	$2 car. & blk.	547
A149	$5 dp. grn. & blk.	524

ISSUES OF 1922-32

A154 Nathan Hale

A155 Franklin

A156 Warren G. Harding

A157 Washington

A158 Lincoln

A159 Martha Washington

A160 Theodore Roosevelt

A161 Garfield

A162 McKinley

A163 Grant

A164 Jefferson

A165 Monroe

A166 Hayes

A167 Cleveland

A168 American Indian

A169 Statue of Liberty

A170 Golden Gate

A171 Niagara Falls

A172 Buffalo

A173 Arlington Amphitheater and Tomb of the Unknown Soldier

A174 Lincoln Memorial

A175 United States Capitol

A176 "America"

Unwmkd.

A154	½c olive brown, perf. 11	551
A154	½c olive brown, perf. 11x10½.	653
A154	½c olive brown, "CANAL ZONE"	C.Z. 70
A155	1c deep green, perf. 11, flat plate	552

A155	1c deep green, booklet pane of 6 . . .	552a
A155	1c green, perf. 11, rotary press 19¾x2¼mm	594
A155	1c green, same, 19¼x22¾mm (used) .	596
A155	1c green, perf. 11x10, rotary press . . .	578
A155	1c green, perf. 10	581
A155	1c green, perf. 11x10½	632
A155	1c green, booklet pane of 6	632a
A155	1c green, overprt. Kans.	658
A155	1c green, overprt. Nebr.	669
A155	1c green, imperf.	575
A155	1c green, perf. 10 vert.	597
A155	1c yellow green, perf. 10 horiz.	604
A155	1c deep green, "CANAL ZONE" type A	C.Z. 71
A55	1c deep green, same, booklet pane of 6	C.Z. 71e
A155	1c green, "CANAL ZONE" type B	C.Z. 100
A156	1½c yellow brown, perf. 11	553
A156	1½c yellow brown, perf. 11x10½	633
A156	1½c brown, overprt. Kans.	659
A156	1½c brown, overprt. Nebr.	670
A156	1½c brown, perf. 10	582
A156	1½c brown, perf. 10 vert.	598
A156	1½c yellow brown, perf. 10 horiz. . . .	605
A156	1½c yellow brown, imperf., flat plate . .	576
A156	1½c yellow brown, imperf., rotary press	631
A156	1½c yellow brown "CANAL ZONE"	C.Z. 72

No heavy hair lines at top center of head. Outline of left acanthus scroll generally faint at top and toward base at left side.

Type I

Three heavy hair lines at top center of head; two being outstanding in the white area. Outline of left acanthus scroll very strong and clearly defined at top (under left edge of lettered panel) and at lower curve (above and to left of numeral oval).

Type II

A157	2c carmine, perf. 11, flat plate	554
A157	2c carmine, same, booklet pane of 6 .	554c
A157	2c carmine, perf. 11, rotary press. . . .	595
A157	2c carmine, perf. 11x10	579
A157	2c carmine, perf. 11x10½, type I	634
A157	2c carmine, perf. 11x10½, type II . .	634A
A157	2c carmine lake, same, type I	634b
A157	2c carmine lake, same, booklet pane of 6	634d
A157	2c carmine, overprt. Molly Pitcher . .	646

A157	2c carmine, overprt. Hawaii 1778-1928.	647
A157	2c carmine, overprt. Kans.	660
A157	2c carmine, overprt. Nebr.	671
A157	2c carmine, perf. 10	583
A157	2c carmine, same, booklet pane of 6	583a
A157	2c carmine, imperf.	577
A157	2c carmine, perf. 10 vert., type I	599
A157	2c carmine, same, type II	599A
A157	2c carmine, perf. 10 horiz.	606
A157	2 carmine, "CANAL ZONE" type A	C.Z. 73
A157	2c carmine, same, booklet pane of 6	C.Z. 73a
A157	2c carmine, "CANAL ZONE" type B, perf. 11	C.Z. 84
A157	2c carmine, same, booklet pane of 6	C.Z. 84d
A157	2c carmine, "CANAL ZONE" type B, perf. 10	C.Z. 97
A157	2c carmine, same, booklet pane of 6	C.Z. 97b
A157	2c carmine, "CANAL ZONE" type B, perf. 11x10½	C.Z. 101
A157	2c carmine, same, booklet pane of 6	C.Z. 101a
A158	3c violet, perf. 11	555
A158	3c violet, perf. 11x10½	635
A158	3c bright violet, same	635a
A158	3c violet, overprt. Kans.	661
A158	3c violet, overprt. Nebr.	672
A158	3c violet, perf. 10	584
A158	3c violet, perf. 10 vert.	600
A158	3c violet, "CANAL ZONE" perf. 11	C.Z. 85
A158	3c violet, "CANAL ZONE" perf. 10	C.Z. 98
A158	3c violet, "CANAL ZONE" perf. 11x10½.	C.Z. 102
A159	4c yellow brown, perf. 11	556
A159	4c yellow brown, perf. 11x10½	636
A159	4c yellow brown, overprt. Kans.	662
A159	4c yellow brown, overprt. Nebr.	673
A159	4c yellow brown, perf. 10	585
A159	4c yellow brown, perf. 10 vert.	601
A160	5c dark blue, perf. 11	557
A160	5c dark blue, perf. 11x10½	637
A160	5c dark blue, overprt. Hawaii 1778-1928.	648
A160	5c deep blue, overprt. Kans.	663
A160	5c deep blue, overprt. Nebr.	674
A160	5c blue, perf. 10	586
A160	5c dark blue, perf. 10 vert.	602
A160	5c dark blue, "CANAL ZONE" type A, perf. 11	C.Z. 74
A160	5c dark blue, same, type B	C.Z. 86
A160	5c dark blue, same, perf. 11x10½	C.Z. 103
A161	6c red orange, perf. 11	558
A161	6c red orange, perf. 11x10½.	638
A161	6c red orange, overprt. Kans.	664
A161	6c red orange, overprt. Nebr.	675
A161	6c red orange, perf. 10	587
A161	6c deep orange, perf. 10 vert.	723
A162	7c black, perf. 11	559
A162	7c black, perf. 11x10½	639
A162	7c black, overprt. Kans.	665
A162	7c black, overprt. Nebr.	676
A162	7c black, perf. 10	588
A163	8c olive green, perf. 11	560
A163	8c olive green, perf. 11x10½	640
A163	8c olive green, overprt. Kans.	666
A163	8c olive green, overprt. Nebr.	677
A163	8c olive green, perf. 10	589
A164	9c rose, perf. 11	561
A164	9c orange red, perf. 11x10½	641
A164	9c light rose, overprt. Kans.	667
A164	9c light rose, overprt. Nebr.	678
A164	9c rose, perf. 10	590
A165	10c orange, perf. 11	562

A165	10c orange, perf. 11x10½	642
A165	10c orange yellow, overprt. Kans.	668
A165	10c orange yellow, overprt. Nebr.	679
A165	10c orange, perf. 10	591
A165	10c orange, perf. 10 vert.	603
A165	10c orange, "CANAL ZONE" type A, perf. 11	C.Z. 75
A165	10c orange, same, type B	C.Z. 87
A165	10c orange, same, perf. 10	C.Z. 99
A165	10c orange, same, perf. 11x10½ . .	C.Z. 104
A166	11c light blue, perf. 11	563
A166	11c light blue, perf. 11x10½	692
A167	12c brown violet, perf. 11	564
A167	12c brown violet, perf. 11x10½	693
A167	12c brown violet, "CANAL ZONE" type A	C.Z. 76
A167	12c brown violet, same, type B . . .	C.Z. 88
A168	14c blue, perf. 11	565
A168	14c dark blue, perf. 11x10½	695
A168	14c dark blue, "CANAL ZONE" type A, perf. 11	C.Z. 77
A168	14c dark blue, same, type B	C.Z. 89
A168	14c dark blue, same, perf. 11x10½	C.Z. 116
A169	15c gray, perf. 11	566
A169	15c gray, perf. 11x10½	696
A169	15c gray, "CANAL ZONE"	C.Z. 90
A170	20c carmine rose, perf. 11	567
A170	20c carmine rose, perf. 10½x11	698
A170	20c carmine rose, "CANAL ZONE"	C.Z. 92
A171	25c yellow green, perf. 11	568
A171	25c blue green, perf. 10½x11	699
A172	30c olive brown, perf. 11	569
A172	30c brown, perf. 10½x11	700
A172	30c olive brown, "CANAL ZONE" type A	C.Z. 79
A172	30c olive brown, "CANAL ZONE" type B	C.Z. 93
A173	50c lilac, perf. 11	570
A173	50c lilac, perf. 10½x11	701
A173	50c lilac, "CANAL ZONE" type A	C.Z. 80
A173	50c lilac, "CANAL ZONE" type B	C.Z. 94
A174	$1 violet black, perf. 11	571
A174	$1 violet brown, "CANAL ZONE" type A	C.Z. 81
A174	$1 violet brown, "CANAL ZONE" type B	C.Z. 95
A175	$2 deep blue, perf. 11	572
A176	$5 car. & blue, perf. 11	573

REGULAR ISSUES OF 1925-26, 1930 and 1932

A186 Harrison

A187 Wilson

A186	13c green, perf. 11.	622
A186	13c yellow green, perf. 11x10½	694
A187	17c black, perf. 11.	623
A187	17c black, perf. 10½x11	697
A187	17c black, "CANAL ZONE"	C.Z. 91

A203 Harding

A204 Taft

A203	1½c brown, perf. 11x10½	684
A203	1½c brown, perf. 10 vert.	686

| A204 | 4c brown, perf. 11x10½ .... | **685** |
| A204 | 4c brown, perf. 10 vert. .... | **687** |

A226 Washington

A226	3c deep violet, perf. 11x10½	**720**
A226	3c deep violet, booklet pane of 6...	**720b**
A226	3c deep violet, perf. 10 vert.	**721**
A226	3c deep violet, perf. 10 horiz.......	**722**
A226	3c deep violet, "CANAL ZONE"	**C.Z. 115**

PRESIDENTIAL ISSUE OF 1938

A275 Benjamin Franklin

A276 George Washington

A277 Martha Washington

A278 John Adams

A279 Thomas Jefferson

A280 James Madison

A281 The White House

A282 James Monroe

A283 John Quincy Adams

A284 Andrew Jackson

A285 Martin Van Buren

A286 William H. Harrison

A287 John Tyler

A288 James K. Polk

A289 Zachary Taylor

A290 Millard Fillmore

A291 Franklin Pierce

A292 James Buchanan

A293 Abraham Lincoln

A294 Andrew Johnson

A295 Ulysses S. Grant

A296 Rutherford B. Hayes

A297 James A. Garfield

A298 Chester A. Arthur

A299 Grover Cleveland

A300 Benjamin Harrison

A301 William McKinley

A302 Theodore Roosevelt

A303 William Howard Taft

A304 Woodrow Wilson

A305 Warren G. Harding

A306 Calvin Coolidge

Rotary Press Printing
Unwmkd.

A275	½c deep orange, perf. 11x10½......	**803**
A275	½c red orange, "CANAL ZONE"	**C.Z. 118**
A276	1c green, perf. 11x10½	**804**
A276	1c green, booklet pane of 6........	**804b**
A276	1c green, perf. 10 vert.	**839**
A276	1c green, perf. 10 horiz.	**848**
A277	1½c bister brown, perf. 11x10½	**805**
A277	1½c bister brown, perf. 10 vert.	**840**
A277	1½c bister brown, perf. 10 horiz.	**849**
A277	1½c bister brown, "CANAL ZONE"	**C.Z. 119**
A278	2c rose carmine, perf. 11x10½	**806**
A278	2c booklet pane of 6	**806b**
A278	2c rose carmine, perf. 10 vert.	**841**
A278	2c rose carmine, perf. 10 horiz.	**850**
A279	3c deep violet, perf. 11x10½	**807**
A279	3c deep violet, booklet pane of 6...	**807a**
A279	3c deep violet, perf. 10 vert.	**842**
A279	3c deep violet, perf. 10 horiz.......	**851**
A280	4c red violet, perf. 11x10½........	**808**
A280	4c red violet, perf. 10 vert........	**843**
A281	4½c dark gray, perf. 11x10½	**809**
A281	4½c dark gray, perf. 10 vert.	**844**
A282	5c bright blue, perf. 11x10½........	**810**
A282	5c bright blue, perf. 10 vert........	**845**
A283	6c red orange, perf. 11x10½........	**811**
A283	6c red orange, perf. 10 vert........	**846**
A284	7c sepia, perf. 11x10½	**812**
A285	8c olive green, perf. 11x10½	**813**
A286	9c rose pink, perf. 11x10½..........	**814**
A287	10c brown red, perf. 11x10½........	**815**
A287	10c brown red, perf. 10 vert........	**847**
A288	11c ultramarine, perf. 11x10½.......	**816**
A289	12c bright violet, perf. 11x10½	**817**
A290	13c blue green, perf. 11x10½	**818**
A291	14c blue, perf. 11x10½	**819**
A292	15c blue gray, perf. 11x10½	**820**
A293	16c black, perf. 11x10½	**821**
A294	17c rose red, perf. 11x10½	**822**
A295	18c brn. carmine, perf. 11x10½	**823**
A296	19c bright violet, perf. 11x10½	**824**
A297	20c bright blue green, perf. 11x10½...	**825**
A298	21c dull blue, perf. 11x10½	**826**
A299	22c vermilion, perf. 11x10½	**827**
A300	24c gray black, perf. 11x10½	**828**
A301	25c dp. red lilac, perf. 11x10½.......	**829**
A302	30c deep ultra, perf. 11x10½	**830**
A303	50c lt. red violet, perf. 11x10½	**831**

Flat Plate Printing
Perf. 11

A304	$1 pur. & blk., unwmkd.	**832**
A304	$1 pur. & blk., wmkd. USIR	**832b**
A304	$1 red vio. & blk., thick white paper, smooth colorless gum	**832c**
A305	$2 yel. grn. & blk.	**833**
A306	$5 car. & blk....................	**834**

LIBERTY ISSUE 1954-73

A477 Benjamin Franklin   **A478** George Washington

A478a Palace of the Governors, Santa Fe   **A479** Mount Vernon

A480 Thomas Jefferson   **A481** Bunker Hill Monument and Massachusetts Flag 1776

A482 Statue of Liberty   **A483** Abraham Lincoln

A484 The Hermitage   **A485** James Monroe

A486 Theodore Roosevelt   **A487** Woodrow Wilson

A488 Statue of Liberty (Rotary and flat plate printing)   **A489** Design slightly altered; see position of torch (Giorgi press printing)

A489a John J. Pershing   **A490** The Alamo

A491 Independence Hall   **A491a** Statue of Liberty

A492 Benjamin Harrison   **A493** John Jay

A494 Monticello

A495 Paul Revere   **A496** Robert E. Lee

A497 John Marshall   **A498** Susan B. Anthony

A499 Patrick Henry   **A500** Alexander Hamilton

Unwmkd.

A477	½c red orange, perf. 11x10½		1030
A478	1c dark green, perf. 11x10½		1031
A478	1c dark green, perf. 10 vert.		1054
A478	1c dark green, imperf., pair		1054b
A478a	1¼c turquoise, perf. 10½x11		1031A
A478a	1¼c turquoise, perf. 10 horiz.		1054A
A479	1½c brown carmine, perf. 10½x11		1032
A480	2c carmine rose, perf. 11x10½		1033
A480	2c carmine rose, perf. 10 vert.		1055
A480	2c carmine rose, same, tagged		1055a
A481	2½c gray blue, perf. 11x10½		1034
A481	2½c gray blue, perf. 10 vert.		1056

A482	3c deep violet, perf. 11x10½		1035
A482	3c deep violet, same, tagged		1035b
A482	3c deep violet, booklet pane of 6		1035a
A482	3c deep violet, perf. 10 vert.		1057
A482	3c deep violet, same, tagged		1057b
A482	3c deep violet, imperf., pair		1057a
A482	3c deep violet, imperf., size: 24x28mm		1075a
A483	4c red violet, perf. 11x10½		1036
A483	4c red violet, same, tagged		1036b
A483	4c red violet, booklet pane of 6		1036a
A483	4c red violet, perf. 10 vert.		1058
A483	4c red violet, imperf. pair		1058a
A484	4½c blue green, perf. 10½x11		1037
A484	4½c blue green, perf. 10 horiz.		1059
A485	5c deep blue, perf. 11x10½		1038
A486	6c carmine, same		1039
A487	7c rose carmine, same		1040
A488	8c dk. violet blue & carmine, perf. 11		1041
A488	8c dk. violet blue & carmine, imperf., size: 24x28mm		1075b
A489	8c dk. violet blue & car. rose, perf. 11		1042
A489a	8c brown, perf. 11x10½		1042A
A490	9c rose lilac, perf. 10½x11		1043
A491	10c rose lake, same		1044
A491	10c rose lake, same, tagged		1044b
A491a	11c carmine & dk. vio. blue, perf. 11		1044A
A491a	Same, tagged.		1044c
A492	12c red, perf. 11x10½		1045
A492	12c red, same, tagged		1045a
A493	15c rose lake, same		1046
A493	15c rose lake, same, tagged		1046a
A494	20c ultramarine, perf. 10½x11		1047
A495	25c green, perf. 11x10½		1048
A495	25c green, perf. 10 vert.		1059A
A495	25c green, same, tagged		1059b
A496	30c black, perf. 11x10½		1049
A497	40c brown red, same		1050
A498	50c bright purple, same		1051
A499	$1 purple, same		1052
A500	$5 black, perf. 11		1053

ISSUE OF 1962-66

A646 Andrew Jackson   **A650** George Washington

A646	1c green, perf. 11x10½, untagged		1209
A646	1c green, same, tagged		1209a
A646	1c green, perf. 10 vert., untagged		1225
A646	1c green, same, tagged		1225a
A650	5c dk. bl. gray, perf. 11x10½, untagged		1213
A650	5c dk. bl. gray, same, tagged		1213b
A650	5c dk. bl. gray, booklet pane of 5+ label, untagged		1213a
A650	5c dk. bl. gray, same, tagged		1213c
A650	5c dk. bl. gray, perf. 10 vert. untagged		12129
A650	5c dk. bl. gray, same, tagged		1229a

PROMINENT AMERICANS ISSUE 1965-75

A710 Thomas Jefferson

A711 Albert Gallatin

A712 Frank Lloyd Wright and Guggenheim Museum, New York

A713 Francis Parkman

A714 Abraham Lincoln

A715 George Washington

A715a re-engraved

A716 Franklin D. Roosevelt

A727a Franklin D. Roosevelt (vertical coil)

A816 Benjamin Franklin and his signature

A717 Albert Einstein

A718 Andrew Jackson

A718a Henry Ford and 1909 Model I

A719 John F. Kennedy

A817a Fiorello H. LaGuardia and New York skyline

A720 Oliver Wendell Holmes

A818 Ernest (Ernie) Taylor Pyle

A818a Dr. Elizabeth Blackwell

A721 George C. Marshall

A818b Amadeo P. Giannini

A722 Frederick Douglass

A723 John Dewey

A724 Thomas Paine

A725 Lucy Stone

A726 Eugene O'Neill

A727 John Bassett Moore

Unwmkd.
Rotary Press Printing

A710	1c green, perf. 11x10½, tagged		**1278**
A710	1c green, booklet pane of 8		**1278a**
A710	1c green, booklet pane of 4+2 labels		**1278b**
A710	1c green, perf. 11x10½, untagged		**1278c**
A710	1c green, perf. 10, vert., tagged		**1299**
A710	1c green, untagged (Bureau precanceled)		**1299a**

A711	1¼c light green, perf. 11x10½, untagged	**1279**
A712	2c dk. bl. gray, perf. 11x10½, tagged	**1280**
A712	2c dk. bl. gray, booklet pane of 5+label	**1280a**
A712	2c dk. bl. gray, perf. 11x10½, untagged (Bureau precanceled)	**1280b**
A712	2c dk. bl. gray, booklet pane of 6	**1280c**
A713	3c violet, perf. 10½x11, tagged	**1281**
A713	3c violet, same, untagged (Bureau precanceled)	**1281a**
A713	3c violet, perf. 10 horiz., tagged	**1297**
A713	3c violet, same, untagged (Bureau precanceled)	**1297b**
A714	4c black, perf. 11x10½, untagged	**1282**
A714	4c black, same, tagged	**1282a**
A714	4c black, perf. 10, vert., tagged	**1303**
A714	4c black, same, untagged (Bureau precanceled)	**1303a**
A715	5c blue, perf. 11x10½, untagged	**1283**
A715	5c blue, same, tagged	**1283a**
A715	5c blue, perf. 10 vert., tagged	**1304**
A715	5c blue, same, untagged (Bureau precanceled)	**1304a**
A715a	5c blue, perf. 11x10½, tagged	**1283B**
A715a	5c blue, untagged (Bureau precanceled)	**1283d**
A716	6c gray brown, perf. 10½x11, tagged	**1284**
A716	6c gray brown, tagged	**1284a**
A716	6c gray brown, booklet pane of 8	**1284b**
A716	6c gray brown, booklet pane of 5+label	**1284c**
A716	6c gray brown, perf. 10 horiz., tagged	**1298**
A727a	6c gray brown, perf. 10 vert., tagged	**1305**
A727a	6c gray brown, untagged (Bureau precanceled)	**1305b**
A816	7c bright blue, perf. 10½x11, tagged	**1393D**
A816	7c bright blue, same, untagged (Bureau precanceled)	**1393e**
A717	8c violet, perf. 11x10½, untagged	**1285**
A717	8c violet, tagged	**1285a**
A718	10c lilac, perf. 11x10½, tagged	**1286**
A718	10c lilac, untagged (Bureau precanceled)	**1286b**
A718a	12c black, perf. 10½x11, tagged	**1286A**
A718a	12c black, untagged (Bureau precanceled)	**1286c**
A719	13c brown, perf. 11x10½, tagged	**1287**
A719	13c brown, untagged (Bureau precanceled)	**1287a**
A817a	14c gray brown, perf. 11x10½	**1397**
A817a	14c gray brown, untagged (Bureau precanceled)	**1397a**
A720	15c maroon, perf. 11x10½, tagged	**1288**
A720	15c maroon, untagged (Bureau precanceled)	**1288a**
A720	15c dark rose claret, perf. 10 (bklt. panes only)	**1288B**
A720	15c dark rose claret, booklet pane of 8	**1288c**
A818	16c brown, tagged	**1398**
A818	16c brown, untagged (Bureau precanceled)	**1398a**
A818a	18c violet, perf. 11x10½	**1399**
A721	20c deep olive, perf. 11x10½, untagged	**1289**
A721	20c deep olive, tagged	**1289a**
A818b	21c green, perf. 11x10½	**1400**
A722	25c rose lake, perf. 11x10½, untagged	**1290**
A722	25c rose lake, tagged	**1290a**
A723	30c red lilac, perf. 10½x11, untagged	**1291**
A723	30c red lilac, tagged	**1291a**
A724	40c blue black, perf. 11x10½, untagged	**1292**
A724	40c blue black, tagged	**1292a**
A725	50c rose magenta, perf. 11x10½, untagged	**1293**
A725	50c rose magenta, tagged	**1293a**

A726	$1 dull purple, perf. 11x10½, untagged	1294
A726	$1 dull purple, tagged	1294a
A726	$1 dull purple, perf. 10 vert., tagged	1305C
A727	$5 gray black, perf. 11x10½, untagged	1295
A727	$5 gray black, tagged	1295a

A815 Dwight D. Eisenhower   **A815a**

A815	6c dark blue gray, perf. 11x10½, tagged	1393
A815	6c dk. bl. gray, booklet pane of 8	1393a
A815	6c dk. bl. gray, booklet pane of 5+label	1393b
A815	6c dk. bl. gray, untagged (Bureau precanceled)	1393c
A815	6c dk. bl. gray, perf. 10, vert., tagged	1401
A815	6c dk. bl. gray, same, untagged (Bureau precanceled)	1401a
A815	8c deep claret, perf. 11x10½ (Booklet panes only)	1395
A815	8c deep claret, booklet pane of 8	1395a
A815	8c deep claret, booklet pane of 6	1395b
A815	8c deep claret, booklet pane of 4+2 labels	1395c
A815	8c deep claret, booklet pane of 7+label	1395d
A815	8c deep claret, perf. 10 vert., tagged	1402
A815	8c deep claret, same, untagged (Bureau precanceled)	1402b
A815a	8c blk., red & bl. gray, perf. 11	1394

FLAG ISSUE, 1968-71

A760 Flag and White House

A760	6c dark blue, red & green, perf. 11, size:19x22mm	1338
A760	6c dark blue, red & green, perf. 11x10½, size: 18¼x21mm.	1338D
A760	6c dark blue, red & green, perf. 10 vert., size: 18¼x21mm.	1338A
A760	8c multicolored, perf. 11x10½	1338F
A760	8c multicolored, perf. 10 vert.	1338G

REGULAR ISSUE 1970-76

A817 U.S. Postal Service Emblem

A923 50-Star and 13-Star Flags   **A924** Jefferson Memorial and quotation from Declaration of Independence

A925 Mail Transport and "Zip Code"   **A926** Liberty Bell

A817	8c multicolored, perf. 11x10½	1396
A923	10c red & blue, perf. 11x10½	1509
A923	10c red & blue, perf. 10 vert.	1519
A924	10c blue, perf. 11x10½	1510
A924	10c blue, same, untagged (Bureau precanceled)	1510a
A924	10c blue, booklet pane of 5+label	1510b
A924	10c blue, booklet pane of 8	1510c
A924	10c blue, booklet pane of 6	1510d
A924	10c blue, perf. 10 vert.	1520
A924	10c blue, same, untagged (Bureau precanceled)	1520a
A925	10c multicolored, perf. 11x10½	1511
A926	6.3c brick red, perf. 10 vert.	1518
A926	6.3c brick red, same, untagged (Bureau precanceled)	1518a

AMERICANA ISSUE 1975-81

A984 Inkwell and Quill   **A985** Speaker's Stand

A987 Early Ballot Box   **A988** Books, Bookmark, Eyeglasses

A994 Dome of Capitol   **A995** Contemplation of Justice

A996 Early American Printing Press   **A997** Torch Statue of Liberty

A998 Liberty Bell   **A999** Eagle and Shield

A1001 Ft. McHenry Flag   **A1002** Head Statue of Liberty

A1006 Old North Church   **A1007** Ft. Nisqually

A1008 Sandy Hook Lighthouse   **A1009** Morris Township School No. 2, Devil's Lake

A1001 Iron "Betty" Lamp Plymouth Colony, 17th-18th Centuries   **A1013** Rush Lamp and Candle Holder

A1013a Kerosene Table Lamp   **A1014** Railroad Conductors Lantern, c. 1850

COIL STAMPS

A1014a Six-string guitar   **A1199** Weaver violins

A1015 Saxhorns   **A1016** Drum

A1017 Steinway
Grand Piano, 1857

A984	1c dark blue, greenish, perf. 11x10½	1581
A984	1c dark blue, greenish, same, untagged (Bureau precanceled)	1581a
A984	1c dark blue, greenish, perf. 10 vert.	1811
A985	2c red brown, greenish, perf. 11x10½	1582
A985	2c red brown, greenish, same, untagged (Bureau precanceled)	1582a
A987	3c olive, greenish, perf. 11x10½	1584
A987	3c olive, greenish, same, untagged (Bureau Precanceled)	1584a
A988	4c rose magenta, cream, perf. 11x10½	1585
A988	4c rose magenta, cream, same, untagged (Bureau precanceled)	1585a
A994	9c slate green, perf. 11x10½ (booklet panes only)	1590
A994	9c slate green, perf. 10 (booklet panes only)	1590a
A994	9c slate green, gray, perf. 11x10½	1591
A994	9c slate green, gray, same, untagged (Bureau precanceled)	1591a
A994	9c slate green, gray, perf. 10 vert.	1616
A994	9c slate green, gray, same, untagged (Bureau precanceled)	1616a
A995	10c violet, gray, perf. 10 vert.	1617
A995	10c violet, gray, perf. 11x10½	1592
A995	10c violet, gray, same, untagged (Bureau precanceled)	1592a
A996	11c orange, gray, perf. 11x10½	1593
A997	12c red brown, beige, perf. 10 vert.	1816
A997	12c red brown, beige, same, untagged (Bureau precanceled)	1816a
A998	13c brown, perf. 11x10½	1595
A998	13c brown, booklet pane of 6	1595a
A998	13c brown, booklet pane of 7+label	1595b
A998	13c brown, booklet pane of 8	1595c
A998	13c brown, booklet pane of 5+label	1595d
A998	13c brown, perf. 10 vert.	1618
A998	13c brown, same, untagged (Bureau precanceled)	1618a
A999	13c multicolored, perf. 11x10½	1596
A1001	15c gray, dark blue & red, perf. 11.	1597
A1001	15c gray, dark blue & red, perf. 11x10½ (booklet panes only)	1598
A1001	15c gray, dark blue & red, booklet pane of 8	1598a

A1001	15c gray, dark blue & red, perf. 10 vert.	1618C
A1002	16c blue, perf. 11x10½	1599
A1002	16c blue, perf. 10 vert.	1619
A1006	24c red, blue, perf. 11x10½.	1603
A1007	28c brown, blue, perf. 11x10½	1604
A1008	29c blue, blue, perf. 11x10½	1605
A1009	30c green, perf. 11x10½	1606
A1011	50c black & orange, perf. 11	1608
A1013	$1 brown, orange & yellow, tan, perf. 11	1610
A1013a	$2 dark green & red, tan, perf. 11.	1611
A1014	$5 red brown, yellow & orange, tan, perf. 11	1612
A1014a	3.1c brown, yellow, perf. 10 vert.	1613
A1014a	3.1c brown, yellow, same, untagged (Bureau precanceled)	1613a
A1199	3.5c purple, yellow, perf. 10 vert.	1813
A1199	3.5c purple, yellow, same, untagged (Bureau precanceled)	1813a
A1015	7.7c brown, bright yellow, perf. 10 vert.	1614
A1015	7.7c brown, bright yellow, same, untagged (Bureau precanceled)	1614a
A1016	7.9c carmine, yellow, perf. 10 vert.	1615
A1016	7.9c carmine, yellow, same, untagged (Bureau precanceled)	1615a
A1017	8.4c dark blue, yellow, perf. 10 vert.	1615C
A1017	8.4c dark blue, yellow, same, untagged (Bureau precanceled)	1615d

FLAG ISSUE 1975-77

A1018 13-star Flag over Independence Hall   **A1018a** Flag over Capitol

A1018	13c dark blue & red, perf. 11x10½	1622
A1018	13c dark blue & red, perf. 10 vert.	1625
A1018a	13c blue & red, perf. 11x10½ (booklet panes only)	1623
A1018a	13c blue & red, booklet pane of 7 #1623 + 1 #1590	1623a
A1018a	13c blue & red, perf. 10 (booklet panes only)	1623b
A1018a	13c blue & red, booklet pane of 7 #1623b + 1 #1590a	1623c

REGULAR ISSUE 1978

A1123 Indian Head Penny, 1877   **A1209** Dolley Madison

A1126 Red Masterpiece and Medallion Roses

A1123	13c brown & blue, green, bister, perf. 11	1734
A1126	15c multicolored, perf. 10 (booklet panes only)	1737
A1126	15c multicolored, booklet pane of 8	1737a
A1209	15c red brown & sepia, perf. 11	1822

REGULAR ISSUE 1978-85

A1124 "A" Eagle   **A1207** "B" Eagle

A1332 "C" Eagle   **A1333** "C" Eagle (Booklet)

A1496 "D" Eagle   **A1497** "D" Eagle (Booklet)

A1124	(15c) orange, Perf. 11	1735
A1124	(15c) orange, perf. 11x10½ (booklet panes only)	1736
A1124	(15c) orange, booklet pane of 8	1736a
A1124	(15c) orange, perf. 10 vert.	1743
A1207	(18c) violet, perf. 11x10½	1818
A1207	(18c) violet, perf. 10 (booklet panes only)	1819
A1207	(18c) violet, booklet pane of 8	1819a
A1207	(18c) violet, perf. 10 vert.	1820
A1332	(20c) brown, perf. 11x10½	1946
A1332	(20c) brown, perf. 10 vert.	1947
A1333	(20c) brown, perf. 11x10½ (booklet panes only)	1948
A1333	(20c) brown, booklet pane of 10	1948a
A1496	(22c) green, perf. 11	2111
A1496	(22c) green, perf. 10 vert.	2112
A1497	(22c) green, perf. 11 (booklet panes only)	2113
A1497	(22c) green, booklet pane of 10	2113a

REGULAR ISSUE 1980

A1127 Virginia

A1128 Rhode Island   **A1129** Massachusetts

A1130 Illinois   **A1131** Texas

A1127 15c sepia, yellow, perf. 11 . . . . **1738**
A1128 15c sepia, yellow, perf. 11 . . . . **1739**
A1129 15c sepia, yellow, perf. 11 . . . . **1740**
A1130 15c sepia, yellow, perf. 11 . . . . **1741**
A1131 15c sepia, yellow, perf. 11 . . . . **1742**
A1131 15c sepia, yellow, booklet pane of 10 **1742a**

GREAT AMERICANS ISSUE
1980-86

A1231	A1551	A1232	A1552	A1233	A1553	A1234
A1554	A1235	A1555	A1236	A1237	A1238	A1239
A1240	A1559	A1241	A1242	A1243	A1560	A1561
A1244	A1562	A1245	A1246	A1247	A1248	A1249

A1563	A1250	A1565	A1566	A1251
A1252	A1253	A1254	A1255	A1571
A1256	A1574	A1575	A1577	A1578

A1231	1c black, Perf. 11	1844	A1236	6c orange vermilion, perf. 11	1849
A1551	1c brownish vermilion, perf. 11	2168	A1237	7c bright carmine, perf. 10½x11 . . .	1850
A1232	2c brown black, perf. 10½x11	1845	A1238	8c olive black, perf. 10½x11	1851
A1552	2c brt blue, perf. 11	2169	A1239	9c dark green, perf. 10½x11	1852
A1233	3c olive green, perf. 10½x11	1846	A1240	10c Prussian blue, perf. 10½x11	1853
A1553	3c bright blue, perf. 11	2170	A1559	10c perf. 11	2176
A1234	4c violet, perf. 10½x11	1847	A1241	11c dark blue, perf. 11	1854
A1554	4c blue violet, perf. 11	2171	A1242	13c light maroon, perf. 10½x11	1855
A1235	5c henna brown, perf. 10½x11	1848	A1243	14c slate green, perf. 11	1856
A1555	5c dark olive green, perf. 11	2172	A1560	14c crimson, perf. 11	2177

A1244	17c green, perf. 10½x11	1857
A1562	17c dull blue green, perf. 11	2179
A1245	18c dark blue, perf. 10½x11	1858
A1246	19c brown, perf. 10½x11	1859
A1247	20c claret, perf. 10½x11	1860
A1248	20c green, perf. 10½x11	1861
A1249	20c black, perf. 11	1862
A1563	21c	2180
A1250	22c dark chalky blue, perf. 11	1863
A1565	23c	2182

A1566   25c blue, perf. 11 2183
A1566   25c blue, booklet pane of 10 ...... 2183a
A1566   25c blue, perf. 10 2197
A1566   25c blue, booklet pane of 6 .... 2197a
A1251   30c olive gray, perf. 11 1864
A1252   35c gray, perf. 10½x11 1865
A1253   37c blue, perf. 10½x11 1866
A1254   39c rose lilac, perf. 11 1867
A1255   40c dark green, perf. 11 1868
A1571   45c bright blue, perf. 11 2188
A1256   50c brown, perf. 11 1869
A1574   56c scarlet, perf. 11 2191
A1575   65c 2192
A1577 $1 dk. plus green, perf. 11 2194
A1578 $2 bright violet, perf. 11 2195

REGULAR ISSUE 1981

A1267 Bighorn

A1268 Puma

A1269 Harbor Seal

A1270 Bison

A1271 Brown bear

A1272 Polar bear

A1273 Elk (wapiti)

A1274 Moose

A1275 White-tailed deer

A1276 Pronghorn

From Booklet Panes

A1267   18c dark brown, perf. 11 1880
A1268   18c dark brown, perf. 11 1881
A1269   18c dark brown, perf. 11 1882
A1270   18c dark brown, perf. 11 1883
A1271   18c dark brown, perf. 11 1884
A1272   18c dark brown, perf. 11 1885
A1273   18c dark brown, perf. 11 1886
A1274   18c dark brown, perf. 11 1887
A1275   18c dark brown, perf. 11 1888
A1276   18c dark brown, perf. 11 1889
A1276   18c dark brown, booklet pane of 10   1889a

FLAG ISSUES 1981

A1277

A1278

A1279 Field of 1777 flag

A1280

A1281

A1498

A1499 Of the People, By the People, For the People

A1277   18c multicolored, perf. 11 1890
A1278   18c multicolored, perf. 10 vert. 1891
A1279   6c multicolored, perf. 11 (booklet
       panes only) 1892
A1280   18c multicolored, perf. 11 (booklet
       panes only) 1893
A1280   18c multicolored, booklet pane of 8   1893a
A1281   20c black, dark blue & red, perf. 11.. 1894

A1281 20c black, dark blue & red, perf. 11x10½ (booklet panes only).... **1896**
A1281 20c black, dark blue & red, booklet pane of 6.................. **1896a**
A1281 20c black, dark blue & red, booklet pane of 8.................. **1896b**
A1498 22c blue, red & black, perf. 11...... **2114**
A1498 22c blue, red & black, perf. 10 vert. . **2115**
A1499 22c blue, red & black, perf. 10 horiz. (booklet panes only)........... **2116**
A1499 22c blue, red and black, booklet pane of 5 .... **2116a**

TRANSPORTATION ISSUE 1981-86

A1283 1c violet, perf. 10 vert........ **1897**
A1284 2c black, perf. 10 vert. **1897A**
A1284a 3c dark green, perf. 10 vert..... **1898**
A1506 3.4c dark bluish green, perf. 10 vert. **2123**
A1506 3.4c dark bluish green, same, untagged (Bureau precanceled) .. **2123a**
A1285 4c reddish brown, perf. 10 vert. **1898A**

A1285 4c reddish brown, same, untagged (Bureau precanceled)..... **1898Ab**
A1508 4.9c brown black, perf. 10 vert. .. **2125**
A1508 4.9c brown black, same, untagged (Bureau precanceled)...... **2125a**
A1286 5c gray green, perf. 10 vert. **1899**
A1287 5.2c carmine, perf. 10 vert....... **1900**
A1287 5.2c carmine, same, untagged (Bureau precanceled)........... **1900a**
A1288 5.9c blue, perf. 10 vert......... **1901**
A1288 5.9c blue, same, untagged (Bureau precanceled)............. **1901a**
A1510 6c red brown, perf. 10 vert..... **2127**
A1510 6c red brown, same, untagged (Bureau precanceled)......... **2127a**
A1288a 7.4c brown, perf. 10 vert....... **1902**
A1288a 7.4c brown, same, untagged (Bureau precanceled)............. **1902a**
A1511 8.3c green, perf. 10 vert. **2128**
A1511 8.3c green, same, untagged (Bureau precanceled)............. **2128a**
A1289 9.3c carmine rose, perf. 10 vert... **1903**
A1289 9.3c carmine rose, same, untagged (Bureau precanceled)...... **1903a**

A1512 10.1c slate blue, perf. 10 vert...... **2129**
A1512 10.1c slate blue, same, untagged (Bureau precanceled)...... **2129a**
A1290 10.9c purple, perf. 10 vert....... **1904**
A1290 10.9c purple, same, untagged (Bureau precanceled)...... **1904a**
A1291 11c red, perf. 10 vert........... **1905**
A1291 11c red, same, untagged (Bureau precanceled)............. **1905a**
A1513 11c dark green, perf. 10 vert..... **2130**
A1514 12c dark blue, perf. 10 vert...... **2131**
A1514 12c dark blue, same, untagged (Bureau precanceled)...... **2131a**
A1515 12.5c olive green, perf. 10 vert..... **2132**
A1515 12.5c olive green, same, untagged (Bureau precanceled)...... **2132a**
A1517 14c sky blue, perf. 10 vert....... **2134**
A1292 17c ultramarine, perf. 10 vert.... **1906**
A1292 17c ultramarine, same, untagged (Bureau precanceled)...... **1906a**
A1518 17c sky blue, perf. 10 vert....... **2135**
A1293 18c dark brown, perf. 10 vert.... **1907**
A1294 20c vermilion, perf. 10 vert. **1908**

Omnibus 1880s USA 1c — **A1283**

Locomotive 1870s USA 2c — **A1284**

Handcar 1880s USA 3c — **A1284a**

School Bus 1920s 3.4 USA — **A1506**

Stagecoach 1890s USA 4c — **A1285**

Buckboard 1880s USA 4.9 — **A1508**

Motorcycle 1913 USA 5c — **A1286**

Sleigh 1880s USA 5.2c Auth. Nonprofit Org. — **A1287**

Bicycle 1870s USA 5.9c Auth. Nonprofit Org. — **A1288**

Tricycle 1880s 6 USA — **A1510**

Baby Buggy 1880s USA 7.4c — **A1288a**

Ambulance 1860s 8.3 USA — **A1511**

Mail Wagon 1880s USA 9.3c Bulk Rate — **A1289**

Oil Wagon 1890s 10.1 USA — **A1512**

Hansom Cab 1890s USA 10.9c Bulk Rate — **A1290**

RR Caboose 1890s USA 11c Bulk Rate — **A1291**

Stutz Bearcat 1933 11 USA — **A1513**

Stanley Steamer 1909 USA 12 — **A1514**

Pushcart 1880s 12.5 USA — **A1515**

Iceboat 1880s USA 14 — **A1517**

Electric Auto 1917 USA 17c — **A1292**

Dog Sled 1920s 17 USA — **A1518**

Surrey 1890s USA 18c — **A1293**

Fire Pumper 1860s USA 20c — **A1294**

REGULAR ISSUE 1983-85

A1296 Eagle and Moon

A1505 Eagle and Half Moon

A1296 $9.35 multicolored, perf. 10
vert. (booklet panes only) ... **1909**
A1296 $9.35 multicolored, booklet
pane of 3............... **1909a**
A1505 $10.75 multicolored, perf. 10
vert. (booklet panes only) ... **2122**
A1505 $10.75 multicolored, booklet
pane of 3............... **2122a**

REGULAR ISSUE 1982-85

A1334 Rocky Mountain   A1390 Consumer
Bighorn   Education

A1334 20c dark blue, perf. 11
(bklt. panes only) **1949**
A1334 20c dark blue, booklet pane of 10 .. **1949a**
A1390 20c sky blue, perf. 10 vert.......... **2005**

A1500 Filled Dogwinkle   A1501 Reticulated
Helmet

A1502 New England   A1503 Calico Scallop
Neptune

A1504 Lightning Whelk

From Booklet Pane

A1500 22c black & brown, perf. 10........ **2117**
A1501 22c black & brown, perf. 10........ **2118**
A1502 22c black & brown, perf. 10........ **2119**
A1503 22c black & brown, perf. 10........ **2120**
A1504 22c black & brown, perf. 10........ **2121**
A1504 22c black & brown, booklet
pane of 10................. **2121a**

REGULAR ISSUE 1985-86

A1532 George   A1533 Sealed
Washington   Envelopes
Washington Monument

A1532 18c multicolored, perf. 10 vert... **2149**
A1532 18c multicolored, same, untagged
(Bureau precanceled)...... **2149a**
A1533 21.1c multicolored, perf. 10 vert... **2150**
A1533 21.1c multicolored, same, untagged
(Bureau precanceled)...... **2150a**

A1588 Muskellunge

A1589 Atlantic Cod

A1590 Largemouth Bass

A1591 Bluefin Tuna

A1592 Catfish

From Booklet Pane

A1588 22c multicolored, perf. 10 horiz..... **2205**
A1589 22c multicolored, perf. 10 horiz..... **2206**
A1590 22c multicolored, perf. 10 horiz..... **2207**
A1591 22c multicolored, perf. 10 horiz..... **2208**
A1592 22c multicolored, perf. 10 horiz..... **2209**
A1592 22c multicolored, booklet
pane of 5 #2205-2209 .... **2209a**

INDEX OF COMMEMORATIVE ISSUES

POSTAL CARDS

Unwatermarked

Issued December 1, 1879

UNIVERSAL POSTAL UNION
(Union Postale Universelle)
UNITED STATES OF AMERICA
(États-Unis d'Amérique)
WRITE ONLY THE ADDRESS ON THIS SIDE

Scott UX6

Collect the Scott Way With Scott's

POSTAL CARD ALBUM

Featuring:

- Spaces for all U.S. Postal Cards listed in Scott's U.S. Specialized Catalogue.

- Scott numbers appear with each space in the album. Most spaces are illustrated.

- Chemically neutral paper protects your stamps for generations.

- Special heavy stock paper supports extra weight of cards. Blank pages are separately available.

- Yearly supplements available to keep your album up-to-date.

POSTMASTERS' PROVISIONALS

PROVISIONAL ISSUES BY POSTMASTERS.

The Act of Congress of March 3, 1845, effective July 1, 1845, established rates of postage as follows:

"For every single letter in manuscript or paper of any kind by or upon which information shall be asked or communicated in writing or by marks or signs, conveyed in the mail, for any distance under 300 miles, five cents; and for any distance over 300 miles, ten cents; and for a double letter there shall be charged double these rates; and for a treble letter, treble these rates; and for a quadruple letter, quadruple these rates; and every letter or parcel not exceeding half an ounce in weight shall be deemed a single letter, and every additional weight of half an ounce, shall be charged with an additional single postage. All drop letters, or letters placed in any post office, not for transmission through the mail but for delivery only, shall be charged with postage at the rate of two cents each."

Circulars were charged 2 cents; magazines and pamphlets, 2½ cents; newspapers according to size.

Between the time of the Act of 1845, effecting uniform postage rates, and the Act of Congress of March 3, 1847, authorizing the postmaster-general to issue stamps, postmasters in various cities issued provisional stamps.

Before adhesive stamps were introduced, mail was marked "Paid" or "Due" either with pen and ink or handstamps of various designs. Sometimes the words sufficed, but usually the amount of the postage and date were added. They may be found separately applied and also in one handstamp. These "Stampless Covers" are found in numerous types and usually carry the town postmark.

New York Postmaster Robert H. Morris issued the first postmaster provisional in July, 1845. Other postmasters soon followed. The provisionals served until superseded by the federal governments 5c and 10c stamps issued July 1, 1847.

Postmasters recognized the provisionals as indicating postage prepaid. On several provisionals the signature or initials of the postmaster vouched for their legitimate use.

On July 12, 1845, Postmaster Morris sent examples of his new stamp to the postmasters of Boston, Philadelphia, Albany and Washington, asking that they be treated as unpaid until they reached the New York office. Starting in that year the New York stamps were distributed to other offices. Postmaster General Cave Johnson reportedly authorized this practice with the understanding that these stamps were to be sold for letters directed to or passing through New York. This was an experiment to test the practicality of the use of adhesive postage stamps.

PRICES FOR ENVELOPES ARE FOR ENTIRES

ALEXANDRIA, VA.

Daniel Bryan, Postmaster.

A1

All known copies cut to shape.
Type I-40 asterisks in circle.
Type II-39 asterisks in circle.

1846		Typeset		Imperf.
1X1	A1	5c *buff*, type I		20,000.
a.		5c *buff*, type II	40,000.	
		On cover (I or II)		100,000.
1X2	A1	5c *blue*, type I, on cover		—

CANCELLATIONS.

Red circular	
town	
Black	
"PAID"	
Black ms.	
account-	
ing num-	
ber ("No.	
45," "No.	
70")	

The few copies of Nos. 1X1 and 1X1a known on cover are generally not tied by postmark and some are uncanceled. The price for "on cover" is for a stamp obviously belonging on a cover which bears the proper circular dated town, boxed "5" and straight line "PAID" markings.

No. 1X2 is unique. It is canceled with a black straight line "PAID" marking which is repeated on the cover. The cover also bears a black circular "Alexandria Nov. 25" postmark.

ANNAPOLIS, MD.

Martin F. Revell, Postmaster.
ENVELOPE

E1

1846		Printed in upper right corner of envelope	
2XU1	E1	5c carmine red, *white*	45,000.

No. 2XU1 exists in two sizes of envelope.

Envelopes and letter sheets are known showing the circular design and figure "2" handstamped in blue or red. They were used locally. Price $1,700.

A letter sheet is known showing the circular design and figure "5" handstamped in red. Used from Annapolis to Washington. Price $2,250.

Similar circular design in blue without numeral or "PAID" is known to have been used as a postmark.

BALTIMORE, MD.

James Madison Buchanan, Postmaster

Signature of
Postmaster
A1

Printed from a plate of 12 (2x6) containing nine 5c stamps (Pos. 1-6, 8, 10, 12) and three 10c (Pos. 7, 9, 11).

1845		Engr.		Imperf.
3X1	A1	5c black, *white*		4,000.
		On cover		6,000.
		Vertical pair on cover		25,000.
3X2	A1	10c black, *white*	—	32,500.
		On cover		40,000.
3X3	A1	5c black, *bluish*	25,000.	5,000.
		On cover		7,500.
3X4	A1	10c black, *bluish*		50,000.
		On cover		—

Nos. 3X3-3X4 preceded Nos. 3X1-3X2 in use.

CANCELLATIONS.

Blue circular	Blue "5" in
town	oval
Blue straight	Blue "10" in
line	oval
"PAID"	Black pen

Prices are for stamps canceled by either pen or handstamp, and are general guides to value. Inferior stamps or covers sell for less. Items of superior quality or attractiveness sell for considerably more.

ENVELOPES

E1

Three Separate Handstamps.

The "PAID" and "5" in oval were handstamped in blue or red, always both in the same color on the same entire. "James M. Buchanan" was handstamped in black, blue or red. The paper is manila, buff, white, salmon or grayish. Manila is by far the most frequently found 5c envelope. All 5c envelopes are rare, with manila or buff the more frequent. Of the 10c on salmon, only one example is known.

Prices are intended as guides. The general attractiveness of the envelope and the clarity of the handstamps primarily determine the value.

The color listed is that of the "PAID" and "5" in oval.

1845		Various Papers	Handstamped
3XU1	E1	5c blue	3,000.

3XU2	E1	5c red	3,500.
3XU3	E1	10c blue	13,000.
3XU4	E1	10c red	13,500.

CANCELLATIONS.

Blue circular	Blue "5" in
town	oval
	Red "5" in oval

The second "5" in oval on the unlisted "5 + 5" envelopes is believed not to be part of the basic prepaid marking, but envelopes bearing this marking merit a premium over the prices for Nos. 3XU1-3XU2.

BOSCAWEN, N. H.

Worcester Webster, Postmaster

A1

1846 (?)		Typeset	Imperf.
4X1	A1	5c dull blue, *yellowish*, on cover	100,000.

One copy known, uncanceled on cover with ms. postal markings.

BRATTLEBORO, VT.

Frederick N. Palmer, Postmaster

Initials of Postmaster — A1

Printed from plate of 10 (5x2) separately engraved subjects with imprint "Eng'd by Thos. Chubbuck, Bratto." below the middle stamp of the lower row (Pos. 8).

1846			Imperf.
Thick Softwove Paper Colored Through			
5X1	A1	5c *buff*	15,000. 5,000.
		On cover	9,000.

CANCELLATIONS.

Red straight	
line	
"PAID"	
Red pen	

The red pen-marks are small and lightly applied. They may have been used to invalidate a sample sheet since each plate position is known so canceled.

LOCKPORT, N. Y.

Hezekiah W. Scovell, Postmaster

A1

"Lockport, N.Y." oval and "PAID" separately handstamped in red, "5" in black ms.

1846   *Imperf.*
6X1 A1 5c red, *buff*, on cover   100,000.

CANCELLATIONS.

Black ms.
"X"

One copy of No. 6X1 is known. Small fragments of two other copies adhering to one cover have been found.

MILLBURY, MASS.

Asa H. Waters, Postmaster

George Washington — A1

Printed from a woodcut, singly, on a hand press.

1846   *Imperf.*
7X1 A1 5c *bluish*   —   17,500.
       On cover   35,000.

CANCELLATIONS.

Red straight
   line
   "PAID"
Red circular
   "MILBURY,
   MS.,"
   date in
   center

NEW HAVEN, CONN.

Edward A. Mitchell, Postmaster
ENVELOPES

E1

Impressed from a brass handstamp at upper right of envelope.
Signed in blue, black, magenta or red ms., as indicated in parenthesis.

1845
8XU1 E1 5c red, *white* (Bl or M)   —
       Cut square   5,000.
       Cut to shape   2,000.
8XU2 E1 5c red, *light bluish* (Bk)   35,000.
8XU3 E1 5c dull blue, *buff* (Bl)   25,000.
8XU4 E1 5c dull blue, *white* (Bk)   25,000.
8XU5 E1 5c dull blue, *buff* (R)   —

Prices of Nos. 8XU1-8XU5 are a guide to value. They are based on auction realizations and take condition into consideration. All New Haven envelopes are of almost equal rarity. An entire of No. 8XU2 is the finest example known. The other envelopes and cut squares are priced according to condition as much as rarity.

Reprints

Twenty reprints in dull blue on white paper, signed by E. A. Mitchell in lilac rose ink, were made in 1871 for W. P. Brown and others. Thirty reprints in carmine on hard white paper, signed in dark blue or red, were made in 1874 for Cyrus B. Peets, Chief Clerk for Mitchell. Unsigned reprints were made for N. F. Seebeck and others about 1872.

Edward A. Mitchell, grandson of the Postmaster, in 1923 delivered reprints in lilac on soft white wove paper, dated "1923" in place of the signature.

In 1932, the New Haven Philatelic Society bought the original handstamp and gave it to the New Haven Colony Historical Society. To make the purchase possible (at the $1000 price) it was decided to print 260 stamps from the original handstamp. Of these, 130 were in red and 130 in dull blue, all on hard, white wove paper.

According to Carroll Alton Means' booklet on the New Haven Provisional Envelope, after this last reprinting the brass handstamp was so treated that further reprints cannot be made. The reprints were sold originally at $5 each. A facsimile signature of the postmaster, "E. A. Mitchell," (blue on the red reprints, black on the blue) was applied with a rubber handstamp. These 260 reprints are all numbered to correspond with the number of the booklet issued then.

NEW YORK, N.Y.

Robert H. Morris, Postmaster.

 George Washington — A1

Printed by Rawdon, Wright & Hatch from a plate of 40 (5x8). The die for Washingtons head on the contemporary bank notes was used for the vignette. It had a small flaw-a line extending from the corner of the mouth down the chin-which is quite visible on the paper money. This was corrected for the stamp.

The stamps were usually initialed "ACM" (Alonzo Castle Monson) in magenta ink as a control before being sold or passed through the mails. There are four or five styles of these initials. The most common is "ACM" without periods. The scarcest is "A.C.M." believed written by Marcena Monson. The rare initials "RHM" (Robert H. Morris, the postmaster) and "MMJr" (Marcena Monson) are listed separately.

The stamps were printed on a variety of wove papers varying in thickness from pelure to thick, and in color from gray to bluish and blue. Some stamps appear to have a slight ribbing or mesh effect. A few also show letters of a double-line papermaker's watermark, a scarce variety. The blue paper is listed separately since it is the rarest and most distinctive. All used true blue copies carry "ACM" without periods; of the three unused copies, two lack initials.

Earliest known use: July 15, 1845.

1845   **Engr.**   *Imperf.*
9X1 A1 5c *bluish*   700.00   325.00
      On cover   450.00
      On cover to foreign country   1,500.
      Pair   2,000.   800.00
      Pair on cover   1,250.
      Pair on cover to foreign country   4,000.
      Strip of three   3,500.
      Strip of four   6,000.
      Block of four   —
      Double transfer at bottom (Pos.
       2)   1,000.   425.00
      Double transfer at top (Pos. 7)   1,000.   425.00
      Bottom frame line double (Pos.
       31)   1,000.   425.00
      Top frame line double (Pos. 36)   1,000.   425.00
   a.   Blue paper   6,000.   2,000.
      On cover, blue paper   4,000.
      Pair, blue paper   5,500.
   b.   Signed "RHM"   12,500.   2,500.
   c.   Signed "MMJr", on cover
   d.   Without signature   1,450.   650.00

Known used from Albany, Boston, Jersey City, N.J., New Hamburgh, N.Y., Philadelphia, Sing Sing, N.Y., Washington, D.C., and Hamilton, Canada, as well as by route agents on the Baltimore R.R. Covers originating in New Hamburgh are known only with No. 9X1b; some also bear the U.S. City Despatch Post carrier.

CANCELLATIONS.

Black pen   325.00   Red "U.S." in
                           octagon
                           frame
                           (Carrier)   +650.00
Blue pen   325.00   Red Baltimore
                           R.R.   -
Magenta
   pen   +50.00
Red grid   +50.00
Red town   +100.00

Another plate of nine subjects (3x3) was made from the original die. Each subject differs slightly from the others, with Position 8 showing the white stock shaded by crossed diagonal lines. Prints were struck from this plate in black on deep blue and white papers, as well as in blue, green, scarlet and brown on white bond paper.

ENVELOPES: Postmaster Morris, according to a newspaper report of July 7, 1845, issued envelopes. The design was not stated and no example has been seen.

PROVIDENCE, R. I.

Welcome B. Sayles, Postmaster

A1   A2

Engraved on copper plate containing 12 stamps (3x4). Upper right corner stamp (Pos. 3) "TEN"; all others "FIVE". The stamps were engraved directly on the plate, each differing from the other. The "TEN" and Pos. 4, 5, 6, 9, 11 and 12 have no period after "CENTS".

Yellowish White Handmade Paper

1846, Aug. 24   *Imperf.*
10X1 A1 5c gray black   200.00   1,250.
      On cover, tied by postmark   12,500.
      On cover, pen canceled   4,000.
      Two on cover
      Pair   425.00
      Block of four   875.00
10X2 A2 10c gray black   1,000.
      On cover, pen canceled   —
   a.   Se-tenant with 5c   1,300.
      Complete sheet   3,850.

CANCELLATIONS.

Black pen
   check
   mark
Red circular
   town
Red straight
   line
   "PAID,"
   (2 types)
Red "5"

All canceled copies of Nos. 10X1-10X2, whether or not bearing an additional handstamped cancellation, are obliterated with a black pen check mark. All genuine covers must bear the red straight line "PAID," the red circular town postmark, and the red numeral "5" or "10" rating mark.

Reprints were made in 1898. In general, each stamp bears one of the following letters on the back: B. O. G. E. R. T. D. U. R. B. I. N. However, some reprint sheets received no such printing on the reverse. All reprints are without gum. Price for 5c, $50; for 10c, $125; for sheet, $725.

ST. LOUIS, MO.

John M. Wimer, Postmaster

Missouri Coat of Arms
A1   A2   A3

Printed from a copper plate of 6 (2x3) subjects separately engraved by J. M. Kershaw.

The plate in its first state, referred to as Plate I, comprised: three 5c stamps in the left vertical row and three 10c in the right vertical row. The stamps vary slightly in size, measuring from 17¾ to 18¼ by 22 to 22½mm.

Later a 20c denomination was believed necessary. So two of the 5c stamps, types I (pos. 1) and II (pos. 3) were changed to 20c by placing the plate face down on a hard surface and hammering on the back of the parts to be altered until the face was driven flush at those points. The new numerals were then engraved. Both 20c stamps show broken frame lines and the paw of the right bear on type II is missing. The 20c type II (pos. 3) also shows retouching in the dashes under "SAINT" and "LOUIS." The characteristics of types I and II of the 5c also serve to distinguish the two types of the 20c. This altered, second state of the plate is referred to as Plate II. It is the only state to show the 20c.

The demand for the 20c apparently proved inadequate, and the plate was altered again. The "20" was erased and "5" engraved in its place, resulting in noticeable differences from the 5c stamps from Plate I. In type I (pos. 1) reengraved, the "5" is twice as far from the top frame line as in the original state, and the four dashes under "SAINT" and "LOUIS" have disappeared except for about half of the upper dash under each word. In type II (pos. 3) reengraved, the ornament in the flag of the "5" is a diamond instead of a triangle; the diamond in the bow is much longer than in the first state, and the ball of the "5," originally blank, contains a large dot. At right of the shading of the "5" is a short curved line which is evidently a remnant of the "0" of "20." Type II (pos. 5) of the 5c was slightly retouched. This second alteration of the plate is referred to as Plate III.

Type characteristics common to Plates I, II and III:
5 Cent. Type I (pos. 1). Haunches of both bears almost touch frame lines.
Type II (pos. 3). Bear at right almost touches frame line, but left bear is about ¼mm. from it.
Type III (pos. 5). Haunches of both bears about ½mm. from frame lines. Small spur on "S" of "POST."

10 Cent. Type I (pos. 2). Three dashes below "POST OFFICE."
Type II (pos. 4). Three pairs of dashes.
Type III (pos. 6). Pairs of dashes (with rows of dots between) at left and right. Dash in center with row of dots above it.
20 Cent. Type I. See 5c Type I.
Type II. See 5c Type II.

Wove Paper Colored Through

1845, Nov.-1846				Imperf.
11X1	A1	5c *greenish*	5,000.	2,350.
		On cover		4,000.
		Pair		5,250.
		Two on cover		7,000.
		Strip of three on cover		10,000.
11X2	A2	10c *greenish*	4,500.	2,000.
		On cover		3,000.
		Pair on cover		6,500.
		Strip of three on cover		9,500.
11X3	A3	20c *greenish*		—
		On cover		—

Three varieties of the 5c and three of the 10c were printed from Plate I. One variety of the 5c, three of the 10c, and two of the 20c were printed from Plate II.

1846				
11X4	A1	5c *gray lilac*	—	3,500.
		On cover		5,000.
11X5	A2	10c *gray lilac*	4,500.	1,750.
		On cover		2,750.
		Pair		5,000.
		Strip of 3		8,250.
		Strip of three on cover		13,500.
		Pair (II & III) se-tenant with 5c (III)		18,500.
11X6	A3	20c *gray lilac*	10,000.	
		On cover		13,500.

Pair on cover			30,000.
Se-tenant with 10c, on cover			27,500.
Strip of 3, 20c + 20c + 5c se-tenant			40,000.

One variety of the 5c, three of the 10c and two of the 20c. Printed from Plate II.

1846				Pelure Paper
11X7	A1	5c *bluish*	—	5,000.
		On cover		6,500.
		Pair		—
		Two on cover		12,500.
11X8	A2	10c *bluish*		5,000.
		On cover		6,500.
a.		Impression of 5c on back		—

Three varieties of the 5c and three of the 10c. Printed from Plate III.

CANCELLATIONS. Nos. 11X1-11X8

Black pen
Ms. initials of postmaster (#11X2, type I)
Red circular town
Red straight line "PAID"
Red grid (#11X7)

Prices for used off-cover stamps are for fine to very fine pen-canceled copies. Handstamp canceled copies sell for much more. Prices for stamps on cover are approximate quotations for fine to very fine stamps pen canceled. Covers with the stamps tied by handstamp sell at considerable premiums depending upon the condition of the stamps and the general attractiveness of the cover. In general, covers with multiple frankings (unless separately priced) are valued at the "on cover" price of the highest item, plus the "off cover" price of the other stamps.

TUSCUMBIA, ALA.

ENVELOPE

E1

1858		Handstamped at upper right of envelope	
12XU1	E1	3c *dull red, buff*	9,000.

No. 12XU1 also exists with a 3c 1857 stamp affixed at upper right over the provisional handstamp, tied by black circular "TUSCUMBIA, ALA." town postmark. Price $2,000.
See Confederate States Nos. 84XU1-84XU3.

POSTAGE

GENERAL ISSUES

All issues from 1847 to 1894 are Unwatermarked.

Benjamin Franklin — A1

Double transfer of top frame line. — 80RI(A)

Double transfer of top and bottom frame lines — 90RI(B)

Double transfer of bottom frame line and lower part of left frame line — (C)

Double transfer of top, bottom and left frame lines, also numerals. — (D)

This issue was authorized by an Act of Congress, approved March 3, 1847, to take effect July 1, 1847, from which date the use of Postmasters' Stamps or any which were not authorized by the Postmaster General became illegal.
Earliest known use: 5c, July 7; 10c, July 2, 1847.
This issue was declared invalid as of July 1, 1851.

Produced by Rawdon, Wright, Hatch & Edson.
Plates of 200 subjects in two panes of 100 each.

1847, July 1			Engr.		Imperf.
		Thin Bluish Wove Paper			
1	A1	5c **red brown**		4,500.	700.00
		pale brown		4,500.	700.00
		brown		4,500.	700.00
a.		5c dark brown		4,500.	700.00
		grayish brown		4,500.	700.00
		blackish brown		4,500.	700.00
b.		5c orange brown		5,000.	800.00
		brown orange		—	1,200.
c.		5c red orange		10,000.	1,850.
		On cover			850.00
		Pair		10,000.	1,600.
		Pair on cover			1,750.
		Strip of three		16,500.	3,000.
		Block of four		35,000.	30,000.
		Block of four on cover			

	Dot in S in upper right corner	5,500.	850.00
(A)	Double transfer of top frame line (80RI)		850.00
(B)	Double transfer of top and bottom frame lines (90RI)		850.00
(C)	Double transfer of bottom frame line and lower part of left frame line		850.00
(D)	Double transfer of top, bottom and left frame lines, also numerals		1,100.

CANCELLATIONS.

Red	700.00	U. S. Express	
		Mail	+100.00
Blue	+25.00	"Way"	+250.00
Black	+35.00	"Steamboat"	+350.00
Magenta	+200.00	"Steam"	+200.00
Orange	+200.00	"Steamship"	+300.00
Ultramarine	+175.00	Hotel	+*2000.*
Ultra., town	+300.00	Numeral	+50.00
Violet	+300.00	Canada	+1200.
Green	+750.00	Wheeling, Va., grid	-
"Paid"	+50.00	Pen	375.00
"Free"	+150.00		
Railroad	+200.00		

George Washington — A2

Double transfer in "X" at lower right — 1RI(A)

Double transfer in "Post Office" — 31RI(B)

Double transfer in "X" at lower right — 2RI(C)

Double transfer of left and bottom frame line. — 41RI(D)

2	A2	10c **black**		18,500.	1,750.
		gray black		18,500.	1,750.
		greenish black		—	1,750.
		On cover			2,000.
		On cover with 5c No. 1			18,500.
		Pair		40,000.	4,000.
		Pair on cover			5,500.
		Strip of three		—	10,500.
		Block of four		120,000.	50,000.

- **a.** Diagonal half used as 5 cents on cover — 15,000.
- **b.** Vertical half used as 5 cents on cover — 21,000.
- **c.** Horizontal half used as 5 cents on cover — 25,000.

		Short transfer at top		18,500.	1,750.
		Vertical line through second "F" of "OFFICE" (68RI)		—	2,000.
		With "Stick Pin" in tie (52LI)		—	2,000.
		With "harelip" (57LI)		—	2,000.
(A)	Double transfer in "X" at lower right (1RI)		—	2,000.
(B)	Double transfer in "Post Office" (31RI)		—	2,000.
(C)	Double transfer in "X" at lower right (2RI)		—	2,000.
(D)	Double transfer of left and bottom frame line (41RI)		—	2,000.

CANCELLATIONS.

Red	1,750.	U.S. Express Mail	+350.00
Blue	+50.00	"Way"	+400.00
Orange	+250.00	Numeral	+100.00
Black	+100.00	"Steam"	+350.00
Magenta	+300.00	"Steamship"	+450.00
Violet	+350.00	"Steamboat"	+650.00
Green	+1000.	"Steamer 10"	+1000.
Ultramarine	+400.00	Canada	+1250.
"Paid"	+100.00	Panama	
"Free"	+300.00	Wheeling, Va., grid	+1500.
Railroad	+350.00	Pen	1000.

REPRODUCTIONS

Actually, official imitations made from new plates of 50 subjects made by the Bureau of Engraving and Printing by order of the Post Office Department for display at the Centennial Exposition of 1876. These were not good for postal use.

Reproductions. The letters R. W. H. & E. at the bottom of each stamp are less distinct on the reproductions than on the originals.

Original

Reproduction

5c. On the originals the left side of the white shirt frill touches the oval on a level with the top of the "F" of "Five". On the reproductions it touches the oval about on a level with the top of the figure "5".

Original

Reproduction

10c. On the originals line of coat (A) points to "T" of TEN and (B) it points between "T" and "S" of CENTS. On the reproductions line of coat (A) points to right tip of "X" and line of coat (B) points to center of "S." On the reproductions the eyes have a sleepy look, the line of the mouth is straighter, and in the curl of the hair near the left cheek is a strong black dot, while the originals have only a faint one. (See Nos. 948a and 948b for 1947 reproductions-5c blue and 10c brown orange in larger size.)

A3

A4

1875		**Bluish paper, without gum**	*Imperf.*
3	A3	5c red brown *(4779)*	1,100.
		brown	1,100.
		dark brown	1,100.
		Pair	2,600.
		Block of four	8,000.
4	A4	10c black *(3883)*	1,500.
		gray black	1,500.
		Pair	3,400.
		Block of four	*11,000.*

Produced by Toppan, Carpenter, Casilear & Co.

Stamps of the 1847, 1851-56 series were printed from plates consisting of 200 subjects and the sheets were divided into panes of 100 each. In order that each stamp in the sheet could be identified easily in regard to its relative position it was devised that the stamps in each pane be numbered from one to one hundred, starting with the top horizontal row and numbering consecutively from left to right. Thus the first stamp at the upper left corner would be No. 1 and the last stamp at the bottom right corner, would be No. 100. The left and right panes are indicated by the letters "L" or "R". The number of the plate is last. As an example, the scarce type III, 1c 1851 being the 99th stamp in the right pane of Plate No. 2 is listed as (99 R 2), i.e. 99th stamp, right pane, Plate No. 2.

One plate of the one cent and several plates of the three cents were extensively recut after they had been in use. The original state of the plate is called "Early" and the recut state is termed "Late". Identification of "Early" state or "Late" state is explained by the addition of the letters "E" or "L" after the plate numbers. The sixth stamp of the right pane of Plate No. 1 from the "Early" state would be 6 R 1 E. The same plate position from the "Late" state would be 6 R 1 L.

The position of the stamp in the sheet is placed within parentheses, for example: (99 R 2).

The different values of this issue were intended primarily for the payment of specific rates, though any value might be used in making up a rate. The 1c was to pay the postage on newspapers, drop letters and circulars, and the one cent carrier fee in some cities from 1856. The 3c stamp represented the rate on ordinary letters and two of them made up the rate for distances over 3000 miles. The 5c was originally intended for registration fee but the fee was usually paid in cash. Occasionally two of them were used to pay the rate over 3000 miles, after it was changed in April, 1855. Singles paid the "Shore to ship" rate to certain foreign countries and, from 1857, triples paid the 15c rate to France. Ten cents was the rate to California and points distant more than 3000 miles. The 12c was for quadruple the ordinary rate. The 24c represented the single letter rate to Great Britain. Thirty cents was the rate to Germany. The 90c was apparently intended to facilitate the payment of large amounts of postage.

Act of Congress, March 3, 1851. "From and after June 30, 1851, there shall be charged the following rates: Every single letter not exceeding 3000 miles, prepaid postage, 3 cents; not prepaid, 5 cents; for any greater distance, double these rates. Every single letter or paper conveyed wholly or in part by sea, and to or from a foreign country over 2500 miles, 20 cents; under 2500 miles, 10 cents. Drop or local letters, 1 cent each. Letters uncalled for and advertised, to be charged 1 cent in addition to the regular postage."

Act of Congress, March 3, 1855. "For every single letter, in manuscript or paper of any kind, in writing, marks or signs, conveyed in the mail between places in the United States not exceeding 3000 miles, 3 cents; and for any greater distance, 10 cents. Drop or local letters, 1 cent."

Act of March 3, 1855, effective April 1, 1855, also said: "the foregoing rates to be prepaid on domestic letters." The Act also made the prepayment of postage on domestic letters compulsory.

The Act of March 3, 1855, effective July 1, 1855, authorized the Postmaster to establish a system for the registration of valuable letters, and to require prepayment of postage on such letters as well as registration fee of 5 cents. Stamps to prepay the registry fee were not required until June 1, 1867.

Franklin — A5

ONE CENT. Issued July 1, 1851.

Type I. Has complete curved lines outside the labels with "U. S. Postage" and "One Cent". The scrolls below the lower label are turned under, forming little balls. The ornaments at top are substantially complete.

Type Ib. As I, but balls below bottom label are not so clear. Plume-like scrolls at bottom are incomplete.

1851-57 — *Imperf.*

5	A5 1c **blue**, type I (7 R 1 E)	100,000.	22,500.	
	On cover, single (7 R 1 E)		32,500.	
	On cover, pair, one stamp (7 R 1 E)		—	
	On cover strip of three, one stamp (7 R 1 E)		60.000.	

CANCELLATIONS.

		Red town	-
Blue	+500.00	Red "Paid"	-
Red grid	+1000.		

5A	A5 1c **blue**, type Ib, July 1, 1851 (Best examples, 6R, 8R, 1E)	15,000.	5,000.	
	On cover		6,500.	
	blue, type Ib (Less distinct 3R, 4R, 5R, 9R, Plate 1E)	9,500.	3,750.	
	Pair	21,000.	8,000.	
	On cover		4,500.	
	Block of four, combination pair type Ib and pair type IIIa (8, 9-18, 19 R 1 E)		—	

CANCELLATIONS.

Blue town	+100.00	Pen 6 or 8 R1E	2,250.
Red Carrier	-	Pen (3, 4, 5 or 9 R1E)	1,400.

A6

Type Ia. Same as I at bottom but top ornaments and outer line are partly cut away.

6	A6 1c **blue**, type Ia, *April 19, 1857*	17,500.	6,000.	
	On cover		7,000.	
	Pair		12,500.	
	Vertical pair, combination types Ia and III	—	—	
	Vertical pair, combination types Ia and IIIa	21,000.	—	
	Block of 4, combination types Ia and IIIa	50,000.		
	"Curl on shoulder" (97 L 4)	18,000.	6,750.	
	"Curl in C" (97 R 4)	18,000.	6,750.	

Type Ia comes only from the bottom row of both panes of Plate 4. All type Ia stamps have the flaw below "U" of "U.S." But this flaw also appears on some stamps of types III and IIIa, Plate 4.

CANCELLATIONS.

		Black Carrier	+350.00
Blue	+100.00	Red Carrier	+350.00
		Pen	2350.

A7

Type II. The little balls of the bottom scrolls and the bottoms of the lower plume ornaments are missing. The side ornaments are complete.

7	A7 1c **blue**, type II, (Plates 1, 2); *July 1, 1851, Dec. 5, 1855*	450.00	85.00	
	On cover		100.00	
	Pair	950.00	185.00	
	Strip of three	1,500.	285.00	
	Pair, combination types II and IIIa (Plate 1E)	2,400.	725.00	
	Plate 3, *May, 1856*	—	325.00	
	On cover (Plate 3)		500.00	
	Pair (Plate 3)	—	750.00	
	Plate 4, *April, 1857*	—	500.00	
	On cover (Plate 4)		600.00	
	Pair (Plate 4)	—	1,100.	
	"Curl in hair" (3 R, 4 R 4)	—	650.00	
	Block of four (Plate 1 E)	—		
	Block of four (Plate 2)	2,100.	600.00	
	Block of four (Plate 3)	—		
	Block of four, combination, type II and type III and IIIa	—		
	Margin block of 8, Impt. & P# (Plate 2)	—		
	Double transfer (Plate 1E or 2)	500.00	100.00	
	Double transfer (4 R 1L)	1,000.	250.00	
	Double transfer (89 R 2)	550.00	110.00	
	Double transfer (Plate 3)	—	350.00	
	Double transfer (10 R 4)	—	750.00	
	Double transfer, one inverted (71 L1E)	750.00	225.00	
	Triple transfer, one inverted (91 L1E)	750.00	225.00	
	Cracked Plate (2L, 12L, 13L, 23L and 33L, Plate 2)	650.00	200.00	
	Perf. 12½, unofficial	—	4,000.	

In addition to the cracked plates listed above (Plate 2) there exist a number of surface cracks coming from the rare Plate 3.

CANCELLATIONS.

Blue	+2.50	"Way"	+35.00
Red	+5.00	Numeral	+15.00
Magenta	+20.00	Railroad	+50.00
Ultramarine	+30.00	"Steam"	+50.00
Green	+225.00	"Steamboat"	+70.00
1855 year date	+10.00	Red Carrier	+15.00
		Black Carrier	+25.00
1856 year date	+5.00	U. S. Express Mail	+25.00
1857 year date	+2.50	Printed Precancellation "PAID"	+325.00
1858 year date		Pen	45.00
"Paid"	+5.00		

A8

Type III. The top and bottom curved lines outside the labels are broken in the middle. The side ornaments are substantially complete.

The most desirable examples of type III are those showing the widest breaks in the top and bottom framelines.

The finest example is 99 R 2. All other stamps come from plate 4 and show the breaks in the lines less clearly defined. Some of these breaks, especially of the bottom line, are very small.

Type IIIa. Similar to III with the outer line broken at top or bottom but not both. The outside ornaments are substantially complete.

8	A8 1c **blue**, type III (Plate 4) *April, 1857,* see below for 99 R 2	5,500.	1,500.	
	On cover		1,850.	
	Pair		3,100.	
	Pair, combination types III and IIIa	—	—	
	Strip of three	—	5,500.	
	Block of four, combination types III and IIIa	—		

CANCELLATIONS.

		Red Carrier	+150.00
Blue	+50.00	Black Carrier	+200.00
		Pen	650.00

Examples of type III with wide breaks in outer lines command higher prices than those with small breaks.

8	A8 1c **blue**, type III (99 R 2)	8,000.	2,750.	
	Pair, combination types III (99 R 2) and II	—	—	
	Pair, combination types III (99 R 2) and IIIa	10,500.	—	
	Block of 4, combination type III (99 R 2) and 3 of type II	18,500.	—	
	On cover (99 R 2)		5,000.	

CANCELLATIONS.

		"Paid"	+250.00
Blue	+100.00	Red Carrier	+250.00

8A	A8 1c **blue**, type IIIa (Plate 1E)	1,900.	600.00	
	On cover		750.00	
	Pair	—	1,250.	
	Double transfer, one inverted (81 L 1 E)	2,250.	775.00	
	Plate 1 E (100 R)	—		
	Plate 2 (100 R)	—		
	Plate 4, *April, 1857*	2,000.	650.00	
	On cover (Plate 4)		850.00	
	Pair (Plate 4)	—	1,350.	
	Vertical pair, combination types IIIa and II (Plate 4)	—		
	Block of four (Plate 4)	—	6,000.	

CANCELLATIONS.

		"Paid"	+75.00
Blue	+25.00	Black Carrier	+150.00
Red	+50.00	Red Carrier	+125.00
		Pen	300.00

Stamps of type IIIa with bottom line broken command higher prices than those with top line broken. See note after type III on width of break of outer lines.

A9

Type IV. Similar to II, but with the curved lines outside the labels recut at top or bottom or both.

9	A9 1c **blue**, type IV, *June 8, 1852*	300.00	75.00	
	On cover		95.00	
	Pair	625.00	160.00	
	Strip of three	975.00	265.00	
	Block of four	1,500.	850.00	
	Margin block of 8, Impt. & P# (Plate 1)	—	—	
a.	Printed on both sides, reverse inverted	—	—	
	Double transfer	325.00	77.50	
	Triple transfer, one inverted (71L1L, 81L1L and 91L1L)	450.00	125.00	
	Cracked plate	450.00	125.00	
	Perf. 12½, unofficial	—	3,000.	

VARIETIES OF RECUTTING.

Stamps of this type were printed from Plate 1 after it had been recut in 1852. All but one stamp (4 R) were recut and all varieties of recutting are listed below:

Recut once at top and once at bottom, (113 on plate)	300.00	75.00
Recut once at top, (40 on plate)	310.00	77.50
Recut once at top and twice at bottom, (21 on plate)	320.00	80.00
Recut twice at bottom, (11 on plate)	325.00	85.00
Recut once at bottom, (8 on plate)	335.00	90.00
Recut once at bottom and twice at top, (4 on plate)	350.00	95.00
Recut twice at bottom and twice at top, (2 on plate)	400.00	125.00
Pair, combination, type II (4 R 1 L) and type IV	1750.	700.00

CANCELLATIONS.

		Railroad	+75.00
Blue	+2.50	"Steam"	+60.00
Red	+7.50	Numeral	+10.00
Ultramarine	+15.00	"Steamboat"	+75.00
Brown	+20.00	"Steamship"	+60.00
Green	+200.00	Red Carrier	+10.00
Violet	+50.00	Black Carrier	+25.00
1853 year date	+250.00	U. S. Express Mail	+60.00
1855 year date	+10.00	Express Company	-
1856 year date	+7.50	Packet boat	-
1857 year date	+10.00	Printed precancellation "PAID"	+450.00
"Paid"	+10.00	Printed precancellation "paid"	+450.00
"U. S. PAID"	+50.00	Pen	40.00
"Way"	+35.00		
"Free"	+50.00		

These 1c stamps were often cut apart carelessly, destroying part or all of the top and bottom lines. This makes it difficult to determine whether a stamp is type II or IV without plating the position. Such mutilated examples sell for much less.

Washington — A10

THREE CENTS. Issued July 1, 1851.
Type I. There is an outer frame line on all four sides.

10	A10	3c	**orange brown,** type I	1,200.	45.00
			deep orange brown	1,200.	45.00
			copper brown	1,350.	60.00
			On cover		65.00
			Pair	2,500.	95.00
			Strip of three	3,750.	175.00
			Block of four	8,500.	
			Double transfer		60.00
			Triple transfer		175.00
			Gash on shoulder		55.00
			Dot in lower right diamond block (69 L 5 E)		65.00
			On part-India paper		200.00

VARIETIES OF RECUTTING.

All of these stamps were recut at least to the extent of four outer frame lines and usually much more. Some of the most prominent varieties are listed below (others are described in "The 3c Stamp of U.S. 1851-57 Issue," by Carroll Chase). Prices for No. 10 are for copies with recut inner frame lines:

No inner frame lines	1250.	47.50
Left inner line only recut		52.50
Right inner line only recut		47.50
1 line recut in upper left triangle	1250.	47.50
2 lines recut in upper left triangle		52.50
3 lines recut in upper left triangle		70.00
5 lines recut in upper left triangle (47 L O)		200.00
1 line recut in lower left triangle		65.00
1 line recut in lower right triangle		60.00
2 lines recut in lower right triangle (57 L O)		175.00
2 lines recut in upper left triangle, 1 line recut in lower right triangle		—
1 line recut in upper right triangle		60.00
Upper part of top label and diamond block recut	1250.	50.00
Top label and right diamond block joined		52.50
Top label, left diam, block joined		55.00
Lower label and right diamond block joined		52.50
2 lines recut at top of upper right diamond block		57.50
1 line recut at bottom of lower left diamond block (34 R 2 E)		65.00

CANCELLATIONS.

		"Free"	+50.00
Blue	+2.00	Numeral	+15.00
Red	+5.00	Railroad	+50.00
Orange	+12.50	U. S. Express Mail	+20.00
Brown	+17.50	"Steam"	+35.00
Ultramarine	+25.00	"Steamship"	+60.00
Green	+175.00	"Steamboat"	+60.00
Violet	+50.00	Packet Boat	+300.00
1851 year date	+250.00	Blue Carrier (New Orleans)	+300.00
1852 year date	+250.00	Green Carrier (New Orleans)	+600.00
		"Paid"	+5.00
		"Way"	+40.00	Canadian	-
		"Way" with numeral	+150.00	Territorial	+175.00
			Pen	30.00

11	A10	3c	**dull red** (1853-54-55), type I	130.00	7.00
			orange red (1855)	130.00	7.00
			rose red (1854-55)	130.00	7.00
			brownish carmine (1852 and 1856)	145.00	8.50
a.			3c claret (1857)	160.00	10.00
			deep claret (1857)	185.00	13.50
			On cover, dull red		9.00

	On patriotic cover	200.00	
	On propaganda cover	350.00	
	Pair	270.00	15.00
	Strip of three	425.00	30.00
	Block of four	675.00	300.00
	Margin block of 8, Impt. & P#		
c.	Vertical half used as 1c on cover		6,000.
d.	Diagonal half used as 1c on cover		5,500.
e.	Double impression		—
	Double transfer in "Three Cents"	150.00	8.00
	Double transfer line through "Three Cents" and rosettes double (92 L 1 L)	225.00	35.00
	Triple transfer (92 L 2 L)	200.00	25.00
	Double transfer, "Gents" instead of "Cents" (66 R 2 L)	200.00	25.00
	Gash on shoulder	140.00	7.50
	Dot on lower right diamond block 69 L 5 L)	175.00	20.00
	Cracked plate (51L, 74L, 84L, 94L, 96L, and 9R, Plate 5 L)	375.00	60.00
	Worn plate	130.00	7.00
	Perf. 12½, unofficial		1,500.

VARIETIES OF RECUTTING.

All of these stamps were recut at least to the extent of three frame lines and usually much more. Some of the most prominent varieties are listed below (others are described in "The 3c Stamp of U.S. 1851-57 Issue," by Carroll Chase):

Recut inner frame lines	130.00	7.00
No inner frame lines	130.00	7.00
Right inner line only recut	140.00	7.25
1 line recut in upper left triangle	140.00	7.25
2 lines recut in upper left triangle	140.00	7.25
3 lines recut in upper left triangle	150.00	8.00
5 lines recut in upper left triangle	—	65.00
1 line recut in lower left triangle	160.00	8.00
1 line recut in lower right triangle	140.00	7.50
1 line recut in upper right triangle	—	10.00
Recut button on shoulder (10 R 2 L)	—	40.00
Lines on bust and bottom of medallion circle recut (47 R 6)	300.00	100.00
Upper part of top label and diamond block recut	140.00	7.25
Top label and right diamond block joined	140.00	7.25
Top label and left diamond block joined	150.00	9.50
Lower label and right diamond block joined	150.00	9.50
1 extra vertical line outside of left frame line (29L, 39L, 49L, 59L, 69L, 79L, Plate 3)	145.00	8.50
2 extra vertical lines outside of left frame line 89L, 99L, Plate 3)	180.00	20.00
1 extra vertical line outside of right frame line (58L, 68L, 78L, 88L, 98L, Plate 3)	155.00	9.00
No inner line and frame line close to design at right (9L, 19L, Plate 3)	165.00	12.50
No inner line and frame line close to design at left (70L, 80L, 90L, 100L, Plate 3)	150.00	10.00

CANCELLATIONS.

		"Free"	+25.00
Blue	+.25	Numeral	+7.50
Red	+1.00	Railroad	+20.00
Orange	+5.00	U. S. Express Mail	+5.00
Brown	+3.00	"Steam"	+15.00
Magenta	+15.00	"Ship"	+20.00
Ultramarine	+15.00	"New York Ship"	+35.00
Green	+80.00	"Steamboat"	+45.00
Violet	+25.00	"Steamship"	+45.00
Purple	+25.00	Packet boat	+45.00
Olive	+30.00	Express Company	+120.00
Yellow	+150.00	Black Carrier	+60.00
1852 year date	+250.00	Red Carrier (New York)	+50.00
1853 year date	+90.00	Green Carrier (New Orleans)	+350.00
1855 year date	+10.00	Blue Carrier (New Orleans)	+200.00
1858 year date	+.50	Canada	-
1859 year date		Territorial	+70.00
"Paid"	+1.00	Pen	4.00
"Way"	+10.00		
"Way" with numeral	+60.00		

Thomas Jefferson — A11

FIVE CENTS. Earliest known use Mar. 24, 1856.
Type I. Projections on all four sides.

12	A11	5c	**red brown,** type I	10,000.	1,300.
			dark red brown	10,000.	1,300.
			single on cover		3,000.
			Pair	21,000.	2,750.
			Strip of three	35,000.	4,500.
			Block of four	110,000.	35,000.

CANCELLATIONS.

		"Paid"	+50.00
Red	+50.00	"Steamship"	+200.00
Magenta	+125.00	U.S. Express Mail	+150.00
Blue	+25.00	Express Company	+300.00
Green	+600.00	"Steamboat"	+250.00
1856 year date	+25.00	Railroad	+250.00
1857 year date	+25.00	Pen	600.00
1858 year date	-		

Washington — A12

TEN CENTS. Earliest known use May 12, 1855
Type I. The "shells" at the lower corners are practically complete. The outer line below the label is very nearly complete. The outer lines are broken above the middle of the top label and the "X" in each upper corner.
Types I, II, III and IV have complete ornaments at the sides of the stamps, and three pearls at each outer edge of the bottom panel.
Type I comes only from the bottom row of both panes of Plate 1.

13	A12	10c	**green,** type I	9,000.	700.00
			dark green	9,000.	700.00
			yellowish green	9,000.	700.00
			On cover		1,000.
			On patriotic cover		5,000.
			Pair	19,000.	1,550.
			Strip of three		—
			Pair, combination types I & III	12,000.	—
			Pair, combination type I and type IV		—
			Vertical strip of three, combination types I, II, III		—
			Block of four, combination type I and type III	25,000	
			Block of four, combination types I, III and IV		—
			Double transfer (100 R 1)	9,500.	775.00
			"Curl" in left "X" (99 R 1)	9,500.	775.00

CANCELLATIONS.

		"Paid"	+50.00
Blue	+25.00	"Steamship"	+150.00
Red	+50.00	Railroad	+175.00
Magenta	+150.00	Territorial	+400.00
Orange	—	Numeral	+50.00
1855 year		U.S. Express	
date	+25.00	Mail	-
1856 year		Pen	325.00
date	+25.00		
1857 year			
date	+25.00		

A13

Type II. The design is complete at the top. The outer line at the bottom is broken in the middle. The shells are partly cut away.

14	A13 10c **green,** type II	1,800.	275.00
	dark green	1,800.	275.00
	yellowish green	1,800.	275.00
	On cover		350.00
	Pair	3,700.	600.00
	Strip of 3		
	Block of four	9,000.	4,000.
	Pair, combination type II and type III	3,750.	600.00
	Pair, combination type II and type IV	13,500.	2,000.
	Vertical strip of three, combination types II, III and IV	—	
	Block of four, combination type II and type III	—	2,750.
	Block of four, combination types II and IV	—	
	Block of four, combination types II, III, and IV		9,000.
	Double transfer (31L, 51L, and 20R, Plate 1)	1,850.	325.00
	"Curl" opposite "X" (10 R 1)	1,900.	350.00

CANCELLATIONS.

		"Paid"	+25.00
Blue	+10.00	"Way"	+50.00
Red	+25.00	"Free"	+75.00
Brown	+25.00	Railroad	+75.00
Ultramarine	+75.00	Steamship	+75.00
Magenta	+75.00	Steamboat	+100.00
Green	+200.00	Numeral	+50.00
1855 year date	-	Territorial	+150.00
1856 year date	+50.00	Express Company	+200.00
1857 year date	+10.00	U. S. Express Mail	+75.00
1858 year date	+10.00	Pen	150.00

A14

Type III. The outer lines are broken above the top label and the "X" numerals. The outer line at the bottom and the shells are partly cut away as in Type II.

15	A14 10c **green,** type III	1,850.	285.00
	dark green	1,850.	285.00
	yellowish green	1,850.	285.00
	On cover		400.00
	Pair	3,800.	600.00
	Strip of 3		
	Pair, combination type III and type IV	14,000.	2,000.
	Double transfer at top and at bottom	—	
	"Curl" on forehead (85 L 1)	1,950.	350.00
	"Curl" to right of left "X" (87 R 1)	1,950.	350.00

CANCELLATIONS.

		"Paid"	+25.00
Blue	+10.00	Steamship	+75.00
Red	+25.00	U. S. Express Mail	+75.00
Magenta	+75.00	Express Company	+200.00
Brown	+25.00	Packet boat	-
Orange	+35.00	Canada (on cover)	+1000.
Green	+200.00	Territorial	+150.00
1855 year date	-	Railroad	+75.00
1856 year date	+50.00	Numeral	+50.00
1857 year date	+10.00	Pen	150.00
1858 year date	+10.00		

A15

Type IV. The outer lines have been recut at top or bottom or both.

16	A15 10c **green,** type IV	11,500.	1,500.
	dark green	11,500.	1,500.
	yellowish green	11,500.	1,500.
	On cover		2,250.
	On patriotic cover		
	Pair	—	3,500.
	Block of four (54-55, 64-65L)	—	

VARIETIES OF RECUTTING

Eight stamps on Plate 1 were recut. All are listed below.

Outer line recut at top (65L, 74L, 86L, and 3R, Plate 1)	11,500.	1,500.
Outer line recut at bottom (54L, 55L, 76L, Plate 1)	12,000.	1,550.
Outer line recut at top and bottom (64 L 1)	13,000.	1,650.

Positions 65 L 1 and 86 L 1 have both "X" ovals recut at top, as well as the outer line.

CANCELLATIONS.

		"Paid"	+100.00
Blue	+50.00	Steamship	+300.00
Red	+100.00	Territorial	+500.00
Brown	-	Express Company	+750.00
1857 year date		Numeral	+100.00
1859 year date		Pen	750.00

Types I, II, III and IV occur on the same sheet, so it is possible to obtain pairs and blocks showing combinations of types. For listings of type combinations in pairs and blocks, see Nos. 13-15.

Washington — A16

17	A16 12c **black,** July 1, 1851	2,000.	250.00
	gray black	2,000.	250.00
	intense black	2,000.	250.00
	Single, on cover		1,300.
	Single on cover with No. 11		1,000.
	Pair	4,100.	525.00
	Pair, on cover		625.00
	Block of four	11,000.	2,750.
a.	Diagonal half used as 6c on cover		4,500.
b.	Vertical half used as 6c on cover		8,500.
c.	Printed on both sides		3,500.
	Double transfer	2,100.	275.00
	Triple transfer (5 R 1 & 49 R 1)	2,400.	325.00
	Not recut in lower right corner	2,000.	275.00
	Recut in lower left corner (43L, 53L, 63L, 73L and 100L, Plate 1)	2,200.	300.00
	On part-India paper	—	475.00

CANCELLATIONS.

Red	+20.00	Steamship	+100.00
Blue	+5.00	Steamboat	+125.00
Brown	+20.00	Supplementary Mail Type A	+75.00
Magenta	+65.00	Railroad	+75.00
Orange	+40.00	"Honolulu" in red	+400.00
Green	+300.00	U. S. Express Mail	+125.00
"Paid"	+25.00	Pen	125.00
"Way"	+75.00		

SAME DESIGNS AS 1851-57 ISSUES
Printed by Toppan, Carpenter & Co.

1857-61   **Perf. 15**

18	A5 1c **blue,** type I (Plate 12), Jan. 25, 1861	800.00	375.00
	On cover		475.00
	On patriotic cover		1,000.
	Pair	1,650.	800.00
	Strip of three	2,600.	1,350.
	Block of four	4,750.	
	Pair, combination types I & II	1,400.	600.00
	Pair, combination types I and IIIa	1,600.	650.00
	Block of four, combination types I and II	3,000.	1,750.
	Block of four, combination types I, II and IIIa	3,400.	2,250.
	Double transfer	850.00	450.00
	Cracked plate (91 R 12)		500.00

Plate 12 consists of types I and II. A few positions are type IIIa.

CANCELLATIONS.

		"Paid"	+25.00
Blue	+10.00	Black Carrier	+85.00
Red	+35.00	Red Carrier	+75.00
Violet	+100.00	Pen	200.00

19	A6 1c **blue,** type Ia (Plate 4), July 26, 1857	10,000.	2,500.
	On cover		3,250.
	Pair	21,000.	5,500.
	Strip of three	35,000.	8,500.
	Vertical pair, types Ia & III	16,000.	4,000.
	Vertical pair, types Ia & IIIa	12,500.	3,000.
	Block of four, combination, pair type Ia and types III or IIIa	—	—
	"Curl on shoulder" (97 L 4)	10,500.	2,500.

Copies of this stamp exist with perforations not touching the design at any point. Such copies command very high prices. Type Ia comes only from the bottom row of both panes of Plate 4. Examples called "Ashbrook type Ic" are sometimes offered as varieties of type Ia. Actually they are varieties of type IIIa (No. 22) except 91 R 4 and 96 R 4 which are varieties of type Ia.

CANCELLATIONS.

Red Carrier +200.00	Pen	1200.

20	A7 1c **blue,** type II (Plate 2) July 25, 1857	450.00	140.00
	On cover		175.00
	Pair	950.00	290.00
	Strip of three	1,500.	450.00
	Block of four	2,300.	1,250.
	Double transfer (Plate 2)	500.00	160.00
	Cracked plate (2L, 12L, 13L, 23L & 33L, Plate 2)	700.00	250.00
	Double transfer (4 R 1 L)		450.00
	Plate 4, July 26, 1857	—	600.00
	On cover (Plate 4)		700.00
	Pair (Plate 4)	—	1,250.
	Strip of three (Plate 4)		750.00
	Double transfer (10 R 4)		750.00
	"Curl in hair" (3 R, 4 R 4)		650.00
	Plate 11, Jan. 12, 1861	575.00	190.00
	On cover (Plate 11)		225.00
	On patriotic cover (Plate 11)		650.00
	Pair (Plate 11)	1,200.	400.00
	Strip of three (Plate 11)		—
	Double transfer (Plate 11)		—
	Plate 12, Jan. 25, 1861	450.00	140.00
	On cover (Plate 12)		175.00
	On patriotic cover (Plate 12)		450.00
	Pair (Plate 12)	950.00	300.00
	Strip of three (Plate 12)	1,500.	460.00
	Block of four (Plate 12)	2,400.	1,250.

CANCELLATIONS.

		1863 year date	+200.00
Blue	+5.00	"Paid"	+15.00
Red	+20.00	Railroad	+60.00
Green	+200.00	"Way"	+75.00
1857 year date	+10.00	Steamboat	+75.00
1858 year date	+5.00	Red Carrier	+35.00
1861 year date	+5.00	Black Carrier	+50.00
"FREE"	-	Pen	65.00

21	A8 1c **blue,** type III (Plate 4), July 26, 1857, see below for 99 R 2	4,500.	1,400.
	On cover		1,750.
	Pair	9,250.	2,900.
	Strip of three		4,400.
	Block of four		
	Pair, types III & IIIa	5,250.	1,750.
	Vertical pair, types III & II	—	
	Block of 4, types III & IIIa	—	
	Top & bottom lines broken (46 L 12)	—	—

CANCELLATIONS.

Blue	+25.00	"Paid"	+50.00
Red	+50.00	Black Carrier	+175.00
Green	+350.00	Red Carrier	+150.00
1858 year date	+25.00	Pen	550.00

(21)	A8 1c **blue,** type III, (99 R 2), July 26, 1857	—	6,000.
	On cover		7,500.
	Pair, combination type III (99 R 2) and type II		
	Pair, combination types III (99 R 2) and IIIa		—

Strip of three, combination type III (99R2) and types II and IIIa		
Block of 12, combination one type III (99 R 2), others type II	—	

22	A8 1c **blue**, type IIIa (Plate 4), *July 26, 1857*	700.00	250.00
	On cover		275.00
	On patriotic cover		600.00
	Pair	1,450.	525.00
	Vertical pair, combination types IIIa and II (Plate 4)	—	900.00
	Strip of three	2,400.	800.00
	Block of four	3,750.	3,750.
	Block of four, combination types IIIa and II (Plate 4)		
	Double transfer	750.00	275.00
b.	Horizontal pair, imperf. between	—	
	Plate 2 (100 R), *July 25, 1857*		
	Plate 11, *Jan. 12, 1861,* and Plate 12, *Jan. 25, 1861*	800.00	275.00
	On cover		325.00
	On patriotic cover		800.00
	Pair	1,700.	575.00
	Vertical pair, combination types IIIa and II (Plate 11)	1,700.	550.00
	Strip of three	2,600.	850.00
	Block of four	4,000.	
	Block of four, combination types IIIa and II (Plate 11)	4,250.	2,500.
	Double transfer	800.00	300.00
	Triple transfer (Plate 11)	—	—
	Bottom line broken (46 L 12)	—	—

One pair of No. 22b is reported. Beware of numerous pairs that have blind perforations. These are not to be confused with No. 22b.

CANCELLATIONS.

Blue	+5.00	1861 year date	-
Red	+20.00	1863 year date	-
Green	+225.00	"Paid"	+25.00
1857 year date		Red Carrier	+35.00
		Black Carrier	+50.00
1858 year date		Blue Carrier	+100.00
		Pen	100.00

23	A9 1c **blue**, type IV, *July 25, 1857*	1,850.	300.00
	On cover		450.00
	Pair	3,750.	650.00
	Strip of three	5,750.	1,050.
	Block of four		4,000.
	Double transfer	1,900.	325.00
	Triple transfer, one inverted (71 L 1 L, 81 L 1 L and 91 L 1 L)	2,500.	425.00
	Cracked plate	2,350.	400.00

VARIETIES OF RECUTTING

Recut once at top and once at bottom, (113 on plate)	1,850.	300.00
Recut once at top, (40 on plate)	1,875.	305.00
Recut once at top and twice at bottom, (21 on plate)	1,900.	310.00
Recut twice at bottom, (11 on plate)	1,950.	325.00
Recut once at bottom, (8 on plate)	2,000.	325.00
Recut once at bottom and twice at top, (4 on plate)	2,050.	335.00
Recut twice at top and twice at bottom, (2 on plate)	2,150.	350.00
Pair, combination, type II (4 R 1 L) and type IV		1,200.

CANCELLATIONS.

Blue	+5.00	Black Carrier	+60.00
Red	+25.00	Railroad	+85.00
"Paid"	+25.00	"Way"	+90.00
Red Carrier	+40.00	Steamboat	+135.00
		"Steam"	+100.00
		Pen	140.00

A20

Type V. Similar to type III of 1851-57 but with side ornaments partly cut away. Wide breaks in top and bottom framelines.

Type Va: Stamps from Plate 5 with almost complete ornaments at right side and no side scratches.

24	A20 1c **blue**, type V (Plates 7, 8, 9, 10) *1857*	110.00	22.50
	On cover		35.00
	On patriotic cover		250.00
	Pair	225.00	47.50
	Strip of three	340.00	75.00
	Block of four	475.00	275.00
	Margin block of 8, Impt. & P#	3,250.	—
	Double transfer at top (8R and 10R, Plate 8)	150.00	45.00
	Double transfer at bottom (52 R 9)	185.00	55.00
	Curl on shoulder, (57R, 58R, 59R, 98R, 99R, Plate 7)	150.00	37.50
	With "Earring" below ear (10 L 9)	200.00	55.00
	"Curl" over "C" of "Cent"	160.00	37.50
	"Curl" over "E" of "Cent" (41R and 81R 8)	170.00	45.00
	"Curl in hair," 23L VII; 39, 69L 8; 34, 74R 9	150.00	32.50
	Horizontal dash in hair (24 L 7)	200.00	50.00
	Horizontal dash in hair (36 L 8)	200.00	50.00
	Long double "curl" in hair (52, 92R 8)	185.00	45.00
b.	Laid paper	450.00	150.00
	Plate 5, *Jan. 2, 1858*	300.00	70.00
	On cover (Plate 5)		110.00
	Pair (Plate 5)	—	—
	Strip of three (Plate 5)	—	—
	Block of four (Plate V)	—	—
	"Curl" in "O" of "ONE" (62 L 5)	—	—
	"Curl" on shoulder (48 L 5)	—	—

Earliest known use; Nov. 17.

CANCELLATIONS.

Blue	+1.00	"Free"	+25.00
Red	+5.00	Railroad	+50.00
Green	+100.00	Numeral	+7.50
		Express Company	+90.00
Brown	+10.00	Steamboat	+55.00
Magenta	+20.00	"Steam"	+30.00
Ultramarine	+10.00	Steamship	+40.00
1857 year date	+70.00	Packet boat	-
1858 year date	+1.00	Supplementary Mail Types A, B, or C	+55.00
1859 year date	+1.00	"Way"	+30.00
1860 year date	+1.00	Red Carrier	+7.50
1861 year date	+1.00	Black Carrier	+12.50
1863 year date	+80.00	Blue Carrier	+50.00
		Brown Carrier	
Printed Precancellation "CUMBERLAND, ME." (on cover)		"Old Stamps- Not Recognized"	+1000.
		Territorial	+80.00
"Paid"	+3.50	Pen	10.00

25	A10 3c **rose**, type I (no inner framelines), *Feb. 28, 1857*	675.00	27.50
	rose red	675.00	27.50
	claret	725.00	32.50
	dull red	675.00	27.50
	On cover		37.50
	On patriotic cover		275.00
	Pair	1,400.	57.50
	Strip of three	2,250.	95.00
	Block of four	3,250.	3,500.

All type I stamps were printed from 7 of the plates used for the imperfs, so many varieties exist both imperf. and perf.

a.	Imperf. vertically, pair		—
b.	Imperf. horizontally, pair		—
	Gash on shoulder	700.00	30.00
	Double transfer	725.00	40.00
	Double transfer "Gents" instead of "Cents" (66 R 2 L)	—	250.00
	Triple transfer (92 L 2 L)	—	300.00
	Worn plate	675.00	27.50
	Cracked plate	900.00	100.00

VARIETIES OF RECUTTING

Recut inner frame lines	750.00	35.00
Recut inner frame line only at right		40.00
1 extra vertical line outside of left frame line (29L, 39L, 49L, 59L, 69L, 79L, Plate 3)	—	45.00
2 extra vertical lines outside of left frame line (89L, 99L, Plate 3)	—	55.00
1 extra vertical line outside of right frame line (58L, 68L, 78L, 88L, 98L, Plate 3)	—	45.00
No inner line and frame line close to design at right (9L, 19L, Plate 3)	—	55.00
No inner line and frame line close to design at left (70L, 80L, 90L, 100L, Plate 3)	—	50.00
Lines on bust and bottom of medallion circle recut (47 R 6)	—	175.00
Recut button (10 R 2)		250.00

Other varieties of recutting are described in "The 3c Stamp of U.S. 1851-57 Issue," by Carroll Chase.

CANCELLATIONS.

Blue	+1.00	Steamship	+35.00
Red	+5.00	Steamboat	+45.00
Orange	+7.50	Packet Boat	+50.00
		Supplementary Mail Type A	+40.00
Brown	+7.50	U. S. Express Mail	+5.00
Ultramarine	+12.50	Express Company	+65.00
Green	+150.00	Black Carrier	+30.00
1857 year date	+1.00	"Old Stamps- Not Recognized"	+1000.
1858 year date	+1.00	Territorial	+35.00
1859 year date	+1.00	Printed precancellation "Cumberland, Me." (on cover)	-
"Paid"	+2.50	Pen	15.00
"Way"	+20.00		
Railroad	+25.00		
Numeral	+7.50		
"Steam"	+20.00		

A21

Type II. The outer frame line has been removed at top and bottom. The side frame lines were recut so as to be continuous from the top to the bottom of the plate.

Type IIa. The side frame lines extend only to the top and bottom of the stamp design. All Type IIa stamps are from plates 10 and 11 (each of which exists in three states), and these plates produced only Type IIa. The side frame lines were recut individually for each stamp, thus being broken between the stamp vertically.

26	A21 3c **dull red**, type II, *1857*	45.00	2.75
	red	45.00	2.75
	rose	45.00	2.75
	brownish carmine	50.00	3.00
	claret	60.00	3.50
	orange brown	—	3.50
	On cover		3.50
	On patriotic cover		75.00
	On Confederate patriotic cover		1,200.
	On Pony express cover		—
	Pair	92.50	5.75
	Strip of three	140.00	9.00
	Block of four	200.00	50.00
	Margin block of 8, Impt. & P#	—	—
b.	Imperf. vertically, pair	—	—
c.	Imperf. horizontally, pair	—	—
d.	Horizontal pair, imperf. between	—	—
e.	Double impression	—	—
	Double transfer	100.00	4.00
	Double transfer, rosettes double and line through "Postage"	—	60.00
	Left frame line double	50.00	3.75
	Right frame line double	50.00	3.75
	Cracked plate	375.00	90.00
	Damaged transfer above lower left rosette	50.00	3.25
	Same, retouched	55.00	3.50
	1 line recut in upper left triangle		16.50
	5 lines recut in upper left triangle		60.00
	Inner line recut at right		32.50
	Worn plate	50.00	3.00

CANCELLATIONS.

Blue	+.10	"Steam"	+12.50
Red	+1.50	Steamer	+22.50
Orange	+2.50	Steamboat	+22.50
Brown	+2.50	Steamship	+22.50
Ultramarine	+4.00	"Way"	+12.50
Violet	+12.00	Railroad	+15.00
Green	+50.00	U. S. Express Mail	+20.00
		Express Company	+65.00
1857-1861 year date	+.25	Packet boat	+65.00
Printed Circular Precancellation "Cumberland, Me." (on cover)	-	Supplementary Mail Types A, B or C	+75.00
"Paid"	+.25	Black Carrier	+30.00
"Paid All"	+15.00	Red Carrier	+25.00
"Free"	+20.00	"Southn. Letter Unpaid"	
"Collect"	+40.00	Territorial	+20.00
Numeral	+2.50	"Old Stamps- Not Recognized"	+500.00

26a	A21 3c **dull red**, type IIa, *July 11, 1857*	110.00	20.00
	brownish carmine	110.00	20.00
	rose	110.00	20.00
	claret	120.00	22.50
	On cover		30.00
	On patriotic cover		175.00
	Pair	225.00	42.50
	Strip of three	350.00	70.00
	Block of four	550.00	120.00
	Double transfer	150.00	25.00

Double transfer of rosettes and lower part of stamp (91R 11 L)	—	60.00
Triple transfer	—	55.00
Damaged transfer above lower left rosette	120.00	21.00
Same, retouched	125.00	22.00
Inner line recut at right	—	35.00
Inner line recut at left	—	55.00
Left frame line double	—	40.00
Worn plate	110.00	20.00

CANCELLATIONS.

		"Collect"	+40.00
Blue	+1.00	Numeral	+2.50
Red	+5.00	"Steam"	+15.00
Orange	+7.50	Steamer	-
Brown	+7.50	Steamboat	+25.00
Ultramarine	+10.00	Steamship	+25.00
Violet	+17.50	"Way"	+15.00
Green	+135.00	Railroad	+17.50
1857 year date	+2.50	U. S. Express Mail	+17.50
1858 or 1859 year date	+1.50	Express Company	+65.00
"Paid"	+2.50	Packet boat	+65.00
"Paid All"	+15.00	Black Carrier	+30.00
"Free"	+20.00	Red Carrier	+20.00
		Territorial	+25.00
		Pen	10.00

27 A11 5c **brick red,** type I, *Oct. 6, 1858* 8,500. 1,000.

On cover		1,600.
On patriotic cover		4,000.
Pair	17,500.	2,100.
Strip of three		3,500.
Block of four	—	14,500.

CANCELLATIONS.

		"Paid"	+25.00
Blue	+25.00	Supplementary Mail Type A	+100.00
Red	+50.00	"Steamship"	+100.00
Ultramarine	+150.00	Pen	450.00
1859 year date	+25.00		
1860 year date	+25.00		

28 A11 5c **red brown,** type I, *Aug. 23, 1857* 1,350. 285.00

pale red brown	1,350.	285.00
b. Bright red brown	1,850.	450.00
On cover		525.00
Pair	2,750.	600.00
Strip of three		925.00
Block of four	10,000.	2,500.

CANCELLATIONS.

		"Paid"	+35.00
Blue	+10.00	Railroad	+75.00
Red	+25.00	"Short Paid"	-
1857 year date	+20.00	Pen	120.00
1858 year date	+10.00		

28A A11 5c **Indian red,** type I, *Mar. 31, 1858* 10,000. 1,500.

On cover		2,600.
Pair		3,100.
Strip of three		4,750.
Block of four		—

CANCELLATIONS.

		1858 year date	+50.00
Red	+50.00	1859 year date	+25.00
		Pen	700.00

29 A11 5c **brown,** type I, *July 4, 1859* 750.00 225.00

pale brown	750.00	225.00
deep brown	750.00	225.00
yellowish brown	750.00	225.00
On cover		325.00
Pair	1,550.	475.00
Strip of three	2,500.	725.00
Block of four	4,750.	2,750.

CANCELLATIONS.

		1859 year date	+5.00
Blue	+5.00	1860 year date	+5.00
Red	+15.00	"Paid"	+15.00
Brown	+20.00	"Steam"	+75.00
Magenta	+65.00	Steamship	+85.00
Green	+250.00	Numeral	+50.00
		Pen	95.00

Jefferson — A22

FIVE CENTS.

Type II. The projections at top and bottom are partly cut away. Several minor types could be made according to the extent of cutting of the projections.

30 A22 5c **orange brown,** Type II, *May 8, 1861* 750.00 900.00

deep orange brown	750.00	900.00
On cover		2,250.
On patriotic cover		4,000.
Pair	1,550.	2,250.
Strip of three	2,500.	—
Block of four	4,000.	—

CANCELLATIONS.

Blue	+25.00	Steamship	+110.00
Red	+50.00	Supp. Mail A	+150.00
Green	-	Railroad	-
"Paid"	+75.00	Pen	300.00

30A A22 5c **brown,** type II, *Mar. 4, 1860* 450.00 185.00

dark brown	450.00	185.00
yellowish brown	450.00	185.00
On cover		250.00
On patriotic cover		-
Pair	925.00	380.00
Strip of three	1,450.	600.00
Block of four	2,400.	2,500.
b. Printed on both sides	3,750.	3,000.
Cracked plate		-

CANCELLATIONS.

		"Steamship"	+50.00
Blue	+5.00	"Steam"	+40.00
Red	+20.00	Express Company	+250.00
Magenta	+50.00	Railroad	-
Green	+250.00	Packet boat	-
"Paid"	+20.00	Pen	75.00
Supp. Mail, A	+50.00		

31 A12 10c **green,** type I, *July 27, 1857* 5,250. 525.00

dark green	5,250.	525.00
bluish green	5,250.	525.00
yellowish green	5,250.	525.00
On cover		800.00
On patriotic cover		2,500.
Pair	11,000.	1,100.
Pair combination, type I and type III	7,250.	750.00
Pair, combination, type I and type IV		—
Strip of three		—
Vertical strip of 3, combination, type I, type III, type II		—
Block of four, combination, type I and type III	15,000.	—
Block of four, combination, types I, III and IV		—
Double transfer (100 R 1)	5,750.	600.00
"Curl" in left "X" (99 R 1)	5,750.	600.00

Type I comes only from the bottom row of both panes of Plate 1.

CANCELLATIONS.

		Supplementary Mail Type A	-
Blue	+10.00	"Steamship"	+100.00
Red	+25.00	Pen	250.00
Green	+225.00		

Act of February 27, 1861. Ten cent rate of postage to be prepaid on letters conveyed in the mail from any point in the United States east of the Rocky Mountains to any State or Territory on the Pacific Coast and vice versa, for each half-ounce.

32 A13 10c **green,** type II, *July 27, 1857* 1,750. 175.00

dark green	1,750.	175.00
bluish green	1,750.	175.00
yellowish green	1,750.	175.00
On cover		225.00
On pony express cover		—
Pair	3,600.	375.00
Strip of 3		600.00
Block of four	9,000.	3,500.
Pair, combination, types II & III	3,750.	375.00
Pair, combination, types II & IV	20,000.	2,000.
Vertical strip of three, combination types II, III and IV		—
Block of four, combination, type II and type III	8,000.	1,650.
Block of four, combination types II and IV		—
Block of 4, types II, III, IV	40,000.	—
Double transfer (31L, 51L and 20R, Plate 1)	1,850.	195.00
"Curl opposite left X" (10 R 1)		235.00

CANCELLATIONS.

		1857 year date	+5.00
Blue	+5.00	Steamship	+50.00
Red	+20.00	Packet boat	-
Brown	+25.00	Railroad	-
Green	+225.00	Express Company	-
"Paid"	+20.00	Pen	70.00

33 A14 10c **green,** type III, *July 27, 1857* 1,850. 185.00

dark green	1,850.	185.00
bluish green	1,850.	185.00
yellowish green	1,850.	185.00

On cover		250.00
Pair	3,800.	385.00
Strip of 3		-
Pair, combination types III & IV		2,100.
"Curl" on forehead (85 L 1)	—	235.00
"Curl in left X" (87 R 1)		235.00

CANCELLATIONS.

		"Paid"	+20.00
Blue	+5.00	"Steam"	+45.00
Red	+20.00	Steamboat	-
Brown	+25.00	Steamship	+50.00
Ultramarine	+45.00	Numeral	+15.00
1857 year date	+5.00	Packet boat	-
		Pen	75.00

34 A15 10c **green,** type IV, *July 27, 1857* 17,500. 1,750.

dark green	17,500.	1,750.
bluish green	17,500.	1,750.
yellowish green	17,500.	1,750.
On cover		2,250.
Pair		3,750.
Block of four (54-55, 64-65L)		—

VARIETIES OF RECUTTING

Eight stamps on Plate I were recut. All are listed below.

Outer line recut at top (65L, 74L, 86L and 3R, Plate I)	17,500.	1,750.
Outer line recut at bottom (54L, 55L, 76L, Plate 1)	18,000.	1,800.
Outer line recut at top and bottom (64 L 1)	18,500.	1,850.

CANCELLATIONS.

		Steamship	+150.00
Blue	+25.00	Packet boat	-
Red	+50.00	Pen	750.00

Types I, II, III and IV occur on the same sheet, so it is possible to obtain pairs and blocks showing combinations of types. For listings of type combinations in pairs and blocks, see Nos. 31-33.

(Two typical examples) — A23

Type V. The side ornaments are slightly cut away. Usually only one pearl remains at each end of the lower label, but some copies show two or three pearls at the right side. At the bottom the outer line is complete and the shells nearly so. The outer lines at top are complete except over the right "X".

35 A23 10c **green,** type V, (Plate 2), *May 9, 1859* 175.00 60.00

dark green	175.00	60.00
yellowish green	175.00	60.00
On cover		85.00
On patriotic cover		600.00
On pony express cover		—
Pair	360.00	125.00
Block of four	750.00	500.00
Margin block of 8, Impt. & P#	9,000.	
Double transfer at bottom (47 R 2)	225.00	80.00
Small "Curl" on forehead (37, 78L 2)	210.00	70.00
Curl in "e" of "cents" (93 L 2)	225.00	80.00
Curl in "t" of "cents" (73 R 2)	225.00	80.00

CANCELLATIONS.

		Steamship	+35.00
Red	+2.50	"Steam"	+30.00
Brown	+5.00	Numerals	+15.00
Blue	+1.50	Supplementary Mail Type A or C	+60.00
Orange	+7.50	Express Company	+135.00
Magenta	+30.00	"Southn Letter Unpaid"	-
Green	+125.00	Territorial	-
1859 year date	+5.00	Pen	30.00
"Paid"	+5.00		
Red carrier			
Railroad	+40.00		

TWELVE CENTS. Printed from two plates.
Plate I. Outer frame lines complete.
Plate III. Outer frame lines noticeably uneven or broken, sometimes partly missing. Imperforate stamps, Plate III, are from a trial printing.

36	A16	12c **black** (Plate 1), July 30, 1857	325.00	85.00
		gray black	325.00	85.00
		Single on cover		450.00
		Single on cover with No. 26		150.00
		Pair on cover		200.00
		Pair on patriotic cover		—
		Pair	700.00	175.00
		Block of four	1,750.	750.00
a.		Diagonal half used as 6c on cover		—
c.		Horizontal pair, imperf. between (I)		
		Not recut in lower right corner	350.00	95.00
		Recut in lower left corner (43L, 53L, 63L, 73L and 100L)	375.00	90.00
		Double transfer	375.00	95.00
		Triple transfer	450.00	

CANCELLATIONS.

		Supplementary Mail Type A	+60.00
Blue	+2.50	Express Company	-
Red	+7.50	Railroad	+60.00
Brown	+10.00	Numeral	+20.00
Magenta	+25.00	"Southn Letter Unpaid"	-
Green	+250.00	Pen	40.00
1857 year date	+20.00		
"Paid"	+10.00		

36b	A16	12c **black** (Plate 3), Dec. 3, 1859	260.00	100.00
		intense black	260.00	100.00
		Single on cover		550.00
		Single on cover with No. 26		175.00
		Pair on cover		250.00
		Pair	550.00	210.00
		Block of four	1,200.	1,100.
		Double frame line at right	285.00	110.00
		Double frame line at left	285.00	110.00
		Vertical line through rosette (95 R 3)	375.00	135.00

Washington — A17

37	A17	24c **gray lilac**, 1860	600.00	235.00
a.		24c **gray**	600.00	235.00
		On cover		1,100.
		On patriotic cover		3,500.
		Pair	1,250.	525.00
		Block of four, gray lilac	3,000.	5,000.
		Margin block of 12, Impt. & P#	30,000.	
b.		24c **red lilac**	1,000.	
b.		Block of four, red lilac	6,000.	
c.		Imperforate	1,150.	
c.		Pair, imperforate	4,750.	

CANCELLATIONS.

		"Free"	+100.00
Blue	+10.00	Supplementary Mail Type A	+100.00
Red	+20.00	Railroad	+150.00
Magenta	+45.00	Packet Boat	+200.00
Violet	+75.00	Red Carrier	-
Green	+450.00	Numeral	+40.00
1860 year date	+15.00	"Southn Letter Unpaid"	+2500.
"Paid"	+25.00	Pen	120.00
"Paid All"	+50.00		

Franklin — A18

38	A18	30c **orange**, Aug. 8, 1860	775.00	300.00
		yellow orange	775.00	300.00
		reddish orange	775.00	300.00
		On cover		2,250.
		On patriotic cover		8,500.
		Pair	1,600.	675.00
		Block of four	4,500.	6,500.
a.		Imperforate	2,500.	
a.		Pair, imperforate	6,000.	
		Double transfer (89 L 1 and 99 L 1)	875.00	350.00
		Recut at bottom (52 L 1)	925.00	400.00
		Cracked plate	—	—

CANCELLATIONS.

		"Free"	-
Blue	+10.00	Black town	+25.00
Red	+25.00	Supplementary Mail Type A	+75.00
Magenta	+60.00	Steamship	-
Violet	+75.00	Express Company	-
Green	+450.00	"Southn Letter Unpaid"	-
1860 year date	+25.00	Pen	175.00
"Paid"	+35.00		

The 30c was first printed in black. It was not perforated or gummed. Evidence that any were issued is unsatisfactory. It is listed in the Trial Color Proofs section.

Washington — A19

39	A19	90c **blue**, 1860	1,450.	3,000.
		deep blue	1,450.	3,000.
		On cover		—
		Pair	3,000.	—
		Block of four	10,000.	—
a.		Imperforate	3,500.	
a.		Pair, imperforate	10,000.	
		Double transfer at bottom	1,600.	—
		Double transfer at top	1,600.	—
		Short transfer at bottom right and left (13 L 1 and 68 R 1)	1,550.	

CANCELLATIONS.

		"Paid"	-
Blue	+100.00	Red Carrier	-
Red	+250.00	Pen	1000.
1861 year date	-		

Genuine cancellations on the 90c are rare.
Nos. 37b, 37c, 38a and 39a were probably not regularly issued but came from trial printings.

REPRINTS OF 1857-60 ISSUE.
Issued for the Centennial Exposition of 1876. These were not good for postal use.
Produced by the Continental Bank Note Co.
White paper, without gum.
The 1, 3, 10 and 12c were printed from new plates of 100 subjects each differing from those used for the regular issue.

1875 — **Perf. 12**

40	A5	1c **bright blue** (3846)		550.00
		Pair		1,200.
		Block of four		3,000.
		Cracked plate (91)		700.00
		Double transfer (94)		700.00
41	A10	3c **scarlet** (479)		2,850.
42	A22	5c **orange brown** (878)		950.00

		Pair		2,750.
		Vertical margin strip of 4, Impt. & P#		9,500.
43	A12	10c **blue green** (516)		2,250.
		Pair		6,500.
44	A16	12c **greenish black** (489)		2,600.
		Pair		6,000.
45	A17	24c **blackish violet** (479)		2,850.
46	A18	30c **yellow orange** (480)		2,850.
47	A19	90c **deep blue** (454)		4,250.

Nos. 40 to 47 exist imperforate.
Numbers in parentheses are quantities issued.

Produced by the National Bank Note Co.

Franklin — A24a

Washington A25a

Jefferson A26a / Washington A27a

Washington — A28a

Washington A31a

Plates of 200 subjects in two panes of 100 each.
The paper of Nos. 55-62 is thin and semitransparent. That of the following issues is thicker and more opaque, except Nos. 62B, 70c, and 70d.
Nos. 55-62 were not regularly issued.

1861 — **Perf. 12**

55	A24a	1c **indigo**		20,000.
56	A25a	3c **brown rose**		700.00
		Pair		1,450.
		Block of four		3,000.
		Margin of 8, Impt. & P#		15,000.
a.		Imperf., pair		1,750.
57	A26a	5c **brown**		14,000.
58	A27a	10c **dark green**		6,000.
59	A28a	12c **black**		40,000.
60	A29	24c **dark violet**		6,500.
		Block of four		—
61	A30	30c **red orange**		17,500.
62	A31a	90c **dull blue**		22,500.
a.		Imperf., pair		5,500.

1861

62B	A27a	10c **dark green**, Sept. 17, 1861	6,000.	450.00
		dark yellow green	6,000.	450.00
		On cover		750.00
		On patriotic cover		2,000.
		Pair	12,500.	1,000.

Block of four	26,000.	5,000.
Double transfer 94 R 4	6,500.	525.00

CANCELLATIONS.

Red	+50.00	Steamship	+100.00
Blue	+25.00	Express Company	+200.00
"Paid"	+50.00	Supplementary Mail Type A	+125.00

No. 62B unused cannot be distinguished from No. 58, which does not exist used.

Designs modified (except 24c and 30c)

Franklin — A24

Washington — A25

Jefferson — A26

Washington — A27

Washington — A28

Washington — A29

Franklin — A30

Washington — A31

Prices in the "unused" column are for never-hinged stamps for United States items since 1960.

1c. A dash has been added under the tip of the ornament at right of the numeral in upper left corner.

3c. Ornaments at corners have been enlarged and end in a small ball.

5c. A leaflet has been added to the foliated ornaments at each corner.

10c. A heavy curved line has been cut below the stars and an outer line added to the ornaments above them.

12c. Ovals and scrolls have been added to the corners.

90c. Parallel lines form an angle above the ribbon with "U. S. Postage"; between these lines a row of dashes has been added and a point of color to the apex of the lower line.

Patriotic Covers covering a wide range of historical interest were used during the Civil War period, in the North as well as the South, and are collected in State groups as well as generally. There are known to be over 11,000 varieties.

During the war, these stamps were used as small change until Postage Currency was issued.

The Act of Congress of March 3, 1863, effective July 1, 1863, created a rate of three cents for each half ounce, first class domestic mail. This Act was the first law which established uniform rate of postage regardless of the distance. This rate remained in effect for twenty years.

1861-62   ***Perf. 12***

63	A24	1c **blue,** *Aug. 17, 1861*	125.00	18.00
		pale blue	125.00	18.00
		bright blue	125.00	18.00
a.		1c ultramarine	225.00	40.00
b.		1c dark blue	175.00	25.00
		On cover (single)		27.50
		On prisoner's letter		—
		On patriotic cover		175.00
		Pair	265.00	37.50
		Block of four	525.00	125.00
		Margin block of 8, Impr. & P#	2,400.	
		Double transfer		25.00
		Dot in "U"	120.00	20.00
c.		Laid paper, horiz. or vert.	—	150.00
d.		Vertical pair, imperf. horiz.		—
e.		Printed on both sides	—	2,500.

CANCELLATIONS.

Blue	+1.00	Supp. Mail, A, B	+30.00
Red	+5.00	Steamship	+35.00
Magenta	+10.00	Steam	+30.00
Green	+90.00	Express Company	+85.00
Violet	+25.00	Red Carrier	+5.00
1861 year date	+7.50	Black Carrier	+10.00
1865 year date	+1.00	Railroad	+30.00
1866 year date	+1.00	Numeral	+10.00
"Free"	+20.00	"Steamboat"	+50.00
"Paid"	+2.50	Printed Precancel "CUMBERLAND, ME." (on cover)	1,500.
"Paid All"	+15.00		

64	A25	3c **pink**	4,000.	300.00
		On cover (pink)		400.00
		On patriotic cover (pink)		650.00
		Block of four (pink)	17,500.	
a.		3c pigeon blood pink	—	1,350.
		On cover (pigeon blood pink)		2,250.
		On patriotic cover (pig. bld. pink)		3,500.
b.		3c rose pink	260.00	45.00
		On cover (rose pink)		65.00
		On patriotic cover (rose pink)		150.00
		Block of four (rose pink)	1,300.	275.00

CANCELLATIONS.

Blue No. 64	+10.00	Blue No. 64b	+5.00
"Paid" No. 64	+25.00	"Paid" No. 64b	+10.00
Red No. 64	+25.00	Red No. 64b	+10.00
"Ship" No. 64	+85.00	"Ship" No. 64b	+30.00
Green No. 64	+500.00	Green No. 64b	+150.00
"Free" No. 64	+125.00	"Free" No. 64b	+50.00
1861 date No. 64	—		
Railroad No. 64	+125.00	Railroad No. 64b	+50.00
Steamboat No. 64	+175.00	Steamboat No. 64b	+75.00
Supp. Mail, B No. 64	+150.00		

65	A25	3c **rose,** *1861*	65.00	1.10
		bright rose	65.00	1.10
		dull red	65.00	1.10
		rose red	65.00	1.10
		brown red	65.00	1.10
		pale brown red	65.00	1.10
		On cover		1.50
		On patriotic cover		40.00
		On prisoner's letter		200.00
		On pony express cover		

	Pair	135.00	2.25
	Block of four	275.00	15.00
	Margin block of 8, Impt. & P#	1,750.	
b.	Laid paper, horiz. or vert.	250.00	35.00
c.	Imperf., pair	450.00	
c.	Margin block of 8, Impt. & P#	—	
d.	Vertical pair, imperf. horiz.	1,200.	750.00
e.	Printed on both sides	1,650.	1,000.
f.	Double impression		1,200.
	Double transfer	80.00	2.50
	Cracked plate	—	

CANCELLATIONS.

Blue	+10	"Collect"	+35.00
Ultramarine	+2.75	"Ship"	+15.00
Brown	+2.50	"U. S. Ship"	+35.00
Red	+2.50	"Steam"	+12.00
Violet	+4.50	Steamship	+15.00
Magenta	+4.50	Steamboat	+20.00
Green	+45.00	"Ship Letter"	+35.00
Olive	+12.00	Red Carrier	+15.00
Orange	+10.00	Blue Carrier	+25.00
1861 year		Black Carrier	+20.00
date	+.50		
1867 or		Numeral	+3.00
1868 year			
date	+.50		
"Paid"	+35	Supplementary	
		Mail Types	
		A, B or C	+15.00
"Paid All"	+7.50	Express Com-	
		pany	+40.00
"Mails Sus-		Army Field	
pended"		Post	+60.00
Railroad	+12.50	Packet Boat	+40.00
"Way"	+20.00	"Registered"	+30.00
"Free"	+20.00	"Postage Due"	+25.00
		"Advertised"	+15.00
		Territorial	+25.00
		St. Thomas	-
		China	-

66	A25	3c **lake**	1,650.
		Pair	3,400.
		Block of four	7,000.
a.		Imperf., (pair)	1,850.
a.		Margin block of 8, Impt. & P#	-
		Double transfer	1,900.

Nos. 66 and 66a were not regularly issued. John N. Luff recorded the plate number as 34.

67	A26	5c **buff,** *Aug. 19, 1861*	4,500.	400.00
a.		5c brown yellow	4,500.	400.00
b.		5c olive yellow	4,500.	400.00
		On cover		700.00
		On patriotic cover		3,500.
		Pair	9,250.	850.00
		Block of four	50,000.	9,000.

CANCELLATIONS.

Red	+25.00	"Paid"	+25.00
Blue	+10.00	Supplementary	
		Mail Type A	+100.00
Magenta	+50.00	Express Com-	
		pany	+250.00
Green	-		
1861 year		Numeral	+50.00
date	+10.00		
		"Steamship"	+100.00

68	A27	10c **yellow green,** *Aug. 20, 1861*	250.00	30.00
		deep yellow green on thin pa-		
		per	325.00	40.00
		green	250.00	30.00
a.		10c dark green	265.00	31.00
		blue green	265.00	32.50
		On cover		45.00
		On patriotic cover		350.00
		Pair	510.00	62.50
		Block of four	1,050.	250.00
		Margin block of 8, Impt. & P#	5,000.	
b.		Vertical pair, imperf. horiz.		3,500.
		Double transfer	300.00	40.00

CANCELLATIONS.

Blue	+1.00	"Free"	+25.00
Red	+2.50	Numeral	+7.50
Purple	+5.00	Red Carrier	+45.00
Magenta	+5.00	Railroad	+20.00
Brown	+2.50	Steamship	+15.00
Green	+110.00	"Steamboat"	+35.00
1865 year		Supplementary	
date	+3.50	Mail Types A	
		or D	+30.00
"Paid"	+2.50	Express Com-	
		pany	+70.00
"Collect"	+32.50	China	-
"Short		Japan	+200.00
Paid"	+50.00		
"P.D." in		St. Thomas	-
circle	+30.00		

69	A28	12c **black,** *Aug. 1861*	475.00	55.00
		gray black	475.00	55.00
		intense black	500.00	60.00
		On cover		85.00
		On patriotic cover		800.00
		Pair	975.00	115.00
		Block of four	2,250.	550.00
		Double transfer of top frame		
		line	525.00	65.00
		Double transfer of bottom		
		frame line	525.00	65.00
		Double transfer of top and		
		bottom frame lines	550.00	70.00

CANCELLATIONS.

Blue	+2.00	"Paid"	+5.00
Red	+5.00	"Registered"	+35.00

Purple	+10.00	Supplementary	
		Mail Types	
		A, B or C	+45.00
Magenta	+10.00	Express Com-	
		pany	+175.00
Green	+175.00	Railroad	+50.00
1861 year		Numeral	+15.00
date	+5.00		

70	A29	24c **red lilac,** *Jan. 7, 1862*	575.00	80.00
		On cover		200.00
		On patriotic cover		3,000.
		Pair	1,200.	165.00
		Block of four	3,750.	750.00
a.		24c brown lilac	475.00	67.50
a.		Block of four	3,000.	
b.		24c steel blue ('61)	3,750.	275.00
b.		Block of four	15,500.	
c.		24c violet, *Aug. 20, 1861*	3,750.	550.00
d.		24c grayish lilac	1,250.	275.00
b.		On cover (steel blue)		800.00
		Scratch under "A" of "Post-		
		age"		95.00

There are numerous shades of the 24c stamp in this and the following issue.

Color changelings, especially of No. 78, are frequently offered as No. 70b.

Nos. 70c and 70d are on a thinner, harder and more transparent paper than Nos. 70, 70a, 70b or the latter Nos. 78, 78a, 78b and 78c. No. 60 is distinguished by its distinctive dark color.

CANCELLATIONS. (No. 70)

Blue	+2.50	1865 year date	+5.00
Red	+5.00	"Paid"	+15.00
Magenta	+15.00	Supplementary	
		Mail Types A	
		or B	+75.00
Brown	+7.50	Express	
		Company	+350.00
Green	+300.00		

71	A30	30c **orange,** *Aug. 20, 1861*	475.00	70.00
		deep orange	475.00	70.00
		On cover		500.00
		On patriotic cover		3,500.
		Pair	975.00	160.00
		Block of four	2,250.	900.00
a.		Printed on both sides		

CANCELLATIONS.

Blue	+2.50	Railroad	-
Magenta	+15.00	Packet Boat	-
Brown	+10.00	"Steamship"	+75.00
Red	+15.00	Supplementary	
		Mail Type A	+75.00
"Paid"	+15.00	Express Com-	
		pany	+350.00
"Paid All"	+35.00	Japan	-

72	A31	90c **blue,** *Aug., 1861*	1,300.	250.00
a.		90c pale blue	1,300.	250.00
b.		90c dark blue	1,400.	275.00
		dull blue	1,300.	250.00
		On cover		13,500.
		Pair	2,700.	550.00
		Block of four	6,250.	2,500.

Earliest known use: Nov. 27.

CANCELLATIONS.

Blue	+10.00	"Paid"	+25.00
Red	+25.00	"Registered"	+75.00
Green	+450.00	Express	
		Company	+500.00
1865 year		Supplementary	
date	+35.00	Mail Type A	+100.00

Nos. 65c, 68a, 69, 71 and 72 exist as imperforate sheet-margin singles with pen cancel. They were not regularly issued.

The 90c was distributed to several post offices in the last two weeks of August, 1861.

Owing to the Civil War, stamps and stamped envelopes in current use or available for postage in 1860, were demonetized by various post office orders, beginning in August, 1861, and extending to early January, 1862.

P. O. Department Bulletin.

"A reasonable time after hostilities began in 1861 was given for the return to the Department of all these (1851-56) stamps in the hands of postmasters, and as early as 1863 the Department issued an order declining to longer redeem them."

The Act of Congress, approved March 3, 1863, abolished carriers' fees and established a prepaid rate of two cents for drop letters, making necessary the 2-cent Jackson (No. 73).

Free City Delivery was authorized by the Act of Congress of March 3, 1863, effective in 49 cities with 449 carriers, beginning July 1, 1863.

Produced by the National Bank Note Co.
DESIGNS AS 1861 ISSUE

Andrew
Jackson — A32

Earliest known use: 2c, July 6, 1863.

1861-66				*Perf. 12*
73	A32	2c **black,** *July 1863*	110.00	22.50
		gray black	110.00	22.50
		intense black	120.00	27.50
		On cover		40.00
		On prisoner's letter		—
		On patriotic cover		1,000.
		Pair	235.00	50.00
		Block of four	500.00	400.00
		Margin block of 8, Impt. & P#	8,000.	
a.		Half used as 1c on cover, diagonal,		
		vert. or horiz.		1,650.
d.		Laid paper		—
e.		Printed on both sides		4,000.
		Double transfer	125.00	25.00
		Major double transfer of top left		
		corner		250.00
		Major overall double transfer		
		("Atherton shift")		6,000.
		Triple transfer		—
		Short transfer	115.00	24.00
		Cracked plate	—	

CANCELLATIONS.

Blue	+1.00	"Paid"	+10.00
Brown	+5.00	Numeral	+15.00
Red	+7.50	Railroad	+85.00
Magenta	+12.50	"Steam"	+40.00
Ultramarine	+12.50	Steamship	+65.00
Orange	+10.00	"Steamboat"	+65.00
Green	+265.00	"Ship Letter"	-
1863 year		Black Carrier	+20.00
date	+5.00		
Printed Pre-		Blue Carrier	+35.00
cancella-			
tion			
"Jefferson,			
Ohio"	-		
"PAID		Supplementary	
ALL"	+40.00	Mail Types A	
		or B	+60.00
		Express Com-	
		pany	+200.00
		"Short Paid"	+130.00
		China	-

74	A25	3c **scarlet**	4,500.	
		Block of four	20,000.	
		With 4 horiz. black pen strokes	1,850.	
a.		Imperf., pair	3,750.	

Nos. 74 and 74a were not regularly issued. John N. Luff recorded the plate number as 19.

75	A26	5c **red brown,** *Jan. 2, 1862*	1,300.	225.00
		dark red brown	1,300.	225.00
		On cover		475.00
		On patriotic cover		2,500.
		Pair	2,700.	475.00
		Block of four	—	3,000.
		Double transfer	1,500.	250.00

CANCELLATIONS.

Blue	+10.00	"Paid"	+25.00
Red	+25.00	Supplementary	
		Mail Type A	+50.00
Magenta	+50.00	Express Com-	
		pany	+300.00

76	A26	5c **brown,** *Feb. 3, 1863*	325.00	52.50
		pale brown	325.00	52.50
a.		5c dark brown	375.00	65.00
		On cover		120.00
		On patriotic cover		800.00
		Pair	675.00	110.00
		Block of four	1,500.	450.00
a.		Block of four	1,750.	
		Double transfer of top frame		
		line	400.00	65.00
		Double transfer of bottom frame		
		line	400.00	65.00
		Double transfer of top and bot-		
		tom frame lines	425.00	70.00
b.		Laid paper		—

CANCELLATIONS.

Blue	+2.50	"Paid"	+15.00
Magenta	+5.00	"Short Paid"	+75.00
Red	+5.00	Supplementary	
		Mail Type A	
		or F	+55.00

Brown	+5.00	Express Company	+175.00
Green	+225.00	"Steamship"	+65.00
1865 year		Packet boat	-
date	+10.00		

Abraham
Lincoln — A33

77	A33	15c **black**, *1866*	500.00	67.50
		full black	500.00	67.50
		On cover		175.00
		Pair	1,050.	140.00
		Block of four	14,000.	
		Margin block of 8, Impt. & P#	—	
		Double transfer	500.00	75.00
		Cracked plate	—	

Earliest known use; April 14.

CANCELLATIONS. Apr.14

Blue	+2.50	"Paid"	+15.00
Magenta	+10.00	"Short Paid"	+85.00
Red	+10.00	"Insufficiently	
		Paid"	+150.00
Brown	+10.00	"Ship"	+50.00
Green	+250.00	Steamship	+50.00
Ultramarine	+25.00	Supplementary	
		Mail Type A	+70.00

78	A29	24c **lilac**, *Feb. 20, 1863*	275.00	50.00
		dark lilac	275.00	50.00
a.		24c grayish lilac	275.00	50.00
b.		24c gray	275.00	50.00
c.		24c blackish violet	4,000.	600.00
		On cover		200.00
		Pair	600.00	110.00
		Block of four	1,350.	450.00
d.		Printed on both sides		3,500.
		Scratch under "A" of "Postage"	350.00	65.00

CANCELLATIONS.

Blue	+2.50	"Paid"	+12.50
Red	+7.50	Numeral	+17.50
Magenta	+10.00	Supplementary	
		Mail Type A	+50.00
Green	+275.00	"Free"	+75.00

Nos. 73, 76-78 exist as imperforate sheet-margin singles, all with pen cancel except No. 76 which is uncanceled. They were not regularly issued.

SAME DESIGNS AS 1861-66 ISSUES
Printed by the National Bank Note Co.

Grill

Embossed with grills of various sizes.
A peculiarity of the United States issues from 1867 to 1870 is the grill or embossing. The object was to break the fibre of the paper so that the ink of the canceling stamp would soak in and make washing for a second using impossible. The exact date at which grilled stamps came into use is unsettled. Luff's "Postage Stamps of the United States" places the date as probably August 8, 1867. Some authorities believe that more than one size of grill probably existed on one of the grill rolls.

GRILL WITH POINTS UP
Grills A and C were made by a roller covered with ridges shaped like an inverted V. Pressing the ridges into the stamp paper forced the paper into the pyramidal pits between the ridges, causing irregular breaks in the paper. Grill B was made by a roller with raised bosses.
A. Grill Covering the Entire Stamp.

1867　　　　　　　　　　　　*Perf. 12*

79	A25	3c **rose**	1,750.	425.00
		On cover		750.00
		Pair	3,750.	1,000.
		Block of four	10,000.	
a.		Imperf., pair		1,650.
a.		Block of four		3,750.

a.	Margin block of 8, Impt. & P#	10,000.
b.	Printed on both sides	—

Earliest known use: Aug. 13, 1867.

CANCELLATIONS.

Blue	+25.00	Railroad	-

An essay which is often mistaken for No. 79 shows the points of the grill as small squares faintly impressed in the paper but not cutting through it. On the issued stamp the grill generally breaks through the paper. Copies without defects are rare.
No. 79a was not regularly issued.

80	A26	5c **brown**	40,000.	—
a.		5c dark brown		37,500.
81	A30	30c **orange**		32,500.

B. Grill about 18x15 mm.
(22x18 points.)

82	A25	3c **rose**	45,000.

C. Grill about 13x16 mm.
(16 to 17 by 18 to 21 points.)
The grilled area on each of four C grills in the sheet may total about 18x15mm. when a normal C grill adjoins a fainter grill extending to the right or left edge of the stamp. This is caused by a partial erasure on the grill roller when it was changed to produce C grills instead of the all-over A grill.

83	A25	3c **rose**	1,750.	400.00
		On cover		550.00
		Pair	3,600.	850.00
		Block of four	8,500.	
a.		Imperf., pair		1,650.
		Double grill	3,500.	1,500.
		Grill with points down	3,000.	650.00

CANCELLATIONS.

Blue	+10.00	

No. 83a was not regularly issued.
A 1c blue (A24) with "c" grill points down exists unused. It was not issued. Experts consider it an essay.

GRILL WITH POINTS DOWN
The grills were produced by rollers with the surface covered, or partly covered, by pyramidal bosses. On the D, E and F grills the tips of the pyramids are vertical ridges. On the Z grill the ridges are horizontal.
D. Grill about 12x14mm.
(15 by 17 to 18 points.)

84	A32	2c **black**	3,500.	900.00
		On cover		1,300.
		Pair	7,250.	1,850.
		Block of four	16,000.	—
		Double transfer		—
		Split grill		950.00

CANCELLATIONS.

Red	+75.00	"Paid All"	+100.00

85	A25	3c **rose**	1,500.	450.00
		On cover		550.00
		Pair	3,250.	925.00
		Block of four	8,500.	—
		Double grill		—
		Split grill		500.00

CANCELLATIONS.

Blue	+10.00	"Paid"	+50.00
Green	+200.00		

Z. Grill about 11x14 mm.
(13 to 14 by 18 points.)

85A	A24	1c **blue**		—
85B	A32	2c **black**	1,300.	350.00
		On cover		550.00
		Pair	2,700.	750.00
		Block of four	8,000.	—
		Double transfer	1,400.	375.00
		Double grill		—

CANCELLATIONS.

Blue	+10.00	Black Carrier	+75.00
Red	+50.00	"Paid All"	+75.00

85C	A25	3c **rose**	4,000.	950.00
		On cover		1,250.
		Block of four	17,500.	
		Double grill	5,000.	

CANCELLATIONS.

Green	+250.00	Red	+75.00
Blue	+25.00	"Paid"	+50.00

85D	A27	10c **green**		25,000.
85E	A28	12c **black**	1,650.	575.00
		On cover		900.00
		Strip of three		—
		Block of four		—
		Double transfer of top frame line		625.00
85F	A33	15c **black**		—

E. Grill about 11x13 mm.
(14 by 15 to 17 points.)

86	A24	1c **blue**	800.00	250.00
a.		1c dull blue	800.00	250.00
		On cover		325.00

Pair		1,650.	525.00
Block of four		3,500.	1,250.
Double grill		—	375.00
Split grill		850.00	275.00

CANCELLATIONS.

Blue	+5.00	"Paid"	+20.00
Red	+25.00	Steamboat	+85.00
Green	+140.00	Red Carrier	+60.00

87	A32	2c **black**	350.00	70.00
		intense black	375.00	75.00
		gray black	350.00	70.00
		On cover		100.00
		Pair	725.00	145.00
		Block of four	1,600.	
a.		Half used as 1c on cover, diagonal or vertical		2,000.
		Double grill	475.00	100.00
		Triple grill		—
		Split grill	400.00	80.00
		Grill with points up		—
		Double transfer	375.00	75.00

CANCELLATIONS.

Blue	+2.50	"Paid"	+10.00
Purple	+15.00	Steamship	+60.00
Brown	+10.00	Black Carrier	+35.00
Red	+15.00	"Paid All"	+20.00
Green	+175.00	"Short Paid"	+65.00
		Japan	-

88	A25	3c **rose**	250.00	10.00
		pale rose	250.00	10.00
		rose red	250.00	10.00
a.		3c lake red	300.00	12.50
		On cover		13.50
		Pair	510.00	21.00
		Block of four	1,050.	110.00
		Double grill	375.00	35.00
		Triple grill		—
		Split grill	275.00	11.50
		Very thin paper	265.00	11.00

CANCELLATIONS.

Blue	+.25	"Paid"	+3.00
Red	+3.00	"Way"	+20.00
Ultramarine	+3.00	Numeral	+2.00
Green	+80.00	Steamboat	+35.00
		Railroad	+25.00
		Express Company	+80.00

89	A27	10c **green**	1,300.	175.00
		dark green	1,300.	175.00
		blue green	1,300.	175.00
		On cover		275.00
		Pair	2,700.	360.00
		Block of four	6,500.	1,100.
		Double grill	1,800.	300.00
		Split grill	1,350.	190.00
		Double transfer	—	200.00
		Very thin paper	1,350.	190.00

CANCELLATIONS.

Blue	+5.00	"Paid"	+15.00
Red	+20.00	Steamship	+50.00
		Japan	+225.00

90	A28	12c **black**	1,500.	190.00
		gray black	1,500.	190.00
		intense black	1,500.	190.00
		On cover		325.00
		Pair	3,100.	400.00
		Block of four	7,250.	1,350.
		Double transfer of top frame line	1,600.	210.00
		Double transfer of bottom frame line	1,600.	210.00
		Double transfer of top and bottom frame lines	1,700.	235.00
		Double grill	2,000.	400.00
		Split grill	1,550.	210.00

CANCELLATIONS.

Blue	+5.00	Railroad	+60.00
Red	+20.00	"Paid"	+20.00
Green	+225.00		

91	A33	15c **black**	3,250.	450.00
		gray black	3,250.	450.00
		On cover		700.00
		Pair	6,600.	950.00
		Block of four	14,000.	3,500.
		Double grill	—	700.00
		Split grill	—	500.00

CANCELLATIONS.

Blue	+10.00	"Paid"	+30.00
Red	+50.00	Supplementary Mail Type A	+100.00

F. Grill about 9x13 mm.
(11 to 12 by 15 to 17 points.)

92	A24	1c **blue**	350.00	100.00
a.		1c pale blue	350.00	100.00
		dark blue	350.00	100.00
		On cover		130.00
		Pair	725.00	210.00
		Block of four	1,600.	550.00
		Double transfer	375.00	120.00
		Double grill	—	200.00
		Split grill	375.00	110.00
		Very thin paper	365.00	105.00

CANCELLATIONS.

Blue	+2.50	"Paid"	+10.00
Red	+10.00	Red Carrier	+25.00
Green	+175.00	"Paid All"	+15.00

93	A32	2c **black**	135.00	25.00
		gray black	135.00	25.00

POSTAGE

On cover		35.00
Pair	275.00	52.50
Block of four	600.00	225.00
Margin block of 8, Impr. & P#		—

a. Half used as 1c on cover, diagonal,
vertical or horizontal — *1,600.*

Double transfer	140.00	30.00
Double grill	—	100.00
Split grill	140.00	30.00
Very thin paper	140.00	30.00

CANCELLATIONS.

Blue	+2.50	"Paid"	+5.00
Red	+7.50	"Paid All"	+15.00
Green	+200.00	Black Carrier	+20.00
Japan	-	Red Carrier	+30.00

94	A25	3c **red**	95.00	2.50
		rose red	95.00	2.50
a.		3c rose	95.00	2.50
		On cover		3.25
		Pair	200.00	5.25
		Block of four	425.00	45.00
		Margin block of 8, Impt. & P#	*2,500.*	

b. Imperf., pair — *650.00*
c. Vertical pair, imperf. horiz. — *900.00*
d. Printed on both sides — *950.00*

Double transfer	110.00	4.00
Double grill	175.00	20.00
Triple grill	—	100.00
End roller grill		200.00
Split grill	100.00	2.75
Quadruple split grill	225.00	75.00
Grill with points up		—
Very thin paper	97.50	2.75

CANCELLATIONS.

Blue	+10	"Paid"	+2.25
Ultramarine	+3.00	"Paid All"	+12.50
Red	+3.50	"Free"	+20.00
Violet	+5.50	Railroad	+30.00
Green	+70.00	Steamboat	+40.00
Numeral	+3.00	Packet boat	+60.00
		Express Company	+50.00

95	A26	5c **brown**	900.00	225.00
a.		5c dark brown	950.00	250.00
		On cover		350.00
		Pair	1,850.	475.00
		Block of four	3,900.	1,250.
		Double transfer of top frame line	—	—
		Double grill	—	—
		Split grill	1,000.	250.00
		Very thin paper	925.00	235.00

CANCELLATIONS.

Blue	+5.00	Green	+200.00
Magenta	+30.00	"Paid"	+25.00
Violet	+35.00	"Free"	+50.00
Red	+30.00	"Steamship"	+100.00

96	A27	10c **yellow green**	700.00	110.00
		green	700.00	110.00
a.		10c dark green	700.00	110.00
		blue green	700.00	110.00
		On cover		175.00
		Pair	1,450.	230.00
		Block of four	3,500.	800.00
		Double transfer	—	—
		Double grill	—	200.00
		Split grill	750.00	120.00
		Quadruple split grill		350.00
		Very thin paper	725.00	120.00

CANCELLATIONS.

Blue	+2.50	"Paid"	+10.00
Red	+15.00	"Free"	+50.00
Magenta	+20.00	Steamship	+75.00
Green	+175.00	Japan	+250.00
		China	-

97	A28	12c **black**	700.00	120.00
		gray black	700.00	120.00
		On cover		200.00
		Pair	1,450.	250.00
		Block of four	3,500.	1,200.
		Double transfer of top frame line	750.00	130.00
		Double transfer of bottom frame line	750.00	130.00
		Double transfer of top and bottom frame lines	—	160.00
		Double grill	—	250.00
		Triple grill		400.00
		Split grill	750.00	140.00
		End roller grill		—
		Very thin paper	725.00	125.00

CANCELLATIONS.

Blue	+2.50	"Paid"	+15.00
Red	+15.00	"Insufficiently Prepaid"	+100.00
Magenta	+20.00	"Paid All"	+25.00
Brown	+15.00	Supplementary Mail Type A	+50.00
Green	+200.00		

98	A33	15c **black**	700.00	135.00
		gray black	700.00	135.00
		On cover		200.00
		Pair	1,450.	300.00
		Block of four	3,750.	1,200.
		Margin block of 8, Impt. & P#	25,000.	
		Double transfer of upper right corner	—	—
		Double grill	—	250.00
		Split grill	700.00	145.00
		Quadruple split grill	1,400.	350.00
		Very thin paper	700.00	140.00

CANCELLATIONS.

Blue	+2.50	"Paid"	+20.00
Magenta	+20.00	"Insufficiently Prepaid"	+135.00
Red	+15.00	"Insufficiently Paid"	+135.00
Green	+225.00	Japan	+300.00
Orange	+20.00	Supplementary Mail Type A	+60.00

99	A29	24c **gray lilac**	1,350.	475.00
		gray	1,350.	475.00
		On cover		800.00
		Pair	2,800.	1,000.
		Block of four	6,500.	4,000.
		Margin block of 8, Impt. & P#	30,000.	
		Double grill	1,850.	750.00
		Split grill	1,450.	500.00

CANCELLATIONS.

Blue	+10.00	Red	+50.00
		"Paid"	+50.00

100	A30	30c **orange**	1,500.	375.00
		deep orange	1,500.	375.00
		On cover		1,000.
		Pair	3,100.	775.00
		Block of four	7,500.	3,000.
		Double grill	2,000	700.00
		Split grill	1,600.	425.00

CANCELLATIONS.

Blue	+10.00	"Paid"	+50.00
Red	+50.00	Supplementary Mail Type A	+100.00
Magenta	+75.00	Japan	+400.00

101	A31	90c **blue**	4,400.	950.00
		dark blue	4,400.	950.00
		On cover		—
		Pair	9,000.	1,950.
		Block of four	20,000.	5,000.
		Double grill	6,500.	
		Split grill	4,600.	1,000.

CANCELLATIONS.

Blue	+25.00	Japan	+600.00
Red	+50.00	"Paid"	+50.00

RE-ISSUE OF 1861-66 ISSUES
Issued for the Centennial Exposition of 1876.
Produced by the National Bank Note Co.
Without grill, hard white paper, with white crackly gum.
The 1, 2, 5, 10 and 12c were printed from new plates of 100 subjects each.

1875				**Perf. 12**
102	A24	1c 1c blue *(3195)*	500.00	800.00
		Block of four	3,500.	—
103	A32	2c black *(979)*	2,500.	4,000.
		Block of four	13,500.	
104	A25	3c brown red *(465)*	3,250.	4,250.
		Block of four	16,000.	
105	A26	5c brown *(672)*	1,800.	2,250.
		Block of four	10,000.	
106	A27	10c green *(451)*	2,100.	3,750.
		Block of four	12,500.	
107	A28	12c black *(389)*	3,000.	4,500.
		Block of four	15,000.	
108	A33	15c black *(397)*	3,000.	4,750.
		Block of four	15,000.	
109	A29	24c deep violet *(346)*	4,000.	6,000.
		Block of four	19,000.	
110	A30	30c brownish orange *(346)*	4,500.	7,000.
		Block of four	22,500.	
111	A31	90c blue *(317)*	5,750.	18,500.

These stamps can be distinguished from the 1861-66 issue by the brighter colors, the sharper proof-like impressions and the paper which is very white instead of yellowish.
Numbers in parentheses are quantities issued.

Produced by the National Bank Note Co.
Plates for the 1c, 2c, 3c, 6c, 10c and 12c consisted of 300 subjects in two panes of 150 each. For the 15c, 24c, 30c and 90c plates of 100 subjects each.
NOTE. Stamps of the 1869 issue without grill cannot be guaranteed except when unused and with the original gum.

Franklin — A34

G. Grill measuring 9½x9mm.
(12 by 11 to 11½ points)

1869	**Hard Wove Paper**			**Perf. 12**
112	A34	1c **buff,** *Mar. 27, 1869*	225.00	60.00
		brown orange	225.00	60.00
		dark brown orange	225.00	60.00
		On cover, single		150.00
		Pair	465.00	125.00

Block of four	1,000.	450.00
Margin block of 4, arrow	1,100.	
Margin block of 10, Impt. & P#	—	
Double transfer		

b. Without grill, original gum — *750.00*

Double grill	450.00	150.00
Split grill	250.00	70.00
Double grill, one split	—	

CANCELLATIONS.

Blue	+2.50	"Paid"	+35.00
Ultramarine	+15.00	Steamship	+50.00
Magenta	+15.00	Black town	+10.00
Purple	+15.00	Blue town	+20.00
Red	+17.50	Red town	+50.00
Green	+150.00	Black Carrier	+60.00
		Japan	+225.00

Post Horse and Rider — A35

113	A35	2c **brown,** *Mar. 27, 1869*	160.00	25.00
		pale brown	160.00	25.00
		dark brown	160.00	25.00
		yellow brown	160.00	25.00
		On cover, single		60.00
		Pair	325.00	52.50
		Block of four	725.00	275.00
		Margin block of 4, arrow	775.00	
		Margin block of 10, Impt. & P#	600.00	

b. Without grill, original gum
c. Half used as 1c on cover, diagonal, vertical or horizontal — —
d. Printed on both sides — —

Double grill	—	125.00
Split grill	185.00	35.00
Quadruple split grill	—	200.00
Double transfer		30.00

CANCELLATIONS.

Blue	+1.00	Steamship	+50.00
Red	+15.00	Black town	+10.00
Orange	+15.00	Blue town	+20.00
Magenta	+12.50	Japan	+200.00
Purple	+12.50	Blue Carrier	+75.00
Ultramarine	+15.00	Black Carrier	+60.00
Green	+175.00	China	-
"Paid"	+15.00	Printed Precancellation "Jefferson, Ohio"	-
"Paid All"	+25.00		

Locomotive — A36

114	A36	3c **ultramarine,** *Mar. 27, 1869*	135.00	5.50
		pale ultramarine	135.00	5.50
		dark ultramarine	135.00	5.50
		blue	135.00	5.50
		dark blue	135.00	5.50
		On cover		12.00
		Pair	275.00	11.50
		Block of four	625.00	125.00
		Margin block of 4, arrow	675.00	
		Margin block of 10, Impt. & P#	*7,000.*	

a. Without grill, original gum — *600.00*
b. Vertical one-third used as 1c on cover — —
c. Vertical two-thirds used as 2c on cover — —
d. Double impression — —

Double transfer	150.00	6.50
Double grill	275.00	45.00
Triple grill	—	100.00
Split grill	145.00	6.50
Quadruple split grill	325.00	60.00
Sextuple grill	*2,000.*	
End roller grill	—	—
Gray paper	—	—
Cracked plate	—	—

CANCELLATIONS.

Blue	+.25	"Paid"	+10.00
Ultramarine	+3.00	"Paid All"	+15.00
Magenta	+5.00	"Steamboat"	+40.00
Purple	+5.00	"Steamship"	
Violet	+5.00	Ship	+35.00

Red	+7.00	Railroad	+30.00
Brown	+3.00	Packet Boat	+100.00
Green	+125.00	Black Carrier	+30.00
Orange	+7.00	Blue Carrier	+40.00
Black town	+2.50	Express Company	-
Blue town	+4.00	"Way"	-
Red town	+25.00	"Free"	+30.00
Numeral	+10.00	Alaska	-
		Japan	+150.00

Washington — A37

115 A37	6c **ultramarine,** *1869*	775.00	95.00
	pale ultramarine	775.00	95.00
	On cover		300.00
	Pair	1,600.	200.00
	Block of four	4,000.	1,000.
	Margin block of 4, arrow	4,500.	
	Double grill	—	300.00
	Split grill	825.00	110.00
	Quadruple split grill	—	400.00
	Double transfer		110.00
b.	Vertical half used as 3c on cover		—

Earliest known use: Apr. 26.

CANCELLATIONS.

		"Paid"	+15.00
Blue	+5.00	"Paid All"	+25.00
Brown	+10.00	Black town	+20.00
Magenta	+20.00	"Short Paid"	+75.00
Purple	+20.00	Steamship	+35.00
Red	+30.00	Railroad	+35.00
Green	+225.00	Japan	+175.00

Shield and Eagle — A38

116 A38	10c **yellow,** *Apr. 1, 1869*	850.00	95.00
	yellowish orange	850.00	95.00
	On cover		325.00
	Pair	1,750.	200.00
	Block of four	4,500.	1,150.
	Margin block of 4, arrow	5,000.	
	Double grill	—	275.00
	Split grill	900.00	105.00
	End roller grill		

CANCELLATIONS.

		"Paid"	+15.00
Blue	+5.00	"Paid All"	+30.00
Magenta	+20.00	"Insufficiently Paid"	+125.00
Purple	+20.00	Supplementary Mail Type A	+55.00
Red	+30.00	Express Company	-
Ultramarine	+30.00	St. Thomas	-
Green	+225.00	Hawaii	-
Black town	+20.00	Japan	+200.00
Steamship	+45.00	China	-
Railroad	+45.00		

S.S. "Adriatic" — A39

117 A39	12c **green,** *Apr. 5, 1869*	750.00	90.00
	bluish green	750.00	90.00
	yellowish green	750.00	90.00

		On cover		325.00
		Pair	1,550.	190.00
		Block of four	4,000.	850.00
		Margin block of 4, arrow	4,500.	
		Double grill	—	275.00
		Split grill	800.00	100.00
		End roller grill		

CANCELLATIONS.

		"Paid"	+25.00
Blue	+5.00	"Paid All"	+40.00
Magenta	+20.00	"Too Late"	+100.00
Purple	+20.00	"Insufficiently Paid"	+125.00
Brown	+15.00	Black town	+20.00
Red	+30.00	Japan	+175.00
Green	+225.00		
Numeral	-		

Landing of Columbus — A40

118 A40	15c **brown & blue,** type I, Picture unframed, *Apr. 2, 1869*	1,750.	250.00
	dark brown & blue	1,750.	250.00
	On cover		1,300.
	Pair	3,650.	525.00
	Block of four	12,000.	20,000.
a.	Without grill, original gum	3,500.	
	Double grill	—	450.00
	Split grill	1,900.	300.00

CANCELLATIONS.

		"Paid"	+50.00
Blue	+10.00	"Insufficiently Paid"	+150.00
Red	+40.00	Black town	+50.00
Brown	+25.00	Steamship	+100.00

A40a

119 A40a	15c **brown & blue,** type II, Picture framed	850.00	125.00
	dark brown & blue	850.00	125.00
	On cover		800.00
	Pair	1,750.	275.00
	Block of four	4,000.	3,500.
	Margin block of 8, Impt. & P#	20,000.	
b.	Center inverted	145,000.	17,500.
c.	Center double, one inverted	—	—
	Double transfer	—	—
	Double grill	1,750.	285.00
	Split grill	1,000.	160.00

Earliest known use: May 23, 1869.

CANCELLATIONS.

Blue	+10.00	"Paid"	+20.00
Purple	+35.00	"Paid All"	+35.00
Magenta	+35.00	Black town	+30.00
Red	+35.00	"Steamship"	+60.00
Brown	+20.00	Supp. Mail, A, F	+40.00
Green	+250.00	Japan	+275.00

The Declaration of Independence A41

120 A41	24c **green & violet,** *Apr. 7, 1869*	2,500.	450.00
	bluish green & violet	2,500.	450.00
	On cover		9,500.
	Pair	5,250.	950.00
	Block of four	14,000.	18,000.
a.	Without grill, original gum	5,000.	
b.	Center inverted	125,000.	16,500.
b.	On cover		
b.	Block of four		
b.	Imperf.	—	1,000.
	Double grill	—	1,000.
	Split grill	2,750.	500.00

No. 120b, imperf., is without grill.

CANCELLATIONS.

		Red town	+150.00
Red	+75.00	"Paid All"	+100.00
Blue	+25.00	"Steamship"	+175.00
Black town	+50.00	Supp. Mail, A	+125.00

Shield, Eagle and Flags — A42

121 A42	30c **blue & carmine,** *May 15, 1869*	2,250.	225.00
	blue & dark carmine	2,250.	225.00
	On cover		11,000.
	Pair	4,600.	475.00
	Block of four	12,000.	1,150.
a.	Without grill, original gum	3,750.	
a.	Block of four	18,500.	
b.	Flags inverted	120,000.	45,000.
	Double grill	—	500.00
	Split grill	2,400.	250.00
	Double paper (without grill), original gum	2,750.	

CANCELLATIONS.

		Black town	+35.00
Red	+50.00	Steamship	+75.00
Blue	+10.00	"Steam"	+60.00
Brown	+25.00	Supplementary Mail Type A	+75.00
Green	+400.00	Japan	+400.00
"Paid"	+50.00	China	
"Paid All"	+75.00		

Lincoln — A43

122 A43	90c **carmine & black**	7,000.	1,200.
	carmine rose & black	7,000.	1,200.
	On cover		
	Pair	16,000.	3,000.
	Block of four	65,000.	25,000.
a.	Without grill, original gum	13,500.	
	Split grill		

Earliest known use: May 10, 1869.

CANCELLATIONS.

| | | Red | +200.00 |
| Blue | +100.00 | Black town | +200.00 |

CANCELLATIONS

The common type of cancellation on the 1869 issue is the block or cork similar to illustrations above. Japanese cancellations seen on this issue (not illustrated) resulted from the sale of U. S. stamps in Japanese cities where post offices were maintained for mail going from Japan to the United States.

RE-ISSUE OF 1869 ISSUE
Issued for the Centennial Exposition of 1876.
Produced by the National Bank Note Co.
Without grill, hard white paper, with white crackly gum.
A new plate of 150 subjects was made for the 1c and for the frame of the 15c. The frame on the 15c is the same as type I but without the fringe of brown shading lines around central vignette.

1875				*Perf. 12*
123 A34	1c buff *(+8252)*		325.00	225.00
	Block of four		1,850.	
	On cover			1,250.
124 A35	2c brown *(4755)*		375.00	325.00
	Block of four		2,250.	
125 A36	3c blue *(1406)*		2,750.	—

CANCELLATIONS.

		Supplementary Mail Type F	-
126 A37	6c blue *(2226)*	850.00	550.00
	Block of four	*12,500.*	
127 A38	10c yellow *(1947)*	1,400.	1,200.
	Block of four	*9,000.*	
128 A39	12c green *(1584)*	1,500.	1,200.
	Block of four	*12,500.*	
129 A40	15c brown & blue, Type III, *(1981)*	1,300.	550.00
	Block of four	*20,000.*	
a.	Imperf. horizontally, single	1,600.	—
130 A41	24c green & violet *(2091)*	1,250.	550.00
131 A42	30c blue & carmine *(1535)*	1,750.	1,000.
132 A43	90c carmine & black *(1356)*	5,500.	*6,000.*
	Block of four	*32,500.*	

Numbers in parentheses are quantities issued.
+ This quantity probably includes the 1880 Re-issue No. 133.

RE-ISSUE OF 1869 ISSUE
Produced by the American Bank Note Co.
Without grill, soft porous paper.

1880			
133 A34	1c **buff,** issued with gum	200.00	135.00
	Block of four, with gum	950.00	
a.	1c brown orange, issued without gum	175.00	120.00
a.	Block of four, without gum	800.00	
	Margin block of 10, Impt. & P#	*17,500.*	
	On cover		1,850.

Produced by the National Bank Note Company.
Plates of 200 subjects in two panes of 100 each.

Franklin — A44

Jackson — A45

Washington — A46

Lincoln — A47

Edwin M. Stanton — A48

Jefferson — A49

Henry Clay — A50

Daniel Webster — A51

Two varieties of grill are known on this issue.
H. Grill about 10x12 mm. (11 to 13 by 14 to 16 points.) On all values 1c to 90c.

I. Grill about 8½x10mm. (10 to 11 by 10 to 13 points.) On 1, 2, 3, 6 and 7c.

On the 1870-71 stamps the grill impressions are usually faint or incomplete. This is especially true of the H grill, which often shows only a few points.

Prices are for stamps showing well defined grills.

Killer cancellation of the oval grid type with letters or numeral centers was first used in 1876 Bank Note issues. By order of the Postmaster-General (July 23, 1860) it was prohibited to use the town mark as a canceling instrument, and a joined town and killer cancellation was developed.

Numeral cancellations-see "Postal Markings-Examples."

White Wove Paper, Thin to Medium Thick.

1870-71				*Perf. 12*
134 A44	1c **ultramarine**, *April 1870*		500.00	57.50
	pale ultramarine		500.00	57.50
	dark ultramarine		500.00	57.50
	On cover			80.00
	Pair		1,050.00	120.00
	Block of four		2,200.00	300.00
	Double transfer		525.00	65.00
	Double grill		—	120.00
	Split grill		550.00	60.00
	Quadruple split grill		—	200.00
	End roller grill			300.00

CANCELLATIONS.

		"Paid"	+10.00
Blue	+2.50	"Paid All"	+20.00
Red	+10.00	"Steamship"	+45.00
Green	+100.00		

135 A45	2c **red brown**, *April 1870*		350.00	37.50
	pale red brown		350.00	37.50
	dark red brown		350.00	37.50
	On cover			55.00
	Pair		725.00	80.00
	Block of four		1,500.00	200.00
a.	Diagonal half used as 1c on cover			
	Double grill		500.00	75.00
	Split grill		375.00	45.00
	Quadruple split grill		*1,100.*	120.00
	End roller grill		*700.00*	225.00

CANCELLATIONS.

		"Paid"	+5.00
Blue	+1.00	"Paid All"	+10.00
Red	+5.00	Numeral	+5.00
Brown	+3.00	China	-
Green	+100.00		

136 A46	3c **green**, *April 12, 1870*		285.00	10.00
	pale green		285.00	10.00
	yellow green		285.00	10.00
	deep green		285.00	10.00
	On cover			15.00
	Pair		585.00	21.00
	Block of four		1,200.00	75.00
	Margin block of 10, Impt. & P#		*5,500.*	
	Margin block of 12, Impt. & P#		*6,500.*	
	Printed on both sides			
	Double transfer		—	12.00
	Double grill		450.00	40.00
	Split grill		300.00	11.00
	Quadruple split grill		—	75.00
	End roller grill		—	150.00
	Cracked plate		—	50.00
b.	Imperf., pair		*1,200.*	
b.	Margin block of 12, Impt. & P#		—	

CANCELLATIONS.

Blue	+.25	"Paid"	+2.50
Purple	+2.50	Railroad	+10.00
Magenta	+2.50	"Steamship"	+20.00
Red	+3.50	"Paid All"	+15.00
Orange	+3.50	Numeral	+4.00
Brown	+1.50	"Free"	+25.00
Green	+45.00		

137 A47	6c **carmine**, *April 1870*		1,650.00	250.00
	pale carmine		1,650.00	250.00
	carmine rose		1,650.00	250.00
	On cover			500.00
	Pair		3,400.00	525.00
	Block of four		*7,250.*	
	Double grill		—	450.00
	Split grill		1,700.00	275.00
	Quadruple split grill		—	500.00
	End roller grill		*2,750.*	550.00

CANCELLATIONS.

Blue	+5.00	"Paid"	+35.00
Red	+35.00		

138 A48	7c **vermilion**, *Mar. 1871*		1,100.00	225.00
	deep vermilion		1,100.00	225.00
	On cover			450.00
	Pair		2,300.00	475.00
	Block of four		*4,750.*	—
	Double grill		—	400.00
	Split grill		1,150.00	250.00
	Quadruple split grill		—	450.00
	End roller grill		—	*500.00*

CANCELLATIONS.

Blue	+5.00	Red	+35.00
Purple	+20.00	Green	+200.00
		"Paid"	+25.00

The 7c stamps, Nos. 138 and 149, were issued for a 7c rate of July 1, 1870, to Prussia, German States and Austria, including Hungary, via Hamburg (on the Hamburg-American Line steamers), or Bremen (on North German Lloyd ships), but issue was delayed by the Franco-Prussian War. The rate for this service was reduced to 6c in 1871. For several months there was no 7c rate, but late in 1871 the Prussian closed mail rate via England was reduced to 7c which revived an important use for the 7c stamps. The rate to Denmark direct via

Baltic Lloyd ships, or via Bremen and Hamburg as above, was 7c from Jan. 1, 1872.

139 A49	10c **brown**, *April 1870*		1,450.	400.00
	yellow brown		1,450.	400.00
	dark brown		1,450.	400.00
	On cover			700.00
	Pair		3,000.	825.00
	Block of four		*10,000.*	
	Double grill			750.00
	Split grill		1,600.	450.00
	End roller grill		*1,000.*	

CANCELLATIONS.

Blue	+5.00	"Steamship"	+50.00
Red	+30.00	"Honolulu Paid All"	-

140 A50	12c **dull violet**, *April 18, 1870*		12,000.	1,500.
	On cover			*4,500.*
	Pair		25,000.	3,200.
	Block of four		*55,000.*	
	Split grill			1,600.
	End roller grill			*4,500.*

CANCELLATIONS.

Blue	+50.00	"Paid all"	-
Red	+100.00		

141 A51	15c **orange**, *April 1870*		1,850.	700.00
	bright orange		1,850.	700.00
	deep orange		1,850.	700.00
	On cover			1,350.
	Pair		3,800.	1,500.
	Block of four		*10,000.*	—
	Double grill		—	—
	Split grill		1,850.	750.00

CANCELLATIONS.

Blue	+10.00	Red	+75.00
Purple	+50.00	Green	+300.00

General Winfield
Scott — A52

142 A52	24c **purple**		—	10,500.
	On cover			—
	Block of four			—
	Split grill			—

CANCELLATIONS.

Red	+500.00	

Alexander
Hamilton — A53

143 A53	30c **black**, *April 1870*		4,500.	825.00
	full black		4,500.	825.00
	On cover			2,000.
	Pair		9,250.	1,800.
	Block of four		*20,000.*	
	Double grill		—	—
	End roller grill			*1,750.*

CANCELLATIONS.

Blue	+25.00	
Red	+100.00	

Commodore Oliver
Hazard Perry — A54

144 A54	90c **carmine**, *April 12, 1870*		6,000.	750.00
	dark carmine		6,000.	750.00
	On cover			—
	Pair		12,500.	1,600.
	Block of four		28,500.	4,000.
	Double grill			—
	Split grill			800.00

CANCELLATIONS.

Blue	+25.00	
Red	+75.00	

Produced by the National Bank Note Co.
White Wove Paper, Thin to Medium Thick.
Issued (except 3c and 7c) in April, 1870.
Without Grill.

1870-71				*Perf. 12*
145 A44	1c **ultramarine**		165.00	6.50
	pale ultramarine		165.00	6.50
	dark ultramarine		165.00	6.50
	gray blue		165.00	6.50
	On cover			10.00
	Pair		340.00	14.00
	Block of four		700.00	50.00
	Double transfer		—	9.00
	Worn plate		165.00	6.50

CANCELLATIONS.

Blue	+ 25	"Paid"	+3.00
Ultramarine	+1.50	"Paid All"	+15.00
Magenta	+1.00	"Steamship"	+25.00
Purple	+1.00	Railroad	+20.00
Brown	+1.00	Numeral	+2.00
Red	+3.00		
Green	+55.00		

146 A45	2c **red brown**		57.50	4.50
	pale red brown		57.50	4.50
	dark red brown		57.50	4.50
	orange brown		60.00	4.75
	On cover			6.50
	Pair		120.00	9.25
	Block of four		250.00	30.00
a.	Half used as 1c on cover, diagonal or vertical		—	—
c.	Double impression		—	—
	Double transfer			6.00

CANCELLATIONS.

Blue	+ 10	"Paid"	+2.00
Purple	+ 75	"Paid All"	+10.00
Red	+2.50	Numeral	+2.00
Green	+55.00	"Steamship"	+22.50
Brown	+1.00	Black Carrier	+12.50
		Japan	-
		China	-
		Curacao	-

147 A46	3c **green**, *Mar. 13, 1870*		120.00	50
	pale green		120.00	50
	dark green		120.00	50
	yellow green		125.00	55
	On cover			1.00
	Pair		250.00	1.05
	Block of four		525.00	9.00
	Margin block of 10, Impt. & P#		*1,850.*	
a.	Printed on both sides			1,500.
b.	Double impression			1,000.
	Double transfer			4.50
	Short transfer at bottom		130.00	75
	Cracked plate		—	25.00
	Worn plate		120.00	50
c.	Imperf., pair		*700.00*	
c.	Margin block of 10, Impt. & P#		—	

CANCELLATIONS.

Blue	+5	"Paid"	+2.00
Purple	+35	"Paid All"	+10.00
Magenta	+35	"Free"	+15.00
Brown	+1.50	Numeral	+2.00
Red	+2.50	Railroad	+10.00
Ultramarine	+2.00	Express Company	-
Green	+35.00	"Steamboat"	+20.00
		"Steamship"	+17.50
		Ship	+15.00
		Japan	+75.00

148 A47	6c **carmine**		225.00	12.00
	dark carmine		225.00	12.00
	rose		225.00	12.00
	brown carmine		225.00	12.00
	violet carmine		240.00	12.00
	On cover			30.00
	Pair		475.00	24.50

Block of four	975.00	125.00	

a. Vertical half used as 3c on cover —
b. Double impression 1,250.
Double transfer —
Double paper — —

CANCELLATIONS.

Blue	+ 25	"Paid"	+3.00
Purple	+1.00	"Steamship"	+25.00
Violet	+1.00	"Paid All"	+15.00
Ultramarine	+2.00	Numeral	
Brown	+1.00	Supplementary Mail Type A or D	+25.00
Red	+3.00	China	-
Green	+90.00	Japan	+150.00

149 A48 7c **vermilion**, Mar. 1871   325.00   50.00
deep vermilion   325.00   50.00
On cover   110.00
Pair   675.00   105.00
Block of four   1,450.   450.00
Cracked plate   —

CANCELLATIONS.

Blue	+2.50	Ultramarine	+12.50
Purple	+7.50	Red	+10.00
		Japan	+150.00

150 A49 10c **brown**   225.00   12.00
dark brown   225.00   12.00
yellow brown   225.00   12.00
On cover   27.50
Pair   475.00   25.00
Block of four   1,000.   125.00
Margin block of 10, Impt. & P#   —
Double transfer   47.50

CANCELLATIONS.

Blue	+.25	Brown	+3.00
Purple	+2.00	"Paid All"	+20.00
Magenta	+2.00	"Steamship"	+20.00
Ultramarine	+4.00	Supplementary Mail Type A or D	+25.00
Red	+4.00	Japan	+120.00
Green	+120.00	China	-
Orange	+4.00	St. Thomas	-

151 A50 12c **dull violet**   525.00   60.00
violet   525.00   60.00
dark violet   525.00   60.00
On cover   350.00
Pair   1,100.   125.00
Block of four   2,750.   600.00

CANCELLATIONS.

Blue	+2.50	"Paid All"	+25.00
Magenta	+7.50	"Steamship"	+50.00
Red	+10.00	Supplementary Mail Type A or D	+40.00
Green	+150.00		

152 A51 15c **bright orange**   500.00   60.00
deep orange   500.00   60.00
On cover   225.00
Pair   1,050.   125.00
Block of four   2,200.   550.00

CANCELLATIONS.

Blue	+2.50	"Paid"	+12.50
Magenta	+7.50	"Steamship"	+40.00
Ultramarine	+10.00	Supplementary Mail Type A or F	+30.00
Red	+12.50	China	-

153 A52 24c **purple**   600.00   80.00
bright purple   600.00   80.00
On cover   1,600.
Pair   1,250.   185.00
Block of four   4,500.   2,500.
Double paper   —   —

CANCELLATIONS.

Red	+10.00	"Paid"	+25.00
Blue	+2.50	Town	+15.00
Purple	+7.50	"Steamship"	-
China		Supplementary Mail Types A, D or F	+30.00

154 A53 30c **black**   1,000.   95.00
full black   1,000.   95.00
On cover   700.00
Pair   2,100.   200.00
Block of four   7,000.

CANCELLATIONS.

Magenta	+15.00	"Steamship"	+55.00
Red	+25.00	Supplementary Mail Type A	+40.00
Brown	+15.00		
Blue	+2.50		

155 A54 90c **carmine**   1,350.   175.00
dark carmine   1,350.   175.00
On cover   —
Pair   2,800.   375.00
Block of four   7,000.   1,100.

CANCELLATIONS.

Blue	+5.00	Town	+20.00
Purple	+15.00	Supplementary Mail Type A or F	+40.00
Magenta	+15.00	Japan	-
Green	+275.00		
Red	+30.00		

Printed by the Continental Bank Note Co.
Plates of 200 subjects in two panes of 100 each.
Issued in July (?), 1873.

Designs of the 1870-71 Issue with secret marks on the values from 1c to 15c, as described and illustrated:
The object of secret marks was to provide a simple and positive proof that these stamps were produced by the Continental Bank Note Company and not by their predecessors.

Franklin A44a

1c. In the pearl at the left of the numeral "1" there is a small crescent.

Jackson — A45a

2c. Under the scroll at the left of "U. S." there is a small diagonal line. This mark seldom shows clearly. The stamp, No. 157, can be distinguished by its color.

Washington A46a

3c. The under part of the upper tail of the left ribbon is heavily shaded.

Lincoln — A47a

6c. The first four vertical lines of the shading in the lower part of the left ribbon have been strengthened.

Stanton A48a

7c. Two small semi-circles are drawn around the ends of the lines which outline the ball in the lower right hand corner.

Jefferson A49a

10c. There is a small semi-circle in the scroll at the right end of the upper label.

Clay — A50a

12c. The balls of the figure "2" are crescent shaped.

Webster A51a

15c. In the lower part of the triangle in the upper left corner two lines have been made heavier forming a "V". This mark can be found on some of the Continental and American (1879) printings, but not all stamps show it.

Secret marks were added to the dies of the 24c, 30c and 90c but new plates were not made from them. The various printings of the 30c and 90c can be distinguished only by the shades and paper.

J. Grill about 7x9½mm. exists on all values except 90c. Grill was composed of truncated pyramids and was so strongly impressed that some points often broke through the paper.

White Wove Paper, Thin to Thick.

1873   **Perf. 12**
156 A44a 1c **ultramarine**   55.00   1.75
pale ultramarine   55.00   1.75
dark ultramarine   60.00   1.75
gray blue   55.00   1.75
blue   55.00   1.75
On cover   3.00
Pair   115.00   3.75
Block of four   235.00   20.00
Margin block of 12, Impt. & P#   2,500.
Double transfer   65.00   4.00
Double paper   200.00
Ribbed paper   60.00   2.50
Paper with silk fibers   15.00
e. With grill   1,200.
Cracked plate   —
f. Imperf., pair   —   500.00
Paper cut with "cogwheel" punch   275.00

CANCELLATIONS.

Blue	+ 10	Railroad	+12.00
Purple	+35	"Free"	+12.00
Magenta	+35	Black carrier	+15.00
Ultramarine	+1.00	Numeral	+2.50
Red	+3.50	Alaska	-
Orange	+3.50	Japan	-
Brown	+1.50	Printed "G." Precancellation (Glastonbury, Conn.)	+200.00
Green	+60.00	Printed Star Precancellation (Glen Allen, Va.)	+100.00
"Paid All"	+7.00		
"Paid"	+1.00		

157 A45a 2c **brown**   150.00   7.00
dark brown   150.00   7.00
dark reddish brown   150.00   7.00
yellowish brown   150.00   7.00
With secret mark   160.00   7.50
On cover   12.50
Pair   325.00   14.50
Block of four   700.00   70.00
Margin block of 12, Impt. & P#   —
Margin block of 14, Impt. & P#   —
Double paper   225.00   20.00
Ribbed paper   160.00   8.50
c. With grill   850.00   600.00
d. Double impression   —
e. Vertical half used as 1c on cover   —
Double transfer   9.50
Cracked plate   —

CANCELLATIONS.

Blue	+ 25	"P. D." in circle	+15.00
Magenta	+1.00	Town	+2.00
Purple	+1.00	Numeral	+1.50
Red	+3.00	Black Carrier	+8.50
Orange	+3.50	"Steamship"	+15.00
Green	+60.00	Supplementary Mail Type F	+5.00
"Paid"	+2.50	China	-
"Insufficiently Paid"	-	Japan	+100.00
"Paid All"	+13.50	Printed Star Precancellation (Glen Allen, Va.)	-

158 A46a 3c **green**   45.00   15
bluish green   45.00   15
yellow green   45.00   15
dark yellow green   45.00   15
dark green   45.00   15
olive green   60.00   2.50
On cover   30
Pair   92.50   35
Block of four   225.00   7.50
Margin strip of 5, Impt. & P#   250.00
Margin strip of 6, Impt. & P#   325.00
Margin block of 10, Impt. & P#   1,300.
Margin block of 12, Impt. & P#   2,000.
Margin block of 14, Impt. & P#   2,650.
Double paper   75.00   5.00
Paper cut with "cogwheel" punch   150.00   150.00
Ribbed paper   50.00   1.00
Paper with silk fibers   —   4.00
e. With grill   175.00
End roller grill   400.00   300.00
f. Imperf. with grill (pair)   650.00
g. Imperf. without grill (pair)   750.00
h. Horizontal pair, imperf. vert.   —
i. Horizontal pair, imperf. between   1,300.
j. Double impression   600.00
k. Printed on both sides   —
Cracked plate   —   27.50
Double transfer   —   4.00
Short transfer   2.25

CANCELLATIONS.

Why are ScottMounts Superior?

Because...

- They're completely interchangeable with Showgard® mounts and come with 10% more mounts to the package.
- They're made of two welded sheets of 100 percent inert polystyrol foil.
- They're center-split across the back for easy insertion of your stamps.
- The Black-backed mounts are totally opaque for perfect stamp framing.
- Crystal clear mount faces eliminate distracting distortions.
- Double layers of gum assure stay-put bonding, yet they're easily peeled off.
- They come packed in their own reuseable storage trays.

Available from your local dealer or direct from Scott.

SCOTT®

P.O. Box 828
Sidney, OH 45365

Blue	+2	Railroad		+7.00
Magenta	+20	"R. P. O."		+1.50
Purple	+20	"P. D." in circle		-
Ultramarine	+1.25	"Steamboat"		-
Red	+2.50	"Steamship"		-
Orange	+2.50	Supplementary Mail Type D		+11.00
Green	+25.00	Supplementary Mail Type F		+8.50
Town	+5	Express Company		-
"Paid"	+2.50	Black Carrier		+8.00
"Paid All"	+20.00	Red Carrier		+25.00
"Free"	+15.00	Japan		+65.00
Numeral	+1.00	Alaska		-
China	-			

159 A47a 6c dull pink   200.00   9.00

brown rose	200.00	9.00
On cover		35.00
Pair	425.00	18.50
Block of four	875.00	85.00
Margin block of 12, Impt. & P#	12,000.	—
Double paper	—	
Ribbed paper	—	10.00
Paper with silk fibers	—	25.00
b. With grill	650.00	
End roller grill	1,000.	

CANCELLATIONS.

Blue	+25	"Paid"	+7.00
Magenta	+1.50	"Paid All"	-
Purple	+1.50	Supplementary Mail Types D, E or F	+15.00
Ultramarine	+2.50	Japan	+100.00
Red	+6.50	China	-
Green	+80.00	Railroad	-
Numeral	+1.50	"R. P. O."	+2.00

160 A48a 7c orange vermillion   400.00   55.00

vermilion	400.00	55.00
On cover		300.00
Pair	825.00	115.00
Block of four	1,700.	
Margin block of 12, Impt. & P#		
a. With grill	1,350.	
Double transfer of "7 cents" (1 R 22)	—	150.00
Double transfer in lower left corner	—	70.00
Double paper	—	
Ribbed paper	—	70.00
Paper with silk fibers	—	90.00

CANCELLATIONS.

Blue	+2.50	Purple	+10.00
Red	+7.50	Brown	+5.00
		"Paid"	+15.00

161 A49a 10c brown   225.00   10.00

dark brown	225.00	10.00
yellow brown	225.00	10.00
On cover		25.00
Pair	475.00	21.00
Block of four	975.00	85.00
Margin block of 10, Impt. & P#	6,500.	
Margin block of 12, Impt. & P#	7,500.	
Double paper	300.00	
Ribbed paper	—	15.00
Paper with silk fibers	—	20.00
c. With grill	1,750.	
d. Horizontal pair, imperf. between	—	2,500.
Double transfer	—	25.00

CANCELLATIONS.

Blue	+50	"Paid"	+4.00
Purple	+1.50	"P. D." in circle	+20.00
Red	+4.00	"Steamship"	+15.00
Magenta	+1.50	Supplementary Mail Type E	+7.00
Orange	+4.00	Supplementary Mail Type F	+2.50
Brown	+1.50	Japan	+100.00
Green	+100.00	China	-
		Alaska	-

162 A50a 12c blackish violet   600.00   65.00

On cover		300.00
Pair	1,250.	135.00
Block of four	3,000.	600.00
a. With grill	3,000.	
Ribbed paper	—	70.00

CANCELLATIONS.

Blue	+2.50	Supplementary Mail Type D	+15.00
Ultramarine	+15.00	Japan	+200.00
Brown	+5.00		
Red	+15.00		

163 A51a 15c yellow orange   575.00   60.00

pale orange	575.00	60.00
reddish orange	575.00	60.00
On cover		250.00
Pair	1,200.	125.00
Block of four	2,700.	550.00
Double paper		
Paper with silk fibers	650.00	80.00
Vertical ribbed paper	600.00	70.00
a. With grill	3,000.	

CANCELLATIONS.

Blue	+2.50	Supplementary Mail Type F	+10.00
Purple	+10.00	"Steamship"	-
Red	+15.00	Numeral	+7.50
		Puerto Rico	-
		China	-

It is generally accepted as fact that the Continental Bank Note Co. printed and delivered a quantity of 24c stamps. They are impossible to distinguish from those printed by the National Bank Note Co.

165 A53 30c gray black   650.00   60.00

greenish black	650.00	60.00
On cover		650.00
Pair	1,350.	125.00
Block of four	3,250.	600.00
Double transfer	—	75.00
Double paper		
Ribbed paper	700.00	70.00
Paper with silk fibers		
c. With grill	3,000.	

CANCELLATIONS.

Purple	+7.50	"Steamship"	-
Blue	+2.50	Supplementary Mail Type E	+10.00
Red	+15.00	Supplementary Mail Type F	+5.00
Brown	+7.50		
Magenta	+7.50		

166 A54 90c rose carmine   1,350.   185.00

pale rose carmine	1,350.	185.00
On cover		7,500.
Pair	2,800.	385.00
Block of four	6,000.	1,750.

CANCELLATIONS.

Blue	+10.00	Supplementary Mail Type F	+30.00
Purple	+15.00		
Red	+30.00		

SPECIAL PRINTING OF 1873 ISSUE
Produced by the Continental Bank Note Co.
Issued for the Centennial Exposition of 1876.

1875   *Perf. 12*

Hard, white wove paper, without gum.

167 A44a 1c ultramarine	7,500.	
168 A45a 2c dark brown	3,500.	
169 A46a 3c blue green	9,500.	—
On cover		—
170 A47a 6c dull rose	8,500.	
171 A48a 7c reddish vermilion	2,100.	
172 A49a 10c pale brown	7,750.	
173 A50a 12c dark violet	2,750.	
Horizontal pair		—
174 A51a 15c bright orange	7,750.	
175 A52 24c dull purple	1,850.	
Horizontal pair		—
176 A53 30c greenish black	7,000.	
177 A54 90c violet carmine	7,000.	

Although perforated, these stamps were usually cut apart with scissors. As a result, the perforations are often much mutilated and the design is frequently damaged.

These can be distinguished from the 1873 issue by the shades; also by the paper, which is very white instead of yellowish.

These and the subsequent issues listed under the heading of "Special Printings" are special printings of stamps then in current use which, together with the reprints and re-issues, were made for sale to collectors. They were available for postage.

REGULAR ISSUE
Printed by the Continental Bank Note Co.
Yellowish Wove Paper

1875   *Perf. 12*

178 A45a 2c vermilion, *June 1875*   160.00   5.00

On cover		10.00
Pair	325.00	10.50
Block of four	675.00	60.00
Margin block of 12, Impt. & P#	—	
Margin block of 14, Impt. & P#	—	
a. Imperf., pair	600.00	
a Margin block of 12, Impt. & P#		
b. Half used as 1c on cover	—	
Double transfer	—	
Double paper	—	
Ribbed paper	—	
c. With grill	250.00	
Paper with silk fibers	200.00	7.50

CANCELLATIONS.

Blue	+10	"Paid"	+8.00
Purple	+25	"Steamship"	-
Magenta	+25	Supplementary Mail Type F	+5.50
Red	+6.00	Black Carrier	+15.00
		Railroad	+12.50

> Prices of premium quality never hinged stamps will be in excess of catalogue price.

Zachary Taylor — A55

179 A55 5c blue, *June 1875*   175.00   9.00

dark blue	175.00	9.00
bright blue	175.00	9.00
light blue	175.00	9.00
greenish blue	185.00	11.00
On cover		20.00
Pair	360.00	19.00
Block of four	750.00	100.00
Cracked plate	—	100.00
Double transfer	—	15.00
Double paper	200.00	
Ribbed paper	—	
c. With grill	325.00	
End roller grill	—	
Paper with silk fibers	—	15.00

CANCELLATIONS.

Blue	+25	Railroad	+17.50
Ultramarine	+3.00	"Steamship"	+12.50
Purple	+1.50	Ship	+12.50
Magenta	+1.50	Supplementary Mail Type E	+5.00
Red	+5.00	Supplementary Mail Type F	+2.00
Green	+70.00	China	-
Numeral	+5.00	Japan	+100.00
		Peru	-

The five cent rate to foreign countries in the Universal Postal Union began on July 1, 1875. No. 179 was issued for that purpose.

SPECIAL PRINTING OF 1875 ISSUE
Produced by the Continental Bank Note Co.
Issued for the Centennial Exposition of 1876.
Hard, White Wove Paper, without gum.

1875

180 A45a 2c carmine vermilion	19,000.
181 A55 5c bright blue	32,500.

Printed by the American Bank Note Company.

The Continental Bank Note Co. was consolidated with the American Bank Note Co. on February 4, 1879. The American Bank Note Company used many plates of the Continental Bank Note Company to print the ordinary postage, Departmental and Newspaper stamps. Therefore, stamps bearing the Continental Company's imprint were not always its product.

The A. B. N. Co. also used the 30c and 90c plates of the N. B. N. Co. Some of No. 190 and all of No. 217 were from A. B. N. Co. plate 405.

Early printings of No. 188 were from Continental plates 302 and 303 which contained the normal secret mark of 1873. After these plates were re-entered by the A. B. N. Co. in 1880, pairs or multiple pieces contained combinations of normal, hairline or missing marks. The pairs or other multiples usually found contain at least one hairline mark which tended to disappear as the plate wore.

A. B. N. Co. plates 377 and 378 were made in 1881 from the National transfer roll of 1870. No. 187 from these plates has no secret mark.

SAME AS 1870-75 ISSUES
Soft Porous Paper

1879   *Perf. 12*

182 A44a 1c dark ultramarine   120.00   1.20

blue	120.00	1.20
gray blue	120.00	1.20
On cover		1.75
Pair	250.00	2.50
Block of four	525.00	25.00
Margin block of 10, Impt. & P#	3,250.	
Double transfer		5.00

CANCELLATIONS.

Blue	+5	Railroad	+12.50
Magenta	+10	Printed "G." Precancellation (Glastonbury, Conn.)	+100.00
Purple	+10	Printed Star Precancellation (Glen Allen, Va.)	+75.00
Red	+7.00		
Green	+35.00		
"Paid"	+4.00		
Supplementary Mail Type F	+10.00		

183 A45a 2c vermilion   55.00   1.20

orange vermilion	55.00	1.20

On cover		1.75
Pair	110.00	2.50
Block of four	225.00	20.00
Margin block of 10, Impt. & P#	1,250.	
Margin block of 12, Impt. & P#	1,700.	

a. Double impression — 500.00
Double transfer

CANCELLATIONS.

Blue	+10	Numeral	+4.00
Purple	+20	Railroad	+15.00
Magenta	+20	Supplementary Mail Type F	+8.00
Red	+6.00	China	
"Paid"	+5.00	Printed Star Precancellation (Glen Allen, Va.)	-
"Paid All"	-		
"Ship"	-		

184 A46a 3c **green** 42.50 10
light green 42.50 10
dark green 42.50 10
On cover 20
Pair 85.00 20
Block of four 175.00 6.00
Margin block of 10, Impt. & P# 900.00
Margin block of 12, Impt. & P# 1,100.
Margin block of 14, Impt. & P# 1,400.

a. Imperf., pair 500.00
b. Double impression —
Double transfer — 4.00
Short transfer — 5.00

CANCELLATIONS.

Blue	+2	Numeral	+2.00
Magenta	+15	Railroad	+12.50
Purple	+15	"Steamboat"	-
Violet	+15	Supplementary Mail Type F	+8.00
Brown	+1.00	Printed Star Precancellation (Glen Allen, Va.)	-
Red	+7.50	China	+60.00
Green	+25.00		
"Paid"	+3.00		
"Free"	+15.00		

185 A55 5c **blue** 225.00 7.50
light blue 225.00 7.50
bright blue 225.00 7.50
dark blue 225.00 7.50
On cover 17.50
Pair 460.00 15.50
Block of four 950.00 100.00
Margin block of 12, Impt. & P# 5,000.

CANCELLATIONS.

Blue	+25	Numeral	+2.00
Purple	+1.00	Supplementary Mail Type F	+1.50
Magenta	+1.00	"Steamship"	+35.00
Ultramarine	+3.50	China	+60.00
Red	+7.50	Peru	-
Railroad	+20.00	Panama	-

186 A47a 6c **pink** 450.00 12.00
dull pink 450.00 12.00
brown rose 450.00 12.00
On cover 30.00
Pair 925.00 24.50
Block of four 1,900. 300.00

CANCELLATIONS.

Blue	+50	Supplementary Mail Type F	+4.00
Purple	+1.00	Railroad	+22.50
Magenta	+1.00	Numeral	+4.00
Red	+12.00	China	+70.00

187 A49 10c **brown,** *without secret mark* 750.00 14.00
yellow brown 750.00 14.00
On cover 35.00
Pair 1,550. 29.00
Block of four 3,250.
Double transfer — 30.00

CANCELLATIONS.

Blue	+50	"Paid"	+3.50
Magenta	+1.50	Supplementary Mail Type F	+3.00
Red	+10.00	China	+70.00

188 A49a 10c **brown,** *with secret mark* 475.00 15.00
yellow brown 475.00 15.00
black brown 525.00 22.50
On cover 30.00
Pair 975.00 31.00
Block of four 2,000. 130.00
Pair, one stamp No. 187 — 150.00
Double transfer — 30.00
Cracked plate —

CANCELLATIONS.

Blue	+50	Red	+10.00
Ultramarine	+3.00	Green	+70.00
Purple	+2.00	"Paid"	+7.50
Magenta	+2.00	Supp. Mail Type F	+5.00
		Numeral	+3.00
		Printed Star Precancellation (Glen Allen, Va.)	-

189 A51a 15c **red orange** 165.00 14.00

orange	165.00	14.00
yellow orange	165.00	14.00
On cover		75.00
Pair	340.00	29.00
Block of four	700.00	100.00
Margin block of 12, Impt. & P#	6,000.	

CANCELLATIONS.

Blue	+1.00	"Steamship"	+22.50
		Supplementary Mail Type F	+5.00
Purple	+3.00	Japan	+120.00
Magenta	+3.00	China	-
Ultramarine	+5.00		
Red	+12.00		

190 A53 30c **full black** 475.00 32.50
greenish black 475.00 32.50
On cover 400.00
Pair 975.00 67.50
Block of four 1,950. 225.00
Margin block of 10, Impt. & P# 8,250.

CANCELLATIONS.

		Supplementary Mail Type F	+6.00
Blue	+1.50	"Steamship"	+35.00
Purple	+3.00	Tahiti	-
Magenta	+3.00	Samoa	-
Red	+20.00		

191 A54 90c **carmine** 1,000. 150.00
rose 1,000. 150.00
carmine rose 1,000. 150.00
On cover 5,000.
Pair 2,050. 310.00
Block of four 4,750. 750.00

b. Imperf., pair 3,250.

CANCELLATIONS.

		Red	+35.00
Blue	+10.00	Supplementary Mail Type F	+20.00
Purple	+20.00		

No. 191b, imperforate, was not regularly issued.

SPECIAL PRINTING OF 1879 ISSUE
Produced by the American Bank Note Co.

1880 **Perf. 12**

Soft porous paper, without gum

192	A44a	1c dark ultramarine		10,000.
193	A45a	2c black brown		6,500.
194	A46a	3c blue green		15,000.
195	A47a	6c dull rose		10,500.
196	A48a	7c scarlet vermilion		2,100.
197	A49a	10c deep brown		9,750.
198	A50a	12c blackish purple		4,500.
199	A51a	15c orange		9,250.
200	A52	24c dark violet		3,000.
201	A53	30c greenish black		7,500.
202	A54	90c dull carmine		8,500.
203	A45a	2c scarlet vermilion		18,000.
204	A55	5c deep blue		32,500.

No. 197 was printed from Continental plate 302 (or 303) after plate was re-entered, therefore stamp may show normal, hairline or missing secret mark.

The Post Office Department did not keep separate records of the 1875 and 1880 Special Printings of the 1873 and 1879 issues, but the total quantity sold of both is recorded. The 1880 Special Printing is much the rarer.

Number Issued of 1875 and 1880 Special Printings.

1c ultramarine & dark ultramarine *(388)*
2c dark brown & black brown *(416)*
2c carmine vermilion & scarlet vermilion *(917)*
3c blue green *(267)*
5c bright blue & deep blue *(317)*
6c dull rose *(185)*
7c reddish vermilion & scarlet vermilion *(473)*
10c pale brown & deep brown *(180)*
12c dark violet & blackish purple *(282)*
15c bright orange & orange *(169)*
24c dull purple & dark violet *(286)*
30c greenish black *(179)*
90c violet carmine & dull carmine *(170)*

REGULAR ISSUE
Printed by the American Bank Note Co.

James A. Garfield — A56

1882 **Perf. 12**
205 A56 5c **yellow brown,** *April 10, 1882* 120.00 4.00
brown 120.00 4.00
gray brown 120.00 4.00
On cover 12.50
Pair 245.00 8.25
Block of four 500.00 65.00
Margin strip of 5, Impt. & P# 700.00
Margin strip of 6, Impt. & P# 875.00
Margin block of 12, Impt. & P# 3,750.

CANCELLATIONS.

		Supplementary Mail Type F	+2.50
Purple	+50	Red Express Co.	-
Magenta	+50	China	+125.00
Blue	+25		
Red	+7.00		
"Ship"	-	Samoa	+150.00
Numeral	+2.00	Puerto Rico	-

SPECIAL PRINTING
Printed by the American Bank Note Co.

1882 **Perf. 12**

Soft porous paper, without gum

205C A56 5c gray brown 18,500.
Block of four

DESIGNS OF 1873 RE-ENGRAVED

A44b

1c. The vertical lines in the upper part of the stamp have been so deepened that the background often appears to be solid. Lines of shading have been added to the upper arabesques.

1881-82
206 A44b 1c **gray blue,** *August 1881* 32.50 40
ultramarine 32.50 40
dull blue 32.50 40
slate blue 32.50 40
On cover 75
Pair 67.50 85
Block of four 140.00 10.00
Margin strip of 5, Impt. & P# 225.00
Margin strip of 6, Impt. & P# 275.00
Margin block of 10, Impt. & P# 1,000.
Margin block of 12, Impt. & P# 1,250.
Double transfer 47.50 4.00
Punched with eight small holes in a circle 175.00
Margin block of 10, Impt. & P# (8-hole punch) 3,750.

CANCELLATIONS.

		"Paid"	+4.75
Purple	+10	"Paid All"	+12.00
Magenta	+10	Numeral	+3.50
Blue	+20	Supp. Mail Type F	+5.00
Red	+3.00	Railroad	+10.00
Green	+35.00	Printed Star Precancel (Glen Allen, Va.)	-
Orange	+3.00	China	+55.00

A46b

3c. The shading at the sides of the central oval appears only about one-half the previous width. A short horizontal dash has been cut about 1 mm. below the "TS" of "CENTS".

207 A46b 3c **blue green,** *July 16, 1881* 40.00 12
green 40.00 12
yellow green 40.00 12
On cover 35
Pair 82.50 25
Block of four 170.00 25.00
Margin strip of 5, Impt. & P# 275.00
Margin block of 10, Impt. & P# 1,250.
Double transfer — 7.50
Cracked plate —
Punched with eight small holes in a circle 200.00

CANCELLATIONS.

		Numeral	+2.50
Purple	+10	"Ship"	-
Magenta	+10	Railroad	+5.00
Blue	+25	Supplementary Mail Type F	+8.00
Brown	+1.50	Printed Star Precancellation (Glen Allen, Va.)	-
Red	+2.50		
"Paid"	+3.00		

"Paid All"   - |

Lincoln — A47b

6c. On the original stamps four vertical lines can be counted from the edge of the panel to the outside of the stamp. On the re-engraved stamps there are but three lines in the same place.

208 A47b	6c **rose,** *June, 1882*		225.00	45.00
	dull rose		225.00	45.00
	On cover (rose)			125.00
	Pair (rose)		460.00	95.00
	Block of four (rose)		950.00	300.00
a.	6c brown red		200.00	
	On cover (brown red)			175.00
	Pair (brown red)		410.00	120.00
	Block of four (brown red)		825.00	350.00
a.	Margin strip of 6, Impt. & P#		*1,800.*	
a.	Margin block of 10, Impt. & P#		—	
a.	Margin block of 12, Impt. & P#			
	Double transfer		275.00	60.00

CANCELLATIONS.

		Blue	+4.00
Magenta	+2.50	Red	+15.00
Purple	+2.50	Supp. Mail Type F	+10.00

Jefferson
A49b

10c. On the original stamps there are five vertical lines between the left side of the oval and the edge of the shield. There are only four lines on the re-engraved stamps. In the lower part of the latter, also, the horizontal lines of the background have been strengthened.

209 A49b	10c **brown,** *April, 1882*		75.00	2.50
	yellow brown		75.00	2.50
	orange brown		75.00	2.50
	purple brown		85.00	2.75
	olive brown		85.00	2.75
	On cover			7.50
	Pair		160.00	4.75
	Block of four		325.00	22.50
	Margin strip of 5, Impt. & P#		450.00	
	Margin strip of 6, Impt. & P#		575.00	
	Margin block of 10, Impt. & P#		1,850.	
	Margin block of 12, Impt. & P#		2,250.	
b.	10c black brown		110.00	6.75
	On cover			30.00
	Pair		—	17.50
	Block of four		—	
c.	Double impression		—	

CANCELLATIONS.

		"Paid"	+2.50
Purple	+25	Supplementary Mail Type F	+3.00
Magenta	+25	Express Company	
Blue	+75	Japan	+75.00
Red	+3.50	China	-
Green	+35.00	Samoa	-
Numeral	+2.00		

Printed by the American Bank Note Company.

Washington — A57

Nos. 210-211 were issued to meet the reduced first class rate of 2 cents for each half ounce, and the double rate, which Congress approved Mar. 3, 1883, effective Oct. 1, 1883.

1883   *Perf. 12*

210 A57	2c **red brown,** *Oct. 1, 1883*		32.50	8
	dark red brown		32.50	8
	orange brown		32.50	8
	On cover			25
	Pair		65.00	20

	Block of four	140.00	9.00
	Margin strip of 5, Impt. & P#	200.00	
	Margin strip of 6, Impt. & P#	275.00	
	Margin block of 10, Impt. & P#	950.00	
	Margin block of 12, Impt. & P#	*1,200.*	
b.	Imperf., pair		
	Double transfer	35.00	1.25

CANCELLATIONS.

		Numeral	+2.50
Purple	+10	"Paid"	+3.00
Margenta	+10	Railroad	+5.00
Blue	+20	Express Company	-
Violet	+30	Supplementary Mail Type F	+5.00
Brown	+30	"Ship"	-
Red	+3.50	"Steamboat"	-
Green	+25.00	China	-

Jackson — A58

211 A58	4c **blue green,** *Oct. 1, 1883*		140.00	7.50
	deep blue green		140.00	7.50
	On cover			40.00
	Pair		285.00	16.00
	Block of four		575.00	65.00
	Margin strip of 6, Impt. & P#		1,100.	
	Margin block of 12, Impt. & P#		4,000.	
a.	Imperf., pair		—	—
	Double transfer		—	—
	Cracked plate		—	

CANCELLATIONS.

		Blue	+1.00
Purple	+1.00	Numeral	+2.00
Magenta	+1.00	Supp. Mail Type F	+5.00
Green	+35.00		

SPECIAL PRINTING
Printed by the American Bank Note Company.

1883   **Soft porous paper**   *Perf. 12*

211B A57	2c **pale red brown,** with gum	750.00	—
	Block of four	3,250.	
c.	Horizontal pair, imperf. between	2,250.	
211D A58	4c **deep blue green,** without gum	15,000.	

The quantity issued of Nos. 211B and 211D is not definitely known, but 2,000 of each were delivered.
No. 211B is from a trial operation of a new steam-powered American Bank Note Company press.

REGULAR ISSUE
Printed by the American Bank Note Company.

Franklin — A59

1887   *Perf. 12*

212 A59	1c **ultramarine,** *June 1887*		60.00	65
	bright ultramarine		60.00	65
	On cover			1.50
	Pair		125.00	1.35
	Block of four		260.00	20.00
	Margin strip of 5, Impt. & P#		350.00	
	Margin strip of 6, Impt. & P#		425.00	
	Margin block of 10, Impt. & P#		1,200.	
	Margin block of 12, Impt. & P#		1,500.	
a.	Imperf., pair		750.00	325.00
	Double transfer			

CANCELLATIONS.

		Numeral	+2.00
Purple	+10	Railroad	+10.00
Magenta	+10	Supplementary Mail Type F	+5.00

		Blue	+10	China
		Red	+5.50	

213 A57	2c **green,** *Sept. 10, 1887*		22.50	8
	bright green		22.50	8
	dark green		22.50	8
	On cover			20
	Pair		47.50	18
	Block of four		100.00	7.50
	Margin strip of 5, Impt. & P#		150.00	
	Margin strip of 6, Impt. & P#		185.00	
	Margin block of 10, Impt. & P#		700.00	
	Margin block of 12, Impt. & P#		850.00	
a.	Imperf., pair		750.00	325.00
b.	Printed on both sides		—	
	Double transfer			3.00

CANCELLATIONS.

		Railroad	+12.00
Purple	+10	Numeral	+2.00
Magenta	+10	"Steam"	
Blue	+90	"Steamboat"	
Red	+5.00	Supp. Mail Type F	+7.50
Green	+25.00	China	
"Paid"	+5.00	Japan	

214 A46b	3c **vermilion,** *Oct. 3, 1887*		45.00	37.50
	On cover (single)			85.00
	Pair		92.50	80.00
	Block of four		190.00	200.00
	Margin strip of 5, Impt. & P#		275.00	
	Margin strip of 6, Impt. & P#		325.00	
	Margin block of 10, Impt. & P#		1,100.	
	Margin block of 12, Impt. & P#		1,300.	

CANCELLATIONS.

		Blue	+10.00
Purple	+5.00	Supplementary Mail Type F	+15.00
Magenta	+5.00	Railroad	+30.00
Green	+150.00		

Printed by the American Bank Note Company.
SAME AS 1870-83 ISSUES

1888   *Perf. 12*

215 A58	4c **carmine,** *Nov. 1888*		140.00	11.00
	rose carmine		140.00	11.00
	pale rose		140.00	11.00
	On cover			35.00
	Pair		290.00	23.00
	Block of four		600.00	75.00
	Margin strip of 5, Impt. & P#		800.00	
	Margin strip of 6, Impt. & P#		1,000.	
	Margin block of 10, Impt. & P#		3,500.	
	Margin block of 12, Impt. & P#		4,250.	

CANCELLATIONS.

		Magenta	+2.00
Blue	+1.00	Supplementary Mail Type F	+5.00
Red	+5.00		
Purple	+2.00		

216 A56	5c **indigo,** *Feb. 1888*		140.00	6.50
	deep blue		140.00	6.50
	On cover			25.00
	Pair		290.00	13.50
	Block of four		600.00	60.00
	Margin strip of 5, Impt. & P#		800.00	
	Margin strip of 6, Impt. & P#		1,000.	
	Margin block of 10, Impt. & P#		3,500.	
	Margin block of 12, Impt. & P#		4,250.	
b.	Imperf., pair		1,000.	

CANCELLATIONS.

		Supplementary Mail Type F	+3.00
Purple	+1.00	China	+85.00
Magenta	+1.00	Japan	+85.00
Blue	+1.00	Puerto Rico	+75.00
Samoa			

217 A53	30c **orange brown,** *Jan. 1888*		325.00	75.00
	deep orange brown		325.00	75.00
	On cover			1,400.
	Pair		675.00	160.00
	Block of four		1,500.	350.00
	Margin strip of 5, Impt. & P#		2,100.	
	Margin block of 10, Impt. & P#		6,750.	
	Margin block of 12, Impt. & P#		—	
a.	Imperf., pair		1,350.	

CANCELLATIONS.

		Supplementary Mail Type F	+10.00
Blue	+5.00	"Paid All"	+25.00
Magenta	+10.00	"Paid"	+15.00

218 A54	90c **purple,** *Feb. 1888*		700.00	130.00
	bright purple		700.00	130.00
	On cover			7,500.
	Pair		1,450.	270.00
	Block of four		3,000.	600.00
	Margin strip of 5, Impt. & P#		4,250.	
	Margin block of 10, Impt. & P#		22,500.	
	Margin block of 12, Impt. & P#		—	
a.	Imperf., pair			

CANCELLATIONS.

		Supplementary Mail Type F	+25.00
Blue	+10.00		

Purple   +15.00

Nos. 216b, 217a and 218 were not regularly issued.

Printed by the American Bank Note Company.
Plates for the 1c and 2c were of 400 subjects in four
panes of 100 each. All other values were from
plates of 200 subjects in two panes of 100 each.

Franklin — A60

Washington — A61

Jackson — A62

Lincoln — A63

Grant — A64

Garfield — A65

William T.
Sherman — A66

Daniel Webster — A67

Henry Clay — A68

Jefferson — A69

Perry — A70

1890-93   **Perf. 12**

219	A60	1c **dull blue,** *Feb. 22, 1890*	18.50	10
		deep blue	18.50	10
		ultramarine	18.50	12
		On cover		35
		Block of four	75.00	3.50
		Margin strip of 5, Impt. & P#	120.00	
		Margin strip of 6, Impt. & P#	145.00	
		Margin strip of 7, Impt. & P#	175.00	
		Margin block of 10, Impt. & P#	475.00	
		Margin block of 12, Impt. & P#	600.00	
		Margin block of 14, Impt. & P#	750.00	
c.		Imperf., pair	225.00	
		Double transfer	—	-

CANCELLATIONS.

Samoa   - | China   -

219D	A61	2c **lake,** *Feb. 22, 1890*	150.00	45
		On cover		1.25
		Block of four	625.00	7.00
		Margin strip of 5, Impt. & P#	750.00	
		Margin block of 10, Impt. & P#	2,750.	
e.		Imperf., pair	100.00	
		Double transfer	—	-

CANCELLATIONS.

Supplementary Mail
Type F   3.00

220	A61	2c **carmine,** *1890*	15.00	5
		dark carmine, rose or car rose	15.00	5
		On cover		15
		Block of four	60.00	1.50
		Margin strip of 5, Impt. & P#	100.00	
		Margin strip of 6, Impt. & P#	125.00	
		Margin strip of 7, Impt. & P#	160.00	
		Margin block of 10, Impt. & P#	450.00	
		Margin block of 12, Impt. & P#	550.00	
		Margin block of 14, Impt. & P#	700.00	
a.		Cap on left "2" (Plates 235-236, 246-247-248)	35.00	1.00
		Pair, cap on left, one normal	—	
a.		Margin block of 12, Impt. & P#	1,200.	
c.		Cap on both "2's" (Plates 245, 246)	110.00	8.00
		Pair, cap on left, cap on both	—	
d.		Imperf., pair	100.00	
d.		Imperf., pair, without gum	40.00	
d.		Margin block of 12, Impt. & P#	—	
		Double transfer	—	3.00

CANCELLATIONS.

Blue	+5	Supplementary Mail Types F or G +3.00
Purple	+5	China +20.00

221	A62	3c **purple,** *Feb. 22, 1890*	50.00	4.50
		bright purple	50.00	4.50
		dark purple	50.00	4.50
		On cover		12.50
		Block of four	210.00	30.00
		Margin strip of 5, Impt. & P#	325.00	
		Margin block of 10, Impt. & P#	1,750.	
a.		Imperf., pair	275.00	

CANCELLATIONS.

Samoa   -

222	A63	4c **dark brown,** *June 2, 1890*	50.00	1.50
		blackish brown	50.00	1.50
		On cover		12.50
		Block of four	210.00	13.50
		Margin strip of 5, Impt. & P#	325.00	
		Margin block of 10, Impt. & P#	1,850.	
a.		Imperf., pair	250.00	
		Double transfer	65.00	-

CANCELLATIONS.

China   +40.00

223	A64	5c **chocolate,** *June 2, 1890*	50.00	1.50
		yellow brown	50.00	1.50
		On cover		10.00
		Block of four	210.00	12.50
		Margin strip of 5, Impt. & P#	325.00	
		Margin block of 10, Impt. & P#	1,850.	
b.		Imperf., pair, yellow brown	275.00	
		Double transfer	65.00	1.75

CANCELLATIONS.

China	+35.00	Supplementary Mail Types F or G +3.00
Samoa	-	

224	A65	6c **brown red,** *Feb. 22, 1890*	55.00	15.00
		dark brown red	55.00	15.00
		On cover		30.00
		Block of four	230.00	70.00
		Margin strip of 5, Impt. & P#	375.00	
		Margin block of 10, Impt. & P#	1,850.	
a.		Imperf., pair	275.00	

CANCELLATIONS.

Supplementary Mail Type F   +3.00

225	A66	8c **lilac,** *Mar. 21, 1893*	40.00	8.50
		grayish lilac	40.00	8.50
		magenta	40.00	8.50
		On cover		25.00
		Block of four	165.00	50.00
		Margin strip of 5, Impt. & P#	275.00	
		Margin block of 10, Impt. & P#	1,300.	
a.		Imperf., pair	1,250.	

The 8c was issued because the registry fee was reduced from
10 to 8 cents effective Jan. 1, 1893.

226	A67	10c **green,** *Feb. 22, 1890*	95.00	1.75
		bluish green	95.00	1.75
		dark green	95.00	1.75
		On cover		7.50
		Block of four	390.00	20.00
		Margin strip of 5, Impt. & P#	650.00	
		Margin block of 10, Impt. & P#	3,000.	
a.		Imperf., pair	400.00	
		Double transfer	—	-

CANCELLATIONS.

Samoa	-	Supplementary Mail Types F or G +2.50

227	A68	15c **indigo,** *Feb. 22, 1890*	135.00	15.00
		deep indigo	135.00	15.00
		On cover		60.00
		Block of four	550.00	75.00

	Margin strip of 5, Impt. & P#	900.00	
	Margin block of 10, Impt. &		
	P#	5,750.	
a.	Imperf., pair	750.00	
	Double transfer		—
	Triple transfer		—

CANCELLATIONS.

			Supplementary	
-----	---	----------------------------	Mail Type F	+3.00
228	A69	30c **black,** *Feb. 22, 1890*	200.00	20.00
		gray black	200.00	20.00
		full black	200.00	20.00
		On cover		600.00
		Block of four	825.00	100.00
		Margin strip of 5, Impt. & P#	1,400.	
		Margin block of 10, Impt. &		
		P#	9,000.	
a.		Imperf., pair	1,350.	—
		Double transfer		-

CANCELLATIONS.

			Supplementary	
-----	---	----------------------------	Mail Type F	+5.00
229	A70	90c **orange,** *Feb. 22, 1890*	325.00	95.00
		yellow orange	325.00	95.00
		red orange	325.00	95.00
		On cover		2,500.
		Block of four	1,400.	425.00
		Margin strip of 5, Impt. & P#	2,350.	
		Margin block of 10, Impt. &		
		P#	18,500.	
a.		Imperf., pair	2,750.	—
		Short transfer at bottom		—

CANCELLATIONS.

		Supplementary	
		Mail Type F	
		or G	+10.00

Imperforate stamps of this issue were not regularly issued. The imperforate 1c, 2c, 4c, 5c and 6c values exist in many trial colors. Price slightly less than for those in normal colors.

COLUMBIAN EXPOSITION ISSUE

Issued to commemorate the World's Columbian Exposition held at Chicago, Ill., from May 1, 1893 to October 30, 1893, which was to celebrate the 400th anniversary of the discovery of America by Christopher Columbus.

Columbus in Sight of Land — A71

Landing of Columbus — A72

"Santa Maria," Flagship of Columbus — A73

The lack of a price for a listed item does not necessarily indicate rarity.

Fleet of Columbus — A74

Columbus Soliciting Aid from Queen Isabella — A75

Columbus Welcomed at Barcelona — A76

Columbus Restored to Favor — A77

Columbus Presenting Natives — A78

Columbus Announcing His Discovery — A79

Columbus at La Rabida — A80

Recall of Columbus — A81

Queen Isabella Pledging Her Jewels — A82

Columbus in Chains — A83

Columbus Describing His Third Voyage — A84

Queen Isabella and Columbus — A85

Samuel Shaskan

Philatelist

Superb Used United States

**Want Lists
Promptly Filled
for
Highest Quality
Used U.S.**

**P.O. Box 8145
Stamford, Connecticut 06905
USA**

(203) 359-8144

Member APS, USPCS

Columbus — A86

AMERICAN BANK NOTE COMPANY

No. 57

Type of imprint and plate number

Exposition Station Cancellation

Condition is extremely important in evaluating Nos. 230-245. Prices are for stamps free from faults and with the design well clear of the perforations. Stamps of superior quality command substantial premiums.
Printed by the American Bank Note Company.
Plates of 200 subjects in two panes of 100 each (1c, 2c).
Plates of 100 subjects in two panes of 50 each (2c-$5).
Issued (except 8c) Jan. 2, 1893.

1893			**Perf. 12**	
230 A71	1c **deep blue**	22.50	30
	blue	22.50	30
	pale blue	22.50	30
	On cover		75
	On cover or card, Expo. sta. canc.		175.00
	Block of four	92.50	6.00
	Margin strip of 3, Impt. & P#	85.00	
	Margin strip of 4, Impt. & P#	125.00	
	Margin block of 6, Impt. & P#	350.00	
	Margin block of 8, Impt., letter & P#	550.00	
	Double transfer	30.00	50
	Cracked plate	100.00	

CANCELLATIONS.
	China	
		-

231 A72	2c **brown violet**	21.00	6
	deep brown violet	21.00	6
	gray violet	21.00	6
	On cover		25

	On cover or card, Expo. sta. cancel		150.00
	Block of four	85.00	3.00
	Margin strip of 3, Impt. & P#	80.00	
	Margin strip of 4, Impt. & P#	115.00	
	Margin block of 6, Impt. & P#	300.00	
	Margin block of 8, Impt., letter & P#	500.00	
b.	Imperf., pair	1,200.	
	Double transfer	30.00	25
	Triple transfer	75.00	—
	Quadruple transfer	110.00	
	Third figure to left of Columbus shows broken hat	65.00	20
	Broken frame line	25.00	8
	Recut frame lines	25.00	
	Cracked plate	100.00	—

CANCELLATIONS.
	China	-	Supp. Mail, G	+3.50
232 A73	3c **green**	50.00		15.00
	dull green	50.00		15.00
	dark green	50.00		15.00
	On cover			30.00
	On cover, Expo. station canc.			300.00
	Block of four	205.00		75.00
	Margin strip of 3, Impt. & P#	200.00		
	Margin strip of 4, Impt. & P#	285.00		
	Margin block of 6, Impt. & P#	650.00		
	Margin block of 8, Impt., letter & P#	1,050.		
	Double transfer	75.00		—

CANCELLATIONS.
	China	-	Supp. Mail, F, G	+7.50
233 A74	4c **ultramarine**	70.00		6.00
	dull ultramarine	70.00		6.00
	deep ultramarine	70.00		6.00
	On cover			20.00
	On cover, Expo. station canc.			400.00
	Block of four	285.00		35.00
	Margin strip of 3, Impt. & P#	275.00		
	Margin strip of 4, Impt. & P#	400.00		—
	Margin block of 6, Impt. & P#	950.00		
	Margin block of 8, Impt., letter & P#	1,800.		
a.	4c blue (error)	7,000.		2,500.
a.	Block of four	30,000.		
a.	Margin strip of 4, Impt., letter & P#	37,500.		
	Double transfer	110.00		-

CANCELLATIONS.
		Supp. Mail, G	+3.00

No. 233a exists in two shades.

234 A75	5c **chocolate**	80.00		7.00
	dark chocolate	80.00		7.00
	pale brown	80.00		7.00
	yellow brown	80.00		7.00
	On cover			20.00
	On cover, Expo. station canc.			400.00
	Block of four	325.00		45.00
	Margin strip of 3, Impt. & P#	320.00		
	Margin strip of 4, Impt. & P#	450.00		
	Margin block of 6, Impt. & P#	1,350.		
	Margin block of 8, Impt., letter & P#	2,500.		
	Double transfer	120.00		—

CANCELLATIONS.
	China	-	Supp. Mail, F	+3.00
235 A76	6c **purple**	70.00		20.00
	dull purple	70.00		20.00
a.	6c red violet	70.00		20.00
	On cover			45.00
	On cover, Expo. station canc.			450.00
	Block of four	285.00		85.00
	Margin strip of 3, Impt. & P#	275.00		
	Margin strip of 4, Impt. & P#	400.00		
	Margin block of 6, Impt. & P#	1,050.		
	Margin block of 8, Impt., letter & P#	1,900.		
	Double transfer	100.00		25.00

CANCELLATIONS.
	China	-	Supp. Mail, F	+5.00
236 A77	8c **magenta**, *Mar. 1893*	57.50		8.00
	light magenta	57.50		8.00
	dark magenta	57.50		8.00
	On cover			20.00
	On cover, Expo. station canc.			450.00
	Block of four	240.00		40.00
	Margin strip of 3, Impt. & P#	220.00		
	Margin strip of 4, Impt. & P#	310.00		
	Margin block of 6, Impt. & P#	650.00		
	Margin block of 8, Impt., letter & P#	1,050.		
	Double transfer	75.00		—

CANCELLATIONS. Mar. 3
	China	-	Supp. Mail, F	+4.50
237 A78	10c **black brown**	120.00		6.50
	dark brown	120.00		6.50
	gray black	120.00		6.50
	On cover			30.00
	On cover, Expo. station canc.			500.00
	Block of four	500.00		40.00
	Margin strip of 3, Impt. & P#	475.00		
	Margin strip of 4, Impt. & P#	675.00		
	Margin block of 6, Impt. & P#	3,000.		
	Margin block of 8, Impt., letter & P#	4,500.		
	Double transfer	175.00		10.00
	Triple transfer			

CANCELLATIONS.
	Supplementary Mail Types F or G	+4.00
238 A79	15c **dark green**	200.00		65.00
	green	200.00		65.00
	dull green	200.00		65.00
	On cover			200.00
	On cover, Expo. station canc.			900.00
	Block of four	850.00		300.00
	Margin strip of 3, Impt. & P#	850.00		
	Margin strip of 4, Impt. & P#	1,150.		
	Margin block of 6, Impt. & P#	4,750.		
	Margin block of 8, Impt., letter & P#	7,500.		
	Double transfer			—

CANCELLATIONS.
	China	+75.00	Supp. Mail, F, G	+10.00
239 A80	30c **orange brown**	275.00		90.00
	bright orange brown	275.00		90.00
	On cover			375.00
	On cover, Expo. station canc.			1,500.
	Block of four	1,150.		425.00
	Margin strip of 3, Impt. & P#	1,100.		
	Margin strip of 4, Impt. & P#	1,600.		
	Margin block of 6, Impt. & P#	7,000.		
	Margin block of 8, Impt., letter & P#	10,500.		

CANCELLATIONS.
	Supplementary Mail Types F or G	+25.00
240 A81	50c **slate blue**	350.00		140.00
	dull state blue	350.00		140.00
	On cover			600.00
	On cover, Expo. station canc.			2,250.
	Block of four	1,450.		650.00
	Margin strip of 3, Impt. & P#	1,400.		
	Margin strip of 4, Impt. & P#	2,000.		
	Margin block of 6, Impt. & P#	9,500.		
	Margin block of 8, Impt., letter & P#	14,000.		
	Double transfer	—		—
	Triple transfer	—		—

CANCELLATIONS.
	Supplementary Mail Types F or G	+30.00
241 A82	$1 **salmon**	1,150.		550.00
	dark salmon	1,150.		550.00
	On cover			1,900.
	On cover, Expo. station canc.			4,500.
	Block of four	5,000.		2,500.
	Margin strip of 3, Impt. & P#	4,750.		
	Margin strip of 4, Impt. & P#	6,500.		
	Margin block of 6, Impt. & P#	20,000.		
	Margin block of 8, Impt., letter & P#	27,500.		
	Double transfer	—		—

CANCELLATIONS.
	Supplementary Mail Types F or G	+50.00
242 A83	$2 **brown red**	1,250.		500.00
	deep brown red	1,250.		500.00
	On cover			1,850.
	On cover, Expo. station canc.			4,500.
	Block of four	5,500.		2,250.
	Margin strip of 3, Impt. & P#	5,250.		
	Margin strip of 4, Impt. & P#	7,000.		
	Margin block of 6, Impt. & P#	22,000.		
	Margin block of 8, Impt., letter & P#	30,000.		

		Supplementary Mail Type G	+50.00		
243	A84	$3 **yellow green**		2,600.	1,100.
		pale yellow green		2,600.	1,100.
a.		$3 olive green		2,600.	1,100.
		On cover			2,500.
		On cover, Expo. station canc.			6,250.
		Block of four		11,500.	5,500.
		Margin strip of 3, Impt. & P#		11,000.	
		Margin strip of 4, Impt. & P#		15,000.	
		Margin block of 6, Impt. & P#		45,000.	
		Margin block of 8, Impt., letter & P#		70,000.	
244	A85	$4 **crimson lake**		3,400.	1,450.
a.		$4 rose carmine		3,400.	1,450.
		pale aniline rose		3,400.	1,450.
		On cover			3,750.
		On cover, Expo. station canc.			8,500.
		Block of four		16,000.	7,000.
		Margin strip of 3, Impt. & P#		15,000.	
		Margin strip of 4, Impt. & P#		21,000.	
		Margin block of 6, Impt. & P#		90,000.	
		Margin block of 8, Impt., letter & P#		130,000.	
245	A86	$5 **black**		3,600.	1,700.
		grayish black		3,600.	1,700.
		On cover			4,500.
		On cover, Expo. station canc.			12,000.
		Block of four		16,500.	9,000.
		Margin strip of 3, Impt. & P#		16,000.	
		Margin strip of 4, Impt. & P#		22,500.	
		Margin block of 6, Impt. & P#		100,000.	
		Margin block of 8, Impt., letter & P#		150,000.	

Nos. 230-245 exist imperforate; not issued.

BUREAU ISSUES In the following listings of postal issues mostly printed by the Bureau of Engraving and Printing at Washington, D.C., the editors acknowledge with thanks the use of material prepared by the Catalogue Listing Committee of the Bureau Issues Association.

The Bureau-printed stamps until 1965 were engraved except the Offset Issues of 1918-19 (Nos. 525-536). Engraving and lithography were combined for the first time for the Homemakers 5c (no. 1253). The Bureau used photogravure first in 1971 on the Missouri 8c (No. 1426).

Stamps in this section which were not printed by the Bureau begin with Nos. 909-921 and are so noted.

"*On cover*" listings carry through No. 550. Beyond this point a few covers of special significance are listed. Many Bureau Issue stamps are undoubtly scarce properly used on cover. Most higher denominations exist almost exclusively on pieces of package wrapping and usually in combination with other values. Collector interest in covers is generally limited to fancy cancellations, attractive corner cards, use abroad and other special usages.

Plate number blocks are priced unused. Although many exist used, and are scarcer in that condition, they command only a fraction of the price of the unused examples because they are less sought after.

IMPRINTS AND PLATE NUMBERS
In listing the Bureau of Engraving & Printing Imprints, the editors have followed the classification of types adopted by the Bureau Issues Association. Types I, II, IV, V and VIII occur on postage issues and are illustrated below. Types III, VI and VII occur only on Special Delivery plates, so are illustrated with the listings of those stamps; other types are illustrated with the listings of the issues on which they occur.

Type I	II	IV	V	VIII

In listing Imprint block and strips, the editors have designated for each stamp the various types known to exist. If, however, the Catalogue listing sufficiently describes the Imprint, no type number is given. Thus a listing reading: "Imprint. P# & A" in the 1912-14 series would not be followed by a type number as the description is self-explanatory. Prices are for the commonest types.

PLATE POSTIONS
At the suggestion of the Catalogue Listing Committee of the Bureau Issues Association, all plate positions of these issues are indicated by giving the plate number first, next the pane position, and finally the stamp position. For example: 20234 L.L. 58.

Franklin — A87

Washington — A88

Jackson — A89

Lincoln — A90

Grant — A91

Garfield — A92

Sherman — A93

Webster — A94

Clay — A95

Jefferson — A96

Perry — A97

James Madison — A98

John Marshall — A99

REGULAR ISSUE

Plates for the issues of 1894, 1895 and 1898 were of two sizes:

400 subjects for all 1c, 2c and 10c denominations; 200 subjects for all 6c, 8c, 15c, 50c, $1.00, $2.00 and $5.00, and both 400 and 200 subjects for the 3c, 4c and 5c denominations; all issued in panes of 100 each.

Dates of issue of the 1894, 1895 and 1898 denominations are taken from the Report of the Third Assistant Postmaster General, dated June 30, 1899.

1894	Unwmk.	Perf. 12	
246 A87	1c **ultramarine**, *Oct. 1894*	22.50	3.00
	bright ultramarine	22.50	3.00
	dark ultramarine	22.50	3.00
	On cover		15.00
	Block of four	92.50	17.50
	Margin strip of 3, Impt. & P#, T I	95.00	
	Margin block of 6, Impt. & P#, T I	300.00	
	Double transfer	30.00	4.00

CANCELLATIONS.

China   - |

247 A87	1c **blue**	55.00	1.25
	bright blue	55.00	1.25
	dark blue	55.00	1.25
	On cover		15.00
	Block of four	225.00	12.50
	Margin strip of 3, Impt. & P#, T I or II	225.00	
	Margin block of 6, Impt. & P#, T I or II	600.00	
	Double transfer	—	3.50

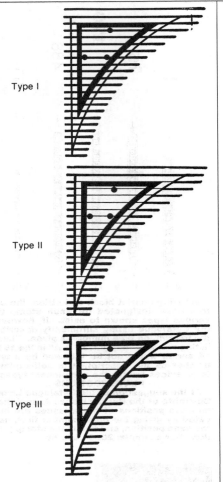

Type I

Type II

Type III

TWO CENTS.

Type I (Triangle I). The horizontal lines of the ground work run across the triangle and are of the same thickness within it as without.

Type II (Triangle II). The horizontal lines cross the triangle but are thinner within it than without.

Type III (Triangle III). The horizontal lines do not cross the double lines of the triangle. The lines within the triangle are thin, as in Type II. Two varieties of Type III are known but the variations are minor. For further information see the March, 1937 issue of the "Bureau Specialist."

248 A88	2c **pink**, type I, *Oct. 1894*	17.50	2.00
	pale pink	17.50	2.00
	On cover		12.50
	Block of four	72.50	15.00
	Margin strip of 3, Impt. & P#, T I or II	75.00	
	Margin block of 6, Impt. & P#, T I or II	200.00	
a.	Vert. pair, imperf. horiz.	*2,000.*	
	Double transfer	—	—
249 A88	2c **carmine lake**, type I	125.00	1.35
	dark carmine lake	125.00	1.35
	On cover		10.00
	Block of four	525.00	15.00
	Margin strip of 3, Impt. & P#, T I or II	525.00	
	Margin block of 6, Impt. & P#, T I or II	1,250.	
	Double transfer	—	2.00
250 A88	2c **carmine**, type I	21.00	25
	dark carmine	21.00	25
	scarlet	21.00	25
	On cover		2.00
	Block of four	85.00	3.00
	Margin strip of 3, Impt. & P#, T I or II	85.00	
	Margin block of 6, Impt. & P#, T I or II	300.00	
a.	Vert. pair, imperf. horiz.	*1,500.*	
b.	Horizontal pair, imperf. between	*1,500.*	
	Double transfer		1.50
251 A88	2c **carmine**, type II	175.00	2.50
	dark carmine	175.00	2.50
	On cover		15.00
	Block of four	750.00	22.50
	Margin strip of 3, Impt. & P#, T II	750.00	
	Margin block of 6, Impt. & P#, T II	2,250.	
252 A88	2c **carmine**, type III	100.00	3.25
	pale carmine	100.00	3.25
	On cover		15.00
	Block of four	425.00	40.00

	Margin strip of 3, Impt. & P#, T II or IV	425.00	
	Margin block of 6, Impt. & P#, T II or IV	1,350.	
a.	Horiz. pair, imperf. vert.	*1,350.*	
b.	Horiz. pair, imperf. between	*1,500.*	
253 A89	3c **purple**, *Sept. 1894*	80.00	6.25
	dark purple	80.00	6.25
	On cover		20.00
	Block of four	325.00	40.00
	Margin block of 4, arrow, R or L	350.00	
	Margin strip of 3, Impt. & P#, T I or II	325.00	
	Margin block of 6, Impt. & P#, T I or II	1,000.	
a.	Imperf., pair	350.00	
a.	Block of four	750.00	
a.	Margin block of 6, Impt. & P#	—	
254 A90	4c **dark brown**, *Sept. 1894*	90.00	2.50
	brown	90.00	2.50
	On cover		20.00
	Block of four	375.00	20.00
	Margin block of 4, arrow, R or L	385.00	
	Margin strip of 3, Impt. & P#, T I or II	375.00	
	Margin block of 6, Impt. & P#, T I or II	1,250.	
a.	Imperf., pair	350.00	
a.	Block of four	750.00	
a.	Margin block of 6, Impt. & P#	—	

CANCELLATIONS.

	Supplementary Mail Type F	+2.00

255 A91	5c **chocolate**, *Sept. 1894*	80.00	3.50
	deep chocolate	80.00	3.50
	yellow brown	80.00	3.50
	On cover		15.00
	Block of four	325.00	20.00
	Margin block of 4, arrow, R or L	340.00	
	Margin strip of 3, Impt. & P#, T I, II or IV	325.00	
	Margin block of 6, Impt. & P#, T I, II or IV	875.00	
b.	Imperf., pair	350.00	
b.	Block of four	750.00	
b.	Margin block of 6, Impt. & P#	—	
c.	Vert. pair, imperf. horiz.	*900.00*	
	Worn plate, diagonal lines missing in oval background	85.00	4.00
	Double transfer	100.00	4.00

CANCELLATIONS.

	Supplementary Mail Type G	+2.00
	China	

256 A92	6c **dull brown**, *July 1894*	140.00	15.00
	On cover		45.00
	Block of four	575.00	80.00
	Margin block of 4, arrow, R or L	600.00	
	Margin strip of 3, Impt. & P#, T I	575.00	
	Margin block of 6, Impt. & P#, T I	1,500.	550.00
a.	Vert. pair, imperf. horiz.	*850.00*	
a.	Margin block of 6, Impt. & P#, T I	*10,000.*	
257 A93	8c **violet brown**, *Mar. 1895*	110.00	11.50
	bright violet brown	110.00	11.50
	On cover		35.00
	Block of four	450.00	65.00
	Margin block of 4, arrow, R or L	475.00	
	Margin strip of 3, Impt. & P#, T I	450.00	
	Margin block of 6, Impt. & P#, T I	1,100.	
258 A94	10c **dark green**, *Sept. 1894*	175.00	7.50
	green	175.00	7.50
	dull green	175.00	7.50
	On cover		35.00
	Block of four	750.00	40.00
	Margin strip of 3, Impt. & P#, T I	750.00	
	Margin block of 6, Impt. & P#, T I	2,400.	
a.	Imperf., pair	650.00	
a.	Block of four	1,400.	
a.	Margin block of 6, Impt. & P#		
	Double transfer	225.00	8.50

CANCELLATIONS.

China	-	Supplementary Mail Types F or G	+2.00

259 A95	15c **dark blue**, *Oct. 1894*	250.00	45.00
	indigo	250.00	45.00
	On cover		120.00
	Block of four	1,050.	250.00
	Margin block of 4, arrow, R or L	1,100.	
	Margin strip of 3, Impt. & P#, T I	1,100.	
	Margin block of 6, Impt. & P#, T I	3,750.	

CANCELLATIONS.

	China	

260 A96	50c **orange**, *Nov. 1894*	325.00	75.00
	deep orange	325.00	75.00
	On cover		750.00
	Block of four	1,400.	450.00
	Margin block of 4, arrow, R or L	1,500.	

Margin strip of 3, Impt. & P#,
  T I   1,400.
Margin block of 6, Impt. & P#,
  T I   6,000.

CANCELLATIONS.

Supplementary Mail Types F or G		-
China		-

Type I

Type II

ONE DOLLAR.

Type I. The circles enclosing "$1" are broken where they meet the curved line below "One Dollar".

Type II. The circles are complete.

The fifteen left vertical rows of impressions from plate 76 are Type I, the balance being Type II.

261	A97	$1 **black**, type I, *Nov. 1894*	850.00	250.00
		grayish black	850.00	250.00
		On cover		1,250.
		Block of four	3,500.	1,100.
		Margin block of 4, arrow, L	3,750.	
		Margin strip of 3, Impt. & P#, T I	3,500.	
		Margin block of 6, Impt. & P#, T II	15,000.	
261A	A97	$1 **black**, type II, *Nov. 1894*	1,850.	475.00
		On cover		3,250.
		Block of four	7,500.	2,750.
		Margin block of 4, arrow, R	7,750.	
		Horizontal pair, types I and II	3,250.	1,000.
		Block of four, two each of types I and II	6,750.	—
		Margin strip of 3, Impt. & P#, T II, one stamp No. 261	6,000.	
		Margin block of 6, Impt. & P#, T II, two stamps No. 261	25,000.	
262	A98	$2 **bright blue**, *Dec. 1894*	2,100.	650.00
		dark blue	2,200.	675.00
		On cover		3,500.
		Block of four	8,500.	2,750.
		Margin block of 4, arrow, R or L	9,000.	
		Margin strip of 3, Impt. & P#, T II	8,750.	
		Margin block of 6, Impt. & P#, T II	35,000.	
263	A99	$5 **dark green**, *Dec. 1894*	3,250.	1,150.
		On cover		6,000.
		Block of four	14,000.	5,500.
		Margin block of 4, arrow, R or L	15,000.	
		Margin strip of 3, Impt. & P#, T II	15,000.	

The Imperf. horizontally variety, No. 248a, and the imperforate varieties Nos. 253a, 254a, 255b and 258a were not regularly issued.

REGULAR ISSUE.

(Actual size of letter)

repeated in rows, thus

The letters stand for "U.S. Postage Stamp."

Plates for the 1895 issue were of two sizes:-
400 subjects for all 1c, 2c and 10c denominations; 200 subjects for all 4c, 5c, 6c, 8c, 15c, 50c, $1, $2 and $5; and both 400 and 200 subjects for the 3c denomination; all issued in panes of 100 each.

Printings from the 400 subject plates show the watermark reading horizontally, on the 200 subject printings the watermark reads vertically (with the tops and bottoms of the letters toward the vertical sides of the stamps.)

Wmk. 191 Horizontally or Vertically

1895			*Perf. 12*	
264	A87	1c **blue**, *Apr. 1895*	5.00	10
		dark blue	5.00	10
		pale blue	5.00	10
		On cover		1.00
		Block of four	20.00	2.00
		Margin strip of 3, Impt. & P#, T I, II, IV or V	20.00	
		Margin block of 6, Impt. & P#, T I, II, IV or V	185.00	
b.		Horiz. pair, imperf. vert.	—	
c.		Imperf., pair	325.00	
c.		Block of four, imperf.	700.00	
		Double transfer	—	1.00

CANCELLATIONS.

China	-	Philippines -
		Samoa -

265	A88	2c **carmine**, type I, *May 1895*	25.00	65
		deep carmine	25.00	65
		On cover		3.00
		Block of four	105.00	6.00
		Margin strip of 3, Impt. & P#, T II	105.00	
		Margin block of 6, Impt. & P#, T II	350.00	
		Double transfer	40.00	5.00
266	A88	2c **carmine**, type II	20.00	2.50
		On cover		6.50
		Block of four	82.50	18.50
		Horizontal pair, types II and III	55.00	10.00
		Margin strip of 3, Impt. & P#, T II or IV	82.50	
		Margin block of 6, Impt. & P#, T II or IV	325.00	
267	A88	2c **carmine**, type III	4.50	5
		deep carmine	4.50	5
		On cover		20
		Block of four	18.50	1.00
		Margin strip of 3, Impt. & P#, T II, IV or V	17.50	
		Margin block of 6, Impt. & P#, T II, IV or V	135.00	
a.		Imperf., pair	300.00	
a.		Block of four, imperf.	650.00	
		Double transfer	15.00	1.50
		Triple transfer	—	
		Triangle at upper right without shading	25.00	7.50

CANCELLATIONS.

China	-	Philippines -
Hawaii	-	Samoa -

The three left vertical rows of impressions from plate 170 are Type II, the balance being Type III.

268	A89	3c **purple**, *Oct. 1895*	35.00	1.00
		dark purple	35.00	1.00
		On cover		10.00
		Block of four	145.00	7.50
		Margin block of 4, arrow, R or L	150.00	
		Margin strip of 3, Impt. & P#, T II or V	145.00	

		Margin block of 6, Impt. & P#, T II or IV	575.00	
a.		Imperf., pair	350.00	
a.		Block of four, imperf.	800.00	
		Double transfer	50.00	3.50

CANCELLATIONS.

Guam	-	Philippines -
China	-	

269	A90	4c **dark brown**, *June 1895*	37.50	1.10
		dark yellow brown	37.50	1.10
		On cover		12.50
		Block of four	155.00	10.00
		Margin block of 4, arrow, R or L	160.00	
		Margin strip of 3, Impt. & P#, T I, II, IV or V	160.00	
		Margin block of 6, Impt. & P#, T I, II, IV or V	600.00	
a.		Imperf., pair	350.00	
a.		Block of four, imperf.	800.00	
		Double transfer	40.00	3.50

CANCELLATIONS.

Philippines	-	Samoa -
China	-	

270	A91	5c **chocolate**, *June 11, 1895*	35.00	1.75
		deep brown	35.00	1.75
		chestnut	35.00	1.75
		On cover		7.50
		Block of four	145.00	10.00
		Margin block of 4, arrow, R or L	155.00	
		Margin strip of 3, Impt. & P#, T I, II, IV or V	145.00	
		Margin block of 6, Impt. & P#, T I, II, IV or V	600.00	
b.		Imperf., pair	350.00	
b.		Block of four, imperf.	800.00	
		Double transfer	50.00	4.00
		Worn plate, diagonal lines missing in oval background	40.00	2.50

CANCELLATIONS.

China	-	Supp. Mail, G +2.50

271	A92	6c **dull brown**, *Aug. 1895*	65.00	3.50
		claret brown	65.00	3.50
		On cover		30.00
		Block of four	265.00	25.00
		Margin block of 4, arrow, R or L	275.00	
		Margin strip of 3, Impt. & P#, T I, IV or V	265.00	
		Margin block of 6, Impt. & P#, T I, IV or V	1,100.	
		Very thin paper	70.00	3.50
a.		Wmkd. USIR	1,850.	350.00
b.		Imperf., pair	400.00	
b.		Block of four, imperf.	850.00	

CANCELLATIONS.

		Philippines -

272	A93	8c **violet brown**, *July 1895*	45.00	1.00
		dark violet brown	45.00	1.00
		On cover		17.50
		Block of four	185.00	7.50
		Margin block of 4, arrow, R or L	190.00	
		Margin strip of 3, Impt. & P#, T I, IV or V	185.00	
		Margin block of 6, Impt. & P#, T I, IV or V	700.00	
a.		Wmkd. USIR	700.00	110.00
a.		Wmkd. USIR, P# strip of 3	3,000.	
b.		Imperf., pair	550.00	
b.		Block of four, imperf.	1,150.	
		Double transfer	65.00	3.00

CANCELLATIONS.

China	-	Puerto Rico, 1898 -
Guam	-	Samoa -
Philippines	-	Supplementary Mail Type G +2.50

273	A94	10c **dark green**, *June 1895*	60.00	1.20
		green	60.00	1.20
		On cover		20.00
		Block of four	245.00	10.00
		Margin strip of 3, Impt. & P#, T I or IV	245.00	
		Margin block of 6, Impt. & P#, T I or IV	1,150.	
a.		Imperf., pair	450.00	
a.		Block of four, imperf.	950.00	
		Double transfer	85.00	4.00

CANCELLATIONS.

China	-	Philippines -
Cuba	-	Supplementary Mail Types F or G +2.00

274	A95	15c **dark blue**, *Sept. 1895*	160.00	8.25
		indigo	160.00	8.25
		On cover		65.00
		Block of four	650.00	50.00
		Margin block of 4, arrow, R or L	700.00	
		Margin strip of 3, Impt. & P#, T I or IV	650.00	
		Margin block of 6, Impt. & P#, T I or IV	3,000.	
a.		Imperf., pair	1,450.	
a.		Block of four, imperf.	3,000.	

CANCELLATIONS.

China	-	Supplementary Mail Type G +3.00
Philippines	-	

275	A96 **50c orange**, *Nov. 1895*	235.00 20.00
a.	50c red orange	250.00 22.50
	On cover	400.00
	Block of four	950.00 100.00
a.	Block of four	1,050. 120.00
	Margin block of 4, arrow, R or L	1,050.
	Margin strip of 3, Impt. & P#, T I	950.00
	Margin block of 6, Impt. & P#, T I	6,000.
b.	Imperf., pair	1,600.
b.	Block of four, imperf.	3,350.

CANCELLATIONS.

China	-	Supplementary Mail Types F or G	+5.00

276	A97 **$1 black**, type I, *Aug. 1895*	550.00 70.00
	greenish black	550.00 70.00
	On cover	1,000.
	Block of four	2,300. 350.00
	Margin block of 4, arrow, L	2,500.
	Margin strip of 3, Impt. & P#, T II	2,400.
	Margin block of 6, Impt. & P#, T II	10,000.
b.	Imperf., pair	2,750.
b.	Block of four, imperf.	6,000.

CANCELLATIONS.

Philippines	-

276A	A97 **$1 black**, type II, *Aug. 1895*	1,200. 135.00
	greenish black	1,200. 135.00
	On cover	1,350.
	Block of four	5,000. 650.00
	Margin block of 4, arrow, R	5,250.
	Horizontal pair, types I and II	2,150. 325.00
	Block of four, two each of types I and II	4,500. 800.00
	Margin strip of 3, Impt. & P#, T II, one stamp No. 276	4,500.
	Margin block of 6, Impt. & P#, T II, two stamps No. 276	20,000.

CANCELLATIONS.

China	-

The fifteen left vertical rows of impressions from plate 76 are Type I, the balance being Type II.

277	A98 **$2 bright blue**, *Aug. 1895*	900.00 290.00
	On cover	2,750.
	Block of four	3,750. 1,400.
	Margin block of 4, arrow, R or L	4,000.
	Margin strip of 3, Impt. & P#, T II	4,000.
	Margin block of 6, Impt. & P#, T II	18,500.
a.	$2 dark blue	950.00 300.00
a.	Block of four	4,000. 1,500.
b.	Imperf., pair	3,500.
b.	Block of four, imperf.	7,500.

CANCELLATIONS.

	-	Supplementary Mail Type G	-

278	A99 **$5 dark green**, *Aug. 1895*	2,000. 425.00
	On cover	5,000.
	Block of four	8,250. 2,250.
	Margin block of 4, arrow, R or L	8,500.
	Margin strip of 3, Impt. & P#, T II	8,500.
	Margin block of 6, Impt. & P#, T II	60,000.
a.	Imperf., pair	6,000.
a.	Block of four, imperf.	13,000.

The Imperf. vertically variety, No. 264b and the imperforate varieties of all the denominations in the 1895 issue were not regularly issued.

REGULAR ISSUE.
Wmk. 191 Horizontally or Vertically
1898   **Perf. 12**

Plates for the 1898 issue were of two sizes:—
400 subjects for the 1c and 2c denominations; 200 subjects for all 5c, 6c and 15c denominations; and both 400 and 200 for the 4c and 0c denominations; all issued in panes of 100 each.
Printings from the 400 subject plates show the watermark reading horizontally, on the 200 subject plate printings the watermark reads vertically.
In January, 1898, the color of the 1-cent stamp was changed to green and in March, 1898, that of the 5-cents to dark blue in order to conform to the colors assigned these values by the Universal Postal Union. These changes necessitated changing the colors of the 10c and 15c denominations in order to avoid confusion.

279	A87 **1c deep green**, *Jan. 1898*	10.00 6
	green	10.00 6
	yellow green	10.00 6
	dark yellow green	10.00 6
	On cover	50
	Block of four	41.00 1.75
	Strip of 3, Impt. & P#, T V	42.50 —
	Block of 6, Impt. & P#, T V	175.00
	Double transfer	15.00 1.25

CANCELLATIONS.

China	-	Puerto Rico, 1898	-

Guam	-	Philippines	-

279B	A88 **2c red**, type III	9.00 5
	On cover	15
	Block of four	36.50 75
	Margin strip of 3, Impt. & P#, T V (red)	35.00
	Margin block of 6, Impt. & P#, T V (red)	160.00
c.	2c rose carmine, type III	150.00 30.00
c.	Block of four	625.00 —
c.	Margin strip of 3, Impt. & P#, T V	625.00
c.	Margin block of 6, Impt. & P#, T V	2,250.
d.	2c orange red, type III	9.50 12
d.	Block of four	38.50 1.25
d.	Margin strip of 3, Impt. & P#, T V	37.50
d.	Margin block of 6, Impt. & P#, T V	175.00
e.	Booklet pane of six	350.00 200.00
	Double transfer	20.00 1.25
f.	2c deep red, type III	20.00 75

CANCELLATIONS.

Puerto Rico, 1898	-	Supplementary Mail Type G	+4.00
Philippines, 1898	-	Cuba, 1898	-
Guam, 1899 or 1900	-	China	-
		Samoa	-

280	A90 **4c rose brown**, *Oct. 1898*	32.50 70
a.	4c lilac brown	32.50 70
	brownish claret	32.50 70
b.	4c orange brown	32.50 70
	On cover	12.50
	Block of four	135.00 7.50
	Margin block of 4, arrow, R or L	140.00
	Margin strip of 3, Impt. & P#, T V	140.00
	Margin block of 6, Impt. & P#, T V	650.00
	Double transfer	40.00 1.50
	Extra frame line at top (Plate 793 R 62)	50.00 5.00

CANCELLATIONS.

	-	Supplementary Mail Type G	+3.00
		China	-
		Philippines	-

281	A91 **5c dark blue**, *Mar. 1898*	35.00 65
	blue	35.00 65
	bright blue	35.00 65
	On cover	10.00
	Block of four	142.50 5.00
	Margin block of 4, arrow, R or L	150.00
	Margin strip of 3, Impt. & P#, T V	145.00
	Margin block of 6, Impt. & P#, T V	650.00
	Double transfer	50.00 2.50
	Worn plate diagonal lines missing in oval background	40.00 85

CANCELLATIONS.

Puerto Rico, 1898	-	Supplementary Mail Type G	+4.00
		China	-
		Cuba	-
		Guam	-
		Philippines	-

282	A92 **6c lake**, *Dec. 1898*	50.00 2.00
	claret	50.00 2.00
	On cover	20.00
	Block of four	205.00 20.00
	Margin block of 4, arrow, R or L	225.00
	Margin strip of 3, Impt. & P#, T V	210.00
	Margin block of 6, Impt. & P#, T V	900.00
a.	6c purplish lake	55.00 2.50
a.	Block of four	225.00 30.00
a.	Margin block of 4, arrow	240.00
a.	Margin strip of 3, Impt. & P#, T V	230.00
a.	Margin block of 6, Impt. & P#, T V	1,100.
	Double transfer	60.00 3.50

CANCELLATIONS.

	-	Supplementary Mail Type G	+4.00
		China	-
		Philippines	-

TEN CENTS.
Type I. The tips of the foliate ornaments do not impinge on the white curved line below "ten cents".

282C	A94 **10c brown**, type I, *Nov. 1898*	160.00 2.00
	dark brown	160.00 2.00
	On cover	17.50
	Block of four	650.00 20.00
	Margin strip of 3, Impt. & P#, T IV or V	650.00
	Margin block of 6, Impt. & P#, T IV or V	2,500.
	Double transfer	200.00 4.50

CANCELLATIONS.

	-	Supplementary Mail Type G	+2.50

Type II. The tips of the ornaments break the curved line below the "e" of "ten" and the "t" of "cents".

283	A94 **10c orange brown**, type II	95.00 1.75
	brown	95.00 1.75
	yellow brown	95.00 1.75
	On cover	20.00
	Block of four	385.00 15.00
	Margin block of 4, arrow, R or L	400.00
	Margin strip of 3, Impt. & P#, T V	385.00
	Margin block of 6, Impt. & P#, T V	1,500.
	Pair, type I and type II	15,000. 850.00

CANCELLATIONS.

Supplementary Mail Type G	+2.50	China	-
		Puerto Rico	-

On the 400 subject plate 932, all the subjects are Type I except the following: U. L. 20; U. R. 11, 12, 13; L. L. 61, 71, 86, these seven being Type II.

284	A95 **15c olive green**, *Nov. 1898*	125.00 7.50
	dark olive green	125.00 7.50
	On cover	35.00
	Block of four	510.00 35.00
	Margin block of 4, arrow, R or L	525.00
	Margin strip of 3, Impt. & P#, T IV	510.00
	Margin block of 6, Impt. & P#, T IV	2,250.

CANCELLATIONS.

Supplementary Mail Types F or G	+2.50	China	-
		Samoa	-

TRANS-MISSISSIPPI EXPOSITION ISSUE
Issued to commemorate the Trans-Mississippi Exposition held in Omaha, Nebraska, June 1 to November 1, 1898.

Jacques Marquette on the Mississippi — A100

Farming in the West — A101

Indian Hunting Buffalo — A102

John Charles Frémont on the Rocky Mountains — A103

Troops Guarding Wagon Train — A104

Hardships of Emigration — A105

Western Mining Prospector — A106

Western Cattle in Storm — A107

Mississippi River Bridge, St. Louis — A108

Exposition Station Cancellation

Condition is extremely important in evaluating Nos. 285-293. Prices are for stamps free from faults and with the design well clear of the perforations. Stamps of superior quality command substantial premiums.

Plates of 100 (10x10) subjects, divided vertically into 2 panes of 50.

1898, June 17   **Wmk. 191**   *Perf. 12*

285	A100	1c	**dark yellow green**	27.50	5.50
			yellow green	27.50	5.50
			green	27.50	5.50
			On cover		10.00
			On card, Expo. station canc.		225.00
			Block of four	112.50	25.00
			Margin block of 4, arrow, R or L	115.00	—
			Margin pair, Impt. & P#, T VIII	70.00	
			Margin strip of 3, Impt. & P#, T VIII	110.00	
			Margin block of 4, Impt. & P#, T VIII	225.00	
			Margin block of 6, Impt. & P#, T VIII	325.00	
			Double transfer	40.00	7.00

CANCELLATIONS.

Supplementary Mail, Types F or G	+1.50	China -
		Philippines -
		Puerto Rico, 1898 -

286	A101	2c	**copper red**	25.00	1.50
			brown red	25.00	1.50
			light brown red	25.00	1.50
			On cover		2.00
			On cover, Expo. station canc.		200.00
			Block of four	102.50	9.00
			Margin block of 4, arrow, R or L	105.00	—
			Margin pair, Impt. & P#, T VIII	65.00	
			Margin strip of 3, Impt. & P#, T VIII	105.00	
			Margin block of 4, Impt. & P#, T VIII	210.00	
			Margin block of 6, Impt. & P#, T VIII	300.00	
			Double transfer	40.00	2.50
			Worn plate	30.00	1.75

CANCELLATIONS.

China	-	Puerto Rico, 1898 -
Hawaii	-	Philippines -

287	A102	4c	**orange**	150.00	22.50
			deep orange	150.00	22.50
			On cover		75.00
			On cover, Expo. station canc.		400.00
			Block of four	625.00	100.00
			Margin block of 4, arrow, R or L	650.00	—
			Margin pair, Impt. & P#, T VIII	350.00	
			Margin strip of 3, Impt. & P#, T VIII	550.00	
			Margin block of four, Impt. & P#, T VIII	1,100.	
			Margin block of 6, Impt. & P#, T VIII	1,700.	

CANCELLATIONS.

Supplementary Mail Types F or G	+5.00	China -
		Philippines -

288	A103	5c	**dull blue**	135.00	20.00
			bright blue	135.00	20.00
			On cover		60.00
			On cover, Expo. station canc.		400.00
			Block of four	575.00	90.00
			Margin block of 4, arrow, R or L	600.00	

		Margin pair, Impt. & P#, T VIII		325.00	—
		Margin strip of 3, Impt. & P#, T VIII		475.00	
		Margin block of four, Impt. & P#, T VIII		1,000.	
		Margin block of 6, Impt. & P#, T VIII		1,500.	

CANCELLATIONS.

Supplementary Mail Types F or G	+5.00	China -
		Philippines -
		Puerto Rico, 1898 -

289	A104	8c	**violet brown**	175.00	40.00
			dark violet brown	175.00	40.00
			On cover		125.00
			On cover, Expo. station canc.		750.00
			Block of four	700.00	185.00
			Margin block of 4, arrow, R or L	725.00	—
			Margin pair, Impt. & P#, T VIII	400.00	
			Margin strip of 3, Impt. & P#, T VIII	650.00	
			Margin block of 4, Impt. & P#, T VIII	1,750.	
			Margin block of 6, Impt. & P#, T VIII	2,650.	
	a.		Vert. pair, imperf. horiz.	12,000.	

CANCELLATIONS.

Philippines	-	Samoa -

290	A105	10c	**gray violet**	200.00	22.50
			blackish violet	200.00	22.50
			On cover		90.00
			On cover, Expo. station canc.		750.00
			Block of four	825.00	100.00
			Margin block of 4, arrow, R or L	850.00	—
			Margin pair, Impt. & P#, T VIII	450.00	
			Margin strip of 3, Impt. & P#, T VIII	700.00	
			Margin block of 4, Impt. & P#, T VIII	2,250.	
			Margin block of 6, Impt. & P#, T VIII	3,500.	

CANCELLATIONS.

China	-	Supplementary Mail Type G +5.00
Philippines	-	

291	A106	50c	**sage green**	725.00	165.00
			dark sage green	725.00	165.00
			On cover		1,200.
			Block of four	3,000.	950.00
			Margin block of 4, arrow, R or L	3,250.	—
			Margin pair, Impt. & P#, T VIII	1,750.	
			Margin strip of 3, Impt. & P#, T VIII	2,850.	
			Margin block of 4, Impt. & P#, T VIII	13,500.	
			Margin block of 6, Impt. & P#, T VIII	20,000.	

CANCELLATIONS.

Cuba	-	Supplementary Mail Types F or G +25.00
Philippines	-	

292	A107	$1	**black**	1,850.	625.00
			On cover		4,000.
			Block of four	8,000.	3,500.
			Margin block of 4, arrow, R or L	8,500.	
			Margin pair, Impt. & P#, T VIII	4,500.	
			Margin strip of 3, Impt. & P#, T VIII	7,500.	
			Margin block of 4, Impt. & P#, T VIII	40,000.	
			Margin block of 6, Impt. & P#, T VIII	52,500.	

CANCELLATIONS.

Philippines	-	

293	A108	$2	**orange brown**	2,850.	875.00
			dark orange brown	2,850.	875.00
			On cover		9,500.
			Block of four	13,000.	4,250.
			Margin block of 4, arrow, R or L	14,000.	
			Margin pair, Impt. & P#, T VII	7,000.	
			Margin strip of 3, Impt. & P#, T VIII	10,500.	
			Margin block of 4, Impt. & P#, T VII	80,000.	
			Margin block of 6, Impt. & P#, T VIII	115,000.	

PAN-AMERICAN EXPOSITION ISSUE

Issued to commemorate the Pan-American Exposition held at Buffalo, N. Y., May 1 to Nov. 1, 1901. On sale May 1-Oct. 31, 1901.

Fast Lake Navigation (Steamship "City of Alpena") A109

Empire State Express A110

Electric Automobile in Washington A111

Bridge at Niagara Falls A112

Canal Locks at Sault Ste. Marie A113

Fast Ocean Navigation (Steamship "St. Paul") A114

Exposition Station Cancellation.

Note on condition and pricing above No. 285 also applies to Nos. 294-299.

Plates of 200 subjects in two panes of 100 each.

1901, May 1		**Wmk. 191**			***Perf. 12***
294	A109	1c	**green & black**	17.50	4.00
			dark blue green & black	17.50	4.00
			On cover		5.50
			On cover or card, Expo. sta. canc.		110.00
			Block of four	70.00	20.00
			Margin block of 4, top arrow & markers	72.50	
			Margin block of 4, bottom arrow & markers & black P#	75.00	
			Margin strip of 3, Impt. & P#, T V	75.00	
			Margin block of 6, Impt. & P#, T V	275.00	
			Margin strip of 5, bottom two P#, T V Impt., arrow & markers	140.00	
			Margin block of 10, bottom, Impt., T V, two P#, arrow & markers	550.00	
a.			Center inverted	*10,000.*	*4,500.*
a.			Center inverted, on cover		*16,500.*
a.			Center inverted, block of 4	*42,500.*	
a.			Same, Margin strip of 3, Impt. & P#	*44,000.*	
			Double transfer	27.50	6.00
295	A110	2c	**carmine & black**	17.50	1.10
			carmine & gray black	17.50	1.10
			rose carmine & black	17.50	1.10
			scarlet & black	17.50	1.10
			On cover		1.75
			On cover or card, Expo. sta. canc.		95.00
			Block of four	70.00	6.00
			Margin block of 4, top arrow & markers	72.50	
			Margin block of 4, bottom arrow & markers and black P#	75.00	
			Margin strip of 3, Impt. & P#, T V	75.00	
			Margin block of 6, Impt. & P#, T V	275.00	
			Margin strip of 5, bottom, Impt., T V, two P#, arrow & markers	140.00	
			Margin block of 10, bottom, Impt., T V, two P#, arrow & markers	525.00	
a.			Center inverted	*45,000.*	*13,500.*
a.			Center inverted, block of 4	*200,000.*	
			Double transfer	27.50	2.50
296	A111	4c	**deep red brown & black**	85.00	20.00
			chocolate & black	85.00	20.00
			On cover		45.00
			On cover, Expo. station canc.		325.00
			Block of four	350.00	85.00
			Margin block of 4, top arrow & markers	360.00	
			Margin block of 4, bottom arrow & markers & black P#	375.00	
			Margin strip of 3, Impt. & P#, T V	350.00	
			Margin block of 6, Impt. & P#, T V	2,500.	
			Margin strip of 5, bottom Impt., T V two P#, arrow & markers	725.00	
			Margin block of 10, bottom, Impt., TV, two P#, arrow & markers	4,750.	
a.			Center inverted	*13,000.*	
a.			Center inverted, block of 4	*57,500.*	
a.			Same, Margin strip of 4, Impt. & P#	*67,500.*	

No. 296a was not regularly issued.
See No. 296a-S, "Specimen" Stamps.

297	A112	5c	**ultramarine & black**	100.00	20.00
			dark ultramarine & black	100.00	20.00
			On cover		45.00
			On cover, Expo. station canc.		325.00
			Block of four	400.00	85.00
			Margin block of 4, top arrow & markers	410.00	
			Margin block of 4, bottom arrow & markers & black P#	425.00	
			Margin strip of 3, Impt. & P#, T V	400.00	
			Margin block of 6, Impt. & P#, T V	2,750.	
			Margin strip of 5, bottom Impt., T V two P#, arrow & markers	800.00	
			Margin block of 10, bottom Impt., T V, two P#, arrow & markers	5,000.	
298	A113	8c	**brown violet & black**	130.00	75.00
			purplish brown & black	130.00	75.00
			On cover		120.00
			On cover, Expo. station canc.		625.00
			Block of four	550.00	375.00
			Margin block of 4, top arrow & markers	560.00	
			Margin block of 4, bottom arrow & markers & black P#	575.00	
			Margin strip of 3, Impt. & P#, T V	550.00	
			Margin block of 6, Impt. & P#, T V	4,750.	
			Margin strip of 5, bottom Impt., T V, two P#, arrow & markers	1,000.	

			Margin block of 10, bottom, Impt., T V, two P#, arrow & markers	8,000.	
299	A114	10c	**yellow brown & black**	200.00	35.00
			dark yellow brown & black	200.00	35.00
			On cover		135.00
			On cover, Expo. station canc.		850.00
			Block of four	825.00	175.00
			Margin block of 4, top arrow & markers	850.00	
			Margin block of 4, bottom arrow & markers & black P#	875.00	
			Margin strip of 3, Impt. & P#, T V	850.00	
			Margin block of 6, Impt. & P#, T V	7,500.	
			Margin strip of 5, bottom Impt., T V, two P#, arrow & markers	1,500.	
			Margin block of 10, bottom Impt., T V, two P#, arrow & markers	11,500.	

Franklin — A115

Washington — A116

Jackson — A117

Grant — A118

Lincoln — A119

Garfield — A120

Martha
Washington — A121

Daniel
Webster — A122

Benjamin
Harrison — A123

Henry Clay — A124

Jefferson — A125

David G.
Farragut — A126

Madison — A127

Marshall — A128

REGULAR ISSUE

Plates of 400 subjects in four
panes of 100 each for all values from 1c to 15c
inclusive. Certain plates of 1c, 2c type A129, 3c and
5c show a round marker in margin opposite the
horizontal guide line at right or left.
Plates of 200 subjects in two panes
of 100 each for 15c, 50c, $1, $2 and $5.

1902-03 **Wmk. 191** *Perf. 12*

Many stamps of this issue are known with blurred printing
due to having been printed on dry paper.

300	A115	1c	**blue green,** *Feb. 1903*	10.00	5
			green	10.00	5
			deep green	10.00	5
			gray green	10.00	5
			yellow green	10.00	6
			On cover		15
			Block of four	40.00	2.00
			Margin strip of 3, Impt. & P#, T V	40.00	
			Margin block of 6, Impt. & P#, T V	185.00	
b.			Booklet pane of six, *Mar. 6, 1907*	*500.00*	*250.00*
			Double transfer	15.00	1.75
			Worn plate	10.50	25
			Cracked plate	—	—
301	A116	2c	**carmine,** *Jan. 17, 1903*	12.50	5
			bright carmine	12.50	5
			deep carmine	12.50	5
			carmine rose	12.50	8
			On cover		15
			Block of four	50.00	2.00
			Margin strip of 3, Impt. & P#, T V	50.00	
			Margin block of 6, Impt. & P#, T V	200.00	
c.			Booklet pane of six, *Jan. 24, 1903*	*425.00*	*250.00*
			Double transfer	20.00	1.50
			Cracked plate	—	
302	A117	3c	**bright violet,** *Feb. 1903*	45.00	3.00
			violet	45.00	3.00
			deep violet	45.00	3.00
			On cover		12.50
			Block of four	185.00	17.50
			Margin strip of 3, Impt. & P#, T V	185.00	
			Margin block of 6, Impt. & P#, T V	850.00	
			Double transfer	85.00	5.00
			Cracked plate	—	
303	A118	4c	**brown,** *Feb. 1903*	45.00	1.00
			dark brown	45.00	1.00
			yellow brown	45.00	1.00
			orange brown	45.00	1.00
			red brown	45.00	1.00
			On cover		12.50
			Block of four	185.00	8.50
			Margin strip of 3, Impt. & P#, T V	185.00	
			Margin block of 6, Impt. & P#, T V	850.00	
			Double transfer	80.00	3.50

304	A119	5c	**blue,** *Jan. 1903*	55.00	1.00
			pale blue	55.00	1.00
			bright blue	55.00	1.00
			dark blue	55.00	1.00
			On cover		8.50
			Block of four	225.00	6.00
			Margin strip of 3, Impt. & P#, T V	225.00	
			Margin block of 6, Impt. & P#, T V	950.00	—
			Double transfer	90.00	4.00
			Cracked plate	—	—
305	A120	6c	**claret,** *Feb. 1903*	60.00	2.25
			deep claret	60.00	2.25
			brownish lake	75.00	2.25
			dull brownish lake	60.00	2.25
			On cover		17.50
			Block of four	245.00	20.00
			Margin strip of 3, Impt. & P#, T V	245.00	
			Margin block of 6, Impt. & P#, T V	1,000.	
			Double transfer	90.00	3.50
306	A121	8c	**violet black,** *Dec. 1902*	35.00	2.00
			black	35.00	2.00
			slate black	35.00	2.00
			gray lilac	35.00	2.00
			lavender	45.00	2.50
			On cover		10.00
			Block of four	145.00	15.00
			Margin strip of 3, Impt. & P#, T V	145.00	
			Margin block of 6, Impt. & P#, T V	700.00	
			Double transfer	47.50	3.00
307	A122	10c	**pale red brown,** *Feb. 1903*	60.00	1.50
			red brown	60.00	1.50
			dark red brown	60.00	1.50
			On cover		10.00
			Block of four	245.00	8.00
			Margin strip of 3, Impt. & P#, T V	245.00	
			Margin block of 6, Impt. & P#, T V	1,150.	
			Double transfer	110.00	15.00
308	A123	13c	**purple black,** *Nov. 18, 1902*	35.00	8.50
			brown violet	35.00	8.50
			On cover		40.00
			Block of four	145.00	40.00
			Margin strip of 3, Impt. & P#, T V	145.00	
			Margin block of 6, Impt. & P#, T V	650.00	
309	A124	15c	**olive green,** *May 27, 1903*	135.00	6.00
			dark olive green	135.00	6.00
			On cover		75.00
			Block of four	550.00	60.00
			Margin block of 4, arrow	575.00	
			Margin strip of 3, Impt. & P#, T V	550.00	
			Margin block of 6, Impt. & P#, T V	3,000.	
			Double transfer	210.00	12.00
310	A125	50c	**orange,** *Mar. 23, 1903*	400.00	27.50
			deep orange	400.00	27.50
			On cover		500.00
			Block of four	1,700.	135.00
			Margin block of 4, arrow	1,800.	
			Margin strip of 3, Impt. & P#, T V	1,700.	
			Margin block of 6, Impt. & P#, T V	6,750.	
311	A126	$1	**black,** *June 5, 1903*	700.00	60.00
			grayish black	700.00	60.00
			On cover		1,350.
			Block of four	2,900.	275.00
			Margin block of 4, arrow	3,000.	
			Margin strip of 3, Impt. & P#, T V	2,900.	
			Margin block of 6, Impt. & P#, T V	*14,500.*	
312	A127	$2	**dark blue,** *June 5, 1903*	950.00	200.00
			blue	950.00	200.00
			On cover		2,500.
			Block of four	4,000.	850.00
			Margin block of 4, arrow	4,200.	
			Margin strip of 3, Impt. & P#, T V	4,100.	
			Margin block of 6, Impt. & P#, T V	*25,000.*	
313	A128	$5	**dark green,** *June 5, 1903*	2,500.	650.00
			On cover		5,000.
			Block of four	10,500.	3,000.
			Margin block of 4, arrow	11,000.	
			Margin strip of 3, Impt. & P#, T V	11,000.	
			Margin block of 6, Impt. & P#, T V	*62,500.*	

*For listings of designs A127 and A128 with Perf. 10 see Nos.
479 and 480.*

1906-08					**Imperf.**
314	A115	1c	**blue green,** *Oct. 2, 1906*	30.00	21.00
			green	30.00	21.00
			deep green	30.00	21.00
			On cover		30.00
			Block of four	120.00	90.00
			Corner margin block of four	125.00	92.50
			Margin block of 4, arrow	130.00	95.00
			Margin block of 4, arrow & round marker	175.00	
			Center line block	250.00	125.00
			Margin block of 6, Impt. & P#	275.00	
			Double transfer	55.00	30.00
314A	A118	4c	**brown,** *April 1908*	*17,500.*	*9,000.*
			On cover		*22,500.*

Pair	45,000.	
Guide line pair	—	

This stamp was issued imperforate but all copies were privately perforated with large oblong perforations at the sides. (Schermack type III).

315	A119	5c **blue**, *May 12, 1908*	500.00	250.00
		On cover	—	
		Block of four	2,100.	1,200.
		Corner margin block of 4	2,200.	
		Margin block of 4, arrow	2,250.	
		Margin block of 4, arrow & round marker	2,650.	
		Center line block	3,000.	
		Margin block of 6, Impt. & P#	4,750.	

COIL STAMPS

Warning! Imperforate stamps have been fraudulently perforated to resemble coil stamps and part-perforate varieties.

1908   *Perf. 12 Horizontally*

316	A115	1c **blue green**, pair, *Feb. 18, 1908*	25,000.	—
		Guide line pair	60,000.	—
317	A119	5c **blue**, pair, *Feb. 24, 1908*	6,000.	—
		Guide line pair	8,000.	

Perf. 12 Vertically

318	A115	1c **blue green**, pair, *July 31, 1908*	4,250.	—
		Guide line pair	6,250.	—
		Double transfer	—	

Coil stamps for use in vending and affixing machines are perforated on two sides only, either horizontally or vertically. They were first issued in 1908, using perf. 12. This was changed to 8½ in 1910, and to 10 in 1914.

Imperforate sheets of certain denominations were sold to the vending machine companies which applied a variety of private perforations and separations. (See Vending and Affixing Machine Perforations section of this catalogue.)

Several values of the 1902 and later issues are found on an apparently coarse-ribbed paper. This is caused by worn blankets on the printing presses and is not a true paper variety.

Washington — A129

Plate of 400 subjects in four panes of 100 each.

Die I   Die II

1903   Wmk. 191   *Perf. 12*

319	A129	2c **carmine**, Die I, *Nov. 12, 1903*	6.00	5
		bright carmine	6.00	5
		carmine lake	6.00	5
		On cover		10
		Block of four	24.50	2.00
		Margin strip of 3, Impt. & P#, T V (carmine)	23.00	
		Margin block of 6, Impt. & P#, T V (carmine)	100.00	
a.		2c lake, Die I	—	—
		On cover		—
		Block of four (lake)	—	
		Margin strip of 3, Impt. & P#, T V (lake)	—	
		Margin block of 6, Impt. & P#, T V (lake)	—	
b.		2c carmine rose, Die I	10.00	20
		On cover		50
		Block of four (carmine rose)	41.00	4.00
		Margin strip of 3, Impt. & P#, T V (carmine rose)	42.50	
		Margin block of 6, Impt. & P#, T V (carmine rose)	200.00	
c.		2c scarlet, Die I	7.00	6
		On cover		10
		Block of four (scarlet)	29.00	4.00
		Margin strip of 3, Impt. & P#, T V (scarlet)	27.50	

		Margin block of 6, Impt. & P#, T V (scarlet)	100.00	
d.		Vert. pair, imperf. horiz.	1,750.	
e.		Vertical pair, imperf. between	950.00	
		Vertical pair, rouletted between	1,000.	
f.		2c lake, Die II	6.50	10
		On cover		20
		Block of four	26.50	3.50
		Double transfer	15.00	2.00
g.		Booklet pane of six, car., Die I	110.00	*20.00*
h.		Booklet pane of six, car., Die II	200.00	
i.		2c carmine, Die II	35.00	—
j.		2c carmine rose, Die II	—	
k.		2c scarlet, Die II	—	
m.		Booklet pane of six, lake (I)	—	
n.		Booklet pane of six, car. rose (I)	—	
p.		Booklet pane of six, scarlet (I)	110.00	
q.		Booklet pane of six, lake, (II)	140.00	

During the use of this stamp, the Postmaster at San Francisco discovered in his stock sheets of No. 319, each of which had the horizontal perforations missing between the two top rows of stamps. To facilitate their separation, the imperf. rows were rouletted, and the stamps sold over the counter. So vertical pairs are found with regular perforations all around and rouletted between.

1906   *Imperf.*

320	A129	2c **carmine**, *Oct. 2, 1906*	27.50	21.00
		On cover		30.00
		Block of four, carmine	110.00	85.00
		Corner margin block of four, carmine	112.50	
		Margin block of 4, arrow, carmine	115.00	—
		Center line block, carmine	225.00	—
		Margin block of 6, Impt. & P#, T V, carmine	300.00	—
a.		2c lake, Die II	90.00	35.00
		On cover		75.00
		Block of four, lake	360.00	160.00
		Corner margin block of four, lake	365.00	
		Margin block of 4, arrow, lake	375.00	—
		Center line block, lake	750.00	—
		Margin block of 6, Impt. & P#, T V, lake	1,100.	
b.		2c scarlet	27.50	21.00
		On cover		30.00
		Block of four, scarlet	110.00	
		Corner margin block of four, scarlet	112.50	
		Margin block of 4, arrow, scarlet	115.00	—
		Center line block, scarlet	225.00	—
		Margin block of 6, Impt. & P#, T V, scarlet	300.00	—
		Die II, scarlet	—	
		Double transfer	40.00	25.00

COIL STAMPS

1908   *Perf. 12 Horizontally*

321	A129	2c **carmine**, pair, *Feb. 18, 1908*	35,000.	—
		Guide line pair	—	

Perf. 12 Vertically

322	A129	2c **carmine**, pair, *July 31, 1908*	6,000.	—
		Guide line pair	8,000.	
		Double transfer	—	

This Government Coil Stamp should not be confused with those of the International Vending Machine Co., which are perforated 12½ to 13.

LOUISIANA PURCHASE EXPOSITION ISSUE

Issued to commemorate the Louisiana Purchase Exposition held at St. Louis, Mo., Apr. 30-Dec. 1, 1904.

Robert R. Livingston — A130

Thomas Jefferson — A131

James Monroe — A132

William McKinley — A133

Map of Louisiana Purchase — A134

Plates of 100 (10x10) subjects, divided vertically into 2 panes of 50.

Exposition Station Cancellation

Note on condition and pricing preceding No. 285 also applies to Nos. 323-327.

1904, Apr. 30   Wmk. 191   *Perf. 12*

323	A130	1c **green**	25.00	5.00
		dark green	25.00	5.00
		On cover		8.50
		On card, Expo. station canc.		55.00
		Block of four	100.00	25.00
		Margin block of 4, arrow, R or L	105.00	—
		Margin pair, Impt. & P#, T V	70.00	
		Margin strip of 3, Impt. & P#, T V	110.00	
		Margin block of 4, Impt. & P#, T V	180.00	
		Margin block of 6, Impt. & P#, T V	275.00	
		Diagonal line through left "1" (2138 L 2)	50.00	15.00
		Double transfer	—	
324	A131	2c **carmine**	22.50	1.50
		bright carmine	22.50	1.50
		On cover		3.00
		On cover, Expo. station canc.		85.00
		Block of four	90.00	12.50
		Margin block of 4, arrow, R or L	95.00	—
		Margin pair, Impt. & P#, T V	65.00	
		Margin strip of 3, Impt. & P#, T V	105.00	
		Margin block of 4, Impt. & P#, T V	180.00	
		Margin block of 6, Impt. & P#, T V	275.00	
a.		Vertical pair, imperf. horiz.	6,000.	
325	A132	3c **violet**	75.00	35.00
		On cover		45.00
		On cover, Expo. station canc.		300.00
		Block of four	300.00	165.00
		Margin block of 4, arrow, R or L	325.00	—
		Margin pair, Impt. & P#, T V	200.00	
		Margin strip of 3, Impt. & P#, T V	300.00	

	Margin block of 4, Impt. & P#, T V	625.00	
	Margin block of 6, Impt. & P#, T V	950.00	
	Double transfer		—
326 A133	5c **dark blue**	110.00	25.00
	On cover		50.00
	On cover, Expo. station canc.		350.00
	Block of four	440.00	120.00
	Margin block of 4, arrow, R or L	450.00	—
	Margin pair, Impt. & P#, T V	275.00	
	Margin strip of 3, Impt. & P#, T V	425.00	
	Margin block of 4, Impt. & P#, T V	750.00	
	Margin block of 6, Impt. & P#, T V	1,100.	
327 A134	10c **red brown**	185.00	35.00
	dark red brown	185.00	35.00
	On cover		100.00
	On cover, Expo. station canc.		525.00
	Block of four	750.00	165.00
	Margin block of 4, arrow, R or L	775.00	—
	Margin pair, Impt. & P#, T V	475.00	
	Margin strip of 3, Impt. & P#, T V	700.00	
	Margin block of 4, Impt. & P#, T V	1,600.	
	Margin block of 6, Impt. & P#, T V	2,500.	

JAMESTOWN EXPOSITION ISSUE

Issued to commemorate the Jamestown Exposition held at Hampton Roads, Va., April 26 to December 1, 1907.

Captain John Smith
A135

Founding of Jamestown
A136

Pocahontas
A137

Plates of 200 subjects in two panes of 100 each.

EXPOSITION STATION

Exposition Station Cancellation

1907		**Wmk. 191**	**Perf. 12**
328 A135	1c **green,** *Apr. 26, 1907*	20.00	4.00
	dark green	20.00	4.00
	On cover		7.50
	On card, Expo. station canc.		75.00
	Block of four	80.00	35.00
	Margin block of 4, arrow	82.50	—
	Margin strip of 3, Impt. & P#, T V	75.00	
	Margin block of 6, Impt. & P#, T V	300.00	
	Double transfer	27.50	6.50
329 A136	2c **carmine,** *Apr. 26, 1907*	27.50	3.00
	bright carmine	27.50	3.00
	On cover		6.00
	On cover, Expo. station canc.		100.00

	Block of four	110.00	17.50
	Margin block of 4, arrow	112.50	—
	Margin strip of 3, Impt. & P#, T V	100.00	
	Margin block of 6, Impt. & P#, T V	425.00	
	Double transfer	40.00	5.00
330 A137	5c **blue**	110.00	30.00
	deep blue	110.00	30.00
	On cover		110.00
	On cover, Expo. station canc.		500.00
	Block of four	450.00	130.00
	Margin block of 4, arrow	460.00	—
	Margin strip of 3, Impt. & P#, T V	400.00	
	Margin block of 6, Impt. & P#, T V	2,750.	
	Double transfer	130.00	45.00

Earliest known use: May 10, 1907.

REGULAR ISSUE

Plates of 400 subjects in four panes of 100 each for all values 1c to 15c inclusive.

Plates of 200 subjects in two panes of 100 each for 50c and $1 denominations.

In 1909 the Bureau prepared certain plates with horizontal spacings of 3mm. between the outer six vertical rows and 2mm. between the others. This was done to try to counteract the effect of unequal shrinkage of the paper. *However, shrinkage did occur and intermediate spacings are frequently found.* The listings of 2mm. and 3mm. spacings are for exact measurements. Intermediate spacings sell for approximately the same as the cheaper of the two listed spacings. All such plates were marked with an open star added to the imprint and exist on the 1c, 2c, 3c, 4c, and 5c denominations only. A small solid star was added to the imprint and plate number for 1c plate No. 4980, 2c plate No. 4988 and for the 2c Lincoln. All other plates for this issue are spaced 2mm. throughout.

There are several types of some of the 2c and 3c stamps of this and succeeding issues. These types are described under the dates at which they first appeared. The differences between the types are usually minute and difficult to distinguish. Illustrations of Types I-VII of the 2c (A140) and Types I-IV of the 3c (A140) are reproduced by permission of H. L. Lindquist.

China Clay Paper. A small quantity of Nos. 331-340 was printed on paper containing a high mineral content (5-20%), instead of the specified 2%. The minerals, principally aluminum silicate, produced China clay paper. It is thick, hard and grayish, often darker than "bluish" paper.

✿ 4968

Imprint, plate number and open star.

★ 4976

Imprint, plate number and small solid star.

A 5557

Imprint, plate number and "A". (Above illustrations reduced in size.)

A 5805
"A" and number only.

988
Number only.

The above illustrations are the several styles used on plates of issues from 1908 to date.

Franklin — A138

Washington — A139

1908-09		**Wmk. 191**	**Perf. 12**
331 A138	1c **green,** *Dec. 1908*	8.00	5
	bright green	8.00	5
	dark green	8.00	5
	yellow green	8.00	5
	On cover		40
	Block of four (2mm. spacing)	32.50	1.50
	Block of four (3mm. spacing)	33.50	1.75
	Margin block of 6, Impt. & P#, T V	90.00	
	Margin block of 6, Impt. & P# & star	80.00	
	Margin block of 6, Impt. & P# & small solid star (plate 4980)	1,000.	
a.	Booklet pane of six, *Dec. 2, 1908*	165.00	35.00
	Double transfer	12.00	1.00
	Cracked plate	—	

No. 331 exists in horizontal pair, imperforate between, a variety resulting from booklet experiments. Not regularly issued.

332 A139	2c **carmine,** *Nov. 1908*	7.50	5
	light carmine	7.50	5
	dark carmine	7.50	5
	On cover		10
	Block of four (2mm. spacing)	31.00	75
	Block of four (3mm. spacing)	32.50	85
	Margin block of 6, Impt. & P#, T V	80.00	
	Margin block of 6, Impt. & P# & star	75.00	
	Margin block of 6, Impt. & P# & small solid star (plate 4988)	950.00	
a.	Booklet pane of six	125.00	35.00
	Double transfer	15.00	1.50
	Double transfer, design of 1c (plate 5299)	1,500.	1,250.
	Rosette crack	—	
	Cracked plate	—	

Washington — A140

TYPE I

TYPE I

THREE CENTS.
Type I. The top line of the toga rope is weak and the rope shading lines are thin. The 5th line from the left is missing. The line between the lips is thin. (For descriptions of 3c types II, III and IV, see notes and illustrations preceding Nos. 484, 529-530.)
Used on both flat plate and rotary press printings.

333 A140	3c **deep violet,** type I, *Dec. 1908*	35.00	3.00
	violet	35.00	3.00
	light violet	35.00	3.00
	On cover		7.50
	Block of four (2mm. spacing)	142.50	16.00
	Block of four (3mm. spacing)	145.00	17.50

	Margin block of 6, Impt. & P#, T V	350.00		
	Margin block of 6, Impt. & P# & star	375.00		
	Double transfer	45.00	7.50	
334 A140	**4c orange brown**, *Dec. 1908*	37.50	1.00	
	brown	37.50	1.00	
	light brown	37.50	1.00	
	dark brown	37.50	1.00	
	On cover		6.00	
	Block of four (2mm. spacing)	155.00	7.50	
	Block of four (3mm. spacing)	160.00	8.50	
	Margin block of 6, Impt. & P#, T V	390.00		
	Margin block of 6, Impt. & P# & star	390.00		
	Double transfer	65.00	4.00	
335 A140	**5c blue**, *Dec. 1908*	50.00	2.00	
	bright blue	50.00	2.00	
	dark blue	50.00	2.00	
	On cover		7.50	
	Block of four (2mm. spacing)	205.00	12.00	
	Block of four (3mm. spacing)	210.00	10.00	
	Margin block of 6, Impt. & P#, T V	600.00		
	Margin block of 6, Impt. & P# & star	625.00		
	Double transfer	55.00	4.50	
336 A140	**6c red orange**, *Jan. 1909*	60.00	4.50	
	pale red orange	60.00	4.50	
	orange	60.00	4.50	
	On cover		20.00	
	Block of four	250.00	30.00	
	Margin block of 6, Impt. & P#, T V	900.00		
337 A140	**8c olive green**, *Dec. 1908*	42.50	2.50	
	deep olive green	42.50	2.50	
	On cover		17.50	
	Block of four	175.00	15.00	
	Margin block of 6, Impt. & P#, T V	475.00		
	Double transfer	65.00	6.00	
338 A140	**10c yellow**, *Jan. 1909*	70.00	1.50	
	On cover		10.00	
	Block of four	285.00	7.50	
	Margin block of 6, Impt. & P#, T V	1,000.	—	
	Double transfer	—	—	
	Very thin paper	—	—	
339 A140	**13c blue green**, *Jan. 1909*	40.00	25.00	
	deep blue green	40.00	25.00	
	On cover		110.00	
	Block of four	165.00	120.00	
	Margin block of 6, Impt. & P#, T V	475.00		
	Line through "TAG" of "POSTAGE" (4948 L. R. 96)	75.00	*40.00*	
340 A140	**15c pale ultramarine**, *Jan. 1909*	65.00	5.75	
	ultramarine	65.00	5.75	
	On cover		125.00	
	Block of four	270.00	40.00	
	Margin block of 6, Impt. & P#, T V	650.00		
341 A140	**50c violet**, *Jan. 13, 1909*	300.00	17.50	
	dull violet	300.00	17.50	
	On cover		*1,750.*	
	Block of four	1,250.	85.00	
	Margin block of 4, arrow, right or left	1,350.		
	Margin block of 6, Impt. & P#, T V	7,500.		
342 A140	**$1 violet brown**, *Jan. 29, 1909*	450.00	90.00	
	light violet brown	450.00	90.00	
	On cover		*2,000.*	
	Block of four	1,900.	425.00	
	Margin block of 4, arrow, right or left	2,000.	450.00	
	Margin block of 6, Impt. & P#, T V	12,500.	—	
	Double transfer	—	—	

For listings of other perforated stamps of A138 A139 and A140 see
Nos. 357 to 366 Bluish paper.
Nos. 374 to 382, 405 to 407 Single line wmk. Perf. 12
Nos. 424 to 430 Single line wmk. Perf. 10
Nos. 461 Single line wmk. Perf. 11
Nos. 462 to 469 unwmk. Perf. 10
Nos. 498 to 507 unwmk. Perf. 11
Nos. 519 Double line wmk. Perf. 11
Nos. 525 to 530 and 536 Offset printing
Nos. 538 to 546 Rotary press printing

Imperf

343 A138	**1c green**, *Dec. 1908*	8.00	3.50	
	dark green	8.00	3.50	
	yellowish green	8.00	3.50	
	On cover		7.50	
	Block of four (2mm. or 3mm. spacing)	32.00	15.00	
	Margin block of 4, arrow, 2mm. or 3mm.	35.00	15.50	
	Corner margin block of four, 2mm. or 3mm.	32.50	15.50	
	Center line block	50.00	20.00	
	Margin block of 6, Impt. & P#, T V	80.00	35.00	
	Margin block of 6, Impt. & P# & star	90.00	37.50	
	Margin block of 6, Impt. & P# & small solid star (plate 4980)	*750.00*		
	Double transfer	20.00	7.00	
344 A139	**2c carmine**, *Dec. 10, 1908*	11.00	3.00	
	light carmine	11.00	3.00	
	dark carmine	11.00	3.00	
	On cover		5.00	
	Block of four (2mm. or 3mm. spacing)	44.00	13.00	

	Margin block of 4, arrow, 2mm. or 3mm.	47.50	14.00	
	Corner margin block of four, 2mm. or 3mm.	45.00	14.00	
	Center line block	65.00	25.00	
	Margin block of 6, Impt. & P#, T V	145.00		
	Margin block of 6, Impt. & P# & star	130.00		
	Double transfer	20.00	5.00	
	Double transfer, design of 1c (plate 5299)	*1,250.*		
345 A140	**3c deep violet**, type I, *Mar. 3, 1909*	20.00	13.50	
	violet	20.00	13.50	
	On cover		30.00	
	Block of four	80.00	57.50	
	Corner margin block of four	85.00	60.00	
	Margin block of 4, arrow	90.00	60.00	
	Center line block	125.00	80.00	
	Margin block of 6, Impt. & P#, T V	300.00	110.00	
	Double transfer	35.00	20.00	
346 A140	**4c orange brown**, *Feb. 25, 1909*	40.00	20.00	
	brown	40.00	20.00	
	On cover		75.00	
	Block of four (2mm. or 3mm. spacing)	160.00	85.00	
	Margin block of 4, arrow, 2mm. or 3mm.	175.00	90.00	
	Corner margin block of four 2mm. or 3 mm.	165.00	90.00	
	Center line block	240.00	100.00	
	Margin block of 6, Impt. & P#, T V	400.00	150.00	
	Margin block of 6, Impt. & P# & star	450.00		
	Double transfer	75.00	30.00	
347 A140	**5c blue**, *Feb. 25, 1909*	60.00	35.00	
	dark blue	60.00	35.00	
	On cover		100.00	
	Block of four	240.00	125.00	
	Corner margin block of four	245.00	135.00	
	Margin block of 4, arrow	260.00	150.00	
	Center line block	400.00	175.00	
	Margin block of 6, Impt. & P#, T V	650.00	250.00	
	Cracked plate	—	—	

For listings of other imperforate stamps of designs A138, A139 and A140 see
Nos. 383, 384, 408, 409 Single line wmk.
Nos. 481 to 485 unwmk.
Nos. 531 to 535 Offset printing

COIL STAMPS

		1908-10	**Perf. 12 Horizontally**	
348 A138	**1c green**, *Dec. 29, 1908*	25.00	13.00	
	dark green	25.00	13.00	
	On cover		25.00	
	Pair	60.00	35.00	
	Guide line pair	175.00	85.00	
349 A139	**2c carmine**, *Jan. 1909*	45.00	6.00	
	dark carmine	45.00	6.00	
	On cover		15.00	
	Pair	110.00	16.00	
	Guide line pair	275.00	40.00	
	Double transfer, design of 1c (plate 5299)	—	—	
350 A140	**4c orange brown**, *Aug. 15, 1910*	110.00	75.00	
	On cover		125.00	
	Pair	250.00	175.00	
	Guide line pair	800.00	275.00	
351 A140	**5c blue**, *Jan. 1909*	130.00	85.00	
	dark blue	130.00	85.00	
	On cover		150.00	
	Pair	290.00	200.00	
	Guide line pair	850.00	350.00	

		1909	**Perf. 12 Vertically**	
352 A138	**1c green**, *Jan. 1909*	55.00	18.50	
	dark green	55.00	18.50	
	On cover		40.00	
	Pair (2mm. spacing)	135.00	45.00	
	Pair (3mm. spacing)	130.00	42.50	
	Guide line pair	325.00	85.00	
	Double transfer	—	—	
353 A139	**2c carmine**, *Jan. 12, 1909*	45.00	6.00	
	dark carmine	45.00	6.00	
	On cover		20.00	
	Pair (2mm. spacing)	110.00	17.50	
	Pair (3mm. spacing)	105.00	15.00	
	Guide line pair	300.00	50.00	
354 A140	**4c orange brown**, *Feb. 23, 1909*	120.00	50.00	
	On cover		85.00	
	Pair (2mm. spacing)	285.00	125.00	
	Pair (3mm. spacing)	275.00	120.00	
	Guide line pair	850.00	200.00	
355 A140	**5c blue**, *Feb. 23, 1909*	130.00	70.00	
	On cover		125.00	
	Pair	300.00	150.00	
	Guide line pair	900.00	250.00	
356 A140	**10c yellow**, *Jan. 7, 1909*	1,300.	400.00	
	On cover		3,000.	
	Pair	3,250.	1,000.	
	Guide line pair	7,500.	2,250.	

These Government Coil Stamps, Nos. 352-355, should not be confused with those of the International Vending Machine Co., which are perf. 12½-13.
For listings of other coil stamps of designs A138 A139 and A140 see
Nos. 385 to 396, 410 to 413, 441 to 459 Single line wmk.
Nos. 486 to 496 unwmk.

BLUISH PAPER

This was made with 35 per cent rag stock instead of all wood pulp. The bluish color goes through the paper showing clearly on the back as well as on the face.

		1909		**Perf. 12**
357 A138	**1c green**, *Feb. 16, 1909*	100.00	90.00	
	On cover		200.00	
	Block of four (2mm. spacing)	410.00	400.00	
	Block of four (3mm. spacing)	*850.00*		
	Margin block of 6, Impt., T V	1,150.		
	Margin block of 6, Impt. & P# & star	*3,250.*		
358 A139	**2c carmine**, *Feb. 16, 1909*	90.00	75.00	
	On cover		200.00	
	Block of four (2mm. spacing)	375.00	325.00	
	Block of four (3mm. spacing)	425.00		
	Margin block of 6, Impt. & P#, T V	1,100.		
	Margin block of 6, Impt. & P# & star	1,750.		
	Double transfer	—	—	
359 A140	**3c deep violet**, type I	1,750.	1,400.	
	On cover		*2,000.*	
	Block of four	7,250.		
	Margin block of 6, Impt., T V	17,500.		
360 A140	**4c orange brown**	15,000.		
	Block of four	62,500.		
	Margin strip of 3, Impt. & P#, T V	65,000.		
361 A140	**5c blue**	3,750.	4,000.	
	Block of four	16,000.	—	
	Margin block of 6, Impt. & P#, T V	37,500.		
362 A140	**6c red orange**	1,050.	650.00	
	Block of four	4,500.		
	Margin block of 6, Impt., T V	12,000.		
363 A140	**8c olive green**	15,000.		
	Block of four	62,500.		
	Margin strip of 3, Impt. & P#, T V	65,000.		
364 A140	**10c yellow**	1,100.	700.00	
	On cover			
	Block of four	4,750.		
	Margin block of 6, Impt., T V	12,500.		
365 A140	**13c blue green**	2,250.	1,100.	
	On cover		1,750.	
	Block of four	9,500.	5,500.	
	Margin block of 6, Impt., T V	18,500.		
366 A140	**15c pale ultramarine**	1,050.	700.00	
	On cover			
	Block of four	4,500.		
	Margin block of 6, Impt., T V	10,000.		

LINCOLN MEMORIAL ISSUE

Issued to commemorate the 100th anniversary of the birth of Abraham Lincoln.

Lincoln — A141

Plates of 400 subjects in four panes of 100 each.

		1909		**Wmk. 191**
		Perf. 12		
367 A141	**2c carmine**, *Feb. 12, 1909*	7.00	2.75	
	bright carmine	7.00	2.75	
	On cover		4.50	
	Block of four (2mm. spacing)	28.00	12.00	
	Block of four (3mm. spacing)	28.00	11.50	
	Margin block of 6, Impt. & P# & small solid star	160.00		
	Double transfer	11.00	4.00	
		Imperf		
368 A141	**2c carmine**, *Feb. 12, 1909*	30.00	25.00	
	On cover		45.00	
	Block of four (2mm. or 3mm. spacing)	120.00	110.00	
	Corner margin block of four	130.00		
	Margin block of 4, arrow	140.00	120.00	
	Center line block	190.00	135.00	
	Margin block of 6, Impt. & P# & small solid star	275.00		
	Double transfer	55.00	35.00	

BLUISH PAPER

Perf. 12

369 A141	**2c carmine**, *Feb. 1909*	225.00	200.00	
	On cover		350.00	

Block of four (2mm. or 3mm
spacing) 950.00 850.00
Margin block of 6, Impt. & P#
& small solid star 4,250.

ALASKA-YUKON-PACIFIC EXPOSITION ISSUE

Issued to commemorate the Alaska-Yukon Pacific Exposition, held at Seattle, Wash., June 1-Oct. 16, 1909.

William H. Seward
A142

Plates of 280 subjects in four panes of 70 each.

1909		Wmk. 191		Perf. 12	
370	A142	2c **carmine,** *June 1, 1909*		12.00	2.25
		bright carmine		12.00	2.25
		On cover		5.00	
		On cover, Expo. station canc.			75.00
		Block of four		52.00	11.00
		Margin block of 6, Impt. & P#, T V		300.00	
		Double transfer (5249 U.L.8)		17.50	5.00

Imperf

371	A142	2c **carmine,** *June 1909*		45.00	35.00
		On cover			50.00
		On cover, Expo. station canc.			175.00
		Block of four		200.00	145.00
		Corner margin block of four		210.00	
		Margin block of 4, arrow		220.00	150.00
		Center line block		275.00	160.00
		Margin block of 6, Impt. & P#, T V		375.00	
		Double transfer		65.00	40.00

Earliest known use: June 13.

HUDSON-FULTON CELEBRATION ISSUE

Issued to commemorate the tercentenary of the discovery of the Hudson River and the centenary of Robert Fulton's steamship, the "Clermont."

Henry Hudson's "Half Moon" and Fulton's
Steamship "Clermont" — A143

Plates of 240 subjects in four panes of 60 each.

1909		Wmk. 191		Perf. 12	
372	A143	2c **carmine,** *Sept. 25, 1909*		14.00	4.75
		On cover			9.00
		Block of four		57.50	20.00
		Margin block of 6, Impt. & P#, T V		350.00	
		Double transfer (5393 and 5394)		20.00	6.00

Imperf

373	A143	2c **carmine,** *Sept. 25, 1909*		50.00	35.00
		On cover			50.00
		Block of four		200.00	145.00
		Corner margin block of four		210.00	
		Margin block of 4, arrow		225.00	155.00
		Center line block		350.00	175.00
		Margin block of 6, Impt. & P#, T V		400.00	
		Double transfer (5393 and 5394)		70.00	40.00

REGULAR ISSUE
DESIGNS OF 1908-09 ISSUES

In this issue the Bureau used three groups of plates:

(1) The old standard plates with uniform 2mm. spacing throughout (6c, 8c, 10c and 15c values);

(2) Those having an open star in the margin and showing spacings of 2mm. and 3mm. between stamps (for all values 1c to 10c); and

(3) A third set of plates with uniform spacing of approximately 2¾mm. between all stamps. These plates have imprints showing
a. "Bureau of Engraving & Printing", "A" and number.
b. "A" and number only.
c. Number only.
(See above No. 331)
These were used for the 1c, 2c, 3c, 4c and 5c values.

On or about Nov. 1, 1910 the Bureau began using paper watermarked with single-lined letters,

(Actual size of letter)

repeated in rows, this way:

Plates of 400 subjects in four panes of 100 each.

1910-11		Wmk. 190		Perf. 12	
374	A138	1c **green,** *Nov. 23, 1910*		6.50	6
		light green		6.50	6
		dark green		6.50	6
		On cover			10
		Block of four (2mm. spacing)		27.50	3.00
		Block of four (3mm. spacing)		27.00	2.75
		Margin block of 6, Impt. & P#, & star		85.00	
		Margin block of 6, Impt. & P# & "A"		100.00	—
a.		Booklet pane of six, *Oct. 7, 1910*		135.00	30.00
		Double transfer		12.50	2.50
		Cracked plate		—	
		Pane of sixty		1,200.	

Panes of 60 of No. 374 were regularly issued in Washington, D. C. during Sept. and Oct., 1912. They were made from the six outer vertical rows of imperforate "Star Plate" sheets that had been rejected for use in vending machines on account of the 3 mm. spacing. These panes have sheet margins on two adjoining sides and are imperforate along the other two sides. Both sheet margins show the plate number, imprint and star.

375	A139	2c **carmine,** *Nov. 23, 1910*		6.00	5
		bright carmine		6.00	5
		dark carmine		6.00	5
		lake		135.00	
		On cover			10
		Block of four (2mm. spacing)		25.00	1.25
		Block of four (3mm. spacing)		24.00	1.00
		Margin block of 6, Impt. & P# & star		85.00	
		Margin block of 6, Impt. & P# & "A"		95.00	
a.		Booklet pane of six, *Nov. 30, 1910*		110.00	25.00
		Cracked plate		—	
		Double transfer		12.50	2.50
		Double transfer, design of 1c (plate 5299)		—	1,000.
376	A140	3c **deep violet,** type I, *Jan. 16, 1911*		20.00	1.50
		violet		20.00	1.50
		lilac		22.50	1.65
		On cover			7.50
		Block of four (2mm. spacing)		85.00	8.50

				Block of four (3mm. spacing)	82.50	8.00
				Margin block of 6, Impt. & P# & star	175.00	
				Margin block of 6, P# only	200.00	
377	A140	4c **brown,** *Jan. 20, 1911*			30.00	50
		dark brown			30.00	50
		orange brown			30.00	50
		On cover				7.50
		Block of four (2mm. spacing)			122.50	3.25
		Block of four (3mm. spacing)			120.00	3.00
		Margin block of 6, Impt. & P# & star			225.00	
		Margin block of 6, P# only			250.00	
		Double transfer			—	
378	A140	5c **blue,** *Jan. 25, 1911*			30.00	50
		light blue			30.00	50
		dark blue			30.00	50
		bright blue			30.00	50
		On cover				5.00
		Block of four (2mm. spacing)			122.50	5.00
		Block of four (3mm. spacing)			120.00	4.00
		Margin block of 6, Impt. & P#, T V			275.00	
		Margin block of 6, Impt. & P# & star			265.00	
		Margin block of 6, "A" & P#			325.00	
		Margin block of 6, P# only			325.00	
		Double transfer			—	
379	A140	6c **red orange,** *Jan. 25, 1911*			37.50	75
		light red orange			37.50	75
		On cover				12.50
		Block of four (2mm. spacing)			155.00	8.50
		Block of four (3mm. spacing)			152.50	8.00
		Margin block of 6, Impt. & P# T V			500.00	
		Margin block of 6, Impt. & P# & star			450.00	
380	A140	8c **olive green,** *Feb. 8, 1911*			115.00	13.50
		dark olive green			115.00	13.50
		On cover				40.00
		Block of four (2mm. spacing)			475.00	60.00
		Block of four (3mm. spacing)			475.00	57.50
		Margin block of 6, Impt. & P# T V			1,250.	
		Margin block of 6, Impt. & P# & star			1,750.	
381	A140	10c **yellow,** *Jan. 24, 1911*			110.00	4.00
		On cover				17.50
		Block of four (2mm. spacing)			450.00	25.00
		Block of four (3mm. spacing)			450.00	22.50
		Margin block of 6, Impt. & P#, T V			1,300.	
		Margin block of 6, Impt. & P# & star			1,250.	
382	A140	15c **pale ultramarine,** *Mar. 1, 1911*			275.00	15.00
		On cover				100.00
		Block of four				1,150.	90.00
		Margin block of 6, Impt. & P#, T V			2,750.	

1911					Imperf.	
383	A138	1c **green,** *Jan. 3, 1911*			4.00	3.00
		dark green			4.00	3.00
		yellowish green			4.00	3.00
		bright green			4.00	3.00
		On cover				5.00
		Block of four (2mm. or 3mm. spacing)			16.00	13.00
		Corner margin block of four			17.00	
		Margin block of 4, arrow			17.50	13.50
		Center line block			35.00	16.00
		Margin block of 6, Impt. & P# & star			65.00	27.50
		Margin block of 6, Impt. & P# & "A"			125.00	
		Double transfer			10.00	6.00
384	A139	2c **carmine,** *Jan. 3, 1911*			6.00	2.00
		light carmine			6.00	2.00
		dark carmine			50.00	20.00
		On cover				2.50
		Horizontal pair			17.50	6.00
		Block of four (2mm. or 3mm. spacing)			36.00	12.00
		Corner margin block of four			37.00	
		Margin block of 4, arrow			37.00	18.00
		Center line block			75.00	30.00
		Margin block of 6, Impt. & P# & star			200.00	
		Margin block of 6, Impt. & P# & "A"			250.00	
		Double transfer, design of 1c (plate 5299)			1,250.	
		Double transfer			12.00	2.75
		Cracked plate			30.00	—

COIL STAMPS

1910				Perf. 12 Horizontally	
385	A138	1c **green,** *Nov. 1, 1910*		25.00	12.00
		dark green		25.00	12.00
		On cover			30.00
		Pair		60.00	27.50
		Guide line pair		250.00	85.00
386	A139	2c **carmine,** *Nov. 1, 1910*		45.00	11.00
		light carmine		45.00	11.00
		On cover			35.00
		Pair		150.00	40.00
		Guide line pair		500.00	100.00

1910-11				Perf. 12 Vertically	
387	A138	1c **green,** *Nov. 1, 1910*		75.00	22.50
		On cover			35.00
		Pair (2mm. spacing)		175.00	50.00
		Pair (3mm. spacing)		185.00	52.50
		Guide line pair		350.00	120.00
388	A139	2c **carmine,** *Nov. 1, 1910*		550.00	75.00
		On cover			250.00

	Pair (2mm. spacing)	1,600.	200.00
	Pair (3mm. spacing)	1,650.	225.00
	Guide line pair	3,750.	550.00

Stamps sold as No. 388 frequently are privately perforated copies of 384, or copies of 375, with horizontal perforations removed.

389	A140	3c **deep vio.,** type I, *Jan. 24, 1911*	15,000.	6,000.
		On cover		12,000.
		Pair	*45,000.*	

This is the rarest coil, only a small supply being used at Orangeburg, N. Y.

(See note above No. 316.)

1910 Perf. 8½ Horizontally

390	A138	1c **green,** *Dec. 12, 1910*	5.00	3.25
		dark green	5.00	3.25
		On cover		6.00
		Pair	11.00	7.00
		Guide line pair	30.00	11.00
		Double transfer	—	
391	A139	2c **carmine,** *Dec. 23, 1910*	30.00	8.50
		light carmine	30.00	8.50
		On cover		20.00
		Pair	75.00	20.00
		Guide line pair	175.00	50.00

1910-13 Perf. 8½ Vertically

392	A138	1c **green,** *Dec. 12, 1910*	20.00	15.00
		dark green	20.00	15.00
		On cover		40.00
		Pair	45.00	35.00
		Guide line pair	125.00	60.00
		Double transfer	—	
393	A139	2c **carmine,** *Dec. 16, 1910*	40.00	6.00
		dark carmine	40.00	6.00
		On cover		18.50
		Pair	90.00	15.00
		Guide line pair	200.00	25.00
394	A140	3c **deep violet,** type I, *Sept. 18, 1911*	50.00	27.50
		violet	50.00	27.50
		red violet	50.00	27.50
		On cover		85.00
		Pair (2mm. spacing)	115.00	65.00
		Pair (3mm. spacing)	110.00	62.50
		Guide line pair	300.00	110.00
395	A140	4c **brown,** *Apr. 15, 1912*	50.00	27.50
		dark brown	50.00	27.50
		On cover		85.00
		Pair (2mm. spacing)	115.00	65.00
		Pair (3mm. spacing)	110.00	62.50
		Guide line pair	300.00	110.00
396	A140	5c **blue,** *Mar. 1913*	50.00	27.50
		dark blue	50.00	27.50
		On cover		85.00
		Pair	110.00	35.00
		Guide line pair	300.00	120.00

PANAMA-PACIFIC EXPOSITION ISSUE

Issued to commemorate the Panama-Pacific Exposition held at San Francisco, Cal., Feb. 20-Dec. 4, 1915.

Vasco Nunez de Balboa A144

Pedro Miguel Locks, Panama Canal A145

Golden Gate A146

Discovery of San Francisco Bay — A147

Exposition Station Cancellation.

```
┌─────────────────────────┐
│ MODEL POST OFFICE │   │
│ PANAMA          │   │
│ PACIFIC         │   │
│ INTERNATIONAL   │   │
│ EXPOSITION      │   │
└─────────────────────────┘
```

Plates of 280 subjects in four panes of 70 each.

1913 Wmk. 190 Perf. 12

397	A144	1c **green,** *Jan. 1, 1913*	17.50	1.75
		deep green	17.50	1.75
		yellowish green	17.50	1.75
		On cover		2.50
		On card, Expo. station 1915 canc.		50.00
		Block of four	70.00	7.50
		Margin block of 6, P# only	175.00	
		Double transfer	27.50	3.00
398	A145	2c **carmine,** *Jan. 1913*	18.00	50
		deep carmine	18.00	50
		lake	250.00	
		On cover		1.00
		On cover, Expo. station 1915 canc.		65.00
		Block of four	75.00	5.00
		Margin block of 6, P# only	300.00	
		Double transfer	35.00	2.00

Earliest known use: Jan. 17.

399	A146	5c **blue,** *Jan. 1, 1913*	75.00	11.00
		dark blue	75.00	11.00
		On cover		25.00
		On cover, Expo. station 1915 canc.		300.00
		Block of four	310.00	55.00
		Margin block of 6, P# only	2,250.	
400	A147	10c **orange yellow,** *Jan. 1, 1913*	145.00	25.00
		On cover		50.00
		On cover, Expo. station 1915 canc.		400.00
		Block of four	590.00	110.00
		Margin block of 6, P# only	3,000.	
400A	A147	10c **orange,** *Aug. 1913*	200.00	20.00
		On cover		60.00
		On cover, Expo. station 1915 canc.		425.00
		Block of four	850.00	85.00
		Margin block of 6, P# only	*9,500.*	

1914-15 Perf. 10

401	A144	1c **green,** *Dec. 1914*	27.50	6.50
		dark green	27.50	6.50
		On cover		15.00
		On card, Expo. station 1915 canc.		120.00
		Block of four	110.00	30.00
		Margin block of 6, P# only	375.00	
402	A145	2c **carmine,** *Jan. 1915*	90.00	1.50
		deep carmine	90.00	1.50
		red	90.00	1.50
		On cover		5.00
		On cover, Expo. station 1915 canc.		185.00
		Block of four	365.00	13.50
		Margin block of 6, P# only	1,850.	
403	A146	5c **blue,** *Feb. 1915*	175.00	17.50
		dark blue	175.00	17.50
		On cover		50.00
		On cover, Expo. station 1915 canc.		450.00
		Block of four	710.00	75.00
		Margin block of 6, P# only	4,500.	
404	A147	10c **orange,** *July 1915*	1,250.	75.00
		On cover		135.00
		On cover, Expo. station 1915 canc.		850.00
		Block of four	*5,100.*	325.00
		Margin block of 6, P# only	*15,000.*	

> A particular stamp may be scarce, but if few collectors want it, its market value may remain relatively low.

REGULAR ISSUE

Washington — A140

1912-14 Wmk. 190 Perf. 12

The plates for this and later issues were the so-called "A" plates with uniform spacing of 2¾mm. between stamps.

Plates of 400 subjects in four panes of 100 each for all values 1c to 50c inclusive.

Plates of 200 subjects in two panes of 100 each for $1 and some of the 50c (No. 422) denomination.

405	A140	1c **green,** *Feb. 1912*	7.50	6
		light green	7.50	6
		dark green	7.50	6
		yellowish green	7.50	6
		On cover		10
		Block of four	30.00	1.00
		Margin block of 6, Impt. & P# & "A"	140.00	
		Margin block of 6, "A" & P#	125.00	
		Margin block of 6, P# only	115.00	
a.		Vert. pair, imperf. horiz.	*650.00*	—
b.		Booklet pane of six, *Feb. 8, 1912*	65.00	7.50
		Cracked plate	25.00	—
		Double transfer	12.00	—

TYPE I

TWO CENTS.

Type I. There is one shading line in the first curve of the ribbon above the left "2" and one in the second curve of the ribbon above the right "2".

The button of the toga has only a faint outline.

The top line of the toga rope, from the button to the front of the throat, is also very faint.

The shading lines of the face terminate in front of the ear with little or no joining, to form a lock of hair.

Used on both flat plate and rotary press printings.

406	A140	2c **carmine,** type I, *Feb. 1912*	6.50	5
		bright carmine	6.50	5
		dark carmine	6.50	5
		lake	150.00	35.00
		On cover		10
		Block of four	26.00	75
		Margin block of 6, Impt. & P# & "A"	165.00	
		Margin block of 6, "A" & P#	150.00	
		Margin block of 6, P# only	140.00	
		Margin block of 6, Electrolytic, (Pl. 6023)	350.00	
a.		Booklet pane of six, *Feb. 8, 1912*	70.00	17.50
b.		Double impression		
		Double transfer	12.50	1.00
407	A140	7c **black,** *Apr. 1914*	85.00	8.00
		grayish black	85.00	8.00
		intense black	85.00	8.00
		On cover		30.00
		Block of four	350.00	45.00
		Margin block of 6, P# only	1,250.	

1912 Imperf.

408	A140	1c **green,** *Mar. 1912*	1.50	60
		yellowish green	1.50	60
		dark green	1.50	60
		On cover		1.10
		Block of four	6.00	2.50
		Corner margin block of four	6.25	2.65
		Margin block of 4, arrow	6.25	2.65
		Center line block	11.00	6.50
		Margin block of 6, Impt. & P# & "A", T, B or L	70.00	13.00
		Margin block of 6, Impt. & P# & "A", at right	*750.00*	
		Margin block of 6, "A" & P#	35.00	
		Margin block of 6, P# only	25.00	5.50
		Double transfer	4.00	1.20

	Cracked plate	—	—
409 A140	2c **carmine**, type I, *Feb. 1912*	1.65	60
	deep carmine	1.65	60
	scarlet	1.65	60
	On cover		1.00
	Block of four	6.60	2.75
	Corner margin block of four	6.75	
	Margin block of 4, arrow	6.75	3.25
	Center line block	12.50	7.00
	Margin block of 6, Impt. & P# & "A"	75.00	10.00
	Margin block of 6, "A" & P#	65.00	
	Margin block of 6, P# only	50.00	
	Cracked plate (Plates 7580, 7582)	25.00	—

In December, 1914, the Post Office at Kansas City, Missouri, had on hand a stock of imperforate sheets of 400 of stamps Nos. 408 and 409, formerly sold for use in vending machines, but not then in demand. In order to make them salable, they were rouletted with ordinary tracing wheels and were sold over the counter with official approval of the Post Office Department given January 5, 1915.

These stamps were sold until the supply was exhausted. Except for one full sheet of 400 of each value, all were cut into panes of 100 before being rouletted and sold. They are known as "Kansas City Roulettes".

COIL STAMPS

1912 — *Perf. 8½ Horizontally*

410 A140	1c **green**, *Mar. 1912*	6.25	3.50
	dark green	6.25	3.50
	On cover		7.50
	Pair	14.00	8.00
	Guide line pair	35.00	14.00
	Double transfer	—	—
411 A140	2c **carmine**, type I, *Mar. 1912*	8.50	3.75
	deep carmine	8.50	3.75
	On cover		10.00
	Pair	20.00	8.50
	Guide line pair	45.00	14.00
	Double transfer	12.00	6.00

Perf. 8½ Vertically

412 A140	1c **green**, *Mar. 18, 1912*	21.00	5.00
	deep green	21.00	5.00
	On cover		12.50
	Pair	45.00	12.00
	Guide line pair	95.00	20.00
413 A140	2c **carmine**, type I, *Mar. 1912*	35.00	60
	dark carmine	35.00	60
	On cover		7.50
	Pair	75.00	4.00
	Guide line pair	190.00	12.50
	Double transfer	60.00	2.50

Franklin — A148

1912-14 — **Wmk. 190** — *Perf. 12*

414 A148	8c **pale olive green**, *Feb. 1912*	37.50	1.50
	olive green	37.50	1.50
	On cover		15.00
	Block of four	155.00	12.00
	Margin block of 6, Impt. & "A"	475.00	
415 A148	9c **salmon red**, *Apr. 1914*	50.00	15.00
	rose red	50.00	15.00
	On cover		45.00
	Block of four	205.00	75.00
	Margin block of 6, P# only	750.00	
416 A148	10c **orange yellow**, *Jan. 1912*	37.50	30
	yellow	37.50	30
	brown yellow	150.00	
	On cover		2.50
	Block of four	155.00	1.75
	Margin block of 6, Impt. & "A"	525.00	
	Margin block of 6, "A" & P#	550.00	
	Double transfer	—	—
417 A148	12c **claret brown**, *Apr. 1914*	45.00	4.50
	deep claret brown	45.00	4.50
	On cover		22.50
	Block of four	185.00	22.50
	Margin block of 6, P# only	550.00	
	Double transfer	60.00	7.50
	Triple transfer	85.00	10.00
418 A148	15c **gray**, *Feb. 1912*	75.00	3.50
	dark gray	75.00	3.50
	On cover		15.00
	Block of four	310.00	20.00
	Margin block of 6, Impt. & "A"	750.00	
	Margin block of 6, "A" & P#	800.00	
	Margin block of 6, P# only	850.00	
	Double transfer	—	—
419 A148	20c **ultramarine**, *Apr. 1914*	175.00	16.00
	dark ultramarine	175.00	16.00
	On cover		150.00
	Block of four	725.00	75.00
	Margin block of 6, P# only	2,000.	

420 A148	30c **orange red**, *Apr. 1914*	125.00	16.00
	dark orange red	125.00	16.00
	On cover		175.00
	Block of four	510.00	75.00
	Margin block of 6, P# only	1,750.	
421 A148	50c **violet**, *Apr. 29, 1914*	500.00	17.50
	bright violet	500.00	17.50
	On cover		1,250.
	Block of four	2,100.	85.00
	Margin block of 6, P# only	9,000.	

1912 — **Wmk. 191**

422 A148	50c **violet**, *Feb. 12, 1912*	250.00	17.50
	On cover		1,250.
	Block of four	1,050.	80.00
	Margin block of 4, arrow, R or L	1,250.	
	Margin block of 6, Impt. & P# & "A"	5,500.	
423 A148	$1 **violet brown**, *Feb. 12, 1912*	575.00	70.00
	On cover		2,500.
	Block of four	2,400.	300.00
	Margin block of 4, arrow, R or L	2,500.	
	Margin block of 6, Impt. & P# & "A"	12,500.	
	Double transfer (5782 L. 66)	650.00	80.00

During the United States occupation of Vera Cruz, Mexico, from April to November, 1914, letters sent from there show Provisional Postmarks.

For other listings of perforated stamps of design A148, see:
Nos. 431 to 440 Single line wmk. Perf. 10
Nos. 460 Double line wmk. Perf. 10
Nos. 470 to 478 unwmk. Perf. 10
Nos. 508 to 518 unwmk. Perf. 11

Plates of 400 subjects in four panes of 100 each.

1913-15 — **Wmk. 190** — *Perf. 10*

424 A140	1c **green**, *Sept. 5, 1914*	2.75	6
	bright green	2.75	6
	deep green	2.75	6
	yellowish green	2.75	6
	On cover		10
	Block of four	11.00	75
	Margin block of 6, P# only	45.00	
	Block of ten with imprint "COIL STAMPS" and number (6581-82, 85, 89)	175.00	
	Cracked plate	—	—
	Double transfer	7.50	1.00
a.	Perf. 12x10	*300.00*	*250.00*
b.	Perf. 10x12		*125.00*
c.	Vert. pair, imperf. horiz.	*425.00*	*250.00*
d.	Booklet pane of six	4.00	75
e.	Vert. pair, imperf. btwn.		

Most copies of No. 424b are precanceled Dayton, Ohio, to which the price applies.
Earliest known use of No. 424d is Dec. 230, 1913.

425 A140	2c **rose red**, type I, *Sept. 5, 1914*	2.50	5
	dark rose red	2.50	5
	carmine rose	2.50	5
	carmine	2.50	5
	dark carmine	2.50	5
	scarlet	2.50	5
	red	2.50	5
	On cover		10
	Block of four	10.00	35
	Margin block of 6, P# only	30.00	
	Block of ten with imprint "COIL STAMPS" and number (6566-73)	175.00	
	Cracked plate	15.00	—
	Double transfer	—	—
c.	Perf. 10x12		
d.	Perf. 12x10		*250.00*
e.	Booklet pane of six, *Jan. 6, 1914*	15.00	*3.00*

The aniline inks used on some printings of Nos. 425, 426 and 435 caused a pink tinge to permeate the paper and appear on the back. These are called "pink backs."

426 A140	3c **deep violet**, type I, *Sept. 18, 1914*	13.50	1.25
	violet	13.50	1.25
	bright violet	13.50	1.25
	reddish violet	13.50	1.25
	On cover		3.00
	Block of four	55.00	6.50
	Margin block of 6, P# only	135.00	
427 A140	4c **brown**, *Sept. 7, 1914*	35.00	40
	dark brown	35.00	40
	orange brown	35.00	40
	yellowish brown	35.00	40
	On cover		5.00
	Block of four	142.50	3.75
	Margin block of 6, P# only	400.00	
	Double transfer	60.00	2.50
428 A140	5c **blue**, *Sept. 14, 1914*	30.00	40
	bright blue	30.00	40
	dark blue	30.00	40
	indigo blue	27.50	50
	On cover		2.50
	Block of four	112.50	2.50
	Margin block of 6, P# only	285.00	
a.	Perf. 12x10		*400.00*
429 A140	6c **red orange**, *Sept. 28, 1914*	37.50	1.20
	deep red orange	37.50	1.20
	pale red orange	37.50	1.20
	On cover		8.50
	Block of four (2mm. spacing)	160.00	11.00
	Block of four (3mm. spacing)	155.00	10.00
	Margin block of 6, Impt. & P# & star	300.00	
	Margin block of 6, P# only	350.00	
430 A140	7c **black**, *Sept. 10, 1914*	90.00	4.25

	gray black	90.00	4.25
	intense black	90.00	4.25
	On cover		35.00
	Block of four	375.00	25.00
	Margin block of 6, P# only	850.00	
431 A148	8c **pale olive green**, *Sept. 26, 1914*	37.50	1.50
	olive green	37.50	1.50
	On cover		7.50
	Block of four	155.00	10.00
	Margin block of 6, Impt. & P# & "A"	400.00	
	Margin block of 6, "A" & P#	450.00	
	Double impression	—	
432 A148	9c **salmon red**, *Oct. 6, 1914*	50.00	8.50
	dark salmon red	50.00	8.50
	On cover		25.00
	Block of four	210.00	40.00
	Margin block of 6, P# only	550.00	
433 A148	10c **orange yellow**, *Sept. 9, 1914*	47.50	25
	golden yellow	47.50	25
	On cover		7.50
	Block of four	195.00	1.50
	Margin block of 6, Impt. & P# & "A"	550.00	
	Margin block of 6, "A" & P#	550.00	
	Margin block of 6, P# only	550.00	
434 A148	11c **dark green**, *Aug. 11, 1915*	22.50	7.00
	bluish green	22.50	7.00
	On cover		22.50
	Block of four	90.00	32.50
	Margin block of 6, P# only	200.00	
435 A148	12c **claret brown**, *Sept. 10, 1914*	25.00	4.50
	deep claret brown	25.00	4.50
	On cover		17.50
	Block of four	100.00	25.00
	Margin block of 6, P# only	250.00	
a.	12c copper red	27.50	4.50
a.	On cover		17.50
a.	Block of four	110.00	25.00
a.	Margin block of 6, P# only	275.00	
b.	Vertical pair, imperf. between	*650.00*	
	Double transfer	40.00	7.50
	Triple transfer	50.00	9.00
437 A148	15c **gray**, *Sept. 16, 1914*	115.00	7.25
	dark gray	115.00	7.25
	On cover		50.00
	Block of four	475.00	40.00
	Margin block of 6, Impt. & P# & "A"	850.00	
	Margin block of 6, "A" & P#	875.00	
	Margin block of 6, P# only	850.00	
438 A148	20c **ultramarine**, *Sept. 19, 1914*	225.00	4.00
	dark ultramarine	225.00	4.00
	On cover		125.00
	Block of four	950.00	25.00
	Margin block of 6, P# only	2,500.	
439 A148	30c **orange red**, *Sept. 19, 1914*	275.00	20.00
	dark orange red	275.00	20.00
	On cover		175.00
	Block of four	1,150.	95.00
	Margin block of 6, P# only	3,500.	
440 A148	50c **violet**, *Dec. 10, 1915*	800.00	20.00
	On cover		1,000.
	Block of four	3,300.	85.00
	Margin block of 6, P# only	11,000.	

COIL STAMPS

1914 — *Perf. 10 Horizontally*

441 A140	1c **green**, *Nov. 14, 1914*	1.00	90
	deep green	1.00	90
	On cover		2.00
	Pair	2.75	2.00
	Guide line pair	7.50	3.50
442 A140	2c **carmine**, type I, *July 22, 1914*	10.00	7.50
	deep carmine	10.00	7.50
	On cover		12.50
	Pair	25.00	17.50
	Guide line pair	57.50	35.00

1914 — *Perf. 10 Vertically*

443 A14	1c **green**, *May 29, 1914*	22.50	6.00
	deep green	22.50	6.00
	On cover		12.00
	Pair	55.00	13.50
	Guide line pair	115.00	30.00
444 A140	2c **carmine**, type I, *Apr. 25, 1914*	30.00	1.50
	deep carmine	30.00	1.50
	red	30.00	1.50
	On cover		10.00
	Pair	75.00	4.00
	Guide line pair	175.00	9.50
445 A140	3c **violet**, type I, *Dec. 18, 1914*	225.00	110.00
	deep violet	225.00	110.00
	On cover		200.00
	Pair	500.00	250.00
	Guide line pair	1,100.	400.00
446 A140	4c **brown**, *Oct. 2, 1914*	130.00	35.00
	On cover		100.00
	Pair	300.00	100.00
	Guide line pair	650.00	140.00
447 A140	5c **blue**, *July 30, 1914*	45.00	22.50
	On cover		50.00
	Pair	105.00	55.00
	Guide line pair	225.00	100.00

No. 443 represents stamps from coils. Part of a sheet of No. 424 is also known which is perforated vertically and imperforate horizontally.

ROTARY PRESS STAMPS

The Rotary Press Stamps are printed from plates that are curved to fit around a cylinder. This curvature produces stamps that are slightly larger, either horizontally or vertically, than those printed from flat plates. Designs of stamps from flat plates measure about 18½-19 mm. wide by 22 mm. high. When the impressions are placed sidewise on the curved plates the designs are 19½-20 mm. wide; when they are placed vertically the designs are 22½ to 23 mm. high. A line of color (not a guide line) shows where the curved plates meet or join on the press.

Rotary Press Coil Stamps were printed from plates of 170 subjects for stamps coiled sidewise, and from plates of 150 subjects for stamps coiled endwise.

Double paper listings of Rotary Press stamps have been discontinued and deleted from this catalogue. Collectors are referred to the note on "Rotary Press Double Paper" in the "Information for Collectors" in the front of the catalogue.

ROTARY PRESS COIL STAMPS
Stamp designs 18½ to 19 mm. wide by 22½ mm. high.

448	A140	1c **green,** *Dec. 12, 1915*	8.50	3.00
		light green	8.50	3.00
		On cover		6.50
		Pair	20.00	7.00
		Joint line pair	50.00	17.50

6568

COIL STAMPS

Type of plate number and imprint used for the 12 special 1c and 2c plates designed for the production of coil stamps.

TYPE II

TWO CENTS.
Type II. Shading lines in ribbons as on type I.
The toga button, rope and rope shading lines are heavy.
The shading lines of the face at the lock of hair end in a strong vertical curved line.
Used on rotary press printings only.

TYPE III

Type III. Two lines of shading in the curves of the ribbons. Other characteristics similar to type II. Used on rotary press printings only.

1915-16   *Perf. 10 Horizontally*

449	A140	2c **red,** type I, *Dec. 5, 1915*	1,600.	175.00
		carmine rose, type I		
		On cover, type I		450.00

		Pair, type I	3,500.	375.00
		Joint line pair, type I	7,500.	750.00
450	A140	2c **carmine,** type III, *Feb. 1916*	12.00	3.00
		carmine rose, type III	12.00	3.00
		red, type III	12.00	3.00
		On cover, type III		7.00
		Pair, type III	25.00	8.00
		Joint line pair, type III	60.00	15.00

1914-16   *Perf. 10 Vertically*
Stamp designs 19½ to 20 mm. wide by 22 mm. high.

452	A140	1c **green,** *Nov. 11, 1914*	12.00	1.75
		On cover		3.00
		Pair	27.50	4.00
		Joint line pair	80.00	8.00
453	A140	2c **carmine rose,** type I, *July 3, 1914*	120.00	4.50
		On cover, type I		10.00
		Pair, type I	250.00	11.00
		Joint line pair, type I	600.00	35.00
		Cracked plate, type I	—	
454	A140	2c **red,** type II, *June, 1915*	115.00	13.50
		carmine, type II	115.00	13.50
		On cover, type II		35.00
		Pair, type II	240.00	35.00
		Joint line pair, type II	575.00	90.00
455	A140	2c **carmine,** type III, *Dec. 1915*	10.00	1.00
		carmine rose, type III	10.00	1.00
		On cover, type III		2.00
		Pair, type III	21.00	2.50
		Joint line pair, type III	60.00	5.00

Fraudulently altered copies of Type III (Nos. 455, 488, 492 and 540) have had one line of shading scraped off to make them resemble Type II (Nos. 454, 487, 491 and 539).

456	A140	3c **violet,** type I, *Feb. 2, 1916*	300.00	95.00
		deep violet	300.00	95.00
		red violet	300.00	95.00
		On cover		175.00
		Pair	650.00	225.00
		Joint line pair	1,300.	400.00
457	A140	4c **brown,** *Feb. 18, 1916*	30.00	18.00
		light brown	30.00	18.00
		On cover		40.00
		Pair	65.00	45.00
		Joint line pair	165.00	75.00
		Cracked plate	60.00	—
458	A140	5c **blue,** *Mar. 9, 1916*	30.00	18.00
		On cover		40.00
		Pair	65.00	45.00
		Joint line pair	165.00	75.00
		Double transfer		

Horizontal Coil

1914   *Imperf.*

459	A140	2c **carmine,** type I, *June 30, 1914*	450.00	600.00
		On cover		
		Pair	950.00	1,350.
		Joint line pair	2,100.	3,250.

Most line pairs of No. 459 are creased. Uncreased pairs command a premium.

FLAT PLATE PRINTINGS

1915   **Wmk. 191**   *Perf. 10*

460	A148	$1 **violet black,** *Feb. 8, 1915*	975.00	95.00
		On cover		
		Block of four	4,100.	425.00
		Margin block of 4, arrow, R or L	4,250.	
		Margin block of 6, Impt. & P# & "A"	12,500.	
		Double transfer (5782 L. 66)	1,050.	105.00

1915   **Wmk. 190**   *Perf. 11*

461	A140	2c **pale car. red,** type I, *June 17, 1915*	100.00	85.00
		On cover		850.00
		Block of four	410.00	375.00
		Margin block of 6, P# only	950.00	

Fraudulently perforated copies of No. 409 are offered as No. 461.

FLAT PLATE PRINTINGS
Plates of 400 subjects in four panes of 100 each for all values 1c to 50c inclusive.
Plates of 200 subjects in two panes of 100 each for $1, $2 and $5 denominations.
The Act of Oct. 3, 1917, effective Nov. 2, 1917, created a 3 cent rate. Local rate, 2 cents.

1916-17   **Unwmk.**   *Perf. 10*

462	A140	1c **green,** *Sept. 27, 1916*	8.50	20
		light green	8.50	20
		dark green	8.50	20
		bluish green	8.50	20
		On cover		40
		Block of four	34.00	2.00
		Margin block of 6, P# only	150.00	
a.		Booklet pane of six, *Oct. 15, 1916*	12.00	1.00
463	A140	2c **carmine,** type I, *Sept. 25, 1916*	5.00	10
		dark carmine	5.00	10
		rose red	5.00	10
		On cover		15
		Block of four	21.00	1.25
		Margin block of 6, P# only	120.00	
a.		Booklet pane of six, *Oct. 8, 1916*	85.00	20.00
		Double transfer	9.00	1.00

464	A140	3c **violet,** type I, *Nov. 11, 1916*	80.00	11.00
		deep violet	80.00	11.00
		On cover		35.00
		Block of four	325.00	60.00
		Margin block of 6, P# only	1,350.	
		Double transfer in "CENTS"	110.00	
465	A140	4c **orange brown,** *Oct. 7, 1916*	50.00	1.75
		deep brown	50.00	1.75
		brown	50.00	1.75
		On cover		10.00
		Block of four	210.00	15.00
		Margin block of 6, P# only	650.00	
		Double transfer	—	
466	A140	5c **blue,** *Oct. 17, 1916*	80.00	1.75
		dark blue	80.00	1.75
		On cover		12.50
		Block of four	325.00	60.00
		Margin block of 6, P# only	900.00	
467	A140	5c **carmine** (error in plate of 2c)	750.00	525.00
		On cover		2,000.
		Block of 9, middle stamp the error	1,000.	850.00
		Block of 12, two middle stamps errors	1,750.	1,500.
		Margin block of six 2c stamps (#463), P#7942	135.00	

No. 467 is an error caused by using a 5c transfer roll in re-entering three subjects: 7942 U. L. 74, 7942 U. L. 84, 7942 L. R. 18; the balance of the subjects on the plate being normal 2c entries. No. 467 imperf. is listed as No. 485.

468	A140	6c **red orange,** *Oct. 10, 1916*	95.00	7.50
		On cover		35.00
		Block of four	385.00	40.00
		Margin block of 6, P# only	1,150.	
		Double transfer	—	
469	A140	7c **black,** *Oct. 10, 1916*	125.00	13.00
		gray black	125.00	13.00
		On cover		40.00
		Block of four	510.00	70.00
		Margin block of 6, P# only	1,350.	
470	A148	8c **olive green,** *Nov. 13, 1916*	55.00	6.50
		dark olive green	55.00	6.50
		On cover		25.00
		Block of four	225.00	35.00
		Margin block of 6, Impt. & P# & "A"	525.00	
		Margin block of 6, "A" & P#	575.00	
471	A148	9c **salmon red,** *Nov. 16, 1916*	60.00	16.00
		On cover		35.00
		Block of four	245.00	65.00
		Margin block of 6, P# only	675.00	
472	A148	10c **orange yellow,** *Oct. 17, 1916*	120.00	1.00
		On cover		7.50
		Block of four	500.00	7.50
		Margin block of 6, P# only	1,350.	
473	A148	11c **dark green,** *Nov. 16, 1916*	32.50	17.50
		On cover		40.00
		Block of four	135.00	85.00
		Margin block of 6, P# only	325.00	
474	A148	12c **claret brown,** *Oct. 10, 1916*	50.00	5.00
		On cover		20.00
		Block of four	200.00	25.00
		Margin block of 6, P# only	550.00	
		Double transfer	60.00	7.50
		Triple transfer	80.00	12.00
475	A148	15c **gray,** *Nov. 16, 1916*	175.00	12.00
		dark gray	175.00	12.00
		On cover		80.00
		Block of four	725.00	75.00
		Margin block of 6, P# only	2,500.	
		Margin block of 6, Impt. & P# & "A"	—	
476	A148	20c **light ultramarine,** *Dec. 5, 1916*	250.00	12.50
		ultramarine	250.00	12.50
		On cover		200.00
		Block of four	1,050.	75.00
		Margin block of 6, P# only	3,500.	
476A	A148	30c **orange red**	—	
		Block of four	—	
		Margin block of 6, P# only	—	
477	A148	50c **light violet,** *Mar. 2, 1917*	1,300.	75.00
		On cover		1,500.
		Block of four	5,300.	375.00
		Margin block of 6, P# only	25,000.	
478	A148	$1 **violet black,** *Dec. 22, 1916*	950.00	22.50
		On cover		2,000.
		Block of four	4,000.	110.00
		Margin block of 4, arrow, R or L	4,250.	
		Margin block of 6, Impt. & P# & "A"	13,000.	
		Double transfer (5782 L. 66)	1,050.	27.50

TYPES OF 1902-03 ISSUE

1917   **Unwmk.**   *Perf. 10*

479	A127	$2 **dark blue,** *Mar. 22, 1917*	500.00	45.00
		On cover (other than first flight)		1,250.
		On flight cover		350.00
		On Zeppelin flight cover		750.00
		Block of four	2,000.	200.00
		Margin block of 4, arrow, R or L	2,100.	
		Margin block of 6, P# only	6,000.	
		Double transfer		
480	A128	$5 **light green,** *Mar. 22, 1917*	400.00	47.50
		On cover		1,250.
		Block of four	1,600.	210.00
		Margin block of 4, arrow, R or L	1,700.	
		Margin block of 6, P# only	4,500.	

1916-17   *Imperf.*

481	A140	1c **green,** *Nov. 1916*	1.00	75

bluish green	1.00	75
deep green	1.00	75
On cover		1.25
Block of four	4.00	3.25
Corner margin block of four	4.25	
Margin block of 4, arrow	4.50	3.75
Center line block	10.00	
Margin block of 6, P# only	15.00	5.00
Margin block of 6, Electrolytic (Pl. 13376-13377)	375.00	
Double transfer	4.00	2.00

During September, 1921, the Bureau of Engraving and Printing issued a 1c stamp printed from experimental electrolytic plates made in accordance with patent granted to George U. Rose. Tests at that time did not prove satisfactory and the method was discontinued. Four plates were made, viz., 13376, 13377, 13389 and 13390 from which stamps were issued. They are difficult to distinguish from the normal varieties. (See No. 498).

TYPE Ia

TWO CENTS.

Type Ia. The design characteristics are similar to type I except that all of the lines of the design are stronger.
The toga button, toga rope and rope and rope shading lines are heavy.
The latter characteristics are those of type II, which, however, occur only on impressions from rotary plates.
Used only on flat plates 10208 and 10209.

482	A140	2c carmine, type I, Dec. 8, 1916	1.25	1.25
		deep carmine	1.25	1.25
		carmine rose	1.25	1.25
		deep rose	1.25	1.25
		On cover		2.25
		Block of four	5.00	5.00
		Corner margin block of four	5.25	5.25
		Margin block of 4, arrow	5.50	5.50
		Center line block	8.00	
		Margin block of 6, P# only	25.00	12.00
		Cracked plate		
482A	A140	2c deep rose, type Ia	6,000.	
		On cover	10,000.	
		Pair		

The imperforate, type Ia, was issued but all known copies were privately perforated with large oblong perforations at the sides. (Schermack type III)
Earliest known use: Feb. 27, 1920.

TYPE II

THREE CENTS.

Type II. The top line of the toga rope is strong and the rope shading lines are heavy and complete.
The line between the lips is heavy.
Used on both flat plate and rotary press printings.

483	A140	3c violet, type I, Oct. 13, 1917	15.00	8.50
		light violet, type I	15.00	8.50
		On cover, type I		15.00
		Block of four, type I	60.00	36.00
		Corner margin block of four, type I	62.50	
		Margin block of 4, arrow, type I	62.50	
		Center line block, type I	90.00	
		Margin block of 6, P# only, type I	175.00	
		Double transfer, type I	25.00	—
		Triple transfer, type I		
484	A140	3c violet, type II	11.00	4.00
		deep violet, type II	11.00	4.00
		On cover, type II		10.00

		Block of four, type II	44.00	17.50
		Corner margin block of four, type I	45.00	
		Margin block of 4, arrow, type II	45.00	
		Center line block, type II	65.00	
		Margin block of 6, P# only, type II	135.00	
		Double transfer, type II	20.00	7.50
485	A140	5c carmine (error), Mar. 1917	13,000.	
		Block of 9, middle stamp the error	15,000.	
		Block of 12, two middle stamps errors	28,500.	
		Margin block of six 2c stamps (#482), P#7942	300.00	

(See note under No. 467.)

ROTARY PRESS COIL STAMPS
(See note over No. 448.)

1916-19   *Perf. 10 Horizontally*
Stamp designs 18½ to 19 mm. wide by 22½ mm. high.

486	A140	1c green, Jan. 1918	1.00	15
		yellowish green	1.00	15
		On cover		35
		Pair	2.25	35
		Joint line pair	4.50	75
		Cracked plate		
		Double transfer	4.00	1.50
487	A140	2c carmine, type II, Nov. 15, 1916	18.00	2.50
		On cover, type II		10.00
		Pair, type II	37.50	6.00
		Joint line pair, type II	135.00	20.00
		Cracked plate		

(See note after No. 455)

488	A140	2c carmine, type III, 1919	3.00	1.50
		carmine rose, type III	3.00	1.50
		On cover, type II		3.00
		Pair, type III	6.50	3.50
		Joint line pair, type III	20.00	8.00
		Cracked plate, type III	20.00	7.50
489	A140	3c violet, type I, Oct. 10, 1917	6.50	1.00
		dull violet	6.50	1.00
		bluish violet	6.50	1.00
		On cover		2.00
		Pair	13.50	2.50
		Joint line pair	37.50	7.00

1916-22   *Perf. 10 Vertically*
Stamp designs 19½ to 20 mm. wide by 22 mm. high.

490	A140	1c green, Nov. 17, 1916	75	15
		yellowish green	75	15
		On cover		25
		Pair	1.75	35
		Joint line pair	4.75	75
		Double transfer		
		Cracked plate (horizontal)	12.00	—
		Cracked plate (vertical) retouched	14.00	—
		Rosette crack	16.50	—
491	A140	2c carmine, type II, Nov. 17, 1916	1,450.	225.00
		On cover, type II		325.00
		Pair, type II	3,100.	500.00
		Joint line pair, type II	7,000.	

(See note after No. 455)

492	A140	2c carmine, type III	11.00	15
		carmine rose, type III	11.00	15
		On cover, type III		25
		Pair, type III	22.50	40
		Joint line pair, type III	65.00	2.00
		Double transfer, type III	—	—
		Cracked plate	—	—
493	A140	3c violet, type I, July 23, 1917	21.00	3.00
		reddish violet, type I	21.00	3.00
		On cover, type I		6.00
		Pair, type I	43.50	7.50
		Joint line pair, type I	140.00	25.00
494	A140	3c violet, type II, Feb. 4, 1918	11.50	60
		dull violet, type II	11.50	60
		gray violet, type II	11.50	60
		On cover, type II		1.00
		Pair, type II	24.00	1.50
		Joint line pair, type II	75.00	3.50
495	A140	4c orange brown, Apr. 15, 1917	12.50	3.50
		On cover		7.50
		Pair	26.00	8.00
		Joint line pair	85.00	13.50
		Cracked plate	35.00	5.00
496	A140	5c blue, Jan. 15, 1919	4.50	60
		On cover		1.00
		Pair	9.50	1.50
		Joint line pair	30.00	4.50
497	A148	10c orange yellow, Jan. 31, 1922	26.50	8.50
		On cover		15.00
		Pair	55.00	18.50
		Joint line pair	150.00	37.50

FLAT PLATE PRINTINGS
Plates of 400 subjects in four panes of 100 each.
TYPES OF 1913-15 ISSUE

1917-19   Unwmk.   *Perf. 11*

498	A140	1c green, Mar. 1917	40	5
		light green	40	5
		dark green	40	5
		yellowish green	40	5
		On cover		10
		Block of four	1.60	25
		Margin block of 6, P# only	17.50	

		Margin block of 6, Electrolytic (Pl. 13376-7, 13389-90) *see note after No. 481*	450.00	
a.		Vertical pair, imperf. horiz.	175.00	
b.		Horizontal pair, imperf. between	75.00	
c.		Vertical pair, imperf. between	450.00	
d.		Double impression	150.00	
g.		Perf. 10 at top or bottom	500.00	—
		Cracked plate (10656 U. L. and 10645 L. R.)	10.00	—
		Double transfer	7.50	2.00
e.		Booklet pane of six, Apr. 6, 1917	1.75	35
f.		Booklet pane of thirty	550.00	
499	A140	2c rose, type I, Mar. 1917	35	5
		dark rose, type I	35	5
		carmine rose, type I	35	5
		deep rose, type I	45	5
		On cover, type I		10
		Block of four, type I	1.40	20
		Margin block of 6, P# only, type I	14.00	
a.		Vertical pair, imperf. horiz., type I	150.00	
b.		Horiz. pair, imperf. vert., type I	150.00	100.00
c.		Vert. pair, imperf. btwn., type I	500.00	225.00
e.		Booklet pane of six, type I, Mar. 31, 1917	2.00	50
f.		Booklet pane of thirty, type I	9,000.	
g.		Double impression, type I	125.00	
		Double impression, type I, 15 mm. wide		
		Cracked plate, type I	—	—
		Recut in hair, type I	—	—
		Double transfer, type I	6.00	—
500	A140	2c deep rose, type Ia	275.00	130.00
		On cover, type Ia		225.00
		Block of four, type Ia	1,150.	550.00
		Margin block of 6, P# only, type Ia	2,250.	
		Margin block of 6, P#, two stamps type I (P# 10208 L.L.)	6,750.	
		Pair, types I and Ia (10208 L. L. 95 or 96)	1,350.	
501	A140	3c light violet, type I, Mar. 1917	17.50	10
		violet, type I	17.50	10
		dark violet, type I	17.50	10
		reddish violet, type I	17.50	10
		On cover, type I		15
		Block of four, type I	70.00	1.60
		Margin block of 6, P# only, type I	175.00	
b.		Blkt. pane of 6, type I, Oct. 17, 1917	75.00	15.00
c.		Vert. pair, imper. horiz., type I	300.00	
d.		Double impression	150.00	
		Double transfer, type I	25.00	
502	A140	3c dark violet, type II	20.00	25
		violet, type II	20.00	25
		On cover, type II		40
		Block of four, type II	80.00	1.75
		Margin block of 6, P# only, type II	210.00	
b.		Bklt. pane of 6, type II, Feb. 25, 1918	50.00	10.00
c.		Vert. pair, imperf. horiz., type II	250.00	125.00
d.		Double impression	125.00	
e.		Perf. 10 at top or bottom	425.00	—
503	A140	4c brown, Mar. 1917	13.00	20
		dark brown	13.00	20
		orange brown	13.00	20
		yellow brown	13.00	20
		On cover		2.00
		Block of four	52.50	85
		Margin block of 6, P# only	185.00	
b.		Double impression		
		Double transfer	30.00	2.00
504	A140	5c blue, Mar. 1917	9.00	8
		light blue	9.00	8
		dark blue	9.00	8
		On cover		20
		Block of four	36.00	75
		Margin block of 6, P# only	150.00	
a.		Horizontal pair, imperf. between	1,250.	—
		Double transfer	20.00	—
505	A140	5c rose (error)	550.00	400.00
		On cover		1,200.
		Block of 9, middle stamp the error	750.00	600.00
		Block of 12, two middle stamps errors	1,300.	
		Margin block of six 2c stamps (#499), P# 7942	35.00	

(See note under No. 467.)

506	A140	6c red orange, Mar. 1917	15.00	30
		orange	15.00	30
		On cover		2.50
		Block of four	60.00	1.35
		Margin block of 6, P# only	210.00	
a.		Perf. 10 at top or bottom	500.00	250.00
		Double transfer		
507	A140	7c black, Mar. 1917	32.50	1.50
		gray black	32.50	1.50
		intense black	32.50	1.50
		On cover		7.50
		Block of four	132.50	8.50
		Margin block of 6, P# only	325.00	
		Double transfer		
508	A148	8c olive bister, Mar. 1917	13.50	70
		dark olive green	13.50	70
		olive green	13.50	70
		On cover		2.50
		Block of four	55.00	4.00
		Margin block of 6, Impt. & P# & "A"	225.00	
		Margin block of 6, "A" & P#	275.00	
		Margin block of 6, P# only	200.00	
b.		Vertical pair, imperf. between		
c.		Perf. 10 at top or bottom		500.00
509	A148	9c salmon red, Mar. 1917	17.50	2.75
		salmon	17.50	2.75

	On cover		12.50
	Block of four	72.50	14.00
	Margin block of 6, P# only	190.00	
	Double transfer	35.00	4.50
a.	Perf. 10 at top or bottom	—	300.00

510 A148 10c **orange yellow**, *Mar. 1917* 20.00 10
golden yellow 20.00 10
On cover 2.00
Block of four 82.50 75
Margin block of 6, "A" & P# 350.00
Margin block of 6, P# only 250.00

511 A148 11c **light green**, *May 1917* 8.00 3.75
green 8.00 3.75
dark green 9.00 3.75
On cover 8.00
Block of four 33.00 17.50
Margin block of 6, P# only 135.00
Double transfer 15.00 5.00
a. Perf. 10 at top or bottom 650.00 275.00

512 A148 12c **claret brown**, *May 1917* 9.50 45
a. brown carmine 10.00 45
On cover 4.00
Block of four 38.50 3.00
Margin block of 6, P# only 150.00
Double transfer 20.00 3.00
Triple transfer 30.00 5.00
b. Perf. 10 at top or bottom — 300.00

513 A148 13c **apple green**, *Jan. 10, 1919* 9.50 7.00
pale apple green 9.50 7.00
deep apple green 11.50 7.50
On cover 17.50
Block of four 38.00 35.00
Margin block of 6, P# only 140.00

514 A148 15c **gray**, *May 1917* 50.00 1.00
dark gray 50.00 1.00
On cover 25.00
Block of four 205.00 10.00
Margin block of 6, P# only 675.00
Double transfer — —

515 A148 20c **light ultramarine**, *May 1917* 60.00 30
deep ultramarine 62.50 30
gray blue 60.00 30
On cover 60.00
Block of four 245.00 2.00
Margin block of 6, P# only 750.00
b. Vertical pair, imperf. between 325.00
c. Double impression 400.00
Double transfer — —
d. Perf. 10 at top or bottom 1,200. —

516 A148 30c **orange red**, *May 1917* 37.50 95
dark orange red 37.50 95
On cover 125.00
Block of four 155.00 6.00
Margin block of 6, P# only 600.00
Double transfer — —
a. Perf. 10 at top or bottom 850.00 —

517 A148 50c **red violet**, *May 1917* 95.00 65
violet 115.00 65
light violet 120.00 75
On cover 250.00
Block of four 385.00 3.00
Margin block of 6, P# only 1,500.
b. Vertical pair, imperf. between 1,750. 750.00
Double transfer 165.00 2.50
c. Perf. 10 at top or bottom 700.00

518 A148 $1 **violet brown**, *May 1917* 75.00 1.75
violet black 75.00 1.75
b. deep brown 750.00 250.00
On cover 250.00
Block of four 310.00 8.00
Margin block of 4, arrow right or left 320.00
Margin block of 6, Impt. & P# & "A" 1,200.
Double transfer (5782 L. 66) 100.00 2.50

TYPE OF 1908-09 ISSUE

1917   **Wmk. 191**   **Perf. 11**

This is the result of an old stock of No. 344 which was returned to the Bureau in 1917 and perforated with the then current gauge 11.

519 A139 2c **carmine**, *Oct. 10, 1917* 250.00 275.00
On cover 1,750.
Block of four 1,050. —
Margin block of 6, T V, Impt. & P# 2,500.

Franklin — A149

Plates of 100 subjects.

1918, Aug.   **Unwmk.**   **Perf. 11**
523 A149 $2 **orange red & black** 850.00 225.00
red orange & black 850.00 225.00
On cover 2,000.
Block of four 3,450. 950.00
Margin block of 4, arrow 3,550.
Center line block 3,700. 1,050.
Margin block of 8, two P# & arrow 18,500.

---

524 A149 $5 **deep green & black** 350.00 30.00
On cover 1,500.
Block of four 1,500. 125.00
Margin block of 4, arrow 1,550. 130.00
Center line block 1,650. 140.00
Margin block of 8, two P# & arrow 6,000.

For other listing of design A149 see No. 547.

OFFSET PRINTING

Plates of 400, 800 or 1600 subjects in panes of 100 each, as follows:
No. 525-400 and 1600 subjects
No. 526-400, 800 and 1600 subjects
No. 529-400 subjects only
No. 531-400 subjects only
No. 532-400, 800 and 1600 subjects
No. 535-400 subjects only
No. 536-400 and 1600 subjects

TYPES OF 1917-19 ISSUE

1918-20   **Unwmk.**   ***Perf. 11.***
525 A140 1c **gray green**, *Dec. 1918* 2.25 60
emerald 4.00 1.50
On cover 1.25
Block of four 9.25 2.75
Margin block of 6, P# only 30.00
a. 1c dark green 2.75 1.25
c. Horizontal pair, imperf. between 60.00
d. Double impression 15.00 15.00
"Flat nose" — —

TYPE IV

TWO CENTS.
Type IV. Top line of the toga rope is broken.
The shading lines in the toga button are so arranged that the curving of the first and last form "DID".
The line of color in the left "2" is very thin and usually broken.
Used on offset printings only.

TYPE V

Type V. Top line of the toga is complete.
There are five vertical shading lines in the toga button.
The line of color in the left "2" is very thin and usually broken.
The shading dots on the nose are as shown on the diagram.
Used on offset printings only.

TYPE Va

Type Va. Characteristics are the same as type V except in the shading dots of the nose. The third row of dots from the bottom has four dots instead of six. The overall height is ⅓ mm. shorter than type V.
Used on offset printings only.

TYPE VI

Type VI. General characteristics the same as type V except that the line of color in the left "2" is very heavy.
Used on offset printings only.

TYPE VII

Type VII. The line of color in the left "2" is invariably continuous, clearly defined and heavier than in type V or Va but not as heavy as type VI.
An additional vertical row of dots has been added to the upper lip.
Numerous additional dots have been added to the hair on top of the head.
Used on offset printings only.
Dates of issue of types after type IV are not known but official records show the first plate of each type to have been certified as follows:
Type IV, Mar. 6, 1920
Type V, Mar. 20, 1920
Type Va, May 4, 1920
Type VI, June 24, 1920
Type VII, Nov. 3, 1920

526 A140 2c **carmine**, type IV, *Mar. 15, 1920* 32.50 4.00
rose carmine, type IV 32.50 4.00
On cover, type IV 10.00
Block of four, type IV 132.50 18.00
Margin block of 6, P# only, type IV 275.00
Gash on forehead, type IV 45.00 6.50
Malformed "2" at left, type IV (10823 L. R. 93) 45.00 7.50

527 A140 2c **carmine**, type V 17.50 1.00
bright carmine, type V 17.50 1.00
rose carmine, type V 17.50 1.00
On cover 2.00
Block of four, type V 71.00 6.50
Margin block of 6, P# only, type V 150.00
a. Double impression, type V 45.00 10.00
b. Vert. pair, imperf. horiz., type V 600.00
c. Horiz. pair, imperf. vert., type V — —

Line through "2" & "EN", type V	32.50	7.50
528 A140 **2c carmine,** type Va	8.00	15
On cover, type Va		35
Block of four, type Va	32.00	2.00
Block of 6, P# only, type Va	65.00	
Block of 6, monogram over P#	90.00	
c. Double impression, type Va	25.00	
g. Vert. pair, imperf. between	—	
Retouches in "P" of Postage type Va	12.00	—
Retouched on toga, type Va	25.00	—
Variety "CRNTS", type Va	22.50	
528A A140 **2c carmine,** type VI	55.00	1.00
bright carmine, type VI	55.00	1.00
On cover, type VI		3.00
Block of four, type VI	220.00	5.00
Margin block of 6, P# only, type VI	400.00	
Block of 6, monogram over P#	500.00	
d. Double impression, type VI	100.00	
f. Vert. pair, imperf. horiz., type VI	—	
h. Vert. pair, imperf. between		
528B A140 **2c carmine,** type VII	20.00	12
On cover, type VII		18
Block of four, type VII	82.50	1.10
Margin block of 6, P# only, type VII	165.00	
e. Double impression, type VII	45.00	—
Retouched on cheek, type VII	35.00	—

TYPE III

THREE CENTS.
Type III. The top line of the toga rope is strong but the 5th shading line is missing as in type I.
Center shading line of the toga button consists of two dashes with a central dot.
The "P" and "O" of "POSTAGE" are separated by a line of color.
The frame line at the bottom of the vignette is complete.
Used on offset printings only.

TYPE IV

Type IV. The shading lines of the toga rope are complete. The second and fourth shading lines in the toga button are broken in the middle and the third line is continuous with a dot in the center.
The "P" and "O" of "POST AGE" are joined.
The frame line at the bottom of the vignette is broken.
Used on offset printings only.

529 A140 **3c violet,** type III, *March 1918*	3.00	10
light violet, type III	3.00	10
dark violet, type III	3.00	10
On cover, type III		15
Block of four, type III	12.00	55
Margin block of 6, P# only, type III	70.00	
a. Double impression, type III	20.00	—
b. Printed on both sides, type III	350.00	
530 A140 **3c purple,** type IV	70	6
light purple, type IV	70	6
deep purple, type IV	70	6
violet, type IV	70	10
On cover, type IV		10
Block of four, type IV	3.00	30
Margin block of 6, P# only, type IV	12.00	
a. Double impression, type IV	12.50	6.00
b. Printed on both sides, type IV	150.00	

"Blister" under "U.S.," type IV	3.50	—
Recut under "U.S.," type IV	3.50	—

Earliest known use, June 30, 1918.

1918-20   *Imperf.*

Dates of issue of 2c types are not known, but official records show that the first plate of each type known to have been issued imperforate was certified as follows:
Type IV, Mar. 1920
Type V, May 4, 1920
Type Va, May 25, 1920
Type VI, July 26, 1920
Type VII, Dec. 2, 1920

531 A140 **1c green,** *Jan. 1919*	10.00	8.00
gray green	10.00	8.00
On cover		12.50
Block of four	40.00	33.50
Corner margin block of four	42.00	
Margin block of 4, arrow	42.00	35.00
Center line block	75.00	
Margin block of 6, P# only	100.00	
532 A140 **2c carmine rose,** type IV	47.50	27.50
On cover, type IV		35.00
Block of four, type IV	190.00	110.00
Corner margin block of four, type IV	200.00	
Margin block of 4, arrow, type IV	200.00	
Center line block, type IV	230.00	
Margin block of 6, P# only, type IV	350.00	
533 A140 **2c carmine,** type V	235.00	70.00
On cover, type V		95.00
Block of four, type V	950.00	300.00
Corner margin block of 4, type V	1,000.	
Margin block of 4, arrow, type V	1,000.	
Center line block, type V	1,150.	375.00
Margin block of 6, P# only, type V	2,000.	
534 A140 **2c carmine,** type Va	12.50	9.00
carmine rose, type Va	12.50	9.00
On cover, type Va		13.50
Block of four, type Va	50.00	40.00
Corner margin block of four, type Va	51.00	
Margin block of 4, arrow, type Va	51.00	
Center line block, type Va	65.00	
Margin block of 6, P# only, type Va	110.00	
Block of 6, monogram over P#	225.00	
534A A140 **2c carmine,** type VI	42.50	25.00
On cover, type VI		35.00
Block of four, type VI	170.00	110.00
Corner block of four, type VI	175.00	
Block of 4, arrow, type VI	175.00	
Center line block, type VI	210.00	
Block of 6, P# only, type VI	375.00	
534B A140 **2c carmine,** type VII	1,550.	425.00
On cover, type VII		625.00
Block of four, type VII	6,250.	1,800.
Corner margin block of four, type VII	6,300.	
Margin block of 4, arrow, type VII	6,400.	
Center line block, type VII	7,250.	
Margin block of 6, P# only, type VII	12,500.	3,000.

Copies of the 2c type VII with Schermack III vending machine perforations, have been cut down at sides to simulate the rarer No. 534B imperforate.

535 A140 **3c violet,** type IV, *1918*	8.50	6.50
On cover		10.00
Block of four	34.00	27.50
Corner margin block of four	35.00	
Margin block of 4, arrow	35.00	
Center line block	50.00	
Margin block of 6, P# only	70.00	
a. Double impression	80.00	—

CANCELLATIONS.

	Haiti	-

1919   *Perf. 12½*

536 A140 **1c gray green,** *Aug. 1919*	15.00	15.00
On cover		50.00
Block of four	62.50	70.00
Margin block of 6, P# only	200.00	
a. Horiz. pair, imperf. vert.	500.00	

VICTORY ISSUE
Victory of the Allies in World War I.

"Victory" and Flags of Allies — A150

Designed by Charles A. Huston.

FLAT PLATE PRINTING
Plates of 400 subjects in four panes of 100 each.

1919, Mar. 3   Unwmk.   *Perf. 11*

537 A150 **3c violet**	11.00	4.25
On cover		6.00
Block of four	45.00	17.50
Margin block of 6, P# only	150.00	
a. deep red violet	325.00	40.00
On cover		150.00
Block of four	1,350.	175.00
Margin block of 6, P# only	3,000.	
b. light reddish violet	11.00	4.25
c. red violet	40.00	11.00
Double transfer		

REGULAR ISSUE
ROTARY PRESS PRINTINGS
(See note over No. 448.)

1919   Unwmk.   *Perf. 11x10*
Issued in sheets of 170 stamps (coil waste).
Stamp designs 19½ to 20mm. wide by 22 to 22¼mm. high.

538 A140 **1c green,** *June 1919*	10.00	9.00
yellowish green	10.00	9.00
bluish green	10.00	9.00
On cover		20.00
Block of four	41.00	37.50
Margin block of 4, P# & "S 30"	100.00	
Margin block of 4, P# only	110.00	
Margin block of 4, star & P#	135.00	
a. Vert. pair, imperf. horiz.	50.00	50.00
a. Margin block of 4, P# only	750.00	
Double transfer	25.00	20.00
539 A140 **2c carmine rose,** type II	2,350.	750.00
On cover, type II		—
Block of four, type II	9,500.	
Margin block of 4, type II, P# & "S 20"	15,000.	

(See note after No. 455)

540 A140 **2c carmine rose,** type III, *June 14, 1919*	11.00	9.00
carmine	11.00	9.00
On cover, type III		22.50
Block of four, type III	45.00	37.50
Margin block of 4, type III, P# & "S 30"	110.00	
Margin block of 4, type III, P# & "S 30" inverted	650.00	
Margin block of 4, type III, P# only	115.00	
Margin block of 4, type III, star & P#	150.00	
a. Vert. pair, imperf. horiz., type III	50.00	50.00
a. Margin block of 4, type III, P# only	500.00	
a. Margin block of 4, type III, Star & P#	550.00	
b. Horiz. pair, imperf. vert., type III	550.00	
Double transfer, type III	30.00	30.00
541 A140 **3c violet,** type II, *June 1919*	37.50	35.00
gray violet, type II	37.50	35.00
On cover		90.00
Block of four	155.00	145.00
Margin block of 4, P# only	400.00	

1920, May 26   *Perf. 10x11*
Plates of 400 subjects in four panes of 100 each.
Stamp design 19mm. wide by 22½ to 22¾mm. high.

542 A140 **1c green**	11.00	1.00
bluish green	11.00	1.00
On cover		5.00
Block of four	44.00	6.00
Vertical margin block of 6, P# opposite center horizontal row	175.00	

1921, May   *Perf. 10*
Plates of 400 subjects in four panes of 100 each.
Stamp design 19mm. wide by 22½ mm. high.

543 A140 **1c green**	60	6
deep green	60	6
On cover		10
Block of four	2.40	25
Vertical margin block of 6, P# opposite center horizontal row	45.00	
Corner margin block of 4, P# only	20.00	
a. Horizontal pair, imperf. between	750.00	
Double transfer	—	—
Triple transfer	—	—

1923   *Perf. 11*
Stamp design 19mm. wide by 22½ mm. high.

544 A140 **1c green**	6,500.	1,750.
On cover		2,500.

1921, May
Issued in sheets of 170 stamps (coil waste).
Stamp designs 19½ to 20mm. wide by 22mm. high.

545 A140 **1c green**	150.00	125.00

	yellowish green	150.00	125.00
	On cover		1,500.
	Block of four	610.00	550.00
	Margin block of 4, P# & "S 30"	1,100.	
	Margin block of 4, P# only	1,150.	
	Margin block of 4, star & P#	1,200.	
546 A140 2c	carmine rose, type III	100.00	90.00
	deep carmine rose	100.00	90.00
	On cover		500.00
	Block of four	410.00	400.00
	Margin block of 4, P# & "S 30"	850.00	
	Margin block of 4, P# only	875.00	
	Margin block of 4, star & P#	900.00	
a.	Perf. 10 on left side	350.00	
	Recut in hair	140.00	120.00

FLAT PLATE PRINTING
Plates of 100 subjects

1920, Nov. 1   *Perf. 11*

547 A149 $2	carmine & black	325.00	40.00
	lake & black	325.00	40.00
	On cover (commercial)		750.00
	On flown cover (philatelic)		250.00
	Block of four	1,350.	165.00
	Margin block of 4, arrow	1,400.	
	Center line block	1,700.	—
	Margin block of 8, two P#, & arrow	6,000.	

PILGRIM TERCENTENARY ISSUE
Issued to commemorate the tercentenary of the Landing of the Pilgrims at Plymouth, Mass.

The "Mayflower" A151

Landing of the Pilgrims A152

Signing of the Compact A153

Designed by Charles A. Huston.

Plates of 280 subjects in four panes of 70 each.

1920, Dec. 21   **Unwmk.**   *Perf. 11*

548 A151 1c	green	4.50	3.00
	dark green	4.50	3.00
	On cover		4.00
	Block of four	18.00	13.00
	Margin block of 6, P# only	55.00	
	Double transfer	—	—
549 A152 2c	carmine rose	8.50	2.25
	carmine	8.50	2.25
	rose	8.50	2.25
	On cover		2.75
	Block of four	34.00	9.25
	Margin block of 6, P# only	80.00	

CANCELLATIONS.
	China	
		-
550 A153 5c	deep blue	52.50	18.50
	dark blue	52.50	18.50
	On cover		25.00
	Block of four	210.00	75.00
	Margin block of 6, P# only	650.00	

REGULAR ISSUE

Nathan Hale — A154

Franklin — A155

Warren G. Harding — A156

Washington — A157

Lincoln — A158

Martha Washington — A159

Theodore Roosevelt — A160

Garfield — A161

McKinley — A162

Grant — A163

Jefferson — A164

Monroe — A165

Demand, as well as supply, determines a stamp's market value. One is as important as the other.

Hayes — A166

Cleveland — A167

American Indian — A168

Statue of Liberty — A169

Golden Gate — A170

Niagara Falls — A171

Buffalo — A172

Arlington Amphitheater A173

Lincoln Memorial — A174

United States Capitol — A175

Head of Freedom Statue, Capitol Dome — A176

Plates of 400 subjects in four panes of 100 each for all values 1c to 50c inclusive.

Plates of 200 subjects for $1 and $2. The sheets were cut along the horizontal guide line into two panes, upper and lower, of 100 subjects each.

Plates of 100 subjects for the $5 denomination, and sheets of 100 subjects were issued intact.

The Bureau of Engraving and Printing in 1925 in experimenting to overcome the loss due to uneven perforations, produced what is known as the "Star Plate". The vertical rows of designs on these plates are spaced 3 mm. apart in place of 2¾ mm. as on the regular plates. These plates were identified with a star added to the plate number.

Designed by Charles Aubrey Huston.

FLAT PLATE PRINTINGS

1922-25		Unwmk.		Perf. 11	
551	A154	½c **olive brown,** *Apr. 4, 1925*	15	6	
		pale olive brown	15	6	
		deep olive brown	15	6	
		Block of four	60	35	
		Margin block of 6, P# only	7.00		
		"Cap" on fraction bar (Pl. 17041)	75	25	
552	A155	1c **deep green,** *Jan. 17, 1923*	1.75	5	
		green	1.75	5	
		pale green	1.75	5	
		Block of four	7.00	35	
		Margin block of 6, P# only	25.00		
a.		Booklet pane of six, *Aug. 11, 1923*	5.50	50	
		Double transfer	6.00	—	
553	A156	1½c **yellow brown,** *Mar. 19, 1925*	3.50	20	
		pale yellow brown	3.50	20	
		brown	3.50	20	
		Block of four	14.00	1.00	
		Margin block of 6, P# only	40.00	2.25	
		Double transfer	—	—	
554	A157	2c **carmine,** *Jan. 15, 1923*	1.75	5	
		light carmine	1.75	5	
		Block of four	7.00	20	
		Margin block of 6, P# only	25.00		
		Margin block of 6, P# & small 5 point star, top only	600.00		
		Margin block of 6, P# & large 5 point star, side only	100.00		
		Same, large 5-pt. star, top	750.00		
		Same, large 6-pt. star, top	1,000.00		
		Same, large 6-pt. star, side only (Pl. 17196)	1,250.		
a.		Horiz. pair, imperf. vert	175.00		
b.		Vert. pair, imperf. horiz.	500.00		
c.		Booklet pane of six, *Feb. 10, 1923*	7.00	1.00	
		Double transfer	4.00	1.00	
d.		Perf. 10 at top or bottom	—		

555	A158	3c **violet,** *Feb. 12, 1923*	21.00	1.25	
		deep violet	21.00	1.25	
		dark violet	21.00	1.25	
		red violet	21.00	1.25	
		bright violet	21.00	1.25	
		Block of four	85.00	5.25	
		Margin block of 6, P# only	210.00		
556	A159	4c **yellow brown,** *Jan. 15, 1923*	22.50	20	
		brown	22.50	20	
		Block of four	90.00	1.35	
		Margin block of 6, P# only	225.00		
a.		Vert. pair, imperf. horiz.	—		
		Double transfer	—		
b.		Perf. 10 at top or bottom	425.00	—	
557	A160	5c **dark blue,** *Oct. 27, 1922*	22.50	8	
		deep blue	22.50	8	
		Block of four	90.00	75	
		Margin block of 6, P# only	250.00		
a.		Imperf., pair	700.00		
b.		Horiz. pair, imperf. vert.	—		
		Double transfer (15571 U.L. 86)	—		
c.		Perf. 10 at top or bottom	—	375.00	
558	A161	6c **red orange,** *Nov. 20, 1922*	40.00	85	
		pale red orange	40.00	85	
		Block of four	160.00	4.25	
		Margin block of 6, P# only	425.00		
		Double transfer (Plate 14169 L. R. 60 and 70)	65.00	3.50	
		Same, recut	65.00	3.50	
559	A162	7c **black,** *May 1, 1923*	10.00	75	
		gray black	10.00	75	
		Block of four	40.00	3.00	
		Margin block of 6, P# only	90.00		
		Double transfer	—	—	
560	A163	8c **olive green,** *May 1, 1923*	55.00	85	
		pale olive green	55.00	85	
		Block of four	220.00	4.25	
		Margin block of 6, P# only	725.00		
		Margin block of 6, P# & large 5 point star, side only	—		
		Double transfer	—		
561	A164	9c **rose,** *Jan. 15, 1923*	18.00	1.25	
		pale rose	18.00	1.25	
		Block of four	72.00	6.00	
		Margin block of 6, P# only	210.00		
		Double transfer	—		
562	A165	10c **orange,** *Jan. 15, 1923*	24.00	10	
		pale orange	24.00	10	
		Block of four	96.00	50	
		Margin block of 6, P# only	300.00		
a.		Vert. pair, imperf. horiz.	500.00		
b.		Imperf., pair	650.00		
c.		Perf. 10 at top or bottom	—	600.00	
563	A166	11c **light blue,** *Oct. 4, 1922*	2.00	25	
		greenish blue	2.00	25	
		light bluish green	2.00	25	
		light yellow green	2.00	40	
		Block of four	8.00	1.25	
		Margin block of 6, P# only	35.00		
d.		Imperf., pair	—		
564	A167	12c **brown violet,** *Mar. 20, 1923*	8.50	8	
		deep brown violet	8.50	8	
		Block of four	34.00	80	
		Margin block of 6, P# only	90.00		
		Margin block of 6, P# & large 5 point star, side only	150.00		
		Margin block of 6, P# & large 6 point star, side only	300.00		
a.		Horiz. pair, imperf. vert.	650.00		
b.		Imperf., pair	—		
		Double transfer, (14404 U.L. 73 & 74)	20.00	1.00	
565	A168	14c **blue,** *May 1, 1923*	5.00	85	
		deep blue	5.00	85	
		Block of four	20.00	3.75	
		Margin block of 6, P# only	60.00		
		Double transfer	—		

Horizontal pairs of No. 565 are known with spacings up to 3¾mm. instead of 2mm. between. These are from the 5th and 6th vertical rows of the upper right pane of Plate 14515 and also between stamps Nos. 3 and 4 of the same pane. A plate block of Pl. 14512 is known with 3 mm. spacing.

566	A169	15c **gray,** *Nov. 11, 1922*	27.50	6	
		light gray	27.50	6	
		Block of four	110.00	40	
		Margin block of 6, P# only	300.00		
		Margin block of 6, P# & large 5 point star, side only	500.00		
567	A170	20c **carmine rose,** *May 1, 1923*	27.50	6	
		deep carmine rose	27.50	6	
		Block of four	110.00	50	
		Margin block of 6, P# only	300.00		
		Margin block of 6, P# & large 5 point star, side only	700.00		
a.		Horiz. pair, imperf. vert.	750.00		
		Double transfer (Pl. 18925)	60.00	2.50	
568	A171	25c **yellow green,** *Nov. 11, 1922*	25.00	50	
		green	25.00	50	
		deep green	25.00	50	
		Block of four	100.00	2.25	
		Margin block of 6, P# only	250.00		
b.		Vert. pair, imperf. horiz.	850.00		
		Perf. 10 at one side	—		
		Double transfer	—	—	
569	A172	30c **olive brown,** *Mar. 20, 1923*	45.00	35	
		Block of four	180.00	2.75	
		Margin block of 6, P# only	450.00		
		Double transfer (16065 U.R. 52)	65.00	2.50	
570	A173	50c **lilac,** *Nov. 11, 1922*	75.00	12	
		dull lilac	75.00	12	
		Block of four	300.00	75	
		Margin block of 6, P# only	900.00		
571	A174	$1 **violet black,** *Feb. 12, 1923*	50.00	45	
		violet brown	50.00	45	
		Block of four	200.00	2.00	

Margin block of 4, arrow, top
 or bottom   210.00
Margin block of 6, P# only   500.00
Double transfers, Pl. 18682 L
 30 and Pl. 18682   110.00   2.50
572 A175   **$2 deep blue**, *Mar. 20, 1923*   135.00   11.00
 Block of four   550.00   45.00
 Margin block of 4, arrow, top
  or bottom   560.00
 Margin block of 6, P# only   1,650.
573 A176   **$5 carmine & blue**, *Mar. 20,*
  1923   325.00   15.00
 carmine lake & dark blue   325.00   15.00
 Block of four   1,300.00   65.00
 Margin block of 4, arrow   1,250.00
 Center line block   1,300.00   *85.00*
 Margin block of 8, two P# &
  arrow   4,000.00

For other listings of perforated stamps of designs A154 to A176 see
 Nos. 578 & 579, Perf. 11x10
 Nos. 581 to 591, Perf. 10
 Nos. 594 to 596, Perf. 11
 Nos. 632 to 642, 653, 692 to 696, Perf. 11x10½
 Nos. 697 to 701, Perf. 10½x11
 This series also includes Nos. 622-623 (perf. 11).

1923-25   *Imperf.*
575 A155   1c **green**, *March 20, 1923*   10.00   3.50
 deep green   10.00   3.50
 Corner margin block of four   41.00
 Margin block of 4, arrow   42.50
 Center line block   50.00
 Margin block of 6, P# only   100.00
576 A156   1½c **yellow brown**, *Apr. 4, 1925*   2.25   1.75
 pale yellow brown   2.25   1.75
 brown   2.25   1.75
 Corner margin block of four   9.50
 Margin block of 4, arrow   10.00
 Center line block   17.50   12.50
 Margin block of 6, P# only   30.00
 Double transfer   —   —

The 1½c A156 Rotary press imperforate is listed as No. 631.

577 A157   2c **carmine**   2.50   2.00
 light carmine   2.50   2.00
 Block of four   10.00   8.50
 Corner margin block of four   10.50
 Margin block of 4, arrow   11.00
 Center line block   20.00
 Margin block of 6, P# only   30.00
 Margin block of 6, P# & large
  5 point star   110.00

ROTARY PRESS PRINTINGS
(See note over No. 448)

1923-26   *Perf. 11x10*
Issued in sheets of 70 or 100 stamps, coil waste.
Stamp designs: 19¾x22¼mm.
578 A155   1c **green**   80.00   65.00
 On cover   175.00
 Margin block of 4, star & P#   750.00
579 A157   2c **carmine**   57.50   50.00
 deep carmine   57.50   50.00
 On cover   200.00
 Margin block of 4, star & P#   450.00
 Recut in eye, plate 14731   75.00   75.00

Perf. 10
Plates of 400 subjects in four panes of 100 each.
Stamp designs: 19x22½mm.
581 A155   1c **green**, *Apr. 21, 1923*   10.00   65
 yellow green   10.00   65
 pale green   10.00   65
 Block of four   40.00   3.00
 Margin block of 4, P# only   125.00
582 A156   1½c **brown**, *Mar. 19, 1925*   5.00   60
 dark brown   5.00   60
 Block of four   20.00   2.75
 Margin block of 4, P# only   45.00
 Pair with full horiz. gutter
  btwn.   *135.00*
 Pair with full vert. gutter
  btwn.   *175.00*

No. 582 was available in full sheets of 400 subjects but was not regularly issued in that form.

583 A157   2c **carmine**, *Apr. 14, 1924*   2.50   5
 deep carmine   2.50   5
 Block of four   10.00   50
 Margin block of 4, P# only   30.00
a.   Booklet pane of six, *Aug. 11, 1926*   75.00   *25.00*
584 A158   3c **violet**, *Aug. 1, 1925*   27.50   1.75
 Block of four   110.00   8.00
 Margin block of 4, P# only   250.00
585 A159   4c **yellow brown**, *Mar. 1925*   17.00   40
 deep yellow brown   17.00   40
 Block of four   68.00   2.00
 Margin block of 4, P# only   175.00
586 A160   5c **blue**, *Dec. 1924*   16.00   18
 deep blue   16.00   18
 Block of four   64.00   90
 Margin block of 4, P# only   165.00
a.   Horizontal pair, imperf. between   —
 Double transfer   —
587 A161   6c **red orange**, *Mar. 1925*   7.50   40
 pale red orange   7.50   40
 Block of four   30.00   2.25
 Margin block of 4, P# only   70.00
588 A162   7c **black**, *May 29, 1926*   11.50   5.00
 Block of four   46.00   25.00
 Margin block of 4, P# only   110.00
589 A163   8c **olive green**, *May 29, 1926*   24.00   3.00

---

 pale olive green   24.00   3.00
 Block of four   96.00   14.00
 Margin block of 4, P# only   250.00
590 A164   9c **rose**, *May 29, 1926*   5.00   2.25
 Block of four   20.00   11.00
 Margin block of 4, P# only   45.00
591 A165   10c **orange**, *June 8, 1925*   75.00   10
 Block of four   300.00   70
 Margin block of 4, P# only   675.00

Perf. 11
Issued in sheets of 70 or 100 stamps, coil waste of Nos. 597, 599.
Stamp designs approximately 19¾x22¼mm.
594 A155   1c **green**   7,000.   2,500.
 On cover   3,250.
595 A157   2c **carmine**   225.00   185.00
 deep carmine   200.00   185.00
 On cover   400.00
 Margin block of 4, star & P#   1,500.
 Recut in eye, plate 14731   —

Perf. 11
Stamp design approximately 19¼x22¾mm.
596 A155   1c **green**   13,500.
Most copies of No. 596 carry the Bureau precancel "Kansas City, Mo."

COIL STAMPS, ROTARY PRESS
1923-29   *Perf. 10 Vertically*
Stamp designs aproximately 19¾x22¼mm.
597 A155   1c **green**, *July 18, 1923*   35   6
 yellow green   35   6
 Pair   75   12
 Joint line pair   2.25   25
 Gripper cracks   3.00   1.00
 Double transfer   3.00   1.00
598 A156   1½c **brown**, *Mar. 19, 1925*   75   10
 deep brown   75   10
 Pair   1.60   25
 Joint line pair   5.25   50

TYPE I

TYPE II

TYPE I   TYPE II

TYPE I-No heavy hair lines at top center of head. Outline of left acanthus scroll generally faint at top and toward base at left side.
TYPE II-Three heavy hair lines at top center of head; two being outstanding in the white area. Outline of left acanthus scroll very strong and clearly defined at top (under left edge of lettered panel) and at lower curve (above and to left of numeral oval). This type appears only on Nos. 599A and 634A.

599 A157   2c **carmine**, type I, *Jan. 1923*   30   5
 deep carmine, type I   30   5
 Pair, type I   65   12
 Joint line pair, type I   2.00   20
 Double transfer, type I   2.00   1.00
 Gripper cracks, type I   2.50   2.50
599A A157   2c **carmine**, type II, *Mar. 1929*   140.00   12.00
 Pair, type II   290.00   25.00
 Joint line pair, type II   800.00   60.00
 Joint line pair, types I & II   900.00   120.00
600 A158   3c **violet**, *May 10, 1924*   8.00   8
 deep violet   8.00   8
 Pair   17.00   20
 Joint line pair   35.00   85
 Cracked plate   —
601 A159   4c **yellow brown**, *Aug. 5, 1923*   4.00   40
 brown   4.00   40
 Pair   8.50

 Joint line pair   27.50   2.00
602 A160   5c **dark blue**, *Mar. 5, 1924*   1.50   18
 Pair   3.25   40
 Joint line pair   10.00   60
603 A165   10c **orange**, *Dec. 1, 1924*   3.50   8
 Pair   7.50   25
 Joint line pair   27.50   1.00

The 6c design A161 coil stamp is listed as No. 723.

1923-25   *Perf. 10 Horizontally*
Stamp designs 19¼-19½mm. wide by 22-22½mm. high.
604 A155   1c **yellow green**   25   8
 green, *July 19, 1924*   25   10
 Pair   55   20
 Joint line pair   3.00   35
605 A156   1½c **yellow brown**, *May 9, 1925*   30   15
 brown   30   15
 Pair   65   35
 Joint line pair   2.75   50
606 A157   2c **carmine**, *Dec. 31, 1925*   30   12
 Pair   65   25
 Joint line pair   2.00   35
 Cracked plate   7.50   3.50

HARDING MEMORIAL ISSUE.
Issued as a tribute to the memory of President Warren G. Harding, who died in San Francisco, Aug. 2, 1923.

Plates of 400 subjects in four panes of 100 each.

Warren Gamaliel
Harding — A177

FLAT PLATE PRINTINGS
Stamp designs 19¼mm. wide by 22¼mm. high.
1923   *Perf. 11*
610 A177   2c **black**, *Sept. 1, 1923*   75   10
 intense black   75   10
 grayish black   75   10
 Margin block of 6, P#   30.00   —
a.   Horiz. pair, imperf. vert.   800.00
 Double transfer   3.00   50

Imperf
611 A177   2c **black**, *Nov. 15, 1923*   10.00   6.00
 Corner margin block of four   42.50   25.00
 Margin block of 4, arrow   42.50   26.00
 Center line block   85.00   55.00
 Margin block of 6, P#   140.00   —

ROTARY PRESS PRINTINGS
Stamp designs 19¼mm. wide by 22¾mm. high.
Perf. 10
612 A177   2c **black**, *Sept. 12, 1923*   18.00   2.50
 gray black   18.00   2.50
 Margin block of 4, P#   375.00
 Pair with full vertical gutter
  between   *350.00*

Perf. 11
613 A177   2c **black**   13,500.

HUGUENOT-WALLOON TERCENTENARY ISSUE
Issued to commemorate the 300th anniversary of the settling of the Walloons, and in honor of the Huguenots.

Ship "Nieu Nederland" — A178

Walloons Landing at Fort Orange (Albany) — A179

Jan Ribault Monument at Mayport, Fla. — A180

Designed by Charles Aubrey Huston.

FLAT PLATE PRINTINGS
Plates of 200 subjects in four panes of 50 each.

1924, May 1				Perf. 11	
614	A178	1c	**dark green**	4.00	4.00
			green	4.00	4.00
			Margin block of 6, P#	50.00	—
			Double transfer	12.00	9.00
615	A179	2c	**carmine rose**	7.00	3.50
			dark carmine rose	7.00	3.50
			Margin block of 6, P#	85.00	—
			Double transfer	17.50	6.00
616	A180	5c	**dark blue**	40.00	22.50
			deep blue	40.00	22.50
			Margin block of 6, P#	450.00	—
			Added line at bottom of white circle around right numeral, so-called "broken circle" (15754 UR 2, 3, 4, 5)	75.00	27.50

LEXINGTON-CONCORD ISSUE

Issued to commemorate the 150th anniversary of the Battle of Lexington-Concord.

Washington at Cambridge — A181

"Birth of Liberty," by Henry Sandham — A182

A little time given to the study of the arrangement of the Scott Catalogue can make it easier to use effectively.

The Minute Man, by Daniel Chester French — A183

Plates of 200 subjects in four panes of 50 each.

1925, Apr. 4				Perf. 11	
617	A181	1c	**deep green**	3.75	3.75
			green	3.75	3.75
			Margin block of 6, P#	50.00	—
618	A182	2c	**carmine rose**	7.00	7.00
			pale carmine rose	7.00	7.00
			Margin block of 6, P#	95.00	—
619	A183	5c	**dark blue**	35.00	20.00
			blue	35.00	20.00
			Margin block of 6, P#	400.00	—
			Line over head (16807 L.L. 48)	75.00	30.00

NORSE-AMERICAN ISSUE

Issued to commemorate the centenary of the arrival in New York, on Oct. 9, 1825, of the sloop "Restaurationen" with the first group of immigrants from Norway.

Sloop "Restaurationen" A184

Viking Ship — A185

Designed by Charles Aubrey Huston.

Plates of 100 subjects.

1925, May 18				Perf. 11	
620	A184	2c	**carmine & black**	6.00	5.00
			deep carmine & black	6.00	5.00
			Margin block of 4, arrow	29.00	
			Center line block	35.00	
			Margin block of 8, two P# & arrow	225.00	—
			Margin block of 8, carmine P# & arrow; black P# omitted	2,750.	—
621	A185	5c	**dark blue & black**	22.50	21.00
			Margin block of 4, arrow	92.50	
			Center line block	110.00	
			Margin block of 8, two P# & arrow	750.00	—

REGULAR ISSUE

Benjamin Harrison — A186

Woodrow Wilson — A187

Plates of 400 subjects in four panes of 100 each.

1925-26				Perf. 11	
622	A186	13c	**green,** Jan. 11, 1926	15.00	65
			light green	15.00	65
			Margin block of 6, P# only	200.00	—
			Margin block of 6, P# & large 5 point star	1,250.	—
623	A187	17c	**black,** Dec. 28, 1925	22.50	35
			gray black	22.50	35
			Margin block of 6, P# only	250.00	—

SESQUICENTENNIAL EXPOSITION ISSUE

Issued in connection with the Sesquicentennial Exposition held at Philadelphia, Pa., from June 1 to Dec. 1, 1926, to commemorate the 150th anniversary of the Declaration of Independence.

Liberty Bell — A188

Designed by Charles Aubrey Huston.

Plates of 200 subjects in four panes of 50 each.

1926				Perf. 11	
627	A188	2c	**carmine rose,** May 10, 1926	4.00	60
			On cover, Expo. station canc.		3.50
			Margin block of 6, P#	50.00	—
			Double transfer	—	

ERICSSON MEMORIAL ISSUE

Issued as a memorial to John Ericsson, builder of the "Monitor" and in connection with the unveiling of his statue by the Crown Prince of Sweden at Washington, D. C., May 29, 1926.

Statue of John Ericsson — A189

Designed by Charles Aubrey Huston.

Plates of 200 subjects in four panes of 50 each.

1926				Perf. 11	
628	A189	5c	**gray lilac,** May 29, 1926	9.00	5.00
			Margin block of 6, P#	110.00	

BATTLE OF WHITE PLAINS ISSUE

Issued to commemorate the 150th anniversary of the Battle of White Plains, N. Y.

Alexander
Hamilton's
Battery — A190

Designed by Charles Aubrey Huston.

Plates of 400 subjects in four panes of 100 each.

1926				Perf. 11	
629	A190	2c	carmine rose, Oct. 18, 1926	2.75	2.25
			Margin block of 6, P#	50.00	—
a.			Vertical pair, imperf. between	1,250.	

INTERNATIONAL PHILATELIC EXHIBITION ISSUE
SOUVENIR SHEET

A190a

Plates of 100 subjects in four panes of 25 each,
separated by one
inch wide gutters with central guide lines.

1926, Oct. 18				Perf. 11	
630	A190a	2c	carmine rose, sheet of 25	500.00	425.00
			Dot over first "S" of "States"		
			18774 LL9 or 18773 LL11,		
			sheet	525.00	450.00

Issued in sheets measuring 158-160 1/4x136-146 1/2mm. containing 25 stamps with inscription "International Philatelic Exhibition, Oct. 16 to 23, 1926" in top margin. Issued to commemorate the International Philatelic Exhibition in New York, Oct. 16 to 23, 1926.

REGULAR ISSUE
ROTARY PRESS PRINTINGS
(See note over No. 448.)
Plates of 400 subjects in four panes of 100 each.
Stamp designs 18 1/2 to 19 mm. wide by 22 1/2 mm. high.

1926				Imperf.	
631	A156	1 1/2c	yellow brown, Aug. 27, 1926	2.25	2.10
			light brown	2.25	2.10
			Gutter block of four	10.00	9.00
			Margin block with dash (left, right, top or bottom)	11.00	9.25
			Center block with crossed gutters and dashes	25.00	
			Margin block of 4, P#	70.00	—
			Without gum breaker ridges	3.25	—

1926-34				Perf. 11x10 1/2	
632	A155	1c	green, June 10, 1927	15	5
			yellow green	15	5
			Margin block of 4, P#	2.00	—
a.			Booklet pane of six, Nov. 2, 1927	4.00	25
			Block of 4 with full gutter btwn.	150.00	
b.			Vertical pair, imperf. between	175.00	100.00
			Cracked plate		
633	A156	1 1/2c	yellow brown, May 17, 1927	2.50	8
			deep brown	2.50	8
			Block of four	10.00	75
			Margin block of 4, P#	90.00	—
634	A157	2c	carmine, type I, Dec. 10, 1926	15	5
			Margin block of 4, type I, P# opposite corner stamp	1.20	—
			Vertical margin block of 10, P# opposite third horizontal row from top or bottom (Experimental Electric Eye plates)	5.00	—
			Margin block of 4, Electric Eye marking	65	25
			Pair with full vertical gutter between	200.00	
b.			2c carmine lake, type I	3.00	1.00
b.			Margin block of 4, P#	30.00	
c.			Horizontal pair, type I, imperf. between	2,000.	
d.			Booklet pane of six, type I, Feb. 25, 1927	1.00	15

Recut face, type I, 20234
LL58 —

No. 634, Type I, exists on a thin, tough experimental paper.

634A	A157	2c	carmine, type II, Dec. 1928	350.00	25.00
			On cover		50.00
			Margin block of 4, type II, P#	2,100.	—
			Pair with full horiz. gutter btwn.	1,000.	—
			Pair with full vert. gutter btwn.	1,000.	—

No. 634A, Type II, was available in full sheet of 400 subjects but was not regularly issued in that form.

635	A158	3c	violet, Feb. 3, 1927	50	5
			Margin block of 4, P#	7.00	—
a.			3c bright violet, Feb. 7, 1934 re-issue, Plates 21185 & 21186	30	5
a.			Margin block of 4, P#	4.00	—
a.			Gripper cracks	4.00	2.00
636	A159	4c	yellow brown, May 17, 1927	3.50	8
			Block of four	14.00	75
			Margin block of 4, P#	100.00	—
			Pair with full vert. gutter btwn.	200.00	
637	A160	5c	dark blue, Mar. 24, 1927	3.00	5
			Margin block of 4, P#	21.00	—
			Pair with full vert. gutter btwn.	275.00	
			Double transfer	—	—
638	A161	6c	red orange, July 27, 1927	3.00	5
			Margin block of 4, P#	21.00	—
			Pair with full horiz. gutter btwn.	—	
			Pair with full vert. gutter btwn.	200.00	
639	A162	7c	black, Mar. 24, 1927	3.00	8
			Margin block of 4, P#	21.00	—
a.			Vertical pair, imperf. between	125.00	80.00
640	A163	8c	olive green, June 10, 1927	3.00	5
			olive bister	3.00	5
			Margin block of 4, P#	21.00	—
641	A164	9c	orange red, 1931	3.00	5
			salmon rose	3.00	5
			rose, May 17, 1927	3.00	5
			Margin block of 4, P#	21.00	—
			Pair with full vert. gutter btwn.	—	
642	A165	10c	orange, Feb. 3, 1927	5.50	5
			Margin block of 4, P#	35.00	—
			Double transfer	—	—

The 2c, 5c and 8c imperf. (dry print) are printer's waste. See No. 653.

VERMONT SESQUICENTENNIAL ISSUE
Battle of Bennington, 150th anniv. and State independence.

Green Mountain
Boy — A191

FLAT PLATE PRINTING
Plates of 400 subjects in four panes of 100 each.

1927				Perf. 11	
643	A191	2c	carmine rose, Aug. 3, 1927	1.50	1.50
			Margin block of 6, P#	45.00	—

BURGOYNE CAMPAIGN ISSUE
Issued to commemorate the Battles of Bennington, Oriskany, Fort Stanwix and Saratoga.

Surrender of Gen. John Burgoyne — A192

Plates of 200 subjects in four panes of 50 each.

1927				Perf. 11	
644	A192	2c	carmine rose, Aug. 3, 1927	5.00	3.75
			Margin block of 6, P#	60.00	—

VALLEY FORGE ISSUE
Issued to commemorate the 150th anniversary of Washingtons encampment at Valley Forge, Pa.

Washington at
Prayer — A193

Plates of 400 subjects in four panes of 100 each.

1928				Perf. 11	
645	A193	2c	carmine rose, May 26, 1928	1.10	65
			Margin block of 6, P#	40.00	—

BATTLE OF MONMOUTH ISSUE
Issued to commemorate the 150th anniversary of the Battle of Monmouth, N.J., and a memorial to Molly Pitcher, the heroine of the battle.

No. 634 Overprinted   **MOLLY PITCHER**

ROTARY PRESS PRINTING

1928				Perf. 11x10 1/2	
646	A157	2c	carmine, Oct. 20, 1928	1.50	1.50
			Margin block of 4, P#	40.00	—
			Wide spacing, vert. pair	35.00	—

The normal space between a vertical pair of the overprints is 18mm., but pairs are known with the space measuring 28mm.

HAWAII SESQUICENTENNIAL ISSUE
Issued to commemorate the Sesquicentennial Celebration of the discovery of the Hawaiian Islands.

Nos. 634 and 637 Overprinted   **HAWAII 1778 - 1928**

ROTARY PRESS PRINTING

1928, Aug. 13				Perf. 11x10 1/2	
647	A157	2c	carmine	7.00	6.00
			Margin block of 4, P#	150.00	—
			Wide spacing, vert. pair	125.00	
648	A160	5c	dark blue	17.50	15.00
			Margin block of 4, P#	300.00	—

Nos. 647-648 were sold at post offices in Hawaii and at the Postal Agency in Washington, D.C. They were valid throughout the nation.

Normally the overprints were placed 18mm. apart vertically, but pairs exist with a space of 28mm. between the overprints.

AERONAUTICS CONFERENCE ISSUE
Issued in commemoration of the International Civil Aeronautics Conference at Washington, D.C., Dec. 12 to 14, 1928, and of the twenty-fifth anniversary of the first airplane flight by the Wright Brothers, Dec. 17, 1903.

Wright Airplane — A194

Globe and Airplane — A195

FLAT PLATE PRINTING

Plates of 200 subjects in four panes of 50 each.

1928, Dec. 12			Perf. 11	
649 A194	2c	**carmine rose**	1.50	1.40
		Margin block of 6, P#	17.50	—
650 A195	5c	**blue**	8.00	5.00
		Margin block of 6, P#	90.00	—
		Plate flaw "prairie dog" (19658 L.L. 50)	50.00	20.00

GEORGE ROGERS CLARK ISSUE

Issued to commemorate the 150th anniversary of the surrender of Fort Sackville, the present site of Vincennes, Ind., to George Rogers Clark.

Surrender of Fort Sackville — A196

Plates of 100 subjects in two panes of 50 each.

1929			Perf. 11	
651 A196	2c	**carmine & black,** *Feb. 25, 1929*	85	80
		Margin block of 4, arrow (line only) right or left	3.50	
		Margin block of 6, two P# & "Top"	16.00	—
		Margin block of 10, red P# only	—	—
		Double transfer (19721 R. 14, 29 & 44)	7.50	5.00

REGULAR ISSUE
Type of 1922-26 Issue
ROTARY PRESS PRINTING

Plates of 400 subjects in four panes of 100 each.

1929			Perf. 11x10½	
653 A154	½c	**olive brown,** *May 25, 1929*	5	5
		Damaged plate, (19652 L.L. 72)	1.50	75
		Retouched plate, (19652 L.L. 72)	1.50	75
		Margin block of 4, P#	1.00	—
		Pair with full horizontal gutter between	150.00	

ELECTRIC LIGHT"S GOLDEN JUBILEE ISSUE

Issued to commemorate the 50th anniversary of the invention of the first incandescent electric lamp by Thomas Alva Edison on October 21, 1879.

Edison's First
Lamp — A197

Designed by Alvin R. Meissner.

FLAT PLATE PRINTING

Plates of 400 subjects in four panes of 100 each.

1929			Perf. 11	
654 A197	2c	**carmine rose,** *June 5, 1929*	90	1.00
		Margin block of 6, P#	35.00	—

ROTARY PRESS PRINTING
Perf. 11x10½

655 A197	2c	**carmine rose,** *June 11, 1929*	85	25
		Margin block of 4, P#	55.00	—

ROTARY PRESS COIL STAMP
Perf. 10 Vertically

656 A197	2c	**carmine rose,** *June 11, 1929*	17.50	2.00
		Pair	37.50	4.50
		Joint line pair	90.00	20.00

SULLIVAN EXPEDITION ISSUE

Issued to commemorate the 150th anniversary of the Sullivan Expedition in New York State during the Revolutionary War.

Major General John
Sullivan — A198

PLAT PLATE PRINTING

Plates of 400 subjects in four panes of 100 each.

1929			Perf. 11.	
657 A196	2c	**carmine rose,** *June 17, 1929*	1.00	90
		lake	40.00	—
		Margin block of 6, P#	35.00	—

REGULAR ISSUE

Nos. 632 to 642 Overprinted **Kans.**

Officially issued May 1, 1929.
Some values are known canceled as early as April 15.

Special issue prepared by overprinting the abbreviations "Kans." and "Nebr." on stamps of the 1926-27 series. This special issue was authorized as a measure of preventing losses from post office burglaries. Approximately a year's supply was printed and issued to postmasters. The P.O. Dept. found it desirable to discontinue the State overprinted stamps after the initial supply was used.

ROTARY PRESS PRINTING

1929			Perf. 11x10½	
658 A155	1c	**green**	2.00	1.65
		Margin block of 4, P#	30.00	—
a.		Vertical pair, one without ovpt.	300.00	
		Wide spacing, pair	40.00	
659 A156	1½c	**brown**	3.00	3.00
		Margin block of 4, P#	45.00	—
a.		Vertical pair, one without ovpt.	325.00	
		Wide spacing, pair	90.00	
660 A157	2c	**carmine**	3.00	65
		Margin block of 4, P#	40.00	—
		Wide spacing, pair	60.00	
661 A158	3c	**violet**	17.50	12.00
		Margin block of 4, P#	175.00	—
a.		Vertical pair, one without ovpt.	400.00	
662 A159	4c	**yellow brown**	17.50	7.50
		Margin block of 4, P#	175.00	—
a.		Vertical pair, one without ovpt.	400.00	
663 A160	5c	**deep blue**	13.00	9.00
		Margin block of 4, P#	150.00	—
664 A161	6c	**red orange**	30.00	17.50
		Margin block of 4, P#	400.00	—
665 A162	7c	**black**	27.50	22.50
		Margin block of 4, P#	400.00	—
a.		Vertical pair, one without ovpt.	400.00	
666 A163	8c	**olive green**	85.00	72.50
		Margin block of 4, P#	800.00	—
667 A164	9c	**light rose**	13.00	11.00
		Margin block of 4, P#	175.00	—
668 A165	10c	**orange yellow**	22.50	11.00
		Margin block of 4, P#	325.00	—
		Pair with full horizontal gutter between	—	

Overprinted **Nebr.**

May 1, 1929				
669 A155	1c	**green**	2.00	2.00
		Margin block of 4, P#	30.00	—
a.		Vertical pair, one without ovpt.	275.00	
		Wide spacing, pair	45.00	45.00

	No period after "Nebr." (19338, 19339 L.R. 26, 36)			
670 A156	1½c	**brown**	3.00	2.25
		Margin block of 4, P#	45.00	—
		Wide spacing, pair	45.00	
671 A157	2c	**carmine**	2.00	85
		Margin block of 4, P#	30.00	—
		Wide spacing, pair	65.00	
672 A158	3c	**violet**	12.00	8.75
		Margin block of 4, P#	150.00	—
a.		Vertical pair, one without ovpt.	400.00	
		Wide spacing, pair	100.00	
673 A159	4c	**yellow brown**	17.50	11.00
		Margin block of 4, P#	200.00	—
		Wide spacing, pair	150.00	
674 A160	5c	**deep blue**	16.00	13.50
		Margin block of 4, P#	210.00	—
675 A161	6c	**red orange**	42.50	19.00
		Margin block of 4, P#	500.00	—
676 A162	7c	**black**	22.50	15.00
		Margin block of 4, P#	275.00	—
677 A163	8c	**olive green**	32.50	22.50
		Margin block of 4, P#	375.00	—
		Wide spacing, pair	225.00	
678 A164	9c	**light rose**	37.50	25.00
		Margin block of 4, P#	400.00	—
a.		Vertical pair, one without ovpt.	600.00	
		Wide spacing, pair	200.00	
679 A165	10c	**orange yellow**	110.00	17.50
		Margin block of 4, P#	900.00	—

Nos. 658, 659, 660, 669, 670, 671, 672, 673, 677 and 678 are known with the overprints on vertical pairs spaced 32mm. apart instead of the normal 22mm.

BATTLE OF FALLEN TIMBERS ISSUE

Issued as a memorial to Gen. Anthony Wayne and to commemorate the 135th anniversary of the Battle of Fallen Timbers, Ohio.

General Wayne
Memorial — A199

FLAT PLATE PRINTING

Plates of 400 subjects in four panes of 100 each.

1929			Perf. 11	
680 A199	2c	**carmine rose,** *Sept. 14, 1929*	1.00	1.00
		deep carmine rose	1.00	1.00
		Margin block of 6, P#	35.00	—

OHIO RIVER CANALIZATION ISSUE

Issued to commemorate the completion of the Ohio River Canalization Project, between Cairo, Ill. and Pittsburgh, Pa.

Lock No. 5,
Monongahela
River — A200

Plates of 400 subjects in four panes of 100 each.

1929			Perf. 11	
681 A200	2c	**carmine rose,** *Oct. 19, 1929*	80	80
		Margin block of 6, P#	27.50	—

MASSACHUSETTS BAY COLONY ISSUE

Issued in commemoration of the 300th anniversary of the founding of the Massachusetts Bay Colony.

The first price column gives the catalogue value of an unused stamp, the second that of a used stamp.

Massachusetts Bay
Colony Seal — A201

Plates of 400 subjects in four panes of 100 each.

1930 **Perf. 11**
682 A201 2c **carmine rose,** *April 8, 1930*   80   60
    Margin block of 6, P#   40.00 —

CAROLINA-CHARLESTON ISSUE

Issued in commemoration of the 260th anniversary of the founding of the Province of Carolina and the 250th anniversary of the city of Charleston, S.C.

Gov. Joseph West and
Chief Shadoo, a
Kiawah — A202

Plates of 400 subjects in four panes of 100 each.

1930 **Perf. 11**
683 A202 2c **carmine rose,** *April 10, 1930*   1.65   1.60
    Margin block of 6, P#   65.00 —

REGULAR ISSUE

Harding — A203

Taft — A204

Type of 1922-26 Issue
ROTARY PRESS PRINTING

1930 **Perf. 11x10½**
684 A203 1½c **brown,** *Dec. 1, 1930*   25   5
    yellow brown   25   5
    Margin block of 4, P#   1.50
    Pair with full horiz. gutter btwn. 175.00
    Pair with full vert. gutter btwn. —
685 A204 4c **brown,** *June 4, 1930*   75   6
    deep brown   75   6
    Margin block of 4, P#   10.00 —
    Gouge on right "4" (20141 U.L. 24)   3.00   90
    Recut right "4" (20141 U.L. 24)   3.00   1.00
    Pair with full horiz. gutter btwn. —

ROTARY PRESS COIL STAMPS
Perf. 10 Vertically
686 A203 1½c **brown,** *Dec. 1, 1930*   2.10   7
    Pair   4.50   16

    Joint line pair   7.50   50
687 A204 4c **brown,** *Sept. 18, 1930*   4.00   50
    Pair   8.25   1.10
    Joint line pair   15.00   1.75

BRADDOCK"S FIELD ISSUE

Issued in commemoration of the 175th anniversary of the Battle of Braddock"s Field, otherwise the Battle of Monongahela.

Statue of Colonel
George
Washington — A205

Designed by Alvin R. Meissner.

FLAT PLATE PRINTING
Plates of 400 subjects in four panes of 100 each.

1930 **Perf. 11**
688 A205 2c **carmine rose,** *July 9, 1930*   1.25   1.25
    Margin block of 6, P#   55.00 —

VON STEUBEN ISSUE

Issued in commemoration of the 200th anniversary of the birth of Baron Friedrich Wilhelm von Steuben (1730-1794) and his participation in the American Revolution.

General von
Steuben — A206

FLAT PLATE PRINTING
Plates of 400 subjects in four panes of 100 each.

1930 **Perf. 11**
689 A206 2c **carmine rose,** *Sept. 17, 1930*   80   75
    Margin block of 6, P#   35.00 —
a.   Imperf., (pair)   2,250.
a.   Margin block of 6, P#, imperf.   10,000.

PULASKI ISSUE

Issued to commemorate the 150th anniversary (in 1929) of the death of Gen. Casimir Pulaski, Polish patriot and hero of the American Revolutionary War.

General Casimir
Pulaski — A207

Plates of 400 subjects in four panes of 100 each.

1931 **Perf. 11**
690 A207 2c **carmine rose,** *Jan. 16, 1931*   25   18
    deep carmine rose   25   18
    Margin block of 6, P#   17.50 —

REGULAR ISSUE
TYPE OF 1922-26 ISSUES
ROTARY PRESS PRINTING

1931 **Perf. 11x10½**
692 A166 11c **light blue,** *Sept. 4, 1931*   3.00   10

    Margin block of 4, P#   19.00 —
    Retouched forehead (20617 L.L. 2, 3)   12.00   1.50
693 A167 12c **brown violet,** *Aug. 25, 1931*   6.50   6
    violet brown   6.50   6
    Margin block of 4, P#   35.00 —
694 A186 13c **yellow green,** *Sept. 4, 1931*   2.50   10
    light yellow green   2.50   10
    blue green   2.50   10
    Block of four   10.00   75
    Margin block of 4, P#   18.00
    Pair with full vert. gutter btwn.   150.00
695 A168 14c **dark blue,** *Sept. 8, 1931*   4.00   30
    Margin block of 4, P#   25.00 —
696 A169 15c **gray,** *Aug. 27, 1931*   10.00   6
    dark gray   10.00   6
    Margin block of 4, P#   60.00 —

    Perf. 10½x11
697 A187 17c **black,** *July 25, 1931*   5.00   25
    Margin block of 4, P#   30.00 —
698 A170 20c **carmine rose,** *Sept. 8, 1931*   12.00   5
    Margin block of 4, P#   65.00 —
    Double transfer (20538 L.R. 26)   35.00 —
699 A171 25c **blue green,** *July 25, 1931*   11.00   8
    Margin block of 4, P#   62.50 —
700 A172 30c **brown,** *Sept. 8, 1931*   18.50   7
    Block of four   74.00   60
    Margin block of 4, P#   100.00 —
    Retouched in head (20552 U.L. 83)   40.00   1.50
    Cracked plate (20552 U.R. 30)   40.00   1.50
701 A173 50c **lilac,** *Sept. 4, 1931*   55.00   7
    red lilac   55.00   7
    Block of four   220.00   50
    Margin block of 4, P#   300.00

RED CROSS ISSUE

Issued in commemoration of the fiftieth anniversary of the founding of the American Red Cross Society.

"The Greatest
Mother" — A208

FLAT PLATE PRINTING
Plates of 200 subjects in two panes of 100 each.

1931 **Perf. 11**
702 A208 2c **black & red,** *May 21, 1931*   15   12
    Margin block of 4, arrow right or left   75
    Margin block of 4, two P#   2.25 —
    Red cross omitted
    Double transfer   2.50   1.00

The cross tends to shift, appearing in many slightly varied positions.

YORKTOWN ISSUE

Issued in commemoration of the Sesquicentennial of the surrender of Cornwallis at Yorktown.

Rochambeau, Washington, de Grasse — A209

First Plate Layout - Border and vignette plates of 100 subjects in two panes of 50 subjects each.
Second Plate Layout - Border plates of 100 subjects in two panes of 50 each, separated by a 1 inch wide vertical gutter with central guide line and vignette plates of 50 subjects.
Issued in panes of 50 subjects.

1931 **Perf. 11**
703 A209 2c **carmine rose & black,** *Oct. 19, 1931*   40   35
    Margin block of 4, arrow marker, right or left   1.70

Center line block	1.85	
Margin block of 4, two P#	3.50	—
Margin block of 4, two P# & arrow & marker block	3.50	—
Margin block of 6, two P# & "TOP", arrow & marker	4.75	—
Margin block of 8, two P# & "TOP"	6.00	—
a. 2c lake & black	3.50	50
b. 2c dark lake & black	300.00	
b. Margin block of 4, two P#	1,750.	
c. Imperf., vertically, pair	2,500.	
Double transfer	3.00	1.25

WASHINGTON BICENTENNIAL ISSUE

200th anniversary of the birth of George Washington. Various Portraits of George Washington.

By Charles Willson
Peale, 1777 — A210

From Houdon Bust,
1785 — A211

By Charles Willson
Peale, 1772 — A212

By Gilbert Stuart,
1796 — A213

By Charles Willson
Peale, 1777 — A214

By Charles Peale
Polk — A215

By Charles Willson
Peale, 1795 — A216

By John Trumbull,
1792 — A217

By John Trumbull,
1780 — A218

By Charles B. J. F.
Saint Memin,
1798 — A219

By W. Williams,
1794 — A220

By Gilbert Stuart,
1795 — A221

Broken Circle

ROTARY PRESS PRINTINGS
Plates of 400 subjects in four panes of 100 each.

1932, Jan. 1			**Perf. 11x10 ½**	
704 A210	½c	**olive brown**	8	5
		Margin block of 4, P#	4.00	—
		Broken circle (20500 U.R. 8)	60	15
705 A211	1c	**green**	13	5
		Margin block of 4, P#	5.00	—
		Gripper cracks (20742 U.L. and U.R.)	3.00	2.00
706 A212	1½c	**brown**	55	8
		Margin block of 4, P#	22.50	—
707 A213	2c	**carmine rose**	10	5
		Margin block of 4, P#	2.00	—
		Pair with full vert. gutter between	—	
		Gripper cracks (20752 L.R., 20755 L.L. & L.R., 20756 L.L., 20774 L.R., 20792 L.L. & L.R., 20796 L.L. & L.R.)	2.00	75

No 708
3 Cent Bicentennial
BROKEN TOP FRAME
L.L. 20847 - Stamp No 8
King

Double Transfer

708 A214	3c	**deep violet**	60	6
		Margin block of 4, P#	16.00	—
		Double transfer	2.00	75
		Broken top frame line (20847 L.L. 8)	4.50	1.00

Retouch in Eyes

709 A215	4c	**light brown**	25	6
		Margin block of 4, P#	5.00	—
		Double transfer (20568 L.R. 60)	1.50	25
		Retouch in eyes (20568 L.R. 89)	2.00	35
		Broken bottom frame line (20568 L.R. 100)	1.50	50

Cracked Plate

710 A216	5c	**blue**	2.25	10
		Margin block of 4, P#	24.00	—
		Cracked plate (20637 U.R. 80)	6.00	1.25
711 A217	6c	**red orange**	6.00	6
		Margin block of 4, P#	75.00	—

Double Transfer

712	A218	7c **black**	30	20
		Margin block of 4, P#	6.00	—
		Double transfer (20563 U.L. 1 or		
		20564 L.L. 91)	1.50	30
713	A219	8c **olive bister**	4.50	90
		Margin block of 4, P#	70.00	—
		Pair, gutter between		—
714	A220	9c **pale red**	4.00	25
		orange red	4.00	25
		Margin block of 4, P#	45.00	—
715	A221	10c **orange yellow**	15.00	10
		Margin block of 4, P#	150.00	—

OLYMPIC WINTER GAMES ISSUE

Issued in honor of the 3rd Olympic Winter Games, held at Lake Placid, N. Y., February 4-13, 1932.

Ski Jumper — A222

FLAT PLATE PRINTING
Plates of 400 subjects in four panes of 100 each.

1932				**Perf. 11**	
716	A222	2c **carmine rose**, *Jan. 25, 1932*		50	25
		carmine		50	25
		Margin block of 6, P#		15.00	—
		Cracked plate (20823 UR 41, 42;			
		UL 48, 49, 50)		6.00	2.50
		Recut (20823 UR 61)		5.00	2.50
		Colored "snowball" (20815 UR 64)		30.00	5.00

ARBOR DAY ISSUE

Issued in commemoration of the sixtieth anniversary of the first observance of Arbor Day in the state of Nebraska in April, 1872, and of the centenary of the birth of Julius Sterling Morton, who conceived the plan and the name "Arbor Day", while he was a member of the Nebraska State Board of Agriculture.

Boy and Girl Planting Tree — A223

ROTARY PRESS PRINTING
Plates of 400 subjects in four panes of 100 each.

1932				**Perf. 11x10½**	
717	A223	2c **carmine rose**, *April 22, 1932*		18	8
		Margin block of 4, P#		10.00	—

OLYMPIC GAMES ISSUE

Issued in honor of the 10th Olympic Games, held at Los Angeles, Calif., July 30 to Aug. 14, 1932.

Runner at Starting Mark — A224

Myron's Discobolus — A225

Designed by Victor S. McCloskey, Jr.

ROTARY PRESS PRINTING
Plates of 400 subjects in four panes of 100 each.

1932, June 15				**Perf. 11x10½**	
718	A224	3c **violet**		2.25	6
		deep violet		2.25	6
		Margin block of 4, P#		20.00	—
		Gripper cracks (20906 UL 1)		5.00	1.00
719	A225	5c **blue**		3.50	30
		deep blue		3.50	30
		Margin block of 4, P#		35.00	—
		Gripper cracks (20868 UL & UR)		5.00	1.25

Washington, by Gilbert Stuart — A226

REGULAR ISSUE
ROTARY PRESS PRINTING
Plates of 400 subjects in four panes of 100 each.

1932				**Perf. 11x10½**	
720	A226	3c **deep violet**, *June 16, 1932*		15	5
		light violet		15	5
		Margin block of 4, P#		1.50	—
		Pair with full vert. gutter btwn.		200.00	
		Pair with full horiz. gutter btwn.		200.00	
b.		Booklet pane of six, *July 25, 1932*		22.50	5.00
c.		Vertical pair, imperf. between		225.00	
		Double transfer		1.50	50
		Recut lines on nose		3.00	1.00
		Gripper cracks		1.75	50

ROTARY PRESS COIL STAMPS

1932				**Perf. 10 Vertically**	
721	A226	3c **deep violet**, *June 24, 1932*		3.00	8
		light violet		3.00	8
		Pair		6.25	20
		Joint line pair		11.00	75
		Gripper cracks		—	—
		Recut lines on nose		—	—
		Recut lines around eyes		—	—

1932				**Perf. 10 Horizontally**	
722	A226	3c **deep violet**, *Oct. 12, 1932*		1.85	45
		light violet		1.85	45
		Pair		3.85	1.00
		Joint line pair		9.00	1.75

TYPE OF 1922-26 ISSUES

1932				**Perf. 10 Vertically**	
723	A161	6c **deep orange**, *Aug. 18, 1932*		12.50	25
		Pair		26.00	60
		Joint line pair		70.00	2.50

WILLIAM PENN ISSUE

Issued in commemoration of the 250th anniversary of the arrival in America of William Penn (1644-1718), English Quaker and founder of Pennsylvania.

William Penn — A227

FLAT PLATE PRINTING
Plates of 400 subjects in four panes of 100 each.

1932			**Perf. 11**	
724	A227	3c **violet**, *Oct. 24, 1932*	35	25
		Margin block of 6, P#	16.00	—
a.	Vert. pair, imperf. horiz.		—	

DANIEL WEBSTER ISSUE

Issued in commemoration of the 150th anniversary of the birth of Daniel Webster (1782-1852), statesman.

Daniel Webster — A228

FLAT PLATE PRINTING
Plates of 400 subjects in four panes of 100 each.

1932			**Perf. 11**	
725	A228	3c **violet**, *Oct. 24, 1932*	50	40
		light violet	50	40
		Margin block of 6, P#	30.00	—

GEORGIA BICENTENNIAL ISSUE

Issued in commemoration of the 200th anniversary of the founding of the Colony of Georgia and in honor of James Edward Oglethorpe, who landed from England, Feb. 12, 1733, and personally supervised the establishing of the colony.

Gen. James Edward Oglethorpe — A229

FLAT PLATE PRINTING
Plates of 400 subjects in four panes of 100 each.

1933			**Perf. 11.**	
726	A229	3c **violet**, *Feb. 12, 1933*	35	25
		Margin block of 6, P#	17.50	—
		Margin block of 10, "CS" & P#	25.00	
		Bottom margin block of 20, no P#		—

PEACE OF 1783 ISSUE

Issued to commemorate the 150th anniversary of the issuance by George Washington of the official order containing the Proclamation of Peace marking officially the ending of hostilities in the War for Independence.

Washington"s
Headquarters at
Newburgh,
N.Y. — A230

ROTARY PRESS PRINTING
Plates of 400 subjects in four panes of 100 each.

1933   *Perf. 10½x11*

727	A230	3c **violet**, April 19, 1933	15	10
		Margin block of 4, P#	6.50	—
		Margin block of 4, horizontal gutter		
		between	75.00	—
		Block of 4, vertical gutter between	85.00	—

No. 727 was available in full sheets of 400 subjects with gum, but was not regularly issued in that form.

CENTURY OF PROGRESS ISSUES

Issued to commemorate the "Century of Progress" International Exhibition at Chicago, which opened June 1, 1933, and the centenary of the incorporation of Chicago as a city.

Restoration of Fort
Dearborn — A231

Federal
Building — A232

ROTARY PRESS PRINTING
Plates of 400 subjects in four panes of 100 each.

1933, May 25   *Perf. 10½x11*

728	A231	1c **yellow green**	12	6
		On cover, Expo. station canc.		50
		Margin block of 4, P#	2.50	—
		Block of 4, horizontal gutter be-		
		tween	100.00	—
		Block of 4, vertical gutter between	100.00	—
		Gripper cracks (21133 UR & LR)	2.00	—
729	A232	3c **violet**	18	5
		On cover, Expo. station canc.		50
		Margin block of 4, P#	3.50	—
		Block of 4, horizontal gutter be-		
		tween	125.00	—
		Block of 4, vertical gutter between	125.00	—

Nos. 728 and 729 were available in full sheets of 400 subjects with gum, but were not regularly issued in that form.

AMERICAN PHILATELIC SOCIETY ISSUE
SOUVENIR SHEETS

A231a

Prices for stamps vary greatly, depending upon centering, gum and condition.

A232a

FLAT PLATE PRINTING
Plates of 225 subjects in nine panes of 25 each.

1933   *Imperf.*

Without Gum

730	A231a	1c **deep yellow green**, sheet of 25,		
		Aug. 25	35.00	35.00
a.		Single stamp	1.00	50
731	A232a	3c **deep violet**, sheet of 25	30.00	30.00
a.		Single stamp	85	50

Issued in sheets measuring 134x120 mm. containing twenty-five stamps, inscribed in the margins:
PRINTED BY THE TREASURY DEPARTMENT, BUREAU OF ENGRAVING AND PRINTING, - UNDER AUTHORITY OF JAMES A. FARLEY, POSTMASTER-GENERAL, AT CENTURY OF PROGRESS, - IN COMPLIMENT TO THE AMERICAN PHILATELIC SOCIETY FOR ITS CONVENTION AND EXHIBITION - CHICAGO, ILLINOIS, AUGUST, 1933. PLATE NO. 21145 (or 21159 (1c) 21146 or 21160 (3c)).
See Nos. 766-767.

NATIONAL RECOVERY ACT ISSUE

Issued to direct attention to and arouse the support of the Nation for the National Recovery Act.

Group of
Workers — A233

ROTARY PRESS PRINTING
Plates of 400 subjects in four panes of 100 each.

1933   *Perf. 10½x11.*

732	A233	3c **violet**, Aug. 15, 1933	14	5
		Margin block of 4, P#	1.75	—
		Gripper cracks (21151 UL & UR,		
		21153 UR & LR)	2.00	—
		Recut at right (21151 UR 47)	2.50	—

BYRD ANTARCTIC ISSUE

Issued in connection with the Byrd Antarctic Expedition of 1933 and for use on letters mailed through the Little America Post Office established at the Base Camp of the Expedition in the territory of the South Pole.

A Map of the World
(on van der
Grinten's
Projection) — A234

Designed by Victor S. McCloskey, Jr.

FLAT PLATE PRINTING
Plates of 200 subjects in four panes of 50 each.

1933   *Perf. 11*

733	A234	3c **dark blue**, Oct. 9, 1933	75	75
		Margin block of 6, P#	25.00	—
		Double transfer (21167 LR 2)	3.50	1.50

In addition to the postage charge of 3 cents, letters sent by the ships of the expedition to be cancelled in Little America were subject to a service charge of 50 cents each.
See No. 753.

KOSCIUSZKO ISSUE

Issued to commemorate Gen. Tadeusz Kosciuszko (1746-1807), Polish soldier and statesman who served in the American Revolution, and to mark the 150th anniversary of the granting to him of American citizenship.

Statue of General
Tadeusz
Kosciuszko — A235

Designed by Victor S. McCloskey, Jr.

FLAT PLATE PRINTING
Plates of 400 subjects in four panes of 100 each

1933   *Perf. 11*

734	A235	5c **blue**, Oct. 13, 1933	85	40
		Margin block of 6, P#	45.00	—
a.		Horiz. pair, imperf. vert.	1,750.	
		Cracked plate		

NATIONAL STAMP EXHIBITION ISSUE
SOUVENIR SHEET

A235a

TYPE OF BYRD ISSUE
Plates of 150 subjects in 25 panes of six each.

1934   *Imperf.*

Without Gum

735	A235a	3c **dark blue**, sheet of six, Feb. 10	19.00	16.50
a.		Single stamp	2.00	2.00

Issued in sheets measuring 87x93mm. containing six stamps, inscribed in the margins: "Printed by the Treasury Department, Bureau of Engraving and Printing, under authority of James A. Farley, Postmaster General, in compliment to the National Stamp Exhibition of 1934. New York, N. Y., February 10-18, 1934. Plate No. 21184." Plate No. 21187 was used for sheets printed at the Exhibition, but all these were destroyed.
See No. 768.

MARYLAND TERCENTENARY ISSUE

Issued to commemorate the 300th anniversary of the founding of Maryland.

"The Ark" and
"The
Dove" — A236

Designed by Alvin R. Meissner.

FLAT PLATE PRINTING
Plates of 400 subjects in four panes of 100 each.

1934			**Perf. 11**
736 A236 3c	**carmine rose**, *Mar. 23, 1934*	20	20
	Margin block of 6, P#	12.50	—
	Double transfer (21190 UL 1)	—	—
a.	Horiz. pair, imperf. between	*1,000.*	

MOTHERS OF AMERICA ISSUE

Issued to commemorate Mother's Day.

Adaptation of Whistler's Portrait of his
Mother — A237

Designed by Victor S. McCloskey, Jr.

Plates of 200 subjects in four panes of 50 each.
ROTARY PRESS PRINTING

1934			**Perf. 11x10½**
737 A237 3c	**deep violet**, *May 2, 1934*	15	6
	Margin block of 4, P#	1.75	

FLAT PLATE PRINTING
Perf. 11

738 A237 3c	**deep violet**, *May 2, 1934*	20	20
	Margin block of 6, P#	7.25	—

See No. 754.

WISCONSIN TERCENTENARY ISSUE

Issued to commemorate the 300th anniversary of the arrival of Jean Nicolet, French explorer, on the shores of Green Bay. According to historical records, Nicolet was the first white man to reach the territory now comprising the State of Wisconsin.

Nicolet's Landing — A238

Designed by Victor S. McCloskey, Jr.

FLAT PLATE PRINTING
Plates of 200 subjects in four panes of 50 each.

1934			**Perf. 11**
739 A238 3c	**deep violet**, *July 7, 1934*	20	12
	violet	20	12
	Margin block of 6, P#	7.00	—
a.	Vert. pair, imperf. horiz.	250.00	
b.	Horiz. pair, imperf. vert.	325.00	

See No. 755.

NATIONAL PARKS ISSUE

Issued to commemorate "National Parks Year".

El Capitan,
Yosemite
(California) — A239

View of Grand Canyon (Arizona) — A240

Mt. Rainier and Mirror Lake (Washington) — A241

Cliff Palace, Mesa Verde Park (Colorado) — A242

Old Faithful,
Yellowstone
(Wyoming) — A243

Crater Lake (Oregon) — A244

Great Head, Acadia Park (Maine) — A245

Great White
Throne, Zion Park
(Utah) — A246

Mt. Rockwell (Mt. Sinopah) and Two Medicine
Lake, Glacier National Park (Montana) — A247

Great Smoky
Mountains (North
Carolina) — A248

FLAT PLATE PRINTING
Plates of 200 subjects in four panes of 50 each.

1934	Unwmk.		Perf. 11	
740	A239	1c **green**, *July 16, 1934*	10	6
		light green	10	6
		Margin block of 6, P#	1.50	—
		Recut	2.00	75
a.		Vert. pair, imperf. horiz., with gum	450.00	
741	A240	2c **red**, *July 24, 1934*	15	6
		orange red	15	6
		Margin block of 6, P#	2.00	
a.		Vert. pair, imperf., horiz., with gum	375.00	
b.		Horiz. pair, imperf. vert., with gum	400.00	
		Double transfer	1.75	—
742	A241	3c **deep violet**, *Aug. 3, 1934*	20	6
		Margin block of 6, P#	3.00	—
		Recut	2.00	—
a.		Vert. pair, imperf. horiz., with gum	500.00	
743	A242	4c **brown**, *Sept. 25, 1934*	55	50
		light brown	55	50
		Margin block of 6, P#	11.00	—
a.		Vert. pair, imperf., with gum	650.00	
744	A243	5c **blue**, *July 30, 1934*	1.10	90
		light blue	1.10	90
		Margin block of 6, P#	16.00	—
a.		Horiz. pair, imperf. vert., with gum	400.00	
745	A244	6c **dark blue**, *Sept. 5, 1934*	2.00	1.25
		Margin block of 6, P#	30.00	—
746	A245	7c **black**, *Oct. 2, 1934*	1.00	1.00
		Margin block of 6, P#	18.00	—
a.		Horiz. pair, imperf. vert., with gum	600.00	
		Double transfer	5.00	2.00
747	A246	8c **sage green**, *Sept. 18, 1934*	2.85	2.50
		Margin block of 6, P#	30.00	—
748	A247	9c **red orange**, *Aug. 27, 1934*	3.00	90
		orange	3.00	90
		Margin block of 6, P#	30.00	—
749	A248	10c **gray black**, *Oct. 8, 1934*	5.00	1.35
		gray	5.00	1.35
		Margin block of 6, P#	50.00	—

Imperforate varieties of the 2c and 5c exist as errors of the perforated Parks set, but are virtually impossible to distinguish from gummed copies from the imperforate sheets of 200. (See note above No. 752).

AMERICAN PHILATELIC SOCIETY ISSUE
SOUVENIR SHEET

A248a

Plates of 120 subjects in 20 panes of 6 stamps each.

1934			Imperf.	
750	A248a	3c **deep violet**, sheet of six, *Aug. 28*	35.00	25.00
a.		Single stamp	3.75	3.75

Issued in sheets measuring 97x99mm. containing six stamps, inscribed in the margins: PRINTED BY THE TREASURY DEPARTMENT, BUREAU OF ENGRAVING AND PRINTING, - UNDER AUTHORITY OF JAMES A. FARLEY, POSTMASTER GENERAL, - IN COMPLIMENT TO THE AMERICAN PHILATELIC SOCIETY FOR ITS CONVENTION AND EXHIBITION, - ATLANTIC CITY, NEW JERSEY, AUGUST, 1934. PLATE NO. 21303.

TRANS-MISSISSIPPI PHILATELIC EXPOSITION ISSUE
SOUVENIR SHEET

A248b

Plates of 120 subjects in 20 panes of 6 stamps each.

1934			Imperf.	
751	A248b	1c **green**, sheet of six, *Oct. 10*	15.00	12.00
a.		Single stamp	1.75	1.75

Issued in sheets measuring 94x99mm. containing six stamps, inscribed in the margins: PRINTED BY THE TREASURY DEPARTMENT, BUREAU OF ENGRAVING AND

PRINTING, - UNDER AUTHORITY OF JAMES A. FARLEY, POSTMASTER GENERAL, - IN COMPLIMENT TO THE TRANS-MISSISSIPPI PHILATELIC EXPOSITION AND CONVENTION, OMAHA, NEBRASKA, - OCTOBER, 1934. PLATE NO. 21341.

SPECIAL PRINTING
(Nos. 752 to 771 inclusive)
Issued March 15, 1935

"Issued for a limited time in full sheets as printed, and in blocks thereof, to meet the requirements of collectors and others who may be interested." - From Postal Bulletin No. 16614.

Issuance of the following 20 stamps in complete sheets resulted from the protest of collectors and others at the practice of presenting, to certain government officials, complete sheets of unsevered panes, imperforate (except Nos. 752 and 753) and generally ungummed.

Gutter or line pairs sell for half the price of gutter or line blocks of four.

Designs of Commemorative Issues
Without Gum
NOTE: In 1940 the P.O. Department offered to and did gum full sheets of Nos. 754 to 771 sent in by owners.

TYPE OF PEACE ISSUE
Issued in sheets of 400, consisting of four panes of 100 each, with vertical and horizontal gutters between panes and plate numbers at outside corners at sides.

ROTARY PRESS PRINTING

1935	Unwmk.		Perf. 10½x11	
752	A230	3c **violet**	15	10
		Horiz. gutter block of four	9.00	—
		Vert. gutter block of four	15.00	—
		Gutter block of four with dash (left or right)	10.00	—
		Gutter block of four with dash (top or bottom)	15.00	—
		Center block with crossed gutters and dashes	42.50	—
		Margin block of 4, P#	16.00	—

No. 752 is similar to No. 727. Positive identification is by blocks or pairs showing wide gutters between stamps. These wide gutters occur only on No. 752.

TYPE OF BYRD ISSUE
Issued in sheets of 200, consisting of four panes of 50 each, with vertical and horizontal guide lines in gutters between panes, and plate numbers centered at top and bottom of each pane. This applies to Nos. 753-765 and 771.

FLAT PLATE PRINTING
Perf. 11

753	A234	3c **dark blue**	85	85
		Horiz. line block of four	7.00	—
		Vert. line block of four	80.00	—
		Margin block of 4, arrow & guide line (left or right)	7.50	—
		Margin block of 4, arrow & guide-line (top or bottom)	82.50	—
		Center line block	87.50	30.00
		Margin block of 6, P# (Number at top or bottom)	25.00	—

No. 753 is similar to No. 733. Positive identification is by blocks or pairs showing guide line between stamps. These lines between stamps are found only on No. 753.

TYPE OF MOTHERS OF AMERICA ISSUE
Issued in sheets of 200
FLAT PLATE PRINTING
Imperf.

754	A237	3c **deep violet**	1.00	60
		Horiz. or vert. line block of four	4.25	—
		Margin block of 4, arrow & guideline (left, right, top or bottom)	4.50	—
		Center line block	10.00	—
		Margin block of 6, P# (Number at top or bottom)	30.00	—

TYPE OF WISCONSIN ISSUE
Issued in sheets of 200
FLAT PLATE PRINTING
Imperf.

755	A238	3c **deep violet**	1.00	60
		Horiz. or vert. line block of four	4.25	—
		Margin block of 4, arrow & guideline (left, right, top or bottom)	4.50	—
		Center line block	10.00	—
		Margin block of 6, P# (Number at top or bottom)	30.00	—

TYPES OF NATIONAL PARKS ISSUE
Issued in sheets of 200
FLAT PLATE PRINTING
Imperf.

756	A239	1c **green**	30	20
		Horiz. or vert. line block of four	1.30	—
		Margin block of 4, arrow & guideline (left, right, top or bottom)	1.40	—
		Center line block	3.50	—
		Margin block of 6, P# (Number at top or bottom)	5.50	—

See note above No. 766.

757	A240	2c **red**	40	35
		Horiz. or vert. line block of four	1.70	—
		Margin block of 4, arrow & guideline (left, right, top or bottom)	1.75	—
		Center line block	5.00	—
		Margin block of 6, P# (Number at top or bottom)	6.50	—
		Double transfer	—	—
758	A241	3c **deep violet**	75	70
		Horiz. or vert. line block of four	3.20	—
		Margin block of 4, arrow & guideline (left, right, top or bottom)	3.25	—
		Center line block	6.50	—
		Margin block of 6, P# (Number at top or bottom)	17.50	—
759	A242	4c **brown**	1.75	1.75
		Horiz. or vert. line block of four	7.25	—
		Margin block of 4, arrow & guideline (left, right, top or bottom)	7.50	—
		Center line block	11.00	—
		Margin block of 6, P# (Number at top or bottom)	24.00	—
760	A243	5c **blue**	2.25	2.25
		Horiz. or vert. line block of four	10.50	—
		Margin block of 4, arrow & guideline (left, right, top or bottom)	11.00	—
		Center line block	17.50	—
		Margin block of 6, P# (Number at top or bottom)	30.00	—
		Double transfer	—	—
761	A244	6c **dark blue**	3.50	2.75
		Horiz. or vert. line block of four	14.50	—
		Margin block of 4, arrow & guideline (left, right, top or bottom)	15.00	—
		Center line block	22.50	—
		Margin block of 6, P# (Number at top or bottom)	47.50	—
762	A245	7c **black**	2.50	2.50
		Horiz. or vert. line block of four	10.50	—
		Margin block of 4, arrow & guideline (left, right, top or bottom)	11.00	—
		Center line block	18.50	—
		Margin block of 6, P# (Number at top or bottom)	40.00	—
		Double transfer	—	—
763	A246	8c **sage green**	2.75	2.75
		Block of four	11.00	11.00
		Horiz. or vert. line block of four	11.50	—
		Margin block of 4, arrow & guideline (left, right, top or bottom)	12.00	—
		Center line block	20.00	—
		Margin block of 6, P# (Number at top or bottom)	50.00	—
764	A247	9c **red orange**	3.00	2.75
		Block of four	12.00	11.00
		Horiz. or vert. line block of four	12.50	—
		Margin block of 4, arrow & guideline (left, right, top or bottom)	13.00	—
		Center line block	21.00	—
		Margin block of 6, P# (Number at top or bottom)	55.00	—
765	A248	10c **gray black**	5.25	5.50
		Block of four	21.00	22.00
		Horiz. or vert. line block of four	21.50	—
		Margin block of 4, arrow & guideline (left, right, top or bottom)	22.00	—
		Center line block	32.50	—
		Margin block of 6, P# (Number at top or bottom)	62.50	—

SOUVENIR SHEETS
TYPE OF CENTURY OF PROGRESS ISSUE

Issued in sheets of 9 panes of 25 stamps each, with vertical and horizontal gutters between panes. This applies to Nos. 766-770.

Note: Single items from these sheets are identical with other varieties, 766 and 730, 766a and 730a, 767 and 731, 767a and 731a, 768 and 735, 768a and 735a, 769 and 756, 770 and 758.

Positive identification is by blocks or pairs showing wide gutters between stamps. These wide gutters occur only on Nos. 766 to 770 and measure, horizontally, 13mm. on Nos. 766-767; 16mm. on No. 768, and 23mm. on Nos. 769-770.

FLAT PLATE PRINTING
Imperf.

766	A231a	1c **yellow green**, pane of 25	30.00	30.00
a.		Single stamp	1.00	50
		Block of four	4.00	2.25

	Horiz. gutter block	13.00	—
	Vert. gutter block	15.00	—
	Block with crossed gutters	17.50	—
	Block of 50 stamps (two panes)	85.00	—
767	A232a 3c **violet,** pane of 25	27.50	27.50
a.	Single stamp	85	50
	Horiz. gutter block	12.00	—
	Vert. gutter block	14.00	—
	Block with crossed gutters	17.50	—
	Block of 50 stamps (two panes)	75.00	—

NATIONAL EXHIBITION ISSUE
TYPE OF BYRD ISSUE
Issued in sheets of 25 panes of 6 stamps each.
FLAT PLATE PRINTING
Imperf.

768	A235a 3c **dark blue,** pane of six	19.00	16.00
a.	Single stamp	2.00	2.00
	Horiz. gutter block	12.50	—
	Vert. gutter block	13.50	—
	Block of four with crossed gutters	16.00	—
	Block of 12 stamps (two panes)	45.00	—

TYPES OF NATIONAL PARKS ISSUE
Issued in sheets of 20 panes of 6 stamps each.
FLAT PLATE PRINTING
Imperf.

769	A248b 1c **green,** pane of six	15.00	12.00
a.	Single stamp	1.75	1.75
	Horiz. or vert. gutter block	14.00	—
	Block of four with crossed gutters	15.00	—
	Block of 12 stamps (two panes)	31.00	—
770	A248a 3c **deep violet,** pane of six	35.00	25.00
a.	Single stamp	3.75	3.75
	Horiz. or vert. gutter block	25.00	—
	Block of four with crossed gutters	26.50	—
	Block of 12 stamps (two panes)	75.00	—

TYPE OF AIR POST SPECIAL DELIVERY
Issued in sheets of 200
FLAT PLATE PRINTING
Imperf.

771	APSD1 16c **dark blue**	3.00	3.00
	Horiz. or vert. line block of four	13.00	13.00
	Margin block of 4, arrow & guide line (left, right, top or bottom)	15.00	15.00
	Center line block	55.00	—
	Margin block of 6, P# (Number at top or bottom)	65.00	—

CONNECTICUT TERCENTENARY ISSUE
Issued in commemoration of the 300th anniversary of the settlement of Connecticut.

The Charter Oak — A249

ROTARY PRESS PRINTING
Plates of 200 subjects in four panes of 50 each.

1935	**Unwmk.**	**Perf. 11x10½**	
772	A249 3c **violet,** *April 26, 1935*	15	6
	rose violet	15	8
	Margin block of 4, P#	2.00	—
	Defect in cent sign (21395 UR 4)	1.00	25

CALIFORNIA PACIFIC EXPOSITION ISSUE
Issued in commemoration of the California Pacific Exposition at San Diego.

View of San Diego Exposition — A250

ROTARY PRESS PRINTING
Plates of 200 subjects in four panes of 50 each.

1935	**Unwmk.**	**Perf. 11x10½**	
773	A250 3c **purple,** *May 29, 1935*	12	6
	On cover, Expo. station canc.		50
	Margin block of 4, P#	1.80	—
	Pair with full vertical gutter between		—

BOULDER DAM ISSUE
Issued to commemorate the dedication of Boulder Dam.

Boulder Dam (Hoover Dam) — A251

FLAT PLATE PRINTING
Plates of 200 subjects in four panes of 50 each.

1935	**Unwmk.**	**Perf. 11**	
774	A251 3c **purple,** *Sept. 30, 1935*	12	6
	deep purple	12	6
	Margin block of 6, P#	2.50	—

MICHIGAN CENTENARY ISSUE
Advance celebration of Michigan Statehood centenary. Michigan was admitted to the Union Jan. 26, 1837.

Michigan State Seal — A252

Designed by Alvin R. Meissner.

ROTARY PRESS PRINTING
Plates of 200 subjects in four panes of 50 each.

1935	**Unwmk.**	**Perf. 11x10½**	
775	A252 3c **purple,** *Nov. 1, 1935*	12	6
	Margin block of 4, P#	1.80	—

TEXAS CENTENNIAL ISSUE
Issued in commemoration of the centennial of Texas independence.

Sam Houston, Stephen F. Austin and the Alamo — A253

Designed by Alvin R. Meissner.

ROTARY PRESS PRINTING
Plates of 200 subjects in four panes of 50 each.

1936	**Unwmk.**	**Perf. 11x10½**	
776	A253 3c **purple,** *Mar. 2, 1936*	12	6
	On cover, Expo. station canc.		50
	Margin block of 4, P#	1.80	—

RHODE ISLAND TERCENTENARY ISSUE
Issued in commemoration of the 300th anniversary of the settlement of Rhode Island.

Statue of Roger Williams — A254

ROTARY PRESS PRINTING
Plates of 200 subjects in four panes of 50 each.

1936	**Unwmk.**	**Perf. 10½x11**	
777	A254 3c **purple,** *May 4, 1936*	15	6
	rose violet	15	6
	Margin block of 4, P#	1.80	—
	Pair with full gutter between	200.00	—

THIRD INTERNATIONAL PHILATELIC EXHIBITION ISSUE
SOUVENIR SHEET

A254a

TYPES OF CONNECTICUT, CALIFORNIA, MICHIGAN AND TEXAS ISSUES
Plates of 120 subjects in thirty panes of 4 each.
FLAT PLATE PRINTING

1936, May 9	**Unwmk.**	**Imperf.**	
778	A254a **violet,** sheet of four	3.00	3.00
a.	3c type A249	60	50
b.	3c type A250	60	50
c.	3c type A252	60	50
d.	3c type A253	60	50

Issued in sheets measuring 98x66mm. containing four stamps, inscribed in the margins: "Printed by the Treasury Department, Bureau of Engraving and Printing, under authority of James A. Farley, Postmaster General, in compliment to the third International Philatelic Exhibition of 1936. New York, N. Y., May 9-17, 1936. Plate No. 21557 (or 21558)."

ARKANSAS CENTENNIAL ISSUE

Issued in commemoration of the 100th anniversary of the State of Arkansas.

Arkansas Post, Old and New State Houses — A255

ROTARY PRESS PRINTING
Plates of 200 subjects in four panes of 50 each.

1936		**Unwmk.**		**Perf. 11x10½**	
782 A255	3c	purple, June 15, 1936		12	6
		Margin block of 4, P#		1.80	—

OREGON TERRITORY ISSUE

Issued in commemoration of the 100th anniversary of the opening of the Oregon Territory, 1836.

Map of Oregon Territory — A256

ROTARY PRESS PRINTING
Plates of 200 subjects in four panes of 50 each.

1936		**Unwmk.**		**Perf. 11x10½**	
783 A256	3c	purple, July 14, 1936		12	6
		Margin block of 4, P#		1.80	—
		Double transfer (21579 UL 3)		1.50	50

SUSAN B. ANTHONY ISSUE

Issued in honor of Susan Brownell Anthony (1820-1906), woman-suffrage advocate, on the 16th anniversary of the ratification of the 19th Amendment which grants American women the right to vote.

Susan B. Anthony — A257

ROTARY PRESS PRINTING
Plates of 400 subjects in four panes of 100 each.

1936		**Unwmk.**		**Perf. 11x10½**	
784 A257	3c	dark violet, Aug. 26, 1936		10	5
		Margin block of 4, P#		75	—
		Period missing after "B" (21590 LR 100)		1.00	25

ARMY ISSUE

Issued in honor of the United States Army.

Generals George Washington, Nathanael Greene and Mt. Vernon — A258

Maj. Gen. Andrew Jackson, Gen. Winfield Scott and the Hermitage — A259

Generals William T. Sherman, Ulysses S. Grant and Philip H. Sheridan — A260

Generals Robert E. Lee, "Stonewall" Jackson and Stratford Hall — A261

U. S. Military Academy, West Point — A262

ROTARY PRESS PRINTING
Plates of 200 subjects in four panes of 50 each.

1936-37		**Unwmk.**		**Perf. 11x10½**	
785 A258	1c	green, Dec. 15, 1936		10	6
		yellow green		10	6
		Margin block of 4, P#		1.00	—
		Pair with full vertical gutter between			
786 A259	2c	carmine, Jan. 15, 1937		15	6
		Margin block of 4, P#		1.10	—
787 A260	3c	purple, Feb. 18, 1937		20	8
		Margin block of 4, P#		1.50	—
788 A261	4c	gray, Mar. 23, 1937		65	15
		Margin block of 4, P#		12.00	—
789 A262	5c	ultramarine, May 26, 1937		1.00	15
		Margin block of 4, P#		13.00	—

NAVY ISSUE

Issued in honor of the United States Navy.

John Paul Jones and John Barry — A263

Stephen Decatur and Thomas MacDonough — A264

Admirals David G. Farragut and David D. Porter — A265

Admirals William T. Sampson, George Dewey and Winfield S. Schley — A266

Seal of U.S. Naval Academy and Naval Cadets — A267

ROTARY PRESS PRINTING
Plates of 200 subjects in four panes of 50 each.

1936-37		**Unwmk.**		**Perf. 11x10½**	
790 A263	1c	green, Dec. 15, 1936		10	6
		yellow green		10	6
		Margin block of 4, P#		1.00	—
791 A264	2c	carmine, Jan. 15, 1937		15	6
		Margin block of 4, P#		1.10	—
792 A265	3c	purple, Feb. 18, 1937		20	8
		Margin block of 4, P#		1.50	—
793 A266	4c	gray, Mar. 23, 1937		65	15
		Margin block of 4, P#		12.00	—

794 A267 5c **ultramarine,** *May 26, 1937*   1.00 15
    Margin block of 4, P#   13.00 —
    Pair with full vert. gutter btwn.   —

ORDINANCE OF 1787 SESQUICENTENNIAL ISSUE

Issued in commemoration of the 150th anniversary of the adoption of the Ordinance of 1787 and the creation of the Northwest Territory.

Manasseh Cutler, Rufus Putnam and Map of
Northwest Territory — A268

ROTARY PRESS PRINTING
Plates of 200 subjects in four panes of 50 each.

1937	Unwmk.	Perf. 11x10 ½
795 A268 3c **red violet,** *July 13, 1937*		12 6
Margin block of 4, P#		1.75 —

VIRGINIA DARE ISSUE

Issued to commemorate the 350th anniversary of the birth of Virginia Dare and the settlement at Roanoke Island. Virginia was the first child born in America of English parents (Aug. 18, 1587).

Virginia Dare
and Parents
A269

FLAT PLATE PRINTING
Plates of 192 subjects in four panes of 48 each, separated by 1 ¼ inch wide gutters with central guide lines.

1937	Unwmk.	Perf. 11
796 A269 5c **gray blue,** *Aug. 18, 1937*		35 25
Margin block of 6, P#		10.00 —

SOCIETY OF PHILATELIC AMERICANS ISSUE
SOUVENIR SHEET

A269a

TYPE OF NATIONAL PARKS ISSUE
Plates of 36 subjects
FLAT PLATE PRINTING

1937	Unwmk.	Imperf.
797 A269a 10c **blue green,** *Aug. 26*		1.00 85

Issued in sheets measuring 67x78mm., one stamp in center of each sheet inscribed in margins: "Printed by the Treasury Department, Bureau of Engraving and Printing - Under the

Authority of James A. Farley, Postmaster General - In Compliment to the 43rd Annual Convention of the Society of Philatelic Americans - Asheville, N.C., August 26-28, 1937. Plate Number 21695 (6)."

CONSTITUTION SESQUICENTENNIAL ISSUE

Issued in commemoration of the 150th anniversary of the signing of the Constitution on September 17, 1787.

"Adoption of the Constitution" — A270

ROTARY PRESS PRINTING
Plates of 200 subjects in four panes of 50 each.

1937	Unwmk.	Perf. 11x10 ½
798 A270 3c **bright red violet,** *Sept. 17, 1937*		15 7
Margin block of 4, P#		1.65 —

TERRITORIAL ISSUES
Hawaii

Statue of
Kamehameha I,
Honolulu — A271

Alaska

Mt. McKinley — A272

Puerto Rico

La Fortaleza, San Juan — A273

Virgin Islands

Charlotte Amalie Harbor, St. Thomas — A274

ROTARY PRESS PRINTING
Plates of 200 subjects in panes of 50 each.

1937	Unwmk.	Perf. 10 ½x11
799 A271 3c **violet,** *Oct. 18, 1937*		15 7
Margin block of 4, P#		1.75 —
		Perf. 11x10 ½
800 A272 3c **violet,** *Nov. 12, 1937*		15 7
Margin block of 4, P#		1.75 —
Pair with full gutter between		—
801 A273 3c **bright violet,** *Nov. 25, 1937*		15 7
Margin block of 4, P#		1.75 —
802 A274 3c **light violet,** *Dec. 15, 1937*		15 7
Margin block of 4, P#		1.75 —
Pair with full vertical gutter between		275.00

PRESIDENTIAL ISSUE

Benjamin
Franklin
A275

George
Washington
A276

Martha
Washington
A277

John Adams
A278

Thomas
Jefferson — A279

James
Madison — A280

The White
House — A281

James
Monroe — A282

John Quincy
Adams — A283

Andrew
Jackson — A284

Martin Van
Buren — A285

William H.
Harrison — A286

William
McKinley
A301

Theodore
Roosevelt
A302

John
Tyler — A287

James K.
Polk — A288

William Howard
Taft — A303

Woodrow
Wilson — A304

Zachary
Taylor — A289

Millard
Fillmore — A290

Warren G.
Harding — A305

Calvin
Coolidge — A306

Franklin Pierce
A291

James Buchanan
A292

ROTARY PRESS PRINTING

Ordinary and Electric Eye Plates of 400 subjects in four panes of 100 each. (For details of Electric Eye Markings, see Information for Collectors in first part of this Catalogue.)

Abraham
Lincoln — A293

Andrew
Johnson — A294

			1938-43	Unwmk.	Perf. 11x10½	
803	A275	½c	**deep orange,** *May 19, 1938*	5	5
			Margin block of 4, P#	40	5
804	A276	1c	**green,** *Apr. 25, 1938*	6	5
			light green	6	5
			Margin block of 4, P#	35	—
b.			Booklet pane of six	1.75	20
			Pair with full vertical gutter between	125.00	—
805	A277	1½c	**bister brown,** *May 5, 1938*	6	5
			buff ('43)	6	5
			Margin block of 4, P#	30	—
b.			Horiz. pair, imperf. between	175.00	15.00
			Pair with full horizontal gutter between	150.00	
			Pair with full vertical gutter between	—	

Used pairs of No. 805b are Bureau precanceled St. Louis, Mo., and generally with gum.

Ulysses S.
Grant — A295

Rutherford B.
Hayes — A296

806	A278	2c	**rose carmine,** *June 3, 1938*	6	5
			rose pink ('43)	6	5
			Margin block of 4, P# opposite corner stamp	40	—
			Vertical margin block of 10, P# opposite third horizontal row (Experimental Electric Eye plates)	4.50	
b.			Booklet pane of six	4.25	50
			Recut at top of head, Pl. 22156 U.L. 3	3.00	1.50
			Pair with full horiz. gutter btwn.	—	
			Pair with full vert. gutter btwn.	—	
807	A279	3c	**deep violet,** *June 16, 1938*	10	5
			Margin block of 4, P# opposite corner stamp	50	25
			Vertical margin block of 10, P# opposite third horizontal row (Experimental Electric Eye plates)	25.00	
a.			Booklet pane of six	8.50	50
b.			Horiz. pair, imperf. between	500.00	—
c.			Imperf., pair	2,500.	
			Pair with full vertical gutter between	150.00	
			Pair with full horizontal gutter between	225.00	

James A.
Garfield — A297

Chester A.
Arthur — A298

808	A280	4c	**red violet,** *July 1, 1938*	1.00	5
			rose violet ('43)	1.00	5
			Margin block of 4, P#	5.00	—
809	A281	4½c	**dark gray,** *July 11, 1938*	20	6
			gray ('43)	20	6
			Block of four	80	50
			Margin block of 4, P#	1.60	—
810	A282	5c	**bright blue,** *July 21, 1938*	40	5
			light blue	40	5
			Margin block of 4, P#	2.00	—
			Pair full vert. gutter btwn.	—	
811	A283	6c	**red orange,** *July 28, 1938*	45	5
			Margin block of 4, P#	2.25	—
812	A284	7c	**sepia,** *Aug. 4, 1938*	50	5
			violet brown	50	5
			Margin block of 4, P#	2.50	—
813	A285	8c	**olive green,** *Aug. 11, 1938*	65	5

Grover
Cleveland
A299

Benjamin
Harrison
A300

			light olive green ('43)	65	5
			olive ('42)	65	5
			Margin block of 4, P#	3.25	
814	A286	9c	**rose pink,** *Aug. 18, 1938*	70	5
			pink ('43)	70	5
			Margin block of 4, P#	3.50	
			Pair with full vertical gutter between	—	
815	A287	10c	**brown red,** *Sept. 2, 1938*	50	5
			pale brown red ('43)	50	5
			Margin block of 4, P#	2.50	
816	A288	11c	**ultramarine,** *Sept. 8, 1938*	1.00	8
			bright ultramarine	1.00	8
			Margin block of 4, P#	6.00	
817	A289	12c	**bright violet,** *Sept. 14, 1938*	1.90	6
			Margin block of 4, P#	9.50	
818	A290	13c	**blue green,** *Sept. 22, 1938*	2.00	8
			deep blue green	2.00	8
			Margin block of 4, P#	10.00	
819	A291	14c	**blue,** *Oct. 6, 1938*	1.75	10
			Margin block of 4, P#	8.75	
820	A292	15c	**blue gray,** *Oct. 13, 1938*	75	5
			Margin block of 4, P#	3.75	
821	A293	16c	**black,** *Oct. 20, 1938*	1.75	35
			Margin block of 4, P#	8.75	
822	A294	17c	**rose red,** *Oct. 27, 1938*	1.50	12
			deep rose red	1.50	12
			Block of four	6.00	60
			Margin block of 4, P#	7.50	
823	A295	18c	**brown carmine,** *Nov. 3, 1938*	3.25	8
			rose brown ('43)	3.25	8
			Block of four	13.00	75
			Margin block of 4, P#	14.00	
824	A296	19c	**bright violet,** *Nov. 10, 1938*	2.00	50
			Margin block of 4, P#	10.00	
825	A297	20c	**bright blue green,** *Nov. 10, 1938*	1.20	5
			deep blue green ('43)	1.20	5
			Margin block of 4, P#	6.00	
826	A298	21c	**dull blue,** *Nov. 22, 1938*	2.25	10
			Block of four	9.00	1.25
			Margin block of 4, P#	12.00	
827	A299	22c	**vermilion,** *Nov. 22, 1938*	2.00	50
			Margin block of 4, P#	12.50	
828	A300	24c	**gray black,** *Dec. 2, 1938*	6.00	25
			Block of four	24.00	1.50
			Margin block of 4, P#	30.00	
829	A301	25c	**deep red lilac,** *Dec. 2, 1938*	1.25	5
			rose lilac ('43)	1.25	5
			Margin block of 4, P#	5.00	
			Pair with full vert. gutter btwn.	—	
830	A302	30c	**deep ultramarine,** *Dec. 8, 1938*	8.00	5
			blue	25.00	—
			deep blue	125.00	—
			Block of four	32.00	50
			Margin block of 4, P#	37.50	
831	A303	50c	**light red violet,** *Dec. 8, 1938*	11.00	6
			Margin block of 4, P#	55.00	

FLAT PLATE PRINTING
Plates of 100 subjects

			1938-54		Perf. 11	
832	A304	$1	**purple & black,** *Aug. 29, 1938*	12.50	10
			Margin block of 4, bottom or side arrow	51.00	—
			Top margin block of 4, 2P#	62.50	—
			Center line block	55.00	4.00
			Top margin block of 20, 2P#, arrow, 2 TOP, 2 registration markers and denomination	265.00	—
a.			Vert. pair, imperf. horiz.	1,000.	
b.			Wmkd. USIR ('51)	300.00	90.00
b.			Margin block of 4, 2P#	1,850.	
c.			red vio. & black, *Aug. 31, 1954*	9.00	15
c.			Top or bottom margin block of 4, 2P#	47.50	—
d.			As "c," vert. pair, imperf. horiz.	1,000.	
e.			Vertical pair, imperf. between	2,500.	
f.			As "c," vert. pair, imperf. btwn.	7,000.	

No. 832c is dry printed from 400-subject flat plates on thick white paper with smooth, colorless gum.

833	A305	$2	**yellow green & black,** *Sept. 29, 1938*	32.50	6.00
			green & black ('43)	32.50	6.00
			Margin block of 4, bottom or side arrow	135.00	—
			Top margin block of 4, 2 P#	165.00	—
			Center line block	140.00	35.00
			Top margin block of 20, 2 P#, arrow, 2 TOP, 2 registration markers and denominations	700.00	—
834	A306	$5	**car. & black,** *Nov. 17, 1938*	125.00	5.50
a.			$5 red brown & black	850.00	175.00
			Margin block of four, bottom or side arrow	510.00	—
			Top margin block of 4, 2 P#	625.00	—
			Center line block	525.00	35.00
			Top margin block of 20, 2 P#, arrow, 2 TOP, 2 registration markers and denominations	2,750.	

Top plate number blocks of Nos. 832, 833 and 834 are found both with and without top arrow or registration markers.

CONSTITUTION RATIFICATION ISSUE

Issued in commemoration of the 150th anniversary of the ratification of the United States Constitution.

Old Courthouse, Williamsburg, Va. — A307

ROTARY PRESS PRINTING
Plates of 200 subjects in four panes of 50 each.

1938		Unwmk.		Perf. 11x10½	
835	A307	3c	deep violet, June 21, 1938	30	8
			Margin block of 4, P#	5.50	—

SWEDISH-FINNISH TERCENTENARY ISSUE

Issued in commemoration of the tercentenary of the founding of the Swedish and Finnish Settlement at Wilmington, Delaware.

"Landing of the First Swedish and Finnish Settlers in America," by Stanley M. Arthurs — A308

FLAT PLATE PRINTING
Plates of 192 subjects in four panes of 48 each, separated by 1¼ inch wide gutters with central guide lines.

1938		Unwmk.		Perf. 11	
836	A308	3c	red violet, June 27, 1938	25	10
			Margin block of 6, P#	4.50	—

NORTHWEST TERRITORY SESQUICENTENNIAL ISSUE

Issued in commemoration of the sesquicentennial of the settlement of the Northwest Territory.

"Colonization of the West," by Gutzon Borglum — A309

ROTARY PRESS PRINTING
Plates of 400 subjects in four panes of 100 each.

1938		Unwmk.		Perf. 11x10½	
837	A309	3c	bright violet, July 15, 1938	20	8
			rose violet	20	8
			Margin block of 4, P#	12.50	—

IOWA TERRITORY CENTENNIAL ISSUE

Issued in commemoration of the 100th anniversary of the establishment of Iowa Territory.

Old Capitol, Iowa City — A310

ROTARY PRESS PRINTING
Plates of 200 subjects in four panes of 50 each.

1938		Unwmk.		Perf. 11x10½	
838	A310	3c	violet, Aug. 24, 1938	25	8
			Margin block of 4, P#	7.00	—
			Pair with full vertical gutter between	—	

REGULAR ISSUE
ROTARY PRESS COIL STAMPS
Types of 1938

1939		Unwmk.		Perf. 10 Vertically	
839	A276	1c	green, Jan. 20, 1939	25	6
			light green	25	6
			Pair	50	14
			Joint line pair	1.25	25
840	A277	1½c	bister brown, Jan. 20, 1939	30	6
			buff	30	6
			Pair	60	12

			Joint line pair	1.30	25
841	A278	2c	rose carmine, Jan. 20, 1939	30	5
			Pair	60	10
			Joint line pair	1.75	15
842	A279	3c	deep violet, Jan. 20, 1939	75	5
			violet	75	5
			Pair	1.50	11
			Joint line pair	2.50	15
			Gripper cracks	—	
			Thin translucent paper	2.00	—
843	A280	4c	red violet, Jan. 20, 1939	9.00	35
			Pair	18.00	70
			Joint line pair	35.00	2.00
844	A281	4½c	dark gray, Jan. 20, 1939	60	45
			Pair	1.20	90
			Joint line pair	4.00	1.50
845	A282	5c	bright blue, Jan. 20, 1939	6.50	35
			Pair	13.00	70
			Joint line pair	30.00	1.50
846	A283	6c	red orange, Jan. 20, 1939	1.40	20
			Pair	2.80	40
			Joint line pair	8.75	80
847	A287	10c	brown red, Jan. 20, 1939	13.00	40
			Pair	26.00	80
			Joint line pair	55.00	2.75

Perf. 10 Horizontally

848	A276	1c	green, Jan. 27, 1939	1.00	12
			Pair	2.00	25
			Joint line pair	3.75	50
849	A277	1½c	bister brown, Jan. 27, 1939	1.50	40
			Pair	3.00	80
			Joint line pair	4.75	1.10
850	A278	2c	rose carmine, Jan. 27, 1939	3.50	50
			Pair	7.00	1.00
			Joint line pair	9.00	1.40
851	A279	3c	deep violet, Jan. 27, 1939	2.75	45
			Pair	5.50	90
			Joint line pair	7.50	1.40

GOLDEN GATE INTERNATIONAL EXPOSITION ISSUE

Issued in commemoration of the Golden Gate International Exposition at San Francisco.

"Tower of the Sun" — A311

ROTARY PRESS PRINTING
Plates of 200 subjects in four panes of 50 each.

1939		Unwmk.		Perf. 10½x11	
852	A311	3c	bright purple, Feb. 18, 1939	12	6
			On cover, Expo. station canc.		6.75
			Margin block of 4, P#	1.75	—

NEW YORK WORLD'S FAIR ISSUE

Issued to commemorate the New York World's Fair.

Trylon and Perisphere — A312

ROTARY PRESS PRINTING
Plates of 200 subjects in four panes of 50 each.

1939		Unwmk.		Perf. 10½x11	
853	A312	3c	deep purple, Apr. 1, 1939	15	6
			On cover, Expo. station canc.		30
			Margin block of 4, P#	2.00	—

WASHINGTON INAUGURATION ISSUE

Issued in commemoration of the sesquicentennial of the inauguration of George Washington as First President.

Washington Taking Oath of Office, Federal Building, New York City — A313

FLAT PLATE PRINTING
Plates of 200 subjects in four panes of 50 each.

1939		Unwmk.		Perf. 11	
854	A313	3c	bright red violet, Apr. 30, 1939	35	10
			Margin block of 6, P#	4.25	—

BASEBALL CENTENNIAL ISSUE

Issued in commemoration of the centennial of Baseball.

Sandlot Baseball Game — A314

Designed by William A. Roach.

ROTARY PRESS PRINTING
Plates of 200 subjects in four panes of 50 each.

1939		Unwmk.		Perf. 11x10½	
855	A314	3c	violet, June 12, 1939	35	8
			Margin block of 4, P#	4.50	—

PANAMA CANAL ISSUE

25th anniversary of the opening of the Panama Canal.

Theodore Roosevelt, Gen. George W. Goethals and Ship in Gaillard Cut — A315

Designed by William A. Roach.

FLAT PLATE PRINTING
Plates of 200 subjects in four panes of 50 each.

1939		Unwmk.		Perf. 11	
856	A315	3c	deep red violet, Aug. 15, 1939	30	8
			Margin block of 6, P#	5.25	—

PRINTING TERCENTENARY ISSUE

Issued in commemoration of the 300th anniversary of printing in Colonial America. The Stephen Daye press is in the Harvard University Museum.

Stephen Daye Press — A316

Designed by William K. Schrage.

ROTARY PRESS PRINTING
E.E. Plates of 200 subjects in four panes of 50 each.

1939		Unwmk.		Perf. 10½x11	
857	A316	3c	violet, Sept. 25, 1939	15	8
			Margin block of 4, P#	1.65	—

50th ANNIVERSARY OF STATEHOOD ISSUE

Issued in commemoration of the 50th anniversary of the admission to statehood of North Dakota, South Dakota, Montana and Washington.

Map of North and South Dakota, Montana and Washington A317

ROTARY PRESS PRINTING

E.E. Plates of 200 subjects in four panes of 50 each.

1939   **Unwmk.**   **Perf. 11x10½**
858 A317 3c **rose violet**, *Nov. 2, 1939*   15 8
     Margin block of 4, P#   1.65 —

FAMOUS AMERICANS ISSUES
ROTARY PRESS PRINTING

E.E. Plates of 280 subjects in four panes of 70 each.

AUTHORS

Issued in honor of famous American authors.

Washington Irving — A318

James Fenimore Cooper — A319

Ralph Waldo Emerson — A320

Louisa May Alcott — A321

Samuel L. Clemens (Mark Twain) — A322

1940   **Unwmk.**   **Perf. 10½x11**
859 A318 1c **bright blue green**, *Jan. 29, 1940* 8 6
    Margin block of 4, P# 1.25 —
860 A319 2c **rose carmine**, *Jan. 29, 1940* 10 8
    Margin block of 4, P# 1.25 —
861 A320 3c **bright red violet**, *Feb. 5, 1940* 12 6
    Block of four 48 40
    Margin block of 4, P# 2.00 —
862 A321 5c **ultramarine**, *Feb. 5, 1940* 35 30
    Margin block of 4, P# 11.00 —
863 A322 10c **dark brown**, *Feb. 13, 1940* 2.00 2.00
    Margin block of 4, P# 50.00 —

POETS

Issued in honor of famous American poets

Henry Wadsworth Longfellow — A323

John Greenleaf Whittier — A324

James Russell Lowell — A325

Walt Whitman — A326

James Witcomb Riley — A327

864 A323 1c **bright blue green**, *Feb. 16, 1940* 12 8
    Margin block of 4, P# 2.25 —
865 A324 2c **rose carmine**, *Feb. 16, 1940* 10 8
    Margin block of 4, P# 2.00 —
866 A325 3c **bright red violet**, *Feb. 20, 1940* 18 6
    Block of four 72 50
    Margin block of 4, P# 3.50 —
867 A326 5c **ultramarine**, *Feb. 20, 1940* 35 25
    Margin block of 4, P# 11.00 —
868 A327 10c **dark brown**, *Feb. 24, 1940* 2.75 2.75
    Margin block of 4, P# 45.00 —

EDUCATORS

Issued in honor of famous American educators.

Horace Mann — A328

Mark Hopkins — A329

Charles W. Eliot — A330

Frances E. Willard — A331

Booker T. Washington — A332

869 A328 1c **bright blue green**, *Mar. 14, 1940* 9 8
    Margin block of 4, P# 2.50 —
870 A329 2c **rose carmine**, *Mar. 14, 1940* 10 6
    Margin block of 4, P# 1.40 —
871 A330 3c **bright red violet**, *Mar. 28, 1940* 30 6
    Block of four 1.20 60
    Margin block of 4, P# 3.25 —
872 A331 5c **ultramarine**, *Mar. 28, 1940* 50 35
    Margin block of 4, P# 14.00 —
873 A332 10c **dark brown**, *Apr. 7, 1940* 1.90 1.90
    Margin block of 4, P# 32.50 —

SCIENTISTS

Issued in honor of famous American scientists.

Prices for well-centered, early U.S. stamps will often exceed catalogue price.

John James Audubon — A333

Dr. Crawford W. Long — A334

Luther Burbank — A335

Dr. Walter Reed — A336

Jane Addams — A337

874 A333 1c **bright blue green**, *Apr. 8, 1940* 8 6
    Margin block of 4, P# 1.00 —
875 A334 2c **rose carmine**, *Apr. 8, 1940* 10 6
    Margin block of 4, P# 1.00 —
876 A335 3c **bright red violet**, *Apr. 17, 1940* 10 6
    Margin block of 4, P# 1.75 —
877 A336 5c **ultramarine**, *Apr. 17, 1940* 30 25
    Block of four 1.20 2.00
    Margin block of 4, P# 9.00 —
878 A337 10c **dark brown**, *Apr. 26, 1940* 1.75 1.75
    Margin block of 4, P# 32.50 —

COMPOSERS

Issued in honor of famous American composers.

Stephen Collins Foster — A338

John Philip Sousa — A339

Victor Herbert — A340

Edward A. MacDowell — A341

Ethelbert Nevin — A342

879 A338 1c **bright blue green**, *May 3, 1940* 8 6
    Margin block of 4, P# 1.50 —
880 A339 2c **rose carmine**, *May 3, 1940* 10 6
    Margin block of 4, P# 1.25 —
881 A340 3c **bright red violet**, *May 13, 1940* 15 6
    Block of four 60 35
    Margin block of 4, P# 1.75 —
882 A341 5c **ultramarine**, *May 13, 1940* 60 30
    Margin block of 4, P# 12.50 —
883 A342 10c **dark brown**, *June 10, 1940* 4.00 2.00
    Margin block of 4, P# 50.00 —

ARTISTS

Issued in honor of famous American artists.

Gilbert Charles
Stuart — A343

James A. McNeill
Whistler — A344

Augustus Saint-
Gaudens
A345

Daniel Chester
French
A346

Frederic Remington — A347

884	A343	1c	**bright blue green,** *Sept. 5, 1940*	8	6
			Margin block of 4, P#	1.25	—
885	A344	2c	**rose carmine,** *Sept. 5, 1940*	10	6
			Margin block of 4, P#	1.10	—
886	A345	3c	**bright red violet,** *Sept. 16, 1940*	10	6
			Margin block of 4, P#	1.25	—
887	A346	5c	**ultramarine,** *Sept. 16, 1940*	40	22
			Margin block of 4, P#	11.50	—
888	A347	10c	**dark brown,** *Sept. 30, 1940*	2.00	2.00
			Margin block of 4, P#	35.00	—

INVENTORS

Issued in honor of famous American inventors.

Eli
Whitney — A348

Samuel F. B.
Morse — A349

Cyrus Hall
McCormick
A350

Elias Howe
A351

Alexander Graham
Bell — A352

889	A348	1c	**bright blue green,** *Oct. 7, 1940*	12	8
			Margin block of 4, P#	2.50	—
890	A349	2c	**rose carmine,** *Oct. 7, 1940*	10	6
			Margin block of 4, P#	1.30	—
891	A350	3c	**bright red violet,** *Oct. 14, 1940*	20	6
			Margin block of 4, P#	2.50	—

892	A351	5c	**ultramarine,** *Oct. 14, 1940*	1.25	40
			Margin block of 4, P#	20.00	—
893	A352	10c	**dark brown,** *Oct. 28, 1940*	12.50	3.00
			Margin block of 4, P#	100.00	—

PONY EXPRESS ISSUE

Issued in commemoration of the 80th anniversary of the Pony Express.

Pony Express
Rider — A353

ROTARY PRESS PRINTING

E.E. Plates of 200 subjects in four panes of 50 each.

1940			**Unwmk.**	***Perf. 11x10½***	
894	A353	3c	**henna brown,** *Apr. 3, 1940*	50	15
			Margin block of 4, P#	5.50	—

PAN AMERICAN UNION ISSUE

Issued in commemoration of the 50th anniversary of the founding of the Pan American Union.

The Three Graces
(Botticelli) — A354

ROTARY PRESS PRINTING

E.E. Plates of 200 subjects in four panes of 50 each.

1940			**Unwmk.**	***Perf. 10½x11***	
895	A354	3c	**light violet,** *Apr. 14, 1940*	40	12
			Margin block of 4, P#	5.00	—

IDAHO STATEHOOD ISSUE

Issued in commemoration of the 50th anniversary of admission of Idaho to statehood.

Idaho State
Capitol — A355

ROTARY PRESS PRINTING

E.E. Plates of 200 subjects in four panes of 50 each.

1940			**Unwmk.**	***Perf. 11x10½***	
896	A355	3c	**bright violet,** *July 3, 1940*	20	8
			Margin block of 4, P#	3.00	—

WYOMING STATEHOOD ISSUE

Issued in commemoration of the 50th anniversary of admission of Wyoming to statehood.

Wyoming State Seal — A356

ROTARY PRESS PRINTING

E.E. Plates of 200 subjects in four panes of 50 each.

1940			**Unwmk.**	***Perf. 10½x11***	
897	A356	3c	**brown violet,** *July 10, 1940*	20	8
			Margin block of 4, P#	2.75	—

CORONADO EXPEDITION ISSUE

Issued in commemoration of the 400th anniversary of the Coronado Expedition.

"Coronado and
His Captains"
Painted by Gerald
Cassidy — A357

ROTARY PRESS PRINTING

E.E. Plates of 200 subjects in four panes of 50 each.

1940			**Unwmk.**	***Perf. 11x10½***	
898	A357	3c	**violet,** *Sept. 7, 1940*	20	8
			Margin block of 4, P#	2.75	—

NATIONAL DEFENSE ISSUE

Issued in connection with the National Defense Program.

Statue of
Liberty — A358

90-millimeter
Anti-aircraft
Gun — A359

Torch of Enlightenment — A360

ROTARY PRESS PRINTING

E.E. Plates of 400 subjects in four panes of 100 each.

1940, Oct. 16			**Unwmk.**	***Perf. 11x10½***	
899	A358	1c	**bright blue green**	5	5
			Margin block of 4, P#	70	—
a.			Vertical pair, imperf. between	500.00	—
b.			Horizontal pair, imperf. between	45.00	—
			Pair with full vertical gutter between	200.00	
			Cracked plate (22684 UR 10)	3.00	
			Gripper cracks	3.00	
900	A359	2c	**rose carmine**	6	5
			Margin block of 4, P#	70	—
a.			Horizontal pair, imperf. between	50.00	—
			Pair with full vertical gutter between	275.00	
901	A360	3c	**bright violet**	12	5
			Margin block of 4, P#	1.40	—
a.			Horizontal pair, imperf. between	25.00	—
			Pair with full vertical gutter between	—	

THIRTEENTH AMENDMENT ISSUE

Issued to commemorate the 75th anniversary of the 13th Amendment to the Constitution abolishing slavery.

Emancipation Monument;
Lincoln and Kneeling Slave, by
Thomas Ball — A361

Designed by William A. Roach.

ROTARY PRESS PRINTING
E.E. Plates of 200 subjects in four panes of 50 each.

1940	Unwmk.	Perf. 10½x11		
902	A361	3c deep violet, *Oct. 20, 1940*	25	15
		dark violet	25	15
		Margin block of 4, P#	5.00	—

VERMONT STATEHOOD ISSUE
Issued in commemoration of the 150th anniversary of the admission of Vermont to statehood.

State Capitol, Montpelier A362

Designed by Alvin R. Meissner.

ROTARY PRESS PRINTING
E.E. Plates of 200 subjects in four panes of 50 each.

1941	Unwmk.	Perf. 11x10½		
903	A362	3c light violet, *Mar. 4, 1941*	22	10
		Margin block of 4, P#	2.50	—

KENTUCKY STATEHOOD ISSUE
Issued in commemoration of the 150th anniversary of the admission of Kentucky to statehood.

Daniel Boone and Three Frontiersmen, from Mural by Gilbert White — A363

Designed by William A. Roach.

ROTARY PRESS PRINTING
E.E. Plates of 200 subjects in four panes of 50 each.

1942	Unwmk.	Perf. 11x10½		
904	A363	3c violet, *June 1, 1942*	15	12
		Margin block of 4, P#	1.75	—

WIN THE WAR ISSUE

American Eagle — A364

ROTARY PRESS PRINTING
E.E. Plates of 400 subjects in four panes of 100 each.

1942	Unwmk.	Perf. 11x10½		
905	A364	3c violet, *July 4, 1942*	10	5
		light violet	10	5
a.		3c purple	20.00	8.00
		Margin block of 4, P#	50	—
		Pair with full vert. or horiz. gutter between	175.00	

CHINESE RESISTANCE ISSUE
Issued to commemorate the Chinese people's five years of resistance to Japanese aggression.

Map of China, Abraham Lincoln and Sun Yat-sen, Founder of the Chinese Republic — A365

ROTARY PRESS PRINTING
E.E. Plates of 200 subjects in four panes of 50 each.

1942	Unwmk.	Perf. 11x10½		
906	A365	5c bright blue, *July 7, 1942*	35	30
		Margin block of 4, P#	16.00	—

ALLIED NATIONS ISSUE

Allegory of Victory — A366

Designed by Leon Helguera.

ROTARY PRESS PRINTING
E.E. Plates of 400 subjects in four panes of 100 each.

1943	Unwmk.	Perf. 11x10½		
907	A366	2c rose carmine, *Jan. 14, 1943*	8	5
		Margin block of 4, P#	40	—
		Pair with full vert. or horiz. gutter between	225.00	

FOUR FREEDOMS ISSUE

Liberty Holding the Torch of Freedom and Enlightenment — A367

Designed by Paul Manship.

ROTARY PRESS PRINTING
E.E. Plates of 400 subjects in four panes of 100 each.

1943	Unwmk.	Perf. 11x10½		
908	A367	1c bright blue green, *Feb. 12, 1943*	6	5
		Margin block of 4, P#	90	—

OVERRUN COUNTRIES ISSUE
Printed by the American Bank Note Co.
FRAMES ENGRAVED, CENTERS OFFSET PRINTING
FLAT PLATE PRINTING
Plates of 200 subjects in four panes of 50 each.

Due to the failure of the printers to divulge detailed information as to printing processes used, the editors omit listings of irregularities, flaws, blemishes and "errors" which are numerous in this issue. These include shifted prints (not true double prints), etc. An exception is made for the widely recognized "KORPA" variety.

Flag of Poland — A368

1943-44	Unwmk.	Perf. 12		
909	A368	5c blue violet, bright red & black, *June 22, 1943*	25	20
		Margin block of 4, Inscribed "Poland"	8.75	—
		Top margin block of 6, with red & blue violet guide markings and "Poland"	9.00	—
		Bottom margin block of 6, with red & black guide markings	2.15	—

Flag of Czechoslovakia A368a

| 910 | A368a | 5c blue violet, blue, bright red & black, *July 12, 1943* | 20 | 15 |

| | Margin block of 4, inscribed "Czechoslovakia" | 4.25 | — |
| | Top margin block of 6, with red & blue violet guide markings and "Czechoslovakia" | 5.00 | — |

Flag of Norway — A368b

911	A368b	5c blue violet, dark rose, deep blue & black, *July 27, 1943*	15	12
		Margin block of 4, inscribed "Norway"	2.25	—
		Bottom margin block of 6 with dark rose & blue violet guide markings	1.75	—

Flag of Luxembourg A368c

912	A368c	5c blue violet, dark rose, light blue & black, *Aug. 10, 1943*	15	12
		Margin block of 4, inscribed "Luxembourg"	2.00	—
		Top margin block of 6 with light blue & blue violet guide markings & "Luxembourg"	3.25	—

Flag of Netherlands A368d

913	A368d	5c blue violet, dark rose, blue & black, *Aug. 24, 1943*	15	12
		Margin block of 4, inscribed "Netherlands"	2.00	—
		Bottom margin block of 6 with blue & blue violet guide markings	1.75	—

Flag of Belgium — A368e

914	A368e	5c blue violet, dark rose, yellow & black, *Sept. 14, 1943*	15	12
		Margin block of 4, inscribed "Belgium"	2.00	—
		Top margin block of 6, with yellow & blue violet guide markings and "Belgium"	3.25	—

Flag of France — A368f

915	A368f	5c blue violet, deep blue, dark rose & black, *Sept. 28, 1943*	15	10
		Margin block of 4, inscribed "France"	2.00	—
		Bottom margin block of 6 with dark rose & blue violet guide markings	1.75	—

Flag of Greece — A368g

916 A368g 5c **blue violet, pale blue & black,** *Oct. 12, 1943*   55 60
   Margin block of 4, inscribed "Greece"   20.00 —
   Top margin block of 6 with pale blue & blue violet guide markings & "Greece"   22.50 —

Flag of Yugoslavia A368h

917 A368h 5c **blue violet, blue, dark rose & black,** *Oct. 26, 1943*   50 40
   Margin block of 4, inscribed "Yugoslavia"   9.00 —
   Bottom margin block of 6 with dark rose & blue violet guide markings   3.25 —

Flag of Albania — A368i

918 A368i 5c **blue violet, dark red & black,** *Nov. 9, 1943*   30 40
   Margin block of 4, inscribed "Albania"   9.00 —
   Top margin block of 6, with dark red & blue violet guide markings & "Albania"   9.00 —

Flag of Austria — A368j

919 A368j 5c **blue violet, red & black,** *Nov. 23, 1943*   30 25
   Margin block of 4, inscribed "Austria"   5.50 —
   Bottom margin block of 6, with red & blue violet guide markings   2.00 —

Flag of Denmark — A368k

920 A368k 5c **blue violet, red & black,** *Dec. 7, 1943*   35 50
   Margin block of 4, inscribed "Denmark"   7.50 —
   Top margin block of 6, with red & blue violet guide markings & "Denmark"   9.00 —

See "Information for Collectors" section at beginning of catalogue for illustrations of types of postmarks and precancels.

Flag of Korea — A368m

921 A368m 5c **blue violet, red, black & light b!ue,** *Nov. 2, 1944*   20 25
   Margin block of 4, inscribed "Korea"   7.00 —
   Top margin block of 6 with blue & black guide markings and "Korea"   7.75 —
   "KORPA" plate flaw   25.00 20.00

TRANSCONTINENTAL RAILROAD ISSUE

Issued to commemorate the 75th anniversary of the completion of the first transcontinental railroad.

"Golden Spike Ceremony" Painted by John McQuarrie A369

ENGRAVED
ROTARY PRESS PRINTING
E.E. Plates of 200 subjects in four panes of 50 each.

1944	Unwmk.	Perf. 11x10½		
922 A369 3c **violet,** *May 10, 1944*			20	15
Margin block of 4, P#			2.50	—

STEAMSHIP ISSUE

Issued to commemorate the 125th anniversary of the first steamship to cross the Atlantic Ocean.

"Savannah" A370

ROTARY PRESS PRINTING
E.E. Plates of 200 subjects in four panes of 50 each.

1944	Unwmk.	Perf. 11x10½		
923 A370 3c **violet,** *May 22, 1944*			15	15
Margin block of 4, P#			2.50	—

TELEGRAPH ISSUE

Issued to commemorate the 100th anniversary of the first message transmitted by telegraph.

Telegraph Wires and Morse's First Transmitted Words "What Hath God Wrought" — A371

ROTARY PRESS PRINTING
E.E. Plates of 200 subjects in four panes of 50 each.

1944	Unwmk.	Perf. 11x10½		
924 A371 3c **bright red violet,** *May 24, 1944*			12	10
Margin block of 4, P#			1.60	—

PHILLIPPINE ISSUE

Issued to commemorate the final resistance of the United States and Philippine defenders on Corregidor to the Japanese invaders in 1942.

Aerial View of Corregidor, Manila Bay — A372

ROTARY PRESS PRINTING
E.E. Plates of 200 subjects in four panes of 50 each.

1944	Unwmk.	Perf. 11x10½		
925 A372 3c **deep violet,** *Sept. 27, 1944*			12	12
Margin block of 4, P#			2.00	—

MOTION PICTURE ISSUE

Issued to commemorate the 50th anniversary of motion pictures.

Motion Picture Showing for Armed Forces in South Pacific — A373

ROTARY PRESS PRINTING
E.E. Plates of 200 subjects in four panes of 50 each.

1944	Unwmk.	Perf. 11x10½		
926 A373 3c **deep violet,** *Oct. 31, 1944*			12	10
Margin block of 4, P#			1.50	—

FLORIDA STATEHOOD ISSUE
Centenary of the admission of Florida to statehood.

State Seal, Gates of St. Augustine and Capitol at Tallahassee A374

ROTARY PRESS PRINTING
E.E. Plates of 200 subjects in four panes of 50 each.

1945	Unwmk.	Perf. 11x10½		
927 A374 3c **bright red violet,** *Mar. 3, 1945*			10	8
Margin block of 4, P#			1.00	—

UNITED NATIONS CONFERENCE ISSUE
United Nations Conference, San Francisco, Calif.

"Toward United Nations, April 25, 1945" — A375

ROTARY PRESS PRINTING
E.E. Plates of 200 subjects in four panes of 50 each.

1945	Unwmk.	Perf. 11x10½		
928 A375 5c **ultramarine,** *Apr. 25, 1945*			12	8
Margin block of 4, P#			70	—

IWO JIMA (MARINES) ISSUE

Issued to commemorate the battle of Iwo Jima and to honor the achievements of the United States Marines.

Marines Raising American Flag on Mount Suribachi, Iwo Jima — A376

ROTARY PRESS PRINTING
E.E. Plates of 200 subjects in four panes of 50 each.

1945	Unwmk.	Perf. 10½x11		
929 A376 3c **yellow green,** *July 11, 1945*			10	5
Margin block of 4, P#			50	—

FRANKLIN D. ROOSEVELT ISSUE

Issued in tribute to Franklin Delano Roosevelt (1882-1945).

Roosevelt and Hyde Park Residence — A377

Roosevelt and the "Little White House" at Warm Springs, Ga. — A378

Roosevelt and White House — A379

Roosevelt, Map of Western Hemisphere and Four Freedoms — A380

ROTARY PRESS PRINTING

E.E. Plates of 200 subjects in four panes of 50 each.

1945-46	Unwmk.	Perf. 11x10½		
930 A377	1c blue green, July 26, 1945		5	5
	Margin block of 4, P#		30	—
931 A378	2c carmine rose, Aug. 24, 1945		8	8
	Margin block of 4, P#		40	—
932 A379	3c purple, June 27, 1945		10	8
	Margin block of 4, P#		55	—
933 A380	5c bright blue, Jan. 30, 1946		12	8
	Margin block of 4, P#		65	—

ARMY ISSUE

Issued to commemorate the achievements of the United States Army in World War II.

United States Troops Passing Arch of Triumph, Paris — A381

ROTARY PRESS PRINTING

E.E. Plates of 200 subjects in four panes of 50 each.

1945	Unwmk.	Perf. 11x10½		
934 A381	3c olive, Sept. 28, 1945		10	5
	Margin block of 4, P#		50	—

NAVY ISSUE

Issued to commemorate the achievements of the United States Navy in World War II.

United States Sailors — A382

ROTARY PRESS PRINTING

E.E. Plates of 200 subjects in four panes of 50 each.

1945	Unwmk.	Perf. 11x10½		
935 A382	3c blue, Oct. 27, 1945		10	5
	Margin block of 4, P#		50	—

COAST GUARD ISSUE

Issued to commemorate the achievements of the United States Coast Guard in World War II.

Coast Guard Landing Craft and Supply Ship — A383

ROTARY PRESS PRINTING

E.E. Plates of 200 subjects in four panes of 50 each.

1945	Unwmk.	Perf. 11x10½		
936 A383	3c bright blue green, Nov. 10, 1945		10	5
	Margin block of 4, P#		50	—

ALFRED E. SMITH ISSUE

Issued in honor of Alfred E. Smith, governor of New York.

Alfred E. Smith — A384

ROTARY PRESS PRINTING

E.E. Plates of 400 subjects in four panes of 100 each.

1945	Unwmk.	Perf. 11x10½		
937 A384	3c purple, Nov. 26, 1945		10	5
	Margin block of 4, P#		50	
	Pair with full vert. gutter btwn.		—	—

TEXAS STATEHOOD ISSUE

Issued to commemorate the 100th anniversary of the admission of Texas to statehood.

Flags of the United States and the State of Texas — A385

ROTARY PRESS PRINTING

E.E. Plates of 200 subjects in four panes of 50 each.

1945	Unwmk.	Perf. 11x10½		
938 A385	3c dark blue, Dec. 29, 1945		10	5
	Margin block of 4, P#		50	—

MERCHANT MARINE ISSUE

Issued to commemorate the achievements of the United States Merchant Marine in World War II.

Liberty Ship Unloading Cargo — A386

ROTARY PRESS PRINTING

E.E. Plates of 200 subjects in four panes of 50 each.

1946	Unwmk.	Perf. 11x10½		
939 A386	3c blue green, Feb. 26, 1946		10	5
	Margin block of 4, P#		50	—

VETERANS OF WORLD WAR II ISSUE

Issued to honor all veterans of World War II.

Honorable Discharge Emblem — A387

ROTARY PRESS PRINTING

E.E. Plates of 400 subjects in four panes of 100 each.

1946	Unwmk.	Perf. 11x10½		
940 A387	3c dark violet, May 9, 1946		10	5
	Margin block of 4, P#		55	—

TENNESSEE STATEHOOD ISSUE

Issued to commemorate the 150th anniversary of the admission of Tennessee to statehood.

Andrew Jackson, John Sevier and State Capitol, Nashville — A388

ROTARY PRESS PRINTING

E.E. Plates of 200 subjects in four panes of 50 each.

1946	Unwmk.	Perf. 11x10½		
941 A388	3c dark violet, June 1, 1946		10	5
	Margin block of 4, P#		50	—

IOWA STATEHOOD ISSUE

Centenary of the admission of Iowa to statehood.

Iowa State Flag and Map — A389

ROTARY PRESS PRINTING

E.E. Plates of 200 subjects in four panes of 50 each.

1946	Unwmk.	Perf. 11x10½		
942 A389	3c deep blue, Aug. 3, 1946		10	5
	Margin block of 4, P#		50	—

SMITHSONIAN INSTITUTION ISSUE

Issued to commemorate the 100th anniversary of the establishment of the Smithsonian Institution, Washington, D.C.

Smithsonian Institution A390

ROTARY PRESS PRINTING

E.E. Plates of 200 subjects in four panes of 50 each.

1946	Unwmk.	Perf. 11x10½		
943 A390	3c violet brown, Aug. 10, 1946		10	5
	Margin block of 4, P#		50	—

KEARNY EXPEDITION ISSUE

Issued to commemorate the 100th anniversary of the entry of General Stephen Watts Kearny into Santa Fe.

"Capture of Santa Fe" by Kenneth M. Chapman — A391

ROTARY PRESS PRINTING

E.E. Plates of 200 subjects in four panes of 50 each.

1946	Unwmk.	Perf. 11x10½		
944 A391	3c brown violet, Oct. 16, 1946		10	5
	Margin block of 4, P#		50	—

THOMAS A. EDISON ISSUE
Centenary of the birth of Thomas Alva Edison
(1847-1931), inventor.

Thomas A. Edison — A392

ROTARY PRESS PRINTING
E.E. Plates of 280 subjects in four panes of 70 each.

1947	Unwmk.		Perf. 10½x11	
945 A392	3c	**bright red violet,** *Feb. 11, 1947*	10	5
		Margin block of 4, P#	50	—

JOSEPH PULITZER ISSUE
Centenary of the birth of Joseph Pulitzer (1847-
1911), journalist.

Joseph Pulitzer
and Statue of
Liberty — A393

Designed by Victor S. McCloskey, Jr.

ROTARY PRESS PRINTING
E.E. Plates of 200 subjects in four panes of 50 each.

1947	Unwmk.		Perf. 11x10½	
946 A393	3c	**purple,** *Apr. 10, 1947*	10	5
		Margin block of 4, P#	50	—

POSTAGE STAMP CENTENARY ISSUE

Issued to commemorate the centenary of the first
postage stamps issued by the United States
Government

Washington and
Franklin, Early
and Modern Mail-
carrying
Vehicles — A394

Designed by Leon Helguera.

ROTARY PRESS PRINTING
E.E. Plates of 200 subjects in four panes of 50 each.

1947	Unwmk.		Perf. 11x10½	
947 A394	3c	**deep blue,** *May 17, 1947*	10	5
		Margin block of 4, P#	50	—

CENTENARY INTERNATIONAL PHILATELIC EXHIBITION ISSUE
SOUVENIR SHEET

A395

FLAT PLATE PRINTING
Plates of 30 subjects

1947	Unwmk.		*Imperf.*	
948 A395		**Sheet of two,** *May 19, 1947*	1.00	1.00
a.		5c blue, type A1	30	30
b.		10c brown orange, type A2	40	30

Sheet inscribed below stamps: "100th Anniversary United
States Postage Stamps" and in the margins:
"PRINTED BY THE TREASURY DEPARTMENT,
BUREAU OF ENGRAVING AND PRINTING. - UNDER
AUTHORITY OF ROBERT E. HANNEGAN, POSTMAS-
TER GENERAL. - IN COMPLIMENT TO THE CENTE-
NARY INTERNATIONAL PHILATELIC EXHIBITION. -
NEW YORK, N.Y., MAY 17-25, 1947."
Sheet size varies: 96-98x66-68mm.

DOCTORS ISSUE

Issued to honor the physicians of America.

"The Doctor" by
Sir Luke
Fildes — A396

Designed by Charles R. Chickering.

ROTARY PRESS PRINTING
E.E. Plates of 200 subjects in four panes of 50 each.

1947	Unwmk.		Perf. 11x10½	
949 A396	3c	**brown violet,** *June 9, 1947*	10	5
		Margin block of 4, P#	50	—

UTAH ISSUE

Issued to commemorate the centenary of the settlement of Utah.

Pioneers Entering
the Valley of
Great Salt
Lake — A397

Designed by Charles R. Chickering.

ROTARY PRESS PRINTING
E.E. Plates of 200 subjects in four panes of 50 each.

1947	Unwmk.		Perf. 11x10½	
950 A397	3c	**dark violet,** *July 24, 1947*	10	5
		Margin block of 4, P#	50	—

U.S. FRIGATE CONSTITUTION ISSUE

Issued to commemorate the 150th anniversary of
the launching of the U.S. frigate Constitution ("Old
Ironsides").

Naval Architect's
Drawing of Frigate
Constitution
A398

Designed by Andrew H. Hepburn.

ROTARY PRESS PRINTING
E.E. Plates of 200 subjects in four panes of 50 each.

1947	Unwmk.		Perf. 11x10½	
951 A398	3c	**blue green,** *Oct. 21, 1947*	10	5
		Margin block of 4, P#	50	—

EVERGLADES NATIONAL PARK ISSUE

Issued to commemorate the dedication of the
Everglades National Park, Florida, December 6,
1947.

Great White Heron and Map
of Florida — A399

Designed by Robert I. Miller, Jr.

ROTARY PRESS PRINTING
E.E. Plates of 200 subjects in four panes of 50 each.

1947	Unwmk.		Perf. 10½x11	
952 A399	3c	**bright green,** *Dec. 5, 1947*	10	5
		Margin block of 4, P#	50	—

GEORGE WASHINGTON CARVER ISSUE

Issued to commemorate the fifth anniversary of
the death of Dr. George Washington Carver, (1864-
1943), botanist.

Dr. George Washington
Carver — A400

ROTARY PRESS PRINTING
E.E. Plates of 280 subjects in four panes of 70 each.

1948	Unwmk.		Perf. 10½x11	
953 A400	3c	**bright red violet,** *Jan. 5, 1948*	10	5
		Margin block of 4, P#	50	—

CALIFORNIA GOLD CENTENNIAL ISSUE
Centenary of the discovery of gold in California.

Sutter's Mill,
Coloma,
California — A401

Designed by Charles R. Chickering.

ROTARY PRESS PRINTING
E.E. Plates of 200 subjects in four panes of 50 each.

1948	Unwmk.		Perf. 11x10½	
954 A401	3c	**dark violet,** *Jan. 24, 1948*	10	5
		Margin block of 4, P#	50	—

MISSISSIPPI TERRITORY ISSUE

Issued to commemorate the 150th anniversary of
the establishment of the Mississippi Territory.

Map, Seal of
Mississippi
Territory and
Gov. Winthrop
Sargent — A402

Designed by William K. Schrage.

ROTARY PRESS PRINTING
E.E. Plates of 200 subjects in four panes of 50 each.

1948	Unwmk.		Perf. 11x10½	
955 A402	3c	**brown violet,** *Apr. 7, 1948*	10	5
		Margin block of 4, P#	50	—

FOUR CHAPLAINS ISSUE

Issued in honor of George L. Fox, Clark V. Poling,
John P. Washington and Alexander D. Goode, the
four chaplains who sacrificed their lives in the sinking of the S.S. Dorchester, February 3, 1943.

Four Chaplains
and Sinking S.S.
Dorchester
A403

Designed by Charles R. Chickering.

ROTARY PRESS PRINTING
E.E. Plates of 200 subjects in four panes of 50 each.

1948		Unwmk.		Perf. 11x10½	
956 A403	3c gray black, May 28, 1948			10	5
	Margin block of 4, P#			50	—

WISCONSIN CENTENNIAL ISSUE
Issued to commemorate the centenary of the admission of Wisconsin to statehood.

Map on Scroll and
State
Capitol — A404

Designed by Victor S. McCloskey, Jr.

ROTARY PRESS PRINTING
E.E. Plates of 200 subjects in four panes of 50 each.

1948		Unwmk.		Perf. 11x10½	
957 A404	3c dark violet, May 29, 1948			10	5
	Margin block of 4, P#			50	—

SWEDISH PIONEER ISSUE
Issued to commemorate the centenary of the coming of the Swedish pioneers to the Middle West.

Swedish Pioneer
with Covered
Wagon Moving
Westward — A405

Designed by Charles R. Chickering.

ROTARY PRESS PRINTING
E.E. Plates of 200 subjects in four panes of 50 each.

1948		Unwmk.		Perf. 11x10½	
958 A405	5c deep blue, June 4, 1948			15	10
	Margin block of 4, P#			90	—

PROGRESS OF WOMEN ISSUE
Issued to commemorate a century of progress of American Women.

Elizabeth Stanton,
Carrie Chapman
Catt and Lucretia
Mott — A406

Designed by Victor S. McCloskey, Jr.

ROTARY PRESS PRINTING
E.E. Plates of 200 subjects in four panes of 50 each.

1948		Unwmk.		Perf. 11x10½	
959 A406	3c dark violet, July 19, 1948			10	5
	Margin block of 4, P#			50	—

WILLIAM ALLEN WHITE ISSUE
Issued to honor William Allen White, (1868-1944), writer and journalist.

Prices paid for stamps on original covers vary greatly in accordance with condition, appearance, cancellation or postmark and usage.

William Allen White — A407

ROTARY PRESS PRINTING
E.E. Plates of 280 subjects in four panes of 70 each.

1948		Unwmk.		Perf. 10½x11	
960 A407	3c bright red violet, July 31, 1948			10	6
	Margin block of 4, P#			60	—

UNITED STATES-CANADA FRIENDSHIP ISSUE
Issued to commemorate a century of friendship between the United States and Canada.

Niagara Railway
Suspension
Bridge — A408

Designed by Leon Helguera, modeled by V. S. McCloskey, Jr.

ROTARY PRESS PRINTING
E.E. Plates of 200 subjects in four panes of 50 each.

1948		Unwmk.		Perf. 11x10½	
961 A408	3c blue, Aug. 2, 1948			10	5
	Margin block of 4, P#			50	—

FRANCIS SCOTT KEY ISSUE
Issued to honor Francis Scott Key (1779-1843), Maryland lawyer and author of "The Star-Spangled Banner" (1813).

Francis Scott Key
and American
Flags of 1814 and
1948 — A409

Designed by Victor S. McCloskey, Jr.

ROTARY PRESS PRINTING
E.E. Plates of 200 subjects in four panes of 50 each.

1948		Unwmk.		Perf. 11x10½	
962 A409	3c rose pink, Aug. 9, 1948			10	5
	Margin block of 4, P#			50	—

SALUTE TO YOUTH ISSUE
Issued to honor the Youth of America and to publicize "Youth Month," September, 1948.

Girl and Boy
Carrying
Books — A410

ROTARY PRESS PRINTING
E.E. Plates of 200 subjects in four panes of 50 each.

1948		Unwmk.		Perf. 11x10½	
963 A410	3c deep blue, Aug. 11, 1948			10	6
	Margin block of 4, P#			50	—

OREGON TERRITORY ISSUE
Issued to commemorate the centenary of the establishment of Oregon Territory.

John McLoughlin,
Jason Lee and
Wagon on Oregon
Trail — A411

ROTARY PRESS PRINTING
E.E. Plates of 200 subjects in four panes of 50 each.

1948		Unwmk.		Perf. 11x10½	
964 A411	3c brown red, Aug. 14, 1948			10	10
	Margin block of 4, P#			50	—

HARLAN F. STONE ISSUE
Issued to honor Harlan Fiske Stone (1872-1946) of New York, associate justice of the Supreme Court, 1925-1941, and chief justice, 1941-1946.

Chief Justice Harlan F.
Stone — A412

ROTARY PRESS PRINTING
E.E. Plates of 280 subjects in four panes of 70 each.

1948		Unwmk.		Perf. 10½x11	
965 A412	3c bright violet, Aug. 25, 1948			10	8
	Margin block of 4, P#			1.00	—

PALOMAR MOUNTAIN OBSERVATORY ISSUE
Issued to commemorate the dedication of the Palomar Mountain Observatory, August 30, 1948.

Observatory, Palomar
Mountain, California — A413

Designed by Victor S. McCloskey, Jr.

ROTARY PRESS PRINTING
E.E. Plates of 280 subjects in four panes of 70 each.

1948		Unwmk.		Perf. 10½x11	
966 A413	3c blue, Aug. 30 1948			12	10
	Margin block of 4, P#			1.75	—
a.	Vert. pair, imperf. btwn.			650.00	

CLARA BARTON ISSUE
Issued to honor Clara Barton (1821-1912), who founded the American Red Cross in 1882.

Clara Barton and
Cross — A414

Designed by Charles R. Chickering.

ROTARY PRESS PRINTING
E.E. Plates of 200 subjects in four panes of 50 each.

1948		Unwmk.		Perf. 11x10½	
967 A414	3c rose pink, Sept. 7, 1948			10	8
	Margin block of 4, P#			50	—

POULTRY INDUSTRY CENTENNIAL ISSUE
Issued to commemorate the centenary of the establishment of the American Poultry Industry.

Light Brahma
Rooster — A415

Designed by Charles R. Chickering.

ROTARY PRESS PRINTING
E.E. Plates of 200 subjects in four panes of 50 each.

1948	Unwmk.	Perf. 11x10½		
968 A415 3c **sepia**, *Sept. 9, 1948*			12	8
Margin block of 4, P#			60	—

GOLD STAR MOTHERS ISSUE

Issued to honor the mothers of deceased members of the United States armed forces.

Star and Palm Frond — A416

Designed by Charles R. Chickering.

ROTARY PRESS PRINTING
E.E. Plates of 200 subjects in four panes of 50 each.

1948	Unwmk.	Perf. 10½x11		
969 A416 3c **orange yellow**, *Sept. 21, 1948*			12	8
Margin block of 4, P#			60	—

FORT KEARNY ISSUE

Centenary of the establishment of Fort Kearny, Neb.

Fort Kearny and
Pioneer
Group — A417

ROTARY PRESS PRINTING
E.E. Plates of 200 subjects in four panes of 50 each.

1948	Unwmk.	Perf. 11x10½		
970 A417 3c **violet**, *Sept. 22, 1948*			12	8
Margin block of 4, P#			60	—

VOLUNTEER FIREMEN ISSUE

Issued to commemorate the 300th anniversary of the organization of the first volunteer firemen in America by Peter Stuyvesant.

Peter Stuyvesant,
Early and
Modern Fire
Engines — A418

ROTARY PRESS PRINTING
E.E. Plates of 200 subjects in four panes of 50 each.

1948	Unwmk.	Perf. 11x10½		
971 A418 3c **bright rose carmine**, *Oct. 4, 1948*			12	8
Margin block of 4, P#			60	—

INDIAN CENTENNIAL ISSUE

Issued to commemorate the centenary of the arrival in Indian Territory, later Oklahoma, of the Five Civilized Indian Tribes: Cherokee, Chickasaw, Choctaw, Muscogee and Seminole.

Map of Indian
Territory and
Seals of Five
Tribes — A419

ROTARY PRESS PRINTING
E.E. Plates of 200 subjects in four panes of 50 each.

1948	Unwmk.	Perf. 11x10½		
972 A419 3c **dark brown**, *Oct. 15, 1948*			12	8
Margin block of 4, P#			60	—

ROUGH RIDERS ISSUE

Issued to commemorate the 50th anniversary of the organization of the Rough Riders of the Spanish-American War.

Statue of Capt.
William O.
(Bucky) O'Neill by
Solon H.
Borglum — A420

Designed by Victor S. McCloskey, Jr.

ROTARY PRESS PRINTING
E.E. Plates of 200 subjects in four panes of 50 each.

1948	Unwmk.	Perf. 11x10½		
973 A420 3c **violet brown**, *Oct. 27, 1948*			12	10
Margin block of 4, P#			65	—

JULIETTE LOW ISSUE

Issued to honor Juliette Gordon Low (1860-1927), founder of the Girl Scouts of America. Mrs. Low organized the first troop of Girl Guides in 1912 at Savannah. The name was changed to Girl Scouts in 1913 and headquarters moved to New York.

Juliette Gordon
Low and Girl
Scout
Emblem -- A421

Designed by William K. Schrage.

ROTARY PRESS PRINTING
E.E. Plates of 200 subjects in four panes of 50 each.

1948	Unwmk.	Perf. 11x10½		
974 A421 3c **blue green**, *Oct. 29, 1948*			12	8
Margin block of 4, P#			60	—

WILL ROGERS ISSUE

Issued to honor Will Rogers, (1879-1935), humorist and political commentator.

Will Rogers — A422

ROTARY PRESS PRINTING
E.E. Plates of 280 subjects in four panes of 70 each.

1948	Unwmk.	Perf. 10½x11		
975 A422 3c **bright red violet**, *Nov. 4, 1948*			12	8
Margin block of 4, P#			80	—

FORT BLISS CENTENNIAL ISSUE

Issued to commemorate the centenary of the establishment of Fort Bliss at El Paso, Texas.

Fort Bliss and Rocket
Firing — A423

Designed by Charles R. Chickering.

ROTARY PRESS PRINTING
E.E. Plates of 280 subjects in four panes of 70 each.

1948	Unwmk.	Perf. 10½x11		
976 A423 3c **henna brown**, *Nov. 5, 1948*			15	8
Margin block of 4, P#			1.75	—

MOINA MICHAEL ISSUE

Issued to honor Moina Michael (1870-1944), educator who originated (1918) the Flanders Field Poppy Day idea as a memorial to the war dead.

Moina Michael
and Poppy
Plant — A424

ROTARY PRESS PRINTING
E.E. Plates of 200 subjects in four panes of 50 each.

1948	Unwmk.	Perf. 11x10½		
977 A424 3c **rose pink**, *Nov. 9, 1948*			12	8
Margin block of 4, P#			60	—

GETTYSBURG ADDRESS ISSUE

Issued to commemorate the 85th anniversary of Abraham Lincoln's address at Gettysburg, Pennsylvania.

Abraham Lincoln
and Quotation
from Gettysburg
Address — A425

Designed by Charles R. Chickering.

ROTARY PRESS PRINTING
E.E. Plates of 200 subjects in four panes of 50 each.

1948	Unwmk.	Perf. 11x10½		
978 A425 3c **bright blue**, *Nov. 19, 1948*			12	8
Margin block of 4, P#			60	—

AMERICAN TURNERS ISSUE

Issued to commemorate the centenary of the formation of the American Turners Society.

Torch and Emblem of
American Turners — A426

Designed by Alvin R. Meissner.

ROTARY PRESS PRINTING
E.E. Plates of 200 subjects in four panes of 50 each.

1948	Unwmk.	Perf. 10½x11		
979 A426 3c **carmine**, *Nov. 20, 1948*			12	8
Margin block of 4, P#			60	—

JOEL CHANDLER HARRIS ISSUE

Issued to commemorate the centenary of the birth of Joel Chandler Harris (1848-1908), Georgia writer, creator of "Uncle Remus" and newspaperman.

Joel Chandler Harris — A427

ROTARY PRESS PRINTING

E.E. Plates of 280 subjects in four panes of 70 each.

1948	Unwmk.		Perf. 10½x11	
980	A427 3c **bright red violet,** *Dec. 9, 1948*		12	8
	Margin block of 4, P#		85	—

MINNESOTA TERRITORY ISSUE

Issued to commemorate the centenary of the establishment of Minnesota Territory.

Pioneer and Red River Oxcart — A428

ROTARY PRESS PRINTING

E.E. Plates of 200 subjects in four panes of 50 each.

1949	Unwmk.		Perf. 11x10½	
981	A428 3c **blue green,** *Mar. 3, 1949*		10	5
	Margin block of 4		50	—

WASHINGTON AND LEE UNIVERSITY ISSUE

Bicentenary of Washington and Lee University.

George Washington, Robert E. Lee and University Building, Lexington, Va. — A429

ROTARY PRESS PRINTING

E.E. Plates of 200 subjects in four panes of 50 each.

1949	Unwmk.		Perf. 11x10½	
982	A429 3c **ultramarine,** *Apr. 12, 1949*		10	5
	Margin block of 4		50	—

PUERTO RICO ELECTION ISSUE

Issued to commemorate the first gubernatorial election in the Territory of Puerto Rico, Nov. 2, 1948.

Puerto Rican Farmer Holding Cogwheel and Ballot Box — A430

ROTARY PRESS PRINTING

E.E. Plates of 200 subjects in four panes of 50 each.

1949	Unwmk.		Perf. 11x10½	
983	A430 3c **green,** *Apr. 27, 1949*		10	5
	Margin block of 4, P#		50	—

ANNAPOLIS TERCENTENARY ISSUE

Issued to commemorate the 300th anniversary of the founding of Annapolis, Maryland.

James Stoddert's 1718 Map of Regions about Annapolis, Redrawn — A431

ROTARY PRESS PRINTING

E.E. Plates of 200 subjects in four panes of 50 each.

1949	Unwmk.		Perf. 11x10½	
984	A431 3c **aquamarine,** *May 23, 1949*		10	5
	Margin block of 4, P#		50	—

G.A.R. ISSUE

Issued to commemorate the final encampment of the Grand Army of the Republic, Indianapolis, August 28 to September 1, 1949.

Union Soldier and G.A.R. Veteran of 1949 — A432

Designed by Charles R. Chickering.

ROTARY PRESS PRINTING

E.E. Plates of 200 subjects in four panes of 50 each.

1949	Unwmk.		Perf. 11x10½	
985	A432 3c **bright rose carmine,** *Aug. 29, 1949*		10	5
	Margin block of 4, P#		50	—

EDGAR ALLAN POE ISSUE

Issued to commemorate the centenary of the death of Edgar Allan Poe (1809-1849), Boston-born poet, story writer and editor.

Edgar Allan Poe — A433

ROTARY PRESS PRINTING

E.E. Plates of 280 subjects in four panes of 70 each.

1949	Unwmk.		Perf. 10½x11	
986	A433 3c **bright red violet,** *Oct. 7, 1949*		10	5
	Margin block of 4, P#		60	—
	Thin outer frame line at top, inner line missing (24143 LL 42)		10.00	

AMERICAN BANKERS ASSOCIATION ISSUE

Issued to commemorate the 75th anniversary of the formation of the American Bankers Association.

Coin, Symbolizing Fields of Banking Service — A434

Designed by Charles R. Chickering.

ROTARY PRESS PRINTING

E.E. Plates of 200 subjects in four panes of 50 each.

1950	Unwmk.		Perf. 11x10½	
987	A434 3c **yellow green,** *Jan. 3, 1950*		10	5
	Margin block of 4, P#		50	—

SAMUEL GOMPERS ISSUE

Issued to commemorate the centenary of the birth of Samuel Gompers (1850-1924), British-born American labor leader.

Samuel Gompers — A435

ROTARY PRESS PRINTING

E.E. Plates of 280 subjects in four panes of 70 each.

1950	Unwmk.		Perf. 10½x11	
988	A435 3c **bright red violet,** *Jan. 27, 1950*		10	5
	Margin block of 4, P#		50	—

NATIONAL CAPITAL SESQUICENTENNIAL ISSUE

Issued to commemorate the 150th anniversary of the establishment of the National Capital, Washington, D.C.

Statue of Freedom on Capitol Dome — A436

Executive Mansion — A437

Supreme Court Building — A438

United States Capitol — A439

ROTARY PRESS PRINTING

E.E. Plates of 200 subjects in four panes of 50 each.

1950	Unwmk.	Perf. 10½x11, 11x10½		
989	A436 3c **bright blue,** *Apr. 20, 1950*		10	5
	Margin block of 4, P#		50	—
990	A437 3c **deep green,** *June 12, 1950*		10	5
	Margin block of 4, P#		50	—
991	A438 3c **light violet,** *Aug. 2, 1950*		10	5
	Margin block of 4, P#		50	—
992	A439 3c **bright red violet,** *Nov. 22, 1950*		10	5
	Margin block of 4, P#		50	—
	Gripper cracks (24285 UL 11)		1.50	50

RAILROAD ENGINEERS ISSUE

Issued to honor the Railroad Engineers of America. Stamp portrays John Luther (Casey) Jones (1864-1900), locomotive engineer killed in train wreck near Vaughn, Miss.

"Casey" Jones and Locomotives of 1900 and 1950 — A440

ROTARY PRESS PRINTING

E.E. Plates of 200 subjects in four panes of 50 each.

1950	Unwmk.	Perf. 11x10½
993 A440 3c **violet brown,** *April 29, 1950*		10 5
Margin block of 4, P#		50 —

KANSAS CITY, MISSOURI, CENTENARY ISSUE

Issued to commemorate the centenary of the incorporation of Kansas City, Missouri.

Kansas City Skyline, 1950 and Westport Landing, 1850 — A441

ROTARY PRESS PRINTING

E.E. Plates of 200 subjects in four panes of 50 each.

1950	Unwmk.	Perf. 11x10½
994 A441 3c **violet,** *June 3, 1950*		10 5
Margin block of 4, P#		50 —

BOY SCOUTS ISSUE

Issued to honor the Boy Scouts of America on the occasion of the second National Jamboree, Valley Forge, Pa.

Three Boys, Statue of Liberty and Scout Badge — A442

ROTARY PRESS PRINTING

E.E. Plates of 200 subjects in four panes of 50 each.

1950	Unwmk.	Perf. 11x10½
995 A442 3c **sepia,** *June 30, 1950*		10 6
Margin block of 4, P#		55 —

INDIANA TERRITORY ISSUE

Issued to commemorate the 150th anniversary of the establishment of Indiana Territory.

Gov. William Henry Harrison and First Indiana Capitol, Vincennes — A443

ROTARY PRESS PRINTING

E.E. Plates of 200 subjects in four panes of 50 each.

1950	Unwmk.	Perf. 11x10½
996 A443 3c **bright blue,** *July 4, 1950*		10 5
Margin block of 4, P#		50 —

CALIFORNIA STATEHOOD ISSUE

Issued to commemorate the centenary of the admission of California to statehood.

Gold Miner, Pioneers and S.S. Oregon — A444

ROTARY PRESS PRINTING

E.E. Plates of 200 subjects in four panes of 50 each.

1950	Unwmk.	Perf. 11x10½
997 A444 3c **yellow orange,** *Sept. 9, 1950*		10 5
Margin block of 4, P#		50 —

UNITED CONFEDERATE VETERANS FINAL REUNION ISSUE

Issued to commemorate the final reunion of the United Confederate Veterans, Norfolk, Virginia, May 30, 1951.

Confederate Soldier and United Confederate Veteran — A445

ROTARY PRESS PRINTING

E.E. Plates of 200 subjects in four panes of 50 each.

1951	Unwmk.	Perf. 11x10½
998 A445 3c **gray,** *May 30, 1951*		10 5
Margin block of 4, P#		50 —

NEVADA CENTENNIAL ISSUE

Issued to commemorate the centenary of the settlement of Nevada.

Carson Valley, c. 1851 — A446

Designed by Charles R. Chickering.

ROTARY PRESS PRINTING

E.E. Plates of 200 subjects in four panes of 50 each.

1951	Unwmk.	Perf. 11x10½
999 A446 3c **light olive green,** *July 14, 1951*		10 5
Margin block of 4, P#		50 —

LANDING OF CADILLAC ISSUE

Issued to commemorate the 250th anniversary of the landing of Antoine de la Mothe Cadillac at Detroit.

Detroit Skyline and Cadillac Landing — A447

ROTARY PRESS PRINTING

E.E. Plates of 200 subjects in four panes of 50 each.

1951	Unwmk.	Perf. 11x10½
1000 A447 3c **blue,** *July 24, 1951*		10 5
Margin block of 4, P#		50 —

COLORADO STATEHOOD ISSUE

Issued to commemorate the 75th anniversary of the admission of Colorado to statehood.

Colorado Capitol, Mount of the Holy Cross, Columbine and Bronco Buster by Proctor — A448

ROTARY PRESS PRINTING

E.E. Plates of 200 subjects in four panes of 50 each.

1951	Unwmk.	Perf. 11x10½
1001 A448 3c **blue violet,** *Aug. 1, 1951*		10 5
Margin block of 4, P#		50 —

AMERICAN CHEMICAL SOCIETY ISSUE

Issued to commemorate the 75th anniversary of the formation of the American Chemical Society.

A.C.S. Emblem and Symbols of Chemistry — A449

ROTARY PRESS PRINTING

E.E. Plates of 200 subjects in four panes of 50 each.

1951	Unwmk.	Perf. 11x10½
1002 A449 3c **violet brown,** *Sept. 4, 1951*		10 5
Margin block of 4, P#		50 —

BATTLE OF BROOKLYN ISSUE

Issued to commemorate the 175th anniversary of the Battle of Brooklyn.

Gen. George Washington Evacuating Army; Fulton Ferry House at Right — A450

ROTARY PRESS PRINTING

E.E. Plates of 200 subjects in four panes of 50 each.

1951	Unwmk.	Perf. 11x10½
1003 A450 3c **violet,** *Dec. 10, 1951*		10 5
Margin block of 4, P#		50 —

BETSY ROSS ISSUE

Issued to commemorate the 200th anniversary of the birth of Betsy Ross, maker of the first American flag.

Betsy Ross Showing Flag to Gen. George Washington, Robert Morris and George Ross — A451

ROTARY PRESS PRINTING

E.E. Plates of 200 subjects in four panes of 50 each.

1952	Unwmk.	Perf. 11x10½
1004 A451 3c **carmine rose,** *Jan. 2, 1953*		10 5
Margin block of 4, P#		50 —

4-H CLUB ISSUE

Issue to honor the 4-H Club movement.

Farm, Club Emblem, Boy and Girl — A452

ROTARY PRESS PRINTING

E.E. Plates of 200 subjects in four panes of 50 each.

1952	Unwmk.	Perf. 11x10½
1005 A452 3c **blue green,** *Jan. 15, 1952*		10 5
Margin block of 4, P#		50 —

B. & O. RAILROAD ISSUE

Issued to commemorate the 125th anniversary of the granting of a charter to the Baltimore and Ohio Railroad Company by the Maryland Legislature.

Charter and Three Stages of Rail Transportation A453

ROTARY PRESS PRINTING

E.E. Plates of 200 subjects in four panes of 50 each.

1952	Unwmk.	Perf. 11x10½		
1006 A453 3c **bright blue**, *Feb. 28, 1952*			10	5
Margin block of 4, P#			55	—

A. A. A. ISSUE.

Issued to commemorate the 50th anniversary of the formation of the American Automobile Association.

School Girls and Safety Patrolman Automobiles of 1902 and 1952 — A454

ROTARY PRESS PRINTING

E.E. Plates of 200 subjects in four panes of 50 each.

1952	Unwmk.	Perf. 11x10½		
1007 A454 3c **deep blue**, *Mar. 4, 1952*			10	5
Margin block of 4, P#			50	—

NATO ISSUE

Issued to commemorate the third anniversary of the signing of the North Atlantic Treaty.

Torch of Liberty and Globe — A455

ROTARY PRESS PRINTING

E.E. Plates of 400 subjects in four panes of 100 each.

1952	Unwmk.	Perf. 11x10½		
1008 A455 3c **deep violet**, *Apr. 4, 1952*			10	5
Margin block of 4, P#			50	—

GRAND COULEE DAM ISSUE

Issued to commemorate 50 years of Federal cooperation in developing the resources of rivers and streams in the West.

Spillway, Grand Coulee Dam — A456

ROTARY PRESS PRINTING

E.E. Plates of 200 subjects in four panes of 50 each.

1952	Unwmk.	Perf. 11x10½		
1009 A456 3c **blue green**, *May 15, 1952*			10	5
Margin block of 4, P#			50	—

LAFAYETTE ISSUE

Issued to commemorate the 175th anniversary of the arrival of Marquis de Lafayette in America.

Marquis de Lafayette, Flags, Cannon and Landing Party — A457

Designed by Victor S. McCloskey, Jr.

ROTARY PRESS PRINTING

E.E. Plates of 200 subjects in four panes of 50 each.

1952	Unwmk.	Perf. 11x10½		
1010 A457 3c **bright blue**, *June 13, 1952*			10	5
Margin block of 4, P#			50	—

MT. RUSHMORE MEMORIAL ISSUE

Issued to commemorate the 25th anniversary of the dedication of the Mt. Rushmore National Memorial in the Black Hills of South Dakota.

Sculptured Heads on Mt. Rushmore — A458

Designed by William K. Schrage.

ROTARY PRESS PRINTING

E.E. Plates of 200 subjects in four panes of 50 each.

1952	Unwmk.	Perf. 10½x11		
1011 A458 3c **blue green**, *Aug. 11, 1952*			10	5
Margin block of 4, P#			60	—

ENGINEERING CENTENNIAL ISSUE

Issued to commemorate the centenary of the founding of the American Society of Civil Engineers.

George Washington Bridge and Covered Bridge of 1850's — A459

ROTARY PRESS PRINTING

E.E. Plates of 200 subjects in four panes of 50 each.

1952	Unwmk.	Perf. 11x10½		
1012 A459 3c **violet blue**, *Sept. 6, 1952*			10	5
Margin block of 4, P#			50	—

SERVICE WOMEN ISSUE

Issued to honor the women in the United States Armed Services.

Women of the Marine Corps, Army, Navy and Air Force — A460

ROTARY PRESS PRINTING

E.E. Plates of 200 subjects in four panes of 50 each.

1952	Unwmk.	Perf. 11x10½		
1013 A460 3c **deep blue**, *Sept. 11, 1952*			10	5
Margin block of 4, P#			50	—

GUTENBERG BIBLE ISSUE

Issued to commemorate the 500th anniversary of the printing of the first book, the Holy Bible, from movable type, by Johann Gutenberg.

Gutenberg Showing Proof to the Elector of Mainz — A461

ROTARY PRESS PRINTING

E.E. Plates of 200 subjects in four panes of 50 each.

1952	Unwmk.	Perf. 11x10½		
1014 A461 3c **violet**, *Sept. 30, 1952*			10	5
Margin block of 4, P#			50	—

NEWSPAPER BOYS ISSUE

Issued to honor the newspaper boys of America.

Newspaper Boy, Torch and Group of Homes — A462

ROTARY PRESS PRINTING

E.E. Plates of 200 subjects in four panes of 50 each.

1952	Unwmk.	Perf. 11x10½		
1015 A462 3c **violet**, *Oct. 4, 1952*			10	5
Margin block of 4, P#			50	—

RED CROSS ISSUE

Issued to honor the International Red Cross.

Globe, Sun and Cross — A463

ROTARY PRESS PRINTING

Cross Typographed

E.E. Plates of 200 subjects in four panes of 50 each.

1952	Unwmk.	Perf. 11x10½		
1016 A463 3c **deep blue & carmine**, *Nov. 21, 1952*			10	5
Margin block of 4, P#			50	—

NATIONAL GUARD ISSUE

Issued to honor the National Guard of the United States.

National Guardsman, Amphibious Landing and Disaster Service — A464

ROTARY PRESS PRINTING

E.E. Plates of 200 subjects in four panes of 50 each.

1953	Unwmk.	Perf. 11x10½		
1017 A464 3c **bright blue**, *Feb. 23, 1953*			10	5
Margin block of 4, P#			50	—

OHIO STATEHOOD ISSUE

Sesquicentennial of Ohio statehood.

Ohio Map, State Seal, Buckeye Leaf — A465

ROTARY PRESS PRINTING

E.E. Plates of 280 subjects in four panes of 70 each.

1953	Unwmk.	Perf. 11x10½		
1018 A465 3c **chocolate**, *Mar. 2, 1953*			10	5
Margin block of 4, P#			60	—

WASHINGTON TERRITORY ISSUE

Issued to commemorate the centenary of the organization of Washington Territory.

Medallion, Pioneers and Washington Scene — A466

ROTARY PRESS PRINTING
E.E. Plates of 200 subjects in four panes of 50 each.

1953	Unwmk.	Perf. 11x10½
1019 A466 3c **green**, *Mar. 2, 1953*		10 5
Margin block of 4, P#		50 —

LOUISIANA PURCHASE ISSUE

Issued to commemorate the 150th anniversary of the Louisiana Purchase, 1803.

James Monroe, Robert R. Livingston and Marquis Francois de Barbe-Marbois A467

ROTARY PRESS PRINTING
E.E. Plates of 200 subjects in four panes of 50 each.

1953	Unwmk.	Perf. 11x10½
1020 A467 3c **violet brown**, *April 30, 1953*		10 5
Margin block of 4, P#		50 —

OPENING OF JAPAN CENTENNIAL ISSUE

Issued to commemorate the centenary of Commodore Matthew Calbraith Perry's negotiations with Japan, which opened her doors to foreign trade.

Commodore Matthew C. Perry and First Anchorage off Tokyo Bay — A468

ROTARY PRESS PRINTING
E.E. Plates of 200 subjects in four panes of 50 each.

1953	Unwmk.	Perf. 11x10½
1021 A468 5c **green**, *July 14, 1953*		15 10
Margin block of 4, P#		1.40 —

AMERICAN BAR ASSOCIATION ISSUE

Issued to commemorate the 75th anniversary of the formation of the American Bar Association.

Section of Frieze, Supreme Court Room — A469

ROTARY PRESS PRINTING
E.E. Plates of 200 subjects in four panes of 50 each.

1953	Unwmk.	Perf. 11x10½
1022 A469 3c **rose violet**, *Aug. 24, 1953*		10 5
Margin block of 4, P#		50 —

SAGAMORE HILL ISSUE

Issued to commemorate the opening of Sagamore Hill, Theodore Roosevelt's home, as a national shrine.

Home of Theodore Roosevelt — A470

ROTARY PRESS PRINTING
E.E. Plates of 200 subjects in four panes of 50 each.

1953	Unwmk.	Perf. 11x10½
1023 A470 3c **yellow green**, *Sept. 14, 1953*		10 5
Margin block of 4, P#		50 —

FUTURE FARMERS ISSUE

Issued to commemorate the 25th anniversary of the organization of Future Farmers of America.

Agricultural Scene and Future Farmer — A471

ROTARY PRESS PRINTING
E.E. Plates of 200 subjects in four panes of 50 each.

1953	Unwmk.	Perf. 11x10½
1024 A471 3c **deep blue**, *Oct. 13, 1953*		10 5
Margin block of 4, P#		50 —

TRUCKING INDUSTRY ISSUE

Issued to commemorate the 50th anniversary of the Trucking Industry in the United States.

Truck, Farm and Distant City — A472

ROTARY PRESS PRINTING
E.E. Plates of 200 subjects in four panes of 50 each.

1953	Unwmk.	Perf. 11x10½
1025 A472 3c **violet**, *Oct. 27, 1953*		10 5
Margin block of 4, P#		50 —

GENERAL PATTON ISSUE

Issued to honor Gen. George S. Patton, Jr. (1885-1945), and the armored forces of the United States Army.

Gen. George S. Patton, Jr., and Tanks in Action — A473

ROTARY PRESS PRINTING
E.E. Plates of 200 subjects in four panes of 50 each.

1953	Unwmk.	Perf. 11x10½
1026 A473 3c **blue violet**, *Nov. 11, 1953*		10 5
Margin block of 4, P#		60 —

NEW YORK CITY ISSUE

Issued to commemorate the 300th anniversary of the founding of New York City.

Dutch Ship in New Amsterdam Harbor — A474

ROTARY PRESS PRINTING
E.E. Plates of 200 subjects in four panes of 50 each.

1953	Unwmk.	Perf. 11x10½
1027 A474 3c **bright red violet**, *Nov. 20, 1953*		10 5
Margin block of 4, P#		60 —

GADSDEN PURCHASE ISSUE

Issued to commemorate the centenary of James Gadsden's purchase of territory from Mexico to adjust the U.S.-Mexico boundary.

Map and Pioneer Group — A475

ROTARY PRESS PRINTING
E.E. Plates of 200 subjects in four panes of 50 each.

1953	Unwmk.	Perf. 11x10½
1028 A475 3c **copper brown**, *Dec. 30, 1953*		10 5
Margin block of 4, P#		50 —

COLUMBIA UNIVERSITY ISSUE

Issued to commemorate the 200th anniversary of the founding of Columbia University.

Low Memorial Library — A476

ROTARY PRESS PRINTING
E.E. Plates of 200 subjects in four panes of 50 each.

1954	Unwmk.	Perf. 11x10½
1029 A476 3c **blue**, *Jan. 4, 1954*		10 5
Margin block of 4, P#		50 —

Wet and Dry Printings

In 1953 the Bureau of Engraving and Printing began experiments in printing on "dry" paper (moisture content 5-10 per cent). In previous "wet" printings the paper had a moisture content of 15-35 per cent.

The new process required a thicker, stiffer paper, special types of inks and greater pressure to force the paper into the recessed plates. The "dry" printings show whiter paper, a higher sheen on the surface, feel thicker and stiffer, and the designs stand out more clearly than on the "wet" printings.

Nos. 832c and 1041 (flat plate) were the first "dry" printings to be issued of flat-plate, regular-issue stamps. No. 1063 was the first rotary press stamp to be produced entirely by "dry" printing.

Stamps printed by both the "wet" and "dry" process are Nos. 1030, 1031, 1035, 1035a, 1036, 1039, 1049, 1050-1052, 1054, 1055, 1057, 1058, C34-C36, C39, C39a, J78, J80-J84, QE1-QE3, RF26. The "wet" printed 4c coil, No. 1058, exists only precanceled.

All postage stamps have been printed by the "dry" process since the late 1950's.

LIBERTY ISSUE

Benjamin Franklin A477

George Washington A478

Palace of the Governors, Santa Fe — A478a

Mount Vernon — A479

Thomas Jefferson — A480

Bunker Hill
Monument and
Massachusetts
Flag,
1776 — A481

Statue of
Liberty — A482

John
Jay — A493

Monticello, Home
of Thomas
Jefferson, near
Charlottesville,
Va. — A494

Abraham
Lincoln — A483

The Hermitage,
Home of Andrew
Jackson, near
Nashville — A484

Paul
Revere — A495

Robert E.
Lee — A496

James Monroe
A485

Theodore
Roosevelt
A486

John Marshall
A497

Susan B.
Anthony
A498

Woodrow
Wilson — A487

Statue of
Liberty — A488

Patrick Henry
A499

Alexander
Hamilton
A500

Statue of Liberty
A489

John J. Pershing
A489a

The Alamo, San
Antonio — A490

Independence
Hall — A491

Statue of Liberty
A491a

Benjamin
Harrison
A492

See table of Territorial and Statehood Dates at
beginning of catalogue. See catalogue index.

ROTARY PRESS PRINTING
E.E. Plates of 400 subjects in
four panes of 100 each.

1954-68			Unwmk.		Perf. 11x10½	
1030	A477	½c	red orange, Oct. 20, 1955		5	5
a.			Dry printing		5	5
			Margin block of 4, P#		30	—
1031	A478	1c	dark green		5	5
			Margin block of 4, P#		25	—
			Pair with full vert. or horiz. gutter between		150.00	
b.			Wet printing, Aug. 26, 1954		8	5

Perf. 10½x11

1031A	A478a	1¼c	turquoise, June 17, 1960		5	5
			Margin block of 4, P#		1.00	—
1032	A479	1½c	brown carmine, Feb. 22, 1956		8	5
			Margin block of 4, P#		5.00	—

Perf. 11x10½

1033	A480	2c	carmine rose, Sept. 15, 1954		5	5
			Margin block of 4, P#		25	—
			Pair with full vert. or horiz. gutter between			
1034	A481	2½c	gray blue, June 17, 1959		8	5
			Margin block of 4, P#		1.25	—
1035	A482	3c	deep violet		8	5
			Margin block of 4, P#		40	—
			Pair with full vert. or horiz. gutter between		150.00	
a.			Booklet pane of 6, June 30, 1954		3.00	50
b.			Tagged, July 6, 1966		25	20
b.			Margin block of 4, P#			—
c.			Imperf., pair		1,500.	
d.			Horiz. pair, imperf. between		1,000.	
e.			Wet printing, June 24, 1954		12	5
f.			As "a," dry printing		4.00	60
1036	A483	4c	red violet		10	5
			Margin block of 4, P#		50	—
			Pair with full vert. gutter between		—	
a.			Booklet pane of 6, July 31, 1958		2.00	50
b.			Tagged, Nov. 2, 1963		75	16
b.			Margin block of 4, P#		10.00	—
c.			Wet printing, Nov. 19, 1954		15	10

Perf. 10½x11

1037	A484	4½c	blue green, Mar. 16, 1959		15	8
			Margin block of 4, P#		1.00	—

Perf. 11x10½

1038	A485	5c	deep blue, Dec. 2, 1954		15	5
			Margin block of 4, P#		75	—

			Pair with full vert. gutter btwn.		200.00	
1039	A486	6c	carmine		40	5
			Margin block of 4, P#		2.00	—
			Wet printing, Nov. 18, 1955		42	6
1040	A487	7c	rose carmine, Jan. 10, 1956		30	5
			Margin block of 4, P#		1.50	—

FLAT PLATE OR ROTARY PRESS PRINTING
Plates of 400 subjects in four panes of 100 each.

Perf. 11

1041	A488	8c	dark violet blue & carmine, Apr. 9, 1954		30	6
			Margin block of 4, 2 P# (flat plate)		5.00	—
			Margin block of 4, 2 P# (rotary)		5.00	—
			Corner margin block of 4, blue P# only		—	
			Corner margin block of 4, red P# only		—	
a.			Carmine dbl. impression		1,200.	

FLAT PRINTING PLATES
Frame: 24912-13-14-15, 24926, 24929-30, 24932-33.
Vignette: 24916-17-18-19-20, 24935-36-37, 24939.

ROTARY PRINTING PLATES
Frame: 24923-24, 24928, 24940, 24942.
Vignette: 24921-22, 24927, 24938.

GIORI PRESS PRINTING
Plates of 400 subjects in four panes of 100 each.
Redrawn design

Perf. 11

1042	A489	8c	dark violet blue & carmine rose, Mar. 22, 1958		30	5
			Margin block of 4, P#		1.75	—

ROTARY PRESS PRINTING
E.E. Plates of 400 subjects in four panes of 100 each.

Perf. 11x10½

1042A	A489a	8c	brown, Nov. 17, 1961		30	5
			Margin block of 4, P#		1.50	—

Perf. 10½x11

1043	A490	9c	rose lilac, June 14, 1956		45	5
			Margin block of 4, P#		2.25	—
1044	A491	10c	rose lake, July 4, 1956		35	5
			Margin block of 4, P#		1.65	—
b.			Tagged, July 6, 1966		1.50	1.25
b.			Margin block of 4, P#		10.00	—

GIORI PRESS PRINTING
Plates of 400 subjects in four panes of 100 each.

Perf. 11

1044A	A491a	11c	carmine & dark violet blue, June 15, 1961		40	6
			Margin block of 4, P#		2.00	—
c.			Tagged, Jan. 11, 1967		2.00	1.60
c.			Margin block of 4, P#		12.50	—

ROTARY PRESS PRINTING
E.E. Plates of 400 subjects in four panes of 100 each.

Perf. 11x10½

1045	A492	12c	red, June 6, 1959		55	5
			Margin block of 4, P#		2.75	—
a.			Tagged, 1968		55	15
a.			Margin block of 4, P#		3.00	—
1046	A493	15c	rose lake, Dec. 12, 1958		1.00	5
			Margin block of 4, P#		5.00	—
a.			Tagged, July 6, 1966		1.10	22
a.			Margin block of 4, P#		6.00	—

Perf. 10½x11

1047	A494	20c	ultramarine, Apr. 13, 1956		75	5
			Margin block of 4, P#		3.75	—

Perf. 11x10½

1048	A495	25c	green, Apr. 18, 1958		2.25	5
			Margin block of 4, P#		11.50	—
1049	A496	30c	black		1.50	8
			Margin block of 4, P#		7.50	—
a.			Wet printing, Sept. 21, 1955		2.00	12
1050	A497	40c	brown red		2.50	10
			Margin block of 4, P#		12.50	—
a.			Wet printing, Sept. 24, 1955		3.00	25
1051	A498	50c	bright purple		2.75	5
			Margin block of 4, P#		14.00	—
			Cracked plate (25231 UL 1)			
a.			Wet printing, Aug. 25, 1955		3.25	8
1052	A499	$1	purple		10.00	6
			Margin block of 4, P#		50.00	—
a.			Wet printing, Oct. 7, 1955		11.00	10

FLAT PLATE PRINTING
Plates of 400 subjects in four panes of 100 each.

Perf. 11

1053	A500	$5	black, Mar. 19, 1956		85.00	8.00
			Margin block of 4, P#		425.00	—

ROTARY PRESS COIL STAMPS

1954-73			Unwmk.		Perf. 10 Vertically	
1054	A478	1c	dark green		35	12
			Pair		70	24
			Joint line pair		1.25	35
b.			Imperf., pair		2,250.	

c.	Wet printing, *Oct. 8, 1954*		52	16

Perf. 10 Horizontally

1054A	A478a	1¼c **turquoise,** *June 17, 1960*	25	20
		Pair	50	40
		Joint line pair	3.50	1.00

Perf. 10 Vertically

1055	A480	2c **carmine rose**	10	5
		Pair	20	10
		Joint line pair	60	20
a.		Tagged, *May 6, 1968*	10	5
a.		Dull finish gum	12	
b.		Imperf., pair (Bureau precanceled)		350.00
c.		As "a," imperf. pair	400.00	
d.		Wet printing, *Oct. 22, 1954*	20	6
1056	A481	2½c **gray blue,** *Sept. 9, 1959*	55	35
		Pair	1.10	70
		Joint line pair	6.50	1.20
1057	A482	3c **deep violet**	15	5
		Pair	30	10
		Joint line pair	80	15
		Gripper cracks	—	—
a.		Imperf., pair	750.00	—
a.		Imperf., joint line pair	1,000.	—
b.		Tagged, *Oct. 1966*	75	25
c.		Wet printing, *July 20, 1954*	24	6

No. 1057a measures about 19½x22mm.; No. 1035c, about 18¾x22½mm.

1058	A483	4c **red violet,** *July 31, 1958*	15	5
		Pair	30	10
		Joint line pair	1.00	20
a.		Imperf. (pair)	100.00	100.00
a.		Imperf., joint line pair	200.00	
b.		Wet printing (Bureau precanceled)		50

Perf. 10 Horizontally

1059	A484	4½c **blue green,** *May 1, 1959*	3.25	1.20
		Pair	6.50	2.40
		Joint line pair	20.00	3.00

Perf. 10 Vertically

1059A	A495	25c **green,** *Feb. 25, 1965*	75	30
		Pair	1.50	60
		Joint line pair	3.00	1.20
b.		Tagged, *April 3, 1973*	55	20
b.		Dull finish gum	55	
		Pair	1.10	40
		Joint line pair	2.50	1.00
c.		Imperf., pair	45.00	

NEBRASKA TERRITORY ISSUE

Issued to commemorate the centenary of the establishment of the Nebraska Territory.

"The Sower," Mitchell Pass and Scotts Bluff — A507

ROTARY PRESS PRINTING
E.E. Plates of 200 subjects in four panes of 50 each.

1954		**Unwmk.**	**Perf. 11x10½**	
1060	A507	3c **violet,** *May 7, 1954*	10	5
		Margin block of 4, P#	50	—

KANSAS TERRITORY ISSUE

Issued to commemorate the centenary of the establishment of the Kansas Territory

Wheat Field and Pioneer Wagon Train — A508

ROTARY PRESS PRINTING
E.E. Plates of 200 subjects in four panes of 50 each.

1954		**Unwmk.**	**Perf. 11x10½**	
1061	A508	3c **brown orange,** *May 31, 1954*	10	5
		Margin block of 4, P#	50	—

GEORGE EASTMAN ISSUE

Issued to commemorate the birth centenary of George Eastman (1854-1932), inventor of photographic dry plates, flexible film and the Kodak camera; Rochester, N.Y., industrialist.

George Eastman — A509

ROTARY PRESS PRINTING
E.E. Plates of 280 subjects in four panes of 70 each.

1954		**Unwmk.**	**Perf. 10½x11**	
1062	A509	3c **violet brown,** *July 12, 1954*	10	5
		Margin block of 4, P#	50	—

LEWIS AND CLARK EXPEDITION

Issued to commemorate the 150th anniversary of the Lewis and Clark expedition.

Meriwether Lewis, William Clark and Sacagawea Landing on Missouri Riverbank A510

ROTARY PRESS PRINTING
E.E. Plates of 200 subjects in four panes of 50 each.

1954		**Unwmk.**	**Perf. 11x10½**	
1063	A510	3c **violet brown,** *July 28, 1954*	10	5
		Margin block of 4, P#	50	—

PENNSYLVANIA ACADEMY OF THE FINE ARTS ISSUE

Issued to commemorate the 150th anniversary of the founding of the Pennsylvania Academy of the Fine Arts, Philadelphia.

Charles Willson Peale in his Museum, Self-portrait — A511

ROTARY PRESS PRINTING
E.E. Plates of 200 subjects in four panes of 50 each.

1955		**Unwmk.**	**Perf. 10½x11**	
1064	A511	3c **rose brown,** *Jan. 15, 1955*	10	5
		Margin block of 4, P#	50	—

LAND GRANT COLLEGES ISSUE

Issued to commemorate the centenary of the founding of Michigan State College and Pennsylvania State University, first of the land grant institutions.

Open Book and Symbols of Subjects Taught — A512

ROTARY PRESS PRINTING
E.E. Plates of 200 subjects in four panes of 50 each.

1955		**Unwmk.**	**Perf. 11x10½**	
1065	A512	3c **green,** *Feb. 12, 1955*	10	5
		Margin block, P#	50	—

ROTARY INTERNATIONAL ISSUE

Issued to commemorate the 50th anniversary of the founding of Rotary International.

Torch, Globe and Rotary Emblem — A513

ROTARY PRESS PRINTING
E.E. Plates of 200 subjects in four panes of 50 each.

1955		**Unwmk.**	**Perf. 11x10½**	
1066	A513	8c **deep blue,** *Feb. 23, 1955*	20	12
		Margin block of 4, P#	1.25	—

ARMED FORCES RESERVE ISSUE

Issued to honor the Armed Forces Reserve.

Marine, Coast Guard, Army, Navy and Air Force Personnel A514

ROTARY PRESS PRINTING
E.E. Plates of 200 subjects in four panes of 50 each.

1955		**Unwmk.**	**Perf. 11x10½**	
1067	A514	3c **purple,** *May 21, 1955*	10	5
		Margin block of 4, P#	50	—

NEW HAMPSHIRE ISSUE

Issued to honor New Hampshire on the occasion of the sesquicentennial of the discovery of the "Old Man of the Mountains."

Great Stone Face — A515

ROTARY PRESS PRINTING
E.E. Plates of 200 subjects in four panes of 50 each.

1955		**Unwmk.**	**Perf. 10½x11**	
1068	A515	3c **green,** *June 21, 1955*	10	5
		Margin block of 4, P#	50	—

SOO LOCKS ISSUE

Centenary of the opening of the Soo Locks.

Map of Great Lakes and Two Steamers — A516

ROTARY PRESS PRINTING
E.E. Plates of 200 subjects in four panes of 50 each.

1955		**Unwmk.**	**Perf. 11x10½**	
1069	A516	3c **blue,** *June 28, 1955*	10	5
		Margin block of 4, P#	50	—

ATOMS FOR PEACE ISSUE

Issued to promote an Atoms for Peace policy.

Atomic Energy Encircling the Hemispheres A517

Designed by George R. Cox.

ROTARY PRESS PRINTING
E.E. Plates of 200 subjects in four panes of 50 each.

1955	Unwmk.	Perf. 11x10½		
1070	A517 3c **deep blue**, *July 28, 1955*		12	5
	Margin block of 4, P#		65	—

FORT TICONDEROGA ISSUE

Issued to commemorate the bicentenary of Fort Ticonderoga, New York.

Map of the Fort, Ethan Allen and Artillery — A518

Designed by Enrico Arno.

ROTARY PRESS PRINTING
E.E. Plates of 200 subjects in four panes of 50 each.

1955	Unwmk.	Perf. 11x10½		
1071	A518 3c **light brown**, *Sept. 18, 1955*		10	5
	Margin block of 4, P#		50	—

ANDREW W. MELLON ISSUE

Issued to commemorate the centenary of the birth of Andrew W. Mellon (1855-1937), U.S. Secretary of the Treasury (1921-32), financier and art collector.

Andrew W. Mellon — A519

Designed by Victor S. McCloskey, Jr.

ROTARY PRESS PRINTING
E.E. Plates of 280 subjects in four panes of 70 each.

1955	Unwmk.	Perf. 10½x11		
1072	A519 3c **rose carmine**, *Dec. 20, 1955*		10	5
	Margin block of 4, P#		50	—

BENJAMIN FRANKLIN ISSUE

Issued to commemorate the 250th anniversary of the birth of Benjamin Franklin.

"Franklin Taking Electricity from the Sky," by Benjamin West — A520

Designed by Charles R. Chickering.

ROTARY PRESS PRINTING
E.E. Plates of 200 subjects in four panes of 50 each.

1956	Unwmk.	Perf. 10½x11		
1073	A520 3c **bright carmine**, *Jan. 17, 1956*		10	5
	Margin block of 4, P#		50	—

BOOKER T. WASHINGTON ISSUE

Issued to commemorate the centenary of the birth of Booker T. Washington (1856-1915), black educator, founder and head of Tuskegee Institute in Alabama.

Log Cabin — A521

Designed by Charles R. Chickering.

ROTARY PRESS PRINTING
E.E. Plates of 200 subjects in four panes of 50 each.

1956	Unwmk.	Perf. 11x10½		
1074	A521 3c **deep blue**, *April 5, 1956*		10	5
	Margin block of 4, P#		50	—

FIFTH INTERNATIONAL PHILATELIC EXHIBITION ISSUES

Issued to commemorate the Fifth International Philatelic Exhibition (FIPEX), New York City, April 28-May 6, 1956.

SOUVENIR SHEET

A522

FLAT PLATE PRINTING
Plates of 24 subjects

1956	Unwmk.	Imperf.		
1075	A522 **Sheet of two**, *Apr. 28, 1956*		4.00	3.50
a.	A482 3c deep violet		1.35	1.10
b.	A488 8c dark violet blue & carmine		1.75	1.50

No. 1075 measures 108x73mm. Nos. 1075a and 1075b measure 24x28mm. Below the stamps appears the signature of Arthur E. Summerfield, Postmaster, General of the United States. Marginal inscription reads: "In compliment to 5th International Philatelic Exhibition, 1956. New York, N.Y. Apr. 28-May 6."
Inscriptions printed in dark viole blue; scrolls and stars in carmine.

New York Coliseum and Columbus Monument A523

Designed by William K. Schrage.

ROTARY PRESS PRINTING
E.E. Plates of 200 subjects in four panes of 50 each.

1956	Unwmk.	Perf. 11x10½		
1076	A523 3c **deep violet**, *April 30, 1956*		10	5
	Margin block of 4, P#		50	—

WILDLIFE CONSERVATION ISSUE

Issued to emphasize the importance of Wildlife Conservation in America.

Wild Turkey — A524

Pronghorn Antelope — A525

King Salmon — A526

Designed by Robert W. (Bob) Hines.

ROTARY PRESS PRINTING
E.E. Plates of 200 subjects in four panes of 50 each.

1956	Unwmk.	Perf. 11x10½		
1077	A524 3c **rose lake**, *May 5, 1956*		12	5
	Margin block of 4, P#		65	5
1078	A525 3c **brown**, *June 22, 1956*		12	5
	Margin block of 4, P#		65	5
1079	A526 3c **blue green**, *Nov. 9, 1956*		12	5
	Margin block of 4, P#		65	5

PURE FOOD AND DRUG LAWS ISSUE

Issued to commemorate the 50th anniversary of the passage of the Pure Food aud Drug Laws.

Harvey Washington Wiley — A527

Designed by Robert L. Miller.

ROTARY PRESS PRINTING
E.E. Plates of 200 subjects in four panes of 50 each.

1956	Unwmk.	Perf. 10½x11		
1080	A527 3c **dark blue green**, *June 27, 1956*		10	5
	Margin block of 4, P#		50	—

WHEATLAND ISSUE

Pres. Buchanan's Home, Lancaster, Pa. — A528

ROTARY PRESS PRINTING
E.E. Plates of 200 subjects in four panes of 50 each.

1956	Unwmk.	Perf. 11x10½		
1081	A528 3c **black brown**, *Aug. 5, 1956*		10	5
	Margin block of 4, P#		50	—

LABOR DAY ISSUE

Issued to commemorate Labor Day.

Mosaic, AFL-CIO
Headquarters — A529

Designed by Victor S. McCloskey, Jr.

ROTARY PRESS PRINTING
E.E. Plates of 200 subjects in four panes of 50 each.

1956	**Unwmk.**	**Perf. 10½x11**	
1082 A529 3c **deep blue,** *Sept. 3, 1956*		10	5
Margin block of 4, P#		50	—

NASSAU HALL ISSUE

Issued to commemorate the 200th anniversary of Nassau Hall, Princeton University.

Nassau Hall,
Princeton,
N.J. — A530

ROTARY PRESS PRINTING
E.E. Plates of 200 subjects in four panes of 50 each.

1956, Sept. 22	**Unwmk.**	**Perf. 11x10½**	
1083 A530 3c **black,** *orange*		10	5
Margin block of 4, P#		50	—

DEVILS TOWER ISSUE

Issued to commemorate the 50th anniversary of the Federal law providing for protection of American natural antiquities. Devils Tower National Monument, Wyoming, is an outstanding example.

Devils Tower — A531

Designed by Charles R. Chickering.

ROTARY PRESS PRINTING
E.E. Plates of 200 subjects in four panes of 50 each.

1956	**Unwmk.**	**Perf. 10½x11**	
1084 A531 3c **violet,** *Sept. 24, 1956*		10	5
Margin block of 4, P#		50	—
Pair with full horiz. gutter btwn.			—

CHILDREN'S ISSUE

Issued to promote friendship among the children of the world.

Children of the
World — A532

Designed by Ronald Dias.

ROTARY PRESS PRINTING
E.E. Plates of 200 subjects in four panes of 50 each.

1956	**Unwmk.**	**Perf. 11x10½**	
1085 A532 3c **dark blue,** *Dec. 15, 1956*		10	5
Margin block of 4, P#		50	—

ALEXANDER HAMILTON ISSUE

Issued to commemorate the 200th anniversary of the birth of Alexander Hamilton (1755-1804).

Alexander
Hamilton and
Federal
Hall — A533

Designed by William K. Schrage.

ROTARY PRESS PRINTING
E.E. Plates of 200 subjects in four panes of 50 each.

1957	**Unwmk.**	**Perf. 11x10½**	
1086 A533 3c **rose red,** *Jan. 11, 1957*		10	5
Margin block of 4, P#		50	—

POLIO ISSUE

Issued to honor "those who helped fight polio," and on the occasion of the 20th anniversary of the National Foundation for Infantile Paralysis and the March of Dimes.

Allegory — A534

Designed by Charles R. Chickering.

ROTARY PRESS PRINTING
E.E. Plates of 200 subjects in four panes of 50 each.

1957	**Unwmk.**	**Perf. 10½x11**	
1087 A534 3c **red lilac,** *Jan. 15, 1957*		10	5
Margin block of 4, P#		50	—

COAST AND GEODETIC SURVEY ISSUE

Issued to commemorate the 150th anniversary of the establishment of the Coast and Geodetic Survey.

Flag of Coast and
Geodetic Survey
and Ships at
Sea — A535

Designed by Harold E. MacEwen.

ROTARY PRESS PRINTING
E.E. Plates of 200 subjects in four panes of 50 each.

1957	**Unwmk.**	**Perf. 11x10½**	
1088 A535 3c **dark blue,** *Feb. 11, 1957*		10	5
Margin block of 4, P#		50	—

ARCHITECTS ISSUE

Issued to commemorate the centenary of the American Institute of Architects.

Corinthian
Capital and
Mushroom Type
Head and
Shaft — A536

Designed by Robert J. Schultz.

ROTARY PRESS PRINTING
E.E. Plates of 200 subjects in four panes of 50 each.

1957	**Unwmk.**	**Perf. 11x10½**	
1089 A536 3c **red lilac,** *Feb. 23, 1957*		10	5
Margin block of 4, P#		50	—

STEEL INDUSTRY ISSUE

Issued to commemorate the centenary of the steel industry in America.

American Eagle and Pouring
Ladle — A537

Designed by Anthony Petruccelli.

ROTARY PRESS PRINTING
E.E. Plates of 200 subjects in four panes of 50 each.

1957	**Unwmk.**	**Perf. 10½x11**	
1090 A537 3c **bright ultramarine,** *May 22, 1957*		10	5
Margin block of 4, P#		50	—

INTERNATIONAL NAVAL REVIEW ISSUE

Issued to commemorate the International Naval Review and the Jamestown Festival.

Aircraft Carrier
and Jamestown
Festival
Emblem — A538

Designed by Richard A. Genders.

ROTARY PRESS PRINTING
E.E. Plates of 200 subjects in four panes of 50 each.

1957	**Unwmk.**	**Perf. 11x10½**	
1091 A538 3c **blue green,** *June 10, 1957*		10	5
Margin block of 4, P#		50	—

OKLAHOMA STATEHOOD ISSUE

Issued to commemorate the 50th anniversary of the admission of Oklahoma to Statehood.

Map of
Oklahoma, Arrow
and Atom
Diagram — A539

Designed by William K. Schrage.

ROTARY PRESS PRINTING
E.E. Plates of 200 subjects in four panes of 50 each.

1957	**Unwmk.**	**Perf. 11x10½**	
1092 A539 3c **dark blue,** *June 14, 1957*		10	5
Margin block of 4, P#		55	—

SCHOOL TEACHERS ISSUE

Issued to honor the school teachers of America.

Teacher and Pupils — A540

ROTARY PRESS PRINTING
E.E. Plates of 200 subjects in four panes of 50 each.

1957	Unwmk.	Perf. 11x10½
1093	A540 3c **rose lake**, *July 1, 1957*	10 5
	Margin block of 4, P#	50 —

FLAG ISSUE

"Old Glory" (48 Stars) — A541

Designed by Victor S. McCloskey, Jr.

GIORI PRESS PRINTING
Plates of 200 subjects in four panes of 50 each.

1957	Unwmk.	Perf. 11
1094	A541 4c **dark blue & deep carmine**, *July 4, 1957*	10 5
	Margin block of 4, P#	55 —

SHIPBUILDING ISSUE

Issued to commemorate the 350th anniversary of shipbuilding in America.

"Virginia of Sagadahock" and Seal of Maine — A542

Designed by Ervine Metzel, Mrs. William Zorach, A. M. Main, Jr., and George F. Cary II.

ROTARY PRESS PRINTING
E.E. Plates of 280 subjects in four panes of 70 each.

1957	Unwmk.	Perf. 10½x11
1095	A542 3c **deep violet**, *Aug. 15, 1957*	10 5
	Margin block of 4, P#	55 —

CHAMPION OF LIBERTY ISSUE

Issued to honor Ramon Magsaysay (1907-1957), President of the Philippines.

Ramon Magsaysay — A543

Designed by Arnold Copeland, Ervine Metzl and William H. Buckley.

GIORI PRESS PRINTING
Plates of 192 subjects in four panes of 48 each.

1957	Unwmk.	Perf. 11
1096	A543 8c **carmine, ultramarine & ocher**, *Aug. 31, 1957*	22 15
	Margin block of 4, two P#	1.25 —
	Margin block of 4, ultra. P# omitted	—

LAFAYETTE BICENTENARY ISSUE

Issued to commemorate the bicentenary of the birth of the Marquis de Lafayette (1757-1834).

Marquis de Lafayette — A544

Designed by Ervine Metzl.

ROTARY PRESS PRINTING
E.E. Plates of 200 subjects in four panes of 50 each.

1957	Unwmk.	Perf. 10½x11
1097	A544 3c **rose lake**, *Sept. 6, 1957*	10 5
	Margin block of 4, P#	50 —

WILDLIFE CONSERVATION ISSUE

Issued to emphasize the importance of Wildlife Conservation in America.

Whooping Cranes — A545

Designed by Bob Hines and C.R. Chickering.

GIORI PRESS PRINTING
Plates of 200 subjects in four panes of 50 each.

1957	Unwmk.	Perf. 11
1098	A545 3c **blue, ocher & green**, *Nov. 22, 1957*	10 5
	Margin block of 4, P#	55 —

RELIGIOUS FREEDOM ISSUE

Issued to commemorate the 300th anniversary of the Flushing Remonstrance.

Bible, Hat and Quill Pen — A546

Designed by Robert Geissmann.

ROTARY PRESS PRINTING
E.E. Plates of 200 subjects in four panes of 50 each.

1957	Unwmk.	Perf. 10½x11
1099	A546 3c **black**, *Dec. 27, 1957*	10 5
	Margin block of 4, P#	50 —

GARDENING HORTICULTURE ISSUE

Issued to honor the garden clubs of America and in connection with the centenary of the birth of Liberty Hyde Bailey, horticulturist.

"Bountiful Earth" — A547

Designed by Denver Gillen.

ROTARY PRESS PRINTING
E.E. Plates of 200 subjects in four panes of 50 each.

1958	Unwmk.	Perf. 10½x11
1100	A547 3c **green**, *March 15, 1958*	10 5
	Margin block of 4, P#	50 —

BRUSSELS EXHIBITION ISSUE

Issued in honor of the opening of the Universal and International Exhibition at Brussels, April 17.

U.S. Pavilion at Brussels — A551

Designed by Bradbury Thompson.

ROTARY PRESS PRINTING
E.E. Plates of 200 subjects in four panes of 50 each.

1958	Unwmk.	Perf. 11x10½
1104	A551 3c **deep claret**, *April 17, 1958*	10 5
	Margin block of 4, P#	50 —

JAMES MONROE ISSUE

Issued to commemorate the bicentenary of the birth of James Monroe (1758-1831), fifth President of the United States.

James Monroe — A552

Designed by Frank P. Conley.

ROTARY PRESS PRINTING
E.E. Plates of 280 subjects in four panes of 70 each.

1958	Unwmk.	Perf. 11x10½
1105	A552 3c **purple**, *April 28, 1958*	10 5
	Margin block of 4, P#	55 —

MINNESOTA STATEHOOD ISSUE

Issued to commemorate the centenary of Minnesota's admission to statehood.

Minnesota Lakes and Pines — A553

Designed by Homer Hill.

ROTARY PRESS PRINTING
E.E. Plates of 200 subjects in four panes of 50 each.

1958	Unwmk.	Perf. 11x10½
1106	A553 3c **green**, *May 11, 1958*	10 5
	Margin block of 4, P#	50 —

GEOPHYSICAL YEAR ISSUE

Issued to commemorate the International Geophysical Year, 1957-58.

Solar Disc and Hands from Michelangelo's "Creation of Adam" — A554

Designed by Ervine Metzl.

GIORI PRESS PRINTING
Plates of 200 subjects in four panes of 50 each.

1958		Unwmk.		Perf. 11	
1107	A554	3c	black & red orange, May 31, 1958	10	5
			Margin block of 4, P#	60	—

GUNSTON HALL ISSUE

Issued for the bicentenary of Gunston Hall and to honor George Mason, author of the Constitution of Virginia and the Virginia Bill of Rights.

Gunston Hall, Virginia — A555

Designed by Rene Clarke.

ROTARY PRESS PRINTING
E.E. Plates of 200 subjects in four panes of 50 each.

1958		Unwmk.		Perf. 11x10½	
1108	A555	3c	light green, June 12, 1958	10	5
			Margin block of 4, P#	50	—

MACKINAC BRIDGE ISSUE

Issued to commemorate the dedication of Mackinac Bridge, Michigan.

Mackinac Bridge — A556

Designed by Arnold J. Copeland.

ROTARY PRESS PRINTING
E.E. Plates of 200 subjects in four panes of 50 each.

1958		Unwmk.		Perf. 10½x11	
1109	A556	3c	bright greenish blue, June 25, 1958	10	5
			Margin block of 4, P#	50	—

CHAMPION OF LIBERTY ISSUE

Issued in honor of Simon Bolívar, South American freedom fighter.

Simon Bolívar — A557

ROTARY PRESS PRINTING
E.E. Plates of 280 subjects in four panes of 70 each.

1958		Unwmk.		Perf. 10½x11	
1110	A557	4c	olive bister, July 24, 1958	10	5
			Margin block of 4, P#	60	—

GIORI PRESS PRINTING
Plates of 288 subjects in four panes of 72 each.

Perf. 11

1111	A557	8c	carmine, ultramarine & ocher, July 24, 1958	25	15
			Margin block of 4, two P#	3.00	—
			Corner block of 4, ocher P# only	—	

ATLANTIC CABLE CENTENNIAL ISSUE

Issued to commemorate the centenary of the Atlantic Cable, linking the Eastern and Western hemispheres.

Neptune, Globe and Mermaid — A558

Designed by George Giusti.

ROTARY PRESS PRINTING
E.E. Plates of 200 subjects in four panes of 50 each.

1958		Unwmk.		Perf. 11x10½	
1112	A558	4c	reddish purple, Aug. 15, 1958	10	5
			Margin block of 4, P#	50	—

LINCOLN SESQUICENTENNIAL ISSUE

Issued to commemorate the sesquicentennial of the birth of Abraham Lincoln. No. 1114 also commemorates the centenary of the founding of Cooper Union, New York City. No. 1115 marks the centenary of the Lincoln-Douglas Debates.

Lincoln by George Healy — A559

Lincoln by Gutzon Borglum — A560

Lincoln and Stephen A. Douglas Debating, from Painting by Joseph Boggs Beale — A561

Daniel Chester French Statue of Lincoln as Drawn by Fritz Busse — A562

Designed by Ervine Metzl.

ROTARY PRESS PRINTING
E.E. Plates of 200 subjects in four panes of 50 each.

1958-59		Unwmk.		Perf. 10½x11	
1113	A559	1c	green, Feb. 12, 1959	5	5
			Margin block of 4, P#	30	—
1114	A560	3c	purple, Feb. 27, 1959	10	6
			Margin block of 4, P#	50	—
			Perf. 11x10½		
1115	A561	4c	sepia, Aug. 27, 1958	10	5
			Margin block, P#	50	—
1116	A562	4c	dark blue, May 30, 1959	10	5
			Margin block of 4, P#	55	—

CHAMPION OF LIBERTY ISSUE

Issued in honor of Lajos Kossuth, Hungarian freedom fighter.

Lajos Kossuth — A563

ROTARY PRESS PRINTING
E.E. Plates of 280 subjects in four panes of 70 each.

1958		Unwmk.		Perf. 10½x11	
1117	A563	4c	green, Sept. 19, 1958	10	5
			Margin block of 4, P#	55	—

GIORI PRESS PRINTING
Plates of 288 subjects in four panes of 72 each.

Perf. 11

1118	A563	8c	carmine, ultramarine & ocher, Sept. 19, 1958	22	12
			Margin block of 4, two P#	2.75	—

FREEDOM OF PRESS ISSUE

Issued in honor of Journalism and freedom of the press in connection with the 50th anniversary of the first School of Journalism at the University of Missouri.

Early Press and Hand Holding Quill — A564

Designed by Lester Beall and Charles Goslin.

ROTARY PRESS PRINTING
E.E. Plates of 200 subjects in four panes of 50 each.

1958		Unwmk.		Perf. 10½x11	
1119	A564	4c	black, Sept. 22, 1958	10	5
			Margin block of 4, P#	50	—

OVERLAND MAIL ISSUE

Issued to commemorate the centenary of Overland Mail Service.

Mail Coach and Map of Southwest U.S. — A565

Designed by William H. Buckley.

ROTARY PRESS PRINTING
E.E. Plates of 200 subjects in four panes of 50 each.

1958		Unwmk.		Perf. 11x10½	
1120	A565	4c	crimson rose, Oct. 10, 1958	10	5
			Margin block of 4, P#	50	—

NOAH WEBSTER ISSUE

Issued to commemorate the bicentenary of the birth of Noah Webster (1758-1843), lexicographer and author.

Noah Webster — A566

Designed by Charles R. Chickering.

ROTARY PRESS PRINTING

E.E. Plates of 280 subjects in four panes of 70 each.

1958	Unwmk.		Perf. 10½x11		
1121	A566	4c dark carmine rose, *Oct. 16, 1958*		10	5
		Margin block of 4, P#		50	—

FOREST CONSERVATION ISSUE

Issued to publicize forest conservation and the protection of natural resources and to honor Theodore Roosevelt, a leading forest conservationist, on the centenary of his birth.

Forest Scene — A567

Designed by Rudolph Wendelin.

GIORI PRESS PRINTING

Plates of 200 subjects in four panes of 50 each.

1958	Unwmk.		Perf. 11		
1122	A567	4c green, yellow & brown, *Oct. 27, 1958*		10	5
		Margin block of 4, P#		55	—

FORT DUQUESNE ISSUE

Issued to commemorate the bicentennial of Fort Duquesne (Fort Pitt) at future site of Pittsburgh.

British Capture of Fort Duquesne, 1758; Brig. Gen. John Forbes on Litter, Colonel Washington Mounted — A568

Designed by William H. Buckley and Douglas Gorsline.

ROTARY PRESS PRINTING

E.E. Plates of 200 subjects in four panes of 50 each.

1958	Unwmk.		Perf. 11x10½		
1123	A568	4c blue, *Nov. 25, 1958*		10	5
		Margin block of 4, P#		50	—

OREGON STATEHOOD ISSUE

Issued to commemorate the centenary of Oregon's admission to Statehood.

Covered Wagon and Mt. Hood — A569

Designed by Robert Hallock.

ROTARY PRESS PRINTING

E.E. Plates of 200 subjects in four panes of 50 each.

1959	Unwmk.		Perf. 11x10½		
1124	A569	4c blue green, *Feb. 14, 1959*		10	5
		Margin block of 4, P#		50	—

CHAMPION OF LIBERTY ISSUE

Issued to honor José de San Martin, South American soldier and statesman.

José de San Martin — A570

ROTARY PRESS PRINTING

E.E. Plates of 280 subjects in four panes of 70 each.

1959, Feb. 25	Unwmk.		Perf. 10½x11		
1125	A570	4c blue		10	5
		Margin block of 4, P#		55	—
a.		Horiz. pair, imperf. between		1,250.	

GIORI PRESS PRINTING

Plates of 288 subjects in four panes of 72 each.

Perf. 11

1126	A570	80c carmine, ultramarine & ocher		20	12
		Margin block of 4, P#		1.50	—

NATO ISSUE

Issued to commemorate the 10th anniversary of the North Atlantic Treaty Organization.

NATO Emblem — A571

Designed by Stevan Dohanos.

ROTARY PRESS PRINTING

E.E. Plates of 280 subjects in four panes of 70 each.

1959	Unwmk.		Perf. 10½x11		
1127	A571	4c blue, *April 1, 1959*		10	5
		Margin block of 4, P#		50	—

ARCTIC EXPLORATIONS ISSUE

Issued to commemorate the conquest of the Arctic by land by Rear Admiral Robert Edwin Peary in 1909 and by sea by the submarine "Nautilus" in 1958.

North Pole, Dog Sled and "Nautilus" A572

Designed by George Samerjan.

ROTARY PRESS PRINTING

E.E. Plates of 200 subjects in four panes of 50 each.

1959, Apr. 6	Unwmk.		Perf. 11x10½		
1128	A572	4c bright greenish blue		13	5
		Margin block of 4, P#		65	—

WORLD PEACE THROUGH WORLD TRADE ISSUE

Issued in conjunction with the 17th Congress of the International Chamber of Commerce, Washington, D.C., April 19-25.

Globe and Laurel — A573

Designed by Robert Baker.

ROTARY PRESS PRINTING

E.E. Plates of 200 subjects in four panes of 50 each.

1959	Unwmk.		Perf. 11x10½		
1129	A573	8c rose lake, *Apr. 20, 1959*		20	12
		Margin block of 4, P#		1.00	—

SILVER CENTENNIAL ISSUE

Issued to commemorate the centenary of the discovery of silver at the Comstock Lode, Nevada.

Henry Comstock at Mount Davidson Site — A574

Designed by Robert L. Miller and W.K. Schrage.

ROTARY PRESS PRINTING

E.E. Plates of 200 subjects in four panes of 50 each.

1959	Unwmk.		Perf. 11x10½		
130	A574	4c black, *June 8, 1959*		10	5
		Margin block of 4, P#		50	—

ST. LAWRENCE SEAWAY ISSUE

Issued to commemorate the opening of the St. Lawrence Seaway.

Great Lakes, Maple Leaf and Eagle Emblems — A575

GIORI PRESS PRINTING

Plates of 200 subjects in four panes of 50 each.

1959			Perf. 11		
1131	A575	4c red & dark blue, *June 26, 1959*		10	5
		Margin block of 4, P#		50	—
		Pair with full horiz. gutter btwn.		—	

49-STAR FLAG ISSUE

U.S. Flag, 1959 — A576

Designed by Stevan Dohanos.

GIORI PRESS PRINTING

Plates of 200 subjects in four panes of 50 each.

1959	Unwmk.		Perf. 11		
1132	A576	4c ocher, dark blue & deep carmine, *July 4, 1959*		10	5
		Margin block of 4, P#		50	—

SOIL CONSERVATION ISSUE

Issued as a tribute to farmers and ranchers who use soil and water conservation measures.

Modern Farm — A577

Designed by Walter Hortens.

GIORI PRESS PRINTING

Plates of 200 subjects in four panes of 50 each.

1959	Unwmk.		Perf. 11		
1133	A577	4c blue, green & ocher, *Aug. 26, 1959*		10	5
		Margin block of 4, P#		55	—

PETROLEUM INDUSTRY ISSUE

Issued to commemorate the centenary of the completion of the nation's first oil well at Titusville, Pa.

Oil Derrick — A578

Designed by Robert Foster.

ROTARY PRESS PRINTING
E.E. Plates of 200 subjects in four panes of 50 each.

1959	Unwmk.	Perf. 10½x11	
1134 A578 4c brown, *Aug. 27, 1959*		10	5
Margin block of 4, P#		50	—

DENTAL HEALTH ISSUE

Issued to publicize Dental Health and for the centenary of the American Dental Association.

Children — A579

Designed by Charles Henry Carter.

ROTARY PRESS PRINTING
E.E. Plates of 200 subjects in four panes of 50 each.

1959	Unwmk.	Perf. 11x10½	
1135 A579 4c green, *Sept. 14, 1959*		10	5
Margin block of 4, P#		50	—

CHAMPION OF LIBERTY ISSUE

Issued to honor Ernst Reuter, Mayor of Berlin, 1948-53.

Ernst Reuter — A580

ROTARY PRESS PRINTING
E.E. Plates of 280 subjects in four panes of 70 each.

1959, Sept. 29	Unwmk.	Perf. 10½x11	
1136 A580 4c gray		10	5
Margin block of 4, P#		55	—

GIORI PRESS PRINTING
Plates of 288 subjects in four panes of 72 each.

Perf. 11

1137 A580 8c carmine, ultramarine & ocher		20	12
Margin block of 4, P#		1.50	—

DR. EPHRAIM McDOWELL ISSUE

Issued to honor Dr. Ephraim McDowell (1771-1830) on the 150th anniversary of the first successful ovarian operation in the United States, performed at Danville, Ky., 1809.

Dr. Ephraim McDowell — A581

Designed by Charles R. Chickering.

ROTARY PRESS PRINTING
E.E. Plates of 280 subjects in four panes of 70 each.

1959	Unwmk.	Perf. 10½x11	
1138 A581 4c rose lake, *Dec. 3, 1959*		10	5
Margin block of 4, P#		50	—
a. Vert. pair, imperf. btwn.		600.00	
b. Vert. pair, imperf. horiz.		500.00	

AMERICAN CREDO ISSUE

Issued to re-emphasize the ideals upon which America was founded and to honor those great Americans who wrote or uttered the credos.

Quotation from Washington's Farewell Address, 1796 — A582

Benjamin Franklin Quotation A583

Thomas Jefferson Quotation A584

Francis Scott Key Quotation A585

Abraham Lincoln Quotation A586

Patrick Henry Quotation A587

Designed by Frank Conley.

GIORI PRESS PRINTING
Plates of 200 subjects in four panes of 50 each.

1960-61	Unwmk.	Perf. 11	
1139 A582 4c dark violet blue, & carmine, *Jan. 20, 1960*		12	5
Margin block of 4, P#		70	—
1140 A583 4c olive bister & green, *Mar. 31, 1960*		12	5
Margin block of 4, P#		70	—
1141 A584 4c gray & vermilion, *May 18, 1960*		15	5
Margin block of 4, P#		75	—
1142 A585 4c carmine & dark blue, *Sept. 14, 1960*		15	5
Margin block of 4, P#		75	—
1143 A586 4c magenta & green, *Nov. 19, 1960*		15	5

1144 A587 4c green & brown, *Jan. 11, 1961*		15	5
Margin block of 4, P#		80	—

BOY SCOUT JUBILEE ISSUE

Issued to commemorate the 50th anniversary of the Boy Scouts of America.

Boy Scout Giving Scout Sign — A588

Designed by Norman Rockwell.

GIORI PRESS PRINTING
Plates of 200 subjects in four panes of 50 each.

1960	Unwmk.	Perf. 11	
1145 A588 4c red, dark blue & dark bister, *Feb. 8, 1960*		10	5
Margin block of 4, P#		50	—

OLYMPIC WINTER GAMES ISSUE

Issued to commemorate the opening of the 8th Olympic Winter Games, Squaw Valley, Feb. 18-29, 1960.

Olympic Rings and Snowflake — A589

Designed by Ervine Metzl.

ROTARY PRESS PRINTING
E.E. Plates of 200 subjects in four panes of 50 each.

1960	Unwmk.	Perf. 10½x11	
1146 A589 4c dull blue, *Feb. 18, 1960*		10	5
Margin block of 4, P#		50	—

CHAMPION OF LIBERTY ISSUE

Issued to honor Thomas G. Masaryk, founder and president of Czechoslovakia (1918-35), on the 110th anniversary of his birth.

Thomas G. Masaryk — A590

ROTARY PRESS PRINTING
E.E. Plates of 280 subjects in four panes of 70 each.

1960	Unwmk.	Perf. 10½x11	
1147 A590 4c blue, *March 7, 1960*		10	5
Margin block of 4, P#		55	—
a. Vert. pair, imperf. between		2,100.	

GIORI PRESS PRINTING
Plates of 288 subjects in four panes of 72 each.

Perf. 11

1148 A590 8c carmine, ultramarine & ocher, *March 7, 1960*		20	12
Margin block of 4, P#		1.50	—
a. Horiz. pair, imperf. between			—

WORLD REFUGEE YEAR ISSUE

Issued to publicize World Refugee Year, July 1, 1959-June 30, 1960.

Family Walking
Toward New
Life — A591

Designed by Ervine Metzl.

ROTARY PRESS PRINTING

E.E. Plates of 200 subjects in four panes of 50 each.

1960   Unwmk.   Perf. 11x10½
1149 A591 4c **gray black**, *Apr. 7, 1960*   10   5
              Margin block of 4, P#   50   —

WATER CONSERVATION ISSUE

Issued to stress the importance of water conservation and to commemorate the 7th Watershed Congress, Washington, D.C.

Water: From
Watershed to
Consumer
A592

Designed by Elmo White.

GIORI PRESS PRINTING

Plates of 200 subjects in four panes of 50 each.

1960   Unwmk.   Perf. 11
1150 A592 4c **dark blue, brown orange & green**, *Apr.
              18, 1960*   10   5
              Margin block of 4, P#   55   —

SEATO ISSUE

Issued to honor the South-East Asia Treaty Organization and to publicize the SEATO Conference, Washington, D.C., May 31-June 3.

SEATO Emblem — A593

Designed by John Maass.

ROTARY PRESS PRINTING

E.E. plates of 280 subjects in four panes of 70 each.

1960   Unwmk.   Perf. 10½x11
1151 A593 4c **blue**, *May 31, 1960*   10   5
              Margin block of 4, P#   50   —
  a.   Vertical pair, imperf. between   200.00

AMERICAN WOMAN ISSUE

Issued to pay tribute to American women and their accomplishments in civic affairs, education, arts and industry.

Mother and
Daughter — A594

Designed by Robert Sivard.

ROTARY PRESS PRINTING

E.E. Plates of 200 subjects in four panes of 50 each.

1960   Unwmk.   Perf. 11x10½
1152 A594 4c **deep violet**, *June 2, 1960*   10   5
              Margin block of 4, P#   50   —

50-STAR FLAG ISSUE

U.S. POSTAGE U.S. Flag, 1960 — A595

Designed by Stevan Dohanos.

GIORI PRESS PRINTING

Plates of 200 subjects in four panes of 50 each.

1960   Unwmk.   Perf. 11
1153 A595 4c **dark blue & red**, *July 4, 1960*   10   5
              Margin block of 4, P#   50   —

PONY EXPRESS CENTENNIAL ISSUE

Issued to commemorate the centenary of the Pony Express.

Pony Express
Rider — A596

Designed by Harold von Schmidt.

ROTARY PRESS PRINTING

E.E. Plates of 200 subjects in four panes of 50 each.
1960   Unwmk.   Perf. 11x10½
1154 A596 4c **sepia**, *July 19, 1960*   10   5
              Margin block of 4, P#   50   —

EMPLOY THE HANDICAPPED ISSUE

Issued to promote the employment of the physically handicapped and to publicize the Eighth World Congress of the International Society for the Welfare of Cripples, New York City.

Man in Wheelchair Operating
Drill Press — A597

Designed by Carl Bobertz.

ROTARY PRESS PRINTING

E.E. Plates of 200 subjects in four panes of 50 each.

1960   Unwmk.   Perf. 10½x11
1155 A597 4c **dark blue**, *Aug. 28, 1960*   10   5
              Margin block of 4, P#   50   —

WORLD FORESTRY CONGRESS ISSUE

Issued to commemorate the Fifth World Forestry Congress, Seattle, Washington, Aug. 29-Sept. 10.

U.S. Proofs are listed and priced in a separate
section of the catalogue. See catalogue index.

World Forestry Congress
Seal — A598

ROTARY PRESS PRINTING

E.E. Plates of 200 subjects in four panes of 50 each.

1960, Aug. 29   Unwmk.   Perf. 10½x11
1156 A598 4c **green**   10   5
              Margin block of 4, P#   50   —

MEXICAN INDEPENDENCE ISSUE

Issued to commemorate the 150th anniversary of Mexican Independence.

Independence Bell — A599

Designed by Leon Helguera and Charles R. Chickering.

GIORI PRESS PRINTING

Plates of 200 subjects in four panes of 50 each.

1960   Unwmk.   Perf. 11
1157 A599 4c **green & rose red**, *Sept. 16, 1960*   10   5
              Margin block of 4, P#   50   —

U.S.-JAPAN TREATY ISSUE

Issued to commemorate the centenary of the United States-Japan Treaty of Amity and Commerce.

Washington Monument and
Cherry Blossoms — A600

Designed by Gyo Fujikawa.

GIORI PRESS PRINTING

Plates of 200 subjects in four panes of 50 each.

1960, Sept. 28   Unwmk.   Perf. 11
1158 A600 4c **blue & pink**   10   5
              Margin block of 4, P#   50   —

CHAMPION OF LIBERTY ISSUE

Issued to honor Ignacy Jan Paderewski, Polish
statesman and musician.

Ignacy Jan
Paderewski — A601

ROTARY PRESS PRINTING

E.E. Plates of 280 subjects in four panes of 70 each.

1960, Oct. 8	Unwmk.	Perf. 10½x11		
1159 A601	4c blue		10	5
	Margin block of 4, P#		50	—

GIORI PRESS PRINTING

Plates of 288 subjects in four panes of 72 each.

Perf. 11

1160 A601	8c carmine, ultramarine & ocher		20	12
	Margin block of 4, P#		1.50	—

SENATOR TAFT MEMORIAL ISSUE

Issued in memory of Senator Robert A. Taft (1889-1953) of Ohio.

Robert A. Taft — A602

Designed by William K. Schrage.

ROTARY PRESS PRINTING

E.E. Plates of 280 subjects in four panes of 70 each.

1960	Unwmk.	Perf. 10½x11		
1161 A602	4c dull violet, Oct. 10, 1960		10	5
	Margin block of 4, P#		50	—

WHEELS OF FREEDOM ISSUE

Issued to honor the automotive industry and in connection with the National Automobile Show, Detroit, Oct. 15-23.

Globe and Steering Wheel with Tractor, Car and Truck — A603

Designed by Arnold J. Copeland.

ROTARY PRESS PRINTING

E.E. Plates of 200 subjects in four panes of 50 each.

1960	Unwmk.	Perf. 11x10½		
1162 A603	4c dark blue, Oct. 15, 1960		10	5
	Margin block of 4, P#		50	—

BOYS' CLUBS OF AMERICA ISSUE

Issued to commemorate the centenary of the Boys' Clubs of America movement.

Profile of Boy — A604

Designed by Charles T. Coiner.

GIORI PRESS PRINTING

Plates of 200 subjects in four panes of 50 each.

1960	Unwmk.	Perf. 11		
1163 A604	4c indigo, slate & rose red, Oct. 18, 1960		10	5
	Margin block of 4, P#		50	—

FIRST AUTOMATED POST OFFICE IN THE U.S.A. ISSUE

Issued to publicize the opening of the first automated post office in the United States at Providence, R.I.

Architect's Sketch of New Post Office, Providence, R.I. — A605

Designed by Arnold J. Copeland and Victor S. McCloskey, Jr.

GIORI PRESS PRINTING

Plates of 200 subjects in four panes of 50 each.

1960	Unwmk.	Perf. 11		
1164 A605	4c dark blue & carmine, Oct. 20, 1960		10	5
	Margin block of 4, P#		50	—

CHAMPION OF LIBERTY ISSUE

Issued to honor Baron Karl Gustaf Emil Mannerheim (1867-1951), Marshal and President of Finland.

Baron Gustaf Mannerheim — A606

ROTARY PRESS PRINTING

E.E. Plates of 280 subjects in four panes of 70 each.

1960, Oct. 26	Unwmk.	Perf. 10½x11		
1165 A606	4c blue		10	5
	Margin block of 4, P#		50	—

GIORI PRESS PRINTING

Plates of 288 subjects in four panes of 72 each.

Perf. 11

1166 A606	8c carmine, ultramarine & ocher		20	12
	Margin block of 4, P#		1.50	—

CAMP FIRE GIRLS ISSUE

Issued to commemorate the 50th anniversary of the Camp Fire Girls' movement and in connection with the Golden Jubilee Convention celebration of the Camp Fire Girls.

Camp Fire Girls Emblem — A607

Designed by H. Edward Oliver.

GIORI PRESS PRINTING

Plates of 200 subjects in four panes of 50 each.

1960, Nov. 1	Unwmk.	Perf. 11		
1167 A607	4c dark blue & bright red		10	5
	Margin block of 4, P#		50	—

CHAMPION OF LIBERTY ISSUE

Issued to honor Giuseppe Garibaldi (1807-1882), Italian patriot and freedom fighter.

Giuseppe Garibaldi — A608

ROTARY PRESS PRINTING

E.E. Plates of 280 subjects in four panes of 70 each.

1960, Nov. 2	Unwmk.	Perf. 10½x11		
1168 A608	4c green		10	5
	Margin block of 4, P#		50	—

GIORI PRESS PRINTING

Plates of 288 subjects in four panes of 72 each.

Perf. 11

1169 A608	8c carmine, ultramarine & ocher		20	12
	Margin block of 4, P#		1.50	—

SENATOR GEORGE MEMORIAL ISSUE

Issued in memory of Senator Walter F. George (1878-1957) of Georgia.

Walter F. George — A609

Designed by William K. Schrage.

ROTARY PRESS PRINTING

E.E. Plates of 280 subjects in four panes of 70 each.

1960	Unwmk.	Perf. 10½x11		
1170 A609	4c dull violet, Nov. 5, 1960		10	5
	Margin block of 4, P#		50	—

ANDREW CARNEGIE ISSUE

Issued to honor Andrew Carnegie (1835-1919), industrialist and philanthropist.

Andrew Carnegie — A610

Designed by Charles R. Chickering.

ROTARY PRESS PRINTING

E.E. Plates of 280 subjects in four panes of 70 each.

1960	Unwmk.	Perf. 10½x11		
1171 A610	4c deep claret, Nov. 25, 1960		10	5
	Margin block of 4, P#		50	—

JOHN FOSTER DULLES MEMORIAL ISSUE

Issued in memory of John Foster Dulles (1888-1959), Secretary of State (1953-1959).

John Foster Dulles — A611

Designed by William K. Schrage.

ROTARY PRESS PRINTING

E.E. Plates of 280 subjects in four panes of 70 each.

1960	Unwmk.	Perf. 10½x11		
1172 A611	4c dull violet, Dec. 6, 1960		10	5
	Margin block of 4, P#		50	—

ECHO I - COMMUNICATIONS FOR PEACE ISSUE

Issued to commemorate the world's first communications satellite, Echo I, placed in orbit by the National Aeronautics and Space Administration, Aug. 12, 1960.

Radio Waves
Connecting Echo I
and Earth — A612

Designed by Ervine Metzl.

ROTARY PRESS PRINTING
E.E. Plates of 200 subjects in four panes of 50 each.

1960, Dec. 15	Unwmk.	Perf. 11x10½		
1173	A612	4c deep violet, *Dec. 15, 1960*	35	12
		Margin block of 4, P#	1.50	—

CHAMPION OF LIBERTY ISSUE

Issued to honor Mohandas K. Gandhi, leader in India's struggle for independence.

Mahatma Gandhi — A613

ROTARY PRESS PRINTING
E.E. Plates of 280 subjects in four panes of 70 each.

1961, Jan. 26	Unwmk.	Perf. 10½x11		
1174	A613	4c red orange	10	5
		Margin block of 4, P#	50	—

GIORI PRESS PRINTING
Plates of 288 subjects in four panes of 72 each.

		Perf. 11		
1175	A613	8c carmine, ultramarine & ocher	20	12
		Margin block of 4, P#	1.65	—

RANGE CONSERVATION ISSUE

Issued to stress the importance of range conservation and to commemorate the meeting of the American Society of Range Management, Washington, D.C. "The Trail Boss" from a drawing by Charles M. Russell is the Society's emblem.

The Trail Boss
and Modern
Range — A614

Designed by Rudolph Wendelin.

GIORI PRESS PRINTING
Plates of 200 subjects in four panes of 50 each.

1961, Feb. 2	Unwmk.	Perf. 11		
1176	A614	4c blue, slate & brown orange	10	5
		Margin block of 4, P#	55	—

HORACE GREELEY ISSUE

Issued to honor Horace Greeley (1811-1872), publisher and editor.

Horace Greeley — A615

Designed by Charles R. Chickering.

ROTARY PRESS PRINTING
E.E. Plates of 280 subjects in four panes of 70 each.

1961	Unwmk.	Perf. 10½x11		
1177	A615	4c dull violet, *Feb. 3, 1961*	10	5
		Margin block of 4, P#	50	—

CIVIL WAR CENTENNIAL ISSUE

Issued to commemorate the centenaries of the firing on Fort Sumter (No. 1178), the Battle of Shiloh (No. 1179), the Battle of Gettysburg (No. 1180), the Battle of the Wilderness (No. 1181) and the surrender at Appomattox (No. 1182).

Sea Coast Gun of
1861 — A616

Rifleman at
Battle of Shiloh,
1862 — A617

Blue and Gray at
Gettysburg,
1863 — A618

Battle of the
Wilderness,
1864 — A619

Appomattox, 1865 — A620

Designed by Charles R. Chickering (Sumter), Noel Sickles (Shiloh), Roy Gjertson (Gettysburg), B. Harold Christenson (Wilderness), Leonard Fellman (Appomattox).

ROTARY PRESS PRINTING
E.E. Plates of 200 subjects in four panes of 50 each.

1961-65	Unwmk.	Perf. 11x10½		
1178	A616	4c light green, *Apr. 12, 1961*	20	5
		Margin block of 4, P#	1.00	—
1179	A617	4c *peach blossom, Apr. 7, 1962*	18	5
		Margin block of 4, P#	1.00	—

GIORI PRESS PRINTING
Plates of 200 subjects in four panes of 50 each.

		Perf. 11		
1180	A618	5c gray & blue, *July 1, 1963*	18	5
		Margin block of 4, P#	1.00	—
1181	A619	5c dark red & black, *May 5, 1964*	18	5
		Margin block of 4, P#	80	—
		Margin block of 4, Mr. Zip and "Use Zip Code"	85	—
1182	A620	5c Prus. blue & black, *Apr. 9, 1965*	30	5
		Margin block of 4, P#	1.50	—
		Margin block of 4, Mr. Zip and "Use Zip Code"	1.35	—
a.		Horiz. pair, imperf. vert.	—	

KANSAS STATEHOOD ISSUE

Issued to commemorate the centenary of the admission of Kansas to statehood.

Souvenir cards are listed and priced in a separate section of the catalogue. See catalogue index.

Sunflower, Pioneer
Couple and
Stockade — A621

GIORI PRESS PRINTING
Plates of 200 subjects in four panes of 50 each.

1961	Unwmk.	Perf. 11		
1183	A621	4c brown, dark red & green, *yellow, May 10, 1961*	10	5
		Margin block of 4, P#	55	—

SENATOR NORRIS ISSUE

Issued to commemorate the centenary of the birth of Senator George W. Norris (1861-1944), of Nebraska.

Senator George W.
Norris and Norris
Dam — A622

Designed by C. R. Chickering.

ROTARY PRESS PRINTING
E.E. Plates of 200 subjects in four panes of 50 each.

1961	Unwmk.	Perf. 11x10½		
1184	A622	4c blue green, *July 11, 1961*	10	5
		Margin block of 4, P#	50	—

NAVAL AVIATION ISSUE

Issued to commemorate the 50th anniversary of Naval Aviation.

Navy's First Plane
(Curtiss A-1 of
1911) and Naval
Air Wings — A623

Designed by John Maass.

ROTARY PRESS PRINTING
E.E. Plates of 200 subjects in four panes of 50 each.

1961	Unwmk.	Perf. 11x10½		
1185	A623	4c blue, *Aug. 20, 1961*	10	5
		Margin block of 4, P#	50	
		Pair with full vertical gutter between	150.00	

WORKMEN'S COMPENSATION ISSUE

Issued to commemorate the 50th anniversary of the first successful Workmen's Compensation Law, enacted by the Wisconsin legislature.

Scales of Justice, Factory,
Worker and Family — A624

Designed by Norman Todhunter.

ROTARY PRESS PRINTING
E.E. Plates of 200 subjects in four panes of 50 each.

1961	Unwmk.	Perf. 10½x11		
1186	A624	4c ultramarine, *grayish, Sept. 4, 1961*	10	5
		Margin block of 4, P#	50	—
		Margin block of 4, P# inverted	75	—

FREDERIC REMINGTON ISSUE

Issued to commemorate the centenary of the birth of Frederic Remington (1861-1909), artist of the West. The design is from an oil painting, Amon Carter Museum of Western Art, Fort Worth, Texas.

"The Smoke Signal" — A625

Designed by Charles R. Chickering.

GIORI PRESS PRINTING

Panes of 200 subjects in four panes of 50 each.

1961	Unwmk.	Perf. 11		
1187 A625	4c **multicolored,** *Oct. 4, 1961*		12	5
	Margin block of 4, P#		60	—

REPUBLIC OF CHINA ISSUE

Issued to commemorate the 50th anniversary of the Republic of China.

Sun Yat-sen — A626

ROTARY PRESS PRINTING

E.E. Plates of 200 subjects in four panes of 50 each.

1961	Unwmk.	Perf. 10½x11		
1188 A626	4c **blue,** *Oct. 10, 1961*		10	5
	Margin block of 4, P#		50	—

NAISMITH - BASKETBALL ISSUE

Issued in honor of basketball and to commemorate the centenary of the birth of James A. Naismith (1861-1939), Canada-born director of physical education, who invented the game in 1891 at Y.M.C.A. College, Springfield, Mass.

Basketball — A627

Designed by Charles R. Chickering.

ROTARY PRESS PRINTING

E.E. Plates of 200 subjects in four panes of 50 each.

1961	Unwmk.	Perf. 10½x11		
1189 A627	4c **brown,** *Nov. 6, 1961*		10	5
	Margin block of 4, P#		55	—

NURSING ISSUE

Issued to honor the nursing profession.

Student Nurse Lighting
Candle — A628

Designed by Alfred Charles Parker.

GIORI PRESS PRINTING

Plates of 200 subjects in four panes of 50 each.

1961, Dec. 28	Unwmk.	Perf. 11		
1190 A628	4c **blue, green, orange & black**		10	5
	Margin block of 4, two P#		55	—

NEW MEXICO STATEHOOD ISSUE

Issued to commemorate the 50th anniversary of New Mexico's admission to statehood.

Shiprock — A629

Designed by Robert J. Jones.

GIORI PRESS PRINTING

Plates of 200 subjects in four panes of 50 each.

1962, Jan. 6	Unwmk.	Perf. 11		
1191 A629	4c **lt. blue, maroon & bister**		10	5
	Margin block of 4, P#		50	—

ARIZONA STATEHOOD ISSUE

Issued to commemorate the 50th anniversary of the admission of Arizona to statehood.

Giant Saguaro
Cactus — A630

Designed by Jimmie E. Ihms and James M. Chemi.

GIORI PRESS PRINTING

Plates of 200 subjects in four panes of 50 each.

1962, Feb. 14	Unwmk.	Perf. 11		
1192 A630	4c **carmine, violet blue & green**		10	5
	Margin block of 4, P#		55	—

PROJECT MERCURY ISSUE

Issued to commemorate the first orbital flight of a U.S. astronaut, Feb. 20, 1962. The flight was made by Lt. Col. John H. Glenn, Jr.

"Friendship 7"
Capsule and
Globe — A631

GIORI PRESS PRINTING

Plates of 200 subjects in four panes of 50 each.

1962	Unwmk.	Perf. 11		
1193 A631	4c **dark blue & yellow,** *Feb. 20, 1962*		10	10
	Margin block of 4, P#		55	—

Imperfs. are printers waste.

MALARIA ERADICATION ISSUE

Issued for the World Health Organization's drive to eradicate malaria.

Great Seal of U.S.
and W.H.O.
Symbol — A632

Designed by Charles R. Chickering.

GIORI PRESS PRINTING

Plates of 200 subjects in four panes of 50 each.

1962	Unwmk.	Perf. 11		
1194 A632	4c **blue & bister,** *March 30, 1962*		10	5
	Margin block of 4, P#		50	—

CHARLES EVANS HUGHES ISSUE

Issued to commemorate the centenary of the birth of Charles Evans Hughes (1862-1948), Governor of New York, Chief Justice of the U.S.

Charles Evans Hughes — A633

Designed by Charles R. Chickering.

ROTARY PRESS PRINTING

E.E. Plates of 200 subjects in four panes of 50 each.

1962	Unwmk.	Perf. 10½x11		
1195 A633	4c **buff,** *Apr. 11, 1962*		10	5
	Margin block of 4, P#		50	—

SEATTLE WORLD'S FAIR ISSUE

Issued to publicize the "Century 21" International Exposition, Seattle, Wash., Apr. 21-Oct. 21.

"Space Needle" and
Monorail — A634

Designed by John Maass.

GIORI PRESS PRINTING

Plates of 200 subjects in four panes of 50 each.

1962	Unwmk.	Perf. 11		
1196 A634	4c **red & dark blue,** *Apr. 25, 1962*		10	5
	Margin block of 4, P#		55	—

LOUISIANA STATEHOOD ISSUE

Issued to commemorate the sesquicentennial of Louisiana statehood.

Riverboat on the Mississippi A635

Designed by Norman Todhunter.

GIORI PRESS PRINTING
Plates of 200 subjects in four panes of 50 each.

1962	**Unwmk.**	**Perf. 11**	
1197	A635 4c **blue, dark slate green & red**, *Apr. 30, 1962*	10	5
	Margin block of 4, P#	50	—

HOMESTEAD ACT ISSUE

Issued to commemorate the centenary of the Homestead Act.

Sod Hut and Settlers — A636

Designed by Charles R. Chickering.

ROTARY PRESS PRINTING
E.E. Plates of 200 subjects in four panes of 50 each.

1962	**Unwmk.**	**Perf. 11x10½**	
1198	A636 4c **slate**, *May 20, 1962*	10	5
	Margin block of 4, P#	50	—

GIRL SCOUTS ISSUE

Issued to commemorate the 50th anniversary of the Girl Scouts of America.

Senior Girl Scout and Flag — A637

Designed by Ward Brackett.

ROTARY PRESS PRINTING
E.E. Plates of 200 subjects in four panes of 50 each.

1962	**Unwmk.**	**Perf. 11x10½**	
1199	A637 4c **rose red**, *July 24, 1962*	10	5
	Margin block of 4, P#	50	—
	Pair with full vertical gutter between	250.00	

SENATOR BRIEN McMAHON ISSUE

Issued to honor Sen. Brien McMahon (1903-1952) of Connecticut for his role in opening the way to peaceful uses of atomic energy through the Atomic Energy Act establishing the Atomic Energy Commission.

Brien McMahon and Atomic Symbol — A638

Designed by V. S. McCloskey, Jr.

ROTARY PRESS PRINTING
E.E. Plates of 200 subjects in four panes of 50 each.

1962	**Unwmk.**	**Perf. 11x10½**	
1200	A638 4c **purple**, *July 28, 1962*	10	5
	Margin block of 4, P#	55	—

APPRENTICESHIP ISSUE

Issued to publicize the National Apprenticeship Program and to commemorate the 25th anniversary of the National Apprenticeship Act.

Machinist Handing Micrometer to Apprentice A639

Designed by Robert Geissmann.

ROTARY PRESS PRINTING
E.E. Plates of 200 subjects in four panes of 50 each.

1962	**Unwmk.**	**Perf. 11x10½**	
1201	A639 4c **yellow bister**, *Aug. 31, 1962*	10	5
	Margin block of 4, P#	50	—

SAM RAYBURN ISSUE

Issued to honor Sam Rayburn (1882-1961), Speaker of the House of Representatives.

Sam Rayburn and Capitol — A640

Designed by Robert L. Miller.

GIORI PRESS PRINTING
Plates of 200 subjects in four panes of 50 each.

1962, Sept. 16	**Unwmk.**	**Perf. 11**	
1202	A640 4c **dark blue & red brown**	10	5
	Margin block of 4, P#	50	—

DAG HAMMARSKJOLD ISSUE

Issued to honor Dag Hammarskjold, Secretary General of the United Nations, 1953-61.

U.N. Headquarters and Dag Hammarskjold A641

Designed by Herbert M. Sanborn.

GIORI PRESS PRINTING
Plates of 200 subjects in four panes of 50 each.

1962	**Unwmk.**	**Perf. 11**	
1203	A641 4c **black, brown & yellow**, *Oct. 23, 1962*	10	5
	Margin block of 4, two P#	60	—

Hammarskjold Special Printing

No. 1204 was issued following discovery of No. 1203 with yellow background inverted.

GIORI PRESS PRINTING
Plates of 200 subjects in four panes of 50 each.

1962	**Unwmk.**	**Perf. 11**	
1204	A641 4c **black, brown & yellow** (yellow inverted), *Nov. 16, 1962*	12	8
	Margin block of 4, two P#, yellow # inverted	2.75	—

The inverted yellow impression is shifted to the right in relation to the black and brown impression. Stamps of first vertical row of UL and LL panes show no yellow at left side for a space of 11-11½mm. in from the perforations. Stamps of first vertical row of UR and LR panes show vertical no-yellow strip 9¾mm. wide, covering UN Building. On all others, the vertical no-yellow strip is 3½mm. wide, and touches UN Building.

CHRISTMAS ISSUE

Wreath and Candles — A642

Designed by Jim Crawford.

GIORI PRESS PRINTING
Plates of 400 subjects in four panes of 100 each.
Panes of 90 and 100 exist without plate numbers due to provisional use of smaller paper.

1962	**Unwmk.**	**Perf. 11**	
1205	A642 4c **green & red**, *Nov. 1, 1962*	10	5
	Margin block of 4, P#	50	—

HIGHER EDUCATION ISSUE

Issued to publicize higher education's role in American cultural and industrial development in connection with the centenary celebrations of the signing of the law creating land-grant colleges and universities.

Map of U.S. and Lamp — A643

Designed by Henry K. Bencsath.

GIORI PRESS PRINTING
Plates of 200 subjects in panes of 50 each.

1962	**Unwmk.**	**Perf. 11**	
1206	A643 4c **blue green & black**, *Nov. 14, 1962*	10	5
	Margin block of 4, two P#	50	—

WINSLOW HOMER ISSUE

Issued to honor Winslow Homer (1836-1910), painter, showing his oil, "Breezing Up," which hangs in the National Gallery, Washington, D.C.

"Breezing Up" — A644

Designed by Victor S. McCloskey, Jr.

GIORI PRESS PRINTING
Plates of 200 subjects in four panes of 50 each.

1962	**Unwmk.**	**Perf. 11**	
1207	A644 4c **multicolored**, *Dec. 15, 1962*	15	5
	Margin block of 4, P#	60	—
a.	Horiz. pair, imperf. between		

FLAG ISSUE

Flag over White House — A645

Designed by Robert J. Jones.

GIORI PRESS PRINTING
Plates of 400 subjects in four panes of 100 each.

1963-66	**Unwmk.**	**Perf. 11**	
1208	A645 5c **blue & red**, *Jan. 9, 1963*	12	5
	Margin block of 4, P#	60	—
a.	Tagged, *Aug. 25, 1966*	25	5
a.	Margin block of 4, P#	1.00	—
b.	Horiz. pair, imperf. between, tagged	1,250.	
	Pair with full horiz. gutter between	—	

REGULAR ISSUE

Andrew Jackson
A646

George
Washington
A650

Designed by William K. Schrage.

ROTARY PRESS PRINTING
E.E. Plates of 400 subjects in four panes of 100 each.

1962-66	Unwmk.		Perf. 11x10½	
1209 A646 1c green, March 22, 1963			5	5
Margin block of 4, P#			25	—
a. Tagged, July 6, 1966			6	5
a. Margin block of 4, P#			35	—
Pair with full vert. gutter btwn.			—	
1213 A650 5c dark blue gray, Nov. 23, 1962			12	5
Margin block of 4, P#			55	—
a. Booklet pane of 5 + label			2.00	75
b. Tagged, Oct. 28, 1963			65	30
b. Margin block of 4, P#			5.00	—
c. As "a," tagged, Oct. 28, 1963			1.25	50
Pair with full vert. gutter btwn.			—	

COIL STAMPS (Rotary Press)

1962-66		Perf. 10 Vertically	
1225 A646 1c green, May 31, 1963		20	5
Pair		40	10
Joint line pair		85	12
a. Tagged, July 6, 1966		12	5
1229 A650 5c dark blue gray, Nov. 23, 1962		1.75	5
Pair		3.50	10
Joint line pair		4.75	15
a. Tagged, Oct. 28, 1963		1.25	6
b. Imperf., pair		350.00	

See Luminescence note in "Information for Collectors" at front of book.

CAROLINA CHARTER ISSUE

Issued to commemorate the tercentenary of the Carolina Charter granting to eight Englishmen lands extending coast-to-coast roughly along the present border of Virginia to the north and Florida to the south. Original charter on display at Raleigh.

First Page of
Carolina
Charter — A662

Designed by Robert L. Miller.

GIORI PRESS PRINTING
Plates of 200 subjects in four panes of 50 each.

1963	Unwmk.		Perf. 11	
1230 A662 5c dk. car. & brown, Apr. 6, 1963			12	5
Margin block of 4, P#			60	—

FOOD FOR PEACE-FREEDOM FROM HUNGER ISSUE

Issued for the American "Food for Peace" program and the "Freedom from Hunger" campaign of the U.N. Food and Agriculture Organization.

Wheat — A663

Designed by Stevan Dohanos.

GIORI PRESS PRINTING
Plates of 200 subjects in four panes of 50 each.

1963	Unwmk.		Perf. 11	
1231 A663 5c green, buff & red, June 4, 1963			12	5
Margin block of 4, P#			60	—

WEST VIRGINIA STATEHOOD ISSUE

Issued to commemorate the centenary of the admission of West Virginia to statehood.

Map of West
Virginia and
State
Capitol — A664

Designed by Dr. Dwight Mutchler.

GIORI PRESS PRINTING
Plates of 200 subjects in four panes of 50 each.

1963	Unwmk.		Perf. 11	
1232 A664 5c green, red & black, June 20, 1963			12	5
Margin block of 4, P#			60	—

EMANCIPATION PROCLAMATION ISSUE

Issued to commemorate the centenary of President Lincoln's Emancipation Proclamation freeing about 3,000,000 slaves in 10 southern states.

Severed
Chain — A665

Designed by Georg Olden.

GIORI PRESS PRINTING
Plates of 200 subjects in four panes of 50 each.

1963, Aug. 16	Unwmk.		Perf. 11	
1233 A665 5c dark blue, black & red			12	5
Margin block of 4, P#			60	—

ALLIANCE FOR PROGRESS ISSUE

Issued to commemorate the second anniversary of the Alliance for Progress, which aims to stimulate economic growth and raise living standards in Latin America.

Alliance
Emblem — A666

Designed by William K. Schrage.

GIORI PRESS PRINTING
Plates of 200 subjects in four panes of 50 each.

1963	Unwmk.		Perf. 11	
1234 A666 5c ultramarine & green, Aug. 17, 1963			12	5
Margin block of 4, P#			60	—

CORDELL HULL ISSUE

Issued to honor Cordell Hull (1871-1955), Secretary of State (1933-44).

Cordell Hull — A667

Designed by Robert J. Jones.

ROTARY PRESS PRINTING
E.E. Plates of 200 subjects in four panes of 50 each.

1963	Unwmk.		Perf. 10½x11	
1235 A667 5c blue green, Oct. 5, 1963			12	5
Margin block of 4, P#			60	—

ELEANOR ROOSEVELT ISSUE

Issued to honor Mrs. Franklin D. Roosevelt (1884-1962).

Eleanor
Roosevelt — A668

Designed by Robert L. Miller.

ROTARY PRESS PRINTING
E.E. Plates of 200 subjects in four panes of 50 each.

1963, Oct. 11	Unwmk.		Perf. 11x10½	
1236 A668 5c bright purple			12	5
Margin block of 4, P#			60	—

SCIENCE ISSUE

Issued to honor the sciences and in connection with the centenary of the National Academy of Science.

"The Universe"
A669

Designed by Antonio Frasconi.

GIORI PRESS PRINTING
Plates of 200 subjects in four panes of 50 each.

1963	Unwmk.		Perf. 11	
1237 A669 5c Prussian blue & black, Oct. 14, 1963			12	5
Margin block of 4, P#			60	—

CITY MAIL DELIVERY ISSUE

Issued to commemorate the centenary of free city mail delivery.

Letter Carrier, 1863 — A670

Designed by Norman Rockwell.

GIORI PRESS PRINTING
Plates of 200 subjects in four panes of 50 each.

1963	Unwmk.	Tagged	*Perf. 11*
1238 A670 5c gray, dk. blue & red, *Oct. 26, 1963*			12 5
Margin block of 4, P#			60 —

RED CROSS CENTENARY ISSUE
Issued to commemorate the centenary of the International Red Cross.

Cuban Refugees on S.S. Morning Light and Red Cross Flag — A671

Designed by Victor S. McCloskey, Jr.

GIORI PRESS PRINTING
Plates of 200 subjects in four panes of 50 each.

1963	Unwmk.	*Perf. 11*
1239 A671 5c bluish black & red, *Oct. 29, 1963*		12 5
Margin block of 4, P#		60 —

CHRISTMAS ISSUE

National Christmas Tree and White House — A672

Designed by Lily Spandorf; modified by Norman Todhunter.

GIORI PRESS PRINTING
Plates of 400 subjects in four panes of 100 each.

1963	Unwmk.	*Perf. 11*
1240 A672 5c dk. blue, bluish black & red, *Nov. 1, 1963*		12 5
Margin block of 4, P#		60 —
a.	Tagged, *Nov. 2, 1963*	1.00 40
a.	Margin block of 4, P#	5.00 —
	Pair with full horiz. gutter between	—

JOHN JAMES AUDUBON ISSUE
Issued to honor John James Audubon (1785-1851), ornithologist and artist. The birds pictured are actually Collie's magpie jays.

"Columbia Jays" by Audubon — A673

Designed by Robert L. Miller.

GIORI PRESS PRINTING
Plates of 200 subjects in four panes of 50 each.

1963	Unwmk.	*Perf. 11*
1241 A673 5c dark blue & multicolored, *Dec. 7, 1963*		12 5
Margin block of 4, P#		60 —

SAM HOUSTON ISSUE
Issued to commemorate the centenary of the death of Sam Houston (1793-1863), soldier, president of Texas, U.S. senator.

Sam Houston — A674

Designed by Tom Lea.

ROTARY PRESS PRINTING
E.E. Plates of 200 subjects in four panes of 50 each.

1964	Unwmk.	*Perf. 10½x11*
1242 A674 5c black, *Jan. 10, 1964*		12 5
Margin block of 4, P#		60 —
Margin block of 4, Mr. Zip and "Use Zip Code"		50 —

CHARLES M. RUSSELL ISSUE
Issued to commemorate the centenary of the birth of Charles M. Russell (1864-1926), painter. The design is from a painting, Thomas Gilcrease Institute of American History and Art, Tulsa, Okla.

"Jerked Down" — A675

Designed by William K. Schrage.

GIORI PRESS PRINTING
Plates of 200 subjects in four panes of 50 each.

1964	Unwmk.	*Perf. 11*
1243 A675 5c multicolored, *March 19, 1964*		15 5
Margin block of 4, P#		75 —
Margin block of 4, Mr. Zip and "Use Zip Code"		70 —

NEW YORK WORLD'S FAIR ISSUE
Issued to publicize the New York World's Fair, 1964-65.

Mall with Unisphere and "Rocket Thrower" by Donald De Lue — A676

Designed by Robert J. Jones.

ROTARY PRESS PRINTING
E.E. Plates of 200 subjects in four panes of 50 each.

1964	Unwmk.	*Perf. 11x10½*
1244 A676 5c blue green, *Apr. 22, 1964*		12 5
On cover, Expo. station canc.		15
Margin block of 4, P#		60 —
Margin block of 4, Mr. Zip and "Use Zip Code"		55 —

JOHN MUIR ISSUE
Issued to honor John Muir (1838-1914), naturalist and conservationist.

John Muir and Redwood Forest — A677

Designed by Rudolph Wendelin.

GIORI PRESS PRINTING
Plates of 200 subjects in four panes of 50 each.

1964	Unwmk.	*Perf. 11*
1245 A677 5c brown, green, yel. grn. & olive, *Apr. 29, 1964*		12 5
Margin block of 4, P#		60 —

KENNEDY MEMORIAL ISSUE
Issued in memory of President John Fitzgerald Kennedy, (1917-1963).

John F. Kennedy and Eternal Flame — A678

Designed by Raymond Loewy/William Snaith, Inc. photograph by William S. Murphy.

ROTARY PRESS PRINTING
E.E. Plates of 200 subjects in four panes of 50 each.

1964		*Perf. 11x10½*
1246 A678 5c blue gray, *May 29, 1964*		12 5
Margin block of 4, P#		60 —

NEW JERSEY TERCENTENARY ISSUE
Issued to commemorate the 300th anniversary of English colonization of New Jersey. The design is from a mural by Howard Pyle in the Essex County Courthouse, Newark, N.J.

Philip Carteret Landing at Elizabethtown, and Map of New Jersey — A679

Designed by Douglas Allen.

ROTARY PRESS PRINTING
E.E. Plates of 200 subjects in four panes of 50 each.

1964	Unwmk.	*Perf. 10½x11*
1247 A679 5c brt. ultramarine, *June 15, 1964*		12 5
Margin block of 4, P#		60 —
Margin block of 4, Mr. Zip and "Use Zip Code"		50 —

NEVADA STATEHOOD ISSUE
Issued to commemorate the centenary of the admission of Nevada to statehood.

Virginia City and Map of Nevada — A680

Designed by William K. Schrage.

GIORI PRESS PRINTING
Plates of 200 subjects in four panes of 50 each.

1964		*Perf. 11*
1248 A680 5c red, yellow & blue, *July 22, 1964*		12 5
Margin block of 4, P#		60 —
Margin block of 4, Mr. Zip and "Use Zip Code"		50 —

REGISTER AND VOTE ISSUE
Issued to publicize the campaign to draw more voters to the polls.

POSTAGE Flag — A681

Designed by Victor S. McCloskey, Jr.

GIORI PRESS PRINTING

Plates of 200 subjects in four panes of 50 each.

1964	Unwmk.	Perf. 11	
1249 A681 5c dk. blue & red, *Aug. 1, 1964*		12	5
Margin block of 4, P#		60	—
Margin block of 4, Mr. Zip and "Use Zip Code"		50	—

SHAKESPEARE ISSUE

Issued to commemorate the 400th anniversary of the birth of William Shakespeare (1564-1616).

William Shakespeare — A682

Designed by Douglas Gorsline.

ROTARY PRESS PRINTING

E.E. Plates of 200 subjects in four panes of 50 each.

1964	Unwmk.	Perf. 10½x11	
1250 A682 5c black brown, *tan, Aug. 14, 1964*		12	5
Margin block of 4, P#		60	—
Margin block of 4, Mr. Zip and "Use Zip Code"		50	—

DOCTORS MAYO ISSUE

Issued to honor Dr. William James Mayo (1861-1939) and his brother, Dr. Charles Horace Mayo (1865-1939), surgeons who founded the Mayo Foundation for Medical Education and Research in affiliation with the University of Minnesota at Rochester, Minn. Heads on stamp are from a sculpture by James Earle Fraser.

Drs. William and Charles Mayo — A683

ROTARY PRESS PRINTING

E.E. Plates of 200 subjects in four panes of 50 each.

1964	Unwmk.	Perf. 10½x11	
1251 A683 5c green, *Sept. 11, 1964*		12	5
Margin block of 4, P#		60	—
Margin block of 4, Mr. Zip and "Use Zip Code"		50	—

AMERICAN MUSIC ISSUE

Issued in tribute to American Music on the 50th anniversary of the founding of the American Society of Composers, Authors and Publishers (ASCAP).

Lute, Horn, Laurel, Oak and Music Score — A684

Designed by Bradbury Thompson.

GIORI PRESS PRINTING

Plates of 200 subjects in four panes of 50 each.

1964	Unwmk.	Perf. 11	
	Gray Paper with Blue Threads		
1252 A684 5c red, black & blue, *Oct. 15, 1964*		12	5
Margin block of 4, P#		60	—
Margin block of 4, Mr. Zip and "Use Zip Code"		50	—
a. Blue omitted		1,500.	

HOMEMAKERS ISSUE

Issued to honor American women as homemakers and to commemorate the 50th anniversary of the passage of the Smith-Lever Act. By providing economic experts under an extension service of the U.S. Department of Agriculture, this legislation helped to improve homelife.

Farm Scene Sampler — A685

Designed by Norman Todhunter.

Plates of 200 subjects in four panes of 50 each.

Engraved (Giori Press); Background Lithographed

1964	Unwmk.	Perf. 11	
1253 A685 5c multicolored, *Oct. 26, 1964*		12	5
Margin block of 4, P#		60	—
Margin block of 4, Mr. Zip and "Use Zip Code"		50	—

CHRISTMAS ISSUE

Holly — A686

Mistletoe — A687

Poinsettia A688

Sprig of Conifer A689

Designed by Thomas F. Naegele.

GIORI PRESS PRINTING

Plates of 400 subjects in four panes of 100 each. Panes contain 25 subjects each of Nos. 1254-1257.

1964	Unwmk.	Perf. 11	
1254 A686 5c green, carmine & black, *Nov. 9*		50	5
Margin block of 4, P# adjoining # 1254		3.00	—
Margin block of 4, Mr. Zip and "Use Zip Code" adjoining #1254		2.75	—
a. Tagged, *Nov. 10*		1.50	50
1255 A687 5c carmine, green & black, *Nov. 9*		50	5
Margin block of 4, P# adjoining # 1255		3.00	—
Margin block of 4, Mr. Zip and "Use Zip Code" adjoining #1255		2.75	—
a. Tagged, *Nov. 10*		1.50	50
1256 A688 5c carmine, green & black, *Nov. 9*		50	5
Margin block of 4, P# adjoining #1256		3.00	—

Margin block of 4, Mr. Zip and "Use Zip Code" adjoining #1256		2.75	—
a. Tagged, *Nov. 10*		1.50	50
1257 A689 5c black, green & carmine, *Nov. 9*		50	5
Margin block of 4, P# adjoining #1257		3.00	—
Margin block of 4, Mr. Zip and "Use Zip Code" adjoining #1257		2.75	—
a. Tagged, *Nov. 10*		1.50	50
a. Margin block of 4, P#		8.50	—
b. Block of four, #1254-1257		2.75	1.25
c. Block of four, tagged		6.50	3.00

VERRAZANO-NARROWS BRIDGE ISSUE

Issued to commemorate the opening of the Verrazano-Narrows Bridge connecting Staten Island and Brooklyn.

Verrazano-Narrows Bridge and Map of New York Bay — A690

ROTARY PRESS PRINTING

E.E. Plates of 200 subjects in four panes of 50 each.

1964	Unwmk.	Perf. 10½x11	
1258 A690 5c blue green, *Nov. 21*		12	5
Margin block of 4, P#		60	—
Margin block of 4, Mr. Zip and "Use Zip Code"		50	—

FINE ARTS ISSUE

Abstract Design by Stuart Davis — A691

GIORI PRESS PRINTING

Plates of 200 subjects in four panes of 50 each.

1964	Unwmk.	Perf. 11	
1259 A691 5c ultra., black & dull red, *Dec. 2*		12	5
Margin block of 4, two P#		60	—
Margin block of 4, Mr. Zip and "Use Zip Code"		50	—

AMATEUR RADIO ISSUE

Issued to honor the radio amateurs on the 50th anniversary of the American Radio Relay League.

Radio Waves and Dial — A692

Designed by Emil J. Willett.

ROTARY PRESS PRINTING

E.E. Plates of 200 subjects in four panes of 50 each.

1964	Unwmk.	Perf. 10½x11	
1260 A692 5c red lilac, *Dec. 15*		12	5
Margin block of 4, P#		60	—
Margin block of 4, Mr. Zip and "Use Zip Code"		50	—

BATTLE OF NEW ORLEANS ISSUE

Issued to commemorate the sesquicentennial of the Battle of New Orleans, Chalmette Plantation, Jan. 8-18, 1815, which established 150 years of peace and friendship between the United States and Great Britain.

General Andrew Jackson and Sesquicentennial Medal — A693

Designed by Robert J. Jones.

GIORI PRESS PRINTING
Plates of 200 subjects in four panes of 50 each.

1965	Unwmk.		Perf. 11
1261 A693 5c dp. carmine, violet blue & gray, *Jan. 8*		12	5
Margin block of 4, P#		60	—
Margin block of 4, Mr. Zip and "Use Zip Code"		50	—

PHYSICAL FITNESS-SOKOL ISSUE

Issued to publicize the importance of physical fitness and to commemorate the centenary of the founding of the Sokol (athletic) organization in America.

Discus Thrower — A694

Designed by Norman Todhunter.

GIORI PRESS PRINTING
Plates of 200 subjects in four panes of 50 each.

1965	Unwmk.		Perf. 11
1262 A694 5c maroon & black, *Feb. 15*		12	5
Margin block of 4, P#		60	—
Margin block of 4, Mr. Zip and "Use Zip Code"		50	—

CRUSADE AGAINST CANCER ISSUE

Issued to publicize the "Crusade Against Cancer" and to stress the importance of early diagnosis.

Microscope and Stethoscope — A695

Designed by Stevan Dohanos.

GIORI PRESS PRINTING
Plates of 200 subjects in four panes of 50 each.

1965	Unwmk.		Perf. 11
1263 A695 5c black, purple & red orange, *Apr. 1*		12	5
Margin block of 4, two P#		60	—
Margin block of 4, Mr. Zip and "Use Zip Code"		50	—

CHURCHILL MEMORIAL ISSUE

Issued in memory of Sir Winston Spencer Churchill (1874-1965), British statesman and World War II leader.

See "Information for Collectors" section at beginning of catalogue for information on printing methods and varieties.

Winston Churchill — A696

Designed by Richard Hurd.

ROTARY PRESS PRINTING
E.E. Plates of 200 subjects in four panes of 50 each.

1965	Unwmk.	Perf. 10½x11	
1264 A696 5c black, *May 13*		12	5
Margin block of 4, P#		60	—
Margin block of 4, Mr. Zip and "Use Zip Code"		50	—

MAGNA CARTA ISSUE

Issued to commemorate the 750th anniversary of the Magna Carta, the basis of English and American common law.

Procession of Barons and King John's Crown — A697

Designed by Brook Temple.

GIORI PRESS PRINTING
Plates of 200 subjects in four panes of 50 each.

1965	Unwmk.		Perf. 11
1265 A697 5c black, yellow ocher & red lilac, *June 15*		12	5
Margin block of 4, two P#		60	—
Margin block of 4, Mr. Zip and "Use Zip Code"		50	—
Corner block of 4, black P# omitted			

INTERNATIONAL COOPERATION YEAR ISSUE

Issued for the International Cooperation Year, 1965, and to commemorate the 20th anniversary of the United Nations.

International Cooperation Year Emblem — A698

Designed by Herbert M. Sanborn and Olav S. Mathiesen.

GIORI PRESS PRINTING
Plates of 200 subjects in four panes of 50 each.

1965	Unwmk.		Perf. 11
1266 A698 5c dull blue & black, *June 26*		12	5
Margin block of 4, P#		60	—
Margin block of 4, Mr. Zip and "Use Zip Code"		50	—

SALVATION ARMY ISSUE

Issued to commemorate the centenary of the founding of the Salvation Army by William Booth in London.

A699

Designed by Sam Marsh.

GIORI PRESS PRINTING
Plates of 200 subjects in four panes of 50 each.

1965	Unwmk.	Perf. 11	
1267 A699 5c red, black & dark blue, *July 2*		12	5
Margin block of 4, P#		60	—
Margin block of 4, Mr. Zip and "Use Zip Code"		50	—

DANTE ISSUE

Issued to commemorate the 700th anniversary of the birth of Dante Alighieri (1265-1321), Italian poet.

Dante after a 16th Century Painting — A700

Designed by Douglas Gorsline.

ROTARY PRESS PRINTING
E.E. Plates of 200 subjects in four panes of 50 each.

1965	Unwmk.	Perf. 10½x11	
1268 A700 5c maroon, *July 17*		12	5
Margin block of 4, P#		60	—
Margin block of 4, Mr. Zip and "Use Zip Code"		50	—

HERBERT HOOVER ISSUE

Issued in memory of President Herbert Clark Hoover, (1874-1964).

Herbert Hoover — A701

Designed by Norman Todhunter; photograph by Fabian Bachrach, Sr.

ROTARY PRESS PRINTING
E.E. Plates of 200 subjects in four panes of 50 each.

1965	Unwmk.	Perf. 10½x11	
1269 A701 5c rose red, *Aug. 10*		12	5
Margin block of 4, P#		60	—
Margin block of 4, Mr. Zip and "Use Zip Code"		50	—

ROBERT FULTON ISSUE

Issued to commemorate the 200th anniversary of the birth of Robert Fulton (1765-1815), inventor of the first commercial steamship.

Robert Fulton and the Clermont — A702

Designed by John Maass; bust by Jean Antoine Houdon.

GIORI PRESS PRINTING
Plates of 200 subjects in four panes of 50 each.

1965			Unwmk.		Perf. 11	
1270	A702	5c	black & blue, *Aug. 19*		12	5
			Margin block of 4, P#		60	—
			Margin block of 4, Mr. Zip and "Use Zip Code"		50	—

FLORIDA SETTLEMENT ISSUE

Issued to commemorate the 400th anniversary of the settlement of Florida, and the first permanent European settlement in the continental United States, St. Augustine, Fla. Similar stamp issued by Spain, No. 1312.

Spanish Explorer, Royal Flag of Spain and Ships — A703

Designed by Brook Temple.

GIORI PRESS PRINTING
Plates of 200 subjects with four panes of 50 each.

1965			Unwmk.		Perf. 11	
1271	A703	5c	red, yellow & black, *Aug. 28*		12	5
			Margin block of 4, three P#		65	—
			Margin block of 4, Mr. Zip and "Use Zip Code"		55	—
a.			Yellow omitted		700.00	

TRAFFIC SAFETY ISSUE

Issued to publicize traffic safety and the prevention of traffic accidents.

Traffic Signal — A704

Designed by Richard F. Hurd.

GIORI PRESS PRINTING
Plates of 200 subjects in four panes of 50 each.

1965			Unwmk.		Perf. 11	
1272	A704	5c	emerald, black & red, *Sept. 3*		12	5
			Margin block of 4, two P#		65	—
			Margin block of 4, Mr. Zip and "Use Zip Code"		55	—

JOHN SINGLETON COPLEY ISSUE

Issued to honor John Singleton Copley (1738-1815), painter. The portrait of the artist's daughter is from the oil painting "The Copley Family," which hangs in the National Gallery of Art, Washington, D.C.

Elizabeth Clarke Copley — A705

Designed by John Carter Brown.

GIORI PRESS PRINTING
Plates of 200 subjects in four panes of 50 each.

1965			Unwmk.		Perf. 11	
1273	A705	5c	black, brown & olive, *Sept. 17*		15	5
			Margin block of 4, P#		75	—
			Margin block of 4, Mr. Zip and "Use Zip Code"		80	—

INTERNATIONAL TELECOMMUNICATION UNION ISSUE

Issued to commemorate the centenary of the International Telecommunication Union.

Galt Projection World Map and Radio Sine Wave — A706

Designed by Thomas F. Naegele.

GIORI PRESS PRINTING
Plates of 200 subjects in four panes of 50 each.

1965			Unwmk.		Perf. 11	
1274	A706	11c	black, carmine & bister, *Oct. 6*		50	25
			Margin block of 4, 2 P#		10.00	—
			Margin block of 4, Mr. Zip and "Use Zip Code"		4.00	—

ADLAI STEVENSON ISSUE

Issued in memory of Adlai Ewing Stevenson (1900-65), governor of Illinois, U.S. ambassador to the U.N.

Adlai E. Stevenson — A707

Designed by George Samerjan; photograph by Philippe Halsman.

LITHOGRAPHED, ENGRAVED (Giori)
Plates of 200 subjects in four panes of 50 each.

1965			Unwmk.		Perf. 11	
1275	A707	5c	pale blue, black, carmine & violet blue, *Oct. 23*		12	5
			Margin block of 4, P#		60	—

CHRISTMAS ISSUE

Angel with Trumpet, 1840 Weather Vane — A708

Designed by Robert Jones after a watercolor by Lucille Gloria Chabot of the 1840 weather vane from the People's Methodist Church, Newburyport, Mass.

GIORI PRESS PRINTING
Plates of 400 subjects in four panes of 100 each.

1965			Unwmk.		Perf. 11	
1276	A708	5c	carmine, dark olive green & bister, *Nov. 2*		12	5
			Margin block of 4, P#		60	—
			Margin block of 4, Mr. Zip and "Use Zip Code"		50	—
			Pair with full vert. gutter btwn.			
a.			Tagged, *Nov. 15*		50	15
a.			Margin block of 4, P#		9.00	—

PROMINENT AMERICANS ISSUE

Thomas Jefferson A710

Albert Gallatin A711

Frank Lloyd Wright and Guggenheim Museum, New York — A712

Francis Parkman — A713

Abraham Lincoln A714

George Washington A715

George Washington (redrawn) A715a

Franklin D. Roosevelt A716

Albert Einstein — A717

Andrew Jackson — A718

Henry Ford and 1909 Model T — A718a

John F. Kennedy — A719

Oliver Wendell
Holmes
A720

George Catlett
Marshall
A721

Frederick
Douglass — A722

John Dewey — A723

Thomas
Paine — A724

Lucy
Stone — A725

Eugene
O'Neill — A726

John Bassett
Moore — A727

Designers: 1c, Robert Geissmann, after portrait by Rembrandt Peale. 1¼c, Robert Gallatin. 2c, Patricia Amarantides; photograph by Blackstone-Shelburne. 3c, Bill Hyde. 4c, Bill Hyde; photograph by Mathew Brady. 5c, Bill Hyde, after portrait by Rembrandt Peale. 5c, No. 1283B, Redrawn by Stevan Dohanos. 6c, 30c, Richard L. Clark. 8c, Frank Sebastiano; photograph by Philippe Halsman. 10c, Lester Beall. 12c, Norman Todhunter. 13c, Stevan Dohanos; photograph by Jacques Lowe. 15c, Richard F. Hurd. 20c, Robert Geissmann. 25c, Walter DuBois Richards. 40c, Robert Geissmann, after portrait by John Wesley Jarvis. 50c, Mark English. $1, Norman Todhunter. $5, Tom Laufer.

ROTARY PRESS PRINTING
E.E. Plates of 400 subjects in four panes of 100 each.

1965-78   Unwmk.   Perf. 11x10½, 10½x11

Types of 15c:
I. Necktie barely touches coat at bottom; crosshatching of tie strong and complete. Flag of "5" is true horizontal. Crosshatching of "15" is colorless when visible.
II. Necktie does not touch coat at bottom; LL to UR crosshatching lines strong, UL to LR lines very faint. Flag of "5" slants down slightly at right. Crosshatching of "15" is colored and visible when magnified.
A third type, used only for No. 1288B, is smaller in overall size and "15¢" is ¾mm. closer to head.

1278	A710	1c **green,** tagged, *Jan. 12, 1968*		5	5
		Margin block of 4, P#		25	—
		Margin block of 4, "Use Zip Codes"		20	—
		Margin block of 6, "Mail Early in the Day"		32	—
a.		Booklet pane of 8, *Jan. 12, 1968*		1.00	25
b.		Bklt. pane of 4+2 labels, *May 10, 1971*		75	20
c.		Untagged (Bureau precanceled)			7
1279	A711	1¼c **light green,** tagged, *Jan. 30, 1967*		10	5
		Margin block of 4, P#		25.00	—
1280	A712	2c **dark blue gray,** tagged, *June 8, 1966*		5	5
		Margin block of 4, P#		30	—
		Margin block of 4, "Use Zip Codes"		20	—
		Margin block of 6, "Mail Early in the Day"		32	—
a.		Bklt. pane of 5+ label, *Jan. 8, 1968*		1.20	40
b.		Untagged (Bureau precanceled)			10
c.		Bklt. pane of 6, *May 7, 1971*		1.00	35
		Pair with full vert. gutter btwn.		—	
1281	A713	3c **violet,** tagged, *Sept. 16, 1967*		6	5
		Margin block of 4, P#		30	—
		Margin block of 4, "Use Zip Codes"		1.20	—

		Margin block of 6, "Mail Early in the Day"	1.40	—
a.		Untagged (Bureau precanceled)		12
1282	A714	4c **black,** *Nov. 19, 1965*	8	5
		Margin block of 4, P#	40	—
a.		Tagged, *Dec. 1, 1965*	8	5
a.		Margin block of 4, P#	50	—
		Pair with full horiz. gutter between	—	
1283	A715	5c **blue,** *Feb. 22, 1966*	10	5
		Margin block of 4, P#	50	—
		Pair with full vert. gutter btwn.	—	
a.		Tagged, *Feb. 23, 1966*	10	5
a.		Margin block of 4, P#	60	—
1283B	A715a	5c **blue,** tagged, *Nov. 17, 1967*	12	5
		Margin block of 4, P#	70	—
		Dull finish gum	20	—
d.		Untagged (Bureau precanceled)		15

No. 1283B is redrawn; highlights, shadows softened.

1284	A716	6c **gray brown,** *Jan. 29, 1966*	18	5
		Margin block of 4, P#	90	—
		Margin block of 4, "Use Zip Codes" (Bureau precanceled)	3.50	
		Margin block of 6, "Mail Early in the Day" (Bureau precanceled)	4.25	
		Pair with full horiz. gutter btwn.	150.00	
		Pair with full vert. gutter btwn.	150.00	
a.		Tagged, *Dec. 29, 1966*	12	5
a.		Margin block of 4, P#	80	—
a.		Margin block of 4, "Use Zip Codes"	55	—
a.		Margin block of 6, "Mail Early in the Day"	80	—
b.		Booklet pane of 8, *Dec. 28, 1967*	1.50	50
c.		Bklt. pane of 5+ label, *Jan. 9, 1968*	1.25	50

For untagged stamps, "Use Zip Codes" and "Mail Early in the Day" marginal markings are found only on panes with Bureau precancels.

1285	A717	8c **violet,** *March 14, 1966*	30	5
		Margin block of 4, P#	1.50	—
a.		Tagged, *July 6, 1966*	16	5
a.		Margin block of 4, P#	90	—
a.		Margin block of 4, "Use Zip Codes"	75	—
a.		Margin block of 6, "Mail Early in the Day"	1.10	—
1286	A718	10c **lilac,** tagged, *March 15, 1967*	25	5
		Margin block of 4, P#	2.00	—
		Margin block of 4, "Use Zip Codes"	1.75	—
		Margin block of 6, "Mail Early in the Day"	2.25	—
b.		Untagged (Bureau precanceled)		20
1286A	718a	12c **black,** tagged, *July 30, 1968*	35	5
		Margin block of 4, P#	1.75	—
		Margin block of 4, "Use Zip Code"	1.50	—
		Margin block of 6, "Mail Early in the Day"	1.90	—
c.		Untagged (Bureau precanceled)		25
1287	A719	13c **brown,** tagged, *May 29, 1967*	30	5
		Margin block of 4, P#	1.65	—
a.		Untagged (Bureau precanceled)		25
1288	A720	15c **maroon,** type I, tagged, *Mar. 8, 1968*	30	6
		Margin block of 4, P#	1.50	—
		Margin block of 4, "Use Zip Codes"	1.45	—
		Margin block of 6, "Mail Early in the Day"	2.00	—
a.		Untagged (Bureau precanceled)		30
d.		Type II	30	6
1288B	A720	15c **dark rose claret,** tagged, perf. 10 (from blkt. pane)	30	5
c.		Booklet pane of 8, *June 14, 1978*	2.40	1.25

No. 1288B issued in booklets only. All stamps have one or two straight edges. Plates made from redrawn die.

1289	A721	20c **deep olive,** *Oct. 24, 1967*	60	6
		Margin block of 4, P#	3.00	—
		Margin block of 4, "Use Zip Codes"	2.50	—
		Margin block of 6, "Mail Early in the Day"	3.75	—
a.		Tagged, *Apr. 3, 1973*	40	6
a.		Margin block of 4, P#	2.00	—
a.		Dull finish gum	50	—
1290	A722	25c **rose lake,** *Feb. 14, 1967*	70	5
		Margin block of 4, P#	3.50	—
		Margin block of 4, "Use Zip Codes"	3.00	—
		Margin block of 6, "Mail Early in the Day"	4.25	—
a.		Tagged, *Apr. 3, 1973*	50	5
a.		Margin block of 4, P#	2.50	—
a.		Dull finish gum	60	—
1291	A723	30c **red lilac,** *Oct. 21, 1968*	85	8
		Margin block of 4, P#	3.75	—
		Margin block of 4, "Use Zip Codes"	3.50	—
		Margin block of 6, "Mail Early in the Day"	5.50	—
a.		Tagged, *Apr. 3, 1973*	60	6
a.		Margin block of 4, P#	3.00	—
1292	A724	40c **blue black,** *Jan. 29, 1968*	1.10	10
		Margin block of 4, P#	5.50	—
		Margin block of 4, "Use Zip Codes"	4.75	—

		Margin block of 6, "Mail Early in the Day"	7.00	—
a.		Tagged, *Apr. 3, 1973*	80	8
a.		Margin block of 4, P#	4.00	—
a.		Dull finish gum	1.00	—
1293	A725	50c **rose magenta,** *Aug. 13, 1968*	1.00	5
		Margin block of 4, P#	5.00	—
		Margin block of 4, "Use Zip Codes"	4.25	—
		Margin block of 6, "Mail Early in the Day"	6.50	—
		Pair with full vert. gutter btwn.	—	
a.		Tagged, *Apr. 3, 1973*	1.00	5
a.		Margin block of 4, P#	5.00	—
1294	A726	$1 **dull purple,** *Oct. 16, 1967*	2.40	8
		Margin block of 4, P#	12.00	—
		Margin block of 4, "Use Zip Codes"	11.00	—
		Margin block of 6, "Mail Early in the Day"	15.00	—
a.		Tagged, *Apr. 3, 1973*	2.00	8
a.		Margin block of 4, P#	10.00	—
1295	A727	$5 **gray black,** *Dec. 3, 1966*	12.50	2.00
		Margin block of 4, P#	62.50	—
a.		Tagged, *Apr. 3, 1973*	10.00	2.00
a.		Margin block of 4, P#	50.00	—

See Luminescence note in "Information for Collectors" at front of book.

COIL STAMPS

1967-75   Tagged   Perf. 10 Horizontally

1297	A713	3c **violet,** *Nov. 4, 1975*	12	5
		Pair	24	10
		Joint line pair	60	8
		Dull finish gum	1.00	—
a.		Imperf., pair	30.00	
a.		Imperf., joint line pair	50.00	—
b.		Untagged (Bureau precanceled)		12
c.		As "b," imperf. pair	10.00	
1298	A716	6c **gray brown,** *Dec. 28, 1967*	25	5
		Pair	60	12
		Joint line pair	2.00	25
a.		Imperf., pair	2,250.	

Franklin D. Roosevelt — A727a

Revised Design by Robert J. Jones and Howard C. Mildner.

COIL STAMPS

1966-78   Tagged   Perf. 10 Vertically

1299	A710	1c **green,** *Jan. 12, 1968*	6	5
		Pair	12	10
		Joint line pair	35	18
a.		Untagged (Bureau precanceled)		7
b.		Imperf., pair	40.00	
b.		Imperf., joint line pair	65.00	
1303	A714	4c **black,** *May 28, 1966*	15	5
		Pair	30	10
		Joint line pair	2.25	20
a.		Untagged (Bureau precanceled)		15
b.		Imperf., pair	500.00	
b.		Imperf., joint line pair	750.00	
1304	A715	5c **blue,** *Sept. 8, 1966*	15	5
		Pair	30	10
		Joint line pair	90	20
a.		Untagged (Bureau precanceled)		15
b.		Imperf., pair	250.00	
b.		Imperf., joint line pair	375.00	
e.		As "a" imperf. pair		300.00
1304C	A715a	5c **blue,** *1981*	15	5
		Pair	35	10
		Joint line pair	75	—
d.		Imperf., pair		
1305	A727a	6c **gray brown,** *Feb. 28, 1968*	20	5
		Pair	40	10
		Joint line pair	1.25	8
a.		Imperf., pair	75.00	
a.		Imperf., joint line pair	120.00	
b.		Untagged (Bureau precanceled)		20
1305E	A720	15c **rose claret,** type I, *June 14, 1978*	30	5
		Pair	60	10
		Joint line pair	1.65	30
		Dull finish gum	60	—
f.		Untagged (Bureau precanceled)		30
g.		Imperf., pair	30.00	
h.		Pair, imperf. between	200.00	
i.		Type II	30	5
i.		Type II, dull finish gum	35	
1305C	A726	$1 **dull purple,** *Jan. 12, 1973*	2.00	20
		Pair	4.00	40
		Joint line pair	6.00	70
		Dull finish gum	2.00	
d.		Imperf., pair	2,000.	

MIGRATORY BIRD TREATY ISSUE

Migratory Birds over Canada-U.S. Border — A728

Designed by Burt E. Pringle.

GIORI PRESS PRINTING
Plates of 200 subjects in four panes of 50 each.

1966	Unwmk.		Perf. 11	
1306 A728	5c black, crimson & dark blue, *March 16*		12	5
	Margin block of 4, two P#		75	—
	Margin block of 4, Mr. Zip and "Use Zip Code"		60	—

HUMANE TREATMENT OF ANIMALS ISSUE

Issued to promote humane treatment of all animals and to commemorate the centenary of the American Society for the Prevention of Cruelty to Animals.

Mongrel — A729

Designed by Norman Todhunter.

LITHOGRAPHED, ENGRAVED (Giori)
Plates of 200 subjects in four panes of 50 each.

1966	Unwmk.		Perf. 11	
1307 A729	5c orange brown & black, *Apr. 9*		12	5
	Margin block of 4, P#		65	—
	Margin block of 4, Mr. Zip and "Use Zip Code"		60	—

INDIANA STATEHOOD ISSUE

Issued to commemorate the sesquicentennial of Indiana statehood.

Sesquicentennial Seal; Map of Indiana with 19 Stars and old Capitol at Corydon — A730

Clown — A731

Designed by Paul A. Wehr.

GIORI PRESS PRINTING
Plates of 200 subjects in four panes of 50 each.

1966	Unwmk.		Perf. 11	
1308 A730	5c ocher, brown & violet blue, *Apr. 16*		12	5
	Margin block of 4, two P#		60	—
	Margin block of 4, Mr. Zip and "Use Zip Code"		55	—

AMERICAN CIRCUS ISSUE

Issued to honor the American Circus on the centenary of the birth of John Ringling.

Designed by Edward Klauck.

GIORI PRESS PRINTING
Plates of 200 subjects in four panes of 50 each.

1966	Unwmk.		Perf. 11	
1309 A731	5c multicolored, *May 2*		12	5

| | Margin block of 4, two P# | | 75 | — |
| | Margin block of 4, Mr. Zip and "Use Zip Code" | | 60 | — |

SIXTH INTERNATIONAL PHILATELIC EXHIBITION ISSUES

Issued to commemorate the Sixth International Philatelic Exhibition (SIPEX), Washington, D.C., May 21-30.

Stamped Cover — A732

Designed by Thomas F. Naegele.

LITHOGRAPHED, ENGRAVED (Giori)
Plates of 200 subjects in four panes of 50 each.

1966			Perf. 11	
1310 A732	5c multicolored, *May 21*		12	5
	Margin block of 4, P#		75	—
	Margin block of 4, Mr. Zip and "Use Zip Code"		60	—

SOUVENIR SHEET
Designed by Brook Temple.

LITHOGRAPHED, ENGRAVED (Giori)
Plates of 24 subjects

1966			Imperf.	
1311 A732	5c multicolored, *May 23*		25	15

No. 1311 measures 108x74mm. Below the stamp appears a line drawing of the Capitol and Washington Monument. Marginal inscriptions and drawing are green.

BILL OF RIGHTS ISSUE

Issued to commemorate the 175th anniversary of the Bill of Rights.

"Freedom" Checking "Tyranny" — A734

Designed by Herbert L. Block (Herblock).

GIORI PRESS PRINTING
Plates of 200 subjects in four panes of 50 each.

1966	Unwmk.		Perf. 11	
1312 A734	5c carmine, dark & light blue, *July 1*		12	5
	Margin block of 4, two P#		75	—
	Margin block of 4, Mr. Zip and "Use Zip Code"		60	—

POLISH MILLENNIUM ISSUE

Issued to commemorate the thousandth anniversary of the adoption of Christianity in Poland.

Polish Eagle and Cross — A735

Designed by Edmund D. Lewandowski.

ROTARY PRESS PRINTING
E.E. Plates of 200 subjects in four panes of 50 each.

1966	Unwmk.		Perf. 10½x11	
1313 A735	5c red, *July 30*		12	5
	Margin block of 4, P#		75	—
	Margin block of 4, Mr. Zip and "Use Zip Code"		60	—

NATIONAL PARK SERVICE ISSUE

Issued to commemorate the 50th anniversary of the National Park Service of the Interior Department. The design "Parkscape U.S.A." identifies National Park Service facilities.

National Park Service Emblem — A736

Designed by Thomas H. Geismar.

LITHOGRAPHED, ENGRAVED (Giori)
Plates of 200 subjects in four panes of 50 each.

1966			Perf. 11	
1314 A736	5c yellow, black & green, *Aug. 25*		12	5
	Margin block of 4, P#		75	—
	Margin block of 4, Mr. Zip and "Use Zip Code"		60	—
a.	Tagged, *Aug. 26.*		30	15
a.	Margin block of 4, P#		3.00	—

MARINE CORPS RESERVE ISSUE

Issued to commemorate the 50th anniversary of the founding of the U.S. Marine Corps Reserve.

Combat Marine, 1966; Frogman; World War II Flier; World War I "Devil Dog" and Marine, 1775 — A737

Designed by Stella Grafakos.

LITHOGRAPHED, ENGRAVED (Giori)
Plates of 200 subjects in four panes of 50 each.

1966			Perf. 11	
1315 A737	5c black, bister, red & ultra., *Aug. 29*		12	5
	Margin block of 4, P#		75	—
	Margin block of 4, Mr. Zip and "Use Zip Code"		60	—
a.	Tagged, *Aug. 29*		30	15
a.	Margin block of 4, P#		3.00	—
b.	Black & bister (engraved) missing		—	

GENERAL FEDERATION OF WOMEN'S CLUBS ISSUE

Issued to honor 75 years of service by the General Federation of Women's Clubs.

Women of 1890 and 1966 — A738

Designed by Charles Henry Carter.

GIORI PRESS PRINTING
Plates of 200 subjects in four panes of 50 each.

1966			Perf. 11	
1316 A738	5c black, pink & blue, *Sept. 12*		12	5
	Margin block of 4, 2 P#		75	—
	Margin block of 4, Mr. Zip and "Use Zip Code"		60	—
a.	Tagged, *Sept. 13*		30	15
a.	Margin block of 4, 2 P#		3.00	—

AMERICAN FOLKLORE ISSUE
Johnny Appleseed

Issued to honor Johnny Appleseed (John Chapman 1774-1845), who wandered over 100,000 square miles planting apple trees, and who gave away and sold seedlings to Midwest pioneers.

Johnny Appleseed — A739

Designed by Robert Bode.

GIORI PRESS PRINTING
Plates of 200 subjects in four panes of 50 each.

1966		Perf. 11	
1317 A739 5c green, red & black, *Sept. 24*		12	5
Margin block of 4, 2 P#		75	—
Margin block of 4, Mr. Zip and "Use Zip Code"		60	—
a.	Tagged, *Sept. 26*	30	15
a.	Margin block of 4, 2 P#	3.00	—

BEAUTIFICATION OF AMERICA ISSUE

Issued to publicize President Johnson's "Plant for a more beautiful America" campaign.

Jefferson Memorial, Tidal Basin and Cherry Blossoms — A740

Designed by Miss Gyo Fujikawa

GIORI PRESS PRINTING
Plates of 200 subjects in four panes of 50 each.

1966		Unwmk.	Perf. 11	
1318 A740 5c emerald, pink & black, *Oct. 5*			12	5
Margin block of 4, two P#			80	—
Margin block of 4, Mr. Zip and "Use Zip Code"			75	—
a.	Tagged, *Oct. 5*		30	15
a.	Margin block of 4, 2 P#		2.00	—

GREAT RIVER ROAD ISSUE

Issued to publicize the 5,600-mile Great River Road connecting New Orleans with Kenora, Ontario, and following the Mississippi most of the way.

Map of Central United States with Great River Road — A741

Designed by Herbert Bayer.

LITHOGRAPHED, ENGRAVED (Giori)
Plates of 200 subjects in four panes of 50 each.

1966			
1319 A741 5c vermilion, yellow, blue & green, *Oct. 21*		12	5
Margin block of 4, P#		75	—
Margin block of 4, Mr. Zip and "Use Zip Code"		60	—
a.	Tagged, *Oct. 22*	30	15
a.	Margin block of 4, P#	3.00	—

SAVINGS BOND-SERVICEMEN ISSUE

Issued to commemorate the 25th anniversary of U.S. Savings Bonds, and to honor American servicemen.

Statue of Liberty and "Old Glory" — A742

Designed by Steven Dohanos, photo by Bob Noble.

LITHOGRAPHED, ENGRAVED (Giori)
Plates of 200 subjects in four panes of 50 each.

1966		Unwmk.	Perf. 11	
1320 A742 5c red, dark blue, light blue & black, *Oct. 26*			12	5
Margin block of 4, P#			75	—
Margin block of 4, Mr. Zip and "Use Zip Code"			60	—
a.	Tagged, *Oct. 27*		30	15
a.	Margin block of 4, P#		3.00	—
b.	Red, dark blue & black omitted		3,500.	

CHRISTMAS ISSUE

Madonna and Child, by Hans Memling — A743

Modeled by Howard C. Mildner after "Madonna and Child with Angels," by the Flemish artist Hans Memling (c.1430-1494), Mellon Collection, National Gallery of Art, Washington, D.C.

LITHOGRAPHED, ENGRAVED (Giori)
Plates of 400 subjects in four panes of 100 each.

1966		Unwmk.	Perf. 11	
1321 A743 5c multicolored, *Nov. 1*			12	5
Margin block of 4, P#			75	—
Margin block of 4, Mr. Zip and "Use Zip Code"			60	—
a.	Tagged, *Nov. 2*		25	10
a.	Margin block of 4, P#		2.50	—

MARY CASSATT ISSUE

Issued to honor Mary Cassatt (1844-1926), painter. The original painting "The Boating Party" is in the National Gallery of Art, Washington, D.C.

"The Boating Party" — A744

Designed by Robert J. Jones.

GIORI PRESS PRINTING
Plates of 200 subjects in four panes of 50 each.

1966		Unwmk.	Perf. 11	
1322 A744 5c multicolored, *Nov. 17*			20	5
Margin block of 4, 2 P#			1.25	—
Margin block of 4, Mr. Zip and "Use Zip Code"			90	—
a.	Tagged, *Nov. 17*		45	15
a.	Margin block of 4, 2 P#		2.50	—

NATIONAL GRANGE ISSUE

Issued to commemorate the centenary of the founding of the National Grange, American farmers' organization.

Grange Poster, 1870 — A745

Designed by Lee Pavao.

GIORI PRESS PRINTING
Plates of 200 subjects in four panes of 50 each.

1967		Unwmk.	Tagged	Perf. 11	
1323 A745 5c orange, yellow, brown, green & black, *April 17*				12	5
Margin block of 4, 2 P#				80	—
Margin block of 4, Mr. Zip and "Use Zip Code"				60	—

CANADA CENTENARY ISSUE

Issued to commemorate the centenary of Canada's emergence as a nation.

Canadian Landscape — A746

Designed by Ivan Chermayeff.

GIORI PRESS PRINTING
Plates of 200 subjects in four panes of 50 each.

1967		Unwmk.	Tagged	Perf. 11	
1324 A746 5c lt. blue, dp. green, ultra., olive & black, *May 25*				12	5
Margin block of 4, 2 P#				75	—
Margin block of 4, Mr. Zip and "Use Zip Code"				60	—

ERIE CANAL ISSUE

Issued to commemorate the 150th anniversary of the Erie Canal ground-breaking ceremony at Rome, N.Y. The canal links Lake Erie and New York City.

Stern of Early Canal Boat — A747

Designed by George Samerjan.

LITHOGRAPHED, ENGRAVED (Giori)
Plates of 200 subjects in four panes of 50 each.

1967		Tagged	Perf. 11	
1325 A747 5c ultra., greenish blue, black & crimson, *July 4*			12	5
Margin block of 4, P#			75	—
Margin block of 4, Mr. Zip and "Use Zip Code"			60	—

"SEARCH FOR PEACE" - LIONS ISSUE

Issued to publicize the search for peace. "Search for Peace" was the theme of an essay contest for young men and women sponsored by Lions International on its 50th anniversary.

Peace Dove — A748

Designed by Bradbury Thompson.

GIORI PRESS PRINTING
Plates of 200 subjects in four panes of 50 each.

1967	Tagged	Perf. 11		
1326	A748 5c **blue, red & black**, *July 5*		12	5
	Margin block of 4, P#		75	—
	Margin block of 4, Mr. Zip and "Use Zip Code"		60	—

HENRY DAVID THOREAU ISSUE

Issued to commemorate the 150th anniversary of the birth of Henry David Thoreau (1817-1862), writer.

Henry David Thoreau — A749

Designed by Leonard Baskin.

GIORI PRESS PRINTING
Plates of 200 subjects in four panes of 50 each.

1967	Tagged	Perf. 11		
1327	A749 5c **carmine, black & blue green**, *July 12*		12	5
	Margin block of 4, P#		75	—
	Margin block of 4, Mr. Zip and "Use Zip Code"		60	—

NEBRASKA STATEHOOD ISSUE

Issued to commemorate the centenary of the admission of Nebraska to Statehood.

Hereford Steer and Ear of Corn — A750

Designed by Julian K. Billings.

LITHOGRAPHED, ENGRAVED (Giori)
Plates of 200 subjects in four panes of 50 each.

1967	Tagged	Perf. 11		
1328	A750 5c **dark red brown, lemon & yellow**, *July 29*		12	5
	Margin block of 4, P#		75	—
	Margin block of 4, Mr. Zip and "Use Zip Code"		60	—

VOICE OF AMERICA ISSUE

Issued to commemorate the 25th anniversary of the radio branch of the United States Information Agency (USIA).

Radio Transmission Tower and Waves — A751

Designed by Georg Olden.

LITHOGRAPHED, ENGRAVED (Giori)
Plates of 200 subjects in four panes of 50 each.

1967	Tagged	Perf. 11		
1329	A751 5c **red, blue, black & carmine**, *Aug. 1*		12	5

	Margin block of 4, P#		75	—
	Margin block of 4, Mr. Zip and "Use Zip Code"		60	—

AMERICAN FOLKLORE ISSUE

Issued to honor Davy Crockett (1786-1836), frontiersman, hunter, and congressman from Tennessee who died at the Alamo.

Davy Crockett and Scrub Pine — A752

Designed by Robert Bode.

LITHOGRAPHED, ENGRAVED (Giori)
Plates of 200 subjects in four panes of 50 each.

1967	Tagged	Perf. 11		
1330	A752 5c **green, black, & yellow**, *Aug. 17*		12	5
	Margin block of 4, P#		80	—
	Margin block of 4, Mr. Zip and "Use Zip Code"		60	—
a.	Vertical pair, imperf. between		—	

ACCOMPLISHMENTS IN SPACE ISSUE

Issued to commemorate United States' accomplishments in space. Nos. 1331-1332 are printed se-tenant in horizontal rows of 5 in panes of 50. In the upper and lower left panes the astronaut stamp is first, third and fifth, the spaceship second and fourth. This arrangement is reversed in the upper and lower right panes.

Space-Walking Astronaut — A753

Gemini 4 Capsule — A754

Designed by Paul Calle.

LITHOGRAPHED, ENGRAVED (Giori)
Plates of 200 subjects in four panes of 50 each.

1967	Tagged	Perf. 11		
1331	A753 5c **multicolored**, *Sept. 29*		70	25
a.	Pair, #1331-1332		1.50	1.25
	Block of four, 2 #1331 + 2 #1332		3.00	3.00
	Margin block of 4, P# adjoining #1331		7.00	—
	Margin block of 4, Mr. Zip and "Use Zip Code" adjoining #1331		4.25	—
1332	A754 5c **multicolored**, *Sept. 29*		70	25
	Margin block of 4, P# adjoining #1332		7.00	—
	Margin block of 4, Mr. Zip and "Use Zip Code" adjoining #1332		4.25	—
	Red stripes of flag on capsule omitted (29322, 29325 UL 19)		250.00	

URBAN PLANNING ISSUE

Issued to publicize the importance of Urban Planning in connection with the International Conference of the American Institute of Planners, Washington, D.C., Oct. 1-6.

View of Model City — A755

Designed by Francis Ferguson.

LITHOGRAPHED, ENGRAVED (Giori)
Plates of 200 subjects in four panes of 50 each.

1967	Tagged	Perf. 11		
1333	A755 5c **dark blue, light blue & black**, *Oct. 2*		15	5
	Margin block of 4, P#		80	—
	Margin block of 4, Mr. Zip and "Use Zip Code"		70	—

FINNISH INDEPENDENCE ISSUE

Issued to commemorate the 50th anniversary of Finland's independence.

Finnish Coat of Arms — A756

Designed by Bradbury Thompson.

ENGRAVED (Giori)
Plates of 200 subjects in four panes of 50 each.

1967	Tagged	Perf. 11		
1334	A756 5c **blue**, *Oct. 6*		15	5
	Margin block of 4, P#		80	—
	Margin block of 4, Mr. Zip and "Use Zip Code"		70	—

THOMAS EAKINS ISSUE

Issued to honor Thomas Eakins (1844-1916), painter and sculptor. The original painting is in the National Gallery of Art, Washington, D.C.

"The Biglin Brothers Racing" (Sculling on Schuylkill River, Philadelphia) A757

Printed by Photogravure & Color Co., Moonachie, N.J.

PHOTOGRAVURE
Plates of 200 subjects in four panes of 50 each.

1967	Tagged	Perf. 12		
1335	A757 5c **gold & multicolored**, *Nov. 2*		18	5
	Margin block of 4, 6 P#		90	—

Plate number blocks from upper left or lower left panes show clipped corner of margin.

CHRISTMAS ISSUE

Madonna and Child, by Hans Memling — A758

LITHOGRAPHED, ENGRAVED (Giori)
Plates of 200 subjects in four panes of 50 each.

1967	Tagged		Perf. 11
1336	A758 5c multicolored, Nov. 6	12	5
	Margin block of 4, P#	60	—
	Margin block of 4, Mr. Zip and "Use Zip Code"	50	—

See note on painting above No. 1321.

MISSISSIPPI STATEHOOD ISSUE

Issued to commemorate the 150th anniversary of Mississippi statehood.

Magnolia — A759

Designed by Andrew Bucci.

GIORI PRESS PRINTING
Plates of 200 subjects in four panes of 50 each.

1967	Unwmk.		Perf. 11
	Tagged		
1337	A759 5c brt. greenish blue, green & red brown, Dec. 11	15	5
	Margin block of 4, 2 P#	75	—
	Margin block of 4, Mr. Zip and "Use Zip Code"	65	—

FLAG ISSUE

Flag and White House — A760

Designed by Stevan Dohanos.

GIORI PRESS PRINTING
Plates of 400 subjects in four panes of 100 each.

1968	Tagged		Perf. 11
	Size: 19x22mm.		
1338	A760 6c dark blue, red & green, Jan. 24	12	5
	Margin block of 4, P#	60	—
	Margin block of 4, "Use Zip Code"	50	—
	Margin block of 6, "Mail Early in the Day"	75	—
c.	Vert. pair, imperf. horiz.	175.00	
k.	Vert. pair, imperf. btwn.	400.00	

MULTICOLOR HUCK PRESS
Panes of 100 (10x10) each.

1970-71	Tagged		Perf. 11x10½
	Size: 18¼x21mm.		
1338D	A760 6c dark blue, red & green, Aug. 7, 1970	20	5
	Margin block of 20+	4.25	—
e.	Horiz. pair, imperf. between	150.00	
1338F	A760 8c dk. blue, red & slate green, May 10, 1971	20	5
	Margin block of 20	4.25	—
i.	Imperf., vert. pair	70.00	
j.	Horiz. pair, imperf. between	70.00	

+ Margin blocks of 20 come in four versions: (1) 2 P#, 3 ME, 3 zip; (2) 3 P#, 2 ME, 2 zip; (3) 2 P#, 3 ME, 2 zip; (4) 3 P#, 2 ME, 3 zip.

COIL STAMPS
MULTICOLOR HUCK PRESS

1969-71	Tagged		Perf. 10 Vertically
	Size: 18¼x21mm.		
1338A	A760 6c dk. blue, red & green, May 30, 1969	20	5
	Pair	40	10
b.	Imperf., pair	650.00	
1338G	A760 8c dk. blue, red & slate green, May 10, 1971	20	5
	Pair	40	10
h.	Imperf., pair	50.00	

ILLINOIS STATEHOOD ISSUE

Issued to commemorate the 150th anniversary of Illinois statehood.

Farm Buildings and Fields of Ripening Grain — A761

Designed by George Barford.

LITHOGRAPHED, ENGRAVED (Giori)
Plates of 200 subjects in four panes of 50 each.

1968	Tagged		Perf. 11
1339	A761 6c dk. blue, blue, red & ocher, Feb. 12	18	5
	Margin block of 4, P#	90	—
	Margin block of 4, Mr. Zip and "Use Zip Code"	80	—

HEMISFAIR '68 ISSUE

Issued to publicize the HemisFair '68 exhibition at San Antonio, Texas, Apr. 6-Oct. 6, commemorating the 250th anniversary of San Antonio.

Map of North and South America and Lines Converging on San Antonio — A762

Designed by Louis Macouillard.

LITHOGRAPHED, ENGRAVED (Giori)
Plates of 200 subjects in four panes of 50 each.

1968	Tagged		Perf. 11
1340	A762 6c blue, rose red & white, Mar. 30	18	5
	Margin block of 4, P#	90	—
	Margin block of 4, Mr. Zip and "Use Zip Code"	80	—
	Margin block of 6, "Mail Early in the Day"	1.10	—
a.	White omitted	1,500.	

AIRLIFT ISSUE

Issued to pay for airlift of parcels from and to U.S. ports to servicemen overseas and in Alaska, Hawaii and Puerto Rico. Valid for all regular postage. On Apr. 26, 1969, the Post Office Department ruled that henceforth No. 1341 "may be used toward paying the postage or fees for special services on airmail articles."

Eagle Holding Pennant — A763

Designed by Steven Dohanos after a late 19th century wood carrying, part of the Index of American Design, National Gallery of Art.

LITHOGRAPHED, ENGRAVED (Giori)
Plates of 200 subjects in four panes of 50 each.

1968	Unwmk.		Perf. 11
1341	A763 $1 sepia, dk. blue, ocher & brown red, Apr. 4	4.00	3.00
	Margin block of 4, P#	20.00	—
	Margin block of 4, Mr. Zip and "Use Zip Code"	17.00	—
	Margin block of 6, "Mail Early in the Day"	25.00	—
	Pair with full horiz. gutter btwn.		

"SUPPORT OUR YOUTH" - ELKS ISSUE

Issued to publicize the Support Our Youth program, and to honor the Benevolent and Protective Order of Elks, which extended its youth service program in observance of its centennial year.

Girls and Boys — A764

Designed by Edward Vebell.

LITHOGRAPHED, ENGRAVED (Giori)
Plates of 200 subjects in four panes of 50 each.

1968	Tagged		Perf. 11
1342	A764 6c ultramarine & orange red, May 1	18	5
	Margin block of 4, P#	90	—
	Margin block of 4, Mr. Zip and "Use Zip Code"	80	—
	Margin block of 6, "Mail Early in the Day"	1.10	—

LAW AND ORDER ISSUE

Issued to publicize the policeman as protector and friend and to encourage respect for law and order.

Policeman and Boy — A765

Designed by Ward Brackett.

GIORI PRESS PRINTING
Plates of 200 subjects in four panes of 50 each

1968	Tagged		Perf. 11
1343	A765 6c blue & black, May 17	18	5
	Margin block of 4, P#	90	—
	Margin block of 4, Mr. Zip and "Use Zip Code"	80	—
	Margin block of 6, "Mail Early in the Day"	1.10	—

REGISTER AND VOTE ISSUE

Issued to publicize the campaign to draw more voters to the polls. The weather vane is from an old house in the Russian Hill section of San Francisco, Cal.

Eagle Weather Vane — A766

Designed by Norman Todhunter and Bill Hyde; photograph by M. Halberstadt.

LITHOGRAPHED, ENGRAVED (Giori)
Plates of 200 subjects in four panes of 50 each.

1968   Unwmk.   *Perf. 11*
Tagged

1344 A766 6c black, yellow & orange, *June 27*   18   5
Margin block of 4, P#   90 —
Margin block of 4, Mr. Zip and "Use Zip Code"   80 —
Margin block of 6, "Mail Early in the Day"   1.10 —

HISTORIC FLAG SERIES

Issued to show flags carried by American colonists and by citizens of the new United States. Nos. 1345-1354 are printed se-tenant in vertical rows of 10 in panes of 50. The flag sequence on the 2 upper panes is as listed. On the 2 lower panes the sequence is reversed with the Navy Jack in the first row and the Fort Moultrie flag in the 10th.

Ft. Moultrie, 1776 — A767

Ft. McHenry, 1795-1818 A768

Washington's Cruisers, 1775 — A769

Bennington, 1777 — A770

Rhode Island, 1775 — A771

First Stars and Stripes, 1777 — A772

Bunker Hill, 1775 — A773

Grand Union, 1776 — A774

Philadelphia Light Horse, 1775 — A775

First Navy Jack, 1775 — A776

ENGR. (Giori) (#1345-1348, 1350);
ENGR. & LITHO. (#1349, 1351-1354)
Plates of 200 subjects in four panes of 50 each.

1968, July 4   Unwmk.   Tagged   *Perf. 11*
1345 A767 6c dark blue   70   50
1346 A768 6c dark blue & red   70   50
1347 A769 6c dark blue & olive green   35   35
1348 A770 6c dark blue & red   35   35
1349 A771 6c dark blue, yellow & red   35   35
1350 A772 6c dark blue & red   40   35
1351 A773 6c dark blue, olive green & red   40   35
1352 A774 6c dark blue & red   40   35
1353 A775 6c dark blue, yellow & red   55   35
1354 A776 6c dark blue, red & yellow   55   40
a. Strip of ten (#1345-#1354)   5.25   5.25
Margin block of 20, P#, inscriptions (#1345-1354)   12.00 —

WALT DISNEY ISSUE

Issued in memory of Walt Disney (1901-1966), cartoonist, film producer and creator of Mickey Mouse.

Walt Disney and Children of the World — A777

Designed by C. Robert Moore; portrait by Paul E. Wenzel. Printed by Achrovure Division of Union-Camp Corp., Englewood, N.J.

PHOTOGRAVURE
Plates of 400 subjects in eight panes of 50 each.

1968   Tagged   Unwmk.   *Perf. 12*
1355 A777 6c multicolored, *Sept. 11*   20   5
Margin block of 4, 5P#   1.25 —
Margin block of 4, 5P# and 5 dashes   1.25 —
Margin block of 4, Mr. Zip and "Use Zip Code"   1.00 —
Margin block of 6, "Mail Early in the Day"   1.35 —
a. Ocher omitted ("Walt Disney," "6c," etc.)   850.00 —
b. Vert. pair, imperf. horiz.   800.00 —
c. Imperf., pair   900.00 —
d. Black omitted   2,250. —
e. Horiz. pair, imperf. between   3,500. —
f. Blue omitted   1,850. —

FATHER MARQUETTE ISSUE

Issued to honor Father Jacques Marquette (1637-1675), French Jesuit missionary, who together with Louis Jolliet explored the Mississippi River and its tributaries.

Father Marquette and Louis Jolliet Exploring the Mississippi A778

Designed by Stanley W. Galli.

GIORI PRESS PRINTING
Plates of 200 subjects in four panes of 50 each.

1968   Tagged   *Perf. 11*
1356 A778 6c black, apple green & orange brown, *Sept. 20*   18   5
Margin block of 4, P#   90 —
Margin block of 4, Mr. Zip and "Use Zip Code"   85 —
Margin block of 6, "Mail Early in the Day"   1.10 —

AMERICAN FOLKLORE ISSUE

Issued to honor Daniel Boone (1734-1820), frontiersman and trapper.

Pennsylvania Rifle, Powder Horn, Tomahawk Pipe and Knife — A779

Designed by Louis Macouillard.

LITHOGRAPHED, ENGRAVED (Giori)
Plates of 200 subjects in four panes of 50 each.

1968   Tagged   *Perf. 11*
1357 A779 6c yellow, deep yellow, maroon & black, *Sept. 26*   18   5
Margin block of 4, P#   90 —
Margin block of 4, Mr. Zip and "Use Zip Code"   85 —
Margin block of 6, "Mail Early in the Day"   1.10 —

ARKANSAS RIVER NAVIGATION ISSUE

Issued to commemorate the opening of the Arkansas River to commercial navigation.

Ship's Wheel, Power Transmission Tower and Barge — A780

Designed by Dean Ellis.

LITHOGRAPHED, ENGRAVED (Giori)
Plates of 200 subjects in four panes of 50 each.

1968, Oct. 1   Tagged   *Perf. 11*
1358 A780 6c bright blue, dark blue & black   18   5
Margin block of 4, P#   90 —
Margin block of 4, Mr. Zip and "Use Zip Code"   85 —
Margin block of 6, "Mail Early in the Day"   1.10 —

LEIF ERIKSON ISSUE

Issued in memory of Leif Erikson, 11th century Norse explorer, called the first European to set foot on the American continent, at a place he called Vinland. The Leif Erikson statue by the American sculptor A. Stirling Calder is in Reykjavik, Iceland.

See "Information for Collectors" section at beginning of catalogue for information on electric eye markings, luminescene and tagging.

Leif Erikson by A. Stirling
Calder — A781

Designed by Kurt Weiner.

LITHOGRAPHED & ENGRAVED
Plates of 200 subjects in four panes of 50 each.

1968, Oct. 9	Tagged	Perf. 11	
1359 A781	6c light gray brown & black brown	18	5
	Margin block of 4, P#	90	—
	Margin block of 4, Mr. Zip and "Use Zip Code"	85	—
	Margin block of 6, "Mail Early in the Day"	1.10	—

The luminescent element is in the light gray brown ink of the background. The engraved parts were printed on a rotary currency press.

CHEROKEE STRIP ISSUE

Issued to commemorate the 75th anniversary of the opening of the Cherokee Strip to settlers, Sept. 16, 1893.

Racing for Homesteads in Cherokee Strip, 1893 — A782

Designed by Norman Todhunter.

ROTARY PRESS PRINTING
E.E. Plates of 200 subjects in four panes of 50 each.

1968	Tagged	Perf. 11x10½	
1360 A782	6c brown, Oct. 15	18	5
	Margin block of 4, P#	90	—
	Margin block of 4, Mr. Zip and "Use Zip Code"	85	—
	Margin block of 6, "Mail Early in the Day"	1.10	—

JOHN TRUMBULL ISSUE

Issued to honor John Trumbull (1756-1843), painter. The stamp design shows Lt. Thomas Grosvenor and his attendant Peter Salem. The original painting hangs at Yale University, New Haven, Connecticut.

Detail from "The Battle of Bunker's Hill" — A783

Modeled by Robert J. Jones.

LITHOGRAPHED, ENGRAVED (Giori)
Plates of 200 subjects in four panes of 50 each.

1968	Tagged	Unwmk.	Perf. 11	
1361 A783	6c multicolored, Oct. 18		20	5
	Margin block of 4, P#		1.00	—
	Margin block of 4, Mr. Zip and "Use Zip Code"		90	—
	Margin block of 6, "Mail Early in the Day"		1.25	—

WATERFOWL CONSERVATION ISSUE

Issued to publicize waterfowl conservation.

Wood Ducks — A784

Designed by Stanley W. Galli.

LITHOGRAPHED, ENGRAVED (Giori)
Plates of 200 subjects in four panes of 50 each.

1968	Tagged	Perf. 11	
1362 A784	6c black & multicolored, Oct. 24	20	5
	Margin block of 4, P#	1.25	—
	Margin block of 4, Mr. Zip and "Use Zip Code"	1.00	—
	Margin block of 6, "Mail Early in the Day"	1.25	—
a.	Vertical pair, imperf. between	750.00	
b.	Red & dark blue omitted	1,750.	

CHRISTMAS ISSUE

"The Annunciation" by the 15th century Flemish painter Jan van Eyck is in the National Gallery of Art, Washington, D.C.

Angel Gabriel, from "The Annunciation" by Jan van Eyck — A785

Designed by Robert J. Jones.

ENGRAVED (Multicolor Huck)
Panes of 50 (10x5)

1968	Tagged	Perf. 11	
1363 A785	6c multicolored, Nov. 1	18	5
	Margin block of 10, 7P# and 3 "Mail Early"	2.75	—
	Margin block of 10, 8P# and 2 "Mail Early"	2.75	—
a.	Untagged, Nov. 2	20	5
a.	Margin block of 10, 7P# and 3 "Mail Early"	4.50	—
a.	Margin block of 10, 8P# and 2 "Mail Early"	4.50	—
b.	Imperf., pair (tagged)	400.00	
c.	Light yellow omitted	200.00	
d.	Imperf. pair, untagged	500.00	

AMERICAN INDIAN ISSUE

Issued to honor the American Indian and to commemorate the opening of the National Portrait Gallery, Washington, D.C. Chief Joseph (Indian name, Thunder Traveling over the Mountains), a leader of the Nez Perce, was born in eastern Oregon agout 1840 and died at the Colesville Reservation in Washington State in 1904.

Chief Joseph, by Cyrenius Hall — A786

Designed by Robert J. Jones; lettering by Crimilda Pontes.

LITHOGRAPHED, ENGRAVED (Giori)
Plates of 200 subjects in four panes of 50 each.

1968	Tagged	Perf. 11	
1364 A786	6c black & multicolored, Nov. 4	25	5
	Margin block of 4, P#	1.25	—

	Margin block of 4, Mr. Zip and "Use Zip Code"	1.10	—
	Margin block of 6, "Mail Early in the Day"	1.60	—

BEAUTIFICATION OF AMERICA ISSUE

Issued to publicize the Natural Beauty Campaign for more beautiful cities, parks, highways and streets. Nos. 1365-1368 are printed in blocks of four in panes of 50. In the upper and lower left panes Nos. 1365 and 1367 appear in first, third and fifth place, Nos. 1366 and 1368 in second and fourth place. This arrangement is reversed in the upper and lower right panes.

Capitol, Azaleas and Tulips — A787

PLANT for more BEAUTIFUL CITIES

Washington Monument, Potomac River and Daffodils — A788

PLANT for more BEAUTIFUL PARKS

Poppies and Lupines along Highway — A789

PLANT for more BEAUTIFUL HIGHWAYS

Blooming Crabapples Lining Avenue — A790

PLANT for more BEAUTIFUL STREETS

Designed by Walter DuBois Richards.

LITHOGRAPHED, ENGRAVED (Giori)
Plates of 200 subjects in four panes of 50 each.

1969, Jan. 16	Tagged	Perf. 11	
1365 A787	6c multicolored	90	15
	Margin block of 4, P# adjoining #1365	5.00	—
	Margin block of 4, Mr. Zip and "Use Zip Code" adjoining #1365	4.50	—
	Margin block of 6, "Mail Early in the Day" adjoining #1365	6.00	—
1366 A788	6c multicolored	90	15
	Margin block of 4, P# adjoining #1366	5.00	—
	Margin block of 4, Mr. Zip and "Use Zip Code" adjoining #1366	4.50	—
	Margin block of 6, "Mail Early in the Day" adjoining #1366	6.00	—
1367 A789	6c multicolored	90	15
	Margin block of 4, P# adjoining #1367	5.00	—
	Margin block of 4, Mr. Zip and "Use Zip Code" adjoining #1367	4.50	—
	Margin block of 6, "Mail Early in the Day" adjoining #1367	6.00	—
1368 A790	6c multicolored	90	15
	Margin block of 4, P# adjoining #1368	5.00	—
	Margin block of 4, Mr. Zip and "Use Zip Code" adjoining #1368	4.50	—
	Margin block of 6, "Mail Early in the Day" adjoining #1368	6.00	—
a.	Block of 4, #1365-1368	4.25	3.50

AMERICAN LEGION ISSUE

Issued to commemorate the 50th anniversary of the American Legion.

Eagle from Great
Seal — A791

Designed by Robert Hallock.

LITHOGRAPHED, ENGRAVED (Giori)
Plates of 200 subjects in four panes of 50 each.

1969	Tagged	Perf. 11	
1369 A791 6c red, blue & black, *Mar. 15*		18	5
Margin block of 4, P#		90	—
Margin block of 4, Mr. Zip and "Use Zip Code"		85	—
Margin block of 6, "Mail Early in the Day"		1.10	—

AMERICAN FOLKLORE ISSUE

Issued to honor Grandma Moses (Anna Mary Robertson Moses, 1860-1961), primitive painter of American life.

July Fourth, by Grandma
Moses — A792

Designed by Robert J. Jones.

LITHOGRAPHED, ENGRAVED (Giori)
Plates of 200 subjects in four panes of 50 each.

1969	Tagged	Perf. 11	
1370 A792 6c multicolored, *May 1*		20	5
Margin block of 4, P#		1.00	—
Margin block of 4, Mr. Zip and "Use Zip Code"		90	—
Margin block of 6, "Mail Early in the Day"		1.25	—
a. Horizontal pair, imperf. between		400.00	
b. Black ("6c U.S. Postage") & Prus. blue ("Grandma Moses") omitted (engraved)		1,000.	

APOLLO 8 ISSUE

Issued to commemorate the Apollo 8 mission, which first put men into orbit around the moon, Dec. 21-27, 1968. The astronauts were: Col. Frank Borman, Capt. James Lovell and Maj. William Anders.

Moon Surface and
Earth — A793

Designed by Leonard E. Buckley after a photograph by the Apollo 8 astronauts.

GIORI PRESS PRINTING

Plates of 200 subjects in four panes of 50 each.

1969	Tagged	Perf. 11	
1371 A793 6c black, blue & ocher, *May 5*		25	6
Margin block of 4, P#		1.25	—

Margin block of 4, Mr. Zip and "Use Zip Code"		1.10	—
Margin block of 6, "Mail Early in the Day"		1.60	—

W.C. HANDY ISSUE

Issued to honor W.C. Handy (1873-1958), jazz musician and composer.

William
Christopher
Handy — A794

Designed by Bernice Kochan.

LITHOGRAPHED, ENGRAVED (Giori)
Plates of 200 subjects in four panes of 50 each.

1969	Tagged	Perf. 11	
1372 A794 6c violet, dp. lilac & blue, *May 17*		18	5
Margin block of 4, P#		90	—
Margin block of 4, Mr. Zip and "Use Zip Code"		85	—
Margin block of 6, "Mail Early in the Day"		1.10	—

CALIFORNIA SETTLEMENT ISSUE

Issued to commemorate the 200th anniversary of the settlement of California.

Carmel Mission Belfry — A795

Designed by Leonard Buckley and Howard C. Mildner.

LITHOGRAPHED, ENGRAVED (Giori)
Plates of 200 subjects in four panes of 50 each.

1969	Tagged	Perf. 11	
1373 A795 6c orange, red, black & light blue, *July 16*		18	5
Margin block of 4, P#		90	—
Margin block of 4, Mr. Zip and "Use Zip Code"		85	—
Margin block of 6, "Mail Early in the Day"		1.10	—

JOHN WESLEY POWELL ISSUE

Issued to honor John Wesley Powell (1834-1902), geologist who explored the Green and Colorado Rivers 1869-1875, and ethnologist.

Major Powell
Exploring
Colorado River,
1869 — A796

Designed by Rudolph Wendelin.

LITHOGRAPHED, ENGRAVED (Giori)
Plates of 200 subjects in four panes of 50 each.

1969	Tagged	Perf. 11	
1374 A796 6c black, ocher & light blue, *Aug. 1*		18	5
Margin block of 4, P#		90	—
Margin block of 4, Mr. Zip and "Use Zip Code"		85	—
Margin block of 6, "Mail Early in the Day"		1.10	—

ALABAMA STATEHOOD ISSUE

Issued to commemorate the 150th anniversary of Alabama statehood.

Camellia and
Yellow-shafted
Flicker — A797

Designed by Bernice Kochan

LITHOGRAPHED, ENGRAVED (Giori)
Plates of 200 subjects in four panes of 50 each.

1969	Tagged	Perf. 11	
1375 A797 6c magenta, rose red, yellow, dark green & brown, *Aug. 2*		18	5
Margin block of 4, P#		90	—
Margin block of 4, Mr. Zip and "Use Zip Code"		85	—
Margin block of 6, "Mail Early in the Day"		1.10	—

BOTANICAL CONGRESS ISSUE

Issued to publicize the 11th International Botanical Congress, Seattle, Wash., Aug. 24-Sept. 2. Nos. 1376-1379 are printed in blocks of four in panes of 50. In upper and lower left panes Nos. 1376 and 1378 appear in first, third and fifth place; Nos. 1377 and 1379 in second and fourth place. This arrangement is reversed in upper and lower right panes.

Douglas Fir
(Northwest)
A798

Lady's-slipper
(Northeast)
A799

Ocotillo
(Southwest)
A800

Franklinia
(Southeast)
A801

Designed by Stanley Galli.

LITHOGRAPHED, ENGRAVED (Giori)
Plates of 200 subjects in four panes of 50 each.

1969, Aug. 23	Tagged	Perf. 11	
1376 A798 6c multicolored		1.10	15
Margin block of 4, P# adjoining #1376		8.50	—
Margin block of 4, Mr. Zip and "Use Zip Code" adjoining #1376		6.50	—
Margin block of 6, "Mail Early in the Day" adjoining #1376		8.50	—
1377 A799 6c multicolored		1.10	15
Margin block of 4, P# adjoining #1377		8.50	—
Margin block of 4, Mr. Zip and "Use Zip Code" adjoining #1377		6.50	—
Margin block of 6, "Mail Early in the Day" adjoining #1377		8.50	—
1378 A800 6c multicolored		1.10	15
Margin block of 4, P# adjoining #1378		8.50	—
Margin block of 4, Mr. Zip and "Use Zip Code" adjoining #1378		6.50	—
Margin block of 6, "Mail Early in the Day" adjoining #1378		8.50	—
1379 A801 6c multicolored		1.10	15

Margin block of 4, P# adjoining
#1379   8.50 —
Margin block of 4, Mr. Zip and
"Use Zip Code" adjoining #1379 6.50 —
Margin block of 6, "Mail Early in
the Day" adjoining #1379   8.50 —
a.   Block of four, #1376-1379   5.50 5.00

DARTMOUTH COLLEGE CASE ISSUE

Issued to commemorate the 150th anniversary of
the Dartmouth College Case, which Daniel Webster
argued before the Supreme Court, reasserting the
sanctity of contracts.

Daniel Webster and
Dartmouth Hall — A802

Designed by John R. Scotford, Jr.

ROTARY PRESS PRINTING
E.E. Plates of 200 subjects in four panes of 50 each.

1969	Tagged	Perf. 10½x11	
1380 A802 6c **green**, *Sept. 22*		18	5
Margin block of 4, P#		1.00	—
Margin block of 4, Mr. Zip and "Use Zip Code"		85	—
Margin block of 6, "Mail Early in the Day"		1.10	—

PROFESSIONAL BASEBALL ISSUE

Issued to commemorate the centenary of professional baseball.

Batter — A803

Designed by Alex Ross.

LITHOGRAPHED, ENGRAVED (Giori)
Plates of 200 subjects in four panes of 50 each.

1969	Tagged	Perf. 11	
1381 A803 6c **yel., red, blk. & grn.**, *Sept. 24*		35	5
Margin block of 4, P#		1.75	—
Margin block of 4, Mr. Zip and "Use Zip Code"		1.50	—
Margin block of 6, "Mail Early in the Day"		2.25	—
a. Black omitted ("1869-1969, United States, 6c, Professional Baseball")		1,250.	

INTERCOLLEGIATE FOOTBALL ISSUE

Issued to commemorate the centenary of intercol-
legiate football.

Football Player
and
Coach — A804

Designed by Robert Peak.

LITHOGRAPHED, ENGRAVED (Giori)
Plates of 200 subjects in four panes of 50 each.

1969	Tagged	Perf. 11	
1382 A804 6c **red & green**, *Sept. 26*		25	5
Margin block of 4, P#		1.25	—
Margin block of 4, Mr. Zip and "Use Zip Code"		1.10	—
Margin block of 6, "Mail Early in the Day"		1.65	—

The engraved parts were printed on a rotary currency press.

DWIGHT D. EISENHOWER ISSUE

Issued in memory of Gen. Dwight David Eisenhower, 34th President (1890-1969).

Dwight D.
Eisenhower — A805

Designed by Robert J. Jones; photograph by Bernie Noble.

GIORI PRESS PRINTING
Plates of 128 subjects in 4 panes of 32 each.

1969	Tagged	Perf. 11	
1383 A805 6c **blue, black & red**, *Oct. 14*		18	5
Margin block of 4, P#		90	—
Margin block of 4, Mr. Zip and "Use Zip Code"		85	—
Margin block of 6, "Mail Early in the Day"		1.10	—

CHRISTMAS ISSUE

The painting, painted about 1870 by an unknown
primitive artist, is the property of the N.Y. State
Historical Association, Cooperstown, N.Y.

Winter Sunday
in Norway,
Maine — A806

Designed by Stevan Dohanos.

ENGRAVED (Multicolor Huck)
Panes of 50 (5x10)

1969	Tagged	Perf. 11x10½	
1384 A806 6c **dark green & multi.**, *Nov. 3*		18	5
Margin block of 10, 5P#, 2-3 zip, 2-3 Mail Early		2.00	—
Precanceled		60	6
b. Imperf., pair		1,500.	
c. Light green omitted		35.00	
d. Lt. grn., red & yel omitted		1,200.	—
e. Yellow omitted			

The precancel price applies to the experimental precancel
printed in four cities with the names between lines 4½mm.
apart: in black or green, "ATLANTA, GA" and in green only
"BALTIMORE, MD", "MEMPHIS, TN" and "NEW
HAVEN, CT". They were sold freely to the public and could
be used on any class of mail at all post offices during the
experimental program and thereafter.

HOPE FOR CRIPPLED ISSUE

Issued to encourage the rehabilitation of crippled
children and adults and to honor the National Society for Crippled Children and Adults (Easter Seal
Society) on its 50th anniversary.

Cured Child — A807

Designed by Mark English.

LITHOGRAPHED, ENGRAVED (Giori)
Plates of 200 subjects in four panes of 50 each.

1969	Tagged	Perf. 11	
1385 A807 6c **multicolored**, *Nov. 20*		18	5
Margin block of 4, P#		90	—
Margin block of 4, Mr. Zip and "Use Zip Code"		80	—
Margin block of 6, "Mail Early in the Day"		1.10	—

WILLIAM M. HARNETT ISSUE

Issued to honor William M. Harnett (1848-1892),
painter. The painting hangs in the Museum of Fine
Arts, Boston.

"Old Models" — A808

Designed by Robert J. Jones.

LITHOGRAPHED, ENGRAVED (Giori)
Plates of 128 subjects in 4 panes of 32 each.

1969	Tagged	Perf. 11	
1386 A808 6c **multicolored**, *Dec. 3*		18	5
Margin block of 4, P#		1.00	—
Margin block of 4, Mr. Zip and "Use Zip Code"		80	—
Margin block of 6, "Mail Early in the Day"		1.10	—

NATURAL HISTORY ISSUE

Issued in connection with the 1969-1970 celebration of the centenary of the American Museum of
Natural History in New York City. Nos. 1387-1390
are printed in blocks of four in panes of 32. Nos.
1387-1388 alternate in first row, Nos. 1389-1390 in
second row. This arrangement is repeated throughout the pane.

American Bald Eagle — A809

African
Elephant
Herd
A810

Tlingit Chief in Haida Ceremonial Canoe — A811

THE AGE OF REPTILES

Brontosaurus, Stegosaurus and Allosaurus from Jurassic Period — A812

Designers: No. 1387 (eagle), Walter Richards; No. 1388 (elephants), Dean Ellis; No. 1389 (Haida canoe), Paul Rabut; No. 1390 (Age of Reptiles) detail from mural by Rudolph Zallinger in Yale's Peabody Museum, adapted by Robert J. Jones.

LITHOGRAPHED, ENGRAVED (Giori)

Plates of 128 subjects in 4 panes of 32 each (4x8).

1970, May 6	Tagged	Perf. 11		
1387	A809 6c **multicolored**	20	12
	Margin block of 4, P# adjoining #1387	1.25	—
	Margin block of 4, Mr. Zip and "Use Zip Code" adjoining #1387	90	—
	Margin block of 6, "Mail Early in the Day" adjoining #1387	1.25	—
1388	A810 6c **multicolored**	20	12
	Margin block of 4, P# adjoining #1388	1.25	—
	Margin block of 4, Mr. Zip and "Use Zip Code" adjoining #1388	90	—
	Margin block of 6, "Mail Early in the Day" adjoining #1388	1.25	—
1389	A811 6c **multicolored**	20	12
	Margin block of 4, P# adjoining #1389	1.25	—
	Margin block of 4, Mr. Zip and "Use Zip Code" adjoining #1389	90	—
	Margin block of 6, "Mail Early in the Day" adjoining #1389	1.25	—
1390	A812 6c **multicolored**	20	12
	Margin block of 4, P# adjoining #1390	1.25	—
	Margin block of 4, Mr. Zip and "Use Zip Code" adjoining #1390	90	—
	Margin block of 6, "Mail Early in the Day" adjoining #1390	1.25	—
a.	Block of four (#1387-1390)	85	85

MAINE STATEHOOD ISSUE

Issued to commemorate the sesquicentennial of Maine Statehood. The painting by Edward Hopper (1882-1967) hangs in the Metropolitan Museum of Art, New York City.

The Lighthouse at Two Lights, Maine, by Edward Hopper — A813

Designed by Stevan Dohanos.

LITHOGRAPHED, ENGRAVED (Giori)

Plates of 200 subjects in four panes of 50 each.

1970	Tagged	Perf. 11		
1391	A813 6c **black & multicolored**, *July 9*	18	5
	Margin block of 4, P#	1.00	—
	Margin block of 4, Mr. Zip and "Use Zip Code"	80	—
	Margin block of 6, "Mail Early in the Day"	1.10	—

WILDLIFE CONSERVATION ISSUE

Issued to emphasize the importance of wildlife conservation in America.

American Buffalo — A814

Designed by Robert Lougheed.

ROTARY PRESS PRINTING

E.E. Plates of 200 subjects in four panes of 50 each.

1970	Tagged	Perf. 11x10½		
1392	A814 6c **light brown**, *July 20*	18	5
	Margin block of 4, P#	1.00	—
	Margin block of 4, Mr. Zip and "Use Zip Code"	80	—
	Margin block of 6, "Mail Early in the Day"	1.10	—

REGULAR ISSUE
Dwight David Eisenhower

Dot between "R" and "U" — A815

No Dot between "R" and "U" — A815a

Benjamin Franklin — A816

U.S. Postal Service Emblem — A817

Fiorello H. LaGuardia A817a

Ernest Taylor Pyle A818

Dr. Elizabeth Blackwell A818a

Amadeo P. Giannini A818b

Designers: Nos. 1393-1395, 1401-1402, Robert Geissman; photograph by George Tames. 7c, Bill Hyde. No. 1396, Raymond Loewy/William Smith, Inc. 14c, Robert Geissman; photograph by George Fayer. 16c, Robert Geissman; photograph by Alfred Eisenstadt. 18c, Robert Geissman; painting by Joseph Kozlowski. 21c, Robert Geissman.

ROTARY PRESS PRINTING

E.E. Plates of 400 subjects in four panes of 100 each.

1970-74	Tagged	Perf. 11x10½		
1393	A815 6c **dark blue gray**, *Aug. 6, 1970*	12	5
	Margin block of 4, P#	60	—
	Margin block of 4, "Use Zip Codes"	50	—
	Margin block of 6, "Mail Early in the Day"	80	—
	Dull finish gum	12	
a.	Booklet pane of 8	1.25	50
b.	Booklet pane of 5 + label	1.20	35
c.	Untagged (Bureau precanceled)		10
	Perf. 10½x11		
1393D	A816 7c **bright blue**, *Oct. 20, 1972*	14	5
	Margin block of 4, P#	1.00	—
	Margin block of 4, "Use Zip Codes"	60	—
	Margin block of 6, "Mail Early in the Day"	95	—
	Dull finish gum	14	
e.	Untagged (Bureau precanceled)		10

GIORI PRESS PRINTING

Plates of 400 subjects in four panes of 100 each.

	Perf. 11			
1394	A815a 8c **black, red & blue gray**, *May 10, 1971*	16	5
	Margin block of 4, P#	1.00	—
	Margin block of 4, "Use Zip Codes"	70	—
	Margin block of 6, "Mail Early in the Day"	1.00	—
	Pair with full vert. gutter btwn.		—

ROTARY PRESS PRINTING

	Perf. 11x10½			
1395	A815 8c **deep claret**, (from blkt. pane)	16	5
a.	Booklet pane of 8, *May 10, 1971*	2.00	1.25
b.	Booklet pane of 6, *May 10, 1971*	1.00	75
c.	Booklet pane of 4 + 2 labels, *Jan. 28, 1972*	1.00	50
d.	Booklet pane of 7 + label, *Jan. 28, 1972*	1.75	1.00

No. 1395 was issued only in booklets. All stamps have one or two straight edges.

PHOTOGRAVURE (Andreotti)

Plates of 400 subjects in four panes of 100 each.

	Perf. 11x10½			
1396	A817 8c **multicolored**, *July 1, 1971*	25	5
	Margin block of 12, 6P#	3.50	
	Margin block of 20, 6P#, "Mail Early in the Day," "Use Zip Codes" and rectangular color contents (UL pane)	6.00	
	Margin block of 4, "Use Zip Codes"	1.20	—
	Margin block of 4, "Mail Early in the Day"	1.20	—

ROTARY PRESS PRINTING

E.E. Plates of 400 subjects in four panes of 100 each.

1397	A817a 14c **gray brown**, *Apr. 24, 1972*	32	5
	Margin block of 4, P#	1.75	—
	Margin block of 4, "Use Zip Codes"	1.30	—
	Margin block of 6, "Mail Early in the Day"	2.00	—
a.	Untagged (Bureau precanceled)		25
1398	A818 16c **brown**, *May 7, 1971*	35	5
	Margin block of 4, P#	1.75	—
	Margin block of 4, "Use Zip Codes"	1.50	—
	Margin block of 6, "Mail Early in the Day"	2.25	—
a.	Untagged (Bureau precanceled)		25
1399	A818a 18c **violet**, *Jan. 23, 1974*	40	6
	Margin block of 4, P#	2.10	—
	Margin block of 4, "Use Zip Codes"	1.70	—
	Margin block of 6, "Mail Early in the Day"	2.50	—
1400	A818b 21c **green**, *June 27, 1973*	45	6
	Margin block of 4, P#	2.25	—
	Margin block of 4, "Use Zip Codes"	2.00	—
	Margin block of 6, "Mail Early in the Day"	2.85	—

COIL STAMPS
ROTARY PRESS PRINTING

1970-71	Tagged	Perf. 10 Vert.		
1401	A815 6c **dark blue gray**, *Aug. 6, 1970*	20	5
	Pair	40	10
	Joint line pair	1.00	15
	Dull finish gum	25	
a.	Untagged (Bureau precanceled)		10
b.	Imperf., pair	1,000.	
1402	A815 8c **deep claret**, *May 10, 1971*	22	5
	Pair	44	10
	Joint line pair	1.00	20
a.	Imperf., pair	50.00	
a.	Joint line pair	75.00	
b.	Untagged (Bureau precanceled)		20
c.	Pair, imperf. between	—	

EDGAR LEE MASTERS ISSUE

Issued to honor Edgar Lee Masters (1869-1950), poet.

Edgar Lee Masters — A819

Designed by Fred Otnes.

LITHOGRAPHED, ENGRAVED (Giori)
E.E. Plates of 200 subjects in four panes of 50 each.

1970 Tagged *Perf. 11*
1405 A819 6c **black & olive bister,** *Aug. 22* 18 5
    Margin block of 4, P# 90 —
    Margin block of 4, Mr. Zip and "Use Zip Code" 80 —
    Margin block of 6, "Mail Early in the Day" 1.10 —

WOMAN SUFFRAGE ISSUE

Issued to commemorate the 50th anniversary of the 19th Amendment, which gave the vote to women.

Suffragettes, 1920, and Woman Voter, 1970 — A820

Designed by Ward Brackett.

GIORI PRESS PRINTING
Plates of 200 subjects in four panes of 50 each.

1970 Tagged *Perf. 11*
1406 A820 6c **blue,** *Aug. 26* 18 5
    Margin block of 4, P# 90 —
    Margin block of 4, Mr. Zip and "Use Zip Code" 80 —
    Margin block of 6, "Mail Early in the Day" 1.10 —

SOUTH CAROLINA ISSUE

Issued to commemorate the 300th anniversary of the founding of Charles Town (Charleston), the first permanent settlement of South Carolina. Against a background of pine wood the line drawings of the design represent the economic and historic development of South Carolina: the spire of St. Phillip's Church, Capitol, state flag, 17th century man and woman, a Fort Sumter cannon, barrels, cotton, tobacco and yellow jasmine.

Symbols of South Carolina — A821

Designed by George Samerjan.

LITHOGRAPHED, ENGRAVED (Giori)
Plates of 200 subjects in four panes of 50 each.

1970 Tagged *Perf. 11*
1407 A821 6c **bister, black & red,** *Sept. 12* 18 5
    Margin block of 4, P# 90 —
    Margin block of 4, Mr. Zip and "Use Zip Code" 80 —
    Margin block of 6, "Mail Early in the Day" 1.10 —

STONE MOUNTAIN MEMORIAL ISSUE

Issued to commemorate the dedication of the Stone Mountain Confederate Memorial, Georgia, May 9, 1970.

Robert E. Lee, Jefferson Davis and "Stonewall" Jackson — A822

Designed by Robert Hallock.

GIORI PRESS PRINTING
Plates of 200 subjects in four panes of 50 each.

1970 Tagged *Perf. 11*
1408 A822 6c **gray,** *Sept. 19* 18 5
    Margin block of 4, P# 90 —
    Margin block of 4, Mr. Zip and "Use Zip Code" 80 —
    Margin block of 6, "Mail Early in the Day" 1.10 —

FORT SNELLING ISSUE

Issued to commemorate the 150th anniversary of Fort Snelling, Minnesota, which was an important outpost for the opening of the Northwest.

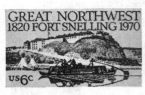

Fort Snelling, Keelboat and Tepees — A823

Designed by David K. Stone.

LITHOGRAPHED, ENGRAVED (Giori)
Plates of 200 in four panes of 50 each.

1970 Tagged *Perf. 11*
1409 A823 6c **yellow & multicolored,** *Oct. 17* 18 5
    Margin block of 4, P# 90 —
    Margin block of 4, Mr. Zip and "Use Zip Code" 80 —
    Margin block of 6, "Mail Early in the Day" 1.10 —

ANTI-POLLUTION ISSUE

Issued to focus attention on the problems of pollution.

Nos. 1410-1413 are printed in blocks of four in panes of 50. In upper and lower left panes Nos. 1410 and 1412 appear in first, third and fifth place; Nos. 1411 and 1413 in second and fourth place. This arrangement is reversed in upper and lower right panes.

Globe and Wheat — A824

Globe and City — A825

Globe and Bluegill — A826

Globe and Seagull — A827

Designed by Arnold Copeland and Walter DuBois Richards. Printed by Bureau of Engraving and Printing at Guilford Gravure, Inc., Guilford, Conn.

PHOTOGRAVURE
Plates of 200 subjects in four panes of 50 each.

1970, Oct. 28 Tagged *Perf. 11x10½*
1410 A824 6c **multicolored** 30 13
    Margin block of 10, 5 P# adjoining #1410, 1412 4.50
    Margin block of 4, Mr. Zip and "Use Zip Code" adjoining #1410 1.50 —
    Margin block of 6, "Mail Early in the Day" adjoining #1410 2.00 —
1411 A825 6c **multicolored** 30 13
    Margin block of 10, 5 P# adjoining #1411, 1413 4.50
    Margin block of 4, Mr. Zip and "Use Zip Code" adjoining #1411 1.50 —
    Margin block of 6, "Mail Early in the Day" adjoining #1411 2.00 —

1412 A826 6c **multicolored** 30 13
    Margin block of 4, Mr. Zip and "Use Zip Code" adjoining #1412 1.50 —
    Margin block of 6, "Mail Early in the Day" adjoining #1412 2.00 —
1413 A827 6c **multicolored** 30 13
    Margin block of 4, Mr. Zip and "Use Zip Code" adjoining #1413 1.50 —
    Margin block of 6, "Mail Early in the Day" adjoining #1413 2.00 —
    a.   Block of four, #1410-1413 1.30 1.30

CHRISTMAS ISSUE

Nos. 1415-1418 are printed in blocks of four in panes of 50. In upper and lower left panes Nos. 1415 and 1417 appear in first, third and fifth place; Nos. 1416 and 1418 in second and fourth place. This arrangement is reversed in upper and lower right panes.

Nativity, by Lorenzo Lotto — A828

Tin and Cast-iron Locomotive A829

Toy Horse on Wheels — A830

Mechanical Tricycle — A831

Doll Carriage — A832

Designers: No. 1414, Howard C. Mildner, from a painting by Lorenzo Lotto (1480-1556) in the National Gallery of Art, Washington, D.C. Nos. 1415-1418, Stevan Dohanos, from a drawing (locomotive) by Charles Hemming and from "Golden Age of Toys" by Fondin and Remise.
Printed by Guilford Gravure, Inc., Guilford, Conn.

PHOTOGRAVURE
Plates of 200 subjects in four panes of 50 each.

1970, Nov. 5 Tagged *Perf. 10½x11*
1414 A828 6c **multicolored** 18 5
    Margin block of 8, 4 P# 1.75
    Margin block of 4, Mr. Zip and "Use Zip Code" 90 —
    Margin block of 6, "Mail Early in the Day" 1.10 —
    a.   Precanceled 18 8
    b.   Black omitted 1,000.
    c.   As "a," blue omitted 1,600.

Perf. 11x10½
1415 A829 6c **multicolored** 85 10

Margin block of 8, 4 P# adjoining #1415, 1417	7.75	
Margin block of 4, Mr. Zip and "Use Zip Code" adjoining #1415	3.50	—
Margin block of 6, "Mail Early in the Day" adjoining #1415	5.50	—
a. Precanceled	1.50	15
b. Black omitted	—	
1416 A830 6c **multicolored**	85	10
Margin block of 8, 4 P# adjoining #1416, 1418	7.75	
Margin block of 4, Mr. Zip and "Use Zip Code" adjoining #1416	3.50	—
Margin block of 6, "Mail Early in the Day" adjoining #1416	5.50	—
a. Precanceled	1.50	15
b. Black omitted	—	
c. Imperf., pair (#1416, 1418)	—	
1417 A831 6c **multicolored**	85	10
Margin block of 4, Mr. Zip and "Use Zip Code" adjoining #1417	3.50	—
Margin block of 6, "Mail Early in the Day" adjoining #1417	5.50	—
a. Precanceled	1.50	15
b. Black omitted	—	
1418 A832 6c **multicolored**	85	10
Margin block of 4, Mr. Zip and "Use Zip Code" adjoining #1418	3.50	—
Margin block of 6, "Mail Early in the Day" adjoining #1418	5.50	—
a. Precanceled	1.50	15
b. Block of four, #1415-1418	3.75	3.50
c. As "b," precanceled	6.50	6.00
d. Black omitted	—	

The precanceled stamps, Nos. 1414a-1418a, were furnished to 68 cities. The plates include two straight (No. 1414a) or two wavy (Nos. 1415a-1418a) black lines that make up the precancellation. Unused prices are for copies with gum and used prices are for copies with an additional cancellation or without gum.

UNITED NATIONS ISSUE

Issued to commemorate the 25th anniversary of the United Nations.

"U.N." and U.N. Emblem — A833

Designed by Arnold Copeland.

LITHOGRAPHED, ENGRAVED (Giori)
Plates of 200 subjects in four panes of 50 each.

1970	Tagged	Perf. 11	
1419 A833 6c **black, verm. & ultra.,** *Nov. 20*		18	5
Margin block of 4, P#		90	—
Margin block of 4, Mr. Zip and "Use Zip Code"		80	—
Margin block of 6, "Mail Early in the Day"		1.10	—
Pair with full horiz. gutter btwn.		—	

LANDING OF THE PILGRIMS ISSUE

Issued to commemorate the 350th anniversary of the landing of the Mayflower.

Mayflower and Pilgrims — A834

Designed by Mark English.

LITHOGRAPHED, ENGRAVED (Giori)
Plates of 200 subjects in four panes of 50 each.

1970	Tagged	Perf. 11	
1420 A834 6c **blk., org., yel., magenta, bl. & brn.,** *Nov. 21*		18	5
Margin block of 4, P#		1.00	—

Margin block of 4, Mr. Zip and "Use Zip Code"	80	
Margin block of 6, "Mail Early in the Day"	1.10	
a. Orange & yellow omitted	1,250.	

DISABLED AMERICAN VETERANS AND SERVICEMEN ISSUE

No. 1421 commemorates the 50th anniversary of the Disabled Veterans of America Organization; No. 1422 honors the contribution of servicemen, particularly those who were prisoners of war, missing or killed in action. Nos. 1421-1422 are printed se-tenant in horizontal rows of 10 in panes of 50, four panes to a sheet.

Disabled American Veterans Emblem — A835

A836

Designed by Stevan Dohanos.

LITHOGRAPHED, ENGRAVED (Giori)
Plates of 200 subjects in four panes of 50 each.

1970, Nov. 24	Tagged	Perf. 11	
1421 A835 6c **dk. blue, red & multicolored**		20	10
a. Pair, #1421-1422		50	50
Margin block of 4, P# No. adjoining #1421		1.75	—
Margin block of 4, Mr. Zip and "Use Zip Code" adjoining #1421		1.05	—
Margin block of 6, "Mail Early in the Day" adjoining #1421		1.45	—

ENGRAVED

1422 A836 6c **dark blue, black & red**		20	10
Margin block of 4, P# adjoining #1422		1.75	—
Margin block of 4, Mr. Zip and "Use Zip Code" adjoining #1422		1.05	—
Margin block of 6, "Mail Early in the Day" adjoining #1422		1.45	—

AMERICAN WOOL INDUSTRY ISSUE

Issued to commemorate the 450th anniversary of the introduction of sheep to the North American continent and the beginning of the American wool industry.

Ewe and Lamb — A837

Designed by Dean Ellis.

LITHOGRAPHED, ENGRAVED (Giori)
Plates of 200 subjects in four panes of 50 each.

1971	Tagged	Perf. 11	
1423 A837 6c **multicolored,** *Jan. 19*		18	5
Margin block of 4, P#		90	—
Margin block of 4, Mr. Zip and "Use Zip Code"		80	—
Margin block of 6, "Mail Early in the Day"		1.10	—

GEN. DOUGLAS MacARTHUR ISSUE

Issued in honor of Gen. Douglas MacArthur (1880-1964), Chief of Staff, Supreme Commander for the Allied Powers in the Pacific Area during World War II and Supreme Commander in Japan after the war.

Gen. Douglas MacArthur — A838

Designed by Paul Calle; Wide World photograph.

GIORI PRESS PRINTING
Plates of 200 subjects in four panes of 50 each.

1971	Tagged	Perf. 11	
1424 A838 6c **black, red & dark blue,** *Jan. 26*		18	5
Margin block of 4, P#		90	—
Margin block of 4, Mr. Zip and "Use Zip Code"		80	—
Margin block of 6, "Mail Early in the Day"		1.10	—

BLOOD DONOR ISSUE

Salute to blood donors and spur to increased participation in the blood donor program.

"Giving Blood Saves Lives" — A839

Designed by Howard Munce.

LITHOGRAPHED, ENGRAVED (Giori)
Plates of 200 subjects in four panes of 50 each.

1971	Tagged	Perf. 11	
1425 A839 6c **blue, scarlet & indigo,** *Mar. 12*		18	5
Margin block of 4, P#		90	—
Margin block of 4, Mr. Zip and "Use Zip Code"		80	—
Margin block of 6, "Mail Early in the Day"		1.10	—

MISSOURI SESQUICENTENNIAL ISSUE

Sesquicentennial of Missouri's admission to the Union. The stamp design shows a Pawnee facing a hunter-trapper and a group of settlers. It is from a mural by Thomas Hart Benton in the Harry S. Truman Library, Independence, Mo.

"Independence and the Opening of the West," Detail, by Thomas Hart Benton — A840

Designed by Bradbury Thompson.

PHOTOGRAVURE (Andreotti)
Plates of 200 subjects in four panes of 50 each.

1971	Tagged	Perf. 11x10½	
1426 A840 8c **multicolored,** *May 8*		20	5
Margin block of 12, 6P#		2.75	—
Margin block of 4, Mr. Zip and "Use Zip Code"		1.10	—
Margin block of 4, "Mail Early in the Day"		1.00	—

See note on Andreotti printings and their color control markings in Information for Collectors under Printing, Photogravure.

WILDLIFE CONSERVATION ISSUE

Nos. 1427-1430 are printed in blocks of 4 in panes of 32. Nos. 1427-1428 alternate in first row, Nos. 1429-1430 in second row. This arrangement repeated throughout pane.

Trout
A841

Alligator
A842

Polar
Bear and
Cubs
A843

California Condor — A844

Designed by Stanley W. Galli.

LITHOGRAPHED, ENGRAVED (Giori)
Plates of 128 subjects in 4 panes of 32 each (4x8).

1971, June 12	Tagged	Perf. 11	
1427 A841 8c multicolored		25	10
Margin block of 4, P# adjoining #1427		1.25	—
Margin block of 4, Mr. Zip and "Use Zip Code" adjoining #1427		1.15	—
Margin block of 6, "Mail Early in the Day" adjoining #1427		1.60	—
1428 A842 8c multicolored		25	10
Margin block of 4, P# adjoining #1428		1.25	—
Margin block of 4, Mr. Zip and "Use Zip Code" adjoining #1428		1.15	—
Margin block of 6, "Mail Early in the Day" adjoining #1428		1.60	—
1429 A843 8c multicolored		25	10
Margin block of 4, P# adjoining #1429		1.25	—
Margin block of 4, Mr. Zip and "Use Zip Code" adjoining #1429		1.15	—
Margin block of 6, "Mail Early in the Day" adjoining #1429		1.60	—
1430 A844 8c multicolored		25	10
Margin block of 4, P# adjoining #1430		1.25	—
Margin block of 4, Mr. Zip and "Use Zip Code" adjoining #1430		1.15	—
Margin block of 6, "Mail Early in the Day" adjoining #1430		1.60	—
a. Block of four, #1427-1430		1.10	1.00
b. As "a", light green & dark green omitted from #1427-1428		3,000.	
c. As "a", red omitted from #1427 1429-1430		—	

ANTARCTIC TREATY ISSUE

Map of
Antarctica
A845

Designed by Howard Koslow; adapted from emblem on official documents of Consultative Meetings.

GIORI PRESS PRINTING
Plates of 200 subjects in four panes of 50 each.

1971	Tagged	Perf. 11	
1431 A845 8c red & dark blue, June 23		25	5
Margin block of 4, P#		1.25	—
Margin block of 4, Mr. Zip and "Use Zip Code"		1.10	—
Margin block of 6, "Mail Early in the Day"		1.65	—

AMERICAN REVOLUTION BICENTENNIAL
Bicentennial of the American Revolution.

Bicentennial Commission
Emblem — A846

Designed by Chermayeff & Geismar.

LITHOGRAPHED, ENGRAVED (Giori)
Plates of 200 subjects in four panes of 50 each.

1971	Tagged	Perf. 11	
1432 A846 8c gray, red, blue & black, July 4		30	5
Margin block of 4, P#		1.75	—
Margin block of 4, Mr. Zip and "Use Zip Code"		1.60	—
Margin block of 6, "Mail Early in the Day"		1.90	—
a. Gray & black omitted		850.00	
b. Gray ("U.S. Postage 8c") omitted		1,500.	

JOHN SLOAN ISSUE

Issued to honor John Sloan (1871-1951), painter. The painting hangs in the Phillips Gallery, Washington, D.C.

The Wake of the
Ferry — A847

Designed by Bradbury Thompson.

LITHOGRAPHED, ENGRAVED (Giori)
Plates of 200 subjects in four panes of 50 each.

1971	Tagged	Perf. 11	
1433 A847 8c multicolored, Aug. 2		20	5
Margin block of 4, P#		1.25	—
Margin block of 4, Mr. Zip and "Use Zip Code"		1.00	—
Margin block of 6, "Mail Early in the Day"		1.30	—

SPACE ACHIEVEMENT DECADE ISSUE

Issued to commemorate a decade of space achievements and the Apollo 15 moon exploration mission, July 26-Aug. 7. Nos. 1434-1435 are printed se-tenant in horizontal rows of 5 in panes of 50. In the upper and lower left panes the earth and sun stamp is first, third and fifth, the rover second and fourth. This arrangement is reversed in the upper and lower right panes.

Earth, Sun and
Landing Craft on
Moon — A848

Lunar Rover and
Astronauts
A849   A DECADE OF ACHIEVEMENT

Designed by Robert McCall.

LITHOGRAPHED, ENGRAVED (Giori)
Plates of 200 subjects in four panes of 50 each.

1971, Aug. 2	Tagged	Perf. 11	
1434 A848 8c black, blue, gray, yellow & red		20	10
a. Pair, #1434-1435		50	35
Block of 4, P# adjoining #1434		1.40	—
Margin block of 4, Mr. Zip and "Use Zip Code" adjoining #1434		1.10	—
Margin block of 6, "Mail Early in the Day" adjoining #1434		1.60	—
b. As "a," blue & red (litho.) omitted		1,250.	
1435 A849 8c black, blue, gray, yellow & red		20	10
Margin block of 4, P# adjoining #1435		1.40	—
Margin block of 4, Mr. Zip and "Use Zip Code" adjoining #1435		1.10	—
Margin block of 6, "Mail Early in the Day" adjoining #1435		1.60	—

EMILY DICKINSON ISSUE

Issued to honor Emily Elizabeth Dickinson (1830-1886), poet.

Emily Dickinson — A850

Designed by Bernard Fuchs after a photograph.

LITHOGRAPHED, ENGRAVED (Giori)
Plates of 200 subjects in four panes of 50 each.

1971	Tagged	Perf. 11	
1436 A850 8c multicolored, greenish, Aug. 28		18	5
Margin block of 4, P#		1.25	—
Margin block of 4, Mr. Zip and "Use Zip Code"		85	—
Margin block of 6, "Mail Early in the Day"		1.20	—
a. Black & olive (engr.) omitted		950.00	
b. Pale rose omitted		—	

SAN JUAN ISSUE

Issued for the 450th anniversary of San Juan, Puerto Rico.

Sentry Box, Morro Castle, San
Juan — A851

Designed as a woodcut by Walter Brooks.

LITHOGRAPHED, ENGRAVED (Giori)
Plates of 200 subjects in four panes of 50 each.

1971	Tagged	Perf. 11	
1437 A851 8c pale brown, black, yellow & dark brown, Sept. 12		18	5
Margin block of 4, P#		1.25	—
Margin block of 4, Mr. Zip and "Use Zip Code"		85	—
Margin block of 6, "Mail Early in the Day"		1.20	—

PREVENT DRUG ABUSE ISSUE
Drug Abuse Prevention Week, Oct. 3-9.

Young Woman Drug
Addict — A852

Designed by Miggs Burroughs.

PHOTOGRAVURE (Andreotti)
Plates of 200 subjects in four panes of 50 each.

1971		Tagged		Perf. 10 ½x11	
1438	A852	8c	blue, deep blue & black, *Oct. 4*	18	5
		Margin block of 6, 3P#		1.50	—
		Margin block of 4, "Use Zip Code"		85	—
		Margin block of 6, "Mail Early in the Day"		1.20	—

CARE ISSUE
25th anniversary of CARE, a U.S.-Canadian Cooperative for American Relief everywhere.

Hands Reaching for
CARE — A853

Designed by Soren Noring.

PHOTOGRAVURE (Andreotti)
Plates of 200 subjects in four panes of 50 each.

1971		Tagged		Perf. 10 ½x11	
1439	A853	8c	blue, blk., vio. & red lilac, *Oct. 27*	18	5
		Margin block of 8, 4P#		1.75	—
		Margin block of 4, Mr. Zip and "Use Zip Code"		85	—
		Margin block of 6, "Mail Early in the Day"		1.20	—

HISTORIC PRESERVATION ISSUE
Nos. 1440-1443 are printed in blocks of 4 in panes of 32. Nos. 1440-1441 alternate in first row, Nos. 1442-1443 in second row. This arrangement is repeated throughout the pane.

Decatur House, Washington, D.C. — A854

Whaling Ship Charles W. Morgan, Mystic, Conn. A855

Cable Car, San Francisco — A856

San Xavier del Bac Mission, Tucson, Ariz. A857

Designed by Melbourne Brindle.

LITHOGRAPHED, ENGRAVED (Giori)

1971, Oct. 29		Tagged		Perf. 11	
1440	A854	8c	black brown & ocher, *buff*	25	12
		Margin block of 4, P# adjoining #1440		1.25	—
		Margin block of 4, Mr. Zip and "Use Zip Code" adjoining #1440		1.10	—
		Margin block of 6, "Mail Early in the Day" adjoining #1440		1.60	—
1441	A855	8c	black brown & ocher, *buff*	25	12
		Margin block of 4, P# adjoining #1441		1.25	—
		Margin block of 4, Mr. Zip and "Use Zip Code" adjoining #1441		1.10	—
		Margin block of 6, "Mail Early in the Day" adjoining #1441		1.60	—
1442	A856	8c	black brown & ocher, *buff*	25	12
		Margin block of 4, P# adjoining #1442		1.25	—
		Margin block of 4, Mr. Zip and "Use Zip Code" adjoining #1442		1.10	—
		Margin block of 6, "Mail Early in the Day" adjoining #1442		1.60	—
1443	A857	8c	black brown & ocher, *buff*	25	12
		Margin block of 4, P# adjoining #1443		1.25	—
		Margin block of 4, Mr. Zip and "Use Zip Code" adjoining #1443		1.10	—
		Margin block of 6, "Mail Early in the Day" adjoining #1443		1.60	—
a.		Block of four (#1440-1443)		1.05	1.05
b.		As "a," black brown omitted		2,500.	
c.		As "a," ocher omitted		—	

CHRISTMAS ISSUE

Adoration of the Shepherds, by Giorgione — A858

"Partridge in a Pear Tree" — A859

Designers: No. 1444, Bradbury Thompson, using a painting by Giorgione in the National Gallery of Art, Washington, D.C. No. 1445, Jamie Wyeth.

PHOTOGRAVURE (Andreotti)
Plates of 200 subjects in four panes of 50 each.

1971, Nov. 10		Tagged		Perf. 10 ½x11	
1444	A858	8c	gold & multicolored	18	5
		Margin block of 12, 6P#		2.50	—
		Margin block of 4, Mr. Zip and "Use Zip Code"		85	—
		Margin block of 4, "Mail Early in the Day"		85	—
a.		Gold omitted		600.00	
1445	A859	8c	dark green, red & multicolored	18	5
		Margin block of 12, 6P#		2.50	—
		Margin block of 4, Mr. Zip and "Use Zip Code"		85	—
		Margin block of 4, "Mail Early in the Day"		85	—

SIDNEY LANIER ISSUE
Issued to honor Sidney Lanier (1842-1881), poet, musician, lawyer and educator.

Sidney Lanier — A860

Designed by William A. Smith.

GIORI PRESS PRINTING
Plates of 200 subjects in four panes of 50 each.

1972		Tagged		Perf. 11	
1446	A860	8c	black, brown & light blue, *Feb. 3*	18	5
		Margin block of 4, P#		90	—
		Margin block of 4, Mr. Zip and "Use Zip Code"		85	—
		Margin block of 6, "Mail Early in the Day"		1.10	—

PEACE CORPS ISSUE
Issued to honor the Peace Corps.

Peace Corps Poster, by David Battle — A861

Designed by Bradbury Thompson.

PHOTOGRAVURE (Andreotti)
Plates of 200 subjects in four panes of 50 each.

1972		Tagged		Perf. 10 ½x11	
1447	A861	8c	dk. blue, lt. blue & red, *Feb. 11*	18	5
		Margin block of 6, 3 P#		1.30	—
		Margin block of 4, Mr. Zip and "Use Zip Code"		85	—
		Margin block of 6, "Mail Early in the Day"		1.10	—

NATIONAL PARKS CENTENNIAL ISSUE
Centenary of Yellowstone National Park, the first National Park, and of the entire National Park System. The four 2c stamps were issued for Cape Hatteras, N.C., National Seashore; 6c for Wolf Trap Farm, Vienna, Va.; 8c for Yellowstone National Park, Wyo., and 15c for Mt. McKinley National Park, Alaska. See No. C84.

A862   A863

A864   A865
Cape Hatteras National Seashore

National Parks Centennial

Wolf Trap Farm, Va. — A866

Old Faithful, Yellowstone — A867

Mt. McKinley, Alaska — A868

Designers: 2c, Walter D. Richards; 6c, Howard Koslow; 8c, Robert Handville; 15c, James Barkley.

LITHOGRAPHED, ENGRAVED (Giori)
Plates of 400 subjects in 4 panes of 100 each. Panes contain 25 subjects each of Nos. 1448-1451.

1972		Tagged	Perf. 11	
1448	A862	2c black & multi., *Apr. 5*	6	6
		Margin block of 4, P# adjoining #1448	1.00	—
		Margin block of 4, "Use Zip Codes" adjoining #1448	40	—
		Margin block of 8, "Mail Early in the Day" adjoining #1448	70	—
1449	A863	2c black & multi., *Apr. 5*	6	6
		Margin block of 4, P# adjoining #1449	1.00	—
		Margin block of 4, "Use Zip Codes" adjoining #1449	40	—
		Margin block of 8, "Mail Early in the Day" adjoining #1449	70	—
1450	A864	2c black & multi., *Apr. 5*	6	6
		Margin block of 4, P# adjoining #1450	1.00	—
		Margin block of 4, "Use Zip Codes" adjoining #1450	40	—
		Margin block of 8, "Mail Early in the Day" adjoining #1450	70	—
1451	A865	2c black & multi., *Apr. 5*	6	6
		Margin block of 4, P# adjoining #1451	1.00	—
		Margin block of 4, "Use Zip Codes" adjoining #1451	40	—
		Margin block of 8, "Mail Early in the Day" adjoining #1451	70	—
a.		Block of four (#1448-1451)	35	30
b.		As "a," black (litho.) omitted	2,000.	

Plates of 200 subjects in four panes of 50 each

1452	A866	6c black & multicolored, *June 26*	16	8
		Margin block of 4, P#	1.00	—
		Margin block of 4, Mr. Zip and "Use Zip Code"	70	—
		Margin block of 6, "Mail Early in the Day"	1.00	—

Plates of 128 subjects in four panes of 32 (8x4)

1453	A867	8c blk., blue, brn. & multi., *Mar. 1*	18	5
		Margin block of 4, P#	1.00	—
		Margin block of 4, Mr. Zip and "Use Zip Code"	85	—
		Margin block of 6, "Mail Early in the Day"	1.20	—

Plates of 200 subjects in four panes of 50 each

1454	A868	15c black & multi., *July 28*	35	22
		Margin block of 4, P#	1.75	—
		Margin block of 4, Mr. Zip	1.50	—
		Margin block of 6, Mail Early	2.25	—

FAMILY PLANNING ISSUE

Family — A869

LITHOGRAPHED, ENGRAVED (Giori)
Plates of 200 subjects in four panes of 50 each.

1972		Tagged	Perf. 11	
1455	A869	8c black & multi., *Mar. 18*	16	5
		Margin block of 4, P#	1.00	—
		Margin block of 4, Mr. Zip and "Use Zip Code"	70	—
		Margin block of 6, "Mail Early in the Day"	1.00	—
a.		Yellow omitted		

AMERICAN BICENTENNIAL ISSUE
Colonial American Craftsmen

Nos. 1456-1459 are printed in blocks of four in panes of 50. In upper and lower left panes Nos. 1456 and 1458 appear in first, third and fifth place; Nos. 1457 and 1459 in second and fourth place. This arrangement is reversed in upper and lower right panes.

Glass Blower — A870

Silversmith A871

Wigmaker A872

Hatter — A873

Designed by Leonard Everett Fisher.

ENGRAVED
E.E. Plates of 200 subjects in four panes of 50 each.

1972, July 4		Tagged	Perf. 11x10½	
1456	A870	8c deep brown, *dull yellow*	25	8
		Margin block of 4, P# adjoining #1456	1.25	—
		Margin block of 4, Mr. Zip and "Use Zip Code" adjoining #1456	1.10	—
		Margin block of 6, Bicentennial emblem+ adjoining #1456	1.60	—
1457	A871	8c deep brown, *dull yellow*	25	8
		Margin block of 4, P# adjoining #1457	1.25	—
		Margin block of 4, Mr. Zip and "Use Zip Code" adjoining #1457	1.10	—
		Margin block of 6, Bicentennial emblem+ adjoining #1457	1.60	—
1458	A872	8c deep brown, *dull yellow*	25	8
		Margin block of 4, P# adjoining #1458	1.25	—
		Margin block of 4, Mr. Zip and "Use Zip Code" adjoining #1458	1.10	—
		Margin block of 6, Bicentennial emblem+ adjoining #1458	1.60	—
1459	A873	8c deep brown, *dull yellow*	25	8
		Margin block of 4, P# adjoining #1459	1.25	—
		Margin block of 4, Mr. Zip and "Use Zip Code" adjoining #1459	1.10	—
		Margin block of 6, Bicentennial emblem+ adjoining #1459	1.60	—
a.		Block of 4, #1456-1459	1.05	1.05

+ Bicentennial Commission emblem and inscription: USA BICENTENNIAL / HONORS COLONIAL / AMERICAN CRAFTSMEN.

OLYMPIC GAMES ISSUE

11th Winter Olympic Games, Sapporo, Japan, Feb. 3-13 and 20th Summer Olympic Games, Munich, Germany, Aug. 26-Sept. 11. See No. C85.

Bicycling and Olympic Rings — A874

Bobsledding and Olympic Rings — A875

Running and Olympic Rings — A876

Designed by Lance Wyman.

PHOTOGRAVURE (Andreotti)
Plates of 200 subjects in four panes of 50 each.

1972, Aug. 17		Tagged	Perf. 11x10½	
1460	A874	6c black, blue, red, emerald & yellow	16	12
		Margin block of 10, 5P#	2.00	—
		Margin block of 4, Mr. Zip and "Use Zip Code"	75	—
		Margin block of 6, "Mail Early in the Day"	1.10	—
		Plate flaw (broken red ring) (33313 UL 43)	7.50	
1461	A875	8c black, blue, red, emerald & yellow	16	5
		Margin block of 10, 5#	2.00	—
		Margin block of 4, Mr. Zip and "Use Zip Code"	70	—
		Margin block of 6, "Mail Early in the Day"	1.00	—
1462	A876	15c black, blue, red, emerald & yel.	35	18
		Margin block of 10, 5P#	4.50	—
		Margin block of 4, Mr. Zip and "Use Zip Code"	1.60	—
		Margin block of 6, "Mail Early in the Day"	2.25	—

PARENT TEACHER ASSN. ISSUE
75th anniversary of the Parent Teacher Association.

Blackboard — A877

Designed by Arthur S. Congdon III.

PHOTOGRAVURE (Andreotti)
Plates of 200 subjects in four panes of 50 each.

1972		Tagged	Perf. 11x10½	
1463	A877	8c yellow & black, *Sept. 15*	16	5
		Margin block of 4, 2 P#	90	—
		Margin block of 4, yel. P# reversed	1.75	—

Margin block of 4, Mr. Zip and "Use
Zip Code" .... 70 —
Margin block of 6, "Mail Early in the
Day" .... 1.00 —

WILDLIFE CONSERVATION ISSUE

Nos. 1464-1467 are printed in blocks of 4 in
panes of 32. Nos. 1464-1465 alternate in first row,
Nos. 1468-1469 in second row. This arrangement
repeated throughout pane.

Fur Seals
A878

Cardinal
A879

Brown
Pelican
A880

Bighorn
Sheep
A881

Designed by Stanley W. Galli.

LITHOGRAPHED, ENGRAVED (Giori)
Plates of 128 subjects in 4 panes of 32 (4x8).

1972, Sept. 20	Tagged	Perf. 11	
1464 A878 8c	multicolored	25	8
	Margin block of 4, P# adjoining #1464	1.25	—
	Margin block of 4, Mr. Zip and "Use Zip Code" adjoining #1464	1.10	—
	Margin block of 6, "Mail Early in the Day" adjoining #1464	1.60	—
1465 A879 8c	multicolored	25	8
	Margin block of 4, P# adjoining #1465	1.25	—
	Margin block of 4, Mr. Zip and "Use Zip Code" adjoining #1465	1.10	—
	Margin block of 6, "Mail Early in the Day" adjoining #1465	1.60	—
1466 A880 8c	multicolored	25	8
	Margin block of 4, P# adjoining #1466	1.25	—
	Margin block of 4, Mr. Zip and "Use Zip Code" adjoining #1466	1.10	—
	Margin block of 6, "Mail Early in the Day" adjoining #1466	1.60	—
1467 A881 8c	multicolored	25	8
	Margin block of 4, P# adjoining #1467	1.25	—
	Margin block of 4, Mr. Zip and "Use Zip Code" adjoining #1467	1.10	—
	Margin block of 6, "Mail Early in the Day" adjoining #1467	1.60	—
a.	Block of four (#1464-1467)	1.05	85
b.	As "a," brown omitted	3,500.	
c.	As "a," green & blue omitted	—	

MAIL ORDER BUSINESS ISSUE

Centenary of mail order business, originated by
Aaron Montgomery Ward, Chicago. Design based
on Headsville, W.Va., post office in Smithsonian
Institution, Washington, D.C.

Rural Post Office
Store — A882

Designed by Robert Lambdin.

PHOTOGRAVURE (Andreotti)
Plates of 200 subjects in four panes of 50 each.

1972	Tagged	Perf. 11x10½	
1468 A882 8c	multicolored, Sept. 27	16	5
	Margin block of 12, 6 P#	2.75	—
	Margin block of 4, Mr. Zip and "Use Zip Code"	70	—
	Margin block of 4, "Mail Early in the Day"	70	—

The tagging on No. 1468 consists of a vertical bar of
phosphor 10 mm. wide.

OSTEOPATHIC MEDICINE ISSUE

75th anniversary of the American Osteopathic
Association, founded by Dr. Andrew T. Still (1828-
1917), who developed the principles of osteopathy
in 1874.

Man's Quest for Health — A883

Designed by V. Jack Ruther.

PHOTOGRAVURE (Andreotti)
Plates of 200 subjects in four panes of 50 each.

1972	Tagged	Perf. 10½x11	
1469 A883 8c	multicolored, Oct. 9	16	5
	Margin block of 6, 3 P#	1.25	—
	Margin block of 4, Mr. Zip and "Use Zip Code"	70	—
	Margin block of 6, "Mail Early in the Day"	1.00	—

AMERICAN FOLKLORE ISSUE
Tom Sawyer

Tom Sawyer, by Norman
Rockwell — A884

Designed by Bradbury Thompson.

LITHOGRAPHED, ENGRAVED (Giori)
Plates of 200 subjects in four panes of 50 each.

1972	Tagged	Perf. 11	
1470 A884 8c	black, red, yellow, tan, blue & rose red, Oct. 13	16	5
	Margin block of 4, P#	1.00	—
	Margin block of 4, Mr. Zip and "Use Zip Code"	70	—
	Margin block of 6, "Mail Early in the Day"	1.00	—
a.	Horiz. pair, imperf. between	2,500.	
b.	Red & black (engr.) omitted	1,250.	
c.	Yellow & tan (litho.) omitted	1,500.	

CHRISTMAS ISSUE

Angels from "Mary,
Queen of
Heaven" — A885

Santa
Claus — A886

Designers: No. 1471, Bradbury Thompson, using detail
from a painting by the Master of the St. Lucy legend, in the
National Gallery of Art, Washington, D.C. No. 1472, Stevan
Dohanos.

PHOTOGRAVURE (Andreotti)
Plates of 200 subjects in four panes of 50 each.

1972, Nov. 9	Tagged	Perf. 10½x11	
1471 A885 8c	multicolored	16	5
	Margin block of 12, 6 P#	2.75	—
	Margin block of 4, Mr. Zip and "Use Zip Code"	70	—
	Margin block of 4, "Mail Early in the Day"	70	—
a.	Pink omitted	500.00	
b.	Black omitted	—	
1472 A886 8c	multicolored	16	5
	Margin block of 12, 6 P#	2.75	—
	Margin block of 4, Mr. Zip and "Use Zip Code"	70	—
	Margin block of 4, "Mail Early in the Day"	70	—

PHARMACY ISSUE

Honoring American druggists in connection with
the 120th anniversary of the American Pharmaceu-
tical Association.

Mortar and Pestle,
Bowl of Hygeia,
19th Century
Medicine
Bottles — A887

Designed by Ken Davies.

LITHOGRAPHED, ENGRAVED (Giori)
Plates of 200 subjects in four panes of 50 each.

1972	Tagged	Perf. 11	
1473 A887 8c	black & multicolored, Nov. 10	16	5
	Margin block of 4, P#	1.00	—
	Margin block of 4, Mr. Zip and "Use Zip Code"	70	—
	Margin block of 6, "Mail Early in the Day"	1.00	—
a.	Blue & orange omitted	1,100.	
b.	Blue omitted	—	

STAMP COLLECTING ISSUE

Issued to publicize stamp collecting.

U.S. No. 1 under
Magnifying
Glass — A888

Designed by Frank E. Livia.

LITHOGRAPHED, ENGRAVED (Giori)
Plates of 160 subjects in four panes of 40 each.

1972	Tagged	Perf. 11	
1474 A888 8c	multicolored, Nov. 17	16	5
	Margin block of 4, P#	1.00	—
	Margin block of 4, Mr. Zip and "Use Zip Code"	70	—
	Margin block of 6, "Mail Early in the Day"	1.00	—
a.	Black (litho.) omitted	1,100.	

LOVE ISSUE

"Love," by Robert Indiana — A889

Designed by Robert Indiana.

PHOTOGRAVURE (Andreotti)
Plates of 200 subjects in four panes of 50 each.

		1973, Jan. 26	Tagged		Perf. 11x10½
1475	A889	8c red, emerald & violet blue		16	5
		Margin block of 6, 3 P#		1.35	—
		Margin block of 4, Mr. Zip and "Use Zip Code"		70	—
		Margin block of 6, "Mail Early in the Day"		1.00	—

AMERICAN BICENTENNIAL ISSUE
Communications in Colonial Times

Printer and Patriots Examining Pamphlet — A890

Posting a Broadside A891

Postrider — A892

Drummer A893

Designed by William A. Smith.

GIORI PRESS PRINTING
Plates of 200 subjects in four panes of 50 each.

		1973	Tagged		Perf. 11
1476	A890	8c ultra., greenish blk. & red, Feb. 16		20	5
		Margin block of 4, P#		1.10	—
		Margin block of 4, Mr. Zip and "Use Zip Code"		90	—
		Margin block of 6, "Mail Early in the Day"		1.30	—
1477	A891	8c black, vermilion & ultra., Apr. 13		20	5
		Margin block of 4, P#		1.10	—
		Margin block of 4, Mr. Zip and "Use Zip Code"		90	—
		Margin block of 6, "Mail Early in the Day"		1.30	—
		Margin block of 6, Bicentennial emblem and "USA Bicentennial Era"		1.30	—
		Pair with full horiz. gutter btwn.		—	

LITHOGRAPHED, ENGRAVED (Giori)

		1478	A892 8c blue, black, red & green, June 22		20	5
			Margin block of 4, P#		1.10	—
			Margin block of 4, Mr. Zip and "Use Zip Code"		90	—
			Margin block of 6, "Mail Early in the Day"		1.30	—
			Margin block of 6, Bicentennial emblem and "USA Bicentennial Era"		1.30	—
		1479	A893 8c blue, black, yellow & red, Sept. 28		20	5
			Margin block of 4, P#		1.10	—
			Margin block of 4, Mr. Zip and "Use Zip Code"		90	—

Margin block of 6, "Mail Early in the Day" 1.30 —
Margin block of 6, Bicentennial emblem and "USA Bicentennial Era" 1.30 —

AMERICAN BICENTENNIAL ISSUE
Boston Tea Party

Nos. 1480-1483 are printed in blocks of four in panes of 50. In upper and lower left panes Nos. 1480 and 1482 appear in first, third and fifth place, Nos. 1481 and 1483 appear in second and fourth place. This arrangement is reversed in upper and lower right panes.

British Merchantman A894

British Three-master A895

Boats and Ship's Hull — A896

Boat and Dock — A897

Designed by William A. Smith.

LITHOGRAPHED, ENGRAVED (Giori)
Plates of 200 subjects in four panes of 50 each.

		1973, July 4	Tagged		Perf. 11
1480	A894	8c black & multicolored		20	10
		Margin block of 4, P# adjoining #1480		1.20	—
		Margin block of 4, Mr. Zip and "Use Zip Code" adjoining #1480		1.00	—
		Margin block of 6, "Mail Early in the Day" adjoining #1480		1.50	—
		Margin block of 6, Bicentennial emblem and "USA Bicentennial Era"		1.50	—
1481	A895	8c black & multicolored		20	10
		Margin block of 4, P# adjoining #1481		1.20	—
		Margin block of 4, Mr. Zip and "Use Zip Code" adjoining #1481		1.00	—
		Margin block of 6, "Mail Early in the Day" adjoining #1481		1.50	—
		Margin block of 6, Bicentennial emblem and "USA Bicentennial Era" adjoining #1481		1.50	—
1482	A896	8c black & multicolored		20	10
		Margin block of 4, P# adjoining #1482		1.20	—
		Margin block of 4, Mr. Zip and "Use Zip Code" adjoining #1482		1.00	—
		Margin block of 6, "Mail Early in the Day" adjoining #1482		1.50	—
		Margin block of 6, Bicentennial emblem and "USA Bicentennial Era" adjoining #1482		1.50	—
1483	A897	8c black & multicolored		20	10
		Margin block of 4, P# adjoining #1483		1.20	—
		Margin block of 4, Mr. Zip and "Use Zip Code" adjoining #1483		1.00	—
		Margin block of 6, "Mail Early in the Day" adjoining #1483		1.50	—
		Margin block of 6, Bicentennial emblem and "USA Bicentennial Era" adjoining #1483		1.50	—
a.		Block of 4, #1480-1483		85	80
b.		As "a," black (engraved) omitted		2,500.	
c.		As "a," black (litho.) omitted		1,800.	

AMERICAN ARTS ISSUE

George Gershwin (1899-1937), composer (No. 1484); Robinson Jeffers (1887-1962), poet (No. 1485); Henry Ossawa Tanner (1859-1937), black painter (No. 1486); Willa Cather (1873-1947), novelist (No. 1487).

Gershwin, Sportin' Life, Porgy and Bess — A898

Robinson Jeffers, Man and Children of Carmel with Burro — A899

Henry Ossawa Tanner, Palette and Rainbow — A900

Willa Cather, Pioneer Family and Covered Wagon — A901

Designed by Mark English.

PHOTOGRAVURE (Andreotti)
Plates of 160 subjects in four panes of 40 each.

		1973	Tagged		Perf. 11
1484	A898	8c dp. green & multi., Feb. 28		16	5
		Margin block of 12, 6 P#		2.75	—
		Margin block of 4, Mr. Zip, "Use Zip Code" and "Mail Early in the Day"		70	—
		Margin block of 16, 6 P#, Mr. Zip and slogans		3.50	—
a.		Vertical pair, imperf. horiz.		350.00	
1485	A899	8c Prussian blue & multi., Aug. 13		16	5
		Margin block of 12, 6 P#		2.75	—
		Margin block of 4, Mr. Zip, "Use Zip Code" "Mail Early in the Day"		70	—
		Margin block of 16, 6 P#, Mr. Zip and slogans		3.50	—
a.		Vertical pair, imperf. horiz.		400.00	
1486	A900	8c yellow brown & multi., Sept. 10		16	5
		Margin block of 12, 6 P#		2.75	—
		Margin block of 4, Mr. Zip, "Use Zip Code" "Mail Early in the Day"		70	—
		Margin block of 16, 6 P#, Mr. Zip and slogans		3.50	—
1487	A901	8c deep brown & multi., Sept. 20		16	5
		Margin block of 12, 6 P#		2.75	—
		Margin block of 4, Mr. Zip, "Use Zip Code" "Mail Early in the Day"		70	—
		Margin block of 16, 6 P#, Mr. Zip and slogans		3.50	—
a.		Vertical pair, imperf. horiz.		450.00	

COPERNICUS ISSUE

500th anniversary of the birth of Nicolaus Copernicus (1473-1543), Polish astronomer.

Nicolaus Copernicus — A902

Designed by Alvin Eisenman after 18th century engraving.

LITHOGRAPHED, ENGRAVED (Giori)
Plates of 200 subjects in four panes of 50 each.

1973		Tagged		Perf. 11	
1488	A902	8c **black & orange**, *Apr. 23*		16	5
		Margin block of 4, P#		1.00	—
		Margin block of 4, Mr. Zip and "Use Zip Code"		70	—
		Margin block of 6, "Mail Early in the Day"		1.00	—
a.		Orange omitted		1,350.	
b.		Black (engraved) omitted		1,750.	

The orange can be chemically removed.

POSTAL SERVICE EMPLOYEES ISSUE

A tribute to U.S. Postal Service employees. Nos. 1489-1498 are printed se-tenant in horizontal rows of 10. Emerald inscription on back, printed beneath gum in water-soluble ink, includes Postal Service emblem, "People Serving You" and a statement, differing for each of the 10 stamps, about some aspect of postal service.

Each stamp in top or bottom row has a tab with blue inscription enumerating various jobs in postal service.

Stamp Counter — A903

Mail Collection — A904

Letter Facing on Conveyor Belt — A905

Parcel Post Sorting — A906

Mail Canceling — A907

Manual Letter Routing — A908

Electronic Letter Routing — A909

Loading Mail on Truck — A910

Mailman — A911

Rural Mail Delivery — A912

Designed by Edward Vebell.

PHOTOGRAVURE (Andreotti)
Plates of 200 subjects in four panes of 50 each.

1973, Apr. 30		Tagged		Perf. 10½x11	
1489	A903	8c **multicolored**		20	12
1490	A904	8c **multicolored**		20	12
1491	A905	8c **multicolored**		20	12
1492	A906	8c **multicolored**		20	12
1493	A907	8c **multicolored**		20	12
1494	A908	8c **multicolored**		20	12
1495	A909	8c **multicolored**		20	12
1496	A910	8c **multicolored**		20	12
1497	A911	8c **multicolored**		20	12
1498	A912	8c **multicolored**		20	12
		Margin block of 20, 5 P# and 10 tabs		4.50	—
a.		Strip of 10 (#1489-1498)		2.20	2.00

The tagging on Nos. 1489-1498 consists of a ½-inch horizontal band of phosphor.

HARRY S. TRUMAN ISSUE

Harry S. Truman, 33rd President, (1884-1972) — A913

Designed by Bradbury Thompson; photograph by Leo Stern.

GIORI PRESS PRINTING
Plates of 128 subjects in four panes of 32 each.

1973		Tagged		Perf. 11	
1499	A913	8c **carmine rose, black & blue**, *May 8*		16	5
		Margin block of 4, P#		90	—

ELECTRONICS PROGRESS ISSUE
See No. C86.

Marconi's Spark Coil and Spark Gap — A914

Transistors and Printed Circuit Board — A915

Microphone, Speaker, Vacuum Tube and TV Camera Tube — A916

Designed by Walter and Naiad Einsel.

LITHOGRAPHED, ENGRAVED (Giori)
Plates of 200 subjects in four panes of 50 each.

1973, July 10		Tagged		Perf. 11	
1500	A914	6c **lilac & multicolored**		12	10
		Margin block of 4, P#		1.00	—
		Margin block of 4, Mr. Zip and "Use Zip Code"		55	—
		Margin block of 6, "Mail Early in the Day"		80	—
1501	A915	8c **tan & multicolored**		16	5
		Margin block of 4, P#		1.00	—
		Margin block of 4, Mr. Zip and "Use Zip Code"		70	—
		Margin block of 6, "Mail Early in the Day"		1.00	—
a.		Black (inscriptions & "U.S. 8c") omitted		850.00	
b.		Tan (background) & lilac omitted		1,750.	
1502	A916	15c **gray green & multicolored**		30	20
		Margin block of 4, P#		3.00	—
		Margin block of 4, Mr. Zip and "Use Zip Code"		1.50	—
		Margin block of 6, "Mail Early in the Day"		1.90	—
a.		Black (inscriptions & "U.S. 15c") omitted		1,900.	

LYNDON B. JOHNSON ISSUE

Lyndon B. Johnson, 36th President (1908-1973) — A917

Designed by Bradbury Thompson, portrait by Elizabeth Shoumatoff.

PHOTOGRAVURE (Andreotti)
Plates of 128 subjects in four panes of 32 each.

1973, Aug. 27				Perf. 11	
1503	A917	8c **black & multicolored**, *Aug. 27*		16	5
		Margin block of 12, 6 P#		2.50	—
a.		Horiz. pair, imperf. vert.		400.00	

RURAL AMERICA ISSUE

Centenary of the introduction of Aberdeen Angus cattle into the United States (No. 1504); of the Chautauqua Institution (No. 1505); and of the introduction of hard winter wheat into Kansas by Mennonite immigrants (No. 1506).

Angus and Longhorn Cattle — A918

A little time given to the study of the arrangement of the Scott Catalogue can make it easier to use effectively.

Chautauqua Tent
and
Buggies — A919

RURAL AMERICA

Wheat Fields and
Train — A920

No. 1504 modeled by Frank Waslick after painting by F. C. "Frank" Murphy. Nos. 1505-1506 designed by John Falter.

LITHOGRAPHED, ENGRAVED (Giori)
Plates of 200 subjects in four panes of 50 each.

1973-74	Tagged	Perf. 11	
1504 A918 8c **multicolored**, *Oct. 5, 1973*		16	5
Margin block of 4, P#		1.00	—
Margin block of 4, Mr. Zip and "Use Zip Code"		70	—
Margin block of 6, "Mail Early in the Day"		1.00	—
a. Green & red brown omitted		600.00	
1505 A919 10c **multicolored**, *Aug. 6, 1974*		20	5
Margin block of 4, P#		1.10	—
Margin block of 4, Mr. Zip and "Use Zip Code"		90	—
Margin block of 6, "Mail Early in the Day"		1.30	—
1506 A920 10c **multicolored**, *Aug. 16, 1974*		20	5
Margin block of 4, P#		1.10	—
Margin block of 4, Mr. Zip and "Use Zip Code"		90	—
Margin block of 6, "Mail Early in the Day"		1.30	—
a. Black and blue (engr.) omitted		750.00	

CHRISTMAS ISSUE

Small Cowper
Madonna, by
Raphael — A921

Christmas Tree in
Needlepoint — A922

Designers: No. 1507, Bradbury Thompson, using a painting in the National Gallery of Art, Washington, D.C. No. 1508, Dolli Tingle.

PHOTOGRAVURE (Andreotti)
Plates of 200 subjects in four panes of 50 each.

1973, Nov. 7	Tagged	Perf. 10½x11	
1507 A921 8c **multicolored**		16	5
Margin block of 12, 6 P#		2.10	—
Margin block of 4, Mr. Zip and "Use Zip Code"		70	—
Margin block of 4, "Mail Early in the Day"		70	—
1508 A922 8c **multicolored**		16	5
Margin block of 12, 6 P#		2.10	—
Margin block of 4, Mr. Zip and "Use Zip Code"		70	—
Margin block of 4, "Mail Early in the Day"		70	—
a. Vertical pair, imperf. between		500.00	
Pair with full horiz. gutter btwn.		—	

The tagging on Nos. 1507-1508 consists of a 20x12mm. horizontal bar of phosphor.

50-Star and
13-Star Flags
A923

Mail Transport
A925

Jefferson
Memorial and
Signature
A924

Liberty Bell
A926

Designers: No. 1509, Ren Wicks. No. 1510, Dean Ellis. No. 1511, Randall McDougall. 6.3c, Frank Lionetti.

MULTICOLOR HUCK PRESS
Panes of 100 (10x10)

1973-74	Tagged	Perf. 11x10½	
1509 A923 10c **red & blue**, *Dec. 8, 1973*		20	5
Margin block of 20, 4-6 P#, 2-3 "Mail Early" and 2-3 "Use Zip Code"		5.50	—
a. Horizontal pair, imperf. between		60.00	
b. Blue omitted		200.00	
c. Imperf., vert. pair		850.00	

ROTARY PRESS PRINTING
E.E. Plates of 400 subjects in four panes of 100 each.

1510 A924 10c **blue**, *Dec. 14, 1973*		20	5
Margin block of 4, P#		1.00	—
Margin block of 4, "Use Zip Codes"		90	—
Margin block of 6, "Mail Early in the Day"		1.30	—
a. Untagged (Bureau precanceled)			20
b. Booklet pane of 5 + label		1.50	30
c. Booklet pane of 8		1.60	30
d. Booklet pane of 6, *Aug. 5, 1974*		2.50	30
e. Vert. pair, imperf. horiz.		250.00	
f. Vert. pair, imperf. between		—	

PHOTOGRAVURE (Andreotti)
Plates of 400 subjects in four panes of 100 each.

1511 A925 10c **multicolored**, *Jan. 4, 1974*		20	5
Margin block of 8, 4 P#		2.25	—
Margin block of 4, "Use Zip Codes"		90	—
Margin block of 6, "Mail Early in the Day"		1.30	—
a. Yellow omitted		60.00	
Pair with full horiz. gutter btwn.		—	

COIL STAMPS
ROTARY PRESS PRINTING

1973-74	Tagged	Perf. 10 Vert.	
1518 A926 6.3c **brick red**, *Oct. 1, 1974*		13	7
Pair		26	14
Joint line pair		35	—
a. Untagged (Bureau precanceled)			13
b. Imperf., pair		150.00	
c. As "a," imperf., pair			90.00

A total of 129 different Bureau precancels were used by 117 cities.

MULTICOLOR HUCK PRESS

1519 A923 10c **red & blue**, *Dec. 8, 1973*		25	5
Pair		50	10
a. Imperf., pair		20.00	

ROTARY PRESS PRINTING

1520 A924 10c **blue**, *Dec. 14, 1973*		20	5
Pair		40	10
Joint line pair		50	—
a. Untagged (Bureau precanceled)			25
b. Imperf., pair		40.00	

VETERANS OF FOREIGN WARS ISSUE

75th anniversary of Veterans of Spanish-American and Other Foreign Wars.

Emblem and
Initials of
Veterans of
Foreign
Wars — A928

Designed by Robert Hallock.

GIORI PRESS PRINTING
Plates of 200 subjects in 4 plates of 50 each.

1974	Tagged	Perf. 11	
1525 A928 10c **red & dark blue**, *Mar. 11*		20	5
Margin block of 4, P#		1.25	—
Margin block of 4, Mr. Zip and "Use Zip Code"		85	—
Margin block of 6, "Mail Early in the Day"		1.25	—

ROBERT FROST ISSUE

Centenary of the birth of Robert Frost (1873-1963), poet.

Robert Frost — A929

Designed by Paul Calle; photograph by David Rhinelander.

ROTARY PRESS PRINTING
E.E. Plates of 200 subjects in four panes of 50 each.

1974	Tagged	Perf. 10½x11	
1526 A929 10c **black**, *Mar. 26*		20	5
Margin block of 4, P#		1.00	—
Margin block of 4, Mr. Zip and "Use Zip Code"		90	—
Margin block of 6, "Mail Early in the Day"		1.30	—

EXPO '74 WORLD'S FAIR ISSUE

EXPO '74 World's Fair "Preserve the Environment," Spokane, Wash., May 4-Nov. 4.

"Cosmic Jumper"
and "Smiling
Sage" — A930

Designed by Peter Max.

PHOTOGRAVURE (Andreotti)
Plates of 160 subjects in four panes of 40 each.

1974	Tagged	Perf. 11	
1527 A930 10c **multicolored**, *Apr. 18*		20	5
Margin block of 12, 6 P#		2.60	—
Margin block of 4, Mr. Zip, "Use Zip Code" and "Mail Early in the Day"		90	—
Margin block of 16, 6 P#, Mr. Zip and slogans		3.50	—

HORSE RACING ISSUE

Centenary of the Kentucky Derby, Churchill Downs.

Horses Rounding
Turn — A931

Designed by Henry Koehler.

PHOTOGRAVURE (Andreotti)
Plates of 200 subjects in four panes of 50 each.

1974	Tagged	Perf. 11x10½	
1528 A931 10c **yellow & multicolored**, *May 4*		20	5
Margin block of 12, 6 P#		3.00	—
Margin block of 4, Mr. Zip and "Use Zip Code"		90	—

Margin block of 4, "Mail Early in
the Day" 90 —
a. Blue ("Horse Racing") omitted 1,750.
b. Red ("U.S. postage 10 cents") omitted

SKYLAB ISSUE

First anniversary of the launching of Skylab I,
honoring all who participated in the Skylab project.

Skylab — A932

Designed by Robert T. McCall.

LITHOGRAPHED, ENGRAVED (Giori)
Plates of 200 subjects in four panes of 50 each.

1974		Tagged	Perf. 11	
1529	A932 10c	**multicolored**, May 14	20	5
		Margin block of 4, P#	1.00	—
		Margin block of 4, Mr. Zip and "Use Zip Code"	90	—
		Margin block of 6, "Mail Early in the Day"	1.30	—
a.		Vert. pair, imperf. between		—

UNIVERSAL POSTAL UNION ISSUE

Centenary of Universal Postal Union. Nos. 1530-
1537 are arranged in blocks of 8 (4x2), four blocks
of a pane (8x4). In the first row Nos. 1530-1537 are
in sequence as listed. In the second row Nos. 1534-
1537 are followed by Nos. 1530-1533. Every row of
8 and every horizontal block of 8 contains all 8
designs. All four panes have this arrangement. The
letter writing designs are from famous works of art;
some are details. The quotation on every second
stamp, "Letters mingle souls," is from a letter by
poet John Donne.

Michelangelo, from
"School of Athens," by
Raphael, 1509 — A933

"Five Feminine
Virtues," by Hokusai, c.
1811 — A934

"Old Scraps," by John
Fredrick Peto,
1894 — A935

"The Lovely Reader,"
by Jean Etienne
Liotard, 1746 — A936

"Lady Writing Letter,"
by Gerard Terborch,
1654 — A937

Inkwell and Quill, from
"Boy with a Top," by
Jean-Baptiste Simeon
Chardin, 1738 — A938

Mrs. John Douglas, by
Thomas Gainsborough,
1784 — A939

Don Antonio Noriega,
by Francisco de Goya,
1801 — A940

Designed by Bradbury Thompson.

PHOTOGRAVURE (Andreotti)
Plates of 128 subjects in four panes of 32 each.

1974, June 6		Tagged	Perf. 11	
1530	A933 10c	**multicolored**	20	18
1531	A934 10c	**multicolored**	20	18
1532	A935 10c	**multicolored**	20	18
1533	A936 10c	**multicolored**	20	18
1534	A937 10c	**multicolored**	20	18
1535	A938 10c	**multicolored**	20	18
1536	A939 10c	**multicolored**	20	18
1537	A940 10c	**multicolored**	20	18
a.		Block or strip of 8 (#1530-1537)	1.60	2.00
b.		As "a," (block), imperf. vert.	6,000.	
		Margin block of 16, 5 P# adjoining #1530-1534, "Mail Early in the Day" adjoining #1535 and Mr. Zip and "Use Zip Code" adjoining #1537	4.00	—
		Margin block of 16, 5 P# adjoining #1533-1537, "Mail Early in the Day" adjoining #1532 and Mr. Zip and "Use Zip Code" adjoining #1530	4.00	—
		Margin block of 16, 5 P# adjoining #1534-1537, 1530, "Mail Early in the Day" adjoining #1531 and Mr. Zip and "Use Zip Code" adjoining #1533	4.00	—
		Margin block of 16, 5 P# adjoining #1537, 1530-1533, "Mail Early in the Day" adjoining #1536 and Mr. Zip and "Use Zip Code" adjoining #1534	4.00	—
		Margin block of 10, 5 P# as above; no slogans	2.60	—

MINERAL HERITAGE ISSUE

Panes contain 12 blocks of 4 (3x4). The
sequence of stamps in first horizontal row is Nos.
1538-1541, 1538-1539. In second row Nos. 1540-
1541 are followed by Nos. 1538-1541. All four
panes have this arrangement.

Petrified
Wood
A941

Tourmaline
A942

Amethyst
A943

Rhodochrosite — A944

Designed by Leonard F. Buckley.

LITHOGRAPHED, ENGRAVED (Giori)
Plates of 192 subjects in four panes of 48 (6x8).

1974, June 13		Tagged	Perf. 11	
1538	A941 10c	**blue & multicolored**	20	10
		Margin block of 4, P# adjoining #1538	1.35	—
		Margin block of 4, Mr. Zip and "Use Zip Code" adjoining #1538	90	—
		Margin block of 6, "Mail Early in the Day" adjoining #1538	1.30	—
a.		Light blue & yellow omitted		
1539	A942 10c	**blue & multicolored**	20	10
		Margin block of 4, P# adjoining #1539	1.35	—
		Margin block of 4, Mr. Zip and "Use Zip Code" adjoining #1539	90	—
		Margin block of 6, "Mail Early in the Day" adjoining #1539	1.30	
a.		Light blue omitted		
b.		Black & purple omitted		—
1540	A943 10c	**blue & multicolored**	20	10
		Margin block of 4, P# adjoining #1540	1.35	—
		Margin block of 4, Mr. Zip and "Use Zip Code" adjoining #1540	90	—
		Margin block of 6, "Mail Early in the Day" adjoining #1540	1.30	—
a.		Light blue & yellow omitted		
1541	A944 10c	**blue & multicolored**	20	10

	Margin block of 4, P# adjoining #1541	1.35	—
	Margin block of 4, Mr. Zip and "Use Zip Code" adjoining #1541	90	—
	Margin block of 6, "Mail Early in the Day" adjoining #1541	1.30	—
a.	Block or strip of 4, #1538-1541	80	80
b.	As "a," lt. blue & yellow omitted	2,000.	
c.	Light blue omitted	—	
d.	Black & red omitted	—	

KENTUCKY SETTLEMENT ISSUE

Bicentenary of Fort Harrod, first settlement in Kentucky.

Covered Wagons at Fort Harrod — A945

Designed by David K. Stone.

LITHOGRAPHED, ENGRAVED (Giori)
Plates of 200 subjects in four panes of 50 each.

1974	**Tagged**	**Perf. 11**	
1542 A945	10c **green & multicolored**, June 15	20	5
	Margin block of 4, P#	1.10	—
	Margin block of 4, Mr. Zip and "Use Zip Code"	90	—
	Margin block of 6, "Mail Early in the Day"	1.30	—
a.	Dull black (litho.) omitted	1,250.	
b.	Green (engr. & litho.), black (engr. & litho.) & blue omitted	3,000.	

AMERICAN REVOLUTION BICENTENNIAL ISSUE

First Continental Congress

Nos. 1543-1546 are printed in blocks of four in panes of 50. Nos. 1543-1544 alternate in first row, Nos. 1545-1546 in second row. This arrangement is repeated throughout the pane.

Carpenters' Hall, Philadelphia A946

"We ask but for peace . . ." A947

"Deriving their just powers . . ." A948

Independence Hall — A949

Designed by Frank P. Conley

GIORI PRESS PRINTING
Plates of 200 subjects in four panes of 50 each.

1974, July 4	**Tagged**	**Perf. 11**	
1543 A946	10c **dark blue & red**	20	10
	Margin block of 4, P# adjoining #1543	1.20	—
	Margin block of 4, Mr. Zip and "Use Zip Code" adjoining #1543	1.15	—
	Margin block of 6, "Mail Early in the Day" adjoining #1543	1.55	—
	Margin block of 6, Bicentennial Emblem and "USA Bicentennial Era" adjoining #1543	1.55	—
1544 A947	10c **gray, dark blue & red**	20	10
	Margin block of 4, P# adjoining #1544	1.20	—
	Margin block of 4, Mr. Zip and "Use Zip Code" adjoining #1544	1.15	—
	Margin block of 6, "Mail Early in the Day" adjoining #1544	1.55	—
	Margin block of 6, Bicentennial Emblem and "USA Bicentennial Era" adjoining #1544	1.55	—
1545 A948	10c **gray, dark blue & red**	20	10
	Margin block of 4, P# adjoining #1545	1.20	—
	Margin block of 4, Mr. Zip and "Use Zip Code" adjoining #1545	1.15	—
	Margin block of 6, "Mail Early in the Day" adjoining #1545	1.55	—
	Margin block of 6, Bicentennial Emblem and "USA Bicentennial Era" adjoining #1545	1.55	—
1546 A949	10c **red & dark blue**	20	10
	Margin block of 4, P# adjoining #1546	1.20	—
	Margin block of 4, Mr. Zip and "Use Zip Code" adjoining #1546	1.15	—
	Margin block of 6, "Mail Early in the Day" adjoining #1546	1.55	—
	Margin block of 6, Bicentennial Emblem and "USA Bicentennial Era" adjoining #1546	1.55	—
a.	Block of four, #1543-1546	1.10	80

ENERGY CONSERVATION ISSUE

Publicizing the importance of conserving all forms of energy.

Molecules and Drops of Gasoline and Oil — A950

Designed by Robert W. Bode.

LITHOGRAPHED, ENGRAVED (Giori)
Plates of 200 subjects in four panes of 50 each.

1974	**Tagged**	**Perf. 11**	
1547 A950	10c **multicolored**, Sept. 23	20	5
	Margin block of 4, P#	1.00	—
	Margin block of 4, Mr. Zip and "Use Zip Code"	90	—
	Margin block of 6, "Mail Early in the Day"	1.30	—
a.	Blue & orange omitted	800.00	
b.	Orange & green omitted	700.00	
c.	Green omitted	800.00	

AMERICAN FOLKLORE ISSUE

Legend of Sleepy Hollow

The Headless Horseman in pursuit of Ichabod Crane from "Legend of Sleepy Hollow," by Washington Irving.

Headless Horseman and Ichabod — A951

Designed by Leonard Everett Fisher.

LITHOGRAPHED, ENGRAVED (Giori)
Plates of 200 subjects in four panes of 50 each.

1974	**Tagged**	**Perf. 11**	
1548 A951	10c **dk. bl., blk., org. & yel.**, Oct. 10	20	5
	Margin block of 4, P#	1.00	—

	Margin block of 4, Mr. Zip and "Use Zip Code"	90	—
	Margin block of 6, "Mail Early in the Day"	1.30	—

RETARDED CHILDREN ISSUE

Retarded Children Can Be Helped, theme of annual convention of the National Association of Retarded Citizens.

Retarded Child — A952

Designed by Paul Calle.

GIORI PRESS PRINTING
Plates of 200 subjects in four panes of 50 each.

1974	**Tagged**	**Perf. 11**	
1549 A952	10c **brown red & dark brown**, Oct. 12	20	5
	Margin block of 4, P#	1.00	—
	Margin block of 4, Mr. Zip and "Use Zip Code"	90	—
	Margin block of 6, "Mail Early in the Day"	1.30	—

CHRISTMAS ISSUE

Angel — A953

"The Road-Winter," by Currier and Ives — A954

Dove Weather Vane atop Mount Vernon — A955

Designers: No. 1550, Bradbury Thompson, using detail from the Perussis altarpiece painted by anonymous French artist, 1480, in Metropolitan Museum of Art, New York City. No. 1551, Stevan Dohanos, using Currier and Ives print from drawing by Otto Knirsch. No. 1552, Don Hedin and Robert Geissman.

PHOTOGRAVURE (Andreotti)
Plates of 200 subjects in four panes of 50 each.

1974, Oct. 23	**Tagged**	**Perf. 10½x11**	
1550 A953	10c **multicolored**	20	5
	Margin block of 10, 5 P#	2.25	—
	Margin block of 4, Mr. Zip and "Use Zip Code"	90	—
	Margin block of 6, "Mail Early in the Day"	1.30	—
	Perf. 11x10½		
1551 A954	10c **multicolored**	20	5
	Margin block of 12, P#	2.60	—
	Margin block of 4, Mr. Zip and "Use Zip Code"	90	—
	Margin block of 4, "Mail Early in the Day"	90	—

Imperf., Paper Backing Rouletted

1974, Nov. 15   **Untagged**

Self-adhesive; Inscribed "Precanceled"

1552 A955 10c **multicolored**   20   8
  Margin block of 20, 6 P# and 5 slo-
    gans   5.50
  Margin block of 12, 6 P# and 5 dif-
    ferent slogans   3.25

Unused price of No. 1552 is for copy on rouletted paper backing as issued. Used price is for copy on piece, with or without postmark. Most copies are becoming discolored, probably from the adhesive. The Catalogue value is for discolored copies.

Die cutting includes crossed slashes through dove, applied to prevent removal and re-use of the stamp. The stamp will separate into layers if soaked.

Two different machines were used to roulette the sheet.

AMERICAN ARTS ISSUE

Benjamin West (1738-1820), painter (No. 1553); Paul Laurence Dunbar (1872-1906), poet (No. 1554); David (Lewelyn) Wark Griffith (1875-1948), motion picture producer (No. 1555).

American artist
10 cents U.S. postage
Self-portrait — A956

A957

A958

Designed by Bradbury Thompson (No. 1553); Walter D. Richards (No. 1554); Fred Otnes (No. 1555).

PHOTOGRAVURE (Andreotti)
Plates of 200 subjects in four panes of 50 each.

1975   **Tagged**   ***Perf. 10½x11***

1553 A956 10c **multicolored,** *Feb. 10*   20   5
  Margin block of 10, 5 P#   2.50 —
  Margin block of 4, Mr. Zip
    and "Use Zip Code"   90 —
  Margin block of 6, "Mail Ear-
    ly in the Day"   1.30 —

    Perf. 11

1554 A957 10c **multicolored,** *May 1*   20   5
  Margin block of 10, 5 P#   2.50 —
  Margin block of 4, Mr. Zip
    and "Use Zip Code"   90 —
  Margin block of 6, "Mail Ear-
    ly in the Day"   1.30 —
  a. Imperf., pair   1,250.

LITHOGRAPHED, ENGRAVED (Giori)
    Perf. 11

1555 A958A 10c **brown & multicolored,** *May 27*   20   5
  Margin block of 4, P#   1.00 —
  Margin block of 4, Mr. Zip
    and "Use Zip Code"   90 —
  Margin block of 6, "Mail Ear-
    ly in the Day"   1.30 —
  a. Brown (engraved) omitted   900.00

SPACE ISSUES

U.S. space accomplishments with unmanned craft. Pioneer 10 passed with 81,000 miles of Jupiter, Dec. 10, 1973. Mariner 10 explored Venus and Mercury in 1974 and Mercury again in 1975.

Pioneer 10
Passing
Jupiter — A959

Mariner 10, Venus and Mercury — A960

Designed by Robert McCall (No. 1556); Roy Gjertson (No. 1557).

LITHOGRAPHED, ENGRAVED (Giori)
Plates of 200 subjects in four panes of 50 each.

1975   **Tagged**   ***Perf. 11***

1556 A959 10c **violet blue, yellow & red,** *Feb. 28*   20   5
  Margin block of 4, P#   1.00 —
  Margin block of 4, Mr. Zip and
    "Use Zip Code"   90 —
  Margin block of 6, "Mail Early in
    the Day"   1.30 —
  a. Red & yellow (litho.) omitted   1,250.
  b. Blue omitted   1,250.
1557 A960 10c **black, red, ultra. & bister,** *Apr. 4*   20   5
  Margin block of 4, P#   1.00 —
  Margin block of 4, Mr. Zip and
    "Use Zip Code"   90 —
  Margin block of 6, "Mail Early in
    the Day"   1.30 —
  a. Red omitted   750.00
  b. Ultra. & bister omitted   2,250.

COLLECTIVE BARGAINING ISSUE

Collective Bargaining law, enacted 1935, in Wagner Act.

"Labor and Management" A961

Designed by Robert Hallock.

PHOTOGRAVURE (Andreotti)
Plates of 200 subjects in four panes of 50 each.

1975   **Tagged**   ***Perf. 11***

1558 A961 10c **multicolored,** *March 13*   20   5
  Margin block of 8, 4 P#   1.80 —
  Margin block of 4, Mr. Zip and
    "Use Zip Code"   90 —
  Margin block of 6, "Mail Early in
    the Day"   1.30 —

Imperfs exist from printer's waste.

AMERICAN BICENTENNIAL ISSUE
Contributors to the Cause

Sybil Ludington, age 16, rallied militia, Apr. 26, 1777; Salem Poor, black freeman, fought in Battle of Bunker Hill; Haym Salomon, Jewish immigrant, raised money to finance Revolutionary War; Peter Francisco, Portuguese-French immigrant, joined Continental Army at 15. Emerald inscription on back, printed beneath gum in water-soluble ink, gives thumbnail sketch of portrayed contributor.

Sybil Ludington A962

Salem Poor — A963

Haym Salomon — A964

Peter Francisco — A965

Peter Francisco   *Fighter Extraordinary*

Designed by Neil Boyle.

PHOTOGRAVURE (Andreotti)
Plates of 200 subjects in four panes of 50 each.

1975, Mar. 25   **Tagged**   ***Perf. 11x10½***

1559 A962 8c **multicolored**   16   13
  Margin block of 10, 5 P#   2.00 —
  Margin block of 4, Mr. Zip and
    "Use Zip Code"   70 —
  Margin block of 6, "Mail Early in
    the Day"   1.10 —
  a. Back inscriptions omitted   350.00
1560 A963 10c **multicolored**   20   5
  Margin block of 10, 5 P#   2.50 —
  Margin block of 4, Mr. Zip and
    "Use Zip Code"   90 —
  Margin block of 6, "Mail Early in
    the Day"   1.30 —
  a. Back inscription omitted   350.00
1561 A964 10c **multicolored**   20   5
  Margin block of 10, 5 P#   2.50 —
  Margin block of 4, Mr. Zip and
    "Use Zip Code"   90 —
  Margin block of 6, "Mail Early in
    the Day"   1.30 —
  a. Back inscription omitted   350.00
  b. Red omitted   325.00
1562 A965 18c **multicolored**   36   20
  Margin block of 10, 5 P#   5.00 —
  Margin block of 4, Mr. Zip and
    "Use Zip Code"   1.65 —
  Margin block of 6, "Mail Early in
    the Day"   2.40 —

Lexington-Concord Battle

Bicentenary of the Battle of Lexington and Concord.

"Birth of Liberty," by Henry Sandham — A966

Designed by Bradbury Thompson.

PHOTOGRAVURE (Andreotti)
Plates of 160 subjects in four panes of 40 each.

1975   **Tagged**   ***Perf. 11***

1563 A966 10c **multicolored,** *Apr. 19*   20   5
  Margin block of 12, 6 P#   2.60 —
  Margin block of 4, Mr. Zip, "Use
    Zip Code" and "Mail Early in
    the Day"   90 —
  Margin block of 16, 6 P#, Mr.
    Zip and slogans   3.50 —
  a. Vert. pair, imperf. horiz.   500.00

Bunker Hill Battle

Bicentenary of the Battle of Bunker Hill.

Battle of Bunker Hill, by John Trumbull — A967

Designed by Bradbury Thompson.

PHOTOGRAVURE (Andreotti)
Plates of 160 subjects in four panes of 40 each.

1975   **Tagged**   ***Perf. 11***

1564 A967 10c **multicolored,** *June 17*   20   5
  Margin block of 12, 6 P#   2.60 —

Margin block of 4, Mr. Zip, "Use Zip Code" and "Mail Early in the Day"   90 —
Margin block of 16, 6 P#, Mr. Zip and slogans   3.50 —

Military Uniforms

Bicentenary of U.S. Military Services. Nos. 1565-1568 are printed in blocks of four in panes of 50. Nos. 1565-1566 alternate in one row, Nos. 1567-1568 in next row.

Soldier with Flintlock Musket, Uniform Button — A968

Sailor with Grappling Hook, First Navy Jack, 1775 — A969

Marine with Musket, Fullrigged Ship — A970

Militaman with Musket and Powder Horn — A971

Designed by Edward Vebell.

PHOTOGRAVURE (Andreotti)

Plates of 200 subjects in four panes of 50 each.

1975, July 4	Tagged	Perf. 11	
1565 A968 10c **multicolored**		20	8
Margin block of 12, 6 P# adjoining Nos. 1565-1566	3.50	—	
Margin block of 20, 6 P# adjoining Nos. 1565-1566, Mr. Zip and slogans	5.75	—	
Margin block of 4, Mr. Zip and "Use Zip Code" adjoining No. 1565	1.10	—	
Margin block of 4, "Mail Early in the Day" adjoining No. 1565	1.10	—	
1566 A969 10c **multicolored**		20	8
Margin block of 4, Mr. Zip and "Use Zip Code" adjoining No. 1566	1.10	—	
Margin block of 4, "Mail Early in the Day" adjoining No. 1566	1.10	—	
1567 A970 10c **multicolored**		20	8
Margin block of 12, 6 P# adjoining Nos. 1567-1568	3.50	—	
Margin block of 20, 6 P# adjoining Nos. 1567-1568, Mr. Zip and slogans	5.75	—	
Margin block of 4, Mr. Zip and "Use Zip Code" adjoining No. 1567	1.10	—	
Margin block of 4, "Mail Early in the Day" adjoining No. 1567	1.10	—	
1568 A971 10c **multicolored**		20	8
Margin block of 4, Mr. Zip and "Use Zip Code" adjoining No. 1568	1.10	—	
Margin block of 4, "Mail Early in the Day" adjoining No. 1568	1.10	—	
a. Block of 4, #1565-1568	1.05	80	

APOLLO SOYUZ SPACE ISSUE

Apollo Soyuz space test project, Russo-American cooperation, launched July 15; link-up, July 17. Nos. 1569-1570 are printed se-tenant in horizontal rows of 3 in panes of 24. In the first row of the pane No. 1569 is in first and third space, No. 1570 is second space; in the second row No. 1570 is in first and third space, No. 1569 in second space, etc. Participating U.S. and U.S.S.R. crews: Thomas P. Stafford, Donald K. Slayton, Vance D. Brand, Aleksei A. Leonov, Valery N. Kubasov.
See Russia Nos. 4339-4340.

Apollo and Soyuz after Link-up, and Earth — A972

Spacecraft before Link-up, Earth and Project Emblem — A973

Designed by Robert McCall (No. 1569) and Anatoly M. Aksamit of USSR (No. 1570).

PHOTOGRAVURE (Andreotti)

Plates of 96 subjects in four panes of 24 each.

1975, July 15	Tagged	Perf. 11	
1569 A972 10c **multicolored**		20	10
a. Pair, #1569-1570	40	25	
Margin block of 12, 6 P#	2.60	—	
Margin block of 4, Mr. Zip, "Use Zip Code" adjoining No. 1569; "Mail Early in the Day" adjoining No. 1570	90	—	
Margin block of 16, 6 P#, Mr. Zip "Use Zip Code" adjoining No. 1569, "Mail Early in the Day" adjoining No. 1570	3.50	—	
b. As "a," vert. pair imperf. horiz.	1,000.		
Pair with full horiz. gutter btwn.	—		
1570 A973 10c **multicolored**		20	10
Margin block of 4, Mr. Zip, "Use Zip Code" adjoining No. 1570; "Mail Early in the Day" adjoining No. 1569	90	—	
Margin block of 16, 6 P#, Mr. Zip, "Use Zip Code" adjoining No. 1570, "Mail Early in the Day" adjoining No. 1569	3.50	—	

INTERNATIONAL WOMEN'S YEAR ISSUE

International Women's Year 1975.

Worldwide Equality for Women — A974

Designed by Miriam Schottland.

PHOTOGRAVURE (Andreotti)

Plates of 200 subjects in four panes of 50 each.

1975	Tagged	Perf. 11x10½	
1571 A974 10c **blue, orange & dark blue,** Aug. 26		20	5
Margin block of 6, 3 P#	1.40	—	
Margin block of 4, Mr. Zip and "Use Zip Code"	90	—	
Margin block of 4, "Mail Early in the Day"	1.30	—	

U.S. POSTAL SERVICE BICENTENNIAL ISSUE

Nos. 1572-1575 are printed in blocks of four in panes of 50. Nos. 1572-1573 alternate in first row, Nos. 1574-1575 in second row. This arrangement is repeated throughout the pane.

Stagecoach and Trailer Truck — A975

Old and New Locomotives A976

Early Mail Plane and Jet — A977

Satellite for Transmission of Mailgrams A978

Designed by James L. Womer.

PHOTOGRAVURE (Andreotti)

Plates of 200 subjects in four panes of 50 each.

1975, Sept. 3	Tagged	Perf. 11x10½	
1572 A975 10c **multicolored**		20	8
Margin block of 12, 6 P# adjoining Nos. 1572, 1574	2.60	—	
Margin block of 20, 6 P# adjoining Nos. 1572, 1574, Mr. Zip and slogans	4.80	—	
Margin block of 4, Mr. Zip and "Use Zip Code" adjoining No. 1572	1.10	—	
Margin block of 4, "Mail Early in the Day" adjoining No. 1572	1.10	—	
1573 A976 10c **multicolored**		20	8
Margin block of 12, 6 P# adjoining Nos. 1573, 1575	2.60	—	
Margin block of 20, 6 P# adjoining Nos. 1573, 1575, Mr. Zip and slogans	4.80	—	
Margin block of 4, Mr. Zip and "Use Zip Code" adjoining No. 1573	1.10	—	
Margin block of 4, "Mail Early in the Day" adjoining No. 1573	1.10	—	
1574 A977 10c **multicolored**		20	8
Margin block of 4, Mr. Zip and "Use Zip Code" adjoining No. 1574	1.10	—	
Margin block of 4, "Mail Early in the Day" adjoining No. 1574	1.10	—	
1575 A978 10c **multicolored**		20	8
Margin block of 4, Mr. Zip and "Use Zip Code" adjoining No. 1575	1.10	—	
Margin block of 4, "Mail Early in the Day" adjoining No. 1575	1.10	—	
a. Block of 4, #1572-1575	1.00	80	
b. As "a," red "10c" omitted	—		

WORLD PEACE THROUGH LAW ISSUE

A prelude to 7th World Law Conference of the World Peace Through Law Center at Washington, D.C., Oct. 12-17.

Law Book, Gavel, Olive Branch and Globe — A979

Designed by Melbourne Brindle.

GIORI PRESS PRINTING

Plates of 200 subjects in four panes of 50 each.

1975	Tagged	Perf. 11	
1576 A979 10c **green, Prussian blue & rose brown,** Sept. 29		20	5
Margin block of 4, P#	1.00	—	
Margin block of 4, Mr. Zip and "Use Zip Code"	90	—	
Margin block of 6, "Mail Early in the Day"	1.30	—	

BANKING AND COMMERCE ISSUE

Banking and commerce in the U.S., and for the Centennial Convention of the American Bankers Association.

Engine Turning, Indian Head Penny, Morgan-type Silver Dollar — A980

Seated Liberty Quarter, $20 Gold Double Eagle and Engine Turning — A981

LITHOGRAPHED, ENGRAVED (Giori)
Plates of 160 subjects in four panes of 40 each.

1975, Oct. 6   **Perf. 11**

1577 A980 10c **multicolored**		20	8
a.	Pair, #1577-1578	40	20
b.	Brown & blue (litho) omitted	1,000.	
	Margin block of 4, P# adjoining #1577	1.00	—
	Margin block of 4, Mr. Zip and "Use Zip Code" adjoining #1577	90	—
	Margin block of 6, "Mail Early in the Day" adjoining #1577	1.30	—
1578 A981 10c **multicolored**		20	8
	Margin block of 4, P# adjoining #1578	1.00	—
	Margin block of 4, Mr. Zip and "Use Zip Code" adjoining #1578	90	—
	Margin block of 6, "Mail Early in the Day" adjoining #1578	1.30	—

CHRISTMAS ISSUE

Madonna and Child, by Domenico Ghirlandaio A982

Christmas Card, by Louis Prang, 1878 A983

Designed by Steven Dohanos.

PHOTOGRAVURE (Andreotti)
Plates of 200 subjects in four panes of 50 each.

1975, Oct. 14   **Tagged**   **Perf. 11**

1579 A982 (10c) **multicolored**		20	5
	Margin block of 12, 6 P#	2.60	—
	Margin block of 4, Mr. Zip and "Use Zip Code"	90	—
	Margin block of 4, "Mail Early in the Day"	90	—
a.	Imperf., pair	125.00	
	Plate flaw ("d" damaged) (36741-36746 LL 47)	5.00	—
1580 A983 (10c) **multicolored**		20	5
	Margin block of 12, 6 P#	2.60	—
	Margin block of 4, Mr. Zip and "Use Zip Code"	90	—
	Margin block of 4, "Mail Early in the Day"	90	—
a.	Imperf., pair	125.00	
b.	Perf. 10½x11	50	5
b.	Margin block of 12, 6P#	12.00	—

AMERICANA ISSUE

Inkwell and Quill — A984

Early Ballot Box A987

Dome of Capitol — A994

Early American Printing Press — A996

Liberty Bell — A998

Fort McHenry Flag (15 Stars) — A1001

Old North Church, Boston — A1006

Speaker's Stand — A985

Books, Bookmark, Eyeglasses A988

Contemplation of Justice, by J. E. Fraser — A995

Torch, Statue of Liberty — A997

Eagle and Shield — A999

Head, Statue of Liberty — A1002

Fort Nisqually, Wash. — A1007

Sandy Hook Lighthouse, N.J. — A1008

Iron "Betty" Lamp, Plymouth Colony, 17th-18th Centuries A1011

Kerosene Table Lamp — A1013a

Morris Township School No. 2, Devils Lake — A1009

Rush Lamp and Candle Holder A1013

Railroad Conductor's Lantern, c. 1850 — A1014

ROTARY PRESS PRINTING
E.E. Plates of 400 subjects in four panes of 100 each.

1975-81   **Tagged**   **Perf. 11x10½**

Size: 18½x22½mm.

1581 A984 1c **dark blue**, *greenish, Dec. 8, 1977*		5	5
	Margin block of 4, P#	25	—
	Margin block of 4, "Use Zip Code"	22	—
	Margin block of 6, "Mail Early in the Day"	32	—
	Dull finish gum	5	
	Pair with full vert. gutter btwn.		
a.	Untagged (Bureau precanceled)		5
1582 A985 2c **red brown**, *greenish, Dec. 8, 1977*		5	5
	Margin block of 4, P#	25	—
	Margin block of 4, "Use Zip Code"	22	—
	Margin block of 6, "Mail Early in the Day"	32	—
	Dull finish gum	10	
a.	Untagged (Bureau precanceled)		6
b.	Cream paper, dull finish gum, *1981*	5	5
1584 A987 3c **olive**, *greenish, Dec. 8, 1977*		6	5
	Margin block of 4, P#	30	—
	Margin block of 4, "Use Zip Code"	28	—
	Margin block of 6, "Mail Early in the Day"	38	—
	Dull finish gum	6	
a.	Untagged (Bureau precanceled)		6
1585 A988 4c **rose magenta**, *cream, Dec. 8, 1977*		8	5
	Margin block of 4, P#	40	—
	Margin block of 4, "Use Zip Code"	35	—
	Margin block of 6, "Mail Early in the Day"	50	—
	Dull finish gum	16	
a.	Untagged (Bureau precanceled)		8

Size: 17½x20½mm.

1590 A994 9c **slate green** (from bklt. pane), *Mar. 11, 1977*		1.00	20
a.	Perf. 10 (from bklt. pane)	27.50	6.00

Size: 18½x22½mm.

1591 A994 9c **slate green**, *gray, Nov. 24, 1975*		18	5
	Margin block of 4, P#	90	—
	Margin block of 4, "Use Zip Code"	80	—
	Margin block of 6, "Mail Early in the Day"	1.20	—
	Dull finish gum	18	
a.	Untagged (Bureau precanceled)		18
1592 A995 10c **violet**, *gray, Nov. 17, 1977*		20	5
	Margin block of 4, P#	1.00	—
	Margin block of 4, "Use Zip Code"	90	—
	Margin block of 6, "Mail Early in the Day"	1.50	—
	Dull finish gum	25	
a.	Untagged (Bureau precanceled)		25
1593 A996 11c **orange**, *gray, Nov. 13, 1975*		22	5

	Margin block of 4, P#	1.10	
	Margin block of 4, "Use Zip Code"	1.00	
	Margin block of 6, "Mail Early in the Day"	1.50	
1594 A997	12c **red brown**, *beige, Apr. 8, 1981*	24	5
	P# block of 4	1.20	
	Zip block of 4	1.10	
	Mail Early block of 6	1.60	
1595 A998	13c **brown** (from bklt. pane), *Oct. 31, 1975*	26	5
a.	Booklet pane of 6	1.60	50
b.	Booklet pane of 7 + label	1.85	50
c.	Booklet pane of 8	2.10	50
d.	Booklet pane of 5 + label, *Apr. 2, 1976*	1.30	50
e.	Vert. pair, imperf. btwn.		

PHOTOGRAVURE (Andreotti)
Plates of 400 subjects in four panes of 100 each.

Perf. 11

1596 A999	13c **multicolored**, *Dec. 1, 1975*	26	5
	Margin block of 12, 6 P#	3.40	—
	Margin block of 20, 6 P# and slogans	5.75	—
	Margin block of 4, "Use Zip Code"	1.10	—
	Margin block of 4, "Mail Early in the Day"	1.10	—
a.	Imperf., pair	40.00	—
b.	Yellow omitted	200.00	—
	Line perforated		
	Pair with full horiz. gutter btwn.		

No. 1596 perforation measures close to 11¼. The entire sheet is perforated at one time so the perforations meet perfectly at the corners of the stamp. The line perforations do not line up perfectly and are perf. 11.

ENGRAVED (Combination Press)
Plates of 460 subjects (20x23) in panes of 100 (10x10)

1597 A1001	15c **gray, dark blue & red**, *June 30, 1978*	30	5
	Margin block of 6, P#	2.10	—
	Margin block of 20, 1 or 2 P#	10.00	—
a.	Imperf., vert. pair	20.00	
b.	Gray omitted		

Plate number appears 3 times on each plate of 23 rows. With no separating gutters, each pane has only left or right sheet margin. Plate numbers appear on both margins; there are no slogans. Margin blocks of 20 have one or two plate numbers.

ENGRAVED
Perf. 11x10½

1598 A1001	15c **gray, dark blue & red** (from bklt. pane), *June 30, 1978*	30	5
a.	Booklet pane of 8	4.25	60
1599 A1002	16c **blue**, *Mar. 31, 1978*	35	5
	Margin block of 4, P#	2.25	—
	Margin block of 4, "Use Correct Zip Code"	1.45	—
	Margin block of 4, copyright	1.45	—
1603 A1006	24c **red**, *blue, Nov. 14, 1975*	60	9
	Margin block of 4, P#	3.00	—
	Margin block of 4, "Use Zip Code"	2.60	—
	Margin block of 6, "Mail Early in the Day"	3.75	—
1604 A1007	28c **brown**, *blue, Aug. 11, 1978*	70	8
	Margin block of 4, P#	3.75	—
	Margin block of 4, "Use Correct Zip Code"	3.00	—
	Margin block of 4, copyright	3.00	—
	Dull finish gum	1.25	
1605 A1008	29c **blue**, *light blue, Apr. 14, 1978*	70	8
	Margin block of 4, P#	3.75	—
	Margin block of 4, "Use Correct Zip Code"	3.00	—
	Margin block of 4, copyright	3.00	—
	Dull finish gum	3.50	
1606 A1009	30c **green**, *blue, Aug. 27, 1979*	75	8
	Margin block of 4, P#	4.00	—
	Margin block of 4, "Use Correct Zip Code"	3.25	—
	Margin block of 4, "United States Postal Service 1979"	3.25	—

Perf. 11
LITHOGRAPHED AND ENGRAVED

1608 A1011	50c **tan, black & orange**, *Sept. 11, 1979*	1.00	25
	Margin block of 4, P#	5.00	—
	Margin block of 4, "Use Correct Zip Code"	4.50	—
	Margin block of 4, "United States Postal Service 1979"	4.50	—
a.	Black omitted		
1610 A1013	$1 **tan, brown, orange & yellow**, *July 2, 1979*	2.00	25
	Margin block of 4, P#	10.00	—
	Margin block of 4, "Use Correct Zip Code"	9.00	—
	Margin block of 4, "United States Postal Service 1979"	9.00	—
a.	Brown (engraved) omitted	600.00	
b.	Tan, orange & yellow omitted	400.00	
c.	Brown inverted		
1611 A1013a	$2 **tan, dark green, orange & yellow**, *Nov. 16, 1978*	4.50	50
	Margin block of 4, P#	22.50	—
	Margin block of 4, "Use Correct Zip Code"	19.00	—
	Margin block of 4, "United States Postal Service 1978"	19.00	—

1612 A1014	$5 **tan, red brown, yellow & orange**, *Aug. 23, 1979*	10.00	2.00
	Margin block of 4, P#	50.00	
	Margin block of 4, "Use Correct Zip Code"	45.00	
	Margin block of 4, "United States Postal Service 1979"	45.00	

Nos. 1590, 1590a, 1595, 1598, 1623 and 1623b were issued only in booklets. All stamps have one or two straight edges.

Six-string Guitar A1014a

Drum — A1016

Saxhorns A1015

Steinway Grand Piano, 1857 — A1017

Designers: 3.1c, George Mercer. 7.7c, Susan Robb. 7.9c, Bernard Glassman. 10c, Walter Brooks. 15c, V. Jack Ruther.

COIL STAMPS

1975-79		Perf. 10 Vertically	
1613 A1014a	3.1c **brown**, *yellow, Oct. 25, 1979*	20	10
	Pair	40	20
	Joint line pair	1.75	—
a.	Untagged (Bureau precanceled)		10
b.	Imperf., pair	950.00	
1614 A1015	7.7c **brown**, *bright yellow, Nov. 20, 1976*	20	8
	Pair	40	16
	Joint line pair	1.00	—
a.	Untagged (Bureau precanceled)		16
b.	As "a," imperf., pair	575.00	

A total of 159 different Bureau precancels were used by 153 cities.

1615 A1016	7.9c **carmine**, *yellow, Apr. 23, 1976*	20	8
	Pair	40	16
	Joint line pair	1.10	—
	Dull finish gum	20	
a.	Untagged (Bureau precanceled)		16
b.	Imperf., pair	500.00	

A total of 108 different Bureau precancels were used by 107 cities.

1615C A1017	8.4c **dark blue**, *yellow, July 13, 1978*	25	8
	Pair	50	16
	Joint line pair	2.00	30
d.	Untagged (Bureau precanceled)		16
e.	As "d," pair, imperf. between	50.00	
f.	As "d," imperf., pair	17.50	

A total of 145 different Bureau precancels were used by 144 cities.

1616 A994	9c **slate green**, *gray, Mar. 5, 1976*	22	5
	Pair	44	10
	Joint line pair	90	20
a.	Imperf., pair	100.00	
b.	Untagged (Bureau precanceled)		18
c.	As "b," imperf., pair	150.00	
1617 A995	10c **violet**, *gray, Nov. 4, 1977*	20	5
	Pair	40	10
	Joint line pair	1.25	—
	Dull finish gum	20	
a.	Untagged (Bureau precanceled)		25
b.	Imperf., pair	65.00	
1618 A998	13c **brown**, *Nov. 25, 1975*	26	5
	Pair	52	10
	Joint line pair	1.00	25
a.	Untagged (Bureau precanceled)		25
b.	Imperf., pair	25.00	
1618C A1001	15c **gray, dark blue & red**, *June 30, 1978*	40	5
	Pair	80	10
d.	Imperf., pair	20.00	
e.	Pair, imperf. between	200.00	
f.	gray omitted	65.00	
1619 A1002	16c **ultramarine**, *Mar. 31, 1978*	32	5
	Pair	65	10
	Joint line pair	1.50	—
	Huck press printing	65	10
	Huck press, pair	1.30	25

No. 1619 was printed on two different presses. Huck press printings have white background without bluish tinge, are a fraction of a millimeter smaller and have block instead of overall tagging. Cottrell press printings show a joint line.
See Nos. 1811, 1813, 1816.

13-Star Flag over Independence Hall A1018

Flag over Capitol A1018a

Designers: No. 1622, Melbourne Brindle. No. 1623, Esther Porter.

Panes of 100 (10x10) each.

1975-81		Perf. 11x10½	
1622 A1018	13c **dark blue & red**, *Nov. 15, 1975*	26	5
	Margin block of 20, 2-3 P#, 2-3 Zip, 2-3 Mail Early	5.50	—
a.	Horiz. pair, imperf. between	60.00	
b.	Vert. pair, imperf.		
c.	Perf. 11, *1981*	30	5
c.	Margin block of 20, 1-2 P#, 1-2 Zip	6.30	—
c.	Margin block of 6, P#	1.85	—

No. 1622 was printed on the Multicolored Huck Press. Plate markings are at top or bottom of pane. See note after No. 1338F for marginal markings.

No. 1622c was printed on the Combination Press. Plate markings are at sides of pane. See note after No. 1703.

	Engr.		
1623 A1018a	13c **blue & red** (from bklt. pane), *Mar. 11, 1977*	26	5
a.	Booklet pane of 8 (1 #1590 + 7 #1623)	3.10	60
b.	Perf. 10 (from bklt. pane)	1.50	1.00
c.	Booklet pane of 8, perf. 10 (1 #1590a + 7 #1623b)	40.00	—
d.	Se-tenant pair, #1590 & #1623	1.50	—
e.	Se-tenant pair, #1590a & #1623b	30.00	

COIL STAMP

1975, Nov. 15		Perf. 10 Vertically	
1625 A1018	13c **dark blue & red**	30	5
	Pair	60	10
a.	Imperf., pair	20.00	

AMERICAN BICENTENNIAL ISSUE
The Spirit of '76

Designed after painting by Archibald M. Willard in Abbot Hall, Marblehead, Massachusetts. Nos. 1629-1631 printed se-tenant in panes of 50 (10x5).

Left panes contain 3 No. 1631a and one No. 1629; right panes contain one No. 1631 and 3 No. 1631a.

Drummer Boy A1019

Old Drummer A1020

Fifer — A1021

Designed by Vincent E. Hoffman.

PHOTOGRAVURE (Andreotti)
Plates of 200 subjects in four panes of 50 each.

1976, Jan. 1		Tagged		Perf. 11	
1629	A1019	13c	blue violet & multi.	26	8
1630	A1020	13c	blue violet & multi.	26	8
1631	A1021	13c	blue violet & multi.	26	8
a.		Strip of 3, #1629-1631		78	60
b.		As "a," imperf.		1,750.	
c.		Imperf., vert. pair		1,100.	
		Margin block of 12, 5 P#		3.40	—
		Margin block of 20, 5 P# and slogans		5.50	—

INTERPHIL ISSUE
Interphil 76 International Philatelic Exhibition, Philadelphia, Pa., May 29-June 6.

"Interphil 76" — A1022

Designed by Terrence W. McCaffrey.

LITHOGRAPHED, ENGRAVED (Giori)
Plates of 200 subjects of four panes of 50 each.

1976		Tagged		Perf. 11	
1632	A1022	13c	dark blue, red & ultra., Jan. 17	26	5
		Margin block of 4, P#		1.30	—
		Margin block of 4, Mr. Zip and "Use Zip Code"		1.20	—
		Margin block of 6, "Mail Early in the Day"		1.70	—

AMERICAN BICENTENNIAL ISSUE

State Flags
A1023-A1072

Designed by Walt Reed.

PHOTOGRAVURE (Andreotti)

Plates of 200 subjects in four panes of 50 each.

1976, Feb. 23			Tagged		Perf. 11	
1633	A1023	13c	Delaware		45	30
1634	A1024	13c	Pennsylvania		45	30
1635	A1025	13c	New Jersey		45	30
1636	A1026	13c	Georgia		45	30
1637	A1027	13c	Connecticut		45	30
1638	A1028	13c	Massachusetts		45	30
1639	A1029	13c	Maryland		45	30
1640	A1030	13c	South Carolina		45	30
1641	A1031	13c	New Hampshire		45	30
1642	A1032	13c	Virginia		45	30
1643	A1033	13c	New York		45	30
1644	A1034	13c	North Carolina		45	30
1645	A1035	13c	Rhode Island		45	30
1646	A1036	13c	Vermont		45	30
1647	A1037	13c	Kentucky		45	30
1648	A1038	13c	Tennessee		45	30
1649	A1039	13c	Ohio		45	30
1650	A1040	13c	Louisiana		45	30
1651	A1041	13c	Indiana		45	30
1652	A1042	13c	Mississippi		45	30
1653	A1043	13c	Illinois		45	30
1654	A1044	13c	Alabama		45	30
1655	A1045	13c	Maine		45	30
1656	A1046	13c	Missouri		45	30
1657	A1047	13c	Arkansas		45	30
1658	A1048	13c	Michigan		45	30
1659	A1049	13c	Florida		45	30
1660	A1050	13c	Texas		45	30
1661	A1051	13c	Iowa		45	30
1662	A1052	13c	Wisconsin		45	30
1663	A1053	13c	California		45	30
1664	A1054	13c	Minnesota		45	30
1665	A1055	13c	Oregon		45	30
1666	A1056	13c	Kansas		45	30
1667	A1057	13c	West Virginia		45	30
1668	A1058	13c	Nevada		45	30
1669	A1059	13c	Nebraska		45	30
1670	A1060	13c	Colorado		45	30
1671	A1061	13c	North Dakota		45	30
1672	A1062	13c	South Dakota		45	30
1673	A1063	13c	Montana		45	30
1674	A1064	13c	Washington		45	30
1675	A1065	13c	Idaho		45	30
1676	A1066	13c	Wyoming		45	30
1677	A1067	13c	Utah		45	30
1678	A1068	13c	Oklahoma		45	30
1679	A1069	13c	New Mexico		45	30
1680	A1070	13c	Arizona		45	30
1681	A1071	13c	Alaska		45	30
1682	A1072	13c	Hawaii		45	30
a.			Pane of 50		25.00	—

Pane of 50, 6 P# adjoining Nos.
1633, 1638, 1643, 1648, 1653,
1658; "Mail Early in the Day"
adjoining No. 1663, Mr. Zip and
"Use Zip Code" adjoining No.
1678 .... 25.00

Pane of 50, 6 P# adjoining Nos.
1637, 1642, 1647, 1652, 1657,
1662; "Mail Early in the Day"
adjoining No. 1667, Mr. Zip and
"Use Zip Code" adjoining No.
1682 .... 25.00

Pane of 50, 6 P# adjoining Nos.
1653, 1658, 1663, 1668, 1673,
1678 "Mail Early in the Day"
adjoining No. 1648, Mr. Zip and
"Use Zip Code" adjoining No.
1633 .... 25.00

Pane of 50, 6 P# adjoining Nos.
1657, 1662, 1667, 1672, 1677,
1682; "Mail Early in the Day"
adjoining No. 1652, Mr. Zip and
"Use Zip Code" adjoining No.
1637 .... 25.00

TELEPHONE CENTENNIAL ISSUE

Centenary of first telephone call by Alexander Graham Bell, March 10, 1876.

Bell's Telephone
Patent
Application,
1876 — A1073

Designed by George Tscherny.

ENGRAVED (Giori)

Plates of 200 subjects in four panes of 50 each.

1976, Mar. 10			Tagged		Perf. 11	
1683	A1073	13c	black, purple & red, tan		26	5
			Margin block of 4, P#		1.30	—
			Margin block of 4, "Mr. Zip and "Use Zip Code"		1.20	—
			Margin block of 6, "Mail Early in the Day"		1.70	—

COMMERCIAL AVIATION ISSUE

50th anniversary of first contract airmail flights: Dearborn, Mich. to Cleveland, Ohio, Feb. 15, 1926; and Pasco, Wash. to Elko, Nev., Apr. 6, 1926.

Ford-Pullman
Monoplane and
Laird Swallow
Biplane — A1074

Designed by Robert E. Cunningham.

PHOTOGRAVURE (Andreotti)

Plates of 200 subjects in four panes of 50 each.

1976, Mar. 19			Tagged		Perf. 11	
1684	A1074	13c	blue & multicolored		26	5
			Margin block of 10, 5 P#		2.90	—
			Margin block of 4, Mr. Zip and "Use Zip Code"		1.20	—
			Margin block of 6, "Mail Early in the Day"		1.70	—

CHEMISTRY ISSUE

Honoring American chemists, in conjunction with the centenary of the American Chemical Society.

Various Flasks,
Separatory Funnel,
Computer
Tape — A1075

Designed by Ken Davies.

PHOTOGRAVURE (Andreotti)

Plates of 200 subjects in four panes of 50 each.

1976, Apr. 6			Tagged		Perf. 11	
1685	A1075	13c	multicolored		26	5
			Margin block of 12, 6 P#		3.40	—
			Margin block of 4, Mr. Zip and "Use Zip Code"		1.20	—
			Margin block of 4, "Mail Early in the Day"		1.20	—

AMERICAN BICENTENNIAL ISSUES
SOUVENIR SHEETS

Designs, from Left to Right, No. 1686: a. Two British officers. b. Gen. Benjamin Lincoln. c. George Washington. d. John Trumbull, Col. Cobb, von Steuben, Lafayette, Thomas Nelson. e. Alexander Hamilton, John Laurens, Walter Stewart (all vert.).

No. 1687: a. John Adams, Roger Sherman, Robert R. Livingston. b. Jefferson, Franklin. c. Thomas Nelson, Jr., Francis Lewis, John Witherspoon, Samuel Huntington. d. John Hancock, Charles Thomson, c. George Read, John Dickinson, Edward Rutledge (a, d, vert., b, c, e, horiz.).

No. 1688: a. Boatsman. b. Washington. c. Flag bearer. d. Men in boat. e. Men on shore (a, d, horiz., b, c, e, vert.).

No. 1689: a. Two officers. b. Washington. c. Officer, black horse. d. Officer, white horse. e. Three soldiers (a, c, e, horiz., b, d, vert.).

Surrender of Cornwallis at Yorktown, by John
Trumbull — A1076

See "Information for Collectors" section at beginning of catalogue for an explanation of paper types, watermarks and grills.

Declaration of Independence, by John
Trumbull — A1077

Washington Crossing the Delaware, by Emmanuel
Leutze / Eastman Johnson — A1078

Washington Reviewing Army at Valley Forge, by
William T. Trego — A1079

Designed by Vincent E. Hoffman.

LITHOGRAPHED

Plates of 30 subjects in six panes of 5 each.

1976, May 29			Tagged		Perf. 11	
1686	A1076	13c	sheet of 5		4.50	—
a.		13c	multicolored		65	40
b.		13c	multicolored		65	40
c.		13c	multicolored		65	40
d.		13c	multicolored		65	40
e.		13c	multicolored		65	40
f.			"USA/13c" omitted on "b," "c" & "d," imperf.		—	—
g.			"USA/13c" omitted on "a" & "e"		—	—
h.			Imperf., untagged		—	—
i.			"USA/13c" omitted on "b," "c" & "d"			—
j.			"USA/13c" double on "b"			—
k.			"USA/13c" omitted on "c" & "d"			—
l.			"USA/13c" omitted on "e"			—
m.			"USA/13c" omitted, imperf. untagged			—
1687	A1077	18c	sheet of 5		6.00	—
a.		18c	multicolored		80	55
b.		18c	multicolored		80	55
c.		18c	multicolored		80	55
d.		18c	multicolored		80	55
e.		18c	multicolored		80	55
f.			Design & marginal inscriptions omitted		—	—
g.			"USA/18c" omitted on "a" & "c"		—	—
h.			"USA/18c" omitted on "b," "d" & "e"		—	—
i.			"USA/18c" omitted on "d"		—	—
j.			Black omitted in design		—	—
k.			"USA/18c" omitted, imperf., untagged		—	—
m.			"USA/18c" omitted on "b" & "e"		—	—
1688	A1078	24c	sheet of 5		7.50	—
a.		24c	multicolored		1.00	75
b.		24c	multicolored		1.00	75
c.		24c	multicolored		1.00	75

d.	24c multicolored		1.00	75
e.	24c multicolored		1.00	75
f.	"USA/24c" omitted, imperf.		—	
g.	"USA/24c" omitted on "d" & "e"		—	—
h.	Design & marginal inscriptions omitted		—	
i.	"USA/24c" omitted on "a," "b" & "c"		—	
j.	Imperf., untagged		—	
k.	"USA/24c" of "d" & "e" inverted		—	
1689	A1079 31c sheet of 5		9.00	—
a.	31c multicolored		1.25	90
b.	31c multicolored		1.25	90
c.	31c multicolored		1.25	90
d.	31c multicolored		1.25	90
e.	31c multicolored		1.25	90
f.	"USA/31c" omitted, imperf.		—	
g.	"USA/31c" omitted on "a" & "c"		—	
h.	"USA/31c" omitted on "b," "d" & "e"		—	—
i.	"USA/31c" omitted on "e"		—	
j.	Black omitted in design		—	
k.	Imperf., untagged		—	
l.	"USA/31c" omitted on "b" & "d"		—	
m.	"USA/31c" omitted on "a," "b" & "e"		—	
n.	As "m," imperf., untagged		—	
p.	As "h," imperf., untagged		—	

Issued in connection with Interphil 76 International Philatelic Exhibition, Philadelphia, Pa., May 29-June 6. Size of sheets: 153x204mm.; size of stamps: 25x39½mm., 39½x25mm.

Nos. 1688-1689 exist with inverted perforations.

Benjamin Franklin

American Bicentennial; Benjamin Franklin (1706-1790), deputy postmaster general for the colonies (1753-1774) and statesman. Design based on marble bust by anonymous Italian sculptor after terra cotta bust by Jean Jacques Caffieri, 1777. Map published by R. Sayer and J. Bennett in London. See Canada No. 691.

Franklin and Map of North America, 1776 — A1080

Designed by Bernard Reilander (Canada).

LITHOGRAPHED, ENGRAVED (Giori)
Plates of 200 subjects in four panes of 50 each.

1976, June 1		**Tagged**	**Perf. 11**	
1690	A1080 13c ultramarine & multicolored		26	5
	Margin block of 4, P#		1.30	—
	Margin block of 4, Mr. Zip and "Use Zip Code"		1.20	—
	Margin block of 6, "Mail Early in the Day"		1.70	—
a.	Light blue omitted		500.00	

Declaration of Independence

Designed after painting in the Rotunda of the Capitol, Washington, D.C. Nos. 1691-1694 printed se-tenant in sheets of 50 (10x5). Left panes contain 10 No. 1694a and 5 each of Nos. 1691-1692; right panes contain 5 each of Nos. 1693-1694 and 10 No. 1694a.

JULY 4,1776
A1081

JULY 4,1776
A1082

JULY 4,1776
A1083

JULY 4,1776
Declaration of Independence, by John Trumbull — A1084

Designed by Vincent E. Hoffman.

PHOTOGRAVURE (Andreotti)
Plates of 200 subjects in four panes of 50 each.

1976, July 4		**Tagged**	**Perf. 11**	
1691	A1081 13c blue & multicolored		26	8
	Margin block of 20, 5 P# adjoining Nos. 1691-1694 & 1691, "Mail Early in the Day" adjoining No. 1693, Mr. Zip and "Use Zip Code" adjoining No. 1692		5.75	—
	Margin block of 16, 5 P# as above, "Mail Early in the Day"		4.50	—
1692	A1082 13c blue & multicolored		26	8
	Margin block of 8, "Mail Early in the Day" adjoining No. 1692		2.30	—
	Margin block of 4, Mr. Zip and "Use Zip Code" adjoining No. 1692		1.15	—
1693	A1083 13c blue & multicolored		26	8
	Margin block of 8, "Mail Early in the Day" adjoining No. 1693		2.30	—
	Margin block of 4, Mr. Zip and "Use Zip Code" adjoining No. 1693		1.15	—
1694	A1084 13c blue & multicolored		26	8
	Margin block of 20, 5 P# adjoining Nos. 1691-1694 & 1694, "Mail Early in the Day" adjoining No. 1692, Mr. Zip and "Use Zip Code" adjoining No. 1693		5.75	—
	Margin block of 16, 5 P# as above, "Mail Early in the Day"		4.50	—
a.	Strip of 4, #1691-1694		1.10	75

OLYMPIC GAMES ISSUE

12th Winter Olympic Games, Innsbruck, Austria, Feb. 4-15, and 21st Summer Olympic Games, Montreal, Canada, July 17-Aug. 1. Nos. 1695-1698 are printed in blocks of four in panes of 50. Nos. 1695-1696 alternate in one row, Nos. 1697-1698 in other row.

Diving — A1085

Running — A1087

Skiing — A1086

Skating — A1088

Designed by Donald Moss.

PHOTOGRAVURE (Andreotti)
Plates of 200 subjects in four panes of 50 each.

1976, July 16		**Tagged**	**Perf. 11**	
1695	A1085 13c multicolored		26	8

	Margin block of 12, 6 P# adjoining Nos. 1695-1696	5.50	—
	Margin block of 20, 6 P# adjoining Nos. 1695-1696, Mr. Zip and slogans	9.25	—
	Margin block of 4, Mr. Zip and "Use Zip Code" adjoining No. 1695	1.80	—
	Margin block of 4, "Mail Early in the Day" adjoining No. 1695	1.80	—
1696 A1086 13c multicolored		26	8
	Margin block of 4, Mr. Zip and "Use Zip Code" adjoining No. 1696	1.80	—
	Margin block of 4, "Mail Early in the Day" adjoining No. 1696	1.80	—
1697 A1087 13c multicolored		26	8
	Margin block of 12, 6 P# adjoining Nos. 1697-1698	5.50	—
	Margin block of 20, 6 P# adjoining Nos. 1697-1698, Mr. Zip and slogans	9.25	—
	Margin block of 4, Mr. Zip and "Use Zip Code" adjoining No. 1697	1.80	—
	Margin block of 4, "Mail Early in the Day" adjoining No. 1697	1.80	—
1698 A1088 13c multicolored		26	8
	Margin block of 4, Mr. Zip and "Use Zip Code" adjoining No. 1698	1.80	—
	Margin block of 4, "Mail Early in the Day" adjoining No. 1698	1.80	—
a. Block of 4, #1695-1698		1.75	1.00
b. As "a," imperf.		1,000.	

CLARA MAASS ISSUE

Clara Louise Maass (1876-1901), volunteer in fight against yellow fever, birth centenary.

Clara Maass and Newark German Hospital Pin — A1089

Designed by Paul Calle.

PHOTOGRAVURE (Andreotti)
Plates of 160 subjects in four panes of 40 each.

1976, Aug. 18		**Tagged**	**Perf. 11**	
1699	A1089 13c multicolored		26	6
	Margin block of 12, 6 P#		3.40	—
	Margin block of 4, Mr. Zip, "Use Zip Code" and "Mail Early in the Day"		1.20	—
	Margin block of 16, 6 P#, Mr. Zip and slogans		4.60	—
a.	Horiz. pair, imperf. vert.		600.00	

ADOLPH S. OCHS ISSUE

Adolph S. Ochs (1858-1935), publisher of the New York Times, 1896-1935.

Adolph S. Ochs — A1090

Designed by Bradbury Thompson; photograph by S. J. Woolf.

GIORI PRESS PRINTING
Plates of 128 subjects in four panes of 32 (8x4).

1976, Sept. 18	Tagged	Perf. 11	
1700 A1090 13c	black & gray	26	5
	Margin block of 4, P#	1.30	—
	Margin block of 4, Mr. Zip and "Use Zip Code"	1.20	—
	Margin block of 6, "Mail Early in the Day"	1.70	—

CHRISTMAS ISSUE

Nativity, by John Singleton Copley — A1091

"Winter Pastime," by Nathaniel Currier — A1092

Designers: No. 1701, Bradbury Thompson after 1776 painting in Museum of Fine Arts, Boston. No. 1702, Stevan Dohanos after 1855 lithograph in Museum of the City of New York.

PHOTOGRAVURE (Andreotti)
Plates of 200 subjects in four panes of 50 each.

1976, Oct. 27	Tagged, Overall	Perf. 11	
1701 A1091 13c	multicolored	26	5
	Margin block of 12, 6 P#	3.40	—
	Margin block of 4, Mr. Zip and "Use Zip Code"	1.20	—
	Margin block of 4, "Mail Early in the Day"	1.20	—
a.	Imperf., pair	100.00	
1702 A1092 13c	multicolored	26	5
	Margin block of 10, 5 P#	3.00	—
	Margin block of 4, Mr. Zip and "Use Zip Code"	1.20	—
	Margin block of 6, "Mail Early in the Day"	1.70	—
a.	Imperf., pair	125.00	

Plates of 230 (10x23) subjects in panes of 50 (5x10)
Tagged, Block

1703 A1092 13c	multicolored	26	5
	Margin block of 20 5-8 P#	5.70	—
a.	Imperf., pair	150.00	
b.	Vert. pair, imperf. btwn.		

No. 1702 has overall tagging. Lettering at base is black and usually ½mm. below design. As a rule, no "snowflaking" in sky or pond. Pane of 50 has margins on 4 sides with slogans. Plate Nos. 37465-37478.

No. 1703 has block tagging the size of printed area. Lettering at base is gray black and usually ¾mm. below design. "Snowflaking" generally in sky and pond. Plate Nos. 37617-37621 or 37634-37638.

COMBINATION PRESS
Cylindrical plates consist of 23 rows of subjects, 10 across for commemoratives (230 subjects), 20 across for definitives (460 subjects), with margins on the two outer edges only. Guillotining through the perforations creates individual panes of 50 or 100 with one margin.

Failure of the guillotine to separate through the perforations resulted in straight edges on some stamps. Perforating teeth along the center column and the tenth rows were removed for issues released on or after May 31, 1984 (the 10c Richard Russell, for definitives; the 20c Horace Moses, for commemoratives), creating panes with straight edged stamps on three sides.

Three sets of plate numbers, copyright notices (starting with No. 1787), and zip insignia (starting with No. 1927) are arranged identically on the left and right sides of the plate so that each pane has at least one of each marking. The markings adjacent to any particular row are repeated either seven or eight rows away on the cylinder.

Fifteen combinations of the three marginal markings and blank rows are possible on panes.

AMERICAN BICENTENNIAL ISSUE
Washington at Princeton

Washington's Victory over Lord Cornwallis at Princeton, N.J., bicentenary.

US Bicentennial 13c

Washington, Nassau Hall, Hessian Prisoners and 13-star Flag, by Charles Willson Peale — A1093

Designed by Bradbury Thompson.

PHOTOGRAVURE (Andreotti)
Plates of 160 subjects in four panes of 40 each.

1977, Jan. 3	Tagged	Perf. 11	
1704 A1093 13c	multicolored	26	5
	Margin block of 10, 5 P#	2.90	—
	Margin block of 4, Mr. Zip and "Use Zip Code", "Mail Early in the Day"	1.20	—
a.	Horiz. pair, imperf. vert.	450.00	

SOUND RECORDING ISSUE
Centenary of the invention of the phonograph by Thomas Alva Edison and development of sophisticated recording industry.

Tin Foil Phonograph A1094

Designed by Walter and Naiad Einsel.

LITHOGRAPHED, ENGRAVED (Giori)
Plates of 200 subjects in four panes of 50 each.

1977, March 23	Tagged	Perf. 11	
1705 A1094 13c	black & multicolored	26	5
	Margin block of 4, P#	1.30	—
	Margin block of 4, Mr. Zip and "Use Zip Code"	1.20	—
	Margin block of 6, "Mail Early in the Day"	1.70	—

AMERICAN FOLK ART ISSUE
Pueblo Pottery

Pueblo art, 1880-1920, from Museums in New Mexico, Arizona and Colorado.

Nos. 1706-1709 are printed in blocks and strips of four in panes of 40. In the first row Nos. 1706-1709 are in sequence as listed. In the second row Nos. 1708-1709 are followed by Nos. 1706-1709, 1708-1709.

Pueblo Art USA 13c   Zia Pot — A1095

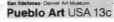

San Ildefonso Pot — A1096   Pueblo Art USA 13c

Pueblo Art USA 13c   Hopi Pot — A1097

Acoma Pot — A1098   Pueblo Art USA 13c

Designed by Ford Ruthling.

PHOTOGRAVURE (Andreotti)
Plates of 160 subjects in four panes of 40 each.

1977, Apr. 13	Tagged	Perf. 11	
1706 A1095 13c	multicolored	26	8
	Margin block of 10, 5 P#	3.00	—
	Margin block of 16, 5 P#; Mr. Zip and slogans adjoining Nos. 1706-1707	5.00	—
	Margin block of 6, Mr. Zip and "Use Zip Code" "Mail Early in the Day" adjoining Nos. 1706-1707	1.70	—
1707 A1096 13c	multicolored	26	8
1708 A1097 13c	multicolored	26	8
	Margin block of 16, 5 P#; Mr. Zip and slogans adjoining Nos. 1708-1709	5.00	—
	Margin block of 6, Mr. Zip and "Use Zip Code" "Mail Early in the Day" adjoining Nos. 1708-1709	1.70	—
1709 A1098 13c	multicolored	26	8
a.	Block or strip of 4, #1706-1709	1.05	1.00
b.	As "a", imperf. vert.	2,500.	

LINDBERGH FLIGHT ISSUE
Charles A. Lindbergh's solo transatlantic flight from New York to Paris, 50th anniversary.

Spirit of St. Louis — A1099

Designed by Robert E. Cunningham.

PHOTOGRAVURE (Andreotti)
Plates of 200 subjects in four panes of 50 each.

1977, May 20	Tagged	Perf. 11	
1710 A1099 13c	multicolored	26	5
	Margin block of 12, 6 P#	3.65	—
	Margin block of 4, Mr. Zip and "Use Zip Code"	1.20	—
	Margin block of 4, "Mail Early in the Day"	1.20	—
a.	Imperf., pair	1,600.	

COLORADO STATEHOOD ISSUE
Issued to honor Colorado as the "Centennial State." It achieved statehood in 1876.

Columbine and Rocky
Mountains — A1100

Designed by V. Jack Ruther.

PHOTOGRAVURE (Andreotti)

Plates of 200 subjects in four panes of 50 each.

1977, May 21	Tagged	Perf. 11	
1711 A1100 13c	**multicolored**	26	5
	Margin block of 12, 6 P#	3.65 —	
	Margin block of 4, Mr. Zip and "Use Zip Code"	1.20 —	
	Margin block of 4, "Mail Early in the Day"	1.20 —	
a.	Horiz. pair, imperf. btwn.	26	
b.	Horiz. pair, imperf. vert.	—	

Perforations do not run through the sheet margin on about 10 percent of the sheets of No. 1711.

BUTTERFLY ISSUE

Nos. 1712-1715 are printed in blocks of 4, in panes of 50. Nos. 1712-1713 alternate in first row, Nos. 1714-1715 in second row. This arrangement is repeated throughout the pane. Butterflies represent different geographic U.S. areas.

Swallowtail
A1101

Checkerspot
A1102

Dogface — A1103

Orange-Tip
A1104

Designed by Stanley Galli.

PHOTOGRAVURE (Andreotti)

Plates of 200 subjects in four panes of 50 each.

1977, June 6	Tagged	Perf. 11	
1712 A1101 13c	**tan & multicolored**	26	8
	Margin block of 12, 6 P# adjoining Nos. 1712, 1714	3.65 —	
	Margin block of 20, 6 P# adjoining Nos. 1712, 1714, Mr. Zip and slogans	6.05 —	
	Margin block of 4, Mr. Zip and "Use Zip Code" adjoining No. 1712	1.20 —	
	Margin block of 4, "Mail Early in the Day" adjoining No. 1712	1.20 —	
1713 A1102 13c	**tan & multicolored**	26	8

	Margin block of 12, 6 P# adjoining Nos. 1713, 1715	3.65 —	
	Margin block of 20, 6 P# adjoining Nos. 1713, 1715	6.05 —	
	Margin block of 4, Mr. Zip and "Use Zip Code" adjoining No. 1713	1.20 —	
	Margin block of 4, "Mail Early in the Day" adjoining No. 1713	1.20 —	
1714 A1103 13c	**tan & multicolored**	26	8
	Margin block of 4, Mr. Zip and "Use Zip Code" adjoining No. 1714	1.20 —	
	Margin block of 4, "Mail Early in the Day" adjoining No. 1714	1.20 —	
1715 A1104 13c	**tan & multicolored**	26	8
	Margin block of 4, Mr. Zip and "Use Zip Code" adjoining No. 1715	1.20 —	
	Margin block of 4, "Mail Early in the Day" adjoining No. 1715	1.20 —	
a.	Block of 4, #1712-1715	1.05	90
b.	As a, imperf. horiz.	—	

AMERICAN BICENTENNIAL ISSUES
Marquis de Lafayette

200th anniversary of Lafayette's Landing on the coast of South Carolina, north of Charleston.

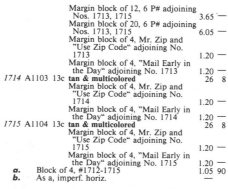

Marquis de
Lafayette — A1105

Designed by Bradbury Thompson.

GIORI PRESS PRINTING

Plates of 160 subjects in four panes of 40 each.

1977, June 13	Tagged	Perf. 11	
1716 A1105 13c	**blue, black & red**	26	5
	Margin block of 4, P#	1.30 —	
	Margin block of 4, Mr. Zip and "Use Zip Code"	1.20 —	
	Margin block of 6, "Mail Early in the Day"	1.70 —	

Skilled Hands for Independence

Nos. 1717-1720 are printed se-tenant in blocks of four, in panes of 50. Nos. 1717-1718 alternate in first row, Nos. 1719-1720 in second row. This arrangement is repeated throughout the pane.

Seamstress
A1106

Blacksmith
A1107

Wheelwright
A1108

Leatherworker
A1109

Designed by Leonard Everett Fisher.

PHOTOGRAVURE (Andreotti)

Plates of 200 subjects in four panes of 50 each.

1977, July 4	Tagged	Perf. 11	
1717 A1106 13c	**multicolored**	26	8
	Margin block of 12, 6 P# adjoining Nos. 1717, 1719	3.65 —	
	Margin block of 20, 6 P# adjoining Nos. 1717, 1719, Mr. Zip and slogans	6.05 —	
	Margin block of 4, Mr. Zip and "Use Zip Code" adjoining No. 1717	1.20 —	
	Margin block of 4, "Mail Early in the Day" adjoining No. 1717	1.20 —	
1718 A1107 13c	**multicolored**	26	8
	Margin block of 12, 6 P# adjoining Nos. 1718, 1720	3.65 —	
	Margin block of 20, 6 P# adjoining Nos. 1718, 1720	6.05 —	
	Margin block of 4, Mr. Zip and "Use Zip Code" adjoining No. 1718	1.20 —	
	Margin block of 4, "Mail Early in the Day" adjoining No. 1718	1.20 —	
1719 A1108 13c	**multicolored**	26	8
	Margin block of 4, Mr. Zip and "Use Zip Code" adjoining No. 1719	1.20 —	
	Margin block of 4, "Mail Early in the Day" adjoining No. 1719	1.20 —	
1720 A1109 13c	**multicolored**	26	8
	Margin block of 4, Mr. Zip and "Use Zip Code" adjoining No. 1720	1.20 —	
	Margin block of 4, "Mail Early in the Day" adjoining No. 1720	1.20 —	
a.	Block of 4, #1717-1720	1.05	90

PEACE BRIDGE ISSUE

50th anniversary of the Peace Bridge, connecting Buffalo (Fort Porter), N.Y. and Fort Erie, Ontario.

Peace Bridge and
Dove — A1110

Designed by Bernard Brussel-Smith (wood-cut).

ENGRAVED

Plates of 200 subjects in four panes of 50 each.

1977, Aug. 4	Tagged	Perf. 11x10½	
1721 A1110 13c	**blue**	26	5
	Margin block of 4, P#	1.30 —	
	Margin block of 4, Mr. Zip and "Use Zip Code"	1.20 —	
	Margin block of 6, "Mail Early in the Day"	1.80 —	

AMERICAN BICENTENNIAL ISSUE
Battle of Oriskany

200th anniversary of the Battle of Oriskany, American Militia led by Brig. Gen. Nicholas Herkimer (1728-1777).

Herkimer at
Oriskany, by
Frederick
Yohn — A1111

Designed by Bradbury Thompson after painting in Utica, N.Y. Public Library.

PHOTOGRAVURE (Andreotti)
Plates of 160 subjects in four panes of 40 each.

1977, Aug. 6		Tagged	Perf. 11	
1722	A1111 13c multicolored		26	5
	Margin block of 10, 5 P#		3.10	—
	Margin block of 6, Mr. Zip and "Use Zip Code" and "Mail Early in the Day"		1.80	—

ENERGY ISSUE
Conservation and development of nations energy resources. Nos. 1723-1724 printed se-tenant vertically.

"Conservation"
A1112

"Development"
A1113

Designed by Terrance W. McCaffrey.

PHOTOGRAVURE (Andreotti)
Plates of 160 subjects in four panes of 40 each.

1977, Oct. 20		Tagged	Perf. 11	
1723	A1112 13c multicolored		26	8
a.	Pair, #1723-1724		60	35
	Margin block of 12, 6 P#		4.00	—
	Margin block of 4, Mr. Zip, "Use Zip Code" and "Mail Early in the Day"		1.25	—
1724	A1113 13c multicolored		26	8

ALTA CALIFORNIA ISSUE
Founding of El Pueblo de San José de Guadalupe, first civil settlement in Alta California, 200th anniversary.

Farm Houses — A1114

Designed by Earl Thollander.

LITHOGRAPHED, ENGRAVED (Giori)
Plates of 200 subjects in four panes of 50 each.

1977, Sept. 9		Tagged	Perf. 11	
1725	A1114 13c black & multicolored		26	5
	Margin block of 4, P#		1.30	—
	Margin block of 4, Mr. Zip and "Use Zip Code"		1.20	—
	Margin block of 6, "Mail Early in the Day"		1.80	—

AMERICAN BICENTENNIAL ISSUE
Articles of Confederation
200th anniversary of drafting the Articles of Confederation, York Town, Pa.

Members of Continental Congress in Conference A1115

Designed by David Blossom.

ENGRAVED (Giori)
Plates of 200 subjects in four panes of 50 each.

1977, Sept. 30		Tagged	Perf. 11	
1726	A1115 13c red & brown, cream		26	5
	Margin block of 4, P#		1.30	—
	Margin block of 4, Mr. Zip and "Use Zip Code"		1.20	—
	Margin block of 6, "Mail Early in the Day"		1.80	—

TALKING PICTURES ISSUE
50th anniversary of talking pictures.

Movie Projector and Phonograph
A1116

Designed by Walter Einsel.

LITHOGRAPHED, ENGRAVED (Giori)
Plates of 200 subjects in four panes of 50 each.

1977, Oct. 6		Tagged	Perf. 11	
1727	A1116 13c multicolored		26	5
	Margin block of 4, P#		1.30	—
	Margin block of 4, Mr. Zip and "Use Zip Code"		1.20	—
	Margin block of 6, "Mail Early in the Day"		1.80	—

AMERICAN BICENTENNIAL ISSUE
Surrender at Saratoga
200th anniversary of Gen. John Burgoyne's surrender at Saratoga.

Surrender at Saratoga 1777 by Trumbull

US Bicentennial 13cents

Surrender of Burgoyne, by John Trumbull
A1117

Designed by Bradbury Thompson.

PHOTOGRAVURE (Andreotti)
Plates of 160 subjects in four panes of 40 each.

1977, Oct. 7		Tagged	Perf. 11	
1728	A1117 13c multicolored		26	5
	Margin block of 10, 5 P#		3.10	—
	Margin block of 6, Mr. Zip, "Use Zip Code" and "Mail Early in the Day"		1.80	—

CHRISTMAS ISSUE

Washington at Valley Forge
A1118

Rural Mailbox
A1119

Designers: No. 1729, Stevan Dohanos, after painting by J. C. Leyendecker. No. 1730, Dolli Tingle.

PHOTOGRAVURE (Combination Press)
Plates of 460 subjects (20x23) in panes of 100 (10x10).

1977, Oct. 21		Tagged	Perf. 11	
1729	A1118 13c multicolored		35	5
	Margin block of 20, 5-8 P#		7.50	—
a.	Imperf., pair		70.00	

See Combination Press note after No. 1703.

PHOTOGRAVURE (Andreotti)
Plates of 400 subjects in 4 panes of 100 each.

1730	A1119 13c multicolored		26	5
	Margin block of 10, 5 P#		3.10	—
	Margin block of 4, Mr. Zip and "Use Zip Code"		1.20	—

	Margin block of 6, "Mail Early in the Day"		1.80	—
a.	Imperf., pair		250.00	

CARL SANDBURG ISSUE
Carl Sandburg (1878-1967), poet, biographer and collector of American folk songs, birth centenary.

Carl Sandburg, by William A. Smith, 1952 — A1120

Designed by William A. Smith.

GIORI PRESS PRINTING
Plates of 200 subjects in four panes of 50 each.

1978, Jan. 6		Tagged	Perf. 11	
1731	A1120 13c black & brown		26	5
	Margin block of 4, P#		1.30	—
	Margin block of 4, Mr. Zip		1.20	—
	Margin block of 4, copyright		1.20	—

CAPTAIN COOK ISSUE
Capt. James Cook, 200th anniversary of his arrival in Hawaii, at Waimea, Kauai, Jan. 20, 1778, and of his anchorage in Cook Inlet, near Anchorage, Alaska, June 1, 1778. Nos. 1732-1733 printed in panes of 50, containing 25 each of Nos. 1732-1733 including 5 No. 1732a.

Alaska 1778
Capt.ⁿ James Cook
13c USA

Capt. Cook, by Nathaniel Dance — A1121

Capt.ⁿ James Cook Hawaii 1778   13c USA

"Resolution" and "Discovery," by John Webber — A1122

GIORI PRESS PRINTING
Plates of 200 subjects in four panes of 50 each.

1978, Jan. 20		Tagged	Perf. 11	
1732	A1121 13c dark blue		26	8
a.	Pair, #1732-1733		55	30
b.	As "a," imperf. between			
	Margin block of 4, P#		1.30	—
	Margin block of 4, Mr. Zip		1.20	—
	Margin block of 4, copyright		1.20	—
	Margin block of 20, 10 each, #1732-1733, P# adjoining #1732, and slogans		6.00	—
1733	A1122 13c green		26	8
a.	Vert. pair, imperf. horiz.		—	
	Margin block of 4, P#		1.30	—
	Margin block of 4, Mr. Zip		1.20	—
	Margin block of 4, copyright		1.20	—
	Margin block of 20, 10 each #1732-1733, P# adjoining #1733, and slogans		6.00	—

USA 13c

Indian Head
Penny, 1877
A1123

Eagle
A1124

15¢

Red Masterpiece and Medallion
Roses — A1126

ENGRAVED (Giori)
Plates of 600 subjects in four panes of 150 each.

1978	**Tagged**	**Perf. 11**	
1734 A1123 13c	**brown & blue green,** *bister, Jan. 11, 1978*	26	10
	Margin block of 4, P#	2.50	—
	Margin block of 4, "Use Correct Zip Code"	1.25	—
	Margin block of 4, copyright	1.25	—
a.	Horiz. pair, imperf. vert.	300.00	

PHOTOGRAVURE (Andreotti)
Plates of 400 subjects in four panes of 100 each.

1735 A1124 (15c)	**orange,** *May 22, 1978*	30	5
	Margin block of 4, P#	1.50	—
	Margin block of 4, "Use Zip Code"	1.30	—
	Margin block of 6, "Mail Early in the Day"	1.90	—
a.	Imperf., vert. pair	65.00	
b.	Vert. pair, imperf. horiz.	350.00	

ENGRAVED
Perf. 11x10½

1736 A1124 (15c)	**orange** (from booklet pane)	30	5
a.	Booklet pane of 8, *May 22, 1978*	2.40	60

Perf. 10

1737 A1126	15c **multicolored** (from booklet pane)	30	6
a.	Booklet pane of 8, *July 11, 1978*	2.40	60
b.	As "a", imperf.	—	

Nos. 1736, 1737 issued in booklets only. All stamps have one or two straight edges.

USA 15¢

A1127

USA 15¢

A1128

USA 15¢

A1129

USA 15¢

A1130

USA 15¢

A1131

Designed by Ronald Sharpe.

ENGRAVED

1980, Feb. 7	**Tagged**	**Perf. 11**	
1738 A1127 15c	**sepia,** *yellow*	30	5
1739 A1128 15c	**sepia,** *yellow*	30	5
1740 A1129 15c	**sepia,** *yellow*	30	5
1741 A1130 15c	**sepia,** *yellow*	30	5
1742 A1131 15c	**sepia,** *yellow*	30	5
a.	Booklet pane of 10, 2 each #1738-1742	4.25	60

Nos. 1738-1742 issued in booklets only. All stamps have one or two straight edges.

COIL STAMP

1978		**Perf. 10 Vert.**	
1743 A1124 (15c)	**orange,** *May 22, 1978*	30	5
	Pair	60	—
	Joint line pair	1.00	—
a.	Imperf. pair	125.00	

BLACK HERITAGE ISSUE
Harriet Tubman

Harriet Tubman (1820-1913), born a slave, helped more than 300 slaves escape to freedom.

Harriet Tubman and Cart
Carrying Slaves — A1133

Designed by Jerry Pinkney after photograph.

PHOTOGRAVURE (Andreotti)
Plates of 200 subjects in four panes of 50 each.

1978, Feb. 1	**Tagged**	**Perf. 10½x11**	
1744 A1133 13c	**multicolored**	26	5
	Margin block of 12, 6 P#	3.65	—
	Margin block of 4, Mr. Zip	1.20	—
	Margin block of 4, copyright	1.20	—

AMERICAN FOLK ART ISSUE
Quilts

Nos. 1745-1748 are printed in blocks of four. Nos. 1745-1746 alternate in first row, Nos. 1747-1748 in second.

Basket Design

13c Folk Art USA: Quilts

A1134

13c Folk Art USA: Quilts

A1135

13c Folk Art USA: Quilts

A1136

13c Folk Art USA: Quilts

A1137

Designed by Christopher Pullman after 1875 quilt made in New York City.

PHOTOGRAVURE (Andreotti)
Plates of 192 subjects in four panes of 48 (6x8).

1978, March 8		**Perf. 11**	
1745 A1134 13c	**multicolored**	26	8
	Margin block of 12, 6 P#, adjoining Nos. 1745, 1747	3.65	—
	Margin block of 16, 6 P# adjoining Nos. 1745, 1747, Mr. Zip and copyright	5.00	—
	Margin block of 4, Mr. Zip adjoining No. 1745, copyright No. 1747	1.20	—
	Margin block of 4, Mr. Zip adjoining No. 1747, copyright No. 1745	1.20	—
1746 A1135 13c	**multicolored**	26	8
	Margin block of 12, 6 P#, adjoining Nos. 1746, 1748	3.65	—
	Margin block of 16, 6 P# adjoining Nos. 1746, 1748, Mr. Zip and copyright	5.00	—
	Margin block of 4, Mr. Zip adjoining No. 1746, copyright No. 1748	1.20	—
	Margin block of 4, Mr. Zip adjoining No. 1748, copyright No. 1746	1.20	—
1747 A1136 13c	**multicolored**	26	8
1748 A1137 13c	**multicolored**	26	8
a.	Block of 4, #1745-1748	1.05	75

AMERICAN DANCE ISSUE

Nos. 1749-1752 printed se-tenant in blocks of four. Nos. 1749-1750 alternate in first row, Nos. 1751-1752 in second.

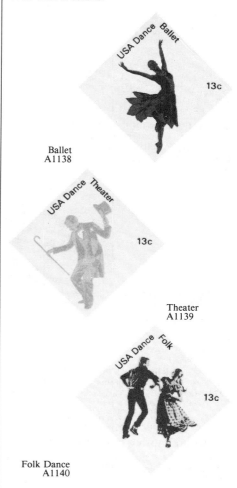

USA Dance Ballet

13c

Ballet
A1138

USA Dance Theater

13c

Theater
A1139

USA Dance Folk

13c

Folk Dance
A1140

Modern Dance
A1141

Designed by John Hill.

PHOTOGRAVURE (Andreotti)
Plates of 192 subjects in four panes of 48 (6x8).

1978, Apr. 26			**Perf. 11**	
1749 A1138 13c multicolored			26	8
Margin block of 12, 6 P#, adjoining Nos. 1749, 1751			3.65	—
Margin block of 16, 6 P#, adjoining Nos. 1749, 1751, Mr. Zip and copyright			5.00	—
Margin block of 4, Mr. Zip adjoining No. 1749, copyright No. 1751			1.20	—
Margin block of 4, Mr. Zip adjoining No. 1751, copyright No. 1749			1.20	—
1750 A1139 13c multicolored			26	8
Margin block of 12, 6 P#, adjoining Nos. 1750, 1752			3.65	—
Margin block of 16, 6 P# adjoining Nos. 1750, 1752, Mr. Zip and copyright			5.00	—
Margin block of 4, Mr. Zip adjoining No. 1750, copyright No. 1752			1.20	—
Margin block of 4, Mr. Zip adjoining No. 1752, copyright No. 1750			1.20	—
1751 A1140 13c multicolored			26	8
1752 A1141 13c multicolored			26	8
a.	Block of 4, #1749-1752		1.05	75

AMERICAN BICENTENNIAL ISSUE
French Alliance

Bicentenary of French Alliance, signed in Paris, Feb. 6, 1778 and ratified by Continental Congress, May 4, 1778.

King Louis XVI and
Benjamin Franklin, by
Charles Gabriel
Sauvage — A1142

Designed by Bradbury Thompson after 1785 porcelain sculpture in Du Pont Winterthur Museum, Delaware.

GIORI PRESS PRINTING
Plates of 160 subjects in four panes of 40 each.

1978, May 4	**Tagged**	**Perf. 11**	
1753 A1142 13c blue, black & red		26	5
Margin block of 4, P#		1.30	—
Margin block of 4, Mr. Zip		1.20	—
Margin block of 4, copyright		1.20	—

EARLY CANCER DETECTION ISSUE

George Papanicolaou, M.D. (1883-1962), cytologist and developer of Pap Test, early cancer detection in women.

Dr. Papanicolaou and
Microscope — A1143

Designed by Paul Calle.

Plates of 200 subjects in four panes of 50 each.

1978, May 18	**Tagged**	**Engr.**	**Perf. 10½x11**	
1754 A1143 13c brown			26	5
Margin block of 4, P#			1.30	—
Margin block of 4, Mr. Zip			1.20	—
Margin block of 4, copyright			1.20	—

PERFORMING ARTS ISSUE

Jimmie Rodgers (1897-1933), the "Singing Brakeman, Father of Country Music" (No. 1755); George M. Cohan (1878-1942), actor and playwright (No. 1756).

Jimmie Rodgers
with Guitar and
Brakeman's Cap,
Locomotive
A1144

George M. Cohan,
"Yankee Doodle
Dandy" and Stars
A1145

Designed by Jim Sharpe.

PHOTOGRAVURE (Andreotti)
Plates of 200 subjects in four panes of 50 each.

1978	**Tagged**	**Perf. 11**	
1755 A1144 13c multicolored, *May 24*		26	5
Margin block of 12, 6 P#		3.65	—
Margin block of 4, Mr. Zip		1.20	—
Margin block of 4, copyright		1.20	—
1756 A1145 15c multicolored, *July 3*		30	5
Margin block of 12, 6 P#		4.20	—
Margin block of 4, Mr. Zip		1.40	—
Margin block of 4, copyright		1.40	—

CAPEX ISSUE

CAPEX '78, Canadian International Philatelic Exhibition, Toronto, Ont., June 9-18. No. 1757 has black inscriptions on green panel: "Canadian International Exhibition, Toronto" and in French and English "This tribute features wildlife that share the Canadian-United States Border." Signature of Postmaster General William F. Bolger. Size: 108x74mm.

Wildlife from Canadian-United States
Border — A1146

Designed by Stanley Galli.

LITHOGRAPHED, ENGRAVED (Giori)
Plates of 24 subjects in four panes of 6 each.

1978, June 10		**Tagged**	**Perf. 11**	
1757 A1146	Block of 8, **multicolored**		2.10	2.00
a.	13c *Cardinal*		26	10
b.	13c *Mallard*		26	10
c.	13c *Canada goose*		26	10
d.	13c *Blue jay*		26	10
e.	13c *Moose*		26	10
f.	13c *Chipmunk*		26	10
g.	13c *Red fox*		26	10
h.	13c *Raccoon*		26	10
i.	Yel., grn., red, brn., bl., blk. (litho) omitted			
	Margin block of 8, P#		2.75	

Margin block of 8, Mr. Zip and copyright	2.75	
Pane of 6 (No. 1757), P#, Mr. Zip and copyright	15.00	

PHOTOGRAPHY ISSUE

Photography's contribution to communications and understanding.

Camera, Lens, Color
Filters, Adapter Ring,
Studio Light Bulb and
Album — A1147

Designed by Ben Somoroff.

PHOTOGRAVURE (Andreotti)
Plates of 160 subjects in four panes of 40 each.

1978, June 26	**Tagged**	**Perf. 11**	
1758 A1147 15c multicolored		30	5
Margin block of 12, 6 P#		4.20	—
Margin block of 4, Mr. Zip and copyright		1.40	—
Margin block of 16, 6 P#, Mr. Zip and copyright		5.60	—

VIKING MISSIONS TO MARS ISSUE

Second anniversary of landing of Viking 1 on Mars.

Viking 1 Lander
Scooping up Soil
on Mars — A1148

Designed by Robert McCall.

LITHOGRAPHED, ENGRAVED (Giori)
Plates of 200 subjects in four panes of 50 each.

1978, July 20	**Tagged**	**Perf. 11**	
1759 A1148 15c multicolored		30	5
Margin block of 4, P#		1.50	—
Margin block of 4, Mr. Zip		1.40	—
Margin block of 4, copyright		1.40	—

AMERICAN OWLS ISSUE

Nos. 1760-1763 are printed in blocks of four. Nos. 1760-1761 alternate in one horizontal row. Nos. 1762-1763 in the next.

Great Gray
Owl — A1149

Saw-whet
Owl — A1150

Barred Owl — A1151

Great Horned Owl — A1152

Designed by Frank J. Waslick.

LITHOGRAPHED, ENGRAVED (Giori)
Plates of 200 subjects in four panes of 50 each.

1978, Aug. 26	Tagged	Perf. 11
1760 A1149 15c multicolored	30	8
Margin block of 4, P# adjoining #1760	1.50	—
Margin block of 4, Mr. Zip adjoining #1760	1.40	—
Margin block of 4, copyright adjoining #1760	1.40	—
1761 A1150 15c multicolored	30	8
Margin block of 4, P# adjoining #1761	1.50	—
Margin block of 4, Mr. Zip adjoining #1761	1.40	—
Margin block of 4, copyright adjoining #1761	1.40	—
1762 A1151 15c multicolored	30	8
Margin block of 4, P# adjoining #1762	1.50	—
Margin block of 4, Mr. Zip adjoining #1762	1.40	—
Margin block of 4, copyright adjoining #1762	1.40	—
1763 A1152 15c multicolored	30	8
Margin block of 4, P# adjoining #1763	1.50	—
Margin block of 4, Mr. Zip adjoining #1763	1.40	—
Margin block of 4, copyright adjoining #1763	1.40	—
a. Block of four, #1760-1763	1.25	85

AMERICAN TREES ISSUE

Nos. 1764-1767 are printed se-tenant in blocks of four. Nos. 1764-1765 alternate in first row, Nos. 1766-1767 in second.

Giant Sequoia — A1153

White Pine — A1154

White Oak — A1155

Gray Birch — A1156

Designed by Walter D. Richards.

PHOTOGRAVURE (Andreotti)
Plates of 160 subjects in four panes of 40 each.

1978, Oct. 9	Tagged	Perf. 11
1764 A1153 15c multicolored	30	8
Margin block of 12, 6 P# adjoining #1764, 1766	4.20	—
Margin block of 16, 6 P# adjoining #1764, 1766, Mr. Zip and copyright	5.60	—
Margin block of 4, Mr. Zip adjoining #1764, copyright #1766	1.40	—
Margin block of 4, Mr. Zip adjoining #1766, copyright #1764	1.40	—
1765 A1154 15c multicolored	30	8
Margin block of 12, 6 P# adjoining #1765, 1767	4.20	—
Margin block of 16, 6 P# adjoining #1765, 1767, Mr. Zip and copyright	5.60	—
Margin block of 4, Mr. Zip adjoining #1765, copyright #1767	1.40	—
Margin block of 4, Mr. Zip adjoining #1767, copyright #1765	1.40	—
1766 A1155 15c multicolored	30	8
1767 A1156 15c multicolored	30	8
a. Block of 4, #1764-1767	1.25	85
b. As "a," imperf. horiz.	—	

CHRISTMAS ISSUE

Madonna and Child with Cherubim, by Andrea della Robbia — A1157

Child on Hobby Horse and Christmas Trees — A1158

Designed by Bradbury Thompson (No. 1768) after terra cotta sculpture in National Gallery, Washington, D.C., and by Dolli Tingle (No. 1769).

PHOTOGRAVURE (Andreotti)
Plates of 400 subjects in four panes of 100 each.

1978, Oct. 18		Perf. 11
1768 A1157 15c blue & multicolored	30	5
Margin block of 12, 6 P#	4.20	—
Margin block of 4, "Use Correct Zip Code"	1.40	—
Margin block of 4, copyright	1.40	—
a. Imperf., pair	125.00	
1769 A1158 15c red & multicolored	30	5
Margin block of 12, 6 P#	4.20	—
Margin block of 4, "Use Correct Zip Code"	1.40	—
Margin block of 4, copyright	1.40	—
a. Imperf., pair	125.00	
b. Vert. pair, imperf. horiz.	—	

ROBERT F. KENNEDY ISSUE

Robert F. Kennedy — A1159

Designed by Bradbury Thompson after photograph by Stanley Tretick.

ENGRAVED
Plates of 192 subjects in four panes of 48 (8x6).

1979, Jan. 12	Tagged	Perf. 11
1770 A1159 15c blue	35	5
Margin block of 4, P#	1.75	—
Margin block of 4, Mr. Zip	1.50	—
Margin block of 4, copyright	1.50	—

BLACK HERITAGE ISSUE
Martin Luther King, Jr.

Dr. Martin Luther King, Jr. (1929-1968), Civil Rights leader.

Martin Luther King, Jr. and Civil Rights Marchers — A1160

Designed by Jerry Pinkney.

PHOTOGRAVURE (Andreotti)
Plates of 200 subjects in four panes of 50 each.

1979, Jan. 13	Tagged	Perf. 11
1771 A1160 15c multicolored	35	5
Margin block of 12, 6 P#	4.75	—
Margin block of 4, Mr. Zip	1.50	—
Margin block of 4, copyright	1.50	—
a. Imperf. pair	—	

INTERNATIONAL YEAR OF THE CHILD ISSUE

Children of Different Races — A1161

Designed by Paul Calle.

ENGRAVED
Plates of 200 subjects in four panes of 50 each.

1979, Feb. 15	Tagged	Perf. 11
1772 A1161 15c orange red	30	5
Margin block of 4, P#	1.50	—
Margin block of 4, Mr. Zip	1.40	—
Margin block of 4, copyright	1.40	—

JOHN STEINBECK ISSUE

John Steinbeck (1902-1968), Novelist — A1162

Designed by Bradbury Thompson after photograph by Philippe Halsman.

ENGRAVED
Plates of 200 subjects in four panes of 50 each.

1979, Feb. 27	Tagged	Perf. 10½x11
1773 A1162 15c dark blue	30	5
Margin block of 4, P#	1.50	—
Margin block of 4, Mr. Zip	1.40	—
Margin block of 4, copyright	1.40	—

ALBERT EINSTEIN ISSUE

Albert Einstein (1879-1955), Theoretical Physicist. — A1163

Designed by Bradbury Thompson after photograph by Hermann Landshoff.

ENGRAVED

Plates of 200 subjects in four panes of 50 each.

1979, Mar. 4		Tagged	*Perf. 10½x11*	
1774 A1163 15c	chocolate		30	5
	Margin block of 4, P#		1.50	—
	Margin block of 4, Mr. Zip		1.40	—
	Margin block of 4, copyright		1.40	—
	Pair, horiz. gutter btwn.			—

AMERICAN FOLK ART ISSUE
Pennsylvania Toleware, c. 1800

Pennsylvania Toleware
Folk Art USA 15c
Coffeepot — A1164

Pennsylvania Toleware
Folk Art USA 15c
Tea Caddy — A1165

Pennsylvania Toleware
Folk Art USA 15c
Sugar Bowl — A1166

Pennsylvania Toleware
Folk Art USA 15c
Coffeepot — A1167

Designed by Bradbury Thompson.

PHOTOGRAVURE (Andreotti)

Plates of 160 subjects in four panes of 40 each.

1979, Apr. 19		Tagged	*Perf. 11*	
1775 A1164 15c	multicolored		30	8
	Margin block of 10, 5 P#		3.50	—
	Margin block of 16, 5 P#; Mr. Zip and copyright adjoining Nos. 1775-1776		5.75	—
	Margin block of 6, Mr. Zip and copyright adjoining Nos. 1775-1776		2.25	—
1776 A1165 15c	multicolored		30	8
1777 A1166 15c	multicolored		30	8
	Margin block of 16, 5 P#; Mr. Zip and copyright adjoining Nos. 1777-1778		5.75	—
	Margin block of 6, Mr. Zip and copyright adjoining Nos. 1777-1778		2.25	—
1778 A1167 15c	multicolored		30	8
a.	Block of 4, #1775-1778		1.25	85
b.	As "a," imperf. horiz.		—	

AMERICAN ARCHITECTURE ISSUE

Nos. 1779-1782 printed se-tenant in blocks of four. Nos. 1779-1780 alternate in first row, Nos. 1781-1782 in second.

Jefferson 1743-1826 Virginia Rotunda
Architecture USA 15c
Virginia Rotunda, by Thomas Jefferson — A1168

Latrobe 1764-1820 Baltimore Cathedral
Architecture USA 15c
Baltimore Cathedral, by Benjamin Latrobe — A1169

Bulfinch 1763-1844 Boston State House
Architecture USA 15c
Boston State House, by Charles Bulfinch — A1170

Strickland 1788-1854 Philadelphia Exchange
Architecture USA 15c
Philadelphia Exchange, by William Strickland — A1171

Designed by Walter D. Richards.

ENGRAVED (Giori)

Plates of 192 subjects in four panes of 48 (6x8).

1979, June 4		Tagged	*Perf. 11*	
1779 A1168 15c	black & brick red		30	8
	Margin block of 4, P# adjoining #1779		1.70	—
	Margin block of 4, Mr. Zip adjoining #1779		1.60	—
	Margin block of 4, copyright adjoining #1779		1.60	—
1780 A1169 15c	black & brick red		30	8
	Margin block of 4, P# adjoining #1780		1.70	—
	Margin block of 4, Mr. Zip adjoining #1780		1.60	—
	Margin block of 4, copyright adjoining #1780		1.60	—
1781 A1170 15c	black & brick red		30	8
	Margin block of 4, P# adjoining #1781		1.70	—
	Margin block of 4, Mr. Zip adjoining #1781		1.60	—
	Margin block of 4, copyright adjoining #1781		1.60	—
1782 A1171 15c	black & brick red		30	8
	Margin block of 4, P# adjoining #1782		1.70	—
	Margin block of 4, Mr. Zip adjoining #1782		1.60	—
	Margin block of 4, copyright adjoining #1782		1.60	—
a.	Block of 4, #1779-1782		1.50	85

ENDANGERED FLORA ISSUE

Nos. 1783-1786 are printed in blocks of four. Nos. 1783-1784 alternate in one horizontal row. Nos. 1785-1786 in the next.

Endangered Flora
PERSISTENT TRILLIUM
Persistent Trillium
A1172

Endangered Flora
HAWAIIAN WILD BROADBEAN
Hawaiian Wild Broadbean
A1173

Endangered Flora
CONTRA COSTA WALLFLOWER
Contra Costa Wallflower
A1174

Endangered Flora
ANTIOCH DUNES EVENING PRIMROSE
Antioch Dunes Evening Primrose
A1175

Designed by Frank J. Waslick.

PHOTOGRAVURE (Andreotti)

Plates of 200 subjects in four panes of 50 each.

1979, June 7		Tagged	*Perf. 11*	
1783 A1172 15c	multicolored		30	8
	Margin block of 12, 6 P# adjoining Nos. 1783-1784		4.20	—

	Margin block of 20, 6 P#; Mr. Zip and copyright adjoining Nos. 1783-1784		7.00	—
	Marginal block of 4, Mr. Zip adjoining No. 1783		1.40	—
	Margin block of 4, copyright adjoining No. 1783		1.40	—
1784 A1173 15c	multicolored		30	8
	Margin block of 4, Mr. Zip adjoining No. 1784		1.40	—
	Margin block of 4, copyright adjoining No. 1784		1.40	—
1785 A1174 15c	multicolored		30	8
	Margin block of 12, 6 P# adjoining Nos. 1785-1786		4.20	—
	Margin block of 20, 6 P#; Mr. Zip and copyright adjoining Nos. 1785-1786		7.00	—
	Margin block of 4, Mr. Zip adjoining No. 1785		1.40	—
	Margin block of 4, copyright adjoining No. 1785		1.40	—
1786 A1175 15c	multicolored		30	8
	Margin block of 4, Mr. Zip adjoining No. 1786		1.40	—
	Margin block of 4, copyright adjoining No. 1786		1.40	—
a.	Block of 4, #1783-1786		1.25	85
b.	As "a," imperf.		1,000.	

SEEING EYE DOGS ISSUE

First guide dog program in the United States, 50th anniversary.

USA 15c
Seeing For Me German Shepherd Leading Man — A1176

Designed by Joseph Csatari.

PHOTOGRAVURE (Combination Press)

Plates of 230 (10x23) subjects in panes of 50 (10x5).

1979, June 15		Tagged	*Perf. 11*	
1787 A1176 15c	multicolored		30	5
	Margin block of 20, 5-8 P#, 1-2 copyright		6.50	—
a.	Imperf. pair		650.00	

See Combination Press note after No. 1703.

Special Olympics
Skill · Sharing · Joy
USA 15c
Child Holding Winner's Medal — A1177

I have not yet begun to fight
John Paul Jones
US Bicentennial 15c
John Paul Jones, by Charles Willson Peale — A1178

SPECIAL OLYMPICS ISSUE

Special Olympics for special children, Brockport, N.Y., Aug. 8-13.

Designed by Jeff Cornell.

PHOTOGRAVURE (Andreotti)

Plates of 200 subjects in four panes of 50 each.

1979, Aug. 9		Tagged	*Perf. 11*	
1788 A1177 15c	multicolored		30	5
	Margin block of 10, 5 P#		3.50	—
	Margin block of 4, Mr. Zip		1.40	—
	Margin block of 4, copyright		1.40	—

JOHN PAUL JONES ISSUE

John Paul Jones (1747-1792), Naval Commander, American Revolution.

Designed by Bradbury Thompson after painting in Independence National Historical Park, Philadelphia.

Printed by J. W. Fergusson and Sons, Richmond, Va.

PHOTOGRAVURE (Champlain)
Plates of 200 subjects in four panes of 50 each.

1979, Sept. 23	Tagged	Perf. 11x12	
1789 A1178 15c **multicolored**		30	5
P# block of 10, 5 P#		3.50	—
Zip block of 4		1.40	—
Copyright block of 4		1.40	—
a. Perf. 11		30	6
a. P# block of 10, 5 P#		3.50	—
b. Perf. 12			
c. Vert. pair, imperf. horiz.		200.00	
d. As "a," vert. pair, imperf. horiz.		150.00	

Imperfs and perforated or imperforate gutter pairs or blocks exist from printer's waste.

OLYMPIC GAMES ISSUE
22nd Summer Olympic Games, Moscow, July 19-Aug. 3, 1980. Nos. 1791-1794 printed se-tenant. Nos. 1791-1792 alternate in one horizontal row, Nos. 1793-1794 in next.

Decathlon, Javelin — A1179

Running — A1180

Swimming, Women's A1181

Rowing — A1182

Equestrian A1183

Designed by Robert M. Cunningham.

PHOTOGRAVURE
Plates of 200 subjects in four panes of 50 each.

1979, Sept. 5	Tagged	Perf. 11	
1790 A1179 10c **multicolored**		25	22
P# block of 12, 6 P#		4.50	—
Zip block of 4		1.10	—
Copyright block of 4		1.10	—

1979, Sept. 28			
1791 A1180 15c **multicolored**		35	8
P# block of 12, 6 P# adjoining Nos. 1791, 1793		4.75	—
Zip block of 4		1.60	—
Copyright block of 4		1.60	—
P# block of 20, 6 P#, zip, copyright adjoining Nos. 1791, 1793		8.00	—
1792 A1181 15c **multicolored**		35	8
P# block of 12, 6 P# adjoining Nos. 1792, 1794		4.75	—
Zip block of 4		1.60	—
Copyright block of 4		1.60	—

P# block of 20, 6 P#, zip, copyright adjoining Nos. 1792, 1794		8.00	—
1793 A1182 15c **multicolored**		35	8
Zip block of 4		1.60	—
Copyright block of 4		1.60	—
1794 A1183 15c **multicolored**		35	8
Zip block of 4		1.60	—
Copyright block of 4		1.60	—
a. Block of 4, #1791-1794		1.50	85
b. As "a," imperf.		2,250.	

OLYMPIC GAMES ISSUE
13th Winter Olympic Games, Lake Placid, N. Y., Feb. 12-24. Nos. 1795-1798 printed se-tenant. Nos. 1795-1796 alternate in one horizontal row, Nos. 1797-1798 in next.

Speed Skating — A1184

Downhill Skiing — A1185

Ski Jump — A1186

Hockey Goaltender A1187

Designed by Robert M. Cunningham

Plates of 200 subject in four panes of 50 each.
PHOTOGRAVURE

1980, Feb. 1	Tagged	Perf. 11x10½	
1795 A1184 15c **multicolored**		45	8
a. Perf. 11		1.50	—
1796 A1185 15c **multicolored**		45	8
a. Perf. 11		1.50	—
1797 A1186 15c **multicolored**		45	8
a. Perf. 11		1.50	—
1798 A1187 15c **multicolored**		45	8
P# block of 12, 6 P#		6.50	—
Zip block of 4		2.00	—
Copyright block of 4		2.00	—
P# block of 20, 6 P#, zip and copyright		10.50	—
a. Perf. 11		1.50	—
a. P# block of 12, 6 P#		19.50	—
a. P# block of 20, 6 P#, zip and copyright		31.50	—
b. Block of 4, #1795-1798		1.90	85
c. Block of 4, #1795a-1798a		6.25	—

CHRISTMAS ISSUE

Virgin and Child by Gerard David A1188

Santa Claus, Christmas Tree Ornament A1189

Designed by Bradbury Thompson (No. 1799) after painting in National Gallery of Art, Washington, D.C. and by Eskil Ohlsson (No. 1800).

PHOTOGRAVURE (Andreotti)
Plates of 400 subjects in four panes of 100 each.

1979, Oct. 18	Tagged	Perf. 11	
1799 A1188 15c **multicolored**		30	5
P# block of 12, 6 P#		4.25	—

Zip block of 4		1.40	—
Copyright block of 4		1.40	—
P# block of 20, 6 P#, zip, copyright		7.05	—
a. Imperf. pair		100.00	
b. Vert. pair, imperf. horiz.		1,000.	
c. Vert. pair, imperf. between			
1800 A1189 15c **multicolored**		30	5
P# block of 12, 6 P#		4.25	—
Zip block of 4		1.40	—
Copyright block of 4		1.40	—
P# block of 20, 6 P#, zip, copyright		7.05	—
a. Green & yellow omitted		750.00	
b. Green, yellow & tan omitted		800.00	

PERFORMING ARTS ISSUE
Will Rogers (1879-1935), actor and humorist.

Will Rogers — A1190

Designed by Jim Sharpe.

Plates of 200 subjects in four panes of 50 each.
PHOTOGRAVURE (Andreotti)

1979, Nov. 4	Tagged	Perf. 11	
1801 A1190 15c **multicolored**		30	5
P# block of 12, 6 P#		4.25	—
Zip block of 4		1.40	—
Copyright block of 4		1.40	—
P# block of 20, 6 P#, zip, copyright		7.05	—
a. Imperf. pair		300.00	

VIETNAM VETERANS ISSUE
A tribute to veterans of the Vietnam War.

Ribbon for Vietnam Service Medal — A1191

Designed by Stevan Dohanos.

PHOTOGRAVURE (Andreotti)
Plates of 200 subjects in four panes of 50 each.

1979, Nov. 11	Tagged	Perf. 11	
1802 A1191 15c **multicolored**		30	5
P# block of 10, 5 P#		3.50	—
Zip block of 4		1.40	—
Copyright block of 4		1.40	—

PERFORMING ARTS ISSUE
W.C. Fields (1800-1946), actor and comedian.

W.C. Fields — A1192

Designed by Jim Sharpe.

Plates of 200 subjects in four panes of 50 each.
PHOTOGRAVURE

1980, Jan. 29	Tagged	Perf. 11	
1803 A1192 15c **multicolored**		30	5
P# block of 12, 6 P#		4.25	—
Zip block of 4		1.40	—

Copyright block of 4		1.40	—
P# block of 20, 6 P#, zip, copyright		7.05	—

BLACK HERITAGE ISSUE

Benjamin Banneker (1731-1806), astronomer and mathematician.

Benjamin Banneker — A1193

Designed by Jerry Pinkney.

Plates of 200 subjects in four panes of 50 each.

PHOTOGRAVURE

1980, Feb. 15	Tagged	Perf. 11	
1804 A1193 15c multicolored		30	5
P# block of 12, 6 P#		4.25	—
Zip block of 4		1.40	—
Copyright block of 4		1.40	—
Plate block of 20, 6 P#, zip, copyright		7.05	—
a. Horiz. pair, imperf. vert.			

Imperfs, including gutter pairs and blocks, exist from printer's waste.

NATIONAL LETTER WRITING WEEK ISSUE

National Letter Writing Week, Feb. 24-Mar. 1. Nos. 1805-1810 are printed vertically se-tenant.

Letters Preserve
Memories — A1194

P.S. Write
Soon — A1195

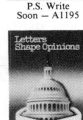

Letters Lift
Spirits — A1196

Letters Shape
Opinions — A1197

Designed by Randall McDougall.

Plates of 240 subjects in four panes of 60 (10x6) each.

PHOTOGRAVURE

1980, Feb. 25	Tagged	Perf. 11	
1805 A1194 15c multicolored		35	8
P# block of 36, 6 P# adjoining #1805		16.50	—
Zip block of 12, adjoining #1805		5.75	—
Copyright block of 12, adjoining #1805		5.75	—
1806 A1195 15c purple & multi		35	8
1807 A1196 15c multicolored		35	8
1808 A1195 15c green & multi		35	8
1809 A1195 15c multicolored		35	8
1810 A1195 15c red & multi		35	8
P# block of 36, 6 P# adjoining #1810		16.50	—

Zip block of 12, adjoining #1810		5.75	—
Copyright block of 12, adjoining #1810		5.75	—
a. Vertical strip of 6, #1805-1810		2.75	1.25

AMERICANA TYPE

Weaver Violins — A1199

Designer: 3.5c, George Mercer.

COIL STAMPS

1980-81	Engr.	Perf. 10 Vertically	
1811 A984 1c dark blue, greenish, Mar. 6, 1980		5	5
Pair		10	10
Joint line pair		15	15
Dull finish gum		5	
a. Imperf., pair		175.00	
1813 A1199 3.5 purple, yellow, June 23, 1980		8	5
Pair		16	10
Joint line pair		30	
a. Untagged (Bureau precanceled, lines only			10
b. Imperf., pair		275.00	
1816 A997 12c red brown, beige, Apr. 8, 1981		24	5
Pair		50	10
Joint line pair		75	
a. Untagged (Bureau precanceled, lines only)			25
b. Imperf., pair		175.00	

Eagle — A1207

PHOTOGRAVURE

Plates of 400 subjects in four panes of 100 each.

1981, Mar. 15	Tagged	Perf. 11x10½	
1818 A1207 (18c) violet		36	5
P# block of 4		1.80	—
Zip block of 4		1.60	—
Mail Early block of 6		2.50	—

ENGRAVED
Perf. 10

1819 A1207 (18c) violet (from booklet pane)		36	5
a. Booklet pane of 8		4.50	1.50

COIL STAMP
Perf. 10 Vert.

1820 A1207 (18c) violet		45	5
Pair		90	10
Joint line pair		1.50	—
a. Imperf., pair		90.00	

Frances Perkins
A1208

Dolley
Madison
A1209

FRANCES PERKINS ISSUE

Frances Perkins (1882-1965), Secretary of Labor, 1933-1945 (first woman cabinet member).

Designed by F.R. Petrie.

ENGRAVED

Plates of 200 subjects in four panes of 50 each.

1980, Apr. 10	Tagged	Perf. 10½x11	
1821 A1208 15c Prussian blue		30	5
P# block of 4		1.50	—

Zip block of 4		1.40	—
Copyright block of 4		1.40	—

DOLLEY MADISON ISSUE

Dolley Madison (1768-1849), First Lady, 1809-1817.

Designed by Esther Porter.

ENGRAVED

Plates of 600 subjects in four panes of 150 each.

1980, May 20	Tagged	Perf. 11	
1822 A1209 15c red brown & sepia		30	5
P# block of 4		1.50	—
Zip block of 4		1.40	—
Copyright block of 4		1.40	—

Emily
Bissell — A1210

Helen Keller and
Anne
Sullivan — A1211

EMILY BISSELL ISSUE

Emily Bissell (1861-1948), social worker; introduced Christmas seals in United States.

Designed by Stevan Dohanos.

ENGRAVED

Plates of 200 subjects in four panes of 50 each.

1980, May 31	Tagged	Perf. 11	
1823 A1210 15c black & red		30	5
P# block of 4		1.50	—
Zip block of 4		1.40	—
Copyright block of 4		1.40	—
a. Vert. pair, imperf. horiz.		400.00	

HELEN KELLER ISSUE

Helen Keller (1880-1968), blind and deaf writer and lecturer taught by Anne Sullivan (1867-1936).

Designed by Paul Calle.

LITHOGRAPHED AND ENGRAVED

Plates of 200 subjects in four panes of 50 each.

1980, June 27	Tagged	Perf. 11	
1824 A1121 15c multicolored		30	5
P# block of 4		1.50	—
Zip block of 4		1.40	—
Copyright block of 4		1.40	—

Veterans
Administration
Emblem — A1212

Gen. Bernardo de
Galvez — A1213

VETERANS ADMINISTRATION ISSUE

Veterans Administration, 50th anniversary.

Designed by Malcolm Grear.

PHOTOGRAVURE

Plates of 200 subjects in four panes of 50 each.

1980, July 21	Tagged	Perf. 11	
1825 A1212 15c carmine & violet blue		30	5
P# block of 4, 2 P#		1.50	—
Zip block of 4		1.40	—
Copyright block of 4		1.40	—
a. Horiz. pair, imperf. vert.		650.00	

BERNARDO DE GALVEZ ISSUE

Gen. Bernardo de Galvez (1746-1786), helped defeat British in Battle of Mobile, 1780.

Designed by Roy H. Andersen.

LITHOGRAPHED & ENGRAVED

Plates of 200 subjects in four panes of 50 each.

1980, July 23	Tagged	Perf. 11	
1826 A1213 15c **multicolored**		30	5
P# block of 4		1.50	—
Zip block of 4		1.40	—
Copyright block of 4		1.40	—
a. Red, brown & blue (engr.) omitted			—
b. Blue, brown, red (engr.) & yellow (litho.) omitted			—

CORAL REEFS ISSUE

Nos. 1827-1830 are printed in blocks of four.
Nos. 1827-1828 alternate in one horizontal row.
Nos. 1829-1830 in the next.

Brain Coral, Beaugregory Fish — A1214

Elkhorn Coral, Porkfish — A1215

Chalice Coral, Moorish Idol — A1216

Finger Coral, Sabertooth Blenny — A1217

Designed by Chuck Ripper.

PHOTOGRAVURE

Plates of 200 subjects in four panes of 50 each.

1980, Aug. 26	Tagged	Perf. 11	
1827 A1214 15c **multi**		30	8
P# block of 12, 6 P# adjoining #1827, 1828		4.50	—
Zip block of 4, adjoining #1827		1.40	—
Copyright block of 4, adjoining #1827		1.40	—
1828 A1215 15c **multi**		30	8
Zip block of 4, adjoining #1828		1.40	—
Copyright block of 4, adjoining #1828		1.40	—
1829 A1216 15c **multi**		30	8
P# block of 12, 6 P# adjoining #1829, 1830		4.50	—
Zip block of 4, adjoining #1829		1.40	—
Copyright block of 4, adjoining #1829		1.40	—
1830 A1217 15c **multi**		30	8
Zip block of 4, adjoining #1830		1.40	—
Copyright block of 4, adjoining #1830		1.40	—
a. Block of 4, #1827-1830		1.20	85
b. As "a," imperf.		2,000.	
c. As "a," imperf. btwn., vert			—
d. As "a," imperf. vert.			—

American Bald Eagle — A1218

Edith Wharton — A1219

ORGANIZED LABOR ISSUE

Designed by Peter Cocci.

PHOTOGRAVURE

Plates of 200 subjects in four panes of 50 each.

1980, Sept. 1	Tagged	Perf. 11	
1831 A1218 15c **multi**		30	5
P# block of 12, 6 P#		4.50	—
Zip block of 4		1.40	—
Copyright block of 4		1.40	—
a. Imperf., pair		600.00	

EDITH WHARTON ISSUE

Edith Wharton (1862-1937), novelist.

Designed by Bradbury Thompson after 1905 photograph.

ENGRAVED

Plates of 200 subjects in four panes of 50 each.

1980, Sept. 5	Tagged	Perf. 10½x11	
1832 A1219 15c **purple**		30	5
P# block of 4		1.50	—
Zip block of 4		1.40	—
Copyright block of 4		1.40	—

EDUCATION ISSUE

"Homage to the Square: Glow" by Josef Albers — A1220

Designed by Bradbury Thompson

PHOTOGRAVURE

Plates of 200 subjects in four panes of 50 each.

1980, Sept. 12	Tagged	Perf. 11	
1833 A1220 15c **multi**		30	5
P# block of 6, 3 P#		2.25	—
Zip block of 4		1.40	—
Copyright block of 4		1.40	—
a. Horiz. pair, imperf. vert.		325.00	

AMERICAN FOLK ART ISSUE

Pacific Northwest Indian Masks

Heiltsuk, Bella Bella Tribe — A1221

Chilkat Tlingit Tribe — A1222

Tlingit Tribe — A1223

Bella Coola Tribe — A1224

Designed by Bradbury Thompson after photographs.

PHOTOGRAVURE

Plates of 160 subjects in four panes of 40 each.

1980, Sept. 25	Tagged	Perf. 11	
1834 A1221 15c **multi**		30	8
1835 A1222 15c **multi**		30	8
1836 A1223 15c **multi**		30	8
1837 A1224 15c **multi**		30	8
P# block of 10, 5 P#		3.50	—
Zip, copyright block of 6		2.25	—
a. Block of 4, #1834-1837		1.20	85

AMERICAN ARCHITECTURE ISSUE

Smithsonian A1225

Trinity Church — A1226

Penn Academy A1227

Lyndhurst A1228

Designed by Walter D. Richards.

ENGRAVED (Giori)

Plates of 160 subjects in four panes of 40 each.

1980, Oct. 9	Tagged	Perf. 11	
1838 A1225 15c **black & red**		30	8
1839 A1226 15c **black & red**		30	8
1840 A1227 15c **black & red**		30	8
1841 A1228 15c **black & red**		30	8
P# block of 4		1.75	—
Zip block of 4		1.65	—
Copyright block of 4		1.65	—
a. Block of 4, #1838-1841		1.50	85

CHRISTMAS ISSUE

Christmas USA 15c
Madonna and
Child — A1229

Wreath and
Toys — A1230

Designed by Esther Porter (No. 1842) after Epiphany Window, Washington Cathedral, and by Bob Timberlake (No. 1843).

PHOTOGRAVURE
Plate of 200 subjects in four panes of 50 each.

1980, Oct. 31		Tagged	Perf. 11	
1842	A1229 15c multi		30	5
	P# block of 12, 6 P#		4.25	—
	Zip block of 4		1.40	—
	Copyright block of 4		1.40	—
a.	Imperf., pair		100.00	
	Pair with full vert. gutter btwn.		—	

PHOTOGRAVURE (Combination Press)
Plates of 230 subjects (10x23) in panes of 50 (10x5).

1843	A1230 15c multi	30	5
	P# block of 20, 5-8 P#, 1-2 copyright	6.50	—
	Copyright block of 4	1.40	—
a.	Imperf., pair	100.00	

See Combination Press note after No. 1703.

GREAT AMERICANS ISSUE

Dorothea Dix
USA 1c
A1231

Igor Stravinsky
USA 2c
A1232

Henry Clay
USA 3c
A1233

Carl Schurz
4c USA
A1234

Pearl Buck
USA 5c
A1235

Walter Lippmann
6 USA
A1236

Abraham Baldwin
USA 7
A1237

Henry Knox
USA 8
A1238

Sylvanus Thayer
USA 9
A1239

Richard Russell
USA 10c
A1240

Alden Partridge
USA 11
A1241

Sinclair Lewis
USA 14
A1243

George Mason
USA 18c
A1245

Ralph Bunche
USA 20c
A1247

Harry S Truman
USA 20c
A1249

Frank C. Laubach
USA 30c
A1251

Robert Millikan
37c USA
A1253

Lillian M. Gilbreth
USA 40c
A1255

USA 13c Crazy Horse
A1242

Rachel Carson
USA 17c
A1244

USA 19c
Sequoyah
A1246

Thomas H Gallaudet
USA 20c
A1248

John J. Audubon
USA 22
A1250

Charles R Drew MD
USA 35c
A1252

Grenville Clark
USA 39
A1254

USA 50 Chester W. Nimitz
A1256

Designers: 1c, Bernie Fuchs. 2c, Burt Silverman, 3c, 17c, 40c, Ward Brackett. 4c, 7c, 10c, 18c, 30c, Richard Sparks. 6c, No. 1862, Dennis Lyall. 8c, Arthur Lidov. 9c, 11c, Robert Alexander Anderson. 13c, Brad Holland. 14c, Bradbury Thompson. 19c, 39c, Roy H. Andersen. No. 1860, Jim Sharpe. No. 1861, 22c, 50c, 37c, Christopher Calle. 35c, Nathan Jones.

ENGRAVED
Perf. 10½x11 Perf. 11 (1c, 6c-11c, 14c, No. 1862, 22c, 30c, 39c, 40c, 50c)

1980-85			Tagged	
1844	A1231 1c black, Sept. 23, 1983		5	5
	P# block of 6, P#		35	—
	P# block of 20, 1-2 P 1-2 copyright		1.00	—
a.	Imperf., pair		250.00	
b.	Vert. pair, imperf. between			
1845	A1232 2c brn blk, Nov. 18, 1982		5	5
	P# block of 4		25	—
	Zip block of 4		20	—
	Copyright block of 4		20	—
1846	A1233 3c olive green, July 13, 1983		8	5
	P# block of 4		40	—
	Zip block of 4		35	—
	Copyright block of 4		35	—
1847	A1234 4c violet, June 3, 1983		10	5
	P# block of 4		50	—
	Zip block of 4		45	—
	Copyright block of 4		45	—
1848	A1235 5c henna brown, June 25, 1983		12	5
	P# block of 4		60	—
	Zip block of 4		50	—
	Copyright block of 4		50	—
1849	A1236 6c orange vermilion, Sept. 19, 1985		12	5
	P# block of 6, P#		85	—
	P# block of 20, 1-2 P 1-2 copyright		2.75	—
1850	A1237 7c bright carmine, Jan. 25, 1985		14	5
	P# block of 6, P#		1.00	—
	P# block of 20, 1-2 P 1-2 zip, 1-2 copyright		3.00	—
1851	A1238 8c olive black, July 25, 1985		16	5
	P# block of 6, P#		80	—
	Zip block of 4		70	—
	Copyright block of 4		70	—
1852	A1239 9c dark green, June 7, 1985		18	5
	P# block of 6, P#		1.30	—
	P# block of 20, 1-2 P 1-2 zip, 1-2 copyright		4.00	—
1853	A1240 10c Prus. blue, May 31, 1984		20	5
	P# block of 6, P#		1.40	—
	P# block of 20, 1-2 P 1-2 copyright, 1-2 zip		5.50	—
a.	Vert. pair, imperf. between			

Completely imperforate and untagged stamps are from printer's waste.

1854	A1241 11c dark blue, Feb. 12, 1985		22	5
	P# block of 4		1.10	—
	Zip block of 4		1.00	—
	Copyright block of 4		1.00	—
1855	A1242 13c lt. maroon, Jan. 15, 1982		30	5
	P# block of 4		1.50	—
	Zip block of 4		1.30	—
	Copyright block of 4		1.30	—
1856	A1243 14c slate green, Mar. 21, 1985		32	5
	P# block of 6, P#		2.25	—
	P# block of 20, 1-2 P 1-2 zip, 1-2 copyright		7.00	—
a.	Vert. pair, imperf. horiz.		175.00	
b.	Horiz. pair, imperf. btwn.		15.00	
c.	Vert. pair, imperf. btwn.			
1857	A1244 17c green, May 28, 1981		40	5
	P# block of 4		2.00	—
	Zip block of 4		1.70	—
	Copyright block of 4		1.70	—
1858	A1245 18c dark blue, May 7, 1981		44	5
	P# block of 4		2.20	—
	Zip block of 4		1.80	—
	Copyright block of 4		1.80	—
1859	A1246 19c brown, Dec. 27, 1980		38	7
	P# block of 4		2.00	—
	Zip block of 4		1.80	—
	Copyright block of 4		1.80	—
1860	A1247 20c claret, Jan. 12, 1982		50	5
	P# block of 4		2.50	—
	Zip block of 4		2.10	—
	Copyright block of 4		2.10	—
1861	A1248 20c green, June 10, 1983		50	5
	P# block of 4		2.50	—
	Zip block of 4		2.10	—
	Copyright block of 4		2.10	—
1862	A1249 20c black, Jan. 26, 1984		40	5
	P# block of 6, P#		2.80	—
	P# block of 20, 1-2 P 1-2 copyright, 1-2 zip		10.00	—
	Corner P# block of 4		2.00	—
1863	A1250 22c dark chalky blue, Apr. 23, 1985		44	5
	P# block of 6, P#		3.10	—
	P# block of 20, 1-2 P 1-2 zip, 1-2 copyright		10.00	—
	Corner P# block of 4		2.20	—
a.	Vert. pair, imperf. horiz.			
1864	A1251 30c olive gray, Sept. 2, 1984		60	8
	P# block of 6, P#		4.25	—
	P# block of 20, 1-2 P 1-2 copyright, 1-2 zip		14.00	—
	Corner P# block of 4		3.00	—
1865	A1252 35c gray, June 3, 1981		70	8
	P# block of 4		3.50	—
	Zip block of 4		3.25	—
	Copyright block of 4		3.25	—
1866	A1253 37c blue, Jan. 26, 1982		75	5
	P# block of 4		3.75	—
	Zip block of 4		3.35	—
	Copyright block of 4		3.35	—
1867	A1254 39c rose lilac, May 20, 1985		80	5
	P# block of 6, P#		5.75	—
	P# block of 20, 1-2 P 1-2 zip, 1-2 copyright		20.00	—
	Perf. 11.2		80	8
	Corner P# block of 4, perf. 11.2		4.00	—
a.	Vert. pair, imperf. horiz.			
b.	Vert. pair, imperf. between			

1868 A1255 40c **dark green,** *Feb. 24, 1984*	80	10
P# block of 6, P#	5.75	—
P# block of 20, 1-2 P 1-2 copyright, 1-2 zip	17.50	—
Corner P# block of 4	4.00	—
1869 A1256 50c **brown,** *Feb. 22, 1985*	1.00	10
P# block of 4	5.00	—
Zip block of 4	4.50	—
Copyright block of 4	4.50	—

USA 15c
Everett Dirksen

A1261

Whitney Moore Young

Black Heritage USA 15c

A1262

EVERETT DIRKSEN (1896-1969)

Senate minority leader, 1960-1969.

Designed by Ron Adair

ENGRAVED
Plates of 200 subjects in four panes of 50 each.

1981, Jan. 4	**Tagged**	**Perf. 11**	
1874 A1261 15c **gray**		30	5
P# block of 4		1.50	—
Zip block of 4		1.40	—
Copyright block of 4		1.40	—

BLACK HERITAGE

Whitney Moore Young, Jr. (1921-1971), civil rights leader.

Designed by Jerry Pinkney.

PHOTOGRAVURE
Plates of 200 subjects in four panes of 50 each.

1981, Jan. 30	**Tagged**	**Perf. 11**	
1875 A1262 15c **multi**		30	5
P# block of 4		1.50	—
Zip block of 4		1.40	—
Copyright block of 4		1.40	—

FLOWER ISSUE

Rose — A1263

Camellia — A1264

Dahlia — A1265

Lily — A1266

Designed by Lowell Nesbitt.

PHOTOGRAVURE
Plates of 192 subjects in four panes of 48 (8x6).

1981, Apr. 23	**Tagged**	**Perf. 11**	
1876 A1263 18c **multicolored**		36	8
1877 A1264 18c **multicolored**		36	8
1878 A1265 18c **multicolored**		36	8
1879 A1266 18c **multicolored**		36	8
P# block of 4		2.10	—
Zip block of 4		2.00	—
Copyright block of 4		2.00	—
a. Block of 4, #1876-1879		1.90	85

A1267-A1276

Designs from photographs by Jim Brandenburg.

ENGRAVED

1981, May 14	**Tagged**	**Perf. 11**	
	Dark brown		
1880 A1267 18c Bighorn		36	5
1881 A1268 18c Puma		36	5
1882 A1269 18c Harbor seal		36	5
1883 A1270 18c Bison		36	5
1884 A1271 18c Brown bear		36	5
1885 A1272 18c Polar bear		36	5
1886 A1273 18c Elk (wapiti)		36	5
1887 A1274 18c Moose		36	5
1888 A1275 18c White-tailed deer		36	5
1889 A1276 18c Pronghorn		36	5
a. Booklet pane of 10		9.00	—

Nos. 1880-1889 issued in booklet only. All stamps have one or two straight edges.

FLAG AND ANTHEM ISSUE

A1277

A1278

A1279

A1280

Designed by Peter Cocci.

ENGRAVED
Plates of 460 subjects (20x23) in panes of 100 (10x10).

1981, Apr. 24	**Tagged**	**Perf. 11**	
1890 A1277 18c **multi**		36	5
P# block of 6, P#		2.60	—
P# block of 20, 1-2 P#		10.00	—
a. Imperf., pair		100.00	

See Combination Press note after No. 1703.

Coil Stamp
Perf. 10 Vert.

1891 A1278 18c **multi**		36	5
Pair		72	10
P# strip of 3, P# 4, 5		6.50	
P# strip of 3, P# 1		140.00	
P# strip of 3, P# 2		25.00	

P# strip of 3, P# 3		300.00	
P# strip of 3, P# 6			
P# strip of 3, P# 7		25.00	
a. Imperf., pair		20.00	

Booklet Stamps
Perf. 11

1892 A1279 6c **multi**		50	10
1893 A1280 18c **multi**		36	5
a. Booklet pane of 8 (2 #1892, 6 #1893)		3.50	—
b. As "a," vert. imperf. btwn.		75.00	

FLAG OVER SUPREME COURT ISSUE

USA 20c

A1281

Designed by Dean Ellis

ENGRAVED
Plates of 460 subjects (20x23) in panes of 100 (10x10)

1981, Dec. 17	**Tagged**	**Perf. 11**	
1894 A1281 20c **blk., dk. blue & red**		45	5
P# block of 6, P#		3.25	—
P# block of 20, 1-2 P#		9.50	—
a. Vert. pair, imperf.		25.00	
b. Vert. pair, imperf. horiz.			
c. Dark blue omitted		—	
d. Black omitted		—	

Coil Stamp
Perf. 10 Vert.

1895 A1281 20c **blk., dk. blue & red**		40	5
Pair		80	10
P# strip of 3, P# 13, 14		6.50	
P# strip of 3, P# 2, 3, 5, 9, 10, 12		7.50	
P# strip of 3, P# 1		12.00	
P# strip of 3, P# 4		65.00	
P# strip of 3, P# 6		50.00	
P# strip of 3, P# 8		9.00	
P# strip of 3, P# 11		13.00	
a. Imperf., pair		6.00	
b. Black omitted		75.00	
c. Blue omitted		—	
d. Pair, imperf. btwn.		—	
e. Untagged (Bureau precanceled)			45
P# strip of 3, P# 14		8.00	

BOOKLET STAMP
Perf. 11x10½

1896 A1281 20c **blk., dk. blue & red**		40	5
a. Booklet pane of 6		2.50	—
b. Booklet pane of 10, *June 1, 1982*		4.25	—

Booklets containing two panes of ten were issued Nov. 17, 1983.

TRANSPORTATION ISSUE

Omnibus 1880s
USA 1c

A1283

Locomotive 1870s
USA 2c

A1284

Handcar 1880s
USA 3c

A1284a

Stagecoach 1890s
USA 4c

A1285

Motorcycle 1913
USA 5c

A1286

Sleigh 1880s
USA 5.2c
Auth Nonprofit Org

A1287

Bicycle 1870s
USA 5.9c
Auth.
Nonprofit
Org.
A1288

Baby Buggy 1880s
USA 7.4c
A1288a

Mail Wagon 1880s
USA 9.3c
Bulk
Rate
A1289

Hansom Cab 1890s
USA 10.9c
Bulk
Rate
A1290

RR Caboose 1890s
USA 11c
Bulk Rate
A1291

Electric Auto 1917
USA 17c
A1292

Surrey 1890s
USA 18c
A1293

Fire Pumper
1860s
USA 20c
A1294

Designers: 1c, 2c, 5.9c, 10.9c, 18c, David Stone. 3c, 5c, 5.2c, Walter Brooks. 4c, 7.4c, 9.3c, 11c, 20c, Jim Schleyer. 17c Chuck Jaquays.

COIL STAMPS
ENGRAVED

1981-84		Tagged	Perf. 10 Vert.	
1897	A1283	1c violet, Aug. 19, 1983	5	5
		Pair	10	10
		P# strip of 3, line, P# 1, 2, 5, 6	70	
		P# strip of 3, line, P# 3, 4	75	
b.		Imperf., pair		
1897A	A1284	2c black, May 20, 1982	10	5
		Pair	20	10
		P# strip of 3, line, P# 3, 4, 8, 10	65	
		P# strip of 3, line, P# 2, 6	85	
e.		Imperf., pair	75.00	
1898	A1284a	3c dark green, Mar. 25, 1983	15	5
		Pair	30	10
		P# strip of 3, line, P# 1, 2	1.00	
		P# strip of 3, line, P# 3, 4	1.25	
1898A	A1285	4c reddish brown, Aug. 19, 1982	12	5
		Pair	24	10
		P# strip of 3, line, P# 3, 4	1.50	
		P# strip of 3, P# 1, 2, 5, 6	2.00	
b.		Untagged (Bureau precanceled)		12
		P# strip of 3, line, P# 3-6	2.25	
c.		As "b," imperf. pair	600.00	
1899	A1286	5c gray green, Oct. 10, 1983	15	5
		Pair	30	10
		P# strip of 3, line, P# 1, 2	1.50	
		P# strip of 3, line, P# 3, 4	1.75	
a.		Imperf., pair	—	
1900	A1287	5.2c carmine, Mar. 21, 1983	20	5
		Pair	40	10
		P# strip of 3, line, P# 1, 2	9.00	
		P# strip of 3, line, P# 3, 5	100.00	
a.		Untagged (Bureau precanceled)		20
		P# strip of 3, line, P# 1, 3-6	8.00	
		P# strip of 3, line, P# 3-6	10.00	
1901	A1288	5.9c blue, Feb. 17, 1982	20	5
		Pair	40	10
		P# strip of 3, line, P# 3, 4	12.00	
a.		Untagged (Bureau Precanceled, lines only)		20

		P# strip of 3, line, P# 3, 4	15.00	
		P# strip of 3, line, P# 5, 6	50.00	
b.		As "a,", imperf. pair	250.00	
1902	A1288a	7.4c brown, Apr. 7, 1984	20	8
		Pair	40	16
		P# strip of 3, P# 2	10.00	
a.		Untagged (Bureau precanceled)		20
		P# strip of 3, P# 2	4.00	
1903	A1289	9.3c carmine rose, Dec. 15	20	8
		Pair	40	16
		P# strip of 3, line, P# 1, 2	15.00	
		P# strip of 3, line, P# 3, 4	25.00	
		P# strip of 3, line, P# 5, 6	200.00	
a.		Untagged (Bureau precanceled, lines only)		20
		P# strip of 3, line, P# 5, 6	5.00	
		P# strip of 3, line, P# 1, 3	25.00	
		P# strip of 3, line, P# 2, 4	16.00	
		P# strip of 3, line, P# 8	95.00	
b.		As "a," imperf. pair	100.00	
1904	A1290	10.9c purple, Mar. 26, 1982	25	5
		Pair	50	10
		P# strip of 3, line, P# 1, 2	20.00	
a.		Untagged (Bureau precanceled, lines only)		25
		P# strip of 3, line, P# 1, 2	20.00	
		P# strip of 3, line, P# 3, 4	450.00	
b.		As "a," imperf. pair	175.00	
1905	A1291	11c red, Feb. 3, 1984	25	8
		Pair	50	16
		P# strip of 3, P# 1	6.00	
a.		Untagged (Bureau precanceled)		25
		P# strip of 3, P# 1	5.00	
1906	A1292	17c ultramarine, June 25	34	5
		Pair	70	10
		P# strip of 3, line, P# 1-5	4.50	
		P# strip of 3, line, P# 6	22.50	
		P# strip of 3, line, P# 7	7.00	
a.		Untagged (Bureau precanceled, Presorted First Class)		35
		P# strip of 3, line, P# 3-6	6.00	
		P# strip of 3, line, P# 1, 2	12.50	
		P# strip of 3, line, P# 7	11.00	

Three different precancel styles exist: "PRESORTED" measuring 11.3mm, 12.8mm and 13.4mm.

b.		Imperf., pair	175.00	
c.		As "a," imperf. pair	250.00	
1907	A1293	18c dark brown, May 18	36	5
		Pair	72	10
		P# strip of 3, line, P# 2, 5, 6, 8-10	5.00	
		P# strip of 3, line, P# 1	65.00	
		P# strip of 3, line, P# 3, 4, 7	30.00	
		P# strip of 3, line, P# 11-18	9.00	
a.		Imperf., pair	110.00	
1908	A1294	20c vermilion, Dec. 10	40	5
		Pair	80	10
		P# strip of 3, line, P# 3-5, 9, 10	5.00	
		P# strip of 3, line, P# 1	60.00	
		P# strip of 3, line, P# 2	200.00	
		P# strip of 3, line, P# 6, 13, 15, 16	6.50	
		P# strip of 3, line, P# 7, 8	65.00	
		P# strip of 3, line, P# 11	35.00	
		P# strip of 3, line, P# 12, 14	20.00	
a.		Imperf., pair	110.00	

See Nos. 2225-2228.

Eagle
and
Moon
A1296

Booklet Stamp
PHOTOGRAVURE

1983, Aug. 12			Perf. 10 Vert.	
1909	A1296	$9.35 multi	25.00	6.00
a.		Booklet pane of 3	77.50	—

AMERICAN RED CROSS CENTENNIAL

The Gift of Self
USA 18c
American Red Cross
1881-1981
A1297

Designed by Joseph Csatari.

PHOTOGRAVURE
Plates of 200 subjects in four panes of 50.

1981, May 1		Tagged	Perf. 10½x11	
1910	A1297	18c multi	36	5
		P# block of 4	1.80	—
		Zip block of 4	1.60	—
		Copyright block of 4	1.60	—

SAVINGS & LOAN SESQUICENTENNIAL

SAVINGS AND LOANS
SAVE
USA 18c
A1298

Designed by Don Hedin.

PHOTOGRAVURE
Plates of 200 subjects in four panes of 50.

1981, May 8		Tagged	Perf. 11	
1911	A1298	18c multi	36	5
		P# block of 4	1.80	—
		Zip block of 4	1.60	—
		Copyright block of 4	1.60	—

SPACE ACHIEVEMENT ISSUE

Exploring
the Moon
USA 18c
A1299

Benefiting Mankind
USA 18c
A1300

Benefiting Mankind

USA 18c

A1301

Understanding the Sun

USA 18c

A1302

Probing the Planets

USA 18c

A1303

USA 18c

A1304

Benefiting Mankind

USA 18c

Benefiting Mankind

A1305

Comprehending the Universe

USA 18c

A1306

Designs: A1299, Moon walk. A1300-A1301, A1304-A1305, Columbia space shuttle. A1302, Skylab. A1303, Pioneer II. A1306, Telescope. Se-tenant in blocks of 8.
Designed by Robert McCall.

PHOTOGRAVURE
Plates of 192 subjects in four panes of 48 each.

			Tagged	Perf. 11	
1981, May 21					
1912	A1299	18c **multi**		36	10
1913	A1300	18c **multi**		36	10
1914	A1301	18c **multi**		36	10
1915	A1302	18c **multi**		36	10
1916	A1303	18c **multi**		36	10
1917	A1304	18c **multi**		36	10
1918	A1305	18c **multi**		36	10
1919	A1306	18c **multi**		36	10
		P# block of 8, 6 P#		4.25	—
		Zip, copyright block of 8		4.00	—
a.		Block of 8, #1912-1919		3.75	2.25
b.		As "a," imperf.			

PROFESSIONAL MANAGEMENT ISSUE

Professional Management

USA 18c

Joseph Wharton (Founder of Wharton School of Business) — A1307

Professional management education centenary.
Designed by Rudolph de Harak.

PHOTOGRAVURE
Plates of 200 subject in four panes of 50 each.

			Tagged	Perf. 11	
1981, June 18					
1920	A1307	18c **blue & black**		36	5
		P# block of 4, 2 P#		1.80	—
		Zip block of 4		1.60	—
		Copyright block of 4		1.60	—

PRESERVATION OF WILDLIFE HABITATS ISSUE

Save Wetland Habitats

USA 18c

Great Blue Heron — A1308

Save Grassland Habitats

USA 18c

Badger — A1309

USA 18c

Grizzly Bear — A1310
Save Mountain Habitats

USA 18c

Save Woodland Habitats

Ruffed Grouse — A1311

Designed by Chuck Ripper.

PHOTOGRAVURE
Plates of 200 subjects in four panes of 50 each.

			Tagged	Perf. 11	
1981, June 26					
1921	A1308	18c **multi**		36	8
1922	A1309	18c **multi**		36	8
1923	A1310	18c **multi**		36	8
1924	A1311	18c **multi**		36	8
		P# block of 4, 5 P#		2.10	—
		Zip block of 4		2.00	—
		Copyright block of 4		2.00	—
a.		Block of 4, #1921-1924		1.90	85

INTERNATIONAL YEAR OF THE DISABLED ISSUE

USA 18c

Man Using Microscope A1312

Disabled doesn't mean Unable

Designed by Martha Perske.

PHOTOGRAVURE
Plates of 200 subjects in four panes of 50 each.

			Tagged	Perf. 11	
1981, June 29					
1925	A1312	18c **multi**		36	5
		P# block of 4, 6 P#		1.80	—
		Zip block of 4		1.60	—
		Copyright block of 4		1.60	—
a.		Vert. pair, imperf. horiz.		2,500.	

EDNA ST. VINCENT MILLAY ISSUE

Edna St Vincent Millay

American Poet   USA 18c

A1313

Designed by Glenora Case Richards.

LITHOGRAPHED AND ENGRAVED
Plates of 200 subjects in four panes of 50 each.

			Tagged	Perf. 11	
1981, July 10					
1926	A1313	18c **multi**		36	5
		P# block of 4, 7 P#		1.80	—
		Zip block of 4		1.60	—
		Copyright block of 4		1.60	—
a.		Black (engr., inscriptions) omitted		800.00	

ALCOHOLISM

Alcoholism You can beat it! USA 18c

A1314

Designed by John Boyd.

ENGRAVED
Plates of 230 (10x23) subjects in panes of 50 (5x10)

			Tagged	Perf. 11	
1981, Aug. 19					
1927	A1314	18c **blue & black**		45	5
		P# block of 6, P#		3.25	—
		P# block of 20, 1-2 P#, 1-2 copyright, 1-2 Zip		42.50	—
a.		Imperf., pair		350.00	

See Combination Press note after No. 1703.

AMERICAN ARCHITECTURE

Stanford White 1853-1906 NYU Library New York

Architecture USA 18c

New York University Library by Stanford White — A1315

Richard Morris Hunt 1828-1895 Biltmore Asheville NC

Architecture USA 18c

Biltmore House By Richard Morris Hunt — A1316

Bernard Maybeck 1862-1957 Palace of Arts San Francisco

Architecture USA 18c

Palace of the Arts by Bernard Maybeck A1317

Louis Sullivan 1856-1924 Bank Owatonna Minn

Architecture USA 18c

National Farmer's Bank by Louis Sullivan A1318

Designed by Walter D. Richards.

ENGRAVED
Plates of 160 subjects in four panes of 40 each.

			Tagged	Perf. 11	
1981, Aug. 28					
1928	A1315	18c **black & red**		36	8
1929	A1316	18c **black & red**		36	8
1930	A1317	18c **black & red**		36	8
1931	A1318	18c **black & red**		36	8
		P# block of 4		1.80	—

	Zip block of 4	1.60	—
	Copyright block of 4	1.60	—
a.	Block of 4, #1928-1931	1.50	85

SPORTS PERSONALITIES

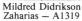

Mildred Didrikson
Zaharias — A1319

Robert Tyre
Jones — A1320

Designed by Richard Gangel

ENGRAVED
Plates of 200 subjects in four panes of 50.

1981, Sept. 22	**Tagged**		**Perf.** *10½x11*	
1932 A1319 18c	**purple**		36	5
	P# block of 4		1.80	—
	Zip block of 4		1.60	—
	Copyright block of 4		1.60	—
1933 A1320 18c	**green**		36	5
	P# block of 4		1.80	—
	Zip block of 4		1.60	—
	Copyright block of 4		1.60	—

Coming Through
the
Rye — A1321

Designed by Paul Calle

LITHOGRAPHED AND ENGRAVED
Plates of 200 in four panes of 50.

1981, Oct. 9	**Tagged**	**Perf.** *11*	
1934 A1321 18c	**gray, olive green & brown**	36	5
	P# block of 4, 3 P#	1.80	—
	Zip block of 4	1.60	—
	Copyright block of 4	1.60	—
a.	Vert. pair, imperf. btwn.	300.00	
b.	Brown omitted	750.00	

JAMES HOBAN

Irish-American
Architect of the
White
House — A1322

Designed by Ron Mercer and Walter D. Richards

PHOTOGRAVURE
Plates of 200 in four panes of 50.

1981, Oct. 13	**Tagged**	**Perf.** *11*	
1935 A1322 18c	**multi**	50	25
	P# block of 4, 6 P#	3.00	—
	Zip block of 4	2.25	—
	Copyright block of 4	2.25	—
1936 A1322 20c	**multi**	40	5
	P# block of 4, 6 P#	2.00	—
	Zip block of 4	1.75	—
	Copyright block of 4	1.75	—

AMERICAN BICENTENNIAL

Battle of
Yorktown
A1323

Battle of the
Virginia Capes
A1324

Designed by Cal Sacks

LITHOGRAPHED AND ENGRAVED
Plates of 200 in four panes of 50.

1981, Oct. 16	**Tagged**	**Perf.** *11*	
1937 A1323 18c	**multicolored**	36	6
1938 A1324 18c	**multicolored**	36	6
	P# block of 4, 7 P#	2.00	—
	Zip block of 4	1.90	—
	Copyright block of 4	1.90	—
a.	Pair, #1937-1938	90	15
b.	As "a," black (engr., inscriptions) omitted	800.00	

CHRISTMAS

Madonna and
Child, Botticelli
A1325

Felt Bear on Sleigh
A1326

Designed by Bradbury Thompson (No. 1939) and by Naiad
Einsel (No. 1940)

PHOTOGRAVURE
Plates of 400 in four panes of 100 (No. 1939)
Plates of 200 in four panes of 50 (No. 1940)

1981, Oct. 28	**Tagged**	**Perf.** *11*	
1939 A1325 (20c)	**multi**	40	5
	P# block of 4, 6 P#	2.00	—
	Zip block of 4	1.75	—
	Copyright block of 4	1.75	—
a.	Imperf. pair	125.00	
1940 A1326 (20c)	**multi**	40	5
	P# block of 4, 5 P#	2.00	—
	Zip block of 4	1.75	—
	Copyright block of 4	1.75	—
a.	Imperf. pair	175.00	
b.	Vert. pair, horiz. imperf.	—	

JOHN HANSON

First President of the
Continental Congress — A1327

Designed by Ron Adair

PHOTOGRAVURE
Plates of 200 in panes of 50

1981, Nov. 5	**Tagged**	**Perf.** *11*	
1941 A1327 20c	**multicolored**	40	5
	P# block of 4, 5 P#	2.00	—
	Zip block of 4	1.75	—
	Copyright block of 4	1.75	—

DESERT PLANTS

Barrel
Cactus — A1328

Agave — A1329

Beavertail
Cactus — A1330

Saguaro — A1331

Designed by Frank J. Waslick.

LITHOGRAPHED AND ENGRAVED
Plates of 160 in four panes of 40

1981 Dec. 11	**Tagged**	**Perf.** *11*	
1942 A1328 20c	**multi**	40	6
1943 A1329 20c	**multi**	40	6
1944 A1330 20c	**multi**	40	6
1945 A1331 20c	**multi**	40	6
	P# block of 4, 7 P#	2.50	—
	Zip block of 4	2.25	—
	Copyright block of 4	2.25	—
a.	Block of 4, #1942-1945	2.10	85

A1332

A1333

Designed by Bradbury Thompson.

PHOTOGRAVURE
Plates of 400 in panes of 100.

1981, Oct. 11	**Tagged**	**Perf.** *11x10½*	
1946 A1332 (20c)	**brown**	45	5
	P# block of 4	2.25	—
	Zip block of 4	2.00	—
	Copyright block of 4	2.00	—

COIL STAMP
Perf. 10 Vert.

1947 A1332	(20c) **brown**	45	5
	Pair	90	10
	Joint line pair	1.10	—
a.	Imperf. pair		

BOOKLET STAMPS
Perf. 11x10½

1948 A1333	(20c) **brown**	40	5
a.	Booklet pane of 10	4.25	—

Rocky Mountain
Bighorn — A1334

ENGRAVED

1982, Jan. 8	Tagged	Perf. 11

1949 A1334	20c **dark blue** (from bklt. pane)	40	5
a.	Booklet pane of 10	5.50	—
	As "a," imperf. between	85.00	

Franklin D. Roosevelt A1335

Designed by Clarence Holbert.

ENGRAVED
Plates of 192 in four panes of 48

1982, Jan. 30	Tagged	Perf. 11

1950 A1335	20c **blue**	40	5
	P# block of 4	2.00	—
	Zip block of 4	1.75	—
	Copyright block of 4	1.75	—

LOVE ISSUE

A1336

Designed by Mary Faulconer.

PHOTOGRAVURE
Plates of 200 in four panes of 50.

1982, Feb. 1	Tagged	Perf. 11x10½

1951 A1336	20c **Multicolored**	45	5
	P# block of 4, 5 P#	2.25	—
	Zip block of 4	2.00	—
	Copyright block of 4	2.00	—
a.	Perf. 11	50	5
a.	P# block of 4, 5 P#	3.00	—
b.	Imperf. pair	300.00	
c.	Blue omitted	—	

GEORGE WASHINGTON

A1337

Designed by Mark English.

PHOTOGRAVURE
Plates of 200 in four panes of 50.

1982, Feb. 22	Tagged	Perf. 11

1952 A1337	20c **multicolored**	45	5
	P# block of 4, 6 P#	2.25	—
	Zip block of 4	2.00	—
	Copyright block of 4	2.00	—

STATE BIRDS AND FLOWERS ISSUE

State Birds and Flowers
A1338-A1387

Designed by Arthur and Alan Singer.

PHOTOGRAVURE (Andreotti)
Plates of 200 subjects in four panes of 50 each.

1982, Apr. 14	Tagged	Perf. 10½x11

1953 A1338	20c	*Alabama*	45	25
1954 A1339	20c	*Alaska*	45	25
1955 A1340	20c	*Arizona*	45	25
1956 A1341	20c	*Arkansas*	45	25
1957 A1342	20c	*California*	45	25
1958 A1343	20c	*Colorado*	45	25
1959 A1344	20c	*Connecticut*	45	25
1960 A1345	20c	*Delaware*	45	25
1961 A1346	20c	*Florida*	45	25
1962 A1347	20c	*Georgia*	45	25
1963 A1348	20c	*Hawaii*	45	25
1964 A1349	20c	*Idaho*	45	25
1965 A1350	20c	*Illinois*	45	25
1966 A1351	20c	*Indiana*	45	25
1967 A1352	20c	*Iowa*	45	25
1968 A1353	20c	*Kansas*	45	25
1969 A1354	20c	*Kentucky*	45	25
1970 A1355	20c	*Louisiana*	45	25
1971 A1356	20c	*Maine*	45	25
1972 A1357	20c	*Maryland*	45	25
1973 A1358	20c	*Massachusetts*	45	25
1974 A1359	20c	*Michigan*	45	25
1975 A1360	20c	*Minnesota*	45	25
1976 A1360	20c	*Mississippi*	45	25
1977 A1361	20c	*Missouri*	45	25
1978 A1362	20c	*Montana*	45	25
1979 A1363	20c	*Nebraska*	45	25
1980 A1364	20c	*Nevada*	45	25
1981 A1364	20c	*New Hampshire*	45	25
1982 A1365	20c	*New Jersey*	45	25
1983 A1366	20c	*New Mexico*	45	25
1984 A1369	20c	*New York*	45	25
1985 A1370	20c	*North Carolina*	45	25
1986 A1371	20c	*North Dakota*	45	25
1987 A1372	20c	*Ohio*	45	25
1988 A1373	20c	*Oklahoma*	45	25
1989 A1374	20c	*Oregon*	45	25
1990 A1375	20c	*Pennsylvania*	45	25
1991 A1376	20c	*Rhode Island*	45	25
1992 A1377	20c	*South Carolina*	45	25
1993 A1378	20c	*South Dakota*	45	25
1994 A1379	20c	*Tennessee*	45	25
1995 A1380	20c	*Texas*	45	25
1996 A1381	20c	*Utah*	45	25
1997 A1382	20c	*Vermont*	45	25
1998 A1383	20c	*Virginia*	45	25
1999 A1384	20c	*Washington*	45	25
2000 A1385	20c	*West Virginia*	45	25
2001 A1386	20c	*Wisconsin*	45	25
2002 A1387	20c	*Wyoming*	45	25
a.	1953a-2002a, any single, perf. 11		50	30
b.	Pane of 50, perf. 10½x11		22.50	—
c.	Pane of 50, perf. 11		25.00	—
d.	Pane of 50, imperf.		—	

US-NETHERLANDS

200th Anniv. of
Diplomatic
Recognition by
The Netherlands
A1388

Designed by Heleen Tigler Wybrandi-Raue.

PHOTOGRAVURE
Plates of 230 (10x23) subjects in panes of 50 (5x10).

1982, Apr. 20	Tagged	Perf. 11

2003 A1388	20c **verm., brt. blue & gray blk.**	45	5
	P# block of 6, P#	3.25	—
	P# block of 20, 1-2 P#, 1-2 copyright, 1-2 zip	12.50	—
a.	Imperf. pair	500.00	

See Combination Press note after No. 1703.

LIBRARY OF CONGRESS

A1389

Designed by Bradbury Thompson.

ENGRAVED
Plates of 200 subjects in four panes of 50.

1982, Apr. 21	Tagged	Perf. 11

2004 A1389	20c **red & black**	40	5
	P# block of 4	2.00	—
	Zip block of 4	1.75	—
	Copyright block of 4	1.75	—

A1390

Designed by John Boyd.

ENGRAVED
Coil Stamp

1982, Apr. 27	Tagged		Perf. 10 Vert.	
2005 A1390 20c	**sky blue**		50	5
	Pair		1.00	10
	P# strip of 3, line, P# 1-4		60.00	
a.	Imperf. pair		100.00	

KNOXVILLE WORLD'S FAIR

A1391

A1392

A1393

A1394

Designed by Charles Harper.

PHOTOGRAVURE
Plates of 200 in four panes of 50.

1982, Apr. 29	Tagged		Perf. 11	
2006 A1391 20c	**multi**		40	8
2007 A1392 20c	**multi**		40	8
2008 A1393 20c	**multi**		40	8
2009 A1394 20c	**multi**		40	8
	P# block of 4, 5 P#		2.50	—
	Zip block of 4		2.25	—
	Copyright block of 4		2.25	—
a.	Block of 4, #2006-2009		2.10	85

AMERICAN AUTHOR, 1832-1899

A1395

Designed by Robert Hallock.

ENGRAVED
Plates of 200 in four panes of 50.

1982, Apr. 30	Tagged		Perf. 11	
2010 A1395 20c	**red & black**, *tan*		40	5
	P# block of 4		2.00	—
	Zip block of 4		1.75	—
	Copyright block of 4		1.75	—

AGING TOGETHER

A1396

Designed by Paul Calle.

ENGRAVED
Plates of 200 in four panes of 50.

1982, May 21	Tagged		Perf. 11	
2011 A1396 20c	**brown**		40	5
	P# block of 4		2.00	—
	Zip block of 4		1.75	—
	Copyright block of 4		1.75	—

John, Lionel and Ethel
Barrymore — A1397

Dr. Mary Walker
Army Surgeon
Medal of Honor
USA 20c

A1398

PERFORMING ARTS
Designed by Jim Sharpe.

PHOTOGRAVURE
Plates of 200 in four panes of 50.

1982, June 8	Tagged		Perf. 11	
2012 A1397 20c	**multicolored**		40	5
	P# block of 4, 6 P#		2.00	—
	Zip block of 4		1.75	—
	Copyright block of 4		1.75	—

WOMENS RIGHTS
Designed by Glenora Richards.

PHOTOGRAVURE
Plate of 200 in four panes of 50.

1982, June 10	Tagged		Perf. 11	
2013 A1398 20c	**multicolored**		40	5
	P# block of 4, 6 P#		2.00	—
	Zip block of 4		1.75	—
	Copyright block of 4		1.75	—

International Peace Garden
1932 1982 USA 20c
Dunseith, ND-
Boissevain,
Manitoba
A1399

Designed by Gyo Fujikawa.

LITHOGRAPHED AND ENGRAVED
Plate of 200 in four panes of 50.

1982, June 30	Tagged		Perf. 11	
2014 A1399 20c	**multicolored**		40	5
	P# block of 4, 5 P#		2.00	—
	Zip block of 4		1.75	—
	Copyright block of 4		1.75	—
a.	Black, green & brown (engr.) omitted		550.00	

A1400

A1401

AMERICA'S LIBRARIES
Designed by Bradbury Thompson.

ENGRAVED
Plate of 200 subjects in four panes of 50.

1982, July 13	Tagged		Perf. 11	
2015 A1400 20c	**red & black**		40	5
	P# block of 4		2.00	—
	Zip block of 4		1.75	—
	Copyright block of 4		1.75	—
a.	Vert. pair, imperf. horiz.		400.00	

JACKIE ROBINSON
Designed by Jerry Pinkney.

PHOTOGRAVURE
Plate of 200 subjects in four panes of 50.

1982, Aug. 2	Tagged		Perf. 10½x11	
2016 A1401 20c	**multicolored**		45	5
	P# block of 4, 5 P#		2.25	—
	Zip block of 4		2.00	—
	Copyright block of 4		2.00	—

TOURO SYNAGOGUE

Oldest Existing
Synagogue
Building in the
U.S. — A1402

Designed by Donald Moss and Bradbury Thompson.

PHOTOGRAVURE AND ENGRAVED
Plates of 230 (10x23) subjects in panes of 50 (5x10).

1982, Aug. 22	Tagged		Perf. 11	
2017 A1402 20c	**multi**		45	5
	P# block of 20, 6-12, #, 1-2 copyright, 1-2 zip		12.50	—
a.	Imperf. pair		600.00	

See Combination Press note after No. 1703.

WOLF TRAP FARM PARK

A1403

Designed by Richard Schlecht.

PHOTOGRAVURE
Plates of 200 in four panes of 50.

1982, Sept. 1	Tagged		Perf. 11	
2018 A1403 20c	**multi**		40	5
	P# block of 4, 5 P#		2.00	—
	Zip block of 4		1.75	—
	Copyright block of 4		1.75	—

A1404

A1405

A1406

Architecture USA 20c   A1407

Designed by Walter D. Richards.

ENGRAVED
Plates of 160 subjects in four panes of 40.

1982, Sept. 30		Tagged		Perf. 11	
2019	A1404 20c black & brown			40	8
2020	A1405 20c black & brown			40	8
2021	A1406 20c black & brown			40	8
2022	A1407 20c black & brown			40	8
	P# block of 4			2.75	—
	Zip block of 4			2.50	—
	Copyright block of 4			2.50	—
a.	Block of 4, #2019-2022			2.25	85

FRANCIS OF ASSISI

FRANCIS OF ASSISI 1182-1982 USA 20c

A1408

Designed by Ned Seidler.
Printed by American Bank Note Co. and J.W. Ferguson and Sons.

Plates of 200 subjects in four panes of 50 each.
PHOTOGRAVURE

1982, Oct. 7		Tagged		Perf. 11	
2023	A1408 20c multi			40	5
	P# block of 4, 6 P#			2.00	—
	Zip block of 4			1.75	—
	Copyright block of 4			1.75	—

PONCE DE LEON

Ponce de León   USA 20c

A1409

Designed by Richard Schlecht.

PHOTOGRAVURE (Combination press)
Plates of 230 subjects (10x23) in panes of 50 (5x10).

1982, Oct. 12		Tagged		Perf. 11	
2024	A1409 20c multi			45	5
	P# block of 6, 5P#			3.25	—
	P# block of 20, 5 or 10 P#, 1-2 zip, 1-2 copyright			12.50	—
a.	Imperf. pair			800.00	

See Combination Press note after No. 1703.

CHRISTMAS

USA 13c

A1410

Christmas USA 20c

Tiepolo National Gallery of Art   A1411

Season's Greetings USA 20c   A1412

Season's Greetings USA 20c   A1413

Season's Greetings USA 20c   A1414

Season's Greetings USA 20c   A1415

PHOTOGRAVURE
Plates of 200 subjects in four panes of 50
Designed by Chuck Ripper.

1982, Nov. 3		Tagged			
2025	A1410 13c multi			26	5
	P# block of 4			1.30	
	Zip block of 4			1.20	
	Copyright block of 4			1.20	
a.	Imperf. pair				

PHOTOGRAVURE (Combination Press)
Plates of 230 subjects (10x23) in panes of 50 (5x10).
Designed by Bradbury Thompson.

1982, Oct. 28		Tagged			
2026	A1411 20c multi			40	5
	P# block of 20, 5 or 10 P#, 1-2 copyright, 1-2 zip			11.50	—
a.	Imperf. pair			175.00	
b.	Horiz. pair, imperf. vert.				

See Combination Press note after No. 1703.

PHOTOGRAVURE
Plates of 200 in four panes of 50.
Designed by Dolli Tingle.

1982, Oct. 28		Tagged			
2027	A1412 20c multi			40	5
2028	A1413 20c multi			40	5
2029	A1414 20c multi			40	5
2030	A1415 20c multi			40	5
	P# block of 4, 4 P#			3.00	
	Zip block of 4			2.75	
	Copyright block of 4			2.75	
a.	Block of 4, #2027-2030			2.50	85
b.	As "a," imperf.				
c.	As "a," imperf. horiz.			—	

SCIENCE & INDUSTRY

Science & Industry USA 20c

Designed by Saul Bass.   A1416

LITHOGRAPHED AND ENGRAVED
Plates of 200 in four panes of 50.

1983, Jan. 19		Tagged		Perf. 11	
2031	A1416 20c multi			40	5
	P# block of 4, 4P#			2.00	—
	Zip block of 4			1.75	—

	Copyright block of 4			1.75	—
a.	Black (engr.) omitted			1,000.	

BALLOONS

Intrepid — A1417

A1418

A1419

Explorer II — A1420

Designed by David Meltzer.
PHOTOGRAVURE
Plates of 160 in four panes of 40.

1983, Mar. 31		Tagged		Perf. 11	
2032	A1417 20c multi			40	8
2033	A1418 20c multi			40	8
2034	A1419 20c multi			40	8
2035	A1420 20c multi			40	8
	P# block of 4, 5P#			2.75	—
	Zip block of 4			2.50	—
	Copyright block of 4			2.50	—
a.	Block of 4, #2032-2035			2.25	85
b.	As "a," imperf.				

US-SWEDEN

20c USA

Benjamin Franklin — A1421

Designed by Czeslaw Slania, court engraver of Sweden.

ENGRAVED
Plates of 200 in four panes of 50.

1983, Mar. 24		Tagged		Perf. 11	
2036	A1421 20c blue, blk & red brn			40	5
	P# block of 4			2.00	—

Zip block of 4	1.75 —
Copyright block of 4	1.75 —

CCC, 50th ANNIV.

A1422

Designed by David K. Stone.

PHOTOGRAVURE
Plates of 200 in four panes of 50.

1983, Apr. 5	Tagged	**Perf. 11**
2037 A1422 20c **multi**		40 5
P# block of 4, 6P#		2.00 —
Zip block of 4		1.75 —
Copyright block of 4		1.75 —
a. Imperf. pair		—

JOSEPH PRIESTLEY

Discoverer of Oxygen — A1423

Designed by Dennis Lyall.
Printed by American Bank Note Company and J.W. Ferguson And Sons.

PHOTOGRAVURE
Plates of 200 in four panes of 50.

1983, Apr. 13	Tagged	**Perf. 11**
2038 A1423 20c **multi**		40 5
P# block of 4, 6P#		2.00 —
Zip block of 4		1.75 —
Copyright block of 4		1.75 —

VOLUNTARISM

A1424

Designed by Paul Calle.

ENGRAVED (Combination Press)
Plates of 230 (10x23) subjects in panes of 50 (5x10).

1983, Apr. 20	Tagged	**Perf. 11**
2039 A1424 20c **red & black**		40 5
P# block of 6, P#		3.00 —
P# block of 20, 1-2 P#, 1-2 copyright, 1-2 zip		11.50 —
a. Imperf., pair		—

See Combination Press note after No. 1703.

US-GERMANY

A1425

Designed by Richard Schlecht.

ENGRAVED
Plates of 200 in four panes of 50.

1983, Apr. 29	Tagged	**Perf. 11**
2040 A1425 20c **brown**		40 5

P# block of 4	2.00 —
Zip block of 4	1.75 —
Copyright block of 4	1.75 —

BROOKLYN BRIDGE

A1426

Designed by Howard Koslow.

ENGRAVED
Plates of 200 in four panes of 50.

1983, May 5	Tagged	**Perf. 11**
2041 A1426 20c **blue**		40 5
P# block of 4		2.00 —
Zip block of 4		1.75 —
Copyright block of 4		1.75 —

TVA

Norris Hydroelectric Dam — A1427

Designed by Howard Koslow.

PHOTOGRAVURE AND ENGRAVED
(Combination Press)
Plates of 230 in panes of 50

1983, May 18	Tagged	**Perf. 11**
2042 A1427 20c **multi**		40 5
P# block of 20, 5-10 P#, 1-2 copyright, 1-2 zip		10.00 —

Runners, Electrocardiograph Tracing — A1428

Designed by Donald Moss.

PHOTOGRAVURE (Combination Press)
Plates of 230 in panes of 50.

1983, May 14	Tagged	**Perf. 11**
2043 A1428 20c **multi**		40 5
P# block of 6, 4 P#		3.00 —
P# block of 20, 4-8 P#, 1-2 copyright, 1-2 zip		11.50 —

SCOTT JOPLIN (1868-1917)
Black Heritage

A1429

Designed by Jerry Pinkney.

PHOTOGRAVURE
Plates of 200 in four panes of 50.

1983, June 9	Tagged	**Perf. 11**
2044 A1429 20c **multi**		40 5
P# block of 4, 6P#		2.00 —
Zip block of 4		1.75 —
Copyright block of 4		1.75 —
a. Imperf. pair		600.00

MEDAL OF HONOR

Medal of Honor — A1430

Designed by Dennis J. Hom.

LITHOGRAPHED AND ENGRAVED
Plates of 160 in four panes of 40.

1983, June 7	Tagged	**Perf. 11**
2045 A1430 20c **multi**		40 5
P# block of 4, 5P#		2.00 —
Zip block of 4		1.75 —
Copyright block of 4		1.75 —
a. Red omitted		400.00

A1431

A1432

GEORGE HERMAN RUTH (1895-1948)

Designed by Richard Gangel.

ENGRAVED
Plates of 200 in four panes of 50.

1983, July 6	Tagged	**Perf. 10½x11**
2046 A1431 20c **blue**		45 5
P# block of 4		2.25 —
Zip block of 4		2.00 —
Copyright block of 4		2.00 —

NATHANIEL HAWTHORNE (1804-1864)

Designed by Bradbury Thompson after 1851 painting by Cephus Giovanni Thompson.

PHOTOGRAVURE
Plates of 200 in four panes of 50.

1983, July 8	Tagged	**Perf. 11**
2047 A1432 20c **multi**		40 5
P# block of 4, 4P#		2.00 —
Zip block of 4		1.75 —
Copyright block of 4		1.75 —

LOS ANGELES OLYMPICS
July 28-August 12, 1984

A1433

A1434

A1435

A1436

Designed by Bob Peake.

PHOTOGRAVURE
Plates of 200 in four panes of 50.

1983, July 28		Tagged	Perf. 11	
2048	A1433 13c **multi**		26	5
2049	A1434 13c **multi**		26	5
2050	A1435 13c **multi**		26	5
2051	A1436 13c **multi**		26	5
	P# block of 4, 4P#		1.75	—
	Zip block of 4		1.65	—
	Copyright block of 4		1.65	—
a.	Block of 4, #2048-2051		1.50	65

SIGNING OF TREATY OF PARIS

John Adams, B.
Franklin, John
Jay, David
Hartley — A1437

Designed by David Blossom based on unfinished painting by Benjamin West in Winterthur Museum.

PHOTOGRAVURE
Plates of 160 in four panes of 40.

1983, Sept. 9		Tagged	Perf. 11	
2052	A1437 20c **multi**		40	5
	P# block of 4, 4P#		2.00	—
	Zip block of 4		1.75	—
	Copyright block of 4		1.75	—

CIVIL SERVICE

A1438

Designed by MDB Communications, Inc.

PHOTOGRAVURE AND ENGRAVED
Plates of 230 in four panes of 50.

1983, Sept. 9		Tagged	Perf. 11	
2053	A1438 20c **buff, blue & red**		40	5
	P# block of 6, P#		3.00	—
	P# block of 20, 1-2P#, 1-2 Zip, 1-2 Copyright		11.50	—

METROPOLITAN OPERA

Original State
Arch and Current
5-arch Entrance
A1439

Designed by Ken Davies.

LITHOGRAPHED AND ENGRAVED
Plates of 200 in four panes of 50.

1983, Sept. 14		Tagged	Perf. 11	
2054	A1439 20c **yel & maroon**		40	5
	P# block of 4		2.00	—
	Zip block of 4		1.75	—
	Copyright block of 4		1.75	—

AMERICAN INVENTORS

Charles Steinmetz
and Curve on
Graph — A1440

Edwin Armstrong
and Frequency
Modulator
A1441

Nikola Tesla and
Induction
Motor — A1442

Philo T.
Farnsworth and
First Television
Camera — A1443

Designed by Dennis Lyall.

LITHOGRAPHED AND ENGRAVED
Plates of 200 in four panes of 50.

1983, Sept. 21		Tagged	Perf. 11	
2055	A1440 20c **multi**		40	8
2056	A1441 20c **multi**		40	8
2057	A1442 20c **multi**		40	8
2058	A1443 20c **multi**		40	8
	P# block of 4, 2 P#		2.50	—
	Zip block of 4		2.25	—
	Copyright block of 4		2.25	—
a.	Block of 4, #2055-2058		2.10	85
b.	As "a," black omitted		650.00	

STREET CARS

A1444

A1445

A1446

A1447

Designed by Richard Leech.

PHOTOGRAVURE AND ENGRAVED
Plates of 200 in four panes of 50.

1983, Oct. 8		Tagged	Perf. 11	
2059	A1444 20c **multi**		40	8
2060	A1445 20c **multi**		40	8
2061	A1446 20c **multi**		40	8
2062	A1447 20c **multi**		40	8
	P# block of 4, 5#		2.50	—
	Zip block of 4		2.25	—
	Copyright block of 4		2.25	—
a.	Block of 4, #2059-2062		2.10	85
b.	As "a," black omitted		700.00	

CHRISTMAS

Niccolini-
Cowper
Madonna, by
Raphael
A1448

Santa Claus
A1449

Designed by Bradbury Thompson (No. 2063), and John Berkey (No. 2064).

PHOTOGRAVURE
Plates of 200 in four panes of 50 (No. 2063),
Plates of 230 in panes of 50 (Combination Press, No. 2064).

1983, Oct. 28		Tagged	Perf. 11	
2063	A1448 20c **multi**		40	5
	P# block of 4, 5#		2.00	—
	Zip block of 4		1.75	—
	Copyright block of 4		1.75	—
2064	A1449 20c **multi**		40	5
	P# block of 6, 5 P#		3.00	—
	P# block of 20, 5-10 P#, 1-2 copyright, 1-2 zip		11.50	—
a.	Imperf. pair		175.00	

See Combination Press note after No. 1703.

German Religious
Leader, Founder of
Lutheran Church
(1483-1546)
A1450

Caribou and Alaska
Pipeline
A1451

MARTIN LUTHER

Designed by Bradbury Thompson.
Printed by American Bank Note Company and J.W. Fergusson And Sons.

PHOTOGRAVURE
Plates of 200 in four panes of 50.

1983, Nov. 11		Tagged	Perf. 11	
2065	A1450 20c **multi**		40	5
	P# block of 4, 5#		2.00	—
	Zip block of 4		1.75	—
	Copyright block of 4		1.75	—

25th ANNIVERSARY OF ALASKA STATEHOOD

Designed by Bill Bond.
Printed by American Bank Note Company and J.W. Fergusson And Sons.

PHOTOGRAVURE
Plates of 200 in four panes of 50.

1984, Jan. 3		Tagged	Perf. 11	
2066	A1451 20c **multi**		40	5
	P# block of 4, 5#		2.00	—
	Zip block of 4		1.75	—
	Copyright block of 4		1.75	—

14th WINTER OLYMPIC GAMES, SARAJEVO, JUGOSLAVIA, FEB. 8-19

Ice Dancing
A1452

Alpine Skiing
A1453

Nordic
Skiing — A1454

Hockey — A1455

Designed by Bob Peak.

PHOTOGRAVURE
Plates of 200 in four panes of 50.

				Tagged		Perf. 10 ½x11
2067	A1452	20c	multi		40	8
2068	A1453	20c	multi		40	8
2069	A1454	20c	multi		40	8
2070	A1455	20c	multi		40	8
			P# block of 4, 4#		2.75	—
			Zip block of 4		2.50	—
			Copyright block of 4		2.50	—
a.			Block of 4, #2067-2070		2.25	85

1984, Jan. 6

Pillar, Dollar
Sign — A1456

LO♥E
LO♥E
LO♥E
LO♥E
LO♥E
USA 20c
A1457

FEDERAL DEPOSIT INSURANCE CORPORATION, 50TH ANNIVERSARY

Designed by Michael David Brown.

PHOTOGRAVURE
Plates of 200 in four panes of 50
(1 pane each #2071, 2074, 2075 and 2081)

				Tagged		Perf. 11
1984, Jan. 12						
2071	A1456	20c	multi		40	5
			P# block of 4, 6#, UL only		2.00	—
			Zip block of 4		1.75	—
			Copyright block of 4		1.75	—

LOVE
Designed by Bradbury Thompson.

PHOTOGRAVURE AND ENGRAVED
(Combination Press)
Plates of 230 in four panes of 50.

				Tagged		Perf. 11 x 10 ½
1984, Jan. 31						
2072	A1457	20c	multi		45	5
			P# block of 20, 6-12#, 1-2 copyright, 1-2 zip		12.50	—
a.			Horiz. pair, imperf. vert.		300.00	

See Combination Press note after No. 1703.

Carter G. Woodson (1875-1950), Black Historian — A1458

A1459

BLACK HERITAGE

Designed by Jerry Pinkney.
Printed by American Bank Note Company.

PHOTOGRAVURE
Plates of 200 in four panes of 50.

				Tagged		Perf. 11
1984, Feb. 1						
2073	A1458	20c	multi		40	5
			P# block of 4, 6#		2.00	—
			Zip block of 4		1.75	—
			Copyright block of 4		1.75	—
a.			Horiz. pair, imperf. vert.			

SOIL & WATER CONSERVATION

Designed by Michael David Brown.

See No. 2071 for printing information.

				Tagged		Perf. 11
1984, Feb. 6						
2074	A1459	20c	multi		40	5
			P# block of 4, 6#, UR only		2.00	—
			Zip block of 4		1.75	—
			Copyright block of 4		1.75	—

50TH ANNIVERSARY OF CREDIT UNION ACT

Dollar Sign, Coin — A1460

Designed by Michael David Brown.

See No. 2071 for printing information.

				Tagged		Perf. 11
1984, Feb. 10						
2075	A1460	20c	multi		40	5
			P# block of 4, 6#, LR only		2.00	—
			Zip block of 4		1.75	—
			Copyright block of 4		1.75	—

ORCHIDS

Wild Pink — A1461

Yellow Lady's-slipper — A1462

Spreading
Pogonia — A1463

Pacific
Calypso — A1464

Designed by Manabu Saito.

PHOTOGRAVURE
Plates of 192 in four panes of 48.

				Tagged		Perf. 11
1984, Mar. 5						
2076	A1461	20c	multi		40	8
2077	A1462	20c	multi		40	8
2078	A1463	20c	multi		40	8
2079	A1464	20c	multi		40	8
			P# block of 4, 5#		2.25	—
			Zip block of 4		2.00	—
			Copyright block of 4		2.00	—
a.			Block of 4, #2076-2079		1.90	85

25th ANNIVERSARY OF HAWAII STATEHOOD

Eastern Polynesian Canoe, Golden Plover, Mauna Loa Volcano — A1465

Designed by Herb Kane.
Printed by American Bank Note Company.

PHOTOGRAVURE
Plates of 200 in four panes of 50.

				Tagged		Perf. 11
1984, Mar. 12						
2080	A1465	20c	multi		40	5
			P# block of 4, 5#		2.00	—
			Zip block of 4		1.75	—
			Copyright block of 4		1.75	—

50TH ANNIVERSARY, NATIONAL ARCHIVES

Abraham Lincoln, George Washington — A1466

Designed by Michael David Brown.

See No. 2071 for printing information.

				Tagged		Perf. 11
1984, Apr. 16						
2081	A1466	20c	multi		40	5
			P# block of 4, 6#, LL only		2.00	—
			Zip block of 4		1.75	—
			Copyright block of 4		1.75	—

LOS ANGELES SUMMER OLYMPICS
July 28-August 12

Diving — A1467

Long
Jump — A1468

Wrestling — A1469

Kayak — A1470

Designed by Bob Peak.

PHOTOGRAVURE
Plates of 200 in four panes of 50.

1984, May 4		Tagged		Perf. 11	
2082	A1467 20c	multi		40	8
2083	A1468 20c	multi		40	8
2084	A1469 20c	multi		40	8
2085	A1470 20c	multi		40	8
		P# block of 4, 4#		3.25	—
		Zip block of 4		3.00	—
		Copyright block of 4		3.00	—
a.		Block of 4, #2082-2085		2.75	85

LOUISIANA WORLD EXPOSITION
New Orleans, May 12-Nov. 11

Bayou
Wildlife — A1471

Designed by Chuck Ripper.

PHOTOGRAVURE
Plates of 160 in four panes of 40.

1984, May 11		Tagged		Perf. 11	
2086	A1471 20c	multi		40	5
		P# block of 4, 5#		2.00	—
		Zip block of 4		1.75	—
		Copyright block of 4		1.75	—

HEALTH RESEARCH

Lab Equipment
A1472

Designed by Tyler Smith.
Printed by American Bank Note Company.

PHOTOGRAVURE
Plates of 200 in four panes of 50.

1984, May 17		Tagged		Perf. 11	
2087	A1472 20c	multi		40	5
		P# block of 4, 5#		2.00	—
		Zip block of 4		1.75	—
		Copyright block of 4		1.75	—

Actor Douglas Fairbanks
(1883-1939) — A1473

A1474

PERFORMING ARTS
Designed by Jim Sharpe.

PHOTOGRAVURE AND ENGRAVED
(Combination Press)
Plates of 230 in panes of 50.

1984, May 23		Tagged		Perf. 11	
2088	A1473 20c	multi		40	5
		P# block of 20, 5-10#, 1-2 copyright, 1-2 zip		12.50	—

See Combination Press note after No. 1703.

JIM THORPE, 1888-1953
Designed by Richard Gangel.

ENGRAVED
Plates of 200 in four panes of 50.

1984, May 24		Tagged		Perf. 11	
2089	A1474 20c	dark brown		45	5
		P# block of 4		2.25	—
		Zip block of 4		2.00	—
		Copyright block of 4		2.00	—

PERFORMING ARTS

John McCormack (1884-1945),
Operatic Tenor — A1475

Designed by Jim Sharpe (U.S.) and Ron Mercer (Ireland).

PHOTOGRAVURE
Plates of 200 in four panes of 50.

1984, June 6		Tagged		Perf. 11	
2090	A1475 20c	multi		40	5
		P# block of 4, 5#		2.00	—
		Zip block of 4		1.75	—
		Copyright block of 4		1.75	—

See Ireland No. 594.

25TH ANNIVERSARY OF ST. LAWRENCE SEAWAY

Aerial View of
Seaway, Freighters
A1476

Designed by Ernst Barenscher (Canada).
Printed by American Bank Note Company.

PHOTOGRAVURE
Plates of 200 in four panes of 50.

1984, June 26		Tagged		Perf. 11	
2091	A1476 20c	multi		40	5
		P# block of 4, 4#		2.00	—
		Zip block of 4		1.75	—
		Copyright block of 4		1.75	—

50TH ANNIVERSARY OF WATERFOWL PRESERVATION ACT

"Mallards
Dropping In" by
Jay N.
Darling — A1477

Design adapted from Darling's work (No. RW1) by Donald M. McDowell.

ENGRAVED
Plates of 200 in four panes of 50.

1984, July 2		Tagged		Perf. 11	
2092	A1477 20c	multi		40	5
		P# block of 4		2.00	—
		Zip block of 4		1.75	—
		Copyright block of 4		1.75	—
a.		Horiz. pair, imperf. vert.		600.00	—

The
Elizabeth — A1478

A1479

ROANOKE VOYAGES
Designed by Charles Lundgren.
Printed by American Bank Note Company.

PHOTOGRAVURE
Plates of 200 in four panes of 50.

1984, July 13		Tagged		Perf. 11	
2093	A1478 20c	multi		40	5
		P# block of 4, 5#		2.00	—
		Zip block of 4		1.75	—
		Copyright block of 4		1.75	—

HERMAN MELVILLE (1819-1891), AUTHOR
Designed by Bradbury Thompson.

ENGRAVED
Plates of 200 in four panes of 50.

1984, Aug. 1		Tagged		Perf. 11	
2094	A1479 20c	sage green		40	5
		P# block of 4		2.00	—
		Zip block of 4		1.75	—
		Copyright block of 4		1.75	—

Founder of Junior
Achievement
A1480

Smokey the Bear
A1481

HORACE MOSES (1862-1947)
Designed by Dennis Lyall.

PHOTOGRAVURE AND ENGRAVED
(Combination Press)
Plates of 200 in panes of 50.

1984, Aug. 6		Tagged		Perf. 11	
2095	A1480 20c	orange & dark brown		40	5
		P# block of 6, P#		3.00	—
		P# block of 20, 1-2#, 1-2 copyright, 1-2 zip		11.50	—

See Combination Press note after No. 1703.

SMOKEY THE BEAR

Designed by Rudolph Wendelin.

LITHOGRAPHED AND ENGRAVED
Plates of 200 in panes of 50.

1984, Aug. 13	Tagged	Perf. 11	
2096 A1481 20c **multi**		40	5
	P# block of 4, 5#	2.00	—
	Zip block of 4	1.75	—
	Copyright block of 4	1.75	—
a.	Horiz. pair, imperf. btwn.	450.00	
b.	Vert. pair, imperf. btwn.	300.00	
c.	Block of 4, imperf. btwn. vert. and horiz.	3,500.	

ROBERTO CLEMENTE (1934-1972)

Clemente Wearing Pittsburgh Pirates Cap, Puerto Rican Flag — A1482

Designed by Juan Lopez-Bonilla.

PHOTOGRAVURE
Plates of 200 in panes of 50.

1984, Aug. 17	Tagged	Perf. 11	
2097 A1482 20c **multi**		45	5
	P# block of 4, 6#	2.25	—
	Zip block of 4	2.00	—
	Copyright block of 4	2.00	—
a.	Horiz. pair, imperf. vert.	—	

DOGS

Beagle and Boston Terrier — A1483

Chesapeake Bay Retriever and Cocker Spaniel — A1484

Alaskan Malamute and Collie — A1485

Black and Tan Coonhound and American Foxhound A1486

Designed by Roy Andersen.

PHOTOGRAVURE
Plates of 160 in panes of 40.

1984, Sept. 7	Tagged	Perf. 11	
2098 A1483 20c **multi**		40	8
2099 A1484 20c **multi**		40	8
2100 A1485 20c **multi**		40	8
2101 A1486 20c **multi**		40	8
	P# block of 4, 4#	2.50	—
	Zip block of 4	2.25	—
	Copyright block of 4	2.25	—
a.	Block of 4, #2098-2101	2.10	85

CRIME PREVENTION

McGruff, the Crime Dog — A1487

Designed by Randall McDougall.
Printed by American Bank Note Company.

PHOTOGRAVURE
Plates of 200 in panes of 50.

1984, Sept. 26	Tagged	Perf. 11	
2102 A1487 20c **multi**		40	5
	P# block of 4, 4#	2.00	—
	Zip block of 4	1.75	—
	Copyright block of 4	1.75	—

HISPANIC AMERICANS

A1488

Designed by Robert McCall.

PHOTOGRAVURE
Plates of 160 in four panes of 40.

1984, Oct. 31	Tagged	Perf. 11	
2103 A1488 20c **multi**		40	5
	P# block of 4, 5 #	2.00	—
	Zip block of 4	1.75	—
	Copyright block of 4	1.75	—
a.	Vert. pair, imperf. horiz.	—	

FAMILY UNITY

Stick Figures — A1489

Designed by Molly LaRue.

PHOTOGRAVURE AND ENGRAVED
(Combination Press)
Plates of 230 in panes of 50.

1984, Oct. 1	Tagged	Perf. 11	
2104 A1489 20c **multi**		40	5
	P# block of 20, 3-6#, 1-2 copyright, 1-2 zip	12.50	—
a.	Horiz. pair, imperf. vert.	750.00	

See Combination Press note after No. 1703.

ELEANOR ROOSEVELT (1884-1962)

A1490

Designed by Bradbury Thompson.

ENGRAVED
Plates of 192 in panes of 48.

1984, Oct. 11	Tagged	Perf. 11	
2105 A1490 20c **deep blue**		40	5
	P# block of 4	2.00	—
	Zip block of 4	1.75	—
	Copyright block of 4	1.75	—

NATION OF READERS

Abraham Lincoln Reading to Son, Tad — A1491

Designed adapted from Matthew Brady daguerrotype by Bradbury Thompson.

ENGRAVED
Plates of 200 in panes of 50.

1984, Oct. 16	Tagged	Perf. 11	
2106 A1491 20c **brown & maroon**		40	5
	P# block of 4	2.00	—
	Zip block of 4	1.75	—
	Copyright block of 4	1.75	—

CHRISTMAS

Madonna and Child by Fra Filippo Lippi — A1492

Season's Greetings Santa Claus — A1493

Designed by Bradbury Thompson (No. 2107) andb Danny La Boccetta (No. 2108).

PHOTOGRAVURE
Plates of 200 in panes of 50.

1984, Oct. 30	Tagged	Perf. 11	
2107 A1492 20c **multi**		40	5
	P# block of 4, 5 #	2.00	—
	Zip block of 4	1.75	—
	Copyright block of 4	1.75	—
2108 A1493 20c **multi**		40	5
	P# block of 4, 5 #	2.00	—
	Zip block of 4	1.75	—
	Copyright block of 4	1.75	—

VIETNAM VETERANS' MEMORIAL

Vietnam Veterans Memorial USA 20c
Memorial and Visitors — A1494

Designed by Paul Calle.

ENGRAVED
Plates of 160 in panes of 40.

1984, Nov. 10		**Tagged**		**Perf. 10½**	
2109	A1494	20c **multi**		40	5
		P# block of 4		2.00	—
		Zip block of 4		1.75	—
		Copyright block of 4		1.75	—

PERFORMING ARTS

Jerome Kern (1885-1945), Composer — A1495

Designed by Jim Sharpe.
Printed by the American Bank Note Company.

PHOTOGRAVURE
Plates of 200 in four panes of 50.

1985, Jan. 23		**Tagged**		**Perf. 11**	
2110	A1495	22c **multi**		44	5
		P# block of 4, 5 #		2.20	—
		Zip block of 4		2.00	—
		Copyright block of 4		2.00	—

A1496   A1497

Designed by Bradbury Thompson.

PHOTOGRAVURE
Plates of 460 (20x23) in panes of 100.

1985, Feb. 1		**Tagged**		**Perf. 11**	
2111	A1496	(22c) **green**		50	5
		P# block of 6, P#		3.00	—
		P# block of 20, 1-2 #, 1-2 Zip, 1-2 Copyright		12.00	—
a.		Vert. pair, imperf.		50.00	
b.		Vert. pair, imperf. horiz.		—	

COIL STAMP
Perf. 10 Vert.

2112	A1496	(22c) **green**		44	5
		Pair		88	10
		P# strip of 3, line, P# 1, 2		6.00	
a.		Imperf. pair		40.00	

BOOKLET STAMP
Perf. 11

2113	A1497	(22c) **green**		44	5
a.		Booklet pane of 10		5.50	—

A1498

Flag Over Capitol Dome — A1499

Designed by Frank Waslick.

ENGRAVED
Plates of 400 subjects in panes of 100.

1985, Mar. 29		**Tagged**		**Perf. 11**	
2114	A1498	22c **blue, red & black**		44	5
		P# block of 4		2.20	—
		Zip block of 4		2.00	—
		Copyright block of 4		2.00	—
		Pair with full horizontal gutter			

COIL STAMP
Perf. 10 Vert.

2115	A1498	22c **blue, red & black**		44	5
		Pair		88	10
		P# strip of 3, P# 2, 4, 5, 8, 10, 12, 15, 16, 18, 19, 21, 22		5.00	
		P# strip of 3, P# 1, 6		11.00	
		P# strip of 3, P# 3		15.00	
		P# strip of 3, P# 7, 11, 13, 14, 17, 20		9.00	
a.		Imperf. pair		17.50	
b.		Inscribed "T" at bottom, *May 23, 1987*		44	8
b.		P# strip of 3, P# T1		4.50	

BOOKLET STAMP
Perf. 10 Horiz.

2116	A1499	22c **blue, red & black**		44	5
a.		Booklet pane of 5		2.20	—

BOOKLET STAMPS

Frilled Dogwinkle
A1500

Reticulated Helmet
A1501

New England Neptune
A1502

Calico Scallop
A1503

Lightning Whelk — A1504

Designed by Pete Cocci.

ENGRAVED

1985, Apr. 4		**Tagged**		**Perf. 10**	
2117	A1500	22c **black & brown**		44	5
2118	A1501	22c **black & multi**		44	5
2119	A1502	22c **black & brown**		44	5
2120	A1503	22c **black & violet**		44	5
2121	A1504	22c **black & multi**		44	5
a.		Booklet pane of 10		4.40	—
b.		As "a," violet omitted on both Nos. 2120		—	
c.		As "a," vert. imperf. between		—	
d.		As "a," imperf.		—	
e.		Strip of 5, Nos. 2117-2121		2.20	—

Eagle and Half Moon
A1505

Designed by Young & Rubicam.

PHOTOGRAVURE

1985, Apr. 29		**Tagged**		**Perf. 10 Vert.**	
2122	A1505	$10.75 **multi**		22.00	—
a.		Booklet pane of 3		67.50	—

TRANSPORTATION ISSUE

A1506

A1507

A1508

A1509

A1510

A1511

A1512

A1513

A1514

A1515

A1516

A1517

A1518

A1519

Designers: 3.4c, 17c, Lou Nolan. 4.9c, 8.5c, 14c, 25c, William H. Bond. 5.5c, David K. Stone. 6c, 8.3c, 10.1c, 12.5c. James Schleyer. 7.1c, 11c, 12c, Ken Dallison.

COIL STAMPS
ENGRAVED

1985-87		**Tagged**		**Perf. 10 Vert.**
2123	A1506	3.4c **dark bluish green**, *June 8*	8	5
		Pair	16	10
		P# strip of 3, line, P# 1, 2	1.50	
a.		Untagged (Bureau precancel)		20
		P# strip of 3, line, P# 1, 2	1.75	
2124	A1507	4.9c **brown black**, *June 21*	10	5
		Pair	20	10
		P# strip of 3, line, P# 3, 4	1.25	
a.		Untagged (Bureau precancel)		10
		P# strip of 3, line, P# 1-6	2.00	
2125	A1508	5.5c **deep magenta**, *Nov. 1, 1986*	11	5
		Pair	22	10
		P# strip of 3, P# 1	1.75	
a.		Untagged (Bureau precancel)		11
		P# strip of 3, P# 1, 2	2.00	
2126	A1509	6c **red brown**, *May 6*	12	5
		Pair	24	10
		P# strip of 3, P# 1	2.00	
a.		Untagged (Bureau precancel)		12
		P# strip of 3, P# 1, 2	2.50	
b.		As "a", imperf. pair		—
2127	A1510	7.1c **lake**, *Feb. 6, 1987*	15	5
		Pair	30	10
		P# strip of 3, P# 1	2.25	
a.		Untagged (Bureau precancel)		15
		P# strip of 3, P# 1	2.25	
2128	A1511	8.3c **green**, *June 21*	18	5
		Pair	36	10
		P# strip of 3, line, P# 1, 2	1.90	
a.		Untagged (Bureau precancel)		16
		P# strip of 3, line, P# 1, 2	2.00	
		P# strip of 3, line, P# 3, 4	5.00	
2129	A1512	8.5c **dark Prussian green**, *Jan. 24, 1987*	18	5
		Pair	36	10
		P# strip of 3, P# 1	2.50	
a.		Untagged (Bureau precancel)		18
		P# strip of 3, P# 1, 2	3.00	
2130	A1513	10.1c **slate blue**, *Apr. 18*	22	5
		Pair	44	10
		P# strip of 3, P# 1	2.50	
a.		Untagged (Bureau precancel in black)		22
a.		P# strip of 3, P# 1, 2	2.75	
a.		Untagged (Bureau precancel "Bulk Rate Carrier Route Sort" in red)		22
a.		P# strip of 3, P# 2	3.50	
b.		As "a", imperf. pair		—
2131	A1514	11c **dark green**, *June 11*	22	5
		Pair	44	10
		P# strip of 3, line, P# 1-4	2.50	
2132	A1515	12c **dark blue**, *Apr. 2*	24	5
		Pair	48	10
		P# strip of 3, line, P# 1, 2	2.75	
a.		Untagged (Bureau precancel)		24
		P# strip of 3, line, P# 1, 2	3.50	
		P# strip of 3, no line, P# 1	3.00	
2133	A1516	12.5c **olive green**, *Apr. 18*	25	5
		Pair	50	10
		P# strip of 3, P# 1	3.00	
a.		Untagged (Bureau precancel)		25
		P# strip of 3, P# 1, 2	3.00	
b.		As "a", imperf. pair		75.00
2134	A1517	14c **sky blue**, *Mar. 23*	28	5
		Pair	56	10
		P# strip of 3, line, P# 1-4	2.00	
		P# strip of 3, no line, P# 2	3.00	
a.		Imperf., pair	75.00	
2135	A1518	17c **sky blue**, *Aug. 20, 1986*	34	5
		Pair	68	10
		P# strip of 3, P# 2	3.25	
a.		Imperf., pair	—	
2136	A1519	25c **orange brown**, *Nov. 22, 1986*	50	5
		Pair	100	10
		P# strip of 3, P# 1-5	5.00	
a.		Imperf., pair	—	

Precancellations on Nos. 2125a, 2127a do not have lines. Precancellation on No. 2129a is in red. See No. 2231.

BLACK HERITAGE

Mary McLeod Bethune (1875-1955), Educator — A-1520

Designed by Jerry Pinkney from a photograph.
Printed by American Bank Note Company.

PHOTOGRAVURE
Plates of 200 in four panes of 50.

1985, Mar. 5		**Tagged**		**Perf. 11**
2137	A1520	22c **multi**	44	5
		P# block of 4, 6 #	2.20	—
		Zip block of 4	2.00	—
		Copyright block of 4	2.00	—

AMERICAN FOLK ART ISSUE
Duck Decoys

Folk Art USA 22 Broadbill A1521

Mallard — A1522 **Folk Art USA 22**

Folk Art USA 22 Canvasback A1523

Redhead A1524 **Folk Art USA 22**

Designed by Stevan Dohanos.
Printed by American Bank Note Company and J.W. Fergusson & Sons.

PHOTOGRAVURE
Plates of 200 in four panes of 50.

1985, Mar. 22		**Tagged**		**Perf. 11**
2138	A1521	22c **multi**	44	8
2139	A1522	22c **multi**	44	8
2140	A1523	22c **multi**	44	8
2141	A1524	22c **multi**	44	8
		P# block of 4, 5 #	2.75	—
		Zip block of 4	2.50	—
		Copyright block of 4	2.50	—
a.		Block of 4, #2138-2141	2.25	1.00

WINTER SPECIAL OLYMPICS

Ice Skater, Emblem, Skier — A1525

Designed by Jeff Carnell.

PHOTOGRAVURE
Plates of 160 in four panes of 40.

1985, Mar. 25		**Tagged**		**Perf. 11**
2142	A1525	22c **multi**	44	5
		P# block of 4, 6 #	2.20	—
		Zip block of 4	2.00	—
		Copyright block of 4	2.00	—
a.		Vert. pair, imperf. horiz.	850.00	

LOVE

A1526

Designed by Corita Kent.

PHOTOGRAVURE
Plates of 200 in four panes of 50.

1985, Apr. 17		**Tagged**		**Perf. 11**
2143	A1526	22c **multi**	44	5
		P# block of 4, 6 #	2.20	—
		Zip block of 4	2.00	—
		Copyright block of 4	2.00	—
a.		Imperf., pair	—	

RURAL ELECTRIFICATION ADMINISTRATION

REA Power Lines, Farmland A1527

Designed by Howard Koslow.

PHOTOGRAVURE & ENGRAVED (Combination Press)
Plates of 200 in four panes of 50.

1985, May 11		**Tagged**		**Perf. 11**
2144	A1527	22c **multi**	44	5
		P# block of 20, 5-10 P#, 1-2 Zip, 1-2 Copyright	11.50	—

See Combination Press note after No. 1703.

AMERIPEX '86

U.S. No. 134 — A1528

Designed by Richard D. Sheaff.

LITHOGRAPHED & ENGRAVED
Plates of 192 in four panes of 48.

1985, May 25		**Tagged**		**Perf. 11**
2145	A1528	22c **multi**	44	5
		P# block of 4, 3 #	2.20	—
		Zip block of 4	2.00	—
		Copyright block of 4	2.00	—
a.		Red, black & blue (engr.) omitted	275.00	

Abigail Adams (1744-1818) — A1529

Designed by Bart Forbes.

PHOTOGRAVURE
Plates of 200 in four panes of 50.

1985, June 14		**Tagged**		**Perf. 11**
2146	A1529	22c **multi**	44	5
		P# block of 4, 4 #	2.20	—
		Zip block of 4	2.00	—
		Copyright block of 4	2.00	—
a.		Imperf., pair	500.00	

FREDERIC AUGUSTE BARTHOLDI (1834-1904)

Architect and Sculptor, Statue of Liberty — A1530

F.A. Bartholdi, Statue of Liberty Sculptor

Designed by Howard Paine from paintings by Jose Frappa and James Dean.

LITHOGRAPHED & ENGRAVED
Plates of 200 in four panes of 50.

1985, July 18	Tagged	Perf. 11	
2147 A1530 22c **multi**		44	5
P# block of 4, 5 #		2.20	—
Zip block of 4		2.00	—
Copyright block of 4		2.00	—

COIL STAMPS

George
Washington,
Washington
Monument
A1532

Sealed Envelopes
A1533

Designed by Thomas Szumowski (#2149) based on a portrait by Gilbert Stuart, and Richard Sheaff (#2150).

PHOTOGRAVURE

1985		Perf. 10 Vertically	
2149 A1532 18c **multi**, *Nov. 6*		36	8
Pair		72	16
P# strip of 3, P# 1112, 3333		3.25	
a. Untagged (Bureau Precancel)		36	
P# strip of 3, P# 11121, 33333, 43444		4.00	
b. Imperf., pair		—	
c. As "a," imperf. pair		—	
2150 A1533 21.1c **multi**, *Oct. 22*		45	8
Pair		90	16
P# strip of 3, P# 111111, 111121		4.50	
a. Untagged (Bureau Precancel)		45	
P# strip of 3, P# 111111, 111121		5.00	

Precancellations on Nos. 2149a ("PRESORTED FIRST-CLASS") and 2150a ("ZIP+4") do not have lines.

KOREAN WAR VETERANS

American Troops
Marching
A1535

Designed by Dick Sheaff from a photograph by David D. Duncan.

ENGRAVED
Plates of 200 in four panes of 50.

1985, July 26	Tagged	Perf. 11	
2152 A1535 22c gray green & rose red		44	5
P# block of 4		2.20	—
Zip block of 4		2.00	—
Copyright block of 4		2.00	—

SOCIAL SECURITY ACT, 50th ANNIV.

Men, Women,
Children,
Corinthian
Columns — A1536

Designed by Robert Brangwynne.
Printed by American Bank Note Company and J.W. Fergusson & Sons.

PHOTOGRAVURE
Plates of 200 in four panes of 50.

1985, Aug. 14	Tagged	Perf. 11	
2153 A1536 22c deep & light blue		44	5
P# block of 4, 2 #		2.20	—
Zip block of 4		2.00	—
Copyright block of 4		2.00	—

WORLD WAR I VETERANS

The Battle of
Marne,
France — A1537

Designed by Dick Sheaff from Harvey Dunn's charcoal drawing.

ENGRAVED
Plates of 200 in four panes of 50.

1985, Aug. 26	Tagged	Perf. 11	
2154 A1537 22c gray green & rose red		44	5
P# block of 4		2.20	—
Zip block of 4		2.00	—
Copyright block of 4		2.00	—

HORSES

Quarter
Horse — A1538

Morgan — A1539

Saddlebred
A1540

Appaloosa
A1541

Designed by Roy Andersen.

PHOTOGRAVURE
Plates of 160 in four panes of 40.

1985, Sept. 25	Tagged	Perf. 11	
2155 A1538 22c **multi**		44	8
2156 A1539 22c **multi**		44	8
2157 A1540 22c **multi**		44	8
2158 A1541 22c **multi**		44	8
P# block of 4, 5#		2.50	—
Zip block of 4		2.25	—
Copyright block of 4		2.25	—
a. Block of 4, #2155-2158		2.10	1.00

PUBLIC EDUCATION IN AMERICA

Quill Pen, Apple, Spectacles,
Penmanship Quiz — A1542

Designed by Uldis Purins.
Printed by American Bank Note Company and J.W. Fergusson & Sons.

PHOTOGRAVURE
Plates of 200 in four panes of 50.

1985, Oct. 1	Tagged	Perf. 11	
2159 A1542 22c **multi**		44	5
P# block of 4, 5 #		2.20	—
Zip block of 4		2.00	—
Copyright block of 4		2.00	—

INTERNATIONAL YOUTH YEAR

YMCA Youth
Camping,
Cent. — A1543

Boy Scouts, 75th
Anniv. — A1544

Big Brothers / Big
Sisters Federation,
40th
Anniv. — A1545

Camp Fire Inc.,
75th
Anniv. — A1546

Designed by Dennis Luzak.
Printed by American Bank Note Company and J.W. Fergusson & Sons.

PHOTOGRAVURE
Plates of 200 in four panes of 50.

1985, Oct. 7	Tagged	Perf. 11	
2160 A1543 22c **multi**		44	8
2161 A1544 22c **multi**		44	8
2162 A1545 22c **multi**		44	8
2163 A1546 22c **multi**		44	8
P# block of 4, 5 #		2.50	—
Zip block of 4		2.25	—
Copyright block of 4		2.25	—
a. Block of 4, #2160-2163		2.10	1.00

HELP END HUNGER

Youths and
Elderly Suffering
from
Malnutrition
A1547

Designed by Jerry Pinkney.
Printed by the American Bank Note Company.

PHOTOGRAVURE
Plates of 200 in four panes of 50.

1985, Oct. 15			Tagged		Perf. 11	
2164	A1547	22c	**multi**		44	5
			P# block of 4, 5 #		2.20	—
			Zip block of 4		2.00	—
			Copyright block of 4		2.00	—

CHRISTMAS

Genoa Madonna, Enameled
Terra-Cotta by Luca Della
Robbia (1400-1482) — A1548

Poinsettia
Plants — A1549

Designed by Bradbury Thompson (No. 2165) and James Dean (No. 2166).

PHOTOGRAVURE
Plates of 200 in panes of 50.

1985, Oct. 30			Tagged		Perf. 11	
2165	A1548	22c	**multi**		44	5
			P# block of 4, 4 #		2.20	—
			Zip block of 4		2.00	—
			Copyright block of 4		2.00	—
a.			Imperf., pair		150.00	
2166	A1549	22c	**multi**		44	5
			P# block of 4, 5 #		2.20	—
			Zip block of 4		2.00	—
			Copyright block of 4		2.00	—
a.			Imperf., pair		150.00	

ARKANSAS STATEHOOD
SESQUICENTENARY

Old State House,
Little
Rock — A1550

Designed by Roger Carlisle.
Printed by the American Bank Note Company and J.W. Fergusson & Sons.

PHOTOGRAVURE
Plates of 200 in four panes of 50.

1986, Jan. 3			Tagged		Perf. 11	
2167	A1550	22c	**multi**		44	5
			P# block of 4, 6 #		2.25	—
			Zip block of 4		2.00	—
			Copyright block of 4		2.00	—
a.			Vert. pair, imperf. horiz.		—	

GREAT AMERICANS ISSUE

A1551

A1552

A1553

A1555

A1560

A1562

A1565

A1571

A1575

A1578

A1554

A1559

A1561

A1563

A1566

A1574

A1577

A1579

Designers: 1c, 2c, Ron Adair. 3c, 4c, 5c, 17c, 65c, Christopher Calle. 10c, 56c, Robert Anderson. 14c, Ward Brackett. 15c, Jack Rosenthal. 21c, Susan Sanford. 23c, Dennis Lyall. 25c, Richard Sparks. 45c, Bradbury Thompson. $1, $2, Tom Broad. $5, Arthur Lidov.

ENGRAVED

1986-88			Tagged		Perf. 11	
2168	A1551	1c	**brownish vermilion**, *June 30*		5	5
			P# block of 4		25	—
			Zip block of 4		22	—

2169	A1552	2c	**bright blue**, *Feb. 28, 1987*	5	5
			P# block of 4	25	—
			Zip block of 4	22	—
			Copyright block of 4	22	—
2170	A1553	3c	**bright blue**, *Sept. 15*	6	5
			P# block of 4	30	—
			Zip block of 4	28	—
			Copyright block of 4	28	—
2171	A1554	4c	**blue violet**, *July 14*	8	5
			P# block of 4	40	—
			Zip block of 4	35	—
			Copyright block of 4	35	—
2172	A1555	5c	**dark olive green**, *Feb. 27*	10	5
			P# block of 4	50	—
			Copyright block of 4	45	—
2176	A1559	10c	**lake**, *Aug. 15, 1987*	20	5
			P# block of 4	1.00	—
			Zip block of 4	90	—
			Copyright block of 4	90	—
2177	A1560	14c	**crimson**, *Feb. 12, 1987*	28	5
			P# block of 4	1.40	—
			Zip block of 4	1.25	—
			Copyright block of 4	1.25	—
2178	A1561	15c	**claret**, *June 6, 1988*	30	5
			P# block of 4	1.50	—
			Zip block of 4	1.35	—
			Copyright block of 4	1.35	—
2179	A1562	17c	**dull blue green**, *June 18*	34	6
			P# block of 4	1.75	—
			Zip block of 4	1.60	—
			Copyright block of 4	1.60	—
2180	A1563	21c	*Oct. 21, 1988*	42	5
			P# block of 4	2.10	—
			Copyright block of 4	1.90	—
2182	A1565	23c	*Nov. 4, 1988*	46	5
			P# block of 4	2.30	—
			Zip block of 4	2.05	—
			Copyright block of 4	2.05	—
2183	A1566	25c	**blue**, *Jan. 11*	50	6
			P# block of 4	2.50	—
			Zip block of 4	2.25	—
			Copyright block of 4	2.25	—
a.			Booklet pane of 10, *May 3, 1988*	5.00	—
2188	A1571	45c	**bright blue**, *June 17, 1988*	90	6
			P# block of 4	4.50	—
			Zip block of 4	4.00	—
			Copyright block of 4	4.00	—
2191	A1574	56c	**scarlet**, *Sept. 3*	1.10	8
			P# block of 4	5.50	—
			Zip block of 4	5.00	—
			Copyright block of 4	5.00	—
2192	A1575	65c	*Nov. 5, 1988*	1.30	18
			P# block of 4	6.50	—
			Zip block of 4	5.75	—
			Copyright block of 4	5.75	—
2194	A1577	$1	**dark Prussian green**, *Sept. 23*	2.00	50
			P# block of 4	10.00	—
			Zip block of 4	9.00	—
			Copyright block of 4	9.00	—
2195	A1578	$2	**bright violet**, *Mar. 19*	4.00	50
			P# block of 4	20.00	—
			Zip block of 4	18.00	—
			Copyright block of 4	18.00	—

Plates of 320 in sixteen panes of 20 (5x4).
The first and fifth rows of horizontal perforations extend into the side selvage.
Copyright information appears in the center of the top or bottom selvage.

2196	A1579	$5	**copper red**, *Aug. 25, 1987*	10.00	1.00
			P# block of 4	50.00	—

Booklet Stamp
Perf. 10 on 2 or 3 sides

2197	A1566	25c	**blue**, *May 3, 1988*	50	5
a.			Bklt. pane of 6	3.00	—

This is an expanding set. Numbers will change if necessary.

UNITED STATES - SWEDEN STAMP
COLLECTING

Handstamped Cover,
Philatelic
Memorabilia
A1581

Boy Examining Stamp
Collection — A1582

No. 836 Under
Magnifying Glass,
Sweden Nos. 268,
271 — A1583

1986 Presidents
Miniature
Sheet — A1584

Designed by Richard Sheaff and Eva Jern (No. 2200).

BOOKLET STAMPS
LITHOGRAPHED & ENGRAVED
Perf. 10 Vert. on 1 or 2 Sides

1986, Jan. 23		Tagged		
2198	A1581	22c **multi**	44	5
2199	A1582	22c **multi**	44	5
2200	A1583	22c **multi**	44	5
2101	A1584	22c **multi**	44	5
a.	Bklt. pane of 4, #2198-2201		1.80 —	
b.	As "a," black omitted on Nos. 2198, 2201		60.00	
c.	As "a," blue (litho.) omitted on Nos. 2198-2200		—	
d.	As "a," buff (litho.) omitted		—	

LOVE ISSUE

A1585

Designed by Saul Mandel.

Plates of 200 in four panes of 50.
PHOTOGRAVURE

1986, Jan. 30		Tagged		Perf. 11
2202	A1585	22c **multi**	44	5
	P# block of 4, 5#		2.25 —	
	Zip block of 4		2.00 —	
	Copyright block of 4		2.00 —	

BLACK HERITAGE ISSUE

Sojourner Truth (c. 1797-1883),
Human Rights
Activist — A1586

Designed by Jerry Pinkney.

Plates of 200 in four panes of 50.
PHOTOGRAVURE

1986, Feb. 4		Tagged		Perf. 11
2203	A1586	22c **multi**	44	5
	P# block of 4, 6#		2.25 —	
	Zip block of 4		2.00 —	
	Copyright block of 4		2.00 —	

REPUBLIC OF TEXAS, 150th Anniv.

Republic of Texas　Texas State Flag and Silver
Spur — A1587

Designed by Don Adair.
Printed by the American Bank Note Co. and J.W. Fergusson
& Sons.

PHOTOGRAVURE
Plates of 200 in four panes of 50.

1986, Mar. 2		Tagged		Perf. 11
2204	A1587	22c **dark blue, dark red & grayish black**	44	5
	P# block of 4, 3 #		2.20 —	
	Zip block of 4		2.00 —	
	Copyright block of 4		2.00 —	
a.	Horiz. pair, imperf. vert.		—	

FISH

Muskellunge
A1588

Atlantic
Cod — A1589

Largemouth
Bass — A1590

Bluefin
Tuna — A1591

Catfish
A1592

Designed by Chuck Ripper.

BOOKLET STAMPS
PHOTOGRAVURE

1986, Mar. 21		Tagged		Perf. 10 Horiz.
2205	A1588	22c **multi**	44	5
2206	A1589	22c **multi**	44	5
2207	A1590	22c **multi**	44	5
2208	A1591	22c **multi**	44	5
2209	A1592	22c **multi**	44	5
a.	Bklt. pane of 5, #2205-2209		3.00 —	

PUBLIC HOSPITALS

A1593

Designed by Uldis Purins.
Printed by the American Bank Note Co. and J.W. Fergusson
& Sons.

PHOTOGRAVURE
Plates of 200 in four panes of 50.

1986, Apr. 11		Tagged		Perf. 11
2210	A1593	22c **multi**	44	5
	P# block of 4, 5#		2.20 —	
	Zip block of 4		2.00 —	
	Copyright block of 4		2.00 —	
a.	Vert. pair. imperf. horiz.		—	

PERFORMING ARTS

Edward Kennedy "Duke"
Ellington (1899-1974), Jazz
Composer — A1594

Designed by Jim Sharpe.
Printed by the American Bank Note Co. and J.W. Fergusson
& Sons.

PHOTOGRAVURE
Plates of 200 in four panes of 50.

1986, Apr. 29		Tagged		Perf. 11
2211	A1594	22c **multi**	44	5
	P# block of 4, 6#		2.20 —	
	Zip block of 4		2.00 —	
	Copyright block of 4		2.00 —	
a.	Vert. pair. imperf. horiz.		—	

AMERIPEX '86 ISSUE
Miniature Sheets

Presidents of the United States: I

AMERIPEX 86
International
Stamp Show
Chicago, Illinois
May 22-June 1, 1986

35 Presidents — A1599a

Presidents of the United States: II

AMERIPEX 86
International
Stamp Show
Chicago, Illinois
May 22-June 1, 1986

A1599b

Presidents of the United States: III

AMERIPEX 86
International
Stamp Show
Chicago, Illinois
May 22-June 1, 1986

A1599c

Presidents of the United States: IV

AMERIPEX 86
International
Stamp Show
Chicago, Illinois
May 22-June 1, 1986

A1599d

Designs: No. 2216a, George Washington. No. 2216b, John Adams. No. 2216c, Thomas Jefferson. No. 2216d, James Madison. No. 2216e, James Monroe. No. 2216f, John Quincy Adams. No. 2216g, Andrew Jackson. No. 2216h, Martin Van Buren. No. 2216i, William H. Harrison. No. 2217a, John Tyler. No. 2217b, James Knox Polk. No. 2217c, Zachary Taylor. No. 2217d, Millard Fillmore. No. 2217e, Franklin Pierce. No. 2217f, James Buchanan. No. 2217g, Abraham Lincoln. No. 2217h, Andrew Johnson. No. 2217i, Ulysses S. Grant. No. 2218a, Rutherford B. Hayes. No. 2218b, James A. Garfield. No. 2218c, Chester A. Arthur. No. 2218d, Grover Cleveland. No. 2218e, Benjamin Harrison. No. 2218f, William McKinley. No. 2218g, Theodore Roosevelt. No.

2218h, William H. Taft. No. 2218i, Woodrow Wilson. No. 2219a, Warren G. Harding. No. 2219b, Calvin Coolidge. No. 2219c, Herbert Hoover. No. 2219d, Franklin Delano Roosevelt. No. 2219e, White House. No. 2219f, Harry S. Truman. No. 2219g, Dwight D. Eisenhower. No. 2219h, John F. Kennedy. No. 2219i, Lyndon B. Johnson.
Designed by Jerry Dadds

LITHOGRAPHED & ENGRAVED

1986, May 22	Tagged		Perf. 11	
2216 A1599a	Sheet of 9		4.00	—
a.-i.	22c, any single		44	20
j.	Blue (engr.) omitted		—	
2217 A1599b	Sheet of 9		4.00	—
a.-i.	22c, any single		44	20
2218 A1599c	Sheet of 9		4.00	—
a.-i.	22c, any single		44	20
j.	Brown (engr.) omitted		—	
2219 A1599d	Sheet of 9		4.00	—
a.-i.	22c, any single		44	20

Issued in conjunction with AMERIPEX '86 Intl. Philatelic Exhibition, Chicago, IL May 22-June 1. Sheet size: 120x207mm.

ARCTIC EXPLORERS

Elisha Kent Kane — A1600

Adolphus W. Greely — A1601

Vilhjalmur Stefansson A1602

Robert E. Peary, Matthew Henson — A1603

Designed by Dennis Lyall.
Printed by the American Bank Note Company and J.W. Ferguson & Sons.

PHOTOGRAVURE
Plates of 200 in four panes of 50.

1986, May 28	Tagged		Perf. 11	
2220 A1600	22c **multi**		44	8
2221 A1601	22c **multi**		44	8
2222 A1602	22c **multi**		44	8
2223 A1603	22c **multi**		44	8
	P# block of 4, 5#		2.75	—
	Zip block of 4		2.50	—
	Copyright block of 4		2.50	—
a.	Block of 4, #2220-2223		2.25	1.00
b.	As "a," black (engr.) omitted		—	

STATUE OF LIBERTY, CENT.

A1604

Designed by Howard Paine.

ENGRAVED
Plates of 200 in four panes of 50.

1986, July 4	Tagged	Perf. 11	
2224 A1604 22c scar & dk bl		44	5
P# block of 4, 2#		2.20	—
Zip block of 4		2.00	—
Copyright block of 4		2.00	—

TRANSPORTATION ISSUE

Omnibus 1880s 1 USA

A1604a

Locomotive 1870s 2 USA

A1604b

Designers: 1c, 2c, David Stone.

COIL STAMPS
ENGRAVED

1986-87	Tagged	Perf. 10 Vert.	
2225 A1604a 1c violet, Nov. 26		5	5
Pair		10	10
P# strip of 3, P# 1, 2		90	
2226 A1604b 2c black, Mar. 6, 1987		5	5
Pair		10	10
P# strip of 3, P# 1		95	

REDUCED SIZE

2228 A1285 4c reddish brown, Aug.		8	5
Pair		16	10
P# strip of 3, P#1		1.75	

UNTAGGED

2231 A1511 8.3c green (Bureau precancel), Aug.			
29			16
Pair			32
P# strip of 3, P# 1, 2			2.75

Earliest known usage of No. 2228: Aug. 15, 1986.
On No. 2228 "Stagecoach 1890s" is 17mm long; on No. 1898A, 19½ mm long.
On No. 2231 "Ambulance 1860s" is 18mm long; on No. 2128, 18½mm long.
Joint lines do not appear on Nos. 2225-2231.
This is an expanding set. Numbers will change if necessary.

NAVAJO ART

Navajo Art USA 22

A1605

Navajo Art USA 22

A1606

Navajo Art USA 22

A1606

Navajo Art USA 22

A1607

Navajo Art USA 22

A1608

Designed by Derry Noyes.

LITHOGRAPHED & ENGRAVED
Plates of 200 in four panes of 50.

1986, Sept. 4	Tagged	Perf. 11	
2235 A1605 22c multi		44	8
2236 A1606 22c multi		44	8
2237 A1607 22c multi		44	8
2238 A1608 22c multi		44	8
P# block of 4, 5#		2.20	—
Zip block of 4		2.00	—
Copyright block of 4		2.00	—
a.	Block of 4, #2235-2238	1.80	1.00
b.	As "a," black (engr.) omitted	600.00	

LITERARY ARTS

T.S.Eliot

22 USA

T.S. Eliot (1888-1965),
Poet — A1609

Designed by Bradbury Thompson.

ENGRAVED
Plates of 200 in four panes of 50.

1986, Sept. 26	Tagged	Perf. 11	
2239 A1609 22c copper red		44	5
P# block of 4		2.20	—
Zip block of 4		2.00	—
Copyright block of 4		2.00	—

AMERICAN FOLK ART ISSUE
Woodcarved Figurines

Wood Carving: Highlander Figure

Folk Art USA 22

A1610

Wood Carving: Ship Figurehead

Folk Art USA 22

A1611

Wood Carving: Nautical Figure

Folk Art USA 22

A1612

Wood Carving: Cigar-Store Figure

Folk Art USA 22

A1613

Designed by Bradbury Thompson.
Printed by the American Bank Note Company and J.W. Ferguson & Sons.

PHOTOGRAVURE
Plates of 200 in four panes of 50.

1986, Oct. 1	Tagged	Perf. 11	
2240 A1610 22c multi		44	8
2241 A1611 22c multi		44	8
2242 A1612 22c multi		44	8
2243 A1613 22c multi		44	8
P# block of 4, 5#		2.20	—
Zip block of 4		2.00	—
Copyright block of 4		2.00	—
a.	Block of 4, #2240-2243	1.80	1.00
b.	As "a," imperf. vert.	—	

CHRISTMAS

CHRISTMAS 22 USA

Perugino, National Gallery

Madonna,
National Gallery,
by Perugino (c.
1450-1513)
A1614

USA 22

GREETINGS
Village Scene
A1615

Designed by Dolli Tingle (No. 2244) and Bradbury Thompson (No. 2245).

PHOTOGRAVURE
Plates of 200 in four panes of 50.

1986, Oct. 24	Tagged	Perf. 11	
2244 A1614 22c multi		44	5
P# block of 4, 6#		2.20	—
Zip block of 4		2.00	—
Copyright block of 4		2.00	—
2245 A1615 22c multi		44	5
P# block of 4, 5#		2.20	—
Zip block of 4		2.00	—
Copyright block of 4		2.00	—

MICHIGAN STATEHOOD SESQUICENTENARY

USA 22

1837-1987 Michigan Statehood

White Pine — A1616

Designed by Robert Wilbert.

PHOTOGRAVURE
Plates of 200 in four panes of 50.

1987, Jan. 26	Tagged	Perf. 11	
2246 A1616 22c multi		44	5
P# block of 4, 4#		2.20	—
Zip block of 4		2.00	—
Copyright block of 4		2.00	—

PAN AMERICAN GAMES, INDIANAPOLIS, AUG. 7-25

22 USA

Pan American Games Indianapolis 1987

Runner in Full
Stride — A1617

Designed by Lon Busch.

PHOTOGRAVURE
Plates of 200 in four panes of 50.

1987, Jan. 29	Tagged	Perf. 11	
2247 A1617 22c multi		44	5
P# block of 4, 5#		2.20	—
Zip block of 4		2.00	—
Copyright block of 4		2.00	—
a.	Silver omitted	—	

LOVE ISSUE

LOVE
USA 22

A1618

Designed by John Alcorn.

PHOTOGRAVURE
Panes of 100

1987, Jan. 30	Tagged	Perf. 11½x11	
2248 A1618 22c multi		44	5
P# block of 4, 5#		2.20	—
Zip block of 4		2.00	—
Copyright block of 4		2.00	—

BLACK HERITAGE

Jean Baptiste Pointe du Sable
(c. 1750-1818), Pioneer Trader,
Founder of Chicago — A1619

Designed by Thomas Blackshear.

PHOTOGRAVURE
Plates of 200 in four panes of 50.

1987, Feb. 20	Tagged		Perf. 11
2249 A1619 22c **multi**		44	5
	P# block of 4, 5#	2.20	—
	Zip block of 4	2.00	—
	Copyright block of 4	2.00	—

PERFORMING ARTS

Enrico Caruso (1873-1921),
Opera Tenor — A1620

Designed by Jim Sharpe.

PHOTOGRAVURE
Plates of 200 in four panes of 50.

1987, Feb. 27	Tagged		Perf. 11
2250 A1620 22c **multi**		44	5
	P# block of 4, 4#	2.20	—
	Zip block of 4	2.00	—
	Copyright block of 4	2.00	—
a.	Black (engr.) omitted	—	

GIRL SCOUTS, 75TH ANNIVERSARY

Fourteen Achievement
Badges — A1621

Designed by Richard D. Sheaff.

LITHOGRAPHED & ENGRAVED
Plates of 200 in four panes of 50.

1987, Mar. 12	Tagged		Perf. 11
2251 A1621 22c **multi**		44	5
	P# block of 4, 6#	2.20	—
	Zip block of 4	2.00	—
	Copyright block of 4	2.00	—

TRANSPORTATION ISSUE

A1622

A1623

A1624

A1626

A1628

A1630

A1632

A1634

A1636

A1625

A1627

A1629

A1631

A1633

A1635

Designers: 3c, 7.6c, 13.2c, 15c, Richard Schlect. 5c, 5.3c 16.7c, Lou Nolan. 8.4c, 20.5c, 24.1c, Christopher Calle. 10c, William F. Bond. 13c, Joe Brockert. 17.5c, Tom Broad. 20c, Dan Romano. 21c, David Stone.

COIL STAMPS
ENGRAVED

1987-88			Perf. 10 Vert.
Tagged, Untagged (5.3c, 7.6c, 8.4c, 13c, 13.2c, 16.7c, 20.5c, 21c, 24.1c)			
2252 A1622	3c **claret**, *Feb. 29, 1988*	6	5
	Pair	12	10
	P# strip of 3, P# 1	1.00	
2253 A1623	5c **black**, *Sept. 25*	10	5
	Pair	20	10
	P# strip of 3, P# 1	1.75	
2254 A1624	5.3c **black** (Bureau precancel), *Sept. 16, 1988*	11	
	Pair	22	
	P# strip of 3, P# 1	1.85	
"Nonprofit Carrier Route Sort" is in scarlet.			
2255 A1625	7.6c **brown** (Bureau precancel), *Aug. 30, 1988*	16	
	Pair	32	
	P# strip of 3, P# 1	2.25	
"Nonprofit" is in scarlet.			

2256 A1626	8.4c **deep claret** (Bureau precancel), *Aug. 12, 1988*	17	
	Pair	35	
	P# strip of 3, P# 1	2.50	
"Nonprofit" is in red.			
2257 A1627	10c **sky blue**, *Apr. 11*	20	5
	pair	40	10
	P# strip of 3, P# 1	2.75	
2258 A1628	13c (Bureau precancel), *Oct. 29, 1988*	26	
	Pair	52	
	P# strip of 3, P#	3.00	
"Presorted First-Class" is in red.			
2259 A1629	13.2c **slate green** (Bureau precancel), *July 19, 1988*	28	
	Pair	56	
	P# strip of 3, P# 1	3.00	
a.	Imperf., pair	—	
"Bulk Rate" is in red.			
2260 A1630	15c **violet**, *July 12, 1988*	30	5
	Pair	60	10
	P# strip of 3, P# 1	1.50	
2261 A1631	16.7c **rose** (Bureau precancel), *July 7, 1988*	34	
	Pair	68	
	P# strip of 3, P# 1	3.25	
"Bulk Rate " is in black.			
2262 A1632	17.5c **dark vio**, *Sept. 25*	35	5
	Pair	70	10
	P# strip of 3, P# 1	3.50	
a.	Untagged (Bureau Precancel)	35	
	P# strip of 3, P# 1	4.00	
b.	Imperf., pair	—	
2263 A1633	20c *Oct. 28, 1988*	40	5
	Pair	80	10
	P# strip of 3, P#	3.75	
2264 A1634	20.5c (Bureau precancel), *Sept. 28, 1988*	42	
	Pair	85	
	P# strip of 3, P# 1	3.75	
"ZIP + 4 Presort" is in black.			
2265 A1635	21c **olive green** (Bureau precancel), *Aug. 16, 1988*	42	
	Pair	85	
	P# strip of 3, P# 1	4.00	
"Presorted First-Class" is in red.			
2266 A1636	24.1c (Bureau precancel), *Oct. 26, 1988*	50	
	Pair	1.00	
	P# strip of 3, P#	4.25	

5.3c, 7.6c, 8.4c, 13.2c, 16.7c, 20.5c, 21c and 24.1c only available precanceled.

SPECIAL OCCASIONS

A1637

A1638

A1639

A1640

A1641

A1642

A1643

A1644

Designed by Oren Sherman.

BOOKLET STAMPS
PHOTOGRAVURE

1987, Apr. 20   **Tagged**   *Perf. 10 on 1, 2 or 3 Sides*

2267	A1637	22c multi	44	5
2268	A1638	22c multi	44	5
2269	A1639	22c multi	44	5
2270	A1640	22c multi	44	5
2271	A1641	22c multi	44	5
2272	A1642	22c multi	44	5
2273	A1643	22c multi	44	5
2274	A1644	22c multi	44	5
a.	Bklt. pane of 10 (#2268-2271, 2273-2274, 2 of each #2267, 2272)		4.50 —	

UNITED WAY CENTENARY

Six Profiles — A1645

Designed by Jerry Pinkney.

LITHOGRAPHED & ENGRAVED
Plates of 200 in four panes of 50.

1987, Apr. 28   **Tagged**   *Perf. 11*

2275	A1645	22c multi	44	5
	P# block of 4, 6#		2.20 —	

A1646

A1648

A1649a

A1649c

Zip block of 4	2.00 —
Copyright block of 4	2.00 —

A1647

A1649

A1649b

A1649d

Designs: Nos. 2276, 2278, 2280, Peter Cocci. Nos. 2277, 2279, 2282, Robert McCall. Nos. 2281, 2283-2285, Chuck Ripper.

PHOTOGRAVURE (Nos. 2276-2279), Panes of 100

1987-88   **Tagged**   *Perf. 11*

2276	A1646	22c multi, *May 9*	44	5

	P# block of 4, 4#		2.20	
	Zip block of 4		2.00	
	Copyright block of 4		2.00	
a.	Booklet pane of 20, *Nov. 30*		8.80 —	
2277	A1647	(25c) multi, *Mar. 22, 1988*	50	5
	P# block of 4, 4#		2.50	
	Zip block of 4		2.25	
	Copyright block of 4		2.25	
2278	A1648	25c multi, *May 6, 1988*	50	5
	P# block of 4, 4#		2.50	
	Zip block of 4		2.25	
	Copyright block of 4		2.25	

COIL STAMPS
Perf. 10 Vert.

2279	A1647	(25c) multi, *Mar. 22, 1988*	50	5
	Pair		1.00	10
	P# strip of 3, P# 1111, 1211, 1222, 2222		2.25	

ENGRAVED

2280	A1649	25c multi, *May 20, 1988*	50	5
	Pair		1.00	10
	P# strip of 3, P# 1-3		2.25	
a.	Imperf., pair		—	

LITHOGRAPHED AND ENGRAVED

2281	A1649d	25c multi, *Sept. 2, 1988*	50	5
	Pair		1.00	10
	P# strip of 3, P# 1, 2		2.25	

BOOKLET STAMPS
PHOTOGRAVURE
Perf. 10 on 2 or 3 Sides

2282	A1647	(25c) multi, *Mar. 22, 1988*	50	5
a.	Bklt. pane of 10		5.00	
2283	A1649a	25c multi, *Apr. 29, 1988*	50	5
a.	Bklt. pane of 10		5.00	
2284	A1649b	25c multi, *May 28, 1988*	50	5
2285	A1649c	25c multi, *May 28, 1988*	50	5
b.	Bklt. pane of 10, 5 each Nos. 2284-2285		5.00	
2285A	A1648	25c multi, *July 5, 1988*	50	5
c.	Bklt. pane of 6		3.00	

NORTH AMERICAN WILDLIFE ISSUE

Fauna and Flora
A1650-A1699

Designed by Chuck Ripper.

PHOTOGRAVURE
Plates of 200 in four panes of 50.

1987, June 13			Tagged		Perf. 11
2286	A1650	22c	Barn swallow	44	15
2287	A1651	22c	Monarch butterfly	44	15
2288	A1652	22c	Bighorn sheep	44	15
2289	A1653	22c	Broad-tailed hummingbird	44	15
2290	A1654	22c	Cottontail	44	15
2291	A1655	22c	Osprey	44	15
2292	A1656	22c	Mountain lion	44	15
2293	A1657	22c	Luna moth	44	15
2294	A1658	22c	Mule deer	44	15
2295	A1659	22c	Gray squirrel	44	15
2296	A1660	22c	Armadillo	44	15
2297	A1661	22c	Eastern chipmunk	44	15
2298	A1662	22c	Moose	44	15
2299	A1663	22c	Black bear	44	15
2300	A1664	22c	Tiger swallowtail	44	15
2301	A1665	22c	Bobwhite	44	15
2302	A1666	22c	Ringtail	44	15
2303	A1667	22c	Red-winged blackbird	44	15
2304	A1668	22c	American lobster	44	15
2305	A1669	22c	Black-tailed jack rabbit	44	15
2306	A1670	22c	Scarlet tanager	44	15
2307	A1671	22c	Woodchuck	44	15
2308	A1672	22c	Roseate spoonbill	44	15
2309	A1673	22c	Bald eagle	44	15
2310	A1674	22c	Alaskan brown bear	44	15
2311	A1675	22c	Iiwi	44	15
2312	A1676	22c	Badger	44	15
2313	A1677	22c	Pronghorn	44	15
2314	A1678	22c	River otter	44	15
2315	A1679	22c	Ladybug	44	15
2316	A1680	22c	Beaver	44	15
2317	A1681	22c	White-tailed deer	44	15
2318	A1682	22c	Blue jay	44	15
2319	A1683	22c	Pika	44	15
2320	A1684	22c	Bison	44	15
2321	A1685	22c	Snowy egret	44	15
2322	A1686	22c	Gray wolf	44	15
2323	A1687	22c	Mountain goat	44	15
2324	A1688	22c	Deer mouse	44	15
2325	A1689	22c	Black-tailed prairie dog	44	15
2326	A1690	22c	Box turtle	44	15
2327	A1691	22c	Wolverine	44	15
2328	A1692	22c	American elk	44	15
2329	A1693	22c	California sea lion	44	15
2330	A1694	22c	Mockingbird	44	15
2331	A1695	22c	Raccoon	44	15
2332	A1696	22c	Bobcat	44	15
2333	A1697	22c	Black-footed ferret	44	15
2334	A1698	22c	Canada goose	44	15
2335	A1699	22c	Red fox	44	15
a.			Pane of 50, #2286-2335	22.00	

RATIFICATION OF THE CONSTITUTION BICENTENNIAL
13 States

Dec 7, 1787   USA
Delaware 22
A1700

Dec 12, 1787
Pennsylvania 22
A1701

Dec 18, 1787   USA
New Jersey 22
A1702

22 USA
January 2, 1788
Georgia
A1703

22 USA
January 9, 1788
Connecticut
A1704

22 USA
Feb 6, 1788
Massachusetts
A1705

Maryland 22 USA
April 28, 1788
A1706

25 USA
May 23, 1788
South Carolina
A1707

25 USA
June 21, 1788
New Hampshire
A1708

June 25, 1788 USA
Virginia 25
A1709

July 26, 1788 USA
New York 25 A1710

Designers: Nos. 2336-2337, Richard D. Sheaff. No. 2338, Jim Lamb. No. 2339, Greg Harlin. No. 2340, Christopher Calle, No. 2342, Stephen Hustuedt. No. 2343, Bob Timberlake. No. 2344, Thomas Szumowski. No. 2345, Pierre Mion. No. 2346, Bradbury Thompson.

Printed by the Bureau of Engraving or the American Banknote Company
and J.W. Fergusson and sons (Nos. 2343-2344).
LITHOGRAPHED & ENGRAVED,
PHOTOGRAVURE (#2337, 2339, 2343-2344),
ENGRAVED (Nos. 2341).
Plates of 200 in four panes of 50.

1987-88			Tagged		Perf. 11
2336	A1700	22c	**multi,** *July 4*	44	5
			P# block of 4, 5#	2.20	—
			Zip block of 4	2.00	—
			Copyright block of 4	2.00	—
2337	A1701	22c	**multi,** *Aug. 26*	44	5
			P# block of 4, 5#	2.20	—
			Zip block of 4	2.00	—
			Copyright block of 4	2.00	—
2338	A1702	22c	**multi,** *Sept. 11*	44	5
			P# block of 4, 5#	2.20	—
			Zip block of 4	2.00	—
			Copyright block of 4	2.00	—
2339	A1703	22c	**multi,** *Jan. 6, 1988*	44	5
			P# block of 4, 5#	2.20	
			Zip block of 4	2.00	
			Copyright block of 4	2.00	
2340	A1704	22c	**multi,** *Jan. 9, 1988*	44	5
			P# block of 4, 4#	2.20	
			Zip block of 4	2.00	
			Copyright block of 4	2.00	
2341	A1705	22c	**dark blue & dark red,** *Feb. 6, 1988*	44	5
			P# block of 4, 1#	2.20	
			Zip block of 4	2.00	
			Copyright block of 4	2.00	
2342	A1706	22c	**multi,** *Feb. 15, 1988*	44	5
			P# block of 4, 6#	2.20	
			Zip block of 4	2.00	
			Copyright block of 4	2.00	
2343	A1707	25c	**multi,** *May 23, 1988*	50	5
			P# block of 4, 5#	2.50	
			Zip block of 4	2.00	
			Copyright block of 4	2.00	
2344	A1708	25c	**multi,** *June 21, 1988*	50	5
			P# block of 4, 4#	2.50	
			Zip block of 4	2.00	
			Copyright block of 4	2.00	
2345	A1709	25c	**multi,** *June 25, 1988*	50	5
			P# block of 4, 5#	2.50	
			Zip block of 4	2.00	
			Copyright block of 4	2.00	
2346	A1710	25c	**multi,** *July 23, 1988*	50	5
			P# block of 4, 5#	2.50	
			Zip block of 4	2.00	
			Copyright block of 4	2.00	

US-MOROCCO DIPLOMATIC RELATIONS BICENTENNIAL

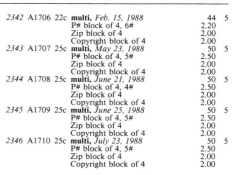

Arabesque, Dar Batha Palace
Door, Fez — A1713

Designed by Howard Paine.

LITHOGRAPHED & ENGRAVED
Plates of 200 in four panes of 50.

1987, July 17			Tagged		Perf. 11
2349	A1713	22c	**scarlet & black**	44	5
			P# block of 4, 2#	2.20	—
			Zip block of 4	2.00	—
			Copyright block of 4	2.00	—
a.			Black (engr.) omitted	—	

LITERARY ARTS

William Faulkner

William Cuthbert Faulkner
(1897-1962), Novelist — A1714

Designed by Bradbury Thompson.

ENGRAVED
Plates of 200 in four panes of 50

1987, Aug. 3			Tagged		Perf. 11
2350	A1714	22c	**bright green**	44	5
			P# block of 4	2.20	—
			Zip block of 4	2.00	—
			Copyright block of 4	2.00	—

FOLK ART ISSUE
Lacemaking

A1715   Lacemaking USA 22

Demand, as well as supply, determines a stamp's market value. One is as important as the other.

Lacemaking USA 22 A1716

A1717 Lacemaking USA 22

Lacemaking USA 22 A1718

Designed by Libby Thiel.

LITHOGRAPHED & ENGRAVED
Plates of 160 in four panes of 40.

1987, Aug. 14		Tagged		Perf. 11	
2351	A1715	22c	ultra & white	44	8
2352	A1716	22c	ultra & white	44	8
2353	A1717	22c	ultra & white	44	8
2354	A1718	22c	ultra & white	44	8
		P# block of 4, 4#		2.20	—
		Zip block of 4		2.00	—
		Copyright block of 4		2.00	—
a.		Block of 4, #2351-2354		1.80	1.00
b.		As "a," white omitted			

DRAFTING OF THE CONSTITUTION BICENTENNIAL
Excerpts from the Preamble

The Bicentennial of the Constitution of the United States of America
1787-1987   USA 22
A1719

We the people of the United States, in order to form a more perfect Union...
Preamble, U.S. Constitution   USA 22   A1720

Establish justice, insure domestic tranquility, provide for the common defense, promote the general welfare...
A1721   Preamble, U.S. Constitution   USA 22

And secure the blessings of liberty to ourselves and our posterity...
Preamble, U.S. Constitution   USA 22   A1722

Do ordain and establish this Constitution for the United States of America
A1723   Preamble, U.S. Constitution   USA 22

Designed by Bradbury Thompson.

BOOKLET STAMPS
PHOTOGRAVURE

1987, Aug. 28		Tagged	Perf. 10 Horiz.	
2355	A1719	22c multi	44	8
2356	A1720	22c multi	44	8
2357	A1721	22c multi	44	8
2358	A1722	22c multi	44	8
2359	A1723	22c multi	44	8
a.		Bklt. pane of 5, #2355-2359	2.25	

SIGNING OF THE CONSTITUTION

U.S. Constitution
We the People
1787-1987 22 USA
A1724

Designed by Howard Koslow.

LITHOGRAPHED & ENGRAVED
Plates of 200 in four panes of 50.

1987, Sept. 17		Tagged	Perf. 11	
2360	A1724	22c multi	44	5
		P# block of 4, 5#	2.20	—
		Zip block of 4	2.00	—
		Copyright block of 4	2.00	—

CERTIFIED PUBLIC ACCOUNTING

CPA
Certified Public Accountant
22 USA
A1725

Designed by Lou Nolan.

LITHOGRAPHED & ENGRAVED
Plates of 200 in four panes of 50.

1987, Sept. 21		Tagged	Perf. 11	
2361	A1725	22c multi	44	5
		P# block of 4, 4#	2.20	—
		Zip block of 4	2.00	—
		Copyright block of 4	2.00	—
a.		Black (engr.) omitted	—	

LOCOMOTIVES

Stourbridge Lion 1829   USA 22
Stourbridge Lion, 1829
A1726

Best Friend of Charleston 1830   USA 22
Best Friend of Charleston, 1830
A1727

John Bull 1831   USA 22
John Bull, 1831
A1728

Brother Jonathan 1832   USA 22
Brother Jonathan, 1832
A1729

Gowan & Marx 1839   USA 22
Gowan & Marx, 1839
A1730

Designed by Richard Leech.

BOOKLET STAMPS
LITHOGRAPHED & ENGRAVED

1987, Oct. 1		Tagged	Perf. 10 Horiz.	
2362	A1726	22c multi	44	8
2363	A1727	22c multi	44	8
2364	A1728	22c multi	44	8
2365	A1729	22c multi	44	8
2366	A1730	22c multi	44	8
a.		Bklt. pane of 5, #2362-2366	2.25	

CHRISTMAS

CHRISTMAS 22 USA
Moroni, National Gallery
Moroni Madonna
A1731

USA 22 GREETINGS
Christmas Ornaments
A1732

Designed by Bradbury Thompson (No. 2367) and Jim Dean (No. 2368).

PHOTOGRAVURE
Plates of 200 in four panes of 50.

1987, Oct. 23		Tagged	Perf. 11	
2367	A1731	22c multi	44	5
		P# block of 4, 6#	2.20	—
		Zip block of 4	2.00	—
		Copyright block of 4	2.00	—
2368	A1732	22c multi	44	5
		P# block of 4, #	2.20	—
		Zip block of 4	2.00	—
		Copyright block of 4	2.00	—

1988 WINTER OLYMPICS, CALGARY

Skiing — A1733
OLYMPICS 88   22 USA

Designed by Bart Forbes.
Printed by the American Bank Note Company and J.W. Fergusson and Sons.

PHOTOGRAVURE
Plates of 200 in four panes of 50.

1988, Jan. 10		Tagged	Perf. 11	
2369	A1733	22c multi	44	5
		P# block of 4, 4#	2.20	—
		Zip block of 4	2.00	—
		Copyright block of 4	2.00	—

AUSTRALIA BICENTENNIAL

Caricature of an Australian Koala and an American Bald Eagle — A1734

Designed by Roland Harvey.

PHOTOGRAVURE
Plates of 160 in four panes of 40.

1988, Jan. 26			Tagged	
2370 A1734 22c	multi		44	5
	P# block of 4, 5		2.20	—
	Zip block of 4		2.00	—
	Copyright block of 4		2.00	—

Set Australia No. 1052.

BLACK HERITAGE

James Weldon Johnson (1871-1938), Author and Lyricist — A1735

Designed by Thomas Blackshear.
Printed by the American Bank Note Company and J.W. Fergusson and Sons.

PHOTOGRAVURE
Plates of 200 in four panes of 50.

1988, Feb.2			Tagged	
2371 A1735 22c	multi		44	5
	P# block of 4, 5#		2.20	—
	Zip block of 4		2.00	—
	Copyright block of 4		2.00	—

CATS

Siamese and Exotic Shorthair A1736

Abyssianian and Himalayan A1737

Maine Coon and Burmese A1738

American Shorthair and Persian — A1739

Designed by John Dawson.
Printed by the American Bank Note Company and J.W. Fergusson and Sons.

PHOTOGRAVURE
Plates of 160 in four panes of 40.

1988, Feb. 5			Tagged	
2372 A1736 22c	multi		44	8
2373 A1737 22c	multi		44	8
2374 A1738 22c	multi		44	8
2375 A1739 22c	multi		44	8
	P# block of 4, 5#		2.20	—
	Zip block of 4		2.00	—
	Copyright block of 4		2.00	—
a.	Block of 4, # 2372-2375		1.80	1.00

AMERICAN SPORTS

Knute Rockne (1883-1931), Notre Dame Football Coach — A1740

Designed by Peter Cocci and Thomas Hipschen.

LITHOGRAPHED & ENGRAVED
Plates of 200 in four panes of 50.

1988, Mar. 9			Tagged	
2376 A1740 22c	multi		44	5
	P# block of 4, 7#		2.20	—
	Zip block of 4		2.00	—
	Copyright block of 4		2.00	—

Francis Ouimet (1893-1967), 1st Amateur Golfer to Win the U.S. Open Championship — A1741

Designed by M. Gregory Rudd.
Printed by the American Bank Note Company and J.W. Fergusson and Sons.

PHOTOGRAVURE
Plates of 200 in four panes of 50.

1988, June 13			Tagged	
2377 A1741 25c	multi		50	5
	P# block of 4, 5#		2.50	—
	Zip block of 4		2.25	—
	Copyright block of 4		2.25	—

LOVE ISSUE
Roses

A1742

A1743

Designed by Richard Sheaff.

PHOTOGRAVURE
Panes of 100 (25c) and panes of 200 in four panes of 50 (45c).

1988			Tagged	
2378 A1742 25c	multi, *July 4*		50	5
	P# block of 4, 5#		2.50	—
	Zip block of 4		2.25	—
	Copyright block of 4		2.25	—
2379 A1743 45c	multi, *Aug. 8*		90	20
	P# block of 4, 4#		4.50	—
	Zip block of 4		4.00	—
	Copyright block of 4		4.00	—

1988 SUMMER OLYMPICS, SEOUL

Gymnastic Rings — A1744

Desinged by Bart Forbes.

PHOTOGRAVURE
Plates of 200 in four panes of 50.

1988, Aug. 19			Tagged	
2380 A1744 25c	multi		50	5
	P# block of 4, 5#		2.50	—
	Zip block of 4		2.25	—
	Copyright block of 4		2.25	—

CLASSIC AUTOMOBILES

1928 Locomobile A1745

1929 Pierce-Arrow A1746

1931 Cord — A1747

1932 Packard A1748

See ''Information for Collectors'' section at beginning of catalogue for an explanation of perforation types, imperforates and coils.

1935 Duesenberg A1749

Designed by Ken Dallison.

LITHOGRAPHED & ENGRAVED
BOOKLET STAMPS

1988, Aug. 25	Tagged	Perf. 10 Horiz.
2381 A1745 25c multi		50 8
2382 A1746 25c multi		50 8
2383 A1747 25c multi		50 8
2384 A1748 25c multi		50 8
2385 A1749 25c multi		50 8
a. Bklt. pane of 5, Nos. 2381-2385		2.50 —

ANTARCTIC EXPLORERS

Nathaniel Palmer (1799-1877) A1750

Lt. Charles Wilkes (1798-1877) A1751

Richard E. Byrd (1888-1957) A1752

Lincoln Ellsworth (1880-1951) A1753

Designed by Dennis Lyall.
Printed by the American Bank Note Company and J.W. Fergusson and Sons.

PHOTOGRAVURE
Plates of 160 in four panes of 40.

1988, Sept. 14	Tagged	Perf. 11
2386 A1750 25c multi		50 8
2387 A1751 25c multi		50 8
2388 A1752 25c multi		50 8
2389 A1753 25c multi		50 8
	P# block of 4, 6#	2.50 —
	Zip block of 4	2.25 —
	Copyright block of 4	2.25 —
a. Block of 4, Nos. 2386-2389		2.00 1.25

FOLK ART ISSUE
Carousel Animals

Deer — A1754   Horse — A1755

Camel — A1756   Goat — A1757

Designed by Paul Calle.

LITHOGRAPHED & ENGRAVED
Plates of 200 in four panes of 50.

1988, Oct. 1	Tagged	Perf. 11
2390 A1754 25c multi		50 8
2391 A1755 25c multi		50 8
2392 A1756 25c multi		50 8
2393 A1757 25c multi		50 8
	P# block of 4,7#	2.50 —
	Zip block of 4	2.25 —
	Copyright block of 4	2.25 —
a. Block of 4, Nos. 2390-2393		2.00 1.25

Eagle and Moon A1758

Designed by Ned Seidler.

LITHOGRAPHED & ENGRAVED
Panes of 20

1988, Oct. 4	Tagged	Perf.11
2394 A1758 $8.75 multi		17.50 —
	P# block of 4, 6#	87.50 —

SPECIAL OCCASIONS

Love You A1759

Happy Birthday A1760

Thinking of You A1761

Best Wishes A1762

Designed by Harry Zelenko.
Printed by the American Bank Note Company and J.W. Fergusson and Sons.

BOOKLET STAMPS
PHOTOGRAVURE

1988, Oct. 22	Tagged	Perf.
2395 A1759 25¢ multi		50 5
2396 A1760 25¢ multi		50 5
a. Bklt. pane of 6, 3# 2395+ 3 #2396 with gutter between		3.00 —
2397 A1761 25¢ multi		50 5
2398 A1762 25¢ multi		50 5
a. Bklt. pane of 6, 3 #2397+ 3 #2398 with gutter between		3.00 —

CHRISTMAS

Madonna and Child, by Botticelli A1763

One-horse Open Sleigh and Village Scene A1764

Designed by Bradbury Thompson (No. 2399) and Joan Landis (No. 2400).

LITHOGRAPHED & ENGRAVED (No. 2399), PHOTOGRAVURE (No. 2400)
Plates of 300 in 6 Panes of 50.

1988, Oct 20	Tagged	Perf.
2399 A1763 25c multi		50 5
	P# block of 4, #	2.50 —
2400 A1764 25c multi		50 5
	P# block of 4, #	2.50 —

AIR POST STAMPS

Air mail in the U. S. Post Office system developed in three stages: pioneer period (with many unofficial or semi-official flights before 1918), government flights and contract air mail (C.A.M.). Contract air mail began on Feb. 15, 1926. All C.A.M. contracts were canceled on Feb. 19, 1934, and air mail was carried by Army planes for six months. After that the contract plan was resumed.

Curtiss Jenny — AP1

No. C3 first used on airplane mail service between Washington, Philadelphia and New York, on May 15, 1918, but was valid for ordinary postage. The rate of postage was 24 cents per ounce, which included immediate individual delivery.

Rate of postage was reduced to 16 cents for the first ounce and 6 cents for each additional ounce, which included 10 cents for immediate individual delivery, on July 15, 1918, by Postmaster General's order of June 26, 1918. No. C2 was first used for air mail in the tri-city service on July 15.

Rate of postage was reduced on December 15, 1918, by Postmaster General's order of November 30, 1918, to 6 cents per ounce. No. C1 was first used for air mail (same three-way service) on Dec. 16.

FLAT PLATE PRINTINGS
Plates of 100 subjects.

1918		Unwmk.		Engr.	Perf. 11
C1	AP1	6c **orange**, *Dec. 10*		100.00	45.00
		pale orange		100.00	45.00
		On cover			65.00
		First flight cover, *Dec. 16*			2,750.
		Margin block of 4, arrow top or left		425.00	195.00
		Center line block		475.00	210.00
		Margin block of 6, arrow & P#		1,200.	500.00
		Double transfer (#9155-14)		150.00	65.00
C2	AP1	16c **green**, *July 11*		150.00	52.50
		dark green		150.00	52.50
		On cover			70.00
		First flight cover, *July 15*			800.00

		Margin block of 4, arrow top or left		625.00	230.00
		Center line block		675.00	250.00
		Margin block of 6, arrow & P#		2,250.	700.00
C3	AP1	24c **carmine rose & blue**, *May 13*		145.00	65.00
		dark carmine rose & blue		145.00	65.00
		On cover			80.00
		First flight cover, *May 15*			750.00
		Margin block of 4, arrow top or left		625.00	285.00
		Margin block of 4, arrow bottom		650.00	300.00
		Margin block of 4, arrow right		725.00	350.00
		Center line block		700.00	325.00
		Margin block of 4, red P# only		725.00	375.00
		Margin block of 12, two P#, arrow & two "TOP"		2,600.	1,200.
		Margin block of 12, two P#, arrow & blue "TOP" only		10,000.	
a.		Center inverted		125,000.	
a.		Same, in block of four		525,000.	
a.		Same, center line block		575,000.	
a.		Same, margin block of 4, blue P#		575,000.	

Airplane Radiator and Wooden Propeller — AP2

Air Service Emblem — AP3

DeHavilland Biplane — AP4

Nos. C4 to C6 were issued primarily for use in the new night-flying air mail service between New York and San Francisco, but valid for all purposes. Three zones were established; the first from New York to Chicago, the second from Chicago to Cheyenne, and the third from Cheyenne to San Francisco, and the rate of postage was 8 cents an ounce for each zone. Service was inaugurated on July 1, 1924.

These stamps were placed on sale at the Philatelic Agency at Washington on the dates indicated in the listings but were not issued to postmasters at that time.

Plates of 400 subjects in four panes of 100 each.

1923			Perf. 11	
C4	AP2	8c **dark green**, *Aug. 15*	40.00	20.00
		deep green	40.00	20.00
		On cover		35.00
		Margin block of 6, P#	600.00	300.00
		Double transfer	70.00	35.00
C5	AP3	16c **dark blue**, *Aug. 17*	145.00	50.00
		On cover		65.00
		Margin block of 6, P#	3,250.	650.00
		Double transfer	185.00	70.00
C6	AP4	24c **carmine**, *Aug. 21*	165.00	40.00
		On cover		55.00
		Margin block of 6, P#	4,250.	850.00
		Double transfer (Pl. 14841)	210.00	55.00

Map of United States and Two Mail Planes AP5

The Act of Congress of February 2, 1925, created a rate of 10 cents per ounce for distances to 1000 miles, 15 cents per ounce for 1500 miles and 20 cents for more than 1500 miles on contract air mail routes.

Plates of 200 subjects in four panes of 50 each.

1926-27		Unwmk.	Perf. 11	
C7	AP5	10c **dark blue**, *Feb. 13, 1926*	4.50	50
		light blue	4.50	50
		Margin block of 6, P#	55.00	20.00

		Double transfer (11 UL 18246)		10.00	2.00
C8	AP5	15c **olive brown**, *Sept. 18, 1926*		5.50	2.75
		light brown		5.50	2.75
		Margin block of 6, P#		65.00	25.00
C9	AP5	20c **yellow green**, *Jan. 25, 1927*		14.00	2.25
		green		14.00	2.25
		Margin block of 6, P#		165.00	40.00

Lindbergh's Plane "Spirit of St. Louis" and Flight Route — AP6

A tribute to Col. Charles A. Lindbergh, who made the first non-stop (and solo) flight from New York to Paris, May 20-21, 1927.

Plates of 200 subjects in four panes of 50 each.

1927		Unwmk.	Perf. 11	
C10	AP6	10c **dark blue**, *June 18*	11.00	3.00
		Margin block of 6, P#	200.00	35.00
a.		Bklt. pane of 3, *May 26, 1928*	110.00	60.00
		Double transfer	20.00	5.00

First day covers of No. C10a and other airmail booklet panes are listed in the Booklet Panes section of this catalogue.

Beacon on Rocky Mountains AP7

Issued to meet the new rate, effective August 1, of 5 cents per ounce.

Plates of 100 subjects in two panes of 50 each.

1928		Unwmk.	Perf. 11	
C11	AP7	5c **carmine and blue**, *July 25*	6.00	65
		On cover, first day of 5c airmail rate, *Aug. 1*		3.00
		Margin block of 4, arrow, (line) right or left	30.00	3.00
		Margin block of 8, two P# only	250.00	25.00
		Margin block of 6, two P# & red "TOP"	65.00	10.00
		Margin block of 6, two P# & blue "TOP"	65.00	10.00
		Margin block of 6, two P# & double "TOP"	150.00	15.00
a.		Vert. pair, imperf. btwn.	5,500.	
		Recut frame line at left	12.00	1.50
		Double transfer	—	—

Winged Globe AP8

Plates of 200 subjects in four panes of 50 each.

1930		Unwmk.	Perf. 11	
		Stamp design: 46½x19mm.		
C12	AP8	5c **violet**, *Feb. 10*	15.00	45
		Margin block of 6, P#	250.00	40.00
a.		Horiz. pair, imperf. btwn.	4,500.	
		Double transfer (Pl. 20189)	27.50	1.75

See Nos. C16-C17, C19.

GRAF ZEPPELIN ISSUE

Zeppelin Over Atlantic Ocean AP9

Zeppelin Between Continents — AP10

Zeppelin Passing Globe AP11

Issued for use on mail carried on the first Europe-Pan-America round trip flight of the Graf Zeppelin in May, 1930. They were withdrawn from sale June 30, 1930.

Plates of 200 subjects in four panes of 50 each.

1930, Apr. 19		Unwmk.		Perf. 11	
C13 AP9	65c	green		450.00	275.00
		On cover or card			325.00
		Block of four		1,850.	1,300.
		Margin block of 6, P#		3,850.	2,500.
C14 AP10	$1.30	brown		1,000.	550.00
		On cover			600.00
		Block of four		4,100.	2,300.
		Margin block of 6, P#		8,250.	4,750.
C15 AP11	$2.60	blue		1,600.	800.00
		On cover			850.00
		Block of four		6,500.	3,350.
		Margin block of 6, P#		13,000.	7,000.

ROTARY PRESS PRINTING
Plates of 200 subjects in four panes of 50 each.

1931-32		Unwmk.	Perf. 10½x11	
		Stamp design: 47½x19mm.		
C16 AP8	5c	violet, Aug. 19, 1931	10.00	50
		Block of four	40.00	2.75
		Margin block of 4, P#	135.00	25.00

Issued to conform with new air mail rate of 8 cents per ounce which became effective July 6, 1932.

C17 AP8	8c	olive bister, Sept. 26, 1932	4.00	30
		Block of four	16.00	1.65
		Margin block of 4, P#	45.00	5.00

CENTURY OF PROGRESS ISSUE

"Graf Zeppelin," Federal Building at Chicago Exposition and Hangar at Friedrichshafen — AP12

Issued in connection with the flight of the airship "Graf Zeppelin" in October, 1933, to Miami, Akron and Chicago and from the last city to Europe.

FLAT PLATE PRINTING
Plates of 200 subjects in four panes of 50 each.

1933		Unwmk.	Perf. 11	
C18 AP12	50c	green, Oct. 2	115.00	95.00
		On cover		110.00
		Block of four	460.00	400.00
		Margin block of 6, P#	1,050.	700.00

Type of 1930 Issue.

ROTARY PRESS PRINTING.

Issued to conform with new air mail rate of 6 cents per ounce which became effective July 1, 1934.

Plates of 200 subjects in four panes of 50 each.

1934		Unwmk.	Perf. 10½x11	
C19 AP8	6c	dull orange, June 30	4.25	12
		On cover, first day of 6c airmail rate, July 1	10.00	

			18.00	70
		Block of four	18.00	
		Margin block of 4, P#	27.50	
		Pair with full vert. gutter btwn.	425.00	

TRANSPACIFIC ISSUES

"China Clipper" over Pacific — AP13

Issued to pay postage on mail transported by the Transpacific air mail service, inaugurated Nov. 22, 1935.

FLAT PLATE PRINTING
Plates of 200 subjects in four panes of 50 each.

1935		Unwmk.	Perf. 11	
C20 AP13	25c	blue, Nov. 22	1.50	1.25
		Margin block of 6, P#	20.00	

"China Clipper" over Pacific — AP14

Issued primarily for use on the Transpacific service to China, but valid for all air mail purposes.

FLAT PLATE PRINTING
Plates of 200 subjects in four panes of 50 each.

1937		Unwmk.	Perf. 11.	
C21 AP14	20c	green, Feb. 15	12.50	2.25
		dark green	12.50	2.25
		Block of four	50.00	12.50
		Margin block of 6, P#	150.00	
C22 AP14	50c	carmine, Feb. 15	12.00	6.50
		Block of four	48.00	27.50
		Margin block of 6, P#	140.00	

Eagle Holding Shield, Olive Branch and Arrows — AP15

FLAT PLATE PRINTING

Frame plates of 100 subjects in two panes of 50 each separated by a 1½-inch wide vertical gutter with central guide line, and vignette plates of 50 subjects. Some plates were made of iron, then chromed; several of these carry an additional imprint, "E.I." (Electrolytic Iron).

1938		Unwmk.		Perf. 11	
C23	AP15	6c	dark blue & carmine, *May 14*	50	6
			Margin block of 4, bottom or side arrow	2.25	55
			Margin block of 4, 2 P#	11.00	—
			Center line block	2.75	95
			Top margin block of 10, with two P#, arrow, two "TOP" and two registration markers	17.50	
a.			Vert. pair, imperf. horiz.	350.00	
b.			Horiz. pair, imperf. vert.	8,500.	
c.			ultramarine & carmine	200.00	

Top plate number blocks of No. C23 are found both with and without top arrow.

TRANSATLANTIC ISSUE

Winged Globe AP16

Inauguration of Transatlantic air mail service.
FLAT PLATE PRINTING
Plates of 200 subjects in four panes of 50 each.

1939		Unwmk.		Perf. 11	
C24	AP16	30c	dull blue, *May 16*	14.00	1.50
			Margin block of 6, P#	200.00	—

Twin-Motored Transport Plane — AP17

ROTARY PRESS PRINTING
E. E. Plates of 200 subjects in four panes of 50 each.

1941-44		Unwmk.		Perf. 11x10½	
C25	AP17	6c	carmine, *June 25, 1941*	15	5
			Margin block of 4, P#	1.00	—
			Pair with full vertical gutter between	225.00	
a.			Booklet pane of three, *March 18, 1943*	6.50	1.00
b.			Horiz. pair, imperf. between	2,000.	
C26	AP17	8c	olive green, *Mar. 21, 1944*	20	5
			Margin block of 4, P#	1.25	—
			Pair with full horiz. gutter btwn.	325.00	
C27	AP17	10c	violet, *Aug. 15, 1941*	1.65	20
			Margin block of 4, P#	12.50	—
C28	AP17	15c	brown carmine, *Aug. 19, 1941*	3.75	35
			Margin block of 4, P#	19.00	—
C29	AP17	20c	bright green, *Aug. 27, 1941*	2.75	30
			Margin block of 4, P#	16.50	—
C30	AP17	30c	blue, *Sept. 25, 1941*	3.50	30
			Margin block of 4, P#	17.50	—
C31	AP17	50c	orange, *Oct. 29, 1941*	16.00	4.00
			Margin block of 4, P#	100.00	—

DC-4 Skymaster AP18

ROTARY PRESS PRINTING
E. E. Plates of 200 subjects in four panes of 50 each.

1946		Unwmk.		Perf. 11x10½	
C32	AP18	5c	carmine, *Sept. 25*	15	5
			Margin block of 4, P#	75	—

DC-4 Skymaster — AP19

ROTARY PRESS PRINTING
E. E. Plates of 400 subjects in four panes of 100 each.

1947		Unwmk.		Perf. 10½x11	
C33	AP19	5c	carmine, *March 26*	12	5
			Margin block of 4, P#	75	—

Pan American Union Building, Washington, D.C., and Martin 2-0-2 — AP20

Statue of Liberty, New York Skyline and Lockheed Constellation AP21

San Francisco-Oakland Bay Bridge and Boeing B377
Stratocruiser — AP22

Designed by Victor S. McCloskey, Jr., Leon Helguera and
William K. Schrage.

ROTARY PRESS PRINTING

E. E. Plates of 200 subjects in four panes of 50 each.

1947	Unwmk.	Perf. 11x10½	
C34 AP20 10c *black, Aug. 30*		30	6
Margin block of 4, P#		2.25	—
a. Dry printing		38	6
C35 AP21 15c **bright blue green,** *Aug. 20*		35	5
blue green		35	5
Margin block of 4, P#		2.50	—
Pair with full horiz. gutter btwn.		400.00	
a. Horiz. pair, imperf. between		2,000	
b. Dry printing		55	5
C36 AP22 25c **blue,** *July 30*		1.60	12
Margin block of 4, P#		8.00	—
a. Dry printing		2.00	12

See note on wet and dry printings following No. 1029.

ROTARY PRESS COIL STAMP
Type of 1947

1948	Unwmk.	Perf. 10 Horizontally	
C37 AP19 5c **carmine,** *Jan. 15*		2.00	1.10
Pair		4.00	2.25
Joint line pair		13.50	3.00

NEW YORK CITY ISSUE

Map of Five Boroughs, Circular
Band and Planes — AP23

Issued to commemorate the 50th anniversary of the consolidation of the five boroughs of New York City.

ROTARY PRESS PRINTING

E. E. Plates of 400 subjects in four panes of 100
each.

1948	Unwmk.	Perf. 11x10½	
C38 AP23 5c **bright carmine,** *July 31*		18	18
Margin block of 4, P#		13.50	—

Type of 1947
ROTARY PRESS PRINTING

E. E. Plates of 400 subjects in four panes of 100
each.

1949	Unwmk.	Perf. 10½x11	
C39 AP19 6c **carmine,** *Jan. 18*		18	5
Margin block of 4, P#		90	—
a. Booklet pane of 6, *Nov. 18*		12.00	—
b. 6c carmine, dry printing		50	6
c. as "a," dry printing		15.00	—

See note on wet and dry printings following No. 1029.

ALEXANDRIA BICENTENNIAL ISSUE

Home of John
Carlyle,
Alexandria Seal
and Gadsby's
Tavern — AP24

Issued to commemorate the 200th anniversary of
the founding of Alexandria, Virginia.

ROTARY PRESS PRINTING

E. E. Plates of 200 subjects in four panes of 50 each.

1949	Unwmk.	Perf. 11x10½	
C40 AP24 6c **carmine,** *May 11*		16	10
Margin block of 4, P#		85	—

ROTARY PRESS COIL STAMP
Type of 1947

1949	Unwmk.	Perf. 10 Horizontally	
C41 AP19 6c **carmine,** *Aug. 25*		4.50	5
Pair		9.00	15
Joint line pair		20.00	1.35

UNIVERSAL POSTAL UNION ISSUE

Post Office
Department
Building — AP25

Globe and Doves
Carrying
Messages — AP26

Boeing
Stratocruiser and
Globe — AP27

Issued to commemorate the 75th anniversary of the formation of the Universal Postal Union.

ROTARY PRESS PRINTING

E. E. Plates of 200 subjects in four panes of 50 each.

1949	Unwmk.	Perf. 11x10½	
C42 AP25 10c **violet,** *Nov. 18*		35	35
Margin block of 4, P#		2.50	—
C43 AP26 15c **ultramarine,** *Oct. 7*		50	50
Margin block of 4, P#		2.50	—
C44 AP27 25c **rose carmine,** *Nov. 30*		85	85
Margin block of 4, P#		10.00	—

WRIGHT BROTHERS ISSUE

Wilbur and Orville
Wright and their
Plane,
1903 — AP28

Issued to commemorate the 46th anniversary of the first
successful flight in a motor-powered airplane, made Dec. 17,
1903, at Kill Devil Hill near Kitty Hawk, N.C., by Wilbur
Wright (1867-1912) and his brother Orville (1871-1948) of
Dayton, O. The plane flew 852 feet in 59 seconds.

ROTARY PRESS PRINTING

E. E. Plates of 200 subjects in four panes of 50 each.

1949	Unwmk.	Perf. 11x10½	
C45 AP28 6c **magenta,** *Dec. 17*		16	10
Margin block of 4, P#		85	—

Diamond Head,
Honolulu,
Hawaii — AP29

ROTARY PRESS PRINTING

E. E. Plates of 200 subjects in four panes of 50 each.

1952, Mar. 26	Unwmk.	Perf. 11x10½	
C46 AP29 80c **bright red violet**		10.00	1.50
Margin block of 4, P#		50.00	—

*United States Air Mail stamps can be mounted in
Scott's annually supplemented National, American,
Minuteman, U.S. Commemorative and Commemorative
Air Mail Plate Blocks, U.S. Blocks of Four and U.S.
Regular and Regular Air Plate Blocks.*

POWERED FLIGHT ISSUE

First Plane and Modern Plane — AP30

Issued to commemorate the 50th anniversary of powered flight.
ROTARY PRESS PRINTING
E. E. Plates of 200 subjects in four panes of 50 each.

1953	Unwmk.	Perf. 11x10 1/2		
C47 AP30 6c carmine, May 29			16	10
Margin block of 4, P#			85	—

Eagle in Flight — AP31

Issued primarily for use on domestic post cards.
ROTARY PRESS PRINTING
E. E. Plates of 400 subjects in four panes of 100 each.

1954	Unwmk.	Perf. 11x10 1/2		
C48 AP31 4c bright blue, Sept. 3			12	8
Margin block of 4, P#			3.75	—

AIR FORCE ISSUE

B-52 Stratofortress and F-104 Starfighters AP32

Designed by Alexander Nagy, Jr.

Issued to commemorate the 50th anniversary of the U. S. Air Force.
ROTARY PRESS PRINTING
E. E. Plates of 200 subjects in four panes of 50 each.

1957	Unwmk.	Perf. 11x10 1/2		
C49 AP32 6c blue, Aug. 1			16	10
Margin block of 4, P#			1.25	—

Type of 1954
Issued primarily for use on domestic post cards.

1958	Unwmk.	Perf. 11x10 1/2		
C50 AP31 5c red, July 31			22	15
Margin block of 4, P#			5.00	—

Silhouette of Jet Airliner — AP33

Designed by William H. Buckley and Sam Marsh.
ROTARY PRESS PRINTING
E. E. Plates of 400 subjects in four panes of 100 each.

1958	Unwmk.	Perf. 10 1/2x11		
C51 AP33 7c blue, July 31			22	5
Margin block of 4, P#			1.30	—
a. Booklet pane of 6			15.00	6.50

ROTARY PRESS COIL STAMP
Perf. 10 Horizontally

C52 AP33 7c blue, July 31			4.50	20
Pair			9.00	50
Joint line pair			22.50	1.25

ALASKA STATEHOOD ISSUE

Big Dipper, North Star and Map of Alaska — AP34

Designed by Richard C. Lockwood.

Issued to commemorate Alaska"s admission to statehood
ROTARY PRESS PRINTING
E. E. Plates of 200 subjects in four panes of 50 each.

1959	Unwmk.	Perf. 11x10 1/2		
C53 AP34 7c dark blue, Jan. 3			25	12
Margin block of 4, P#			1.50	—

BALLOON JUPITER ISSUE

Balloon and Crowd — AP35

Designed by Austin Briggs.

Issued to commemorate the centenary of the carrying of mail by the balloon Jupiter from Lafayette to Crawfordsville, Ind.
GIORI PRESS PRINTING
Plates of 200 subjects in four panes of 50 each.

1959	Unwmk.	Perf. 11		
C54 AP35 7c dark blue & red, Aug. 17			25	12
Margin block of 4, P#			1.50	—

HAWAII STATEHOOD ISSUE

Alii Warrior, Map of Hawaii and Star of Statehood AP36

Designed by Joseph Feher.

Issued to commemorate Hawaii's admission to statehood.
ROTARY PRESS PRINTING
E. E. Plates of 200 subjects in four panes of 50 each.

1959	Unwmk.	Perf. 11 x 10 1/2		
C55 AP36 7c rose red, Aug. 21			25	12
Margin block of 4, P#			1.50	—

PAN AMERICAN GAMES ISSUE

Runner Holding Torch — AP37

Designed by Suren Ermoyan.

Issued to commemorate the 3rd Pan American Games at Chicago, Aug. 27-Sept. 7, 1959.
GIORI PRESS PRINTING
Plates of 200 subjects in four panes of 50 each.

1959	Unwmk.	Perf. 11		
C56 AP37 10c violet blue & bright red, Aug. 27			40	40
Margin block of 4, P#			3.00	—

Liberty Bell — AP38

Statue of Liberty — AP39

Abraham Lincoln — AP40

GIORI PRESS PRINTING
Plates of 200 subjects in four panes of 50 each.

1959-66	Unwmk.	Perf. 11		
C57 AP38 10c black & green, June 10, 1960			2.75	1.00
Margin block of 4, P#			14.00	—
C58 AP39 15c black & orange, Nov. 20, 1959			60	6
Margin block of 4, P#			3.25	—
C59 AP40 25c black & maroon, Apr. 22, 1960			75	6
Margin block of 4, P#			4.00	—
a. Tagged, Dec. 29, 1966			75	15

See Luminescence data in Information for Collectors section.

Type of 1958
ROTARY PRESS PRINTING
E. E. Plates of 400 subjects in four panes of 100 each.

1960	Unwmk.	Perf. 10 1/2x11		
C60 AP33 7c carmine, Aug. 12			30	5
Margin block of 4, P#			1.50	—
Pair with full horiz. gutter btwn.				
a. Booklet pane of 6, Aug. 19			20.00	7.00

Type of 1958
ROTARY PRESS COIL STAMP

1960	Unwmk.	Perf. 10 Horizontally		
C61 AP33 7c carmine, Oct. 22			8.00	25
Pair			16.00	55
Joint line pair			50.00	3.25

Type of 1959-60 and

Statue of Liberty — AP41

GIORI PRESS PRINTING
Plates of 200 subjects in four panes of 50 each.

1961-67	Unwmk.	Perf. 11	
C62 AP38 13c	**black & red**, June 28, 1961	65	10
	Margin block of 4, P#	3.50	—
a.	Tagged, Feb. 15, 1967	80	25
C63 AP41 15c	**black & orange**, Jan. 13, 1961	40	8
	Margin block of 4, P#	2.25	—
a.	Tagged, Jan. 11, 1967	50	12
b.	As "a," horiz. pair, imperf. vert.	15,000.	

Jet Airliner over Capitol — AP42

Designed by Henry K. Bencsath.

ROTARY PRESS PRINTING
E.E. Plates of 400 subjects in four panes of 100 each.

1962-65	Unwmk.	Perf. 10½x11	
C64 AP42 8c	**carmine**, Dec. 5, 1962	22	5
	Margin block of 4, P#	1.10	—
a.	Tagged, Aug. 1, 1963	22	5
a.	Pair with full horiz. gutter between		
b.	Booklet pane of 5 + label	7.50	1.25
c.	As "b," tagged, 1964	2.25	50

Nos. C64a and C64c were made by overprinting Nos. C64 and C64b with phosphorescent ink. No. C64a was first issued at Dayton, O., for experiments in high speed mail sorting. The tagging is visible in ultraviolet light.

COIL STAMP; ROTARY PRESS
Perf. 10 Horizontally

C65 AP42 8c	**carmine**, Dec. 5, 1962	50	8
	Pair	1.00	20
	Joint line pair	4.00	35
a.	Tagged, Jan. 14, 1965	60	10

MONTGOMERY BLAIR ISSUE

Montgomery Blair — AP43

Designed by Robert J. Jones

Issued to honor Montgomery Blair (1813-1883), Postmaster General (1861-64), who called the first International Postal Conference, Paris, 1863, forerunner of the U.P.U.

GIORI PRESS PRINTING
Plates of 200 subjects in four panes of 50 each.

1963	Unwmk.	Perf. 11	
C66 AP43 15c	**dull red, dk. brn. & bl.**, May 3	1.20	75
	Margin block of 4, P#	6.00	—

Bald Eagle — AP44

Designed by V. S. McCloskey, Jr.

Issued primarily for use on domestic post cards.

ROTARY PRESS PRINTING
E.E. Plates of 400 subjects in four panes of 100 each.

1963-67	Unwmk.	Perf. 11x10½		
C67 AP44 6c	**red**, *July 12, 1963*		20	15
	Margin block of 4, P#		3.50	—
a.	Tagged, *Feb. 15, 1967*		3.00	50

AMELIA EARHART ISSUE

Amelia Earhart and Lockheed Electra — AP45

Designed by Robert J. Jones.

Issued to honor Amelia Earhart (1898-1937), first woman to fly across the Atlantic.

GIORI PRESS PRINTING
Plates of 200 subjects in four panes of 50 each.

1963	Unwmk.	Perf. 11		
C68 AP45 8c	**carmine & maroon**, *July 24*		30	15
	Margin block of 4, P#		2.50	

ROBERT H. GODDARD ISSUE

Robert H. Goddard, Atlas Rocket and Launching tower, Cape Kennedy — AP46

Designed by Robert J. Jones.

Issued to honor Dr. Robert H. Goddard (1882-1945), physicist and pioneer rocket researcher.

GIORI PRESS PRINTING
Plates of 200 subjects in four panes of 50 each.

1964	Tagged	Perf. 11		
C69 AP46 8c	**blue, red & bister**, *Oct. 5*		90	15
	Margin block of 4, P#		4.00	—
	Margin block of 4, Mr. Zip and "Use Zip Code"		3.75	—

Luminescence
Air Post stamps issued after mid-1964 are tagged.

ALASKA PURCHASE ISSUE

Tlingit Totem, Southern Alaska — AP47

Designed by Willard R. Cox

Issued to commemorate the centenary of the Alaska Purchase. The totem pole shown is in the Alaska State Museum, Juneau.

GIORI PRESS PRINTING
Plates of 200 subjects in four panes of 50 each.

1967	Unwmk.	Perf. 11		
C70 AP47 8c	**brown**, *March 30*		45	20
	Margin block of 4, P#		3.50	—
	Margin block of 4, Mr. Zip and "Use Zip Code"		2.00	—

"Columbia Jays" by John James Audubon — AP48

Fifty-Star Runway — AP49

GIORI PRESS PRINTING

Designed by Robert J. Jones.

Plates of 200 subjects in four panes of 50 each.

1967		Perf. 11		
C71 AP48 20c	**multicolored**, *Apr. 26*		1.50	15
	Margin block of 4, P#		7.50	—
	Margin block of 4, Mr. Zip and "Use Zip Code"		6.50	—

See note over No. 1241.

ROTARY PRESS PRINTING

Designed by Jaan Born.

E. E. Plates of 400 subjects in four panes of 100 each.

1968	Unwmk.	Perf. 11x10½		
C72 AP49 10c	**carmine**, *Jan. 5*		30	5
	Margin block of 4, P#		2.25	—
	Margin block of 4, "Use Zip Codes"		1.40	—
	Margin block of 6, "Mail Early in the Day"		2.00	—
b.	Booklet pane of 8		4.00	75
c.	Booklet pane of 5 + label, *Jan. 6*		2.50	75

ROTARY PRESS COIL STAMP
Perf. 10 Vertically

1968				
C73 AP49 10c	**carmine**, *Jan. 5*		65	5
	Pair		1.30	10
	Joint line pair		3.50	20
a.	Imperf., pair		500.00	

$1 Air Lift
This stamp, listed as No. 1341, was issued Apr. 4, 1968, to pay for airlift of parcels to and from U.S. ports to servicemen overseas and in Alaska, Hawaii and Puerto Rico. It was "also valid for paying regular rates for other types of mail," the Post Office Department announced to the public in a philatelic release dated Mar. 10, 1968. The stamp is inscribed "U.S. Postage" and is untagged.

On Apr. 26, 1969, the P.O.D. stated in its Postal Manual (for postal employees) that this stamp "may be used toward paying the postage or fees for special services on *airmail* articles." On Jan. 1, 1970, the Department told postal employees through its Postal Bulletin that this $1 stamp "can only be used to pay the airlift fee or toward payment of postage or fees on *airmail* articles."

Some collectors prefer to consider No. 1341 an airmail stamp.

50th ANNIVERSARY OF AIR MAIL ISSUE

Curtiss Jenny — AP50

Designed by Hordur Karlsson.

Issued to commemorate the 50th anniversary of regularly scheduled air mail service.

LITHOGRAPHED, ENGRAVED (GIORI)
Plates of 200 subjects in four panes of 50 each.

1968		Perf. 11		
C74 AP50 10c	**blue, black & red**, *May 15*		50	15
	Margin block of 4, P#		5.00	—
	Margin block of 4, Mr. Zip and "Use Zip Code"		2.60	—
	Margin block of 6, "Mail Early in the Day"		3.75	—
a.	Red (tail stripe) omitted			

"USA" and Jet — AP51

Designed by John Larrecq.

LITHOGRAPHED, ENGRAVED (GIORI)
Plates of 200 subjects in four panes of 50 each.

1968		Perf. 11		
C75 AP51 20c	**red, blue & black**, *Nov. 22*		85	6
	Margin block of 4, P#		4.25	—
	Margin block of 4, Mr. Zip and "Use Zip Code"		4.00	—
	Margin block of 6, "Mail Early in the Day"		5.25	—

MOON LANDING ISSUE

First Man on the Moon AP52

Designed by Paul Calle.

Issued to commemorate man"s first landing on the moon July 20, 1969, by U.S. astronauts Neil A. Armstrong and Col. Edwin E. Aldrin, Jr., with Lieut. Col. Michael Collins piloting Apollo 11.

LITHOGRAPHED, ENGRAVED (GIORI)
Plates of 128 subjects in four panes of 32 each.

1969		Perf. 11		
C76 AP52 10c	**yellow, black, lt. blue, ultra., rose red & carmine**, *Sept. 9*		30	15
	Margin block of 4, P#		1.75	—
	Margin block of 4, Mr. Zip and "Use Zip Code"		1.40	—
	Margin block of 6, "Mail Early in the Day"		2.10	—
a.	Rose red (litho.) omitted		350.00	—

On No. C76a, the lithographed rose red is missing from the entire vignette-the dots on top of the yellow areas as well as the flag shoulder patch.

Silhouette of Delta Wing Plane — AP53

Silhouette of Jet Airliner — AP54

Winged Airmail Envelope — AP55

Statue of Liberty — AP56

Designed by George Vander Sluis (9c, 11c), Nelson Gruppo (13c) and Robert J. Jones (17c).

ROTARY PRESS PRINTING
E. E. Plates of 400 subjects in four panes of 100 each.

1971-73	**Perf. 10½x11**	
C77 AP53 9c **red,** *May 15, 1971*	22	15
Margin block of 4, P#	1.50	—
Margin block of 4, "Use Zip Codes"	1.00	—
Margin block of 6, "Mail Early in the Day"	1.50	—

No. C77 issued primarily for use on domestic post cards.

	Perf. 11x10½	
C78 AP54 11c **carmine,** *May 7, 1971*	30	5
Margin block of 4, P#	1.75	—
Margin block of 4, "Use Zip Codes"	1.30	—
Margin block of 6, "Mail Early in the Day"	2.00	—
Pair with full vert. gutter btwn.	—	
a. Booklet pane of 4+2 labels	1.50	40
b. Untagged (Bureau precanceled)		25
C79 AP55 13c **carmine,** *Nov. 16, 1973*	32	10
Margin block of 4, P#	1.65	—
Margin block of 4, "Use Zip Codes"	1.35	—
Margin block of 6, "Mail Early in the Day"	2.00	—
a. Booklet pane of 5 + label, *Dec. 27, 1973*	1.35	70
b. Untagged (Bureau precanceled)		30

No. C78b precanceled "WASHINGTON D.C." (or "DC"), No. C79b "WASHINGTON DC" only; both for use of Congressmen, but available to any permit holder.

GIORI PRESS PRINTING
Panes of 200 subjects in four panes of 50 each.

	Perf. 11	
C80 AP56 17c **bluish black, red, & dark green,** *July 13, 1971*	55	15
Margin block of 4, P#	2.75	—
Margin block of 4, Mr. Zip and "Use Zip Code"	2.35	—
Margin block of 6, "Mail Early in the day"	3.40	—

"USA" & Jet Type of 1968
LITHOGRAPHED, ENGRAVED (GIORI)
Plates of 200 subjects in four panes of 50 each.

	Perf. 11	
C81 AP51 21c **red, blue & black,** *May 21, 1971*	55	10
Margin block of 4, P#	2.75	—
Margin block of 4, Mr. Zip and "Use Zip Code"	2.35	—
Margin block of 6, "Mail Early in the Day"	3.40	—

COIL STAMPS
ROTARY PRESS PRINTING

1971-73	**Perf. 10 Vertically**	
C82 AP54 11c **carmine,** *May 7, 1971*	40	6
Pair	80	24
Joint line pair	2.25	32
a. Imperf., pair	200.00	
a. Joint line pair	300.00	
C83 AP55 13c **carmine,** *Dec. 27, 1973*	40	10
Pair	80	25
Joint line pair	2.10	—
a. Imperf., pair	90.00	
a. Joint line pair	125.00	

NATIONAL PARKS CENTENNIAL ISSUE
City of Refuge, Hawaii

Kii Statue and Temple — AP57

Designed by Paul Rabut.

Issued to commemorate the centenary of national parks. This 11c honors the City of Refuge National Historical Park, established in 1961 at Honaunau, island of Hawaii.

LITHOGRAPHED, ENGRAVED (GIORI)
Plates of 200 subjects in four panes of 50 each.

1972	**Perf. 11**	
C84 AP57 11c **orange & multicolored,** *May 3*	30	15
Margin block of 4, P#	1.75	—
Margin block of 4, Mr. Zip and "Use Zip Code"	1.50	—
Margin block of 6, "Mail Early in the Day"	2.00	—
Blue & green (litho.) omitted	1,750.	

OLYMPIC GAMES ISSUE

Skiing and Olympic Rings — AP58

Designed by Lance Wyman.

Issued to commemorate the 11th Winter Olympic Games, Sapporo, Japan, Feb. 3-13, and the 20th Summer Olympic Games, Munich, Germany, Aug. 26-Sept. 11.

PHOTOGRAVURE (Andreotti)
Plates of 200 subjects in four panes of 50 each.

1972	**Perf. 11x10½**	
C85 AP58 11c **black, blue, red, emerald & yellow,** *Aug. 17*	30	15
Margin block of 10, 5 P#	3.50	—
Margin block of 4, "Use Zip Code"	1.25	—
Margin block of 6, "Mail Early in the Day"	1.90	—

ELECTRONICS PROGRESS ISSUE

De Forest Audions — AP59

Designed by Walter and Naiad Einsel.

LITHOGRAPHED, ENGRAVED (GIORI)
Plates of 200 subjects in four panes of 50 each.

1973	**Perf. 11**	
C86 AP59 11c **vermilion, lilac, pale lilac, olive, brown, dp. carmine & black,** *July 10*	30	15
Margin block of 4, P#	1.75	—
Margin block of 4, Mr. Zip and "Use Zip Code"	1.35	—
Margin block of 6, "Mail Early in the Day"	2.00	—
a. Verm. & olive (litho.) omitted	2,000.	

Statue of Liberty — AP60

Mt. Rushmore National Memorial AP61

Designed by Robert (Gene) Shehorn.

GIORI PRESS PRINTING
Panes of 200 subjects in four panes of 50 each.

1974	**Perf. 11**	
C87 AP60 18c **carmine, black & ultramarine,** *Jan. 11*	45	45
Margin block of 4, 2 P#	2.50	—
Margin block of 4, Mr. Zip and "Use Zip Code"	1.90	—
Margin block of 6, "Mail Early in the Day"	2.85	—
C88 AP61 26c **ultramarine, black & carmine,** *Jan. 2*	60	15
Margin block of 4, P#	3.00	—
Margin block of 4, Mr. Zip and "Use Zip Code"	2.50	—
Margin block of 6, "Mail Early in the Day"	3.75	—

Plane and Globes — AP62

Plane, Globes and Flags — AP63

Designed by David G. Foote.

GIORI PRESS PRINTING
Panes of 200 subjects in four panes of 50 each.

1976, Jan. 2	**Perf. 11**	
C89 AP62 25c **red, blue & black**	60	18
Margin block of 4, P#	3.25	—
Margin block of 4, Mr. Zip and "Use Zip Code"	2.60	—
Margin block of 6, "Mail Early in the Day"	3.75	—
C90 AP63 31c **red, blue & black**	62	10
Margin block of 4, P#	3.25	—
Margin block of 4, Mr. Zip and "Use Zip Code"	2.75	—
Margin block of 6, "Mail Early in the Day"	4.00	—

WRIGHT BROTHERS ISSUE

Orville and Wilbur Wright, and Flyer A — AP64

Wright Brothers, Flyer A and Shed — AP65

Designed by Ken Dallison.
75th anniversary of first powered flight, Kill Devil Hill, N.C., Dec. 17, 1903. Nos. C91-C92 printed se-tenant vertically.

LITHOGRAPHED, ENGRAVED (GIORI)
Plates of 400 subjects in four panes of 100 each.

1978, Sept. 23	**Perf. 11**	
C91 AP64 31c **ultra. & multicolored**	90	15
C92 AP65 31c **ultra. & multicolored**	90	15
a. Pair, #C91-C92	1.85	65
Margin block of 4, P#	4.50	—
Margin block of 4, "Use Correct Zip Code"	3.75	—
Margin block of 4, copyright	3.75	—
b. As "a," ultra. & black (engr.) omitted	1,500.	
c. As "a," black (engr.) omitted	—	

OCTAVE CHANUTE ISSUE

Chanute and Biplane Hang-glider AP66

Biplane Hang-glider and Chanute AP67

Designed by Ken Dallison.
Octave Chanute (1832-1910), civil engineer and aviation pioneer. Nos. C93-C94 printed se-tenant vertically.

LITHOGRAPHED, ENGRAVED (GIORI)
Plates of 400 subjects in four panes of 100 each.

1979, Mar. 29	**Tagged**	**Perf. 11**
C93 AP66 21c **blue & multicolored**	1.25	32
C94 AP67 21c **blue & multicolored**	1.25	32
a. Pair, #C93-C94	2.60	75
Margin block of 4, P#	6.50	—
Margin block of 4, Mr. Zip	5.50	—

Margin block of 4, copyright 5.50 —
b. As "a." ultra & black (engr.) omitted 3,000.

WILEY POST ISSUE

Wiley Post and "Winnie Mae" — AP68

NR-105-W, Post in Pressurized Suit, Portrait — AP69

Designed by Ken Dallison.
Wiley Post (1899-1935), first man to fly around the world alone and high-altitude flying pioneer. Nos. C95-C96 printed se-tenant vertically.

LITHOGRAPHED, ENGRAVED (GIORI)
Plates of 400 subjects in four panes of 100 each.

1979, Nov. 20	Tagged	Perf. 11	
C95 AP68 25c blue & multicolored		1.50	35
C96 AP69 25c blue & multicolored		1.50	35
a. Pair, #C95-C96		3.25	85
Margin block of 4, P#		12.50	—
Margin block of 4, Mr. Zip		6.50	—
Margin block of 4, copyright		6.50	—

OLYMPIC GAMES ISSUE

High Jump — AP70

Designed by Robert M. Cunningham.

PHOTOGRAVURE
22nd Olympic Games, Moscow, July 19-Aug. 3, 1980.
Plates of 200 subjects in four panes of 50 each.

1979, Nov. 1	Tagged	Perf. 11	
C97 AP70 31c multi		90	30
P# block of 12, 6 P#		12.00	—
Zip block of 4		3.75	—
Copyright block of 4		3.75	—

PHILIP MAZZEI (1730-1816)

Philip Mazzei
Patriot Remembered

Italian-born Political Writer — AP71

Designed by Sante Graziani

PHOTOGRAVURE
Plates of 200 subjects in four panes of 50 each.

1980, Oct. 13	Tagged	Perf. 11	
C98 AP71 40c multi		90	30
P# block of 12, 6 P#		12.00	—
Zip block of 4		3.75	—
Copyright block of 4		3.75	—
a. Perf.10½x11 ('82)		2.00	—
b. Imperf. pair		2,250.	

BLANCHE STUART SCOTT (1886-1970)

First Woman Pilot — AP72

Designed by Paul Calle.

PHOTOGRAVURE
Plates of 200 subjects in four panes of 50.

1980, Dec. 30	Tagged	Perf. 11	
C99 AP72 28c multi		70	15
P# block of 12, 6 P#		9.25	—
Zip block of 4		3.00	—
Copyright block of 4		3.00	—

GLENN CURTISS (1878-1930)

Aviation Pioneer and Aircraft Designer — AP73

Designed by Ken Dallison.

PHOTOGRAVURE
Plates of 200 subjects in four panes of 50.

1980, Dec. 30	Tagged	Perf. 11	
C100 AP73 35c multi		75	15
P# block of 12, 6 P#		10.00	—
Zip block of 4		3.25	—
Copyright block of 4		3.25	—

SUMMER OLYMPICS 1984

Women's Gymnastics AP74

Hurdles AP75

Women's Basketball — AP76

Soccer — AP77

Shot Put — AP78

Men's Gymnastics AP79

Women's Swimming AP80

Weight Lifting — AP81

Women's Fencing — AP82

Cycling — AP83

Women's Volleyball — AP84

Pole Vaulting — AP85

Designed by Robert Peak.
23rd Olympic Games, Los Angeles, July 28-Aug. 12, 1984.

PHOTOGRAVURE
Plates of 200 subjects in four panes of 50.

1983, June 17	Tagged	Perf. 11	
C101 AP74 28c multi		56	28
C102 AP75 28c multi		56	28
C103 AP76 28c multi		56	28
C104 AP77 28c multi		56	28
P# block of 4, 4 P#		3.75	—
Zip block of 4		3.50	—
Copyright block of 4		3.50	—
a. Block of 4, #C101-C104		3.25	1.75
b. As "a," imperf.			

1983, Apr. 8	Tagged	Perf. 11	
C105 AP78 40c multi		80	40
a. Perf. 11x10½		90	45
C106 AP79 40c multi		80	40
a. Perf. 11x10½		90	45
C107 AP80 40c multi		80	40
a. Perf. 11x10½		90	45
C108 AP81 40c multi		80	40
P# block of 4, 4 P#		5.25	
Zip block of 4		5.00	—
Copyright block of 4		5.00	—
c. Perf. 11x10½		90	45
c. P# block of 4, 4 P#		6.00	—
a. Block of 4, #C105-C108		4.75	2.00
b. As "a," imperf.			
d. As "a," perf. 11x10½		4.00	—

1983, Nov. 4	Tagged	Perf. 11	
C109 AP82 35c multi		70	35
C110 AP83 35c multi		70	35
C111 AP84 35c multi		70	35
C112 AP85 35c multi		70	35
P# block of 4, 4#		5.00	—
Zip block of 4		4.75	
Copyright block of 4		4.75	—
a. Block of 4, #C109-C112		4.50	1.85

AVIATION PIONEERS

Alfred V. Verville (1890-1970), Inventor, Verville-Sperry R-3 Army Racer — AP86

Lawrence (1892-1931), Aircraft Designer, and Elmer (1860-1930), Designer and Pilot, Sperry, First Seaplane — AP87

Designed by Ken Dallison (No. C113) and Howard Koslow (No. C114)

PHOTOGRAVURE

Plates of 200 in four panes of 50 (2 panes each, No. C113 and No. C114)

Plates of 200 in four panes of 50 (No. C114)

1985, Feb. 13	Tagged	Perf. 11	
C113 AP86 33c **multi**		66	20
	P# block of 4, 5 #, UL, LR	3.50	—
	Zip block of 4	3.00	—
	Copyright block of 4	3.00	—
a.	Imperf. pair		—
C114 AP87 39c **multi**		78	20
	P# block of 4, 5 #, UR, LL	4.00	—
	P# block of 4, 4 #	4.00	—
	Zip block of 4	3.50	—
	Copyright block of 4	3.50	—
a.	Imperf. pair		—

TRANSPACIFIC AIRMAIL
50th Anniversary

Martin M-130 China Clipper — AP88

Designed by Chuck Hodgson.

PHOTOGRAVURE

Plates of 200 in four panes of 50

1985, Feb. 15	Tagged	Perf. 11	
C115 AP88 44c **multi**		88	20

	P# block of 4, 5 #	4.50	—
	Zip block of 4	4.00	—
	Copyright block of 4	4.00	—
a.	Imperf. pair		—

FR. JUNIPERO SERRA (1713-1784)
California Missionary

Outline Map of Southern California, Portrait, San Gabriel Mission — AP89

Designed by Richard Schlecht from a Spanish stamp.

PHOTOGRAVURE

Plates of 200 in four panes of 50

1985, Aug. 22	Tagged	Perf. 11	
C116 AP89 44c **multi**		1.00	20
	P# block of 4	6.50	—
	Zip block of 4	4.50	—
	Copyright block of 4	4.50	—
a.	Imperf. pair		—

SETTLING OF NEW SWEDEN, 350th ANNIV.

Settler, Two Indians, Map of New Sweden, Swedish Ships "Kalmar Nyckel" and "Fogel Grip" — AP90

Designed by Goran Osterland based on an 18th century illustration from a Swedish book about the Colonies.

LITHOGRAPHED AND ENGRAVED

Plates of 200 in four panes of 50

1988, Mar. 29	Tagged	Perf. 11	
C117 AP90 44c **multi**		88	20
	P# block of 4, 5#	4.50	—

	Zip block of 4	4.00	—
	Copyright block of 4	4.00	—

SAMUEL P. LANGLEY (1834-1906)

Langley and Unmanned Aerodrome No. 5 — AP91

Designed by Ken Dallison.

LITHOGRAPHED AND ENGRAVED

Plates of 200 in four panes of 50

1988, May 14	Tagged	Perf. 11	
C118 AP91 45c **multi**		90	20
	P# block of 4, 7#	4.50	—
	Zip block of 4	4.00	—
	Copyright block of 4	4.00	—

IGOR SIKORSKY (1889-1972)

Sikorsky and 1939 VS300 Helicopter AP92

Designed by Ren Wicks.

PHOTOGRAVURE AND ENGRAVED

Plates of 200 in four panes of 50

1988, June 23	Tagged	Perf. 11	
C119 AP92 36c **multi**		72	20
	P# block of 4, 6#	3.60	—
	Zip block of 4	3.25	—
	Copyright block of 4	3.25	—

AIR POST SPECIAL DELIVERY STAMPS

Great Seal of United States — APSD1

No. CE1 was issued for the prepayment of the air postage and the special delivery fee in one stamp. First day sale was at the American Air Mail Society Convention.

FLAT PLATE PRINTING

Plates of 200 subjects in four panes of 50 each.

1934, Aug. 30	Unwmk.	Perf. 11	
CE1 APSD1 16c **dark blue**		75	85
	blue	75	85
	First day cover, Chicago (40,171)		25.00
	First day cover, Washington, D.C., Aug. 31		
	Margin block of 6, P#	20.00	—

For imperforate variety see No. 771.

Type of 1934

Frame plates of 100 subjects in two panes of 50 each separated by a 1½ inch wide vertical gutter with central guide line, and vignette plates of 50 subjects.

The "seal" design for No. CE2 was from a new engraving, slightly smaller than that used for No. CE1.

Top plate number blocks of No. CE2 are found both with and without top arrow.

Issued in panes of 50 each.

1936, Feb. 10			
CE2 APSD1 16c **red & blue**		40	25
	First day cover Washington, D.C. (72,981)		17.50
	Margin block of 4, two P#	8.50	—
	Margin block of 4, two P#, blue dotted registration marker	65.00	
	Same, arrow, red registration marker	50.00	
	Margin block of 4, bottom or side arrow	2.00	1.75
	Center line block	2.25	2.75
	Margin block of 10, two P#, two "TOP" and two registration markers	15.00	6.00
a.	Horiz. pair, imperf. vert.	3,750.	

Quantities issued: No. CE1, 9,215,750. No. CE2, 72,517,850.

United States Air Post Special Delivery stamps can be mounted in Scott's National Album.

AIR POST SEMI-OFFICIAL

Buffalo Balloon

This stamp was privately issued by John F. B. Lillard, a Nashville reporter. It was used on covers carried on a balloon ascension of June 18, 1877, which began at Nashville and landed at Gallatin, Tenn., and possibly on other flights. The balloon was owned and piloted by Samuel Archer King. The stamp was reported to have been engraved by (Mrs.?) J. H. Snively and printed in strips from a single die. Lillard wrote that 300 were printed and 23 used.

Buffalo Balloon — CS1

1877, June 18	Typo.	Imperf.
CL1 CS1	5c **deep blue**	6,000.
	On cover with 3c #158	—

	On cover with 1c, #156 & 2c #178	—
a.	Tête bêche pair, vertical	13,000.

A black proof exists of No. CL1.

R.F. OVERPRINTS

Authorized as a control mark by the United States Fleet Post Office during 1944-45 for the accommodation of and exclusive use by French naval personnel on airmail correspondence to the United States and Canada. All "R.F.' (Republique Francaise) mail had to be posted at the North African naval bases and had to bear the return address, rank and/or serial number of a French officer or seaman. It also had to be censored.

All "R.F." overprints were handstamped by the French naval authorities after the stamps were affixed for mailing. The stamps had to be cancelled by a special French naval cancellation. The status of unused copies seems questionable; they are alleged to have been handstamped at a later date. Several types of "R.F." overprints other than those illustrated are known, but their validity is doubtful.

United States No. C25 Handstamped in Black

R. F. a	R.F. b	RF h
R.F c	R.F d	
	R.F. g	
RF e	RF f	RF i
		R. F. j

1944-45		Unwmk.		Perf. 11x10½
CM1	AP17	*(a)*	6c carmine, on cover	200.00
CM2	AP17	*(b)*	6c carmine, on cover	275.00
CM3	AP17	*(c)*	6c carmine, on cover	350.00
CM4	AP17	*(d)*	6c carmine, on cover	250.00

CM5	AP17	*(e)*	6c carmine, on cover	500.00
CM6	AP17	*(f)*	6c carmine, on cover	275.00
CM7	AP17	*(g)*	6c carmine, on cover	475.00
CM8	AP17	*(h)*	6c carmine, on cover	500.00
CM9	AP17	*(i)*	6c carmine, on cover	500.00
CM10	AP17	*(j)*	6c carmine, on cover	—

Counterfeits of several types exist.

No. 907 is known with type "c" overprint; No. C19 with type "e" or "h"; No. C25a (single) with type "c", and No. C26 with type "b" or "f." Type "i" exists in several variations.

STAMPED ENVELOPES
No. UC5 Handstamped in Black

1944-45

UCM1	UC2	*(a)*	6c orange, *white,* entire	300.00
UCM2	UC2	*(b)*	6c orange, *white,* entire	400.00
UCM3	UC2	*(d)*	6c orange, *white,* entire	450.00
UCM4	UC2	*(f)*	6c orange, *white,* entire	450.00
UCM5	UC2	*(h)*	6c orange, *white,* entire	500.00

SPECIAL DELIVERY

Special Delivery service was instiuted by the Act of Congress of Congress of March 3, 1885, and put into operation on October 1, 1885. The Act limited the service to free delivery offices and such others as served places with a population of 400 or more, and its privileges werethus operative in but 555 post offices. The Act of August 4, 1886 made the stamps and service available at all post offices and upon any article of mailable matter. To consume the supply of stamps of the first issue, No. E2 was withheld until Sept. 6 1888.

A Special Delivery stamp, when affixed to any stamped letter or article of mailable matter, secures later delivery during daytime and evening at most post offices.

Messenger Running — SD1

ENGRAVED
Printed by the American Bank Note Co.
Plates of 100 subjects in two panes of 50 each.

1885		Unwmk.		Perf. 12	
E1	SD1	10c **blue,** *Oct. 1, 1885*		275.00	30.00
		deep blue		275.00	30.00
		On cover			50.00
		First day cover		8,000.	
		Margin block of 8, Impt. & P# 495 or 496		12,000.	
		Margin strip of 4, same		1,700.	
		Double transfer at top		350.00	50.00

United States Special Delivery stamps can be mounted in Scott's National and Minuteman Albums.

Messenger Running — SD2

1888
E2　SD2　10c **blue**, *Sept. 6, 1888*　　　275.00　7.50
　　　deep blue　　　　　　　　　275.00　7.50
　　　On cover　　　　　　　　　　　　　25.00
　　　Margin block of 8, Impt. & P#
　　　73 or 552　　　　　　　　12,000.
　　　Margin strip of 4, same　　　1,700.

Earliest known use: Dec. 18, 1888.

COLUMBIAN EXPOSITION ISSUE

From January 24, 1893, until January 5, 1894, the special delivery stamp was printed in orange; the issue in that color continued until May 19, 1894, when the stock on hand was exhausted. The stamp in blue was not issued from January 24, 1893 to May 19, 1894. However, on January 5, 1894, printing of the stamp in blue was resumed. Presumably it was reissued from May 19, 1894 until the appearance of E4 on October 10, 1894. The emissions of the blue stamp of this design before January 24, 1893 and after January 5, 1894 are indistinguishable.

1893
E3　SD2　10c **orange**, *Jan. 24, 1893*　　175.00　14.00
　　　deep orange　　　　　　　　175.00　14.00
　　　On cover　　　　　　　　　　　　　60.00
　　　Margin block of 8, Impt. & P#
　　　73 or 552　　　　　　　　7,250.
　　　Margin strip of 4, same　　　1,200.

Earliest known use: Feb. 11, 1893.

Messenger Running — SD3

Printed by the Bureau of Engraving and Printing.
1894
Line under "TEN CENTS"
E4　SD3　10c **blue**, *Oct. 10, 1894*　　750.00　17.50
　　　dark blue　　　　　　　　　750.00　17.50
　　　bright blue　　　　　　　　750.00　17.50
　　　On cover　　　　　　　　　　　　100.00
　　　Block of four　　　　　　　3,250.
　　　Margin block of 4, arrow　　3,350.
　　　Margin block of 6, T III Impt.
　　　& P# 77　　　　　　　　14,500.
　　　Margin strip of 3, same　　3,500.
　a.　Imperf., pair　　　　　　5,500.
　　　Double transfer　　　　　　　—

Earliest known use: Nov. 21, 1894.

1895　　　　　　　　　　　　Wmk. 191
E5　SD3　10c **blue**, *Aug. 16, 1895*　　135.00　2.50
　　　dark blue　　　　　　　　　135.00　2.50
　　　deep blue　　　　　　　　　135.00　2.50
　　　On cover　　　　　　　　　　　　17.50
　　　Margin block of 4, arrow　　600.00
　　　Margin block of 6, T III, VI or
　　　VII Impt. & P#　　　　　4,500.
　　　Margin strip of 3, same　　625.00
　a.　Imperf., pair　　　　　　4,500.
　b.　Printed on both sides　　1,250.
　　　Double transfer　　　　　　—　25.00
　　　Line of color through "POSTAL
　　　DELIVERY", from bottom row
　　　of Plates 1257-1260　　200.00　15.00
　　　Dots in curved frame above
　　　messenger (Pl. 882)　　175.00　10.00

No. E5a was not regularly issued.
Earliest known use: Oct. 3, 1895.

Messenger on Bicycle — SD4

1902
E6　SD4　10c **ultramarine**, *Dec. 9, 1902*　90.00　2.50
　　　dark ultramarine　　　　　90.00　2.50
　　　pale ultramarine　　　　　90.00　2.50
　　　blue　　　　　　　　　　　90.00　2.50
　　　On cover　　　　　　　　　　　　10.00
　　　P# block of 6, "09"　　　2,750.
　　　Margin block of 4, arrow　450.00
　　　Margin block of 6, T VII Impt.
　　　& P#　　　　　　　　3,000.
　　　Margin strip of 3, same　400.00
　　　Double transfer　　　　　　—
　　　Damaged transfer under "N" of
　　　"CENTS"　　　　　　　150.00　5.00

Earliest known use: Jan. 22, 1903.
No. E6 was re-issued in 1909 from new plates 5240, 5243-5245. After a few months use the Bureau added "09" to these plate numbers. The stamp can be identified only by plate number.

Helmet of Mercury SD5

1908
Plates of 280 subjects in four panes of 70 each.
E7　SD5　10c **green**, *Dec. 12, 1908*　　60.00　27.50
　　　dark green　　　　　　　　60.00　27.50
　　　yellowish green　　　　　60.00　27.50
　　　On cover　　　　　　　　　　　　85.00
　　　Margin block of 6, T V Impt. &
　　　P#　　　　　　　　　925.00　—
　　　Margin strip of 3, same　250.00
　　　Double transfer　　　　　85.00　35.00

Earliest known use: Dec. 14, 1908.

1911　　　Wmk. 190　　　Perf. 12
Plates of 200 subjects in four panes of 50 each.
E8　SD4　10c **ultramarine**, *Jan., 1911*　90.00　4.00
　　　pale ultramarine　　　　　90.00　4.00
　　　dark ultramarine　　　　　90.00　4.00
　b.　10c violet blue　　　　　90.00　4.00
　　　On cover　　　　　　　　　　　17.50
　　　Margin block of 6, T VII Impt.
　　　& P#　　　　　　　　2,750.
　　　Margin block of 6, P# only　2,500.
　　　Top frame line missing (Pl.
　　　5514)　　　　　　　120.00　5.00

Earliest known use: Jan. 14, 1911.

1914　　　　　　　　　　　Perf. 10
E9　SD4　10c **ultramarine**, *Sept., 1914*　175.00　5.25
　　　pale ultramarine　　　　　175.00　5.25
　　　blue　　　　　　　　　　175.00　5.25
　　　On cover　　　　　　　　　　　30.00
　　　Margin block of 6, T VII Impt.
　　　& P#　　　　　　　　5,000.　—
　　　Margin block of 6, P# only　4,250.　—
　　　Margin block of 8, T VII Impt.
　　　& P# (side)　　　　　　—

Earliest known use: Oct. 26, 1914.

1916　　　Unwmk.　　　Perf. 10
E10　SD4　10c **pale ultramarine**, *Oct. 19, 1916*　325.00　21.00
　　　ultramarine　　　　　　　325.00　21.00
　　　blue　　　　　　　　　　325.00　21.00
　　　On cover　　　　　　　　　　　65.00
　　　Margin block of 6, T VII Impt.
　　　& P# 5520　　　　　　6,250.　—
　　　Margin block of 6, P# only　5,750.　—

Earliest known use: Nov. 4, 1916.

1917　　　Unwmk.　　　Perf. 11
E11　SD4　10c **ultramarine**, *May 2, 1917*　15.00　30
　　　pale ultramarine　　　　　15.00　30
　　　dark ultramarine　　　　　15.00　30
　a.　10c gray violet　　　　　15.00　30
　c.　10c blue　　　　　　　　30.00　50
　　　On cover　　　　　　　　　　　3.00
　　　Margin block of 6, T VII Impt. &
　　　P#　　　　　　　　850.00　—
　　　Margin block of 6, P# only　200.00　—
　　　Margin block of 8, T VII Impt. &
　　　P# (side)　　　　　　—
　d.　Perf. 10 at left　　　　　—

Earliest known use: June 12, 1917.
The aniline ink used on some printings of No. E11 permeated the paper causing a pink tinge to appear on the back. Such stamps are called "pink backs."

Motorcycle Delivery — SD6

FLAT PLATE PRINTING
1922　　　Unwmk.　　　Perf. 11
E12　SD6　10c **gray violet**, *July 12, 1922*　22.50　15
　a.　10c deep ultramarine　　30.00　20
　　　On cover　　　　　　　　　　　1.00
　　　First day cover　　　　　　500.00
　　　Margin block of 6, P# only　375.00
　　　Double transfer　　　　　45.00　1.00

Post Office Truck — SD7

1925　　　Unwmk.　　　Perf. 11
Issued to facilitate special delivery service for parcel post.
E13　SD6　15c **deep orange**, *April 11, 1925*　24.00　65
　　　On cover　　　　　　　　　　　10.00
　　　First day cover　　　　　　250.00
　　　Margin block of 6, P# only　250.00
　　　Double transfer　　　　　35.00　1.50
E14　SD7　20c **black**, *April 25, 1925*　　3.00　1.75
　　　On cover　　　　　　　　　　　2.25
　　　First day cover　　　　　　125.00
　　　Margin block of 6, P# only　37.50

Motorcycle Type of 1922
ROTARY PRESS PRINTING
1927　　　Unwmk.　　　Perf. 11x10½
E15　SD6　10c **gray violet**, *Nov. 29, 1927*　70　5
　a.　10c red lilc　　　　　　70　5
　b.　10c gray lilac　　　　　70　5
　　　violet　　　　　　　　　70　5
　　　On cover　　　　　　　　　　　25
　　　First day cover　　　　　　90.00
　　　Margin block of 4, P# only　6.50
　c.　Horizontal pair, imperf. between　275.00
　　　Gouged plate　　　　　　—
　　　Cracked plate 19280 LR　50.00

The design of No. E15 (rotary printing) measures 36½x21¾ mm. Design of stamps from the flat plates measures 36x21½ mm.

Motorcycle Type of 1922
ROTARY PRESS PRINTING
1931　　　Unwmk.　　　Perf. 11x10½
E16　SD6　15c **orange**, *Aug. 13, 1931*　　80　8
　　　On cover　　　　　　　　　　　25
　　　First day cover, Washington,
　　　D.C.　　　　　　　　125.00
　　　First day cover, Easton, Pa., *Aug.
　　　6, 1931*　　　　　　1,000.
　　　Margin block of 4, P# only　5.50

Design of No. E16 measures 36¾x22¼mm.
Design of No. E13 measures 36½x22½mm.

Motorcycle Type of 1922
ROTARY PRESS PRINTING
E. E. Plates of 200 subjects in four panes of 50 each.
1944, Oct. 30　　Unwmk.　　Perf. 11x10½
E17　SD6　13c **blue**　　　　　　65　6
　　　First day cover　　　　　　12.00
　　　Margin block of 4, P#　　4.00　—
E18　SD6　17c **orange yellow**　　5.00　2.25
　　　First day cover　　　　　　12.00
　　　First day cover, Nos. E17 & E18　30.00
　　　Margin block of 4, P#　　28.50

Truck Type of 1925
ROTARY PRESS PRINTING.
E. E. Plates of 200 subjects in four panes of 50 each.

1951	Unwmk.	Perf. 11x10½		
E19 SD7 20c	black, *Nov. 30, 1951*		2.00	12
	First day cover		5.00	
	Margin block of 4, P#		10.00	—

Design of No. E19 measures 36¼x22mm.
Design of No. E14 measures 35½x21½mm.

Special Delivery Letter, Hand to Hand — SD8

ROTARY PRESS PRINTING
E. E. Plates of 200 subjects in four panes of 50 each.

1954	Unwmk.	Perf. 11x10½		
E20 SD8 20c	deep blue, *Oct. 13, 1954*		60	8
	light blue		—	—
	First day cover, Boston *(194,043)*			3.00
	Margin block of 4, P#		4.00	—

1957				
E21 SD8 30c	lake, *Sept. 3, 1957*		90	5
	First Day cover, Indianapolis *(111,451)*			2.25
	Margin block of 4, P#		5.00	—

Arrows — SD9

Designed by Norman Yves.

GIORI PRESS PRINTING
Plates of 200 subjects in four panes of 50 each.

1969	Unwmk.	Perf. 11		
E22 SD9 45c	carmine & violet blue, *Nov. 21*		2.25	20
	First day cover, New York, N.Y.		3.50	
	Margin block of 4, P#		11.50	-
	Margin block of 4, Mr. Zip and "Use Zip Code"		9.50	—
	Margin block of 6, "Mail Early in the Day"		14.00	—

1971		Perf. 11		
E23 SD9 60c	vio. blue & carmine, *May 10*		1.20	12
	First day cover, Phoenix, Ariz. *(129,562)*		3.50	—
	Margin block of 4, P#		6.00	—
	Margin block of 4, Mr. Zip and "Use Zip Code"		5.00	—
	Margin block of 6, "Mail Early in the Day"		7.50	—

(Vertical side-text labels: BUREAU ENGRAVING & PRINTING)

	77	257	381
Type	III	VI	VII

CERTIFIED MAIL

Certified Mail service was started on June 6, 1955, for use on first-class mail for which no indemnity value is claimed but for which proof of mailing and proof of delivery are available at less cost than registered mail. The mailer receives one receipt and the addressee signs another when the postman delivers the letter. The second receipt is kept on file at the Post Office for six months. The 15c Certified Mail charge is in addition to regular postage, whether surface mail, air mail or special delivery.

Letter Carrier — CM1

ROTARY PRESS PRINTING
E. E. Plates of 200 subjects in four panes of 50 each.

1955	Unwmk.	Perf. 10½x11		
FA1 CM1 15c	red, *June 6, 1955*		50	30
	First day cover		3.25	
	Margin block of 4, P#		6.25	—

> United States Certified Mail stamp can be mounted in Scott's National and Minuteman Albums.

POSTAGE DUE

For affixing, by a postal clerk, to any piece of mailable matter, to denote the amount to be collected from the addressee because of insufficient prepayment of postage.

Prior to July, 1879, whenever a letter was unpaid, or insufficiently prepaid, the amount of postage due was written by hand or handstamped on the envelope, and the deficiency collected by the carrier. No vouchers were given for money thus collected.

Postage Due Stamps were authorized by the Act of Congress, approved March 3, 1879, effective July 1, 1879.

Printed by the American Bank Note Co.
Plates of 200 subjects in two panes of 100 each.

Figure of Value in Oval — D1

1879		Unwmk.	Engr.		Perf. 12	
J1	D1	1c **brown**			30.00	5.00
		pale brown			30.00	5.00
		deep brown			30.00	5.00
		Block of four			125.00	25.00
J2	D1	2c **brown**			200.00	4.00
		pale brown			200.00	4.00
		Block of four			825.00	—
J3	D1	3c **brown**			25.00	2.50
		pale brown			25.00	2.50
		deep brown			25.00	2.50
		yellowish brown			27.50	3.50
		Block of four			105.00	11.00
J4	D1	5c **brown**			300.00	25.00
		pale brown			300.00	25.00
		deep brown			300.00	25.00
		Block of four			1,250.	—
J5	D1	10c **brown**, *Sept. 19*			350.00	12.50
		pale brown			350.00	12.50
		deep brown			350.00	12.50
		Block of four			1,500.	
a.		Imperf., pair			1,600.	
J6	D1	30c **brown**, *Sept. 19*			175.00	25.00
		pale brown			175.00	25.00
		Block of four			725.00	—
J7	D1	50c **brown**, *Sept. 19*			225.00	30.00
		pale brown			225.00	30.00
		Block of four			925.00	—

Special Printing

1879		Unwmk.		Perf. 12

Soft porous paper
Printed by the American Bank Note Co.

J8	D1	1c **deep brown** *(4,420)*	5,750.
J9	D1	2c **deep brown** *(1,361)*	3,750.
J10	D1	3c **deep brown** *(436)*	3,500.
J11	D1	5c **deep brown** *(249)*	3,000.
J12	D1	10c **deep brown** *(174)*	1,850.
J13	D1	30c **deep brown** *(179)*	1,850.
J14	D1	50c **deep brown** *(179)*	2,000.

1884		Unwmk.		Perf. 12	
J15	D1	1c **red brown**		30.00	2.50
		pale red brown		30.00	2.50
		deep red brown		30.00	2.50
		Block of four		125.00	12.00
J16	D1	2c **red brown**		37.50	2.50
		pale red brown		37.50	2.50
		deep red brown		37.50	2.50
		Block of four		160.00	12.00
J17	D1	3c **red brown**		500.00	100.00
		deep red brown		500.00	100.00
		Block of four		2,100.	—
J18	D1	5c **red brown**		250.00	12.50
		pale red brown		250.00	12.50
		deep red brown		250.00	12.50
		Block of four		1100.	—
J19	D1	10c **red brown**		225.00	7.00
		deep red brown		225.00	7.00
		Block of four		925.00	—
J20	D1	30c **red brown**		110.00	22.50
		deep red brown		110.00	22.50
		Block of four		450.00	110.00
J21	D1	50c **red brown**		1000.	125.00
		Block of four		4,250.	

1891		Unwmk.		Perf. 12.	
J22	D1	1c **bright claret**		12.50	50
		light claret		12.50	50
		dark claret		12.50	50
		Block of four		52.50	2.25
a.		Imperforate, pair		450.00	
J23	D1	2c **bright claret**		15.00	45
		light claret		15.00	45
		dark claret		15.00	45
		Block of four		62.50	2.25
a.		Imperforate, pair		450.00	
J24	D1	3c **bright claret**		32.50	4.00
		dark claret		32.50	4.00
		Block of four		135.00	17.50
a.		Imperforate, pair		450.00	
J25	D1	5c **bright claret**		35.00	4.00
		light claret		35.00	4.00
		dark claret		35.00	4.00
		Block of four		145.00	17.50
a.		Imperforate, pair		450.00	
J26	D1	10c **bright claret**		70.00	10.00
		light claret		70.00	10.00
		Block of four		300.00	45.00
a.		Imperforate, pair		450.00	
J27	D1	30c **bright claret**		250.00	85.00
		Block of four		1050.	
a.		Imperforate, pair		525.00	
J28	D1	50c **bright claret**		275.00	85.00
		dark claret		275.00	85.00
		Block of four		1,200.	
a.		Imperforate, pair		525.00	

The imperforate varieties, Nos. J22a-J28a, were not regularly issued.

Printed by the Bureau of Engraving and Printing.

D2

1894		Unwmk.		Perf. 12	
J29	D2	1c **vermilion**		575.00	100.00
		pale vermilion		575.00	100.00
		Block of four		2,400.	425.00
		Margin block of 6, Impt. & P#		5,250.	
J30	D2	2c **vermilion**		250.00	50.00
		deep vermilion		250.00	50.00
		Block of four		1,050.	
		Margin block of 6, Impt. & P#		2,400.	

1894					
J31	D2	1c **deep claret**, *Aug. 14, 1894*		20.00	3.00
		claret		20.00	3.00
		lake		20.00	3.00
		Block of four		82.50	13.00
		Margin block of 6, Impt. & P#		375.00	
a.		Imperf., pair		225.00	
a.		Block of four		500.00	
b.		Vertical pair, imperf. horiz.		—	

J32	D2	2c **deep claret**, *July 20, 1894*		17.50	1.75
		claret		17.50	1.75
		lake		17.50	1.75
		Block of four		72.50	8.00
		Margin block of 6, Impt. & P#		325.00	
J33	D2	3c **deep claret**, *Apr. 27, 1895*		75.00	20.00
		lake		75.00	20.00
		Block of four		325.00	
		Margin block of 6, Impt. & P#		850.00	
J34	D2	5c **deep claret**, *Apr. 27, 1895*		100.00	22.50
		claret		100.00	22.50
		Block of four		450.00	
		Margin block of 6, Impt. & P#		950.00	
J35	D2	10c **deep claret**, *Sept. 24, 1894*		100.00	17.50
		Block of four		450.00	
		Margin block of 6, Impt. & P#		950.00	
J36	D2	30c **deep claret**, *Apr. 27, 1895*		225.00	50.00
		claret		225.00	50.00
		Block of four		950.00	
a.		30c carmine		225.00	50.00
a.		Block of four (carmine)		950.00	
b.		30c pale rose		210.00	45.00
b.		Block of four (pale rose)		850.00	
		Margin block of 6, Impt. & P#		2,100.	
J37	D2	50c **deep claret**, *Apr. 27, 1895*		500.00	150.00
		Block of four		2,250.	
a.		50c pale rose		450.00	135.00
a.		Block of four (pale rose)		1,750.	
		Margin block of 6, Impt. & P#		5,000.	

Shades are numerous in the 1894 and later issues.

Wmk. 191 Horizontally or Vertically

1895-97				Perf. 12	
J38	D2	1c **deep claret**, *Aug. 29, 1895*		5.00	30
		claret		5.00	30
		carmine		5.00	30
		lake		5.00	30
		Block of four		21.00	1.40
		Margin block of 6, Impt. & P#		190.00	
J39	D2	2c **deep claret**, *Sept. 14, 1895*		5.00	20
		claret		5.00	20
		carmine		5.00	20
		lake		5.00	20
		Block of four		21.00	1.00
		Margin block of 6, Impt. & P#		190.00	
		Double transfer		—	

In October, 1895, the Postmaster at Jefferson, Iowa, surcharged a few 2 cent stamps with the words "Due 1 cent" in black on each side, subsequently dividing the stamps vertically and using each half as a 1 cent stamp. Twenty of these were used.

J40	D2	3c **deep claret**, *Oct. 30, 1895*		35.00	1.00
		claret		35.00	1.00
		rose red		35.00	1.00
		carmine		35.00	1.00
		Block of four		150.00	4.50
		Margin block of 6, Impt. & P#		425.00	
J41	D2	5c **deep claret**, *Oct. 15, 1895*		37.50	1.00
		claret		37.50	1.00
		carmine rose		37.50	1.00
		Block of four		160.00	4.50
		Margin block of 6, Impt. & P#		450.00	
J42	D2	10c **deep claret**, *Sept. 14, 1895*		40.00	2.00
		claret		40.00	2.00
		carmine		40.00	2.00
		lake		40.00	2.00
		Block of four		170.00	8.50
		Margin block of 6, Impt. & P#		550.00	
J43	D2	30c **deep claret**, *Aug. 21, 1897*		300.00	25.00
		claret		300.00	25.00
		Block of four		1,250.	
		Margin block of 6, Impt. & P#		3,750.	
J44	D2	50c **deep claret**, *Mar. 17, 1896*		190.00	20.00
		claret		190.00	20.00
		Block of four		775.00	90.00
		Margin block of 6, Impt. & P#		2,250.	

1910-12		**Wmk. 190**		Perf. 12	
J45	D2	1c **deep claret**, *Aug. 30, 1910*		20.00	2.00
a.		1c rose carmine		17.50	1.75
		Block of four (2 or 3mm spacing)		82.50	9.00
		Margin block of 6, Impt. & P# & star		400.00	
J46	D2	2c **deep claret**, *Nov. 25, 1910*		20.00	15
		lake		20.00	15
a.		2c rose carmine		17.50	15
		Block of four (2 or 3mm spacing)		82.50	75
		Margin block of 6, Impt. & P# & star		350.00	—
		Margin block of 6, P# only		375.00	—
		Double transfer		—	
J47	D2	3c **deep claret**, *Aug. 31, 1910*		350.00	17.50
		lake		350.00	17.50
		Block of four (2 or 3mm spacing)		1,450.	70.00
		Margin block of 6, Impt. & P# & star		3,850.	
J48	D2	5c **deep claret**, *Aug. 31, 1910*		60.00	3.50
a.		5c rose carmine			
		Block of four (2 or 3mm spacing)		250.00	15.00
		Margin block of 6, Impt. & P# & star		600.00	
J49	D2	10c **deep claret**, *Aug. 31, 1910*		75.00	7.50
a.		10c rose carmine			
		Block of four (2 or 3mm spacing)		310.00	32.50
		Margin block of 6, Impt. & P# & star		1,150.	
J50	D2	50c **deep claret**, *Sept. 23, 1912*		600.00	75.00

United States Postage Due stamps can be mounted in Scott's National, American and Minuteman Albums.

Block of four (2 or 3mm spacing) 2,500.
Margin block of 6, Impt. & P# & star 7,500.

1914   ***Perf. 10***
J52 D2 1c **carmine lake** 40.00 7.50
    deep carmine lake 40.00 7.50
a. 1c dull rose 40.00 7.50
    Block of four (2 or 3mm spacing) 165.00 32.00
    Margin block of 6, Impt. & P# & star 550.00 75.00
J53 D2 2c **carmine lake** 32.50 20
a. 2c dull rose 32.50 20
b. 2c vermilion 32.50 20
    Block of four 135.00 1.00
    Margin block of 6, P# only 350.00 7.50
J54 D2 3c **carmine lake** 425.00 20.00
a. 3c dull rose 425.00 20.00
    Block of four (2 or 3mm spacing) 1,800. —
    Margin block of 6, Impt. & P# & star 4,500. —
J55 D2 5c **carmine lake** 25.00 1.50
a. 5c dull rose 25.00 1.50
    carmine rose 25.00 1.50
    deep claret
    Block of four (2 or 3mm spacing) 105.00 7.00
    Margin block of 6, Impt. & P# & star 285.00 30.00
J56 D2 10c **carmine lake** 40.00 1.00
a. 10c dull rose 40.00 1.00
    carmine rose 40.00 1.00
    Block of four (2 or 3mm spacing) 165.00 4.75
    Margin block of 6, Impt. & P# & star 600.00 30.00
J57 D2 30c **carmine lake** 140.00 12.00
    Block of four (2 or 3mm spacing) 575.00 50.00
    Margin block of 6, Impt. & P# & star 2,100. 125.00
J58 D2 50c **carmine lake** 5,500. 375.00
    Block of four (2 or 3mm spacing) 23,000. 1,600.
    Margin block of 6, Impt. & P# & star 40,000.

1916   Unwmk.   ***Perf. 10***
J59 D2 1c **rose** 1,100. 175.00
    Block of four (2 or 3mm spacing) 4,500. 750.00
    Margin block of 6, Impt. & P# & star 8,750.
J60 D2 2c **rose** 85.00 10.00
    Block of four 350.00
    Margin block of 6, P# only 800.00 75.00

1917   Unwmk.   ***Perf. 11***
J61 D2 1c **carmine rose** 1.75 8
    dull rose 1.75 8
a. 1c rose red 1.75 8
b. 1c deep claret 1.75 8
    claret brown 1.75 8
    Block of four (2 or 3mm spacing) 7.25 35
    Margin block of 6, Impt. & P# & star 85.00 75
    Margin block of 6, P# only 40.00 65
J62 D2 2c **carmine rose** 1.50 5
a. 2c rose red 1.50 5
b. 2c deep claret 1.50 5
    claret brown 1.50 5
    Block of four 6.25 20
    Margin block of 6, P# only 35.00 60
    Double transfer
J63 D2 3c **carmine rose** 8.50 8
a. 3c rose red 8.50 7
b. 3c deep claret 8.50 25
    claret brown 8.50 25
    Block of four (2 or 3mm spacing) 35.00 30
    Margin block of 6, Impt. & P# & star 100.00 2.25
    Margin block of 6, P# only 85.00 1.50
J64 D2 5c **carmine** 8.50 8
    carmine rose 8.50 8
a. 5c rose red 8.50 8
b. 5c deep claret 8.50 5
    claret brown 8.50 10
    Block of four (2 or 3mm spacing) 35.00 32
    Margin block of 6, Impt. & P# & star 100.00 2.85
    Margin block of 6, P# only 85.00 1.50
J65 D2 10c **carmine rose** 12.50 20
a. 10c rose red 12.50 6
b. 10c deep claret 12.50 6
    claret brown 12.50 6
    Block of four (2 or 3mm spacing) 52.50 85
    Margin block of 6, Impt. & P# & star 125.00 4.50
    Margin block of 6, P# only 135.00 2.00
    Double transfer
J66 D2 30c **carmine rose** 55.00 40
a. 30c deep claret 55.00 40
    claret brown 55.00 40
    Block of four (2 or 3mm spacing) 225.00 1.75
    Margin block of 6, Impt. & P# & star 525.00 —
    Margin block of 6, P# only 550.00
J67 D2 50c **carmine rose** 75.00 12
a. 50c rose red 75.00 12
b. 50c deep claret 75.00 15
    claret brown 75.00 15
    Block of four (2 or 3mm spacing) 325.00 50
    Margin block of 6, Impt. & P# & star 750.00 7.50
    Margin block of 6, P# only 800.00 8.50

1925
J68 D2 ½c **dull red**, *Apr. 13, 1925* 50 6
    Block of four 2.00 24
    Margin block of 6, P# only 11.00 50

D3

D4

1930-31   Unwmk.   ***Perf. 11***
Design measures 19x22 mm.
J69 D3 ½c **carmine** 3.50 70
    Margin block of 6, P# 35.00 7.50
J70 D3 1c **carmine** 2.50 15
    Margin block of 6, P# 27.50 2.00
J71 D3 2c **carmine** 3.50 15
    Margin block of 6, P# 40.00 2.00
J72 D3 3c **carmine** 30.00 1.00
    Margin block of 6, P# 250.00 10.00
J73 D3 5c **carmine** 25.00 1.50
    Margin block of 6, P# 225.00 15.00
J74 D3 10c **carmine** 50.00 50
    Margin block of 6, P# 425.00 7.50
J75 D3 30c **carmine** 135.00 1.00
    Margin block of 6, P# 1,000. 15.00
J76 D3 50c **carmine** 175.00 30
    Margin block of 6, P# 1,250. 10.00

Design measures 22x19 mm.
J77 D4 $1 **carmine** 35.00 6
a. $1 scarlet 27.50 6
    Margin block of 6, P# 275.00
J78 D4 $5 **carmine** 45.00 12
a. $5 scarlet 40.00 12
b. as "a," wet printing 42.50 12
    Margin block of 6, P# 375.00

See note on Wet and Dry Printings following No. 1029.

Type of 1930-31 Issue
Rotary Press Printing
Ordinary and Electric Eye Plates
Design measures 19x22½ mm.

1931-32   Unwmk.   ***Perf. 11x10½***
J79 D3 ½c **dull carmine** 1.25 8
a. ½c scarlet 1.25 8
    Margin block of 4, P# 22.50 1.00
J80 D3 1c **dull carmine** 15 5
a. 1c scarlet 15 5
b. as "a," wet printing 18 5
    Margin block of 4, P# 2.00 25
    Pair with full vertical gutter between
J81 D3 2c **dull carmine** 15 5
a. 2c scarlet 15 5
b. as "a," wet printing 18 5
    Margin block of 4, P# 2.00 25
J82 D3 3c **dull carmine** 25 5
a. 3c scarlet 25 5
b. as "a," wet printing 28 5
    Margin block of 4, P# 3.00 30
J83 D3 5c **dull carmine** 35 5
a. 5c scarlet 35 5
b. as "a," wet printing 45 5
    Margin block of 4, P# 4.00 35
J84 D3 10c **dull carmine** 1.10 5
a. 10c scarlet 1.10 5
b. as "a," wet printing 1.25 5
    Margin block of 4, P# 8.50 45
J85 D3 30c **dull carmine** 8.50 8
a. 30c scarlet 8.50 8
    Margin block of 4, P# 45.00 90
J86 D3 50c **dull carmine** 9.50 6
a. 50c scarlet 9.50 6
    Margin block of 4, P# 57.50 90

Design measures 22½x19mm.

1956   ***Perf. 10½x11***
J87 D4 $1 **scarlet** 40.00 20
    Margin block of 4, P# 300.00 2.50

D5

Rotary Press Printing
Denominations added in black by rubber plates in an operation similar to precanceling.

1959, June 19   Unwmk.   ***Perf. 11x10½***
J88 D5 ½c **carmine rose** 1.25 85
    Margin block of 4, P# 150.00
J89 D5 1c **carmine rose** 5 5
    Margin block of 4, P# 50
a. "1 CENT" omitted 400.00
b. Pair, one without "1 CENT"
J90 D5 2c **carmine rose** 6 5
    Margin block of 4, P# 60
J91 D5 3c **carmine rose** 7 5
    Margin block of 4, P# 70
a. Pair, one without "3 CENTS"
J92 D5 4c **carmine rose** 8 5
    Margin block of 4, P# 1.25
J93 D5 5c **carmine rose** 10 5
    Margin block of 4, P# 75
a. Pair, one without "5 CENTS"
J94 D5 6c **carmine rose** 12 5
    Margin block of 4, P# 1.40
a. Pair, one without "6 CENTS"
    Pair with full vert. gutter between
J95 D5 7c **carmine rose** 14 6
    Margin block of 4, P# 1.60
J96 D5 8c **carmine rose** 16 5
    Margin block of 4, P# 1.75
a. Pair, one without "8 CENTS"
J97 D5 10c **carmine rose** 20 5
    Margin block of 4, P# 1.25
J98 D5 30c **carmine rose** 70 5
    Margin block of 4, P# 5.50
J99 D5 50c **carmine rose** 1.10 5
    Margin block of 4, P# 6.50

Straight Numeral Outlined in Black
J100 D5 $1 **carmine rose** 2.00 5
    Margin block of 4, P# 10.00
J101 D5 $5 **carmine rose** 8.00 15
    Margin block of 4, P# 40.00

The 2c, 4c, 7c and 8c exist in vertical pairs with numerals widely spaced. This spacing was intended to accommodate the gutter, but sometimes fell within the pane.

Rotary Press Printing
1978-85   ***Perf. 11x10½***
Denomination in Black
J102 D5 11c **carmine rose**, *Jan. 2, 1978* 22 5
    Margin block of 4, P# 3.50
J103 D5 13c **carmine rose**, *Jan. 2, 1978* 26 5
    Margin block of 4, P# 3.00
J104 D5 17c **carmine rose**, *June 10, 1985* 50 5
    Margin block of 4, P# 12.50

OFFICES IN CHINA

Postage stamps of the 1917-19 U.S. series (then current) were issued to the U. S. Postal Agency, Shanghai, China, surcharged (as illustrated) at double the original value of the stamps. The surcharges on the 1919 issue are in black, except on the 7-cent and $1 which are surcharged in red ink.

These stamps were intended for sale at Shanghai at their surcharged value in local currency, valid for prepayment on mail despatched from the United States Postal Agency at Shanghai to addresses in the United States.

Stamps were first issued May 24, 1919, and were placed on sale at Shanghai on July 1, 1919. These stamps were not issued to postmasters in the United States. The Shanghai post office, according to the U. S. P. O. Bulletin was closed in December, 1922. After the closing of the Shanghai office, the stamps were on sale at the Philatelic Agency in Washington, D. C. for a short time.

The postmarks of the China office were "U.S. Postal Agency Shanghai China" and "U.S.Pos. Service Shanghai China".

U. S. POSTAL AGENCY IN CHINA.

SHANGHAI 2¢ CHINA

United States Stamps Nos. 498 to 518 Surcharged

1919   Unwmk.   *Perf. 11*

K1	A140	2c on 1c **green**	20.00	22.50
		Block of four	82.50	100.00
		Margin block of six, P#	275.00	—
K2	A140	4c on 2c **rose**, type I	20.00	22.50
		Block of four	82.50	100.00
		Margin block of six, P#	275.00	—
K3	A140	6c on 3c **violet**, type II	37.50	50.00
		Block of four	155.00	235.00
		Margin block of six, P#	450.00	—
K4	A140	8c on 4c **brown**	45.00	50.00
		Block of four	185.00	235.00
		Margin block of six, P#	550.00	—
K5	A140	10c on 5c **blue**	50.00	57.50
		Block of four	210.00	250.00
		Margin block of six, P#	525.00	—
K6	A140	12c on 6c **red orange**	60.00	72.50
		Block of four	250.00	325.00
		Margin block of six, P#	700.00	
K7	A140	14c on 7c **black**	65.00	80.00
		Block of four	270.00	375.00
		Margin block of six, P#	800.00	
K8	A148	16c on 8c **olive bister**	50.00	55.00
a.		16c on 8c olive green	45.00	47.50
		Block of four	210.00	275.00
		Margin block of six, P#	600.00	
K9	A148	18c on 9c **salmon red**	50.00	60.00
		Block of four	210.00	300.00
		Margin block of six, P#	650.00	
K10	A148	20c on 10c **orange yellow**	45.00	52.50
		Block of four	190.00	250.00
		Margin block of six, P#	600.00	
K11	A148	24c on 12c **brown carmine**	52.50	62.50
a.		24c on 12c claret brown	67.50	77.50
		Block of four (brown carmine)	220.00	300.00
		Margin block of six, P#	800.00	
K12	A148	30c on 15c **gray**	65.00	80.00
		Block of four	270.00	375.00
		Margin block of six, P#	1,000.	
K13	A148	40c on 20c **deep ultramarine**	100.00	125.00
		Block of four	425.00	600.00
		Margin block of six, P#	1,300.	
K14	A148	60c on 30c **orange red**	90.00	110.00
		Block of four	375.00	525.00
		Margin block of six, P#	1,000.	

K15	A148	$1 on 50c **light violet**	600.00	500.00
		Block of four	2,500.	2,250.
		Margin block of six, P#	10,000.	
K16	A148	$2 on $1 **violet brown**	425.00	425.00
		Block of four	1,750.	2,000.
		Margin block of four, arrow, right or left	1,850.	
		Margin block of six, P#	7,500.	
a.		Double surcharge	2,500.	2,250.

SHANGHAI 2 Cts. CHINA

United States Stamps Nos. 498 and 528B Locally Surcharged

1922, July 3

K17	A140	2c on 1c **green**	90.00	75.00
		Block of four	365.00	350.00
		Margin block of six, P#	725.00	
K18	A140	4c on 2c **carmine**, type VII	80.00	70.00
		Block of four	325.00	350.00
		Margin block of six, P#	675.00	
		"SHANGHAI" omitted		
		"CHINA" only		—

> *United States Offices in China stamps can be mounted in Scott's National and Minuteman Albums.*

OFFICIAL

Official stamps were authorized by Act of Congress, approved March 3, 1873, abolishing the franking privilege. Stamps of special design for each government department to prepay postage on official matter were issued July 1, 1873. These stamps were supplanted on May 1, 1879, by penalty envelopes and on July 5, 1884, were declared obsolete.

DESIGNS. All Official stamps have name of department at top. Large numerals form the central design of the Post Office Department stamps. Those for the other departments picture the same busts used in the regular postage issue: 1c Franklin, 2c Jackson, 3c Washington, 6c Lincoln, 7c Stanton, 10c Jefferson, 12c Clay, 15c Webster, 24c Scott, 30c Hamilton, 90c Perry, $2, $10 and $20 Seward.

Designs of the various denominations are not identical, but resemble those illustrated.

PLATES. Plates of 200 subjects in two panes of 100 were used for Post Office Department 1c, 3c, 6c: Treasury Department 1c, 2c, 3c, and War Department 2c, 3c. Plates of 10 subjects were used for State Department $2, $5, $10 and $20. Plates of 100 subjects were used for all other Official stamps.

CANCELLATIONS. Odd or Town cancellations on Departmental stamps are relatively much scarcer than those appearing on the general issues of the same period. Town cancellations, especially on the 1873 issue, are scarce. The "Kicking Mule" cancellation is found used on stamps of the War Department and has also been seen on some stamps of the other Departments. Black is usual.

CONDITION. Examples that are fresh, well centered and (if unused) have original gum, sell at much higher prices.

Practically all official stamps exist imperforate but little is known of their history.

SPECIAL PRINTING. In 1875 a Special printing of the Official stamps was made along with those of the regular issues. These stamps were overprinted "SPECIMEN". They are listed in the "Specimen" Stamps section.

Printed by the Continental Bank Note Co.
Thin Hard Paper
AGRICULTURE

Franklin — O1

1873		Engr.	Unwmk.		Perf. 12
O1	O1	1c **yellow**		65.00	30.00
		golden yellow		67.50	32.50
		olive yellow		70.00	35.00
		On cover			—
		Block of four		300.00	
		Ribbed paper		75.00	35.00

CANCELLATIONS.

Magenta	+7.50	Town		+7.50
Purple	+7.50			
Blue	+5.00			

O2	O1	2c **yellow**		45.00	13.50
		golden yellow		47.50	14.50
		olive yellow		52.50	15.50
		On cover			1,100.
		Block of four		200.00	
		Ribbed paper		55.00	18.50

CANCELLATIONS.

Blue	+ 3.00	Town		+5.00
Red	+15.00			
Magenta	+ 5.00			

O3	O1	3c **yellow**		40.00	3.50
		golden yellow		42.50	4.00
		olive yellow		45.00	4.50
		On cover			600.00
		Block of four		185.00	
		Ribbed paper		50.00	6.00
		Double transfer		—	

CANCELLATIONS.

Blue	+ .50	Town		+ 4.00
Purple	+ 1.00	"Paid"		+27.50
Magenta	+ 1.00	Railroad		+75.00
Violet	+ 1.00	Numeral		+35.00
Red	+ 12.00			
Green	+125.00			

O4	O1	6c **yellow**		50.00	12.50
		golden yellow		52.50	13.50
		olive yellow		55.00	15.00
		On cover			700.00
		Pair on cover			—
		Block of four		225.00	

CANCELLATIONS.

Blue	+3.00	Town		+7.00
Magenta	+4.00	Express Company		—
Violet	+4.00			

O5	O1	10c **yellow**		110.00	47.50
		golden yellow		115.00	50.00
		olive yellow		125.00	52.00
		On cover			—
		Block of four		500.00	

CANCELLATIONS.

Purple	+5.00	Town		+15.00
Blue	+5.00			

O6	O1	12c **yellow**		140.00	70.00
		golden yellow		170.00	75.00
		olive yellow		180.00	85.00
		On cover			—
		Block of four		700.00	

CANCELLATIONS.

Purple	+10.00	Town		+20.00
Blue	+10.00			

O7	O1	15c **yellow**		110.00	47.50
		golden yellow		115.00	50.00
		olive yellow		120.00	55.00
		Block of four		500.00	

CANCELLATIONS.

Purple	+10.00		

O8	O1	24c **yellow**		125.00	55.00
		golden yellow		140.00	60.00
		Block of four		550.00	

CANCELLATIONS.

	Purple	+10.00

O9	O1	30c **yellow**		165.00	85.00
		golden yellow		175.00	90.00

		oliven yellow		185.00	100.00
		Block of four		725.00	

CANCELLATIONS.

	Red	+35.00

EXECUTIVE

Franklin — O2

1873					
O10	O2	1c **carmine**		250.00	85.00
		deep carmine		250.00	85.00
		On cover			1,300.
		Block of four		5,000.	

CANCELLATIONS.

Purple	+10.00	Town		+30.00
Blue	+10.00			
Red	+50.00			

O11	O2	2c **carmine**		165.00	70.00
		deep carmine		165.00	70.00
		On cover			1,500.
		Block of four		1,500.	
		Double transfer		—	—

CANCELLATIONS.

Blue	+10.00	Red		+50.00

O12	O2	3c **carmine**		190.00	65.00
a.		3c violet rose		165.00	65.00
		On cover			700.00
		Block of four		950.00	

CANCELLATIONS.

Blue	+10.00	Town		+25.00
Purple	+10.00			

O13	O2	6c **carmine**		300.00	140.00
		pale carmine		300.00	140.00
		deep carmine		300.00	140.00
		On cover			2,000.
		Block of four		2,250.	

CANCELLATIONS.

Purple	+15.00	Town		+50.00

O14	O2	10c **carmine**		275.00	150.00
		pale carmine		275.00	150.00
		deep carmine		275.00	150.00
		On cover			—
		Block of four		2,250.	

CANCELLATIONS.

Blue	+15.00	Purple		+15.00

INTERIOR

Franklin — O3

1873					
O15	O3	1c **vermilion**		17.50	3.50
		dull vermilion		17.50	3.50
		bright vermilion		17.50	3.50
		On cover			125.00
		Block of four		75.00	—
		Ribbed paper		21.00	4.50

CANCELLATIONS.

Purple	+ 1.00	Town		+3.00
Blue	+ 1.00			
Red	+12.50			
Ultramarine	+ 8.00			

O16	O3	2c **vermilion**		15.00	2.00

		dull vermilion		15.00	2.00
		bright vermilion		15.00	2.00
		On cover			60.00
		Block of four		60.00	12.50

CANCELLATIONS.

Purple	+ .75	Town		+2.00
Blue	+ .75			
Red	+ 6.00			

O17	O3	3c **vermilion**		22.50	2.00
		dull vermilion		22.50	2.00
		bright vermilion		22.50	2.00
		On cover			40.00
		Block of four		95.00	—
		Ribbed paper		30.00	4.00

CANCELLATIONS.

Purple	+ 1.00	Town		+ 2.00
Blue	+ 1.00	Express Company		+75.00
Red	+15.00	"Paid"		+20.00
Green	+65.00	Fort		—

O18	O3	6c **vermilion**		17.50	2.00
		dull vermilion		17.50	2.00
		bright vermilion		17.50	2.00
		scarlet vermilion		17.50	3.00
		On cover			85.00
		Block of four		75.00	

CANCELLATIONS.

Purple	+ 1.00	Town		+2.00
Blue	+ 1.00	Express Company		—
Red	+15.00	Railroad		—
		Fort		—

O19	O3	10c **vermilion**		16.00	5.00
		dull vermilion		16.00	5.00
		bright vermilion		16.00	5.00
		On cover			225.00
		Block of four		70.00	

CANCELLATIONS.

Purple	+ 1.00	Town		+4.00
Blue	+ 1.00	Fort		—

O20	O3	12c **vermilion**		25.00	5.00
		bright vermilion		25.00	5.00
		On cover			275.00
		Block of four		110.00	

CANCELLATIONS.

Purple	+ 1.00	Town		+4.00
Magenta	+ 1.00	Fort		—
Blue	+ 1.00			
Red	+15.00			

O21	O3	15c **vermilion**		40.00	10.00
		bright vermilion		40.00	10.00
		On cover			450.00
		Block of four		170.00	
		Double transfer		60.00	17.50

CANCELLATIONS.

Blue	+1.50	Town		+5.00
Purple	+1.50			

O22	O3	24c **vermilion**		30.00	7.00
		dull vermilion		30.00	7.00
		bright vermilion		30.00	7.00
		On cover			500.00
		Block of four		135.00	

CANCELLATIONS.

Purple	+ 1.50	Town		+5.00
Blue	+ 1.50			
Red	+15.00			

O23	O3	30c **vermilion**		40.00	8.00
		bright vermilion		40.00	8.00
		On cover			—
		Block of four		170.00	

CANCELLATIONS.

Purple	+ 2.00	Town		+5.00
Blue	+ 2.00			
Red	+15.00			

O24	O3	90c **vermilion**		90.00	15.00
		bright vermilion		90.00	15.00
		On cover			—
		Block of four		400.00	120.00
		Double transfer		—	

CANCELLATIONS.

Purple	+4.00	Town		+7.50
Blue	+4.00			

JUSTICE

Franklin — O4

1873

O25	O4	1c	**purple**	40.00	17.50
			dark purple	40.00	17.50
			On cover		*600.00*
			Block of four	185.00	—

CANCELLATIONS.

Violet	+ 3.00	Town	+ 7.50
Blue	+ 3.00		
Red	+20.00		

O26	O4	2c	**purple**	65.00	20.00
			light purple	65.00	20.00
			On cover		—
			Block of four	280.00	

CANCELLATIONS.

Violet	+ 4.00	Town	+10.00
Blue	+ 4.00		
Red	+20.00		

O27	O4	3c	**purple**	65.00	8.00
			dark purple	65.00	8.00
			bluish purple	65.00	8.00
			On cover		*400.00*
			Block of four	280.00	—
			Double transfer	—	

CANCELLATIONS.

Purple	+ 2.00	Town	+5.00
Magenta	+ 2.00		
Blue	+ 2.00		
Red	+ 12.00		
Green	+100.00		

O28	O4	6c	**purple**	60.00	11.00
			light purple	60.00	11.00
			bluish purple	60.00	11.00
			On cover		*500.00*
			Block of four	260.00	—

CANCELLATIONS.

Violet	+ 2.00	Town	+7.50
Purple	+ 2.00		
Blue	+ 2.00		
Red	+15.00		

O29	O4	10c	**purple**	70.00	25.00
			bluish purple	70.00	25.00
			On cover		*1,200.*
			Block of four	325.00	—
			Double transfer	—	—

CANCELLATIONS.

| Violet | +4.00 | Town | +10.00 |
| Blue | +4.00 | | |

O30	O4	12c	**purple**	50.00	15.00
			dark purple	50.00	15.00
			On cover		*800.00*
			Block of four	225.00	

CANCELLATIONS.

| Purple | +2.00 | Town | +7.50 |
| Blue | +2.00 | | |

O31	O4	15c	**purple**	110.00	47.50
			On cover		*900.00*
			Block of four	575.00	—
			Double transfer	—	

CANCELLATIONS.

| Blue | +5.00 | Town | +10.00 |
| Purple | +5.00 | | |

O32	O4	24c	**purple**	300.00	120.00
			On cover		*1,100.*
			Block of four	—	

CANCELLATIONS.

Violet	+ 10.00	Town	+30.00
Purple	+ 10.00		
Blue	+ 10.00		
Red	+ 35.00		

O33	O4	30c	**purple**	275.00	85.00
			On cover		—
			Block of four	*1,400.*	
			Double transfer at top	—	

CANCELLATIONS.

Blue	+ 10.00	Town	+30.00
Purple	+ 10.00		
Red	+ 35.00		

O34	O4	90c	**purple**	400.00	175.00
			dark purple	400.00	175.00
			Block of four	—	

CANCELLATIONS.

| Blue | +25.00 | Violet | +25.00 |

NAVY

Franklin — O5

1873

O35	O5	1c	**ultramarine**	35.00	10.00
			dark ultramarine	35.00	10.00
a.			1c dull blue	42.50	12.00
			On cover		*250.00*
			Block of four	150.00	

CANCELLATIONS.

Violet	+ 2.00	Town	+ 7.50
Blue	+ 2.00	Steamship	+100.00
Red	+20.00		

O36	O5	2c	**ultramarine**	25.00	9.00
			dark ultramarine	25.00	9.00
a.			2c dull blue	32.50	11.00
			gray blue	27.50	11.00
			On cover		*200.00*
			Block of four	100.00	—
			Double transfer	—	

The 2c deep green, both perforated and imperforate, is a trial color proof.

CANCELLATIONS.

Purple	+ 1.50	Town	+10.00
Violet	+ 1.50	Steamship	+85.00
Blue	+ 1.50		
Red	+15.00		
Green	+75.00		

O37	O5	3c	**ultramarine**	27.50	4.00
			pale ultramarine	27.50	4.00
			dark ultramarine	27.50	4.00
a.			3c dull blue	32.50	5.50
			On cover		*150.00*
			Block of four	120.00	—
			Double transfer	—	

CANCELLATIONS.

Violet	+ 1.50	Town	+ 5.00
Blue	+ 1.50	Blue town	+15.00
Red	+15.00	Steamship	+50.00

O38	O5	6c	**ultramarine**	25.00	6.00
			bright ultramarine	25.00	6.00
a.			6c dull blue	32.50	7.50
			On cover		*225.00*
			Block of four	110.00	—
			Vertical line through "N" of		
			"Navy" (Pos. 2 & 6, plate 53)	57.50	15.00
			Double transfer	—	

CANCELLATIONS.

Violet	+ 1.50	Town	+ 5.00
Purple	+ 1.50	Steamship	+65.00
Blue	+ 1.50		
Red	+17.50		
Green	+75.00		

O39	O5	7c	**ultramarine**	165.00	65.00
			dark ultramarine	165.00	65.00
a.			7c dull blue	185.00	85.00
			On cover		—
			Block of four	750.00	—
			Double transfer	—	

CANCELLATIONS.

Blue	+10.00	Town	+15.00
Violet	+10.00		
Magenta	+10.00		
Red	+40.00		

O40	O5	10c	**ultramarine**	35.00	11.00
			dark ultramarine	35.00	11.00
a.			10c dull blue	40.00	13.00
			On cover		*1,350.*
			Block of four	150.00	—
			Cracked plate	70.00	—
			Ribbed paper	45.00	15.00

CANCELLATIONS.

Violet	+ 2.00	Town	+10.00
Blue	+ 2.00	Steamship	+85.00
Brown	+20.00		
Purple	+ 2.00		
Red	+25.00		

O41	O5	12c	**ultramarine**	45.00	10.00
			pale ultramarine	45.00	10.00
			dark ultramarine	45.00	10.00
			On cover		*1,500.*
			Block of four	200.00	—
			Double transfer of left side	90.00	—

CANCELLATIONS.

Purple	+ 2.50	Town	+10.00
Magenta	+ 2.50	Supplementary	
		Mail	+80.00
Blue	+ 2.50	Steamship	+100.00

			Red	+25.00	
O42	O5	15c	**ultramarine**	75.00	25.00
			dark ultramarine	75.00	25.00
			Block of four	400.00	

CANCELLATIONS.

| Blue | + 2.50 | Town | +20.00 |
| Red | +35.00 | | |

O43	O5	24c	**ultramarine**	75.00	30.00
			dark ultramarine	75.00	30.00
a.			24c dull blue	85.00	—
			Block of four	400.00	

CANCELLATIONS.

Magenta	+ 5.00	Town	+ 20.00
Blue	+ 5.00	Steamship	+100.00
Green	+150.00		

O44	O5	30c	**ultramarine**	65.00	15.00
			dark ultramarine	65.00	15.00
			Block of four	325.00	
			Double transfer	95.00	30.00

CANCELLATIONS.

Blue	+ 4.00	Town	+ 10.00
Red	+30.00	Supplementary	
		Mail	+125.00
Purple	+ 4.00		
Violet	+ 4.00		

O45	O5	90c	**ultramarine**	300.00	80.00
			Block of four	1,400.	
a.			Double impression		*2,000.*

CANCELLATIONS.

| Purple | +15.00 | Town | +25.00 |

POST OFFICE

Numeral of Value — O6

Stamps of the Post Office Department are often on paper with a gray surface. This is due to insufficient wiping of the plates during printing.

1873

O47	O6	1c	**black**	7.25	3.00
			gray black	7.25	3.00
			On cover		50.00
			Block of four	32.50	—

CANCELLATIONS.

Purple	+ 1.00	Town	+3.50
Magenta	+ 1.00		
Blue	+ 1.00		
Red	+12.50		

O48	O6	2c	**black**	7.00	2.50
			gray black	7.00	2.50
			On cover		50.00
			Block of four	32.50	—
a.			Double impression	300.00	

CANCELLATIONS.

Magenta	+ 1.00	Town	+3.50
Purple	+ 1.00	Blue town	+7.50
Blue	+ 1.00		
Red	+12.50		

O49	O6	3c	**black**	2.50	75
			gray black	2.50	75
			On cover		25.00
			Block of four	11.50	5.00
			Cracked plate	—	—
			Double transfer at bottom	—	—
			Double paper	—	—
			Vertical ribbed paper	—	—

CANCELLATIONS.

Purple	+ .75	Town	+1.50
Magenta	+ .75	Railroad	+25.00
Violet	+ .75	"Paid"	+12.00
Blue	+ .75		
Ultramarine	+ 1.50		
Red	+10.00		
Green	+60.00		

O50	O6	6c	**black**	8.00	1.65
			gray black	8.00	1.65
			On cover		75.00
			Block of four	35.00	—
a.			Diagonal half used as 3c on cover		*2,750.*
			Vertical ribbed paper	—	7.50

CANCELLATIONS.

Purple	+ .75	Town	+ 2.50
Magenta	+ .75	"Paid"	+15.00
Blue	+ .75		
Red	+12.00		

| O51 | O6 | 10c | **black** | 40.00 | 16.50 |
| | | | gray black | 40.00 | 16.50 |

On cover *400.00*
Block of four 180.00 —
CANCELLATIONS.
Purple +3.50 | Red +15.00
Magenta +3.50 | Town +10.00
Blue +3.50 |

O52 O6 12c **black** 22.50 5.00
gray black 22.50 5.00
On cover *425.00*
Block of four 100.00 —
CANCELLATIONS.
Purple + 1.00 | Town +4.00
Magenta + 1.00
Blue + 1.00
Red + 12.50

O53 O6 15c **black** 25.00 8.50
gray black 25.00 8.50
On cover *1,000.*
Block of four 110.00 —
a. Imperf., pair 600.00
Double transfer 32.50 *12.00*
CANCELLATIONS.
Purple +1.50 | Town +7.50
Magenta +1.50
Blue +1.50

O54 O6 24c **black** 32.50 10.00
gray black 32.50 10.00
On cover *600.00*
Block of four 140.00 —
Double paper — —
CANCELLATIONS.
Purple + 1.50 | Town +7.50
Blue + 1.50
Red +20.00

O55 O6 30c **black** 32.50 9.00
gray black 32.50 9.00
On cover *800.00*
Block of four 140.00 —
CANCELLATIONS.
Purple + 1.50 | Town +12.50
Blue + 1.50
Red +20.00
Magenta + 1.50

O56 O6 90c **black** 47.50 12.50
gray black 47.50 12.50
Block of four 210.00 —
Double transfer — —
Double paper — —
CANCELLATIONS.
Purple +1.50 | Town +6.50
Magenta +1.50
Blue +1.50

STATE

Franklin — O7

1873
O57 O7 1c **dark green** 42.50 13.00
dark yellow green 42.50 13.00
light green 42.50 13.00
On cover —
Block of four 225.00
CANCELLATIONS.
Violet +2.00 | Town +7.50
Purple +2.00
Blue +2.00
Red +17.50

O58 O7 2c **dark green** 85.00 27.50
dark yellow green 85.00 27.50
yellow green —
On cover *650.00*
Block of four — —
Double transfer — —
CANCELLATIONS.
Purple + 5.00 | Town +10.00
Blue + 5.00 | Blue town +20.00
Red +30.00
Green +75.00

O59 O7 3c **bright green** 35.00 9.00
yellow green 35.00 9.00
dark green 35.00 9.00
On cover *450.00*
First day cover, *July 1, 1873* —
Block of four 165.00 —
Double paper — —
CANCELLATIONS.

Purple + 1.50 | Town + 6.50
Blue + 1.50 | Blue town +10.00
Red +10.00

O60 O7 6c **bright green** 32.50 9.00
dark green 32.50 9.00
yellow green 32.50 9.00
On cover *550.00*
Block of four 140.00 —
Double transfer — —
CANCELLATIONS.
Purple + 2.00 | Town +7.50
Red +10.00

O61 O7 7c **dark green** 60.00 18.50
dark yellow green 60.00 18.50
On cover *1,000.*
Block of four 425.00 —
Ribbed paper 75.00 22.50
CANCELLATIONS.
Purple + 2.00 | Town +10.00
Blue + 2.00
Red +25.00

O62 O7 10c **dark green** 50.00 15.00
bright green 50.00 16.00
yellow green —
On cover *1,200.*
Block of four 325.00
CANCELLATIONS.
Purple + 2.50 | Town + 5.00
Magenta + 2.50 | Blue town +10.00
Blue + 2.50 | Numeral +15.00
Red +25.00

O63 O7 12c **dark green** 75.00 27.50
dark yellow green —
On cover *1,400.*
Block of four 400.00
CANCELLATIONS.
Purple +5.00 | Town +15.00
Blue +5.00
Red +30.00

O64 O7 15c **dark green** 70.00 20.00
dark yellow green 70.00 20.00
On cover —
Block of four 350.00
CANCELLATIONS.
Purple + 2.50 | Town +15.00
Blue + 2.50
Red +20.00

O65 O7 24c **dark green** 175.00 75.00
On cover *1,750.*
dark yellow green 175.00 75.00
Block of four *850.00* —
CANCELLATIONS.
Purple +15.00 | Town +25.00
Blue +15.00
Red +65.00

O66 O7 30c **dark green** 160.00 60.00
dark yellow green 160.00 60.00
On cover —
Block of four — —
CANCELLATIONS.
Purple + 5.00 | Town +20.00
Blue + 5.00 | Blue town +30.00
Red +35.00

O67 O7 90c **dark green** 300.00 125.00
dark yellow green —
Block of four
CANCELLATIONS.
Purple +15.00 | Town +40.00
Blue +15.00
Red +75.00

William H. Seward — O8

O68 O8 $2 **green & black** 550.00 250.00
yellow green & black 550.00 250.00
On cover —
Block of four *17,000.*

CANCELLATIONS.
Blue + 25.00 | Town + 75.00
Red +125.00 | Blue town +150.00
Purple + 25.00 | Manuscript *125.00*

O69 O8 $5 **green & black** 4,250. 2,000.
dark green & black 4,250. 2,000.
yellow green & black 4,250. 2,000.
Block of four *20,000.*
CANCELLATIONS.
Blue +250.00 | Manuscript *1,000.*

O70 O8 $10 **green & black** 3,000. 1,300.
dark green & black 3,000. 1,300.
yellow green & black 3,000. 1,300.
Block of four *14,000.*
CANCELLATIONS.
Blue +200.00 | Manuscript *700.00*

O71 O8 $20 **green & black** 2,250. 1,100.
dark green & black 2,250. 1,100.
yellow green & black 2,250. 1,100.
Block of four *12,500.*
Block of four, ms. cancel *4,000.*
CANCELLATIONS.
Blue +200.00 | Manuscript *550.00*

The design of Nos. O68 to O71 measures 25½x39½mm.

TREASURY

Franklin — O9

1873
O72 O9 1c **brown** 17.50 1.75
dark brown 17.50 1.75
yellow brown 17.50 1.75
On cover 85.00
Block of four 75.00 —
Double transfer 25.00 3.50
CANCELLATIONS.
Purple + 1.00 | Town +2.00
Magenta + 1.00 | Blue town +4.00
Blue + 1.00
Red +10.00

O73 O9 2c **brown** 20.00 1.75
dark brown 20.00 1.75
yellow brown 20.00 1.75
On cover 75.00
Block of four 90.00 —
Double transfer 5.00
Cracked plate 35.00
CANCELLATIONS.
Purple + 1.00 | Town +2.00
Magenta + 1.00 | Blue town +4.00
Blue + 1.00
Red +10.00

O74 O9 3c **brown** 12.50 1.00
dark brown 12.50 1.00
yellow brown 12.50 1.00
On cover 40.00
First day cover, *July 1, 1873* —
Block of four 55.00 —
Double paper —
Shaded circle outside of right
frame line — —
CANCELLATIONS.
Purple + .50 | Town + 1.00
Magenta + .50 | Railroad +20.00
Blue + .50 | "Paid" +10.00
Ultramarine +2.00
Red +3.50

O75 O9 6c **brown** 17.50 1.00
dark brown 17.50 1.00
yellow brown 17.50 1.00
On cover 125.00
Block of four 80.00 —
Worn plate 18.50 2.00
Double transfer — —
CANCELLATIONS.
Purple + .50 | Town +1.50
Magenta + .50
Blue + .50
Ultramarine + 1.50
Red + 5.00
Green +20.00

O76 O9 7c **brown** 42.50 12.50
dark brown 42.50 12.50
yellow brown 42.50 12.50
On cover 750.00
Block of four 185.00

CANCELLATIONS.

Purple	+ 2.00	Town	+ 7.50
Blue	+ 2.00	Blue town	+12.50
Green	+60.00		

O77 O9 10c **brown** 42.50 4.50
dark brown 42.50 4.50
yellow brown 42.50 4.50
On cover 375.00
Block of four 185.00 —
Double paper —
Double transfer —

CANCELLATIONS.

Purple	+ 1.00	Town	+4.00
Magenta	+ 1.00	Blue town	+8.50
Blue	+ 1.00		
Ultramarine	+ 4.00		
Red	+12.00		

O78 O9 12c **brown** 42.50 3.00
dark brown 42.50 3.00
yellow brown 42.50 3.00
On cover 500.00
Block of four 185.00

CANCELLATIONS.

Purple	+ .50	Town	+2.50
Blue	+ .50		
Red	+10.00		
Green	+35.00		

O79 O9 15c **brown** 37.50 4.50
yellow brown 37.50 4.50
On cover 850.00
Block of four 160.00

CANCELLATIONS.

Blue	+ 1.00	Town	+ 2.50
Purple	+ 1.00	Blue town	+ 7.50
Red	+10.00	Numeral	+15.00

O80 O9 24c **brown** 185.00 55.00
dark brown 185.00 55.00
yellow brown 185.00 55.00
Block of four 800.00
Double transfer at top —

CANCELLATIONS.

Blue	+5.00	Town	+15.00
Magenta	+5.00	Blue town	+25.00

O81 O9 30c **brown** 62.50 5.00
dark brown 62.50 5.00
yellow brown 62.50 5.00
On cover 1,000.
Block of four 270.00 —
Short transfer at top right —

CANCELLATIONS.

Blue	+ 1.00	Black town	+3.50
Red	+12.00	Blue town	+7.50
Purple	+ 1.00		

O82 O9 90c **brown** 67.50 5.00
dark brown 67.50 5.00
yellow brown 67.50 5.00
Block of four 300.00 45.00
Double paper —

CANCELLATIONS.

Purple	+1.00	Town	+3.50
Magenta	+1.00	Blue town	+7.50
Blue	+1.00		
Brown	+7.50		

WAR

Franklin — O10

1873

O83 O10 1c **rose** 60.00 4.00
rose red 60.00 4.00
On cover 125.00
Pair on cover 125.00
Block of four 260.00

CANCELLATIONS.

Purple	+ 1.00	Town	+ 3.50
Blue	+ 1.00	Fort	+50.00
Red	+15.00	Numeral	+12.50
		"Paid"	—

O84 O10 2c **rose** 55.00 6.00
rose red 55.00 6.00
On cover 60.00
Block of four 235.00 —
Ribbed paper 67.50 7.50

CANCELLATIONS.

Purple	+ 1.50	Town	+ 4.00
Magenta	+ 1.50	Fort	+50.00
Blue	+ 1.50		

Red +15.00

O85 O10 3c **rose** 50.00 1.50
rose red 50.00 1.50
On cover 30.00
Block of four 220.00

CANCELLATIONS.

Blue	+ 1.00	Town	+ 1.50
Purple	+ 1.00	Fort	+40.00
Magenta	+ 1.00	"Paid"	+12.00
Green	+35.00		

O86 O10 6c **rose** 240.00 4.00
pale rose 240.00 4.00
On cover 50.00
Block of four 950.00 —

CANCELLATIONS.

Purple	+ 1.50	Town	+ 3.50
Blue	+ 1.50	Blue town	+ 6.50
Red	+15.00	Fort	+40.00

O87 O10 7c **rose** 52.50 30.00
pale rose 52.50 30.00
rose red 52.50 30.00
On cover —
Block of four 220.00 —

CANCELLATIONS.

Purple	+2.50	Town	+7.50
Blue	+3.50		

O88 O10 10c **rose** 19.00 4.00
rose red 19.00 4.00
On cover —
Block of four 82.50 —
Cracked plate —

CANCELLATIONS.

Purple	+1.00	Town	+ 3.50
Blue	+1.00	Fort	+40.00

O89 O10 12c **rose** 52.50 4.00
On cover 300.00
Block of four 220.00 —
Ribbed paper 67.50 6.50

CANCELLATIONS.

Purple	+ 1.00	Town	+ 3.00
Magenta	+ 1.00	Fort	+35.00
Blue	+ 1.00		
Red	+10.00		

O90 O10 15c **rose** 15.00 2.50
pale rose 15.00 2.50
rose red 15.00 2.50
On cover 325.00
Block of four 65.00 20.00
Ribbed paper 20.00 4.50

CANCELLATIONS.

Purple	+ 1.00	Town	+ 2.50
Blue	+ 1.00	Fort	+30.00
Red	+10.00	Express Company	—

O91 O10 24c **rose** 15.00 3.00
pale rose 15.00 3.00
rose red 15.00 3.00
On cover —
Block of four 65.00 —

CANCELLATIONS.

Purple	+1.00	Town	+2.50
Blue	+1.00	Fort	+3.50

O92 O10 30c **rose** 17.50 2.50
rose red 17.50 2.50
On cover —
Block of four 72.50 25.00
Ribbed paper 22.50 5.00

CANCELLATIONS.

Purple	+1.00	Town	+ 2.50
Magenta	+1.00	Fort	+35.00
Blue	+1.00		

O93 O10 90c **rose** 40.00 12.50
rose red 40.00 12.50
On cover 1,000.
Block of four 170.00 —

CANCELLATIONS.

Purple	+2.00	Town	+ 7.50
Magenta	+2.00	Fort	+90.00
Blue	+2.00		

Printed by the American Bank Note Co.

1879   **Soft Porous Paper**

AGRICULTURE

O94 O1 1c **yellow** (issued without gum) 1,350.
6,000.

O95 O1 3c **yellow** 175.00 37.50
On cover —
Block of four 775.00

CANCELLATIONS.

Purple	+5.00	Town	+17.50
Blue	+5.00		

INTERIOR

O96 O3 1c **vermilion** 125.00 65.00
pale vermilion 125.00 65.00
Block of four 550.00 —

CANCELLATIONS.

Blue	+5.00	Town	+15.00

O97 O3 2c **vermilion** 2.50 75
pale vermilion 2.50 75
scarlet vermilion 2.50 75
On cover 35.00
Block of four 12.00 —

CANCELLATIONS.

Purple	+ .50	Town	+ 1.50
Blue	+ .50	Blue town	+ 3.00
Red	+5.00	Fort	+25.00

O98 O3 3c **vermilion** 2.00 60
pale vermilion 2.00 60
On cover 30.00
Block of four 9.00

CANCELLATIONS.

Purple	+ .50	Town	+1.50
Blue	+ .50	Blue town	+3.00
Red	+5.00	Numeral	+5.00

O99 O3 6c **vermilion** 3.00 1.00
pale vermilion 3.00 1.00
scarlet vermilion 3.00 1.00
On cover 200.00
Block of four 14.00 —

CANCELLATIONS.

Purple	+ .50	Town	+1.50
Blue	+ .50		
Red	+5.00		

O100 O3 10c **vermilion** 32.50 17.50
pale vermilion 32.50 17.50
On cover 350.00
Block of four 135.00

CANCELLATIONS.

Purple	+5.00	Town	+10.00
Blue	+5.00		

O101 O3 12c **vermilion** 65.00 30.00
pale vermilion 65.00 30.00
On cover 550.00
Block of four 275.00

O102 O3 15c **vermilion** 150.00 70.00
Block of four 625.00
On cover —
Double transfer 200.00 —

CANCELLATIONS.

Purple	+5.00	

O103 O3 24c **vermilion** 1,200.
Block of four 5,000.

JUSTICE

1879

O106 O4 3c **bluish purple** 50.00 17.50
deep bluish purple 50.00 17.50
On cover 550.00
Block of four 220.00

CANCELLATIONS.

Blue	+5.00	

O107 O4 6c **bluish purple** 110.00 60.00
Block of four 475.00

CANCELLATIONS.

Blue	+10.00	Town	+20.00

POST OFFICE

O108 O6 3c **black** 7.50 1.40
gray black 7.50 1.40
On cover 35.00
Block of four 32.50 10.00

CANCELLATIONS.

Blue	+ 1.00	Town	+ 2.00
Purple	+ 1.00	"Paid"	+12.00
Violet	+ 1.00		
Magenta	+ 1.00		
Green	+40.00		

TREASURY

O109 O9 3c **brown** 27.50 3.50
yellow brown 27.50 3.50
On cover 110.00
Block of four 120.00

CANCELLATIONS.

Purple	+1.50	Town	+2.00
Blue	+1.50	Numeral	+7.50

O110 O9 6c **brown** 50.00 17.50
yellow brown 50.00 17.50
dark brown 50.00 17.50
On cover 300.00
Block of four 210.00

CANCELLATIONS.

Purple	+6.00	
Magenta	+6.00	
Blue	+6.00	

O111 O9 10c **brown** 65.00 15.00
yellow brown 65.00 15.00
dark brown 65.00 15.00
On cover 900.00
Block of four 275.00 —

CANCELLATIONS.

Purple	+2.50	Town	+7.50
Blue	+2.50		

O112 O9 30c **brown** 750.00 135.00
Block of four 3,500.

CANCELLATIONS.

Blue	+25.00	Town	+50.00

O113 O9 90c **brown** 775.00 135.00
dark brown 775.00 135.00
Block of four 3,750.

CANCELLATIONS.

Purple	+25.00	Town	+75.00
Blue	+25.00		

WAR

1879

O114 O10 1c **rose red** 2.00 75

	rose			2.00	75
	dull rose red			2.00	75
	brown rose			2.00	75
	On cover				50.00
	Block of four			9.00	4.00

CANCELLATIONS.

Purple	+.50	Town		+ 1.00
Blue	+.50	Fort		+25.00

O115	O10	2c **rose red**		3.00	1.00
		dark rose red		3.00	1.00
		dull vermilion		3.00	1.25
		On cover			40.00
		Pair on cover			—
		Block of four		13.00	6.00

CANCELLATIONS.

Blue	+ .50	Town		+ 2.00
Purple	+ .50	Fort		+25.00
Magenta	+ .50			
Green	+35.00			

O116	O10	3c **rose red**		3.00	65
		dull rose red		3.00	65
		On cover			35.00
		Pair on cover			40.00
		Block of four		13.00	4.00
a.		Imperf., pair		*800.00*	
b.		Double impression		*500.00*	
		Double transfer		6.00	4.00

CANCELLATIONS.

Purple	+ .50	Town		+ 1.00
Violet	+ .50	Fort		+25.00
Blue	+ .50			
Red	+5.00			

O117	O10	6c **rose red**		2.50	70
		dull rose red		2.50	70
		dull vermilion			
		On cover			50.00
		Block of four		10.50	6.00

CANCELLATIONS.

Purple	+ .50	Town		+ 1.00
Blue	+ .50	Fort		+25.00
		Numeral		+ 7.50

O118	O10	10c **rose red**		20.00	6.00
		dull rose red		20.00	6.00
		On cover			
		Block of four		85.00	

CANCELLATIONS.

	Town		+ 5.00
	Fort		+45.00

O119	O10	12c **rose red**		15.00	3.00
		dull rose red		15.00	3.00
		brown rose		15.00	3.00
		On cover			
		Block of four		62.50	20.00

CANCELLATIONS.

Purple	+ 1.00	Town		+ 2.50
Violet	+ 1.00	Fort		+40.00
Red	+10.00			

O120	O10	30c **rose red**		47.50	25.00
		dull rose red		47.50	25.00
		On cover			
		Block of four		200.00	—

CANCELLATIONS.

	Town		+10.00
	Fort		+80.00

POSTAL SAVINGS MAIL

The Act of Congress, approved June 25, 1910, establishing postal savings depositories, provided:
"Sec. 2. That the Postmaster General is hereby directed to prepare and issue special stamps of the necessary denominations for use, in lieu of penalty or franked envelopes, in the transmittal of free mail resulting from the administration of this act."

The use of postal savings official stamps was discontinued by the Act of Congress, approved September 23, 1914. The unused stamps in the hands of postmasters were returned and destroyed.

O11

1910-11	**Engr.**		**Wmk. 191**
O121	O11	2c **black,** *Dec. 22, 1910*	9.00	1.10

	On cover		10.00
	Block of four (2mm. spacing)	40.00	6.00
	Block of four (3mm. spacing)	38.50	5.00
	Margin block of 6, Impt. & P# & Star	225.00	
	Double transfer	12.50	2.00
O122	O11	50c **dark green,** *Feb. 1, 1911*	110.00	32.50
	On cover		150.00

	Block of four (2mm. spacing)	465.00	175.00
	Block of four (3mm. spacing)	450.00	175.00
	Margin block of 4, arrow	475.00	
	Margin block of 6, Impt. & P# & Star	2,200.	
O123	O11	$1 **ultramarine,** *Feb. 1, 1911*	100.00	9.50
	On cover		85.00
	Block of four (2mm. spacing)	425.00	50.00
	Block of four (3mm. spacing)	410.00	50.00
	Margin block of 4, arrow	450.00	
	Margin block of 6, Impt. & P# & Star	2,000.	350.00

Wmk. 190

O124	O11	1c **dark violet,** *March 27, 1911*	4.00	1.00
	On cover		10.00
	Block of four (2mm. spacing)	17.50	4.50
	Block of four (3mm. spacing)	17.00	4.25
	Margin block of 6, Impt. & P# & Star	120.00	
O125	O11	2c **black**	30.00	3.50
	On cover		17.50
	Block of four (2mm. spacing)	125.00	17.50
	Block of four (3mm. spacing)	122.50	17.50
	Margin block of 6, Impt. & P# & Star	550.00	
	Double transfer	35.00	4.50
O126	O11	10c **carmine,** *Feb. 1, 1911*	8.50	1.00
	On cover		10.00
	Block of four (2mm. spacing)	37.50	5.50
	Block of four (3mm. spacing)	36.00	5.00
	Margin block of 6, Impt. & P# & Star	250.00	
	Double transfer	15.00	2.50

OFFICIAL MAIL

O12

Designed by Bradbury Thompson

ENGRAVED

1983, Jan. 12-1985			*Perf. 11x10 ½, 11 (14c)*	
O127	O12	1c **red, blue & blk**	5	—
		FDC, Washington, DC		75
		P# block of 4, UL or UR	25	
O128	O12	4c **red, blue & blk**	8	—
		FDC, Washington, DC		75
		P# block of 4, LR only	40	
O129	O12	13c **red, blue & blk**	26	—
		FDC, Washington, DC		60
		P# block of 4, UR only	1.30	
O129A	O12	14c **red, blue & blk,** *May 15, 1985*	28	—
		FDC, Washington, DC		65
O130	O12	17c **red, blue & blk**	34	—
		FDC, Washington, DC		75
		P# block of 4, LL only	1.70	
O132	O12	$1 **red, blue & blk**	2.00	—
		FDC, Washington, DC		2.25
		P# block of 4, UL only	10.00	
O133	O12	$5 **red, blue & blk**	10.00	—
		FDC, Washington, DC		12.50
		P# block of 4, LL only	50.00	

Coil Stamp
Perf. 10 Vert.

O135	O12	20c **red, blue & blk**	50	40
		FDC, Washington, DC		75
		Pair	1.00	
		P# strip of 3, P# 1	20.00	
a.		Imperf pair	—	
O136	O12	22c **red, blue & blk,** *May 15, 1985*	44	—
		FDC, Washington, DC		80
		Pair	90	

O13

1985, Feb. 4			*Perf. 11*	
O138	O13	(14c) **red, blue & blk**	3.50	—
		FDC, Washington, DC		65
		P# block of 4, LR only	30.00	

No. O138 is inscribed "Postal Card Rate D."

Coil Stamps
Perf. 10 Vert.

O138A	O13	15c **red, blue & blk,** *June 11, 1988*	30	—
		FDC, Corpus Christi, TX		65
		Pair	60	
		P# strip of 3, P# 1	1.50	
O138B	O13	20c **red, blue & blk,** *May 19, 1988*	40	—
		FDC, Washington		75
		Pair	80	
		P# strip of 3, P# 1	2.00	

O139	O13	(22c) **red, blue & blk**	4.50	—
		FDC, Washington, DC		80
		Pair	9.00	
		P# strip of 3, P# 1	30.00	
O140	O13	(25c) **red, blue & blk,** *Mar. 22, 1988*	50	—
		FDC, Washington		85
		Pair	1.00	
		P# strip of 3, P# 1	3.00	
O141	O13	25c **red, blue & blk,** *June 11, 1988*	50	—
		FDC, Corpus Christi, TX		85
		Pair	1.00	
		P# strip of 3, P# 1	3.00	

NEWSPAPER

First issued in September, 1865, for prepayment of postage on bulk shipments of newspapers and periodicals. From 1875 on, the stamps were affixed to memorandums of mailing, cancelled and retained by the post office. Discontinued on July 1, 1898.

Washington — N1

Franklin — N2

Lincoln — N3

(Illustrations N1, N2 and N3 are half the size of the stamps.)

Printed by the National Bank Note Co.
Plates of 20 subjects in two panes of 10 each.
Typographed and Embossed

1865		Unwmk.		**Perf. 12**

Thin hard paper, without gum
Size of design: 51x95mm.
Colored Border

PR1	N1	5c **dark blue**	185.00	—
a.		5c light blue	200.00	—
		blue	175.00	—
		Block of four	850.00	—
PR2	N2	10c **blue green**	85.00	—
a.		10c green	85.00	—
		Block of four	400.00	—
b.		Pelure paper	90.00	—
PR3	N3	25c **orange red**	85.00	—
a.		25c carmine red	85.00	—
		Block of four	400.00	—
b.		Pelure paper	90.00	

White Border
Yellowish paper

PR4	N1	5c **light blue**	50.00	30.00
		blue	50.00	30.00
a.		5c dark blue	50.00	30.00
		Block of four	220.00	
b.		Pelure paper	55.00	—

REPRINTS OF 1865 ISSUE
Printed by the Continental Bank Note Co.

1875			**Perf. 12**

Hard white paper, without gum
5c White Border, 10c and 25c Colored Border

PR5	N1	5c **dull blue** (6395)	75.00
		dark blue	75.00
		Block of four	350.00
a.		Printed on both sides	—
PR6	N2	10c **dark bluish green** (8515)	60.00
		deep green	60.00
		Block of four	250.00
a.		Printed on both sides	1,500.
PR7	N3	25c **dark carmine** (7434)	80.00
		dark carmine red	80.00
		Block of four	350.00

Printed by the American Bank Note Co.
Soft porous paper
White Border

1880			
PR8	N1	5c **dark blue**	150.00
		Block of four	625.00

The Continental Bank Note Co. made another special printing from new plates, which did not have the colored border. These exist imperforate and perforated, but they were not regularly issued.

Statue of Freedom on Capitol Dome, by Thomas Crawford — N4

"Justice" — N5

Ceres — N6

"Victory" — N7

Clio — N8

Minerva — N9

Vesta — N10

"Peace" — N11

"Commerce" N12

Hebe — N13

The lack of a price for a listed item does not necessarily indicate rarity.

Indian Maiden — N14

Printed by the Continental Bank Note Co.
Plates of 100 subjects in two panes of 50 each.
Size of design: 24x35mm.

1875, Jan. 1 — Engr. — **Perf. 12**
Thin hard paper

PR9	N4	2c	black	12.50	11.00
			gray black	12.50	11.00
			greenish black	12.50	11.00
			Block of four	57.50	65.00
PR10	N4	3c	black	16.00	14.50
			gray black	16.00	14.50
			Block of four	70.00	65.00
PR11	N4	4c	black	14.00	12.50
			gray black	14.00	12.50
			greenish black	14.00	12.50
			Block of four	60.00	
PR12	N4	6c	black	18.00	17.00
			gray black	18.00	17.00
			greenish black	18.00	17.00
			Block of four	80.00	
PR13	N4	8c	black	25.00	22.50
			gray black	25.00	22.50
			greenish black	25.00	22.50
PR14	N4	9c	black	55.00	50.00
			gray black	55.00	50.00
			Double transfer at top	65.00	60.00
PR15	N4	10c	black	25.00	20.00
			gray black	25.00	20.00
			greenish black	25.00	20.00
			Block of four	120.00	
PR16	N5	12c	rose	55.00	40.00
			pale rose	55.00	40.00
PR17	N5	24c	rose	67.50	45.00
			pale rose	67.50	45.00
PR18	N5	36c	rose	72.50	50.00
			pale rose	72.50	50.00
PR19	N5	48c	rose	135.00	85.00
			pale rose	135.00	85.00
PR20	N5	60c	rose	65.00	45.00
			pale rose	65.00	45.00
PR21	N5	72c	rose	165.00	110.00
			pale rose	165.00	110.00
PR22	N5	84c	rose	250.00	135.00
			pale rose	250.00	135.00
PR23	N5	96c	rose	135.00	100.00
			pale rose	135.00	100.00
PR24	N6	$1.92	dark brown	185.00	125.00
PR25	N7	$3	vermilion	240.00	135.00
PR26	N8	$6	ultramarine	400.00	
			dull ultramarine	400.00	165.00
PR27	N9	$9	yellow	525.00	225.00
PR28	N10	$12	blue green	650.00	300.00
PR29	N11	$24	dark gray violet	650.00	325.00
PR30	N12	$36	brown rose	675.00	375.00
PR31	N13	$48	red brown	875.00	500.00
PR32	N14	$60	violet	875.00	425.00

Special Printing of 1875 Issue
Hard white paper, without gum

1875 — **Perf. 12**

PR33	N4	2c	gray black (19,514+)	70.00
			Horizontally ribbed paper	70.00
PR34	N4	3c	gray black (6952)	75.00
			Block of four	
			Horizontally ribbed paper	85.00
PR35	N4	4c	gray black (4451)	90.00
			Block of four	450.00
PR36	N4	6c	gray black (2348)	125.00
PR37	N4	8c	gray black (1930)	140.00
PR38	N4	9c	gray black (1795)	165.00
PR39	N4	10c	gray black (1499)	200.00
			Horizontally ribbed paper	220.00
PR40	N5	12c	pale rose (1313)	225.00
PR41	N5	24c	pale rose (411)	300.00
PR42	N5	36c	pale rose (330)	425.00
PR43	N5	48c	pale rose (268)	475.00
PR44	N5	60c	pale rose (222)	550.00
PR45	N5	72c	pale rose (174)	700.00
PR46	N5	84c	pale rose (164)	725.00
PR47	N5	96c	pale rose (141)	875.00
PR48	N6	$1.92	dark brown (41)	2,750.
PR49	N7	$3	vermilion (20)	5,750.
PR50	N8	$6	ultramarine (14)	6,750.
PR51	N9	$9	yellow (4)	13,500.
PR52	N10	$12	blue green (5)	12,500.
PR53	N11	$24	dark gray violet (2)	—

PR54	N12	$36	brown rose (2)	—
PR55	N13	$48	red brown (1)	—
PR56	N14	$60	violet (1)	—

All values of this issue, Nos. PR33 to PR56, exist imperforate but were not regularly issued.
Numbers in parenthesis are quantities issued.
+ This quantity may include the 1883 Re-issue.

Printed by the American Bank Note Co.
Soft porous paper

1879 — **Unwmk.** — **Perf. 12**

PR57	N4	2c	black	6.00	4.50
			gray black	6.00	4.50
			greenish black	6.00	4.50
			Block of four	27.50	
			Imperf., (pair)		
			Double transfer at top	8.50	8.50
			Cracked plate		
PR58	N4	3c	black	7.50	5.00
			gray black	7.50	5.00
			intense black	7.50	5.00
			Block of four	35.00	
			Imperf., (pair)		
			Double transfer at top	9.00	9.00
PR59	N4	4c	black	7.50	5.00
			gray black	7.50	5.00
			intense black	7.50	5.00
			greenish black	7.50	5.00
			Block of four	35.00	
			Imperf., (pair)		
			Double transfer at top	9.00	9.00
PR60	N4	6c	black	15.00	11.00
			gray black	15.00	11.00
			intense black	15.00	11.00
			greenish black	15.00	11.00
			Block of four	65.00	
			Imperf., (pair)		
			Double transfer at top	17.50	17.50
PR61	N4	8c	black	15.00	11.00
			gray black	15.00	11.00
			greenish black	15.00	11.00
			Block of four	65.00	
			Imperf., (pair)		
			Double transfer at top	17.50	15.00
PR62	N4	10c	black	15.00	11.00
			gray black	15.00	11.00
			greenish black	15.00	11.00
			Block of four	65.00	
			Imperf., (pair)		
			Double transfer at top	17.50	
PR63	N5	12c	red	45.00	25.00
			Block of four	200.00	
PR64	N5	24c	red	45.00	22.50
			Block of four	200.00	
PR65	N5	36c	red	150.00	95.00
			Block of four	650.00	
PR66	N5	48c	red	115.00	60.00
PR67	N5	60c	red	85.00	60.00
			Block of four	350.00	
a.		Imperf., (pair)		600.00	
PR68	N5	72c	red	185.00	115.00
PR69	N5	84c	red	140.00	85.00
			Block of four		
PR70	N5	96c	red	100.00	60.00
			Block of four	450.00	
PR71	N6	$1.92	pale brown	80.00	55.00
			brown	80.00	55.00
			Block of four	375.00	
			Cracked plate	125.00	
			Imperf., (pair)		
PR72	N7	$3	red vermilion	80.00	55.00
			Block of four	375.00	
			Imperf., (pair)		
PR73	N8	$6	blue	140.00	90.00
			ultramarine	140.00	90.00
			Imperf., (pair)		
PR74	N9	$9	orange	95.00	60.00
			Imperf., (pair)		
PR75	N10	$12	yellow green	140.00	85.00
			Imperf., (pair)		
PR76	N11	$24	dark violet	185.00	110.00
			Imperf., (pair)		
PR77	N12	$36	Indian red	225.00	135.00
			Imperf., (pair)		
PR78	N13	$48	yellow brown	300.00	165.00
			Imperf., (pair)		
PR79	N14	$60	purple	325.00	165.00
			bright purple	325.00	165.00
			Imperf., (pair)		

Imperforate stamps of this issue, except No. PR67a, were not regularly issued.

Special Printing of 1879 Issue

1883

PR80	N4	2c	intense black	175.00
			Block of four	700.00

Printed by the American Bank Note Co.

1885, July 1 — **Unwmk.** — **Perf. 12**

PR81	N4	1c	black	8.50	5.00
			gray black	8.50	5.00
			intense black	8.50	5.00
			Block of four	40.00	
			Imperf., (pair)		
			Double transfer at top	11.00	8.50
PR82	N5	12c	carmine	27.50	12.50
			deep carmine	27.50	12.50
			rose carmine	27.50	12.50
			Block of four	120.00	
			Imperf., (pair)		
PR83	N5	24c	carmine	30.00	15.00
			deep carmine	30.00	15.00
			rose carmine	30.00	15.00

			Block of four	130.00	
			Imperf, (pair)		
PR84	N5	36c	**carmine**	42.50	17.50
			deep carmine	42.50	17.50
			rose carmine	42.50	17.50
			Block of four	180.00	
			Imperf, (pair)		
PR85	N5	48c	**carmine**	60.00	30.00
			deep carmine	60.00	30.00
			Block of four	250.00	
			Imperf, (pair)		
PR86	N5	60c	**carmine**	85.00	40.00
			deep carmine	85.00	40.00
			Block of four	375.00	
			Imperf, (pair)		
PR87	N5	72c	**carmine**	95.00	45.00
			deep carmine	95.00	45.00
			rose carmine	95.00	45.00
			Block of four	425.00	
			Imperf, (pair)		
PR88	N5	84c	**carmine**	200.00	110.00
			rose carmine	200.00	110.00
			Block of four	825.00	
			Imperf, (pair)		
PR89	N5	96c	**carmine**	140.00	85.00
			rose carmine	140.00	85.00
			Block of four	600.00	
			Imperf, (pair)		

Imperforate stamps of the 1885 issue were not regularly issued.

Printed by the Bureau of Engraving and Printing

1894			**Unwmk.**	**Perf. 12**	
			Soft wove paper		
PR90	N4	1c	**intense black**	42.50	
			Block of four	185.00	
			Double transfer at top	52.50	
PR91	N4	2c	**intense black**	42.50	
			Block of four	185.00	
			Double transfer at top	52.50	
PR92	N4	4c	**intense black**	60.00	
			Block of four	275.00	
PP93	N4	6c	**intense black**	850.00	
			Block of four		
PR94	N4	10c	**intense black**	110.00	
			Block of four	500.00	
PR95	N5	12c	**pink**	450.00	—
			Block of four	2,000.	
PR96	N5	24c	**pink**	400.00	
			Block of four	1,750.	
PR97	N5	36c	**pink**	2,750.	
			Block of four		
PR98	N5	60c	**pink**	2,750.	—
			Block of four		
PR99	N5	96c	**pink**	4,000.	
PR100	N7	$3	**scarlet**	5,500.	
			Block of four		
PR101	N8	$6	**pale blue**	6,250.	3,000.

Statue of Freedom
on Capitol Dome, by
Thomas
Crawford — N15

"Justice" — N16

"Victory" N17

Clio — N18

Vesta — N19

"Peace" — N20

"Commerce" N21

Indian
Maiden
N22

1895, Feb. 1			**Unwmk.**	**Perf. 12**	
			Size of designs:		
			1c to 50c, 21x34 mm.		
			$2 to $100, 24x35 mm.		
PR102	N15	1c	**black**	25.00	7.50
			Block of four	105.00	32.50
PR103	N15	2c	**black**	25.00	7.50
			gray black	25.00	7.50
			Block of four	110.00	
			Double transfer at top	32.50	—
PR104	N15	5c	**black**	35.00	12.50
			gray black	35.00	12.50
			Block of four	150.00	
PR105	N15	10c	**black**	75.00	32.50
			Block of four	325.00	
PR106	N16	25c	**carmine**	100.00	35.00
			Block of four	425.00	
PR107	N16	50c	**carmine**	235.00	95.00
			Block of four	970.00	
PR108	N17	$2	**scarlet**	275.00	65.00
PR109	N18	$5	**ultramarine**	375.00	150.00
PR110	N19	$10	**green**	350.00	165.00
PR111	N20	$20	**slate**	675.00	300.00
PR112	N21	$50	**dull rose**	700.00	300.00
PR113	N22	$100	**purple**	775.00	350.00

1895-97			**Wmk. 191**	**Perf. 12**	
PR114	N15	1c	**black,** *Jan. 11, 1896*	3.50	3.00
			gray black	3.50	3.00
			Block of four	15.00	
PR115	N15	2c	**black,** *Nov. 21, 1895*	4.00	3.50
			gray black	4.00	3.50
			Block of four	17.50	
PR116	N15	5c	**black,** *Feb. 12, 1896*	6.00	5.00
			gray black	6.00	5.00
			Block of four	25.00	
PR117	N15	10c	**black,** *Sept. 13, 1895*	4.00	3.50
			gray black	4.00	3.50
			Block of four	18.00	
PR118	N16	25c	**carmine,** *Oct. 11, 1895*	8.00	8.00
			lilac rose	8.00	8.00
			Block of four	35.00	
PR119	N16	50c	**carmine,** *Sept. 19, 1895*	10.00	12.50
			rose carmine	10.00	12.50
			lilac rose	10.00	12.50
			Block of four	45.00	
PR120	N17	$2	**scarlet,** *Jan. 23, 1897*	12.00	15.00
			scarlet vermilion	12.00	15.00
			Block of four	55.00	
PR121	N18	$5	**dark blue,** *Jan. 16, 1896*	20.00	25.00
a.		$5	**light blue**	100.00	45.00
			Block of four	85.00	
PR122	N19	$10	**green,** *Mar. 5, 1896*	18.00	25.00
			Block of four	75.00	
PR123	N20	$20	**slate,** *Jan. 27, 1896*	20.00	27.50
			Block of four	82.50	
PR124	N21	$50	**dull rose,** *July 31, 1897*	25.00	30.00
			Block of four	105.00	

PR125 N22 $100 **purple**, *Jan. 23, 1896*   30.00 37.50
     Block of four   130.00

Nos. PR102-PR125 were printed from plates with guide lines and arrows both vertical and horizontal.

In 1899 the Government sold 26,989 sets of these stamps, but, as the stock of high values was not sufficient to make up the required number, an additional printing was made of the $5, $10, $20, $50 and $100. These are virtually indistinguishable from earlier printings.

The use of newspaper and periodical stamps was discontinued on July 1, 1898.

POSTAL NOTE

Postal notes were issued in amounts up to $10 to supplement the regular money order service. Postal note stamps were affixed and cancelled by the clerk to make up fractions of a dollar. They were discontinued March 31, 1951.

UNITED STATES OF AMERICA — POSTAL NOTE — 1 CENT — MO1

ROTARY PRESS PRINTING

1945, Feb. 1   Unwmk.   *Perf. 11x10½*

PN1	MO1	1c **black**	10	5
PN2	MO1	2c **black**	15	5
PN3	MO1	3c **black**	20	5
PN4	MO1	4c **black**	25	5
PN5	MO1	5c **black**	35	5
PN6	MO1	6c **black**	40	5
PN7	MO1	7c **black**	50	5
PN8	MO1	8c **black**	65	5
PN9	MO1	9c **black**	70	5
PN10	MO1	10c **black**	85	5
PN11	MO1	20c **black**	1.65	5
PN12	MO1	30c **black**	2.25	5
PN13	MO1	40c **black**	2.75	6
PN14	MO1	50c **black**	3.25	5
PN15	MO1	60c **black**	4.50	5
PN16	MO1	70c **black**	5.00	5
PN17	MO1	80c **black**	6.00	8
PN18	MO1	90c **black**	6.50	8

Blocks of four and plate number blocks of four are priced at 4 and 15 times the unused single price.

Postal note stamps exist on postal note cards with first day cancellation.

Plate Nos.:

1c	155950-51
2c	156003-04
3c	156062-63
4c	155942-43
5c	156261-62
6c	156064-65
7c	156075-76
8c	156077-78
9c	156251-52
10c	156274-75
20c	156276-77
30c	156303-04
40c	156283-84
50c	156322-23
60c	156324-25
70c	156344-45
80c	156326-27
90c	156352-53

PARCEL POST

The Act of Congress approved Aug. 24, 1912, created postage rates on fourth-class mail weighing 4 ounces or less at 1 cent per ounce or fraction. On mail over 4 ounces, the rate was by the pound. These rates were to be prepaid by distinctive postage stamps. Under this provision, the Post Office Dept. prepared 12 parcel post and 5 parcel post due stamps, usable only on parcel post packages starting Jan. 1, 1913.

With the approval of the Interstate Commerce Commission, the Postmaster General directed, in Order No. 7241 dated June 26, 1913, and effective July 1, 1913, that regular postage stamps should be valid on parcels. Parcel post stamps then became usable as regular stamps.

Parcel post and parcel post due stamps remained on sale, but no further printings were made. Remainders, consisting of 3,510,345 of the 75c, were destroyed in September, 1921.

The 20c was the first postage stamp of any country to show an airplane.

Post Office Clerk — PP1

City Carrier — PP2

Railway Postal Clerk — PP3

Rural Carrier — PP4

Mail Train and Mail Bag on Rack — PP5

Steamship "Kronprinz Wilhelm" and Mail Tender, New York — PP6

Automobile Service — PP7

Airplane Carrying Mail — PP8

Manufacturing (Steel Plant, South Chicago) — PP9

Dairying — PP10

Harvesting — PP11

Fruit Growing (Florida Orange Grove) — PP12

TEN

6161

Plate number and imprint consisting of value in words.

Marginal imprints, consisting of value in words, were added to the plates on January 27, 1913. Plates of 180 subjects in four panes of 45 each.

1913   Wmk. 190   Engr.   Perf. 12

Q1	PP1	1c **carmine rose** (209,691,094)	4.00	90
		carmine	4.00	90
		First day cover, *July 1, 1913*		1,500.
		On cover, 1913-25		5.00
		Block of four	16.50	5.00
		Margin block of 4, Impt. & P#	30.00	
		Margin block of 6, Impt. & P#	85.00	
		Margin block of 6, P# only	95.00	
		Double transfer	9.00	3.00
Q2	PP2	2c **carmine rose** (206,417,253)	4.50	70
		carmine	4.50	70
		lake	—	
		First day cover, *July 1, 1913*		1,500.
		On cover, 1913-25		5.00
		Block of four	18.50	3.50
		Margin block of 4, Impt. & P#	35.00	
		Margin block of 6, Impt. & P#	95.00	
		Margin block of 6, P# only	115.00	
		Double transfer	—	
Q3	PP3	3c **carmine,** *Apr. 5, 1913* (29,027,433)	10.00	5.00
		deep carmine	10.00	5.00
		First day cover, *July 1, 1913*		3,000.
		On cover, 1913-25		17.50
		Block of four	40.00	25.00
		Margin block of 4, Impt. & P#	65.00	
		Margin block of 6, Impt. & P#	185.00	
		Margin block of 6, P# only	175.00	
		Margin block of 8, Impt. & P# (side)	225.00	
		Retouched at lower right corner (No. 6257 LL 7)	25.00	12.50
		Double transfer (No. 6257 LL 6)	25.00	12.50
Q4	PP4	4c **carmine rose** (76,743,813)	25.00	2.00
		carmine	25.00	2.00
		First day cover, *July 1, 1913*		3,000.
		On cover, 1913-25		60.00
		Block of four	105.00	
		Margin block of 4, Impt. & P#	250.00	
		Margin block of 6, Impt. & P#	775.00	
		Margin block of 6, P# only	750.00	
		Double transfer	—	—
Q5	PP5	5c **carmine rose** (108,153,993)	25.00	1.25
		carmine	25.00	1.25
		First day cover, *July 1, 1913*		3,000.
		On cover, 1913-25		40.00
		Block of four	105.00	10.00
		Margin block of 4, Impt. & P#	250.00	
		Margin block of 6, Impt. & P#	775.00	
		Margin block of 6, P# only	750.00	
		Double transfer	50.00	5.00
Q6	PP6	10c **carmine rose** (56,896,653)	40.00	1.75
		carmine	40.00	1.75
		On cover, 1913-25		50.00
		Block of four	165.00	20.00
		Margin block of 4, Impt. & P#	300.00	
		Margin block of 6, Impt. & P#	1,000.00	
		Margin block of 6, P# only	950.00	—
		Double transfer	—	
Q7	PP7	15c **carmine rose** (21,147,033)	65.00	9.00
		carmine	65.00	9.00
		First day cover, *July 1, 1913*		—
		On cover, 1913-25		350.00
		Block of four	265.00	60.00
		Margin block of 4, Impt. & P#	500.00	
		Margin block of 6, Impt. & P#	2,100.00	
		Margin block of 8, Impt. & P#	2,650.00	
		Margin block of 6, P# only	2,000.00	
Q8	PP8	20c **carmine rose** (17,142,393)	140.00	17.50
		carmine	140.00	17.50
		On cover, 1913-25		750.00
		Block of four	575.00	100.00
		Margin block of 4, Impt. & P#	1,050.00	
		Margin block of 6, Impt. & P#	5,750.	
		Margin block of 8, Impt. & P# (side)	6,250.	
		Margin block of 6, P# only	5,750.	
Q9	PP9	25c **carmine rose** (21,940,653)	80.00	4.50
		carmine	80.00	4.50
		On cover, 1913-25		300.00
		Block of four	325.00	35.00
		Margin block of 6, Impt. & P#	2,500.	
		Margin block of 8, Impt. & P# (side)	3,000.	
		Margin block of 6, P# only	2,350.	
Q10	PP10	50c **carmine rose,** *Mar. 15, 1913* (2,117,793)	210.00	35.00
		carmine	210.00	35.00
		On cover, 1913-25		
		Block of four	850.00	200.00
		Margin block of 4, Impt. & P#	1,500.	
		Margin block of 6, Impt. & P#	13,500.	
Q11	PP11	75c **carmine rose** (2,772,615)	80.00	30.00
		carmine	80.00	30.00
		On cover, 1913-25		
		Block of four	325.00	140.00
		Margin block of 6, Impt. & P#	3,000.	
		Margin block of 8, Impt. & P# (side)	3,500.	
		Margin block of 6, P# only	2,900.	
Q12	PP12	$1 **carmine rose,** *Jan. 3, 1913* (1,053,273)	400.00	20.00
		carmine	400.00	20.00
		On cover, 1913-25		1,100.00
		Block of four	1,650.00	100.00
		Margin block of 6, Impt. & P#	16,000.	
		Margin block of 8, Impt. & P# (side)	17,500.	
		Margin block of 6, P# only	16,000.	

The 1, 2, 4 and 5c are known in parcel post usage postmarked Jan. 1, 1913.

P.P. POSTAGE DUE

Parcel Post Due stamps were prepared in conformity with the Act of Congress, approved August 24, 1912, at the same time the Parcel Post stamps were issued. (See note over Q1).

PPD1

Plates of 180 subjects in four panes of 45.

1912   Wmk. 190   Engr.   Perf. 12

JQ1	PPD1	1c **dark green,** *Nov. 27, 1912* (7,322,400)	9.00	3.00
		yellowish green	9.00	3.00
		On cover, 1913-25		150.00
		Block of four	36.50	20.00
		Margin block of 6, P#	550.00	
JQ2	PPD1	2c **dark green,** *Dec. 9, 1912* (3,132,000)	80.00	15.00
		yellowish green	80.00	15.00
		On cover, 1913-25		200.00
		Block of four	325.00	85.00
		Margin block of 6, P#	2,750.	
JQ3	PPD1	5c **dark green,** *Nov. 27, 1912* (5,840,100)	11.50	3.50
		yellowish green	11.50	3.50
		On cover, 1913-25		185.00
		Block of four	47.50	20.00
		Margin block of 6, P#	675.00	
JQ4	PPD1	10c **dark green,** *Dec. 12, 1912* (2,124,540)	150.00	35.00
		yellowish green	150.00	35.00
		On cover, 1913-25		650.00
		Block of four	625.00	200.00
		Margin block of 6, P#	6,750.	
JQ5	PPD1	25c **dark green,** *Dec. 16, 1912* (2,117,700)	85.00	3.50
		yellowish green	85.00	3.50
		On cover, 1913-25		
		Block of four	350.00	20.00
		Margin block of 6, P#	3,000.	

> *United States Parcel Post Postage Due stamps can be mounted in Scott's National and Minuteman Albums.*

SPECIAL HANDLING

The Postal Service Act, approved February 28, 1925, provided for a special handling stamp of the 25 cent denomination for use on fourth-class mail matter, which would secure for such mail matter the expeditious handling accorded to mail matter of the first class.

PP13

FLAT PLATE PRINTING
Plates of 200 subjects in four panes of 50

1925-29		Unwmk.		Perf. 11
QE1	PP13	10c **yellow green**	1.50	90
		First day cover		55.00
		Block of four	6.00	5.00
		Margin block of 6, P# only	25.00	
a.		Wet printing, *June 25, 1928*	3.00	90
QE2	PP13	15c **yellow green**	1.65	90
		First day cover		55.00
		Block of four	6.60	5.00
		Margin block of 6, P# only	35.00	
a.		Wet printing, *June 25, 1928*	3.00	90
QE3	PP13	20c **yellow green**	2.00	1.75
		First day cover		55.00
		Block of four	8.00	9.00
		Margin block of 6, P# only	40.00	
a.		Wet printing, *June 25, 1928*	3.00	1.75
QE4	PP13	25c **yellow green** ('29)	20.00	7.50
		Block of four	80.00	35.00
		Margin block of 6, P# only	240.00	
a.		25c **deep green**, *Apr. 11, 1925*	25.00	4.50
a.		First day cover		225.00
a.		Block of four	100.00	25.00
a.		Margin block of 6, P# only	325.00	
		"A" and "T" of "States" joined at top (Pl. 17103)	45.00	20.00
		"A" and "T" of "States" and "T" and "A" of "Postage" joined at top (Pl. 17103)	45.00	45.00

See note on Wet and Dry Printings following No. 1029.

POSTAL INSURANCE

Postal insurance labels were issued to pay insurance on parcels for loss or damage. The label comes in a booklet of one which also carries instructions for use and a receipt form for possible claim. The booklets were sold by vending machine.

PPI1

1965, Aug. **Typo.** ***Rouletted 9 at Top***
QI1 PPI1 (10c) **dark red** 120.00 —

No. QI1 paid insurance up to $10. It was sold at the Canoga Park, Calif., automatic post office which opened Aug. 19, 1965. The "V" stands for "Vended."

PPI2

1966, March 26 **Litho.** ***Perf. 11 at Top***
QI2 PPI2 (20c) **red** 75 —

No. QI2 paid insurance up to $15. The rate increased from 20c to 25c on Apr. 18, 1976, and to 40c on July 18, 1976.
No 25c labels were printed. Existing copies of No. QI2 had 5c stamps added and the value on the cover was changed to 25c, usually by hand. Twenty-cent stamps were added to make the 40c rate since new labels were not issued until 1978.

POSTMARK OF

MAILING OFFICE

PPI3

FEE PAID THROUGH
VENDING MACHINE

1978-81 **Litho.** ***Perf. 11 at Top***
QI3 PPI3 (40c) **black** 80 —
QI4 PPI3 (50c) **green** 1.00 —

The rate increased to 50c on May 29, 1978.

QI5 PPI3 (45c) **red**, *1981* 90 —

FIRST DAY COVERS

All envelopes or cards are postmarked Washington, D.C., unless otherwise stated.

Prices are for covers bearing single stamps. Blocks of 4 on first day covers usually sell for about 1½ the price for singles; Plate Number blocks of 4 at about 3 times; Plate Number blocks of 6 at about 4 times; coil line pairs at about 3 times.

Dates given are those on which the stamps were first *officially* placed on sale. Instances are known of stamps being sold in advance, contrary to regulations.

Numbers in parentheses are quantities canceled on first day.

Listings since 1922 are all exclusively for covers canceled at cities officially designated by the Post Office Department or Postal Service. Some tagged varieties are exceptions.

Airmail first day covers are listed in the Air Post section of this catalogue. Booklet pane first day covers are listed in the Booklet Panes section.

Printed cachets on covers before No. 772 sell at a substantial premium. Prices for covers from No. 772 and C20 onward are for those with the most common cachets and addressed. Unaddressed covers command a premium. Those without cachets sell at a substantial discount.

1851-57

5A	1c	blue, type Ib, *July 1, 1851,* Boston, Mass.	18,500.
7	1c	blue, type II, *July 1, 1851, any city*	13,000.
		same on printed circular	2,500.
10	3c	orange brown, *July 1, 1851, any city*	7,500.

1883

210	2c	red brown, *Oct. 1, 1883, any city*	2,000.
211	4c	blue green, *Oct. 1, 1883, any city*	8,500.
		210 to 211 on one cover	10,000.

1890

219D	2c	lake, *Feb. 22, 1890, any city*	14,500.

1893

COLUMBIAN EXPOSITION ISSUE

230	1c	deep blue, *Jan. 2, 1893, any city*	3,500.
231	2c	brown violet, *Jan. 2, 1893, any city*	2,600.
232	3c	green, *Jan. 2, 1893, any city*	6,000.
233	4c	ultramarine, *Jan. 2, 1893, any city*	6,000.
234	5c	chocolate, *Jan. 2, 1893, any city*	6,250.
235	6c	purple, *Jan. 2, 1893, any city*	6,750.
237	10c	black brown, *Jan. 2, 1893, any city*	7,500.
242	$2	brown red, *Jan. 2, 1893, any city*	18,000.

Jan. 1, 1893, postmarks are known on the Columbian issue. As that day was a Sunday, specialists recognize both Jan. 1 and 2 as "first day."

1898

TRANS-MISSISSIPPI EXPOSITION ISSUE

285	1c	green, *June 17, 1898, any city*	4,500.
286	2c	copper red, *June 17, 1898, any city*	4,000.
288	5c	dull blue, *June 17, 1898, any city*	5,000.
289	8c	violet brown, *June 17, 1898, any city*	7,500.
		285 to 290, all six on one cover, June 17, 1898, any city	13,000.
291	50c	sage green, *June 17, 1898, any city*	9,000.
292	$1	black, *June 17, 1898, any city*	12,500.

1901

PAN AMERICAN EXPOSITION ISSUE

294	1c	green & black, *May 1, 1901, any city*	3,750.
295	2c	carmine & black, *May 1, 1901, any city*	3,250.
296	4c	deep red brown & black, *May 1, 1901*	4,250.
297	5c	ultra. & blk., *May 1, 1901, any city*	450.00
		294 to 299, Complete set of six on one cover *May 1, 1901, any city*	10,000.

1903

301	2c	carmine, *Jan. 17, 1903, any city*	2,750.

1904

LOUISIANA PURCHASE EXPOSITION ISSUE

323	1c	green, *Apr. 30, 1904, any city*	3,000.
324	2c	carmine, *Apr. 30, 1904, any city*	2,750.
325	3c	violet, *Apr. 30, 1904, any city*	3,750.
326	5c	dark blue, *Apr. 30, 1904, any city*	5,500.
327	10c	red brown, *Apr. 30, 1904, any city*	8,500.
		323 to 327, all five on one cover, *Apr. 30, 1904, any city*	12,500.

1907

JAMESTOWN EXPOSITION ISSUE

328	1c	green, *Apr. 26, 1907, any city*	375.00
329	2c	carmine, *Apr. 26, 1907, any city*	5,500.

1909

LINCOLN ISSUE

367	2c	carmine, *Feb. 12, 1909, any city*	350.00

Imperf

368	2c	carmine, *Feb. 12, 1909, any city*	5,000.

1909

ALASKA-YUKON ISSUE

370	2c	carmine, *June 1, 1909, any city*	1,800.

1909

HUDSON-FULTON ISSUE

372	2c	carmine, *Sept. 25, 1909, any city*	900.00

Imperf

373	2c	carmine, *Sept. 25, 1909, any city*	2,000.

1913

PANAMA-PACIFIC ISSUE

397	1c	green, *Jan. 1, 1913, any city*	3,250.
399	5c	blue, *Jan. 1, 1913*	4,000.
400	10c	orange yellow, *Jan. 1, 1913*	
		397, 399 & 400, all 3 on one cover, San Francisco	5,000.

1916-22

COIL STAMP

497	10c	orange yellow, *Jan. 31, 1922, any city*	2,000.

1918-20

OFFSET PRINTING

526	2c	carmine, type IV, *Mar. 15, 1920*	950.00

1919

VICTORY ISSUE

537	3c	violet, *Mar. 3, 1919, any city*	750.00

1920

REGULAR ISSUE

Perf. 10x11

542	1c	green, *May 26, 1920*	950.00

1920

PILGRIM TERCENTENARY ISSUE

548	1c	green, *Dec. 21, 1920, any city*	800.00
549	2c	carmine rose, *Dec. 21, 1920, any city*	650.00
		Plymouth, Mass.	900.00
		548 to 550, Complete set of three on one cover, *Dec. 21, 1920, any city*	2,500.
		Washington, D.C.	3,000.

1922-26

Perf. 11

551	½c	Hale, *April 4, 1925,* (Block of 4)	25.00
		New Haven, Conn.	35.00
552	1c	Franklin, *Jan. 17, 1923*	35.00
		Philadelphia, Pa.	65.00
553	1½c	Harding, *Mar. 19, 1925*	35.00
554	2c	Washington, *Jan. 15, 1923*	45.00
555	3c	Lincoln, *Feb. 12, 1923*	37.50
		Hodgenville, Ky.	275.00
556	4c	Martha Washington, *Jan. 15, 1923*	50.00
557	5c	Roosevelt, *Oct. 27, 1922*	150.00
		New York, N.Y.	250.00
		Oyster Bay, N.Y.	675.00
558	6c	Garfield, *Nov. 20, 1922*	225.00
559	7c	McKinley, *May 1, 1923*	125.00
		Niles, O.	200.00
560	8c	Grant, *May 1, 1923*	125.00
561	9c	Jefferson, *Jan. 15, 1923*	125.00
562	10c	Monroe, *Jan. 15, 1923*	140.00
563	11c	Hayes, *Oct. 4, 1922*	550.00
		Fremont, O.	1,200.
564	12c	Cleveland, *Mar. 20, 1923*	175.00
		Boston, Mass. (Philatelic Exhibition)	175.00
		Caldwell, N.J.	200.00
565	14c	Indian, *May 1, 1923*	350.00
		Muskogee, Okla.	1,100.
566	15c	Statue of Liberty, *Nov. 11, 1922*	400.00
567	20c	Golden Gate, *May 1, 1923*	400.00
		San Francisco, Cal.	1,200.
568	25c	Niagara Falls, *Nov. 11, 1922*	625.00
569	30c	Bison, *Mar. 20, 1923*	750.00
570	50c	Arlington, *Nov. 11, 1922*	1,100.
571	$1	Lincoln Memorial, *Feb. 12, 1923*	4,500.
		Springfield, Ill.	5,500.

572	$2	U.S. Capitol, *Mar. 20, 1923*	10,000.
573	$5	America, *Mar. 20, 1923*	14,000.

Imperf

576	1½c	Harding, *April 4, 1925*	45.00

Perf. 10

581	1c	Franklin, *Oct. 17, 1923,* not pre-canceled	2,000.
582	1½c	Harding, *May 19, 1925*	47.50
584	3c	Lincoln, *Aug. 1, 1925*	55.00
585	4c	Martha Washington, *Apr. 4, 1925*	55.00
586	5c	Roosevelt, *April 4, 1925*	60.00
587	6c	Garfield, *April 4, 1925*	70.00
588	7c	McKinley, *May 29, 1926*	72.50
589	8c	Grant, *May 29, 1926*	75.00
590	9c	Jefferson, *May 29, 1926*	77.50
591	10c	Monroe, *June 8, 1925*	100.00

ROTARY PRESS COIL STAMPS

Perf. 10 Vertically

597	1c	Franklin, *July 18, 1923*	550.00
598	1½c	Harding, *Mar. 19, 1925*	55.00
599	2c	Washington, *Jan. 15, 1923*	850.00
600	3c	Lincoln, *May 10, 1924*	77.50
602	5c	Roosevelt, *Mar. 5, 1924*	82.50
603	10c	Monroe, *Dec. 1, 1924*	100.00

Perf. 10 Horizontally

604	1c	Franklin, *July 19, 1924*	100.00
605	1½c	Harding, *May 9, 1925*	70.00
606	2c	Washington, *Dec. 31, 1923*	125.00

1923

610	2c	Harding, *Sept. 1, 1923* (Perf. 11)	40.00
		Marion, O.	22.50
611	2c	Harding, *Nov. 15, 1923* (Imperf.)	100.00
612	2c	Harding, *Sept. 12, 1923* (Perf. 10)	110.00

1924

Perf. 11

614	1c	Huguenot—Walloon, *May 1, 1924*	
		Albany, N.Y.	
		Allentown, Pa.	
		Charleston, S.C.	
		Jacksonville, Fla.	
		Lancaster, Pa.	
		Mayport, Fla.	
		New Rochelle, N.Y.	
		New York, N.Y.	
		Philadelphia, Pa.	
		Reading, Pa.	@32.50
615	2c	Huguenot—Walloon, *May 1, 1924*	
		Albany, N.Y.	
		Allentown, Pa.	
		Charleston, S.C.	
		Jacksonville, Fla.	
		Lancaster, Pa.	
		Mayport, Fla.	
		New Rochelle, N.Y.	
		New York, N.Y.	
		Philadelphia, Pa.	
		Reading, Pa.	@37.50
616	5c	Huguenot—Walloon, *May 1, 1924*	
		Albany, N.Y.	
		Allentown, Pa.	
		Charleston, S.C.	
		Jacksonville, Fla.	
		Lancaster, Pa.	
		Mayport, Fla.	
		New Rochelle, N.Y.	
		New York, N.Y.	
		Philadelphia, Pa.	
		Reading, Pa.	@70.00
		614 to 616, set of three on one cover, *any city*	150.00

1925

617	1c	Lexington—Concord, *April 4, 1925*	32.50
		Boston, Mass.	32.50
		Cambridge, Mass.	32.50
		Concord, Mass.	37.50
		Concord Junction, Mass.	37.50
		Lexington, Mass.	37.50
618	2c	Lexington—Concord, *April 4, 1925*	37.50
		Boston, Mass.	37.50
		Cambridge, Mass.	37.50
		Concord, Mass	37.50
		Concord Junction, Mass.	37.50
		Lexington, Mass.	50.00

619	5c	Lexington—Concord, *April 4, 1925*	65.00
		Boston, Mass.	80.00
		Combridge, Mass.	80.00
		Concord, Mass.	80.00
		Concord Junction, Mass.	80.00
		Lexington, Mass.	80.00
		617 to 619, set of three on one cover, Concord Junction, Mass., or Lexington, Mass.	175.00
		Set of three on one cover, any other city	130.00

1925

620	2c	Norse—American, *May 18, 1925*	
		Algona, Iowa	
		Benson, Minn.	
		Decorah, Iowa	
		Minneapolis, Minn.	
		Northfield, Minn.	
		St. Paul, Minn.	@27.50
621	5c	Norse—American, *May 18, 1925*	
		Algona, Iowa	
		Benson, Minn.	
		Decorah, Iowa	
		Minneapolis, Minn.	
		Northfield, Minn.	
		St. Paul, Minn.	@47.50
		620 and 621, set of two on one cover, *any city*	72.50

1925-26

622	13c	Harrison, *Jan. 11, 1926*	35.00
		Indianapolis, Ind.	47.50
		North Bend, Ohio *(500)*	300.00
623	17c	Wilson, *Dec. 28, 1925*	
		New York, N.Y.	
		Princeton, N.J.	
		Staunton, Va.	@30.00

1926

627	2c	Sesquicentennial, *May 10, 1926*	
		Boston, Mass.	
		Philadelphia, Pa.	@15.00
628	5c	Ericsson, *May 29, 1926*	
		Chicago, Ill.	
		Minneapolis, Minn.	
		New York, N.Y.	@22.50
629	2c	White Plains, New York, N.Y., *Oct. 18, 1926*	6.25
		New York, N.Y., Inter—Philatelic Exhibition Agency cancellation	6.25
		White Plains, N.Y.	6.25
		Washington, D.C., *Oct. 28, 1926*	3.50
630		Sheet of 25, *Oct. 18, 1926*	1,400.
		Sheet of 25, *Oct. 28, 1926*	600.00

1926-34 — *Imperf.*

631	1½c	Harding, *Aug. 27, 1926*	35.00

Perf. 11x10½

632	1c	Franklin, *June 10, 1927*	55.00
633	1½c	Harding, *May 17, 1927*	55.00
634	2c	Washington, *Dec. 10, 1926*	57.50
635	3c	Lincoln, *Feb. 3, 1927*	47.50
635a	3c	bright violet, *Feb. 7, 1934*	25.00
636	4c	Martha Washington, *May 17, 1927*	55.00
637	5c	Roosevelt, *Mar. 24, 1927*	55.00
638	6c	Garfield, *July 27, 1927*	65.00
639	7c	McKinley, *Mar. 24, 1927*	67.50
640	8c	Grant, *June 10, 1927*	70.00
641	9c	Jefferson, *May 17, 1927*	85.00
642	10c	Monroe, *Feb. 3, 1927*	90.00

1927 — *Perf. 11*

643	2c	Vermont, *Aug. 3, 1927*	
		Bennington, Vt.	@7.00
644	2c	Burgoyne, *Aug. 3, 1927*	
		Albany, N.Y.	
		Rome, N.Y.	
		Syracuse, N.Y.	
		Utica, N.Y.	@17.50

1928

645	2c	Valley Forge, *May 26, 1928*	6.00
		Cleveland, O.	60.00
		Lancaster, Pa.	6.00
		Norristown, Pa.	6.00
		Philadelphia, Pa.	6.00
		Valley Forge, Pa.	6.00
		West Chester, Pa.	6.00
		Cleveland, Midwestern Philatelic Sta. cancellation	6.00

Perf. 11x10½

646	2c	Molly Pitcher, *Oct. 20, 1928*	
		Freehold, N.J.	
		Red Bank, N.J.	@22.50

1928 — *Perf. 11x10½*

647	2c	Hawaii, *Aug. 13, 1928*	17.50
		Honolulu, Hawaii	22.50
648	5c	Hawaii, *Aug. 13, 1928*	32.50
		Honolulu, Hawaii	40.00
		647 and 648, set of two on one cover	60.00

Perf. 11

649	2c	Aero Conf., *Dec. 12, 1928*	12.50
650	5c	Aero Conf., *Dec. 12, 1928*	17.50
		649 and 650, set of two on one cover	27.50

1929

651	2c	**Clark,** Vincennes, Indiana, *Feb. 25, 1929*	10.00
		Washington, *Feb. 26, 1929,* first day of sale by Philatelic Agency	3.00
		Charlottesville, Va., *Feb. 26, 1929*	7.50
		Perf. 11x10 ½	
653	½c	**olive brown,** *May 25, 1929* (Block of Four)	30.00
		Perf. 11	
654	2c	**Electric Light,** Menlo Park, N.J., *June 5, 1929*	15.00
		Washington, *June 6, 1929,* first day of sale by Philatelic Agency	6.00
		Perf. 11x10 ½	
655	2c	**Electric Light,** *June 11, 1929*	90.00
		Perf. 10 Vertically	
656	2c	**Electric Light,** *June 11, 1929*	100.00
		Perf. 11 Vertically	
657	2c	**Sullivan,** Auburn, N.Y., *June 17, 1929*	
		Binghamton, N.Y.	
		Canajoharie, N.Y.	
		Canandaigua, N.Y.	
		Elmira, N.Y.	
		Geneva, N.Y.	
		Geneseo, N.Y.	
		Horseheads, N.Y.	
		Owego, N.Y.	
		Penn Yan, N.Y	
		Perry, N.Y.	
		Seneca Falls, N.Y.	
		Waterloo, N.Y.	
		Watkins Glen, N.Y.	
		Waverly, N.Y.	@5.00
		Washington, D.C., *June 18, 1929*	2.00

1929

KANSAS AND NEBRASKA

658	1c	**Kansas,** *May 1, 1929*	27.50
		Newton, Kan., *April 15, 1929*	200.00
659	1½c	**Kansas,** *May 1, 1929*	27.50
		Colby, Kan., *April 16, 1929*	—
660	2c	**Kansas,** *May 1, 1929*	27.50
		Colby, Kan., *April 16, 1929*	—
661	3c	**Kansas,** *May 1, 1929*	30.00
		Colby, Kan., *April 16, 1929*	—
662	4c	**Kansas,** *May 1, 1929*	32.50
		Colby, Kan., *April 16, 1929*	—
663	5c	**Kansas,** *May 1, 1929*	35.00
		Colby, Kan., *April 16, 1929*	—
664	6c	**Kansas,** *May 1, 1929*	42.50
		Newton, Kan., *April 15, 1929*	350.00
665	7c	**Kansas,** *May 1, 1929*	42.50
		Colby, Kan., *April 16, 1929*	—
666	8c	**Kansas,** *May 1, 1929*	80.00
		Newton, Kan., *April 15, 1929*	350.00
667	9c	**Kansas,** *May 1, 1929*	72.50
		Colby, Kan., *April 16, 1929*	—
668	10c	**Kansas,** *May 1, 1929*	85.00
		Colby, Kan., *April 16, 1929*	—
		658 to 668, set of eleven on one cover, Washington, D.C., *May 1, 1929*	950.00
669	1c	**Nebraska,** *May 1, 1929*	27.50
		Beatrice, Neb., *April 15, 1929*	—
670	1½c	**Nebraska,** *May 1, 1929*	25.00
		Hartington, Neb., *April 15, 1929*	160.00
671	2c	**Nebraska,** *May 1, 1929*	25.00
		Auburn, Neb., *April 15, 1929*	—
		Beatrice, Neb., *April 15, 1929*	—
		Hartington, Neb., *April 15, 1929*	160.00
672	3c	**Nebraska,** *May 1, 1929*	32.50
		Beatrice, Neb., *April 15, 1929*	175.00
		Hartington, Neb., *April 15, 1929*	175.00
673	4c	**Nebraska,** *May 1, 1929*	37.50
		Beatrice, Neb., *April 15, 1929*	175.00
		Hartington, Neb., *April 15, 1929*	175.00
674	5c	**Nebraska,** *May 1, 1929*	37.50
		Beatrice, Neb., *April 15, 1929*	175.00
		Hartington, Neb., *April 15, 1929*	175.00
675	6c	**Nebraska,** *May 1, 1929*	55.00
		Ravenna, Neb., *April 17, 1929*	—
		Wahoo, Neb., *April 17, 1929*	—
676	7c	**Nebraska,** *May 1, 1929*	57.50
		Auburn, Neb., *April 17, 1929*	—
677	8c	**Nebraska,** *May 1, 1929*	60.00
		Humbolt, Neb., *April 17, 1929*	—
		Pawnee City, Neb., *April 17, 1929*	—
678	9c	**Nebraska,** *May 1, 1929*	62.50
		Cambridge, Neb., *April 17, 1929*	—
679	10c	**Nebraska,** *May 1, 1929*	70.00
		Tecumseh, Neb., *April 18, 1929*	—
		669 to 679, set of eleven on one cover, Washington, D.C., *May 1, 1929*	950.00
		Perf. 11	
680	2c	**Fallen Timbers,** Erie, Pa., *Sept. 14, 1929*	
		Maumee, O.	
		Perrysburg, O.	
		Toledo, O.	
		Waterville, O.	
		Washington, D.C., *Sept. 16, 1929*	@5.00
681	2c	**Ohio River,** Cairo, Ill., *Oct. 19, 1929*	
		Cincinnati, O.	
		Evansville, Ind.	
		Homestead, Pa.	
		Louisville, Ky.	
		Pittsburgh, Pa.	
		Wheeling, W. Va.	

| | | Washington, D.C., *Oct. 21, 1929* | @4.50 |

1930

682	2c	**Massachusetts Bay Colony,** Boston, Mass. *April 8, 1930* (60,000)	5.25
		Salem, Mass.	5.25
		Washington, D.C., *April 11, 1930*	2.00
683	2c	**Carolina—Charleston,** Charleston, S.C. *April 10, 1930*	5.50
		Washington, D.C., *April 11, 1930*	2.00
		Perf. 11x10 ½	
684	1½c	**Harding,** Marion, O., *Dec. 1, 1930*	6.25
		Washington, D.C., *Dec. 2, 1930*	2.50
685	4c	**Taft,** Cincinnati, O., *June 4, 1930*	10.00
		Washington, D.C., *June 5, 1930*	4.00
		Perf. 10 Vertically	
686	1½c	**Harding,** Marion, Ohio, *Dec. 1, 1930*	7.50
		Washington, D.C., *Dec. 2, 1930*	3.00
687	4c	**Taft,** *Sept. 18, 1930*	30.00
		Perf. 11	
688	2c	**Braddock,** Braddock, Pa., *July 9, 1930*	6.00
		Washington, D.C., *July 10, 1930*	2.75
689	2c	**Von Steuben,** New York, N.Y., *Sept. 17, 1930*	6.00
		Washington, D.C., *Sept. 18, 1930*	2.75

1931

690	2c	**Pulaski,** Brooklyn, N.Y., *Jan. 16, 1931*	
		Buffalo, N.Y.	
		Chicago, Ill.	
		Cleveland, O.	
		Detroit, Mich.	
		Gary, Ind.	
		Milwaukee, Wis.	
		New York, N.Y.	
		Pittsburgh, Pa.	
		Savannah, Ga.	
		South Bend, Ind.	
		Toledo, O.	@5.00
		Washington, D.C., *Jan. 17, 1931*	2.75

1931

Perf. 11x10 ½

692	11c	**Hayes,** *Sept. 4, 1931*	110.00
693	12c	**Cleveland,** *Aug. 25, 1931*	110.00
694	13c	**Harrison,** *Sept. 4, 1931*	110.00
695	14c	**Indian,** *Sept. 8, 1931*	110.00
696	15c	**Liberty,** *Aug. 27, 1931*	150.00
		Perf. 10 ½x11	
697	17c	**Wilson,** *July 25, 1931,* Brooklyn, N.Y.	*1,250.*
		Washington, D.C., *July 27*	325.00
698	20c	**Golden Gate,** *Sept. 8, 1931*	185.00
699	25c	**Niagara Falls,** *July 25, 1931,* Brooklyn, N.Y.	*1,250.*
		Washington, D.C., *July 27*	350.00
		697, 699 on one cover	*700.00*
700	30c	**Bison,** *Sept. 8, 1931*	300.00
701	50c	**Arlington,** *Sept. 8, 1931*	450.00

1931

702	2c	**Red Cross,** *May 21, 1931*	4.00
		Dansville, N.Y.	4.00
703	2c	**Yorktown,** *Oct. 19, 1931,* Wethersfield, Conn.	5.00
		Yorktown, Va.	5.00
		Washington, D.C., *Oct. 20*	3.00

1932

WASHINGTON BICENTENNIAL ISSUE

704	½c	*Jan. 1932*	5.00
705	1c	*Jan. 1, 1932*	5.50
706	1½c	*Jan. 1, 1932*	5.50
707	2c	*Jan. 1, 1932*	5.50
708	3c	*Jan. 1, 1932*	5.75
709	4c	*Jan. 1, 1932*	5.75
710	5c	*Jan. 1, 1932*	6.00
711	6c	*Jan. 1, 1932*	6.75
712	7c	*Jan. 1, 1932*	6.75
713	8c	*Jan. 1, 1932*	6.75
714	9c	*Jan. 1, 1932*	8.75
715	10c	*Jan. 1, 1932*	12.00
		704 to 715, Complete set of twelve on one cover, Washington, D.C., *Jan. 1, 1932*	100.00

1932

716	2c	**Olympic Winter Games,** *Jan. 25, 1932,* Lake Placid, N.Y.	7.50
		Washington, D.C., *Jan. 26*	1.50
717	2c	**Arbor Day,** *April 22, 1933,* Nebraska City, Neb.	5.00
		Washington, D.C., *April 23*	1.50
		Adams, N.Y., *April 23*	6.50
718	3c	**Olympis Summer Games,** *June 15, 1932,* Los Angeles, Cal.	7.50
		Washington, D.C., *June 16*	2.75
719	5c	**Olympic Summer Games,** *June 15, 1932,* Los Angeles, Cal.	9.50
		Washington, D.C., *June 16*	2.75
		718, 719 on one cover, Los Angeles, Cal.	16.00
		718, 719 on one cover, Washington, D.C.	4.50
720	3c	**Washington,** *June 16, 1932*	10.00
721	3c	**Washington Coil,** Sideways, *June 24, 1932*	20.00

722	3c	Washington Coil, Endways, Oct. 12, 1932	20.00
723	6c	Garfield Coil, Sideways, Aug. 18, 1932	
		Los Angeles, Cal.	20.00
		Washington, D.C., Aug. 19	6.00
724	3c	William Penn, Oct. 24, 1932, New Castle, Del.	
		Chester, Pa.	
		Philadelphia, Pa.	@3.25
		Washington, D.C., Oct. 25	1.25
725	3c	Daniel Webster, Oct. 24, 1932, Franklin, N.H.	
		Exeter, N.H.	@3.25
		Hanover, N.H.	
		Washington, D.C., Oct. 25	1.25

1933

726	3c	Gen. Oglethorpe, Feb. 12, 1933, Savannah, Ga., (200,000)	3.25
		Washington, D.C., Feb. 13	1.25
727	3c	Peace Proclamation, April 19, 1933, Newburgh, N.Y. (349,571)	3.50
		Washington, D.C., April 20	1.20
728	1c	Century CProgress, May 25, 1933,Chicago, Ill.	3.00
		Washington, D.C., May 26	1.00
729	3c	Century of Progress, May 25, 1933,Chicago, Ill.	3.00
		Washington, D.C., May 26	1.00
		728, 729 on one cover	6.50

Covers mailed May 25, bearing Nos. 728 and 729 total 232,251.

730	1c	American Philatelic Society, sheet of 25, Aug. 25, 1933, Chicago, Ill.	120.00
730a	1c	A.P.S.,single, imperf., Chicago, Ill.	3.25
		Washington, D.C., Aug. 28	1.25
731	3c	American Philatelic Society, sheet of 25, Aug. 25, 1933, Chicago, Ill.	120.00
731a	3c	A.P.S.,single, imperf., Chicago, Ill.	3.25
		Washington, D.C., Aug. 28	1.25
		730a, 731a on one cover	5.50

Covers mailed Aug. 25 bearing Nos. 730a and 731a total 65,218.

732	3c	National Recovery Administration, Aug. 15, 1933, Washington, D.C. (65,000)	3.25
		Nira, Iowa, Aug. 17	2.50
733	3c	Byrd Antarctic, Oct. 9, 1933	6.00
734	5c	Kosciuszko, Oct. 13, 1933, Boston, Mass. (23,025)	5.50
		Buffalo, N.Y. (14,981)	7.00
		Chicago, Ill, (26,306)	5.50
		Detroit, Mich. (17,792)	6.50
		Pittsburgh, Pa. (6,282)	40.00
		Kosciuszko, Miss. (27,093)	6.50
		St. Louis, Mo. (17,872)	6.50
		Washington, D.C., Oct. 14	2.00

1934

735	3c	National Exhibition, sheet of 6, Byrd imperf., Feb. 10, 1934, New York, N.Y.	55.00
		Washington, D.C., Feb. 19	27.50
735a	3c	National Exhibition, single, imperf., New York, N.Y., Feb. 10, 1934 (450,715)	6.00
		Washington, D.C., Feb. 19	2.75
736	3c	Maryland Tercentenary, Mar. 23, 1934 St. Mary's City, Md. (148,785)	1.60
		Washington, D.C., Mar. 24	.60

Perf. 11x10½

| 738 | 3c | Mothers of America, May 2, 1934, any city | 1.60 |

Perf. 11

| 738 | 3c | Mothers of America, May 2, 1934, any city | 1.60 |
| | | 737, 738 on one cover | 4.00 |

Covers mailed at Washington, May 2 bearing Nos. 737 and 738 total 183,359.

739	3c	Wisconsin, July 7, 1934, Green Bay, Wisconsin (130,000)	1.60
		Washington, D.C., July 9	.75
740	1c	Parks, Yosemite, July 16, 1934	3.25
		Yosemite, California (60,000)	3.75
741	2c	Parks, Grand Canyon, July 24, 1934	3.25
		Grand Canyon, Arizona (75,000)	3.75
742	3c	Parks, Mt. Rainier, August 3, 1934	3.50
		Longmire, Washington, (64,500)	4.00
743	4c	Parks, Mesa Verde, Sept. 25, 1934	4.25
		Mesa Verde, Colorado (51,882)	4.50
744	5c	Parks, Yellowstone, July 30, 1934	4.25
		Yellowstone, Wyoming (87,000)	4.50
745	6c	Parks, Crater Lake, Sept. 5, 1934	5.00
		Crater Lake, Oregon (45,282)	5.25
746	7c	Parks, Arcadia, October 2, 1934	5.00
		Bar Harbor, Maine (51,312)	5.25
747	8c	Parks, Zion, Sept. 18, 1934	5.25
		Zion, Utah, (43,650)	5.75
748	9c	Parks, Glacier Park, August 27, 1934	5.50
		Glacier Park, Montana (52,626)	5.75
749	10c	Parks, Smoky Mountains, Oct. 8, 1934	11.00
		Sevierville, Tennessee (39,000)	13.00

Imperf

750	3c	American Philatelic Society, sheet of 6, Aug. 28, 1934, Atlantic City, N.Y.	55.00
750a	3c	A.P.S., single, Aug. 28, 1934, Atlantic City, N.J. (40,000)	6.25
		Washington, D.C., Sept. 4	4.00
751	1c	Trans—Mississippi Philatelic Expo., sheet of 6, Oct. 10, 1934, Omaha, Neb.	40.00
751a	1c	Trans—Miss. Phil. Expo., single, Omaha. Neb., Oct. 10, 1934 (125,000)	4.50
		Washington, D.C., Oct. 15	2.00

1935

SPECIAL PRINTING
Nos. 752 to 771 inclusive issued March 15, 1935.

752	3c	Peace Commemoration	10.00
753	3c	Byrd	12.00
754	3c	Mothers of America	12.00
755	3c	Wisconsin Tercentenary	12.00
756	1c	Parks, Yosemite	12.00
757	2c	Parks, Grand Canyon	12.00
758	3c	Parks, Mount Rainier	13.00
759	4c	Parks, Mesa Verde	13.00
760	5c	Parks, Yellowstone	13.00
761	6c	Parks, Crater Lake	13.00
762	7c	Parks, Acadia	13.00
763	8c	Parks, Zion	15.00
764	9c	Parks, Glacier Park	15.00
765	10c	Parks, Smoky Mountains	15.00
766a	1c	Century of Progress	11.00
		Pane of 25	250.00
767a	3c	Century of Progress	11.00
		Pane of 25	250.00
768a	3c	Byrd	13.00
		Pane of 6	250.00
769a	1c	Parks, Yosemite	8.00
		Pane of 6	250.00
770a	3c	Parks, Mount Rainier	10.00
		Pane of 6	250.00
771	15c	Airmail Special Delivery	25.00
772	3c	Connecticut Tercentenary, April 26, 1935,Hartford, Conn. (217,800)	8.00
		Washington, D.C., April 27	1.25
773	3c	California Exposition, May 29, 1935,San Diego, Cal. (214,042)	8.00
		Washington, D.C., May 31	1.25
774	3c	Boulder Dam, Sept. 30, 1935, Boulder City, Nev. (166,180)	10.00
		Washington, D.C., Oct. 1	2.00
775	3c	Michigan Centenary, Nov. 1, 1935, Lansing, Mich. (176,962)	8.00
		Washington, D.C., Nov. 2	1.25

1936

776	3c	Texas Centennial, March 2, 1936, Gonzales, Texas (319,150)	12.50
		Washington, D.C., March 3	1.25
777	3c	Rhode Island Tercentenary, May 4, 1936, Providence, R.I. (245,400)	8.00
		Washington, D.C., May 5	1.25
778		TIPEX souvenir sheet, May 9, 1936 (297,194) New York, N.Y. (TIPEX cancellation)	13.00
		Washington, D.C., May 11	3.50
782	3c	Arkansas Centennial, June 15, 1936, Little Rock, Ark. (376,693)	8.00
		Washington, D.C., June 16	1.00
783	3c	Oregon Territory Centennial, July 14, 1936, Astoria, Ore. (91,110)	8.00
		Daniel, Wyo. (67,013)	8.50
		Lewiston, Idaho. (86,100)	8.00
		Missoula, Mont. (59,883)	8.50
		Walla Walla, Wash. (106,150)	8.00
		Washington, D.C., July 15	1.25
784	3c	Susan Anthony, August 26, 1936 (178,500)	17.50

1936-37

785	1c	Army, December 15, 1936	5.00
786	2c	Army, January 15, 1937	5.00
787	3c	Army, February 18, 1937	5.00
788	4c	Army, March 23, 1937	5.50
789	5c	Army, May 26, 1937, West Point, N.Y., (160,000)	5.50
		Washington, D.C., May 27	1.25
790	1c	Navy, December 15, 1936	5.00
791	2c	Navy, January 15, 1937	5.00
792	3c	Navy, February 17, 1937	5.00
793	4c	Navy, March 23, 1937	5.50
794	5c	Navy, May 26, 1937, Annapolis, Md., (202,806)	1.25
		Washington, D.C., May 27	1.25

Covers for both Nos. 785 and 790 total 390, 749; Nos. 786 and 791 total 292,570; Nos. 787 and 792 total 320,888; Nos. 788 and 793 total 331,000.

1937

795	3c	Ordinance of 1787, July 13, 1937	6.00
		Marietta, Ohio (130,531)	
		New York, N.Y. (125,134)	6.00
		Washington, D.C., July 14	1.20
796	5c	Virginia Dare, Aug. 18, 1937, Manteo, N.C. (226,730)	7.00
797	10c	Souvenir Sheet, Aug. 26, 1937, Asheville, N.C. (164,215)	6.00
798	3c	Constitution, Sept. 17, 1937, Philadelphia, Pa. (281,478)	6.50
799	3c	Hawaii, Oct. 18, 1937, Honolulu, Hawaii (320,334)	7.00
800	3c	Alaska, Nov. 12, 1937, Juneau, Alaska (230,370)	7.00
801	3c	Puerto Rico, Nov. 25, 1937, San Juan, P.R. (244,054)	7.00
802	3c	Virgin Islands, Dec. 15, 1937, Charlotte Amalie, V.I. (225,469)	7.00

1938

PRESIDENTIAL ISSUE

803	½c	May 19, 1938, Philadelphia, Pa. (224,901)	1.50
804	1c	April 25, 1938 (124,037)	2.25
805	1½c	May 5, 1938 (128,339)	2.25
806	2c	June 3, 1938 (127,806)	2.25
807	3c	June 16, 1938 (118,097)	2.25
808	4c	July 1, 1938 (118,765)	2.25
809	4½c	July 11, 1938 (115,820)	2.75
810	5c	July 21, 1938 (98,282)	2.50
811	6c	July 28, 1938 (97,428)	2.50
812	7c	Aug. 4, 1938 (98,414)	2.75
813	8c	Aug. 11, 1938 (94,857)	2.75
814	9c	Aug. 18, 1938 (91,229)	3.00
815	10c	Sept. 2, 1938 (83,707)	3.00
816	11c	Sept. 8, 1938 (63,966)	3.00
817	12c	Sept. 14, 1938 (62,935)	3.25
818	13c	Sept. 22, 1938 (58,965)	3.25
819	14c	Oct. 6, 1938 (49,819)	3.50
820	15c	Oct. 13, 1938 (52,209)	3.50
821	16c	Oct. 20, 1938 (59,566)	3.75
822	17c	Oct. 27, 1938 (55,024)	4.00
823	18c	Nov. 3, 1938 (53,124)	4.50
824	19c	Nov. 10, 1938 (54,124)	4.50
825	20c	Nov. 10, 1938 (51,971)	4.75
821	21c	Nov. 22, 1938 (44,367)	5.25
827	22c	Nov. 22, 1938 (44,358)	5.50
828	24c	Dec. 2, 1938 (46,592)	5.50
829	25c	Dec. 2, 1938 (45,691)	6.75
830	30c	Dec. 8, 1938 (43,528)	10.00
831	50c	Dec. 8, 1938 (41,984)	20.00
832	$1	Aug. 29, 1938 (24,618)	60.00
832c	$1	Aug. 31, 1954 (20,202)	30.00
833	$2	Sept. 29, 1938 (19,895)	125.00
834	$5	Nov. 17, 1938 (15,615)	190.00

1938

835	3c	Constitution, June 21, 1938, Philadelphia, Pa. (232,873)	6.50
836	3c	Swedes and Finns, June 27, 1938Wilmington, Del. (225,617)	6.00
837	3c	Northwest Sesqui., July 15, 1938, Marietta, Ohio (180,170)	6.00
838	3c	Iowa, Aug. 24, 1938, Des Moines, Iowa (209,860)	6.00

1939

COIL STAMPS
Perf. 10 Vertically

839	1c	Pair, Jan. 20, 1939	7.00
840	1½c	Pair, Jan. 20, 1939	7.00
841	2c	Pair, Jan. 20, 1939	7.00
842	3c	Pair, Jan. 20, 1939	8.00
843	4c	Pair, Jan. 20, 1939	10.00
844	4½c	Pair, Jan. 20, 1939	10.00
845	5c	Pair, Jan. 20, 1939	11.00
846	6c	Pair, Jan. 20, 1939	16.00
847	10c	Pair, Jan. 20, 1939	22.00
		839 to 847, set of 9 pairs on one cover, Jan. 20, 1939	125.00

Perf. 10 Horizontally

848	1c	Pair, Jan. 27, 1939	7.00
849	1½c	Pair, Jan. 27, 1939	9.00
850	2c	Pair, Jan. 27, 1939	11.00
851	3c	Pair, Jan. 27, 1939	13.50
		848 to 851, set of 4 pairs on one cover, Jan. 27, 1939	55.00

1939

852	3c	Golden Gate Expo, Feb. 18, 1939, San Francisco, Cal. (352,165)	5.00
853	3c	N.Y. World's Fair, Apr. 1, 1939, New York, N.Y. (585,565)	8.00
854	3c	Washington Inauguration, Apr. 30, 1939, New York, N.Y. (395,644)	5.00
855	3c	Baseball Centennial, June 12, 1939, Cooperstown, N.Y. (398,199)	25.00
856	3c	Panama Canal, Aug. 15, 1939, U.S.S. Charleston, Canal Zone (230,974)	5.00
857	3c	Printing Tercentenary, Sept. 25, 1939, New York, N.Y. (295,270)	5.00
858	3c	50th Statehood Anniversary, Bismarck, N.D. Nov. 2, 1939 (142,106)	
		Pierre, S.D., Nov. 2, 1939 (150,429)	
		Helena, Mont., Nov. 8, 1939 (130,273)	
		Olympia, Wash., Nov. 11, 1939 (150,429)	@5.00

1940

FAMOUS AMERICANS

| 859 | 1c | Washington Irving, Jan. 29, 1940, Tarrytown, N.Y. (170,969) | 1.90 |

860	2c	James Fenimore Cooper, Jan. 29, 1940, Cooperstown, N.Y. (154,836)	1.90
861	3c	Ralph Waldo Emerson, Feb. 5, 1940, Boston, Mass. (185,148)	1.90
862	5c	Louisa May Alcott, Feb. 5, 1940, Concord, Mass. (134,325)	4.50
863	10c	Samuel L. Clemens, Feb. 13, 1940, Hannibal, Mo. (150,492)	7.50
864	1c	Henry W. Longfellow, Feb. 16, 1940, Portland, Me. (160,508)	1.90
865	2c	John Greenleaf Whittier, Feb. 16, 1940, Haverhill, Mass. (148,423)	1.90
866	3c	James Russell Lowell, Feb. 20, 1940, Cambridge, Mass. (148,735)	1.90
867	5c	Walt Whitman, Feb. 20, 1940, Camden, N.J. (134,185)	4.00
868	10c	James Whitcomb Riley, Feb. 24, 1940, Greenfield, Ind. (131,760)	7.50
869	1c	Horace Mann, March 14, 1940, Boston, Mass. (186,854)	1.90
870	2c	Mark Hopkins, March 14, 1940, Williamstown, Mass. (140,286)	1.90
871	3c	Charles W. Eliot, March 28, 1940, Cambridge, Mass. (155,708)	1.90
872	5c	Frances E. Willard, March 28, 1940, Evanston, Ill. (140,483)	4.00
873	10c	Booker T. Washington, April 7, 1940, Tuskegee Institute, Ala. (163,507)	7.50
874	1c	John James Audubon, April 8, 1940, St. Francisville, La. (144,123)	1.90
875	2c	Dr. Crawford W. Long, April 8, 1940, Jefferson, Ga. (158,128)	1.90
876	3c	Luther Burbank, April 17, 1940, Santa Rosa, Cal. (147,033)	2.75
877	5c	Dr. Walter Reed, April 17, 1940, Washington, D.C. (154,464)	4.00
878	10c	Jane Addams, April 26, 1940, Chicago, Ill. (132,375)	7.50
879	1c	Stephen Collins Foster, May 3, 1940, Bardstown, Ky. (183,461)	1.90
880	2c	John Philip Sousa, May 3, 1940, Washington, D.C. (131,422)	1.90
881	3c	Victor Herbert, May 13, 1940, New York, N.Y. (168,200)	1.90
882	5c	Edward A. MacDowell, May 13, 1940, Peterborough, N.H. (135,155)	4.00
883	10c	Ethelbert Nevin, June 10, 1940, Pittsburgh, Pa. (121,951)	7.00
884	1c	Gilbert Charles Stuart, Sept. 5, 1940, Narragansett, R.I. (131,965)	1.90
885	2c	James A. McNeill Whistler, Sept. 5, 1940, Lowell, Mass. (130,962)	1.90
886	3c	Augustus Saint—Gaudens, Sept. 16, 1940, New York, N.Y. (138,200)	1.90
887	5c	Daniel Chester French, Sept. 16, 1940, Stockbridge, Mass. (124,608)	3.50
888	10c	Frederic Remington, Sept. 30, 1940, Canton, N.Y. (116,231)	7.00
889	1c	Eli Whitney, Oct. 7, 1940, Savannah, Ga. (140,868)	1.90
890	2c	Samuel F.B. Morse, Oct. 7, 1940, New York, N.Y. (135,388)	1.90
891	3c	Cyrus Hall McCormick, Oct. 14, 1940, Lexington, Va. (137,415)	1.90
892	5c	Elias Howe, Oct. 14, 1940, Spencer, Mass. (126,334)	4.50
893	10c	Alexander Graham Bell, Oct. 28, 1940, Boston, Mass. (125,372)	12.50

1940

894	3c	Pony Express, April 3, 1940, St. Joseph, Mo. (194,589)	6.00
		Sacramento, Cal. (160,849)	6.00
895	3c	Pan American Union, April 14, 1940 (182,401)	4.50
896	3c	Idaho Statehood, July 3, 1940, Boise, Idaho (156,429)	4.50
897	3c	Wyoming Statehood, July 10, 1940 Cheyenne, Wyo. (156,709)	4.50
898	3c	Coronado Expedition, Sept. 7, 1940, Albuquerque, N.M. (161,012)	4.50
899	1c	Defense, Oct. 16, 1940	4.25
900	2c	Defense, Oct. 16, 1940	4.25
901	3c	Defense, Oct. 16, 1940	4.25
		899 to 901 on one cover (450,083)	12.50
902	3c	Thirteenth Amendment, Oct. 20, 1940, Worlds Fair, N.Y. (156,146)	5.00

1941

| 903 | 3c | Vermont Statehood, March 4, 1941, Montpelier, Vt. (182,423) | 4.50 |

1942

904	3c	Kentucky Statehood, June 1, 1942, Frankfort, Ky. (155,730)	4.00
905	3c	"Win the War", July 4, 1942 (191,168)	3.75
906	5c	Chinese Resistance, July 7, 1942, Denver, Colo. (168,746)	5.75

1943

| 907 | 2c | United Nations, Jan. 14, 1943 (178,865) | 3.50 |

908	1c	Four Freedoms, Feb. 12, 1943 (193,800)	3.50
909	5c	Poland, June 22, 1943, Chicago, Ill. (88,170)	6.00
		Washington, D.C. (136,002)	5.00
910	5c	Czechoslovakia, July 12, 1943 (145,112)	5.00
911	5c	Norway, July 27, 1943 (130,054)	4.00
912	5c	Luxemborg, Aug. 10, 1943 (166,367)	4.00
913	5c	Netherlands, Aug. 24, 1943 (148,763)	4.00
914	5c	Belgium, Sept. 14, 1943 (154,220)	4.00
915	5c	France, Sept. 28, 1943 (163,478)	4.00
916	5c	Greece, Oct. 12, 1943 (166,553)	4.00
917	5c	Yugoslavia, Oct. 26, 1943 (161,835)	4.00
918	5c	Albania, Nov. 9, 1943 (162,275)	4.00
919	5c	Austria, Nov. 23, 1943 (172,285)	4.00
920	5c	Denmark, Dec. 7, 1943 (173,784)	4.00

1944

921	5c	Korea, Nov. 2, 1944 (192,860)	5.00
922	3c	Railroad, May 10, 1944, Ogden, Utah (151,324)	
		Omaha, Neb. (171,000)	
		San Francisco, Cal. (125,000)	@6.00
923	3c	Steamship, May 22, 1944, Kings Point, N.Y. (152,324)	
		Savannah, Ga. (181,472)	@4.00
924	3c	Telegraph, May 24, 1944, Washington, D.C. (141,907)	
		Baltimore, Md. (136,480)	@3.50
925	3c	Philippines, Sept. 27, 1944 (214,865)	3.50
926	3c	Motion Picture, Oct. 31, 1944, Hollywood, Cal. (190,660)	
		New York, N.Y. (176,473)	@3.50

1945

927	3c	Florida, March 3, 1945, Tallahassee, Fla. (228,435)	3.50
928	5c	United Nations Conference, April 25, 1945, San Francisco, Cal. (417,450)	3.50
929	3c	Iwo Jima, July 11, 1945 (391,650)	5.25

1945-46

930	1c	Roosevelt, July 26, 1945, Hyde Park, N.Y. (390,219)	2.50
931	2c	Roosevelt, Aug. 24, 1945, Warm Springs, Ga. (426,142)	2.50
932	3c	Roosevelt, June 27, 1945 (391,650)	2.50
933	5c	Roosevelt, Jan. 30, 1946 (466,766)	3.00
		930 to 933 on one cover	10.00
934	3c	Army, Sept. 28, 1945 (392,300)	3.50
935	3c	Navy, Oct. 27, 1945, Annapolis, Md. (460,352)	3.50
936	3c	Coast Guard, Nov. 10, 1945 New York, N.Y. (405,280)	3.50
937	3c	Alfred E. Smith, Nov. 26, 1945 New York, N.Y. (424,950)	2.50
938	3c	Texas, Dec. 29, 1945, Austin, Tex. (397,860)	3.50

1946

939	3c	Merchant Marine, Feb. 26, 1946 (432,141)	2.50
940	3c	Veterans of WWII, May 9, 1946 (492,786)	2.50
941	3c	Tennessee, June 1, 1946, Nashville, Tenn. (463,512)	2.50
942	3c	Iowa, Aug. 3, 1946, Iowa City, Iowa (517,505)	2.50
943	3c	Smithsonian, Aug. 10, 1946 (402,448)	2.50
944	3c	Kearny Expedition, Oct. 16, 1946, Santa Fe, N.M. (384,300)	2.50

1947

945	3c	Thomas A. Edison, Feb. 11, 1947, Milan, Ohio (632,473)	2.50
946	3c	Joseph Pulitzer, Apr. 10, 1947, New York, N.Y. (580,870)	2.50
947	3c	Stamp Centenary, May 17, 1947, New York, N.Y. (712,873)	2.50
948	5c	and 10c Centenary Exhibition Sheet, May 19, 1947, New York, N.Y. (502,175)	3.00
949	3c	Doctors, June 9, 1947, Atlantic City, N.J. (508,016)	1.50
950	3c	Utah, July 24, 1947, Salt Lake City, Utah (456,416)	1.50
951	3c	"Constitution", Oct. 21, 1947, Boston, Mass. (683,416)	1.50
952	3c	Everglades Park, Dec. 5, 1947, Florida City, Fla. (466,647)	1.50

1948

953	3c	Carver, Jan. 5, 1948, Tuskegee Institute, Ala. (402,179)	1.50
954	3c	California Gold, Jan. 24, 1948, Coloma, Calif. (526,154)	1.50
955	3c	Mississippi Territory, April 7, 1948, Natchez, Miss. (434,804)	1.50
956	3c	Four Chaplains, May 28, 1948, Washington, D.C. (459,070)	1.50
957	3c	Wisconsin Centennial, May 29, 1948, Madison, Wis. (470,280)	1.50
958	5c	Swedish Pioneers, June 4, 1948 Chicago, Ill. (364,318)	1.50
959	3c	Women's Progress, July 19, 1948, Seneca Falls, N.Y. (401,923)	1.50

960	3c	William Allen White, July 31, 1948, Emporia, Kans. (385,648)	1.50
961	3c	U.S.—Canada Friendship, Aug. 2, 1948, Niagara Falls, N.Y. (406,467)	1.50
962	3c	Francis Scott Key, Aug. 2, 1948, Frederick, Md. (505,930)	1.50
963	3c	Salute to Youth, Aug. 11, 1948, Washington, D.C. (347,070)	1.50
964	3c	Oregon Territory Establishment, Aug. 14, 1948, Oregon City, Ore. (365,898)	1.50
965	3c	Harlan Fiske Stone, Aug. 25, 1948, Chesterfield, N.H. (362,170)	1.50
966	3c	Palomar Observatory, Aug. 30, 1948, Palomar Mountain, Calif. (401,365)	1.50
967	3c	Clara Barton, Sept. 7, 1948, Oxford, Mass. (362,000)	1.25
968	3c	Poultry Industry, Sept. 9, 1948, New Haven, Conn. (475,000)	1.25
969	3c	Gold Star Mothers, Sept. 21, 1948, Washington, D.C. (386,064)	1.50
970	3c	Fort Kearny, Sept. 22, 1948, Minden, Neb. (429,633)	1.50
971	3c	Volunteer Firemen, Oct. 4, 1948, Dover, Del. (399,630)	1.50
972	3c	Indian Centennial, Oct. 15, 1948, Muskogee, Okla. (459,528)	1.25
973	3c	Rough Riders, Oct. 27, 1948, Prescott, Ariz. (399,198)	1.25
974	3c	Juliette Low, Oct. 29, 1948, Savannah, Ga. (476,573)	1.25
975	3c	Will Rogers, Nov. 4, 1948, Claremore, Okla. (450,350)	1.25
976	3c	Fort Bliss, Nov. 5, 1948, El Paso, Tex. (421,000)	1.25
977	3c	Moina Michael, Nov. 9, 1948, Athens, Ga. (374,090)	1.25
978	3c	Gettysburg Address, Nov. 19, 1948, Gettysburg, Pa. (511,990)	1.25
979	3c	American Turners Society, Nov. 20, 1948, Cincinnati, Ohio (434,090)	1.25
980	3c	Joel Chandler Harris, Dec. 9, 1948, Eatonton, Ga. (426,199)	1.25
981	3c	Minnesota Territory, May 3, 1949, St. Paul, Minn. (458,750)	1.25
982	3c	Washington and Lee University, April 12, 1949, Lexington, Va. (447,910)	1.25
983	3c	Puerto Rico Election, April 27, 1949, San Juan, P.R. (390,416)	1.25
984	3c	Annapolis, Md., May 23, 1949, Annapolis, Md. (441,802)	1.25
985	3c	G.A.R., Aug. 29, 1949, Indianapolis, Ind. (471,696)	1.25
986	3c	Edgar Allan Poe, Oct. 7, 1949, Richmond, Va. (371,020)	1.25

1950

987	3c	American Bankers Association, Jan. 3, 1950, Saratoga Springs, N.Y. (388,622)	1.25
988	3c	Samuel Gompers, Jan. 27, 1950, Washington, D.C. (332,023)	1.25
989	3c	National Capital Sesquicentennial (Freedom), April 20, 1950, Washington, D.C. (371,743)	1.25
990	3c	National Capital Sesquicentennial (Executive), June 12, 1950, Washington, D.C. (376,789)	1.25
991	3c	National Capital Sesquicentennial (Judicial), Aug. 2, 1950, Washington, D.C. (324,007)	1.25
992	3c	National Capital Sesquicentennial, (Legislative), Nov. 22, 1950, Washington, D.C. (352,215)	1.25
993	3c	Railroad Engineers, April 29, 1950, Jackson, Tenn. (420,830)	1.25
994	3c	Kansas City Centenary, June 3, 1950, Kansas City, Mo. (405,390)	1.25
995	3c	Boy Scouts, June 30, 1950, Valley Forge, Pa. (622,972)	2.00
996	3c	Indiana Territory Sesquicentennial, July 4, 1950, Vincennes, Ind. (359,643)	1.25
997	3c	California Statehood, Sept. 9, 1950, Sacramento, Cal. (391,919)	1.25

1951

998	3c	United Confederate Veterans, May 30, 1951, Norfolk, Va. (374,235)	1.25
999	3c	Nevada Centennial, July 14, 1951, Genoa, Nev. (336,890)	1.25
1000	3c	Landing of Cadillac, July 24, 1951, Detroit, Mich. (323,094)	1.25
1001	3c	Colorado Statehood, Aug. 1, 1951, Minturn, Colo. (311,568)	1.25
1002	3c	American Chemical Society, Sept. 4, 1951, New York, N.Y. (436,419)	1.25
1003	3c	Battle of Brooklyn, Dec. 10, 1951, Brooklyn, N.Y. (420,000)	1.25

1952

1004	3c	Betsy Ross, Jan. 2, 1952, Philadelphia, Pa. (314,312)	1.25
1005	3c	4—H Club, Jan. 15, 1952, Springfield, Ohio (383,290)	1.25
1006	3c	B. & O. Railroad, Feb. 28, 1952, Baltimore, Md. (441,600)	1.50

1007	3c	**American Automobile Association,** *March 4, 1952,* Chicago, Ill. *(520,123)*	85
1008	3c	**NATO,** *April 4, 1952,* Washington, D.C. *(313,518)*	85
1009	3c	**Grand Coulee Dam,** *May 15, 1952,* Grand Coulee, Wash. *(341,680)*	85
1010	3c	**Lafayette,** *June 13, 1952,* Georgetown, S.C. *(349,102)*	85
1011	3c	**Mt. Rushmore Memorial,** *Aug. 11, 1952,* Keystone, S.D. *(337,027)*	85
1012	3c	**Civil Engineers,** *Sept. 6, 1952,* Chicago, Ill. *(318,483)*	85
1013	3c	**Service Women,** *Sept. 11, 1952,* Washington, D.C. *(308,062)*	85
1014	3c	**Gutenberg Bible,** *Sept. 30, 1952,* Washington, D.C. *(387,078)*	85
1015	3c	**Newspaper Boys,** *Oct. 4, 1952,* Philadelphia, Pa. *(626,000)*	85
1016	3c	**Red Cross,** *Nov. 21, 1952,* New York, N.Y. *(439,252)*	85

1953

1017	3c	**National Guard,** *Feb. 23, 1953,* Washington, D.C. *(387,618)*	85
1018	3c	**Ohio Sesquicentennial,** *March 2, 1953,* Chillicothe, Ohio *(407,983)*	85
1019	3c	**Washington Territory,** *March 2, 1953,* Olympia, Wash. *(344,047)*	85
1020	3c	**Louisiana Purchase,** *April 30, 1953,* St. Louis, Mo *(425,600)*	85
1021	5c	**Opening of Japan,** *July 14, 1953,* Washington, D.C. *(320,541)*	85
1022	3c	**American Bar Association,** *Aug. 24, 1953,* Boston, Mass. *(410,036)*	85
1023	3c	**Sagamore Hill,** *Sept. 14, 1953,* Oyster Bay, N.Y. *(379,750)*	1.00
1024	3c	**Future Farmers,** *Oct. 13, 1953,* Kansas City, Mo. *(424,193)*	85
1025	3c	**Trucking Industry,** *Oct. 27, 1953,* Los Angeles, Calif. *(875,021)*	85
1026	3c	**Gen. G.S. Patton, Jr.,** *Nov. 11, 1953,* Fort Knox, Ky. *(342,600)*	85
1027	3c	**New York City,** *Nov. 20, 1953,* New York, N.Y. *(387,914)*	85
1028	3c	**Gadsden Purchase,** *Dec. 30, 1953,* Tucson, Ariz. *(363,250)*	85

1954

1029	3c	**Columbia University,** *Jan. 4, 1954,* New York, N.Y. *(550,745)*	85

1954-67

LIBERTY ISSUE

1030	½c	*Oct. 20, 1955,* Washington, D.C. *(223,122)*Block of four	85
1031	1c	*Aug. 26, 1954,* Chicago, Ill. *(272,581)*	85
1031A	1¼c	*June 17, 1960,* Santa Fe, N.M. (total for #1031A, 1054A and combination covers, 501,848)	85
		1031A and 1054A on one cover	1.50
1031	1½c	*Feb. 22, 1956,* Mount Vernon, Va. *(270,109)*	60
1033	2c	*Sept. 15, 1954,* San Francisco, Cal. *(307,300)*	60
1034	2½c	*June 17, 1959,* Boston, Mass. *(315,060)*	60
1035	3c	*June 24, 1954,* Albany, N.Y. *(340,001)*	60
1035b	3c	Tagged, *July 6, 1966*	15.00
1036	4c	*Nov. 19, 1954,* New York, N.Y. *(374,064)*	60
1036b	4c	Tagged, *Nov. 2, 1963,* Washington, D.C.	50.00

No. 1036b was supposed to have been issued at Dayton Nov. 2, but a mix-up delayed its issuance there until Nov. 4. About 510 Covers received the Nov. 2 cancellation.

1037	4½c	*Mar. 16, 1959,* Hermitage, Tenn. *(320,000)*	60
1038	5c	*Dec. 2, 1954,* Fredericksburg, Va. *(255,650)*	60
1039	6c	*Nov. 18, 1955,* New York, N.Y. *(257,551)*	65
1040	7c	*Jan. 10, 1956,* Staunton, Va. *(200,111)*	70
1041	8c	*April 9, 1954,* Washington, D.C. *(340,077)*	80
1042	8c	(Giori press), *Mar. 22, 1958,* Cleveland, O. *(223,899)*	60
1042A	8c	**Pershing,** *Nov. 17, 1961,* New York, N.Y. *(321,031)*	60
1043	9c	*June 14, 1956,* San Antonio, Texas *(207,086)*	1.50
1044	10c	*July 4, 1956,* Philadelphia, Pa., *(220,930)*	90
1044b	10c	Tagged, *July 6, 1966*	15.00
1044A	11c	*June 15, 1961,* Washington, D.C. *(238,905)*	90
1044c	11c	Tagged, *Jan. 11, 1967*	22.50
1045	12c	*June 6, 1959,* Oxford, O. *(225,869)*	90
1045a	12c	Tagged, *May 6, 1968*	25.00
1046	15c	*Dec. 12, 1958,* Washington, D.C. *(205,680)*	1.00
1046a	15c	Tagged, *July 6, 1966*	20.00
1047	20c	*Apr. 13, 1956,* Charlottesville, Va. *(147,860)*	1.20
1048	25c	*April 18, 1958,* Boston, Mass. *(196,530)*	1.30

1049	30c	*Sept. 21, 1955,* Norfolk, Va. *(120,166)*	1.50
1050	40c	*Sept. 24, 1955,* Richmond, Va. *(113,972)*	1.75
1051	50c	*Aug. 25, 1955,* Louisville, Ky. *(110,220)*	6.00
1052	$1	*Oct. 7, 1955,* Joplin, Mo. *(80,191)*	13.00
1053	$5	*Mar. 19, 1956,* Paterson, N.J. *(34,272)*	75.00

1954-65

COIL STAMPS

1054	1c	*Oct. 8, 1954,* Baltimore, Md. *(196,318)*Strip of three	75
1054A	1¼c	*June 17, 1960,* Santa Fe, N.M. (total for #1054A, 1031A and combination covers, 501,848)	1.00
1055	2c	*Oct. 22, 1954,* St. Louis, Mo. *(162,050)*Pair	75
1055a	2c	Tagged, *May 6, 1968* pair	11.00
1056	2½c	*Sept. 9, 1959,* Los Angeles, Calif. *(198,680)*	1.20
1057	3c	*July 20, 1954,* Washington, D.C. *(137,139)*	75
1058	4c	*July 31, 1958,* Mandan, N.D. *(184,079)*	75
1059	4½c	*May 1, 1959,* Denver, Colo. *(202,454)*	1.75
1059A	25c	*Feb. 25, 1965,* Wheaton, Md. *(184,954)*	1.20
1059b	25c	Tagged, *Apr. 3, 1973,* New York, N.Y.	14.00

1954

1060	3c	**Nebraska Territory,** *May 7, 1954,* Nebraska City, Neb. *(401,015)*	75
1061	3c	**Kansas Territory,** *May 31, 1954,* Fort Leavenworth, Kans. *(349,145)*	75
1062	3c	**George Eastman,** *July 12, 1954,* Rochester, N.Y. *(630,448)*	75
1063	3c	**Lewis & Clark Expedition,** *July 28, 1954,* Sioux City, Iowa *(371,557)*	75

1955

1064	3c	**Pennsylvania Academy of the Fine Arts,** *Jan. 15, 1955,* Philadelphia, Pa. *(307,040)*	75
1065	3c	**Land Grant Colleges,** *Feb. 12, 1955,* East Lansing, Mich. *(419,241)*	75
1066	8c	**Rotary International,** *Feb. 23, 1955,* Chicago, Ill. *(350,625)*	90
1067	3c	**Armed Forces Reserve,** *May 21, 1955,* Washington, D.C. *(300,436)*	75
1068	3c	**New Hampshire,** *June 21, 1955,* Franconia, N.H. *(330,630)*	75
1069	3c	**Soo Locks,** *June 28, 1955,* Sault Sainte Marie, Mich. *(316,616)*	75
1070	3c	**Atoms for Peace,** *July 28, 1955,* Washington, D.C. *(351,940)*	75
1071	3c	**Fort Ticonderoga,** *Sept. 18, 1955,* Fort Ticonderoga, N.Y. *(342,946)*	75
1072	3c	**Andrew W. Mellon,** *Dec. 20, 1955,* Washington, D.C. *(278,897)*	75

1956

1073	3c	**Benjamin Franklin,** *Jan. 17, 1956,* Philadelphia, Pa. *(351,260)*	75
1074	3c	**Booker T. Washington,** *Apr. 5, 1956,* Booker T. Washington Birthplace, Va. *(272,659)*	75
1075	11c	**FIPEX Souvenir Sheet,** *Apr. 28, 1956,* New York, N.Y. *(429,327)*	6.50
1076	3c	**FIPEX,** *Apr. 30, 1956,* New York, N.Y. *(526,090)*	75
1077	3c	**Wildlife (Turkey),** *May 5, 1956,* Fond du Lac, Wis. *(292,121)*	1.10
1078	3c	**Wildlife (Antelope),** *June 22, 1956,* Gunnison, Colo. *(294,731)*	1.10
1079	3c	**Wildlife (Salmon),** *Nov. 9, 1956,* Seattle, Wash. *(346,800)*	1.10
1080	3c	**Pure Food and Drug Laws,** *June 27, 1956,* Washington, D.C. *(411,761)*	80
1081	3c	**Wheatland,** *Aug. 5, 1956,* Lancaster, Pa. *(340,142)*	80
1082	3c	**Labor Day,** *Sept. 3, 1956,* Camden, N.J. *(338,450)*	80
1083	3c	**Nassau Hall,** *Sept. 22, 1956,* Princeton, N.J. *(350,756)*	80
1084	3c	**Devils Tower,** *Sept. 24, 1956,* Devils Tower, Wyo. *(285,090)*	80
1085	3c	**Children,** *Dec. 15, 1956,* Washington, D.C. *(305,125)*	80

1957

1086	3c	**Alexander Hamilton,** *Jan. 11, 1957,* New York, N.Y. *(305,117)*	80
1087	3c	**Polio,** *Jan. 15, 1957,* Washington, D.C. *(307,630)*	80
1088	3c	**Coast & Geodetic Survey,** *Feb. 11, 1957,* Seattle, Wash. *(309,931)*	80
1089	3c	**Architects,** *Feb. 23, 1957,* New York, N.Y. *(368,840)*	80
1090	3c	**Steel Industry,** *May 22, 1957,* New York, N.Y. *(473,284)*	80

1091	3c	**Naval Review,** *June 10, 1957,* U.S.S. Saratoga, Norfolk, Va. *(365,933)*	80
1092	3c	**Oklahoma Statehood,** *June 14, 1957,* Oklahoma City, Okla. *(327,172)*	80
1093	3c	**School Teachers,** *July 1, 1957,* Philadelphia, Pa. *(357,986)*	80
		(Spelling error) Philadelpia	5.00
1094	4c	**Flag,** *July 4, 1957,* Washington, D.C. *(523,879)*	80
1095	3c	**Shipbuilding,** *Aug. 15, 1957,* Bath, Maine *(347,432)*	80
1096	8c	**Ramon Magsaysay,** *Aug. 31, 1957,* Washington, D.C. *(334,558)*	80
1097	3c	**Lafayette Bicentenary,** *Sept. 6, 1957,* Easton, Pa. *(260,421)*	80
		Fayetteville, N.C. *(230,000)*	
		Louisville, Ky. *(207,856)*	@80
1098	3c	**Wildlife (Whooping Cranes),** *Nov. 22, 1957,* New York, N.Y. *(342,970)*	80
		New Orleans, La. *(154,327)*	
		Corpus Christi, Tex. *(280,990)*	@1.00
1099	3c	**Religious Freedom,** *Dec. 27, 1957,* Flushing, N.Y. *(357,770)*	80

1958

1100	3c	**Gardening—Horticulture,** *Mar. 15, 1958,* Ithaca, N.Y. *(451,292)*	80
1104	3c	**Brussels Exhibition,** *April 17, 1958,* Detroit, Mich. *(428,073)*	80
1105	3c	**James Monroe,** *April 28, 1958,* Montross, Va. *(326,988)*	80
1106	3c	**Minnesota Statehood,** *May 11, 1958,* Saint Paul, Minn. *(475,552)*	80
1107	3c	**International Geophysical Year,** *May 31, 1958,* Chicago, Ill. *(397,000)*	80
1108	3c	**Gunston Hall,** *June 12, 1958,* Lorton, Va. *(349,801)*	80
1109	3c	**Mackinac Bridge,** *June 25, 1958,* "Mackinac Bridge, Mich." *(445,605)*	80
1110	4c	**Simon Bolivar,** *July 24, 1958,* Washington, D.C.	80
1111	8c	**Simon Bolivar,** *July 24, 1958* Washington, D.C.	80
		1110 and 1111, set of two on one cover	2.25

First day cancellation was applied to 708, 777 covers bearing No. 1110, No. 1111, or both.

1112	4c	**Atlantic Cable,** *Aug. 15, 1958,* New York, N.Y. *(365,072)*	80

1958-59

1113	1c	**Lincoln Sesquicentennial,** *Feb. 12, 1959,* Hodgenville, Ky. *(379,862)*	80
1114	3c	**Lincoln Sesquicentennial,** *Feb. 12, 1959,* New York, N.Y. *(437,537)*	80
1115	4c	**Lincoln—Douglas Debates,** *Aug. 27, 1958,* Freeport, Ill. *(373,063)*	80
1116	4c	**Lincoln Sesquicentennial,** *May 30, 1959,* Washington, D.C. *(894,887)*	80

1958

1117	4c	**Lajos Kossuth,** *Sept. 19, 1958,* Washington, D.C.	80
1118	8c	**Lajos Kossuth,** *Sept. 19, 1958,* Washington, D.C.	80
		1117 and 1118, set of two on one cover	2.25

First day cancellation was applied to 722, 188 covers bearing No. 1117, No. 1118, or both.

1119	4c	**Freedom of Press,** *Sept. 22, 1958,* Columbia, Mo. *(411,752)*	80
1120	4c	**Overland Mail,** *Oct. 10, 1958,* San Francisco, Cal. *(352,760)*	80
1121	4c	**Noah Webster,** *Oct. 16, 1958,* West Hartford, Conn. *(364,608)*	80
1122	4c	**Forest Conservation,** *Oct. 27, 1958,* Tucson, Ariz. *(405,959)*	80
1123	4c	**Fort Duquesne,** *Nov. 25, 1958,* Pittsburgh, Pa. *(421,764)*	80

1959

1124	4c	**Oregon Statehood,** *Feb. 14, 1959,* Astoria, Ore. *(452,764)*	80
1125	4c	**San Martin,** *Feb. 25, 1959,* Washington, D.C.	80
1126	8c	**San Martin,** *Feb. 25, 1959,* Washington, D.C.	80
		1125 and 1126, set of two on one cover	2.25

First day cancellation was applied to 910, 208 covers bearing No. 1125, No. 1126, or both.

1127	4c	**NATO** *April, 1, 1959,* Washington, D.C. *(361,040)*	80
1128	4c	**Arctic Exploration,** *April 6, 1959,* Cresson, Pa. *(397,770)*	80
1129	8c	**World Trade,** *April 20, 1959,* Washington, D.C. *(503,618)*	80
1130	4c	**Silver Centennial,** *June 8, 1959,* Virginia City, Nev. *(337,233)*	80
1131	4c	**St. Lawrence Seaway,** *June 26, 1959,* Massena, N.Y. *(543,211)*	80
1132	4c	**Flag (49 stars),** *July 4, 1959,* Auburn, N.Y. *(523,773)*	80

1133	4c	**Soil Conservation,** *Aug. 26, 1959,* Rapid City, S.D. *(400,613)*	80
1134	4c	**Petroleum Industry,** *Aug. 27, 1959,* Titusville, Pa. *(801,859)*	80
1135	4c	**Dental Health,** *Sept. 14, 1959,* New York, N.Y. *(649,813)*	80
1136	4c	**Reuter,** *Sept. 29, 1959,* Washington, D.C.	80
1137	8c	**Reuter,** *Sept. 29, 1959,* Washington, D.C.	80
		1136 and 1137, set of two on one cover	2.25

First day cancellation was applied to 1,207,933 covers bearing No. 1136, No. 1137, or both.

1138	4c	**Dr. Ephraim McDowell,** *Dec. 3, 1959,* Danville, Ky. *(344,603)*	80

1960-61

1139	4c	**Washington "Credo,"** *Jan. 20, 1960,* Mount Vernon, Va. *(438,335)*	1.25
1140	4c	**Franklin "Credo,"** *March 31, 1960,* Philadelphia, Pa. *(497,913)*	1.00
1141	4c	**Jefferson "Credo,"** *May 18, 1960,* Charlottesville, Va. *(454,903)*	1.00
1142	4c	**Francis Scott Key "Credo,"** *Sept. 14, 1960,* Baltimore, Md. *(501,129)*	1.25
1143	4c	**Lincoln "Credo,"** *Nov. 19, 1960,* New York, N.Y. *(467,780)*	1.25
1144	4c	**Patrick Henry "Credo,"** *Jan. 11, 1961,* Richmond, Va. *(415,252)*	1.25
1145	4c	**Boy Scouts,** *Feb. 8, 1960,* Washington, D.C. *(1,419,955)*	1.25
1146	4c	**Olympic Winter Games,** *Feb. 18, 1960,* Olympic Valley, Calif, *(516,456)*	80
1147	4c	**Masaryk,** *Mar. 7, 1960,* Washington, D.C.	80
1148	4c	**Masaryk,** *Mar. 7, 1960,* Washington, D.C.	80
		1147 and 1148, set of two on one cover	2.25

First day cancellation was applied to 1,710,726 covers bearing No. 1147, No. 1148, or both.

1149	4c	**World Refugee Year,** *Apr. 7, 1960,* Washington, D.C. *(413,298)*	80
1150	4c	**Water Conservation,** *Apr. 18, 1960,* Washington, D.C. *(648,988)*	80
1151	4c	**SEATO,** *May 31, 1960,* Washington, D.C. *(514,926)*	80
1152	4c	**American Woman,** *June 2, 1960,* Washington, D.C. *(830,385)*	80
1153	4c	**50—Star Flag,** *July 4, 1960,* Honolulu, Hawaii *(820,900)*	80
1154	4c	**Pony Express Centennial,** *July 19, 1960,* Sacramento, Calif, *(520,223)*	80
1155	4c	**Employ the Handicapped,** *Aug. 28, 1960,* New York, N.Y. *(439,638)*	80
1156	4c	**World Forestry Congress,** *Aug. 29, 1960,* Seattle, Wash. *(350,848)*	80
1157	4c	**Mexican Independence,** *Sept. 16, 1960,* Los Angeles, Calif, *(360,297)*	80
1158	4c	**U.S.—Japan Treaty,** *Sept. 28, 1960,* Washington, D.C. *(545,150)*	80
1159	4c	**Paderewski,** *Oct. 8, 1960,* Washington, D.C.	80
1160	8c	**Paderewski,** *Oct. 8, 1960,* Washington, D.C.	80
		1159 and 1160 on one cover	2.25

First day cancellation was applied to 1,057,438 covers bearing No. 1159, No. 1160, or both.

1161	4c	**Robert A. Taft,** *Oct. 10, 1960,* Cincinnati, Ohio *(312,116)*	80
1162	4c	**Wheels of Freedom,** *Oct. 15, 1960,* Detroit, Mich. *(380,551)*	80
1163	4c	**Boys' Clubs,** *Oct. 18, 1960,* New York, N.Y. *(435,009)*	80
1164	4c	**Automated P.O.,** *Oct. 20, 1960,* Providence, R.I. *(458,237)*	80
1165	4c	**Mannerheim,** *Oct. 26, 1960,* Washington, D.C.	80
1166	8c	**Mannerheim,** *Oct. 26, 1960,* Washington, D.C.	80
		1165 and 1166 on one cover	2.25

First day cancellation was applied to 1,168,770 covers bearing No. 1165, No. 1166, or both.

1167	4c	**Camp Fire Girls,** *Nov. 1, 1960,* New York, N.Y. *(324,944)*	80
1168	4c	**Garibaldi,** *Nov. 2, 1960,* Washington, D.C.	80
1169	4c	**Garibaldi,** *Nov. 2, 1960,* Washington, D.C.	80
		1168 and 1169 on one cover	2.25

First day cancellation was applied to 1,001,490 covers bearing No. 1168, No. 1169, or both.

1170	4c	**Senator George,** *Nov. 5, 1960,* New York, N.Y. *(318,180)*	80
1171	4c	**Andrew Carnegie,** *Nov. 25, 1960,* New York, N.Y. *(318,180)*	80
1172	4c	**John Foster Dulles,** *Dec. 6, 1960,* Washington, D.C. *(400,055)*	80
1173	4c	**Echo I,** *Dec. 15, 1960,* Washington, D.C. *(583,747)*	2.00

1961-65

1174	4c	**Gandhi,** *Jan. 26, 1961,* Washington, D.C.	80
1175	8c	**Gandhi,** *Jan. 26, 1961,* Washington, D.C.	80
		1174 and 1175 on one cover	2.25

First day cancellation was applied to 1,013,515 covers bearing No. 1174, No. 1175, or both.

1176	4c	**Range Conservation,** *Feb. 2, 1961,* Salt Lake City, Utah *(357,101)*	75
1177	4c	**Horace Greeley,** *Feb. 3, 1961,* Chappaqua, N.Y. *(359,205)*	75
1178	4c	**Fort Sumter,** *Apr. 12, 1961,* Charleston, S.C. *(602,599)*	1.75
1179	4c	**Battle of Shiloh,** *Apr. 7, 1962,* Shiloh, Tenn. *(526,062)*	1.75
1180	5c	**Battle of Gettysburg,** *July 1, 1963,* Gettysburg, Pa. *(600,205)*	1.75
1181	5c	**Battle of Wilderness,** *May 5, 1964,* Fredericksburg, Va. *(450,904)*	1.75
1182	5c	**Appomattox,** *Apr. 9, 1965,* Appomattox, Va. *(653,121)*	1.75
1183	4c	**Kansas Statehood,** *May 10, 1961,* Council Grove, Kansas *(480,561)*	75
1184	4c	**Senator Norris,** *July 11, 1961,* Washington, D.C. *(482,875)*	75
1185	4c	**Naval Aviation,** *Aug. 20, 1961,* San Diego, Calif. *(416,391)*	90
1186	4c	**Workmen's Compensation,** *Sept. 4, 1961,* Milwaukee, Wis, *(410,236)*	75
1187	4c	**Frederic Remington,** *Oct. 4, 1961,* Washington, D.C. *(723,443)*	75
1188	4c	**China Republic,** *Oct. 10, 1961,* Washington, D.C. *(463,900)*	75
1189	4c	**Naismith—Basketball,** *Nov. 6, 1961,* Springfield, Mass. *(479,917)*	1.50
1190	4c	**Nursing,** *Dec. 28, 1961,* Washington, D.C. *(964,005)*	75

1962

1191	4c	**New Mexico Statehood,** *Jan. 6, 1962,* Sante Fe, N.M. *(365,330)*	75
1192	4c	**Arizona Statehood,** *Feb. 14, 1962,* Phoenix, Ariz. *(508,216)*	75
1193	4c	**Project Mercury,** *Feb. 20, 1962,* Cape Canaveral, Fla. *(3,000,000)*	2.00
		Any city	5.00
1194	4c	**Malaria Eradication,** *Mar. 30, 1962,* Washington, D.C. *(554,175)*	75
1195	4c	**Charles Evans Hughes,** *Apr. 11, 1962,* Washington, D.C. *(544,424)*	75
1196	4c	**Seattle World's Fair,** *Apr. 25, 1962,* Seattle, Wash. *(771,856)*	75
1197	4c	**Louisiana Statehood,** *Apr. 30, 1962,* New Orleans, La. *(436,681)*	75
1198	4c	**Homestead Act,** *May 20, 1962,* Beatrice, Nebr. *(487,450)*	75
1199	4c	**Girl Scouts,** *July 24, 1962,* Burlington, VT *(634,347)*	1.00
1200	4c	**Brien McMahon,** *July 28, 1962,* Norwalk, Conn. *(384,419)*	75
1201	4c	**Apprenticeship,** *Aug. 31, 1962,* Washington, D.C. *(1,003,548)*	75
1202	4c	**Sam Rayburn,** *Sept. 16, 1962,* Bonham, Texas *(401,042)*	75
1203	4c	**Dag Hammarskjold,** *Oct. 23, 1962,* New York, N.Y. *(500,683)*	75
1204	4c	**Hammarskjold,** yellow inverted, *Nov. 16, 1962,* Washington, D.C. (about 75,000)	6.00
1205	4c	**Christmas,** *Nov. 1, 1962,* Pittsburgh, Pa. *(491,312)*	75
1206	4c	**Higher Education,** *Nov. 14, 1962,* Washington, D.C. *(627,347)*	75
1207	4c	**Winslow Homer,** *Dec. 15, 1962,* Gloucester, Mass. *(498,866)*	75

1963-66

1208	5c	**Flag,** *Jan. 9, 1963,* Washington, D.C. *(696,185)*	75
1208a	5c	Tagged, *Aug. 25, 1966*	11.50

1962-66

REGULAR ISSUE

1209	1c	**Jackson,** *Mar. 22, 1963,* New York, N.Y. *(392,363)*	75
1209a	1c	Tagged, *July 6, 1966,* Washington, D.C.	5.75
1213	5c	**Washington,** *Nov. 23, 1962* New York, N.Y. *(360,531)*	75
1213b	5c	Tagged, *Oct. 28, 1963* Dayton, Ohio, (about 15,000)	5.75
1225	1c	Coil, *May 31, 1963.* Chicago, Ill. *(238,952)*	75
1225a	1c	Coil, tagged, *July 6, 1966,* Washington, D.C., Pair	5.75
1229	5c	Coil, *Nov. 23, 1962,* New York, N.Y. *(184,627)*	75
1229a	5c	Coil, tagged, *Oct. 28, 1963,* Dayton, Ohio, (about 2,000)	20.00

1963

1230	5c	**Carolina Charter,** *Apr. 6, 1963,* Edenton, N.C. *(426,200)*	75
1231	5c	**Food for Peace,** *June 4, 1963,* Washington, D.C. *(624,342)*	75
1232	5c	**West Virginia Statehood,** *June 20, 1963,* Wheeling, W. Va. *(413,389)*	75
1233	5c	**Emancipation Proclamation,** *Aug. 16, 1963,* Chicago, Ill, *(494,886)*	75
1234	5c	**Alliance for Progress,** *Aug. 17, 1963,* Washington, D.C. *(528,095)*	75
1235	5c	**Cordell Hull,** *Oct. 5, 1963* Carthage, Tenn. *(391,631)*	75
1236	5c	**Eleanor Roosevelt,** *Oct. 11, 1963,* Washington, D.C. *(860,155)*	75
1237	5c	**Science,** *Oct. 14, 1963,* Washington, D.C. *(504,503)*	75
1238	5c	**City Mail Delivery,** *Oct. 26, 1963,* Washington, D.C. *(544,806)*	75
1239	5c	**Red Cross,** *Oct. 29, 1963,* Washington, D.C. *(557,678)*	75
1240	5c	**Christmas,** *Nov. 1, 1963,* Santa Claus, Ind. *(458,619)*	75
1240a	5c	**Christmas, tagged,** *Nov. 2, 1963,* Washington, D.C. (about 500)	75.00

Note below No. 1036b also applies to No. 1240a.

1241	5c	**Audubon,** *Dec. 7, 1963,* Henderson, Ky. *(518,855)*	75

1964

1242	5c	**Sam Houston,** *Jan. 10, 1964,* Houston, Tex. *(487,986)*	75
1243	5c	**Charles Russel,** *Mar. 19, 1964,* Great Falls, Mont. *(658,745)*	75
1244	5c	**N.Y. World's Fair,** *Apr. 22, 1964,* World's Fair, N.Y. *(1,656,346)*	75
1245	5c	**John Muir,** *Apr. 29, 1964,* Martinez, Calif. *(446,925)*	75
1246	5c	**John F. Kennedy,** *May 29, 1964,* Boston, Mass. *(2,003,096)*	75
		Any city	75
1247	5c	**New Jersey Tercentenary,** *June 15, 1964,* Elizabeth, N.J. *(526,879)*	75
1248	5c	**Nevada Statehood,** *July 22, 1964,* Carson City, Nev. *(584,973)*	75
1249	5c	**Register & Vote,** *Aug. 1, 1964,* Washington, D.C. *(533,439)*	75
1250	5c	**Shakespeare,** *Aug. 14, 1964,* Stratford, Conn. *(524,053)*	75
1251	5c	**Drs. Mayo,** *Sept. 11, 1964,* Rochester, Minn. *(674,846)*	75
1252	5c	**American Music,** *Oct. 15, 1964,* New York, N.Y. *(466,107)*	75
1253	5c	**Homemakers,** *Oct. 26, 1964,* Honolulu, Hawaii *(435,392)*	75
1254	5c	**Christmas (holly),** *Nov. 9, 1964,* Bethlehem, Pa.	75
1254a	5c	Tagged, *Nov. 10, 1964,* Dayton, O.	12.50
1255	5c	**Christmas (mistletoe),** *Nov. 9, 1964,* Bethlehem, Pa.	75
1255a	5c	Tagged, *Nov. 10, 1964,* Dayton, O.	12.50
1256	5c	**Christmas (poinsettia),** *Nov. 9, 1964,* Bethlehem, Pa.	75
1256a	5c	Tagged, *Nov. 10, 1964,* Dayton, O.	12.50
1257	5c	**Christmas (conifer),** *Nov. 9, 1964,* Bethlehem, Pa.	75
1257a	5c	Tagged, *Nov. 10, 1964,* Dayton, O.	12.50
		1257b	3.00
		1257c	57.50

First day cancellation was applied to 794,900 covers bearing Nos. 1254 to 1257 in singles or block and (at Dayton) to about 2,700 covers bearing Nos. 1254a to 1257a in singles or multiples.

1258	5c	**Verrazano—Narrows Bridge,** *Nov. 21, 1964,* Staten Island, N.Y. *(619,780)*	75
1259	5c	**Fine Arts,** *Dec. 2, 1964,* Washington, D.C. *(558,046)*	75
1260	5c	**Amateur Radio,** *Dec. 15, 1964,* Anchorage, Alaska *(452,255)*	75

1965

1261	5c	**Battle of New Orleans,** *Jan. 8,* New Orleans, La. *(466,029)*	75
1262	5c	**Physical Fitness—Sokol,** *Feb. 15,* Washington, D.C. *(864,848)*	75
1263	5c	**Cancer Crusade,** *Apr. 1,* Washington, D.C. *(744,485)*	75
1264	5c	**Churchill,** *May 13,* Fulton, Mo. *(773,580)*	75
1265	5c	**Magna Carta,** *June 15,* Jamestown, Va. *(479,065)*	75
1266	5c	**Intl. Cooperation Year,** *June 26,* San Francisco, Cal. *(402,925)*	75
1267	5c	**Salvation Army,** *July 2,* New York, N.Y. *(634,228)*	75
1268	5c	**Dante,** *July 17,* San Francisco, Cal. *(424,893)*	75
1269	5c	**Herbet Hoover,** *Aug. 10,* West Branch, Iowa *(698,182)*	75
1270	5c	**Robert Fulton,** *Aug. 19,* Clermont, N.Y. *(550,330)*	75
1271	5c	**Florida Settlement,** *Aug. 28,* St. Augustine, Fla. *(465,000)*	75
1272	5c	**Traffic Safety,** *Sept. 3,* Baltimore, Md. *(527,075)*	75
1273	5c	**Copley,** *Sept. 17,* Washington, D.C. *(613,484)*	75

Cat#	Denom	Description	Price
1274	11c	**Intl. Telecommunication Union,** *Oct. 6,* Washington, D.C. *(332,818)*	75
1275	5c	**Adlai Stevenson,** *Oct. 23,* Bloomington, Ill. *(755,656)*	75
1276	5c	**Christmas,** *Nov. 2,* Silver Bell, Ariz. *(705,039)*	75
1276a	5c	Tagged, *Nov. 15,* Washington, D.C. (about *300*)	42.50

1965-78

PROMINENT AMERICANS ISSUE

Cat#	Denom	Description	Price
1278	1c	*Jan. 12, 1968,* Jeffersonville, Ind.	60

First day cancellation was applied to 655,680 covers bearing Nos. 1278, 1278a or 1299.

Cat#	Denom	Description	Price
1279	1¼c	*Jan. 30, 1967,* Gallatin, Mo. *(439,010)*	60
1280	2c	*June 8, 1966,* Spring Green, Wis. *(460,427)*	60
1281	3c	*Sept. 16, 1967,* Boston, Mass. *(518,355)*	60
1282	4c	*Nov. 19, 1965,* New York, N.Y. *(445,629)*	60
1282a	4c	Tagged, *Dec. 1, 1965,* Dayton, O. (about *2,000*)	20.00
		Washington, D.C. *(1,200)*	32.50
1283	5c	*Feb. 22, 1966,* Washington, D.C. *(525,372)*	60
1283a	5c	Tagged, *Feb. 23, 1966,* Washington, D.C. (about *900*)	22.50
		Dayton, Ohio (about *200*)	57.50
1283B	5c	Redrawn, *Nov. 17, 1967,* New York, N.Y. *(328,983)*	45
1284	6c	*Jan. 29, 1966,* Hyde Park, N.Y. *(448,631)*	45
1284a	6c	Tagged, *Dec. 29, 1966,* Washington, D.C.	20.00
1285	8c	*Mar. 14, 1966,* Princeton, N.J. *(366,803)*	50
1285a	8c	Tagged, *July 6, 1966*	14.00
1286	10c	*Mar. 15, 1967,* Hermitage, Tenn. *(255,945)*	60
1286A	12c	*July 30, 1968,* Greenfield Village, Mich. *(342,850)*	50
1287	13c	*May 29, 1967,* Brookline, Mass. *(391,195)*	65
1288	15c	*Mar. 8, 1968,* Washington, D.C. *(322,970)*	60
1288B	15c	*June 14, 1978,* Boston, Mass.	65

First day cancellation was applied to 387,119 covers bearing Nos. 1288B or 1305E.

Cat#	Denom	Description	Price
1289	20c	*Oct. 24, 1967,* Lexington, Va. *(221,206)*	80
1289a	20c	Tagged, *Apr. 3, 1973,* New York, N.Y.	12.50
1290	25c	*Feb. 14, 1967,* Washington, D.C. *(213,730)*	1.00
1290a	25c	Tagged, *Apr. 3, 1973,* New York, N.Y.	14.00
1291	30c	*Oct. 21, 1968,* Burlington, Vt. *(162,790)*	1.20
1291a	30c	Tagged, *Apr. 3, 1973,* New York, N.Y.	14.00
1292	40c	*Jan. 29, 1968,* Philadelphia, Pa. *(157,947)*	1.60
1292a	40c	Tagged, *Apr. 3, 1973,* New York, N.Y.	15.00
1293	50c	*Aug. 13, 1968,* Dorchester, Mass. *(140,410)*	3.25
1293a	50c	Tagged, *Apr. 3, 1973,* New York, N.Y.	20.00
1294	$1	*Oct. 16, 1967,* New London, Conn. *(103,102)*	7.50
1294a	$1	Tagged, *Apr. 3,* New York, N.Y.	22.50
1295	$5	*Dec. 3, 1966,* Smyrna, Del. *(41,130)*	60.00
1295a	$5	Tagged, *Apr. 3, 1973,* New York, N.Y.	70.00

First day cancellation was applied to 17,533 covers bearing one or more of Nos. 1059b, 1289a, 1290a, 1291a, 1292a, 1293a, 1294a and 1295a.

Cat#	Denom	Description	Price
1297	3c	*Nov. 4, 1975,* Pendleton, Ore. *(166,798)*	75
1298	6c	Perf. 10 Horiz., *Dec. 28, 1967,* Washington, D.C.	75

First day cancellation was applied to 312,330 covers bearing Nos. 1298 and 1284b.

Cat#	Denom	Description	Price
1299	1c	*Jan. 12, 1968,* Jeffersonville, Ind.	75
1303	4c	*May 28, 1966,* Springfield, Ill. *(322,563)*	75
1304	5c	*Sept. 8, 1966,* Cincinnati, O. *(245,400)*	75
1305	6c	Perf. 10 vert., *Feb. 28, 1968,* Washington, D.C. *(317,199)*	75
1305E	15c	*June 14, 1978,* Boston, Mass.	75
1305C	$1	*Jan. 12, 1973,* Hempstead, N.Y. *(121,217)*	3.00

1966

Cat#	Denom	Description	Price
1306	5c	**Migratory Bird Treaty,** *Mar. 16, 1966,* Pittsburgh, Pa. *(555,485)*	75
1307	5c	**Humane Treatment of Animals,** *Apr. 9, 1966,* New York, N.Y. *(524,420)*	75
1308	5c	**Indiana Statehood,** *Apr. 16, 1966,* Corydon, Ind. *(575,557)*	75
1309	5c	**Circus,** *May 2, 1966,* Delavan, Wis. *(754,076)*	75
1310	5c	**SIPEX,** *May 21, 1966,* Washington, D.C. *(637,802)*	75

Cat#	Denom	Description	Price
1311	5c	**SIPEX, Souvenir Sheet,** *May 23, 1966,* Washington, D.C. *(700,882)*	75
1312	5c	**Bill of Rights,** *July 1, 1966,* Miami Beach, Fla. *(562,920)*	75
1313	5c	**Polish Millennium,** *July 30, 1966,* Washington, D.C. *(715,603)*	75
1314	5c	**National Park Service,** *Aug. 25, 1966,* Yellowstone National Park, Wyo. *(528,170)*	75
1314a	5c	Tagged, *Aug. 26, 1966*	20.00
1315	5c	**Marine Corps Reserve,** *Aug. 29, 1966* Washington, D.C. *(585,923)*	75
1315a	5c	Tagged, *Aug. 29, 1966,* Washington, D.C.	20.00
1316	5c	**Gen. Fed. of Womens Clubs,** *Sept. 12, 1966,* New York, N.Y. *(383,334)*	75
1316a	5c	Tagged, *Sept. 13, 1966*	22.50
1317	5c	**Johnny Appleseed,** *Sept. 24, 1966,* Leominster, Mass. *(794,610)*	75
1317a	5c	Tagged, *Sept. 26, 1966*	22.50
1318	5c	**Beautification of America,** *Oct. 5, 1966,* Washington, D.C. *(564,440)*	75
1318a	5c	Tagged, *Oct. 5, 1966,* Washington, D.C.	20.00
1319	5c	**Great River Road,** *Oct. 21, 1966,* Baton Rouge, La. *(330,933)*	75
1319a	5c	Tagged, *Oct. 22, 1966*	22.50
1320	5c	**Savings Bond—Servicemen,** *Oct. 26, 1966,* Sioux City, Iowa *(444,421)*	75
1320a	5c	Tagged, *Oct. 27, 1966*	22.50
1321	5c	**Christmas,** *Nov. 1, 1966,* Christmas, Mich. *(537,650)*	75
1321a	5c	Tagged, *Nov. 2, 1966*	9.50
1322	5c	**Mary Cassatt,** *Nov. 17, 1966,* Washington, D.C. *(593,389)*	75
1322a	5c	Tagged, *Nov. 17, 1966,* Washington, D.C.	20.00

1967

Cat#	Denom	Description	Price
1323	5c	**National Grange,** *Apr. 17, 1967,* Washington, D.C. *(603,460)*	75
1324	5c	**Canada Centenary,** *May 25, 1967,* Montreal, Canada *(711,795)*	75
1325	5c	**Erie Canal,** *July 4, 1967,* Rome, N.Y. *(784,611)*	75
1326	5c	**Search for Peace—Lions,** *July 5, 1967,* Chicago, Ill. *(393,197)*	75
1327	5c	**Thoreau,** *July 12, 1967,* Concord, Mass. *(696,789)*	75
1328	5c	**Nebraska Statehood,** *July 29, 1967,* Lincoln, Nebr. *(1,146,957)*	75
1329	5c	**Voice of America,** *Aug. 1, 1967,* Washington, D.C. *(455,190)*	75
1330	5c	**Davy Crockett,** *Aug. 17, 1967,* San Antonio, Tex. *(462,291)*	75
1331 to 1332	5c	**Space Accomplishments,** *Sept. 29, 1967,* Kennedy Space Center, Fla. *(667,267)*	@3.00
		1331a	8.00
1333	5c	**Urban Planning,** *Oct. 2, 1967,* Washington, D.C. *(389,009)*	75
1334	5c	**Finland Independence,** *Oct. 6, 1967,* Finland, Minn. *(408,532)*	75
1335	5c	**Thomas Eakins,** *Nov. 2, 1967,* Washington, D.C. *(648,054)*	75
1336	5c	**Christmas,** *Nov. 6, 1967,* Bethlehem, Ga. *(462,118)*	75
1337	5c	**Mississippi Statehood,** *Dec. 11, 1967,* Natchez, Miss. *(379,612)*	75

1968-71

Cat#	Denom	Description	Price
1338	6c	**Flag**(Giori), *Jan. 24, 1968,* Washington, D.C. *(412,120)*	75
1338A	6c	**Flag coil,** *May 30, 1969,* Chicago, Ill. *(248,434)*	75
1338D	6c	**Flag**(Huck) *Aug. 7, 1970,* Washington, D.C. *(365,280)*	75
1338F	8c	**Flag,** *May 10, 1971,* Washington, D.C.	75
1338G	8c	**Flag coil,** *May 10, 1971,* Washington, D.C.	75

First day cancellation (May 10) was applied to 235,543 covers bearing either No. 1338F or 1338G.

Cat#	Denom	Description	Price
1339	6c	**Illinois Statehood,** *Feb. 12, 1968,* Shawneetown, Ill. *(761,640)*	75
1340	6c	**HemisFair'68,** *Mar. 30, 1968,* San Antonio, Tex. *(469,909)*	75
1341	$1	**Airlift,** *Apr. 4, 1968,* Seattle, Wash. *(105,088)*	6.50
1342	6c	**Youth—Elks,** *May 1, 1968,* Chicago, Ill. *(354,711)*	75
1343	6c	**Law and Order,** *May 17, 1968,* Washington, D.C. *(407,081)*	75
1344	6c	**Register and Vote,** *June 27, 1968,* Washington, D.C. *(355,685)*	75
1345 to 1354	6c	**Historic Flag series of 10,** *July 4, 1968,* Pittsburgh, Pa.	@4.00
		1354a	12.00

First day cancellation was applied to 2,924,962 covers bearing one or more of Nos. 1345 to 1354.

Cat#	Denom	Description	Price
1355	6c	**Disney,** *Sept. 11, 1968,* Marceline, Mo. *(909,505)*	1.00
1356	6c	**Marquette,** *Sept. 20, 1968,* Sault Ste. Marie, Mich. *(379,710)*	75
1357	6c	**Daniel Boone,** *Sept. 26, 1968,* Frankfort, Ky. *(333,440)*	75
1358	6c	**Arkansas River,** *Oct. 1, 1968,* Little Rock, Ark. *(358,025)*	75

Cat#	Denom	Description	Price
1359	6c	**Leif Erikson,** *Oct. 9, 1968,* Seattle, Wash. *(376,565)*	75
1360	6c	**Cherokee Strip,** *Oct. 15, 1968,* Ponca, Okla. *(339,330)*	75
1361	6c	**John Trumbull,** *Oct. 18, 1968,* New Haven, Conn. *(378,285)*	75
1362	6c	**Waterfowl Conservation,** *Oct. 24, 1968,* Cleveland, Ohio *(349,719)*	75
1363	6c	**Christmas,** tagged, *Nov. 1, 1968,* Washington, D.C. *(739,055)*	75
1363a	6c	Untagged, *Nov. 2, 1968,* Washington, D.C.	6.50
1364	6c	**American Indian,** *Nov. 4, 1968,* Washington, D.C. *(415,964)*	75

1969

Cat#	Denom	Description	Price
1365 to 1368	6c	**Beautification of America,** *Jan. 16, 1969,* Washington, D.C.	@2.00
		1368a	5.00

First day cancellation was applied to 1,094,184 covers bearing one or more of Nos. 1365 to 1368.

Cat#	Denom	Description	Price
1369	6c	**American Legion,** *Mar. 15, 1959,* Washington, D.C. *(632,035)*	75
1370	6c	**Grandma Moses,** *May 1, 1969,* Washington, D.C. *(367,880)*	75
1371	6c	**Apollo 8,** *May 5, 1969,* Houston, Texas *(908,634)*	2.00
1372	6c	**W.C. Handy,** *May 17, 1969,* Memphis, Tenn. *(398,216)*	75
1373	6c	**California Bicentenary,** *July 16, 1969,* San Diego, Calif. *(530,210)*	75
1374	6c	**J.W. Powell,** *Aug. 1, 1969,* Page, Ariz. *(434,433)*	75
1375	6c	**Alabama Statehood,** *Aug. 2, 1969,* Huntsville, Ala. *(485,801)*	75
1376 to 1379	6c	**Botanical Congress,** *Aug. 23, 1969,* Seattle, Wash.	@2.00
		1379a	7.00

First day cancellation was applied to 737,935 covers bearing one or more of Nos. 1376 to 1379.

Cat#	Denom	Description	Price
1380	6c	**Dartmouth Case,** *Sept. 22, 1969,* Hanover N.H. *(416,327)*	75
1381	6c	**Professional Baseball,** *Sept. 24, 1969,* Cincinnati, Ohio *(414,942)*	1.50
1382	6c	**Intercollegiate Football,** *Sept. 26, 1969,* New Brunswick, N.J. *(414,860)*	1.50
1383	6c	**Dwight D. Eisenhower,** *Oct. 14, 1969,* Abilene, Kans. *(1,009,560)*	75
1384	6c	**Christmas,** *Nov. 3, 1969,* Christmas, Fla. *(555,500)*	75
1385	6c	**Hope for Crippled,** *Nov. 20, 1969,* Columbus, Ohio *(342,676)*	75
1386	6c	**William M. Harnett,** *Dec. 3, 1969,* Boston, Mass. *(408,860)*	75

1970-74

Cat#	Denom	Description	Price
1387 to 1390	6c	**National History,** *May 6, 1970,* New York, N.Y.	@2.00
		1390a	3.00

First day cancellation was applied to 834,260 covers bearing one or more of Nos. 1387 to 1390.

Cat#	Denom	Description	Price
1391	6c	**Maine Statehood,** *July 9, 1970,* Portland, Maine, *(472,165)*	75
1392	6c	**Wildlife Conservation,** *July 20, 1970,* Custer, S.D. *(309,418)*	1.00
1393	6c	**Eisenhower,** *Aug. 6, 1970,* Washington, D.C.	75

First day cancellations were applied to 823,540 covers bearing one or more of Nos. 1393 and 1401.

Cat#	Denom	Description	Price
1393D	7c	**Franklin,** *Oct. 20, 1972,* Philadelphia, Pa. *(309,276)*	75
1394	8c	**Eisenhower**(multi), *May 10, 1971,* Washington, D.C.	75
1395	8c	**Eisenhower**(claret), *May 10, 1971,* Washington, D.C.	75

First day cancellations were applied to 813,947 covers bearing one or more of Nos. 1394, 1395 and 1402.

Cat#	Denom	Description	Price
1396	8c	**Postal Service Emblem,** *July 1, 1971,* any city (est. *16,300,000*)	75
1397	14c	**Fiorello H. LaGuardia,** *Apr. 24, 1972,* New York, N.Y. *(180,114)*	85
1398	16c	**Ernie Pyle,** *May 7, 1971,* Washington, D.C. *(444,410)*	75
1399	18c	**Elizabeth Blackwell,** *Jan. 23, 1974,* Geneva, N.Y. *(217,938)*	1.25
1400	21c	**Amadeo Giannini,** *June 27, 1973,* San Mateo, Calif. *(282,520)*	1.00
1401	6c	**Eisenhower coil,** *Aug. 6, 1970,* Washington, D.C.	75
1402	8c	**Eisenhower coil,** *May 10, 1971,* Washington, D.C.	75
1405	6c	**Edgar Lee Masters,** *Aug. 22, 1970,* Petersburg Ill. *(372,804)*	75
1406	6c	**Woman Suffrage,** *Aug. 26, 1970,* Adams, Mass. *(508,142)*	75
1407	6c	**South Carolina Anniv.,** *Sept. 12, 1970,* Charleston, S.C. *(533,000)*	75
1408	6c	**Stone Mt. Memorial,** *Sept. 19, 1970,* Stone Mountain, Ga. *(558,546)*	75
1409	6c	**Fort Snelling,** *Oct. 17, 1970,* Fort Snelling, Minn. *(497,611)*	75
1410 to 1413	6c	**Anti—Pollution,** *Oct. 28, 1970,* San Clemente, Calif.	@1.40
		1413a	4.25

First day cancellation was applied to 1,033, 147 covers bearing one or more of Nos. 1410 to 1413.

1414 to *1418*	6c	**Christmas**, *Nov. 5, 1970*, Washington, D.C.	@1.40
		1414 to 1418 on one cover	3.50

First day cancellation was applied to 2,014,450 covers bearing one or more of Nos. 1414 to 1418 or 1414a to 1418a.

1419	6c	**United Nations**, *Nov. 20, 1970*, New York, N.Y. *(474,070)*	75
1420	6c	**Pilgrims Landing**, *Nov. 21, 1970*, Plymouth, Mass. *(629,850)*	75
1421	6c	**Disabled Veterans**, *Nov. 24, 1970*, Cincinnati, Ohio, or Montgomery, Ala.	75
1422	6c	**U.S. Servicemen**, *Nov. 24, 1970*, Cincinnati, Ohio, or Montgomery, Ala.	75
		1421 to 1422 se—tenant on one cover	1.20

First day cancellation was applied to 476,610 covers at Cincinnati and 336,417 at Montgomery, each cover bearing one or both of Nos. 1421 to 1422.

1971

1423	6c	**Wool Industry**, *Jan. 19, 1971*, Las Vegas, Nev. *(379,911)*	75
1424	6c	**MacArthur**, *Jan. 26, 1971*, Norfolk, Va. *(720,035)*	75
1425	6c	**Blood Donor**, *Mar. 12, 1971*, New York, N.Y. *(644,497)*	75
1426	8c	**Missouri Sesquicentennial**, *May 8, 1971*, Independence, Mo. *(551,000)*	75
1427 to *1430*	8c	**Wildlife Conservation**, *June 12, 1971*, Avery Island, La.	@1.75
		1430a	3.00

First day cancellation was applied to 679,483 covers bearing one or more of Nos. 1427 to 1430.

1431	8c	**Antarctic Treaty**, *June 23, 1971*, Washington D.C. *(419,200)*	75
1432	8c	**American Revolution Bicentennial**, *July 4, 1971*, Washington, D.C. *(434,930)*	75
1433	8c	**John Sloan**, *Aug. 2, 1971*, Lock Haven, Pa. *(482,265)*	75
1434 to *1435*	8c	**Space Achievement Decade**, *Aug. 2, 1971*, se—tenant, Kennedy Space Center, Fla. *(1,403,644)*	1.75
		Houston, Texas *(811,560)*	2.00
		Huntsville, Ala. *(524,000)*	2.25
1436	8c	**Emily Dickinson**, *Aug. 28, 1971*, Amherst, Mass. *(498,180)*	75
1437	8c	**San Juan**, *Sept. 12, 1971*, San Juan, P.R. *(501,668)*	75
1438	8c	**Drug Abuse**, *Oct. 4, 1971*, Dallas, Texas *(425,330)*	75
1439	8c	**CARE**, *Oct. 27, 1971*, New York, N.Y. *(402,121)*	75
1440 to *1443*	8c	**Historic Preservation**, *Oct. 29, 1971*, San Diego, Calif.	@1.50
		1443a	3.00

First day cancellation was applied to 783,242 covers bearing one or more of Nos. 1440 to 1443.

1444 to *1445*	8c	**Christmas**, *Nov. 10, 1971*, Washington, D.C.	@75
		1444 to 1445 on one cover	1.20

First day cancellation was applied to 348,038 covers with No. 1444 (Nativity) and 580,062 with No. 1445 (partridge).

1972

1446	8c	**Sidney Lanier**, *Feb. 3, 1972*, Macon Ga. *(394,800)*	75
1447	8c	**Peace Corps**, *Feb. 11, 1972*, Washington, D.C. *(453,660)*	75
1448 to *1451*	2c	**National Parks Centennial**, *Apr. 5, 1972*, Hatteras, N.C., block of 4 *(505,697)*	1.25
1452	6c	**National Parks**, *June 26, 1972*, Vienna, Va. *(403,396)*	75
1453	8c	**National Parks**, *Mar. 1, 1972* Yellowstone National Park, Wyo. Washington, D.C. *(847,500)*	75 75
1454	15c	**National Parks**, *July 28, 1972*, Mt. McKinley National Park, Alaska *(491,456)*	75
1455	8c	**Family Planning**, *Mar. 18, 1972*, New York, N.Y. *(691,385)*	75
1456 to *1459*	8c	**Colonial Craftsmen** (Rev. Bicentennial), *July 4, 1972*, Williamsburg, Va. *(1,914,976)*	@1.00
		1459a	2.50
1460	6c	**Olympics**, *Aug. 17, 1972*, Washington, D.C.	75
1461	8c	**Winter Olympics**, *Aug. 17, 1972*, Washington, D.C.	85
1462	15c	**Olympics**, *Aug. 17, 1972*, Washington, D.C.	1.00
		1460 to 1462 and C85 on one cover	2.75

First day cancellation was applied to 971,536 covers bearing one or more of Nos. 1460 to 1462 and C85.

1463	8c	**P.T.A.**, *Sept. 15, 1972*, San Francisco, Cal. *(523,454)*	75
1464 to *1467*	8c	**Wildlife**, *Sept. 20, 1972*, Warm Springs, Ore.	@2.00
		1467a	3.00

First day cancellation was applied to 733,778 covers bearing one or more of Nos. 1464 to 1467.

1468	8c	**Mail Order**, *Sept. 27, 1972*, Chicago, Ill. *(759,666)*	75
1469	8c	**Osteopathy**, *Oct. 9, 1972*, Miami, Fla. *(607,160)*	75
1470	8c	**Tom Sawyer**, *Oct. 13, 1972*, Hannibal, Mo. *(459,013)*	75
1471 to *1472*	8c	**Christmas**, *Nov. 9, 1972*, Washington, D.C.	@75
		1471 to 1472 on one cover	1.00

First day cancellation was applied to 713,821 covers bearing one or more of Nos. 1471 to 1472.

1473	8c	**Pharmacy**, *Nov. 10, 1972*, Cincinnati, Ohio *(804,320)*	75
1474	8c	**Stamp Collecting**, *Nov. 17, 1972*, New York, N.Y. *(434,680)*	75

1973

1475	8c	**Love**, *Jan. 26, 1973*, Philadelphia, Pa. *(422,492)*	75
1476	8c	**Pamphleteer** (Rev. Bicentennial), *Feb. 16, 1973*, Portland, Ore. *(431,784)*	75
1477	8c	**Broadside** (Rev. Bicentennial), *April 13, 1973*, Atlantic City, N.J. *(423,437)*	75
1478	8c	**Post Rider** (Rev. Bicentennial), *June 22, 1973*, Rochester, N.Y. *(586,850)*	75
1479	8c	**Drummer** (Rev. Bicentennial), *Sept. 28, 1973*, New Orleans, La. *(522,427)*	75
1480 to *1483*	8c	**Boston Tea Party** (Rev. Bicentennial), *July 4, 1973*, Boston, Mass.	@1.75
		1483a	3.75

First day cancellation was applied to 897,870 covers bearing one or more of Nos. 1480 to 1483.

1484	8c	**George Gershwin**, *Feb. 28, 1973*, Beverly Hills, Calif. *(448,814)*	75
1485	8c	**Robinson Jeffers**, *Aug. 13, 1973*, Carmel, Calif. *(394,261)*	75
1486	8c	**Henry O. Tanner**, *Sept. 10, 1973*, Pittsburgh, Pa. *(424,065)*	75
1487	8c	**Willa Cather**, *Sept. 20, 1973*, Red Cloud, Nebr. *(435,784)*	75
1488	8c	**Nicolaus Copernicus**, *April 23, 1973*, Washington, D.C. *(734,190)*	75
1489 to *1498*	8c	**Postal People**, *April 30, 1973*, any city	@1.10
		1498a	6.00

First day cancellation was applied at Boston to 1,205,212 covers bearing one or more of Nos. 1489 to 1498. Cancellations at other cities unrecorded.

1499	8c	**Harry S. Truman**, *May 8, 1973*, Independence, Mo. *(938,636)*	75
1500	6c	**Electronics**, *July 10, 1973*, New York, N.Y.	75
1501	8c	**Electronics**, *July 10, 1973*, New York, N.Y.	75
1502	15c	**Electronics**, *July 10, 1973*, New York, N.Y.	80
		1500 to 1502 and C86 on one cover	3.50

First day cancellation was applied to 1,197,700 covers bearing one or more of Nos. 1500 to 1502 and C86.

1503	8c	**Lyndon B. Johnson**, *Aug. 27, 1973*, Austin Texas *(701,490)*	75

1973-74

1504	8c	**Angus Cattle**, *Oct. 5, 1973*, St. Joseph, Mo. *(521,427)*	75
1505	10c	**Chautauqua**, *Aug. 6, 1974*, Chautauqua, N.Y. *(411,105)*	75
1506	10c	**Wheat**, *Aug. 16, 1974*, Hillsboro, Kans. *(468,280)*	75
1507 to *1508*	8c	**Christmas**, *Nov. 7, 1973*, Washington, D.C.	@75
		1507 to 1508 on one cover	1.00

First day cancellation was applied to 807,468 covers bearing one or both of Nos. 1507 to 1508.

1509	10c	**Crossed Flags**, *Dec. 8, 1973*, San Francisco, Calif.	75

First day cancellation was applied to 341,528 covers bearing one or more of Nos. 1509 and 1519.

1510	10c	**Jefferson Memorial**, *Dec. 14, 1973*, Washington, D.C.	75

First day cancellation was applied to 686,300 covers bearing one or more of Nos. 1510, 1510b, 1510c, 1520.

1511	10c	**Zip Code**, *Jan. 4, 1974*, Washington, D.C. *(335,220)*	75
1518	6.3c	**Bell Coil**, *Oct. 1, 1974*, Washington, D.C. *(221,141)*	75
1519	10c	**Crossed Flags coil**, *Dec. 8, 1973*, San Francisco, Calif.	75
1520	10c	**Jefferson Memorial coil**, *Dec. 14, 1973*, Washington, D.C.	75

1974

1525	10c	**Veterans of Foreign Wars**, *Mar. 11, 1974*, Washington, D.C. *(543,598)*	75
1526	10c	**Robert Frost**, *Mar. 26, 1974*, Derry, N.H. *(500,425)*	75
1527	10c	**EXPO '74**, *April 18, 1974*, Spokane, Wash. *(565,548)*	75

1528	10c	**Horse Racing**, *May 4, 1974*, Louisville, Ky. *(623,983)*	75
1529	10c	**Skylab**, *May 14, 1974*, Houston, Tex. *(972,326)*	1.25
1530 to *1537*	10c	**UPU Centenary**, *June 6, 1974*, Washington, D.C.	@1.10
		1537a	4.25

First day cancellation was applied to 1,374,765 covers bearing one or more of Nos. 1530 to 1537.

1538 to *1541*	10c	**Mineral Heritage**, *June 13, 1974*, Lincoln, Neb.	@1.50
		1541a	3.00

First day cancellation was applied to 865,368 covers bearing one or more of Nos. 1538 to 1541.

1542	10c	**Kentucky Settlement**, *June 15, 1974*, Harrodsburg, Ky. *(478,239)*	75
1543 to *1546*	10c	**Continental Congress** (Rev. Bicentennial), *July 4, 1974*, Philadelphia	@90
		1546a	2.75

First day cancellation was applied to 2,124,957 covers bearing one or more of Nos. 1543 to 1546.

1547	10c	**Energy Conservation**, *Sept. 23, 1974*, Detroit, Mich. *(587,210)*	75
1548	10c	**Sleepy Hollow**, *Oct. 10, 1974*, North Tarrytown, N.Y. *(514,836)*	75
1549	10c	**Retarded Children**, *Oct. 12, 1974*, Arlington Tex. *(412,882)*	75
1550 to *1551*	10c	**Christmas**, *Oct. 23, 1974*, New York, N.Y. *(634,990)*	@75
		1550 to 1551 on one cover	1.10
1552	10c	**Christmas**, *Nov. 15, 1974*, New York, N.Y. *(477,410)*	75

1975

1553	10c	**Benjamin West**, *Feb. 10, 1975*, Swarthmore, Pa. *(465,017)*	75
1554	10c	**Paul L. Dunbar**, *May 1, 1975*, Dayton, Ohio *(397,347)*	75
1555	10c	**D.W. Griffith**, *May 27, 1975*, Beverly Hills, Calif. *(424,167)*	75
1556	10c	**Pioneer—Jupiter**, *Feb. 28, 1975*, Mountain View, Calif. *(594,896)*	1.25
1557	10c	**Mariner 10**, *Apr. 4, 1975*, Pasadena, Calif. *(563,636)*	1.25
1558	10c	**Collective Bargaining**, *Mar. 13, 1975*, Washington, D.C. *(412,329)*	75
1559	8c	**Sybil Ludington** (Rev. Bicentennial), *Mar. 25, 1975*, Carmel, N.Y. *(394,550)*	75
1560	10c	**Salem Poor** (Rev. Bicentennial), *Mar. 25, 1975*, Cambridge, Mass. *(415,565)*	75
1561	10c	**Haym Salomon** (Rev. Bicentennial), *Mar. 25, 1975*, Chicago, Ill. *(442,630)*	75
1562	18c	**Peter Francisco** (Rev. Bicetennial), *Mar. 25, 1975*, Greensboro, N.C. *(415,000)*	75
1563	10c	**Lexington—Concord** (Rev. Bicentennial), *Apr. 19, 1975*, Lexington, Mass., or Concord, Mass, *(975,020)*	75
1564	10c	**Bunker Hill** (Rev. Bicentennial), *June 17, 1975*, Charlestown, Mass. *(557,130)*	75
1565 to *1568*	10c	**Military Services** (Rev. Bicentennial), *July 4, 1975*, Washington, D.C.	@90
		1568a	2.40

First day cancellation was applied to 1,134,831 covers bearing one or more of Nos. 1565 to 1568.

1569 to *1470*	10c	**Apollo—Soyuz**, *July 15, 1975*, Kennedy Space Center, Fla. *(1,427,046)*	@1.25
		1569a	3.00
1571	10c	**International Women's Year**, *Aug. 26, 1975*, Seneca Falls, N.Y. *(476,769)*	75
1572 to *1575*	10c	**Postal Service Bicentenary**, *Sept. 3, 1975*, Philadelphia, Pa.	@75
		1575a	2.40

First day cancellation was applied to *(969,999)* covers bearing one or more of Nos. 1572 to 1575.

1576	10c	**World Peace through Law**, *Sept. 29, 1975*, Washington, D.C. *(386,736)*	75
1577 to *1578*	10c	**Banking—Commerce**, *Oct. 6, 1975*, New York, N.Y. *(555,580)*	@75
		1577a	1.00
1579 to *1580*	10c	**Christmas**, *Oct. 14, 1975*, Washington	@75
		1579 to 1580 on one cover	1.10

First day cancellation was applied to 730,079 covers bearing one or more of Nos. 1579 to 1580.

1975-79

AMERICANA ISSUE

1581	1c	*Dec. 8, 1977*, St. Louis, Mo.	60
1582	2c	*Dec. 8, 1977*, St. Louis, Mo.	60
1584	3c	*Dec. 8, 1977*, St. Louis, Mo.	60

1585	4c	Dec. 8, 1977, St. Louis, Mo.	60

First day cancellation was applied to 530,033 covers bearing one or more of Nos. 1581 to 1582, 1584 to 1585.

1590	9c	Mar. 11, 1977, New York, N.Y.	1.00
1591	9c	Nov. 24, 1975, Washington, D.C. (190,117)	60
1592	10c	Nov. 17, 1977, New York, N.Y. (359,050)	60
1594	11c	Nov. 13, 1975, Philadelphia, Pa. (217,755)	60
1594	12c	Apr. 8, 1981, Dallas, TX	60

First day cancellation was applied to 280,930 covers bearing Nos. 1594 or 1816.

1595	13c	Oct. 31, 1975, Cleveland, Ohio (256,734)	60
1596	13c	Dec. 1, 1975, Juneau, Alaska (418,272)	60
1597	15c	June 30, 1978, Baltimore, Md.	65
1598	15c	June 30, 1978, Baltimore, Md.	65

First day cancellation was applied to 315,359 covers bearing Nos. 1597, 1598, or 1618C.

1599	16c	Mar. 31, 1978, New York, N.Y.	65
1603	24c	Nov. 14, 1975, Boston, Mass. (208,973)	75
1604	28c	Aug. 11, 1978, Tacoma, Wash. (159,639)	1.20
1605	29c	Apr. 14, 1978, Atlantic City, N.J. (193,476)	1.10
1606	30c	Aug. 27, 1979, Devils Lake, N.D. (186,882)	1.10
1608	50c	Sept. 11, 1979, San Juan, P.R. (159,540)	1.50
1610	$1	July 2, 1979, San Francisco, Calif. (255,575)	3.00
1611	$2	Nov. 16, 1978, New York, N.Y. (173,596)	5.00
1612	$5	Aug. 23, 1989, Boston, Mass. (129,192)	10.00

COIL STAMPS

1613	3.1c	Oct. 25, 1979, Shreveport, La. (230,403)	60
1614	7.7c	Nov. 20, 1976, New York, N.Y. (285,290)	60
1615	7.9c	Apr. 23, 1976, Miami, Fla. (193,270)	60
1615C	8.4c	July 13, 1978, Interlochen, Mich. (200,392)	60
1616	9c	Mar. 5, 1976, Milwaukee, Wis. (128,171)	60
1617	10c	Nov. 4, 1977, Tampa, Fla. (184,954)	60
1618	13c	Nov. 25, 1975, Allentown, Pa. (320,387)	65
1618C	15c	June 30, 1978, Boston, Mass.	65
1619	16c	Mar. 31, 1978, New York, N.Y.	60

First day cancellation was applied to 376,338 covers bearing one or more of Nos. 1599 or 1619.

1975

1622	13c	13—Star Flag, Nov. 15, 1975, Philadelphia, Pa.	65
1623	13c	Mar. 11, 1977, New York, N.Y. (242,208)	1.00
1625	13c	13—Star Flag coil, Nov. 15, 1975, Philadelphia, PA	65

First day cancellation was applied to 362,959 covers bearing Nos. 1622 or 1625.

1976

1629 to 1631	13c	Spirit of '76, Jan. 1, 1976, Pasadena, CA	65
		1631a	1.75

First day cancellation was applied to 1,013,067 covers bearing one or more of Nos. 1629 to 1631.

1632	13c	Interphil '76, Jan. 17, 1976, Philadelphia, Pa. (519,902)	65
1633 to 1682	13c	State Flags, Feb. 23, 1976, Washington, D.C.	@1.75
		1682a	32.50
1683	13c	Telephone, Mar. 10, 1976, Boston, Mass. (662,515)	65
1684	13c	Commercial Aviation, Mar. 19, 1976, Chicago Ill. (631,555)	65
1685	13c	Chemistry, April 6, 1976, New York, N.Y. (557,600)	65
1686	13c	Bicentennial Souvenir Sheet of 5, Surrender of Cornwallis, May 29, 1976, Philadelphia, Pa.	6.00
1687	18c	Bicentennial Souvenir Sheet of 5, Declaration of Independence, May 29, 1976, Philadelphia, Pa.	7.50
1688	24c	Bicentennial Souvenir Sheet of 5, Declaration of Independence, May 29, 1976, Philadelphia, Pa.	8.50
1689	31c	Bicentennial Souvenir Sheet of 5, Washington at Valley Forge, May 29, 1976, Philadelphia, Pa.	9.50

First day cancellation was applied to 879,890 covers bearing one of Nos. 1686 to 1689.

1690	13c	Franklin, June 1, 1976, Philadelphia, Pa. (588,740)	65

1691 to 1694	13c	Declaration of Independence, July 4, 1976, Philadelphia, Pa.	@65
		1694a	2.00

First day cancellation was applied to 2,093,880 covers bearing one or more of Nos. 1691 to 1694.

1695 to 1698	13c	Olympic Games, July 16, 1976, Lake Placid, N.Y. (1,140,189)	@75
		1698a	2.00
1699	13c	Clara Maass, Aug. 18, 1976, Belleville, N.J. (646,506)	75
1700	13c	Adolph S. Ochs, Sept. 18, 1976, New York, N.Y. (582,580)	75
1701 to 1703	13c	Christmas, Oct. 27, 1976, Boston, Mass. (No. 1701, 540,050; No. 1702, 181,410; No. 1703, 330,450)	@65
		1701 and 1702 or 1703 on one cover	1.20

1977

1704	13c	Washington at Princeton, Jan. 3, 1977, Princeton, N.J. (695,335)	65
1705	13c	Sound Recording, Mar. 23, 1977, Washington, D.C. (632,216)	65
1706 to 1709	13c	Pueblo Art, Apr. 13, 1977, Santa Fe, N.M. (1,194,554)	@75
		1709a	2.00
1710	13c	Lindbergh Flight, May 20, 1977, Roosevelt Sta., N.Y. (3,985,989)	75
1711	13c	Colorado Statehood, May 21, 1977, Denver, Colo. (510,880)	65
1712 to 1715	13c	Butterflies, June 6, 1977, Indianapolis, Ind. (1,218,278)	@75
		1715a	2.00
1716	13c	Lafayettes Landing, June 13, 1977, Charleston, S.C. (514,506)	65
1717 to 1720	13c	Skilled Hands, July 4, 1977, Cincinnati, Ohio (1,263,568)	@65
		1720a	1.75
1721	13c	Peace Bridge, Aug. 4, 1977, Buffalo, N.Y. (512,995)	65
1722	13c	Battle of Oriskany, Aug. 6, 1977, Utica, N.Y. (605,906)	65
1723 to 1724	13c	Energy Conservation, Oct. 20, 1977, Washington, D.C. (410,290)	@65
		1723a	1.00
1725	13c	Alta California, Sept. 9, 1977, San Jose, Calif. (709,457)	65
1726	13c	Articles of Confederation, Sept. 30, 1977, York, Pa. (605,455)	65
1727	13c	Talking Pictures, Oct. 6, 1977, Hollywood, Calif. (570,195)	75
1728	13c	Surrender at Saratoga, Oct. 7, 1977, Schuylerville, N.Y. (557,529)	65
1729	13c	Christmas (Valley Forge), Oct. 21, 1977, Valley Forge, Pa. (583,139)	65
1730	13c	Christmas (mailbox), Oct. 21, 1977, Omaha, Nebr. (675,786)	65

1978

1731	13c	Carl Sandburg, Jan. 6, Galesburg, Ill. (493,826)	65
1732 to 1733	13c	Captain Cook, Jan. 20, Honolulu, Hawaii, or Anchorage, Alaska	@75
		1732a	1.50

First day cancellation was applied to 823,855 covers at Honolulu, and 672,804 at Anchorage, each cover bearing one or both of Nos. 1732 to 1733.

1734	13c	Indian Head Penny, Jan. 11, Kansas City, Mo. (512,426)	1.00

1978-80

REGULAR ISSUE

1735	(15c)	"A" Eagle, May 22, Memphis, Tenn.	65
1736	(15c)	"A" Eagle, May 22, Memphis, Tenn.	65
1737	15c	Roses, July 11, Shreveport, La. (445,003)	65
1738 to 1742	15c	Windmills, Feb. 7, 1980, Lubbock, TX (708,411)	65
1743	15c	"A" Eagle coil, May 22, Memphis, Tenn.	65

First day cancellation was applied to 689,049 covers bearing Nos. 1735, 1736 or 1743.

1978

1744	13c	Harriet Tubman, Feb. 1, Washington, D.C. (493,495)	1.00
1745 to 1748	13c	American Quilts, Mar. 8, Charleston, W.Va.	@75
		1748a	2.00

First day cancellation was applied to 1,081,827 covers bearing one or more of Nos. 1745 to 1748.

1749 to 1752	13c	American Dance, April 26, New York, N.Y. (1,626,493)	@75
		1752a	1.75
1753	13c	French Alliance, May 4, York, Pa. (705,240)	65
1754	13c	Papanicolaou, May 18, Washington, D.C. (535,584)	65
1755	13c	Jimmie Rodgers, May 24, Meridian, Miss. (599,287)	65
1756	13c	George M. Cohan, July 3, Providence, R.I. (740,750)	65
1757		CAPEX souv. sheet, June 10, Toronto, Canada (1,994,067)	2.75

1758	15c	Photography, June 26, Las Vegas, Nev. (684,987)	65
1759	15c	Viking Missions, July 20, Hampton, Va. (805,051)	1.10
1760 to 1763	15c	American Owls, Aug. 26, Fairbanks, Alas. (1,690,474)	@75
		1763a	2.00
1764 to 1767	15c	American Trees, Oct. 9, Hot Springs National Park, Ark. (1,139,100)	@75
		1767a	2.00
1768	15c	Christmas (Madonna), Oct. 18, Washington, D.C. (553,064)	65
1769	15c	Christmas (Hobby Horse), Oct. 18, Holly, Mich. (603,008)	65

1979-80

1770	15c	Robert Kennedy, Jan. 12, Washington, D.C. (624,582)	65
1771	15c	Martin L. King, Jan. 13, Atlanta, Ga. (726,149)	65
1772	15c	Year of Child, Feb. 15, Philadelphia, Pa. (716,782)	65
1773	15c	John Steinbeck, Feb. 27, Salinas, Calif. (709,073)	65
1774	15c	Albert Einstein, Mar. 4, Princeton, N.J. (641,423)	65
1775 to 1778	15c	Toleware, Apr. 19, Lancaster, Pa. (1,581,962)	@75
		1778a	2.00
1779 to 1782	15c	American Architecture, June 4, Kansas City, Mo. (1,219,258)	@75
		1782a	2.00
1783 to 1786	15c	Endangered Flora, June 7, Milwaukee, Wis. (1,436,268)	@75
		1786a	2.00
1787	15c	Guide Dogs, June 15, Morristown, N.J. (588,826)	65
1788	15c	Special Olympics, Aug. 9, Brockport, N.Y. (651,344)	65
1789	15c	John Paul Jones, Sept. 23, Annapolis, Md. (587,018)	65
1790	10c	Olympic Javelin, Sept. 5, Olympia, Wash. (305,122)	1.00
1791 to 1794	15c	Olympics 1980, Sept. 28, Los Angeles, Calif. (1,561,366)	@75
		1794a	2.00
1795 to 1798	15c	Winter Olympics, Feb. 1, 1980, Lake Placid, N.Y. (1,166,302)	@75
		1798b	2.00
1799	15c	Christmas (Madonna), Oct. 18, Washington, D.C. (686,990)	65
1800	15c	Christmas (Santa Claus), Oct. 18, North Pole, Alaska (511,829)	65
1801	15c	Will Rogers, Nov. 4, Claremore, Okla. (1,643,151)	65
1802	15c	Viet Nam Veterans, Nov. 11, Washington, D.C. (445,934)	1.25

1980

1803	15c	W.C. Fields, Jan. 29, Beverly Hills, CA (633,303)	65
1804	15c	Benjamin Banneker, Feb. 15, Annapolis, MD (647,126)	65
1805 to 1810	15c	Letter Writing, Feb. 25, Washington, DC (1,083,360)	@65
		1810a	3.00

1980-81

DEFINITIVES

1811	1c	Quill Pen, coil, Mar. 6, 1980, New York, NY (262,921)	60
1813	3.5c	Violins, coil, June 23, 1980, Williamsburg, PA	60

FD cancel was applied to 716,988 covers bearing Nos. 1813 or U590.

1816	12c	Torch, coil, Apr. 8, 1981, Dallas, TX	60
1818	(18c)	"B" Eagle, Mar. 15, 1981, San Francisco, CA	75

FD cancel was applied to 511,688 covers bearing Nos. 1818 to 1820, U592 or UX88.

1819	(18c)	"B" Eagle, bklt. single, Mar. 15, 1981, San Francisco, CA	75
1820	(18c)	"B" Eagle, coil, Mar. 15, 1981, San Francisco, CA	75

1980

1821	15c	Frances Perkins, Apr. 10, Washington, DC (678,966)	65
1822	15c	Dolley Madison, May 20, Washington, DC (331,048)	65
1823	15c	Emily Bissel, May 31, Wilmington, DE (649,509)	65
1824	15c	Helen Keller, Anne Sullivan, June 27, Tuscumbia, AL (713,061)	80
1825	15c	Veterans Administration, July 21, Washington, DC (634,101)	65
1826	15c	Bernardo de Galvez, July 23, New Orleans, LA (658,061)	65
1827 to 1830	15c	Coral Reefs, Aug. 26, Charlotte Amalie, VI (1,195,126)	@85
		1830a	2.00
1831	15c	Organized Labor, Sept. 1, Washington, DC (759,973)	65
1832	15c	Edith Wharton, Sept. 5, New Haven, CT (633,917)	65
1833	15c	Education, Sept. 12, Washington, DC (672,954)	65
1834 to 1837	15c	Indian Masks, Sept. 25, Spokane, WA (2,195,136)	@75
		1837a	2.00

1838 to 1841	15c	**Architecture**, *Oct. 9*, New York, NY *(2,164,721)*	@75
		1841a	2.00
1842	15c	**Christmas (Madonna)**, *Oct. 31*, Washington, DC *(718,614)*	65
1843	15c	**Christmas (Toys)**, *Oct. 31*, Christmas, MI *(755,108)*	65

1980-85

GREAT AMERICANS ISSUE

1844	1c	**Dorothea Dix**, *Sept. 23, 1983*, Hampden, ME *(164,140)*	60
1845	2c	**Igor Stravinsky**, *Nov. 18, 1982*, New York, NY *(501,719)*	60
1846	3c	**Henry Clay**, *July 13, 1983*, Washington, DC *(204,320)*	60
1847	4c	**Carl Schurz**, *June 3, 1983*, Watertown, WI *(165,010)*	60
1848	5c	**Pearl Buck**, *June 23, 1983*, Hillsboro, WV *(231,852)*	60
1849	6c	**Walter Lippman**, *Sept. 19, 1985*, Minneapolis, MN *(371,990)*	60
1850	7c	**Abraham Baldwin**, *Jan. 25, 1985*, Athens, GA *(402,285)*	60
1851	8c	**Henry Knox**, *July 25, 1985*, Thomaston, ME *(315,937)*	60
1852	9c	**Sylvanus Thayer**, *June 7, 1985*, Braintree, MA *(345,649)*	60
1853	10c	**Richard Russell**, *May 31, 1984*, Winder, GA *(183,581)*	65
1854	11c	**Alden Partridge**, *Feb. 12, 1985*, Northfield, VT *(442,311)*	65
1855	13c	**Crazy Horse**, *Jan. 15, 1982*, Crazy Horse, SD	65
1856	14c	**Sinclair Lewis**, *Mar. 21, 1985*, Sauk Centre, MN *(308,612)*	65
1857	17c	**Rachel Carson**, *May 28, 1981*, Springdale, PA *(273,686)*	75
1858	18c	**George Mason**, *May 7, 1981*, Gunston Hall, VA *(461,937)*	75
1859	19c	**Sequoyah**, *Dec. 27, 1980*, Tahlequah, OK *(241,325)*	80
1860	20c	**Ralph Bunche**, *Jan. 12, 1982*, New York, NY	75
1861	20c	**Thomas Gallaudet**, *June 10, 1983*, West Hartford, CT *(261,336)*	75
1862	20c	**Harry S. Truman**, *Jan. 26, 1984*, Washington, DC *(267,631)*	75
1863	22c	**John J. Audubon**, *Apr. 23, 1985*, New York, NY *(516,249)*	80
1864	30c	**Frank Laubach**, *Sept. 2, 1984*, Benton, PA *(118,974)*	85
1865	35c	**Charles Drew**, *June 3, 1981*, Washington, DC *(383,882)*	1.00
1866	37c	**Robert Millikan**, *Jan. 26, 1982*, Pasadena, CA	1.00
1867	39c	**Grenville Clark**, *Mar. 20, 1985*, Hanover, NH *(297,797)*	1.00
1868	40c	**Lillian Gilbreth**, *Feb. 24, 1984*, Montclair, NJ *(110,588)*	1.00
1869	50c	**Chester W. Nimitz**, *Feb. 22, 1985*, Fredericksburg, TX *(376,166)*	1.25

1981

1874	15c	**Everett Dicksen**, *Jan. 4*, Pekin, IL *(665,755)*	65
1875	15c	**Whitney M. Young**, *Jan. 30*, New York, NY *(963,870)*	65
1876 to 1879	15c	**Flowers**, *Apr. 23*, Fort Valley, GA *(1,966,599)*	@75
		1879a	2.50

DEFINITIVES

1880 to 1889	18c	**Animals**, *May 14*, Boise, ID	75
1890	18c	**Flag—Anthem (grain)**, *Apr. 24*, Portland, ME	75
1891	18c	**Flag—Anthem (sea)**, *Apr. 24*, Portland, ME	75
1892	6c	**Star Circle**, *Apr. 24*, Portland, ME	75
1893	18c	**Flag—Anthem (mountain)**, *Apr. 24*, Portland, ME	75

FDC cancel was applied to 691,526 covers bearing Nos. 1890 to 1893 & 1893a.

1894	20c	**Flag—Court**, *Dec. 17*, Washington, DC	75
1895	20c	**Flag—Court**, coil, *Dec. 17*, Washington, DC	75
1896	20c	**Flag—Court**, p. 11x10½, *Dec. 17*, Washington, DC *(185,543)*	75

First day cancellations were applied to 598,169 covers bearing one or more of Nos. 1894 to 1896.

1981-84

TRANSPORTATION ISSUE

1897	1c	**Omnibus**, *Aug. 19, 1983*, Arlington, VA *(109,463)*	60
1897A	2c	**Locomotive**, *May 20, 1982*, Chicago, IL *(290,020)*	60
1898	3c	**Handcar**, *Mar. 25, 1983*, Rochester, NY *(77,900)*	60
1898A	4c	**Stagecoach**, *Aug. 19, 1982*, Milwaukee, WI *(152,940)*	60
1899	5c	**Motorcycle**, *Oct. 10, 1983*, San Francisco, CA *(188,240)*	60
1900	5.2c	**Sleigh**, *Mar. 21, 1983*, Memphis, TN *(141,979)*	60
1901	5.9c	**Bicycle**, *Feb. 17, 1982*, Wheeling, WV *(814,419)*	60

1902	7.4c	**Baby Buggy**, *Apr. 7, 1984*, San Diego, CA	65
1903	9.3c	**Mail Wagon**, *Dec. 15, 1981*, Shreveport, LA *(199,645)*	65
1904	10.9c	**Hansom**, *May 26, 1982*, Chattanooga, TN	65
1905	11c	**Railroad Caboose**, *Feb. 3, 1984*, Chicago, IL *(172,753)*	65
1906	17c	**Electric Auto**, *June 25, 1982*, Greenfield Village, MI *(239,458)*	75
1907	18c	**Surrey**, *May 18, 1981*, Notch, MO *(207,801)*	75
1908	20c	**Fire Pumper**, *Dec. 10, 1981*, Alexandria, VA *(304,668)*	65
1909	$9.35	**Eagle**, *Aug. 12, 1983*, Kennedy Space Center, FL *(77,858)*	25.00

1981

1910	18c	**Red Cross**, *May 1*, Washington, DC *(874,972)*	75
1911	18c	**Savings & Loan**, *May 8*, Chicago, IL *(740,910)*	75
1912 to 1919	18c	**Space Achievement**, *May 21*, Kennedy Space Center, FL *(7,027,549)*	@75
		1919a	5.00
1920	18c	**Professional Management**, *June 18*, Philadelphia, PA *(713,096)*	75
1921 to 1924	18c	**Wildlife Habitats**, *June 26*, Reno, NV *(2,327,609)*	@75
		1924a	2.50
1925	18c	**Year of Disabled**, *June 29*, Milford, MI *(714,244)*	75
1926	18c	**Edna St. V. Millay**, *July 10*, Austerlitz, NY *(725,978)*	75
1927	18c	**Alcoholism**, *Aug. 19*, Washington, DC *(874,972)*	75
1928 to 1931	18c	**Architecture**, *Aug. 28*, New York, NY *(1,998,208)*	@75
		1931a	2.00
1932	18c	**Babe Zaharias**, *Sept. 22*, Pinehurst, NC	75
1933	18c	**Bobby Jones**, *Sept. 22*, Pinehurst, NC	75

FD cancel was applied to 1,231,543 covers bearing No. 1932 or 1933.

1934	18c	**Frederic Remington**, *Oct. 9*, Oklahoma City, OK *(1,367,099)*	75
1935	18c	**James Hoban**, *Oct. 13*, Washington, DC	75
1936	20c	**James Hoban**, *Oct. 13*, Washington, DC	75

FD cancel was applied to 635,012 covers bearing No. 1935 or 1936.

1937 to 1938	18c	**Yorktown—Va. Capes Battle**, *Oct. 16*, Yorktown, VA *(1,098,278)*	@75
		1938a	1.00
1939	(20c)	**Christmas (Madonna)**, *Oct. 28*, Chicago, IL *(481,395)*	75
1940	(20c)	**Christmas (Teddy Bear)**, *Oct. 28*, Christmas Valley, OR *(517,898)*	75
1941	20c	**John Hanson**, *Nov. 5*, Frederick, MD *(605,616)*	75
1942 to 1945	20c	**Desert Plants**, *Dec. 11*, Tucson, AZ 1945a *(1,770,187)*	2.50

REGULAR ISSUE

1946	(20c)	**"C" Eagle**, *Oct. 11*, Memphis, TN	75
1947	(20c)	**"C" Eagle**, coil, *Oct. 11*, Memphis, TN	75
1948	(20c)	**"C" Engle**, bklt. single, *Oct. 11*, Memphis, TN	75

First day cancellations were applied to 304,404 covers bearing Nos. 1946 to 1948.

1982

1949	20c	**Bighorn**, *Jan. 8*, Bighorn, MT	
1950	20c	**F.D. Roosevelt**, *Jan. 30*, Hyde Park, NY	75
1951	20c	**Love**, *Feb. 1*, Boston, MA *(325,727)*	75
1952	20c	**Washington**, *Feb. 22*, Mt. Vernon, VA	75
1953 to 2002	20c	**Birds—Flowers**, *Apr. 14*, Washington, DC, or State Capital	@1.00
		2002b	—
2003	20c	**U.S.—Netherlands**, *Apr. 20*, Washington, DC	75
2004	20c	**Library of Congress**, *Apr. 21*, Washington, DC	75
2005	20c	**Consumer Education**, *Apr. 27*, Washington, DC	75
2006 to 2009	20c	**Knoxville Fair**, *Apr. 29*, Knoxville, TN	@75
		2009a	2.50
2010	20c	**Horatio Alger**, *Apr. 30*, Willow Grove, PA	75
2011	20c	**Aging**, *May 21*, Sun City, AZ *(510,677)*	75
2012	20c	**Barrymores**, *June 8*, New York, NY	75
2013	20c	**Dr. Mary Walker**, *June 10*, Oswego, NY	75
2014	20c	**Peace Garden**, *June 30*, Dunseith, ND	75
2015	20c	**Americas Libraries**, *July 13*, Philadelphia, PA	75
2016	20c	**Jackie Robinson**, *Aug. 2*, Cooperstown, NY	75

2017	20c	**Touro Synagogue**, *Aug. 22*, Newport, RI *(517,264)*	85
2018	20c	**Wolf Trap Farm Parks**, *Sept. 1*, Vienna, VA *(704,361)*	75
2019 to 2022	20c	**Architecture**, *Sept. 30*, Washington, DC *(1,552,567)*	75
		2022a	2.50
2023	20c	**St. Francis**, *Oct. 7*, San Francisco, CA *(530,275)*	75
2024	20c	**Ponce de Leon**, *Oct. 12*, San Juan, PR *(530,275)*	75
2025	13c	**Puppy, Kitten**, *Nov. 3*, Danvers, MA *(239,219)*	75
2026	20c	**Christmas (Madonna)**, *Oct. 28*, Washington, DC *(462,982)*	75
2027 to 2030	20c	**Christmas (Children)**, *Oct. 28*, Snow, OK *(676,950)*	@75
		2030a	2.50

1983

2031	20c	**Science & Industry**, *Jan. 19*, Chicago, IL *(526,693)*	75
2032 to 2035	20c	**Balloon**, *Mar. 31*, Albuquerque, NM or Wash., DC *(989,305)*	@75
		2035a	2.50
2036	20c	**U.S.—Sweden**, *Mar. 24*, Philadelphia, PA *(526,373)*	75
2037	20c	**Civilian Conservation Corps.**, *Apr. 5*, Luray, VA *(483,824)*	75
2038	20c	**Joseph Priestley**, *Apr. 13*, Northumberland, PA *(673,266)*	75
2039	20c	**Voluntarism**, *Apr. 20*, Washington, DC *(574,708)*	75
2040	20c	**U.S.—Germany**, *Apr. 29*, Germantown, PA *(611,109)*	75
2041	20c	**Brooklyn Bridge**, *May 17*, Brooklyn, NY *(815,085)*	75
2042	20c	**TVA**, *May 18*, Knoxville, TN *(837,588)*	75
2043	20c	**Physical Fitness**, *May 14*, Houston, TX *(501,336)*	75
2044	20c	**Scott Joplin**, *June 9*, Sedalia, MO *(472,667)*	75
2045	20c	**Medal of Honor**, *June 7*, Washington, DC *(1,623,995)*	75
2046	20c	**Babe Ruth**, *July 6*, Chicago, IL *(1,277,907)*	75
2047	20c	**Nathaniel Hawthorne**, *July 8*, Salem, MA *(442,793)*	75
2048 to 2051	13c	**Summer Olympics**, *July 28*, South Bend, IN *(909,332)*	@75
		2051a	2.50
2052	20c	**Treaty of Paris**, *Sept. 2*, Washington, DC *(651,208)*	75
2053	20c	**Civil Service**, *Sept. 9*, Washington, DC *(422,206)*	75
2054	20c	**Metropolitan Opera**, *Sept. 14*, New York, NY *(807,600)*	75
2055 to 2058	20c	**American Inventors**, *Sept. 21*, Washington, D.C. *(1,006,516)*	@75
		2058a	2.50
2059 to 2062	20c	**Streetcars**, *Oct. 8*, Kennebunkport, ME	75
		2062a *(1,116,909)*	2.50
2063	20c	**Christmas (Madonna)**, *Oct. 28*, Washington, DC *(361,874)*	75
2064	20c	**Christmas (Santa)**, *Oct. 28*, Santa Claus, IN *(388,749)*	75
2065	20c	**Martin Luther**, *Nov. 11*, Washington, DC *(463,777)*	75

1984

2066	20c	**Alaska Statehood**, *Jan. 3*, Fairbanks, AK *(816,591)*	75
2067 to 2070	20c	**Winter Olympics**, *Jan. 6*, Lake Placid, NY *(1,245,807)*	@75
		2070a	2.50
2071	20c	**Federal Deposit Ins. Corp.**, *Jan. 12*, Washington, DC *(536,329)*	75
2072	20c	**Love**, *Jan. 31*, Washington, DC *(327,727)*	75
2073	20c	**Carter Woodson**, *Feb. 1*, Washington, DC *(387,583)*	75
2074	20c	**Soil & Water Conservation**, *Feb. 6*, Denver, CO *(426,101)*	75
2075	20c	**Credit Union Act**, *Feb. 10*, Salem, MA *(383,583)*	75
2076 to 2079	20c	**Orchids**, *Mar. 5*, Miami FL	@75
		2079a *(1,063,237)*	2.50
2080	20c	**Hawaii Statehood**, *Mar. 12*, Honolulu, HI *(546,930)*	75
2081	20c	**National Archives**, *Apr. 16*, Washington, DC *(414,415)*	75
2082 to 2085	20c	**Olympics 1984**, *May 4*, Los Angeles, CA	@75
		2085a *(1,172,313)*	2.50
2086	20c	**Louisiana Exposition**, *May 11*, New Orleans, LA *(467,408)*	75
2087	20c	**Health Research**, *May 17*, New York, NY *(845,007)*	75
2088	20c	**Douglas Fairbanks**, *May 23*, Denver CO *(547,134)*	75
2089	20c	**Jim Thorpe**, *May 24*, Shawnee, OK *(568,544)*	75
2090	20c	**John McCormack**, *June 6*, Boston, MA *(464,117)*	75
2091	20c	**St. Lawrence Seaway**, *June 26*, Massena, NY *(550,173)*	75
2092	20c	**Waterfowl Preservation Act**, *July 2*, Des Moines, IA *(549,388)*	75
2093	20c	**Roanoke Voyages**, *July 13*, Manteo, NC *(443,725)*	75
2094	20c	**Herman Melville**, *Aug. 1*, New Bedford, MA *(378,293)*	75
2095	20c	**Horace A. Moses**, *Aug. 6*, Bloomington, IN *(459,386)*	75

2096	20c	**Smokey the Bear,** *Aug. 13,* Capitan, NM *(506,833)*	75
2097	20c	**Roberto Clemente,** *Aug. 17,* Carolina, PR *(547,387)*	75
2098 to 2101	20c	**Dogs,** *Sept. 7,* New York, NY *(1,157,373)*	@75
		2101a	2.50
2102	20c	**Crime Prevention,** *Sept. 26,* Washington, DC *(427,564)*	75
2103	20c	**Hispanic Americans,** *Oct. 31,* Washington, DC *(416,796)*	75
2104	20c	**Family Unity,** *Oct. 1,* Shaker Heights, OH *(400,659)*	75
2105	20c	**Eleanor Roosevelt,** *Oct. 11,* Hyde Park, NY *(479,919)*	75
2106	20c	**Nation of Readers,** *Oct. 16,* Washington, DC *(437,559)*	75
2107	20c	**Christmas (Madonna),** *Oct. 30,* Washington, DC *(386,385)*	75
2108	20c	**Christmas (Santa),** *Oct. 30,* Jamaica, NY *(430,843)*	75
2109	20c	**Vietnam Veterans' Memorial,** *Nov. 10,* Washington, DC *(434,489)*	75

1985

2110	22c	**Jerome Kern,** *Jan. 23,* New York, NY *(503,855)*	80

REGULAR ISSUE

2111	(22c)	**"D" Eagle,** *Feb. 1,* Los Angeles, CA	80
2112	(22c)	**"D" Eagle, coil,** *Feb. 1,* Los Angeles, CA	80
2113	(22c)	**"D" Eagle, bklt. single,** *Feb. 1,* Los Angeles, CA	80

First Day cancel was applied to 513,027 covers bearing Nos. 2111 to 2113.

DEFINITIVES

2114	22c	**Flag over Capitol Dome,** *Mar. 29,* Washington, DC	80
2115	22c	**Flag Over Capitol Dome, coil,** *Mar. 29,* Washington, DC	80

First Day Cancel was applied to 268,161 covers bearing Nos. 2114 to 2115.

2116	22c	**Flag Over Capitol Dome, bklt. single,** *Mar. 29,* Waubeka, WI *(234,318)*	80
2117 to 2121	22c	**Seashells,** *Apr. 4,* Boston, MA *(426,290)*	@80
2122	$10.75	**Eagle and Half Moon,** *Apr. 29,* San Francisco, CA *(93,154)*	30.00

1985-87

TRANSPORTATION ISSUE

2123	3.4c	**School Bus,** *June 8, 1985* Arlington, VA *(131,480)*	70
2124	4.9c	**Buckboard,** *June 21, 1985,* Reno, NV	70
2125	5.5c	**Star Route Truck,** *Nov. 1, 1986,* Fort Worth, TX *(136,021)*	70
2126	6c	**Tricycle,** *May 6, 1985,* Childs, MD *(151,494)*	70
2127	7.1c	**Tractor,** *Feb. 6, 1987,* Sarasota, FL *(167,555)*	70
2128	8.3c	**Ambulance,** *June 21, 1986,* Reno, NV	70
2129	8.5c	**Tow Truck,** *Jan. 24, 1987,* Tucson, AZ *(224,285)*	70
2130	10.1c	**Oil Wagon,** *Apr. 18, 1985,* Oil Center, NM	75
2131	11c	**Stutz Super Bearcat,** *June 11, 1985,* Baton Rouge, LA *(135,037)*	75
2132	12c	**Stanley Steamer,** *Apr. 2, 1985,* Kingfield, ME *(173,998)*	75
2133	12.5c	**Pushcart,** *Apr. 18, 1985,* Oil Center, NM	75
2134	14c	**Ice Boat,** *Mar. 23, 1985,* Rochester, NY *(324,710)*	80
2135	17c	**Dog Sled,** *Aug. 20, 1986,* Anchorage, AK	80
2136	25c	**Bread Wagon,** *Nov. 22, 1986,* Virginia Beach, VA *(151,950)*	85

1985

2137	22c	**Mary McLeod Bethune,** *Mar. 5,* Washington, DC *(413,244)*	80
2138 to 2141	22c	**Duck Decoys,** *Mar. 22,* Shelburne, VT *(932,249)*	@80
		2141a	2.75
2142	22c	**Winter Special Olympics,** *Mar. 25,* Park City, UT *(253,074)*	80
2143	22c	**Love,** *Apr. 17,* Hollywood, CA *(283,072)*	80
2144	22c	**Rural Electrification Administration,** *May 11,* Madison, SD *(472,895)*	80
2145	22c	**AMERIPEX '86,** *May 25,* Rosemont, IL *(457,038)*	80
2146	22c	**Abigail Adams,** *June 14,* Quincy, MA *(491,026)*	80
2147	22c	**Frederic Auguste Bartholdi,** *July 18,* New York, NY *(594,896)*	80
2149	18c	**George Washington, Washington Monument,** *Nov. 6,* Washington, DC *(376,238)*	80
2150	21.1c	**Sealed Envelopes,** *Oct. 22,* Washington, DC *(119,941)*	80
2152	22c	**Korean War Veterans,** *July 26,* Washington, DC *(391,754)*	80
2153	22c	**Social Security Act,** *Aug. 14,* Baltimore, MD *(265,143)*	80

2154	22c	**World War I Veterans,** *Aug. 26,* Milwaukee, WI	80
2155 to 2158	22c	**Horses,** *Sept. 25,* Lexington, KY *(1,135,368)*	@80
		2158a	2.75
2159	22c	**Public Education in America,** *Oct. 1,* Boston, MA *(356,030)*	80
2160 to 2163	22c	**International Youth Year,** *Oct. 7,* Chicago, IL *(1,202,541)*	@80
		2163a	2.75
2164	22c	**Help End Hunger,** *Oct. 15,* Washington, DC *(299,485)*	80
2165	22c	**Christmas (Madonna & Child),** *Oct. 30,* Detroit, MI	80
2166	22c	**Christmas (Poinsettia),** *Oct. 30,* Nazareth, MI *(524,929)*	80

1986

2167	22c	**Arkansas Statehood,** *Jan. 3,* Little Rock, AR *(364,729)*	80

1986-88

GREAT AMERICANS ISSUE

2168	1c	**Margaret Mitchell,** *June 30, 1986,* Atlanta, GA *(316,764)*	80
2169	2c	**Mary Lyon,** *Feb. 28, 1987,* South Hadley, MA *(349,831)*	80
2170	3c	**Dr. Paul Dudley White,** *Sept. 15, 1986,* Washington, DC	80
2171	4c	**Father Flanagan,** *July 14, 1986,* Boys Town, NE *(367,883)*	80
2172	5c	**Hugo Black,** *Feb. 27, 1986,* Washington, DC *(303,012)*	80
2176	10c	**Red Cloud,** *Aug. 15, 1987,* Red Cloud, NE *(300,472)*	80
2177	14c	**Julia Ward Howe,** *Feb. 12, 1987,* Boston, MA *(454,829)*	80
2178	15c	**Buffalo Bill Cody,** *June 6, 1988,* Cody, WY	75
2179	17c	**Belva Ann Lockwood,** *June 18, 1986,* Middleport, NY *(249,215)*	80
2180	21c	**Chester Carlson,** *Oct. 21, 1988,* Rochester, NY	80
2182	23c	**Mary Cassat,** *Nov. 4, 1988,* Philadelphia, PA	80
2183	25c	**Jack London,** *Jan. 11, 1986,* Glen Ellen, CA *(358,686)*	85
2188	45c	**Harvey Cushing,** *June 17, 1988,* Cleveland, OH	1.05
2191	56c	**John Harvard,** *Sept. 3, 1986,* Boston, MA	1.25
2192	65c	**Hap Arnold,** *Nov. 5, 1988,* Gladwyne, PA	1.50
2194	$1	**Dr. Bernard Revel,** *Sept. 23, 1986,* New York, NY	2.00
2195	$2	**William Jennings Bryan,** *Mar. 19, 1986,* Salem, IL *(123,430)*	4.00
2196	$5	**Bret Harte,** *Aug. 25, 1987,* Twain Harte, CA *(111,431)*	10.00
2197	25c	**Jack London, bklt. single,** *May 3, 1988,* San Francisco, CA	85

1986

2198 to 2201	22c	**Stamp Collecting,** *Jan. 23,* State College, PA *(675,924)*	@80
2202	22c	**Love,** *Jan. 30,* New York, NY	80
2203	22c	**Sojourner Truth,** *Feb. 4,* New Paltz, NY *(342,985)*	80
2204	22c	**Republic of Texas,** *Mar. 2,* San Antonio, TX *(380,450)*	80
2205 to 2209	22c	**Fish,** *Mar. 21,* Seattle, WA *(988,184)*	@80
2210	22c	**Public Hospitals,** *Apr. 11,* New York, NY *(403,665)*	80
2211	22c	**Duke Ellington,** *Apr. 29,* New York, NY *(397,894)*	80
2216 to 2219	22c	**Presidents Souvenir Sheets of 9,** *May 22,* Chicago, IL *(9,009,599)*	@4.00
		2216a to 2219i	@80
2220 to 2223	22c	**Polar Explorers,** *May 28,* North Pole, AK *(760,999)*	@80
		2223a	2.75
2224	22c	**Statue of Liberty,** *July 4,* New York, NY *(1,540,308)*	80

1986-87

TRANSPORTATION ISSUE

2225	1c	**Omnibus,** *Nov. 26, 1986,* Washington, DC *(57,845)*	70
2226	2c	**Locomotive,** *Mar. 6, 1987,* Milwaukee, WI *(169,484)*	70

1986

2235 to 2238	22c	**Navajo Art,** *Sept. 4,* Window Rock, AZ *(1,102,520)*	@80
		2238a	2.75
2239	22c	**T.S. Eliot,** *Sept. 26,* St. Louis, MO *(304,764)*	80
2240 to 2243	22c	**Woodcarved Figurines,** *Oct. 1,* Washington, DC *(629,399)*	@80
		2243a	2.75
2244	22c	**Christmas (Madonna),** *Oct. 24,* Washington, DC *(467,999)*	80
2245	22c	**Christmas (Winter Village),** *Oct. 24,* Snow Hill, MD *(504,851)*	80

1987

2246	22c	**Michigan Statehood Sesquicent.,** *Jan. 26,* Lansing, MI *(379,117)*	80
2247	22c	**Pan American Games,** *Jan. 29,* Indianapolis, IN *(344,731)*	80
2248	22c	**Love,** *Jan. 30,* San Francisco, CA *(333,329)*	80

2249	22c	**Pointe du Sable,** *Feb. 20,* Chicago, IL *(313,054)*	80
2250	22c	**Enrico Caruso,** *Feb. 27,* New York, NY *(389,834)*	80
2251	22c	**Girl Scouts of America,** *Mar. 12,* Washington, DC *(556,391)*	80

1987-88

TRANSPORTATION ISSUE

2252	3c	**Conestoga Wagon,** *Feb. 29, 1988,* Conestoga, PA	65
2253	5c	**Milk Wagon,** *Sept. 25, 1987,* Indianapolis, IN	70

First day cancel was applied to 162,571 covers bearing Nos. 2253 and 2262.

2254	5.3c	**Elevator,** *Sept. 16, 1988,* New York, NY	70
2255	7.6c	**Carretta,** *Aug. 30, 1988,* San Jose, CA	70
2256	8.4c	**Wheelchair,** *Aug. 12, 1988,* Tucson, AZ	70
2257	10c	**Canal Boat,** *Apr. 11, 1987,* Buffalo, NY *(171,952)*	75
2258	13c	**Police Patrol Wagon,** *Oct. 29, 1988,* Anaheim, CA	75
2259	13.2c	**Railway Coal Car,** *July 19, 1988,* Pittsburgh, PA	75
2260	15c	**Tugboat,** *July 12, 1988,* Long Beach, CA	75
2261	16.7c	**Popcorn Wagon,** *July 7, 1988,* Chicago, IL	75
2262	17.5c	**Marmon Wasp,** *Sept. 25, 1987,* Indianapolis, IN	80
2263	20c	**Cable Car,** *Oct. 28, 1988,* San Francisco, CA	80
2264	20.5c	**Fire Engine,** *Sept. 28, 1988,* San Angelo, TX	80
2265	21.5c	**Railway Mail Car,** *Aug. 16, 1988,* Santa Fe, NM	80
2266	24.1c	**Tandem Bicycle,** *Oct. 26, 1988,* Redmond, WA	80

1987

2267 to 2274	22c	**Special Occasions,** *Apr. 20,* Atlanta, GA *(1,588,129)*	@80
2275	22c	**United Way,** *Apr. 28,* Washington, DC *(556,391)*	80

1987-88

2276	22c	**Flag and Fireworks,** *May 9,* Denver, CO	80
2277	(25c)	**'E' Earth,** *Mar. 22, 1988,* Washington, DC	85
2278	25c	**Flag and Clouds,** *May 6, 1988,* Boxborough, MA	85
2279	(25c)	**'E' Earth, coil,** *Mar. 22, 1988,* Washington, DC	85
2280	25c	**Flag over Yosemite,** *May 20, 1988,* Yosemite, CA	85
2281	25c	**Honey Bee,** *Sept. 2, 1988,* Omaha, NE	85
2282	(25c)	**'E' Earth, bklt. single,** *Mar. 22, 1988,* Washington, DC	85
2283	25c	**Pheasant,** *Apr. 29, 1988,* Rapid City, SD	85
2284 to 2285	25c	**Owl and Grosbeak,** *May 28, 1988,* Arlington, VA	@85
2285A	25c	**Flag and Clouds, bklt. single,** *July 5, 1988,* Washington, DC	85
2286 to 2335	22c	**American Wildlife,** *June 13, 1987,* Toronto, Canada	@80
		2335a	—

1987-88

RATIFICATION OF THE CONSTITUTION

2336	22c	**Delaware,** *July 4, 1987,* Dover, DE *(505,770)*	80
2337	22c	**Pennsylvania,** *Aug. 26, 1987,* Harrisburg, PA *(367,184)*	80
2338	22c	**New Jersey,** *Sept. 11, 1987,* Trenton, NJ *(432,899)*	80
2339	22c	**Georgia,** *Jan. 6, 1988,* Atlanta, GA	80
2340	22c	**Connecticut,** *Jan. 9, 1988,* Hartford, CT	80
2341	22c	**Massachusetts,** *Feb. 6, 1988,* Boston, MA	80
2342	22c	**Maryland,** *Feb. 15, 1988,* Annapolis, MD	80
2343	25c	**South Carolina,** *May 23, 1988,* Columbia, SC	85
2344	25c	**New Hampshire,** *June 21, 1988,* Concord, NH	85
2345	25c	**Virginia,** *June 25, 1988,* Williamsburg, VA	85
2346	25c	**New York,** *July 26, 1988,* Albany, NY	85

1987

2349	22c	**U.S.—Morocco Diplomatic Relations Bicent.,** *July 17,* Washington, DC *(372,814)*	80
2350	22c	**William Faulkner,** *Aug. 3,* Oxford, MS *(480,024)*	80
2351 to 2354	22c	**Lacemaking,** *Aug. 14,* Ypsilanti, MI	@80
2355 to 2359	22c	**Drafting of Constitution Bicent.,** *Aug. 28,* Washington, DC *(1,008,799)*	@80
2360	22c	**Signing of Constitution Bicent.,** *Sept. 17,* Philadelphia, PA *(719,975)*	80
2361	22c	**Certified Public Accounting,** *Sept. 21,* New York, NY *(362,099)*	80

2362 to 2366	22c	**Locomotives,** *Oct. 1,* Baltimore, MD *(976,694)*	80
2367	22c	**Christmas (Madonna),** *Oct. 23,* Washington, DC *(320,406)*	80
2368	22c	**Christmas (Ornaments),** *Oct. 23,* Holiday—Anaheim, CA *(375,858)*	80

1988

2369	22c	**Winter Olympics,** Calgary, *Jan. 10,* Anchorage, AK	80
2370	22c	**Australia Bicentennial,** *Jan. 26,* Washington, DC	80
2371	22c	**James Weldon Johnson,** *Feb. 2,* Nashville, TN	80

2372 to 2375	22c	**Cats,** *Feb. 5,* New York, NY	@80
		2375a	2.75
2376	22c	**Knute Rockne,** *Mar. 9,* Notre Dame, IN	80
2377	25c	**Francis Ouimet,** *June 13,* Brookline, MA	85
2378	25c	**Love,** *July 4,* Pasadena, CA	85
2379	45c	**Love,** *Aug. 8,* Shreveport, LA	1.05
2380	25c	**Summer Olympics,** Seoul, *Aug. 19,* Colorado Springs, CO	85
2381 to 2385	25c	**Classic Automobiles,** *Aug. 25,* Detroit, MI	@85
2386 to 2389	25c	**Antartic Explorers,** *Sept. 14,* Washington, DC	@85

2390 to 2393	25c	**Carousel Animals,** *Oct. 1,* Sandusky, OH	@85
		2393a	3.00
2394	$8.75	**Express Mail,** *Oct. 6,* Terre Haute, IN	25.00
2395 to 2398	25c	**Special Occasions,** *Oct. 22,* King of Prussia, PA	@85
2399	25c	**Christmas (Madonna),** *Oct. 20,* Washington, DC	85
2400	25c	**Christmas (Contemporary),** *Oct. 20,* Berlin, NH	85

AIR POST FIRST DAY COVERS

See first day cover pages for postage issues for introductory notes.

1918

C1	6c	**orange,** *Dec. 10*	17,500.
C2	16c	**green,** *July 11*	22,500.
C3	24c	**carmine rose & blue,** *May 13*	27,500.

1923

C4	8c	**dark green,** *Aug. 15*	450.00
C5	16c	**dark blue,** *Aug. 17*	850.00
C6	24c	**carmine,** *Aug. 21*	1,000.

1926-27

C7	10c	**dark blue,** *Feb. 13, 1926,*	65.00
		Chicago, Ill.	75.00
		Detroit, Mich.	75.00
		Cleveland, Ohio	135.00
		Dearborn, Mich.	135.00
C8	15c	**olive brown,** *Sept. 18, 1926,*	110.00
C9	20c	**yellow green,** *Jan. 25, 1927,*	115.00
		New York, N.Y.	125.00
C10	10c	**dark blue,** *June 18, 1927,*	25.00
		St. Louis, Mo.	25.00
		Little Falls, Minn.	35.00
		Detroit, Mich.	35.00

1928-30

C11	5c	**carmine & blue,** *July 25, 1928,* pair	50.00
		single stamp	250.00
C12	5c	**violet,** *Feb. 10, 1930*	20.00
C13	65c	**green,** *April 19, 1930*	1,850.
C14	$1.30	**brown,** *April 19, 1930*	1,400.
C15	$2.60	**blue,** *April 19, 1930*	2,000.
		C13 to C15 on one cover	12,500.

1931-33

C16	5c	**violet,** *Aug. 19, 1931*	200.00
C17	8c	**olive bister,** *Sept. 26, 1932*	20.00
C18	50c	**green,** *Oct. 2, 1933,* New York, N.Y. *(3,500)*	275.00
		Akron, Ohio, *Oct. 4*	425.00
		Washington, D.C., *Oct. 5*	375.00
		Miami, Fla., *Oct. 6*	225.00
		Chicago, Ill., *Oct. 7*	350.00

1934-37

C19	6c	**dull orange,** *June 30, 1934,* Baltimore, Md.	200.00
		New York, N.Y.	950.00
C20	25c	**blue,** *Nov. 22, 1935 (10,910)*	40.00
		San Francisco, Cal. *(15,000)*	35.00
C21	20c	**green,** *Feb. 15, 1937*	40.00
C22	50c	**carmine,** *Feb. 15, 1937*	40.00
		C21 to C22 on one cover	75.00

First day covers of Nos. C21 and C22 total 40,000.

1938-39

C23	6c	**dark blue & carmine,** *May 14, 1938,* Dayton, Ohio *(116,443)*	15.00
		St. Petersburg, Fla. *(95,121)*	15.00
		Washington, D.C., *May 15*	3.50
C24	30c	**dull blue,** *May 16, 1939,* New York, N.Y. *(68,634)*	45.00

1941-44

C25	6c	**carmine,** *June 25, 1941 (99,986)*	2.25
C26	8c	**olive green,** *March 21, 1944 (147,484)*	3.75
C27	10c	**violet,** *Aug. 15, 1941,* Atlantic City, N.J. *(87,712)*	10.00
C28	15c	**brown carmine,** *Aug. 19, 1941,* Baltimore, Md. *(74,000)*	12.00
C29	20c	**bright green,** *Aug. 27, 1941,* Philadelphia, Pa. *(66,232)*	15.00
C30	30c	**blue,** *Sept. 25, 1941,* Kansas City, Mo. *(57,175)*	22.50
C31	50c	**orange,** *Oct. 29, 1941,* St. Louis, Mo. *(54,580)*	45.00

1946-48

C32	5c	**carmine,** *Sept. 25, 1946*	2.00

First day covers of both Nos. C32 and UC14 (5c stamped envelope) total 396,669.

C33	5c	**carmine,** *March 26, 1947 (342,634)*	2.00
C34	10c	**black,** *Aug. 30, 1947 (265,773)*	2.00
C35	15c	**bright blue green,** *Aug. 20, 1947,* New York, N.Y. *(230,338)*	2.75
C36	25c	**blue,** *July 30, 1947,* San Francisco, Cal. *(201,762)*	3.75
C37	5c	**carmine, coil,** *Jan. 15, 1948 (192,084)*	2.00
C38	5c	**New York City,** *July 31, 1948,* New York, N.Y. *(371,265)*	1.75

1949

C39	6c	**carmine,** *Jan. 18 (266,790)*	1.50
C40	6c	**Alexandria Bicentennial,** *May 11,* Alexandria, Va. *(386,717)*	1.25
C41	6c	**carmine coil,** *Aug. 25 (240,386)*	1.25
C42	10c	**U.P.U.,** *Nov. 18,* New Orleans, La. *(270,000)*	1.75
C43	15c	**U.P.U.,** *Oct. 7,* Chicago, Ill. *(246,833)*	2.25
C44	25c	**U.P.U.,** *Nov. 30,* Seattle, Wash. *(220,215)*	3.00
C45	6c	**Wright Brothers,** *Dec. 17,* Kitty Hawk, N.C. *(378,585)*	4.25

1952-59

C46	80c	**Hawaii,** *March 26, 1952,* Honolulu, Hawaii, *(89,864)*	17.50
C47	6c	**Powered Flight,** *May 29, 1953,* Dayton, Ohio *(359,050)*	1.50
C48	4c	**bright blue,** *Sept. 3, 1954,* Philadelphia, Pa. *(295,720)*	75
C49	6c	**Air Force,** *Aug. 1, 1957 (356,683)*	1.75
C50	5c	**red,** *July 31, 1958,* Colorado Springs, Colo. *(207,954)*	80
C51	7c	**blue,** *July 31, 1958,* Philadelphia, Pa. *(204,401)*	75
C52	7c	**blue coil,** *July 31, 1958,* Miami, Fla. *(181,603)*	90
C53	7c	**Alaska Statehood,** *Jan. 3, 1959,* Juneau, Alaska *(489,752)*	65
C54	7c	**Balloon Jupiter,** *Aug. 17, 1959,* Lafayette, Ind. *(383,556)*	1.10
C55	7c	**Hawaii Statehood,** *Aug. 21, 1959,* Honolulu, Hawaii *(533,464)*	1.00
C56	10c	**Pan American Games,** *Aug. 27, 1959,* Chicago, Ill. *(302,306)*	90

1959-66

C57	10c	**Liberty Bell,** *June 10, 1960,* Miami, Fla. *(246,509)*	1.25
C58	15c	**Statue of Liberty,** *Nov. 20, 1959,* New York, N.Y. *(259,412)*	1.25
C59	25c	**Abraham Lincoln,** *April 22, 1960,* San Francisco, Cal. *(211,235)*	1.75
C59a	25c	**Tagged,** *Dec. 29, 1966 (about 3,000)*	12.50
C60	7c	**carmine,** *Aug. 12, 1960,* Arlington, Va. *(247,190)*	70
C61	7c	**carmine coil,** *Oct. 22, 1960,* Atlantic City, N.J. *(197,995)*	1.00

1961-67

C62	13c	**Liberty Bell,** *June 28, 1961,* New York, N.Y. *(316,166)*	80
C62a	13c	**Tagged,** *Feb. 15, 1967*	10.00
C63	15c	**Redrawn Statue of Liberty,** *Jan. 13, 1961,* Buffalo, N.Y. *(192,976)*	1.00
C63a	15c	**Tagged,** *Jan. 11, 1967*	12.00
C64	8c	**carmine,** *Dec. 5, 1962 (288,355)*	60
C64a	8c	**Tagged,** *Aug. 1, 1963,* Dayton, Ohio *(262,720)*	50
C65	8c	**carmine coil,** *Dec. 5, 1962 (220,173)*	80
C65a	8c	**Tagged,** *Jan. 14, 1965,* New Orleans, La.	—

1963-69

C66	15c	**Montgomery Blair,** *May 3, 1963,* Silver Spring, Md. *(260,031)*	1.35

C67	6c	**Bald Eagle,** *July 12, 1963,* Boston, Mass. *(268,265)*	50
C67a	6c	**Tagged,** *Feb. 15, 1967*	12.50
C68	8c	**Amelia Earhart,** *July 24, 1963,* Atchison, Kan. *(437,996)*	2.75
C69	8c	**Robert H. Goddard,** *Oct. 5, 1964,* Roswell, N.M. *(421,020)*	2.75
C70	8c	**Alaska Purchase,** *March 30, 1967,* Sitka, Alaska *(554,784)*	70
C71	20c	**Audubon,** *April 26, 1967,* Audubon (Station of N.Y.C.), N.Y. *(227,930)*	2.00
C72	10c	**carmine,** *Jan. 5, 1968,* San Francisco, Cal.	60
C73	10c	**carmine coil,** *Jan. 5, 1968,* San Francisco, Cal.	60
C74	10c	**Air Mail Service,** *May 15, 1968 (521,084)*	1.50
C75	20c	**USA and Jet,** *Nov. 22, 1968,* New York, N.Y. *(276,244)*	1.10
C76	10c	**Moon Landing,** *Sept. 9, 1969 (8,743,070)*	3.50

1971-73

C77	9c	**red,** *May 15, 1971,* Kitty Hawk, N.C.	50

First day cancellation was applied to 379,442 covers of Nos. C77 and UXC10.

C78	11c	**carmine,** *May 7, 1971,* Spokane, Wash.	50
C79	13c	**carmine,** *Nov. 16, 1973,* New York, N.Y. *(282,550)*	55

First day cancellation was applied to 464,750 covers of Nos. C78, C78a and C82, and to 204,756 covers of Nos. C79a and C83.

C80	17c	**Statue of Liberty,** *July 13, 1971,* Lakehurst, N.J. *(172,269)*	60
C81	21c	**USA and Jet,** *May 21, 1971 (293,140)*	75
C82	11c	**carmine coil,** *May 7, 1971,* Spokane, Wash.	50
C83	13c	**carmine coil,** *Dec. 27, 1973,* Chicago, Ill.	50
C84	11c	**National Parks Centennial,** *May 3, 1972,* Honaunau, Hawaii *(364,816)*	65
C85	11c	**Olympics,** *Aug. 17, 1972*	50

First day cancellation was applied to 971,536 covers of Nos. 1460 to 1462 and C85.

C86	11c	**Electronics,** *July 10, 1973,* New York, N.Y.	50

First day cancellation was applied to 1,197,700 covers of Nos. 1500 to 1502 and C86.

1974-79

C87	18c	**Statue of Liberty,** *Jan. 11, 1974,* Hempstead, N.Y. *(196,902)*	65
C88	26c	**Mt. Rushmore,** *Jan. 2, 1974,* Rapid City, S.D. *(210,470)*	85
C89	25c	**Plane and Globes,** *Jan. 2, 1976,* Honolulu, Hawaii	85
C90	31c	**Plane, Globes and Flag,** *Jan. 2, 1976,* Honolulu, Hawaii	85
C91 to C92	31c	**Wright Brothers,** *Sept. 23, 1978,* Dayton, Ohio	@1.15
		C92a	2.30
C93 to C94	21c	**Octave Chanute,** *Mar. 29, 1979,* Chanute, Kan.	@1.00
		C94a	2.00

First day cancellation was applied to 459,235 covers bearing Nos. C93, C94 or pair.

C95 to C96	25c	**Wiley Post,** *Nov. 20, 1979,* Oklahoma City, Okla.	@1.00
		C96a	2.00
C97	31c	**Olympics,** *Nov. 1, 1979,* Colorado Springs, CO	1.15

1980-83

C98	40c	**Philip Mazzei,** *Oct. 13, 1980*	1.35
C99	28c	**Blanche Stuart Scott,** *Dec. 30, 1980,* Hammondsport, NY *(238,502)*	1.10

C100	**35c**	**Glenn Curtiss**, *Dec. 30, 1980,* Hammondsport, NY)208,502)	1.25
C101 to *C104*	**28c**	**Olympics**, *June 17, 1983,* San Antonio, TX *(901,028)*	@1.10
		C104a	3.75
C105 to *C108*	**40c**	**Olympics**, *April 8, 1983,* Los Angeles, CA *(1,001,657)*	@1.35
		C108a	5.00
C109 to *C112*	**35c**	**Olympics**, *Nov. 4, 1983,* Colorado Springs, CO*(897,729)*	@1.25
		C112a	4.50

1985

C113	**33c**	**Alfred V. Verville**, *Feb. 13,* Garden City, NY	1.25
C114	**39c**	**Lawrence & Elmer Sperry**, *Feb. 13,* Garden City, NY	1.35

First dat cancellation was applied to 429,290 covers bearing Nos. C113 and C114.

C115	**44c**	**Transpacific Air Mail**, *Feb. 15,* San Francisco, CA *(269,229)*	1.35

A total of 269,229 first day cancels were applied for Nos. C115 and UXC22.

C116	**44c**	**Junipero Serra**, *Aug. 22,* San Diego, CA *(254,977)*	1.35

1988

C117	**44c**	**Settling of New Sweden**, *Mar. 29,* Wilmington, DE	1.35
C118	**45c**	**Samuel P. Langley**, *May 14,* San Diego, CA	1.40
C119	**36c**	**Igor Sikorsky**, *June 23,* Stratford, CT	1.30

BOOKLETS: PANES & COVERS

Most booklet panes issued before 1962 consist of a vertical block of 6 stamps perforated vertically through the center. The panes are perforated horizontally on all but the bottom edge. The two sides and bottom are straight edged. Exceptions for panes issued before 1962 are the 1917 American Expeditionary Forces panes (30 stamps); Lindbergh and 6¢ 1943 air mails (3), and the Savings Stamps (10). Since 1962, panes have been issued with 3 to 10 stamps and various configurations. They have included one or more labels and two or more stamps se-tenant.

Flat plate booklet panes, with the exceptions noted above, were made from specially designed plates of 180 or 360 subjects. They are collected in plate positions. There are nine collectible positions on the 180-subject plate and 12 on the 360-subject plate.

Rotary booklet panes issued from 1926 to May 1978 (except for Nos. 1623a and 1623c) were made from specially designed plates of 180, 320, 360, and 400 subjects. They also are collected in plate positions. There are five collectible positions on the 360-subject plates which were printed before electric eye plates came into use, and 20 collectible positions on the Type II "new design" 360-subject rotary plates. There are 21 collectible positions in the rotary air mail 180-subject plate as well as the Type IV "modified design" 360-subject plate. There are 16 collectible positions on the 320-subject plates and 20 on the 400 subject plates. There are five collectible positions on Defense and War Savings 300-subject plates.

The generally accepted methods of designating pane positions as illustrated and explained hereafter are those suggested by George H. Beans in the May 1913 issue of "Everybody's Philatelist" and by B. H. Mosher in his monograph "Discovering U.S. Rotary Pane Varieties 1926-78". Some collectors take all varieties possible, but the majority collect unused (A) panes and plate number (D) panes from flat plate issues, and plain panes and panes with electric eye bars and electric eye dashes where available from rotary plates.

Starting in 1977, BEP made two major changes in booklet production. Printing of panes was gradually moved from rotary plates to sleeves for modern high speed presses. Also, booklet production was transferred to Goebel booklet-forming machines. These changes virtually eliminated collectible pane positions. Also, because of the requirements of the Goebel machine, the subject size of printing plates or sleeves varied widely. For these reasons, plate layouts are not shown for each issue. The plate layout for No. 1288c and the sleeve layout for No. 1623a are shown as typical. The subject size of the plates or sleeves will be given with each issue.

The following panes, issued after March 11, 1977, were printed from rotary plates and assembled into booklets on the Goebel machine: Nos. 1288c, 1736a, 1742a, 1819a, 1889a, and most printings of No. 1949a. All other issues from March 11, 1977 on were printed from sleeves. Except for No. 1736a; one pane in 12 of the plate issues may have a plate join line along either long side of the pane, creating three collectible positions: no join line, join line top (or right), and join line bottom (or left).

All panes printed for booklet assembly on the Goebel machine contain two register marks in the tab: a cross register mark 1.5mm wide which runs across the tab and a length register mark (LRM), 1.5x5mm, usually placed vertically above the right hand (or top) stamp on the pane. Nos. 1623a and 1623c were regularly issued with the LRM over either stamp. Some copies of No. 1893a were issued with the LRM over the left stamp.

Starting with No. 1889a (except for 1948a), plate numbers (1 to 5 digits) were placed in the tab, normally over the left stamp. On Nos. 1889a and 1893a, the plate numbers are 3mm high. On all subsequent issues, the numbers are 1 mm high. On booklets containing Nos. 1889a and 1949a, the plate number is only on the top pane, the second pane in each case not having a number. All subsequent multi-pane booklets have the plate number on each pane.

Panes in all booklets assembled on the Goebel machine will be folded at least once.

Dr. William R. Bush, Robert E. Kitson, Richard F. Larkin, Dr. Robert Marks, Bruce H. Mosher, the Bureau Issues Association, and the Booklet Collectors Club helped the editors extensively in compiling the listings and preparing the illustrations of booklets, covers and plate layouts.

The 180-Subject Plate —— 9 Collectible Positions

Beginning at upper left and reading from left to right, the panes are designated from 1 to 30. All positions not otherwise identifiable are designated by the letter A: Pane 1A, 2A, 3A, 4A, etc.

The identifiable positions are as follows:

A The ordinary booklet pane without distinguishing features. Occurs in Position 1, 2, 3, 4, 8, 9, 10, 21, 22, 23, 24, 27, 28, 29, 30.
B Split arrow and guide line at right. Occurs in Position 5 only.
C Split arrow and guide line at left. Occurs in Position 6 only.
D Plate number pane. Occurs in Position 7 only.
E Guide line pane showing horizontal guide line between stamps 1-2 and 3-4 of the pane. Occurs in Positions 11, 12, 13, 14, 17, 18, 19, and 20.
F Guide line through pane and at right. Occurs in Position 15 only.
G Guide line through pane and at left. Occurs in Position 16 only.
H Guide line at right. Occurs in Position 25 only.
I Guide line at left. Occurs in Position 26 only.

Only positions B, F and H or C, G and I may be obtained from the same sheet, depending on whether the knife which separated the panes fell to right or left of the line.

Side arrows, bottom arrows, or bottom plate numbers are seldom found because the margin of the sheets is usually cut off, as are the sides and bottom of each pane.

In the illustrations, the dotted lines represent the rows of perforations, the unbroken lines represents the knife cut.

The 360-Subject Plate —— 12 Collectible Positions

As with the 180-Subject Sheets, the position of the various panes is indicated by numbers beginning in the upper left corner with the No. 1 and reading from left to right to No. 60.

The identifiable positions are as follows:

A The ordinary booklet pane without distinguishing features. Occurs in Positions 1, 2, 3, 4, 8, 9, 10, 11, 12, 13, 14, 17, 18, 19, 20, 41, 42, 43, 44, 47, 48, 49, 50, 51, 52, 53, 54, 57, 58, 59, and 60.

B Split arrow and guide line at right. Occurs in Position 5 only.

C Split arrow and guide line at left. Occurs in Position 6 only.

D Plate number pane. Occurs in Position 7 only.

E, F, G Do not occur in the 360-Subject Plate.

H Guide line at right. Occurs in Positions 15, 45, and 55.

I Guide line at left. Occurs in Positions 16, 46, and 56.

J Guide line at bottom. Occurs in Positions 21, 22, 23, 24, 27, 28, 29 and 30.

K Guide line at right and bottom. Occurs in Position 25 only.

L Guide line at left and bottom. Occurs in Position 26 only.

M Guide line at top. Occurs in Positions 31, 32, 33, 34, 37, 38, 39 and 40.

N Guide line at top and right. Occurs in Position 35 only.

O Guide line at top and left. Occurs in Position 36 only.

The 360-Subject Rotary Press Plate (before Electric Eye) Position A only

The 360-Subject Rotary Press Plate —— Electric Eye
A modified design was put into use in 1956. The new plates have 20 frame bars instead of 17.

The A.E.F. Plate —— 360-Subject Flat Plate —— 10 Collectible Positions

The 320-Subject Plate

The 400-Subject Plate —— The 300-Subject Plate with double labels has the same layout

1 A	2 A	3 A	4 A	5 B	6 C	7 A	8 A	9 A	10 A
11 A	12 A	13 A	14 A	15 H	16 I	17 A	18 A	19 A	20 A
21 J	22 J	23 J	24 J	25 K	26 L	27 J	28 J	29 J	30 J
31 M	32 M	33 M	34 M	35 N	36 O	37 M	38 M	39 M	40 M
41 A	42 A	43 A	44 A	45 H	46 I	47 A	48 A	49 A	50 A
51 A	52 A	53 A	54 A	55 H	56 I	57 A	58 A	59 A	60 A

Lindbergh Booklet Plate —— 180 Subjects —— 11 Collectible Positions

Airmail 180-Subject Rotary Press Plate —— Electric Eye

Prices are for complete panes with selvage, and for panes of six unless otherwise stated.

Plate Sizes

1288c	288
1598a	832
1623a, c	832
1736a	400
1737a	832
1742a	480
1819a	288
1889a	480
1893a	832
1896a	780
1896b	780, 960
1909a	78
1948a	1040
1949a	480, 1040
2113a	1040
2116a	390, 480
2121a	960
2122a	78
2197a	864
2201a	96
2209a	120
2282a	480
2285b	480

Booklet Covers

Front covers of booklets of postage and airmail issues are illustrated and numbered. Included are the Booklet Cover number (BC2A); and the catalogue numbers of the Booklet Panes (300b, 331a). The text of the inside and back covers changes. When more than one combination of covers exists, the number of possible booklets is noted in parenthesis after the booklet listing.

1900
Text only cover

25c   booklet contains 2 panes of six 2c stamps.
49c   booklet contains 4 panes of six 2c stamps.
97c   booklet contains 8 panes of six 2c stamps.

Booklets sold for 1c more than the face value of the stamps.

279e — BC1A

279e — BC1B

279e — BC1C

1900-1908
Text cover with price added in upper corners

25c   booklets contain 4 panes of six 1c stamps or 2 panes of six 2c stamps.
49c   booklets contain 4 panes of six 2c stamps.
97c   booklet contains 8 panes of six 2c stamps.

300b, 331a — BC2A

279e, 301c, 319, 332a — BC2B

279e, 301c, 319, 332a — BC2C

279e, 301c, 319, 332a — BC2D

1908-1912
Postrider

25c   booklet contains 2 panes of six 2c stamps.
49c   booklet contains 4 panes of six 2c stamps.
97c   booklet contains 8 panes of six 2c stamps.

331a, 374a, 405b — BC3A

332a, 375a, 406a — BC3B

> United States Booklet Panes can be mounted in Scott's U.S. Booklet Panes Album.

332a, 375a, 406a — BC3C

332a, 375a, 406a — BC3D

1912-1939
Washington P.O.
Price of booklet in large numerals behind contents information

25c   booklet contains 4 panes of six 1c stamps.
73c   booklet contains 4 panes of six 1c stamps and 4 panes of six 2c stamps.
97c   booklet contains 16 panes of six 1c stamps.

405b, 424d, 462a, 498e — BC4A

405b, 424d, 462a, 498e, 552a, 632a — BC4B

405b, 424d, 462a, 498e, 552a, 632a, 804b — BC4C

1912-1939
Small Postrider
Large background numerals

25c   booklets contain 4 panes of six 1c stamps or 2 panes of six 2c stamps.
49c   booklets contain 4 panes of six 2c stamps.
73c   booklets contain 4 panes of six 1c stamps and 2 panes of six 2c stamps.
97c   booklets contain 16 panes of six 1c stamps or 8 panes of six 2c stamps.

632a, 804b — BC5A

406a, 425e, 463a, 499e, 554c, 583a, 634d, 806b — BC5B

406a, 425e, 463a, 499e, 554c, 583a, 634d, 806b — BC5C

632a, 804b — BC5D

632a, 804b — BC5E

406a, 425e, 463a, 499e, 634d 806b — BC5F

1917-1927   **Oval designs**

25c	booklet contains 4 panes of six 1c stamps.
37c	booklet contains 2 panes of six 3c stamps.
97c	booklet contains 8 panes of six 2c stamps.

498e, 552a — BC6A

501b, 502b — BC6B

97c  97c

499e, 554c, 583a, 634d — BC6C

1918   **A.E.F.**

$3	booklet contains 10 panes of thirty 1c stamps.
$6	booklet contains 10 panes of thirty 2c stamps.

Booklets sold for face value.

498f
BC7A

300
1 CENT POSTAGE STAMPS
$3.

300
2 CENT POSTAGE STAMPS
$6.

499f
BC7B

1928   **Postrider and Wings**

61c   booklet contains 2 panes of three 10c stamps.

C10a
BC8

Large background numerals

1932-1954   **Post Office Seal**

25c   booklet contains 2 panes of six 2c stamps.
37c   booklet contains 2 panes of six 3c stamps.
49c   booklet contains 4 panes of six 2c stamps.
73c   booklets contain 4 panes of six 3c stamps or 4
       panes of six 1c stamps and 4 panes of six 2c
       stamps.

806b — BC9A

720b, 807a, 1035a — BC9B

806b — BC9C

720b, 807a, 1035a — BC9D

804b — BC9E

1958

97c   booklet contains 4 panes of six 4c stamps.

1036a — BC9F

1036a — BC9G

1036a — BC9H

Large background numerals

1943   **Postrider and Wings**

37c   booklet contains 2 panes of three 6c stamps.
73c   booklet contains 4 panes of three 6c stamps.

C25a — BC10A

C25a — BC10B

1949-1963   **U.S. Airmail Wings**

    The 73c and 85c booklets were the last sold for 1c over face
value.

73c   booklet contains 2 panes of six 6c stamps.
85c   booklet contains 2 panes of six 7c stamps.
80c   booklet contains 2 panes of five 8c stamps.
$2   booklet contains 5 panes of five 8c stamps.

C39a — BC11A

C51a — BC11B

C51a, C60a — BC11C

C64b, C64c — BC11D

C64b — BC11E

1962-1963   **Small Postrider**

$1   booklet contains 4 panes of five 5c stamps.

1213a — BC12A

1963-1964   **Mr. Zip**

$1   booklet contains 4 panes of five 5c stamps.
$2   booklet contains 5 panes of five 8c stamps.

1213a, 1213c — BC13A

C64b, C64c — BC13B

1967-1968

$2   booklet contains 4 panes of eight 6c stamps and 1 pane of eight 1c stamps.
$4   booklet contains 5 panes of eight 10c stamps.

1284b — BC14A

C72b — BC14B

1968-1971

$1   booklets contain 2 panes of five 10c stamps or 2 panes of six 8c stamps and 1 pane of four 1c stamps; 3 panes of five 6c stamps and 1 pane of five 2c stamps or 2 panes of four 11c stamps and 1 pane of six 2c stamps.

C72c — BC15A

1395b — BC15B

1284c, 1393b — BC15C

C78a — BC15D

1970-1971   **Eisenhower**

$2   booklet contains 4 panes of eight 6c stamps and 1 pane of eight 1c stamps.
$1.92   booklet contains 3 panes of eight 8c stamps.

1393a — BC16A

1395a — BC16B

1972-1974   **Postal Service Emblem**

$2   booklet contains 3 panes of seven 8c stamps and 1 pane of four 8c stamps.
$1   booklet contains 2 panes of five 10c stamps.
$4   booklet contains 5 panes of eight 10c stamps.
$1.25   booklet contains 1 pane of five 13c stamps and 1 pane of six 10c stamps.

1395d — BC17A

1510b — BC17B

1510c — BC17C

1510d — BC17D

1973

$1.30   booklet contains 2 panes of five 13c stamps.

C79a — BC18

1975-1976

90c   booklet contains 1 pane of six 13c stamps and 1 pane of six 2c stamps.
$1.30   booklet contains 2 panes of five 13c stamps.
$2.99   booklet contains 2 panes of eight 13c stamps and 1 pane of seven 13c stamps.

1595a, 1595d — BC19A

1595c — BC19B

1977-1978

$1   booklet contains 1 pane of one 9c stamp and seven 13c stamps.
$1.20   booklet contains 1 pane of eight 15c stamps.
$2.40   booklet contains 2 panes of eight 15c stamps.
$3.60   booklet contains 3 panes of eight 15c stamps.

1623a — BC20

1598a — BC21

1738a — BC22

1288c — BC23

1736c — BC24

1980

$3   booklet contains 2 panes of ten 15c stamps.

1742a — BC25

1981-82

$4.32   booklet contains 3 panes of eight B stamps.
$4   booklet contains 2 panes of ten C stamps.
$4.40   booklet contains 2 panes of ten D stamps.

1819a, 1948a, 2113a — BC26

1981

$1.20   booklet contains 1 pane of two 6c and six 18c stamps.
$3.60   booklet contains 2 panes of ten 18c stamps.

1893a
BC27

1889a
BC28

1982

$1.20   booklet contains 2 panes of six 20c stamps.
$2   booklet contains 1 pane of ten 20c stamps.
$4   booklet contains 2 panes of ten 20c stamps.

1896a — BC29

1896b — BC29B

1949a — BC30

1983

$28.05 booklet contains 1 pane of three $9.35 stamps.
$32.25 booklet contains 1 pane of three $10.75 stamps.

1909a, 2121a — BC31

1985

$1.10 booklet contains one pane of five 22c stamps.
$2.20 booklet contains two panes of five 22c stamps.
$4.40 booklet contains two panes of ten 22c stamps.

2116a — BC32

2121a — BC33A

2121a — BC33B

Many different seashell configurations are possible on BC33A. Seven adjacent covers are necessary to show all 25 shells.

2116a — BC33C

1986

$1.76 booklet contains 2 panes of four 22c stamps.
$2.20 booklet contains 2 panes of five 22c stamps.

2201a — BC34

2209a — BC35

1987

$2.20 booklet contains 1 pane of ten 22c stamps.

2274a — BC36

1987

$4.40 booklet contains four panes of five 22c stamps.

2359a — BC37

1987

$4.40 booklet contains four panes of five 22c stamps.

2366a — BC38

1987

$4.40 booklet contains one pane of twenty 22c stamps.

2276a — BC39

1988

$5   booklet contains two panes of ten E stamps.

2282a — BC40

1988

$5   booklet contains two panes of ten 25c stamps.

2283a — BC41

1988

$1.50   booklet contains one pane of six 25c stamps.
$3   booklet contains two panes of six 25c stamps.
$5   booklet contains two panes of ten 25c stamps.

2197a — BC43

1988

$5   booklet contains two panes of ten 25c stamps.

2285b — BC45

1988

$3   booklet contains two panes of six 25c stamps.

2285c — BC46

1988

$5   booklet contains four panes of five 25c stamps.

2385a — BC47

2396a, 2398a — BC48

1988

$3   booklet contains two panes of six 25c stamps.

———————

A particular stamp may be scarce, but if few collectors want it, its market value may remain relatively low.

BOOKLET PANES

Washington — A88

Wmk. 191 Horizontally or Vertically

1900				Perf. 12
279e	A88	2c orange red, *April 16*	350.00	200.00
		2c red	350.00	200.00
		With plate number		
		(D)		750.00

180- and 360-Subject Plates. All plate positions exist, except J, K, and L, due to the horizontal guide line being placed too far below stamps to appear on the upper panes.

Booklets

BK1	BC1A	25c black, *cream*	—
BK2	BC1A	25c black, *buff*	—
BK3	BC1B	49c green, *cream*	—
BK4	BC1B	49c black, *buff*	—
BK5	BC1C	97c red, *cream*	—
BK6	BC1C	97c black, *gray*	—
BK7	BC2B	25c black, *cream* (3)	—
BK8	BC2C	49c black, *buff* (3)	—
BK9	BC2D	97c black, *gray* (3)	—

BK1-BK6 and one type each of BK7-BK9 exist with specimen overprints handstamped on cover and individual stamps.

All covers of BK7-BK9 exist with "Philippines" overprint in 50mm or 48mm.

Franklin — A115

Washington — A116

1903-07   **Wmk. 191 Vertically**
300b   A115   1c blue green, *March 6,*
1907   500.00   250.00
    With plate number
    (D)   1000.

180-Subject Plates only. All plate positions exist.

Booklet

BK10   BC2A   25c black, *green* (6)   —

301c   A116   2c carmine, *Jan. 24,*
1903   425.00   250.00
    With plate number
    (D)   1100.

180-Subject Plates only. All plate positions exist.

Booklets

BK11   BC2B   25c black, *cream*   —
BK12   BC2C   49c black, *buff*   —
BK13   BC2D   97c black, *gray*   —

Washington — A129

1903   **Wmk. 191 Vertically**
319g   A129   2c carmine, Die I, *Dec.*
3, 1903   110.00   20.00
319m   A129   2c lake (I)   —
319n   A129   2c carmine rose (I)   —
319p   A129   2c scarlet (I)   110.00
319h   A129   2c carmine, Die II   200.00
319q   A129   2c lake (II)   140.00
    With plate number,
    Die I (D)   200.00
    With plate number,
    Die II (D)   300.00
    Wmk. horizontal   135.00   30.00

180-Subject Plates only. All plate positions exist.

Booklet

BK14   BC2B   25c black, *cream* (11)   —
BK15   BC2C   49c black, *buff,* (11)   —
BK16   BC2C   49c black, *pink*   —
BK17   BC2D   97c black, *gray* (11)   —

Franklin — A138

Washington — A139

1908   **Wmk. 191 Vertically**
331a   A138   1c green, *Dec. 2, 1908*   165.00   35.00
    With plate number
    (D)   225.00

180- and 360-Subject Plates. All plate positions exist.

Booklets

BK18   BC2A   25c black, *green* (3)   —
BK19   BC3A   25c black, *green*   —

332a   A139   2c carmine, *Nov. 16,*
1908   125.00   35.00
    With plate number
    (D)   175.00

180- and 360-Subject Plates. All plate positions exist.

Booklets

BK20   BC2B   25c black, *cream* (2)   —
BK21   BC2C   49c black, *buff* (2)   —
BK22   BC2C   49c black, *pink*   —
BK23   BC2D   97c black, *gray* (3)   —
BK24   BC3B   25c black, *cream*   —
BK25   BC3C   49c black, *pink*   —
BK26   BC3D   97c black, *gray*   —

1910   **Wmk. 190 Vertically**   *Perf. 12*
374a   A138   1c green, *Oct. 7, 1910*   135.00   30.00
    With plate number
    (D)   175.00

360-Subject Plates only. All plate positions exist.

Booklet

BK27   BC3A   25c black, *green* (2)   —

375a   A139   2c carmine, *Nov. 30,*
1910   110.00   25.00
    With plate number
    (D)   150.00

360-Subject Plates only. All plate positions exist.

Booklets

BK28   BC3B   25c black, *cream* (2)   —
BK29   BC3C   49c black, *pink* (2)   —
BK30   BC3D   97c black, *gray* (2)   —

Washington — A140

1912   **Wmk. 190 Vertically**
405b   A140   1c green, *Feb. 8, 1912*   65.00   7.50
    With plate number
    (D)   90.00

360-Subject Plates only. All plate positions exist.

Ordinary Booklets

BK31   BC3A   25c black, *green* (2)   —
BK32   BC4A   25c green, *green* (3)   —
BK33   BC4C   97c green, *lavender*   —

Combination Booklet

BK34   BC4B   73c red, 4 #405b (1c) + 4
       #406a (2c)   —

406a   A140   2c carmine, *Feb. 8, 1912*   70.00   17.50
    With plate number
    (D)   90.00

360-Subject Plates only. All plate positions exist.

Ordinary Booklets

BK35   BC3B   25c black, *cream* (2)   —
BK36   BC3C   49c black, *pink* (2)   —
BK37   BC3D   97c black, *gray* (2)   —
BK38   BC5B   25c red, *buff* (3)   —
BK39   BC5C   49c red, *pink* (3)   —
BK40   BC5F   97c red, *blue,* (3)   —

Combination Booklet

See No. BK34.

1914   **Wmk. 190 Vertically**   *Perf. 10*
424d   A140   1c green   4.00   75
    Double transfer, Plate
    6363   —
    With plate number
    (D)   7.00
    Cracked plate   —
    Imperf.   —

360-Subject Plates only. All plate positions exist.

Ordinary Booklets

BK41   BC4A   25c green, *green* (3)   —
BK42   BC4C   97c green, *lavender* (2)   —

Combination Booklet

BK43   BC4B   73c red, 4 #424d (1c) + 4
       #425e (2c) (3)   —

425e   A140   2c carmine, *Jan. 6, 1914*   15.00   3.00
    With plate number
    (D)   22.50

360-Subject Plates only. All plate positions exist.

Ordinary Booklets

BK44   BC5B   25c red, *buff* (3)   —
BK45   BC5C   49c red, *pink* (3)   —
BK46   BC5F   97c red, *blue* (3)   —

Combination Booklet

See No. BK43.

1916   **Unwmk.**   **Perf. 10**

462a	A140	1c green, *Oct. 15, 1916*	12.00	1.00
		Cracked plate at right	50.00	—
		Cracked plate at left	50.00	
		With plate number		
		(D)	17.50	

360-Subject Plates only. All plate positions exist.

Ordinary Booklets

BK47	BC4A	25c green, *green*	—
BK48	BC4C	97c green, *lavender*	—

Combination Booklets

BK49	BC4B	73c red, 4 #462a (1c) + 4 #463a (2c) (2)	—

463a	A140	2c carmine, *Oct. 8, 1916*	85.00	20.00
		With plate number		
		(D)	120.00	

360-Subject Plates only. All plate positions exist.

Ordinary Booklets

BK50	BC5B	25c red, *buff*	—
BK51	BC5C	49c red, *pink*	—
BK52	BC5F	97c red, *blue*	—

Combination Booklets

See No. BK49.

1917-18   **Unwmk.**   **Perf. 11**

498e	A140	1c green, *Apr. 6, 1917*	1.75	35
		Double transfer	—	—
		With plate number		
		(D)	2.75	60

360-Subject Plates only. All plate positions exist.

Ordinary Booklets

BK53	BC4A	25c green, *green* (2)	—
BK54	BC4C	97c green, *lavender* (4)	—
BK55	BC6A	25c green, *green* (5)	—

Combination Booklets

BK56	BC4B	73c red, 4 #498e (1c) + 4 #499e (2c) (4)	—
BK57	BC4B	73c red, 4 #498e (1c) + 4 #554c (2c) (3)	—

499e	A140	2c rose, type I, *Mar. 31, 1917*	2.00	50
		With plate number		
		(D)	3.00	90

360-Subject Plates only. All plate positions exist.

Ordinary Booklets

BK58	BC5B	25c red, *buff* (5)	—
BK59	BC5C	49c red, *pink* (4)	—
BK60	BC5F	97c red, *blue* (3)	—
BK61	BC6C	97c red, *blue* (2)	—

Combination Booklets

See No. BK56.

501b	A140	3c violet, type I, *Oct. 17, 1917*	75.00	15.00
		With plate number		
		(D)	100.00	

360-Subject Plates only. All plate positions exist.

Booklet

BK62	BC6B	37c violet, *sage*	—

502b	A140	3c violet, type II, *Mar. 1918*	50.00	10.00
		With plate number		
		(D)	70.00	

360-Subject Plates only. All plate positions exist.

Booklet

BK63	BC6B	37c violet, *sage*	—

Washington — A140

A.E.F. Panes of 30

498f	A140	1c green (pane of 30) *Sept. 1917*	550.00

Booklet

BK64	BC7A	$3 black, *green*	—

499f	A140	2c rose, (pane of 30) type I, *Sept. 1917*	9,000.

Booklet

BK65	BC7B	$6 black, *pink*	—

Nos. 498f and 499f were for use of the American Expeditionary Force in France.

They were printed from the ordinary 360-Subject Plates, the sheet being cut into 12 leaves of 30 stamps each in place of 60 leaves of 6 stamps each, and, of course, the lines of perforations changed accordingly.

The same system as used for designating plate positions on the ordinary booklet panes is used for designating the war booklet, only each war booklet pane is composed of 5 ordinary panes. Thus, No. 1 was booklet pane would be composed of positions 1, 2, 3, 4, and 5 of an ordinary pane.

The following varieties are noted, the figures in parentheses indicating the number of ordinary booklet panes:

W 1 (1 to 5) Split arrow and guide line at right.
W 2 (6 to 10) Split arrow and guide line at left. Plate number over fourth stamp.
W 3 (11 to 15) Guide line at right.
W 4 (16 to 20) Guide line at left.
W 5 (21 to 25) Guide line at right and at bottom. Arrow at lower left.
W 6 (26 to 30) Guide line at left and at bottom. Arrow at lower right.
W 7 (31 to 35) Guide line at right and top. Arrow at upper left.
W 8 (36 to 40) Guide line at left and top. Arrow at upper right.
W 9 (41 to 45) Guide line at right.
W10 (46 to 50) Guide line at left.
W11 (51 to 55) Guide line at right. Arrow at lower right. Initials.
W12 (56 to 60) Guide line at left. Arrow at lower left. Initials.

The A. E. F. booklet panes were bound at side margins which accounts for arrows being found. More often than not, the positions are not found on the sheets as when knifing them apart, very little attention was paid to the location of the margins. Positions W3 and W4 cannot be distinguished from W9 and W10.

Franklin — A155

Washington — A157

1923   **Unwmk.**   **Perf. 11**

552a	A155	1c deep green, *Aug. 1923*	5.50	50
		With plate number		
		(D)	8.50	

360-Subject Plates only. All plate positions exist.

Ordinary Booklets

BK66	BC6A	25c green, *green* (2)	—
BK67	BC4C	97c green, *lavender* (3)	—

Combination Booklet

BK68	BC4B	73c white, *red*, 4 #552a (1c) + 4 #554c (2c) (3)	—

554c	A157	2c carmine	7.00	1.00
		With plate number		
		(D)	11.00	

360-Subject Plates only. All plate positions exist.

Ordinary Booklets

BK69	BC5B	25c red, *buff* (3)	—
BK70	BC5C	49c red, *pink* (3)	—
BK71	BC6C	97c red, *blue* (3)	—

Combination Booklets

See Nos. BK57 and BK68.

ROTARY PRESS PRINTINGS

The rotary press booklet panes were printed from specially prepared plates of 360-subjects in arrangement as before, but without the guide lines and the plate numbers are at the sides instead of at the top as on the flat plates. The only varieties possible are the ordinary pane (A) and Partial plate numbers appearing at the right or left of the upper or lower stamps of a booklet pane when the trimming of the sheets is off center. The note applies to Nos. 583a, 632a, 634d, 720b, 804b, 806b and 807a, before Electric Eyes.

1926   **Perf. 10**

583a	A157	2c carmine, *Aug. 1926*	75.00	25.00
		First day cover		1,200.00

Ordinary Booklets

BK72	BC5B	25c red, *buff* (3)	—
BK73	BC5C	49c red, *pink*	—
BK74	BC6C	97c red, *blue*	—

1927   **Perf. 11x10½**

632a	A155	1c green, *Nov. 2, 1927*	4.00	25

Ordinary Booklets

BK75	BC5A	25c green, *green* (3)	—
BK76	BC4C	97c green, *lavender*	—
BK77	BC5E	97c green, *lavender*	—

Combination Booklets

BK78	BC4B	73c red, 4 #632a (1c) + 4 #634d (2c)	—
BK79	BC5D	73c red, 4 #632a (1c) + 4 #634d (2c) (2)	—

634d	A157	2c carmine, type I, *Feb. 25, 1927*	1.00	15

Ordinary Booklets

BK80	BC5B	25c red, *buff* (2)	—
BK81	BC5C	49c red, *pink* (2)	—
BK82	BC5F	97c red, *blue* (3)	—
BK83	BC6C	97c red, *blue*	—

Combination Booklets

See Nos. BK78 and BK79.

Washington — A226

1932

720b	A226	3c deep violet, *July 25, 1932*	22.50	5.00
		First day cover		100.00

Ordinary Booklets

BK84	BC9B	37c violet, *buff* (2)	—
BK85	BC9D	73c violet, *pink* (2)	—

Washington — A276

Adams — A278

Jefferson — A279

In 1942 plates were changed to the Type II "new design" and the E. E. marks may appear at the right or left margins of panes of Nos. 804b, 806b and 807a. Panes printed from E. E. plates have 2½mm. vertical gutter; those from pre-E. E. plates have 3mm. vertical gutter.

1939-42   *Perf. 11x10½*

804b	A276	1c green (3mm. vert. gutter), *Jan. 27, 1939*	1.75	*30*
		First day cover		20.00

Ordinary Booklets

BK86	BC5A	25c green, *green*	—	
BK87	BC5E	97c green, *lavender*	—	
BK88	BC4C	97c green, *lavender*	—	

Combination Booklet

BK89	BC5D	73c red, 4 #804b (1c) + 4 #806b (2c)	—	

804b	A276	1c green (2½mm. vert. gutter), *April 14, 1942*	1.75	*20*
		Horiz. pair, perf. only at bottom		—

Ordinary Booklets

BK90	BC5A	25c green, *green*	—	
BK91	BC5E	97c green, *lavender*	—	

Combination Booklets

BK92	BC5D	73c red, 4 #804b (1c) + 4 #806b (2c)	—	
BK93	BC9E	73c red, 4 #804b (1c) + 4 #806b (2c)	—	

806b	A278	2c rose carmine (3mm. vert. gutter), *Jan. 27, 1939*	4.50	*85*
		First day cover		20.00

Ordinary Booklets

BK94	BC5F	97c red, *blue*	—	

Combination Booklets

See No. BK89.

806b	A278	2c rose carmine, (2½mm. vert. gutter), *April 25, 1942*	4.25	*50*

Ordinary Booklets

BK95	BC5F	97c red, *blue*	—	
BK96	BC5B	25c red, *buff*	—	
BK97	BC9A	25c red, *buff*	—	
BK98	BC5C	49c red, *pink*	—	
BK99	BC9C	49c red, *pink*	—	

Combination Booklets

See Nos. BK92 and BK93.

807a	A279	3c deep violet (3mm. vert. gutter), *Jan. 27, 1939*	9.50	*1.50*
		First day cover		24.00

Booklets

BK100	BC9B	37c violet, *buff*	—	
BK101	BC9D	73c violet, *pink*	—	

807a	A279	3c deep violet, (2½mm. vert. gutter), *Mar. 6, 1942*	8.50	*50*
		With full vert. gutter (6mm.) btwn.		—

Booklets

BK102	BC9B	37c violet, *buff* (3)	—	
BK103	BC9D	73c violet, *pink* (3)	—	

Statue of Liberty — A482

Lincoln — A483

1954-58   *Perf. 11x10½*

1035a	A482	3c deep violet, *June 30, 1954*	3.00	*50*
		First day cover		6.00
1035f		Dry printing	4.00	*60*

Booklets

BK104	BC9B	37c violet, *buff*	9.00	
BK105	BC9D	73c violet, *pink*	15.00	

1036a	A483	4c red violet, *July 31, 1958*	2.00	*50*
		First day cover, Wheeling, W. Va. (135,825)		5.00
		Imperf. horizontally	—	

Booklets

BK106	BC9F	97c on 37c violet, *buff*	—	
BK107	BC9G	97c on 73c violet, *pink*	—	
BK108	BC9H	97c blue, *yellow*	10.00	
BK109	BC9H	97c blue, *pink* (3)	10.00	

Washington (Slogan 1) — A650

(Slogan 2)

(Slogan 3)

1962-64   *Perf. 11x10½*

Plate of 300 stamps, 60 labels

1213a	A650	5c dark blue gray, pane of 5+label, slogan 1, *Nov. 23, 1962*	5.50	*2.00*
		First day cover, New York, N. Y. (111,452)		5.00
		With slogan 2, *1963*	10.00	*3.50*
		With slogan 3, *1964*	2.00	*75*
		Imperf. vertically	—	

Booklets

BK110	BC12A	$1 blue, slogan 1	—	
BK111	BC12A	$1 blue, slogan 2	—	
BK112	BC13A	$1 blue, slogan 2	—	
BK113	BC13A	$1 blue, slogan 3 (4)	10.00	

1213c	A650	As No. 1213a, tagged, slogan 2, *Oct. 28, 1963*	55.00	*7.50*
		First day cover, Dayton, O.		100.00
		Washington, D.C. (750)		115.00
		With slogan 3, *1964*	1.25	*50*

Booklets

BK114	BC13A	$1 blue, slogan 2	—	
BK115	BC13A	$1 blue, slogan 3 (4)	6.00	

The first price column gives the catalogue value of an unused stamp, the second that of a used stamp.

Jefferson — A710

Wright — A712

(Slogan 4)

(Slogan 5)

1967-78   **Tagged**   **Perf. 11x10½**

1278a	A710	1c green, pane of 8, *Jan. 12, 1968*	1.00	*25*
		First day cover, Jeffersonville, Ind.	2.50	
		Dull finish gum	2.00	

Combination Booklets

See Nos. BK116, BK117B, BK118 and BK119.

1278b	A710	1c green, pane of 4+2 labels, slogans 5 & 4, *May 10, 1971*	75	*20*
		First day cover, Washington, D.C.	15.00	

Combination Booklet

See No. BK122.

1280a	A712	2c dark blue gray, pane of 5+label, slogan 4, *Jan. 8, 1968*	1.20	*40*
		First day cover, Buffalo, N.Y. *(147,244)*	2.50	
		With slogan 5	1.20	*40*

Combination Booklets

See Nos. BK117 and BK120.

1280c	A712	2c dark blue gray, pane of 6, *May 7, 1971*	1.00	*35*
		First day cover, Spokane, Wash.	15.00	
		Dull finish gum	1.00	

Combination Booklets

See Nos. BK127 and BKC22.

The 1c and 6c panes of 8, Nos. 1278a and 1284b, were printed from 320-subject plates and from 400-subject plates, both with electric eye markings. The 2c and 6c panes of 5 stamps plus label, Nos. 1280a and 1284c, were printed from 360-subject plates.

An experimental moisture-resistant gum was used on 1,000,000 panes of No. 1278a and 4,000,000 of No. 1393a released in March, 1971. This dull finish gum shows no breaker ridges. The booklets lack interleaving. This gum was also used for Nos. 1395c, 1395d, 1288c and all panes from No. 1510b on unless noted.

Oliver Wendell
Holmes — A720

Roosevelt — A716

Perf. 10½x11

1284b	A716	6c gray brown, pane of 8, *Dec. 28, 1967*	1.50	*50*
		First day cover, Washington, D.C.	3.50	

Combination Booklet

BK116	BC14A	$2 brown, 4 #1284b (6c)+1 #1278a(1c)(2)	8.50	

1284c	A716	6c gray brown, pane of 5+label, slogan 4, *Jan. 9, 1968*	1.25	*50*
		First day cover, Washington, D.C.	110.00	
		With slogan 5	1.25	*50*

Combination Booklet

BK117	BC15C	$1 brown, 3 #1284c (6c) + 1 #1280a (2c) (2)	6.00	

No. BK117 contains panes with slogan 4, slogan 5 or combinations of 4 and 5.

Perf. 10

1288c	A720	15c dark rose claret, pane of 8, *June 24, 1978*	2.40	*1.25*
		First day cover, Boston, Mass.	4.00	
1288e		As "c," vert. imperf. btwn.	—	

Booklet

BK117A	BC23	$3.60 red & light blue	8.00	

Eisenhower — A815

Plate of 400 subjects for No. 1393a. Plate of 300 stamps and 60 labels for No. 1393b.

1970   **Tagged**   **Perf. 11x10½**

1393a	A815	6c dark gray, pane of 8, *Aug. 6*	1.25	*50*
		First day cover, Washington, D.C.	3.75	
		Dull finish gum	1.75	

Combination Booklets

BK117B	BC14A	$2 blue, 4 #1393a (6c) + 1 #1278a (1c)	—	

BK118	BC16A	$2 blue, 4 #1393a (6c) + 1 #1278a (1c)	7.00	
BK119	BC16A	$2 blue, dull finish gum, 4 #1393a (6c) + 1 #1278a (1c) (2)	10.00	
1393b	A815	6c dark blue gray, pane of 5+label, slogan 4, *Aug. 6*	1.20	*35*
		With slogan 5	1.20	*35*
		First day cover, Washington, D.C. (either slogan)	2.00	

Combination Booklet

BK120	BC15C	$1 blue, 3 #1393b (6c) + 1 #1280a (2c)	5.50	

No. BK120 contains panes with slogan 4, slogan 5 or combinations of 4 and 5.

Stamps in this book have been gummed with a matte finish adhesive which permits the elimination of the separation tissues.

This book contains 25— 8¢ stamps — four on this pane and seven each on three additional panes. Selling price $2.00.

Slogans 6 and 7

Eisenhower — A815a

1971-72		Tagged	Perf. 11x10½	
1395a	A815a	8c deep claret, pane of 8, *May 10, 1971*	2.00	*1.25*
		First day cover, Washington, D.C.	3.50	

Booklet

BK121	BC16B	$1.92 claret (2)	7.00	
1395b	A815a	8c deep claret, pane of 6, *May 10, 1971*	1.00	*75*

| | | First day cover, Washington, D.C. | 3.00 | |

Combination Booklet

BK122	BC15B	$1 claret, 2 #1395b (8c) + 1 #1278a (1c) (2)	4.75	

Dull Finish Gum

1395c	A815a	8c deep claret, pane of 4+2 labels, slogans 6 and 7, *Jan. 28, 1972*	1.00	*50*
		First day cover, Casa Grande, Ariz.	2.25	
1395d	A815	8c deep claret, pane of 7+label, slogan 4, *Jan. 28, 1972*	1.75	*1.00*
		With slogan 5	1.75	*1.00*
		First day cover, Casa Grande, Ariz.	2.50	

The first day cancellation was applied to 181,601 covers bearing Nos. 1395c or 1395d.

Combination Booklet

BK123	BC17A	$2 claret, *yellow*, 3 #1395d + 1 #1395c	7.50	

Plate of 400 subjects for No. 1395a. Plate of 360 subjects for No. 1395b. Plate of 300 subjects (200 stamps and 100 double-size labels) for No. 1395c. Plate of 400 subjects (350 stamps and 50 labels) for No. 1395d.

Slogan 8

Jefferson Memorial — A924

1973-74		Tagged	Perf. 11x10½	
1510b	A924	10c blue, pane of 5+label, slogan 8, *Dec. 14, 1973*	1.50	*30*
		First day cover, Washington, D.C.	2.75	

Booklet

BK124	BC17B	$1 red & blue	3.50	
1510c	A924	10c blue, pane of 8, *Dec. 14, 1973*	1.60	*30*
		First day cover, Washington, D.C.	3.00	

Booklet

BK125	BC17C	$4 red & blue	9.00	
1510d	A924	10c blue, pane of 6, *Aug. 5, 1974*	2.50	*30*
		First day cover, Oakland, Calif.	3.00	

Combination Booklet

BK126	BC17D	$1.25 red & blue, 1 #1510d (10c) + 1 #C79a (13c)	6.00	

Slogan 9

Liberty Bell — A998

1975-78   **Tagged**   **Perf. 11x10½**

1595a	A998	13c brown, pane of 6, *Oct. 31, 1975*	1.60	50
		First day cover, Cleveland, Ohio		2.00

Combination Booklet

BK127	BC19A	90c red & blue, 1 #1595a (13c) + 1 #1280c (2c) (2)	3.00	
1595b	A998	13c brown, pane of 7+label, slogan 8, *Oct. 31, 1975*	1.85	50
		First day cover, Cleveland, Ohio		2.75
1595c	A998	13c brown, pane of 8, *Oct. 31, 1975*	2.10	50
		First day cover, Cleveland, Ohio		2.50

Combination Booklet

BK128	BC19B	$2.99 red & blue, 2 #1595c (13c) + 1 #1595b (13c) (2)	6.50	
1595d	A998	13c brown, pane of 5+label, slogan 9, *Apr. 2, 1976*	1.30	50
		First day cover, Liberty, Mo.		2.25

Booklet

BK129	BC19A	$1.30 red & blue	3.00	

Fort McHenry Flag (15 Stars) — A1001

1977-78   **Tagged**   **Perf. 11x10½**

1598a	A1001	15c gray, dark blue & red, pane of 8, *June 30, 1978*	4.25	60
		First day cover, Baltimore, Md.		3.00

Booklet

BK130	BC21	$1.20 red & light blue	4.50	
1623a	A1018a	Pane of 8 (1 #1590 + 7 #1623), *Mar. 11, 1977*	3.10	60
		First day cover, New York, N.Y.		30.00

Booklet

BK131	BC20	$1 red & light blue (3)	3.25	

Perf. 10

1623c	A1018a	Pane of 8 (1 #1590a + 7 #1623b), *Mar. 11, 1977*	40.00	—
		First day cover, New York, N.Y.		15.00

First day cancellation was applied to 242,208 covers bearing Nos. 1623a or 1623c.

Booklet

BK132	BC20	$1 red & light blue (2)	45.00	

Eagle — A1124

1978   **Tagged**   **Perf. 11x10½**

1736a	A1124	A orange, pane of 8, *May 22, 1978*	2.40	60
		First day cover, Memphis, Tenn.		3.00

Booklet

BK133	BC24	$3.60 deep orange	8.00	

Red Masterpiece and Medallion Roses — A1126

Perf. 10

1737a	A1126	15c multicolored, pane of 8, *July 11, 1978*	2.40	60
		First day cover, Shreveport, La.		3.00
1737b		As "a," imperf.	—	

Booklet

BK134	BC22	$2.40 rose red & yellow green	5.00	

See the "Information for Collectors" section at beginning of catalogue for information on printing methods and varieties.

Windmills — A1127-A1131

1980   **Tagged**   **Perf. 11**

1742a	A1131	15c sepia, *yellow,* pane of 10, *Feb. 7*	4.25	60

Booklet

BK135	BC25	$3 lt. blue & dark blue, *blue*	8.75	

A1207

A1279-A1280

A1267-A1276

1981

1819a	A1207	B violet, pane of 8, *Mar. 15*	4.50	*1.50*
		First day cover, San Francisco, CA	4.00	
Booklet				
BK136	BC26	$4.32 dull violet	14.50	
1889a	A1267-A1276	18c dark brown, pane of 10, *May 14*	9.00	—
		First day cover, Boise, ID	7.00	
Booklet				
BK137	BC28	$3.60 gray & olive	18.50	
1893a	A1279-A1280	Pane of 8 (2 #1892, 6 #1893), *Apr. 24*	3.50	—
		First day cover, Portland, ME	3.00	
1893b		As "a," vert. imperf. btwn.	75.00	
Booklet				
BK138	BC27	$1.20 blue & red	3.60	

A1281

1896a	A1281	20c black, dark blue & red, pane of 6, *Dec. 17, 1981*	2.50	—
		First day cover, Washington, D.C.	8.00	

Booklet

BK139	BC29	$1.20 blue & red (2)	2.75	
1896b	A1281	20c black, dark blue & red, pane of 10, *June 1, 1982*	4.25	—
		First day cover, Washington, D.C.		*12.00*
		Scored perforation	4.25	

Booklets

BK140	BC29	$2 blue & red (4)	4.50	
BK140A	BC29B	$4 blue & red	8.50	

A1296

1983

1909a	A1296	$9.35 multi, pane of 3, *Aug. 12, 1983*	77.50	—
		First day cover, Kennedy Space Center, FL		*90.00*

Booklet

BK140B	BC31	$28.05 blue & red	80.00	

A1333

1981

1948a	A1333	C brown, pane of 10, *Oct. 11, 1981*	4.25	—
		First day cover, Memphis, TN		*4.00*

Booklet

BK141	BC26	$4 brown, *blue*	9.00	

A1334

1982

1949a	A1334	20c dark blue, pane of 10, *Jan. 8, 1982*	4.00	—
		First day cover, Bighorn, MI		*8.00*
1949b		As "a," vert. imperf. btwn.	85.00	
Booklet				
BK142	BC30	$4 blue, *yellow green*	8.50	

A1497

1985   *Perf. 11*

2113a	A1497	D green, pane of 10 *Feb. 1, 1985*	4.40	—
		First day cover, Los Angeles, CA		*9.00*
Booklet				
BK143	BC26	$4.40 green	9.50	

A1499

Perf. 10 Horiz.

2116a	A1499	22c blue, red & black, pane of 5, *Mar. 29, 1985*	2.20	—
		First day cover, Waubeka, WI		*4.50*
Booklets				
BK144	BC33C	$1.10 blue & red	2.50	
BK145	BC33C	$2.20 blue & red	5.00	

A little time given to the study of the arrangement of the Scott Catalogue can make it easier to use effectively.

A1500-A1504

Perf. 10

2121a	A1500-A1504	22c multicolored, pane of 10, *Apr. 4, 1985*	4.40	—
		First day cover, Boston, MA		9.00
2121b		As "a," violet omitted	—	
2121c		As "a," vert. imperf. between	—	
2121d		As "a," imperf.	—	

Booklets

BK146	BC33A	$4.40 multi	9.50
BK147	BC33B	$4.40 multi	9.50

A1505

Perf. 10 Vert.

2122a	A1505	$10.75 multicolored, pane of 3, *Apr. 29, 1985*	67.50	—
		First day cover, San Francisco, CA		75.00

Booklet

BK148	BC31	$32.25	70.00

A1566

1988   Perf. 11

2183a	A1566	25c blue, pane of 10, *May 3, 1988*	5.00	—
		First day cover, San Francisco, CA		8.50

Booklet

BK148A	BC43	$5	10.50

Perf. 10

2197a	A1566	25c blue, pane of 6, *May 3, 1988*	3.00	—
		First day cover, San Francisco, CA		5.25

Booklets

BK148B	BC43	$1.50	3.25
BK148C	BC43	$3 brown & blue	6.50

A1581-A1584

1986

2201a	A1581-A1584	22c multicolored, pane of 4, *Jan. 23, 1986*	1.80	—
		First day cover, State College, PA		3.75
2201b		As "a," black omitted on Nos. 2198, 2201	60.00	
2201c		As "a," blue (litho.) omitted on Nos. 2198-2200	—	
2201d		As "a," buff (litho.) omitted	—	

Booklet

BK149	BC34	$1.76 purple & black	4.25

A1588-A1592

2209a	A1588-A1592	22c multicolored, pane of 5, *Mar. 21, 1986*	3.00	—
		First day cover, Seattle, WA		4.00

Booklet

BK150	BC35	$2.20 blue green and red	6.50

A1637-A1644

1987

2274a	A1637- A1644	22c multicolored, pane of 10, *Apr. 20, 1987*	4.50	—
		First day cover, At- lanta, GA		7.00
		Booklet		
BK151	BC36	$2.20 blue & red	4.75	

A1646

2276a	A1646	22c multicolored, pane of 20, *Nov. 30, 1987*	8.80	—
		First day cover, Washington, DC		15.00
		Booklet		
BK151A	BC39	$4.40 multicolored	9.25	

A1647

1988

2282a	A1647	E multicolored, pane of 10, *Mar. 22, 1988*	5.00	—
		First day cover, Washington, DC		8.50
		Booklet		
BK151B	BC40	$5 blue	10.50	

A1649a

2283a	A1649a	25c multicolored, pane of 10, *Apr. 29, 1988*	5.00	—
		First day cover, Rap- id City, SD		8.50
		Booklet		
BK151C	BC41	$5 multicolored	10.50	

A1649b-A1649c

2285b	A1649b- A1649c	25c multicolored, pane of 10, *May 28, 1988*	5.00	—
		First day cover, Ar- lington, VA		8.50
		Booklet		
BK151D	BC45	$5 red & black	10.50	

A1648

2285c	A1648	25c multicolored, pane of 6, *July 5, 1988*	3.00	—
		First day cover, Washington, DC		5.25
		Booklet		
BK151E	BC46	$3 blue & red	6.50	

Prices for stamps vary greatly, depending upon
centering, gum and condition.

A1719-A1723

2359a	A1719- A1723	22c multicolored, pane of 5, *Aug. 28, 1987*	2.25	—
		First day cover, Washington, DC		4.00
		Booklet		
BK152	BC37	$4.40 red & blue	9.50	

A1726-A1730

2366a	A1726- A1730	22c multicolored, pane of 5, *Oct. 1, 1987*	2.25	—
		First day cover, Balti- more, MD		4.00
		Booklet		
BK153	BC38	$4.40 black & yellow	9.50	

1928 Locomobile

1929 Pierce-Arrow

1931 Cord

1932 Packard

1935 Duesenberg

A1745-A1749

1988

2385a	A1745- A1749	25c multicolored, pane of 5, *Aug. 25, 1988*	2.50	—
		First day cover, De- troit, MI		4.00
		Booklet		
BK154	BC47	$5 black & red	10.50	

A1759-A1760

A1761-A1762

2396a	A1759- A1760	25c multicolored, pane of 6, *Oct. 22, 1988*	3.00	—
		First day cover, King of Prussia, PA		5.25
2398a	A1761- A1762	25c multicolored, pane of 6, *Oct. 22, 1988*	3.00	—
		First day cover, King of Prussia, PA		5.25
		Combination Booklet		
BK155	BC48	$3 multicolored, 1 #2396a, 1 #2398a	6.50	

AIR POST STAMPS

Spirit of St.
Louis — AP6

FLAT PLATE PRINTING

1928			**Perf. 11**	
C10a	AP6	10c dark blue, *May 26*	110.00	*60.00*
		First day cover, Washington, D.C.		925.00
		First day cover, Cleveland Midwestern Philatelic Sta. cancel		900.00
		Tab at bottom		

No. C10a was printed from specially designed 180-subject
plates arranged exactly as a 360-subject plate-each pane of
three occupying the relative position of a pane of six in a 360-
subject plate. Plate numbers appear at the sides, therefore
Position D does not exist except partially on panes which have
been trimmed off center All other plate positions common to a
360-subject plate are known.

Booklet

| BKC1 | BC8 | 61c blue | | — |

AP17

AP42

AP54

ROTARY PRESS PRINTINGS

1943

C25a	AP17	6c carmine, *Mar. 18, 1943*	6.50	1.00
		First day cover, Washington, D.C.		25.00

180-Subject Plates Electric Eye Convertible.

Booklets

BKC2	BC10A	37c red	—
BKC3	BC10B	37c red	—

AP19

1949 *Perf. 10½x11*

C39a	AP19	6c carmine, *Nov. 18, 1949*	12.00	5.00
		First day cover, New York, N.Y.		10.00

Booklet

BKC4	BC11A	73c red (3)	—

AP33

1958

C51a	AP33	7c blue, *July 31, 1958*	15.00	6.50
		First day cover, San Antonio, Tex. *(119,769)*		9.50

Booklets

BKC5	BC11B	85c on 73c red	—
BKC6	BC11C	85c blue	—

1960

C60a	AP33	7c carmine, *Aug. 19, 1960*	20.00	7.00
		First day cover, St. Louis, Mo. *(143,363)*		9.50

Booklets

BKC7	BC11C	85c blue	—
BKC8	BC11C	85c red	—

1962-64

C64b	AP42	8c carmine, pane of 5+label, slogan 1, *Dec. 5, 1962*	7.50	1.25
		First day cover, Washington, D.C. *(146,835)*		2.00
		With slogan 2, *1963*	30.00	5.00
		With slogan 3, *1964*	12.50	1.25

Booklets

BKC9	BC11D	80c black, *pink,* slogan 1	—
BKC10	BC11E	$2 red, *pink,* slogan 1	—
BKC11	BC11D	80c black, *pink,* slogan 3 (2)	—
BKC12	BC11E	$2 red, *pink,* slogan 2	—
BKC13	BC13B	$2 red, *pink,* slogan 2	—
BKC14	BC13B	$2 red, slogan 3	—
BKC15	BC13B	$2 red, *pink,* slogan 3	—

C64c	AP42	As No.C64b, tagged, slogan 3, *1964*	2.25	50

Plate of 360 subjects (300 stamps, 60 labels).

Booklets

BKC16	BC11D	80c black (2)	6.00
BKC17	BC11D	80c black, *pink*	6.00
BKC18	BC13B	$2 red, *pink*	13.00
BKC19	BC13B	$2 red (3)	13.00

AP49

AP55

1968-73 **Tagged** *Perf. 11x10½*

C72b	AP49	10c carmine, pane of 8, *Jan. 5, 1968*	4.00	75
		First day cover, San Francisco, Cal.		3.00

Booklet

BKC20	BC14B	$4 red (2)	21.00

C72c	AP49	10c carmine, pane of 5+label, slogan 4, *Jan. 6, 1968*	2.50	75
		First day cover, Washington, D.C.		115.00
		With slogan 5	2.50	75
		First day cover, Washington, D.C.		115.00

Booklet

BKC21	BC15A	$1 red (2)	7.00

C78a	AP54	11c carmine, pane of 4+2 labels, slogans 5 & 4, *May 7, 1971*	1.50	40
		First day cover, Spokane, Wash.		1.75

Combination Booklet

BKC22	BC15D	$1 red, 2 #C78a (11c) + 1 #1280c (2c) (2)	5.00

C79a	AP55	13c carmine, pane of 5+label, slogan 8, *Dec. 27, 1973*	1.35	70
		First day cover, Chicago, Ill.		1.75

Booklet

BKC23	BC18	$1.30 blue & red	3.00

Combination Booklet

See No. BK126.

No. C72b, the 8-stamp pane, was printed from 320-subject plate and from 400-subject plate; No. C72c, C78a and C79a from 360-subject plates.

VENDING AND AFFIXING MACHINE PERFORATIONS

Imperforate sheets of 400 were first issued in 1906 on the request of several makers of vending and affixing machines. The machine manufacturers made coils from the imperforate sheets and applied various perforations to suit the particular needs of their machines. These privately applied perforations were used for many years and form a chapter of postal history.

Unused prices are for pairs, used prices for singles. "On cover" prices are for single stamps commercially used in the proper period.

The 2mm. and 3mm. spacings refer only to the 1908-11 issues. Prices for intermediate spacings would roughly correspond to the lower-priced of the two listed spacings.

Many varieties are suspected or known to have been perforated for philatelic purposes and not actually used in machines. These are indicated by an asterisk before the number. Several of these privately applied perforation varieties exist in blocks, which were not produced in the regular course of business. They are generally valued as a multiple of the coil pairs contained with a slight premium for plate numbers attached.

Counterfeits are prevalent, especially of items having a basic imperf. priced far lower than the vending machine coil.

The Vending and Affixing Machine Perforations Committee of the Bureau Issues Association compiled these listings.

THE BRINKERHOFF COMPANY
Sedalia, Mo.
Manufacturers of Vending Machines.

Perforations Type I

Stamps were cut into strips and joined before being perforated.

			Unused Pair	Used Single
On Issue of 1906-08				
314	1c	blue green	90.00	12.00
		Guide line pair	105.00	
320	2c	carmine	80.00	12.00
		Guide line pair	105.00	
*320a	2c	lake	70.00	10.00
		Guide line pair	95.00	
On Issue of 1908-09				
*343	1c	green	60.00	9.00
		Guide line pair	80.00	
*344	2c	carmine	60.00	9.00
		Guide line pair	80.00	
		On cover		125.00
*345	3c	deep violet	75.00	
		Guide line pair	95.00	
*346	4c	orange brown	95.00	35.00
		Guide line pair	135.00	
*347	5c	blue	105.00	35.00
		Guide line pair	140.00	
On Lincoln Issue of 1909				
*368	2c	carmine, coiled endwise	60.00	15.00
		Guide line pair	90.00	
On Alaska-Yukon Issue of 1909				
*371	2c	carmine, coiled sideways	200.00	
On Issue of 1912				
*408	1c	green	25.00	7.00
		Guide line or pasteup pair	40.00	
*409	2c	carmine	25.00	7.00
		Guide line or pasteup pair	40.00	

Type IIa. One knife cut.

Type IIb. Two knife cuts.

Perforations Type II

The Type II perforations consist of two holes. The knife cuts separating the stamps were applied by the vending machine and were of two types as illustrated above. All items listed below are known without knife cuts, but did not pass through the vending machine.

	Type			Unused Pair	Used Single
On Issue of 1906-08					
314	II	1c	blue green	70.00	
	IIa	1c	blue green	60.00	4.00
			Guide line pair	75.00	
	*IIb	1c	blue green	110.00	
320	II	2c	carmine	90.00	
	IIa	2c	carmine	25.00	5.00
			Guide line pair	40.00	
320a	II	2c	lake	65.00	
	IIa	2c	lake	40.00	5.00
			On cover		350.00
			Guide line or pasteup pair	60.00	
	*IIb	2c	lake	150.00	
On Issue of 1908-09					
343	II	1c	green	45.00	
			Guide line pair	65.00	
	IIa	1c	green	15.00	1.25
			Paste-up pair	20.00	
	IIb	1c	green	15.00	
			Paste-up pair	20.00	
344	II	2c	carmine	50.00	
			Paste-up pair	70.00	
			On cover, pair		550.00
	IIa	2c	carmine	10.00	1.00
			Guide line pair	15.00	
			On cover		175.00
	IIb	2c	carmine	15.00	2.00
			Guide line or pasteup pair	20.00	
*345	II	3c	deep violet	65.00	
	*IIa	3c	deep violet	60.00	4.00
			Guide line pair	75.00	
	*IIb	3c	deep violet	110.00	
*346	II	4c	orange brown	105.00	
			Guide line pair	125.00	
	*IIa	4c	orange brown	85.00	
			Guide line or pasteup pair	110.00	
	*IIb	4c	orange brown	120.00	15.00
*347	II	5c	blue	135.00	
			Guide line pair	165.00	
	*IIa	5c	blue	100.00	40.00
			On cover		750.00
	*IIb	5c	blue	110.00	
On Lincoln Issue of 1909					
368	II	2c	carmine	70.00	
			Guide line pair	90.00	
	IIa	2c	carmine	60.00	6.00
			Guide line pair	75.00	
	IIb	2c	carmine	65.00	7.50
			Guide line pair	85.00	

				Unused Pair	Used Single
On Alaska-Yukon Issue of 1909					
371	II	2c	carmine, coiled sideways	100.00	
			Guide line or pasteup pair	125.00	
	II	2c	carmine, coiled endwise	225.00	
			Guide line pair	250.00	
	IIa	2c	carmine, coiled sideways	110.00	10.00
			On cover		500.00
			Guide line or pasteup pair	135.00	
On Hudson-Fulton Issue of 1909					
*373	II	2c	carmine, coiled sidewise	165.00	
			Guide line pair	225.00	
On Issue of 1911					
383	II	1c	green	15.00	
			Guide line pair	20.00	
	IIa	1c	green	20.00	4.00
	IIb	1c	green	15.00	
			Guide line pair	20.00	
384	II	2c	carmine	10.00	
			Guide line pair	13.50	
	IIa	2c	carmine	50.00	
	IIb	2c	carmine	45.00	3.50
On Issue of 1912					
408	II	1c	green	50.00	
			Guide line pair	80.00	
			On cover		200.00
	*IIa	1c	green	70.00	
			Guide line pair	85.00	
	IIb	1c	green	10.00	2.25
			Guide line pair	15.00	
409	II	2c	carmine	60.00	
			Guide line pair	100.00	
	*IIa	2c	carmine	75.00	
			Guide line pair	110.00	
	IIb	2c	carmine	10.00	
			Guide line pair	15.00	

THE FARWELL COMPANY
Chicago, Ill.

A wholesale dry goods firm using Schermack (Mailometer) affixing machines. In 1911 the Farwell Company began to make and perforate their own coils. These were sometimes wrongly called "Chambers" perforations.

Type A

Type B

Stamps were perforated in sheets, then cut into strips and coiled. Blocks exist. The following listings are grouped according to the number of holes, further divided into two types of spacing, narrow and wide. The type symbols (3A2) indicate 3 holes over 2 holes with narrow, type A, spacing between groups. Types A and B occurred in different rows on the same sheet. Left margin or pasteup stamps.

sometimes show different perforation type on the two sides.

Group I, no spacing
On Issue of 1911

			Unused Pair Spacing 2 mm.	3 mm.	Used Single
384	2c	carmine, 7 holes	500.00		200.00
		On cover			1,250.
384	2c	carmine, 6 holes	600.00		

Group 2, two and three holes
On Issue of 1911

	Type					
383	2B3	1c	green	225.00		100.00
	3A2	1c	green	225.00		
			Guide line pair	350.00		
384	2A3	2c	carmine	225.00	225.00	
			On cover			950.00
	2B3	2c	carmine		250.00	100.00
			On cover			—
	3A2	2c	carmine	250.00	250.00	85.00
			On cover			950.00
			Guide line pair	350.00		
	3B2	2c	carmine		250.00	—
			Guide line pair	350.00		

Group 3, three and four holes
On Issue of 1911

383	3B4	1c	green			135.00
	4B3	1c	green	200.00	200.00	50.00
384	3B4	2c	carmine	100.00		
			On cover			600.00
			Guide line pair	200.00		
	4B3	2c	carmine		275.00	75.00
			On cover			650.00

Group 4, four and four holes
On Issue of 1908-09

343	*A	1c	green	125.00		
	*B	1c	green	115.00		
344	*A	2c	carmine	125.00		
	*B	2c	carmine	110.00		

On Lincoln Issue of 1909

368	*A	2c	carmine	300.00		
	*B	2c	carmine	—		

On Issue of 1911

383	A	1c	green	20.00	18.00	
			Guide line pair	30.00		
	B	1c	green	20.00	18.00	—
			Guide line pair	30.00		
384	A	2c	carmine	25.00	20.00	2.50
			Guide line pair	35.00		
	B	2c	carmine	27.50	22.50	2.50
			Guide line pair	37.50		
			On cover			225.00

On Issue of 1912

408	A	1c	green	15.00		1.00
			On cover			75.00
			Guide line pair	20.00		
	B	1c	green	15.00		1.25
			Guide line pair	20.00		
409	A	2c	carmine	7.50		75
			On cover			75.00
			Guide line	10.00		
	B	2c	carmine	10.00		1.00
			On cover			75.00
			Guide line pair	12.50		

On Issue of 1916-17

482	A	2c	carmine	100.00		10.00
	B	2c	carmine	120.00		10.00

Group 5, four and five holes
On Issue of 1911

383	4A5	1c	green			125.00
			Guide line pair	160.00		
384	4A5	2c	carmine	100.00	105.00	—
			Guide line pair	135.00		

On Issue of 1912

408	4A5	1c	green	110.00		
			Guide line pair	135.00		
	*5A4	1c	green	140.00		
			Guide line pair	190.00		
409	*4A5	2c	carmine	140.00	140.00	
	*5A4	2c	carmine	140.00		
			Guide line pair	190.00		

INTERNATIONAL VENDING MACHINE CO.
Baltimore, Md.

Similar to the Government Coil stamp No. 322, but perforated 12½ to 13.

On Issue of 1906

320b	2c	scarlet	750.00

On Issue of 1908-09

343	1c	green	—
344	2c	carmine	—
345	3c	deep violet	—
346	4c	orange brown	—
347	5c	blue	—

THE MAILOMETER COMPANY
Detroit, Mich.

Formerly the Schermack Mailing Machine Co., then Mail-om-eter Co., and later the Mail-O-Meter Co. Their round-hole perforations were developed in an attempt to get the Bureau of Engraving and Printing to adopt a larger perforation for coil stamps.

Perforations Type I

Used experimentally in Detroit and Chicago in August, 1909. Later used regularly in the St. Louis branch.

On Issue of 1906-08

			Unused Pair Spacing 2mm	3mm	Used Single
*320	2c	carmine	135.00		
*320a	2c	lake	75.00		
		Guide line pair	90.00		
*320b	2c	scarlet	75.00		

On Issue of 1908-09

343	1c	green	15.00	16.00	10.00
		On cover			175.00
		Guide line pair	18.50		
344	2c	carmine	15.00	16.00	1.50
		On cover, St. Louis			75.00
		On cover, Detroit or Chicago			150.00
		Guide line pair	18.50		
345	3c	deep violet	40.00		5.00
		Guide line pair	50.00		
346	4c	orange brown	75.00	65.00	9.00
		Guide line pair	100.00		
347	5c	blue	100.00		10.00
		Guide line pair	125.00		

On Lincoln Issue of 1909

*368	2c	carmine	100.00	85.00	40.00
		Guide line or pasteup	120.00		

On Alaska-Yukon Issue of 1909

*371	2c	carmine		100.00	30.00
		Guide line pair		125.00	

On Hudson-Fulton Issue of 1909

*373	2c	carmine		100.00	30.00
		Guide line or pasteup pair		125.00	

On Issue of 1911

383	1c	green	7.50	6.25	1.00
		Guide line pair	9.00		
384	2c	carmine	11.50	10.00	1.50
		On cover			65.00
		Guide line pair	15.00		

On Issue of 1912

*408	1c	green	7.00		1.25
		Guide line pair	9.00		
*409	2c	carmine	7.00		1.25
		Guide line pair	9.00		

Perforations Type II

Used experimentally in Detroit from 1909 to 1911.

On Issue of 1906-08

*320	2c	carmine	115.00		
*320b	2c	scarlet	210.00		

On Issue of 1908-09

343	1c	green	20.00	19.00	4.00
		Guide line pair	25.00		
344	2c	carmine	27.50	26.00	4.00
		On cover			225.00
		Guide line pair	35.00		
*345	3c	deep violet	110.00		15.00
*346	4c	orange brown	150.00	140.00	
*347	5c	blue	185.00		

On Lincoln Issue of 1909

*368	2c	carmine	105.00	100.00	

On Alaska-Yukon Issue of 1909

*371	2c	carmine	110.00		

On Hudson-Fulton Issue of 1909

*373	2c	carmine	120.00		
		Guide line pair	140.00		

On Issue of 1911

383	1c	green	50.00	45.00	10.00
		Guide line or pasteup pair	60.00		
384	2c	carmine		60.00	12.50
		On cover			200.00

Perforations Type III

Used experimentally in Detroit in 1910.

On Issue of 1906-08

*320	2c	carmine	125.00		
*320b	2c	scarlet	140.00		

On Issue of 1908-09

343	1c	green	40.00	30.00	
		Guide line pair	50.00		
344	2c	carmine	50.00	45.00	
		Guide line pair	65.00		
*345	3c	deep violet	90.00		
*346	4c	orange brown	130.00	120.00	
*347	5c	blue	325.00		

On Lincoln Issue of 1909

*368	2c	carmine	110.00	100.00	25.00

On Alaska-Yukon Issue of 1909

*371	2c	carmine	130.00		

On Hudson-Fulton Issue of 1909

*373	2c	carmine	120.00		

Perforations Type IV

Used in St. Louis branch office. Blocks exist but were not regularly produced or issued.

On Issue of 1906-08

*320	2c	carmine	120.00		35.00
*320b	2c	scarlet	100.00		25.00

On Issue of 1908-09

			2mm.	3mm.	Used Single
343	1c	green	20.00	18.00	4.00
		Guide line pair	27.50		
344	2c	carmine	27.50	25.00	3.50
		Guide line or pasteup pair	37.50		
345	3c	deep violet	75.00		
		Guide line or pasteup pair	90.00		
346	4c	orange brown	95.00	90.00	
		Guide line pair	125.00		
347	5c	blue	150.00		
		Guide line pair	190.00		

On Lincoln Issue of 1909

*368	2c	carmine	75.00	65.00	12.50
		Guide line or pasteup pair	100.00		

On Alaska-Yukon Issue of 1909

*371	2c	carmine	*200.00*		
		Guide line pair	*250.00*		

On Hudson-Fulton Issue of 1909

*373	2c	carmine	*200.00*		
		Guide line pair	*250.00*		

On Issue of 1911

383	1c	green	4.00	3.75	60
		On cover			*85.00*
		Guide line pair	5.00		
384	2c	carmine	9.00	8.00	40
		On cover			*85.00*
		Guide line pair	11.50		

On Issue of 1912

408	1c	green	3.00		40
		On cover			15.00
		Guide line or pasteup pair	4.00		
409	2c	carmine	3.25		25
		On cover			15.00
		Guide line or pasteup pair	4.75		

On Issue of 1916-17

482	2c	carmine	80.00		25.00
		On cover			275.00
		Guide line pair	*110.00*		
483	3c	violet, type I	85.00		—
		On cover			250.00
		Pasteup pair	*110.00*		

THE SCHERMACK COMPANY
Detroit, Mich.

These perforations were developed by the Schermack Mailing Machine Co. before it became the Mailometer Co. The Type III perforation was used in Mailometer affixing machines from 1909 through 1927.

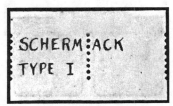

Perforations Type I. Eight Holes.

Perforated in sheets, then cut into strips and coiled.

On Issue of 1906-08

			Unused Pair 2mm.	3mm.	Used Single
314	1c	blue green	100.00		*15.00*
		Guide line pair	125.00		
		*Seven holes	325.00		
		*Six holes	225.00		
		*Guide line pair	300.00		
320	2c	carmine	65.00		*15.00*
		On cover			
		Guide line pair	90.00		
		Seven holes	225.00		
		On cover			—
		Guide line or pasteup pair	300.00		
		*Six holes	175.00		
*320a	2c	lake	150.00		*45.00*
		*Seven holes	225.00		
		*Six holes	200.00		
*315	5c	blue	*1,350.*		

On Issue of 1908-09

*343	1c	green			*20.00*
		Guide line pair	75.00		
*344	2c	carmine	75.00		
		Guide line pair			
*345	3c	deep violet	85.00		
		Guide line pair	85.00		
*346	4c	orange brown	125.00		
		Guide line pair	85.00		
*347	5c	blue	110.00		
		Guide line pair			

On Lincoln Issue of 1909

*368	2c	carmine	100.00	95.00	*30.00*

	Unused Pair 2mm.	3mm.	Used Single
Guide line pair	110.00		
*Seven holes	300.00		
*Six holes	300.00		

Perforations Type II

Cut into strips and joined before being perforated.

On Issue of 1906-08

314	1c	blue green	80.00		30.00
		Guide line pair	100.00		
320	2c	carmine	60.00		25.00
		Guide line pair	75.00		
*320a	2c	lake	100.00		40.00
		Guide line pair	120.00		
*315	5c	blue	*1,350.*		550.00
		Guide line pair			

On Issue of 1908-09

*343	1c	green	85.00	80.00	
		Guide line pair	110.00		
*344	2c	carmine	85.00		
		Guide line pair	110.00		
*345	3c	deep violet	95.00		
		Guide line pair	120.00		
*346	4c	orange brown	105.00		
		Guide line pair	130.00		
*347	5c	blue	160.00		
		Guide line pair	200.00		

On Issue of 1912

*368	2c	carmine	95.00	90.00	20.00
		Guide line pair	115.00		

On Issue of 1912

*383	1c	green	—		

Perforations Type III

Blocks exist but were not regularly produced or issued.

On Issue of 1906-08

			Unused Pair 2mm.	3mm.	Used Single
314	1c	blue green	15.00		1.00
		On cover			*75.00*
		Guide line or pasteup pair	20.00		
320	2c	carmine	20.00		2.50
		On cover			*75.00*
		Guide line pair	30.00		
320a	2c	lake	25.00		1.00
		On cover			*75.00*
		Guide line or pasteup pair	30.00		
*320b	2c	scarlet	25.00		2.75
		Guide line pair	30.00		
314A	4c	brown	45,000.		*9,000.*
		On cover			*22,500.*
		Guide line pair			
*315	5c	blue	1,100.		

On Issue of 1908-09

343	1c	green	5.00	6.00	40
		On cover			25.00
		Guide line or pasteup pair	7.00		
344	2c	carmine	5.00	6.00	40
		On cover			25.00
		Guide line or pasteup pair	7.00		
345	3c	deep violet	20.00	*150.00*	2.50
		Guide line pair	25.00		
346	4c	orange brown	30.00	20.00	2.50
		Guide line or pasteup pair	40.00		
347	5c	blue	40.00		7.50
		Guide line pair	50.00		

On Lincoln Issue of 1909

			Unused Pair 2mm.	3mm.	Used Single
368	2c	carmine	50.00	45.00	4.00
		On cover			*200.00*
		Guide line or pasteup pair	65.00		

On Alaska-Yukon Issue of 1909

*371	2c	carmine	70.00		
		Guide line or pasteup pair	85.00		

On Hudson-Fulton Issue of 1909

*373	2c	carmine	70.00		
		Guide line or pasteup pair	85.00		

On Issue of 1911

383	1c	green	2.25	2.00	40
		On cover			17.50
		Guide line or pasteup pair	5.00		
384	2c	carmine	6.00	5.00	30
		On cover			17.50
		Guide line pair	7.50		

On Issue of 1912

408	1c	green	75		20
		On cover			15.00
		Guide line or pasteup pair	1.00		
409	2c	carmine	75		15
		On cover			15.00
		Guide line or pasteup pair	1.00		

On Issue of 1916-17

481	1c	green	2.25		15
		On cover			15.00
		Guide line or pasteup pair	3.00		
482	2c	carmine, type I	2.75		30
		On cover			15.00
		Guide line or pasteup pair	3.75		
482A	2c	carmine, type I a			*6,000.*
		On cover			*10,000.*
483	3c	violet, type I	10.00		1.50
		On cover			55.00
		Guide line pair	15.00		
484	3c	violet, type II	15.00		2.00
		On cover			75.00
		Guide line or pasteup pair	20.00		

On Issue of 1918-20

531	1c	green	10.00		2.00
		On cover			65.00
		Guide line or pasteup pair	15.00		
532	2c	carmine, type IV	35.00		2.00
		On cover			85.00
		Guide line or pasteup pair	45.00		
533	2c	carmine, type V	*350.00*		40.00
		On cover			*300.00*
		Guide line or pasteup pair	500.00		
534	2c	carmine, type Va	15.00		1.00
		On cover			85.00
		Guide line or pasteup pair	20.00		
534A	2c	carmine, type VI	35.00		2.00
		On cover			85.00
		Guide line or pasteup pair	45.00		
534B	2c	carmine, type VII	800.00	140.00	
		On cover			*450.00*
		Guide line pair	*1,500.*		
535	3c	violet, type IV	12.50		2.00
		On cover			60.00
		Guide line or pasteup pair	15.00		

On Issue of 1923-26

575	1c	green	*125.00*		4.00
		Unused single	6.50		
		On cover			65.00
		Precanceled		3.00	50
576	1½c	yellow brown		4.50	60
		Guide line or pasteup pair	6.25		
		Precanceled		3.00	20
577	2c	carmine	6.00	4.25	20
		On cover			20.00
		Guide line or pasteup pair	6.00		

On Harding Issue of 1923

611	2c	black	70.00		12.50
		On cover			*75.00*
		Guide line or pasteup pair	90.00		

U. S. AUTOMATIC VENDING COMPANY
New York City

This firm also used coil strips of manila paper, folded so as to form small "pockets", each "pocket" containing one 1c stamp and two 2c stamps, usually imperforate. The manila "pockets" were perforated type II, coiled sideways.

Separations Type I

Cut into strips and joined before being perforated.

On Issue of 1906-08
Coiled Endwise

			Unused Pair	Used Single
314	1c	blue green	40.00	5.00
		On cover		250.00
		Guide line or pasteup pair	50.00	
320	2c	carmine	45.00	4.00
		Guide line pair	55.00	
*320a	2c	lake	60.00	4.50
		Guide line or pasteup pair	70.00	
320b	2c	scarlet	45.00	3.50
		On cover		250.00
		Guide line pair	55.00	
315	5c	blue	1,150.	—
		On cover		
		Guide line pair	1,350.	

On Issue of 1908-09
Coiled Endwise

343	1c	green	6.00	75
		On cover		50.00
		Guide line or pasteup pair	8.00	
344	2c	carmine	7.00	75
		On cover		50.00
		Guide line or pasteup pair	9.00	
*345	3c	deep violet	30.00	4.00
		On cover		200.00
		Guide line or pasteup pair	40.00	
*346	4c	orange brown	45.00	4.50
		Guide line or pasteup pair	55.00	
347	5c	blue	85.00	15.00
		On cover		325.00
		Guide line or pasteup pair	110.00	

On Lincoln Issue of 1909

368	2c	carmine, coiled endwise	50.00	4.00
		On cover		200.00
		Guide line or pasteup pair	75.00	

On Alaska-Yukon Issue of 1909

*371	2c	carmine, coiled sideways	60.00	5.00
		Guide line pair	90.00	

On Issue of 1911

383	1c	green	4.00	1.25
		On cover		30.00
		Guide line or pasteup pair	6.00	
*384	2c	carmine	10.00	2.25
		Guide line pair	15.00	

On Issue of 1912

*408	1c	green	5.00	—
		Guide line pair	7.00	
*409	2c	carmine	6.00	1.25
		Guide line pair	8.00	

Separations Type II

Similar to Type I but with notches further apart and a longer slit. Cut into strips and joined before being perforated.

Coiled Sideways

			Unused Pair Spacing 2mm.	3mm.	Used Single
On Issue of 1906-08					
*314	1c	blue green	37.50		4.00
		Guide line or pasteup pair	47.50		
*320	2c	carmine	55.00		
*320b	2c	scarlet	42.50		2.75
		Guide line pair	50.00		
*315	5c	blue	1,050.		
		Guide line pair	1,250.		
On Issue of 1908-09					
343	1c	green	10.00		2.00
		Guide line pair	11.50		
344	2c	carmine	12.50		
		Guide line pair	16.00		
*345	3c	deep violet	50.00		
		Guide line pair	65.00		
*346	4c	orange brown	65.00	55.00	
		Guide line pair	80.00		
*347	5c	blue	110.00		
		Guide line pair	130.00		
On Lincoln Issue of 1909					
368	2c	carmine	60.00	55.00	10.00
		Guide line or pasteup pair	75.00		
On Alaska-Yukon Issue of 1909					
*371	2c	carmine	85.00		
		Guide line or pasteup pair	100.00		
On Hudson-Fulton Issue of 1909					
*373	2c	carmine	70.00		6.00
		On cover			250.00
		Guide line or pasteup pair	85.00		
On Issue of 1911					
383	1c	green	10.00		9.00
		Guide line pair	12.50		
384	2c	carmine	15.00		13.00
		Guide line pair	20.00		
On Issue of 1912					
408	1c	green	4.50		1.00
		Guide line or pasteup pair	7.00		
409	2c	carmine	6.00		2.00
		Guide line pair	8.50		

Perforations Type III

Cut into strips and joined before being perforated.

On Issue of 1906-08

*314	1c	blue green	50.00		5.00
		Guide line pair	60.00		
*320	2c	carmine	70.00		
*320b	2c	scarlet	60.00		5.00
		Guide line pair	75.00		
*315	5c	blue	1,150.		
		Guide line pair	1,350.		

On Issue of 1908-09

343	1c	green	12.50	11.50	2.50
		Guide line or pasteup pair	16.50		
344	2c	carmine	12.50		2.00
		Guide line pair	16.50		
*345	3c	deep violet	50.00		
		Guide line pair	60.00		
*346	4c	orange brown	65.00	60.00	6.00
		Guide line pair	80.00		

*347	5c	blue	90.00		
		Guide line pair	105.00		
On Lincoln Issue of 1909					
*368	2c	carmine	60.00	50.00	10.00
		Guide line pair	90.00		
On Alaska-Yukon Issue of 1909					
*371	2c	carmine	70.00		10.00
		Guide line or pasteup pair	100.00		
On Hudson-Fulton Issue of 1909					
*373	2c	carmine	70.00		10.00
		Guide line or pasteup pair	100.00		
On Issue of 1911					
383	1c	green	8.00	8.00	1.25
		Guide line pair	10.50		
384	2c	carmine	9.00	9.00	1.25
		Guide line pair	11.00		
On Issue of 1912					
408	1c	green	2.75		
		Guide line pair	3.75		
409	2c	carmine	3.50		
		Guide line pair	4.75		
On 1914 Rotary Press Coil					
459	2c	carmine	9,000.		5,000.

IMPERFORATE COIL

The imperforate coil stamps were made from imperforate sheets of the regular issues, and were issued in coils of 500 or 1,000. The numbers assigned below are those of the regular imperforate stamps to which "S" or "E" has been added to indicate that the stamps are coiled horizontally (side by side), or vertically (end to end). These coil stamps are virtually indistinguishable from the corresponding imperforate stamps, although they can be authenticated by experts, particularly when in strips of four or longer. Many genuine imperforate coil stamps bear authenticating signatures of contemporary experts and professionals.

FLAT PLATE PRINTING

1908		**Wmk. 191**		*Imperf.*
314E A115	1c blue green, pair		250.00	—
	Strip of 4		650.00	—
	Guide line pair		—	
	Guide line strip of 4		—	—
314S A115	1c blue green, pair		—	—
	Strip of 4		—	—
	Guide line pair		—	
	Guide line strip of 4		—	—
320E A129	2c carmine, pair		—	—
	Strip of 4		—	—
	Guide line pair		—	
	Guide line strip of 4		—	—
320S A129	2c carmine, pair		—	—
	Strip of 4		—	—
	Guide line pair		—	
	Guide line strip of 4		—	

1908-10				*Imperf.*
343E A138	1c green, pair		22.00	8.50
	Strip of 4		50.00	—
	Guide line pair		30.00	—
	Guide line strip of 4		65.00	
343S A138	1c green, pair		42.50	—
	Strip of 4		105.00	—
	Guide line pair		70.00	—
	Guide line strip of 4		—	
344E A139	2c carmine, pair		27.50	20.00
	Strip of 4		65.00	—
	Guide line pair		40.00	—
	Guide line strip of 4		75.00	—
	Double transfer, design of 1c		*1,250.*	
344S A139	2c carmine, pair (2mm. spacing)		27.50	20.00
	Strip of 4		—	

	Guide line pair		—	
	Guide line strip of 4		—	
	Pair (3mm. spacing)		30.00	—
	Strip of 4		—	
	Guide line pair		45.00	—
	Guide line strip of 4		—	
346E A140	4c orange brown, pair		110.00	—
	Strip of 4		250.00	—
	Guide line pair		135.00	75.00
	Guide line strip of 4		—	
347E A140	5c blue, pair		150.00	—
	Strip of 4		325.00	—
	Guide line pair		185.00	—
	Guide line strip of 4		375.00	

1909				*Imperf.*
368E A141	2c carmine, *Lincoln,* pair		85.00	—
	Strip of 4		200.00	—
	Guide line pair		150.00	—
	Guide line strip of 4		325.00	—
368S A141	2c carmine, *Lincoln,* pair		150.00	—
	Strip of 4		—	
	Guide line pair		—	
	Guide line strip of 4		—	

1910		**Wmk. 190**		*Imperf.*
383E A138	1c green, pair		11.00	—
	Strip of 4		25.00	—
	Guide line pair		15.00	—
	Guide line strip of 4		50.00	—
383S A138	1c green, pair (2mm. spacing)		12.00	—
	Strip of 4		26.00	—
	Guide line pair		—	
	Guide line strip of 4		—	
	Pair (3mm. spacing)		12.00	—
	Strip of 4		26.00	—

	Guide line pair		15.00	—
	Guide line strip of 4		—	
384E A139	2c carmine, pair		12.50	—
	Strip of 4		27.50	—
	Guide line pair		17.50	—
	Guide line strip of 4		32.50	—
	Double transfer, design of 1c		*1,000.*	
384S A139	2c carmine, pair (2mm. spacing)		25.00	—
	Strip of 4		60.00	—
	Guide line pair		—	—
	Guide line strip of 4		—	
	Pair (3mm. spacing)		22.50	—
	Strip of 4		55.00	—
	Guide line pair		30.00	—
	Guide line strip of 4		—	—

1912		**Wmk. 190**		*Imperf.*
408E A140	1c green, pair		3.50	
	Strip of 4		7.75	
	Guide line pair		5.50	
	Guide line strip of 4		10.00	
408S A140	1c green, pair		3.75	
	Strip of 4		—	
	Guide line pair		—	
	Guide line strip of 4		—	
409E A140	2c carmine, pair		3.75	
	Strip of 4		8.25	
	Guide line pair		6.00	
	Guide line strip of 4		10.50	
409S A140	2c carmine, pair		5.00	
	Strip of 4		—	
	Guide line pair		—	
	Guide line strip of 4		—	
	Double transfer		—	

COMMEMORATIVE

QUANTITIES ISSUED

Cat. No.		Quantity
230		449,195,550
231		1,464,588,750
232		11,501,250
233		19,181,550
234		35,248,250
235		4,707,550
236		10,656,550
237		16,516,950
238		1,576,950
239		617,250
240		243,750
241		55,050
242		45,550
243		27,650
244		26,350
245		27,350
285		70,993,400
286		159,720,800
287		4,924,500
288		7,694,180
289		2,927,200
290		4,629,760
291		530,400
292		56,900
293		56,200
294		91,401,500
295		209,759,700
296		5,737,100
297		7,201,300
298		4,921,700
299		5,043,700
323		79,779,200
324		192,732,400
325		4,542,600
326		6,926,700
327		4,011,200
328		77,728,794
329		149,497,994
330		7,980,594
367		148,387,191
368		1,273,900
369		637,000
370		152,887,311
371		525,400
372		72,634,631
373		216,480
397 & 401		334,796,926
398 & 402		503,713,086
399 & 403		29,088,726
400 & 404		16,968,365

Cat. No.		Quantity
537		99,585,200
548		137,978,207
549		196,037,327
550		11,321,607
610		1,459,487,085
611		770,000
612		99,950,300
614		51,378,023
615		77,753,423
616		5,659,023
617		15,615,000
618		26,596,600
619		5,348,800
620		9,104,983
621		1,900,983
627		307,731,900
628		20,280,500
629		40,639,485
630	(sheet of 25)	107,398
643		39,974,900
644		25,628,450
645		101,330,328
646		9,779,896
647		5,519,897
648		1,459,897
649		51,342,273
650		10,319,700
651		16,684,674
654		31,679,200
655		210,119,474
656		133,530,000
657		51,451,880
658		13,390,000
659		8,240,000
660		87,410,000
661		2,540,000
662		2,290,000
663		2,700,000
664		1,450,000
665		1,320,000
666		1,530,000
667		1,130,000
668		2,860,000
669		8,220,000
670		8,990,000
671		73,220,000
672		2,110,000
673		1,600,000
674		1,860,000
675		980,000
676		850,000
677		1,480,000
678		530,000

Cat. No.		Quantity
679		1,890,000
680		29,338,274
681		32,680,900
682		74,000,774
683		25,215,574
688		25,609,470
689		66,487,000
690		96,559,400
702		99,074,600
703		25,006,400
704		87,969,700
705		1,265,555,100
706		304,926,800
707		4,222,198,300
708		456,198,500
709		151,201,300
710		170,565,100
711		111,739,400
712		83,257,400
713		96,506,100
714		75,709,200
715		147,216,000
716		51,102,800
717		100,869,300
718		168,885,300
719		52,376,100
724		49,949,000
725		49,538,500
726		61,719,200
727		73,382,400
728		348,266,800
729		480,239,300
730	(sheet of 25)	456,704
730a		11,417,600
731	(sheet of 25)	441,172
731a		11,029,300
732		1,978,707,300
733		5,735,944
734		45,137,700
735	(sheet of six)	811,404
735a		4,868,424
736		46,258,300
737		193,239,100
738		15,432,200
739		64,525,400
740		84,896,350
741		74,400,200
742		95,089,000
743		19,178,650
744		30,980,100
745		16,923,350
746		15,988,250
747		15,288,700

Cat. No.		Quantity	Cat. No.	Quantity	Cat. No.	Quantity
748		17,472,600	906	21,272,800	1023	115,780,000
749		18,874,300	907	1,671,564,200	1024	115,244,600
750	(sheet of six)	511,391	908	1,227,334,200	1025	123,709,600
750a		3,068,346	909	19,999,646	1026	114,789,600
751	(sheet of six)	793,551	910	19,999,646	1027	115,759,600
751a		4,761,306	911	19,999,646	1028	116,134,600
752		3,274,556	912	19,999,646	1029	118,540,000
753		2,040,760	913	19,999,646	1060	115,810,000
754		2,389,288	914	19,999,646	1061	113,603,700
755		2,294,948	915	19,999,646	1062	128,002,000
756		3,217,636	916	14,999,646	1063	116,078,150
757		2,746,640	917	14,999,646	1064	116,139,800
758		2,168,088	918	14,999,646	1065	120,484,800
759		1,822,684	919	14,999,646	1066	53,854,750
760		1,724,576	920	14,999,646	1067	176,075,000
761		1,647,696	921	14,999,646	1068	125,944,400
762		1,682,948	922	61,303,000	1069	122,284,600
763		1,638,644	923	61,001,450	1070	133,638,850
764		1,625,224	924	60,605,000	1071	118,664,600
765		1,644,900	925	50,129,350	1072	112,434,000
766	(pane of 25)	98,712	926	53,479,400	1073	129,384,550
766a		2,467,800	927	61,617,350	1074	121,184,600
767	(pane of 25)	85,914	928	75,500,000	1075	2,900,731
767a		2,147,850	929	137,321,000	1076	119,784,200
768	(pane of six)	267,200	930	128,140,000	1077	123,159,400
768a		1,603,200	931	67,255,000	1078	123,138,800
769	(pane of six)	279,960	932	133,870,000	1079	109,275,000
769a		1,679,760	933	76,455,400	1080	112,932,200
770	(pane of six)	215,920	934	128,357,750	1081	125,475,000
770a		1,295,520	935	138,863,000	1082	117,855,000
771		1,370,560	936	111,616,700	1083	122,100,000
772		70,726,800	937	308,587,700	1084	118,180,000
773		100,839,600	938	170,640,000	1085	100,975,000
774		73,610,650	939	135,927,000	1086	115,299,450
775		75,823,900	940	260,339,100	1087	186,949,627
776		124,324,500	941	132,274,500	1088	115,235,000
777		67,127,650	942	132,430,000	1089	106,647,500
778	(sheet of four)	2,809,039	943	139,209,500	1090	112,010,000
778a		2,809,039	944	114,684,450	1091	118,470,000
778b		2,809,039	945	156,540,510	1092	102,230,000
778c		2,809,039	946	120,452,600	1093	102,410,000
778d		2,809,039	947	127,104,300	1094	84,054,400
782		72,992,650	948	10,299,600	1095	126,266,000
783		74,407,450	949	132,902,000	1096	39,489,600
784		269,522,200	950	131,968,000	1097	122,990,000
785		105,196,150	951	131,488,000	1098	174,372,800
786		93,848,500	952	122,362,000	1099	114,365,000
787		87,741,150	953	121,548,000	1100	122,765,200
788		35,794,150	954	131,109,500	1104	113,660,200
789		36,839,250	955	122,650,500	1105	120,196,580
790		104,773,450	956	121,953,500	1106	120,805,200
791		92,054,550	957	115,250,000	1107	125,815,200
792		93,291,650	958	64,198,500	1108	108,415,200
793		34,552,950	959	117,642,500	1109	107,195,200
794		36,819,050	960	77,649,600	1110	115,745,280
795		84,825,250	961	113,474,500	1111	39,743,640
796		25,040,400	962	120,868,500	1112	114,570,200
797		5,277,445	963	77,800,500	1113	120,400,200
798		99,882,300	964	52,214,000	1114	91,160,200
799		78,454,450	965	53,958,100	1115	114,860,200
800		77,004,200	966	61,120,010	1116	126,500,000
801		81,292,450	967	57,823,000	1117	120,561,280
802		76,474,550	968	52,975,000	1118	44,064,576
835		73,043,650	969	77,149,000	1119	118,390,200
836		58,564,368	970	58,332,000	1120	125,770,200
837		65,939,500	971	56,228,000	1121	114,114,280
838		47,064,300	972	57,832,000	1122	156,600,200
852		114,439,600	973	53,875,000	1123	124,200,200
853		101,699,550	974	63,834,000	1124	120,740,200
854		72,764,550	975	67,162,200	1125	133,623,280
855		81,269,600	976	64,561,000	1126	45,569,088
856		67,813,350	977	64,079,500	1127	122,493,280
857		71,394,750	978	63,388,000	1128	131,260,200
858		66,835,000	979	62,285,000	1129	47,125,200
859		56,348,320	980	57,492,610	1130	123,105,000
860		53,177,110	981	99,190,000	1131	126,105,050
861		53,260,270	982	104,790,000	1132	209,170,000
862		22,104,950	983	108,805,000	1133	120,835,000
863		13,201,270	984	107,340,000	1134	115,715,000
864		51,603,580	985	117,020,000	1135	118,445,000
865		52,100,510	986	122,633,000	1136	111,685,000
866		51,666,580	987	130,960,000	1137	43,099,200
867		22,207,780	988	128,478,000	1138	115,444,000
868		11,835,530	989	132,090,000	1139	126,470,000
869		52,471,160	990	130,050,000	1140	124,560,000
870		52,366,440	991	131,350,000	1141	115,455,000
871		51,636,270	992	129,980,000	1142	122,060,000
872		20,729,030	993	122,315,000	1143	120,540,000
873		14,125,580	994	122,170,000	1144	113,075,000
874		59,409,000	995	131,635,000	1145	139,325,000
875		57,888,600	996	121,860,000	1146	124,445,000
876		58,273,180	997	121,120,000	1147	113,792,000
877		23,779,000	998	119,120,000	1148	44,215,200
878		15,112,580	999	112,125,000	1149	113,195,000
879		57,322,790	1000	114,140,000	1150	121,805,000
880		58,281,580	1001	114,490,000	1151	115,353,000
881		56,398,790	1002	117,200,000	1152	111,080,000
882		21,147,000	1003	116,130,000	1153	153,025,000
883		13,328,000	1004	116,175,000	1154	119,665,000
884		54,389,510	1005	115,945,000	1155	117,855,000
885		53,636,580	1006	112,540,000	1156	118,185,000
886		55,313,230	1007	117,415,000	1157	112,260,000
887		21,720,580	1008	2,899,580,000	1158	125,010,000
888		13,600,580	1009	114,540,000	1159	119,798,000
889		47,599,580	1010	113,135,000	1160	42,696,000
890		53,766,510	1011	116,255,000	1161	106,610,000
891		54,193,580	1012	113,860,000	1162	109,695,000
892		20,264,580	1013	124,260,000	1163	123,690,000
893		13,726,580	1014	115,735,000	1164	123,970,000
894		46,497,400	1015	115,430,000	1165	124,796,000
895		47,700,000	1016	136,220,000	1166	42,076,800
896		50,618,150	1017	114,894,600	1167	116,210,000
897		50,034,400	1018	118,706,000	1168	126,252,000
898		60,943,700	1019	114,190,000	1169	42,746,400
902		44,389,550	1020	113,990,000	1170	124,117,000
903		54,574,550	1021	89,289,600	1171	119,840,000
904		63,558,400	1022	114,865,000	1172	117,187,000

Cat. No.	Quantity	Cat. No.	Quantity	Cat. No.	Quantity
1173	124,390,000	1356	132,560,000	1557	158,600,000
1174	112,966,000	1357	130,385,000	1558	153,355,000
1175	41,644,200	1358	132,265,000	1559	63,205,000
1176	110,850,000	1359	128,710,000	1560	157,865,000
1177	98,616,000	1360	124,775,000	1561	166,810,000
1178	101,125,000	1361	128,295,000	1562	44,825,000
1179	124,865,000	1362	142,245,000	1563	144,028,000
1180	79,905,000	1363	1,410,580,000	1564	139,928,000
1181	125,410,000	1364	125,100,000	1565—1568	179,855,000
1182	112,845,000	1365—1368	192,570,000	1569—1570	161,863,200
1183	106,210,000	1369	148,770,000	1571	145,640,000
1184	110,810,000	1370	139,475,000	1572—1575	168,655,000
1185	116,995,000	1371	187,165,000	1576	146,615,000
1186	121,015,000	1372	125,555,000	1577—1578	146,196,000
1187	111,600,000	1373	144,425,000	1579	739,430,000
1188	110,620,000	1374	135,875,000	1580	878,690,000
1189	109,110,000	1375	151,110,000	1629—1631	219,455,000
1190	145,350,000	1376—1379	159,195,000	1632	157,825,000
1191	112,870,000	1380	129,540,000	1633—1682	436,005,000
1192	121,820,000	1381	130,925,000	1683	159,915,000
1193	289,240,000	1382	139,055,000	1684	156,960,000
1194	120,155,000	1383	150,611,200	1685	158,470,000
1195	124,595,000	1384	1,709,795,000	1686	1,990,000
1196	147,310,000	1385	127,545,000	1687	1,983,000
1197	118,690,000	1386	145,788,800	1688	1,953,000
1198	122,730,000	1387—1390	201,794,200	1689	1,903,000
1199	126,515,000	1391	171,850,000	1690	164,890,000
1200	130,960,000	1392	142,205,000	1691—1694	208,035,000
1201	120,055,000	1405	137,660,000	1695—1698	185,715,000
1202	120,715,000	1406	135,125,000	1699	130,592,000
1203	121,440,000	1407	135,895,000	1700	158,332,800
1204	40,270,000	1408	132,675,000	1701	809,955,000
1205	861,970,000	1409	134,795,000	1702—1703	963,370,000
1206	120,035,000	1410—1413	161,600,000	1704	150,328,000
1207	117,870,000	1414—1414a	683,730,000	1705	176,830,000
1230	129,945,000	1415—1418,	489,255,000	1706—1709	195,976,000
1231	135,620,000	1415a—1418a		1710	208,820,000
1232	137,540,000	1419	127,610,000	1711	192,250,000
1233	132,435,000	1420	129,785,000	1712—1715	219,830,000
1234	135,520,000	1421—1422	134,380,000	1716	159,852,000
1235	131,420,000	1423	136,305,000	1717—1720	188,310,000
1236	133,170,000	1424	134,840,000	1721	163,625,000
1237	130,195,000	1425	130,975,000	1722	156,296,000
1238	128,450,000	1426	161,235,000	1723—1724	158,676,000
1239	118,665,000	1427—1430	175,679,600	1725	154,495,000
1240	1,291,250,000	1431	138,700,000	1726	168,050,000
1241	175,175,000	1432	138,165,000	1727	156,810,000
1242	125,995,000	1433	152,125,000	1728	153,736,000
1243	128,025,000	1434—1435	176,295,000	1729	882,260,000
1244	145,700,000	1436	142,845,000	1730	921,530,000
1245	120,310,000	1437	148,755,000	1731	156,560,000
1246	511,750,000	1438	139,080,000	1732—1733	202,155,000
1247	123,845,000	1439	130,755,000	1744	156,525,000
1248	122,825,000	1440—1443	170,208,000	1745—1748	165,182,400
1249	453,090,000	1444	1,074,350,000	1749—1752	157,598,400
1250	123,245,000	1445	979,540,000	1753	102,856,000
1251	123,355,000	1446	137,355,000	1754	152,270,000
1252	126,970,000	1447	150,400,000	1755	94,600,000
1253	121,250,000	1448—1451	172,730,000	1756	151,570,000
1254—1257	1,407,760,000	1452	104,090,000	1757	15,170,400
1258	120,005,000	1453	164,096,000	1758	161,228,000
1259	125,800,000	1454	53,920,000	1759	158,880,000
1260	122,230,000	1455	153,025,000	1760—1763	186,550,000
1261	115,695,000	1456—1459	201,890,000	1764—1767	168,136,000
1262	115,095,000	1460	67,335,000	1768	963,120,000
1263	119,560,000	1461	179,675,000	1769	916,800,000
1264	125,180,000	1462	46,340,000	1770	159,297,600
1265	120,135,000	1463	180,155,000	1771	166,435,000
1266	115,405,000	1464—1467	198,364,800	1772	162,535,000
1267	115,855,000	1468	185,490,000	1773	155,000,000
1268	115,340,000	1469	162,335,000	1774	157,310,000
1269	114,840,000	1470	162,789,950	1775—1778	174,096,000
1270	116,140,000	1471	1,003,475,000	1779—1782	164,793,600
1271	116,900,000	1472	1,017,025,000	1783—1786	163,055,000
1272	114,085,000	1473	165,895,000	1787	161,860,000
1273	114,880,000	1474	166,508,000	1788	165,775,000
1274	26,995,000	1475	320,055,000	1789	160,000,000
1275	128,495,000	1476	166,005,000	1790	67,195,000
1276	1,139,930,000	1477	163,050,000	1791—1794	186,905,000
1306	116,835,000	1478	159,005,000	1795—1798	208,295,000
1307	117,470,000	1479	147,295,000	1799	873,710,000
1308	123,770,000	1480—1483	196,275,000	1800	931,880,000
1309	131,270,000	1484	139,152,000	1801	161,290,000
1310	122,285,000	1485	128,048,000	1802	172,740,000
1311	14,680,000	1486	146,008,000	1803	168,995,000
1312	114,160,000	1487	139,608,000	1804	160,000,000
1313	128,475,000	1488	159,475,000	1805—1810	232,134,000
1314	119,535,000	1489—1498	486,020,000	1821	163,510,000
1315	125,110,000	1499	157,052,800	1822	256,620,000
1316	114,853,200	1500	53,005,000	1823	95,695,000
1317	124,290,000	1501	159,775,000	1824	153,975,000
1318	128,460,000	1502	39,005,000	1825	160,000,000
1319	127,585,000	1503	152,624,000	1826	103,850,000
1320	115,875,000	1504	145,840,000	1827—1830	204,715,000
1321	1,173,547,420	1505	151,335,000	1831	166,545,000
1322	114,015,000	1506	141,085,000	1832	163,310,000
1323	121,105,000	1507	885,160,000	1833	160,000,000
1324	132,045,000	1508	939,835,000	1834—1837	152,404,000
1325	118,780,000	1525	143,930,000	1838—1841	152,420,000
1326	121,985,000	1526	145,235,000	1842	692,500,000
1327	111,850,000	1527	135,052,000	1843	718,715,000
1328	117,225,000	1528	156,750,000	1874	160,155,000
1329	111,515,000	1529	164,670,000	1875	159,505,000
1330	114,270,000	1530—1537	190,156,800	1876—1879	210,633,000
1331—1332	120,865,000	1538—1541	167,212,800	1910	165,175,000
1333	110,675,000	1542	156,265,000	1911	107,240,000
1334	110,670,000	1543—1546	195,585,000	1912—1919	337,819,000
1335	113,825,000	1547	148,850,000	1920	99,420,000
1336	1,208,700,000	1548	157,270,000	1921—1924	178,930,000
1337	113,330,000	1549	150,245,000	1925	100,265,000
1339	141,350,000	1550	835,180,000	1926	99,615,000
1340	144,345,000	1551	882,520,000	1927	97,535,000
1342	147,120,000	1552	213,155,000	1928—1931	167,308,000
1343	130,125,000	1553	156,995,000	1932	101,625,000
1344	158,700,000	1554	146,365,000	1922	99,170,000
1345—1354	228,040,000	1555	148,805,000	1934	101,155,000
1355	153,015,000	1556	173,685,000	1935	101,200,000

Cat. No.	Quantity
1936	167,360,000
1937—1938	162,420,000
1939	597,720,000
1940	792,600,000
1941	167,130,000
1942—1945	191,560,000
1950	163,939,200
1952	180,700,000
1953—2002	666,950,000
2003	109,245,000
2004	112,535,000
2006—2009	124,640,000
2010	107,605,000
2011	173,160,000
2012	107,285,000
2013	109,040,000
2014	183,270,000
2015	169,495,000
2016	164,235,000
2017	110,130,000
2018	110,995,000
2019—2022	165,340,000
2023	174,180,000
2024	110,261,000
2026	703,295,000
2027—2030	788,880,000
2031	118,555,000
2032—2035	226,128,000
2036	118,225,000
2037	114,290,000
2038	165,000,000
2039	120,430,000
2040	117,025,000
2041	181,700,000
2042	114,250,000
2043	111,775,000
2044	115,200,000
2045	108,820,000
2046	184,950,000
2047	110,925,000
2048—2051	395,424,000
2052	104,340,000
2053	114,725,000
2054	112,525,000
2055—2058	193,055,000
2059—2062	207,725,000
2063	715,975,000
2064	848,525,000
2065	165,000,000
2066	120,000,000
2067—2070	319,675,000
2071	103,975,000
2072	554,675,000
2073	120,000,000
2074	106,975,000
2075	107,325,000
2076—2079	306,912,000
2080	120,000,000
2081	108,000,000
2082—2085	313,350,000
2086	130,320,000
2087	120,000,000
2088	117,050,000
2089	115,725,000
2090	116,600,000
2091	120,000,000
2092	123,575,000
2093	120,000,000
2094	117,125,000
2095	117,225,000
2096	95,525,000
2097	119,125,000
2098—2101	216,260,000
2102	120,000,000
2103	108,140,000

Cat. No.	Quantity
2104	117,625,000
2105	112,896,000
2106	116,500,000
2107	751,300,000
2108	786,225,000
2109	105,300,000
2110	124,500,000
2137	120,000,000
2138—2141	300,000,000
2142	120,580,000
2143	729,700,000
2144	124,750,000
2145	203,496,000
2146	126,325,000
2147	130,000,000
2152	119,975,000
2153	120,000,000
2154	119,975,000
2155—2158	147,940,000
2159	120,000,000
2160—2163	130,000,000
2164	120,000,000
2165	759,200,000
2166	757,600,000
2198—2201	67,996,800
2202	947,450,000
2203	130,000,000
2204	136,500,000
2205—2209	219,990,000
2210	130,000,000
2211	130,000,000
2216	5,825,050
2217	5,825,050
2218	5,825,050
2219	5,825,050
2220—2223	130,000,000
2224	220,725,000
2235—2238	240,525,000
2239	131,700,000
2240—2243	240,000,000
2244	690,100,000
2245	882,150,000

AIRPOST STAMPS

Cat. No.	Quantity
C1	3,395,854
C2	3,793,887
C3	2,134,888
C4	6,414,576
C5	5,309,275
C6	5,285,775
C7	42,092,800
C8	15,597,307
C9	17,616,350
C10	20,379,179
C11	106,887,675
C12	97,641,200
C13	93,536
C14	72,428
C15	61,296
C16	57,340,050
C17	76,648,803
C18	324,070
C19	302,205,100
C20	10,205,400
C21	12,794,600
C22	9,285,300
C23	349,946,500
C24	19,768,150

Cat. No.	Quantity
C25	4,746,527,700
C26	1,744,878,650
C27	67,117,400
C28	78,434,800
C29	42,359,850
C30	59,880,850
C31	11,160,600
C32	864,753,100
C33	971,903,700
C34	207,976,550
C35	756,186,350
C36	132,956,100
C37	33,244,500
C38	38,449,100
C39	5,070,095,200
C40	75,085,000
C41	260,307,500
C42	21,061,300
C43	36,613,100
C44	16,217,100
C45	80,405,000
C46	18,876,800
C47	78,415,000
C48	50,483,977
C49	63,185,000
C50	72,480,000
C51	1,326,960,000
C52	157,035,000
C53	90,055,200
C54	79,290,000
C55	84,815,000
C56	38,770,000
C57	39,960,000
C58	98,160,000
C59	
C60	1,289,460,000
C61	87,140,000
C62	
C63	
C64	
C65	
C66	42,245,000
C67	
C68	63,890,000
C69	62,255,000
C70	55,710,000
C71	+50,000,000
C72	
C73	
C74	+60,000,000
C75	
C76	152,364,800
C77	
C78	
C79	
C80	
C81	
C82	
C83	
C84	78,210,000
C85	96,240,000
C86	58,705,000
C87	
C88	
C89	
C90	
C91—C92	
C93—C94	
C95—C96	
C97	

+ Quantity ordered printed.

CARRIERS'

The term "Carriers' Stamps" is applied to certain stamps of the United States used to defray delivery to a post office on letters going to another post office, and for collection and delivery in the same city (local letters handled only by the carrier department). A less common usage was for collection fee to the addressee at the post office ("drop letters"). During the period when these were in use, the ordinary postage fee defrayed the carriage of mail matter from post office to post office only.

In many of the larger cities the private ("Local") posts delivered mail to the post office or to an addressee in the city direct for a fee of 1 or 2 cents (seldom more), and adhesive stamps were often employed to indicate payment. In some cases mail was delivered by private posts from the post office to the addressee as well. (See introduction to "Local Stamps" section.)

In 1851 the Federal Government, under the acts of 1825 and 1836, undertook to deliver letters in many cities and so issued Carriers' stamps for local delivery service. This Act of Congress of Mar. 3, 1851, effective July 1, 1851 (succeeding Act of 1836) provided for the collecting and delivering of letters to the post office by carriers, "for which not exceeding 1 or 2 cents shall be charged."

Carriers' stamps were issued under the authority of, or derived from, the postmaster general. The "Official Issues" (Nos. L01-L02) were general issues of which No. L02 was valid for postage at face value, and No. L01 at the value set upon sale, in any post office. They were issued under the direct authority of the postmaster general. The "Semi-official Issues" were valid in the city in which they were issued either directly by or sanctioned by the local postmaster under authority derived from the postmaster general.

These "Official" and "Semi-official" Carriers' stamps prepaid the fees of official letter carriers who were appointed by the postmaster general and were under heavy bond to the United States for the faithful performance of their duties. Some of the letter carriers received fixed salaries from the government. Others were paid from the fees received for the delivery and collection of letters carried by them. After discontinuance of carrier fees on June 30, 1863, all carriers of the United States Post Office were government employees, paid by salary at a yearly rate.

Some Carriers' stamps are often found on cover with the regular government stamps and have the official post office cancellation applied to them as well. Only Williams' City Post in Cincinnati used its own cancellation, which is sometimes found on No. L02. Honour's City Express and the other Charleston, S. C., Carrier stamps almost always have the stamp uncanceled or canceled with pen, or less frequently pencil.

Prices for Carriers' stamps on cover are for covers having the stamp tied by a handstamped cancellation.

Carriers' stamps, either uncanceled or pen-canceled, **on covers to which they apparently belong** deserve **a premium of approximately 25 percent** over the prices for the respective uncanceled or canceled off-cover stamps.

Stamps are listed "On cover" **only** when they are known to exist tied by a handstamped cancellation.

All Carriers' stamps are imperforate and on wove paper, either white or colored through, unless otherwise stated.

Counterfeits exist of many Carriers' stamps.

OFFICIAL ISSUES
Franklin Carrier

Franklin — OC1

Engraved and printed by Toppan, Carpenter, Casilear & Co. Plate of 200 subjects divided into two panes of 100 each, one left, one right.

1851		Unwmk.		Imperf.	
LO1	OC1 (1c)	dull blue (shades), rose, Sept., 1851		1,500.	2,000.
		On cover			4,500.
		Cracked plate		2,000.	—
		Double transfer			—
		Pair		3,500.	5,000.
		Strip of three		6,250.	9,500.

CANCELLATIONS.

Philadelphia		New Orleans	—
Red star	2,000.	Blue grid	—
Blue town	—	Black grid	—
New York	—	Green grid	—
Red town	—		

Of the entire issue of 310,000 stamps, 250,000 were sent to New York, 50,000 to New Orleans, 10,000 to Philadelphia. However, the quantity sent to each city is not indicative of proportionate use. More appear to have been used in Philadelphia than in the other two cities. The use in all three cities was notably limited.

Eagle Carrier

Eagle — OC2

Engraved and printed by Toppan, Carpenter, Casilear & Co. Plate of 200 subjects divided into two panes of 100 each, one upper, one lower.

1851		Unwmk.		Imperf.	
LO2	OC2	1c blue (shades), Nov. 17, 1851		20.00	20.00
		On cover, used alone			100.00
		On cover with block of 3, 1c #9			1,000.
		On cover with 3c #11			150.00
		On cover with 3c #26			150.00
		On cover with strip of 3, 3c #26			400.00
		On 3c envelope #U2, #U9 or U10			175.00
		Pair		42.50	
		Block of four		90.00	
		Double transfer			—

CANCELLATIONS.

Red star	20.00	Red town	—
Black grid	+5.00	Blue squared target	—
Red grid	—	Red squared target	+100.00
Black town	+5.00	Railroad	—
Blue town	+5.00	Black carrier (Type C32)	—
		Red carrier (Type C32)	—

Used principally in Philadelphia. Also known used from Cincinnati, Baltimore, Boston, Washington, D. C., and Kensington, Pa. One cover bearing a strip of 3 is known used from Andalusia, Pa.

GOVERNMENT REPRINTS
Made for the Centennial Exposition of 1876.
Printed by the Continental Bank Note Co.
First reprinting-10,000 copies, on April 2, 1875.
Second reprinting-10,000 copies, on Dec. 22, 1875.

The first reprinting of the Franklin stamp was on the rose paper of the original, obtained from Toppan, Carpenter, Casilear & Co. The second was on slightly thicker, softer paper of paler tint. The Franklin reprints are in dark blue instead of the dull or deep blue of the originals. First and second reprints and originals all differ under ultraviolet light.

Reprints of the Eagle stamp are on the same hard white paper used for reprints and special printings of the postage issue, and on a coarse wove paper. Originals are on yellowish paper with brown gum.

Franklin Reprints

1875			Imperf.
LO3	OC1 (1c)	blue, rose	40.00
		Block of four	175.00
		Cracked plate	60.00

SPECIAL PRINTING
Perf. 12

LO4	OC1 (1c)	blue	2,500.
		Pair	8,500.

Eagle Reprints.
Imperf.

LO5	OC2	1c blue	20.00
		Block of four	90.00

SPECIAL PRINTING
Perf. 12

LO6	OC2	1c blue	120.00
		Block of four	550.00

Nos. LO3-LO6 were issued without gum.

SEMI-OFFICIAL ISSUES
All are imperforate.
Baltimore, Md.

C1

1850-55		Typo.	Settings of 10 (2x5) varieties.	
1LB1	C1	1c red (shades), bluish	100.00	60.00
		On cover		250.00
1LB2	C1	1c blue (shades), bluish	125.00	90.00
		On cover		300.00
a.		Bluish laid paper		
1LB3	C1	1c blue (shades)	75.00	50.00
		On cover		250.00
		Block of four	500.00	
a.		Laid paper	150.00	100.00
		On cover		300.00
1LB4	C1	1c green	—	600.00
		On cover		1,000.
		Pair		—
1LB5	C1	1c red	350.00	275.00
		On cover		550.00
		On cover with 3c #11		650.00

CANCELLATIONS. Nos. 1LB1-1LB5

Black grid	—	Blue town	—
Blue grid	—	Black numeral	—
Black cross	—	Blue numeral	—
Black town	—	Black pen	—

C2

1856				Typo.	
1LB6	C2	1c blue (shades)		90.00	60.00
		On cover with 3c #26			250.00
1LB7	C2	1c red (shades)		65.00	40.00
		On cover			350.00
		On cover with 3c #26			250.00
		Block of four		600.00	

C3

Plate of 10 (2x5); 10 Varieties

The sheet consisted of at least four panes of 10 placed horizontally, the two center panes tete beche. This makes possible five horizontal tete beche gutter pairs.

1857				Typo.	
1LB8	C3	1c black (shades)		25.00	20.00
		On cover			150.00
		On cover with 3c #26			150.00
		On 3c envelope #U10			150.00
		Block of four		125.00	
a.		"SENT", Pos. 7		35.00	25.00
b.		Short rays, Pos. 2		35.00	25.00
		Tete beche gutter pair		400.00	

CANCELLATIONS.

Black pen (or pencil)	20.00	Black town	22.50
Blue town	22.50	Black Steamship	—

1LB9	C3	1c red (shades)		40.00	30.00
		On cover with 3c #26			150.00
		On 3c envelope #U9			200.00
		On 3c envelope #U10			—
a.		"SENT", Pos. 7		50.00	40.00
b.		Short rays, Pos. 2		50.00	40.00

CANCELLATIONS. Nos. 1LB6-1LB7, 1LB9:

Black town	—	Blue numeral	—
Blue town	—	Black pen	—

Boston, Mass.

C6

Several Varieties

1849-50		Pelure Paper		Typeset	
3LB1	C6	1c blue		120.00	75.00
		On cover			200.00
		On cover with 5c #1			1,200.

C7

Typeset
Several Varieties
Wove Paper Colored Through

3LB2	C7	1c blue (shades), grayish		135.00	65.00
		On cover			175.00
		On cover with 3c #10			300.00
		On cover with 3c #11			150.00
3LB3	C7	1c blue (shades), bluish		125.00	65.00
		On cover			200.00
		On cover with 3c #11			225.00
		On 3c envelope #U9			275.00

CANCELLATIONS. Nos. 3LB1-3LB3:

Black small fancy circle	—	Black diamond grid	—
Red small fancy circle	—	Red diamond grid	—
		Red town	—

Charleston, S. C.

John H. Honour was appointed a letter carrier at Charleston, in 1849, and engaged his brother-in-law, E. J. Kingman, to assist him. They separated in 1851, dividing the carrier business of the city between them. At the same time Kingman was appointed a letter carrier. In March, 1858, Kingman retired, being replaced by Joseph G. Martin. In the summer of 1858, John F. Steinmeyer, Jr., was added to the carrier force. When Honour retired in 1860, John C. Beckman was appointed in his place.

Each of these carriers had stamps prepared. These stamps were sold by the carriers. The Federal Government apparently encouraged their use.

Honour's City Express

C8

1849		Typo.	Wove Paper Colored Through	
4LB1	C8	2c *brown rose*	1,300.	1,300.
		Cut to shape		600.00
4LB2	C8	2c *yellow*		1,300.
		On cover with 10c #2		5,500.

CANCELLATIONS. Nos. 4LB1-4LB2:

Red grid — | Red town —

C10

1854		Wove Paper	Typeset	
4LB3	C10	2c *black*		650.00
		On cover with 3c #11		1,400.

CANCELLATIONS.

Black — | Black pen 650.00
"PAID"

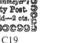

C11

Several Varieties

1849-50		Wove Paper Colored Through	Typeset	
4LB5	C11	2c *bluish*, pelure	400.00	300.00
		On cover with pair 5c #1b		3,500.
		On cover with 3c #11		600.00
4LB7	C11	2c *yellow*	400.00	400.00
		On cover		1,500.

CANCELLATIONS. Nos. 4LB5, 4LB7:

Red town —
Black pen —
Red crayon —

The varieties of type C11 on bluish wove (thicker) paper and pink, pelure paper are not believed genuine.

C13 C14

C15

Several varieties of each type

1851-58		Wove Paper Colored Through	Typeset	
4LB8	C13	2c *bluish*	175.00	100.00
		On cover		250.00
		On cover with 3c #10		350.00
		On cover with 3c #11		350.00
		On cover with 3c #26		350.00
		Horiz. pair		1,000.
a.		Period after "PAID"	350.00	150.00
		On cover		375.00
b.		"Cens"		700.00
c.		"Conours" and "Bents"		
4LB9	C13	2c *bluish*, pelure	375.00	425.00
4LB11	C14	(2c) *bluish*	—	250.00
		On cover with 3c #11		2,500.
4LB12	C14	(2c) *bluish*, pelure	—	250.00
4LB13	C15	(2c) *bluish* ('58)	250.00	125.00
		On cover with 3c #26		1,200.
a.		Comma after "PAID"		300.00
b.		No period after "Post"		300.00

A 2c of type C13 exists on pink pelure paper. It is believed not to have been issued by the post, but to have been created later and perhaps accidentally.

CANCELLATIONS. Nos. 4LB8-4LB13

Black town	—	Black pen	—
Blue town	—	Black pencil	—
Red town	—	Red crayon	—

Kingman's City Post

C16 C17

Several varieties of each

1851(?)-58(?)			Typeset	
		Wove Paper Colored Through		
4LB14	C16	2c *bluish*	450.00	450.00
		On cover with 3c #26		1,250.
4LB15	C17	2c *bluish*	500.00	500.00
		On cover		1,400.
		Vertical pair		
		Vertical strip of three	2,200.	

CANCELLATIONS. Nos. 4LB14-4LB15

Black town —
Black pen — |

Martin's City Post

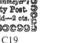

C18

Several varieties

1858		Wove Paper Colored Through	Typeset
4LB16	C18	2c *bluish*	2,750

Beckman's City Post

Same as C19, but inscribed "Beckmann's City Post."

1860			
4LB17	C19	2c **black**, on cover	—

No. 4LB17 is unique. It is on cover with 3c No. 26, both tied by black circle townmark: "CHARLESTON, S.C. JUN 18, 1860".

Steinmeyer's City Post

C19 C20

Several varieties of C19; C20 printed from plate of 10 (2x5) varieties.

1859		Wove Paper Colored Through	Typeset	
4LB18	C19	2c *bluish*	2,500	
4LB19	C20	2c *bluish*	1,500	—
4LB20	C20	2c *pink*	100.00	—
		Block of four	450.00	
		Sheet of ten	1,250.	
4LB21	C20	2c *yellow*	85.00	
		Block of four	400.00	
		Sheet of ten	1,500.	

Cancellation on Nos. 4LB19-4LB21: Black pen.

Cincinnati, Ohio

Williams' City Post

Organized by C. C. Williams, who was appointed and commissioned by the Postmaster General.

C20a

1854		Wove Paper	Litho.	
9LB1	C20a	2c *brown*	500.00	500.00
		On cover		1,000.
		On cover with 1c #9		2,250.
		Pair	1,500.	

CANCELLATIONS.

Red squared target	—	Blue company circle	—
Black pen	—		

Cleveland, Ohio

Bishop's City Post.
Organized by Henry S. Bishop, "Penny Postman" who was appointed and commissioned by the Postmaster General.

C20b C20c

1854		Wove Paper	Litho.	
10LB1	C20b	2c *blue*	400.00	400.00
		On cover		1,500.
		Vertically Laid Paper		
10LB2	C20c	2c *bluish*	400.00	400.00
		On cover		1,250.
		Pair		1,750.

CANCELLATIONS. #10LB1-10LB2

Red town	—	Black pencil	—
Red boxed numeral	—	Black pen	—

Louisville, Ky.

Carrier Service was first established by the Louisville Post Office about 1854, with one carrier. David B. Wharton, appointed a carrier in 1856, issued an adhesive stamp in 1857, but as he was soon thereafter replaced in the service, it is not believed that any of these stamps were used. Brown & McGill, carriers who succeeded Wharton, issued stamps in April, 1858.

Wharton's U.S.P.O. Despatch

C21

Sheet of 50 subjects in two panes of 25 (5x5) each, one upper, one lower

1857			Lithographed by Robyn & Co.
5LB1	C21	(2c) *bluish green*	35.00
		Block of four	150.00
		Pane of 25	950.00
		Sheet of 50	2,000.

Brown & McGill's U. S. P. O. Despatch

C22

1858			Litho. by Hart & Maypother	
5LB2	C22	(2c) *blue* (shades)	100.00	150.00
		On cover with 3c #26		1,100.
		Block of four	650.00	
5LB3	C22	(2c) *black*	600.00	1,750.

CANCELLATIONS. #5LB2-5LB3

Blue town —
Black pencil — |

New York, N. Y.
UNITED STATES CITY DESPATCH POST

By an order made on August 1, 1842, the Postmaster General established a carrier service in New York known as the "United States City Despatch Post". Local delivery service had been authorized by the Act of Congress of July 2, 1836. Greig's City Despatch Post was sold to the U. S. P. O. Department and on August 16, 1842, began operation as the "United States City Despatch Post" under the superintendence of Alexander M. Greig who was appointed a U. S. letter carrier for that purpose.

The Greig circular introducing this service stated that letter boxes had been placed throughout the city, that letters might be sent prepaid or collect, and that registry service was available for an extra 3 cents.

The City Despatch Post stamps were accepted for the service of the United States City Despatch Post. The stamps thus used bear the cancellation of the New York Post Office, usually "U.S." in an octagon:

Occasionally they bear a circle with the date and the words "U.S. CITY DESPATCH POST" or infrequently a New York town postmark. No. 6LB3 was the first stamp issued by authority of the U.S.P.O. Department. The 3c denomination included 1 cent in lieu of drop letter postage until June 30, 1845, and the maximum legal carrier fee of 2 cents. Service was discontinued late in November, 1846.

C23

Engraved and printed by Rawdon, Wright & Hatch.

Plate of 42 (6x7) subjects
Wove Paper Colored Through

1842

6LB1	C23	3c *grayish*	750.00	
		On cover		2,500.

CANCELLATIONS.

Red circle "U.S." City Despatch	Red "U.S." in octagon —

Used copies which do not bear the official cancellation of the New York Post Office and unused copies are classed as Local stamps. See No. 40L1.

C24

Plate of 100 subjects.

1842-45 Engraved by Rawdon, Wright & Hatch

Wove Paper (unsurfaced) Colored Through

6LB2	C24	3c *rosy buff*	550.00	
6LB3	C24	3c *light blue*	300.00	200.00
		On cover		500.00
		Pair	700.00	
6LB4	C24	3c *green*	2,000	

Some authorities consider No. 6LB2 to be an essay, and No. 6LB4 a color changeling.

Glazed Paper, Surface Colored

6LB5	C24	3c *darkblue* (shades)	100.00	75.00
		On cover		300.00
		Pair	—	300.00
		Strip of three	—	500.00
		Block of four	2,000.	
a.		Double impression		500.00
		Ribbed paper	—	
		Double transfer	—	

6LB6	C24	3c *bluish green*	125.00	75.00
		On cover		300.00
		Five on cover		2,500.
		Pair		250.00
		Strip of three	—	
		Strip of four	—	
		Strip of five	—	
a.		Double impression		550.00
		Ribbed paper	—	
		Double transfer	—	

No. 6LB6 has been noted on cover with the 5c New York signed "R.H.M.", No. 9X1b.

C25

1846
No. 6LB6 Surcharged in Red

6LB7	C25	2c on 3c *bluish green*, on cover	5,000.

The City Dispatch 2c red formerly listed as No. 6LB8 is now listed under Local Stamps as No. 160L1.

U.S. MAIL

C27

Issued by the Postmaster at New York, N.Y.

1849 Wove Paper, Colored Through Typo.

6LB9	C27	1c *rose*	50.00	25.00
		On cover		150.00
		On cover with 5c #1		1,250.
		Pair	—	
		Block of four	—	

1849-50
Glazed Surface Paper

6LB10	C27	1c *yellow*	45.00	25.00
		On cover		125.00
		On cover with 5c #1		
		Pair	—	
		Block of four	—	
6LB11	C27	1c *buff*	40.00	25.00
		On cover		100.00
		On cover with 5c #1		
a.		Pair, one stamp sideways	1,000.	

CANCELLATIONS. #6LB9-6LB11

Red town —	Red "N.Y. U.S. CITY MAIL" in circle —
Red grid —	Black pen —
Red "PAID" —	Black pen —
Black numeral in circle	

Philadelphia, Pa.

C28

Several Varieties
Thick Wove Paper Colored Through

1849-50 Typeset

7LB1	C28	1c *rose* (with "L P")	175.00
		On cover	500.00
7LB2	C28	1c *rose* (with "S")	500.00
7LB3	C28	1c *rose* (with "H")	175.00
		On cover	400.00
7LB4	C28	1c *rose* (with "L S")	175.00
7LB5	C28	1c *rose* (with "J J")	2,000.

C29

Several Varieties

7LB6	C29	1c *rose*	150.00	125.00
		On cover		400.00
7LB7	C29	1c *blue*, glazed	600.00	

7LB8	C29	1c *vermilion*, glazed	600.00	
7LB9	C29	1c *yellow*, glazed	1,350.	

Cancellations on Nos. 7LB1-7LB9: Normally these stamps were left uncanceled on the letter, but occasionally were accidentally tied by the Philadelphia town postmark which was normally struck in blue ink.

A 1c black on buff (unglazed) of type C29 is believed to be a color changeling.

C30

Settings of 25 (5x5) varieties (Five basic types)

1850-52 Litho.

7LB11	C30	1c *gold, black*, glazed	60.00	55.00
		On cover		200.00
		On cover with 5c #1		—
		On cover with 3c #10		—
		Block of four	500.00	
7LB12	C30	1c *blue*	200.00	100.00
		On cover		250.00
		Pair	—	
7LB13	C30	1c *black*	—	500.00
		On cover		1,000.
		On cover with 3c #11		1,200.

CANCELLATIONS. #7LB11-7LB13

Red star —	

C31

Handstamped

7LB14	C31	1c *blue*, *buff*	1,000.

No. 7LB14 was handstamped on coarse dark buff paper on which rectangles in the approximate size of the type C31 handstamp had been ruled in pencil. The stamps so produced were later cut out and show traces of the adjoining handstamp markings as well as parts of the penciled rectangle.

1855(?)

7LB16	C31	1c *black*	1,650.
		On cover with strip of 3, 1c #9	—

C32

1856(?) Handstamped

7LB18	C32	1c *black*	1,200.	1,300.
		On cover (cut diamond-shaped) with pair 1c #7 and single 1c #9		2,750.
		On cover with strip of 3, 1c #9		—
		On cover with 3c #11		2,750.

CANCELLATIONS. #7LB16, 7LB18

Black circled grid	Black town —

Nos. 7LB16 and 7LB18 were handstamped on the sheet margins of U.S. 1851 1c stamps, cut out and used as adhesives. The paper therefore has some surface bluing, and some stamps show parts of the plate imprint. Prices are for stamps cut square unless otherwise mentioned.

The authenticity of stamps of these designs, typeset and on thin wove paper, is in doubt. Those seen are uncanceled, either off cover or affixed to stampless covers of the early 1850's.

ENVELOPES

Handstamps of types C31 and C32 were also used to make stamped envelopes and letter sheets or circulars. These same types were also used as postmarks or cancellations in the same period. A handstamp similar to C32, but with "U.S.P. DESPATCH" in serif capitals, is believed to have been used only as a postmark.

Type C31 exists struck in blue or red, type C32 in blue, black or red. When found on cover, on various papers, struck alone, they are probably postmarks and not prepaid stamped envelopes. As such, these entire covers, depending upon the clarity of the handstamp and the general attractiveness of the letter are priced between $100 and $200.

When found on envelopes with the Carrier stamp canceled by a handstamp (such as type C31 struck in blue on a buff envelope canceled by the red solid star cancellation) they can be regarded as probably having been sold as prepaid envelopes. Price approximately $600.

St. Louis, Mo.

C36   C37

1849		White Wove Paper Two Types	Litho.	
8LB1	C36	2c **black**	2,000.	2,750.
		CANCELLATIONS.		
		Black town	—	

1857			Litho.	
8LB2	C37	2c **blue**		2,500.
		On cover		
		CANCELLATIONS.		
		Black boxed	—	
		"1ct"	—	
		Black pen	—	

United States Carrier stamps can be mounted in Scott's National Album.

LOCAL

This listing of Local stamps includes stamps issued by Local Posts (city delivery), Independent Mail Routes and Services, Express Companies and other private posts which competed with, or supplemented, official services.

The Independent Mail Routes began using stamps early in 1844 and were put out of business by an Act of March, 1845, which became effective July 1, 1845. By this Act, the Government reduced the zones to two, reduced the rates to 5c and 10c and applied them to weight instead of the number of sheets of paper which composed a letter.

Most of the Local Posts still in business were forced to discontinue service by an Act of 1861, except Boyd's and Hussey's which were able to continue about 20 years longer because of the particular nature of their business. Other posts appeared illegally and sporadically after 1861 and were quickly suppressed.

City posts generally charged 1c to deliver a letter to the Post Office (usually the letter bore a government stamp as well) and 2c for intracity delivery (such letters naturally bore only local stamps). These usages are not catalogued separately because the value of a cover is determined as much by its attractiveness as its franking, rarity being the basic criterion.

Only a few Local Posts used special handstamps for canceling. The stamps frequently were left uncanceled, were canceled by pen, or less often by pencil. **Prices for stamps on cover are for covers having the stamp tied by a handstamped cancellation, either private or governmental.** Local stamps, either uncanceled or pen canceled, **on covers to which they apparently belong** deserve **a premium of about 25 percent** over the prices for the respective uncanceled or canceled off-cover stamp.

The absence of any specific cancellation listed indicates that no company handstamp is known so used, and that the canceling, if any, was done by pen, pencil or government handstamp.

Stamps are listed "on cover" **only** when they are known to exist tied by private or governmental handstamp. Local stamps used on letters directed out of town (and consequently bearing government stamps) sometimes, because of their position, are tied together with the government stamp by the cancellation used to cancel the latter.

Prices for envelopes are for entires unless specifically mentioned where entires are unknown.

All Local stamps are imperforate and on wove paper, either white or colored through, unless otherwise stated.

Counterfeits exist of many Local stamps, but most of these are crude reproductions and would deceive only the novice.

Adams & Co.'s Express, California

This post started in September, 1849, operating only on the Pacific Coast.

See the "Information for Collectors" section at beginning of catalogue for an explanation of paper types, watermarks and grills.

D. H. Haskell, Manager
L1   L2

Nos. 1L2-1L5 Printed in Sheets of 40 (8x5).

1854				Litho.	
1L1	L1	25c	*blue*	175.00	—
			On cover		—
1L2	L2	25c	black (initials in black)	50.00	—
			Block of four	225.00	
a.			Initials in red		—
b.			Without initials		—

Cancellation (1L1-1L2): Black Express Co.

Nos. 1L1-1L2 were the earliest adhesive franks issued west of the Mississippi River.

Glazed Surface Cardboard

1L3	L2	25c *pink*	20.00	
		Block of four	90.00	
		Retouched flaw above LR "25"	100.00	

No. 1L3 was probably never placed in use as a postage stamp.

L3

Overprinted in red "Over our California lines only"

1L4	L3	25c black	175.00	—

L4

L5

1L5	L4	25c black (black surcharge)	300.00	—
1L6	L5	25c black	300.00	
		Pair	750.00	

NEWSPAPER STAMP

L6

1LP1	L6	*claret*	350.00	450.00

Cancellation: Blue company oval.

ENVELOPES

L6a

L6b

Typo.

1LU1	L6a	25c blue (cut square)		
1LU2	L6b	25c black (on U.S. #U9)	250.00	400.00
1LU3	L6b	50c black (on U.S. #U9)	250.00	400.00
1LU4	L6b	50c black, *buff*	—	—

No. 1LU2 exists cut out and apparently used as an adhesive.
Cancellation: Blue company oval.

USPS Souvenir pages are now listed and priced in a separate section of the catalogue. See catalogue index.

Adams' City Express Post, New York, N.Y.

L7

L8

1850-51				**Typo.**
2L2	L7	2c *buff*	250.00	250.00
2L3	L8	1c *gray*	300.00	300.00
2L4	L8	2c *gray*	275.00	275.00

Nos. 2L3-2L4 were reprinted in black and in blue on white wove paper. Some students claim that the 1c and 2c in blue exist as originals.

Allen's City Dispatch, Chicago, Ill.

Established by Edwin Allen for intracity delivery of letters and circulars. The price of the stamps is believed to have been determined on a quantity basis. Uncanceled and canceled remainders were sold to collectors after suppression of the post.

L9

1882		**Typo.**		**Perf. 10.**
		Sheet of 100		
3L1	L9	pink	3.00	8.00
		On cover		225.00
3L2	L9	black	7.00	
		On cover		200.00
a.		Horizontal pair, imperf. between	—	
3L3	L9	red, *yellow*	50	2.00
		On cover		200.00
a.		Imperf., pair	—	
b.		Horizontal pair, imperf. between	—	
3L4	L9	purple	50.00	

Cancellations: Violet company oval. Violet "eagle."

American Express Co., New York, N.Y.

Believed by some researchers to have been established by Smith & Dobson in 1856, and short-lived.

L10

Typeset
Glazed Surface Paper

4L1	L10	2c *green*	—

American Letter Mail Co.

Lysander Spooner established this independent mail line operating to and from New York, Philadelphia and Boston.

L12

1844				**Engr.**
		Sheet of 20 (5x4)		
5L1	L12	5c black, thin paper (2nd printing)	4.00	15.00
		Thick paper (1st printing)	15.00	25.00
		On cover		85.00
		Pair on cover		

	Block of four, thin paper	20.00
	Sheet of 20, thin paper	100.00

No. 5L1 has been extensively reprinted in several colors.
Cancellations: Red dotted star (2 types). Red "PAID".

L13

		Engr.		
5L2	L13	black, *gray*	45.00	45.00
		On cover		150.00
		Pair on cover		250.00
		Block of four	250.00	
5L3	L13	blue, *gray*	225.00	225.00
		On cover		300.00

Cancellations: Red "PAID". Red company oval.

A. W. Auner's Despatch Post, Philadelphia, Pa.

L13a

1851				**Typeset**
		Cut to shape		
154L1	L13a	black, *grayish*	1,000.	1,000.

Baker's City Express Post, Cincinnati, Ohio

L14

1849				
6L1	L14	2c *pink*		750.00

Barnard's Cariboo Express, British Columbia

The adhesives were used on British Columbia mail and the post did not operate in the United States, so the formerly listed PAID and COLLECT types are omitted. This company had an arrangement with Wells, Fargo & Co. to exchange mail at San Francisco.

Barnard's City Letter Express, Boston, Mass.

Established by Moses Barnard

L19

1845				
7L1	L19	*yellow*, glazed paper	300.00	300.00
7L2	L19	red		750.00

Barr's Penny Dispatch, Lancaster, Pa.

Established by Elias Barr.

L20

1855   **Typeset**
Five varieties of each

8L1	L20	red	250.00	250.00
		On cover		2,500.
8L2	L20	black, *green*	45.00	
		Pair	100.00	

Bayonne City Dispatch, Bayonne City, N.J.

Organized April 1, 1883, to carry mail, with three daily deliveries. Stamps sold at 80 cents per 100.

L21

1883   **Electrotyped**
Sheet of 10

9L1	L21	1c black	100.00	100.00
		On cover		300.00

Cancellation: Purple concentric circles.

ENVELOPE

1883, May 15   **Handstamped**

9LU1	L21	1c purple, *amber*	100.00	500.00

Bentley's Dispatch, New York, N.Y.

Established by H. W. Bentley, who acquired Cornwell's Madison Square Post Office, operating until 1856, when the business was sold to Lockwood. Bentley's postmark was double circle handstamp.

L22   L22a

1856(?)   **Glazed Surface Paper**

10L1	L22	gold	1,500.	1,500.
10L2	L22a	gold		1,500.

Cancellation: Black "PAID."

Berford & Co.'s Express, New York, N.Y.

Organized by Richard G. Berford and Loring L. Lombard.

Carried letters, newspapers and packages by steamer to Panama and points on the West Coast, North and South America. Agencies in West Indies, West Coast of South America, Panama, Hawaii, etc.

L23

1851

11L1	L23	3c black	500.00	500.00
		On cover		500.00
11L2	L23	6c green	500.00	500.00
		On cover		750.00
11L3	L23	10c violet	500.00	500.00
		On cover		—
		Pair	1,250.	
		Horiz. tete beche pair	1,500.	
11L4	L23	25c red	500.00	500.00
		On cover		—

Prices of out to shape copies are about half of those quoted.
Cancellation: Red "B & Co. Paid" (sometimes impressed without ink). Dangerous counterfeits exist of Nos. 11L1-11L4.

Bicycle Mail Route, California.

During the American Railway Union strike, Arthur C. Banta, Fresno agent for Victor bicycles, established this post to carry mail from Fresno to San Francisco and return, employing messengers on bicycles. The first trip was made from Fresno on July 6, 1894. Service was discontinued on July 18 when the strike ended. In all, 380 letters were carried. Stamps were used on covers with U.S. Government adhesive stamps and on stamped envelopes.

(Illustration reduced size.) — L24

Printed from single die. Sheet of six.
Error of spelling "SAN FRANSISCO"

1894   **Typo.**   **Rouletted 10**

12L1	L24	25c green	50.00	75.00
		On cover		1,100.

(Illustration reduced size.) — L25

Retouched die. Spelling error corrected.

12L2	L25	25c green	20.00	40.00
		On cover		1,400.
		Block of 4	85.00	
		Pane of 6	165.00	
a.		"Horiz." pair, imperf. "vert"	65.00	

ENVELOPES

12LU1	L25	25c brown, on 2c No. U311	85.00	1,350.
12LU2	L25	25c brown, on 2c No. U312	85.00	1,350.

Cancellation: Two black parallel bars 2mm. apart.
Stamps and envelopes were reprinted from the defaced die.

Bigelow's Express, Boston, Mass.

Authorities consider items of this design to be express company labels rather than stamps.

Bishop's City Post, Cleveland, Ohio

See Carriers' Stamps, Nos. 10LB1-12LB2.

Blizzard Mail

Organized March, 1888, to carry mail to New York City during the interruption of U.S. mail by the Blizzard of 1888. Used March 12-16.

L27

1888, Mar. 12   **Quadrille Paper**   **Typo.**

163L1	L27	5c black	300.00

D.O. Blood & Co., Philadelphia, Pa.
I. Philadelphia Despatch Post

Operated by Robertson & Co., predecessor of D.O. Blood & Co.

L28

L29

Initialed "R & Co."

1843   **Handstamped**
Cut to Shape

15L1	L28	3c red, *bluish*	750.00
		On cover	2,500.
15L2	L28	3c black	750.00
		On cover	—

Cancellations on Nos. 15L1-15L2: Red "3". Red pattern of segments.

Without shading in background.
Initialed "R & Co"

1843   **Litho.**

15L3	L29	(3c) *grayish*	225.00
		On cover	500.00
a.		Double impression	

Cancellation on No. 15L3: Red "3"
The design shows a messenger stepping over the Merchants' Exchange Building, which then housed the Government Post Office, implying that the private post gave faster service.

II. D.O. Blood & Co.

Formed by Daniel Otis Blood and Walter H. Blood in 1845. Successor to Philadelphia Despatch Post which issued Nos. 15L1-15L3.

L30

Initialed "Dob & Cos" or "D.O.B. & Co."

1845
Shading in background

15L4	L30	(3c) *grayish*	125.00
		On cover	500.00

L31

L32

1845

15L5	L31	(2c) black	75.00	100.00
		On cover		350.00
		Block of four	350.00	

1846

15L6	L32	(2c) black	—	125.00
		On cover		500.00

Cancellations on Nos. 15L4-15L6: Black dot pattern. Black cross. Red "PAID".

Dangerous counterfeits exist of Nos. 15L3-15L6.

L33

L34

L35

1846-47

15L7	L33	(1c) black	85.00	60.00
		On cover		300.00
15L8	L34	(1c) black	60.00	40.00
		On cover		275.00
15L9	L35	(1c) black	40.00	30.00
		On cover		275.00
		Block of four	275.00	—

Prices for Nos. 15L7-15L9 cut to shape are half of those quoted.

"On cover" listings of Nos. 15L7-15L9 are for stamps tied by government town postmarks, either Philadelphia, or rarely Baltimore.

L36

L37

1848

15L10	L36	black and blue	85.00	85.00
		On cover		250.00
15L11	L37	pale green	—	50.00
		On cover		150.00

Cancellation: Black grid.

L38

L39

L40

L41

1848-54

15L12	L38	(1c) gold, *black*, glazed	40.00	25.00
		On cover		100.00
15L13	L39	1c bronze, *black*, glazed ('50)	7.50	6.00
		On cover		75.00
		On cover, acid tied		25.00
		Block of four	50.00	
15L14	L40	(1c) bronze, *lilac* ('54)	3.50	2.50
		On cover		75.00
		On cover, acid tied		25.00
		Block of four	35.00	
a.		Laid paper	—	—
15L15	L40	(1c) blue & pink, *bluish* ('53)	9.00	6.00
		On cover		85.00
		On cover, acid tied		40.00
		Block of four	60.00	
a.		Laid paper	—	—
15L16	L40	(1c) bronze, *black*, glazed ('54)	12.00	9.00
		On cover		90.00
		On cover, acid tied		40.00
15L17	L41	(1c) bronze, *black*, glazed	15.00	8.00
		On cover		90.00
		On cover, acid tied		40.00

Cancellations: Black grid (No. 15L12, 15L17). Nos. 15L13-15L16 were almost always canceled with an acid which discolored both stamp and cover.

"On cover" prices for Nos. 15L13-15L17 are minimum quotations for stamps tied by government postmarks to stampless covers or covers bearing contemporary government stamps, usually the 3c denomination. Covers with less usual frankings such as 5c or 10c 1847, or 1c or 10c 1851-57, merit substantial premiums.

III. Blood's Penny Post

Blood's Penny Post was acquired by the general manager, Charles Kochersperger, in 1855, when Daniel O. Blood died.

Henry Clay — L42

1855   Engr. by Draper, Welsh & Co.

15L18	L42	(1c) black	10.00	5.00
		On cover		75.00
		Block of four	60.00	

Cancellations: Black circular "Blood's Penny Post". Black "1" in frame. Red "1" in frame.

ENVELOPES

L43

L44

1850-60   Embossed

15LU1	L43	red, *white*	30.00	50.00
a.		pink, *white*		50.00
b.		Impressed on U.S. Env. No. U9		200.00
15LU2	L43	red, *buff*	—	65.00
15LU3	L44	red, *white*	30.00	45.00
15LU4	L44	red, *buff*	30.00	45.00

L45

15LU5	L45	red, *white*	20.00	50.00
		Used with 3c No. 11		125.00
a.		Impressed on U.S. Env. #U7		175.00
b.		Impressed on U.S. Env. #U9		175.00
c.		Impressed on U.S. Env. #U1		250.00
d.		Impressed on U.S. Env. #U3		200.00
e.		Impressed on U.S. Env. #U2		200.00
15LU6	L45	red, *amber*	20.00	30.00
15LU6A	L45	red, *buff*		65.00

	b.	red, *brown*		=
		Used with 10c No. 2		=

Laid Paper

15LU7	L45	red, *white*	20.00	60.00
15LU8	L45	red, *amber*	20.00	60.00
		Used with 3c No. 25		125.00
15LU9	L45	red, *buff*	20.00	60.00
15LU10	L45	red, *blue*	200.00	200.00

Nos. 15LU1-15LU9 exist in several envelope sizes.

Cancellations: Black grid (Nos. 15LU1-15LU4). Black company circle (2 sizes and types). When on government envelope, the Blood stamp was often left uncanceled.

Bouton's Post, New York, N.Y.
I. Franklin City Despatch Post

Organized by John R. Bouton

L46

1847   **Glazed Surface Paper**   **Typo.**

16L1	L46	(2c) *green*		500.00
a.		"Bouton" in blk. ms. vert. at side		500.00

II. Bouton's Manhattan Express

Acquired from William V. Barr

L47

1847   **Typo.**

17L1	L47	2c *pink*		350.00
		Cut to shape		80.00

III. Bouton's City Dispatch Post

(Sold to Swart's in 1849.)

Zachary Taylor

1848   **Litho.**

18L1	L48	2c black	—	150.00
		On cover		600.00
18L2	L49	2c *gray blue*	125.00	100.00
		On cover		550.00

Cancellations on Nos. 18L1-18L2: Red "PAID BOUTON".

Boyce's City Express Post, New York, N.Y.

L50

Center background has 17 parallel lines

1852   **Glazed Surface Paper**   **Typo.**

19L1	L50	2c *green*	350.00	300.00
		On cover		1,250.00

Boyd's City Express, New York, N.Y.

Boyd's City Express, as a post, was established by John T. Boyd, on June 17, 1844. In 1860 the post was briefly operated by John T. Boyd, Jr., under whose management No. 20L15 was issued. For about six months in 1860 the post was suspended. It was then sold to William and Mary Blackham who resumed operation on Dec. 24, 1860. The Blackham issues began with No. 20L16. Boyd's had arrangements to handle local delivery mail for Pomeroy, Letter Express, Brooklyn City

249

Express Post, Staten Island Express Post and possibly others.

L51 (Type I)

Types I to VI, IX and X have a rectangular frame of fine lines surrounding the design.

1844   **Glazed Surface Paper**   **Litho.**
20L1   L51   2c *green*, type I   175.00
         On cover   *400.00*

Cancellation: Red "FREE".

L52 (Type II)

1844   **Plain background. Map on globe.**
20L2   L52   2c *yellow green*, type II   75.00
         On cover   *150.00*

Cancellation: Red "FREE".

L53 (Type III)

1845   **Plain background. Only globe shaded.**
20L3   L53   2c *bluish green*, type III   —   95.00
         On cover   *150.00*

Cancellation: Red "FREE".

L54 (Type IV)

1845
   Inner oval frame of two thin lines. Netted background, showing but faintly on late impressions.
20L4   L54   2c *green*, type IV   10.00   10.00
         On cover   *75.00*
         On cover with 5c #1   *1,000.*
         Double transfer   20.00
         Diagonal half used as
           1c on cover   —

Cancellations: Red "FREE". Black grid.

1847
20L5   L54   2c *gold*, *cream*, type IV   60.00

Types IV to IX (except No. 20L23) were also obtainable die cut. An extra charge was made for such stamps. In general, genuine Boyd die-cuts sell for 75% of rectangular cut copies. Stamps hand cut to shape are worth much less.

L55 (Type V)

1848
   No period after "CENTS". Inner oval frame has heavy inner line.
20L7   L55   2c *green*, type V (glazed)   5.00   8.00
         On cover   75.00
         Block of four   25.00
    a.   2c *yellow green*, type V   8.00
         On cover   85.00

Cancellation: Black grid.
No. 20L7a is on unglazed surface-colored paper.

L56 (Type VI)

Period after "CENTS." Inner frame as in type V.

1852   **Litho.**
20L8   L56   2c *green*, type VI   15.00   20.00
         On cover   75.00
         Vert. strip of 3 on
           cover   300.00
20L9   L56   2c *gold*, type VI   8.00   20.00
         On cover   75.00
         Block of four   35.00

Cancellations on Nos. 20L8-20L9: Black cork. Black "PAID J.T.B."
No. 20L8 was reprinted in 1862 on unglazed paper, and about 1880 on glazed paper without rectangular frame.

L57 (Type VII)

1854

Period after "CENTS." Inner oval frame has heavy outer line. Eagle's tail pointed. Upper part of "2" open, with heavy downstroke at left shorter than one at right. "2C" closer than "T2".
20L10   L57   2c *green*, type VII   20.00   15.00
         On cover   75.00

Cancellation: Black "PAID J.T.B."

L58 (Type VIII)

1856   **Unglazed Paper Colored Through**   **Typo.**

Outer oval frame of three lines, outermost heavy. Solid background.
20L11   L58   2c *olive green*, type VIII   20.00   15.00
         On cover   80.00

1857
20L12   L58   2c *brick red*, *white*, type
           VIII   17.50   17.50
         On cover   100.00
20L13   L58   2c *dull orange*, *white*,
           type VIII   20.00   20.00
         On cover   110.00

Cancellation on Nos. 20L11-20L13: Black "PAID J.T.B.'
Nos. 20L11-20L13 were reprinted in the 1880s for sale to collectors. They were printed from a new small plate of 25 on lighter weight paper and in colors of ink and paper lighter than the originals.

L59 (Type IX)

1857   **Glazed Surface Paper**   **Litho.**

Similar to type VII, but eagles tail square. Upper part of "2" closed (in well printed specimens) forming a symmetrical "o" with downstrokes equal. "T2" closer than "2C".
20L14   L59   2c *green*, type IX   6.00   5.00
         On cover   75.00
         Pair on cover   —
         Block of four   30.00
    a.   Serrate perf.   —

The serrate perf. is probably of private origin.
No. 20L15 was made by altering the stone of type IX, and many traces of the "S" of "CENTS" remain.

1860
20L15   L59   1c *green*, type IX   1.00   15.00
         On cover   *90.00*
         Block of four   5.00
    a.   "CENTS" instead of "CENT"   —

Cancellation on Nos. 20L14-20L15: Black "PAID J.T.B."

(Type X) — L60

Center dots before "POST" and after "CENTS".

1860
20L16   L60   2c *red*, type X   5.00   7.00
         On cover   75.00
         Block of four   25.00
    a.   Tete beche pair   20.00
20L17   L60   1c *lilac*, type X   5.00   7.00
         On cover   125.00
         Block of four   20.00
    a.   "CENTS" instead of "CENT"   15.00   20.00
         Two on cover (No.
           20L17a)   —
    b.   Tete beche pair   35.00
    c.   "1" inverted   —
20L18   L60   1c *blue gray*, type X   5.00   10.00
         On cover   100.00
         Block of four   25.00
    a.   "CENTS" instead of "CENT"   15.00   20.00
    a.   On cover   200.00
    b.   Tete beche pair   35.00

Cancellations on Nos. 20L16-20L18: Black company oval. Black company circle. Black "PAID" in circle.

1861
20L19   L60   2c *gold*, type X   50.00
         Block of four   —
    a.   Tete beche pair   —
20L20   L60   2c *gold*, *green*, type X   15.00
         Block of four   65.00
    a.   Tete beche pair   50.00
20L21   L60   2c *gold*, *dark blue*, type
           X   5.00
         On cover   *100.00*
         Block of four   22.50
    a.   Tete beche pair   25.00
20L22   L60   2c *gold*, *crimson*, type X   12.00
         Block of four   50.00
    a.   Tete beche pair   40.00

1863   **Typo.**
20L23   L58   2c *red*, type VIII   5.00   10.00
         On cover   100.00
         Block of four   25.00
    a.   Tete beche pair   35.00

Cancellations: Black company. Black "PAID" in circle.
No. 20L23 was reprinted from a new stone on paper of normal color. See note after No. 20L13.

(Type XI) — L61

No period or center dots.

1867   **Typo.**
20L24   L61   1c *lilac*, type XI   6.00   12.00
         On cover   100.00
         Block of four   25.00
20L25   L61   1c *blue*, type XI   4.00   10.00
         On cover   100.00
         Block of four   20.00

Cancellation on Nos. 20L24-20L25: Black company.

Boyd's City Dispatch
(Change in Name.)

L62

1874　　　Glazed Surface Paper　　　Litho.

20L26	L62	2c light blue	12.00	12.00
		On cover		100.00
		Block of four	60.00	

The 2c black on wove paper, type L62, is a cut-out from the Bank Notices envelope, No. 20LU45.

Surface Colored Paper

20L28	L62	2c *red*		*40.00*
20L29	L62	2c blue, *red*		*40.00*

The adhesives of type L62 were made from the third state of the envelope die.

Nos. 20L28 and 20L29 are color trials, possibly used postally.

L63　　　　　　　　L64

1876　　　　　　　　　　　　Litho.

20L30	L63	2c lilac, *roseate*		—

Laid Paper

20L31	L63	2c lilac, *roseate*		—

Perf. 12½.

20L32	L63	2c lilac, *roseate*	10.00	15.00
		On cover		*150.00*
a.		2c lilac, *grayish*	10.00	15.00

Laid Paper

20L33	L63	2c lilac, *roseate*		10.00
a.		2c lilac, *grayish*		12.00

Glazed Surface Paper

20L34	L63	2c brown, *yellow*	15.00	15.00
a.		Imperf. horizontally		—

1877　　　Laid Paper　　　Perf. 11, 12, 12½

20L35	L64	(1c) violet, *lilac*	10.00	10.00
		On cover		*150.00*
a.		(1c) red lilac, *lilac*	10.00	10.00
b.		(1c) gray lilac, *lilac*	8.00	8.00
c.		Vert. pair, imperf. horiz.	*100.00*	
20L36	L64	(1c) gray, *roseate*	10.00	10.00
		On cover		*150.00*
a.		(1c) gray, *grayish*		10.00

Boyd's Dispatch
(Change in Name.)

Mercury Series-Type I — L65

Printed in sheets of 100.
Inner frame line at bottom broken below foot of Mercury.
Printed by C.O. Jones.

1878　　　Litho.　　　Wove Paper　　　*Imperf.*

20L37	L65	*pink*	50.00	50.00

Surface Colored Wove Paper

20L38	L65	*orange red*	*110.00*	*110.00*
20L39	L65	*crimson*	*110.00*	*110.00*

Laid Paper

20L40	L65	*salmon*		*150.00*

20L41	L65	*lemon*	*150.00*	*150.00*
20L42	L65	*lilac pink*	*150.00*	

Nos. 20L37-20L42 are color trials, some of which may have been used postally.

Surface Colored Paper
Perf. 12

20L43	L65	*crimson*	20.00	20.00
		On cover		*100.00*
20L43A	L65	*orange red*	50.00	

Wove Paper
Perf. 11, 11½, 12, 12½ and Compound

20L44	L65	*pink*	1.00	1.00
		On cover		*75.00*
a.		Horizontal pair, imperf. between	—	—

1879　　　　　　　　Perf. 11, 11½, 12

20L45	L65	*blue*	5.00	5.00
		On cover		*85.00*
20L46	L65	blue, *blue*	12.00	15.00
		On cover		*125.00*

1880　　　　　　　　Perf. 11, 12, 13½

20L47	L65	*lavender*	2.50	2.50
		On cover		*100.00*
20L48	L65	blue, *lavender*		—

1881　　　Laid Paper　　　Perf. 12, 12½, 14

20L49	L65	*pink*		—
20L50	L65	*lilac pink*	4.00	4.00
		On cover		*100.00*

Mercury Series-Type II — L65a

No break in frame, the great toe raised, other toes touching line.
Printed by J. Gibson.

1881　　　Wove Paper　　　Perf. 12, 16 & Compound.

20L51	L65a	*blue*	7.50	7.50
20L52	L65a	*pink*		—
		On cover		*100.00*

Laid Paper

20L53	L65a	*pink*	3.00	3.00
		On cover		*100.00*
20L54	L65a	*lilac pink*	4.00	4.00
		On cover		*100.00*

Mercury Series-Type III — L65b

No break in frame, the great toe touching.
Printed by the "Evening Post".

Perf. 10, 11½, 12, 16 & Compound.

				Wove Paper
20L55	L65b	*blue*	3.00	3.00
		On cover		*100.00*
20L56	L65b	*pink*	35	2.00
		On cover		*100.00*

Cancellation on Nos. 20L37-20L56: Purple company.

Boyd's City Post
ENVELOPES

L66

Imprinted in upper right corner.
Used envelopes show Boyds handstamps.

1864　　　Laid Paper　　　Embossed

20LU1	L66	red, *white*	40.00
20LU2	L66	red, *amber*	35.00
20LU3	L66	red, *yellow*	—
20LU4	L66	blue, *white*	60.00
20LU5	L66	blue, *amber*	50.00
20LU6	L66	blue, *yellow*	—

Several shades of red and blue.

20LU7	L66	deep blue, *orange*	—	350.00

Reprinted on pieces of white, fawn and oriental buff papers, vertically, horizontally or diagonally laid.

Wove Paper

20LU8	L66	red, *cream*	65.00	—
20LU9	L66	red, *orange*	—	150.00
20LU10	L66	blue, *cream*	65.00	150.00
20LU11	L66	blue, *orange*	—	—
20LU11A	L66	blue, *amber*	—	1,250.

Boyd's City Dispatch

A. First state of die. Lines and letters sharp and clear. Trefoils at sides pointed and blotchy, middle leaf at right long and thick at end.

B. Second state. Lines and letters thick and rough. Lobes of trefoils rounded and definitely outlined. Stamp impressed normally in upper right corner of envelope; in second state rarely in upper left.

1867　　　Laid Paper　　　Typo.

20LU12	L67	2c red, *white* (A) (B)	25.00	40.00
20LU13	L67	2c red, *amber* (B)	25.00	10.00
20LU14	L67	2c red, *cream* (B)	25.00	40.00
20LU15	L67	2c red, *yellow* (A) (B)	25.00	50.00
20LU16	L67	2c red, *orange* (B)	30.00	50.00

Wove Paper

20LU17	L67	2c red, *white* (A) (B)	25.00	—
20LU18	L67	2c red, *cream* (A) (B)	25.00	40.00
20LU19	L67	2c red, *yellow* (A)	25.00	40.00
20LU20	L67	2c red, *orange* (A)	30.00	50.00
20LU21	L67	2c red, *blue* (A) (B)	50.00	75.00

Design as Type L62
First state of die, showing traces of old address.

1874

Laid Paper

20LU22	L62	2c red, *amber*		
20LU23	L62	2c red, *cream*	30.00	30.00

Wove Paper

20LU24	L62	2c red, *amber*		
20LU25	L62	2c red, *yellow*		30.00

Second state of die, no traces of address.

1875

Laid Paper

20LU26	L62	2c red, *amber*		—
20LU27	L62	2c red, *cream*	30.00	30.00

Wove Paper

20LU28	L62	2c red, *amber*		—

L68　　　　　　　　L69

1877

Laid Paper

20LU29	L68	2c red, *amber*		90.00

Stamp usually impressed in upper left corner of envelope.

1878

Laid Paper

20LU30	L69	(1c) red, *amber*	25.00	45.00

Wove Paper

20LU31	L69	(1c) red, *cream*		—
20LU32	L69	(1c) red, *yellow*		

Boyd's Dispatch

L70

Mercury Series-
Type IV — L71

Shading omitted in banner. No period after "Dispatch." Short line extends to left from great toe.

1878

Laid Paper

20LU33	L70	black, *white*	25.00	60.00
20LU34	L70	black, *amber*		45.00
20LU35	L70	black, *cream*	30.00	60.00
20LU36	L70	red, *white*		30.00
20LU37	L70	red, *amber*	20.00	25.00
20LU38	L70	red, *cream*	20.00	45.00
20LU39	L70	red, *yellow green*		—
20LU40	L70	red, *orange*		80.00
20LU41	L70	red, *fawn*		—

Wove Paper

20LU42	L70	red, *white*		10.00

Mercury Series-Type V
Colorless crosshatching lines in frame work

1878

Laid Paper

20LU43	L71	red, *white*		—
20LU44	L71	red, *cream*	6.00	20.00

BANK NOTICES

IMPORTERS' AND TRADERS' NATIONAL BANK

1874

**Thin to Thick White Wove Paper
Incomplete Year Date on Card**

20LU45	L62	2c black	40.00

1875-83

Complete Year Date on Card

20LU46	L62	2c black	40.00
20LU47	L63	2c black ('76-'77)	40.00
20LU48	L69	2c black ('78)	40.00
20LU49	L70	2c black ('79)	40.00
20LU50	L70	2c black ('80)	40.00
20LU51	L71	2c black ('81)	—
20LU52	L71	2c black ('82)	—
20LU53	L71	2c black ('83)	—

NATIONAL PARK BANK

1880

20LU54	L71	black, 120x65mm.	—

The Bank Notices are in the class of postal cards. No postmarks or cancellations were used on Bank Notices.

Bradway's Despatch, Millville, N.J.

Operated by Isaac Bradway

L72

1857

21L1	L72	gold, lilac	750.00	750.00

Typo.

Brady & Co., New York, N.Y.

Operated by Abner S. Brady at 97 Duane St. Successor to Clark & Co.

L73

1857

22L1	L73	1c red, *yellow*	175.00	150.00
		On cover		1,000.

Typo.

Cancellations: Blue boxed "PAID". Blue company oval.
Reprints exist.

Brady & Co.s Penny Post, Chicago, Ill.

L74

1860(?)

23L1	L74	1c violet	100.00	

Litho.

The authenticity of this stamp has not been fully established.

Brainard & Co.

Established by Charles H. Brainard in 1844, operating between New York, Albany and Troy, Exchanged mail with Hale & Co. by whom Brainard had been employed.

L75

1844

24L1	L75	black	100.00	125.00
24L2	L75	blue	150.00	175.00
		On Cover		350.00

Typo.

Prices for Nos. 21L1-24L2 cut to shape are one half of prices quoted.

Brigg's Despatch, Philadelphia, Pa.

Established by George W. Briggs

L76

L77

1847

25L1	L76	(2c) *yellow buff*	500.00
25L2	L76	(2c) *blue*, cut to shape	1,000.

1848

25L4	L77	(2c) gold, *yellow*, glazed	400.00
25L5	L77	(2c) gold, *black*, glazed	400.00
25L6	L77	(2c) gold, *pink*	—

Handstamps formerly illustrated as types L78 and L79 are included in the section "Local Handstamped Covers" at the end of the Local Stamp listings. They were used as postmarks and there is no evidence that any prepaid handstamped envelopes or letter sheets were ever sold.

Broadway Post Office, New York, N.Y.

Started by James C. Harriott in 1848. Sold to Dunham & Lockwood in 1855.

L80

1849(?)

26L1	L80	(1c) gold, *black*, glazed	300.00	250.00
		Cut to shape		150.00
		On cover		—
		Pair on cover		2,500.

Typo.

1851(?)

26L2	L80	(1c) black	40.00	60.00
		On cover		750.00

Pair on cover		2,000.
Block of four	300.00	

Cancellation: Black oval "Broadway City Express Post-Office 2 Cts".

Bronson & Forbes' City Express Post, Chicago, Ill.

Operated by W.H. Bronson and G.F. Forbes.

L81

1855

27L1	L81	*green*	100.00	110.00
		On cover		2,500.
27L2	L81	*lilac*		750.00

Typo.

Cancellation: Black circle "Bronson & Forbes' City Express Post" (2 types).

Brooklyn City Express Post, Brooklyn, N.Y.

According to the foremost students of local stamps, when this concern was organized its main asset was the business of Kidder's City Express Post, of which Isaac C. Snedeker was the proprietor.

L82

1855-64

Glazed Surface Paper

28L1	L82	1c *blue* (shades)	15.00	30.00
		On cover		150.00
a.		Tete beche pair	50.00	
28L2	L82	1c *green*	15.00	30.00
		On cover		150.00
a.		Tete beche pair	50.00	

Typo.

L83

No. 28L5 has frame (dividing) lines around design.

28L3	L83	2c *crimson*	—	40.00
		On cover		150.00
28L4	L83	2c *pink*	15.00	30.00
		On cover		200.00
		Block of four	55.00	
a.		Tete beche pair	50.00	
28L5	L83	2c *dark blue*	40.00	30.00
		On cover		175.00
		Block of four	225.00	
28L6	L83	2c *orange*	—	—
		On cover		—
a.		Tete beche pair	100.00	

Unsurfaced Paper Colored Through

28L7	L83	2c *pink*	100.00

Cancellation: Black ring.
Reprints exist of Nos. 28L1-28L4, 28L6.

Browne & Co.'s City Post Office, Cincinnati, Ohio

Operated by John W.S. Browne

L84

L85

1852-55   **Litho.**

29L1	L84	1c black (Brown & Co.)	85.00	50.00
		On cover		600.00
		Pair	350.00	
29L2	L85	2c black (Browne & Co.)	120.00	100.00
		On cover		750.00
		Pair	500.00	

Cancellations: Black, blue or red circle "City Post*". Red, bright blue or dull blue circle "Browne & Co. City Post Paid".

Browne's Easton Despatch, Easton, Pa.

Established by William J. Browne

L87   L88

1857   **Glazed Surface Paper**   **Typeset**

30L1	L87	2c red	—	500.00
30L2	L88	2c red	—	600.00

George Washington — L89

Wove Paper   **Engr.**

30L3	L89	2c black	125.00	350.00
		Pair	325.00	
		Block of four	1,000.	

Cancellation on No. 30L3: Black oval "Browne's Despatch Easton Pa."

Brown's City Post, New York, N.Y.

Established by stamp dealer William P. Brown for philatelic purposes.

L86

1876   **Glazed Surface Paper**   **Typo.**

31L1	L86	1c bright red	45.00	60.00
		On cover		250.00
31L2	L86	1c yellow	45.00	60.00
		On cover		250.00
31L3	L86	1c green	45.00	60.00
		On cover		250.00
31L4	L86	1c violet	45.00	60.00
		On cover		250.00
31L5	L86	1c vermilion	45.00	60.00
		On cover		250.00

Cancellation: Black circle "Brown's Despatch Paid".

Bury's City Post, New York, N.Y.

L90   L91

1857   **Embossed without color**

32L1	L90	1c blue	1,250.00

Handstamped

32L2	L91	blue	200.00

See table of Territorial and Statehood Dates at beginning of catalogue. See catalogue index.

Bush's Brooklyn City Express, Brooklyn, N.Y.

L91a

1848(?)   **Cut to shape**   **Handstamped**

157L1	L91a	2c red, green, glazed	1,500.00

See Bush handstamp in Local Handstamped Covers section.

California City Letter Express Co., San Francisco, Calif.

Organized by J.W. Hoag, proprietor of the Contra-Costa Express, for local delivery. Known also as the California Letter Express Co.

L92

L93

1862-66   **Typeset**

33L1	L92	10c red	—	750.00
33L2	L92	10c blue	—	1,000.00
33L3	L92	10c green	—	—
33L4	L93	10c red	—	—
33L5	L93	10c blue	—	—
33L6	L93	10c green	1,000.	750.00
33L7	L93	10c red (no side ornaments, "Hoogs & Madison's" in one line)		1,000.
33L8	L93	10c blue (Same as 33L7)		1,000.

California Penny Post Co.

Established in 1855 by J. P. Goodwin and partners. At first confined its operations to San Francisco, Sacramento, Stockton and Marysville, but branches were soon established at Benicia, Coloma, Nevada, Grass Valley and Mokelumne Hill. Operation was principally that of a city delivery post, as it transported mail to the General Post Office and received mail for local delivery. Most of the business of this post was done by means of prepaid envelopes

L94   L95

1855   **Litho.**

34L1	L94	2c blue	200.00	250.00
		On cover		1,500.00
		Block of four	900.00	
34L1A	L95	3c blue	600.00	
34L2	L95	5c blue	60.00	125.00
		On cover		1,000.00
		Block of four	300.00	
34L3	L95	10c blue	225.00	—
		On cover		3,000.00

Cancellation: Blue circle "Penny Post Co."

L96

34L4	L96	5c blue	300.00	325.00
		On cover		2,000.
		Strip of three	1,000.	

ENVELOPES

L97

(Illustration reduced size.)

1855-59

34LU1	L97	2c black, white	150.00	750.00
a.		Impressed on 3c U.S. env. No. U10	200.00	750.00
34LU2	L97	5c blue, blue	120.00	—
34LU3	L97	5c black, buff	120.00	—
a.		Impressed on 3c U.S. env. No. U10		750.00
34LU4	L97	7c black, buff	120.00	—

L98

34LU6	L98	7c verm. on 3c U.S. env. No. U9	90.00	500.00
34LU7	L98	7c verm. on 3c U.S. env. No. U10	90.00	600.00

PENNY-POSTAGE PAID, 5.

L98A

34LU8	L98A	5c black, white	100.00	400.00
34LU9	L98A	5c black, buff	100.00	400.00
a.		Impressed on 3c U.S. env. No. U10		600.00
34LU10	L98A	7c black, white	100.00	400.00
a.		Impressed on 3c U.S. env. No U10		750.00
34LU11	L98A	7c black, buff		400.00
a.		Impressed on 3c U.S. env. No U10		1,000.
34LU11C	L98A	black, buff, "Collect Penny Postage" (no denomination)		750.00

Penny Postage Paid, 7.

L98B

34LU11B	L98B	7c black on 3c U.S. env. No. U10	850.00
34LU12	L98B	7c black on 3c U.S. env. No. U9	600.00

L98C

| 34LU13 | L98C | 5c black, *buff* | 750.00 |

L98D

34LU13A	L98D	5c black, *buff*	—	
34LU14	L98D	7c black, *buff*	100.00	2,500.
34LU15	L98D	7c black on 3c U.S. env.	125.00	2,500.
		No. U9		

The non-government envelopes of types L97, L98A, L98C and L98D bear either 1c No. 9 or 3c No. 11 adhesives. These adhesives are normally canceled with the government post-mark of the town of original mailing. Prices are for covers of this kind. The U.S. adhesives are seldom canceled with the Penny Post cancellation. When they are, the cover brings a higher price.

Carnes' City Letter Express, San Francisco, Calif.

Established by George A. Carnes, former P.O. clerk.

L99

L100

1864   **Typo.**
| 35L1 | L99 | (5c) rose | 30.00 | 50.00 |
| | | On cover | | 1,500. |

Cancellations: Black dots. Blue dots. Blue "Paid". Blue oval "Wm. A. Frey".

Overprinted "X" in Blue
| 35L2 | L99 | 10c rose | 40.00 |

Litho.
35L3	L100	5c bronze	15.00
a.		Tete beche pair	40.00
35L4	L100	5c gold	15.00
a.		Tete beche pair	40.00
35L5	L100	5c silver	15.00
a.		Tete beche pair	40.00
35L6	L100	5c black	15.00
a.		Tete beche pair	40.00
35L7	L100	5c blue	15.00
a.		Tete beche pair	40.00
35L8	L100	5c red	15.00
a.		Tete beche pair	40.00

Printed in panes of 15 (3x5), the last two horizontal rows being tete beche.

G. Carter's Despatch, Philadelphia, Pa.

Operated by George Carter

L101

1849-51
36L1	L101	2c black	—	45.00
		On cover		150.00
a.		Ribbed paper		75.00

No. 36L1 exists on paper with a blue, green, red or maroon wash. The origin and status are unclear.
Cancellation: Black circle "Carter's Despatch".

ENVELOPE

L102

| 36LU1 | L102 | blue, *buff* | 500.00 |

Known only used with 3c No. 11.

Cheever & Towle, Boston, Mass.

Sold to George H. Barker in 1851

L104

1849(?)
| 37L1 | L104 | 2c blue | 200.00 | 200.00 |
| | | On cover | | 750.00 |

Cancellation: Red oval "Towle's City Despatch Post 7 State Street".

Chicago Penny Post, Chicago, Ill.

L105

1862   **Typo.**
| 38L1 | L105 | (1c) orange brown | 185.00 | 350.00 |
| | | On cover | | 3,000. |

Cancellation: Black circle "Chicago Penny Post A. E. Cooke Sup't".

Cincinnati City Delivery, Cincinnati, Ohio

Operated by J. Staley, who also conducted the St. Louis City Delivery Co. He established the Cincinnati post in January, 1883. The government suppressed both posts after a few weeks. Of the 25,000 Cincinnati City Delivery stamps printed, about 5,000 were sold for postal use. The remainders, both canceled and uncanceled, were sold to collectors.

L106

1883   **Typo.**   **Perf. 11**
| 39L1 | L106 | (1c) carmine | 2.00 | 20.00 |
| a. | | Imperf., pair | — | — |

Cancellation: Purple target.

City Despatch Post, New York, N.Y.

The City Despatch Post was started Feb. 1, 1842, by Alexander M. Greig. Greig's Post extended to 23rd St. Its operations were explained in a circular which throws light on the operations of all Local Posts:

New York City Despatch Post, Principal Office, 46 William Street.

"The necessity of a medium of communication by letter from one part of the city to another being universally admitted, and the Penny Post, lately existing having been relinquished, the opportunity has been embraced to reorganize it under an entirely new proprietary and management, and upon a much more comprehensive basis, by which Despatch, Punctuality and Security-those essential elements of success-may at once be attained, and the inconvenience now experienced be entirely removed."

"*** Branch Offices-Letter boxes are placed throughout every part of the city in conspicuous places; and all letters deposited therein not exceeding two ounces in weight, will be punctually delivered three times a day *** at three cents each."

"*** Post-Paid Letters.-Letters which the writers desire to send free, must have a free stamp affixed to them. An ornamental stamp has been prepared for this purpose *** 36 cents per dozen or 2 dolls. 50c per hundred. ****"

"No money must be put in boxes. All letters intended to be sent forward to the General Post Office for the inland mails must have a free stamp affixed to them."

"Unpaid Letters.-Letters not having a free stamp will be charged three cents, payable by the party to whom they are addressed, on delivery."

"Registry and Despatch.-A Registry will be kept for letters which it may be wished to place under special charge. Free stamps must be affixed for such letters for the ordinary postage, and three cents additional be paid (or an additional fee stamp be affixed), for the Registration."

The City Despatch Post ceased to operate as a private carrier on August 15, 1842. It was replaced by the "United States City Despatch Post" which began operation on August 16, 1842, as a Government carrier.

No. 40L1 was issued by Alexander M. Greig; No. 40L2 and possibly No. 40L3 by Abraham Mead; Nos. 40L4-40L8 probably by Charles Cole.

L106a

Cancellation   FREE

Plate of 42 (6x7) subjects.

The City Despatch Post was started Feb. 1, 1842, by Alexander M. Greig. Greig's Post extended to 23rd St. Its operations were explained in a circular which throws light on the operations of all Local Posts: This was the first adhesive stamp used in the United States. Issued on Feb. 1, 1842. This stamp was also used as a carrier stamp-see No. 6LB1.

1842   **Engraved by Rawdon, Wright & Hatch**
40L1	L106a	3c *grayish*	300.00	150.00
		On cover		600.00
		First day cover		4,500.00
		Block of four	1,400.	

Cancellations: Red framed "FREE" (see illustration above). Red circle "City Despatch Post" (2 types).

1847

Glazed Surface Paper
40L2	L106a	2c *green*	100.00	60.00
		On cover		150.00
40L3	L106a	2c *pink*	600.00	
		On cover		1,750.

Cancellations: Red framed "FREE". Black framed "FREE". Red circle "City Despatch Post".
Die reprints of No. 40L1 were made in 1892 on various colored papers.

L107

Similar to L106a with "CC" at sides.

1847-50
40L4	L107	2c *green*	350.00	90.00
		On cover		225.00
a.		"C" at right inverted		200.00
b.		"C" at left sideways		200.00
c.		"C" at right only		—
40L5	L107	2c *grayish*		165.00
		On cover		650.00
a.		"C" at right inverted		250.00
b.		"C" at left sideways		250.00
c.		"C" in ms. between "Two" and "Cents"		200.00
40L6	L107	2c *vermilion*	450.00	175.00
		On cover		500.00
a.		"C" at right inverted		250.00
b.		"C" at left sideways		250.00
40L7	L107	2c *yellow*	1,000.	
40L8	L107	2c *buff*		650.00
a.		"C" at right inverted		750.00
b.		"C" at left sideways		750.00

Cancellations: Red framed "FREE". Black framed "FREE". Black "PAID". Red "PAID". Red circle company. Black grid of 4 short parallel bars.

City Dispatch, New York, N.Y.

L107a

1846   Typo.
160L1	L107a	2c red	800.00	750.00
		On cover		1,750.
		Pair	2,000.	

Cancellation: Red "PAID".

City Dispatch, Philadelphia, Pa.

Justice — L108

1860   Thick to Thin Wove Paper   Litho.
41L1	L108	1c black	5.00	20.00
		On cover		350.00
		Block of four	25.00	

Cancellations: Black circle "Penny Post Philada." Black circled grid of X's.

City Dispatch, St. Louis, Mo.

L109

Initials in black ms.

1851   Litho.
42L1	L109	2c blue	1,750.

City Dispatch Post Office, New Orleans, La.
Stamps sold at 5c each, or 30 for $1.

L110

1847   Glazed Surface Paper   Typeset
43L1	L110	(5c) *green*	1,000.	
		On cover		—
43L2	L110	(5c) *pink*	1,000.	
		On cover		—

City Express Post, Philadelphia, Pa.

L111   L112

184-(?)   Typeset
44L1	L111	2c black	1,000.
44L2	L112	(2c) pink	500.00
44L3	L112	(2c) red, yellow	3,000.

City Letter Express Mail, Newark, N.J.

Began business under the management of Augustus Peck at a time when there was no free city delivery in Newark.

L113

1856   Litho.
45L1	L113	1c red	125.00	200.00
		On cover		500.00
45L2	L113	2c red (on cover)		—

On No. 45L2, the inscription reads "City Letter/Express/City Delivery" in three lines across the top.

City Mail Co., New York, N.Y.

There is evidence that Overton & Co. owned this post.

L114

1845
46L1	L114	(2c) *grayish*	1,500.	1,000.
		On cover		1,500.

Cancellation: Red "PAID".

City One Cent Dispatch, Baltimore, Md.

L115

1851
47L1	L115	1c *pink* (on cover)	—

Clark & Co., New York, N.Y.
(See Brady & Co.)

L116

1857   Typo.
48L1	L116	1c red, *yellow*	150.00	150.00
		On cover		750.00

Cancellation: Blue boxed "PAID".

Clark & Hall, St. Louis, Mo.

Established by William J. Clark and Charles F. Hall.

L117

Several varieties

1851   Typeset
49L1	L117	1c *pink*	750.00

Clarke's Circular Express, New York, N.Y.
Established by Marion M. Clarke

George Washington — L118

Impression handstamped through inked ribbon. Cut squares from envelopes or wrappers.

1865-68(?)
50LU1	L118	blue, wove paper	350.00	
a.		diagonally laid paper		—
50LU2	L118	black, diag. laid paper		350.00

Cancellation: Blue dated company circle.

Clinton's Penny Post, Philadelphia, Pa.

L118a

Typo.
161L1	L188a	(1c) black	—

Cook's Dispatch, Baltimore, Md.
Established by Isaac Cook

L119

1853
51L1	L119	(1c) green, *white*	500.00
		On cover	3,000.

Cancellation: Red straight-line "I cook"

Cornwell's Madison Square Post Office, New York, N.Y.

Established by Daniel H. Cornwell. Sold to H.W. Bentley.

L120

1856   Typo.
52L1	L120	(1c) red, *blue*	75.00	—
52L2	L120	(1c) red	100.00	100.00
		On cover		1,000.
		Pair	250.00	

Cancellation: Black oval "Cornwell's Madison Square Post Office". Covers also bear black boxed "Paid Swarts".

Cressman & Co.'s Penny Post, Philadelphia, Pa.

L121

1856
Glazed Surface Paper
53L1	L121	(1c) gold, *black*	—	125.00
		Pair		400.00
53L2	L121	(1c) gold, *lilac*		1,750.
		On cover		3,750.

Cancellation: Acid. (See D.O. Blood & Co. Nos. 15L13-15L16.)

Crosby's City Post, New York, N.Y.

Established by Oliver H. Crosby. Stamps printed by J.W. Scott & Co.

L123

1870   **Typo.**
Printed in sheets 25 (5x5), imprint at left.
54L1	L123	2c carmine (shades)	1.00	25.00
		On cover		250.00
		Sheet of 25	25.00	

Cancellation: Black oval "Crosby's City Post".

Cummings' City Post, New York, N.Y.

Established by A. H. Cummings.

L124

1844   **Glazed Surface Paper**   **Typo.**
55L1	L124	2c *rose*		500.00
		On cover		—
55L2	L124	2c *green*		250.00
		On cover		600.00
55L3	L124	2c *yellow*		275.00
		On cover		750.00

Cancellations: Red boxed "FREE". Red boxed "PAID AHC". Black cork (3 types).

L125

55L4	L125	2c *green*	750.00	750.00
55L5	L125	2c *olive*	750.00	750.00

L126

55L7	L126	2c *vermilion*	2,000.
		On cover	3,500.

As L124, but "Cummings" erased on cliche
55L8	L124	2c *vermilion*	5,000.

Cutting's Despatch Post, Buffalo, N.Y.

Established by Thomas S. Cutting

L127

Cut to shape

1847
Glazed Surface Paper
56L1	L127	2c *vermilion*	2,500.

Davis's Penny Post, Baltimore, Md.

Established by William D. Davis and brother.

L128

1856   **Typeset**
Several varieties
57L1	L128	(1c) *lilac*	400.00
		On cover	1,500.

Cancellation: Red company circle.

Deming's Penny Post, Frankford, Pa.

Established by Sidney Deming

L129

1854   **Litho.**
58L1	L129	(1c) *grayish*	750.00	750.00

Douglas' City Despatch, New York, N.Y.

Established by George H. Douglas

L130   L131

Printed in sheets of 25

1879   **Typo.**   **Perf. 11**
59L1	L130	(1c) pink	4.00	5.00
		On cover		150.00
59L2	L130	(2c) blue	4.00	5.00
a.		Imperf.	10.00	—
b.		Printed on both sides		—

Perf. 11, 12 & Compound
59L3	L131	1c vermilion	3.50	8.00
		On cover		100.00
a.		Imperf.	40	
59L4	L131	1c orange	5.00	8.00
59L5	L131	1c blue	8.00	10.00
		On cover		100.00
a		Imperf.	40	
59L6	L131	1c slate blue	10.00	12.50
a.		Imperf.	75	—

Imperforates are believed to be remainders sold by the printer.

Dupuy & Schenck, New York, N.Y.

Established by Henry J. Dupuy and Jacob H. Schenck, formerly carriers for City Despatch Post and U. S. City Despatch Post.

Beehive — L132

1846-48   **Engr.**
60L1	L132	(1c) black, glazed paper	125.00	125.00
60L2	L132	(1c) *gray*	85.00	75.00
		On cover		500.00

Cancellation: Red "PAID".

Eagle City Post, Philadelphia, Pa.

Established by W. Stait, an employee of Adams' Express Co.

L133

Black "WS" manuscript control
1847   **Pelure Paper**   **Typeset**
61L1	L133	(2c) *grayish*	1,500.
		Cut to shape	500.00

L134   L135

Two types: 39 and 46 points around circle
1848   **Litho.**
61L2	L134	(2c) black	50.00	65.00
		On cover		350.00
		Block of four	225.00	
a.		Tete beche pair		175.00

Paper varies in thickness.

1850
61L3	L135	(1c) red, *bluish*	75.00	75.00
		On cover		200.00
61L4	L135	(1c) blue, *bluish*	65.00	65.00
		On cover		200.00
		Block of four	450.00	

Cancellations on Nos. 61L2-61L4: Red "PAID" in large box. Red circular "Stait's at Adams Express."

East River Post Office, New York, N. Y.

Established by Jacob D. Clark and Henry Wilson in 1850, and sold to Sigmund Adler in 1852.

L136   L137

1852   **Typo.**
62L1	L136	(1c) *rose* (on cover)	—

1852-54   **Litho.**
62L3	L137	(1c) *green*, glazed	200.00

L138

1855
62L4	L138	(1c) *green*, glazed	100.00	125.00
		On cover		750.00
		Pair	300.00	

Eighth Avenue Post Office. New York, N. Y.

L139

1852				Typo.
63L1	L139	red		2,500.

Empire City Dispatch, New York, N. Y.

Established by J. Bevan & Son and almost immediately suppressed by the Government.

L140

1881		Typo.	Laid Paper	Perf. 12
64L1	L140	green		1.00
		Block of four		5.00
a.	Imperf.			—
b.	Horiz. or vert. pair, imperf. between			35.00

Essex Letter Express, New York, N. Y.

L141

1856		Glazed Surface Paper		Typo.
65L1	L141	2c red		250.00

Some authories doubt that No. 65L1 was placed in use.

Faunce's Penny Post, Atlantic City, N. J.

Established in 1884 by Ancil Faunce to provide local delivery of letters to and from the post office. Discontinued in 1887.

L141a

1885				Die cut
152L1	L141a	(1c) black, red	110.00	175.00
		On cover		900.00

Jabez Fearey & Co.'s Mustang Express, Newark, N. J.

Established by Jabez Fearey, Local Agent of the Pacific & Atlantic Telegraph Co.

L142

1870		Glazed Surface Paper	Typeset
66L1	L142	red	100.00

Some authorities consider this item to be an express company label rather than a stamp.

Fiske & Rice

Fiske

Authorities consider items of this design to be express company labels rather than stamps.

Floyd's Penny Post, Chicago, Ill.

Established by John R. Floyd early in 1860, operated by him until June 20, 1861, then continued by Charles W. Mappa.

John R. Floyd — L144

1860				Typo.
68L1	L144	(1c) blue (shades)	—	65.00
		On cover		2,500.
		Pair		200.00
68L2	L144	(1c) brown	—	90.00
		On cover		4,250.
68L3	L144	(1c) green	—	100.00
		On cover		4,250.
		On cover with U.S. #11		3,000.

Cancellations: Black circle "Floyd's Penny Post Chicago". Black circle "Floyd's Penny Post" and sunburst. Black or blue oval "Floyd's Penny Post Chicago".

Franklin City Despatch Post, N. Y.
(See Bouton's Manhattan Express.)
Frazer & Co., Cincinnati, Ohio.

Established by Hiram Frazer. Stamps used while he was a Cincinnati letter carrier.

L145

Cut to shape

1845		Glazed Surface Paper		
69L1	L145	2c green		750.00
		On cover		1,250.

L146

1845-51		Wove Paper		Litho.
69L2	L146	2c pink	—	200.00
69L3	L146	2c green	200.00	200.00
69L4	L146	2c yellow	200.00	200.00
69L5	L146	2c grayish	200.00	200.00

Some stamps of type L146 show manual erasure of "& Co."

L147

1848-51				
69L6	L147	2c rose		600.0
69L7	L147	2c blue (shades)	600.00	600.00
69L8	L147	2c yellow		1,000.

Freeman & Co.'s Express, New York, N. Y.

L147a

1855 (?)				Litho.
164L1	L145a	(25c) blue		500.00

Friend's Boarding School, Barnesville, Ohio.

(Barclay W. Stratton, Supt.)

On Nov. 6, 1877 the school committee decided to charge the students one cent for each letter carried to or from the post office, one and a half miles away. Adhesive labels were prepared and sold for one cent each. Their sale and use continued until 1884.

L147b

Several varieties and sizes of frame

1877				Typo.
151L1	L147b	(1c) black	75.00	
		On cover		150.00

No. 151L1 was usually affixed to the back of the envelope and left uncanceled.

Gahagan & Howe City Express, San Francisco, Calif.

Established by Dennis Gahagan and C. E. B. Howe, as successors to John C. Robinson, proprietor of the San Francisco Letter Express. Sold in 1865 to William E. Loomis, who later purchased the G. A. Carnes business. Loomis used the adhesive stamps and handstamps of these posts, changing the Carnes stamp by erasing his name.

L148   L149

1849-70				Typeset
70L1	L148	5c light blue	60.00	75.00
70L2	L149	(5c) blue	60.00	75.00
a.	Tete beche pair		150.00	

Sheets of No. 70L2 contain five vertical rows of four, the first two rows being reversed against the others, making horizontal tete beche pairs with wide margins between. The pairs were not evenly locked up in the form.

L150

70L3	L150	(5c) black	25.00	20.00
		Pair		45.00
		Strip of three		75.00
Overprinted "X" in Blue				
70L4	L150	10c black		85.00

Cancellations: Blue or black oval "Gahagan & Howe". Blue or black oval "San Francisco Letter Express" and horseman (Robinson). Blue or black oval "PAID" (Loomis).

Glen Haven Daily Mail, Glen Haven, N.Y.

Glen Haven was located at the head of Skaneateles Lake, Cayuga County, N.Y., until 1910 when the City of Syracuse, having purchased the land for reservoir purposes, razed all the buildings.

Glen Haven, by 1848, had become a famous Water Cure resort, with many sanitariums conducted there. The hamlet had a large summer colony interested in dress reform under the leadership of Amelia Jenks Bloomer; also antislavery, and other reform movements.

A local post was established by the hotel and sanitarium managements for their guests' convenience to deliver mail to the U.S. post offices at Homer or Scott, N.Y. The local stamps were occasionally pen canceled. They are known tied to cover with the Homer or Scott town postmark when the local stamp was placed adjacent to the government stamp and received the cancellation accidentally. The local stamps are only known used in conjunction with government stamps.

L151   L152

1854-58   **Typeset**
Several varieties of each
71L1   L151   1c *dark green*   300.00
  a.   "Gien" instead of "Glen"   500.00
Glazed Surface Paper
71L2   L152   1c *green*   400.00 400.00
                 On cover   750.00

Links at   Varying
corners — L153   ornaments at
                  corners — L153a

Several varieties of each
Glazed Surface Paper
71L3   L153   1c *green*   125.00   125.00
                 On cover   1,500.00
                 Pair   500.00
71L4   L153a 1c *green*   200.00   200.00
                 On cover   600.00

Gordon's City Express, New York, N. Y.
Established by Samuel B. Gordon

L154

1848-52   **Typo.**   **Surface Colored Paper**
72L1   L154   2c *vermilion*   750.00   750.00
              On cover   1,000.00
72L2   L154   2c *green*   75.00   75.00
              On cover   400.00
Glazed Surface Paper
72L3   L154   2c *green*   85.00   85.00
              On cover   450.00

Cancellation: Small black or red "PAID".

Grafflin's Baltimore Despatch, Baltimore, Md.
Established by Joseph Grafflin

L155

1856   **Litho.**
73L1   L155   1c black   85.00   125.00
              On cover   400.00
              Block of four   600.00

Originals show traces of a fine horizontal line through tops of most of the letters in "BALTIMORE".

Guy's City Despatch, Philadelphia, Pa.
Established by F. A. Guy, who employed 8 carriers

L156

Sheets of 25 (5x5)
1879   **Typo.**   **Perf. 11, 12, 12½**
74L1   L156   (1c) pink   12.00   12.00
              On cover   300.00
  a.   Imperf., pair   —
74L2   L156   (1c) blue   15.00   20.00
              On cover   300.00
  a.   Imperf., pair   —

When Guy's City Despatch was suppressed, the remainders were sold to a New York stamp dealer.

Hackney & Bolte Penny Post, Atlantic City, N. J.

Established in 1886 by Evan Hackney and Charles Bolte to provide delivery of mail to and from the post office. Discontinued in 1887.

L156a

Die cut
153L1   L156a (1c) black on red   125.00   175.00
              On cover   900.00
              On cover with 2c No.
              210   1,000.

Hale & Co.
Established by James W. Hale at New York, N.Y., to carry mail to points in New England, New York State, Philadelphia and Baltimore. Stamps sold at 6 cents each or "20 for $1.00."

L157

1844   **Wove Paper (several thicknesses)**   **Typo.**
75L1   L157 (6c) light blue (shades)   40.00   25.00
            Cut to shape   15.00
            On cover   150.00
            Cut to shape on cov-
            er   50.00
            Strip of 3 on cover   250.00
75L2   L157 (6c) red, *bluish*   100.00   85.00
            Cut to shape   40.00
            On cover   400.00
            Cut to shape on cov-
            er   100.00
            Pair on cover   —

Same Handstamped in Black or Red,
"City Despatch Office, 23 State St."
75L3   L157 (6c) red, *bluish* (Bk), cut
            to shape   400.00
            Pair, partly cut to
            shape   1,000.00
75L4   L157 (6c) blue (R), cut to shape 400.00

L158

Same as Type L157 but street
address omitted
75L5   L158 (6c) blue (shades)   15.00   10.00
            Cut to shape   5.00
            On cover   175.00
            Cut to shape on cov-
            er   40.00
            Pair on cover   175.00
            Block of four   75.00
            Sheet of 20 (5x4)   450.00

Cancellations on Nos. 75L1-75L5: Large red "PAID". Red, black or blue oval "Hale & Co." (several types and cities). Small red ornamental framed box (several types). Red negative monogram "WE".

Hall & Mills' Despatch Post, New York, N.Y.
Established by Gustavus A. Mills and A. C. Hall.

L159

Several Varieties
1847   **Glazed Surface Paper**   **Typeset**
76L1   L159 (2c) *green*   250.00   250.00
            On cover   500.00
            On cover with 5c #1   2,000.

T.A. Hampton City Despatch, Philadelphia, Pa.

L159a   L159b

Several Varieties of L159a
1847   **Cut to shape**   **Typeset**
77L1   L159a (2c) black   350.00   350.00
            On cover   900.00
77L2   L159b black

A handstamp similar to type L159b with denomination "2cts" or "3c" instead of "PAID." in center has been used as a postmark.

Hanford's Pony Express, New York, N.Y.
Established by John W. Hanford.

L160

1845   **Glazed Surface Paper**   **Typo.**
78L1   L160 2c *orange yellow*
            (shades)   65.00   85.00
            Cut to shape   35.00
            On cover   500.00

Cancellation: Small red "PAID".

The handstamp in black or red formerly listed as Nos. 78LU1-78LU6 is illustrated in the Local Handstamped Covers section. It was used as a postmark and there is no evidence that any prepaid handstamped envelopes or lettersheets were ever sold.

George S. Harris City Despatch Post, Philadelphia, Pa.

L160a

L160b

1847 (?)   **Typeset**
79L1   L160a (2c) black   500.00
79L2   L160b   black   750.00

Hartford, Conn. Mail Route

L161

Plate of 12 (6x2) varieties

1844   **Glazed Surface Paper**   **Engr.**
80L1   L161   (5c) *yellow*   250.00   150.00
           Pair   400.00
           On cover   *1,000.*
80L3   L161   *pink*   300.00   300.00

Chemically affected copies of No. 80L1 appear as buff, and of No. 80L3 as salmon.

Cancellations are usually initials or words ("S", "W", "South", etc.) in black ms. This may indicate destination or routing.

Hill's Post, Boston, Mass.

Established by Oliver B. Hill

L162

1849   **Typo.**
81L1   L162   1c *rose*   750.00

A. M. Hinkley's Express Co., New York, N.Y.

Organized by Abraham M. Hinkley, Hiram Dixon and Hiram M. Dixon, in 1855, and business transferred to the Metropolitan Errand & Carrier Express Co. in same year.

L163

Sheets of 64 (8x8)

1855   **Litho.**
82L1   L163   1c red, *bluish*   200.00

It is doubtful that No. 82L1 was ever placed in use. *Reprints exist on white paper somewhat thicker than the originals.*

Homan's Empire Express, New York, N.Y.

Established by Richard S. Homan

L164

Several varieties

1852   **Typeset**
83L1   L164   *yellow*   400.00   400.00
     a.   "1" for "I" in "PAID"   500.00

Hopedale Penny Post, Milford, Mass.

Hopedale was a large farm community southwest of Milford, Mass. The community meeting of Feb. 2, 1849, voted to arrange for regular transportation of mail to the nearest post office, which was at Milford, a mile and a half distant, at a charge of 1c a letter. A complete history of this community may be found in "The Hopedale Community," published in 1897.

Rayed   Plain asterisks
asterisks in   in corners
corners   L166
L165

Several varieties of Types L165-L166

1849   **Glazed Surface Paper**   **Typeset**
84L1   L165   (1c) *pink*   300.00   300.00
84L2   L166   (1c) *pink*   300.00   300.00

Types L165 and L166 probably were printed together in a single small plate.

L167

       Wove Paper   **Typo.**
84L3   L167   (1c) *yellow*   400.00   400.00
           On cover   *1,250.*
84L4   L167   (1c) *pink*   450.00   450.00
           Pair   *1,100.*

J. A. Howell's City Despatch, Philadelphia, Pa.

L167a

184 ?   **Typo.**
165L1   L167a   black   —

Hoyt's Letter Express, Rochester, N.Y.

David Hoyt, agent at Rochester for the express company of Livingston, Wells & Pomeroy, operated a letter and package express by boats on the Genesee Canal between Dansville, N.Y., and Rochester, where connection was also made with Pomeroy's Letter Express.

L168

Several varieties

1844   **Glazed Surface Paper**   **Typeset**
85L1   L168   (5c) *vermilion*   300.00   300.00
     a.   "LETTCR" instead of "LET-
         TER"   450.00

Humboldt Express, Nevada

A branch of Langton's Pioneer Express, connecting with the main line of Pioneer Express at Carson City, Nevada, and making tri-weekly trips to adjacent points.

L169

1863   **Litho.**
86L1   L169   25c brown   250.00   300.00

        Pair   700.00
        On cover (U.S. Enve-
           lopes Nos. U34 or
           U35)   *50,000.*

Cancellations: Blue oval "Langton's Pioneer Express Unionville". Red "Langton & Co."

Hussey's Post, New York City, N.Y.

Established by George Hussey.
Reprints available for postage are so described.

L170   L171

1854   **Litho.**
87L1   L170   (1c) blue   50.00
           On cover   250.00

1856
87L2   L171   (1c) black   150.00   50.00
           On cover   300.00
87L3   L171   (1c) red   35.00
           On cover   275.00

Cancellation on Nos. 87L1-87L3: Black "FREE".

L172   L173

1858
87L4   L172   1c brown red   17.50   25.00
           On cover   150.00
           Pair   400.00
87L5   L172   1c black   50.00
           On cover   —

Cancellation on Nos. 87L4-87L5: Black circle "1ct PAID HUSSEY 50 Wm. ST", date in center.

1858
87L6   L173   (1c) black   2.00
           On cover   —
87L7   L173   (1c) rose red   2.00
           On cover   —
87L8   L173   (1c) red   8.00
           On cover   —

Type L173 was printed in sheets of 46: 5 horizontal rows of 8, one row of 6 sideways at bottom. Type L173 saw little, if any, commercial use and was probably issued mainly for collectors. Covers exist, many with apparently contemporary corner cards. On cover stamps bear a black HUSSEY'S POST handstamp, but most if not all of Nos. 87L6-87L8 were canceled after the post ceased to operate.

L174   L175

1858   **Typo.**
87L9   L174   (1c) blue   2.00

1859   **Litho.**
87L10   L175   1c rose red   10.00   20.00
           On cover   200.00

No. 87L10 in orange red is not known to have been placed in use.
Cancellations: Black "FREE". Black company circle "1 CT PAID HUSSEY 50 WM. ST.", no date in center (smaller than cancel on Nos. 87L4-87L5).

87L11   L175   1c lake   —
87L12   L175   1c black   —

L176

L177

1862

87L13	L176	1c black	15.00	
87L14	L176	1c blue	7.00	10.00
		On cover		125.00
87L15	L176	1c green	8.00	
		On cover		125.00
87L16	L176	1c red	15.00	
87L17	L176	1c red brown	15.00	
87L18	L176	1c brown	15.00	
87L19	L176	1c lake	17.50	
87L20	L176	1c purple	12.00	
87L21	L176	1c yellow	12.00	

1862

Similar to L174 but has condensed "50"
and shows a short
flourish line over the "I" of "DELIVERY".

| 87L22 | L177 | (1c) blue | 70 | — |
| | | On cover | | — |

L178

Similar to L171, but no dots in
corners — L179

1863

87L23	L178	(1c) blue	5.00	
87L24	L179	(1c) black	2.00	
87L25	L179	(1c) red	5.00	

See No. 87L52.

L180

L182

87L26	L180	1c brown red	4.00	—
		Block of four	20.00	
		On cover		125.00

A so-called "reprint" of No. 87L26, made for J. W. Scott, has a colored flaw extending diagonally upward from the "I" in "CITY."

Reprints of types L173, L174, L178, L179 and L180 were made in 1875-76 on thicker paper in approximately normal colors and were available for postage.

1863

Dated 1863

87L27	L182	1c blue	8.00	10.00
		On cover		125.00
87L28	L182	1c green	12.00	
		On cover		—
87L29	L182	1c yellow	15.00	
		On cover		—
87L30	L182	1c brown	10.00	
87L31	L182	1c red brown	10.00	
87L32	L182	1c red	10.00	
87L33	L182	1c black	20.00	
87L34	L182	1c violet	20.00	
87L35	L182	2c brown	10.00	12.00
		On cover		125.00

The 2c blue dated 1863 exists only as a counterfeit.

1865

Dated 1865

| 87L38 | L182 | 2c blue | 12.00 | 12.00 |
| | | On cover | | 225.00 |

1867

Dated 1867

| 87L39 | L182 | 2c blue | 20.00 | 20.00 |
| | | On cover | | 225.00 |

1868

Dated 1868

| 87L40 | L182 | 2c blue | 17.50 | 17.50 |
| | | On cover | | 225.00 |

1869

Dated 1870

| 87L41 | L182 | 2c blue | 20.00 | 20.00 |
| | | On cover | | 225.00 |

1871

Dated 1871

| 87L42 | L182 | 2c blue | 22.50 | 22.50 |
| | | On cover | | 225.00 |

L183

L184

1872

Wove Paper

87L43	L183	black	3.00	5.00
		On cover		125.00
87L44	L183	red lilac	6.00	—
		On cover		125.00
87L45	L183	blue	5.00	
87L46	L183	green	6.00	
		On cover		125.00

Sheets contain four panes of 28 each. Double periods after "A.M." on two stamps in two panes, and on four stamps in the other two panes.
Covers show postmark reading: "HUSSEY'S SPECIAL-MESSENGER EXPRESS-PAID-54 PINE ST."

1872

Thick Laid paper

87L47	L184	black	5.00	8.00
		Block of four	22.50	
		On cover		—
87L48	L184	yellow	9.00	10.00
87L49	L184	red brown	7.00	
		On cover		125.00
87L50	L184	red	6.00	8.00
		On cover		—

L185

1873

Thin Wove Paper

| 87L51 | L185 | 2c black | 10.00 | 10.00 |
| | | On cover | | 100.00 |

A reprint of No. 87L51, believed to have been made for J. W. Scott, shows a 4mm. break in the bottom frameline under "54."

Type of 1863

1875

Thick Wove Paper

| 87L52 | L179 | (1c) blue | | — |

L186

L186 in imitation of L180, but no corner dots, "S" for "$", etc.

1875

| 87L53 | L186 | 1c black | 1.00 | |

Some authorities believe Nos. 87L52-87L53 are imitations made from new stones. Attributed to J. W. Scott.

"Copyright
1877" — L188

L188a

1877

Thick Wove Paper

| 87L55 | L188 | black | 75.00 | — |
| | | On cover | | 500.00 |

Error of design, used provisionally. Stamp was never copyrighted. Printed singly.

| 87L56 | L188a | black | 50.00 | |

Thin Wove Paper

87L57	L188a	blue	10.00	
87L58	L188a	rose	6.00	
		On cover		—

Perf. 12½

87L59	L188a	blue	2.00	5.00
a.		Imperf. horizontally, pair		—
		On cover		125.00
87L60	L188a	rose	2.00	5.00
		On cover		125.00

L189

L190

L191

L189-"TRADE MARK" small.
L190-"TRADE MARK" medium.
L191-"TRADE MARK" larger, touching "s" of "Easson".

1878	**Wove Paper**		**Perf. 11, 11½, 11x12, 12**	
87L61	L189	blue	5.00	
		On cover		125.00
87L62	L189	carmine	8.50	
		On cover		100.00
87L63	L189	black	50.00	

Nos. 87L61-87L63 exist imperforate.

Perf. 11, 12, 12½, 14, 16 and Compound

87L64	L190	blue	2.00	5.00
		On cover		100.00
87L65	L190	red	2.00	5.00
		On cover		75.00
87L66	L190	black	—	

Nos. 87L64-87L66 imperf. are reprints.

1879

Perf. 11, 12, and Compound

87L67	L191	blue	2.00	5.00
		On cover		100.00
87L69	L191	black	—	

1880

Imperf.

87L70	L191	blue		225.00
		On cover		
87L71	L191	red	—	
87L72	L191	black	—	

The authenticity of Nos. 87L69-87L72 has not been fully established.

L192

Two types of L192: I. Imprint "N. F. Seebeck, 97 Wall St. N. Y." is in lower tablet below "R Easson, etc." II. Imprint in margin below stamp.

1880		**Glazed Surface Wove Paper**	**Perf. 12**	
87L73	L192	brown, type I	5.00	8.00
a.		brown, type II	5.00	8.00
b.		Horiz. pair, imperf. between	20.00	
c.		Imperf., pair	20.00	
		On cover		150.00
		Block of four, type I		
87L74	L192	ultramarine, type I	7.00	8.00
a.		Imperf., pair	—	
b.		deep blue, type II	20.00	
87L75	L192	red, type II	1.00	—
		On cover		100.00
		Block of four	5.00	

1882			**Perf. 16, 12x16**	
87L76	L192	brown, type I	6.00	10.00
		On cover		100.00
87L77	L192	ultramarine, type I	6.00	10.00
		On cover		100.00

Cancellations: Violet 3-ring target. Violet ornamental "T". Imperforate impressions of Type I in various colors, on horizontally laid paper, ungummed, are color trials.

SPECIAL DELIVERY STAMPS

 L181

Typographed; Numerals Inserted Separately

1863				**Glazed Surface Paper**	
87LE1	L181	5c	red	1.50	7.50
			On cover		150.00
87LE2	L181	10c	gold, green	1.50	8.50
			On cover		150.00
87LE3	L181	15c	gold, black	1.50	10.00
			On cover		200.00
87LE4	L181	20c	black	1.50	10.00
			On cover		200.00
87LE5	L181	25c	gold, blue	1.50	8.50
			On cover		200.00
87LE6	L181	30c	gold, red		—
87LE7	L181	50c	black, green		—

Nos. 87LE1-87LE7 on cover show Hussey handstamp cancellations in various types.
Nos. 87LE4 and 87LE5 are on unglazed paper, the latter surface colored. Ten minor varieties of each value, except the 30c and 50c, which have the figures in manuscript. Printed in two panes of 10, certain values exist in horizontal cross-gutter tete beche pairs.
Originals of the 5c to 20c have large figures of value. The 25c has condensed figures with decimal point. Reprints exist with both large and condensed figures. Reprints of the 25c also exist with serifs on large figures.
Most of the Hussey adhesives are known on cover, tied with Hussey Express postmarks. Many of these were canceled after the post ceased to operate as a mail carrier. "On cover" prices are for original stamps used while the post was operating.

WRAPPERS

 L192a

1856	**Handstamped**	**Inscribed: "82 Broadway"**		
87LUP1	L192	black, white	—	175.00

1858		**Inscribed: "50 William St. Basement"**		
87LUP2	L192a	black, manila	—	175.00
87LUP3	L192a	black, white	—	175.00

Jefferson Market P. O., New York, N. Y.

Established by Godfrey Schmidt

 L193

1850		**Glazed Surface Paper**	**Litho.**	
88L1	L193	(2c) pink	600.00	450.00
88L2	L193	(2c) blue	—	500.00
		On cover		1,250.

Jenkins' Camden Dispatch, Camden, N. J.

Established by Samuel H. Jenkins and continued by William H. Jenkins.

 George Washington — L194

 L195

1853			**Litho.**	
89L1	L194	black (fine impression)	70.00	70.00
		On cover		700.00
		Block of four	350.00	
89L2	L194	yellow (coarse impression)		350.00
		Typeset		
89L3	L195	1c bluish	—	—

Type L194 printed on envelopes at upper left is considered a corner card.
Some authorities believe No. 89L3 is bogus.

Johnson & Co.'s City Despatch Post, Baltimore, Md.

Operated by Ezekiel C. Johnson, letter carrier

 L196

1848			**Typeset**	
90L1	L196	2c black, lavender	2,000.	

Jones' City Express, Brooklyn, N. Y.

George Washington — L197

1845		**Glazed Surface Paper**	**Engr.**	
91L1	L197	2c black, pink	350.00	350.00
		On cover		850.00

Cancellation: Red oval "Boyd's City Express Post".

Kellogg's Penny Post & City Despatch, Cleveland, Ohio

 L198

1853			**Typo.**	
92L1	L198	(1c) vermilion	400.00	
		On cover		600.00

Cancellation: Black grid.

Kidder's City Express Post, Brooklyn, N.Y.

In 1847, Henry A. Kidder took over the post of Walton & Co., and with the brothers Isaac C.

Snedeker and George H. Snedeker increased its scope. In 1851, the business was sold to the Snedekers. It was operated under the old name until 1853 when the Brooklyn City Express Post was founded.

 L199

Stamps bear black manuscript "I S" control in two styles.

1847		**Glazed Surface Paper**	**Typo.**	
93L1	L199	2c pale blue	275.00	225.00
		On cover		450.00
		Block of four	1,400.	

Cancellation: Red "PAID".
Reprinted on green paper.

Kurtz Union Despatch Post, New York, N. Y.

 L200

Typeset; "T" in Black Ms.

1853		**Glazed Surface Paper**		
94L1	L200	2c green	3,500.	

Langton & Co.
(See Humboldt Express.)
Ledger Dispatch, Brooklyn, N.Y.

Established by Edwin Pidgeon. Stamps reported to have been sold at 80 cents per 100. Suppressed after a few months.

 L201

1882		**Typo.**	**Rouletted 12 in color**	
95L1	L201	rose (shades)	65.00	
		Block of four	350.00	

Letter Express

Established by Henry Wells. Carried mail for points in Western New York, Chicago, Detroit and Duluth.

 L202   L203

1844		**Glazed Surface Paper**	**Typo.**	
96L1	L202	5c pink	100.00	75.00
		Pair	250.00	200.00
		Block of four	750.00	
96L2	L202	5c green	—	75.00
		Pair		200.00
96L3	L203	10c Pink	150.00	100.00
		Pair		300.00
a.		Bisect on cover		750.00

No. 96L3a was sold as a horizontal or vertical bisect. It is known used singly for 5c (rare), or as two bisects for 10c (extremely rare). Stamps are known almost exclusively tied with black ms. "X" covering the cut, and can be authenticated by experts.

L204

96L4   L204   10c *scarlet*   —   300.00

Cancellations: Red large partly boxed "PAID". Red boxed "Boyd's City Express Post".

Locomotive Express Post

L205

1847 (?)   **Handstamped**
97L1   L205   black   —

Wm. E. Loomis Letter Express, San Francisco, Calif.

William E. Loomis established this post as the successor to the Gahagan & Howe City Express, which he bought in 1865. He continued to use the Gahagan & Howe stamps unchanged. Later Loomis bought Carnes' City Letter Express. He altered the Carnes stamp by erasing "CARNES" from the plate and adding the address below the oval: "S.E. cor. Sans'e & Wash'n."

L206

1868   **Typo.**
98L1   L206   (5c) rose   45.00   125.00

McGreely's Express, Alaska

Established in 1898 by S. C. Marcuse to carry letters and packages by motorboat between Dyea and Skagway, Alaska.

L208

1898   **Typo.**   **Perf. 14**
155L1   L208   25c blue   12.00
    Block of four   60.00

The status of No. 155L1 is questioned.

McIntires's City Express Post, New York, N. Y.

Established by William H. McIntire

Mercury — L207

1859   **Litho.**
99L1   L207   2c pink   10.00   30.00
    Block of four   60.00
    On cover   300.00
    a.   Period after CENTS omitted   —

Cancellation: Black oval "McIntires's City Express Post Paid".

McMillan's City Dispatch Post, Chicago, Ill.

L208a

1855   **Typeset**
100L1   L208a   *rose*   —

Magic Letter Express, Richmond, Va.
Established by Evans, Porter & Co.

L209

1865   **Typo.**
101L1   L209   2c *brown*   1,000.
101L2   L209   5c *brown*   —   —

Mason's New Orleans City Express, New Orleans, La.
J. Mason, proprietor

L210

1850-57   **Typeset**
102L1   L210   ½c *blue* (value changed
        to "1" in black ms.)   750.00
    On cover   2,000.
102L2   L210   2c *yellow*   —   250.00
    On cover   1,250.

Cancellations: Red grid. Small red circle "Mason's City Express".

Mearis' City Despatch Post, Baltimore, Md.
Established by Malcom W. Mearis

L211

L212

Black ms. initials "M W M" control on all stamps

1846   **Typeset**
103L1   L211   1c *gray*   300.00   300.00
    On cover   750.00
103L2   L212   1c *gray*   400.00
103L3   L212   2c *gray*   400.00
    a.   Horiz. pair, Nos. 103L2-
        103L3 se-tenant   1,500.

L213

103L4   L213   1c *gray*   400.00

103L5   L213   2c *gray*   400.00
    a.   Horiz. pair, Nos. 103L4-
        103L5 se-tenant   1,500.

L214

103L6   L214   1c *gray*   500.00

Corner ornaments of Nos. 103L1-103L6 differ on each stamp. All varieties probably contained in one plate.

Menant & Co.'s Express, New Orleans, La.

L215

1853 (?)   **Typo.**
104L1   L215   2c dark red   750.00

Mercantile Library Association, New York, N. Y.

Stamps paid for special delivery service of books ordered from the library, and of forms especially provided to subscribers. The forms bore a government stamp on the outside, a library stamp inside.

L216

1870-75   **Litho.**
105L1   L216   5c maroon   55.00   55.00
105L2   L216   5c *yellow*   75.00   75.00
105L3   L216   5c *blue*   75.00   75.00
    Pair   175.00
105L5   L216   6c *maroon*   150.00
105L6   L216   10c *yellow*   100.00   125.00

No. 105L5 is slightly larger than the 5c and 10c stamps.
The stamps "on cover" are affixed to cutouts from order blanks showing order number, title of book desired, and subscriber's name and address. When canceled, the stamps and order blanks show a dull blue double-lined oval inscribed "MERCANTILE LIBRARY ASSOCIATION" and date in center. The stamps are really more a form of receipt for a prepaid parcel delivery service than postage stamps.

POSTAL CARD
Printed on U. S. Postal Card, First Issue
105LU1   L216   10c *yellow*   500.00

Messenkope's Union Square Post Office, New York, N. Y.

Established by Charles F. Messenkope in 1849 and sold to Joseph E. Dunham in 1850

L217

1849   **Glazed Surface Paper**   **Litho.**
106L1   L217   (1c) *green*   70.00   70.00
    On cover   250.00
    Two on cover (2c
    rate)   350.00
    On cover with 5c #1   1,200.
106L2   L217   (2c) *pink*   400.00   350.00
    On cover   500.00

Some examples of No. 106L1 are found with "MESSENKOPES" crossed through in black ms. in an apparent attempt (by Dunham ?) to obliterate it.
Cancellations: Red "PAID". Red oval "DUNHAMS UNION SQUARE POST OFFICE". Red grid of dots.

Metropolitan Errand and Carrier Express Co., New York, N. Y.

Organized Aug. 1, 1855, by Abraham M. Hinkley, Hiram Dixon, and others

L218

Printed in sheets of 100 (10x10), each stamp separated by thin ruled lines.

1855		Thin to Medium Wove Paper		Engr.
107L1	L218	1c red orange (shades)	10.00	15.00
		Cut to shape	2.50	3.50
		Pair	30.00	
		Block of four	75.00	
		On cover		225.00
107L2	L218	5c red orange	85.00	
		Cut to shape	30.00	
107L3	L218	10c red orange	85.00	
		Cut to shape	30.00	
107L4	L218	20c red orange	125.00	
		Cut to shape	40.00	

Cancellations: Black, blue or green boxed "PAID".
Nos. 107L1-107L4 have been extensively reprinted in brown and in blue on paper much thicker than the originals.

ENVELOPE

L219

Embossed
Wide Diagonally Laid Paper

107LU1	L219	2c red, *amber*	65.00

No. 107LU1 has been reprinted on amber wove, diagonally laid or horizontally laid paper with narrow lines. The embossing is sharper than on the original.

Metropolitan Post Office, New York, N. Y.

Established by Lemuel Williams who later took William H. Laws as a partner.

L220

L221

L222

Nos. 108L1-108L5 were issued die cut, and only exist thus.

1852-53		Glazed Surface Paper	Embossed	
108L1	L220	(2c) red (L. Williams)	350.00	350.00
108L2	L221	(2c) red (address and name erased)	400.00	400.00
108L3	L222	(2c) red	100.00	75.00
		On cover		1,000.
108L3A	L222	(2c) blue	350.00	350.00
		On cover		2,500.

L223

Wove Paper

108L4	L223	1c red	60.00	70.00
		On cover		225.00
108L5	L223	1c blue	60.00	70.00
		On cover		200.00

Cancellations: Black circle "METROPOLITAN P. O." Black boxed "PAID W. H. LAWS."

G. A. Mills' Despatch Post, New York, N. Y.

Established by Gustavus A. Mills at 6 Wall St., succeeding Hall & Mills.

L224

Several varieties

1847		Glazed Surface Paper		Typeset
109L1	L224	(2c) *green*	200.00	200.00
		On cover		500.00

Moody's Penny Dispatch, Chicago, Ill.

Robert J. Moody, proprietor

L225

Several varieties

1856		Glazed Surface Paper		Typeset
110L1	L225	(1c) *red,* "CHICAGO" 8mm.	200.00	175.00
		Vert. strip of 3 showing 3 varieties:period, colon, comma after "Dispatch"	1,500.	
		On cover		4,500.
a.		"CHICAGO" 12½mm.		200.00

Cancellations: Black or blue circle "Moody's Despatch".

New York City Express Post, New York, N.Y.

L226

Several varieties

1847		Glazed Surface Paper		Engr.
111L1	L226	2c *green*	250.00	150.00
		Cut to shape	60.00	60.00
		On cover		600.00
		Cut to shape on cover		125.00
		Wove Paper		
111L2	L226	2c orange	500.00	500.00
		On cover		1,000.

One Cent Despatch, Baltimore, Md., Washington, D.C.

Established by J.H. Wiley to deliver mail in Washington, Georgetown and Baltimore. Made as many as five deliveries daily at 1 cent if prepaid, or 2 cents payable on delivery.

Souvenir cards are listed and priced in a separate section of the catalogue. See catalogue index.

L227

Two types: I. Courier's letter points to "O" of "ONE."
II. Letter points to "N" of "ONE."

1856	**Washington, D.C.**		Litho.	
	Inscribed at bottom "Washington City"			
112L1	L227	1c violet	125.00	85.00
		On cover		1,000.
		Horiz. pair, Types I && II se-tenant	600.00	

	Baltimore, Maryland			
	No name at bottom			
112L2	L227	1c red	125.00	100.00
		On cover		750.00

Cancellation on Nos. 112L1-112L2: Black circle "City Despatch".

Overton & Co.

Carried mail principally between New York and Boston; also to Albany. Stamps sold for 6c each, 20 for $1.

L229

1844				
113L1	L229	(6c) *greenish*	200.00	150.00
		On cover		350.00
		Pair		400.00

Cancellation: Black "PAID".
A variety of this stamp has "FREE" below the design.

Penny Express Co.

Little information is available on this post, but a sheet is known carrying the ms. initials of Henry Reed of the Holladay staff. The post was part of the Holladay Overland Mail and Express Co. system.

In 1866 in the West the "short-bit" or 10 cents was the smallest currency generally used. The word "penny" is believed to refer to the "half-bit" or 5 cents (nickel)

L230

Printed in sheets of 32 (8x4)

1866				Litho.
114L1	L230	5c black	100.00	
a.		Initialed "HR", black ms.		—
		As "a," block of four		—
114L2	L230	5c blue	5.00	
		Block of four	21.00	
114L3	L230	5c red	5.00	
		Block of four	21.00	

Little information is available on this post, but a sheet is known carrying the ms. initials of Henry Reed of the Holladay staff. The post was part of the Holladay Overland Mail and Express Co. system. Nos. 114L1-114L3 lack gum and probably were never placed in use.

Philadelphia Despatch Post, Philadelphia, Pa.
See D.O. Blood & Co.

Pinkney's Express Post, New York, N.Y.

L231

1851   **Glazed Surface Paper**   **Typo.**
115L1   L231   2c *green*   *1,000.*
     Cut to shape   600.00

Pips Daily Mail, Brooklyn, N.Y.

L232

1862 (?)   **Litho.**
116L1   L232   1c black   85.00
116L2   L232   1c *buff*   65.00
116L3   L232   1c *yellow*   80.00
116L4   L232   1c *dark blue*   80.00
116L5   L232   1c *rose*   80.00
     Block of four   —

Pomeroy's Letter Express.

Established in 1844 by George E. Pomeroy. Carried mail principally to points in New York State. Connected with Letter Express for Western points.

L233

Engraved by John E. Gavit, Albany, N. Y. (Seen as "GAVIT" in bottom part of stamp). Sheets of 40 (8x5).

1844
     Surface Colored Wove Paper
117L1   L233   5c *yellow*   3.00   15.00
     On cover   125.00
     Pair   100.00
     Pair on cover   300.00
117L2   L233   *yellow* (value incomplete)   100.00
     On cover   200.00
     Thin Bond Paper
117L3   L233   5c blue   1.50   25.00
     On cover   100.00
     Pair on cover   300.00
117L4   L233   5c black   1.50   25.00
     On cover   125.00
     Strip of four on cover   500.00
117L5   L233   5c red   1.50   35.00
     On cover   125.00
     Strip of three on cover   600.00
117L6   L233   5c lake   100.00   100.00
     On cover   —
     Pair on cover   —
117L7   L233   5c orange   5.00   —

Cancellations: Large red partly boxed "PAID" (Nos. 117L1, 117L6). Red "Cd" (Nos. 117L1-117L2, 117L4); stamps are considered "tied to cover" by this "Cd" when the impression shows through the letter paper.

All stamps except No. 117L2 have "20 for $1" in tablet at the bottom. On No. 117L2 the value is incomplete.

Remainders (reprints?) of Nos. 117L1, 117L3, 117L4 and 117L5 are plentiful in unused condition, including multiples and sheets. A 5c black on yellow paper colored through and a 5c brown were prepared for use but never issued. No. 117L2 was never reprinted.

P. O. Paid, Philadelphia, Pa.
See note in Carriers' Stamps Section.

Price's City Express, New York, N. Y.

L235   L236

1857-58   **Glazed Surface Paper**   **Litho.**
119L1   L235   2c *vermilion*   100.00
     On cover   750.00
119L2   L235   2c *green*   85.00

1858
     Sheets of 108 (12x9)
119L3   L236   2c *green*   5.00   55.00
     On cover   —
     Block of four   25.00

Cancellation on No. 119L3: Black oval "Price's City Express".

Price's Eighth Avenue Post Office, New York, N. Y.
Established by James Price at 350 Eighth Avenue, in 1854, and sold to Russell in the same year.

L237

1854   **Litho.**
120L1   L237   (2c) red, *bluish*   200.00

Priest's Despatch Philadelphia, Pa.
Established by Solomon Priest

L238   L239

1851   **Glazed Surface Paper**   **Typo.**
121L1   L238   (2c) silver, *vermilion*   300.00   300.00
121L2   L238   (2c) gold, *dark blue*   500.00
     Wove Paper
121L2A   L238   (2c) bronze, *bluish*   250.00   250.00
121L3   L238   (2c) *yellow*   150.00
121L4   L238   (2c) *rose*   150.00
121L5   L238   (2c) *blue*   150.00
121L6   L239   (2c) *yellow*   150.00
121L7   L239   (2c) *blue*   150.00
121L8   L239   (2c) *rose*   150.00
121L9   L239   (2c) *emerald*   250.00

Prince's Letter Dispatch, Portland, Maine.
Established by J. H. Prince of Portland. Mail carried nightly by messenger travelling by steamer to Boston. Stamp engraved by Lowell of Lowell & Brett, Boston, his name appearing in the design below the steamship.

L240

Printed in sheets of 40 (5x8)

1861   **Litho.**
122L1   L240   black   5.00   50.00
     On cover   750.00
     Block of four   25.00
     Sheet of forty   275.00

Private Post Office, San Francisco, Calif.
ENVELOPES

L241

(Illustration reduced size.)

Impressed on U. S. Envelopes, 1863-64 Issue

1864   **Typo.**
123LU1   L241   15c blue, *orange* (on U. S. No. U56)   350.00
123LU2   L241   15c blue, *buff* (on U. S. No. U54)   350.00
   a.   15c blue, *buff* (on U. S. No. U58)   150.00
   b.   15c blue, *buff* (on U. S. No. U59)   150.00
123LU3   L241   25c blue, *buff* (on U. S. No. U54)   350.00

Providence Despatch, Providence, R.I.

L242

1849   **Typeset**
124L1   L242   black   *2,000.*

Public Letter Office, San Francisco, Calif.
ENVELOPES

L243

(Illustration reduced size.)

Impressed on U. S. Envelopes, 1863-64 Issue

1864   **Typeset**
125LU1   L243   black   200.00
125LU2   L243   blue   200.00
125LU3   L243   15c blue   250.00
125LU4   L243   25c blue   250.00

Reed's City Despatch Post, San Francisco, Calif.
Pioneer San Francisco private post. Also serving Adams & Co. for city delivery.

L244

1853-54   **Glazed Surface Paper**   **Litho.**
126L1   L244   *green*, on cover   —
126L2   L244   *blue*   *3,000.*

Cancellation: Blue double-circle "Adams & Co. San Francisco".

Ricketts & Hall, Baltimore, Md.
Successors to Cook's Dispatch

L244a

1857   **Cut to shape**   **Typo.**
127L1   L244a   1c red, *bluish*   750.00   1,500.

Robison & Co., Brooklyn, N. Y.

L245

1855-56				Typo.	
128L1	L245	1c blue		300.00	300.00
		On cover			4,000.

Cancellation: Blue "PAID".

Roche's City Dispatch, Wilmington, Del.

L246

1850		Glazed Surface Paper		Typo.	
129L1	L246	(2c) green		750.00	
		Cut to shape		400.00	
		On cover			1,250.

A black negative handstamp similar to type L246 served solely as a postmark and no evidence exists that any prepaid handstamped envelopes or lettersheets were ever sold.

Rogers' Penny Post, Newark, N.J.

Established by Alfred H. Rogers, bookseller, at 194 Broad St., Newark, N.J.

L246a

Cut to shape

1856		Glazed Surface Paper		Handstamped	
162L1	L246a	(1c) green			—

See Rogers' handstamp in Local Handstamp Covers section.

Russell 8th Ave. Post Office, New York, N. Y.

(See Price's Eighth Avenue Post Office.)

L247

1854-58				Wood Engraving	
130L1	L247	(2c) blue, rose		150.00	125.00
		On cover			400.00
130L2	L247	(2c) yellow		175.00	150.00
		On cover			400.00
130L3	L247	(2c) red, bluish		250.00	200.00
		On cover			500.00
130L4	L247	(2c) blue green, green			—

St. Louis City Delivery Company, St. Louis, Mo.

(See Cincinnati City Delivery)

L249

1883				Typo.	Perf. 12
131L1	L249	(1c) red		1.50	2.50

	Block of four		8.50	
	On cover			200.00
a.	Imperf., pair		—	

Cancellation: Purple target.

Smith & Stephens' City Delivery, St. Louis, Mo.

L284

			Typeset	
158L1	L284	1c pale rose		—

Spaulding's Penny Post, Buffalo, N. Y.

L283   L283a

1848-49			
156L1	L283	2c vermilion	1,250.
156L2	L283a	2c carmine	2,000.

Spence & Brown Express Post, Philadelphia, Pa.

L285   L286

(Illustrations reduced size)

1847 (?)				Typeset	
159L1	L285	2c bluish		900.00	900.00

1848				Litho.	
159L2	L286	(2c) black		800.00	800.00

Squier & Co. City Letter Dispatch, St. Louis, Mo.

(Jordan & Co.)

This post began to operate as a local carrier on July 6, 1859 and was discontinued in the early part of 1860. Squier & Co. used imperforate stamps; their successors (Jordan & Co.) about Jan. 1 1860, used the roulettes.

L248

1859			Litho.	Imperf.
132L1	L248	1c green		— 75.00
		On cover		500.00

1860				Rouletted 19
132L2	L248	1c rose brown	75.00	75.00
		On cover		400.00
132L3	L248	1c brownish purple	75.00	75.00
		On cover		400.00
132L4	L248	1c green	75.00	75.00
		On cover		400.00

Cancellation: Black circle "Jordan's Penny Post Saint Louis".

Staten Island Express Post, Staten Island, N. Y.

Established by Hagadorn & Co., with office at Stapleton, Staten Island. Connected with Boyd for delivery in New York City.

L250

1849				Typo.	
133L1	L250	3c vermilion		350.00	300.00
133L2	L250	6c vermilion		—	1,250.

Stringer & Morton's City Despatch, Baltimore, Md.

According to an advertisement in the Baltimore newspapers, dated October 19, 1850, this post aimed to emulate the successful posts of other cities, and divided the city into six districts, with a carrier in each district. Stamps were made available throughout the city.

L251

1850			Glazed Surface Paper	
134L1	L251	(1c) gold, black	100.00	—
		On cover		750.00

Cancellation: Black circle "Baltimore City Despatch & Express Paid".

Sullivan's Dispatch Post, Cincinnati, Ohio

L252

1853		Glazed Surface Paper		Litho.	
135L1	L252	(2c) green		1,500.	
		Wove Paper			
135L2	L252	(2c) bluish black		1,500.	
135L3	L252	(2c) green		—	1,200.

Nos. 135L1-135L2 are either die cut octagonally or cut round. They do not exist cut square.

Swarts' City Dispatch Post, New York, N. Y.

Established by Aaron Swarts, at Chatham Square, in 1847, becoming one of the largest local posts in the city.

The postmarks of Swarts' Post Office are often found on stampless covers, as this post carried large quantities of mail without using adhesive stamps.

Zachary Taylor   George
L253   Washington
          L254

1849-53		Glazed Surface Paper		Litho.	
136L1	L253	(2c) light green		—	100.00
		On cover			250.00
136L2	L253	(2c) dark green		—	75.00
		On cover			200.00
		Wove Paper			
136L3	L253	(2c) pink		—	20.00
		On cover			125.00
136L4	L253	(2c) red (shades)		20.00	15.00
		On cover			125.00
136L5	L253	(2c) pink, blue		—	35.00
		On cover			175.00
136L6	L253	(2c) red, blue		—	35.00
		On cover			175.00
136L7	L253	(2c) black, blue gray		100.00	85.00
		On cover			175.00
136L8	L253	(2c) blue		—	90.00
		On cover			300.00
136L9	L254	(1c) red		—	20.00
		On cover			150.00
136L10	L254	(1c) pink		—	15.00
		On cover			150.00
136L11	L254	(1c) red, bluish		—	25.00

136L12	L254	(1c) *pink, bluish*	—	175.00
		On cover		175.00
		On cover	—	175.00

Bouton's Stamp with Red ms. "Swarts" at Top

136L13	L149	2c *gray blue*	250.00	250.00
		On cover		500.00

L255

Printed in sheets of 25 (5x5). Five minor varieties, the stamps in each vertical row being identical.

136L14	L255	1c blue	—	40.00
		On cover		200.00
a.		Thin paper	5.00	
		As "a," block of four	25.00	
136L15	L255	1c red	—	50.00
		On cover		250.00
136L16	L255	1c red, *bluish*	—	75.00
		On cover		350.00
136L17	L255	1c black, on cover		1250.00

Nos. 136L3-136L4, 136L9-136L10, 136L14-136L15 have been reprinted.

Cancellations: Red boxed "PAID" (mostly on Nos. 136L1-136L8, 136L13). Black boxed "PAID SWARTS" (mostly on Nos. 136L9-136L12). Black oval "Swarts Post Office Chatham Square" (Nos. 136L9-136L12). Black oval "Swarts B Post Chatham Square". Black grids (5-bar rectangle, 6-bar circle, solid star, hollow star, star in circle, etc.) Other handstamp postmarks of the post have been found as cancellations. Government town postmarks exist on almost all Swarts stamps.

Feese & Co. Penny Post, Philadelphia, Pa.

 L256

Printed in sheet of 200 divided into two panes of 100. Each pane includes setting of 20, repeated 5 times. Vertical or horizontal tete beche pairs appear twice in each setting. Twenty varieties.

1852		**Wove Paper**		**Litho.**
137L1	L256	(1c) blue, *bluish*	6.50	35.00
		On cover		400.00
		Block of four	35.00	
a.		Tete beche pair	45.00	

Telegraph Despatch P. O., Philadelphia, Pa.

 L257

1848				
138L1	L257	1c black, *yellowish*		600.00
138L2	L257	2c black, *yellowish*		2,000.

The 2c differs in design, including the address, "Office No. 6 Sth 8 St" at bottom.

Third Avenue Post Office, New York, N. Y.

Established by S. Rotheneim, a former carrier for Boyd's City Express. All stamps were cut to shape by hand before being sold and exist only in that form.

L258

1855		**Glazed Surface Paper**		**Handstamped**
139L1	L258	2c green	250.00	250.00
		On cover		700.00
139L1A	L258	2c blue, *green*	400.00	
139L2	L258	2c maroon	400.00	
		Unsurfaced Paper colored through		
139L3	L258	2c yellow		200.00
139L4	L258	2c blue		450.00
139L5	L258	2c brown		450.00
139L6	L258	2c buff		250.00

139L7	L258	2c *pink*	450.00	
139L8	L258	2c *green*	400.00	400.00

Cancellation on No. 139L1: Black "PAID".

Union Post, New York, N. Y.

L259

1846		**Thick Glazed Surface Paper**		**Handstamped**
140L3	L259	blue, *green* ("UNOIN")		3,000.
140L4	L259	red, *blue* ("UNION")		2,000.
		On cover		—

Type L259 was used also as a postmark, usually struck in blue.

Union Square Post Office, New York, N. Y.

Established by Joseph E. Dunham about 1850. In 1851 Dunham acquired Messenkope's Union Square Post Office, operating the combined posts until 1854 or 1855. The business was sold in 1855 to Phineas C. Godfrey.

L259a   L260

1852				**Typo.**
141L1	L259a	1c *dark green*	6.00	20.00
		On cover		250.00
141L2	L259a	1c *light apple green*	30.00	40.00
		On cover		200.00
141L3	L260	2c *rose*	1.75	
		Block of four	8.50	

Walton & Co.'s City Express, Brooklyn, N. Y.

Operated by Wellington Walton

 L261

1846		**Glazed Surface Paper**		**Litho.**
142L1	L261	2c *pink*	400.00	300.00
		On cover		700.00

Cancellations: Black "PAID / W. W." Black oblong quad (ties stamp "through" to cover).

Wells, Fargo and Co.

Wells, Fargo & Company entered the Western field about July 1, 1852, to engage in business on the Pacific Coast, and soon began to acquire other express businesses, eventually becoming the most important express company in its territory.

The Central Overland, California and Pikes Peak Express Company, inaugurated in 1860, was the pioneer Pony Express system and was developed to bring about quicker communication between the extreme portions of the United States. Via water the time was 28 to 30 days, with two monthly sailings, and by the overland route the time was 28 days. In 1860 the pioneer Pony Express carried letters only, reducing the time for the 2,100 miles (St. Joseph to San Francisco) to about 12 days. The postage rate was originally $5 the half-ounce.

About April 1, 1861, Wells, Fargo & Company became agents for the Central Overland, California and Pikes Peak Express Company and issued $2 red and $4 green stamps.

The rates were cut in half about July 1, 1861, and new stamps were issued: the $1 red, $2 green and $4 black, and the $1 garter design.

The revival of the Pony Express in 1862, known as the "Virginia City Pony" resulted in the appearance of the "cents" values, first rate.

Advertisement in the Placerville newspaper, Aug. 7, 1862: "Wells, Fargo & Co.'s Pony Express. On and after Monday, the 11th inst., we will run a Pony Express Daily between Sacramento and Virginia City, carrying letters and exchange papers, through from San Francisco in 24 hours, Sacramento in 15 hours and Placerville in 10 hours. Rates: All letters to be enclosed in our franks, and TEN CENTS PRE-PAID, in addition, for each letter weighing half an ounce or less, and ten cents for each additional half-ounce."

Wells, Fargo & Company used various hand-stamps to indicate mail transit. These are illustrated and described in the handbook, "Wells, Fargo & Co.'s Handstamps and Franks" by V. M. Berthold, published by Scott Stamp & Coin Co., Ltd. (out of print). The history of the Pony Express, a study of the stamps and reprints, and a survey of existing covers are covered in "The Pony Express," by M. C. Nathan and Winthrop S. Boggs, published by the Collectors Club, 22 E. 35th., New York, N.Y. 10016.

Wells Fargo stamps of types L262-L264 were lithographed by Britton & Rey, San Francisco.

L262

Printed in sheets of 40 (8x5), two panes of 20 (4x5) each.

1861		**(April to July 1)**		**Litho.**
143L1	L262	$2 red	100.00	250.00
		On U. S. envelope No. U10		—
		On U. S. envelope No. U16		—
		On U. S. envelope No. U17		6,000.
		On U. S. envelope No. U18		6,000.
		On U. S. envelope No. U32 (patriotic cover)		13,000.
		On U. S. envelope No. U33		6,000.
		On U. S. envelope No. U65		—
143L2	L262	$4 green	200.00	400.00
		Block of four	—	
		On U. S. envelope No. U33		—
1861		**(July 1 to Nov.)**		
143L3	L262	$1 red	60.00	135.00
		Block of four	325.00	
		On U. S. envelope No. U11		—
		On U. S. envelope No. U15		4,500.
		On U. S. envelope No. U17		4,500.
		On U. S. envelope No. U32		6,000.
		On U. S. envelope No. U33		6,000.
		On U. S. envelope No. U35		4,500.
		On U. S. envelope No. U40		6,000.
		On U. S. envelope No. U41		5,000.
143L4	L262	$2 green	150.00	250.00
		Block of four	900.00	
		On U. S. envelope No. U41		11,000.
143L5	L262	$4 black	125.00	500.00
		Block of four	—	
		On cover		—

Cancellations: Blue, black or magenta express company. Nos. 143L1-143L5 and 143L7-143L9 were reprinted in 1897. The reprints are retouched. Shades vary from originals. Originals and reprints are fully described in "The Pony Express," by M. C. Nathan and W. S. Boggs (Collectors Club).

L263

Printed in sheets of 16 (4x4)

1861

Thin Wove Paper

143L6	L263	$1 blue	300.00	600.00
		On 10c U.S. envel-ope No. U40		17,500.

No. 143L6 apparently used only from east to west. One counterfeit has a horizontal line bisecting the shield. Another, without the line, is sometimes called a reprint.

L264

Printed in sheets of 40 (8x5), four panes of 10, each pane 2x5.

1862-64

143L7	L264	10c brown (shades)	30.00	75.00
		Pair	75.00	350.00
		Block of four	250.00	
		On U.S. envelope No. U26		5,000.
		On U.S. envelope No. U34		4,500.
		On U.S. envelope No. U35		3,500.
		On cover with 3c #65		—
143L8	L264	25c blue	50.00	75.00
		Pair	125.00	
		Block of four	350.00	
		On plain cover		2,250.
		On U.S. envelope No. U10		—
		On U.S. envelope No. U34		3,500.
		On U.S. envelope No. U35		4,000.
143L9	L264	25c red	20.00	40.00
		Pair	60.00	
		Block of four	150.00	
		On U.S. envelope No. U9		—
		On U.S. envelope No. U10		4,000.
		On U.S. envelope No. U34		4,000.
		On U.S. envelope No. U35		4,000.
		Pair on U.S. envel-ope No. U35		9,000.

Cancellations on Nos. 143L7-143L9: Blue or black express company. Black town.

NEWSPAPER STAMPS

L265

L266

L267

L268

L269

L270

1861-70

143LP1	L265	black	250.00	300.00
143LP2	L266	blue	350.00	
143LP3	L267	blue	10.00	
a.		Thin paper	20.00	
143LP4	L268	blue	25.00	

Perf. Rouletted 10

143LP5	L267	blue	15.00	25.00
		On wrapper		
		Block of four	75.00	
a.		Thin paper	15.00	
143LP6	L268	blue	15.00	
a.		Tete beche	100.00	

Type L267 was printed in sheets of 50 (5x10).

1883-88   **Perf. 11, 12, 12½**

143LP7	L268	blue		7.50
143LP8	L269	blue	12.50	17.50
143LP9	L270	blue	2.00	2.50
		On wrapper		
a.		Vertical pair, imperf. between	60.00	
b.		Horiz. pair, imperf. vert.	—	
		Double transfer	—	

FOR PUBLISHERS' USE

L271

1876   **Typo.**

143LP10	L271	blue	6.00	15.00
		Block of four	30.00	
		On wrapper		500.00

Cancellation: Blue company

ENVELOPES

1862

143LU1	L264	10c red	—	750.00
143LU2	L264	10c blue	—	750.00
143LU3	L264	25c red	350.00	
		On "Gould & Curry" overall advertising envelope	350.00	

Westervelt's Post, Chester, N. Y.

Operated by Charles H. Westervelt. Rate was 1 cent for letters and 2 cents for packages carried to the post office. Local and government postage required prepayment.

L273

Several varieties

1863 (?)   **Typeset**

144L1	L273	(1c) *flesh*	20.00	
		On cover		500.00
144L2	L273	*lavender*	25.00	
		On cover		—

Indian Chief — L274

General U. S. Grant — L275

Six varieties

1864 (?)   **Typeset**

144L9	L274	(1c) red, *pink*	20.00	
		On cover		500.00

Six varieties

1865   **Typo.**

144L29	L275	2c *yellow*	20.00	—
144L30	L275	2c *gray green*	25.00	—
144L40	L275	2c red, *pink*	25.00	—

All of the Westervelt stamps are believed to have a philatelic flavor, although it is possible that Nos. 144L1-144L2 were originally issued primarily for postal purposes. It is possible that Nos. 144L9, 144L29-144L30 and 144L40 were used in the regular course of business, particularly No. 144L9.

However, the large number of varieties on various colors of paper, which exist both as originals as well as contemporary and near-contemporary reprints, are believed to have been produced solely for sale to collectors. Type L275 was certainly issued primarily for sale to collectors. Many of the unlisted colors in all three types exist only as reprints. Forgeries of all three types also exist.

L276

ENVELOPES

Impressed at top left

1865   **Typo.**

144LU1	L276	red, *white*	—	
144LU2	L276	red brown, *orange*	—	200.00
144LU3	L276	black, *bluish*	—	
144LU4	L276	black, *buff*	—	
144LU5	L276	black, *white*	—	

It is possible that Nos. 114LU1-144LU5 were corner cards and had no franking value.

Westtown, Westtown, Pa.

The Westtown School at Westtown, Pa., is the oldest of the secondary schools in America, managed by the Society of Friends. It was established in 1799. In 1853 the school authorities decided that all outgoing letters carried by stage should pay a fee of 2 cents. Prepaid stamps were placed on sale at the school. Stamps were usually affixed to the reverse of the letter sheets or envelopes.

At first, letters were usually mailed at West Chester, Pa. After March 4, 1859, letters were sent from Street Road Post Office, located at the railroad station. Later this became the Westtown Post Office. The larger stamp was the first used. The smaller stamp came into use about 1867.

L277

L277a

Several types of each, with and without hyphen

1853-67(?)   **Litho.**

145L1	L277	(2c) gold	30.00	
145L2	L277a	(2c) gold	12.50	30.00
		On cover		110.00
		Block of four	500.00	
a.		Tete beche pair	100.00	

No. 145L1 in red brown is a color changeling.

Whittelsey's Express, Chicago, Ill.

Operated by Edmund A. and Samuel M. Whittelsey

George Washington — L278

1857   **Typo.**
146L1   L278   2c red   600.00   1,000.
           Block of four   —
Cancellation: Blue oval "Whittelsey's Express".

Williams' City Post, Cincinnati, Ohio.
See Carriers' Stamps, No. 9LB1.

Wood & Co. City Despatch, Baltimore, Md.
Operated by W. Wood

 L280

1856   **Typeset**
148L1   L280   (1c) *yellow*   750.00

W. Wyman, Boston, Mass.
Established to carry mail between Boston and New
York

     L281

1844   **Litho.**
149L1   L281   5c black   —   150.00
           On cover   750.00
No. 149L1 may have been sold singly at 6 cents each.

Zieber's One Cent Dispatch, Pittsburgh, Pa.

 L282

1851   **Typeset**
150L1   L282   1c *gray blue*   3,000.
         Cancellation: Acid

For Local 151L1 see under **Friend's Boarding School.**

For Local 152L1 see under **Faunce's Penny Post.**

For Local 153L1 see under **Hackney & Bolte Penny Post.**

For Local 154L1 see under **A. W. Auner's Despatch Post.**

For Local 155L1 see under **McGreely's Express.**

For Local 156L1-2 see under **Spaulding's Penny Post.**

For Local 157L1 see under **Bush's Brooklyn City Express.**

For Local 158L1 see under **Smith & Stephens City Delivery.**

For Local 159L1-2 see under **Spence & Brown Express Post.**

For Local 160L1 see under **City Dispatch, New York City.**

For Local 161L1 see under **Clinton's Penny Post.**

For Local 162L1 see under **Rogers' Penny Post.**

For Local 163L1 see under **Blizzard Mail.**

For Local 164L1 see under **Freeman & Co.'s Express, New York City.**

For Local 165L1 see under **J. A. Howell's City Despatch**

LOCAL HANDSTAMPED COVERS

Accessory Transit Co. of Nicaragua

Black

Red, Black or Blue

A sub-variety shows "Leland" below "MAILS" in lower right corner.

Blue

1853

Barker's City Post, Boston, Mass.

Black

1856-57

Also known with "10" instead of "34" Court Square.

E. N. Barry's Despatch Post, New York City, N.Y.

Black

1852 (?)

See the "Information for Collectors" section at beginning of catalogue for an explanation of perforation types, imperforates and coils.

Bates & Co., New Bedford, Mass.
(Agent for Hale & Co. at New Bedford)

Red

1845

Branch Post Office, New York City, N. Y.
(Swarts' Chatham Square Post Office)

Red

1847

Brigg's Despatch, Philadelphia, Pa.

Black, Red or Blue

1848

Bush's Brooklyn City Express, Brooklyn, N. Y.

Red

1848

Cover shows red PAID.

City Despatch & Express, Baltimore, Md.

Black

1856

Cover shows black PAID.

City Despatch Post, New York City, N. Y.
(Used by Mead, successor to United States City Despatch Post.)

Black

1848

City Dispatch Post, Baltimore, Md.

Red brown

City Despatch & Express, Baltimore, Md.

Black

1850

United States postage and air mail first day covers are listed and priced in a separate section of the catalogue. See catalogue index.

Cole's City Despatch P. O., New York City, N. Y.
(Used by Cole with some of the City Despatch Post stamps.)

Black or Red

1848

Dunhams Post Office, New York City, N. Y.
(See Union Square Post Office).

Red

Gay, Kinsley & Co., Boston, Mass.
(A package express)

Red

Hanford's Pony Express Post, New York, N.Y.

Black or Red

1845

Hartford Penny Post, Hartford, Conn.

Black

1853

Hudson Street Post Office, New York City, N. Y.

Red

1850

Cover shows red PAID.

Jones & Russell's Pikes Peak Express Co., Denver, Colo.

Black

1859-60

Kenyon's Letter Office, 91 Wall St., New York City

Red

1859

Letter Express, San Francisco, Cal.
(See Gahagan & Howe, San Francisco, Cal.)

Blue

Libbey & Co.'s City Post, Boston, Mass.

**LIBBEY & CO'S
CITY POST.**
10 COURT SQUARE   Black or Red

1852

Cover has 3c 1851 postmarked Boston, Mass.

Manhattan Express, New York City, N. Y.
(W. V. Barr. See also Bouton's Manhattan Express.)

Red

1847

**New York Penny Post,
New York City, N. Y.**

Black or Red

1840-41

Also known with hour indicated.

Noisy Carriers, San Francisco, Cal.

Blue or Green

Blue

Black or Red

Pony Express

Blue or Red

1860

Blue (Enlarged)

Black or Carmine

Blue or Red

Black, Blue or Green

Black

Black or Blue

1853-56

Northern Liberties News Rooms, Philadelphia, Pa.

Black

Black

1836

Two types.   Press printed.

**Overton & Co.'s City Mail,
New York City, N. Y.**

Red

1845

from
St. Joseph, Mo.   Black or Green
Denver City, K. T.   Black
Leavenworth City, K. T. Black
San Francisco, Cal.   Blue

Black or Green

Red

Blue

1860

Rogers' Penny Post, Newark, N. J.

Black or Red

1856

Spark's Post Office, New York City, N. Y.

Spaulding's Penny Post, Buffalo, N. Y.

Black

1848

Spence & Brown Express Post, Philadelphia, Pa.

Black

1848

Stait's Despatch Post, Philadelphia, Pa. (Eagle City Post)

Black

1850

Red

Stone's City Post, New York City, N. Y.

Red

1859

J. W. Sullivan's Newspaper Office, San Francisco, Cal.

Black
or
Red

1854

Towle & Co. Letter Delivery, Boston, Mass.

Red

1847

Towle's City Dispatch Post, Boston, Mass.

Red

1849

Towle's City Post, Boston, Mass.

(Also 10
Court Sq.)
Red

1849
Cover shows PAID.

TELEGRAPH

These stamps were issued by the individual companies for use on their own telegrams, and can usually be divided into three classes: Free franking privileges issued to various railroad, newspaper and express company officials, etc., whose companies were large users of the lines; those issued at part cost to to the lesser officials of the same type companies; and those bearing values which were usually sold to the general public. Some of the companies on occasions granted the franking privilege to stockholders and minor State (not Federal) officials. Most Telegraph Stamps were issued in booklet form and will be found with one or more straight edges.

American Rapid Telegraph Company

Organized February 21st, 1879, in New York State. Its wires extended as far north as Boston, Mass., and west to Cleveland, Ohio. It was amalgamated with the Bankers and Merchants Telegraph Co., but when that company was unable to pay the fixed charges, the properties of the American Rapid Telegraph Company were sold on March 11th, 1891, to a purchasing committee comprised of James W. Converse and others. This purchasing committee deeded the property and franchise of the American Rapid Telegraph Company to the Western Union Telegraph Company on June 25th, 1894. Issued three types of stamps: Telegram, Collect and Duplicate. Telegram stamps were issued in sheets of 100 and were used to prepay messages which could be dropped in convenient boxes for collection. Collect and duplicate stamps were issued in alternate rows on the same sheet of 100 subjects. Collect stamps were attached to telegrams sent collect, the receiver of which paid the amount shown by the stamps, while the Duplicate stamps were retained by the Company as vouchers. Remainders with punched cancellations were bought up by a New York dealer.

T1

"Prepaid Telegram" Stamps
Engraved and Printed by the American Bank Note Co.

1881   **Perf. 12**

				Unused	Used	Punched
1T1	T1	1c	black	5.00	3.00	10
			Block of four	25.00		1.00
1T2	T1	3c	orange	17.50	12.50	1.00
			Block of four			10.00
1T3	T1	5c	bister brown	1.00	40	8
			Block of four	5.00		40
a.			5c brown	1.00	40	10
			Block of four	5.00		1.00
1T4	T1	10c	purple	7.00	4.00	10
			Block of four	35.00		1.00
1T5	T1	15c	green	2.50	75	10
			Block of four	12.50		1.00
1T6	T1	20c	red	2.50	60	8
			Block of four			80
1T7	T1	25c	rose	3.00	75	10
			Block of four	15.00		1.00
1T8	T1	50c	blue	6.00	4.00	60
			Block of four			6.00

T2

"Collect" Stamps

				Unused	Used	Punched
1T9	T2	1c	brown	3.00	2.50	10
1T10	T2	5c	blue	1.50	65	10
1T11	T2	15c	red brown	1.00	50	25
1T12	T2	20c	olive green	75	50	10

T3

"Office Coupon" Stamps

1T13	T3	1c	brown	5.00	1.75	10
a.			Pair, se-tenant with "Collect"			1.50
			Block of four, same as "a"			3.25
1T14	T3	5c	blue	4.00	1.50	10
a.			Pair, se-tenant with "Collect"	12.50		2.25
			Block of four, same as "a"	25.00		5.00
1T15	T3	15c	red brown	7.50	2.00	20
a.			Pair, se-tenant with "Collect"	12.50		2.50
			Block of four, same as "a"	27.50		5.50
1T16	T3	20c	olive green	7.50	2.50	10
a.			Pair, se-tenant with "Collect"			2.75
			Block of four, same as "a"			6.00

Atlantic Telegraph Company

Organized 1884 at Portland, Maine. Its lines extended from Portland, Me., to Boston, Mass., and terminated in the office of the Baltimore and Ohio Telegraph Company at Boston. Later bought out by the Baltimore and Ohio Telegraph Co. Stamps issued by the Atlantic Telegraph Company could also be used for messages destined to any point on the Baltimore and Ohio system. Stamps were printed in panes of six and a full book sold for $10. Remainders of these stamps, without control numbers, were purchased by a Boston dealer and put on the market about 1932.

T4

1888   **Perf. 13**

				Unused	Used	Remainders (no control numbers)
2T1	T4	1c	green	3.50	—	2.00
			Pane of six	—		14.00
2T2	T4	5c	blue	3.50	—	2.00
			Pane of six	—		14.00
a.			Imperf. vert., pair	—		
b.			Imperf. horiz., pair	20.00	—	
2T3	T4	10c	purple brown	3.50	—	2.00
			Pane of six	—		14.00
a.			Horiz. pair, imperf. between	30.00		
2T4	T4	25c	carmine	3.50	—	2.25
			Pane of six			16.00

Baltimore & Ohio Telegraph Companies

"The Baltimore & Ohio Telegraph Co. of the State of New York" was incorporated May 17, 1882. Organization took place under similar charter in 26 other states. It absorbed the National Telegraph Co. and several others. Extended generally along the lines of the Baltimore & Ohio Railroad, but acquired interests in other states. Company absorbed in 1887 by the Western Union Telegraph Co. Stamps were issued in booklet form and sold for $5.00 and $10.00, containing all denominations.

T5   T6

Engraved by the American Bank Note Co.

1885   **Perf. 12**

3T1	T5	1c	vermilion	25.00	10.00
			Pane of six	160.00	
3T2	T5	5c	blue	25.00	20.00
3T3	T5	10c	red brown	12.00	8.00
			Pane of six	75.00	
3T4	T5	25c	orange	25.00	12.00
3T5	T6		brown	1.00	
			Pane of four	6.00	

1886

3T6	T6		black	1.00	
			Pane of four	6.00	

Imprint of Kendall Bank Note Co.
Thin Paper

1886   **Perf. 14**

3T7	T5	1c	green	5.00	50
a.			Thick paper	7.00	85
b.			Imperf., pair	60.00	
3T8	T5	5c	blue	3.00	75
a.			Thick paper	5.00	75
b.			Imperf. pair		50.00
3T9	T5	10c	brown	5.00	60
a.			Thick paper	7.00	85
3T10	T5	25c	deep orange	15.00	75
a.			Thick paper	15.00	1.00

Used copies of Nos. 3T7-3T20 normally have heavy grid cancellations. Lightly canceled copies command a premium.

Litho. by A. Hoen & Co.

1886   **Imprint of firm**   **Perf. 12**

3T11	T5	1c	green	2.50	25
			Pane of six	17.50	
3T12	T5	5c	blue	6.50	25
			Pane of six	40.00	
a.			Imperf., pair	75.00	
3T13	T5	10c	dark brown	5.00	40
			Pane of six	32.50	—
a.			Vertical pair, imperf. between		50.00

Wmk. "A HOEN AND CO. BALTIMORE" in double lined capitals in sheet
Perf. 12

3T14	T5	1c	green	7.00	1.00
			Pane of six	45.00	—
3T15	T5	5c	blue	12.50	1.00
			Pane of six	80.00	—
a.			Imperf., pair	40.00	
3T16	T5	10c	dark brown	9.00	85
			Pane of six	60.00	—

Lithographed by Forbes Co., Boston

1887   **Imprint of firm**   **Perf. 12½**

3T17	T5	1c	green	21.00	1.00
3T18	T5	5c	blue	22.50	1.50
3T19	T5	10c	brown	16.00	1.50
3T20	T5	25c	yellow	21.00	1.00
a.			25c orange	21.00	1.00

Baltimore & Ohio-Connecticut River Telegraph Companies

The Connecticut River Telegraph Co. ran from New Haven to Hartford. An agreement was entered wherein the Baltimore &, Ohio System had mutual use of their lines. This agreement terminated when the Baltimore & Ohio System was absorbed by the Western Union. The Connecticut River Telegraph Company then joined the United Lines. In 1885 stamps (black on yellow) were issued and sold in booklets for $10. In 1887 the Connecticut River Telegraph Co. had extended its lines to New Boston, Mass., and new books of stamps (black on blue) were issued for use on this extension. Remainders were cancelled with bars and sold to a New York dealer.

T7

1885 — Perf. 11

			Unused	Used	Remainders (Bar canc.)
4T1	T7	1c yellow	3.00	7.50	30
		Pane of ten	35.00		4.00
	a.	Imperf., pair	40.00		—
	b.	Imperf. horizontally, pair			—
4T2	T7	5c yellow	3.00	7.50	25
		Pane of ten	35.00		3.00
	a.	Horizontal pair, imperf. between			—
	b.	Vertical pair, imperf. between			35.00
	c.	Imperf., pair			35.00
4T3	T7	1c blue	7.00	—	2.00
		Pane of ten	80.00		22.50
4T4	T7	5c blue	6.00	—	2.00
		Pane of ten	65.00		22.50

California State Telegraph Company

Incorporated June 17, 1854 as the California Telegraph Company and constructed a line from Nevada through Grass Valley to Auburn. Extended to run from San Francisco to Marysville via San Jose and Stockton. Later absorbed Northern Telegraph Co. and thus extended to Eureka. It was incorporated as the California State Telegraph Company on April 6, 1861. At the time of its lease to the Western Union on May 16, 1867 the California State consisted of the following companies which had been previously absorbed: Alta California Telegraph Co., Atlantic and Pacific States Telegraph Co., National Telegraph Co., Northern California Telegraph Co., Overland Telegraph Co., Placerville and Humboldt Telegraph Co., Tuolumne Telegraph Co. Stamps were issued in booklets, six to a pane. Remainders of Nos. 5T1 and 5T4, without frank numbers are known.

T8

1870 — Perf. 13½

5T1	T8	black & blue	65.00	
		Pane of six	400.00	
	a.	Without number	55.00	

T9

T10

1870 — Perf. 12, 13

5T2	T9	black & red, without number	135.00	135.00

1871 — Dated "1871"

5T3	T9	black & red, without number	225.00	
	a.	Imperf., pair		—
5T4	T10	black & salmon, blue number	125.00	—
		Pane of six		—
	a.	Without number	90.00	

1872

5T5	T10	green & red, red number (No year date)	100.00	—
		Pane of six		—

1873 — Dated "1873"

5T6	T10	red & salmon, blue number	140.00	140.00

1874 — Dated "1874"

5T7	T10	blue & salmon, black number	75.00	—
		Pane of six		—

1875 — Dated "1875"

5T8	T10	brown & green, black number	100.00	—
		Pane of six		—

City & Suburban Telegraph Company
(New York City and Suburban Printing Telegraph Company)

Organized 1855. Extended only through New York City and Brooklyn. Sold out to the American Telegraph Co. Stamps were sold to the public for prepayment of messages, which could be dropped in convenient boxes for collection. Stamps were issued in sheets of 60 having a face value of $1.00. These were arranged in six vertical rows of ten, the horizontal rows having the following denominations: 2c, 1c, 1c, 1c, 2c, 3c.

Counterfeits are known both in black and blue, mostly on pelure or hard white paper. Originals are on soft wove paper, somewhat yellowish. Scalloped edge is more sharply etched on the counterfeits.

T11

			Typo.	Imperf.
6T1	T11	1c black	120.00	100.00
		Pair	—	
		Block of four	—	
6T2	T11	2c black	200.00	140.00
		Pair	—	
		Pair, 2c + 1c	375.00	
6T3	T11	3c black	325.00	225.00
		Pair	—	
		Strip of three, 1c, 2c and 3c	1100.	

Colusa, Lake & Mendocino Telegraph Company

Was organized in California early in 1873. First known as the Princeton, Colusa and Grand Island Telegraph Co. In May, 1873 they completed their line from Princeton through Colusa, at which point it was connected with the Western Union office, to Grand Island. On Feb. 10, 1875 it was incorporated as the Colusa, Lake & Mendocino Telegraph Co. Its lines were extended into the counties of Colusa, Lake, Mendocino and Napa. Eventually reached a length of 260 miles. Went out of business in 1892. Stamps were issued for prepayment of messages and were sold in books. When sold they were stamped "P.L.W." (the superintendent's initials) in blue. The 5c value was printed 10 to a pane, being two horizontal rows of five. Of the 10c and 25c nothing definite is known about the settings.

T11a

1876 — Perf. 12

7T1	T11a	5c black	175.00	—
		Block of four	750.00	
		Pane of ten	2000.	
		Without "P.L.W."	225.00	
7T2	T11a	10c black	9000.	—
7T3	T11a	25c red	9000.	—

Commercial Union Telegraph Company

Incorporated in New York State on March 31, 1886. Its lines ran from Albany through Troy to Berlin, N.Y., thence to North Adams, Mass. The lines of this Company, which was controlled by the Postal Telegraph Company, were later extended throughout Northern New York and the States of Massachusetts, Vermont, New Hampshire and Maine. Stamps issued in panes of four.

T12

T13

T14

1891 — Lithographed by A. C. Goodwin — Perf. 12

8T1	T12	25c yellow	12.50	—
		Pane of four	55.00	
8T2	T13	25c green	10.00	—
		Pane of four	45.00	
	a.	Imperf. vertically (pair)	40.00	
8T3	T14	lilac rose	25.00	—

Mutual Union Telegraph Company

Incorporated October 4, 1880. Extended over 22 states. Absorbed about 1883 by the Western Union Telegraph Co. Franks issued for use of stockholders, in books, four to a pane.

T15

Engr. by Van Campen Engraving Co., New York
1882-83 — Perf. 14

9T1	T15	blue	20.00	20.00
		Pane of four	90.00	
	a.	Imperf. horizontally (pair)	60.00	
	b.	Imperf., pair	60.00	
9T2	T15	carmine	20.00	—
		Pane of four	90.00	

North American Telegraph Company

Incorporated October 15, 1885 to run from Chicago to Minneapolis, later being extended into North and South Dakota. Absorbed In 1929 by the Postal System.

Apparently these stamps were not cancelled when used. Issued in panes of four.

T15a

1899-1907 — Perf. 12

10T1	T15a	violet (1899)	50.00	
		Pane of four	210.00	
10T2	T15a	green (1901)	70.00	
10T3	T15a	dark brown (1902)	100.00	
10T4	T15a	blue (1903)	70.00	
10T5	T15a	violet (1904)	65.00	
		Pane of four	275.00	
	a.	Imperf. vertically (pair)	200.00	
10T6	T15a	red brown (1905)	50.00	
10T7	T15a	rose (1906)	65.00	
10T8	T15a	red brown (1907)	325.00	

Nos. 10T1 to 10T8 are known imperforate.

Northern Mutual Telegraph Company

Incorporated in New York State as the Northern Mutual Telegraph and Telephone Company on June 20, 1882. Its line, which consisted of a single wire, extended from Syracuse to Ogdensburg via Oswego, Watertown and Clayton, a distance of 170 miles. It was sold to the Bankers and Merchants Telegraph Company in 1883. Stamps were in use for a few days only in April, 1883. Issued in panes of 35 having a face value of $5.00. Seven horizontal rows of five covering all denominations as follows: 2 rows of 25c, 1 of 20c, 2 of 10c, 2 of 5c. The remainders and plates were purchased by a New York dealer in 1887.

T16

			1883			**Perf. 14**
11T1	T16	5c	yellow brown		4.00	—
			Block of four		17.50	
11T2	T16	10c	yellow brown		4.00	—
			Block of four		17.50	
11T3	T16	20c	yellow brown		10.00	—
			Horizontal pair		22.50	
11T4	T16	25c	yellow brown		4.00	—
			Block of four		17.50	
			Pane of 35		225.00	

The first reprints are lighter in color than the originals, perf. 14 and the gum is yellowish instead of white. The pane makeup differs in the reprints. The second reprints are darker than the original, perf. 12. Price 75c each.

Northern New York Telegraph Company

Organized about 1892. Extended from Malone, N. Y. to Massena, N.Y. Re-incorporated as the New York Union Telegraph Co. on April 2, 1896.

T16a

Typo. by Charles H. Smith, Brushton, N.Y.

		1894-95			**Rouletted**
12T1	T16a	green (overprinted in red "Frank 1894")		45.00	
		Pane of six		275.00	
	a.	Imperf. pair		50.00	
12T2	T16a	red (overprinted in black "Frank 1895")		150.00	
		Pane of six		1000.	
	a.	Imperf. pair		50.00	
12T3	T16a	1c yellow (overprinted in black "One")		80.00	
		Pane of 6		500.00	
	a.	Imperf. pair		50.00	
12T4	T16a	10c blue (overprinted in red "10")		125.00	
		Pane of six		800.00	
	a.	Imperf. pair		50.00	

Some specialists believe that Nos. 12T1-12T4 were not issued and probably are essays.

Pacific Mutual Telegraph Company

Incorporated in Missouri on June 21, 1883. Operated between St. Louis and Kansas City, Mo., during the years 1884 and 1885. It had 15 offices, 425 miles of poles and 850 miles of wire. The controlling interests were held by the Bankers and Merchants Telegraph Company. The name was changed on Sept. 10, 1910 to Postal Telegraph-Cable Company of Missouri. Stamps were issued in booklets having a face value of $10 and containing 131 stamps as follows: 50-1c, 20-5c, 45-10c, 16-25c. They are not known used.

T17

		1883			**Perf. 12**
13T1	T17	1c black		22.50	
13T2	T17	1c slate		35	
		Block of four		1.50	
	a.	1c gray		35	
		Block of four		1.50	
13T3	T17	5c buff		40	
		Block of four		1.75	

13T4	T17	10c green		25
		Block of four		1.25
	a.	Horizontal pair, imperf. between		—
13T5	T17	25c salmon buff		30
		Block of four		1.50

Pacific Postal Telegraph-Cable Company

The Pacific Postal Telegraph-Cable Company was the Pacific Coast Department of the Postal Telegraph-Cable Company, and was organized in 1886. Its first wire ran from San Francisco to New Westminster, B.C., where it touched the lines of the Canadian Pacific Railway Company, then the only connection between the Eastern and Western Postal systems. Later the Postal's own wires spanned the continent and the two companies were united.

Stamps issued in booklet form in vertical panes of five.

T16b

Perf. 12xImperf.

14T1	T16b	10c brown		30.00	25.00
		Pane of five		150.00	
14T2	T16b	15c black		20.00	15.00
		Pane of five		105.00	
14T3	T16b	25c rose red		30.00	25.00
		Pane of five		160.00	
14T4	T16b	40c green		25.00	20.00
		Pane of five		135.00	
14T5	T16b	50c blue		30.00	25.00
		Pane of five		160.00	

These stamps were issued with three sizes of frank numbers; large closely spaced, small closely spaced and small widely spaced figures.

They also exist without frank numbers.

Postal Telegraph Company

Organized in New York in 1881. Reorganized in 1891 as the Postal Telegraph-Cable Co. The Postal Telegraph Co stamps of 1885 were issued in sheets of 100. Some years after the reorganization a New York dealer purchased the remainders which were cancelled with a purple star. The Postal Telegraph-Cable Co. issued frank stamps in booklets, usually four stamps to a pane. This company was merged with the Western Union Telegraph Company in 1943.

T18

T19

T20

T21

Engraved by Hamilton Bank Note Co.

		1885				**Perf. 14**
				Unused	Used	Remainders (Purple Star)
15T1	T18	10c green		1.75	—	25
		Block of four		8.00		1.25
	a.	Horizontal pair, imperf. between				20.00
	b.	10c deep green		1.75	—	25
		Block of four		8.00		1.25
15T2	T19	15c orange red		2.50	—	60
		Block of four		12.00		3.00
	a.	Horizontal pair, imperf. between		25.00		
15T3	T20	25c blue		1.00	4.00	15
		Block of four		5.00		75
	a.	Horizontal pair, imperf. between		30.00		
15T4	T21	50c brown		1.50	—	60
		Block of four		7.00		3.00

The 25c in ultramarine and the 50c in black were printed and perforated 16 but are not known to have been issued. Price about $5 each.

T22

T22a

Typographed by Moss Engraving Co.

		1892-1920			**Perf. 14**

Signature of A.B. Chandler

15T5	T22	blue gray	(1892)	15.00	
	a.	Imperf., pair		50.00	

Perf. 13 to 14½ and Compound

15T6	T22	gray lilac	(1892)	15.00	
15T7	T22	red	(1893)	12.00	10.00
		Pane of four		50.00	
15T8	T22	red brown	(1893)	4.00	3.00

Perf. 12

15T9	T22	violet brown	(1894)	6.00	
15T10	T22	gray green	(1894)	4.00	
	a.	Imperf., pair		20.00	
15T11	T22	blue	(1895)	20.00	
15T12	T22	rose	(1895)	100.00	
15T13	T22a	slate green	(1896)	5.00	
		Pane of four		17.50	
15T14	T22	brown	(1896)	80.00	

Nos. 15T11 and 15T12 are from a new die resembling T22 but without shading under "Postal Telegraph Co."

Signature of Albert B. Chandler

15T15	T22a	lilac brown	(1897)	1.50	
		Pane of four		6.50	
15T16	T22a	orange	(1897)	65.00	

Typographed by Knapp & Co.

15T17	T22a	pale blue	(1898)	1.25	
		Pane of four		5.50	
15T18	T22a	rose	(1898)	85.00	

Typographed by Moss Engraving Co.

Perf. 12

15T19	T22a	orange brown	(1899)	1.25	
		Pane of four		5.50	

Perf. 11

15T20	T22a	blue	(1900)	3.00	3.00
	a.	"I" "Complimentary" omitted		40	80
		Pane of four		2.50	

The variety 15T20a represents a different die with many variations in the design.

Perf. 14

15T21	T22a	sea green	(1901)	40	40
		Pane of four		1.75	
	a.	Horiz. pair, imperf. between			

Signature of John W. Mackay

15T22	T22a	chocolate	(1902)	50	60
		Pane of four		2.50	

Signature of Clarence H. Mackay

15T23	T22a	blue	(1903)	2.50	2.50
		Pane of four		2.50	

Perf. 12

15T24	T22a	blue, blue	(1904)	2.00	2.00
		Pane of four		9.00	
15T25	T22a	blue, yellow	(1905)	4.50	
		Pane of four		20.00	
15T26	T22a	blue, light blue	(1906)	3.00	
		Pane of four		13.00	
	a.	Imperf. vertically, pair		—	

T22b

T22c

Perf. 12

15T27	T22b	yellow (laid paper)	(1907)	25.00	
		Pane of four		105.00	
15T28	T22b	blue, pink (laid paper)	(1907)	17.50	
		Pane of four		75.00	

"One Telegram of 10 Words"

15T29	T22c	blue	(1908)	25.00	
		Pane of four		105.00	
15T30	T22c	yellow	(1908)	85.00	

	Pane of four			350.00
15T31	T22c black		(1908)	22.50
	Pane of four			95.00
15T32	T22c brown		(1909)	20.00
	Pane of four			85.00
a.	Date reads "1908"			100.00
15T33	T22c olive green		(1909)	12.50
	Pane of four			55.00
15T34	T22c dark blue		(1910)	17.50
15T35	T22c dark brown		(1910)	15.00
15T36	T22c violet		(1911)	120.00
15T37	T22c blue		(1912)	130.00
15T38	T22c violet		(1913)	130.00

Perf. 14

15T39	T22c violet (not dated)		(1914)	40.00
a.	Red violet			40.00
	Pane of four			170.00

"One Telegram"
Perf. 12

15T40	T22c blue,		(1908)	30.00
	Pane of four			125.00
15T41	T22c lilac		(1909)	15.00
	Pane of four			60.00
15T42	T22c yellow (laid paper)		(1910)	85.00
15T43	T22c violet		(1910)	10.00
a.	Red violet			10.00
	Pane of four			—
	Pane of eight			90.00
15T44	T22c dark blue,		(1911)	25.00
	Pane of four			100.00
15T45	T22c light violet,		(1912)	20.00
	Pane of four			85.00

Perf. 14

15T46	T22c dark blue		(1913)	60.00
	Pane of eight			500.00
a.	Imperf. vertically, pair			100.00
b.	Perf. 12			40.00
15T47	T22c dark blue, (not dated)		(1914)	20
	Pane of four			1.50
	Pane of eight			2.50

In panes of four the stamps are 4½mm. apart horizontally, panes of eight 5½mm. There are two types of design T22c, one with and one without spurs on colored curved lines above "O" of "Postal" and below "M" of "Company". Both types are known of 15T47.

Nos. 15T39 and 15T47 handstamped with date in double line numerals, all four numerals complete on each stamp.

15T47A	T22c violet		(1916)	300.00
15T48	T22c dark blue		(1917)	600.00
15T49	T22c dark blue		(1918)	700.00
15T49A	T22c dark blue		(1919)	70.00
15T49B	T22c dark blue		(1920)	60.00

No. 15T49B is handstamped "1920" in small single line numerals.

T22d

1907　　　　　　　　　　　*Perf. 12*

15T50	T22d 1c dark brown		20.00	20.00
	Pane of four		85.00	
15T51	T22d 2c dull violet		20.00	20.00
	Pane of four		85.00	
15T52	T22d 5c green		20.00	20.00
	Pane of four		85.00	
15T53	T22d 25c light red		20.00	20.00
	Pane of four		85.00	

T22e

1931　　　　　　　　　　　*Perf. 14*

15T54	T22e 25c gray blue (1931)		25
	Pane of six		1.50

1932

Stamp of 1931 overprinted "1932" and control number in red.

15T55	T22e 25c gray blue		30.00
	Pane of six		200.00

Many varieties between Nos. 15T5 and 15T55 are known without frank numbers.

OFFICIAL

1900　　　Inscribed "Supts."　　　*Perf. 11, 12*

15TO1	T22c magenta		75 75

For Use of Railroad Superintendents
Perf. 12
"C. G. W." (Chicago, Great Western Railroad) at top

15TO2	T22c carmine		(1908)	30.00
	Pane of four			120.00
15TO3	T22c carmine		(1909)	45.00
15TO4	T22c carmine		(1910)	65.00
15TO5	T22c carmine		(1911)	40.00
15TO6	T22c carmine		(1912)	45.00

Perf. 14

15TO7	T22c carmine		(1913)	75.00
a.	Perf. 12			—
15TO8	T22c dull red (not dated)		(1914)	20
	Pane of eight			2.00

Perf. 12
"E. P." (El Paso and Northeastern Railroad) at top

15TO9	T22c orange		(1908)	60.00

"I. C." (Illinois Central Railroad) at top

15TO10	T22c green		(1908)	25.00
	Pane of four			110.00
15TO11	T22c yellow green		(1909)	9.00
	Pane of four			—
	Pane of eight			75.00
15TO12	T22c dark green		(1910)	50.00
15TO13	T22c dark green		(1911)	35.00
	Pane of four			140.00
	Pane of eight			285.00
15TO14	T22c dark green		(1912)	75.00
15TO15	T22c dark green		(1913)	125.00

Perf. 14

15TO16	T22c dark green (not dated)		(1914)	2.00
	Pane of four			9.00
	Pane of eight			17.50
a.	Green (spurs)			1.25
	Pane of four			6.00
b.	Line under "PRESI-DENT" (no spurs)			20
	Pane of eight			2.00

(See note after No. 15T47.)
Both types of design T22c are known of 15TO16.

Perf. 12
"O. D." (Old Dominion Steamship Co.) at top

15TO17	T22c violet		(1908)	225.00

"P. R." (Pennsylvania Railroad) at top

15TO18	T22c orange brown		(1908)	10.00
	Pane of four			42.50
	Pane of eight			90.00
15TO19	T22c orange brown		(1909)	25.00
	Pane of four			110.00
	Pane of eight			225.00
15TO20	T22c orange brown		(1910)	15.00
	Pane of four			65.00
	Pane of eight			125.00
15TO21	T22c orange brown		(1911)	55.00
15TO22	T22c orange brown		(1912)	45.00

Perf. 14

15TO23	T22c orange brown		(1913)	17.50
	Pane of eight			145.00
a.	Perf. 12			85.00

"P. R. R." (Pennsylvania Rail Road) at top

15TO24	T22c orange (not dated)		(1914)	20.00
	Pane of four			175.00

Perf. 12
"S. W." (El Paso Southwestern Railroad) at top

15TO25	T22c yellow		(1909)	90.00
15TO26	T22c yellow		(1910)	275.00
15TO27	T22c yellow		(1911)	85.00
15TO28	T22c yellow		(1912)	90.00
	Pane of four			375.00

Nos. 15TO1 to 15TO17 and 15TO25 to 15TO28 are without frank numbers.

TO1

1942　　　Litho.　　　Unwmk.

15TO29	TO1 5c pink		6.00	3.00
	Pane of eight		50.00	
15TO30	TO1 25c pale blue		7.00	4.00
	Pane of eight		57.50	

The stamps were issued in booklets to all Postal Telegraph employees in the Armed Forces for use in the United States.

They were discontinued Oct. 8, 1943. Used copies normally bear manuscript cancellations.

Western Union Telegraph Company

Organized by consolidation in 1856.
Now extends throughout the United States. Frank stamps have been issued regularly since 1871 in booklet form. The large size, early issues, were in panes of four, 1871-1913; the medium size, later issues, were in panes of six, 1914-32; and the recent small size issues are in panes of nine, 1933 to 1946.

T23　　　　　　　　　T24

Engraved by the National Bank Note Co.
1871-94　　　　　　　　　*Perf. 12*

Signature of William Orton

16T1	T23	green (not dated)	(1871)	20.00	
16T2	T23	red (not dated)	(1872)	20.00	
		Pane of four		85.00	
16T3	T23	blue (not dated)	(1873)	20.00	
		Pane of four		85.00	
16T4	T23	brown (not dated)	(1874)	20.00	
		Pane of four		85.00	
16T5	T24	deep green	(1875)	20.00	
16T6	T24	red	(1876)	17.50	
		Pane of four		75.00	
16T7	T24	violet	(1877)	20.00	
16T8	T24	gray brown	(1878)	22.50	

Signature of Norvin Green

16T9	T24	blue	(1879)	22.50	
		Pane of four		100.00	

Engraved by the American Bank Note Co.

16T10	T24	lilac rose	(1880)	15.00	
		Pane of four		65.00	
16T11	T24	green	(1881)	12.00	
		Pane of four		50.00	
16T12	T24	blue	(1882)	7.50	
		Pane of four		35.00	
16T13	T24	yellow brown	(1883)	15.00	
		Pane of four		65.00	
16T14	T24	gray violet	(1884)	40	30
		Pane of four		2.00	
16T15	T24	green	(1885)	2.00	1.25
		Pane of four		10.00	
16T16	T24	brown violet	(1886)	2.25	
		Pane of four		11.00	
16T17	T24	red brown	(1887)	4.00	
		Pane of four		20.00	
16T18	T24	blue	(1888)	2.00	
		Pane of four		10.00	
16T19	T24	olive green	(1889)	1.25	80
		Pane of four		5.00	
16T20	T24	purple	(1890)	60	40
		Pane of four		3.00	
16T21	T24	brown	(1891)	80	
		Pane of four		4.00	
16T22	T24	vermilion	(1892)	1.25	
		Pane of four		6.00	
16T23	T24	blue	(1893)	60	25
		Pane of four		3.00	

Signature of Thos. T. Eckert

16T24	T24	green	(1894)	50	40
		Pane of four		2.50	

T25

Engraved by the International Bank Note Co.
1895-1913　　　　　　　　　*Perf. 14*

16T25	T25	dark brown	(1895)	50	35
		pane of four		2.50	
16T26	T25	violet	(1896)	50	35
		Pane of four		2.50	
16T27	T25	rose red	(1897)	50	40
		Pane of four		2.50	

```
16T28  T25  yellow green          (1898)   50   40
            Pane of four                   2.50
      a.    Vert. pair, imperf.
            between                          —
16T29  T25  olive green           (1899)   40   40
            Pane of four                   2.00
16T30  T25  red violet, perf. 13  (1900)   50   45
            Pane of four                   2.25
16T31  T25  brown, perf. 13       (1901)   40
            Pane of four                   2.00
16T32  T25  blue                  (1902)   5.00
            Pane of four                  25.00
```

Signature of R.C. Clowry

```
16T33  T25  blue                  (1902)   5.00
            Pane of four                  25.00
16T34  T25  green                 (1903)   50   40
            Pane of four                   2.25
16T35  T25  red violet            (1904)   50
            Pane of four                   2.25
16T36  T25  carmine rose          (1905)   40   30
            Pane of four                   1.75
16T37  T25  blue                  (1906)   40   30
            Pane of four                   2.00
      a.    Vertical pair, imperf.,
            between                       30.00
16T38  T25  orange brown          (1907)   40   30
            Pane of four                   2.00
16T39  T25  violet                (1908)   75   40
            Pane of four                   4.00
16T40  T25  olive green           (1909)   1.00
            Pane of four                   5.00
```

Perf. 12

```
16T41  T25  buff                  (1910)   50   40
            Pane of four                   2.25
```

Engraved by the American Bank Note Co.
Signature of Theo. N. Vail

```
16T42  T24  green                 (1911)  10.00
            Pane of four                  50.00
16T43  T24  violet                (1912)   6.00
            Pane of four                  30.00
```

Imprint of Kihn Brothers Bank Note Company
Perf. 14

```
16T44  T24  brown                 (1913)  10.00
            Pane of four                  50.00
      a.    Vert. pair, imperf. be-
            tween                         35.00
      b.    Horiz. pair, imperf. be-
            tween                         40.00
```

T26   T27

Engraved by the E.A. Wright Bank Note Co.
1914-15 Signature of Theo. N. Vail Perf. 12

```
16T45  T26  5c  brown            (1914)   1.00
            Pane of six                   7.00
      a.    Vert. pair, imperf.
            between                         —
      b.    Horiz. pair, imperf.
            between                         —
16T46  T26  25c slate            (1914)   4.00  4.00
            Pane of six                  25.00
```

Signature of Newcomb Carlton

```
16T47  T26  5c  orange           (1915)   1.25
            Pane of six                   8.00
            orange yellow                 5.00
16T48  T26  25c olive green      (1915)   4.00
            Pane of six                  25.00
      a.    Imperf. horizontally
            (pair)                        45.00
```

Engraved by the American Bank Note Co.
1916-32

```
16T49  T27  5c  light blue       (1916)   1.50
            Pane of six                  10.00
16T50  T27  25c carmine lake     (1916)   1.50
            Pane of six                  10.00
```

Engraved by the Security Bank Note Co.
Perf. 11

```
16T51  T27  5c  yellow brown     (1917)   1.00
            Pane of six                   6.50
16T52  T27  25c deep green       (1917)   2.75
            Pane of six                  18.00
16T53  T27  5c  olive green      (1918)    60
            Pane of six                   4.00
16T54  T27  25c dark violet      (1918)   1.75
            Pane of six                  11.00
16T55  T27  5c  brown            (1919)   1.25
            Pane of six                   8.00
16T56  T27  25c blue             (1919)   3.00
            Pane of six                  20.00
```

Engraved by the E.A. Wright Bank Note Co.
Perf. 12

```
16T57  T27  5c  dark green       (1920)    50
            Pane of six                   3.25
```

```
      a.    Vert. pair, imperf
            between                         —
16T58  T27  25c olive green      (1920)    60
            Pane of six                   4.00
```

Engraved by the Security Bank Note Co.

```
16T59  T27  5c  carmine rose     (1921)    40
            Pane of six                   2.75
16T60  T27  25c deep blue        (1921)   1.00
            Pane of six                   6.50
16T61  T27  5c  yellow brown     (1922)    40
            Pane of six                   2.75
      a.    Horizontal pair, im-
            perf. between                12.00
16T62  T27  25c claret           (1922)   1.25
            Pane of six                   8.50
16T63  T27  5c  olive green      (1923)    50
            Pane of six                   3.25
16T64  T27  25c dull violet      (1923)   1.00
            Pane of six                   7.00
16T65  T27  5c  brown            (1924)   1.25
            Pane of six                   8.00
16T66  T27  25c ultramarine      (1924)   3.00
            Pane of six                  20.00
16T67  T27  5c  olive green      (1925)    40
            Pane of six                   2.75
16T68  T27  25c carmine rose     (1925)    75
            Pane of six                   5.00
16T69  T27  5c  blue             (1926)    50
            Pane of six                   3.50
16T70  T27  25c light brown      (1926)   1.25
            Pane of six                   8.00
16T71  T27  5c  carmine          (1927)    60
            Pane of six                   4.00
16T72  T27  25c green            (1927)   4.50
            Pane of six                  30.00
```

Engraved by the E. A. Wright Bank Note Co.
Without Imprint

```
16T73  T27  5c  yellow brown     (1928)    35
            Pane of six                   2.25
16T74  T27  25c dark blue        (1928)    75
            Pane of six                   5.00
```

Engraved by the Security Bank Note Co.
Without Imprint

```
16T75  T27  5c  dark green       (1929)    25   25
            Pane of six                   1.50
16T76  T27  25c red violet       (1929)    75   50
            Pane of six                   5.00
16T77  T27  5c  olive green      (1930)    20   15
            Pane of six                   1.25
16T78  T27  25c carmine          (1930)    20   12
            Pane of six                   1.40
      a.    Imperf. vertically
            (pair)                        35.00
16T79  T27  5c  brown            (1931)    15   10
            Pane of six                   1.00
16T80  T27  25c blue             (1931)    15   10
            Pane of six                   1.00
16T81  T27  5c  green            (1932)    15   10
            Pane of six                   1.00
16T82  T27  25c rose carmine     (1932)    15   10
            Pane of six                   1.00
```

T28

Perf. 14x12½ Lithographed by Oberly & Newell Co.
1933-40
Without Imprint

```
16T83  T28  5c  pale brown       (1933)    25
            Pane of nine                  2.50
16T84  T28  25c green            (1933)    25
            Pane of nine                  2.50
```

Lithographed by Security Bank Note Co.
Without Imprint
Perf. 12
Signature of R. B. White

```
16T85  T28  5c  lake             (1934)    15
            Pane of nine                  1.50
16T86  T28  25c dark blue        (1934)    15
            Pane of nine                  1.75
16T87  T28  5c  yellow brown     (1935)    12
            Pane of nine                  1.50
16T88  T28  25c lake             (1935)    15
            Pane of nine                  1.50
16T89  T28  25c blue             (1936)    20   15
            Pane of nine                  2.00
16T90  T28  25c apple green      (1936)    15   10
            Pane of nine                  1.50
16T91  T28  5c  bister brown     (1937)    20
            Pane of nine                  2.00
16T92  T28  25c carmine rose     (1937)    20
            Pane of nine                  2.00
16T93  T28  5c  green            (1938)    20   15
            Pane of nine                  2.00
16T94  T28  25c blue             (1938)    25   15
            Pane of nine                  2.50
16T95  T28  25c dull vermilion   (1939)    60
            Pane of nine                  6.00
```

```
      a.    Horiz. pair, imperf.
            between                         —
16T96  T28  25c bright violet    (1939)    50
            Pane of nine                  5.00
16T97  T28  5c  light blue       (1940)    40
            Pane of nine                  4.00
16T98  T28  25c bright green     (1940)    40
            Pane of nine                  4.00
```

Samuel F. B. Morse — T29

Plates of 90 stamps.
Stamp designed by Nathaniel Yontiff.
Unlike the frank stamps, Nos. 16T99 to 16T103 were sold to the public in
booklet form for use in prepayment of telegraph services.

Engraved by Security Bank Note Co. of Philadelphia

1940   Unwmk.   Perf. 12.

```
16T99  T29  1c  yellow green               1.00
            Pane of five                   6.00
      a.    Imperf. pair                     —
16T100 T29  2c  chestnut                   1.75  1.00
            Pane of five                  12.00
      a.    Imperf. pair                     —
16T101 T29  5c  deep blue                  3.00
            Pane of five                  18.00
      a.    Vert. pair, imperf. btwn.     65.00
      b.    Iperf. pair                     —
16T102 T29  10c orange                     3.50
            Pane of five                  20.00
      a.    Imperf. pair                     —
16T103 T29  25c bright carmine             4.00
            Pane of five                  25.00
      a.    Imperf. pair                     —
```

Type of 1933-40

1941   Litho.   Perf. 12½
Without Imprint
Signature of R.B. White

```
16T104 T28  5c  dull rose lilac            25
            Pane of nine                  2.50
16T105 T28  25c vermilion                  25
            Pane of nine                  2.50
```

1942   Signature of A.N. Williams

```
16T106 T28  5c  brown                      30
            Pane of nine                  3.00
16T107 T28  25c ultramarine                30
            Pane of nine                  3.00
```

1943

```
16T108 T28  5c  salmon                     30
            Pane of nine                  3.00
16T109 T28  25c red violet                 25
            Pane of nine                  2.50
```

1944

```
16T110 T28  5c  light green                30
            Pane of nine                  3.00
16T111 T28  25c buff                       25
            Pane of nine                  2.50
```

1945

```
16T112 T28  5c  light blue                 35
            Pane of nine                  3.50
      a.    Pair, imperf. between           —
16T113 T28  25c light green                35
            Pane of nine                  3.50
```

1946

```
16T114 T28  5c  light bister brown        1.00
            Pane of nine                 10.00
16T115 T28  25c rose pink                 1.00
            Pane of nine                 10.00
```

Many of the stamps between 16T1 and 16T98 and 16T104 to 16T115 are known without frank numbers. Several of them are also known with more than one color used in the frank number and with handstamped and manuscript numbers. The numbers are also found in combination with various letters: O, A, B, C, D, etc.

Western Union discontinued the use of Telegraph stamps with the 1946 issue.

United States
Telegraph-Cable-Radio Carriers

Booklets issued to accredited representatives to the World Telecommunications Conferences, Atlantic City, New Jersey, 1947. Valid for messages to points outside the United States. Issued by All America Cables & Radio, Inc., The Commercial Cable Company, Globe Wireless, Limited, Mackay Radio and Telegraph Company, Inc., R C A Communications, Inc., Tropical Radio Telegraph Company and The Western Union Telegraph Company.

TX1

1947	Litho.	Unwmk.		Perf. 12½
17T1	TX1	5c	olive bister	5.00
			Pane of nine	50.00
			Pane of 8+1 No. 17T2	350.00
17T2	TX1	10c	olive bister	250.00
17T3	TX1	50c	olive bister	7.00
			Pane of nine	75.00

American Telegraph Typewriter Co.
Continental Telegraph Co.
Marconi Wireless Telegraph Co.
Telepost Co.
Tropical Radio Telegraph Co.
United Fruit Co. Wireless Service.
United Wireless Telegraph Co.

UNLISTED ISSUES

Several telegraph or wireless companies other than those listed above have issued stamps or franks, but as evidence of actual use is lacking, they are not listed. Among these are: American District Telegraph Co.

SANITARY FAIR

The United States Sanitary Commission was authorized by the Secretary of War on June 9, 1861, and approved by President Lincoln on June 13, 1861. It was a committee of inquiry, advice and aid dealing with the health and general comfort of Union troops, supported by public contributions.

Many Sanitary Fairs were held to raise funds for the Commission, and eight issued stamps. The first took place in 1863 at Chicago when no stamp was issued. Some Sanitary Fairs advertised on envelopes.

Sanitary Fair stamps occupy a position midway between United States semi-official carrier stamps and the private local posts. Although Sanitary Fair stamps were not valid for U.S. postal service, they were prepared for, sold and used at the fair post offices, usually with the approval and participation of the local postmaster.

The Commission undertook to forward soldiers' unpaid and postage due letters. These letters were handstamped "Forwarded by the U.S. Sanitary Commission."

Details about the Sanitary Fair stamps may be found in the following publications:
American Journal of Philately, Jan. 1889, by J. W. Scott
The Collector's Journal, Aug-Sept. 1909, by C. E. Severn
Scott's Monthly Journal, Jan. 1927 (reprint, Apr. 1973), by Elliott Perry
Stamps, April 24th, 1937, by Harry M. Konwiser
Pat Paragraphs, July, 1939, by Elliott Perry
Covers, Aug. 1952, by George B. Wray
The listings were compiled originally by H. M. Konwiser and Dorsey F. Wheless.

Albany, New York
Army Relief Bazaar

SF1

Panes of 12 (Narrow Spacing), or 25 (Wide Spacing)
1864, Feb. 22-Mar. 30   **Litho.**   *Imperf.*
Thin White Paper

WV1	SF1	10c rose	40.00	
		Block of four	175.00	
		Pane of 12	675.00	
		Pane of 25	1,100.	
		Used on cover (tied "Albany")		850.00
WV2	SF1	10c black	175.00	
		Block of five	1,100.	

Imitations are typographed in red, blue, black or green on a thin white or ordinary white paper, also on colored papers and are:
(a) Eagle with topknot, printed in sheets of 30 (6x5).
(b) Eagle without shading around it.
(c) Eagle with shading around it, but with a period instead of a circle in "C" of "Cents", and "Ten Cents" is smaller.

Boston, Mass.
National Sailors' Fair

SF2

1864, Nov. 9-22   **Litho.**
Die Cut

WV3	SF2	10c green	150.00

Brooklyn, N. Y.
Brooklyn Sanitary Fair

SF3

1864, Feb. 22-Mar. 8   **Litho.**   *Imperf.*

WV4	SF3	green	350.00	—
		Block of four	1,350.	
		Block of six	2,000.	
		On cover, Fair postmark on envelope		1,100.
WV5	SF	black		—
		On cover, Fair postmark on envelope		1,500.

Imitations: (a) Typographed and shows "Sanitary" with a heavy cross bar to "T" and second "A" with a long left leg. (b) Is a rough typograph print without shading in letters of "Fair".

SF4

SF5

1863, Dec.   **Typeset**   *Imperf.*

WV6	SF4	5c	black, *rosy buff*	375.00
WV7	SF5	10c	green	500.00
	a.		Tete beche pair	1,250.

New York, N. Y.
Metropolitan Fair

SF6

1864, Apr. 4-27   **Engr.**   *Imperf.*
Thin White Paper

WV8	SF6	10c blue	35.00	
		Sheet of four	185.00	
WV9	SF6	10c red	375.00	
		Pair	900.00	
WV10	SF6	10c black	750.00	

Engraved and printed by John E. Gavit of Albany, N.Y. from a steel plate composed of four stamps, 2x2. Can be plated by the positions of scrolls and dots around "Ten Cents".

Philadelphia, Pa.
Great Central Fair

SF7

1864, June 7-28   **Engr.**   *Perf. 12*
Printed by Butler & Carpenter, Philadelphia
Sheets of 126 (14x9)

WV11	SF7	10c blue	15.00	110.00
		Block of four	67.50	
		On cover tied with Fair postmark		900.00

	On cover with 3c #65, Fair and Philadelphia postmarks		*1500.00*
WV12 SF7	20c green	7.50	90.00
	Block of four	32.50	
	Block of 12	135.00	
	On cover tied with Fair postmark		*800.00*
WV13 SF7	30c black	16.50	75.00
	Block of four	75.00	
	On cover tied with Fair postmark		*750.00*

Imprint "Engraved by Butler & Carpenter, Philadelphia" on right margin adjoining three stamps.
Used examples of Nos. WV11-WV13 have Fair cancellation.
Imitation of No. WV13 comes typographed in blue or green on thick paper.
White and amber envelopes were sold by the fair inscribed "Great Central Fair for the Sanitary Commission," showing picture of wounded soldier, doctors and ambulance marked "U. S. Sanitary Commission." Same design and inscription are known on U.S. envelope No. U46.

Springfield, Mass.
Soldiers' Fair

SF8

1864, Dec. 19-24   **Typo.**   *Imperf.*

WV14 SF8	10c lilac	75.00	
	Horizontal strip of four	350.00	
	On unaddressed cover, Fair postmark on envelope		250.00

Design by Thomas Chubbuck, engraver of the postmaster provisional stamp of Brattleboro, Vt.
Imitations: (a) Without designer's name in lower right corner, in lilac on laid paper. *(b)* With designer's name, but roughly typographed, in lilac on white wove paper. Originals show 5 buttons on uniform.

Stamford, Conn.
Soldiers' Fair

SF9

Sheets of 8

1864

WV15 SF9	15c pale brown	450.00	475.00

Originals have tassels at ends of ribbon inscribed "SOLDIERS FAIR."
Imitations have leaning "s" in "CENTS" and come in lilac, brown, green, also black on white paper, green on pinkish paper and other colors.

PROOFS
New York Metropolitan Fair

1864

		Plate on India Mounted on Card
WV10P	10c black	225.00

Philadelphia Great Central Fair

1864

		LARGE DIE Card	PLATE Wove, Imperf.	Wove, Perf.
WV11P	10c blue	40.00		
	Block of four	200.00		
WV11TC to WV13TC	10c 30c greenish black, setenant vert., glazed paper	450.00		
WV12P	20c green	45.00		

		LARGE DIE Card	PLATE Wove, Imperf.	Wove, Perf.
	Block of four	200.00		
WV12TC	20c carmine			35.00
	Block of four			175.00
WV12TC	20c vermilion, India on card	275.00		
WV12TC	20c vermilion		22.50	35.00
	Block of four		115.00	175.00
WV12TC	20c orange		22.50	
	Block of four		115.00	
WV12TC	20c brown orange, opaque paper		22.50	
	Block of four		115.00	
WV12TC	20c red brown			35.00
	Block of four			175.00
WV12TC	20c black brown		25.00	
	Block of four		125.00	
WV12TC	20c olive		22.50	
	Block of four		100.00	
WV12TC	20c yellow green		22.50	
	Block of four		125.00	
WV12TC	20c light green			35.00
	Block of four			175.00
WV12TC	20c blue, India on card	275.00		
WV12TC	20c bright blue		22.50	35.00
	Block of four		125.00	175.00
WV12TC	20c lt. ultramarine		22.50	
	Block of four		125.00	
WV12TC	20c purple		22.50	
	Block of four		125.00	
WV12TC	20c claret			35.00
	Block of four			200.00
WV12TC	20c brown black			35.00
	Block of four			175.00
WV12TC	20c greenish black, glazed paper	225.00		
WV12TC	20c gray black, opaque paper		22.50	
	Block of four		125.00	
WV12TC	20c gray black			35.00
	Block of four			175.00
WV12TC	20c black, experimental double paper		25.00	
	Block of four		140.00	
WV13P	30c black	22.50		
	Block of four	125.00		

STAMPED ENVELOPES AND WRAPPERS

STAMPED ENVELOPES were first issued on July 1, 1853. They have always been made by private contractors, after public bidding, usually at four year intervals. They have always been sold to the public at postage value plus cost of manufacture. They have appeared in many sizes and shapes, made of a variety of papers, with a number of modifications.

George F. Nesbitt & Co. made the government envelopes during the 1853-70 period. The Nesbitt seal or crest on the tip of the top flap was officially ordered discontinued July 7, 1853.

Watermarks in envelope paper, illustrated on opposite page, have been mandatory since their first appearance in 1853. One important exception, started in 1919 and lasted until the manila newspaper wrappers were discontinued in October 1934. The envelope contractor, due to inability to obtain watermarked Manila paper, was permitted to buy unwatermarked stock in the open market, a procedure that accounts for the wide range of shades and weights in this paper, including glazed and unglazed brown (kraft) paper. A diagonally laid paper has been used for some envelopes beginning with number U571.

A few stamped envelopes, in addition to the Manila items noted above, have been found without watermarks or with unauthorized watermarks. Such unusual watermarks or lack of watermarks are errors, bidders' samples or "specimen" envelopes, and most of them are quite rare.

Watermarks have usually been changed with every four year contract, and thus serve to identify the envelope contractor, and since 1911, the manufacturer of the paper.

Envelope paper watermarks can be seen by spreading the Envelope open and holding it against the light.

COLORS IN ENVELOPE PAPER.

Stamped envelopes have usually been supplied in several colors and qualities of paper, some of which blend into each other and require study for identification. The following are the principal colors and their approximate years of use for stamped envelopes and wrappers:

Amber: 1870-1920 and 1929-1943; in two qualities; a pale yellow color; its intentional use in the Nesbitt series is doubtful.

Amber-Manila: 1886-98; same as Manila-amber.

Blue: 1874-1943; usually in two qualities; light and dark shades.

Buff: 1853-70; called cream, 1870-78; and oriental buff, 1886-1920; varies widely in shades.

Canary: 1873-78; another designation given to lemon.

Cream: 1870-78; see buff; second quality in 1c and 2c envelopes.

Fawn: 1874-86; very dark buff, almost light chocolate.

Lemon: 1873-78; Post Office official envelopes only, same as canary.

Manila: 1861-1934; second quality envelopes 1886-1928, and most wrappers; light and dark shades 1920-34; also kraft colored paper in later years.

Manila-Amber: 1886-98; amber shade of Manila quality.

Orange: 1861-83; second and third qualities only.

Oriental Buff: 1886-1920; see buff.

White: 1853-date; two qualities 1915-date; three qualities 1915-25; many shades including ivory, light gray, and bluish; far more common than any other color of paper.

Laid paper was used almost exclusively from 1853 to 1915, but there were a few exceptions, mostly in the Manila papers. Wove paper has been the rule since 1915.

EMBOSSING AND PRINTING DIES.

Stamped envelopes have always been embossed, with the colorless areas slightly raised above the colored (or printed) flat background. While this process was not made mandatory in the original act, custom and tradition have firmly established this policy. It is an unusual procedure, seldom seen in other printed matter. Embossed impressions without color and those where the colored lines are raised are not unusual. The method of making envelope embossings has few counterparts in the typographic industries, and hence is not well understood, even by stamp collectors.

Three types of dies are used, closely inter-related in their derivation, MASTER dies, HUB dies and WORKING (or PRINTING) dies. These types and the ways in which they are made, have undergone many changes with the years, and some of the earlier techniques are unrecorded and rather vague. No attempt will be made to describe other than the present day methods. As an aid to clarity, the design illustrated herewith is the interlocked monogram US, within a single circular border. Dies with curved faces for rotary printing are extensively used, as well as with straight faces for flat printing; only the latter will be described, since the basic principles are the same for both.

Fig. 1

Master Die for Envelope Stamps
Colorless Lines are Recessed Below the Printing Surface.
It Reads Backward.

The MASTER die (Fig. 1) is engraved on the squared end of a small soft steel cylinder, before hardening. The lines that are to remain colorless are cut or engraved into the face of this die, leaving the flat area of the face to carry the printing ink. The monogram is reversed, reading backward, as with any printing type or plate Instead of engraving, a master die may be made by transfer under heavy pressure, usually for some modification in design, in which case it is called a sub-master or supplementary-master die. Sub-master dies are sometimes made without figures of value, when the balance of the design is as desired, and only the figures of value engraved by hand. Various other combinations of transfer and engraving are known, always resulting in a reversed design, with recessed lines and figures, from which proofs can be pulled, and which accurately represents the printing surface that is desired in the eventual working die. The soft steel of a master die, after engraving and transferring is completed, is hardened by heat treatments before it can be used for making hubs.

Fig. 2

Hub Die for Envelope Stamps
Colorless Lines Protrude above the Surface.
The Monogram Reads Forward.

The HUB die (Fig. 2), also called HOB die, is made from soft steel by transfer under pressure from the hardened master or sub-master die, which serves as a matrix or pattern. Since it is a transfer from the master die, the colorless lines protrude from the surface and it reads forward. This transfer impression of the hub die is made in a depression at the end of a sturdy cylinder, as it is subject to extremely hard service in making many working dies.

Fig. 3

Pressure Transfer from Master Die to Hub Die
Above, Hardened Steel Master Die with Recessed Monogram.
Below, Soft Steel Hub Die Blank.

Fig. 3 shows the relative position of the hardened steel master die as it enters the depression in the soft steel hub die blank. Some surplus metal may be squeezed out as the master die is forced into the hub blank, and require removal, leading to possible minor differences between the hub and master dies. At the completion of the pressure transfer the engraver may need to touch up the protruding surfaces to eliminate imperfections, to make letters and figures more symmetrical, and to improve the facial lines of the bust.

A hub die may be made by normal transfer, as above, the figures of value then ground off, and thus be ready for use in making a sub-master die without figures of value, and in which the figures of value may be engraved or punched. Since a hub die may be used to make a hundred or more working dies, it must be exceedingly sturdy and withstand terrific punishment without damage. Duplicate hub dies are frequently made from master dies, as stand-bys or reserves. After completion, hub dies are hardened. Hub dies cannot be engraved, nor can proof impressions be taken from them.

Fig. 4

Working or Printing Die for Envelope Stamps
An exact Replica of the Master Die, except for size and shape of shank, which is designed for Printers lock-up.
It Reads Backward.

The WORKING, or PRINTING, die (Fig. 4) is like the type or plate that printers use, and may be thin to clamp to a base block, or type-high with square sides to lock in a printer's form. Its face reads backward, i.e., in reverse, and it is an exact replica of the master die as well as an exact matrix of the hub die.

Fig. 5

Pressure Transfer from Hub to Working Die

Above, Soft Steel Blank for Working Die.

Below, Hardened Steel Hub Die with Protruding Lines.

The process of pressure transfer is shown in Fig. 5. where the soft steel blank of the working die is entering the depression on the top end of the hardened hub die. In fact the pressure transfer of working dies from hub dies closely resembles that of minting coins, and many of these envelope stamp dies are made at the United States Mint in Philadelphia.

In some cases even working dies may be made without figures of value, and the figures of value individually engraved thereon. This is known to be the case in Die B of the 6c orange airmail stamped envelope die, where the size and position of the "6" has eleven variations.

There are some known instances, as in the case of the 4c and 5c envelopes dies of 1903 and 1907, where the engraved master dies were used as printing dies, since the anticipated demand did not justify the expense of making hub dies.

While working envelope dies are heat treated to the hardest temper known, they do wear down eventually to a point where impressions deteriorate and are unsatisfactory, due to shallow recesses or to broken areas, and such dies are destroyed. In many cases these printing dies can be reworked, or deepened, by annealing the steel, touching up the lines or busts by hand engraving to restore the letters or renew the facial contour lines, and then rehardened for subsequent use. This recutting is the principal cause for minor die varieties in envelope stamps. When working dies are no longer useful, they are mutilated and eventually melted down into scrap metal.

The average "life" (in number of good impressions obtained) of a hardened steel working die, as used in envelope printing and embossing machines is around 30,000,000 on flat bed presses, and 43,000,000 on rotary presses. The present production of stamped envelopes is approximately 2,000,000,000 annually, indicating that 60 to 75 working dies are worn out each year, and require replacement with new dies or a reworking of old dies. Some 200 to 250 working dies are in constant use, since most envelope printing presses are set up for a special size, type or value, and few can be operated continuously at maximum capacity.

Master and hub dies of obsolete envelope issues are kept in the vaults of the Bureau of Engraving and printing in Washington, as are the original dies of adhesive stamps, revenue paper, government securities and paper currency.

PRINTING ENVELOPE STAMPS.

Embossed envelope stamps are not printed against a rigid flat platen, as is the normal printed page, but against a somewhat flexible or resilient platen or make-ready (Fig. 6). This resilient platen is hard enough to produce a clear full impression from the ink on the face of the working die, and soft enough to push the paper into the uninked recesses that correspond to the engraved lines cut into the master die. The normal result is raised lines or embossments without ink or color, standing out in relief against an inked or colored background. The method differs from the usual embossing technique, where rigid dies are used on both sides of the paper, as in notarial seals. The use of the resilient platen in envelope embossing permits far higher operating speeds than can be obtained with rigid embossing dies, without the need of such accurate register between the printing surface and the platen.

Fig. 6

Printing Process for embossed

A. Working Die, Carrying ink on its surface.

B. Resilient Platen, or Make-ready, Pushing Paper into uninked recesses, so that lines of Embossed Monogram receive no color.

C. Paper of Envelope Blank, after Printing and Embossing. Heavy line shows deposit of ink on surface of paper, but Embossed Lines are not inked.

D. Front view of Embossed impression.

When these recessed lines in a working die become filled with ink or other foreign material, the paper is not pushed in, the plugged area receives ink, and the corresponding colorless line does not appear on the stamp. This accounts for missing letters, lines or figures, and is a printing error, not a die variety.

An ALBINO impression is where two or more envelope blanks are fed into the printing press. The one adjacent to the printing die receives the color and the embossing, while the others are embossed only. Albinos are printing errors and are worth more than normal, inked impressions. Albinos of earlier issues, canceled while current, are scarce.

Before Jan. 1, 1965, stamped envelopes were printed by two processes: (1.) The rotary, with curved dies, on Huckins and Harris presses. (2.) The flat process, with straight dies, as illustrated, on the O'Connell-type press, which is a redesigned Hartford press. The flat bed presses include a gumming and folding attachment, while the rotary presses, running at higher speeds, require separate folding machines.

Different master dies in every denomination are required for Huckins, Harris and flat bed presses. This difference gives rise to most of the major die varieties in envelope stamps.

Web-fed equipment which converts paper from a roll into finished envelopes in a continuous operation has produced envelopes starting with Nos. U547 and UC37. Albino impressions do not occur on envelopes produced by web-fed equipment.

Some authorities claim that Nos. U37, U48, U49, U110, U124, U125, U130, U133A, U137A, U137B, U137C, W138, U145, U162, U178A, U185, U220, U285, U286, U298, U299, UO3, UO32, UO38, UO45 and UO45A (with plus sign + before number), were not regularly issued and are not known to have been used.

Wrappers are listed with envelopes of corresponding design, and are numbered with the prefix "W" instead of "U."

Prices for cut squares are for copies with fine margins on all sides. Prices for unused entires are for those without printed or manuscript address. Prices for letter sheets are for folded entires. Unfolded copies sell for more. A "full corner" includes back and side flaps and commands a premium.

ENVELOPE WATERMARKS

Watermark Illustrations 5, 6, 17 and 18 are condensed. Watermark 4 was used only on Officials. Watermarks 9 and 10 are found on Specimens and Errors. Watermarks 17-18 were the last laid paper watermarks; watermarks 19-21 the first wove paper watermarks.

1-(1853-70)

2-(1870-78)

3-(1876)

4-(1877-82)

5-(1878-82)

6-(1882-86)

7-(1886-90)

8-(1890-94)

9-(1886-87)

10-(1886-99)

11-(1893)

12-(1894-98)

13-(1899-1902)

14-(1903-07)

15-(1907-11)

See the "Information for Collectors" section at beginning of catalogue for illustrations of types of postmarks and precancels.

15A-(1907-11)

16-(1911-15)

U S S E
1911
17-(1911-15)

US-S E
1911
18-(1911-15)

19-(1915-19)

20-(1915-19)

21-(1915-19)

22-(1919-20)

23-(1919-20)

24-(1921-24)

25-(1921-24)

26-(1925-28)

27-(1925-28)

28-(1929-32)

28A-(1929-32)

29-(1929-32)

30-(1929-32)

30A-(1929-32)

31-(1933-36)

32-(1933-36)

33-(1933-36)

35-(1937-40)

36-(1937-40)

38-(1941-44)

39-(1941-44)

40-(1945-48)

41-(1945-48)

42-(1949-52)

43-(1949-52)

44-(1953-56)

45-(1953-56)

46-(1957-60)

☆USA
47-(1961-64)

USA☆
48-(1961-64)

USA
☆
49-(1965-68)

☆
USA
50-(1965-68)

Letter Sheet (1886-94)

Washington — U1

Die 1 - "THREE" in short label with curved ends; 13mm. wide at top. (Twelve varieties.)

U2

Die 2 - "THREE" in short label with straight ends; 15½mm. wide at top. (Three varieties.)

U3

Die 3 - "THREE" in short label with octagon ends. (Two varieties.)

U4

Die 4 - "THREE" in wide label with straight ends; 20 mm. wide at top.

U5

Die 5 - "THREE" in medium wide label with curved ends; 14½mm. wide at top (10 varieties). A sub-variety shows curved lines at either end of label omitted; both T's have longer cross stroke; R is smaller (20 varieties).

U6

Four varieties.

U7

Die 1 - "TEN" in short label; 15½mm. wide at top.

U8

Die 2 - "TEN" in wide label; 20 mm. wide at top.

Printed by George F. Nesbitt & Co., New York, N.Y.

1853-55

On Diagonally Laid Paper (Early printings of Nos. U1, U3 on Horizontally Laid Paper)

U1	U1	3c **red,** die 1, *white*	175.00	15.00
		Entire	950.00	25.00
U2	U1	3c **red,** die 1, *buff*	65.00	6.00
		Entire	625.00	12.00
U3	U2	3c **red,** die 2, *white*	600.00	30.00
		Entire	2,500.	55.00
U4	U2	3c **red,** die 2, *buff*	175.00	12.00
		Entire	1,200.	25.00
U5	U3	3c **red,** die 3, *white* ('54)	3,000.	375.00
		Entire	9,000.	500.00
U6	U3	3c **red,** die 3, *buff* ('54)	125.00	25.00
		Entire	800.00	60.00
U7	U4	3c **red,** die 4, *white*	525.00	60.00
		Entire	4,500.	100.00
U8	U4	3c **red,** die 4, *buff*	1,000.	85.00
		Entire	4,000.	125.00
U9	U5	3c **red,** die 5, *white* ('54)	15.00	1.50
		Entire	55.00	5.00
U10	U5	3c **red,** die 5, *buff* ('54)	9.50	1.00
		Entire	45.00	3.00
U11	U6	6c **red,** *white*	125.00	85.00
		Entire	200.00	110.00
U12	U6	6c **red,** *buff*	85.00	50.00
		Entire	185.00	160.00
U13	U6	6c **green,** *white*	165.00	85.00
		Entire	275.00	150.00
U14	U6	6c **green,** *buff*	165.00	75.00

		Entire	300.00	150.00
U15	U7	10c **green,** die 1, *white* ('55)	125.00	50.00
		Entire	250.00	100.00
U16	U7	10c **green,** die 1, *buff* ('55)	55.00	40.00
		Entire	165.00	80.00
a.		10c pale green, die 1, *buff*	55.00	40.00
		Entire	175.00	85.00
U17	U8	10c **green,** die 2, *white* ('55)	175.00	90.00
		Entire	300.00	150.00
a.		10c pale green, die 2, *white*	150.00	90.00
		Entire	200.00	125.00
U18	U8	10c **green,** die 2, *buff* ('55)	90.00	50.00
		Entire	150.00	75.00
a.		10c pale green, die 2, *buff*	90.00	50.00
		Entire	150.00	80.00

Nos. U9, U10, U11, U12, U13, U14, U17, and U18 have been reprinted on white and buff paper, vertically laid, and are not known entire. The originals are on diagonally laid paper. Price, set of 8 reprints, $125.

Franklin — U9

Die 1 - Period after "POSTAGE." (Eleven varieties.)

Franklin — U10

Die 2 - Bust touches inner frame-line at front and back.

Franklin — U11

Die 3 - No period after "POSTAGE." (Two varieties.)

Washington
U12

Nine varieties of type U12.

Envelopes are on diagonally laid paper.
Wrappers on vertically or horizontally laid paper.

Wrappers of the 1 cent denomination were authorized by an Act of Congress, February 27, 1861, and were issued in October, 1861. These were suspended in 1863, and their use resumed in June, 1864.

1860-61

U19	U9	1c **blue**, die 1, *buff*		22.50	10.00
		Entire		50.00	25.00
W20	U9	1c **blue**, die 1, *buff*		50.00	45.00
		Entire		90.00	65.00
W21	U9	1c **blue**, die 1, *manila*			
		('61)		35.00	35.00
		Entire		70.00	70.00
W22	U9	1c **blue**, die 1, *orange*			
		('61)		1,250.	
		Entire		2,000.	
U23	U10	1c **blue**, die 2, *orange*		400.00	400.00
		Entire		450.00	450.00
U24	U11	1c **blue**, die 3, *buff*		180.00	90.00
		Entire		300.00	175.00
W25	U11	1c **blue**, die 3, *manila*			
		('61)		1,200.	950.00
		Entire		7,000.	2,750.
U26	U12	3c **red**, *white*		17.50	10.00
		Entire		25.00	20.00
U27	U12	3c **red**, *buff*		15.00	9.00
		Entire		25.00	17.50
U28	U12 + U9	3c + 1c **red & blue**, *white*		350.00	250.00
		Entire		500.00	400.00
U29	U12 + U9	3c + 1c **red & blue**, *buff*		250.00	200.00
		Entire		450.00	475.00
U30	U12	6c **red**, *white*		2,250.	1,250.
		Entire		2,900.	
U31	U12	6c **red**, *buff*		1,500.	900.00
		Entire		2,750.	3,750.
U32	U12	10c **green**, *white*		800.00	275.00
		Entire		8,000.	375.00
U33	U12	10c **green**, *buff*		750.00	225.00
		Entire		2,250.	400.00

Nos. U26, U27, U30 to U33 have been reprinted on the same papers as the reprints of the 1853-55 issue, and are not known entire. Price, set of 6 reprints, $160.

Washington
U13

17 varieties for Nos. U34-U35; 2 varieties for No. U36.

Washington
U14

Washington — U15

Washington — U16

Envelopes are on diagonally laid paper.

U36 comes on vertically or horizontally laid paper. It appeared in August, 1861, and was withdrawn in 1864. Total issue 211,800.

1861

U34	U13	3c **pink**, *white*		14.00	4.00
		Entire		35.00	10.00
U35	U13	3c **pink**, *buff*		12.50	4.00
		Entire		35.00	10.00
U36	U13	3c **pink**, *blue* (Letter Sheet)		65.00	45.00
		Entire		175.00	85.00
+U37	U13	3c **pink**, *orange*		2,300.	
		Entire		3,750.	
U38	U14	6c **pink**, *white*		90.00	75.00
		Entire		140.00	150.00
U39	U14	6c **pink**, *buff*		55.00	55.00
		Entire		100.00	150.00
U40	U15	10c **yellow green**, *white*		25.00	22.50
		Entire		50.00	42.50
a.		10c blue green, *white*		25.00	25.00
		Entire		50.00	37.50
U41	U15	10c **yellow green**, *buff*		22.50	19.00
		Entire		50.00	37.50
a.		10c blue green, *buff*		20.00	20.00
		Entire		35.00	40.00
U42	U16	12c **red & brown**, *buff*		175.00	140.00
		Entire		400.00	600.00
a.		12c lake & brown, *buff*		800.00	
U43	U16	20c **red & blue**, *buff*		150.00	140.00
		Entire		400.00	750.00
U44	U16	24c **red & green**, *buff*		150.00	140.00
		Entire		500.00	750.00
a.		24c lake & green, *salmon*		190.00	150.00
		Entire		500.00	950.00
U45	U16	40c **black & red**, *buff*		225.00	275.00
		Entire		650.00	1,250.

Nos. U38 and U39 have been reprinted on the same papers as the reprints of the 1853-55 issue, and are not known entire. Price, set of 2 reprints, $30.

Jackson — U17

Die 1 - "U.S. POSTAGE" above. Downstroke and tail of "2" unite near the point (seven varieties.)

Jackson — U18

Die 2 - "U.S. POSTAGE" above. The downstroke and tail of the "2" touch but do not merge.

Jackson
U19

Die 3 - "U.S. POST" above. Stamp 24-25mm. wide. (Sixteen varieties.)

Jackson
U20

Die 4 - "U.S. POST" above. Stamp 25½-26¼mm. wide. (Twenty-five varieties.)

Envelopes are on diagonally laid paper.
Wrappers on vertically or horizontally laid paper.

1863-64

U46	U17	2c **black**, die 1, *buff*		25.00	12.00
		Entire		50.00	30.00
W47	U17	2c **black**, die 1, *dark manila*			
				35.00	30.00

+U48	U18	2c **black,** die 2, *buff*	55.00	50.00
		Entire	1,500.	3,250.
+U49	U18	2c **black,** die 2, *orange*	950.00	
		Entire	2,000.	
U50	U19	2c **black,** die 3, *buff* ('64)	8.00	7.00
		Entire	22.50	14.00
W51	U19	2c **black,** die 3, *buff* ('64)	140.00	140.00
		Entire	225.00	200.00
U52	U19	2c **black,** die 3, *orange* ('64)	9.50	6.00
		Entire	20.00	10.00
W53	U19	2c **black,** die 3, *dark manila* ('64)	25.00	17.50
		Entire	100.00	60.00
U54	U20	2c **black,** die 4, *buff* ('64)	9.50	8.00
		Entire	20.00	12.00
W55	U20	2c **black,** die 4, *buff* ('64)	65.00	40.00
		Entire	115.00	95.00
U56	U20	2c **black,** die 4, *orange* ('64)	7.50	6.00
		Entire	12.00	10.00
W57	U20	2c **black,** die 4, *light manila* ('64)	10.00	8.00
		Entire	20.00	17.50

Washington
U21

79 varieties for Nos. U58-U61; 2 varieties for Nos. U63-U65

Washington — U22

1864-65

U58	U21	3c **pink,** *white*	5.00	1.25
		Entire	8.00	3.00
U59	U21	3c **pink,** *buff*	3.50	80
		Entire	7.50	2.25
U60	U21	3c **brown,** *white* ('65)	35.00	20.00
		Entire	70.00	80.00
U61	U21	3c **brown,** *buff* ('65)	35.00	20.00
		Entire	70.00	60.00
U62	U21	6c **pink,** *white*	40.00	22.50
		Entire	75.00	50.00
U63	U21	6c **pink,** *buff*	27.50	20.00
		Entire	75.00	50.00
U64	U21	6c **purple,** *white* ('65)	35.00	20.00
		Entire	60.00	50.00
U65	U21	6c **purple,** *buff* ('65)	30.00	17.50
		Entire	50.00	50.00
U66	U22	9c **lemon,** *buff* ('65)	300.00	200.00
		Entire	525.00	450.00
U67	U22	9c **orange,** *buff* ('65)	75.00	70.00
		Entire	175.00	250.00
a.		9c **orange yellow,** *buff*	85.00	80.00
		Entire	150.00	275.00
U68	U22	12c **brown,** *buff* ('65)	300.00	190.00
		Entire	525.00	900.00
U69	U22	12c **red brown,** *buff* ('65)	75.00	50.00
		Entire	125.00	200.00
U70	U22	18c **red,** *buff* ('65)	75.00	75.00
		Entire	200.00	750.00
U71	U22	24c **blue,** *buff* ('65)	70.00	70.00
		Entire	200.00	750.00
U72	U22	30c **green,** *buff* ('65)	50.00	50.00
		Entire	175.00	750.00
a.		30c **yellow green,** *buff*	50.00	60.00
		Entire	175.00	850.00

U73	U22	40c **rose,** *buff* ('65)	60.00	200.00
		Entire	250.00	1,250.

Printed by George H. Reay, Brooklyn, N. Y.
The engravings in this issue are finely executed.

Franklin
U23

Bust points to the end of the "N" of "ONE".

Jackson
U24

Bust narrow at back. Small, thick figures of value.

Washington — U25

Queue projects below bust.

Lincoln
U26

Neck very long at the back.

Stanton
U27

Bust pointed at the back; figures "7" are normal.

Jefferson
U28

Queue forms straight line with the bust.

Clay
U29

Ear partly concealed by hair, mouth large, chin prominent.

Webster
U30

Has side whiskers.

Scott
U31

Straggling locks of hair at top of head; ornaments around the inner oval end in squares.

Hamilton
U32

Back of bust very narrow, chin almost straight; labels containing figures of value are exactly parallel.

Perry
U33

Front of bust very narrow and pointed; inner lines of shields project very slightly beyond the oval.

1870-71

U74	U23	1c **blue**, *white*	25.00	20.00
		Entire	50.00	30.00
a.		1c ultramarine, *white*	50.00	25.00
		Entire	75.00	50.00
U75	U23	1c **blue**, *amber*	25.00	20.00
		Entire	50.00	25.00
a.		1c ultramarine, *amber*	40.00	25.00
		Entire	60.00	50.00
U76	U23	1c **blue**, *orange*	12.00	9.00
		Entire	25.00	18.00
W77	U23	1c **blue**, *manila*	35.00	25.00
		Entire	60.00	55.00
U78	U24	2c **brown**, *white*	30.00	12.00
		Entire	50.00	14.00
U79	U24	2c **brown**, *amber*	13.00	6.00
		Entire	26.00	15.00
U80	U24	2c **brown**, *orange*	7.00	4.50
		Entire	11.00	6.50
W81	U24	2c **brown**, *manila*	17.50	15.00
		Entire	35.00	35.00
U82	U25	3c **green**, *white*	5.00	60
		Entire	10.00	2.25
U83	U25	3c **green**, *amber*	3.50	1.50
		Entire	10.00	2.50
U84	U25	3c **green**, *cream*	6.50	2.50
		Entire	14.00	4.00
U85	U26	6c **dark red**, *white*	14.00	15.00
		Entire	25.00	15.00
a.		6c vermilion, *white*	12.00	12.00

		Entire	25.00	16.00
U86	U26	6c **dark red**, *amber*	16.00	12.00
		Entire	30.00	15.00
a.		6c vermilion, *amber*	16.00	12.00
		Entire	30.00	15.00
U87	U26	6c **dark red**, *cream*	20.00	12.00
		Entire	40.00	20.00
a.		6c vermilion, *cream*	22.50	12.00
		Entire	35.00	20.00
U88	U27	7c **vermilion**, *amber* ('71)	35.00	*165.00*
		Entire	50.00	*600.00*
U89	U28	10c **olive black**, *white*	300.00	300.00
		Entire	425.00	*800.00*
U90	U28	10c **olive black**, *amber*	300.00	300.00
		Entire	425.00	*800.00*
U91	U28	10c **brown**, *white*	45.00	60.00
		Entire	70.00	75.00
U92	U28	10c **brown**, *amber*	60.00	45.00
		Entire	80.00	70.00
a.		10c dark brown, *amber*	60.00	50.00
		Entire	80.00	75.00
U93	U29	12c **plum**, *white*	85.00	60.00
		Entire	180.00	*350.00*
U94	U29	12c **plum**, *amber*	90.00	90.00
		Entire	185.00	*500.00*
U95	U29	12c **plum**, *cream*	200.00	190.00
		Entire	350.00	
U96	U30	15c **red orange**, *white*	50.00	65.00
		Entire	150.00	
a.		15c orange, *white*	50.00	
		Entire	150.00	
U97	U30	15c **red orange**, *amber*	140.00	175.00
		Entire	375.00	
a.		15c orange, *amber*	140.00	
		Entire	375.00	
U98	U30	15c **red orange**, *cream*	200.00	200.00
		Entire	300.00	
a.		15c orange, *cream*	200.00	
		Entire	300.00	
U99	U31	24c **purple**, *white*	110.00	75.00
		Entire	160.00	
U100	U31	24c **purple**, *amber*	160.00	275.00
		Entire	350.00	
U101	U31	24c **purple**, *cream*	160.00	275.00
		Entire	350.00	
U102	U32	30c **black**, *white*	65.00	80.00
		Entire	275.00	
U103	U32	30c **black**, *amber*	155.00	225.00
		Entire	500.00	
U104	U32	30c **black**, *cream*	200.00	350.00
		Entire	400.00	
U105	U33	90c **carmine**, *white*	125.00	200.00
		Entire	170.00	
U106	U33	90c **carmine**, *amber*	275.00	350.00
		Entire	775.00	
U107	U33	90c **carmine**, *cream*	300.00	450.00
		Entire	850.00	

Printed by Plimpton Manufacturing Co.

U34

Die 1 - Bust forms an angle at the back near the frame. Lettering poorly executed. Distinct circle in "O" of "Postage".

U35

Die 2 - Lower part of bust points to the end of the "E" in "ONE". Head inclined downward.

U36

Die 1 - Bust narrow at back. Thin numerals. Head of "P" narrow. Bust broad at front, ending in sharp corners.

U37

Die 2 - Bust broad. Figures of value in long ovals.

U38

Die 3 - Similar to die 2 but the figure "2" at the left touches the oval.

U39

Die 4 - Similar to die 2 but the "O" of "TWO" has the center netted instead of plain and the "G" of "POSTAGE" and the "C" of "CENTS" have diagonal crossline.

U40

Die 5 - Bust broad: numerals in ovals short and thick.

U41

Die 6 - Similar to die 5 but the ovals containing the numerals are much heavier. A diagonal line runs from the upper part of the "U" to the white frame-line.

U42

Die 7 - Similar to die 5 but the middle stroke of "N" in "CENTS" is as thin as the vertical strokes.

U43

Die 8 - Bottom of bust cut almost semi-circularly.

U44

Die 1 - Thin lettering, long thin figures of value.

U45

Die 2 - Thick lettering, well-formed figures of value, queue does not project below bust.

U46

Die 3 - Top of head egg-shaped; knot of queue well marked and projects triangularly.

Taylor
U47

Die 1 - Figures of value with thick, curved tops.

Die 2 - Figures of value with long, thin tops.

U48

Neck short at back.

U49

Figures of value turned up at the ends.

Prices for cancellation varieties are for specimens off cover.

U50

Die 1 - Very large head.

U51

Die 2 - Knot of queue stands out prominently.

U52

Ear prominent, chin receding.

U53

No side whiskers, forelock projects above head.

U54

Hair does not project; ornaments around the inner oval end in points.

U55

Back of bust rather broad, chin slopes considerably; labels containing figures of value are not exactly parallel.

U56

Front of bust sloping; inner lines of shields project considerably into the inner oval.

1874-86

U108	U34	1c **dark blue**, die 1, *white*	70.00	35.00
		Entire	95.00	75.00
a.		light blue, die 1, *white*		
U109	U34	1c **dark blue**, die 1, *amber*	85.00	55.00
		Entire	120.00	80.00
+U110	U34	1c **dark blue**, die 1, *cream*	600.00	
U111	U34	1c **dark blue**, die 1, *orange*	15.00	12.50
		Entire	25.00	20.00
a.		1c light blue, die 1, *orange*	17.00	8.00
		Entire	18.00	15.00
W112	U34	1c **dark blue**, die 1, *manila*	35.00	27.50
		Entire	60.00	60.00
U113	U35	1c **light blue**, die 2, *white*	1.00	60
		Entire	1.75	1.00
a.		1c dark blue, die 2, *white*	5.50	4.00
		Entire	15.00	10.00
U114	U35	1c **light blue**, die 2, *amber*	3.00	2.50
		Entire	4.00	3.00
a.		1c dark blue, die 2, *amber*	11.00	8.00
		Entire	18.00	10.00
U115	U35	1c **blue**, die 2, *cream*	3.00	3.00
		Entire	5.00	3.00
a.		1c dark blue, die 2, *cream*	14.00	4.00
		Entire	20.00	15.00
U116	U35	1c **light blue**, die 2, *orange*	40	30
		Entire	50	40
a.		1c dark blue, die 2, *orange*	1.50	85
		Entire	6.00	5.00

U117	U35	1c **light blue**, die 2, *blue* ('80)	4.00	3.00
		Entire	6.00	5.00
U118	U35	1c **light blue**, die 2, *fawn* ('79)	4.00	3.00
		Entire	5.00	5.00
U119	U35	1c **light blue**, die 2, *manila* ('86)	4.00	2.50
		Entire	5.00	5.00
W120	U35	1c **light blue**, die 2, *manila*	1.00	80
		Entire	1.50	1.50
a.		1c dark blue, die 2, *manila*	3.50	2.00
		Entire	7.00	5.00
U121	U35	1c **light blue**, die 2, *amber manila* ('86)	8.00	7.50
		Entire	10.00	10.00
U122	U36	2c **brown**, die 1, *white*	75.00	30.00
		Entire	90.00	80.00
U123	U36	2c **brown**, die 1, *amber*	40.00	30.00
		Entire	65.00	65.00
+U124	U36	2c **brown**, die 1, *cream*	500.00	
+U125	U36	2c **brown**, die 1, *orange*	6,500.	
		Entire	12,500.	
W126	U36	2c **brown**, die 1, *manila*	75.00	35.00
		Entire	80.00	60.00
W127	U36	2c **vermilion**, die 1, *manila*	1,000.	275.00
		Entire	1,500.	
U128	U37	2c **brown**, die 2, *white*	35.00	22.50
		Entire	70.00	70.00
U129	U37	2c **brown**, die 1, *amber*	55.00	30.00
		Entire	65.00	40.00
+U130	U37	2c **brown**, die 2, *cream*	18,500.	
W131	U37	2c **brown**, die 2, *manila*	12.00	12.00
		Entire	18.00	12.00
U132	U38	2c **brown**, die 3, *white*	50.00	20.00
		Entire	70.00	70.00
U133	U38	2c **brown**, die 3, *amber*	175.00	55.00
		Entire	200.00	100.00
+U133A	U38	2c **brown**, die 3, *cream*	—	
U134	U39	2c **brown**, die 4, *white*	600.00	100.00
		Entire	700.00	150.00
U135	U39	2c **brown**, die 4, *amber*	375.00	100.00
		Entire	500.00	150.00
U136	U39	2c **brown**, die 4, *orange*	27.50	25.00
		Entire	50.00	40.00
W137	U39	2c **brown**, die 4, *manila*	45.00	27.50
		Entire	55.00	40.00
+U137A	U39	2c **vermilion**, die 4, *white*	17,500.	
+U137B	U39	2c **vermilion**, die 4, *amber*	17,500.	
		Entire	—	
+U137C	U39	2c **vermilion**, die 4, *orange*	17,500.	
+W138	U39	2c **vermilion**, die 4, *manila*	6,000.	
U139	U40	2c **brown**, die 5, *white* ('75)	35.00	30.00
		Entire	45.00	40.00
U140	U40	2c **brown**, die 5, *amber* ('75)	60.00	50.00
		Entire	75.00	60.00
W141	U40	2c **brown**, die 5, *manila* ('75)	30.00	20.00
		Entire	35.00	35.00
U142	U40	2c **vermilion**, die 5, *white* ('75)	4.00	2.00
		Entire	5.00	2.50
a.		2c pink, die 5, *white*	7.00	5.00
		Entire	12.00	7.50
U143	U40	2c **vermilion**, die 5, *amber* ('75)	4.00	2.00
		Entire	5.00	4.00
U144	U40	2c **vermilion**, die 5, *cream* ('75)	9.00	4.00
		Entire	10.00	5.00
+U145	U40	2c **vermilion**, die 5, *orange* ('75)	8,000.	
		Entire	11,500.	
U146	U40	2c **vermilion**, die 5, *blue* ('80)	110.00	27.50
		Entire	175.00	150.00
U147	U40	2c **vermilion**, die 5, *fawn* ('75)	5.00	3.50
		Entire	9.00	6.00
W148	U40	2c **vermilion**, die 5, *manila* ('75)	2.50	2.50
		Entire	5.00	5.00
U149	U41	2c **vermilion**, die 6, *white* ('78)	30.00	20.00
		Entire	45.00	35.00
a.		2c pink, die 6, *white*	30.00	20.00
		Entire	40.00	30.00
U150	U41	2c **vermilion**, die 6, *amber* ('78)	17.00	12.00
		Entire	25.00	16.00
U151	U41	2c **vermilion**, die 6, *blue* ('80)	7.00	6.00
		Entire	9.00	9.00
a.		2c pink, die 6, *blue*	7.00	6.00
		Entire	10.00	7.50
U152	U41	2c **vermilion**, die 6, *fawn* ('78)	7.50	3.00
		Entire	10.00	9.00
U153	U42	2c **vermilion**, die 7, *white* ('76)	40.00	25.00
		Entire	65.00	35.00
U154	U42	2c **vermilion**, die 7, *amber* ('76)	250.00	70.00
		Entire	300.00	110.00
W155	U42	2c **vermilion**, die 7, *manila* ('76)	12.00	7.00
		Entire	30.00	10.00
U156	U43	2c **vermillion**, die 8, *white* ('81)	600.00	110.00
		Entire	650.00	300.00
U157	U43	2c **vermilion**, die 8, *amber* ('81)	14,000.	14,000.
		Entire	45,000.	
W158	U43	2c **vermilion**, die 8, *manila* ('81)	60.00	50.00
		Entire	125.00	100.00
U159	U44	3c **green**, die 1, *white*	16.00	4.00
		Entire	30.00	10.00

U160	U44	3c **green**, die 1, *amber*	18.00	7.50
		Entire	35.00	12.00
U161	U44	3c **green**, die 1, *cream*	30.00	8.00
		Entire	40.00	15.00
+U162	U44	3c **green**, die 1, *blue*	—	
U163	U45	3c **green**, die 2, *white*	75	25
		Entire	1.50	75
U164	U45	3c **green**, die 2, *amber*	1.00	40
		Entire	2.00	1.00
U165	U45	3c **green**, die 2, *cream*	4.50	4.00
		Entire	8.00	6.00
U166	U45	3c **green**, die 2, *blue*	5.00	3.00
		Entire	9.00	7.00
U167	U45	3c **green**, die 2, *fawn* ('75)	3.00	2.00
		Entire	6.00	3.00
U168	U46	3c **green**, die 3, *white* ('81)	400.00	30.00
		Entire	1,750.	75.00
U169	U46	3c **green**, die 3, *amber*	175.00	90.00
		Entire	275.00	125.00
U170	U46	3c **green**, die 3, *blue* ('81)	1,500.	1,500.
		Entire	15,000.	4,000.
U171	U46	3c **green**, die 3, *fawn* ('81)	24,000.	1,250.
		Entire		12,500.
U172	U47	5c **blue**, die 1, *white* ('75)	7.00	6.00
		Entire	9.00	8.00
U173	U47	5c **blue**, die 1, *amber* ('75)	7.50	6.50
		Entire	9.00	6.00
U174	U47	5c **blue**, die 1, *cream* ('75)	75.00	37.50
		Entire	90.00	85.00
U175	U47	5c **blue**, die 1, *blue* ('75)	12.50	12.50
		Entire	15.00	14.00
U176	U47	5c **blue**, die 1, *fawn* ('75)	90.00	50.00
		Entire	175.00	
U177	U47	5c **blue**, die 2, *white* ('75)	4.75	4.75
		Entire	9.00	11.00
U178	U47	5c **blue**, die 2, *amber* ('75)	5.50	5.00
		Entire	10.00	12.00
+U178A	U47	5c **blue**, die 2, *cream* ('76)	1,500.	
		Entire	4,000.	
U179	U47	5c **blue**, die 2, *blue* ('75)	10.00	6.00
		Entire	14.00	12.00
U180	U47	5c **blue**, die 2, *fawn* ('75)	70.00	40.00
		Entire	95.00	90.00
U181	U48	6c **red**, *white*	4.00	4.00
		Entire	8.00	7.00
a.		6c **vermilion**, *white*	4.00	4.00
		Entire	8.00	7.00
U182	U48	6c **red**, *amber*	4.00	4.00
		Entire	12.00	10.00
a.		6c **vermilion**, *amber*	7.00	4.00
		Entire	12.00	10.00
U183	U48	6c **red**, *cream*	14.00	9.00
		Entire	18.00	18.00
a.		6c **vermilion**, *cream*	14.00	9.00
		Entire	18.00	18.00
U184	U48	6c **red**, *fawn* ('75)	14.00	9.00
		Entire	20.00	16.00
+U185	U49	7c **vermilion**, *white*	1,000.	
U186	U49	7c **vermilion**, *amber*	75.00	55.00
		Entire	110.00	
U187	U50	10c **brown**, die 1, *white*	25.00	15.00
		Entire	45.00	
U188	U50	10c **brown**, die 1, *amber*	50.00	25.00
		Entire	75.00	
U189	U51	10c **chocolate**, die 2, *white* ('75)	4.00	2.50
		Entire	7.00	7.00
a.		bister brown, die 2, *white*	5.00	3.00
		Entire	8.00	8.00
b.		yellow ocher	1,000.	
		Entire	1,200.	
U190	U51	10c **chocolate**, die 2, *amber* ('75)	5.50	5.00
		Entire	7.50	7.00
a.		bister brown, die 2, *amber*	5.50	5.00
		Entire	7.50	7.50
b.		yellow ocher	1,000.	
		Entire	1,200.	
U191	U51	10c **brown**, die 2, *oriental buff* ('86)	7.00	6.00
		Entire	8.50	7.00
U192	U51	10c **brown**, die 2, *blue* ('86)	8.00	6.00
		Entire	9.00	7.00
a.		10c gray black, die 2, *blue*	8.00	6.00
		Entire	9.00	7.00
b.		10c red brown, die 2, *blue*	8.00	6.00
		Entire	9.00	7.00
U193	U51	10c **brown**, die 2, *manila* ('86)	8.50	6.00
		Entire	10.00	10.00
a.		10c red brown, die 2, *manila*	9.00	6.00
		Entire	10.00	8.00
U194	U51	10c **brown**, die 2, *amber manila* ('86)	10.00	5.00
		Entire	10.00	10.00
a.		10c red brown, die 2, *amber manila*	10.00	5.00
		Entire	12.00	12.00
U195	U52	12c **plum**, *white*	150.00	75.00
		Entire	150.00	
U196	U52	12c **plum**, *amber*	140.00	140.00
		Entire	250.00	
U197	U52	12c **plum**, *cream*	175.00	150.00
		Entire	750.00	
U198	U53	15c **orange**, *white*	30.00	25.00
		Entire	75.00	45.00
U199	U53	15c **orange**, *amber*	110.00	90.00
		Entire	175.00	
U200	U53	15c **orange**, *cream*	350.00	350.00
		Entire	900.00	
U201	U54	24c **purple**, *white*	150.00	100.00
		Entire	225.00	
U202	U54	24c **purple**, *amber*	155.00	100.00
		Entire	225.00	
U203	U54	24c **purple**, *cream*	150.00	110.00
		Entire	750.00	
U204	U55	30c **black**, *white*	50.00	25.00
		Entire	65.00	75.00
U205	U55	30c **black**, *amber*	55.00	50.00

		Entire	110.00	250.00
U206	U55	30c **black**, *cream* ('75)	400.00	375.00
		Entire	750.00	
U207	U55	30c **black**, *oriental buff* ('81)	80.00	70.00
		Entire	125.00	
U208	U55	30c **black**, *blue* ('81)	85.00	70.00
		Entire	110.00	
U209	U55	30c **black**, *manila* ('81)	75.00	70.00
		Entire	110.00	
U210	U55	30c **black**, *amber manila* ('86)	100.00	70.00
		Entire	125.00	
U211	U56	90c **carmine**, *white* ('75)	100.00	70.00
		Entire	110.00	100.00
U212	U56	90c **carmine**, *amber* ('75)	150.00	200.00
		Entire	200.00	
U213	U56	90c **carmine**, *cream* ('75)	1,250.	
		Entire	2,000.	
U214	U56	90c **carmine**, *oriental buff* ('86)	175.00	250.00
		Entire	250.00	
U215	U56	90c **carmine**, *blue* ('86)	150.00	200.00
		Entire	250.00	
U216	U56	90c **carmine**, *manila* ('86)	100.00	200.00
		Entire	190.00	
U217	U56	90c **carmine**, *amber manila* ('86)	100.00	175.00
		Entire	200.00	

Note: No. U206 has watermark #2; No. U207 watermark #6 or #7. No U213 has watermark #2; No. U214 watermark #7. These envelopes cannot be positively identified except by the watermark.

U57

Single line under "POSTAGE".

U58

Double line under "POSTAGE".

1876
Printed by Plimpton Manufacturing Co.

U218	U57	3c **red**, *white*	60.00	20.00
		Entire	65.00	40.00
U219	U57	3c **green**, *white*	45.00	12.50
		Entire	55.00	30.00
U220	U58	3c **red**, *white*	20,000.	
		Entire	27,500.	
U221	U58	3c **green**, *white*	55.00	15.00
		Entire	75.00	45.00

Garfield
U59

1882-86
Printed by Plimpton Manufacturing Co. and Morgan Envelope Co.

U222	U59	5c **brown**, *white*	2.75	1.50
		Entire	5.00	5.00
U223	U59	5c **brown**, *amber*	3.00	1.75
		Entire	6.00	6.00
U224	U59	5c **brown**, *oriental buff* ('86)	85.00	45.00
		Entire	90.00	
U225	U59	5c **brown**, *blue*	40.00	30.00
		Entire	75.00	40.00
U226	U59	5c **brown**, *fawn*	200.00	
		Entire	275.00	

Washington — U60

1883, October

U227	U60	2c **red**, *white*	2.75	1.25
		Entire	5.00	1.50
a.		2c brown (error), *white*, entire	2,000.	
U228	U60	2c **red**, *amber*	3.50	1.50
		Entire	6.00	3.00
U229	U60	2c **red**, *blue*	5.00	3.50
		Entire	6.50	5.00
U230	U60	2c **red**, *fawn*	3.75	2.00
		Entire	7.00	3.00

Washington — U61

Wavy lines fine and clear.

1883, November
Four Wavy Lines in Oval

U231	U61	2c **red**, *white*	2.00	1.00
		Entire	5.00	1.50

U232	U61	2c **red**, *amber*	2.00	1.25
		Entire	5.00	2.75
U233	U61	2c **red**, *blue*	5.00	3.50
		Entire	9.00	4.50
U234	U61	2c **red**, *fawn*	3.00	2.00
		Entire	5.00	3.00
W235	U61	2c **red**, *manila*	6.00	3.00
		Entire	10.00	6.00

U62

Retouched die. Wavy lines thick and blurred.

1884, June

U236	U62	2c **red**, *white*	4.00	2.00
		Entire	7.00	4.00
U237	U62	2c **red**, *amber*	7.50	5.50
		Entire	12.00	6.50
U238	U62	2c **red**, *blue*	10.00	5.50
		Entire	15.00	7.00
U239	U62	2c **red**, *fawn*	7.50	5.00
		Entire	11.00	7.50

U63

3½ links over left "2".

U240	U63	2c **red**, *white*	35.00	25.00
		Entire	60.00	45.00
U241	U63	2c **red**, *amber*	550.00	275.00
		Entire	900.00	600.00
U242	U63	2c **red**, *fawn*		6,250.
		Entire		—

U64

2 links below right "2".

U243	U64	2c **red**, *white*	50.00	35.00
		Entire	75.00	70.00
U244	U64	2c **red**, *amber*	100.00	60.00
		Entire	150.00	100.00
U245	U64	2c **red**, *blue*	250.00	95.00
		Entire	400.00	150.00
U246	U64	2c **red**, *fawn*	250.00	100.00
		Entire	300.00	225.00

U65

Round "O" in "TWO".

U247	U65	2c **red**, *white*	800.00	225.00
		Entire	1,200.00	600.00
U248	U65	2c **red**, *amber*	1,500.00	600.00
		Entire	2,500.00	800.00
U249	U65	2c **red**, *fawn*	450.00	275.00
		Entire	750.00	350.00

Jackson,
Die
1 — U66

Die 1 - Numeral at left is 2¾mm. wide.

Die 2 - Numeral at left is 3¼mm. wide

1883-86

U250	U66	4c **green**, die 1, *white*	2.00	2.00
		Entire	4.00	4.00
U251	U66	4c **green**, die 1, *amber*	3.00	2.00
		Entire	4.50	4.00
U252	U66	4c **green**, die 1, *oriental buff* ('86)	5.00	5.00
		Entire	8.50	6.00
U253	U66	4c **green**, die 1, *blue* ('86)	5.00	3.50
		Entire	8.50	6.00
U254	U66	4c **green**, die 1, *manila* ('86)	6.00	3.50
		Entire	9.00	7.00
U255	U66	4c **green**, die 1, *amber manila* ('86)	15.00	7.50
		Entire	20.00	12.00
U256	U66	4c **green**, die 2, *white*	3.00	2.75
		Entire	8.50	5.00
U257	U66	4c **green**, die 2, *amber*	7.00	4.00
		Entire	10.00	8.00
U258	U66	4c **green**, die 2, *manila* ('86)	6.00	4.00
		Entire	9.00	9.00
U259	U66	4c **green**, die 2, *amber manila* ('86)	6.00	4.00
		Entire	10.00	8.00

1884, May

U260	U61	2c **brown**, *white*	9.00	3.00
		Entire	12.00	7.50

U261	U61	2c **brown**, *amber*	8.00	3.50
		Entire	11.00	4.00
U262	U61	2c **brown**, *blue*	8.50	4.00
		Entire	12.00	6.00
U263	U61	2c **brown**, *fawn*	7.50	4.00
		Entire	9.00	6.50
W264	U61	2c **brown**, *manila*	7.50	6.50
		Entire	15.00	10.00

1884, June

Retouched Die

U265	U62	2c **brown**, *white*	10.00	3.00
		Entire	14.00	8.00
U266	U62	2c **brown**, *amber*	40.00	16.00
		Entire	50.00	25.00
U267	U62	2c **brown**, *blue*	7.00	4.00
		Entire	10.00	6.00
U268	U62	2c **brown**, *fawn*	8.00	6.50
		Entire	11.00	8.00
W269	U62	2c **brown**, *manila*	15.00	10.00
		Entire	25.00	11.00

2 Links Below Right "2"

U270	U64	2c **brown**, *white*	60.00	35.00
		Entire	80.00	80.00
U271	U64	2c **brown**, *amber*	165.00	85.00
		Entire	250.00	175.00
U272	U64	2c **brown**, *fawn*	2,100.	1,000.
		Entire	3,750.	2,250.

Round "O" in "Two"

U273	U65	2c **brown**, *white*	110.00	60.00
		Entire	125.00	85.00
U274	U65	2c **brown**, *amber*	125.00	60.00
		Entire	125.00	75.00
U275	U65	2c **brown**, *blue*		4,500.
U276	U65	2c **brown**, *fawn*	600.00	400.00
		Entire	850.00	600.00

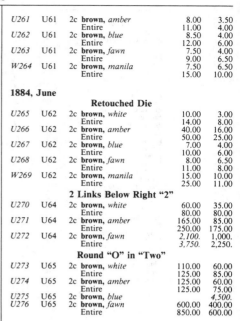

Washington — U67

Die 1 - Extremity of bust below the queue forms a point.

U68

Die 2 - Extremity of bust is rounded. Similar to U61. Two wavy lines in oval.

1884-86

U277	U67	2c **brown**, die 1, *white*	25	15
		Entire	60	25
a.		2c brown lake, die 1, *white*	17.50	10.00
		Entire	17.50	12.00
U278	U67	2c **brown**, die 1, *amber*	40	30
		Entire	1.00	50
a.		2c brown lake, die 1, *amber*	30.00	10.00
		Entire	32.50	11.00
U279	U67	2c **brown**, die 1, *oriental buff* ('86)	2.00	1.25
		Entire	3.00	2.25
U280	U67	2c **brown**, die 1, *blue*	1.50	1.00
		Entire	2.00	1.50

U281	U67	2c **brown,** die 1, *fawn*	2.00	1.25
		Entire	2.50	1.50
U282	U67	2c **brown,** die 1, *manila* ('86)	7.00	2.50
		Entire	8.00	3.00
W283	U67	2c **brown,** die 1, *manila*	4.00	3.50
		Entire	6.00	5.00
U284	U67	2c **brown,** die 1, *amber manila* ('86)	4.00	4.00
		Entire	7.50	5.00
U285	U67	2c **red,** die 1, *white*	500.00	
		Entire	750.00	
U286	U67	2c **red,** die 1, *blue*	200.00	
		Entire	300.00	
W287	U67	2c **red,** die 1, *manila*	90.00	
		Entire	125.00	
U288	U68	2c **brown,** die 2, *white*	150.00	30.00
		Entire	400.00	75.00
U289	U68	2c **brown,** die 2, *amber*	10.00	9.00
		Entire	14.00	12.00
U290	U68	2c **brown,** die 2, *blue*	675.00	125.00
		Entire	750.00	175.00
U291	U68	2c **brown,** die 2, *fawn*	17.00	14.00
		Entire	25.00	17.50
W292	U68	2c **brown,** die 2, *manila*	17.00	14.00
		Entire	19.00	17.50

Gen. U.S.
Grant — US1

1886
Printed by American Bank Note Co.
Issued August 18, 1886. Withdrawn June 30, 1894.
Letter Sheet, 160x271mm. Stamp in upper right corner.
Creamy White Paper.

U293	US1	2c **green,** *white,* entire	20.00	8.50

Perforation varieties:

83 perforations at top	20.00	8.50
41 perforations at top	20.00	8.50
33 perforations at top	35.00	10.50

All with 41 perforations at top.

Inscribed: Series 1	20.00	8.50
Inscribed: Series 2	20.00	8.50
Inscribed: Series 3	20.00	8.50
Inscribed: Series 4	20.00	8.50
Inscribed: Series 5	20.00	8.50
Inscribed: Series 6	20.00	8.50
Inscribed: Series 7	20.00	8.50

Franklin
U69

Washington
U70

Die 1 - Bust points between third and fourth notches of inner oval "G" of "POSTAGE" has no bar.

U71

Die 2 - Bust points between second and third notches of inner oval; "G" of "POSTAGE" has a bar; ear is indicated by one heavy line; one vertical line at corner of mouth.

U72

Die 3 - Frame same as die 2; upper part of head more rounded; ear indicated by two curved lines with two locks of hair in front; two vertical lines at corner of mouth.

U.S. Proofs are listed and priced in a separate
section of the catalogue. See catalogue index.

Jackson
U73

Grant — U74

Die 1 - There is a space between the beard and the collar of the coat. A button is on the collar.

U75

Die 2 - The collar touches the beard and there is no button.

1887-94
Printed by Plimpton Manufacturing Co. and
Morgan Envelope Co., Hartford,
Conn.; James Purcell, Holyoke, Mass.

U294	U69	1c **blue,** *white*	40	20
		Entire	60	30
U295	U69	1c **dark blue,** *white* ('94)	5.50	2.00
		Entire	8.50	5.50
U296	U69	1c **blue,** *amber*	2.00	1.00
		Entire	3.50	2.50
U297	U69	1c **dark blue,** *amber* ('94)	35.00	17.50
		Entire	45.00	22.50
+U298	U69	1c **blue,** *oriental buff*	2,250.	
		Entire	4,000.	
+U299	U69	1c **blue,** *blue*	3,000.	
		Entire	4,250.	
U300	U69	1c **blue,** *manila*	50	25
		Entire	85	40
W301	U69	1c **blue,** *manila*	30	25
		Entire	65	40
U302	U69	1c **dark blue,** *manila* ('94)	17.50	7.00
		Entire	25.00	15.00
W303	U69	1c **dark blue,** *manila* ('94)	10.00	8.50
		Entire	20.00	15.00
U304	U69	1c **blue,** *amber manila*	3.00	2.25
		Entire	5.00	3.50
U305	U70	2c **green,** die 1, *white*	7.00	6.00
		Entire	15.00	10.00
U306	U70	2c **green,** die 1, *amber*	16.00	10.50
		Entire	22.50	12.00
U307	U70	2c **green,** die 1, *oriental buff*	55.00	25.00

U308	U70	2c **green**, die 1, *blue*	75.00 2,750.	40.00 650.00
		Entire		4,000.
U309	U70	2c **green**, die 1, *manila*	1,700.	400.00
		Entire	5,500.	600.00
U310	U70	2c **green**, die 1, *amber manila*		
			1,500.	500.00
		Entire	5,000.	2,500.
U311	U71	2c **green**, die 2, *white*	25	10
		Entire	40	20
U312	U71	2c **green**, die 2, *amber*	30	10
		Entire	50	25
U313	U71	2c **green**, die 2, *oriental buff*	40	20
		Entire	75	35
U314	U71	2c **green**, die 2, *blue*	40	20
		Entire	80	30
U315	U71	2c **green**, die 2, *manila*	75	35
		Entire	1.65	80
W316	U71	2c **green**, die 2, *manila*	1.90	1.65
		Entire	5.00	4.00
U317	U71	2c **green**, die 2, *amber manila*	1.50	1.25
		Entire	3.50	2.00
U318	U72	2c **green**, die 3, *white*	90.00	10.00
		Entire	125.00	35.00
U319	U72	2c **green**, die 3, *amber*	115.00	15.00
		Entire	130.00	35.00
U320	U72	2c **green**, die 3, *oriental buff*	125.00	30.00
		Entire	150.00	60.00
U321	U72	2c **green**, die 3, *blue*	140.00	40.00
		Entire	150.00	60.00
U322	U72	2c **green**, die 3, *manila*	125.00	60.00
		Entire	150.00	100.00
U323	U72	2c **green**, die 3, *amber manila*	300.00	75.00
		Entire	325.00	110.00
U324	U73	4c **carmine**, *white*	1.10	95
		Entire	2.50	1.00
a.		4c lake, *white*	1.50	90
		Entire	3.50	2.50
b.		4c scarlet, *white* ('94)	1.50	90
		Entire	3.00	2.00
U325	U73	4c **carmine**, *amber*	1.75	1.50
		Entire	3.50	2.00
a.		4c lake, *amber*	1.75	1.50
		Entire	3.50	2.00
b.		4c scarlet, *amber* ('94)	1.75	2.00
		Entire	4.00	2.00
U326	U73	4c **carmine**, *oriental buff*	4.00	2.00
		Entire	7.00	3.00
a.		4c lake, *oriental buff*	4.00	2.00
		Entire	7.00	3.50
U327	U73	4c **carmine**, *blue*	3.00	3.00
		Entire	5.00	4.00
a.		4c lake, *blue*	3.50	3.00
		Entire	7.50	3.00
U328	U73	4c **carmine**, *manila*	5.00	4.00
		Entire	7.00	5.00
a.		4c lake, *manila*	5.00	4.00
		Entire	7.00	5.00
b.		4c pink, *manila*	6.00	3.00
		Entire	8.00	5.00
U329	U73	4c **carmine**, *amber manila*	3.00	2.00
		Entire	6.00	3.00
a.		4c lake, *amber manila*	3.00	2.00
		Entire	6.00	3.50
b.		4c pink, *amber manila*	4.00	2.00
		Entire	7.00	7.00
U330	U74	5c **blue**, die 1, *white*	2.50	2.25
		Entire	4.50	8.50
U331	U74	5c **blue**, die 1, *amber*	3.00	1.50
		Entire	6.00	11.00
U332	U74	5c **blue**, die 1, *oriental buff*	3.00	2.50
		Entire	7.50	12.00
U333	U74	5c **blue**, die 1, *blue*	4.00	3.00
		Entire	8.00	10.00
U334	U75	5c **blue**, die 2, *white* ('94)	7.00	4.00
		Entire	9.50	12.00
U335	U75	5c **blue**, die 2, *amber* ('94)	7.50	4.00
		Entire	11.00	14.00
U336	U55	30c **red brown**, *white*	30.00	35.00
		Entire	40.00	200.00
a.		30c yellow brown, *white*	40.00	27.50
		Entire	50.00	300.00
b.		30c chocolate, *white*	40.00	45.00
		Entire	50.00	300.00
U337	U55	30c **red brown**, *amber*	35.00	50.00
		Entire	45.00	300.00
a.		30c yellow brown, *amber*	40.00	40.00
		Entire	60.00	300.00
b.		30c chocolate, *amber*	40.00	40.00
		Entire	60.00	300.00
U338	U55	30c **red brown**, *oriental buff*	30.00	40.00
		Entire	40.00	300.00
a.		30c yellow brown, *oriental buff*	30.00	40.00
		Entire	40.00	300.00
U339	U55	30c **red brown**, *blue*	30.00	40.00
		Entire	35.00	300.00
a.		30c yellow brown, *blue*	30.00	40.00
		Entire	35.00	300.00
U340	U55	30c **red brown**, *manila*	35.00	35.00
		Entire	40.00	250.00
a.		30c brown, *manila*	35.00	35.00
		Entire	45.00	250.00
U341	U55	30c **red brown**, *amber manila*	40.00	25.00
		Entire	45.00	250.00
a.		30c yellow brown, *amber manila*	40.00	25.00
		Entire	45.00	250.00
U342	U56	90c **purple**, *white*	50.00	60.00
		Entire	65.00	400.00
U343	U56	90c **purple**, *amber*	60.00	60.00
		Entire	80.00	400.00
U344	U56	90c **purple**, *oriental buff*	60.00	65.00
		Entire	80.00	400.00
U345	U56	90c **purple**, *blue*	65.00	70.00
		Entire	90.00	400.00

U346	U56	90c **purple**, *manila*	65.00	70.00
		Entire	90.00	400.00
U347	U56	90c **purple**, *amber manila*	65.00	70.00
		Entire	95.00	400.00

Columbus and Liberty — U76

Four dies were used for the 1c, 2c and 5c:
1. Meridian behind Columbus' head. Period after "CENTS".
2. No meridian. With period.
3. With meridian. No period.
4. No meridian. No period.

1893

U348	U76	1c **deep blue**, *white*	1.75	75
		Entire	2.25	80
U349	U76	2c **violet**, *white*	1.50	40
		Entire	1.75	50
a.		2c dark slate (error), *white*	1,000.	
		Entire		
U350	U76	5c **chocolate**, *white*	7.50	6.50
		Entire	12.00	10.00
a.		5c slate brown (error), *white*	600.00	600.00
		Entire	650.00	1,000.
U351	U76	10c **slate brown**, *white*	35.00	25.00
		Entire	55.00	45.00

Franklin
U77

Washington
U78

Die 1 - Bust points to first notch of inner oval and is only slightly concave below.

U79

Die 2 - Bust points to middle of second notch of inner oval and is quite hollow below. Queue has ribbon around it.

U80

Die 3 - Same as die 2, but hair flowing. No ribbon on queue.

Lincoln
U81

Die 1 - Bust pointed but not draped.

U82

Die 2 - Bust broad and draped.

U83

Die 3 - Head larger, inner oval has no notches.

Grant
U84

Similar to design of 1887-95 but smaller.

1899

U352	U77	1c	**green**, white	40	20
			Entire	65	50
U353	U77	1c	**green**, amber	3.50	1.25
			Entire	5.75	2.50
U354	U77	1c	**green**, oriental buff	7.00	2.00
			Entire	9.00	3.50
U355	U77	1c	**green**, blue	7.50	2.00
			Entire	9.00	5.25
U356	U77	1c	**green**, manila	1.50	75
			Entire	4.50	1.75
W357	U77	1c	**green**, manila	1.50	75
			Entire	6.25	2.50
U358	U78	2c	**carmine**, die 1, white	1.65	75
			Entire	5.50	2.50
U359	U78	2c	**carmine**, die 1, amber	13.00	9.00
			Entire	17.50	11.00
U360	U78	2c	**carmine**, die 1, oriental buff	13.00	7.50
			Entire	20.00	8.75
U361	U78	2c	**carmine**, die 1, blue	45.00	22.50
			Entire	50.00	32.50
U362	U79	2c	**carmine**, die 2, white	25	20
			Entire	50	30
a.		2c	dark lake, die 2, white	25.00	30.00
			Entire	30.00	35.00
U363	U79	2c	**carmine**, die 2, amber	75	15
			Entire	2.00	60
U364	U79	2c	**carmine**, die 2, oriental buff	75	15
			Entire	1.90	60
U365	U79	2c	**carmine**, die 2, blue	95	45
			Entire	2.50	1.65
W366	U79	2c	**carmine**, die 2, manila	3.50	2.25
			Entire	7.50	5.00
U367	U80	2c	**carmine**, die 3, white	3.00	1.50
			Entire	6.75	6.00
U368	U80	2c	**carmine**, die 3, amber	6.00	4.50
			Entire	10.00	9.00
U369	U80	2c	**carmine**, die 3, oriental buff	18.00	9.00
			Entire	24.00	18.00
U370	U80	2c	**carmine**, die 3, blue	8.00	6.00
			Entire	17.50	8.50
U371	U81	4c	**brown**, die 1, white	13.00	9.00
			Entire	16.00	14.00
U372	U81	4c	**brown**, die 1, amber	13.00	9.00
			Entire	25.00	22.50
U373	U82	4c	**brown**, die 2, white	3,500.	350.00
			Entire	4,000.	
U374	U83	4c	**brown**, die 3, white	7.50	5.00
			Entire	15.00	10.00
U375	U83	4c	**brown**, die 3, amber	32.50	10.00
			Entire	37.50	15.00
W376	U83	4c	**brown**, die 3, manila	12.00	6.00
			Entire	15.00	9.50
U377	U84	5c	**blue**, white	7.50	7.00
			Entire	8.50	8.00
U378	U84	5c	**blue**, amber	10.00	8.50
			Entire	13.00	13.00

Franklin — U85

Washington
U86

One short and two long vertical lines at the right of "CENTS".

Grant
U87

Lincoln — U88

1903
Printed by Hartford Manufacturing Co., Hartford, Conn.

U379	U85	1c	**green**, white	50	10
			Entire	75	30
U380	U85	1c	**green**, amber	10.00	1.75
			Entire	13.00	2.25
U381	U85	1c	**green**, oriental buff	8.00	1.65
			Entire	11.50	2.00
U382	U85	1c	**green**, blue	10.00	1.75
			Entire	13.00	2.25
U383	U85	1c	**green**, manila	2.00	75
			Entire	3.00	1.00

W384	U85	1c	**green**, manila	80	30
			Entire	1.00	75
U385	U86	2c	**carmine**, white	30	15
			Entire	50	35
		2c	pink, white	1.25	75
U386	U86	2c	**carmine**, amber	1.25	20
			Entire	2.50	80
		2c	pink, amber	2.50	1.10
U387	U86	2c	**carmine**, oriental buff	1.25	30
			Entire	1.75	35
		2c	pink, oriental buff	1.90	85
U388	U86	2c	**carmine**, blue	1.00	50
			Entire	2.50	60
		2c	pink, blue	2.50	1.50
W389	U86	2c	**carmine**, manila	12.00	6.00
			Entire	14.00	7.25
U390	U87	4c	**chocolate**, white	14.00	8.00
			Entire	17.00	12.50
U391	U87	4c	**chocolate**, amber	14.00	8.50
			Entire	17.00	12.00
W392	U87	4c	**chocolate**, manila	14.00	9.50
			Entire	17.00	12.00
U393	U88	5c	**blue**, white	14.00	7.50
			Entire	17.00	15.00
U394	U88	5c	**blue**, amber	14.00	8.00
			Entire	17.00	18.00

U89

Re-cut die - The three lines at the right of "CENTS" and at the left of "TWO" are usually all short; the lettering is heavier and the ends of the ribbons slightly changed.

1904

Re-cut Die

U395	U89	2c	**carmine**, white	35	15
			Entire	70	45
		2c	pink, white	4.00	2.00
U396	U89	2c	**carmine**, amber	6.00	45
			Entire	7.50	1.25
		2c	pink, amber	7.00	2.00
U397	U89	2c	**carmine**, oriental buff	4.00	1.00
			Entire	5.00	1.50
		2c	pink, oriental buff	5.00	2.00
U398	U89	2c	**carmine**, blue	2.50	75
			Entire	3.50	1.25
		2c	pink, amber	4.00	2.00
W399	U89	2c	**carmine**, manila	9.50	5.50
			Entire	14.00	6.00
		2c	pink, manila	13.00	5.00

Franklin
U90

U90 Die 1

U90 Die 2

U90 Die 3   U90 Die 4

U91 Die 5   U91 Die 6

U91 Die 7   U91 Die 8

Die 1. Wide "D" in "UNITED".
Die 2. Narrow "D" in "UNITED".
Die 3. Wide "S-S" in "STATES" (1910).
Die 4. Sharp angle at back of bust, "N" and "E" of "ONE" are parallel (1912).

Die 1. Oval "O" in "TWO" and "C" in "CENTS". front of bust broad.
Die 2. Similar to 1 but hair re-cut in two distinct locks at top of head.
Die 3. Round "O" in "TWO" and "C" in "CENTS", coarse lettering.
Die 4. Similar to 3 but lettering fine and clear, hair lines clearly embossed. Inner oval thin and clear.
Die 5. All "S's" wide (1910).
Die 6. Similar to 1 but front of bust narrow (1913).
Die 7. Similar to 6 but upper corner of front of bust cut away (1916).
Die 8. Similar to 7 but lower stroke of "S" in "CENTS" is a straight line. Hair as in Die 2 (1916).

1907-16

Printed by Mercantile Corp. and Middle West Supply Co., Dayton, Ohio.

U400	U90	1c **green**, *white*, die 1	25	10
		Entire	30	30
a.	Die 2		40	15
		Entire	50	25
b.	Die 3		50	25
		Entire	75	45
c.	Die 4		50	20
		Entire	60	25
U401	U90	1c **green**, *amber*, die 1	60	40
		Entire	90	60
a.	Die 2		75	50
		Entire	1.10	70
b.	Die 3		75	50
		Entire	1.40	70
c.	Die 4		70	45
		Entire	1.00	60
U402	U90	1c **green**, *oriental buff*, die 1	2.50	1.00
		Entire	3.25	1.75
a.	Die 2		2.50	1.00
		Entire	3.25	1.00
b.	Die 3		4.00	1.50
		Entire	4.50	1.75
c.	Die 4		3.00	1.25
		Entire	3.50	1.75
U403	U90	1c **green**, *blue*, die 1	3.00	1.25
		Entire	3.50	2.25
a.	Die 2		3.00	1.00
		Entire	4.00	1.40
b.	Die 3		3.00	1.50
		Entire	3.50	1.75
c.	Die 4		2.75	75
		Entire	4.50	1.25
U404	U90	1c **green**, *manila*, die 1	2.25	1.75
		Entire	3.25	2.75
a.	Die 2		2.50	2.00
		Entire	5.50	3.50
W405	U90	1c **green**, *manila*, die 1	40	25
		Entire	50	30
a.	Die 2		30.00	20.00
		Entire	32.50	22.50
b.	Die 3		3.50	2.00
		Entire	7.50	4.50
c.	Die 4		25.00	20.00
		Entire	25.00	22.50

Washington — U91

U91 Die 1

U91 Die 3

U91 Die 2 *(top)* / U91 Die 4 *(bottom)*

U406	U91	2c **brown red**, *white*, die 1	35	15
		Entire	70	30
a.	Die 2		20.00	7.50
		Entire	30.00	22.50
b.	Die 3		30	20
		Entire	40	25
U407	U91	2c **brown red**, *amber*, die 1	4.00	2.00
		Entire	5.75	5.00
a.	Die 2		85.00	40.00
		Entire	100.00	65.00
b.	Die 3		1.75	60
		Entire	2.50	90
U408	U91	2c **brown red**, *oriental buff*, die 1	5.50	1.25
		Entire	7.50	3.00
a.	Die 2		110.00	50.00
		Entire	125.00	80.00
b.	Die 3		4.50	2.00
		Entire	5.00	4.00
U409	U91	2c **brown red**, *blue*, die 1	3.00	1.50
		Entire	4.25	3.00
a.	Die 2		110.00	80.00
		Entire	140.00	100.00
b.	Die 3		3.50	1.50
		Entire	5.00	3.00
W410	U91	2c **brown red**, *manila*, die 1	35.00	22.50
		Entire	40.00	27.50
U411	U91	2c **carmine**, *white*, die 1	20	15
		Entire	50	35
a.	Die 2		20	8
		Entire	50	35
b.	Die 3		40	25
		Entire	75	40
c.	Die 4		20	15
		Entire	40	25
d.	Die 5		30	20
		Entire	60	45
e.	Die 6		20	8
		Entire	40	25
f.	Die 7		11.00	9.00
		Entire	13.00	11.00
g.	Die 8		11.00	9.00
		Entire	13.00	11.00
h.		2c carmine, die 1, with added impression of 1c green (#U400), die 1, entire	225.00	
i.		2c carmine, die 1, with added impression of 4c black (#U416a), entire	175.00	
U412	U91	2c **carmine**, *amber*, die 1	20	10
		Entire	80	16
a.	Die 2		12	10
		Entire	40	15
b.	Die 3		1.00	30
		Entire	1.40	60
c.	Die 4		20	15
		Entire	40	35
d.	Die 5		35	20
		Entire	70	40
e.	Die 6		15	10
		Entire	50	20
f.	Die 7		9.00	7.00
		Entire	11.00	9.00
U413	U91	2c **carmine**, *oriental buff*, die 1	40	20
		Entire	50	25
a.	Die 2		45	45
		Entire	60	35
b.	Die 3		5.00	2.50
		Entire	9.00	5.25
c.	Die 4		10	10
		Entire	35	15
d.	Die 5		35	25
		Entire	80	45
e.	Die 6		30	25
		Entire	75	45
f.	Die 7		30.00	15.00
		Entire	37.50	22.50
g.	Die 8		9.00	7.00
		Entire	12.50	9.00

U414	U91	2c **carmine**, *blue*, die 1	30	10
		Entire	90	16
a.	Die 2		25	20
		Entire	55	30
b.	Die 3		50	35
		Entire	1.10	55
c.	Die 4		10	8
		Entire	30	15
d.	Die 5		50	30
		Entire	1.10	40
e.	Die 6		25	15
		Entire	70	30
f.	Die 7		10.00	6.00
		Entire	15.00	14.00
g.	Die 8		10.00	6.00
		Entire	12.50	11.50
W415	U91	2c **carmine**, *manila*, die 1	3.00	1.75
		Entire	6.00	4.25
a.	Die 2		2.00	90
		Entire	2.75	1.15
b.	Die 5		2.00	90
		Entire	3.25	2.25
c.	Die 7		35.00	30.00
		Entire	42.50	37.50

U90 4c Die 1   U90 4c Die 2

4c-Die 1. "F" close to (1 mm.) left "4".
4c-Die 2. "F" far from (1¼ mm.) left "4".

U416	U90	4c **black**, *white*, die 2	2.75	1.50
		Entire	7.25	3.00
a.	Die 1		3.75	2.75
		Entire	6.75	5.00
U417	U90	4c **black**, *amber*, die 2	4.00	2.00
		Entire	8.00	3.75
a.	Die 1		4.00	2.00
		Entire	7.00	4.00

U91 5c Die 1   U91 5c Die 2

5c-Die 1. Tall "F" in "FIVE".
5c-Die 2. Short "F" in "FIVE".

U418	U91	5c **blue**, *white*, die 2	5.00	1.75
		Entire	9.00	4.25
a.	Die 1		5.00	1.75
		Entire	10.00	4.50
a.		5c blue, *buff*, die 2 (error)	700.00	
c.		5c blue, *blue*, die 2 (error)	700.00	
d.		5c blue, *blue*, die 1 (error)	800.00	
		Entire	1,250.	
U419	U91	5c **blue**, *amber*, die 2	10.00	9.00
		Entire	13.00	10.00
a.	Die 1		10.00	9.00
		Entire	13.00	12.00

On July 1, 1915 the use of laid paper was discontinued and wove paper was substituted. Nos. U400 to W405 and U411 to U419 exist on both papers; U406 to W410 come on laid only. Nos. U429 and U430 exist on laid paper.

Franklin U92

Die 1

Die 2

Die 3

Die 5

(The 1c and 4c dies are the same except for figures of value.)
Die 1. UNITED nearer inner circle than outer circle.
Die 2. Large U; large NT closely spaced.
Die 3. Knob of hair at back of neck. Large NT widely spaced.
Die 4. UNITED nearer outer circle than inner circle.
Die 5. Narrow oval C, (also O and G).
Some of the engraved dies of this series represent printing methods now obsolete, others are still in service. Some are best distinguished in the entire envelope. Many electrotypes were used.

Printed by Middle West Supply Co. and International Envelope Corp., Dayton, Ohio.

1916-32

U420	U92	1c **green,** *white,* die 1	6	5
		Entire	20	10
a.	Die 2		60.00	45.00
		Entire, size 8	80.00	60.00
b.	Die 3		8	5
		Entire	25	10
c.	Die 4		12	10
		Entire	30	15
d.	Die 5		12	10
		Entire	50	25
U421	U92	1c **green,** *amber,* die 1	30	30
		Entire	40	35
a.	Die 2		250.00	150.00
		Entire, size 8	400.00	175.00
b.	Die 3		1.00	50
		Entire	1.50	85
c.	Die 4		1.00	40
		Entire	1.50	1.05
d.	Die 5		80	30
		Entire	1.00	70
U422	U92	1c **green,** *oriental buff,* die 1	1.25	75
		Entire	1.50	1.20
a.	Die 4		3.00	1.00
		Entire	4.00	2.50
U423	U92	1c **green,** *blue,* die 1	35	8
		Entire	45	15
a.	Die 3		60	40
		Entire	90	65
b.	Die 4		1.00	40
		Entire	1.50	75
c.	Die 5		60	30
		Entire	90	50
U424	U92	1c **green,** *manila,* (unglazed) die 1	5.00	3.00
		Entire	6.00	4.00
W425	U92	1c **green,** *manila,* (unglazed) die 1	8	6
		Entire	10	8
a.	Die 3		125.00	110.00
		Entire	140.00	125.00
U426	U92	1c **green,** (glazed) *brown* ('20), die 1	20.00	12.50
		Entire	30.00	17.50
W427	U92	1c **green,** (glazed) *brown* ('20), die 1	60.00	
		Entire	70.00	
U428	U92	1c **green,** (unglazed) *brown* ('20), die 1	6.00	6.00
		Entire	9.00	8.00

All manila envelopes of circular dies are unwatermarked. Manila paper, including that of Nos. U424 and W425, exists in many shades.

Washington — U93

Die 1

Die 2

Die 3

Die 4

Die 5

Die 6

Die 7

Die 8

Die 9

(The 1½c, 2c, 3c, 5c, and 6c dies are the same except for figures of value.)
Die 1. Letters broad. Numerals vertical. Large head (9¼ mm.) from tip of nose to back of neck. E closer to inner circle than N of cents.
Die 2. Similar to 1; but U far from left circle.
Die 3. Similar to 2; but all inner circles very thin (Rejected die).
Die 4. Similar to 1; but C very close to left circle.
Die 5. Small head (8¾ mm.) from tip of nose to back of neck. T and S of CENTS close at bottom.
Die 6. Similar to 5; but T and S of CENTS far apart at bottom. Left numeral slopes to right.
Die 7. Large head. Both numerals slope to right. Clean cut lettering. All letters T have short to strokes.
Die 8. Similar to 7; but all letters T have long top strokes.
Die 9. Narrow oval C (also O and G).

U429	U93	2c **carmine,** *white,* die 1	5	5
		Entire	20	5
a.	Die 2		7.00	5.00
		Entire	14.00	7.50
b.	Die 3		25.00	20.00
		Entire	35.00	25.00
c.	Die 4		7.00	6.00
		Entire	10.00	7.50
d.	Die 5		25	15
		Entire	40	35
e.	Die 6		25	15
		Entire	60	35
f.	Die 7		30	15
		Entire	60	40
g.	Die 8		25	10
		Entire	50	35
h.	Die 9		15	6

		Entire	40	30
i.	2c green, die 1 (error), *white,* entire		4,250.	
j.	carmine, die 1, with added impression of 1c green (#U420), die 1, entire		500.00	
k.	2c carmine, die 1, with added impression of 4c black (#U416a), entire		500.00	
l.	2c carmine, die 1, with added impression of 1c green (#U400), die 1, entire		400.00	
U430	U93	2c **carmine,** *amber,* die 1	12	6
		Entire	30	10
a.	Die 2		8.50	6.00
		Entire	14.00	9.50
b.	Die 4		17.50	9.00
		Entire	22.50	11.50
c.	Die 5		25	25
		Entire	80	60
d.	Die 6		45	15
		Entire	85	40
e.	Die 7		35	20
		Entire	70	35
f.	Die 8		35	20
		Entire	65	35
g.	Die 9		25	8
		Entire	60	35
U431	U93	2c **carmine,** *oriental buff,* die 1	1.25	35
		Entire	3.00	85
a.	Die 2		80.00	30.00
		Entire	80.00	60.00
b.	Die 4		25.00	25.00
		Entire	30.00	30.00
c.	Die 5		2.00	1.00
		Entire	4.25	1.25
d.	Die 6		2.50	1.10
		Entire	4.75	1.50
e.	Die 7		2.50	1.10
		Entire	3.75	1.50
U432	U93	2c **carmine,** *blue,* die 1	10	5
		Entire	40	20
b.	Die 2		20.00	15.00
		Entire	25.00	25.00
c.	Die 3		85.00	75.00
		Entire	125.00	92.50
d.	Die 4		20.00	20.00
		Entire	25.00	22.50
e.	Die 5		30	10
		Entire	75	30
f.	Die 6		20	16
		Entire	95	45
g.	Die 7		30	15
		Entire	95	45
h.	Die 8		35	20
		Entire	60	45
i.	Die 9		30	20
		Entire	1.65	45
U432A	U93	2c **car,** *manila,* die 1, entire	—	
W433	U93	2c **carmine,** *manila,* die 1	20	15
		Entire	25	20
W434	U93	2c **carmine,** (glazed) *brown* ('20), die 1	75.00	50.00
		Entire	90.00	55.00
W435	U93	2c **carmine,** (unglazed) *brown* ('20), die 1	75.00	50.00
		Entire	90.00	55.00
U436	U93	3c **dark violet,** *white,* die 1	40	15
		Entire	60	10
a.	3c purple ('32), die 1		25	15
		Entire	30	20
b.	3c dark violet, die 5		1.00	10
		Entire	1.75	30
c.	3c dark violet, die 6		1.25	25
		Entire	2.00	35
d.	3c dark violet, die 7		1.00	10
		Entire	1.75	30
e.	3c purple ('32), die 7		30	10
		Entire	1.25	20
f.	3c purple ('32), die 9		10	5
		Entire	35	10
g.	3c carmine (error), die 1		25.00	25.00
		Entire	30.00	30.00
h.	3c carmine (error), die 5		25.00	25.00
		Entire	30.00	30.00
i.	3c dark violet, die 1, with added impression of 1c green (#U420), die 1, entire		500.00	
j.	3c dark violet, die 1, with added impression of 2c carmine (#U429), die 1, entire		600.00	—
U437	U93	3c **dark violet,** *amber,* die 1	1.90	75
		Entire	3.00	1.75
a.	3c purple ('32), die 1		15	5
		Entire	45	25
b.	3c dark violet, die 5		4.00	1.25
		Entire	6.00	2.75
c.	3c dark violet, die 6		4.50	1.25
		Entire	6.50	2.75
d.	3c dark violet, die 7		3.25	80
		Entire	4.50	1.75
e.	3c purple ('32), die 7		50	10
		Entire	80	50
f.	3c purple ('32), die 9		35	10
		Entire	60	25
g.	3c carmine (error), die 5		300.00	225.00
		Entire	350.00	250.00
h.	3c black (error), die 1		140.00	
		Entire	175.00	—
U438	U93	3c **dark violet,** *oriental buff,* die 1	18.00	1.00
		Entire	22.50	1.25
a.	Die 5		18.00	75
		Entire	21.00	85
b.	Die 6		20.00	1.25
		Entire	30.00	2.00
c.	Die 7		30.00	3.00

		Entire	37.50	7.00
U439	U93	3c **dark violet**, *blue*, die 1	5.25	1.00
		Entire	8.00	5.00
a.		3c purple ('32), die 1	18	5
		Entire	40	10
b.		3c dark violet, die 5	5.00	2.00
		Entire	7.75	3.00
c.		3c dark violet, die 6	4.50	2.50
		Entire	7.50	2.75
d.		3c dark violet, die 7	7.50	2.75
		Entire	11.00	6.00
e.		3c purple ('32), die 7	30	20
		Entire	60	30
f.		3c purple ('32), die 9	30	10
		Entire	80	40
g.		3c carmine (error), die 5	275.00	275.00
		Entire	325.00	325.00
U440	U92	4c **black**, *white*, die 1	60	35
		Entire	1.75	1.50
a.		4c black with added impression of 2c carmine (#U429), die 1, entire	225.00	
U441	U92	4c **black**, *amber*, die 1	2.00	55
		Entire	3.50	1.40
U442	U92	4c **black**, *blue*, ('21) die 1	2.00	40
		Entire	4.00	1.50
U443	U93	5c **blue**, *white*, die 1	2.00	50
		Entire	4.25	2.50
U444	U93	5c **blue**, *amber*, die 1	2.50	75
		Entire	5.00	2.75
U445	U93	5c **blue**, *blue*, ('21) die 1	2.75	75
		Entire	6.00	3.00

The provisional 2c surcharges of 1920-21 were made at central post offices with canceling machines using slugs provided by the Post Office Department.

Double or triple surcharge listings of 1920-25 are for specimens with surcharge directly or partly upon the stamp.

Type 1

1920-21

Surcharged on 1874-1920 Envelopes indicated by Numbers in Parentheses

Surcharged in Black

U446	U93	2c on 3c **dark violet**, *white* (U436, die 1)	8.50	9.00
		Entire	10.00	9.50
a.		Die 5	8.50	9.00
		Entire	10.00	9.50

Surcharged

Type 2

Rose Surcharge

U447	U93	2c on 3c **dark violet**, *white* (U436, die 1)	4.75	5.00
		Entire	6.00	6.00
b.		Die 6	4.75	5.00
		Entire	8.25	8.00

Black Surcharge

U447A	U93	2c on 2c **carmine**, *white* (U429)	1,500.	
U447C	U93	2c on 2c **carmine**, *amber* (U430)	—	
U448	U93	2c on 3c **dark violet**, *white* (U436)	1.75	1.75
		Entire	2.00	2.00
U449	U93	2c on 3c **dark violet**, *amber* (U437)	4.00	4.00
		Entire	4.50	4.50
U450	U93	2c on 3c **dark violet**, *oriental buff* (U438)	12.00	12.00
		Entire	13.00	13.00
U451	U93	2c on 3c **dark violet**, *blue* (U439)	9.50	10.00
		Entire	10.50	10.50

Type 2 exists in three city sub-types.

Surcharged

Type 3

Bars 2 mm. apart

U451A	U90	2c on 1c **green**, *white* (U400, die 1)	1,500.	
U452	U92	2c on 1c **green**, *white* (U420)	750.00	

		Entire	850.00	
a.		Double surcharge, type 3	900.00	
U453	U91	2c on 2c **carmine**, *white* (U411, die 1)	750.00	
		Entire	850.00	
a.		Die 4	750.00	
		Entire	850.00	
U453B	U91	2c on 2c **carmine**, *blue* (U414e, die 6)	625.00	
		Entire	675.00	
U453C	U91	2c on 2c **carmine**, *oriental buff* (U413e, die 6)	650.00	600.00
		Entire	700.00	
d.		Die 1	650.00	
		Entire	700.00	
U454	U93	2c on 2c **carmine**, *white* (U429)	75.00	
		Entire	85.00	
U455	U93	2c on 2c **carmine**, *amber* (U430, die 1)	850.00	
		Entire	900.00	
U456	U93	2c on 2c **carmine**, *oriental buff* (U431)	150.00	
		Entire	200.00	
a.		Double surcharge, type 3	225.00	
U457	U93	2c on 2c **carmine**, *blue* (U432)	175.00	
		Entire	200.00	
U458	U93	2c on 3c **dark violet**, *white* (U436)	30	30
		Entire	50	45
a.		Double surcharge	12.00	6.00
b.		Triple surcharge	27.50	
c.		Double surcharge, one in magenta	55.00	
d.		Double surcharge, types 2 & 3	85.00	
U459	U93	2c on 3c **dark violet**, *amber* (U437)	2.00	75
		Entire	3.25	1.50
a.		Double surcharge, type 3	15.00	
b.		Double surcharge, types 2 & 3	67.50	
U460	U93	2c on 3c **dark violet**, *oriental buff* (U438)	2.00	75
		Entire	2.75	1.10
a.		Double surcharge	9.00	
b.		Triple surcharge	22.50	
U461	U93	2c on 3c **dark violet**, *blue* (U439)	3.25	75
		Entire	4.75	1.25
a.		Double surcharge	12.00	
U462	U87	2c on 4c **chocolate**, *white* (U390)	300.00	150.00
		Entire	325.00	175.00
U463	U93	2c on 4c **chocolate**, *amber* (U391)	300.00	75.00
		Entire	350.00	150.00
U463A	U90	2c on 4c **black**, *white* (U416)	650.00	375.00
		Entire	750.00	
U464	U93	2c on 5c **blue**, *white* (U443)	800.00	
		Entire	925.00	

Type 3 exists in 11 city sub-types.

Type 4

Same as Type 3, but bars 1½ mm. apart.

U465	U92	2c on 1c **green**, *white* (U420)	750.00	
		Entire	900.00	
U466	U91	2c on 2c **carmine**, *white* (U411e, die 6)	2,750.	
		Entire	3,250.	
U466A	U91	2c on 2c **carmine**, *white* (U429)	190.00	
		Entire	250.00	
c.		Die 5	350.00	
U466B	U93	2c on 2c **carmine**, *amber* (U430, die 1)	1,500.	
		Entire	1,750.	
U467	U45	2c on 3c **green**, die 2, *white* (U163)	210.00	
		Entire	250.00	
U468	U93	2c on 3c **dark violet**, *white* (U436)	45	30
		Entire	65	40
a.		Double surcharge	12.00	
b.		Triple surcharge	15.00	
c.		Inverted surcharge	60.00	
d.		Double surcharge, types 2 & 4	60.00	
e.		2c on 3c carmine (error), *white* (U436h)	375.00	
		Entire	400.00	
U469	U93	2c on 3c **dark violet**, *amber* (U437)	2.50	1.50
		Entire	3.25	2.00
a.		Double surcharge, types 2 & 4	50.00	
U470	U93	2c on 3c **dark violet**, *oriental buff* (U438)	3.50	2.00
		Entire	4.50	3.25
a.		Double surcharge, type 4	15.00	
b.		Double surcharge, types 2 & 4	50.00	
U471	U93	2c on 3c **dark violet**, *blue* (U439)	3.50	1.00
		Entire	10.50	2.50
a.		Double surcharge, type 4	15.00	
b.		Double surcharge, types 2 & 4	125.00	
U472	U87	2c on 4c **chocolate**, *white* (U390)	9.50	8.00

		Entire	19.00	12.00
a.		Double surcharge	30.00	
U473	U93	2c on 4c **chocolate**, *amber* (U391)	11.00	7.50
		Entire	15.00	11.50

Type 4 exists in 30 city sub-types.

1
CENT

Double Surcharge, Type 4 and 1 c as above.

U474	U93	2c on 1c **dark violet**, *white* (U436)	200.00	
		Entire	225.00	
U475	U93	2c on 1c on 3c **dark violet**, *amber* (U437, die 1)	200.00	
		Entire	225.00	

Type 5

U476	U93	2c on 3c **dark violet**, *amber* (U437, die 1)	85.00	
		Entire	95.00	
a.		Double surcharge	—	

Surcharged

Type 6

U477	U93	2c on 3c **dark violet**, *white* (U436)	85.00	
		Entire	95.00	
U478	U93	2c on 3c **dark violet**, *amber* (U437, die 1)	175.00	
		Entire	200.00	

Handstamped Surcharged in Black or Violet

Type 7

U479	U93	2c on 3c **dark violet**, *white* (Bk) (U436)	275.00	
		Entire	325.00	
U480	U93	2c on 3c **dark violet**, *white* (V) (U436, die 7)	1,000.	
		Entire	1,100.	

1925

Type of 1916-32 Issue

U481	U93	1½c **brown**, die 1, *white* (Washington)	10	6
		Entire	50	10
a.		Die 8	15	10
		Entire	55	15
b.		1½c purple, die 1, *white* (error) ('34)	75.00	
		Entire	90.00	
U482	U93	1½c **brown**, die 1, *amber*	75	20
		Entire	1.25	45
a.		Die 8	85	35
		Entire	1.40	65
U483	U93	1½c **brown**, die 1, *blue*	1.25	60
		Entire	1.50	90
a.		Die 8	1.40	65
		Entire	1.65	1.00
U484	U93	1½c **brown**, die 1, *manila*	5.00	2.00
		Entire	10.00	5.00
W485	U93	½c **brown**, die 1, *manila*	60	10
		Entire	90	40
a.		With added impression of #W433	100.00	—

The manufacture of newspaper wrappers was discontinued in 1934.

New rates on printed matter effective Apr. 15, 1925, resulted in revaluing some of the current envelopes.

Under the caption "Revaluation of Surplus Stocks of the 1 cent envelopes", W. Irving Glover, Third Assistant Postmaster-General, distributed through the Postal Bulletin a notice to postmasters authorizing the surcharging of envelopes under stipulated conditions.

Surcharging was permitted "at certain offices where the excessive quantities of 1 cent stamped envelopes remained in stock on April 15, 1925."

Envelopes were revalued by means of post office cancelling machines equipped with special dies designed to imprint "1½" in the center of the embossed stamp and four vertical bars over the original numerals "1" in the lower corners.

Postmasters were notified that the revaluing dies would be available for use only in the International and "Universal" Model G machines and that the overprinting of surplus envelopes would be restricted to post offices having such cancelling equipment available.

Envelopes of Preceding Issues Surcharged

Type 8

1925

On Envelopes of 1887

			unused	used
U486	U71	1½c on 2c **green**, *white* (U311)	575.00	
		Entire	625.00	
U487	U71	1½c on 2c **green**, *amber* (U312)	675.00	
		Entire	725.00	

On Envelopes of 1899

U488	U77	1½c on 1c **green**, *white* (U352)	500.00	
		Entire	600.00	
U489	U77	1½c on 1c **green**, *amber* (U353)	75.00	70.00
		Entire	92.50	87.50

On Envelopes of 1907-16

U490	U90	1½c on 1c **green**, *white* (U400, die 1)	3.00	3.00
		Entire	4.50	4.50
a.		Die 2	10.00	8.00
		Entire	12.00	10.00
b.		Die 4	5.00	2.50
		Entire	6.75	3.50
U491	U90	1½c on 1c **green**, *amber* (U401, die 1)	6.00	2.00
		Entire	10.00	5.25
a.		Die 2	60.00	60.00
		Entire	65.00	65.00
a.		Die 4	3.50	1.75
		Entire	6.00	4.00
U492	U90	1½c on 1c **green**, *oriental buff* (U402a, die 2)	175.00	75.00
		Entire	185.00	82.50
a.		Die 4	175.00	75.00
		Entire	185.00	82.50
U493	U90	1½c on 1c **green**, *blue* (U403c, die 4)	75.00	55.00
		Entire	85.00	62.50
a.		Die 2	75.00	55.00
		Entire	90.00	65.00
U494	U90	1½c on 1c **green**, *manila* (U404, die 1)	190.00	75.00
		Entire	215.00	90.00

On Envelopes of 1916-20

U495	U92	1½c on 1c **green**, *white* (U420, die 1)	25	15
		Entire	50	25
a.		Die 3	1.10	50
b.		Die 4	1.50	50
c.		Double surcharge	3.00	1.50
U496	U92	1½c on 1c **green**, *amber* (U421)	12.00	12.00
		Entire	17.00	14.00
U497	U92	1½c on 1c **green**, *oriental buff* (U422, die 1)	2.50	1.50
		Entire	4.00	1.75
U498	U92	1½c on 1c **green**, *blue* (U423)	75	50
		Entire	1.50	80
U499	U92	1½c on 1c **green**, *manila* (U424, die 1)	9.00	6.00
		Entire	15.00	6.50
U500	U92	1½c on 1c **green**, *brown* (unglazed) (U428, die 1)	50.00	30.00
		Entire	55.00	32.50
U501	U92	1½c on 1c **green**, *brown* (glazed) (U426, die 1)	50.00	25.00
		Entire	52.50	27.50
U502	U93	1½c on 2c **carmine**, *white* (U429, die 1)	225.00	—
		Entire	250.00	
U503	U93	1½c on 2c **carmine**, *oriental buff* (U431c, die 5)	250.00	—
		Entire	275.00	
a.		Double surcharge		—
U504	U93	1½c on 2c **carmine**, *blue* (U432f, die 6)	225.00	—
		Entire	275.00	

On Envelopes of 1925

U505	U93	1½c on 1½c **brown**, *white* (U481, die 1)	375.00	
		Entire	475.00	
a.		Die 8	450.00	
		Entire	500.00	
U506	U93	1½c on 1½c **brown**, *blue* (U483a, die 8)	300.00	
		Entire	325.00	

The paper of No. U500 is not glazed and appears to be the same as that used for the wrappers of 1920.
Type 8 exists in 20 city sub-types.

Surcharged

Type 9

Black Surcharge
On Envelope of 1887

U507	U69	1½c on 1c **blue**, *white* (U294)	1,000.	
		Entire	1,100.	

On Envelope of 1899

U508	U77	1½c on 1c **green**, *amber* (U353)	45.00	
		Entire	55.00	

On Envelope of 1903

U508A	U85	1½c on 1c **green**, *white* (U379)	1,150.	
		Entire	1,400.	
U509	U85	1½c on 1c **green**, *amber* (U380)	10.00	10.00
		Entire	22.50	12.00
a.		Double surcharge	20.00	
		Entire	25.00	
U509B	U69	1½c on 1c **green**, *oriental buff* (U381)	45.00	40.00
		Entire	50.00	42.50

On Envelopes of 1907-16

U510	U90	1½c on 1c **green**, *white* (U400, die 1)	1.50	1.00
		Entire	2.50	1.25
a.		Double surcharge	5.00	
b.		Die 2	5.00	3.00
		Entire	7.00	5.00
c.		Die 3	14.00	7.00
		Entire	20.00	10.00
d.		Die 4	2.50	1.00
		Entire	5.00	2.00
U511	U90	1½c on 1c **green**, *amber* (U401, die 1)	150.00	75.00
		Entire	175.00	87.50
U512	U90	1½c on 1c **green**, *oriental buff* (U402, die 1)	5.00	3.00
		Entire	8.25	6.00
a.		Die 4	15.00	12.00
		Entire	20.00	14.00
U513	U90	1½c on 1c **green**, *blue* (U403, die 1)	4.00	2.00
		Entire	6.50	3.50
a.		Die 4	4.00	3.00
		Entire	4.00	3.00
U514	U90	1½c on 1c **green**, *manila* (U404, die 1)	15.00	7.50
		Entire	27.50	22.50
a.		Die 3	50.00	50.00
		Entire	57.50	57.50

On Envelopes of 1916-20

U515	U92	1½c on 1c **green**, *white* (U420)	25	15
		Entire	50	25
a.		Double surcharge	5.00	
b.		Inverted surcharge	7.50	
c.		Triple surcharge	8.50	
U516	U92	1½c on 1c **green**, *amber* (U421)	35.00	25.00
		Entire	45.00	32.50
U517	U92	1½c on 1c **green**, *oriental buff* (U422)	3.50	1.00
		Entire	4.25	1.25
U518	U92	1½c on 1c **green**, *blue* (U423)	3.50	1.00
		Entire	4.25	1.25
a.		Double surcharge	7.00	
U519	U92	1½c on 1c **green**, *manila* (U424, die 1)	15.00	10.00
		Entire	18.00	12.00
a.		Double surcharge	20.00	
U520	U93	1½c on 2c **carmine**, *white* (U429)	150.00	—
		Entire	175.00	—

Magenta Surcharge

U521	U92	1½c on 1c **green**, *white* (U420)	3.50	3.00
		Entire	3.75	4.00
a.		Double surcharge	20.00	

Sesquicentennial Exposition Issue
Issued to commemorate the 150th anniversary of the Declaration of Independence.

Liberty Bell — U94

Die 1. The center bar of "E" of "postage" is shorter than top bar.
Die 2. The center bar of "E" of "postage" is of same length as top bar.

1926, July 27

U522	U94	2c **carmine**, *white*, die 1	1.50	50
		Entire	2.50	95
		Entire, 1st day cancel, Washington, D.C.		32.50
		Entire, 1st day cancel, Philadelphia		30.00
a.		Die 2	8.50	6.00
		Entire	12.00	9.50

Washington Bicentennial Issue.
200th anniversary of the birth of George Washington.

Mount Vernon — U95

2c Die 1. "S" of "Postage" normal.
2c Die 2. "S" of "Postage" raised.

1932

U523	U95	1c **olive green**, *white*, Jan. 1	1.75	1.25
		Entire	2.75	2.50
		Entire, 1st day cancel		18.00
U524	U95	1½c **chocolate**, *white*, Jan. 1	3.50	1.50
		Entire	4.00	2.00
		Entire, 1st day cancel		18.00
U525	U95	2c **carmine**, die 1, *white*, Jan. 1	40	5
		Entire	60	10
		Entire, 1st day cancel		15.00
a.		2c carmine, die 2, *white*	90.00	15.00
		Entire	125.00	55.00
b.		2c carmine, die 1, *blue* (error) entire	10,000.	
U526	U95	3c **violet**, *white*, June 16	3.50	35
		Entire	4.00	40
		Entire, 1st day cancel		18.00
U527	U95	4c **black**, *white*, Jan. 1	25.00	15.00
		Entire	32.50	21.00
		Entire, 1st day cancel		30.00
U528	U95	5c **dark blue**, *white*, Jan. 1	5.00	4.00
		Entire	6.50	6.00
		Entire, 1st day cancel		20.00

1932, Aug. 18

Type of 1916-32 Issue

U529	U93	6c **orange**, die 7, *white*	4.50	2.75
		Entire	7.00	4.50
		Entire, 1st day cancel		17.50
U530	U93	6c **orange**, die 7, *amber*	10.00	7.50
		Entire	13.00	9.25
		Entire, 1st day cancel		17.50
U531	U93	6c **orange**, die 7, *blue*	10.00	7.50
		Entire	13.00	9.25
		Entire, 1st day cancel		17.50

Franklin U96

Washington U97

Die 1

Die 2

Die 3

Die 1. Short (3½ mm.) and thick "I" in thick circle.
Die 2. Tall (4½ mm.) and thin "1" in thin circle; upper and lower bars of E in ONE long and 1 mm. from circle
Die 3. As in Die 2, but E normal and 1½ mm. from circle.

Printed by International Envelope Corp.

1950

U532	U96	1c **green**, *white*, die 1, *Nov. 16, 1950*	5.00	1.75
		Entire	6.25	2.25
		Entire, 1st day cancel		2.50
a.	Die 2		5.00	3.00
		Entire	7.50	3.75
b.	Die 3		5.00	3.00
		Entire	7.50	3.75
b.	Precanceled			60
		Entire, precanceled		90

Die 1

Die 2

Die 3

Die 4

Die 1. Thick "2" in thick circle; toe of "2" is acute right angle.
Die 2. Thin "2" in thin circle; toe of "2" is almost right angle; line through left stand of "N" in UNITED and stand of "E" in POSTAGE goes considerably below tip of chin; "N" of UNITED is tall; "O" of TWO is high.
Die 3. Figure "2" as in Die 2. Short UN in UNITED thin crossbar in A of STATES.
Die 4. Tall UN in UNITED; thick crossbar in A of STATES; otherwise like Die 3.

U533	U97	2c **carmine**, *white*, die 3	65	8
		Entire	95	10
a.	Die 1, *Nov. 17, 1950*		75	25
		Entire	1.25	40
		Entire, 1st day cancel		85
b.	Die 2		1.30	80
		Entire	1.70	85
c.	Die 4		1.20	50
		Entire	1.40	60

Die 1

Die 2

Die 3

Die 4   Die 5

Die 1. Thick and tall (4½mm.) "3" in thick circle; long top bars and short stems in T's of STATES.
Thin and tall (4½ mm.) "3" in medium circle; short top bars and long stems in T's of STATES
Die 3. Thin and short (4 mm.) "3" in thin circle; lettering wider than Dies 1 and 2; line from left stand of N to stand of E is distinctly below tip of chin.
Die 4. Figure and letters as in Die 3. Line hits tip of chin; short N in UNITED and thin crossbar in A of STATES.
Die 5. Figure, letter and chin line as in Die 4; but tall N in UNITED and thick crossbar in A of STATES.

U534	U97	3c **dark violet**, *white*, die 4	35	10
		Entire	40	15
a.	Die 1, *Nov. 18, 1950*		1.25	30
		Entire	1.75	80
		Entire, 1st day cancel		2.00
b.	Die 2, *Nov. 19, 1950*		65	25
		Entire	1.25	30
c.	Die 3		50	25
		Entire	95	35
d.	Die 5		50	30
		Entire	75	35

Washington — U98

1952

U535	U98	1½c **brown**, *white*	4.50	3.50
		Entire	5.25	4.25
		Precanceled		35
		Entire, precanceled		75

Die 1

Die 2

Die 3

Die 1. Head high in oval (2mm. below T of STATES). Circle near (1 mm.) bottom of colored oval.
Die 2. Head low in oval (3 mm.). Circle 1½ mm. from edge of oval. Right leg of A in POSTAGE shorter than left. Short leg on P.
Die 3. Head centered in oval (2½mm.). Circle as in Die 2. Legs of A of POSTAGE about equal. Long leg on P.

1958

U536	U96	4c **red violet**, *white*, die 1, *July 31*	75	10
		Entire	90	12
		Entire, 1st day cancel, Montpelier, Vt. *(163,746)*		1.50
a.	Die 2		1.00	10
		Entire	1.25	10
b.	Die 3		1.00	10
		Entire	1.25	12

Nos. U429, U429f, U429h, U533, U533a-U533c
Surcharged in Red at Left of Stamp

b

1958

U537	U93	2c + 2c **carmine**, *white*, die 1	3.00	1.50
		Entire	3.50	
a.	Die 7		10.00	7.00
		Entire	12.50	
b.	Die 9		5.00	4.00
		Entire	6.50	—
U538	U97	2c + 2c **carmine**, *white*, die 1	75	18
		Entire	80	25
a.	Die 2		1.00	25
		Entire	1.20	
b.	Die 3		80	15
		Entire	1.00	20
c.	Die 4		80	
		Entire	1.00	

Nos. U436a, U436e-U436f, U534, U534b-U534d
Surcharged in Green at Left of Stamp

a

U539	U93	3c + 1c **purple**, *white*, die 1	14.00	11.50
		Entire	15.00	
a.	Die 7		12.00	10.00
		Entire	14.00	
b.	Die 9		30.00	16.00
		Entire	32.50	
U540	U97	3c + 1c **dark violet**, *white*, die 3	50	10
		Entire	60	12
a.	Die 2		—	
		Entire	900.00	
b.	Die 4		75	10
		Entire	85	15
c.	Die 5		75	10
		Entire	85	15

Benjamin
Franklin
U99

George
Washington
U100

Die 1   Die 2

Dies of 1¼c
Die 1. The "4" is 3 mm. high. Upper leaf in left cluster is 2 mm. from "U."
Die 2. The "4" is 3½ mm. high. Leaf clusters are larger. Upper leaf at left is 1 mm. from "U."

1960

U541	U99	1¼c **turquoise**, *white*, die 1, *June 25, 1960*	70	50
		Entire	80	55
		Entire, 1st day cancel, Birmingham, Ala. *(211,500)*		1.50
		Precanceled		5
		Entire, precanceled		10
a.		Die 2, precanceled		2.00
		Entire, precanceled		2.25
U542	U100	2½c **dull blue**, *white, May 28, 1960*	80	50
		Entire	90	60
		Entire, 1st day cancel, Chicago, Ill. *(196,977)*		1.50
		Precanceled		10
		Entire, precanceled		12

Pony Express Centennial Issue

Pony Express Rider — U101

White Outside, Blue Inside.

1960

U543	U101	4c **brown**, *July 19, 1960*	60	30
		Entire	72	40
		Entire, 1st day cancel, St. Joseph, Mo. *(407,160)*		2.25

Abraham Lincoln — U102

Die 1

Die 2

Die 3

Die 1. Center bar of E of POSTAGE is above the middle. Center bar of E of STATES slants slightly upward. Nose sharper, more pointed. No offset ink specks inside envelope on back of die impression.

Die 2. Center bar of E of POSTAGE in middle. P of POSTAGE has short stem. Ink specks on back of die impression.

Die 3. Fl of FIVE closer than Die 1 or 2. Second T of STATES seems taller than ES. Ink specks on back of die impression.

1962

U544	U102	5c **dark blue**, *white*, die 2, *Nov. 19, 1962*	80	20
		Entire	90	25
		Entire, 1st day cancel, Springfield, Ill. *(163,258)*		1.50
a.		Die 1	85	25
		Entire	95	30
b.		Die 3	90	30

		Entire	1.00	35
c.		Die 2 with albino 4c impression, entire	45.00	—
d.		Die 3 with albino 4c impression, entire	67.50	—

No. U536 Surcharged in Green at left of Stamp

a

Two types of surcharge:

Type I. "U.S. POSTAGE" 18½ mm. high. Serifs on cross of T both diagonal. Two lines of shading in C of CENT.

Type II. "U.S. POSTAGE" 17½ mm. high. Right serif on cross of T is vertical. Three shading lines in C.

1962

U545	U96	4c + 1c **red vio.**, *white*, die 1, type I, *Nov. 1962*	1.30	50
		Entire	1.50	60
a.		Type II	1.30	50
		Entire	1.50	60

New York World's Fair Issue

Issued to publicize the New York World's Fair, 1964-65.

Globe with Satellite Orbit — U103

1964

U546	U103	5c **maroon**, *Apr. 22, 1964*	60	40
		Entire	72	50
		Entire, 1st day cancel World's Fair N.Y. *(466,422)*		1.50

Liberty Bell — U104

Old Ironsides — U105

Eagle — U106

Head of Statue of Liberty — U107

Printed by the United States Envelope Company, Williamsburg, Pa. Designed (6c) by Howard C. Mildner and (others) by Robert J. Jones.

1965-69

U547	U104	1¼c **brown**, *Jan. 6, 1965*	—	15
		Entire	90	35
		Entire, 1st day cancel, Washington, D.C.		1.50
U548	U104	1⁴⁄₁₀c **brown**, *March 26, 1968*	—	10
		Entire	1.00	25
		Entire, 1st day cancel, Springfield, Mass. *(134,832)*		1.50
U548A	U104	1⁶⁄₁₀c **orange**, *June 16, 1969*	—	10
		Entire	85	18
		Entire, 1st day cancel, Washington, D.C.		1.50
U549	U105	4c **bright blue**, *Jan. 6, 1965*	75	10
		Entire	95	15
		Entire, 1st day cancel, Washington, D.C.		1.50
U550	U106	5c **bright purple**, *Jan. 5, 1965*	75	8
		Entire	85	8
		Entire, 1st day cancel, Williamsburg, Pa. *(246,496)*		1.50
a.		Tagged, *Aug. 15, 1967*	60	5
		Entire	1.25	20
		Entire, tagged, 1st day cancel		5.00

Tagged

U551	U107	6c **light green**, *Jan. 4, 1968*	70	5
		Entire	80	8
		Entire, 1st day cancel, New York, N.Y. *(184,784)*		1.75

No. U550a has a 9x29 mm. panel at left of stamp that glows yellow green under ultraviolet light.

First day covers of the 1¼c and 4c total 451,960.

Nos. U549-U550 Surcharged Types "b" and "a" in Red or Green at Left of Stamp

1968, Feb. 5

U552	U105	4c + 2c **bright blue** (R)	3.75	1.50
		Entire	4.00	2.25
		Entire, 1st day cancel		7.00
U553	U106	5c + 1c **bright purple** (G)	3.50	2.50
		Entire	4.00	3.00
a.		Tagged	3.50	2.50
		Entire	4.00	2.50
		Entire, 1st day cancel		7.00

Tagged

Envelopes from No. U554 onward are tagged, with the tagging element in the ink unless otherwise noted.

Herman Melville Issue

Issued to honor Herman Melville (1819-1891), writer, and the whaling industry.

Moby Dick — U108

1970, Mar. 7

U554	U108	6c **blue**	50	15
		Entire	60	25
		Entire, 1st day cancel, New Bedford, Mass. *(433,777)*		1.75

Youth Conference Issue

Issued to publicize the White House Conference on Youth, Estes Park, Colo., Apr. 18-22.

Conference Emblem Symbolic of Man's Expectant Soul and of Universal Brotherhood U109

Printed by United States Envelope Company, Williamsburg, Pa. Designed by Chermayeff and Geismar Associates.

1971, Feb. 24

U555	U109	6c light blue	75	15
		Entire	85	80
		Entire, 1st day cancel, Washington, D.C.		1.50
		(264,559)		

Liberty Bell Type of 1965 and U110

Eagle — U110

Printed by the United States Envelope Co., Williamsburg, Pa. Designed (8c) by Bradbury Thompson.

1971

U556	U104	1⁷/₁₀c deep lilac, untagged, *May 10*	—	8
		Entire	30	10
		Entire, 1st day cancel, Baltimore, Md. *(150,767)*		1.50
U557	U110	8c ultramarine, *May 6*	40	5
		Entire	50	8
		Entire, 1st day cancel, Williamsburg, Pa. *(193,000)*		1.75

Nos. U551 and U555 Surcharged in Green at Left of Stamp

c

1971

U561	U107	6c + (2c) light green, *May 16*	1.00	30
		Entire	1.10	45
		Entire, 1st day cancel, Washington, D.C.		3.00
U562	U109	6c + (2c) light blue, *May 16*	2.50	1.00
		Entire	2.75	75
		Entire, 1st day cancel, Washington, D.C.		4.00

Bowling Issue

Issued as a salute to bowling and in connection with the 7th World Tournament of the International Bowling Federation, Milwaukee, Wis.

Bowling Ball and Pin — U111

Designed by George Giusti.

1971, Aug. 21

U563	U111	8c rose red	50	15
		Entire	65	18
		Entire, 1st day cancel, Milwaukee, Wis. *(281,242)*		2.00

Aging Conference Issue

White House Conference on Aging, Washington, D.C., Nov. 28-Dec. 2, 1971.

Conference Symbol — U112

Designed by Thomas H. Geismar.

1971, Nov. 15

U564	U112	8c light blue	50	15
		Entire	65	18
		Entire, 1st day cancel, Washington, D.C. *(125,000)*		1.75

International Transportation Exhibition Issue

U.S. International Transportation Exhibition, Dulles International Airport, Washington, D.C., May 27-June 4.

Transportation Exhibition Emblem — U113

(Size of actual stamp: 64x70 mm.)

Emblem designed by Toshihiki Sakow.

1972, May 2

U565	U113	8c ultramarine & rose red	50	5
		Entire	75	15
		Entire, 1st day cancel, Washington, D.C.		1.75

No. U557 Surcharged Type "b" in Ultramarine at Left of Stamp

1973, Dec. 1

U566	U110	8c + 2c brt. ultramarine	40	5
		Entire	50	10
		Entire, 1st day cancel, Washington, D.C.		2.00

Liberty Bell — U114

1973, Dec. 5

U567	U114	10c emerald	35	5
		Entire	40	8
		Entire, 1st day cancel, Philadelphia, Pa. *(142,141)*		1.25

"Volunteer Yourself" — U115

Designed by Norman Ives.

1974, Aug. 23

Untagged

U568	U115	1⁸/₁₀c blue green	—	8
		Entire	30	12
		Entire, 1st day cancel, Cincinnati, Ohio		1.25

Tennis Centenary Issue

Centenary of tennis in the United States.

Tennis Racquet — U116

Designed by Donald Moss.

1974, Aug. 31

U569	U116	10c yellow, brt. blue & light green	24	15
		Entire	35	20
		Entire, 1st day cancel, Forest Hills, N.Y. *(245,000)*		2.00

Bicentennial Era Issue

The Seafaring Tradition - Compass Rose — U118

The American Homemaker - Quilt Pattern U119

The American Farmer - Sheaf of Wheat U120

The American Doctor - Mortar U121

See the "Information for Collectors" section at beginning of catalogue for information on electric eye markings, luminescene and tagging.

The American Craftsman - Tools, c. 1750 — U122

Designs (in brown on left side of envelope): 10c, Norwegian sloop Restaurationen. No. U572, Spinning wheel. No. U573, Plow. No. U574, Colonial era medical instruments and bottle. No. U575, Shaker rocking chair.
Designed by Arthur Congdon.

1975-76

Diagonally Laid Paper   Embossed

U571	U118	10c **brown & blue,** *light brown, Oct. 13, 1975*		24	15
		Entire		40	20
		Entire, 1st day cancel, Minneapolis, Minn. *(255,304)*			1.50
a.		Brown ("10c/USA") omitted, entire		125.00	
U572	U119	13c **brown & blue green,** *light brown, Feb. 2, 1976*		30	15
		Entire		50	20
		Entire, 1st day cancel, Biloxi, Miss. *(196,647)*			80
a.		Brown ("13c/USA") omitted, entire		125.00	
U573	U120	13c **brown & bright green,** *light brown, Mar. 15, 1976*		30	15
		Entire		50	20
		Entire, 1st day cancel, New Orleans, La. *(214,563)*			1.50
a.		Brown ("13c/USA") omitted, entire		—	
U574	U121	13c **brn. & org.,** *light brown, June 30, 1976*		30	15
		Entire		50	20
		Entire, 1st day cancel, Dallas, Texas			1.50
U575	U122	13c **brn. & car.,** *lt. brown, Aug. 6, 1976*		30	13
		Entire		50	15
		Entire, 1st day cancel, Hancock, Mass.			1.50
a.		Brown ("13c/USA") omitted, entire		—	

Liberty Tree, Boston, 1646 — U123

Designed by Leonard Everett Fisher.

1975, Nov. 8   Embossed

U576	U123	13c **orange brown**	30	13
		Entire	40	15
		Entire, 1st day cancel, Memphis, Tenn. *(226,824)*		80

Star and Pinwheel — U124

U125

U126

Eagle — U127

Uncle Sam — U128

Designers: 2c, Rudolph de Harak. 2.1c, Norman Ives. 2.7c, Ann Sforza Clementino. 15c, George Mercer.

1976-78   Embossed

U577	U124	2c **red,** untagged, *Sept. 10, 1976*	—	5
		Entire	30	10
		Entire, 1st day cancel, Hempstead, N.Y. *(81,388)*		70
U578	U125	2.1c **green,** untagged, *June 3, 1977*	—	5
		Entire	30	10
		Entire, 1st day cancel, Houston, Tex. *(120,280)*		70
U579	U126	2.7c **green,** untagged, *July 5, 1978*	—	5
		Entire	35	15
		Entire, 1st day cancel, Raleigh, N.C. *(92,687)*		75
U580	U127	(15c) **orange,** *May 22, 1978*	35	15
		Entire	48	18
		Entire, 1st day cancel, Memphis, Tenn.		85
U581	U128	15c **red,** *June 3, 1978*	35	15
		Entire	48	18
		Entire, 1st day cancel, Williamsburg, Pa. *(176,000)*		85

Bicentennial Issue

Centennial Envelope, 1876 — U129

1976, Oct. 15   Embossed

U582	U129	13c **emerald**	30	13
		Entire	40	15
		Entire, 1st day cancel, Los Angeles, Cal. *(277,222)*		80

Golf Issue

Golf Club in Motion and Golf Ball — U130

Designed by Guy Salvato.

1977, Apr. 7   **Photograve and Embossed**

U583	U130	13c **black, blue & yellow green**	30	13
		Entire	40	10
		Entire, 1st day cancel, Augusta, Ga. *(252,000)*		1.10
a.		Black omitted, entire	—	
b.		Black & blue omitted, entire	—	

Energy Issue

Conservation and development of national resources.

"Conservation" U131

"Development" U132

Designed by Terrance W. McCaffrey.

1977, Oct. 20   Embossed

U584	U131	13c **black, red & yellow**	30	13
		Entire	40	15
		Entire, 1st day cancel, Ridley Park, Pa.		80
a.		Red & yellow omitted, entire	—	
b.		Yellow omitted, entire	—	
c.		Black omitted, entire	—	
d.		Black & red omitted, entire	—	
U585	U132	13c **black, red & yellow**	30	13
		Entire	40	15
		Entire, 1st day cancel, Ridley Park, Pa.		80

First day cancellation a applied to 353,515 of Nos. U584 and U585.
Envelopes exist with black omitted, and with red and black omitted.
Nos. U584-U585 have a luminescent panel at left of stamp which glows green under ultraviolet light.

Olive Branch and Star — U133

Designed by George Mercer.

1978, July 28   Embossed

Black Surcharge

U586	U133	15c on 16c **blue**	35	15
		Entire	48	18

Entire, 1st day cancel,
Williamsburg, Pa.
(193,153) ... 75
a. Surcharge omitted, entire — —
b. Surch. on No. U581, entire — —

Auto Racing Issue

Indianapolis 500 Racing Car — U134

Designed by Robert Peak.

1978, Sept. 2		Embossed	
U587	U134 15c **red, blue & black**	35	15
	Entire	48	18
	Entire, 1st day cancel, Ontario, Cal. *(209,147)*		1.00
a.	Black omitted, entire	200.00	
b.	Black & blue omitted, entire	—	
c.	Red omitted, entire	—	

No. U576 Surcharged Like No. U586

1978, Nov. 28		Embossed	
U588	U123 15c on 13c **orange brown**	35	15
	Entire	48	18
	Entire, 1st day cancel, Williamsburg, Pa. *(137,500)*		75

U135

Weaver
Violins — U136

U137

Eagle — U138

Eagle — U140

1979, May 18		Untagged	Embossed
U589	U135 3.1c **ultramarine**, untagged	—	5
	Entire	12	5
	Entire, 1st day cancel, Denver, Colo. *(117,575)*		60

1980, June 23		Untagged	Embossed
U590	U136 3.5c **purple**, untagged	—	8
	Entire	25	15
	Entire, 1st day cancel, Williamsburg, Pa.		65

1982, Feb. 17		Untagged	Embossed
U591	U137 5.9c **brown**, untagged	—	8
	Entire	20	10
	Entire, 1st day cancel, Wheeling, WV		70

1981, Mar. 15			Embossed
U592	U138 (18c) **violet**	45	18
	Entire	55	22
	Entire, 1st day cancel, Memphis, TN *(179,171)*		80

1981, Apr. 2			Embossed
U593	U139 18c **dark blue**	45	18
	Entire	55	22
	Entire, 1st day cancel, Star City, IN *(160,439)*		80

1981, Oct. 11			Embossed
U594	U140 (20c) **brown**	40	10
	Entire	48	15
	Entire, 1st day cancel, Memphis, TN *(304,404)*		80

Veterinary Medicine Issue

Seal of Veterinarians
U141

Design at left side of envelope shows 5 animals and bird in brown, "Veterinary Medicine" in gray.
Designed by Guy Salvato.

1979, July 24			Embossed
U595	U141 15c **brown & gray**	35	15
	Entire	48	18
	Entire, 1st day cancel, Seattle, WA *(209,658)*		75

Olympic Games Issue

22nd Olympic Games, Moscow, July 19-Aug. 3, 1980.

U142

Design (multicolored on left side of envelope) shows two soccer players with ball.
Designed by Robert M. Cunningham.

1979, Dec. 10			Embossed
U596	U142 15c **red, green & black**	60	15
	Entire	75	18

Entire, 1st day cancel,
East Rutherford, NJ
(179,336) ... 75
a. Red & grn omitted, untagged 200.00
b. Black omitted, untagged 200.00
c. Black & green omitted 200.00

Highwheeler Bicycle — U143

Design (blue on left side of envelope) shows racing bicycle.
Designed by Robert Hallock.

1980, May 16		Embossed	
U597	U143 15c **blue & rose claret**	35	15
	Entire	35	15
	Entire, 1st day cancel, Baltimore, MD *(173,978)*		75
a.	Blue ("15c USA") omitted	—	

AMERICA'S CUP Yacht — U144

Designed by Cal Sachs.

1980, Sept. 15		Embossed	
U598	U144 15c **blue & red**	35	15
	Entire	48	18
	Entire, 1st day cancel, Newport, RI *(192,220)*		75

Italian
Honeybee
and Orange
Blossoms
U145

Honeybee

Bee and petals colorless embossed.

Designed by Jerry Pinkney.

1980, Oct. 10		Photogravure and Embossed	
U599	U145 15c **brown, green & yel.**	35	15
	Entire	48	18
	Entire, 1st day cancel, Pairs, IL *(202,050)*		75
a.	Brown ("USA 15c") omitted	—	

Hand and Braille
U146

Hand and braille colorless embossed.
Designed by John Boyd.

United States Envelopes can be mounted in Scott's U.S. Postal Stationery and American Albums.

1981, Aug. 13

			Embossed	
U600	U146 18c blue & red		45	18
	Entire		55	22
	Entire, 1st day cancel, Arlington, VA			80
	(175,966)			

Capital Dome — U147

1981, Nov. 13

			Embossed	
U601	U147 20c deep magenta		45	10
	Entire		48	15
	Entire, first day cancel, Los Angeles, CA			80

The Great Seal of the United States 1782-1982 USA 20c

U148

Designed by Bradbury Thompson.

1982, June 15

			Embossed	
U602	U148 20c dark blue, black & magenta		45	10
	Entire		48	15
	Entire, first day cancel, Washington, DC			80
	(163,905)			
a.	Dark blue omitted, entire		—	

The Purple Heart 1782 1982 USA 20c U149

Designed by John Boyd.

1982, Aug. 6

			Embossed	
U603	U149 20c purple & black		45	10
	Entire		45	10
	Entire, first day cancel, Washington, DC			80
	(110,679)			

U150

1983, Mar. 21

			Embossed	
U604	U150 5.2c orange		—	10
	Entire		20	15
	Entire, first day cancel, Memphis, TN			80

Remember Our Paralyzed Veterans USA 20c

U151

1983, Aug. 3

			Embossed	
U605	U151 20c red, blue & black		45	10
	Entire		50	15
	Entire, first day cancel, Portland, OR			80

U152 **Small Business USA 20c**

Designed by Peter Spier and Pat Taylor. Design shows storefronts at lower left. Stamp and design continue on back of envelope.

1984, May 7

			Embossed	
U606	U152 20c multi		50	10
	Entire		55	15
	Entire, first day cancel, Washington, DC			80

U153

Designed by Bradbury Thompson.

1985, Feb. 1

			Embossed	
U607	U153 (22c) deep green		55	12
	Entire		60	18
	Entire, first day cancel, Washington, DC			1.10

Bison — U154

Designed by George Mercer.

1985, Feb. 25

			Embossed	
U608	U154 22c violet brown		50	10
	Entire		55	15
	Entire, first day cancel, Washington, DC			1.10
a.	Untagged, 3 precancel lines		—	15
	Entire		60	20

Original printings of No. U608 were printed with luminescent ink. later printings have a luminescent vertical bar to the left of the stamp.

Frigate U.S.S. Constitution — U155

Designed by Cal Sacks.

1985, May 3

			Embossed	
U609	U155 6c green blue		—	5
	Entire		22	6
	Entire, first day cancel, Washington, DC			30

The Mayflower — U156

Designed by Robert Brangwynne.

1986, Dec. 4

			Embossed	Precanceled
U610	U156 8.5c black & gray		—	10
	Entire		28	14
	Entire, first day cancel, Plymouth, MA			44
	(105,164)			

Star U157

Designed by Joe Brockert.

1988, Mar. 26

			Typo. & Embossed	
U611	U157 25c dark red & deep blue		50	25
	Entire		60	30
	Entire, first day cancel, Star, MS			75

U.S Frigate Constellation — U158

Designed by Jerry Dadds.

1988, Apr. 12

			Typo. & Embossed	Precanceled
U612	U158 8.4c black & bright blue		—	10
	Entire		28	14
	Entire, first day cnacel, Baltimore, MD			44

Snowflake — U159

Designed by Randall McDougall. "Holiday Greetings!" inscribed in lower left.

1988, Sept. 8   **Typo.**
U613   U159 25c **dark red & green**   50   25
              Entire   60   30
              Entire, first day cancel,
              Snowflake, AZ   75

AIR POST STAMPED ENVELOPES AND AIR LETTER SHEETS

All envelopes have carmine and blue borders, unless noted. There are seven types of borders:
Carmine Diamond in Upper Right Corner.
a. Diamonds measure 9 to 10 mm. paralled to edge of envelope and 11 to 12 mm. along oblique side (with top flap open). Sizes 5 and 13 only.
b. Like "a" except diamonds measure 7 to 8 mm. along oblique side (with top flap open). Sizes 5 and 13 only.
c. Diamonds measure 11 to 12 mm. parallel to edge of envelope. Size 5 only.
Blue Diamond in Upper Right Corner.
d. Lower points of top row of diamonds point to left. Size 8 only.
e. Lower points of top row of diamonds point to right. Size 8 only.
Diamonds Omitted in Upper Right Corner (1965 Onward)
f. Blue diamond above at left of stamp.
g. Red diamond above at left of stamp.

UC1

Die 1 (5c) - Vertical rudder is not semi-circular but slopes down to the left. The tail of the plane projects into the G of POSTAGE. Border types a, b, c, d and e.

UC2

Die 2 (5c and 8c): Vertical rudder is semi-circular. The tail of the plane touches but does not project into the G of POSTAGE. Border types b, d, and e for the 5c; b and d for the 8c.

Die 2 (6c): Same as UC2 except three types of numeral.
2a. The numeral "6" is 6½ mm. wide.
2b. The numeral "6" is 6 mm. wide.
2c. The numeral "6" is 5½mm. wide.
Eleven working dies were used in printing the 6c. On each, the numeral "6" was engraved by hand, producing several variations in position, size and thickness.
Nos. UC1 and UC2 occur with varying size blue blobs, caused by a shallow printing die. They are not constant.
Border types b and d for dies 2a and 2b; also without border (June 1944 to Sept. 1945) for dies 2a, 2b and 2c.
Die 3 (6c): Vertical rudder leans forward. S closer to O than to T of POSTAGE. E of POSTAGE has short center bar. Border types b and d, also without border.
No. UC1 with 1933 and 1937 watermarks and No. UC2 with 1929 and 1933 watermarks were issued in Puerto Rico.
No. UC1 in blue black, with 1925 watermark #26 and border type a, is a proof.

1929-44
UC1   UC1   5c **blue**, white, die 1, Jan.
                 12, 1929   3.00   1.75
              Entire, border a or b   4.25   2.25
              Entire, border c, d or e   8.00   5.75
              First day cancel, border
                 a, entire   40.00
              1933 wmk. #33, border
                 d, entire   700.00   700.00
              1933 wmk. #33, border
                 b, entire   —   —
              1937 wmk. #36, border
                 d, entire   950.00
              1937 wmk. #36, border
                 b, entire   —   —
              Bicolored border omit-
                 ted, entire   600.00
UC2   UC2   5c **blue**, white, die 2   12.50   5.00
              Entire, border b   15.00   6.50
              Entire, border e   21.00   12.50
              1929 wmk. #28, border
                 d, entire   —   1,500.
              1933 wmk. #33, border
                 b, entire   600.00
              1933 wmk. #33, border
                 d, entire   300.00   —
UC3   UC2   6c **orange**, white, die 2a,
                 July 1, 1934   1.25   25
              Entire, bicolored border   1.50   50
              Entire, without border   1.75   1.25
              Entire, 1st day cancel   14.00
    a.   6c orange, white, die 2a, with
                 added impression of 3c purple
                 (#U436a), entire without bor-
                 der   3,000.
UC4   UC2   6c **orange**, white, die 2b
                 ('42)   2.00   1.25
              Entire, bicolored border,
                 1941 wmk. #39   50.00   12.50
              Entire, without border   4.00   2.00
UC5   UC2   6c **orange**, white, die 2c
                 ('44)   75   30
              Entire, without border   1.00   40
UC6   UC2   6c **orange**, white, die 3 ('42) 1.00 35
              Entire, bicolored border   1.50   75
              Entire, without border   2.50   60
              Entire, carmine of bor-
                 der omitted   1,000.
              Double impression, en-
                 tire   350.00
    a.   6c orange, blue, die 3 (error) En-
                 tire, without border   3,500.   2,250.
UC7   UC2   8c **olive green**, white, die 2,
                 Sept. 26, 1932   12.50   3.00
              Entire, bicolored border   16.00   6.00
              Entire, 1st day cancel   11.00

Surcharged in black on envelopes indicated by number in parenthesis

1945
UC8   U93   6c on 2c **carmine**, white
                 (U429)   1.00   55
              Entire   1.50   1.00
    a.   6c on 1c green (error), white
                 (U420)   1,750.
              Entire   2,500.
    b.   6c on 3c purple (error), white
                 (U436a)   1,750.
              Entire   2,500.
    c.   6c on 3c purple (error), amber
                 (U437a)   3,000.
              Entire   3,500.
    d.   6c on 3c violet (error), white
                 (U526)   3,000.
              Entire   3,500.
UC9   U95   6c on 2c **carmine**, white
                 (U525)   75.00   40.00
              Entire   100.00   50.00

Ten surcharge varieties are found on Nos. UC8-UC9.

Surcharged in Black on 6c Air Post Envelopes without borders

REVALUED 5¢ P.O. DEPT.

1946
UC10   UC2   5c on 6c **orange**, white, die
                 2a   2.50   1.25
              Entire   3.75   2.50
    a.   Double surcharge   60.00
UC11   UC2   5c on 6c **orange**, white, die
                 2b   9.00   5.00
              Entire   10.50   6.25
UC12   UC2   5c on 6c **orange**, white, die
                 2c   75   50
              Entire   1.25   60
    a.   Double surcharge   60.00   20.00
UC13   UC2   5c on 6c **orange**, white, die
                 3   80   60
              Entire   95   75
    a.   Double surcharge   60.00

The 6c borderless envelopes and the revalued envelopes were issued primarily for use to and from members of the armed forces. The 5c rate came into effect Oct. 1, 1946.
Ten surcharge varieties are found on Nos. UC10-UC13.

DC-4 Skymaster — UC3

Envelopes with borders types b and d.
Die 1. The end of the wing at the right is a smooth curve. The juncture of the front end of the plane and the engine forms an acute angle. The first T of STATES and the E's of UNITED STATES lean to the left.
Die 2. The end of the wing at the right is a straight line. The juncture of the front end of the plane and the engine is wide open. The first T of STATES and the E's of UNITED STATES lean to the right.

1946
UC14   UC3   5c **carmine**, white, die 1,
                 Sept. 25, 1946   75   20
              Entire, bicolored border   1.10   40
              Entire, 1st day cancel   2.50
              Entire, bicolored border
                 omitted   —
UC15   UC3   5c **carmine**, white, die 2   85   25
              Entire, bicolored border   1.10   40

No. UC14, printed on flat bed press, measures 21½ mm. high. No. UC15, printed on rotary press, measures 22 mm. high.

DC-4 Skymaster UC4

**1947-55   Typographed, Without Embossing
                 Letter Sheets for Foreign Postage**
UC16   UC4   10c **bright red**, pale blue,
                 "Air Letter" on face, 2-
                 line inscription on
                 back, entire   7.50   6.00
              Entire, 1st day cancel,
                 Apr. 29, 1947   7.50
              Die cutting reversed,
                 entire   110.00
UC16a UC4   10c **bright red**, pale blue,
                 Sept. 1951, "Air Let-
                 ter" on face, 4-line in-
                 scription on back,
                 entire   12.50   10.00

Die cutting reversed, entire	275.00	
b. 10c chocolate, *pale blue,* entire	400.00	
UC16c UC4 10c **bright red,** *pale blue,* Nov. 1953, "Air Letter" and "Aerogramme" on face, 4-line inscription on back, entire	55.00	10.00
Die cutting reversed, entire	—	
UC16d UC4 10c **bright red,** *pale blue,* 1955, "Air Letter" and "Aerogramme" on face, 3-line inscription on back, entire	8.00	8.00
Die cutting reversed, entire	60.00	
Dark blue (inscriptions & border diamonds) omitted	—	

Printed on protective tinted paper containing colorless inscription.

UNITED STATES FOREIGN AIR MAIL multiple, repeated in parallel vertical or horizontal lines.

Postage Stamp Centenary Issue

Issued to commemorate the centenary of the first postage stamps issued by the United States Government.

Washington and Franklin, Early and Modern Mail-carrying Methods — UC5

Two dies: Rotary, design measures 22¼ mm. high; and flat bed press, design 21¾mm. high.

1947, May 21	**For Domestic Postage**	**Embossed**	
UC17 UC5 5c **carmine,** *white* (rotary)	40	25
Entire, bicolored border b	50	30
Entire, 1st day cancel		2.00
a. Flat plate printing	50	30
a. Entire	60	40

Type of 1946

Type I: 6's lean to right.
Type II: 6's upright.

1950			
UC18 UC3 6c **carmine,** *white,* type I, *Sept. 22, 1950*	25	8
Entire, bicolored border	50	15
Entire, 1st day cancel		1.25
a. Type II	75	25
Entire	1.00	30

Several other types differ slightly from the two listed.

Nos. UC14, UC15, UC18 Surcharged in Red at Left of Stamp

REVALUED 6¢ P. O. DEPT.

1951			
UC19 UC3 6c on 5c **carmine,** *white,* die 1	85	50
Entire	1.25	75
UC20 UC3 6c on 5c **carmine,** *white,* die 2	80	50
Entire	1.15	70
a. 6c on 6c car. *white* (error) entire	1,500.	
b. Double surcharge	250.00	—

Nos. UC14 and UC15 Surcharged in Red at Left of Stamp

REVALUED 6¢ P. O. DEPT.

1952			
UC21 UC3 6c on 5c **carmine,** *white,* die 1	30.00	15.00
Entire	35.00	18.00
UC22 UC3 6c on 5c **carmine,** *white,* die 2, *Aug. 29, 1952*	3.50	2.50
Entire	4.50	4.25
a. Double surcharge	75.00	

Same Surcharge in Red on No. UC17

UC23 UC5 6c on 5c **carmine,** *white*		
Entire	1,000.	

The 6c on 4c black (No. U440) is believed to be a favor printing.

Fifth International Philatelic Exhibition Issue

FIPEX, the Fifth International Philatelic Exhibition, New York, N.Y., Apr. 28-May 6, 1956.

Eagle in Flight — UC6

1956, May 2			
UC25 UC6 6c **red**	75	50
Entire	1.10	80
Entire, 1st day cancel, New York, N.Y. *(363,239)*		1.10

Two types exist, differing slightly in the clouds at top.

Skymaster Type of 1946

1958, July 31			
UC26 UC3 7c **blue,** *white*	65	50
Entire	1.10	1.00
Entire, 1st day cancel, Dayton, O. *(143,428)*		2.00

Nos. UC3-UC5, UC18 and UC25 Surcharged in Green at Left of Stamp

1958			
UC27 UC2 6c + 1c **orange,** *white,* die 2a	175.00	200.00
Entire, without border	225.00	225.00
UC28 UC2 6c + 1c **orange,** *white,* die 2b	60.00	75.00
Entire, without border	70.00	110.00
UC29 UC2 6c + 1c **orange,** *white,* die 2c	35.00	50.00
Entire	40.00	75.00
UC30 UC3 6c + 1c **carmine,** *white,* type I	1.00	50
Entire	1.25	65
a. Type II	1.00	50
Entire	1.10	65
UC31 UC6 6c + 1c **red,** *white*	1.00	50
Entire	1.40	85

Jet Airliner — UC7

Letter Sheet for Foreign Postage

Type I: Back inscription in 3 lines.

Type II: Back inscription in 2 lines

1958-59	**Typographed, Without Embossing**		
UC32 UC7 10c **blue & red,** *blue,* II, *May, 1959,* entire	6.00	5.00
b. Red omitted, II, entire	—	
c. Blue omitted, II, entire	850.00	
UC32a UC7 10c **blue & red,** *blue,* I, *Sept. 12, 1958,* entire	10.00	5.00
Entire, 1st day cancel, St. Louis, Mo. *(92,400)*		3.25
Die cutting reversed, entire	75.00	

Silhouette of Jet Airliner — UC8

1958, Nov. 21		**Embossed**	
UC33 UC8 7c **blue,** *white*	60	12
Entire	70	15
Entire, 1st day cancel, New York, N.Y. *(208,980)*		1.50

1960, Aug. 18			
UC34 UC8 7c **carmine,** *white*	60	12
Entire	70	15
Entire, 1st day cancel, Portland, Ore. *(196,851)*		1.50

Jet Airliner and Globe — UC9

Letter Sheet for Foreign Postage

1961, June 16	**Typographed, Without Embossing**		
UC35 UC9 11c **red & blue,** *blue,* entire	2.25	1.50
Entire, 1st day cancel, Johnstown, Pa. *(163,460)*		2.50
a. Red omitted, entire	850.00	
b. Blue omitted, entire	850.00	
Die cutting reversed, entire	35.00	

Jet Airliner — UC10

1962, Nov. 17		**Embossed**	
UC36 UC10 8c **red,** *white*	50	8
Entire	80	15
Entire, 1st day cancel, Chantilly, Va. *(194,810)*		80

Jet Airliner
UC11

1965-67

UC37	UC11 8c **red**, *Jan. 7*		35	6
	Entire, border "f"		50	10
	Entire, border "g"		*9.00*	
	Entire, 1st day cancel, Chicago, Ill. *(226,178)*			60
a.	Tagged, *Aug. 15, 1967*		85	30
	Entire		1.75	75
	Tagged, 1st day cancel			6.00

No. UC37a has a ⅜x1-inch panel at left of stamp that glows orange red under ultraviolet light.

Pres. John F. Kennedy and Jet Plane — UC12

Letter Sheets for Foreign Postage

1965, May 29   Typographed, Without Embossing

UC38	UC12 11c **red & dark blue**, *blue*, entire		3.25	1.00
	Entire, 1st day cancel, Boston, Mass. *(337,422)*			1.50
	Die cutting reversed, entire		50.00	

1967, May 29

UC39	UC12 13c **red & dark blue**, *blue*, entire		3.00	75
	Entire, 1st day cancel, Chicago, Ill. *(211,387)*			1.50
a.	Red omitted		*500.00*	
b.	Dark blue omitted		*500.00*	
	Die cutting reversed, entire		—	

Jet Liner
UC13

Designed by Robert J. Jones.

1968, Jan. 8   Tagged   Embossed

UC40	UC13 10c **red**		50	6
	Entire		80	15
	Entire, 1st day cancel, Chicago, Ill. *(157,553)*			75

No. UC37 Surcharged in Red at Left of Stamp

1968, Feb. 5

UC41	UC11 8c + 2c **red**		55	15
	Entire		90	40
	Entire, 1st day cancel, Washington, D.C.			8.50

Human Rights Year Issue

Issued for International Human Rights Year, and to commemorate the 20th anniversary of the United Nations' Declaration of Human Rights.

Globes and Flock of Birds — UC14

Printed by Acrovure Division of Union-Camp Corporation, Englewood, N.J. Designed by Antonio Frasconi.

Letter Sheet for Foreign Postage

1968, Dec. 3   Tagged   Photo.

UC42	UC14 13c **gray, brown, orange & black**, *blue*, entire		7.50	2.00
	Entire, 1st day cancel, Washington, D.C. *(145,898)*			2.75
a.	Orange omitted		—	
b.	Brown omitted		—	
c.	Black omitted		—	

No. UC42 has a luminescent panel ⅜x1 inch on the right globe. The panel glows orange red under ultraviolet light.

Jet Plane — UC15

Printed by United States Envelope Co., Williamsburg, Pa. Designed by Robert Geissmann.

1971, May 6   Embossed (Plane)
Center Circle Luminescent

UC43	UC15 11c **red & blue**		50	10
	Entire		60	13
	Entire, 1st day cancel, Williamsburg, Pa. *(187,000)*			90

Birds in Flight — UC16

Printed by Bureau of Engraving and Printing. Designed by Soren Noring.

Letter Sheet for Foreign Postage

1971   Tagged   Photo.

UC44	UC16 15c **gray, red, white & blue**, *blue*, entire, *May 28*		1.50	90
	Entire, 1st day cancel, Chicago, Ill. *(130,669)*			1.35
	Die cutting reversed, entire		30.00	
a.	"AEROGRAMME" added to inscription, entire, *Dec. 13*		1.50	90
	Entire, 1st day cancel, Philadelphia, Pa.			1.35
	Die cutting reversed, entire		30.00	

Folding instructions (2 steps) in capitals on No. C44; (4 steps) in upper and lower case on No. UC44a.
On Nos. UC44-UC44a the white rhomboid background of "USA postage 15c" is luminescent. No. UC44 is inscribed: "VIA AIR MAIL-PAR AVION". "postage 15c" is in gray. See No. UC46.

No. UC40 Surcharged in Green at Left of Stamp

1971, June 28   Embossed

UC45	UC13 10c + (1c) **red**		1.50	20
	Entire		1.90	25
	Entire, 1st day cancel, Washington, D.C.			8.50

HOT AIR BALLOONING CHAMPIONSHIPS ISSUE

Hot Air Ballooning World Championships, Albuquerque, N.M., Feb. 10-17, 1973.

"usa" Type of 1971

Design: Three balloons and cloud at left in address section; no birds beside stamp. Inscribed "INTERNATIONAL HOT AIR BALLOONING." "postage 15c" in blue.
Printed by Bureau of Engraving and Printing. Designed by Soren Noring (vignette) and Esther Porter (balloons).

Letter Sheet for Foreign Postage

1973, Feb. 10   Tagged   Photo.

UC46	UC16 15c **red, white & blue**, *blue*, entire		75	40
	Entire, 1st day cancel, Albuquerque, N.M. *(210,000)*			70

Folding instructions as on No. UC44a. See notes after No. UC44.

Bird in Flight — UC17

1973, Dec. 1   Luminescent Ink

UC47	UC17 13c **rose red**		28	10
	Entire		40	13
	Entire, 1st day cancel, Memphis, Tenn. *(132,658)*			55

"usa" — UC18

Printed by the Bureau of Engraving and Printing. Designed by Bill Hyde.

Letter Sheet for Foreign Postage

1974, Jan. 4   Tagged   Photo.

UC48	UC18 18c **red & blue**, *blue*, entire		70	30
	Entire, 1st day cancel, Atlanta, Ga. *(119,615)*			80
a.	Red omitted, entire		—	
	Die cutting reversed, entire		—	

25TH ANNIVERSARY OF NATO ISSUE

"USA" — UC19

Design: "NATO" and NATO emblem at left in address section.
Printed by Bureau of Engraving and Printing. Designed by Soren Noring.

Letter Sheet for Foreign Postage

1974, Apr. 4   Tagged   Photo.

UC49	UC19 18c **red & blue**, *blue*, entire		70	25
	Entire, 1st day cancel, Washington, D.C.			80

"USA" — UC20

Printed by Bureau of Engraving and Printing. Designed by Robert Geissmann.

Letter Sheet for Foreign Postage

1976, Jan. 16	Tagged		Photo.
UC50 UC20 22c **red & blue,** *blue,* entire		70	25
Entire, 1st day cancel, Tempe, Ariz. *(118,303)*			90
Die cutting reversed, entire		25.00	

"USA" — UC21

Printed by Bureau of Engraving and Printing. Designed by Soren Noring.

Letter Sheet for Foreign Postage

1978, Nov. 3	Tagged		Photo.
UC51 UC21 22c **blue,** *blue,* entire		70	25
Entire, 1st day cancel, St. Petersburg, Fla. *(86,099)*			90
Die cutting reversed, entire		25.00	

22nd OLYMPIC GAMES, MOSCOW, JULY 19- AUG. 3, 1980.

UC22

Design (multicolored in bottom left corner) shows discus thrower.
Printed by Bureau of Engraving and Printing. Designed by Robert M. Cunningham.

Letter Sheet for Foreign Postage

1979, Dec. 5	Tagged		Photo.
UC52 UC22 22c **red, black & green,** *bluish,* entire		1.50	22
Entire, 1st day cancel, Bay Shore, N.Y.			90

"USA" — UC23

Design (brown): lower left, Statue of Liberty. Inscribed "Tour the United States." Folding area shows tourist attractions.
Printed by Bureau of Engraving and Printing. Designed by Frank J. Waslick.

Letter Sheet for Foreign Postage

1980, Dec. 29	Tagged		Photo.
UC53 UC23 30c **blue, red & brn.,** *blue,* entire		60	30
Entire, 1st day cancel, San Francisco, CA			1.10
a. Red ("30") omitted		—	
Die cutting reversed, entire		20.00	

1981, Sept. 21	Tagged		Photo.
UC54 UC23 30c **yel., mag., blue & black,** *blue,* entire		60	30

	First day cancel, Honolulu, HI	1.10
	Die cutting reversed, entire	20.00

UC24

Design: "Made in USA . . . world's best buys!" on flap, ship, tractor in lower left. Reverse folding area shows chemicals, jet silhouette, wheat, typewriter and computer tape disks. Printed by Bureau of Engraving and Printing.
Design by Frank J. Waslick.

Letter Sheet for Foreign Postage

1982, Sept. 16	Tagged		Photo.
UC55 UC24 30c **multi.,** *blue,* entire		60	30
First day cancel, Seattle, WA			1.10

WORLD COMMUNICATIONS YEAR

World Map Showing Locations of Satellite Tracking Stations — UC25

Design: Reverse folding area shows satellite, tracking station.
Printed by Bureau of Engraving and Printing.
Designed by Esther Porter.

Letter Sheet for Foreign Postage

1983, Jan. 7	Tagged		Photo.
UC56 UC25 30c **multi,** *blue,* entire		60	30
First day cancel, Anaheim, CA			1.10
Die cutting reversed, entire		25.00	

1984 OLYMPICS

UC26

Design: Woman equestrian at lower left with montage of competitive events on reverse folding area.
Printed by the Bureau of Engraving & Printing.
Designed by Bob Peak.

Letter Sheet for Foreign Postage

1983, Oct. 14	Tagged		Photo.
UC57 UC26 30c **multi,** *blue,* entire		60	30
First day cancel, Los Angeles, CA			1.10

WEATHER SATELLITES, 25TH ANNIV.

Landsat Infrared and Thermal Mapping Bands — UC27

Design: Landsat orbiting the earth at lower left with three Landsat photographs on reverse folding area. Inscribed: "Landsat views the Earth."
Printed by the Bureau of Engraving & Printing.
Designed by Esther Porter.

Letter Sheet for Foreign Postage

1985, Feb. 14	Tagged		Photo.
UC58 UC27 36c **multi,** *blue,* entire		72	36
First day cancel, Goddard Flight Center, MD			1.35
Die cutting reversed, entire		30.00	

NATIONAL TOURISM WEEK

Urban Skyline — UC28

Design: Inscribed "Celebrate America" at lower left and "Travel. . . the perfect freedom" on folding area. Skier, Indian chief, cowboy, jazz trumpeter and pilgrims on reverse folding area.
Printed by the Bureau of Engraving & Printing.
Designed by Dennis Luzak.

Letter Sheet for Foreign Postage

1985, May 21	Tagged		Photo.
UC59 UC28 36c **multi,** *blue,* entire		72	36
First day cancel, Washington, DC			1.35
Die cutting reversed, entire		25.00	

MARK TWAIN AND HALLEY'S COMET

Comet Tail Viewed from Space — UC29

Design: Portrait of Twain at lower left and inscribed "I came in with Halley's Comet in 1835. It is coming again next year, and I expect to go out with it. It will be the greatest disappointment of my life if I don't go out with Halley's Comet." "1835 . Mark Twain . 1910 . Halley's Comet . 1985" and Twain, Huckleberry Finn, steamboat and comet on reverse folding areas.
Printed by the Bureau of Engraving & Printing.
Designed by Dennis Luzak.

Letter Sheet for Foreign Postage

1985, Dec. 4	Tagged		Photo.
UC60 UC29 36c **multi,** entire		72	36
First day cancel, Washington, DC			1.35

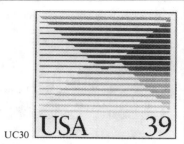

UC30

Printed by the Bureau of Engraving & Printing.

Letter Sheet for Foreign Postage

1988, May 9   Litho.   Tagged

UC61	UC30 39c **multi,** entire		78	39
	First day cancel, Miami, FL			1.55

OFFICIAL ENVELOPES

By the Act of Congress, January 31, 1873, the franking privilege of officials was abolished as of July 1, 1873 and the Postmaster General was authorized to prepare official envelopes. At the same time official stamps were prepared for all Departments. Department envelopes became obsolete July 5, 1884. After that, government offices began to use franked envelopes of varied design. These indicate no denomination and lie beyond the scope of this Catalogue.

Post Office Department

UO1

Numeral 9mm. high.

UO2

Numeral 9mm. high

UO3

Numeral 9½mm. high.

Printed by George H. Reay, Brooklyn, N.Y.

1873

UO1	UO1	2c **black,** lemon		9.00	5.00
		Entire		12.00	8.75
UO2	UO2	3c **black,** lemon		3.00	3.00
		Entire		8.00	6.00
+UO3	UO2	3c **black,** white		6,000.	
		Entire		15,000.	
UO4	UO3	6c **black,** lemon		9.00	8.00
		Entire		13.00	14.00

UO4

Numeral 9¼mm. high.

UO5

Numeral 9¼mm. high.

UO6

Numeral 10½mm. high.

Printed by Plimpton Manufacturing Co., Hartford, Conn.

1874-79

UO5	UO4	2c **black,** lemon		3.00	2.50
		Entire		6.00	3.75
UO6	UO4	2c **black,** white		45.00	30.00
		Entire		57.50	32.50
UO7	UO5	3c **black,** lemon		2.00	50
		Entire		2.50	1.00
UO8	UO5	3c **black,** white		700.00	750.00
		Entire		825.00	
UO9	UO5	3c **black,** amber		35.00	25.00
		Entire		45.00	27.50
UO10	UO5	3c **black,** blue		15,000.	
		Entire		18,000.	
UO11	UO5	3c **blue,** blue ('75)		14,000.	
		Entire		16,000.	
UO12	UO6	6c **black,** lemon		3.00	2.00
		Entire		6.00	6.00
UO13	UO6	6c **black,** white		525.00	
		Entire		675.00	

Fakes exist of Nos. UO3, UO8 and UO13.

Postal Service

UO7

1877

UO14	UO7	**black,** white		3.00	2.50
		Entire		4.00	4.00
UO15	UO7	**black,** amber		20.00	15.00
		Entire		80.00	24.00
UO16	UO7	**blue,** amber		25.00	16.00
		Entire		75.00	26.00
UO17	UO7	**blue,** blue		4.00	4.00
		Entire		6.50	4.50

War Department

Franklin
UO8

Bust points to the end of "N" of "ONE".

Jackson
UO9

Bust narrow at the back.

Washington
UO10

Queue projects below the bust.

Lincoln
UO11

Neck very long at the back.

Jefferson
UO12

Queue forms straight line with bust.

Clay
UO13

Ear partly concealed by hair, mouth large, chin prominent.

Webster
UO14

Has side whiskers.

Scott
UO15

Hamilton
UO16

Back of bust very narrow; chin almost straight; the labels containing the letters "U S" are exactly parallel.

Printed by George H. Reay.

1873

UO18	UO8	1c	**dark red**, *white*	500.00	225.00
			Entire	625.00	300.00
UO19	UO9	2c	**dark red**, *white*	550.00	275.00
			Entire	625.00	
UO20	UO10	3c	**dark red**, *white*	45.00	30.00
			Entire	60.00	32.50
UO21	UO10	3c	**dark red**, *amber*	9,000.	

			Entire	15,000.	
UO22	UO10	3c	**dark red**, *cream*	350.00	150.00
			Entire	450.00	175.00
UO23	UO11	6c	**dark red**, *white*	150.00	50.00
			Entire	175.00	
UO24	UO11	6c	**dark red**, *cream*	1,250.	300.00
			Entire	2,000.	1,050.
UO25	UO12	10c	**dark red**, *white*	2,250.	250.00
			Entire	4,000.	475.00
UO26	UO13	12c	**dark red**, *white*	95.00	35.00
			Entire	115.00	
UO27	UO14	15c	**dark red**, *white*	95.00	40.00
			Entire	115.00	
UO28	UO15	24c	**dark red**, *white*	110.00	30.00
			Entire	140.00	
UO29	UO16	30c	**dark red**, *white*	325.00	90.00
			Entire	375.00	140.00

1873

UO30	UO8	1c	**vermilion**, *white*	135.00	
			Entire	215.00	
WO31	UO8	1c	**vermilion**, *manila*	6.00	2.50
			Entire	10.00	5.50
+UO32	UO9	2c	**vermilion**, *white*	200.00	
			Entire	4,000.	
WO33	UO9	2c	**vermilion**, *manila*	150.00	
			Entire	200.00	
UO34	UO10	3c	**vermilion**, *white*	60.00	30.00
			Entire	125.00	
UO35	UO10	3c	**vermilion**, *amber*	75.00	
			Entire	210.00	
UO36	UO10	3c	**vermilion**, *cream*	9.00	2.75
			Entire	27.50	11.00
UO37	UO11	6c	**vermilion**, *manila*	65.00	
			Entire	90.00	
+UO38	UO11	6c	**vermilion**, *cream*	300.00	
			Entire	6,000.	
UO39	UO12	10c	**vermilion**, *white*	175.00	
			Entire	325.00	
UO40	UO13	12c	**vermilion**, *white*	110.00	
			Entire	175.00	
UO41	UO14	15c	**vermilion**, *white*	175.00	
			Entire	2,000.	
UO42	UO15	24c	**vermilion**, *white*	300.00	
			Entire	325.00	
UO43	UO16	30c	**vermilion**, *white*	350.00	
			Entire	475.00	

UO17

Bottom serif on "S" is thick and short; bust at bottom below hair forms a sharp point.

UO18

Bottom serif on "S" is thick and short; front part of bust is rounded.

UO19

Bottom serif on "S" is short; queue does not project below bust.

UO20

Neck very short at the back.

UO21

Knot of queue stands out prominently.

UO22

Ear prominent, chin receding.

UO23

Has no side whiskers; forelock projects above head.

UO24

Back of bust rather broad; chin slopes considerably; the label containing letters "U S" are not exactly parallel.

Printed by Plimpton Manufacturing Co.

1875

UO44	UO17	1c	**red,** *white*	90.00	75.00
			Entire	100.00	—
+UO45	UO17	1c	**red,** *amber*	600.00	
+UO45A	UO17	1c	**red,** *orange*	17,500.	
WO46	UO17	1c	**red,** *manila*	2.00	75
			Entire	5.00	2.00
UO47	UO18	2c	**red,** *white*	75.00	
			Entire	87.50	
UO48	UO18	2c	**red,** *amber*	20.00	6.00
			Entire	25.00	18.00
UO49	UO18	2c	**red,** *orange*	30.00	10.00
			Entire	32.50	20.00
WO50	UO18	2c	**red,** *manila*	60.00	45.00
			Entire	80.00	—
UO51	UO19	3c	**red,** *white*	8.00	5.00
			Entire	8.75	8.25
UO52	UO19	3c	**red,** *amber*	9.00	5.00
			Entire	10.50	8.25
UO53	UO19	3c	**red,** *cream*	4.00	2.00
			Entire	5.00	3.00
UO54	UO19	3c	**red,** *blue*	2.00	1.50
			Entire	2.50	3.00
UO55	UO19	3c	**red,** *fawn*	3.00	50
			Entire	4.00	1.25
UO56	UO20	6c	**red,** *white*	27.50	17.50
			Entire	65.00	
UO57	UO20	6c	**red,** *amber*	60.00	20.00
			Entire	70.00	
UO58	UO20	6c	**red,** *cream*	150.00	60.00
			Entire	175.00	
UO59	UO21	10c	**red,** *white*	110.00	75.00
			Entire	125.00	
UO60	UO21	10c	**red,** *amber*	1,000.	
			Entire	1,150.	
UO61	UO22	12c	**red,** *white*	30.00	30.00
			Entire	77.50	
UO62	UO22	12c	**red,** *amber*	600.00	
			Entire	650.00	
UO63	UO22	12c	**red,** *cream*	500.00	
			Entire	625.00	
UO64	UO23	15c	**red,** *white*	125.00	90.00
			Entire	150.00	
UO65	UO23	15c	**red,** *amber*	600.00	
			Entire	650.00	
UO66	UO23	15c	**red,** *cream*	550.00	
			Entire	575.00	
UO67	UO24	30c	**red,** *white*	125.00	90.00
			Entire	140.00	—
UO68	UO24	30c	**red,** *amber*	850.00	
			Entire	900.00	
UO69	UO24	30c	**red,** *cream*	800.00	
			Entire	875.00	

POSTAL SAVINGS ENVELOPES

Issued under the Act of Congress, approved June 25, 1910, in lieu of penalty or franked envelopes.

Unused remainders, after October 5, 1914, were overprinted with the Penalty Clause. Regular stamped envelopes, redeemed by the Government, were also overprinted for official use.

UO25

1911

UO70	UO25	1c	**green,** *white*	50.00	7.50
			Entire	60.00	30.00
UO71	UO25	1c	**green,** *oriental buff*	145.00	45.00
			Entire	165.00	57.50
UO72	UO25	2c	**carmine,** *white*	6.00	1.50
			Entire	8.00	6.00
a.		2c	carmine, *manila* (error)	1,400.	—
			Entire	1,900.	

OFFICIAL MAIL

UO26

1983, Jan. 12   **Embossed**

UO73	UO26	20c	**blue,** entire	50
			First day cancel, Washington, DC	75

UO27

1985, Feb. 26   **Embossed**

UO74	UO27	22c	**blue,** entire	55 —
			First day cancel, Washington, DC	80

UO28

1987, Mar. 2   **Typo.**

UO75	UO28	22c	**blue,** entire	55 —
			First day cancel, Washington, DC	80

Used exclusively to mail U.S. Savings Bonds.

UO29

UO30

UO31

1988, Mar. 22   **Typo.**
UO76   UO29 (25c) **black & blue,** entire   60   —
    First day cancel, Washington, DC   85
   Used exclusively to mail U.S. Savings Bonds.

1988, Apr. 11   **Typo. & Embossed**
UO77   UO30 25c **black & blue,** entire   60   —
    First day cancel, Washington, DC   85

1988, Apr. 11   **Typo.**
UO78   UO31 25c **black & blue,** entire   60   —
    First day cancel, Washington, DC   85
   Used exclusively to mail U.S. Savings Bonds.

OFFICIAL WRAPPERS
Included in listings of Official Envelopes
with prefix letters WO instead of UO.

POSTAL CARDS

Prices are for (1), unused cards as sold by the Post Office, without printed or written address or message.
(2), unused cards with printed or written address or message. Used price applies after 1952.
*(3), used cards with Post Office cancellation, when current.
Starting with No. UX21, all postal cards have been printed by the Government Printing Office.
Nos. UX1-UX48 are typographed; others are lithographed (offset) unless otherwise stated.
Numerous printing varieties exist. Varieties of surcharged cards include (a) inverted surcharge at lower left, (b) double surcharge, one inverted at lower left, (c) surcharge in other abnormal positions, including back of card. Such varieties command a premium.
Colored cancellations sell for more than black in some instances.
All prices are for entire cards.
* Used prices for international rate cards are for proper usage. Those domestically used sell for less.

Liberty — PC1

Size: 130x76mm.

Wmk. Large "U S P O D" in Monogram,
(90x60mm.)

1873

              (1)   (2)   (3)

UX1   PC1   1c   brown on buff,   275.00   50.00   17.50
      May 13
      First day cancel,   2250.
      Boston, New
      York or
      Washington

Wmk. Small "U S P O D" in Monogram,
(53x36mm.)

UX3   PC1   1c   brown on buff,   60.00   13.00   1.50
      July 6, 1873
   a.   Without   —
       watermark

The watermarks on Nos. UX1, UX3 and UX4 are found in normal position, inverted, reversed, and inverted and reversed. They are often dim, especially on No. UX4.
No. UX3a is not known unused. Cards offered as such are either unwatermarked proofs, or have partial or vague watermarks. See No. UX65.

U.S. Proofs are listed and priced in a separate section of the catalogue. See catalogue index.

Liberty
PC2

Since 1875 it has been possible to purchase postal cards in sheets for multiple printing, hence pairs, strips and blocks are available.

Inscribed: "WRITE THE ADDRESS . . ."

1875   **Wmk. Small "U S P O D" in Monogram**

UX4   PC2   1c   black on buff,   1,500.   575.00   200.00
      Sept. 28

Unwmk.

UX5   PC2   1c   black on buff,   50.00   5.00   40
      Sept. 30

For other postal card of type PC2 see No. UX7.

Liberty — PC3

1879

UX6   PC3   2c   blue on buff,   17.50   7.50   15.00
      Dec. 1, 1879
   a.   2c dark blue on   22.50   9.00   17.50
      buff

See Nos. UX13 and UX16.

Design of PC2, Inscribed "NOTHING BUT THE ADDRESS."

1881

UX7   PC2   1c   black on buff,   45.00   3.50   30
      Oct. 17 (?)
   a.   23 teeth below   500.00   175.00   25.00
      "ONE CENT"
   b.   Printed on both   525.00   350.00
      sides

Jefferson — PC4

1885

UX8   PC4   1c   brown on buff,   30.00   6.00   1.00
      Aug. 24
   a.   1c orange brown   30.00   6.00   1.00
      on buff
   b.   1c red brown on   30.00   6.00   1.00
      buff
   c.   1c chocolate on   60.00   15.00   6.00
      buff
   d.   Double   —
      impression
   e.   Double   525.00
      impression, one
      inverted

f. Printed both   *500.00*
     sides

PC5

Head of Jefferson facing right, centered on card.

1886

UX9	PC5	1c	black on buff, *Dec. 1, 1886*	9.00	1.00	50
	a.		1c black on dark buff	15.00	4.00	1.00
	b.		Double impression	*400.00*		
	c.		Double impression, one inverted	*850.00*		

Grant — PC6

1891   **Size: 155x95mm.**

UX10	PC6	1c	black on buff, *Dec. 16, 1891*	25.00	5.00	1.25
	a.		Double impression, one inverted	*550.00*		
	b.		Double impression	*550.00*		

Two types exist of No. UX10.

Size: 117x75mm.

UX11	PC6	1c	blue on grayish white, *Dec. 16, 1891*	9.00	3.00	1.50
	b.		Double impression, one inverted	170.00		

Cards printed in black instead of blue are invariably proofs.

PC7

Head of Jefferson facing left.
Small wreath and name below.
Size: 140x89mm.

1894

UX12	PC7	1c	black on buff, *Jan. 2, 1894*	27.50	1.50	35
	a.		Double impression	*200.00*		

1897   **Design of PC3**

Size: 140x89mm.

UX13	PC3	2c	bl. on cream, *Jan. 25, 1897*	110.00	60.00	65.00

PC8

Head same as PC7. Large wreath and name below.

1897

Size: 139x82mm.

UX14	PC8	1c	black on buff, *Dec. 1, 1897*	20.00	2.00	25
	a.		Double impression, one inverted	—	600.00	650.00
	b.		Printed both sides	—	—	—
	c.		Double impression	*300.00*	—	—

John
Adams
PC9

1898   **Size: 126x74mm.**

UX15	PC9	1c	black on buff, *Mar. 31*	27.50	7.50	12.50

United States Postal Cards can be
mounted in Scott's U.S. Postal Cards
Album.

Design same as PC3, without frame around card.
Size: 140x82mm.

UX16	PC3	2c	black on buff, *1898*	8.50	4.50	8.50

McKinley — PC10

1902

UX17	PC10	1c	black on buff	*5,000.*	*3,250.*	*2,500.*

Earliest known use: May 27, 1902.

McKinley
PC11

1902

UX18	PC11	1c	black on buff	9.00	1.00	30

Earliest known use: July 14, 1902.
Two types exist of Nos. UX18-UX20.

McKinley — PC12

1907

UX19	PC12	1c	black on buff	27.50	1.50	40

Earliest known use: June 28, 1907.

1908

Same design,
correspondence space at left.

UX20 PC12 1c black on buff, 40.00 6.50 4.50
Jan. 2, 1908

PC13

McKinley, background shaded.

1910

UX21	PC13 1c	blue on bluish	90.00	15.00	5.00
a.		1c bronze blue on bluish	150.00	25.00	10.00
b.		Double impression	275.00	—	
c.		Triple impression	325.00		
d.		Double impression, one inverted	400.00		
e.		Four arcs above and below "IS" of inscription to left of stamp impression are pointed	700.00	400.00	400.00

A No. UX21 card exists with Philippines No. UX11 printed on the back.

PC14

Same design, white background.

1910

UX22	PC14 1c	blue on bluish, Apr. 13, 1910	11.00	1.25	25
a.		Double impression	175.00		
b.		Triple impression	200.00		
c.		Triple impression, one inverted	—		

See No. UX24.

PC15

Head of Lincoln solid background.

1911

Size: 127x76mm.

UX23	PC15 1c	red on cream, Jan. 21	6.00	2.50	5.00
a.		Triple impression	450.00		

For other postal card of type PC15 see No. UX26.

Design same as PC14

Size: 140x82mm.

UX24	PC14 1c	red on cream, Aug. 10	7.50	1.00	25
a.		Double impression	200.00		
b.		Triple impression	250.00		

Grant — PC16

UX25	PC16 2c	red on cream, Oct. 27, 1911	1.25	50	7.50
a.		Double impression	—		

For other postal card of type PC16 see No. UX36.

1913

Size: 127x76mm.

UX26	PC15 1c	green on cream, July 29	6.50	1.75	5.00

Jefferson — PC17

Die I—End of queue small, sloping sharply downward to right.

Die II (re-cut)—End of queue large and rounded.

1914-16

Size: 140x82mm.

UX27	PC17 1c	green on buff, Die I, June 4, 1914	25	20	10
a.		1c green on cream	3.00	1.00	50
b.		Double impression	125.00		

On gray, rough surfaced card

UX27C	PC17 1c	green, Die I, 1916	1,750.	—	
UX27D	PC17 1c	dark green, Die II, Dec. 22, 1916	1,750.	200.00	100.00

Lincoln — PC19

1917-18 **Size: 127x76mm.**

UX28	PC19 1c	green on cream, Mar. 14, 1917	60	30	30
a.		1c green on dk. buff	1.25	50	50
b.		Double impression	—	—	

No. UX28 was printed also on light buff and canary.

Jefferson — PC20

Die I. Rough, coarse impression. End of queue slopes sharply downward to right. Left basal ends of "2" form sharp points.

Size: 140x82mm.

Die II. Clear fine lines in hair. Left basal ends of "2" form balls.

UX29	PC20 2c	red on buff, Die I, Oct. 22, 1917	32.50	4.50	1.25
a.		2c lake on cream, DieI	40.00	7.50	2.00
c.		2c vermilion on buff, Die I	250.00	60.00	50.00
UX30	PC20 2c	red on cream, Die II, Jan. 23, 1918	17.50	3.00	1.25

2c Postal Cards of 1917-18 Revalued.

Surcharged in one line by canceling machine at Washington, D. C.

1920

UX31	PC20	1c	on 2c red on cream, Die II, *April, 1920*	3,250.	2,500.	3,250.

Surcharged in two lines by canceling machine (46 Types)

UX32	PC20	1c	on 2c red on buff, Die I, *April, 1920*	37.50	10.00	9.00
	a.		1c on 2c vermilion on buff	85.00		55.00
	b.		Double surcharge	—		75.00
UX33	PC20	1c	on 2c red on cream, Die II, *April, 1920*	6.00	1.50	1.25
	a.		Inverted surcharge	50.00		—
	b.		Double surcharge	40.00	30.00	30.00
	c.		Double surcharge, one inverted			300.00
	d.		Triple surcharge	300.00		

Prices for surcharge varieties of Nos. UX32 and UX33 are for cards having the surcharges *on the stamp.* Copies having the surcharge inverted in the lower left corner, either alone or in combination with a normal surcharge, exist in many of the 46 types.

Surcharged in Two Lines by Press Printing

UX34	PC20	1c	on 2c red on buff, Die I	350.00	85.00	35.00
	g.		Double surcharge	500.00		
UX35	PC20	1c	on 2c red on cream, Die II	175.00	40.00	25.00

Surcharges were prepared from (a) special dies fitting International and Universal post office canceling machines (Nos. UX31-UX33), and (b) printing press dies (Nos. UX34-UX35). There are 38 canceling machine types on Die I, and 44 on Die II. There are two printing press types of each die.

UX36	PC16	1c	on 2c red on cream (#UX25)			3,500.

Unused copies of No. UX36 (New York surcharge) were probably made by favor. Used copies of No. UX36 (Los Angeles surcharge) are unquestionably authentic. Surcharges on other numbers exist, but their validity is doubtful.

McKinley — PC21

Franklin — PC22

1926

For International Use

UX37	PC21	3c	red on buff, *Feb. 1, 1926*	3.00	1.50	7.50
			First day cancel, Washington, D.C.			200.00
	a.		3c red on yellow	3.50	1.50	10.00

1951

UX38	PC22	2c	carmine rose on buff, *Nov. 16, 1951*	30	25	25

		First day cancel	4.00
	a.	Double impression	200.00

Nos. UX27 and UX28 Surcharged by Canceling Machine at Left of Stamp in Light Green

REVALUED 2¢ P. O. DEPT.

1952, Jan. 1

UX39	PC17	2c	on 1c green on buff	50	25	25
			First day cancel, any city			20.00
	a.		Surcharged vertically, reading down	6.00	2.50	7.50
	b.		Double surcharge	15.00		17.50
UX40	PC19	2c	on 1c green on cream, *Mar. 22, 1952*	60	40	30
	a.		Surcharged vertically, reading down	7.50	4.00	5.00

Nos. UX27 and UX28 with Similar Surcharge Typographed at Left of Stamp in Dark Green.

1952

UX41	PC17	2c	on 1c green on buff	3.50	1.40	1.50
	a.		Inverted surcharge at lower left	85.00	40.00	110.00
UX42	PC19	2c	on 1c green on cream	4.50	2.50	2.00
	a.		Surcharged on back	75.00		

Type of 1917
Size: 127x76mm.

UX43	PC19	2c	carmine on buff, *July 31, 1952*	25	15	20
			First day cancel			2.50

Torch and Arm of Statue of Liberty PC23

Issued to commemorate the Fifth International Philatelic Exhibition (FIPEX), New York City, Apr. 28-May 6, 1956.

1956

UX44	PC23	2c	deep carmine & dark violet blue on buff, *May 4, 1956*	25	20	
			First day cancel, New York, N. Y. *(537,474)*			1.25
	a.		2c lilac rose & dark violet blue on buff	1.50	50	
	b.		Dark violet blue omitted	350.00	225.00	
	c.		Double impression of dark violet blue	16.00	10.00	

Statue of Liberty
PC24   PC25

For International Use

1956

				(1)	(3)
UX45	PC24	4c	deep red & ultramarine on buff, *Nov. 16, 1956*	1.25	*30.00*
			First day cancel, New York, N. Y. *(129,841)*		1.25

Issued at the American Stamp Dealers' Association National Postage Stamp Show, New York, N.Y., Nov. 16-18.

1958-61

UX46	PC25	3c	purple on buff, *Aug. 1, 1958*	40	20
			First day cancel, Philadelphia, Pa. *(180,610)*		1.25
	a.		"N GOD WE TRUST"	12.50	15.00
	b.		Double impression	325.00	
	c.		Precanceled with 3 printed purple lines, *1961*	3.50	2.50

Issued at the convention and exhibition of the American First Day Cover Society, Philadelphia, Pa.

On No. UX46c, the precanceling lines are incorporated with the design. The earliest known postmark on this experimental card is Sept. 15, 1961.

No. UX38 Surcharged by Canceling Machine at Left of Stamp in Black

ONE CENT ADDITIONAL PAID

1958

UX47	PC22	2c	+1c carmine rose on buff	160.00	225.00

The surcharge was applied to 750,000 cards for the use of the General Electric Co., Owensboro, Ky. A variety of the surcharge shows the D of PAID beneath the N of ADDITIONAL. All known examples of No. UX47 have a printed advertisement on the back and a small punch hole near lower left corner.

Lincoln — PC26

1962-66

Precanceled with 3 printed red violet lines.

UX48	PC26	4c	red violet on white, *Nov. 19, 1962*	25	20
			First day cancel, Springfield, Ill. *(162,939)*		1.50
	a.		Tagged, *June 25, 1966*	50	20
			Tagged, first day cancel, Bellevue, Ohio		—

No. UX48a was printed with luminescent ink.

The lack of a price for a listed item does not necessarily indicate rarity.

See note on Luminescence in "Information for Collectors."

Map of Continental
United States — PC27

Designed by Suren H. Ermoyan.

For International Use

1963

			(1)	(3)
UX49	PC27 7c	bl. & red on white, *Aug. 30*	2.00	20.00
		First day cancel, New York, N. Y.		1.00
a.		Blue omitted		—

First day cancellation was applied to 270,464 of Nos. UX49 and UY19. See Nos. UX54, UX59.

Flags and Map of U.S. — PC28

Designed by Gerald N. Kurtz.

1964   **Precanceled with 3 printed blue lines.**

175th anniv. of the U.S. Customs Service.

UX50	PC28 4c	red & blue on white, *Feb. 22*	40	50
		First day cancel, Washington, D.C. *(313,275)*		1.00
a.		Blue omitted	450.00	
b.		Red omitted	—	

Americans "Moving Forward" (Street
Scene) — PC29

Designed by Gerald N. Kurtz.

1964

Precanceled with a blue and 2 red printed lines

Issued to publicize the need to strengthen the U.S. Social Security system. Released in connection with the 15th conference of the International Social Security Association at Washington, D.C.

UX51	PC29 4c	dull blue & red on white, *Sept. 26*	40	20
		First day cancel, Washington, D.C. *(293,650)*		1.00

a.	Red omitted	—
b.	Blue omitted	550.00

Coast Guard Flag — PC30

Designed by Muriel R. Chamberlain.

1965   **Precanceled with 3 printed red lines**

175th anniv. of the U.S. Coast Guard.

UX52	PC30 4c	blue & red on white, *Aug. 4*	30	20
		First day cancel, Newburyport, Mass. *(338,225)*		1.00
a.		Blue omitted	—	

Crowd and Census Bureau Punch Card — PC31

Designed by Emilio Grossi.

1965   **Precanceled with 3 bright blue printed lines**

UX53	PC31 4c	bright blue & black on white, *Oct. 21*	30	20
		First day cancel, Philadelphia, Pa. *(275,100)*		1.00

Map Type of 1963

1967, Dec. 4

For International Use

UX54	PC27 8c	blue & red on white	2.00	20.00
		First day cancel, Washington, D.C.		50

First day cancellation was applied to 268,077 of Nos. UX54 and UY20.

Lincoln — PC33

Designed by Robert J. Jones.

Luminescent Ink

1968   **Precanceled with 3 printed green lines**

UX55	PC33 5c	emerald on white, *Jan. 4*	25	15

First day cancel, Hodgenville, Ky.	1.00
a.	Double impression	—

First day cancellation was applied to 274,000 of Nos. UX55 and UY21.

Woman Marine, 1968,
and Marines of Earlier
Wars — PC34

Designed by Muriel R. Chamberlain.

1968, July 26

25th anniv. of the Women Marines.

UX56	PC34 5c	rose red & grn. on white	35	20
		First day cancel, San Francisco, Cal. *(203,714)*		1.00

Weather Vane — PC35

Designed by Robert Geissmann.

1970   **Tagged**

Issued to commemorate the centenary of the Army's Signal Service, the Weather Services (Weather Bureau).

UX57	PC35 5c	blue, yellow, red & black on white, *Sept. 1*	30	15
		First day cancel, Fort Myer, Va. *(285,800)*		1.00
a.		Yellow & black omitted	700.00	
b.		Blue omitted	500.00	
c.		Black omitted	600.00	

Paul Revere — PC36

Designed by Howard C. Mildner after statue near Old North Church, Boston.

Luminescent Ink

1971   **Precanceled with 3 printed brown lines.**

Issued to honor Paul Revere, Revolutionary War patriot.

UX58	PC36 6c	brown on white, *May 15*	25	20
		First day cancel, Boston, Mass.		1.00
a.		Double impression	300.00	

First day cancellation was applied to 340,000 of Nos. UX58 and UY22.

Map Type of 1963

1971   **Tagged**

For International Use

UX59	PC27 10c	bl. & red on white, *June 10*	2.00	20.00
		First day cancel, New York, N.Y.		1.00

First day cancellation was applied to 297,000 of Nos. UX59 and UXC11.

New York Hospital, New York City — PC37

Designed by Dean Ellis.
Issued as a tribute to America's hospitals in connection with the 200th anniversary of New York Hospital.

1971				Tagged	
UX60	PC37 6c	bl. & multi. on white, Sept. 16		25	20
		First day cancel, New York, N.Y. (218,200)			1.00
a.		Blue & yellow omitted	700.00		

U.S. POSTAGE 6 CENTS

U.S.F. Constellation — PC38

MONUMENT VALLEY
U.S. POSTAGE 6 CENTS
Monument Valley PC39

Gloucester, Mass. PC40
U.S. POSTAGE 6 CENTS

Tourism Year of the Americas
Designed by Melbourne Brindle.

1972, June 29
Tagged
Size: 152½x108½mm.

UX61	PC38 6c	black on buff (Yosemite, Mt. Rushmore, Niagara Falls, Williamsburg on back)		30	50
		First day cancel, any city			40
a.		Address side blank	300.00		
UX62	PC39 6c	black on buff (Monterey, Redwoods, Gloucester, U.S.F. Constellation on back)		30	50
		First day cancel, any city			40
UX63	PC40 6c	black on buff (Rodeo, Mississippi Riverboat, Grand Canyon, Monument Valley on back)		30	50
		First day cancel, any city			40

Nos. UX61-UX63, UXC12-UXC13 went on sale throughout the United States. They were sold as souvenirs without postal validity at Belgica Philatelic Exhibition in Brussels and were displayed at the American Embassies in Paris and Rome. This is reflected in the first day cancel.

Nos. UX61-UX63 have a luminescent panel at left of stamp which glows green under ultraviolet light.
Varieties of the pictorial back printing include: black omitted (UX62), black and pale salmon omitted (UX63), and back inverted in relation to address side (UX63).

John Hanson — PC41

Designed by Thomas Kronen after statue by Richard Edwin Brooks in Maryland Capitol.

1972 Luminescent Ink
Precanceled with 3 printed blue lines.

UX64	PC41 6c	blue on white, Sept. 1	25	15
		First day cancel, Baltimore, Md.		1.00

Liberty Type of 1873

1973 Centenary of first U.S. postal card.
Tagged

UX65	PC1 6c	magenta on white, Sept. 14	25	15
		First day cancel, Washington, D.C. (289,950)		1.00

Samuel Adams — PC42

Designed by Howard C. Mildner.

1973 Luminescent Ink
Precanceled with 3 printed orange lines

UX66	PC42 8c	orange, Dec. 16	25	15
		First day cancel, Boston, Mass. (147,522)		1.00

Ship's Figurehead, 1883 — PC43

Design is after a watercolor by Elizabeth Moutal of the oak figurehead by John Rogerson from the barque Edinburgh.

1974 Tagged
For International Use

UX67	PC43 12c	multicolored, Jan. 4	35	15.00
		First day cancel, Miami, Fla. (138,500)		1.00

No. UX67 has a luminescent panel at left of stamp which glows green under ultraviolet light.

Charles Thomson — PC44

John Witherspoon — PC45

Caesar Rodney — PC46

Designed by Howard C. Mildner.
Luminescent Ink

1975-76
Precanceled with 3 printed emerald lines

UX68	PC44 7c	emerald, Sept. 14, 1975	25	10
		First day cancel, Bryn Mawr, Pa.		75

Precanceled with 3 printed brown lines

UX69	PC45 9c	yellow brown, Nov. 10, 1975	25	10
		First day cancel, Princeton, N.J.		75

Precanceled with 3 printed blue lines

UX70	PC46 9c	blue on white, July 1, 1976	25	10
		First day cancel, Dover, Del.		75
a.		Double impression	—	

First day cancellation applied to 231,919 of Nos. UX68 and UY25; 254,239 of Nos. UX69 and UY26; 304,061 of Nos. UX70 and UY27.

Federal Court House, Galveston, Texas — PC47

Designed by Donald Moss.
The Court House, completed in 1861, is on the National Register of Historic Places.

1977, July 20 Tagged

UX71	PC47 9c	multicolored on white	25	16
		First day cancel, Galveston, Tex. (245,535)		75

Nathan Hale — PC48

Designed by Howard C. Mildner.

Luminescent Ink

1977, Oct. 14
Precanceled with 3 printed green lines

UX72 PC48 9c green   25   10
              First day cancel,   75
              Coventry, Conn.

First day cancellation applied to 304,592 of Nos. UX72 and UY28.

Cincinnati Music Hall — PC49

Designed by Clinton Orlemann.

1978, May 12   **Tagged**
Centenary of Cincinnati Music Hall, Cincinnati, Ohio.

UX73 PC49 10c multicolored   25   16
               First day cancel,   75
               Cincinnati, O.
               (300,000)

John Hancock — PC50

Designed by Howard Behrens.

Luminescent Ink

1978
Precanceled with 3 printed brown orange lines.

UX74 PC50 (10c) brown orange, *May 19*   25   10
                 First day cancel,   75
                 Quincy, Mass.
                 (299,623)
       Inscribed "U.S. Postage 10¢"
UX75 PC50 10c brown orange on white,   25   10
                 June 20   75
                 First day cancel, Quin-
                 cy, Mass. (187,120)

US Coast Guard Eagle USA 14c
Coast Guard Cutter Eagle — PC51

Designed by Carl G. Evers.

For International Use

1978, Aug. 4   **Tagged**

UX76 PC51 14c multicolored   35   8.00
                 First day cancel, Seattle,   75
                 Wash. (196,400)

Molly Pitcher, Monmouth, 1778
Molly Pitcher Firing Cannon at Monmouth — PC52

Designed by David Blossom.

Bicentennial of Battle of Monmouth, June 28, 1778, and to honor Molly Pitcher (Mary Ludwig Hays).

1978, Sept. 8   **Tagged**   **Litho.**

UX77 PC52 10c multicolored   25   16
                 First day cancel,   75
                 Freehold, N.J.
                 (180,280)

George Rogers Clark, Vincennes, 1779
Clark and his Frontiersmen Approaching Fort Sackville — PC53

Designed by David Blossom.

Bicentenary of capture of Fort Sackville from the British by George Rogers Clark.

1979, Feb. 23   **Tagged**   **Litho.**

UX78 PC53 10c multicolored   25   16
                 First day cancel,   75
                 Vincennes, Ind.

Casimir Pulaski, Savannah, 1779
Gen. Casimir Pulaski — PC54

Bicentenary of the death of Gen. Casimir Pulaski (1748-1779), Polish nobleman who served in American Revolutionary Army.

1979, Oct. 11   **Tagged**   **Litho.**

UX79 PC54 10c multicolored   25   16
                 First day cancel,   75
                 Savannah. GA
                 (210,000)
       Olympic Games Issue

Sprinter
PC55

Designed by Robert M. Cunningham.

22nd Olympic Games, Moscow, July 19-Aug. 3, 1980.

1979, Dept. 17   **Tagged**   **Litho.**

UX80 PC55 10c multicolored   50   25
                 First day cancel, Eugene,   75
                 Ore.

Iolani Palace, Honolulu
PC56

1979, Oct. 1   **Tagged**   **Litho.**

UX81 PC56 10c multicolored   25   16
                 First day cancel,   75
                 Honolulu, HI (242,804)

Women's
Figure Skating
PC57

13th Winter Olympic Games, Lake Placid, N.Y., Feb. 12-24.

Designed by Robert M. Cunningham.

For International Use

1980, Jan. 15   **Tagged**   **Litho.**

UX82 PC57 14c multicolored   50   1.00
                 First day cancel,   75
                 Atlanta, GA (160,977)

Salt Lake Temple, Salt Lake City — PC58

1980, Apr. 5   **Tagged**   **Litho.**

UX83 PC58 10c multicolored   22   15
                 First day cancel, Salt   75
                 Lake City, UT
                 (325,260)

Landing of Rochambeau, 1780

Rochambeau's Fleet — PC59

Count Jean-Baptiste de Rochambeau's landing at Newport, R.I. (American Revolution) bicentenary.

Designed by David Blossom.

1980, July 11   **Tagged**   **Litho.**

UX84 PC59 10c multicolored   22   15
                First day cancel,   75
                Newport, R.I. *(180,567)*

Battle of Kings Mountain, 1780

Whig Infantrymen — PC60

Bicentenary of the Battle of Kings Mountain (American Revolution).

Designed by David Blossom.

1980, Oct. 7   **Tagged**   **Litho.**

UX85 PC60 10c multicolored   22   15
                First day cancel, Kings   75
                Mountain, NC
                (136,130)

Golden
Hinde — PC61

300th anniv. of Sir Francis Drake's circumnavigation (1578-1580).

Designed by Charles J. Lundgren.

For International Use

1980, Nov. 21

UX86 PC61 19c multicolored   50   5.00
                First day cancel, San   75
                Rafael, CA *(290,547)*

See the "Information for Collectors" section at beginning of catalogue for information on printing methods and varieties.

Battle of Cowpens, 1781

Cols. Washington and Tarleton — PC62

Bicentenary of the Battle of Cowpens (American Revolution).

Designed by David Blossom.

1981, Jan. 17

UX87 PC62 10c multicolored   22   15
                First day cancel,   75
                Cowpens, SC *(160,000)*

Eagle — PC63

Luminescent Ink

1981, Mar. 15
Precanceled with 3 printed violet lines

UX88 PC63 (12c) violet   28   18
                First day cancel,   75
                Memphis, TN

See No. 1818, FDC section.

Isaiah Thomas — PC64

Designed by Chet Jezierski.

1981, May 5   **Precanceled with 3 printed lines**

UX89 PC64 12c lt blue   28   12
                First day cancel,   75
                Worchester, MA
                (185,610)

Nathanael Greene, Eutaw Springs, 1781

PC65

Bicentenary of the Battle at Eutaw Springs (American Revolution)

Designed by David Blossom

1981, Sept. 8   **Litho.**

UX90 PC65 12c multicolored   28   18
                First day cancel, Eutaw   75
                Springs, SC *(115,755)*

Lewis and Clark Expedition, 1806

PC66

Designed by David Blossom

1981, Sept. 23

UX91 PC66 12c multicolored   28   18
                First day cancel, Saint   75
                Louis, MO

Robert Morris — PC67

1981   **Precanceled with 3 printed lines**

UX92 PC67 (13c) buff, *Oct. 11*   30   20
                First day cancel,   55
                Memphis, TN

   See No. 1946, FDC section.

Inscribed: U.S. Postage 13¢

UX93 PC67 13c buff, *Nov. 10*   30   12
                First day cancel,   55
                Philadelphia, PA

"Swamp Fox" Francis Marion, 1782

General Francis Marion (1732?-1795) — PC68

Designed by David Blossom

1982, Apr. 3   **Litho.**

UX94 PC68 13c multicolored   30   20
                First day cancel,   55
                Marion, SC *(141,162)*

La Salle claims Louisiana, 1682
Rene Robert Cavelier, Sieur de la Salle (1643-1687) — PC69

Designed by David Blossom

1982, Apr. 7 **Litho.**

UX95 PC69 13c multicolored 30 20
First day cancel, New 55
Orleans, LA

PC70

Designed by Melbourne Brindle

1982, June 18 **Litho.**

UX96 PC70 13c brown, red & cream on 30 20
buff
First day cancel, 55
Philadelphia, PA
a. Brown & cream omitted —

PC71 Historic Preservation

Designed by Clint Orlemann

1982, Oct. 14 **Litho.**

UX97 PC71 13c multicolored 30 20
First day cancel, St. 55
Louis, MO

Landing of Oglethorpe, Georgia, 1733
Gen. Oglethorpe Meeting Chief Tomo-Chi-Chi of the Yamacraw — PC72

Designed by David Blossom

1983, Feb. 12 **Litho.**

UX98 PC72 13c multicolored 30 20
First day cancel, 55
Savannah, GA

Old Post Office, Washington, D.C. PC73

Designed by Walter Brooks

1983, Apr. 19 **Litho.**

UX99 PC73 13c multicolored 30 20
First day cancel, 55
Washington, DC
(125,056)

Olympics 84, Yachting — PC74

Designed by Bob Peak

1983, Aug. 5 **Litho.**

UX100 PC74 13c multicolored 30 20
First day cancel, Long 55
Beach, CA

Ark and Dove, Maryland, 1634
The Ark and the Dove — PC75

Designed by David Blossom

1984, Mar. 25 **Litho.**

UX101 PC75 13c multicolored 30 20
First day cancel, St. 55
Clement's Island, MD

Runner Carrying Olympic Torch — PC76

Designed by Robert Peak

1984, Apr. 30 **Litho.**

UX102 PC76 13c multicolored 30 20
First day cancel, Los 55
Angeles, CA

Frederic Baraga, Michigan, 1835
Father Baraga and Indian Guide in Canoe — PC77

Designed by David Blossom

1984, June 29 **Litho.**

UX103 PC77 13c multicolored 30 20
First day cancel, 55
Marquette, MI

Dominguez Adobe at Rancho San Pedro — PC78

Designed by Earl Thollander

1984, Sept. 16 **Litho.**

UX104 PC78 13c multicolored 30 20
First day cancel, 55
Compton, CA
a. Black & blue omitted —

Charles Carroll (1737-1832) — PC79

Designed by Richard Sparks

1985, Feb. 1
Precanceled with 3 printed lines

UX105 PC79 (14c) pale grn 28 18
First day cancel, New 58
Carrollton, MD
Inscribed: USA 14

1985, Mar. 6
Precanceled with 3 printed lines

UX106 PC79 14c pale grn 28 14
First day cancel, 58
Annapolis, MD

Clipper *Flying Cloud* 1852   USA 25

Clipper Flying Cloud — PC80

Designed by Richard Schlecht

For International Use

1985, Feb. 27   Litho.

UX107 PC80 25c multi   60   5.00
              First day cancel, Salem,   95
              MA

No. UX107 was sold by the U.S.P.S. at CUP-PEX 87, Perth, Western Australia, with a cachet honoring CUP-PEX 87 and the America's Cup race.

George Wythe (1726-1806) — PC81

Designed by Chet Jezierski from a portrait by John Fergusson

1985, June 20

Precanceled with 3 printed lines

UX108 PC81 14c brt apple grn   28   14
              First day cancel,   58
              Williamsburg, VA

Settling of Connecticut, 1636

Arrival of Thomas Hooker and Hartford
Congregation — PC82

Settlement of Connecticut, 350th Anniv. Designed by David Blossom

1986, Apr. 18   Litho.

UX109 PC82 14c multi   28   18
              First day cancel,   58
              Hartford, CT

Stamp Collecting — PC83

Designed by Ray Ameijide

1986, May 23   Litho.

UX110 PC83 14c multi   28   18

              First day cancel,   58
              Chicago, IL

No. UX110 was sold by the U.S.P.S. at "najubria 86" with a show cachet.

USA 14

Francis Vigo, Vincennes, 1779

Francis Vigo (1747-1836) — PC84

Designed by David Blossom

1986, May 24   Litho.

UX111 PC84 14c multi   28   18
              First day cancel,   58
              Vincennes, IN

USA 14

Settling of Rhode Island, 1636

Roger Williams (1603-1683), Clergyman, Landing at
Providence — PC85

Settling of Rhode Island, 350th Anniv. Designed by David Blossom

1986, June 26   Litho.

UX112 PC85 14c multi   28   18
              First day cancel,   58
              Providence, RI

14 USA

Wisconsin Territory, 1836

Miners, Shake Rag Street Housing — PC86

Wisconsin Territory Sesquicentennial Designed by David Blossom

1986, July 3   Litho.

UX113 PC86 14c multi   28   18
              First day cancel,   58
              Mineral Point, WI

14 USA

National Guard Heritage, 1636-1986

The First Muster, by Don Troiani — PC87

Designed by Bradbury Thompson

1986, Dec. 12   Litho.

UX114 PC87 14c multi   28   18
              First day cancel, Boston,   58
              MA (72,316)

USA 14

Self-scouring steel plow, 1837

PC88

Design by William H. Bond.
The self-scouring steel plow invented by blacksmith John Deere in 1837 pictured at lower left.

1987, May 22   Litho.

UX115 PC88 14c multi   28   18
              First day cancel, Moline,   58
              IL (160,009)

USA 14

Constitutional Convention, 1787

Convening of the Constitutional Convention,
1787 — PC89

Designed by David K. Stone
George Mason, Gouverneur Morris, James Madison, Alexander Hamilton and Charles C. Pinckney are listed in the lower left corner of the card.

1987, May 25   Litho.

UX116 PC89 14c multi   28   18
              First day cancel,   58
              Philadelphia, PA
              (138,207)

Stars and
Stripes — PC90   USA 14

Designed by Steven Dohanos

1987, June 14   Litho.

UX117 PC90 14c black, blue & red   28   14
              First day cancel,   58
              Baltimore, MD

No. UX117 was sold by the U.S.P.S. at Cologne, Germany, with a cachet for Philatelia'87.

Take Pride in America — PC91

Designed by Lou Nolan

1987, Sept. 22   Litho.

UX118   PC91 14c   multicolored   28   18
First day cancel,   58
Jackson, WY (47,281)

Timberline Lodge, 50th Anniversary — PC92

Designed by Walter DuBois Richards

1987, Sept. 28   Litho.

UX119   PC92 14c   multi   28   18
First day cancel,   58
Timberline, OR
(63,595)

Bison and Prairie — PC93

Designed by Bart Forbes

1988, Mar. 28   Litho.

UX120   PC93 15c   multi   30   15
First day cancel, Buffalo,   60
WY

Blair House — PC94

Designed by Pierre Mion

1988, May 4   Litho.

UX121   PC94 15c   multi   30   15
First day cancel,   60
Washington, DC

Yorkshire, Squarerigged Packet — PC95

Designed by Richard Schlect
Inscribed: Yorkshire, Black Ball Line, Packet Ship, circa
1850 at lower left.

1988, June 29   Litho.

UX122   PC95 28c   multi   60   28
First day cancel, Mystic,   1.00
Ct

Harvesting Corn Fields — PC96

Designed by Greg Hargreaves
Iowa Territory Sesquicentennial

1988, July 2   Litho.

UX123   PC96 15c   multi   30   15
First day cancel,   60
Burlington, IA

Flatboat Ferry Transporting Settlers Down the Ohio
River — PC97

Designed by James M. Gurney and Susan Sanford
Bicentenary of the settlement of Ohio, the Northwest Terri-
tory. Design at lower left shows map of the eastern United
States with Northwest Territory highlighted.

1988, July 15   Litho.

UX124   PC97 15c   multi   30   15
First day cancel,   60
Marietta, OH

Hearst Castle — PC98

Designed by Robert Reynolds

1988, Sept. 20   Litho.

UX125   PC98 15c   multi   30   15
First day cancel, San   60
Simeon, CA

Pressman, New Yorker Reading Newspaper,
1787 — PC99

Designed by Roy Andersen

1988, Oct. 27   Litho.

UX126   PC99 15c   multi   30   15
First day cancel, New
York, NY

PAID REPLY POSTAL CARDS

These are sold to the public as two unsevered cards, one for
message and one for reply. These are listed first as unsevered
cards and then as severed cards. Prices are for
(1) unused cards (both unsevered and severed) without
printed or written address or message.
(2) unused cards (both unsevered and severed) with printed
or written address or message. Used price applies after 1952.
(3) used unsevered cards, Message Card with Post Office
cancellation and Reply Card uncanceled (from 1968 price is for
a single used severed card); and used severed cards with cancellation when current.
Unsevered cards sell for a premium if never folded.
Used prices for International Paid Reply Cards are for
proper usage. Those domestically used sell for less than the
unused price.

PM1

PR1

Head of Grant, card framed.

1892, Oct. 25   **Size: 140x89mm.**

			(1)	(2)	(3)
UY1	PM1+PR1	1c+1c black on buff, unsevered	30.00	12.50	7.50
	a.	Message card printed on both sides, reply card blank	225.00		
	b.	Message card blank, reply card printed on both sides	275.00		
	c.	Cards joined at bottom	150.00	60.00	75.00
	m.	PM1 Message card detached	5.00	2.50	1.25
	r.	PR1 Reply card detached	5.00	2.50	1.25

For other postal cards of types PM1 and PR1 see No. UY3.

PM2

Liberty — PR2

1893, Mar. 1   **For International Use**

		(1)	(2)	(3)
UY2	PM2+PR2 2c +2c blue on grayish white, unsevered	15.00	9.00	*20.00*
a.	2c+2c dark blue on grayish white, unsevered	15.00	9.00	*20.00*
b.	Message card printed on both sides, reply card blank	275.00		
c.	Message card blank, reply card printed on both sides	—		
d.	Message card normal, reply card blank	275.00		
m.	PM2 Message card detached	4.00	2.00	*6.00*
r.	PR2 Reply card detached	4.00	2.00	*7.50*

For other postal cards of types PM2 and PR2 see No. UY11.

Design same as PM1 and PR1, without frame around card.

1898, Sept.

Size: 140x82mm.

		(1)	(2)	(3)
UY3	PM1+PR1 1c +1c black on buff, unsevered	55.00	15.00	9.00
a.	Message card normal, reply card blank	225.00		
b.	Message card printed on both sides, reply card blank	225.00		
c.	Message card blank, reply card printed on both sides	225.00		
d.	Message card without "Detach annexed card/for answer"	225.00	—	150.00
e.	Message card blank, reply card normal	225.00		
m.	PM1 Message card detached	10.00	4.00	2.00

r.	PR1 Reply card detached	10.00	4.00	2.00

PM3

PR3

1904, Mar, 31

		(1)	(2)	(3)
UY4	PM3+PR3 1c +1c black on buff, unsevered	40.00	7.50	2.50
a.	Message card normal, reply card blank	250.00		
b.	Message card printed on both sides, reply card blank	—		
c.	Message card blank, reply card normal	250.00		
d.	Message card blank, reply card printed on both sides	—	175.00	150.00
m.	PM3 Message card detached	7.50	3.00	75
r.	PR3 Reply card detached	7.50	3.00	75

PM4

PR4

1910, Sept. 14

Double frame line around instructions

		(1)	(2)	(3)
UY5	PM4+PR4 1c +1c blue on bluish, unsevered	125.00	30.00	17.50
a.	Message card normal, reply card blank	175.00		
m.	PM4 Message card detached	7.50	5.00	2.50
r.	PR4 Reply card detached	7.50	5.00	2.50

1911, Oct. 27

Same designs

		(1)	(2)	(3)
UY6	PM4+PR4 1c +1c green on cream, unsevered	100.00	50.00	20.00
a.	Message card normal, reply card blank	—		
m.	PM4 Message card detached	20.00	10.00	4.00
r.	PR4 Reply card detached	20.00	10.00	4.00

1915, Sept. 18

Same designs

Single frame line around instructions

		(1)	(2)	(3)
UY7	PM4+PR4 1c +1c green on cream, unsevered	1.00	50	50
a.	1c+1c dark green on buff, unsevered	1.00	50	50
m.	PM4 Message card detached	25	15	20
r.	PR4 Reply card detached	25	15	20

PM5

PR5

1918, Aug. 2

		(1)	(2)	(3)
UY8	PM5+PR5 2c +2c red on buff, unsevered	65.00	25.00	35.00

	(1)	(2)	(3)
m. PM5 Message card detached	17.50	8.00	6.00
r. PR 5 Reply card detached	17.50	8.00	6.00

1

CENT

Same Surcharged — UY9

1920, April

Fifteen canceling machine types

UY9 PM5+PR5	1c on 2c+1c on 2c red on buff, unsevered	15.00	7.50	7.50
a.	Message card normal, reply card no surcharge	75.00	—	—
b.	Message card normal, reply card double surcharge	65.00	—	—
c.	Message card double surcharge, reply card normal	65.00	—	—
d.	Message card no surcharge, reply card normal	65.00	—	—
e.	Message card no surcharge, reply card double surcharge	65.00	—	—
m.	PM5 Message card detached	4.00	2.00	2.00
r.	PR5 Reply card detached	4.00	2.00	2.00

One press printed type

UY10 PM5+PR5	1c on 2c+1c on 2c red on buff, unsevered	275.00	125.00	150.00
a.	Message card no surcharge, reply card normal	—	—	—
m.	PM5 Message card detached	75.00	35.00	35.00
r.	PR5 Reply card detached	75.00	35.00	35.00

Designs same as PM2 and PR2

1924, Mar. 18   **For International Use**
Size: 139x89mm.

UY11 PM2+PR2	2c +2c red on cream, unsevered	1.50	1.25	*20.00*
m.	PM2 Message card detached	50	40	*8.00*
r.	PR2 Reply card detached	50	40	*8.00*

PM6

PR6

1926, Feb. 1

For International Use

UY12 PM6+PR6	3c +3c red on buff, unsevered	7.50	4.00	*15.00*
a.	3c+3c red on yellow, unsevered	9.00	5.00	*17.50*
	First day cancel			—
m.	PM6 Message card detached	2.50	1.25	*6.00*
r.	PR6 Reply card detached	2.50	1.25	*6.00*

Type of 1910

1951, Dec. 29

Single frame line around instructions.

UY13 PM4+PR4	2c +2c carmine rose on buff, unsevered	1.00	50	50
	First day cancel, Washington, D.C.			3.00
m.	PM4 Message card detached	35	25	20
r.	PR4 Reply card detached	35	25	20

> REVALUED 2¢ P. O. DEPT.

No. UY7a Surcharged by Canceling Machine Below Stamp in Green

1952, Jan. 1

		(1)	(2)	(3)
UY14 PM4+PR4	2c on 1c+2c on 1c green on buff, unsevered	1.00	50	50
a.	Surcharge vertical at left of stamps	6.00	5.00	5.00
b.	Surcharge horizontal at left of stamps	12.50	7.50	10.00
c.	Inverted surcharge horizontal at left of stamps	125.00	65.00	85.00
d.	Message card normal, reply card no surcharge	30.00	—	35.00
e.	Message card normal, reply card double surcharge	35.00	—	20.00
f.	Message card no surcharge, reply card normal	30.00	—	35.00
g.	Message card double surcharge, reply card normal	35.00	—	20.00
h.	Both cards, dbl. surch.	40.00	—	30.00
m.	PM4 Message card detached	40	30	25
r.	PR4 Reply card detached	40	30	25

No. UY7a with Similar Surcharge (horizontal)
Typographed at Left of Stamp in Dark Green.

1952

UY15 PM4+PR4	2c on 1c+2c on 1c green on buff, unsevered	80.00	30.00	40.00
a.	Surcharge on message card only	100.00		
m.	PM4 Message card detached	15.00	7.50	8.00
r.	PR4 Reply card detached	15.00	7.50	8.00

On No. UY15a, the surcharge also appears on blank side of card.

Liberty Type of Postal Card, 1956

1956

		(1)	(3)

For International Use

UY16 PC24	4c+4c carmine & dark violet blue on buff, unsevered, *Nov. 16, 1956*	1.00	*35.00*
	First day cancel, New York, N. Y. (127,874)		1.50
a.	Message card printed on both halves	110.00	
b.	Reply card printed on both halves	110.00	—
m.	Message card detached	40	*30.00*
r.	Reply card detached	40	*25.00*

See note after UX45.

Liberty Type of Postal Card, 1956

1958

UY17 PC25	3c+3c purple on buff, unsevered, *July 31, 1958*	3.00	60
	First day cancel, Boise, Idaho (136,768)		1.00
a.	One card blank	125.00	—

Both halves of No. UY17 are identical, inscribed as No. UX46, "This side of card is for address."

Lincoln Type of Postal Card, 1962
Precanceled with 3 printed red violet lines.

1962

UY18 PC26	4c+4c red violet on white, unsevered, *Nov. 19, 1962*	2.50	75
	First day cancel, Springfield, Ill. (107,746)		2.25
a.	Tagged, *Mar. 7, 1967*	6.00	3.00
a.	First day cancel, Dayton, OH		30.00

Both halves of No. UY18 are identical, inscribed as No. UX48, "This side of card is for address."
No. UY18a was printed with luminescent ink.

Map Type of Postal Card, 1963

1963   **For International Use**

UY19 PC27	7c+7c blue & red on white, unsevered, *Aug. 30, 1963*	2.00	*25.00*
	First day cancel, New York		1.50
a.	Message card normal, reply card blank	125.00	100.00
b.	Message card blank, reply card normal	125.00	
m.	Message card detached	75	*20.00*
r.	Reply card detached	75	*17.50*

Message card inscribed "Postal Card With Paid Reply" in English and French. Reply card inscribed "Reply Postal Card Carte Postale Reponse".

Map Type of Postal Card, 1963

1967, Dec. 4

For International Use

UY20 PC27	8c+8c blue & red on white, unsevered	2.00	*25.00*
	First day cancel, Washington, D.C.		1.50
m.	Message card detached	75	*20.00*
r.	Reply card detached	75	*17.50*

Message card inscribed "Postal Card With Paid Reply" in English and French. Reply card inscribed "Reply Postal Card Carte Postale Response."

Lincoln Type of Postal Card, 1968

1968

Tagged

UY21 PC33	5c+5c emerald on white, unsevered, *Jan. 4, 1968*	1.00	40
	First day cancel, Hodgenville, Ky.		1.50

Paul Revere Type of Postal Card, 1971
Luminescent Ink

1971

Precanceled with 3 printed brown lines.

UY22 PC36	6c+6c brown on white, unsevered, *May 15*	75	25

	First day cancel,		1.25	
	Boston, Mass			

John Hanson Type of Postal Card, 1972
Luminescent Ink

1972

Precanceled with 3 printed blue lines.

UY23	PC41	6c+6c	blue on white,	75	25
			unsevered, *Sept. 1*		
			First day cancel,		75
			Baltimore, Md.		

Samuel Adams Type of Postal Card, 1973
Luminescent Ink

1973

Precanceled with 3 printed orange lines

UY24	PC42	8c+8c	orange on white,	75	25
			unsevered, *Dec. 16*		
			First day cancel,		1.00
			Boston, Mass.		
			(105,369)		

Thomson, Witherspoon, Rodney, Hale &
Hancock Types of Postal Cards, 1975-78
Luminescent Ink

1975-78

Precanceled with 3 printed emerald lines

UY25	PC44	7c+7c	emerald, unsevered,	75	40
			Sept. 14, 1975		
			First day cancel,		80
			Bryn Mawr, Pa.		

Precanceled with 3 printed yellow brown lines

UY26	PC45	9c+9c	yellow brown, un-	75	25
			severed, *Nov. 10,*		
			1975		
			First day cancel,		1.25
			Princeton, N.J.		

Precanceled with 3 printed blue lines

UY27	PC46	9c+9c	blue on white, un-	75	30
			severed, *July 1,*		
			1976		
			First day cancel,		1.00
			Dover, Del.		

Precanceled with 3 printed green lines

UY28	PC48	9c+9c	green on white, un-	75	25
			severed, *Oct. 14,*		
			1977		
			First day cancel,		1.25
			Coventry, Conn.		

Inscribed "U.S. Domestic Rate"
Precanceled with 3 printed brown orange lines

UY29	PC50	(10c+10c)	brn. orange on	8.50	4.50
			white, unsevered,		
			May 19, 1978		
			First day cancel,		2.00
			Quincy, Mass.		

Inscribed "U.S. Postage 10¢"
Precanceled with 3 printed brown orange lines

UY30	PC50	10c+10c	brn. orange on	75	25
			white, unsevered,		
			June 20, 1978		
			First day cancel,		1.50
			Quincy, Mass.		
	a.		One card "Domestic		
			Rate," other "Post-		
			age 10¢"		

Eagle Type of 1981
Inscribed "U. S. Domestic Rate"
Luminescent Ink

1981, Mar. 15

Precanceled with 3 printed violet lines

UY31	PC63	(12c+12c)	violet, unsevered	75	25
			First day cancel,		1.10
			Memphis, TN		

Isaiah Thomas Type
Luminescent Ink

1981, May 5

Precanceled with 3 printed lines

UY32	PC64	12c+12c	lt blue, unsevered	75	15
			First day cancel,		1.10
			Worcester, MA		
	a.		Small die on one	3.00	2.00
			side		

Morris Type of 1981
Inscribed "U.S. Domestic Rate"

1981

Precanceled with 3 printed lines

UY33	PC67	(13c+13c)	buff, *Oct. 11*, unsev-	1.25	25
			ered		
			First day cancel,		85
			Memphis, TN		

Inscribed "U.S. Postage 13¢"

UY34	PC67	13c+13c	buff, *Nov. 10*, unsev-	75	15
			ered		

	First day cancel,		85	
	Philadelphia, PA			

Charles Carroll Type of 1985
Inscribed: U.S. Domestic Rate

1985

Precanceled with 3 printed lines

UY35	PC79	(14c+14c)	pale grn, *Feb. 1,* un-	1.00	25
			severed		
			First day cancel,		90
			New Carrollton,		
			MD		

Inscribed: USA

UY36	PC79	14c+14c	pale green, *Mar. 6,*	56	18
			unsevered		
			First day cancel,		90
			Annapolis, MD		

George Wythe Type of 1985

1985, June 20

Precanceled with 3 printed lines

UY37	PC81	14c+14c	brt apple grn, unsev-	56	18
			ered		
			First day cancel,		90
			Williamsburg, VA		

Flag Type of 1987

1987, Sept. 1

UY38	PC90	14c+14c	black, blue & red	56	18
			First day cancel,		90
			Baltimore, MD		
			(22,314)		

America the Beautiful Type

1988, July 1

UY39	PC9	15c+15c	multi	60	20
			First day cancel,		90
			Buffalo, WY		

AIR POST POSTAL CARDS

Eagle in Flight — APC1

1949					**Typo.**

				(1)	(2)	(3)
UXC1	APC1	4c orange red on buff, *Jan.*		40	30	35
		10, 1949				
		First day cancel,				4.00
		Washington, D.C.				
		(236,620)				

Type of Air Post Stamp, 1954

1958

				(1)	(3)
UXC2	AP31	5c red on buff, *July 31,*		1.50	60
		1958			
		First day cancel,			3.00
		Wichita, Kans.			
		(156,474)			

Type of 1958 Redrawn

1960				**Lithographed (Offset)**

UXC3	AP31	5c red on buff, bicolored		6.00	1.75
		border, *June 18, 1960*			
		First day cancel,			2.75
		Minneapolis, Minn.			
		(228,500)			

Size of stamp of No. UXC3: 18½x21mm.; on No. UXC2:
19x22mm. White cloud around eagle enlarged and finer detail
of design on No. UXC3. Inscription "AIR MAIL-POSTAL
CARD" has been omitted and blue and red border added on
No. UXC3.

Bald Eagle — APC2

1963   **Precanceled with 3 printed red lines**

UXC4	APC2	6c	red on white, bicolored	40	20
			border, *Feb. 15, 1963*		
			First day cancel,		2.25
			Maitland, Fla.		
			(216,203)		

Emblem of Commerce Department's Travel
Service — APC3

1966   **For International Use**

Issued at the Sixth International Philatelic Exhibition
(SIPEX), Washington, D.C., May 21-30.

UXC5	APC3	11c blue & red on white,	50	8.00
		May 27		
		First day cancel,		2.00
		Washington, D.C.		
		(272,813)		

Four photographs at left on address side show: Mt. Rainier,
New York skyline, Indian on horseback and Miami Beach.
The card has blue and red border.
See No. UXC8, UXC11.

Virgin Islands and Territorial Flag — APC4

Designed by Burt Pringle.

1967   **Litho.**

50th anniv. of the purchase of the Virgin Islands.

UXC6	APC4	6c	multi. on white, *Mar.*	40	25
			31		
			First day cancel,		1.75
			Charlotte Amalie, V.		
			I. *(346,906)*		
	a.		Red & yellow omitted	—	

Borah Peak, Lost River Range, Idaho, and Scout
Emblem — APC5

Designed by Stevan Dohanos.

1967, Aug. 4   Litho.

Issued to commemorate the 12th Boy Scout World Jamboree, Farragut State Park, Idaho, Aug. 1-9.

UXC7	APC5	6c bl., yel., blk. & red on white	40	20
		First day cancel, Farragut State Park, ID *(471,585)*		1.50
a.		Blue omitted		—
b.		Blue & black omitted		—
c.		Red & yellow omitted		—

Travel Service Type of 1966

1967   **For International Use**

Issued in connection with the American Air Mail Society Convention, Detroit, Mich.

UXC8	APC3	13c blue & red on white, *Sept. 8*	1.25	8.00
		First day cancel, Detroit, Mich. *(178,189)*		1.75

Stylized Eagle — APC6

Designed by Muriel R. Chamberlain.

1968-69   **Precanceled with 3 printed red lines**

UXC9	APC6	8c blue & red, *Mar. 1*	60	35
		First day cancel, New York, N.Y. *(179,923)*		1.50
a.		Tagged, *Mar. 19, 1969*	1.75	2.50
		Tagged, first day cancel		15.00

1971   **Tagged**

Precanceled with 3 printed blue lines

UXC10	APC6	9c red & blue, *May 15*	45	30
		First day cancel, Kitty Hawk, N.C.		2.00

Travel Service Type of 1966

1971   **Tagged**

For International Use

UXC11	APC3	15c blue & red, *June 10*	1.50	8.00
		First day cancel, New York, N.Y.		1.75

Grand Canyon APC7

Niagara Falls — APC8

Tourism Year of the Americas 1972.

Designed by Melbourne Brindle.

1972, June 29   **Tagged**   Litho.
Size: 152½x108½mm.

UXC12	APC7	9c black on buff *(Statue of Liberty, Hawaii, Alaska, San Francisco on back)*	45	1.00
		First day cancel, any city		1.50

For International Use

UXC13	APC8	15c black on buff *(Mt. Vernon, Washington, D.C., Lincoln, Liberty Bell on back)*	55	15.00
		First day cancel, any city		1.50
a.		Address side blank	400.00	—

See note after No. UX63. Nos. UXC12-UXC13 have a luminescent panel at left of stamp which glows orange under ultraviolet light.

Stylized Eagle — APC9

Eagle Weather Vane — APC10

Designed by David G. Foote (11c) and Stevan Dohanos (18c).

1974, Jan. 4   **Tagged**   Litho.

UXC14	APC9	11c ultramarine & red	70	40
		First day cancel, State College, Pa. *(160,500)*		1.25

For International Use

UXC15	APC10	18c multicolored	85	7.00
		First day cancel, Miami, Fla. *(132,114)*		1.50

All following issues are for international use.

Angel Gabriel Weather Vane — APC11

Designed by Stevan Dohanos.

1975, Dec. 17   **Tagged**   Litho.

UXC16	APC11	21c multicolored	80	5.00
		First day cancel, Kitty Hawk, N.C.		1.50

Nos. UXC14-UXC16 have a luminescent panel at left of stamp which glows orange under ultraviolet light.

Curtiss (JN4H) Jenny — APC12

Designed by Keith Ferris.

1978, Sept. 16   **Tagged**   Litho.

UXC17	APC12	21c multicolored	75	3.00
		First day cancel, San Diego, Cal. *(174,886)*		1.75

No. UXC17 has luminescent panel at left of stamp which glows green under ultraviolet light.

Gymnast APC13

22nd Olympic Games, Moscow, July 19-Aug. 3, 1980.

Designed by Robert M. Cunningham.

1979, Dec. 1   **Tagged**   Litho.

UXC18	APC13	21c multicolored	75	10.00
		First day cancel, Fort Worth, Tex.		1.25

Pangborn, Herndon and Miss Veedol — APC14

First non-stop transpacific flight by Clyde Pangborn and Hugh Herndon, Jr., 50th anniversary
Designed by Ken Dallison

1981, Jan. 2   **Tagged**   Litho.

UXC19	APC14	28c multicolored	75	1.00
		First day cancel, Wenatchee, WA		1.00

Gliders APC15

Designed by Robert E. Cunningham

1982, Mar. 5   **Tagged**   Litho.

UXC20	APC15	28c magenta, yel, blue & black	75	1.00
		FDC, Houston, TX *(106,932)*		1.00

Speedskater — APC16

Designed by Robert Peak

1983, Dec. 29 — **Litho.**

UXC21 APC16 28c multicolored   75   *1.00*
     First day cancel,   *1.00*
     Milwaukee, WI

Martin M-130 China Clipper Seaplane — APC17

Designed by Chuck Hodgson

1985, Feb. 15 — **Litho.**

UXC22 APC17 33c multi   66   *1.00*
     First day cancel, San   *1.10*
     Francisco, CA

Chicago Skyline — APC18

AMERIPEX '86, Chicago, May 22-June 1

Designed by Ray Ameijide

1986, Feb. 1 — **Tagged** — **Litho.**

UXC23 APC18 33c multi   66   *1.00*
     First day cancel,   *1.10*
     Chicago, IL

No. UXC23 was sold at Sudposta '87 by the U.S.P.S. with a show cachet.

DC-3 — APC19

Designed by Chuck Hodgson

1988, May 14 — **Litho.** — **Tagged**

UXC24 APC19 36c multi   72   *1.00*
     First day cancel, San   *1.15*
     Diego, CA

No. UXC24 was sold at SYDPEX '88 by the U.S.P.S. with a cachet for Australia's bicentennial and SYDPEX '88.

OFFICIAL POSTAL CARDS

PO1

1913

Size: **126x76mm.**

UZ1 PO1 1c black on white, *July,*   300.00 150.00
     1913

All No. UZ1 cards have printed address and printed form on message side.

PO2

1983-85

UZ2 PO2 13c blue, *Jan. 12*   40   —
     First day cancel,   75
     Washington, DC

UZ3 PO2 14c blue, *Feb. 26, 1985*   45   —
     First day cancel,   80
     Washington, DC

PO3

Designed by Bradbury Thompson

1988, June 10 — **Litho.**

UZ4 PO3 15c   30   —
     First day cancel,   85
     Washington, DC

REVENUE

The Commissioner of Internal Revenue advertised for bids for revenue stamps in August, 1862, and the contract was awarded to Butler & Carpenter of Philadelphia.

Nos. R1-R102 were used to pay taxes on documents and proprietary articles including playing cards. Until Dec. 25, 1862, the law stated that a stamp could be used only for payment of the tax upon the particular instrument or article specified on its face. After that date, stamps, except the Proprietary, could be used indiscriminately.

Most stamps of the first issue appeared in the latter part of 1862 or early in 1863. The 5c and 10c Proprietary were issued in the fall of 1864, and the 6c Proprietary on April 13, 1871.

Plate numbers and imprints are usually found at the bottom of the plate on all denominations except 25c and $1 to $3.50. On these it is nearly always at the left of the plate. The imprint reads "Engraved by Butler & Carpenter, Philadelphia" or "Jos. R. Carpenter".

Plates were of various sizes: 1c and 2c, 210 subjects (14x15); 3c to 20c, 170 subjects (17x10); 25c to 30c, 102 subjects (17x6); 50c to 70c, 85 subjects (17x5); $1 to $1.90, 90 subjects (15x6); $2 to $10, 73 subjects (12x6); $15 to $50, 54 subjects (9x6); $200, 8 subjects (2x4). No. R132, one subject.

The paper varies, the first employed being thin, hard and brittle until September, 1869, from which time it acquired a softer texture and varied from medium to very thick. Early printings of some revenue stamps occur on paper which appears to have laid lines. Some are found on experimental silk paper, first employed about August, 1870.

Canceling was usually done with pen and ink and all values quoted are for stamps canceled in that way. Handstamped cancellations as a rule sell for more than pen. Printed cancellations are scarce and command much higher prices. Herringbone, punched or other types of cancellation which break the surface of the paper adversely affect prices.

Some of the stamps were in use eight years and were printed several times. Many color variations occurred, particularly if unstable pigments were used and the color was intended to be purple or violet, such as the 4c Proprietary, 30c and $2.50 stamps. Before 1868 dull colors predominate on these and the early red stamps. In later printings of the 4c Proprietary, 30c and $2.50 stamps, red predominates in the mixture and on the dollar values of red is brighter. The early $1.90 stamp is dull purple, imperforate or perforated. In a later printing, perforated only, the purple is darker. Where a stamp is known in a given form or variety but insufficient information is available on which to base a price, its existence is indicated by a dash.

Part perforate stamps are understood to be imperforate horizontally unless otherwise stated.

Part perforate stamps with an asterisk (*) exist imperforate horizontally or vertically.

Part perforate PAIRS should be imperforate between the stamps as well as imperforate at opposite ends. See illustration **Type A** under "Information For Collectors-Perforations."

All imperforate or part perforate stamps listed are known in pairs or larger multiples. Certain unlisted varieties of this nature exist as singles and specialists believe them genuine.

Prices are for fine specimens. Imperforates and part-perforate singles in very fine or better condition and with large margins usually command substantial premiums.

Documentary revenue stamps were no longer required after Dec. 31, 1967.

First Issue

George Washington
R1   R2

1862-71   **Engr.**   *Imperf. or Perf. 12*

			a. Imperf.	b. Part Perf.	Perforated Old Paper	d. Silk Paper
R1	R1	1c **Express, red**	50.00	35.00*	1.00	50.00
		Pair	130.00	100.00	2.50	
		Block of four	400.00	425.00	10.00	
		Double transfer			—	
		Short transfer, No. 156		—	100.00	
R2	R1	1c **Playing Cards, red**	800.00	400.00	125.00	
		Pair	*1,700.*	950.00	275.00	
		Block of four	—		675.00	
		Cracked plate			—	
R3	R1	1c **Proprietary, red**	500.00	100.00	35	6.00
		Pair	*1,750.*	325.00	75	
		Block of four		800.00	2.00	
R4	R1	1c **Telegraph, red**	275.00		8.00	
		Pair	700.00		20.00	
		Block of four			70.00	

Double transfer (T5)

			a. Imperf.	b. Part Perf.	Perforated Old Paper	d. Silk Paper
R5	R2	2c **Bank Check, blue**	75	90*	6	
		Pair	15.00	4.00	25	
		Block of four	75.00	40.00	1.50	
		Double transfer (T5)	55.00	60.00	45.00	
		Cracked plate		—	—	
		Double impression			—	
	e.	Vertical pair, imperf. between			—	
R6	R2	2c **Bank Check, orange**		75.00*	5	150.00
		Pair		—	20	
		Block of four			1.00	
		Double transfer (T5)			100.00	
		Vertical half used as 1c			—	
	e.	2c orange, *green*			325.00	

Double transfer (T7)

				a. Imperf.	b. Part Perf.	Perforated Old d. Silk Paper Paper	
R7	R2	2c	**Certificate, blue**	10.00		21.00	
			Pair	30.00		50.00	
			Block of four	125.00		150.00	
			Double transfer (T7)	160.00		175.00	
			Cracked plate			30.00	
R8	R2	2c	**Certificate, orange**			20.00	
			Pair			125.00	
			Block of four			—	
			Double transfer (T7)			275.00	
R9	R2	2c	**Express, blue**	10.00	12.00*	25	
			Pair	30.00	30.00	90	
			Block of four	90.00	125.00	3.00	
			Double transfer	50.00		15.00	
			Cracked plate			—	
R10	R2	2c	**Express, orange**			6.00	30.00
			Pair			14.00	
			Block of four			35.00	

			Double transfer		21.00		
R11	R2	2c	**Playing Cards, blue**	130.00	3.00		
			Pair	400.00	10.00		
			Block of four		40.00		
			Cracked plate		—		
R12	R2	2c	**Playing Cards, orange**		25.00		
			Pair		—		

Double transfer (T13)

Double transfer (T13a)

R13	R2	2c	**Proprietary, blue**	120.00	35	12.50	
			Pair	260.00	80		
			Block of four	750.00	5.00		
			Double transfer (T13)		70.00		
			Complete double transfer (T13a)		100.00		
			Cracked plate		25.00		
			Horizontal half used as 1c		—		
		e.	2c ultramarine		150.00		
			Pair		325.00		
			Block of four		875.00		
			Double transfer		—		
R14	R2	2c	**Proprietary, orange**		30.00		
			Pair		—		
			Block of four		—		
			Double transfer (T13)		110.00		
			Complete double transfer (T13a)		350.00		

Double transfer (T15)

Double transfer (T15a)

				a. Imperf.	b. Part Perf.	Perforated Old d. Silk Paper Paper	
R15	R2	2c	**U.S. Internal Revenue, orange ('64)**			5	12
			Pair		—	10	—
			Block of four			40	
			Double transfer (T15)			60.00	
			Double transfer (T15a)			45.00	
			Double transfer			12.00	

			Triple transfer		40.00		
			Cracked plate		—		
			Half used as 1c		—		
		e.	2c orange, green		350.00		

R3

R16	R3	3c	**Foreign Exchange, green**	150.00	2.50	17.50	
			Pair	—	5.75		
			Block of four		45.00		
			Double transfer		—		
R17	R3	3c	**Playing Cards, green ('63)**	6,750.	100.00		
			Pair	17,000.	275.00		
			Block of four		700.00		
R18	R3	3c	**Proprietary, green**	175.00	1.75	15.00	
			Pair		4.50	—	
			Block of four	400.00	15.00		
			Double transfer	—	8.00		
			Double impression		—		
		e.	Printed on both sides		—		
R19	R3	3c	**Telegraph, green**	45.00	16.00	2.25	
			Pair	160.00	35.00	6.00	
			Block of four	600.00	150.00	50.00	
R20	R3	4c	**Inland Exchange, brown ('63)**		1.50	17.50	
			Pair		4.50		
			Block of four		20.00		
			Double transfer at top		4.00		
R21	R3	4c	**Playing Cards, slate ('63)**		350.00		
			Pair		875.00		
			Block of four		2,000.		
R22	R3	4c	**Proprietary, purple**	200.00	2.50	22.50	
			Pair	450.00	6.00		
			Block of four	—	25.00		
			Double transfer at top		7.50		
			Double transfer at bottom		11.00		

There are shade and color variations of Nos. R21-R22. See foreword of Revenue Stamps section.

				a. Imperf.	b. Part Perf.	Perforated Old d. Silk Paper Paper	
R23	R3	5c	**Agreement, red**			20	1.00
			Pair			40	2.50
			Block of four			1.25	12.50
			Double transfer in numerals			25.00	
R24	R3	5c	**Certificate, red**	2.00	8.00	10	30
			Pair	25.00	60.00	20	90
			Block of four	125.00	200.00	60	6.00
			Double transfer in upper label			10.00	
			Double transfer throughout			70.00	
			Triple transfer (No. 121)			35.00	

Cat	Type	Denom	Description	a. Imperf.	b. Part Perf.	Perforated Old Paper	Perforated d. Silk Paper
			Impression of No. R3 on back				—
R25	R3	5c	Express, red	3.50	4.00*	25	
			Pair	12.00	40.00	60	
			Block of four	60.00	100.00	2.00	
			Double transfer			5.00	
R26	R3	5c	Foreign Exchange, red		—	25	100.00
			Pair		—	75	
			Block of four			10.00	
			Double transfer at top			—	
			Double transfer at bottom			—	
R27	R3	5c	Inland Exchange, red	3.50	3.00	10	7.00
			Pair	20.00	15.00	20	
			Block of four	50.00	50.00	1.25	
			Dbl. transfer at top	60.00	40.00	25.00	
			Cracked plate	60.00	60.00	30.00	
R28	R3	5c	Playing Cards, red ('63)			12.00	
			Pair			26.00	
			Block of four			60.00	
			Double impression			250.00	
R29	R3	5c	Proprietary, red ('64)			16.00	40.00
			Pair			40.00	
			Block of four			120.00	
R30	R3	6c	Inland Exchange, orange ('63)			90	25.00
			Pair			10.00	
			Block of four			60.00	

Cat	Type	Denom	Description	a. Imperf.	b. Part Perf.	Perforated Old Paper	Perforated d. Silk Paper
R31	R3	6c	Proprietary, orange ('71)			2,000.	
R32	R3	10c	Bill of Lading, blue	45.00	150.00	85	
			Pair	125.00	500.00	2.00	
			Block of four	325.00		7.00	
			Double transfer (Nos. 33 & 143)			—	
			Half used as 5c			200.00	
R33	R3	10c	Certificate, blue	90.00	95.00*	20	3.00
			Pair	225.00	225.00	45	
			Block of four	1,000.	—	1.50	
			Double transfer			7.00	
			Cracked plate			15.00	
			Half used as 5c			200.00	
R34	R3	10c	Contract, blue	100.00		20	2.00
			Pair	275.00		50	5.00
			Block of four		—	2.00	50.00
			Complete double transfer			70.00	
			Vertical half used as 5c			200.00	
e.		10c	ultramarine	225.00			
f.		10c	ultramarine			50	
			Pair			1.25	
			Block of four			15.00	
R35	R3	10c	Foreign Exchange, blue			3.00	—
			Pair			7.00	
			Block of four			35.00	
e.		10c	ultramarine			6.50	
			Pair			15.00	
			Block of four			35.00	

Cat	Type	Denom	Description	a. Imperf.	b. Part Perf.	Perforated Old Paper	Perforated d. Silk Paper
R36	R3	10c	Inland Exchange, blue	120.00	3.00*	15	15.00
			Pair	275.00	10.00	35	—
			Block of four	750.00	50.00	1.50	
			Half used as 5c			200.00	
R37	R3	10c	Power of Attorney, blue	300.00	17.00	25	
			Pair	650.00	65.00	60	
			Block of four	1,800.	200.00	3.50	
			Half used as 5c			200.00	
R38	R3	10c	Proprietary, blue ('64)			13.00	
			Pair			30.00	
			Block of four			75.00	
R39	R3	15c	Foreign Exchange, brown ('63)			12.00	
			Pair			45.00	
			Block of four			225.00	
			Double impression			500.00	
R40	R3	15c	Inland Exchange, brown	25.00	10.00	1.00	
			Pair	95.00	30.00	2.25	
			Block of four	325.00	150.00	8.00	
			Double transfer			5.00	
			Cracked plate	40.00		—	
			Double impression			—	550.00
R41	R3	20c	Foreign Exchange, red	40.00		30.00	
			Pair	125.00		70.000	
			Block of four	500.00		200.00	
R42	R3	20c	Inland Exchange, red	12.00	16.00	30	—
			Pair	50.00	45.00	70	
			Block of four	160.00	150.00	12.50	

			a. Imperf.	b. Part Perf.	Perforated Old Paper	d. Silk Paper
		Half used as 10c			*200.00*	

R4

R5

			a. Imperf.	b. Part Perf.	Perforated Old Paper	d. Silk Paper
R43	R4	25c Bond, red	80.00	5.00	1.75	
		Pair	400.00	35.00	4.50	
		Block of four		200.00	40.00	
R44	R4	25c Certificate, red	5.00	5.00*	10	2.00
		Pair	35.00	30.00	20	—
		Block of four	300.00	150.00	2.50	—
		Double transfer, top or bottom			2.00	
		Triple transfer			—	
	e.	Printed on both sides			—	
	f.	Impression of No. R48 on back			—	
R45	R4	25c Entry of Goods, red	15.00	30.00*	40	8.00
		Pair	55.00	—	35.00	
		Block of four	300.00		2.50	
		Top frame line double	60.00	75.00	10.00	
R46	R4	25c Insurance, red	8.00	9.00	20	3.00
		Pair	35.00	20.00	50	—
		Block of four	*500.00*	175.00	5.00	
		Double impression			—	
		Cracked plate			15.00	
R47	R4	25c Life Insurance, red	30.00	100.00	5.00	
		Pair	90.00	525.00	75.00	
		Block of four				
R48	R4	25c Power of Attorney, red	5.00	15.00	25	
		Pair	40.00	55.00	60	
		Block of four	300.00	200.00	6.00	
		Double transfer			1.00	
		Bottom frame line double			3.00	
R49	R4	25c Protest, red	20.00	125.00	6.00	
		Pair	80.00	300.00	25.00	
		Block of four	350.00		100.00	
R50	R4	25c Warehouse Receipt, red	35.00	125.00	21.00	
		Pair	100.00	350.00	65.00	
		Block of four	*750.00*		200.00	
R51	R4	30c Foreign Exchange, lilac	60.00	350.00	35.00	—
		Pair	250.00	850.00	150.00	
		Block of four				
		Double transfer			70.00	

			a. Imperf.	b. Part Perf.	Perforated Old Paper	d. Silk Paper
		Top frame line double	—			
R52	R4	30c Inland Exchange, lilac	35.00	40.00	2.25	
		Pair	125.00	150.00	25.00	
		Block of four	—		100.00	
		Double transfer				

There are shade and color variations of Nos. R51-R52. See foreword of "Revenues" section.

			a. Imperf.	b. Part Perf.	Perforated Old Paper	d. Silk Paper
R53	R4	40c Inland Exchange, brown	425.00	3.50	2.25	—
		Pair	—	15.00	5.50	
		Block of four		150.00	100.00	
		Double transfer		35.00	30.00	
R54	R5	50c Conveyance, blue	10.00	1.00	10	2.75
		Pair	50.00	30.00	25	6.00
		Block of four	250.00	100.00	2.50	
		Double transfer			6.00	
		Cracked plate			15.00	
	e.	50c ultramarine			20	
		Pair			1.00	
		Block of four			10.00	
	f.	50c ultramarine			—	
R55	R5	50c Entry of Goods, blue		10.00	20	12.00
		Pair		60.00	50	
		Block of four		—	20.00	
		Double transfer			5.00	
		Cracked plate			20.00	
R56	R5	50c Foreign Exchange, blue	35.00	30.00	4.50	
		Pair	85.00	80.00	30.00	
		Block of four			100.00	
		Double impression			—	
		Double transfer at left			10.00	
		Half used as 25c			*200.00*	
R57	R5	50c Lease, blue	20.00	50.00	6.50	
		Pair	80.00	130.00	100.00	
		Block of four	650.00	400.00	225.00	
R58	R5	50c Life Insurance, blue	25.00	50.00	60	
		Pair	80.00		5.00	
		Block of four	400.00		30.00	
		Double transfer	25.00		10.00	
		Double impression			—	

Cracked Plate (C59)

			a. Imperf.	b. Part Perf.	Perforated Old Paper	d. Silk Paper
R59	R5	50c Mortgage, blue	10.00	1.50	30	25.00
		Pair	40.00	40.00	70	
		Block of four	160.00	150.00	5.00	
		Cracked plate (C59)		40.00	15.00	
		Scratched plate, diagonal	40.00	30.00	15.00	
		Double transfer			3.00	

			a. Imperf.	b. Part Perf.	Perforated Old Paper	d. Silk Paper
		Double impression	—			
R60	R5	50c Original Process, blue	2.50		25	1.50
		Pair	45.00		60	—
		Block of four	300.00		2.50	—
		Double transfer at top			5.00	
		Double transfer at bottom			8.00	
		Cracked plate			10.00	
R61	R5	50c Passage Ticket, blue	60.00	100.00	50	
		Pair	175.00	250.00	5.00	
		Block of four	—		90.00	
R62	R5	50c Probate of Will, blue	30.00	40.00	15.00	
		Pair	80.00	90.00	40.00	
		Block of four	375.00	350.00	—	
R63	R5	50c Surety Bond, blue	120.00	2.00	15	
		Pair	*800.00*	12.00	1.00	
		Block of four		75.00	8.00	
	e.	50c ultramarine			80	
		Pair			5.00	
		Block of four			50.00	
R64	R5	60c Inland Exchange, orange	75.00	40.00	5.00	22.50
		Pair	175.00	90.00	12.00	—
		Block of four	*600.00*	300.00	75.00	
R65	R5	70c Foreign Exchange, green	300.00	80.00	5.00	22.50
		Pair		225.00	20.00	60.00
		Block of four		*1,000.*	150.00	
		Cracked plate			25.00	
	e.	Vert. pair, imperf. between			—	

R6

R7

			a. Imperf.	b. Part Perf.	Perforated Old Paper	d. Silk Paper
R66	R6	$1 Conveyance, red	10.00	250.00	2.00	
		Pair	40.00	*1,250.*	6.00	
		Block of four	250.00		20.00	
		Double transfer	25.00		6.00	
		Right frame line double	70.00		15.00	
		Top frame line double			12.00	
R67	R6	$1 Entry of Goods, red	25.00		1.25	
		Pair	80.00		4.00	
		Block of four	275.00		40.00	
R68	R6	$1 Foreign Exchange, red	45.00		5	
		Pair	120.00	—	1.2	
		Block of four			9	
		Double transfer			4	

		Left frame line double	125.00		15.00		
		Diagonal half used as 50c					200.00
R69	R6	$1	**Inland Exchange, red**	10.00	225.00*	35	2.00
			Pair	45.00	1,500.	1.50	6.50
			Block of four	425.00	—	8.00	20.00
			Double transfer at bottom				3.50
			Double transfer of top shields	75.00		30.00	
R70	R6	$1	**Lease, red**	30.00		1.50	
			Pair	80.00		5.00	
			Block	350.00		40.00	
			Double transfer at bottom	40.00		7.50	
			Cracked plate			25.00	
R71	R6	$1	**Life Insurance, red**	130.00		4.50	—
			Pair	275.00		12.00	
			Block of four	600.00		45.00	
			Right frame line double	250.00		17.50	
R72	R6	$1	**Manifest, red**	50.00		21.00	
			Pair	120.00		50.00	
			Block	275.00		120.00	
R73	R6	$1	**Mortgage, red**	18.00		125.00	
			Pair	50.00		275.00	
			Block of four	250.00		600.00	
			Double transfer at left	—		150.00	
			Bottom frame line double	75.00		200.00	
R74	R6	$1	**Passage Ticket, red**	150.00		125.00	
			Pair	325.00		275.00	
			Block of four	700.00		700.00	
R75	R6	$1	**Power of Attorney, red**	60.00		1.50	
			Pair	140.00		4.00	
			Block of four	325.00		18.00	
			Double transfer			7.50	
			Recut			10.00	
R76	R6	$1	**Probate of Will, red**	55.00		30.00	
			Pair	140.00		75.00	
			Block of four	550.00		200.00	
			Right frame line double	125.00		60.00	
R77	R7	$1.30	**Foreign Exchange, orange ('63)**	2,000.		45.00	
			Pair			125.00	
			Block of four			—	

Double transfer (T78)

R78	R7	$1.50	**Inland Exchange, blue**	20.00	2.75
			Pair	80.00	40.00
			Block of four	250.00	225.00
			Double transfer (T78)		8.50
R79	R7	$1.60	**Foreign Exchange, green ('63)**	600.00	85.00
			Pair	3,000.	—
R80	R7	$1.90	**Foreign Exchange, purple ('63)**	1,900.	60.00 125.00
			Pair	—	130.00
			Block of four		350.00

There are many shade and color variations of No. R80. See foreword of "Revenues" section.

R8

R81	R8	$2	**Conveyance, red**	85.00	800.00	1.50	12.00
			Pair	200.00	—	5.00	
			Block of four	600.00		35.00	
			Cracked plate			—	
			Half used as $1			—	
R82	R8	$2	**Mortgage, red**	75.00		2.50	27.50
			Pair	180.00		6.00	
			Block of four	450.00		35.00	
			Double transfer			10.00	
			Half used as $1			—	
R83	R8	$2	**Probate of Will, red ('63)**	2,100.		40.00	
			Pair	4,400.		90.00	
			Block of four			225.00	

			Double transfer		60.00
R84	R8	$2.50	**Inland Exchange, purple ('63)**	850.00	3.00 12.50
			Pair	—	8.00 35.00
			Block of four		75.00 350.00
			Double impression	—	

There are many shade and color variations of Nos. R84c and R84d. See foreword of "Revenues" section.

R85	R8	$3	**Charter Party, green**	90.00	3.00 30.00
			Pair	260.00	40.00 75.00
			Block of four	—	150.00
			Double transfer at top		—
			Double transfer at bottom		9.00
			Half used as $1.50		—
	e.		Printed on both sides		2,000.
	g.		Impression of No. RS208 on back		4,000.
R86	R8	$3	**Manifest, green**	85.00	20.00
			Pair	210.00	50.00
			Block of four	1,000.	150.00
			Double transfer		30.00
R87	R8	$3.50	**Inland Exchange, blue ('63)**	925.00	45.00
			Pair	2,500.	120.00
			Block of four		350.00

R9

R10

					Perforated		
				a. Imperf.	b. Part Perf.	Old Paper	d. Silk Paper
R88	R9	$5	**Charter Party, red**	225.00		4.50	27.50
			Pair	500.00		50.00	
			Block of four	—		150.00	
			Right frame line double	375.00		50.00	
			Top frame line double	350.00		50.00	
R89	R9	$5	**Conveyance, red**	30.00		3.50	25.00
			Pair	95.00		10.00	
			Block of four	500.00		25.00	

A particular stamp may be scarce, but if few collectors want it, its market value may remain relatively low.

				a. Imperf.	b. Part Perf.	Perforated Old Paper	d. Silk Paper
R90	R9	$5	**Manifest, red**	80.00		80.00	
			Pair	225.00		200.00	
			Block of four	1,000.		500.00	
			Left frame line double	135.00		135.00	
R91	R9	$5	**Mortgage, red**	80.00		16.00	
			Pair	400.00		60.00	
			Block of four	—		—	
R92	R9	$5	**Probate of Will, red**	375.00		16.00	
			Pair	800.00		70.00	
			Block of four	1,750.		300.00	
R93	R9	$10	**Charter Party, green**	400.00		20.00	
			Pair	1,000.		60.00	
			Block of four	—		300.00	
			Double transfer			60.00	
R94	R9	$10	**Conveyance, green**	70.00		50.00	
			Pair	160.00		120.00	
			Block of four	400.00		600.00	
			Double transfer at top	100.00		80.00	
			Right frame line double	135.00			
R95	R9	$10	**Mortgage, green**	325.00		20.00	
			Pair	700.00		80.00	
			Block of four	—		—	
			Top frame line double	375.00		55.00	
R96	R9	$10	**Probate of Will, green**	900.00		20.00	
			Pair	—		60.00	
			Block of four			250.00	
			Double transfer at top			45.00	
R97	R10	$15	**Mortgage, blue**	900.00		100.00	
			Pair	2,100.		275.00	
			Block of four	4,500.		2,500.	
	e.		$15 ultra marine			150.00	
			Pair			300.00	
			Block of four			—	
			Milky blue			150.00	
R98	R10	$20	**Conveyance, orange**	50.00		27.50	45.00
			Pair	130.00		70.00	100.00
			Block of four	300.00		225.00	
R99	R10	$20	**Probate of Will, orange**	900.00		850.00	
			Pair	1,900.		1,750.	
			Block of four	4,250.		3,750.	
R100	R10	$25	**Mortgage, red** ('63)	750.00		80.00	125.00
			Pair	1,600.		190.00	
			Block of four	—		900.00	
	e.		Horiz. pair, imperf. between			1,100.	
R101	R10	$50	**U.S. Internal Revenue, green** ('63)	150.00		85.00	
			Pair	325.00		190.00	
			Block of four	800.00		450.00	
			Cracked plate			—	

R11

					a. Imperf.	Perforated Old Paper	d. Silk Paper
R102	R11	$200	**U.S. Internal Revenue, green & red** ('64)		1,000.	550.00	
			Pair		2,250.	1,200.	
			Block of four		5,500.	2,750.	

DOCUMENTARY STAMPS
Second Issue

After release of the First Issue revenue stamps, the Bureau of Internal Revenue received many reports of fraudulent cleaning and re-use. The Bureau ordered a Second Issue with new designs and colors, using a patented "chameleon" paper which is usually violet or pinkish, with silk fibers.

While designs are different from those of the first issue, stamp sizes and make up of the plates are the same as for corresponding denominations.

George Washington
R12　　　R12a

Engraved and printed by Jos. R. Carpenter, Philadelphia.
Various Frames and Numeral Arrangements
1871　　　　　　　　　　**Perf. 12**

				Single	Pair	Block of Four
R103	R12	1c	blue & black	25.00	60.00	150.00
	a.		Inverted center	1,300.		
R104	R12	2c	blue & black	1.00	3.00	15.00
	a.		Inverted center	4,500.		
R105	R12a	3c	blue & black	12.00	27.50	60.00
R106	R12a	4c	blue & black	45.00	110.00	—
			Horiz. or vert. half used as 2c			
R107	R12a	5c	blue & black	1.00	2.50	10.00
	a.		Inverted center	1,850.		
R108	R12a	6c	blue & black	65.00	150.00	450.00
R109	R12a	10c	blue & black	75	2.00	6.00
			Double impression of medallion	—		
			Half used as 5c	—		
	a.		Inverted center	1,650.		
R110	R12a	15c	blue & black	20.00	42.50	95.00
R111	R12a	20c	blue & black	4.00	9.00	35.00
	a.		Inverted center	7,500.		

R13　　　　　　　R13a

				Old Paper	Silk Paper	Perforated
R112	R13	25c	blue & black	50	1.50	7.50
			Double transfer, position 57	15.00		
	a.		Inverted center	9,500.		
	b.		Sewing machine perf.	90.00	250.00	750.00
	c.		Perf. 8	250.00		
R113	R13	30c	blue & black	45.00	100.00	275.00
R114	R13	40c	blue & black	27.50	90.00	
R115	R13a	50c	blue & black	50	1.25	6.50
			Double transfer	15.00		
	a.		Sewing machine perf.	90.00	200.00	1,200.
	b.		Inverted center	650.00	1,800.	
			Inverted center, punch cancellation	200.00	500.00	
R116	R13a	60c	blue & black	60.00	160.00	
			Double transfer, design of 70c	125.00		
R117	R13a	70c	blue & black	25.00	80.00	
	a.		Inverted center	3,000.		

R13b　　　　　　　R13c

				Old Paper	Silk Paper	Perforated
R118	R13b	$1	blue & black	2.50	6.00	20.00
	a.		Inverted center	5,250.		
			Inverted center, punch cancellation	1,000.		
R119	R13b	$1.30	blue & black	225.00	500.00	
R120	R13b	$1.50	blue & black	10.00	30.00	—
	a.		Sewing machine perf.	350.00	—	
R121	R13b	$1.60	blue & black	325.00	750.00	
R122	R13b	$1.90	blue & black	150.00	325.00	—
R123	R13c	$2	blue & black	10.00	25.00	100.00
			Double transfer	15.00		
R124	R13c	$2.50	blue & black	18.00	45.00	525.00
R125	R13c	$3	blue & black	30.00	80.00	—
			Double transfer			

R126 R13c $3.50 blue &   110.00   250.00
                   black

R13d   R13e

R127 R13d $5   blue & black   15.00   40.00   150.00
        a. Inverted   2,150.
             center
             Inverted   600.00
             center,
             punch cancel
R128 R13d $10 blue & black   100.00   225.00   —
R129 R13e $20 blue & black   300.00   650.00   —
R130 R13e $25 blue & black   300.00   650.00   —
R131 R13e $50 blue & black   325.00   700.00   —

R13f

R132 R13f $200 blue, black   5,250.
              & red

R13g

R133 R13g $500 blk., green   15,000.
              & red

Inverted Centers: Fraudulently produced inverted centers exist, some excellently made.

Third Issue

Confusion resulting from the fact that all denominations of the Second Issue were uniform in color, caused the ordering of a new printing with values in distinctive colors.

Plates used were those of the preceding issue.

Engraved and printed by Jos. R. Carpenter, Philadelphia.
Various Frames and Numeral Arrangements.
Violet "Chameleon" Paper with Silk Fibers.

1871-72   *Perf. 12*

				Single	Pair	Block of Four
R134	R12	1c	claret & black ('72)	20.00	50.00	175.00
R135	R12	2c	orange & black	5	12	1.00
			Double transfer	—		
			Double impression of frame	—		
			Frame printed on both sides	1,000.		
			Double impression of head	150.00		
	a.		2c vermilion & black (error)	400.00		
	b.		Inverted center	250.00	600.00	—
R136	R12a	4c	brown & black ('72)	27.50	70.00	
R137	R12a	5c	orange & black	20	40	1.00
	a.		Inverted center	3,500.		
R138	R12a	6c	orange & black ('72)	30.00	70.00	150.00
R139	R12a	15c	brown & black ('72)	7.50	20.00	110.00
	a.		Inverted center	8,000.		
R140	R13	30c	orange & black ('72)	11.00	30.00	—

				Single	Pair	Block of Four
			Double transfer	—		
	a.		Inverted center	1,350.		
R141	R13	40c	brown & black ('72)	20.00	55.00	125.00
R142	R13	60c	orange & black ('72)	45.00	100.00	225.00
			Double transfer, design of 70c	150.00		
R143	R13	70c	green & black ('72)	30.00	75.00	—
R144	R13b	$1	green & black ('72)	1.00	3.00	25.00
	a.		Inverted center	7,000.		
R145	R13c	$2	vermilion & black ('72)	18.00	40.00	140.00
			Double transfer	25.00		
R146	R13c	$2.50	claret & black	30.00	70.00	175.00
	a.		Inverted center	15,000.		
R147	R13c	$3	green & black ('72)	30.00	80.00	250.00
			Double transfer	—		
R148	R13d	$5	vermilion & black ('72)	17.50	45.00	125.00
R149	R13d	$10	green & black ('72)	85.00	200.00	700.00
R150	R13e	$20	orange & black ('72)	375.00	800.00	—
	a.		$20 vermilion & black (error)	525.00		

(See note on Inverted Centers after No. R133.)

1874   *Perf. 12*

R151 R12   2c orange & black,   6   12   60
                 green
        a. Inverted center   325.00

Liberty — R14

1875-78

			Silk Paper a. Perf.	Wmkd. USIR 191R b. Perf. c. Rouletted 6	
R152	R14	2c blue, *blue*	6	6	32.50
		Pair	15	15	150.00
		Block of four	50	60	
		Double transfer	5.00	5.00	
	d.	Vert. pair, imperf. horiz.	100.00		
	e.	Imperf., pair	250.00		

The watermarked paper came into use in 1878.

Postage Stamps of 1895-98 Overprinted:

a

b

Overprint "a" exists in two or possibly more settings, with upright rectangular periods, as illustrated, or with square periods, taller thicker letters and a slight upturn to the right leg of the "R.". The latter are from the right row of the plate. Overprint "b" has 4 stamps with small period in each sheet of 100.

1898   **Wmk. 191**   *Perf. 12*

				Unused	Used
R153	A87	1c	green, red overprint *(a)*	1.25	1.25
			Block of four	7.50	7.50
			Margin strip of 3, Impt. & P #	17.50	

See the ''Information for Collectors'' section at beginning of catalogue for an explanation of paper types, watermarks and grills.

				Unused	Used
			Margin block of 6, Impt. & P #	50.00	
R154	A87	1c	green, red overprint (b)	12	10
			Block of four	50	45
			Margin strip of 3, Impt. & P #	9.00	
			Margin block of 6, Impt. & P #	40.00	
		a.	Overprint inverted	10.00	7.50
		a.	Block of four	45.00	—
		a.	Margin strip of 3, Impt. & P #	50.00	
		a.	Margin block of 6, Impt. & P #	125.00	
		b.	Overprint on back instead of face, inverted	—	
		c.	Pair, one without overprint	—	
R155	A88	2c	carmine, blue overprint (b)	15	6
			Block of four	65	30
			Margin strip of 3, Impt. & P #	8.50	
			Margin block of 6, Impt. & P #	30.00	
		a.	Overprint inverted	1.25	1.00
		a.	Block of four	6.00	5.00
		b.	Pair, one without overprint	400.00	
		c.	Overprint on back instead of face, inverted	400.00	

Handstamped Type "b" in Magenta

R156	A93	8c	violet brown	2,000.
R157	A94	10c	dark green	2,250.
R158	A95	15c	dark blue	2,750.

Nos. R156-R158 were emergency provisionals, privately prepared, not officially issued.

Privately Prepared Provisionals

No. 285 Overprinted in Red

I. R.
L. H. C.

1898		Wmk. 191			Perf. 12

| R158A | A100 | 1c | dark yellow green | — | 3,500. |

Same Overprinted "I.R./P.I.D. & Son" in Red

| R158B | A100 | 1c | dark yellow green | — | 6,000. |

Nos. R158A-R158B were overprinted with federal government permission by the Purvis Printing Co. upon order of Capt. L. H. Chapman of the Chapman Steamboat Line. Both the Chapman Line and P. I. Daprix & Son operated freight-carrying steamboats on the Erie Canal. The Chapman Line touched at Syracuse, Utica, Little Falls and Fort Plain; the Daprix boat ran between Utica and Rome. Overprintings of 250 of each stamp were made.

Dr. Kilmer & Co. provisional overprints are listed under "Private Die Medicine Stamps," Nos. RS307-RS315.

Newspaper Stamp No. PR121
Surcharged in Red:

INT. REV. $5. DOCUMENTARY.

1898					Perf. 12

				Unused	Used
R159	N18	$5	dark blue, surcharge reading down	150.00	125.00
			Block of four	650.00	550.00
			Margin strip of 3, Impt. & P #	—	
		a.	"OCUMENTARY"	300.00	200.00
R160	N18	$5	dark blue, surcharge reading up	80.00	55.00
			Block of four	350.00	—
			Margin strip of 3, Impt. & P #	—	
		a.	"OCUMENTARY"	300.00	200.00

Battleship — R15

There are two styles of rouletting for the proprietary and documentary stamps of the 1898 issue, an ordinary rouletting 5½ and one by which small rectangles of the paper are cut out, usually called hyphen-hole perforation 7. Several stamps are known with an apparent roulette 14 caused by slippage of a hyphen-hole 7 rouletting wheel.

1898		Wmk. 191R		Rouletted 5½, 7	

				Rouletted 5½		p. Hyphen Hole Perf. 7	
				Unused	Used	Unused	Used
R161	R15	½c	orange	1.50	5.00		
			Block of four	7.00	35.00		
R162	R15	½c	dark gray	15	10		
			Block of four	75	50		
			Double transfer	—			
		a.	Vert. pair, imperf. horiz.	40.00			
R163	R15	1c	pale blue	8	5	25	15
			Block of four	40	25	2.50	1.25
			Double transfer	—			
		a.	Vert. pair, imperf. horiz.	7.50			
R164	R15	2c	carmine rose	10	5	30	10
			Block of four	45	25	2.50	50
			Double transfer	1.00	25		
		a.	Vert. pair, imperf. horiz.	30.00			
		b.	Imperf., pair	125.00			
		c.	Horiz. pair, imperf. vert.	—			
R165	R15	3c	dark blue	70	12	2.00	25
			Block of four	3.50	75	9.00	1.50
			Double transfer	—			
R166	R15	4c	pale rose	25	10	60	25
			Block of four	1.25	50	3.00	1.50
		a.	Vert. pair, imperf. horiz.	75.00			
R167	R15	5c	lilac	15	6	40	15
			Block of four	75	30	2.00	1.00
		a.	Pair, imperf. horiz. or vert.	125.00	75.00		
R168	R15	10c	dark brown	20	6	40	15
			Block of four	1.00	30	2.00	75
		a.	Vert. pair, imperf. horiz.	20.00	20.00		
		b.	Horiz. pair, imperf. vert.	—			
R169	R15	25c	purple brown	20	10	50	20
			Block of four	1.00	50	2.50	1.00
			Double transfer	—			
R170	R15	40c	blue lilac	30.00	1.00	40.00	10.00
			Block of four	150.00	50.00	175.00	100.00
			Cut cancellation		15		
R171	R15	50c	slate violet	2.75	12	4.50	20
			Block of four	12.50	2.00	25.00	2.00
		a.	Imperf., pair	300.00			
		b.	Horiz. pair, imperf. between	—			
R172	R15	80c	bister	17.50	25	45.00	15.00
			Block of four	80.00	30.00	200.00	100.00
			Cut cancellation		8		

Numerous double transfers exist on this issue.

Commerce — R16

R173	R16	$1	dark green	3.50	10	—	50

			Block of four	—	50		2.50
		a.	Vert. pair, imperf. horiz.	—			
		b.	Horiz. pair, imperf. vert.	—	250.00		
R174	R16	$3	dark brown	6.50	20	—	1.25
			Block of four	—	1.25		6.00
			Cut cancellation		12		25
		a.	Horiz. pair, imperf. vert.	325.00			

Rouletted 5½.

				Unused	Used
R175	R16	$5	orange red	—	1.00
			Block of four		6.00
			Cut cancellation		18
R176	R16	$10	black	27.50	2.50
			Block of four		12.00
			Cut cancellation		50
		a.	Horiz. pair, imperf. vert.	—	
R177	R16	$30	red	110.00	70.00
			Block of four		325.00
			Cut cancellation		25.00
R178	R16	$50	gray brown	45.00	2.75
			Block of four		12.00
			Cut cancellation		1.25

John Marshall — R17

Alexander Hamilton — R18

James Madison — R19

Various Portraits in Various Frames, Each Inscribed "Series of 1898."

1899			Without Gum		Imperf.

				Unused	Used
R179	R17	$100	yellow brown & black	50.00	27.50
			Vertical strip of four	—	125.00
			Cut cancellation		13.00
			Vertical strip of four, cut canc.	—	45.00
R180	R18	$500	carmine lake & black	—	400.00
			Vertical strip of four	—	1,700.
			Cut cancellation		175.00
			Vertical strip of four, cut canc.		750.00
R181	R19	$1000	green & black	400.00	300.00
			Vertical strip of four	—	1,300.
			Cut cancellation		90.00
			Vertical strip of four, cut canc.		400.00

1900					Hyphen-hole perf. 7

Allegorical Figure of Commerce

R182	R16	$1	carmine	5.50	50
			Block of four		2.25
			Cut cancellation		10
			Block of four, cut canc.		50
R183	R16	$3	lake (fugitive ink)	55.00	40.00
			Block of four		200.00
			Cut cancellation		7.00

Block of four, cut canc. | 30.00

Surcharged in Black with Open Numerals of Value

R184	R16	$1	gray	3.75	12
			Block of four	—	55
			Cut cancellation		6
			Block of four, cut canc.		30
a.			Horiz. pair, imperf. vert	—	
b.			Surcharge omitted	125.00	
			Surcharge omitted, cut canc.		80.00
R185	R16	$2	gray	3.00	12
			Block of four	14.00	50
			Cut cancellation		6
			Block of four, cut canc.		30
R186	R16	$3	gray	25.00	11.00
			Block of four	—	50.00
			Cut cancellation		2.00
			Block of four, cut canc.		9.00
R187	R16	$5	gray	15.00	4.50
			Block of four	—	20.00
			Cut cancellation		25
			Block of four, cut canc.		1.25
R188	R16	$10	gray	35.00	10.00
			Block of four	—	45.00
			Cut cancellation		3.00
			Block of four, cut canc.		14.00
R189	R16	$50	gray	500.00	350.00
			Block of four	—	1,500.
			Cut cancellation		70.00
			Block of four, cut canc.		300.00

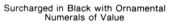

Surcharged in Black with Ornamental Numerals of Value

1902

Warning: If Nos. R190-R194 are soaked, the center part of the surcharged numeral may wash off. Before the surcharging, a square of soluble varnish was applied to the middle of some stamps.

R190	R16	$1	green	6.00	2.25
			Block of four	—	10.00
			Cut cancellation		20
			Block of four, cut canc.		85
a.			Inverted surcharge	150.00	
R191	R16	$2	green	5.50	1.00
			Block of four	—	5.00
			Cut cancellation		20
			Block of four, cut canc.		1.00
a.			Surcharged as No. R185	75.00	75.00
b.			Surcharged as No. R185, in violet	—	—
c.			Double surcharge	100.00	
R192	R16	$5	green	30.00	12.50
			Block of four	—	55.00
			Cut cancellation		1.75
			Block of four, cut canc.		8.00
a.			Surcharge omitted	50.00	
b.			Pair, one without surcharge	300.00	
R193	R16	$10	green	225.00	125.00
			Block of four	—	550.00
			Cut cancellation		25.00
			Block of four, cut canc.		110.00
R194	R16	$50	green	900.00	700.00
			Block of four	—	
			Cut cancellation		225.00
			Block of four, cut canc.		950.00

R20

Wmk. 190

Inscribed "Series of 1914"

1914   **Wmk. 190**   **Offset Printing**   **Perf. 10**

R195	R20	½c	rose	5.00	2.50
			Block of four	22.50	11.00
R196	R20	1c	rose	1.25	12
			Block of four	5.50	50
			Creased transfer, left side	—	

R197	R20	2c	rose	1.25	10
			Block of four	5.50	45
			Double impression	—	
R198	R20	3c	rose	27.50	20.00
			Block of four	125.00	90.00
R199	R20	4c	rose	6.50	1.00
			Block of four	30.00	4.50
			Recut U. L. corner	—	
R200	R20	5c	rose	2.50	12
			Block of four	11.00	75
R201	R20	10c	rose	2.25	8
			Block of four	10.00	35
R202	R20	25c	rose	12.50	40
			Block of four	55.00	1.75
R203	R20	40c	rose	7.50	50
			Block of four	35.00	2.25
R204	R20	50c	rose	3.50	10
			Block of four	16.00	45
R205	R20	80c	rose	40.00	6.00
			Block of four	175.00	26.00

Wmk. 191R

R206	R20	½c	rose	1.25	45
			Block of four	5.50	2.00
R207	R20	1c	rose	12	5
			Block of four	55	18
			Double impression	—	—
R208	R20	2c	rose	15	5
			Block of four	65	20
R209	R20	3c	rose	1.25	20
			Block of four	5.50	85
R210	R20	4c	rose	2.25	30
			Block of four	10.00	1.35
R211	R20	5c	rose	1.25	.10
			Block of four	5.50	45
R212	R20	10c	rose	40	6
			Block of four	1.75	30
R213	R20	25c	rose	3.50	60
			Block of four	16.00	2.75
R214	R20	40c	rose	35.00	7.00
			Block of four	150.00	30.00
			Cut cancellation		45
R215	R20	50	rose	7.50	12
			Block of four	32.50	45
R216	R20	80c	rose	40.00	7.50
			Block of four	175.00	35.00
			Cut cancellation		1.00

Liberty — R21

Inscribed "Series 1914"
Engr.

R217	R21	$1	green	12.50	15
			Block of four	—	75
			Cut cancellation		5
			Block of four, cut canc.		25
a.			$1 yellow green	—	12
R218	R21	$2	carmine	25.00	20
			Block of four	—	1.00
			Cut cancellation		6
			Block of four, cut canc.		25
R219	R21	$3	purple	35.00	1.25
			Block of four	—	6.00
			Cut cancellation		20
			Block of four, cut canc.		1.00
R220	R21	$5	blue	30.00	2.00
			Block of four	135.00	9.00
			Cut cancellation		50
			Block of four, cut canc.		2.50
R221	R21	$10	orange	57.50	4.50
			Block of four	—	20.00
			Cut cancellation		75
			Block of four, cut canc.		3.50
R222	R21	$30	vermilion	100.00	10.00
			Block of four	—	45.00
			Cut cancellation		2.00
			Block of four, cut canc.		10.00
R223	R21	$50	violet	800.00	600.00
			Block of four	—	
			Cut cancellation		250.00

Portrait Types of 1899 Inscribed "Series of 1915" (#R224), or "Series of 1914"

1914-15   **Without Gum**   **Perf. 12**

R224	R19	$60	brown (Lincoln)	—	100.00
			Cut cancellation		45.00
			Vertical strip of four, cut canc.		200.00
R225	R17	$100	green (Washington)	—	40.00
			Cut cancellation		15.00
			Vertical strip of four, cut canc.		65.00
R226	R18	$500	blue (Hamilton)	—	450.00
			Cut cancellation		200.00
			Vertical strip of four, cut canc.		850.00
R227	R19	$1000	orange (Madison)	—	450.00
			Cut cancellation		200.00

Vertical strip of four, cut canc. | | 850.00

The stamps of types R17, R18 and R19 in this and subsequent issues are issued in vertical strips of four which are imperforate at the top, bottom and right side; therefore, single copies are always imperforate on one or two sides.

R22

1917   **Offset Printing**   **Wmk. 191R**   **Perf. 11**
Size: 21x18mm.

Two types of design R22 are known.
Type I - With dot in centers of periods before and after "CENTS".
Type II - Without such dots.
First printings were done by commercial companies, later printings by the Bureau of Engraving and Printing.

R228	R22	1c	carmine rose	12	8
			Block of four	55	40
			Double impression	7.00	4.00
R229	R22	2c	carmine rose	8	5
			Block of four	40	25
			Double impression	7.50	5.00
R230	R22	3c	carmine rose	25	15
			Block of four	1.10	70
			Double impression	—	
R231	R22	4c	carmine rose	12	5
			Block of four	60	25
			Double impression	—	
R232	R22	5c	carmine rose	15	5
			Block of four	70	25
R233	R22	8c	carmine rose	1.50	12
			Block of four	7.00	55
R234	R22	10c	carmine rose	15	5
			Block of four	75	25
			Double impression		5.00
R235	R22	20c	carmine rose	30	5
			Block of four	1.40	25
			Double impression	—	
R236	R22	25c	carmine rose	60	5
			Block of four	2.60	25
			Double impression	—	
R237	R22	40c	carmine rose	1.00	8
			Block of four	—	35
			Double impression	8.00	5.00
R238	R22	50c	carmine rose	1.25	5
			Block of four	5.25	25
			Double impression	—	
R239	R22	80c	carmine rose	3.00	8
			Block of four	13.00	35
			Double impression	40.00	

Liberty Type of 1914 without "Series 1914"
1917-33   Size: 18½x27½mm.   **Engr.**

R240	R21	$1	yellow green	4.00	5
			Block of four	—	25
a.			$1 green	4.50	5
R241	R21	$2	rose	8.50	8
			Block of four	—	35
R242	R21	$3	violet	20.00	40
			Block of four	—	1.75
			Cut cancellation		8
R243	R21	$4	yellow brown ('33)	11.00	1.00
			Block of four	—	4.50
			Cut cancellation		12
			Block of four, cut canc.		50
R244	R21	$5	dark blue	9.00	15
			Block of four	—	75
			Cut cancellation		6
R245	R21	$10	orange	17.50	50
			Block of four	—	3.00
			Cut cancellation		12
			Block of four, cut canc.		60

Portrait Types of 1899 without "Series of" and Date
1917   **Without Gum**   **Perf. 12**

R246	R17	$30	deep orange, green numerals (Grant)	25.00	2.00
			Vertical strip of four		—
			Cut cancellation		55
			Vertical strip of four, cut canc.		3.00
a.			Imperf., pair	—	
b.			Numerals in blue		1.75
			Numerals in blue, cut canc.		90
R247	R19	$60	brown (Lincoln)	30.00	7.00
			Vertical strip of four		—
			Cut cancellation		80
			Vertical strip of four cut canc.		5.00
R248	R17	$100	green (Washington)	20.00	75
			Vertical strip of four		—
			Cut cancellation		35
			Vertical strip of four, cut canc.		1.90
R249	R18	$500	blue, red numerals (Hamilton)	—	30.00
			Vertical strip of four		—
			Cut cancellation		7.00

	Vertical strip of four, cut canc.	45.00		
	Double transfer	—	50.00	
a.	Numerals in orange		70.00	
R250 R19 $1000	orange (Madison)	80.00	11.00	
	Vertical strip of four Cut cancellation		4.00	
	Vertical strip of four, cut canc.		17.50	
a.	Imperf., pair		—	

See note after No. R227.

1928-29   Offset Printing   Perf. 10

				Unused	Used
R251	R22	1c	carmine rose	2.00	1.10
			Block of four	9.00	5.00
R252	R22	2c	carmine rose	60	20
			Block of four	3.00	1.00
R253	R22	4c	carmine rose	5.50	3.75
			Block of four	25.00	17.50
R254	R22	5c	carmine rose	1.10	35
			Block of four	5.00	1.75
R255	R22	10c	carmine rose	1.75	1.00
			Block of four	8.00	4.50
R256	R22	20c	carmine rose	5.50	4.50
			Block of four	25.00	20.00
			Double impression	—	

Engr.

R257	R21	$1	green	45.00	25.00
			Block of four	—	
			Cut cancellation		5.00
R258	R21	$2	rose	15.00	2.00
			Block of four	—	10.00
R259	R21	$10	orange	70.00	32.50
			Block of four	—	
			Cut cancellation		20.00

1929   Offset Printing   Perf. 11x10

R260	R22	2c	carmine rose ('30)	2.75	2.25
			Block of four	12.00	10.00
			Double impression	—	
R261	R22	5c	carmine rose ('30)	2.00	1.75
			Block of four	10.00	8.00
R262	R22	10c	carmine rose	7.50	6.50
			Block of four	35.00	30.00
R263	R22	20c	carmine rose	15.00	9.00
			Block of four	70.00	40.00

Types of 1917-33 Overprinted in Black

SERIES 1940

1940   Wmk. 191R   Offset Printing   Perf. 11

				Unused	Used (uncut)	Used (cut canc.)	Used (perf. initials)
R264	R22	1c	rose pink	1.75	1.25	35	20
R265	R22	2c	rose pink	1.75	1.25	40	30
R266	R22	3c	rose pink	5.00	3.00	70	50
R267	R22	4c	rose pink	2.00	35	12	8
R268	R22	5c	rose pink	2.50	60	25	15
R269	R22	8c	rose pink	12.00	11.00	3.00	2.00
R270	R22	10c	rose pink	1.00	25	8	5
R271	R22	20c	rose pink	1.50	30	10	5
R272	R22	25c	rose pink	2.75	40	10	6
R273	R22	40c	rose pink	3.00	40	8	5
R274	R22	50c	rose pink	3.50	30	8	5
R275	R22	80c	rose pink	5.00	50	20	10

Engr.

R276	R21	$1	green	14.00	30	10	8
R277	R21	$2	rose	14.00	60	10	8
R278	R21	$3	violet	15.00	12.00	2.25	1.25
R279	R21	$4	yellow brown	35.00	17.50	3.00	1.25
R280	R21	$5	dark blue	20.00	5.00	50	15
R281	R21	$10	orange	45.00	15.00	1.25	35

Types of 1917 Handstamped in Green "Series 1940".

1940   Wmk. 191R   Perf. 12   Without Gum

R282	R17	$30	vermilion	425.00	325.00	
R283	R19	$60	brown	600.00	450.00	
a.			As #R285a		—	
R284	R17	$100	green	900.00	725.00	
R285	R18	$500	blue	1,200.	1,000.	800.00
			Double transfer		1,250.	
a.			With black 2-line handstamp in larger type	1,600.	1,200.	
			Double transfer	—		
b.			Blue handstamp; double transfer	—		
R286	R19	$1000	orange	550.00	325.00	200.00

Alexander
Hamilton — R23

Levi
Woodbury — R24

Overprinted in Black   SERIES 1940

Various Portraits

1940   Engr.   Wmk. 191R   Perf. 11
Plates of 400 subjects, issued in panes of 100
Size: 19x22mm.

The "sensitive ink" varieties are in a bluish-purple overprint showing minute flecks of gold.

R288	R23	1c	carmine	3.00	2.25	1.25	65
			Sensitive ink	20.00	—		
R289	R23	2c	carmine (Oliver Wolcott, Jr.)	3.25	2.25	1.25	80
			Sensitive ink	20.00	—		
R290	R23	3c	carmine (Samuel Dexter)	12.50	5.50	3.25	2.25
			Sensitive ink	30.00	—		
R291	R23	4c	carmine (Albert Gallatin)	27.50	20.00	4.50	3.75
R292	R23	5c	carmine (G.W. Campbell)	2.75	60	25	18
R293	R23	8c	carmine (Alexander Dallas)	37.50	32.50	17.50	12.00
R294	R23	10c	carmine (William H. Crawford)	1.75	30	12	10
R295	R23	20c	carmine (Richard Rush)	2.25	1.75	1.00	75
R296	R23	25c	carmine (S.D. Ingham)	2.00	20	12	10
R297	R23	40c	carmine (Louis McLane)	20.00	12.00	4.00	2.25
R298	R23	50c	carmine (Wm. J. Duane)	3.00	20	6	5
R299	R23	80c	carmine (Roger B. Taney)	50.00	45.00	22.50	16.50

Plates of 200 subjects, issued in panes of 50
Size: 21½x36¼mm.

				Unused	Used (uncut)	Used (cut canc.)	Used (perf. initials)
R300	R24	$1	carmine	—	15	6	5
			Sensitive ink	50.00	—		
R301	R24	$2	carmine (Thomas Ewing)	—	25	8	6
			Sensitive ink	70.00	—		
R302	R24	$3	carmine (Walter Forward)	—	50.00	10.00	7.00
			Sensitive ink	120.00	—		
R303	R24	$4	carmine (J.C. Spencer)	—	20.00	5.00	1.50
R304	R24	$5	carmine (G.M. Bibb)	—	80	30	20
R305	R24	$10	carmine (R.J. Walker)	—	3.00	70	25
R305A	R24	$20	carmine (Wm.M. Meredith)	600.00	500.00	300.00	175.00
b.			Imperf. pair	750.00			

Thomas Corwin — R25

(Overprint: "SERIES 1940")

Perf. 12
Various Frames and Portraits
Plates of 16 subjects, issued in strips of 4
Without Gum
Size: 28½x42 mm.

R306	R25	$30	carmine	75.00	35.00	15.00	10.00
R306A	R25	$50	carmine (James Guthrie)	—	800.00	650.00	—
R307	R25	$60	carmine (Howell Cobb)	—	40.00	25.00	15.00
a.			Vert. pair, imperf. between	—			
R308	R25	$100	carmine (P.F. Thomas)	—	37.50	17.50	9.00
R309	R25	$500	carmine (J.A. Dix)	—	500.00	275.00	160.00
R310	R25	$1000	carmine (S.P. Chase)	—	250.00	110.00	85.00

The $30 to $1,000 denominations in this and following similar issues, and the $2,500, $5,000 and $10,000 stamps of 1952-58 have straight edges on one or two sides. They were issued without gum through No. R723.

Documentary Stamps of 1940 Overprinted in Black

SERIES 1941

1941   Wmk. 191R   Perf. 11
Size: 19x22 mm.

R311	R23	1c	carmine	2.00	1.75	70	60
R312	R23	2c	carmine	2.00	75	40	35
R313	R23	3c	carmine	5.00	3.00	1.25	85
R314	R23	4c	carmine	3.00	75	30	12
R315	R23	5c	carmine	75	15	8	6
R316	R23	8c	carmine	12.00	5.00	3.00	2.50
R317	R23	10c	carmine	1.00	20	10	8
R318	R23	20c	carmine	2.25	40	20	15
R319	R23	25c	carmine	1.25	10	5	5
R320	R23	40c	carmine	7.00	2.00	1.00	60
R321	R23	50c	carmine	2.00	10	5	5
R322	R23	80c	carmine	32.50	6.00	2.25	1.65

Size: 21½x36¼mm.

R323	R24	$1	carmine	5.00	10	6	5
R324	R24	$2	carmine	6.00	12	5	5
R325	R24	$3	carmine	10.00	1.75	35	30
R326	R24	$4	carmine	15.00	8.00	85	70
R327	R24	$5	carmine	20.00	30	10	8
R328	R24	$10	carmine	30.00	2.00	25	20
R329	R24	$20	carmine	100.00	80.00	30.00	20.00

Perf. 12
Without Gum
Size: 28½x42mm.

R330	R25	$30	carmine	—	16.00	9.00	6.00
R331	R25	$50	carmine	110.00	80.00	50.00	25.00
R332	R25	$60	carmine	—	30.00	7.50	5.00
R333	R25	$100	carmine	—	13.00	4.00	2.75
R334	R25	$500	carmine	—	135.00	75.00	40.00

R335	R25	$1000	carmine	—	100.00	30.00	20.00

Documentary Stamps of 1940 Overprinted in Black

SERIES 1942

1942   **Wmk. 191R**   *Perf. 11*
Size: 19x22mm.

R336	R23	1c	carmine	30	25	10	8
R337	R23	2c	carmine	30	25	10	8
R338	R23	3c	carmine	50	35	22	15
R339	R23	4c	carmine	80	40	25	20
R340	R23	5c	carmine	35	10	6	5
R341	R23	8c	carmine	3.50	2.25	1.00	1.00
R342	R23	10c	carmine	70	10	6	5
R343	R23	20c	carmine	95	25	15	15
R344	R23	25c	carmine	1.25	15	5	5
R345	R23	40c	carmine	3.50	75	50	30
R346	R23	50c	carmine	2.25	10	5	5
R347	R23	80c	carmine	8.50	6.00	2.50	1.75

Size: 21½x36¼mm.

R348	R24	$1	carmine	4.50	10	5	5
R349	R24	$2	carmine	5.50	10	5	5
R350	R24	$3	carmine	9.00	1.50	25	20
R351	R24	$4	carmine	11.00	3.25	30	25
R352	R24	$5	carmine	18.00	50	7	5
R353	R24	$10	carmine	30.00	1.75	10	8
R354	R24	$20	carmine	50.00	25.00	14.00	10.00

Perf. 12
Without Gum
Size: 28½x42mm.

R355	R25	$30	carmine	—	18.00	6.00	5.00
R356	R25	$50	carmine	150.00	110.00	70.00	50.00
R357	R25	$60	carmine	160.00	135.00	65.00	50.00
R358	R25	$100	carmine	—	50.00	25.00	16.00
R359	R25	$500	carmine	—	150.00	100.00	45.00
R360	R25	$1000	carmine	—	100.00	50.00	40.00

Documentary Revenue Stamps of 1940 Overprinted in Black

SERIES 1943

1943   **Wmk. 191R**   *Perf. 11*
Size: 19x22 mm.

R361	R23	1c	carmine	50	25	12	10
R362	R23	2c	carmine	40	20	8	6
R363	R23	3c	carmine	1.75	1.50	50	30
R364	R23	4c	carmine	80	50	25	20
R365	R23	5c	carmine	35	20	8	5
R366	R23	8c	carmine	3.00	2.50	1.50	1.00
R367	R23	10c	carmine	40	15	7	6
R368	R23	20c	carmine	1.25	40	25	20
R369	R23	25c	carmine	1.00	20	8	6
R370	R23	40c	carmine	4.00	1.50	1.00	60
R371	R23	50c	carmine	1.10	10	5	5
R372	R23	80c	carmine	7.00	4.50	1.10	90

Size: 21½x36¼mm.

R373	R24	$1	carmine	3.75	8	5	5
R374	R24	$2	carmine	5.50	10	6	5
R375	R24	$3	carmine	9.00	1.75	30	10
R376	R24	$4	carmine	11.00	2.50	40	30
R377	R24	$5	carmine	16.00	40	8	6
R378	R24	$10	carmine	25.00	2.00	50	35
R379	R24	$20	carmine	45.00	10.00	3.50	2.25

Perf. 12
Without Gum
Size: 28½x42mm.

R380	R25	$30	carmine	—	15.00	4.00	3.00
R381	R25	$50	carmine	—	22.00	8.00	5.00
R382	R25	$60	carmine	—	35.00	11.00	6.00
R383	R25	$100	carmine	—	10.00	5.50	3.50
R384	R25	$500	carmine	—	110.00	75.00	60.00

R385	R25	$1000	carmine	—	140.00	45.00	37.50

Documentary Revenue Stamps of 1940 Overprinted in Black

Series 1944

1944   **Wmk. 191R**   *Perf. 11*
Size: 19x22mm.

R386	R23	1c	carmine	25	20	12	10
R387	R23	2c	carmine	25	20	8	8
R388	R23	3c	carmine	25	20	10	8
R389	R23	4c	carmine	40	35	12	10
R390	R23	5c	carmine	30	10	6	5
R391	R23	8c	carmine	1.25	75	45	40
R392	R23	10c	carmine	40	6	5	5
R393	R23	20c	carmine	65	20	15	12
R394	R23	25c	carmine	1.10	10	6	5
R395	R23	40c	carmine	2.25	30	25	20
R396	R23	50c	carmine	2.25	10	5	5
R397	R23	80c	carmine	7.00	3.50	1.00	80

Size: 21½x36¼mm.

R398	R24	$1	carmine	3.75	8	5	5
R399	R24	$2	carmine	5.00	10	7	5
R400	R24	$3	carmine	7.50	1.50	45	10
R401	R24	$4	carmine	12.00	8.00	1.00	90
R402	R24	$5	carmine	12.00	25	10	7
R403	R24	$10	carmine	25.00	90	25	10
R404	R24	$20	carmine	45.00	12.50	3.00	2.00

Perf. 12
Without Gum
Size: 28½x42mm.

R405	R25	$30	carmine	50.00	20.00	4.50	3.00
R406	R25	$50	carmine	20.00	7.50	3.00	2.50
R407	R25	$60	carmine	90.00	35.00	7.00	5.00
R408	R25	$100	carmine	—	8.00	4.00	3.00
R409	R25	$500	carmine	—	450.00	325.00	250.00
R410	R25	$1000	carmine	—	125.00	50.00	40.00

Documentary Revenue Stamps of 1940 Overprinted in Black

Series 1945

1945   **Wmk. 191R**   *Perf. 11*
Size: 19x22mm.

R411	R23	1c	carmine	15	10	8	5
R412	R23	2c	carmine	15	10	8	6
R413	R23	3c	carmine	40	30	15	10
R414	R23	4c	carmine	25	15	10	8
R415	R23	5c	carmine	25	6	5	5
R416	R23	8c	carmine	3.00	1.25	60	30
R417	R23	10c	carmine	50	10	5	5
R418	R23	20c	carmine	3.50	75	40	15
R419	R23	25c	carmine	90	15	6	5
R420	R23	40c	carmine	3.00	75	40	35
R421	R23	50c	carmine	2.00	10	5	5
R422	R23	80c	carmine	11.00	6.00	3.00	1.75

Size: 21½x36¼mm.

R423	R24	$1	carmine	3.75	10	6	6
R424	R24	$2	carmine	5.00	15	8	6
R425	R24	$3	carmine	7.50	2.25	80	60
R426	R24	$4	carmine	11.00	2.50	50	30
R427	R24	$5	carmine	12.00	30	15	10
R428	R24	$10	carmine	25.00	1.10	25	18
R429	R24	$20	carmine	40.00	8.00	3.00	2.50

Perf. 12
Without Gum
Size: 28½x42mm.

R430	R25	$30	carmine	—	17.50	4.50	2.00
R431	R25	$50	carmine	—	20.00	10.00	5.50
R432	R25	$60	carmine	75.00	30.00	10.00	8.00
R433	R25	$100	carmine	—	10.00	6.00	4.00
R434	R25	$500	carmine	150.00	110.00	60.00	50.00

R435	R25	$1000	carmine	100.00	70.00	25.00	17.50

Documentary Stamps of 1940 Overprinted in Black

Series 1946

1946   **Wmk. 191R**   *Perf. 11*
Size: 19x22mm.

R436	R23	1c	carmine	15	10	5	5
R437	R23	2c	carmine	20	18	6	5
R438	R23	3c	carmine	25	15	10	8
R439	R23	4c	carmine	35	30	8	6
R440	R23	5c	carmine	25	8	6	5
R441	R23	8c	carmine	90	75	25	10
R442	R23	10c	carmine	60	8	6	5
R443	R23	20c	carmine	1.00	40	12	6
R444	R23	25c	carmine	1.10	15	8	6
R445	R23	40c	carmine	1.25	70	30	15
R446	R23	50c	carmine	2.50	10	6	5
R447	R23	80c	carmine	5.50	3.25	60	45

Size: 21½x36¼mm.

R448	R24	$1	carmine	3.75	15	8	5
R449	R24	$2	carmine	5.50	20	10	8
R450	R24	$3	carmine	8.00	4.50	85	35
R451	R24	$4	carmine	10.00	8.00	2.00	1.00
R452	R24	$5	carmine	11.00	40	15	10
R453	R24	$10	carmine	22.00	1.25	30	18
R454	R24	$20	carmine	40.00	7.50	2.00	1.50

Without Gum   *Perf. 12*
Size: 28½x42mm.

				Unused	Used (uncut)	Used (cut canc.)	Used (perf. initials)
R455	R25	$30	carmine	40.00	10.00	4.00	2.50
R456	R25	$50	carmine	20.00	8.00	4.00	2.50
R457	R25	$60	carmine	40.00	12.00	8.00	6.00
R458	R25	$100	carmine	—	8.00	3.00	3.00
R459	R25	$500	carmine	—	75.00	30.00	22.50
R460	R25	$1000	carmine	—	70.00	25.00	15.00

Documentary Stamps of 1940 Overprinted in Black

Series 1947

1947   **Wmk. 191R**   *Perf. 11*
Size: 19x22mm.

R461	R23	1c	carmine	40	25	8	5
R462	R23	2c	carmine	35	25	8	5
R463	R23	3c	carmine	40	25	15	5
R464	R23	4c	carmine	40	35	12	5
R465	R23	5c	carmine	30	15	5	5
R466	R23	8c	carmine	75	35	20	10
R467	R23	10c	carmine	70	15	8	5
R468	R23	20c	carmine	1.00	35	15	5
R469	R23	25c	carmine	1.25	35	12	8
R470	R23	40c	carmine	2.25	60	20	10
R471	R23	50c	carmine	2.00	15	8	5
R472	R23	80c	carmine	4.00	3.50	60	20

Size: 21½x36¼mm.

R473	R24	$1	carmine	3.75	20	6	6
R474	R24	$2	carmine	5.00	20	10	8
R475	R24	$3	carmine	6.75	4.00	1.00	60
R476	R24	$4	carmine	8.00	3.50	40	30
R477	R24	$5	carmine	11.00	40	12	10
R478	R24	$10	carmine	25.00	2.00	60	20
R479	R24	$20	carmine	40.00	7.50	1.00	70

Perf. 12
Without Gum
Size: 28½x42mm.

R480	R25	$30	carmine	60.00	17.50	4.00	2.00
R481	R25	$50	carmine	30.00	9.00	4.00	2.50
R482	R25	$60	carmine	—	22.50	14.00	6.00
R483	R25	$100	carmine	30.00	8.00	4.00	2.00
R484	R25	$500	carmine	—	100.00	50.00	35.00

				Unused	Used (uncut)	(cut canc.)	Used (perf. initials)
R485	R25	$1000	carmine	—	70.00	35.00	22.50

Documentary Stamps of 1940 Overprinted in Black

Series 1948

1948   Wmk. 191R   Perf. 11
Size: 19x22mm.

				Unused	Used (uncut)	(cut canc.)	Used (perf. initials)
R486	R23	1c	carmine	15	12	8	6
R487	R23	2c	carmine	18	15	8	6
R488	R23	3c	carmine	30	25	12	10
R489	R23	4c	carmine	25	25	10	8
R490	R23	5c	carmine	25	10	6	5
R491	R23	8c	carmine	50	30	18	12
R492	R23	10c	carmine	50	10	6	5
R493	R23	20c	carmine	1.00	30	12	8
R494	R23	25c	carmine	1.00	15	8	6
R495	R23	40c	carmine	2.25	1.00	30	20
R496	R23	50c	carmine	2.00	12	6	5
R497	R23	80c	carmine	4.50	3.50	1.50	50

Size: 21½x36¼mm.

				Unused	Used (uncut)	(cut canc.)	Used (perf. initials)
R498	R24	$1	carmine	3.75	20	8	6
R499	R24	$2	carmine	5.00	15	8	6
R500	R24	$3	carmine	7.00	2.00	40	25
R501	R24	$4	carmine	10.00	2.50	75	40
R502	R24	$5	carmine	11.00	50	20	10
R503	R24	$10	carmine	20.00	1.00	25	15
a.		Pair one dated "1946"		—			
R504	R24	$20	carmine	40.00	7.50	3.00	1.25

Perf. 12
Without Gum
Size: 28½x42mm.

				Unused	Used (uncut)	(cut canc.)	Used (perf. initials)
R505	R25	$30	carmine	40.00	15.00	5.00	2.50
R506	R25	$50	carmine	40.00	12.50	6.00	2.50
a.		Vertical pair, imperf. between carmine		—			
R507	R25	$60	carmine	50.00	17.50	9.00	5.00
a.		Vertical pair, imperf. between carmine		—			
R508	R25	$100	carmine	—	10.00	4.00	2.50
a.		Vertical pair, imperf. between		350.00			
R509	R25	$500	carmine	125.00	75.00	40.00	20.00
R510	R25	$1000	carmine	80.00	50.00	27.50	18.00

Documentary Stamps of 1940 Overprinted in Black

Series 1949

1949   Wmk. 191R   Size: 19x22mm.   Perf. 11

				Unused	Used (uncut)	(cut canc.)	Used (perf. initials)
R511	R23	1c	carmine	10	10	6	6
R512	R23	2c	carmine	20	15	8	6
R513	R23	3c	carmine	20	15	10	8
R514	R23	4c	carmine	30	25	10	8
R515	R23	5c	carmine	30	15	10	8
R516	R23	8c	carmine	50	30	20	18
R517	R23	10c	carmine	35	20	12	10
R518	R23	20c	carmine	50	40	30	25
R519	R23	25c	carmine	75	45	25	20
R520	R23	40c	carmine	2.25	1.25	40	30
R521	R23	50c	carmine	2.00	25	6	5
R522	R23	80c	carmine	3.75	3.00	1.50	75

Size: 21½x36¼mm.

				Unused	Used (uncut)	(cut canc.)	Used (perf. initials)
R523	R24	$1	carmine	3.75	30	12	10
R524	R24	$2	carmine	4.50	1.25	40	25
R525	R24	$3	carmine	7.50	5.00	2.00	1.00
R526	R24	$4	carmine	7.50	4.75	2.75	1.50
R527	R24	$5	carmine	10.00	1.75	60	40
R528	R24	$10	carmine	20.00	2.50	1.00	85
R529	R24	$20	carmine	40.00	6.00	2.00	1.00

Perf. 12
Without Gum
Size: 28½x42mm.

				Unused	Used (uncut)	(cut canc.)	Used (perf. initials)
R530	R25	$30	carmine	50.00	18.00	5.00	3.00
R531	R25	$50	carmine	—	30.00	10.00	6.00
R532	R25	$60	carmine	—	35.00	18.00	7.00
R533	R25	$100	carmine	—	15.00	3.00	2.50
R534	R25	$500	carmine	—	140.00	75.00	40.00
R535	R25	$1000	carmine	—	80.00	35.00	20.00

Documentary Stamps of 1940 Overprinted in Black

Series 1950

1950   Wmk. 191R   Perf. 11
Size: 19x22mm.

				Unused	Used (uncut)	(cut canc.)	Used (perf. initials)
R536	R23	1c	carmine	10	6	5	5
R537	R23	2c	carmine	20	10	5	5
R538	R23	3c	carmine	20	15	6	5
R539	R23	4c	carmine	25	20	10	8
R540	R23	5c	carmine	25	12	8	6
R541	R23	8c	carmine	50	30	20	12
R542	R23	10c	carmine	60	15	10	8
R543	R23	20c	carmine	75	35	25	12
R544	R23	25c	carmine	1.10	35	25	20
R545	R23	40c	carmine	2.50	1.25	40	25
R546	R23	50c	carmine	3.00	20	8	5
R547	R23	80c	carmine	4.00	3.50	85	50

Size: 21½x36¼mm.

				Unused	Used (uncut)	(cut canc.)	Used (perf. initials)
R548	R24	$1	carmine	3.50	20	12	8
R549	R24	$2	carmine	4.00	2.00	35	15
R550	R24	$3	carmine	5.50	3.00	1.25	75
R551	R24	$4	carmine	8.00	4.00	2.50	1.25
R552	R24	$5	carmine	10.00	75	30	18
R553	R24	$10	carmine	20.00	6.50	80	50
R554	R24	$20	carmine	40.00	7.00	2.50	1.50

Perf. 12
Without Gum
Size: 28½x42mm.

				Unused	Used (uncut)	(cut canc.)	Used (perf. initials)
R555	R25	$30	carmine	—	30.00	10.00	8.00
R556	R25	$50	carmine	—	11.00	6.00	3.50
a.		Vert. pair, imperf. horiz.		—			
R557	R25	$60	carmine	—	40.00	12.00	6.00
R558	R25	$100	carmine	—	17.50	5.00	3.00
R559	R25	$500	carmine	—	100.00	40.00	30.00
R560	R25	$1000	carmine	—	60.00	25.00	18.00

Documentary Stamps of 1940 Overprinted in Black

Series 1951

1951   Wmk. 191R   Perf. 11
Size: 19x22mm.

				Unused	Used (uncut)	(cut canc.)	Used (perf. initials)
R561	R23	1c	carmine	10	10	6	5
R562	R23	2c	carmine	20	10	5	5
R563	R23	3c	carmine	15	15	8	6
R564	R23	4c	carmine	15	15	8	6
R565	R23	5c	carmine	30	15	8	6
R566	R23	8c	carmine	50	30	20	15
R567	R23	10c	carmine	55	15	10	8
R568	R23	20c	carmine	1.00	35	25	15
R569	R23	25c	carmine	1.00	35	25	15
R570	R23	40c	carmine	2.00	70	40	25
R571	R23	50c	carmine	2.00	30	10	6
R572	R23	80c	carmine	2.75	2.25	1.50	70

Size: 21½x36¼mm.

				Unused	Used (uncut)	(cut canc.)	Used (perf. initials)
R573	R24	$1	carmine	3.50	20	15	10
R574	R24	$2	carmine	4.00	25	18	12
R575	R24	$3	carmine	7.00	3.50	1.75	1.00
R576	R24	$4	carmine	9.00	4.50	2.50	1.25
R577	R24	$5	carmine	9.00	40	30	20
R578	R24	$10	carmine	20.00	2.25	1.00	75
R579	R24	$20	carmine	40.00	6.50	3.00	3.50

Perf. 12
Without Gum
Size: 28½x42mm.

				Unused	Used (uncut)	(cut canc.)	Used (perf. initials)
R580	R25	$30	carmine	—	10.00	5.00	3.50
a.		Imperf., pair		750.00			
R581	R25	$50	carmine	—	12.50	6.00	4.00
R582	R25	$60	carmine	—	30.00		12.50
R583	R25	$100	carmine	—	12.50	6.00	5.00
R584	R25	$500	carmine	125.00	70.00	37.50	22.50
R585	R25	$1000	carmine	—	75.00	30.00	25.00

Documentary Stamps and Types of 1940 Overprinted in Black

Series 1952

Designs: 55c, $1.10, $1.65, $2.20, $2.75, $3.30, L. J. Gage; $2500, William Windom; $5000, C. J. Folger; $10,000, W. Q. Gresham.

1952   Wmk. 191R   Perf. 11
Size: 19x22mm.

				Unused	Used (uncut)	(cut canc.)	Used (perf. initials)
R586	R23	1c	carmine	10	6	5	5
R587	R23	2c	carmine	20	10	5	5
R588	R23	3c	carmine	15	15	6	5
R589	R23	4c	carmine	15	15	8	6
R590	R23	5c	carmine	20	10	6	5
R591	R23	8c	carmine	40	30	12	8
R592	R23	10c	carmine	35	15	8	6
R593	R23	20c	carmine	60	35	20	18
R594	R23	25c	carmine	1.00	40	25	20
R595	R23	40c	carmine	1.75	80	50	40
R596	R23	50c	carmine	2.00	20	8	6
R597	R23	55c	carmine	10.00	5.00	1.25	1.00
R598	R23	80c	carmine	4.50	2.25	75	65

Size: 21½x36¼mm.

				Unused	Used (uncut)	(cut canc.)	Used (perf. initials)
R599	R24	$1	carmine	3.00	1.50		35
R600	R24	$1.10	carmine	18.00	12.50		
R601	R24	$1.65	carmine	75.00	40.00		
R602	R24	$2	carmine	5.00	40		10
R603	R24	$2.20	carmine	55.00	45.00		
R604	R24	$2.75	carmine	75.00	40.00		
R605	R24	$3	carmine	8.00	3.50	1.50	1.25
a.		Horiz. pair, imperf. btwn.		—			
R606	R24	$3.30	carmine	55.00	40.00		
R607	R24	$4	carmine	10.00	3.50	2.00	1.50
R608	R24	$5	carmine	10.00	1.25	40	35
R609	R24	$10	carmine	22.00	1.25	40	35
R610	R24	$20	carmine	35.00	8.00	2.75	2.25

Perf. 12
Without Gum
Size: 28½x42mm.

				Unused	Used (uncut)	(cut canc.)	Used (perf. initials)
R611	R25	$30	carmine	—	12.00	5.00	4.00
R612	R25	$50	carmine	—	12.00	5.00	4.00
R613	R25	$60	carmine	—	30.00	10.00	8.00
R614	R25	$100	carmine	—	8.00	3.00	2.00
R615	R25	$500	carmine	—	75.00	50.00	30.00
R616	R25	$1000	carmine	—	30.00	15.00	10.00
R617	R25	$2500	carmine	—	125.00	100.00	75.00
R618	R25	$5000	carmine	—	850.00	650.00	550.00

The Demand, as well as supply, determines a stamp's market value. One is as important as the other.

R619	R25	$10,000	carmine	—	400.00	300.00	225.00

Documentary Stamps and Types of 1940 Overprinted in Black

Series 1953

1953 Wmk. 191R Perf. 11
Size: 19x22mm.

R620	R23	1c	carmine	15	10	5	5
R621	R23	2c	carmine	15	10	5	5
R622	R23	3c	carmine	15	10	6	5
R623	R23	4c	carmine	15	10	8	5
R624	R23	5c	carmine	15	10	6	5
R625	R23	8c	carmine	35	20	15	12
R626	R23	10c	carmine	40	18	6	5
R627	R23	20c	carmine	50	40	20	15
R628	R23	25c	carmine	75	50	25	20
R629	R23	40c	carmine	1.50	75	40	30
R630	R23	50c	carmine	1.65	15	6	5
R631	R23	55c	carmine	2.25	1.50		
a.		Horiz. pair, imperf. vert.		275.00			
R632	R23	80c	carmine	2.75	1.65	1.40	1.10

Size: 21½x36¼mm.

R633	R24	$1	car-mine	2.75	25	12	10
R634	R24	$1.10	car-mine	4.00	2.50	2.00	1.50
a.		Horiz. pair, imperf. vert.		300.00			
b.		Imperf. pair		450.00			
R635	R24	$1.65	car-mine	5.00	3.50		
R636	R24	$2	car-mine	4.50	50	25	20
R637	R24	$2.20	car-mine	6.00	5.00	2.50	2.00
R638	R24	$2.75	car-mine	8.00	6.00	3.50	
R639	R24	$3	car-mine	6.00	3.00	1.50	1.25
R640	R24	$3.30	car-mine	12.00	7.00		
R641	R24	$4	car-mine	8.00	5.50	1.75	1.50
R642	R24	$5	car-mine	10.00	75	40	30
R643	R24	$10	car-mine	20.00	1.75	1.00	85
R644	R24	$20	car-mine	40.00	15.00	3.00	2.00

Perf. 12
Without Gum
Size: 28½x42mm.

R645	R25	$30	car-mine	—	12.00	5.00	4.00
R646	R25	$50	car-mine	—	20.00	5.00	4.00
R647	R25	$60	car-mine	—	45.00		
R648	R25	$100	car-mine	35.00	12.00	5.00	3.50
R649	R25	$500	car-mine	—	90.00	30.00	20.00
R650	R25	$1000	car-mine	100.00	50.00	20.00	15.00
R651	R25	$2500	car-mine	400.00	300.00	225.00	200.00
R652	R25	$5000	car-mine	—	850.00	750.00	600.00
R653	R25	$10,000	car-mine	—	600.00	400.00	150.00

Types of 1940
Without Overprint

1954 Wmk. 191R Perf. 11
Size: 19x22mm.

R654	R23	1c	car-mine	6	5	5	5
a.		Horiz. pair, imperf. vert.		—			
R655	R23	2c	car-mine	8	6	5	5
R656	R23	3c	car-mine	12	10	5	5
R657	R23	4c	car-mine	12	10	5	5
R658	R23	5c	car-mine	13	8	5	5
R659	R23	8c	car-mine	25	20	12	10
R660	R23	10c	car-mine	25	15	6	5
R661	R23	20c	car-mine	50	35	15	12
R662	R23	25c	car-mine	60	40	18	15
R663	R23	40c	car-mine	90	60	40	35

R664	R23	50c	car-mine	1.00	15	10	8
a.		Horiz. pair, imperf. vert.		200.00			
R665	R23	55c	car-mine	1.25	1.10		
R666	R23	80c	car-mine	1.75	1.65	1.00	80

Size: 21½x36¼mm.

R667	R24	$1	car-mine	1.00	20	10	8
R668	R24	$1.10	car-mine	2.75	2.35		
R669	R24	$1.65	car-mine	100.00	75.00		
R670	R24	$2	car-mine	1.75	45	25	20
R671	R24	$2.20	car-mine	4.50	3.75		
R672	R24	$2.75	car-mine	100.00	75.00		
R673	R24	$3	car-mine	3.00	2.00	1.00	75
R674	R24	$3.30	car-mine	6.50	5.00		
R675	R24	$4	car-mine	4.50	3.50	2.00	1.50
R676	R24	$5	car-mine	10.00	50	30	20
R677	R24	$10	car-mine	15.00	1.50	80	70
R678	R24	$20	car-mine	40.00	6.00	3.00	1.50

Documentary Stamps and Type of 1940 Overprinted in Black

Series 1954

1954 Wmk. 191R Perf. 12
Without Gum
Size: 28½x42mm.

R679	R25	$30	carmine	—	12.00	4.00	3.00
R680	R25	$50	carmine	—	15.00	9.00	4.50
R681	R25	$60	carmine	—	17.50	10.00	6.00
R682	R25	$100	carmine	—	7.00	4.00	3.00
R683	R25	$500	carmine	—	60.00	22.50	15.00
R684	R25	$1000	carmine	—	40.00	15.00	12.00
R685	R25	$2500	carmine	—	125.00	70.00	35.00
R686	R25	$5000	carmine	—	400.00	325.00	225.00
R687	R25	$10,000	carmine	—	350.00	100.00	90.00

Documentary Stamps and Type of 1940 Overprinted in Black

Series 1955

1955 Wmk. 191R Perf. 12
Without Gum
Sizes: 28½x42mm.

R688	R25	$30	carmine	—	9.00	4.00
R689	R25	$50	carmine	—	13.50	9.00	4.00
R690	R25	$60	carmine	—	16.50	5.00	4.00
R691	R25	$100	carmine	—	7.00	5.00	3.50
R692	R25	$500	carmine	—	90.00	30.00	20.00
R693	R25	$1000	carmine	—	35.00	17.50	12.50
R694	R25	$2500	carmine	—	100.00	60.00	40.00
R695	R25	$5000	carmine	—	550.00	350.00	225.00
R696	R25	$10,000	carmine	—	300.00	150.00	80.00

Documentary Stamps and Type of 1940 Overprinted in Black "Series 1956"

1956 Wmk. 191R Without Gum Perf. 12
Size: 28½x42mm.

				Unused	Used (uncut)	(cut canc.)	Used (perf. initials)
R697	R25	$30	carmine	—	13.50	9.00	3.50
R698	R25	$50	carmine	—	15.00	10.00	3.50
R699	R25	$60	carmine	—	30.00	5.00	3.50
R700	R25	$100	carmine	—	10.00	5.00	4.00
R701	R25	$500	carmine	—	62.50	25.00	15.00
R702	R25	$1000	carmine	—	50.00	15.00	9.00
R703	R25	$2500	carmine	—	200.00	90.00	60.00
R704	R25	$5000	carmine	—	1,050.	700.00	600.00
R705	R25	$10,000	carmine	—	350.00	150.00	100.00

Documentary Stamps and Type of 1940 Overprinted in Black "Series 1957"

1957 Wmk. 191R Perf. 12
Without Gum
Size: 28½x42mm.

R706	R25	$30	carmine	—	27.50	10.00	5.00
R707	R25	$50	carmine	—	15.00	6.00	4.00
R708	R25	$60	carmine	—	85.00		40.00
R709	R25	$100	carmine	—	12.50	8.00	4.00
R710	R25	$500	carmine	175.00	75.00	50.00	30.00
R711	R25	$1000	carmine	—	65.00	30.00	
R712	R25	$2500	carmine	—	450.00	375.00	225.00
R713	R25	$5000	carmine	—	450.00	375.00	100.00
R714	R25	$10,000	carmine	—	350.00	150.00	100.00

Documentary Stamps and Type of 1940 Overprinted in Black "Series 1958"

1958 Wmk. 191R Perf. 12
Without Gum
Size: 28½x42mm.

R715	R25	$30	carmine	—	15.00	10.00	
R716	R25	$50	carmine	—	16.00	14.00	6.00
R717	R25	$60	carmine	—	25.00		10.00
R718	R25	$100	carmine	—	10.00	5.00	
R719	R25	$500	carmine	100.00	45.00		18.00
R720	R25	$1000	carmine	—	55.00	30.00	
R721	R25	$2500	carmine	—	600.00	375.00	275.00
R722	R25	$5000	carmine	—	1,250.	1,100.	1,000.
R723	R25	$10,000	carmine	—	650.00	550.00	300.00

Documentary Stamps and Type of 1940 Without Overprint

1958 Wmk. 191R Perf. 12
With Gum
Size: 28½x42mm.

R724	R25	$30	car	35.00	6.00	4.50	3.00
a.		Vert. pair, imperf. horiz.		—			
R725	R25	$50	car	35.00	5.00	2.50	2.00
a.		Vert. pair, imperf. horiz.		—			
R726	R25	$60	carmine	—	20.00	10.00	
R727	R25	$100	car	17.50	4.75	3.00	2.25
R728	R25	$500	car	80.00	25.00	10.00	7.50
R729	R25	$1000	car	50.00	20.00	10.00	7.50
a.		Vert. pair, imperf. horiz.		—			
R730	R25	$2500	carmine	—	125.00	75.00	
R731	R25	$5000	carmine	—	125.00	85.00	60.00
R732	R25	$10,000	carmine	—	100.00	50.00	25.00

Internal Revenue Building, Washington, D.C. — R26

Centenary of the Internal Revenue Service.

Giori Press Printing
1962, July 2 Unwmk. Perf. 11

R733	R26	10c	vio.bl.& brt.grn.	1.00	20	10	8
			Margin block of 4, P#	15.00			

1963

"Established 1862" Removed

R734	R26	10c	vio.bl. & brt.grn.	3.00	10	5	5
			Margin block of 4, P #	35.00			

Documentary revenue stamps were no longer required after Dec. 31, 1967.

PROPRIETARY STAMPS

Stamps for use on proprietary articles were included in the first general issue of 1862-71. They are R3, R13, R14, R18, R22, R29, R31 and R38.

Several varieties of "violet" paper were used in printing Nos. RB1-RB10. One is grayish with a slight greenish tinge, called "intermediate" paper by specialists. It should not be confused with the "green" paper, which is truly green.

All prices prior to 1898 are for used copies. Printed cancellations on proprietary stamps command sizable premiums.

RB1   RB1a
George Washington

Engraved and printed by Jos. R. Carpenter, Philadelphia.

1871-74 Perf. 12

			a. Violet Paper (1871)	b. Green Paper (1874)
RB1	RB1	1c green & black	4.00	6.00
		Pair	9.00	14.00
		Block of four	20.00	35.00
	c.	Imperf.	100.00	
		Imperf. pair	250.00	
		Imperf. block of four	600.00	
	d.	Inverted center	2,500.	
RB2	RB1	2c green & black	4.50	13.00
		Pair	10.00	30.00
		Block of four	22.50	65.00
		Double transfer	—	
	c.	Inverted center	40,000.	9,500.
		Vert. half used as 1c	—	
RB3	RB1a	3c green & black	12.00	35.00
		Pair	30.00	80.00
		Block of four	60.00	175.00
		Double transfer	—	
	c.	Sewing machine perf.	125.00	
	d.	Inverted center	15,000.	
RB4	RB1a	4c green &. black	7.00	12.50
		Pair	18.00	30.00
		Block of four	40.00	70.00
		Double transfer	—	
	c.	Inverted center	16,500.	
		Vert. half used as 2c	—	
RB5	RB1a	5c green & black	90.00	95.00
		Pair	225.00	225.00
		Block of four	500.00	500.00
	c.	Inverted center	40,000.	
RB6	RB1a	6c green & black	27.50	70.00
		Pair	65.00	150.00
		Block of four	150.00	400.00
		Double transfer	—	
RB7	RB1a	10c green & black ('73)	125.00	35.00
		Pair	300.00	75.00
		Block of four	—	175.00
		Double transfer	—	

(See note on Inverted Centers after No. R133.)

RB1b

			a. Violet Paper	b. Green Paper (1874)
RB8	RB1b	50c green & black ('73)	550.00	800.00
		Pair	1,300.	
RB9	RB1b	$1 green & black ('73)	1,200.	3,000.
		Pair	—	

RB1c

			a. Violet Paper	b. Green Paper (1874)
RB10	RB1c	$5 green & black ('73)	2,500.	—
		Pair	5,500.	

When the Carpenter contract expired Aug. 31, 1875, the proprietary stamps remaining unissued were delivered to the Bureau of Internal Revenue. Until the taxes expired, June 30, 1883, the B.I.R. issued 34,315 of the 50c, 6,585 of the $1 and 2,109 of the $5, Nos. RB8-RB10. No. RB19, the 10c blue, replaced No. RB7b, the 10c on green paper, after 336,000 copies were issued, exhausting the supply in 1881.

George Washington
RB2   RB2a

Engraved and printed by the National Bank Note Co.

1875-81

			Silk Paper a. Perf.	Wmkd. USIR 191R b. Perf.	c. Rouletted 6
RB11	RB2	1c green	1.50	35	30.00
		Pair	3.00	1.00	65.00
		Block of four	8.00	2.50	150.00
	d.	Vertical pair, imperf. between		250.00	
RB12	RB2	2c brown	2.00	1.25	45.00
		Pair	5.00	3.00	100.00

			Silk Paper a. Perf.	Wmkd. USIR 191R b. Perf.	c. Rouletted 6
		Block of four	10.00	7.00	250.00
RB13	RB2a	3c orange	9.00	2.25	45.00
		Pair	20.00	5.00	100.00
		Block of four	45.00	12.00	225.00
	d.	Horizontal pair, imperf. between			—
RB14	RB2a	4c red brown	4.50	4.00	
		Pair	10.00	9.00	
		Block of four	22.00	20.00	
RB15	RB2a	4c red		3.50	45.00
		Pair		8.00	100.00
		Block of four		20.00	
RB16	RB2a	5c black	80.00	70.00	725.00
		Pair	170.00	150.00	—
		Block of four	375.00	325.00	
RB17	RB2a	6c violet blue	20.00	13.00	125.00
		Pair	45.00	30.00	275.00
		Block of four	100.00	65.00	
RB18	RB2a	6c violet		20.00	150.00
		Pair		45.00	325.00
		Block of four		100.00	
RB19	RB2a	10c blue ('81)		175.00	
		Pair		375.00	
		Block of four		800.00	

No. RB19 was produced by the Bureau of Engraving and Printing after taking over the stamp printing contract in 1880.

 Battleship — RB3

Inscribed "Series of 1898." and "Proprietary."
1898   Wmk. 191R   Engr.   Rouletted 5½, 7
See note on rouletting preceding No. R161.

			Rouletted 5½ Unused	Used	p. Hyphen Hole Perf. 7 Unused	Used
RB20	RB3	⅛c yellow green	6	6	12	10
		Block of four	25	25	55	50
		Double transfer	—			
	a.	Vert. pair, imperf. horiz.	—			
RB21	RB3	¼c brown	6	6	12	10
	a.	¼c red brown	6	6		
	b.	¼c yellow brown	6	6	12	10
	c.	¼c orange brown	6	6	12	10
	d.	¼c bister	6	6		
		Block of four	25	25	55	50
		Double transfer	—	—		
	e.	Vert. pair, imperf. horiz.	—	—		
	f.	Printed on both sides	—			
RB22	RB3	⅜c deep orange	12	8	25	15
		Block of four	60	32	1.25	
	a.	Horiz. pair, imperf. vert.	9.00			
	b.	Vert. pair, imperf. horiz.	—			
RB23	RB3	⅝c deep ultramarine	12	10	25	15
		Block of four	60	40	1.25	75
		Double transfer	1.50			
	a.	Vert. pair, imperf. horiz.	50.00			
	b.	Horiz. pair, imperf. vert.	200.00			

				Rouletted 5½ Unused	Used	p. Hyphen Hole Perf. 7 Unused	Used
RB24	RB3	1c	dark green	30	15	12.00	5.00
			Block of four	1.50	75	—	—
a.			Vert. pair, imperf. horiz.	—			
RB25	RB3	1¼c	violet	10	8	20	12
			Block of four	45	35	90	90
a.			1¼c brown violet	12	10	20	12
b.			Vertical pair, imperf. between	—			
RB26	RB3	1⁷⁄₈c	dull blue	2.00	65	7.50	—
			Block of four	10.00	—	50.00	—
			Double transfer	—			
RB27	RB3	2c	violet brown	35	18	75	25
			Block of four	1.75	—	4.00	—
			Double transfer	—			
a.			Horiz. pair, imperf. vert.	25.00			
RB28	RB3	2½c	lake	40	12	50	20
			Block of four	2.00	60		
a.			Vert. pair, imperf. horiz.	30.00			
RB29	RB3	3¾c	olive gray	5.00	2.50	10.00	5.00
			Block of four	25.00	—	55.00	25.00
RB30	RB3	4c	purple	2.00	75	—	—
			Block of four	10.00	3.75	—	—
			Double transfer	—			
RB31	RB3	5c	brown orange	2.00	75	10.00	6.00
			Block of four	10.00	4.00	—	—
a.			Vert. pair, imperf. horiz.	—	*225.00*		
b.			Horiz. pair, imperf. vert.	—			

See note after No. RS315 regarding St. Louis Provisional Labels of 1898.

RB4

Inscribed "Series of 1914"

1914		Wmk. 190	Offset Printing		Perf. 10
RB32	RB4	⅛c	black	20	15
			Block of four	1.00	75
RB33	RB4	¼c	black	1.25	1.00
			Block of four	6.00	
RB34	RB4	⅜c	black	20	15
			Block of four	90	75
RB35	RB4	⅝c	black	2.50	1.75
			Block of four	11.00	
RB36	RB4	1¼c	black	1.75	80
			Block of four	8.00	
RB37	RB4	1⁷⁄₈c	black	25.00	15.00
			Block of four	110.00	
RB38	RB4	2½c	black	3.50	2.50
			Block of four	16.00	11.00
RB39	RB4	3⅛c	black	70.00	50.00
			Block of four	300.00	
RB40	RB4	3¾c	black	25.00	19.00
			Block of four	110.00	
RB41	RB4	4c	black	45.00	27.50
			Block of four	200.00	
RB42	RB4	4⅜c	black	*900.00*	—
			Block of four		
RB43	RB4	5c	black	90.00	65.00
			Block of four	375.00	
		Wmk. 191R			
RB44	RB4	⅛c	black	15	10
			Block of four	75	45
RB45	RB4	¼c	black	15	10
			Block of four	75	45
RB46	RB4	⅜c	black	60	30
			Block of four	3.00	1.50
			Double impression	12.50	
RB47	RB4	½c	black	2.75	2.00
			Block of four	12.00	
RB48	RB4	⅝c	black	15	10
			Block of four	70	45
RB49	RB4	1c	black	3.50	2.75
			Block of four	15.00	12.00
RB50	RB4	1¼c	black	35	25
			Block of four	1.50	1.10

RB51	RB4	1½c	black	3.00	2.25
			Block of four	14.00	10.00
RB52	RB4	1⁷⁄₈c	black	1.00	60
			Block of four	4.50	2.25
RB53	RB4	2c	black	5.00	4.00
			Block of four	22.50	
RB54	RB4	2½c	black	1.25	1.00
			Block of four	5.50	4.50
RB55	RB4	3c	black	3.50	2.75
			Block of four	15.00	
RB56	RB4	3⅛c	black	4.50	3.00
			Block of four	20.00	
RB57	RB4	3¾c	black	9.00	7.50
			Block of four	37.50	
RB58	RB4	4c	black	30	20
			Block of four	1.50	1.00
			Double impression	—	
RB59	RB4	4⅝c	black	11.00	7.50
			Block of four	45.00	
RB60	RB4	5c	black	2.75	2.50
			Block of four	12.50	
RB61	RB4	6c	black	45.00	37.50
			Block of four	210.00	
RB62	RB4	8c	black	13.50	11.00
			Block of four	60.00	
RB63	RB4	10c	black	9.00	7.00
			Block of four	40.00	
RB64	RB4	20c	black	17.50	15.00
			Block of four	80.00	

RB5

1919		Offset Printing			Perf. 11
RB65	RB5	1c	dark blue	10	8
			Block of four	50	40
			Double impression	17.50	—
RB66	RB5	2c	dark blue	12	8
			Block of four	55	40
			Double impression	—	
RB67	RB5	3c	dark blue	1.00	60
			Block of four	4.50	2.75
			Double impression	—	
RB68	RB5	4c	dark blue	1.00	50
			Block of four	4.50	
RB69	RB5	5c	dark blue	1.25	60
			Block of four	5.50	2.75
RB70	RB5	8c	dark blue	11.00	9.00
			Block of four	46.00	
RB71	RB5	10c	dark blue	2.25	1.75
			Block of four	10.00	7.50
RB72	RB5	20c	dark blue	4.00	3.00
			Block of four	17.50	
RB73	RB5	40c	dark blue	22.50	8.00
			Block of four	95.00	

FUTURE DELIVERY STAMPS

Issued to facilitate the collection of a tax upon each sale, agreement of sale or agreement to sell any products or merchandise at any exchange or board of trade, or other similar place for future delivery.

Documentary Stamps of 1917 Overprinted in Black or Red

Type I

FUTURE

DELIVERY

1918-1934		Wmk. 191R	Offset Printing	Perf. 11
		Overprint Horizontal (Lines 8mm. apart)		
RC1	R22	2c	carmine rose	1.25	10
			Block of four	6.00	50
RC2	R22	3c	carmine rose ('34)	25.00	22.50
			Cut cancellation		12.50
RC3	R22	4c	carmine rose	1.25	10
			Block of four	6.00	50
			Double impression of stamp		10.00
RC3A	R22	5c	carmine rose ('33)	—	3.00
			Block of four		15.00
RC4	R22	10c	carmine rose	2.50	15
			Block of four	11.00	75
a.			Double overprint	—	5.00
b.			"FUTURE" omitted	—	
c.			"DELIVERY FUTURE"		35.00
RC5	R22	20c	carmine rose	2.75	10
			Block of four	12.00	50
a.			Double overprint		20.00
RC6	R22	25c	carmine rose	10.00	40
			Block of four	42.50	1.75
			Cut cancellation		6
			Block of four, cut canc.		25
RC7	R22	40c	carmine rose	10.00	75
			Block of four	45.00	3.50
			Cut cancellation		6
			Block of four, cut canc.		25
RC8	R22	50c	carmine rose	3.00	12

			Block of four	14.00	55
	a.		"DELIVERY" omitted	—	
RC9	R22	80c	carmine rose	20.00	7.50
			Block of four	85.00	35.00
			Cut cancellation		1.00
			Block of four, cut canc.		4.50
	a.		Double overprint		25.00
	a.		Cut cancellation		6.00
		Engr.			

Overprint Vertical, Reading Up (Lines 2mm. apart)

RC10	R21	$1	green (R)	—	25
			Block of four	—	1.25
			Cut cancellation		5
	a.		Overprint reading down		*275.00*
	b.		Black overprint	—	
			Black ovpt., cut canc.	—	125.00
RC11	R21	$2	rose	—	25
			Block of four	—	1.25
			Cut cancellation		5
RC12	R21	$3	violet (R)	—	1.25
			Block of four	—	6.00
			Cut cancellation		12
			Block of four, cut canc.		50
	a.		Overprint reading down	—	50.00
RC13	R21	$5	dark blue (R)	—	35
			Block of four	—	1.50
			Cut cancellation		8
			Block of four, cut canc.		35
RC14	R21	$10	orange	—	60
			Block of four	—	3.00
			Cut cancellation		15
			Block of four, cut canc.		75
	a.		"DELIVERY FUTURE"		
RC15	R21	$20	olive bister	—	3.75
			Block of four	—	17.50
			Cut cancellation		50
			Block of four, cut canc.		2.25

Overprint Horizontal (Lines 11⅔mm. apart)
Perf. 12
Without Gum

RC16	R17	$30	vermilion, green numerals	—	3.00
			Vertical strip of four	—	
			Cut cancellation		1.25
			Vertical strip of four, cut canc.		6.00
	a.		Numerals in blue	50.00	3.00
			Cut cancellation		1.50
	b.		Imperf., blue numerals		
RC17	R19	$50	olive green (Cleveland)	—	1.00
			Vertical strip of four	—	
			Cut cancellation		40
			Vertical strip of four, cut canc.		1.75
	a.		$50 olive bister	—	1.00
			Cut cancellation		40
RC18	R19	$60	brown	—	2.00
			Vertical strip of four	—	
			Cut cancellation		75
			Vertical strip of four, cut canc.		3.50
	a.		Vert. pair, imperf. horiz.		*400.00*
RC19	R17	$100	yellow green ('34)	55.00	22.50
			Vertical strip of four	—	
			Cut cancellation		6.00
			Vertical strip of four, cut canc.		25.00
RC20	R18	$500	blue, red numerals (R)	50.00	10.00
			Vertical strip of four	—	
			Cut cancellation		4.50
			Vertical strip of four, cut canc.		20.00
			Double transfer		15.00
	a.		Numerals in orange	—	60.00
	a.		Cut cancellation		10.00
	a.		Double transfer		125.00
RC21	R19	$1000	orange	—	4.00
			Vertical strip of four	—	20.00
			Cut cancellation		1.50
			Vertical strip of four, cut canc.		7.50
	a.		Vert. pair, imperf. horiz.		*500.00*

See note after No. R227.

1923-24		Offset Printing		Perf. 11
		Overprint Horizontal. (Lines 2mm. apart)		
RC22	R22	1c	carmine rose	75	15
			Block of four	3.50	70
RC23	R22	80c	carmine rose	—	1.75
			Block of four	—	8.00
			Cut cancellation		25
			Block of four, cut canc.		1.10

Documentary Stamps of 1917 Overprinted

FUTURE

Type II

DELIVERY

1925-34 — Engr.

				Unused	Used
RC25	R21	$1	green (R)	8.00	60
			Block of four	—	2.75
			Cut cancellation		6
			Block of four, cut canc.		30
RC26	R21	$10	orange (Bk) ('34)	—	12.00
			Cut cancellation		7.00

Overprint Type I

1928-29 — Offset Printing — Perf. 10

					Used
RC27	R22	10c	carmine rose		850.00
RC28	R22	20c	carmine rose		850.00

STOCK TRANSFER STAMPS

Issued to facilitate the collection of a tax on all sales or agreements to sell, or memoranda of sales or delivery of, or transfers of legal title to shares or certificates of stock.

STOCK

Documentary Stamps of 1917 Overprinted in Black or Red

TRANSFER

1918-22 — Offset Printing — Wmk. 191R — Perf. 11
Overprint Horizontal (Lines 8mm. apart)

				Unused	Used
RD1	R22	1c	carmine rose	30	10
			Block of four	1.50	45
a.			Double overprint	—	—
RD2	R22	2c	carmine rose	15	5
			Block of four	—	20
a.			Double overprint		5.00
a.			Cut cancellation		2.50
			Double impression of stamp	—	
RD3	R22	4c	carmine rose	12	5
			Block of four	50	20
a.			Double overprint		4.00
a.			Cut cancellation		2.00
b.			"STOCK" omitted		10.00
d.			Ovpt. lines 10mm. apart	—	
			Double impression of stamp		6.00
RD4	R22	5c	carmine rose	20	5
			Block of four	90	25
RD5	R22	10c	carmine rose	12	5
			Block of four	—	25
a.			Double overprint		5.00
a.			Cut cancellation		2.50
b.			"STOCK" omitted		—
			Double impression of stamp		—
RD6	R22	20c	carmine rose	20	5
			Block of four	95	25
a.			Double overprint		6.00
b.			"STOCK" double		6.00
			Double impression of stamp		6.00
RD7	R22	25c	carmine rose	75	10
			Block of four	—	50
			Cut cancellation		5
RD8	R22	40c	carmine rose ('22)	65	6
			Block of four	—	30
RD9	R22	50c	carmine rose	25	5
			Block of four	70	25
a.			Double overprint		—
			Double impression of stamp		—
RD10	R22	80c	carmine rose	90	25
			Block of four		1.25
			Cut cancellation		5

Engr.
Overprint Vertical, Reading Up (Lines 2mm. apart)

				Unused	Used
RD11	R21	$1	green (R)	30.00	7.75
			Block of four	—	
			Cut cancellation		45
			Block of four, cut canc.		2.25
a.			Overprint reading down	—	11.00
a.			Cut cancellation		4.00
RD12	R21	$1	green (Bk)	1.50	5
			Block of four	—	25
a.			Pair, one without overprint	—	
b.			Overprinted on back instead of face, inverted	—	
c.			Overprint reading down		5.00
d.			$1 yellow green	—	6
RD13	R21	$2	rose	1.50	5
			Block of four	—	25
a.			Overprint reading down		10.00
a.			Cut cancellation		1.50
b.			Vert. pair, imperf. horiz.	500.00	
c.			"TRANSFER STOCK"		—
RD14	R21	$3	violet (R)	5.50	1.00
			Block of four	—	
			Cut cancellation		20
			Block of four, cut canc.		1.00
RD15	R21	$4	yellow brown	4.00	5
			Block of four	—	25
			Cut cancellation		5
RD16	R21	$5	dark blue (R)	2.25	5
			Block of four	—	25
			Cut cancellation		5
			Block of four, cut canc.		15
a.			Overprint reading down		1.00
a.			Cut cancellation		15
RD17	R21	$10	orange	3.25	12
			Block of four	17.50	75
			Cut cancellation		5
			Block of four, cut canc.		20
a.			"TRANSFER STOCK"		—
b.			"TRANSFER" omitted		—
RD18	R21	$20	olive bister ('21)	30.00	15.00
			Block of four	125.00	75.00
			Cut cancellation		3.00
			Block of four, cut canc.		15.00

Overprint Horizontal (Lines 11½mm. apart)
1918 — Without Gum — Perf. 12

				Unused	Used
RD19	R17	$30	vermilion, green numerals	12.50	4.00
			Vertical strip of four		17.50
			Cut cancellation		1.00
			Vertical strip of four, cut canc.		6.00
a.			Numerals in blue		50.00
RD20	R19	$50	olive green (*Cleveland*)	75.00	50.00
			Vertical strip of four		225.00
			Cut cancellation		15.00
			Vertical strip of four, cut canc.		70.00
RD21	R19	$60	brown	50.00	16.00
			Vertical strip of four		70.00
			Cut cancellation		6.00
			Vertical strip of four, cut canc.		26.00
RD22	R17	$100	green	15.00	5.00
			Vertical strip of four		22.50
			Cut cancellation		2.00
			Vertical strip of four, cut canc.		9.00
RD23	R18	$500	blue (R)	—	100.00
			Vertical strip of four		
			Cut cancellation		45.00
			Vertical strip of four, cut canc.		200.00
			Double transfer		125.00
a.			Numerals in orange		125.00
RD24	R19	$1000	orange	—	65.00
			Vertical strip of four		275.00
			Cut cancellation		22.50
			Vertical strip of four, cut canc.		100.00

See note after No. R227.

1928 — Offset Printing — Perf. 10
Overprint Horizontal (Lines 8mm. apart)

				Unused	Used
RD25	R22	2c	carmine rose	50	5
			Block of four	2.25	25
RD26	R22	4c	carmine rose	45	25
			Block of four	2.00	25
RD27	R22	10c	carmine rose	50	6
			Block of four	2.25	25
a.			Inverted overprint		*1,000.*
RD28	R22	20c	carmine rose	60	6
			Block of four	2.50	25
			Double impression of stamp		—
RD29	R22	50c	carmine rose	1.25	10
			Block of four	6.00	45

Engr.
Overprint Vertical, Reading Up (Lines 2mm. apart)

				Unused	Used
RD30	R21	$1	green	2.00	5
			Block of four	—	25
a.			$1 yellow green	—	—
RD31	R21	$2	carmine rose	2.00	5
			Block of four	—	25
a.			Pair, one without overprint	*150.00*	
RD32	R21	$10	orange	8.00	15
			Block of four	—	75
			Cut cancellation		5
			Perf. 11 at top or bottom	—	

STOCK

Overprinted Horizontally in Black

TRANSFER

1920 — Offset Printing — Perf. 11

				Unused	Used
RD33	R22	2c	carmine rose	3.00	50
			Block of four	13.00	2.25
RD34	R22	10c	carmine rose	50	5
			Block of four	2.25	20
a.			"TRANSFER STOCK"		40.00
RD35	R22	20c	carmine rose	60	5
			Block of four	2.75	25
a.			Pair, one without overprint	*175.00*	—
b.			"TRANSFER STOCK"		75.00
c.			"TRANSFER" omitted		65.00
RD36	R22	50c	carmine rose	1.25	8
			Block of four	5.25	35

Engr.

				Unused	Used
RD37	R21	$1	green	12.50	6.50
			Block of four	—	22.50
			Cut cancellation		25
			Block of four, cut canc.		65
RD38	R21	$2	rose	10.00	6.00
			Block of four	45.00	27.50
			Cut cancellation		25
			Block of four, cut canc.		1.10

Offset Printing — Perf. 10

				Unused	Used
RD39	R22	2c	carmine rose	2.75	35
			Block of four	12.00	1.65
			Double impression of stamp		—
RD40	R22	10c	carmine rose	90	10
			Block of four	4.00	50
RD41	R22	20c	carmine rose	1.25	6
			Block of four	6.00	25

SERIES 1940

Documentary Stamps of 1917-33 Overprinted in Black

STOCK
TRANSFER

1940 — Offset Printing — Wmk. 191R — Perf. 11

				Unused	Used (uncut)	Used (cut canc.)	Used (perforated initials)
RD42	R22	1c	rose pink	1.75	45	20	15
a.			"Series 1940" inverted	—	225.00	100.00	
RD43	R22	2c	rose pink	1.10	50	8	6
RD45	R22	4c	rose pink	1.10	10	5	5
RD46	R22	5c	rose pink	1.25	10	5	5
RD48	R22	10c	rose pink	1.75	10	5	5
RD49	R22	20c	rose pink	5.00	15	5	5
RD50	R22	25c	rose pink	5.00	35	12	10
RD51	R22	40c	rose pink	2.50	60	15	10
RD52	R22	50c	rose pink	3.50	15	6	5
RD53	R22	80c	rose pink	45.00	25.00	7.50	5.50

Engr.

				Unused	Used (uncut)	Used (cut canc.)	Used (perforated initials)
RD54	R21	$1	green	9.00	25	8	5
RD55	R21	$2	rose	9.00	25	8	6
RD56	R21	$3	violet	—	2.00	8	6
RD57	R21	$4	yellow brown	10.00	30	5	5
RD58	R21	$5	dark blue	12.00	30	12	5
RD59	R21	$10	orange	30.00	3.50	50	40
RD60	R21	$20	olive bister	55.00	17.50	6.00	4.00

Nos. RD19-RD24 Handstamped in Blue "Series 1940"

1940 — Wmk. 191R — Perf. 12
Without Gum

				Unused	Used (uncut)	Used (cut canc.)
RD61	R17	$30	vermilion	350.00	175.00	125.00
RD62	R19	$50	olive green	450.00	100.00	80.00
a.			Double overprint		*325.00*	
RD63	R19	$60	brown	400.00	100.00	85.00
RD64	R17	$100	green	350.00	100.00	60.00
RD65	R18	$500	blue	1,250.	800.00	350.00
RD66	R19	$1000	orange	1,750.	1,500.	1,250.

Alexander
Hamilton — ST1

Levi
Woodbury — ST2

Overprinted in Black

RD67

Various Portraits

1940		**Engr.**	**Wmk. 191R** **Size: 19x22mm.**		**Perf. 11**	
RD67	ST1	1c	bright green	4.75	1.75	50 30
RD68	ST1	2c	bright green (Oliver Wolcott, Jr.)	2.00	75	12 10
RD70	ST1	4c	bright green (Albert Gallatin)	4.50	2.25	50 25
RD71	ST1	5c	bright green (G. W. Campbell)	3.00	1.00	15 8
a.			Without overprint			—
RD73	ST1	10c	bright green (William H. Crawford)	4.00	90	20 8
RD74	ST1	20c	bright green (Richard Rush)	4.00	75	15 10
RD75	ST1	25c	bright green (S. D. Ingham)	15.00	4.50	60 35
RD76	ST1	40c	bright green (Louis McLane)	30.00	21.00	1.75 85
RD77	ST1	50c	bright green (Wm. J. Duane)	4.00	90	30 25
RD78	ST1	80c	bright green (R. B. Taney)	40.00	25.00	12.00 1.75
			Size: 21 1/2x36 1/4mm.			
RD79	ST2	$1	bright green	7.00	1.25	35 25
a.			Without overprint			150.00
RD80	ST2	$2	bright green (Thomas Ewing)	8.50	3.50	35 25
RD81	ST2	$3	bright green (Walter Forward)	16.00	5.00	50 8
RD82	ST2	$4	bright green (J. C. Spencer)	—	100.00	50.00 40.00
RD83	ST2	$5	bright green (G. M. Bibb)	16.00	7.00	30 20
RD84	ST2	$10	bright green (R. J. Walker)	—	16.00	50 40

RD85	ST2	$20	bright green (Wm. M. Meredith)	—	22.50	4.50 2.50

Nos. RD67-RD85 exist imperforate, without overprint.

Thomas Corwin — ST3

Overprinted "SERIES 1940"
Various Frames and Portraits

Perf. 12
Without Gum
Size: 28 1/2x42mm.

RD86	ST3	$30	bright green	—	80.00	40.00 22.50
RD87	ST3	$50	bright green (James Guthrie)	—	100.00	35.00 30.00
RD88	ST3	$60	bright green (Howell Cobb)	—	140.00	55.00 40.00
RD89	ST3	$100	bright green (P. F. Thomas)	—	110.00	50.00 30.00
RD90	ST3	$500	bright green (J. A. Dix)	—	375.00	300.00
RD91	ST3	$1000	bright green (S. P. Chase)	—	275.00	250.00 225.00

Stock Transfer Stamps of 1940 Overprinted in Black

SERIES 1941

1941			**Wmk. 191R** **Size: 19x22mm.**		**Perf. 11**	
RD92	ST1	1c	bright green	50	25	15 10
RD93	ST1	2c	bright green	25	8	6 5
RD95	ST1	4c	bright green	25	6	5 5
RD96	ST1	5c	bright green	25	6	5 5
RD98	ST1	10c	bright green	35	6	5 5
RD99	ST1	20c	bright green	80	6	5 5
RD100	ST1	25c	bright green	1.00	20	8 6
RD101	ST1	40c	bright green	1.10	25	8 6
RD102	ST1	50c	bright green	2.25	15	5 5
RD103	ST1	80c	bright green	9.00	3.75	25 12
			Size: 21 1/2x36 1/4mm.			
RD104	ST2	$1	bright green	5.00	10	5 5
RD105	ST2	$2	bright green	6.00	15	8 5
RD106	ST2	$3	bright green	8.00	1.00	30 5
RD107	ST2	$4	bright green	15.00	4.50	25 15
RD108	ST2	$5	bright green	18.00	40	10 6
RD109	ST2	$10	bright green	40.00	2.50	70 15
RD110	ST2	$20	bright green	—	27.50	7.50 1.00

Perf. 12
Without Gum
Size: 28 1/2x42mm.

RD111	ST3	$30	bright green	85.00	70.00	16.00 9.00
RD112	ST3	$50	bright green	—	75.00	18.00 9.00
RD113	ST3	$60	bright green	160.00	100.00	
RD114	ST3	$100	bright green	—	45.00	18.00 8.00

RD115	ST3	$500	bright green	—	325.00	150.00
RD116	ST3	$1000	bright green	—	275.00	165.00

Stock Transfer Stamps of 1940 Overprinted in Black

SERIES 1942

1942			**Wmk. 191R** **Size: 19x22mm.**		**Perf. 11**	
RD117	ST1	1c	bright green	35	15	10 7
RD118	ST1	2c	bright green	20	15	6 5
RD119	ST1	4c	bright green	2.25	70	50 40
RD120	ST1	5c	bright green	30	10	5 5
a.			Overprint inverted (Cut cancel.)		225.00	
RD121	ST1	10c	bright green	75	10	5 5
RD122	ST1	20c	bright green	1.10	10	6 5
RD123	ST1	25c	bright green	1.25	10	6 5
RD124	ST1	40c	bright green	2.25	25	10 8
RD125	ST1	50c	bright green	3.00	10	5 5
RD126	ST1	80c	bright green	7.00	3.50	1.00 20
			Size: 21 1/2x36 1/4mm.			
RD127	ST2	$1	bright green	5.50	10	5 5
RD128	ST2	$2	bright green	9.50	15	8 6
RD129	ST2	$3	bright green	11.00	55	10 6
RD130	ST2	$4	bright green	17.50	11.00	35 18
RD131	ST2	$5	bright green	13.00	25	10 5
a.			Double ovpt.			—
RD132	ST2	$10	bright green	27.50	4.50	65 20
RD133	ST2	$20	bright green	55.00	21.00	3.25 1.00

Perf. 12
Without Gum
Size: 28 1/2x42mm.

RD134	ST3	$30	bright green	—	35.00	12.00 6.00
RD135	ST3	$50	bright green	—	55.00	16.00 6.00
RD136	ST3	$60	bright green	—	75.00	30.00
RD137	ST3	$100	bright green	—	60.00	20.00 10.00
RD138	ST3	$500	bright green	—	—	
RD139	ST3	$1000	bright green	—	200.00	150.00

Stock Transfer Stamps of 1940 Overprinted in Black

SERIES 1943

1943			**Wmk. 191R** **Size: 19x22mm.**		**Perf. 11**	
RD140	ST1	1c	bright green	30	20	15 10
RD141	ST1	2c	bright green	40	20	6 5
RD142	ST1	4c	bright green	1.10	10	8 5
RD143	ST1	5c	bright green	40	10	6 5
RD144	ST1	10c	bright green	45	10	5 5
RD145	ST1	20c	bright green	1.00	10	6 5
RD146	ST1	25c	bright green	2.25	25	12 8
RD147	ST1	40c	bright green	2.25	25	10 8
RD148	ST1	50c	bright green	2.25	10	5 5
RD149	ST1	80c	bright green	6.00	2.50	1.25 75
			Size: 21 1/2x36 1/4mm.			
RD150	ST2	$1	bright green	4.50	10	6 5
RD151	ST2	$2	bright green	7.00	20	10 5
RD152	ST2	$3	bright green	7.50	75	10 5
RD153	ST2	$4	bright green	16.00	10.00	35 15
RD154	ST2	$5	bright green	26.00	35	20 6
RD155	ST2	$10	bright green	27.50	3.00	75 8
RD156	ST2	$20	bright green	45.00	22.50	10.00 2.75

USPS Souvenir pages are now listed and priced in a separate section of the catalogue. See catalogue index.

Perf. 12
Without Gum
Size: 28½x42mm.

RD157	ST3	$30	bright green	175.00	75.00	20.00	17.50
RD158	ST3	$50	bright green	—	75.00	20.00	12.00
RD158	ST3	$60	bright green	—	90.00	40.00	35.00
RD160	ST3	$100	bright green	—	45.00	15.00	10.00
RD161	ST3	$500	bright green	—	175.00	90.00	
RD162	ST3	$1000	bright green	—	165.00	125.00	90.00

Stock Transfer Stamps of 1940 Overprinted in Black

Series 1944

1944   **Wmk. 191R**   **Perf. 11**
Size: 19x22mm.

RD163	ST1	1c	bright green	50	40	15	12
RD164	ST1	2c	bright green	35	15	10	8
RD165	ST1	4c	bright green	50	20	15	12
RD166	ST1	3c	bright green	40	10	5	5
RD167	ST1	10c	bright green	40	10	6	5
RD168	ST1	20c	bright green	60	15	10	8
RD169	ST1	25c	bright green	1.25	30	16	10
RD170	ST1	40c	bright green	4.50	3.75	1.50	1.25
RD171	ST1	50c	bright green	2.50	15	10	6
RD172	ST1	80c	bright green	4.00	3.00	1.50	1.25

Size: 21½x36¼mm.

RD173	ST2	$1	bright green	3.50	30	10	8
RD174	ST2	$2	bright green	—	35	15	8
RD175	ST2	$3	bright green	9.00	75	25	8
RD176	ST2	$4	bright green	13.00	3.50	18	10
RD177	ST2	$5	bright green	11.00	60	30	15
RD178	ST2	$10	bright green	25.00	3.00	45	20
RD179	ST2	$20	bright green	50.00	5.50	3.00	1.50

Perf. 12
Without Gum
Size: 28½x42mm.

RD180	ST3	$30	bright green	50.00	35.00	11.00	9.00
RD181	ST3	$50	bright green	50.00	30.00	11.00	8.00
RD182	ST3	$60	bright green	125.00	75.00		30.00
RD183	ST3	$100	bright green	—	35.00	15.00	8.00
RD184	ST3	$500	bright green	—	300.00	225.00	175.00
RD185	ST3	$1000	bright green	—		175.00	150.00
RD185A	ST3	$2500	bright green (William Windom)	—	—		
RD185B	ST3	$5000	bright green (C.J. Folger)	—	—		
RD185C	ST3	$10,000	bright green (W.Q. Gresham)	—	800.00		

Stock Transfer Stamps of 1940 Overprinted in Black

Series 1945

1945   **Wmk. 191R**   **Perf. 11**
Size: 19x22mm.

RD186	ST1	1c	bright green	12	10	6	5
RD187	ST1	2c	bright green	20	15	8	6
RD188	ST1	4c	bright green	15	10	6	5
RD189	ST1	5c	bright green	18	10	5	5
RD190	ST1	10c	bright green	40	30	10	8
RD191	ST1	20c	bright green	60	25	20	12
RD192	ST1	25c	bright green	1.00	35	25	20
RD193	ST1	40c	bright green	1.65	20	12	8
RD194	ST1	50c	bright green	1.75	20	8	6

RD195	ST1	80c	bright green	2.75	2.00	70	65

Size: 21½x36¼mm.

RD196	ST2	$1	bright green	6.00	20	8	6
RD197	ST2	$2	bright green	8.50	25	10	8
RD198	ST2	$3	bright green	12.00	50	12	10
RD199	ST2	$4	bright green	12.00	1.25	45	40
RD200	ST2	$5	bright green	10.00	30	15	8
RD201	ST2	$10	bright green	20.00	3.75	75	60
RD202	ST2	$20	bright green	35.00	4.25	1.00	85

Perf. 12
Without Gum
Size: 28½x42mm.

RD203	ST3	$30	bright green	60.00	30.00	16.00	13.00
RD204	ST3	$50	bright green	40.00	10.00	4.00	3.00
RD205	ST3	$60	bright green	100.00	65.00	20.00	15.00
RD206	ST3	$100	bright green	—	20.00	12.00	7.00
RD207	ST3	$500	bright green	—	200.00	135.00	100.00
RD208	ST3	$1000	bright green	—	225.00		125.00
RD208A	ST3	$2500	bright green	—	—		
RD208B	ST3	$5000	bright green	—	—		
RD208C	ST3	$10,000	bright green	—	800.00		

Stock Transfer Stamps and Type of 1940 Overprinted in Black

Series 1946

1946   **Wmk. 191R**   **Perf. 11**
Size: 19x22mm.

RD209	ST1	1c	bright green	15	10	6	5
a.		Pair, one dated "1945"	375.00				
RD210	ST1	2c	bright green	20	10	5	5
RD211	ST1	4c	bright green	15	10	6	5
RD212	ST1	5c	bright green	30	10	5	5
RD213	ST1	10c	bright green	40	10	5	5
RD214	ST1	20c	bright green	90	15	10	8
RD215	ST1	25c	bright green	85	20	10	8
RD216	ST1	40c	bright green	1.50	40	15	12
RD217	ST1	50c	bright green	1.75	20	12	10
RD218	ST1	80c	bright green	3.00	2.75	90	80

Size: 21½x36¼mm.

RD219	ST2	$1	bright green	3.00	30	8	6
RD220	ST2	$2	bright green	4.00	30	15	12
RD221	ST2	$3	bright green	7.00	75	30	18
RD222	ST2	$4	bright green	7.50	3.00	1.00	85
RD223	ST2	$5	bright green	11.00	50	30	18
RD224	ST2	$10	bright green	20.00	1.00	25	15
RD225	ST2	$20	bright green	35.00	21.00	7.00	5.00

Perf. 12
Without Gum
Size: 28½x42mm.

RD226	ST3	$30	bright green	45.00	25.00	12.00	9.00
RD227	ST3	$50	bright green	45.00	25.00	10.00	7.00
RD228	ST3	$60	bright green	100.00	60.00	22.50	10.00
RD229	ST3	$100	bright green	60.00	30.00	10.00	8.00
RD230	ST3	$500	bright green	—	125.00		65.00
RD231	ST3	$1000	bright green	—	110.00		75.00
RD232	ST3	$2500	bright green	—	—		
RD233	ST3	$5000	bright green	—	—		

RD234	ST3	$10,000	bright	—	—		800.00

Stock Transfer Stamps and Type of 1940 Overprinted in Black

Series 1947

1947   **Wmk. 191R**   **Perf. 11**
Size: 19x22mm.

RD235	ST1	1c	bright green	50	40	8	6
RD236	ST1	2c	bright green	40	25	8	8
RD237	ST1	4c	bright green	30	25	6	5
RD238	ST1	5c	bright green	25	20	5	5
RD239	ST1	10c	bright green	40	25	6	5
RD240	ST1	20c	bright green	60	30	15	12
RD241	ST1	25c	bright green	90	35	18	15
RD242	ST1	40c	bright green	1.25	45	25	18
RD243	ST1	50c	bright green	1.65	15	5	5
RD244	ST1	80c	bright green	7.50	5.50	2.25	2.00

Size: 21½x36¼mm.

RD245	ST2	$1	bright green	3.00	35	15	12
RD246	ST2	$2	bright green	4.50	50	15	12
RD247	ST2	$3	bright green	7.00	90	35	30
RD248	ST2	$4	bright green	15.00	3.75	85	70
RD249	ST2	$5	bright green	10.00	90	30	20
RD250	ST2	$10	bright green	17.50	3.00	1.10	90
RD251	ST2	$20	bright green	35.00	17.50		4.50

Perf. 12
Without Gum
Size: 28½x42mm.

RD252	ST3	$30	bright green	50.00	22.50	7.00	4.00
RD253	ST3	$50	bright green	100.00	70.00	20.00	12.50
RD254	ST3	$60	bright green	100.00	75.00	30.00	25.00
RD255	ST3	$100	bright green	—	21.00	10.00	8.00
RD256	ST3	$500	bright green	—	175.00	75.00	60.00
RD257	ST3	$1000	bright green	—	75.00	35.00	25.00
RD258	ST3	$2500	bright green	—		300.00	
RD259	ST3	$5000	bright green	—		350.00	
RD260	ST3	$10,000	bright green	—		65.00	
a.		Horiz. pair, imperf. vert.	—				

Stock Transfer Stamps of 1940 Overprinted in Black

Series 1948

1948   **Wmk. 191R**   **Perf. 11**
Size: 19x22mm.

RD261	ST1	1c	bright green	15	15	6	5
RD262	ST1	2c	bright green	15	15	6	5
RD263	ST1	4c	bright green	25	20	12	8
RD264	ST1	5c	bright green	20	15	6	5
RD265	ST1	10c	bright green	25	15	6	5
RD266	ST1	20c	bright green	65	25	10	8
RD267	ST1	25c	bright green	75	30	15	12
RD268	ST1	40c	bright green	1.10	40	25	20
RD269	ST1	50c	bright green	2.00	20	8	8
RD270	ST1	80c	bright green	6.00	5.00	1.10	1.00

Size: 21½x36¼mm.

RD271	ST2	$1	bright green	3.50	30	12	10
RD272	ST2	$2	bright green	6.00	40	15	15
RD273	ST2	$3	bright green	7.00	2.50	50	40
RD274	ST2	$4	bright green	8.00	6.00	1.50	1.50
RD275	ST2	$5	bright green	12.00	1.25	25	20

No.	Type	Denom.	Color				
RD276	ST2	$10	bright green	18.00	3.00	75	60
RD277	ST2	$20	bright green	35.00	12.00	4.50	

Perf. 12
Without Gum
Size: 28½x42mm.

No.	Type	Denom.	Color				
RD278	ST3	$30	bright green	50.00	25.00	18.00	10.00
RD279	ST3	$50	bright green	40.00	25.00	9.00	6.00
RD280	ST3	$60	bright green	75.00	55.00	20.00	15.00
RD281	ST3	$100	bright green	—	12.00	6.00	4.00
RD282	ST3	$500	bright green	—	125.00	75.00	35.00
RD283	ST3	$1000	bright green	—	75.00	30.00	25.00
RD284	ST3	$2500	bright green	250.00	200.00	150.00	
RD285	ST3	$5000	bright green	—	200.00	150.00	
RD286	ST3	$10,000	bright green	—	60.00		

Stock Transfer Stamps of 1940 Overprinted in Black

Series 1949

1949 Wmk. 191R Perf. 11
Size: 19x22mm.

No.	Type	Denom.	Color				
RD287	ST1	1c	bright green	25	20	6	5
RD288	ST1	2c	bright green	25	20	5	5
RD289	ST1	4c	bright green	30	25	6	5
RD290	ST1	5c	bright green	30	25	6	5
RD291	ST1	10c	bright green	50	25	5	5
RD292	ST1	20c	bright green	1.00	30	10	8
RD293	ST1	25c	bright green	1.25	50	12	10
RD294	ST1	40c	bright green	2.50	90	20	15
RD295	ST1	50c	bright green	2.50	25	6	5
RD296	ST1	80c	bright green	5.00	3.50	1.75	1.20

Size: 21½x36¼mm.

No.	Type	Denom.	Color				
RD297	ST2	$1	bright green	3.50	40	10	8
RD298	ST2	$2	bright green	6.00	60	18	15
RD299	ST2	$3	bright green	10.00	3.50	45	40
RD300	ST2	$4	bright green	12.00	6.00	2.00	1.50
RD301	ST2	$5	bright green	17.50	1.75	25	20
RD302	ST2	$10	bright green	25.00	3.00	1.25	1.00
RD303	ST2	$20	bright green	50.00	12.00	5.00	4.00

Perf. 12
Without Gum
Size: 28½x42mm.

No.	Type	Denom.	Color				
RD304	ST3	$30	bright green	—	35.00	12.00	
RD305	ST3	$50	bright green	—	35.00	12.00	9.00
RD306	ST3	$60	bright green	125.00	70.00	25.00	
RD307	ST3	$100	bright green	—	35.00	20.00	12.00
RD308	ST3	$500	bright green	—	110.00	45.00	35.00
RD309	ST3	$1000	bright green	—	60.00	40.00	25.00
RD310	ST3	$2500	bright green	—	325.00		
RD311	ST3	$5000	bright green	—	300.00	225.00	
RD312	ST3	$10,000	bright green	—	30.00		
	a.	Pair, one without overprint		—			

Stock Transfer Stamps of 1940 Overprinted in Black

Series 1950

1950 Wmk. 191R Perf. 11
Size: 19x22mm.

No.	Type	Denom.	Color				
RD313	ST1	1c	bright green	25	20	5	5
RD314	ST1	2c	bright green	25	20	5	5
RD315	ST1	4c	bright green	25	20	6	5
RD316	ST1	5c	bright green	30	15	5	5
RD317	ST1	10c	bright green	1.00	20	5	5
RD318	ST1	20c	bright green	1.25	30	6	5
RD319	ST1	25c	bright green	2.25	40	12	10
RD320	ST1	40c	bright green	2.50	60	20	18
RD321	ST1	50c	bright green	4.00	30	6	5
RD322	ST1	80c	bright green	3.50	3.50	2.00	1.10

Size: 21½x36¼mm.

No.	Type	Denom.	Color				
RD323	ST2	$1	bright green	4.00	35	8	6
RD324	ST2	$2	bright green	7.50	50	12	10
RD325	ST2	$3	bright green	11.00	3.00	60	50
RD326	ST2	$4	bright green	12.50	7.50	2.25	1.75
RD327	ST2	$5	bright green	17.50	1.25	20	18
RD328	ST2	$10	bright green	30.00	4.00	85	75
RD329	ST2	$20	bright green	40.00	14.00	4.00	

Perf. 12
Without Gum
Size: 28½x42mm.

No.	Type	Denom.	Color				
RD330	ST3	$30	bright green	60.00	35.00	20.00	12.00
RD331	ST3	$50	bright green	70.00	50.00	18.00	
RD332	ST3	$60	bright green	—	75.00	30.00	
RD333	ST3	$100	bright green	—	30.00	20.00	10.00
RD334	ST3	$500	bright green	—	100.00	75.00	
RD335	ST3	$1000	bright green	—	65.00	30.00	20.00
RD336	ST3	$2500	bright green		425.00		
RD337	ST3	$5000	bright green	—	350.00	225.00	
RD338	ST3	$10,000	bright green	—	60.00		

Stock Transfer Stamps of 1940 Overprinted in Black

Series 1951

1951 Wmk. 191R Perf. 11
Size: 19x22mm.

No.	Type	Denom.	Color				
RD339	ST1	1c	bright green	30	25	5	5
RD340	ST1	2c	bright green	30	25	5	5
RD341	ST1	4c	bright green	40	30	5	5
RD342	ST1	5c	bright green	40	25	5	5
RD343	ST1	10c	bright green	50	25	5	5
RD344	ST1	20c	bright green	1.25	50	12	10
RD345	ST1	25c	bright green	1.75	50	15	12
RD346	ST1	40c	bright green	3.00	2.75	50	40
RD347	ST1	50c	bright green	3.00	50	8	6
RD348	ST1	80c	bright green	4.50	3.50	1.50	1.10

Size: 21½x36¼mm.

No.	Type	Denom.	Color				
RD349	ST2	$1	bright green	6.00	50	6	5
RD350	ST2	$2	bright green	7.00	75	18	12
RD351	ST2	$3	bright green	11.00	5.50		
RD352	ST2	$4	bright green	13.00	7.50		1.50
RD353	ST2	$5	bright green	18.00	2.00	25	20
RD354	ST2	$10	bright green	30.00	7.50	2.00	1.50
RD355	ST2	$20	bright green	45.00	12.50	6.00	4.50

Perf. 12
Without Gum
Size: 28½x42mm.

No.	Type	Denom.	Color				
RD356	ST3	$30	bright green	—	27.50	10.00	
RD357	ST3	$50	bright green	—	25.00	10.00	
RD358	ST3	$60	bright green	—	150.00	70.00	
RD359	ST3	$100	bright green	—	20.00	15.00	
RD360	ST3	$500	bright green	—	90.00	50.00	
RD361	ST3	$1000	bright green	—	50.00	30.00	
RD362	ST3	$2500	bright green	—	500.00	200.00	150.00
RD363	ST3	$5000	bright green	—	500.00	175.00	
RD364	ST3	$10,000	bright green	—	100.00	50.00	

Stock Transfer Stamps of 1940 Overprinted in Black

Series 1952

1952 Wmk. 191R Perf. 11
Size: 19x22mm.

No.	Type	Denom.	Color		
RD365	ST1	1c	bright green	20.00	10.00	1.50	1.25
RD366	ST1	10c	bright green	15.00	7.50	1.00	90
RD367	ST1	20c	bright green	350.00	—		
RD368	ST1	25c	bright green	475.00	—		
RD369	ST1	40c	bright green	40.00	15.00	6.00	3.00

Size: 21½x36¼mm.

No.	Type	Denom.	Color		
RD370	ST2	$4	bright green	750.00	350.00
RD371	ST2	$10	bright green	1500.	—
RD372	ST2	$20	bright green	2000.	—

Stock Transfer Stamps were discontinued in 1952.

CORDIALS, WINES, Etc.

RE1

Inscribed "Series of 1914"

Size: 19½x22¼mm.
1914 Wmk. 190 Offset Printing Perf. 10

No.	Type	Denom.	Color		
RE1	RE1	¼c	green	40	30
RE2	RE1	½c	green	30	20
RE3	RE1	1c	green	35	25
RE4	RE1	1½c	green	1.75	75
RE5	RE1	2c	green	3.00	2.00
RE6	RE1	3c	green	1.50	55
RE7	RE1	4c	green	1.75	1.25
RE8	RE1	5c	green	55	30
RE9	RE1	6c	green	3.50	1.75
RE10	RE1	8c	green	2.25	75
RE11	RE1	10c	green	2.25	2.00
RE12	RE1	20c	green	2.00	90
RE13	RE1	24c	green	7.50	4.50
RE14	RE1	40c	green	1.75	50

RE1a

Without Gum Imperf.
Size: 47x40mm.

No.	Type	Denom.	Color		
RE15	RE1a	$2	green	2.75	20
	a.	Double impression		90.00	

1914 Wmk. 191R Perf. 10

No.	Type	Denom.	Color		
RE16	RE1	¼c	green	2.50	2.25
RE17	RE1	½c	green	1.25	1.00
RE18	RE1	1c	green	25	8
RE19	RE1	1½c	green	30.00	25.00
RE20	RE1	2c	green	10	8
RE21	RE1	3c	green	1.50	1.25
RE22	RE1	4c	green	75	60
RE23	RE1	5c	green	7.00	6.00
RE24	RE1	6c	green	50	25
RE25	RE1	8c	green	80	30
RE26	RE1	10c	green	35	12
RE27	RE1	20c	green	55	25
RE28	RE1	24c	green	7.00	55
RE29	RE1	40c	green	15.00	8.50

Imperf
Without Gum

No.	Type	Denom.	Color		
RE30	RE1a	$2	green	15.00	2.00

RE31	RE1	2c				
			Perf. 11			
			green		40.00	30.00

WINE STAMPS

RE2

Inscribed: "Series of 1916"

1916   Wmk. 191R   Offset Printing   *Rouletted 3½*
Without Gum
Plates of 100 subjects
Size: Approximately 40x47mm.

RE32	RE2	1c	green	35	30
RE33	RE2	3c	green	3.50	3.00
RE34	RE2	4c	green	30	25
RE35	RE2	6c	green	1.00	75
RE36	RE2	7½c	green	6.00	3.50
RE37	RE2	10c	green	1.00	40
RE38	RE2	12c	green	1.75	1.65
RE39	RE2	15c	green	1.75	1.50
RE40	RE2	18c	green	24.00	21.00
RE41	RE2	20c	green	30	25
RE42	RE2	24c	green	2.75	2.00
RE43	RE2	30c	green	3.00	2.25
RE44	RE2	36c	green	15.00	11.00
RE45	RE2	50c	green	60	40
RE46	RE2	60c	green	2.75	2.00
RE47	RE2	72c	green	30.00	27.50
RE48	RE2	80c	green	75	55
RE49	RE2	$1.20	green	6.00	5.00
RE50	RE2	$1.44	green	5.00	2.50
RE51	RE2	$1.60	green	20.00	15.00
RE52	RE2	$2	green	1.25	1.25

RE3

Engr.
Plates of 50 subjects

RE53	RE3	$4	green	60	18
RE54	RE3	$4.80	green	2.75	2.50
RE55	RE3	$9.60	green	90	25

Nos. RE32 to RE55 exist in many shades. Size variations of 1c to $2 are believed due to offset printing. These designs in

Prices for well-centered, early U.S. stamps will often exceed catalogue price.

light green, rouletted 7, were re-issued in 1933-34. See Nos. RE60 to RE83.

RE4

Perf. 11½ at left.
Size: Approximately 51x81mm.
Plates of 6 subjects

RE56	RE4	$20	green	75.00	35.00
RE57	RE4	$40	green	150.00	45.00
RE58	RE4	$50	green	35.00	30.00
RE59	RE4	$100	green	200.00	125.00

Stamps of design RE4 have an adjoining tablet at right for affixing additional stamps. See Nos. RE107A-RE107D.

Same designs as Issue of 1916-18

1933   Wmk. 191R   Offset Printing   *Rouletted 7*

RE60	RE2	1c	light green	2.00	25
RE61	RE2	3c	light green	6.00	1.75
RE62	RE2	4c	light green	75	15
RE63	RE2	6c	light green	9.00	3.50
RE64	RE2	7½c	light green	1.50	25
RE65	RE2	10c	light green	1.25	10
RE66	RE2	12c	light green	4.50	90
RE67	RE2	15c	light green	2.00	10
RE69	RE2	20c	light green	2.25	5
	a.		Double impression		—
RE70	RE2	24c	light green	2.25	5
	a.		Double impression		—
RE71	RE2	30c	light green	2.25	10
RE72	RE2	36c	light green	6.50	45
RE73	RE2	50c	light green	3.75	25
RE74	RE2	60c	light green	4.00	10
RE75	RE2	72c	light green	7.50	30
RE76	RE2	80c	light green	7.00	10
RE77	RE2	$1.20	light green	9.00	1.25
RE78	RE2	$1.44	light green	6.00	3.50
RE79	RE2	$1.60	light green	175.00	65.00
RE80	RE2	$2	light green	27.50	3.00
			Engr.		
RE81	RE3	$4	light green	20.00	6.00
RE82	RE3	$4.80	light green	22.50	13.00
RE83	RE3	$9.60	light green	125.00	60.00

RE5

Perf. Rouletted 7
1934-40   Offset Printing   Wmk. 191R
Inscribed: "Series of 1934"
Size: Approximately 28x25mm.
Plates of 200 and 224 subjects
Issued With and Without Gum

RE83A	RE5	⅕c	green ('40)	70	20
RE84	RE5	⅕c	green	55	25
RE85	RE5	1c	green	65	15

RE86	RE5	1¼c	green	1.50	75
RE87	RE5	1½c	green	6.00	3.25
RE88	RE5	2c	green	1.65	35
RE89	RE5	2½c	green	1.65	50
RE90	RE5	3c	green	5.50	4.00
RE91	RE5	4c	green	1.50	15
RE92	RE5	5c	green	55	10
RE93	RE5	6c	green	1.75	25
RE94	RE5	7½c	green	1.25	15
RE95	RE5	10c	green	35	6
RE96	RE5	12c	green	1.25	10
RE96A	RE5	14⅖c	green ('40)	80.00	3.00
RE97	RE5	15c	green	75	10
RE98	RE5	18c	green	1.40	12
RE99	RE5	20c	green	1.25	6
RE100	RE5	24c	green	1.40	10
RE101	RE5	30c	green	1.25	8

Size: Approximately 39x45mm.
Plates of 100 subjects
Issued Without Gum

RE102	RE2	40c	green	1.50	25
RE102A	RE2	43⅕c	green ('40)	8.00	2.00
RE103	RE2	48c	green	8.00	1.25
RE104	RE2	$1	green	13.00	10.00
RE105	RE2	$1.50	green	22.50	13.00
			Perforated initials		5.50

Engr.

Size: Approximately 39x46mm.
Plates of 50 subjects.

RE106	RE3	$2.50	green	27.50	15.00
			Perforated initials		6.00
RE107	RE3	$5	green	20.00	7.50
			Perforated initials		2.50

Stamps of types RE5 and RE2 overprinted "Rectified Spirits / Puerto Rico" are listed under Puerto Rico.

Inscribed: "Series of 1916"
Size: Approximately 51x81mm.
Plates of 6 subjects

1934   *Perf. 11½ at left*

| RE107A | RE4 | $20 | yellow green | | 1,300. |
| RE107B | RE4 | $40 | yellow green | | 1,750. |

Perf. 12½ at left

| RE107C | RE4 | $50 | yellow green | | 575.00 |
| RE107D | RE4 | $100 | yellow green | | 300.00 |

The serial numbers of Nos. RE107A-RE107D are much thinner than on Nos. RE56-RE59.

RE6

Offset Printing
Size: 28x25mm.
Inscribed "Series of 1941"

1942-44   **Wmk. 191R**   *Rouletted 7*

RE108	RE6	⅕c	green & black	65	35
RE109	RE6	¼c	green & black	1.25	60
RE110	RE6	½c	green & black	1.25	90
	a.		Imperf. vertically (pair)	90.00	
RE111	RE6	1c	green & black	60	30
RE112	RE6	2c	green & black	2.50	2.00
RE113	RE6	3c	green & black	2.50	2.00
RE114	RE6	3½c	green & black		2,400.
RE115	RE6	3¾c	green & black	4.00	2.00
RE116	RE6	4c	green & black	1.50	1.25
RE117	RE6	5c	green & black	1.50	1.25
RE118	RE6	6c	green & black	1.50	1.25
RE119	RE6	7c	green & black	2.00	1.50
RE120	RE6	7½c	green & black	2.50	2.00
RE121	RE6	8c	green & black	2.50	1.50
RE122	RE6	9c	green & black	3.50	2.75

RE123	RE6	10c	green & black	3.00	90
RE124	RE6	11¼c	green & black	3.25	2.50
RE125	RE6	12c	green & black	4.00	3.00
RE126	RE6	14c	green & black	14.00	8.00
RE127	RE6	15c	green & black	3.25	1.75
	a.		Imperf. vert., pair	—	
RE128	RE6	16c	green & black	4.25	3.00
RE129	RE6	19¹⁄₅c	green & black	90.00	4.00
RE130	RE6	20c	green & black	3.50	1.00
RE131	RE6	24c	green & black	3.25	10
RE132	RE6	28c	green & black	1,200.	525.00
RE133	RE6	30c	green & black	90	10
RE134	RE6	32c	green & black	50.00	3.25
RE135	RE6	36c	green & black	2.00	10
RE136	RE6	40c	green & black	1.50	15
RE137	RE6	45c	green & black	2.25	20
RE138	RE6	48c	green & black	7.00	2.25
RE139	RE6	50c	green & black	8.00	4.00
RE140	RE6	60c	green & black	2.00	15
RE141	RE6	72c	green & black	6.50	75
RE142	RE6	80c	green & black	25.00	3.50
RE143	RE6	84c	green & black	—	35.00
RE144	RE6	90c	green & black	10.00	15
RE145	RE6	96c	green & black	10.00	15

See Nos. RE182D-RE194.

Denomination Spelled Out in Two Lines — RE7

1942-47   Size: **39x45½mm.**   Engr.

RE146	RE7	$1.20	yellow green & black	3.00	10
RE147	RE7	$1.44	yellow green & black	1.50	6
RE148	RE7	$1.50	yellow green & black	90.00	50.00
RE149	RE7	$1.60	yellow green & black	6.50	1.00
RE150	RE7	$1.68	yellow green & black	60.00	45.00
RE151	RE7	$1.80	yellow green & black	2.25	8
	a.		Vertical pair, one without denomination	—	
RE152	RE7	$1.92	yellow green & black	37.50	32.50
RE153	RE7	$2.40	yellow green & black	6.50	60
RE154	RE7	$3	yellow green & black	45.00	25.00
RE155	RE7	$3.36	yellow green & black	—	27.50
RE156	RE7	$3.60	yellow green & black	—	6.00
RE157	RE7	$4	yellow green & black	16.00	5.00

RE158	RE7	$4.80	yellow green & black	—	3.00
RE159	RE7	$5	yellow green & black	11.00	8.00
RE160	RE7	$7.20	yellow green & black	17.50	50
RE161	RE7	$10	yellow green & black	100.00	60.00
RE162	RE7	$20	yellow green & black	110.00	70.00
RE163	RE7	$50	yellow green & black	100.00	50.00
			Perforated initials		18.00
RE164	RE7	$100	yellow green & black	250.00	30.00
			Perforated initials		12.00
RE165	RE7	$200	yellow green & black	90.00	20.00
			Perforated initials		8.50
RE165B	RE7	$400	yellow green & black	—	1,200.
RE166	RE7	$500	yellow green & black	—	125.00
			Perforated initials		25.00
RE167	RE7	$600	yellow green & black	—	125.00
RE168	RE7	$900	yellow green & black		1,250.
			Perforated initials		750.00
RE169	RE7	$1000	yellow green & black		150.00
RE170	RE7	$2000	yellow green & black		600.00
RE171	RE7	$3000	yellow green & black		160.00
RE172	RE7	$4000	yellow green & black		575.00

Denomination Repeated, Spelled Out in One Line
1949-54

RE173	RE7	$1	yellow green & black	2.75	1.50
RE174	RE7	$2	yellow green & black	4.50	1.75
RE175	RE7	$4	yellow green & black	425.00	275.00
RE176	RE7	$5	yellow green & black		60.00
RE177	RE7	$6	yellow green & black		375.00
RE178	RE7	$7	yellow green & black		45.00
RE179	RE7	$8	yellow green & black	400.00	250.00
RE180	RE7	$10	yellow green & black	15.00	5.00
			Perforated initials		1.00
RE181	RE7	$20	yellow green & black	15.00	3.00
			Perforated initials		1.00
RE182	RE7	$30	yellow green & black	550.00	500.00

Other denominations of engraved stamps, type RE7, that were printed and delivered to the Internal Revenue Service were: $7.14, $9, $12, $40, $60, $70, $80, $300, $700 and $800. None are reported in collectors' hands.

Types of 1941-54
1951-54   Size: **28x25mm.**   Offset Printing

RE182D	RE6	1⁷⁄₁₀c	green & black		3250.00
RE183	RE6	3²⁄₅c	green & black	40.00	27.50
RE184	RE6	8½c	green & black	20.00	17.50
RE185	RE6	13²⁄₅c	green & black	60.00	50.00
RE186	RE6	17c	green & black	12.00	12.00
RE187	RE6	20²⁄₅c	green & black	60.00	35.00

RE188	RE6	33½c	green & black	60.00	45.00
RE189	RE6	38¼c	green & black	65.00	45.00
RE190	RE6	40⁴⁄₅c	green & black	3.50	65
RE191	RE6	51c	green & black	3.50	75
RE192	RE6	67c	green & black	10.00	4.00
RE193	RE6	68c	green & black	3.00	65
RE194	RE6	80²⁄₅c	green & black	75.00	70.00

Engr.
Size: **39x45½mm.**
Denomination Spelled Out in Two Lines in Small Letters

Two types of $1.60⁴⁄₅:
I. The "4" slants sharply. Loop of "5" almost closes to form oval. Each numeral 2mm. high.
II. The "4" is less slanted. Loop of "5" more open and nearly circular. Each numeral 2½mm high.

RE195	RE7	$1.50¾	yellow green & black	40.00	30.00
RE196	RE7	$1.60⁴⁄₅	yellow green & black (I)	3.50	35
	a.		"DOL-LAR"	40.00	12.50
	b.		As "a," horiz. pair, one without denomination	500.00	
	c.		Type II	350.00	100.00
RE197	RE7	$1.88³⁄₁₀	yellow green & black	90.00	50.00

Denomination Spelled Out in Two Lines in Slightly Larger Letters Same as Nos. RE146-RE172

RE198	RE7	$1.60⁴⁄₅	yellow green & black (II)	25.00	5.00
	a.		First line larger letters, second line small letters		500.00
	b.		Type I ('53)	50.00	20.00
RE199	RE7	$2.01	yellow green & black	3.50	35
RE200	RE7	$2.68	yellow green & black	3.50	35
RE201	RE7	$4.08	yellow green & black	40.00	25.00
RE202	RE7	$5.76	yellow green & black	200.00	85.00
RE203	RE7	$8.16	yellow green & black	12.00	4.00
RE204	RE7	$9.60	yellow green & black		2,250.

Other denominations that were printed out not delivered to the Internal Revenue Service were: 6⁷⁄₁₀c, 10¹⁄₅c and $90. None are reported in collectors' hands.
Wine stamps were discontinued on Dec. 31, 1954.

PLAYING CARD STAMPS

Stamps for use on packs of playing cards were included in the first general issue of 1862-71. They are Nos. R2, R11, R12, R17, R21 and R28.
The tax on playing cards was repealed effective June 22, 1965.

"ON HAND . . ."
RF1

"ACT OF . . ."
RF2

1894   Engr.   Unwmk.   Rouletted 5½

RF1	RF1	2c	lake	50	30
	a.		Horizontal pair, imperf. between	150.00	

	b.	Horiz. pair, imperf. vert.	—	
RF2	RF2 2c	ultramarine	4.50	2.50
	a.	2c blue		3.50
	b.	Imperf., pair	125.00	
	c.	Imperf horizontally	100.00	100.00
	d.	Rouletted 12½	50.00	50.00
	e.	Imperf. horizontally, rouletted 12½ vertically, pair	80.00	80.00

 Wmk. 191R

1896-99		**Wmk. 191R**		***Rouletted 5½, 7***
RF3	RF2 2c	blue	4.00	50
	a.	2c ultramarine ('99)	5.50	1.25
	b.	Imperf., pair	65.00	

1902				***Perf. 12***
RF4	RF2 2c	deep blue		27.50

No. RF4 is known with cancellation date "1899" but that is due to the use of an old cancelling plate. The stamp was first used in 1902.

ACT OF 1917
7 CENTS

Stamp of 1896-99 Surcharged in Rose

1917		**Wmk. 191R**		***Rouletted 7***
RF5	RF2 7c	on 2c ultramarine	*750.00*	600.00
	a.	Inverted surcharge		—

The surcharge on No. RF5 was handstamped at the Internal Revenue Office in New York City.

The surcharges on Nos. RF6 to RF13 inclusive, and No. RF15 were applied by the manufacturers, together with their initials, dates, etc., thus forming a combination of surcharge and precancellation. The surcharge on No. RF16 was made by the Bureau of Engraving and Printing. After it appeared the use of the combinations was continued but only as cancellations.

Surcharged in Black 17

1917				
RF6	RF2 (7c)	on 2c blue		32.50
	a.	Inverted surcharge		32.50

The "17" indicated that the 7 cent tax had been paid according to the Act of 1917.

Surcharged in Black 7

1917				
RF7	RF2 7c	on 2c blue		275.00
	a.	Inverted surcharge		275.00

Surcharged Vertically in Red or Violet 7 CTS.

RF8	RF2 7c	on 2c blue		450.00

---

	a.	Double surcharge		500.00

Surcharged Vertically, Reading up in Black, Violet or Red

7 CENTS

RF9	RF2 7c	on 2c blue	8.00
	a.	Double surcharge	45.00
	b.	Numeral omitted	30.00
	c.	Surcharge reading down	10.00
	d.	As "c", numeral omitted	30.00
	e.	As "c", double surcharge	110.00
	f.	Double surcharge, one inverted	110.00
	g.	Surcharge and "A.D." in violet	110.00
	h.	Surcharge and "A.D." in red, "U.S.P.C." in black	250.00
	i.	Surcharge and "A.D." in red reading up, "U.S.P.C." in black reading down	*300.00*

"A.D." stands for Andrew Dougherty, the name of a playing card company. "U.S.P.C." stands for United States Playing Card Co.

On Nos. RF9g-RF9i, surcharge and company initials were applied simultaneously.

Surcharged in Carmine 7c

RF10	RF2 7c	on 2c blue	35.00
	a.	Inverted surcharge	25.00
	b.	Double surcharge	175.00
	c.	Double surcharge, inverted	135.00
	d.	Triple surcharge	—

RF3

1918		**Size: 21x40mm.**		***Imperf.***
RF11	RF3	blue	35.00	25.00
		Block of four	150.00	110.00
RF12	RF3	***Private Roulette 14*** blue	125.00	
	a.	Rouletted 13 in red	500.00	
	b.	Rouletted 6½	150.00	
	c.	Perf. 12 horiz., imperf. vert.	90.00	

---

	d.	Perf. 12 on 4 sides		—

Nos. RF11 and RF12 served as 7c stamps when used before April 1, 1919, and as 8c stamps when used after that date.

Surcharged like No. RF9 in Violet, Red or Black
Private Roulette 9½

RF13	RF3 7c	blue	27.50
	a.	Inverted surcharge	27.50
	b.	Double surcharge	160.00
	c.	Double surcharge, inverted	160.00

REVENUE ACT OF 1918 8 CENTS

Stamp of 1896-99 Surcharged in Magenta or Rose

1919				***Rouletted 7***
RF14	RF2 8c	on 2c ultramarine		70.00
	a.	Double surcharge		125.00
	b.	Inverted surcharge		125.00

The surcharge on No. RF14 was handstamped at the Internal Revenue Office in New York City.

Surcharged in Carmine ○8

RF15	RF2 8c	on 2c blue (inverted surcharge)		325.00
	a.	Double surcharge, inverted		*425.00*

No. RF15 is surcharged only with large "8c" inverted, and overprinted with date and initials. No. RF16 is often found with additional impression of large "8c," as on No. RF15, but in this usage the large "8c" is a cancellation.

Surcharged in Carmine 8 Cts.

RF16	RF2 8c	on 2c blue	30.00	75
	a.	Inverted surcharge		

See note after No. RF5.

RF4

1922		**Size: 19x22mm.**		***Rouletted 7***
RF17	RF4 (8c)	blue	11.00	1.25

Surcharged in Carmine, Blue or Black 8c

RF18	RF4 8c	blue		32.50
	a.	Inverted surcharge		27.50

RF5

1924				***Rouletted 7***
RF19	RF5 10c	blue	7.50	40
		Block of four	32.50	

ROTARY PRESS COIL STAMP

1926			**Perf. 10 Vertically**		
RF20	RF5	10c	blue		25

No. RF20 exists only precanceled.

FLAT PLATE PRINTING

1927				**Perf. 11**	
RF21	RF5	10c	blue	10.00	5.00
			Block of four	45.00	
1929				**Perf. 10**	
RF22	RF5	10c	blue	8.50	4.00

RF6

ROTARY PRESS COIL STAMP

1929			**Perf. 10 Horizontally**		
RF23	RF6	10c	light blue		15

No. RF23 exists only precanceled.

FLAT PLATE PRINTING

1930				**Perf. 10**	
RF24	RF6	10c	blue	8.50	1.25
			Block of four	40.00	10.00
	a.		Horiz. pair, imperf. vert.	150.00	
1931				**Perf. 11**	
RF25	RF6	10c	blue	8.50	1.25

RF7

ROTARY PRESS COIL STAMP

1940			**Perf. 10 Vertically**		
RF26	RF7		blue, wet printing	—	40
			Dry printing	—	40

See note after No. 1029.

RF8

ROTARY PRESS COIL STAMP

1940		**Wmk. 191R**	**Perf. 10 Horizontally**		
RF27	RF8		blue		15

FLAT PLATE PRINTING
Perf. 11

RF28	RF8		blue	5.00	1.25

ROTARY PRESS PRINTING.
Perf. 10x11

RF29	RF8		blue	125.00	75.00
	a.		Imperforate (P.C. Co.)		150.00

PLAYING CARD STAMPS FOR THE VIRGIN ISLANDS

These stamps were overprinted by the Bureau of Engraving and Printing. Shipments of 10,000 each of Nos. RFV1-RFV3 were sent to the Virgin Islands on June 17, 1920, Jan. 16, 1926, and Mar. 5, 1934, respectively.

U. S. Playing Card Stamp No. RF3 Overprinted in Carmine

VIRGIN ISLANDS
4 CTS.

1920	**Engr.**	**Wmk. 191R**		**Rouletted 7**	
RFV1	RF2	4c	on 2c blue		140.00

U. S. Playing Card Stamp No. RF17 Overprinted in Carmine

VIRGIN ISLANDS
4 cts.

1926				**Rouletted 7**	
RFV2	RF4	4c	blue		35.00

Same Overprint on U.S. Type RF4

1934				**Perf. 11**	
RFV3	RF4	4c	light blue		100.00

The above stamp with perforation 11 was not issued in the United States without the overprint.

SILVER TAX STAMPS

The Silver Purchase Act of 1934 imposed a 50 per cent tax on the net profit realized on a transfer of silver bullion. The tax was paid by affixing stamps to the transfer memorandum. Congress authorized the Silver Tax stamps on Feb. 20, 1934. They were discontinued on June 4, 1963.

Documentary Stamps of 1917 Overprinted

SILVER TAX

1934	**Offset Printing**	**Wmk. 191R**		**Perf. 11**	
RG1	R22	1c	carmine rose	60	30
RG2	R22	2c	carmine rose	85	35
	a.		Double impression of stamp	—	
RG3	R22	3c	carmine rose	1.00	45
RG4	R22	4c	carmine rose	1.00	50
RG5	R22	5c	carmine rose	1.25	75
RG6	R22	8c	carmine rose	1.75	1.00
RG7	R22	10c	carmine rose	1.75	1.00
RG8	R22	20c	carmine rose	3.50	2.50
RG9	R22	25c	carmine rose	3.50	3.00
RG10	R22	40c	carmine rose	5.00	4.25
RG11	R22	50c	carmine rose	6.00	5.00
	a.		Double impression of stamp	30.00	
RG12	R22	80c	carmine rose	9.00	6.00

Engr.

RG13	R21	$1	green	10.00	7.50
RG14	R21	$2	rose	13.00	11.00
RG15	R21	$3	violet	27.50	21.00
RG16	R21	$4	yellow brown	20.00	14.00
RG17	R21	$5	dark blue	25.00	13.00
RG18	R21	$10	orange	40.00	13.00

Perf. 12
Without Gum

RG19	R17	$30	vermilion	—	30.00
			Cut cancellation		17.50
RG20	R19	$60	brown	—	50.00
			Vertical strip of four		210.00
			Cut cancellation		25.00
RG21	R17	$100	green	90.00	30.00
			Vertical strip of four		125.00
RG22	R18	$500	blue	250.00	200.00
			Vertical strip of four		
			Cut cancellation		95.00
RG23	R19	$1000	orange	—	100.00

		Cut cancellation			60.00

See note after No. R227.

Same Overprint, spacing 11 mm. between words "SILVER TAX"

Without Gum

1936				**Perf. 12**	
RG26	R17	$100	green	110.00	50.00
			Vertical strip of four		
RG27	R19	$1000	orange		475.00

Documentary Stamps of 1917 Handstamped "SILVER TAX" in Violet, Large Block Letters, in Two Lines

1939	**Wmk. 191R**	**Offset Printing**		**Perf. 11**	
RG28	R22	3c	rose pink		—
RG30	R22	10c	rose pink		—
RG32	R22	80c	rose pink		—

Other handstamps exist on various values. One has letters 4mm. high, 2mm. wide with "SILVER" and "TAX" applied in separate operations. Another has "Silver Tax" in two lines in a box.

Engr.
Overprint Typewritten in Black
Perf. 11

RG35	R21	$3	violet		—
RG36	R21	$5	dark blue		—

Typewritten overprints also exist on 2c, 3c, 20c, 50c and in red on $5.

SERIES 1940

Type of Documentary Stamps 1917, Overprinted in Black

SILVER TAX

1940		**Offset Printing**		**Perf. 11**	
RG37	R22	1c	rose pink	11.00	—
RG38	R22	2c	rose pink	11.00	—
RG39	R22	3c	rose pink	11.00	—
RG40	R22	4c	rose pink	12.50	—
RG41	R22	5c	rose pink	7.50	—
RG42	R22	8c	rose pink	12.50	—
RG43	R22	10c	rose pink	11.00	—
RG44	R22	20c	rose pink	12.50	—
RG45	R22	25c	rose pink	11.00	—
RG46	R22	40c	rose pink	20.00	—
RG47	R22	50c	rose pink	20.00	—
RG48	R22	80c	rose pink	20.00	—

Engr.

RG49	R21	$1	green	45.00	—
RG50	R21	$2	rose	65.00	—
RG51	R21	$3	violet	100.00	—
RG52	R21	$4	yellow brown	225.00	—
RG53	R21	$5	dark blue	250.00	—
RG54	R21	$10	orange	325.00	—

Nos. RG19-RG20, RG26 Handstamped in Blue "Series 1940"

1940		**Without Gum**		**Perf. 12**	
RG55	R17	$30	vermilion	—	1,250.
RG56	R19	$60	brown	—	1,900.
RG57	R17	$100	green	—	1,500.

Alexander Hamilton
RG1

Levi Woodbury
RG2

Thomas Corwin — RG3

Overprinted in Black   **SERIES 1941**

1941		Wmk. 191R	Engr.	Perf. 11	
		Size: 19x22mm.			
RG58	RG1	1c	gray	1.10	—
RG59	RG1	2c	gray (Oliver Wolcott, Jr.)	1.10	—
RG60	RG1	3c	gray (Samuel Dexter)	1.25	—
RG61	RG1	4c	gray (Albert Gallatin)	1.65	—
RG62	RG1	5c	gray (G.W. Campbell)	2.00	—
RG63	RG1	8c	gray (A.J. Dallas)	2.50	—
RG64	RG1	10c	gray (Wm. H. Crawford)	3.00	—
RG65	RG1	20c	gray (Richard Rush)	4.75	—
RG66	RG1	25c	gray (S.D. Ingham)	7.00	—
RG67	RG1	40c	gray (Louis McLane)	11.00	—
RG68	RG1	50c	gray (Wm. J. Duane)	15.00	—
RG69	RG1	80c	gray (Roger B. Taney)	25.00	20.00
		Size: 21½x36¼mm.			
RG70	RG2	$1	gray	25.00	—
RG71	RG2	$2	gray (Thomas Ewing)	70.00	35.00
RG72	RG2	$3	gray (Walter Forward)	55.00	40.00
RG73	RG2	$4	gray (J.C. Spencer)	65.00	—
RG74	RG2	$5	gray (G.M. Bibb)	70.00	50.00
RG75	RG2	$10	gray (R.J. Walker)	100.00	60.00
RG76	RG2	$20	gray (Wm. M. Meredith)	175.00	—

Perf. 12
Without Gum
Size: 28½x42mm.

RG77	RG3	$30	gray	125.00	60.00
			Cut cancellation		45.00
RG78	RG3	$50	gray (James Guthrie)	—	—
RG79	RG3	$60	gray (Howell Cobb)	600.00	100.00
			Cut cancellation		75.00
RG80	RG3	$100	gray (P.F. Thomas)	—	175.00
			Vertical strip of four	—	
			Cut cancellation		75.00
RG81	RG3	$500	gray (J.A. Dix)	—	—
RG82	RG3	$1000	gray (S.P. Chase)	—	650.00
			Cut cancellation		325.00

Silver Purchase Stamps of 1941 Overprinted in Black

SERIES 1942

1942		Wmk. 191R		Perf. 11	
		Size: 19x22mm.			
RG83	RG1	1c	gray	60	—
RG84	RG1	2c	gray	75	—
RG85	RG1	3c	gray	75	—
RG86	RG1	4c	gray	80	—
RG87	RG1	5c	gray	90	—

RG88	RG1	8c	gray	1.25	—
RG89	RG1	10c	gray	2.75	—
RG90	RG1	20c	gray	4.00	—
RG91	RG1	25c	gray	7.75	—
RG92	RG1	40c	gray	9.00	—
RG93	RG1	50c	gray	9.00	—
RG94	RG1	80c	gray	25.00	—
		Size: 21½x36¼mm.			
RG95	RG2	$1	gray	25.00	—
	a.		Overprint "SERIES 5942"	275.00	
RG96	RG2	$2	gray	27.50	—
	a.		Overprint "SERIES 5942"	250.00	
RG97	RG2	$3	gray	50.00	—
	a.		Overprint "SERIES 5942"		
RG98	RG2	$4	gray	50.00	—
	a.		Overprint "SERIES 5942"	—	
RG99	RG2	$5	gray	55.00	—
	a.		Overprint "SERIES 5942"	250.00	
RG100	RG2	$10	gray	125.00	—
RG101	RG2	$20	gray	250.00	—
	a.		Overprint "SERIES 5942"	—	

Perf. 12
Without Gum
Size: 28½x42mm.

RG102	RG3	$30	gray	325.00	300.00
RG103	RG3	$50	gray	325.00	300.00
RG104	RG3	$60	gray	—	300.00
			Cut cancellation		250.00
RG105	RG3	$100	gray		225.00
			Cut cancellation		175.00
RG106	RG3	$500	gray	—	—
RG107	RG3	$1000	gray	—	—
			Cut cancellation		

Silver Purchase Stamps of 1941 without Overprint

1944		Wmk. 191R		Perf. 11	
		Size: 19x22mm.			
RG108	RG1	1c	gray	25	15
RG109	RG1	2c	gray	30	—
RG110	RG1	3c	gray	45	—
RG111	RG1	4c	gray	60	—
RG112	RG1	5c	gray	1.10	—
RG113	RG1	8c	gray	1.50	—
RG114	RG1	10c	gray	1.50	—
RG115	RG1	20c	gray	3.75	—
RG116	RG1	25c	gray	3.75	—
RG117	RG1	40c	gray	6.50	—
RG118	RG1	50c	gray	6.50	—
RG119	RG1	80c	gray	9.00	—
		Size: 21½x36¼mm.			
RG120	RG2	$1	gray	16.00	8.00
RG121	RG2	$2	gray	27.50	18.00
RG122	RG2	$3	gray	32.50	11.00
RG123	RG2	$4	gray	40.00	32.50
RG124	RG2	$5	gray	40.00	15.00
RG125	RG2	$10	gray	55.00	27.50
			Cut cancellation		11.00
RG126	RG2	$20	gray	225.00	—

Perf. 12
Without Gum
Size: 28½x42mm.

RG127	RG3	$30	gray	110.00	85.00
			Vertical strip of four		—
			Cut cancellation		50.00
RG128	RG3	$50	gray	375.00	325.00
			Vertical strip of four		—
			Cut cancellation		225.00
RG129	RG3	$60	gray		125.00
			Cut cancellation		75.00
RG130	RG3	$100	gray		30.00
			Vertical strip of four		—
			Cut cancellation		15.00
RG131	RG3	$500	gray		250.00
			Cut cancellation		175.00
RG132	RG3	$1000	gray		150.00
			Vertical strip of four		—
			Cut cancellation		75.00

CIGARETTE TUBES STAMPS

These stamps were for a tax on the hollow tubes of cigarette paper, each with a thin cardboard mouthpiece attached. They were sold in packages so buyers could add loose tobacco to make cigarettes.

Documentary Stamp of 1917 Overprinted

1919	Offset Printing		Wmk. 191R	Perf. 11	
RH1	R22	1c	carmine rose	50	25
			Block of four	2.25	
	a.		Without period	10.00	6.00
1929				Perf. 10	
RH2	R22	1c	carmine rose	17.50	6.00

RH1

1933		Wmk. 191R		Perf. 11	
RH3	RH1	1c	rose	1.50	50
			Block of four	7.50	
RH4	RH1	2c	rose	3.00	1.25

POTATO TAX STAMPS

These stamps were required under the Agricultural Adjustment Act of Dec. 1, 1935. Their use ended Jan. 6, 1936, when this act was declared unconstitutional. Potato growers were given allotments and for excess had to pay ¾ cent a pound.

Young Woman — RI1

		Engr.	Unwmk.	Perf. 11	
RI1	RI1	¾c	carmine rose	25	
RI2	RI1	1½c	black brown	40	
RI3	RI1	2¼c	yellow green	40	
RI4	RI1	3c	light violet	50	
RI5	RI1	3¾c	olive bister	50	
RI6	RI1	7½c	orange brown	1.25	
RI7	RI1	11¼c	deep orange	1.50	
RI8	RI1	18¾c	violet brown	3.25	
RI9	RI1	37½c	red orange	3.50	
RI10	RI1	75c	blue	4.00	
RI11	RI1	93¾c	rose lake	5.50	
RI12	RI1	$1.12½	green	7.50	
RI13	RI1	$1.50	yellow	8.50	

TOBACCO SALE TAX STAMPS

These stamps were required to pay the tax on the sale of tobacco in excess of quotas set by the Secretary of Agriculture. The tax was 25 per cent of the price for which the excess tobacco was sold. It was intended to affect tobacco harvested after June 28, 1934 and sold before May 1, 1936. The tax was stopped when the Agricultural Adjustment Act was declared unconstitutional by the Supreme Court on Dec. 1, 1935.

Prices for unused stamps are for copies with original gum.

Stamps and Types of 1917
Documentary Issue Overprinted

1934		Offset Printing		Wmk. 191R	Perf. 11	
RJ1	R22	1c	carmine rose		30	15
RJ2	R22	2c	carmine rose		35	20
RJ3	R22	5c	carmine rose		1.20	40
RJ4	R22	10c	carmine rose		1.50	40
		a.	Inverted overprint		9.00	6.50
RJ5	R22	25c	carmine rose		4.00	1.50
RJ6	R22	50c	carmine rose		4.00	1.50

		Engr.			
RJ7	R21	$1	green	7.00	1.60
RJ8	R21	$2	rose	12.50	1.75
RJ9	R21	$5	dark blue	15.00	4.00
RJ10	R21	$10	orange	25.00	10.00
RJ11	R21	$20	olive bister	60.00	12.00

On No. RJ11 the overprint is vertical, reading up.

NARCOTIC TAX STAMPS

The Revenue Act of 1918 imposed a tax of 1 cent per ounce or fraction thereof on opium, coca leaves and their derivatives. The tax was paid by affixing Narcotic stamps to the drug containers. The tax lasted from Feb. 25, 1919, through Apr. 30, 1971.

Members of the American Revenue Association compiled the listings in this section.

Documentary Stamps of 1914 Handstamped "NARCOTIC" in Magenta, Blue or Black

1919		Wmk. 191R	Offset Printing		Perf. 10
RJA1	R20	1c	rose	55.00	40.00

The overprint was applied by District Collectors of Internal Revenue. It is always in capital letters and exists in various type faces and sizes, including: 21 1/2x2 1/2mm., serif; 21x2 1/4mm., sans-serif boldface; 15 1/2x2 1/2mm., sans-serif; 13x2mm., sans-serif.

The 1/2c, 2c, 3c, 4c, 5c, 10c, 25c and 50c with similar handstamp in serif capitals measuring about 20x2 1/4mm. are bogus.

Documentary Stamps of 1917 Handstamped "NARCOTIC" "Narcotic", "NARCOTICS" or "ACT/NARCOTIC/1918" in Magenta, Black, Blue, Violet or Red

1919		Wmk. 191R	Offset Printing		Perf. 11
RJA9	R22	1c	carmine rose	1.50	1.00
RJA10	R22	2c	carmine rose	4.00	3.00
RJA11	R22	3c	carmine rose	15.00	12.00
RJA12	R22	4c	carmine rose	7.00	5.00
RJA13	R22	5c	carmine rose	10.00	10.00
RJA14	R22	8c	carmine rose	7.50	12.00
RJA15	R22	10c	carmine rose	35.00	6.00
RJA16	R22	20c	carmine rose	35.00	30.00
RJA17	R22	25c	carmine rose	30.00	25.00
RJA18	R22	40c	carmine rose	65.00	55.00
RJA19	R22	50c	carmine rose	15.00	15.00
RJA20	R22	80c	carmine rose	75.00	55.00

		Engr.			
RJA21	R21	$1	green	35.00	25.00
RJA22	R21	$2	rose	—	
RJA23	R21	$3	violet	—	
RJA24	R21	$5	dark blue	—	
RJA25	R21	$10	orange	—	

The overprints were applied by District Collectors of Internal Revenue. They are known in at least 20 type faces and sizes of which the majority read "NARCOTIC" in capital letters. Two are in upper and lower case letters. Experts have identified 14 by city. The 3-line handstamp was used in Seattle; "NARCOTICS" in Philadelphia. Most handstamps are not found on all denominations.

No. R228 Overprinted in Black: "NARCOTIC / E.L. CO. / 3-19-19"

1919		Wmk. 191R		Perf. 11

"NARCOTIC" 14 1/2mm. wide.

RJA26	R22	1c	carmine rose	325.00

Overprinted by Eli Lilly Co., Indianapolis, for that firm's use.

No. R228 Overprinted in Black: "J W & B / NARCOTIC"

1919		Wmk. 191R		Perf. 11

"NARCOTIC" 14 1/2mm. wide.

RJA27	R22	1c	carmine rose	250.00

Overprinted by John Wyeth & Brother, Philadelphia, for that firm's use.

Nos. R228, R231-R232 Handstamped in Blue: "P-W-R-Co. / NARCOTIC"

1919		Wmk. 191R		Perf. 11
RJA28	R22	1c	carmine rose	225.00
RJA28A	R22	4c	carmine rose	—
RJA29	R22	5c	carmine rose	—

The handstamp was applied by the Powers-Weightmann-Rosengarten Co., Philadelphia, for that firm's use.

Proprietary Stamps of 1919 Handstamped "NARCOTIC" in Blue

1919		Wmk. 191R	Offset Printing		Perf. 11
RJA30	RB5	1c	dark blue	—	—
RJA31	RB5	2c	dark blue	—	
RJA32	RB5	4c	dark blue	—	

No. RB65 is known with "Narcotic" applied in red ms.

Documentary Stamps of 1917 Overprinted in Black, "Narcotic" **NARCOTIC** 17 1/2mm. wide

1919		Wmk. 191R	Offset Printing		Perf. 11
RJA33	R22	1c	carmine rose (6,900,000)	75	50
RJA34	R22	2c	carmine rose (3,650,000)	1.50	1.00
RJA35	R22	3c	carmine rose (388,400)	25.00	15.00
RJA36	R22	4c	carmine rose (2,400,000)	5.00	3.50
RJA37	R22	5c	carmine rose (2,400,000)	12.00	10.00
RJA38	R22	8c	carmine rose (1,200,000)	17.50	13.00
RJA39	R22	10c	carmine rose (3,400,000)	3.00	2.50
RJA40	R22	25c	carmine rose (700,000)	17.50	13.00

		Overprint Reading Up Engr.			
RJA41	R21	$1	green (270,000)	20.00	12.00

The overprint of Nos. RJA33-RJA41 has been counterfeited. In the genuine the C's are not slanted.

 NT1

		Imperf., Rouletted			
1919-70		Offset Printing		Wmk. 191R	
				a. Imperf.	b. Rouletted 7
RJA42	NT1	1c	violet	3.50	10
		d.	1c purple		6.00

NT2

RJA43	NT2	1c	violet	50	15
		d.	1c purple	3.00	3.00
RJA44	NT2	2c	violet	1.00	40
		d.	2c purple		5.00
RJA45	NT2	3c	violet ('64)	—	80.00

Souvenir cards are listed and priced in a separate section of the catalogue. See catalogue index.

NT3

NT4

				a. Imperf.	b. Rouletted 7
RJA46	NT3	1c	violet	2.00	65
		d.	1c purple		5.00
RJA47	NT3	2c	violet	1.50	50
		d.	2c purple		7.00
RJA48	NT3	3c	violet	400.00	
RJA49	NT3	4c	violet ('42)	—	7.50
		d.	4c purple		27.50
RJA50	NT3	5c	violet	40.00	3.25
		d.	5c purple		11.00
RJA51	NT3	6c	violet		65
		d.	6c purple		8.00
RJA52	NT3	8c	violet	55.00	3.00
		d.	8c purple		22.50
RJA53	NT3	9c	violet ('53)	65.00	6.50
RJA54	NT3	10c	violet	30.00	50
		d.	10c purple		6.00
RJA55	NT3	16c	violet	50.00	2.50
		d.	16c purple		11.50
RJA56	NT3	18c	violet ('61)	80.00	5.00
RJA57	NT3	19c	violet ('61)	110.00	15.00
RJA58	NT3	20c	violet	275.00	110.00

Nos. RJA47-RJA58 have "CENTS" below the value.

				a. Imperf.	b. Roul. 7	c. Roul. 3 1/2
RJA59	NT4	1c	violet	45.00	10.00	4.00
RJA60	NT4	2c	violet		20.00	
RJA61	NT4	3c	violet	40.00	18.50	
RJA62	NT4	5c	violet		25.00	
RJA63	NT4	6c	violet	60.00	20.00	
RJA64	NT4	8c	violet		45.00	
RJA65	NT4	9c	violet ('61)	12.50	10.00	
RJA66	NT4	10c	violet	11.00	15.00	
RJA67	NT4	16c	violet	15.00	10.00	
RJA68	NT4	18c	violet ('61)	325.00	375.00	
RJA69	NT4	19c	violet	10.00	110.00	
RJA70	NT4	20c	violet	300.00	110.00	
RJA71	NT4	25c	violet	—	20.00	4.00
RJA72	NT4	40c	violet	325.00	65.00	
RJA73	NT4	$1	green		1.25	
RJA74	NT4	$1.28	green	20.00	10.00	

		b. Roul.	c. Roul.
a. Imperf.	7	3 ½

RJA75 NT4 $4   green,   *750.00*
                   unwmkd.
                   ('70)

On Nos. RJA60-RJA75 the value tablet is solid.

NT5

Denomination added in black by rubber plate in an operation similar to precanceling.

1963		**Engr.**	**Unwmk.**		***Imperf.***
RJA76	NT5	1c	violet		50.00
1964		**Denomination on Stamp Plate**			
		Offset Printing			***Imperf.***
RJA77	NT5	1c	violet		5.00

CONSULAR SERVICE FEE

Act of Congress, April 5, 1906, effective June 1, 1906, provided that every consular officer should be provided with special adhesive stamps printed in denominations determined by the Department of State.

Every document for which a fee was prescribed had to have attached a stamp or stamps representing the amount collected, and such stamps were used to show payment of these prescribed fees.

These stamps were usually affixed close to the signature, or at the lower left corner of the document. If no document was issued, the stamp or stamps were attached to a receipt for the amount of the fee and canceled either with pen and ink or rubber stamp showing the date of cancellation and bearing the initials of the canceling officer or name of the Consular Office. These stamps were not sold to the public uncanceled. Their use was discontinued Sept. 30, 1955.

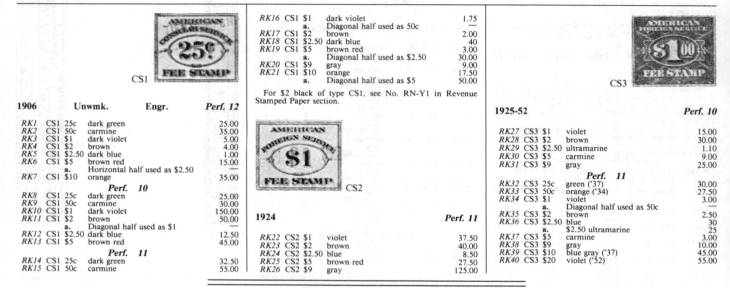

CS1

1906		**Unwmk.**	**Engr.**	**Perf. 12**
RK1	CS1	25c	dark green	25.00
RK2	CS1	50c	carmine	35.00
RK3	CS1	$1	dark violet	5.00
RK4	CS1	$2	brown	4.00
RK5	CS1	$2.50	dark blue	1.00
RK6	CS1	$5	brown red	15.00
a.			Horizontal half used as $2.50	35.00
RK7	CS1	$10	orange	35.00
		Perf. 10		
RK8	CS1	25c	dark green	25.00
RK9	CS1	50c	carmine	30.00
RK10	CS1	$1	dark violet	150.00
RK11	CS1	$2	brown	50.00
a.			Diagonal half used as $1	
RK12	CS1	$2.50	dark blue	12.50
RK13	CS1	$5	brown red	45.00
		Perf. 11		
RK14	CS1	25c	dark green	32.50
RK15	CS1	50c	carmine	55.00

RK16	CS1	$1	dark violet	1.75
a.			Diagonal half used as 50c	—
RK17	CS1	$2	brown	2.00
RK18	CS1	$2.50	dark blue	40
RK19	CS1	$5	brown red	3.00
a.			Diagonal half used as $2.50	30.00
RK20	CS1	$9	gray	9.00
RK21	CS1	$10	orange	17.50
a.			Diagonal half used as $5	50.00

For $2 black of type CS1, see No. RN-Y1 in Revenue Stamped Paper section.

CS2

1924				**Perf. 11**
RK22	CS2	$1	violet	37.50
RK23	CS2	$2	brown	40.00
RK24	CS2	$2.50	blue	8.50
RK25	CS2	$5	brown red	27.50
RK26	CS2	$9	gray	125.00

CS3

1925-52				***Perf. 10***
RK27	CS3	$1	violet	15.00
RK28	CS3	$2	brown	30.00
RK29	CS3	$2.50	ultramarine	1.10
RK30	CS3	$5	carmine	9.00
RK31	CS3	$9	gray	25.00
		Perf. 11		
RK32	CS3	25c	green ('37)	30.00
RK33	CS3	50c	orange ('34)	27.50
RK34	CS3	$1	violet	3.00
a.			Diagonal half used as 50c	—
RK35	CS3	$2	brown	2.50
RK36	CS3	$2.50	blue	30
a.			$2.50 ultramarine	25
RK37	CS3	$5	carmine	3.00
RK38	CS3	$9	gray	10.00
RK39	CS3	$10	blue gray ('37)	45.00
RK40	CS3	$20	violet ('52)	55.00

CUSTOMS FEE

New York Custom House

Issued to indicate the collection of miscellaneous customs fees. Use was discontinued on February 28, 1918. The stamps were not utilized in the collection of customs duties.

Silas Wright
CF1

Size: 48mm.x34mm.

1887		**Engr.**		**Rouletted 5 ½**
RL1	CF1	20c	dull rose	50
a.			20c red, perf. 10	—
b.			Vertical half used as 10c	—
c.			20c red, rouletted 7	*100.00*
RL2	CF1	30c	orange	1.25
RL3	CF1	40c	green	2.25
RL4	CF1	50c	dark blue	4.50
RL5	CF1	60c	red violet	1.25
RL6	CF1	70c	brown violet	25.00

RL7	CF1	80c brown	55.00
RL8	CF1	90c black	75.00

Each of these eight stamps has its own distinctive background.

EMBOSSED REVENUE STAMPED PAPER

Some of the American Colonies of Great Britain used embossed stamps in raising revenue, as Britain had done from 1694. The British government also imposed stamp taxes on the Colonies, and in the early 19th century the U.S. government and some of the states enacted similar taxes.

Under one statute or another, these stamps were required on such documents as promissory notes, bills of exchange, insurance policies, bills of lading, bonds, protests, powers of attorney, stock certificates, letters patent, writs, conveyances, leases, mortgages, charter parties, commissions and liquor licenses.

A few of these stamps were printed, but most were colorless impressions resembling a notary publics seal.

The scant literature of these stamps includes E. B. Sterlings revenue catalogue of 1888, and "New Discovery from British Archives on the 1765 Tax Stamps for America," edited by Adolph Koeppel and published (1962) by the American Revenue Association.

Prices are for stamps of clear impression on entire documents in good condition. Parts of documents, cut squares or poor impressions sell for much less. Prices represent actual sales wherever possible. Prices in italics are tentative. A dash in the price column indicates that few copies are known or information for pricing is inadequate.

Colin MacR. Makepeace originally compiled the listings in this section.

INCLUDING COLONIAL EMBOSSED REVENUES
I. COLONIAL ISSUES
A. MASSACHUSETTS
Act of January 8, 1755
In effect May 1, 1755-April 30, 1757

EP1

EP2

EP3

EP4

Typo.

RM1	EP1	½p red	2,000.

Embossed

RM2	EP2	2p	450.00
RM3	EP3	3p	110.00
RM4	EP4	4p	500.00

A second die of EP2 with no fin on the under side of the codfish has been seen. There were at least two dies of the ½p.

B. NEW YORK
Act of December 1, 1756
In effect January 1, 1757-December 31, 1760

EP9

Typo.

RM9	EP9	½p red	2,500.

Embossed

RM10	EP9	1p	450.00
RM11	EP9	2p	200.00
RM12	EP9	3p	400.00
RM13	EP9	4p	300.00

II. BRITISH REVENUES FOR USE IN AMERICA
Act of March 22, 1765
In effect November 1, 1765-May 1, 1766.
A. ALMANAC STAMPS

EP15

Engr.

RM15	EP15	2p red	
RM16	EP15	4p red	—
RM17	EP15	8p red	

Proofs of all of these stamps printed in the issued color are known. Full size facsimile reproductions in the color of the originals were made about 1876 of the proof sheets of the 8p stamp, Plates 1 and 2, Dies 1 to 50 inclusive.

B. PAMPHLETS AND NEWSPAPER STAMPS

EP18

Engr.

RM18	EP18	½p red	1,750.
RM19	EP18	1p red	
RM20	EP18	2p red	

Proofs of all of these stamps printed in the issued color are known. Full size facsimile reproductions in the color of the originals were made about 1876 of the proof sheets of the 1p stamp, Plates 3 and 4, Dies 51 to 100 inclusive.

C. GENERAL ISSUE

EP24

EP25

EP26

EP27

EP28

EP29

EP30

EP31

See the "Information for Collectors" section at beginning of catalogue for an explanation of perforation types, imperforates and coils.

EP33

EP34

EP35

Embossed

RM24	EP24	3p	1,250.
RM25	EP25	4p	3,000.
RM26	EP26	6p	2,000.
RM27	EP27	1sh	1,000.
RM28	EP28	1sh 6p	1,250.
RM29	EP29	2sh	3,000.
RM30	EP30	2sh 3p	2,250.
RM31	EP31	2sh 6p	800.00
	a.	Not on document	500.00
RM33	EP33	4sh	2,500.
RM34	EP34	5sh	2,500.
RM35	EP35	10sh	3,250.

Proofs exist of similar 1sh, 1sh6p and 2sh6p stamps inscribed "AMERICA CONT.& c."

Various Similar Designs

RM36	£1	—
RM37	£2	—
RM38	£3	—
RM39	£4	—
RM40	£6	—
RM41	£10	—

The £1 to £10 denominations probably exist only as proofs.

D. PLAYING CARDS STAMP
Type similar to EP29, with Arms of George III Encircled by Garter.

RM42	1sh	—

All of these were embossed without color and most of them were embossed directly on the document except the 2sh 6p which was general embossed on a rectangular piece of bluish or brownish stiff paper or cardboard only slightly larger than the stamp which was attached to the document by a small piece of metal. Three dies exist of the 3p; two of the 4p, 6p, 1sh, 1sh 6p, 2sh and 2sh 3p.

All of these stamps have the word "America" somewhere in the design and this is the feature which distinguishes them from the other British revenues. The stamps of the general issue are occasionally found with a design of a British revenue stamp struck over the American design, as a number of them were afterwards re-struck and used elsewhere as British revenues.

These stamps are sometimes called the "Teaparty" or "Tax on Tea" stamps. This, however, is a misnomer, as the act under which these stamps were issued laid no tax on tea. The tax on tea was levied by an act passed two years later, and the duties imposed by that act were not collected by stamps.

It must be remembered that these stamps were issued under an act applicable to all of the British colonies in America which included many which are not now part of the United States. Copies have been seen which were used in Quebec, Nova Scotia and in the West Indies. So great was the popular clamor against taxation by a body in which the colonists had no representation that ships bringing the stamps from England were not allowed to land them in some of the colonies, the stamps were destroyed in others, and in practically all of those which are now a part of the United States the "Stamp Masters" who were to administer the act were forced to resign and to take oath that they would never carry out the duties of the offices. Notwithstanding the very general feeling about these stamps there is evidence that a very small number of them were actually used on ships' documents for one vessel clearing from New York and for a very small number of vessels clearing from the Savannah River. Florida was at this time under military government and the only known copy of these stamps used in what is now the United States, a 4p (#RM25), was used there.

III. ISSUES OF THE UNITED STATES
A. FIRST FEDERAL ISSUE
Act of July 6, 1797
In effect July 1, 1798-February 28, 1801

The distinguishing feature of the stamps of this issue is the name of a state in the design. These stamps were issued by the Federal Government, however, and not by the states. The design, with the exception of the name of the state, was the same for each denomination; but different denominations had the shield and the eagle in different positions. The design of only one denomination of these stamps is illustrated.

In addition to the eagle and shield design on the values from four cents to ten dollars there are two other stamps for each state, similar in design to one another, one of which is illustrated. All of these stamps are embossed without color.

Prices are for clearly impressed examples.

RM45	4c	Connecticut	21.00
RM46	10c	Connecticut	21.00
RM47	20c	Connecticut	160.00
RM48	25c	Connecticut	25.00
RM49	30c	Connecticut	—
RM50	50c	Connecticut	125.00
RM51	75c	Connecticut	—
RM52	$1	Connecticut	750.00
RM54	$4	Connecticut	—
RM58	4c	Delaware	90.00
RM59	10c	Delaware	135.00
RM60	20c	Delaware	225.00
RM61	25c	Delaware	135.00
RM62	30c	Delaware	—
RM63	50c	Delaware	250.00
RM64	75c	Delaware	—
RM65	$1	Delaware	—
RM71	4c	Georgia	135.00
RM72	10c	Georgia	55.00
RM73	20c	Georgia	—
RM74	25c	Georgia	65.00
RM75	30c	Georgia	—
RM76	50c	Georgia	120.00
RM77	75c	Georgia	—
RM78	$1	Georgia	—
RM84	4c	Kentucky	15.00
RM85	10c	Kentucky	15.00
RM86	20c	Kentucky	145.00
RM87	25c	Kentucky	15.00
RM88	30c	Kentucky	475.00
RM89	50c	Kentucky	90.00
RM90	75c	Kentucky	70.00
RM91	$1	Kentucky	—
RM97	4c	Maryland	32.50
RM98	10c	Maryland	11.00
RM99	20c	Maryland	175.00
RM100	25c	Maryland	11.00
RM101	30c	Maryland	325.00
RM102	50c	Maryland	25.00
RM103	75c	Maryland	25.00
RM104	$1	Maryland	375.00
RM106	$4	Maryland	—
RM110	4c	Massachusetts	8.00
RM111	10c	Massachusetts	8.00
RM112	20c	Massachusetts	75.00
RM113	25c	Massachusetts	8.00
RM114	30c	Massachusetts	—
RM115	50c	Massachusetts	50.00
RM116	75c	Massachusetts	160.00
RM117	$1	Massachusetts	90.00
RM123	4c	New Hampshire	25.00
RM124	10c	New Hampshire	25.00
RM125	20c	New Hampshire	75.00
RM126	25c	New Hampshire	32.50
RM127	30c	New Hampshire	190.00
RM128	50c	New Hampshire	110.00
RM129	75c	New Hampshire	100.00
RM130	$1	New Hampshire	425.00
RM136	4c	New Jersey	250.00
RM137	10c	New Jersey	135.00
RM138	20c	New Jersey	—
RM139	25c	New Jersey	100.00
RM140	30c	New Jersey	425.00
RM141	50c	New Jersey	250.00
RM142	75c	New Jersey	—
RM143	$1	New Jersey	—
RM147	$10	New Jersey	—
RM149	4c	New York	25.00
RM150	10c	New York	15.00
RM151	20c	New York	25.00
RM152	25c	New York	10.00
RM153	30c	New York	18.00
RM154	50c	New York	22.50
RM155	75c	New York	55.00
RM156	$1	New York	110.00
RM157	$2	New York	—
RM159	$5	New York	—
RM160	$10	New York	—
RM162	4c	North Carolina	27.50
RM163	10c	North Carolina	22.50
RM164	20c	North Carolina	300.00

RM165	25c	North Carolina	40.00
RM166	30c	North Carolina	—
RM167	50c	North Carolina	110.00
RM168	75c	North Carolina	150.00
RM169	$1	North Carolina	275.00
RM175	4c	Pennsylvania	30.00
RM176	10c	Pennsylvania	17.50
RM177	20c	Pennsylvania	22.50
RM178	25c	Pennsylvania	17.50
RM179	30c	Pennsylvania	20.00
RM180	50c	Pennsylvania	17.50
RM181	75c	Pennsylvania	17.50
RM182	$1	Pennsylvania	70.00
RM187		Pennsylvania, "Ten cents per centum"	—
RM188	4c	Rhode Island	30.00
RM189	10c	Rhode Island	25.00
RM190	20c	Rhode Island	90.00
RM191	25c	Rhode Island	45.00
RM192	30c	Rhode Island	225.00
RM193	50c	Rhode Island	100.00
RM194	75c	Rhode Island	325.00
RM195	$1	Rhode Island	165.00
RM201	4c	South Carolina	45.00
RM202	10c	South Carolina	35.00
RM203	20c	South Carolina	—
RM204	25c	South Carolina	75.00
RM205	30c	South Carolina	—
RM206	50c	South Carolina	90.00
RM207	75	South Carolina	425.00
RM208	$1	South Carolina	—
RM211	$5	South Carolina	—
RM214	4c	Tennessee	165.00
RM215	10c	Tennessee	70.00
RM216	20c	Tennessee	—
RM217	25c	Tennessee	185.00
RM218	30c	Tennessee	—
RM219	50c	Tennessee	475.00
RM220	75c	Tennessee	—
RM221	$1	Tennessee	—
RM227	4c	Vermont	50.00
RM228	10c	Vermont	25.00
RM229	20c	Vermont	165.00
RM230	25c	Vermont	40.00
RM231	30c	Vermont	135.00
RM232	50c	Vermont	110.00
RM233	75c	Vermont	375.00
RM234	$1	Vermont	750.00
RM238	$10	Vermont	—
RM240	4c	Virginia	17.50
RM241	10c	Virginia	15.00
RM242	20c	Virginia	65.00
RM243	25c	Virginia	17.50
RM244	30c	Virginia	250.00
RM245	50c	Virginia	25.00
RM246	75c	Virginia	25.00
RM247	$1	Virginia	—

The Act calls for a $2, $4, $5 and $10 stamp for each state, only the listed ones have been seen.

The Act also calls for a "Ten cents per centum" and a "Six mills per dollar" stamp for each state, none of which has been seen except RM187.

A press and a set of dies, one die for each denomination, were prepared and sent to each state where it was the duty of the Supervisors of the Revenue to stamp all documents presented to them upon payment of the proper tax. The Supervisors were also to have on hand for sale blank paper stamped with the different rates of duty to be sold to the public upon which the purchaser could later write or print the proper type of instrument corresponding with the value of the stamp impressed thereon. So far as is now known there was no distinctive watermark for the paper sold by the government. The Vermont set of dies is in the Vermont Historical Society at Montpelier.

B. SECOND FEDERAL ISSUE
Act of April 23, 1800
In effect March 1, 1801-June 30, 1802

	(a)Government watermark in italics; laid paper	(b)Government watermark in Roman; wove paper	(c)No Government watermark
RM260	4c	15.00	15.00	50.00
RM261	10c	15.00	15.00	50.00
RM262	20c	55.00	50.00	85.00
RM263	25c	15.00		17.50
RM264	30c	15.00	15.00	500.00
RM265	50c	37.50	55.00	500.00
RM266	75c	55.00	45.00	85.00
RM267	$1	30.00	40.00	100.00
RM269	$4	100.00	120.00	90.00
RM271	$10			500.00
			500.00	

The distinguishing feature of this issue is the counter stamp, the left stamp shown in the illustration which usually appears on a document below the other stamp. In the right stamp the design of the eagle and the shield are similar to their design in the same denomination of the First Federal

Issue but the name of the state is omitted and the denomination appears below instead of above the eagle and the shield. All of these stamps were embossed without color.

All the paper which was furnished by the government contained the watermark vertically along the edge of the sheet, "GEN STAMP OFFICE", either in Roman capitals on wove paper or in italic capitals on laid paper. The wove paper also had in the center of each half sheet either the watermark "W. Y. & Co." or "Delaware". William Young & Co. who owned the Delaware Mills made the government paper. The laid paper omitted the watermark "Delaware". The two stamps were separately impressed. The design of the eagle and shield differed in each value.

All the stamping was done in Washington, the right stamp being put on in the General Stamp Office and the left one or counter stamp in the office of the Commissioner of the Revenue as a check on the stamping done in the General Stamp Office. The "Com. Rev. C. S." in the design of the counter stamp stands for "Commissioner of the Revenue, Counter Stamp."

The Second Federal issue was intended to include $2 and $5 stamps, but these denominations have not been seen.

C. THIRD FEDERAL ISSUE
Act of August 2, 1813
In effect January 1, 1814-December 31, 1817

		a.Watermark	b.Unwmkd.
RM275	5c	10.00	15.00
RM276	10c	10.00	10.00
RM277	25c	10.00	10.00
RM278	50c	10.00	10.00
RM279	75c	13.00	17.50
RM280	$1	13.00	27.50
RM281	$1.50	13.00	32.50
RM282	$2	27.50	27.50
RM283	$2.50	27.50	55.00
RM284	$3.50	65.00	45.00
RM285	$4		110.00
RM286	$5	37.50	50.00

The distinguishing features of the stamps of this issue are the absence of the name of a state in the design and the absence of the counter stamp. Different values show different positions of the eagle.

All stamps of this issue were embossed without color at Washington. The paper with the watermark "Stamp U. S." was sold by the government. Unwatermarked paper may be either wove or laid.

IV. ISSUES BY VARIOUS STATES
A. DELAWARE
Act of June 19, 1973
In effect October 1, 1793-February 7, 1794

EP50   EP51

EP53

RM291	EP50	5c	850.00
RM292	EP51	20c	1,100.—
RM294	EP53	50c	

In some cases a reddish ink was used in impressing the stamp and in other cases the impressions are colorless.
Besides the denominations listed, 3c, 33c, and $1 stamps were called for by the taxing act. Stamps of these denominations have not been seen.

B. VIRGINIA
Act of February 20, 1813
In effect May 1, 1813-April 30, 1815 Act of
December 21, 1814
In effect May 1, 1815-February 27, 1816

EP60

EP61

			a. Die cut	b. On Document
RM305	EP61	4c	17.50	—
RM306	EP60	6c	17.50	—
RM307	EP61	10c		—
RM308	EP60	12c	17.50	—
RM309	EP61	20c		—
RM310	EP61	25c	17.50	125.00
RM311	EP61	37c	17.50	—
RM312	EP61	45c		—
RM313	EP61	50c	17.50	—
RM314	EP61	70c		—
RM315	EP61	75c	17.50	—
RM316	EP61	95c		—
RM317	EP61	100c	—	—
RM318	EP61	120c		—
RM319	EP61	125c	17.50	—
RM323	EP60	175c	17.50	—
RM325	EP61	200c	17.50	—

All of these stamps are colorless impressions and with some exceptions as noted below those issued the 1813 Act cannot be distinguished from those issued under the 1814 Act. The 10c, 20c, 45c, 70c, 95c, 120c, 145c, 150c, 170c and 190c denominations were issued only under the 1813 Act and the 6c, 12c, and 37c denominations were issued only under the 1814 Act. The other denominations were common to both Acts.

RM311, the 37c denomination, has the large lettering of EP60 but the 37 is to the left and the XXXVII to the right as in EP61. The design of the dogwood branch and berries is similar but not identical in all values.

When the tax on the document exceeded "two hundred cents", two or more stamps were impressed or attached to the document. For instance a document has been seen with RM312 and RM325 both impressed on it to make up the $2.45 rate, and another with RM315 and RM325.

Since both the Virginia and the Third Federal Acts to some extent taxed the same kind of document, and since during the period from an. 1, 1814, to Feb. 27, 1816, both Acts were in effect in Virginia, some instruments have both Virginia and Third Federal stamps on them.

The circular die cut Virginia stamps about 29mm. in diameter were cut out of previously stamped paper which after the Act was repealed, was presented for redemption at the office of the Auditor of Public Accounts. They were threaded on fine

twine and until recently preserved in his office as required by law. Watermarked die cut Virginia stamps are all cut out of Third Federal watermarked paper.

Besides the denominations listed, 145c, 150c, and 170c stamps were called for by the 1813 Act, and a 195c by both the 1813 and 1814 Acts. Stamps of these four denominations have not been seen.

C. MARYLAND
1. Act of February 11, 1818
In effect May 1, 1818-March 7, 1819

EP70

RM362	EP70	30c red (printed), unused	150.00
		Sheet of 4, unused	700.00

The Act called for six other denominations, none of which has been seen. The Act imposing this tax was held unconstitutional by the United States Supreme Court in the case of McCulloch vs. Maryland.

2. Act of March 10, 1845
In effect May 10, 1845-March 10, 1856

EP71

RM370	EP71	10c	8.00
RM371	EP71	15c	6.00
RM372	EP71	25c	6.00
RM373	EP71	50c	6.00
RM374	EP71	75c	6.00
RM375	EP71	$1	6.00
RM376	EP71	$1.50	12.00
RM377	EP71	$2	15.00
RM378	EP71	$2.50	15.00
RM379	EP71	$3.50	35.00
RM380	EP71	$4	60.00
RM381	EP71	$5.50	35.00
RM382	EP71	$6	35.00

Nos. RM370-RM382 are embossed without color with a similar design for each value. They vary in size from 20 mm. in diameter for the 10c to 33 mm. for the $6.

V. FEDERAL LICENSES TO SELL LIQUOR, ETC.
1. Act of June 5, 1794
In effect September 1, 1794-June 30, 1802

EP80

RM400	EP80	$5	350.00

Provisionals are in existence using the second issue Connecticut Supervisors' stamp with the words "Five Dollars" written or printed over it or the second issue of the New Hampshire Supervisors' stamp without the words "Five Dollars".

2. Act of August 2, 1813
In effect January 1, 1814-December 31, 1817

EP81

RM451	EP81	$10	375.00
RM452	EP81	$12	300.00
RM453	EP81	$15	250.00
RM454	EP81	$18	275.00
RM455	EP81	$20	275.00
RM456	EP81	$22.50	300.00
RM457	EP81	$25	250.00
RM458	EP81	$30	—
RM459	EP81	$37.50	325.00

The Act of December 23, 1814, increased the basic rates of $10, $12, $15, $20 and $25 by 50 per cent, effective February 1, 1815. This increase applied to the unexpired portions of the year so far as licenses then in effect were concerned and these licenses were required to be brought in and to have the payment of the additional tax endorsed on them.

VI. FEDERAL LICENSES TO WORK A STILL
Act of July 24, 1813
In effect January 1, 1814-December 31, 1817

(Embossed)
EP82

(Printed)
EP83

		a. Embossed	b. Printed
RM466	4½c		800.00
RM468	9c	550.00	
RM471	18c	—	375.00
RM480	52c	350.00	
RM488	$1.08	350.00	

The statute under which these were issued provided for additional rates of 2½c, 5c, 10c, 16c, 21c, 25c, 26c, 32c, 35c, 36c, 42c, 50c, 54c, 60c, 64c, 70c, 84c, $1.04, $1.05, $1.20, $1.35, $1.40, $2.10, $2.16 and $2.70 per gallon of the capacity of the still. Stamps of these denominations have not been seen.

VII. SUPERVISORS' AND CUSTOM HOUSE SEALS
1. Supervisors' Seals Act of March 3, 1791.
In effect July 1, 1792-March 2, 1799.

EP90

		Check Letter	State	
RM501	EP90	"B"	South Carolina	30.00
RM503	EP90	"D"	Virginia	—
RM506	EP90	"G"	Pennsylvania	70.00
RM508	EP90	"I"	New York	22.50
RM509	EP90	"K"	Connecticut	25.00
RM510	EP90	"L"	Rhode Island	75.00
RM511	EP90	"M"	Massachusetts	22.50
RM512	EP90	"N"	New Hampshire	
RM514	EP90	"P"	Kentucky	—

2. Supervisors' Seals Act of March 2, 1799
In effect from March 2, 1799

EP91

RM552	EP91	North Carolina	—
RM553	EP91	Virginia	
RM554	EP91	Maryland	50.00
RM556	EP91	Pennsylvania	—
RM558	EP91	New York	22.50
RM559	EP91	Connecticut	22.50
RM560	EP91	Rhode Island	27.50
RM561	EP91	Massachusetts	22.50
RM562	EP91	New Hampshire	70.00

3. Custom House Seals

EP92

| RM575 | EP92 | Custom House, Philadelphia | 60.00 |

Although no value is expressed in the Supervisors' and Custom House seals, and they do not evidence the payment of a tax in the same way that the other stamps do, some collectors of stamped paper include them in their collections if they are on instruments evidencing the payment of a tax. They were all embossed without color and, as to Supervisors' seals issued under the Act of 1791, the only difference in design is that at the left of the eagle there was a different check letter for each state. Custom House seals used in the other cities are in existence, but, in view of the doubtful status of Custom House seals as revenue stamps, it is not proposed to list them.

REVENUE STAMPED PAPER

These stamps were printed in various denominations and designs on checks, drafts, receipts, insurance policies, bonds, stock certificates, etc. They were authorized by Act of Congress of July 1, 1862, effective Oct. 1, 1862, and were used until July 1, 1882, except for the Spanish-American War series of 1898.

Most of these stamps were lithographed; some were engraved. They were printed by private firms under supervision of government representatives from stones or dies loaned by the Bureau of Internal Revenue. Types A-F were printed by, or the stones originated with, the American Phototype Co., New York (1865-75); type G, American Graphic Co., New York (1875); types H-L, Joseph R. Carpenter, Philadelphia (1869-75); types M-N, Bureau of Engraving and Printing (1874); type O, St. Louis Lithograph Co., St. Louis.

Samples of these stamps were produced with special dies for types B-G and P. For each sample die a section of the design was removed and replaced by the word "Sample." Types G and P-W exist with a redemption clause added by typography or rubber stamp.

Multiples or single impressions on various plain papers are usually considered proofs or printers' waste.

For further information see "Handbook for United States Revenue Stamped Paper," published (1979) by the American Revenue Association.

Illustration size varies, with actual size quoted for each type.

Prices for types A-O are for clear impressions on plain entire checks and receipts. Attractive documents with vignettes sell for more. Prices for types P-W are for stamps on documents with attractive engravings, usually stock certificates, bonds and insurance policies. Examples on plain documents and cut squares sell for less.

Type A

Size: 22x25mm.

				Unused	Used
RN—A1	A	2c	black	65.00	50.00
	a.		Printed on both sides		30.00
RN—A2	A	2c	orange		100.00
RN—A8	A	2c	purple (shades)		750.00
RN—A9	A	2c	green		600.00

Same Type with 1 Entire and 53 to 57 Partial Impressions in Vertical Format ("Tapeworm")

				Full Document	Strip with Bank Names
RN—A10A		2c	orange, 56 partial impressions	900.00	150.00
	a.		53 partial impressions	1,100.	250.00
	b.		54 partial impressions	1,250.	350.00
	d.		57 partial impressions	1,250.	350.00
			Cut square, stamp only		50.00

No. RN-A10 was used by the Mechanics' National Bank of New York on a bank specie clerk's statement. It was designed so that the full stamp or one of the repeated bottom segments fell on each line opposite the name of a bank.

Eagle Type B

Size: 31x48mm.

RN—B1	B	2c	orange	3.00	1.00
			yellow orange	3.00	1.00
			deep orange	3.00	1.00
	a.		Printed on both sides	—	20.00
	b.		Double impression	350.00	
	c.		Printed on back	300.00	—
	d.		With 10 centimes blue French handstamp, right	300.00	
RN—B2	B	2c	black	65.00	30.00
			slate	75.00	35.00

RN—B3	B	2c	blue	75.00	25.00
			light blue	75.00	15.00
RN—B4	B	2c	brown	—	45.00
RN—B5	B	2c	bronze	65.00	25.00
RN—B6	B	2c	green (shades)	75.00	20.00
RN—B7	B	2c	yellow	6.00	2.50
RN—B10B		2c	red	75.00	20.00
			pale red	75.00	15.00
RN—B11B		2c	purple	75.00	40.00
RN—B13B		2c	violet (shades)	85.00	50.00
	a.		2c violet brown	100.00	75.00

"Good only for checks and drafts payable at sight." in Rectangular Tablet at Base

RN—B16B		2c	orange	40.00	12.50
	a.		With 2c org. red Nevada	325.00	200.00

"Good only for checks and drafts payable at sight." in Octagonal Tablet at Base

RN—B17B		2c	orange	40.00	12.50
	a.		Tablet inverted		650.00
	b.		With 2c org. red Nevada	85.00	35.00
	c.		With 2c green Nevada	100.00	35.00
	d.		With 2c dull vio. Nevada	—	

"Good when issued for the payment of money." in Octagonal Tablet at Base

RN—B20B		2c	orange	60.00	5.00
	a.		Printed on both sides	30.00	7.50
	b.		As "a," one stamp inverted	—	

"Good when issued for the payment of money" in two lines at base in orange

RN—B23B		2c	orange		600.00

"Good when the amount does not exceed $100." in Octagonal Tablet at Base

RN—B24B		2c	orange	175.00	60.00

Washington-Type C

Size: 108x49mm.

RN—C1	C	2c	orange	5.00	2.00
			red orange	5.00	2.00
			yellow orange	5.00	2.00
			salmon	6.00	2.50
			brown orange	6.00	2.50
	a.		"Good when used . . ." vert. at left black		—
RN—C2	C	2c	brown	30.00	10.00
	a.		2c buff	30.00	10.00
RN—C5	C	2c	pale red	50.00	17.50
			red	50.00	22.50
	a.		2c pink		17.50
RN—C6	C	2c	yellow	7.50	3.00
RN—C8	C	2c	green		

"Good only for Sight Draft" in two lines in color of stamp

RN—C9	C	2c	orange, legend at lower right	75.00	35.00
RN—C11C		2c	brown, legend at lower left	75.00	35.00
RN—C13C		2c	orange, legend at lower left	40.00	15.00

"Good only for Receipt for Money Paid" in two lines in color of stamp

RN—C15C		2c	orange, legend at lower right		—
RN—C16C		2c	orange, legend at lower left		200.00

"Good when issued for the payment of money" in one line at base in color of stamp.

RN—C17C		2c	orange (shades)		300.00

"Good when issued for the/Payment of Money" in two tablets at lower left and right.

RN—C19C		2c	orange		300.00
	a.		Printed on both sides		30.00

"Good/only for Bank/Check" in 3-part Band

RN—C21C		2c	orange	50.00	10.00
			yellow		20.00
	a.		Inverted		650.00
	b.		With 2c red org. Nevada	70.00	30.00
	c.		Printed on back		—
RN—C22C		2c	brown	—	22.50
	a.		Printed on back		125.00
RN—C23C		2c	red		650.00

"Good when the amount does not exceed $100" in tablet at lower right.

RN—C26C		2c	orange		175.00

Franklin Type D

Size: 80x43mm.

RN—D1	D	2c	orange (shades)	2.00	60
	a.		Double impression		
	b.		Printed on back	—	300.00
	c.		Inverted		350.00
RN—D2	D	2c	yellow	10.00	4.00
RN—D3	D	2c	brown	7.50	3.00
			light brown	7.50	3.00
	a.		2c buff	7.50	3.00
RN—D5	D	2c	red		

"Good only for/Bank Check" in panels within circles at left and right

RN—D7	D	2c	orange	20.00	7.50
	a.		Printed on back		

"Good only for/Bank Check" in two lines at lower right in color of stamp

RN—D8	D	2c	orange		325.00

See the "Information for Collectors" section at beginning of catalogue for illustrations of types of postmarks and precancels.

"Good only for Sight Draft" in two lines at lower left in color of stamp

RN—D9 D 2c orange   150.00   50.00

Franklin Type E

Size: 28x50mm.

RN—E4 E 2c orange   5.00   3.00
     a.   Double impression   350.00
     Broken die, lower   40.00   20.00
     R or L

"Good only for sight draft" in two lines at base in orange

RN—E5 E 2c orange   65.00   17.50

"Good only for/Bank Check" in colorless letters in two lines above and below portrait

RN—E7 E 2c orange   50.00   15.00

Franklin Type F

Size: 56x34mm.

RN—F1 F 2c orange   8.00   3.00
RN—F2 F 2c yellow   10.00   5.00
     a.   Inverted   —

Liberty Type G

Size: 80x48mm.

RN—G1 G 2c orange   1.25   25
     a.   Printed on back   50.00   35.00
RN—G2 G 2c yellow   10.00   10.00

Imprint: "Graphic Co., New York" at left and right in minute type

RN—G3 G 2c orange   100.00   85.00

Eagle Type H

Size: 32x50mm.

RN—H3 H 2c orange   7.50   2.00
     a.   Inverted   —
     b.   Double impression   400.00
     c.   "Good when used . . ." added in 2 lines at base, black   400.00
     d.   As "c," legend added in 1 line upward at left, black   —
     e.   As "c," legend added in 1 line horiz., black   500.00
     f.   "Good for bank check . . ." added in black   125.00

"Good for check or sight draft only" at left and right in color of stamp

RN—H5 H 2c orange   800.00

Type I
Design R2 of 1862-72 adhesive revenues
Size: 20x23mm.
"BANK CHECK"

RN—I1 R2 2c orange   175.00

"U.S. INTER. REV."

RN—I2 R2 2c orange   750.00   300.00

Washington Type J

Size: 105x40mm.
Background of medallion crosshatched, filling oval except for bust

RN—J4 J 2c orange   10.00   4.00
     pale orange   10.00   4.00
     deep orange   20.00   7.50
     a.   Double impression   —
     b.   "Good only for . . ." added vert. at left in red org.   450.00
RN—J5 J 2c red   35.00   12.00

"Good for check or sight draft only" curved, below

RN—J9 J 2c red   700.00

Background shaded below bust and at left.

RN—J11 J 2c orange   50.00   15.00

Washington Type K

Size: 84x33mm.

RN—K4 K 2c gray   35.00   7.50
     pale gray   35.00   7.50
RN—K5 K 2c brown   150.00   100.00
RN—K6 K 2c orange   15.00   7.50
RN—K8 K 2c red   275.00
RN—K11K 2c olive   175.00   150.00
     pale olive   125.00

Washington Type L

Size: 50x33mm.

RN—L1 L 2c blue (shades)   200.00   140.00
RN—L3 L 2c gray   25.00   10.00
     pale gray   25.00   10.00
RN—L4 L 2c green   300.00   225.00
     light green   300.00   225.00
RN—L5 L 2c orange   12.50   5.00
RN—L6 L 2c olive   65.00
     gray olive   30.00
RN—L10L 2c red   15.00   5.00
     a.   2c violet red   15.00   5.00
RN—L13L 2c brown   —   125.00

Washington Type M

Size: 68x37mm.

RN—M1 M 2c yellow   40.00   10.00
RN—M2 M 2c orange   35.00   7.50
     a.   Printed on back, inverted   —
RN—M3 M 2c green   225.00
RN—M4 M 2c gray   500.00

Eagle, Numeral and Monitor Type N

Size: 107x48mm.

RN—N3 N 2c orange   50.00   12.00
     a.   Printed on back   150.00   100.00
     b.   Inverted   —
RN—N4 N 2c light brown   150.00

Liberty Type O

Size: 75x35mm.

RN—O2 O 2c orange   1,000. 1,250.

Type P
Frame as Type B, Lincoln in center
Size: 32x49mm.

			Unused (full document)	Used (full document)	Cut Square
RN—P2	P	5c brown		300.00	50.00
RN—P4	P	5c yellow		40.00	6.00
RN—P5	P	5c orange	40.00	35.00	4.00
RN—P6	P	5c red (shades)	—	175.00	30.00

The 5c green, type P, only exists in combination with a 25c green or 50c green. See Nos. RN-T2, RN-V1.

Madison Type Q

Size: 28x56mm.

RN—Q1	Q	5c orange	100.00	85.00	15.00
		brownish orange	100.00	85.00	
RN—Q2	Q	5c brown			300.00

Type R
Frame as Type B, Lincoln in center
Size: 32x49mm.

RN—R2	R	10c red	—	600.00	100.00
RN—R3	R	10c orange		475.00	50.00

"Good when the premium does not exceed $10" in tablet at base

RN—R6 R 10c orange   350.00 50.00

RN—R7 R 10c orange, motto without tablet   450.00

Washington Type S

"Good when the premium does not exceed $10" in tablet at base
Size: 33x54mm.

			Unused (full doc.)	Used (full doc.)	Cut Square
RN—S1	S	10c orange no motto or tablet		4,000.	
RN—S2	S	10c orange		3,250.	250.00

Eagle Type T

Size: 33x40mm.

RN—T1	T	25c black	—		—
RN—T2	T	25c green		700.00	
RN—T3	T	25c red	150.00	75.00	7.50
RN—T4	T	25c orange	125.00	60.00	6.00
		light orange	125.00	60.00	6.00
		brown orange		70.00	7.50

RN-T2 includes a 5c green, type P, and a 25c green, type T, obliterating an RN-V4.

"Good when the premium does not exceed $50" in tablet at base

RN—T6	T	25c orange	450.00	350.00	50.00
RN—T7	T	25c org., motto without tablet		400.00	

"Good when the amount insured shall not exceed $1000" in tablet at base

RN—T8 T 25c deep orange 550.00 500.00 75.00

Franklin Type U

Size: 126x65mm.

RN—U1	U	25c orange	35.00	25.00	4.00
RN—U2	U	25c brown	45.00	30.00	5.00

"Good when the premium does not exceed $50" in tablet at lower right

			Unused (full document)	Used (full document)	Cut Square
RN—U3	U	25c orange			400.00

Tablet at lower left.

RN—U4	U	25c yellow	550.00	450.00	75.00
RN—U5	U	25c red	600.00		250.00
RN—U6	U	25c orange	500.00	400.00	60.00

Tablet at base.

RN—U7	U	25c brown		500.00	175.00
RN—U9	U	25c orange		550.00	200.00

Type V
As Type T, Lincoln in center
Size: 32x41mm.

RN—V1	V	50c green		135.00	40.00
RN—V2	V	50c brown	—	400.00	50.00
RN—V4	V	50c orange	125.00	75.00	10.00
		deep orange	125.00	75.00	10.00
RN—V5	V	50c red	600.00		200.00

RN-V1 includes a 50c green, type V, and a 5c green, type P, obliterating an RN-W2.

"Good when the amount insured shall not exceed $5000" in tablet at base

RN—V6	V	50c orange	450.00	350.00	60.00
RN—V9	V	50c red	—	500.00	
RN—V10	V	50c orange, motto without tablet		350.00	

Washington Type W

Size: 34x73mm.

			Unused (full document)	Used (full document)	Cut Square
RN—W2	W	$1 orange (shades)	125.00	65.00	10.00
RN—W4	W	$1 light brown	175.00	150.00	30.00

SPANISH-AMERICAN WAR SERIES

Many of these stamps were used for parlor car tax and often were torn in two or more parts.

Liberty Type X

1898   **Size: 68x38mm.**

			New	Used	Partial
RN—X1 X	1c	rose	500.00		50.00

			New	Used	Partial
		dark red			50.00
RN—X4 X	1c	orange	120.00		
a.		On pullman ticket	350.00		20.00
b.		As "a," printed on back			50.00
RN—X5 X	1c	green	50.00	30.00	
a.		On parlor car ticket	50.00	15.00	
b.		On pullman ticket	500.00		15.00
RN—X6 X	2c	yellow	5.00	2.00	
		pale olive		1,000.	
RN—X7 X	2c	orange	75	25	
		pale orange	75	25	
a.		Printed on back only	125.00	100.00	

			New	Used	Partial
c.		Printed on front and back	—	—	
d.		Vertical		85.00	
e.		Double impression		—	
f.		On pullman ticket	500.00	200.00	
g.		Inverted		—	

No. RN-X1 exists only as a four-part unused pullman ticket or as a used half of a two-part ticket. Nos. RN-X4a and RN-X5b exist as unused two-part tickets and as used half portions. No. RN-X7f exists as an unused four-part ticket and as a used two-piece portion with nearly complete stamp design.

CONSULAR FEE
Type of Consular Fee Stamps

1906 (?)

RN—Y1	CS1	$2	black	—

PRIVATE DIE PROPRIETARY

The extraordinary demands of the Civil War upon the Federal Treasury resulted in Congress devising and passing the Revenue Act of 1862. The Government provided revenue stamps to be affixed to boxes or packages of matches, and to proprietary medicines, perfumery, playing cards-as well as to documents, et cetera.

But manufacturers were permitted, at their expense, to have dies engraved and plates made for their exclusive use. Many were only too willing to do this because a discount or premium of from 5% to 10% was allowed on orders from the dies which often made it possible for them to undersell their competitors and too, the considerable advertising value of the stamps could not be overlooked. These are now known as private die proprietary stamps.

The face value of the stamp used on matches was determined by the number, i.e., 1c for each 100 matches or fraction thereof. Medicines and perfumery were taxed at the rate of 1c for each 25 cents of the retail price or fraction thereof up to $1 and 2c for each 50 cents or fraction above that amount. Playing cards were first taxed at the same rate but subsequently the tax was 5c for a deck of 52 cards and 10c for a greater number of cards or double decks.

The stamp tax was repealed on Mar. 3, 1883, effective July 1, 1883.

The various papers were:

a. **Old paper, 1862-71. First Issue. Hard and brittle varying from thick to thin.**
b. **Silk paper, 1871-77. Second Issue. Soft and porous with threads of silk, mostly red, blue and black, up to ¼inch in length.**
c. **Pink paper, 1877-78. Third Issue. Soft paper colored pink ranging from pale to deep shades.**
d. **Watermarked paper, 1878-83. Fourth Issue. Soft porous paper showing part of "USIR".**
e. **Experimental silk paper. Medium smooth paper, containing minute fragments of silk threads either blue alone or blue and red (infrequent), widely scattered, sometimes but a single fiber on a stamp.**

Early printings of some private die revenue stamps are on paper which appears to have laid lines.

These stamps were usually torn in opening the box or container. Prices quoted are for specimens which are damaged, but are reasonably attractive. Specimens in fine to very fine condition sell for 30% to 100% more.

PRIVATE DIE MATCH STAMPS

Arnold & Co. — RO14

Thos. Allen — RO5

Wm. Bond & Co. — RO32/RO33

1864-83   **Perf. 12**

			a. Old Paper	b. Silk Paper	c. Pink Paper	d. Wmkd. USIR 191R
A						
RO1	1c	blue, Akron Match Co.	120.00			
RO2	1c	orange, Alexander's Matches	7.00	60.00		
RO3	1c	blue, Alexander's Matches	1,250.			

			a. Old Paper	b. Silk Paper	c. Pink Paper	d. Wmkd. USIR 191R
RO4	1c	blue, Allen's, J. J., Sons				2.00
RO5	1c	green, Allen, Thos.	50.00			
RO6	1c	blue, Allen & Powers		3.50	15.00	3.00
RO7	1c	blue, Alligator Match Co.				15.00
RO8	1c	blue, Alligator Match Co. (Rouletted)				60.00
RO9	1c	black, American Fusee Co.		2.50	4.50	2.50
RO10	1c	black, American Match Co.	75.00	15.00		
RO11	3c	black, American Match Co.	325.00	90.00		
e.		Experimental silk paper	400.00			
f.		Double transfer		135.00		
RO12	1c	black, American Match Co. (Eagle)	40.00			
RO13	3c	green, American Match Co. (Rock Island)	1,500.			
RO14	1c	black, Arnold & Co.		22.50		
B						
RO15	1c	green, Bagley & Dunham				12.50
RO16	1c	blue, Barber, Geo. & O. C.	50.00			
RO17	1c	blue, Barber Match Co.	15.00	50	9.00	50
u.		1c ultramarine	135.00			
e.		Experimental silk paper	45.00			
		Double transfer	—		—	—

			a. Old Paper	b. Silk Paper	c. Pink Paper	d. Wmkd. USIR 191R
RO18	1c	blue, Barber Match Co. (Rouletted)				900.00
RO19	3c	black, Barber Match Co.	125.00	75.00		
e.		Experimental silk paper	175.00			
RO20	1c	blue, Barber & Peckham	30.00			
RO21	3c	black, Barber & Peckham	150.00			
RO22	1c	blue, Bauer & Beudel	50.00	90.00		
u.		1c ultramarine	80.00			
RO23	1c	orange, A. B. & S. (A. Beecher & Son)	4.50	40.00		
e.		Experimental silk paper	35.00			
RO24	1c	brown, Bendel, B. & Co.		2.25		275.00
RO25	12c	brown, Bendel, B. & Co.	100.00			
RO26	1c	brown, Bendel, H.		4.00	1.50	50
RO27	12c	brown, Bendel, H.	350.00			

Nos. RO26-RO27 are RO24-RO25 altered to read "H. Bendel doing business as B. Bendel & Co."

			a. Old Paper	b. Silk Paper	c. Pink Paper	d. Wmkd. USIR 191R
RO28	1c	blue, Bentz, H. & M.	20.00			
RO29	1c	black, Bent & Lea	25.00			
e.		Experimental silk paper	15.00			
		Double transfer at left				
RO30	1c	green, B. J. & Co. (Barber, Jones & Co.)		50.00		

			a. Old Paper	b. Silk Paper	c. Pink Paper	d. Wmkd. USIR 191R
RO31	1c	black, Bock, Schneider & Co.	5.00			
RO32	4c	black, Bond, Wm. & Co.	175.00			
RO33	4c	green, Bond, Wm. & Co.	90.00	100.00	10.00	

Charles
Busch — RO47

W.D. Curtis — RO68

Eichele &
Co. — RO78

Excelsior
Match — RO83

Gardner, Beer
& Co. — RO86

Charles S.
Hale — RO106

			a. Old Paper	b. Silk Paper	c. Pink Paper	d. Wmkd. USIR 191R
RO34	1c	lilac, Bousfield & Poole	80.00			
RO35	1c	black, Bousfield & Poole	10.00	3.00		
e.		Experimental silk paper	30.00			
		Double transfer	—			
RO36	3c	lilac, Bousfield & Poole	1,350.			
RO37	3c	black, Bousfield & Poole	120.00	75.00		
e.		Experimental silk paper	200.00			
RO38	1c	black, Boutell & Maynard		90.00		
RO39	1c	green, Bowers & Dunham				150.00
RO40	1c	blue, Bowers & Dunham				50.00
RO41	1c	lake, B. & N. (Brocket & Newton) die I	25.00			
RO42	1c	lake, B. & N. (Brocket & Newton) die II	4.50			

The initials "B. & N." measure 5¼mm. across the top in Die I, and 4¾mm. in Die II.

RO43	1c	black, Brown & Durling	800.00			
RO44	1c	green, Brown & Durling	50.00			
RO45	1c	black, Buck, L. W. & Co.	600.00			
e.		Experimental silk paper	400.00			
RO46	1c	black, Burhans, D. & Co.	100.00	1,000.		
e.		Experimental silk paper	350.00			
RO47	1c	black, Busch, Charles				15.00
RO48	1c	black, Byam, Carlton & Co., (41x75mm.) (Two heads to left) (Imperf.)	1,300.			
RO49	1c	black, Byam, Carlton & Co., (19x23mm.)	20.00	3.00		40
e.		Experimental silk paper	35.00			

			a. Old Paper	b. Silk Paper	c. Pink Paper	d. Wmkd. USIR 191R
i.		Imperf. horizontally (pair)				150.00
		Double transfer				—
RO50	1c	black, Byam, Carlton & Co., 2 heads to left, buff wrapper, 131x99 mm.	1,100.			
RO51	1c	black, Byam, Carlton & Co., 2 heads to left, buff wrapper 131x89 mm.	150.00			
RO52	1c	black, Byam, Carlton & Co., 1 head to right, white wrapper (94x54mm.)	50.00			
RO53	1c	black, Byam, Carlton & Co., 1 head to right, buff wrapper (94x54mm.)	125.00			
RO54	1c	black, Byam, Carlton & Co., 2 heads to right, buff wrapper (81x50mm.)	5.00			
h.		Right block reading up	20.00			
RO55	1c	black, Byam, Carlton & Co., 1 head to left, white wrapper (94x56mm.)	17.50			
RO56	1c	black, Byam, Carlton & Co., 2 heads to left, buff wrapper (95x57mm.)	2.25			

C

RO57	1c	green, Cannon Match Co.				15.00
RO58	1c	lake, Cardinal Match Co.				4.00
RO59	1c	lake, C., F.E. (Frank E. Clark)	50.00	50.00		
e.		Experimental silk paper	50.00			
RO60	3c	black, Chicago Match Co.	150.00			
RO61	1c	green, Clark, Henry A.		50.00		
RO62	1c	green, Clark, James L.		60	15.00	60
		Double transfer				—
RO63	1c	green, Clark, James L. (Rouletted)				275.00
RO64	1c	lake, Clark Match Co.				4.00
RO65	1c	black, Cramer & Kemp	22.50			
RO66	1c	blue, Cramer & Kemp	50.00	3.00		
e.		Experimental silk paper	125.00			
u.		1c ultramarine	150.00			
RO67	1c	black, Crown Match Co				15.00
RO68	1c	green, Curtis, W.D.	100.00	75.00		
e.		Experimental silk paper	110.00			

D

RO69	1c	black, Davis, G.W.H.		35.00		
RO70	1c	carmine, Davis, G.W.H.				30.00
RO71	1c	blue, Doolittle, W.E.	225.00			
RO72	1c	green, Dunham, E.P.				50.00

E

RO73	1c	black, Eaton, James	25.00	85	7.00	85
e.		Experimental silk paper	65.00			
RO74	1c	black, Eaton, James (Rouletted)				35.00
RO75	1c	carmine, Eddy, E.B., die I				8.00
r.		Die II				25.00

Die II shows eagle strongly recut; ribbon across bottom is narrower; color is deeper.

RO76	1c	black, Eichele, Aug.	45.00			
RO77	1c	blue, Eichele, P., & Co.	45.00	4.50		
u.		1c ultramarine	160.00			
e.		Experimental silk paper	70.00			
RO78	1c	blue, Eichele & Co.		2.00	10.00	1.50
RO79	1c	blue, Eichele & Co. (Rouletted)				125.00
RO80	1c	blue, Eisenhart, J.W.		27.50	60.00	17.50

			a. Old Paper	b. Silk Paper	c. Pink Paper	d. Wmkd. USIR 191R
RO81	1c	black, Excelsior M. Co., Watertown		65.00		
RO82	1c	black, Excelsior M. Co., Syracuse		4.00	8.50	4.00
RO83	1c	blue, Excelsior Match, Baltimore	35.00	70.00		
u.		1c ultramarine	160.00			

F

| RO84 | 1c | black, Farr, G., & Co. | 50.00 | | | |
| RO85 | 1c | brown, Frank, L. | | 40.00 | | |

G

RO86	1c	black, Gardner, Beer & Co.				90.00
RO87	1c	black, Gates, Wm. die 1	4.00	2.50		
RO88	1c	black, Gates, Wm. die 2	25.00	2.50		
		Double transfer				—
e.		Experimental silk paper	55.00			

The shirt collar is colorless in Die 1, and shaded in Die 2. Other differences exist.

RO89	3c	black, Gates, Wm.	40.00	30.00		
e.		Experimental silk paper	125.00			
		Double transfer		65.00		
RO90	6c	black, Gates, Wm.	75.00			
RO91	3c	black, Gates, Wm. (three 1c stamps)		80.00		
RO92	1c	black, Gates, Wm., Sons		15.00	4.00	50
RO93	1c	black, Gates, Wm., Sons (Rouletted)				850.00
RO94	3c	black, Gates, Wm., Sons (three 1c stamps)		75.00	110.00	60.00
RO95	1c	green, Goldback, A. & Co.		25.00		
RO96	1c	green, Goldback, A.		50.00	1,750.	
RO97	1c	black, Gorman, T. & Bro.	200.00			
		Double transfer	—			
RO98	1c	green, Gorman, T. & Bro.	20.00	13.00		
		Double transfer	—			
RO99	1c	green, Gorman, Thomas		2.75	15.00	35.00
RO100	1c	green, Greenleaf & Co.	50.00	50.00		
RO101	3c	carmine, Greenleaf & Co.	75.00	110.00		
RO102	5c	orange, Greenleaf & Co.	100.00	900.00		
RO103	1c	black, Griggs & Goodwill		20.00		
RO104	1c	green, Griggs & Goodwill		8.50		
		Double transfer		—		
RO105	1c	black, Griggs & Scott	5.00	25.00		
e.		Experimental silk paper	35.00			

H

RO106	1c	green, Hale, Charles S.		100.00		
RO107	1c	blue, Henning & Bonhack	85.00			
RO108	1c	red, Henry, W.E. & Co.				20.00
RO109	1c	black, Henry, W.E. & Co.				5.00
RO110	1c	green, Hotchkiss, J.G.		4.00	30.00	6.00
RO111	1c	lake, Howard, B. & H.D.	65.00			
RO112	1c	blue, Howard, B. & H.D.	6.00			
u.		1c ultramarine	90.00			
RO113	1c	black, Hunt, L.G.	125.00	600.00		
e.		Experimental silk paper	100.00			
RO114	1c	lake, Hutchinson, D.F., Jr.				8.00

I

RO115	1c	blue, Ives Matches	3.50	3.50		
u.		1c ultramarine	75.00			
		Double transfer				—
RO116	1c	blue, Ives, P.T.		2.50	15.00	2.50
RO117	1c	blue, Ives, P.T. (Rouletted)				200.00
RO118	8c	blue, Ives, P.T.	80.00			
u.		8c ultramarine	450.00			
RO119	1c	green, Ives & Judd		8.00	30.00	65.00
RO120	1c	green, Ives & Judd Match Co.		65.00		
		Double transfer		200.00		

		a. Old Paper	b. Silk Paper	c. Pink Paper	d. Wmkd. USIR 191R

———— K ————

RO121	1c	green, Kirby & Sons		30.00	
RO122	1c	black, Kyle, W.S.	10.00	6.00	
		Double transfer	—		

———— L ————

RO123	1c	black, Lacour's Matches	10.00	35.00	
	e.	Experimental silk paper	50.00		
RO124	1c	green, Leeds, Robinson & Co.			45.00
RO125	1c	blue, Leigh, H.			4.50
RO126	1c	black, Leigh & Palmer	20.00	45.00	30.00
RO127	1c	blue, Loehr, John	15.00		
RO128	1c	blue, Loehr, Joseph	1.50	8.00	1.75

———— M ————

RO129	1c	black, Macklin, J.J. & Co. (Rouletted)	3,500.		
RO130	1c	blue, Mansfield, F. & Co.	2.50	5.00	6.50
RO131	1c	blue, Maryland M. Co.	70.00		2,500.
RO132	1c	blue, Matches, (head Franklin)	2.25	2.00	
	u.	1c ultramarine	*150.00*		
		Double transfer	80.00		
	e.	Experimental silk paper	50.00		
RO133	1c	black, Messinger, A.		1.00	8.00	1.00

———— N ————

RO134	1c	blue, National M. Co.			50.00
RO135	1c	lake, Newton, F.P.		1.00	4.50	1.00
RO136	1c	blue, N.Y. Match Co. (Shield)	125.00	4.00	
RO137	1c	vermilion, N.Y. Match Co. (Eagle)	45.00	2,500.	
	e.	Experimental silk paper	110.00		
RO138	1c	green, N.Y. Match Co. (Size 22x60mm.)	25.00	4.00	
	e.	Experimental silk paper	30.00		
RO139	5c	blue, N.Y. Match Co. (Size 22x60mm.)		950.00	
RO140	4c	green, N. & C. (Newbauer & Co.)		2.50	85.00	2.50

———— O ————

| RO141 | 1c | blue, Orono Match Co. | 20.00 | 20.00 | |
| | u. | 1c ultramarine | 200.00 | | |

———— P ————

RO142	1c	green, Park City Match Co.	30.00	30.00	
	e.	Experimental silk paper	85.00		
RO143	3c	orange, Park City Match Co.	30.00		
RO144	1c	blue, Penn Match Co.			25.00
RO145	1c	green, Pierce Match Co.	1,000.		
RO146	1c	black, P.M. Co. (Portland M. Co.)	20.00		
RO147	1c	black, Portland M. Co. (wrapper)	45.00		

Price of No. RO147 applies to commonest date (Dec. 1866); all others are much rarer.

RO148	1c	blue, Powell, V.R.	2.50	6.00	
	u.	1c ultramarine	150.00		
	e.	Experimental silk paper	40.00		
		Double transfer	—		

Ives & Judd Match Co. — RO120

Leeds, Robinson & Co. — RO124

"Matches" RO132

Standard Match Co. — RO170

RO149	1c	black, Powell, V.R. (buff wrapper) uncut	1,500.		
RO150	1c	black, Powell, V. R. (buff wrapper) cut to shape	650.00		
RO151	1c	black, Powell, V. R. (white wrapper) cut to shape	1,000.		

———— R ————

RO152	1c	black, Reading M. Co.			5.00
RO153	1c	black, Reed & Thompson			4.50
RO154	1c	red, Richardson, D. M.	80.00		
RO155	1c	black, Richardson, D. M.	2.50	1.50	
	e.	Experimental silk paper	25.00		
		Double transfer		30.00	
RO156	3c	vermilion, Richardson, D.M.	90.00		
RO157	3c	blue, Richardson, D. M.	3.50	2.00	
	e.	Experimental silk paper	30.00		
RO158	1c	black, Richardson Match Co.		75	3.50	75
RO159	3c	blue, Richardson Match Co.	55.00		
RO160	1c	blue, Roeber, H. & W.	6.00	1.50	
	u.	1c ultramarine	75.00		
		Double transfer	175.00		
RO161	1c	blue, Roeber, Wm.		1.25	4.00	1.25
RO162	1c	blue, Roeber, Wm. (Rouletted)			80.00
RO163	1c	black, Russell, E. T.	3.00	9.00	
	e.	Experimental silk paper	30.00		
RO164	1c	lake, R. C. & W. (Ryder, Crouse & Welch)			40.00

———— S ————

San Francisco Match Co. — RO165

RO165	12c	blue, San Francisco Match Co.	350.00		
RO166	1c	vermilion, Schmitt & Schmittdiel		2.00	40.00	2.00
RO167	3c	blue, Schmitt & Schmittdiel	30.00		
RO168	1c	blue, Smith, E. K.	8.00	30.00	12.00
RO169	1c	blue, Smith, E. K. (Rouletted)			950.00

V.R. Powell RO148

Washington Match Co. — RO181

RO170	1c	black, Standard Match Co.			22.50
RO171	1c	black, Stanton, H.	8.00	3.50	9.50	5.00
	e.	Experimental silk paper	35.00		
RO172	1c	black, Star Match	3.00	10	25	10
	e.	Experimental silk paper	15.00		
		Double transfer	—			12.50
RO173	1c	blue, Swift & Courtney	1.25	1.25	
	u.	1c ultramarine	30.00		
	e.	Experimental silk paper	10.00		
		Double transfer	—		
RO174	1c	blue, Swift & Courtney & Beecher Co.		40	1.50	40
		Double transfer				60.00
RO175	1c	black, S. C. B. C. (Flag)				60.00

———— T ————

RO176	1c	blue, Trenton M. Co.			4.00
RO177	1c	green, T., E. R. (E. R. Tyler)	8.00	2.75	
	e.	Experimental silk paper	25.00		
		Double transfer	—		

———— U ————

RO178	1c	green, Underwood, Alex. & Co.	45.00	80.00	
	e.	Experimental silk paper	125.00		
RO179	1c	black, Union Match Co.			30.00
RO180	1c	black, U. S. M. Co. (Universal Safety M. Co.)	1.50	15.00	
	e.	Experimental silk paper	20.00		

———— W ————

RO181	1c	black, Washington Match Co.			30.00
RO182	1c	black, Wilmington Parlor Match Co.	60.00	2,500.	
	e.	Experimental silk paper	55.00		
RO183	1c	black, Wise & Co.	800.00		

———— Z ————

RO184	1c	black, Zaiss, F. & Co.		75	2.00	1.00
RO185	1c	green, Zisemann, Griesheim & Co.	500.00		
RO186	1c	blue, Zisemann, Griesheim & Co.	90.00	15.00	
		1c ultramarine	175.00		

PRIVATE DIE CANNED FRUIT STAMP

T. Kensett & Co. — RP1

1867   *Perf. 12*

| RP1 | 1c | green, Kensett, T. & Co. | 650.00 | | |

PRIVATE DIE MEDICINE STAMPS

Anglo-American Drug Co. — RS1

1862-83   *Perf. 12*

		a. Old Paper	b. Silk Paper	c. Pink Paper	d. Wmkd. USIR 191R

———— A ————

RS1	1c	black, Anglo—American Drug Co.			45.00
RS2	1c	brown, carmine, Ayer J. C. & Co. (imperf.)	*2,000.*		
RS3	1c	green, Ayer, J. C. & Co. (imperf.)	*2,000.*		
RS4	1c	black, Ayer, J. C. & Co. (imperf.)	45.00	45.00	725.00	35.00

			a. Old Paper	b. Silk Paper	c. Pink Paper	d. Wmkd. USIR 191R
		Double transfer				—
RS5	1c	blue, Ayer, J. C. & Co. (imperf.)	2,000.			
RS6	1c	orange Ayer, J. C. & Co. (imperf.)	2,000.			
RS7	1c	gray lilac, Ayer, J.C. & Co. (imperf.)	2,000.			
RS8	4c	red, Ayer, J.C. & Co. (die cut)	2,000.			
RS9	4c	blue, Ayer, J.C. & Co. (die cut)	3.00	3.00		3.00
u.		4c ultramarine (die cut)	225.00			
RS10	4c	blue, Ayer, J.C. & Co. (imperf.)	350.00	325.00		375.00
RS11	4c	purple, Ayer, J.C. & Co. (die cut)	2,500.			
RS12	4c	green, Ayer, J.C. & Co. (die cut)	1,750.			
RS13	4c	vermilion, Ayer, J.C. & Co. (die cut)	2,000.			

The 4c in black was printed and sent to Ayer & Co. It may exist but has not been seen by collectors.

B

			a. Old Paper	b. Silk Paper	c. Pink Paper	d. Wmkd. USIR 191R
RS14	4c	green, Barham, P.C. Co., wmkd. lozenges				60.00
RS15	1c	vermilion, Barnes, D.S.	100.00			
RS16	2c	vermilion, Barnes, D.S.	60.00			
RS17	4c	vermilion, Barnes, D.S.	250.00			
RS18	1c	black, Barnes, D.S.	17.50			
RS19	2c	black, Barnes, D.S.	50.00			
RS20	4c	black, Barnes, D.S.	65.00			
RS21	1c	black, Barnes, Demas	15.00			
RS22	2c	black, Barnes, Demas	40.00			
RS23	4c	black, Barnes, Demas	15.00			
RS24	1c	black, Barnes & Co., Demas	9.00	300.00		
RS25	2c	black, Barnes, Demas & Co.	5.00	250.00		
e.		Experimental silk paper	35.00			
RS26	4c	black, Barnes, Demas & Co.	5.00			
RS27	4c	black, Barr, T.H. & Co.	7.50			
		Double transfer	75.00			
RS28	2c	green, Barry's Tricopherous	9.00	10.00		
RS29	2c	green, Barry's Proprietary		2.25	95.00	3.00
		Double transfer				—
RS30	1c	lake, Bennett, D.M.	5.00			
e.		Experimental silk paper	45.00			
RS31	1c	green, Blow, W.T.	200.00	55.00	275.00	45.00
e.		Experimental silk paper	250.00			
RS32	1c	black, Brandreth, (perf.)	250.00	300.00		
RS33	1c	black, Brandreth, (imperf.)	2.00	1.50		
e.		Experimental silk paper	12.50			
RS34	1c	black, Brandreth, Allcock's (41x50 mm. imperf.)		100.00		
RS35	1c	black, Brandreth, Allcock's (24x30 mm. imperf.)		85	3.00	85
p.		Perf.				—
RS36	1c	blue, Brown, C.F.	150.00	45.00		60.00
RS37	2c	black, Brown, Fred Co. (imperf.) die I, "E" of "Fred" incomplete	85.00	45.00	800.00	45.00
e.		Experimental silk paper	150.00			
RS38	2c	black, Brown, Fred Co. (imperf.) die II, "E" of "Fred" normal		60.00		

Die II shows recutting in the "E" of "Fred" and "Genuine".

			a. Old Paper	b. Silk Paper	c. Pink Paper	d. Wmkd. USIR 191R
RS39	1c	black, Brown, John I. & Son	6.00	20.00		4.00
RS40	2c	green, Brown, John I. & Son	7.00	7.00	150.00	175.00
e.		Experimental silk paper	40.00			
		Double transfer				
RS41	4c	brown, Brown, John I. & Son	150.00	70.00		800.00
RS42	1c	black, Bull, John	100.00	10.00	275.00	8.50
e.		Experimental silk paper	150.00			
RS43	4c	blue, Bull, John	125.00	8.00	175.00	6.00

			a. Old Paper	b. Silk Paper	c. Pink Paper	d. Wmkd. USIR 191R
u.		4c ultramarine	350.00			
e.		Experimental silk paper	200.00			
RS44	1c	black, Burdsal, J.S. & Co., wrapper white paper		40.00		25.00
RS45	1c	black, Burdsal, J.S. & Co., wrapper orange paper		500.00		275.00
RS46	4c	black, Burnett, Joseph & Co.	65.00	5.00	165.00	5.00

C

			a. Old Paper	b. Silk Paper	c. Pink Paper	d. Wmkd. USIR 191R
RS47	4c	black, Campion, J.W. & Co. (imperf.)		300.00		250.00
p.		Pair, perf. horiz.				850.00
RS48	4c	black, Campion, J.W. & Co. (die cut)		120.00	175.00	70.00
RS49	4c	green, Cannon & Co. (imperf.)		75.00	200.00	55.00
RS50	1c	vermilion, Centaur Co.			40.00	5.00
RS51	2c	black, Centaur Co.			10.00	1.00
RS52	4c	black, Centaur Co.				40.00
RS53	1c	black, Chase, A.W., Son & Co.		55.00		1,500.
RS54	2c	black, Chase, A.W., Son & Co.		65.00		
RS55	4c	black, Chase, A.W., Son & Co.		95.00		
RS56	3c	blue, Clarke, Wm. E				70.00
RS57	6c	black, Clarke, Wm. E.				60.00
RS58	4c	black, Clark, R.C. & C.S. (A.B.C.)		9.00		15.00
RS59	1c	black, Collins Bros.	10.00	150.00		
RS60	1c	black, Comstock, W.H.				2.00
RS61	4c	blue, Cook & Bernheimer				75.00
RS62	1c	black, Crittenton, Chas. N.		4.00		
RS63	1c	blue, Crittenton, Chas. N.			10.00	3.50
RS64	2c	black, Crittenton, Chas. N.		50.00	25.00	3.00
RS65	4c	black, Crook, Oliver & Co.	55.00	10.00		
e.		Experimental silk paper	10.00			
RS66	1c	black, Curtis, Jeremiah, & Son, die I, small numerals	55.00			
RS67	1c	black, Curtis, Jeremiah, & Son, die II, large numerals				80.00
RS68	2c	black, Curtis, Jeremiah, & Son	8.00	8.00	80.00	150.00
		Double transfer				—
RS69	1c	black, Curtis & Brown	3.50	2.50		
RS70	2c	black, Curtis & Brown		75.00		
RS71	1c	black, Curtis & Brown Mfg. Co.			100.00	2.50
RS72	2c	black, Curtis & Brown Mfg. Co.		1,000.		450.00

D

			a. Old Paper	b. Silk Paper	c. Pink Paper	d. Wmkd. USIR 191R
RS73	2c	green, Dalley's Horse Salve	60.00	60.00		60.00
RS74	1c	black, Dalley's Pain Ext.	5.00	5.00		6.00
h.		Error, $100 instead of $1.00	250.00			7.50
RS75	1c	blue, Davis, Perry & Son	5.00	2.00	150.00	2.00
u.		1c ultramarine	65.00			
e.		Experimental silk paper	50.00			
RS76	2c	brown red, Davis, Perry & Son	90.00			

Barry's Tricopherous RS28

Dr. C.F. Brown RS36

Wm. E. Clarke — RS56

Herrick's Pills & Plasters — RS118

Holman Liver Pad Co. — RS126

			a. Old Paper	b. Silk Paper	c. Pink Paper	d. Wmkd. USIR 191R
RS77	2c	black, Davis, Perry & Son	50.00			
RS78	2c	dull purple, Davis, Perry & Son		4.50		
RS78A	2c	slate, Davis, Perry & Son		8.00		2.50
RS79	2c	dull red, Davis, Perry & Son		50.00		
RS80	2c	brown, Davis, Perry & Son		—		
RS81	4c	brown, Davis, Perry & Son	7.00	2.00		1.50
RS82	2c	black, Drake, P. H. & Co.	850.00			
RS83	4c	black, Drake, P. H. & Co.	25.00	45.00		
e.		Experimental silk paper	85.00			

F

			a. Old Paper	b. Silk Paper	c. Pink Paper	d. Wmkd. USIR 191R
RS84	1c	lake, Fahnestock, B. A. (imperf.)	100.00	85.00		
RS85	4c	black, Father Mathew T. M. Co.				3.50
RS86	1c	green, Flanders, A. H. (perf.)		10.00	—	9.00
RS87	1c	green, Flanders, A. H. (part perf.)	20.00	1.25	25.00	1.25
RS88	1c	black, Fleming Bros. (Vermifuge) (imperf.)	8.50	15.00		30.00
e.		Experimental silk paper	50.00			
RS89	1c	black, Fleming Bros. (L. Pills) (imperf.)	1,500.			
RS90	1c	blue, Fleming Bros. (L. Pills) (imperf.)	2.50	2.50		2.00
u.		1c ultramarine	150.00			
		Double transfer		40.00		40.00
RS91	4c	black, Fowle, Seth W. & Son.	10.00	2.00		3.00
i.		Vertical pair, imperf. between				—

G

			a. Old Paper	b. Silk Paper	c. Pink Paper	d. Wmkd. USIR 191R
RS92	3c	black, Green, G. G.				2.25
h.		Tete beche pair				250.00
RS93	3c	black, Green, G. G. (rouletted)				100.00

H

			a. Old Paper	b. Silk Paper	c. Pink Paper	d. Wmkd. USIR 191R
RS94	4c	black, Hall & Co. Reuben P.	15.00	14.00		16.00
RS95	1c	green, Hall & Ruckel	60	60	17.50	75
e.		Experimental silk paper	10.00			
RS96	3c	black, Hall & Ruckel	1.25	1.25	45.00	1.50
RS97	1c	black, Harter, Dr. & Co.	15.00	10.00		
e.		Experimental silk paper	60.00			
RS98	1c	black, Harter, Dr.		85	8.00	85
		Double impression				
RS99	4c	black, Hartman, S. B. & Co.	175.00	40.00	175.00	800.00
RS100	6c	black, Hartman, S. B. & Co.	200.00	150.00		
RS101	1c	black, Hazeltine, E. T.				10.00
RS102	2c	blue, Hazeltine, E. T.		22.50		
RS103	4c	black, Hazeltine, E. T.	250.00	15.00		12.00
e.		Experimental silk paper	275.00			
i.		Imperf. (pair)	800.00			
RS104	3c	black, H., E (Edward Heaton)				30.00
RS105	3c	brown, H., E. (Edward Heaton)				9.00

RS106 2c blue, Helmbold   65   175.00
  t. Double transfer   —
RS107 3c green, Helmbold   30.00   25.00
RS108 4c black, Helmbold   3.00   100.00
  Double transfer   —
RS109 6c black, Helmbold   2.00   2.50
  e. Experimental silk   15.00
RS110 2c blue, Helmbold, A. L.   85.00   100.00   85.00
RS111 4c black, Helmbold, A.L.   20.00   100.00   6.00
RS112 2c violet, Henry, John F.   150.00
RS113 4c bistre, Henry, John F.   400.00
RS114 1c black, Henry, John F.   40.00   35   3.50   35
  e. Experimental silk paper   75.00
RS115 2c blue, Henry, John F.   27.50   4.00   90.00   4.00
  u. 2c ultramarine
RS116 4c red, Henry, John F.   125.00   60   10.00   60
  e. Experimental silk paper   35.00
RS117 1c black, Herrick's Pills   60.00   25.00   60.00   25.00
  e. Experimental silk paper   110.00
RS118 1c red, Herrick's Pills & Plasters   1.00   2.50   50.00   1.25
RS119 1c black, Hetherington, J. E.   10.00
RS120 2c black, Hetherington, J. E.   250.00
RS121 3c black, Hetherington, J. E.   15.00
  i. Imperf.   175.00
RS122 2c black, Hiscox & Co.   10.00
RS123 4c black, Hiscox & Co.   75.00   150.00   950.00
RS124 1c blue, Holloway's Pills, (perf.)   6.50
RS125 1c blue, Holloway's Pills, (imperf.)   165.00
RS126 1c green, Holman Liver Pad Co.   15.00
RS127 1c green, Holman Liver Pad Co.   6.00
RS128 2c blue, Home Bitters Co.   125.00
  Double transfer   —
RS129 3c green, Home Bitters Co.   80.00   100.00   65.00
RS130 4c green, Home Bitters Co.   150.00   175.00
RS131 4c black, Hop Bitters   5.00
RS132 4c black, Hostetter & Smith (imperf.)   50.00   30.00   65.00   20.00
  Double transfer   —   —   —   —
RS133 6c black, Hostetter & Smith (imperf.)   70.00
  e. Experimental silk paper   150.00
RS134 4c black, Howe, S. D. (Duponco's Pills)   75.00   135.00
RS135 4c red, Howe, S. D. (Duponco's Pills)   225.00
RS136 4c green, Howe, S. D. (Duponco's Pills)   225.00

Nos. RS135 and RS136 were never used.

RS137 4c blue, Howe, S. D. (Arabian Milk)   4.00   110.00
RS138 1c black, Hull, C. E. & Co.   90.00   3.00   25.00   4.00
RS139 2c violet, Husband, T. J. (imperf.)   375.00
RS140 2c vermilion, Husband, T. J. (imperf.)   7.50   4.00   5.00
RS141 4c green, Hutchings & Hillyer (imperf.)   15.00   17.50
  e. Experimental silk paper   80.00

I

RS142 1c black, Ingham, H. A. & Co.   45.00

J

RS143 4c green, Jackson, J. A. & Co.   450.00   150.00
RS144 1c blue, Jayne, D. & Son (imperf.)   900.00   325.00
  p. Perf.   800.00   —
RS145 2c black, Jayne, D. & Son (imperf.)   1,500.   1,000.   700.00
  p. Perf.   2,000.   —
RS146 4c green, Jayne, D. & Son (imperf.)   1,750.   900.00   850.00   300.00
  p. Perf.   2,000.   —
RS147 1c blue, Jayne, D. & Son (die cut)   2.00   4.00   150.00   3.00
  p. Perf. and die cut   55.00
  On horizontally laid paper   —
RS148 2c black, Jayne, D. & Son (die cut)   3.50   4.00   65.00   4.50

  e. Experimental silk paper   25.00
  p. Perf. and die cut   20.00
  Double transfer   40.00   40.00   100.00   40.00
RS149 4c green, Jayne, D. & Son (die cut)   3.00   3.00   65.00   3.00
  e. Experimental silk paper   50.00
  p. Perf. and die cut   35.00
  On vertically laid paper   —
  Double transfer   —
RS150 1c vermilion, Johnson, I. S. & Co.   35   8.50   30
  Double transfer   15.00   15.00
RS151 1c black, Johnston, Holloway & Co.   2.00   2.50
RS152 2c green, Johnston, Holloway & Co.   1.25   1.25

K

RS153 4c black, Kelly, J.B. & Co. (imperf.)   1,250.
  e. Experimental silk   1,250.
RS154 4c blue, Kendall, B. J. & Co.   20.00
RS155 2c green, Kennedy, Dr.   35.00   2.50   22.50   2.50
  Double transfer
RS156 6c black, Kennedy, Dr.   4.00   50.00   4.00
RS157 2c black, Kennedy & Co.   2.50   75.00   2.50
RS158 1c green, Kennedy, (K & Co.)   3.50
RS159 4c blue, Kerr, Jas. C.   2,500.   120.00   12.00
RS160 6c black, Kerr, Jas. C.   300.00

L

RS161 4c black, Lawrence & Martin   20.00
RS162 1c blue, Lee & Osgood   6.00   7.50   8.00
RS163 4c blue, Lippman, J. & Bro.   1,000.   1,250.
  e. Experimental silk paper   1,000.
  Double transfer   35.00
RS164 1c black, Littlefield, Alvah   75   75   15.00
  e. Experimental silk paper   15.00
  Double transfer   35.00
RS165 4c green, Littlefield, Alvah   500.00   120.00
RS166 1c black, Low, Prof.   1.50   10.00   1.50
  Double transfer   —   50.00   40.00
RS167 1c black, Lyon Mfg. Co.   10.00   150.00   12.00
RS168 2c black, Lyon Mfg. Co.   4.50   100.00   4.50
  i. Vertical pair, imperf. between   500.00

M

RS169 4c black, McCullough, J.   60.00   75.00
RS170 1c black, McLean, J.H.   2.00   75   10.00   75
  e. Experimental silk paper   40.00
  i. Imperf. horizontally   —
  Double transfer   —   35.00
RS171 1c violet, Manhattan Med. Co.   20.00
  u. 1c purple   40.00
RS172 2c black, Manhattan Med. Co.   20.00   27.50   10.00
RS173 1c blue, Mansfield & Higbee   12.00
  i. Pair, imperf. between   125.00
  j. Block of four, imperf. between   120.00
RS174 1c blue, Mansfield, S. & Co.   22.50   125.00   10.00
  i. Pair, imperf. between   90.00   225.00   150.00
  j. Block of four, imperf. between   150.00   300.00   150.00

Nos. RS173-RS174 are perf. on 4 sides. The i. and j. varieties served as 2c or 4c stamps. Straightedged copies from severed pairs or blocks are worth much less.

RS175 2c blue, Marsden, T.W.   2,500.
RS176 4c black, Marsden, T.W.   225.00
RS177 2c black, Mercado & Seully (imperf.)   2,000.
RS178 1c black, Merchant's Gargling Oil   175.00   15.00   225.00   17.50
  e. Experimental silk paper   250.00
RS179 2c green, Merchant's Gargling Oil   135.00   17.50   250.00   20.00
  e. Experimental silk paper   200.00
  Double transfer, over design of RO11   —   2,000.
RS180 3c black, Mette & Kanne   250.00
RS181 4c black, Mishler Herb Bitters Co.   75.00
  p. Imperf. at ends   80.00

RS182 4c black, Moody Michel & Co. (imperf.)   125.00
RS183 1c vermilion, Moore, C. C.   3.50
RS184 2c black, Moore C.C.   50.00   2,000.   22.50
RS185 1c black, Morehead's Mag. Plaster   17.50
RS186 4c black, Morehead's Neurodyne   750.00

N

RS187 4c black, New York Pharmacal Assn.   8.50   25.00   4.00

P

RS188 6c black, Perl, Dr. M. & Co. (cut to shape)   950.00
RS189 1c green, Pierce, R.V.   10.00   110.00   20.00
RS190 2c green, Pierce, R.V.   20.00   3.00   22.50   3.50
  e. Experimental silk paper   60.00
  Double transfer   —
RS191 4c black, Pieters, Bennett & Co.   300.00   1,000.
  e. Experimental silk paper   300.00
RS192 6c black, Pieters, Bennett & Co.   850.00
  i. Imperf.

R

RS193 2c black, Radway & Co.   2.50   2.50   8.00   3.00
  e. Experimental silk paper   35.00
  Double transfer   50.00   125.00   —
RS194 1c blue, Ransom, D. & Co.   2.00   1.75
  e. Experimental silk paper   40.00
  Double transfer   —
RS195 2c black, Ransom, D. & Co.   12.50   14.00
  e. Experimental silk paper   55.00
RS196 1c blue, Ransom, D., Son & Co.   2.50   10.00   1.50
  Double transfer   —
RS197 2c black, Ransom, D., Son & Co.   8.00   50.00   7.00
RS198 1c black, Redding's Russia Salve   4.50   4.50
  Double transfer   75.00
RS199 2c blue, Ring's Veg. Ambrosia (imperf.)   1,500.
  p. Perf.   1,000.
RS200 4c black, Ring's Veg. Ambrosia (imperf.)   1,000.   950.00
RS201 2c blue, Ring's Veg. Ambrosia (die cut)   15.00
RS202 4c black, Ring's Veg. Ambrosia (die cut)   10.00   10.00   15.00
  e. Experimental silk paper   55.00
RS203 4c black, Ring's Veg. Ambrosia (perf.)   900.00   950.00
  k. Perf. and die cut   —
  p. Part perf.   1,000.
RS204 2c black, Rose, J.B. & Co.   2.50   20.00   2,250.
  Double transfer   40.00   —
RS205 4c black, Rose, J.B. & Co.   85.00
  Double transfer   —
RS206 2c green, Rumford Chemical Works   2.25
RS207 2c green, Rumford Chemical Works (imperf.)   17.50

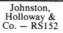

Johnston, Holloway & Co. — RS152

S. Mansfield & Co. — RS174

New York Pharmacal Association — RS187

Merchant's Gargling Oil — RS178

Redding's Russia Salve RS198

J.B. Rose & Co. RS205

Seabury & Johnson — RS216

			a. Old Paper	b. Silk Paper	c. Pink Paper	d. Wmkd. USIR 191R
RS222	8c	black, Seelye, D.H. & Co. (imperf.)	8.50			
RS223	1c	black, Simmons, M.A., Iuka, Miss.		60.00		2,000.
RS224	1c	black, Simmons, M.A., St. Louis, Mo.		85.00		
RS225	4c	black, Smith, S.N. & Co.		27.50		22.50
RS226	1c	blue, Soule, E.L. & Co., New York (wrapper)	45.00			
RS227	1c	blue, Soule, E.L. & Co. Syracuse (wrapper)	50.00	20.00		
u.		1c ultramarine	150.00			
RS228	1c	brown, Stevens, H.R.				12.00
RS229	2c	chocolate, Stevens, H.R.				3.50
RS230	6c	black, Stevens, H.R.			80.00	2.50
RS231	6c	orange, Swaim, Jas. (die cut), manuscript signature	1,250.			
RS232	8c	orange, Swaim, Jas. (imperf.)	750.00			
h.		Manuscript signature	700.00	—		
RS233	8c	orange, Swaim, Jas. (die cut)	225.00			
h.		Manuscript signature	700.00	—		
RS234	8c	orange, Swaim, Wm. (imperf.)	1,750.	1,500.		850.00
k.		Without signature	400.00	400.00		
RS235	8c	orange, Swaim, Wm. (die cut)	500.00	150.00		140.00
k.		Signature inverted	950.00			
i.		Manuscript signature	—			
RS236	4c	black, Swett, G.W. (die cut)	8.00			
RS237	4c	green, Swett, G.W. (perf.)		180.00		700.00
RS238	4c	green, Swett, G.W. (perf. and die cut)		225.00		950.00

John L. Thompson RS242

H.H. Warner & Co. RS254

J.H. Zeilin & Co. — RS277

T

			a. Old Paper	b. Silk Paper	c. Pink Paper	d. Wmkd. USIR 191R
RS239	2c	vermilion, Tallcot, Geo				8.00
RS240	4c	black, Tallcot, Geo		50.00	1,500.	15.00
RS241	4c	red, Tarrant & Co.		1.50	60.00	1.50
RS242	1c	black, Thompson, John L.	2.25	2.50		2.25
e.		Experimental silk paper	50.00			
		Double transfer	—			

U

			a.	b.	c.	d.
RS243	4c	black, U.S. Prop. Med. Co.	45.00	75.00		
e.		Experimental silk paper	75.00			
RS244	6c	black, U.S. Prop. Med. Co.	600.00			
RS245	1c	black, U.S. Prop. Med. Co. white wrapper	13.00	13.00		
e.		Experimental silk paper	500.00			

			a. Old Paper	b. Silk Paper	c. Pink Paper	d. Wmkd. USIR 191R
RS246	1c	black, U.S. Prop. Med. Co. yellow wrapper	60.00	135.00		
RS247	1c	black, U.S. Prop. Med. Co. orange wrapper	135.00	700.00		
RS248	1c	black, U.S. Prop. Med. Co. orange red wrapper	400.00	1,000.		

V

			a.	b.	c.	d.
RS249	4c	blk., Van Duzer, S.R.	25.00	20.00		125.00
RS250	6c	black, Van Duzer, S.R.				45.00
RS251	1c	black, Vogeler, A. & Co.		50		50
RS252	1c	vermilion, Vogeler, Meyer & Co.			2.50	25

W

			a.	b.	c.	d.
RS253	4c	black, Walker, J.	25.00	12.50		12.50
e.		Experimental silk paper	60.00			
		Double transfer	—			
RS254	1c	brown, W., H.H. & Co. (H.H. Warner & Co.)				4.00
RS255	6c	brown, W., H.H. & Co. (H.H. Warner & Co.) (19x26mm.)				55.00
RS256	2c	brown, W., H.H. & Co. (H.H. Warner & Co.) (88x11 mm.)				22.50
RS257	4c	brown, W., H.H. & Co. (H.H. Warner & Co.) (95x18 mm.)				30.00
RS258	6c	brown, same				3.50
		Double transfer				40.00
RS259	1c	black, Weeks & Potter		4.50		1.50
RS260	2c	black, Weeks & Potter		80.00		
RS261	4c	black, Weeks & Potter		17.50	20.00	5.00
RS262	2c	red, Weeks & Potter			25.00	5.00
RS263	4c	black, Wells, Richardson & Co.				17.50
RS264	4c	black, West India Mfg. Co., die I	225.00	180.00	300.00	
r.		Die II				180.00

Die II shows evidence of retouching, particularly in the central disk.

			a.	b.	c.	d.
RS265	1c	green, Wilder, Edward (imperf.)	600.00	150.00		200.00
RS266	1c	green, Wilder, Edward (die cut)	40.00	30.00		17.50
e.		Experimental silk paper	135.00			
RS266A	4c	vermilion, Wilder, Edward (imperf.)				
e.		Experimental silk paper	—			
RS267	4c	vermilion, Wilder, Edward (die cut)	100.00	300.00		
e.		Experimental silk paper	100.00			
RS268	4c	lake, Wilder, Edward (imperf.)		150.00		450.00
RS269	4c	lake, Wilder, Edward (die cut)	375.00	6.00		6.00
RS270	12c	blue, Wilson, E.A.		50.00		250.00
RS271	4c	black, Wilson, Thos. E.	2,750.			
RS272	1c	green, World Dispen. Med. Assn.				17.50
RS273	2c	black, World Dispen. Med. Assn.				2.50
RS274	1c	green, Wright's Indian Veg. Pills	1.00	1.00	20.00	1.00
e.		Experimental silk paper	30.00			
		Double transfer	—			

Z

			a.	b.	c.	d.
RS275	2c	red, Zeilin, J.H. & Co. (perf.)	400.00			
RS276	2c	green, Zeilin, J.H. & Co. (perf.)	30.00			
RS277	2c	green, Zeilin, J.H. & Co. (imperf.)	200.00	3.50	100.00	2.00

1898-1900

		Rouletted 5½		Hyphen Hole Perf. 7	
		Unused	Used	Unused	Used

See rouletting note preceding No. R161.

RS278	2½c	carmine, Antikamnia Co.		1.50		1.50

S

			a. Old Paper	b. Silk Paper	c. Pink Paper	d. Wmkd. USIR 191R
RS208	1c	green, Sands, A.B. & D.	9.00	9.00		
e.		Experimental silk paper	50.00			
RS209	2c	green, Sands, M.P. J. & H.M.		12.00	85.00	10.00
RS210	4c	black, Scheetz's Bitter Cordial (perf.)		250.00		
RS211	4c	black, Scheetz's Bitter Cordial (imperf.)		1,000.		
RS212	1c	green, Schenck's Mandrake Pills (imperf.)	3.50	6.00.	100.00	3.00
e.		Experimental silk paper	—			
		Double transfer		30.00		—
RS213	6c	black, Schenck' Pulmonic Syrup (imperf.)	3.00	3.00	85.00	85.00
e.		Experimental silk paper	50.00			
p.		Perforated	—			
		Double transfer		50.00		—
RS214	4c	black, Schenck, J.H. & Son				5.00
RS215	1c	lake, Schwartz, J.E. & Co. (imperf.)		70.00	225.00	55.00
RS216	1c	black, Seabury & Johnson				45.00
RS217	1c	black, Seabury & Johnson ("porous" obliterated by pen)				2.00
h.		Printed obliteration				1.50
RS218	1c	lake, Seabury & Johnson				1,100.
RS219	4c	blue, Sigesmond, S. Brown				75.00
RS220	1c	black, Scovill, A.L. & Co.	75	1.25		
e.		Experimental silk paper	15.00			
r.		Printed on both sides		750.00		
		Double transfer				
RS221	4c	green, Scovill, A.L. & Co.	1.50	2.25		
e.		Experimental silk paper	10.00			

			Rouletted 5½		Hyphen Hole Perf. 7	
			Unused	Used	Unused	Used
RS279	4c	black, Branca Bros	6.00	6.00	5.00	5.00
RS280	¼c	carmine, Emerson Drug Co.			3.50	.75
RS281	⅝c	green, Emerson Drug Co.			3.50	1.00
RS282	1¼c	violet brown, Emerson Drug Co.			4.00	2.50
RS283	2½c	brown orange, Emerson Drug Co.			4.00	2.50
RS284	1¼c	black, Fletcher, C.H.	25	25	20	20
RS285	2½c	black, Hostetter Co. (imperf.)	40	40		
RS286	⅝c	carmine, Johnson & Johnson	10	10	10	10
RS287	⅝c	green, Lanman & Kemp	6.00	2.00	8.00	2.00
RS288	1¼c	brown, Lanman & Kemp	10.00	6.00	10.00	6.00
RS289	1⅞c	blue, Lanman & Kemp	10.00	3.00	12.00	3.00
RS290	¼c	dark blue, Lee, J. Ellwood, Co.			1.75	1.75
RS291	⅝c	carmine, Lee, J. Ellwood, Co.			75	75
RS292	1¼c	dark green, Lee, J. Ellwood, Co.			1.50	1.50
RS293	2½c	orange, Lee, J. Ellwood, Co.			1.75	1.75
RS294	5c	chocolate, Lee. J. Ellwood, Co.			1.75	1.75
RS295	⅝c	black, Marchand, Chas.	4.00	4.00	5.00	5.00
RS296	1¼c	black, Marchand, Chas.	1.00	1.00	1.00	1.00
RS297	1⅞c	black, Marchand, Chas.	1.50	1.50	2.00	2.00
RS298	2½c	black, Marchand, Chas.	75	75	1.00	1.00
RS299	3⅛c	black, Marchand, Chas	5.00	5.00	5.00	5.00
RS300	4⅜c	black, Marchand, Chas.	10.00	10.00	10.00	10.00
RS301	7½c	black, Marchand, Chas.	8.00	8.00	8.00	8.00
RS302	2½c	carmine, Od Chemical Co.				75
RS303	⅝c	blue, Piso Co.	15	15	15	15
RS304	⅝c	blue, Radway & Co.	60	60	60	60
RS305	3⅛c	brown, Warner's Safe Cure Co.	60	60	60	60
RS306	1¼c	pink, Williams Medicine Co., Dr.			1.25	1.25

Dr. Kilmer & Co., Provisionals.

Postage Stamps of 1895-98, Nos. 279, 279B and 268, Precancel Overprinted in Black:

Dr. K. & Co.   Dr. K. & Co.
I. R.   **I. R.**
7-5-'98.   Binghamton, N. Y.
    7-11-'98.
a   b

Dr. K. & Co.
I. R.
Binghamton, N. Y.
7-7-'98   c

1898		Wmk. 191		Perf. 12

Overprint "a," Large "I.R." Dated July 5, 1898

RS307	A87	1c	deep green	60.00
RS308	A88	2c	red	35.00
RS309	A89	3c	purple	40.00

Overprint "b," Small "I.R.," "Dr. K. & Co." with Serifs Dated July 6, 7, 9, 11 to 14, 1898

RS310	A87	1c	deep green	40.00
RS311	A88	2c	red	20.00
RS312	A89	3c	purple	35.00

Overprint "c," Small "I.R.," "Dr. K. & Co." without Serifs Dated July 7, 9, 11 to 14, 1898

RS313	A87	1c	deep green	50.00
RS314	A88	2c	red	20.00

RS315	A89	3c		purple	25.00

Many varieties of the Kilmer overprints exist. For the complete listing see "The Case of Dr. Kilmer," by Morton Dean Joyce.

St. Louis Provisional Labels, 1898

Ten proprietary drug companies of St. Louis prepared and used labels to denote payment of July 1, 1898, Proprietary Revenue tax because the government issue of "Battleship" stamps (Nos. RB20-RB31) was not available on the effective date. An illustrated descriptive list of these labels, compiled by Morton Dean Joyce, appeared in the December, 1970, issue of Scott's Monthly Journal.

PRIVATE DIE PERFUMERY STAMPS

Corning & Tappan — RT4

C.B. Woodworth & Son — RT20

R. & G.A. Wright — RT23

1864-81				Perf. 12

			a. Old Paper	b. Silk Paper	c. Pink Paper	d. Wmkd. USIR 191R
RT1	2c	blue, Bazin X, (die cut)	450.00			

This stamp was never placed in use.

RT2	1c	black, Corning & Tappan (imperf.)				650.00
h.		Die cut, 19mm. diameter				85.00
k.		Die cut, 21mm. diameter				95.00
RT3	1c	black, Corning & Tappan, (perf.)				250.00
RT4	1c	blue, Corning & Tappan, (perf.)				1.50
RT5	2c	vermilion, Fetridge & Co. (cut to shape)	100.00			
RT6	1c	black, Hoyt, E. W. & Co. (imperf.)	1,500.	900.00	100.00	
RT7	1c	black, Hoyt, E. W. & Co. (die cut)	20.00	20.00		8.00
RT8	1c	black, Hoyt, E. W. & Co. (imperf.)				250.00
RT9	2c	black, Hoyt, E. W. & Co. (die cut)				55.00
RT10	4c	black, Hoyt, E. W. & Co. (imperf.)	900.00	225.00	650.00	
RT11	4c	black, Hoyt, E. W. & Co. (die cut)	65.00	50.00	50.00	
RT12	1c	vermilion, Kidder & Laird				6.00
RT13	2c	vermilion, Kidder & Laird				8.00
RT14	3c	black, Laird, Geo. W (imperf.)	400.00	600.00	475.00	
		Double transfer	600.00	800.00		
p.		perf.	1,000.	—		
		As "p," double transfer				
RT15	3c	black, Laird, Geo. W (die cut)	900.00	70.00	450.00	75.00
p.		Perf. and die cut	900.00			
		Double transfer	—	750.00		
RT16	1c	black, Lanman & Kemp	3.50	150.00	3.50	
		Double transfer				
RT17	2c	brown, Lanman & Kemp	22.50		6.00	
RT18	3c	green, Lanman & Kemp	3.50		7.00	
RT19	1c	vermilion, Tetlow's Perfumery				1.50
RT20	1c	green, Woodworth, C. B. & Son	4.00	12.00	4.00	

			a. Old Paper	b. Silk Paper	c. Pink Paper	d. Wmkd. USIR 191R
		Double transfer		100.00	800.00	6.00
RT21	2c	blue, Woodworth, C. B. & Son				
RT22	1c	blue, Wright, R. & G. A.	4.00	4.00		45.00
e.		Experimental silk paper	25.00			
RT23	2c	black, Wright, R. & G. A.	8.50	15.00		125.00
RT24	3c	lake, Wright, R. & G. A.	22.50	70.00		175.00
RT25	4c	grn. Wright, R. & G. A.	60.00	75.00		150.00
RT26	1c	green, Young, Ladd & Coffin (imperf.)		65.00	65.00	60.00
RT27	1c	green, Young, Ladd & Coffin (perf.)		15.00	12.50	10.00
RT28	2c	blue, Young, Ladd & Coffin (imperf.)		90.00	75.00	45.00
RT29	2c	blue, Young, Ladd & Coffin (perf.)		50.00	60.00	10.00
RT30	3c	vermilion Young, Ladd & Coffin (imperf.)		80.00	90.00	50.00
RT31	3c	vermilion Young, Ladd & Coffin (perf.)		25.00	3.50	1.50
RT32	4c	brown, Young, Ladd & Coffin (imperf.)			90.00	35.00
RT33	4c	brown, Young, Ladd & Coffin (perf.)		30.00	9.00	3.00

PRIVATE DIE PLAYING CARD STAMPS

Eagle Card Co. — RU7

Victor E. Mauger & Petrie — RU13

Russell, Morgan & Co. — RU16

1864-83					

			a. Old Paper	b. Silk Paper	c. Pink Paper	d. Wmkd. USIR 191R
RU1	5c	brown, Caterson Brotz & Co.				2,500.

This stamp was never placed in use.

RU2	2c	orange, Dougherty, A	40.00			
RU3	4c	black, Dougherty, A	30.00			
RU4	5c	blue, Dougherty, A (20x26mm.)	35	35	7.50	
u.		5c ultramarine Double transfer	75.00	—		
RU5	5c	blue, Dougherty, A (18x23mm.)				50
RU6	10c	blue, Dougherty, A	30.00			
RU7	5c	black, Eagle Card Co.				70.00
RU8	5c	black, Goodall, Chas.	140.00	1.50		
e.		Experimental silk paper	200.00			
RU9	5c	black, Hart, Samuel & Co.	4.00	4.00		
RU10	2c	blue, Lawrence & Cohen	50.00			
RU11	5c	green, Lawrence & Cohen	3.00	2.00		
e.		Experimental silk paper	40.00			
RU12	5c	black, Levy, John J.	15.00	20.00		
e.		Experimental silk paper	60.00			
RU13	5c	blue, Mauger, Victor E., & Petrie		1.00	1.00	30

			a. Old Paper	b. Silk Paper	c. Pink Paper	d. Wmkd. USIR 191R				a. Old Paper	b. Silk Paper	c. Pink Paper	d. Wmkd. USIR 191R
RU14	5c	black, N. Y. Con- solidated Card Co.		2.00	10.00	2.00	RU16	5c	black, Russell, Morgan & Co.				6.00
RU15	5c	black, Paper Fabrique Co.		3.50	12.00	4.00							

MOTOR VEHICLE USE REVENUE

When affixed to a motor vehicle, permitted use of that vehicle for a stated period.

RV1

OFFSET PRINTING
1942   Wmk. 191R   With Gum on Back   *Perf. 11*
RV1   RV1 $2.09 light green *(February)*   1.25   40

With Gum on Face
Inscriptions on Back
RV2   RV1 $1.67 light green *(March)*   12.50   7.00
RV3   RV1 $1.25 light green *(April)*   11.00   6.00
RV4   RV1   84c light green *(May)*   12.50   6.00
RV5   RV1   42c light green *(June)*   11.00   6.00

With Gum and Control Number on Face
1942   Inscriptions on Back
RV6   RV1 $5 rose red *(July)*   2.50   75
RV7   RV1 $4.59 rose red *(August)*   20.00 10.00
RV8   RV1 $4.17 rose red *(September)*   25.00 10.00
RV9   RV1 $3.75 rose red *(October)*   22.50 10.00
RV10   RV1 $3.34 rose red *(November)*   21.00 10.00
RV11   RV1 $2.92 rose red *(December)*   20.00   —

1943
RV12   RV1 $2.50 rose red *(January)*   25.00   8.00
RV13   RV1 $2.09 rose red *(February)*   18.00   6.00
RV14   RV1 $1.67 rose red *(March)*   15.00   —
RV15   RV1 $1.25 rose red *(April)*   15.00   6.00
RV16   RV1   84c rose red *(May)*   15.00   6.00

RV17   RV1   42c rose red *(June)*   12.50   —
RV18   RV1 $5 yellow *(July)*   3.00   75
RV19   RV1 $4.59 yellow *(August)*   25.00 10.00
RV20   RV1 $4.17 yellow *(September)*   37.50 10.00
RV21   RV1 $3.75 yellow *(October)*   35.00 10.00
RV22   RV1 $3.34 yellow *(November)*   40.00 10.00
RV23   RV1 $2.92 yellow *(December)*   50.00 10.00

1944
RV24   RV1 $2.50 yellow *(January)*   50.00 12.50
RV25   RV1 $2.09 yellow *(February)*   32.50   8.00
RV26   RV1 $1.67 yellow *(March)*   25.00   8.00
RV27   RV1 $1.25 yellow *(April)*   25.00   6.00
RV28   RV1   84c yellow *(May)*   20.00   —
RV29   RV1   42c yellow *(June)*   20.00   —

Gum on Face
Control Number and Inscriptions on Back
RV30   RV1 $5 violet *(July)*   2.50   50
RV31   RV1 $4.59 violet *(August)*   40.00 12.50
RV32   RV1 $4.17 violet *(September)*   30.00 12.50
RV33   RV1 $3.75 violet *(October)*   30.00 10.00
RV34   RV1 $3.34 violet *(November)*   20.00   8.00
RV35   RV1 $2.92 violet *(December)*   22.50   8.00

1945
RV36   RV1 $2.50 violet *(January)*   22.50   7.00
RV37   RV1 $2.09 violet *(February)*   20.00   6.00
RV38   RV1 $1.67 violet *(March)*   17.50   6.00
RV39   RV1 $1.25 violet *(April)*   17.50   5.00
RV40   RV1   84c violet *(May)*   15.00   4.00
RV41   RV1   42c violet *(June)*   12.50   4.00

Daniel
Manning
RV2

Gum on Face
Control Number and Inscriptions on Back
1945   Wmk. 191R   Offset Printing   *Perf. 11*
RV42   RV2 $5 bright blue green & yellow
             green *(July)*   2.50   50
RV43   RV2 $4.59 bright blue green & yellow
             green *(August)*   30.00   —
RV44   RV2 $4.17 bright blue green & yellow
             green *(Sept.)*   30.00   —
RV45   RV2 $3.75 bright blue green & yellow
             green *(October)*   25.00   —
RV46   RV2 $3.34 bright blue green & yellow
             green *(November)*   20.00   —
RV47   RV2 $2.92 bright blue green & yellow
             green *(December)*   17.50   —

1946
RV48   RV2 $2.50 bright blue green & yellow
             green *(January)*   20.00   —
RV49   RV2 $2.09 bright blue green & yellow
             green *(February)*   20.00   —
RV50   RV2 $1.67 bright blue green & yellow
             green *(March)*   15.00   —
RV51   RV2 $1.25 bright blue green & yellow
             green *(April)*   12.00   —
RV52   RV2   84c bright blue green & yellow
             green *(May)*   12.00   —
RV53   RV2   42c bright blue green & yellow
             green *(June)*   8.00   —

BOATING

Required on applications for the certificate of number for motorboats of more than 10hp, starting April 1, 1960. The pictorial upper part of the $3 stamp is attached to the temporary certificate and kept by the boat owner. The lower part (stub), showing number only, is affixed to the application and sent by the Post Office to the Coast Guard which issues permanent certificate. The $3 fee is for three years. The $1 stamp covers charges for reissuance of a lost or destroyed certificate of number.

Outboard and
Inboard
Motorboats — B1

Offset Printing, Number Typographed
1960   Unwmk.   *Rouletted*
RVB1B1 $1 rose red, black number   30.00
         Margin block of 4, P#   130.00
RVB2B1 $3 blue, red number   45.00   25.00
         Margin block of 4, P#   200.00

HUNTING PERMIT

Authorized by Act of Congress, approved March 16, 1934, to license hunters, the receipts going to maintain waterfowl life in the United States. Sales to collectors were made legal June 15, 1935. The 1934 issue was designed by J. N. Darling, 1935 by Frank W. Benson, 1936 by Richard E. Bishop, 1937 by J. D. Knap, 1938 by Roland Clark, 1939 by Lynn Bogue Hunt, 1940 by Francis L. Jaques, 1941 by E. R. Kalmbach, 1942 by A. Lassell Ripley, 1943 by Walter E. Bohl, 1944 by Walter A. Weber, 1945 by Owen J. Gromme, 1946 by Robert W. Hines, 1947 by Jack Murray, 1948 by Maynard Reece, 1949 by "Roge" E. Preuss, 1950 by Walter A. Weber, 1951 by Maynard Reece, 1952 by John H. Dick, 1953 by Clayton B. Seagears, 1954 by Harvey D. Sandstrom, 1955 by Stanley Stearns, 1956 by Edward J. Bierly, 1957 by Jackson Miles Abbott, 1958 by Leslie C. Kouba, 1959 by Maynard Reece, 1960 by John A. Ruthven, 1961-62 by Edward A. Morris, 1963 by Edward J. Bierly, 1964 by Stanley Stearns, 1965 by Ron Jenkins, 1966 by Stanley Stearns, 1967 by Leslie C. Kouba, 1968 by C. G. Pritchard, 1969 by Maynard Reece, 1970 by Edward J. Bierly, 1971 by Maynard Reece, 1972 by Arthur M. Cook, 1973 by Lee LeBlanc, 1975 by James L. Fisher, 1976 by Alderson Magee, 1977 by Martin R. Murk, 1978 by Albert Earl Gilbert, 1979 by Kenneth L. Michaelsen, 1980 by Richard W. Plasschaert, 1981 by John S. Wilson, 1982 by David A. Maass, 1983 by Phil Scholer, 1984 by William C. Morris, 1985 by Gerald Mobely, 1986 by Burton E. Moore, Jr. 1987 by Arthur G. Anderson, 1988 by Daniel Smith.
Used price is for stamp with signature. Plate number blocks of six have margins on two sides.

Department of Agriculture

Mallards
Alighting — HP1

Issued in panes of 28 subjects.
Various Designs
Engraved: Flat Plate Printing

1934	**Unwmk.**		**Perf. 11**
	Inscribed "Void after June 30, 1935".		
RW1 HP1	$1 **blue**	425.00	110.00
	P# block of 6	6,000.	
a.	Imperf., pair	*4,000.*	
b.	Vert. pair, imperf. horiz.	—	
1935	Inscribed "Void after June 30, 1936"		
RW2	$1 **rose lake** (*Canvasbacks Taking to Flight*)	450.00	125.00
	P# block of 6	7,000.	

1936	Inscribed "Void after June 30, 1937"		
RW3	$1 **brown black** (*Canada Geese in Flight*)	250.00	60.00
	P# block of 6	3,000.	
1937	Inscribed "Void after June 30, 1938"		
RW4	$1 **light green** (*Scaup Ducks Taking to Flight*)	160.00	35.00
	P# block of 6	1,750.	
1938	Inscribed "Void after June 30, 1939"		
RW5	$1 **light violet** (*Pintail Drake and Hen Alighting*)	200.00	35.00
	P# block of 6	2,000.	

Department of the Interior

Green-winged
Teal — HP2

1939	Inscribed "Void after June 30, 1940"		
RW6 HP2	$1 **chocolate**	130.00	30.00
	P# block of 6	1,200.	
1940	Inscribed "Void after June 30, 1941"		
RW7	$1 **sepia** (*Black Mallards*)	120.00	30.00
	P# block of 6	1,100.	
1941	Inscribed "Void after June 30, 1942"		
RW8	$1 **brown carmine** (*Family of Ruddy Ducks*)	120.00	25.00
	P# block of 6	1,000.	
1942	Inscribed "Void after June 30, 1943"		
RW9	$1 **violet brown** (*Baldpates*)	120.00	25.00
	P# block of 6	1,000.	
1943	Inscribed "Void After June 30, 1944"		
RW10	$1 **deep rose** (*Wood Ducks*)	60.00	20.00
	P# block of 6	425.00	
1944	Inscribed "Void after June 30, 1945"		
RW11	$1 **red orange** (*White-fronted Geese*)	60.00	20.00
	P# block of 6	400.00	
1945	Inscribed "Void after June 30, 1946"		
RW12	$1 **black** (*Shoveller Ducks in Flight*)	35.00	10.00
	P# block of 6	250.00	
1946	Inscribed "Void after June 30, 1947"		
RW13	$1 **red brown** (*Redhead Ducks*)	35.00	10.00
	P# block of 6	250.00	
1947	Inscribed "Void after June 30, 1948"		
RW14	$1 **black** (*Snow Geese*)	35.00	10.00
	P# block of 6	250.00	
1948	Inscribed "Void after June 30, 1949"		
RW15	$1 **bright blue** (*Buffleheads in Flight*)	35.00	10.00
	P# block of 6	250.00	

Goldeneye
Ducks — HP3

1949	Inscribed "Void after June 30, 1950"		
RW16 HP3	$2 **bright green**	35.00	10.00
	P# block of 6	250.00	
1950	Inscribed "Void after June 30, 1951"		
RW17	$2 **violet** (*Trumpeter Swans in Flight*)	55.00	7.00
	P# block of 6	375.00	
1951	Inscribed "Void after June 30, 1952"		
RW18	$2 **gray black** (*Gadwall Ducks*)	55.00	7.00
	P# block of 6	375.00	
1952	Inscribed "Void after June 30, 1953"		
RW19	$2 **deep ultramarine** (*Harlequin Ducks*)	55.00	7.00
	P# block of 6	375.00	
1953	Inscribed "Void after June 30, 1954"		
RW20	$2 **dark rose brown** (*Blue-winged Teal*)	55.00	5.00
	P# block of 6	375.00	

1954 RW21	Inscribed "Void after June 30, 1955"			
	$2 black (Ring-necked Ducks)		55.00	5.00
	P# block of 6		400.00	
1955 RW22	Inscribed "Void after June 30, 1956"			
	$2 dark blue (Blue Geese)		55.00	5.00
	P# block of 6		400.00	
1956 RW23	Inscribed: "Void after June 30, 1957"			
	$2 black (American Merganser)		55.00	5.00
	P# block of 6		400.00	
1957 RW24	Inscribed: "Void after June 30, 1958"			
	$2 emerald (American Eider)		55.00	5.00
	P# block of 6		400.00	
1958 RW25	Inscribed: "Void after June 30, 1959"			
	$2 black (Canada Geese)		55.00	5.00
	P# block of 6		400.00	

Labrador Retriever Carrying Mallard Drake — HP4

Giori Press Printing
Issued in panes of 30 subjects

1959 RW26 HP4	Inscribed: "Void after June 30, 1960"			
	$3 blue, ocher & black		65.00	5.00
	P# block of 4		325.00	

Redhead Ducks — HP5

1960 RW27 HP5	Inscribed: "Void after June 30, 1961"			
	$3 red brown, dark blue & bister		65.00	5.00
	P# block of 4		325.00	
1961 RW28	Inscribed: "Void after June 30, 1962"			
	$3 Mallard Hen and Ducklings		70.00	5.00
	P# block of 4		350.00	

Pintail Drakes Coming in for Landing — HP6

1962 RW29 HP6	Inscribed: "Void after June 30, 1963"			
	$3 dark blue, dark red brown & black		85.00	6.00
	P# block of 4		425.00	
1963 RW30	Inscribed: "Void after June 30, 1964"			
	$3 Pair of Brant Landing		80.00	6.00
	P# block of 4		400.00	
1964 RW31	Inscribed: "Void after June 30, 1965"			
	$3 Hawaiian Nene Geese		80.00	6.00
	P# block of 6		2,250.00	
1965 RW32	Inscribed: "Void after June 30, 1966"			
	$3 Three Canvasback Drakes		80.00	6.00
	P# block of 4		400.00	

United States Hunting Permit stamps can be mounted in Scott's National, American, Minuteman, U.S. Federal and State Duck Stamps and U.S. Federal Duck Plate Block Albums.

Whistling Swans — HP7

1966 RW33 HP7	Inscribed: "Void after June 30, 1967"			
	$3 multicolored		80.00	6.00
	P# block of 4		400.00	
1967 RW34	Inscribed: "Void after June 30, 1968"			
	$3 Old Squaw Ducks		80.00	6.00
	P# block of 4		400.00	
1968 RW35	Inscribed: "Void after June 30, 1969"			
	$3 Hooded Mergansers		50.00	6.00
	P# block of 4		250.00	

White-winged Scoters — HP8

1969 RW36 HP8	Inscribed: "Void after June 30, 1970"			
	$3 multicolored		50.00	4.00
	P# block of 4		250.00	
1970 RW37	Engraved & Lithographed Inscribed: "Void after June 30, 1971"			
	$3 Ross's Geese		45.00	4.00
	P# block of 4		225.00	
1971 RW38	Inscribed: "Void after June 30, 1972"			
	$3 Three Cinnamon Teal		30.00	4.00
	P# block of 4		140.00	
1972 RW39	Inscribed: "Void after June 30, 1973"			
	$5 Emperor Geese		25.00	4.00
	P# block of 4		110.00	
1973 RW40	Inscribed: "Void after June 30, 1974"			
	$5 Steller's Eiders		20.00	4.00
	P# block of 4		90.00	
1974 RW41	Inscribed: "Void after June 30, 1975"			
	$5 Wood Ducks		15.00	4.00
	P# block of 4		70.00	
1975 RW42	Inscribed: "Void after June 30, 1976"			
	$5 Canvasback Decoy, 3 Flying Canvasbacks		12.00	4.00
	P# block of 4		55.00	
1976 RW43	Inscribed "Void after June 30, 1977" Engr.			
	$5 Family of Canada Geese		10.00	4.00
	P# block of 4		50.00	
1977 RW44	Inscribed: "Void after June 30, 1978"			
	$5 Pair of Ross's Geese		10.00	4.00
	P# block of 4		50.00	

Hooded Merganser Drake — HP9

1978 RW45 HP9	Inscribed: "Void after June 30, 1979"			
	$5 multicolored		10.00	4.00
	P# block of 4		50.00	
1979 RW46	Inscribed: "Void after June 30, 1980"			
	$7.50 Green-winged Teal		15.00	4.00
	P# block of 4		75.00	
1980 RW47	Inscribed: "Void after June 30, 1981"			
	$7.50 Mallards		15.00	4.00
	P# block of 4		75.00	
1981 RW48	Inscribed: "Void after June 30, 1982"			
	$7.50 Ruddy Ducks		15.00	4.00
	P# block of 4		75.00	

1982
RW49   Inscribed: "Void after June 30, 1983"
    $7.50 **Canvasbacks**   15.00   4.00
    P# block of 4   75.00

1983
RW50   Inscribed: "Void after June 30, 1984"
    $7.50 **Pintails**   15.00   3.50
    P# block of 4   75.00

1984
RW51   Inscribed: "Void after June 30, 1985"
    $7.50 **Wigeons**   15.00   3.50
    P# block of 4   75.00

After No. RW51 became void, uncut sheets of 120 (4 panes of 30 separated by gutters) were overprinted in the margins and auctioned.

1985
RW52   Inscribed: "Void after June 30, 1986"
    $7.50 **Cinnamon teal**   15.00   3.50
    P# block of 4   75.00

1986
RW53   Inscribed: "Void after June 30, 1987"
    $7.50 **Fulvous whistling duck**   15.00   3.50
    P# block of 4   75.00
    a.   Black omitted   —

1987
RW54   Inscribed: "Void after June 30, 1988"
    $10 **Redheads**   20.00   3.50
    P# block of 4   100.00

1988
RW55   Inscribed: "Void after June 30, 1989"
    $10 **Snow Goose**   20.00   3.50
    P# block of 4   100.00

Gray inscription on back of Nos. RW13-RW34: "It is unlawful to hunt waterfowl unless you sign your name in ink on the face of this stamp". Additional wording on Nos. RW26-RW27: "Duck stamp dollars buy wetlands to perpetuate waterfowl," and on Nos. RW28-RW34: "Duck stamp dollars buy wetlands for waterfowl.' Back inscription on Nos. RW35-RW36 reads: "Buy duck stamps/Save wetlands /Send in all bird bands/Sign your duck stamps."
Back inscription of Nos. RW37-RW55 repeats 4-line message of Nos. RW35-RW36 and also includes in two added lines the "It is unlawful . . ." warning.
No. RW21 and following issues are printed on dry, pregummed paper and the back inscription is printed on top of the gum.

QUANTITIES ISSUED

RW1	635,001
RW2	448,204
RW3	603,623
RW4	783,039
RW5	1,002,715
RW6	1,111,561
RW7	1,260,810
RW8	1,439,967
RW9	1,383,629
RW10	1,169,352
RW11	1,487,029
RW12	1,725,505
RW13	2,016,841
RW14	1,722,677
RW15	2,127,603
RW16	1,954,734
RW17	1,903,644
RW18	2,167,767
RW19	2,296,628
RW20	2,268,446
RW21	2,184,550
RW22	2,369,940
RW23	2,332,014
RW24	2,355,190
RW25	2,176,425
RW26	1,626,115
RW27	1,725,634
RW28	1,344,236
RW29	1,147,212
RW30	1,448,191
RW31	1,573,155
RW32	1,558,197
RW33	1,805,341
RW34	1,934,697
RW35	1,837,139
RW36	2,072,108
RW37	2,420,244
RW38	2,441,664
RW39	2,179,628
RW40	2,113,594
RW41	2,190,268
RW42	2,218,589
RW43	2,248,394
RW44	2,180,625
RW45	2,196,758
RW46	2,209,572
RW47	2,103,021
RW48	1,907,114
RW49	1,926,253
RW50	1,867,998
RW51	1,913,509

DISTILLED SPIRITS

Charles S. Fairchild, Secretary of Treasury 1887-89 — DS1

Actual size: 89½x63½mm.

1950   **Wmk. 191R**   **Offset Printing**   *Rouletted 7*
Inscribed "STAMP FOR SERIES 1950"

			Used	Punched Cancel
RX1	DS1	1c yellow green & black	25.00	20.00
RX2	DS1	3c yellow green & black	100.00	90.00
RX3	DS1	5c yellow green & black	25.00	20.00
RX4	DS1	10c yellow green & black	20.00	15.00
RX5	DS1	25c yellow green & black	8.00	6.00
RX6	DS1	50c yellow green & black	8.00	6.00
RX7	DS1	$1 yellow green & black	1.50	1.00
RX8	DS1	$3 yellow green & black	20.00	15.00
RX9	DS1	$5 yellow green & black	7.00	5.00
RX10	DS1	$10 yellow green & black	2.50	1.25
RX11	DS1	$25 yellow green & black	12.50	9.00
RX12	DS1	$50 yellow green & black	8.00	5.00
RX13	DS1	$100 yellow green & black	3.00	2.00
RX14	DS1	$300 yellow green & black	30.00	25.00
RX15	DS1	$500 yellow green & black	20.00	15.00
RX16	DS1	$1,000 yellow green & black	9.00	7.50
RX17	DS1	$1,500 yellow green & black	65.00	50.00
RX18	DS1	$2,000 yellow green & black	4.00	3.00
RX19	DS1	$3,000 yellow green & black	25.00	20.00
RX20	DS1	$5,000 yellow green & black	25.00	20.00
RX21	DS1	$10,000 yellow green & black	35.00	25.00
RX22	DS1	$20,000 yellow green & black	40.00	35.00
RX23	DS1	$30,000 yellow green & black	80.00	60.00
RX24	DS1	$40,000 yellow green & black	700.00	500.00
RX25	DS1	$50,000 yellow green & black	100.00	75.00

Type of 1950

1952

Inscription "STAMP FOR SERIES 1950" omitted

RX28	DS1	5c yellow green & black		40.00
RX29	DS1	10c yellow green & black	—	4.00
RX30	DS1	25c yellow green & black		17.50
RX31	DS1	50c yellow green & black		15.00

RX32	DS1	$1 yellow green & black	20.00	1.00
RX33	DS1	$3 yellow green & black	35.00	22.50
RX34	DS1	$5 yellow green & black	40.00	27.50
RX35	DS1	$10 yellow green & black		1.50
RX36	DS1	$25 yellow green & black	25.00	10.00
RX37	DS1	$50 yellow green & black		30.00
RX38	DS1	$100 yellow green & black	20.00	2.50
RX39	DS1	$300 yellow green & black		7.00
RX40	DS1	$500 yellow green & black		35.00
RX41	DS1	$1,000 yellow green & black	—	6.00
RX43	DS1	$2,000 yellow green & black	—	65.00
RX44	DS1	$3,000 yellow green & black	—	600.00
RX45	DS1	$5,000 yellow green & black		45.00
RX46	DS1	$10,000 yellow green & black		90.00

Seven other denominations with "Stamp for Series 1950" omitted were prepared but are not known to have been put into use: 1c, 3c, $1,500, $20,000, $30,000, $40,000 and $50,000.
Copies listed as used have staple holes.
Distilled Spirits Excise Tax stamps were discontinued in 1959.

FIREARMS TRANSFER TAX

Documentary Stamp of 1917 Overprinted Vertically in Black. Reading Up

NATIONAL FIREARMS ACT

1934   Engr.   Wmk. 191R   Without Gum   *Perf. 11*
RY1 R21 $1 green 300.00 300.00

Eagle, Shield and Stars from U.S. Seal
RY1 (Type I)   RY2

Two types of $200:
I. Serial number with serifs, not preceded by zeros. Tips of 6 lines project into left margin.
II. Gothic serial number preceded by zeros. Five line tips in left margin.

1934-74   Wmk. 191R   Size: 28x42mm.
Without Gum
RY2 RY1 $200 dull blue & red, type II, #3001-up, unmkd. ('74)   250.00   120.00
  a. $200 dark blue & red, type I, #1-1500   2,000.   —
  b. $200 dull blue & red, type II, #1501-3000 ('50)   750.00   —

Issued in vertical strips of 4 which are imperforate at top, bottom and right side.

1938   Size: 28x33½mm.   *Perf. 11*
RY3 RY2 $1 green   75.00   —

1960, July 1   Size: 29x34mm.   *Perf. 11*
RY4 RY2 $5 red   10.00   —

No. RY4 was issued in sheets of 50 (10x5) with straight edge on four sides of sheet.
The watermark is hard to see on many copies of Nos. RY2-RY4.

RECTIFICATION TAX

RT1

Actual size: 89½x64mm.

1946   Offset Printing   Wmk. 191R   *Rouletted 7*

			Unused	Used	Punched Cancel
RZ1	RT1	1c blue & black	7.00	3.00	1.50
RZ2	RT1	3c blue & black	25.00	8.00	7.50
RZ3	RT1	5c blue & black	15.00	2.50	1.25
RZ4	RT1	10c blue & black	15.00	2.50	1.25
RZ5	RT1	25c blue & black	15.00	3.00	2.00
RZ6	RT1	50c blue & black	20.00	5.00	3.00
RZ7	RT1	$1 blue & black	20.00	4.00	2.00
RZ8	RT1	$3 blue & black	—	18.00	9.00
RZ9	RT1	$5 blue & black	30.00	10.00	6.00

			Unused	Used	Punched Cancel
RZ10	RT1	$10 blue & black	25.00	3.00	1.00
RZ11	RT1	$25 blue & black	—	9.00	4.00
RZ12	RT1	$50 blue & black	—	6.50	3.00
RZ13	RT1	$100 blue & black	—	9.00	3.50
RZ14	RT1	$300 blue & black	—	10.00	7.50
RZ15	RT1	$500 blue & black	—	10.00	7.00
RZ16	RT1	$1000 blue & black	—	16.50	15.00
RZ17	RT1	$1500 blue & black	—	45.00	35.00
RZ18	RT1	$2000 blue & black	—	75.00	55.00

Copies listed as used have staple holes.

DIE AND PLATE PROOFS

PROOFS are known in many styles other than those noted in this section. For the present, however, listings are restricted to die proofs, large and small, and plate proofs on India paper and cardboard. The listing of normal color proofs includes several that differ somewhat from the colors of the issued stamps.

Large Die Proofs are so termed because of the relatively large piece of paper on which they are printed which is about the size of the die block, 40 mm. by 50 mm. or larger. The margins of this group of proofs usually are from 15 to 20 mm. in width though abnormal examples prevent the acceptance of these measurements as a complete means of identification.

These proofs were prepared in most cases by the original contracting companies and often show the imprint thereof and letters and numbers of identification. They are listed under "DIE-Large (1)." The India paper on which these proofs are printed is of an uneven texture and in some respects resembles hand-made paper. These large die proofs were mounted on cards though many are found removed from the card. Large Die Proofs autographed by the engraver or officially approved are worth much more.

Values for die proofs of the bicolored 1869 issue are for examples which are completely printed. Occasionally the vignette has been cut out and affixed to an impression of the border.

Die Proofs of all United States stamps of later issues exist. Only those known outside of government ownership are listed.

Small Die Proofs are so called because of the small piece of paper on which they are printed. Proofs of stamps issued prior to 1904, are reprints, and not in all cases from the same dies as the large die proofs. The margins are extremely narrow, seldom being more than from 3 to 5mm. in width. These 302 small die proofs are from sets prepared for 85 ("Roosevelt presentation") albums in 1904 by the Bureau of Engraving and Printing but bear no imprint to this effect. The white wove paper on which they are printed is of a fibrous nature. These are listed under "DIE-Small (2)."

A special printing of 413 different small die proofs was made in 1915 for the Panama-Pacific Exposition. These have small margins (2½ to 3 mm.) and are on soft yellowish wove paper. They are extremely scarce as only 3 to 5 of each are known and a few, such as the 1861 5c buff, exist only in this special printing. They are listed under "DIE-Small (2a)."

Plate Proofs are, quite obviously, impressions taken from finished plates and differ from the stamps themselves chiefly in their excellence of impression and the paper on which they are printed. Some of the colors vary.

Hybrids are plate proofs of all issues before 1894 which have been cut to shape, mounted and pressed on large cards to resemble large die proofs. These sell for somewhat less than the corresponding large die proofs.

India Paper is a thin, soft, opaque paper which wrinkles when wet. It varies in thickness and shows particles of bamboo.

Card is a plain, clear white card of good quality, which is found in varying thicknesses for different printings. Plate proofs on cardboard were made in five printings in 1879-93. Quantities range from 500 to 2,500 of the cardboard proofs listed between Nos. 3P and 245P.

Margin blocks with full imprint and plate number are indicated by the abbreviation "P # blk. of -."

Numbers have been assigned to all proofs consisting of the number of the regular stamp with the suffix letter "P" to denote Proof.

Proofs in other than accepted or approved colors exist in a large variety of shades, colors and papers produced at various times by various people for many different reasons. The field is large. The task of listing has been begun under "Trial Colors" following the regular proofs.

Values are for items in very fine condition.

The editors are indebted to the Essay-Proof Society, through co-operation of its catalogue advisory committee, for help in preparing this section.

NORMAL COLORS

1845

New York

		DIE		PLATE	
		(1) Large	(2) Small	(2a)	(3) In-dia	(4) Card

			Large	Small	(2a)	In-dia	Card
9X1P	5c	black on India paper	500.00	300.00		250.00	
a.		With scar on neck		275.00			
b.		Dot in "P" of "POST" and scar on neck	375.00	275.00			
c.		As "b" on Bond	375.00	275.00			225.00
d.		As "b" on glazed paper	375.00				

The above listed Large Die varieties have an additional impression of the portrait medallion. Plate proofs from the sheet of 9 also exist on white and bluish bond paper. Price $125.

Providence, R.I.

10X1P	5c	black					325.00
10X2P	10c	black					425.00
		Sheet of 12					4,000.

General Issues

1847

			Large	Small	(2a)	In-dia	Card
1P	5c	red brown on India paper	950.00	750.00		500.00	
a.		White bond paper	950.00	750.00			
b.		Colored bond paper	950.00				
c.		White laid paper	950.00	750.00			
d.		Bluish laid paper	950.00	750.00			
e.		Yellowish wove paper	950.00				
f.		Bluish wove paper	950.00				
g.		White wove paper	950.00				
h.		Card		750.00			
i.		Glazed paper	950.00				
2P	10c	black on India paper	950.00	750.00		750.00	
a.		White bond paper	950.00	750.00			
b.		Colored bond paper	950.00				
c.		White laid paper	950.00				
d.		Bluish laid paper	950.00				
e.		Yellowish wove paper	950.00				
g.		White wove paper	950.00				
h.		Card		750.00			
i.		Glazed paper	950.00				

Original die proofs are generally found cut to stamp size. Plate proofs overprinted "Specimen" sell for about half the above figures.

Reproductions of 1847 Issue

Actually, official imitations made about 1875 from new dies and plates by order of the Post Office Department.

3P	5c	red brown	900.00	400.00	1,300.	285.00	200.00
		Block of four				1,350.	900.00
a.		On bond paper		650.00			

4P	10c	black	900.00	400.00	1,300.	285.00	200.00
		Block of four				1,350.	900.00
a.		On bond paper		650.00			

1851-60

			Large	Small	(2a)	In-dia	Card
5P	1c	blue, type I		5,000.			
11P	3c	red, type I		5,000.			
		brush obliteration				600.00	
		Block of four				3,000.	
12P	5c	brown, type I		5,000.	575.00	1,650.	
13P	10c	green, type I		5,000.			
17P	12c	black		5,000.			
24P	1c	blue, type V (pl. 9)				825.00	
		Pair				2,300.	
26P	3c	red, type II (pl. 20)				650.00	
30P	5c	brown, type II				575.00	
35P	10c	green, type V				625.00	
36P	12c	black, plate III (broken frame lines)				525.00	
		Block of four				2,700.	
37P	24c	lilac	2,200.		1,500.	525.00	
		Pair				1,400.	
38P	30c	orange	2,200.	550.00	1,500.	525.00	
		Pair				1,400.	
39P	90c	blue	2,200.	550.00	1,500.	775.00	
		Pair				1,650.	

Plate proofs of 24P to 39P are from the original plates. They may be distinguished from the 40P to 47P by the type in the case of the 1c, 3c, 10c and 12c, and by the color in the case of the 5c, 24c, 30c and 90c.

The 3c plate proofs (No. 11) are on proof paper and nearly all known copies have a vertical brush stroke obliteration.

Reprints of 1857-60 Issue

			Large	Small	(2a)	In-dia	Card
40P	1c	bright blue, type I (new plate)	400.00	425.00	1,400.	110.00	80.00
		Block of four				550.00	400.00
41P	3c	scarlet, type I (new plate)	400.00	425.00	1,400.	110.00	80.00
		Block of four				550.00	400.00
42P	5c	orange brown type II (plate II)	400.00	425.00		110.00	80.00
		Block of four				550.00	400.00
		P# blk. of 8				1,500.	—
43P	10c	blue green, type I (new plate)	400.00	425.00	1,400.	110.00	80.00
		Block of four				550.00	400.00
44P	12c	greenish black (new plate, frame line complete)	400.00	425.00	1,400.	160.00	80.00
		Block of four				650.00	400.00
45P	24c	blksh vio (pl.I)	400.00	425.00	1,400.	110.00	80.00
		Block of four				550.00	400.00
		P# blk. of 8				1,500.	
46P	30c	yel org (pl. I)	400.00	425.00	1,400.	110.00	80.00
		Block of four				550.00	400.00
		P# blk. of 8				1,750.	—
47P	90c	deep blue (pl. I)	400.00	425.00	1,400.	160.00	110.00
		Block of four				650.00	550.00
		P# blk. of 8				1,750.	1,700.

Nos. 40P-47P, large die, exist only as hybrids.

FIRST DESIGNS

1861

			Large	Small	(2a)	In-dia	Card
55P	1c	indigo	1,350.	350.00		350.00	
		Block of four				1,750.	
56P	3c	red	1,350.	350.00	1,750.	225.00	
		Block of four				1,300.	
57P	5c	brown		350.00	1,750.	225.00	
		Block of four				1,300.	
		P# blk. of 12				5,000.	
58P	10c	dark green		350.00		225.00	
		Block of four				1,300.	
59P	12c	black	1,350.	500.00	1,750.	450.00	
		Block of four				2,200.	
60P	24c	violet	900.00	400.00	1,750.	225.00	
		Block of four				1,300.	
61P	30c	red orange	1,750.	400.00	1,750.	450.00	
		Block of four				2,500.	
62P	90c	blue	1,350.	400.00	1,750.	450.00	
		Block of four				2,500.	

SECOND DESIGNS (Regular Issue)

1861

			Large	Small	(2a)	In-dia	Card
63P	1c	blue	700.00	275.00	1,600.	85.00	55.00
		Block of four				375.00	400.00
		P# blk. of 8				2,000.	—
		Indigo			1,600.		
64P	3c	pink	3,500.	—			
					1,600.		
65P	3c	rose	1,000.	—	1,600.	160.00	150.00
		Block of four				950.00	
		P# blk. of 8				2,500.	
a.		3c dull red				160.00	

66P	3c	lake	325.00		1,600.	175.00	
		Block of four				1,000.	
		P# blk. of 8				2,500.	
67P	5c	buff			1,600.		
76P	5c	brown	700.00	250.00	1,600.	75.00	45.00
		Block of four				350.00	200.00
		P# blk.				1,400.	—
68P	10c	green	650.00	250.00	1,600.	110.00	45.00
		Block of four				500.00	200.00
		P# blk. of 8				1,600.	—
69P	12c	black	700.00	250.00	1,600.	110.00	45.00
		Block of four				500.00	200.00
		P# blk. of 8				1,600.	—
70P	24c	red lilac			2,100.		400.00
78P	24c	lilac		250.00	2,100.	135.00	115.00
		Block of four				700.00	550.00
		P# blk. of 8				2,000.	—
71P	30c	orange	500.00	300.00	1,600.	85.00	45.00
		Block of four				400.00	225.00
		P# blk. of 8				1,800.	—
72P	90c	blue	500.00	300.00	1,600.	85.00	45.00
		Block of four				400.00	225.00
		P# blk. of 8				1,800.	—

1861-66

73P	2c	black, die I	3,000.			175.00	
		Block of four				850.00	
		P# blk. of 8				2,500.	—
a.		Die II	2,500.	1,500.	5,000.	150.00	120.00
a.		Block of four				750.00	650.00
a.		P# blk. of 8				2,250.	
74P	3c	scarlet	2,250.	450.00	1,600.	150.00	180.00
		Block of four				750.00	825.00
		P# blk. of 8					—
77P	15c	black	1,250.	550.00	2,500.	85.00	60.00
		Block of four				400.00	275.00
		P# blk. of 8				1,600.	

The listed plate proofs of the 1c (63P), 5c (76P), 10c (68P) and 12c (69P) are from the 100 subject re-issue plates of 1875. The 2c Die II has a small dot on the left cheek.

1869

112P	1c	buff	1,400.	650.00	1,800.	90.00	100.00
		Block of four				400.00	450.00
		P# blk. of 10				1,350.	
113P	2c	brown	1,400.		1,800.	62.50	67.50
		Block of four				275.00	300.00
		P# blk. of 10				1,100.	—
114P	3c	ultra.	1,750.	650.00	1,800.	72.50	77.50
		Block of four				300.00	350.00
		P# blk. of 10				1,450.	—
115P	6c	ultra.	1,500.	650.00	1,800.	72.50	82.50
		Block of four				300.00	425.00
		P# blk. of 10				1,450.	—
116P	10c	yellow	1,500.	650.00	1,800.	72.50	82.50
		Block of four				300.00	425.00
		P# blk. of 10				1,450.	—
117P	12c	green	1,500.	650.00	1,800.	77.50	90.00
		Block of four				350.00	475.00
		P# blk. of 10				1,600.	—
119P	15c	brown & blue (type II)	850.00	700.00	2,100.	200.00	
		Block of four				1,000.	
		P# blk. of 8				2,650.	
129P	15c	Reissue (type III)	850.00	700.00	2,100.	400.00	115.00
		Block of four				1,900.	625.00
		P# blk. of 8				5,500.	—
a.		Center inverted (100)				5,250.	
a.		Block of four				22,500.	

a.		P# blk. of 8				60,000.	
120P	24c	green & violet	850.00	700.00	2,100.	225.00	200.00
		Block of four				1,000.	1,000.
		P# blk. of 8				2,650.	—
a.		Center inverted (100)				5,250.	
a.		Block of four				22,500.	
a.		P# blk. of 8				60,000.	
121P	30c	bl. & carmine	1,400.	700.00	2,100.	225.00	250.00
		Block of four				1,000.	1,350.
		P# blk. of 8				2,650.	—
a.		Flags inverted (100)				5,250.	
a.		Block of four				22,500.	
a.		P# blk. of 8				60,000.	
122P	90c	carmine & black	850.00	700.00	2,100.	300.00	250.00
		Block of four				1,350.	1,350.
		P# blk. of 8				3,200.	—
a.		Center inverted (100)				5,250.	
a.		Block of four				22,500.	
a.		P# blk. of 8				60,000.	

Large die proofs of Nos. 119, 129, 120 and 122 exist only as hybrids.

1880

133P	1c	dark buff	1,400.		125.00
		Block of four			625.00
		P# blk. of 10			2,000.

1870-71   **National Bank Note Co.**

145P	1c	ultra	450.00	250.00	800.00	30.00	
		Block of four				130.00	
		P# blk. of 12				700.00	
146P	2c	red brown	450.00			30.00	
		Block of four				130.00	
		P# blk. of 12				700.00	
147P	3c	green	500.00			35.00	
		Block of four				150.00	
		P# blk. of 12				725.00	
148P	6c	carmine	600.00			65.00	
		Block of four				275.00	
		P# blk. of 12				1,200.	
149P	7c	vermilion	375.00			27.50	
		Block of four				125.00	
		P# blk. of 12				650.00	
150P	10c	brown	500.00			70.00	
		Block of four				300.00	
		P# blk. of 12				1,350.	
151P	12c	violet	400.00			30.00	
		Block of four				125.00	
		P# blk. of 12				700.00	
152P	15c	orange	450.00			55.00	
		Block of four				250.00	
		P# blk. of 12				1,000.	
153P	24c	purple	450.00			55.00	
		Block of four				250.00	
		P# blk. of 12				1,000.	
154P	30c	black	450.00			70.00	
		Block of four				300.00	
		P# blk. of 12				1,350.	
155P	90c	carmine	450.00			80.00	
		Block of four				350.00	
		P# blk. of 12				1,450.	

Secret Marks on 24, 30 and 90c Dies of the Bank Note Issues

National 24c - Rays of lower star normal.

Continental 24c - Rays of lower star strengthened.

National 30c - Lower line does not join point of shield.

Continental and American 30c - Lower line joins point of shield and bottom line of shield thicker.

National 90c - Rays of star in upper right normal.

Continental and American 90c - Rays of star in upper right strengthened.

1873   **Continental Bank Note Co.**

			DIE			PLATE	
			(1) Large	(2) Small	(2a)	(3) India	(4) Card
156P	1c	ultra.	750.00			100.00	175.00
		Block of four				450.00	
		P# blk. of 14				2,100.	
157P	2c	brown	600.00	265.00	800.00	65.00	30.00
		Block of four				300.00	150.00
		P# blk. of 12				1,200.	—
158P	3c	green	600.00	265.00	800.00	100.00	200.00
		Block of four				450.00	
		P# blk. of 14				2,100.	
159P	6c	pink	1,000.	300.00	800.00	200.00	275.00
		Block of four				950.00	
		P# blk. of 12				3,750.	
160P	7c	orange vermilion	450.00	265.00	800.00	65.00	20.00
		Block of four				300.00	100.00
		P# blk. of 14				1,500.	—
161P	10c	brown	750.00	285.00	800.00	110.00	275.00
		Block of four				550.00	
		P# blk. of 14				2,400.	
162P	12c	blackish violet	400.00	265.00	800.00	70.00	30.00
		Block of four				350.00	140.00
		P# blk. of 14				1,750.	—
163P	15c	yellow orange	650.00	265.00	800.00	100.00	35.00
		Block of four				450.00	180.00
		P# blk. of 12				1,800.	—
164P	24c	violet	650.00	265.00	800.00	90.00	50.00

No.	Denom	Color	DIE Large (1)	DIE Small (2)	DIE (2a)	PLATE India (3)	PLATE Card (4)
		Block of four				400.00	225.00
		P# blk. of 12				1,750.	
165P	30c	gray black	650.00	265.00	800.00	70.00	30.00
		Block of four				350.00	140.00
		P# blk. of 12				1,500.	
166P	90c	rose carmine	650.00	265.00	800.00	100.00	70.00
		Block of four				450.00	325.00
		P# blk. of 12				1,850.	

Die proofs of the 24c, 30c and 90c show secret marks, as illustrated, but as plates of these denominations were not made from these dies, plate proofs can be identified only by color.

No.	Denom	Color	Large	Small	(2a)	India	Card
182P	1c	gray blue	850.00			110.00	
		Block of four				500.00	
		P# blk. of 12				1,850.	
183P	2c	vermilion	500.00	275.00	750.00	45.00	20.00
		Block of four				200.00	110.00
		P# blk. of 12				825.00	—
185P	5c	blue	600.00	275.00	750.00	100.00	35.00
		Block of four				450.00	165.00
		P# blk. of 12				1,800.	—

1881-82   American Bank Note Co.

No.	Denom	Color	Large	Small	(2a)	India	Card
205P	5c	yellow brown	350.00	275.00	750.00	65.00	25.00
		Block of four				290.00	125.00
		P# blk. of 12				1,100.	—
206P	1c	blue	550.00	275.00	750.00	65.00	30.00
		Block of four				290.00	140.00
		P# blk. of 12				1,100.	—
207P	3c	blue green	550.00	275.00	750.00	65.00	30.00
		Block of four				290.00	140.00
		P# blk. of 12				1,100.	—
208P	6c	rose	1,100.	275.00	750.00	160.00	80.00
		Block of four				750.00	350.00
		P# blk. of 12				—	—
a.	6c	brown red		750.00			90.00
209P	10c	brown	1,100.	275.00	750.00	70.00	40.00
		Block of four				300.00	175.00
		P# blk. of 12				1,200.	—

1883

No.	Denom	Color	Large	Small	(2a)	India	Card
210P	2c	red brown	550.00	275.00	750.00	60.00	35.00
		Block of four				260.00	150.00
		P# blk. of 12				1,100.	—
211P	4c	green	550.00	275.00	750.00	70.00	45.00
		Block of four				300.00	200.00
		P# blk. of 12				1,350.	—

1887-88

No.	Denom	Color	Large	Small	(2a)	India	Card
212P	1c	ultra.	950.00	275.00	750.00	175.00	1,850.
		Block of four				800.00	
		P# blk. of 12				3,250.	
213P	2c	green	600.00	275.00	750.00	65.00	35.00
		Block of four				290.00	150.00
		P# blk. of 12				1,150.	—
214P	3c	vermilion	650.00	275.00	750.00	70.00	45.00
		Block of four				300.00	200.00
		P# blk. of 12				—	—

Nos. 207P-1 & 214P-1 inscribed: "Worked over by new company, June 29th, 1881."

No.	Denom	Color	Large	Small	(2a)	India	Card
215P	4c	carmine	900.00	275.00	750.00	175.00	70.00
		Block of four				850.00	300.00
		P# blk. of 12				—	—
216P	5c	indigo	900.00	275.00	750.00	110.00	45.00
		Block of four				550.00	200.00
		P# blk. of 12				—	
217P	30c	org. brown	1,000.	275.00	750.00	110.00	45.00
		Block of four				550.00	200.00
		P# blk. of 10				—	
218P	90c	purple	1,000.	275.00	750.00	160.00	70.00
		Block of four				750.00	300.00
		P# blk. of 10					

1890-93

No.	Denom	Color	Large	Small	(2a)	India	Card
219P	1c	ultra.	300.00	275.00	550.00	45.00	65.00
		Block of four				175.00	290.00
		P# blk. of 12				900.00	1,200.
219DP	2c	lake	800.00	275.00	550.00	150.00	300.00
		Block of four				700.00	1,300.
		P# blk. of 12				3,000.	6,000.
220P	2c	carmine	700.00	275.00		400.00	275.00
		Block of four				1,800.	1,200.
		P# blk. of 12				7,000.	4,500.
221P	3c	purple	300.00	275.00	550.00	65.00	40.00
		Block of four				290.00	175.00
		P# blk. of 12				1,200.	1,100.
222P	4c	dark brown	300.00	275.00	550.00	65.00	40.00
		Block of four				290.00	175.00
		P# blk. of 12				1,200.	1,100.
223P	5c	chocolate	300.00	275.00	550.00	60.00	35.00
		Block of four				250.00	150.00
		P# blk. of 12				1,100.	1,150.
224P	6c	brown red	300.00	275.00	550.00	60.00	35.00
		Block of four				250.00	150.00
		P# blk. of 12				1,100.	1,400.
225P	8c	lilac	850.00	275.00	550.00	100.00	200.00
		Block of four				450.00	900.00
		P# blk. of 12				2,000.	3,750.
226P	10c	green	300.00	275.00	550.00	70.00	70.00
		Block of four				300.00	300.00
		P# blk. of 12				1,300.	1,350.
227P	15c	indigo	400.00	275.00	550.00	80.00	70.00
		Block of four				350.00	300.00
		P# blk. of 12				1,500.	1,600.
228P	30c	black	400.00	275.00	550.00	80.00	80.00
		Block of four				350.00	350.00
		P# blk. of 12				1,500.	1,600.
229P	90c	orange	400.00	275.00	550.00	110.00	90.00
		Block of four				500.00	400.00
		P# blk. of 12				2,000.	2,100.

COLUMBIAN ISSUE

1893

No.	Denom	Color	Large	Small	(2a)	India	Card
230P	1c	blue	800.00	450.00	1,100.	75.00	40.00
		Block of four				325.00	200.00
		P# blk. of 8				850.00	625.00
231P	2c	violet	800.00	450.00	1,100.	450.00	150.00
		Block of four				2,000.	650.00
		P# blk. of 8				4,500.	1,900.
232P	3c	green	800.00	450.00	1,100.	100.00	90.00
		Block of four				450.00	400.00
		P# blk. of 8				1,200.	1,000.
233P	4c	ultra.	800.00	450.00	1,100.	100.00	90.00
		Block of four				450.00	400.00
		P# blk. of 8				1,200.	1,000.
233aP	4c	blue (error) on thin card	2,750.				
234P	5c	chocolate	800.00	450.00	1,100.	100.00	90.00
		Block of four				450.00	400.00
		P# blk. of 8				1,200.	1,000.
235P	6c	purple	800.00	450.00	1,100.	110.00	90.00
		Block of four				500.00	400.00
		P# blk. of 8				1,500.	1,000.
236P	8c	magenta	800.00	450.00	1,100.	110.00	200.00
		Block of four				500.00	950.00
		P# blk. of 8				1,500.	2,500.
237P	10c	black brown	800.00	450.00	1,100.	110.00	90.00
		Block of four				500.00	400.00
		P# blk. of 8				1,500.	1,000.
238P	15c	dark green	800.00	450.00	1,100.	110.00	110.00
		Block of four				500.00	500.00
		P# blk. of 8				1,500.	1,500.
239P	30c	orange brown	800.00	450.00	1,100.	150.00	130.00
		Block of four				700.00	600.00
		P# blk. of 8				2,250.	2,250.
240P	50c	slate blue	800.00	450.00	1,100.	225.00	150.00
		Block of four				1,000.	700.00
		P# blk. of 8				2,750.	2,200.
241P	$1	salmon	1,000.	550.00	1,200.	275.00	225.00
		Block of four				1,300.	950.00
		P# blk. of 8				3,500.	
242P	$2	brown red	1,000.	550.00	1,200.	300.00	250.00
		Block of four				1,250.	1,100.
		P# blk. of 8				3,750.	3,000.
243P	$3	yellow green	1,000.	550.00	1,200.	375.00	300.00
		Block of four				1,800.	1,350.
		P# blk of 8				5,000.	3,750.
244P	$4	crimson lake	1,000.	550.00	1,200.	450.00	350.00
		Block of four				2,000.	1,600.
		P# blk. of 8				5,500.	4,750.
245P	$5	black	1,000.	550.00	1,200.	550.00	450.00
		Block of four				2,300.	2,000.
		P# blk. of 8				6,250.	5,750.

This set also exists as Large Die proofs, not die sunk, but printed directly on thin card. Set price $8,650. 1c through 50c, $400 each; $1 through $5, $850 each. Nos. 234P1, 234P2 differ from issued stamp.

Bureau of Engraving and Printing

1894

No.	Denom	Color	Large	Small	(2a)	India	Card
246P	1c	ultra	450.00				
247P	1c	blue	250.00	250.00	650.00		150.00
		Block of four					650.00
		P# blk. of 6					1,200.
250P	2c	carmine (triangle I)	250.00	250.00			150.00
		Block of four					700.00
		P# blk. of 6					1,350.
251P	2c	carmine (triangle II)	250.00	—			
252P	2c	carmine (triangle III)	400.00			650.00	275.00
		Block of four				1,200.	
253P	3c	purple (triangle I)	400.00				
253P	3c	purple (triangle II)	325.00	250.00	650.00		
254P	4c	dark brown	250.00	250.00	650.00		
255P	5c	chocolate	250.00	250.00	650.00		
256P	6c	brown					350.00
		Block of four					1,600.
		P# blk. of 6					2,750.
257P	8c	violet brown	275.00	250.00	650.00		
258P	10c	green	275.00	250.00	650.00		
259P	15c	dark blue	300.00	250.00	650.00		
260P	50c	orange	450.00	210.00	650.00		
261AP	$1	black	475.00	350.00	725.00		
262P	$2	dark blue	475.00	350.00			600.00
		Block of four					2,500.
		P# blk. of 6					4,000.
263P	$5	dark green	650.00	375.00	725.00		650.00
		Block of four					2,700.

P# blk. of 6					4,250.

258P to 263P (small die) are from the type II die.

1898-99

279P	1c	green	700.00	375.00 700.00
279BP	2c	orange red		700.00
280P	4c	rose brown	700.00	700.00
281P	5c	blue	700.00	375.00 700.00
282P	6c	lake		700.00
283P	10c	orange brown (type II)	800.00	375.00 700.00
283aP	10c	brown (type II)	800.00	
284P	15c	olive green (type II)	800.00	375.00 700.00

TRANS-MISSISSIPPI ISSUE

1898

285P	1c	green	1,000.	650.00 1,000.	
286P	2c	copper red	1,000.	650.00 1,000.	1,350.
287P	4c	orange	1,000.	650.00 1,000.	
288P	5c	dull blue	1,000.	650.00 1,000.	
289P	8c	violet brown	1,000.	650.00 1,000.	
290P	10c	gray violet	1,000.	650.00 1,000.	
291P	50c	sage green	1,000.	650.00 1,000.	
292P	$1	black	1,100.	650.00 1,000.	
293P	$2	orange brown	1,100.	650.00 1,000.	2,750.
		Block of four			11,500.

PAN-AMERICAN ISSUE

1901

294P	1c	green & black	575.00	575.00 800.00
295P	2c	carmine & black	575.00	575.00 800.00
296P	4c	chocolate & black	575.00	575.00 800.00
297P	5c	ultra & black	575.00	575.00 800.00
298P	8c	brown violet & black	575.00	575.00 800.00
299P	10c	yellow brown & black	575.00	575.00 800.00

1902-03

300P	1c	green	750.00	300.00 650.00
301P	2c	carmine	750.00	300.00 650.00
302P	3c	purple	750.00	300.00 650.00
303P	4c	orange brown	750.00	300.00 650.00
304P	5c	blue	750.00	300.00 650.00
305P	6c	lake	750.00	300.00 650.00
306P	8c	violet black	750.00	300.00 650.00
307P	10c	orange brown	750.00	300.00 650.00
308P	13c	deep violet brown	750.00	300.00 650.00
309P	15c	olive green	750.00	300.00 650.00
310P	50c	orange	750.00	300.00 650.00
311P	$1	black	750.00	300.00 650.00
312P	$2	blue	750.00	300.00 650.00
313P	$5	green	850.00	375.00 800.00

1903

319P	2c	carmine, Die I	950.00	900.00
319iP	2c	carmine, Die II	950.00	700.00

LOUISIANA PURCHASE ISSUE

1904

323P	1c	green	1,400.	750.00 900.00
324P	2c	carmine	1,400.	750.00 900.00
325P	3c	violet	1,400.	750.00 900.00
326P	5c	dark blue	1,400.	750.00 900.00
327P	10c	brown	1,400.	750.00 900.00

JAMESTOWN EXPOSITION ISSUE

1907

328P	1c	green	1,300.	900.00 1,100.
329P	2c	carmine	1,300.	900.00 1,100.
330P	5c	blue	1,300.	900.00 1,100.

1908-09

331P	1c	green	1,050.	725.00 800.00
332P	2c	carmine	1,050.	725.00 800.00
333P	3c	deep violet	1,050.	725.00 800.00
334P	4c	brown	1,050.	725.00 800.00
335P	5c	blue	1,050.	725.00 800.00
336P	6c	red orange	1,050.	725.00 800.00
337P	8c	olive green	1,050.	725.00 800.00
338P	10c	yellow	1,050.	725.00 800.00
339P	13c	blue green	1,050.	725.00 800.00
340P	15c	pale ultramarine	1,050.	725.00 800.00
341P	50c	violet	1,050.	725.00 800.00
342P	$1	violet black	1,050.	725.00 800.00

LINCOLN MEMORIAL ISSUE

1909

367P	2c	carmine	1,100.	900.00 1,000.

ALASKA-YUKON ISSUE

1909

370P	2c	carmine	1,100.	900.00 1,000.

HUDSON-FULTON ISSUE

1909

372P	2c	carmine	1,100.	900.00 1,000.

PANAMA-PACIFIC ISSUE

1912-13

397P	1c	green	1,250.	1,100. 1,100.
398P	2c	carmine	1,250.	1,100. 1,100.
399P	5c	blue	1,250.	1,100. 1,100.
400P	10c	org. yellow	1,250.	1,100. 1,100.
400AP	10c	orange	1,350.	1,100. 1,200.
398AP	2c	carmine *(Inscribed "Gatun Locks")*	4,750.	

Plates were made of this design. It was discovered that the view shown did not in fact represent the Gatun Locks, but those of San Pedro Miguel. The stamps and plates were destroyed and the die altered to read Panama Canal. Only three impressions of the original die exist.

1912-19

			DIE		
			(1) Large	(2) Small	(2a)
405P	1c	green	825.00	650.00	875.00
406P	2c	carmine	825.00	650.00	875.00
407P	7c	black	825.00	650.00	875.00
414P	8c	olive green	825.00	650.00	875.00
415P	9c	salmon red	825.00	650.00	875.00
416P	10c	orange yellow	825.00	650.00	875.00
434P	11c	dark green	825.00		
417P	12c	claret brown	825.00	650.00	875.00
513P	13c	apple green	825.00		
418P	15c	gray	825.00	650.00	875.00
419P	20c	ultramarine	825.00	650.00	875.00
420P	30c	orange red	825.00	650.00	875.00
421P	50c	violet	825.00	650.00	875.00
423P	$1	violet black	825.00	650.00	875.00

1918-20

524P	$5	deep green & black	1,500.
547P	$2	carmine & black	1,500.

VICTORY ISSUE

1919

537P	3c	violet	1,100.	850.00

PILGRIM ISSUE

1920

548P	1c	green	1,250.	1,000.
549P	2c	carmine rose	1,250.	1,000.
550P	5c	deep blue	1,250.	1,000.

1922-26

			LARGE DIE (1) India	(1a) White Wove	PLATE (3) White Wove	(4) Card
551P	½c	olive brown	800.00			
552P	1c	deep green	800.00	500.00	—	—
553P	1½c	yellow brown	800.00			
554P	2c	carmine	800.00	500.00	—	
555P	3c	violet	800.00	500.00	—	
556P	4c	yellow brown	800.00	500.00	—	
557P	5c	dark blue	800.00	500.00	—	
558P	6c	red orange	800.00	500.00	—	
559P	7c	black	800.00	500.00	—	
560P	8c	olive green	800.00	500.00	—	
561P	9c	rose	800.00	500.00	—	
562P	10c	orange	800.00	500.00	—	
563P	11c	light blue	1,200.	500.00	—	
564P	12c	brown violet	750.00	500.00	—	
622P	13c	green	1,000.	500.00	—	
565P	14c	dark blue	750.00	500.00	—	
566P	15c	gray	800.00			
623P	17c	black	800.00			
567P	20c	carmine rose	800.00	500.00	—	
568P	25c	deep green	800.00	500.00	—	

			LARGE DIE (1) India	(1a) White Wove	PLATE (3) White Wove	(4) Card
569P	30c	olive brown	800.00	500.00	—	
570P	50c	lilac	800.00	500.00	—	
571P	$1	violet brown	800.00	500.00	—	
572P	$2	deep blue	1,100.	500.00		
573P	$5	carmine & dark blue	1,100.			

			SMALL DIE (2) India
572P	$2	deep blue	—

No. 573P1 exists only as a hybrid.

1923-26

			LARGE DIE (1) India	(1a) White Wove	SMALL DIE (2) White or Yellowish Wove
611P	Harding, 2c black		1000.	700.00	700.00
614P	Huguenot Walloon, 1c dark green		650.00	600.00	600.00
615P	Huguenot Walloon, 2c carmine rose		650.00	600.00	600.00
616P	Huguenot Walloon, 5c dark blue		650.00	600.00	600.00
617P	Lexington Concord, 1c deep green		650.00	600.00	600.00
618P	Lexington Concord, 2c carmine rose		650.00	600.00	600.00
619P	Lexington Concord, 5c dark blue		650.00	600.00	600.00
620P	Norse American, 2c car. & blk.		750.00	750.00	750.00
621P	Norse American, 5c dk. bl. & blk.		750.00	750.00	750.00
627P	Sesquicentennial, 2c carmine rose		700.00		750.00
628P	Ericsson, 5c gray lilac		700.00	650.00	750.00
629P	White Plains, 2c carmine rose		700.00	650.00	750.00

1927-29

643P	Vermont, 2c carmine rose	700.00	650.00	750.00
644P	Burgoyne, 2c carmine rose	700.00	650.00	750.00
645P	Valley Forge, 2c carmine rose	700.00	650.00	750.00
649P	Aeronautics, 2c carmine rose	1,250.	900.00	900.00
650P	Aeronautics, 5c blue	1,250.	900.00	900.00
651P	Clark, 2c carmine & black	800.00	700.00	650.00
654P	Edison, 2c carmine rose	800.00	700.00	650.00
657P	Sullivan, 2c carmine rose	750.00	700.00	650.00
680P	Fallen Timbers, 2c carmine rose	750.00	700.00	650.00
681P	Ohio River Canalization, 2c carmine rose	750.00	700.00	650.00

1930-31

682P	Massachusetts Bay, 2c carmine rose	750.00	700.00	650.00
683P	Carolina Charleston, 2c carmine rose	750.00	700.00	650.00
684P	1½c brown	650.00		
685P	4c brown	650.00		
688P	Braddock's Field, 2c carmine rose	750.00	700.00	650.00
689P	von Steuben, 2c carmine rose	750.00	700.00	650.00
690P	Pulaski, 2c carmine rose	750.00	700.00	650.00
702P	Red Cross, 2c black & red		700.00	650.00
703P	Yorktown, 2c carmine rose & black	1,000.	700.00	650.00

1932

704P	Bicentennial, ½c olive brown	850.00	800.00	750.00
705P	Bicentennial, 1c green	850.00	800.00	750.00
706P	Bicentennial, 1½c brown	850.00	800.00	750.00
707P	Bicentennial, 2c carmine rose	850.00	800.00	750.00
708P	Bicentennial, 3c deep violet	850.00	800.00	750.00
709P	Bicentennial, 4c light brown	850.00	800.00	750.00
710P	Bicentennial, 5c blue	850.00	800.00	750.00
711P	Bicentennial, 6c red orange	850.00	800.00	750.00
712P	Bicentennial, 7c black	850.00	800.00	750.00
713P	Bicentennial, 8c olive bister	850.00	800.00	750.00
714P	Bicentennial, 9c pale red	850.00	800.00	750.00
715P	Bicentennial, 10c org. yellow	850.00	800.00	750.00
716P	Winter Games, 2c carmine rose	1,000.	850.00	800.00
717P	Arbor Day, 2c carmine rose	800.00	800.00	700.00
718P	Olympic Games, 3c violet	1,100.	850.00	800.00
719P	Olympic Games, 5c blue	1,100.	850.00	800.00
720P	3c deep violet	700.00		
724P	Penn, 3c violet	700.00	650.00	650.00
725P	Webster, 3c violet	700.00	650.00	650.00

1933-34

726P	Georgia, 3c violet	700.00	650.00	650.00
727P	Peace, 3c violet	700.00	650.00	650.00
728P	Century of Progress, 1c yellow green	700.00	650.00	650.00
729P	Century of Progress, 3c violet	700.00	650.00	650.00
732P	N.R.A., 3c violet		650.00	650.00
733P	Byrd Antarctic, 3c dark blue		650.00	650.00
734P	Kosciuszko, 5c blue		650.00	650.00
736P	Maryland, 3c carmine rose		650.00	650.00
737P	Mothers Day, 3c deep violet	800.00	650.00	650.00
739P	Wisconsin, 3c deep violet		650.00	650.00
740P	Parks, 1c green			650.00
741P	Parks, 2c red			650.00
742P	Parks, 3c violet			650.00
743P	Parks, 4c brown			650.00
744P	Parks, 5c blue			650.00
745P	Parks, 6c dark blue			650.00
746P	Parks, 7c black			650.00
747P	Parks, 8c sage green			650.00
748P	Parks, 9c red orange	800.00		650.00
749P	Parks, 10c gray black			650.00

1935-37

772P	Conn., 3c violet			650.00
773P	San Diego, 3c purple			650.00
774P	Boulder Dam, 3c purple			650.00
775P	Michigan, 3c purple			650.00
776P	Texas, 3c purple			650.00
777P	Rhode Is., 3c purple			650.00
782P	Arkansas, 3c pur.	800.00		650.00
783P	Oregon, 3c purple	—	600.00	650.00
784P	Anthony, 3c violet			650.00
785P	Army, 1c green			650.00
786P	Army, 2c carmine			650.00
787P	Army, 3c purple	800.00		650.00
788P	Army, 4c gray			650.00
789P	Army, 5c ultramarine		800.00	650.00
790P	Navy, 1c green			650.00
791P	Navy, 2c car.	800.00		650.00
792P	Navy, 3c purple			650.00
793P	Navy, 4c gray			650.00
794P	Navy, 5c ultramarine			650.00
795P	Ordinance, 3c red violet			650.00
796P	Virginia Dare, 5c gray blue	800.00		650.00
797P	S.P.A. Sheet, 10c blue green			650.00
798P	Constitution, 3c red violet	800.00		650.00
799P	Hawaii, 3c violet			650.00
800P	Alaska, 3c violet			650.00
801P	Puerto Rico, 3c bright violet	800.00		650.00
802P	Virgin Is., 3c light violet	—		650.00

PRESIDENTIAL ISSUE

1938

803P	½c deep orange	1,000.	650.00
804P	1c green		650.00
805P	1½c bister brown		650.00
806P	2c rose carmine		650.00
807P	3c deep violet		650.00
808P	4c red violet		650.00
809P	4½c dark gray		650.00
810P	5c bright blue	1,000.	650.00
811P	6c red orange		650.00
812P	7c sepia		650.00
813P	8c olive green		650.00
814P	9c olive green		650.00
815P	10c brown red		650.00
816P	11c ultramarine		650.00
817P	12c bright violet	1,000.	650.00
818P	13c blue green		650.00
819P	14c blue		650.00
820P	15c blue gray		650.00
821P	16c black	1,000.	650.00
822P	17c rose red		650.00
823P	18c brown carmine		650.00
824P	19c bright violet		650.00
825P	20c bright blue green		650.00
826P	21c dull blue		650.00
827P	22c vermilion		650.00
828P	24c gray black		650.00
829P	25c deep red lilac		650.00
830P	30c deep ultramarine		650.00
831P	50c light red violet		650.00
832P	$1 purple & black		650.00
833P	$2 yellow green & black		800.00
834P	$5 carmine & black		800.00

1938

835P	Constitution, 3c deep violet		600.00
836P	Delaware, 3c red violet		600.00
837P	N.W. Territory, 3c bright violet		600.00
838P	Iowa, 3c violet	850.00	600.00

1939

852P	Golden Gate, 3c bright purple		600.00
853P	World's Fair, 3c deep purple		600.00
854P	Inauguration, 3c bright red violet	850.00	600.00
855P	Baseball, 3c violet		600.00
856P	Panama Canal, 3c deep red violet		600.00
857P	Printing, 3c violet		600.00
858P	Statehood, 3c rose violet		600.00

FAMOUS AMERICANS ISSUE

1940

859P	Authors, 1c bright blue green		800.00
860P	Authors, 2c rose carmine		800.00
861P	Authors, 3c bright red violet		800.00
862P	Authors, 5c ultramarine	850.00	800.00
863P	Authors, 10c dark brown		800.00
864P	Poets, 1c bright blue green		800.00
865P	Poets, 2c rose carmine		800.00
866P	Poets, 3c bright red violet		800.00
867P	Poets, 5c ultramarine		800.00
868P	Poets, 10c dark brown		800.00
869P	Educators, 1c bright blue green		800.00
870P	Educators, 2c rose carmine		800.00
871P	Educators, 3c bright red violet		800.00
872P	Educators, 5c ultramarine		800.00
873P	Educators, 10c dark brown		800.00
874P	Scientists, 1c bright blue green		800.00
875P	Scientists, 2c rose carmine	900.00	800.00
876P	Scientists, 3c bright red violet		800.00
877P	Scientists, 5c ultramarine		800.00
878P	Scientists, 10c dark brown		800.00
879P	Composers, 1c bright blue green		800.00
880P	Composers, 2c rose carmine		800.00
881P	Composers, 3c bright red violet		800.00
882P	Composers, 5c ultramarine	900.00	800.00
883P	Composers, 10c dark brown		800.00
884P	Artists, 1c bright blue green		800.00
885P	Artists, 2c rose carmine		800.00
886P	Artists, 3c bright red violet		800.00
887P	Artists, 5c ultramarine		800.00
888P	Artists, 10c dark brown		800.00
889P	Inventors, 1c bright blue green		800.00
890P	Inventors, 2c rose carmine		800.00
891P	Inventors, 3c bright red violet	900.00	800.00
892P	Inventors, 5c ultramarine		800.00
893P	Inventors, 10c dark brown		800.00

1940

894P	Pony Express, 3c henna brown		500.00
895P	Pan American, 3c light violet		500.00
896P	Idaho, 3c bright violet		500.00
897P	Wyoming, 3c brown violet		500.00
898P	Coronado, 3c violet		500.00
899P	Defense, 1c bright blue green	600.00	500.00
900P	Defense, 2c rose carmine		500.00
901P	Defense, 3c bright violet		500.00
902P	Emancipation, 3c deep violet	600.00	500.00

1941-44

903P	Vermont, 3c light violet		500.00
904P	Kentucky, 3c violet		500.00
905P	Win the War, 3c violet		500.00
906P	China, 5c bright blue		500.00
907P	Allied Nations, 2c rose carmine		500.00
908P	Four Freedoms, 1c bright blue green	600.00	500.00
922P	Railroad, 3c violet	600.00	500.00
923P	Steamship, 3c violet		500.00
924P	Telegraph, 3c bright red violet	600.00	500.00
925P	Corregidor, 3c deep violet		500.00
926P	Motion Picture, 3c deep violet	600.00	500.00

1945-46

927P	Florida, 3c bright red violet		500.00
928P	United Nations, 5c ultramarine		500.00
929P	Iwo Jima, 3c yellow green		500.00
930P	Roosevelt, 1c blue green		500.00
931P	Roosevelt, 2c carmine rose	600.00	500.00
932P	Roosevelt, 3c purple		500.00
934P	Army, 3c olive	600.00	500.00
935P	Navy, 3c blue	600.00	500.00
941P	Tennessee	600.00	
942P	Iowa	600.00	
944P	Kearny	600.00	

1947-50

945P	Edison	600.00
946P	Pulitzer	600.00
949P	Doctors	600.00
951P	Constitution	600.00
958P	Wisconsin	600.00
959P	Women	600.00
962P	Key	600.00
965P	Stone	600.00
973P	Rough Riders	600.00
981P	Minnesota Terr., 3c blue green	600.00 —

983P	Puerto Rico	600.00
991P	Supreme Court	600.00
992P	Capitol	600.00

1951-53

1000P	Cadillac	600.00	
1001P	Colorado	600.00	
1002P	Chemical, 3c violet brown	600.00	
1003P	Brooklyn	600.00	
1004P	Betsy Ross	600.00	
1005P	4H Clubs	600.00	
1007P	A.A.A., 3c deep blue	600.00	—
1009P	Grand Coulee Dam, 3c blue green	600.00	
1011P	Mt. Rushmore, 3c blue green	600.00	
1017P	National Guard 3c bright blue	600.00	
1018P	Ohio Statehood, 3c chocolate	600.00	
1019P	Washington	600.00	
1020P	Louisiana	600.00	
1021P	Japan	600.00	
1022P	American Bar	600.00	
1026P	Gen. Patton, 3c blue violet	600.00	—

1954

1029P	Columbia	600.00

LIBERTY ISSUE

1031P	Washington	600.00
1032P	Mount Vernon	600.00
1033P	Jefferson	
1036P	Lincoln	600.00
1038P	Monroe	600.00
1039P	Roosevelt	
1047P	Monticello	600.00
1050P	Marshall	600.00
1051P	Anthony	600.00
1052P	Henry	600.00

1954-57

1053P	Hamilton	600.00	
1060P	Nebraska	600.00	
1062P	Eastman	600.00	
1063P	Lewis & Clark	600.00	
1068P	New Hampshire	600.00	
1073P	Franklin	600.00	
1074P	Washington	600.00	
1076P	FIPEX, 3c deep violet	600.00	—
1077P	Turkey	600.00	
1078P	Antelope	600.00	
1079P	Salmon	600.00	
1081P	Wheatland	600.00	
1082P	Labor Day	600.00	
1083P	Nassau Hall	600.00	
1085P	Children	600.00	
1086P	Hamilton, 3c rose red	600.00	—
1087P	Polio	600.00	
1090P	Steel	600.00	

AIR POST

1918

			DIE	
			(1) Large	(2) Small
C1P	6c	orange	9,500.	
C2P	16c	green	8,000.	
C3P	24c	carmine rose & blue	9,500.	

1923

C4P	8c	dark green	5,500.	
C5P	16c	dark blue	5,500.	
C6P	24c	carmine	5,500.	

1926-27

C7P	10c	dark blue	4,000.	
C8P	15c	olive brown	4,000.	
C9P	20c	yellow green	4,000.	

LINDBERGH ISSUE

1927

C10P	10c	dark blue	4,000.	4,000.

1930

C11P	5c	car. & blue	4,250.	
C12P	5c	violet	3,300.	

ZEPPELIN ISSUE

1930

C13P	65c	green	9,250.	8,250.
a.		on wove	9,250.	
C14P	$1.30	brown	9,500.	8,500.
a.		on wove	9,500.	
C15P	$2.60	blue	9,500.	8,500.
a.		on wove	9,500.	

1932

C17P	8c	olive bister	2,750.	

CENTURY OF PROGRESS ISSUE

1933

C18P	50c	green	5,750.	5,750.

1935-39

C20P	25c	blue on wove		2,750.
C21P	20c	green on wove		2,750.

C22P	50c	carmine on wove			2,750.
C23P	6c	dark blue & carm. on wove			2,750.
C24P	30c	dull blue		3,500.	2,750.

1941-53

C25P	6c	carmine on wove		2,750.
C26P	8c	olive green on wove		2,750.
C27P	10c	violet on wove		2,750.
C28P	15c	brown carmine on wove		2,750.
C29P	20c	brt. grn. on wove		2,750.
C30P	30c	blue on wove		2,750.
C31P	50c	orange on wove		2,750.
C46P	80c	brt. red violet		1,650.
C47P	6c	carmine		1,650.
C48P	4c	brt. blue		—

AIR POST SPECIAL DELIVERY

1934

CE1P	16c	dk. blue on wove	2,600.
CE2P	16c	red & blue on wove	2,600.

SPECIAL DELIVERY

1885

			DIE			PLATE	
			(1) Large	(2) Small	(2a)	(3) India	(4) Card
E1P	10c	blue	500.00	250.00	1,000.	60.00	50.00
		Block of four				275.00	225.00
		P# blk. of 8					—

1888

E2P	10c	blue	750.00	250.00	1,000.	60.00	50.00
		Block of four				275.00	225.00
		P# blk. of 8				700.00	—

1893

E3P	10c	orange	1,100.	300.00	1,100.	110.00	120.00
		Block of four				475.00	525.00
		P# blk. of 8					1,500.

1894

E4P	10c	blue	400.00	250.00	1,100.

1902

E6P	10c	ultra.	900.00	250.00	750.00

1908

E7P	10c	green	1,750.	1,000.	1,100.

1922

			LARGE DIE	
			(1) India	(1a) White Wove
E12P	10c	deep ultra.	1,250.	1,100.

1925-54

E13P	15c	deep orange	1,250.
E14P	20c	black	1,250.
E20P	20c	deep blue	1,000.

REGISTRATION

1911

			DIE		PLATE	
			(1) Large	(2) Small	(2a)	(3) India	(4) Card
F1P	10c	ultra	2,500.	1,000.	1,100.		

POSTAGE DUE

1879

J1P	1c	brown	115.00	100.00	400.00	35.00	15.00
		Block of four				175.00	100.00
		P# blk. of 12				750.00	
J2P	2c	brown	115.00	100.00	400.00	32.50	15.00
		block of four				150.00	100.00
		P# blk. of 12				750.00	
		2c dark brown		—			
J3P	3c	brown	115.00	100.00	400.00	32.50	15.00
		block of four				150.00	100.00
		P# blk. of 12				750.00	
		3c dark brown		—			
J4P	5c	brown	115.00	100.00	400.00	32.50	15.00
		block of four				150.00	100.00
		P# blk. of 12				750.00	
		5c dark brown		—			
J5P	10c	brown	115.00	100.00	400.00		15.00

	10c dark brown		—			50.00	
		block of four				250.00	100.00
		P# blk. of 12				1,200.	
J6P	30c	brown	115.00	100.00	400.00		15.00
		30c dark brown		—			50.00
		block of four				250.00	100.00
		P# blk. of 12				1,200.	
J7P	50c	brown	115.00	100.00	400.00		15.00
		50c dark brown		—			50.00
		block of four				250.00	100.00
		P# blk. of 12				1,200.	

1887

J15P	1c	red brown		400.00	20.00
		Block of four			
		P# blk. of 12			
J16P	2c	red brown		400.00	20.00
		Block of four			
		P# blk. of 12			
J17P	3c	red brown		400.00	30.00
		Block of four			
		P# blk. of 12			
J18P	5c	red brown		400.00	20.00
		Block of four			
		P# blk. of 12			
J19P	10c	red brown		400.00	30.00	40.00
		Block of four			150.00	
		P# blk. of 12			600.00	
J20P	30c	red brown		400.00	30.00	25.00
		Block of four			150.00	
		P# blk. of 12			600.00	
J21P	50c	red brown		400.00	75.00	40.00
		Block of four			350.00	
		P# blk. of 12			1,500.	

1891-93

J22P	1c	bright claret	140.00	125.00	400.00	20.00	25.00
		Block of four				110.00	125.00
		P# blk. of 12					—
J23P	2c	bright claret	140.00	125.00	400.00	20.00	25.00
		Block of four				110.00	125.00
		P# blk. of 12					—
J24P	3c	bright claret	140.00	125.00	400.00	20.00	25.00
		Block of four				110.00	125.00
		P# blk. of 12					—
J25P	5c	bright claret	140.00	125.00	400.00	20.00	25.00
		Block of four				110.00	125.00
		P# blk. of 12					—
J26P	10c	bright claret	140.00	125.00	400.00	20.00	25.00
		Block of four				110.00	125.00
		P# blk. of 12					—
J27P	30c	bright claret	140.00	125.00	400.00	45.00	25.00
		Block of four				225.00	125.00
		P# blk. of 12					—
J28P	50c	bright claret	140.00	125.00	400.00	30.00	25.00
		Block of four				140.00	125.00
		P# blk. of 12					—

1894

J31P	1c	claret	165.00	120.00	350.00		
J32P	2c	claret	165.00	120.00	350.00		125.00
		Block of four				650.00	
		P# blk. of 6					1,200.
J33P	3c	claret	165.00	120.00	350.00		
J34P	5c	claret	165.00	120.00	350.00		
J35P	10c	claret	165.00	120.00	350.00		
J36P	30c	claret	165.00	120.00	350.00		
J37P	50c	claret	165.00	120.00	350.00		

1930-31

J69P	½c	deep carmine	450.00
J70P	1c	deep carmine	450.00
J71P	2c	deep carmine	450.00
J72P	3c	deep carmine	450.00
J73P	5c	deep carmine	450.00
J74P	10c	deep carmine	450.00
J75P	30c	deep carmine	450.00
J76P	50c	deep carmine	450.00
J77P	$1	deep carmine	450.00
J78P	$5	deep carmine	450.00

PARCEL POST POSTAGE DUE

1912

			DIE			PLATE	
			(1) Large	(2) Small	(2a)	(3) India	(4) Cards
JQ1P	1c	dark green	600.00	500.00	700.00		
JQ2P	2c	dark green	600.00	500.00	700.00		
JQ3P	5c	dark green	600.00	500.00	700.00		
JQ4P	10c	dark green	600.00	500.00	700.00		
JQ5P	25c	dark green	600.00	500.00	700.00		

CARRIERS

1851

LO1P	1c	bl. (Franklin)	700.00	200.00	700.00	60.00	30.00
		Block of four				300.00	150.00
		Cracked plate				—	—
LO2P	1c	blue (Eagle)	700.00	200.00	700.00	60.00	30.00
		Block of four				300.00	150.00
		P # blk. of 8				1,200.	

Nos. LO1P (1) and LO2P (1) exist only as hybrids.

OFFICIAL
AGRICULTURE

1873

O1P	1c	yellow	80.00	55.00	275.00	9.00	7.00
		Block of four				45.00	55.00
		P# blk. of 12					—
O2P	2c	yellow	80.00	55.00	275.00	9.00	7.00
		Block of four				45.00	55.00
		P# blk. of 10					—
O3P	3c	yellow	80.00	55.00	275.00	9.00	7.00
		Block of four				45.00	55.00
		P# blk. of 12					—
O4P	6c	yellow	80.00	55.00	275.00	9.00	7.00
		Block of four				45.00	55.00
		P# blk. of 12					—
O5P	10c	yellow	80.00	55.00	275.00	9.00	7.00
		Block of four				45.00	55.00
		P# blk. of 12					—
O6P	12c	yellow	80.00	55.00	275.00	9.00	7.00
		Block of four				45.00	55.00
		P# blk. of 12					—
O7P	15c	yellow	80.00	55.00	275.00	9.00	7.00
		Block of four				45.00	55.00
		P# blk. of 12					—
O8P	24c	yellow	80.00	55.00	275.00	9.00	7.00
		Block of four				45.00	55.00
		P# blk. of 12					—
O9P	30c	yellow	80.00	55.00	275.00	9.00	7.00
		Block of four				45.00	55.00
		P# blk. of 12					—

EXECUTIVE

O10P	1c	carmine	100.00	70.00	275.00	14.00	10.00
		Block of four				65.00	55.00
		P# blk. of 14					—
O11P	2c	carmine	100.00	70.00	275.00	14.00	10.00
		Block of four				65.00	55.00
		P# blk. of 12					—
O12P	3c	carmine	100.00	70.00	275.00	14.00	10.00
		Block of four				65.00	55.00

	P# blk. of 12						—
O13P 6c	carmine	100.00	70.00	275.00	25.00	15.00	
	Block of four				125.00	80.00	
	P# blk. of 10						—
O14P 10c	carmine	100.00	70.00	275.00	20.00	10.00	
	Block of four				100.00	55.00	
	P# blk. of 12						—

INTERIOR

O15P 1c	vermilion	80.00	55.00	275.00	9.00	7.00	
	Block of four				65.00	55.00	
	P# blk. of 12						—
O16P 2c	vermilion	80.00	55.00	275.00	9.00	7.00	
	Block of four				65.00	55.00	
	P# blk. of 10						—
O17P 3c	vermilion	80.00	55.00	275.00	9.00	7.00	
	Block of four				65.00	55.00	
	P# blk. of 10						—
O18P 6c	vermilion	80.00	55.00	275.00	17.50	15.00	
	Block of four				85.00	75.00	
	P# blk. of 12						—
O19P 10c	vermilion	80.00	55.00	275.00	9.00	7.00	
	Block of four				65.00	55.00	
	P# blk. of 12						—
O20P 12c	vermilion	80.00	55.00	275.00	9.00	7.00	
	Block of four				65.00	55.00	
	P# blk. of 10						—
O21P 15c	vermilion	80.00	55.00	275.00	9.00	7.00	
	Block of four				65.00	55.00	
	P# blk. of 12						—
O22P 24c	vermilion	80.00	55.00	275.00	9.00	7.00	
	Block of four				65.00	55.00	
	P# blk. of 12						—
O23P 30c	vermilion	80.00	55.00	275.00	9.00	7.00	
	Block of four				65.00	55.00	
	P# blk. of 12						—
O24P 90c	vermilion	80.00	55.00	275.00	11.00	9.00	
	Block of four				95.00	85.00	
	P# blk. of 12						—

JUSTICE

O25P 1c	purple	80.00	55.00	275.00	9.00	7.00	
	Block of four				55.00	55.00	
	P# blk. of 12						—
O26P 2c	purple	80.00	55.00	275.00	9.00	7.00	
	Block of four				55.00	55.00	
	P# blk. of 12						—
O27P 3c	purple	80.00	55.00	275.00	9.00	7.00	
	Block of four				55.00	55.00	
	P# blk. of 12						—
O28P 6c	purple	80.00	55.00	275.00	9.00	7.00	
	Block of four				55.00	55.00	
	P# blk. of 12						—
O29P 10c	purple	80.00	55.00	275.00	9.00	7.00	
	Block of four				55.00	55.00	
	P# blk. of 12						—
O30P 12c	purple	80.00	55.00	275.00	9.00	7.00	
	Block of four				55.00	55.00	
	P# blk. of 12						—
O31P 15c	purple	80.00	55.00	275.00	9.00	7.00	
	Block of four				55.00	55.00	
	P# blk. of 10						—
O32P 24c	purple	80.00	55.00	275.00	12.00	9.00	
	Block of four				85.00	65.00	
	P# blk. of 12						—
O33P 30c	purple	80.00	55.00	275.00	12.00	9.00	
	Block of four				85.00	65.00	
	P# blk. of 12						—
O34P 90c	purple	80.00	55.00	275.00	15.00	9.00	
	Block of four				90.00	65.00	
	P# blk. of 10						

NAVY

O35P 1c	ultramarine	80.00	55.00	275.00	10.00	7.00	
	Block of four				55.00	55.00	
	P# blk. of 12						—
O36P 2c	ultramarine	80.00	55.00	275.00	10.00	7.00	
	Block of four				55.00	55.00	
	P# blk. of 12						—
O37P 3c	ultramarine	80.00	55.00	275.00	10.00	7.00	
	Block of four				55.00	55.00	
	P# blk. of 10						—
O38P 6c	ultramarine	80.00	55.00	275.00	25.00	18.00	
	Block of four				125.00	90.00	
	P# blk. of 10						—
O39P 7c	ultramarine	80.00	55.00	275.00	12.00	12.00	
	Block of four				75.00	75.00	
	P# blk. of 10						—
O40P 10c	ultramarine	80.00	55.00	275.00	10.00	7.00	
	Block of four				55.00	55.00	
	P# blk. of 12						—
O41P 12c	ultramarine	80.00	55.00	275.00	10.00	7.00	
	Block of four				55.00	55.00	
	P# blk. of 12						—
O42P 15c	ultramarine	80.00	55.00	275.00	10.00	7.00	
	Block of four				55.00	55.00	
	P# blk. of 12						—
O43P 24c	ultramarine	80.00	55.00	275.00	12.00	7.00	
	Block of four				75.00	55.00	
	P# blk. of 12						—
O44P 30c	ultramarine	80.00	55.00	275.00	20.00	10.00	
	Block of four				105.00	75.00	
	P# blk. of 12						—
O45P 90c	ultramarine	80.00	55.00	275.00	13.00	10.00	
	Block of four				80.00	75.00	
	P# blk. of 12						—

POST OFFICE

O47P 1c	black	80.00	55.00	275.00	8.00	7.00	
	Block of four				55.00	55.00	
	P# blk. of 10						—
O48P 2c	black	80.00	55.00	275.00	8.00	7.00	
	Block of four				55.00	55.00	
	P# blk. of 14						—
O49P 3c	black	80.00	55.00	275.00	8.00	7.00	
	Block of four				55.00	55.00	
	P# blk. of 12						—
O50P 6c	black	80.00	55.00	275.00	8.00	7.00	
	Block of four				55.00	55.00	
	P# blk. of 12						—
O51P 10c	black	80.00	55.00	275.00	10.00	10.00	
	Block of four				65.00	65.00	
	P# blk. of 12						—
O52P 12c	black	80.00	55.00	275.00	8.00	8.00	
	Block of four				55.00	55.00	
	P# blk. of 12						—
O53P 15c	black	80.00	55.00	275.00	8.00	10.00	
	Block of four				55.00	65.00	
	P# blk. of 12						—
O54P 24c	black	80.00	55.00	275.00	8.00	7.00	
	Block of four				55.00	55.00	
	P# blk. of 12						—
O55P 30c	black	80.00	55.00	275.00	8.00	7.00	
	Block of four				55.00	55.00	
	P# blk. of 12						—
O56P 90c	black	80.00	55.00	275.00	8.00	7.00	
	Block of four				55.00	55.00	
	P# blk. of 12						—

STATE

O57P 1c	green	80.00	55.00	275.00	10.00	9.00	
	Block of four				70.00	60.00	
	P# blk. of 12						
O58P 2c	green	80.00	55.00	275.00	10.00	9.00	
	Block of four				70.00	60.00	
	P# blk. of 10						—
O59P 3c	green	80.00	55.00	275.00	10.00	9.00	
	Block of four				70.00	60.00	
	P# blk. of 10						—
O60P 6c	green	80.00	55.00	275.00	30.00	20.00	
	Block of four				150.00	115.00	
	P# blk. of 12						—
O61P 7c	green	80.00	55.00	275.00	10.00	9.00	
	Block of four				70.00	60.00	
	P# blk. of 12						—
O62P 10c	green	80.00	55.00	275.00	10.00	9.00	
	Block of four				70.00	60.00	
	P# blk. of 12						—
O63P 12c	green	80.00	55.00	275.00	10.00	9.00	
	Block of four				70.00	60.00	
	P# blk. of 10						—
O64P 15c	green	80.00	55.00	275.00	10.00	9.00	
	Block of four				70.00	60.00	
	P# blk. of 12						—
O65P 24c	green	80.00	55.00	275.00	20.00	9.00	
	Block of four				100.00	55.00	
	P# blk. of 12						—
O66P 30c	green	80.00	55.00	275.00	20.00	13.00	
	Block of four				100.00	80.00	
	P# blk. of 12						—
O67P 90c	green	80.00	55.00	275.00	20.00	13.00	
	Block of four				100.00	80.00	
	P# blk. of 12						—
O68P $2	green & black	150.00	125.00	300.00	90.00	55.00	
	Block of four				400.00	275.00	
	Sheet of ten				1,200.	—	
a.	Invtd. center					1,250.	
O69P $5	green & black	150.00	125.00	300.00	90.00	55.00	
	Block of four				400.00	275.00	
	Sheet of ten				1,200.	—	
a.	Invtd. center					1,250.	
O70P $10	green & black	150.00	125.00	350.00	90.00	55.00	
	Block of four				400.00		
	Sheet of ten				1,200.	—	
O71P $20	green & black	150.00	125.00	350.00	90.00	55.00	
	Block of four				400.00	275.00	
	Sheet of ten				1,200.	—	
a.	Invtd. center					1,250.00	

O68P to O71P Large Dies exist as hybrids only.

TREASURY

O72P 1c	brown	80.00	55.00	275.00	8.00	7.00	
	Block of four				55.00	55.00	
	P# blk. of 12						—
O73P 2c	brown	80.00	55.00	275.00	8.00	7.00	
	Block of four				55.00	55.00	
	P# blk. of 12						—
O74P 3c	brown	80.00	55.00	275.00	8.00	7.00	
	Block of four				55.00	55.00	
	P# blk. of 14						—
O75P 6c	brown	80.00	55.00	275.00	22.50	22.50	
	Block of four				115.00	115.00	
	P# blk. of 12						—
O76P 7c	brown	80.00	55.00	275.00	8.00	7.00	
	Block of four				55.00	55.00	
	P# blk. of 12						—
O77P 10c	brown	80.00	55.00	275.00	8.00	7.00	
	Block of four				55.00	55.00	
	P# blk. of 12						—
O78P 12c	brown	80.00	55.00	275.00	8.00	7.00	
	Block of four				55.00	55.00	

P# blk. of 12					—	
O79P 15c	brown	80.00	55.00	275.00	8.00	7.00
Block of four					55.00	55.00
P# blk. of 12					—	
O80P 24c	brown	80.00	55.00	275.00	20.00	15.00
Block of four					100.00	80.00
P# blk. of 12					—	
O81P 30c	brown	80.00	55.00	275.00	20.00	15.00
Block of four					100.00	80.00
P# blk. of 12					—	
O82P 90c	brown	80.00	55.00	275.00	12.00	7.00
Block of four					85.00	55.00
P# blk. of 12					—	

WAR

O83P 1c	rose	80.00	55.00	275.00	15.00	7.00
Block of four					75.00	55.00
P# blk. of 12					—	
O84P 2c	rose	80.00	55.00	275.00	15.00	7.00
Block of four					75.00	55.00
O85P 3c	rose	80.00	55.00	275.00	15.00	7.00
Block of four					75.00	55.00
O86P 6c	rose	80.00	55.00	275.00	15.00	7.00
Block of four					75.00	55.00
P# blk. of 12					—	
O87P 7c	rose	80.00	55.00	275.00	15.00	7.00
Block of four					75.00	55.00
P# blk. of 10					—	
O88P 10c	rose	80.00	55.00	275.00	15.00	7.00
Block of four					75.00	55.00
P# blk. of 10					—	
O89P 12c	rose	80.00	55.00	275.00	15.00	7.00
Block of four					75.00	55.00
P# blk. of 12					—	
O90P 15c	rose	80.00	55.00	275.00	15.00	7.00
Block of four					75.00	55.00
P# blk. of 12					—	
O91P 24c	rose	80.00	55.00	275.00	15.00	7.00
Block of four					75.00	55.00
P# blk. of 10					—	
O92P 30c	rose	80.00	55.00	275.00	15.00	18.00
Block of four					75.00	100.00
P# blk. of 10					—	
O93P 90c	rose	80.00	55.00	275.00	15.00	7.00
Block of four					75.00	55.00
P# blk. of 12					—	

O83-O93 exist in a plum snade.

POSTAL SAVINGS MAIL

1911

O124P 1c	dark violet	385.00	275.00	500.00
O121P 2c	black	385.00	275.00	500.00
O126P 10c	carmine	385.00	275.00	500.00
O122P 50c	dark green	385.00	275.00	500.00
O123P $1	ultramarine	385.00	275.00	500.00

POSTAL SAVINGS

1911

PS1P 10c	orange	1,000.		500.00
PS4P 10c	deep blue			500.00

POST OFFICE SEALS

1872

OX1P	green	275.00	165.00	100.00	65.00
Block of four				450.00	
a. Wove paper		100.00			
b. Glazed paper		190.00			

1877

OX3P	brown		30.00
Block of four			135.00

1879

OX4P	brown	2,500.	110.00	25.00
Block of four				110.00

1888-94

		DIE (2) Small
OX6bP	chocolate	140.00

1901-03

		DIE
OX10P	yellow brown	100.00
OX10aP	gray brown	100.00
OX10bP	red brown	100.00
OX10cP	dark brown	100.00
OX10dP	orange brown	100.00

NEWSPAPERS

1865

			DIE			PLATE	
			(1) Large	(2) Small	(2a)	(3) Wove Paper	(4) Card
PR2P 10c	green		275.00	125.00		60.00	72.50
Block of four						300.00	375.00
P# blk. of 6						—	
PR3P 25c	orange red		275.00	125.00		65.00	72.50
Block of four						325.00	375.00
P# blk. of 6						—	
PR4P 5c	blue		275.00	125.00		60.00	72.50
Block of four						300.00	375.00
P# blk. of 6						—	

1875

PR5P 5c	dark blue				475.00		40.00
PR6P 10c	deep green				475.00		45.00
PR7P 25c	dark carmine red				475.00		45.00
PR9P 2c	black		80.00	40.00	250.00	10.00	6.00
Block of four						45.00	35.00
P# blk. of 8						—	
PR10P 3c	black		80.00	40.00	250.00	10.00	6.00
Block of four						45.00	35.00
P# blk. of 8						—	
PR11P 4c	black		80.00	40.00	250.00	10.00	6.00
Block of four						45.00	35.00
P# blk. of 8						—	
PR12P 6c	black		80.00	40.00	250.00	10.00	6.00
Block of four						45.00	35.00
P# blk. of 8						—	
PR13P 8c	black		80.00	40.00	250.00	10.00	6.00
Block of four						45.00	35.00
P# blk. of 8						—	
PR14P 9c	black		80.00	40.00	250.00	10.00	6.00
Block of four						45.00	35.00
P# blk. of 8						—	
PR15P 10c	black		80.00	40.00	250.00	10.00	6.00
Block of four						45.00	35.00
P# blk. of 8						—	
PR16P 12c	rose		80.00	40.00	250.00	10.00	8.00
Block of four						45.00	45.00
P# blk. of 8						—	
PR17P 24c	rose		80.00	40.00	250.00	10.00	8.00
Block of four						45.00	45.00
P# blk. of 8						—	
PR18P 36c	rose		80.00	40.00	250.00	10.00	8.00
Block of four						45.00	45.00
P# blk. of 8						—	
PR19P 48c	rose		80.00	40.00	250.00	10.00	8.00
Block of four						45.00	45.00
P# blk. of 8						—	
PR20P 60c	rose		80.00	40.00	250.00	10.00	8.00

Block of four						45.00	45.00
P# blk. of 8						—	
PR21P 72c	rose		80.00	40.00	250.00	10.00	8.00
Block of four						45.00	45.00
P# blk. of 8						—	
PR22P 84c	rose		80.00	40.00	250.00	10.00	8.00
Block of four						45.00	45.00
P# blk. of 8						—	
PR23P 96c	rose		80.00	40.00	250.00	10.00	8.00
Block of four						45.00	45.00
P# blk. of 8						—	
PR24P $1.92	dark brown		80.00	40.00	250.00	14.00	10.00
Block of four						70.00	55.00
P# blk. of 8						—	
PR25P $3	ver		80.00	40.00	250.00	14.00	10.00
Block of four						70.00	55.00
P# blk. of 8						—	
PR26P $6	ultra		80.00	40.00	250.00	14.00	10.00
Block of four						70.00	55.00
P# blk. of 8						—	
PR27P $9	yellow		80.00	40.00	250.00	14.00	10.00
Block of four						70.00	55.00
P# blk. of 8						—	
PR28P $12	blue green		80.00	40.00	250.00	16.00	10.00
Block of four						80.00	55.00
P# blk. of 8						—	
PR29P $24	dark gray violet		80.00	40.00	250.00	18.00	12.00
Block of four						90.00	75.00
P# blk. of 8						—	
PR30P $36	brown rose		80.00	40.00	250.00	20.00	12.00
Block of four						100.00	75.00
P# blk. of 8						—	
PR31P $48	red brown		80.00	40.00	250.00	25.00	12.00
Block of four						125.00	75.00
P# blk. of 8						—	
PR32P $60	violet		80.00	40.00	250.00	30.00	15.00
Block of four						150.00	85.00
P# blk. of 8						—	

1879

PR57P 2c	deep black		80.00			12.00	6.00
Block of four						60.00	35.00
PR58P 3c	deep black		80.00			12.00	6.00
Block of four						60.00	35.00
PR59P 4c	deep black		90.00			12.00	6.00
Block of four						60.00	35.00
PR60P 6c	deep black		90.00			12.00	6.00
Block of four						60.00	35.00
PR61P 8c	deep black		90.00			12.00	6.00
Block of four						60.00	35.00
PR62P 10c	deep black		90.00			12.00	6.00
Block of four						60.00	35.00
PR63P 12c	red		90.00			12.00	8.00

	Block of four					60.00	50.00
PR64P	24c	red	90.00			12.00	8.00
	Block of four					60.00	50.00
PR65P	36c	red	90.00			12.00	8.00
	Block of four					60.00	50.00
PR66P	48c	red	90.00			12.00	8.00
	Block of four					60.00	50.00
PR67P	60c	red	90.00			12.00	8.00
	Block of four					60.00	50.00
PR68P	72c	red	90.00			12.00	8.00
	Block of four					60.00	50.00
PR69P	84c	red	90.00			12.00	8.00
	Block of four					60.00	50.00
PR70P	96c	red	90.00			12.00	8.00
	Block of four					60.00	50.00
PR71P	$1.92	pale brown	90.00			14.00	11.00
	Block of four					70.00	65.00
PR72P	$3	red verm.	90.00			14.00	11.00
	Block of four					70.00	65.00
PR73P	$6	blue	90.00			14.00	11.00
	Block of four					70.00	65.00
PR74P	$9	orange	90.00			14.00	11.00
	Block of four					70.00	65.00
PR75P	$12	yel. green	90.00			14.00	11.00
	Block of four					70.00	65.00
PR76P	$24	dark violet	90.00			18.00	11.00
	Block of four					90.00	65.00
PR77P	$36	Indian red	90.00			19.00	11.00
	Block of four					100.00	65.00
PR78P	$48	yel. brown	90.00			25.00	11.00
	Block of four					125.00	65.00
PR79P	$60	purple	90.00			25.00	11.00
	Block of four					125.00	65.00

1885

PR81P	1c	black	100.00	60.00	250.00	16.00	11.00
	Block of four					70.00	55.00
	P # blk. of 8						275.00
PR82P	12c	carmine		80.00	250.00	25.00	11.00
	Block of four					120.00	
PR83P	24c	carmine		80.00	250.00	25.00	11.00
	Block of four					120.00	
PR84P	36c	carmine		80.00	250.00	25.00	11.00
	Block of four					120.00	
PR85P	48c	carmine		80.00	250.00	25.00	11.00
	Block of four					120.00	
PR86P	60c	carmine		80.00	250.00	25.00	11.00
	Block of four					120.00	
PR87P	72c	carmine		80.00	250.00	25.00	11.00
	Block of four					120.00	
PR88P	84c	carmine		80.00	250.00	25.00	11.00
	Block of four					120.00	
PR89P	96c	carmine		80.00	250.00	25.00	11.00
	Block of four					120.00	

1895

PR102P	1c	blk	125.00	100.00	275.00

PR103P	2c	blk	125.00	100.00	275.00
PR104P	5c	blk	125.00	100.00	275.00
PR105P	10c	blk	125.00	100.00	275.00
PR106P	25c	carm	125.00	100.00	275.00
PR107P	50c	carm	125.00	100.00	275.00
PR108P	$2	scar	125.00	100.00	275.00
PR109P	$5	bl	125.00	100.00	275.00
PR110P	$10	grn	125.00	100.00	275.00
PR111P	$20	sl	125.00	100.00	275.00
PR112P	$50	carm	125.00	100.00	275.00
PR113P	$100	pur	125.00	100.00	275.00

POSTAL SAVINGS

1940

PS7P	10c	deep ultra. on wove		1,200.
PS8P	25c	dk. car. rose on wove		1,200.
PS9P	50c	dk. bl. green on wove		1,200.
PS10P	$1	gray black on wove		1,200.

1941

PS11P	10c	rose red on wove		1,000.
PS12P	25c	blue green on wove		1,000.
PS13P	50c	ultramarine on wove		1,000.
PS14P	$1	gray black on wove		1,000.
PS15P	$5	sepia on wove		1,000.

PARCEL POST

1912-13

			DIE ON INDIA			PLATE	
			(1) Large	(2) Small	(2a)	(3) India	(4) Card
Q1P	1c	carmine rose	900.00	700.00	900.00		
Q2P	2c	carmine rose	900.00	700.00	900.00		
Q3P	3c	carmine rose	900.00	700.00	900.00		
Q4P	4c	carmine rose	900.00	700.00	900.00		
Q5P	5c	carmine rose	900.00	700.00	900.00		
Q6P	10c	carmine rose	900.00	700.00	900.00		
Q7P	15c	carmine rose	900.00	700.00	900.00		
Q8P	20c	carmine rose	900.00	700.00	900.00		
Q9P	25c	carmine rose	900.00	700.00	900.00		
Q10	50c	carmine rose	900.00	700.00	900.00		
Q11P	75c	carmine rose	900.00	700.00	900.00		
Q12P	$1	carmine rose	900.00	700.00	900.00		

SPECIAL HANDLING

1925-28

QE1P	10c	yellow grn.	900.00
QE2P	15c	yellow grn.	900.00
QE3P	20c	yellow grn.	900.00
QE4aP	25c	deep green	900.00

REVENUE PROOFS
NORMAL COLORS
1862-68 by Butler & Carpenter, Philadelphia.
1868-75 by Joseph R. Carpenter, Philadelphia.

In the following listings the so-called small die proofs on India paper may be, in fact probably are, plate proofs. The editors shall consider them die proofs, however, until they see them in pairs or blocks. Many revenue proofs on India are mounted on card.

FIRST ISSUE

1862-71

			DIE ON INDIA		PLATE	
			(1) Large	(2) Small	(3) India	(4) Card
R1P	1c	Express, red			170.00	160.00
	Block of four					675.00
R2P	1c	Playing Cards, red	600.00		140.00	160.00
	Block of four				600.00	675.00
R3P	1c	Proprietary, red			130.00	100.00
	Block of four					450.00
R4P	1c	Telegraph, red				60.00
	Block of four					250.00
R5P	2c	Bank Check, blue		525.00		65.00
	Block of four					275.00

			DIE ON INDIA		PLATE	
			(1) Large	(2) Small	(3) India	(4) Card
R6P	2c	Bank Check, orange			140.00	
	Block of four				600.00	
R7P	2c	Certificate, blue				60.00
	Block of four					250.00
R8P	2c	Certificate, orange			160.00	
	Block of four				650.00	
R9P	2c	Express, blue				60.00
	Block of four					250.00
R10P	2c	Express, orange	600.00		140.00	
	Pair				600.00	
R11P	2c	Playing Cards, blue				80.00
	Block of four					350.00
R13P	2c	Proprietary, blue		400.00		60.00
	Block of four					250.00
R15P	2c	U.S.I.R., orange			700.00	
R16P	3c	Foreign Exchange, green	600.00		400.00	80.00
	Block of four					350.00
R17P	3c	Playing Cards, green		400.00		225.00
	Block of four					950.00
R18P	3c	Proprietary, green			140.00	60.00
	Block of four				600.00	250.00
R19P	3c	Telegraph, green	600.00		500.00	60.00
	Block of four					250.00
R20P	4c	Inland Exchange, brown			450.00	60.00
	Block of four					250.00
R21P	4c	Playing Cards, violet		400.00		200.00
	Block of four					875.00
R22P	4c	Proprietary, violet	600.00		250.00	135.00
	Block of four				1,100.	600.00
R23P	5c	Agreement, red				75.00
	Block of four					350.00
R24P	5c	Certificate, red			200.00	250.00
	Block of four				825.00	
R25P	5c	Express, red		250.00		70.00
	Block of four					325.00
R26P	5c	Foreign Exchange, red				450.00
R27P	5c	Inland Exchange, red		250.00		60.00
	Block of four					275.00
R28P	5c	Playing Cards, red		—	235.00	450.00
	Block of four				900.00	
R30P	6c	Inland Exchange, orange			130.00	75.00
	Block of four				550.00	325.00
R32P	10c	Bill of Lading, blue				75.00
	Block of four					325.00
R33P	10c	Certificate, blue			300.00	75.00
	Block of four					325.00
R34P	10c	Contract, blue				75.00
	Block of four					325.00
R35P	10c	Foreign Exchange, blue				75.00
	Block of four					325.00
R36P	10c	Inland Exchange, blue				75.00
	Block of four					325.00
R37P	10c	Power of Attorney, blue				75.00
	Block of four					325.00
R38P	10c	Proprietary, blue			160.00	
	Block of four				650.00	
R39P	15c	Foreign Exchange, brown			210.00	475.00
	Block of four				875.00	
R40P	15c	Inland Exchange, brown			275.00	75.00
	Block of four					325.00
R41P	20c	Foreign Exchange, red	600.00		200.00	225.00
	Block of four				825.00	925.00
R42P	20c	Inland Exchange, red	600.00	250.00	350.00	75.00
	Block of four					325.00
R43P	25c	Bond, red				375.00
	Block of four					—
R44P	25c	Certificate, red				75.00
	Block of four					325.00
R45P	25c	Entry of Goods, red				450.00
R46P	25c	Insurance, red			145.00	75.00

FIRST ISSUE (continued)

No.	Denom	Description	Die on India Large	Die on India Small	Plate India	Plate Card
R47P	25c	Life Insurance, red			600.00	325.00
		Block of four				75.00
R48P	25c	Power of Attorney, red				325.00
		Block of four				75.00
R49P	25c	Protest, red				325.00
		Block of four				75.00
R50P	25c	Warehouse Receipt, red				325.00
		Block of four				75.00
R51P	30c	Foreign Exchange, lilac			250.00	225.00
		Block of four			1,050.	1,000.
R52P	30c	Inland Exchange, lilac			140.00	120.00
		Block of four			600.00	500.00
R53P	40c	Inland Exchange, brown			200.00	140.00
		Block of four			600.00	600.00
R54P	50c	Conveyance, blue		250.00		140.00
		Block of four			600.00	400.00
R55P	50c	Entry of Goods, blue			140.00	90.00
		Block of four			600.00	400.00
R56P	50c	Foreign Exchange, blue			140.00	90.00
		Block of four			600.00	400.00
R57P	50c	Lease, blue			140.00	80.00
		Block of four			600.00	350.00
R58P	50c	Life Insurance, blue			140.00	80.00
		Block of four			600.00	350.00
R59P	50c	Mortgage, blue			140.00	200.00
		Block of four				850.00
R60P	50c	Original Process, blue			140.00	80.00
		Block of four			600.00	350.00
R61P	50c	Passage Ticket, blue				120.00
		Block of four				500.00
R62P	50c	Probate of Will, blue			140.00	120.00
		Block of four			600.00	500.00
R63P	50c	Surety Bond, blue				120.00
		Block of four				500.00
R64P	60c	Inland Exchange, orange			120.00	90.00
		Block of four				400.00
R65P	70c	Foreign Exchange, green			275.00	125.00
		Block of four				525.00
R66P	$1	Conveyance, red				100.00
		Block of four				425.00
R67P	$1	Entry of Goods, red	500.00			100.00
		Block of four				425.00
R68P	$1	Foreign Exchange red				80.00
		Block of four				350.00
R69P	$1	Inland Exchange, red				120.00
		Block of four				500.00
R70P	$1	Lease, red				750.00
R71P	$1	Life Insurance, red				80.00
		Block of four				350.00
R72P	$1	Manifest, red	130.00			80.00
		Block of four			—	350.00
R73P	$1	Mortgage, red				120.00
		Block of four				500.00
R74P	$1	Passage Ticket, red				750.00
		Block of four				3,100.
R75P	$1	Power of Attorney, red				210.00
		Block of four				900.00
R76P	$1	Probate of Will, red				80.00
		Block of four				350.00
R77P	$1.30	Foreign Exchange, orange			300.00	225.00
		Block of four			1,250.	950.00
R78P	$1.50	Inland Exchange, blue			250.00	100.00
		Block of four			1,050.	425.00
R79P	$1.60	Foreign Exchange green			300.00	225.00
		Block of four				950.00
R80P	$1.90	Foreign Exchange, violet			300.00	225.00
		Block of four			1,300.	950.00
R81P	$2	Conveyance, red			275.00	80.00
		Block of four				350.00
R82P	$2	Mortgage, red			275.00	80.00
		Block of four			—	350.00
R83P	$2	Probate of Will, red				250.00
		Block of four				—
R84P	$2.50	Inland Exchange, violet			400.00	350.00
		Block of four				—
R85P	$3	Charter Party, green			275.00	140.00
		Block of four			1,150.	600.00
R86P	$3	Manifest, green	350.00		400.00	140.00
		Block of four				600.00
R87P	$3.50	Inland Exchange, blue			400.00	225.00
		Block of four				950.00
R88P	$5	Charter Party, red			160.00	120.00
		Block of four			150.00	500.00
R89P	$5	Conveyance, red			600.00	120.00
		Block of four				500.00
R90P	$5	Manifest, red			300.00	120.00
		Block of four				500.00
R91P	$5	Mortgage, red			600.00	120.00
		Block of four				500.00
R92P	$5	Probate of Will, red			300.00	120.00
		Block of four				500.00
R93P	$10	Charter Party, green			275.00	120.00
		Block of four				500.00
R94P	$10	Conveyance, green				120.00
		Block of four				500.00
R95P	$10	Mortgage, green				120.00
		Block of four				500.00
R96P	$10	Probate of Will, green			300.00	160.00
		Block of four				600.00
R97P	$15	Mortgage, dark blue			—	250.00
		Block of four				1,100.
R97eP	$15	Mortgage, ultramarine			—	475.00
		Block of four				—
	$15	Mortgage, milky blue			400.00	
R98P	$20	Conveyance, orange			475.00	225.00
		Block of four			2,000.	950.00
R99P	$20	Probate of Will, orange				500.00
		Block of four				—
R100P	$25	Mortgage, red			400.00	300.00
		Block of four				1,250.
R101P	$50	U.S.I.R., green			500.00	525.00
		Block of four				2,200.
R102P	$200	U.S.I.R., green & red				1,900.

SECOND ISSUE

1871-72

No.	Denom	Description	Die on India Large	Die on India Small	Plate India	Plate Card
R105P	3c	blue & black			27.50	20.00
		Block of four			120.00	90.00
R109P	10c	blue & black			27.50	20.00
		Block of four			120.00	90.00
R111P	20c	blue & black			27.50	20.00
		Block of four			120.00	90.00
R112P	25c	blue & black			27.50	20.00
		Block of four			120.00	90.00
R115P	50c	blue & black			65.00	20.00
		Block of four			300.00	90.00
R119P	$1.30	blue & black			65.00	50.00
		Block of four			300.00	225.00
R120P	$1.50	blue & black			35.00	30.00
		Block of four			160.00	130.00
R121P	$1.60	blue & black			80.00	80.00
		Block of four			350.00	350.00
R122P	$1.90	blue & black			65.00	50.00
		Block of four			300.00	225.00
R126P	$3.50	blue & black			120.00	135.00
		Block of four			525.00	575.00
R130P	$25	blue & black			210.00	160.00
		Block of four			900.00	700.00
R131P	$50	blue & black			225.00	200.00
		Block of four			1,000.	900.00
R132P	$200	blue, red & black	3,500.	2,750.		2,500.
R133P	$500	green, red & black	3,500.	2,750.		
	$5000	green, orange & black	6,500.			
	$5000	light green, yellow & black	6,500.			
	$5000	blue, red & black	8,500.			
	$5000	light green, scarlet & black	8,500.			

The $5000 revenue stamp was approved but never issued. The "small die proofs" formerly listed under Nos. R103P–R131P are plate proofs from the sheets listed under "Trial Color Proofs."

THIRD ISSUE

1871-72

No.	Denom	Description	Plate India	Plate Card
R134P	1c	claret & black		22.50
		Block of four		100.00
R135P	2c	orange & black	24.00	22.50
		Block of four	105.00	100.00
R136P	4c	brown & black	27.50	22.50
		Block of four	120.00	100.00
R137P	5c	orange & black	27.50	22.50
		Block of four	120.00	100.00
R138P	6c	orange & black	27.50	22.50
		Block of four	120.00	100.00
R139P	15c	brown & black	27.50	22.50
		Block of four	120.00	100.00
R140P	30c	orange & black	35.00	27.50
		Block of four	150.00	120.00
R141P	40c	brown & black	35.00	27.50
		Block of four	150.00	120.00
R142P	60c	orange & black	95.00	80.00
		Block of four	400.00	350.00
a.		Center inverted		450.00
		Same, block of four		2,000.
		Double transfer, design of 70c		2,000.
R143P	70c	green & black	65.00	55.00
		Block of four	285.00	250.00
R144P	$1	green & black	55.00	55.00
		Block of four	250.00	250.00
R145P	$2	vermilion & black	120.00	160.00
		Block of four	500.00	675.00
R146P	$2.50	claret & black	70.00	55.00
		Block of four	300.00	250.00
R147P	$3	green & black	95.00	100.00
		Block of four	400.00	425.00
R148P	$5	vermilion & black	95.00	80.00
		Block of four	400.00	350.00
R149P	$10	green & black	120.00	80.00
		Block of four	500.00	350.00
R150P	$20	orange & black	175.00	225.00
		Block of four	750.00	950.00

The "small die proofs" formerly listed under Nos. R134P–R150P are plate proofs from the sheets listed under "Trial Color Proofs."

1875   National Bank Note Co., New York City

No.	Denom	Description	Die on India Large	Die on India Small	Plate India
R152P	2c	blue (Liberty)	450.00		110.00
		Block of four			475.00

DOCUMENTARY

1898

No.	Denom	Description	Plate India
R173P	$1	dark green	475.00
R176P	$10	black	575.00

1899

R180P	$500	carmine lake & black	1,200.

1914

R197P	2c	rose	—

1914-15

R226P	$500	blue	675.00

1952

R597P	55c	carmine	675.00

PROPRIETARY

1871-75   Joseph R. Carpenter, Philadelphia

No.	Denom	Description	Die on India Small	Plate India	Plate Card	Plate Bond
RB1P	1c	green & black		—	18.00	18.00
		Block of four			80.00	80.00
RB2P	2c	green & black	175.00		18.00	
		Block of four			80.00	
RB3P	3c	green & black		22.50	18.00	
		Block of four		100.00	80.00	
RB4P	4c	green & black		22.50	18.00	
		Block of four		100.00	80.00	
RB5P	5c	green & black		22.50	18.00	
		Block of four		100.00	80.00	
RB6P	6c	green & black		22.50	18.00	
		Block of four		100.00	80.00	
RB7P	10c	green & black		22.50	18.00	
		Block of four		100.00	80.00	
RB8P	50c	green & black	600.00		725.00	

	DIE ON INDIA		PLATE	
	(2) Small	(3) India	(4) Card	(5) Bond
RB9P $1 green & black	700.00			
RB10P $5 green & black	850.00		1,000.	

The "small die proofs" formerly listed under Nos. RB1P-RB7P are from the composite plate proofs listed under "Trial Color Proofs."

National Bank Note Co., New York City
1875-83

	DIE ON INDIA		PLATE	
	(1) Large	(2) Small	(3) India	(4) Card
RB11P 1c green	600.00		70.00	—
Block of four			300.00	
RB12P 2c brown	600.00		70.00	—
Pair			150.00	
RB13P 3c orange	600.00		75.00	—
Pair			165.00	
Block of four				—
RB14P 4c red brown	600.00		70.00	—
Pair			150.00	
Block of four				—
RB15P 4c red	600.00			—
RB16P 5c black	600.00		75.00	—
Pair			165.00	
Block of four				—
RB17P 6c violet blue	600.00		70.00	—
Pair			150.00	
RB18P 6c blue	600.00		200.00	
Pair			425.00	
RB19P 10c blue	600.00			

No. RB19P was produced by the Bureau of Engraving and Printing.

PLAYING CARDS
1896   **Bureau of Engraving & Printing**

RF2P 2c ultramarine	145.00
a. 2c blue	145.00

HUNTING PERMIT

	DIE (Wove)	
	(1) Large	(2) Small
RW1P 1934 $1 blue	—	2,750.
RW2P 1935 $1 rose lake		2,750.
RW3P 1936 $1 brown black		2,750.
RW4P 1937 $1 light green	—	2,750.
RW5P 1938 $1 light violet		2,750.
RW6P 1939 $1 chocolate		2,750.
RW7P 1940 $1 sepia		2,750.
RW8P 1941 $1 brown carmine		2,750.
RW9P 1942 $1 violet brown		2,750.
RW10P 1943 $1 deep rose		2,750.
RW11P 1944 $1 red orange		2,750.
RW12P 1945 $1 black	3,850.	2,750.
RW13P 1946 $1 red brown	3,850.	
RW14P 1947 $1 black	3,850.	
RW15P 1948 $1 bright blue	3,850.	
RW19P 1952 $2 deep ultra.	3,850.	
RW23P 1956 $2 black	3,850.	

TELEGRAPH
AMERICAN RAPID TELEGRAPH CO.
1881

	DIE (2) Small	PLATE (3) India
1T1P 1c black	77.50	32.50
Pair		67.50
1T2P 3c orange		32.50
Pair		67.50
1T3P 5c bister brown	77.50	32.50
Pair		67.50
1T4P 10c purple		32.50
Pair		67.50
1T5P 15c green	77.50	32.50
Pair		67.50
1T6P 20c red	77.50	32.50
Pair		67.50
1T7P 25c rose	77.50	32.50
Pair		67.50
1T8P 50c blue		32.50
Pair		67.50

"Collect"

	DIE		PLATE
	(1) Large	(2) Small	(3) India
1T9P 1c brown			32.50
Pair, setenant with 1T13P			67.50
Same, block of four			145.00
1T10P 5c blue			32.50
Pair, setenant with 1T14P			67.50
Same, block of four			145.00
1T11P 15c red brown			32.50
Pair, setenant with 1T15P			67.50
Same, block of four			145.00
1T12P 20c olive green			32.50
Pair, setenant with 1T16P			67.50
Same, block of four			145.00

Office Coupon

1T13P 1c brown	32.50
1T14P 5c blue	32.50
1T15P 15c red brown	32.50
1T16P 20c olive green	32.50

BALTIMORE & OHIO TELEGRAPH CO.
1885

3T1P 1c vermilion	32.50
Pair	67.50
3T2P 5c blue	32.50
Pair	67.50
3T3P 10c red brown	32.50
Pair	67.50
3T4P 25c orange	32.50
Pair	67.50

1886

3T6P black	32.50
Pair	67.50
3T7P 1c green	32.50
3T8P 5c blue	32.50
3T9P 10c brown	32.50
3T10P 25c orange	32.50

POSTAL TELEGRAPH CO.
1885

15T1P 10c green	55.00	32.50

15T2P 15c orange red		32.50
15T3P 25c blue	65.00	32.50
15T4P 50c brown	65.00	32.50

WESTERN UNION TELEGRAPH CO.

16T1P (1871) green	16.50
Pair	35.00
16T2P (1872) red	16.50
Pair	35.00
16T3P (1873) blue	16.50
Pair	35.00
16T4P (1874) brown	16.50
Pair	35.00
16T5P (1875) deep green	16.50
16T6P (1876) red	16.50
16T7P (1877) violet	—
16T8P (1878) gray brown	20.00
16T9P (1879) blue	14.00
16T10P (1880) lilac rose	16.00
16T11P (1881) green	16.00
16T12P (1882) blue	20.00
16T13P (1883) yellow brown	16.00
16T14P (1884) gray violet	20.00
16T15P (1885) green	20.00
16T16P (1886) brown violet	13.00
Pair	27.50
16T17P (1887) red brown	13.00
Pair	27.50
16T18P (1888) blue	13.00
Pair	27.50
16T19P (1889) olive green	16.00
16T22P (1892) vermilion	16.00
16T30P (1900) red violet	27.50
16T44P (1913) brown	— — —

TRIAL COLOR PROOFS

The listings of trial color proofs include several that are similar to the colors of the issued stamps.

New York
All on India paper unless otherwise stated.
Original Die
1845

	DIE		PLATE
	(1) Large	(2) Small	(5) Bond
9X1TC 5c dull dark violet		250.00	
9X1TC 5c brown violet		250.00	
9X1TC 5c deep rose violet		250.00	
9X1TC 5c deep blue		250.00	175.00
9X1TC 5c dark green		250.00	175.00
9X1TC 5c orange yellow		250.00	
9X1TC 5c brown		250.00	175.00
9X1TC 5c scarlet			175.00

With "Scar" on Neck

9X1TC 5c dull blue	175.00
9X1TC 5c vermilion	175.00

With "Scar" and dot in "P" of "POST"

9X1TC 5c sapphire	450.00	
9X1TC 5c dull gray blue		300.00

	DIE		PLATE
	(1) Large	(2) Small	(5) Bond
9X1TC 5c deep blue on Bond			250.00
9X1TC 5c deep ultramarine on thin glazed card	450.00		
9X1TC 5c deep green	450.00	300.00	
9X1TC 5c deep green on Bond			250.00
9X1TC 5c dull dark green		300.00	
9X1TC 5c org. verm.	450.00		
9X1TC 5c orange vermilion on thin glazed card	450.00		
9X1TC 5c dark red org.	450.00		
9X1TC 5c dull brown red on Bond		250.00	
9X1TC 5c dark brown red		300.00	
9X1TC 5c dull dark brown		300.00	
9X1TC 5c dull dark brown on Bond		250.00	
9X1TC 5c sepia	450.00		

	DIE		PLATE
	(1) Large	(2) Small	(5) Bond
9X1TC 5c brown black on thin glazed card	450.00		

The above listed Large Die varieties, except those on thin glazed card, have an additional impression of the portrait medallion. Plate proofs are from the small sheet of 9.

Providence, R. I.
1846

	Plate on Card
10X1TC 5c gray blue	275.00
10X1TC 5c green	275.00
10X1TC 5c brown carmine	275.00
10X1TC 5c brown	275.00
10X2TC 10c gray blue	400.00
10X2TC 10c green	400.00
10X2TC 10c brown carmine	400.00
10X2TC 10c brown	400.00
Sheet of 12, any color	3,750.

General Issues

1847

			DIE LARGE				DIE SMALL	
			India	Bond	Wove	Thin Glazed Card	India	Bond
1TC	5c	vio	900.00					
1TC	5c	dull bl.	900.00					
1TC	5c	deep blue		800.00	800.00		625.00	
1TC	5c	deep ultra.			800.00			
1TC	5c	bl green	900.00				625.00	
1TC	5c	dull blue green		800.00				
1TC	5c	dull grn.	900.00					600.00
1TC	5c	dk grn.	900.00					
1TC	5c	yellow green					625.00	
1TC	5c	org yel	900.00	800.00	800.00		625.00	
1TC	5c	deep yellow			800.00			
1TC	5c	org vermilion	900.00	800.00	800.00			
1TC	5c	scar vermilion	900.00	800.00		800.00		
1TC	5c	rose lake	900.00				625.00	
1TC	5c	black brown			800.00			
1TC	5c	dull rose lake					625.00	
1TC	5c	brn red	900.00					
1TC	5c	blk	900.00	800.00		800.00	675.00	
2TC	10c	vio	900.00					
2TC	10c	dull blue						
2TC	10c	dp blue	900.00	800.00	800.00	800.00	675.00	
2TC	10c	dull gray blue	900.00				625.00	
2TC	10c	blue green		800.00				
2TC	10c	dull blue green		800.00				
2TC	10c	dull green		800.00				
2TC	10c	dk grn	900.00					
2TC	10c	yel grn					675.00	
2TC	10c	dull yel			800.00			
2TC	10c	org yel	900.00		800.00			
2TC	10c	org vermilion	900.00	800.00	800.00		675.00	
2TC	10c	scar verm			800.00			
2TC	10c	gld brown	900.00	800.00		800.00		
2TC	10c	lt brn	900.00					
2TC	10c	dk brn	900.00	800.00				
2TC	10c	red brown					675.00	
2TC	10c	dull red					675.00	
2TC	10c	rose lake	900.00				625.00	
2TC	10c	dull rose lake					625.00	
2TC	10c	blk brn			800.00			
2TC	10c	yel grn on blue pelure paper	900.00					

			DIE (1) Large	DIE (2) Small	PLATE (3) India	PLATE (4) Card
1TC	5c	orange				600.00
1TC	5c	black				600.00
2TC	10c	orange				600.00
2TC	10c	deep brown				600.00

1875

			DIE (1) Large	DIE (2) Small	PLATE (3) India	PLATE (4) Card
3TC	5c	dull rose lake				550.00
3TC	5c	black		900.00		
3TC	5c	green		900.00		
4TC	10c	green		900.00		750.00

1856-60

			DIE (1) Large	DIE (2) Small	PLATE (3) India	PLATE (5) Wove Paper
11TC	3c	black				1,500.
12TC	5c	pale brown				300.00
12TC	5c	rose brown				300.00
12TC	5c	dp. red brown				1,500.
12TC	5c	dark olive bister				300.00
12TC	5c	olive brown				300.00
12TC	5c	olive green				300.00
12TC	5c	deep orange				300.00
12TC	5c	black				2,000.
13TC	10c	black	2,650.			—
37TC	24c	claret brown				600.00
37TC	24c	red brown				600.00
37TC	24c	orange				600.00
37TC	24c	deep yellow				600.00
37TC	24c	yellow				600.00
37TC	24c	deep blue				600.00
37TC	24c	black				600.00
37TC	24c	violet black				600.00
38TC	30c	black	2,350.		1,400.	600.00
		Block of four			9,000.	
39TC	90c	rose lake				625.00
39TC	90c	henna brown				625.00
39TC	90c	orange red				625.00
39TC	90c	brown orange	2,350.			625.00
39TC	90c	sepia				625.00
39TC	90c	dark green				625.00
39TC	90c	dark violet brown				625.00
39TC	90c	black	2,350.	1,250.		675.00

1875

			DIE (1) Large	DIE (2) Small	PLATE (3) India	PLATE (5) Wove Paper
40TC	1c	orange vermilion				400.00
40TC	1c	orange				400.00
40TC	1c	yellow orange				400.00
40TC	1c	orange brown				400.00
40TC	1c	dark brown				400.00
40TC	1c	dull violet				400.00
40TC	1c	violet				400.00
40TC	1c	red violet				400.00
40TC	1c	gray				400.00
41TC	3c	red				—

1861

			PLATE (5) Wove Paper, Imperf.	PLATE (6) Wove Paper, Perf.
63TC	1c	rose	30.00	32.50
63TC	1c	deep orange red	30.00	32.50
63TC	1c	deep red orange	30.00	
63TC	1c	dark orange		32.50
63TC	1c	yellow orange	30.00	
63TC	1c	orange brown	30.00	32.50
63TC	1c	dark brown	30.00	
63TC	1c	yellow green		32.50
63TC	1c	green	30.00	32.50
63TC	1c	blue green	30.00	32.50
63TC	1c	gray lilac	30.00	32.50
63TC	1c	gray black	30.00	32.50
63TC	1c	slate black	30.00	
63TC	1c	blue	30.00	
63TC	1c	light blue	30.00	

There are many trial color impressions of the issues of 1861 to 1883 made for experimentation with various patent papers, grills, etc. Some are fully perforated, gummed and with grill.

1861

			DIE (1) Large	DIE (2) Small	PLATE (3) India	PLATE (4) Card
55TC	1c	ultramarine	2,250.		400.00	
56TC	3c	black	2,000.			
56TC	3c	black on regular paper				400.00
56TC	3c	scarlet	2,000.		300.00	
56TC	3c	pink	2,850.			
56TC	3c	orange red	2,000.			
56TC	3c	dk. org. red	2,000.			
57TC	5c	black	1,750.			
57TC	5c	light brown			300.00	
57TC	5c	dark brown			300.00	
58TC	10c	black	1,750.			
58TC	10c	green			300.00	
58TC	10c	light green			300.00	
59TC	12c	scarlet	1,750.			
60TC	24c	scarlet	1,750.			
60TC	24c	green	1,750.			
60TC	24c	orange	1,750.			
60TC	24c	red brown	1,750.			
60TC	24c	orange brown	1,750.			
60TC	24c	orange yellow	1,750.			
60TC	24c	rose red	1,750.			
60TC	24c	gray	1,750.			
60TC	24c	steel blue	2,250.			
60TC	24c	blue	1,750.			
61TC	30c	black	1,750.			
61TC	30c	green	1,750.			
61TC	30c	dull gray blue	1,750.			
61TC	30c	violet brown	1,750.			
61TC	30c	scarlet	1,750.			
61TC	30c	dull rose	1,750.			
62TC	90c	black	1,750.			
62TC	90c	blue green on regular paper				275.00

1861-62

			PLATE (3) India
63TC	1c	black	600.00
63TC	1c	red	600.00
63TC	1c	brown	600.00
65TC	3c	black	1,400.

			DIE (1) Large	DIE (2) Small	PLATE (3) India	PLATE (5) Wove Paper
65TC	3c	blk. on glazed	1,400.			
65TC	3c	blue green	1,400.			
65TC	3c	orange	1,400.			
65TC	3c	brown	1,400.			
65TC	3c	dark blue	1,400.			
65TC	3c	ocher	1,400.			
65TC	3c	green	1,400.			
65TC	3c	dull red	1,400.			
65TC	3c	slate	1,400.			
65TC	3c	red brown	1,400.			
65TC	3c	deep pink	1,400.			
65TC	3c	rose pink	1,400.			
65TC	3c	dark rose	1,400.			
68TC	10c	orange	1,400.			
68TC	10c	red brown	1,400.			
68TC	10c	dull pink	1,400.			
68TC	10c	scarlet	1,400.			
68TC	10c	black	1,400.	550.00		
69TC	12c	scarlet verm.	1,400.			
69TC	12c	brown	1,400.			
69TC	12c	red brown	1,400.			
69TC	12c	green	1,400.			
69TC	12c	orange yellow	1,400.			
69TC	12c	black		550.00		
71TC	30c	rose	1,400.			
71TC	30c	black		600.00		
72TC	90c	black	1,400.	600.00		
72TC	90c	ultramarine	1,400.			
72TC	90c	bluish gray	1,400.			
72TC	90c	violet gray	1,400.			
72TC	90c	red brown	1,400.			
72TC	90c	orange	1,400.			
72TC	90c	yellow orange	1,400.			
72TC	90c	scarlet	1,400.			
72TC	90c	green	1,400.			

1863

			DIE (1) Large	DIE (2) Small	PLATE (3) India	PLATE (5) Wove Paper
73TC	2c	light blue				335.00
73TC	2c	dull chalky bl.	4,500.			335.00
73TC	2c	green	4,500.			335.00
73TC	2c	olive green				335.00
73TC	2c	dull yellow	4,500.			
73TC	2c	dark orange	4,500.			
73TC	2c	vermilion				335.00
73TC	2c	scarlet	4,500.			335.00
73TC	2c	dull red				335.00
73TC	2c	dull rose	4,500.			335.00
73TC	2c	brown	4,500.			
73TC	2c	gray black				335.00
73TC	2c	ultramarine	4,500.			
76TC	5c	black	1,500.	550.00		
76TC	5c	orange yellow	1,550.			
76TC	5c	dark orange	1,500.			
76TC	5c	green	1,500.			
76TC	5c	ultramarine	1,500.			
76TC	5c	gray	1,500.			
78TC	24c	black		550.00		

1866

			DIE (1) Large	DIE (2) Small	PLATE (3) India	PLATE (5) Wove Paper
77TC	15c	deep blue	1,900.			335.00
		Block of four				1,650.
77TC	15c	dark red	1,900.			
77TC	15c	orange red	1,900.			
77TC	15c	dark orange	1,900.			
77TC	15c	yellow orange	1,900.			
77TC	15c	yellow				
77TC	15c	sepia				
77TC	15c	orange brown	1,900.			
77TC	15c	red brown	1,900.			
77TC	15c	blue green	1,900.			
77TC	15c	dusky blue	1,900.			
77TC	15c	gray black	1,900.			

1869

			DIE (1) Large	DIE (2) Small	PLATE (3) India	PLATE (5) Wove Paper
112TC	1c	black	2,250.			
113TC	2c	black	2,250.			
114TC	3c	black	2,250.			
115TC	6c	deep dull blue	2,250.			
115TC	6c	black	2,250.			
116TC	10c	black	2,250.			
116TC	10c	dull dk. violet	2,250.			
116TC	10c	deep green	2,250.			
116TC	10c	dull dk. orange	2,250.			
116TC	10c	dull rose	2,250.			
116TC	10c	copper red	2,250.			
116TC	10c	chocolate	2,250.			
116TC	10c	dk. Pruss. bl.	2,250.			
117TC	12c	black	2,250.			
118TC	15c	dull dk. violet	2,250.			
118TC	15c	deep blue	2,250.			
118TC	15c	dull red brown	2,250.			
118TC	15c	black	2,250.			
118TC	15c	dark blue gray	2,250.			
120TC	24c	black	2,250.			
121TC	30c	deep blue & deep green	2,250.			
121TC	30c	dp. brn. & blue	2,250.			
121TC	30c	golden brown & carmine lake	2,250.			
121TC	30c	carmine lake & dull violet	2,250.			
121TC	30c	carmine lake & green	2,250.			
121TC	30c	carmine lake & brown	2,250.			
121TC	30c	carmine lake & black	2,250.			
121TC	30c	dull orange red & dp. green	2,250.			
121TC	30c	deep ocher & golden brown	2,250.			
121TC	30c	dull violet & golden brown	2,250.			
121TC	30c	blk. & dp. green	2,250.			
122TC	90c	brn. & dp. grn.	2,250.			

122TC	90c	green & black		1,500.

1870-71

			DIE		PLATE	
			(1) Large	(2) Small	(3) India	(4) Card
145TC	1c	yellow orange	800.00			
145TC	1c	red brown	800.00			
145TC	1c	red violet	800.00			
145TC	1c	green	800.00			
146TC	2c	black	800.00			
147TC	3c	brown			200.00	
147TC	3c	dark brown			200.00	
147TC	3c	dark red			200.00	
147TC	3c	light ultramarine			200.00	
147TC	3c	violet brown			200.00	
147TC	3c	bister			200.00	
147TC	3c	dull red violet			200.00	
147TC	3c	orange			200.00	
148TC	6c	deep magenta	800.00			
148TC	6c	ultramarine	800.00			
148TC	6c	carmine	800.00			
148TC	6c	maroon	800.00			
149TC	7c	black	800.00			
150TC	10c	blue	800.00			
150TC	10c	dull pale blue	800.00			
150TC	10c	ultramarine	800.00			
150TC	10c	blue green	800.00			
150TC	10c	carmine	800.00			
150TC	10c	bister	800.00			
150TC	10c	dull red	800.00			
150TC	10c	red orange	800.00			
150TC	10c	yellow brown	800.00			
150TC	10c	brown orange	800.00			
151TC	12c	orange	800.00			
151TC	12c	orange brown	800.00			
151TC	12c	brown red	800.00			
151TC	12c	dull red	800.00			
151TC	12c	carmine	800.00			
151TC	12c	blue	800.00			
151TC	12c	light blue	800.00			
151TC	12c	ultramarine	800.00			
151TC	12c	green	800.00			
153TC	24c	dark brown	800.00			
155TC	90c	carmine	800.00			
155TC	90c	ultramarine	800.00			
155TC	90c	black	800.00			

1873

156TC	1c	black			15.00	
		Block of four			65.00	
156TC	1c	scarlet			—	
157TC	2c	black			15.00	
		Block of four			65.00	
157TC	2c	dull blue	800.00			
158TC	3c	black			12.00	
		Block of four			55.00	
159TC	6c	black		250.00	30.00	
		Block of four			150.00	
159TC	6c	deep green		225.00		
159TC	6c	deep brown		225.00		
159TC	6c	dull red		225.00		
159TC	6c	dull gray blue		225.00		
160TC	7c	black		250.00	75.00	
		Block of four			325.00	
160TC	7c	deep green		225.00		
160TC	7c	deep brown		225.00		
160TC	7c	dull gray blue		225.00		
160TC	7c	dull red		225.00		
161TC	10c	black		250.00		
161TC	10c	deep green		225.00		
161TC	10c	deep brown		225.00		
161TC	10c	dull gray blue		225.00		
161TC	10c	dull red		225.00		
162TC	12c	black		250.00		
162TC	12c	deep green		225.00		
162TC	12c	dull gray blue		225.00		
162TC	12c	deep brown		225.00		
162TC	12c	dull red		225.00		
163TC	15c	black		250.00		
163TC	15c	deep green		225.00		
163TC	15c	dull gray blue		225.00		
163TC	15c	deep brown		225.00		
163TC	15c	dull red		225.00		
164TC	24c	black		250.00		
164TC	24c	deep green		225.00		
164TC	24c	dull gray blue		225.00		
164TC	24c	deep brown		225.00		
164TC	24c	dull red		225.00		
165TC	30c	black		250.00		
165TC	30c	deep green		225.00		
165TC	30c	deep brown		225.00		
165TC	30c	dull red		225.00		
166TC	90c	black		250.00		
166TC	90c	deep green		225.00		
166TC	90c	dull gray blue		225.00		
166TC	90c	deep brown		225.00		
166TC	90c	dull red		225.00		

1875

179TC	5c	black	850.00	250.00	25.00	
		Block of four			125.00	
179TC	5c	deep green			225.00	
179TC	5c	dull gray blue			225.00	
179TC	5c	deep brown			225.00	
179TC	5c	dull red			225.00	
179TC	5c	scarlet	1,000.			

Small die proofs of 1873-75 issues are "Goodall" prints.

1881-82

206TC	1c	deep green	900.00	200.00	
206TC	1c	black	900.00		125.00

206TC	1c	ultramarine	900.00	
206TC	1c	dk. yel. green	900.00	

1882-87

			LARGE DIE		PLATE	
			(1) India	(2) Card	(3) India	(4) Card
212TC	1c	indigo	800.00			
212TC	1c	carmine	800.00			
212TC	1c	green	800.00	700.00		
212TC	1c	deep green	800.00	700.00		
212TC	1c	copper brown	800.00	700.00		
212TC	1c	chestnut brown	800.00			
210TC	2c	brown red	800.00	700.00		
210TC	2c	dp. dull orange	800.00			
210TC	2c	chestnut brown	800.00	700.00		
210TC	2c	violet rose	800.00	700.00		
210TC	2c	indigo	800.00	700.00		
210TC	2c	black	800.00			
210TC	2c	pale ultramarine	800.00			
210TC	2c	olive green	800.00	700.00		
210TC	2c	olive brown		700.00		
210TC	2c	lake				140.00
210TC	2c	rose lake				140.00
210TC	2c	dark carmine				140.00
210TC	2c	deep red				140.00
214TC	3c	green	750.00	700.00		
214TC	3c	dark brown	750.00	700.00		
214TC	3c	chestnut brown	750.00	700.00		
214TC	3c	dull red brown	750.00	700.00		

All of 214TC above bear inscription "Worked over by new company, June 29th, 1881."

211TC	4c	green	900.00	700.00		
211TC	4c	chestnut brown	900.00	700.00		
211TC	4c	orange brown	900.00	700.00		
211TC	4c	pale ultra.	900.00	700.00		
211TC	4c	dark brown	900.00			
211TC	4c	black	900.00	700.00		
205TC	5c	chestnut brown	900.00			
205TC	5c	dp. dull orange	900.00			
205TC	5c	pale ultra.	900.00			
205TC	5c	deep green	900.00			
205TC	5c	green	900.00	700.00	200.00	
205TC	5c	carmine	900.00	700.00		
205TC	5c	carmine lake	900.00		225.00	
205TC	5c	blue black	900.00			
205TC	5c	black on glazed	900.00			
208TC	6c	indigo	900.00	700.00		
208TC	6c	dp. dull orange	900.00			
208TC	6c	org. vermilion	900.00	700.00		
208TC	6c	dark violet	900.00	700.00		
208TC	6c	chestnut brown	900.00	700.00		
208TC	6c	carmine	900.00			
209TC	10c	carmine	900.00	700.00		
209TC	10c	orange brown	900.00	700.00		
209TC	10c	dp. dull orange	900.00	700.00		
209TC	10c	chestnut brown	900.00	700.00		
209TC	10c	indigo	900.00	700.00		
209TC	10c	pale ultra.	900.00	700.00		
209TC	10c	black (glazed)	900.00			
189TC	15c	org. vermilion	900.00	700.00		
189TC	15c	orange brown	900.00	700.00		
189TC	15c	chestnut brown	900.00	700.00		
189TC	15c	dark brown	900.00	700.00		
189TC	15c	deep green	900.00	700.00		
189TC	15c	black	900.00	700.00		
190TC	30c	black	900.00			
190TC	30c	org. vermilion	900.00	700.00		
190TC	30c	dark brown	900.00	700.00		
190TC	30c	deep green	900.00	700.00		
190TC	30c	dull red brown	900.00	700.00		
190TC	30c	green	900.00	700.00		
191TC	90c	carmine	900.00	700.00		
191TC	90c	dark brown	900.00	700.00		
191TC	90c	dp. dull orange	900.00	700.00		
191TC	90c	indigo	900.00	700.00		
191TC	90c	dull red brown	900.00	700.00		
191TC	90c	black	900.00	700.00		

1890-93

			DIE		PLATE	
			(1) India	(2) Card	(3) India	(4) Card
219TC	1c	green	550.00			
	1c	dull violet	550.00			
220TC	2c	dull violet	550.00			
220TC	2c	blue green	550.00			
220TC	2c	slate black	550.00			
222TC	4c	org. brn. on wove				—
222TC	4c	yel. brn. on wove				
222TC	4c	green	550.00			
223TC	5c	bl. on glossy wove	550.00			
223TC	5c	dark brown on glossy wove	550.00			
223TC	5c	bister on wove				—
223TC	5c	sepia on wove				—
223TC	5c	blk. brn. on wove				—
224TC	6c	deep orange red	550.00			
224TC	6c	org. red on wove				120.00
224TC	6c	vio. blk. on wove				120.00
224TC	6c	yellow on wove				120.00
224TC	6c	olive grn. on wove				120.00
224TC	6c	purple on wove				120.00
224TC	6c	red org. on wove				120.00

			DIE		PLATE	
			(1) India	(2) Card	(3) India	(4) Card
224TC	6c	brown on wove				120.00
224TC	6c	red brn. on wove				120.00
224TC	6c	org. brn. on wove				120.00
224TC	6c	blk. brn. on wove				120.00
224TC	6c	slate grn. on wove				120.00
224TC	6c	brn. olive on wove				120.00
225TC	8c	dark violet red		550.00		
225TC	8c	metallic green		550.00		
225TC	8c	salmon		550.00		
225TC	8c	orange brown		550.00		
225TC	8c	light green		550.00		
225TC	8c	blue		550.00		
225TC	8c	steel blue		550.00		

1893

231TC	2c	sepia	850.00	850.00		
231TC	2c	orange brown		850.00		
231TC	2c	deep orange		850.00		
231TC	2c	light brown		850.00		
231TC	2c	blue green		850.00		
231TC	2c	bright rose red		850.00		
231TC	2c	rose violet		850.00		
232TC	3c	sepia		850.00		
232TC	3c	blackish green		850.00	800.00	
232TC	3c	black		850.00		
233TC	4c	sepia		850.00		
233TC	4c	deep orange		850.00		
233TC	4c	light brown		850.00		
233TC	4c	blue green		850.00		
233TC	4c	rose red		850.00		
233TC	4c	rose violet		850.00		
234TC	5c	black	850.00			
234TC	5c	dark violet	850.00	850.00		
234TC	5c	rose violet	850.00	850.00		
234TC	5c	red violet	850.00			
234TC	5c	brown violet	850.00			
234TC	5c	deep blue	850.00			
234TC	5c	deep ultra.	850.00			
234TC	5c	green	850.00			
234TC	5c	deep green	850.00			
234TC	5c	blue green		850.00		
234TC	5c	dk. olive green	850.00			
234TC	5c	deep orange	850.00			
234TC	5c	orange red	850.00			
234TC	5c	orange brown	850.00	850.00		
234TC	5c	bright rose red	850.00			
234TC	5c	claret	850.00			
234TC	5c	brown rose	850.00			
234TC	5c	dull rose brown		850.00		
234TC	5c	sepia	850.00	850.00		

The 5c trial color proofs differ from the issued stamp.

237TC	10c	bright rose red	1,000.			
237TC	10c	claret	1,000.			
239TC	30c	sepia		1,000.		
239TC	30c	black		1,000.		350.00
240TC	50c	sepia		1,000.		
242TC	$2	blackish brown			1,000.	

1894

			DIE	
			(1) Large	(2) Small
255TC	5c	black	900.00	
257TC	8c	black	900.00	
258TC	10c	olive	900.00	
259TC	15c	red violet	900.00	
259TC	15c	dark red orange	1,000.	
261ATC	$1	lake	1,000.	
262TC	$2	black	1,000.	
262TC	$2	dull violet	1,000.	
262TC	$2	violet	1,000.	
262TC	$2	turquoise blue	1,000.	
262TC	$2	orange brown	1,000.	
262TC	$2	olive green	1,000.	
262TC	$2	sepia	1,000.	
262TC	$2	greenish black	1,000.	
263TC	$5	black	1,000.	
263TC	$5	dark yellow	1,000.	
263TC	$5	orange brown	1,000.	
263TC	$5	olive green	1,000.	
263TC	$5	dull violet	1,000.	
263TC	$5	rose red	1,000.	
263TC	$5	brown red	1,000.	

1898

283TC	10c	orange	1,000.	
283TC	10c	sepia	1,000.	

1898

286TC	2c	purple				1,200.
286TC	2c	black				1,200.
286TC	2c	blue				1,200.
286TC	2c	brown				1,200.
286TC	2c	deep carmine rose				1,200.
290TC	10c	black	1,200.	1,000.		
291TC	50c	black	1,200.	1,000.		
293TC	$2	black	5,000.			

1903

319TC	2c	black, Die I	900.00	

1907

330TC	5c	ultramarine	1,600.
330TC	5c	black	1,700.

1908

332TC	2c	dull violet	450.00
332TC	2c	light ultra.	450.00
332TC	2c	bright ultra.	450.00
332TC	2c	light green	450.00
332TC	2c	dark olive green	450.00
332TC	2c	golden yellow	450.00
332TC	2c	dull orange	450.00
332TC	2c	rose carmine	450.00
332TC	2c	ultramarine	450.00
332TC	2c	ultra. on buff	450.00
332TC	2c	ultra. on green	450.00
332TC	2c	green on pink	450.00
332TC	2c	green on rose	450.00
332TC	2c	dk. green on grn	450.00

1909

342TC	$1	carmine lake	1,200.	1,100.
342TC	$1	pink	1,200.	1,100.

1912-13

400TC	10c	brown red	1,350.	1,100.

1918

524TC	$5	carmine & blk.	1,350.

1919

513TC	13c	violet	550.00
513TC	13c	lilac	550.00
513TC	13c	violet brown	550.00
513TC	13c	light ultra.	550.00
513TC	13c	ultramarine	550.00
513TC	13c	deep ultra.	550.00
513TC	13c	green	550.00
513TC	13c	dark green	550.00
513TC	13c	olive green	550.00
513TC	13c	orange yellow	550.00
513TC	13c	orange	550.00
513TC	13c	red orange	550.00
513TC	13c	ocher	550.00
513TC	13c	salmon red	550.00
513TC	13c	brown carmine	550.00
513TC	13c	claret brown	550.00
513TC	13c	brown	550.00
513TC	13c	black brown	550.00
513TC	13c	gray	550.00
513TC	13c	black	550.00

1920

547TC	$2	green & black	1,300.

1922-25

554TC	2c	black (bond paper)		500.00
561TC	9c	red orange	900.00	
563TC	11c	deep green	900.00	
565TC	14c	dark brown	900.00	
566TC	15c	black	900.00	

1923

611TC	2c	Harding, green	1,000.

1926

622TC	13c	black	1,000.	
628TC	5c	Ericsson, dull dusky blue	1,000.	
628TC		gray blue		1,000.

1932

718TC	3c	Olympic, car.	1,000.	
720TC	3c	black (bond paper)		750.00

1935

773TC	3c	San Diego, org. red (yel. glazed card)	1,000.	

1936-43

785TC	1c	Army, black (bond paper)		750.00
788TC	4c	Army, dk. brn.	900.00	
789TC	5c	Army, blue	900.00	
793TC	4c	Navy, dk. brn.	900.00	
798TC	3c	Constitution, blk. (bond paper)		750.00
799TC	3c	Hawaii, black (bond paper)		750.00
800TC	3c	Alaska, black (bond paper)		750.00
800TC		(India paper)	800.00	
801TC	3c	Puerto Rico, blk (bond paper)	800.00	750.00
801TC		(India paper)	800.00	
802TC	3c	Virgin Islands, black (bond paper)		750.00
815TC	10c	sepia	800.00	
836TC	3c	Swedes & Finns, purple	800.00	
837TC	3c	Northwest Terr., dark purple	800.00	
854TC	3c	Inauguration, purple	800.00	
862TC	5c	Authors, dull bl.	800.00	
866TC	3c	Poets, dark blue violet	800.00	
963TC	3c	Youth, violet	650.00	
964TC	3c	Oregon, dull violet	650.00	
968TC	3c	Poultry, red brown	650.00	

1923-47

Air Post

C5TC	16c	dark green	5,000.
C8TC	15c	orange	4,500.
C32TC	5c	blue	4,500.
C35TC	15c	brown violet	4,500.

1934

Air Post Special Delivery

CE1TC	16c	black	4,000.

1885-1902

Special Delivery

E1TC	10c	black	1,000.	
E1TC	10c	dark brown	1,000.	
E1TC	10c	org. yellow (wove paper)		1,100.
E2TC	10c	black	900.00	
E2TC	10c	green	900.00	
E2TC	10c	olive yellow		600.00
E6TC	10c	orange	1,000.	
E6TC	10c	black	1,000.	
E6TC	10c	rose red	1,500.	

1922-25

E12TC	10c	black	1,100.

1911

Registration

F1TC	10c	black (glazed card)	900.00

		DIE		PLATE	
		(1) Large	(2) Small	(3) India	(4) Card

Carriers

LO1TC		deep green		200.00	
		Block of four		950.00	
		a. orange (wove paper)			350.00
LO2TC		deep green		200.00	
		Block of four		950.00	
		a. orange (wove paper)			350.00

1879

Postage Due

J1TC	1c	black	250.00			25.00
J1TC	1c	gray black	250.00			
J1TC	1c	ultramarine	250.00			
J1TC	1c	blue	250.00			
J1TC	1c	blue green	250.00			
J1TC	1c	orange	250.00		80.00	
J1TC	1c	red orange	250.00			
J1TC	1c	olive bister	250.00			
J2TC	2c	black	250.00			
J2TC	2c	gray black	250.00			
J2TC	2c	ultramarine	250.00			
J2TC	2c	blue	250.00			
J2TC	2c	blue green	250.00			
J2TC	2c	orange	250.00		80.00	
J2TC	2c	red orange	250.00			
J2TC	2c	sepia	250.00			
J3TC	3c	black	250.00			
J3TC	3c	gray black			80.00	
J3TC	3c	ultramarine	250.00			
J3TC	3c	blue	250.00			
J3TC	3c	blue green	250.00			
J3TC	3c	orange	250.00		80.00	
J3TC	3c	red orange	250.00			
J3TC	3c	light brown	250.00			
J4TC	5c	black	250.00			
J4TC	5c	gray black	250.00			
J4TC	5c	ultramarine	250.00			
J4TC	5c	blue	250.00			
J4TC	5c	blue green	250.00			
J4TC	5c	orange	250.00		80.00	
J4TC	5c	red orange	250.00			
J5TC	10c	black	250.00			
J5TC	10c	gray black	250.00			
J5TC	10c	blue	250.00			
J5TC	10c	blue green	250.00			
J5TC	10c	orange	250.00		80.00	
J5TC	10c	red orange	250.00			
J5TC	10c	olive bister	250.00			
J5TC	10c	sepia	250.00			
J5TC	10c	gray	250.00			
J6TC	30c	black	250.00			
J6TC	30c	gray black	250.00			
J6TC	30c	olive yellow			80.00	
J6TC	30c	blue green	250.00			
J6TC	30c	orange	250.00		80.00	
J6TC	30c	red orange	250.00			
J6TC	30c	olive bister	250.00			
J6TC	30c	sepia			80.00	
J7TC	50c	black	250.00			
J7TC	50c	gray black	250.00			
J7TC	50c	blue	250.00		80.00	
J7TC	50c	olive yellow			80.00	
J7TC	50c	blue green	250.00			
J7TC	50c	orange	250.00		80.00	
J7TC	50c	red orange	250.00			
J7TC	50c	olive bister	250.00			
J7TC	50c	sepia	250.00			
J7TC	50c	gray	250.00			

Official

Agriculture

O1TC	1c	black	190.00	65.00
O2TC	2c	black	190.00	65.00
O3TC	3c	deep green	190.00	
O4TC	6c	black	190.00	125.00
O5TC	10c	black	190.00	
O6TC	12c	black	190.00	65.00
O9TC	30c	black	190.00	

Executive

O11TC	2c	black	190.00	65.00	
O11TC	2c	deep brown	190.00		
O11TC	2c	brown carmine			75.00
O12TC	3c	black	190.00	65.00	
O12TC	3c	deep green	190.00		
O13TC	6c	black		80.00	
O14TC	10c	black		80.00	

Interior

O16TC	2c	black	190.00	
O16TC	2c	deep brown	190.00	
O17TC	3c	black	190.00	80.00
O17TC	3c	deep green	190.00	

Justice

O27TC	3c	black	190.00	80.00
O27TC	3c	deep green	190.00	
O27TC	3c	bister yellow		80.00
O27TC	3c	dull orange		80.00
O27TC	3c	black violet		80.00

Navy

O35TC	1c	black		80.00	
O36TC	2c	black	190.00		
O36TC	2c	deep brown	190.00		
O36TC	2c	dp. green on wove paper, perf.			250.00
O36TC	2c	dp. green on wove paper, imperf.			250.00
O37TC	3c	black	190.00	80.00	
O37TC	3c	deep green	190.00		

Post Office

O48TC	2c	deep brown	190.00
O49TC	3c	deep green	190.00
O50TC	6c	deep brown	190.00
O50TC	6c	brown carmine	190.00

State

O57TC	1c	black	190.00
O57TC	1c	lt. ultramarine	190.00
O58TC	2c	black	190.00
O58TC	2c	deep brown	190.00
O59TC	3c	black	190.00
O67TC	90c	black	190.00
O68TC	$2	violet & black	1,000.
O68TC	$2	brown red & black	1,000.
O68TC	$2	orange red & slate blue	1,000.

Treasury

O72TC	1c	black	190.00
O72TC	1c	lt. ultramarine	190.00
O73TC	2c	black	190.00
O74TC	3c	black	190.00
O74TC	3c	deep green	190.00
O75TC	6c	black	190.00
O77TC	10c	black	190.00
O78TC	12c	black	190.00
O79TC	15c	black	190.00
O82TC	90c	black	190.00

War

O83TC	1c	black	190.00	80.00	
O83TC	1c	lt. ultramarine	190.00		
O84TC	2c	black	190.00	80.00	75.00
O84TC	2c	deep brown	190.00		
O85TC	3c	black	190.00		
O85TC	3c	deep green	190.00		
O86TC	6c	black		80.00	
O89TC	12c	black		80.00	

1910

Postal Savings Mail

O121TC	2c	lake	300.00

The so-called "Goodall" set of Small Die proofs on India Paper in five colors

Agriculture

		(a) Black	(b) Deep green	(c) Dull gray blue	(d) Deep brown	(e) Dull red
O1TC	1c	150.00	140.00	140.00	140.00	140.00
O2TC	2c	150.00	140.00	140.00	140.00	140.00
O3TC	3c	150.00	140.00	140.00	140.00	140.00
O4TC	6c	150.00	140.00	140.00	140.00	140.00
O5TC	10c	150.00	140.00	140.00	140.00	140.00
O6TC	12c	150.00	140.00	140.00	140.00	140.00

		(a) Black	(b) Deep green	(c) Dull gray blue	(d) Deep brown	(e) Dull red
O7TC	15c	150.00	140.00	140.00	140.00	140.00
O8TC	24c	150.00	140.00	140.00	140.00	140.00
O9TC	30c	150.00	140.00	140.00	140.00	140.00

Executive

O10TC	1c	150.00	140.00	140.00	140.00	140.00
O11TC	2c	150.00	140.00	140.00	140.00	140.00
O12TC	3c	150.00	140.00	140.00	140.00	140.00
O13TC	6c	150.00	140.00	140.00	140.00	140.00
O14TC	10c	150.00	140.00	140.00	140.00	140.00

Interior

O15TC	1c	150.00	140.00	140.00	140.00	140.00
O16TC	2c	150.00	140.00	140.00	140.00	140.00
O17TC	3c	150.00	140.00	140.00	140.00	140.00
O18TC	6c	150.00	140.00	140.00	140.00	140.00
O19TC	10c	150.00	140.00	140.00	140.00	140.00
O20TC	12c	150.00	140.00	140.00	140.00	140.00
O21TC	15c	150.00	140.00	140.00	140.00	140.00
O22TC	24c	150.00	140.00	140.00	140.00	140.00
O23TC	30c	150.00	140.00	140.00	140.00	140.00
O24TC	90c	150.00	140.00	140.00	140.00	140.00

Justice

O25TC	1c	150.00	140.00	140.00	140.00	140.00
O26TC	2c	150.00	140.00	140.00	140.00	140.00
O27TC	3c	150.00	140.00	140.00	140.00	140.00
O28TC	6c	150.00	140.00	140.00	140.00	140.00
O29TC	10c	150.00	140.00	140.00	140.00	140.00
O30TC	12c	150.00	140.00	140.00	140.00	140.00
O31TC	15c	150.00	140.00	140.00	140.00	140.00
O32TC	24c	150.00	140.00	140.00	140.00	140.00
O33TC	30c	150.00	140.00	140.00	140.00	140.00
O34TC	90c	150.00	140.00	140.00	140.00	140.00

Navy

O35TC	1c	150.00	140.00	140.00	140.00	140.00
O36TC	2c	150.00	140.00	140.00	140.00	140.00
O37TC	3c	150.00	140.00	140.00	140.00	140.00
O38TC	6c	150.00	140.00	140.00	140.00	140.00
O39TC	7c	150.00	140.00	140.00	140.00	140.00
O40TC	10c	150.00	140.00	140.00	140.00	140.00
O41TC	12c	150.00	140.00	140.00	140.00	140.00
O42TC	15c	150.00	140.00	140.00	140.00	140.00
O43TC	24c	150.00	140.00	140.00	140.00	140.00
O44TC	30c	150.00	140.00	140.00	140.00	140.00
O45TC	90c	150.00	140.00	140.00	140.00	140.00

Post Office

O47TC	1c	150.00	140.00	140.00	140.00	140.00
O48TC	2c	150.00	140.00	140.00	140.00	140.00
O49TC	3c	150.00	140.00	140.00	140.00	140.00
O50TC	6c	150.00	140.00	140.00	140.00	140.00
O51TC	10c	150.00	140.00	140.00	140.00	140.00
O52TC	12c	150.00	140.00	140.00	140.00	140.00
O53TC	15c	150.00	140.00	140.00	140.00	140.00
O54TC	24c	150.00	140.00	140.00	140.00	140.00
O55TC	30c	150.00	140.00	140.00	140.00	140.00
O56TC	90c	150.00	140.00	140.00	140.00	140.00

State

O57TC	1c	150.00	140.00	140.00	140.00	140.00
O58TC	2c	150.00	140.00	140.00	140.00	140.00
O59TC	3c	150.00	140.00	140.00	140.00	140.00
O60TC	6c	150.00	140.00	140.00	140.00	140.00
O61TC	7c	150.00	140.00	140.00	140.00	140.00
O62TC	10c	150.00	140.00	140.00	140.00	140.00
O63TC	12c	150.00	140.00	140.00	140.00	140.00
O64TC	15c	150.00	140.00	140.00	140.00	140.00
O65TC	24c	150.00	140.00	140.00	140.00	140.00
O66TC	30c	150.00	140.00	140.00	140.00	140.00
O67TC	90c	150.00	140.00	140.00	140.00	140.00

O68TC	$2	scarlet frame, green center	900.00
O68TC	$2	scarlet frame, black center	900.00
O68TC	$2	scarlet frame, blue center	900.00
O68TC	$2	green frame, brown center	900.00
O68TC	$2	brown frame, green center	900.00
O68TC	$2	brown frame, black center	900.00

Treasury

O72TC	1c	150.00	140.00	140.00	140.00	140.00
O73TC	2c	150.00	140.00	140.00	140.00	140.00
O74TC	3c	150.00	140.00	140.00	140.00	140.00
O75TC	6c	150.00	140.00	140.00	140.00	140.00
O76TC	7c	150.00	140.00	140.00	140.00	140.00
O77TC	10c	150.00	140.00	140.00	140.00	140.00
O78TC	12c	150.00	140.00	140.00	140.00	140.00
O79TC	15c	150.00	140.00	140.00	140.00	140.00
O80TC	24c	150.00	140.00	140.00	140.00	140.00
O81TC	30c	150.00	140.00	140.00	140.00	140.00
O82TC	90c	150.00	140.00	140.00	140.00	140.00

War

O83TC	1c	150.00	140.00	140.00	140.00	140.00
O84TC	2c	150.00	140.00	140.00	140.00	140.00
O85TC	3c	150.00	140.00	140.00	140.00	140.00
O86TC	6c	150.00	140.00	140.00	140.00	140.00
O87TC	7c	150.00	140.00	140.00	140.00	140.00
O88TC	10c	150.00	140.00	140.00	140.00	140.00
O89TC	12c	150.00	140.00	140.00	140.00	140.00
O90TC	15c	150.00	140.00	140.00	140.00	140.00
O91TC	24c	150.00	140.00	140.00	140.00	140.00
O92TC	30c	150.00	140.00	140.00	140.00	140.00
O93TC	90c	150.00	140.00	140.00	140.00	140.00

Official Seals

1872

OX1TC	ultramarine	Die on India	250.00
OX1TC	blue	Die on card, colored border	350.00
OX1TC	deep blue	Die on card, colored border	350.00
OX1TC	deep green	Die on card, colored border	350.00
OX1TC	chocolate	Die on glossy bond	250.00
OX1TC	chocolate	Die on card, colored border	350.00

OX1TC	carmine	Die on India	250.00
OX1TC	brown	Die on India	250.00
OX1TC	red violet	Die on India	—

1877

OX3TC	blue	Die on India	150.00
OX3TC	green	Die on India	150.00
OX3TC	green	Plate on bond	150.00
OX3TC	orange	Die on India	150.00
OX3TC	red orange	Die on India	150.00
OX3TC	black	Die on India	150.00

Newspapers

1865

			(2) Small Die	(5) Thick, cream, wove paper
PR2TC	10c	black		70.00
PR2TC	10c	lake		70.00
PR2TC	10c	blue green		70.00
PR2TC	10c	blue		70.00
PR3TC	25c	black		70.00
PR3TC	25c	lake		70.00
PR3TC	25c	blue green		70.00
PR3TC	25c	blue		70.00
PR3TC	25c	ocher	200.00	
PR3TC	25c	brick red	200.00	
PR4TC	5c	black		70.00
PR4TC	5c	lake		70.00
PR4TC	5c	blue green		70.00
PR4TC	5c	blue		70.000

1875

			(1) Die on India	(3) Plate on India
PR9TC	2c	dark carmine		35.00
PR9TC	2c	brown rose		35.00
PR9TC	2c	scarlet		35.00
PR9TC	2c	orange brown	110.00	35.00
PR9TC	2c	black brown	110.00	
PR9TC	2c	sepia		35.00
PR9TC	2c	orange yellow		35.00
PR9TC	2c	dull orange		35.00
PR9TC	2c	green		35.00
PR9TC	2c	blue green	110.00	35.00
PR9TC	2c	light ultramarine		35.00
PR9TC	2c	light blue		35.00
PR9TC	2c	dark violet		35.00
PR9TC	2c	violet black		35.00
PR10TC	3c	rose lake	110.00	
PR16TC	12c	dark carmine		35.00
PR16TC	12c	brown rose	110.00	35.00
PR16TC	12c	scarlet	110.00	35.00
PR16TC	12c	orange brown		35.00
PR16TC	12c	sepia	110.00	35.00
PR16TC	12c	orange yellow		35.00
PR16TC	12c	dull orange		35.00
PR16TC	12c	green	110.00	35.00
PR16TC	12c	light ultramarine	110.00	35.00
PR16TC	12c	light blue		35.00
PR16TC	12c	dark violet	110.00	35.00
PR16TC	12c	violet black	110.00	35.00
PR16TC	12c	black	110.00	35.00
PR17TC	24c	dark carmine		35.00
PR17TC	24c	green	110.00	
PR17TC	24c	black	110.00	35.00
PR18TC	36c	black	110.00	
PR18TC	36c	sepia	110.00	
PR18TC	36c	green	110.00	
PR19TC	48c	black	110.00	35.00
PR19TC	48c	sepia	110.00	
PR19TC	48c	green	110.00	
PR20TC	60c	black	110.00	35.00
PR21TC	72c	black	110.00	35.00
PR22TC	84c	black	110.00	35.00
PR23TC	96c	black		35.00
PR24TC	$1.92	dark carmine		35.00
PR24TC	$1.92	brown rose		35.00
PR24TC	$1.92	scarlet		35.00
PR24TC	$1.92	orange brown	110.00	35.00
PR24TC	$1.92	sepia		35.00
PR24TC	$1.92	orange yellow		35.00
PR24TC	$1.92	dull orange		35.00
PR24TC	$1.92	green	110.00	35.00
PR24TC	$1.92	light ultramarine		35.00
PR24TC	$1.92	dark violet		35.00
PR24TC	$1.92	violet black		35.00
PR24TC	$1.92	black		35.00
PR25TC	$3	dark carmine	110.00	
PR25TC	$3	brown rose		35.00
PR25TC	$3	scarlet		35.00
PR25TC	$3	orange brown		35.00
PR25TC	$3	sepia		35.00
PR25TC	$3	orange yellow	110.00	35.00
PR25TC	$3	dull orange	110.00	35.00
PR25TC	$3	green	110.00	35.00
PR25TC	$3	light ultramarine	110.00	35.00
PR25TC	$3	light blue		35.00
PR25TC	$3	dark violet	110.00	35.00
PR25TC	$3	violet black	110.00	35.00
PR25TC	$3	black	110.00	35.00
PR26TC	$6	dark carmine	110.00	35.00
PR26TC	$6	brown rose	110.00	35.00
PR26TC	$6	scarlet	110.00	35.00
PR26TC	$6	orange brown		35.00
PR26TC	$6	dark brown		35.00
PR26TC	$6	sepia	110.00	35.00
PR26TC	$6	orange yellow	110.00	35.00
PR26TC	$6	dull orange	110.00	35.00
PR26TC	$6	green	110.00	35.00
PR26TC	$6	light ultramarine	110.00	35.00
PR26TC	$6	light blue	110.00	35.00

			(1) Die on India	(3) Plate on India
PR26TC	$6	dark violet	110.00	35.00
PR26TC	$6	violet black	110.00	35.00
PR26TC	$6	black	110.00	35.00
PR27TC	$9	dark carmine	110.00	35.00
PR27TC	$9	brown rose	110.00	35.00
PR27TC	$9	scarlet	110.00	35.00
PR27TC	$9	orange brown		35.00
PR27TC	$9	sepia	110.00	35.00
PR27TC	$9	orange yellow	110.00	35.00
PR27TC	$9	dull orange	110.00	35.00
PR27TC	$9	green	110.00	35.00
PR27TC	$9	light ultramarine	110.00	35.00
PR27TC	$9	light blue		35.00
PR27TC	$9	dark violet	110.00	35.00
PR27TC	$9	violet black	110.00	35.00
PR27TC	$9	black	110.00	35.00
PR28TC	$12	black	110.00	
PR28TC	$12	sepia	110.00	
PR28TC	$12	orange brown	110.00	
PR29TC	$24	black	110.00	35.00
PR29TC	$24	black brown	110.00	
PR29TC	$24	orange brown	110.00	
PR29TC	$24	green	110.00	
PR30TC	$36	dark carmine	110.00	
PR30TC	$36	black	110.00	35.00
PR30TC	$36	black brown	110.00	
PR30TC	$36	orange brown	110.00	
PR30TC	$36	sepia	110.00	
PR30TC	$36	violet	110.00	
PR30TC	$36	green	110.00	
PR31TC	$48	violet brown	110.00	35.00
PR31TC	$48	black	110.00	35.00
PR31TC	$48	sepia	110.00	
PR31TC	$48	green	110.00	
PR32TC	$60	dark carmine	110.00	40.00
PR32TC	$60	scarlet	110.00	40.00
PR32TC	$60	sepia	110.00	40.00
PR32TC	$60	green	110.00	40.00
PR32TC	$60	light ultramarine	110.00	40.00
PR32TC	$60	black	110.00	40.00
PR32TC	$60	violet black	110.00	
PR32TC	$60	orange brown	110.00	
PR32TC	$60	orange yellow	110.00	
PR32TC	$60	dull orange	110.00	
PR32TC	$60	brown rose	110.00	

1885

			(1) Die on India	(3) Plate on India
PR18TC	1c	salmon	110.00	
PR18TC	1c	scarlet		120.00
PR18TC	1c	dark brown		120.00
PR18TC	1c	violet brown		120.00
PR18TC	1c	dull orange		120.00
PR18TC	1c	green		120.00
PR18TC	1c	light blue		120.00

1894

			(1) Die on India	(3) Plate on India
PR106TC	25c	deep carmine		150.00
PR106TC	25c	dark carmine		150.00
PR107TC	50c	black		150.00
PR108TC	$2	deep scarlet		150.00
PR108TC	$2	dark scarlet		150.00
PR109TC	$5	light ultramarine		150.00
PR109TC	$5	dark ultramarine		150.00
PR110TC	$10	black		150.00
PR112TC	$50	black		150.00
PR112TC	$50	deep rose		150.00
PR112TC	$50	dark rose		150.00
PR113TC	$100	black		150.00

The so-called "Goodall" set of Small Die proofs on India Paper in five colors

		(a) Black	(b) Deep green	(c) Dull gray blue	(d) Deep brown	(e) Dull red
PR9TC	2c	150.00	125.00	125.00	125.00	125.00
PR10TC	3c	150.00	125.00	125.00	125.00	125.00
PR11TC	4c	150.00	125.00	125.00	125.00	125.00
PR12TC	6c	150.00	125.00	125.00	125.00	125.00
PR13TC	8c	150.00	125.00	125.00	125.00	125.00
PR14TC	9c	150.00	125.00	125.00	125.00	125.00
PR15TC	10c	150.00	125.00	125.00	125.00	125.00
PR16TC	12c	150.00	125.00	125.00	125.00	125.00
PR17TC	24c	150.00	125.00	125.00	125.00	125.00
PR18TC	36c	150.00	125.00	125.00	125.00	125.00
PR19TC	48c	150.00	125.00	125.00	125.00	125.00
PR20TC	60c	150.00	125.00	125.00	125.00	125.00
PR21TC	72c	150.00	125.00	125.00	125.00	125.00
PR22TC	84c	150.00	125.00	125.00	125.00	125.00
PR23TC	96c	150.00	125.00	125.00	125.00	125.00
PR24TC	$1.92	150.00	125.00	125.00	125.00	125.00
PR25TC	$3	150.00	125.00	125.00	125.00	125.00
PR26TC	$6	150.00	125.00	125.00	125.00	125.00
PR27TC	$9	150.00	125.00	125.00	125.00	125.00
PR28TC	$12	150.00	125.00	125.00	125.00	125.00
PR29TC	$24	150.00	125.00	125.00	125.00	125.00
PR30TC	$36	150.00	125.00	125.00	125.00	125.00
PR31TC	$48	150.00	125.00	125.00	125.00	125.00
PR32TC	$60	150.00	125.00	125.00	125.00	125.00

1925

Special Handling

QE4TC	25c	apple green	700.00
QE4TC	25c	olive green	700.00
QE4TC	25c	light blue green	700.00
QE4TC	25c	dark blue	700.00
QE4TC	25c	orange yellow	700.00
QE4TC	25c	orange	700.00

QE4TC	25c dull rose	700.00
QE4TC	25c carmine lake	700.00
QE4TC	25c brown	700.00
QE4TC	25c gray brown	700.00
QE4TC	25c dark violet brown	700.00
QE4TC	25c gray black	700.00
QE4TC	25c black	700.00

THE "ATLANTA" SET OF PLATE PROOFS

A set in five colors on thin card
reprinted in 1881 for display at the International Cotton Exhibition
in Atlanta, Ga.

1847 Designs (Reproductions)

		Black	Scarlet	Brown	Green	Blue
3TC	5c	300.00	300.00	300.00	300.00	300.00
4TC	10c	300.00	300.00	300.00	300.00	300.00

1851-60 Designs

		Black	Scarlet	Brown	Green	Blue
40TC	1c	150.00	135.00	135.00	135.00	135.00
41TC	3c	150.00	135.00	135.00	135.00	135.00
42TC	5c	150.00	135.00	135.00	135.00	135.00
43TC	10c	150.00	135.00	135.00	135.00	135.00
44TC	12c	150.00	135.00	135.00	135.00	135.00
45TC	24c	150.00	135.00	135.00	135.00	135.00
46TC	30c	150.00	135.00	135.00	135.00	135.00
47TC	90c	150.00	135.00	135.00	135.00	135.00

1861-66 Designs

		Black	Scarlet	Brown	Green	Blue
102TC	1c	125.00	115.00	115.00	115.00	115.00
103TC	2c	200.00	200.00	200.00	200.00	200.00
104TC	3c	125.00	115.00	115.00	115.00	115.00
105TC	5c	125.00	115.00	115.00	115.00	115.00
106TC	10c	125.00	115.00	115.00	115.00	115.00
107TC	12c	125.00	115.00	115.00	115.00	115.00
108TC	15c	125.00	115.00	115.00	115.00	115.00
109TC	24c	125.00	115.00	115.00	115.00	115.00
110TC	30c	125.00	115.00	115.00	115.00	115.00
111TC	90c	125.00	115.00	115.00	115.00	115.00

1869 Designs

		Black	Scarlet	Brown	Green	Blue
123TC	1c	200.00	175.00	175.00	175.00	175.00
124TC	2c	200.00	175.00	175.00	175.00	175.00
125TC	3c	200.00	175.00	175.00	175.00	175.00
126TC	6c	200.00	175.00	175.00	175.00	175.00
127TC	10c	200.00	175.00	175.00	175.00	175.00
128TC	12c	200.00	175.00	175.00	175.00	175.00

129TC	15c black frame, scarlet center	450.00
129TC	15c black frame, green center	450.00
129TC	15c scarlet frame, black center	450.00
129TC	15c scarlet frame, blue center	450.00
129TC	15c brown frame, black center	450.00
129TC	15c brown frame, green center	450.00
129TC	15c brown frame, blue center	450.00
129TC	15c green frame, black center	450.00
129TC	15c green frame, blue center	450.00
129TC	15c blue frame, black center	450.00
129TC	15c blue frame, brown center	450.00
129TC	15c blue frame, green center	450.00
130TC	24c black frame, scarlet center	450.00
130TC	24c black frame, green center	450.00
130TC	24c black frame, blue center	450.00
130TC	24c scarlet frame, black center	450.00
130TC	24c scarlet frame, blue center	450.00
130TC	24c brown frame, black center	450.00
130TC	24c brown frame, blue center	450.00
130TC	24c green frame, black center	450.00
130TC	24c green frame, brown center	450.00
130TC	24c green frame, blue center	450.00
130TC	24c blue frame, brown center	450.00
130TC	24c blue frame, green center	450.00
131TC	30c black frame, scarlet center	450.00
131TC	30c black frame, green center	450.00
131TC	30c black frame, blue center	450.00
131TC	30c scarlet frame, black center	450.00
131TC	30c scarlet frame, green center	450.00
131TC	30c scarlet frame, blue center	450.00
131TC	30c brown frame, black center	450.00
131TC	30c brown frame, scarlet center	450.00
131TC	30c brown frame, blue center	450.00
131TC	30c green frame, black center	450.00
131TC	30c green frame, brown center	450.00
131TC	30c blue frame, scarlet center	450.00
131TC	30c blue frame, brown center	450.00
131TC	30c blue frame, green center	450.00
132TC	90c black frame, scarlet center	500.00
132TC	90c black frame, brown center	500.00
132TC	90c black frame, green center	500.00
132TC	90c scarlet frame, blue center	500.00
132TC	90c brown frame, black center	500.00
132TC	90c brown frame, blue center	500.00
132TC	90c green frame, brown center	500.00
132TC	90c green frame, blue center	500.00
132TC	90c blue frame, brown center	500.00
132TC	90c blue frame, green center	500.00

1873-75 Designs

		Black	Scarlet	Brown	Green	Blue
156TC	1c	60.00	55.00	55.00	55.00	55.00
157TC	2c	60.00	55.00	55.00	55.00	55.00
158TC	3c	65.00	60.00	60.00	60.00	60.00
159TC	6c	65.00	60.00	60.00	60.00	60.00
160TC	7c	60.00	55.00	55.00	55.00	55.00
161TC	10c	60.00	55.00	55.00	55.00	55.00
162TC	12c	60.00	55.00	55.00	55.00	55.00
163TC	15c	60.00	55.00	55.00	55.00	55.00
164TC	24c	60.00	55.00	55.00	55.00	55.00
165TC	30c	65.00	60.00	60.00	60.00	60.00
166TC	90c	60.00	55.00	55.00	55.00	55.00
179TC	5c	75.00	70.00	70.00	70.00	70.00

Postage Due

		Black	Scarlet	Brown	Green	Blue
J1TC	1c	60.00	55.00	55.00	55.00	55.00

(continued)

		Black	Scarlet	Brown	Green	Blue
J2TC	2c	60.00	55.00	55.00	55.00	55.00
J3TC	3c	60.00	55.00	55.00	55.00	55.00
J4TC	5c	60.00	55.00	55.00	55.00	55.00
J5TC	10c	60.00	55.00	55.00	55.00	55.00
J6TC	30c	60.00	55.00	55.00	55.00	55.00
J7TC	50c	60.00	55.00	55.00	55.00	55.00

Carriers

		Black	Scarlet	Brown	Green	Blue
LO1TC	1c Franklin	100.00	90.00	90.00	90.00	90.00
LO2TC	1c Eagle	100.00	90.00	90.00	90.00	90.00

Agriculture

		Black	Scarlet	Brown	Green	Blue
O1TC	1c	45.00	40.00	40.00	40.00	40.00
O2TC	2c	45.00	40.00	40.00	40.00	40.00
O3TC	3c	45.00	40.00	40.00	40.00	40.00
O4TC	6c	55.00	50.00	50.00	50.00	50.00
O5TC	10c	45.00	40.00	40.00	40.00	40.00
O6TC	12c	45.00	40.00	40.00	40.00	40.00
O7TC	15c	45.00	40.00	40.00	40.00	40.00
O8TC	24c	45.00	40.00	40.00	40.00	40.00
O9TC	30c	45.00	40.00	40.00	40.00	40.00

Executive

O10TC	1c	45.00	40.00	40.00	40.00	40.00
O11TC	2c	45.00	40.00	40.00	40.00	40.00
O12TC	3c	45.00	40.00	40.00	40.00	40.00
O13TC	6c	55.00	50.00	50.00	50.00	50.00
O14TC	10c	45.00	40.00	40.00	40.00	40.00

Interior

O15TC	1c	45.00	40.00	40.00	40.00	40.00
O16TC	2c	45.00	40.00	40.00	40.00	40.00
O17TC	3c	45.00	40.00	40.00	40.00	40.00
O18TC	6c	55.00	50.00	50.00	50.00	50.00
O19TC	10c	45.00	40.00	40.00	40.00	40.00
O20TC	12c	45.00	40.00	40.00	40.00	40.00
O21TC	15c	45.00	40.00	40.00	40.00	40.00
O22TC	24c	45.00	40.00	40.00	40.00	40.00
O23TC	30c	60.00	55.00	55.00	55.00	55.00
O24TC	90c	45.00	40.00	40.00	40.00	40.00

Justice

O25TC	1c	45.00	40.00	40.00	40.00	40.00
O26TC	2c	45.00	40.00	40.00	40.00	40.00
O27TC	3c	45.00	40.00	40.00	40.00	40.00
O28TC	6c	55.00	50.00	50.00	50.00	50.00
O29TC	10c	45.00	40.00	40.00	40.00	40.00
O30TC	12c	45.00	40.00	40.00	40.00	40.00
O31TC	15c	45.00	40.00	40.00	40.00	40.00
O32TC	24c	45.00	40.00	40.00	40.00	40.00
O33TC	30c	60.00	55.00	55.00	55.00	55.00
O34TC	90c	45.00	40.00	40.00	40.00	40.00

Navy

O35TC	1c	45.00	40.00	40.00	40.00	40.00
O36TC	2c	45.00	40.00	40.00	40.00	40.00
O37TC	3c	45.00	40.00	40.00	40.00	40.00
O38TC	6c	55.00	50.00	50.00	50.00	50.00
O39TC	7c	45.00	40.00	40.00	40.00	40.00
O40TC	10c	45.00	40.00	40.00	40.00	40.00
O41TC	12c	45.00	40.00	40.00	40.00	40.00
O42TC	15c	45.00	40.00	40.00	40.00	40.00
O43TC	24c	45.00	40.00	40.00	40.00	40.00
O44TC	30c	60.00	55.00	55.00	55.00	55.00
O45TC	90c	45.00	40.00	40.00	40.00	40.00

Post Office

O48TC	2c	45.00	40.00	40.00	40.00	40.00
O49TC	3c	45.00	40.00	40.00	40.00	40.00
O50TC	6c	45.00	40.00	40.00	40.00	40.00
O51TC	10c	45.00	40.00	40.00	40.00	40.00
O52TC	12c	45.00	40.00	40.00	40.00	40.00
O53TC	15c	45.00	40.00	40.00	40.00	40.00
O54TC	24c	45.00	40.00	40.00	40.00	40.00
O55TC	30c	45.00	40.00	40.00	40.00	40.00
O56TC	90c	45.00	40.00	40.00	40.00	40.00

State

O57TC	1c	45.00	40.00	40.00	40.00	40.00
O58TC	2c	45.00	40.00	40.00	40.00	40.00
O59TC	3c	45.00	40.00	40.00	40.00	40.00
O60TC	6c	55.00	50.00	50.00	50.00	50.00
O61TC	7c	45.00	40.00	40.00	40.00	40.00
O62TC	10c	45.00	40.00	40.00	40.00	40.00
O63TC	12c	45.00	40.00	40.00	40.00	40.00
O64TC	15c	45.00	40.00	40.00	40.00	40.00
O65TC	24c	45.00	40.00	40.00	40.00	40.00
O66TC	30c	60.00	55.00	55.00	55.00	55.00
O67TC	90c	45.00	40.00	40.00	40.00	40.00

O68TC	$2 scarlet frame, black center	850.00
O68TC	$2 scarlet frame, blue center	850.00
O68TC	$2 brown frame, black center	850.00
O68TC	$2 brown frame, blue center	850.00
O68TC	$2 green frame, brown center	850.00
O68TC	$2 blue frame, brown center	850.00
O68TC	$2 blue frame, green center	850.00
O69TC	$5 scarlet frame, black center	850.00
O69TC	$5 scarlet frame, blue center	850.00
O69TC	$5 brown frame, black center	850.00
O69TC	$5 brown frame, blue center	850.00
O69TC	$5 green frame, brown center	850.00
O69TC	$5 blue frame, brown center	850.00
O69TC	$5 blue frame, green center	850.00
O70TC	$10 scarlet frame, black center	850.00
O70TC	$10 scarlet frame, blue center	850.00
O70TC	$10 brown frame, black center	850.00
O70TC	$10 brown frame, blue center	850.00
O70TC	$10 green frame, brown center	850.00
O70TC	$10 blue frame, brown center	850.00
O70TC	$10 blue frame, green center	850.00
O71TC	$20 scarlet frame, black center	850.00
O71TC	$20 scarlet frame, blue center	850.00
O71TC	$20 brown frame, black center	850.00
O71TC	$20 brown frame, blue center	850.00
O71TC	$20 green frame, brown center	850.00
O71TC	$20 blue frame, brown center	850.00
O71TC	$20 blue frame, green center	850.00

Treasury

		Black	Scarlet	Brown	Green	Blue
O72TC	1c	45.00	40.00	40.00	40.00	40.00
O73TC	2c	45.00	40.00	40.00	40.00	40.00
O74TC	3c	45.00	40.00	40.00	40.00	40.00
O75TC	6c	55.00	50.00	50.00	50.00	50.00
O76TC	7c	45.00	40.00	40.00	40.00	40.00
O77TC	10c	45.00	40.00	40.00	40.00	40.00
O78TC	12c	45.00	40.00	40.00	40.00	40.00
O79TC	15c	45.00	40.00	40.00	40.00	40.00
O80TC	24c	45.00	40.00	40.00	40.00	40.00
O81TC	30c	60.00	55.00	55.00	55.00	55.00
O82TC	90c	45.00	40.00	40.00	40.00	40.00

War

O83TC	1c	45.00	40.00	40.00	40.00	40.00
O84TC	2c	45.00	40.00	40.00	40.00	40.00
O85TC	3c	45.00	40.00	40.00	40.00	40.00
O86TC	6c	55.00	50.00	50.00	50.00	50.00
O87TC	7c	45.00	40.00	40.00	40.00	40.00
O88TC	10c	45.00	40.00	40.00	40.00	40.00
O89TC	12c	45.00	40.00	40.00	40.00	40.00
O90TC	15c	45.00	40.00	40.00	40.00	40.00
O91TC	24c	45.00	40.00	40.00	40.00	40.00
O92TC	30c	60.00	55.00	55.00	55.00	55.00
O93TC	90c	45.00	40.00	40.00	40.00	40.00

Newspapers

PR9TC	2c	45.00	30.00	30.00	30.00	30.00
PR10TC	3c	45.00	30.00	30.00	30.00	30.00
PR11TC	4c	45.00	30.00	30.00	30.00	30.00
PR12TC	6c	45.00	30.00	30.00	30.00	30.00
PR13TC	8c	45.00	30.00	30.00	30.00	30.00
PR14TC	9c	45.00	30.00	30.00	30.00	30.00
PR15TC	10c	45.00	30.00	30.00	30.00	30.00
PR16TC	12c	45.00	30.00	30.00	30.00	30.00
PR17TC	24c	45.00	30.00	30.00	30.00	30.00
PR18TC	36c	45.00	30.00	30.00	30.00	30.00
PR19TC	48c	45.00	30.00	30.00	30.00	30.00
PR20TC	60c	45.00	30.00	30.00	30.00	30.00
PR21TC	72c	45.00	30.00	30.00	30.00	30.00
PR22TC	84c	45.00	30.00	30.00	30.00	30.00
PR23TC	96c	45.00	30.00	30.00	30.00	30.00
PR24TC	$ 1.92	45.00	30.00	30.00	30.00	30.00
PR25TC	$ 3	45.00	30.00	30.00	30.00	30.00
PR26TC	$ 6	45.00	30.00	30.00	30.00	30.00
PR27TC	$ 9	45.00	30.00	30.00	30.00	30.00
PR28TC	$12	45.00	30.00	30.00	30.00	30.00
PR29TC	$24	45.00	30.00	30.00	30.00	30.00
PR30TC	$36	45.00	30.00	30.00	30.00	30.00
PR31TC	$48	45.00	30.00	30.00	30.00	30.00
PR32TC	$60	45.00	30.00	30.00	30.00	30.00

REVENUES

Several lists of revenue proofs in trial colors have been published, but the accuracy of some of them is questionable. The following listings are limited to items seen by the editors. The list is not complete.

1862-71   **FIRST ISSUE**

R3TC	1c	Proprietary, black	Plate on India	80.00
R3TC	1c	Proprietary, carmine	Plate on Card	110.00
R3TC	1c	Proprietary, dull red	Plate on Bond	110.00
R3TC	1c	Proprietary, dull yel.	Plate on Bond	110.00
R3TC	1c	Proprietary, vio. rose	Plate on Bond	110.00
R3TC	1c	Proprietary, deep blue	Plate on Bond	110.00
R3TC	1c	Proprietary, red on blue	Plate on Bond	110.00
R3TC	1c	Proprietary, blue, perf. & gum	Plate on Bond	110.00
R7TC	2c	Certificate, ultra.	Plate on Card	65.00
R11TC	2c	Playing Cards, black	Die on India	400.00
R13TC	2c	Proprietary, black	Plate on India	75.00
R15TC	2c	U.S.I.R., violet rose	Plate on Bond	110.00
R15TC	2c	U.S.I.R., light green	Plate on Bond	110.00
R15TC	2c	U.S.I.R., pale blue	Plate on Bond	110.00
R15TC	2c	U.S.I.R., black	Plate on India	110.00
R16TC	3c	Foreign Exchange, green on blue	Plate on Bond	110.00
R16TC	3c	Foreign Exchange, blue	Plate on Goldbeater's Skin	110.00
R18TC	3c	Proprietary, black	Die on India	300.00
R21TC	4c	Playing Cards, black	Die (?) on India	300.00
R22TC	4c	Proprietary, black	Plate on India	110.00
R22TC	4c	Proprietary, black	Die on India	350.00
R22TC	4c	Proprietary, red lilac	Plate on Card	110.00
R24TC	5c	Certificate, carmine	Plate on India	110.00
R26TC	5c	Foreign Exchange, orange	Plate on India	110.00
R28TC	5c	Playing Cards, black	Die (?) on India	300.00
R30TC	6c	Inland Exchange, black	Die on India	350.00

R31TC	6c	Proprietary, black	Die on India	—
R32TC	10c	Bill of Lading, greenish blue	Die on India	350.00
R35TC	10c	Foreign Exchange, black	Die (?) on India	350.00
R37TC	10c	Power of Attorney, greenish blue	Die on India	350.00
R38TC	10c	Proprietary, black	Die on India	350.00
R43TC	25c	Bond, carmine	Plate on Card	90.00
R46TC	25c	Insurance, dull red	Plate on Bond	150.00
R46TC	25c	Insurance, dull red	Plate on Goldbeater's Skin	210.00
R46TC	25c	Insurance, vermilion	Plate on Goldbeater's Skin	210.00
R46TC	25c	Insurance, vermilion	Plate on Bond	170.00
R46TC	25c	Insurance, blue	Plate on Bond	170.00
R46TC	25c	Insurance, blue	Plate on Goldbeater's Skin	215.00
R46TC	25c	Insurance, dark blue	Plate on Bond	155.00
R46TC	25c	Insurance, dark blue	Plate on Goldbeater's Skin	215.00
R46TC	25c	Insurance, green	Plate on Goldbeater's Skin	215.00
R51TC	30c	Foreign Exchange, violet	Plate on India	130.00
R51TC	30c	violet gray	Plate on India	130.00
R51TC	30c	black	Plate on India	155.00
R51TC	30c	red	Plate on India	155.00
R52TC	30c	Inland Exchange, deep red lilac	Plate on India	155.00
R55TC	50c	Entry of Goods, orange	Plate on Bond	275.00
R55TC	50c	green	Plate on Bond	275.00
R55TC	50c	red	Plate on Bond	340.00
R58TC	50c	Life Insurance, ultramarine	Plate on India	85.00
R60TC	50c	Original Process, black	Die (?) on India	280.00
R64TC	60c	Inland Exchange, green	Die (?) on India	—
R65TC	70c	Foreign Exchange, orange	Die (?) on India	—
R65TC	70c	Foreign Exchange, black	Die (?) on India	285.00
R66TC	$1	Conveyance, carmine	Plate on India	85.00
R67TC	$1	Entry of Goods, carmine	Plate on India	60.00
R68TC	$1	Foreign Exchange, carmine	Plate on India	60.00
R69TC	$1	Inland Exchange, carmine	Plate on India	60.00
R70TC	$1	Lease, carmine	Plate on India	130.00
R71TC	$1	Life Insurance, carmine	Plate on India	75.00
R72TC	$1	Manifest, carmine	Plate on India	80.00
R73TC	$1	Mortgage, carmine	Plate on India	85.00
R74TC	$1	Passage Ticket, carmine	Plate on India	120.00
R75TC	$1	Power of Attorney, carmine	Plate on India	120.00
R76TC	$1	Probate of Will, carmine	Plate on India	60.00
R78TC	$1.50	Inland Exchange, black	Die on India	475.00
R80TC	$1.90	Foreign Exchange, black	Plate on India	155.00
R81TC	$2	Conveyance, carmine	Plate on Card	85.00
R82TC	$2	Mortgage, carmine	Plate on Card	85.00
R84TC	$2.50	Inland Exchange, black	Die (?) on India	120.00
R87TC	$3.50	Inland Exchange, black	Die on India	400.00
R88TC	$5	Charter Party, carmine	Plate on India	85.00
R89TC	$5	Conveyance, carmine	Plate on India	90.00
R91TC	$5	Mortgage, carmine	Plate on India	90.00
R95TC	$10	Mortgage, yel. green	Plate on India	—
R98TC	$20	Conveyance, red orange	Plate on Card	120.00
R98TC	$20	red orange	Plate on India	220.00
R99TC	$20	Probate of Will, red orange	Plate on Card	275.00
R99TC	$20	black	Plate on Card	275.00
R101TC	$50	U.S.I.R., orange	Plate on Bond	275.00
R101TC	$50	U.S.I.R., deep blue	Plate on Bond	275.00
R102TC	$200	U.S.I.R., black & red	Plate on India	1,400.
R102TC	$200	gray brown & red	Plate on India	1,400.
R102TC	$200	green & brown red	Plate on India	1,400.

SECOND ISSUE

R104TC	2c	pale blue & black	Plate on Bond	60.00
R132TC	$200	green, red & black	Die on India	2,500.
R132TC	$200	orange	Die on India	2,500.
R132TC	$200	blue	Die on India	2,500.
R132TC	$200	green	Die on India	2,500.
R133TC	$500	green, yel. & black	Die on India	2,500.
R133TC	$500	black	Plate on Card	3,250.
R133TC	$500	yellow & black	Plate on Card	2,500.
R133TC	$500	red, green & black	Plate on Bond	3,000.
R133TC	$500	blue, scarlet & black	Plate on Bond	2,500.

THIRD ISSUE

R134TC	1c	brown & black	Plate on Card	60.00

1875 National Bank Note Co., New York City

R152TC	2c	(Liberty), green	Die on India	600.00
R152TC	2c	(Liberty), brown	Die on India	600.00
R152TC	2c	(Liberty), black	Die on India	600.00

1898

R161TC	½c	green	Large die on India	750.00
R163TC	1c	green	Large die on India	750.00
R163TC	1c	black	Large die on India	750.00
R165TC	3c	green	Small die on India	650.00
R169TC	25c	green	Large die on India	650.00
R170TC	40c	black	Large die on India	650.00
R172TC	80c	green	Large die on India	650.00

1898

R174TC	$3	black	Die on India	650.00
R176TC	$10	green	Die on India	650.00

1899

R179TC	$100	dark green & black	Die on India	850.00
R181TC	$1000	dark blue & black	Die on India	850.00

1914

R195TC	½c	black	Small die on Wove	—
R196TC	1c	blue green	Small die on Wove	—
R198TC	3c	ultramarine	Small die on Wove	—
R199TC	4c	brown	Small die on Wove	—
R200TC	5c	blue	Small die on Wove	—
R201TC	10c	yellow	Small die on Wove	—
R202TC	25c	dull violet	Small die on Wove	—
R203TC	40c	blue green	Small die on Wove	—
R204TC	50c	red brown	Small die on Wove	—
R205TC	80c	orange	Small die on Wove	—

Proprietary

1871-75

RB1TC	1c	blue & black	Plate on Bond	70.00
RB1TC	1c	scarlet & black	Plate on Bond	70.00
RB1TC	1c	orange & black	Plate on Bond	70.00
RB1TC	1c	orange & ultramarine	Plate on Granite Bond	60.00
RB3TC	3c	blue & black, with gum	Plate on Bond	60.00
RB3TC	3c	blue & black	Plate on Gray Bond	60.00
RB8TC	50c	green & brown	Die on India	675.00
RB8TC	50c	green & purple	Die on India	675.00
RB8TC	50c	green & brown red	Die on India	675.00
RB8TC	50c	green & violet	Die on India	675.00
RB8TC	50c	green & dk. carmine	Die on India	675.00
RB8TC	50c	ultramarine & red	Die on India	675.00
RB9TC	$1	green & brown	Die on India	675.00
RB9TC	$1	green & purple	Die on India	675.00
RB9TC	$1	green & violet brown	Die on India	675.00
RB9TC	$1	green & brown red	Die on India	675.00
RB9TC	$1	green & violet	Die on India	675.00
RB9TC	$1	green & dk. carmine	Die on India	675.00

1875-83

RB11TC	1c	brown	Die on India	500.00
RB11TC	1c	black	Die on India	500.00
RB12TC	2c	green	Die on India	500.00
RB12TC	2c	black	Die on India	500.00
RB12TC	2c	brown	Die on India	500.00
RB13TC	3c	brown	Die on India	500.00
RB13TC	3c	green	Die on India	500.00

RB13TC	3c	black	Plate on India	150.00
RB14TC	4c	dark brown	Die on India	450.00
RB14TC	4c	green	Die on India	450.00
RB14TC	4c	black	Die on India	450.00
RB14TC	4c	black	Die on India	150.00
RB16TC	5c	green	Die on India	450.00
RB17TC	6c	green	Plate on India	150.00
RB17TC	6c	black	Die on India	450.00
RB17TC	6c	black	Plate on India	150.00
RB17TC	6c	violet brown	Die on India	550.00
RB19TC	10c	black	Die on India	550.00

SECOND, THIRD AND PROPRIETARY ISSUES
Stamps Nos. R103 to R131, R134 to R150 and RB1 to RB7.

A special composite plate was made and impressions taken in various colors and shades. Although all varieties in all colors must have been made, only those seen by the editors are listed.

PLATE PROOFS ON INDIA PAPER. CENTERS IN BLACK.

1871-75

R103TC 1c

a. dark purple	60.00
b. dull purple	60.00
d. brown	60.00
e. black brown	60.00
g. light blue	60.00
h. dark blue	70.00
i. ultramarine	70.00
k. yellow green	70.00
n. green	65.00
o. dark green	65.00
p. blue green	65.00
q. light orange	65.00
r. dark orange	65.00
s. deep orange	65.00
t. scarlet	65.00
u. carmine	65.00
x. dark brown red	65.00
y. dark brown orange, goldbeater's skin	90.00

R104TC 2c

a. dark purple	60.00
b. dull purple	60.00
d. brown	60.00
e. black brown	60.00
g. light blue	60.00
h. dark blue	70.00
i. ultramarine	70.00
k. yellow green	70.00
l. dark yellow green	70.00
n. green	65.00
o. dark green	65.00
p. blue green	65.00
q. light orange	65.00
r. dark orange	65.00
s. deep orange	65.00
t. scarlet	65.00
u. carmine	65.00
x. dark brown red	65.00
y. dark brown orange, goldbeater's skin	90.00

R105TC 3c

a. dark purple	60.00
b. dull purple	60.00
d. brown	60.00
e. black brown	60.00
g. light blue	60.00
h. dark blue	70.00
i. ultramarine	70.00
k. yellow green	70.00
n. green	65.00
o. dark green	65.00
p. blue green	65.00
q. light orange	65.00
r. dark orange	65.00
s. deep orange	65.00
t. scarlet	65.00
u. carmine	65.00
x. dark brown red	65.00
y. dark brown orange, goldbeater's skin	90.00

R106TC 4c

a. dark purple	60.00
b. dull purple	60.00
d. brown	60.00
e. black brown	60.00
f. orange brown	65.00
g. light blue	60.00
h. dark blue	70.00
i. ultramarine	70.00
k. yellow green	70.00
n. green	65.00
o. dark green	65.00
p. blue green	65.00
q. light orange	65.00
r. dark orange	65.00
s. deep orange	65.00
t. scarlet	65.00
u. carmine	65.00
x. dark brown red	65.00
y. dark brown orange, goldbeater's skin	90.00

R107TC 5c

a. dark purple	60.00
b. dull purple	60.00
d. brown	60.00
e. black brown	60.00
f. orange brown	65.00
g. light blue	60.00
h. dark blue	70.00
i. ultramarine	70.00
k. yellow green	70.00

n. green 65.00
o. dark green 65.00
p. blue green 65.00
q. light orange 65.00
r. dark orange 65.00
s. deep orange 65.00
t. scarlet 65.00
u. carmine 65.00
v. dark carmine 65.00
w. purplish carmine 65.00
x. dark brown red 65.00
y. dark brown orange, goldbeater's skin 90.00

R108TC 6c
a. dark purple 60.00
b. dull purple 60.00
d. brown 60.00
e. black brown 60.00
f. orange brown 65.00
g. light blue 60.00
h. dark blue 70.00
i. ultramarine 70.00
k. yellow green 70.00
n. green 65.00
o. dark green 65.00
p. blue green 65.00
q. light orange 65.00
r. dark orange 65.00
s. deep orange 65.00
t. scarlet 65.00
u. carmine 65.00
v. dark carmine 65.00
w. purplish carmine 65.00
x. dark brown red 65.00
y. dark brown orange, goldbeater's skin

R109TC 10c
a. dark purple 60.00
b. dull purple 60.00
d. brown 60.00
e. black brown 60.00
g. light blue 60.00
h. dark blue 70.00
i. ultramarine 70.00
k. yellow green 70.00
n. green 65.00
o. dark green 65.00
p. blue green 65.00
q. light orange 65.00
r. dark orange 65.00
s. deep orange 65.00
t. scarlet 65.00
u. carmine 65.00
x. dark brown red 65.00

R110TC 15c
a. dark purple 60.00
b. dull purple 60.00
d. brown 60.00
e. black brown 60.00
f. orange brown 65.00
g. light blue 60.00
h. dark blue 70.00
i. ultramarine 70.00
k. yellow green 70.00
n. green 65.00
o. dark green 65.00
p. blue green 65.00
q. light orange 65.00
r. dark orange 65.00
s. deep orange 65.00
t. scarlet 65.00
u. carmine 65.00
w. purplish carmine 65.00
x. dark brown red 65.00

R111TC 20c
a. dark purple 60.00
b. dull purple 60.00
d. brown 60.00
e. black brown 60.00
g. light blue 60.00
h. dark blue 70.00
i. ultramarine 70.00
k. yellow green 70.00
n. green 65.00
o. dark green 65.00
p. blue green 65.00
q. light orange 65.00
r. dark orange 65.00
s. deep orange 65.00
t. scarlet 65.00
u. carmine 65.00
w. purplish carmine 65.00
x. dark brown red 65.00
y. dark brown orange, goldbeater's skin 90.00

R112TC 25c
a. dark purple 60.00
b. dull purple 60.00
d. brown 60.00
e. black brown 60.00
g. light blue 60.00
h. dark blue 70.00
i. ultramarine 70.00
k. yellow green 70.00
l. dark yellow green 70.00
n. green 65.00
o. dark green 65.00
p. blue green 65.00
q. light orange 65.00
r. dark orange 65.00
s. deep orange 65.00
t. scarlet 65.00
u. carmine 65.00
x. dark brown red 65.00
y. dark brown orange, goldbeater's skin 90.00

R113TC 30c
a. dark purple 60.00
b. dull purple 60.00

d. brown 60.00
e. black brown 60.00
g. light blue 60.00
h. dark blue 70.00
i. ultramarine 70.00
k. yellow green 70.00
n. green 65.00
o. dark green 65.00
p. blue green 65.00
q. light orange 65.00
r. dark orange 65.00
s. deep orange 65.00
t. scarlet 65.00
u. carmine 65.00
v. dark carmine 65.00
w. purplish carmine 65.00
x. dark brown red 65.00
y. dark brown orange, goldbeater's skin 90.00

R114TC 40c
a. dark purple 60.00
b. dull purple 60.00
d. brown 60.00
e. black brown 60.00
f. orange brown 65.00
g. light blue 60.00
h. dark blue 70.00
i. ultramarine 70.00
k. yellow green 70.00
n. green 65.00
o. dark green 65.00
p. blue green 65.00
q. light orange 65.00
r. dark orange 65.00
s. deep orange 65.00
t. scarlet 65.00
u. carmine 65.00
x. dark brown red 65.00

R115TC 50c
a. dark purple 60.00
b. dull purple 60.00
d. brown 60.00
e. black brown 60.00
g. light blue 60.00
h. dark blue 70.00
i. ultramarine 70.00
k. yellow green 70.00
n. green 65.00
o. dark green 65.00
p. blue green 65.00
q. light orange 65.00
r. dark orange 65.00
s. deep orange 65.00
t. scarlet 65.00
u. carmine 65.00
x. dark brown red 65.00

R116TC 60c
a. dark purple 60.00
b. dull purple 60.00
d. brown 60.00
e. black brown 60.00
g. light blue 60.00
h. dark blue 70.00
i. ultramarine 70.00
k. yellow green 70.00
n. green 65.00
o. dark green 65.00
p. blue green 65.00
q. light orange 65.00
r. dark orange 65.00
s. deep orange 65.00
t. scarlet 65.00
u. carmine 65.00
v. dark carmine 65.00
x. dark brown red 65.00
y. dark brown orange, goldbeater's skin 90.00

R117TC 70c
a. dark purple 60.00
b. dull purple 60.00
d. brown 60.00
e. black brown 60.00
g. light blue 60.00
h. dark blue 70.00
i. ultramarine 70.00
k. yellow green 70.00
n. green 65.00
o. dark green 65.00
p. blue green 65.00
q. light orange 65.00
r. dark orange 65.00
s. deep orange 65.00
t. scarlet 65.00
u. carmine 65.00
x. dark brown red 65.00

R118TC $1
a. dark purple 70.00
b. dull purple 70.00
d. brown 70.00
e. black brown 70.00
g. light blue 80.00
h. dark blue 82.50
i. ultramarine 82.50
k. yellow green 77.50
n. green 72.50
o. dark green 72.50
p. blue green 72.50
q. light orange 72.50
r. dark orange 72.50
s. deep orange 72.50
t. scarlet 77.50
u. carmine 77.50
w. purplish carmine 77.50
x. dark brown red 77.50
y. dark brown orange, goldbeater's skin 90.00

R119TC $1.30
a. dark purple 70.00
b. dull purple 70.00

d. brown 70.00
e. black brown 70.00
g. light blue 80.00
h. dark blue 82.50
i. ultramarine 82.50
j. bright yellow green, on card 72.50
k. yellow green 77.50
n. green 72.50
o. dark green 72.50
p. blue green 72.50
q. light orange 72.50
r. dark orange 72.50
s. deep orange 72.50
t. scarlet 77.50
u. carmine 77.50
x. dark brown red 77.50

R120TC $1.50
a. dark purple 70.00
b. dull purple 70.00
d. brown 70.00
e. black brown 70.00
g. light blue 80.00
h. dark blue 82.50
i. ultramarine 82.50
j. bright yellow green, on card 72.50
k. yellow green 77.50
n. green 72.50
o. dark green 72.50
p. blue green 72.50
q. light orange 72.50
r. dark orange 72.50
s. deep orange 72.50
t. scarlet 77.50
u. carmine 77.50
x. dark brown red 77.50

R121TC $1.60
a. dark purple 70.00
b. dull purple 70.00
d. brown 70.00
e. black brown 70.00
g. light blue 80.00
h. dark blue 82.50
i. ultramarine 82.50
k. yellow green 77.50
n. green 72.50
o. dark green 72.50
p. blue green 72.50
q. light orange 72.50
r. dark orange 72.50
s. deep orange 72.50
t. scarlet 77.50
u. carmine 77.50
x. dark brown red 77.50

R122TC $1.90
a. dark purple 70.00
b. dull purple 70.00
d. brown 70.00
e. black brown 70.00
g. light blue 80.00
h. dark blue 82.50
i. ultramarine 82.50
j. bright yellow green, on card 72.50
k. yellow green 77.50
n. green 72.50
o. dark green 72.50
p. blue green 72.50
q. light orange 72.50
r. dark orange 72.50
s. deep orange 72.50
t. scarlet 77.50
u. carmine 77.50
x. dark brown red 77.50

R123TC $2
a. dark purple 70.00
b. dull purple 70.00
d. brown 70.00
e. black brown 70.00
g. light blue 80.00
h. dark blue 82.50
i. ultramarine 82.50
j. bright yellow green, on card 72.50
k. yellow green 77.50
n. green 72.50
o. dark green 72.50
p. blue green 72.50
q. light orange 72.50
r. dark orange 72.50
s. deep orange 72.50
t. scarlet 77.50
u. carmine 77.50
w. purplish carmine 77.50
x. dark brown red 77.50
y. dark brown orange, goldbeater's skin 100.00

R124TC $2.50
a. dark purple 70.00
b. dull purple 70.00
d. brown 70.00
e. black brown 70.00
g. light blue 80.00
h. dark blue 82.50
i. ultramarine 82.50
k. yellow green 77.50
n. green 72.50
o. dark green 72.50
p. blue green 72.50
q. light orange 72.50
r. dark orange 72.50
s. deep orange 72.50
t. scarlet 77.50
u. carmine 77.50
v. dark carmine 77.50

R125TC $3
a. dark purple 70.00
b. dull purple 70.00
d. brown 70.00
e. black brown 70.00
g. light blue 80.00

h. dark blue	82.50	
i. ultramarine	82.50	
j. bright yellow green, on card	72.50	
k. yellow green	77.50	
n. green	72.50	
o. dark green	72.50	
p. blue green	72.50	
q. light orange	72.50	
r. dark orange	72.50	
s. deep orange	72.50	
t. scarlet	77.50	
u. carmine	77.50	
x. dark brown red	77.50	

R126TC $3.50

a. dark purple	70.00
b. dull purple	70.00
c. red purple	75.00
d. brown	70.00
e. black brown	70.00
g. light blue	80.00
h. dark blue	82.50
i. ultramarine	82.50
k. yellow green	77.50
n. green	72.50
o. dark green	72.50
p. blue green	72.50
q. light orange	72.50
r. dark orange	72.50
s. deep orange	72.50
t. scarlet	87.50
u. carmine	77.50
x. dark brown red	77.50

R127TC $5

a. dark purple	70.00
b. dull purple	70.00
d. brown	70.00
e. black brown	70.00
g. light blue	80.00
h. dark blue	82.50
i. ultramarine	82.50
k. yellow green	77.50
n. green	72.50
o. dark green	72.50
p. blue green	72.50
q. light orange	72.50
r. dark orange	72.50
s. deep orange	72.50
t. scarlet	72.50
u. carmine	72.50
w. purplish carmine	72.50
x. dark brown red	77.50
y. dark brown orange, goldbeater's skin	100.00

R128TC $10

a. dark purple	70.00
b. dull purple	70.00
d. brown	70.00
e. black brown	70.00
g. light blue	80.00
h. dark blue	82.50
i. ultramarine	82.50
j. bright yellow green, on card	72.50
k. yellow green	75.00
n. green	72.50
o. dark green	72.50
p. blue green	72.50
q. light orange	72.50
r. dark orange	72.50
s. deep orange	72.50
t. scarlet	72.50
u. carmine	77.50
x. dark brown red	77.50

R129TC $20

a. dark purple	95.00
b. dull purple	95.00
d. brown	95.00
e. black brown	95.00
g. light blue	87.50
h. dark blue	87.50
i. ultramarine	87.50
k. yellow green	85.00
m. emerald green	85.00
n. green	72.50
o. dark green	72.50
p. blue green	72.50
q. light orange	72.50
r. dark orange	85.00
s. deep orange	85.00
t. scarlet	87.50
u. carmine	77.50
v. dark carmine	87.50
x. dark brown red	77.50

R130TC $25

a. dark purple	100.00
b. dull purple	100.00
d. brown	100.00
e. black brown	100.00
g. light blue	90.00
h. dark blue	87.50
i. ultramarine	87.50
k. yellow green	85.00
m. emerald green	85.00
n. green	72.50
o. dark green	72.50
p. blue green	72.50
q. light orange	72.50
r. dark orange	85.00
s. deep orange	85.00
t. scarlet	87.50
u. carmine	77.50
w. purplish carmine	87.50
x. dark brown red	300.00
y. dark brown orange, goldbeater's skin	100.00

R131TC $50

a. dark purple	95.00
b. dull purple	95.00
d. brown	95.00
e. black brown	95.00

g. light blue	87.50	
h. dark blue	87.50	
i. ultramarine	87.50	
j. bright yellow green, on card	85.00	
k. yellow green	85.00	
m. emerald green	85.00	
n. green	72.50	
o. dark green	72.50	
p. blue green	72.50	
q. light orange	72.50	
r. dark orange	85.00	
s. deep orange	85.00	
t. scarlet	87.50	
u. carmine	77.50	
x. dark brown red	77.50	

RB1TC 1c

a. dark purple	67.50
b. dull purple	67.50
d. brown	65.00
e. black brown	65.00
g. light blue	75.00
h. dark blue	75.00
i. ultramarine	75.00
k. yellow green	70.00
l. dark yellow green	70.00
n. green	65.00
o. dark green	65.00
p. blue green	65.00
q. light orange	65.00
r. dark orange	65.00
s. deep orange	65.00
t. scarlet	65.00
u. carmine	65.00
x. dark brown red	65.00

RB2TC 2c

a. dark purple	67.50
b. dull purple	67.50
d. brown	65.00
e. black brown	65.00
g. light blue	70.00
h. dark blue	70.00
i. ultramarine	70.00
j. bright yellow green, on card	70.00
k. yellow green	70.00
n. green	65.00
o. dark green	65.00
p. blue green	65.00
q. light orange	65.00
r. dark orange	65.00
s. deep orange	65.00
t. scarlet	65.00
u. carmine	65.00
x. dark brown red	65.00

RB3TC 3c

a. dark purple	67.50
b. dull purple	67.50
d. brown	65.00
e. black brown	65.00
g. light blue	70.00
h. dark blue	70.00
i. ultramarine	70.00
k. yellow green	70.00
l. dark yellow green	70.00
n. green	65.00
o. dark green	65.00
p. blue green	65.00
q. light orange	65.00
r. dark orange	65.00
s. deep orange	65.00
t. scarlet	65.00
u. carmine	65.00
x. dark brown red	65.00

RB4TC 4c

a. dark purple	67.50
b. dull purple	67.50
d. brown	65.00
e. black brown	65.00
g. light blue	70.00
h. dark blue	70.00
i. ultramarine	70.00
k. yellow green	70.00
n. green	65.00
o. dark green	65.00
p. blue green	65.00
q. light orange	65.00
r. dark orange	65.00
s. deep orange	65.00
t. scarlet	65.00
u. carmine	65.00
x. dark brown red	65.00

RB5TC 5c

a. dark purple	67.50
b. dull purple	67.50
d. brown	65.00
e. black brown	65.00
g. light blue	70.00
h. dark blue	70.00
i. ultramarine	70.00
j. bright yellow green, on card	70.00
k. yellow green	70.00
l. dark yellow green	70.00
n. green	65.00
o. dark green	65.00
p. blue green	65.00
q. light orange	65.00
r. dark orange	65.00
s. deep orange	65.00
t. scarlet	65.00
u. carmine	65.00
x. dark brown red	65.00

RB6TC 6c

a. dark purple	67.50
b. dull purple	67.50
d. brown	65.00
e. black brown	65.00
g. light blue	70.00
h. dark blue	70.00
i. ultramarine	70.00
k. yellow green	70.00

l. dark yellow green	70.00	
n. green	65.00	
o. dark green	65.00	
p. blue green	65.00	
q. light orange	65.00	
r. dark orange	65.00	
s. deep orange	65.00	
t. scarlet	65.00	
u. carmine	65.00	
x. dark brown red	65.00	

RB7TC 10c

a. dark purple	67.50
b. dull purple	67.50
d. brown	65.00
e. black brown	65.00
g. light blue	70.00
h. dark blue	70.00
i. ultramarine	70.00
k. yellow green	70.00
l. dark yellow green	70.00
n. green	65.00
o. dark green	65.00
p. blue green	65.00
q. light orange	65.00
r. dark orange	65.00
s. deep orange	65.00
t. scarlet	65.00
u. carmine	65.00
x. dark brown red	65.00

1898

RB21TC	¼c	green	Large die on India	500.00
RB22TC	⅜c	green	Large die on India	500.00
RB26TC	1⅞c	green	Large die on India	500.00
RB26TC	1⅞c	black	Large die on India	500.00
RB27TC	2c	green	Small die on India	350.00
RB31TC	5c	green	Small die on India	350.00

1918-29

Stock Transfer

RD20TC	$50	black	Die on India	400.00
RD20TC	$50	blue	Die on India	400.00

1894

Playing Cards

RF1TC	2c	black (On hand)	Die on India	400.00
RF2TC	2c	lake (Act of)	Die on India	400.00

Telegraph
American Rapid Telegraph Co.

			DIE (2) Small	PLATE (3) India	(4) Card
1T1TC	1c	green	55.00		
1T1TC	1c	brown	55.00		
1T1TC	1c	red	55.00		
1T1TC	1c	blue	55.00		
1T1TC	1c	bluish green	55.00		
1T3TC	5c	green	55.00		
1T3TC	5c	black	55.00		
1T3TC	5c	red	55.00		
1T3TC	5c	blue	55.00		
1T3TC	5c	bluish green	55.00		
1T5TC	15c	red	55.00		
1T5TC	15c	black	55.00		
1T5TC	15c	brown	55.00		
1T5TC	15c	bluish green	55.00		
1T6TC	20c	green	55.00		
1T6TC	20c	black	55.00		
1T6TC	20c	brown	55.00		
1T6TC	20c	blue	55.00		
1T6TC	20c	bluish green	55.00		

Collect

			DIE (1) Large	(2) Small	PLATE (3) India	(4) Card
1T10TC	5c	red		55.00		
1T10TC	5c	black		55.00		
1T10TC	5c	brown		55.00		
1T10TC	5c	green		55.00		
1T10TC	5c	bluish green		55.00		
1T11TC	15c	red		55.00		
1T11TC	15c	black		55.00		
1T11TC	15c	brown		55.00		
1T11TC	15c	green		55.00		
1T11TC	15c	blue		55.00		
1T11TC	15c	bluish green		55.00		

Office Coupon

1T14TC	5c	red		55.00	
1T14TC	5c	black		55.00	
1T14TC	5c	brown		55.00	
1T14TC	5c	green		55.00	
1T14TC	5c	bluish green		55.00	
1T15TC	15c	red		55.00	
1T15TC	15c	black		55.00	
1T15TC	15c	brown		55.00	
1T15TC	15c	green		55.00	
1T15TC	15c	blue		55.00	
1T15TC	15c	bluish green		55.00	

Baltimore & Ohio Telegraph Co.

3T2TC	5c	dark olive		65.00
3T4TC	25c	dark olive		65.00

Postal Telegraph Co.

15T1TC	10c	brown red		65.00	
15T1TC	10c	red			65.00
15T1TC	10c	blue			65.00

	DIE (1) Large	(2) Small	PLATE (3) India	(4) Card
15T1TC 10c black	65.00			
15T1TC 10c orange		65.00		
15T2TC 15c black	65.00	55.00		
15T2TC 15c red	65.00	55.00		
15T2TC 15c blue	65.00	55.00		
15T2TC 25c brown red		65.00		
15T3TC 25c black	65.00			
15T3TC 25c red	65.00			
15T3TC 25c ultramarine				40.00
15T3TC 25c brown		65.00		40.00
15T4TC 50c dull blue	65.00			
15T4TC 50c black	65.00			40.00
15T4TC 50c red	65.00			
15T4TC 50c blue	65.00			

	DIE (1) Large	(2) Small	PLATE (3) India	(4) Card
15T6TC red brown			40.00	

Western Union Telegraph Co.

	(3) India	(4) Card
16T1TC lilac (1871)	20.00	20.00
Pair	45.00	45.00
16T1TC orange	20.00	20.00
Pair	45.00	45.00
16T1TC black	20.00	20.00
Pair	45.00	45.00
16T1TC violet brown		20.00
Pair		45.00
16T1TC light olive		20.00
Pair		45.00
16T1TC brown		20.00
Pair		45.00

16T1TC orange brown		20.00
Pair		45.00
16T1TC blue green		20.00
Pair		45.00
16T6TC violet blue (1876)	20.00	20.00
16T7TC orange yellow (1877)		20.00
Pair		45.00
16T7TC dark brown		20.00
Pair		45.00
16T7TC black		20.00
Pane of four		—
16T8TC dark brown (1878)		—
16T9TC blue (1879)		—
16T10TC violet brown (1880)		—
16T10TC rose		—
16T22TC black (1892)		—

SPECIMEN

These are regular stamps overprinted "Specimen." Each number has a suffix letter "S" to denote Specimen. The number is that of the regular stamp, and the second letter "A", etc., indicates the type of overprint.

Specimen — Type A; 12 mm. long.

Specimen. — Type B; 15 mm. long.

Specimen. — Type C; 30 mm. long.

SPECIMEN — Type D; Capital Letters.

Specimen. — Type E; Initial Capital.

Specimen. — Type F; 22 mm. long

SPECIMEN — Type G; 14 mm. long

SPECIMEN — Type H; 16 mm. long

Specimen — Type I; 20 mm. long.

REGULAR ISSUES

Overprinted in Black **Specimen**

Type A. Overprint 12mm. long

1851-56

7S	A	1c blue, Type II	200.00
11S	A	3c dull red, Type I	—

1857-60

21S	A	1c blue, Type III	1,500.
24S	A	1c blue, Type V	1,000.
26S	A	3c dull red, Type II	1,000.
30S	A	5c orange brown, Type II	1,000.
35S	A	10c green, Type V	1,100.
36bS	A	12c black	1,000.
37S	A	24c lilac	1,000.
38S	A	30c orange	1,000.
26S	F	3c dull red, Type II	1,500.
26S	I	3c dull red, Type II	1,500.

1861

63S	A	1c blue	425.00
65S	A	3c rose	425.00
68S	A	10c dark green	425.00
70S	A	24c red lilac	425.00
72S	A	90c blue	425.00
73S	A	2c black	525.00
76S	A	5c brown	425.00

Specimen.

1861-66 — Type B. Overprint 15mm. long
Black, except as noted

63S	B	1c blue (1300)	120.00

		Without period	—
65S	B	3c rose (1500)	120.00
68S	B	10c dark green (1600)	120.00
69S	B	12c black (Orange) (1300)	120.00
71S	B	30c orange (1400)	120.00
72S	B	90c blue (1394)	120.00
73S	B	2c black (Vermilion) (1306)	275.00
		Without period	—
76S	B	5c brown (1306)	120.00
77S	B	15c black (Vermilion) (1208)	200.00
78S	B	24c lilac (1300)	120.00

1867-68

86S	A	1c blue	400.00
85E—S	A	12c black	400.00
93S	A	2c black	500.00
94S	A	3c rose	400.00
95S	A	5c brown	400.00
98S	A	15c black	450.00
100S	A	30c orange	400.00

1869

112S	A	1c buff	525.00
113S	A	2c brown	525.00
115S	A	6c ultramarine	525.00
116S	A	10c yellow	525.00
117S	A	12c green	525.00
119S	A	15c brown & blue	675.00
120S	A	24c green & violet	675.00
		a. Without grill	—
121S	A	30c blue & carmine	675.00
		a. Without grill	—
122S	A	90c carmine & black	950.00
		a. Without grill	—

1870-71

145S	A	1c ultramarine	350.00
146S	A	2c red brown	350.00
147S	A	3c green	350.00
147S	B	3c green	450.00
148S	A	6c carmine	350.00
149S	A	7c vermilion	350.00
150S	A	10c brown	350.00
151S	A	12c dull violet	350.00
152S	A	15c bright orange	350.00
155S	A	90c carmine	350.00
155S	B	90c carmine (Blue)	450.00

1873

159S	B	6c dull pink	375.00
160S	B	7c orange vermilion (Blue)	350.00
162S	B	12c blackish violet (Blue)	—

Overprinted in Red **SPECIMEN.**

1879

Type D

189S	D	15c red orange	80.00
190S	D	30c full blue	80.00
191S	D	90c carmine	80.00
		a. Overprint in black brown	80.00

1881-82

205S	D	5c yellow brown	80.00
206S	D	1c gray blue	80.00
207S	D	3c blue green	80.00
208S	D	6c brown red	80.00
209S	D	10c brown	80.00

1883

210S	D	2c red brown	100.00
211S	D	4c blue green	100.00

Handstamped in Dull Purple **Specimen.**

1890-93

Type E

219S	E	1c dull blue	100.00
220S	E	2c carmine	100.00
221S	E	3c purple	100.00
222S	E	4c dark brown	100.00
223S	E	5c chocolate	100.00
224S	E	6c dull red	100.00
225S	E	8c lilac	100.00
226S	E	10c green	100.00
227S	E	15c blue	100.00
228S	E	30c black	100.00
229S	E	90c orange	135.00

COLUMBIAN ISSUE

1893

230S	E	1c deep blue	400.00
		Double overprint	400.00
231S	E	2c violet	400.00
232S	E	3c green	400.00
233S	E	4c ultramarine	400.00
234S	E	5c chocolate	400.00
235S	E	6c purple	400.00
236S	E	8c magenta	400.00
237S	E	10c black brown	400.00
238S	E	15c dark green	400.00
239S	E	30c orange brown	400.00
240S	E	50c slate blue	400.00
241S	E	$1 salmon	500.00
242S	E	$2 brown red	500.00
243S	E	$3 yellow green	550.00
244S	E	$4 crimson lake	575.00
245S	E	$5 black	675.00

Overprinted in Magenta **Specimen.**

Type F

230S	F	1c deep blue	550.00
232S	F	3c green	550.00
233S	F	4c ultramarine	550.00
234S	F	5c chocolate	550.00
235S	F	6c purple	550.00
237S	F	10c black brown	550.00
243S	F	3c yellow green	700.00

Overprinted Type H in Black or Red

231S	H	2c violet (Bk)	625.00
233S	H	4c ultramarine (R)	625.00
234S	H	5c chocolate (R)	625.00

Overprinted Type I in Black or Red

231S	I	2c violet (R)	625.00
232S	I	3c green (R)	625.00
233S	I	4c ultramarine (R)	625.00
234S	I	5c chocolate (Bk)	625.00
235S	I	6c purple (R)	625.00
236S	I	8c magenta (Bk)	625.00
237S	I	10c black brown (R)	625.00
238S	I	15c dark green (R)	625.00
239S	I	30c orange brown (Bk)	625.00
240S	I	50c slate blue (R)	625.00

1895

Type E

264S	E	1c blue	90.00
267S	E	2c carmine	90.00
268S	E	3c purple	90.00
269S	E	4c dark brown	100.00
270S	E	5c chocolate	90.00
271S	E	6c dull brown	90.00
272S	E	8c violet brown	90.00
273S	E	10c dark green	90.00
274S	E	15c dark blue	90.00
275S	E	50c orange	90.00

276S	E	$1 black, Type I	325.00
277S	E	$2 dark blue	300.00
278S	E	$5 dark green	400.00

1898-99

279S	E	1c deep green	90.00
279B—SE		2c orange red	90.00
	a.	Booklet pane of 6	525.00
280S	E	4c rose brown	160.00
281S	E	5c dark blue	80.00
282S	E	6c lake	80.00
282C—SE		10c brown, Type I	80.00
283S	E	10c brown, Type II	80.00
284S	E	15c olive green	80.00

TRANS-MISSISSIPPI ISSUE

1898

285S	E	1c dark yellow green	250.00
286S	E	2c copper red	250.00
287S	E	4c orange	250.00
288S	E	5c dull blue	250.00
289S	E	8c violet brown	250.00
290S	E	10c gray violet	250.00
291S	E	50c sage green	300.00
292S	E	$1 black	450.00
293S	E	$2 orange brown	625.00

PAN-AMERICAN ISSUE

1901

294S	E	1c green & black	235.00
295S	E	2c carmine	235.00
296S	E	4c chocolate & black	235.00
	a.	Center inverted	4,500.
297S	E	5c ultramarine & black	235.00
298S	E	8c brown violet & black	235.00
299S	E	10c yellow brown & black	235.00

1902

300S	E	1c blue green	90.00
301S	E	2c carmine	90.00
302S	E	3c bright violet	90.00
303S	E	4c brown	90.00
304S	E	5c blue	90.00
305S	E	6c claret	90.00
306S	E	8c violet black	90.00
307S	E	10c pale red brown	90.00
308S	E	13c purple black	90.00
309S	E	15c olive green	90.00
310S	E	50c orange	90.00
311S	E	$1 black	200.00
312S	E	$2 dark blue	300.00
313S	E	$5 dark green	400.00

1903

319S	E	2c carmine	110.00

LOUISIANA PURCHASE ISSUE

1904

323S	E	1c green	350.00
324S	E	2c carmine	350.00
325S	E	3c violet	350.00
326S	E	5c dark blue	350.00
327S	E	10c red brown	350.00

SPECIAL DELIVERY STAMPS

Overprinted in Red   **SPECIMEN.**

1885

Type D

E1S	D	10c blue	110.00

Handstamped in Dull Purple   **Specimen.**

1888

Type E

E2S	E	10c blue	110.00

1893

E3S	E	10c orange	150.00

1894

E4S	E	10c blue	225.00

1895

E5S	E	10c blue	150.00

1902

E6S	E	10c ultramarine	150.00

POSTAGE DUE STAMPS

Overprinted in Red   **SPECIMEN·**

1879

Type D.

J1S	D	1c brown	250.00
J2S	D	2c brown	250.00
J3S	D	3c brown	250.00
J4S	D	5c brown	250.00

1884

J15S	D	1c red brown	45.00
J16S	D	2c red brown	45.00
J17S	D	3c red brown	45.00
J18S	D	5c red brown	45.00
J19S	D	10c red brown	45.00
J20S	D	30c red brown	45.00
J21S	D	50c red brown	45.00

Overprinted in Dull Purple   **Specimen.**

1895

Type E

J38S	E	1c deep claret	85.00
J39S	E	2c deep claret	85.00
J40S	E	3c deep claret	85.00
J41S	E	5c deep claret	85.00
J42S	E	10c deep claret	85.00
J43S	E	30c deep claret	85.00
J44S	E	50c deep claret	85.00

Official Stamps

Special printings of Official stamps were made in 1875 at the time the other Reprints, Re-issues and Special Printings were printed. They are ungummed.

Although perforated, these stamps were sometimes (but not always) cut apart with scissors. As a result the perforations may be mutilated and the design damaged.

Number issued indicated in brackets.

All values exist imperforate.

Overprinted in Block Letters   **SPECIMEN**

Type D

1875   **Thin, hard white paper**   *Perf. 12*

AGRICULTURE
Carmine Overprint

O1S	D	1c yellow (15,234)	5.00
	a.	"Sepcimen" error	475.00
	b.	Small dotted "i" in "Specimen"	165.00
	c.	Ribbed paper	15.00
O2S	D	2c yellow (4,192)	11.00
	a.	"Sepcimen" error	525.00
O3S	D	3c yellow (389)	45.00
	a.	"Sepcimen" error	1,900.
O4S	D	6c yellow (373)	80.00
	a.	"Sepcimen" error	—
O5S	D	10c yellow (390)	80.00
	a.	"Sepcimen" error	1,900.
O6S	D	12c yellow (379)	75.00
	a.	"Sepcimen" error	1,900.
O7S	D	15c yellow (370)	75.00
	a.	"Sepcimen" error	1,900.
O8S	D	24c yellow (352)	75.00
	a.	"Sepcimen" error	1,900.
O9S	D	30c yellow (354)	75.00
	a.	"Sepcimen" error	1,900.

EXECUTIVE
Blue Overprint

O10S	D	1c carmine (14,652)	7.00
	a.	Small dotted "i" in "Specimen"	175.00
	b.	Ribbed paper	13.50
O11S	D	2c carmine (7,430)	10.00
O12S	D	3c carmine (3,735)	15.00
O13S	D	6c carmine (3,485)	15.00
O14S	D	10c carmine (3,461)	15.00

INTERIOR
Blue Overprint

O15S	D	1c vermilion (7,194)	9.50
O16S	D	2c vermilion (1,263)	15.00
	a.	"Sepcimen" error	1,150.
O17S	D	3c vermilion (88)	325.00
O18S	D	6c vermilion (83)	300.00
O19S	D	10c vermilion (82)	300.00
O20S	D	12c vermilion (75)	325.00
O21S	D	15c vermilion (78)	325.00
O22S	D	24c vermilion (77)	325.00
O23S	D	30c vermilion (75)	325.00
O24S	D	90c vermilion (77)	325.00

JUSTICE
Blue Overprint

O25S	D	1c purple (19,729)	8.00
	a.	"Sepcimen" error	450.00
	b.	Small dotted "i" in "Specimen"	150.00
	c.	Ribbed paper	10.00
O26S	D	2c purple (3,395)	10.00
	a.	"Sepcimen" error	750.00
O27S	D	3c purple (178)	140.00
	a.	"Sepcimen" error	2,450.
O28S	D	6c purple (163)	140.00
O29S	D	10c purple (163)	135.00
O30S	D	12c purple (154)	135.00
	a.	"Sepcimen" error	2,450.
O31S	D	15c purple (157)	160.00
	a.	"Sepcimen" error	2,450.
O32S	D	24c purple (150)	175.00
	a.	"Sepcimen" error	2,450.
O33S	D	30c purple (150)	175.00
	a.	"Sepcimen" error	2,450.
O34S	D	90c purple (152)	175.00

NAVY
Carmine Overprint

O35S	D	1c ultramarine (9,182)	8.25
	a.	"Sepcimen" error	375.00

	b.	Broken "i" in "Specimen"	165.00
O36S	D	2c ultramarine (1,748)	13.00
	a.	"Sepcimen" error	475.00
	b.	Broken "i" in "Specimen"	575.00
O37S	D	3c ultramarine (126)	175.00
O38S	D	6c ultramarine (116)	200.00
O39S	D	7c ultramarine (501)	80.00
	a.	"Sepcimen" error	1,200.
O40S	D	10c ultramarine (112)	200.00
	a.	"Sepcimen" error	2,400.
O41S	D	12c ultramarine (107)	185.00
	a.	"Sepcimen" error	2,400.
O42S	D	15c ultramarine (107)	185.00
	a.	"Sepcimen" error	2,400.
O43S	D	24c ultramarine (106)	180.00
	a.	"Sepcimen" error	2,400.
O44S	D	30c ultramarine (104)	180.00
	a.	"Sepcimen" error	2,400.
O45S	D	90c ultramarine (102)	180.00

POST OFFICE
Carmine Overprint

O47S	D	1c black (6,015)	9.00
	a.	"Sepcimen" error	450.00
	b.	Inverted overprint	375.00
O48S	D	2c black (590)	32.00
	a.	"Sepcimen" error	1,200.
O49S	D	3c black (91)	240.00
	a.	"Sepcimen" error	2,400.
O50S	D	6c black (87)	240.00
O51S	D	10c black (177)	165.00
	a.	"Sepcimen" error	2,000.
O52S	D	12c black (93)	240.00
O53S	D	15c black (82)	260.00
	a.	"Sepcimen" error	2,400.
O54S	D	24c black (84)	240.00
	a.	"Sepcimen" error	2,400.
O55S	D	30c black (81)	250.00
O56S	D	90c black (82)	250.00
	a.	"Sepcimen" error	2,400.

STATE.
Carmine Overprint.

O57S	D	1c bluish green (21,672)	8.00
	a.	"Sepcimen" error	275.00
	b.	Small dotted "i" in "Specimen"	225.00
	c.	Ribbed paper	10.00
O58S	D	2c bluish green (5,145)	11.00
	a.	"Sepcimen" error	375.00
O59S	D	3c bluish green (793)	23.00
	a.	"Sepcimen" error	1,200.
O60S	D	6c bluish green (467)	55.00
	a.	"Sepcimen" error	1,300.
O61S	D	7c bluish green (791)	23.00
	a.	"Sepcimen" error	1,200.
O62S	D	10c bluish green (346)	100.00
O63S	D	12c bluish green (280)	110.00
	a.	"Sepcimen" error	2,000.
O64S	D	15c bluish green (257)	110.00
O65S	D	24c bluish green (253)	110.00
	a.	"Sepcimen" error	2,000.
O66S	D	30c bluish green (249)	110.00
	a.	"Sepcimen" error	2,000.
O67S	D	90c bluish green (245)	110.00
	a.	"Sepcimen" error	2,000.
O68S	D	$2 green & black (32)	2,000.
O69S	D	$5 green & black (12)	3,750.
O70S	D	$10 green & black (8)	4,450.
O71S	D	$20 green & black (7)	4,750.

TREASURY
Blue Overprint

O72S	D	1c dark brown (2,185)	12.00
O73S	D	2c dark brown (309)	75.00
O74S	D	3c dark brown (84)	240.00
O75S	D	6c dark brown (85)	275.00
O76S	D	7c dark brown (198)	155.00
O77S	D	10c dark brown (82)	240.00
O78S	D	12c dark brown (75)	250.00
O79S	D	15c dark brown (75)	250.00
O80S	D	24c dark brown (99)	240.00
O81S	D	30c dark brown (74)	360.00
		Short transfer at top right	—
O82S	D	90c dark brown (72)	360.00

WAR
Blue Overprint

O83S	D	1c deep rose (4,610)	10.00
	a.	"Sepcimen" error	375.00
O84S	D	2c deep rose (1,618)	15.00
	a.	"Sepcimen" error	675.00
O85S	D	3c deep rose (118)	200.00
	a.	"Sepcimen" error	2,000.
O86S	D	6c deep rose (111)	240.00
	a.	"Sepcimen" error	2,000.
O87S	D	7c deep rose (539)	40.00
	a.	"Sepcimen" error	1,000.
O88S	D	10c deep rose (119)	190.00
	a.	"Sepcimen" error	2,000.
O89S	D	12c deep rose (105)	240.00
	a.	"Sepcimen" error	2,000.
O90S	D	15c deep rose (105)	240.00
	a.	"Sepcimen" error	2,000.
O91S	D	24c deep rose (106)	240.00
	a.	"Sepcimen" error	2,000.
O92S	D	30c deep rose (104)	240.00
	a.	"Sepcimen" error	2,000.
O93S	D	90c deep rose (106)	240.00
	a.	"Sepcimen" error	2,000.

SOFT POROUS PAPER

EXECUTIVE
Blue Overprint

O10xS	D	1c violet rose	25.00
		Broken "i" in "Specimen"	200.00

NAVY
Carmine Overprint

O35xS	D	1c gray blue	30.00
		deep blue	35.00
		Broken "i" in "Specimen"	200.00
	a.	Double overprint	550.00

STATE

O57xS	D	1c yellow green	110.00

The total number issued of the 1c Executive, 1c Navy, 1c State Departments possibly includes the soft paper "Specimen" printings.

SAVINGS STAMPS
Overprinted Vertically Reading Down in Red   [SPECIMEN]

1911

PS4S	10c deep blue	—

1917-18   Handstamped "SPECIMEN" in Violet

WS1S	25c deep green	—
WS2S	$5 deep green	—

NEWSPAPER STAMPS

Overprinted in Red   **Specimen.**

1865

Type C. Overprint 30mm. long

PR5S	C	5c dark blue	150.00
	a.	Triple overprint	260.00
PR2S	C	10c blue green	165.00
RP3S	C	25c carmine red	175.00

Handstamped in Black   **Specimen**

1875

Type A

PR9S	A	2c black	225.00
PR11S	A	4c black	225.00
PR12S	A	6c black	225.00
PR16S	A	12c rose	225.00

Overprinted in Black, except as noted   **Specimen.**

1875

Type B. Overprint 15mm. long

PR9S	B	2c black	45.00
PR10S	B	3c black	45.00
PR11S	B	4c black	45.00
PR12S	B	6c black	45.00
PR13S	B	8c black	45.00
PR14S	B	9c black	45.00
	a.	Overprint in blue	—
PR15S	B	10c black	45.00
PR16S	B	12c rose	45.00
PR17S	B	24c rose	45.00
PR18S	B	36c rose	45.00
PR19S	B	48c rose	45.00
	a.	Overprint in blue	62.50
PR20S	B	60c rose	45.00
PR21S	B	72c rose	45.00
	a.	Overprint in blue	62.50
PR22S	B	84c rose	45.00
	a.	Overprint in blue	—
PR23S	B	96c rose	45.00
	a.	Overprint in blue	—
PR24S	B	$1.92 dark brown	45.00
PR25S	B	$3 vermilion	45.00
	a.	Overprint in blue	62.50
PR26S	B	$6 ultramarine	45.00
	a.	Overprint in blue	250.00
PR27S	B	$9 yellow	45.00
	a.	Overprint in blue	250.00
PR28S	B	$12 dark green	45.00
	a.	Overprint in blue	250.00
PR29S	B	$24 dark gray violet	45.00
	a.	Overprint in blue	60.00
PR30S	B	$36 brown rose	62.00
PR31S	B	$48 red brown	62.00
PR32S	B	$60 violet	62.00

Overprinted in Red   **SPECIMEN.**

1875

Type D

PR14S	D	9c black	30.00

1879

PR57S	D	2c black	25.00

PR58S	D	3c black	25.00
PR59S	D	4c black	25.00
PR60S	D	6c black	25.00
PR61S	D	8c black	25.00
PR62S	D	10c black	25.00
	a.	Double overprint	250.00
PR63S	D	12c red	25.00
PR64S	D	24c red	25.00
PR65S	D	36c red	25.00
PR66S	D	48c red	25.00
PR67S	D	60c red	25.00
PR68S	D	72c red	25.00
PR69S	D	84c red	25.00
PR70S	D	96c red	25.00
PR71S	D	$1.92 pale brown	25.00
PR72S	D	$3 red vermilion	25.00
PR73S	D	$6 blue	25.00
PR74S	D	$9 orange	25.00
PR75S	D	$12 yellow green	25.00
PR76S	D	$24 dark violet	25.00
PR77S	D	$36 Indian red	25.00
PR78S	D	$48 yellow brown	25.00
PR79S	D	$60 purple	25.00

1885

PR81S	D	1c black	25.00

Handstamped in Dull Purple   **Specimen.**

1879

Type E

PR57S	E	2c black	22.50
PR58S	E	3c black	22.50
PR59S	E	4c black	22.50
PR60S	E	6c black	22.50
PR61S	E	8c black	22.50
PR62S	E	10c black	22.50
PR63S	E	12c red	22.50
PR64S	E	24c red	22.50
PR65S	E	36c red	22.50
PR66S	E	48c red	22.50
PR67S	E	60c red	22.50
PR68S	E	72c red	22.50
PR69S	E	84c red	22.50
PR70S	E	96c red	22.50
PR71S	E	$1.92 pale brown	22.50
PR72S	E	$3 red vermilion	22.50
PR73S	E	$6 blue	22.50
PR74S	E	$9 orange	22.50
PR75S	E	$12 yellow green	22.50
PR76S	E	$24 dark violet	22.50
PR77S	E	$36 Indian red	22.50
PR78S	E	$48 yellow brown	22.50
PR79S	E	$60 purple	22.50

1885

PR81S	E	1c black	22.50

1895   Wmk. 191

PR114S	E	1c black	35.00
PR115S	E	2c black	35.00
PR116S	E	5c black	35.00
PR117S	E	10c black	35.00
PR118S	E	25c carmine	35.00
PR119S	E	50c carmine	35.00
PR120S	E	$2 scarlet	35.00
PR121S	E	$5 dark blue	35.00
PR122S	E	$10 green	42.50
PR123S	E	$20 slate	42.50
PR124S	E	$50 dull rose	42.50
PR125S	E	$100 purple	42.50

REVENUE STAMPS

SPECIMEN
Type G

1862

Overprint 14mm long

R5S	G	2c Bank Check, blue (Red)	375.00
R15S	A	2c U. S. I. R., orange	—

SPECIMEN
Type H

Overprint 16mm. long

R23S	H	5c Agreement, red (Black)	375.00
R34S	H	10c Contract, blue (Red)	375.00
R35eS	H	10c Foreign Exchange, ultramarine (Red)	375.00
R36S	H	10c Inland Exchange, blue (Red)	375.00
R46S	H	25c Insurance, red (Black)	375.00
R52S	H	30c Inland Exchange, lilac (Red)	375.00
R53S	H	40c Inland Exchange, brown (Red)	375.00
R68S	H	$1 Foreign Exchange, red (Black)	375.00

Specimen
Type I

1898   Overprint 20mm. long

R153S	I	1c green (Red)	475.00

1875

RB11S	H	1c green (Red)	300.00

PRIVATE MATCH STAMP

Overprinted with Type G in Red — RO133dS   **SPECIMEN**

RO133bS	G	1c black, A.Messinger	300.00

VARIOUS OVERPRINTS

Overprinted with control numbers in carmine   **7890**

1861   Type J

63S	J	A24	1c pale blue (overprint 9012)	200.00
65S	J	A25	3c brown red (overprint 7890)	200.00
68S	J	A27	10c green (overprint 5678)	200.00
69S	J	A28	12c gray black (overprint 4567)	200.00
71S	J	A30	30c orange (overprint 2345)	200.00
72S	J	A31	90c pale blue (overprint 1234)	200.00
	a.		Pair, one without overprint	

1861-66

73S	J	A32	2c black (overprint 8901)	275.00
76S	J	A26	5c brown (overprint 6789)	250.00
77S	J	A33	15c black (overprint 235)	250.00
78S	J	A29	24c gray lilac (overprint 3456)	200.00

Special Printings Overprinted in Red or Blue   **SAMPLE.**

1889   Type K

212S	K	A59	1c ultramarine (red)	75.00
210S	K	A57	2c red brown (blue)	75.00
210S	K	A57	2c lake (blue)	75.00
210S	K	A57	2c rose lake (blue)	75.00
210S	K	A57	2c scarlet (blue)	75.00
214S	K	A46b	3c vermilion (blue)	75.00
211S	K	A58	4c blue green (red)	75.00
205S	K	A56	5c yellow brown (red)	75.00
208S	K	A47b	6c red brown (blue)	75.00
209S	K	A49b	10c brown (red)	75.00
			Without overprint	80.00
189S	K	A51a	15c orange (blue)	75.00
190S	K	A53	30c full black (red)	75.00
191S	K	A54	90c carmine (blue)	75.00

Special Printings Overprinted in Red or Blue   **SAMPLE. A.**

Type L

212S	L	A59	1c ultramarine (red)	75.00
210S	L	A57	2c rose lake (blue)	75.00
214S	L	A46b	3c purple (red)	75.00
211S	L	A58	4c dark brown (red)	75.00
205S	L	A56	5c gray brown (blue)	75.00
208S	L	A47b	6c vermilion (blue)	75.00
209S	L	A49b	10c green (red)	75.00
			Without overprint	100.00
189S	L	A51a	15c blue (red)	75.00
			Without overprint	100.00
190S	L	A53	30c full black (red)	75.00
191S	L	A54	90c orange (blue)	75.00

Overprinted with Type K together with "A" in Black manuscript

191S	M	A54	90c carmine (blue)	140.00
209S	M	A49b	10c brown (red)	140.00
211S	M	A58	4c blue green (red)	140.00

"SAMPLE A" in manuscript (red or black)

216S	N	A56	5c indigo	160.00

Regular Issues Overprinted in Blue or Red   **UNIVERSAL POSTAL (CONGRESS**

1897   Type O

125 sets were distributed to delegates to the Universal Postal Congress held in Washington, D. C., May 5 to June 15, 1897.

264S	O	A87	1c blue	135.00
267S	O	A88	2c carmine	135.00
268S	O	A89	3c purple	135.00
269S	O	A90	4c dark brown	135.00
270S	O	A91	5c chestnut	135.00
271S	O	A92	6c claret brown	135.00
272S	O	A93	8c violet brown	135.00
273S	O	A94	10c dark green	135.00
274S	O	A95	15c dark blue	135.00
275S	O	A96	50c red orange	135.00
276S	O	A97	$1 black, Type I	500.00
276A—S	O	A97	$1 black, Type II	450.00

277S	O A98	$2 dark blue	325.00
278S	O A99	$5 dark green	500.00

SPECIAL DELIVERY

E5S	O SD3	10c blue (R)	250.00

POSTAGE DUE

J38S	O D2	1c deep claret	125.00
J39S	O D2	2c deep claret	125.00
J40S	O D2	3c deep claret	125.00
J41S	O D2	5c deep claret	125.00
J42S	O D2	10c deep claret	125.00
J43S	O D2	30c deep claret	125.00
J44S	O D2	50c deep claret	125.00

NEWSPAPERS

PR114S	O N15	1c black	85.00
PR115S	O N15	2c black	85.00
PR116S	O N15	5c black	85.00
PR117S	O N15	10c black	85.00
PR118S	O N16	25c carmine	85.00
PR119S	O N16	50c carmine	85.00
PR120S	O N17	$2 scarlet	85.00
PR121S	O N18	$5 dark blue	85.00
PR122S	O N19	$10 green	85.00
PR123S	O N20	$20 slate	85.00
PR124S	O N21	$50 dull rose	85.00

PR125S	O N22	$100 purple	85.00

ENVELOPES

UNIVERSAL

Overprinted **POSTAL**

CONGRESS

Type P

U294S	P	1c blue on white	100.00
U296S	P	1c blue on amber	100.00
U300S	P	1c blue on manila	100.00
W301S	P	1c blue on manila	100.00
U304S	P	1c blue on amber manila	100.00
U311S	P	2c green, Die 2, on white	100.00
U312S	P	2c green, Die 2, on amber	100.00
U313S	P	2c green, Die 2, on oriental buff	100.00
U314S	P	2c green, Die 2, on blue	100.00
U315S	P	2c green, Die 2, on manila	100.00
W316S	P	2c green, Die 2, on manila	100.00
U317S	P	2c green, Die 2, on amber manila	100.00

U324S	P	4c carmine on white	100.00
U325S	P	4c carmine on amber	120.00
U330S	P	5c blue, Die 1, on white	110.00
U331S	P	5c blue, Die 1, on amber	110.00

Two settings of type P overprint are found.

POSTAL CARDS

Overprinted **UNIVERSAL POSTAL CONGRESS.**

Type Q

UX12S	Q	1c black on buff	400.00
UX13S	Q	2c blue on cream	400.00

PAID REPLY POSTAL CARDS

Overprinted with Type Q

UY1S	Q	1c black on buff	400.00
UY2S	Q	2c blue on grayish white	400.00

As Nos. UY1S-UY2S were made by overprinting unsevered reply cards, prices are for unsevered cards.

SOUVENIR CARDS

These cards were issued as souvenirs of the philatelic gatherings at which they were distributed by the United States Postal Service, its predecessor the United States Post Office Department, or the Bureau of Engraving and Printing. They were not valid for postage.

Most of the cards bear reproductions of United States stamps with the design enlarged or altered by removal of denomination, country name and "Postage" or "Air Mail." The cards are not perforated.

A forerunner of the souvenir cards is the 1938 Philatelic Truck souvenir sheet which the Post Office Department issued and distributed in various cities visited by the Philatelic Truck. It shows the White House, printed in blue on white paper. Issued with and without gum. Price, with gum, $85; without gum, $15.

1954

1   Postage Stamp Design Exhibition, National   *1,750.*
Philatelic Museum, Mar. 13, 1954, Philadelphia. Card of 4. Monochrome views of Washington, D.C. Inscribed: "Souvenir sheet designed, engraved and printed by members, Bureau, Engraving and Printing. Reissued by popular request".

1960

2   Barcelona, 1st International Philatelic Congress,   375.00
Mar. 26—Apr. 5, 1960. Enlarged vignette, Landing of Columbus from No. 231. Printed in black. (P.O.D.)

1966

3   SIPEX, 6th International Philatelic Exhibition,   200.00
May 21—30, 1966, Washington, D.C. Card of 3. Multicolored views of Washington, D.C. Inscribed: "Sixth International Phialtelic Exhibition / Washington, D.C. / Designed, Engraved, and Printed by Union Members of Bureau of Engraving and Printing".

1968

4   EFIMEX, International Philatelic Exhibition,   4.00
Nov. 1—9, 1968, Mexico City. No. 292 enlarged to 58x37½mm. Card inscribed in Spanish. (P.O.D.)

1969

5   SANDIPEX, San Diego Philatelic Exhibition,   85.00
July 16—20, 1969, San Diego, Cal. Card of 3. Multicolored views of Washington, D.C. Inscribed: "Sandipex—San Diego 200th Anniversary—1769—1969". (B.E.P.)

6   A.S.D.A. National Postage Stamp Show, Nov.   30.00
21—23, 1969, New York. Card of 4. No. E4 reengraved. Denomination and "United States" removed. (B.E.P.)

1970

7   INTERPEX, Mar. 13—15, 1970, New York.   70.00
Card of 4. Nos. 1027, 1035, C35 and C38 reengraved. Denomination, etc. removed. (B.E.P.)

8   COMPEX, Combined Philatelic Exhibition of   20.00
Chicagoland, May 29—31, 1970, Chicago. Card of 4 No. C18 reengraved. Denomination, etc. removed. (B.E.P.)

9   PHILYMPIA, London International Stamp Exhibition, Sept. 18—26 1970. Card of 3. Nos.   3.00
548—550 enlarged 1½ times. (P.O.D.)

10   HAPEX, American Philatelic Society Convention, Nov. 5—8, 1970, Honolulu, Hawaii.   20.00
Card of 3, Nos. 799, C46 and C55 reengraved. Denomination, etc. removed. (B.E.P.)

1971

11   INTERPEX, Mar. 12—14, 1971, New York.   3.50
Card of 4 No. 1193 reengraved. Denomination removed. Background tint includes enlargements of Nos. 1331—1332, 1371 and C76. (B.E.P.)

12   WESTPEX, Western Philatelic Exhibition, Apr.   3.50
23—25, 1971, San Francisco. Card of 4, Nos. 740, 852, 966 and 997. Denomination, etc. removed. (B.E.P.)

13   NAPEX 71, National Philatelic Exhibition,   3.50
May 21—23, 1971, Washington, D.C. Card of 3, Nos. 990, 991, 992. Denomination, etc. removed. (B.E.P.)

14   TEXANEX 71, Texas Philatelic Association   4.00
and American Philatelic Society conventions, Aug. 26—29, 1971, San Antonio, Tex. Card of 3, Nos. 938, 1043 and 1242. Denomination, etc. removed. (B.E.P.)

15   EXFILIMA 71, 3rd Inter—American Philatelic   2.25
Exhibition, Nov. 6—14, 1971, Lima, Peru. Card of 3. Nos. 1111 and 1126 with denomination, etc. removed. Reproduction of Peru No. 360. Card inscribed in Spanish. (U.S.P.S.)

16   A.S.D.A. National Postage Stamp Show, Nov.   3.50
19—21, 1971, New York. Card of 3, Nos. C13—C15. Denomination, etc. removed. (B.E.P.)

17   ANPHILEX '71, Anniversary Philatelic Exhibition, Nov. 26—Dec. 1, 1971, New York. Card   2.00
of 2, Nos. 1—2. Denomination, etc. removed. (B.E.P.)

1972

18   INTERPEX, Mar. 17—19, 1972, New York.   2.00
Card of 4 No. 1173. Denomination, etc. removed. Background tint includes enlargements of Nos. 976, 1434—1435 and C20. (B.E.P.)

19   NOPEX, Apr. 6—9, 1972, New Orleans. Card   2.00
of 4 No. 1020. Denomination, etc. removed. Background tint includes enlargements of Nos. 323—327. (B.E.P.)

20   BELGICA 72, Brussels International Philatelic   2.25
Exhibition, June 24—July 9, 1972, Brussels, Belgium. Card of 3. No. 914 enlarged to 56x34mm. Nos. 1026 and 1104 with denomination, etc. removed. Card inscribed in Flemish and French. (U.S.P.S.)

21   Olympia Philatelie Munchen 72, Aug.   2.25
18—Sept. 10, 1972, Munich, Germany. Card of 4, Nos. 1460—1462 and C85 enlarged to 54x32mm. Card inscribed in German. (U.S.P.S.)

22   EXFILBRA 72, 4th Inter—American Philatelic   2.25
Exhibition, Aug. 26—Sept. 2, 1972, Rio de Janeiro, Brazil. Card of 3. No. C14 enlarged to 69½x28½mm. and reproductions of Brazil Nos. C18—C19. Card inscribed in Portuguese. (U.S.P.S.)

23   National Philatelic Forum VI, Aug. 28—30,   2.50
1972, Washington, D.C. Card of 4 No. 1396 enlarged to 26x31mm. (B.E.P.)

24   SEPAD '72, Oct. 20—22, 1972, Philadelphia.   3.00
Card of 4 No. 1044 reengraved, denomination, etc. removed. (B.E.P.)

25   A.S.D.A. National Postage Stamp Show, Nov.   2.00
17—19, 1972, New York. Card of 4, Nos. 883, 863, 868 and 888. Denomination, etc. removed. (B.E.P.)

26   STAMP EXPO, Nov. 24—26, 1972, San Francisco. Card of 4 No. C36 re—engraved with   2.50
denomination, etc. removed. (B.E.P.)

1973

27   INTERPEX, Mar. 9—11, 1973, New York.   3.00
Card of 4 No. 976. Denomination, etc. removed. (B.E.P.)

28   IBRA 73 International Philatelic Exhibition,   3.00
Munich, May 11—20, 1973. No. C13 enlarged to 70x29mm. (U.S.P.S.)

29   COMPEX 73, May 25—27, 1973, Chicago.   2.00
Card of 4 No. 245. Denomination, etc. removed. (B.E.P.)

30   APEX 73, International Airmail Exhibition,   2.00
Manchester, England, July 4—7, 1973. Card of 3. No. C3a enlarged to 34x29mm., enlarged reproductions of Newfoundland No. C4 and Honduras No. C12. (U.S.P.S.)

31   POLSKA 73, World Philatelic Exhibition, Poznan, Poland, Aug. 19—Sept. 2, 1973. Card of   3.50
3. No. 1488 enlarged to 32x55mm., enlarged reproductions of Poland Nos. 1944—1945. Card inscribed in Polish. (U.S.P.S.)

32   NAPEX 73, Sept. 14—16, 1973, Washington,   2.50
D.C. Card of 4 No. C3. Denomination, etc. removed. Background tint includes montage of enlarged reproductions of C4—C6. (B.E.P.)

33   A.S.D.A. National Postage Stamp Show, Nov.   2.50
16—18, 1973, New York. Card of 4 No. 908 reengraved. Denomination, etc. removed. Foreground includes enlarged reproductions of Nos. 1139—1144. (B.E.P.)

34   STAMP EXPO NORTH, Dec. 7—9, 1973, San   2.50
Francisco. Card of 4 No. C20. Denomination, etc. removed. (B.E.P.)

A card of 10, Nos. 1489-1498, was distributed to postal employees. Not available to public. Size: about 14x11 inches.

1974

35   National Hobby Industry Trade Show, Feb.   3.50
3—6, 1974, Chicago. Card of 4, block of Nos. 1456—1459 reduced to 61x39mm. Enlarged reproductions of silversmith (from No. 1457) and glassmaker (from No. 1456). (U.S.P.S.)

36   MILCOPEX 1974, Mar. 8—10, 1974,   3.50
Milwaukee. Card of 4 No. C43. Denomination, etc. removed. (B.E.P.)

37   INTERNABA 1974, June 6, 1974, Basel,   4.00
Switzerland. Card of 8, strip of Nos. 1530—1537 reduced to 175x35mm. Card inscribed in German, French, and Italian. (U.S.P.S.)

38   STOCKHOLMIA 74, International Philatelic   4.00
Exhibition, September 21—29, 1974, Stockholm, Sweden. Card of 3 No. 836 enlarged to 34x35mm., enlarged reproductions of Sweden Nos. 300 and 767. Card inscribed in Swedish. (U.S.P.S.)

39 EXFILMEX 74, Interamerican Philatelic Exposition, Oct. 26—Nov. 3, 1974, Mexico City. Card of 2. No. 1157 enlarged to 39x61 mm. Enlarged reproduction of Mexico No. 910. Card inscribed in Spanish. (U.S.P.S.) — 4.00

1975

40 ESPANA 75, World Stamp Exhibition, Apr. 4—13, Madrid. Card of 3 No. 233 enlarged to 52x34 mm., No. 1271 and Spain No. 1312 reduced to 16x27mm. Card inscribed in Spanish. (U.S.P.S.) — 3.00

41 NAPEX 75, May 9—11, 1975, Washington, D.C. Card of 4 No. 708. Denomination, etc. removed. (B.E.P.) — 10.00

42 ARPHILA 75, June 6—16, 1975, Paris. Card of 3. Designs of No. 1187 enlarged to 32x55 mm., No. 1207 enlarged to 55x32 mm. Reproduction of France No. 1117. Card inscribed in French. (U.S.P.S.) — 3.00

43 International Women's Year, 1975. Card of 3 Nos. 872, 878, and 959. Denomination, etc. removed. Reproduction of 1886 dollar bill. (B.E.P.) — 35.00

44 A.S.D.A. National Postage Stamp Show, Nov. 21—23, 1975. Bicentennial series. Card of 4 No. 1003 reengraved. Denomination, etc. removed. Bicentennial insignia, Trumbull's Washington with his words, ". . . and maintain the liberty which we have derived from our ancestors". (B.E.P.) — 50.00

1976

45 WERABA 76, Third International Space Stamp Exhibition, April 1—4, 1976, Zurich, Switzerland. Card of 2, Nos. 1434 and 1435 se—tenant enlarged to 114x32 mm. Quotation "Man is his own star . . .". (U.S.P.S.) — 5.00

46 INTERPHIL 76, Seventh International Philatelic Exhibition, May 29—June 6, 1976. Philadelphia, Pa. Bicentennial series. Card of 4 No. 120. Denominations, etc. removed. Bicentennial insignia. Bust of Jefferson with words ". . . that all men are created equal." Reading of the Declaration of Independence. (B.E.P.) — 10.00

An Interphil '76 card issued by the American Revolution Bicentennial Administration was bound into the Interphil program. It shows an altered No. 1044 in black brown, the Bicentennial emblem and a view of Independence Hall. Printed by B.E.P.

48 Bicentennial Exposition on Science and Technology, May 30—Sept. 6, 1976, Kennedy Space Center, Fla. No. C76 enlarged to 75x41mm. (U.S.P.S.) — 5.00

49 STAMP EXPO 76, June 11—13, 1976, Los Angeles, Calif. Bicentennial series. Card of 4, Nos. 1351, 1352, 1345 and 1348 se—tenant vertically. Denominations, etc. removed. (B.E.P.) — 9.00

50 Colorado Statehood Centennial, August 1, 1976. Card of 3, Nos. 743 and 288 denominations, etc. removed and No. 1670 (Colorado state flag) enlarged. (B.E.P.) — 5.00

51 HAFNIA 76, International Stamp Exhibition, Copenhagen, Denmark, August 20—29, 1976. Card of 2. No. 5 and Denmark No. 2 enlarged. Card inscribed in Danish and English. (U.S.P.S.) — 4.50

52 ITALIA 76, International Philatelic Exhibition, Oct. 14—24, Milan, Italy. Card of 3. No. 1168 and Italy Nos. 578 and 601. Card inscribed in Italian. (U.S.P.S.) — 4.50

53 NORDPOSTA 76, North German Stamp Exhibition, Oct. 30—31, Hamburg, Germany. Card of 3. No. 689 and Germany Nos. B366 and B417. Card inscribed in German. (U.S.P.S.) — 4.50

1977

54 MILCOPEX, Milwaukee Philatelic Society, Mar. 4—6, Milwaukee. Card of 2, Nos. 733 and 1128. (B.E.P.) — 3.75

55 ROMPEX 77, Rocky Mountain Philatelic Exhibition, May 20—22, Denver. Card of 4. No. 1001. (B.E.P.) — 4.00

56 AMPHILEX 77, International Philatelic Exhibition, May 26—June 5, Amsterdam, Netherlands. Card of 3. No. 1027 and Netherlands Nos. 41 and 294. Card inscribed in Dutch. (U.S.P.S.) — 4.50

57 SAN MARINO 77, International Philatelic Exhibition, San Marino, Aug. 28—Sept. 4. Card of 3. Nos. 1—2 and San Marino No. 1. Card inscribed in Italian. (U.S.P.S.) — 4.50

58 PURIPEX 77, Silver Anniversary Philatelic Exhibit, Sept. 2—5, San Juan, Puerto Rico. Card of 4 No. 801. (B.E.P.) — 3.50

59 A.S.D.A. National Postage Stamp Show, Nov. 15—20, New York. Card of 4 No. C45. (B.E.P.) — 4.50

1978

60 ROCPEX 78, International Philatelic Exhibition, Mar. 20—29, Taipei, Taiwan. Card of 6. Nos. 1706—1709 and China Nos. 1812 and 1816. Card inscribed in Chinese. (U.S.P.S.) — 5.50

61 NAPOSTA '78 Philatelic Exhibition, May 20—25, Frankfurt, Germany. Card of 3. Nos. 555, 563 and Germany No. 1216. Card inscribed in German. (U.S.P.S.) — 5.50

62 CENJEX 78, Federated Stamp Clubs of New Jersey, 30th annual exhibition, June 23—25, Freehold, N.J. Card of 9. Nos. 646, 680, 689, 1086, 1716 and 4 No. 785. (B.E.P.) — 5.50

1979

63 BRASILIANA 79, International Philatelic Exhibition, Sept. 15—23, Rio de Janeiro. Card of 3. Nos. C91—C92 and Brazil No. 1295. Card inscribed in Portuguese. (U.S.P.S.) — 7.50

64 JAPEX 79, International Philatelic Exhibition, Nov. 2—4, Tokyo. Card of 2. No. 1158 and Japan No. 1024. Card inscribed in Japanese. (U.S.P.S.) — 7.50

1980

65 LONDON 1980, International Philatelic Exhibition, May 6—14, London. No. 329 enlarged. (U.S.P.S.) — 6.50

66 NORWEX 80, International Stamp Exhibition, June 13—22, Oslo. Card of 3. Nos. 620—621 and Norway No. 658. Card inscribed in Norwegian. (U.S.P.S.) — 5.50

67 NAPEX 80, July 4—6, Washington, D.C. Card of 4. No. 573. (B.E.P.) — 15.00

68 A.S.D.A. Stamp Festival, Sept. 25—28, 1980, New York, N.Y. Card of 4 No. 962. (B.E.P.) — 17.50

69 ESSEN 80, Third International Stamp Fair, Nov. 15—19, Essen, West Germany. Card of 2. No. 1014 and Germany No. 723. Card inscribed in German. (U.S.P.S.) — 5.50

1981

70 STAMP EXPO '81 SOUTH, Mar. 20—22, Anaheim, Calif. Card of 6. Nos. 1331—1332, 4 of No. 1287. (B.E.P.) — 15.00

71 WIPA 1981, International Stamp Exhibition, May 22—31, Vienna, Austria. Card of 2. No. 1252 and Austria No. 789. Card inscribed in German. (U.S.P.S.) — 5.00

72 National Stamp Collecting Month, October, 1981. Card of 2. Nos. 245 and 1918, enlarged. (U.S.P.S.) — 5.00

73 PHILATOKYO '81, International Stamp Exhibition, Oct. 9—18. Tokyo. Card of 2. No. 1531 and Japan No. 800. Card inscribed in Japanese. (U.S.P.S.) — 6.00

74 NORDPOSTA 81, North German Stamp Exhibition, Nov. 7—8. Hamburg, Germany. Card of 2. No. 923 and Germany No. B538. Card inscribed in German. (U.S.P.S.) — 5.00

1982

75 MILCOPEX '82, Milwaukee Philatelic Association Exhibition, Mar. 5—7, Milwaukee, Wis. Card of 4. No. 1137. (B.E.P.) — 15.00

76 CANADA 82, international philatelic youth exhibition, May 20—24, Toronto. Card of 2. No. 116 and Canada No. 15. Card inscribed in French and English. (U.S.P.S.) — 5.00

77 PHILEXFRANCE '82, International Philatelic Exhibition, June 11—21, Paris, Card of 2. No. 1753 and France No. 1480. Card inscribed in French. (U.S.P.S.) — 4.00

78 National Stamp Collecting Month, October. Card of 1. No. C3a. (U.S.P.S.) — 6.00

79 ESPAMER '82, International Philatelic Exhibition, Oct. 12—17, San Juan, P.R. Card of 4. No. 244. Card inscribed in English and Spanish. (B.E.P.) — 30.00

80 ESPAMER '82, International Philatelic Exhibition, Oct. 12—17, San Juan, P.R. Card of 3. Nos. 801, 1437 and 2024. Card inscribed in Spanish and English. (U.S.P.S.) — 6.00

1983

81 Joint stamp issues, Sweden and U.S.A. Mar. 24. Card of 3. Nos. 958, 2036 and Sweden No. 1453, all enlarged. Card inscribed in Swedish and English. (U.S.P.S.) — 5.00

82 Joint stamp issues, Germany and U.S.A. Apr. 29. Card of 2. No. 2040 and Germany No. 1397, both enlarged. Card inscribed in German and English. (U.S.P.S.) — 5.00

83 TEMBAL 83, International Philatelic Exhibition, Mar. 21—29, Basel Card of 2. No. C71 and Switzerland, Basel No. 3L1, both enlarged. Card inscribed in German. (U.S.P.S.) — 5.00

84 TEXANEX—TOPEX '83 Exhibition, June 17—19, San Antonio, Texas. Card of 5. No. 1660, enlarged, and No. 776, block of 4, both with denomination removed. (B.E.P.) — 15.00

85 BRASILIANA 83, International Philatelic Exhibition, July 29—Aug. 7, Rio de Janeiro. Card of 2. No. 2 and Brazil No. 1, both enlarged. Card inscribed in Portuguese (U.S.P.S.) — 5.00

86 BANGKOK 83, International Philatelic Exhibition, Aug. 4—13, Bangkok, Thailand. Card of 2. No. 210 and Thailand No. 1, both enlarged. Card inscribed in Thai. (U.S.P.S.) — 5.00

87 International Philatelic Memento, 1983—84. Card of one. No. 1387, enlarged. (U.S.P.S.) — 2.50

88 National Stamp Collecting Month, October. Card of 1. No. 293, enlarged and bicolored. (U.S.P.S.) — 5.00

89 Philatelic Show '83, Boston, Oct. 21—23. Card of 2, Nos. 2178—719. (B.E.P.) — 15.00

90 ASDA 1983, National Postage Stamp Show, New York, Nov. 17—20. Card of 4, No. 881. Denominations, etc. removed. (B.E.P.) — 15.00

1984

91 ESPANA 84, World Exhibition of Philately. Madrid, Apr. 27—May 6. Card of 4, No. 241. Denominations removed. Enlarged vignette, Landing of Columbus, from No. 231 at right. Card inscribed in English and Spanish. (B.E.P.) — 12.00

92 ESPANA 84, International Philatelic Exhibition, Madrid, Apr. 27—May 6. Card of 2, No. 233 and Spain No. 428, both enlarged. Card inscribed in Spanish. (U.S.P.S.) — 5.00

93 Stamp Expo '84 South, Anaheim, Calif., Apr. 27—29. Card of 4, Nos. 1791—1794, with Olympic torch. (B.E.P.) — 12.00

94 COMPEX '84, Rosemont, Ill., May 25—27. Card of 4, No. 728. (B.E.P.) — 12.00

95 HAMBURG '84, International Exhibition for 19th UPU Congress, Hamburg, Germany, June 19—26. Card of 2, inscribed in English, French and German. (U.S.P.S.) — 5.00

96 St. Lawrence Seaway, 25th anniversary, June 26. Card of 2, No. 1131 and Canada No. 387, both enlarged. Card inscribed in English and French. (U.S.P.S.) — 5.00

97 AUSIPEX '84, Australia's first international exhibition, Melbourne, Sept. 21—30. Card of 2, No. 290 and Western Australia No. 1, both enlarged. Card inscribed in English. (U.S.P.S.) — 5.00

98 National Stamp Collecting Month, October. Card of 1, No. 2104, enlarged and tricolored. Card inscribed in English. (U.S.P.S.) — 5.00

99 PHILAKOREA '84, Seoul, Oct. 22—31. Card of 2, No. 741 and Korea No. 994, both enlarged. Card inscribed in Korean and English. (U.S.P.S.) — 5.00

100 ASDA 1984, National Postage Stamp Show, New York, NY, Nov. 15—18. Card of 4, No. 1470. Denominations removed. (B.E.P.) — 10.00

1985

101 International Philatelic Memento, 1985. Card of 1, No. 2, enlarged. (U.S.P.S.) — 3.00

102 OLYMPHILEX '85. International Philatelic Exhibition, Lausanne, Switzerland, Mar. 18—24. Card of 2, No. C106 and Switzerland No. 746, both enlarged. Card inscribed in French and English. (U.S.P.S.) — 5.00

103 ISRAPHIL '85. International Philatelic Exhibition, Tel Aviv, Israel, May 14—22. Card of 2, No. 566 and Israel No. 33, both enlarged. Card inscribed in Hebrew and English. (U.S.P.S.) — 5.00

104 LONG BEACH '85, Numismatic and Philatelic Exposition, Long Beach, CA, Jan. 31—Feb. 3. Card of 4, No. 954, plus a Series 1865 $20 Gold Certificate. Stamp denominations removed. (B.E.P.) — 10.00

105 MILCOPEX '85, Milwaukee Philatelic Society annual stamp show, Milwaukee, WI, Mar. 1—3. Card of 4, No. 880. Denominations, etc., removed. (B.E.P.) — 10.00

106 NAPEX '85, National Philatelic Exhibition, Arlington, VA, June 7—9. Card of 4, No. 2014. Denominations defaced with diagonal lines. (B.E.P.) — 10.00

107 ARGENTINA '85, International Philatelic Exhibition, Buenos Aires, July 5—14. Card of 2, No. 1737 and Argentina No. B27, both enlarged. Card inscribed in Spanish. (U.S.P.S.) — 4.00

108 MOPHILA '85, International Philatelic Exhibition, Hamburg, Sept. 11—15. Card of 2, No. 296 and Germany No. B595, both enlarged. Card inscribed in German. (U.S.P.S.) — 4.00

109 ITALIA '85, International Philatelic Exhibition, Rome, Oct. 25—Nov. 3. Card of 2, No. 1107 and Italy No. 830, both enlarged. Card inscribed in Italian. (U.S.P.S.) — 4.00

1986

110 Statue of Liberty Centennial, National Philatelic Memento, 1986. Card of 1, No. C87, enlarged. (U.S.P.S.) — 2.00

111 Garfield Perry Stamp Club, National Stamp Show, Cleveland, OH, Mar. 21—23. Card of 4, No. 306. Denominations, etc., removed. (B.E.P.) — 8.00

112 AMERIPEX '86, International Philatelic Exhibition, Chicago, IL, May 22—June 1. Card of 3, Nos. 134, 2052 and 1474. Denominations, etc., removed, or stamp enlarged. (B.E.P.) — 8.00

113 STOCKHOLMIA '86, International Philatelic Exhibition, Stockholm, Sweden, Aug. 28—Sept. 7. Card of 2, No. 113 and Sweden No. 253, both enlarged. Card inscribed in Swedish. (U.S.P.S.) — 4.00

114 HOUPEX '86, National Stamp Show, Houston, TX. Sept. 5—7. Card of 3: Nos. 1035, 1042 and 1044A. Denominations, etc., removed. (B.E.P.) — 8.00

115 LOBEX '86, Numismatic and Philatelic Exhibition, Long Beach, CA, Oct. 2—5. Long Beach Stamp Club 60th anniv. Card of 4, No. 291, plus a series 1907 $10 Gold Certificate. Stamp denominations removed. (B.E.P.) — 8.00

116 DCSE '86, Dallas Coin and Stamp Exhibition, Dallas, TX, Dec. 11—14. Card of 4, No. 550, plus $10,000 Federal Reserve Note. Stamp denominations removed. (B.E.P.) — 8.00

1987

117 CAPEX '87, International Philatelic Exhibition, Toronto, Ontario, Canada, June 13—21. Card of 2, No. 569 and Canada No. 883. Denominations removed and/or stamps enlarged. Card inscribed in English and French. (U.S.P.S.)   4.00

118 HAFNIA '87, International Philatelic Exhibition, Copenhagen, Denmark, Oct. 16—25. Card of 2, No. 299 and Denmark No. B52. Denominations removed and/or stamps enlarged. Card inscribed in English and Danish. (U.S.P.S.)   4.00

119 SESCAL '87, Stamp Exhibition of Southern California, Los Angeles, CA, Oct. 16—18. Card of 1, No. 798 defaced by diagonal bars over denominations. (B.E.P.)   8.00

120 HSNA '87, Hawaii State Numismatic Association Exhibition, Honolulu, Hawaii, Nov. 12—15. Card of 1, No. 799 defaced by a diagonal bar(LR) plus a Series 1923 $5 Silver Certificate. (B.E.P.)   8.00

121 MONTE CARLO, International Philatelic Exhibition, Monte Carlo, Monaco, Nov. 13—17. Card of 3, Nos. 2287, 2300 and Monaco No. 1589. Denominations removed and/or stamps enlarged. Card inscribed in French and English. (U.S.P.S.)   4.00

1988

122 FINLANDIA '88, International Philatelic Exhibition, Helsinki, Finland, June 1—12. Card of 2, No. 836 and Finland No. 768 defaced by diagonal bars over denominations. Card inscribed in English and Finnish. (U.S.P.S.)   4.00

123 STAMPSHOW '88, American Philatelic Society national stamp show, Detroit, MI, Aug. 25—28. Card of 1, No. 835 defaced by diagonal bars over denominations. (B.E.P.)   8.00

COMMEMORATIVE PANELS

The Postal Service began issuing commemorative panels Sept. 20, 1972, with the Wildlife Conservation issue, Nos. 1464-1467. Each panel is devoted to a separate issue. It includes unused examples of the stamp or stamps, usually a block of four; reproductions of steel engravings, and background information on the subject of the issue.

1972

1CP	Wildlife Conservation, #1467a	11.00
2CP	Mail Order, #1468	11.00
3CP	Osteopathic Medicine, #1469	11.00
4CP	Tom Sawyer, #1470	11.00
5CP	Pharmacy, #1473	11.00
6CP	Christmas, 1972 (angel), #1471	15.00
7CP	Santa Claus, #1472	15.00
8CP	Stamp Collecting, #1474	11.00

1973

9CP	Love, #1475	11.00
10CP	Pamphleteers, #1476	12.50
11CP	George Gershwin, #1484	12.50
12CP	Posting a Broadside, #1477	12.50
13CP	Copernicus, #1488	11.00
14CP	Postal Service Employees, #1489—1498	12.50
15CP	Harry S. Truman, #1499	15.00
16CP	Postrider, #1478	12.50
17CP	Boston Tea Party, #1483a	33.00
18CP	Electronics Progress, #1500—1502, C86	12.50
19CP	Robinson Jeffers, #1485	12.50
20CP	Lyndon B. Johnson, #1503	15.00
21CP	Henry O. Tanner, #1486	12.50
22CP	Willa Cather, #1487	12.50
23CP	Drummer, #1479	15.00
24CP	Angus and Longhorn Cattle, #1504	11.00
25CP	Christmas, 1973 (Madonna), #1507	12.50
26CP	Christmas Tree, needlepoint, #1508	12.50

1974

27CP	Veterans of Foreign Wars, #1525	11.00
28CP	Robert Frost, #1526	11.00
29CP	EXPO 74, #1527	11.00
30CP	Horse Racing, #1528	11.00
31CP	Skylab, #1529	12.50
32CP	Universal Postal Union, #1537a	12.50
33CP	Mineral Heritage, #1541a	12.50
34CP	Kentucky Settlement (Ft. Harrod), #1542	11.00
35CP	First Continental Congress, #1546a	11.00
36CP	Chautauqua, #1505	11.00
37CP	Kansas Wheat, #1506	11.00
38CP	Energy Conservation, #1547	11.00
39CP	Sleepy Hollow Legend, #1548	11.00
40CP	Retarded Children, #1549	11.00
41CP	Christmas, 1974 (Currier—Ives), #1551	18.00
42CP	Christmas, 1974 (angel), #1550	18.00

1975

43CP	Benjamin West, #1553	11.00
44CP	Pioneer 10, #1556	13.50
45CP	Collective Bargaining, #1558	11.00
46CP	Contributors to the Cause, #1559—1562	11.00
47CP	Mariner 10, #1557	13.50
48CP	Lexington—Concord Battle, #1563	13.50
49CP	Paul Laurence Dunbar, #1554	11.00
50CP	D. W. Griffith, #1555	11.00
51CP	Battle of Bunker Hill, #1564	13.50
52CP	Military Services (uniforms), #1568a	13.50
53CP	Apollo Soyuz, #1569a	13.50
54CP	World Peace through Law, #1576	11.00
55CP	International Women's Year, #1571	11.00
56CP	Postal Service 200 Years, #1575a	13.50
57CP	Banking and Commerce, #1577a	11.00
58CP	Early Christmas Card, #1580	13.75
59CP	Christmas, 1975 (Madonna), #1579	13.75

1976

60CP	Spirit of '76, #1631a	16.50
61CP	Interphil '76, #1632	13.50
62CP	State Flags, block of 4 from #1633—1682	25.00
63CP	Telephone Centenary, #1683	11.00
64CP	Commercial Aviation, #1684	11.00
65CP	Chemistry, #1685	11.00
66CP	Benjamin Franklin, #1690	13.50
67CP	Declaration of Independence, #1694a	13.50
68CP	12th Winter Olympics, #1698a	12.50
69CP	Clara Maass, #1699	12.50
70CP	Adolph S. Ochs, #1700	11.00
71CP	Christmas, 1976 (Currier print), #1702	13.50
72CP	Christmas, 1976 (Copley Nativity), #1701	13.50

1977

73CP	Washington at Princeton, #1704	19.00
74CP	Sound Recording, #1705	22.50
75CP	Pueblo Art, #1709a	100.00
76CP	Lindbergh Flight, #1710	100.00
77CP	Colorado Statehood, #1711	22.50
78CP	Butterflies, #1715a	22.50
79CP	Lafayette, #1716	22.50
80CP	Skilled Hands for Independence, #1720a	22.50
81CP	Peace Bridge, #1721	22.50
82CP	Battle of Oriskany, #1722	22.50
83CP	Energy Conservation—Development, #1723a	22.50
84CP	Alta California, #1725	22.50
85CP	Articles of Confederation, #1726	22.50
86CP	Talking Pictures, #1727	22.50
87CP	Surrender at Saratoga, #1728	22.50
88CP	Christmas, 1977 (Washington at Valley Forge), #1729	22.50
89CP	Christmas, 1977 (rural mailbox), #1730	22.50

1978

90CP	Carl Sandburg, #1731	11.00
91CP	Captain Cook, #1732a	25.00
92CP	Harriet Tubman, #1744	11.00
93CP	American Quilts, #1748a	22.50
94CP	American Dance, #1752a	11.00
95CP	French Alliance, #1753	11.00
96CP	Pap Test, #1754	11.00
97CP	Jimmie Rodgers, #1755	11.00
98CP	Photography, #1758	11.00
99CP	George M. Cohan, #1756	11.00
100CP	Viking Missions, #1759	40.00
101CP	American Owls, #1763a	40.00
102CP	American Trees, #1767a	40.00
103CP	Christmas, 1978 (Madonna), #1768	15.00
104CP	Christmas, 1978 (hobby—horse), #1769	15.00

1979

105CP	Robert F. Kennedy, #1770	12.50
106CP	Martin Luther King, Jr., #1771	12.50
107CP	Year of the Child, #1772	10.00
108CP	John Steinbeck, #1773	10.00
109CP	Albert Einstein, #1774	10.00
110CP	Pennsylvania Toleware, #1778a	12.50
111CP	American Architecture, #1782a	12.50
112CP	Endangered Flora, #1786a	10.00
113CP	Seeing Eye Dogs, #1787	10.00
114CP	Special Olympics, #1788	10.00
115CP	John Paul Jones, #1789	12.50
116CP	Olympic Games, #1794a	20.00
117CP	Christmas, 1979 (Madonna), #1799	15.00
118CP	Christmas, 1979 (Santa Claus), #1800	15.00
119CP	Will Rogers, #1801	15.00
120CP	Viet Nam Veterans, #1802	15.00
121CP	10c, 31c Olympics, #1790, C97	15.00

1980

122CP	Winter Olympics, #1798a	15.00
123CP	W.C Fields, #1803	10.00
124CP	Benjamin Banneker, #1804	10.00
125CP	Frances Perkins, #1821	10.00
126CP	Emily Bissell, #1823	10.00
127CP	Helen Keller, #1824	10.00
128CP	Veterans Administration, #1825	10.00
129CP	Galvez, #1826	10.00
130CP	Coral Reefs, #1830a	12.50
131CP	Organized Labor, #1831	10.00
132CP	Edith Wharton, #1832	10.00
133CP	Education, #1833	10.00
134CP	Indian Masks, #1837a	12.50
135CP	Architecture, #1841a	10.00
136CP	Christmas Window, #1842	14.00
137CP	Christmas Toys, #1843	14.00

1981

138CP	Dirkson, #1874	10.00
139CP	Young, #1875	10.00
140CP	Flowers, #1879a	10.00
141CP	Red Cross, #1910	10.00
142CP	Savings and Loan, #1911	10.00
143CP	Space Achievements, #1919a	15.00
144CP	Management, #1920	10.00

145CP	Wildlife, #1924a	15.00
146CP	Disabled, #1925	10.00
147CP	Millay, #1926	10.00
148CP	Architecture, #1931a	10.00
149CP	Zaharias, Jones, #1932, 1933	12.50
150CP	Remington, #1934	10.00
151CP	18c, 20c Hoban, #1935, 1936	10.00
152CP	Yorktown, Va. Capes, #1938a	10.00
153CP	Madonna and Child, #1939	15.00
154CP	Teddy Bear, #1940	15.00
155CP	John Hanson, #1941	10.00
156CP	Desert Plants, #1945a	11.00

1982

157CP	FDR, #1950	20.00
158CP	Love, #1951	20.00
159CP	Washington, #1952	20.00
160CP	Birds and Flowers, block of 4 from #1953—2002	25.00
161CP	US—Netherlands, #2003	20.00
162CP	Library of Congress, #2004	20.00
163CP	Knoxville World's Fair, #2009a	20.00
164CP	Horatio Alger, #2010	20.00
165CP	Aging, #2011	20.00
166CP	Barrymores, #2012	20.00
167CP	Dr. Mary Walker, #2013	20.00
168CP	Peace Garden, #2014	20.00
169CP	Libraries, #2015	20.00
170CP	Jackie Robinson, #2016	20.00
171CP	Tuoro Synagogue, #2017	20.00
172CP	Wolf Trap Farm, #2018	20.00
173CP	Architecture, #2022a	20.00
174CP	Francis of Assisi, #2023	20.00
175CP	Ponce de Leon, #2024	20.00
176CP	Puppy, Kitten, #2025	25.00
177CP	Madonna and Child, #2026	25.00
178CP	Children Playing, #2030a	25.00

1983

179CP	Science, #2031	9.00
180CP	Ballooning, #2035a	12.00
181CP	US—Sweden, #2036	9.00
182CP	CCC, #2037	9.00
183CP	Priestley, #2038	9.00
184CP	Voluntarism, #2039	8.00
185CP	German Immigration, #2040	9.00
186CP	Brooklyn Bridge, #2041	10.00
187CP	TVA, #2042	9.00
188CP	Fitness, #2043	8.00
189CP	Scott Joplin, #2044	10.00
190CP	Medal of Honor, #2045	10.00
191CP	Babe Ruth, #2046	20.00
192CP	Hawthorne, #2047	9.00
193CP	13c Olympics, #2051a	15.00
194CP	28c Olympics, #C104a	12.50
195CP	40c Olympics, #C108a	12.50
196CP	35c Olympics, #C112a	15.00
197CP	Treaty of Paris, #2052	10.00
198CP	Civil Service, #2053	10.00
199CP	Metropolitan Opera, #2054	10.00
200CP	Inventors, #2058a	10.00
201CP	Streetcars, #2062a	10.00
202CP	Madonna and Child, #2063	15.00
203CP	Santa Claus, #2064	15.00
204CP	Martin Luther, #2065	10.00

1984

205CP	Alaska, #2066	8.00
206CP	Winter Olympics, #2070a	10.00
207CP	FDIC, #2071	8.00
208CP	Love, #2072	8.00
209CP	Woodson, #2073	8.00
210CP	Conservation, #2074	8.00
211CP	Credit Union, #2075	8.00
212CP	Orchids, #2079a	9.00
213CP	Hawaii, #2080	9.00
214CP	National Archives, #2081	8.00
215CP	Olympics, #2085a	12.50
216CP	World Expo, #2086	9.00
217CP	Health Research, #2087	8.00
218CP	Fairbanks, #2088	8.00
219CP	Thorpe, #2089	10.00
220CP	McCormack, #2090	8.00
221CP	St. Lawrence Seaway, #2091	8.00

222CP Waterfowl, #2092	12.50	
223CP Roanoke Voyages, #2093	8.00	
224CP Melville, #2094	8.00	
225CP Horace Moses, #2095	8.00	
226CP Smokey the Bear, #2096	10.00	
227CP Roberto Clemente, #2097	16.00	
228CP Dogs, #2101a	10.00	
229CP Crime Prevention, #2102	8.00	
230CP Hispanic Americans, #2103	8.00	
231CP Family Unity, #2104	8.00	
232CP Eleanor Roosevelt, #2105	8.00	
233CP Readers, #2106	8.00	
234CP Madonna and Child, #2107	12.50	
235CP Child's Santa, #2108	12.50	
236CP Vietnam Memorial, #2109	12.50	

1985

237CP Jerome Kern, #2110	8.00
238CP Bethune, #2137	8.00
239CP Duck Decoys, #2141a	9.00
240CP Winter Special Olympics, #2142	8.00
241CP Love, #2143	8.00
242CP REA, #2144	8.00
243CP AMERIPEX '86, #2145	8.00

244CP Abigail Adams, #2146	8.00
245CP Bartholdi, #2147	10.00
246CP Korean Veterans, #2152	8.00
247CP Social Security, #2153	8.00
248CP World War I Veterans, #2154	8.00
249CP Horses, #2158a	10.00
250CP Education, #2159	7.00
251CP Youth Year, #2163a	8.00
252CP Hunger, #2164	8.00
253CP Madonna and Child, #2165	11.00
254CP Poinsettias, #2166	11.00

1986

255CP Arkansas, #2167	8.00
256CP Stamp Collecting booklet pane, #2201a	8.00
257CP Love, #2202	8.00
258CP Sojourner Truth, #2203	8.00
259CP Texas Republic, #2204	8.00
260CP Fish booklet pane, #2209a	8.00
261CP Hospitals, #2210	8.00
262CP Duke Ellington, #2211	8.00
263CP Presidents Souvenir Sheet No. 1, #2216	8.00
264CP Presidents Souvenir Sheet No. 2, #2217	8.00

265CP Presidents Souvenir Sheet No. 3, #2218	8.00
266CP Presidents Souvenir Sheet No. 4, #2219	8.00
267CP Arctic Explorers, #2223a	8.00
268CP Statue of Liberty, #2224	8.00
269CP Navajo Art, #2238a	8.00
270CP T.S. Eliot, #2239	8.00
271CP Woodcarved Figurines, #2243a	8.00
272CP Madonna and Child, #2244	10.00
273CP Village Scene, #2245	10.00

1987

274CP Michigan, #2246	8.00
275CP Pan American Games, #2247	8.00
276CP Love, #2248	8.00
277CP du Sable, #2249	8.00
278CP Caruso, #2250	8.00
279CP Girl Scouts, #2251	8.00
280CP Special Occasions booklet pane, #2274a	8.00
281CP United Way, #2275	8.00

SOUVENIR PAGES

Liberty Issue

1960-65

1	1031A, 1054A	1¼c	Palace of Governors, sheet, coil	75.00
2	1042A	8c	Pershing	50.00
3	1044A	11c	Statue of Liberty	50.00
4	1059A	25c	Revere coil	10.00

1959

5	1132	4c	49 Star Flag	—
6	C55	7c	Hawaii Statehood	—
7	1133	4c	Soil Conservation	—
8	C56	10c	Pan American Games	—
9	1134	4c	Petroleum	—
10	1135	4c	Dental Health	—
11	1136, 1137	4c, 8c	Reuter	—
12	1138	4c	McDowell	—

1960

13	1139	4c	Washington Credo	100.00
14	1140	4c	Franklin Credo	100.00
15	1141	4c	Jefferson Credo	100.00
16	1142	4c	F.S. Key Credo	100.00
17	1143	4c	Lincoln Credo	90.00
18	1144	4c	P. Henry Credo	50.00
19	1145	4c	Boy Scout	100.00
20	1146	4c	Winter Olympics	100.00
21	1147, 1148	4c, 8c	Masaryk	100.00
22	1149	4c	Refugee Year	100.00
23	1150	4c	Water Consevation	30.00
24	1151	4c	SEATO	30.00
25	1152	4c	American Women	30.00
26	C57	10c	Liberty Bell	—
27	C58	15c	Statue of Liberty	—
28	C59	25c	Lincoln	—
29	1153	4c	50 Star Flag	75.00
30	1154	4c	Pony Express	75.00
31	C60	7c	Jet, carmine	17.50
32	C60a	7c	Booklet pane of 6	40.00
33	C61	7c	Jet coil	25.00
34	1155	4c	Handicapped	75.00
35	1156	4c	Forestry Congress	75.00
36	1157	4c	Mexican Independence	50.00
37	1158	4c	U.S., Japan Treaty	30.00
38	1159, 1160	4c, 8c	Paderewski	40.00
39	1161	4c	Sen. Taft	60.00
40	1162	4c	Wheels of Freedom	60.00
41	1163	4c	Boys' Clubs	60.00
42	1164	4c	Automated Post Office	60.00
43	1165, 1166	4c, 8c	Mannerheim	60.00
44	1167	4c	Camp Fire Girls	60.00
45	1168, 1169	4c, 8c	Garibaldi	60.00
46	1170	4c	Sen. George	60.00
47	1171	4c	Carnegie	60.00
48	1172	4c	Dulles	60.00
49	1173	4c	Echo I	30.00

1961

50	1174, 1175	4c, 8c	Gandhi	30.00
51	1176	4c	Range Conservation	30.00
52	1177	4c	Greeley	30.00
53	1178	4c	Ft. Sumpter	30.00
54	1179	4c	Shiloh	30.00
55	1180	5c	Gettysburgh	7.50
56	1181	5c	Wilderness	8.00
57	1182	5c	Appomattox	8.00
58	1183	4c	Kansas	17.50
59	C62	15c	Statue of Liberty	30.00
60	1184	4c	Sen. Norris	15.00
61	1185	4c	Naval Aviation	30.00
62	1186	4c	Workmen's Compensation	30.00
63	1187	4c	Remington	15.00
64	1188	4c	Sun Yat sen	30.00
65	1189	4c	Basketball	30.00
66	1190	4c	Nursing	15.00

1962

67	1191	4c	New Mexico	17.50
68	1192	4c	Arizona	17.50
69	1193	4c	Project Mercury	15.00
70	1194	4c	Malaria	17.50
71	1195	4c	Hughes	17.50
72	1196	4c	Seattle World's Fair	25.00
73	1197	4c	Louisiana	25.00
74	1198	4c	Homestead Act	25.00
75	1199	4c	Girl Scouts	30.00
76	1200	4c	McMahon	25.00
77	1201	4c	Apprenticeship	25.00
78	1202	4c	Rayburn	25.00
79	1203	4c	Hammarskmjold	25.00
80	1204	4c	Hammarskjold, yellow inverted	55.00
81	1205	4c	Christmas	75.00
82	1206	4c	Higher Education	15.00
83	C64, C65	8c	Capitol	12.50
83a	C64, C64b, C65	8c	Capitol sheet, booklet, coil	20.00
84	C64a	8c	Capitol, tagged	35.00
85	C64b	8c	Capitol booklet single	40.00
86	C65	8c	Capitol coil	20.00
87	1207	4c	Winslow Homer	20.00
88	1208	5c	Flag	17.50
89	1209	1c	Jackson	17.50
90	1213	5c	Washington	25.00
91	1213a	5c	Washington booklet pane of 5 + label	40.00
92	1225	1c	Jackson coil	25.00
93	1229	5c	Washington coil	25.00
94	C66	15c	Montgomery Blair	—

1963

96	1231	5c	Food for Peace	8.00
97	1232	5c	West Virginia	7.00
98	1233	5c	Emancipation Proclamation	20.00
99	1234	5c	Alliance for Progress	7.50
100	1235	5c	Cordell Hall	7.00
101	1236	5c	Eleanor Roosevelt	8.00
102	1237	5c	Science	7.50
103	1238	5c	City Mail Delivery	7.50
104	1239	5c	Red Cross	7.00
105	1240	5c	Christmas	7.50
106	1241	5c	Audubon	8.50

1964

107	1242	5c	Sam Houston	13.50
108	1243	5c	C.M. Russell	7.00
109	1244	5c	N.Y. World's Fair	8.50
110	1245	5c	John Muir	13.50
111	1246	5c	Kennedy (Boston, Mass.) (At least 4 other cities known)	8.00
112	1247	5c	New Jersey	7.00
113	1248	5c	Nevada	6.00
114	1249	5c	Register and Vote	6.00
115	1250	5c	Shakespeare	6.00
116	1251	5c	Mayo Brothers	6.00
117	C69	8c	Goddard	7.00
118	1252	5c	Music	6.00
119	1253	5c	Homemakers	6.00
120	1257b	5c	Christmas Plants	15.00
121	1257c	5c	Christmas, tagged	120.00
122	1258	5c	Verrazano Narrows Bridge	7.00
123	1259	5c	Fine Arts	6.00
124	1260	5c	Amateur Radio	8.00

1965

125	1261	5c	New Orleans	5.00
126	1262	5c	Sokols	5.00
127	1263	5c	Cancer	6.00
128	1264	5c	Churchill	6.50
129	1265	5c	Magna Carta	6.50
130	1266	5c	I.C.Y.	6.50
131	1267	5c	Salvation Army	6.50

132	1268	5c	Dante	7.00
133	1269	5c	Hoover	8.00
134	1270	5c	Fulton	6.00
135	1271	5c	Florida	6.50
136	1272	5c	Traffic Safety	6.00
137	1273	5c	Copley	6.00
138	1274	11c	I.T.U.	8.50
139	1275	5c	Stevenson	7.00
140	1276	5c	Christmas	7.00

Prominent Americans

1965-73

141	1278	1c	Jefferson	6.00
141a	1278, 1278a, 1299	1c	Jefferson sheet, booklet, coil	10.00
142	1278a	1c	Jefferson booklet pane of 8	11.00
143	1279	1¼c	Gallatin	6.00
144	1280	2c	Wright	5.00
145	1280a	2c	Wright booklet pane of 5 + label	10.00
146	1281	3c	Parkman	5.00
147	1282	4c	Lincoln	7.00
148	1283	5c	Washington	5.00
149	1283B	5c	Washington redrawn	6.00
150	1284	6c	Roosevelt	5.00
151	1284b	6c	Roosevelt booklet pane of 8	11.00
151a	1284b, 1298	6c	Roosevelt booklet, vert. coil	7.00
151b	1284b, 1305	6c	Roosevelt booklet, horiz. coil	7.00
152	1285	8c	Einstein	11.00
153	1286	10c	Jackson	7.00
154	1286A	12c	Ford	6.00
155	1287	13c	Kennedy	25.00
156	1288	15c	Holmes	5.00
157	1289	20c	Marshall	7.00
158	1290	25c	Douglas	8.00
159	1291	30c	Dewey	30.00
160	1292	40c	Paine	60.00
161	1293	50c	Stone	50.00
162	1294	$1	O'Neill	60.00
163	1295	$5	Moore	160.00
164	1298	6c	Roosevelt vert. coil	5.00
165	1299	1c	Jefferson coil	6.00
166	1303	4c	Lincoln coil	5.25
167	1304	5c	Washington coil	6.00
168	1305	6c	Roosevelt horiz. coil	5.25

Nos. 1297, 1305C and 1305E are known on unofficial pages. They are not listed here. For official pages of these issues, see Nos. 296-298.

1966

169	1306	5c	Migratory Bird Treaty	6.00
170	1307	5c	ASPCA	6.50
171	1308	5c	Indiana	7.00
172	1309	5c	Circus	5.00
173	1310	5c	SIPEX	5.00
174	1311	5c	SIPEX Souvenir Sheet	7.00
175	1312	5c	Bill of Rights	5.00
176	1313	5c	Poland	5.00
177	1314	5c	National Park Service	5.00
178	1315	5c	Marine Corps Reserve	5.00
179	1316	5c	Women's Clubs	6.50
180	1317	5c	Johnny Appleseed	7.00
181	1318	5c	Beautifcation of America	10.00
182	1319	5c	Great River Road	7.00
183	1320	5c	Savings Bonds Servicemen	6.00
184	1321	5c	Christmas	5.00
185	1322	5c	Mary Cassatt	7.00

1967

186	C70	8c	Alaska	8.00
187	1323	5c	Grange	

No.	Scott	Denom.	Description	Price
188	C71	20c	Audubon	6.00
189	1324	5c	Canada	5.50
190	1325	5c	Erie Canal	5.00
191	1326	5c	Search for Peace	5.75
192	1327	5c	Thoreau	5.00
193	1328	5c	Nebraska	5.00
194	1329	5c	VOA	5.00
195	1330	5c	Crockett	5.00
196	1331a	5c	Space	27.50
197	1333	5c	Urban Planning	5.00
198	1334	5c	Finland	5.00
199	1335	5c	Eakins	5.00
200	1336	5c	Christmas	6.00
201	1337	5c	Mississippi	5.00

1968-71

202	1338	6c	Flags, Giori Press	4.00
203	1338D	6c	Flag, Huck Press	4.00
204	1338F	8c	Flag	5.00
205	1338A	6c	Flag coil	4.00

1968

206	C72	10c	50 star Runway	7.00
206a	C72, C72b, C73	10c	sheet, booklet, coil	10.00
207	C72, C72b, C73	10c	sheet, coil, booklet pane of 8	35.00
208	C73	10c	50 star Runway coil	12.00
209	1339	6c	Illinois	5.00
210	1340	6c	HemisFair	5.00
211	1341	$1	Airlift	65.00
212	1342	6c	Youth	4.00
213	C74	10c	Air Mail Service	6.00
214	1343	6c	Law and Order	5.00
215	1344	6c	Register and Vote	6.00
216	1345—1354	6c	Historic Flags	100.00
217	1355	6c	Disney	6.00
218	1356	6c	Marquette	3.50
219	1357	6c	Daniel Boone	4.00
220	1358	6c	Arkansas River Navigation	3.50
221	1359	6c	Leif Erikson	11.00
222	1360	6c	Cherokee Strip	11.00
223	1361	6c	John Trumbull	5.00
224	1362	6c	Waterfowl	6.00
225	1363	6c	Christmas	6.50
226	1364	6c	Chief Joseph	5.00
227	C75	20c	USA	7.00

1969

228	1368a	6c	Beautification	20.00
229	1369	6c	American Legion	3.50
230	1370	6c	Grandma Moses	5.00
231	1371	6c	Apollo 8	7.00
232	1372	6c	W.C. Handy	3.50
233	1373	6c	California	3.50
234	1374	6c	Powell	3.50
235	1375	6c	Alabama	3.50
236	1379a	6c	Botanical Congress	15.00
237	C76	10c	Man on the Moon	6.00
238	1380	6c	Dartmouth	3.50
239	1381	6c	Baseball	65.00
240	1382	6c	Football	6.00
241	1383	6c	Eisenhower	3.50
242	1384	6c	Christmas	5.00
243	1385	6c	Hope	4.00
244	E22	45c	Special Delivery	35.00
245	1386	6c	Harnett	4.00

1970

246	1390a	6c	Natural History	35.00
247	1391	6c	Maine	3.50
248	1392	6c	Wildlife Conservation	3.50

Regular Issue

1970-71

249	1393	6c	Eisenhower	5.00
249a	1393, 1393a, 1401	6c	sheet, booklet, coil stamps	8.00
249b	1393, 1401	6c	sheet, coil stamps	8.00
250	1393a	6c	Eisenhower booklet pane of 8	16.00
250a	1393a, 1401	6c	booklet, coil	8.00
251	1393b	6c	Eisenhower booklet pane of 5 + label	8.00
252	1394	8c	Eisenhower	5.00
252a	1394, 1395, 1402	8c	sheet, booklet, coil	8.00
253	1395a	8c	Eisenhower booklet pane of 8	20.00
254	1395b	8c	Eisenhower booklet pane of 8	20.00
255	1396	8c	U.S.P.S.	15.00
256	1398	16c	Pyle	5.00
257	1401	6c	Eisenhower coil	5.00
258	1402	8c	Eisenhower coil	5.00

1970

259	1405	6c	Masters	3.50
260	1406	6c	Suffrage	3.50
261	1407	6c	S. Carolina	3.50
262	1408	6c	Stone Mountain	3.50
263	1409	6c	Ft. Snelling	3.50
264	1413a	6c	Anti pollution	7.00
265	1414	6c	Christmas Nativity	5.50
266	1418b	6c	Christmas Toys	8.00
267	1418c	6c	Toys precanceled	50.00
268	1419	6c	U.N.	3.50
269	1420	6c	Mayflower	5.00
270	1421a	6c	DAV, Servicemen	20.00

1971

271	1423	6c	Wool	3.50
272	1424	6c	MacArthur	3.50

273	1425	6c	Blood Donors	3.50
274	1426	8c	Missouri	3.50
275	C77	9c	Delta Wing	8.00
276	C78	11c	Jet	5.00
276a	C78, C78a, C82	11c	sheet, booklet, coil	8.00
277	C78a	11c	Jet booklet pane of 4 + 2 labels	17.50
278	E23	60c	Special Delivery	25.00
279	1430a	8c	Wildlife	20.00
280	1431	8c	Antarctic Treaty	15.00
281	1432	8c	Bicentennial Emblem	17.50
282	C80	17c	Statue of Liberty	22.50
283	C81	21c	USA	22.50
284	C82	11c	Jet coil	5.00
285	1433	8c	Sloan	15.00
286	1434a	8c	Space	22.50
287	1436	8c	Dickenson	15.00
288	1437	8c	San Juan	15.00
289	1438	8c	Drug Abuse	15.00
290	1439	8c	CARE	15.00
291	1443a	8c	Historic Preservation	18.00
292	1444	8c	Adoration	15.00
293	1445	8c	Patridge	15.00

1972

294	1446	8c	Lanier	15.00
295	1447	8c	Peace Corps	15.00

OFFICIAL SOUVENIR PAGES

In 1972 the USPS began issuing "official" Souvenir pages by subscription. A few more "unofficials" were produced.

Prominent Americans

1970-74

296	1297	3c	Parkman coil	3.50
297	1305C	$1	O'Neill coil	25.00
298	1305E	15c	Holmes coil	4.50
299	1393D	7c	Franklin	11.00
300	1397	14c	LaGuardia	135.00
301	1399	18c	Blackwell	4.50
302	1400	21c	Giannini	7.00

1972

303	1451a	2c	Cape Hatteras	125.00
304	1452	6c	Wolf Trap Farm	50.00
305	1453	8c	Yellowstone	110.00
306	C84	11c	City of Refuge	130.00
307	1454	15c	Mt. McKinley	50.00
308	1455	8c	Family Planning	—
309	1459a	8c	Colonial Craftsmen	27.50
310	1460—1462, C85	8c	Olympics	30.00
311	1463	8c	PTA	11.00
312	1467a	8c	Wildlife	15.00
313	1468	8c	Mail Order	11.00
314	1469	8c	Osteopathic	12.50
315	1470	8c	Tom Sawyer	12.50
316	1471, 1472	8c	Christmas	17.50
317	1473	8c	Pharmacy	10.00
318	1474	8c	Stamp Collecting	10.00

1973

319	1475	8c	Love	25.00
320	1476	8c	Printing	10.00
321	1477	8c	Broadside	11.00
322	1478	8c	Postrider	10.00
323	1479	8c	Drummer	9.00
324	1483a	8c	Tea Party	11.00
325	1484	8c	Gershwin	7.00
326	1485	8c	Jeffers	6.00
327	1486	8c	Tanner	5.00
328	1487	8c	Cather	5.00
329	1488	8c	Copernicus	9.00
330	1489—1498	8c	Postal People	12.00
331	1499	8c	Truman	7.00
332	1500—1502, C86	8c	Electronics	10.00
333	1503	8c	L.B. Johnson	6.00

1973-74

334	1504	8c	Cattle	5.00
335	1505	10c	Chautauqua	5.00
336	1506	10c	Train	5.00

1973

337	1507, 1508	8c	Christmas	11.00

REGULAR ISSUES

1973-74

338	1509	10c	Crossed Flags	5.00
339	1510	10c	Jefferson Memorial	5.00
340	1511	10c	ZIP	5.00
341	1518	6.3c	Liberty Bell coil	6.00

1974

342	C87	18c	Statue of Liberty	5.00
343	C88	26c	Mt. Rushmore	10.00
344	1525	10c	VFW	5.00
345	1526	10c	Robert Frost	5.00
346	1527	10c	EXPO '74	5.00
347	1528	10c	Horse Racing	6.00
348	1529	10c	Skylab	9.00
349	1537a	10c	UPU	11.00
350	1541a	10c	Minerals	8.00
351	1542	10c	Ft. Harrod	5.00
352	1546a	10c	Continental Congress	7.50
353	1547	10c	Energy	5.00
354	1548	10c	Sleepy Hollow	5.00
355	1549	10c	Retarded Children	5.00
356	1550—1552	10c	Christmas	9.00

1975

357	1553	10c	Benjamin West	4.00
358	1554	10c	Dunbar	4.00
359	1555	10c	D.W. Griffith	4.00
360	1556	10c	Pioneer	8.00
361	1557	10c	Mariner	8.00
362	1558	10c	Collective Bargaining	4.00
363	1559	8c	Sybil Ludington	4.00
364	1560	10c	Salem Poor	4.00
365	1561	10c	Hyam Salomon	4.00
366	1562	15c	Peter Francisco	4.00
367	1563	10c	Lexington Concord	5.00
368	1564	10c	Bunker Hill	5.00
369	1568a	10c	Military Uniforms	8.00
370	1569a	10c	Apollo Soyuz	8.00
371	1571	10c	Women's Year	4.00
372	1575a	10c	Postal Service	6.00
373	1576	10c	Peace through Law	4.00
374	1577a	10c	Banking and Commerce	4.50
375	1579, 1580	10c	Christmas	7.50

Americana Issue

1975-81

376	1581, 1582, 1584, 1585	1c, 2c, 3c, 4c	Americana	4.00
377	1591	9c	Capitol Dome	4.00
378	1592	10c	Justice	4.00
379	1593	11c	Printing Press	4.00
380	1594, 1816	12c	Torch sheet, coil	4.50
381	1596	13c	Eagle and Shield	4.00
382	1597, 1618C	15c	Flag sheet, coil	4.00
383	1599, 1619	16c	Statue of Liberty sheet, coil	4.50
384	1603	24c	Old North Church	4.00
385	1604	28c	Ft. Nisqually	5.00
386	1605	29c	Lighthouse	4.50
387	1606	30c	Schoolhouse	6.00
388	1608	50c	"Betty" Lamp	6.00
389	1610	$1	Candle Holder	10.00
390	1611	$2	Kerosene Lamp	10.00
391	1612	$5	R.R. Lantern	27.50
392	1811	1c	Inkwell coil	3.50
393	1813	3.1c	Guitar coil	5.00
394	1813	3.5c	Violin coil	5.00
395	1614	7.7c	Saxhorns coil	4.00
396	1615	7.9c	Drum coil	4.00
397	1615C	8.4c	Piano coil	4.00
398	1616	9c	Capitol Dome coil	3.75
399	1618	13c	Liberty Bell coil	3.75
400	1622, 1625	13c	13 star Flag sheet, coil	4.00
401	1623c	9c, 13c	Booklet pane, perf. 10	25.00

1976

402	1631a	13c	Spirit of '76	7.00
403	C89, C90	25c, 31c	Plane and Globes	5.00
404	1632	13c	Interphil 76	4.00
405	1633—1642	13c	State Flags	12.50
406	1643—1652	13c	State Flags	12.50
407	1653—1662	13c	State Flags	12.50
408	1663—1672	13c	State Flags	12.50
409	1673—1682	13c	State Flags	12.50
410	1683	13c	Telephone	3.75
411	1684	13c	Aviation	3.75
412	1685	13c	Chemistry	3.75
413	1686	13c	Bicentennial Souvenir Sheet	15.00
414	1687	18c	Bicentennial Souvenir Sheet	15.00
415	1688	24c	Bicentennial Souvenir Sheet	15.00
416	1689	31c	Bicentennial Souvenir Sheet	15.00
417	1690	13c	Franklin	3.75
418	1694a	13c	Declaration of Independence	6.00
419	1698a	13c	Olympics	7.00
420	1699	13c	Clara Maass	3.50
421	1700	13c	Adolph Ochs	3.50
422	1701—1703	13c	Christmas	7.00

1977

423	1704	13c	Washington at Princeton	4.00
424	1705	13c	Sound Recording	4.00
425	1709a	13c	Pueblo Pottery	5.00
426	1710	13c	Lindbergh Flight	3.50
427	1711	13c	Colorado	3.50
428	1715a	13c	Butterflies	4.75
429	1716	13c	Lafayette	3.50
430	1720a	13c	Skilled Hands	5.00
431	1721	13c	Peace Bridge	3.50
432	1722	13c	Oriskany	4.00
433	1723a	13c	Energy	3.75
434	1725	13c	Alta California	3.50
435	1726	13c	Articles of Confederation	3.50
436	1727	13c	Talking Pictures	3.50
437	1728	13c	Saratoga	4.00
438	1729, 1730	13c	Christmas	4.00

1978

439	1731	13c	Sandburg	3.50
440	1732, 1733	13c	Capt. Cook	3.50
441	1734	13c	Indian Head Penny	3.50
442	1735, 1743	15c	A Sheet, coil	4.00
443	1737	15c	Roses booklet single	3.50
444	1742a	15c	Windmills booklet pane of 10	7.50
445	1744	13c	Tubman	3.50
446	1748a	13c	Quilts	4.50
447	1752a	13c	American Dance	4.50
448	1753	13c	French Alliance	4.50

449	1754	13c	Cancer Detection	3.50
450	1755	13c	Jimmy Rogers	3.50
451	1756	15c	George M. Cohan	3.50
452	1757	13c	CAPEX '78 Souvenir Sheet	7.50
453	1758	15c	Photography	3.50
454	1759	15c	Viking Missions	4.50
455	1763a	15c	Owls	4.25
456	C92a	31c	Wright Brothers	5.00
457	1767a	15c	Trees	4.25
458	1768	15c	Madonna and Child	4.00
459	1769	15c	Hobby Horse	4.00

1979

460	1770	15c	Robert F. Kennedy	3.50
461	1771	15c	Martin Luther King Jr.	3.25
462	1772	15c	Year of the Child	3.50
463	1773	15c	John Steinbeck	3.50
464	1774	15c	Einstein	4.00
465	C94a	21c	Chanute	5.00
466	1778a	15c	Toleware	4.25
467	1782a	15c	Architecture	4.25
468	1786a	15c	Endangered Flora	4.50
469	1787	15c	Seeing Eye Dogs	3.50
470	1788	15c	Special Olympics	4.00
471	1789	15c	John Paul Jones	4.25
472	1790	10c	Olympics	4.00
473	1794a	15c	Olympics	7.50
474	C97	31c	Olympics	8.50

1980

475	1798a	15c	Winter Olympics	7.50

1979

476	1799	15c	Madonna and Child	3.75
477	1800	15c	Santa Claus	3.75
478	1801	15c	Will Rogers	3.50
479	1802	15c	Vietnam Veterans	3.75
480	C96a	25c	Wiley Post	5.00

1980

481	1803	15c	W.C. Fields	4.00
482	1804	15c	Benjamin Banneker	3.00
483	1805—1810	15c	Letter Writing Week	5.00
484	1818, 1820	18c	B sheet, coil	3.25
485	1819a	18c	B booklet pane of 8	4.50
486	1821	15c	Frances Perkins	3.00
487	1822	15c	Dolley Madison	3.00
488	1823	15c	Emily Bissell	3.00
489	1824	15c	Helen Keller	3.25
490	1825	15c	Veterans Administration	3.00
491	1826	15c	Galvez	3.00
492	1830a	15c	Coral Reefs	4.00
493	1831	15c	Organized Labor	3.00
494	1832	15c	Edith Wharton	3.00
495	1833	15c	Education	3.00
496	1837a	15c	Indian Masks	4.00
497	1841a	15c	Architecture	3.50
498	C98	40c	Mazzei	4.00
499	1842	15c	Christmas Window	3.25
500	1843	15c	Christmas Toys	3.25
501	C99	28c	Blanche Stuart Scott	3.25
502	C100	35c	Curtiss	3.25

Great Americans

1980-85

503	1844	1c	Dix	2.75
504	1845	2c	Stravinsky	2.75
505	1846	3c	Clay	2.75
506	1847	4c	Schurz	2.75
507	1848	5c	Buck	2.75
508	1849	6c	Lippmann	2.75
509	1850	7c	Baldwin	2.75
510	1851	8c	Knox	2.75
511	1852	9c	Thayer	2.75
512	1853	10c	Russell	2.75
513	1854	11c	Partridge	2.75
514	1855	13c	Crazy Horse	2.75
515	1856	14c	Lewis	2.75
516	1857	17c	Carson	2.75
517	1858	18c	Mason	2.75
518	1859	19c	Sequoyah	2.75
519	1860	20c	Bunche	2.75
520	1861	20c	Gallandet	2.75
521	1862	20c	Truman	2.75
522	1863	22c	Audubon	2.75
523	1864	30c	Laubach	2.75
524	1865	35c	Drew	2.75
525	1866	37c	Milikan	2.75
526	1867	39c	Clark	2.75
527	1868	40c	Gilbert	2.75
528	1869	50c	Nimitz	2.75

1981

529	1874	15c	Dirksen	2.75
530	1875	15c	Young	2.75
531	1879a	18c	Flowers	3.50
532	1889a	18c	Animals booklet pane of 10	6.00
533	1890, 1891	18c	Flag sheet, coil	3.25
534	1893a	6c, 18c	Booklet pane	4.00
535	1894, 1895	20c	Flag sheet, coil	3.00
536	1896a	20c	Flag booklet pane of 6	3.50

1982

537	1896b	20c	Flag booklet pane of 10	5.75

Transporation Coils

1981-84

538	1897	1c	Omnibus	2.75
539	1897A	2c	Locomotive	2.75
540	1898	3c	Handcar	2.75
541	1898A	4c	Stagecoach	2.75
542	1899	5c	Motorcycle	2.75
543	1900	5.2c	Sleigh	2.75
544	1901	5.9c	Bicycle	2.75
545	1902	7.4c	Baby Buggy	2.75
546	1903	9.3c	Mail Wagon	2.75
547	1904	10.9c	Hansom Cab	2.75
548	1905	11c	Caboose	2.75
549	1906	12c	Electric Auto	3.00
550	1907	18c	Surrey	3.00
551	1008	20c	Fire Pumper	3.00

1983

552	1909	$9.35	Express Mail single	60.00
552a	1909a	$9.35	Express Mail booklet pane of 3	150.00

1981

553	1910	18c	Red Cross	2.75
554	1911	18c	Savings and Loan	2.75
555	1919a	18c	Space Achievements	7.50
556	1920	18c	Management	2.75
557	1924a	18c	Wildlife	3.50
558	1925	18c	Disabled	2.75
559	1926	18c	Millay	2.75
560	1927	18c	Alcoholism	2.75
561	1931a	18c	Architecture	3.50
562	1932	18c	Zaharias	3.00
563	1933	18c	Jones	3.00
564	1934	18c	Remington	2.75
565	1935, 1936	18c, 20c	Hoban	3.00
566	1938a	18c	Yorktown, Va. Capes	2.75
567	1939	20c	Madonna and Child	3.00
568	1940	20c	Teddy Bear	3.00
569	1941	20c	John Hanson	2.75
570	1945a	20c	Desert Plants	3.25
571	1946, 1947	20c	C sheet, coil	2.75
572	1948a	20c	C Booklet pane of 10	5.25

1982

573	1949a	20c	Bighorn Sheep booklet pane of 10	5.00
574	1950	20c	FDR	2.75
575	1951	20c	Love	2.75
576	1952	20c	Washington	2.75
577	1953—1962	20c	Birds and Flowers	7.50
578	1963—1972	20c	Birds and Flowers	7.50
579	1973—1982	20c	Birds and Flowers	7.50
580	1983—1992	20c	Birds and Flowers	7.50
581	1993—2002	20c	Birds and Flowers	7.50
582	2003	20c	US Netherlands	2.75
583	2004	20c	Library of Congress	2.75
584	2005	20c	Consumer Education	2.75
585	2009a	20c	Knoxville World's Fair	3.50
586	2010	20c	Horatio Alger	2.75
587	2011	20c	Aging	2.75
588	2012	20c	Barrymores	2.75
589	2013	20c	Dr. Mary Walker	2.75
590	2014	20c	Peace Garden	2.75
591	2015	20c	Librarian	2.75
592	2016	20c	Jackie Robinson	4.00
593	2017	20c	Tuoro Synagogue	2.75
594	2018	20c	Wolf Trap Farm	2.75
595	2022a	20c	Architecture	3.25
596	2023	20c	Francis of Assisi	2.75
597	2024	20c	Ponce de Leon	2.75
598	2025	13c	Puppy, Kitten	2.75
599	2026	20c	Madonna and Child	2.75
600	2030a	20c	Children Playing	4.00

1983

601	O127—O129	1c, 4c, 13c	Official Mail	5.00
602	O130	17c	Official Mail	5.00
603	O132	$1	Official Mail	7.50
604	O133	$5	Official Mail	15.00
605	O135	20c	Official Mail coil	5.00
606	2031	20c	Science	2.75
607	2035a	20c	Ballooning	4.50
608	2036	20c	US Sweden	2.75
609	2037	20c	CCC	2.75
610	2038	20c	Priestley	2.75
611	2039	20c	Voluntarism	2.75
612	2040	20c	German Immigration	2.75
613	2041	20c	Brooklyn Bridge	2.75
614	2042	20c	TVA	2.75
615	2043	20c	Fitness	2.75
616	2044	20c	Scott Joplin	2.75
617	2045	20c	Medal of Honor	2.75
618	2046	20c	Babe Ruth	5.00
619	2047	20c	Hawthorne	2.75
620	2051a	13c	Olympics	4.00
621	C104a	28c	Olympics	4.00
622	C108a	40c	Olympics	5.00
623	C112a	35c	Olympics	4.50
624	2052	20c	Treaty of Paris	2.75
625	2053	20c	Civil Service	2.75
626	2054	20c	Metropolitan Opera	2.75
627	2058a	20c	Inventors	4.00
628	2062a	20c	Streetcars	4.00
629	2063	20c	Madonna and Child	3.00
630	2064	20c	Santa Claus	3.00
631	2065	20c	Martin Luther	2.75

1984

632	2066	20c	Alaska	2.75
633	2070a	20c	Winter Olympics	3.00
634	2071	20c	FDIC	2.75
635	2072	20c	Love	2.75
636	2073	20c	Woodson	2.75
637	O138, O139	14c, 22c	D sheet, coil	4.00

638	2074	20c	Conservation	2.75
639	2075	20c	Credit Union	2.75
640	2079a	20c	Orchids	3.25
641	2080	20c	Hawaii	2.75
642	2081	20c	National Archives	2.75
643	2085a	20c	Olympics	4.00
644	2086	20c	World Expo	2.75
645	2087	20c	Health Research	2.75
646	2088	20c	Fairbanks	2.75
647	2089	20c	Thorpe	2.75
648	2090	20c	McCormack	2.75
649	2091	20c	St. Lawrence Seaway	2.75
650	2092	20c	Waterfowl	2.75
651	2093	20c	Roanoke Voyages	2.75
652	2094	20c	Melville	2.75
653	2095	20c	Horace Moses	2.75
654	2096	20c	Smokey the Bear	2.75
655	2097	20c	Clemente	4.00
656	2101a	20c	Dogs	4.00
657	2102	20c	Crime Prevention	2.75
658	2103	20c	Hispanic Americans	2.75
659	2104	20c	Family Unity	2.75
660	2105	20c	Eleanor Roosevelt	2.75
661	2106	20c	Readers	2.75
662	2107	20c	Madonna and Child	2.75
663	2108	20c	Child's Santa	2.75
664	2109	20c	Vietnam Memorial	2.75

1985

665	2110	20c	Jerome Kern	2.75
666	2111, 2112	22c	D sheet, coil	2.75
667	2113a	22c	D booklet pane of 10	7.00
668	C113	33c	Verville	3.00
669	C114	39c	Sperry	3.00
670	C115	44c	Transpacific	3.00
671	2114, 2115	22c	Flags sheet, coil	2.75
672	2116a	22c	Flag booklet pane of 5	4.00
673	2121a	22c	Seashells booklet pane of 10	7.00
674	2122	$10.75	Express Mail single	40.00
674a	2122a	$10.75	Express Mail booklet pane of 3	80.00

Transporation Coils

1985-87

675	2123	3.4c	School Bus	2.75
676	2124	4.9c	Buckboard	2.75
677	2125	5.5c	Star Route Truck	2.75
678	2126	6c	Tricycle	2.75
679	2127	7.1c	Tractor	2.75
680	2128	8.3c	Ambulance	2.75
681	2129	8.5c	Tow Truck	2.75
682	2130	10.1c	Oil Wagon	2.75
683	2131	11c	Stutz Bearcat	2.75
684	2132	12c	Stanley Steamer	2.75
685	2133	12.5c	Pushcart	2.75
686	2134	14c	Iceboat	2.75
687	2135	17c	Dog Sled	2.75
688	2136	25c	Bread Wagon	2.75

1985

689	2137	22c	Bethune	2.75
690	2141a	22c	Duck Decoys	3.50
691	2142	22c	Winter Special Olympics	2.75
692	2143	22c	Love	2.75
693	2144	22c	REA	2.75
694	O129A, O136	14c, 22c	Official Mail	4.00
695	2145	22c	AMERIPEX '86	2.75
696	2146	22c	Abigail Adams	2.75
697	2147	22c	Bartholdi	2.75
698	2149	18c	Washington coil	2.75
699	2150	21.1c	Letters coil	2.75
700	2152	22c	Korean Veterans	2.75
701	2153	22c	Social Security	2.75
702	C116	44c	Serra	2.75
703	2154	22c	World War I Veterans	2.75
704	2158a	22c	Horses	3.50
705	2159	22c	Education	2.75
706	2163a	22c	Youth Year	2.75
707	2164	22c	Hunger	2.75
708	2165	22c	Madonna and Child	2.75
709	2166	22c	Poinsettias	2.75

1986

710	2167	22c	Arkansas	2.75

Great Americans

1986-87

711	2168	1c	Mitchell	2.75
712	2169	2c	Lyon	2.75
713	2170	3c	White	2.75
714	2171	4c	Flanagan	2.75
715	2172	5c	Black	2.75
716	2176	10c	Red Cloud	2.75
717	2177	14c	Howe	2.75
718	2179	17c	Lockwood	2.75
719	2183	25c	London	2.75
720	2191	56c	Harvard	2.75
721	2194	$1	Revel	3.50
722	2195	$2	Bryan	4.50
723	2196	$5	Harte	8.00

1986

724	2201a	22c	Stamp Collecting booklet pane of 4	4.50
725	2202	22c	Love	2.75
726	2203	22c	Sojourner Truth	2.75
727	2204	22c	Texas Republic	2.75
728	2209a	22c	Fish booklet pane of 5	4.50
729	2210	22c	Hospitals	2.75

730	2211	22c	Duke Ellington	2.75	736	2224	22c	Statue of Liberty	2.75	746	2246	22c	Michigan	2.75

No.	Scott	Denom	Name	Price
730	2211	22c	Duke Ellington	2.75
731	2216	22c	Presidents Souvenir Sheet #1	7.50
732	2217	22c	Presidents Souvenir Sheet #2	7.50
733	2218	22c	Presidents Souvenir Sheet #3	7.50
734	2219	22c	Presidents Souvenir Sheet #4	7.50
735	2223a	22c	Arctic Explorers	4.50
736	2224	22c	Statue of Liberty	2.75
741	2238a	22c	Navajo Art	4.50
742	2239	22c	T.S. Elliot	2.75
743	2243a	22c	Woodcarved Figurines	4.50
744	2244	22c	Madonna and Child	2.75
745	2245	22c	Village Scene	2.75
1987				
746	2246	22c	Michigan	2.75
747	2247	22c	Pan American Games	2.75
748	2248	22c	Love	2.75
749	2249	22c	du Sable	2.75
750	2250	22c	Caruso	2.75
751	2251	22c	Girl Scouts	2.75

SAVINGS

POSTAL SAVINGS STAMPS.
Issued by the Post Office Department.

Redeemable in the form of credits to Postal Savings accounts. The Postal Savings system was discontinued Mar. 28, 1966.

PS1

Plates of 400 subjects in four panes of 100 each
FLAT PLATE PRINTING

1911   Wmk. 191   Engr.   Perf. 12
Size of design: 18x21½mm.

PS1 PS1 **10c orange,** *Jan. 3, 1911* — 10.00 — 75
Block of four, 2 mm. spacing — 40.50
Block of four, 3 mm. spacing — 41.50
Margin strip of 3, Impt. open star & P# — 50.00
Margin block of 6, Impt. open star & P# — 500.00

Plate Nos.
5504 — 5505 — 5506 — 5507
5698 — 5700 — 5703 — 5704

1911   Unwmk.
Imprinted on Deposit Card. Size of design: 137x79mm.

PS2 PS1 **10c orange,** *Jan. 3, 1911* — 90.00 — 35.00

A 10c deep blue with head of Washington in circle imprinted on deposit card (design 136x79mm.) exists, but there is no evidence that it was ever placed in use.

1911   Wmk. 190   Perf. 12

PS4 PS1 **10c deep blue,** *Aug. 14, 1911* — 5.50 — 75
Block of four, 2 mm. spacing — 22.50
Block of four, 3 mm. spacing — 24.00
Margin strip of 3, Impt. open star & P# — 30.00
Margin block of 6, Impt. open star & P# — 185.00

Plate Nos.
5504 — 5505 — 5506 — 5507
5698 — 5700 — 5703 — 5704

1911   Unwmk.
Imprinted on Deposit Card. Size of design: 133x78mm.

PS5 PS1 **10c deep blue** — 90.00 — 25.00

1936   Unwmk.   Perf. 11

PS6 PS1 **10c deep blue** — 4.50 — 1.00
a. **10c violet blue** — 4.50 — 1.00
Block of four — 18.50
Margin block of 6, Impt. solid star & P# — 125.00
Plate Nos. 21485 21486

PS2

Plates of 400 subjects in four panes of 100 each
FLAT PLATE PRINTING

1940   Unwmk.   Engr.   Perf. 11
Size of design: 19x22mm.

PS7 PS2 **10c deep ultramarine,** *April 3, 1940* — 12.00
Block of four — 48.00
Margin block of 6, P# — 225.00
Plate Nos. 22540, 22541

PS8 PS2 **25c dark carmine rose,** *April 1, 1940* — 16.00
Block of four — 64.00
Margin block of 6, P# — 300.00
Plate Nos. 22542 22543

PS9 PS2 **50c dark blue green,** *April 1, 1940* — 45.00
Block of four — 180.00
Margin block of 6, P# — 775.00
Plate No. 22544

PS10 PS2 **$1 gray black,** *April 1, 1940* — 85.00
Block of four — 340.00
Margin block of 6, P# — 1,750.
Plate No. 22545

Nos. PS11-PS15 redeemable in the form of United States Treasury Defense, War or Savings Bonds.

Minute Man — PS3

E.E. Plates of 400 subjects in four panes of 100 each
ROTARY PRESS PRINTING

1941   Unwmk.   Perf. 11x10½
Size of design: 19x22½mm.

PS11 PS3 **10c rose red,** *May 1, 1941* — 65
a. **10c carmine rose** — 65
Block of four — 2.60
Margin block of 4, P# — 9.00
b. Bklt. pane of 10, *July 30, 1941*, trimmed horizontal edges — 50.00
As "b," with Electric Eye marks at left — 55.00
c. Booklet pane of 10, perf. horizontal edges — 110.00
As "c," with Electric Eye marks at left — 125.00

Plate Nos. of sheet stamps
22714 — 22722 — 148245
22715 — 22723 — 148246

Plate Nos. of booklet panes
147084 — 147085 — 148241 — 148242

PS12 PS3 **25c blue green,** *May 1, 1941* — 3.00
Block of four — 12.00
Margin block of 4, P# — 22.00
b. Bklt. pane of 10, *July 30, 1941* — 60.00
Booklet pane with Electric Eye marks at left — 65.00

Plate Nos. of sheet stamps
22716 — 22717 — 22724
22725 — 148247 — 148248

Plate Nos. of booklet panes
147087 — 147088 — 148243 — 148244

PS13 PS3 **50c ultramarine,** *May 1, 1941* — 9.00
Block of four — 36.00
Margin block of 4, P# — 50.00

Plate Nos.
22718 — 22719 — 22726 — 22727

PS14 PS3 **$1 gray black,** *May 1, 1941* — 16.00
Block of four — 64.00
Margin block of 4, P# — 110.00

Plate Nos.
22720 — 22728

FLAT PLATE PRINTING
Plates of 100 subjects in four panes of 25 each
Size: 36x46mm.   Perf. 11

PS15 PS3 **$5 sepia,** *May 1, 1941* — 45.00
Block of four — 180.00
Margin block of 6, P# at top or bottom — 550.00

Plate Nos.
22730 — 22731 — 22732
22733 — 22734 — 22735
22736 — 22737 — 22740

SAVINGS STAMPS
Issued by the Post Office Department.

Redeemable in the form of United States Savings Bonds. Sale of Savings Stamps was discontinued June 30, 1970.

Minute Man — S1

E.E. Plates of 400 subjects in four panes of 100 each
ROTARY PRESS PRINTING

1954-57		Unwmk.		*Perf. 11x10 1/2*

Size of design: 19x22 1/2mm.

S1	S1	**10c rose red,** *Nov. 30, 1954*	60
		Block of four	2.40
		Margin block of 4, P#	3.50
	a.	Booklet pane of 10, *Apr. 22, 1955*	135.00
		Booklet pane with Electric Eye marks at left	150.00

Plate Nos. of sheet stamps

164991	164992	165917	165918	166643
166644	167089	167090	168765	168766

Plate Nos. of booklet panes

165218		165219		165954
165955		167001		167002

S2	S1	**25c blue green,** *Dec. 30, 1954*	3.00
		Block of four	12.00
		Margin block of 4, P#	30.00
	a.	Booklet pane of 10, *Apr. 15, 1955*	450.00
		Booklet pane with Electric Eye marks at left	475.00

Plate Nos. of sheet stamps

165007		165008		165919		165920

Plate Nos. of booklet panes

165220		165221		165956		165957

S3	S1	**50c ultramarine,** *Dec. 31, 1956*	6.00
		Block of four	24.00
		Margin block of 4, P#	35.00

Plate Nos.

165050		165051		166741
166742		166941		166942

S4	S1	**$1 gray black,** *March 13, 1957*	18.00
		Block of four	72.00
		Margin block of 4, P#	90.00

Plate Nos.

166097				166098
166683				166684

FLAT PLATE PRINTING
Plates of 100 subjects in four panes of 25 each
Size: 36x46mm.

				Perf. 11

S5	S1	**$5 sepia,** *Nov. 30, 1956*	65.00
		Block of four	260.00
		Margin block of 6, P# at top or bottom	800.00

Plate No. 166068

Minute Man and 48-Star Flag — S2

GIORI PRESS PRINTING
Plates of 400 subjects in four panes of 100 each

1958		Unwmk.		*Perf. 11*

S6	S2	**25c dark blue & carmine,** *Nov. 18, 1958*	75
		Block of four	3.00
		Margin block of 4, P#	7.50
	a.	Booklet pane of 10, *Nov. 18, 1958*	65.00

Plate Nos. of sheet stamps

166921	166925	166946	166949	167014

Minute Man and 50-Star Flag — S3

Plates of 400 subjects in four panes of 100 each

1961		Unwmk.		*Perf. 11*

S7	S3	**25c dark blue & carmine**	75
		Block of four	3.00
		Margin block of 4, P #	7.50
	a.	Booklet pane of 10	300.00

Plate Nos. of sheet stamps

167473	167476	167486	167489	169089

Plate Nos. of booklet panes

167495				167502

WAR SAVINGS STAMPS
Issued by the Treasury Department.

Redeemable in the form of United States Treasury War Certificates, Defense Bonds or War Bonds.

WS1

Plates of 300 subjects in six panes of 50 each
FLAT PLATE PRINTING

1917		Unwmk.	Engr.	*Perf. 11*

Size of design: 28x18 1/2mm.

WS1	WS1	**25c deep green,** *Dec. 1, 1917*	10.00
		Block of four	42.50
		Margin strip of 3, P# only	50.00
		Margin block of 6, P# only	500.00

Plate Nos.

56800	56810	56811	56817	57074
57075	57076	57077	57149	57150
57151	57152	57336	57382	57395
57396	57399	57443	58801	58802
58803	58804	59044	59045	59156
61207	61208	61209	61210	

George Washington — WS2

Plates of 80 subjects in four panes of 20 each
FLAT PLATE PRINTING

1918		Unwmk.	Engr.	*Perf. 11*

Size of design: 39x55mm.

WS2	WS2	**$2 deep green,** *Nov. 17, 1917*	90.00
		Block of four	375.00
		Margin copy with P# only	125.00
	b.	Vertical pair, imperf. horizontally	—

Plate Nos.

56914	57170	58434	60662	61265
56915	57171	58435	60665	61266
56916	57172	58436	60666	61267
56917	57173	58437	60667	61268
57066	57174	58438	60668	61360
57067	57175	58726	60846	61361
57068	57176	58727	60847	61362
57069	57333	58728	60848	61363
57070	57334	58729	60849	61364
57071	57343	59071	60850	61365
57072	57344	60257	60851	61366
57073	57345	60258	60852	61367
57145	57346	60259	60899	61388
57146	57347	60260	61203	61435
57147	57348	60659	61204	61502
57148	58431	60660	61205	
57169	58433	60661	61206	

Rouletted 7				

WS3	WS2	**$5 deep green**	1,000.
		Block of four	4,250.
		Margin copy with P# only	1,250.

Benjamin Franklin — WS3

Plates of 150 subjects in six panes of 25 each
FLAT PLATE PRINTING

1919		Unwmk.	Engr.	*Perf. 11*

Size of design: 27x36mm.

WS4	WS3	**$5 deep blue,** *July 3, 1919*	275.00
		Block of four	1,150.
		Margin copy with P# only	300.00
		Margin copy with inverted P#	325.00

Plate Nos.

61882	61910	61970	61998	62010
61883	61911	61971	62007	62011
61884	61912	61972	62008	62012
61885	61913	61997	62009	62013

George Washington — WS4

Plates of 100 subjects in four panes of 25 each
FLAT PLATE PRINTING

1920		Unwmk.	Engr.	*Perf. 11*

Size of design: 36x41 1/2mm.

WS5	WS4	**$5 carmine,** *Dec. 11, 1919*	475.00
		Block of four	2,000.
		Margin copy with P# only	500.00

Plate Nos.

67545	67549	69349	69673	69678
67546	67550	69350	69674	68679
67547	67551	69351	69675	69680
67548	67552	69352	69677	69829

Abraham
Lincoln — WS5

Plates of 100 subjects in four panes of 25 each
FLAT PLATE PRINTING

1921   Unwmk.   Engr.   **Perf. 11**
Size of design: 39 1/2x42mm.

WS6	WS5	$5 orange, green, *Dec. 21, 1920*	2,500.
		Block of four	11,000.
		Margin copy with P# only	2,650.

Plate Nos.

73129	73131	73133	73135
73130	73132	73134	73136

Minute Man — WS6

Plates of 400 subjects in four panes of 100 each
ROTARY PRESS PRINTING

1942   Unwmk.   **Perf. 11x10 1/2**
Size of design: 19x22 1/2mm.

WS7	WS6	10c rose red, *Oct. 29, 1942*	50
	a.	10c carmine rose	50
		Block of four	2.00
		Margin block of 4, P#	5.00
	b.	Booklet pane of 10, *Oct. 27, 1942*	40.00
		Booklet pane with Electric Eye marks at left	45.00

Plate Nos. of sheet stamps

149492	149495	150706	155311
149493	150206	150707	155312
149494	150207		

Plate Nos. of booklet panes

149655	149656	149657	150664

WS8	WS6	25c dark blue green, *Oct. 15, 1942*	1.25
		Block of four	5.00
		Margin block of 4, P#	12.50
	b.	Booklet pane of 10, *Nov. 6, 1942*	55.00
		Booklet pane with Electric Eye marks at left	60.00

Plate Nos. of sheet stamps

149587	150320	155313	155813
149588	150321	155314	156517
149589	150708	155812	156518
149590	150709		

Plate Nos. of booklet panes

149658	149659	149660	150666

WS9	WS6	50c deep ultramarine, *Nov. 12, 1942*	4.50
		Block of four	18.00
		Margin block of 4, P#	32.50

Plate Nos.

149591	149592	149593	149594

WS10	WS6	$1 gray black, *Nov. 17, 1942*	12.50
		Block of four	50.00
		Margin block of 4, P#	65.00

Plate Nos.

149595	149596	149597	149598

Type of 1942
FLAT PLATE PRINTING
Plates of 100 subjects in four panes of 25 each

1945   Unwmk.   Size: 36x46mm.   **Perf. 11**

WS11	WS6	$5 violet brown	55.00
		Block of four	220.00
		Margin block of 6, P# at top or bottom	600.00

Plate Nos.

150131	150132	150133	150134
150291			

Type of 1942
Coil Stamps

1943   Unwmk.   **Perf. 10 Vertically**

WS12	WS6	10c rose red, *Aug. 5, 1943*	2.00
		Pair	4.25
		Line pair	12.00

Plate Nos.

153286	153287

WS13	WS6	25c dark blue green, *Aug. 5, 1943*	4.00
		Pair	8.50
		Line pair	20.00

Plate Nos.

153289	153290

TREASURY SAVINGS STAMP
Issued by the Treasury Department.

Redeemable in the form of War Savings Stamps or Treasury Savings Certificates.

Alexander Hamilton — TS1

FLAT PLATE PRINTING

1921   Unwmk.   Engr.   **Perf. 11**
Size of design: 33 1/2x33 1/2mm.

TS1	TS1	$1 red, green, *Dec. 21, 1920*	2,750.
		Block of four	11,500.
		Margin copy with P#	2,850.

Plate Nos.

73196	73198	73200	73202
73197	73199	73201	73203

ENCASED POSTAGE

In 1862 John Gault of Boston patented the idea of encasing postage stamps in metal frames behind a shield of transparent mica, and using them for advertising. The scarcity of small change during the Civil War made these encased stamps popular. Many firms impressed their names and products on the back of these stamp frames in embossed letters. Prices are for fine specimens with mica intact, although signs of circulation and handling are to be expected.

Values are for fine specimens. Grading encompasses three areas: 1. Case will show signs of wear or handling and signs of original toning. 2. Mica will be intact with no pieces missing. 3. Stamp will be fresh with no signs of toning or wrinkling.

Examples that came with silvered cases and still have some or all of the original silvering will sell for more than the values shown.

Aerated Bread Co., New York

1	1c	1,500.

Ayer's Cathartic Pills, Lowell, Mass.

Varieties with long and short arrows below legend occur on all denominations.

2	1c	185.00
3	3c	165.00
4	5c	275.00
5	10c	350.00
6	12c	700.00
7	24c	1,900.

Take Ayer's Pills

8	1c	175.00
9	3c	150.00
10	5c	225.00
	a. Ribbed frame	900.00
11	10c	300.00
12	12c	900.00

Ayer's Sarsaparilla

Three varieties: "AYER'S"; small, medium and large.

13	1c	medium "Ayer's"	200.00
	a.	Small	450.00
14	2c		—
15	3c	medium "Ayer's"	160.00
	a.	Small	350.00
	b.	Large	325.00
	c.	Ribbed frame, medium	650.00
16	5c	medium "Ayer's"	300.00
	a.	Large	600.00
17	10c	medium "Ayer's"	275.00
	a.	Ribbed frame, medium	850.00
	b.	Small	600.00
	c.	Large	475.00
18	12c	medium "Ayer's"	800.00
	a.	Small	1200.00
19	24c	medium "Ayer's"	1,500.
20	30c	medium "Ayer's"	1,750.

The authenticity of No. 14 is questioned.

Bailey & Co., Philadelphia

21	1c	650.00
22	3c	675.00
23	5c	700.00
24	10c	700.00
25	12c	1600.00

Joseph L. Bates, Boston

Two varieties: FANCY GOODS as one word or two.

26	1c	one word	225.00
	a.	Two words	275.00
27	3c	one word	450.00
	a.	Two words	500.00
28	5c	Two word	600.00
	a.	One words	750.00
	b.	Ribbed frame, one word	850.00
29	10c	Two word	400.00
	a.	One words	500.00
	b.	Ribbed frame, one word	900.00
30	12c	two words	900.00

Brown's Bronchial Troches

31	1c	700.00
32	3c	325.00
33	5c	300.00
34	10c	500.00
35	12c	850.00
36	24c	2,200.
37	30c	3,500.

F. Buhl & Co., Detroit

38	1c	800.00
39	3c	900.00
40	5c	850.00
41	10c	1,000.
42	12c	1,300.

| 43 | 24c | 2,500. |

Burnett's Cocoaine Kalliston

44	1c	275.00
45	3c	275.00
46	5c	375.00
47	10c	400.00
48	12c	950.00
49	24c	2,250.
50	30c	3,000.
51	90c	7,500.

Burnett's Cooking Extracts

52	1c	200.00
53	3c	200.00
54	5c	250.00
55	10c	275.00
	a. Ribbed frame	800.00
56	12c	850.00
57	24c	2,000.
58	30c	3,000.

A. M. Claflin, Hopkinton, Mass.

59	1c	6,000.
60	3c	3,750.
61	5c	5,000.
62	10c	4,500.
63	12c	5,500.

H. A. Cook, Evansville, Ind.

| 64 | 5c | 750.00 |
| 65 | 10c | 750.00 |

Dougan, Hatter, New York

66	1c	1,500.
67	3c	900.00
68	5c	1,000.
69	10c	1,750.

Drake's Plantation Bitters

70	1c	225.00
71	3c	200.00
72	5c	300.00
	a. Ribbed frame	750.00
73	10c	350.00
	a. Ribbed frame	850.00
74	12c	500.00
75	24c	2,000.
76	30c	3,000.
77	90c	8,500.

Ellis, McAlpin & Co., Cincinnati

78	1c	1,250.
79	3c	1,250.
80	5c	900.00
81	10c	900.00
82	12c	1,500.
83	24c	1,500.

C. G. Evans, Philadelphia

84	1c	550.00
85	3c	550.00
86	5c	1,000.
87	10c	1,000.

Gage Bros. & Drake, Tremont House, Chicago

88	1c	300.00
89	3c	375.00
90	5c	300.00
91	10c	400.00
	a. Ribbed frame	900.00
92	12c	1,250.

J. Gault

93	1c	275.00
	a. Ribbed frame	600.00
94	2c	8,500.
95	3c	150.00
	a. Ribbed frame	550.00
96	5c	200.00
	a. Ribbed frame	525.00
97	10c	300.00
	a. Ribbed frame	550.00
98	12c	675.00
	a. Ribbed frame	1,500.
99	24c	1,500.
	a. Ribbed frame	2,500.
100	30c	2,000.
	a. Ribbed frame	3,500.
101	90c	6,500.

L. C. Hopkins & Co., Cincinnati

102	1c	1,500.
103	3c	850.00
104	5c	1,100.
105	10c	1,500.

Hunt & Nash, Irving House, New York

106	1c	500.00
107	3c	400.00
	a. Ribbed frame	800.00
108	5c	400.00
	a. Ribbed frame	450.00
109	10c	425.00

	a. Ribbed frame	550.00
110	12c	900.00
	a. Ribbed frame	1,250.
111	24c	1,500.
	a. Ribbed frame	2,500.
112	30c	3,250.

Kirkpatrick & Gault, New York

113	1c	325.00
114	3c	375.00
115	5c	350.00
116	10c	325.00
117	12c	550.00
118	24c	1,500.
119	30c	2,250.
120	90c	6,000.

Lord & Taylor, New York

121	1c	650.00
122	3c	800.00
123	5c	800.00
124	10c	800.00
125	12c	1,250.
126	24c	2,250.
127	30c	3,000.
128	90c	8,500.

Mendum's Family Wine Emporium, New York

129	1c	450.00
130	3c	800.00
131	5c	600.00
132	10c	650.00
	a. Ribbed frame	1,250.
133	12c	1,000.

B. F. Miles, Peoria

134	1c	3,000.
135	5c	3,000.

John W. Norris, Chicago

136	1c	1,000.
137	3c	1,000.
138	5c	1,350.
139	10c	1,750.

No. America Life Insurance Co., N. Y.

Two varieties: "Insurance" in curved line or straight line.

140	1c curved	325.00
	a. Straight	350.00
141	3c curved	475.00
	a. Straight	400.00
142	5c straight	500.00
	a. Ribbed frame	950.00
143	10c straight	450.00
	a. Curved	600.00
	b. Curved, ribbed frame	1,400.
144	12c straight	1,200.

Pearce, Tolle & Holton, Cincinnati

145	1c	1,750.
146	3c	1,750.
147	5c	1,500.
148	10c	2,200.
149	12c	2,500.
150	24c	3,000.

Sands Ale

151	5c	1,700.
152	10c	2,000.
153	12c	2,300.
154	30c	4,250.

Schapker & Bussing, Evansville, Ind.

155	1c	550.00
156	3c	600.00
157	5c	550.00

158	10c	550.00
150	12c	1,250.

John Shillito & Co., Cincinnati

160	1c	600.00
161	3c	500.00
162	5c	500.00
163	10c	600.00
164	12c	1,750.

S. Steinfeld, New York

165	1c	1,250.
166	5c	1,350.
167	10c	1,600.
168	12c	2,500.

N. G. Taylor & Co., Philadelphia

169	1c	1,250.
170	3c	1,200.
171	5c	1,500.
172	10c	1,800.
173	12c	2,500.

Weir and Larminie, Montreal

174	1c	1,500.
175	3c	1,750.
176	5c	1,600.
177	10c	1,500.

White, the Hatter, New York

178	1c	1,500.
179	3c	1,400.
180	5c	1,400.
181	10c	2,000.

POSTAGE CURRENCY

Small coins disappeared from circulation in 1861-62 as cash was hoarded. To ease business transactions, merchants issued notes of credit, promises to pay, tokens, store cards, etc. U.S. Treasurer Francis E. Spinner made a substitute for small currency by affixing postage stamps, singly and in multiples, to Treasury paper. He arranged with the Post office to replace worn stamps with new when necessary.

The next step was to print the stamps on Treasury paper. On July 17, 1862, Congress authorized the issue of such "Postage Currency." It was not money, but a means of making stamps negotiable.

Postage Currency remained in use until 1876 when Congress authorized the minting of silver coins to redeem the outstanding fractional currency.

Prices quoted are for notes in crisp, new condition, not creased or worn.

Creased or worn copies sell for 25 to 75 per cent less.

August 21, 1862 to May 27, 1863

Front Engraved and Printed by the National Bank Note Co.

This series has on each note a facsimile of the postage stamp then current. In the 25c and 50c denominations the 5c and 10c stamps are engraved overlapping each other, five in a row, respectively.

Back Engraved and Printed by The American Bank Note Co.
"A B Co." on Back
Perforated Edges-Perf. 12

1	5c Bust of Jefferson on 5c stamp, brown	50.00
	a. Inverted back	200.00
2	10c Bust of Washington on 10c stamp, green	35.00
3	25c Five 5c stamps, brown	45.00
4	50c Five 10c stamps, green	50.00
	a. Perforated 14	100.00
	b. Inverted back	200.00

Imperforate Edges

5	5c Bust of Jefferson on 5c stamp	17.50
	a. Inverted back	200.00
6	10c Bust of Washington on 10c stamp	15.00
	a. Inverted back	200.00
7	25c Five 5c stamps	30.00
	a. Inverted back	200.00
8	50c Five 10c stamps	50.00

	a. Inverted back	200.00

Back Printed by the the National Bank Note Co.
Without "A B Co." on Back

Perforated Edges-Perf. 12

9	5c Bust of Jefferson on 5c stamp	50.00
	a. Inverted back	250.00
10	10c Bust of Washington on 10c stamp	50.00
	a. Inverted back	250.00
11	25c Five 5c stamps	100.00
	a. Inverted back	250.00
12	50c Five 10c stamps	120.00

	a.	Inverted back	250.00
15	25c	Five 5c stamps	120.00
16	50c	Five 10c stamps	135.00

a.	Inverted back	250.00

INTERNATIONAL REPLY COUPONS

Coupons produced by the Universal Postal Union for member countries to provide for payment of postage on a return letter from a foreign country. Exchangeable for a stamp representing single-rate ordinary postage to a foreign country under the terms of contract as printed on the face of the coupon in French and the language of the issuing country and on the reverse in four, five or six other languages.

Postmasters are instructed to apply a postmark indicating date of sale to the left circle on the coupon. When offered for exchange for stamps, the receiving postmaster is instructed to cancel the right circle.

The following is a list of all varieties issued by the Universal Postal Union for any or all member countries.

Type A- Face

Wmk. "25c Union Postale Universelle 25c".

1907-20

A1 Face   Name of country in letters 1½mm. high.
    Reverse   Printed rules between paragraphs German text contains four lines.

1907-20

A2 Face   Same as A1.
    Reverse   Same as A1 but without rules between paragraphs.

1910-20

A3 Face   Same as A1 and A2.
    Reverse   Same as A2 except German text has but three lines.

1912-20

A4 Face   Name of country in bold face type; letters 2 mm. to 2½ mm. high.
    Reverse   Same as A3.

1922-25

A5 Face   French words "le mois d'émission écoulé, deux mois encore".
    Reverse   As A3 and A4 but overprinted with new contract in red; last line of red German text has five words.

Wmk. "50c Union Postale Universelle 50c"

1925-26

A6 Face   Same as A5.
    Reverse   Four paragraphs of five lines each.

1926-29

A7 Face   French words "il est valable pendent un delai de six mois".
    Reverse   As A6 but overprinted with new contract in red; last line of red German text has two words.

Wmk. "40c Union Postale Universelle 40c"

1926-29

A8 Face   Design redrawn. Without lines in hemispheres.
    Reverse   Four paragraphs of four lines each.

Type B- Face

1931-35   **Wmk. Double-lined "UPU"**

B1 Face   French words "d'une lettre simple".
    Reverse   Four paragraphs of three lines each.

1935-36

B2 Face   French words "d'une lettre ordinaire de port simple".
    Reverse   Last line of German text contains two words.

1936-37

B3 Face   Same as B2.
    Reverse   Last line of German text contains one word.

1937-40

B4 Face   Same as B2 and B3. "Any Country of the Union."
    Reverse   German text is in German Gothic type.

1945

B5 Face   "Any Country of the Universal Postal Union."
    Reverse   Each paragraph reads "Universal Postal Union."

    Type B5 exists without central printing on face.

1950

B6 Face   Same as B5.
    Reverse   Five paragraphs (English, Arabic, Chinese, Spanish, Russian).

1954

B7 Face   Same as B5.
    Reverse   Six paragraphs (German, English, Arabic, Chinese, Spanish, Russian).

Type C- Face

1968   **Wmk. Single-lined "UPU" Multiple**

C1 Face   French words "d'une lettre ordinaire de port simple".
    Reverse   Six paragraphs (German, English, Arabic, Chinese, Spanish, Russian).

1971

C2 Face   French words "d'une lettre ordinaire du premier echelon de poids."
    Reverse   Six paragraphs (German, English, Arabic, Chinese, Spanish, Russian).

Foreign coupons, but not U.S., of type C1 are known with large double-lined "UPU" watermark, as on type B coupons.

Type D- Face

1975   **Wmk. Single-lined "UPU" Multiple**

D1 Face   French words "d'une lettre ordinaire, expediee a l'etranger par voie de surface."
    Reverse   Six paragraphs (German, English, Arabic, Chinese, Spanish, Russian).

REPLY COUPONS ISSUED FOR THE UNITED STATES

1907

1	A1	6c	slate green & gray green (2 line English paragraph on face. Rules between paragraphs on reverse.)	12.00
2	A2	6c	slate green & gray green (Rules omitted on reverse.)	6.00

1912

3	A4	6c	slate green & gray green (3 line English paragraph on face.)	6.00

1922

4	A5	11c	slate green & gray green, name 81½mm. long	6.00
	a.		Name 88½mm. long (5 line English paragraph on face. Red overprint on reverse.)	6.00

1925-26

5	A6	11c	slate green & gray green (5 line English paragraph on face. No overprint on reverse.)	6.00
6	A6	9c	slate green & gray green	6.00

1926

7	A7	9c	slate green & gray green (4 line English paragraph on face. Red overprint on reverse.)	6.00
8	A8	9c	slate green & gray green (Without lines in hemispheres.)	6.00

1935

9	B2	9c	blue & yellow (On reverse, last line of German text contains two words.)	2.00

1936

10	B3	9c	blue and yellow (On reverse, last line of German text contains one word.)	2.00

1937

11	B4	9c	blue & yellow (On reverse, German text in German Gothic type.)	2.00

1945

12	B5	9c	blue & yellow (On face, "Universal Postal Union" replaces "Union")	2.00

1948

13	B5	11c	blue & yellow (On face, "Universal Postal Union" replaces "Union")	2.00

1950

   14 B6 11c blue & yellow   2.00
          (On reverse, text in English, Arabic,
            Chinese, Spanish, Russian)

1954

   15 B7 13c blue & yellow   2.00
          (On reverse, text in German, English,
            Arabic, Chinese, Spanish, Russian.)
      No. 15 Surcharged in Various Manners.

1959

   16 B7 15c on 13c blue & yellow   2.00

   Individual post offices were instructed to surcharge the 13c coupon, resulting in many types of surcharge in various inks. For example, "REVALUED 15 CENTS," reading vertically; "15," etc.

1959

   17 B7 15c blue & yellow   2.00

1964

   18 B7 15c blue & yellow   2.00
          On face, box at lower left: "Empreinte
           de controle/du Pays d'origine/(date
           facultative)" replaces "Timbre
           du/Bureau/d'Emission"
      a. Reverse printing 60mm. deep instead of 2.00
          65mm. (smaller Arabic characters)

1969

   19 C1 15c blue & yellow   1.00

1971

   20 C2 22c blue & yellow   1.00
      No. 20 Surcharged in Various Manners

1974

   21 C2 26c on 22c blue & yellow   1.00
          See note after No. 16.

1975

   22 D1 26c blue & yellow   80
      No. 22 Surcharged in Various Manners

1976

   23 D1 42c on 26c blue & yellow   85
          See note after No. 16.

1976

   24 D1 42c blue & yellow   85

REGISTRATION

The Registry System for U.S. mail went into effect July 1, 1855, the fee being 5 cents. On June 30, 1863, the fee was increased to 20 cents. On Jan. 1, 1869, the fee was reduced to 15 cents and on Jan. 1, 1874, to 8 cents. On July 1, 1875, the fee was increased to 10 cents. On Jan. 1, 1893 the fee was again reduced to 8 cents and again it was increased to 10 cents on Nov. 1, 1909.

Early registered covers with various stamps, rates and postal markings are receiving the attention of collectors.

Registry stamps (10c ultramarine) were issued on Dec. 1, 1911, to prepay registry fees (not postage), but ordinary stamps were valid for registry fees then as now. These special stamps were abolished May 28, 1913, by order of the Postmaster General, who permitted their use until supplies on hand were exhausted.

Eagle — RS1

		ENGRAVED		
1911		**Wmk. 190**	***Perf. 12***	
F1	RS1	10c **ultramarine,** *Dec. 1, 1911*	75.00	4.50
		pale ultramarine	75.00	4.50
		On cover		40.00
		First day cover		8,000.
		Block of four	310.00	75.00
		block of 6, Impt., P# & "A"	1,850.	350.00

POST OFFICE SEALS

Official Seals begin to appear in 1872. They do not express any value, having no franking power.
The first seal issued was designed to prevent tampering with registered letters while in transit. It was intended to be affixed over the juncture of the flaps of the large official envelopes in which registered mail letters were enclosed and was so used exclusively. Beginning in 1877, official seals were used to repair damaged letters or to close those received by the Post Office unsealed.

POS1

National Bank Note Co.
Typographed from a steel plate

Two or more plates: 9 subjects (3x3), 30 subjects (3x10)

	1872	Unwmk.	White Wove Paper	Perf. 12	
OX1	POS1		green	17.50	5.00
			On cover		20.00
			Block of four	75.00	
a.			Yellow green, pelure paper	30.00	
b.			Printed on both sides	250.00	
c.			Double impression		—
d.			Imperf. pair	500.00	
e.			Horizontally laid paper		—

Special Printing
American Bank Note Co.
Plate of 30 subjects (5x6)

	1880 (?)		Soft Porous Paper	Perf. 12
OX2	POS1		bluish green	550.00

POS2

("Post Obitum" in background.)
National Bank Note Co.
Plate of 100 subjects (10x10)
Silk Paper

	1877		Engr.	Perf. 12.	
OX3	POS2		brown	25.00	12.50
			Block of four	200.00	
			On cover		250.00

No. OX3 was intended for use in the Dead Letter Office.

POS3

American Bank Note Co.
Engraved
Plate of 100 subjects (10x10) bearing imprint of
American Bank Note Co.

Also plates of 50 subjects with or without imprint

	1879			Perf. 12	
OX4	POS3		brown	50	25
a.			dark brown	3.00	5.00
b.			yellow brown	1.00	50
c.			red brown	50	25
			Block of four	5.00	
			On cover		60.00
			Margin block with imprint	20.00	

A so-called "special printing" exists in deep brown on hard white paper.

POS4

Typographed
Without words in lower label.
Outer frame line at top and left is thick and heavy.
Plate of 42 subjects (7x6)
Thin to Thick Paper

	1888			Imperf.	
OX6	POS4		light brown	75	
a.			yellow brown	75	—
b.			chocolate, thin paper	5.00	
			Block of four	3.00	
c.			Toned paper		—

No. 0X6 was not regularly used.

Thin to Thick Paper
Perf. 12

	OX7	POS4	bister brown	25	15
a.			light brown	25	15
b.			chocolate	25	15
c.			gray brown	25	15
d.			dark brown	25	15
e.			rose brown	25	15
			Block of four	2.00	
			On cover		20.00
f.			Imperf. vertically, pair	15.00	
g.			Imperf. horizontally, pair	15.00	
h.			Vertical pair, imperf. between	10.00	
i.			Double impression		—
j.			Toned paper		—

	1892			Rouletted 5½	
OX8	POS4		light brown	7.50	7.50
a.			brown	7.50	7.50
			Block of four	35.00	
			On cover		50.00

	1895 (?)			Hyphen Hole Perf. 7	
OX9	POS4		gray brown	2.75	2.25
			Block of four	15.00	
			On cover		35.00

POS5

Plate of 143 (11x13)

Outer frame line at top and left is thin. Otherwise similar to POS4.

	1900		Litho.	Perf. 12	
OX10	POS5		red brown	20	20
			Block of four, red brown	1.00	
			On cover, red brown		10.00
a.			gray brown	1.50	1.50
b.			yellow brown	80	80
c.			dark brown	90	85
d.			orange brown	60	60
e.			Imperf., (pair), red brown	1.50	
f.			Imperf. vertically (pair)	3.50	—

g.			Imperf. horizontally (pair)	5.00	
h.			Horiz. or vert. pair, imperf. btwn.	5.00	

Design similar to POS5 but smaller.
Issued in panes of 10 and 20

	1907		Typo.	Perf. 12	
OX11	POS5		blue	10	10
a.			dark blue	10	10
b.			violet blue	10	10
			Block of four	40	
			On cover		5.00
c.			Imperf., (pair)	1.00	—
d.			Imperf. horizontally (pair)	2.00	—
e.			Imperf. vertically (pair)	2.00	—
f.			Horiz. or vert. pair, imperf. between	5.00	
h.			Tête bêche pair, perf.		—
i.			Tête bêche pair, imperf.	20.00	
j.			Tête bêche pair, imperf. between	35.00	
k.			Double impression, imperf., (pair)	75.00	
l.			Double impression, tete beche pair	200.00	
m.			Wmkd. Seal of U.S. in sheet	1.35	1.35
n.			Wmkd. "Rolleston Mills" in sheet	1.35	1.35
p.			Vert. pair with horiz. gutter btwn.	20.00	

	1912			Rouletted 6½	
OX12	POS5		blue	75	75
			Block of four	3.25	
			On cover		15.00
a.			Wmkd. Seal of U.S. in sheet	2.00	1.50
b.			Wmkd. "Rolleston Mills" in sheet	2.00	1.50

	1913			12 x Rouletted 6½	
OX13	POS5		blue	2.00	2.00
			Block of four	12.00	
			On cover		15.00
a.			Rouletted 6½ x Perf. 12	4.00	4.00
			Block of four	17.50	
b.			Wmkd. Seal of U.S. in sheet	2.50	2.25
c.			As "a" and "b"	4.50	4.50

	1916			Perf. 12	
OX14	POS5		black, pink	50	75
			Block of four	2.00	
			On cover		15.00
a.			Imperf. horizontally, pair	2.50	

	1917			Perf. 12	
OX15	POS5		black	25	40
a.			gray black	25	40
			Block of four	1.00	
			On cover		15.00
b.			Imperf. horizontally, (pair)	5.00	
c.			Vertical pair, imperf. between	10.00	
d.			Horizontal pair, imperf. between	3.50	
e.			Imperf. vertically, (pair)	5.00	
f.			Wmkd. Seal of U.S. in sheet		—
g.			Imperf., pair	15.00	

POS6

Quartermaster General's Office
Issued in sheets of 10.

	1919			Perf. 12
OX16	POS6		indigo	100.00
			Block of four	410.00
				Rouletted 7
OX17	POS6		indigo	—

See the "Information for Collectors" section at beginning of catalogue for information on electric eye markings, luminescene and tagging.

POS7

Issued in panes of 10, 16 and 20

1919   *Perf. 8½, 9, 12, 12½ and Compound*

OX18	POS7	black	5	5
a.		gray black	5	5
		Block of four	25	
		On cover		2.50
b.		Imperf., pair	2.00	1.50
c.		Horiz. pair, imperf. vert.	1.00	
d.		Vert. pair, imperf. horiz.	1.00	
e.		Horiz. or vert. pair, imperf. btwn.	2.00	
g.		Wmkd. Seal of U.S. in sheet	1.00	1.00
h.		Wmkd. letters	3.00	

1949   *Hyphen Hole Perf. 9½x Imperf.*
Issued in vertical panes of 5
Design width: 37½mm.

OX19	POS7	black	20	20
		Pane of 5	1.25	
		On cover		1.50
a.		Vert. pair, imperf. between	2.00	
b.		Imperf., pane of 5	5.00	

Tab inscribed, "16-56164-1 GPO"

Design width: 38½mm.
Issued in vertical panes of 5

1970 (?)   *Hyphen Hole Perf. 9½ x Imperf.*

OX19C	POS7	black	20	20
		Pane of 5	1.75	
		On cover		3.00
d.		Vert. pair, imperf. btwn	4.00	
e.		Imperf., pane of 5	7.50	

Tab inscribed, "c43-16-56164-1 GPO"

POS8

Rouletted 6½, 8½ or 9½ x Imperf., Hyphen Hole Perf. 7 x Imperf. Perf. 12½ x Imperf.

1972   **Issued in vertical panes of 5**   Litho.

OX20	POS8	black	20	20
		Pane of 5	1.25	
		On cover		2.00
a.		Imperf., pair	2.00	

Tab inscribed, "LABEL 21, JULY 1971"

TYPESET SEALS.

Little is known of the history and origin, but it is believed that they were privately made for sale to postmasters. Many are extremely rare. Unquestioned varieties are listed.

"U. S. POST OFFICE DEPARTMENT" in capital letters

TSS1

Imperf.

OX25	TSS1	black		135.00 135.00

TSS1a

Imperf.

OX25A	TSS1a	black	175.00	—
		"OFFICALLY"		

TSS2

Imperf.

OX26	TSS2	black		—

"U.S. Post Office Department" with initial capitals

TSS3

Imperf.

OX27	TSS3	black, *pink*		—

TSS4

Imperf.

OX28	TSS4	black		135.00

TSS4a

Imperf.

OX28A	TSS4a	black	

Form D.
U. S. Post Office Department
OFFICIALLY SEALED.
Opened through mistake by

TSS5

Rouletted 9½ horizontally

OX29	TSS5	black		175.00

TSS6

Printed in panes of 4, two tete beche pairs
Rouletted 11½, 12½, 16½ in black at top & side

OX30	TSS6	black	35.00	35.00
		Tete beche pair	70.00	
		Sheet of four	150.00	

TSS7

Solid lines above and below "OFFICIALLY SEALED"
Printed in panes of four, two tete beche pairs.

Rouletted 12½, 16½ in black between

OX31	TSS7	black	125.00	150.00
		Tete beche pair	—	
		Sheet of four		

TSS8

Dotted lines above and below "OFFICIALLY SEALED"
Printed in panes of four.

Rouletted, 11½, 12½ or 16½ in black

OX32	TSS8	black, *pink*	175.00	
OX33	TSS8	black	75	
a.		Tete beche pair	1.50	
b.		Tete beche sheet of four	3.00	
c.		Period after "OFFICIALLY"	1.00	
d.		As "c" in pair	2.00	
e.		As "c" in tete beche pair	2.50	
f.		Tete beche sheet of four, one stamp with period	5.00	
g.		As "c", printed in blue		—

"U. S. Postoffice Dept."

U. S. Postoffice Dept.

OFFICIALLY SEALED

Opened through mistake by

TSS9

Imperf.

OX34   TSS9   **black or blue**   135.00

U. S. Postoffice Dept.

OFFICIALLY SEALED

Opened through mistake by

TSS10

Imperf.

OX35   TSS10   **blue**   —   —

𝔘. 𝔖. 𝔓ostoffice 𝔇ept.

OFFICIALLY SEALED

Opened through mistake by

TSS11

Imperf.

OX36   TSS11   **black**   —   —
              blue

"United States Post Office"

𝔘nited 𝔖tates 𝔓ost 𝔒ffice.

OFFICIALLY SEALED.

Opened by Mistake by

TSS12

Imperf.

OX37   TSS12   **blue**   —   —

𝔘. 𝔖. 𝔓ostoffice.

Officially Sealed.

Opened by Mistake by

TSS13

Imperf.

OX38   TSS13   **dark blue**   40.00   40.00

           On cover   —
a.   Printed on both sides   325.00
b.   2mm. btwn. "y" & "S", no period
         after "d"   85.00
OX39   TSS13   **black**   100.00   —

OFFICIALLY SEALED
BY
Birmingham, Ala., Post Office

TSS14

Imperf.

OX40   TSS14   **black,** *light green*   —   —

U. S. Postoffice

PETALUMA, CAL.

Officially Sealed

Opened by Mistake by

TSS15

Imperf.

OX41   TSS15   **black,** *blue*   —   —

U. S. POST OFFICE,

NORTHFIELD, MASS.

OFFICIALLY SEALED.

OPENED THROUGH MISTAKE BY

TSS16

Imperf.

OX42   TSS16   **black**   —   —

U. S. Post Office,

NORTHFIELD, MASS.

OFFICIALLY SEALED.

OPENED BY MISTAKE BY

Rec'd open

TSS17

Imperf.

OX43   TSS17   **black**   —   —

U. S. Post Office Department.

Ipswich, Mass.

OFFICIALLY SEALED.

Opened through mistake by

TSS18

Imperf.

OX44   TSS18   **black**   —   —

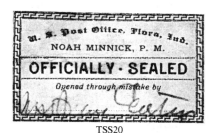

POST OFFICE DEPARTMENT

Officially Sealed

Berkeley, Cal.

TSS19

Imperf.

OX45   TSS19   **black**   —
a.   Top line 4mm. high   —   *275.00*

𝔘. 𝔖. 𝔓ost 𝔒ffice, 𝔉lora, 𝔍nd.

NOAH MINNICK, P. M.

OFFICIALLY · SEALED

Opened through mistake by

TSS20

Imperf.

OX46   TSS20   **black**   —

U. S. POST OFFICE, BERWICK, PA.

Opened through mistake, *Aug 18* by

D. C. McHenry

OFFICIALLY SEALED

TSS21

Imperf.

OX47   TSS21   **black,** *dark brown red*   —

The first price column gives the catalogue value
of an unused stamp, the second that of a used
stamp.

CHRISTMAS SEALS

Issued by the American National Red Cross (1907-1919), the National Tuberculosis Association (1920-1967), the National Tuberculosis and Respiratory Disease Association (1968-1972) and the American Lung Association (1973-).

While the Christmas Seal is not a postage stamp, it has long been associated with the postal service because of its use on letters and packages.

Einar Holboell, an employee of the Danish Post Office, created the Christmas Seal. He believed that seal sales could raise money for charity. The post offices of Denmark, Iceland and Sweden began to sell such seals in the 1904 Christmas season. In the United States, Christmas Seals were first issued in 1907 under the guidance of Emily P. Bissell, following the suggestion of Jacob Riis, social service worker.

Until 1975, all seals (except those of 1907 and 1908 type I) were issued in sheets of 100. The grilled gum (1908) has small square depressions like a waffle. The broken gum (1922), devised to prevent paper curling, consists of depressed lines in the gum, ½mm. apart, forming squares. The vertical and horizontal broken gum (1922, 1923, 1925, 1927-1932) forms diamonds. The perf. 12.00 (1917-1919, 1923, 1925, 1931) has two larger and wider-spaced holes between every 11 smaller holes.

Prices are for seals with original gum.

SEALS ISSUED AND SOLD BY THE DELAWARE CHAPTER OF THE AMERICAN NATIONAL RED CROSS

CS1 (Type II)

Both types designed by Miss Emily P. Bissell.
Nearly $4,000.00 worth of seals were sold, $3,000.00 cleared.

1907   *Perf. 14*

Red

WX1	CS1	Type I. Inscribed "Merry Christmas" only	15.00
WX2	CS1	Type II. Inscribed "Merry Christmas" and "Happy New Year"	12.00

Types I and II. Lithographed by Theo. Leonhardt & Son, Philadelphia, Pa. The first seals were sold December 7, 1907, in Wilmington, Del. Both types were issued in sheets of 228 seals, 19 horizontal by 12 vertical. Type II was issued to extend the sale of seals until New Year's Day, 1908. Counterfeits of both types exist (perf. 12).

SEALS ISSUED AND SOLD BY THE AMERICAN NATIONAL RED CROSS

CS2 (Type II)

Designed by Howard Pyle.
Realized from sales $135,000.00.

1908   *Perf. 12, 14*

Red and Green

WX3	CS2	Type I. Frame lines with square corners. Small "C" in "Christmas." Perf. 14 Smooth gum	35.00
	a.	Perf. 12 Smooth gum	35.00
	c.	Perf. 14 Grilled gum	35.00
	d.	Perf. 12 Grilled gum	35.00
	e.	Perf. 14 Booklet pane of six. Smooth gum	300.00
	f.	Perf. 14 Booklet pane of six. Grilled gum	300.00
	g.	Perf. 14 Booklet pane of three. Smooth gum	300.00
WX4	CS2	Type II. Perf. 12 Frame lines have rounded corners. Large "C" in "Christmas", and leaves veined	35.00
	a.	Booklet pane of six	150.00
	b.	Booklet pane of three	150.00

Type I. Lithographed by Theo. Leonhardt & Son. Sheets of 250 seals, 14 horizontal by 18 vertical, with the first space in the ninth and eighteenth rows left blank.

Type II. Lithographed by the American Bank Note Co., New York, N. Y. in sheets of 100 seals, 10 horizontal by 10 vertical.

Booklet panes have straight edges on three sides and perforated on left side where there is a stub, except No. WX4b which is a vertical strip of three with stub at top. The panes of six were made up in books of 24 and 48 seals and sold for 25c and 50c, and panes of three in books of 9 seals and sold for 10c. The grilled gum has small square depressions like on a waffle.

CS3

Designed by Carl Wingate.
Realized from sales $250,000.00.

1909   *Perf. 12*

Red and Green

WX5	CS3	One type only	50

Lithographed by The Strobridge Lithographing Company, Cincinnati, Ohio. Seals with a round punched hole of 3½mm. are printers' samples.

CS4

Designed by Mrs. Guion Thompson.
Realized from sales $300,000.00.

1910   *Perf. 12*

Red and Green

WX6	CS4	One type only	8.00

Lithogrpahed by The Strobridge Lithographing Co.

SEALS ISSUED BY THE AMERICAN NATIONAL RED CROSS BUT SOLD BY THE NATIONAL ASSOCIATION FOR THE STUDY AND PREVENTION OF TUBERCULOSIS.

"The Old Home Among the Cedars" — CS5 (Type II)

Designed by Anton Rudert under directions of F. D. Millet.
Realized from sales $320,000.00.

1911   *Perf. 12*

Red and Green

WX7	CS5	Type I. Diameter of circle 22mm. Solid end in house	45.00
WX8	CS5	Type II. Same circle but thinner. Lined end to house	55.00

COIL STAMP

Perf. 8½ Vertically

WX9	CS5	Type III. Diameter of circle 20mm. Lined end to house	75.00

All three types were typographed by Eureka Specialty Printing Co. Scranton, Pa. Type I has name and address of printer and union label in red in top margin. Type II has union label only in green on left margin.

CS6

Designed by John H. Zeh.
Realized from sales $402,256.00.

1912   *Perf. 12*

Red, Green & Black

WX10	CS6	One type only	8.00

Lithographed by The Strobridge Lithographing Co.

CS7 (Type I)

Designed by C. J. Budd.
Realized from sales $449,505.00.

1913   *Perf. 12*

Red and Green

WX11	CS7	Type I. With Poinsettia flowers and green circles around red crosses at either side	600.00
WX12	CS7	Type II. The Poinsettia flowers have been removed	6.00
WX13	CS7	Type III. The Poinsettia flowers and green circles have been removed	6.50

Lithograped by American Bank Note Co.

CS8

Designed by Benjamin S. Nash.
Realized from sales $555,854.00.

1914　　　　　　　　　　　　　　　*Perf. 12*

Red, Green & Black

WX15	CS8	One type only	8.50

Lithogrpahed by The Strobridge Lithographing Co.

CS9

Designed by Benjamin S. Nash.
Realized from sales $760,000.00.

1915

Red, Green & Black

WX16	CS9	One type only. Perf. 12½	5.50
	a.	Perf. 12	65.00

Lithographed by Andrew B. Graham Co., Washington, D.C.

CS10

Designed by T. M. Cleland.
Realized from sales $1,040,810.00.

1916

Red and Green

WX18	CS10	One type only. Perf. 12	2.50
	a.	Perf. 12x12½	2.50
	b.	Perf. 12½x12	7.50
	c.	Perf. 12½	7.50

Lithographed by the Strobridge Lithographing Co.

Seals of 1917-21 are on coated paper.

CS11

Designed by T. M. Cleland.
Realized from sales $1,815,110.00.

1917

Red and Green

WX19	CS11	One type only, perf. 12	30
	a.	Perf. 12½	7.50
	b.	Perf. 12x12.00	35
	c.	Perf. 12x12½	15.00

Typographed by Eureka Specialty Printing Co. The Perf. 12 has two larger and wider spaced holes between every eleven smaller holes. Sheets come with straight edged margins on all

four sides also with perforated margins at either right or left. Perforated margins have the union label imprint in green.

SEALS ISSUED BY THE AMERICAN NATIONAL RED CROSS AND DISTRIBUTED BY THE NATIONAL TUBERCULOSIS ASSOCIATION

CS12

Designed by Charles A. Winter.
These seals were issued but not sold. They were given to members and others in lots of 10, the National Tuberculosis Association being subsidized by a gift of $2,500,000 from the American National Red Cross.

1918

Red, Green and Brown

WX21	CS12	Type I. "American Red Cross" 15 mm. long. Heavy circles between date. Perf. 11½x12.00	5.00
	a.	Perf. 12	5.00
	b.	Perf. 12.00 Booklet pane of ten	2.00
	c.	Perf. 12x12.00 Booklet pane of ten	2.00
	d.	Perf. 12 Booklet pane of ten	2.00
	e.	Perf. 12.00x12 Booklet pane of ten	50.00
WX22	CS12	Type II. "American Red Cross" 15½ mm. long. Periods between date. Booklet pane of ten. Perf. 12½xRoulette 9½	2.00
	a.	Perf. 12½ Booklet pane of ten	2.00
	b.	Perf. 12½x12 Booklet pane of ten	—
	d.	Roulette 9½xPerf. 12½ Booklet pane of ten	—
	e.	Perf. 12½xRoulette 9½ Booklet pane of ten	12.50
	f.	Perf. 12½ Booklet pane of ten	12.50
	h.	Roulette 9½xPerf. 12½ Booklet pane of ten	12.50
	i.	Roulette 9½xPerf. 12½ and Roulette 12½ Booklet pane of ten	—
	j.	Perf. 12½x12½ Booklet pane of ten	60.00
	k.	Perf. 12½x12½ and 12 Booklet pane of ten	—
	l.	Roulette 9½xPerf. 12½ Booklet pane of ten	—
	m.	Perf. 12½ Booklet pane of ten	—
	n.	Perf. 12½, stub at bottom Booklet pane of ten	60.00

Type I. Typographed by Eureka Specialty Printing Co.

Type II. Lithographed by Strobridge Lithographing Co.

Nos. WX21-WX21a are from sheet of 100, no straight edges.

Type I. Booklet panes are of 10 seals, 2 horizontal by 5 vertical and normally have straight edges on all four sides. They were cut from the sheets of 100 and can be plated by certain flaws which occur on both. Sheets have union label imprint on top margin in brown.

Type II. Booklet panes are the same but normally have a perforated margin at top and stub attached. These too can be plated by flaws. One or both vertical sides are rouletted on Number WX22e; perforated on Numbers WX22f and WX22h. Number WX22i is rouletted 12½ on left perforated 12½ on right. Numbers WX22j, WX22k and WX22l are booklet panes of 10 seals arranged 5x2. Number WX22m has a perforated margin at left.

The seal with "American Red Cross" 17¼ mm. long is believed to be an essay.

CS13 (Type II)

Designed by Ernest Hamlin Baker.
Realized from sales $3,872,534.00.

1919

Ultramarine, Red and Green

WX24	CS13	Type I. Plume at right side of Santa's cap. Perf. 12	20
	a.	Perf. 12x12.00	25
	b.	Perf. 12½x12	20
	c.	Perf. 12½x12.00	2.00

WX25	CS13	Type II. No plume but a white dot in center of band on Santa's cap. Perf. 12½	25

This is the first time the double barred cross, the emblem of the National Tuberculosis Association, appeared in the design of the seals. It is also the last time the red cross emblem of the American National Red Cross was used on seals.

Type I. Typographed by Eureka Specialty Printing Co., and has union label on margin at left in dark blue.

Type II lithographed by The Strobridge Lithographing Co.

SEALS ISSUED AND SOLD BY THE NATIONAL TUBERCULOSIS ASSOCIATION

CS14

Designed by Ernest Hamlin Baker.
Realized from sales $3,667,834.00.

1920

Ultramarine, Red and Green

WX26	CS14	Type I. Size of seal 18x22 mm. Perf. 12x12½	35
	a.	Perf. 12	35
	b.	Perf. 12½x12	7.50
	c.	Perf. 12½x12½	5.00
WX27	CS14	Type II. Size of seal 18½x23½ mm. Letters larger and numerals heavier than Type I. Perf. 12½	30

Type I typographed by Eureka Speciality Printing Co., and has union label imprint and rings on margin at left in dark blue. Type II lithographed and offset printing by The Strobridge Lithographing Co.

CS15

Designed by George V. Curtis.
Realized from sales $3,520,303.00

1921

Ultramarine, Red and Green

WX28	CS15	Type I. The dots in the shading of the chimney and faces are arranged in diagonal lines. The dots on chimney are separate except between the two top rows of bricks where they are a solid mass. Perf. 12½	35
WX29	CS15	Type II. The dots in the shading of the chimney and faces are arranged in horizontal lines. Perf. 12½	35
WX29A	CS15	Type III. The same as Type I except the red dots on chimney are mostly joined and form lines. The dots between the two top rows of bricks are not a solid mass. Perf. 12	35

Type I typographed by Eureka Specialty Printing Co. Type II offset printing by The Strobridge Lithographing Co. Type III typographed by Zeese-Wilkinson Company Inc., Long Island City, N.Y.

CS16

Designed by T. M. Cleland.
Realized from sales $3,857,086.00.

1922

Pale Ultramarine, Red and Yellow

WX30	CS16 One type only. Perf. 12½, broken gum	50
	a. Perf. 12, broken gum	2.00
	b. Perf. 12x12½, broken gum	5.00
	c. Perf. 12, smooth gum	2.00
	d. Perf. 12½, vertical broken gum	5.00

Typographed by Eureka Specialty Printing Co.

The broken gum on this issue, which was devised to prevent curling of paper, consists of depressed lines in the gum ½ mm. apart, forming squares, or vertical broken gum forming diamonds.

CS17

Designed by Rudolph Ruzicka.
Realized from sales $4,259,660.00.

1923

Green and Red

WX31	CS17 One type only. Perf. 12½. Vertical broken gum	20
	a. Perf. 12 Horizontal broken gum	2.50
	b. Perf. 12x12.00 Vertical broken gum	2.50
	c. Perf. 12½x12 Vertical broken gum	5.00
	d. Perf. 12 Vertical broken gum	1.00
	e. Perf. 12.00x12 Vertical broken gum	2.50

Typographed by Eureka Specialty Printing Co.

The broken gum on this and issues following printed by the Eureka Co. consists of very fine depressed lines forming diamonds. The brown color in seals is due to the overlapping of the two colors.

CS18

Designed by George V. Curtis.
Realized from sales $4,479,656.00.

1924

Red, Ultramarine and Yellow

| WX32 | CS18 One type only | 10 |

Offset printing by The Strobridge Lithographing Co., Edwards & Deutsch Lithographing Co., Chicago, Ill., and The United States Printing & Lithograph Co., Brooklyn, N.Y.

CS19 (Type II)

Designed by Robert G. Eberhard.
Realized from sales $4,937,786.00.

1925

Green, Red and Pale Green

WX35	CS19 Type I. Red lines at each side of "1925" do not join red tablet below. Perf. 12½ Vertical broken gum	10
	a. Perf. 12x12, vertical broken gum	2.50
	b. Perf. 12x12½ vertical broken gum	35
	c. Perf. 12.00x12½ vertical broken gum	—
WX36	CS19 Type II. Red lines, as in Type I, join red tablet below. Perf. 12½	10
WX37	CS19 Same as Type I but shorter rays around flames and "ea" of "Health" smaller. Perf. 12½	50

Type I typographed by Eureka Specialty Printing Co. Type II offset printing by Edwards & Deutsch Lithographing Co.

Type III lithographed by Gugler Lithographing Co., Milwaukee, Wis.

CS20

Designed by George V. Curtis.
Realized from sales $5,121,872.00.

1926   *Perf. 12½*

Black, Red, Blue and Yellow

| WX38 | CS20 One type only | 10 |

Offset printing by Edwards & Deutsch Lithographing Co., and The United States Printing & Lithograph Co.

Printers' marks on sheets: E.& D. has a red dot at upper right on seal No. 91 on some sheets. U.S.P.&L. has a black dot at upper left on seal No. 56 on some sheets.

CS21

Designed by John W. Evans.
Realized from sales $5,419,959.00.

1927

Red, Ultramarine, Green and Black

WX39	CS21 One type only. Perf. 12. Horizontal broken gum	10
	a. Perf. 12. Smooth gum. (See also No. WX43)	1.00
WX40	CS21 Perf. 12½. No dot as on No. WX41	10
WX41	CS21 Perf. 12½. This seal has one larger red dot in background 1mm. above right post of dashboard on sleigh	10
WX42	CS21 "Bonne Sante" added to design under reindeer and sleigh. For French Canadians. Perf. 12	50
WX43	CS21 Same as WX39a but body of sleigh a myrtle green instead of green. For English Canadians. Perf. 12	50

All seals of 1927 are offset printing. Nos. WX39 and WX39a by Eureka Specialty Printing Co. No. WX40 by Edwards & Deutsch Lithographing Co. No. WX41 by The United States Printing & Lithograph Co. Nos. WX42 and WX43 by Canadian Bank Note Co., Ottawa, Ont. Canada.

Printer's marks on sheets: Eureka has no mark but can be identified by the Perf. 12. E.&D. has red dot to left of knee of first reindeer on seal No. 92. U.S.P.&Lithograph Co. has two red dots in white gutter, one at lower left of seal No. 46 (and sometimes No. 41) and the other at upper right of seal No. 55. The perforations often strike out one of these dots.

The Gallant Ship
"Argosy" — CS22

Designed by John W. Evans.
Realized from sales $5,465,738.00.

1928   *Perf. 12½.*

Black, Blue, Red, Orange and Green

WX44	CS22 Type I. Shading on sails broken. Dots in flag regular. Vertical broken gum	10
WX45	CS22 Type II. Shading on sails broken. Dots in flag spotty	10
WX46	CS22 Type III. Shading on sails unbroken. Dots in flag regular	10
WX47	CS22 Type IV. Inscribed "Bonne Annee 1929" For French Canadians	35

| WX48 | CS22 Type V. Same as Type II but green in water, and black lines of ship heavier and deeper color. For English Canadians | 35 |

All seals of 1928 are offset printing. Type I by Eureka Specialty Printing Co., Type II by The Strobridge Lithographing Co., Type III by Edwards & Deutsch Lithographing Co., and Types IV and V by The Copp Clark Co., Ltd., Toronto, Ont., Canada.
Printers' mark on sheets: Type I comes with and without a blue dash above seal No. 10, also with a blue and a black dash. Type II has two blue dashes below seal No. 100. Type III has red dot in crest of first wave on seal No. 92.

CS23

Designed by George V. Curtis.
Realized from sales $5,546,147.00.

1929

Blue, Red, Yellow and Black

WX49	CS23 One type only. Perf. 12½. Vertical broken gum	10
	a. Perf. 12. Vertical broken gum	50
	b. Perf. 12½x12. Vertical broken gum	75
WX50	CS23 Perf. 12½. Smooth gum	10
WX53	CS23 Inscribed "Bonne Sante 1929" for French Canadians. Perf. 12½	35
	a. Perf. 14x12½	—
WX54	CS23 Inscribed "Christmas Greetings 1929" for English Canadians. Perf. 12½	35

All seals of 1929 are offset printing. Nos. WX49 to WX49b by Eureka Specialty Printing Co. No. WX50 by Edwards & Deutsch Lithographing Co., The United States Printing and Lithograph Co., and R.R. Heywood Co., Inc., New York, N.Y. Nos. WX53 and WX54 by the Copp Clark Co., Ltd.

Printers' marks on sheets: Eureka is without mark but identified by broken gum. E.&D. has a black dot in lower left corner of seal No. 92. U.S.P.&L. Co. has blue dot above bell on seal No. 56. Heywood has a blue dot at lower right corner of seal No. 100.

CS24

Designed by Ernest Hamlin Baker, and redrawn by John W. Evans.
Realized from sales $5,309,352.00.

1930

Green, Red, Gray and Black

WX55	CS24 One type only. Perf. 12½. Vertical broken gum	10
	a. Perf. 12. Vertical broken gum	50
	b. Perf. 12.00x12. Vertical broken gum	25
	c. Perf. 12½x12. Vertical broken gum	2.50
	d. Perf. 12. Bklt. pane of 10, horiz. broken gum	50
WX56	CS24 Perf. 12½. Smooth gum	10
WX59	CS24 Inscribed "Bonne Sante," on red border of seal, for French Canadians. Perf. 12½	50
WX60	CS24 Inscribed "Merry Christmas," on red border of seal for English Canadians. Perf. 12½	25

All seals of 1930 are offset printing. Nos. WX55 to WX55d by Eureka Specialty Printing Co. No. WX56 by The Strobridge Lithographing Co. and Edwards & Deutsch Lithographing Co. and by The United States Printing & Lithograph Co. Nos. WX59 and WX60 by the Copp Clark Co., Ltd.

Printers' marks on sheets: Eureka has a dot between the left foot and middle of "M" of "Merry" on seal No. 1. Strobridge has two dashes below "ALL" on seal No. 100. E.&D. printed on Nashua paper has dot on coat just under elbow on seal No. 92, and on Gummed Products Co. paper has the dot on seals Nos. 91 and 92. U.S.P.& Litho. Co. has a dash which joins ree to top frame line just under "MA" of "Christmas" on seal No. 55.

The plate for booklet panes was made up from the left half of the regular plate and can be plated by certain flaws which occur on both.

CS25

Designed by John W. Evans.
Realized from sales $4,526,189.00.

1931

Green, Black, Red and Cream

WX61	CS25 One type only. Perf. 12½.	50
	Horizontal broken gum (see footnote)	
WX62	CS25 Perf. 12½. Horizontal broken gum	5
a.	Perf. 12x12½. Horizontal broken gum	35
b.	Perf. 12.00x12½. Horizontal broken gum	2.50
c.	Perf. 12 Horizontal broken gum	1.00
g.	Perf. 12. Vertical broken gum. Booklet pane of 10 seals	50
h.	Perf. 12x12.00. Vertical broken gum. Booklet pane of 10 seals	50
WX63	CS25 Perf. 12½. Smooth gum	5

All seals of 1931 are offset printing. Nos. WX61 to WX62h by Eureka Specialty Printing Co. No. WX63 by the Strobridge Lithographing Co. No. WX61 has a green dash across inner green frame line at bottom center on each seal in sheet except those in first and last vertical rows and the two rows at bottom. This dash is omitted on all other numbers.

Printers' marks on sheets: Eureka has none. Strobridge has the usual two dashes under seal No. 100.

The plate for booklet panes was made up from transfers of sixty seals-twelve horizontal by five vertical. The six panes of the transfer can be plated by minor flaws.

CS26

Designed by Edward F. Volkmann.
Realized from sales $3,470,637.00.

1932

Red, Ultramarine, Blue, Green and Yellow

WX64	CS26 One type only. Perf. 12½x12¾.	5
a.	Perf. 12½x12¾. Vertical broken gum	40
WX65	CS26 Perf. 12	5
WX66	CS26 Perf. 12½	5
WX67	CS26 Perf. 12½	5

All seals of 1932 are offset printing. No. WX64 by Eureka Specialty Printing Co. No. WX65 by Edwards & Deutsch Lithographing Co. No. WX66 by The United States Printing & Lithograph Co. No. WX67 by Columbian Bank Note Co., Chicago, Ill. Nos. WX64, WX66 and WX67 have a little red spur on bottom inner frame line of each seal, at left corner. Nos. WW65 and WX66 come without the spur.

Printers' marks on sheets: Eureka has a red dash, in each corner of the sheet, which joins the red border to the red inner frame line. E.&D. has a blue dot at lower left on seal No. 91. U.S.P.& L. Co. has a blue dot on top of post on seal No. 56. Columbian Bank Note Co. has small "C" in lower part of girl's coat on seal No. 82.

CS27

Designed by Hans Axel Walleen.
Realized from sales $3,429,311.00.

1933

Red, Black, Green and Yellow

WX68	CS27 One type only. Perf. 12	5
WX69	CS27 Perf. 12½	5

All seals of 1933 are offset printing. No. WX68 by Eureka Specialty Printing Co. No. WX69 by The Strobridge Lithographing Co., The United States Printing & Lithograph Co., and the Columbian Bank Note Co.

Printers' marks on sheets; Eureka has rope joining elbow of figure to left on seals Nos. 11, 20, 91 and 100. Strobridge has the usual two dashes under seal No. 100. U.S.P.&L. Co. has green dot on tail of "s" of "Greetings" on seal No. 55. Columbian has white "c" on margin, under cross, on seal No. 93.

CS28

Designed by Herman D. Giesen.
Realized from sales $3,701,344.00.

1934

Carmine, Ultramarine, Green, Blue and Yellow

WX72	CS28 One type only. Perf. 12½x12¼	5
WX73	CS28 Perf. 12½. (see footnote)	5
WX74	CS28 Perf. 12½. (see footnote)	5
WX75	CS28 Perf. 12½. (see footnote)	5

All seals of 1934 are offset printing. No. WX72 by Eureka Specialty Printing Co., No. WX73 by The Strobridge Lithographing Co., No. WX74 by Edwards & Deutsch Lithographing Co. and No. WX75 by The United States Printing & Lithograph Co.

Cutting of blue plate for the under color: Nos. WX72, WX73 (early printing) and WX74 have lettering and date cut slightly larger than ultramarine color. No. WX73 (later printing) has square cutting around letters and date, like top part of letter "T". No. WX75 has cutting around letters and date cut slightly larger.

Printers' marks on sheets. Eureka has five stars to right of cross on seal No. 10. Strobridge has two blue dashes in lower left corner of seal No. 91 or same dashes in lower right corner of seal No. 100. E.&D. has a red dot in lower left corner of seal No. 99. U.S.P.& L. Co. has five stars to left of cross on seal No. 56.

Great Britain issued seals of this design which can be distinguished by the thinner and whiter paper. Sheets have perforated margins on all four sides but without any lettering on bottom margin. The perforation is 12½.

CS29

Designed by Ernest Hamlin Baker.
Realized from sales $3,946,498.00.

1935

Blue, Carmine, Red Brown and Green

WX76	CS29 One type only. Perf. 12½x12¼	5
WX77	CS29 Perf. 12½	5

All seals of 1935 are offset printing. No. WX76 by Eureka Specialty Printing Co., No. WX77 by The Strobridge Lithographing Co., The United States Printing & Lithograph Co. and Columbian Bank Note Co.
Eureka recut their blue plate and eliminated the faint blue shading around cross, girl's head and at both sides of the upper part of post. U.S.P.&L. Co. eliminated the two brown spurs which pointed to the base of cross, in all four corners of the sheet.
Printers' marks on sheets: Eureka has an extra vertical line of shading on girl's skirt on seal No. 60. Strobridge has two brown dashes in lower right corner of position No. 100 but sheets from an early printing are without this mark. U.S.P.&L. Co. has a blue dot under post on seal No. 55. Columbian has a blue "c" under post on seal No. 99.

The four corner seals in each sheet carry slogans: Seal 1, "Help Fight Tuberculosis." Seal 10, "Protect Your Home from Tuberculosis." Seal 91, "Tuberculosis Is Preventable." Seal 100, "Tuberculosis Is Curable."

Printers' marks appear on seal 56 on sheets of 100 unless otherwise noted:
E Eureka Specialty Printing Co.
S Strobridge Lithographing Co. (1930-1958).
S Specialty Printers of America (1975-).
D Edwards & Deutsch Lithographing Co.
U United States Printing & Lithographing Co.
F Fleming-Potter Co., Inc.
W Western Lithograph Co.
B Berlin Lithographing Co. (1956-1969); I. S. Berlin Press (1970-1976); Barton-Cotton (1977-).
R Bradford-Robinson Printing Co.
N Sale-Niagara, Inc.
Printers of Canadian seals, unmarked:
Arthurs-Jones Lithographing, Toronto (1943-1949).
Rolph, Clarke and Stone, Toronto (1950-1955).
Seals from 1936 onward are printed by offset.
Seals with tropical gum (dull), starting in 1966, were used in Puerto Rico.

CS30

Designed by Walter I. Sasse.
Realized from sales $4,522,269.00.

1936

Gray, Red, Green and Yellow
Pair

WX80	CS30 Perf. 12½x12, red & grn. backgrounds (E)	5
WX81	CS30 Perf. 12½, red & grn. backgrounds (S,D,U)	5

Seals with red background and green cap-band alternate with seals showing green background and red cap-band. The four corner seals, positions 1, 10, 91 and 100, carry the same slogans as those of 1935.

Two of the three Strobridge printings show vertical green dashes in margin below seal 100, besides "S" on seal 56.

CS31

Designed by A. Robert Nelson.
Realized from sales $4,985,697.00.

1937

Blue, Red, Black and Yellow

WX88	CS31 Perf. 12x12½ (E)	5
WX89	CS31 Perf. 12½ (S,D,U)	5

Four seals in each sheet, positions 23, 28, 73 and 78, carry slogans: "Health for all," "Protect your home," "Preventable" and "Curable."

The "U" printer's mark of United States Printing & Lithographing Co. appears on seal 55. It is omitted on some sheets.

CS32

Designed by Lloyd Coe.
Realized from sales $5,239,526.00.

1938

Red, Brown, Green and Black

WX92 CS32 Perf. 12½x12 (E) 5
WX93 CS32 Perf. 12½ (S,D,U) 5
   a. Miniature sheet, imperf. 3.50

The corner seals of each sheet bear portraits of Rene T. H. Laennec, Robert Koch, Edward Livingston Trudeau and Einar Holboll.

No. WX93a contains the four corner seals, with the regular seal in the center. Inscriptions in black include slogans and "They made landmarks in the fight against tuberculosis," with brief statements on the contributions of Laennec, Koch, Trudeau and Holboll. Size of sheet: 140x86mm. It sold for 25 cents.

CS33

Designed by Rockwell Kent.
Realized from sales $5,593,399.00.

1939
Red, Ultramarine and Pale Red

WX96 CS33 Perf. 12½x12 (E) 5
   a. Booklet pane of 20, Perf. 12 35
WX97 CS33 Perf. 12½ (S,D,U) 5

The four center seals in each sheet, positions 45, 46, 55 and 56, carry slogans: "Health to All," "Protect Your Home." "Tuberculosis Preventable Curable" and "Holiday Greetings." Printers' marks appear on seal 57.

CS34

Designed by Felix L. Martini.
Realized from sales $6,305,979.00.

1940
Blue, Ultramarine, Red and Yellow

WX100 CS34 Perf. 12½x12 (E) 5
WX101 CS34 Perf. 12½x13 (E) 5
WX103 CS34 Perf. 12½ (S,D,U) 5

Three seals in each sheet-positions 23, 32 and 34-carry the slogan "Protect Us from Tuberculosis." Each slogan seal shows one of the three children separately.

CS35

Designed by Stevan Dohanos.
Realized from sales $7,530,496.00.

1941
Blue, Black, Red and Yellow

WX104 CS35 Perf. 12½x12 (E) 5
WX105 CS35 Perf. 12½ (S,D,U) 5

"S" and "U" printers' marks exist on same sheet.

CS36

Designed by Dale Nichols.
Realized from sales $9,390,117.00.

1942
Yellow, Blue, Red and Black

WX108 CS36 Perf. 12x12½ (E) 5
WX109 CS36 Perf. 12½ (S,D,U) 5

CS37

Designed by Andre Dugo.
Realized from U. S. sales $12,521,494.00.

1943
Blue, Red, Buff and Black
Pair

WX112 CS37 Perf. 12½x12 (E) 5
WX113 CS37 Perf. 12½ (S,D,U) 5
WX116 CS37 "Joyeux Noel" replaces "Greetings 1943" and "1943" added on curtain. For French Canadians. Perf. 12½. 10
WX117 CS37 Same as WX113 but darker colors. For English Canadians and Great Britain. Perf. 12½. 10

On alternate seals, the vertical frame colors (blue and red) are transposed and the horizontal frame colors (buff and black) are transposed.

CS38

Designed by Spence Wildey.
Realized from U. S. sales $14,966,227.00.

1944
Gray, Blue, Red and Yellow

WX118 CS38 Perf. 12½x12 (E) 5
WX119 CS38 Perf. 12½ (S,D,U) 5
WX122 CS38 "Joyeux Noel" replaces "Merry Christmas" and "USA" omitted. For French Canadians. Perf. 12½ 10
WX123 CS38 Same as WX119 but "USA" omitted. For English Canadians. Perf. 12½ 10

CS39

Designed by Park Phipps.
Realized from U.S. sales $15,638,755.00.

1945
Blue, Red, Black and Yellow
"USA" at Lower Right Corner.

WX124 CS39 Perf. 12½x12 (E) 5
WX125 CS39 Perf. 12½ (S,D,U) 5
WX128 CS39 "Bonne Sante" replaces "Greetings" and "USA" omitted. For French Canadians. Perf. 12½ 10

WX129 CS39 Same as WX125 but "USA" omitted. For English Canadians. Perf. 12½ 10

CS40

Designed by Mary Louise Estes and Lloyd Coe.
Realized from U.S. sales $17,075,608.44.

1946
Blue, Black, Red and Olive
"USA" at Left of Red Cross.

WX130 CS40 Perf. 12½x12 (E) 5
WX131 CS40 Perf. 12½ (S,D,U) 5
WX132 CS40 "Bonne Sante" replaces "Greetings" and "USA" omitted. For French Canadians. Perf. 12½ 10
WX133 CS40 Same as WX131 but "USA" omitted. For English Canadians and Great Britain. Perf. 12½ 10
   a. Same, overprinted "NEWFOUNDLAND" 1.25
WX134 CS40 "Bermuda" replaces seven stars and "USA" omitted. For Bermuda. Perf. 12½x12 (E) 25

Printers' marks are on seal 86.

The four center seals (45, 46, 55, 56) of Nos. WX130 and WX131 bear portraits of Jacob Riis, Emily P. Bissell, E. A. Van Valkenburg and Leigh Mitchell Hodges.

CS41

Designed by Raymond H. Lufkin.
Realized from U. S. sales $18,665,523.00.

1947
Red, Blue, Green and Brown

WX135 CS41 Perf. 12x12½ (E) 5
WX136 CS41 Perf. 12½ (S,D,U) 5
WX137 CS41 "Bonne Sante" replaces "Merry Christmas" and "USA" omitted. For French Canadians. Perf. 12½ 5
WX138 CS41 Same as WX136 but "USA" omitted. For English Canadians and Great Britain. Perf. 12½ 5
WX139 CS41 "BERMUDA" overprinted in red on WX138. For Bermuda. Perf. 12½ 20

The "U" printer's mark of United States Printing & Lithographing Co. appears on seal 46.

CS42

Designed by Jean Barry Bart.
Realized from U. S. sales $20,153,834.47.

1948
Blue, Red, Light Blue and Yellow

WX140 CS42 Perf. 12x12½ (E) 5
WX141 CS42 Perf. 12½ (S,D,U) 5
WX142 CS42 "Bonne Sante" replaces "Merry Christmas", date in white and "USA" omitted. For French Canadians. Perf. 12½
WX143 CS42 Same as WX141 but date in white and "USA" omitted. For English Canadians, Great Britain and Newfoundland. Perf. 12½ 5

WX144 CS42 "BERMUDA" overprinted in black on WX143. Perf. 12½   20

CS43

Designed by Herbert Meyers.
Realized from U.S. sales $20,226,794.15.

1949

Green, Light Blue, Red and Ultramarine

WX145 CS43 Perf. 12x12½ (E)   5
WX146 CS43 Perf. 12½ (S,D,U)   5
WX147 CS43 "Bonne Sante" replaces "Greetings" and "USA" omitted. For French Canadians. Perf. 12½   5
WX148 CS43 Same as WX146 but "USA" omitted. For English Canadians, Great Britain and Newfoundland. Perf. 12½   5
WX149 CS43 "BERMUDA" replaces "USA" on WX145. For Bermuda. Perf. 12x12½ (E)   15

CS44

Designed by Andre Dugo.
Realized from U. S. sales $20,981,540.77.

1950

Red, Green, Orange and Black

WX150 CS44 Perf. 12½x12 (E)   5
WX151 CS44 Perf. 12½ (S,D,U,F)   5
WX152 CS44 "Bonne Sante" replaces "Greetings" and "USA" omitted. For French Canadians. Perf. 12½   5
WX153 CS44 Same as WX151 but "USA" omitted. For English Canadians and Great Britain. Perf 12½   5
WX154 CS44 Same as WX150 but "BERMUDA" in larger letters replaces "USA" at bottom (E)   15

CS45

Designed by Robert K. Stephens.
Realized from U.S. sales $21,717,953.09.

1951

Blue Green, Red, Flesh and Black

WX155 CS45 Perf. 12½x12 (E)   5
WX156 CS45 Perf. 12½ (S,D,U,F)   5
WX157 CS45 Same as WX156 but "USA" omitted. For English Canadians. Perf. 12½.   5
WX158 CS45 "BERMUDA" replaces "USA" on WX155. For Bermuda. Perf 12½x12 (E)   15

CS46

Designed by Tom Darling.
Realized from U. S. sales $23,238,148.12.

1952

Green, Yellow, Red and Black

WX159 CS46 Perf. 12½x12 (E)   5
WX160 CS46 Perf. 12½ (S,D,U,F)   5
WX161 CS46 "CANADA" replaces "Christmas Greetings." Copyright mark and "USA" eliminated. Perf. 12½   5
WX162 CS46 "BERMUDA" in vertical lettering at right. "USA" eliminated. Perf. 12½x12 (E)   15
WX163 CS46 Overprinted "Ryukyus" (in Japanese characters) in black. Perf. 12½x12, 12½ (U)   1.50

CS47

Designed by Elmer Jacobs and E. Willis Jones.
Realized from U. S. sales $23,889,044.50.

1953

Gold, Red, Green and Black

WX164 CS47 Perf. 13 (E)   5
WX165 CS47 Perf. 12½ (S,D,U,F)   5
WX166 CS47 "CANADA" replaces "Greetings." Copyright mark, "NTA" and "USA" eliminated. Perf. 12½   5
WX167 CS47 "BERMUDA" replaces "NTA" and "USA." Perf. 13 (E)   15

CS48

Designed by Jorgen Hansen.
Realized from U. S. sales $24,670,202.85.

1954

Yellow, Black, Green and Red
Block of Four

WX168 CS48 Perf. 13 (E)   10
WX169 CS48 Perf. 12½ (S,U,F,W)   10
WX170 CS48 Perf. 11 (D)   10
WX171 CS48 CANADA, perf. 12½   20
WX172 CS48 BERMUDA, perf. 13 (E)   1.00

CS49

Designed by Miss Jean Simpson.
Realized from U.S. sales $25,780,365.96.

1955

Ultramarine, Olive Green, Red and Blue
Pair

WX173 CS49 Perf. 13 (E)   5
WX174 CS49 Perf. 12½ (S,U,F,W)   5
WX175 CS49 Perf. 11 (D)   5
WX176 CS49 CANADA, perf. 10½   10

United States postage and air mail first day covers are listed and priced in a separate section of the catalogue. See catalogue index.

WX177 CS49 BERMUDA, perf. 13 (E)   30

CS50

Designed by Heidi Brandt.
Realized from U. S. sales $26,310,491.

1956

Dull Yellow, Red, Green and Black
Block of Four

WX178 CS50 Perf. 12½x12 (E)   10
WX179 CS50 Perf. 12½ (E,S,U,F,W)   10
WX180 CS50 Perf. 11 (D,b)   10
WX181 CS50 "Canada," perf. 11, pair   10
WX182 CS50 BERMUDA, perf. 12½   75
WX183 CS50 "Puerto Rico," perf. 12½   1.25

CS51

Designed by Clinton Bradley.
Realized from U.S. sales $25,959,998.51.

1957

Dark Green, Light Green, Red and Yellow
Block of Four

WX184 CS51 Perf. 13 (E)   10
WX185 CS51 Perf. 12½ (S,U,F,W,R)   10
WX186 CS51 Perf. 11 (D,B)   10
WX187 CS51 Perf. 10½x11 (D)   10
WX188 CS51 Perf. 10½ (D)   10
WX189 CS51 "Bermuda," perf. 13, pair   30
WX190 CS51 "Puerto Rico," perf. 13   1.25

CS52

Designed by Alfred Guerra.
Realized from U.S. sales $25,955,390.47

1958

Red, Green, Yellow and Black
Pair

WX191 CS52 Perf. 13 (E)   5
WX192 CS52 Perf. 12½ (S,U,F,W,R)   5
WX193 CS52 Perf. 10½x11 (B,D)   5
WX194 CS52 Perf. 11 (B,D)   5
WX195 CS52 "Bermuda," perf. 13   30

WX196   CS52 "Puerto Rico," perf. 13   60

CS53

Designed by Katherine Rowe.
Realized from U.S. sales $26,740,906.16.

1959

Crimson, Green, Bister & Black
Pair

WX197	CS53 Perf. 13 (E)	5
WX198	CS53 Perf. 12½ (F,R,W)	5
a.	Horiz. pair, imperf. btwn. (D)	1.50
WX199	CS53 Perf. 10½x11 (B)	5
WX200	CS53 Perf. 11 (B,D)	5
WX201	CS53 Perf. 10½(B)	5
WX202	CS53 "Bermuda," perf. 13	30
WX203	CS53 "Puerto Rico," perf. 13	60

Edwards & Deutsch Lithographing Co. omitted every other
vertical row of perforation on a number of sheets which were
widely distributed as an experiment. No. WX198a is from one
of these sheets.

CS54

Designed by Philip Richard Costigan.
Realized from U.S. sales $26,259,030.37.

1960

Red, Bister, Green & Black
Block of Four

WX204	CS54 Perf. 12½ (E,F,R,W)	10
WX205	CS54 Perf. 12½x12 (E)	10
WX206	CS54 Perf. 11x10½ (B)	10
WX207	CS54 Perf. 11 (D)	10
WX208	CS54 "Bermuda," perf. 12½	75

Puerto Rico used No. WX204 (E).

CS55

Designed by Heidi Brandt.
Realized from U.S. sales $26,529,517.20.

1961

Dark Blue, Yellow, Green and Red
Block of Four

WX209	CS55 Perf. 12½ (E,F,R,W)	10
WX209A	CS55 Perf. 12½x12 (E)	10
WX210	CS55 Perf. 11x10½ (B)	10

WX211	CS55 Perf. 11 (D)	10
WX212	CS55 "Bermuda," perf. 12½	75

Puerto Rico used No. WX209 (E).

CS56

Designed by Paul Dohanos.
Realized from U.S. sales $27,429,202.18.

1962

Emerald, Red, Prussian Blue & Yellow
Block of Four

WX213	CS56 Perf. 12½ (F,R,W)	10
WX214	CS56 Perf. 13 (E)	10
WX215	CS56 Perf. 10½x11 (B)	10
WX216	CS56 Perf. 11 (D,B)	10
WX217	CS56 "Bermuda," perf. 13	75

Puerto Rico used No. WX214.

CS57

Designed by Judith Campbell Piussi.
Realized from U.S. sales $27,411,806.

1963

Bright Ultra., Yel., Red, Green, Orange & Black
Block of Four

WX218	CS57 Perf. 12½ (E,F,R,W)	10
WX219	CS57 Perf. 11 (B,D)	10

Puerto Rico used No. WX218 (E).

CS58

Designed by Gaetano di Palma.
Realized from U.S. sales $28,784,043.

1964

Bister, Red, Emerald & Black
Block of Four

WX220	CS58 Perf. 12½ (E,F,R,W)	10
WX221	CS58 Perf. 11 (B,D)	10

Puerto Rico used No. WX221 (B).

CS59

Designed by Frede Salomonsen.
Realized from U.S. sales $29,721,878.

1965

Blue, Red, Yellow, Green & Black
Block of Four

WX222	CS59 Perf. 12½ (F,W)	10
WX223	CS59 Perf. 11 (B,D)	10
WX224	CS59 Perf. 13 (E)	10

Puerto Rico used No. WX223 (B).

CS60

Designed by Heidi Brandt.
Realized from U.S. sales $30,776,586.

1966

Yellow Green, Black, Red & Yellow
Block of Eight

WX225	CS60 Perf. 12½ (E,F,W)	25
WX226	CS60 Perf. 10½x11 (B)	25
WX227	CS60 Perf. 11 (D)	25

Blocks of four seals with yellow green and white backgrounds alternate in sheet in checkerboard style.
Puerto Rico used No. WX226.

Holiday Train — CS61

Designed by L. Gerald Snyder.
Realized from U.S. sales $31,876,773.
The seals come in 10 designs showing a train filled with
Christmas gifts and symbols. The direction of the train is
reversed in alternating rows as are the inscriptions "Christmas
1967" and "Greetings 1967". The illustration shows first two
seals of top row. Each listing stands for two horizontal rows of
10 seals.

1967

Red, Green, Black, Blue & Yellow
Block of 20 (10x2)

WX228	CS61 Perf. 13 (E)	30
WX229	CS61 Perf. 12½ (F,W)	30
WX230	CS61 Perf. 10½(B)	30

WX231	CS61 Perf. 11 (D)	30
WX232	CS61 Perf. 11x10½ (B)	30

Puerto Rico used No. WX229 (F).

SEALS ISSUED BY NATIONAL TUBERCULOSIS AND RESPIRATORY DISEASE ASSOCIATION

CS62

Designed by William Eisele.
Realized from U.S. sales $33,059,107.

1968

Bluish Green, Yellow, Blue, Black & Red
Block of Four

WX233	CS62 Perf. 13 (E)	10
WX234	CS62 Perf. 10½x11 (B)	10
WX234A	CS62 Perf. 10½ (B)	10
WX235	CS62 Perf. 11 (D)	10
WX236	CS62 Perf. 12½ (F,W)	10

Blocks of four seals with bluish green and yellow backgrounds alternate in sheet in checkerboard style.
Puerto Rico used No. WX236 (F).

CS63

Designed by Bernice Kochan.
Realized from U.S. sales $34,437,591.

1969

Blue Grn., Verm., Emerald, Magenta & Black
Block of Four

WX237	CS63 Perf. 13 (E)	10
WX238	CS63 Perf. 12½ (F,W)	10
WX239	CS63 Perf. 10½x11 (B)	10
WX240	CS63 Perf. 11 (B)	10

Puerto Rico used No. WX238 (F).

CS64

Designed by L. Gerald Snyder.
Realized from U.S. sales $36,237,977.
Sheets of 100 show different design for each seal, Christmas symbols, toys, decorated windows; inscribed alternately "Christmas 1970" and "Greetings 1970." The illustration shows 6 seals from the center of the sheet.

1970

Ultramarine, Black, Red, Yellow & Olive
Sheet of 100 (10x10)

WX242	CS64 Perf. 12½ (E,F,W)	1.00
WX243	CS64 Perf. 11 (B)	1.00
WX244	CS64 Perf. 11x10½ (B)	1.00

Puerto Rico used No. WX242 (F).

CS65

Designed by James Clarke.
Realized from U.S. sales $36,120,000.

1971

Lilac Rose, Yellow, Green & Blue
Block of Eight (2x4)

WX245	CS65 Perf. 12½ (E,F)	20
WX246	CS65 Perf. 11 (B)	20

The four illustrated seals each come in a second design arrangement: cross at left, inscriptions transposed, and reversed bugler, candle and tree ornaments. Each sheet of 100 has six horizontal rows of seals as shown and four rows with second designs.
Puerto Rico used No. WX245 (F).
Eureka printings are found with large "E", small "E" and without "E".

CS66

Designed by Linda Layman
Realized from U.S. sales $38,000,557.
The seals come in 10 designs showing various holiday scenes with decorated country and city houses, carolers, Christmas trees and snowman. Inscribed alternately "1972 Christmas" and "Greetings 1972." Illustration shows seals from center of row.

1972

Bright Blue, Red, Green, Yellow & Black
Strip of 10

WX247	CS66 Perf. 13 (E)	30
	Blue, Red, Green, Yellow & Black	
WX248	CS66 Perf. 12½ (F)	30
	Ultramarine, Red, Green, Yellow & Black	
WX249	CS66 Perf. 11 (B)	30

Seal 100 has designer's name. Puerto Rico used No. WX248.

SEALS ISSUED BY AMERICAN LUNG ASSOCIATION

CS67

Designed by Cheri Johnson.
Realized from U.S. sales $36,902,439.
The seals are in 12 designs representing "The 12 Days of Christmas." Inscribed alternately "Christmas 1973" and "Greetings 1973." Illustration shows block from center of top two rows.

1973

Multicolored
Block of 12

WX250	CS67 Perf. 12½ (F), 18x22mm.	35
	a. Size 16½x20½mm. (E)	35
WX251	CS67 Perf. 11 (B,W)	35

Seal 100 has designer's name. Puerto Rico used No. WX250 (F).

CS68

Designed by Rubidoux.
Realized from U.S. sales $37,761,745.

1974

Green, Black, Red, Yellow & Blue
Block of Four

WX252   CS68 Perf. 12½ (E,F)   10
WX253   CS68 Perf. 11 (B)   10

Seal 99 has designer's name. Puerto Rico used No. WX252 (F).

CS69

Children's paintings of holiday scenes. Different design for each seal, inscribed with name of state or territory. Paintings by elementary school children were selected in a nationwide campaign ending in January, 1974.
Realized from U.S. contributions $34,710,107.

1975

Multicolored
Sheet of 54 (6x9)

WX254   CS69 Perf. 12½ (S,F)   75
WX255   CS69 Perf. 11 (B)   75

Printers' marks are on seal 28 (New Mexico). Specialty Printers' seals (S) carry union labels: "Scranton 4", "Scranton 7", "E. Stroudsburg".
Puerto Rico used No. WX254 (F).

CS70

Continuous village picture covers sheet with Christmas activities and Santa crossing the sky with sleigh and reindeer. No inscription on 34 seals. Others inscribed "Christmas 1976", "Greetings 1976", and (on 9 bottom-row seals) "American Lung Association". Illustration shows seals 11-12, 20-21.
Realized from U.S. contributions $36,489,207.

1976

Multicolored
Sheet of 54 (9x6)

WX256   CS70 Perf. 12½ (F,N)   75
WX257   CS70 Perf. 11 (B)   75
WX258   CS70 Perf. 13 (S)   75

Printers' marks (N, B, S) on seal 32 and (F) on seal 23.
Puerto Rico used No. WX256 (F).

CS71

Children's paintings of holiday scenes. Different design for each seal, inscribed with name of state or territory.
Realized from U.S. contributions $37,583,883.

1977

Multicolored
Sheet of 54 (6x9)

WX259   CS71 Perf. 12½ (F)   75
WX260   CS71 Perf. 11 (B)   75
WX261   CS71 Perf. 13 (S)   75

Printers' marks on seal 28 (Georgia).
Puerto Rico used No. WX259.

CS72

Children's paintings of holiday scenes. Different design for each seal, inscribed with name of state or territory.
Realized from U.S. contributions $37,621,466.

1978

Multicolored
Sheet of 54 (6x9)

WX262   CS72 Perf. 12½ (F)   75
WX263   CS72 Perf. 11 (B)   75
WX264   CS72 Perf. 13 (S)   75

Printers' marks on seal 29 (New Hampshire).
Puerto Rico used No. WX262.

Type of 1978 Inscribed 1979

Children's paintings of holiday scenes. Different design for each seal, inscribed with name of state or territory.

1979

Multicolored
Sheet of 54 (6x9)

WX265   CS72 Perf. 12½ (F)   75
WX266   CS72 Perf. 11 (B)   75
WX267   CS72 Perf. 13 (S)   75

Printer's marks on seal 22 (Virgin Islands). Puerto Rico used No. WX265.

Beginning in 1979 there is no longer one national issue. Additional designs are issued on a limited basis as test seals to determine the designs to be used the following year.

CONFEDERATE STATES

These stamps and envelopes were issued by individual postmasters generally during the interim between June 1, 1861, when the use of United States stamps stopped in the Confederacy, and Oct. 16, 1861, when the first Confederate Government stamps were issued. They were occasionally issued at later periods, especially in Texas, when regular issues of Government stamps were unavailable.

Canceling stamps of the post offices were often used to produce envelopes, some of which were supplied in advance by private citizens. These envelopes and other stationery therefore may be found in a wide variety of papers, colors, sizes and shapes, including patriotic and semi-official types. It is often difficult to determine whether the impression made by the canceling stamp indicates provisional usage or merely postage paid at the time the letter was deposited in the post office. Occasionally the same mark was used for both purposes.

The *press-printed* provisional envelopes are in a different category. They were produced in quantity, using envelopes procured in advance by the postmaster, such as those of Charleston, Lynchburg, Memphis, etc. The *press-printed* envelopes are listed and priced on all known papers.

The *handstamped* provisional envelopes are listed and priced according to type and variety of handstamp, but not according to paper. Many exist on such a variety of papers that they defy accurate, complete listing. The value of a handstamped provisional envelope is determined primarily by the clarity of the markings and its overall condition and attractiveness, rather than the type of paper. All handstamped provisional envelopes, when used, should also show the postmark of the town of issue.

Most handstamps are impressed at top right, although they exist from some towns in other positions.
Many illustrations in this section are reduced in size.

Prices for envelopes are for entires.

PROVISIONAL ISSUES
Aberdeen, Miss.
Envelopes

E1

Handstamped

1XU1	E1	5c black	2,000.
1XU2	E1	10c (ms.) on 5c black	—

Abingdon, Va.
Envelopes

E1

Handstamped

2XU1	E1	2c black	11,000.
2XU2	E1	5c black	900.00
		On patriotic cover	3,000.
2XU3	E1	10c black	2,500.

One example known of No. 2XU1.

Albany, Ga.
Envelopes

E1

E2

Handstamped

3XU1	E1	5c greenish blue	750.00
3XU2	E1	10c greenish blue	1,250.
3XU3	E1	10c on 5c greenish blue	1,750.
3XU5	E2	5c greenish blue	—
3XU6	E2	10c greenish blue	1,350.

Anderson Court House, S.C.
Envelopes

E1

Handstamped

4XU1	E1	5c black		1,000.
4XU2	E1	10c (ms.) black	700.00	3,000.

Athens, Ga.

A1 (type I)

A1 (type II)

Printed from woodcuts of two types. Pairs, both
horizontal and vertical, always show one of each
type.

5X1	A1	5c purple (shades)	750.00	800.00
		Pair	—	1,750.
		On cover		2,000.
		Pair on cover		3,250.
		Strip of four on cover		
		(horiz.)		*10,000.*
a.		Tête bêche pair (vertical)		*4,000.*
		Tête bêche pair on cover		*7,500.*
5X2	A1	5c red	—	*2,500.*
		On cover		*8,000.*
		Pair on cover		—

CANCELLATIONS.

Black grid	Black "Paid"
Black town	

Atlanta, Ga.
Envelopes

E1

E2

Handstamped

6XU1	E1	5c red		2,000.
6XU2	E1	5c black	150.00	750.00
		On patriotic cover		*4,000.*
		On U. S. envelope No.		
		U28		—
6XU3	E1	10c on 5c black		1,500.
6XU4	E2	2c black		*3,500.*
6XU5	E2	5c black		800.00
		On patriotic cover		2,250.
6XU6	E2	10c black		700.00
6XU7	E2	10c on 5c black		2,500.

E3

Handstamped

6XU8	E3	5c black	3,250.
6XU9	E3	10c black ("10" upright)	2,250.

Augusta, Ga.
Envelope

E1

Handstamped

7XU1	E1	5c black	—

Provisional status questioned.

Austin, Miss.
Envelope

E1

Typographed Impressed at top right

8XU1	E1	5c red, *amber*	*14,500.*

Cancellation is black "Paid".
One example known.

Austin, Texas
Envelope

E1

Handstamped

9XU1	E1	10c black	1,350.

Cut squares of No. 9XU1 are known as adhesives on cover.

Autaugaville, Ala.
Envelopes

E1

E2

Handstamped

10XU1	E1	5c black	8,000.
10XU2	E2	5c black	5,000.

Baton Rouge, La.

A1

A2

Ten varieties of each
Typeset

11X1	A1	2c green	5,000.	3,500.
		On cover		10,000.
a.		"McCcrmick"	8,000.	7,500.
a.		On cover		12,000.
11X2	A2	5c green & carmine (Maltese cross border)	1,100.	800.00
		On cover		3,000.
		Strip of three		4,000.
		Strip of five		8,500.
		Used in New Orleans, on cover		8,000.
a.		"McCcrmick"	—	2,000.
a.		On cover		6,500.

A3

A4

Ten varieties of each

11X3	A3	5c green & car. (crisscross border)	3,000.	1,750.
		On cover		6,250.
a.		"McCcrmick"		3,250.
11X4	A4	10c blue		15,000.
		On cover		95,000.

Cancellation on Nos. 11X1-11X4: black town.

Beaumont, Texas

A1

A2

Typeset
Several varieties of each

12X1	A1	10c black, *yellow*	—	4,500.
		On cover		8,000.
12X2	A1	10c black, *pink*	—	4,000.
		On cover		6,500.
12X3	A2	10c black, *yellow,* on cover		150,000.

Cancellations: black pen; black town.
One example known of No. 12X3.

Bridgeville, Ala.

A1

Handstamped in black within red pen-ruled squares

13X1	A1	5c black & red, pair on cover	20,000.

Cancellation is black pen.

Canton, Miss.
Envelopes

E1

"P" in star is initial of Postmaster William Priestly.

Handstamped

14XU1	E1	5c black	1,850.
14XU2	E1	10c (ms.) on 5c black	3,500.

Carolina City, N.C.
Envelope

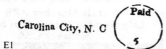

Carolina City, N. C

E1

Handstamped

118XU1	E1	5c black	—

Chapel Hill, N. C.
Envelope

E1

Handstamped

15XU1	E1	5c black	1,750.
		On patriotic cover	4,500.

Charleston, S. C.

A1

Litho.

16X1	A1	5c blue	550.00	500.00
		Pair	1,500.	1,200.
		On cover		1,350.
		On patriotic cover		5,000.
		Pair, on cover		5,000.

Cancellation: black town (two types).

Envelopes

E1

E2

Typographed from Woodcut

16XU1	E1	5c blue, *white*	300.00	1,000.
16XU2	E1	5c blue, *amber*	300.00	1,000.
16XU3	E1	5c blue, *orange*	300.00	1,000.
16XU4	E1	5c blue, *buff*	300.00	1,000.
16XU5	E1	5c blue, *blue*	300.00	1,000.
16XU6	E2	10c blue, *orange*		16,500.

One example known of No. 16XU6.

Handstamped

16XU7	E2	10c black	3,000.

Chattanooga, Tenn.
Envelopes

E1

Handstamped

17XU2	E1	5c black	1,750.
17XU3	E1	5c on 2c black	—

Christiansburg, Va.
Envelopes

E1

Typeset
Impressed at top right

99XU1	E1	5c black, *blue*	1,250.

99XU2	E1	5c blue, *white*		1,250.
99XU3	E1	5c black, *orange*		1,250.
99XU4	E1	5c green on U.S. envelope No. U27		4,500.
99XU5	E1	10c black, *blue*		—

Colaparchee, Ga.
Envelope

E1

Control

Handstamped

119XU1	E1	5c black	—

Columbia, S.C.
Envelopes

E1

E2

Handstamped

18XU1	E1	5c blue	135.00	750.00
18XU2	E1	5c black	235.00	750.00
18XU3	E1	10c on 5c blue		—

Three types of "PAID", one in circle

18XU4	E2	5c blue (seal on front)	1,000.
a.		Seal on back	900.00
18XU5	E2	10c blue (seal on back)	1,400.

Circular Seal similar to E2, 27mm. diameter

18XU6	E2	5c blue (seal on back)	1,000.

Columbia, Tenn.
Envelope

E1

Handstamped

113XU1	E1	5c red	2,250.

Columbus, Ga.
Envelopes

E1

Handstamped

19XU1	E1	5c blue	1,000.
19XU2	E1	10c red	2,500.

Courtland, Ala.
Envelopes

E1

Handstamped from Woodcut

103XU1 E1 5c black   —
103XU2 E1 5c red   10,000.

Provisional status of No. 103XU1 questioned.

Dalton, Ga.
Envelopes

E1

Handstamped

20XU1 E1 5c black   500.00
20XU2 E1 10c black   700.00
20XU3 E1 10c (ms.) on 5c black   1,000.

Danville, Va.

A1

Typeset
Wove Paper

21X1 A1 5c red   5,500.
            Cut to shape   4,000.
            On cover   15,000.
            On cover, cut to shape   6,000.

            Two varieties known.

Laid Paper

21X2 A1 5c red   6,500.
            On cover, cut to shape   10,000.

Cancellation: black town.

Envelopes

E2

curved

                                                  500.
                                                  500.
                                                  00.

Demopolis, Ala.
Envelopes

E1

Handstamped. Signature in ms.

22XU1 E1 5c black ("Jno. Y. Hall")   1,250.
22XU2 E1 5c black ("J. Y. Hall")   1,250.
22XU3 E1 5c (ms.) black ("J. Y. Hall")   1,000.

Eatonton, Ga.
Envelopes

E1

Handstamped

23XU1 E1 5c black   3,000.
23XU2 E1 5c + 5c black   1,250.

Emory, Va.

A1

Handstamped on margins of sheets of U.S. 1c stamps, 1857 issue. Also known with "5" above "PAID."

Perf. 15 on three sides

24X1 A1 5c blue   —   4,000.
            On cover   6,000.

Cancellation: blue town.

Envelopes

E1   E2

Handstamped

24XU1 E1 5c blue   1,000.
24XU2 E1 10c blue   2,000.

Fincastle, Va.
Envelope

E1

Typeset
Impressed at top right

104XU1 E1 10c black   25,000.

One example known.

Forsyth, Ga.
Envelope

  E1

Handstamped

120XU1 E1 10c black   450.00

Franklin, N. C.
Envelope

E1

Typographed
Impressed at top right

25XU1 E1 5c blue, *buff*   30,000.

The one known envelope shows black circular Franklin postmark with manuscript date.

Fredericksburg, Va.

   A1

Sheets of 20, two panes of 10 varieties each

		Typeset	Thin bluish paper
26X1	A1	5c blue, *bluish*	200.00	600.00
		Block of four	950.00	
		On cover		2,000.
		Pair on cover		7,000.
26X2	A1	10c red, *bluish*	650.00	
		Brown red, *bluish*	650.00	
		Block of four	—	

Cancellation: black town.

Gainesville, Ala.
Envelopes

E1   E2

Handstamped

27XU1 E1 5c black   1,500.
27XU2 E2 10c ("01") black   7,500.

Postmark spells town name "Gainsville".

Galveston, Tex.
Envelopes

E1

Handstamped

98XU1 E1 5c black   500.00   2,000.
98XU2 E1 10c black   2,250.

E2

Handstamped

98XU3 E2 10c black   550.00   1,000.
98XU4 E2 20c black   3,500.

Georgetown, S.C.
Envelope

Control

E1

ped

750.00

d, Texas

28XU1 E1 5c bla

A2

Typeset

29X1	A1	5c	black	5,000.
29X2	A1	5c	*gray*	4,500.
29X3	A1	5c	*rose*	5,000.
			On cover	8,000.
29X4	A1	10c	black	—
				5,000.
29X5	A1	10c	*rose*	5,000.
			On cover	7,500.
			On patriotic cover	—

Type A1 stamps are signed "Clarke-P.M." vertically in black.

29X6	A2	5c	*gray*	5,000.
			Pair	—
			On cover	7,250.
a.			"GOILAD"	5,500.
			Pair, left stamp the error	15,000.
29X7	A2	10c	*gray*	5,000.
			On cover	7,500.
a.			"GOILAD"	5,500.
a.			On cover	8,500.
29X8	A2	5c	*dark blue*	6,000.
			On cover	8,000.
29X9	A2	10c	*dark blue*	6,500.

Cancellations in black: pen, town, "Paid"

Gonzales, Texas

Colman & Law were booksellers when John B. Law (of the firm) was appointed Postmaster. The firm used a small lithographed label on the front or inside of books they sold. One variety was used, as listed.

A1

Lithographed on colored glazed paper

30X1	A1	(5c) gold, *dark blue*		7,500.
			Pair on cover	15,000.

Cancellation: black town. No. 30X1 must bear double-circle town cancel as validating control. All items of type A1 without this control are book labels. The control was applied to the labels in the sheet before their sale as stamps. When used, the stamps bear the additional Gonzales double-circle postmark.

Similar labels in gold on garnet and on black paper are known on cover. Some authorities believe Postmaster Law sold them for use as 10c stamps.

Greensboro, Ala.
Envelopes

E1

E2

Handstamped

31XU1	E1	5c	black	1,000.
31XU2	E1	10c	black	1,000.
31XU3	E2	10c	black	1,250.

Greensboro, N.C.
Envelope

E1

Handstamped

32XU1 E1 10c red   1,500.

Greenville, Ala.

A1   A2

Typeset
Two varieties of each
On pinkish surface-colored glazed paper.
Type I-"Greenville, Ala." in Roman type.
Type II-"Greenville, Ala." in script type.

33X1	A1	5c red & blue, type I		4,500.
a.		Type II		4,500.
		On cover, type I or II	18,000.	
33X2	A2	10c red & blue, type II		5,000.
		On cover, type II	20,000.	

Greenville Court House, S.C.
Envelopes

PAID 5

E1

Control

Handstamped (Several types)

34XU1	E1	5c	black	800.00
34XU2	E1	10c	black	900.00
34XU3	E1	20c	(ms.) on 10c black	1,000.

Envelopes usually bear the black control on the back.

Greenwood Depot, Va.

A1

"PAID" Handstamped; Value and Signature ms.
Laid Paper

35X1	A1	10c black, *gray blue*	4,500.	—
		On cover		16,000.

Cancellation: black town.

Griffin, Ga.
Envelope

E1

Handstamped
102XU1 E1 5c black   1,350.

Grove Hill, Ala.

A1

Handstamped woodcut
36X1 A1   5c black, on cover   125,000.

Cancellations: black town, magenta pen.

Hallettsville, Texas

A1

Handstamped
Ruled Letter Paper
37X1 A1   10c black, *gray blue*, on cover   15,000.

Cancellation: black ms.
One example known.

Hamburgh, S.C.
Envelope

E1

Handstamped
112XU1 E1 5c black
On cover with No. 16X1 (forwarded)

Helena, Texas

A1

Typeset
Several varieties

38X1	A1	5c	black, *buff*
38X2	A1	10c	black, *gray*

On 10c "Helena" is in upper and
Cancellation: black town.

Hillsboro, N

Hands
39X1 A1   5c black, on co

Cancellatio

Houston, Texas
Envelopes

E1

Handstamped

40XU1	E1	5c red	600.00
		On patriotic cover	—
40XU2	E1	10c red	1,000.
40XU3	E1	10c black	750.00
40XU4	E1	5c +10c red	1,500.
40XU5	E1	10c +10c red	1,500.
40XU6	E1	10c (ms.) on 5c red	3,000.

Nos. 40XU2-40XU5 show "TEX" instead of "TXS".

Huntsville, Texas
Envelope

E1

Control

Handstamped

E1   5c black   1,350.

E1 exists with "5" outside or within control circle.

Independence, Texas

A1

...ped

3,250.	
8,000.	
3,500.	
8,500.	

manuscript
4,000.
10,000.

...ANCE").

| 7,500. | 5,000. |
| 5,000. | |

...ower case italics.

...C.

A1   15,000.

...tamped

...over

...: black town.

Confederate stamps can be ...tt's National Album.

Jacksonville, Ala.
Envelope

E1

Handstamped

110XU1   E1   5c black   —   1,500.

Jetersville, Va.

A1

Typeset ("5"); ms. ("AHA.")
Laid Paper

44X1   A1   5c black, Vert. pair on cover, uncanceled   16,000.

Initials are those of Postmaster A. H. Atwood.
Cancellation: black town.

Jonesboro, Tenn.
Envelopes

E1

Handstamped

45XU1	E1	5c black	4,000.
45XU2	E1	5c dark blue	4,250.

Kingston, Ga.
Envelopes

PAID **5** CENTS
E1

PAID c**5**s CENTS
E2

E3

E4

Typographed (E1-E3); Handstamped (E4)

46XU1	E1	5c black	800.00	—
46XU2	E2	5c black		1,500.
46XU3	E2	5c black, amber		1,500.
46XU4	E3	5c black		—
46XU5	E4	5c black		5,000.

Knoxville, Tenn.

A1

Woodcut
Grayish Laid Paper

47X1	A1	5c brick red	1,000.	550.00
		Horizontal pair	3,000.	1,300.
		Vertical pair	2,500.	
		Vertical strip of three	5,000.	

47X2	A1	5c	On cover	3,500.
			Pair on cover	7,500.
		5c carmine		1,500.
			Vertical strip of three	1,000.
			On cover	—
47X3		10c	Pair on cover	3,500.
		10c green		—
			On cover	8,500.

CANCELLATIONS.
Black ... | Black pen or pencil

The 5c has been re... white and bluish wove a...
The authenticity of No. ...red, brown and chocolate on Envelo... questioned.

E1

E2

Typo.

47XU1	E1	5c blue, white	500.00	1,500.
47XU2	E1	5c blue, orange	500.00	1,500.
47XU3	E1	10c red, white (cut to shape)		1,000.
47XU4	E1	10c red, orange (cut to shape)		1,000.

Handstamped

47XU5	E2	5c black	500.00	2,000.
		On patriotic cover		3,000.
47XU6	E2	10c on 5c black		3,500.

Type E2 exists with "5" above or below "PAID".

La Grange, Texas
Envelopes

E1

Handstamped

48XU1	E1	5c black	— 1,250.
48XU2	E1	10c black	1,500.

Lake City, Florida
Envelope

PAID **10**
E1

Control

Handstamped

96XU1   E1   10c black   3,500.

Envelopes have black circle control mark, or printed name of E. R. Ives, postmaster, on face or back.

Laurens Court House, S.C.
Envelope

E1

Handstamped

116XU1   E1   5c black   —

Lenoir, N.C.

A1

Handstamped from woodcut
White wove paper with cross-ruled orange lines

49X1	A1	5c blue & orange	3,250.	3,000.
		Pair		
		On cover		10,000.

CANCELLATIONS.

Blue town	Blue "Paid" in
Black pen	circle

Envelopes

E1

Handstamped

49XU1	A1	5c black		—
49XU2	A1	10c (5c+5c) blue		
49XU3	E1	5c blue		3,500.
49XU4	E1	5c black		900.00

Lexington, Miss.
Envelopes

E1

Handstamped

50XU1	E1	5c black	3,000.
50XU2	E1	10c black	4,000.

Liberty, Va.

PAID

5cts.

A1

Typeset
Laid Paper

74X1	A1	5c black	—

No. 74X1 is on cover and uncanceled.
A cover with Salem, Va., postmark is known.

Limestone Springs, S.C.

5 A1

Handstamped

121X1	A1	5c black, on cover	4,000.
		pair on cover	7,500.

Stamps are round, square or rectangular. Covers are not postmarked.

Livingston, Ala.

A1

Litho.

51X1	A1	5c blue	7,000.
		On cover	30,000.
		Pair on cover	—

Cancellation: black town.

Lynchburg, Va.

A1

Stereotype from Woodcut

52X1	A1	5c blue (shades)	500.00	650.00
		Pair		1,800.
		On cover		5,000.
		Pair on cover		8,000.

Cancellations: black town, blue town.

Envelopes

E1

Typo.
Impressed at top right or left

52XU1	E1	5c black, *white*		1,500.
52XU2	E1	5c black, *amber*	650.00	1,500.
52XU3	E1	5c black, *buff*		1,500.
52XU4	E1	5c black, *brown*	900.00	1,500.
		On patriotic cover		

Macon, Ga.

A1

A2

A3

A4

	Typeset	Wove Paper

Several varieties of type A1, 10 of A2, 5 of A3.

53X1	A1	5c *light blue green* (shades)	800.00	600.00
		On cover		3,500.
		Pair on cover		8,000.
53X3	A2	5c *yellow*	2,250.	750.00
		On cover		4,000.
		On patriotic cover		8,000.
		Pair on cover		6,000.
53X4	A3	5c *yellow* (shades)	2,250.	1,000.
		On cover		3,500.
		Pair on cover		8,000.
a.		Vertical tete beche pair		12,000.
53X5	A4	2c *gray green*		6,500.
		On cover		15,000.

Laid Paper

53X6	A2	5c *yellow*	3,000.	3,500.
		On cover		6,000.
53X7	A3	5c *yellow*	6,000.	
		On cover		9,000.
53X8	A1	5c *light blue green*	1,750.	2,000.
		On cover		3,750.

Cancellations: black town, black "PAID" (2 types).

Envelope

E1

Handstamped
Two types: PAID over 5, 5 over PAID

53XU1	E1	5c black	250.00 500.00

Marietta, Ga.
Envelopes

E1

E2

Handstamped
Two types of "PAID" and numerals

54XU1	E1	5c black		400.00
54XU2	E1	10c on 5c black E1		1,200.
54XU3	E2	10c black		750.00
54XU4	E2	5c black		450.00

Marion, Va.

A1

Typeset frame, with handstamped numeral in center

55X1	A1	5c black		5,000.
		On cover		8,000.
55X2	A1	10c black	16,500.	8,000.
		On cover		12,000.

Bluish Laid Paper

55X3	A1	5c black	—

Cancellations: black town, black "PAID".
The 2c, 3c, 15c and 20c are believed to be bogus.

Memphis, Tenn.

A1

A2

Stereotype from woodcut

Plate of 50 (5x10) for the 2c. The stereotypes for the 5c stamps were set in 5 vertical rows of 8, with at least 2 rows set sideways to the right (see Thomas H. Pratt's monograph, "The Postmaster's Provisionals of Memphis").

56X1	A1	2c blue (shades)	75.00	750.00
		Block of four	500.00	
		On cover		7,500.
		Cracked plate (16, 17, 18)	125.00	850.00

The "cracking off" (breaking off) of the plate at right edge caused incomplete printing of stamps in positions 5, 10, 15, 20, and 50. Poor make-ready also caused incomplete printing in position 50.

56X2	A2	5c red (shades)	150.00	200.00
		Pair	350.00	500.00
		Block of four	800.00	
		On cover		1,000.
		Pair on cover		2,250.
		Strip of four on cover		7,000.
		On patriotic cover		4,000.
a.		Tete beche pair		1,500.
		Tete beche pair on cover		10,000.
b.		Pair, one sideways	750.00	
c.		Pelure paper	—	—

Cancellation on Nos. 56X1-56X2: black town.

Envelopes
Typo.

56XU1	A2	5c red, *white*		2,500.
56XU2	A2	5c red, *amber*		2,500.
		With No. 1		5,000.
56XU3	A2	5c red, *orange*		2,750.
		On patriotic cover		4,000.

Micanopy, Fla.
Envelope

E1

Handstamped

105XU1   E1   5c black   11,500.

One example known.

Milledgeville, Ga.
Envelopes

E1

Handstamped

57XU1	E1	5c black		300.00
57XU2	E1	5c blue		400.00
57XU3	E1	10c on 5c black		850.00

E2   E3

57XU4	E2	10c black	225.00	750.00
57XU5	E3	10c black		750.00

Mobile, Ala.

 A1

Litho.

58X1	A1	2c black	1,250.	700.00
		Pair		1,500.
		On cover		2,500.
		Pair on cover		4,000.
		Three singles on one cover		5,000.
		Five copies on one cover		17,500.
58X2	A1	5c blue	250.00	150.00
		Pair	600.00	400.00
		On cover		750.00
		Pair on cover		1,500.
		Strip of three on cover		4,000.
		Strip of four on cover		5,000.
		Strip of five on cover		

Cancellations: black town, express company.

Montgomery, Ala.
Envelopes

 E1

Handstamped

59XU1	E1	5c red		1,000.
59XU2	E1	5c blue	400.00	1,200.
59XU3	E1	10c red		1,000.
59XU4	E1	10c blue		1,250.
59XU5	E1	10c black		1,000.
59XU6	E1	10c on 5c red		2,000.

The 10c design is larger than the 5c.

E2   E3

59XU7	E2	2c red		3,000.
59XU7A	E2	2c blue		1,000.
59XU8	E2	5c black		1,500.
59XU9	E3	10c black		1,500.
59XU10	E3	10c red		

Mt. Lebanon, La.

 A1

Woodcut, Design Reversed

60X1	A1	5c red brown, on cover		100,000.

Cancellation black pen. One example known.

Nashville, Tenn.

A1   A2

Typeset (5 varieties of 3c)

61X1	A1	3c carmine		125.00
		Horizontal strip of five		750.00

No. 61X1 was not placed in use.

Stereotype from Woodcut
Gray Blue Ribbed Paper

61X2	A2	5c carmine (shades)	700.00	400.00
		Pair		1,000.
		On cover		1,750.
		On patriotic cover		4,500.
		Pair on cover		6,000.
		On cover with U.S. 3c 1857 (express)		5,000.
a.		Vertical tete beche pair		2,000.
61X3	A2	5c brick red	700.00	400.00
		On cover		1,500.
		On patriotic cover		5,000.
		Pair on cover		4,500.
		On U.S. envelope No. U26		—
		On U.S. #U27 with #26 (express)		26,000.
61X4	A2	5c gray (shades)	700.00	500.00
		On cover		2,000.
		Pair on cover		5,000.
61X5	A2	5c violet brown	600.00	400.00
		Block of four		
		On cover		1,750.
		On patriotic cover		
		Pair on cover		4,500.
a.		Vertical tete beche pair	4,000.	5,000.
		Vert. tete beche pair on cover		—
61X6	A2	10c green	3,000.	2,250.
		On cover		10,000.
		On cover with U.S. 3c 1857		
		On cover with No. 61X2		12,000.

CANCELLATIONS. Nos. 61X2 to 61X5.

Blue "Paid"	Blue express company
Blue "Postage Paid"	
Blue town	Black express company
Blue numeral "5"	
Blue numeral "10"	

Envelopes

E1

Handstamped

61XU1	E1	5c blue		900.00
		On patriotic envelope		1,750.
61XU2	E1	5c +10c blue		1,500.

New Orleans, La.

A1   A2

Plate of 40
Stereotype from Woodcut

62X1	A1	2c blue, *July 14, 1861*	100.00	400.00
		Pair	400.00	900.00
		Block of four	4,000.	
		On cover		3,000.
		On patriotic cover		7,500.
		Pair on cover		7,500.
		Three singles on one cover		8,500.
		Strip of five on cover		17,500.
		On U.S. envelope No. U27		—
a.		Printed on both sides		—
62X2	A1	2c red (shades), *Jan. 6, 1862*	100.00	650.00
		Pair	250.00	
		Block of four	1,200.	
		On cover		16,000.
62X3	A2	5c brown, *white, June 12, 1861*	200.00	125.00
		Pair	425.00	275.00
		Block of four	1,000.	
		On cover		375.00
		On patriotic cover		3,000.
		Pair on cover		750.00
		Strip of 5 on cover		5,000.
		On cover with U.S. No. 30A		—
a.		Printed on both sides		1,000.
b.		5c ocher, *June 18, 1861*	500.00	350.00
		Pair		1,000.
		On cover		1,000.
		On patriotic cover		5,000.
		Pair on cover		2,500.
62X4	A2	5c red brown, *bluish, Aug. 22, 1861*	220.00	95.00
		Pair	475.00	195.00
		Horizontal strip of 6		2,000.
		Block of four		1,250.
		On cover		300.00
		On patriotic cover		3,500.
		Pair on cover		850.00
		Block of four on cover		5,000.
		On cover with No. 1		4,000.
a.		Printed on both sides		1,050.
62X5	A2	5c yel brn, *off-white, Dec. 3, 1861*	90.00	200.00
		Pair	200.00	450.00
		Block of four	600.00	
		On cover		425.00
		On patriotic cover		2,500.
		Pair on cover		1,000.
		Strip of 5 on cover		
62X6	A2	5c red	—	7,500.
62X7	A2	5c red, *bluish*		10,000.

CANCELLATIONS. Nos. 62X3-62X5.

Black town (single or double circle New Orleans)	Black "Paid"
Red town (double circle New Orleans)	Express Company
Town other than New Orleans	Packet boat, cover "STEAM" "Southn Letter Unpaid" on cover with U.S. No. 26
Postmaster's handstamp	

Envelopes

J.L.RIDDELL. P.M

PD 5 CTS

N O.P.O   E1

Handstamped

62XU1	E1	5c black	3,500.
62XU2	E1	10c black	5,000.

"J. L. RIDDELL, P. M." omitted

62XU3	E1	2c black	7,500.

New Smyrna, Fla.

 A1

Handstamped
On white paper with blue ruled lines

63X1   A1   10c ("O1") on 5c black   25,000.

One example known. It is uncanceled on a postmarked patriotic cover.

Oakway, S.C.

 A1

Handstamped

115X1   A1   5c black, on cover   —   12,000.

Pensacola, Fla.
Envelopes

 E1

Handstamped

106XU1	E1	5c black	4,000.
106XU2	E1	10c (ms.) on 5c black	4,250.
		On patriotic cover	13,500.

Petersburg, Va.

 A1

Typeset
Ten varieties
Thick white paper

65X1	A1	5c red	600.00	400.00
		Pair	1,500.	1,000.
		Block of four	4,500.	
		On cover		1,500.
		On patriotic cover		
		Pair on cover		5,500.
		On cover with General Issue stamp No. 1		7,500.

Cancellation: blue town.

Pittsylvania Court House, Va.

 A1

Typeset
Wove Paper

66X1	A1	5c dull red	6,000.	5,000.
		octagonally cut		4,000.
		On cover		20,000.
		On cover, octagonally cut		15,000.
		On patriotic cover, octagonally cut		17,500.

Laid Paper

66X2	A1	5c dull red		6,500.
		Octagonally cut		5,500.
		On cover		20,000.
		On cover, octagonally cut		15,000.

Cancellation: black town.

Pleasant Shade, Va.

 A1

Typeset
Five varieties

67X1	A1	5c blue	2,500.	4,500.
		On cover		15,000.
		Pair on cover		65,000.
		Pair	5,500.	
		Block of six	25,000.	

Cancellation: blue town.

Port Lavaca, Tex.

 A1

Typeset

107X1   A1   10c black   25,000.

One example known. It is uncanceled on a postmarked cover.

Raleigh, N. C.
Envelopes

 E1

Handstamped

68XU1	E1	5c red	425.00
		On patriotic cover	2,500.
		On U.S. envelope No. U10	1,500.
68XU2	E1	5c blue	1,000.

Rheatown, Tenn.

 A1

Typeset
Three varieties

69X1	A1	5c red	2,000.	2,750.

	On cover	8,500.
	Pair	5,000.
	Pen cancellation	2,000.

Cancellations: red town or black pen.

Richmond, Texas
Envelopes or Letter Sheets

 E1

Handstamped

70XU1	E1	5c red	2,500.
70XU2	E1	10c red	2,500.
70XU3	E1	10c on 5c red	5,000.
70XU4	E1	15c (ms.) on 10c red	—

Ringgold, Ga.
Envelope

 E1

Handstamped

71XU1   E1   5c blue black   4,000.

Rutherfordton, N.C.

A1

Handstamped; "Paid 5cts" in ms.

72X1   A1   5c black, cut round   25,000.

No. 72X1 is on cover and uncanceled.

Salem, N.C.
Envelopes

E1   E2

Handstamped

73XU1	E1	5c black	750.00
73XU2	E1	10c black	850.00
73XU3	E2	5c black	750.00
73XU4	E2	10c on 5c black	1,600.

Reprints exist on various papers. They either lack the "Paid" and value or have them counterfeited.

Salem, Va.
See No. 74X1 under Liberty, Va.

Salisbury, N.C.
Envelope

E1

Typographed
Impressed at top left

75XU1	E1	5c black, *greenish*	5,000.

One example known. Part of envelope is torn away, leaving part of design missing. Illustration E1 partly suppositional.

San Antonio, Texas
Envelopes

E2

E1

Control

Handstamped

76XU1	E1	10c black	275.00	1,100.
76XU2	E2	10c black		1,250.

Black circle control mark is on front or back.

Savannah, Ga.
Envelopes

E1

E2   Control

Handstamped

101XU1	E1	5c black	300.00
101XU2	E2	5c black	450.00
101XU3	E1	10c black	500.00
101XU4	E2	10c black	500.00
101XU5	E1	10c on 5c black	1,500.
101XU6	E2	20c on 5c black	3,000.

Envelopes must have octagonal control mark.

Selma, Ala.
Envelopes

E1

Handstamped; Signature in ms.

77XU1	E1	5c black	1,500.

77XU2	E1	10c black	2,500.
77XU3	E1	10c on 5c black	3,000.

Signature is that of Postmaster William H. Eagar.

Sparta, Ga.
Envelopes

E1

Handstamped

93XU1	E1	5c red	— 750.00
93XU2	E1	10c red	1,000.

Spartanburg, S.C.

A1

A2

Handstamped on Ruled or Plain Wove Paper

78X1	A1	5c black		2,500.
		On cover		12,500.
		Pair on cover		—
		On patriotic cover		15,000.
a.		"5" omitted (on cover)		—
78X2	A2	5c black, *bluish*		3,000.
		On cover		12,500.
78X3	A2	5c black, *brown*		3,000.
		On cover		15,000.

Most examples of Nos. 78X1-78X3 are cut round. Cut square examples are worth much more.
Cancellations: black "PAID", black town.

Statesville, N.C.
Envelopes

E1

Handstamped

79XU1	E1	5c black	135.00	700.00
79XU2	E1	10c on 5c black		1,500.

Sumter, S.C.
Envelopes

E1

Handstamped

80XU1	E1	5c black	150.00	
80XU2	E1	10c black	100.00	
80XU3	E1	10c on 5c black		175.00
80XU4	E1	2c (ms.) on 10c black		800.00

Used examples of Nos. 80XU1-80XU2 are indistinguishable from handstamped "Paid" covers.

Talbotton, Ga.
Envelopes

E1

94XU1	E1	5c black	750.00
		On U.S. envelope No. U27	—
94XU2	E1	10c black	500.00
94XU3	E1	10c on 5c black	1,000.

Tellico Plains, Tenn.

A1

Typeset
Settings of two 5c and one 10c
Laid Paper

81X1	A1	5c red	800.00
		On cover	17,500.
81X2	A1	10c red	1,500.
		Se-tenant with 5c	2,500.
		Strip of three (5c+5c+10c)	3,500.

Cancellation: black pen.

Thomasville, Ga.
Envelopes

PAID   5

E1   Control

Handstamped

82XU1	E1	5c black	1,000.

E2

82XU2	E2	5c black	900.00

Tullahoma, Tenn.
Envelope

E1   Control

Handstamped

111XU1	E1	10c black	3,000.

Tuscaloosa, Ala.
Envelopes

E1

Handstamped

83XU1	E1	5c black	250.00
83XU2	E1	10c black	250.00

Used examples of Nos. 83XU1-83XU2 are indistinguishable from handstamped "Paid" covers. Some authorities question the use of E1 to produce provisional envelopes.

Tuscumbia, Ala.
Envelopes

E1

Handstamped

84XU1	E1	5c	black	550.00
			On patriotic cover	—
84XU2	E1	5c	red	650.00
84XU3	E1	10c	black	1,100.

See U.S. Postmasters' Provisional No. 12XU1.

Union City, Tenn.

E1

The use of E1 to produce provisional envelopes is doubtful.

Uniontown, Ala.

A1

Typeset in settings of four (2x2)
Four varieties of each value
Laid Paper

86X1	A1	2c	dark blue, *gray blue*	10,000.	—
86X2	A1	2c	dark blue, *white*	5,500.	—
			Block of four	30,000.	
86X3	A1	5c	green, *gray blue*	2,750.	2,000.
			Pair	—	
			On cover		6,500.
86X4	A1	5c	green, *white*	2750.	2,000.
			On cover		6,500.
			Pair on cover		18,500.
86X5	A1	10c	red, *gray blue*	8,000	5,000.
			On cover		22,500.

Two examples known of No. 86X1, both on cover (drop letters), one uncanceled and one pen canceled. Cancellation on Nos. 86X3-86X5: black town.

Unionville, S.C.

A1

Handstamped in two impressions
Paper with Blue Ruled Lines

87X1	A1	5c	black, *grayish*, on cover	13,500.
			Pair on patriotic cover	32,500.

Cancellation: black town.

Valdosta, Ga.
Envelope

E1   Control

Handstamped

100XU1	E1	10c	black	800.00

The black circle control is usually on back of envelope.

Victoria, Texas

A1

Typeset
Surface colored paper

88X1	A1	5c	red brown, *green*	4,000.	
88X2	A1	10c	red brown, *green*	4,250.	4,500.
			On cover		17,500.
88X3	A1	10c	red brown, *green* ("10" in bold face type), pelure paper	5,500.	5,250.

Walterborough, S.C.
Envelopes

E1

Typeset

108XU1	E1	10c	black, *buff*	2,000.
108XU2	E1	10c	carmine	4,000.

Warrenton, Ga.
Envelopes

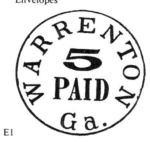

E1

Handstamped

89XU1	E1	5c	black	1,250.
89XU2	E1	10c (ms.) on 5c	black	1,000.

Washington, Ga.
Envelope

 E1

Handstamped

117XU1	E1	10c	black	1,500.

Envelopes must have black circle control on front or back.

Weatherford, Tex.
Envelopes

E1

Woodcut with "PAID" inserted in type.

Handstamped

109XU1	E1	5c	black	2,000.
109XU2	E1	5c +5c	black	16,000.

Winnsborough, S.C.
Envelopes

E1   Control

Handstamped

97XU1	E1	5c	black	1,000.
97XU2	E1	10c	black	1,000.

Envelopes must have black circle control on front or back.

Wytheville, Va.
Envelope

E1   Control

Handstamped

114XU1	E1	5c	black	900.00

For later additions, listed out of numerical sequence, see—
#74X1, Liberty, Va.
#92XU1, Huntsville, Tex.
#93XU1, Sparta, Ga.
#94XU1, Talbotton, Ga.
#96XU1, Lake City, Fla.
#97XU1, Winnsborough, S. C.
#98XU1, Galveston, Tex.
#99XU1, Christiansburg, Va.
#100XU1, Valdosta, Ga.
#101XU1, Savannah, Ga.
#102XU1, Griffin, Ga.
#103XU1, Courtland, Ala.
#104XU1, Fincastle, Va.
#105XU1, Micanopy, Fla.
#106XU1, Pensacola, Fla.
#107X1, Port Lavaca, Tex.
#108XU1, Walterborough, S. C.
#109XU1, Weatherford, Tex.
#110XU1, Jacksonville, Ala.
#111XU1, Tullahoma, Tenn.
#112XU1, Hamburgh, S. C.
#113XU1, Columbia, Tenn.
#114XU1, Wytheville, Va.
#115X1, Oakway, S. C.
#116XU1, Laurens Court House, S. C.
#117XU1, Washington, Ga.
#118XU1, Carolina City, N.C.
#119XU1, Colaparchee, Ga.
#120XU1, Forsyth, Ga.
#121XU1, Limestone Springs, S.C.

GENERAL ISSUES

For explanations of various terms used see the notes at the end of these listings.

Jefferson Davis — A1

1861   Litho.   Soft Porous Paper   *Imperf.*

All 5c Lithographs were printed by Hoyer & Ludwig, of Richmond, Va.

Stones A or B-First stones used. Earliest dated cancellation October 16, 1861. Plating not completed hence size of sheets unknown. These stones had imprints. Stamps from Stones A or B are nearly all in the olive green shade. Sharp, clear impressions. Distinctive marks are few and minute.

Stone 1-Earliest dated cancellation October 18, 1861. Plating completed. Sheet consists of four groups of fifty varieties arranged in two panes of one hundred each without imprint. The first small printing was in olive green and later small printings appeared in light and dark green; the typical shade, however, is an intermediate shade of bright green. The impressions are clear though not as sharp as those from Stones A or B. Distinctive marks are discernible.

Stone 2-Earliest dated cancellation December 2, 1861. Plating completed. Sheet consists of four groups of fifty varieties arranged in two panes of one hundred each without imprint. All shades other than olive green are known from this stone, the commonest being a dull green. Poor impressions. Many noticeable distinctive marks.

UNUSED

				Stones A or B	Stone 1	Stone 2
1	A1	5c	green		200.00	175.00
			bright green		200.00	175.00
			dull green		200.00	175.00
		a.	5c light green		175.00	180.00
		b.	5c dark green		180.00	190.00
		c.	5c olive green	250.00	190.00	
			Pair	550.00	450.00	450.00
			Block of four	1,300.	1,000.	1,000.

USED

				Stones A or B	Stone 1	Stone 2
1	A1	5c	green		125.00	125.00
			bright green		125.00	125.00
			dull green		125.00	125.00
		a.	5c light green		125.00	125.00
		b.	5c dark green		135.00	135.00
		c.	5c olive green	175.00	150.00	
			On cover	225.00	175.00	175.00
			Single on cover (overpaid drop letter)			275.00
			On wallpaper cover			500.00
			On prisoner's cover			—
			On prisoner's cover with U.S. #65			—
			On prisoner's cover with U.S. #U34			—
			On patriotic cover	1,200.	1,100.	1,100.
			Pair	350.00	275.00	275.00
			Pair on cover	400.00	335.00	285.00
			Block of four	900.00	750.00	750.00
			Horiz. pair, vert. gutter between			—

CANCELLATIONS

	Stones A or B	Stone 1	Stone 2
Blue town	+10.00	+10.00	+10.00
Red town	+110.00	+80.00	+80.00
Green town		+175.00	+150.00
Orange town			+100.00
Texas town		+35.00	+35.00
Arkansas town		+90.00	+90.00
Florida town		+110.00	+110.00
Kentucky town		+200.00	+200.00
October, 1861, year date		+50.00	+40.00
Blue gridiron	+5.00	+5.00	+5.00
Red gridiron		+50.00	+50.00
Blue concentric	+5.00	+5.00	+5.00
Star or flowers			+100.00
Numeral	+60.00	+50.00	+50.00
"Paid"	+50.00	+50.00	+50.00
"Steam"	+150.00	+150.00	
"Steamboat"		+150.00	+150.00
Express Company	+400.00	+350.00	+350.00
Railroad		+300.00	+300.00

VARIETIES

	Unused	Used
White curl back of head (S A or B)	225.00	175.00
Imprint (S A or B)	450.00	350.00
Acid flaw (S 1)	225.00	135.00
Arrow between panes (S 1)	350.00	235.00
Flaw on "at" of "States" (38 S 1)	235.00	175.00
Spur on upper left scroll (21 S 2)	235.00	175.00
Bottom scrolls doubled (re—entry 50 S 2)	325.00	235.00
Side margin copy showing initials (41 S 2 or 50 S 2)	650.00	450.00
Misplaced transfer (S 2)	425.00	625.00
Rouletted unofficially	—	325.00

Thomas Jefferson — A2

1861-62   Litho.   Soft Porous Paper

Hoyer & Ludwig-First stone used. Earliest dated cancellation November 8, 1861. Sheet believed to consist of four groups of fifty varieties each arranged in two panes of one hundred each with imprint at bottom of each pane. Two different imprints are known. Hoyer & Ludwig printings are always in a uniform shade of dark blue. Impressions are clear and distinct, especially so in the early printings. Plating marks are distinct.

J. T. Paterson & Co.-Earliest dated cancellation July 25, 1862. Sheet consists of four groups of fifty varieties each arranged in two panes of one hundred each with imprint at bottom of each pane. Two different imprints are known and at least one pane is known without an imprint. Wide range of shades. Impressions are less clear than those from the Hoyer & Ludwig stone. Paterson stamps show small vertical colored dash below the lowest point of the upper left triangle.

Stone "Y"-Supposedly made by J. T. Paterson & Co., as it shows the distinctive mark of that firm. Plating not completed hence size of sheet unknown. No imprint found. Color is either a light milky blue or a greenish blue. Impressions are very poor and have a blurred appearance. Stone Y stamps invariably show a large flaw back of the head as well as small vertical colored dash beneath the upper left triangle.

UNUSED

				Hoyer	Paterson	Stone Y
2	A2	10c	blue		225.00	
		a.	10c light blue		225.00	
			light milky blue			
		b.	10c dark blue	325.00	275.00	
		c.	10c indigo			
		e.	10c greenish blue			350.00
			Pair	700.00	575.00	1,000.
			Block of four	1,750.	1,350.	
			Horiz. pair, gutter btwn.			750.00

USED

				Hoyer	Paterson	Stone Y
2	A2	10c	blue		175.00	
		a.	10c light blue		175.00	
			light milky blue			200.00
		b.	10c dark blue	200.00	160.00	
		c.	10c indigo			
		e.	10c greenish blue			275.00
			On cover	375.00	225.00	375.00
			On wallpaper cover	700.00	650.00	
			On patriotic cover	1,500.	1,350.	1,750.
			On prisoner's cover with U.S. #65	—	—	
			Pair	575.00	500.00	—
			Pair on cover	1,200.	800.00	—
			Strip of 3 on cover	3,500.		—
			Block of four	—		1,850.

	Hoyer	Paterson	Stone Y
Blue town	+30.00	+10.00	+10.00
Red town	+75.00	+75.00	+100.00
Green town		+200.00	+300.00
Violet town			
Texas town	+125.00	+125.00	+125.00
Arkansas town	+275.00	+275.00	+275.00
Florida town	+325.00	+325.00	
Kentucky town	+400.00		
Nov., 1861, date	+300.00		
July, 1862, date		+300.00	
Straight line town	+500.00	+500.00	+500.00
Blue gridiron	+10.00	+10.00	+10.00
Red gridiron	+50.00	+50.00	+50.00
Blue concentric	+10.00	+10.00	+10.00
Numeral	+75.00	+80.00	+100.00
"Paid"	+50.00	+75.00	+100.00
Star or flower		+150.00	
Railroad	+350.00	+350.00	
Express Company	+300.00	+300.00	

VARIETIES

	Unused	Used
Malformed "T" of "TEN" (No. 4 Hoyer)	325.00	250.00
"G" and "E" of "POSTAGE" joined (No. 10 Hoyer)	325.00	250.00
Circular flaw, upper left star (No. 11 Hoyer)	325.00	250.00
Third spiked ornament at right, white (No. 45 Hoyer)	325.00	250.00

		Unused	Used
	Hoyer & Ludwig imprint	500.00	550.00
d.	Printed on both sides (Hoyer)	—	—
d.	Printed on both sides (Pat.)	—	—
	Malformed "O" of "POSTAGE" (No. 25 Pat.)	275.00	225.00
	J. T. Paterson & Co. imprint	550.00	850.00

Andrew Jackson — A3

1862 (March)   Soft Porous Paper.   Litho.

Sheet consists of four groups of fifty varieties arranged in two panes of 100 each.

One stone only was used. Date of issue, probably March, 1862. Printed by Hoyer & Ludwig, of Richmond, Va. Issued to prepay drop letter and circular rates. Strips of five used to prepay regular 10c rate, which was changed from 5c on July 1, 1862. Earliest known cancellation, March 21, 1862.

				Unused	Used
3	A3	2c	green	500.00	625.00
			light green	500.00	625.00
			dark green	550.00	625.00
			dull yellow green	550.00	
			On cover		
			Pair on cover (double circular rate)		4,000.
			Strip of five on cover		8,000.
			On patriotic cover		10,000.
			Pair		
			Block of four	1,200.	1,500.
			Block of five	2,750.	3,250.
		a.	2c bright yellow green	1,500.	2,000.
		a.	On cover		
		a.	Strip of five on cover		
			Diagonal half used as 1c with unsevered pair, on cover		
			Horiz. pair, vert. gutter between	—	—
			Mark between stamps (between Nos. 4 and 5)	1,200.	1,600.
			Mark above upper right corner (No. 30)	600.00	750.00
			Mark above upper left corner (No. 31)	600.00	750.00
			Acid flaw	575.00	700.00

CANCELLATIONS.

Blue town	+500.00	Blue gridiron	+250.00
Red town	+800.00	"Paid"	
Arkansas town		Express Company	
Texas town	+1,250.	Railroad	+3,000.
		Pen	500.00

1862   Soft Porous Paper.   Litho.

Stone 2-First stone used for printing in blue. Plating is the same as Stone 2 in green. Earliest dated cancellation Feb. 28, 1862. Printings from Stone 2 are found in all shades of blue. Rough, coarse impressions are typical of printings from Stone 2.

Stone 3-A new stone used for printings in blue only. Earliest dated cancellation April 10, 1862. Sheet consists of four groups of fifty varieties each arranged in two panes of one hundred each without imprint. Impressions are clear and sharp, often having a proof-like appearance, especially in the deep blue printing. Plating marks, while not so large as on Stone 2 are distinct and clearly defined.

UNUSED

				Stone 2	Stone 3
4	A1	5c	blue	125.00	
			light blue	130.00	
		a.	5c dark blue	150.00	175.00
		b.	5c light milky blue	150.00	200.00
			Pair	300.00	425.00
			Block of four	700.00	900.00
			Horiz. pair, wide gutter between	725.00	
			Vert. pair, narrow gutter between		

USED

				Stone 2	Stone 3
4	A1	5c	blue	100.00	
			light blue	105.00	
		a.	5c dark blue	125.00	150.00
		b.	5c light milky blue	125.00	175.00
			On cover	225.00	300.00

Single on cover (overpaid drop letter)	300.00	
Pair on cover	325.00	425.00
On wallpaper cover	600.00	
On patriotic cover	1,250.	1,500.
On prisoner's cover	2,000.	
On prisoner's cover with U.S. #65		
Pair	250.00	400.00
Block of four	1,400.	1,500.
Horiz. pair, wide gutter btwn.		—

CANCELLATIONS	Stone 2	Stone 3
Blue town	+20.00	+40.00
Red town	+75.00	+75.00
Texas town	+300.00	+300.00
Arkansas town	+325.00	+325.00
Florida town	+200.00	
Straight line town	+300.00	+325.00
Blue gridiron	+10.00	+10.00
Red gridiron	+65.00	
Star or Flowers	+100.00	+100.00
Numeral	+85.00	
Railroad	—	
"Paid"	+25.00	+50.00
"Steamboat"	+400.00	
Express Company	—	
"Way"	+250.00	

VARIETIES

	Unused	Used
Spur on upper left scroll (21 S 2)	140.00	115.00
Thin hard paper (S 2)		110.00
Tops of "C" and "E" of "cents" joined by flaw (33 S 3)	210.00	210.00
"Flying bird" above lower left corner ornament (19 S 3)	200.00	200.00

1862 (March)   Soft Porous Paper.   Litho.

Settings of fifty varieties repeated.

Printed by Hoyer & Ludwig, of Richmond, Va. One stone used, being the same as that used for the Hoyer & Ludwig 10c value in blue. Color change occured probably in March, 1862.

There are many shades of this stamp. The carmine is a very dark, bright color and should not be confused with the deeper shade of rose.

Earliest known cancellation, March 10, 1862. The earliest date of usage of the carmine shade is May 1, 1862.

		Unused	Used
5	A2	**10c rose**	800.00	500.00
		dull rose	800.00	500.00
		brown rose	1,100.	650.00
		deep rose	850.00	550.00
		carmine rose	1,050.	600.00
		On cover		825.00
		On wallpaper cover		2,000.
		On patriotic cover		2,500.
		On prisoner's cover		5,500.
		On prisoner's cover with U.S. #65		
		Pair	2,250.	2,000.
		Strip of three	—	4,000.
		Block of four	9,000.	7,500.
a.		10c carmine	—	1,000.
a.		On cover		3,000.
		Malformed "T" of "TEN" (No. 4)	1,050.	600.00
		"G" and "E" of "POSTAGE" joined (No. 10)	1,050.	600.00
		Circ. flaw, upper left star (No.11)	1,050.	600.00
		Third spiked ornament at right, white (No. 45)	1,050.	600.00
		Scratched stone (occurring on Nos. 40, 39, 49 and 48, one pane)	1,150.	700.00
		Imprint		1,250.
		Horiz. pair, vert. gutter between		—
		Side margin copy, initials (No. 41)		1,750.

CANCELLATIONS.

Blue town	+ 50.00		
Red town	+100.00	April, 1862, year date	—
Green town	+350.00	Blue gridiron	+50.00
Texas town	+150.00	Black concentric	+50.00
Arkansas town	—	Blue concentric	+50.00
Straight line town	+500.00	"Paid"	—
		Railroad	—
		Express Company	

Jefferson Davis — A4

Typographed by De La Rue & Co. in London, England.

1862 (April)   Hard Medium Paper

Plate of 400 in four panes of 100 each. No imprint.

No. 6 represents London printings from De La Rue & Co., a number of sheets being sent over by blockade runners. Fine clear impressions. The gum is light and evenly distributed. Exact date of issue unknown. Earliest known cancellation, April 16, 1862.

6	A4	**5c light blue**	10.00	20.00
		Single on cover used before July 1, 1862		150.00
		Single on cover (overpaid drop letter)		350.00
		Single on patriotic cover used before July 1, 1862		1,000.
		Single on prisoner's cover used before July 1, 1862		—
		On wallpaper cover		400.00
		On patriotic cover		1,000.
		On prisoner's cover		1,250.
		On prisoner's cover with U.S. #65		1,250.
		Pair	22.00	50.00
		Pair on cover		75.00
		Block of four	55.00	350.00
		Block of four on cover		1,000.

CANCELLATIONS.

Blue town	+2.00	Blue gridiron	+2.00
Red town	+45.00	Red gridiron	+35.00
Green town	+75.00	Blue concentric	+2.00
Texas town	+65.00	Express Company	+350.00
Arkansas town	+85.00	Railroad	+250.00
Straight line town	+150.00	"Paid"	+50.00

1862 (August)   Typo.   Thin to Thick Paper

Plate of 400 in four panes of 100 each. No imprint.

Locally printed by Archer & Daly of Richmond, Va., from plates made in London, England, by De La Rue & Co. Printed on both imported English and local papers. Earliest known cancellation, August 15, 1862.

No. 7 shows coarser impressions than No. 6, and the color is duller and often blurred. Gum is light or dark and unevenly distributed.

7	A4	**5c blue**	12.00	10.00
	a.	5c deep blue	12.00	10.00
		Single on cover (overpaid drop letter)		300.00
		On wallpaper cover		350.00
		On patriotic cover		800.00
		On prisoner's cover		1,000.
		On prisoner's cover with U.S. #65		—
		Pair	25.00	25.00
		Pair on cover		100.00
		Block of four	60.00	300.00
		Block of four on cover		800.00
		Eight on cover (Trans—Miss. rate)		—
		White tie (U.R. 30)	140.00	150.00
		White tie on cover		375.00
		De La Rue paper (thin)	20.00	25.00
		White tie, De La Rue paper	195.00	240.00
		Thick paper	15.00	18.00
		Horiz. pair, vert. gutter between	200.00	
	b.	Printed on both sides	1,000.	700.00

CANCELLATIONS.

Blue town	+2.00	Blue gridiron	+2.00
Red town	+60.00	Red gridiron	+60.00
Brown town	+30.00		
Violet town	+110.00		
Green town	+125.00	Blue concentric	+2.00
Texas town	+90.00	Railroad	+250.00
Arkansas town	+110.00	Express Company	+400.00
Florida town	+140.00	Design (stars, etc.)	+75.00
Straight line town	+140.00	"Paid"	+50.00

The unissued 10c type A4 was privately printed in various colors for philatelic purposes. (See note below No. 14.) Counterfeits of the 10c exist.

Andrew Jackson — A5

1863 (April)   Soft Porous Paper   Line Engraved

Sheet of 200 (two panes of 100 each).

One plate. Printed by Archer & Daly of Richmond, Va. Earliest known cancellation. Apr. 21, 1863. Issued to prepay drop letter and circular rates. Strips of five used to prepay regular 10c rate.

8	A5	**2c brown red**	50.00	350.00
	a.	2c pale red	60.00	375.00
		Single on cover		1,300.
		On prisoner's cover		3,000.
		On prisoner's cover with U.S. #65		4,000.
		Pair	110.00	750.00
		Pair on cover		3,000.
		On wallpaper cover		—
		Block of four	250.00	—
		Block of five		—
		Strip of five on cover		5,500.
		Strip of five on wallpaper cover		—
		Strip of ten on cover		13,000.
		Double transfer	125.00	400.00
		Horiz. pair, vert. gutter between	275.00	

CANCELLATIONS.

Blue town	+35.00	Blue gridiron	+35.00
Red town	+225.00	Black numeral	—
Army of Tenn.	—	Railroad	+325.00

Jefferson Davis "TEN CENTS" — A6

1863, Apr.   Soft Porous Paper   Line Engraved

One plate of 200 subjects all of which were probably recut as every copy examined to date shows distinct recutting. Plating not completed.

Printed by Archer & Daly of Richmond, Va. First printings in milky blue. First issued in April, 1863. Earliest known cancellation, April 23, 1863.

9	A6	**10c blue**	700.00	500.00
	a.	10c milky blue (first printing)	750.00	550.00
	b.	10c gray blue	700.00	500.00
		On cover		1,000.
		On wallpaper cover		3,000.
		On patriotic cover		3,500.
		On prisoner's cover		4,250.
		On prisoner's cover with U.S. #65		—
		Pair	1,550.	2,000.
		Pair on cover		3,000.
		Block of four	3,500.	
		Four stamps on one cover (Trans—Mississippi rate)		13,500.
		Curved lines outside the labels at top and bottom are broken in the middle (No. 63R)	800.00	600.00
		Double transfer	850.00	850.00
		Damaged plate	900.00	900.00

CANCELLATIONS.

Blue town	+25.00	Black gridiron	+25.00
Red town	+150.00	Blue gridiron	+50.00
Green town	+600.00	Red gridiron	+200.00
Violet town	—	Railroad	+400.00
Straight line town	+500.00	Circle of wedges	+1,000.
April, 1863, year date	—	Pen	350.00

Frame Line "10 CENTS"
(Illustration actual size) — A6a

1863, Apr.   Soft Porous Paper   Line Engraved

Printed by Archer & Daly of Richmond, Va.
One copper plate of 100 subjects, all but one of which were recut. First issued in April, 1863. Earliest known use April 19, 1863.
Stamp design same as Die A (No. 11).
Prices are for copies showing parts of lines on at least two of the four sides. Copies showing lines on three or four sides sell for more.

10	A6a	10c blue	2,750.	1,250.
	a.	10c milky blue	3,000.	1,500.
	b.	10c greenish blue	2,750.	1,250.
	c.	10c dark blue	2,750.	1,250.
		On cover		2,250.
		On wallpaper cover		4,500.
		On patriotic cover		6,000.
		On prisoner's cover		7,000.
		On prisoner's cover with U.S. #65		—
		Pair	7,000.	5,500.
		Pair on cover		7,000.
		Block of four	15,000.	
		Strip of four	17,000.	
		Strip of seven	28,500.	
		Double transfer (No. 74)	3,250.	1,750.

CANCELLATIONS.

Blue town	+100.00	Blue gridiron	+100.00
Red town	+500.00	Pen	900.00
Straight line town	+750.00		
April, 1863, year date	—		

No Frame Line "10
CENTS" — A7 (Die A)

1863-64   Thick or Thin Paper   Line Engraved

There are many slight differences between A7 (Die A) and A8 (Die B), the most noticeable being the additional line outside the ornaments at the four corners of A8 (Die B).

Jefferson Davis — A8 (Die B)

1863-64   Thick or Thin Paper   Line Engraved

Plates bore Nos. 3 and 4, otherwise notes on No. 11 apply.

Stamps were first printed by Archer & Daly, of Richmond, Va. In 1864 the plates were transferred to the firm of Keatinge & Ball in Columbia, S. C., who made further printings from them. Two plates, each with two panes of 100, numbered 1 and 2. First state shows numbers only, later states show various styles of Archer & Daly imprints, and latest show Keatinge & Ball imprints. Archer & Daly stamps show uniformly clear impressions and a good quality of gum evenly distributed (Earliest known cancellation, April 21, 1863); Keatinge & Ball stamps generally show filled in impressions in a deep blue, and the gum is brown and unevenly distributed. (Earliest known cancellation, Oct. 4, 1864. The so-called laid paper is probably due to thick streaky gum. (These notes also apply to No. 12.)

11	A7	10c blue	10.00	15.00
	a.	10c milky blue	25.00	30.00
	b.	10c dark blue	10.00	15.00
	c.	10c greenish blue	10.00	15.00
	d.	10c green	35.00	45.00
		deep blue, Keatinge & Ball ('64)	15.00	30.00
		On cover		65.00
		Single on cover (overpaid drop letter)		225.00
		On wallpaper cover		400.00
		On patriotic cover		750.00
		On prisoner's cover		600.00
		On prisoner's cover with U.S. #65		1,100.
		On cover, dp. blue (K. & B.) ('64)		125.00
		On prisoner's cover (K. & B.) with U.S. #65 ('64)		—
		Pair	22.00	35.00
		Pair on cover		200.00
		Block of four	50.00	325.00
		Strip of four on cover (Trans—Mississippi rate)		4,500.
		Margin block of 12, Archer & Daly impt. & P#	325.00	
		Margin block of 12, Keatinge & Ball impt. & P#	300.00	
		Double transfer	60.00	75.00
		Horiz. pair, vert. gutter between	100.00	
	e.	Perforated	150.00	165.00
	e.	On cover		450.00
	e.	On wallpaper cover		—
	e.	Block of four	650.00	

CANCELLATIONS.

Blue town	+5.00	April, 1863 year date	+75.00
Red town	+35.00	"FREE"	+250.00
Brown town	+60.00	Blue gridiron	+5.00
Green town	+110.00	Black concentric circles	+20.00
Violet town	+85.00	Crossroads	+150.00
Texas town	+60.00	"Paid"	+100.00
Arkansas town	+125.00	Numeral	+100.00
Florida town	+200.00	Railroad	+175.00
Straight line town	+350.00	Steamboat	+1,500.
Army of Tenn.	+300.00		

Earliest known cancellation May 1, 1863.

12	A8	10c blue	11.00	16.00
	a.	10c milky blue	25.00	30.00
	b.	10c light blue	11.00	16.00
	c.	10c greenish blue	11.00	16.00
	d.	10c dark blue	11.00	16.00
	e.	10c green	35.00	45.00
		deep blue, Keatinge & Ball ('64)	15.00	30.00
		On cover		70.00
		Single on cover (overpaid drop letter)		225.00
		On wallpaper cover		400.00
		On patriotic cover		750.00
		On prisoner's cover		600.00
		On prisoner's cover with U.S. #65		1,000.
		On cover, dp. blue (K. & B.) ('64)		125.00
		Pair	23.00	35.00
		Pair on cover		225.00
		Block of four	50.00	325.00
		Strip of four on cover (Trans—Mississippi rate)		4,500.
		Margin block of 12, Archer & Daly impt. & P#	350.00	
		Margin block of 12, Keatinge & Ball impt. & P#	300.00	
		Double transfer	60.00	75.00
		Horiz. pair, vert. gutter between	100.00	
	f.	Perforated	150.00	165.00
	f.	On cover		500.00
	f.	Block of four	675.00	

CANCELLATIONS.

Blue town	+5.00	Army of Tenn.	+350.00
Red town	+35.00	May, 1863, year date	+60.00
Brown town	+60.00	Blue gridiron	+5.00
Green town	+120.00	Black concentric circles	+15.00
Violet town	+85.00	Railroad	+175.00
Texas town	+125.00		
Arkansas town	+150.00		
Florida town	+200.00		
Straight line town	+350.00		

George
Washington — A9

1863 (June 1)   Line Engraved by Archer & Daly

One plate which consisted of two panes of 100 each. First printings were from plates with imprint in Old English type under each pane, which was later removed. Printed on paper of varying thickness and in many shades of green. This stamp was also used as currency. Earliest known cancellation, June 1, 1863. Forged cancellations exist.

13	A9	20c green	40.00	450.00
	a.	20c yellow green	40.00	450.00
	b.	20c dark green	50.00	500.00
		On cover		1,000.
		On wallpaper cover		1,500.
		On prisoner's cover		4,000.
		On prisoner's cover with U.S. #65		5,000.
		Pair	85.00	1,000.
		Pair on cover (Trans—Mississippi rate)		6,000.
		Block of four	190.00	3,000.
		Strip of four with imprint	400.00	
	c.	Diagonal half used as 10c on cover		4,000.
	c.	On prisoner's cover		—
	d.	Horizontal half used as 10c on cover		4,500.
		Double transfer, 20 doubled (24L and 35R)	110.00	—
		Horiz. pair, vert. gutter between	250.00	
		"20" on forehead	1,750.	—

CANCELLATIONS.

Blue town	+50.00	Pen	250.00
Red town	+200.00	Railroad	—
Violet town	—		
Texas town	+100.00		

John C. Calhoun — A10

Typographed by De La Rue & Co., London, England 1862

14	A10	1c	orange	125.00
	a.		1c deep orange	150.00
			Pair	275.00
			Block of four	600.00

This stamp was never put in use.

Upon orders from the Confederate Government, De La Rue & Co. of London, England, prepared Two Cents and Ten Cents typographed plates by altering the One Cent (No. 14) and the Five Cents (Nos. 6-7) designs previously made by them. Stamps were never officially printed from these plates although privately made prints exist in various colors.

Explanatory Notes

The following notes by Lawrence L. Shenfield explain the various routes, rates and usages of the general issue Confederate stamps.

"Across the Lines"
Letters Carried by Private Express Companies

Express Company Handstamps Used on "Across the Lines" Letters

About two months after the outbreak of the Civil War, in June, 1861, postal service between North and South and vice versa was carried on largely by Adams Express Company, and the American Letter Express Company. Northern terminus for the traffic was Louisville, Ky.; Southern terminus was Nashville, Tenn. Letters for transmission were delivered to any office of the express company, together with a fee, usually 20c or 25c per ½ ounce to cover carriage. The express company messengers carried letters across the lines and delivered them to their office on the other side, where they were deposited in the Government mail for transmission to addressees, postage paid out of the fee charged. Letters from North to South, always enclosed in 3c U. S. envelopes, usually bear the handstamp of the Louisville office of the express company, and in addition the postmark and "Paid 5" of Nashville, Tenn., indicating its acceptance for delivery at the Nashville Post Office. Letters from South to North sometimes bear the origin postmark of a Southern post office, but more often merely the handstamp of the Louisville express company office applied as the letters cleared through Louisville. In addition, they bear the 3c 1857 U.S. adhesive stamp, cancelled with the postmark and grid of Louisville, Ky., where they went into the Government mail for delivery. Some across-the-lines letters show the handstamp of various express company offices, according to the particular routing the letters followed.

1861, the traffic ceased by order of the U. S. Post Office Dept. (Prices are for full covers bearing the usual Louisville, Ky., or Nashville, Tenn., handstamps of the express company. Unusual express office markings are rarer and worth more.)

North to South 3c U.S. Envelope, Adams Exp. Co. Louisville, Ky., handstamp	1,250.
North to South 3c U.S. Envelope, American Letter Express Co., Ky., handstamp	2,000.
South to North 3c 1857, Adams Exp. Co., Louisville, Ky., handstamp	1,500.
South to North 3c 1857, American Letter Exp. Co., Nashville, Tenn., handstamp	2,500.
South to North 3c 1861, Adams Exp. Co., Louisville, Ky., handstamp	3,500.

Blockade-Run Letters from Europe to the Confederate States

Charleston "STEAM-SHIP" in Oval Handstamp

As the Federal Fleet gradually extended its blockade of the Confederate States coastal regions, the South was forced to resort to blockade runners to carry letters to and from outside ports. These letters were all private-ship letters and never bore a foreign stamp if from Europe, nor a Confederate stamp if to Europe. The usual route from Europe was via a West Indies port, Nassau, Bahamas; Hamilton, Bermuda, or Havana, into the Southern ports of Wilmington, N.C. and Charleston, S.C. More rarely such letters came in to Savannah, Mobile and New Orleans. Letters from Europe are the only ones which are surely identified by their markings. They bore either the postmark of Wilmington, N.C., straightline "SHIP" and "12", "22", "32", etc., in manuscript; or the postmark of Charleston, S. C., "STEAMSHIP" in oval, and "12", "22", "32", etc., in manuscript. Very rarely Charleston used a straightline "SHIP" instead of "STEAMSHIP" in oval. All such letters were postage due; the single letter rate of 12c being made up of 2c for the private ship captain plus 10c for the regular single letter Confederate States rate. Over-weight letters were 22c (due), 32c, 42c, etc. A few examples are known on which Confederate General Issue stamps were used, usually as payment for forwarding postage. Covers with such stamps, or with the higher rate markings, 22c, 32, etc., are worth more.
(Prices are for all full covers in fine condition.)

Charleston, S.C. "6" handstamp	2,000.
Charleston, S.C., postmark, "STEAMSHIP," and "12" in ms.	2,000.
Charleston, S.C., postmark, "SHIP," and "12" in ms.	1,500.
Wilmington, N.C., postmark, "SHIP," and "12" in ms.	2,500.
Savannah, Ga., postmark "SHIP," and "7" in ms. (*)	4,000.
New Orleans, La. postmark "SHIP" and "10" in ms.	5,000.

(* 7c rate: 5c postage before July 1, 1862, plus 2c for ship captain.)

Express Company Mail in the Confederacy

Southern Express Company Handstamps

Shortly after the outbreak of war in 1861, the Adams Express Company divisions operating in the South were forced to suspend operations and turned their Southern lines over to a new company organized under the title Southern Express Company. This express did the bulk of the express business in the Confederacy despite the continued opposition of the Post Office Dept. of the C.S.A. and the ravages of the contending armies upon railroads. Other companies operating in the Confederacy were: South Western Express Co. (New Orleans), Pioneer Express Company, White's Southern Express (only one example known) and some local expresses of limited operation. The first three used handstamps of various designs usually bearing the city name of the office. Postal regulation necessitated the payment of regular Confederate postal rates on letters carried by express companies, express charges being paid in addition. Important letters, particularly money letters, were entrusted to these express companies as well as goods and wares of all kinds. The express rates charged for letters are not known; probably they varied depending on the difficulty and risk of transmittal. Covers bearing stamps and express company handstamps are very rare.

Prisoner-of-War and Flag-of-Truce Letters

Prison Censor Handstamps

By agreement between the United States and the Confederate States, military prisoners and imprisoned civilians of both sides were permitted to send censored letters to their respective countries. Such letters, if from North to South, usually bore a U.S. 3c 1861 adhesive, postmarked at a city near the prison, to pay the postage to the exchange ground near Old Point Comfort, Va.; and a 10c Confederate stamp, canceled at Richmond, Va. (or "due" handstamp) to pay the Confederate postage to destination. It from South to North, letters usually bore a 10c Confederate stamp canceled at a Southern city (or "paid" handstamp) and a U. S. 3c 1861 adhesive (or "due 3" marking) and the postmark of Old Point Comfort, Va. In addition, prison censor markings, handstamped or manuscript, the name and rank of the soldier, and "Flag of Truce, via Fortress Monroe" in manuscript usually appear on these covers. Federal prison censor handstamps of various designs are known from these prisons:

Camp Chase, Columbus, O.
David's Island, Pelham, N.Y.
Fort Delaware, Delaware City, Del.
Camp Douglas, Chicago, Ill.
Elmira Prison, Elmira, N.Y.
Johnson's Island, Sandusky, O.
Fort McHenry, Baltimore, Md.
Camp Morton, Indianapolis, Ind.
Fort Oglethorpe, Macon, Ga.
Old Capitol Prison, Washington, D.C.
Point Lookout Prison, Point Lookout, Md.
Fort Pulaski, Savannah, Ga.
Rock Island Prison, Rock Island, Ill.
Ship Island, New Orleans, La.
West's Hospital, Baltimore, Md.
U.S. General Hospital, Gettysburg, Pa.

Several other Federal prisons used manuscript censor markings.

Southern prison censor markings are always in manuscript, and do not identify the prison. The principal Southern prisons were at Richmond and Danville, Va.; Andersonville and Savannah, Ga.; Charleston, Columbia and Florence S.C.; Salisbury, N.C.; Hempstead and Tyler, Tex.

Civilians residing in both the North and the South were also, under exceptional circumstances, permitted to send Flag of Truce letters across the lines. Such covers bore no censor marking nor prison markings, but were always endorsed "via Flag of Truce".

Prices will be found under various individual stamps for "on prisoner's cover" and are for the larger prisons. Prisoners' letters from the smaller prisons are much rarer. Only a very small percentage of prisoners' covers bore *both* a U.S. stamp and a Confederate stamp.

The "SOUTHERN LETTER UNPAID" Marking On Northbound Letters of Confederate Origin

DUE 3

SOUTHᴺ LETTER UNPAID.

By mid-May, 1861, correspondence between the North and South was difficult. In the South, postmasters were resigning and closing their accounts with Washington as the Confederacy prepared to organize its own postal system by June 1. From that date on, town marks and "paid" handstamps (and later postmasters' provisional stamps) were used in all post offices of the seceded states. The three most important Southern cities for clearing mail to the North were Memphis, Nashville and Richmond. The Richmond-Washington route was closed in April; Memphis was closed by June 1st, and mail attempting to cross the lines at these points generally ended up at the dead letter office. However, at Louisville, Kentucky, mail from the South via Nashville continued to arrive in June, July and August. On June 24, 1861, the Post Office Department advised the Louisville post office, "You will forward letters from the South for the Loyal States as unpaid, after removing postage stamps, but foreign letters in which prepayment is compulsory must come to the Dead Letter Office." However, Louisville avoided the task of "removing postage stamps," and instead prepared the "Southern Letter Unpaid" handstamp and special "due 3" markers for use. These markings were applied in the greenish-blue color of the Louisville office to letters of Southern origin that had accumulated, in addition to the usual town mark and grid of Louisville. The letters were delivered in the North at abroad as unpaid. Probably Louisville continued to forward such unpaid mail until about July 15. The marking is very rare. Other Southern mail was forwarded from Louisville as late as Aug. 27.

For listings see under U.S. 1857-61 issue, Nos. 26, 35-38. Prices shown there are generally for this marking on off-cover stamps. Complete covers bearing stamps showing the full markings are valued from $7,500 upward depending upon the stamps, other postal markings and unusual usages. Fraudulent covers exist.

Trans-Mississippi Express Mail-the 40c Rate

Prices paid for stamps on original covers vary greatly in accordance with condition, appearance, cancellation or postmark and usage.

From the fall of New Orleans on April 24, 1862, the entire reach of the Mississippi River was threatened by the Federal fleets. Late in 1862 the Confederacy experienced difficulty in maintaining regular mail routes trans-Mississippi to the Western states. Private express companies began to carry some mail, but by early 1863 when the Meridian-Jackson-Vicksburg-Shreveport route was seriously menaced, the Post Office Department of the Confederate States was forced to inaugurate an express mail service by contracting with a private company the name of which remains undisclosed. The eastern termini were at Meridian and Brandon, Miss.; the western at Shreveport and Alexandria, La. Letters, usually endorsed "via Meridian (or Brandon)" if going West; "via Shreveport (or Alexandria)" if going East were deposited in any Confederate post office. The rate was 40c per ½ ounce or less. Such Trans-Mississippi Express Mail upon arrival at a terminus was carried by couriers in a devious route across the Mississippi and returned to the regular mails at the nearest terminus on the other side of the river. The precise date of the beginning of the Trans-Mississippi service is not known. The earliest date of use so far seen is November 2, 1863 and the latest use February 9, 1865. These covers can be identified by the written endorsement of the route, but particularly by the rate since many bore no route endorsements.

Strips of four of 10c engraved stamps, pairs of the 20c stamp and various combinations of 10c stamps and the 5c London or Local prints are known; also handstamped Paid 40c marking. No identifying handstamps were used, merely the postmark of the office which received the letter originally. Prices for Trans-Mississippi Express covers will be found under various stamps of the General Issues.

A 50c Preferred Mail Express rate, announced in April, 1863, preceded the Trans-Mississippi Express Mail 40c rate. Covers have been reported.

Packet and Steamboat Covers and Markings

Letters carried on Confederate packets operating on coastal routes or up and down the inland waterways were usually handstamped with the name of the packet or marked STEAM or STEAMBOAT. Either United States stamps of the 1857 issue or stamped envelopes of the 1853 or 1860 issues have been found so used, as well as Confederate Postmasters' Provisional and General Issue stamps. Some specially designed pictorial or imprinted packet boat covers also exist. All are scarce and command prices from $500 upward for handstamped United States envelopes and from $1,000 up for covers bearing Confederate stamps.

TABLE OF SECESSION

States in Order of Secession	Ordinance of Secession Passed	Admitted to Confederacy	Period for Use of U.S. Stamps As Independent State	Total to May 31, 1861*
S. Carolina	12/20/1860	2/4/1861	1 mo 15 da	5 mo 11 da
Mississippi	1/9/1861	2/4/1861	26 da	4 mo 22 da
Florida	1/10/1861	2/4/1861	25 da	4 mo 21 da
Alabama	1/11/1861	2/4/1861	24 da	4 mo 20 da
Georgia	1/18/1861	2/4/1861	17 da	4 mo 13 da
Louisiana	1/26/1861	2/4/1861	9 da	4 mo 5 da
Texas	2/1/1861	3/6/1861	1 mo 6 da	4 mo 0 da
Virginia	4/17/1861	5/7/1861	20 da	1 mo 14 da
Arkansas	5/6/1861	5/18/1861	12 da	25 da
N. Carolina	5/20/1861	5/27/1861	7 da	11 da
Tennessee	6/8/1861	7/2/1861	0*	0*

* The use of United States stamps in the seceded States was prohibited after May 31, 1861.
Ordinance of Secession adopted. Popular vote to secede Feb. 23, effective March 2, 1861.
Secession data by courtesy of August Dietz, Sr.

The Confederate postal laws did not provide the franking privilege for any mail except official correspondence of the Post Office Department. Such letters could be sent free only when enclosed in officially imprinted envelopes individually signed by the official using them. These envelopes were prepared and issued for Post Office Department use.

The imprints were on United States envelopes of 1853-61 issue, and also on commercial envelopes of various sizes and colors. When officially signed and mailed, they were postmarked, usually at Richmond, Va., with printed or handstamped "FREE". Envelopes are occasionally found unused and unsigned, and more rarely, signed but unused. When such official envelopes were used on other than official Post Office Department business, Confederate stamps were used.

Semi-official envelopes also exist bearing imprints of other government departments, offices, armies, states, etc. Regular postage was required to carry such envelopes through the mails.

OFFICIAL ENVELOPES

The Confederate postal laws did not provide the franking privilege for any mail except official correspondence of the Post Office Department. Such letters could be sent free only when enclosed in officially imprinted envelopes individually signed by the official using them. These envelopes were prepared and issued for Post Office Department use.

The imprints were on United States envelopes of 1853-61 issue, and also on commercial envelopes of various sizes and colors. When officially signed and mailed, they were postmarked, usually at Richmond, Va., with printed or handstamped "FREE". Envelopes are occasionally found unused and unsigned, and more rarely, signed but unused. When such official envelopes were used on other than official Post Office Department business, Confederate stamps were used.

Semi-official envelopes also exist bearing imprints of other government departments, offices, armies, states, etc. Regular postage was required to carry such envelopes through the mails.

CONFEDERATE STATES OF AMERICA,
POST OFFICE DEPARTMENT,
OFFICIAL BUSINESS.

John H. Reagan
POSTMASTER GENERAL.

Confederate States of America,
POST OFFICE DEPARTMENT,
OFFICIAL BUSINESS.

John B. A. Dimitry
Ast. CHIEF CLERK P. O. DEPARTMENT.

Typical Imprints of Official Envelopes of the Post Office Department. (Many variations of type, style and wording exist.)

Office	Signature
Postmaster General	John H. Reagan
Chief of the Contract Bureau	H. St. Geo. Offutt
Chief of the Appointment Bureau	B. N. Clements
Chief of the Finance Bureau	Jno. L. Harrell
Chief of the Finance Bureau	J. L. Lancaster
Chief of the Finance Bureau	A. Dimitry
Dead Letter Office	A. Dimitry
Dead Letter Office	Jno. L. Harrell
Chief Clerk, P. O. Department	B. Fuller
Chief Clerk	W. D. Miller
Auditor's Office	W. W. Lester
Auditor's Office	B. Baker
Auditor's Office	J. W. Robertson
First Auditor's Office, Treasury Department	J. W. Robertson
First Auditor's Office, Treasury Department	B. Baker
Third Auditor's Office	A. Moise
Third Auditor's Office	I. W. M. Harris
Agency, Post Office Dept. Trans—Miss.	Jas. H. Starr

PROOFS

			DIE		PLATE
			(1) Glazed card	*(1a)* Wove paper	*(5)* Wove paper
1861					
1P	5c	green			*1,500.*
2P	10c	blue			*1,500.*
2TC	10c	black (stone y)			*3,000.*
1862					
6P	5c	blight blue	1,000.		
6P	5c	dark blue		1,000.	
6P	5c	gray blue			600.00
6TC	5c	black	750.00		1,000.
6TC	5c	pink	1,250.		

			DIE (1) Glazed card	(1a) Wove paper	PLATE (5) Wove paper
7P	5c	carmine			850.00
1863					
8TC	2c	black		1,000.	
9TC	10c	black		1,200.	
11TC	10c	black		900.00	
13P	20c	green		900.00	
13TC	20c	red brown		800.00	
1862					
14P	1c	orange	700.00		
14TC	1c	black	700.00		
14TC	1c	light yellow brown			600.00

Essay Die Proofs

In working up the final dies, proofs of incomplete designs in various stages were made. Usually dated in typeset lines, they are very rare. Others, of the 10c (No. 12) and the 20c (No. 13) were proofs made as essays from the dies. They are deeply engraved and printed in deep shades of the issued colors, but show only small differences from the stamps as finally issued. All are very rare.

Specimen Overprints

The De La Rue typographed 5c and 1c are known with "SPECIMEN" overprinted diagonally, also horizontally for 1c.

Counterfeits

In 1935 a set of 12 lithographed imitations, later known as the "Springfield facsimiles," appeared in plate form. They are in approximately normal colors on yellowish soft wove paper of modern manufacture.

CANAL ZONE

The Canal Zone, a strip of territory with an area of about 552 square miles following generally the line of the Canal, was under the jurisdiction of the United States, 1904-1979.

The Canal organization underwent two distinct and fundamental changes. The construction of the Canal and the general administration of civil affairs were performed by the Isthmian Canal Commission under the provisions of the Spooner Act. This was supplanted in April, 1914, by the Panama Canal Act which established the organization known as The Panama Canal. This was an independent Government Agency which included both the operation and maintenance of the waterway and civil government in the Canal Zone. Most of the quasi-business enterprises relating to the Canal operation were conducted by the Panama Railroad, an adjunct of the Panama Canal.

A basic change in the mode of operations took effect July 1, 1951, under provisions of Public Law 841 of the 81st Congress. This in effect transferred the canal operations to the Panama Railroad Co., which had been made a federal government corporation in 1948, and changed its name to the Panama Canal Co. Simultaneously the civil government functions of The Panama Canal, including the postal service, were renamed the Canal Zone Government. The organization therefore consisted of two units-the Panama Canal Co. and Canal Zone Government-headed by an individual who was president of the company and governor of the Canal Zone. His appointment as governor was made by the President of the United States, subject to confirmation by the Senate, and he was ex-officio president of the company.

The Canal Zone Governmen functioned as an independent government agency, and was under direct supervision of the President of the United States who delegated this authority to the Secretary of the Army.

The Panama Canal is 50 miles long from deep water in the Atlantic to deep water in the Pacific. Its runs from northwest to southeast with the Atlantic entrance being 33.5 miles north and 27 miles west of the Pacific entrance. The airline distance between the two entrances is 43 miles. It requires about eight hours for an average ship to transit the Canal. Transportation between the Atlantic and Pacific sides of the Isthmus is available by railway or highway.

The U.S. Canal Zone Postal Service began operating June 24, 1904, when nine post offices were opened in connection with the construction of the Panama Canal. It ceased Sept. 30, 1979, and the Panama Postal Service took over.

Numbers in parentheses indicate quantity issued.

100 CENTAVOS = 1 PESO
100 CENTESIMOS = 1 BALBOA
100 CENTS = 1 DOLLAR

Map of Panama — A1

Violet to Violet Blue Handstamp on Panama Nos. 72, 72a-72c, 78, 79.

On the 2c "PANAMA" is normally 13mm. long. On the 5c and 10c it measures about 15mm.

On the 2c, "PANAMA" reads up on the upper half of the sheet and down on the lower half. On the 5c and 10c, "PANAMA" reads up at left and down at right on each stamp.

On the 2c only, varieties exist with inverted "V" for "A", accent on "A", inverted "N", etc., in "PANAMA."

1904, June 24   Unwmk.   Perf. 12

1	A1	2c rose, both "PANAMA" reading up or down *(2600)*	450.00	425.00
		Single on cover		850.00
		Strip of three on cover		1,600.
		Block of four	2,100.	2,100.
a.		"CANAL ZONE" inverted *(100)*	750.00	750.00
b.		"CANAL ZONE" double	2,000.	2,000.
c.		"CANAL ZONE" double, both inverted	4,000.	
d.		"PANAMA" reading down and up *(52)*	550.00	550.00
e.		As "d," "CANAL ZONE" invtd.	3,500.	3,500.
f.		Vert. pair, "PANAMA" reading up on top 2c, down on other	1,500.	1,500.
		"PANAMA" 15mm. long *(260)*	500.00	500.00
		"P NAMA"	500.00	500.00
2	A1	5c blue *(7800)*	275.00	225.00
		On cover		450.00
		First day cover		2,500.
		Block of four	1,450.	1,450.
a.		"CANAL ZONE" inverted	500.00	500.00
b.		"CANAL ZONE" double	1,000.	1,000.
c.		Pair, one without "CANAL ZONE" overprint	2,250.	2,250.
d.		"CANAL ZONE" overprint diagonal, reading down to right	500.00	500.00
		Left "PANAMA" 2¼mm. below bar *(156)*	450.00	450.00
		Colon between right "PANAMA" and bar *(156)*	450.00	450.00

3	A1	10c yellow *(4946)*	325.00	300.00
		On cover		500.00
		First day cover		2,500.
		Block of four	1,600.	1,600.
a.		"CANAL ZONE" inverted *(200)*	500.00	500.00
b.		"CANAL ZONE" double		3,000.
c.		Pair, one without "CANAL ZONE" overprint	2,750.	2,750.
		Left "PANAMA" 2¼mm. below bar *(100)*	550.00	550.00
		Colon between right "PANAMA" and bar *(100)*	500.00	500.00

Cancellations consist of town and/or bars in magenta or black, or a mixture of both colors.

Nos. 1-3 were withdrawn July 17, 1904.

Forgeries of the "Canal Zone" overprint and cancellations are numerous.

CANAL ZONE   PANAMA

United States Nos. 300, 319, 304, 306 and 307 Overprinted in Black

1904, July 18   Wmk. 191

4	A115	1c blue green *(43,738)*	27.50	22.50
		green	27.50	22.50
		On cover		60.00
		Block of four	125.00	125.00
		Margin strip of three, Impt. & P#	135.00	
		Margin block of six, Impt. & P#	875.00	
5	A129	2c carmine *(68,414)*	22.50	20.00
		On cover		60.00
		Block of four	100.00	100.00
		Margin strip of three, Impt. & P#	100.00	
		Margin block of six, Impt. & P#	800.00	
a.		2c scarlet	27.50	22.50
6	A119	5c blue *(20,858)*	100.00	70.00
		On cover		125.00
		Block of four	475.00	375.00
		Margin strip of three, Impt. & P#	500.00	
		Margin block of six, Impt. & P#	1,850.	
7	A121	8c violet black *(7932)*	150.00	130.00
		On cover		225.00
		Block of four	700.00	700.00
		Margin strip of three, Impt. & P#	700.00	

	Margin block of six, Impt. & P#	2,500.		
8	A122 10c pale red brown *(7856)*	175.00	130.00	
	On cover		225.00	
	Block of four	825.00	700.00	
	Margin strip of three, Impt. & P#	825.00		
	Margin block of six, Impt. & P#	3,000.		

Nos. 4 to 8 frequently show minor broken letters.

Cancellations consist of circular town and/or bars in black, blue or magenta.

A2

A3

CANAL ZONE
Regular Type

CANAL ZONE
Antique Type

The Canal Zone overprint on stamps Nos. 9-15 and 18-20 was made with a plate which had six different stages, each with its peculiar faults and errors of which there was generally only one in each sheet. Stage 1: Broken CA-L, broken L, A-L spaced, on Nos. 9, 10, 12-15. Stage 2: broken L, Z, N, E, on Nos. 9, 10, 12-14. Stage 3: same as 2 with additional antique ZONE, on Nos. 9, 11-14, 18. Stage 4: same as 3 with additional antique CANAL on Nos. 9, 12, 13. Stage 5: broken E and letters L, Z, N, and words CANAL and ZONE in antique type on Nos. 12-14, 19, 20. Stage 6: same as 5 except for additional antique Z on stamp which had antique L, on No. 12. The Panama overprints can be distinguished by the different shades of the red overprint, the width of the bar, and the word PANAMA. No. 11 has two different Panama overprints; No. 12 has six; No. 13 five; No. 14 two; and Nos. 15, 18-20, one each. In the "8cts" surcharge of Nos. 14 and 15, there are three varieties of the figure "8". The bar is sometimes misplaced so that it appears on the bottom of the stamp instead of the top.

1904-06   Unwmk.

Black Overprint on Stamps of Panama

9	A2 1c green *(319,800)* Dec. 12, 1904	2.25	1.75	
	On cover		5.00	
	Block of four	10.00	9.00	
a.	"CANAL" in antique type *(500)*	125.00	125.00	
b.	"ZONE" in antique type *(1500)*	75.00	75.00	
c.	Inverted overprint	—	2,000.	
d.	Double overprint	1,200.	800.00	
	Spaced "A L" in "CANAL" *(700)*	125.00	125.00	
	"ON" of "ZONE" dropped	275.00	275.00	
10	A2 2c rose *(367,500)* Dec. 12, 1904	5.00	3.00	
	On cover		7.25	
	Block of four	25.00	18.00	
a.	Inverted overprint	250.00	250.00	
b.	"L" of "CANAL" sideways	1,100.	1,100.	
	Spaced "A L" of "CANAL" *(1700)*	85.00	85.00	
	"ON" of "ZONE" dropped	250.00	250.00	

"PANAMA" (15mm. long) reading up at left, down at right

Overprint "CANAL ZONE" in Black, "PANAMA" and Bar in Red

11	A3 2c rose *(150,000)* Dec. 9, 1905	6.50	4.50	
	On cover		9.50	
	Block of four	32.50	25.00	
a.	"ZONE" in antique type *(1500)*	125.00	125.00	
b.	"PANAMA" overprint inverted, bar at bottom *(200)*	350.00	350.00	
	Inverted "M" in "PANAMA" *(3,000)*	60.00	60.00	
	"PANAMA" 16mm. long *(3000)*	60.00	60.00	
12	A3 5c blue *(400,000)* Dec. 12, 1904	8.50	4.25	
	On cover		11.50	
	Block of four	42.50	22.50	
a.	"CANAL" in antique type *(2750)*	75.00	75.00	
b.	"ZONE" in antique type *(2950)*	75.00	75.00	
c.	"CANAL ZONE" double *(200)*	500.00	500.00	
d.	"PANAMA" double *(120)*	650.00	650.00	
e.	"PANAMA" inverted, bar at bottom	950.00	950.00	
	Spaced "A L" in "CANAL" *(300)*	90.00	90.00	
	"PAMANA" reading up *(2800)*	70.00	70.00	
	"PAMANA" reading down *(400)*	200.00	200.00	
	"PANAMA" 16mm. long *(1300)*	50.00	50.00	
	Inverted "M" in "PANAMA" *(1300)*	50.00	50.00	
	Right "PANAMA" 5mm. below bar *(600)*	75.00	75.00	
	"PANAMA"	70.00	70.00	
	"PANAAM" at right	650.00	650.00	
	"PAN MA"	75.00	75.00	
	"ANAMA"	80.00	80.00	
13	A2 10c yellow *(64,900)* Dec. 12, 1904	20.00	15.00	
	On cover		30.00	

	Block of four	100.00	80.00	
a.	"ZONE" in antique type *(200)*	200.00	200.00	
b.	"ZONE" in antique type *(400)*	175.00	175.00	
c.	"PANAMA" ovpt. double *(80)*	600.00	600.00	
	Spaced "A L" in "CANAL" *(200)*	150.00	150.00	
	"PANAMA" 16mm. long *(400)*	90.00	90.00	
	"PANAMA" reading down *(200)*	150.00	150.00	
	Invtd. "M" in "PANAMA" *(400)*	125.00	125.00	
	Right "PANAMA" 5mm. below bar *(398)*	125.00	125.00	
	Left "PANAMA" touches bar *(400)*	125.00	125.00	
d.	"PANAMA" overprint in red brown *(5000)*	25.00	25.00	
	"PANAMA" ovpt. in org. red	30.00	30.00	

With Additional Surcharge in Red

a

8 cts

There are three varieties of "8" in the surcharge on Nos. 14-15.

14	A3 8c on 50c bister brown *(27,900)* Dec. 12, 1904	35.00	25.00	
	On cover		42.50	
	Block of four	165.00	125.00	
a.	"ZONE" in antique type *(25)*	750.00	700.00	
b.	"CANAL ZONE" inverted *(200)*	325.00	325.00	
	Spaced "A L" in "CANAL" *(194)*	125.00	125.00	
	Right "PANAMA" 5mm. below bar *(438)*	110.00	110.00	
c.	"PANAMA" overprint in rose brown *(6000)*	37.50	37.50	
d.	As "c", "CANAL" in antique type *(10)*	1,500.		
e.	As "c", "ZONE" in antique type *(10)*	1,500.		
f.	As "c", "8cts" double *(30)*	700.00		
g.	As "c", "8" omitted	4,000.		

Nos. 11-14 are overprinted or surcharged on Panama Nos. 77, 77e, 78, 78c, 78d, 78f, 78g, 78h, 79 79c, 79e, 79g and 81 respectively.

Panama No. 74a, 74b Overprinted "CANAL ZONE" in Regular Type and Surcharged "a" in Red

Both "PANAMA" (13mm. long) Reading Up

15	A3(a) 8c on 50c bister brown *(500)* Dec. 12, 1904	2,400.	2,400.	
	On cover		6,000.	
	Block of four	10,000.	10,000.	
a.	"PANAMA" reading down and up *(10)*	3,300.	3,300.	
	"PANAMA" 15mm. long *(50)*	2,750.	2,750.	
	"P NAMA"	2,800.		
	Spaced "A L" in "CANAL" *(5)*	3,100.		

Map of Panama — A4

Panama Nos. 19 and 21 Surcharged in Black:

CANAL ZONE 1 ct.	CANAL ZONE 1 ct.	
a	b	
CANAL ZONE 1 ct.	CANAL ZONE 2 cts.	
c	d	
CANAL ZONE 2 cts.	CANAL ZONE 2 cts.	
e	f	

1906

There were three printings of each denomination, differing principally in the relative position of the various parts of the surcharges. Varieties occur with inverted "v" for the final "a" in "Panama", "CA" spaced, "ZO" spaced, "2c" spaced, accents in various positions, and with bars shifted so that two bars appear on top or bottom of the stamp (either with or without the corresponding bar on the top or bottom) and sometimes with only one bar at top or bottom.

16	A4 1c on 20c violet, type a *(100,000)*	1.75	1.20	
	March			
	On cover		4.00	
	Block of four	7.75	6.00	
a.	1c on 20c violet, type b *(100,000)* May	1.75	1.20	
	On cover		4.00	
	Block of four	7.75	6.00	
b.	1c on 20c violet, type c *(300,000)* Sept.	1.50	1.20	
	On cover		4.00	
	Block of four	7.75	6.00	
	Spaced C-A	12.50		
17	A4 2c on 1p lake, type d *(200,000)*	2.50	1.75	
	Mar.			
	On cover		7.00	
	Block of four	13.00	9.00	
a.	2c on 1p lake, type e *(200,000)* May	2.50	1.75	
	On cover		7.00	
	Block of four	13.00	9.00	
b.	2c on 1p lake, type f *(50,000)* Sept.	22.50	22.50	
	On cover		27.50	
	Block of four	95.00	95.00	

Panama Nos. 74, 74a and 74b Overprinted "CANAL ZONE" in Regular Type in Black and Surcharged in Red

8 cts.
b

8 cts
c

1905-06

Both "Panama" Reading Up

18	A3(b) 8c on 50c bister brown *(17,500)*	70.00	70.00	
	Nov. 1905			
	On cover		100.00	
	Block of four	300.00	300.00	
a.	"ZONE" in antique type *(175)*	200.00	200.00	
b.	"PANAMA" reading down and up *(350)*	125.00	125.00	
	"PANAMA" 15mm. long *(1750)*	90.00	90.00	
	"P NAMA"	125.00	125.00	
19	A3(c) 8c on 50c bister brown *(19,000)*	70.00	65.00	
	April 23, 1906			
	On cover		100.00	
	Block of four	300.00	300.00	
a.	"CANAL" in antique type *(190)*	175.00	175.00	
b.	"ZONE" in antique type *(190)*	175.00	175.00	
c.	"8 cts" double	1,000.	1,000.	
d.	"PANAMA" reading down and up *(380)*	100.00	100.00	
	"PANAMA" 15mm. long *(1900)*	75.00	65.00	
	"P NAMA"	80.00		

Panama No. 81 Overprinted "CANAL ZONE" in Regular Type in Black and Surcharged in Red Type "c" plus Period "Panama" reading up and down

20	A3(c) 8c on 50c bis. brown *(19,600)*	60.00	50.00	
	Sept. 1906			
	On cover		75.00	
	Block of four	240.00	200.00	
a.	"CANAL" antique type *(196)*	175.00	175.00	
b.	"ZONE" in antique type *(196)*	175.00	175.00	
c.	"8 cts" omitted *(50)*	700.00	700.00	
d.	"8 cts" double	1,250.		
	"PANAMA" reading up *(392)*	80.00	80.00	

Nos. 14 and 18-20 exist without CANAL ZONE overprint but were not regularly issued. Forgeries of the overprint varieties of Nos. 9-15 and 18-20 are known.

Vasco Núñez de Balboa
A5

Fernández de Córdoba
A6

Justo Arosemena
A7

Manuel J. Hurtado
A8

José de Obaldía — A9

Engraved by Hamilton Bank Note Co. Overprinted in black by Isthmian Canal Commission Press.

1906-07   **Unwmk.**   **Perf. 12**

Overprint Reading Up

21	A6	2c red & black *(50,000)* Oct. 29, 1906	35.00	30.00
		On cover		45.00
		Block of four	175.00	160.00
a.		"CANAL" only	4,500.	

Overprint Reading Down

22	A5	1c green & black *(2,000,000) Jan. 14, 1907*	2.25	1.25
		dull green & black	2.25	1.25
		On cover		3.00
		Block of four	10.00	6.00
a.		Horiz. pair, imperf. btwn. *(50)*	900.00	900.00
b.		Vert. pair, imperf. btwn. *(20)*	1,500.	1,500.
c.		Vert. pair, imperf. horiz. *(20)*	1,500.	1,500.
d.		Inverted overprint reading up *(100)*	300.00	300.00
e.		Double overprint *(300)*	225.00	225.00
f.		Double overprint, one inverted	1,100.	1,100.
g.		Invtd. center, ovpt. reading up	2,250.	2,250.
		"ANA" for "CANAL" *(1000)*	70.00	70.00
		"CAN L" for "CANAL"	80.00	80.00
		"ONE" for "ZONE" *(3000)*	60.00	60.00
23	A6	2c red & black *(2,370,000)* Nov. 25, 1906	2.75	1.25
		scarlet & black, *1907*	2.75	1.25
		On cover		3.00
		Block of four	12.00	7.00
a.		Horizontal pair, imperf. between *(20)*	1,000.	1,000.
b.		Vertical pair, one without overprint	1,500.	1,500.
c.		Double overprint *(100)*	400.00	400.00
d.		Double overprint, one diagonal	550.00	550.00
e.		Double overprint, one diagonal in pair with normal	1,300.	
f.		2c carmine red & black, Sept. 9, 1907	6.00	4.00
g.		As "f", inverted center and overprint reading up		5,500.
h.		As "d," one "ZONE CANAL"	2,250.	
i.		"CANAL" double	2,750.	
		"CAN L" for "CANAL"	45.00	
24	A7	5c ultramarine & black *(1,390,000)* Dec. 1906	7.25	2.75
		light ultramarine & black	7.25	2.75
		blue & black, Sept. 16, 1907	7.25	2.75
		dark blue & black	7.25	2.75
		On cover		10.00
		Block of four	35.00	20.00
a.		5c dull blue & black	7.25	2.75
b.		5c light blue & black	6.00	2.25
c.		Double overprint *(200)*	350.00	250.00
d.		"CANAL" only *(10)*	1,750.	
e.		"ZONE CANAL"	3,000.	
		"CAN L" for "CANAL"	60.00	
25	A8	8c purple & black *(170,000)* Dec. 1906	27.50	12.50
		On cover		12.50
		Block of four	135.00	62.50
a.		Horizontal pair, imperf. between and at left margin *(34)*	700.00	700.00
26	A9	10c violet & black *(250,000)* Dec. 1906	27.50	10.00
		On cover		37.50
		Block of four	135.00	62.50
a.		Dbl. ovpt., one reading up *(10)*	2,000.	
b.		Overprint reading up	2,250.	

The early printings of this series were issued on soft, thick, porous-textured paper, while later printings of all except No. 25 appear on hard, thin, smooth-textured paper. Normal spacing of the early printings is 7¼mm. between the words; later printings, 6¾mm. Nos. 22 and 26 exist imperf. between stamp and sheet margin. Nos. 22-25 occur with "CA" of "CANAL" spaced ½mm. further apart on position No. 50 of the setting.

Córdoba
A11

Arosemena
A12

Hurtado
A13

José de
Obaldía
A14

Engraved by American Bank Note Co.

1909

Overprint Reading Down

27	A11	2c vermilion & black *(500,000)* May 11, 1909	17.50	9.00
		On cover		14.00
		First day cover		400.00
		Block of four	82.50	47.50
a.		Horizontal pair, one without overprint	2,250.	
b.		Vert. pair, one without ovpt.	2,400.	
28	A12	5c deep blue & black *(200,000)* May 28, 1909	62.50	14.00
		On cover		25.00
		Block of four	275.00	75.00
29	A13	8c violet & black *(50,000)* May 25, 1909	55.00	12.50
		On cover		40.00
		Block of four	250.00	85.00
30	A14	10c violet & black *(100,000)* Jan. 19, 1909	55.00	15.00
		On cover		45.00
		Block of four	250.00	100.00
a.		Horizontal pair, one without overprint	3,250.	
b.		Vertical pair, one without overprint	3,750.	

Nos. 27-30 occur with "CA" spaced (position 50).

Vasco Núñez de Balboa — A15

Engraved, Printed and Overprinted by American Bank Note Co.

Black Overprint Reading Up

CANAL ZONE

Type I

Type I Overprint: "C" with serifs both top and bottom. "L," "Z" and "E" with slanting serifs.
Illustrations of Types I to V are considerably enlarged and do not show actual spacing between lines of overprint.

1909-10

31	A15	1c dark green & black *(4,000,000)* Nov. 8, 1909	3.50	2.00
		On cover		3.00
		Block of four	16.00	10.50
a.		Inverted center and overprint reading down		12,000.
b.		Booklet pane of 6 handmade, perf. margins	550.00	
32	A11	2c vermilion & black, *(4,000,000)* Nov. 8, 1909	4.25	2.00
		On cover		3.00
		Block of four	19.00	10.50
a.		Vert. pair, imperf. horiz.	700.00	700.00
b.		Bklt. pane of 6 handmade, perf. margins	700.00	
33	A12	5c deep blue & black, *(2,000,000)* Nov. 8, 1909	13.00	4.50
		On cover		8.00
		Block of four	65.00	25.00
a.		Double overprint *(200)*	275.00	275.00
34	A13	8c violet & black, *(200,000)* Mar. 18, 1910	9.50	5.00
		On cover		10.00
		Block of four	50.00	25.00
a.		Vertical pair, one without overprint *(10)*	1,750.	
35	A14	10c violet & black, *(100,000)* Nov. 8, 1909	65.00	25.00
		On cover		40.00
		Block of four	300.00	100.00

Normal spacing between words of overprint on No. 31 is 10mm. and on Nos. 32 to 35, 8½mm. Minor spacing variations are known.

A16

A17

1911

36	A16	10c on 13c gray *(476,700)* Jan. 14, 1911	5.00	2.00
		On cover		5.00

		Block of four	24.00	11.00
a.		"10 cts" inverted	300.00	225.00
b.		"10 cts" omitted	250.00	—

The "10 cts" surcharge was applied by the Isthmian Canal Commission Press after the overprinted stamps were received from the American Bank Note Co.
Many of the stamps offered as No. 36b are merely No. 36 from which the surcharge has been removed with chemicals.

1914

37	A17	10c gray *(200,000)* Jan. 6, 1914	50.00	12.00
		On cover		22.50
		Block of four	240.00	55.00

CANAL ZONE

Type II

Type II Overprint: "C" with serifs at top only. "L" and "E" with vertical serifs. Inner oval of "O" tilts to left.

1912-16

38	A15	1c green & black *(3,000,000)* July 1913	12.00	2.75
		On cover		5.00
		Block of four	55.00	18.00
a.		Vertical pair, one without overprint	1,250.	1,250.
b.		Booklet pane of six, imperf. margins *(120,000)*	525.00	
c.		Booklet pane of 6 handmade, perf. margins	900.00	
39	A11	2c vermilion & black *(7,500,000)* Dec. 1912	7.00	1.25
		orange vermilion & black, *1916*	7.00	1.25
		On cover		3.50
		Block of four	35.00	7.00
a.		Horizontal pair, one without overprint	700.00	
b.		"CANAL" only		1,000.
c.		Booklet pane of 6, imperf. margins *(194,868)*	500.00	
d.		Overprint reading down	150.00	
e.		As "d" inverted center	750.00	750.00
f.		As "e" booklet pane of 6 handmade, perf. margins	5,000.	
g.		As "c," handmade, perf. margins	850.00	
40	A12	5c deep blue & black *(2,300,000)* Dec. 1912	25.00	2.75
		On cover		10.00
		Block of four	125.00	13.00
a.		With Cordoba portrait of 2c	7,000.	
41	A14	10c violet & black *(200,000)* Feb. 1916	50.00	10.00
		On cover		25.00
		Block of four	250.00	55.00

Normal spacing between words of overprint on the first printing of Nos. 38-40 is 8½mm. and on the second printing 9¼mm. The spacing of the single printing of No. 41 and the imperf. margin booklet panes printing of Nos. 38 and 39 is 7¾mm. Minor spacing variations are known.

Map of Panama
Canal — A18

Balboa Taking
Possession of the
Pacific Ocean — A19

Gatun Locks — A20

Culebra Cut — A21

Engraved, Printed and Overprinted by American Bank Note Co.

1915, Mar. 1

Blue Overprint, Type II

42	A18	1c dark green & black *(100,000)*	8.25	5.00
		On cover		7.00
		Block of four	35.00	22.50
		First day cover		150.00
43	A19	2c carmine & black *(100,000)*	10.00	5.50
		vermilion & black	10.00	5.50
		On cover		8.00
		First day cover		150.00
		Block of four	42.50	25.00
44	A20	5c blue & black *(100,000)*	10.00	5.00
		On cover		13.00
		Block of four	45.00	27.50
		First day cover		150.00
45	A21	10c orange & black *(50,000)*	22.50	15.00
		On cover		24.00

Block of four	100.00	72.50
First day cover		150.00

Normal spacing between words of overprint is 9¼mm. on all four values except position No. 61 which is 10mm.

Type III

Type III Overprint: Similar to Type I but letters appear thinner, particularly the lower bar of "L," "Z" and "E." Impressions are often light, rough and irregular.

Engraved and Printed by American Bank Note Co.
Black overprint reading up applied by Panama Canal Press, Mount Hope, C. Z.

1915-20

46	A15	1c green & black, *Dec. 1915*	200.00	120.00
		light green & black, *1920*	225.00	175.00
		On cover		175.00
		Block of four	950.00	575.00
a.		Overprint reading down *(200)*	350.00	
b.		Double overprint *(180)*	375.00	
c.		"ZONE" double *(2)*	3,250.	
d.		Double overprint, one reads "ZONE CANAL" *(18)*	1,000.	
47	A11	2c orange vermilion & black, *Aug. 1920*	2,500.	100.00
		On cover		350.00
		Block of four	12,000.	550.00
48	A12	5c deep blue & black, *Dec. 1915*	700.00	200.00
		On cover		500.00
		Block of four	3,000.	900.00

Normal spacing between words of overprint on Nos. 46-48 is 9¼mm. This should not be confused with an abnormal 9¼mm. spacing of the 2c and 5c values of type I, which are fairly common in singles, particularly used. Blocks of the abnormal spacing are rare.

S. S. "Panama" in Culebra Cut
A22   A23

S. S. "Cristobal" in Gatun Locks — A24

Engraved, Printed and Overprinted by American Bank Note Co.

1917, Jan.

Blue Overprint, Type II

49	A22	12c purple & black *(314,914)*	20.00	7.00
		On cover		15.00
		Block of four	90.00	30.00
50	A23	15c bright blue & black	55.00	35.00
		On cover		57.50
		Block of four	250.00	150.00
51	A24	24c yellow brown & black	50.00	17.50
		On cover		35.00
		Block of four	225.00	90.00

Formal spacing between words of overprint is 11¼mm.

Type IV

Type IV Overprint: "C" thick at bottom, "E" with center bar same length as top and bottom bars.

Engraved, Printed and Overprinted by American Bank Note Co.

1918-20

Black Overprint, Reading Up

52	A15	1c green & black *(2,000,000)* Jan. 1918	37.50	6.50
		On cover		11.00

		Block of four	175.00	32.50
a.		Overprint reading down	125.00	
b.		Booklet pane of 6 *(60,000)*	600.00	
c.		Booklet pane of 6, left vertical row of 3 without overprint	2,250.	
d.		Booklet pane of 6, right vertical row of 3, with double overprint	2,250.	
e.		Pair, one without overprint	850.00	
53	A11	2c vermilion & black *(2,000,000)* *Nov. 1918*	150.00	10.00
		On cover		15.00
		Block of four	675.00	52.50
a.		Overprint reading down	140.00	140.00
b.		Horiz. pair, one without ovpt.	1,250.	
c.		Booklet pane of 6 *(34,000)*	700.00	
d.		Booklet pane of 6, left vertical row of 3, without overprint	2,250.	
54	A12	5c deep blue & black *(500,000)* *Apr. 1920*	250.00	45.00
		On cover		130.00
		Block of four	1,050.	210.00

Normal spacing between words of overprint on Nos. 52 and 53 is 9¼mm. On No. 54 and the booklet printings of Nos. 52 and 53, the normal spacing is 9mm. Minor spacing varieties are known.

Type V

Type V Overprint: Smaller block type 1¾mm. high. "A" with flat top.

1920-21

Black Overprint, Reading Up

55	A15	1c light green & black, *Apr. 1921*	25.00	4.50
		On cover		7.00
		Block of four	110.00	20.00
a.		Overprint reading down	140.00	140.00
b.		Pair, one without ovpt.	800.00	
c.		"CANAL" double	1,100.	
d.		"ZONE" only	2,250.	—
e.		Booklet pane of 6	2,750.	
56	A11	2c orange vermilion & black, *Sept. 1920*	9.00	3.00
		On cover		4.00
		Block of four	40.00	14.00
a.		Double overprint *(100)*	350.00	
b.		Double overprint, one reading down *(100)*	350.00	
c.		Horizontal pair, one without overprint	800.00	
d.		Vertical pair, one without overprint	1,750.	
e.		"CANAL" double	900.00	
f.		"ZONE" double	1,000.	
g.		Booklet pane of 6	850.00	
57	A12	5c deep blue & black, *Apr. 1921*	325.00	50.00
		On cover		150.00
		Block of four	1,500.	235.00
a.		Horizontal pair, one without overprint *(20)*		

Normal spacing between words of overprint on Nos. 55-57 is 9½mm. On booklet printings of Nos. 55 and 56 the normal spacing is 9¼mm.

Drydock at Balboa — A25

U.S.S. "Nereus" in Pedro Miguel Locks — A26

1920, Sept.

Black Overprint Type V

58	A25	50c orange & black	350.00	200.00
		On cover		350.00
		Block of four	1,650.	1,050.
59	A26	1b dark violet & black *(23,014)*	180.00	75.00
		On cover		175.00
		Block of four	825.00	350.00

José Vallarino
A27

"Land Gate"
A28

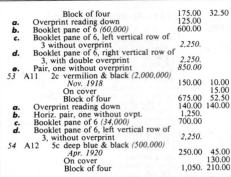

Bolivar's Tribute — A29

Municipal Building in 1821 and 1921 — A30

Statue of Balboa A31

Tomás Herrera A32

José de Fábrega — A33

Engraved, Printed and Overprinted by American Bank Note Co.

Type V overprint in black, reading up, on all values except the 5c which is overprinted with larger type in red

1921, Nov. 13

60	A27	1c green	3.50	1.50
		On cover		2.50
		Block of four	17.00	7.00
a.		"CANAL" double	1,200.	
b.		Booklet pane of six	750.00	
61	A28	2c carmine	2.50	1.40
		On cover		2.50
		Blocks of four	11.00	6.00
a.		Invtd. overprint, reading down	175.00	175.00
b.		Double overprint	650.00	
c.		Vertical pair, one without overprint	3,500.	
d.		"CANAL" double	1,750.	
e.		"ZONE" only	3,500.	
f.		Booklet pane of six	1,200.	
62	A29	5c blue (R)	10.00	4.00
		On cover		7.00
		Block of four	45.00	22.50
a.		Overprint reading down (R)	80.00	
63	A30	10c violet	17.50	7.50
		On cover		15.00
		Block of four	80.00	35.00
a.		Invtd. overprint, reading down	100.00	
64	A31	15c light blue	60.00	17.50
		On cover		35.00
		Block of four	275.00	87.50
65	A32	24c black brown	70.00	27.50
		On cover		55.00
		Block of four	325.00	165.00
66	A33	50c black	150.00	110.00
		On cover		250.00
		Block of four	725.00	575.00

Experts question the status of the 5c with a small type V overprint in red or black.

Engraved and printed by the American Bank Note Co.

1924, Jan. 28

Type III overprint in black, reading up, applied by the Panama Canal Press, Mount Hope, C. Z.

67	A27	1c green	475.00	200.00
		On cover		300.00
		Block of four	2000.00	1500.00
a.		"ZONE CANAL" reading down	750.00	
b.		"ZONE" only, reading down	1500.00	

Arms of Panama — A34

1924, Feb.

68	A34	1c dark green	12.50	4.00
		On cover		6.00
		Block of four	55.00	18.00
69	A34	2c carmine	10.00	3.50
		carmine rose	10.00	3.50

On cover		5.00
Block of four	42.50	15.00

The following were prepared for use, but not issued.

A34 5c dark blue *(600)*		225.00
Block of four		800.00
A34 10c dark violet *(600)*		225.00
Block of four		800.00
A34 12c olive green *(600)*		225.00
Block of four		800.00
A34 15c ultramarine *(600)*		225.00
Block of four		800.00
A34 24c yellow brown *(600)*		225.00
Block of four		800.00
A34 50c orange *(600)*		225.00
Block of four		800.00
A34 1b black *(600)*		225.00
Block of four		800.00

The 5c to 1b values were prepared for use but never issued due to abrogation of the Taft Agreement which required the Canal Zone to use overprinted Panama stamps. Six hundred of each denomination were not destroyed, as they were forwarded to the Director General of Posts of Panama for transmission to the U.P.U. which then required about 400 sets.

All Panama stamps overprinted "CANAL ZONE" were withdrawn from sale June 30, 1924, and were no longer valid for postage after Aug. 31, 1924.

CANAL

United States Nos. 551 to 554, 557, 562, 564 to 566, 569, 570 and 571 Overprinted in Red or Black

ZONE

Printed and Overprinted by the U.S. Bureau of Engraving and Printing.
Type A
Letters "A" with Flat Tops

1924-25		Unwmk.		Perf. 11	
70	A154	½c olive brown (R) *(399,500) Apr. 15, 1925*		1.00	1.00
		On cover			1.65
		Block of four		4.50	4.50
		Margin block of six, P#		25.00	
71	A155	1c deep green *(1,985,000) July 1, 1924*		1.75	80
		On cover			1.25
		Block of four		7.50	3.60
		Margin block of six, P#		47.50	
a.		Inverted overprint		500.00	500.00
b.		"ZONE" inverted		350.00	350.00
c.		"CANAL" only *(20)*		1,000.	
d.		"ZONE CANAL" *(180)*		300.00	
e.		Booklet pane of six *(43,152)*		125.00	
72	A156	1½c yellow brown *(180,599) Apr. 15, 1925*		2.25	1.25
		brown		2.25	1.25
		On cover			2.50
		Block of four		9.50	7.00
		Margin block of six, P#		35.00	
73	A157	2c carmine *(2,975,000) July 1, 1924*		10.00	1.50
		On cover			2.00
		Block of four		42.50	7.00
		Margin block of six, P#		250.00	
a.		Booklet pane of six *(140,000)*		150.00	
74	A160	5c dark blue *(500,000) July 1, 1924*		22.50	9.00
		On cover			14.00
		Block of four		95.00	40.00
		Margin block of six, P#		425.00	
75	A165	10c orange *(60,000) July 1, 1924*		45.00	20.00
		On cover			35.00
		Block of four		190.00	90.00
		Margin block of six, P#		850.00	
76	A167	12c brown violet *(80,000) July 1, 1924*		40.00	22.50
		On cover			35.00
		Block of four		175.00	100.00
		Margin block of six, P#		600.00	
a.		"ZONE" inverted		3,000.	2,000.
77	A168	14c dark blue *(100,000) June 27, 1925*		25.00	17.50
		On cover			32.50
		Block of four		110.00	87.50
		Margin block of six, P#		450.00	
78	A169	15c gray *(55,000) July 1, 1924*		55.00	35.00
		On cover			70.00
		Block of four		250.00	175.00
		Margin block of six, P#		850.00	
79	A172	30c olive brown *(40,000) July 1, 1924*		30.00	20.00
		On cover			40.00
		Block of four		135.00	100.00
		Margin block of six, P#		550.00	
80	A173	50c lilac *(25,000) July 1, 1924*		65.00	40.00
		On cover			80.00
		Block of four		275.00	200.00
		Margin block of six, P#		1,750.	
81	A174	$1 violet brown *(10,000) July 1, 1924*		350.00	180.00
		On cover			325.00
		Block of four		1,600.	875.00
		Margin block of four, arrow, top or bottom		1,700.	
		Margin block of six, P#		4,000.	

Normal spacing between words of the overprint is 9¼mm. Minor spacing variations are known. The overprint of the early printings used on all values of this series except No. 77 is a sharp, clear impression. The overprint of the late printings, used only on Nos. 70, 71, 73, 76, 77, 78 and 80 is heavy and smudged, with many of the letters, particularly the "A" practically filled.

Booklet panes Nos. 71e, 73a, 84d, 97b, 101a, 106a and 117a were made from 360 subject plates. The handmade booklet panes Nos. 102a, 115c and a provisional lot of 117b were made from Post Office sheets from regular 400-subject plates.

CANAL

United States Nos. 554, 555, 567, 562, 564 to 567, 569, 570, 571 and 623 Overprinted in Red or Black

ZONE

Type B
Letters "A" with Sharp Pointed Tops

1925-28				Perf. 11	
84	A157	2c carmine *(1,110,000) May 1926*		35.00	8.50
		On cover			10.00
		Block of four		150.00	40.00
		Margin block of six, P#		450.00	
		Margin block of 6, P# & large 5 point star, side only		1,250.	
a.		"CANAL" only *(20)*		1,000.	
b.		"ZONE CANAL" *(180)*		300.00	
c.		Horizontal pair, one without overprint		2,750.	
d.		Booklet pane of six *(82,000)*		200.00	
85	A158	3c violet *(199,200) June 27, 1925*		4.75	2.50
		On cover			4.25
		Block of four		20.00	11.00
		Margin block of six, P#		225.00	
a.		"ZONE ZONE"		500.00	500.00
86	A160	5c dark blue *(1,343,147) Jan. 7, 1926*		4.50	2.50
		On cover			3.25
		Block of four		20.00	11.00
		Margin block of six, P#		200.00	
a.		"ZONE ZONE" (LR18)		900.00	
b.		"CANAL" inverted (LR7)		900.00	
c.		Inverted overprint *(80)*		450.00	
d.		Horizontal pair, one without overprint		3,250.	
e.		Overprinted "ZONE CANAL" *(90)*		325.00	
f.		"ZONE" only *(10)*		2,000.	
g.		Vertical pair, one without overprint, other overprint inverted *(10)*		2,000.	
h.		"CANAL" only		2,000.	
		Double transfer (15571 UL 86)		50.00	50.00
87	A165	10c orange *(99,510) Aug., 1925*		40.00	10.00
		On cover			15.00
		Block of four		180.00	60.00
		Margin block of six, P#		600.00	
a.		"ZONE ZONE" (LR18)		3,250.	
b.		"ZONE" only		3,500.	
88	A167	12c brown violet *(58,062) Feb., 1926*		30.00	15.00
		On cover			30.00
		Block of four		130.00	70.00
		Margin block of six, P#		450.00	
a.		"ZONE ZONE" (LR18)		3,250.	
89	A168	14c dark blue *(55,700) Dec., 1928*		22.50	18.00
		On cover			30.00
		Block of four		100.00	80.00
		Margin block of six, P#		400.00	
90	A169	15c gray *(204,138) Jan., 1926*		7.75	2.75
		On cover			6.00
		Block of four		32.50	13.00
		Margin block of six, P#		250.00	
		Margin block of 6, P# & large 5 point star, side only		3,500.	
a.		"ZONE ZONE" (LR18)		3,500.	
91	A187	17c black (R) *(199,500) Apr. 5, 1926*		4.25	2.00
		On cover			5.00
		Block of four		19.00	9.00
		Margin block of six, P#		200.00	
a.		"ZONE" only *(20)*		1,100.	
b.		"CANAL" only		1,400.	
c.		"ZONE CANAL" *(270)*		200.00	
92	A170	20c carmine rose *(259,807) Apr. 5, 1926*		9.00	4.25
		On cover			8.50
		Block of four		37.50	18.50
		Margin block of six, P#		300.00	
a.		"CANAL" inverted (UR48)		3,500.	
b.		"ZONE" inverted (LL76)		3,500.	
c.		"ZONE CANAL" (LL91)		3,500.	
93	A172	30c olive brown *(154,700) Dec., 1926*		7.00	3.75
		On cover			7.00
		Block of four		30.00	18.50
		Margin block of six, P#		350.00	
94	A173	50c lilac *(13,533) July, 1928*		300.00	130.00
		On cover			250.00
		Block of four		1,300.	625.00
		Margin block of six, P#		3,500.	
95	A174	$1 violet brown *(20,000) Apr., 1926*		150.00	55.00
		On cover			140.00
		Block of four		650.00	265.00
		Margin block of four, arrow, top or bottom		700.00	
		Margin block of six, P#		2,000.	

Nos. 85-88, 90 and 93-95 exist with wrong-font "CANAL" and "ZONE". Positions are: Nos. 85-88 and 90, UL51 (CANAL) and UL82 (ZONE); Nos. 93-95, U51 (CANAL) and U82 (ZONE).

Normal spacing between words of the overprint is 11mm. on No. 84; 9mm. on Nos. 85-88, 90, first printing of No. 91 and the first, third and fourth printing of No. 92; 7mm. on the second printings of Nos. 91-92. Minor spacing varieties exist on Nos. 84-88, 90-92.

Overprint Type B on United States Sesquicentennial Stamp No. 627

1926					
96	A188	2c carmine rose *(300,000) July 6, 1926*		5.00	4.50
		On cover			5.75
		Block of four		22.50	19.00
		Margin block of six, P#		130.00	

On this stamp there is a space of 5mm. instead of 9 mm. between the two words of the overprint.

The authorized date, July 4, fell on a Sunday with the next day also a holiday, so No. 96 was not regularly issued until July 6. But the postmaster sold some copies and canceled some covers on July 4 for a few favored collectors.

Overprint Type B in Black on United States Nos. 583, 584 and 591

1926-27		Rotary Press Printings		Perf. 10	
97	A157	2c carmine *(1,290,000) Dec., 1926*		65.00	10.00
		On cover			15.00
		Block of four		275.00	45.00
		Margin block of four, P#		500.00	
a.		Pair, one without overprint *(10)*		2,000.	
b.		Booklet pane of six *(58,000)*		650.00	
c.		"CANAL" only *(10)*		1,400.	
d.		"ZONE" only		2,500.	
98	A158	3c violet *(239,600) May 9, 1927*		8.50	4.00
		On cover			7.00
		Block of four		35.00	17.50
		Margin block of four, P#		135.00	
99	A165	10c orange *(128,400) May 9, 1927*		14.00	6.50
		On cover			12.50
		Block of four		60.00	30.00
		Margin block of four, P#		200.00	

Overprint Type B in Black on United States Nos. 632, 634 (Type I), 635, 637 and 642

1927-31		Rotary Press Printings		Perf. 11x10½	
100	A155	1c green *(434,892) June 28, 1927*		2.00	1.50
		On cover			2.25
		Block of four		8.50	7.00
		Margin block of four, P#		25.00	
a.		Vertical pair, one without overprint *(10)*		2,000.	
101	A157	2c carmine *(1,628,195) June 28, 1927*		2.25	80
		On cover			1.25
		Block of four		10.00	4.00
		Margin block of four, P#		27.50	
a.		Booklet pane of six *(82,108)*		190.00	
102	A158	3c violet *(1,250,000) Feb., 1931*		4.50	1.75
		On cover			3.00
		Block of four		24.00	8.00
		Margin block of four, P#		110.00	
a.		Booklet pane of six, handmade, perf. margins		2,500.	
103	A160	5c dark blue *(60,000) Dec. 13, 1927*		27.50	15.00
		On cover			25.00
		Block of four		125.00	65.00
		Margin block of four, P#		250.00	
104	A165	10c orange *(119,800) July, 1930*		20.00	8.00
		On cover			16.00
		Block of four		85.00	37.50
		Margin block of four, P#		225.00	

Maj. Gen. William Crawford Gorgas — A35

Maj. Gen. George Washington Goethals — A36

Canal Zone stamps can be mounted in Scott's U.S. Possessions Album.

Gaillard Cut — A37

Maj. Gen. Harry Foote
Hodges — A38

Lt. Col. David Du Bose
Gaillard — A39

Maj. Gen. William
Luther Sibert — A40

Jackson Smith — A41

Rear Admiral Harry
Harwood
Rousseau — A42

Col. Sydney Bacon
Williamson — A43

Joseph Clay Styles
Blackburn — A44

Printed by the U. S. Bureau of Engraving and Printing.
Plates of 400 subjects (except 5c), issued in panes of 100.
The 5c was printed from plate of 200 subjects, issued in panes
of 50. The 400-subject sheets were originally cut by knife into
Post Office panes of 100, but beginning in 1948 they were
seprated by perforations to eliminate straight edges.

		1928-40 Flat Plate Printing Unwmk. Perf. 11		
105	A35	1c yel grn (22,392,147)	10	8
		green	10	8
		First day cover		10.00
		Margin block of six, P#	75	
a.		Wet printing Oct. 3, 1928	15	12
106	A36	2c carmine (7,191,600) Oct. 1, 1928	20	10
		First day cover		10.00
		Margin block of six, P#	2.50	
a.		Booklet pane of six (284,640)	17.50	7.50
107	A37	5c blue (4,187,028) June 25, 1929	1.50	60
		First day cover		6.00
		Margin block of six, P#	14.00	
108	A38	10c orange (4,559,788)	30	15
		First day cover		6.00
		Margin block of six, P#	60.00	
a.		Wet printing Jan. 11, 1932	40	25
109	A39	12c violet brown (844,635)	1.00	60
		brown violet	1.00	60
		First day cover		10.00
		Margin block of six, P#	12.00	
a.		Wet printing July 1, 1929	1.50	1.00
110	A40	14c blue (406,131) Sept. 27, 1937	1.10	85
		First day cover		6.50
		Margin block of six, P#	13.00	
111	A41	15c gray (3,356,500)	50	35
		gray black	50	35
		First day cover		10.00
		Margin block of six, P#	8.00	
a.		Wet printing Jan. 11, 1932	80	50
112	A42	20c olive brown (3,619,080)	75	20
		First day cover		10.00
		Margin block of six, P#	8.00	
a.		Wet printing Jan. 11, 1932	1.00	30
113	A43	30c brown black (2,376,491)	1.00	70
		First day cover		10.00
		Margin block of six, P#	11.00	
a.		Wet printing Apr. 15, 1940	1.25	1.00
114	A44	50c lilac	2.00	65
		rose lilac	2.00	65
		First day cover		10.00
		Margin block of six, P#	20.00	
a.		Wet printing July 1, 1929	2.50	85

Coils are listed as Nos. 160-161.

Wet and Dry Printings
Canal Zone stamps printed by both the "wet"
and "dry" process are Nos. 105, 108-109, 111-
114, 117, 138-140, C21-C24, C26, J25, J27.
Starting with Nos. 147 and C27, the Bureau of
Engraving and Printing used the "dry" method
exclusively.
See note on Wet and Dry Printings following
U.S. No. 1029.

United States Nos. 720 and 695 Overprinted

CANAL

Type B

ZONE

Rotary Press Printing

		1933, Jan. 14	Perf. 11x10½	
115	A226	3c deep violet (3,150,000)	3.00	25
		First day cover		7.50
		Margin block of four, P#	22.50	
b.		"CANAL" only	3.000.	
c.		Booklet pane of six, handmade, perf. margins	325.00	—
116	A168	14c dark blue (104,800)	7.00	3.50
		First day cover		25.00
		Margin block of four, P#	55.00	
a.		"ZONE CANAL" (16)	1,250.	

Maj. Gen. George
Washington
Goethals — A45

Issued in commemoration of the twentieth anniversary of
the opening of the Panama Canal.

Flat Plate Printing

		1934, Aug. 15 Unwmk.	Perf. 11	
117	A45	3c deep violet	10	6
		red violet	10	6
		First day cover		1.00
		Margin block of six, P#	2.00	
a.		Booklet pane of six	45.00	20.00
b.		As "a," handmade, perf. margins	250.00	
c.		Wet printing	12	8

Coil is listed as No. 153.

United States Nos. 803 and 805   **CANAL**
Overprinted in Black   **ZONE**

Rotary Press Printing

		1939, Sept. 1 Unwmk.	Perf. 11x10½	
118	A275	½c red orange, (1,030,000)	15	10
		First day cover		75
		Margin block of four, P#	3.00	—
119	A277	1½c bister brown (935,000)	20	20
		brown	20	20
		First day cover		75
		Margin block of four, P#	3.50	

Balboa-Before — A46

Balboa-After — A47

Gaillard Cut-Before — A48

Canal Channel-Before — A54

Gatun Spilway-Before — A60

Gaillard Cut-After — A49

Canal Channel-After — A55

Gatun Spilway-After — A61

Bas Obispo-Before — A50

Gamboa-Before — A56

Issued in commemoration of the 25th anniversary of the opening of the Panama Canal.

Withdrawn Feb. 28, 1941; remainders burned Apr. 12, 1941.

Flat Plate Printing

1939, Aug. 15   Unwmk.   Perf. 11

120	A46	1c yellow green (1,019,482)	40	30
		First day cover		1.00
		Margin block of six, P#	10.00	—
121	A47	2c rose carmine (227,065)	50	35
		First day cover		1.00
		Margin block of six, P#	11.00	—
122	A48	3c purple (2,523,735)	40	15
		First day cover		1.00
		Margin block of six, P#	10.00	—
123	A49	5c dark blue (460,213)	1.00	90
		First day cover		2.50
		Margin block of six, P#	17.50	—
124	A40	6c red orange (68,290)	2.25	1.50
		First day cover		5.50
		Margin block of six, P#	35.00	—
125	A51	7c black (71,235)	2.25	1.50
		First day cover		5.50
		Margin block of six, P#	35.00	—
126	A52	8c green (41,576)	3.25	2.25
		First day cover		5.50
		Margin block of six, P#	45.00	—
127	A53	10c ultramarine (83,571)	3.25	2.00
		First day cover		5.50
		Margin block of six, P#	45.00	—
128	A54	11c blue green (34,010)	7.50	6.00
		First day cover		11.00
		Margin block of six, P#	110.00	—
129	A55	12c brown carmine (66,735)	6.00	5.00
		First day cover		11.00
		Margin block of six, P#	85.00	—
130	A56	14c dark violet (37,365)	6.75	4.50
		First day cover		11.00
		Margin block of six, P#	100.00	—
131	A57	15c olive green (105,058)	11.00	3.75
		First day cover		10.00
		Margin block of six, P#	125.00	—
132	A58	18c rose pink (39,255)	9.00	6.00
		First day cover		10.00
		Margin block of six, P#	120.00	—
133	A59	20c brown (100,244)	13.00	8.00
		First day cover		10.00
		Margin block of six, P#	150.00	—
134	A60	25c orange (34,283)	20.00	9.00
		First day cover		20.00
		Margin block of six, P#	250.00	—
135	A61	50c violet brown (91,576)	22.50	3.50
		First day cover		25.00
		Margin block of six, P#	275.00	—

Bas Obispo-After — A51

Gamboa-After — A57

Gatun Locks-Before — A52

Pedro Miguel Locks-Before — A58

Gatun Locks-After — A53

Pedro Miguel Locks-After — A59

Maj. Gen. George W. Davis — A62

Gov. Charles E. Magoon — A63

Theodore Roosevelt — A64

John F. Stevens — A65

John F. Wallace — A66

1946-49   Unwmk.   *Perf. 11*
Size: 19x22mm.

136 A62 ½c bright red *(1,020,000)* Aug. 16, 1948   35   15
First day cover   1.25
Margin block of six, P#   3.00   —
137 A63 1½c chocolate *(603,600)* Aug. 16, 1948   35   15
First day cover   1.25
Margin block of six, P#   3.00   —
138 A64 2c rose carmine *(6,951,755)*   10   5
First day cover   50
Margin block of six, P#   75   —
a. Wet printing *Oct. 27, 1949*   15   8
139 A65 5c deep blue   40   10
First day cover   1.00
Margin block of six, P#   4.00   —
a. Wet printing *Apr. 25, 1946*   1.00   10
140 A66 25c yellow green *(1,520,000)*   2.25   1.00
First day cover   3.50
Margin block of six, P#   20.00   —
a. Wet printing *Aug. 16, 1948*   5.00   1.75

See Nos. 155, 162, 164.

Map of Biological Area and Coatimundi — A67

Issued to commemorate the 25th anniversary of the establishment of the Canal Zone Biolgical Area on Barro Colorado Island.
Withdrawn Mar. 30, 1951, and remainders destroyed April 10, 1951.

1948, Apr. 17   Unwmk.   *Perf. 11*
141 A67 10c black *(521,200)*   1.75   1.35
First day cover   2.00
Margin block of six, P#   14.00

"Forty-niners" Arriving at Chagres — A68

Journeying in "Bungo" to Las Cruces — A69

Las Cruces Trail to Panama — A70

Departure for San Francisco — A71

Issued to commemorate the centenary of the California Gold Rush.
Stocks on hand were processed for destruction on Aug. 11, 1952 and destroyed Aug. 13, 1952.

1949, June 1   Unwmk.   *Perf. 11*
142 A68 3c blue *(500.000)*   85   35
First day cover   1.00
Margin block of six, P#   7.50   —
143 A69 6c violet *(481,600)*   90   45
First day cover   1.00
Margin block of six, P#   10.00   —
144 A70 12c bright blue green *(230,200)*   2.50   1.40
First day cover   1.75
Margin block of six, P#   22.50   —
145 A71 18c deep red lilac *(240,200)*   3.25   2.00
First day cover   3.00
Margin block of six, P#   30.00   —

Workers in Culebra Cut — A72

Issued to commemorate the contribution of West Indian laborers in the construction of the Panama Canal. Entire issue sold, none withdrawn and destroyed.

1951, Aug. 15   Unwmk.   *Perf. 11*
146 A72 10c carmine *(480,000)*   4.00   1.65
First day cover   2.25
Margin block of six, P#   35.00

Early Railroad Scene — A73

Issued to commemorate the centenary of the completion of the Panama Railroad and the first transcontinental railroad trip in the Americas.

1955, Jan. 28   Unwmk.   *Perf. 11*
147 A73 3c violet *(994,000)*   1.10   50
First day cover   1.25
Margin block of six, P#   9.00   —

Gorgas Hospital and Ancon Hill — A74

Issued to commemorate the 75th anniversary of Gorgas Hospital.

1957, Nov. 17   Unwmk.   *Perf. 11*
148 A74 3c *dull blue green (1,010,000)*   60   35
Light blue green paper   60   35
First day cover   75
Margin block of four, P#   5.00   —

S.S. Ancon — A75

1958, Aug. 30   Engr.   Unwmk.   *Perf. 11*
149 A75 4c greenish blue *(1,749,700)*   45   20
First day cover   75
Margin block of four, P#   3.50   —

Roosevelt Medal and Canal Zone Map — A76

Issued to commemorate the centenary of the birth of Theodore Roosevelt (1858-1919).

1958, Nov. 15	**Unwmk.**	**Perf. 11**
150 A76	4c brown *(1,060,000)*	60 30
	First day cover	75
	Margin block of four, P#	4.00 —

Boy Scout
Badge — A77

Issued to commemorate the 50th anniversary of the Boy Scouts of America.

	Giori Press Printing	
1960, Feb. 8	**Unwmk.**	**Perf. 11**
151 A77	4c dark blue, red & bister *(654,933)*	75 40
	First day cover	1.00
	Margin block of four, P#	5.00 —

Administration
Building, Balboa
Heights — A78

1960, Nov. 1	**Engr.**	**Unwmk.**	**Perf. 11**
152 A78	4c rose lilac *(2,486,725)*		20 12
	First day cover		85
	Margin block of four, P#		1.25 —

Coil Stamps
Types of 1934, 1960 and 1946

1960-62	**Unwmk.**	**Perf. 10 Vertically**
153 A45	3c deep violet *(3,743,959)* Nov. 1, 1960	15 12
	First day cover	1.00
	Pair	30 25
	Joint line pair	1.00 —

	Perf. 10 Horizontally	
154 A78	4c dull rose lilac *(2,776,273)* Nov. 1, 1960	20 12
	First day cover	1.00
	Pair	40 25
	Joint line pair	1.25 —

	Perf. 10 Vertically	
155 A65	5c deep blue *(3,288,264)* Feb. 10, 1962	30 20
	First day cover	1.00
	Pair	60 50
	Joint line pair	1.50 —

Girl Scout Badge and Camp at Gatun Lake — A79

Issued to commemorate the 50th anniversary of the Girl Scouts.

	Giori Press Printing	
1962, Mar. 12	**Unwmk.**	**Perf. 11**
156 A79	4c blue, dark green & bister *(640,000)*	40 30
	First day cover *(83,717)*	1.25
	Margin block of four, P#	4.00 —

Thatcher Ferry Bridge and Map of Western
Hemisphere — A80

Issued to commemorate the opening of the Thatcher Ferry Bridge, spanning the Panama Canal.

	Giori Press Printing	
1962, Oct. 12	**Unwmk.**	**Perf. 11**
157 A80	4c black & silver *(775,000)*	35 25
	First day cover *(65,833)*	1.00
	Margin block of 4, two P#	4.00 —
a.	Silver (bridge) omitted *(50)*	9,000.
a.	Margin block of 10, black P# only	—

Goethals Memorial,
Balboa — A81

Fort San Lorenzo — A82

	Giori Press Printing	
1968-71		**Perf. 11**
158 A81	6c green & ultra. *(1,890,000)* Mar. 15, 1968	40 30
	First day cover	75
	Margin block of 4, P#	2.50 —
159 A82	8c slate green, blue, dark brown & ocher *(3,460,000)* July 14, 1971	45 25
	First day cover	75
	Margin block of 4, P#	3.00 —

Coil Stamps
Types of 1928, 1932 and 1948

1975, Feb. 14	**Engr.**	**Unwmk.**	**Perf. 10 Vertically**
160 A35	1c green *(1,090,958)*		20 10
	First day cover		35
	Pair		40 20
	Joint line pair		1.00 —
161 A38	10c orange *(590,658)*		85 25
	First day cover		50
	Pair		1.70 50
	Joint line pair		4.00 —
162 A66	25c yellow green *(129,831)*		4.00 1.00
	First day cover		1.50
	Pair		8.00 2.00
	Joint line pair		20.00 —

Dredge
Cascadas — A83

	Giori Press Printing	
1976		**Perf. 11**
163 A83	13c multi *(3,653,950)* Feb. 23	40 20
	First day cover	1.00
	Margin block of 4, P#	2.50 —
a.	Bklt. pane of 4 *(1,032,400)* Apr. 19	3.00 —

Stevens Type of 1946

	Rotary Press Printing	**Perf. 11x10 ½**
1977	**Size: 19x22 ½mm.**	
164 A65	5c deep blue *(1,009,612)*	60 25
	Margin block of 4, P#	4.00 —

No. 164 exists tagged.

Towing
Locomotive, Ship
in Lock, by Alwyn
Sprague — A84

1978, Oct. 25	**Engr.**		**Perf. 11**
165 A84	15c dp grn & bl grn *(2,921,083)*		40 20
	First day cover *(81,405)*		75
	Margin block of 4, P#		2.00 —

AIR POST STAMPS

AIR MAIL

Regular Issue of 1928 Surcharged
in Dark Blue

25 CENTS 25

Type I - Flag of "5" pointing up. **15**

15 Type II - Flag of "5" curved.

1929-31	**Flat Plate Printing**	**Unwmk.**	**Perf. 11**
C1 A35	15c on 1c green, type I, 1929		10.00 6.50
	First day cover		25.00
	Block of four		42.50 30.00
	Margin block of six, P#		175.00 —
C2 A35	15c on 1c yellow green, type II, Mar. 1931		135.00 85.00
	On cover		125.00
	Block of four		575.00 375.00
	Margin block of six, P#		1,350.
C3 A36	25c on 2c carmine *(223,880)* Jan. 11, 1929		4.00 2.25
	First day cover		17.50
	Block of four		17.00 10.50
	Margin block of six, P#		115.00 —

AIR MAIL

Nos. 114 and 106 Surcharged
in Black

≡10c

1929, Dec. 31			
C4 A44	10c on 50c lilac *(116,666)*		10.00 9.00
	First day cover		25.00
	Block of four		42.50 40.00
	Margin block of six, P#		150.00 —
C5 A36	20c on 2c carmine *(638,395)*		7.00 2.00
	First day cover		20.00
	Block of four		29.00 8.00
	Margin block of six, P#		120.00 55.00
a.	Dropped "2" in surch. *(7,000)*		100.00 —

The Demand, as well as supply, determines a stamp's market value. One is as important as the other.

Gaillard Cut — AP1

Printed by the U. S. Bureau of Engraving and Printing.
Plates of 200 subjects, issued in panes of 50.

1931-49 Unwmk. *Perf. 11*

C6	AP1	4c red violet *(525,000)* Jan. 3, 1949		75	60
		First day cover			2.00
		Margin block of six, P#	6.50		
C7	AP1	5c yellow green *(9,988,800)* Nov. 18, 1931		50	30
		green		50	30
		First day cover			10.00
		Margin block of six, P#	4.00		
C8	AP1	6c yellow brown *(9,440,000)* Feb. 15, 1946		70	30
		First day cover			2.00
		Margin block of six, P#	6.00		
C9	AP1	10c orange *(5,140,000)* Nov. 18, 1931		85	30
		First day cover			10.00
		Margin block of six, P#	10.00		
C10	AP1	15c blue *(11,961,500)* Nov. 18, 1931		1.00	25
		pale blue		1.00	25
		First day cover			10.00
		Margin block of six, P#	10.00		
C11	AP1	20c red violet *(3,214,600)* Nov. 18, 1931		2.00	25
		deep violet		2.00	25
		First day cover			20.00
		Margin block of six, P#	17.50		
C12	AP1	30c rose lake *(1,150,000)* July 15, 1941		3.50	1.00
		dull rose		3.50	1.00
		First day cover			22.50
		Margin block of six, P#	30.00		
C13	AP1	40c yellow *(826,100)* Nov. 18, 1931		3.00	1.00
		lemon		3.00	1.00
		First day cover			30.00
		Margin block of six, P#	30.00		
C14	AP1	$1 black *(406,000)* Nov. 18, 1931		10.00	2.25
		First day cover			50.00
		Margin block of six, P#	85.00		

Douglas Plane over Sosa Hill — AP2

Planes and Map of Central America — AP3

Pan American Clipper and Scene near Fort Amador — AP4

Pan American Clipper at Cristobal Harbor — AP5

Pan American Clipper over Gaillard Cut — AP6

Pan American Clipper Landing — AP7

Issued in commemoration of the 10th anniversary of Air Mail service and the 25th anniversary of the opening of the Panama Canal.
Withdrawn February 28, 1941 and remainders burned April 12, 1941.

Flat Plate Printing

1939, July 15 Unwmk. *Perf. 11*

C15	AP2	5c greenish black *(86,576)*		3.75	3.25
		black		10.00	10.00
		First day cover			5.00
		Margin block of six, P#	35.00		
C16	AP3	10c dull violet *(117,644)*		3.75	3.00
		First day cover			5.00
		Margin block of six, P#	40.00		
C17	AP4	15c light brown *(883,742)*		4.00	1.25
		First day cover			3.00
		Margin block of six, P#	45.00		
C18	AP5	25c blue *(82,126)*		17.50	11.00
		First day cover			17.50
		Margin block of six, P#	165.00		
C19	AP6	30c rose carmine *(121,382)*		12.50	8.00
		First day cover			15.00
		Margin block of six, P#	120.00		
C20	AP7	$1 green *(40,051)*		45.00	35.00
		First day cover			50.00
		Margin block of six, P#	400.00		

Globe and
Wing — AP8

Flat Plate Printing

1951, July 16 Unwmk. *Perf. 11*

C21	AP8	4c red violet *(1,315,000)*		80	30
		Margin block of six, P#	7.50		
a.		Wet printing		1.25	40
C22	AP8	6c brown *(22,657,625)*		65	25
		Margin block of six, P#	7.00		
a.		Wet printing		95	35
C23	AP8	10c red orange *(1,049,130)*		1.10	40
		Margin block of six, P#	11.00		
a.		Wet printing		2.00	50
C24	AP8	21c blue *(1,460,000)*		9.50	3.50
		Margin block of six, P#	85.00		
a.		Wet printing		15.00	5.00
C25	AP8	31c cerise *(375,000)*		9.00	3.25
		Margin block of six, P#	90.00		
a.		Horiz. pair, imperf. vert. *(98)*	750.00		—
C26	AP8	80c gray black *(827,696)*		6.50	1.25
		Margin block of six, P#	60.00		
a.		Wet printing		12.50	1.65

See note after No. 114.

Type of 1951
Flat Plate Printing

1958, Aug. 16 Unwmk. *Perf. 11*

C27	AP8	5c yellow green *(899,923)*		1.50	50
		First day cover *(2,176)*			1.50
		Margin block of four, P#	10.00		
C28	AP8	7c olive *(9,381,797)*		1.40	40
		First day cover *(2,815)*			1.25
		Margin block of four, P#	8.50		
C29	AP8	15c brown violet *(359,923)*		6.00	1.50
		First day cover *(2,040)*			2.50
		Margin block of four, P#	40.00		
C30	AP8	25c orange yellow *(600,000)*		13.00	2.00
		First day cover *(2,115)*			4.50
		Margin block of four, P#	90.00		
C31	AP8	35c dark blue *(283,032)*		11.50	2.00
		First day cover *(1,868)*			6.00
		Margin block of four, P#	60.00		

Emblem of U.S. Army Caribbean School — AP9

Issued to honor the U.S. Army Caribbean School for Latin America at Fort Gulick.

Giori Press Printing

1961, Nov. 21 Unwmk. *Perf. 11*

C32	AP9	15c red & blue *(560,000)*		2.00	1.25
		First day cover *(25,949)*			1.75
		Margin block of four, P#	17.50		

Malaria Eradication Emblem and Mosquito — AP10

Issued for the World Health Organization drive to eradicate malaria.

Giori Press Printing

1962, Sept. 24   **Unwmk.**   *Perf. 11*
C33 AP10   7c yellow & black *(862,349)*   75   50
    First day cover *(44,433)*   1.00
    Margin block of four, P#   4.50

Globe-Wing Type of 1951

1963, Jan. 7   **Rotary Press Printing**   *Perf. 10¹/₂x11*
C34 AP8   8c carmine *(5,054,727)*   75   30
    First day cover *(19,128)*   1.00
    Margin block of four, P#   6.00

Alliance for Progress Emblem — AP11

Issued to commemorate the second anniversary of the Alliance for Progress, which aims to stimulate economic growth and raise living standards in Latin America.

Giori Press Printing

1963, Aug. 17   **Unwmk.**   *Perf. 11*
C35 AP11 15c gray, grn. & dk. ultra.
    (405,000)   1.50   1.00
    First day cover *(29,594)*   1.50
    Margin block of four, P#   15.00

Jet over Cristobal — AP12

Issued to commemorate the 50th anniversary of the Panama Canal.
    Designs: 8c, Gatun Locks. 15c, Madden Dam. 20c, Gaillard Cut. 30c, Miraflores Locks. 80c, Balboa.

Giori Press Printing

1964, Aug. 15   **Unwmk.**   *Perf. 11*
C36 AP12   6c green & black *(257,193)*   60   35
    Margin block of four, P#   3.75
C37 AP12   8c rose red & black *(3,924,283)*   70   35
    Margin block of four, P#   4.25
C38 AP12 15c blue & black *(472,666)*   1.65   50
    Margin block of four, P#   10.50
C39 AP12 20c rose lilac & black *(399,784)*   2.75   85
    Margin block of four, P#   14.00
C40 AP12 30c reddish brown & black
    (204,524)   4.00   2.00
    Margin block of four, P#   21.00
C41 AP12 80c olive bister & black *(186,809)*   7.00   3.00
    Margin block of four, P#   32.50

Canal Zone Seal and Jet Plane — AP13

Giori Press Printing

1965, July 15   **Unwmk.**   *Perf. 11*
C42 AP13   6c green & black *(548,250)*   45   20
    Margin block of four, P#   3.00
C43 AP13   8c rose red & black *(8,357,700)*   35   10
    Margin block of four, P#   3.00
C44 AP13 15c blue & black *(2,385,000)*   45   20
    Margin block of four, P#   3.00
C45 AP13 20c lilac & black *(2,290,699)*   75   30
    Margin block of four, P#   4.50

C46 AP13 30c redsh brn & blk *(2,332,255)*   1.00   35
    Margin block of four, P#   5.50
C47 AP13 80c bister & black *(1,456,596)*   3.25   90
    Margin block of four, P#   16.50

1968-76
C48 AP13 10c dull orange & black
    (10,055,000) Mar. 15, 1968   35   15
    Margin block of 4, P#   2.00
a.   Bklt. pane of 4 *(713,390) Feb. 18,*
    1970   4.25
C49 AP13 11c olive & black *(3,335,000)*
    Sept. 24, 1971   40   18
    Margin block of 4, P#   2.00
a.   Bklt. pane of 4 *(1,277,760) Sept. 24,*
    1971   3.50
C50 AP13 13c emerald & black *(1,865,000)*
    Feb. 11, 1974   1.10   30
    First day cover   55
    Margin block of 4, P#   6.00
a.   Booklet pane of 4 *(619,200) Feb. 11,*
    1974   6.00
C51 AP13 22c vio & blk *(363,720) May 10,*
    1976   1.25   50
    Margin block of four, P#   8.00
C52 AP13 25c pale yellow green & black
    (1,640,441) Mar. 15, 1968   1.10   35
    Margin block of four, P#   7.00
C53 AP13 35c salmon & black *(573,822)*
    May 10, 1976   2.00   60
    Margin block of four, P#   10.00

AIR POST OFFICIAL STAMPS

(See note above No. O1)

Air Post Stamps of 1931-41   OFFICIAL
Overprinted in Black   PANAMA CANAL

Two types of overprint.
Type I - "PANAMA CANAL" 19-20mm. long.
1941-42   **Unwmk.**   *Perf. 11*
CO1 AP1   5c yellow green *(42,754) Mar. 31,*
    1941   4.25   1.50
    green   4.25   1.50
    On cover   40.00
    Block of four   18.50   6.00
CO2 AP1 10c orange *(49,723) Mar. 31, 1941*   9.00   2.00
    On cover   30.00
    Block of four   40.00   9.00
CO3 AP1 15c blue *(56,898) Mar. 31, 1941*   11.00   2.75
    On cover   25.00
    Block of four   47.50   25.00
CO4 AP1 20c red violet *(22,107) Mar. 31,*
    1941   16.00   4.50
    deep violet   16.00   4.50
    On cover   110.00
    Block of four   75.00   22.50
CO5 AP1 30c rose lake *(22,100) June, 4,*
    1942   20.00   4.50
    dull rose   20.00   4.50
    On cover   40.00
    Block of four   90.00   20.00
CO6 AP1 40c yellow *(22,875) Mar. 31, 1941*   22.50   7.00
    lemon yellow   22.50   7.00
    On cover   50.00
    Block of four   100.00   35.00
CO7 AP1 $1 black *(29,525) Mar. 31, 1941*   30.00   10.00
    On cover   150.00
    Block of four   135.00   45.00

Overprint varieties occur on Nos. CO1-CO7 and CO14: "O" of "OFFICIAL" over "N" of "PANAMA" (entire third row). "O" of "OFFICIAL" broken at top (position 31). "O" of "OFFICIAL" over second "A" of "PANAMA" (position 45). First "F" of "OFFICIAL" over second "A" of "PANAMA" (position 50).

1941, Sept. 22
Type II - "PANAMA CANAL" 17mm. long
CO8 AP1   5c yellow green *(2,000)*   — 200.00
    On cover   400.00
    Block of four   850.00
CO9 AP1 10c orange *(2,000)*   — 250.00
    On cover   400.00
    Block of four   1,250.
CO10 AP1 20c red violet *(2,000)*   — 200.00
    On cover   850.00
    Block of four   850.00
CO11 AP1 30c rose lake *(5,000)*   — 60.00
    On cover   125.00
    Block of four   250.00
CO12 AP1 40c yellow *(2,000)*   — 200.00
    On cover   400.00
    Block of four   850.00

1947, Nov.
Type I - "PANAMA CANAL" 19-20mm. long.
CO14 AP1   6c yellow brown *(33,450)*   11.00   3.50
    On cover   50.00
    Block of four   50.00   15.00
a.   Inverted overprint *(50)*   1,200.

POSTAGE DUE STAMPS

Prior to 1914, many of the postal issues were handstamped "Postage Due" and used as postage due stamps.

Postage Due Stamps of the United
States Nos. J45a, J46a, and J49a   **CANAL ZONE**
Overprinted in Black

1914, Mar.   **Wmk. 190**   *Perf. 12*
J1   D2   1c rose carmine *(23,533)*   80.00   17.00
    On cover   150.00
    Block of four (2 mm. spacing)   350.00 80.00
    Block of four (3 mm. spacing)   375.00 90.00
    Margin block of six, imprint, star
    and P#   650.00   —
J2   D2   2c rose carmine *(32,312)*   250.00 50.00
    On cover   175.00
    Block of four   1,050. 225.00
    Margin block of six, P#   1,750.
J3   D2 10c rose carmine *(92,493)*   700.00 50.00
    On cover   450.00
    Block of four (2 mm. spacing)   3,000. 225.00
    Block of four (3 mm. spacing)   3,000. 225.00
    Margin block of six, imprint, star
    and P#   5,250.   —

Many examples of Nos. J1-J3 show one or more letters of the overprint out of alignment, principally the "E".

San Geronimo Castle Gate,
Portobelo (See footnote) — D1

Statue of
Columbus
D2

Pedro J. Sosa
D3

1915, March   **Unwmk.**   *Perf. 12*
Blue Overprint, Type II, on Postage Due Stamps of Panama
J4   D1   1c olive brown *(50,000)*   10.00   4.25
    On cover   75.00
    Block of four   42.50   20.00
J5   D2   2c olive brown *(50,000)*   140.00 22.50
    On cover   100.00
    Block of four   600.00 120.00
J6   D3 10c olive brown *(200,000)*   40.00   11.00
    On cover   90.00
    Block of four   175.00 50.00

Type D1 was intended to show a gate of San Lorenzo Castle, Chagres, and is so labeled. By error the stamp actually shows the main gate of San Geronimo Castle, Portobelo.
    Experts believe that examples of the 1c with overprint type V, reading up or down, are bogus.

Surcharged in Red   **CANAL 2 ZONE**

1915, Nov.   **Unwmk.**   *Perf. 12*
J7   D1   1c on 1c olive brown *(60,614)*   110.00 20.00
    On cover   100.00
    Block of four   475.00 100.00
J8   D2   2c on 2c olive brown   25.00   7.50
    On cover   85.00
    Block of four   105.00 35.00
J9   D3 10c on 10c olive brown *(175,548)*   22.50   4.50
    On cover   70.00
    Block of four   100.00 22.50

One of the printings of No. J9 shows wider spacing between "1" and "0". Both spacings occur on the same sheet.

D4

Capitol,
Panama — D5

1919, Dec.
Surcharged in Carmine at Mount Hope

J10	D4	2c on 2c olive brown	27.50 11.00
		On cover	85.00
		Block of four	120.00 50.00
J11	D5	4c on 4c olive brown *(35,695)*	35.00 15.00
		On cover	100.00
		Block of four	150.00 65.00
a.		"ZONE" omitted	3,250.
b.		"4" omitted	2,750.

CANAL

United States Postage Due Stamps
Nos. J61, J62b and J65b Overprinted

ZONE

Type A
Letters "A" with Flat Tops

1924, July 1   ***Perf. 11***

J12	D2	1c carmine rose *(10,000)*	140.00 30.00
		On cover	75.00
		Block of four	600.00 130.00
		Margin block of six, P#	1,400.
J13	D2	2c deep claret *(25,000)*	85.00 15.00
		On cover	75.00
		Block of four	375.00 55.00
		Margin block of six, P#	750.00
J14	D2	10c deep claret *(30,000)*	325.00 50.00
		On cover	200.00
		Block of four (2 mm. spacing)	1,400. 225.00
		Block of four (3 mm. spacing)	1,400. 225.00
		Margin block of six, imprint, star and P#	3,000.

United States Nos. 552, 554 and 562
Overprinted Type A and Additionally
Overprinted at Mount Hope in Red or Blue

POSTAGE DUE

1925, Feb.   ***Perf. 11***

J15	A155	1c deep green (R) *(15,000)*	100.00 17.50
		On cover	75.00
		Block of four	425.00 75.00
		Margin block of 6, P#	825.00
J16	A157	2c carmine (Bl) *(21,335)*	27.50 7.00
		On cover	50.00
		Block of four	125.00 30.00
		Margin block of 6, P#	250.00
J17	A165	10c orange (R) *(39,819)*	55.00 11.00
		On cover	75.00
		Block of four	250.00 47.50
		Margin block of 6, P#	500.00
a.		"POSTAGE DUE" double	400.00
b.		"E" of "POSTAGE" omitted	350.00
c.		As "b," double	2,750.

Overprinted Type B
Letters "A" with Sharp Pointed Tops
On United States Postage Due Stamps Nos. J61,
J62, J65 and J65a

1925, June 24

J18	D2	1c carmine rose *(80,000)*	9.00 3.00
		On cover	35.00
		Block of four	40.00 15.00
		Margin block of 6, P#	90.00
a.		"ZONE ZONE" (LR18)	1,400.
J19	D2	2c carmine rose *(146,430)*	20.00 5.00
		On cover	35.00
		Block of four	85.00 21.00
		Margin block of 6, P#	200.00
a.		"ZONE ZONE" (LR18)	1,400.
J20	D2	10c carmine rose *(153,980)*	130.00 20.00
		On cover	100.00
		Block of four, 2 mm. spacing	525.00 85.00
		Block of four, 3 mm. spacing	550.00 90.00
		Margin block of 6, Imprint, star and P#	1,200.
a.		Vert. pair, one without ovpt. *(10)*	1,750.
		Margin block of 6, imprint, Star and P#	
b.		10c rose red	165.00 70.00
		On cover	110.00
c.		Double overprint	325.00

Nos. J18-J20 exist with wrong font "CANAL" (UL51) and "ZONE" (UL82).

POSTAGE DUE

Regular Issue of
1928-29 Surcharged

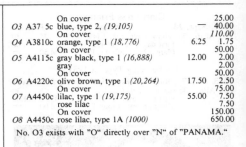

≡ **10** ≡

1929-30

J21	A37	1c on 5c blue *(35,990)* Mar. 20, 1930	3.00 1.75
		On cover	15.00
		Margin block of 6, P#	30.00
a.		"POSTAGE DUE" omitted *(5)*	2,250.
J22	A37	2c on 5c blue *(40,207)* Oct. 18, 1930	6.00 2.50
		On cover	15.00
		Margin block of 6, P#	50.00
J23	A37	5c on 5c blue *(35,464)* Dec. 1, 1930	6.00 2.75
		On cover	15.00
		Margin block of 6, P#	60.00
J24	A371	0c on 5c blue *(90,504)* Dec. 16, 1929	5.00 2.75
		On cover	15.00
		Margin block of 6, P#	60.00

On No. J23 the three short horizontal bars in the lower corners of the surcharge are omitted.

Canal Zone Seal — D6

Printed by the U.S. Bureau of Engraving and
Printing.
Plates of 400 subjects, issued in panes of 100.

1932-41   **Flat Plate Printing**

J25	D6	1c claret *(378,300)* Jan. 2, 1932	10 10
a.		red violet, dry printing	20 10
		Margin block of 6, P#	3.00
J26	D6	2c claret *(413,800)* Jan. 2, 1932	15 10
		Margin block of 6, P#	4.00
J27	D6	5c claret Jan. 2, 1932	35 20
a.		red violet, dry printing	1.00 30
		Margin block of 6, P#	6.00
J28	D6	10c claret *(400,600)* Jan. 2, 1932	1.40 1.25
		Margin block of 6, P#	15.00
J29	D6	15c claret Apr. 21, 1941	1.10 90
		Margin block of 6, P#	12.00

See note after No. 114.

OFFICIAL STAMPS

Beginning in March, 1915, stamps for use on official mail were identified by a large "P" perforated through each stamp. These were replaced by overprinted issues in 1941. The use of official stamps was discontinued December 31, 1951. During their currency, they were not for sale in mint condition and were sold to the public only when cancelled with a parcel post rotary canceller reading "Balboa Heights, Canal Zone" between two wavy lines.

After having been withdrawn from use, mint stamps (except Nos. O3, O8 and CO8-CO12) were made available to the public at face value for three months beginning Jan. 2, 1952. Prices for used stamps are for cancelled-to-order specimens, postally used copies being worth more. Sheet margins were removed to facilitate overprinting and plate numbers are, therefore, unknown.

Regular Issues of 1928-34 Overprinted in Black by
the Panama Canal Press, Mount Hope, C.Z.

OFFICIAL

PANAMA	OFFICIAL
CANAL	PANAMA CANAL
Type 1	Type 2

Type 1 - "PANAMA" 10 mm. long.
Type 1A - "PANAMA" 9 mm. long.
Type 2 - "PANAMA CANAL" 19½ mm. long.

1941, Mar. 31   **Unwmk.**   ***Perf. 11***

O1	A35	1c yellow green, type 1 *(87,198)*	2.00 35
		On cover	35.00
O2	A45	3c deep violet, type 1 *(34,958)*	3.75 70

		On cover	25.00
O3	A37	5c blue, type 2, *(19,105)*	— 40.00
			110.00
O4	A38	10c orange, type 1 *(18,776)*	6.25 1.75
			50.00
O5	A41	15c gray black, type 1 *(16,888)*	12.00 2.00
		gray	2.00
		On cover	50.00
O6	A42	20c olive brown, type 1 *(20,264)*	17.50 2.50
		On cover	75.00
O7	A44	50c lilac, type 1 *(19,175)*	55.00 7.50
		rose lilac	7.50
		On cover	150.00
O8	A44	50c rose lilac, type 1A *(1000)*	650.00

No. O3 exists with "O" directly over "N" of "PANAMA."

No. 139 Overprinted in Black

1947, Feb.

O9	A65	5c deep blue, type 1 *(21,639)*	8.00 3.00
		On cover	70.00

POST OFFICE SEALS

POS1

Issued in sheets of 8 without gum, imperforate
margins.

1907   **Typo.**   **Unwmk.**   ***Perf. 11½***

OX1	POS1	blue	40.00
		Block of four	175.00
a.		Wmkd. seal of U.S. in sheet	55.00

No. OX1 clichés are spaced 3½mm. apart.

1910

OX2	POS1	ultramarine	70.00
a.		Wmkd. "Rolleston Mills" in sheet	90.00
b.		Wmkd. U.S. Seal in sheet	225.00
		Block of four, cliches ½mm apart	325.00
		Block of four, cliches 1½mm apart horiz., 4mm vert.	800.00

POS2

Printed by the Panama Canal Press, Mount Hope, C.Z.

Issued in sheets of 25, without gum, imperforate margins.

Rouletted 6 horizontally in color of seal, vertically without color

1917, Sept. 22

OX3	POS2	dark blue	4.00
		Block of four	17.50
a.		Wmkd. double lined letters in sheet ("Sylvania")	35.00

1946   *Rouletted 6, without color*

Issued in sheets of 20, without gum, imperforate margins.

OX4	POS2	slate blue	7.00
		Block of four	30.00

POS3

Typographed by the Panama Canal Press
Issued in sheets of 32, without gum, imperforate margins except at top.

Size: 46x27mm.
Seal Diameter: 13mm.

1954, Mar. 8	Unwmk.	Perf. 12½	
OX5 POS3	black *(16,000)*	5.00	—
a.	Wmkd. Seal of U. S. in sheet	20.00	—

Seal Diameter: 11½mm.

1961-74		Rouletted 5	
OX6 POS3	black, *July 1, 1974*	2.50	—
a.	Perf. 12½ *May 16, 1961 (48,000)*	2.50	—
b.	Wmkd. Seal of U.S. in sheet, perf. 12½	6.00	
c.	As "a," double impression	80.00	
d.	As "b," double impression	100.00	

ENVELOPES

Prices for cut squares are for copies with fine margins on all sides. Prices for unused entries are for those without printed or manuscript address. A "full corner" includes black and side flaps and commands a premium.

Vasco Núñez de Balboa — E1   Fernandez de Cordoba — E2

Envelopes of Panama Lithographed and Overprinted by American Bank Note Co.

1916, April 24
On White Paper

U1	E1	1c green & black	15.00	10.00
		Entire	110.00	60.00
a.		Head and overprint only		
		Entire	1,750.	1,750.
b.		Frame only		
		Entire	2,250.	2,250.
U2	E2	2c carmine & black	12.50	5.00
		Entire	90.00	45.00
a.		2c red & black	12.50	5.00
		Entire	85.00	45.00
b.		Head and overprint only		
		Entire	1,600.	1,400.
c.		Frame only (red)		
		Entire	1,600.	1,400.
d.		Frame double (carmine)		
		Entire	2,250.	2,000.

José Vallarino — E3   "The Land Gate" — E4

1921, Nov. 13
On White Paper

U3	E3	1c green	140.00	100.00
		Entire	1,000.	450.00
U4	E4	2c red	35.00	20.00
		Entire	250.00	120.00

Arms of Panama — E5

Typographed and embossed by American Bank Note Co. with "CANAL ZONE" in color of stamp.

1923, Dec. 15
On White Paper

U5	E5	2c carmine	55.00	32.50
		Entire	200.00	125.00

CANAL

U.S. Nos. U420 and U429 Overprinted in Black by Bureau of Engraving and Printing, Washington, D.C.

ZONE

1924, July 1

U6	U92	1c green *(50,000)*	5.00	3.00
		Entire	40.00	22.50
U7	U93	2c carmine *(100,000)*	5.00	3.00
		Entire	40.00	22.50

Seal of Canal Zone — E6

Printed by the Panama Canal Press, Mount Hope, C.Z.

1924, Oct.
On White Paper

U8	E6	1c green *(205,000)*	2.00	1.00
		Entire	35.00	17.50
U9	E6	2c carmine *(1,997,658)*	75	40
		Entire	30.00	9.00

Gorgas E7

Goethals E8

Typographed and Embossed by International Envelope Corp., Dayton, O.

1932, April 8

U10	E7	1c green *(1,300,000)*	15	10
		Entire	2.75	1.00
U11	E8	2c carmine *(400,250)*	25	15
		Entire	3.50	1.50

No. U9 Surcharged in Violet by Panama Canal Press, Mount Hope, C.Z. Numerals 3 mm. high   **3   3**

1932, July 20

U12	E6	3c on 2c carmine *(20,000)*	17.50	7.50
		Entire	275.00	120.00

No. U11 Surcharged in Violet, Numerals 5 mm. high   **3   3**

1932, July 20

U13	E8	3c on 2c carmine *(320,000)*	2.00	1.00
		Entire	25.00	14.00

1934, Jan. 17
Numerals with Serifs

U14	E6	3c on 2c carmine (Numerals 4mm. high) *(8,000)*	115.00	60.00
		Entire	600.00	500.00
U15	E8	3c on 2c carmine (Numerals 5mm. high) *(23,000)*	25.00	15.00
		Entire	300.00	135.00

Typographed and Embossed by International Envelope Corp., Dayton, O.

1934, June 18

U16	E8	3c purple *(2,450,000)*	15	10
		Entire	1.10	55

1958, Nov. 1

U17	E8	4c blue *(596,725)*	20	15
		Entire	1.25	50

Surcharged at Left of Stamp in Ultra. as No. UX13

1969, Apr. 28

U18	E8	4c +1c blue *(93,850)*	15	10
		Entire	1.25	95
U19	E8	4c +2c blue *(23,125)*	50	30
		Entire	2.50	1.50

Ship Passing through Gaillard Cut — E9

Typographed and Embossed by United States Envelope Co., Williamsburg, Pa.

1971, Nov. 17

U20	E9	8c emerald *(121,500)*	25	12
		Entire	75	35

Surcharged at Left of Stamp in Emerald as No. UX13

1974, Mar. 2

U21	E9	8c +2c emerald	30	15
		Entire	1.00	35

1976, Feb. 23

U22	E9	13c violet *(638,350)*	35	20
		Entire	75	40

A little time given to the study of the arrangement of the Scott Catalogue can make it easier to use effectively.

Surcharged at Left of Stamp in Violet as No. UX13

1978, July 5
U23 E9 13c +2c violet *(245,041)*   35   20
      Entire   75   40

AIR POST ENVELOPES

No. U9 Overprinted with Horizontal Blue and Red Bars
Across Entire Face.

Overprinted by Panama Canal Press, Mount Hope, C.Z.

Boxed inscription in lower left with nine lines of instructions.

Additional adhesives required for air post rate.

1928, May 21
UC1 E6 2c red, entire *(15,000)*   120.00 60.00
      First day cancel   80.00

No. U9 with Similar Overprint of Blue and Red Bars, and "VIA AIR MAIL" in Blue, Centered, no box.

1929
UC2 E6 2c red, entire *(10,000)* Jan. 11,
      1929   250.00 100.00
  a. Inscription at left *(60,200)* Feb. 6, 1929 80.00 30.00

DC-4 Skymaster — UC1

Typographed and Embossed by International Envelope Corp., Dayton, O.

1949, Jan. 3
UC3 UC1 6c blue *(4,400,000)*   25   15
      Entire   3.75 1.50
      Entire, 1st day cancel   2.00

1958, Nov. 1
UC4 UC1 7c carmine *(1,000,000)*   25   15
      Entire   4.00 1.00
      Entire, 1st day cancel   1.50

No. U16 Surcharged at Left of Stamp and Imprinted "VIA AIR MAIL" in Dark Blue

Surcharged by Panama Canal Press, Mount Hope, C.Z.

1963, June 22
UC5 E8 3c +5c purple *(105,000)*   75   35
      Entire   8.50 4.00
  a. Double surcharge   700.00

Jet Liner and Tail Assembly — UC2

Typographed and Embossed by International Envelope Corp., Dayton, O.

1964, Jan. 6
UC6 UC2 8c deep carmine *(600,000)*   35   20
      Entire   1.75 1.25

No. U17 Surcharged at Left of Stamp as No. UC5 and Imprinted "VIA AIR MAIL" in Vermilion
Surcharged by Canal Zone Press, La Boca, C.Z.

1965, Oct. 15
UC7 E8 4c +4c blue *(100,000)*   50   25
      Entire   4.00 2.75

Jet Liner and Tail Assembly — UC3

Typographed and Embossed by United States Envelope Co., Williamsburg, Pa.

1966, Feb. 25 (?)
UC8 UC3 8c carmine *(224,000)*   50   35
      Entire   3.50 1.75

No. UC8 Surcharged at Left of Stamp as No. UX13 in Vermilion
Surcharged by Canal Zone Press, La Boca, C.Z.

1968, Jan. 18
UC9 UC3 8c +2c carmine *(376,000)*   40   25
      Entire   2.75 1.10

No. UC7 with Additional Surcharge at Left of Stamp as No. UX13 and Imprinted "VIA AIR MAIL" in Vermilion
Surcharged by Canal Zone Press, La Boca, C.Z.

1968, Feb. 12
UC10 E8 4c +4c +2c blue *(224,150)*   60   40
      Entire   2.25 1.50

Type of 1966
Typographed and Engraved by United States Envelope Co., Williamsburg, Pa.

1969, Apr. 1
Luminescent Ink
UC11 UC3 10c ultramarine *(448,000)*   60   30
      Entire   3.50 1.40

No. U17 Surcharged at Left of Stamp as Nos. UC5 and UX13, and Imprinted "VIA AIR MAIL" in Vermilion

1971, May 17
UC12 E8 4c +5c +2c blue *(55,775)*   60   30
      Entire   3.00 2.25

No. UC11 Surcharged in Ultra. at Left of Stamp as No. UX13

1971, May 17
Luminescent Ink
UC13 UC3 10c +1c ultramarine *(152,000)*   45   30
      Entire   3.25 1.25

Type of 1966
Typographed and Engraved by United States Envelope Co., Williamsburg, Pa.

1971, Nov. 17
UC14 UC3 11c rose red *(553,000)*   30   15
      Entire   1.00 60
  a. 11c carmine, tagged   30   15
      Entire   1.00 60

Surcharged at Left of Stamp in Rose Red as No. UX13

1974, Mar. 2
UC15 UC3 11c +2c carmine, tagged *(387,000)*   35   20
      Entire   1.50 80
  a. 11c +2c rose red, untagged   35   20
      Entire   2.00 80

No. U21 with Additional Surcharge in Vermilion at Left of Stamp as No. UX 13 and Imprinted "VIA AIR MAIL" in Vermilion

1975, May 3
UC16 E9 8c +2c +3c emerald *(75,000)*   50   25
      Entire   1.25 1.00

REGISTRATION ENVELOPES

RE1

Panama Registration Envelope surcharged by Panama Canal Press, Mount Hope, C.Z.

1918, Oct.   **8mm. btwn. CANAL & ZONE**
UF1 RE1 10c on 5c black & red, *cream*
      (10,000), entire   1,750. 1,500.
  a. 9¼ mm. btwn. CANAL & ZONE
      (25,000), entire ('19)   1,500. 1,250.

Stamped envelopes inscribed "Diez Centesimos," surcharged with numerals "5" and with solid blocks printed over "Canal Zone," were issued by the Republic of Panama after being rejected by the Canal Zone. Parts of "Canal Zone" are often legible under the surcharge blocks. These envelopes exist without surcharge.

POSTAL CARDS

Prices are for Entires

Map of Panama — PC1

Panama Card Lithographed by American Bank Note Co., revalued and surcharged in black by the Isthmian Canal Commission.

1907, Feb. 9
On White
UX1 PC1 1c on 2c carmine, "CANAL"
      15mm. *(50,000)*   45.00 35.00
  a. Double surcharge   1,500. 1,500.
  b. Double surcharge, one reading down   2,750.
  c. Triple surcharge, one reading down   2,750.
  d. "CANAL" 13 mm. *(10,000)*   250.00 200.00
  e. As "d," double surch.   2,750.

Balboa — PC2

Panama card lithographed by Hamilton Bank Note Co. Overprinted in black by Isthmian Canal Commission.

At least six types of overprint, reading down.

1908, March 3
UX2 PC2 1c green & black, "CANAL"
      13mm. *(295,000)*   200.00 100.00
  a. Double overprint   1,750. 1,750.
  b. Triple overprint   1,750. —
  c. Period after "ZONE" *(40,000)*   200.00 125.00
  d. "CANAL" 15 mm. *(30,000)*   200.00 125.00
  e. "ZONE CANAL", reading up   2,750.

Balboa
PC3   PC4

Lithographed by Hamilton Bank Note Co.
Overprinted in Black by Panama Canal Press,
Mount Hope, C.Z.

1910, Nov. 10
UX3 PC3 1c green & black *(40,000)*   175.00 100.00
    a.   Double overprint   2,750.

    This card, with overprint reading up, is actually the fourth of
seven settings of UX2.

Lithographed and Overprinted by American Bank
Note Co.

1913, March 27
UX4 PC4 1c green & black *(634,000)* 175.00 80.00

Design of Canal Zone Envelopes
Overprinted in black by the American Bank Note
Co.

1921-24
UX5 E3 1c green, *Oct. 1921*   1,100. 700.00

Typographed and embossed by American Bank
Note Co. with "CANAL ZONE" in color of stamp.

UX6 E5 1c green, *Jan. 1924*   1,000. 700.00

CANAL

U.S. No. UX27 Overprinted by U.S.
Gov't. Printing Office at Washington,
D.C.

ZONE

1924, July 1
UX7 PC17 1c green on buff *(Jefferson)*
      (50,000)   85.00 40.00

Design of Canal Zone Envelope
Printed by Panama Canal Press.

1925, Jan.
UX8 E6 1c green on buff *(25,000)*   85.00 40.00
    a. Background only   2,250.

CANAL

U.S. No. UX27 Overprinted

ZONE

1925, May
UX9 PC17 1c green on buff *(Jefferson)*
      (850,000)   8.50 2.50

CANAL

U.S. No. UX27 Overprinted

ZONE

1935, Oct.
UX10 PC17 1c green on buff *(Jefferson)*
      (2,900,000)   1.50 60
    a. Double overprint   2,500.

Same on U.S. No. UX38

1952, May 1
UX11 PC22 2c carmine rose on buff *(Frank-*
      lin) (800,000)   1.75 75

Ship in Lock — PC5

Printed by Bureau of Engraving & Printing,
Washington, D.C.

1958, Nov. 1
UX12 PC5 3c dark blue on buff *(335,116)* 1.50 75

No. UX12 Surcharged at Left of
Stamp in Green by Panama Canal
Press, Mount Hope, C.Z.

1963, July 27
UX13 PC5 3c +1c dark blue on buff *(78,000)* 4.00 3.00

Ship Passing through
Panama Canal — PC6

Printed by Panama Canal Press, Mount Hope, C.Z.
1964, Dec. 1
UX14 PC6 4c violet blue on buff *(74,200)* 3.50 2.50

Ship in Lock (Tow car at right redrawn) — PC7

Printed by Bureau of Engraving & Printing,
Washington, D.C.

1965, Aug. 12
UX15 PC7 4c emerald on white *(95,500)* 1.00 65

No. UX15 Surcharged at Left of Stamp in Green
as No. UX13 by Canal Zone Press, La Boca, C.Z.
1968, Feb. 12
UX16 PC7 4c +1c emerald on white *(94,775)* 1.00 65

Ship-in-Lock Type of 1965
1969, Apr. 1
UX17 PC7 5c light ultra. on white *(63,000)* 90 50

No. UX17 Surcharged at Left of Stamp in Light
Ultramarine as No. UX13
1971, May 24
UX18 PC7 5c +1c light ultra. on white
      (100,500)   80 40

Ship-in-Lock Type of 1965
Printed by Bureau of Engraving & Printing,
Washington, D.C.
1974, Feb. 11
UX19 PC7 8c brown on white *(90,895)* 65 40

No. UX19 Surcharged at left of Stamp in Brown as
No. UX13
1976, June 1
UX20 PC7 8c +1c brown on white *(60,249)* 50 40

No. UX19 Surcharged at Left of Stamp in Brown as
No. UX13
1978, July 5
UX21 PC7 8c +2c brown on white *(74,847)* 60 40

AIR POST POSTAL CARDS

Plane, Flag and Map — APC1

Printed by Bureau of Engraving & Printing,
Washington, D.C.

1958, Nov. 1
UXC1 APC1 5c blue & carmine rose on
      white *(104,957)*   3.50 3.00

No. UXC1 Surcharged at Left of Stamp in Green
as No. UX13 by Panama Canal Press,
Mount Hope, C.Z.

1963, July 27
UXC2 APC1 5c +1c blue & carmine rose
      on white *(48,000)*   9.50 6.00
    a.   Inverted surcharge   1,500.

No. UX15 Surcharged at Left of Stamp as
No. UX13 and Imprinted "AIR MAIL" in
Vermilion

1965, Aug. 18
UXC3 PC7 4c +2c emerald on white
      (41,700)   4.00 3.00

No. UX15 Surcharged at Left of Stamp as No. UC5 and Imprinted "AIR MAIL" in Vermilion by Canal Zone Press, La Boca, C.Z.

1968, Feb. 2

UXC4	PC7	4c +4c emerald on white (60,100)	2.75	1.50

No. UX17 Surcharged at Left of Stamp as No. UC5 and Imprinted "AIR MAIL" in Vermilion

1971, May 24

UXC5	PC7	5c +4c light ultramarine on white (68,000)	75	50

PROOFS

1928-40

			DIE (1) Large	(2) Small
106TC	2c	black	750.00	
113P	30c	brown black		650.00

1934

117P	3c	deep violet	350.00	

1939

120P	1c	yellow green		650.00
121P	2c	rose carmine		650.00
122P	3c	purple	750.00	650.00
123P	5c	dark blue	750.00	650.00
124P	6c	red orange		650.00
125P	7c	black		650.00
126P	8c	green		650.00
127P	10c	ultramarine		650.00
128P	11c	blue green	750.00	650.00
129P	12c	brown carmine	750.00	650.00
130P	14c	dark violet		650.00
131P	15c	olive green		650.00
132P	18c	rose pink		650.00
133P	20c	brown	750.00	650.00
134P	25c	orange	750.00	650.00
135P	50c	violet brown	750.00	650.00

1946-48

136P	½c	bright red	750.00
137P	1½c	chocolate	750.00
139P	5c	deep blue	750.00
140P	25c	yellow blue	750.00
141P	10c	black	750.00

1949

142P	3c	blue	750.00
143P	6c	violet	750.00
144P	12c	bright blue green	750.00

145P	18c	deep red lilac	750.00

Air Post

1931-49

C6P	4c	red violet	850.00
C7P	5c	light green	850.00
C8P	6c	yellow brown	850.00
C13P	40c	yellow	850.00

1939

C15P	5c	greenish black		750.00
C15TC	5c	scarlet	850.00	
C16P	10c	dull violet	850.00	750.00
C17P	15c	light brown		750.00
C18P	25c	blue		750.00
C19P	30c	rose carmine	850.00	750.00
C20P	$1	green		750.00

1951

C21P	4c	red violet	850.00

The Small Die proofs listed are on soft yellowish wove paper.

CUBA

AFTER the U. S. battleship "Maine" was destroyed in Havana harbor with a loss of 266 lives in February, 1898, the United States demanded the withdrawal of Spanish troops from Cuba. The Spanish-American War followed. By the peace treaty of Dec. 10, 1898, Spain relinquished Cuba to the United States in trust for its inhabitants. On Jan. 1, 1899, Spanish authority was succeeded by U. S. military rule which lasted until May 20, 1902, when Cuba, as a republic, assumed self-government.

The listings in this catalogue cover the U. S. Administration issue of 1899, the Republic's 1899-1902 issues under U. S. military rule and the Puerto Principe issue of provincial provisionals.

100 CENTS = 1 DOLLAR

Puerto Principe Issue

In December, 1898, Puerto Principe, a provincial capital now called Camagüey, ran short of 1c, 2c, 3c, 5c and 10c stamps. The Postmaster ordered Cuban stamps to be surcharged on Dec. 19, 1898.

The surcharging was done to horizontal strips of five stamps, so vertical pairs and blocks do not exist. Five types are found in each setting, and five printings were made. Counterfeits are plentiful.

First Printing
Black Surcharge, 17½ mm. high

HABILITADO
2
cents.
Position 1

HABILITADO
2
cents.
Position 2

HABILITADO
2
cents.
Position 3

HABILITADO
2
cents.
Position 4

HABILITADO
2
cents.
Position 5

Position 1	-No serif at right of "t".
Position 2	-Thin numeral except on 1c on 17 No. 176.
Position 3	-Broken right foot of "n".
Position 4	-Up-stroke of "t" broken.
Position 5	-Broken "DO".

This printing consisted of the following stamps:

176	1c on 1m orange brown, Pos. 1, 2, 3, 4 and 5
178	2c on 2m orange brown, Pos. 1, 3, 4 and 5
179	2c on 2m orange brown, Pos. 2
180	3c on 3m orange brown, Pos. 1, 3, 4 and 5
181	3c on 3m orange brown, Pos. 2

188	5c on 5m orange brown, Pos. 1, 3, 4 and 5
189	5c on 5m orange brown, Pos. 2

Surcharge measures 17½mm. high and is roughly printed in dull black ink.

Second Printing
Black Surcharge, 17½mm. high

This printing was from the same setting as used for the first printing, but the impression is much clearer and the ink quite shiny.

The printing consisted of the following stamps:

179F	3c on 2m orange brown, Pos. 1, 3, 4 and 5
179G	3c on 2m orange brown, Pos. 2
182	5c on 1m orange brown, Pos. 1, 3, 4 and 5
183	5c on 1m orange brown, Pos. 2
184	5c on 2m orange brown, Pos. 1, 3, 4 and 5
185	5c on 2m orange brown, Pos. 2
186	5c on 3m orange brown, Pos. 1, 3, 4 and 5
187	5c on 3m orange brown, Pos. 2
188	5c on 5m orange brown, Pos. 1, 3, 4 and 5
189	5c on 5m orange brown, Pos. 2
190	5c on ½m blue green, Pos. 1, 3, 4 and 5
191	5c on ½m blue green, Pos. 2

Third Printing
Red Surcharge, 20mm. high

The same setting as for the first and second was used for the third printing. The 10c denomination first appeared in this printing and position 2 of that value has numerals same as on positions 1, 3, 4 and 5, while position 4 has broken "1" in "10".

The printing consisted of the following stamps:

196	3c on 1c black violet, Pos. 1, 3, 4 and 5
197	3c on 1c black violet, Pos. 2
198	5c on 1c black violet, Pos. 1, 3, 4 and 5
199	5c on 1c black violet, Pos. 2
200	10c on 1c black violet, Pos. 1, 2, 3 and 5
200a	10c on 1c black violet, Pos. 4

Fourth Printing
Black Surcharge, 19½mm. high

The same type as before but spaced between so that the surcharge is 2mm. taller. Clear impression, shiny ink.

HABILITADO
1
cents.
Position 1

HABILITADO
1
cents.
Position 2

HABILITADO
1
cents.
Position 3

HABILITADO
1
cents.
Position 4

HABILITADO
1
cents. Position 5

Position 1	-No serif at right of "t".
Position 2	-Broken "1" on No. 177.
Position 2	-Thin numerals on 5c stamps.
Position 3	-Broken right foot of "n".
Position 4	-Up-stroke of "t" broken.
Position 4	-Thin numeral on 3c stamps.
Position 5	-Broken "DO".

This printing consisted of the following stamps:

177	1c on 1m orange brown, Pos. 1, 3, 4 and 5
177a	1c on 1m orange brown, Pos. 2
179B	3c on 1m orange brown, Pos. 1, 2, 3 and 5
179D	3c on 1m orange brown, Pos. 4
183B	5c on 1m orange brown, Pos. 1, 3, 4 and 5
189C	5c on 5m orange brown, Pos. 1, 3, 4 and 5
192	5c on ½m blue green, Pos. 1, 3, 4 and 5
193	5c on ½m blue green, Pos. 2

Fifth Printing
Black Surcharge, 19½mm. high

HABILITADO

3

cents.
Position 1

HABILITADO

3

cents.
Position 2

HABILITADO

3

eents.
Position 3

HABILITADO

3

cents.
Position 4

HABILITADO

3

cents.
Position 5

Position 1	-Nick in bottom of "e"and lower serif of "s".
Position 2	-Normal surcharge.
Position 3	-"eents".
Position 4	-Thin numeral.
Position 5	-Nick in upper part of right stroke of "n".

This printing consisted of the following stamps:

201	3c on 1m blue green, Pos. 1, 2 and 5
201b	3c on 1m blue green, Pos. 3
202	3c on 1m blue green, Pos. 4
203	3c on 2m blue green, Pos. 4
203a	3c on 2m blue green, Pos. 3
204	3c on 2m blue green, Pos. 4
205	3c on 3m blue green, Pos. 1, 2 and 5
205b	3c on 3m blue green, Pos. 3
206	3c on 3m blue green, Pos. 4
211	5c on 1m blue green, Pos. 1, 2 and 5
211a	5c on 1m blue green, Pos. 3
212	5c on 1m blue green, Pos. 4
213	5c on 2m blue green, Pos. 1, 2 and 5
213a	5c on 2m blue green, Pos. 3
214	5c on 2m blue green, Pos. 4
215	5c on 3m blue green, Pos. 1, 2 and 5
215a	5c on 3m blue green, Pos. 3
216	5c on 3m blue green, Pos. 4
217	5c on 4m blue green, Pos. 1, 2 and 5
217a	5c on 4m blue green, Pos. 3
218	5c on 4m blue green, Pos. 4
219	5c on 8m blue green, Pos. 1, 2 and 5
219b	5c on 8m blue green, Pos. 3
220	5c on 8m blue green, Pos. 4

Counterfeits exist of all Puerto Principe surcharges. Illustrations have been altered to discourage further counterfeiting.

Regular Issues of Cuba of 1896 and 1898 Surcharged:

HABILITADO

1

cent.
a

Numerals in ( ) after color indicate printings.

1898-99   **Puerto Principe Issue**
Black Surcharge on Nos. 156-158, 160

| 176 | (a) | 1 cent on 1m orange brown (1) | 55.00 | 37.50 |

HABILITADO

1

cents.
b

177	(b)	1 cents on 1m orange brown (4)	45.00	30.00
a.		Broken figure "1"	75.00	60.00
b.		Inverted surcharge		200.00
d.		Same as "a" inverted		250.00

HABILITADO

2

cents.
c

| 178 | (c) | 2c on 2m orange brown (1) | 22.50 | 15.00 |
| a. | | Inverted surcharge | 250.00 | 50.00 |

HABILITADO

2

cents.
d

| 179 | (d) | 2c on 2m orange brown (1) | 40.00 | 25.00 |
| a. | | Inverted surcharge | 350.00 | 100.00 |

HABILITADO

3

cents.
k

| 179B | (k) | 3c on 1m orange brown (4) | 450.00 | 150.00 |
| c. | | Double surcharge | 1,500. | 750.00 |

HABILITADO

3

cents.
l

| 179D | (l) | 3c on 1m orange brown (4) | 1,500. | 600.00 |
| e. | | Double surcharge | — | — |

HABILITADO

3

cents.
e

| 179F | (e) | 3c on 2m orange brown (2) | | 2,000. |

HABILITADO

3

cents.
f

179G	(f)	3c on 2m orange brown (2)	—	2,500.
180	(e)	3c on 3m orange brown (1)	27.50	22.50
a.		Inverted surcharge		100.00
181	(f)	3c on 3m orange brown (1)	75.00	50.00
a.		Inverted surcharge		300.00

HABILITADO

5

cents.
g

| 182 | (g) | 5c on 1m orange brown (2) | 700.00 | 175.00 |
| a. | | Inverted surcharge | | 500.00 |

HABILITADO

5

cents.
h

| 183 | (h) | 5c on 1m orange brown (2) | 1,500. | 400.00 |
| a. | | Inverted surcharge | | 700.00 |

HABILITADO

5

cents.
i

184	(g)	5c on 2m orange brown (2)	750.00	200.00
185	(h)	5c on 2m orange brown (2)	1,500.	400.00
186	(g)	5c on 3m orange brown (2)		165.00
a.		Inverted surcharge		700.00
187	(h)	5c an 3m orange brown (2)		400.00
a.		Inverted surcharge		1,000.
188	(g)	5c on 5m orange brown (1) (2)	70.00	55.00
a.		Inverted surcharge	400.00	175.00
b.		Double surcharge	—	—
189	(h)	5c on 5m orange brown (1) (2)	350.00	225.00
a.		Inverted surcharge		400.00
b.		Double surcharge	—	—
189C	(i)	5c on 5m orange brown (4)		8,000.

Black Surcharge on No. P25

190	(g)	5c on ½m blue green (2)	250.00	75.00
a.		Inverted surcharge	500.00	150.00
b.		Pair, one without surcharge		700.00
191	(h)	5c on ½m blue green (2)	300.00	90.00
a.		Inverted surcharge		200.00
192	(i)	5c on ½m blue green (4)	550.00	200.00
a.		Double surcharge, one diagonal		6,000.

HABILITADO

5

cents.
j

| 193 | (j) | 5c on ½m blue green (4) | 700.00 | 300.00 |

Red Surcharge on No. 161

196	(k)	3c on 1c black violet (3)	60.00	25.00
a.		Inverted surcharge		200.00
197	(l)	3c on 1c black violet (3)	125.00	45.00
a.		Inverted surcharge		300.00
198	(i)	5c on 1c black violet (3)	20.00	20.00
a.		Inverted surcharge		100.00
b.		Vertical surcharge		2,000.
c.		Double surcharge	400.00	600.00
d.		Double inverted surcharge		—
199	(j)	5c on 1c black violet (3)	50.00	40.00
a.		Inverted surcharge		250.00
b.		Vertical surcharge		2,000.
c.		Double surcharge	1,000.	600.00

HABILITADO

10

cents.
m

| 200 | (m) | 10c on 1c black violet (3) | 20.00 | 50.00 |
| a. | | Broken figure "1" | 40.00 | 100.00 |

Black Surcharge on Nos. P26-P30

201	(k)	3c on 1m blue green (5)	300.00	200.00
a.		Inverted surcharge		400.00
b.		"EENTS"	550.00	400.00
c.		Same as "b", inverted		850.00
202	(l)	3c on 1m blue green (5)	500.00	400.00
a.		Inverted surcharge		850.00
203	(k)	3c on 2m blue green (5)	850.00	250.00
a.		"EENTS"	1,250.	450.00
b.		Inverted surcharge		600.00
c.		Same as "a", inverted		750.00
204	(l)	3c on 2m blue green (5)	1,000.	450.00
a.		Inverted surcharge		750.00
205	(k)	3c on 3m blue green (5)	900.00	250.00
a.		Inverted surcharge		500.00
b.		"EENTS"	1,250.	375.00
c.		Same as "b", inverted		700.00
206	(l)	3c on 3m blue green (5)	1,250.	375.00
a.		Inverted surcharge		700.00
211	(i)	5c on 1m blue green (5)		2,000.
a.		"EENTS"	—	2,500.
212	(j)	5c on 1m blue green (5)		2,500.
213	(i)	5c on 2m blue green (5)		1,500.
a.		"EENTS"	—	2,000.
214	(j)	5c on 2m blue green (5)		1,750.
215	(i)	5c on 3m blue green (5)		500.00
a.		"EENTS"		1,000.
216	(j)	5c on 3m blue green (5)	—	1,000.
217	(i)	5c on 4m blue green (5)	2,500.	700.00
a.		"EENTS"	3,000.	1,500.
b.		Inverted surcharge		1,400.
c.		Same as "a", inverted		2,000.
218	(j)	5c on 4m blue green (5)	1,500.	
a.		Inverted surcharge		2,000.
219	(i)	5c on 8m blue green (5)	3,000.	1,000.
a.		Inverted surcharge		1,500.
b.		"EENTS"	—	2,000.
c.		Same as "b", inverted		2,500.
220	(j)	5c on 8m blue green (5)		2,000.
a.		Inverted surcharge		2,500.

Puerto Principe pairs, strips and stamps properly canceled on cover are scarce and command high premiums.

Most copies of all but the most common varieties are faulty or have tropical toning. Prices are for copies where they exist.

CUBA

United States Stamps Nos. 279a, 267, 279B, 268, 281a, 282C and 283a Surcharged in Black

1 c.
de PESO.

1899		Wmk. 191		Perf. 12	
221	A87	1c on 1c yellow green	4.25	60
		On cover		15.00
		Block of four	20.00	6.00
		Margin strip of 3, Impt. & P#	50.00	
		Margin block of 6, Impt. & P#	225.00	
222	A88	2c on 2c carmine, type III	4.25	50
		On cover		12.50
		Block of four	20.00	6.00
		Margin strip of 3, Impt. & P#	50.00	
		Margin block of 6, Impt. & P#	350.00	
a.		2c on 2c red, type III	5.00	40
b.		"CUPA"	135.00	120.00
c.		Inverted surcharge	3,000.	3,000.
		"CUBA" at bottom	450.00	
223	A88	2½c on 2c red, type III	3.00	60
		On cover		12.50
		Block of four	15.00	6.00
		Margin strip of 3, Impt. & P#	50.00	
		Margin block of 6, Impt. & P#	225.00	
a.		2½ on 2c carmine, type III	3.50	2.00

The 2½c was sold and used as a 2c stamp.

224	A89	3c on 3c purple	8.50	1.25
		On cover		20.00
		Block of four	40.00	17.50
		Margin strip of 3, Impt. & P#	85.00	
		Margin block of 6, Impt. & P#	500.00	
a.		Period between "B" and "A"	27.50	27.50

Two types of surcharge
I "3" directly over "P"
II "3" to left over "P"

225	A91	5c on 5c blue	8.50	1.25
		On cover		20.00
		Block of four	40.00	15.00
		Margin strip of 3, Impt. & P#	150.00	
		Margin block of 6, Impt. & P#	650.00	
a.		"CUPA"	75.00	50.00
		"CUBA" at bottom		
226	A94	10c on 10c brown, type I	22.50	8.00
		On cover		100.00
		Block of four	90.00	50.00
		Margin strip of 3, Impt. & P#	300.00	
		Margin block of 6, Impt. & P#	1,250.	
b.		"CUBA" omitted	3,500.	3,500.
		"CUBA" at bottom	350.00	350.00
226A	A94	10c on 10c brown, type II	5,000.	
		Block of four		

No. 226A exists only in the special printing.

Special Printing

In 1899 one sheet each of Nos. 221 to 225, 226A; E1 (three sheets), and J1 to J4 (two sheets each) were specially printed for display at the Paris Exposition. All but a few copies, however, were later destroyed. Nearly all copies remaining bear impression of handstamp reading "Special Surcharge" on the back. Price: Nos. 221-225, J1-J4, each $250; No. E1, $400.

Issues of the Republic under U. S. Military Rule

Statue of
Columbus
A20

Royal Palms
A21

Allegory,
"Cuba"
A22

Ocean Liner
A23

Cane Field — A24

Printed by the U.S. Bureau of Engraving and Printing

1899		Wmk. US-C (191C)		Perf. 12	
227	A20	1c yellow green	3.00	15
		On cover		2.00
		Block of four	12.50	1.50
		Margin block of 10, Impt. & P#, type VII	225.00	
228	A21	2c carmine	3.00	15
		On cover		2.00
		Block of four	12.50	1.50
		Margin block of 10, Impt. & P#, type VII	175.00	
a.		2c scarlet	3.00	15
b.		Booklet pane of six	1,750.	
229	A22	3c purple	3.00	25
		On cover		4.00
		Block of four	12.50	4.00
		Margin block of 10, Impt. & P#, type VII	250.00	—
230	A23	5c blue	4.50	30
		On cover		4.00
		Block of four	20.00	4.00
		Margin block of 10, Impt. & P#, type VII	650.00	—
231	A24	10c brown	10.00	75
		On cover		6.50
		Block of four	45.00	8.00
		Margin block of 10, Impt. & P#, type VII	1,000.	—

Re-engraved

The re-engraved stamps issued by the Republic of Cuba in 1905-07 may be distinguished from the Issue of 1899 as follows:
Nos. 227 to 231 are watermarked U S-C
The re-engraved stamps are unwatermarked.

No. 227

Re-engraved.

No. 228

Re-engraved.

No. 230

Re-engraved.

No. 231

Re-engraved.
   1c: The ends of the label inscribed "Centavo" are rounded instead of square.
   2c: The foliate ornaments, inside the oval disks bearing the numerals of value, have been removed.
   5c: Two lines forming a right angle have been added in the upper corners of the label bearing the word "Cuba".
   10c: A small ball has been added to each of the square ends of the label bearing the word "Cuba".

SPECIAL DELIVERY

Issued under Administration of the United States.

CUBA.

Special Delivery Stamp of the United States No. E5 Surcharged in Red

10c.
de PESO.

1899		Wmk. 191		Perf. 12	
E1	SD3	10c on 10c blue	120.00	80.00
		On cover		450.00
		Block of four	500.00	
		Margin block of four, arrow	550.00	
		Margin strip of 3, Impt. & P#	900.00	
		Margin block of 6, Impt. & P#	5,000.	
a.		No period after "CUBA"	350.00	400.00
		Dots in curved frame above messenger (Pl. 882)		

Issue of the Republic under U. S. Military Rule

Special Delivery
Messenger — SD2

Printed by the U. S. Bureau of Engraving and
Printing

1899   **Wmk. US-C (191C)**
Inscribed: "Immediata"

E2	SD2 10c orange		45.00	12.00
	On cover			125.00
	Block of four		200.00	—
	Margin strip of 3, Impt. & P #, type VII		300.00	
	Margin block of 6, Impt. & P #, type VII		1,000.	

Re-engraved

In 1902 the Republic of Cuba issued a stamp of design SD2 re-engraved with word correctly spelled "Immediata." The corrected die was made in 1899 (See No. E3P). It was printed by the U.S. Bureau of Engraving and Printing.

POSTAGE DUE

Issued under Administration of the United States. Postage Due Stamps of the United States Nos. J38, J39, J41 and J42 Surcharged in Black Like Regular Issue of Same Date.

1899   **Wmk. 191**   *Perf. 12*

J1	D2 1c on 1c deep claret		25.00	3.50
	Block of four		110.00	30.00
	Margin block of 6, Impt. & P#		650.00	
J2	D2 2c on 2c deep claret		22.50	3.50
	Block of four		100.00	30.00
	Margin block of 6, Impt. & P#		650.00	
a.	Inverted surcharge			2,000.
J3	D2 5c on 5c deep claret		25.00	3.50
	Block of four		110.00	30.00
	Margin block of 6, Impt. & P#		600.00	
a.	"CUPA"		175.00	160.00
J4	D2 10c on 10c deep claret		22.50	1.25
	Block of four		100.00	12.50
	Margin block of 6, Impt. & P#		750.00	

ENVELOPES

Prices are for Cut Squares
U. S. Envelopes of 1887-99 Surcharged

CUBA.   CUBA.

1c. DE PESO.   2c. DE PESO.
      a   b

1899

U1	U77 (a)	1c on 1c green on buff (No. U354)	5.00	4.00
		Entire	15.00	20.00
U2	U77 (a)	1c on 1c green on blue (No. U355)	3.50	3.00
		Entire	6.00	8.00
a.		Double surch., entire	2,000.	
U3	U71 (b)	2c on 2c green on white (No. U311)	1.50	1.25
		Entire	3.50	4.50
a.		Double surch., entire	2,000.	2,000.
U4	U71 (b)	2c on 2c green on amber (No. U312)	2.50	2.00
		Entire	6.00	7.50
a.		Double surch., entire	2,000.	
U5	U71 (a)	2c on 2c green on buff (No. U313)	17.50	10.00
		Entire	60.00	60.00
U6	U79 (a)	2c on 2c carmine on amber (No. U363)	17.50	17.50
		Entire	60.00	60.00
U7	U79 (a)	2c on 2c carmine on buff (No. U364)	25.00	25.00
		Entire	85.00	95.00
U8	U79 (a)	2c on 2c carmine on blue (No. U365)	3.00	2.50

	Entire	9.00	10.00
a.	Double surch., entire		2,000.

In addition to the envelopes listed above, several others are known but were not regularly issued. They are:
1c on 1c green on white
1c on 1c green on manila
2c on 2c carmine on white
2c on 2c carmine on oriental buff
2c on 2c carmine on blue
4c on 4c brown on white
5c on 5c blue on white

Issue of the Republic under U. S. Military Rule

Columbus — E1

Similar envelopes without watermark on white and amber papers, were issued by the Republic after Military Rule ended in 1902.

1899   **Wmk. "US POD '99" in Monogram**

U9	E1	1c green on white	75	60
		Entire	1.75	1.75
U10	E1	1c green on amber	75	60
		Entire	1.75	1.75
U11	E1	1c green on buff	17.50	12.00
		Entire	60.00	30.00
U12	E1	1c green on blue	25.00	15.00
		Entire	60.00	30.00
U13	E1	2c carmine on white	75	50
		Entire	1.50	1.25
U14	E1	2c carmine on amber	75	50
		Entire	1.50	1.25
U15	E1	2c carmine on buff	10.00	8.00
		Entire	25.00	15.00
U16	E1	2c carmine on blue	25.00	18.00
		Entire	60.00	30.00
U17	E1	5c blue on white	1.00	70
		Entire	2.50	1.00
U18	E1	5c blue on amber	4.00	2.50
		Entire	8.50	5.00

WRAPPERS
Issue of the Republic under U. S. Military Rule

1899

W1	E1	1c green on manila	3.00	10.00
		Entire	11.00	50.00
W2	E1	2c carmine on manila	8.00	10.00
		Entire	22.50	50.00

POSTAL CARDS

Prices are for Entires
U. S. Postal Cards Nos. UX14, UX16 Surcharged

CUBA. 1c. de Peso.

UX1	PC8 1c on 1c black on buff, *Jefferson*		
	(1,000,000)	25.00	25.00
a.	No period after "1c"	60.00	60.00
b.	No period after "Peso"	50.00	
UX2	PC3 2c on 2c black on buff, *Liberty*		
	(583,000)	25.00	25.00
a.	No period after "Peso"	60.00	60.00
b.	Double surcharge		

In 1904 the Republic of Cuba revalued remaining stocks of No. UX2 by means of a perforated numeral "1".

PROOFS

1899

			DIE	
			(1) Large	*(2)* Small
227P	1c	yellow green	225.00	150.00
227TC	1c	blue green	400.00	
227TC	1c	black	400.00	
228P	2c	carmine	225.00	150.00
228TC	2c	black	400.00	
229P	3c	purple	225.00	150.00
229TC	3c	black	400.00	
230P	5c	blue	225.00	150.00
230TC	5c	black	400.00	
231P	10c	brown	225.00	150.00
231TC	10c	gray	400.00	
231TC	10c	black	400.00	

1902

Special Delivery

E2TC	10c blue	650.00	
E3P	10c orange	350.00	250.00

SPECIMEN STAMPS

Overprinted Type E in black   Specimen.

1899

221SE	1	on 1c yellow green	175.00
222SE	2	on 2c carmine	175.00
223SE	2	on 2c orange red	175.00
224SE	3½	on 3c purple	175.00
225SE	5	on 5c blue	175.00
226SE	10	on 10c brown, type I	175.00
226ASE	10	on 10c brown, type II	2,500.

1899

227SE		yellow green	300.00
228SE		carmine	300.00
229SE		purple	300.00
230SE		blue	300.00
231SE		brown	300.00

Special Delivery

1899

E1SE	on 10c blue	350.00
E2SE	orange	500.00

Postage Due

1899

J1SE	on 1c deep claret	250.00
J2SE	on 2c deep claret	250.00
J3SE	on 5c deep claret	250.00
J4SE	on 10c deep claret	250.00

"Specimen" overprint known on all stamps of the Special Printing.

DANISH WEST INDIES

FORMERLY a Danish colony, these islands were purchased by the United States in 1917 and have since been known as the U.S. Virgin Islands. They lie east of Puerto Rico, have an area of 132 square miles and had a population of 27,086 in 1911. The capital is Charlotte Amalie (also called St. Thomas). Stamps of Danish West Indies were replaced by those of the United States in 1917.

100 CENTS = 1 DOLLAR
100 BIT = 1 FRANC (1905)

Coat of Arms — A1

Wmk. 111- Small Crown

Wmk. 112- Crown

1856　Typo.　Wmk. 111　Imperf.
Yellowish Paper
Yellow Wavy-line Burelage, UL to LR

1	A1	3c dark carmine, brown gum	175.00	200.00
		On cover		2,500.
		Block of four	1,300.	
a.		3c dark carmine, yellow gum	225.00	210.00
a.		On cover		3,000.
a.		Block of four	4,500.	
b.		3c carmine, white gum	2,250.	

Reprint: 1981, carmine, back-printed across two stamps ("Reprint by Dansk Post og Telegrafmuseum 1978"), price, pair, $7.

1866
White Paper
Yellow Wavy-line Burelage UR to LL

2	A1	3c rose	80.00	70.00
		On cover		2,500.
		Block of four	375.00	925.00
		Rouletted 4½ privately	400.00	200.00
		On cover, rouletted 4½		2,750.
		Rouletted 9	400.00	200.00

No. 2 reprints, unwatermarked: 1930, carmine, price $120. 1942, rose carmine, back-printed across each row ("Nytryk 1942 G. A. Hagemann Danmark og Dansk Vestindiens Frimaerker Bind 2"), price $80.

1872　　　　Perf. 12½

3	A1	3c rose	160.00	170.00
		On cover		4,750.
		Block of four	1,100.	

1873
Without Burelage

4	A1	4c dull blue	300.00	350.00
		On cover		7,000.
		Block of four	1,750.	
a.		Imperf., pair	950.00	1,200.
b.		Horiz. pair, imperf. vert.	750.00	900.00

The 1930 reprint of No. 4 is ultramarine, unwatermarked and imperf., price $120.
The 1942 4c reprint is blue, unwatermarked, imperf. and has printing on back (see note below No. 2), price $80.

Numeral of Value — A2

NORMAL FRAME　　　　　INVERTED FRAME

The arabesques in the corners have a main stem and a branch. When the frame is in normal position, in the upper left corner the branch leaves the main stem half way between two little leaflets. In the lower right corner the branch starts at the foot of the second leaflet. When the frame is inverted the corner designs are, of course, transposed.

Danish West Indies stamps can be mounted in Scott's U.S. Possessions Album.

1874-79　　Wmk. 112　　Perf. 14x13½
Printings on White Wove Paper, Varying from Thin to Thick

1c.	Nine printings
3c.	Eight printings
4c.	Two printings
5c.	Six printings
7c.	Two printings
10c.	Seven printings
12c.	Two printings
14c.	One printing
50c.	Two printings

Prices for inverted frames, covers and blocks are for the cheapest variety.

5	A2	1c green & brown red	25.00	20.00
		On cover		200.00
		Block of four	110.00	—
a.		1c green & rose lilac	37.50	37.50
b.		1c green & red violet	37.50	37.50
c.		1c green & violet	80.00	110.00
		green & claret	25.00	20.00
e.		Inverted frame	25.00	25.00

No. 5 exists with "b" surcharge, "10 CENTS 1895." See note below No. 15.

6	A2	3c blue & carmine	27.50	17.00
		On cover		160.00
		Block of four	140.00	—
		Dull blue & rose	27.50	17.00
		Dull blue & red	27.50	17.00
		Blue & lake	27.50	17.00
d.		Imperf., pair	600.00	
e.		Inverted frame	27.50	16.00
		White "wedge" flaw	50.00	40.00
7	A2	4c brown & dull blue	17.00	17.00
		On cover		160.00
		Block of four	85.00	—
		Brown & bright blue	17.00	17.00
b.		4c brown & ultramarine	250.00	175.00
c.		Diagonal half used as 2c on cover		225.00
d.		Inverted frame	1,000.	1,000.
8	A2	5c green & gray	30.00	22.50
		On cover		275.00
		Block of four	150.00	—
		Green & dark gray	30.00	22.50
b.		Inverted frame	30.00	22.50
9	A2	7c lilac & orange	27.50	60.00
		On cover		1,000.
		Block of four	140.00	—
a.		7c lilac & yellow	70.00	90.00
b.		Inverted frame	65.00	100.00
10	A2	10c blue & brown	30.00	18.00
		On cover		175.00
		Block of four	150.00	—
		Blue & black brown	30.00	18.00
b.		Period between "t" & "s" of "cents"	45.00	35.00
c.		Inverted frame	30.00	20.00
11	A2	12c red lilac & yellow green	35.00	47.50
		On cover		1,000.
		Block of four	180.00	—
a.		12c lilac & deep green	100.00	70.00
12	A2	14c lilac & green	700.00	825.00
		On cover		8,500.
		Block of four	4,500.	
a.		Inverted frame	2,000.	2,750.
13	A2	50c violet	120.00	130.00
		On cover		2,000.
		Block of four	575.00	—
a.		50c gray violet	160.00	200.00

Issue dates: 1c, 3c, 4c, 14c, Jan. 15, 1874. 7c, July 22, 1874. 5c, 10c, 1876; 12c, 1877; 50c, 1879. Colors of major numbers are generally those of the least expensive of two or more shades, and do not indicate the shade of the first printing.

Nos. 9 and 13 Surcharged in Black:

10 CENTS

1 CENT
a

1895
b

1887
14	A2 (a)	1c on 7c lilac & orange	75.00	90.00
		On cover		1,500.
		Block of four	450.00	—
a.		1c on 7c lilac & yellow	120.00	175.00
b.		Double surcharge	250.00	350.00
c.		Inverted frame	115.00	135.00

1895
15	A2	10c on 50c violet		
	(b)		35.00	40.00
		On cover		325.00
		Block of four	165.00	—

The "b" surcharge also exists on No. 5, with "10" found in two sizes. These are essays.

1896-1901　　　　　Perf. 13
16	A2	1c green & red violet ('98)	15.00	15.00
		On cover		160.00
		Block of four	72.50	—
a.		Normal frame	300.00	350.00
17	A2	3c blue & lake ('98)	13.00	13.00
		On cover		160.00
		Block of four	60.00	—
a.		Normal frame	260.00	300.00
		White "wedge" flaw	50.00	50.00
18	A2	4c bister & dull blue ('01)	13.00	13.00
		On cover		160.00
		Block of four	65.00	—
a.		Diagonal half used as 2c on cover		45.00
b.		Inverted frame	60.00	60.00
b.		On cover		200.00
		As "a" and "b" on cover		225.00
19	A2	5c green & gray	37.50	32.50
		On cover		375.00
		Block of four	200.00	—
a.		Normal frame	750.00	750.00
20	A2	10c blue & brown ('01)	85.00	100.00
		On cover		1,750.
		Block of four	425.00	—
a.		Inverted frame	1,100.	1,600.
b.		Period between "t" and "s" of "cents"	85.00	100.00

Two printings each of Nos. 18-19.

Arms — A5

1900
21	A5	1c light green	2.50	2.50
		On cover		60.00
		Block of four	11.00	12.00
22	A5	5c light blue	13.00	13.00
		On cover		260.00
		Block of four	60.00	—

2

Nos. 6, 17 and 20 Surcharged in Black — c

CENTS

1902

1902　　　　Perf. 14x13½
23	A2	2c on 3c blue & carmine	500.00	650.00
		Block of four	2,500.	
a.		"2" in date with straight tail	525.00	675.00
b.		Normal frame	1,500.	

Perf. 13
24	A2	2c on 3c blue & lake	8.00	10.00
		On cover		160.00
		Block of four	32.50	—
a.		"2" in date with straight tail	9.00	11.00
b.		Dated "1901"	450.00	500.00
c.		Normal frame	225.00	275.00
d.		Dark green surcharge	1,600.	
e.		As "d." & "a."	1,750.	
f.		As "d." & "c."	3,000.	
		White "wedge" flaw	50.00	50.00
25	A2	8c on 10c blue & brown	25.00	25.00
		On cover		260.00
		Block of four	100.00	—
a.		"2" with straight tail	27.50	37.50
b.		On No. 20b	42.50	52.50
c.		Inverted frame	350.00	350.00

1902

Nos. 17 and 20 Surcharged in Black — d **8 Cents 1902**

1902					**Perf. 13**
27	A2	2c on 3c blue & lake		12.50	25.00
		On cover			225.00
		Block of four		50.00	
a.		Normal frame		275.00	300.00
		White "wedge" flaw		52.50	52.50
28	A2	8c on 10c blue & brown		11.00	11.00
		On cover			200.00
		Block of four		45.00	
a.		On No. 20b		20.00	20.00
b.		Inverted frame		275.00	275.00

Wmk. 113- Crown

1903					**Wmk. 113**
29	A5	2c carmine		13.00	13.00
		On cover			160.00
		Block of four		52.50	
30	A5	8c brown		27.50	27.50
		On cover			400.00
		Block of four		120.00	

King Christian IX — A8

1905		**Typo.**			**Perf. 12½**
31	A8	5b green		7.50	4.00
		On cover			60.00
		Block of four		35.00	
32	A8	10b red		7.50	4.00
		On cover			75.00
		Block of four		35.00	
33	A8	20b green & blue		13.00	13.00
		On cover			180.00
		Block of four		60.00	
34	A8	25b ultramarine		13.00	13.00
		On cover			140.00
		Block of four		60.00	
35	A8	40b red & gray		12.50	12.50
		On cover			170.00
		Block of four		60.00	
36	A8	50b yellow & gray		11.00	13.00
		On cover			275.00
		Block of four		55.00	

St. Thomas Harbor — A9

Frame Typographed, Center Engraved

1905		**Wmk. Two Crowns (113)**			**Perf. 12**
37	A9	1fr green & blue		20.00	30.00
		On cover			275.00
		Block of four		85.00	
38	A9	2fr orange red & brown		42.50	75.00
		On cover			425.00
		Block of four		180.00	
39	A9	5fr yellow & brown		110.00	250.00
		On cover			550.00
		Block of four		475.00	

Nos. 18, 22 and 30 Surcharged in Black **5 BIT 1905**

1905		**Wmk. 112**			**Perf. 13**
40	A2	5b on 4c bister & dull blue		22.50	45.00
		On cover			450.00
		Block of four		100.00	
a.		Inverted frame		42.50	75.00
41	A5	5b on 5c light blue		15.00	27.50
		On cover			450.00
		Block of four		65.00	
		Wmk. 113			
42	A5	5b on 8c brown		14.00	30.00

	On cover		450.00
	Block of four	60.00	—

King Frederik VIII — A10

Frame Typographed, Center Engraved

1908		**Wmk. 113**			**Perf. 13**
43	A10	5b green		2.50	1.50
		On cover			45.00
		Block of four		12.50	
44	A10	10b red		2.50	1.50
		On cover			52.50
		Block of four		12.50	
45	A10	15b violet & brown		6.00	6.00
		On cover			110.00
		Block of four		30.00	
46	A10	20b green & blue		47.50	20.00
		On cover			170.00
		Block of four		200.00	
47	A10	25b blue & dark blue		3.25	2.00
		On cover			45.00
		Block of four		14.00	
48	A10	30b claret & slate		70.00	30.00
		On cover			350.00
		Block of four		300.00	125.00
49	A10	40b vermilion & gray		6.50	10.00
		On cover			225.00
		Block of four		27.50	
50	A10	50b yellow & brown		7.00	10.00
		On cover			225.00
		Block of four		32.50	

King Christian X — A11

Wmk. 114- Multiple Crosses

Frame Typographed, Center Engraved

1915-17		**Wmk. 114**			**Perf. 14x14½**
51	A11	5b yellow green		3.00	7.00
		On cover			55.00
		Block of four		14.00	60.00
52	A11	10b red		3.00	60.00
		On cover			175.00
		Block of four		14.00	60.00
53	A11	15b lilac & red brown		3.00	60.00
		On cover			200.00
		Block of four		14.00	60.00
54	A11	20b green & blue		3.00	60.00
		On cover			260.00
		Block of four		14.00	60.00
55	A11	25b blue & dark blue		3.00	15.00
		On cover			90.00
		Block of four		14.00	60.00
56	A11	30b claret & black		3.00	60.00
		On cover			350.00
		Block of four		14.00	60.00
57	A11	40b orange & black		3.00	60.00
		On cover			350.00
		Block of four		14.00	60.00
58	A11	50b yellow & brown		3.00	60.00
		On cover			350.00
		Block of four		14.00	

Forged and favor cancellations exist.

POSTAGE DUE

Royal Cipher "Christian Rex" D1

Numeral of Value D2

1902		**Litho.**	**Unwmk.**		**Perf. 11½**
J1	D1	1c dark blue		10.00	15.00
		Block of four		42.50	
J2	D1	4c dark blue		14.00	20.00
		Block of four		60.00	
J3	D1	6c dark blue		35.00	60.00

	Block of four		170.00	
J4	D1	10c dark blue	25.00	35.00
		Block of four	110.00	

There are five types of each value. On the 4c they may be distinguished by differences in the figure "4"; on the other values differences are minute.

Used prices of Nos. J1-J8 are for canceled copies. Uncanceled examples without gum have probably been used. Price 60% of unused.

Excellent counterfeits of Nos. J1 to J4 exist.

1905-13					
J5	D2	5b red & gray		7.00	9.00
		Block of four		32.50	
J6	D2	20b red & gray		14.00	20.00
		Block of four		60.00	
J7	D2	30b red & gray		8.50	13.00
		Block of four		37.50	
J8	D2	50b red & gray		12.50	20.00
		Block of four		55.00	
a.		Perf. 14x14½ ('13)		25.00	125.00
a.		Block of four		120.00	
b.		Perf. 11½		325.00	

Nos. J5-J8 are known imperforate but were not regularly issued. Excellent counterfeits exist.

ENVELOPES

E1

1877-78				**On White Paper**
U1	E1	2c light blue ('78)	10.00	30.00
		Entire	30.00	100.00
a.		2c ultramarine	30.00	125.00
		Entire	100.00	650.00
U2	E1	3c orange	8.00	30.00
		Entire	25.00	100.00
a.		3c red orange	8.00	30.00
		Entire	25.00	100.00

Three different Crown watermarks are found on entires of No. U1, four on entires of No. U2. Envelope watermarks do not show on cut squares.

POSTAL CARDS

Prices are for entire cards
Designs of Adhesive Stamps
"BREV-KORT" at top

1877

Inscription in Three Lines

UX1	A2	6c violet	30.00	300.00

1878-85

Inscription in Four Lines

UX2	A2	2c light blue (8,800)	30.00	60.00
UX3	A2	3c carmine rose (17,700)	30.00	60.00

1888

Inscription in Five Lines

UX4	A2	2c light blue (30,500)	10.00	35.00
UX5	A2	3c red (26,500)	15.00	45.00

Card UX5 Locally Surcharged with type "c" but with date "1901"

1901

UX6	A2	1c on 3c red (2,000)	75.00	250.00

1902

Card UX4 Locally Surcharged with type "c"

UX7	A2	1c on 2c light blue (3,000)	60.00	200.00

Card UX5 Surcharged similar to type "c" but heavy letters

1902

UX8	A2	1c on 3c red (7,175)	12.50	65.00

1903

UX9	A5	1c light green (10,000)	20.00	60.00
UX10	A5	2c carmine (10,000)	30.00	150.00

1905

UX11	A8	5b green (16,000)	17.50	35.00
UX12	A8	10b red (14,000)	20.00	85.00

1907-08					**Unwmk.**
UX13	A10	5b green ('08) (30,750)		16.00	35.00
UX14	A10	10b red (19,750)		25.00	70.00

1913   **Wmk. Wood-grain**
UX15 A10 5b green *(10,000)* 175.00 400.00
UX16 A10 10b red *(10,000)* 200.00 750.00

1915-16   **Wmk. Wood-grain**
UX17 A11 5b yellow green *(8,200)* 150.00 350.00
UX18 A11 10b red ('16) *(2,000)* 200.00 850.00

PAID REPLY POSTAL CARDS
Designs similar to Nos. UX2 and UX3 with added
inscriptions in Danish and French:
Message Card-Four lines at lower left.
Reply Card-Fifth line centered, "Svar. Réponse."

1883
UY1 A2 2c+2¢2c light blue, unsevered
           (2,600) 40.00 150.00
  m. Message card, detached 12.50   60.00
  r. Reply card, detached 12.50   80.00
UY2 A2 3c +3c carmine rose, unsevered 30.00 100.00
  m. Message card, detached 10.00   40.00
  r. Reply card, detached 10.00   55.00

Designs similar to Nos. UX4 and UX5 with added
inscription in fifth line, centered in French:
Message Card-"Carte postale avec réponse payée."
Reply Card-"Carte postale-réponse."

1888-98
UY3 A2 2c +2c light blue, unsevered
           (26,000) 20.00   90.00
  m. Message card, detached 8.00   35.00
  r. Reply card, detached 8.00   45.00

UY4 A2 3c +3c carmine rose, unsevered
           (5,000) 35.00 110.00
  m. Message card, detached 12.50   40.00
  r. Reply card, detached 12.50   55.00

No. UY4 Locally Surcharged with type "c" but with
date "1901"

1902
UY5 A2 1c on 3c+1c on 3c carmine rose,
           unsevered *(1,000)* 65.00 250.00
  m. Message card, detached 22.50   90.00
  r. Reply card, detached 22.50 125.00

No. UY4 Surcharged in Copenhagen with type
similar to "c" but heavy letters

UY6 A2 1c on 3c+1c on 3c carmine rose,
           unsevered *(975)* 80.00 275.00
  m. Message card, detached 27.50 110.00
  r. Reply card, detached 27.50 150.00

Designs similar to Nos. UX9 and UX10 with added
inscriptions in Danish and English

1903
UY7 A5 1c +1c light green, unsevered
           (5,000) 35.00 110.00
  m. Message card, detached 12.50   40.00
  r. Reply card, detached 12.50   55.00
UY8 A5 2c +2c carmine, unsevered
           (5,000) 80.00 325.00
  m. Message card, detached 30.00 125.00
  r. Reply card, detached 30.00 175.00

Designs similar to Nos. UX11 and UX12 with
added inscriptions

1905
UY9 A8 5b +5b green, unsevered *(5,000)* .. 35.00   80.00
  m. Message card, detached 12.50   32.50
  r. Reply card, detached 12.50   40.00
UY10 A8 10b +10b red, unsevered *(4,000)* . 60.00 110.00
  m. Message card 20.00   45.00
  r. Reply card, detached 20.00   60.00

Designs similar to Nos. UX13, UX14 and UX15
with added inscriptions

1908   **Unwmk.**
UY11 A10 5b +5b green, unsevered *(7,150)* . 60.00 140.00
  m. Message card, detached 20.00   55.00
  r. Reply card, detached 20.00   70.00
UY12 A10 10b +10b red, unsevered *(6,750)* . 60.00 140.00
  m. Message card, detached 20.00   55.00
  r. Reply card, detached 20.00   70.00

1913   **Wmk. Wood-grain**
UY13 A10 5b +5b green, unsevered *(5,000)* 900.00
  m. Message card, detached 450.00
  r. Reply card, detached 450.00

The 10b + 10b red type A10 with wood-grain watermark was
authorized and possibly printed, but no example is known.

GUAM

A former Spanish island possession in the Pacific Ocean, one of the Mariana group, about 1,450 miles east of the Philippines. Captured June 20, 1898, and ceded to the United States by treaty after the Spanish-American War. Stamps overprinted "Guam" were used while the post office was under the jurisdiction of the Navy Department from July 7, 1899, until March 29, 1901, when a Postal Agent was appointed by the Post Office Department and the postal service passed under that Department's control. From this date on Guam was supplied with regular United States postage stamps, although the overprints remained in use for several more years. Population 9,000 (est. 1899).

100 CENTS = 1 DOLLAR

United States Nos. 279, 267, 279c, 268, 280a, 281a,
282, 272, 282C, 283a, 284, 275, 275a, 276 and 276A
Overprinted

GUAM

1899   **Wmk. 191**   **Perf. 12**
Black Overprint

1   A87 1c deep green *(25,000)* 27.50   35.00
       On cover 200.00
       Block of four 125.00 200.00
       Margin strip of 3, Impt. & P# 140.00
       Margin block of 6, Impt. &
         P# 450.00
  a. Inverted overprint ....   —
2   A88 2c carmine, type III *(105,000)* . 25.00   35.00
       On cover 200.00
       Block of four 120.00 200.00
       Margin strip of 3, Impt. & P# 120.00
       Margin block of 6, Impt. &
         P# 400.00
  a. 2c rose carmine, type III 30.00   40.00
3   A89 3c purple *(5000)* 125.00 175.00
       On cover 400.00
       Block of four 550.00 850.00
       Margin strip of 3, Impt. & P# 550.00
       Margin block of 6, Impt. &
         P# 1,600.00
4   A90 4c lilac brown *(5000)* 125.00 175.00
       On cover 450.00
       Block of four 550.00 850.00
       Margin strip of 3, Impt. & P# 550.00
       Margin block of 6, Impt. &
         P# 1,600.00
       Extra frame line at top (Plate
         793 R62) ....   —
5   A91 5c blue *(20,000)* 35.00   45.00
       On cover 200.00
       Block of four 150.00 250.00
       Margin strip of 3, Impt. & P# 160.00
       Margin block of 6, Impt. &
         P# 700.00
6   A92 6c lake *(5000)* 125.00 175.00
       On cover 450.00
       Block of four 550.00 800.00
       Margin strip of 3, Impt. & P# 500.00
       Margin block of 6, Impt. &
         P# 1,600.00
7   A93 8c violet brown *(5000)* 125.00 175.00
       On cover 450.00
       Block of four 550.00 850.00
       Margin strip of 3, Impt. & P# 550.00
       Margin block of 6, Impt. &
         P# 1,600.00
8   A94 10c brown, type I *(10,000)* 55.00   70.00
       On cover 275.00
       Block of four 250.00 350.00
       Margin strip of 3, Impt. & P# 275.00
       Margin block of 6, Impt. &
         P# 950.00

9   A94 10c brown, type II .... 5,000.
10 A95 15c olive green *(5000)* 135.00 175.00
       On cover 900.00
       Block of four 600.00 900.00
       Margin strip of 3, Impt. & P# 600.00
       Margin block of 6, Impt. &
         P# .... 2,100.
11 A96 50c orange *(4000)* 250.00 350.00
       On cover 1250.00
       Block of four 1,150.00 1750.00
       Margin strip of 3, Impt. & P# 1,150.00
       Margin block of 6, Impt. &
         P# 4,000.00
  a. 50c red orange .... 300.00   —

Red Overprint

12 A97 $1 black, type I *(3000)* 400.00 550.00
       On cover ....   2,000.
       Block of four .... 1,850. 2,500.
       Margin strip of 3, Impt. & P# 1,850.
       Margin block of 6, Impt. &
         P# 7,000.00
13 A97 $1 black, type II *(3000)* .... 3,000.
       Block of four ....   —

No. 13 exists only in the special printing.

Special Printing

In 1899 a special printing of all values Nos. 1 to 8, 10, 11, 12,
and E1, was made for display at the Paris Exposition. Price:
Nos. 1-8, 10, each $350; Nos. 11, E1, each $400; No. 12, $650.
Counterfeits of overprint exist.

SPECIAL DELIVERY STAMP
Special Delivery Stamp of the
United States, No. E5 Overprinted **GUAM**
diagonally in Red

1899   **Wmk. 191**   **Perf. 12**
E1 SD3 10c blue *(5000)* 150.00 200.00
       On cover 600.00
       Block of four 650.00
       Margin block of four, arrow ... 700.00
       Margin strip of 3, Impt. & P# 750.00
       Margin block of 6, Impt. &
         P# 4,000.00
       Dots in curved frame above
         messenger (Plate 882) 275.00

Counterfeits of overprint exist.
The special stamps for Guam were replaced by the regular
issues of the United States.

> Guam stamps can be mounted in Scott's
> U.S. Possessions Album.

GUAM GUARD MAIL
LOCAL POSTAL SERVICE
Inaugurated April 8, 1930, by Commander Willis
W. Bradley, Jr., U.S.N., Governor of Guam, for the
conveyance of mail between Agana and the other
smaller towns.

Philippines Nos. 290 and 291   **GUAM**
Overprinted   **GUARD**
                                    MAIL

1930, Apr. 8   **Unwmk.**   **Perf. 11**
M1 A40 2c green *(2000)* 400.00 350.00
       On cover 500.00
       Block of four .... 1,700.
M2 A40 4c carmine *(3000)* 350.00 300.00
       On cover 500.00
       Block of four .... 1,500.

Counterfeits of overprint exist.

Seal of Guam — A1

1930, July   **Unwmk.**   **Perf. 12**
Without Gum
M3 A1 1c red & black 125.00 150.00
       On cover 300.00
       Block of four 550.00
M4 A1 2c black & red 125.00 150.00
       On cover 525.00
       Block of four 550.00

Copies are often found showing parts of watermark "Cleveland Bond".

Philippines Nos. 290 and 291   **GUAM**
Overprinted in Black   **GUARD**
                                    MAIL

1930, Aug. 10		Unwmk.		Perf. 11	
M5	A40	2c green *(20,000)*		4.00	4.50
		On cover			75.00
		Block of four		17.50	
a.		2c yellow green		3.75	4.00
M6	A40	4c carmine *(80,000)*		75	2.75
		On cover			75.00
		Block of four		3.25	

Same Overprint in Red on Philippines Nos. 290, 291, 292, 293a, and 294

1930, Dec.					
M7	A40	2c green *(50,000)*		1.25	1.25
		On cover			50.00
		Block of four		5.25	
a.		GRAUD (No. 63 in sheet) *(500)*		375.00	
b.		MIAL (No. 84 in sheet) *(500)*		375.00	
M8	A40	4c carmine *(50,000)*		1.25	1.25
		On cover			50.00
		Block of four		5.25	
M9	A40	6c deep violet *(25,000)*		3.50	4.00
		On cover			60.00
		Block of four		15.00	
M10	A40	8c orange brown *(25,000)*		3.50	4.00
		On cover			60.00
		Block of four		15.00	
M11	A40	10c deep blue *(25,000)*		3.50	4.00
		On cover			60.00
		Block of four		15.00	

The local postal service was discontinued April 8th, 1931, and replaced by the service of the United States Post Office Department.

SPECIMEN STAMPS

Overprinted United States Type E in Violet — **Specimen.**

1899			
1S		1c deep green	250.00
2S		2c carmine	250.00
3S		3c purple	250.00
4S		4c lilac brown	250.00
5S		5c blue	250.00
6S		6c lake	250.00
7S		8c violet brown	250.00
8S		10c brown, type I	250.00
10S		15c olive green	250.00
11S		50c orange	250.00
12S		$1 black, type I	500.00
13S		$1 black, type II	—

Special Delivery

1899			
E1S		10c blue	500.00

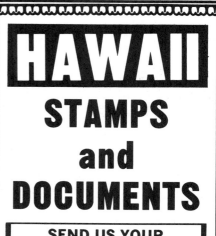
HAWAII

Until 1893, Hawaii was an independent kingdom. From 1893-1898 it was a republic. At the request of the inhabitants, Hawaii was annexed to the United States in 1898. Hawaiian stamps remained in use through June 13, 1900, and were replaced by U.S. stamps on June 14. In 1959 Hawaii became the 50th State of the Union. Hawaii consists of about 20 islands in the Pacific, about 2,000 miles southwest of San Francisco. The area is 6,434 square miles and the population was estimated at 150,000 in 1899. Honolulu is the capital.

100 CENTS = 1 DOLLAR

Prices of early Hawaii stamps vary according to condition. Quotations for Nos. 5-18 are for fine copies. Very fine to superb specimens sell at much higher prices, and inferior or poor copies sell at reduced prices, depending on the condition of the individual specimen.

A1	A2	A3

1851-52		Unwmk.	Typeset	Pelure Paper	*Imperf.*
1	A1	2c blue		350,000.	250,000.
		On cover			300,000.
2	A1	5c blue		35,000.	15,000.
		On cover			25,000.
3	A2	13c blue		17,500.	9,000.
		On cover			15,000.
4	A3	13c blue		45,000.	21,000.
		On cover			27,500.

Nos. 1-4 are known as the "Missionaries." Two varieties of each. Nos. 1-4, off cover, are almost invariably damaged.

King Kamehameha III
A4　　　　A5

Printed in Sheets of 20 (4x5).

1853		**Thick White Wove Paper**		**Engr.**
5	A4	5c blue	650.00	450.00
		On cover		2,250.
		On cover with U.S. #17		12,000.
		Line through "Honolulu" (No. 2 in sheet)	1,350.	900.00
6	A5	13c dark red	325.00	350.00
		On cover		2,500.
		On cover with U.S. #17		7,500.
		On cover with #5 and U.S. #17		—
		Pair	900.00	1,200.
		Block of four	2,400.	

A6

1857				
7	A6	5c on 13c dark red	4,500.	5,500.
		On cover		10,000.
		On cover with pair U.S. #7 and U.S. #15		—
		On cover with U.S. #14		15,000.
		On cover with U.S. #17		15,000.

1857				
		Thin White Wove Paper		
8	A4	5c blue	250.00	250.00
		On cover		1,250.
		On cover with U.S. #15 and #7		
		On cover with U.S. #17		5,000.
		On cover with U.S. #26		—
		On cover with U.S. #36		5,000.
		On cover with U.S. #69		5,500.
		On cover with U.S. #76		—
		Pair	650.00	
a.		Double impression	2,000.	—
		Line through "Honolulu" (No. 2 in sheet)	700.00	

1861				
		Thin Bluish Wove Paper		
9	A4	5c blue	110.00	110.00
		On cover		850.00
		On cover with U.S. #36		
		On cover with U.S. #65 and #73		3,500.
		On cover with U.S. #68		4,250.
		On cover with U.S. #76		—
		Block of four	700.00	
a.		Double impression		
		Line through "Honolulu" (No. 2 in sheet)	325.00	325.00

RE-ISSUE

1868

Ordinary White Wove Paper

10	A4	5c blue	25.00	
		Block of four	125.00	
		Line through "Honolulu"		
		(No. 2 in sheet)	40.00	
11	A5	13c dull rose	225.00	
		Block of four	1,100.	

Remainders of Nos. 10 and 11 were overprinted "SPECI-MEN." See Nos. 10S-11Sb.

Nos. 10 and 11 were never placed in use but copies (both with and without overprint) were sold at face value at the Honolulu post office.

REPRINTS (Official Imitations) 1889

5c Originals have two small dots near the left side of the square in the upper right corner. These dots are missing in the reprints.

13c The bottom of the 3 of 13 in the upper left corner is flattened in the originals and rounded in the reprints. The "t" of "Cts" on the left side is as tall as the "C" in the reprints, but shorter in the originals.

10R	A4	5c blue	50.00
11R	A5	13c orange red	200.00

On August 19, 1892, the remaining supply of reprints was overprinted in black "REPRINT." The reprints (both with and without overprint) were sold at face value. Quantities sold (including overprints) were 5c-3634 and 13c-1696. See Nos. 10R-S and 11R-S.

Numerals of Value
A7   A8   A9

1859-62   **Typeset from settings of 10 varieties**

12	A7	1c light blue, *bluish white*	2,750.	3,000.
		Pair		6,250.
a.		"1 Ce" omitted	—	
13	A7	2c light blue, *bluish white*	2,250.	1,250.
		On cover		3,500.
		Block of four	10,000.	
a.		2c dark blue, *grayish white*	—	
b.		Comma after "Cents"	—	
14	A7	2c black, *greenish blue* ('62)	3,250.	1,250.
		On cover		4,000.
a.		"2-Cents."	—	

1863

15	A7	1c black, *grayish*	225.00	275.00
		On cover		—
		Block of four	1,100.	
a.		Tête bêche pair	3,500.	
b.		"NTER"	—	
16	A7	2c black, *grayish*	375.00	325.00
		On cover		2,500.
		Pair	—	
a.		"2" at top of rectangle	1,800.	1,800.
b.		Printed on both sides	—	
c.		"NTER"	1,400.	1,400.
d.		2c black, *grayish white*	375.00	325.00
e.		Period omitted after "Cents"	—	
f.		Double impression	—	
g.		"tage."	—	
17	A7	2c dark blue, *bluish*	3,500.	1,600.
		On cover		5,000.
		Pair	7,500.	
18	A7	2c black, *blue gray*	700.00	1,100.
		On cover		4,000.
		Pair		3,000.
		Thick paper	—	

1864-65

19	A7	1c black	275.00	425.00
		Pair	650.00	
		Block of four	1,500.	
20	A7	2c black	325.00	425.00
		On cover		1,250.
		Pair	800.00	
		Block of four	2,250.	
21	A8	5c blue, *blue* ('65)	275.00	275.00
		On cover with U.S. #65		—
		On cover with U.S. #76		5,000.
		Block of four	1,400.	
a.		Tête bêche pair	4,500.	
b.		5c black, *grayish white*	—	
22	A9	5c blue, *blue* ('65)	225.00	250.00
		On cover		1,100.
		On cover with U.S. #76		4,500.
		On cover with U.S. #63 and 76		—
		Block of four	1,100.	
a.		Tête bêche pair	3,500.	
b.		5c blue, *grayish white*	—	

1864

Laid Paper

23	A7	1c black	150.00	500.00
		On cover with U.S. #76		—

		Block of four	675.00	
a.		"HA" instead of "HAWAIIAN"	1,750.	
b.		Tête bêche pair	3,500.	
24	A7	2c black	150.00	500.00
		Block of four	750.00	
a.		"NTER"	700.00	
b.		"S" of "POSTAGE" omitted	700.00	
c.		Tête bêche pair	3,500.	

A10

King
Kamehameha
IV — A11

1865

Wove Paper

25	A10	1c dark blue	150.00	
		Block of four	750.00	
		Double impression	—	
		With inverted impression of No. 21 on face	—	
26	A10	2c dark blue	125.00	
		Block of four	600.00	

Nos. 12 to 26 were typeset and were printed in sheets of 50 (5 settings of 10 varieties each). The sheets were cut into panes of 25 (5x5) before distribution to the post offices.

1861-63   **Litho.**

Horizontally Laid Paper

27	A11	2c pale rose	175.00	110.00
		On cover		550.00
		Pair		—
a.		2c carmine rose ('63)	600.00	500.00

Vertically Laid Paper

28	A11	2c pale rose	175.00	110.00
		On cover		500.00
		Block of four	800.00	750.00
a.		2c carmine rose ('63)	135.00	135.00
a.		Block of four	650.00	

1869   **Engr.**   **Thin Wove Paper**

29	A11	2c red	50.00	
		Block of four	250.00	

No. 29 is a re-issue. It was not issued for postal purposes although canceled copies are known. It was sold only at the Honolulu post office, at first without overprint and later with overprint "CANCELLED." See No. 29S.
See note following No. 51.

Princess Victoria Kamamalu — A12

King Kamehameha IV — A13

King Kamehameha V — A14

Kamehameha V — A15

Mataio Kekuanaoa — A16

1864-71   **Wove Paper**   *Perf. 12*

30	A12	1c purple ('71)	7.50	6.00
a.		1c violet	7.50	6.00
		On cover		125.00
		Block of four	40.00	
31	A13	2c rose vermilion	11.00	7.00
a.		2c vermilion	11.00	7.00
		On cover		125.00
		On cover with U.S. #76		250.00
		Block of four	55.00	50.00
b.		Half used as 1c on cover		—
32	A14	5c blue ('66)	50.00	19.00
		On cover		125.00
		On cover with any U.S. issues of 1861-67		1,250.
		On cover with U.S. #116		1,500.
		Block of four	225.00	100.00
33	A15	6c green ('71)	17.50	6.00
a.		6c yellow green	17.50	6.00
		On cover		125.00
		On cover with U.S. #179		500.00
		Block of four	95.00	
34	A16	18c dull rose ('71)	85.00	14.00
		On cover		300.00
		Block of four	375.00	
		Without gum	17.50	
		Block of four without gum	85.00	

Half of No. 31 was used with a 5c stamp to make up the 6-cent rate to the United States.

No. 32 has traces of rectangular frame lines surrounding the design. Nos. 39 and 52C have no such frame lines.

King David
Kalakaua
A17

Prince
William Pitt
Leleiohoku
A18

1875

35	A17	2c brown	6.00	2.25
		On cover		30.00
		Block of four	30.00	30.00
36	A18	12c black	40.00	20.00
		On cover		250.00
		Block of four	200.00	

Princess
Likelike
(Mrs.
Archibald
Cleghorn)
A19

King David
Kalakaua
A20

Queen Kapiolani — A21

Statue of King Kamehameha I — A22

King
William
Lunalilo
A23

Queen
Emma
Kaleleonalani
A24

1882

37	A19	1c blue	4.00	7.50
		On cover		32.50
		Block of four	22.50	40.00

38	A17	2c lilac rose	90.00	30.00
		On cover		150.00
		Block of four	450.00	
a.		Half used as 1c on cover		*1,250.*
39	A14	5c ultramarine	12.00	2.25
		On cover		27.50
		Block of four	60.00	42.50
a.		Vert. pair, imperf. horiz.	*3,500.*	
40	A20	10c black	22.50	15.00
		On cover		125.00
		Block of four	100.00	100.00
41	A21	15c red brown	40.00	22.50
		On cover		175.00
		Block of four	200.00	175.00

1883-86

42	A19	1c green	2.25	1.50
		On cover		25.00
		Block of four	11.00	11.00
43	A17	2c rose ('86)	3.50	75
		On cover		25.00
		Block of four	17.50	10.00
44	A20	10c red brown ('84)	17.50	7.00
		On cover		110.00
		Block of four	85.00	65.00
45	A20	10c vermilion	20.00	12.50
		On cover		125.00
		Block of four	100.00	75.00
46	A18	12c red lilac	60.00	30.00
		On cover		300.00
		Block of four	300.00	200.00
47	A22	25c dark violet	85.00	42.50
		On cover		300.00
		Block of four	400.00	275.00
48	A23	50c red	135.00	75.00
		On cover		500.00
		Block of four	700.00	
49	A24	$1 rose red	200.00	85.00
		On cover		600.00
		Block of four	950.00	
		Maltese cross cancellation		25.00

Reproduction and Reprint
Yellowish Wove Paper

1886-89			**Engr.**	**Imperf.**
50	A11	2c orange vermilion	150.00	
		Block of four	750.00	
51	A11	2c carmine ('89)	25.00	
		Block of four	110.00	

In 1885 the Postmaster General wished to have on sale complete sets of Hawaii's portrait stamps, but was unable to find either the stone from which Nos. 27 and 28, or the plate from which No. 29 was printed. He therefore sent a copy of No. 29 to the American Bank Note Company, with an order to engrave a new plate like it and print 10,000 stamps therefrom, of which 5000 were overprinted "SPECIMEN" in blue.

The original No. 29 was printed in sheets of fifteen (5x3), but the plate of these "Official Imitations" was made up of fifty stamps (10x5). Later, in 1887, the original die for No. 29 was discovered, and, after retouching, a new plate was made and 37,500 stamps were printed (No. 51). These, like the originals, were printed in sheets of fifteen. They were delivered during 1889 and 1890. In 1892 all remaining unsold in the Post Office were overprinted "Reprint".

No. 29 is red in color, and printed on very thin white wove paper. No. 50 is orange vermilion in color, on medium, white to buff paper. In No. 50 the vertical line on the left side of the portrait touches the horizontal line over the label "Elua Keneta", while in the other two varieties, Nos. 29 and 51, it does not touch the horizontal line by half a millimeter. In No. 51 there are three parallel lines on the left side of the King's nose, while in No. 29 and No. 50 there are no such lines. No. 51 is carmine in color and printed on thick, yellowish to buff, wove paper.

It is claimed that both Nos. 50 and 51 were available for postage, although not made to fill a postal requirement. They exist with favor cancellation. See Nos. 50S-51S.

Queen Liliuokalani — A25

1890-91				**Perf. 12**
52	A25	2c dull violet, *Nov. 8, 1891*	6.50	1.25
		On cover		25.00
		Block of four	27.50	9.00
a.		Vert. pair, imperf. horiz.	*2,750.*	
52C	A14	5c deep indigo	110.00	75.00
		On cover		275.00
		Block of four	475.00	

Stamps of 1864-1891 Overprinted in Red

Provisional GOVT. 1893

1893

53	A12	1c purple	4.00	3.50
		On cover		35.00
		Block of four	20.00	20.00
a.		"189" instead of "1893"	225.00	
b.		No period after "GOVT"	35.00	
c.		Double overprint	*300.00*	
54	A19	1c blue	4.00	6.50

		On cover		40.00
		Block of four	20.00	35.00
a.		Double overprint	175.00	
b.		No period after "GOVT"	35.00	
55	A19	1c green	1.50	3.00
		On cover		25.00
		Block of four	7.50	15.00
a.		Pair, one without overprint	*1,250.*	
b.		Double overprint	400.00	150.00
56	A17	2c brown	5.00	10.00
		On cover		60.00
		Block of four	25.00	70.00
a.		No period after "GOVT"	100.00	
b.		Double overprint	—	
57	A25	2c dull violet	1.50	1.25
		On cover		25.00
		Block of four	6.50	6.50
a.		Inverted overprint	*1,000.*	*1,000.*
b.		Double overprint	350.00	250.00
c.		"18 3" instead of "1893"	125.00	90.00
58	A14	5c deep indigo	9.00	*17.50*
		On cover		100.00
		Block of four	45.00	*100.00*
a.		No period after "GOVT"	100.00	
b.		Double overprint	*1,400.*	
59	A14	5c ultramarine	5.00	2.50
		On cover		40.00
		Block of four	25.00	20.00
a.		Inverted overprint	900.00	700.00
b.		Double overprint	*1,200.*	
60	A15	6c green	10.00	*17.50*
		On cover		135.00
		Block of four	50.00	90.00
a.		Double overprint	650.00	
61	A20	10c black	7.00	10.00
		On cover		125.00
		Block of four	35.00	55.00
a.		Double overprint	900.00	800.00
61B	A20	10c red brown	16,500.	17,500.
		Block of four	—	
		Strip of five, plate imprint	—	
62	A18	12c black	7.50	*12.00*
		On cover		125.00
		Block of four	40.00	75.00
a.		Double overprint	750.00	
63	A18	12c red lilac	*125.00*	160.00
		On cover		450.00
		Block of four	750.00	900.00
64	A22	25c dark violet	20.00	22.50
		On cover		175.00
		Block of four	100.00	110.00
a.		No period after "GOVT"	165.00	
b.		Double overprint	*1,000.*	

Same Overprint in Black

65	A13	2c rose vermilion	50.00	55.00
		On cover		250.00
		Block of four	250.00	275.00
a.		No period after "GOVT"	200.00	175.00
66	A17	2c rose	1.25	2.25
		On cover		25.00
		Block of four	6.50	11.00
a.		Double overprint	*1,100.*	
b.		No period after "GOVT"	50.00	45.00
66C	A15	6c green	16,500.	—
		On cover		—
		Block of four	—	
67	A20	10c vermilion	11.00	20.00
		On cover		125.00
		Block of four	60.00	120.00
a.		Double overprint	*1,100.*	
68	A20	10c red brown	6.00	10.00
		On cover		100.00
		Block of four	30.00	60.00
a.		Double overprint	—	
69	A18	12c red lilac	225.00	*275.00*
		On cover		900.00
		Block of four	*1,000.*	*1,300.*
70	A21	15c red brown	17.50	*30.00*
		On cover		185.00
		Block of four	95.00	150.00
a.		Double overprint	800.00	
71	A16	18c dull rose	22.50	*35.00*
		On cover		225.00
		Block of four	110.00	175.00
a.		Double overprint	175.00	
b.		Pair, one without overprint	*1,000.*	
c.		No period after "GOVT"	125.00	125.00
72	A23	50c red	55.00	*85.00*
		On cover		600.00
		Block of four	250.00	*450.00*
a.		Double overprint	750.00	
b.		No period after "GOVT"	250.00	
73	A24	$1 rose red	100.00	*140.00*
		On cover		750.00
		Block of four	450.00	*700.00*
a.		No period after "GOVT"	350.00	*450.00*

Coat of Arms — A26

View of Honolulu — A27

Statue of King Kamehameha I — A28

Star and Palms — A29

S.S. "Arawa" — A30

President Sanford Ballard Dole — A31

Statue of King Kamehameha I — A32

1894

74	A26	1c yellow	1.85	1.25
		On cover		25.00
75	A27	2c brown	2.00	60
		On cover		25.00
		Block of four	9.00	7.00
		"Flying goose" flaw (48 LR II)	275.00	250.00
		Double transfer	—	
76	A28	5c rose lake	3.75	1.50
		On cover		25.00
		Block of four	18.50	15.00
77	A29	10c yellow green	5.00	4.50
		On cover		45.00
		Block of four	25.00	25.00
78	A30	12c blue	10.00	*12.00*
		On cover		125.00
		Block of four	45.00	—
79	A31	25c deep blue	10.00	*12.00*
		On cover		100.00

Numerous double transfers exist on Nos. 75 and 81.

1899

80	A26	1c dark green	1.50	1.25
		On cover		25.00
		Block of four	7.00	7.00
81	A27	2c rose	1.35	1.00
		On cover		20.00
		Double transfer	—	
a.		2c salmon	1.50	1.25
b.		Vert. pair, imperf. horiz.	*2,750.*	
		"Flying goose" flaw (48 LR II)	275.00	250.00
82	A32	5c blue	5.00	3.00
		On cover		25.00
		Block of four	25.00	20.00

OFFICIAL

Lorrin Andrews Thurston — O1

1896			**Engr.**	**Unwmk.**	**Perf. 12**
O1	O1	2c green		27.50	17.50
		On cover			200.00
		Block of four		120.00	
O2	O1	5c black brown		27.50	17.50
		On cover			200.00
		Block of four		120.00	
O3	O1	6c deep ultramarine		27.50	17.50
		On cover			200.00
		Block of four		120.00	
O4	O1	10c bright rose		27.50	17.50
		On cover			200.00
		Block of four		120.00	
O5	O1	12c orange		27.50	17.50
		On cover			200.00
		Block of four		120.00	
O6	O1	25c gray violet		27.50	17.50
		On cover			200.00
		Block of four		120.00	

ENVELOPES
All printed by American Bank Note Co., N.Y.

View of Honolulu Harbor — E1

Envelopes of White Paper, Outside and Inside

1884

U1	E1	1c light green *(109,000)*	2.50	3.00
		Entire	6.00	15.00
a.		1c green *(10,000)*	5.00	5.00
		Entire	17.50	27.50
U2	E1	2c carmine *(386,000 including U2a, U2b)*	2.50	4.00
		Entire	6.00	17.50
a.		2c red	2.50	4.00
		Entire	6.00	17.50
b.		2c rose	2.50	4.00
		Entire	6.00	17.50
c.		2c pale pink *(5,000)*	10.00	12.50
		Entire	35.00	60.00
U3	E1	4c red *(18,000)*	12.50	15.00
		Entire	45.00	65.00
U4	E1	5c blue *(90,775)*	6.50	7.50
		Entire	15.00	30.00
U5	E1	10c black *(3,500 plus)*	25.00	25.00
		Entire	75.00	100.00

Envelopes White Outside, Blue Inside

U6	E1	2c rose	175.00	150.00
		Entire	550.00	*750.00*
U7	E1	4c red	175.00	150.00
		Entire	500.00	—
U8	E1	5c blue	175.00	150.00
		Entire	500.00	600.00
U9	E1	10c black	350.00	325.00
		Entire	700.00	—

Nos. U1, U2, U4 & U5 Overprinted Locally
"Provisional Government 1893" in Red or Black

1893

U10	E1	1c light green (R) *(16,000)*	3.50	6.50
		Entire	7.50	20.00
a.		Double overprint		
		Entire	1,000.	
U11	E1	2c carmine (Bk) *(37,000)*	2.50	3.50
		Entire	6.00	15.00
a.		Double overprint		
		Entire	750.00	
b.		Double overprint, one inverted entire	900.00	
U12	E1	5c blue (R) *(34,891)*	5.00	5.00
		Entire	12.00	15.00
a.		Double overprint, entire	600.00	
U13	E1	10c black (R) *(17,707 incl. No. U14)*	10.00	15.00
		Entire	25.00	75.00
a.		Double overprint, entire	900.00	700.00

Envelope U9 with same overprint

U14	E1	10c black	225.00	—
		Entire	600.00	—

SPECIAL DELIVERY ENVELOPE
Price is for Entire.
Envelope U5 with added inscription "Special
Despatch Letter" etc. in red at top left corner

1885

UE1	E1	10c black, white inside *(2,000)*	250.00

Envelope UE1 was prepared for use but never issued for
postal purposes. Favor cancellations exist.

POSTAL CARDS

All printed by American Bank Note Co., N.Y.
Prices are for Entires.

Queen
Liliuokalani — PC1

View of Diamond
Head — PC2

Royal Emblems — PC3

1882-92   Engr.

UX1	PC1	1c red on buff *(125,000)*	45.00	60.00
UX2	PC2	2c black on white *(45,000)*	70.00	80.00
a.		Litho. ('92)	150.00	
UX3	PC3	3c blue green on white *(21,426)*	100.00	110.00

1889   Litho.

UX4	PC1	1c red on flesh *(171,240)*	40.00	50.00

Cards UX4, UX2a and UX3 overprinted locally
"Provisional Government 1893" in red or black.

1893

UX5	PC1	1c red on flesh (Bk) *(28,760)*	55.00	80.00
a.		Double overprint	1,650.	
UX6	PC2	2c black on white (R) *(10,000)*	75.00	90.00
UX7	PC3	3c blue green on white (R) *(8,574)*	100.00	110.00
a.		Double ovpt.	1,100.	

Iolani
Palace — PC4

POSTAL CARDS (continued)

Map of Pacific Ocean, Mercator's Projection — PC5

1894-97   Litho.
Border Frame 131 ½x72 ½mm.

UX8	PC4	1c red on flesh *(100,000)*	30.00	37.50
a.		Border frame 132½x74mm. ('97) *(200,000)*	27.50	37.50
UX9	PC5	2c green on white *(60,000)*	60.00	75.00
a.		Border frame 132½x74mm. ('97) *(190,000)*	55.00	75.00

PAID REPLY POSTAL CARDS
Double cards, same designs as postal cards
with added inscriptions on reply cards.

1883   Litho.

UY1	PC1	1c +1c purple on buff, unsevered *(5,000)*	250.00	300.00
m.		Message card, detached	30.00	40.00
r.		Reply card, detached	30.00	40.00
UY2	PC2	2c +2c black on white, un-severed *(5,000)*	300.00	375.00
m.		Message card, detached	55.00	65.00
r.		Reply card, detached	55.00	65.00

1889

UY3	PC1	1c +1c gray violet on flesh, un-severed *(5,000)*	250.00	300.00
m.		Message card, detached	30.00	40.00
r.		Reply card, detached	30.00	40.00
UY4	PC2	2c +2c sapphire on white, un-severed *(5,000)*	250.00	300.00
m.		Message card, detached	30.00	40.00
r.		Reply card, detached	30.00	40.00

REVENUE

R1   R2

R3   R4

R5	R6

Printed by the American Bank Note Co.
Sheets of 70

1877		Engr.	Unwmk.		*Rouletted 8*
R1	R1	25c green *(160,000)*		7.50	7.50
R2	R2	50c yellow orange *(190,000)*		7.50	7.50
R3	R3	$1 black *(580,000)*		12.50	5.00
a.		$1 gray		12.50	5.00

Denominations Typo.

R4	R4	$5 vermilion & violet blue *(21,000)*	25.00	25.00
R5	R5	$10 reddish brown & green *(14,000)*	50.00	25.00
R6	R6	$50 slate blue & carmine *(3,500)*	250.00	250.00

No. R1 Surcharged in Black or Gold

REPUBLIC

OF

TWENTY
CENTS

HAWAII
b

TWENTY

CENTS
a

1893-94				
R7	R1(a)	20c on 25c green	10.00	10.00
a.		Inverted surcharge	110.00	110.00
R8	R1(b)	20c on 25c green (G)	30.00	30.00
a.		Double surcharge	—	—
b.		Double surch., one black	—	—

R7	Kamehameha I — R8

Sheets of 50

1894		Litho.		*Perf. 14*
R9	R7	20c red *(10,000)*	125.00	125.00
a.		Imperf. *(25,000)*	125.00	125.00
R10	R7	25c violet brown	175.00	175.00
a.		Imperf.	175.00	175.00

Printed by the American Bank Note Co.
Sheets of 100

1897		Engr.		*Perf. 12*
R11	R8	$1 dark blue *(60,000)*	7.00	4.00

No. R6 Inscribed "Territory of Hawaii"

1901			*Rouletted 8*	
R12	R6	$50 slate blue & carmine *(7,000)*	37.50	—

Types of 1877
Printed by the American Bank Note Co.
Sheets of 70

1910-13		Engr.		*Perf. 12*
R13	R2	50c yellow orange ('13) *(70,000)*	12.50	—
R14	R3	$1 black ('13) *(35,000)*	15.00	—
R15	R4	$5 vermilion & violet blue *(14,000)*	27.50	—
R16	R5	$10 reddish brown & green *(14,000)*	27.50	—

PROOFS

1853

			LARGE DIE *(1)*	PLATE *(3)* India
5TC	5c	black on wove		—
6TC	13c	black on wove		—

1868

10TC	5c	orange red	600.00	
11TC	13	orange red	600.00	400.00

1861-63

27TC	2c	black		550.00

1864-71

30P	1c	purple	550.00	125.00
		Block of four		550.00
31P	2c	rose vermilion	550.00	125.00
		Block of four		—
32P	5c	blue	550.00	125.00
32TC	5c	black	550.00	
32TC	5c	dark red		150.00
32TC	5c	orange red		150.00
32TC	5c	orange		150.00
32TC	5c	red brown		150.00
32TC	5c	green		150.00
32TC		Block of four		—
33P	5c	dark violet		150.00
33P	6c	green	550.00	125.00
34P	18c	dull rose	550.00	125.00
		Block of four		125.00
34TC	18c	orange red	550.00	550.00
34TC	18c	dark orange	550.00	

1875

35P	2c	brown	550.00	125.00
		Block of four		550.00
35TC	2c	black	550.00	
36P	12c	black	550.00	125.00
36TC	12c	violet blue	550.00	

1882

37P	1c	blue		125.00
		Block of four		550.00
37TC	1c	black	550.00	
39P	5c	ultramarine	475.00	125.00
40P	10c	black	475.00	125.00
		Block of four		475.00
41P	15c	red brown		125.00

1883-86

42P	1c	green		75.00
		Block of four		325.00
43P	2c	rose		100.00
		Block of four		400.00
47P	25c	dark violet	450.00	100.00
48P	50c	red	450.00	100.00
49P	$1	rose red		100.00
		Block of four		400.00
49TC	$1	black		150.00
49TC	$1	orange red	450.00	

1886-89

50P	2c	orange vermilion	550.00	125.00
51P	2c	carmine	550.00	

1890-91

52P	2c	dull violet	475.00	100.00
52CP	5c	deep indigo		100.00

1894

74P	1c	yellow	450.00	100.00
75P	2c	brown	450.00	100.00
75TC	2c	dark green	550.00	
76P	5c	rose lake	500.00	100.00
77P	10c	yellow green	500.00	100.00
		Block of four		400.00
78P	12c	blue	500.00	125.00
79P	25c	deep blue	500.00	100.00

1899

82P	5c	blue		150.00

1896   **Official**

O1P	2c	green	300.00	100.00
O2P	5c	black brown	300.00	100.00
O3P	6c	deep ultramarine	300.00	100.00
O4P	10c	bright rose	300.00	100.00
		Block of four		—
O4TC	10c	black	300.00	
O5P	12c	orange	300.00	100.00
O5TC	12c	black	300.00	
O6P	25c	gray violet	300.00	100.00
O6TC	25c	black	300.00	

SPECIMEN

Overprinted in Black or Red   **SPECIMEN.**

1868

10S	5c	blue (R)	20.00

		Line through "Honolulu"	45.00
11Sa	13c	dull rose	20.00

Overprinted in Black   **SPECIMEN.**

11Sb	13c	dull rose	50.00
		Dbl. ovpt., one as #11Sa, one as #11Sb	1,100.
		Period omitted	80.00

Overprinted in Black   REPRINT

1889			
10RS	5c	blue	45.00
11RS	13c	orange red	80.00

Overprinted in Black   **CANCELLED.**

1869			
29S	2c	red	50.00

Overprinted in Blue   **SPECIMEN.**

1886			
50S	2c	orange vermilion	60.00

Overprinted in Black   REPRINT

1889			
51S	2c	carmine	25.00

A group of 32 atolls and more than 867 reefs in the west Pacific Ocean, about 2,500 miles southeast of Tokyo. The islands, comprised of two major chains, the Ralik chain in the west, and the Ratak chain in the east, were annexed by Germany in 1885. Stamps issued under German Dominion (Nos. 1-27) are listed in Vol. III of the Scott Standard Postage Stamp Catalogue. Japan seized the islands in 1914. They were taken by the U.S. in World War II and became part of the U.S. Trust Territory of the Pacific in 1947. By agreement with the U.S. Postal Service, the islands began issuing their own stamps in 1984, with the U.S.P.S. continuing to carry the mail to and from the islands. Islands and atolls include Kwajalein, Jaluit and Majuro, site of the government headquarters. Land area: 70 sq. mi. Population: 31,042 (1980).

100 CENTS = 1 DOLLAR

Inauguration of Postal Service — A5

1984, May 2   Litho.   Perf. 14x13½

31	A5	20c Outrigger canoe	40	40
32	A5	20c Fishnet	40	40
33	A5	20c Navigational stick chart	40	40
34	A5	20c Islet	40	40
a.		Block of 4, #31-34	1.60	
				1.60

Mili Atoll, Astrolabe — A6

Maps and Navigational Instruments.

1984-85   Litho.   Perf. 15x14

35	A6	1c shown	5	5
36	A6	3c Likiep, Azimuth compass	6	6
37	A6	5c Ebon, 16th cent. compass	10	10
38	A6	10c Jaluit, anchor buoys	20	20
39	A6	13c Ailinginae, Nocturnal	26	26
a.		Booklet pane of 10	2.60	
40	A6	14c Wotho Atoll, navigational stick chart ('85)	28	28
a.		Bklt. pane of 10	2.80	
41	A6	20c Kwajalein and Ebeye, stick chart	40	40
a.		Booklet pane of 10	4.00	
b.		Booklet pane of 5 each, 13c, 20c	3.30	
42	A6	22c Enewetak, 18th cent. lode stone storage case ('85)	44	44
a.		Bklt. pane of 10	4.40	
b.		Blkt. pane of 5 each, 14c, 22c	3.60	
43	A6	28c Ailinglaplap, printed compass	56	56
44	A6	30c Majuro, navigational stick-chart	60	60
45	A6	33c Namu, stick chart ('85)	66	66
46	A6	37c Rongelap, quadrant	74	74
47	A6	39c Taka, map compass, 16th cent. sea chart ('85)	78	78
48	A6	44c Ujelang, chronograph ('85)	88	88
49	A6	50c Maloelap and Aur, nocturlabe ('85)	1.00	1.00
49A	A6	$1 Arno, 16th cent. sector compass	2.00	2.00
		Nos. 35-49A (16)	9.01	9.01

Issue dates: 1c, 3c, 10c, 30c and $1, June 12. 13c, 20c, 28c and 37c. Dec. 19, 1984. 14c, 22c, 33c, 39c, 44c and 50c, June 5, 1985.
See Nos. 107-109.

No. 7 — A7

1984, June 19   Perf. 14½x15

50	A7	40c shown	80	80
51	A7	40c No. 13	80	80
52	A7	40c No. 4	80	80
53	A7	40c No. 25	80	80
a.		Block of 4, #50-53	3.20	3.20

Philatelic Salon, 19th UPU Congress, Hamburg, June 19-26.

Ausipex '84
A8

Dolphins.

1984, Sept. 5   Litho.   Perf. 14

54	A8	20c Common	40	40
55	A8	20c Risso's	40	40
56	A8	20c Spotter	40	40
57	A8	20c Bottlenose	40	40
a.		Block of 4, #54-57	1.60	1.60

Christmas 1984 — A9

1984, Nov. 7   Litho.   Perf. 14

58		Strip of 4	1.60	1.60
a.-d.	A9	20c Any single	40	40

Printed in sheets of 16; background shows text from Marshallese New Testament, giving each stamp on the sheet a different background.

Marshalls Constitution, 5th Anniv. — A10

1984, Dec. 19   Litho.   Perf. 14

59	A10	20c Traditional chief	40	40
60	A10	20c Amata Kabua	40	40
61	A10	20c Chester Nimitz	40	40
62	A10	20c Trygve Lie	40	40
a.		Block of 4, #59-62	1.60	1.60

Audubon Bicentenary
A11

1985, Feb. 15   Litho.   Perf. 14

63	A11	22c Forked-tailed Petrel	44	44
64	A11	22c Pectoral Sandpiper	44	44
a.		Pair, #63-64	90	90

See Nos. C1-C2.

Sea Shells — A12

1985, Apr. 17   Litho.   Perf. 14

65	A12	22c Cymatium lotorium	44	44
66	A12	22c Chicoreus cornucervi	44	44
67	A12	22c Strombus aurisdanae	44	44
68	A12	22c Turbo marmoratus	44	44

69	A12	22c Chicoreus palmarosae	44	44
a.		Strip of 5, #65-69	2.20	2.20
		Nos. 65-69 (5)	2.20	2.20

See Nos. 119-123, 152-156.

Decade for Women — A13

Marshallese women and: No. 70, Native drum. No. 71, Palm branches. No. 72, Pounding stone. No. 73, Ak bird.

1985, June 5			**Litho.**	**Perf. 14**	
70	A13	22c multi		44	44
71	A13	22c multi		44	44
72	A13	22c multi		44	44
73	A13	22c multi		44	44
a.		Block of 4, #70-73		1.80	1.80

Reef and Lagoon Fish — A14

1985, July 15			**Litho.**	**Perf. 14**	
74	A14	22c Acanthurus dussumieri		44	44
75	A14	22c Adioryx caudimaculatus		44	44
76	A14	22c Ostracion meleacaris		44	44
77	A14	22c Chaetodon ephippium		44	44
a.		Block of 4, #74-77		1.80	1.80

Intl. Youth Year — A15

IYY and Alele Nautical Museum emblems and: No. 78, Marshallese youths and Peace Corps volunteers playing basketball. No. 79, Legend teller reciting local history, girl listening to recording. No. 80, Islander explaining navigational stick charts. No. 81, Jabwa stick dance.

1985, Aug. 31			**Litho.**	**Perf. 14**	
78	A15	22c multi		44	44
79	A15	22c multi		44	44
80	A15	22c multi		44	44
81	A15	22c multi		44	44
a.		Block of 4, #78-81		1.80	1.80

1856 American Board of Commissions Stock Certificate for Foreign Missions A16

Missionary ship Morning Star I: 22c, Launch, Jothan Stetson Shipyard, Chelsea, MA, Aug. 7, 1857. 33c, First voyage, Honolulu to the Marshalls, 1857. 44c, Marshall islanders pulling Morning Star I into Ebon Lagoon, 1857.

1985, Oct. 21			**Litho.**	**Perf. 14**	
82	A16	14c multi		28	28
83	A16	22c multi		44	44
84	A16	33c multi		66	66
85	A16	44c multi		88	88

Christmas 1985.

U.S. Space Shuttle, Astro Telescope, Halley's Comet — A17

Comet tail and research spacecraft: No. 87, Planet A Space Probe, Japan. No. 88, Giotto spacecraft, European Space Agency. No. 89, INTERCOSMOS Project Vega spacecraft, Russia, France, etc. No. 90, U.S. naval tracking ship, NASA observational aircraft, cameo portrait of Edmond Halley (1656-1742), astronomer. Se-tenant in continuous design.

1985, Nov. 21					
86	A17	22c multi		44	44
87	A17	22c multi		44	44
88	A17	22c multi		44	44
89	A17	22c multi		44	44
90	A17	22c multi		44	44
a.		Strip of 5, #86-90		2.25	2.25

Medicinal Plants — A18

1985, Dec. 31			**Litho.**	**Perf. 14**	
91	A18	22c Sida fallax		44	44
92	A18	22c Scaevola frutescens		44	44
93	A18	22c Guettarda speciosa		44	44
94	A18	22c Cassytha filiformis		44	44
a.		Block of 4, #91-94		1.80	1.80

Maps Type of 1984

1986-87			**Perf. 15x14, 14 ($10)**		
107	A6	$2 Wotje and Erikub, terrestrial globe, 1571		4.00	4.00
108	A6	$5 Bikini, Stick chart		10.00	10.00
		Size: 31x31mm.			
109	A6	$10 Stick chart of the atolls		20.00	20.00

Issue dates: $2, $5, Mar 7, 1986. $10, Mar. 31, 1987.

Marine Invertebrates — A19

1986, Mar. 31			**Litho.**	**Perf. 14½x14**	
110	A19	14c Triton's trumpet		28	28
111	A19	14c Giant clam		28	28
112	A19	14c Small giant clam		28	28
113	A19	14c Coconut crab		28	28
a.		Block of 4, #110-113		1.15	1.15

Souvenir Sheet

AMERIPEX '86, Chicago, May 22-June 1 — A20

1986, May 22			**Litho.**	**Perf. 14**	
114	A20	$1 Douglas C-54 Globester		2.00	2.00

1st Around-the-world scheduled flight, 40th anniv. No. 114 has multicolored margin continuing the design and picturing

US Air Transport Command Base, Kwajalein Atoll and souvenir card. Size: 89x63mm.
See Nos. C3-C6.

Operation Crossroads, Atomic Bomb Tests, 40th Anniv. — A21

Designs: No. 115, King Juda, Bikinians sailing tibinal canoe. No. 116, USS Sumner, amphibious DUKW, advance landing. No. 117, Evacuating Bikinians. No. 118, Land reclamation, 1986.

1986, July 1			**Litho.**	**Perf. 14**	
115	A21	22c multi		44	44
116	A21	22c multi		44	44
117	A21	22c multi		44	44
118	A21	22c multi		44	44
a.		Block of 4, #115-118		1.80	1.80

See No. C7.

Seashells Type of 1985

1986, Aug. 1			**Litho.**	**Perf. 14**	
119	A12	22c Ramose murex		44	44
120	A12	22c Orange spider		44	44
121	A12	22c Red-mouth frog shell		44	44
122	A12	22c Laciniate conch		44	44
123	A12	22c Giant frog shell		44	44
a.		Strip of 5, #119-123		2.20	2.20
		Nos. 119-123 (5)		2.20	2.20

Game Fish — A22

1986, Sept. 10			**Litho.**		
124	A22	22c Blue marlin		44	44
125	A22	22c Wahoo		44	44
126	A22	22c Dolphin fish		44	44
127	A22	22c Yellowfin tuna		44	44
a.		Block of 4, #124-127		1.80	1.80

Christmas 1986, Intl. Peace Year — A23

1986, Oct. 28   Litho.   Perf. 14
128	A23	22c United Nations UR	44	44
129	A23	22c United Nations UL	44	44
130	A23	22c United Nations LR	44	44
131	A23	22c United Nations LL	44	44
a.		Block of 4, #128-131	1.80	1.80

See No. C8.

U.S. Whaling Ships — A24

1987, Feb. 20   Litho.   Perf. 14
132	A24	22c James Arnold, 1854	44	44
133	A24	22c General Scott, 1859	44	44
134	A24	22c Charles W. Morgan, 1865	44	44
135	A24	22c Lucretia, 1884	44	44
a.		Block of 4, #132-135	1.80	1.80

Historic and Military Flights — A25

Designs: No. 136, Charles Lindbergh commemorative medal, Spirit of St. Louis crossing the Atlantic, 1927. No. 137, Lindbergh flying in the Battle of the Marshalls, 1944. No. 138, William Bridgeman flying in the Battle of Kwajalein, 1944. No. 139, Bridgeman testing the Douglas Skyrocket, 1951. No. 140, John Glenn flying in the Battle of the Marshalls. No. 141, Glenn, the first American to orbit the Earth, 1962.

1987, Mar. 12   Litho.   Perf. 14½
136	A25	33c multi	66	66
137	A25	33c multi	66	66
a.		Pair, Nos. 136-137	1.35	1.35
138	A25	39c multi	78	78
139	A25	39c multi	78	78
a.		Pair, Nos. 138-139	1.60	1.60
140	A25	44c multi	88	88
141	A25	44c multi	88	88
a.		Pair, Nos. 140-141	1.80	1.80
		Nos. 136-141 (6)	4.64	4.64

Souvenir Sheet

CAPEX '87 — A26

1987, June 15   Litho.   Perf. 14
142	A26	$1 Map of flight	2.00	2.00

Amelia Earhart (1897-1937), American aviator who died during attempted round-the-world flight, 50th anniv. No. 142 has multicolored margin picturing Earhart's flight pattern from Calcutta, India, to the crash site near Barre Is., Marshall Isls. Size: 88x63mm.

U.S. Constitution Bicentennial A27

Excerpts from the Marshall Islands and U.S. Constitutions.

1987, July 16   Litho.   Perf. 14
143	A27	14c We,... Marshall	28	28
144	A27	14c National seals	28	28
145	A27	14c We,... United States	28	28
a.		Triptych, Nos. 143-145	85	85
146	A27	22c All we have...	44	44
147	A27	22c Flags	44	44
148	A27	22c to establish...	44	44
a.		Triptych, Nos. 146-148	1.35	1.35
149	A27	44c With this Constitution...	88	88
150	A27	44c Stick chart, Liberty Bell	88	88
151	A27	44c to promote...	88	88
a.		Triptych, Nos. 149-151	2.65	2.65
		Nos. 143-151 (9)	4.80	4.80

Triptychs printed in continuous designs.

Seashells Type of 1985

1987, Sept. 1   Litho.   Perf. 14
152	A12	22c Magnificent cone	44	44
153	A12	22c Partridge tun	44	44
154	A12	22c Scorpion spider conch	44	44
155	A12	22c Hairy triton	44	44
156	A12	22c Chiragra spider conch	44	44
a.		Strip of 5, Nos. 152-156	2.20	2.20
		Nos. 152-156 (5)	2.20	2.20

Copra Industry — A28

Contest-winning crayon drawings by Amram Enox; design contest sponsored by the Tobular Copra Processing Co.

1987, Dec. 10   Litho.   Perf. 14
157	A28	44c Planting coconut	88	88
158	A28	44c Making copra	88	88
159	A28	44c Bottling coconut oil	88	88
a.		Triptych, Nos. 157-159	2.65	

Biblical Verses A29

1987, Dec. 10
160	A29	14c Matthew 2:1	28	28
161	A29	22c Luke 2:14	44	44
162	A29	33c Psalms 33:3	66	66
163	A29	44c Pslams 150:5	88	88

Christmas 1987.

Marine Birds — A30

1988, Jan. 27
164	A30	44c Pacific reef herons	88	88
165	A30	44c Bar-tailed godwit	88	88
166	A30	44c Masked booby	88	88
167	A30	44c Northern shoveler	88	88

Fish — A31

1988   Litho.   Perf. 14½X14
168	A31	1c Damselfish	5	5
169	A31	3c Blackface butterflyfish	6	6
170	A31	14c Hawkfish	28	28
a.		Bklt. pane of 10	2.80	
171	A31	15c Balloonfish	30	30
172	A31	17c Trunk fish	34	34
173	A31	22c Lyretail wrasse	44	44
a.		Bklt. pane of 10	4.40	
b.		Bklt. pane of 10 (5 each 14c, 22c)	3.60	
174	A31	25c Parrotfish	50	50
175	A31	33c White-spotted boxfish	66	66
176	A31	36c Spotted boxfish	72	72
177	A31	39c Surgeonfish	78	78
178	A31	44c Long-snouted butterflyfish	88	88
179	A31	45c Trumpetfish	90	90
180	A31	56c Sharp-nosed puffer	1.12	1.12
181	A31	$1 Seahorse	2.00	2.00
182	A31	$2 Ghost pipefish	4.00	4.00
183	A31	$5 Big-spotted triggerfish	10.00	10.00
		Nos. 168-183 (16)	23.03	23.03

Issue dates: Nos. 170a, 173a, 173b, Mar. 31, 1988. 15c, 25c, 36c, 45c, July 19. Others, Mar. 17.

A32

1988 Summer Olympics, Seoul — A33

Athletes in motion: 15c Javelin thrower (Nos. 188a-188e as shown). 25c, Runner (Nos. 189a-189e as shown).

1988, June 30   Litho.   Perf. 14
188		Strip of 5	1.50	1.50
a.-e.		A32 15c any single	30	30
189		Strip of 5	2.50	2.50
a.-e.		A33 25c any single	50	50

Souvenir Sheet

Pacific Voyages of Robert Louis Stevenson A34

Stick chart of the Marshalls and: No. 190a, *Casco* sailing through the Golden Gate. No. 190b, At the Needles of Ua-Pu, Marquesas. No. 190c, *Equator* departing from Honolulu and

Kajulani, an Hawaiian princess. No. 190d, Chief's canoe, Majuro Lagoon. No. 190e, Bronze medallion, 1887, by Augustus St. Gaudens in the Tate Gallery, London. No. 190f, Outrigger canoe and *S.S. Janet Nicoll* in Majuro Lagoon. No. 190g, View of Apemama, Gilbert Is. No. 190h, Samoan outrigger canoe, Apia Harbor. No. 190i, Stevenson riding horse Jack at his estate, Vallima, Samoa.

1988, July 19   **Litho.**   *Perf. 14*

190		Sheet of 9	4.50 4.50
a.-i.		A34 25c any single	50 50

Robert Louis Stevenson (1850-1894), Scottish novelist, poet and essayist. No. 190 has multicolored decorative margin. Size: 215x152mm.

AIR POST STAMPS

Audubon Type of 1985

1985, Feb. 15   **Litho.**   *Perf. 14*

C1	A11	44c Booby Gannet, vert.	88 88
C2	A11	44c Esquimaux Curlew, vert.	88 88
a.		Pair, #C1-C2	1.80 1.80

AMERIPEX Type of 1986

Designs: No. C3, Consolidated PBY-5A Catalina Amphibian. No. C4, Grumman SA-16 Albatross. No. C5, McDonnell Douglas DC-6B Super Cloudmaster. No. C6, Boeing 727-100.

1986, May 22   **Litho.**   *Perf. 14*

C3	A20	44c multi	88 88
C4	A20	44c multi	88 88
C5	A20	44c multi	88 88
C6	A20	44c multi	88 88
a.		Block of 4, #C3-C6	3.60 3.60

Operation Crossroads Type of 1986
Souvenir Sheet

1986, July 1   **Litho.**   *Perf. 14*

C7	A21	44c USS Saratoga	88 88

No. C7 has multicolored margin inscribed "Baker Day Atomic Bomb Test, 25 July 1946," and picturing mushroom cloud. Size: 106x72mm.

AIRMAIL   REPUBLIC OF THE   44c MARSHALL ISLANDS   Statue of Liberty Cent., Intl. Peace Year — AP1

1986, Oct. 28   **Litho.**

C8	AP1	44c multi	88 88

Natl. Girl Scout Movement, 20th Anniv. — AP2

1986, Dec. 8   **Litho.**

C9	AP2	44c Community service	88 88
C10	AP2	44c Salute	88 88
C11	AP2	44c Health care	88 88
C12	AP2	44c Learning skills	88 88
a.		Block of 4, #C9-C12	3.55 3.55

Girl Scout Movement in the US, 75th anniv. (1912-1987).

Marine Birds — AP3

1987, Jan. 12   **Litho.**   *Perf. 14*

C13	AP3	44c Wedge-tailed shearwater	88 88
C14	AP3	44c Red-footed booby	88 88
C15	AP3	44c Red-tailed tropicbird	88 88
C16	AP3	44c Great frigatebird	88 88
a.		Block of 4, #C13-C16	3.55 3.55

CAPEX '87 AP4

Last flight of Amelia Earhart: No. C17, Take-off at Lae, New Guinea, July 2, 1937. No. C18, USCG Itasca cutter at Howland Is. No. C19, Purported crash landing of the Electra at Mili Atoll. No. C20, Recovery of the Electra by the Koshu, a Japanese survey ship.

1987, June 15   **Litho.**   *Perf. 14*

C17	AP4	44c multi	88 88
C18	AP4	44c multi	88 88
C19	AP4	44c multi	88 88
C20	AP4	44c multi	88 88
a.		Block of 4, Nos. C17-C20	3.55 3.55

MICRONESIA, FEDERATED STATES OF

A group of more than 600 islands in the west Pacific Ocean, north of the equator. These islands, also known as the Caroline Islands, were bought by Germany from Spain in 1899. Caroline Islands stamps issued as a German colony are listed in Vol. II of the Scott Standard Postage Stamp Catalogue. The islands were seized by Japan in 1914. They were taken by the U.S. in World War II and became part of the U.S. Trust Territory of the Pacific in 1947. By agreement with the U.S. Postal Service, the islands began issuing their own stamps in 1984, with the U.S.P.S. continuing to carry the mail to and from the islands. Yap, Truk, Pohnpei and Kosrae are the four states of Micronesia. All but Kosrae are island groups. Kolonia, on Pohnpei, is the seat of government. Land area: 271 sq. mi. Population: 73,755 (1980).

100 CENTS = 1 DOLLAR

Map of State of Yap A1

1984, July 12   **Litho.**   *Perf. 14*

1	A1	20c shown	40 40
2	A1	20c Truk	40 40
3	A1	20c Pohnpei	40 40
4	A1	20c Kosrae	40 40
a		Block of 4, #1-4	1.60 1.60

Postal service inauguration.

Fernandez de Quiros — A2

Men's House, Yap — A3

Designs: 1c, 19c, Pedro Fernandez de Quiros, Spanish explorer, first discovered Pohnpei, 1595. 2c, 20c, Louis Duperrey, French explorer. 3c, 30c, Fyedor Lutke, Russian explorer. 4c, 37c, Dumont d'Urville. 10c, Sleeping Lady, Kosrae. 13c, Liduduhriap Waterfall, Pohnpei. 17c, Tonachau Peak, Truk.

50c, Devil mask, Truk. $1, Sokeh's Rock, Pohnpei. $2, Canoes, Kosrae. $5, Stone money, Yap.

1984, July 12   *Perf. 13½x13*

5	A2	1c Prus bl	5 5
6	A2	2c dp cl	5 5
7	A2	3c dk bl	6 6
8	A2	4c green	8 8
9	A3	5c yel brn	10 10
10	A3	10c dk vio	20 20
11	A3	13c dk bl	26 26
12	A3	17c brn lake	34 34
13	A2	19c dk vio	38 38
14	A2	20c ol grn	40 40
15	A2	30c rose lake	60 60
16	A2	37c dp vio	75 75
17	A3	50c brown	1.00 1.00
18	A3	$1 olive	2.00 2.00
19	A3	$2 Prus bl	4.00 4.00
20	A3	$5 brn lake	10.00 10.00
		Nos. 5-20 (16)	20.27 20.27

See Nos. 30-42.

Ausipex '84 A4

1984, Sept. 21   **Litho.**   *Perf. 13½*

21	A4	20c Truk Post Office	40 40

See Nos. C4-C6.

Christmas — A5

Child's drawing.

1984, Dec. 20

22	A5	20c Child in straw manger	40 40

See Nos. C7-C9.

Ships — A6

1985, Aug. 19

23	A6	22c U.S.S. Jamestown	44 44

See Nos. C10-C12.

Federated States of Micronesia Christmas — A7

1985, Oct. 15   Litho.   *Perf. 13 1/2*
24   A7   22c Lelu Protestant Church, Kosrae   44   44

See Nos. C13-C14.

Audubon Birth Bicentenary — A8

1985, Oct. 30   *Perf. 14 1/2*
25   A8   22c Noddy tern   44   44
26   A8   22c Turnstone   44   44
27   A8   22c Golden plover   44   44
28   A8   22c Black-bellied plover   44   44
a.   Block of 4, #25-28   1.80   1.80

See No. C15.

Birds — A8a

Tall Ship
Senyavin — A9

Natl. Seal — A10

Perf. 13 1/2x13, 13 1/2 (3c, 14c, No. 35)
1985-88   Litho.
30   A8a   3c Long-billed white-eye ('88)   6   6
32   A8a   14c Truk monarch ('88)   28   28
33   A3   15c Liduduhriap Waterfall, Pohnpei   ('88)   30   30
34   A9   22c brt bl grn ('86)   44   44
35   A8a   22c Pohnpei mountain starling ('88)   44   44
36   A3   25c Tonachau Peak, Truk ('88)   50   50
39   A9   36c ultra ('88)   72   72
40   A3   45c Sleeping Lady, Kosrae ('88)   90   90
42   A10 $10 brt ultra   20.00   20.00
    Nos. 30-42,C34-C36 (12)   27.18   27.18

Issue dates: 3c, 14c, No. 35, Aug. 1, 1988. 15c, 25c, 36c, 45c, Sept. 1, 1988. No. 34, Apr. 14, 1986. $10, Oct. 15, 1985.

Nan Madol Ruins,
Pohnpei — A16

1985, Dec.   Litho.   *Perf. 13 1/2*
45   A16   22c Land of the Sacred Masonry   44   44

See Nos. C16-C18.

Intl. Peace
Year — A17

1986, May 16
46   A17   22c multi   44   44

Nos. 1-4 Surcharged

1986, May 19   Litho.   *Perf. 14*
48   A1   22c on 20c No. 1   44   44
49   A1   22c on 20c No. 2   44   44
50   A1   22c on 20c No. 3   44   44
51   A1   22c on 20c No. 4   44   44
a.   Block of 4, #48-51   1.80   1.80

AMERIPEX '86 — A18

Bully Hayes (1829-1877), Buccaneer.

1986, May 22   *Perf. 13 1/2*
52   A18   22c At ships helm   44   44
    Nos. 52,C21-C24 (5)   4.26   4.26

First
Passport — A19

1986, Nov. 4   Litho.   *Perf. 13 1/2*
53   A19   22c multi   44   44

Christmas — A20

Virgin and child paintings: 5c, Italy, 18th cent. 22c, Germany, 19th cent.

1986, Oct. 15   Litho.   *Perf. 14 1/2*
54   A20   5c multi   10   10
55   A20   22c multi   44   44

See Nos. C26-C27.

Anniversaries
and
Events — A21

1987, June 13   Litho.   *Perf. 14 1/2*
56   A21   22c Intl. Year of Shelter for the Homeless   44   44

Souvenir Sheet
57   A21 $1 CAPEX '87   2.00   2.00

See Nos. C28-C30. No. 57 has inscribed multicolored margin picturing Toronto landmarks. Size: 85x55m.

Federated States of Micronesia   Christmas — A22

Design: 22c, Archangel Gabriel appearing before Mary.

1987, Nov. 16   Litho.   *Perf. 14 1/2*
58   A22   22c multi   44   44

See. Nos. C31-C33.

Colonial
Eras — A23

1988, July 20   Litho.   *Perf. 13x13 1/2*
59   A23   22c German   44   44
60   A23   22c Spanish   44   44
61   A23   22c Japanese   44   44
62   A23   22c U.S. Trust Territory   44   44
a.   Block of 4, Nos. 59-62   1.80   1.80
    Nos. 59-62,C37-C38 (6)   3.52   3.52

Nos. 59-62 printed se-tenant in sheets of 28 plus 4 center labels picturing flags of Spain (UL), Germany (UR), Japan (LL), and the United States (LR).

25   1988 Summer Olympics, Seoul — A24

1988, Sept. 1   Litho.   *Perf. 14*
63   A24   25c Running   50   50
64   A24   25c Women's hurdles   50   50
a.   Pair, Nos. 63-64   1.00   1.00
65   A24   45c Basketball   90   90
66   A24   45c Women's volleyball   90   90
a.   Pair, Nos. 65-66   1.80   1.80

AIR POST STAMPS

Boeing 727,
1968 — AP1

1984, July 12   Litho.   *Perf. 13 1/2*
C1   AP1   28c shown   56   56
C2   AP1   35c SA-16 Albatross, 1960   70   70
C3   AP1   40c PBY-5A Catalina, 1951   80   80

Ausipex Type of 1984

Ausipex '84 emblem and: 28c, Caroline Islands No. 4. 35c, No. 7. 40c, No. 19.

1984, Sept. 21		**Litho.**	**Perf. 13½**
C4	A4 28c multi		56 56
C5	A4 35c multi		70 70
C6	A4 40c multi		80 80

Christmas Type of 1984

Children's drawings.

1984, Dec. 20			
C7	A5 28c Illustrated Christmas text		56 56
C8	A5 35c Decorated palm tree		70 70
C9	A5 40c Feast preparation		80 80

Ships Type of 1985

1985, Aug. 19			
C10	A6 33c L'Astrolabe		66 66
C11	A6 39c La Coquille		78 78
C12	A6 44c Shenandoah		88 88

Christmas Type of 1985

1985, Oct. 15		**Litho.**	**Perf. 13½**
C13	A7 33c Dublon Protestant Church		66 66
C14	A7 44c Pohnpei Catholic Church		88 88

Audubon Type of 1985

1985, Oct. 31			**Perf. 14½**
C15	A8 44c Sooty tern		88 88

Ruins Type of 1985

1985, Dec.		**Litho.**	**Perf. 13½**
C16	A16 33c Nan Tauas inner courtyard		66 66
C17	A16 39c Outer wall		78 78
C18	A16 44c Tomb		88 88

Halley's Comet — AP2

1986, May 16

C19 AP2 44c dk bl, bl & blk		88 88

Return of Nauruans from Truk, 40th Anniv. — AP3

1986, May 16

C20 AP3 44c Ship in port		88 88

AMERIPEX '86 Type of 1986

Bully Hayes (1829-1877), buccaneer.

1986, May 22			
C21	A18 33c Hawaii No. 5		66 66
C22	A18 39c Sinking of the Leonora, Kosrae		78 78
C23	A18 44c Hayes escapes capture		88 88
C24	A18 75c Biography, by Louis Becke		1.50 1.50

Souvenir Sheet

C25	A18 $1 Hayes ransoming chief		2.00 2.00

No. C25 has multicolored inscribed margin continuing the design and picturing exhibition emblem. Size: 128x71mm.

Christmas Type of 1986

Virgin and child paintings: 33c, Austria, 19th cent. 44c, Italy, 18th cent., diff.

1986, Oct. 15		**Litho.**	**Perf. 14½**
C26	A20 33c multi		66 66
C27	A20 44c multi		88 88

Anniversaries and Events Type of 1987

1987, June 13		**Litho.**	**Perf. 14½**
C28	A21 33c U.S. currency, bicent.		66 66
C29	A21 39c 1st American in orbit, 25th anniv.		78 78
C30	A21 44c U.S. Constitution, bicent.		88 88

Christmas Type of 1987

1987, Nov. 16		**Litho.**	**Perf. 14½**
C31	A22 33c Holy Family		66 66
C32	A22 39c Shepherds		78 78
C33	A22 44c Three Wise Men		88 88

Bird Type of 1988

1988, Aug. 1		**Litho.**	**Perf. 13½**
C34	A8a 33c Great Truk white-eye		66 66
C35	A8a 44c Blue-faced parrotfinch		88 88
C36	A8a $1 Yap monarch		2.00 2.00

Colonial Era Type of 1988

1988, July 20			**Perf. 13x13½**
C37	A23 44c Traditional skills (boat building)		88 88
C38	A23 44c Modern Micronesia (tourism)		88 88
a.	Pair, Nos. C37-C38		1.80 1.80

Nos. C37-C38 printed se-tenant in sheets of 28 plus 4 center labels picturing flags of Kosrae (UL), Truk (UR), Pohnpei (LL), and Yap (LR).

ENVELOPES

National Flag — U1

1984, July 12		**Litho.**
U1 U1 20c blk, gray & bl, entire		50 50

PALAU

A group of about 100 islands and islets forming part of the western Caroline Islands in the west Pacific Ocean, 1,000 miles southeast of Manila. Part of the U.S. Trust Territory of the Pacific established in 1947, Palau became a republic in 1981. By agreement with the U.S. Postal Service, Palau began issuing its own stamps in 1983 with the U.S.P.S. continuing to carry the mail to and from Palau. Islands include Babelthuap, Angaur, Eli Malk, Peleliu, Urukthapel and Koror, site of government headquarters. Area: 179 sq. mi. Population: 16,000 (est. 1983).

Inauguration of Postal Service — A1

1983, Mar. 10		**Litho.**	**Perf. 14**
1	A1 20c Constitution preamble		50 50
2	A1 20c Hunters		50 50
3	A1 20c Fish		50 50
4	A1 20c Preamble, diff.		50 50
a.	Block of 4, #1-4		2.00 2.00

Palau Fruit Dove — A2

1983, May 16			**Perf. 15**
5	A2 20c shown		40 40

6	A2 20c Palau morningbird		40 40
7	A2 20c Giant white-eye		40 40
8	A2 20c Palau fantail		40 40
a.	Block of 4, #5-8		1.60 1.60

Sea Fan — A3

1983-84		**Litho.**	**Perf. 13½x14**
9	A3 1c shown		5 5
10	A3 3c Map cowrie		6 6
11	A3 5c Jellyfish		10 10
12	A3 10c Hawksbill turtle		20 20
13	A3 13c Giant Clam		26 26
a.	Booklet pane of 10		2.60
b.	Booklet pane of 10 (5 #13, 5 #14)		3.30
14	A3 20c Parrotfish		40 40
b.	Booklet pane of 10		4.00
15	A3 28c Chambered Nautilus		56 56
16	A3 30c Dappled sea cucumber		60 60
17	A3 37c Sea Urchin		74 74
18	A3 50c Starfish		1.00 1.00
19	A3 $1 Squid		2.00 2.00

Perf. 15x14

20	A3 $2 Dugong		4.00 4.00
21	A3 $5 Pink sponge		10.00 10.00
	Nos. 9-21 (13)		19.97 19.97

See Nos. 75-85.

Humpback Whale, World Wildlife Emblem — A4

1983, Sept. 21			**Perf. 14**
24	A4 20c shown		40 40
25	A4 20c Blue whale		40 40
26	A4 20c Fin whale		40 40
27	A4 20c Great sperm whale		40 40
a.	Block of 4, #24-27		1.60 1.60

Christmas — A5

Paintings by Charlie Gibbons, 1971.

1983, Oct.		**Litho.**	**Perf. 14½**
28	A5 20c First Child ceremony		40 40
29	A5 20c Spearfishing from Red Canoe		40 40
30	A5 20c Traditional feast at the Bai		40 40
31	A5 20c Taro gardening		40 40
32	A5 20c Spearfishing at New Moon		40 40
a.	Strip of 5, #28-32		2.00 2.00
	Nos. 28-32 (5)		2.00 2.00

Capt. Wilson's Voyage, Bicentennial — A7

1983, Dec. 14   **Perf. 14x15**
33	A6	20c Capt. Henry Wilson	40	40
34	A7	20c Approaching Pelew	40	40
35	A7	20c Englishman's Camp on Ulong	40	40
36	A6	20c Prince Lee Boo	40	40
37	A7	20c King Abba Thulle	40	40
38	A7	20c Mooring in Koror	40	40
39	A7	20c Village scene of Pelew Islands	40	40
40	A6	20c Ludee	40	40
a.		Block or strip of 8	3.20	3.20
		Nos. 33-40 (8)	3.20	3.20

Local Seashells — A8

Shell paintings (dorsal and ventral) by Deborah Dudley Max. Se-tenant.

1984, Mar. 15   **Litho.**   **Perf. 14**
41	A8	20c Triton trumpet, d.	40	40
42	A8	20c Horned helmet, d.	40	40
43	A8	20c Giant clam, d.	40	40
44	A8	20c Laciniate conch, d.	40	40
45	A8	20c Royal cloak scallop, d.	40	40
46	A8	20c Triton trumpet, v.	40	40
47	A8	20c Horned helmet, v.	40	40
48	A8	20c Giant clam, v.	40	40
49	A8	20c Laciniate conch, v.	40	40
50	A8	20c Royal cloak scallop, v.	40	40
		Nos. 41-50 (10)	4.00	4.00

Explorer Ships — A9

1984, June 19   **Litho.**   **Perf. 14**
51	A9	40c Oroolong, 1783	80	80
52	A9	40c Duff, 1797	80	80
53	A9	40c Peiho, 1908	80	80
54	A9	40c Albatross, 1885	80	80
a.		Block of 4, #51-54	3.25	3.25

UPU Congress.

Ausipex '84 A10

Fishing Methods. Nos. 55-58 se-tenant.

1984, Sept. 6   **Litho.**   **Perf. 14**
55	A10	20c Throw spear fishing	40	40
56	A10	20c Kite fishing	40	40
57	A10	20c Underwater spear fishing	40	40
58	A10	20c Net fishing	40	40
a.		Block of 4, #55-58	1.60	1.60

Christmas Flowers — A11

1984, Nov. 28   **Litho.**   **Perf. 14**
59	A11	20c Mountain Apple	40	40
60	A11	20c Beach Morning Glory	40	40
61	A11	20c Turmeric	40	40
62	A11	20c Plumeria	40	40
a.		Block of 4, #59-62	1.60	1.60

Audubon Bicentenary A12

1985, Feb. 6   **Litho.**   **Perf. 14**
63	A12	22c Shearwater chick	44	44
64	A12	22c Shearwater's head	44	44
65	A12	22c Shearwater in flight	44	44
66	A12	22c Shearwater swimming	44	44
a.		Block of 4, #63-66	1.80	1.80

See No. C5.

Canoes and Rafts — A13

1985, Mar. 27   **Litho.**
67	A13	22c Cargo canoe	44	44
68	A13	22c War canoe	44	44
69	A13	22c Bamboo raft	44	44
70	A13	22c Racing/sailing canoe	44	44
a.		Block of 4, #67-70	1.80	1.80

Marine Life Type of 1983

1985, June 11   **Litho.**   **Perf. 14½x14**
75	A3	14c Trumpet triton	28	28
a.		Bklt. pane of 10	2.80	
76	A3	22c Bumphead parrotfish	44	44
a.		Bklt. pane of 10	4.40	
b.		Bklt. pane of 10 (5 14c, 5 22c)	3.60	
77	A3	25c Soft coral, damsel fish	50	50
79	A3	33c Sea anemone, clownfish	66	66
80	A3	39c Green sea turtle	78	78
81	A3	44c Pacific sailfish	88	88
		Perf. 15x14		
85	A3	$10 Spinner dolphins	20.00	20.00
		Nos. 75-85 (7)	23.54	23.54

Intl. Youth Year — A14

IYY emblem and children of all nationalities joined in a circle.

1985, July 15   **Litho.**   **Perf. 14**
86	A14	44c multi	88	88
87	A14	44c multi	88	88
88	A14	44c multi	88	88
89	A14	44c multi	88	88
a.		Block of 4, #86-89	3.55	3.55

Nos. 86-89 printed se-tenant in a continuous design.

Christmas — A15

Island mothers and children.

1985, Oct. 21   **Litho.**   **Perf. 14**
90	A15	14c multi	28	28
91	A15	22c multi	44	44
92	A15	33c multi	66	66
93	A15	44c multi	88	88

Souvenir Sheet

Pan American Airways Martin M-130 China Clipper — A16

1985, Nov. 21   **Litho.**   **Perf. 14**
94	A16	$1 multi	2.00	2.00

1st Trans-Pacific Mail Flight, Nov. 22, 1935. No. 94 has multicolored decorative margin continuing the design and picturing the S.S. North Haven support ship at sea, the flight map and China Clipper emblem. Size: 96x70mm.
See Nos. C10-C13.

Return of Halley's Comet — A17

Fictitious local sightings.

1985, Dec. 21   **Litho.**   **Perf. 14**
95	A17	44c Kaeb canoe, 1758	88	88
96	A17	44c U.S.S. Vincennes, 1835	88	88
97	A17	44c S.M.S. Scharnhorst, 1910	88	88
98	A17	44c Yacht, 1986	88	88
a.		Block of 4, #95-98	3.75	3.75

Songbirds — A18

1986, Feb. 24   Litho.   Perf. 14
99 A18 44c Mangrove flycatcher   88   88
100 A18 44c Cardinal honeyeater   88   88
101 A18 44c Blue-faced parrotfinch   88   88
102 A18 44c Dusky and bridled white-eyes 88   88
  a.   Block of 4, #99-102   3.75 3.75

World of Sea and Reef — A19

1986, May 22   Litho.   Perf. 15x14
103   Sheet of 40   11.25
  a.   A19 14c, any single   28   28

AMERIPEX '86, Chicago, May 22-June 1

Seashells — A20

1986, Aug. 1   Litho.   Perf. 14
104 A20 22c Commercial trochus   44   44
105 A20 22c Marble cone   44   44
106 A20 22c Fluted giant clam   44   44
107 A20 22c Bullmouth helmet   44   44
108 A20 22c Golden cowrie   44   44
  a.   Strip of 5, #104-108   2.20 2.20
       Nos. 104-108 (5)   2.20 2.20

See Nos. 150-154

Intl. Peace Year — A21

1986, Sept. 19   Litho.
109 A21 22c Soldier's helmet   44   44
110 A21 22c Plane wreckage   44   44
111 A21 22c Woman playing guitar   44   44
112 A21 22c Airai vista   44   44
  a.   Block of 4, #109-112   1.80 1.80
       Nos. 109-112,C17 (5)   2.64 2.64

Reptiles — A22

1986, Oct. 28   Litho.   Perf. 14
113 A22 22c Gecko   44   44
114 A22 22c Emerald tree skink   44   44
115 A22 22c Estuarine crocodile   44   44
116 A22 22c Leatherback turtle   44   44
  a.   Block of 4, #113-116   1.80 1.80

Christmas — A23

Joy to the World, carol by Isaac Watts and Handel: No. 117, Girl playing guitar, boys, goat. No. 118, Girl carrying bouquet, boys singing. No. 119, Palauan mother and child. No. 120, Children, baskets of fruit. No. 121, Girl, fairy tern. Nos. 117-121 printed in a continuous design.

1986, Nov. 26   Litho.
117 A23 22c multi   44   44
118 A23 22c multi   44   44
119 A23 22c multi   44   44
120 A23 22c multi   44   44
121 A23 22c multi   44   44
  a.   Strip of 5, #117-121   2.20 2.20

Butterflies — A23a

1987, Jan. 5   Litho.   Perf. 14
121B A23a 44c Tangadik, soursop   88   88
121C A23a 44c Dira amartal, sweet orange 88   88
121D A23a 44c Ilhuochel, swamp cabbage   88   88
121E A23a 44c Bauosech, fig   88   88
  f.   Block of 4, #121B-121E   3.55 3.55

Fruit Bats — A24

1987, Feb. 23   Litho.
122 A24 44c In flight   88   88
123 A24 44c Hanging   88   88
124 A24 44c Eating   88   88
125 A24 44c Head   88   88
  a.   Block of 4, #122-125   3.55 3.55

Indigenous Flowers — A25

1987-88   Litho.   Perf. 14
126 A25 1c Ixora casei   5   5
127 A25 3c Lumnitzera littorea   6   6
128 A25 5c Sonneratia alba   10   10
129 A25 10c Tristellateria australasiae 20   20
130 A25 14c Bikkia palauensis   28   28
  a.   Bklt. pane of 10   2.80
131 A25 15c Limnophila aromatica   30   30
  a.   Bklt. pane of 10   3.00
132 A25 22c Bruguiera gymnorhiza   44   44
  a.   Bklt. pane of 10   4.40
  b.   Bklt. pane of 10 (5 14c, 5 22c) 3.60
133 A25 25c Fragraea ksid   50   50
  a.   Bklt. pane of 10   3.00
  b.   Bklt. pane of 10 (5 15c, 5 25c) 5.00
137 A25 36c Ophiorrhiza palauensis   72   72
138 A25 39c Cerbera manghas   78   78
140 A25 44c Sandera indica   88   88
141 A25 45c Maesa canfieldiae   90   90
142 A25 50c Dolichandrone spathacea 1.00 1.00
143 A25 $1 Barringtonia racemosa   2.00 2.00
144 A25 $2 Nepenthes mirabilis   4.00 4.00
145 A25 $5 Dendrobium palawense   10.00 10.00
145A A25 $10 Bouquet   20.00 20.00
       Nos. 126-145A (17)   42.21 42.21

Issue dates: Nos. 130a, 132a, 132b, Mar. 31, 1987. 15c, 25c, 36c, 45c, July 1, 1988. Nos. 131a, 133a, 133b, July 5, 1988. $10, Mar. 17, 1988. Others, Mar. 12, 1987.

CAPEX '87 A26

1987, June 15   Litho.   Perf. 14
146 A26 22c Babeldaob Is.   44   44
147 A26 22c Floating Garden Isls.   44   44
148 A26 22c Rock Is.   44   44
149 A26 22c Koror   44   44
  a.   Block of 4, Nos. 146-149   1.80 1.80

Seashells Type of 1986

1987, Aug. 25   Litho.   Perf. 14
150 A20 22c Black-striped triton   44   44
151 A20 22c Tapestry turban   44   44
152 A20 22c Adusta murex   44   44
153 A20 22c Little fox miter   44   44
154 A20 22c Cardinal miter   44   44
  a.   Strip of 5, Nos. 150-154   2.25 2.25
       Nos. 150-154 (5)   2.20 2.20

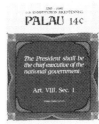

U.S. Constitution Bicentennial — A27

Excerpts from Articles of the Palau and U.S. Constitutions and Seals.

1987, Sept. 17   Litho.   Perf. 14
155 A27 14c Art. VIII, Sec. 1, Palau   28   28
156 A27 14c Presidential seals   28   28
157 A27 14c Art. II, Sec. 1, U.S.   28   28
  a.   Triptych + label, Nos. 155-157 85 85
158 A27 22c Art. IX, Sec. 1, Palau   44   44
159 A27 22c Legislative seals   44   44
160 A27 22c Art. I, Sec. 1, U.S.   44   44
  a.   Triptych + label, Nos. 158-160 1.40 1.40
161 A27 44c Art X, Sec. 1, Palau   88   88
162 A27 44c Supreme Court seals   88   88

163	A27 44c Art. III, Sec. 1, U.S.	88	88
a.	Triptych + label, Nos. 161-163	2.75	2.75
	Nos. 155-163 (9)	4.80	4.80

Triptychs printed se-tenant with inscribed label picturing national flags.

Japanese Links to Palau — A28

Japanese stamps, period cancellations and installations: 14c, No. 257 and 1937 Datsun sedan used as mobile post office, near Ngerchelechuus Mountain. 22c, No. 347 and phosphate mine at Angaur. 33c, No. B1 and Japan Airways DC-2 over stone monuments at Badrulchau. 44c, No. 201 and Japanese post office, Koror. $1, Aviator's Grave, Japanese Cemetary, Peleliu, vert.

1987, Oct. 16		Litho.	Perf. 14x13½	
164	A28 14c multi		28	28
165	A28 22c multi		44	44
166	A28 33c multi		66	66
167	A28 44c multi		88	88

Souvenir Sheet
Perf. 13½x14

168	A28 $1 multi	2.00	2.00

No. 168 has multicolored margin continuing the design and picturing Japan Nos. 547 and B7. Size: 81x94mm.

Christmas — A30

Verses from carol "I Saw Three Ships," Biblical characters, landscape and Palauans in outrigger canoes.

1987, Nov. 24		Litho.	Perf. 14	
173	A30 22c I saw...		44	44
174	A30 22c And what was...		44	44
175	A30 22c 'Twas Joseph...		44	44
176	A30 22c Saint Michael...		44	44
177	A30 22c And all the bells...		44	44
a.	Strip of 5, Nos. 173-177		2.20	2.20

Symbiotic Marine
Species — A31

Designs: No. 178, Snapping shrimp, goby. No. 179, Mauve vase sponge, sponge crab. No. 180, Pope's damselfish, cleaner wrasse. No. 181, Clown anemone fish, sea anemone. No. 182, Four-color nudibranch, banded coral shrimp.

1987, Dec. 15			
178	A31 22c multi	44	44
179	A31 22c multi	44	44
180	A31 22c multi	44	44

181	A31 22c multi	44	44
182	A31 22c multi	44	44
a.	Strip of 5, Nos. 178-182	2.20	2.20

Butterflies and Flowers Type of 1987

Designs: No. 183, Dannaus plexippus, Tournefotia argentia. No. 184, Papilio machaon, Citrus reticulata. No. 185, Captopsilia, Crataeva speciosa. No. 186, Colias philodice, Crataeva speciosa.

1988, Jan. 25			
183	A23a 44c multi	88	88
184	A23a 44c multi	88	88
185	A23a 44c multi	88	88
186	A23a 44c multi	88	88
a.	Block of 4, Nos. 183-186	3.55	3.55

Ground-dwelling
Birds — A32

1988, Feb. 29		Litho.	Perf. 14	
187	A32 44c Whimbrel		88	88
188	A32 44c Yellow Bittern		88	88
189	A32 44c Rufous night-heron		88	88
190	A32 44c Banded rail		88	88
a.	Block of 4, Nos. 187-190		3.55	3.55

Seashells Type of 1986

1988, May 11		Litho.	Perf. 14	
191	A20 25c Striped engina		50	50
192	A20 25c Ivory cone		50	50
193	A20 25c Plaited miter		50	50
194	A20 25c Episcopal miter		50	50
195	A20 25c Isabelle cowrie		50	50
a.	Strip of 5, Nos. 191-195		2.50	2.50
	Nos. 191-195 (5)		2.50	2.50

Souvenir Sheet

Postal
Independence,
5th
Anniv. — A33

Designs: a. Kaeb (pre-European outrigger sailboat). b. Spanish colonial cruiser. c. German colonial cruiser SMS Cormoran, circa 1885. d. Japanese mailbox, World War II machine gun, Koror museum. e. U.S. Trust Territory ship, Malakal Harbor. f. Koror post office.

1988, June 8		Litho.	Perf. 14	
196		Souv. sheet of 6	3.00	3.00
a.-f.	A33 25c multi		50	50

FINLANDIA '88. No. 196 has multicolored inscribed margin picturing Palau flag and exhibition emblem. Size: 150x97mm.

Souvenir Sheet

U.S.
Possessions
Philatelic Soc.,
10th
Anniv. — A34

Designs: a. "Collect Palau Stamps," original artwork for No. 196f and head of a man. b. Society emblem. c. Nos. 1-4. d. China Clipper original artwork and covers. f. Girl at show cancel booth.

1988, Aug. 26		Litho.	Perf. 14	
197	A34	Sheet of 6	5.40	5.40
a.-f.	45c any single		90	90

PRAGA '88. No. 197 has multicolored margin picturing exhibition and FIP emblems. Size:149x97mm.

AIR POST STAMPS

White-tailed
Tropicbird
AP1

1984, June 12		Litho.	Perf. 14	
C1	AP1 40c shown		80	80
C2	AP1 40c Fairy tern		80	80
C3	AP1 40c Black noddy		80	80
C4	AP1 40c Black-naped tern		80	80
a.	Block of 4, #C1-C4		3.25	3.25

Audubon Type of 1985

1985, Feb. 6		Litho.	Perf. 14	
C5	A12 44c Audubon's Shearwater		88	88

Palau-Germany Political, Economic & Cultural
Exchange Cent. — AP2

Germany Nos. 40, 65, Caroline Islands Nos. 19, 13 and: No. C6, German flag-raising at Palau, 1885. No. C7, Early German trading post in Angaur. No. C8, Abai architecture recorded by Prof. & Frau Kramer, 1908-1910. No. C9, S.M.S. Cormoran.

1985, Sept. 19		Litho.	Perf. 14x13½	
C6	AP2 44c multi		88	88
C7	AP2 44c multi		88	88
C8	AP2 44c multi		88	88
C9	AP2 44c multi		88	88
a.	Block of 4, #C6-C9		3.55	3.55

Trans-Pacific Airmail Anniv. Type of 1985

Aircraft: No. C10, 1951 Trans-Ocean Airways PBY-5A Catalina Amphibian. No. C11, 1968 Air Micronesia DC-6B Super Cloudmaster. No. C12, 1960 Trust Territory Airline SA-16 Albatross. No. C13, 1967 Pan American Douglas DC-4.

1985, Nov. 21		Litho.	Perf. 14	
C10	A16 44c multi		88	88
C11	A16 44c multi		88	88
C12	A16 44c multi		88	88
C13	A16 44c multi		88	88
a.	Block of 4, #C10-C13		3.75	3.75

Haruo I.
Remeliik
(1933-1985),
1st President
AP3

Designs: No. C14, Presidential seal, excerpt from 1st inaugural address. No. C15, War canoe, address excerpt, diff. No. C16, Remeliik, U.S. Pres. Reagan, excerpt from Reagan's speech, Pacific Basin Conference, Guam, 1984.

1986, June 30		Litho.	Perf. 14	
C14	AP3 44c multi		88	88
C15	AP3 44c multi		88	88

C16 AP3 44c multi 88 88
   a. Strip of 3, #C14-C16 .... 2.65 2.65

Intl. Peace Year, Statue of
Liberty Cent. — AP4

1986, Sept. 19   **Litho.**
C17 AP4 44c multi 88 88

SEMI-POSTAL STAMPS

Olympic
Sports — SP1

1988, Aug. 8   **Litho.**   *Perf. 14*
B1 SP1 25c +5c Baseball glove, player 60 60
B2 SP1 25c +5c Running shoe, athlete 60 60
   a. Pair, Nos. B1-B2 .... 1.20 1.20
B3 SP1 45c +5c Goggles, swimmer 1.00 1.00
B4 SP1 45c +5c Gold medal, diver 1.00 1.00
   a. Pair, Nos. B3-B4 .... 2.00 2.00

ENVELOPES

Marine Life Type of 1983
1985, Feb. 14   **Litho.**
U1 A3 22c Parrotfish, entire 55 55

Paintings Type of 1983 without Inscription for
Christmas
1985, Feb. 14   **Litho.**
U2 A5 22c Spear Fishing from Red Canoe, entire 55 55

AIR LETTER SHEETS

Bird Type of 1983
Letter sheet for foreign postage.
1985, Feb. 14   **Litho.**
UC1 A2 36c multi, entire 72 72

Designs of Nos. C1-C4 (without inscriptions) and text on
reverse folding area.

POSTAL CARDS

Marine Life Type of 1983
1985, Feb. 14   **Litho.**
UX1 A3 14c Giant Clam 28 28

PHILIPPINES

Issued under U.S. Administration.

Following the American occupation of the Philippines, May 1, 1898, after Admiral Dewey's fleet entered Manila Bay, an order was issued by the U. S. Postmaster General (No. 201, May 24, 1898) establishing postal facilities with rates similar to the domestic rates.

Military postal stations were established as branch post offices, each such station being placed within the jurisdiction of the nearest regular post office. Supplies were issued to these military stations through the regular post office of which they were branches.

Several post office clerks were sent to the Philippines and the San Francisco post office was made the nearest regular office for the early Philippine mail and the postmarks of the period point out this fact.

U.S. stamps overprinted "PHILIPPINES" were placed on sale in Manila June 30, 1899. Regular U.S. stamps had been in use from early March, and at the Manila post office Spanish stamps were also acceptable.

The first regular post office was established at Cavite on July 30, 1898, as a branch of the San Francisco post office. The first cancellation was a dated handstamp with "PHILIPPINE STATION" and "SAN FRANCISCO, CAL."

On May 1, 1899, the entire Philippine postal service was separated from San Francisco and numerous varieties of postmarks resulted. Many of the early used stamps show postmarks and cancellations of the Military Station, Camp or R.P.O. types, together with "Killers" of the types employed in the U.S. at the time.

The Philippines became a commonwealth of the United States on November 15, 1935, the High Commissioner of the United States taking office on the same day. The official name of the government was "Commonwealth of the Philippines" as provided by Article 17 of the Constitution. Upon the final and complete withdrawal of sovereignty of the United States and the proclamation of Philippine independence on July 4, 1946, the Commonwealth of the Philippines became the "Republic of the Philippines."

Numbers in parenthesis indicate quantities issued.

Authority for dates of issue, stamps from 1899 to 1911, and quantities issued-"The Postal Issues of the Philippines," by F. L. Palmer (New York, 1912).

100 CENTS = 1 DOLLAR
100 CENTAVOS = 1 PESO (1906)

Regular Issues of the United States Overprinted in Black

Printed and overprinted by the U.S. Bureau of Engraving and Printing.

1899, June 30   **Unwmk.**   **Perf. 12**

On U.S. Stamp No. 260

212	A96	50c orange	425.00	250.00
		On cover		—
		Block of four	2,000.	
		Margin strip of 3, Impt. & P#	2,000.	
		Margin block of 6, Impt. & P#	6,000.	

On U.S. Stamps

Nos. 279a, 279d, 267, 268, 281a, 282C, 283, 284, 275 and 275a.

Wmk. Double-lined USPS (191)

213	A87	1c yellow green *(5,500,000)*	3.75	90
		On cover		15.00
		Block of four	17.00	6.00
		Margin strip of 3, Impt. & P#	30.00	
		Margin block of 6, Impt. & P#	200.00	
214	A88	2c orange red, type III *(6,970,000)*	1.75	60
		On cover		12.50
		Block of four	7.50	5.00
		Margin strip of 3, Impt. & P#	22.50	
		Margin block of 6, Impt. & P#	150.00	
a.		2c carmine, type III	2.50	1.00
b.		Booklet pane of six ('00)	325.00	175.00
215	A89	3c purple *(673,814)*	6.50	1.75
		On cover		45.00
		Block of four	30.00	20.00
		Margin strip of 3, Impt. & P#	65.00	
		Margin block of 6, Impt. & P#	500.00	
216	A91	5c blue *(1,700,000)*	6.50	1.50
		On cover		30.00
		Block of four	30.00	15.00
		Margin strip of 3, Impt. & P#	60.00	
		Margin block of 6, Impt. & P#	425.00	
a.		Inverted overprint		3,000.
217	A94	10c brown, type I *(750,000)+*	20.00	5.00
		On cover		90.00
		Block of four	100.00	65.00
		Margin strip of 3, Impt. & P#	100.00	
		Margin block of 6, Impt. & P#	700.00	

(+ Quantity includes Nos. 217, 217A)

217A	A94	10c orange brown, type II	250.00	50.00
		On cover		250.00
		Block of four	1,100.	350.00
		Margin strip of 3, Impt. & P#	1,100.	
		Margin block of 6, Impt. & P#	3,000.	
218	A95	15c olive green *(200,000)*	35.00	8.75
		On cover		175.00
		Block of four	160.00	100.00
		Margin strip of 3, Impt. & P#	160.00	
		Margin block of 6, Impt. & P#	650.00	
a.		15c light olive green	45.00	12.50
219	A96	50c orange *(50,000)+*	125.00	50.00
		On cover		350.00
		Block of four	550.00	300.00
		Margin strip of 3, Impt. & P#	550.00	
		Margin block of 6, Impt. & P#	1,500.	
a.		50 red orange	250.00	

(+ Quantity includes Nos. 212, 219, 219a)

Special Printing

In 1899 a special printing of Nos. 213 to 217, 218, 219 and J1 to J5 was made for display at the Paris Exposition. All but a few copies were destroyed. Most of the existing copies bear the handstamp "Special Surcharge" on the back. Price each $350.

1901, Aug. 30   **Regular Issue**

Same Overprint in Black On U.S. Stamps Nos. 280b, 282 and 272

220	A90	4c orange brown *(404,907)*	22.50	6.00
		On cover		75.00
		Block of four	100.00	65.00

		Margin strip of 3, Impt. & P#	100.00	
		Margin block of 6, Impt. & P#	600.00	
221	A92	6c lake *(223,465)*	27.50	8.00
		On cover		100.00
		Block of four	125.00	75.00
		Margin strip of 3, Impt. & P#	125.00	
		Margin block of 6, Impt. & P#	800.00	
222	A93	8c violet brown *(248,000)*	30.00	8.00
		On cover		75.00
		Block of four	135.00	80.00
		Margin strip of 3, Impt. & P#	135.00	
		Margin block of 6, Impt. & P#	900.00	

Same Overprint in Red On U.S. Stamps Nos. 276, 276A, 277a and 278

223	A97	$1 black, type I *(3,000)+*	475.00	275.00
		On cover		1,000.
		Block of four	2,250.	
		Margin strip of 3, Impt. & P#	2,250.	
		Margin block of 6, Impt. & P#	—	
		Horiz. pair, types I & II	4,000.	

(+ Quantity includes Nos. 223, 223A)

223A	A97	$1 black, type II	2,750.	1,350.
		On cover		—
		Block of four	12,000.	—
		Margin strip of 3, Impt. & P#, one stamp No. 223	11,000.	
		Margin block of 6, Impt. & P#, two stamps No. 223	—	
224	A98	$2 dark blue *(1800)*	700.00	350.00
		On cover		3,500.
		Block of four	3,250.	
		Margin strip of 3, Impt. & P#	3,250.	
		Margin block of 6, Impt. & P#	—	
225	A99	$5 dark green *(782)*	1,650.	1,100.
		On cover		3,250.
		Block of four	7,500.	
		Margin strip of 3, Impt. & P#	7,500.	
		Margin block of 6, Impt. & P#	—	

Special Printing

Special printings exist of Nos. 227, 221, 223-225, made from defaced plates. These were made for display at the St. Louis Exposition. All but a few copies were destroyed. Most of the existing copies have the handstamp "Special Printing" on the back. Price: Nos. 227, 221, each $400; No. 223, $850; No. 224, $1,200; No. 225, $2,000.

1903-04   **Regular Issue**

Same Overprint in Black On U.S. Stamps Nos. 300 to 310 and shades

226	A115	1c blue green *(9,631,172)*	4.50	50
		On cover		12.50
		Block of four	20.00	3.00
		Margin strip of 3, Impt. & P#	22.50	
		Margin block of 6, Impt. & P#	175.00	
227	A116	2c carmine *(850,000)*	7.50	1.75
		On cover		15.00
		Block of four	32.50	10.00
		Margin strip of 3, Impt. & P#	35.00	
		Margin block of 6, Impt. & P#	250.00	
228	A117	3c bright violet *(14,500)*	85.00	20.00
		On cover		85.00
		Block of four	375.00	110.00
		Margin strip of 3, Impt. & P#	375.00	
		Margin block of 6, Impt. & P#	1,000.	
229	A118	4c brown *(13,000)*	90.00	30.00
		On cover		60.00
		Block of four	400.00	150.00
		Margin strip of 3, Impt. & P#	400.00	
		Margin block of 6, Impt. & P#	1,100.	
a.		4c orange brown	90.00	25.00
230	A119	5c blue *(1,211,844)*	12.00	1.25
		On cover		35.00
		Block of four	50.00	7.00
		Margin strip of 3, Impt. & P#	50.00	
		Margin block of 6, Impt. & P#	325.00	
231	A120	6c brownish lake *(11,500)*	95.00	25.00
		On cover		85.00
		Block of four	425.00	200.00
		Margin strip of 3, Impt. & P#	425.00	
		Margin block of 6, Impt. & P#	1,200.	

232	A121	8c violet black *(49,033)*	40.00	15.00
		On cover		85.00
		Block of four	200.00	120.00
		Margin strip of 3, Impt. & P#	200.00	
		Margin block of 6, Impt. & P#	950.00	
233	A122	10c pale red brown *(300,179)*	22.50	3.50
		On cover		40.00
		Block of four	110.00	30.00

		Margin strip of 3, Impt. & P#	110.00	
		Margin block of 6, Impt. & P#	750.00	
a.		10c red brown	27.50	5.00
b.		Pair, one without overprint		1,350.
234	A123	13c purple black (91,341)	35.00	17.50
a.		13c brown violet	35.00	17.50
		On cover		80.00
		Block of four	175.00	100.00
		Margin strip of 3, Impt. & P#	175.00	
		Margin block of 6, Impt. & P#	1,000.	
235	A124	15c olive green (183,965)	60.00	13.00
		On cover		150.00
		Block of four	275.00	85.00
		Margin strip of 3, Impt. & P#	275.00	
		Margin block of 6, Impt. & P#	1,100.	
236	A125	50c olive green (57,641)	175.00	55.00
		On cover		350.00
		Block of four	800.00	400.00
		Margin strip of 3, Impt. & P#	800.00	
		Margin block of 6, Impt. & P#	3,750.	

Same Overprint in Red On U. S. Stamps Nos. 311, 312 and 313

237	A126	$1 black (5617)	650.00	300.00
		On cover		600.00
		Block of four	2,750.	1,850.
		Margin strip of 3, Impt. & P#	2,750.	
		Margin block of 6, Impt. & P#	9,000.	
238	A127	$2 dark blue (695)	2,000.	1,200.
		Block of four	9,000.	—
		Margin strip of 3, Impt. & P#	9,000.	
		Margin block of 6, Impt. & P#	15,000.	
239	A128	$5 dark green (746)	2,400.	1,400.
		Block of four	10,500.	—
		Margin strip of 3, Impt. & P#	10,500.	
		Margin block of 6, Impt. & P#	—	

Same Overprint in Black On U.S. Stamp No. 319

240	A129	2c carmine (862,245)	5.50	2.50
		On cover		5.00
		Block of four	24.00	12.50
		Margin strip of 3, Impt. & P#	40.00	
		Margin block of 6, Impt. & P#	250.00	
a.		Booklet pane of six	1,200.	
b.		scarlet	6.50	2.75

Dates of issue:
Sept. 20, 1903, Nos. 226, 227, 236.
Jan. 4, 1904, Nos. 230, 234, 235, 237.
Nov. 1, 1904, Nos. 228, 229, 231, 232, 233, 238, 239, 240.
Nos. 212 to 240 became obsolete on Sept. 8, 1906, the remainders being destroyed.

Special Printing

Two sets of special printings exist of the 1903-04 issue. The first consists of Nos. 226, 230, 234, 235, 236, 237 and 240. These were made for display at the St. Louis Exposition. All but a few copies were destroyed. Most of the existing copies have the handstamp "Special Surcharge" on the back. Price: No. 237, $750; others $400; J6; J7, $450:

In 1907 the entire set Nos. 226, 228 to 240, J1 to J7 were specially printed for the Bureau of Insular Affairs on very white paper. They are difficult to distinguish from the ordinary stamps except the Special Delivery stamp which is on U.S. No. E6 (see Philippines No. E2A). Price: No. 237, $750; No. 238, $1500; No. 239, $2000; others, $350

Regular Issue

José Rizal — A40

Arms of City of
Manila — A41

Printed by the U.S. Bureau of Engraving and Printing.
Plates of 400 subjects in four panes of 100 each.

Booklet panes Nos. 240a, 241b, 242b, 261a, 262b, 276a, 277a, 285a, 286a, 290e, 291b and 292c were made from plates of 180 subjects.

No. 214b came from plates of 360 subjects.

Wmk. Double-lined PIPS (191)

1906, Sept. 8   *Perf. 12*

241	A40	2c deep green (51,125,010)	30	6
		Block of four	1.25	30
a.		2c yellow green ('10)	50	6
		Double transfer		50.00
b.		Booklet pane of six	225.00	
242	A40	4c carmine (McKinley) (14,150,030)	40	6
		Block of four	1.75	25
a.		4c carmine lake ('10)	75	6
b.		Booklet pane of six	225.00	
243	A40	6c violet (Fernando Magellan) (1,980,000)	1.25	15
		Block of four	5.50	70
244	A40	8c brown (Miguel Lopez de Legaspi) (770,000)	2.25	75
		Block of four	10.00	5.00
245	A40	10c blue (Gen. Henry W. Lawton) (5,550,000)	1.65	10
		Dark blue	1.65	10
		Block of four	7.00	45
246	A40	12c brown lake (Lincoln) (670,000)	5.00	2.25
		Block of four	23.00	15.00
247	A40	16c violet black (Adm. William T. Sampson) (1,300,000)	3.25	25
		Block of four	13.50	1.75
248	A40	20c orange brown (Washington) (2,100,000)	3.75	40
		Block of four	17.00	2.50
249	A40	26c violet brown (Francisco Carriedo) (480,000)	6.00	2.50
		Block of four	27.50	16.00
250	A40	30c olive green (Franklin) (1,256,000)	4.50	1.60
		Block of four	19.00	8.50
251	A41	1p orange (200,000)	25.00	11.00
		Block of four	105.00	60.00
252	A41	2p black (100,000)	35.00	1.50
		Block of four	150.00	12.50
253	A41	4p dark blue (10,000)	100.00	17.50
		Block of four	450.00	85.00
254	A41	10p dark green (6,000)	200.00	85.00
		Block of four	950.00	400.00

1909

Change of Colors

255	A40	12c red orange (300,000)	8.00	3.00
		Block of four	37.50	14.00
256	A40	16c olive green (500,000)	2.00	50
		Block of four	9.00	2.25
257	A40	20c yellow (800,000)	7.50	1.50
		Block of four	32.50	9.00
258	A40	26c blue green	1.50	80
		Block of four	6.50	4.50
259	A40	30c ultramarine (600,000)	10.00	4.00
		Block of four	45.00	22.50
260	A41	1p pale violet (100,000)	30.00	6.00
		Block of four	150.00	40.00
260A	A41	2p violet brown (50,000)	80.00	3.00
		Block of four	375.00	20.00

1911   Wmk. Single-lined PIPS (190)   *Perf. 12*

261	A40	2c green	60	10
		Block of four	2.75	50
a.		Booklet pane of six	200.00	
262	A40	4c carmine lake	3.00	12
		Block of four	13.00	55
a.		4c carmine	—	—
b.		Booklet pane of six	200.00	
263	A40	6c deep violet	1.75	10
		Block of four	8.00	45
264	A40	8c brown	8.00	50
		Block of four	35.00	2.25
265	A40	10c blue	3.00	10
		Block of four	14.00	50
266	A40	12c orange	2.00	50

267	A40	16c olive green	2.25	20
		Block of four	9.00	2.50
		Pale olive green	2.25	20
		Block of four	10.00	1.00
268	A40	20c yellow	2.00	15
		Block of four	8.50	65
a.		20c orange	2.00	15
269	A40	26c blue green	2.75	30
		Block of four	11.00	1.50
270	A40	30c ultramarine	3.25	50
		Block of four	15.00	2.75
271	A41	1p pale violet	20.00	50
		Block of four	85.00	3.00
272	A41	2p violet brown	25.00	1.00
		Block of four	110.00	5.50
273	A41	4p deep blue	650.00	60.00
		Block of four	3,000.	325.00
274	A41	10p deep green	200.00	22.50
		Block of four	950.00	110.00

1914

275	A40	30c gray	10.00	65
		Block of four	45.00	3.75

1914   *Perf. 10*

276	A40	2c green	1.50	12
		Block of four	6.25	55
a.		Booklet pane of six	200.00	
277	A40	4c carmine	1.50	15
		Block of four	6.25	65
a.		Booklet pane of six	200.00	
278	A40	6c light violet	35.00	15.00
		Block of four	150.00	85.00
a.		6c deep violet	37.50	7.00
279	A40	8c brown	35.00	12.50
		Block of four	150.00	70.00
280	A40	10c dark blue	22.50	25
		Block of four	95.00	1.25
281	A40	16c olive green	70.00	5.00
		Block of four	300.00	30.00
282	A40	20c orange	20.00	1.00
		Block of four	90.00	6.00
283	A40	30c gray	50.00	3.50
		Block of four	225.00	20.00
284	A41	1p pale violet	110.00	4.00
		Block of four	475.00	22.50

1918   *Perf. 11*

285	A40	2c green	20.00	5.00
		Block of four	85.00	22.50
a.		Booklet pane of six	600.00	
286	A40	4c carmine	27.50	3.00
		Block of four	125.00	15.00
a.		Booklet pane of six	600.00	
287	A40	6c deep violet	37.50	2.00
		Block of four	150.00	10.00
287A	A40	8c light brown	225.00	40.00
		Block of four	925.00	250.00
288	A40	10c dark blue	50.00	1.75
		Block of four	210.00	10.00
289	A40	16c olive green	100.00	8.00
		Block of four	425.00	35.00
289A	A40	20c orange	55.00	10.00
		Block of four	235.00	50.00
289C	A40	30c gray	50.00	17.50
		Block of four	210.00	85.00
289D	A41	1p pale violet	60.00	15.00
		Block of four	250.00	85.00

1917   Unwmk.   *Perf. 11*

290	A40	2c yellow green	10	5
		Block of four	45	20
a.		2c dark green	12	5
		Green	15	5
		Double transfer	—	
b.		Vert. pair, imperf. horiz.	1,000.	
c.		Horiz. pair, imperf. between	1,200.	—
d.		Vertical pair, imperf. btwn.	1,850.	
e.		Booklet pane of six	25.00	
291	A40	4c carmine	10	5
		Block of four	45	25
a.		4c light rose	25	5
b.		Booklet pane of six	17.50	—
292	A40	6c deep violet	30	8
		Block of four	1.25	45
a.		6c lilac	40	8
b.		6c red violet	40	10
c.		Booklet pane of six	250.00	
293	A40	8c yellow brown	20	12
		Block of four	90	50
a.		8c orange brown	20	12
294	A40	10c deep blue	20	8
		Block of four	85	35
295	A40	12c red orange	40	15
		Block of four	1.75	75
296	A40	16c light olive green	50.00	25
		Block of four	250.00	95
a.		16c olive bister	50.00	50
297	A40	20c orange yellow	35	10
		Block of four	1.50	45
298	A40	26c green	55	25
		Block of four	2.50	2.75
a.		26c blue green	70	40
299	A40	30c gray	50	10
		Block of four	2.20	50
		Dark gray	50	10
300	A41	1p pale violet	32.50	1.25
		Block of four	135.00	5.50
a.		1p red lilac	32.50	1.25
b.		1p pale rose lilac	32.50	1.50
301	A41	2p violet brown	30.00	75
		Block of four	125.00	3.50
302	A41	4p blue	21.00	50
		Block of four	87.50	2.25
a.		4p dark blue	21.00	50

1923-26

303	A40	16c olive bister *(Adm. George Dewey)*	75	20
		Block of four	3.25	90
a.		16c olive green	1.35	20
304	A41	10p deep green ('26)	60.00	8.00
		Block of four	250.00	35.00

Legislative Palace Issue

Issued to commemorate the opening of the Legislative Palace.

Legislative Palace — A42

Printed by the Philippine Bureau of Printing.

1926, Dec. 20		**Unwmk.**		**Perf. 12**
319	A42	2c green & black *(502,550)*	50	30
		First day cover		5.00
		Block of four	3.50	1.50
a.		Horiz. pair, imperf. between	275.00	
b.		Vert. pair, imperf. between	425.00	
320	A42	4c carmine & black *(304,400)*	50	40
		First day cover		5.00
		Block of four	2.25	1.75
a.		Horiz. pair, imperf. between	275.00	
b.		Vert. pair, imperf. between	350.00	
321	A42	16c olive green & black *(203,750)*	1.00	85
		First day cover		15.00
		Block of four	5.00	4.00
a.		Horiz. pair, imperf. between	325.00	
b.		Vert. pair, imperf. between	425.00	
c.		Double impression of center	550.00	
322	A42	18c light brown & black *(103,950)*	1.25	75
		First day cover		15.00
		Block of four	5.50	3.50
a.		Double impression of center *(150)*	550.00	
b.		Vertical pair, imperf. between	425.00	
323	A42	20c orange & black *(103,450)*	1.75	1.25
		Block of four	7.50	6.00
a.		20c orange & brown *(100)*	400.00	—
b.		Imperf. (pair), orange & black *(50)*	450.00	450.00
c.		Imperf. (pair), orange & brown *(100)*	375.00	
d.		Vert. pair, imperf. between	425.00	
324	A42	24c gray & black *(103,350)*	1.50	1.00
		Block of four	6.50	4.50
a.		Vert. pair, imperf. between	425.00	
325	A42	1p rose lilac & black *(11,050)*	70.00	35.00
		Block of four	300.00	200.00
a.		Vert. pair, imperf. between	475.00	
		First day cover, #319-325		125.00

Coil Stamp
Rizal Type of 1906

Printed by the U.S. Bureau of Engraving and Printing.

1928		**Unwmk.**		**Perf. 11 Vertically**
326	A40	2c green	8.50	*10.00*
		Pair	20.00	*25.00*
		Line pair	60.00	

Types of 1906-1923

1925-31		**Unwmk.**		**Imperf.**

Two issues of imperforate stamps were made, in 1925 and in 1931. They differ in shade.

340	A40	2c yellow green ('31)	12	12
		Block of four	50	50
		green	50	—
341	A40	4c carmine rose ('31)	20	20
		Block of four	80	80
		carmine	75	
342	A40	6c violet ('31)	2.00	2.00
		Block of four	8.50	8.50
		deep violet	8.00	
343	A40	8c brown ('31)	1.75	1.75
		Block of four	7.50	7.50
		yellow brown	6.00	
344	A40	10c blue ('31)	2.00	2.00
		Block of four	8.00	8.00
		deep blue	8.50	—
345	A40	12c deep orange ('31)	3.00	3.00
		Block of four	12.50	12.50
		red orange	10.00	—
346	A40	16c olive green *(Dewey)* ('31)	2.25	

		Block of four bister green	9.50	9.50
			8.50	—
347	A40	20c orange yellow ('31)	2.25	2.25
		Block of four	9.50	9.50
		yellow	8.50	—
348	A40	26c green ('31)	2.25	2.25
		Block of four	9.50	9.50
		blue green	8.50	—
349	A40	30c light gray ('31)	2.50	2.50
		Block of four	10.50	10.50
		gray	8.50	—
350	A41	1p light violet ('31)	8.00	8.00
		Block of four	33.00	33.00
		violet	35.00	—
351	A41	2p brown violet ('31)	20.00	20.00
		Block of four	85.00	85.00
		violet brown	85.00	—
352	A41	4p blue ('31)	60.00	60.00
		Block of four	250.00	—
		deep blue *(200)*	300.00	—
353	A41	10p green ('31)	175.00	175.00
		Block of four	725.00	—
		deep green *(200)*	375.00	—

Mount Mayon, Luzon — A43

Post Office, Manila — A44

Pier No. 7, Manila Bay — A45

Vernal Falls, Yosemite Park, California (See Footnote) — A46

Rice Planting — A47

Rice Terraces — A48

Baguio Zigzag — A49

1932, May 3		**Unwmk.**		**Perf. 11**
354	A43	2c yellow green	75	35
		First day cover		3.00
		Block of four	3.25	1.50
355	A44	4c rose carmine	50	35
		First day cover		3.00
		Block of four	2.25	1.75
356	A45	12c orange	75	75
		First day cover		10.00
		Block of four	3.50	3.25
357	A46	18c red orange	25.00	12.50
		First day cover		20.00
		Block of four	100.00	50.00
358	A47	20c yellow	1.00	80
		First day cover		10.00
		Block of four	4.00	3.50
359	A48	24c deep violet	1.50	1.00
		First day cover		10.00
		Block of four	6.00	5.50
360	A49	32c olive brown	1.50	1.15
		First day cover		10.00
		Block of four	6.50	5.00
		First day cover, #354-360		75.00

The 18c vignette was intended to show Pagsanjan Falls in Laguna, central Luzon, and is so labeled. Through error the stamp pictures Vernal Falls in Yosemite National Park, California.

Nos. 302, 302a Surcharged in Orange or Red

1932				
368	A41	1p on 4p blue (O)	2.50	50
		On cover		70
		Block of four	10.00	2.50
a.		1p on 4p dark blue (O)	3.50	1.50
369	A41	2p on 4p dark blue (R)	4.50	1.00
		On cover		1.25
		Block of four	17.00	4.50
a.		2p on 4p blue (R)	4.50	1.00

Far Eastern Championship
Issued in commemoration of the Tenth Far Eastern Championship Games.

Baseball Players — A50

Tennis Player — A51

Basketball Players — A52

Printed by the Philippine Bureau of Printing.

1934, Apr. 14		Unwmk.	Perf. 11½	
380	A50	2c yellow brown	20	20
		brown	20	20
		First day cover		1.50
		"T" of "Eastern" malformed	2.50	2.00
381	A51	6c ultramarine	40	35
		pale ultramarine	40	35
		First day cover		2.50
a.		Vertical pair, imperf. between	900.00	
382	A52	16c violet brown	90	90
		dark violet	90	90
		First day cover		3.50
a.		Imperf. horizontally, pair	900.00	

José Rizal — A53

Woman and Carabao — A54

La Filipina — A55

Pearl Fishing — A56

Fort Santiago — A57

Salt Spring — A58

Magellan's Landing, 1521 — A59

"Juan de la Cruz" — A60

Rice Terraces — A61

Miguel Lopez de Legaspi and Chief Sikatuna Signing "Blood Compact," 1565 — A62

Barasoain Church, Malolos — A63

Battle of Manila Bay, 1898 — A64

United States Administration of the Philippines stamps can be mounted in Scott's U.S. Possessions Album.

Montalban Gorge — A65

George Washington A66

Printed by U. S. Bureau of Engraving and Printing.

1935, Feb. 15   Unwmk.   *Perf. 11*

383	A53	2c rose	5	5
		First day cover		75
384	A54	4c yellow green	5	5
		Light yellow green	8	5
		First day cover		75
385	A55	6c dark brown	9	6
		First day cover		75
386	A56	8c violet	12	12
		First day cover		2.50
387	A57	10c rose carmine	25	20
		First day cover		2.50
388	A58	12c black	18	15
		First day cover		2.50
389	A59	16c dark blue	18	12
		First day cover		2.50
390	A60	20c light olive green	25	6
		First day cover		3.50
391	A61	26c indigo	35	35
		First day cover		4.50
392	A62	30c orange red	35	35
		First day cover		4.50
393	A63	1p red orange & black	2.50	1.85
		First day cover		12.50
394	A64	2p bister brown & black	5.00	1.75
		First day cover		20.00
395	A65	4p blue & black	5.00	3.75
		First day cover		30.00
396	A66	5p green & black	10.00	2.25
		First day cover		40.00

Issues of the Commonwealth
Commonwealth Inauguration Issue
Issued to commemorate the inauguration of the Philippine Commonwealth Nov. 15, 1935.

"The Temples of Human Progress"
A67

1935, Nov. 15   Unwmk.   *Perf. 11*

397	A67	2c carmine rose	15	10
		First day cover		1.00
398	A67	6c deep violet	20	15
		First day cover		1.00
399	A67	16c blue	30	20
		First day cover		1.50
400	A67	36c yellow green	50	45
		First day cover		2.00
401	A67	50c brown	80	80
		First day cover		3.00

José Rizal Issue
Issued to commemorate the 75th anniversary of the birth of Jose Rizal (1861-1896), national hero of the Filipinos.

José Rizal — A68

Printed by the Philippine Bureau of Printing.

1936, June 19   Unwmk.   *Perf. 12*

402	A68	2c yellow brown	10	10
		light yellow brown	10	10
		First day cover		75
403	A68	6c slate blue	15	10
		light slate green	15	10
		First day cover		1.50
a.		Imperf. vertically, pair	900.00	
404	A68	36c red brown	75	70
		light red brown	75	70
		First day cover		3.50

Commonwealth Anniversary Issue
Issued in commemoration of the first anniversary of the Commonwealth.

President Manuel L. Quezon — A69

Printed by U.S. Bureau of Engraving and Printing.

1936, Nov. 15   Unwmk.   *Perf. 11*

408	A69	2c orange brown	6	6
		First day cover		75
409	A69	6c yellow green	12	10
		First day cover		1.25
410	A69	12c ultramarine	18	15
		First day cover		2.25

Stamps of 1935 Overprinted in Black:

COMMON-WEALTH
a

COMMONWEALTH
b

1936-37   Unwmk.   *Perf. 11*

411	A53(a)	2c rose, Dec. 28, 1936	6	5
		First day cover		50.00
a.		Bklt. pane of 6, Jan. 15 1937	5.00	1.00
a.		First day cover		60.00
412	A54(b)	4c yellow green, Mar. 29, 1937	75	40
		On cover		50
413	A55(a)	6c dark brown, Oct. 7, 1936	25	10
		On cover		12
414	A56(b)	8c violet, Mar. 29, 1937	35	30
		On cover		35
415	A57(b)	10c rose carmine, Dec. 28, 1936	20	6
		First day cover		50.00
a.		"COMMONWEALT"		—
416	A58(b)	12c black, Mar. 29, 1937	20	8
				10
417	A59(b)	16c dark blue, Oct. 7, 1936	25	20
		On cover		25
418	A60(a)	20c lt. olive green, Mar. 29, 1937	75	50
		On cover		55
419	A61(b)	26c indigo, Mar. 29, 1937	65	45
		On cover		55
420	A62(b)	30c orange red, Dec. 28, 1936	30	15
		First day cover		50.00
421	A63(b)	1p red org. & blk., Oct. 7, 1936	1.00	30
		On cover		50
422	A64(b)	2p bis. brn. & blk., Mar. 29, 1937	7.00	3.00
		On cover		4.00
423	A65(b)	4p blue & blk., Mar. 29, 1937	25.00	4.00
		On cover		5.00
424	A66(b)	5p green & blk., Mar. 29, 1937	2.50	1.65
		On cover		2.00

Eucharistic Congress Issue

Issued to commemorate the 33rd International Eucharistic Congress held at Manila, Feb. 3-7, 1937.

Map, Symbolical of the Eucharistic Congress Spreading Light of Christianity — A70

FLAT PLATE PRINTING

Plates of 256 subjects in four panes of 64 each.

1937, Feb. 2   Unwmk.   *Perf. 11*

425	A70	2c yellow green	10	6
		First day cover		75
426	A70	6c light brown	18	10
		First day cover		75
427	A70	12c sapphire	20	10
		First day cover		1.25
428	A70	20c deep orange	35	5
		First day cover		1.50
429	A70	36c deep violet	60	50
		First day cover		2.00
430	A70	50c carmine	70	35
		First day cover		3.00

Arms of City of Manila — A71

1937, Aug. 27   Unwmk.   *Perf. 11*

431	A71	10p gray	6.50	3.00
432	A71	20p henna brown	3.50	2.00

Nos. 431-432 exist on one first day cover. Price $75.

Stamps of 1935 Overprinted in Black:

COMMON-
WEALTH
a

COMMONWEALTH
b

1938-40   Unwmk.   *Perf. 11*

433	A53(a)	2c rose ('39)	8	5
a.		Booklet pane of six	5.00	1.00
b.		"WEALTH COMMON-"	3,000.	
c.		Hyphen omitted	—	—
434	A54(b)	4c yellow green ('40)	60	50
435	A55(a)	6c dark brown, *May 12, 1939*	8	8
		First day cover		50.00
a.		6c golden brown	15	8
436	A56(b)	8c violet ('39)	10	10
a.		"COMMONWEALT"	100.00	
437	A57(b)	10c rose carmine, *May 12, 1939*	10	6
438	A58(b)	12c black ('40)	10	9
439	A59(b)	16c Dark blue	18	10
440	A60(a)	20c light olive green ('39)	20	10
441	A61(b)	26c indigo ('40)	30	30
442	A62(b)	30c orange red *May 23, 1939*	1.60	85
443	A63(b)	1p red org. & blk., *Aug. 29, 1938*	60	25
		First day cover		60.00
444	A64(b)	2p bister brown & black ('39)	4.00	1.00
445	A65(b)	4p blue & black ('40)	65.00	65.00
446	A66(b)	5p green & black ('40)	7.00	4.00

Overprint *"b"* measures 18½x1¼mm.
No. 433b occurs in booklet pane, No. 433a, position 5; all copies are straight-edged, left and bottom.

First Foreign Trade Week Issue

Nos. 384, 298a and 432 Surcharged in Red, Violet or Black:

FIRST
FOREIGN

TRADE
WEEK

MAY 21-27, 1939
a

2
CENTAVOS

FIRST FOREIGN
TRADE WEEK

MAY 21-27, 1939
6 CENTAVOS 6
b

50 CENTAVOS 50

c

FIRST FOREIGN
TRADE WEEK

MAY 21-27, 1939

1939, July 5

449	A54(a)	2c on 4c yellow green (R)	10	8
		First day cover		2.00
450	A40(b)	6c on 26c blue green (V)	20	20
		First day cover		3.00
a.		6c on 26c green	1.00	45
451	A71(c)	50c on 20p henna brown (Bk)	1.25	1.25
		First day cover		7.50

Commonwealth 4th Anniversary Issue

Nos. 452-460 were issued to commemorate the fourth anniversary of the Commonwealth.

Triumphal Arch — A72

Printed by U. S. Bureau of Engraving and Printing.

1939, Nov. 15   Unwmk.   *Perf. 11*

452	A72	2c yellow green	10	8
		First day cover		1.00
453	A72	6c carmine	15	10
		First day cover		1.00
454	A72	12c bright blue	25	10
		First day cover		2.00

Malacañan Palace — A73

1939, Nov. 15   Unwmk.   *Perf. 11*

455	A73	2c green	10	6
		First day cover		1.00
456	A73	6c orange	15	10
		First day cover		1.00
457	A73	12c carmine	25	8
		First day cover		2.00

President Quezon Taking Oath of Office — A74

1940, Feb. 8   Unwmk.   *Perf. 11*

458	A74	2c dark orange	10	8
		First day cover		1.00
459	A74	6c dark green	15	12
		First day cover		1.00
460	A74	12c purple	30	15
		First day cover		2.00

José Rizal — A75

ROTARY PRESS PRINTING

1941, April 14   Unwmk.   *Perf. 11x10½*
Size: 19x22½mm.

461	A75	2c apple green	5	5
		First day cover		1.00
		Margin block of 4, P#	1.50	

FLAT PLATE PRINTING

1941-43   Unwmk.   Size: 18¾x22mm.   *Perf. 11*

462	A75	2c apple green	12	6
a.		2c pale apple green ('41)	25	6
b.		Booklet pane of six (apple green)	1.50	1.50
c.		Booklet pane of six (pale apple green) ('41)	4.00	3.50

This stamp was issued only in booklet panes and all copies have one or two straight edges.

Further printings were made in 1942 and 1943 in different shades from the first supply of stamps sent to the islands.

Stamps of 1935-41 Handstamped **VICTORY** in Violet

1944   Unwmk.   *Perf. 11, 11x10½*

463	A53	2c rose (On 411), *Dec. 3*	225.00	125.00
a.		Booklet pane of six	1,850.	
463B	A53	2c rose (On 433), *Dec. 14*	1,450.	1,450.
464	A75	2c apple green (On 461), *Nov. 8*	2.50	2.50
		On cover		5.00
465	A54	4c yellow green (On 384), *Nov. 8*	25.00	25.00
		On cover		—
466	A55	6c dark brown (On 385), *Dec. 14*	1,350.	750.00
		On cover		—
467	A69	6c yellow green (On 409), *Dec. 3*	100.00	85.00
		On cover		—
468	A55	6c dark brown (On 413), *Dec. 28*	550.00	300.00
		On cover		—
469	A72	6c carmine (On 453), *Dec. 14*	125.00	100.00
		On cover		—
470	A73	6c orange (On 456), *Dec. 14*	500.00	300.00
		On cover		—
471	A74	6c dark green (On 459), *Nov. 8*	150.00	90.00
		On cover		—
472	A56	8c violet (On 436), *Nov. 8*	12.50	15.00
		On cover		—
473	A57	10c carmine rose (On 415), *Nov. 8*	100.00	60.00
		On cover		—
474	A57	10c carmine rose (On 437), *Nov. 8*	125.00	80.00
		On cover		

475	A69	12c ultramarine (On 410), *Dec. 3*	300.00	110.00
		On cover		—
476	A72	12c bright blue (On 454), *Dec. 14*	3,500.	1,400.
		On cover		—
477	A74	12c purple (On 460), *Nov. 8*	175.00	100.00
		On cover		—
478	A59	16c dark blue (On 389), *Dec. 3*	700.00	
479	A59	16c dark blue (On 417), *Nov. 8*	350.00	120.00
		On cover		—
480	A59	16c dark blue (On 439), *Nov. 8*	130.00	100.00
		On cover		—
481	A60	20c light olive green (On 440), *Nov. 8*	27.50	27.50
		On cover		—
482	A62	30c orange red (On 420), *Dec. 3*	200.00	125.00
		On cover		—
483	A62	30c orange red (On 442), *Dec. 3*	275.00	135.00
		On cover		—
484	A63	1p red orange & black (On 443) *Dec. 3*	7,000.	4,500.
		On cover		—

No. 463 comes only from the booklet pane. All copies have one or two straight edges.

Types of 1935-37 Overprinted

VICTORY

VICTORY

COMMON-WEALTH
a

COMMONWEALTH
b

c

V̶I̶CTORY

1945		**Unwmk.**		**Perf. 11**
485	A53(a)	2c rose, *Jan. 19*	10	6
		First day cover		4.00
486	A54(b)	4c yellow green, *Jan. 19*	12	8
		First day cover		4.00
487	A55(a)	6c golden brown, *Jan. 19*	15	10
		First day cover		4.00
488	A56(b)	8c violet, *Jan. 19*	20	18
		First day cover		4.50
489	A57(b)	10c rose carmine, *Jan. 19*	20	15
		First day cover		4.50
490	A58(b)	12c black, *Jan. 19*	30	18
		First day cover		5.00
491	A59(b)	16c dark blue, *Jan. 19*	40	15
		First day cover		6.00
492	A60(a)	20c light olive green, *Jan. 19*	45	12
		First day cover		6.50
493	A62(b)	30c orange red, *May 1*	60	50
		First day cover		4.00
494	A63(b)	1p red orange & black, *Jan. 19*	1.75	40
		First day cover		10.00
495	A71(c)	10p gray, *May 1*	60.00	20.00
		First day cover		30.00
496	A71(c)	20p henna brown, *May 1*	50.00	22.50
		First day cover		40.00

José Rizal — A76

ROTARY PRESS PRINTING

1946, May 28		**Unwmk.**		**Perf. 11x10½**
497	A76	2c sepia	10	6
		Margin block of 4, P#	75	

Later issues, released by the Philippine Republic on July 4, 1946, and thereafter, are listed in Scotts Standard Postage Stamp Catalogue, Vol. IV.

AIR POST

Madrid-Manila Flight Issue
Issued to commemorate the flight of Spanish aviators Gallarza and Loriga from Madrid to Manila.

Regular Issue of 1917-26 Overprinted in Red or Violet by the Philippine Bureau of Printing

1926, May 13		**Unwmk.**		**Perf. 11**
C1	A40	2c green (R) *(10,000)*	5.00	4.00
		First day cover		35.00
		Block of four	22.50	20.00
C2	A40	4c carmine (V) *(9,000)*	6.50	4.50
		First day cover		35.00
		Block of four	27.50	21.00
a.		Inverted overprint *(100)*	1,200.	
C3	A40	6c lilac (R) *(5,000)*	35.00	12.00
		First day cover		50.00
		Block of four	150.00	
C4	A40	8c orange brown (V) *(5,000)*	35.00	12.00
		First day cover		50.00
		Block of four	150.00	
C5	A40	10c deep blue (R) *(5,000)*	35.00	12.00
		First day cover		50.00
		Block of four	125.00	
C6	A40	12c red orange (V) *(4,000)*	40.00	17.50
		First day cover		50.00
		Block of four	175.00	
C7	A40	16c light olive green *(Sampson)* (V) *(300)*	1,350.	1,000.
		Block of four	—	
C8	A40	16c olive bister *(Sampson)* (R) *(100)*	2,000.	1,650.
C9	A40	16c olive green *(Dewey)* (V) *(4,000)*	40.00	17.50
		First day cover		50.00
		Block of four	175.00	
C10	A40	20c orange yellow (V) *(4,000)*	40.00	17.50
		First day cover		50.00
		Block of four	175.00	
C11	A40	26c blue green (V) *(4,000)*	40.00	17.50
		First day cover		50.00
		Block of four	175.00	
C12	A40	30c gray (V) *(4,000)*	40.00	17.50
		First day cover		50.00
		Block of four	175.00	
C13	A41	2p violet brown (R) *(900)*	350.00	250.00
		On cover		325.00
		Block of four	—	
C14	A41	4p dark blue (R) *(700)*	600.00	350.00
		On cover		425.00
		Block of four	—	
C15	A41	10p deep green (V) *(500)*	900.00	600.00
		On cover		750.00
		Block of four	—	

Same Overprint on No. 269
Wmk. Single-lined PIPS (190)
Perf. 12

C16	A40	26c blue green (V) *(100)*	2,000.	
		Block of four	—	

Same Overprint on No. 284
Perf. 10

C17	A41	1p pale violet (V) *(2,000)*	120.00	85.00
		On cover		100.00
		First day cover		140.00
		Block of four	525.00	

Overprintings of Nos. C1-C6, C9-C15 and C17 were made from two plates. Position No. 89 of the first printing shows broken left blade of propeller.

London-Orient Flight Issue
Issued Nov. 9, 1928, to celebrate the arrival of a British squadron of hydroplanes.

Regular Issue of 1917-25 Overprinted in Red

1928, Nov. 9		**Unwmk.**		**Perf. 11**
C18	A40	2c green *(101,200)*	60	40
		First day cover		10.00
C19	A40	4c carmine *(50,500)*	60	50
		First day cover		12.00
C20	A40	6c violet *(12,600)*	2.25	1.75
		On cover		2.00
C21	A40	8c orange brown *(10,000)*	2.50	2.25
		On cover		2.75
C22	A40	10c deep blue *(10,000)*	2.50	2.25
		On cover		2.75
C23	A40	12c red orange *(8,000)*	3.50	3.00
		On cover		4.00
C24	A40	16c olive green (No. 303a) *(12,600)*	2.75	2.25
		On cover		3.00
C25	A40	20c orange yellow *(8,000)*	3.50	3.00
		On cover		3.75
C26	A40	26c blue green *(7,000)*	10.00	7.50

		On cover		10.00
C27	A40	30c gray *(7,000)*	10.00	7.50
		On cover		10.00

Same Overprint on No. 271
Wmk. Single-lined PIPS (190)
Perf. 12

C28	A41	1p pale violet *(6,000)*	35.00	35.00
		On cover		40.00

Von Gronau Issue
Issued commemoration of the visit of Capt. Wolfgang von Gronau's airplane on its round-the-world flight.

Nos. 354-360 Overprinted by the Philippine Bureau of Printing

1932, Sept. 27		**Unwmk.**		**Perf. 11**
C29	A43	2c yellow green *(100,000)*	45	45
		First day cover		3.00
C30	A44	4c rose carmine *(80,000)*	50	50
		First day cover		3.00
C31	A45	12c orange *(55,000)*	80	80
		On cover		1.00
C32	A46	18c red orange *(30,000)*	4.00	4.00
		On cover		4.75
C33	A47	20c yellow *(30,000)*	2.25	2.25
		On cover		2.50
C34	A48	24c deep violet *(30,000)*	2.25	2.25
		On cover		2.75
C35	A49	32c olive brown *(30,000)*	2.25	2.25
		On cover		2.50
		First day cover, #C29-C35		50.00

Rein Issue
Commemorating the flight from Madrid to Manila of the Spanish aviator Fernando Rein y Loring.

Regular Issue of 1917-25 Overprinted in Black

1933, Apr. 11				
C36	A40	2c green *(95,000)*	45	45
		First day cover		2.50
C37	A40	4c carmine *(75,000)*	50	50
		First day cover		—
C38	A40	6c deep violet *(65,000)*	80	80
		First day cover		4.50
C39	A40	8c orange brown *(35,000)*	1.75	1.65
C40	A40	10c dark blue *(35,000)*	1.50	1.25
C41	A40	12c orange *(35,000)*	1.25	1.25
C42	A40	16c olive green *(Dewey)* *(35,000)*	1.25	1.25
C43	A40	20c yellow *(35,000)*	1.25	1.25
C44	A40	26c green *(35,000)*	1.50	1.50
a.		26c blue green	2.50	2.50
C45	A40	30c gray *(30,000)*	2.00	1.85
		First day cover, #C36-C45		50.00

No. 290b Overprinted by the Philippine Bureau of Printing

1933, May 26		**Unwmk.**		**Perf. 11**
C46	A40	2c green	65	50

Regular Issue of 1932 Overprinted

C47	A44	4c rose carmine	10	8
C48	A45	12c orange	50	18
C49	A47	20c yellow	50	30
C50	A48	24c deep violet	50	35
C51	A49	32c olive brown	75	45
		First day cover, #C46-C51		50.00

Transpacific Issue
Issued to commemorate the China Clipper flight from Manila to San Francisco, Dec. 2-5, 1935.

Nos. 387, 392 Overprinted in Gold

1935, Dec. 2   **Unwmk.**   *Perf. 11*

C52	A57	10c rose carmine *(500,000)*	25	25
		First day cover		3.00
C53	A62	30c orange red *(350,000)*	50	50
		First day cover		5.00

Manila-Madrid Flight Issue

Issued to commemorate the Manila-Madrid flight by aviators Antonio Arnaiz and Juan Calvo.

Nos. 291, 295, 298a, 298 Surcharged in Various Colors by Philippine Bureau of Printing

1936, Sept. 6

C54	A40	2c on 4c carmine (Bl) *(2,000,000)*	8	6
		First day cover		1.50
C55	A40	6c on 12c red orange (V) *(500,000)*	15	12
		First day cover		5.00
C56	A40	16c on 26c blue green (Bk) *(300,000)*	30	30
		First day cover		7.50
a.		16c on 26c green	1.50	1.00

Air Mail Exhibition Issue

Issued to commemorate the first Air Mail Exhibition, held Feb. 17-19, 1939.

Nos. 298a, 298, 431 Surcharged in Black or Red by Philippine Bureau of Printing

1939, Feb. 17

C57	A40	8c on 26c blue green (Bk) *(200,000)*	1.00	55
		First day cover		5.00
a.		8c on 26c green (Bk)	2.00	75
C58	A71	1p on 10p gray (R) *(30,000)*	3.00	2.50
		First day cover		12.50

Moro Vinta and Clipper — AP1

Printed by the U. S. Bureau of Engraving and Printing.

1941, June 30   **Unwmk.**   *Perf. 11*

C59	AP1	8c carmine	1.10	70
		First day cover		2.50
C60	AP1	20c ultramarine	1.40	55
		First day cover		3.00
C61	AP1	60c blue green	2.00	1.00
		First day cover		4.50
C62	AP1	1p sepia	1.00	65
		First day cover		3.50

No. C47 Handstamped in Violet   **VICTORY**

1944, Dec. 3   **Unwmk.**   *Perf. 11*

C63	A44	4c rose carmine	*1,650.*	*1,000.*
		On cover		—

SPECIAL DELIVERY

U.S. No. E5 Overprinted in Red

a   **PHILIPPINES**

Printed by U.S. Bureau of Engraving & Printing
Wmk. Double-lined USPS (191)

1901, Oct. 15   *Perf. 12*

E1	SD3	10c dark blue *(15,000)*	110.00	125.00
		On cover		350.00
		Block of four	475.00	
		Margin strip of 3, Impt. & P#	750.00	

Margin block of 6, Impt. & P#	*3,250.*	
Dots in curved frame above messenger (Pl. 882)	*135.00*	

Special Delivery Messenger — SD2

Wmk. Double-lined PIPS (191)

1906, Sept. 8   *Perf. 12*

E2	SD2	20c deep ultramarine *(40,000)*	30.00	8.00
		On cover		17.50
		Block of four	125.00	
b.		20c pale ultramarine	30.00	10.00

SPECIAL PRINTING

U.S. No. E6 Overprinted Type "a" in Red

1907   **Wmk. Double-lined USPS (191)**   *Perf. 12*

E2A	SD4	10c ultramarine	*1,600.*	
		Block of four	*7,000.*	
		Margin block of 6, Impt. & P#	—	

This stamp was part of the set specially printed for the Bureau of Insular Affairs in 1907. See note following No. 240.

1911, Apr.   **Wmk. Single-lined PIPS (190)**   *Perf. 12*

E3	SD2	20c deep ultramarine *(90,000)*	20.00	2.00
		On cover		15.00
		Block of four	85.00	

1916   *Perf. 10*

E4	SD2	20c deep ultramarine	165.00	40.00
		On cover		80.00
		Block of four	700.00	
		pale ultramarine	—	

Early in 1919 the supply of Special Delivery stamps in the Manila area was exhausted. A Government decree permitted the use of regular issue postage stamps for payment of the special delivery fee when so noted on the cover. This usage was permitted until the new supply of Special Delivery stamps arrived.

1919   **Unwmk.**   *Perf. 11*

E5	SD2	20c ultramarine	60	25
		On cover		35
		Block of four	2.50	
a.		20c pale blue	1.00	50
b.		20c dull violet	60	25

Type of 1906 Issue

1925-31   **Unwmk.**   *Imperf.*

E6	SD2	20c dull violet ('31)	20.00	*25.00*
		violet blue	25.00	*30.00*
		On cover		*30.00*
		Block of four	85.00	

Type of 1919 Overprinted in Black   **COMMONWEALTH**

1939, Apr. 27   **Unwmk.**   *Perf. 11*

E7	SD2	20c blue violet	30	30
		First day cover		50.00

Nos. E5b and E7 Handstamped in Violet   **VICTORY**

1944   **Unwmk.**   *Perf. 11*

E8	SD2	20c dull violet (On E5b)	400.00	300.00
E9	SD2	20c blue violet (On E7)	200.00	165.00
		On cover		—

Type SD2 Overprinted "VICTORY" As No. 486

1945, May 1   **Unwmk.**   *Perf. 11*

E10	SD2	20c blue violet	85	85
		First day cover		15.00
a.		"IC" close together	3.50	3.50

SPECIAL DELIVERY OFFICIAL STAMP

Type of 1906 Issue Overprinted

1931   **Unwmk.**   *Perf. 11*

EO1	SD2	20c dull violet	85	65
a.		No period after "B"	25.00	20.00
b.		Double overprint	—	

POSTAGE DUE

U.S. Nos. J38-J44 Overprinted in Black

Printed by the U. S. Bureau of Engraving and Printing.

Wmk. Double-lined USPS (191)

1899, Aug. 16   *Perf. 12.*

J1	D2	1c deep claret *(340,892)*	5.00	2.00
		On Cover		35.00
		Margin block of 6, Impt. & P#	*500.00*	
J2	D2	2c deep claret *(306,983)*	5.00	1.75
		On cover		40.00
		Margin block of 6, Impt. & P#	500.00	
J3	D2	5c deep claret *(34,565)*	11.00	3.75
		On cover		*50.00*
		Margin block of 6, Impt. & P#	*750.00*	
J4	D2	10c deep claret *(15,848)*	15.00	7.00
		On cover		60.00
		Margin block of 6, Impt. & P#	*850.00*	
J5	D2	50c deep claret *(6,168)*	165.00	100.00
		On cover		—
		Margin block of 6, Impt. & P#	*3,000.*	

No. J1 was used to pay regular postage Sept. 5th to 19th, 1902.

1901, Aug. 31

J6	D2	3c deep claret *(14,885)*	15.00	10.00
		On cover		50.00
		Margin block of 6, Impt. & P#	*850.00*	
J7	D2	30c deep claret *(2,140)*	225.00	100.00
		On cover		—
		Margin block of 6, Impt. & P#	*3,500.*	

Post Office Clerk — D3

1928, Aug. 21   **Unwmk.**   *Perf. 11*

J8	D3	4c brown red	15	15
J9	D3	6c brown red	15	15
J10	D3	8c brown red	15	15
J11	D3	10c brown red	20	20
J12	D3	12c brown red	20	20
J13	D3	16c brown red	25	25
J14	D3	20c brown red	20	20

No. J8 Surcharged in Blue   **3 CVOS. 3**

1937, July 29   **Unwmk.**   *Perf. 11*

J15	D3	3c on 4c brown red	25	15
		First day cover		50.00

Nos. J8 to J14 Handstamped in Violet   **VICTORY**

1944, Dec. 3   **Unwmk.**   *Perf. 11*

J16	D3	4c brown red	*130.00*	—
J17	D3	6c brown red	*90.00*	—
J18	D3	8c brown red	*100.00*	—
J19	D3	10c brown red	*90.00*	—
J20	D3	12c brown red	*90.00*	—
J21	D3	16c brown red	*100.00*	—
J22	D3	20c brown red	*100.00*	—

OFFICIAL

Official Handstamped Overprints

"Officers purchasing stamps for government business may, if they so desire, surcharge them with the letters O.B. either in writing with black ink or by rubber stamps but in such a manner as not to obliterate the stamp that postmasters will be unable to determine whether the stamps have been previously used." C. M. Cotterman, Director of Posts, December 26, 1905.

Beginning with January 1, 1906, all branches of the Insular Government, used postage stamps to prepay postage instead of franking them as before. Some officials used manuscript, some utilized the typewriting machines but by far the larger number provided themselves with rubber stamps. The majority of these read "O. B." but other forms were: "OFFICIAL BUSINESS" or "OFFICIAL MAIL" in two lines, with variations on many of these.

These "O. B." overprints are known on U. S. 1899-1901 stamps; on 1903-06 stamps in red and blue; on 1906 stamps in red, blue, black, yellow and green.

"O. B." overprints were also made on the centavo and peso stamps of the Philippines, per order of May 25, 1907.

Beginning in 1926 the stamps were overprinted and issued by the Government, but some post offices continued to handstamp "O.B."

During the Japanese occupation period 1942-45, the same system of handstamped official overprints prevailed, but the handstamp usually consisted of "K.P.", initials of the Tagalog words, "Kagamitang Pampamahalaan" (Official Business), and the two Japanese characters used in the printed overprint on Nos. NO1 to NO4.

Legislative Palace Issue of 1926 **OFFICIAL** Overprinted in Red

Printed and overprinted by the Philippine Bureau of Printing.

1926, Dec. 20   **Unwmk.**   *Perf. 12*

O1	A42	2c green & black *(90,500)*	2.50	1.75
		On cover		3.00
		Block of four	10.50	7.25
O2	A42	4c carmine & black *(90,450)*	2.50	1.60
		On cover		3.00
		First day cover		15.00
		Block of four	10.00	7.00
a.		Vertical pair, imperf. between	375.00	
O3	A42	18c light brown & black *(70,000)*	7.00	6.00
		On cover		10.00
		Block of four	35.00	30.00
O4	A42	20c orange & black *(70,250)*	6.00	2.00
		On cover		3.00
		Block of four	30.00	10.00
		First day cover, #O1-O4		75.00

Regular Issue of 1917-25 Overprinted **O.B.**

Printed and overprinted by the U.S. Bureau of Engraving and Printing.

1931   **Unwmk.**   *Perf. 11*

O5	A40	2c green	6	5
a.		No period after "B"	10.00	5.00
b.		No period after "O"		—
O6	A40	4c carmine	8	5
a.		No period after "B"	10.00	5.00
O7	A40	6c deep violet	10	8
O8	A40	8c yellow brown	10	8
O9	A40	10c deep blue	40	12
O10	A40	12c red orange	25	15
a.		No period after "B"	30.00	
O11	A40	16c light olive green *(Dewey)*	25	10
a.		16c olive bister	1.50	30
O12	A40	20c orange yellow	30	10
a.		No period after "B"	15.00	15.00
O13	A40	26c green	45	45
a.		26c blue green	1.25	1.00
O14	A40	30c gray	40	35

Regular Issue of 1935 Overprinted in Black **O.B.**

1935   **Unwmk.**   *Perf. 11*

O15	A53	2c rose	6	5
a.		No period after "B"	10.00	5.00
O16	A54	4c yellow green	6	5
a.		No period after "B"	10.00	7.50
O17	A55	6c dark brown	10	6
a.		No period after "B"	17.50	17.50
O18	A56	8c violet	12	12
O19	A57	10c rose carmine	15	6
O20	A58	12c black	20	15
O21	A59	16c dark blue	20	15
O22	A60	20c light olive green	20	15
O23	A61	26c indigo	40	35
O24	A62	30c orange red	45	40

Nos. 411 and 418 with Additional Overprint in Black **O.B.**

1937-38   **Unwmk.**   *Perf. 11*

O25	A53	2c rose, *Apr. 10, 1937*	8	5
		First day cover		75.00
a.		No period after "B"	6.50	3.50
O26	A60	20c light olive green, *Apr. 26, 1938*	1.00	75

Regular Issue of 1935 Overprinted In Black:

O.B.   **O. B.**

COMMON-WEALTH   COMMONWEALTH

a   b

1938-40   **Unwmk.**   *Perf. 11*

O27	A53(a)	2c rose	8	5
a.		Hyphen omitted	17.50	15.00
b.		No period after "B"	20.00	15.00
O28	A54(b)	4c yellow green	10	8
O29	A55(a)	6c dark brown	15	6
O30	A56(b)	8c violet	15	10
O31	A57(b)	10c rose carmine	17	10
a.		No period after "O"	25.00	25.00
O32	A58(b)	12c black	18	18
O33	A59(b)	16c dark blue	25	12
O34	A60(a)	20c light olive green ('40)	35	35
O35	A61(b)	26c indigo	45	45
O36	A62(b)	30c orange red	40	40

No. 461 Overprinted in Black

c   **O.   B.**

ROTARY PRESS PRINTING

1941, Apr. 14   **Unwmk.**   *Perf. 11x10 ½*

O37	A75	2c apple green	6	6
		First day cover		5.00
		Margin block of four, P#	35	

Nos. O27, O37, O16, O29, O31, O22 and O26 Handstamped in Violet **VICTORY**

1944   **Unwmk.**   *Perf. 11, 11x10 ½*

O38	A53	2c rose (On O27)	*130.00*	85.00
O39	A75	2c apple green (On O37)	5.00	3.00
		On cover		10.00
		Block of four	25.00	
O40	A54	4c yellow green (On O16)	25.00	20.00
		Block of four	125.00	
O40A	A55	6c dark brown (On O29)	*3,000.*	—
O41	A57	10c rose carmine (On O31)	100.00	
		Block of four	*425.00*	
O42	A60	20c light olive green (On O22)	*3,500.*	
O43	A60	20c light olive green (On O26)	*1,400.*	

No. 497 Overprinted Type "c" in Black.

1946, June 19   **Unwmk.**   *Perf. 11x10 ½*

O44	A76	2c sepia	6	5
		Margin block of 4, P#	40	

POST OFFICE SEALS

POS1

1906		**Litho.** **Unwmk.**	*Perf. 12*	
OX1	POS1	light brown	40.00	—

Wmk. "PIRS" in Double-lined Capitals

1907			*Perf. 12*	
OX2	POS1	light brown	70.00	—
		Hyphen-hole Perf. 7		
OX3	POS1	orange brown	35.00	—
1911			*Hyphen-hole Perf. 7*	
OX4	POS1	yellow brown	30.00	
OX5	POS1	olive bister	60.00	—
a.		Unwatermarked		
OX6	POS1	yellow	70.00	
1913		**Unwmk.**	*Hyphen-hole Perf. 7*	
OX7	POS1	lemon yellow	1.25	1.25
		Perf. 12		
OX8	POS1	yellow		—

Wmk. "USPS" in Single-lined Capitals
Hyphen-hole Perf. 7

OX9	POS1	yellow	70.00	30.00
1934		**Unwmk.**	*Rouletted*	
OX10	POS1	dark blue	1.25	1.25

United States Administration of the Philippines stamps can be mounted in Scott's U.S. Possessions Album.

POS2

OX11	POS2	dark blue	1.00	1.00

POS3

1938			*Hyphen-hole Perf. 7*	
OX12	POS3	dark blue	8.50	3.50
a.		Perforated 12	—	—

ENVELOPES

U.S. Envelopes of 1899 Issue Overprinted below stamp in color of the stamp, except where noted

PHILIPPINES.

1899-1900

Note: Many envelopes for which there was no obvious need were issued in small quantities. Anyone residing in the Islands could, by depositing with his postmaster the required amount, order any envelopes in quantities of 500, or multiples thereof, provided it was on the schedule of U.S. envelopes. Such special orders are indicated by an plus sign.

U1	U77	1c green on white (No. U352) *(370,000)*	2.50	2.00
		Entire	10.00	11.00
U2	U77	1c green on amber (No. U353) *(1,000)+*	17.50	15.00
		Entire	65.00	45.00
U3	U77	1c green on amber (No. U353) red overprint *(500)+*	25.00	22.50
		Entire	70.00	65.00
U4	U77	1c green on oriental buff (No. U354) *(1,000)+*	15.00	15.00
		Entire	32.50	32.50
U5	U77	1c green on oriental buff (No. U354) red overprint *(500)+*	40.00	40.00
		Entire	87.50	*87.50*
U6	U77	1c green on blue (No. U355) *(1,000)+*	10.00	10.00
		Entire	35.00	35.00
U7	U77	1c green on blue (No. U355) red overprint *(500)+*	22.50	20.00
		Entire	80.00	72.50
U8	U79	2c carmine on white (No. U362) *(1,180,000)*	1.50	1.50
		Entire	4.25	3.00
U9	U79	2c carmine on amber (No. U363) *(21,000)*	5.50	5.00
		Entire	16.00	14.00
U10	U79	2c carmine on oriental buff (No. U364) *(10,000)*	5.50	5.00
		Entire	17.50	14.00
U11	U79	2c carmine on blue (No. U365) *(10,000)*	6.50	6.50
		Entire	14.00	14.00
U12	U81	4c brown on amber (No. U372), Die 1 *(500)+*	45.00	40.00

	a.	Entire	130.00	*110.00*
		Double overprint	—	
		Entire		*2,100.*
U13	U83	4c brown on white (No. U374),		
		Die 3 *(10,500)*	12.00	10.00
		Entire	50.00	*45.00*
U14	U83	4c brown on amber (No. U375),		
		Die 3 *(500)+*	60.00	55.00
		Entire	190.00	140.00
U15	U84	5c blue on white (No. U377)		
		(20,000)	7.00	6.50
		Entire	14.00	14.00
U16	U84	5c blue on amber (No. U378)		
		(500)+	35.00	35.00
		Entire	110.00	*125.00*

1903   **Same Overprint on U.S. Issue of 1903**

U17	U85	1c green on white (No. U379)		
		(300,000)	1.50	1.25
		Entire	4.25	4.25
U18	U85	1c green on amber (No. U380)		
		(1,000)+	14.00	13.00
		Entire	25.00	*27.50*
U19	U85	1c green on oriental buff (No.		
		U381) *(1,000)+*	15.00	14.00
		Entire	27.50	*30.00*
U20	U85	1c green on blue (No. U382)		
		(1,500)+	12.50	12.00
		Entire	27.50	*30.00*
U21	U85	1c green on manila (No. U383)		
		(500)+	20.00	20.00
		Entire	50.00	*55.00*
U22	U86	2c carmine on white (No. U385)		
		(150,500)	5.00	3.50
		Entire	7.50	7.50
U23	U86	2c carmine on amber (No.		
		U386) *(500)+*	20.00	15.00
		Entire	50.00	47.50
U24	U86	2c carmine on oriental buff (No.		
		U387) *(500)+*	20.00	*27.50*
		Entire	50.00	—
U25	U86	2c carmine on blue (No. U388)		
		(500)+	20.00	18.00
		Entire	50.00	
U26	U87	4c chocolate on amber (No.		
		U391) *(500)+*	60.00	*75.00*
		Entire	150.00	*175.00*
	a.	Double overprint, entire		*2,000.*
U27	U88	5c blue on amber (No. U394)		
		(500)+	60.00	—
		Entire	150.00	150.00

1906

Same Overprint on Re-cut U.S. issue of 1904

U28	U89	2c carmine on white (No. U395)	50.00	35.00
		Entire	175.00	160.00
U29	U89	2c carmine on oriental buff (No.		
		U397)	80.00	*135.00*
		Entire	250.00	*275.00*

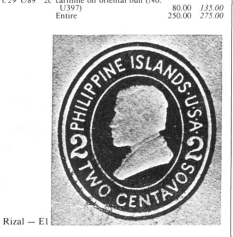

Rizal — E1

1908

U30	E1	2c green on white	40	20
		Entire	2.00	2.00
U31	E1	2c green on amber	5.00	3.00
		Entire	12.50	12.00
U32	E1	2c green on oriental buff	6.00	4.00
		Entire	12.00	12.00
U33	E1	2c green on blue	6.00	4.00
		Entire	12.00	12.00
U34	E1	2c green on manila *(500)*	10.00	
		Entire	25.00	32.50
U35	E1	4c carmine on white, *McKinley*	45	30
		Entire	2.00	1.50
U36	E1	4c carmine on amber	5.00	3.00
		Entire	12.50	10.00
U37	E1	4c carmine on oriental buff	6.00	4.50
		Entire	12.00	22.50
U38	E1	4c carmine on blue	5.50	3.50
		Entire	12.00	12.00
U39	E1	4c carmine on manila *(500)*	12.50	—
		Entire	25.00	42.50

Rizal — E2

1927, Apr. 5

U40	E2	2c green on white	15.00	12.50
		Entire	37.50	35.00
		Entire, 1st day cancel		*60.00*

"Juan de la Cruz" — E3

1935, June 19

U41	E3	2c carmine on white	30	20
		Entire	1.25	1.00
U42	E3	4c olive green on white	45	35
		Entire	1.75	1.50

Nos. U30, U35, U41 and U42 Handstamped in Violet **VICTORY**

1944

U42A	E1	2c green on white (On U30), Entire		—
U43	E3	2c green on white (On U41)	20.00	15.00
		Entire	45.00	*60.00*
U44	E1	4c carmine on white, *McKinley* (On U35)		—
		Entire	750.00	*750.00*
U45	E3	4c olive green on white (On U42)	90.00	85.00
		Entire	140.00	*150.00*

WRAPPERS

U. S. Wrappers Overprinted in **PHILIPPINES.** Color of Stamp

1901

W1	U77	1c green on manila (No. W357)		
		(320,000)	1.50	1.25
		Entire	5.00	6.00

1905

W2	U85	1c green on manila (No. W384)	12.50	10.00
		Entire	25.00	20.00
	a.	Double overprint, entire		*2,000.*
W3	U86	2c carmine on manila (No. W389)	12.50	12.00
		Entire	25.00	24.00

Design of Philippine Envelopes

1908

W4	E1	2c green on manila	2.00	2.00
		Entire	12.50	12.50

POSTAL CARDS

Prices are for Entires.
U.S. Cards Overprinted in Black below Stamp

a   **PHILIPPINES.**

1900, Feb.

UX1	(a)	1c black (Jefferson) (UX14)		
		(100,000)	17.50	15.00
	a.	Without period	45.00	
UX2	(a)	2c black (Liberty) (UX16)		
		(20,000)	40.00	22.50

b   **PHILIPPINES**

1903, Sept. 15

UX3	(b)	1c black (McKinley) (UX18)	*1,350.*	*1,100.*
UX4	(b)	2c black (Liberty) (UX16)	*750.00*	*600.00*

c   PHILIPPINES.

1903, Nov. 10

UX5	(c)	1c black (McKinley) (UX18)	65.00	40.00
UX6	(c)	2c black (Liberty) (UX16)	75.00	65.00

d   **PHILIPPINES**

1906

UX7	(d)	1c black (McKinley) (UX18)	325.00	325.00
UX8	(d)	2c black (Liberty) (UX16)	*1,750.*	*1,350.*

Designs same as postage issue of 1906

1907

UX9	A40	2c black on buff (Rizal)	12.50	10.00
UX10	A40	4c black on buff (McKinley)	30.00	22.50

Color changes

1911

UX11	A40	2c blue on light blue (Rizal)	10.00	10.00
	a.	2c blue on white	25.00	22.50
UX12	A40	4c blue on light blue (McKinley)	30.00	25.00

An impression of No. UX11 exists on the back of a U.S. No. UX21.

1915

UX13	A40	2c green on buff (Rizal)	4.00	2.50
UX14	A40	2c yellow green on amber	3.00	1.50
UX15	A40	4c green on buff (McKinley)	20.00	15.00

Design of postage issue of 1935

1935

UX16	A53	2c red on pale buff (Rizal)	3.00	2.00

No. UX16 Overprinted at left of Stamp **COMMONWEALTH**

1938

UX17	A53	2c red on pale buff	3.00	2.00

No. UX16 Overprinted **COMMONWEALTH**

UX18	A53	2c red on pale buff	55.00	45.00

No. UX16 Overprinted **COMMONWEALTH**

UX19	A53	2c red on pale buff	5.00	5.00

Nos. UX13, UX18 and UX19 Handstamped in Violet **VICTORY**

1944

UX20	A40	2c green on buff, *Rizal* (On UX13)	*175.00*	*175.00*
UX21	A53	2c red on pale buff (On UX18)	*700.00*	—
UX22	A53	2c red on pale buff (On UX19)	*275.00*	—

Overprinted in Black at left **VICTORY**

1945, Jan. 19

UX23	A76	2c gray brown on pale buff	1.50	75
		First day cancel		4.00
	a.	"IC" of "Victory" very close	6.00	3.50

This card was not issued without overprint.

PAID REPLY POSTAL CARDS
U.S. Paid Reply Cards of 1892-93 issues
Overprinted with type "a" in blue

1900, Feb.

UY1		2c +2c blue on white, unsevered *(5,000)*	*175.00*	*175.00*
m.		PM2, Message card, detached	30.00	30.00
r.		PR2, Reply card, detached	30.00	30.00

Overprinted type "c" in black

1903

UY2		1c +1c black on buff, unsevered *(20,000)*	*175.00*	*185.00*
m.		PM1, Message card, detached	30.00	35.00
r.		PR1, Reply card, detached	30.00	35.00
UY3		2c +2c blue on white, unsevered *(20,000)*	375.00	
m.		PM2, Message card, detached	65.00	60.00
r.		PR2, Reply card, detached	65.00	60.00

OFFICIAL CARDS

Overprinted at left of stamp   **O. B.**

1925   **On postal card No. UX13**

UZ1	A40	2c green on buff (Rizal)	35.00 30.00

1935   **On postal card No. UX16**

UZ2	A53	2c red on pale buff	15.00 16.00

Overprinted at Left of Stamp   **O. B.**

1938   **On postal card No. UX19**

UZ3	A53	2c red on pale buff	15.00 16.00

Overprinted Below Stamp   **O. B.**

1941   **Design of postage issue of 1941**

UZ4	A75	2c light green on pale buff	150.00 160.00

This card was not issued without overprint.

Postal Card No. UX19 Overprinted at   **O. B.**
Left of Stamp

1941

UZ5	A53	2c red on pale buff	25.00 25.00

OCCUPATION

Issued Under Japanese Occupation
Nos. 461, 438 and 439 Overprinted with Bars in Black

1942-43   **Unwmk.**   **Perf. 11x10½, 11**

N1	A75	2c apple green, *Mar. 4, 1942*	6	6
a.		Margin block of 4, P#	30	
		Pair, one without overprint	—	
N2	A58	12c black, *Apr. 30, 1943*	15	15
N3	A59	16c dark blue, *Mar. 4, 1942*	4.50	3.50

Nos. 435a, 435, 442, 443, and 423 Surcharged in Black

 (50 CENTAVOS 50)

ONE PESO

1942-43   **Perf. 11**

N4	A55(a)	5(c) on 6c golden brown *Sept. 1, 1942*	10	10
		First day cover		1.50
a.		Top bar shorter and thinner	20	20
b.		5(c) on 6c dark brown	20	20
c.		As "b", top bar shorter and thinner	20	20
N5	A62(b)	16(c) on 30c orange red, *Jan. 11, 1943*	20	20
		First day cover		1.75
N6	A63(c)	50c on 1p red orange & black, *April 30, 1943*	60	60
a.		Double surcharge		250.00
N7	A65(d)	1p on 4p blue & black, *April 30, 1943*	67.50	52.50
		Inverted "S" in "PESO"; position 4	80.00	80.00

On Nos. N4 and N4b, the top bar measures 1½x22½ mm. On Nos. N4a and N4c, the top bar measures 1 x 21 mm. and the "5" is smaller and thinner.

CONGRATULATIONS
FALL OF
BATAAN AND
CORREGIDOR
1942   **2**

1942, May 18

N8	A54	2(c) on 4c yellow green	2.50	2.00
		First day cover		4.00

Issued to commemorate Japan's capture of Bataan and Corregidor. The American-Filipino forces finally surrendered May 7, 1942. No. N8 exists with "R" for "B" in BATAAN.

No. 384 Surcharged   ダイトーアセンソー
in Black   イッシューネンキネン
     12-8-1942 5

1942, Dec. 8

N9	A54	5(c) on 4c yellow green	45	30
		First day cover		1.50

Issued to commemorate the first anniversary of the "Greater East Asia War".

     ヒトー ギョーセイフ
     イッシューオン キネン
Nos. C59 and C62   **1-23-43**
Surcharged in Black   **2**

1943, Jan. 23

N10	AP1	2(c) on 8c carmine	20	20
N11	AP1	5c on 1p sepia	40	40
		First day cover, #N10-N11		2.00

Issued to commemorate the first anniversary of the Philippine Executive Commission.

Nipa Hut   Rice
OS1   Planting
             OS2

Mt. Mayon   Moro Vinta
and Mt. Fuji   OS4
OS3

Wmk. 257

Engraved; Typographed (2c, 6c, 25c)

1943-44   **Wmk. 257**   **Perf. 13**

N12	OS1	1c deep orange, *June 7, 1943*	5	5
N13	OS2	2c bright green, *Apr. 1, 1943*	5	5
N14	OS1	4c slate green, *June 7, 1943*	5	5
N15	OS3	5c orange brown, *Apr. 1, 1943*	5	5
N16	OS2	6c red, *July 14, 1943*	8	8
N17	OS3	10c blue green, *July 14, 1943*	6	6
N18	OS4	12c steel blue, *July 14, 1943*	75	75
N19	OS4	16c dark brown, *July 14, 1943*	6	6
N20	OS1	20c rose violet, *Aug. 16, 1943*	85	85
N21	OS3	21c violet, *Aug. 16, 1943*	15	15
N22	OS2	25c pale brown, *Aug. 16, 1943*	6	5
N23	OS3	1p deep carmine, *June 7, 1943*	18	15
N24	OS4	2p dull violet, *Sept. 16, 1943*	1.75	1.50
		First day cover		7.50
N25	OS4	5p dark olive, *Apr. 10, 1944*	6.00	5.00
		First day cover		7.50

Map of Manila Bay Showing
Bataan and
Corregidor — OS5

1943, May 7   **Photo.**   **Unwmk.**

N26	OS5	2c carmine red	12	12
N27	OS5	5c bright green	18	18
		Colorless dot after left "5"	1.50	—
		First day cover, #N26-N27		2.00

Issued to commemorate the first anniversary of the fall of Bataan and Corregidor.

Limbagan
1593 - 1943

No. 440 Surcharged in Black

12   12

1943, June 20   **Engr.**   **Perf. 11**

N28	A60	12(c) on 20c light olive green	25	20
		First day cover		1.75
a.		Double surcharge		

Issued to commemorate the 350th anniversary of the printing press in the Philippines. "Limbagan" is Tagalog for "printing press."

Rizal Monument, Filipina and
Philippine Flag — OS6

1943, Oct. 14   **Photo.**   **Unwmk.**   **Perf. 12**

N29	OS6	5c light blue	10	10
a.		Imperf.	12	12
N30	OS6	12c orange	14	14
a.		Imperf.	16	16
N31	OS6	17c rose pink	16	16
		First day cover, #N29-N31		1.25
a.		Imperf.	22	22
		First day cover, #N29a-N31a		1.25

Issued to commemorate the "Independence of the Philippines." Japan granted "independence" Oct. 14, 1943, when the puppet republic was founded.

The imperforate stamps were issued without gum.

José Rizal
OS7

Rev. José
Burgos
OS8

Apolinario Mabini — OS9

1944, Feb. 17   Litho.   Unwmk.   Perf. 12

N32	OS7	5c blue	22	22
a.		Imperf.	22	22
N33	OS8	12c carmine	12	12
a.		Imperf.	12	12
N34	OS9	17c deep orange	16	16
		First day cover, #N32-N34		1.50
a.		Imperf.	16	16
		First day cover, #N32a-N34a, Apr. 17		2.25

REPÚBLIKÁ
NG PILIPINAS
5-7-44

Nos. C60 and C61
Surcharged in
Black

1944, May 7   Unwmk.   Perf. 11

N35	AP1	5(c) on 20c ultramarine	50	50
N36	AP1	12(c) on 60c blue green	1.00	1.00
		First day cover, #N35-N36		3.00

Issued to commemorate the second anniversary of the fall of Bataan and Corregidor.

José P. Laurel — OS10

**1945, Jan. 12   Litho.   Unwmk.   Imperf.
Without Gum**

N37	OS10	5c dull violet brown	7	6
N38	OS10	7c blue green	10	8
N39	OS10	20c chalky blue	15	12
		First day cover, #N37-N39		1.00

Issued belatedly on Jan. 12, 1945, to commemorate the first anniversary of the puppet Philippine Republic, Oct. 14, 1944. "S" stands for "sentimos".

The special cancellation devices prepared for use on Oct. 14, 1944, were employed on "First Day" covers Jan. 12, 1945.

OCCUPATION SEMI-POSTAL

Woman, Farming and
Cannery — OSP1

1942, Nov. 12   Litho.   Unwmk.   Perf. 12

NB1	OSP1	2c +1c pale violet	15	15
NB2	OSP1	5c +1c bright green	10	10
NB3	OSP1	16c +2c orange	13.00	10.00
		First day cover, #NB1-NB3		17.50

Issued to promote the campaign to produce and conserve food. The surtax aided the Red Cross.

Souvenir Sheet

OSP2

1943, Oct. 14   Without Gum   Imperf.

NB4	OSP2	Sheet of three	35.00	2.00
		First day cover, Manila		5.00

Issued to commemorate the "Independence of the Philippines."

No. NB4 contains one each of Nos. N29a-N31a. Marginal inscription is from Rizal's "Last Farewell". Size: 127x177mm. Sold for 2.50p.

BAHÂ
1943
+21

Nos. N18, N20 and N21 Surcharged
in Black

1943, Dec. 8   Wmk. 257   Perf. 13

NB5	OS4	12c +21 (c) steel blue	15	15
NB6	OS1	20c +36 (c) rose violet	12	12
NB7	OS3	21c +40 (c) violet	15	15
		First day cover, #NB5-NB7		1.75

The surtax was for the benefit of victims of a Luzon flood. "Baha" is Tagalog for "flood."

Souvenir Sheet

OSP3

**1944, Feb. 9   Litho.   Unwmk.   Imperf.
Without Gum**

NB8	OSP3	Sheet of three	2.00	2.50
		First day cover		5.00

No. NB8 contains one each of Nos. N32a-N34a. The sheet sold for 1p, the surtax going to a fund for the care of heroes' monuments. Size: 101x143mm. No. NB8 exists with 5c inverted.

OCCUPATION POSTAGE DUE

No. J15 Overprinted with Bar in Blue

1942, Oct. 14   Unwmk.   Perf. 11

NJ1	D3	3c on 4c brown red	27.50	12.00
		First day cover		30.00
		Double bar		

On copies of No. J15, two lines were drawn in India ink with a ruling pen across "United States of America" by employees of the Short Paid Section of the Manila Post Office to make a provisional 3c postage due stamp which was used from Sept. 1, 1942 (when the letter rate was raised from 2c to 5c) until Oct. 14 when No. NJ1 went on sale. Price on cover, $150.

OCCUPATION OFFICIAL

Nos. 461, 413, 435, 435a and 442
Overprinted or Surcharged in Black with
Bars and

公用
(K. P.)

1943-44   Unwmk.   Perf. 11x10½, 11

NO1	A75	2c apple green, Apr. 7, 1943	8	8
		Margin block of 4, P#	40	
a.		Double overprint		

NO2	A55	5(c) on 6c dark brown (On No. 413), June 26, 1944	20.00	20.00
		First day cover		45.00
NO3	A55	5(c) on 6c golden brown (On No. 435a), Apr. 7, 1943	15	15
a.		Narrower spacing between bars	20	20
b.		5(c) on 6c dark brown (On No. 435)	15	12
c.		As "b", narrower spacing between bars	20	20
NO4	A62	16(c) on 30c orange red, Apr. 7, 1943	45	45
a.		Wider spacing between bars	45	45
		First day cover (#NO1, NO3-NO4)		50.00

On Nos. NO3 and NO3b the bar deleting "United States of America" is 9¾ to 10mm. above the bar deleting "Common". On Nos. NO3a and NO3c, the spacing is 8 to 8½mm.

On No. NO4, the center bar is 19mm. long, 3½mm. below the top bar and 6mm. above the Japanese characters. On No. NO4a, the center bar is 20½mm. long, 9mm. below the top bar and 1mm. above the Japanese characters.

"K.P." stands for Kagamitang Pampamahalaan, "Official Business" in Tagalog.

Nos. 435 and 435a Surcharged
in Black

REPUBLIKA NG
PILIPINAS
(K. P.)

1944, Aug. 28   Unwmk.   Perf. 11

NO5	A55	(5c) on 6c golden brown	10	10
a.		5(c) on 6c dark brown	10	10

Nos. O34 and C62 Overprinted in Black

Pilipinas
REPUBLIKA

REPUBLIKA NG PILIPINAS

(K. P.)

K. P.

a   b

NO6	A60(a)	20c light olive green	35	35
NO7	AP1(b)	1p sepia	1.00	1.00
		First day cover, #NO5-NO7		3.00

OCCUPATION ENVELOPES

No. U41 Surcharged in Black

5   5

1943, Apr. 1

NU1	E3	5c on 2c carmine on white	50	30
		Entire	2.50	1.50
		Entire, 1st day cancel		5.00

No. U41 Surcharged in
Black

REPUBLIKA NG PILIPINAS

5   5

1944, Feb. 17

NU2	E3	5c on 2c carmine on white	50	30
		Entire	2.50	1.50
		Entire, 1st day cancel		7.50
a.		Inverted surcharged	—	
b.		Double surcharge	—	
c.		Both 5's missing	—	

OCCUPATION POSTAL CARDS

Prices are for entire cards.
Nos. UX19 and UZ4 Overprinted with Bars in Black

1942

NUX1	A53	2c red on pale buff, *Mar. 4, 1942*	7.50	4.00
		First day cancel		100.00
a.		Vertical obliteration bars reversed	200.00	
NUX2	A75	2c light green on pale buff, *Dec. 12, 1942*	4.00	3.00
		First day cancel		9.00

Rice Planting — A77

1943, May 17

NUX3	A77	2c green	1.50	*1.50*
		First day cancel, Manila		3.00

OCCUPATION OFFICIAL CARDS

Nos. UX19, UX17 and UX18 Overprinted in Black with Bars and 公 [印] **(K. P.)**

1943-44

NUZ1	A53	2c red on pale buff, *Apr. 7, 1943*	4.00	3.00
		First day cancel		100.00
a.		On No. UX17	—	
b.		On No. UX18	—	

REPUBLIKA NG PILIPINAS (K. P.)

No. NUX3 Overprinted in Black

NUZ2	A77	2c green, *Aug. 28, 1944*	1.50	*1.00*
		First day cancel		2.00
a.		Double overprint	—	

FILIPINO REVOLUTIONARY GOVERNMENT

The Filipino Republic was instituted by Gen. Emilio Aguinaldo on June 23, 1899. At the same time he assumed the office of President. Aguinaldo dominated the greater part of the island of Luzon and some of the smaller islands until late in 1899. He was taken prisoner by United States Troops on March 23, 1901.

The devices composing the National Arms, adopted by the Filipino Revolutionary Government, are emblems of the Katipunan political secret society or of Katipunan origin. The letters "K K K" on these stamps are the initials of this society whose complete name is "Kataas-taasang, Kagalang-galang Katipunan nang Manga Anak nang Bayan," meaning "Sovereign Worshipful Association of the Sons of the Country."

The regular postage and telegraph stamps were in use on Luzon as early as Nov. 10, 1898. Owing to the fact that stamps for the different purposes were not always available together with a lack of proper instructions, any of the adhesives were permitted to be used in the place of the other. Hence telegraph and revenue stamps were accepted for postage and postage stamps for revenue or telegraph charges. In addition to the regular postal emission, there are a number of provisional stamps, issues of local governments of islands and towns.

POSTAGE ISSUES

Coat of Arms
A1   A2   A3

1898-99   Unwmk.   *Perf. 11½*

Y1	A1	2c red	11.00	9.00
a.		Double impression	*300.00*	
Y2	A2	2c red	6	40
a.		Imperf., pair	—	
b.		Double impression	—	
c.		Imperf. horizontally, pair	—	—
d.		Horiz. pair, imperf. between	—	
Y3	A3	2c red	3.00	

REGISTRATION STAMP

RS1

YF1	RS1	8c green	18	2.00
a.		Imperf., pair	—	
b.		Imperf. vertically, pair	—	

NEWSPAPER STAMP

N1

YP1	N1	1m black	6	
a.		Imperf., pair	15	

PROOFS

1906

			DIE			PLATE (4)
			(1) Large	*(2)* Small	*(2a)*	Glazed Card
241P	2c	yellow green		225.00	400.00	
242P	4c	carmine lake	600.00	225.00	400.00	
243P	6c	violet	600.00	225.00	400.00	
244P	8c	brown	600.00	225.00	400.00	
245P	10c	dark blue		225.00	400.00	
246P	12c	brown lake		225.00	400.00	
247P	16c	violet black	600.00	225.00	400.00	
248P	20c	orange brown		225.00	400.00	
249P	26c	violet brown		225.00	400.00	
250P	30c	olive green	600.00	225.00	400.00	
251P	1p	orange		225.00	400.00	
252P	2p	black		225.00	400.00	
253P	4p	dark blue		225.00	400.00	
254P	10p	dark green		225.00	400.00	

1909-13

255P	12c	red orange		225.00	400.00
256P	16c	olive green		225.00	400.00
257P	20c	yellow		225.00	400.00
258P	26c	blue green		225.00	400.00
259P	30c	ultramarine		225.00	400.00
260P	1p	pale violet		225.00	400.00
260AP	2p	violet brown		225.00	400.00
275P	30c	gray		225.00	400.00

1923

303P	16c	olive bister	600.00
303TC	16c	olive green	600.00

1926

322P	18c	light brown & black	600.00

1932

357P	18c	red orange	600.00
357TC	18c	orange red	600.00

1935

383P	2c	rose	600.00
384P	4c	yellow green	600.00
385P	6c	dark brown	600.00
386P	8c	violet	600.00
387P	10c	rose carmine	600.00
388P	12c	black	600.00
389P	16c	dark blue	600.00
390P	20c	light olive green	600.00
390TC	20c	black	—
391P	26c	indigo	600.00
392P	30c	orange red	600.00
393P	1p	red orange & black	600.00
394P	2p	bister brown & black	600.00
395P	4p	blue & black	600.00
396P	5p	green & black	600.00

1936

408P	2c	orange brown	600.00
408TC	2c	yellow green	600.00

1937

425P	2c	yellow green	300.00

1939

452P	2c	yellow green	300.00
453P	6c	carmine	300.00
454P	12c	bright blue	300.00

1939

455P	2c	green	500.00	300.00
456P	6c	orange		300.00
457P	12c	carmine		300.00

1940

458P	2c	dark orange	500.00	300.00
459P	6c	dark green		300.00
460P	12c	purple		300.00

1941

461P	2c	apple green	300.00

1946

497P	2c	sepia	—

AIR POST

1941

C59P	8c	carmine	500.00
C60P	20c	ultramarine	500.00
C61P	60c	blue green	500.00
C62P	1p	sepia	500.00

SPECIAL DELIVERY

1906

E2P	20c	ultramarine	600.00	200.00	350.00
E2TC	20c	green		225.00	

POSTAGE DUE

1899

J1P	1c	deep claret	500.00
J2P	2c	deep claret	500.00
J3P	5c	deep claret	500.00
J4P	10c	deep claret	500.00
J5P	50c	deep claret	500.00

1901

J6P	3c	deep claret	500.00
J7P	30c	deep claret	500.00

SPECIMEN STAMPS

Overprinted in Black   Specimen.

1899

Type E

213S E	1c	yellow green	150.00
214S E	2c	orange red	150.00
215S E	3c	purple	150.00
216S E	5c	blue	150.00
217S E	10c	brown, type I	150.00
218S E	15c	olive brown	150.00
219S E	50c	orange	150.00

Special Printings (Paris 1899) with "Specimen" overprints exist. Price, each $350.

Overprinted in Black   *Specimen*

1917-25

Type R

290S R	2c	green	40.00
291S R	4c	carmine	40.00
292S R	6c	deep violet	40.00
293S R	8c	yellow brown	40.00
294S R	10c	deep blue	40.00
295S R	12c	red orange	40.00
297S R	20c	orange yellow	40.00
298S R	26c	green	40.00
299S R	30c	gray	40.00
300S R	1p	pale violet	40.00
301S R	2p	violet brown	40.00
302S R	4p	blue	40.00

1923-26

303S R	16c	olive bister	40.00
304S R	10p	deep green	40.00

1926   **Overprinted Type R in Red**

319S R	2c	green & black	50.00
320S R	4c	carmine & black	50.00
321S R	16c	olive green & black	50.00
322S R	18c	light brown & black	50.00
323S R	20c	orange & black	50.00
324S R	24c	gray & black	50.00
325S R	1p	rose lilac & black	50.00

Overprinted in Red   *Cancelled*

1926

Type S

319S S	2c	green & black	50.00
320S S	4c	carmine & black	50.00
321S S	16c	olive green & black	50.00
322S S	18c	light brown & black	50.00
323S S	20c	orange & black	50.00
324S S	24c	gray & black	50.00
325S S	1p	rose lilac & black	50.00

Imperforate copies of this set, on glazed cards with centers in brown, are known with the "Cancelled" overprint.

Handstamped "SPECIMEN" in Red Capitals, 13x3mm.

1925

340S	2c	green	30.00
341S	4c	carmine	30.00
342S	6c	deep violet	30.00

343S	8c	yellow brown	30.00
344S	10c	deep blue	30.00
345S	12c	red orange	30.00
346S	16c	olive bister	30.00
347S	20c	yellow	30.00
348S	26c	blue green	30.00
349S	30c	gray	30.00
350S	1p	violet	30.00
351S	2p	violet brown	30.00
352S	4p	deep blue	40.00
353S	10p	deep green	50.00

Special Delivery

1919   **Overprinted Type R in Black**

E5S R	20c	ultramarine	250.00

Handstamped "SPECIMEN" in Red Capitals, 13x3mm.

1925

E6aS	20c	violet blue	250.00

Postage Due

1899   **Overprinted Type E in Black**

J1S E	1c	deep claret	150.00
J2S E	2c	deep claret	150.00
J3S E	5c	deep claret	150.00
J4S E	10c	deep claret	150.00
J5S E	50c	deep claret	150.00

Official

1926   **Overprinted Type R in Red**

O1S R	2c	green & black	45.00
O2S R	4c	carmine & black	45.00
O3S R	18c	light brown & black	45.00
O4S R	20c	orange & black	45.00

1926   **Overprinted Type S in Red**

O1S S	2c	green & black	45.00
O2S S	4c	carmine & black	45.00
O3S S	18c	light brown & black	45.00
O4S S	20c	orange & black	45.00

PUERTO RICO

(Porto Rico)

United States troops landed at Guanica Bay, Puerto Rico, on July 25, 1898, and mail service between various points in Puerto Rico began soon after under the authority of General Wilson, acting governor of the conquered territory, who authorized a provisional service early in August, 1898. The first Military Postal Station was opened at La Playa de Ponce on August 3, 1898. Control of the island passed formally to the United States on October 18, 1898. Twenty-one military stations operating under the administration of the Military Postal Service, were authorized in Puerto Rico after the Spanish-American war. After the overprinted provisional issue of 1900, unoverprinted stamps of the United States replaced those of Puerto Rico.
Name changed to Puerto Rico by Act of Congress, approved May 17, 1932.

100 CENTS = 1 DOLLAR.

PROVISIONAL ISSUES

Ponce Issue

A11

1898   Unwmk.   Handstamped   Imperf.

200	A11	5c violet, *yellowish*	6,500.	—

Dangerous counterfeits exist.

Coamo Issue

A12

Types of "5":
I. Curved flag. Pos. 2, 3, 4, 5.
II. Flag turns down at right. Pos. 1, 9, 10.
III. Fancy outlined "5". Pos. 6, 7.
IV. Flag curls into ball at right. Pos. 8.

Typeset, setting of 10

1898, Aug.   Unwmk.   Imperf.

201	A12	5c black, Type I	425.00 425.00
		Type II	450.00 450.00
		Type III	475.00 475.00
		Type IV	500.00 500.00
		Pair	950.00 —
		Block of four	2,200.
		Sheet of ten	6,500.

	On cover	1,250.
	Pair on cover	

The stamps bear the control mark "F. Santiago" in violet. About 500 were issued.
Dangerous counterfeits exist.

Regular Issue

United States Nos. 279, 267, 281, 272 and 282C Overprinted in Black at 36 degree Angle

1899   Wmk. 191   Perf. 12

210	A87	1c yellow green	6.50	1.75
		On cover		20.00
		Block of four	30.00	15.00
		Margin strip of 3, Impt. & P#	50.00	
		Margin block of 6, Impt. & P#	200.00	
a.		Overprint at 25 degree angle	9.00	2.50
		Pair, 36 degree and 25 degree angles	25.00	
		"PORTO RICU"	30.00	—
211	A88	2c carmine, type III	6.00	1.50
		On cover		12.50
		Block of four	30.00	12.50
		Margin strip of 3, Impt. & P#	40.00	
		Margin block of 6, Impt. & P#	200.00	
a.		Overprint at 25 degree angle	7.50	2.00
		Pair, 36 degree and 25 degree angles	22.50	
		"PORTU RICO"	60.00	22.50
		"FORTO RICO"		
212	A91	5c blue	9.00	2.25
		On cover		40.00
		Block of four	42.50	20.00
		Margin strip of 3, Impt. & P#	75.00	
		Margin block of 6, Impt. & P#	300.00	
213	A93	8c violet brown	30.00	17.50
		On cover		175.00
		Block of four	150.00	90.00
		Margin strip of 3, Impt. & P#	250.00	
		Margin block of 6, Impt. & P#	1,000.	
a.		Overprint at 25 degree angle	37.50	20.00
		Pair, 36 degree and 25 degree angles	85.00	
		"FORTO RICO"		—
c.		"PORTO RIC"	125.00	125.00
214	A94	10c brown, type I	21.00	6.00
		On cover		150.00
		Block of four	95.00	45.00
		Margin strip of 3, Impt. & P#	750.00	
		Margin block of 6, Impt. & P#	100.00	100.00
		"FORTO RICO"		

Misspellings of the overprint on Nos. 210-214 (PORTO RICU, PORTU RICO, FORTO RICO) are actually broken letters.

United States Nos. 279, 267 and 279d Overprinted in Black

1900

215	A87	1c yellow green	6.50	1.75
		On cover		17.50
		Block of four	30.00	12.50
		Margin strip of 3, Impt. & P#	35.00	
		Margin block of 6, Impt. & P#	150.00	
216	A88	2c carmine, type III	6.00	1.25
		On cover		15.00
		Block of four	26.00	9.00
		Margin strip of 3, Impt. & P#	35.00	
		Margin block of 6, Impt. & P#	135.00	
a.		2c orange red, type III	6.50	1.25
b.		Inverted overprint		4,500.

Special Printing

In 1899 one sheet each of Nos. 210-212 and 214, and two sheets each of Nos. 213, J1-J3 were specially overprinted "Porto Rico" for display at the Paris Exposition. Price, each $400. Later another special printing of Nos. 212-216, J1-J3 was made reading "Puerto Rico." Price, each $550.
Of both printings, all but a few copies were destroyed. Nearly all existing copies of Nos. 215-216 are handstamped "Special Surcharge" on the back.

AIR POST

In 1938 a series of eight labels, two of which were surcharged, was offered to the public as "Semi-Official Air Post Stamps", the claim being that they had been authorized by the "Puerto Rican postal officials." These labels, printed by the Ever Ready Label Co. of New York, were a private issue of Aerovias Nacionales Puerto Rico, operating a passenger and air express service. Instead of having been authorized by the postal officials, they were at first forbidden but later tolerated by the Post Office Department at Washington.
In 1941 a further set of eight triangular labels was prepared and offered to collectors, and again the Post Office Department officials at Washington objected and forbade their use after September 16, 1941.
These labels represent only the charge for service rendered by a private enterprise for transporting matter outside the mails by plane. Their use did not and does not eliminate the payment of postage on letters carried by air express, which must in every instance be paid by United States postage stamps.

POSTAGE DUE STAMPS

United States Nos. J38, J39 and J42 Overprinted in Black at 36 degree Angle

1899		Wmk. 191			*Perf. 12*
J1	D2	1c deep claret		22.00	8.00
		On cover			
		Block of four		100.00	75.00
		Margin strip of 3, Impt. & P#		150.00	
		Margin block of 6, Impt. & P#		*600.00*	
a.		Overprint at 25 degree angle		27.50	10.00
		Pair, 36 degree and 25 degree angles		80.00	
J2	D2	2c deep claret		15.00	7.50
		On cover		70.00	—
		Block of four		150.00	
		Margin strip of 3, Impt. & P#		*600.00*	
		Margin block of 6, Impt. & P#			
a.		Overprint at 25 degree angle		20.00	8.50
		Pair, 36 degree and 25 degree angles		50.00	
J3	D2	10c deep claret		150.00	55.00
		Block of four		750.00	
		Margin strip of 3, Impt. & P#		800.00	
		Margin block of 6, Impt. & P#		*3,000.*	
a.		Overprint at 25 degree angle		185.00	65.00
		Pair, 36 degree and 25 degree angles		425.00	

ENVELOPES

U.S. Envelopes of 1887 Issue Overprinted in Black

PORTO RICO.

20mm. long.

1899-1900

Note: Some envelopes for which there was no obvious need were issued in small quantities. Anyone residing in Puerto Rico could, by depositing with his postmaster the required amount, order any envelope in quantities of 500, or multiples thereof, provided it was on the schedule of U.S. envelopes. Such special orders are indicated by an plus sign, i. e., Nos. U15 and U18, and half the quantities of Nos. U16 and U17.

U1	U71	2c green on white (No. U311) *(3,000)*	15.00	20.00
		Entire	45.00	55.00
a.		Double overprint, entire		
U2	U74	5c blue on white (No. U330) *(1,000)*	20.00	20.00
		Entire	55.00	55.00
		Double overprint, entire		

U.S. Envelopes of 1899 Overprinted in color of the stamp

PORTO RICO.

21mm. long.

U3	U79	2c carmine on white (No. U362) *(100,000)*	3.00	3.00
		Entire	10.00	12.50
U4	U84	5c blue on white (No. U377) *(10,000)*	8.00	10.00
		Entire	17.50	32.50

Overprinted in Black   **PORTO RICO.**

19mm. long.

U5	U77	1c green on blue (No. U355) *(1,000)*		750.00
		Entire		2,250.
U6	U79	2c carmine on amber (No. U363), Die 2 *(500)*	500.00	600.00
		Entire	1,250.	1,500.
U7	U79	2c carmine on oriental buff (No. U364), Die 2 *(500)*		600.00
		Entire		1,500.
U8	U80	2c carmine on oriental buff (No. U369), Die 3 *(500)*		750.00
		Entire		1,500.
U9	U79	2c carmine on blue (No. U365), Die 2		
		Entire		*4,000.*
U10	U83	4c brown on white (No. U374), Die 3 *(500)*	250.00	
		Entire	400.00	*500.00*

U.S. Envelopes of 1899 Issue Overprinted

PUERTO RICO.

23mm. long.

U11	U79	2c carmine on white (No. U362) red overprint *(100,000)*	4.00	3.00
		Entire	10.00	11.00
U12	U79	2c carmine on oriental buff (No. U364), Die 2, black overprint *(1,000)*	—	350.00
		Entire	*1,250.*	*1,350.*
U13	U80	2c carmine on oriental buff (No. U369), Die 3, black overprint *(1,000)*		350.00
		Entire		*2,000.*
U14	U84	5c blue on white (No. U377) blue overprint *(10,000)*	15.00	15.00
		Entire	45.00	55.00

Overprinted in Black   **PUERTO RICO.**

U15	U77	1c green on oriental buff (No. U354)	20.00	50.00
		(500)+		
		Entire	75.00	80.00
U16	U77	1c green on blue (No. U355)	25.00	50.00
		(1,000)+		
		Entire	95.00	135.00
U17	U79	2c carmine on oriental buff (No. U364) *(1,000)*+	20.00	50.00
		Entire	95.00	135.00
U18	U79	2c carmine on blue (No. U365)	20.00	50.00
		(500)+		
		Entire	75.00	135.00

There were two settings of the overprint, with minor differences, which are found on Nos. U16 and U17.

WRAPPER

U.S. Wrapper of 1899 Issue Overprinted in Green

PORTO RICO.

21mm. long

W1	U77	1c green on manila (No. W357)		
		(15,000)	8.00	30.00
		Entire	17.50	90.00

POSTAL CARDS

Prices are for Entires.

Imprinted below stamp   **PORTO RICO.**

1899-1900   **U.S. Postal Card No. UX14**

UX1	PC8 1c black on buff, imprint 21mm. long	165.00	175.00
b.	Double imprint		*2,500.*

Imprinted below stamp   **PORTO RICO.**

UX1A	PC8 1c black on buff, imprint 20mm. long	1,100.	1,350.

Imprinted below stamp   **PORTO RICO.**

UX2	PC8 1c black on buff, imprint 26mm. long	175.00	190.00

Imprinted below stamp   **PUERTO RICO.**

UX3	PC8 1c black on buff	175.00	190.00

SPECIMEN

Overprinted in black   **Specimen.**

1899

210S	E	1c yellow green	200.00
211S	E	2c carmine	200.00
212S	E	5c blue	200.00
213S	E	8c violet brown	200.00
214S	E	10c brown	200.00

The Special Printing of Nos. 212-214 (5c, 8c, 10c) with "Puerto Rico" overprint received the "Specimen" overprint. Price about $300 each.

Postage Due

1899

J1S	E	1c deep claret	200.00
J2S	E	2c deep claret	200.00
J3S	E	10c deep claret	200.00

Puerto Rico stamps can be mounted in
Scott's U.S. Possessions Album.

REVENUE

U.S. Revenue Stamps Nos. R163, R168-R169, R171 and Type of 1898 Surcharged in Black or Dark Blue

**PORTO RICO
10 c.
Excise Revenue**
a

PORTO RICO $1 EXCISE REVENUE
b

1901		Wmk. 191R		*Hyphen-hole Roulette 7*	
R1	R15(a)	1c on 1c pale blue (Bk)		8.00	7.00
R2	R15(a)	10c on 10c dark brown		11.00	8.00
R3	R15(a)	25c on 25c purple brown		13.00	9.00
R4	R15(a)	50c on 50c slate violet		21.00	12.50
R5	R16(b)	$1 on $1 pale greenish gray		55.00	18.00
R6	R16(b)	$3 on $3 pale greenish gray		65.00	24.00
R7	R16(b)	$5 on $5 pale greenish gray		75.00	32.50
R8	R16(b)	$10 on $10 pale greenish gray		110.00	50.00
R9	R16(b)	$50 on $50 pale greenish gray		325.00	125.00

Lines of 1c surcharge spaced farther apart; total depth of surcharge 15¾mm. instead of 11mm.

RECTIFIED SPIRITS

RECTIFIED

U.S. Wine Stamps of 1933-34 Overprinted in Red or Carmine

SPIRITS

1934		Offset Printing	Wmk. 191R	*Rouletted 7*

Overprint Lines 14mm. Apart, Second Line 25mm. Long

RE1	RE5	2c green	10.00
RE2	RE5	3c green	45.00
RE3	RE5	4c green	12.00
RE4	RE5	5c green	10.00
RE5	RE5	6c green	12.00

Overprint Lines 21½mm. Apart, Second Line 23½mm. Long

RE6	RE2	50c green	22.50
RE7	RE2	60c green	20.00

Handstamped overprints are also found on U.S. Wine stamps of 1933-34.

U.S. Wine Stamps of 1933-34 Overprinted in Black

RECTIFIED

RECTIFIED

SPIRITS   **SPIRITS**
a   b

1934		Offset Printing	Wmk. 191R	*Rouletted 7*
RE8	RE5(a)	1c green		20.00
RE9	RE5(a)	2c green		10.00
RE10	RE5(a)	2c green		50.00
RE11	RE5(a)	5c green		10.00
RE12	RE5(a)	6c green		12.00
RE13	RE2(b)	50c green		15.00
RE14	RE2(b)	60c green		12.00
RE15	RE2(b)	72c green		60.00
RE16	RE2(b)	80c green		35.00

RECTIFIED SPIRITS

U.S. Wine Stamps of 1933-34 Overprinted in Black

PUERTO RICO

1934		Offset Printing	Wmk. 191R	*Rouletted 7*
RE17	RE5	½c green		2.50
RE18	RE5	1c green		60
RE19	RE5	2c green		50

RE20	RE5	3c green	3.50
RE21	RE5	4c green	75
RE22	RE5	5c green	1.00
RE23	RE5	6c green	1.25
RE24	RE5	10c green	3.50
RE25	RE5	30c green	30.00

Overprint Lines 12½mm. Apart

RE26	RE2	36c green	6.00
RE27	RE2	40c green	5.00
RE28	RE2	50c green	2.50
RE29	RE2	60c green	50
a.		Inverted overprint	
RE30	RE2	72c green	3.00
RE31	RE2	80c green	4.00
RE32	RE2	$1 green	7.50

George Sewall
Boutwell — R1

Engr. 8c & 58c; Litho.

| 1942-57 | | **Wmk. 191**
Without Gum | | **Rouletted 7** |
|---|---|---|---|---|
| RE33 | R1 | ½c carmine | 3.00 | 1.25 |
| RE34 | R1 | 1c sepia | 7.50 | 3.50 |
| RE35 | R1 | 2c bright yellow green | 1.00 | 15 |
| RE36 | R1 | 3c lilac | 60.00 | 32.50 |
| RE37 | R1 | 4c olive | 2.00 | 50 |
| RE38 | R1 | 5c orange | 4.50 | 1.00 |
| RE39 | R1 | 6c red brown | 3.50 | 1.25 |
| RE40 | R1 | 8c bright pink ('57) | 7.00 | 3.50 |
| RE41 | R1 | 10c bright purple | 11.00 | 5.00 |
| RE41A | R1 | 30c vermilion | 175.00 | |
| RE42 | R1 | 36c dull yellow | 150.00 | 65.00 |
| RE43 | R1 | 40c deep claret | 18.00 | 7.00 |
| RE44 | R1 | 50c green | 10.00 | 4.00 |
| RE45 | R1 | 58c red orange | 70.00 | 6.00 |
| RE46 | R1 | 60c brown | 1.25 | 15 |
| RE47 | R1 | 62c black | 3.00 | 70 |
| RE48 | R1 | 72c blue | 35.00 | 1.00 |
| RE49 | R1 | 77½c olive gray | 10.00 | 3.50 |

RE50	R1	80c brownish black	12.00	6.00
RE51	R1	$1 violet	75.00	22.50

The 30c is believed not to have been placed in use.

RYUKYU ISLANDS

LOCATION — Chain of 63 islands between Japan and Formosa, separating the East China Sea from the Pacific Ocean.
GOVT. — Semi-autonomous under United States administration.
AREA — 848 sq. mi.
POP. — 945,465 (1970)
CAPITAL — Naha, Okinawa

The Ryukyus were part of Japan until American forces occupied them in 1945. The islands reverted to Japan May 15, 1972.

100 Sen = 1 Yen
100 Cents = 1 Dollar (1958).

Cycad — A1

Sailing
Ship — A3

Lily — A2

Farmer — A4

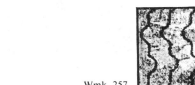

Wmk. 257

1948-49		**Typo.** **Wmk. 257**		**Perf. 13**
		Second Printing		
1	A1	5s magenta	1.25	1.25
2	A2	10s yel grn	3.25	2.75
3	A1	20s yel grn	2.25	2.00
4	A3	30s vermilion	1.25	1.25
5	A2	40s magenta	1.25	1.25
6	A3	50s ultra	2.75	2.75
7	A4	1y ultra	3.00	3.00
		First Printing		
1a	A1	5s magenta	2.25	4.00
2a	A2	10s yel grn	1.40	2.50
3a	A1	20s yel grn	1.40	2.50
4a	A3	30s vermilion	2.25	3.50
5a	A2	40s magenta	45.00	45.00
6a	A3	50s ultra	2.25	4.00

7a	A4	1y ultra	250.00	225.00
		First day covers. #1a-7a, each		300.00

First printing: thick yellow gum, dull colors, rough perforations, grayish paper. Second printing: white gum, sharp colors, cleancut perforations, white paper.
Issue dates: First printing, July 1, 1948: second printing, July 18, 1949.

Imprint Blocks of 10, Unused

1	30.00
1a	40.00
2	60.00
2a	25.00
3	40.00
3a	25.00
4	30.00
4a	40.00
5	25.00
5a	550.00
6	50.00
6a	40.00
7	50.00
7a	3,500.

See the "Information for Collectors" section at beginning of catalogue for an explanation of paper types, watermarks and grills.

Roof Tiles — A5　　　Ryukyu University — A6

Designs: 1y, Ryukyu girl. 2y, Shuri Castle. 3y, Guardian dragon. 4y, Two women. 5y, Sea shells.

1950, Jan. 21　Photo.　Unwmk.　Perf. 13x13½
Off-white Paper

8	A5	50s dk car rose	20	20
		First day cover		30.00
		Imprint block of 6	2.00	
a.		White paper	50	50
		First day cover, *Sept. 6, 1958*		50.00
		Imprint block of 10	6.50	
9	A5	1y dp bl	2.25	2.00
		First day cover		30.00
		Imprint block of 6	15.00	
10	A5	2y rose vio	8.25	5.00
		First day cover		30.00
		Imprint block of 6	60.00	
11	A5	3y car rose	16.00	5.00
		First day cover		30.00
		Imprint block of 6	125.00	
12	A5	4y grnsh gray	10.00	4.25
		First day cover		30.00
		Imprint block of 6	75.00	
13	A5	5y bl grn	4.50	3.75
		First day cover		30.00
		Imprint block of 6	40.00	
		First day cover. #8-13		200.00

No. 8a has colorless gum and an 8-character imprint in the sheet margin. The original 1950 printing on off-white paper has yellowish gum and a 5-character imprint.

1951, Feb. 12　　　　　　　　Perf. 13½x13

14	A6	3y red brn	42.50	18.00
		First day cover		70.00
		Imprint block of 6	325.00	

Opening of Ryukyu University, Feb. 12.

Pine Tree — A7

1951, Feb. 19　　　　　　　　　　Perf. 13

15	A7	3y dk grn	40.00	18.00
		First day cover		70.00
		Imprint block of 6	300.00	

Reforestation Week, Feb. 18-24.

Nos. 8 and 10 Surcharged in Black

改　訂　　　　　　　　　改　訂

*　　　　　　　　　　　　*

10 圓　　　　　　　　　10 圓
━━━━━　　　　　　　━━━━━
Type I　　　　　　　　Type II

改　訂

*

10 圓
━━━━━
Type III

Three types of 10y surcharge:
I.　Narrow-spaced rules, "10" normal spacing.
II.　Wide-spaced rules, "10" normal spacing.
III.　Rules and "10" both wide-spaced.

1952　　　　　　　　　　　　Perf. 13x13½

16	A5	10y on 50s dk car rose (II)	10.50	10.50
		Imprint block of 6	90.00	
a.		Type I	30.00	30.00
		Imprint block of 6	250.00	
b.		Type III	37.50	37.50
		Imprint block of 6	300.00	

17	A5	100y on 2y rose vio	1,500.	1,250.
		Imprint block of 6	12,500.	

These are two types of surcharge on No. 17.

Dove, Bean Sprout　　　　　Madanbashi
and Map — A8　　　　　　　Bridge — A9

1952, Apr. 1　　　　　　　　Perf. 13½x13

18	A8	3y dp plum	85.00	30.00
		First day cover		90.00
		Imprint block of 10	1,300.	

Establishment of the Government of the Ryukyu Islands (GRI), April 1, 1952.

1952-53

Designs: 2y, Main Hall, Shuri Castle. 3y, Shruei Gate. 6y, Stone Gate, Soenji Temple, Naha. 10y, Benzaiten-do Temple. 30y, Sonohan Utaki (altar) at Shuri Castle. 50y, Tamaudun (royal mausoleum). Shuri. 100y, Stone Bridge, Hosho Pond, Enkaku Temple.

19	A9	1y red	30	30
		Imprint block of 10	4.00	
20	A9	2y green	40	40
		Imprint block of 10	5.50	
21	A9	3y aqua	50	50
		First day cover, #19-21		40.00
		Imprint block of 10	7.00	
22	A9	6y blue	2.00	3.00
		First day cover		30.00
		Imprint block of 10	27.50	
23	A9	10y crim rose	3.25	50
		First day cover		50.00
		Imprint block of 10	37.50	
24	A9	30y ol grn	11.00	7.00
		First day cover		90.00
		Imprint block of 10	120.00	
a.		lt ol grn ('58)	40.00	
		Imprint block of 10	600.00	
25	A9	50y rose vio	9.50	5.50
		First day cover		150.00
		Imprint block of 10	110.00	
26	A9	100y claret	12.00	3.50
		First day cover		250.00
		First day cover, #22-26		650.00
		Imprint block of 10	150.00	

Issue dates: 1y, 2y and 3y, Nov. 20, 1952. Others, Jan. 20, 1953.

Reception at Shuri
Castle — A10

Perry and
American
Fleet — A11

1953, May 26　　　　Perf. 13½x13, 13x13½

27	A10	3y dp mag	10.50	6.00
		Imprint block of 6	75.00	
28	A11	6y dl bl	1.00	1.00
		First day cover. #27-28		14.00
		Imprint block of 6	10.00	

Centenary of the arrival of Commodore Matthew Calbraith Perry at Naha, Okinawa.

Ryukyu Islands stamps can be mounted in Scott's Ryukyu Islands Album.

Chofu Ota and　　　　　Shigo Toma and
Pencil-shaped　　　　　　Pen — A13
Matrix — A12

1953, Oct. 1　　　　　　　　Perf. 13½x13

29	A12	4y yel brn	10.00	3.75
		First day cover		20.00
		Imprint block of 10	120.00	

Third Newspaper Week.

1954, Oct. 1

30	A13	4y blue	12.00	6.00
		First day cover		25.00
		Imprint block of 10	140.00	

Fourth Newspaper Week.

Ryukyu　　　　　　Noguni Shrine and
Pottery — A14　　　　Sweet Potato
　　　　　　　　　Plant — A15

Designs: 15y, Lacquerware. 20y, Textile design.

1954-55　　　　Photo.　　　　Perf. 13

31	A14	4y brown	1.00	50
		First day cover		9.00
		Imprint block of 10	12.50	
32	A14	15y ver ('55)	3.50	2.50
		First day cover		15.00
		Imprint block of 10	40.00	
33	A14	20y yel org ('55)	2.50	2.00
		First day cover		15.00
		Imprint block of 10	32.50	
		First day cover, #32-33		40.00

1955, Nov. 26

34	A15	4y blue	12.00	6.00

First day cover 25.00
Imprint block of 10 140.00

350th anniv. of the introduction of the sweet potato to the Ryukyu Islands.

Stylized Trees — A16

Willow Dance — A17

1956, Feb. 18 **Unwmk.**
35 A16 4y bluish grn 10.00 5.00
First day cover 22.50
Imprint block of 6 75.00

Arbor Week, Feb. 18-24.

1956, May 1 **Perf. 13**

Design: 8y, Straw hat dance. 14y, Dancer in warrior costume with fan.

36 A17 5y rose lil 1.00 60
First day cover 10.00
Imprint block of 10 14.00
37 A17 8y vio bl 2.50 2.00
First day cover 10.00
Imprint block of 10 30.00
38 A17 14y redsh brn 3.00 2.50
First day cover 10.00
First day cover, #36-38 35.00
Imprint block of 10 32.50

Telephone A18

1956, June 8
39 A18 4y vio bl 14.00 7.00
First day cover 15.00
Imprint block of 6 90.00

Establishment of dial telephone system.

Garland of Pine, Bamboo and Plum — A19

Map of Okinawa and Pencil Rocket — A20

1956, Dec. 1 **Perf. 13½x13**
40 A19 2y multi 2.00 1.00
First day cover 4.00
Imprint block of 10 25.00

New Year, 1957.

1957, Oct. 1 **Photo.** **Perf. 13½x13**
41 A20 4y dp vio bl 1.00 1.00
First day cover 6.00
Imprint block of 10 11.00

7th annual Newspaper Week, Oct. 1-7.

Phoenix — A21

1957, Dec. 1 **Unwmk.** **Perf. 13**
42 A21 2y multi 25 25
First day cover 2.00
Imprint block of 10 3.50

New Year, 1958.

Ryukyu Stamps A22

1958, July 1 **Perf. 13½**
43 A22 4y multi 1.00 75
First day cover 2.00
Imprint block of 4 4.50

10th anniv. of 1st Ryukyu stamps.

Yen Symbol and Dollar Sign — A23

Perf. 10, 10½, 11 & Compound
1958, Sept. 16
Without Gum **Typo.**
44 A23 ½c orange 55 55
Imprint block of 6 4.00
Horiz. or vert. pair, imperf. btwn. 75.00
a. Imperf., pair 1,250.
45 A23 1c yel grn 1.10 70
Imprint block of 6 7.50
Horiz. pair, imperf. btwn. 100.00
Vert. pair, imperf. btwn. 90.00
46 A23 2c dk bl 1.40 1.25
Imprint block of 6 9.00
Horiz. pair, imperf. btwn. 125.00
Vert. pair, imperf. btwn. 1,000.
47 A23 3c dp car 1.10 70
Imprint block of 6 7.50
Horiz. or vert. pair, imperf. btwn. 75.00
48 A23 4c brt grn 1.25 1.10
First day cover, #44-48 8.00
Imprint block of 6 9.00
Horiz. pair, imperf. btwn. 500.00
Vert. pair, imperf. btwn. 100.00
49 A23 5c orange 2.50 2.50
Imprint block of 6 17.50
Horiz. pair, imperf. btwn. 100.00
Vert. pair, imperf. btwn. 300.00
50 A23 10c aqua 3.50 3.50
Imprint block of 6 27.50
Horiz. pair, imperf. btwn. 200.00
Vert. pair, imperf. btwn. 125.00
51 A23 25c brt vio bl 5.00 5.00
Imprint block of 6 37.50
Horiz. or vert. pair, imperf. btwn. 1,000.
a. Gummed paper ('61) 8.00
Imprint block of 6 85.00
52 A23 50c gray 12.00 8.00
Imprint block of 6 85.00
Horiz. pair, imperf. btwn. 1,000.
a. Gummed paper ('61) 11.00
First day cover, #51a-52a 20.00
Imprint block of 6 85.00
53 A23 $1 rose lil 10.00 3.00
First day cover, #49-53 25.00
First day cover, #44-53 40.00
Imprint block of 6 75.00
Horiz. pair, imperf. btwn. 300.00
Vert. pair, imperf. btwn. 1,000.

Printed locally. Perforation, paper and shade varieties exist.

Gate of Courtesy A24

1958, Oct. 15 **Photo.** **Perf. 13½**
54 A24 3c multi 1.25 1.00
First day cover 2.00
Imprint block of 4 5.50

Restoration of Shureimon, Gate of Courtesy, on road leading to Shuri City.

Lion Dance — A25

Trees and Mountains — A26

1958, Dec. 10 **Unwmk.** **Perf. 13½**
55 A25 1½c multi 25 25
First day cover 1.75
Imprint block of 6 2.25

New Year, 1959.

1959, Apr. 30 **Litho.** **Perf. 13½x13**
56 A26 3c bl, yel grn, grn & red 80 75
First day cover 2.00
Imprint block of 6 6.00
a. Red omitted —

"Make the Ryukyus Green" movement.

Yonaguni Moth — A27

1959, July 23 **Photo.** **Perf. 13**
57 A27 3c multi 1.25 75
First day cover 2.00
Imprint block of 6 8.00

Meeting of the Japanese Biological Education Society in Okinawa.

Hibiscus — A28

Toy (Yakaji) — A29

Designs: 3c, Fish (Moorish idol). 8c, Sea shell (Phalium bandatum). 13c, Butterfly (Kallinia Inachus Eucerca), denomination at left, butterfly going up. 17c, Jellyfish (Dactylometra pacifera Goette).

Inscribed: 琉球郵便

1959, Aug. 10 **Perf. 13x13½**
58 A28 ½c multi 25 25
Imprint block of 10 4.00

59	A28	3c	multi	1.00	50
			Imprint block of 10	13.50	
60	A28	8c	lt ultra, blk & ocher	8.00	7.00
			Imprint block of 10	90.00	
61	A28	13c	lt bl, gray & org	2.75	2.25
			Imprint block of 10	30.00	
62	A28	17c	vio bl, red & yel	18.00	10.00
			First day cover, #58-62		25.00
			Imprint block of 10	225.00	

Four-character inscription measures 10x2 mm. on ½c; 12x3mm. on 3c, 8c; 8½x2 mm. on 13c, 17c. See Nos. 76-80.

1959, Dec. 1   **Litho.**

63	A29	1½c	gold & multi	80	40
			First day cover		1.50
			Imprint block of 10	12.50	

New Year, 1960.

University Badge — A30

1960, May 22   **Photo.**   **Perf. 13**

64	A30	3c	multi	1.10	55
			First day cover		1.50
			Imprint block of 6	8.50	

10th anniv. opening of Ryukyu University.

Dancer — A31

Designs: Various Ryukyu Dances.

1960, Nov. 1   **Photo.**   **Perf. 13**
Dark Gray Background

65	A31	1c	yel, red & vio	1.25	80
			Imprint block of 10	17.50	
66	A31	2½c	crim, bl & yel	2.50	80
			Imprint block of 10	30.00	
67	A31	5c	dk bl, yel & red	80	70
			Imprint block of 10	12.50	
68	A31	10c	dk bl, yel & red	80	80
			First day cover, #65-68		9.50
			Imprint block of 10	12.50	

See Nos. 81-87, 220.

Torch and Nago Bay — A32

Runners at Starting Line — A33

1960, Nov. 8

72	A32	3c	lt bl, grn & red	7.00	3.00
			First day cover		3.50
			Imprint block of 6	50.00	
73	A33	8c	orange & slate green	1.00	1.00
			First day cover		3.00
			First day cover, #72-73		9.00
			Imprint block of 6	7.50	

8th Kyushu Inter-Prefectural Athletic Meet, Nago, Northern Okinawa, Nov. 6-7.

Little Egret and Rising Sun — A34

1960, Dec. 1   **Unwmk.**   **Perf. 13**

74	A34	3c	redsh brn	6.00	3.00
			First day cover		6.00
			Imprint block of 6	40.00	

National census.

Okinawa Bull Fight — A35

1960, Dec. 10   **Perf. 13½**

75	A35	1½c	bis, dk bl & red brn	2.00	75
			First day cover		3.50
			Imprint block of 6	14.00	

New Year, 1961.

Type of 1959 With Japanese Inscription Redrawn: 琉球郵便

1960-61   **Photo.**   **Perf. 13x13½**

76	A28	½c	multi ('61)	35	30
			Imprint block of 10	5.00	
77	A28	3c	multi ('61)	1.00	30
			First day cover		2.50
			Imprint block of 10	12.50	
78	A28	8c	lt ultra, blk & ocher	1.00	50
			Imprint block of 10	12.50	
79	A28	13c	bl, brn & red	1.25	85
			Imprint block of 10	15.00	
80	A28	17c	vio bl, red & yel	8.00	4.50
			First day cover, #78-80		25.00
			Imprint block of 10	100.00	

Size of Japanese inscription on Nos. 78-80 is 10½x1½mm. On No. 79 the denomination is at right, butterfly going down.

Dancer Type of 1960 with "RYUKYUS" Added.

1961-64   **Perf. 13**

81	A31	1c	multi	20	15
			First day cover		1.50
			Imprint block of 10	3.00	
82	A31	2½c	multi ('62)	30	15
			Imprint block of 10	3.50	
83	A31	5c	multi ('62)	35	30
			Imprint block of 10	4.50	
84	A31	10c	multi ('62)	65	50
			First day cover, #82-84		3.00
			Imprint block of 10	7.50	
84A	A31	20c	multi ('64)	1.65	1.25
			First day cover		3.50
			Imprint block of 10	20.00	
85	A31	25c	multi ('62)	1.25	1.10
			First day cover		4.00
			Imprint block of 10	17.50	
86	A31	50c	multi	3.25	1.00
			Imprint block of 10	37.50	
87	A31	$1	multi	4.50	20
			First day cover		45.00
			Imprint block of 10	55.00	

Pine Tree — A36

1961, May 1   **Photo.**   **Perf. 13**

88	A36	3c	yel grn & red	1.50	1.25
			First day cover		2.50
			Imprint block of 6	12.00	

"Make the Ryukyus Green" movement.

Naha, Steamer and Sailboat — A37

1961, May 20

89	A37	3c	aqua	2.50	1.25
			First day cover		2.50
			Imprint block of 6	18.50	

40th anniv. of Naha.

White Silver Temple — A38

Books and Bird — A39

1961, Oct. 1   **Typo.**   **Unwmk.**   **Perf. 11**

90	A38	3c	red brn	2.00	1.75
			First day cover		3.50
			Imprint block of 6	12.00	
a.			Horiz. pair, imperf. between	400.00	
b.			Vert. pair, imperf. between	350.00	

Merger of townships Takamine, Kanegushiku and Miwa with Itoman.

1961, Nov. 12   **Litho.**   **Perf. 13**

91	A39	3c	multi	1.75	1.25
			First day cover		2.50
			Imprint block of 6	14.50	

Book Week.

Rising Sun and Eagles — A40

Symbolic Steps, Trees and Government Building — A41

1961, Dec. 10   **Photo.**   **Perf. 13½**

92	A40	1½c	gold, ver & blk	2.00	1.75
			First day cover		3.00
			Imprint block of 6	15.00	

New Year, 1962.

1962, Apr. 1   **Unwmk.**   **Perf. 13½**

Design: 3c, Government Building.

93	A41	1½c	multi	75	80
			Imprint block of 6	6.00	
94	A41	3c	brt grn, red & gray	1.25	1.00
			First day cover, #93-94		3.00
			Imprint block of 6	9.00	

10th anniv. of the Government of the Ryukyu Islands (GRI).

Anopheles Hyrcanus Sinensis — A42

Design: 8c, Malaria eradication emblem and Shurei gate.

1962, Apr. 7   *Perf. 13¹/₂x13*
95	A42	3c multi	75	80
		Imprint block of 6	6.50	
96	A42	8c multi	1.50	1.00
		First day cover, #95-96		3.50
		Imprint block of 6	12.50	

World Health Organization drive to eradicate malaria.

Dolls and Toys — A43

Linden or Sea Hibiscus — A44

1962, May 5   **Litho.**   *Perf. 13¹/₂*
97	A43	3c red, blk, bl & buff	1.75	1.00
		First day cover		3.00
		Imprint block of 6	14.00	

Children's Day, 1962.

1962, June 1   **Photo.**

Flowers: 3c, Indian coral tree. 8c, Iju (Schima liukiuensis Nakal). 13c, Touch-me-not (garden balsam). 17c, Shell flower (Alpinia speciosa).
98	A44	¹/₂c multi	10	10
		Imprint block of 10	1.50	
99	A44	3c multi	40	15
		Imprint block of 10	4.50	
100	A44	8c multi	45	45
		Imprint block of 10	6.00	
101	A44	13c multi	70	65
		Imprint block of 10	8.00	
102	A44	17c multi	1.00	1.00
		First day cover, #98-102		6.50
		Imprint block of 10	12.50	

See Nos. 107 and 114 for 1¹/₂c and 15c flower stamps.

Earthenware — A45

1962, July 5   *Perf. 13¹/₂x13*
103	A45	3c multi	4.50	3.50
		First day cover		5.50
		Imprint block of 6	30.00	

Philatelic Week.

Japanese Fencing (Kendo) — A46

1962, July 25   *Perf. 13*
104	A46	3c multi	5.00	3.75
		First day cover		5.50
		Imprint block of 6	35.00	

All-Japan Kendo Meeting in Okinawa, July 25, 1962.

Rabbit Playing near Water, Bingata Cloth Design — A47

Young Man and Woman, Stone Relief — A48

1962, Dec. 10   *Perf. 13x13¹/₂*
105	A47	1¹/₂c gold & multi	1.25	1.00
		First day cover		2.50
		Imprint block of 10	15.00	

New Year, 1963.

1963, Jan. 15   **Photo.**   *Perf. 13¹/₂*
106	A48	3c gold, blk & bl	1.25	1.00
		First day cover		2.50
		Imprint block of 6	9.00	

Gooseneck Cactus — A49

Trees and Wooded Hills — A50

1963, Apr. 5   *Perf. 13x13¹/₂*
107	A49	1¹/₂c dk bl grn, yel & pink	10	10
		First day cover		2.50
		Imprint block of 10	1.50	

1963, Mar. 25   *Perf. 13¹/₂x13*
108	A50	3c ultra, grn & red brn	1.25	1.25
		First day cover		2.50
		Imprint block of 6	9.00	

"Make the Ryukyus Green" movement.

Map of Okinawa — A51

Hawks over Islands — A52

1963, Apr. 30   **Unwmk.**   *Perf. 13¹/₂*
109	A51	3c multi	1.50	1.50
		First day cover		3.00
		Imprint block of 6	12.50	

Opening of the Round Road on Okinawa.

1963, May 10   **Photo.**
110	A52	3c multi	1.25	1.25
		First day cover		2.50
		Imprint block of 6	12.50	

Bird Day, May 10.

Shioya Bridge — A53

1963, June 5
111	A53	3c multi	1.25	1.25

First day cover   2.50
Imprint block of 6   9.00

Opening of Shioya Bridge over Shioya Bay.

Tsuikin-wan Lacquerware Bowl — A54

1963, July 1   **Unwmk.**   *Perf. 13¹/₂*
112	A54	3c multi	3.00	2.50
		First day cover		5.50
		Imprint block of 6	22.50	

Map of Far East and JCI Emblem — A55

1963, Sept. 16   **Photo.**   *Perf. 13¹/₂*
113	A55	3c multi	1.10	75
		First day cover		2.50
		Imprint block of 6	8.50	

Meeting of the International Junior Chamber of Commerce (JCI), Naha, Okinawa, Sept. 16-19.

Mamaomoto A56

Site of Nakagusuku Castle A57

1963, Oct. 15   *Perf. 13x13¹/₂*
114	A56	15c multi	1.50	75
		First day cover		2.50
		Imprint block of 10	17.50	

1963, Nov. 1   *Perf. 13¹/₂x13*
115	A57	3c multi	1.00	60
		First day cover		2.25
		Imprint block of 6	7.50	

Protection of national cultural treasures.

Flame — A58

Dragon (Bingata Pattern) — A59

1963, Dec. 10   *Perf. 13¹/₂*
116	A53	3c red, dk bl & yel	1.00	60
		First day cover		2.25
		Imprint block of 6	7.00	

15th anniv. of the Universal Declaration of Human Rights.

1963, Dec. 10   **Photo.**
117	A59	1¹/₂c multi	50	25
		First day cover		2.25
		Imprint block of 10	6.50	

New Year, 1964.

Carnation — A60

Pineapples and
Sugar Cane — A61

1964, May 10   **Perf. 13½**
118 A60   3c bl, yel, blk & car   60   50
    First day cover   2.50
    Imprint block of 6   4.50

Mothers Day.

1964, June 1
119 A61   3c multi   60   50
    First day cover   2.25
    Imprint block of 6   4.50

Agricultural census.

Minsah Obi (Sash Woven of
Kapok) — A62

1964, July 1   **Unwmk.**   **Perf. 13½**
120 A62   3c dp bl, rose pink & ocher   80   60
    First day cover   4.50
    Imprint block of 6   6.00
  a.   dp bl, dp car & ocher   1.00   80
    First day cover   5.50
    Imprint block of 6   7.50

Philatelic Week.

Girl Scout and
Emblem — A63

1964, Aug. 31   **Photo.**
121 A63   3c multi   40   30
    First day cover   2.25
    Imprint block of 6   3.00

10th anniv. of Ryukyuan Girl Scouts.

Shuri Relay
Station — A64

Parabolic Antenna
and Map — A65

1964, Sept. 1   **Unwmk.**
    Black Overprint
122 A64   3c dp grn   1.00   1.00
    Imprint block of 6   8.00
  a.   Figure "1" invtd.   37.50   37.50
123 A65   8c ultra   2.00   2.00

    First day cover, #122-123   9.50
    Imprint block of 6   15.00

Opening of the Ryukyu Islands-Japan microwave system carrying telephone and telegraph messages. Nos. 122-123 not issued without overprint.

Gate of Courtesy, Olympic
Torch and Emblem — A66

1964, Sept. 7   **Photo.**   **Perf. 13½x13**
124 A66   3c ultra, yel & red   40   30
    First day cover   2.50
    Imprint block of 6   2.75

Relaying the Olympic torch on Okinawa en route to Tokyo.

"Naihanchi," Karate
Stance — A67

"Makiwara,"
Strengthening Hands
and Feet — A68

"Kumite," Simulated
Combat — A69

1964-65   **Photo.**   **Perf. 13½**
125 A67   3c dl cl, yel & blk   80   50
    First day cover   2.50
    Imprint block of 6   5.50
126 A68   3c yel & multi ('65)   60   50
    First day cover   2.50
    Imprint block of 6   4.50
127 A69   3c gray, red & blk ('65)   60   50
    First day cover   2.50
    Imprint block of 6   4.50

Karate, Ryukyuan self-defense sport.

Miyara Dunchi — A70

Snake and Iris
(Bingata) — A71

1964, Nov. 1   **Perf. 13½**
128 A70   3c multi   50   40

    First day cover   2.25
    Imprint block of 6   3.50

Protection of national cultural treasures. Miyara Dunchi was built as a residence by Miyara-pechin Toen in 1819.

1964, Dec. 10   **Photo.**
129 A71   1½c multi   25   20
    First day cover   2.25
    Imprint block of 10   4.00

New Year, 1965.

Boy Scouts — A72

1965, Feb. 6   **Perf. 13½**
130 A72   3c lt bl & multi   75   50
    First day cover   2.50
    Imprint block of 6   5.00

10th anniv. of Ryukyuan Boy Scouts.

Main Stadium,
Onoyama
A73

1965, July 1   **Perf. 13x13½**
131 A73   3c multi   30   25
    First day cover   2.00
    Imprint block of 6   3.00

Inauguration of the main stadium of the Onoyama athletic facilities.

Samisen of King
Shoko — A74

1965, July 1   **Photo.**   **Perf. 13½**
132 A74   3c buff & multi   50   40
    First day cover   2.50
    Imprint block of 6   4.00

Philatelic Week.

Kin Power
Plant — A75

ICY Emblem,
Ryukyu Map — A76

1965, July 1
133 A75   3c grn & multi   30   25
    First day cover   2.00
    Imprint block of 6   3.00

Completion of Kin power plant.

1965, Aug. 24   **Photo.**   **Perf. 13½**
134 A76   3c multi   25   20
    First day cover   2.00
    Imprint block of 6   2.50

20th anniv. of the UN and International Cooperation Year, 1964-65.

Naha City
Hall — A77

1965, Sept. 18   Unwmk.   Perf. 13 1/2

135	A77	3c bl & multi	25	20
		First day cover		2.00
		Imprint block of 6	2.50	

Completion of Naha City Hall.

Chinese Box Turtle — A78

Horse
(Bingata) — A79

Turtles: No. 137, Hawksbill turtle (denomination at top, country name at bottom). No. 138, Asian terrapin (denomination and country name on top).

1965-66   Photo.   Perf. 13 1/2

136	A78	3c gldn brn & multi	30	30
		First day cover		2.00
		Imprint block of 6	2.50	
137	A78	3c blk, yel & brn ('66)	30	30
		First day cover		2.00
		Imprint block of 6	2.50	
138	A78	3c gray & multi ('66)	30	30
		First day cover		2.00
		Imprint block of 6	2.50	

Issue dates: No. 136, Oct. 20, 1965. No. 137, Jan. 20, 1966. No. 138, Apr. 20, 1966.

1965, Dec. 10   Photo.   Perf. 13 1/2

139	A79	1 1/2c multi	10	10
		First day cover		2.00
		Imprint block of 10	2.00	
a.		Gold omitted	1,000.	1,000.

New Year, 1966.

NATURE CONSERVATION ISSUE

Noguchi's Okinawa
Woodpecker — A80

Sika Deer — A81

Design: No. 142, Dugong.

1966   Photo.   Perf. 13 1/2

140	A80	3c bl grn & multi	25	25
		First day cover		2.00
		Imprint block of 6	2.00	
141	A81	3c bl, red, blk, brn & grn	30	30
		First day cover		2.00
		Imprint block of 6	2.25	
142	A81	3c bl, yel grn, blk & red	30	30
		First day cover		2.00
		Imprint block of 6	2.25	

Issue dates: No. 140, Feb. 15. No. 141, Mar. 15. No. 142, Apr. 20.

Ryukyu Bungalow
Swallow — A82

1966, May 10   Photo.   Perf. 13 1/2

143	A82	3c sky bl, blk & brn	20	20
		First day cover		2.00
		Imprint block of 6	1.75	

4th Bird Week, May 10-16.

Lilies and
Ruins — A83

1966, June 23   Perf. 13x13 1/2

144	A83	3c multi	20	20
		First day cover		2.00
		Imprint block of 6	1.50	

Memorial Day, end of the Battle of Okinawa, June 23, 1945.

University of
the
Ryukyus — A84

1966, July 1

145	A84	3c multi	20	20
		First day cover		2.00
		Imprint block of 6	1.50	

Transfer of the University of the Ryukyus from U.S. authority to the Ryukyu Government.

Lacquerware, 18th
Century — A85

Tile-Roofed House
and UNESCO
Emblem — A86

1966, Aug. 1   Perf. 13 1/2

146	A85	3c gray & multi	20	20
		First day cover		2.00
		Imprint block of 6	1.75	

Philatelic Week.

1966, Sept. 20   Photo.   Perf. 13 1/2

147	A86	3c multi	20	20
		First day cover		2.00
		Imprint block of 6	1.75	

20th anniv. of UNESCO.

Government Museum
and Dragon
Statue — A87

1966, Oct. 6

148	A87	3c multi	20	20
		First day cover		2.00
		Imprint block of 6	1.50	

Completion of the GRI (Government of the Ryukyu Islands) Museum, Shuri.

Tomb of Nakasone-
Tuimya Genga, Ruler
of Miyako — A88

1966, Nov. 1   Photo.   Perf. 13 1/2

149	A88	3c multi	20	20
		First day cover		2.00
		Imprint block of 6	1.50	

Protection of national cultural treasures.

Ram in Iris
Wreath — A89

Clown Fish — A90

1966, Dec. 10   Photo.   Perf. 13 1/2

150	A89	1 1/2c dk bl & multi	10	10
		First day cover		2.00
		Imprint block of 10	1.75	

New Year, 1967.

1966-67

Fish: No. 152, Young boxfish (white numeral at lower left). No. 153, Forceps fish (pale buff numeral at lower right). No. 154. Spotted triggerfish (orange numeral). No. 155. Saddleback butterflyfish (carmine numeral, lower left).

151	A90	3c org red & multi	25	20
152	A90	3c org yel & multi ('67)	25	20
153	A90	3c multi ('67)	35	30
154	A90	3c multi ('67)	35	30
155	A90	3c multi ('67)	40	30
		First day covers, #151-155		
		each		2.00
		Imprint block of 6, #151-155		
		each	2.50	

Issue dates: No. 151, Dec. 20, 1966. No. 152, Jan. 10, 1967. No. 153, Apr. 10, 1967. No. 154, May 25, 1967. No. 155, June 10, 1967.

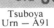

Tsuboya
Urn — A91

Episcopal Miter — A92

1967, Apr. 20

156	A91	3c yel & multi	25	20
		First day cover		2.50
		Imprint block of 6	2.00	

Philatelic Week, 1967.

1967-68   Photo.   Perf. 13 1/2

Seashells: No. 158, Venus comb murex. No. 159, Chiragra spider. No. 160, Green truban. No. 161, Euprotomus bulla.

157	A92	3c lt grn & multi	30	25
		Imprint block of 6	2.25	
158	A92	3c grnsh bl & multi	30	25
		Imprint block of 6	2.25	
159	A92	3c emer & multi ('68)	40	30
		Imprint block of 6	3.00	
160	A92	3c lt bl & multi ('68)	40	30

161 A92	Imprint block of 6		3.00	
	3c brt bl & multi ('68)		70	50
	Imprint block of 6		5.50	
	First day cover, #157-161,			
	each		2.00	

Issue dates: 1967, No. 157, July 20. No. 158, Aug. 30, 1968. No. 159, Jan. 18. No. 160, Feb. 20. No. 161, June 5.

Red-tiled Roofs and ITY Emblem — A93

1967, Sept. 11		**Photo.**	**Perf. 13½**	
162 A93	3c multi		20	20
	First day cover			2.00
	Imprint block of 6		1.50	

International Tourist Year, 1967.

Mobile TB Clinic — A94

1967, Oct. 13		**Photo.**	**Perf. 13½**	
163 A94	3c lil & multi		20	20
	First day cover			2.00
	Imprint block of 6		1.50	

15th anniv. of the Anti-Tuberculosis Society.

Hojo Bridge, Enkaku Temple, 1498 — A95

1967, Nov. 1				
164 A95	3c bl grn & multi		25	20
	First day cover			2.00
	Imprint block of 6		2.00	

Protection of national cultural treasures.

Monkey (Bingata) — A96

TV Tower and Map — A97

1967, Dec. 11		**Photo.**	**Perf. 13½**	
165 A96	1½c sil & multi		15	15
	First day cover			2.00
	Imprint block of 10		2.50	

New Year, 1968.

1967, Dec. 22				
166 A97	3c multi		30	20
	First day cover			2.00
	Imprint block of 6		2.25	

Opening of Miyako and Yaeyama television stations.

Prices for stamps vary greatly, depending upon centering, gum and condition.

Dr. Kijin Nakachi and Helper — A98

Pill Box (Inro) — A99

1968, Mar. 15		**Photo.**	**Perf. 13½**	
167 A98	3c multi		30	20
	First day cover			2.00
	Imprint block of 6		2.25	

120th anniv. of the first vaccination in the Ryukyu Islands, by Dr. Kijin Nakachi.

1968, Apr. 18				
168 A99	3c gray & multi		50	45
	First day cover			2.50
	Imprint block of 6		4.00	

Philatelic Week, 1968.

Young Man, Library, Book and Map of Ryukyu Islands — A100

1968, May 13				
169 A100	3c multi		40	35
	First day cover			2.00
	Imprint block of 6		3.00	

10th International Library Week.

Mailmen's Uniforms and Stamp of 1948 — A101

1968, July 1		**Photo.**	**Perf. 13x13½**	
170 A101	3c multi		40	35
	First day cover			2.00
	Imprint block of 6		3.00	

First Ryukyuan postage stamps, 20th anniv.

Main Gate, Enkaku Temple — A102

1968, July 15		**Photo. & Engr.**	**Perf. 13½**	
171 A102	3c multi		40	35
	First day cover			2.00
	Imprint block of 6		3.00	

Restoration of the main gate Enkaku Temple, built 1492-1495, destroyed during World War II.

Old Man's Dance — A103

1968, Sept. 15		**Photo.**	**Perf. 13½**	
172 A103	3c gold & multi		40	35
	First day cover			2.00
	Imprint block of 6		3.25	

Old People's Day.

Mictyris Longicarpus — A104

Crabs: No. 174, Uca dubia stimpson. No. 175, Baptozius vinosus. No. 176, Cardisoma carnifex. No. 177, Ocypode ceratophthalma pallas.

1968-69		**Photo.**	**Perf. 13½**	
173 A104	3c bl, ocher & blk		60	50
	Imprint block of 6		5.00	
174 A104	3c lt bl grn & multi ('69)		70	50
	Imprint block of 6		5.50	
175 A104	3c lt grn & multi ('69)		70	50
	Imprint block of 6		5.50	
176 A104	3c lt ultra & multi ('69)		90	60
	Imprint block of 6		6.50	
177 A104	3c lt ultra & multi ('69)		90	60
	First day cover, each			2.50
	Imprint block of 6		6.50	

Issue dates: No. 173, Oct. 10, 1968. No. 174, Feb. 5, 1969. No. 175, Mar. 5, 1969. No. 177, June 2, 1969.

Saraswati Pavilion — A105

1968, Nov. 1		**Photo.**	**Perf. 13½**	
178 A105	3c multi		40	30
	First day cover			2.00
	Imprint block of 6		3.25	

Restoration of the Sarawati Pavilion (in front of Enkaku Temple), destroyed during World War II.

Tennis Player — A106

Cock and Iris (Bingata) — A107

1968, Nov. 3		**Photo.**	**Perf. 13½**	
179 A106	3c grn & multi		40	30
	First day cover			2.00
	Imprint block of 6		3.25	

35th All-Japan East-West Men's Soft-ball Tennis Tournament, Naha City, Nov. 23-24.

1968, Dec. 10				
180 A107	1½c org & multi		15	15

First day cover 2.00
Imprint block of 10 2.00

New Year, 1969.

Boxer — A108

Ink Slab
Screen — A109

1969, Jan. 3
181 A108 3c gray & multi 40 35
First day cover 2.00
Imprint block of 6 3.00

20th All-Japan Amateur Boxing Championships held at the University of the Ryukyus, Jan. 3-5.

1969, Apr. 17 **Photo.** **Perf. 13½**
182 A109 3c sal, ind & red 50 35
First day cover 2.50
Imprint block of 6 3.50

Philatelic Week, 1969.

Box Antennas and
Map of Radio
Link — A110

Gate of Courtesy
and
Emblems — A111

1969, July 1 **Photo.** **Perf. 13½**
183 A110 3c multi 25 20
First day cover 2.00
Imprint block of 6 2.00

Opening of the UHF (radio) circuit system between Okinawa and the outlying Miyako-Yaeyama Islands.

1969, Aug. 1 **Photo.** **Perf. 13½**
184 A111 3c Prus. bl, gold & ver 25 20
First day cover 2.00
Imprint block of 6 2.00

22nd All-Japan Formative Education Study Conference, Naha, Aug. 1-3.

FOLKLORE ISSUE

Tug of War
Festival
A112

Hari Boat
Race — A113

Izaiho
Ceremony,
Kudaka
Island — A114

Mortardrum
Dance — A115

Sea God
Dance — A116

1969-70 **Photo.** **Perf. 13**
185 A112 3c multi 50 40
Imprint block of 6 3.50
186 A113 3c multi 60 40
Imprint block of 6 4.00
187 A114 3c multi 60 40
Imprint block of 6 4.00
188 A115 3c multi ('70) 90 60
Imprint block of 6 6.50
189 A116 3c multi ('70) 90 60
First day cover, each 2.50
Imprint block of 6 6.50

Issue dates: No. 185, Aug. 1. No. 186, Sept. 5. No. 187, Oct. 3. No. 188, Jan. 20, 1970. No. 189, Feb. 27, 1970.

No. 99 Surcharged 改訂½¢

1969, Oct. 15 **Photo.** **Perf. 13½**
190 A44 ½c on 3c multi 40 40
First day cover 3.00
Imprint block of 10 5.00

Nakamura-ke Farm
House, Built 1713-
51 — A117

1969, Nov. 1 **Photo.** **Perf. 13½**
191 A117 3c multi 30 20
First day cover 2.00
Imprint block of 6 2.25

Protection of national cultural treasures.

Statue of Kyuzo
Toyama, Maps of
Hawaiian and Ryukyu
Islands — A118

1969, Dec. 5 **Photo.** **Perf. 13½**
192 A118 3c lt ultra & multi 50 40
First day cover 2.50
Imprint block of 6 3.50
a. Without overprint 2,000.
b. Wide-spaced bars 600.00

70th anniv. of Ryukyu-Hawaii emigration Kyuzo Toyama leader.
The overprint "1969" at lower left and bars across "1970" at upper right was applied before No. 192 was issued.

Dog and Flowers
(Bingata) — A119

Sake Flask Made from
Coconut — A120

1969, Dec. 10
193 A119 1½c pink & multi 15 15
First day cover 2.00
Imprint block of 10 2.00

New Year, 1970.

1970, Apr. 15 **Photo.** **Perf. 13½**
194 A120 3c multi 50 40
First day cover 2.50
Imprint block of 6 3.50

Philatelic Week, 1970.

CLASSIC OPERA ISSUE

"The Bell" (Shushin
Kaneiri) — A121

Child and Kidnapper
(Chu-nusudu)
A122

Robe of Feathers
(Mekarushi) — A123

Vengeance of Two
Young Sons
(Nidotichiuchi)
A124

The Virgin and the
Dragon
(Kokonomaki)
A125

1970 **Photo.** **Perf. 13½**
195 A121 3c dl bl & multi 1.00 80
196 A122 3c lt bl & multi 1.00 80
197 A123 3c bluish grn & multi 1.00 80
198 A124 3c dl bl grn & multi 1.00 80
199 A125 3c multi 1.00 80
First day cover, each 3.00
Imprint block of 6, each 7.00

Souvenir Sheets
195a-199a Sheets of 4, each 5.50 8.00
First day covers, each 10.00

Marginal decoration and inscription. Size: 93x102mm.

Underwater
Observatory and
Tropical Fish — A126

1970, May 22
200	A126	3c bl grn & multi	40	35
		First day cover		2.50
		Imprint block of 6	3.00	

Completion of the underwater observatory of Busena-Misaki, Nago.

Noboru Jahana
(1865-1908),
Politician — A127

Map of Okinawa
and People — A128

Portraits: No. 202, Saion Gushichan Bunjaku (1682-1761), statesman. No. 203, Choho Giwan (1823-1876), regent and poet.

1970-71   **Engr.**   *Perf. 13½*
201	A127	3c rose cl	80	50
		Imprint block of 6	5.00	
202	A127	3c dl bl grn	1.25	90
		Imprint block of 6	10.00	
203	A127	3c blk ('71)	80	50
		First day cover, each		2.50
		Imprint block of 6	5.00	

Issue dates: No. 201, Sept. 25, 1970. No. 202, Dec. 22, 1970. No. 203, Jan. 22, 1971.

1970, Oct. 1   **Photo.**
204	A128	3c red & multi	25	20
		First day cover		2.00
		Imprint block of 6	2.00	

1970 census, Oct. 1, 1970.

Great Cycad of
Une — A129

1970, Nov. 2   **Photo.**   *Perf. 13½*
205	A129	3c gold & multi	30	25
		First day cover		2.00
		Imprint block of 6	2.25	

Protection of national treasures.

Japanese Flag, Diet and Map
of Ryukyus — A130

Wild Boar and
Cherry Blossoms
(Bingata) — A131

1970, Nov. 15   **Photo.**   *Perf. 13½*
206	A130	3c ultra & multi	1.00	80
		First day cover		2.50
		Imprint block of 6	7.50	

Citizens participation in national administration to Japanese law of Apr. 24, 1970.

1970, Dec. 10
207	A131	1½c multi	15	15
		First day cover		2.00
		Imprint block of 10	2.50	

New Year, 1971.

Low Hand Loom
(Jibata) — A132

Farmer Wearing
Palm Bark Raincoat
and Kuba Leaf
Hat — A133

Fisherman's Wooden
Box and
Scoop — A134

Designs: No. 209, Woman running a filature (reel). No. 211, Woman hulling rice with cylindrical "Shiri-ushi."

1971   **Photo.**   *Perf. 13½*
208	A132	3c lt bl & multi	45	35
		Imprint block of 6	3.00	
209	A132	3c pale grn & multi	45	35
		Imprint block of 6	3.00	
210	A133	3c lt bl & multi	55	40
		Imprint block of 6	3.25	
211	A132	3c yel & multi	65	50
		Imprint block of 6	5.00	
212	A134	3c gray & multi	55	40
		First day cover, each		2.50
		Imprint block of 6	3.50	

Issue dates: No. 208, Feb. 16. No. 209, Mar. 16. No. 210, Apr. 13. No. 211, May 20. No. 212, June 15.

Water Carrier (Taku) — A135

1971, Apr. 15   **Photo.**   *Perf. 13½*
213	A135	3c bl grn & multi	50	35
		First day cover		2.50
		Imprint block of 6	4.00	

Philatelic Week, 1971.

Old and New
Naha, and City
Emblem
A136

1971, May 20   *Perf. 13*
214	A136	3c ultra & multi	30	25
		First day cover		2.00
		Imprint block of 6	2.00	

50th anniv. of Naha as a municipality.

Caesalpinia
Pulcherrima — A137

Design: 2c, Madder (Sandanka).

1971   **Photo.**   *Perf. 13*
215	A137	2c gray & multi	15	10
216	A137	3c gray & multi	20	15
		First day cover, each		2.00
		Imprint block of 10, each	2.50	

Issue dates: 2c, Sept. 30; 3c, May 10.

GOVERNMENT PARK SERIES

View from Mabuni
Hill — A138

Mt. Arashi from
Haneji Sea — A139

Yabuchi Island from
Yakena Port — A140

1971-72
217	A138	3c grn & multi	40	30
218	A139	3c bl & multi	40	30
219	A140	4c multi ('72)	50	30
		First day cover, each		2.50
		Imprint block of 6, each	3.00	

Issue dates: No. 217, July 30. No. 218, Aug. 30, 1971. No. 219, Jan. 20, 1972.

Dancer — A141

Deva King, Torinji
Temple — A142

1971, Nov. 1   **Photo.**   *Perf. 13*
220	A141	4c Prus bl & multi	20	15
		First day cover		2.00
		Imprint block of 10	2.50	

1971, Dec. 1
221	A142	4c dp bl & multi	25	25
		First day cover		2.00
		Imprint block of 6	2.00	

Protection of national cultural treasures.

Ryukyu Islands stamps can be mounted in Scott's Ryukyu Islands Album.

Rat and Chrysanthemums A143

Student Nurse A144

1971, Dec. 10
222 A143 2c brn org & multi 15 15
First day cover 2.00
Imprint block of 10 2.50

New Year, 1972.

1971, Dec. 24
223 A144 4c lil & multi 35 25
First day cover 2.00
Imprint block of 6 2.50

Nurses' training, 25th anniversary.

A145

A147

Coral Reef — A146

1972   Photo.   Perf. 13
224 A145 5c brt bl & multi 60 40
225 A146 5c gray & multi 60 40
226 A147 5c ocher & multi 60 40
First day cover, each 2.50
Imprint block of 6, each 4.00

Issue dates: No. 224, Apr. 14. No. 225, Mar. 30. No. 226, Mar. 21.

Dove, U.S. and Japanese Flags — A148

1972, Apr. 17   Photo.   Perf. 13
227 A148 5c brt bl & multi 1.00 75
First day cover 3.00
Imprint block of 6 7.50

Antique Sake Pot (Yushibin) — A149

1972, Apr. 20
228 A149 5c ultra & multi 80 50
First day cover 2.50
Imprint block of 6 6.00

Ryukyu stamps were replaced by those of Japan after May 15, 1972.

AIR POST

Dove and Map of Ryukyus — AP1

1950, Feb. 15   Photo.   Unwmk.   Perf. 13x13½
C1 AP1 8y brt bl 62.50 50.00
Imprint block of 6 800.00
C2 AP1 12y green 22.50 20.00
Imprint block of 6 250.00
C3 AP1 16y rose car 18.00 15.00
Imprint block of 6 150.00
First day cover, each 35.00
First day cover #C1-C3 175.00

Heavenly Maiden — AP2

1951-54
C4 AP2 13y blue 2.00 1.75
First day cover 60.00
Imprint block of 6, 5-character 250.00
Imprint block of 6, 8-character 50.00
C5 AP2 18y green 2.75 2.75
First day cover 60.00
Imprint block of 6, 5-character 75.00
Imprint block of 6, 8-character 60.00
C6 AP2 30y cerise 4.25 1.50
First day cover 60.00
First day cover, #C4-C6 250.00
Imprint block of 6, 5-character 80.00
Imprint block of 6, 8-character 140.00
C7 AP2 40y red vio ('54) 7.00 6.50
First day cover 35.00
Imprint block of 6 100.00
C8 AP2 50y yel org ('54) 8.50 7.50
First day cover 35.00
First day cover, #C7-C8 100.00
Imprint block of 6 120.00

Issue dates Nos. C4-C6, Nov. 1. Nos. C7-C8, Aug. 16.

Heavenly Maiden Playing Flute — AP3

1957, Aug. 1   Engr.   Perf. 13½
C9 AP3 15y bl grn 4.00 2.25
Imprint block of 6 45.00
C10 AP3 20y rose car 6.50 3.75
Imprint block of 6 75.00
C11 AP3 35y yel grn 12.00 6.00
Imprint block of 6 125.00
C12 AP3 45y redsh brn 13.00 9.00
Imprint block of 6 150.00
C13 AP3 60y gray 17.00 10.50
Imprint block of 6 240.00
First day cover, #C9-C13 70.00

On one printing of No. C10, position 49 shows an added spur on the right side of the second character from the left.

Same Surcharged in Brown Red or Light Ultramarine   改訂 9 ¢

1959, Dec. 20
C14 AP3 9c on 15y bl grn (BrR) 2.75 2.00
Imprint block of 6 30.00
a. Inverted surch. 600.00
Imprint block of 6 4,000.
C15 AP3 14c on 20y rose car (L.U.) 3.25 3.00
Imprint block of 6 35.00
C16 AP3 19c on 35y yel grn (BrR) 6.50 5.00
Imprint block of 6 75.00
C17 AP3 27c on 45y redsh brn (L.U.) 12.00 7.00
Imprint block of 6 130.00
C18 AP3 35c on 60y gray (BrR) 14.00 9.00
Imprint block of 6 170.00
First day cover, #C14-C18 50.00

No. C15 is found with the variety described below No. C13.

改訂 ====

Nos. 31-33, 36 and 38 Surcharged in Black, Brown, Red, Blue or Green

9¢

1960, Aug. 3   Photo.   Perf. 13
C19 A14 9c on 4y brn 3.25 2.00
Imprint block of 10 45.00
a. Invtd. surch. 10,000. 12,500.
C20 A17 14c on 5y rose lil (Br) 3.25 2.00
Imprint block of 10 45.00
C21 A14 19c on 15y ver (R) 2.50 1.50
Imprint block of 10 35.00
C22 A17 27c on 14y redsh brn (Bl) 7.25 4.00
Imprint block of 10 110.00
C23 A14 35c on 20y yel org (G) 6.50 5.50
Imprint block of 10 110.00
First day cover, #C19-C23 40.00

Wind God — AP4

Designs: 9c, Heavenly Maiden (as on AP2). 14c, Heavenly Maiden (as on AP3). 27c, Wind God at right. 35c, Heavenly Maiden over treetops.

1961, Sept. 21   Unwmk.   Perf. 13½
C24 AP4 9c multi 45 20
Imprint block of 6 3.50
C25 AP4 14c multi 75 75
Imprint block of 6 5.00
C26 AP4 19c multi 80 75
Imprint block of 6 6.00
C27 AP4 27c multi 3.00 50
Imprint block of 6 18.00
C28 AP4 35c multi 2.00 1.00
Imprint block of 6 15.00
First day cover, #C24-C28 60.00

AP5

AP6

1963, Aug. 28   Perf. 13x13½
C29 AP5 5½c multi 20 20
Imprint block of 10 3.00
C30 AP6 7c multi 25 30
Imprint block of 10 3.50
First day cover, each 1.00
First day cover, #C29-C30 2.50

SPECIAL DELIVERY

Dragon and Map of Ryukyus — SD1

1950, Feb. 15   Unwmk.   Photo.   Perf. 13x13½

E1	SD1 5y brt bl	25.00	18.00
	First day cover		100.00
	Imprint block of 6	275.00	

QUANTITIES ISSUED
Regular Postage and Commemorative Stamps

Cat. No.	Quantity
1	90,214
2	55,901
3	94,663
4	55,413
5	76,387
6	117,321
7	291,403
1a	61,000
2a—4a, each	181,000
5a	29,936
6a	99,300
7a	46,000
8	2,859,000
8a	247,943
9	1,198,989
10	589,000
11	479,000
12	598,999
13	397,855
14	499,000
15	498,960
16	200,000
16a	200,000
16b	40,000
17	9,800
18	299,500
19	3,014,427
20	3,141,777
21	2,970,827
22	191,917
23	1,118,617
24	276,218
24a	ca. 1,300
25	231,717
26	220,139
27	398,993
28	386,421
29	498,854
30	298,994
31	4,768,413
32	1,202,297
33	500,059
34	298,994
35	199,000
36	455,896
37	160,518
38	198,720
39	198,199
40	599,000
41	598,075
42	1,198,179
43	1,625,406
44	994,880
45	997,759
46	996,759
47	2,705,955
48	997,542
49	996,609
50	996,928
51	499,000
52	249,000
52a	78,415
53	248,700
54	1,498,991
55	2,498,897
56	1,098,972
57	998,918
58	2,699,000
59	2,499,000
60	199,000
61	499,000
62	199,000
63	1,498,931
64	798,953
65—68, each	999,000
72	598,912
73	398,990
74	598,936
75	1,998,992
76	1,000,000
77	2,000,000
78	500,000
79—80, each	400,000
81	12,599,000
82	11,979,000
83	6,850,000
84	5,099,000
84A	1,699,000
85	4,749,000
86	2,099,000
87	3,019,000
88	298,966
89	298,966
90	398,901
91	398,992
92	1,498,970
93	598,989
94	398,998
95	398,993
96	298,993
97	398,997
98	9,699,000
99	10,991,500
100	1,549,000
101	799,000
102	1,299,000
103	398,995
104	298,892

Cat. No.	Quantity
105	1,598,949
106	348,989
107	10,099,000
108	348,865
109	348,937
110	348,962
111	348,974
112	398,974
113	398,911
114	1,199,000
115	398,948
116	398,943
117	1,698,912
118	550,000
119	549,000
120	749,000
121	799,000
122	389,000
123	319,000
124	1,999,000
125—127, each	999,000
128	799,000
129	1,699,000
130—131, each	799,000
132	849,000
133	799,000
134	1,299,000
135	1,099,000
136	1,299,000
137—138, each	1,598,000
139	3,098,000
140—142, each	1,598,000
143—148, each	2,498,000
149	2,298,000
150	3,798,000
151	2,298,000
152—156, each	1,998,000
157—158, each	1,698,000
159—160, each	1,298,000
161	898,000
162	1,498,000
163—164, each	1,298,000
165	3,998,000
166—167, each	1,298,000
168	998,000
169—179, each	898,000
180	3,198,000
181—189, each	898,000
190	1,773,050
191	898,000
192	864,960
193	3,198,000
194	898,000
195—199, each	598,000
195a—199a, each	124,500
200—206, each	898,000
207	3,198,000
208—210, each	1,098,000
211—212, each	1,298,000
213	1,098,000
214	1,298,000
215—216, each	4,998,000
217	1,498,000
218—219, each	1,798,000
220	2,998,000
221	1,798,000
222	4,998,000
223	1,798,000
224—226, each	2,498,000
227	2,998,000
228	3,998,000

AIR POST STAMPS

Cat. No.	Quantity
C1—C3, each	198,000
C4	1,952,348
C5	331,360
C6	762,530
C7	76,166
C8	122,816
C9	708,319
C10	108,824
C11	164,147
C12	50,335
C13	69,092
C14	597,103
C15	77,951
C16	97,635
C17	98,353
C18	96,650
C19	1,033,900
C19a	100
C20	230,000
C21	185,000
C22	191,000
C23	190,000
C24	17,199,000
C25	1,999,000
C26	1,250,000
C27	3,499,000
C28	1,699,000
C29	1,199,00
C30	1,949,000

SPECIAL DELIVERY STAMP

E1	198,804

PROVISIONAL ISSUES

Stamps of Japan Overprinted by Postmasters in Four Island Districts

Gen. Maresuke Nogi — A84

Admiral Heihachiro Togo — A86

Garambi Lighthouse, Taiwan — A88

Meiji Shrine, Tokyo — A90

Plane and Map of Japan — A92

Kasuga Shrine, Nara — A93

Mount Fuji and Cherry Blossoms — A94

Horyu Temple, Nara — A95

Miyajima Torii, Itsukushima Shrine — A96

Golden Pavilion, Kyoto — A97

Great Budda, Kamakura — A98

Kamatari Fujiwara — A99

War Factory Girl — A144

Palms and Map of "Greater East Asia" — A148

Aviator Saluting and Japanese Flag — A150

Torii of Yasukuni Shrine — A151

Mt. Fuji and Cherry Blossoms — A152

Torii of Miyajima — A153

Garambi Lighthouse,
Taiwan — A154

Coal Miners — A163

"Thunderstorm below Fuji,"
by Hokusai — A167

Prices are for unused stamps.
Used copies sell for considerably more, should be
expertized and are preferred on cover or document.

KUME ISLAND

A1

Mimeographed
Seal Handstamped in Vermilion

1945, Oct. 1   Ungummed   Unwmk.   Imperf.

1X1	A1	7s black, cream (2,400)	1,200.
	"7" & "SEN" one letter space to left		2,500.

Printed on legal-size U.S. military mimeograph paper and
validated by the official seal of the Kume Island postmaster,
Norifume Kikuzato. Valid until May 4, 1946.
Cancellations "20.10.1" (Oct. 1, 1945) or "20.10.6" (Oct. 6,
1945) are by favor. Copies on U.S. official bond paper, white
and water-marked, were not issued.

AMAMI DISTRICT

Inspection Seal ("Ken," abbreviation for
kensa zumi, inspected or examined; five
types)

Stamps of Japan 1937-46 Handstamped in Black,
Blue, Purple, Vermilion
or Red

Typographed, Lithographed, Engraved

1947-48		**Wmk. 257**	**Perf. 13, Imperf**
2X1	A82	½s purple, #257	800.00
2X2	A83	1s fawn, #258	—
2X3	A144	1s orange brown, #325	1,750.
2X4	A84	2s crimson, #259	600.00
a.		2s vermilion, #259c	—
2X5	A84	2s rose red, imperf., #351	2,000.
2X6	A85	3s green, #260	1,700.
2X7	A84	3s brown, #329	—
2X8	A161	3s rose carmine, imperf., #352	1,800.
2X9	A146	4s emrald, #330	650.00
2X10	A86	5s brown lake, #331	700.00
2X11	A162	5s green, imperf., #353	1,500.
2X12	A147	6s light ultramarine, #332	1,250.
2X13	A86	7s orange vermilion, #333	—
2X14	A90	8s dark purple & pale violet, #265	1,500.
2X15	A148	10s crimson & dull rose, #344	500.00
2X16	A152	10s red orange, imperf., #355 (48)	2,500.
2X17	A93	14s rose lake & pale rose, #268	—
2X18	A150	15s dull blue, #336	500.00
2X19	A151	17s gray violet, #337	1,750.
2X20	A94	20s ultramarine, #269	1,750.
2X21	A152	20s blue, #338	600.00
2X22	A152	20s ultramarine, imperf., #356 (48)	1,750.
2X23	A95	25s dark brown & pale brown, #270	900.00
2X24	A151	27s rose brown, #339	—
2X25	A153	30s bluish green, #340	—
2X26	A153	30s bright blue, imperf., #357	2,000.
2X27	A88	40s dull violet, #341	1,750.
2X28	A154	40s dark violet, #342	1,750.
2X29	A97	50s olive & pale olive, #272	—
2X30	A163	50s dark brown, imperf., #358 (48)	2,000.
2X31	A164	1y deep olive green, imperf., #359	2,500.
2X32	A167	1y deep ultramarine, imperf., #364	—
2X33	A99	5y deep gray green, #274	—
2X34	A99	5y deep gray green, imperf., #360	—

MIYAKO DISTRICT

Personal Seal of Postmaster Jojin
Tomiyama

Stamps of Japan 1937-46 Handstamped in
Vermilion or Red

Typographed, Lithographed, Engraved

1946-47		**Wmk. 257**	**Perf. 13**
3X1	A144	1s orange brown, #325	175.00
3X2	A84	2s crimson, #259	125.00
a.		2s vermilion #259c ('47)	150.00
3X3	A84	3s brown, #329	80.00
3X4	A86	4s dark green, #261	80.00
3X5	A86	5s brown lake, #331	550.00
3X6	A88	6s orange, #263	80.00
3X7	A90	8s dark purple & pale violet, #265	100.00
3X8	A148	10s crimson & dull rose, #334	80.00
3X9	A152	10s red orange, imperf., #355 ('47) (1,000)	120.00
3X10	A92	12s indigo, #267	80.00
3X11	A93	14s rose lake & pale rose, #268	80.00
3X12	A150	15s dull blue, #336	80.00
3X13	A151	17s gray violet, #337	80.00
3X14	A94	20s ultramarine, #269	—
3X15	A152	20s blue, #338	80.00
3X16	A152	20s ultramarine, imperf., #356 ('47)	175.00
3X17	A95	25s dark brown & pale brown, #270	80.00
3X18	A153	30s bluish green, #340	80.00
3X19	A88	40s dull violet, #341	250.00
3X20	A154	40s dark violet, #342	90.00
3X21	A97	50s olive & pale olive, #272	80.00
3X22	A163	50s dark brown, #358 ('47) (750)	200.00
3X23	A98	1y brown & pale brown, #273	—
3X24	A167	1y deep ultramarine, #364 ('47) (500)	1,500.

Nos. 3X22 and 3X24 have sewing machine perf.; No. 3X16
exists with that perf. also.

Nos. 3X1-3X2, 3X2a, 3X3-3X5, 3X8 Handstamp
Surcharged with 2 Japanese Characters

1946-47			
3X25	A144	1y on 1s orange brown	140.00
3X26	A84	1y on 2s crimson	2,000.
3X27	A84	1y on 3s brown ('47)	2,000.
3X28	A84	2y on 2s crimson	160.00
a.		2y on 2s vermilion ('47)	160.00
3X29	A86	4y on 4s dark green	140.00
3X30	A86	5y on 5s brown lake	140.00
3X31	A148	10y on 10s crimson & dull rose	120.00

OKINAWA DISTRICT

Personal Seal of Postmaster Shiichi
Hirata

R1

Japan Nos. 355-356, 358, 364 Overprinted
in Black

1947, Nov. 1		**Wmk. 257 Litho.**	**Imperf.**
4X1	A152	10s red orange (13,997)	1,200.
4X2	A152	20s ultramarine (13,611)	500.00
4X3	A163	50s dark brown (6,276)	900.00
4X4	A167	1y deep ultramarine (1,947)	1,750.

On Revenue Stamp of Japan

4X5	R1	30s brown (14,000)	3,500.

No. 4X5 is on Japan's current 30s revenue stamp. The
Hirata seal validated it for postal use.
Nos. 4X1-4X4 are known with rough sewing machine perfo-
rations, full or partial.

YAEYAMA DISTRICT

Personal Seal of Postmaster Kenpuku
Miyara

Stamps of Japan 1937-46 Handstamped in Black
Typographed, Engraved, Lithographed

1948		**Wmk. 257**	**Perf. 13**
5X1	A86	4s dark green, #261	1,200.
5X2	A86	5s brown lake, #331	1,200.
5X3	A86	7s orange vermilion, #333	800.00
5X4	A148	10s crimson & dull rose, #334	5,000.
5X5	A94	20s ultramarine, #269	100.00
5X6	A96	30s peacock blue, #271	1,000.
5X7	A88	40s dull violet, #341	50.00
5X8	A97	50s olive & pale olive, #272	70.00
5X9	A163	50s dark brown, imperf., #358 (250)	1,350.
5X10	A99	5y deep gray green, #274	2,000.

Provisional postal stationery of the four districts also exists.

LETTER SHEETS

Typographed by Japan Printing Bureau. Stamp
is in upper left corner.

Prices are for entires.

Stylized Deigo
Blossom — US1

Banyan
Tree — US2

Designer: Shutaro Higa

1948-49				
U1	US1	50s vermilion, cream, July 18, 1949 (250,000)	50.00	75.00
		First day cancel		—
a.		Orange red, cream, July 1, 1948 (1,000)	550.00	—

Designer: Ken Yabu

1950, Jan. 21				
U2	US2	1y carmine red, cream (250,000)	45.00	60.00
		First day cancel		—

AIR LETTER SHEETS

DC-4 Skymaster and
Shurei Gate — UC1

UC2

Designer: Chosho Ashitomi
"PAR AVION" (Bilingual) below Stamp
Litho. & Typo. by Japan Printing Bureau

1952, Nov. 1				
UC1	UC1	12y dull rose, pale blue green (126,000)	20.00	15.00
		First day cancel		75.00

Printed on tinted paper with colorless overall inscription,
RYUKYU FOREIGN AIRMAIL, repeated in parallel vertical
lines. Model: U.S. No. UC16.

Litho. & Typo. by Nippon Toppan K.K.
"AEROGRAMME" below Stamp

1955, Sept. 10				
UC2	UC2	15y violet blue, pale blue green (200,000)	35.00	20.00
		First day cancel		75.00

See the "Information for Collectors" section at
beginning of catalogue for illustrations of types
of postmarks and precancels.

No. UC2 surcharged in Red

"13" & "¢" aligned at bot.; 2 thick bars — a

"¢" raised; 2 thick bars — b

"13" & "¢" as in "a"; 4 thin bars — c

"¢" raised; 4 thin bars — d

Printers: Type "a," Nakamura Printing Co., "b" and "d," Okinawa Printing Co., "c," Sun Printing Co.

1958-60

UC3	UC2	13c on 15y type "a" (60,000)	20.00	20.00
		First Day Cancel		60.00
a.		Type "b" ('59) (E 10,000)	50.00	30.00
b.		Type "c" ('59) (E 2,000)	100.00	80.00
c.		Type "d," Oct. 1, 1960 (E 3,000)	300.00	300.00
d.		As "b," small "¢"	1,000.	—

No. UC3c has Nos. 55, 58 affixed to make the 15c rate.

UC3

Lithographed by Japan Printing Bureau

1959, Nov. 10

UC4	UC3	15c dark blue, pale blue (560,000)	5.00	3.50
		First day cancel		15.00

POSTAL CARDS

Nos. UX1-UX9 are typo., others litho.
Printed by Japan Printing Bureau unless otherwise stated.
Quantities in parentheses; "E" means estimated.
Prices are for entire cards.

Deigo Blossom Type
Designer: Shutaro Higa

1948, July 1

UX1	US1	10s dull red, grayish tan (100,000)	50.00	90.00

1949, July 1

UX2	US1	15s orange red, gray (E 175,000)	40.00	80.00
		First day cancel	125.00	150.00
a.		15s vermilion, tan (E 50,000)		

Banyan Tree Type
Designer: Ken Yabu

1950, Jan. 21

UX3	US2	50s carmine red, light tan (E 200,000)	15.00	15.00
		First day cancel		90.00
a.		Grayish tan card (E 25,000)	45.00	80.00

Nos. UX2, UX2a Handstamp Surcharged in Vermilion

19-21x23-25mm — a

22-23x26-27mm — b

20-21x24-24½mm c

22-23½x25-26mm d

1951

UX4	US1	(c) 15s + 85s on #UX2 (E 35,000)	100.00	100.00
a.		Type "c" on #UX2a (E 5,000)	150.00	150.00
b.		Type "a" on #UX2 (E39,000)	75.00	100.00
c.		Type "a" on #UX2a	1,000.	—
d.		Type "b" on #UX2	1,000.	1,000.
e.		Type "d" on #UX2 (E 4,000)	150.00	300.00
f.		Type "d" on #UX2a (E 1,000)	250.00	300.00

Type "a" exists on the 15s cherry blossom postal card of Japan.

Crown, Leaf Ornaments

Naha die
21x22mm — PC3

Tokyo die
18½x19mm — PC4

Designer: Masayoshi Adaniya Koshun Printing Co.

1952

UX5	PC3	1y vermilion, tan, Feb. 8 (400,600)	50.00	50.00
UX6	PC4	1y vermilion, off-white, Oct. 6 (1,295,000)	25.00	15.00
a.		Tan card, coarse (50,000)	40.00	25.00
b.		Tan card, smooth (16,000)	500.00	150.00

Naminoue Shrine

PC5 PC6
Naha die Tokyo die
23x25½mm 22x24½mm

Designer: Gensei Agena

1953-57

UX7	PC5	2y green, off-white (1,799,400)	45.00	20.00
		First day cancel, Dec. 2, 1953		100.00
a.		Printed both sides	500.00	
UX8	PC6	2y green, off-white ('55) (2,799,400)	20.00	10.00
b.		Deep blue green ('56) (300,000)	40.00	25.00
c.		Yellow green ('57) (2,400,000)	15.00	5.00
d.		As "a," printed both sides	500.00	
e.		As "b," printed both sides	500.00	

Stylized Pine, Bamboo, Plum Blossoms — PC7

Designer: Koya Oshiro Kotsura and Koshun Printing Companies

1956 New Year Card

1955, Dec. 1

UX9	PC7	2y red, cream	100.00	50.00
		First day cancel		150.00

No. UX9 was printed on rough card (43,400) and smooth-finish card (356,600)

Sun — PC8

Temple Lion — PC9

Designer: Seikichi Tamanaha Kobundo Printing Co.

1957 New Year Card

1956, Dec. 1

UX10	PC8	2y brown carmine & yellow, off-white (600,000)	6.00	5.00
		First day cancel		15.00

Designer: Shin Isagawa Fukuryu Printing Co.

1958 New Year Card

1957, Dec. 1

UX11	PC9	2y lilac rose, off-white (1,000,000)	3.50	4.50
		First day cancel		6.00
a.		"1" omitted in right date	60.00	75.00
b.		Printed both sides	250.00	300.00

Nos. UX8, UX8a and UX8b "Revalued" in Red, Cherry or Pink by Three Naha Printeries

改 訂
1½¢
a

改 訂
1½¢
b

改 訂
1½¢
c

1958-59

UX12	PC6	1½c on 2y green, type "a," Sept. 16 (600,000)	5.00	5.00
		First day cancel		15.00
a.		Shrine stamp omitted	750.00	1,000.
b.		Bar of ½ omitted, top of 2 broken	75.00	100.00
c.		Type "b," Nov. (1,000,000)	10.00	15.00
d.		Type "c" ('59) (200,000)	20.00	30.00
e.		Wrong font "¢," type "c"	30.00	45.00
f.		"¢" omitted, type "c"	1,500.	1,500.
g.		Double surcharge, type "c"	1,000.	
h.		Triple surcharge, type "c"	1,500.	—

Multicolor Yarn Ball — PC10

Toy Pony
19½x23mm — PC11

Designer: Masayoshi Adaniya Kobundo Printing Co.

1959 New Year Card

1958, Dec. 10
UX13 PC10 1½c black, red, yellow & gray
blue, *off-white*
(1,514,000) 2.00 2.50
First day cancel 3.00
a. Black omitted —

Designer: Seikichi Tamanaha Kobundo Printing
Co.

1959, June 20
UX14 PC11 1½c dark blue & brown
(1,140,000) 3.00 2.50
First day cancel 2.00
a. Dark blue omitted 350.00

Toy Carp and
Boy — PC12

Toy Pony
21x25mm — PC13

Designer: Masayoshi Adaniya

1960 New Year Card

1959, Dec. 1
UX15 PC12 1½c violet blue, red & black,
cream (2,000,000) 2.00 2.50
First day cancel 2.00

1959, Dec. 30
UX16 PC13 1½c gray violet & brown,
cream (3,500,000) 3.50 1.00
First day cancel 4.00

Household
Altar — PC14

Coral
Head — PC15

Designer: Shin Isagawa

1961 New Year Card

1960, Nov. 20
UX17 PC14 1½c gray, carmine, yellow &
black, *off-white*
(2,647,591) 2.00 3.00
First day cancel 2.50

Designer: Shinzan Yamada Kidekuni Printing Co.
Summer Greeting Card

1961, July 5
UX18 PC15 1½c ultramarine & cerise, *off-
white (264,900)* 3.00 5.00
First day cancel 6.00

Tiger
PC16

Inscribed
"RYUKYUS"
PC17

Designer: Shin Isagawa

1962 New Year Card

1961, Nov. 15
UX19 PC16 1½c ocher, black & red, *off-
white (2,891,626)* 2.50 4.50

First day cancel 2.50
a. Red omitted 750.00 —
b. Red inverted 500.00 —
c. Red omitted on face, inverted on
back 500.00 —
d. Double impression of red, one inverted 500.00 —
e. Double impression of ocher & black,
red inverted 500.00 —
f. Double impression of ocher & black,
one inverted 500.00 —

Designer: Seikichi Tamanaha

1961-67
UX20 PC17 1½c gray violet & brown, *white*
('67) (18,600,000) 1.50 75
a. Off-white card ('66) *(4,000,000)* 2.00 1.00
b. Cream card, Dec. 23 *(12,500,000)* 1.50 75
First day cancel 2.00

Ie Island — PC18

New Year
Offerings — PC19

Designer: Shinzan Yamada Sakai Printing Co.

Summer Greeting Card

1962, July 10
UX21 PC18 1½c bright blue, yellow &
brown, *off-white*
(221,500) 2.50 3.50
First day cancel 4.50
Square notch at left 35.00 45.00

Designer: Shin Isagawa Sakai Printing Co.
1963 New Year Card; Precanceled

1962, Nov. 15
UX22 PC19 1½c olive brown, carmine &
black *(3,000,000)* 3.00 4.50
First day cancel 3.50
a. Yellow brown background —
b. Brown ocher background —

Ryukyu Temple
Dog and Wine
Flask
Silhouette — PC20

Water Strider — PC21

Designer: Shin Isagawa

International Postal Card

1963, Feb. 15
UX23 PC20 5c vermilion, emerald &
black, *pale yellow*
(150,000) 2.50 3.50
First day cancel 2.50
a. Black & emerald omitted 450.00

Designer: Seikichi Tamanaha
Summer Greeting Card

1963, June 20
UX24 PC21 1½c Prussian green & black,
off-white (250,000) 6.00 7.00
First day cancel 5.00

Princess
Doll — PC22

Bitter Melon
Vine — PC23

Designer: Koya Oshiro

1964 New Year Card; Precanceled

1963, Nov. 15
UX25 PC22 1½c orange red, yellow & ultra.,
off-white (3,200,000) 3.00 3.50
First day cancel 3.00

Designer: Shinzan Yamada
Summer Greeting Card

1964, June 20
UX26 PC23 1½c multicolored, *off-white*
(285,410) 2.00 3.50
First day cancel 2.75

Fighting Kite
with
Rider — PC24

Palm-leaf
Fan — PC25

Designer: Koya Oshiro

1965 New Year Card; Precanceled

1964, Nov. 15
UX27 PC24 1½c multicolored, *off-white*
(4,876,618) 2.00 2.50
First day cancel 2.50

Designer: Koya Oshiro
Summer Greeting Card

1965, June 20
UX28 PC25 1½c multicolored, *off-white*
(340,604) 2.50 3.50
First day cancel 2.50

Toy Pony
Rider — PC26

Fan Palm
Dipper — PC27

Designer: Seikichi Tamanaha

1966 New Year Card; Precanceled

1965, Nov. 15
UX29 PC26 1½c multicolored, *off-white*
(5,224,622) 2.00 2.50
First day cancel 2.00
a. Silver (background) omitted 250.00

Designer: Seikichi Tamanaha
Summer Greeting Card

1966, June 20
UX30 PC27 1½c multicolored, *off-white*
(339,880) 2.50 3.50
First day cancel 2.00

Toy
Dove — PC28

Cycad Insect Cage
and Praying
Mantis — PC29

Designer: Seikichi Tamanaha

1967 New Year Card; Precanceled
1966, Nov. 15
UX31 PC28　1½c multicolored, *off-white*
(5,500,000)　　　2.00　　2.50
First day cancel　　　　　　　2.50
a.　Silver (background) omitted　500.00
b.　Gray blue & green omitted　750.00

Designer: Shin Isagawa
Summer Greeting Card
1967, June 20
UX32 PC29　1½c multicolored, *off-white*
(350,000)　　2.50　　3.50
First day cancel　　　　　　2.50

Paper Doll
Royalty — PC30

Pandanus
Drupe — PC31

Designer: Shin Isagawa
1968 New Year Card; Precanceled
1967, Nov. 15
UX33 PC30　1½c multicolored, *off-white*
(6,200,000)　　2.00　　2.50
First day cancel　　　　　　2.50
a.　Gold omitted　　　　500.00

Designer: Seikan Omine
Summer Greeting Card
1968, June 20
UX34 PC31　1½c multicolored, *off-white*
(350,000)　　2.00　　3.50
First day cancel　　　　　　2.50

Toy Lion — PC32

Ryukyu Trading
Ship — PC33

Designer: Teruyoshi Kinjo
1969 New Year Card; Precanceled
1968, Nov. 15
UX35 PC32　1½c multicolored, *off-white*
(7,000,000)　　2.00　　2.50
First day cancel　　　　　　2.00

Designer: Seikichi Tamanaha
Summer Greeting Card
1969, June 20
UX36 PC33　1½c multicolored, *(349,800)*　2.00　3.50
First day cancel　　　　　　2.50

See the "Information for Collectors" section at beginning of catalogue for an explanation of perforation types, imperforates and coils.

Toy Devil
Mask — PC34

Ripe
Litchis — PC35

Designer: Teruyoshi Kinjo
1970 New Year Card; Precanceled
1969, Nov. 15
UX37 PC34　1½c multicolored *(7,200,000)*　1.50　2.50
First day cancel　　　　　　2.00

Designer: Kensei Miyagi
Summer Greeting Card
1970, June 20
UX38 PC35　1½c multicolored *(400,000)*　2.00　3.50
First day cancel　　　　　　2.00

Thread-winding
Implements for
Dance — PC36

Ripe
Guavas — PC37

Designer: Yoshinori Arakai
1971 New Year Card; Precanceled
1970, Nov. 16
UX39 PC36　1½c multicolored *(7,500,000)*　1.50　2.50
First day cancel　　　　　　2.00

Designer: Kensei Miyagi
Summer Greeting Card
1971, July 10
UX40 PC37　1½c multicolored *(400,000)*　2.00　3.50
First day cancel　　　　　　2.00

Pony Type of 1961
Zip Code Boxes in Vermilion
1971, July 10
UX41 PC17　1½c gray violet & brown
(3,000,000)　　2.00　　5.00
First day cancel　　　　　　2.50

No. UX41 Surcharged below
Stamp in Vermilion

"Revalued 2¢" applied by Nakamura Printing Co.

1971, Sept. 1
UX42 PC17　2c on 1½c gray violet &
brown *(1,699,569)*　1.50　3.00
First day cancel　　　　　　3.00
a.　Inverted surcharge　　500.00
b.　Double surcharge　　　500.00
c.　Surcharge on back　　　500.00
e.　Surcharge on back, inverted　500.00

Tasseled Castanets — PC38

Designer: Yoshinori Arakaki
Zip Code Boxes in Vermilion
1972 New Year Card; Precanceled
1971, Nov. 15
UX43 PC38　2c multicolored *(8,000,000)*　1.50　2.50
First day cancel　　　　　　2.00

Type of 1961
Zip Code Boxes in Vermilion
1971, Dec. 15
UX44 PC17　2c gray violet & brown
(3,500,000)　　2.00　　2.50
First day cancel　　　　　　2.50

PAID REPLY POSTAL CARDS

Sold as two attached cards, one for message, one for reply. The listings are of unsevered cards except Nos. UY4-UY6.

往信　　　　　　返信
Message　　　　Reply

1948, July 1
UY1　US1　10s + 10s dull red, *grayish tan*
(1,000)　　1,400.　1,500. —
m.　Message card　　400.00　—
r.　Reply card　　400.00　—

1949, July 18
UY2　US1　15s + 15s vermilion, *tan (E*
150,000)　35.00　—
First day cancel
a.　Gray card *(E 75,000)*　75.00　—
m.　Message card　10.00　25.00
r.　Reply card　10.00　25.00

1950, Jan. 21
UY3　US2　50s + 50s carmine red, *gray*
cream (E 130,000)　40.00　—
First day cancel
a.　Message card, double impression　—　—
b.　Light tan card *(E 96,000)*　20.00　—
m.　Message card　5.00　20.00
r.　Reply card　5.00　20.00

No. UY2a Handstamp Surcharged in Vermilion
1951
UY4　US1　1y (15s+85s) message, type
"b" *(E 3750)*　350.00　350.00
a.　Reply, type "b" *(E 3750)*　350.00　350.00
b.　Message, type "a" *(E 1500)*　600.00　—
c.　Reply, type "a" *(E 1500)*　600.00　—
d.　Message, type "d" *(E 2250)*　500.00　—
e.　Reply, type "d" *(E 2250)*　500.00　—
f.　Message, UY2, type "a" *(E 250)*　150.00　225.00
g.　Reply, UY2, type "a" *(E 250)*　150.00　225.00
h.　Message, UY2, type "b" *(E 1500)*　275.00　275.00
i.　Reply, UY2, type "b" *(E 1500)*　275.00　275.00
j.　Message, UY2, type "d" *(E 250)*　150.00　250.00
k.　Reply, UY2, type "d" *(E 250)*　150.00　250.00

e　　　　　　f

g　　　　　　h

Typographed Surcharge in Vermilion
UY5　US1　1y (15s+85s) message, type "f"
(E 20,000)　125.00　125.00
a.　Reply, type "f" *(E 20,000)*　125.00　125.00
b.　Message, type "e" *(E 12,500)*　225.00　225.00
c.　Reply, type "e" *(E 12,500)*　225.00　225.00
d.　Message, type "g" *(E 500)*　1,000.　1,000.
e.　Reply, type "g" *(E 500)*　1,000.　1,000.
f.　Message, UY2, type "e" *(E 15,000)*　125.00　125.00
g.　Reply, UY2, type "e" *(E 15,000)*　125.00　125.00
h.　Message, UY2, type "f" *(E 9,000)*　125.00　125.00
i.　Reply, UY2, type "f" *(E 9,000)*　125.00　125.00
j.　Message, UY2, type "g" *(E 500)*　1,000.　1,000.
k.　Reply, UY2, type "g" *(E 500)*　1,000.　1,000.

Nos. UY4-UY5 were also issued as unsevered cards.

Typographed Surcharge Type "h" in Vermilion on No. UY3

UY6	US2	1y (50s+50s) message (E 35,000)	100.00	150.00
a.		Reply (E 35,000)	100.00	150.00
b.		Message, UY3b (E 10,000)	100.00	150.00
c.		Reply, UY3b (E 10,000)	100.00	150.00

Smooth or Coarse Card

1952, Feb. 8

UY7	PC3	1y + 1y vermilion, *gray tan* (60,000)	90.00	—
		First day cancel		250.00
m.		Message card	25.00	50.00
r.		Reply card	25.00	50.00

1953

UY8	PC4	1y + 1y vermilion, *tan* (22,900)	35.00	—
		First day cancel		—
a.		Off-white card (13,800)	40.00	—
m.		Message card	10.00	25.00
r.		Reply card	10.00	35.00

Off-white or Light Cream Card

1953, Dec. 2

UY9	PC5	2y + 2y green (50,000)	60.00	—
		First day cancel		150.00
m.		message card	15.00	25.00
r.		Reply card	15.00	35.00

1955, May

UY10	PC6	2y + 2y green, *off-white* (280,000)	12.50	—
a.		Reply card blank	500.00	—
m.		Message card	4.00	15.00
r.		Reply card	4.00	20.00

No. UY10 Surcharged in Red

1958, Sept. 16

UY11	PC6	1½c on 2y, 1½c on 2y (95,000)	12.50	—
		First day cancel		40.00
a.		Surcharge on reply card only	500.00	—
b.		Surcharge on message card only	500.00	—
c.		Reply card double surcharge	750.00	—
d.		Reply card stamp omitted (surcharge only)	1,000.	—
m.		Message card	4.00	15.00
r.		Reply card	4.00	25.00

Surcharge varieties include: "1" omitted; wrong font "2".

PONY TYPES

1959, June 20

UY12	PC11	1½c + 1½c dark blue & brown (366,000)	5.00	—
		First day cancel		4.00
m.		Message card	1.00	5.00
r.		Reply card	1.00	5.00

1960, Mar. 10

UY13	PC13	1½c + 1½c gray violet & brown, (150,000)	7.00	—
		First day cancel		9.00
m.		Message card	1.50	5.00
r.		Reply card	1.50	5.00

INTERNATIONAL TYPE

1963, Feb. 15

UY14	PC20	5c + 5c vermilion, emerald & black, *pale yellow* (70.000)	2.50	—
		First day cancel		4.50
m.		Message card	1.00	5.00
r.		Reply card	1.00	5.00

PONY ("RYUKYUS" TYPE)

1963-69

UY15	PC17	1½c + 1½c gray violet & brown, *cream Mar. 15,* (800,000)	2.50	—
		First day cancel		3.50
a.		Off-white card, Mar. 13, 1967 (100,000)	3.50	—
b.		White card, Nov. 22, 1969 (700,000)	2.00	—
m.		Message card detached	50	5.00
r.		Reply card detached	50	5.00

No. UY14 Surcharged below Stamp in Vermilion

1971, Sept. 1

UY16	PC17	2c on 1½c + 2c on 1½c gray violet & brown (80,000)	3.00	—
		First day cancel		3.50
m.		Message card	1.00	5.00
r.		Reply card	1.00	5.00

PONY ("RYUKYUS") TYPE
Zip Code Boxes in Vermilion

1971, Nov. 1

UY17	PC17	2c + 2c gray violet & brown (150,000)	3.00	—
		First day cancel		4.00
m.		Message card	1.00	5.00
r.		Reply card	1.00	5.00

REVENUE

Upon its establishment Apr. 1, 1952, the government of the Ryukyu Islands assumed responsibility for the issuing and the profit from revenue stamps. The various series served indiscriminately as evidence of payment of the required fees for various legal, realty and general commercial transactions.

1 yen — R1

3	5	10	50

100	500	1000

Litho. by Japan Printing Bureau.
Designer: Eizo Yonamine

1952, July 15   Wmk. 257   Perf. 13x13½

R1	R1	1y brown	10.00	3.00
R2	R1	3y carmine	15.00	3.00
R3	R1	5y green	20.00	7.50
R4	R1	10y blue	25.00	15.00
R5	R1	50y purple	40.00	17.50
R6	R1	100y yellow brown	60.00	25.00

1954, Apr. 16

R7	R1	500y dark green	150.00	75.00
R8	R1	1,000y carmine	200.00	125.00

Denomination Vertical

"Cent"   "Dollar"

Litho. by Kobundo Printing Co., Naha
Perf. 10, 10½, 11 and combinations

1958, Sept. 16   Without Gum   Unwmk.

R9	R1	1c red brown	20.00	20.00
a.		Horiz. pair, imperf. between	250.00	
R10	R1	3c red	25.00	25.00
a.		Horiz. pair, imperf. between	250.00	
R11	R1	5c green	35.00	35.00
R12	R1	10c blue	60.00	40.00
a.		Horiz. pair, imperf. between	300.00	
R13	R1	50c purple	100.00	60.00
R14	R1	$1 sepia	150.00	100.00
R15	R1	$5 dark green	300.00	100.00
R16	R1	$10 carmine	400.00	150.00

R2   R3

R4 $20

Litho. by Japan Printing Bureau.

1959-69   Wmk. 257   Perf. 13x13½

R17	R2	1c brown	2.50	1.50

R18	R2	3c red	3.00	1.50
R19	R2	5c purple	5.00	3.00
R20	R2	10c green	10.00	6.00
R21	R2	20c sepia ('69)	50.00	30.00
R22	R2	30c light olive ('69)	60.00	35.00
R23	R2	50c blue	20.00	10.00

Engr.

R24	R3	$1 olive	30.00	15.00
R25	R3	$2 vermilion ('69)	125.00	35.00
R26	R3	$3 purple ('69)	150.00	45.00
R27	R3	$5 orange	80.00	50.00
R28	R3	$10 dark green	150.00	70.00
R29	R4	$20 carmine ('69)	600.00	300.00
R30	R4	$30 blue ('69)	750.00	350.00
R31	R4	$50 black ('69)	1,250.	500.00

PROVISIONAL ISSUES MIYAKO

Stamps of Japan 1938-42 Handstamped in Black or Red

1948   Typo., Litho., Engr.   Wmk. 257   Perf. 13

3XR1	A84	3s brown, #329	75.00	—
3XR2	A86	5s brown lake, #331	75.00	—
3XR3	A152	20s blue, #338 (R)	60.00	—
3XR4	A95	25s dark brown & pale brown, #270 (R)	60.00	—
a.		Black overprint	500.00	—
3XR5	A96	30s peacock blue, #271 (R)	60.00	—
3XR6	A154	40s dark violet, #342 (R)	60.00	—
3XR7	A97	50s olive & pale olive, #272 (R)	135.00	—

"SPECIMEN"

Regular stamps and postal cards of 1958-65 overprinted with three cursive syllabics *mi-ho-n* ("specimen"). Two trial color proofs, Nos. 46TC and 48TC, received vermilion mihon overprints in a different cursive type (100 each).

Type A

1961-64

Overprinted in Black

91S		3c multi (1,000)	250.00
118S		3c multi (1,100)	500.00
119S		3c multi (1,100)	450.00

Type B   み ほ ん

1964-65

Overprinted in Red or Black

120aS		3c dp bl, dp car & ocher (R) (1,500)	225.00
121S		3c multi (R) (1,500)	200.00
124S		3c ultra, yel & red (R) (5,000)	45.00
125S		3s dl cl, yel & blk (1,500)	75.00
126S		3c yel & multi (2,000)	60.00
127S		3c gray, red & blk (2,000)	60.00
128S		3c multi (1,500)	75.00
129S		1½c multi (1,500)	60.00
130S		3c lt bl & multi (R) (1,500)	175.00
131S		3c multi (R) (1,500)	60.00
132S		3c buff & multi (2,000)	60.00
133S		3c grn & multi (R) (2,000)	60.00
134S		3c multi (2,000)	60.00
135S		3c bl & multi (2,000)	60.00
136S		3c gldn brn & multi (2,000)	60.00
139S		1½c multi (R) (2,500)	50.00

Postal Cards

1964-65

Overprinted Type A or B in Black or Red

UX26S	A	1½c multi (1,000)	500.00
UX27S	B	1½c multi (1,000)	350.00
UX28S	A	1½c multi (1,000)	300.00
UX29S	A	1½c multi (1,100)	250.00

UNEMPLOYMENT INSURANCE

These stamps, when affixed in an official booklet and canceled, certified a one-day contract for a day laborer. They were available to employers at certain post offices on various islands.

Dove — RQ1   Shield — RQ2

Lithographed in Naha
1961, Jan. 10   Without Gum   Unwmk.   *Rouletted*

RQ1	RQ1	2c pale red	400.00
RQ2	RQ2	4c violet	25.00 25.00

Redrawn
Lithographed by Japan Printing Bureau
1966, Feb.   Unwmk.   *Perf. 13x13½*

RQ3	RQ1	2c pale violet	
RQ4	RQ2	4c violet	20.00 20.00

Redrawn stamps have bolder numerals and inscriptions, and fewer, stronger lines of shading in background.

Cycad — RQ3

Lithographed by Japan Printing Bureau
1968, Apr. 19   Wmk. 257   *Perf. 13x13½*

RQ5	RQ3	8c brown	25.00 25.00

Nos. RQ3-RQ4 Surcharged with New Values and 2 Bars
1967-72

RQ6	RQ1	8c on 2c pale red	40.00 40.00
RQ7	RQ2	8c on 4c violet ('72)	25.00 25.00
RQ8	RQ2	12c on 4c violet ('71)	20.00 20.00

PROOFS AND TRIAL COLOR PROOFS
1948

Salmon Paper

1aP		5s magenta	—
2aP		10s yellow green	—
3aP		20s yellor green	—
5aP		40s magenta	—
6aP		50s ultramarine	—
7aP		1y ultramarine	—

Sheets of the second printing, Nos. 1-7, were overprinted in Tokyo with a swirl-pattern of blue or red dots. These essays sell for about $400 each.

1950

Soft White Paper

8P		50s dark carmine rose	600.00
9P		1y deep blue	600.00
10P		2y rose violet	600.00
11P		3y carmine rose	600.00
12P		4y greenish gray	600.00
12TC		4y olive	600.00
13P		5y blue green	600.00

1951

14P		3y red brown	800.00

1953

27P		3y deep magenta	—
28P		6y dull blue	—

1958

46TC		2c black	500.00
48TC		4c black	500.00

AIR POST
1950

C1P		8y bright blue	900.00
C2P		12y green	900.00
C3P		16y rose carmine	900.00

1951

C6P		30y cerise	800.00

SPECIAL DELIVERY
1950

E1P		5y bright blue	700.00

An official proof folder contains one each of Nos. 8P-13P, 12TC, C1P-C3P and E1P.

UNITED NATIONS

United Nations stamps are used on U.N. official mail sent from U.N. Headquarters in New York City, the U.N. European Office in Geneva, Switzerland, or from the Donaupark Vienna International Center or Atomic Energy Agency in Vienna, Austria to points throughout the world. They may be used on private correspondence sent through the U.N. post offices.

U.N. mail is carried by the U.S., Swiss and Austrian postal systems.

See Switzerland official stamp listings in Scotts Standard Postage Stamp Catalogue for stamps issued by the Swiss Government for official use of the U.N. European Office and other U.N. affiliated organizations. See France official stamp listings for stamps issued by the French Government for official use of UNESCO.

The 1962 U.N. Temporary Executive Authority overprints on stamps of Netherlands New Guinea are listed under West Irian in Scotts Standard Catalogue.

+: When following the quantity, this indicates the total printed to date. Unless otherwise noted, these are the initial printing order.

Blocks of four generally sell for four times the single stamp price.

Peoples of the World — A1

UN Headquarters Building — A2

"Peace, Justice, Security" — A3

UN Flag — A4

UN International Childrens Emergency Fund — A5

World Unity — A6

Printed by Thomas De La Rue & Co., Ltd., London (1c, 3c, 10c, 15c, 20c, 25c), and Joh. Enschedeand Sons, Haarlem, Netherlands (1½c, 2c, 5c, 50c, $1). The 3c, 15c and 25c have frame engraved, center photogravure; other denominations are engraved. Panes of 50. Designed by O. C. Meronti (A1), Leon Helguera (A2), J. F. Doeve (A3), Ole Hamann (A4), S. L. Hartz (5c) and Hubert Woyty-Wimmer (20c).

			Perf. 13x12½, 12½x13		
1951			**Engr. and Photo.**		**Unwmk.**
1	A1	1c magenta, *Oct. 24, 1951*			
		(8,000,000)		5	5
		First day cover			50
		Margin block of 4, UN seal		25	—
2	A2	1½c blue green, *Oct. 24, 1951*			
		(7,450,000)		5	5
		First day cover			50
		Margin block of 4, UN seal		25	—
		Precanceled (361,700)			15.00
3	A3	2c purple, *Nov. 16, 1951*			
		(8,470,000)		6	5
		First day cover			50
		Margin block of 4, UN seal		30	—
4	A4	3c magenta & blue, *Oct. 24, 1951*			
		(8,250,000)		6	5
		First day cover			50
		Margin block of 4, UN seal		30	—
5	A5	5c blue, *Oct. 24, 1951 (6,000,000)*		10	6
		First day cover			75
		Margin block of 4, UN seal		50	—
6	A1	10c chocolate, *Nov. 16, 1951*			
		(2,600,000)		25	15
		First day cover			1.00
		Margin block of 4, UN seal		1.25	—
7	A4	15c violet & blue, *Nov. 16, 1951*			
		(2,300,000)		30	20
		First day cover			1.25
		Margin block of 4, UN seal		1.75	—
8	A6	20c dark brown, *Nov. 16, 1951*			
		(2,100,000)		1.00	65
		First day cover			1.50
		Margin block of 4, UN seal		5.00	—
9	A4	25c olive gray & blue, *Oct. 24, 1951 (2,000,000)*		75	65
		First day cover			2.00
		Margin block of 4, UN seal		3.75	—
10	A2	50c indigo, *Nov. 16, 1951*			
		(1,500,000)		8.00	5.50
		First day cover			8.00
		Margin block of 4, UN seal		40.00	—
11	A3	$1 red, *Oct. 24, 1951 (2,012,500)*		2.50	1.50
		First day cover			9.00
		Margin block of 4, UN seal		12.50	—

First day covers of Nos. 1-11 and C1-C4 total 1,113,216.

The various printings of Nos. 1-11 vary in sheet marginal perforation. Some were perforated through left or right margins, or both; some through all margins.

Most of this issue carry a marginal inscription consisting of the UN seal and "First UN/Issue 1951." This inscription appears four times on each sheet. The listing "Margin block of 4, UN seal" or "Margin block of 4, inscription" in this and following issues refers to a corner block.

Sheets of the 1½c, 2c, 50c and $1 have a cut-out of different shape in one margin. The printer trimmed this off entirely on most of the 1½c third printing, and partially on the 1½c fourth printing and $1 fifth and sixth printings.

For 30c in type A1 and 10fr in type A3, see UN Offices in Geneva Nos. 4 and 14.

Forgeries of the 1½c precancel exist.

Veterans' War Memorial Building, San Francisco — A7

Issued to mark the 7th anniversary of the signing of the United Nations Charter.

Engraved and printed by the American Bank Note Co., New York. Panes of 50. Designed by Jean Van Noten.

1952, Oct. 24				**Perf. 12**
12	A7	5c blue (1,274,670)	60	30
		First day cover (160,117)		75
		Margin block of 4, inscription	3.25	—

Globe and Encircled Flame — A8

Issued to commemorate the 4th anniversary of the adoption of the Universal Declaration of Human Rights.

Engraved and printed by Thomas De La Rue & Co., Ltd., London. Panes of 50. Designed by Hubert Woyty-Wimmer.

1952, Dec. 10				**Perf. 13½x14**
13	A8	3c deep green (1,554,312)	25	20
		First day cover		75
		Margin block of 4, inscription	1.25	—
14	A8	5c blue (1,126,371)	1.25	45
		First day cover		1.00
		First day cover, #13-14		1.25
		Margin block of 4, inscription	6.50	—

First day covers of Nos. 13 and 14 total 299,309.

Refugee Family — A9

Issued to publicize "Protection for Refugees."
Engraved and printed by Thomas De La Rue & Co., Ltd., London. Panes of 50. Designed by Olav Mathiesen.

1953, April 24   *Perf. 12 1/2x13*
15	A9	3c dark red brown & rose brown		
		(1,299,793)	40	15
		First day cover		70
		Margin block of 4, inscription	2.00	—
16	A9	5c indigo & blue (969,224)	2.00	75
		First day cover		1.25
		First day cover, #15-16		1.50
		Margin block of 4, inscription	10.00	—

First day covers of Nos. 15 and 16 total 234,082.

Envelope, U. N. Emblem and Map — A10

Issued to honor the Universal Postal Union.
Engraved and printed by Thomas De La Rue & Co., Ltd., London. Panes of 50. Designed by Hubert Woyty-Wimmer.

1953, June 12   *Perf. 13*
17	A10	3c black brown (1,259,689)	50	20
		First day cover		75
		Margin block of 4, inscription	2.50	—
18	A10	5c dark blue (907,312)	2.50	1.00
		First day cover		1.50
		First day cover, #17-18		1.75
		Margin block of 4, inscription	12.50	—

First day covers of Nos. 17 and 18 total 231,627.
Plate number ("1A" or "1B") in color of stamp appears below 47th stamp of sheet.

Gearwheels and U. N. Emblem — A11

Issued to publicize United Nations activities in the field of technical assistance.
Engraved and printed by Thomas De La Rue & Co. Ltd. London. Panes of 50. Designed by Olav Mathiesen.

1953, Oct. 24   *Perf. 13x12 1/2*
19	A11	3c dark gray (1,184,348)	20	18
		First day cover		75
		Margin block of 4, inscription	1.00	—
20	A11	5c dark green (968,182)	1.75	45
		First day cover		1.00
		First day cover, #19-20		1.25
		Margin block of 4, inscription	8.75	—

First day covers of Nos. 19 and 20 total 229,211.

Hands Reaching Toward Flame — A12

Issued to publicize Human Rights Day.
Engraved and printed by Thomas De La Rue & Co., Ltd., London. Panes of 50. Designed by Leon Helguera.

1953, Dec. 10   *Perf. 12 1/2x13*
21	A12	3c bright blue (1,456,928)	50	25
		First day cover		75
		Margin block of 4, inscription	2.50	—
22	A12	5c rose red (983,831)	3.50	60
		First day cover		1.00
		First day cover, #21-22		1.25
		Margin block of 4, inscription	17.50	—

First day covers of Nos. 21 and 22 total 265,186.

Ear of Wheat — A13

Issued to honor the Food and Agriculture Organization.
and printed by Thomas De La Rue & Co., Ltd., London. Panes of 50. Designed by Dirk Van Gelder.

1954, Feb. 11   *Perf. 12 1/2x13*
23	A13	3c dark green & yellow		
		(1,250,000)	1.00	15
		First day cover		75
		Margin block of 4, inscription	5.00	—
24	A13	8c indigo & yellow (949,718)	2.00	70
		First day cover		1.00
		First day cover, #23-24		1.25
		Margin block of 4, inscription	10.00	—

First day covers of Nos. 23 and 24 total 272,312.

U. N. Emblem and Anvil Inscribed "ILO" — A14

Design: 8c, inscribed "OIT."
Issued to honor the International Labor Organization.
Engraved and printed by Thomas De La Rue & Co., Ltd., London. Panes of 50. Designed by JoseRenau.

1954, May 10   *Perf. 12 1/2x13*
25	A14	3c brown (1,085,651)	40	30
		First day cover		75
		Margin block of 4, inscription	2.00	—
26	A14	8c magenta (903,561)	5.50	1.40
		First day cover		1.50
		First day cover, #25-26		1.75
		Margin block of 4, inscription	27.50	—

First day covers of Nos. 25 and 26 total 252,796.

U. N. European Office, Geneva — A15

Issued on the occasion of United Nations Day.
Engraved and printed by Thomas De La Rue & Co., Ltd., London. Panes of 50. Designed by Earl W. Purdy.

1954, Oct. 25   *Perf. 14*
27	A15	3c dark blue violet (1,000,000)	6.50	1.50
		First day cover		2.00
		Margin block of 4, inscription	32.50	—
28	A15	8c red (1,000,000)	50	50
		First day cover		90
		First day cover, #27-28		2.50
		Margin block of 4, inscription	3.00	—

First day covers of Nos. 27 and 28 total 233,544.

Mother and Child — A16

Issued to publicize Human Rights Day.
Engraved and printed by Thomas De La Rue & Co., Ltd. London. Panes of 50. Designed by Leonard C. Mitchell.

1954, Dec. 10   *Perf. 14*
29	A16	3c red orange (1,000,000)	15.00	3.00
		First day cover		5.00
		Margin block of 4, inscription	75.00	—
30	A16	8c olive green (1,000,000)	60	60
		First day cover		75
		First day cover, #29-30		6.00
		Margin block of 4, inscription	3.00	—

First day covers of Nos. 29 and 30 total 276,333.

Symbol of Flight — A17

Design: 8c, inscribed "OACI."
Issued to honor the International Civil Aviation Organization.
Engraved and printed by Waterlow & Sons, Ltd., London. Panes of 50. Designed by Angel Medina Medina.

1955, Feb. 9   *Perf. 13 1/2x14*
31	A17	5c blue (1,000,000)	6.00	50
		First day cover		1.00
		Margin block of 4, inscription	30.00	—
32	A17	8c rose carmine (1,000,000)	1.75	90
		First day cover		1.50
		First day cover, #31-32		2.25
		Margin block of 4, inscription	8.75	—

First day covers of Nos. 31 and 32 total 237,131.

UNESCO Emblem — A18

Issued to honor the U. N. Educational, Scientific and Cultural Organization.
Engraved and printed by Waterlow & Sons, Ltd., London. Panes of 50. Designed by George Hamori.

1955, May 11   *Perf. 13 1/2x14*
33	A18	3c lilac rose (1,000,000)	2.50	60
		First day cover		1.00
		Margin block of 4, inscription	12.50	—
34	A18	8c light blue (1,000,000)	35	35
		First day cover		75
		First day cover, #33-34		1.50
		Margin block of 4, inscription	1.75	—

First day covers of Nos. 33 and 34 total 255,326.

United Nations Charter — A19

Design: 4c, Spanish inscription. 8c, French inscription.

Issued to commemorate the 10th anniversary of the United Nations.
Engraved and printed by Waterlow & Sons, Ltd., London. Panes of 50. Designed by Claude Bottiau.

1955, Oct. 24				**Perf. 13½x14**	
35	A19	3c deep plum (1,000,000)		8.00	1.25
		First day cover			1.50
		Margin block of 4, inscription		40.00	—
36	A19	4c dull green (1,000,000)		20	20
		First day cover			50
		Margin block of 4, inscription		1.00	—
37	A19	8c bluish black (1,000,000)		35	35
		First day cover			75
		First day cover, #35-37			2.50
		Margin block of 4, inscription		1.75	—

Wmk. 309- Wavy Lines

Souvenir Sheet

1955, Oct. 24		**Wmk. 309**	**Imperf.**	
38	A19	Sheet of three (250,000)	250.00	65.00
a.		3c deep plum	15.00	8.00
b.		4c dull green	15.00	8.00
c.		8c bluish black	15.00	8.00
		First day cover		75.00
		Sheet with retouch on 8c	250.00	65.00

No. 38 measures 108x83mm. and has marginal inscriptions in deep plum.
Two printings were made of No. 38. The first (200,000) may be distinguished by the broken line of background shading on the 8c. It leaves a small white spot below the left leg of the "n" of "Unies." For the second printing (50,000), the broken line was retouched, eliminating the white spot. The 4c was also retouched.
First day covers of Nos. 35-38 total 455,791.
Copies of No. 38 are known with the 4c and 8c stamps misaligned.

Hand Holding Torch — A20

Issued in honor of Human Rights Day.
Engraved and printed by Waterlow & Sons, Ltd., London. Panes of 50. Designed by Hubert Woyty-Wimmer.

1955, Dec. 9		**Unwmk.**	**Perf. 14x13½**	
39	A20	3c ultramarine (1,250,000)	20	20
		First day cover		75
		Margin block of 4, inscription	1.00	—
40	A20	8c green (1,000,000)	2.25	45
		First day cover		1.00
		First day cover, #39-40		1.50
		Margin block of 4, inscription	11.50	—

First day covers of Nos. 39 and 40 total 298,038.

Symbols of Telecommunication — A21

Design: 8c, inscribed "UIT."
Issued in honor of the International Telecommunication Union.
Engraved and printed by Thomas De La Rue & Co., Ltd., London. Panes of 50. Designed by Hubert Woyty-Wimmer.

1956, Feb. 17				**Perf. 14**	
41	A21	3c turquoise blue (1,000,000)		75	25
		First day cover			75
		Margin block of 4, inscription		3.75	—
42	A21	8c deep carmine (1,000,000)		1.75	60
		First day cover			1.00
		First day cover, #41-42			1.50
		Margin block of 4, inscription		8.75	—

Plate number ("1A" or "1B") in color of stamp appears below 47th stamp of sheet.

Globe and Caduceus — A22

Design: 8c, inscribed "OMS."
Issued in honor of the World Health Organization.
Engraved and printed by Thomas De La Rue & Co., Ltd., London. Panes of 50. Designed by Olav Mathiesen.

1956, April 6			**Perf. 14**	
43	A22	3c bright greenish blue (1,250,000)	15	15
		First day cover		75
		Margin block of 4, inscription	75	—
44	A22	8c golden brown (1,000,000)	2.25	75
		First day cover		1.50
		First day cover, #43-44		1.75
		Margin block of 4, inscription	11.50	—

First day covers of Nos. 43 and 44 total 260,853.

General Assembly — A23

Design: 8c, French inscription.
Issued to commemorate United Nations Day.
Engraved and printed by Thomas De La Rue & Co., Ltd., London. Panes of 50. Designed by Kurt Plowitz.

1956, Oct. 24			**Perf. 14**	
45	A23	3c dark blue (2,000,000)	10	5
		First day cover		30
		Margin block of 4, inscription	50	—
46	A23	8c gray olive (1,500,000)	30	12
		First day cover		75
		First day cover, #45-46		75
		Margin block of 4, inscription	1.50	—

First day covers of Nos. 45 and 46 total 303,560.

Flame and Globe — A24

Issued to publicize Human Rights Day.
Engraved and printed by Thomas De La Rue & Co., Ltd., London. Panes of 50. Designed by Rashid-ud Din.

1956, Dec. 10			**Perf. 14**	
47	A24	3c plum (5,000,000)	6	5
		First day cover		25
		Margin block of 4, inscription	30	—
48	A24	8c dark blue (4,000,000)	16	12
		First day cover		45
		First day cover, #47-48		55
		Margin block of 4, inscription	80	—

First day covers of Nos. 47 and 48 total 416,120.

Weather Balloon — A25

Design: 8c, Agency name in French.
Issued to honor the World Meterological Organization.
Engraved and printed by Thomas De La Rue & Co., Ltd., London. Panes of 50. Designed by A. L. Pollock.

1957, Jan. 28			**Perf. 14**	
49	A25	3c violet blue (5,000,000)	6	5
		First day cover		25
		Margin block of 4, inscription	30	—
50	A25	8c dark carmine rose (3,448,985)	16	12
		First day cover		45
		First day cover, #49-50		55
		Margin block of 4, inscription	80	—

First day covers of Nos. 49 and 50 total 376,110.

Badge of U. N. Emergency Force — A26

Issued in honor of the U. N. Emergency Force.
Engraved and printed by Thomas De La Rue & Co., Ltd., London. Panes of 50. Designed by Ole Hamann.

1957, April 8			**Perf. 14x12½**	
51	A26	3c light blue (4,000,000)	6	5
		First day cover		25
		Margin block of 4, inscription	30	—
52	A26	8c rose carmine (3,000,000)	16	12
		First day cover		45
		First day cover, #51-52		55
		Margin block of 4, inscription	80	—

First day covers of Nos. 51 and 52 total 461,772.

Nos. 51-52 Re-engraved

1957, April, May			**Perf. 14x12½**	
53	A26	3c blue (2,736,206)	10	10
		Margin block of 4, inscription	50	—
54	A26	8c rose carmine (1,000,000)	40	30
		Margin block of 4, inscription	2.00	—

On Nos. 53-54 the background within and around the circles is shaded lightly, giving a halo effect. The lettering is more distinct with a line around each letter.

U. N. Emblem and Globe — A27

Design: 8c, French inscription.
Issued to honor the Security Council.
Engraved and printed by Thomas De La Rue & Co., Ltd., London. Panes of 50. Designed by Rashid-ud Din.

1957, Oct. 24			**Perf. 12½x13**	
55	A27	3c orange brown (3,674,968)	6	5
		First day cover		25
		Margin block of 4, inscription	30	—
56	A27	8c dark blue green (2,885,938)	16	12
		First day cover		45
		First day cover, #55-56		55
		Margin block of 4, inscription	80	—

First day covers of Nos. 55 and 56 total 460,627.

Flaming
Torch — A28

Issued in honor of Human Rights Day.
Engraved and printed by Thomas De La Rue & Co., Ltd., London. Panes of 50. Designed by Olav Mathiesen.

1957, Dec. 10   **Perf. 14**

57	A28	3c red brown (3,368,405)	6	5
		First day cover		25
		Margin block of 4, inscription	30	—
58	A28	8c block (2,717,310)	16	12
		First day cover		45
		First day cover, #57-58		55
		Margin block of 4, inscription	80	—

First day covers of Nos. 57 and 58 total 553,669.

U. N. Emblem Shedding
Light on Atom — A29

Design: 8c, French inscription.
Issued in honor of the International Atomic Energy Agency.
Engraved and printed by the American Bank Note Co., New York. Panes of 50. Designed by Robert Perrot.

1958, Feb. 10   **Perf. 12**

59	A29	3c olive (3,663,305)	6	5
		First day cover		25
		Margin block of 4, inscription	30	—
60	A29	8c blue (3,043,622)	16	12
		First day cover		45
		First day cover, #59-60		55
		Margin block of 4, inscription	80	—

First day covers of Nos. 59 and 60 total 504,832.

Central Hall,
Westminster — A30

Design: 8c, French inscription.
Central Hall, Westminster, London, was the site of the first session of the United Nations General Assembly, 1946.
Engraved and printed by the American Bank Note Co., New York. Panes of 50. Designed by Olav Mathiesen.

1958, April 14   **Perf. 12**

61	A30	3c violet blue (3,353,716)	6	5
		First day cover		25
		Margin block of 4, inscription	30	—
62	A30	8c rose claret (2,836,747)	16	12
		First day cover		45
		First day cover, #61-62		55
		Margin block of 4, inscription	80	—

First day covers of Nos. 61 and 62 total 449,401.

U. N. Seal — A31

Engraved and printed by Bradbury, Wilkinson & Co., Ltd., England. Panes of 50. Designed by Herbert M. Sanborn.

1958, Oct. 24   **Perf. 13½x14**

63	A31	4c red orange (9,000,000)	8	6
		First day cover		30
		Margin block of 4, inscription	40	—

1958, June 2   **Perf. 13x14**

64	A31	8c bright blue (5,000,000)	16	12
		First day cover (219,422)		50
		Margin block of 4, inscription	80	—
		Margin block of 4, Bradbury, Wilkinson imprint	5.00	—

Gearwheels — A32

Design: 8c, French inscription.
Issued to honor the Economic and Social Council.
Engraved and printed by the American Bank Note Co., New York. Panes of 50. Designed by Ole Hamann.

1958, Oct. 24   **Unwmk.**   **Perf. 12**

65	A32	4c dark blue green (2,556,784)	8	6
		First day cover		30
		Margin block of 4, inscription	40	—
66	A32	8c vermilion (2,175,117)	16	12
		First day cover		50
		First day cover, #65-66		65
		Margin block of 4, inscription	80	—

First day covers of Nos. 63, 65 and 66 total 626,236.

Hands Upholding
Globe — A33

Issued for Human Rights Day and to commemorate the tenth anniversary of the signing of the Universal Declaration of Human Rights.
Engraved and printed by the American Bank Note Co., New York. Panes of 50. Designed by Leonard C. Mitchell.

1958, Dec. 10   **Unwmk.**   **Perf. 12**

67	A33	4c yellow green (2,644,340)	8	6
		First day cover		30
		Margin block of 4, inscription	40	—
68	A33	8c red brown (2,216,838)	16	12
		First day cover		50
		First day cover, #67-68		65
		Margin block of 4, inscription	80	—

First day covers of Nos. 67 and 68 total 618,124.

New York City
Building,
Flushing
Meadows — A34

Design: 8c, French inscription.
New York City Building at Flushing Meadows, New York, was the site of many General Assembly meetings, 1946-50.
Engraved and printed by Canadian Bank Note Company, Ltd., Ottawa. Panes of 50. Designed by Robert Perrot.

1959, March 30   **Unwmk.**   **Perf. 12**

69	A34	4c light lilac rose (2,035,011)	8	6
		First day cover		35
		Margin block of 4, inscription	40	—
70	A34	8c aquamarine (1,627,281)	16	12
		First day cover		50
		First day cover, #69-70		70
		Margin block of 4, inscription	80	—

First day covers of Nos. 69 and 70 total 440,955.

U. N. Emblem and Symbols of
Agriculture, Industry and
Trade — A35

Issued to honor the Economic Commission for Europe.
Engraved and printed by Canadian Bank Note Company, Ltd., Ottawa. Panes of 50. Designed by Ole Hamann.

1959, May 18   **Unwmk.**   **Perf. 12**

71	A35	4c blue (1,743,502)	15	10
		First day cover		40
		Margin block of 4, inscription	75	—
72	A35	8c red orange (1,482,898)	30	20
		First day cover		60
		First day over, #71-72		90
		Margin block of 4, inscription	1.50	—

First day covers of Nos. 71 and 72 total 433,549.

Figure Adapted from Rodin's
"Age of Bronze" — A36

Design: 8c, French inscription.
Issued to honor the Trusteeship Council.
Engraved and printed by Canadian Bank Note Co., Ltd., Ottawa. Panes of 50. Designed by Leon Helguera; lettering by Ole Hamann.

1959, Oct. 23   **Unwmk.**   **Perf. 12.**

73	A36	4c bright red (1,929,677)	8	6
		First day cover		30
		Margin block of 4, inscription	40	—
74	A36	8c dark olive green (1,587,647)	16	12
		First day cover		50
		First day cover, #73-74		65
		Margin block of 4, inscription	80	—

First day covers of Nos. 73 and 74 total 466,053.

World Refugee Year
Emblem — A37

Design: 8c, French inscription.
Issued to publicize World Refugee Year, July 1, 1959-June 30, 1960.
Engraved and printed by Canadian Bank Note Co., Ltd., Ottawa. Panes of 50. Designed by Olav Mathiesen.

1959, Dec. 10   **Unwmk.**   **Perf. 12**

75	A37	4c olive & red (2,168,963)	8	6
		First day cover		30
		Margin block of 4, inscription	40	—
76	A37	8c olive & bright greenish blue (1,843,886)	16	12
		First day cover		50
		First day cover, #75-76		65
		Margin block of 4, inscription	80	—

First day covers of Nos. 75 and 76 total 502,262.

See table of Territorial and Statehood Dates at beginning of catalogue. See catalogue index.

Chaillot Palace, Paris — A38

Design: 8c, French inscription.
Chaillot Palace in Paris was the site of General Assembly meetings in 1948 and 1951.
Engraved and printed by Thomas De La Rue & Co., Ltd., London. Panes of 50. Designed by Hubert Woyty-Wimmer.

1960, Feb. 29　　　**Unwmk.**　　　**Perf. 14**
77	A38	4c rose lilac & blue *(2,276,678)*		8	6
		First day cover			30
		Margin block of 4, inscription	40		—
78	A38	8c dull green & brown *(1,930,869)*		16	12
		First day cover			50
		First day cover, #77-78			65
		Margin block of 4, inscription	80		—

First day covers of Nos. 77 and 78 total 446,815.

Map of Far East and Steel Beam — A39

Design: 8c, French inscription.
Issued to honor the Economic Commission for Asia and the Far East (ECAFE).
Printed by the Government Printing Bureau, Tokyo. Panes of 50. Designed by Hubert Woyty-Wimmer.

1960, Apr. 11　**Photo.**　**Unwmk.**　**Perf. 13x13½**
79	A39	4c deep claret, blue green & dull yellow *(2,195,945)*		8	6
		First day cover			30
		Margin block of 4, inscription	40		—
80	A39	8c olive green, blue & rose *(1,897,902)*		16	12
		First day cover			50
		First day cover, #79-80			65
		Margin block of 4, inscription	80		—

First day covers of Nos. 79 and 80 total 415,127.

Tree, FAO and U.N. Emblems — A40

Design: 8c, French inscription.
Issued to commemorate the Fifth World Forestry Congress, Seattle, Washington, Aug. 29-Sept. 10.
Printed by the Government Printing Bureau, Tokyo. Panes of 50. Designed by Ole Hamann.

1960, Aug. 29　**Photo.**　**Unwmk.**　**Perf. 13½**
81	A40	4c dark blue, green & orange *(2,188,293)*		8	6
		First day cover			30
		Margin block of 4, inscription	40		—
a.		Imperf., pair			—
82	A40	8c yellow green, black & orange *(1,837,778)*		16	12
		First day cover			50
		First day cover, #81-82			65
		Margin block of 4, inscription	80		—

First day covers of Nos. 81 and 82 total 434,129.

U.N. Headquarters and Preamble to U.N. Charter — A41

Design: 8c, French inscription.
Issued to commemorate the 15th anniversary of the United Nations.
Engraved and printed by the British American Bank Note Co., Ltd., Ottawa, Canada. Panes of 50. Designed by Robert Perrot.

1960, Oct. 24　　　**Unwmk.**　　　**Perf. 11**
83	A41	4c blue *(2,631,593)*		8	6
		First day cover			30
		Margin block of 4, inscription	40		—
84	A41	8c gray *(2,278,022)*		16	12
		First day cover			50
		First day cover, #83-84			65
		Margin block of 4, inscription	80		—

Souvenir Sheet
Imperf.
85	A41	Sheet of two *(1,000,000)*		3.50	3.00
a.		4c blue		1.00	50
b.		8c gray		1.00	50
		First day cover *(256,699)*			3.25

No. 85 has dark gray marginal inscription. Size: 92x71mm. Broken "I" and "V" flaws occur in "ANNIVERSARY" in marginal inscription. Copies are known with the two stamps misaligned.

Block and Tackle — A42

Design: 8c, French inscription.
Issued to honor the International Bank for Reconstruction and Development.
Printed by the Government Printing Bureau, Tokyo. Panes of 50. Designed by Angel Medina Medina.

1960, Dec. 9　**Photo.**　**Unwmk.**　**Perf. 13½x13**
86	A42	4c multicolored *(2,286,117)*		8	6
		First day cover			30
		Margin block of 4, inscription	40		—
87	A42	8c multicolored *(1,882,019)*		16	12
		First day cover			50
		First day cover, #86-87			65
		Margin block of 4, inscription	80		—
a.		Imperf., pair			

First day covers of Nos. 86 and 87 total 559,708.
No. 86 exists imperf.

Scales of Justice from Raphael's Stanze — A43

Design: 8c, French inscription.
Issued to honor the International Court of Justice.
Printed by the Government Printing Bureau, Tokyo, Japan. Panes of 50. Designed by Kurt Plowitz.

1961, Feb. 13　**Photo.**　**Unwmk.**　**Perf. 13½x13**
88	A43	4c yellow, orange brown & black *(2,234,588)*		8	6
		First day cover			30
		Margin block of 4, inscription	40		—
89	A43	8c yellow, green & black *(2,023,968)*		16	12

	First day cover		50
	First day cover, #88-89		65
	Margin block of 4, inscription	80	

First day covers of Nos. 88 and 89 total 447,467.
Nos. 88-89 exist imperf.

Seal of International Monetary Fund — A44

Design: 7c, French inscription.
Issued to honor the International Monetary Fund.
Printed by the Government Printing Bureau, Tokyo, Japan. Panes of 50. Designed by Roy E. Carlson and Hordur Karlsson, Iceland.

1961, Apr. 17　**Photo.**　**Unwmk.**　**Perf. 13x13½**
90	A44	4c bright bluish green *(2,305,010)*		8	6
		First day cover			30
		Margin block of 4, inscription	40		—
91	A44	7c terra cotta & yellow *(2,147,201)*		14	10
		First day cover			50
		First day cover, #90-91			65
		Margin block of 4, inscription	70		—

First day covers of Nos. 90 and 91 total 448,729.

Abstract Group of Flags — A45

Printed by Courvoisier S.A., La Chaux-de-Fonds, Switzerland. Panes of 50. Designed by Herbert M. Sanborn.

1961, June 5　**Photo.**　**Unwmk.**　**Perf. 11½**
92	A45	30c multicolored *(3,370,000)*		60	30
		First day cover *(182,949)*			70
		Margin block of 4, inscription	3.00		—

See U.N. Offices in Geneva No. 10.

Cogwheel and Map of Latin America — A46

Design: 11c, Spanish inscription.
Issued to honor the Economic Commission for Latin America.
Printed by the Government Printing Bureau, Tokyo. Panes of 50. Designed by Robert Perrot.

1961, Sept. 18　**Photo.**　**Unwmk.**　**Perf. 13½**
93	A46	4c blue, red & citron *(2,037,912)*		15	10
		First day cover			30
		Margin block of 4, inscription	75		—
94	A46	11c green, lilac & org vermilion *(1,835,097)*		45	20
		First day cover			80
		First day cover, #93-94			1.00
		Margin block of 4, inscription	2.25		—

First day covers of Nos. 93 and 94 total 435,820.

Africa House, Addis Ababa, and Map — A47

Design: 11c, English inscription.
Issued to honor the Economic Commission for Africa.
Printed by Courvoisier S.A., La Chaux-de-Fonds, Switzerland. Panes of 50. Designed by Robert Perrot.

1961, Oct. 24 Photo. Unwmk. Perf. 11½

95	A47	4c ultramarine, orange, yellow & brown *(2,044,842)*	8	6
		First day cover		30
		Margin block of 4, inscription	40	—
96	A47	11c emerald, orange, yellow & brown *(1,790,894)*	22	18
		First day cover		80
		First day cover, #95-96		1.00
		Margin block of 4, inscription	1.10	—

First day covers of Nos. 95 and 96 total 435,131.

Mother Bird Feeding Young
and UNICEF Seal — A48

Designs: 3c, Spanish inscription. 13c, French inscription.
Issued to commemorate the 15th anniversary of the United Nations Children's Fund.
Printed by Courvoisier S.A., La Chaux-de-Fonds, Switzerland. Panes of 50. Designed by Minoru Hisano.

1961, Dec. 4 Photo. Unwmk. Perf. 11½

97	A48	3c brown, gold, orange & yellow *(2,867,456)*	6	5
		First day cover		30
		Margin block of 4, inscription	30	—
98	A48	4c brown, gold, blue & emerald *(2,735,899)*	8	6
		First day cover		30
		Margin block of 4, inscription	40	—
99	A48	13c dp. grn., gold, purple & pink *(1,951,715)*	26	20
		First day cover		1.20
		First day cover, #97-99		1.60
		Margin block of 4, inscription	1.30	—

First day covers of Nos. 97-99 total 752,979.

Family and
Symbolic
Buildings — A49

Design: 7c, inscribed "Services Collectifs".
Issued to publicize the U.N. program for housing and urban development, and in connection with the expert committee meeting at U.N. headquarters, Feb. 7-21.
Printed by Harrison and Sons, Ltd., London, England. Panes of 50. Designed by Olav Mathiesen.

1962, Feb. 28 Photo. Unwmk. Perf. 14½x14
Central design multicolored

100	A49	4c bright blue *(2,204,190)*	8	6
		First day cover		30
		Margin block of 4, inscription	40	—
a.		Black omitted	550.00	
b.		Yellow omitted	400.00	
c.		Brown omitted	225.00	
101	A49	7c orange brown *(1,845,821)*	14	10
		First day cover		50
		First day cover, #100-101		70
		Margin block of 4, inscription	70	—
a.		Red omitted	400.00	

First day covers of Nos. 100-101 total 466,178.

"The World Against
Malaria" — A50

Issued in honor of the World Health Organization and to call attention to the international campaign to eradicate malaria from the world.
Printed by Harrison and Sons, Ltd., London, England. Panes of 50. Designed by Rashid-ud Din.

1962, Mar. 30 Photo. Unwmk. Perf. 14x14½
Word frame in gray

102	A50	4c orange, yellow, brown, green & black *(2,047,000)*	10	8
		First day cover		30
		Margin block of 4, inscription	50	—
103	A50	11c green, yellow, brown & indigo *(1,683,766)*	30	20
		First day cover		70
		First day cover, #102-103		90
		Margin block of 4, inscription	1.50	—

First day covers of Nos. 102-103 total 522,450.

"Peace" — A51

U.N. Flag — A52

Hands Combining
"UN" and
Globe — A53

U.N. Emblem
over Globe — A54

Printed by Harrison & Sons, Ltd. London, England (1c, 3c and 11c), and by Canadian Bank Note Co., Ltd., Ottawa (5c). Panes of 50. Designed by Kurt Plowitz (1c), Ole Hamann (3c), Renato Ferrini (5c) and Olav Mathiesen (11c).

Photo.; Engr. (5c)

1962, May 25 Unwmk. Perf. 14x14½

104	A51	1c vermilion, blue, blk. & gray *(5,000,000)*	5	5
		First day cover		35
		Margin block of 4, inscription	25	—
105	A52	3c light green, Prussian blue, yellow & gray *(5,000,000)*	6	5
		First day cover		30
		Margin block of 4, inscription	30	—

Perf. 12

106	A53	5c dark carmine rose *(4,000,000)*	20	10
		First day cover		45
		Margin block of 4, inscription	1.00	—

Perf. 12½

107	A54	11c dark & light blue & gold *(4,400,000)*	22	18
		First day cover		70
		First day cover, #104-107		1.25
		Margin block of 4, inscription	1.10	—

First day covers of Nos. 104-107 total 738,985.
Size of 5c, No. 106: 36½x23½mm.
See No. 167.
See U.N. Offices in Geneva Nos. 2 and 6.

Flag at Half-mast and U.N.
Headquarters — A55

Issued on the first anniversary of the death of Dag Hammarskjold, Secretary General of the United Nations 1953-61, in memory of those who died in the service of the United Nations.
Printed by Courvoisier S. A., La Chaux-de-Fonds, Switzerland. Panes of 50. Designed by Ole Hamann.

1962, Sept. 17 Photo. Unwmk. Perf. 11½

108	A55	5c black, light blue & blue *(2,195,707)*	45	15
		First day cover		35
		Margin block of 4, inscription	2.25	—
109	A55	15c black, gray olive & blue *(1,155,047)*	1.50	45
		First day cover		90
		First day cover, #108-109		1.15
		Margin block of 4, inscription	7.50	—

First day covers of Nos. 108-109 total 513,963.

World Map Showing
Congo — A56

Design: 11c inscribed "Operation des Nations Unies au Congo."
Issued to commemorate the United Nations Operation in the Congo.
Printed by Courvoisier S. A., La Chaux-de-Fonds, Switzerland. Panes of 50. Designed by George Hamori.

1962, Oct. 24 Photo. Unwmk. Perf. 11½

110	A56	4c olive, orange, blk. & yellow *(1,477,958)*	25	15
		First day cover		30
		Margin block of 4, inscription	1.25	—
111	A56	11c bl. grn., org., blk. & yel. *(1,171,255)*	1.00	40
		First day cover		80
		First day cover, #110-111		1.00
		Margin block of 4, inscription	5.00	—

First day covers of Nos. 110-111 total 460,675.

Globe in Universe and
Palm Frond — A57

Design: 4c, English inscription.
Issued to honor the Committee on Peaceful Uses of Outer Space.
Printed by Bradbury, Wilkinson and Co., Ltd., England. Panes of 50. Designed by Kurt Plowitz.

1962, Dec. 3 Engr. Unwmk. Perf. 14x13½

112	A57	4c violet blue, *(2,263,876)*	8	6
		First day cover		30
		Margin block of 4, inscription	40	—
113	A57	11c rose claret *(1,681,584)*	22	18
		First day cover		70
		First day cover, #112-113		80
		Margin block of 4, inscription	1.10	—

First day covers of Nos. 112-113 total 529,780.

Development Decade
Emblem — A58

Design: 11c, French inscription.
Issued to publicize the U.N. Development Decade and to commemorate the U.N. Conference on the Application of Science and Technology for the Benefit of the Less Developed Areas, Geneva, Feb. 4-20.
Printed by Courvoisier S.A., La Chaux-de-Fonds, Switzerland. Panes of 50. Designed by Rashid-ud Din.

1963, Feb. 4 Photo. Unwmk. Perf. 11½

114	A58	5c pale grn., maroon, dk. bl. & Prussian blue *(1,802,406)*	15	10
		First day cover		35

	Margin block of 4, inscription	75	—
115 A58	11c yel., maroon, dk. bl. & Prussian blue (1,530,190)	35	20
	First day cover		70
	First day cover, #114-115		1.00
	Margin block of 4, inscription	1.75	—

First day covers of Nos. 114-115 total 460,877.

Stalks of Wheat — A59

Design: 11c, French inscription.
Issued for the "Freedom from Hunger" campaign of the Food and Agriculture Organization.
Printed by Courvoisier S. A., La Chaux-de-Fonds, Switzerland. Panes of 50. Designed by Ole Hamann.

1963, Mar. 22   Photo.   Unwmk.   Perf. 11 1/2

116 A59	5c vermilion, green & yellow (1,666,178)	15	10
	First day cover		35
	Margin block of 4, inscription	75	—
117 A59	11c verm., deep claret & yel. (1,563,023)	35	20
	First day cover		70
	First day cover, #116-117		1.00
	Margin block of 4, inscription	1.75	—

First day covers of Nos. 116-117 total 461,868.

Bridge over Map of New Guinea — A60

Issued to commemorate the first anniversary of the United Nations Temporary Executive Authority (UNTEA) in West New Guinea (West Irian).
Printed by Courvoisier S.A., La Chaux-de-Fonds, Switzerland. Panes of 50. Designed by Henry Bencsath.

1963, Oct. 1   Photo.   Unwmk.   Perf. 11 1/2

118 A60	25c blue, green & gray (1,427,747)	85	50
	First day cover (222,280)		1.20
	Margin block of 4, inscription	4.25	—

General Assembly Building, New York — A61

Design: 11c, French inscription.
Since October 1955 all sessions of the General Assembly have been held in the General Assembly Hall, U.N. Headquarters, N.Y.
Printed by the Government Printing Bureau, Tokyo. Panes of 50. Designed by Kurt Plowitz.

1963, Nov. 4   Photo.   Unwmk.   Perf. 13

119 A61	5c vio. bl., bl., yel. grn. & red (1,892,539)	15	10
	First day cover		35
	Margin block of 4, inscription	75	—
120 A61	11c grn., yel. grn., bl., yel. & red (1,435,079)	35	20
	First day cover		70
	First day cover, #119-120		1.00
	Margin block of 4, inscription	1.75	—

First day covers of Nos. 119-120 total 410,306.

Flame — A62

Design: 11c inscribed "15e Anniversaire."
Issued to commemorate the 15th anniversary of the signing of the Universal Declaration of Human Rights.
Printed by the Government Printing Bureau, Tokyo. Panes of 50. Designed by Rashid-ud Din.

1963, Dec. 10   Photo.   Unwmk.   Perf. 13

121 A62	5c green, gold, red & yellow (2,208,008)	15	10
	First day cover		35
	Margin block of 4, inscription	75	—
122 A62	11c carm., gold, blue & yellow (1,501,125)	35	20
	First day cover		70
	First day cover, #121-122		1.00
	Margin block of 4, inscription	1.75	—

First day covers of Nos. 121-122 total 567,907.

Ships at Sea and IMCO Emblem — A63

Design: 11c, inscribed "OMCI."
Issued to honor the Intergovernmental Maritime Consultative Organization.
Printed by Courvoisier S.A., La Chaux-de-Fonds, Switzerland. Panes of 50. Designed by Henry Bencsath; emblem by Olav Mathiesen.

1964, Jan. 13   Photo.   Unwmk.   Perf. 11 1/2

123 A63	5c blue, olive, ocher & yellow (1,805,750)	15	10
	First day cover		35
	Margin block of 4, inscription	75	—
124 A63	11c dark blue, dark green, emerald & yellow (1,583,848)	35	20
	First day cover		70
	First day cover, #123-124		1.00
	Margin block of 4, inscription	1.75	—

First day covers of Nos. 123-124 total 442,696.

World Map, Sinusoidal Projection — A64

U.N. Emblem — A65

Three Men United Before Globe — A66

Stylized Globe and Weather Vane — A67

Printed by Thomas De La Rue & Co. Ltd., London (2c) and Courvoisier S.A., La Chaux-de-Fonds, Switzerland (7c, 10c and 50c). Panes of 50.
Designed by Ole Hamann (2c), George Hamori (7c, 10c) and Hatim El Mekki (50c).

1964-71   Photo.   Unwmk.   Perf. 14

125 A64	2c light & dark blue, orange & yellow green (3,800,000)	5	5
	First day cover		25
	Margin block of 4, inscription	30	—
a.	Perf. 13x13 1/2, Feb. 24, 1971 (1,500,000)	6	6

Perf. 11 1/2

126 A65	7c dark blue, orange brown & black (2,700,000)	14	10
	First day cover		45
	Margin block of 4, inscription	70	—
127 A66	10c blue green, olive green & black (3,200,000)	20	15
	First day cover		70
	First day cover, #125-127		1.00
	Margin block of 4, inscription	1.00	—
128 A67	50c multicolored (2,520,000)	1.00	75
	First day cover (210,713)		2.00
	Margin block of 4, inscription	5.00	—

Issue dates: 50c, Mar. 6; 2c, 7c and 10c, May 29, 1964.
First day covers of 2c, 7c and 10c total 524,073.
See U.N. Offices in Geneva Nos. 3 and 12.

Arrows Showing Global Flow of Trade — A68

Design: 5c, English inscription.
Issued to commemorate the U.N. Conference on Trade and Development, Geneva, March 23-June 15.
Printed by Thomas De La Rue & Co., Ltd., London. Panes of 50. Designed by Herbert M. Sanborn and Ole Hamann.

1964, June 15   Photo.   Unwmk.   Perf. 13

129 A68	5c black, red & yellow (1,791,211)	15	10
	First day cover		35
	Margin block of 4, inscription	75	—
130 A68	11c black, olive & yellow (1,529,526)	35	20
	First day cover		70
	First day cover, #129-130		1.00
	Margin block of 4, inscription	1.75	—

First day covers of Nos. 129-130 total 422,358.

Poppy Capsule and Reaching Hands — A69

Design: 11c, Inscribed "Echec au Stupéfiants."
Issued to honor international efforts and achievements in the control of narcotics.
Printed by the Canadian Bank Note Co., Ottawa. Panes of 50. Designed by Kurt Plowitz.

1964, Sept. 21   Engr.   Unwmk.   Perf. 12

131 A69	5c rose red & black (1,508,999)	15	10
	First day cover		35
	Margin block of 4, inscription	90	—
132 A69	11c emerald & black (1,340,691)	45	20
	First day cover		70
	First day cover, #131-132		1.00
	Margin block of 4, inscription	2.25	—

First day covers of Nos. 131-132 total 445,274.

Padlocked Atomic Blast — A70

Issued to commemorate the signing of the nuclear test ban treaty pledging an end to nuclear explosions in the atmosphere, outer space and under water.
Printed by Artia, Prague, Czechoslovakia. Panes of 50.
Designed by Ole Hamann.

Litho. and Engr.

1964, Oct. 23		**Unwmk.**	**Perf. 11x11½**	
133 A70	5c	dark red & dark brown		
		(2,422,789)	10	8
		First day cover (298,652)		30
		Margin block of 4, inscription	50	—

Education for Progress — A71

Design: 11c, French inscription.
Issued to publicize the UNESCO world campaign for universal literacy and for free compulsory primary education.
Printed by Courvoisier, S. A., La Chaux-de-Fonds, Switzerland. Panes of 50. Designed by Kurt Plowitz.

1964, Dec. 7		**Photo.**	**Unwmk.**	**Perf. 12½**
134 A71	4c	org. red, bister, grn. & blue		
		(2,375,181)	8	6
		First day cover		30
		Margin block of 4, inscription	40	—
135 A71	5c	bister, red, dk. & lt. blue		
		(2,496,877)	10	8
		First day cover		35
		Margin block of 4, inscription	50	—
136 A71	11c	green, lt. blue, blk. & rose		
		(1,773,645)	22	18
		First day cover		60
		First day cover, #134-136		1.00
		Margin block of 4, inscription	1.10	—

First day covers of Nos. 134-136 total 727,875.

Progress Chart of Special Fund, Key and Globe — A72

Design: 11c, French inscription.
Issued to publicize the Special Fund program to speed economic growth and social advancement in low-income countries.
Printed by the Government Printing Bureau, Tokyo. Panes of 50. Designed by Rashid-ud Din, Pakistan.

1965, Jan. 25		**Photo.**	**Unwmk.**	**Perf. 13½x13**
137 A72	5c	dull bl., dk. bl., yel. & red		
		(1,949,274)	10	8
		First day cover		30
		Margin block of 4, inscription	50	—
138 A72	11c	yel. grn., dk. bl., yel. & red		
		(1,690,908)	22	18
		First day cover		70
		First day cover, #137-138		80
		Margin block of 4, inscription	1.10	—
a.		Black omitted (U.N. emblem on key)	—	

First day covers of Nos. 137-138 total 490,608.

U.N. Emblem, Stylized Leaves and View of Cyprus — A73

Design: 11c, French inscription.
Issued to honor the United Nations Peace-keeping Force on Cyprus.
Printed by Courvoisier S.A., Switzerland. Panes of 50.
Designed by George Hamori, Australia.

1965, Mar. 4		**Photo.**	**Unwmk.**	**Perf. 11½**
139 A73	5c	orange, olive & black		
		(1,887,042)	10	8
		First day cover		30
		Margin block of 4, inscription	50	—
140 A73	11c	yellow green, bl. grn. & blk.		
		(1,691,767)	22	18

First day cover		70
First day cover, #139-140		90
Margin block of 4, inscription	1.10	

First day covers of Nos. 139-140 total 438,059.

"From Semaphore to Satellite" — A74

Design: 11c, French inscription.
Issued to commemorate the centenary of the International Telecommunication Union.
Printed by Courvoisier S.A., Switzerland. Panes of 50.
Designed by Kurt Plowitz, United States.

1965, May 17		**Photo.**	**Unwmk.**	**Perf. 11½**
141 A74	5c	aquamarine, orange, blue &		
		purple (2,432,407)	10	8
		First day cover		35
		Margin block of 4, inscription	50	—
142 A74	11c	light violet, red orange, bister		
		& bright green (1,731,070)	22	18
		First day cover		70
		First day cover, #141-142		90
		Margin block of 4, inscription	1.10	—

First day covers of Nos. 141-142 total 434,393.

ICY Emblem — A75

Design: 15c, French inscription.
Issued to commemorate the 20th anniversary of the United Nations and International Cooperation Year.
Printed by Bradbury, Wilkinson and Co., Ltd., England. Panes of 50. Designed by Olav Mathiesen, Denmark.

1965, June 26		**Engr.**	**Unwmk.**	**Perf. 14x13½**
143 A75	5c	dark blue (2,282,452)	10	8
		First day cover		35
		Margin block of 4, inscription	50	—
144 A75	15c	lilac rose (1,993,562)	30	20
		First day cover		75
		First day cover, #143-144		1.00
		Margin block of 4, inscription	1.50	—

Souvenir Sheet

145 A75		Sheet of two (1,928,366)	90	75
		First day cover		1.25

No. 145 contains one each of Nos. 143-144 with dark blue and ocher marginal inscription, ocher edging. Size: 92x70mm.
First day covers of Nos. 143-145 total: New York, 748,876; San Francisco, 301,435.

"Peace" — A76

Opening Words, U.N. Charter — A77

U.N. Headquarters and Emblem — A78

U.N. Emblem — A79

U.N. Emblem Encircled — A80

Printed by Government Printing Bureau, Tokyo (1c); Government Printing Office, Austria (15c, 20c); Government Printing Office (Bundesdruckerei), Berlin (25c), and Courvoisier S.A., Switzerland ($1). Panes of 50.
Designed by Kurt Plowitz U.S. (1c); Olav S. Mathiesen, Denmark (15c); Vergniaud Pierre-Noel, U.S. (20c); Rashid-ud Din, Pakistan (25c), and Ole Hamann, Denmark ($1).

1965-66		**Photo.**	**Unwmk.**	**Perf. 13½x13**
146 A76	1c	vermilion, blue, blk. & gray		
		(7,000,000)	5	5
		First day cover		20
		Margin block of 4, inscription	25	—
		Perf. 14		
147 A77	15c	olive bister, dull yellow, black		
		& deep claret (2,500,000)	30	25
		First day cover		75
		Margin block of 4, inscription	1.50	—
		Perf. 12		
148 A78	20c	dk. blue, bl., red & yel.		
		(3,000,000)	50	30
		First day cover		80
		First day cover, #147-148		1.25
		Margin block of 4, inscription	2.50	—
a.		Yellow omitted	—	
		Litho. and Embossed		
		Perf. 14		
149 A79	25c	light & dark blue (3,200,000)	90	45
		First day cover		1.00
		First day cover, #146, 149		1.15
		Margin block of 4, inscription	4.50	—
		Margin block of 6,		
		"Bundesdruckerei Berlin" imprint and inscription	35.00	
		Photo.		
		Perf. 11½		
150 A80	$1	aquamarine & sapphire		
		(2,570,000)	2.00	1.50
		First day cover (181,510)		2.50
		Margin block of 4, inscription	10.00	—

Issue dates: 1c and 25c, Sept. 20, 1965; 15c and 20c, Oct. 25, 1965; $1, Mar. 25, 1966.
First day covers of Nos. 146 and 149 total 443,964. Those of Nos. 147-148 total 457,596.
The 25c has the marginal inscription (U.N. emblem and "1965") in two sizes: 1st printing (with Bundesdruckerei imprint), 6mm. in diameter; 2nd printing, 8mm. In 1st printing, "halo" of U.N. emblem is larger, overlapping "25c."
See U.N. Offices in Geneva Nos. 5, 9 and 11.

Fields and People — A81

Design: 11c, French inscription.
Issued to emphasize the importance of the world's population growth and its problems and to call attention to population trends and development.
Printed by Government Printing Office, Austria. Panes of 50. Designed by Olav S. Mathiesen, Denmark.

1965, Nov. 29		**Photo.**	**Unwmk.**	**Perf. 12**
151 A81	4c	multicolored (1,966,033)	8	6
		First day cover		30
		Margin block of 4, inscription	40	—
152 A81	5c	multicolored (2,298,731)	10	8
		First day cover		30
		Margin block of 4, inscription	50	—
153 A81	11c	multicolored (1,557,589)	22	18
		First day cover		50
		First day cover, #151-153		90
		Margin block of 4, inscription	1.10	—

First day covers of Nos. 151-153 total 710,507.

Globe and Flags of U.N.
Members — A82

Design: 15c, French inscription.
Issued to honor the World Federation of United Nations Associations.
Printed by Courvoisier S.A., Switzerland.   Panes of 50.
Designed by Olav S. Mathiesen, Denmark.

1966, Jan. 31	Photo.	Unwmk.	Perf. 11½	
154 A82	5c multicolored (2,462,215)		10	8
	First day cover			30
	Margin block of 4, inscription		50	—
155 A82	15c multicolored (1,643,661)		30	25
	First day cover			70
	First day cover, #154-155			90
	Margin block of 4, inscription		1.50	—

First day covers of Nos. 154-155 total 474,154.

WHO Headquarters,
Geneva — A83

Design: 11c, French inscription.
Issued to commemorate the opening of the World Health Organization Headquarters, Geneva.
Printed by Courvoisier, S.A., Switzerland.   Panes of 50.
esigned by Rashid-ud Din.

Granite Paper

1966, May 26	Photo.	Perf. 12½x12	
156 A83	5c light & dark blue, orange, green & bister (2,079,893)	10	8
	First day cover		30
	Magin block of 4, inscription	50	—
157 A83	11c orange, light & dark blue, green & bister (1,879,879)	22	18
	First day cover		50
	First day cover, #156-157		75
	Margin block of 4, inscription	1.10	—

First day covers of Nos. 156-157 total 466,171.

Coffee — A84

Design: 11c, Spanish inscription.
Issued to commemorate the International Coffee Agreement of 1962.
Printed by the Government Printing Bureau, Tokyo. Panes of 50. Designed by Rashid-ud Din, Pakistan.

1966, Sept. 19	Photo.	Perf. 13½x13	
158 A84	5c orange, light blue, green, red & dark brown (2,020,308)	10	8
	First day cover		30
	Margin block of 4, inscription	50	—
159 A84	11c light blue, yellow, green, red & dark brown (1,888,682)	22	18
	First day cover		40
	First day cover, #158-159		65
	Margin block of 4, inscription	1.10	—

First day covers of Nos. 158-159 total 435,886.

United Nations Observer — A85

Issued to honor the Peace Keeping United Nation Observers.
Printed by Courvoisier, S.A. Panes of 50. Designed by Ole S. Hamann.

Granite Paper

1966, Oct. 24	Photo.	Perf. 11½	
160 A85	15c steel blue, org., blk. & grn. (1,889,809)	30	25
	First day cover (255,326)		40
	Margin block of 4, inscription	1.50	—

Children of Various
Races — A86

Designs: 5c, Children riding in locomotive and tender. 11c, Children in open railroad car playing medical team (French inscription).
Issued to commemorate the 20th anniversary of the United Nations Children's Fund (UNICEF).
Printed by Thomas De La Rue & Co., Ltd. Panes of 50. Designed by Kurt Plowitz.

1966, Nov. 28	Litho.	Perf. 13x13½	
161 A86	4c pink & multicolored (2,334,989)	8	6
	First day cover		25
	Margin block of 4, inscription	40	—
162 A86	5c pale green & multicolored (2,746,941)	10	8
	First day cover		30
	Margin block of 4, inscription	50	—
a.	Yellow omitted	—	
163 A86	11c light ultramarine & multicolored (2,123,841)	22	18
	First day cover		50
	First day cover, #161-163		90
	Margin block of 4, inscription	1.10	—
a.	Imperf., pair	—	
b.	Dark blue omitted	—	

First day covers of Nos. 161-163 total 987,271.

Hand Rolling up Sleeve
and Chart Showing
Progress — A87

Design: 11c, French inscription.
United Nations Development Program.
Printed by Courvoisier, S.A. Panes of 50. Designed by Olav S. Mathiesen.

1967, Jan. 23	Photo.	Perf. 12½	
164 A87	5c grn., yel., pur. & org. (2,204,679)	10	8
	First day cover		30
	Margin block of 4, inscription	50	—
165 A87	11c bl., choc., lt. grn. & org. (1,946,159)	22	20
	First day cover		40
	First day cover, #164-165		60
	Margin block of 4, inscription	1.10	—

First day covers of Nos. 164-165 total 406,011.

Type of 1962 and

U.N. Headquarters, New York,
and World Map — A88

Printed by Courvoisier, S.A. Panes of 50. Designed by Jozsef Vertel, Hungary (1½c); Renato Ferrini, Italy (5c).

1967	Photo.	Perf. 11½	
166 A88	1½c ultra., black, orange & ocher (4,000,000)	5	5
	First day cover (199,751)		25
	Margin block of 4, inscription	25	—
	Size: 33x23mm.		
167 A53	5c red brn., brn. & org. yel (5,500,000)	10	8
	First day cover (212,544)		35
	Margin block of 4, inscription	50	—

Issue dates: 1½c, March 17; 5c, Jan. 23.
For 5c of type A88, see U.N. Offices in Geneva No. 1.

Fireworks — A89

Design: 11c, French inscription.
Issued to honor all nations which gained independence since 1945.
Printed by Harrison & Sons, Ltd. Panes of 50. Designed by Rashid-ud Din.

1967, Mar. 17	Photo.	Perf. 14x14½	
168 A89	5c dark blue & multi. (2,445,955)	10	8
	First day cover		30
	Margin block of 4, inscription	50	—
169 A89	11c brown lake & multi. (2,011,004)	22	18
	First day cover		50
	First day cover, #168-169		60
	Margin block of 4, inscription	1.10	—

First day covers of Nos. 168-169 total 390,499.

"Peace" — A90

U.N. Pavilion, EXPO
'67 — A91

Designs: 5c, Justice. 10c, Fraternity. 15c, Truth.
Issued to commemorate EXPO '67, International Exhibition, Montreal, Apr. 28-Oct. 27, 1967.
Under special agreement with the Canadian Government Nos. 170-174 were valid for postage only on mail posted at the U.N. pavilion during the Fair.   The denominations are expressed in Canadian currency.
Printed by British American Bank Note Co., Ltd., Ottawa.
The 8c was designed by Olav S. Mathiesen after a photograph by Michael Drummond. The others were adapted by Ole S. Hamann from reliefs by Ernest Cormier on doors of General Assembly Hall, presented to U.N. by Canada.

1967, Apr. 28	Engr. & Litho.	Perf. 11	
170 A90	4c red & red brown (2,464,813)	10	10
	First day cover		30
	Margin block of 4, inscription	50	—
171 A90	5c blue & red brown (2,177,073)	15	15

| | First day cover | | 35 |
| | Margin block of 4, inscription | 75 | — |

Litho.

172 A91 8c multicolored (2,285,440) 20 20
First day cover 45
Margin block of 4, inscription 1.00 —

Engr. and Litho.

173 A90 10c green & red brown (1,955,352) 20 20
First day cover 1.30
Margin block of 4, inscription 1.00 —
174 A90 15c dark brown & red brown (1,899,185) 30 30
First day cover 1.65
First day cover, #170-174 3.75
Margin block of 4, inscription 1.50 —

First day covers of Nos. 170-174 total 901,625.

Luggage Tags and U.N. Emblem — A92

Issued to publicize International Tourist Year, 1967.
Printed by Government Printing Office, Berlin. Panes of 50.
Designed by David Dewhurst.

1967, June 19   Litho.   Perf. 14

175 A92 5c reddish brown & multi. (2,593,782) 10 8
First day cover 30
Margin block of 4, inscription 50 —
176 A92 15c ultramarine & multi. (1,940,457) 30 25
First day cover 75
First day cover, #175-176 90
Margin block of 4, inscription 1.50 —

First day covers of Nos. 175-176 total 382,886.

Quotation from Isaiah 2:4 — A93

Design: 13c, French inscription.
Issued to publicize the U.N. General Assembly's resolutions on general and complete disarmament and for suspension of nuclear and thermonuclear tests.
Printed by Heraclio Fournier S.A., Spain. Panes of 50.
Designed by Ole Hamann.

1967, Oct. 24   Photo.   Perf. 14

177 A93 6c ultra., yel., gray & brown (2,462,277) 12 8
First day cover 35
Margin block of 4, inscription 60 —
178 A93 13c magenta, yel., gray & brown (2,055,541) 26 20
First day cover 50
First day cover, #177-178 75
Margin block of 4, inscription 1.30 —

First day covers of Nos. 177-178 total 403,414.

Art at U.N. Issue
Miniature Sheet

Stained Glass Memorial Window by Marc Chagall, at U.N. Headquarters — A94

"The Kiss of Peace" by Marc Chagall — A95

Printed by Joh. Enschedé and Sons, Netherlands. No. 180 issued in panes of 50. Design adapted by Ole Hamann from photograph by Hans Lippmann.

1967, Nov. 17   Litho.   Rouletted 9

179 A94 Sheet of six (3,178,656) 75 60
First day cover 1.25
a. 6c multi., 41x46mm. 12 8
b. 6c multi., 24x46mm. 12 8
c. 6c multi., 41½x33½mm. 12 8
d. 6c multi., 36x33½mm. 12 8
e. 6c multi., 29x33½mm. 12 8
f. 6c multi., 41½x47mm. 12 8

Perf. 13x13½

180 A95 6c multicolored (3,438,497) 12 8
First day cover 30
Margin block of 4, inscription 60 —

No. 179 is divisible into six 6c stamps, each rouletted on 3 sides, imperf. on fourth side. Size: 124x80mm. On Nos. 179a-179c, "United Nations 6c" appears at top; on Nos. 179d-179f, at bottom. No. 179f includes name "Marc Chagall."
First day covers of Nos. 179-180 total 617,225.

Globe and Major U.N. Organs — A96

Design: 13c, French inscriptions.
Issued to honor the United Nations Secretariat.
Printed by Courvoisier, S. A., Switzerland. Panes of 50.
Designed by Rashid-ud Din.

1968, Jan. 16   Photo.   Perf. 11½

181 A96 6c multicolored (2,772,965) 12 8
First day cover 35
Margin block of 4, inscription 60 —
182 A96 13c multicolored (2,461,992) 26 20
First day cover 50
First day cover, #181-182 75
Margin block of 4, inscription 1.30 —

First day covers of Nos. 181-182 total 411,119.

Art at U.N. Issue

Statue by Henrik Starcke — A97

The 6c is part of the "Art at the U.N." series. The 75c belongs to the regular definitive series. The teakwood Starcke statue, which stands in the Trusteeship Council Chamber, represents mankind's search for freedom and happiness.
Printed by Courvoisier, S.A., Switzerland. Panes of 50.

1968, Mar. 1   Photo.   Perf. 11½

183 A97 6c blue & multicolored (2,537,320) 12 10
First day cover 35
Margin block of 4, inscription 60 —
184 A97 75c rose lake & multicolored (2,300,000) 4.00 2.00
First day cover 6.00
First day cover, #183-184 6.50
Margin block of 4, inscription 20.00 —

First day covers of Nos. 183-184 total 413,286.

No. 183 exists imperforate.
For 3fr in type A97, see U.N. Offices in Geneva No. 13.

Factories and Chart — A98

Design: 13c, French inscription ("ONUDI," etc.).
Issued to publicize the U.N. Industrial Development Organization.
Printed by Canadian Bank Note Co., Ltd., Ottawa. Panes of 50. Designed by Ole Hamann.

1968, Apr. 18   Litho.   Perf. 12

185 A98 6c greenish blue, lt. greenish blue, black & dull claret (2,439,656) 12 8
First day cover 35
Margin block of 4, inscription 60 —
186 A98 13c dull red brown, lt. red brown, black & ultra. (2,192,453) 26 20
First day cover 50
First day cover, #185-186 75
Margin block of 4, inscription 1.30 —

First day covers of Nos. 185-186 total 396,447.

U.N. Headquarters — A99

Printed by Aspioti Elka-Chrome Mines, Ltd., Athens. Panes of 50. Designed by Olav S. Mathiesen.

1968, May 31   Litho.   Perf. 12x13½

187 A99 6c green, blue, black & gray (4,000,000) 12 10
First day cover (241,179) 35
Margin block of 4, inscription 60 —

Radarscope and Globe — A100

Design: 20c, French inscription.
Issued to publicize World Weather Watch, a new weather system directed by the World Meteorological Organization.
Printed by the Government Printing Bureau, Tokyo. Designed by George A. Gundersen and George Fanais, Canada.

1968, Sept. 19   Photo.   Perf. 13x13½

188 A100 6c grn., blk., ocher, red & bl. (2,245,078) 12 10
First day cover 35
Margin block of 4, inscription 60 —
189 A100 20c lilac, blk., ocher, red & bl. (2,069,966) 40 30
First day cover 80
First day cover, #188-189 1.00
Margin block of 4, inscription 2.00 —

First day covers of Nos. 188-189 total 620,510.

Human Rights
Flame — A101

Design: 13c, French inscription.
Issued for International Human Rights Year, 1968.
Printed by Harrison & Sons, Ltd., England. Designed by
Robert Perrot, France.

1968, Nov. 22   Photo.; Foil Embossed   Perf. 12½
190 A101   6c brt. bl., dp. ultra. & gold
                (2,394,235)   15   10
             First day cover   75
             Margin block of 4, inscription   75   —
191 A101 13c rose red, dk. red & gold
                (2,284,838)   25   20
             First day cover   60
             First day cover, #190-191   1.20
             Margin block of 4, inscription   1.25   —

First day covers of Nos. 190-191 total 519,012.

Books and U.N.
Emblem — A102

Design: 13c, French inscription in center, denomination
panel at bottom.
Issued to publicize the United Nations Institute for Training
and Research (UNITAR).
Printed by the Government Printing Bureau, Tokyo. Panes
of 50. Designed by Olav S. Mathiesen.

1969, Feb. 10   Litho.   Perf. 13½
192 A102   6c yellow green & multicolored
                (2,436,559)   12   10
             First day cover   35
             Margin block of 4, inscription   60   —
193 A102 13c bluish lilac & multicolored
                (1,935,151)   25   20
             First day cover   60
             First day cover, #192-193   85
             Margin block of 4, inscription   1.25   —

First day covers of Nos. 192-193 total 439,606.

U.N. Building,
Santiago,
Chile — A103

Design: 15c, Spanish inscription.
The U.N. Building in Santiago, Chile, is the seat of the U.N.
Economic Commission for Latin America and of the Latin
American Institute for Economic and Social Planning.
Printed by Government Printing Office, Berlin. Panes of 50.
Design by Ole Hamann, adapted from a photograph.

1969, Mar. 14   Litho.   Perf. 14
194 A103   6c light blue, violet blue & light
                green (2,543,992)   12   10
             First day cover   35
             Margin block of 4, inscription   60   —
195 A103 15c pink, cream & red brown
                (2,030,733)   30   25
             First day cover   55
             First day cover, #194-195   85
             Margin block of 4, inscription   1.50   —

First day covers of Nos. 194-195 total 398,227.

"UN" and U.N.
Emblem — A104

Printed by Government Printing Bureau, Tokyo. Panes of
50. Designed by Leszek Holdanowicz and Marek
Freudenreich, Poland.

1969, Mar. 14   Photo.   Perf. 13½
196 A104 13c brt. blue, black & gold
                (4,000,000)   26   20
             First day cover (177,793)   50
             Margin block of 4, inscription   1.30   —

For 70c in type A104, see U.N. Offices in Geneva No. 7.

U.N. Emblem and Scales of
Justice — A105

Design: 13c, French inscription.
Issued to publicize the 20th anniversary session of the U.N.
International Law Commission.
Printed by Courvoisier S.A., Switzerland. Panes of 50.
Designed by Robert Perrot, France.

Granite Paper
1969, Apr. 21   Photo.   Perf. 11½
197 A105   6c brt. green, ultra. & gold
                (2,501,492)   12   10
             First day cover   35
             Margin block of 4, inscription   70   —
198 A105 13c crimson, lilac & gold
                (1,966,994)   26   20
             First day cover   50
             First day cover, #197-198   80
             Margin block of 4, inscription   1.30   —

First day covers of Nos. 197-198 total 439,324.

Allegory of Labor,
Emblems of U.N.
and ILO — A106

Design: 20c, French inscription.
Printed by Government Printing Bureau, Tokyo. Panes of
50. Designed by Nejat M. Gur, Turkey.
Issued to publicize "Labor and Development" and to com-
memorate the 50th anniversary of the International Labor
Organization.

1969, June 5   Photo.   Perf. 13
199 A106   6c blue, dp. blue, yel. & gold
                (2,078,381)   12   10
             First day cover   35
             Margin block of 4, inscription   60   —
200 A106 20c orange vermilion, magenta,
                yellow & gold (1,751,100)   40   30
             First day cover   80
             First day cover, #199-200   1.00
             Margin block of 4, inscription   2.00   —

First day covers of Nos. 199-200 total 514,155.

Art at U.N. Issue

Ostrich, Tunisian Mosaic,
3rd Century — A107

Design: 13c, Pheasant; French inscription.
The mosaic "The Four Seasons and the Genius of the Year"
was found at Haidra, Tunisia. It is now at the Delegates'
North Lounge, U.N. Headquarters, New York.
Printed by Heraclio Fournier, S. A., Spain. Panes of 50.
Designed by Olav S. Mathiesen.

1969, Nov. 21   Photo.   Perf. 14
201 A107   6c blue & multicolored
                (2,280,702)   12   10
             First day cover   35
             Margin block of 4, inscription   60   —
202 A107 13c red & multicolored (1,918,554)   26   20
             First day cover   60
             First day cover, #201-202   85
             Margin block of 4, inscription   1.30   —

First day covers of Nos. 201-202 total 612,981.

Art at U.N. Issue

Peace Bell, Gift of
Japanese — A108

Design: 25c, French inscription.
The Peace Bell was a gift of the people of Japan in 1954, cast
from donated coins and metals. It is housed in a Japanese
cypress structure at U.N. Headquarters, New York.
Printed by Government Printing Bureau, Tokyo. Panes of
50. Designed by Ole Hamann.

1970, Mar. 13   Photo.   Perf. 13½x13
203 A108   6c violet blue & multi (2,604,253)   12   10
             First day cover   35
             Margin block of 4, inscription   60   —
204 A108 25c claret & multi. (2,090,185)   50   40
             First day cover   1.00
             First day cover, #203-204   1.25
             Margin block of 4, inscription   2.50   —

First day covers of Nos. 203-204 total 502,384.

Mekong River,
Power Lines and
Map of Mekong
Delta — A109

Design: 13c, French inscription.
Issued to publicize the Lower Mekong Basin Development
project under U.N. auspices.
Printed by Heraclio Fournier, S.A., Spain. Panes of 50.
Designed by Ole Hamann.

1970, Mar. 13   Perf. 14
205 A109   6c dark blue & multi. (2,207,309)   12   10
             First day cover   35
             Margin block of 4, inscription   60   —
206 A109 13c deep plum & multi.
                (1,889,023)   26   20
             First day cover   60
             First day cover, #205-206   85
             Margin block of 4, inscription   1.30   —

First day covers of Nos. 205-206 total 522,218.

"Fight Cancer" — A110

Design: 13c, French inscription.
Issued to publicize the fight against cancer in connection with the 10th International Cancer Congress of the International Union Against Cancer, Houston, Texas, May 22-29.
Printed by Government Printing Office, Berlin. Panes of 50. Designed by Leonard Mitchell.

1970, May 22		**Litho.**	**Perf. 14**	
207 A110	6c blue & black (2,157,742)		12	10
	First day cover			35
	Margin block of 4, inscription		60	—
208 A110	13c olive & black (1,824,714)		26	20
	First day cover			60
	First day cover, #207-208			85
	Margin block of 4, inscription	1.30		

First day covers of Nos. 207-208 total 444,449.

U.N. Emblem and Olive Branch — A111

U.N. Emblem — A112

Design: 13c, French inscription.
Issued to commemorate the 25th anniversary of the United Nations. First day covers were postmarked at U.N. Headquarters, New York, and at San Francisco.
Printed by Courvoisier, S.A., Switzerland. Designed by Ole Hamann and Olav S. Mathiesen (souvenir sheet).

1970, June 26		**Photo.**	**Perf. 11½**	
209 A111	6c red, gold, dk. & lt. blue (2,365,229)		12	10
	First day cover			45
	Margin block of 4, inscription		60	—
210 A111	13c dk. blue, gold, green & red (1,861,613)		26	20
	First day cover			60
	Margin block of 4, inscription	1.30		—
			Perf. 12½	
211 A112	25c dark blue, gold & lt. blue (1,844,669)		50	40
	First day cover			1.10
	First day cover, #209-211			2.00
	Margin block of 4, inscription	2.50		—

Souvenir Sheet

Imperf

212	Sheet of 3 (1,923,639)		90	60
a.	A111 6c red, gold & multicolored		12	8
b.	A111 13c vio. blue, gold & multi.		26	20
c.	A112 25c vio. blue, gold & lt. blue		50	30
	First day cover			1.00

No. 212 contains 3 imperf. stamps, gold border and violet blue marginal inscription. Size: 94½x78mm.
First day covers of Nos. 209-212 total: New York, 846,389; San Francisco, 471,100.

Scales, Olive Branch and Symbol of Progress — A113

Design: 13c, French inscription.
Issued to publicize "Peace, Justice and Progress" in connection with the 25th anniversary of the United Nations.
Printed by Government Printing Bureau, Tokyo. Panes of 50. Designed by Ole Hamann.

1970, Nov. 20		**Photo.**	**Perf. 13½**	
213 A113	6c gold & multicolored (1,921,441)		12	10
	First day cover			35
	Margin block of 4, inscription		60	—
214 A113	13c silver & multicolored (1,663,669)		26	20
	First day cover			60
	First day cover, #213-214			85
	Margin block of 4, inscription	1.30		—

First day covers of Nos. 213-214 total 521,419.

Sea Bed, School of Fish and Underwater Research — A114

Issued to publicize peaceful uses of the sea bed.
Printed by Setelipaino, Finland. Panes of 50. Designed by Pentti Rahikainen, Finland.

1971, Jan. 25		**Photo. & Engr.**	**Perf. 13**	
215 A114	6c blue & multicolored (2,354,179)		12	10
	First day cover (405,554)			35
	Margin block of 4, inscription		60	—

See U.N. Offices in Geneva No. 15.

Refugees, Sculpture by Kaare K. Nygaard — A115

International support for refugees.
Printed by Joh. Enschede and Sons, Netherlands. Panes of 50. Designed by Dr. Kaare K. Nygaard and Martin J. Weber.

1971, Mar. 2		**Litho.**	**Perf. 13x12½**	
216 A115	6c brown, ocher & black (2,247,232)		12	10
	First day cover			35
	Margin block of 4, inscription		60	—
217 A115	13c ultra., greenish blue & black (1,890,048)		26	20
	First day cover			60
	First day cover, #216-217			85
	Margin block of 4, inscription	1.30		—

First day covers of Nos. 216-217 total 564,785.
See U.N. Offices in Geneva No. 16.

Wheat and Globe — A116

Publicizing the U.N. World Food Program.
Printed by Heraclio Fournier, S.A., Spain. Panes of 50. Designed by Olav S. Mathiesen.

1971, Apr. 13		**Photo.**	**Perf. 14**	
218 A116	13c red & multicolored (1,968,542)		26	20
	First day cover (409,404)			60
	Margin block of 4, inscription	1.30		—

See U.N. Offices in Geneva No. 17.

UPU Headquarters, Bern — A117

Opening of new Universal Postal Union Headquarters, Bern.
Printed by Courvoisier, S.A. Panes of 50. Designed by Olav S. Mathiesen.

1971, May 28		**Photo.**	**Perf. 11½**	
219 A117	20c brown orange & multi. (1,857,841)		40	30
	First day cover (375,119)			80
	Margin block of 4, inscription	2.00		—

See U.N. Offices in Geneva No. 18.

A118

"Eliminate Racial Discrimination" — A119

International Year Against Racial Discrimination.
Printed by Government Printing Bureau, Tokyo. Panes of 50. Designers: Daniel Gonzague (8c); Ole Hamann (13c).

1971, Sept. 21		**Photo.**	**Perf. 13½**	
220 A118	8c yellow green & multi. (2,324,349)		16	12
	First day cover			32
	Margin block of 4, inscription		80	—
221 A119	13c blue & multicolored (1,852,093)		26	20
	First day cover			60
	First day cover, #220-221			85
	Margin block of 4, inscription	1.30		—

First day covers of Nos. 220-221 total 461,103.
See U.N. Offices in Geneva Nos. 19-20.

U.N. Headquarters, New York — A120

U.N. Emblem and Symbolic Flags — A121

No. 222 printed by Heraclio Fournier, S.A., Spain. No. 223 printed by Government Printing Bureau, Tokyo. Panes of 50. Designers: O. S. Mathiesen (8c); Robert Perrot (60c).

1971, Oct. 22		**Photo.**	**Perf. 13½**	
222 A120	8c violet blue & multi. (5,300,000)+		16	12
	First day cover			35
	Margin block of 4, inscription		80	—
			Perf. 13	
223 A121	60c ultramarine & multi. (3,500,000)+		1.20	90
	First day cover			2.40
	First day cover, #222-223			2.50
	Margin block of 4, inscription	6.00		—

First day covers of Nos. 222-223 total 336,013.
+ Printing orders to Apr. 1982.

Maia, by Pablo Picasso — A122

To publicize the U.N. International School.
Printed by Courvoisier, S.A. Panes of 50. Designed by Ole Hamann.

1971, Nov. 19   Photo.   Perf. 11½
224 A122   8c olive & multicolored
                 (2,668,214)   16   12
             First day cover   35
             Margin block of 4, inscription   80   —
225 A122   21c ultra. & multicolored
                 (2,040,754)   42   30
             First day cover   80
             First day cover, #224-225   2.10   1.00
             Margin block of 4, inscription

First day covers of Nos. 224-225 total 579,594.
See U.N. Offices in Geneva No. 21.

Letter Changing
Hands — A123

Printed by Bundesdruckerei, Berlin. Panes of 50. Designed by Olav S. Mathiesen.

1972, Jan. 5   Litho.   Perf. 14
226 A123   95c carmine & multi (2,000,000)   1.90   1.50
             First day cover (188,193)   3.50
             Margin block of 4, inscription   9.50   —

"No More
Nuclear
Weapons"
A124

To promote non-proliferation of nuclear weapons.
Printed by Heraclio Fournier, S. A., Spain. Panes of 50.
Designed by Arne Johnson, Norway.

1972, Feb. 14   Photo.   Perf. 13½x14
227 A124   8c dull rose, black, blue & gray
                 (2,311,515)   16   12
             First day cover (268,789)   40
             Margin block of 4, inscription   80   —

See U.N. Offices in Geneva No. 23.

Proportions of Man, by
Leonardo da Vinci — A125

World Health Day, Apr. 7.
Printed by Setelipaino, Finland. Panes of 50. Designed by George Hamori.

1972, Apr. 7   Litho. & Engr.   Perf. 13x13½
228 A125   15c black & multicolored
                 (1,788,962)   30   25
             First day cover (322,724)   55
             Margin block of 4, inscription   1.50   —

See U.N. Offices in Geneva No. 24.

"Human
Environment" — A126

U.N. Conference on Human Environment, Stockholm, June 5-16, 1972.
Printed by Joh. Enschedé and Sons, Netherlands. Panes of 50. Designed by Robert Perrot.

1972, June 5   Litho. & Embossed   Perf. 12½x14
229 A126   8c red, buff, green & blue
                 (2,124,604)   16   12
             First day cover   35
             Margin block of 4, inscription   80   —
230 A126   15c bl. green, buff, green & bl.
                 (1,589,943)   30   25
             First day cover   55
             First day cover, #229-230   80
             Margin block of 4, inscription   1.50   —

First day covers of Nos. 229-230 total 437,222.
See U.N. Offices in Geneva Nos. 25-26.

"Europe" and U.N.
Emblem — A127

Economic Commission for Europe, 25th anniversary.
Printed by Government Printing Bureau, Tokyo. Panes of 50. Designed by Angel Medina Medina.

1972, Sept. 11   Litho.   Perf. 13x13½
231 A127   21c yellow brown & multi
                 (1,748,675)   42   30
             First day cover (271,128)   80
             Margin block of 4, inscription   2.10   —

See U.N. Offices in Geneva No. 27.

Art at U.N. Issue

The Five Continents by José
Maria Sert — A128

Design shows part of ceiling mural of the Council Hall, Palais des Nations, Geneva. It depicts the five continents joining in space.
Printed by Courvoisier, S. A. Panes of 50. Designed by Ole Hamann.

1972, Nov. 17   Photo.   Perf. 12x12½
232 A128   8c gold, brn. & golden brn.
                 (2,573,478)   16   12
             First day cover   35
             Margin block of 4, inscription   80   —
233 A128   15c gold, blue green & brown
                 (1,768,432)   30   25
             First day cover   55
             First day cover, #232-233   80
             Margin block of 4, inscription   1.50   —

First day covers of Nos. 232-233 total 589,817.
See U.N. Offices in Geneva Nos. 28-29.

Olive Branch and
Broken
Sword — A129

Disarmament Decade, 1970-79.
Printed by Ajans-Turk, Turkey. Panes of 50. Designed by Kurt Plowitz.

1973, Mar. 9   Litho.   Perf. 13½x13
234 A129   8c blue & multi. (2,272,716)   16   12
             First day cover   35
             Margin block of 4, inscription   1.00   —
235 A129   15c lilac rose & multi. (1,643,712) 35   30
             First day cover   55
             First day cover, #234-235   80
             Margin block of 4, inscription   1.75   —

First day covers of Nos. 234-235 total 548,336.
See U.N. Offices in Geneva Nos. 30-31.

Poppy Capsule and
Skull — A130

Fight against drug abuse.
Printed by Heraclio Fournier, S.A., Spain. Panes of 50.
Designed by George Hamori.

1973, Apr. 13   Photo.   Perf. 13½
236 A130   8c dp. orange & multi.
                 (1,846,780)   20   15
             First day cover   35
             Margin block of 4, inscription   1.00   —
237 A130   15c pink & multi. (1,466,806)   40   30
             First day cover   55
             First day cover, #236-237   80
             Margin block of 4, inscription   2.00   —

First day covers of Nos. 236-237 total 394,468.
See U.N. Offices in Geneva No. 32.

Honeycomb — A131

5th anniversary of the United Nations Volunteer Program.
Printed by Heraclio Fournier, S.A., Spain. Panes of 50.
Designed by Courvoisier, S.A.

1973, May 25   Photo.   Perf. 14
238 A131   8c olive bister & multi.
                 (1,868,176)   16   12
             First day cover   35
             Margin block of 4, inscription   80   —
239 A131   21c gray blue & multi. (1,530,114)   42   30
             First day cover   55
             First day cover, #238-239   80
             Margin block of 4, inscription   2.10   1.00

First day covers of Nos. 238-239 total 396,517.
See U.N. Offices in Geneva No. 33.

Map of Africa with
Namibia — A132

To publicize Namibia (South-West Africa) for which the U.N. General Assembly ended the mandate of South Africa and established the U.N. Council for Namibia to administer the territory until independence.

Printed by Heraclio Fournier, S.A., Spain. Panes of 50.
Designed by George Hamori.

1973, Oct. 1   **Photo.**   **Perf. 14**
240 A132 8c emerald & multi. *(1,775,260)*   16   12
          Margin block of 4, inscription   75   —
241 A132 15c bright rose & multi.
          (1,687,782)   35   30
          First day cover   55
          First day cover, #240-241   80
          Margin block of 4, inscription   1.75

First day covers of Nos. 240-241 total 385,292.
See U.N. Offices in Geneva No. 34.

U.N. Emblem and
Human Rights
Flame — A133

25th anniversary of the adoption and proclamation of the
Universal Declaration of Human Rights.
Printed by Government Printing Bureau, Tokyo. Panes of
50. Designed by Alfred Guerra.

1973, Nov. 16   **Photo.**   **Perf. 13½**
242 A133 8c dp. carmine & multi.
          (2,026,245)   16   12
          First day cover   35
          Margin block of 4, inscription   80   —
243 A133 21c bl. green & multi. *(1,558,201)*   42   35
          First day cover   80
          First day cover, #242-243   1.00
          Margin block of 4, inscription   2.10

First day covers of Nos. 242-243 total 398,511.
See U.N. Offices in Geneva Nos. 35-36.

ILO Headquarters,
Geneva — A134

New Headquarters of International Labor Organization.
Printed by Heraclio Fournier, S.A., Spain. Panes of 50.
Designed by Henry Bencsath.

1974, Jan. 11   **Photo.**   **Perf. 14**
244 A134 10c ultra. & multi. *(1,734,423)*   22   15
          First day cover   40
          Margin block of 4, inscription   1.10   —
245 A134 21c blue green & multi. *(1,264,447)*   48   40
          First day cover   90
          First day cover, #244-245   1.10
          Margin block of 4, inscription   2.50   —

First day covers of Nos. 244-245 total 282,284.
See U.N. Offices in Geneva Nos. 37-38.

UPU Emblem and
Post Horn
Encircling
Globe — A135

Centenary of Universal Postal Union.
Printed by Ashton-Potter Ltd., Canada. Panes of 50.
Designed by Arne Johnson.

1974, Mar. 22   **Litho.**   **Perf. 12½**
246 A135 10c gold & multicolored
          (2,104,919)   20   15
          First day cover *(342,774)*   40
          Margin block of 4, inscription   1.00   —

See U.N. Offices in Geneva Nos. 39-40.

Art at U.N. Issue

Peace Mural, by
Candido
Portinari — A136

The mural, a gift of Brazil, is in the Delegates' Lobby, Gen-
eral Assembly Building.
Printed by Heraclio Fournier, S.A., Spain. Panes of 50.
Design adapted by Ole Hamann.

1974, May 6   **Photo.**   **Perf. 14**
247 A136 10c gold & multi. *(1,769,342)*   22   18
          First day cover   40
          Margin block of 4, inscription   1.10   —
248 A136 18c ultramarine & multi.
          (1,477,500)   38   32
          First day cover   70
          First day cover, #247-248   1.00
          Margin block of 4, inscription   1.90

First day covers of Nos. 247-248 total 271,440.
See U.N. Offices in Geneva Nos. 41-42.

Dove and U.N. Emblem
A137

U.N. Headquarters
A138

Globe, U.N. Emblem,
Flags — A139

Printed by Heraclio Fournier, S.A., Spain. Panes of 50.
Designed by Nejut M. Gur (2c); Olav S. Mathiesen (10c);
Henry Bencsath (18c).

1974, June 10   **Photo.**   **Perf. 14**
249 A137 2c dark & light blue *(6,500,000)*   5   5
          First day cover   30
          Margin block of 4, inscription   25   —
250 A138 10c multicolored *(4,000,000)*   20   15
          First day cover   40
          Margin block of 4, inscription   1.00   —
251 A139 18c multicolored *(2,300,000)*   36   25
          First day cover   70
          First day cover, #249-251   1.00
          Margin block of 4, inscription   1.80

Printing orders to Nov. 1985.
First day covers of Nos. 249-251 total 307,402.

Children of the
World — A140

World Population Year
Printed by Heraclio Fournier, S.A., Spain. Panes of 50.
Designed by Henry Bencsath.

1974, Oct. 18   **Photo.**   **Perf. 14**
252 A140 10c light blue & multi. *(1,762,595)*   22   20

          First day cover   35
          Margin block of 4, inscription   1.10
253 A140 18c lilac & multi. *(1,321,574)*   38   35
          First day cover   70
          First day cover, #252-253   1.00
          Margin block of 4, inscription   1.90

First day covers of Nos. 253-254 total 354,306.
See U.N. Offices in Geneva Nos. 43-44.

Law of the Sea — A141

Declaration of U.N. General Assembly that the sea bed is
common heritage of mankind, reserved for peaceful purposes.
Printed by Heraclio Fournier, S.A., Spain. Panes of 50.
Designed by Asher Kalderon.

1974, Nov. 22   **Photo.**   **Perf. 14**
254 A141 10c green & multicolored
          (1,621,328)   25   25
          First day cover   40
          Margin block of 4, inscription   1.25   —
255 A141 26c orange red & multicolored
          (1,293,084)   60   50
          First day cover   1.00
          First day cover, #254-255   1.25
          Margin block of 4, inscription   3.00   —

First day covers of Nos. 254-255 total 280,686.
See U.N. Offices in Geneva No. 45.

Satellite and
Globe — A142

Peaceful uses (meteorology, industry, fishing, communica-
tions) of outer space.
Printed by Setelipaino, Finland. Panes of 50. Designed by
Henry Bencsath.

1975, Mar. 14   **Litho.**   **Perf. 13**
256 A142 10c multicolored *(1,681,115)*   20   15
          First day cover   35
          Margin block of 4, inscription   1.00   —
257 A142 26c multicolored *(1,463,130)*   60   50
          First day cover   1.00
          First day cover, #256-257   1.25
          Margin block of 4, inscription   3.00   —

First day covers of Nos. 256-257 total 330,316.
See U.N. Offices in Geneva Nos. 46-47.

Equality Between Men
and Women — A143

International Women's Year
Printed by Questa Colour Security Printers, Ltd., England.
Panes of 50. Designed by Asher Kalderon and Esther Kurti.

1975, May 9   **Litho.**   **Perf. 15**
258 A143 10c multicolored *(1,402,542)*   22   20
          First day cover   35
          Margin block of 4, inscription   1.10   —
259 A143 18c multicolored *(1,182,321)*   45   35
          First day cover   70
          First day cover, #258-259   1.00
          Margin block of 4, inscription   2.25   —

First day covers of Nos. 258-259 total 285,466.
See U.N. Offices in Geneva Nos. 48-49.

U.N. Flag and
"XXX" — A144

30th anniversary of the United Nations.
  Printed by Ashton-Potter, Ltd., Canada. Panes of 50.
Stamps designed by Asher Calderon, sheets by Olav S.
Mathiesen.

1975, June 26	**Litho.**	**Perf. 13**	
260 A144	10c olive bister & multi.		
	(1,904,545)	20	15
	First day cover		35
	Margin block of 4, inscription	1.00	—
261 A144	26c purple & multicolored		
	(1,547,766)	52	40
	First day cover		1.00
	First day cover, #260-261		1.25
	Margin block of 4, inscription	2.60	—

Souvenir Sheet

Imperf

262 A144	Sheet of 2 (1,196,578)	1.25	1.00
a.	10c olive bister & multicolored	30	25
b.	26c purple & multicolored	60	55
	First day cover		1.75

  No. 262 has blue and bister margin with inscription and
U.N. emblem. Size: 92x70mm.
  First day covers of Nos. 260-262 total: New York 477,912;
San Francisco, 237,159.
  See Offices in Geneva Nos. 50-52.

Hand Reaching up over
Map of Africa and
Namibia — A145

  "Namibia-United Nations direct responsibility." See note
after No. 241.
  Printed by Heraclio Fournier S.A., Spain. Panes of 50.
Designed by Henry Bencsath.

1975, Sept. 22	**Photo.**	**Perf. 13½**	
263 A145	10c multicolored (1,354,374)	22	20
	First day cover		35
	Margin block of 4, inscription	1.10	—
264 A145	18c multicolored (1,243,157)	38	35
	First day cover		35
	First day cover, #263-264		1.00
	Margin block of 4, inscription	1.90	—

  First day covers of Nos. 263-264 total 281,631.
  See U.N. Offices in Geneva Nos. 53-54.

Wild Rose Growing from
Barbed Wire — A146

United Nations Peace-keeping Operations
  Printed by Setelipaino, Finland. Panes of 50. Designed by
Mrs. Eeva Oivo.

1975, Nov. 21	**Engr.**	**Perf. 12½**	
265 A146	13c ultramarine (1,628,039)	26	15
	First day cover		45
	Margin block of 4, inscription	1.30	—
266 A146	26c rose carmine (1,195,580)	55	40
	First day cover		90
	First day cover, #265-266		1.15
	Margin block of 4, inscription	2.75	—

  First day covers of Nos. 265-266 total 303,711.
  See U.N. Offices in Geneva Nos. 55-56.

Symbolic Flags Forming
Dove — A147

People of All
Races — A148

U.N.
Emblem — A149

United Nations
Flag — A150

Dove and Rainbow — A151

  Printed by Ashton-Potter, Ltd., Canada (3c, 4c, 30c, 50c),
and Questa Colour Security Printers, Ltd., England (9c). Panes
of 50.
  Designed by Waldemar Andrzesewski (3c); Arne Johnson
(4c); George Hamori (9c, 30c); Arthur Congdon (50c).

1976	**Litho.**	**Perf. 13x13½, 13½x13**	
267 A147	3c multicolored (4,000,000)	6	5
	First day cover		30
	Margin block of 4, inscription	30	—
268 A148	4c multicolored (4,000,000)	8	6
	First day cover		30
	Margin block of 4, inscription	40	—

Photo.

Perf. 14

269 A149	9c multicolored (3,270,000)	18	15
	First day cover		40
	Margin block of 4, inscription	90	—

Litho.

Perf. 13x13½

270 A150	30c blue, emerald & black		
	(2,500,000)	60	45
	First day cover		1.00
	Margin block of 4, inscription	3.00	—
271 A151	50c yellow green & multicolored		
	(2,000,000)	1.00	75

	First day cover	2.00	
	Margin block of 4, inscription	5.00	—

  Issue dates: 3c, 4c, 30c, 50c, Jan. 6; 9c, Nov. 19.
  First day covers of Nos. 267-268, 270-271 total 355,165.
  First day covers of Nos. 269 and 280 total 366,556.
  See U.N. Offices in Vienna No. 8.

Interlocking Bands and U.N.
Emblem — A152

World Federation of United Nations Associations.
  Printed by Heraclio Fournier, S.A., Spain. Panes of 50.
Designed by George Hamori.

1976, Mar. 12	**Photo.**	**Perf. 14**	
272 A152	13c blue, green & black (1,331,556)	30	25
	First day cover		45
	Margin block of 4, inscription	1.50	—
273 A152	26c green & multi. (1,050,145)	55	40
	First day cover		90
	First day cover, #272-273		1.15
	Margin block of 4, inscription	2.75	—

  First day covers of Nos. 272-273 total 300,775.
  See U.N. Offices in Geneva No. 57.

Cargo, Globe and
Graph — A153

U.N. Conference on Trade and Development (UNCTAD),
Nairobi, Kenya, May 1976.
  Printed by Courvoisier, S.A. Panes of 50. Designed by
Henry Bencsath.

1976, Apr. 23	**Photo.**	**Perf. 11½**	
274 A153	13c dp. magenta & multi.		
	(1,317,900)	30	25
	First day cover		45
	Margin block of 4, inscription	1.50	—
275 A153	31c dull blue & multi. (1,216,959)	65	50
	First day cover		1.00
	First day cover, #274-275		1.25
	Margin block of 4, inscription	3.25	—

  First day covers of Nos. 274-275 total 234,657.
  See U.N. Offices in Geneva No. 58.

Houses Around Globe — A154

Habitat, U.N. Conference on Human Settlements, Vancou-
ver, Canada, May 31-June 11.
  Printed by Heraclio Fournier, S.A., Spain. Panes of 50.
Designed by Eliezer Weishoff.

1976, May 28	**Photo.**	**Perf. 14**	
276 A154	13c red brn. & multi (1,346,589)	30	25
	First day cover		45
	Margin block of 4, inscription	1.50	—
277 A154	25c green & multicolored		
	(1,057,924)	50	40
	First day cover		85
	First day cover, #276-277		1.10
	Margin block of 4, inscription	2.50	—

  First day covers of Nos. 276-277 total 232,754.

Magnifying Glass, Sheet of Stamps, U.N. Emblem — A155

See U.N. Offices in Geneva Nos. 59-60.

United Nations Postal Administration, 25th anniversary. Printed by Courvoisier, S.A. Panes of 20 (5x4). Designed by Henry Bencsath.

1976, Oct. 8   **Photo.**   **Perf. 11½**
278 A155 13c blue & multicolored
(1,996,309)   75   50
First day cover   1.25
Margin block of 4, inscription   3.75
279 A155 31c green & multicolored
(1,767,465)   7.50   4.00
First day cover   7.00
First day cover, #278-279   8.00
Margin block of 4, inscription   37.50

First day covers of Nos. 278-279 total 366,784.
Upper margin blocks are inscribed "XXV ANNIVERSARY"; lower margin blocks "UNITED NATIONS POSTAL ADMINISTRATIONS."
See U.N. Offices in Geneva Nos. 61-62.

Grain — A156

World Food Council. Printed by Questa Colour Security Printers, Ltd., England. Panes of 50. Designed by Eliezer Weishoff.

1976, Nov. 19   **Litho.**   **Perf. 14½**
280 A156 13c multicolored (1,515,573)   30   25
First day cover   45
Margin block of 4, inscription   1.50

See U.N. Offices in Geneva No. 63.

WIPO Headquarters, Geneva — A157

World Intellectual Property Organization (WIPO). Printed by Heraclio Fournier, S. A., Spain. Panes of 50. Designed by Eliezer Weishoff.

1977, Mar. 11   **Photo.**   **Perf. 14**
281 A157 13c citron & multi. (1,330,272)   30   25
First day cover   45
Margin block of 4, inscription   1.50
282 A157 31c brt. green & multi. (1,115,406)   65   50
First day cover   1.00
First day cover, #281-282   1.25
Margin block of 4, inscription   3.25

First day covers of Nos. 281-282 total 364,184.
See U.N. Offices in Geneva No. 64.

Drops of Water Falling into Funnel — A158

U.N. Water Conference, Mar del Plata, Argentina, Mar. 14-25.
Printed by Government Printing Bureau, Tokyo. Panes of 50. Designed by Elio Tomei.

1977, Apr. 22   **Photo.**   **Perf. 13½x13**
283 A158 13c yellow & multi. (1,317,536)   30   25
First day cover   45
Margin block of 4, inscription   1.50
284 A158 25c salmon & multi. (1,077,424)   55   45
First day cover   85
First day cover, #283-284   1.10
Margin block of 4, inscription   2.75

First day covers of Nos. 283-284 total 321,585.
See U.N. Offices in Geneva Nos. 65-66.

Burning Fuse Severed — A159

U.N. Security Council.
Printed by Heraclio Fournier, S.A., Spain. Panes of 50. Designed by Witold Janowski and Marek Freudenreich.

1977, May 27   **Photo.**   **Perf. 14**
285 A159 13c purple & multi. (1,321,527)   30   20
First day cover   50
Margin block of 4, inscription   1.50
286 A159 31c dark blue & multi. (1,137,195)   65   50
First day cover   1.00
First day cover, #285-286   1.25
Margin block of 4, inscription   3.25

First day covers of Nos. 285-286 total 309,610.
See U.N. Offices in Geneva Nos. 67-68.

"Combat Racism" — A160

Fight against racial discrimination.
Printed by Setelipaino, Finland. Panes of 50. Designed by Bruno K. Wiese.

1977, Sept. 19   **Litho.**   **Perf. 13½x13**
287 A160 13c black & yellow (1,195,739)   30   25
First day cover   50
Margin block of 4, inscription   1.50
288 A160 25c black & vermilion (1,074,639)   50   40
First day cover   85
First day cover, #287-288   1.10
Margin block of 4, inscription   2.50

First day covers of Nos. 287-288 total 356,193.
See U.N. Offices in Geneva Nos. 60-70.

Atom, Grain, Fruit and Factory — A161

Peaceful uses of atomic energy.
Printed by Heraclio Fournier, S.A., Spain. Panes of 50. Designed by Henry Bencsath.

1977, Nov. 18   **Photo.**   **Perf. 14**
289 A161 13c yel. bister & multi. (1,316,473)   30   25
First day cover   50
Margin block of 4, inscription   1.50
290 A161 18c dull green & multi. (1,072,246)   40   30
First day cover   75
First day cover, #289-290   1.50
Margin block of 4, inscription   2.00

First day covers of Nos. 289-290 total 325,348.
See U.N. Offices in Geneva Nos. 71-72.

Opening Words of U.N. Charter — A162

"Live Together in Peace" — A163

People of the World — A164

Printed by Questa Colour Security Printers, United Kingdom. Panes of 50. Designed by Salahattin Kanidic (1c); Elio Tomei (25c); Paula Schmidt ($1).

1978, Jan. 27   **Litho.**   **Perf. 14½**
291 A162 1c gold, brown & red
(4,800,000)+   5   5
First day cover   30
Margin block of 4, inscription   25
292 A163 25c multicolored (3,000,000)+   50   25
First day cover   90
Margin block of 4, inscription   2.50
293 A164 $1 multicolored (3,000,000)+   2.00   1.00
First day cover   3.00
Margin block of 4, inscription   10.00

+ Printing order to Dec. 1984.
First day covers of Nos. 291-293 total 264,782.
See U.N. Offices in Geneva No. 73.

Smallpox Virus — A165

Global eradication of smallpox.
Printed by Courvoisier, S.A. Panes of 50. Designed by Herbert Auchli.

1978, Mar. 31   **Photo.**   **Perf. 12x11½**
294 A165 13c rose & black (1,188,239)   30   25
First day cover   50
Margin block of 4, inscription   1.50
295 A165 31c blue & black (1,058,688)   65   50
First day cover   1.00
First day cover, #294-295   1.25
Margin block of 4, inscription   3.25

First day covers of Nos. 294-295 total 306,626.
See U.N. Offices in Geneva Nos. 74-75.

Open Handcuff — A166

Liberation, justice and cooperation for Namibia.
Printed by Government Printing Office, Austria. Panes of 50. Designed by Cafiro Tomei.

1978, May 5   **Photo.**   **Perf. 12**
296 A166 13c multicolored (1,203,079)   30   25
First day cover   50
Margin block of 4, inscription   1.50

297 A166 18c multicolored *(1,066,738)*   38   30
           First day cover   75
           First day cover, #296-297   1.10
           Margin block of 4, inscription   1.90   —

First day covers of Nos. 296-297 total 324,471.
See U.N. Offices in Geneva No. 76.

Multicolored Bands and
Clouds — A167

International Civil Aviation Organization for "Safety in the
Air."
Printed by Heraclio Fournier, S.A., Spain. Panes of 50.
Designed by Cemalettin Mutver.

1978, June 12   **Photo.**   **Perf. 14**
298 A167 13c multicolored *(1,295,617)*   30   25
           First day cover   50
           Margin block of 4, inscription   1.50
299 A167 25c multicolored *(1,101,256)*   50   40
           First day cover   90
           First day cover, #298-299   1.25
           Margin block of 4, inscription   2.50

First day covers of Nos. 298-299 total 329,995.
See U.N. Offices in Geneva Nos. 77-78.

General
Assembly — A168

Printed by Government Printing Bureau, Tokyo. Panes of
50. Designed by Jozsef Vertel.

1978, Sept. 15   **Photo.**   **Perf. 13½**
300 A168 13c multicolored *(1,093,005)*   30   25
           First day cover   50
           Margin block of 4, inscription   1.50
301 A168 18c multicolored *(1,065,934)*   38   30
           First day cover   75
           First day cover, #300-301   1.10
           Margin block of 4, inscription   1.90

First day covers of Nos. 300-301 total 283,220.
See U.N. Offices in Geneva Nos. 79-80.

Hemispheres as
Cogwheels — A169

Technical Cooperation Among Developing Countries Con-
ference, Buenos Aires, Argentina, Sept. 1978.
Printed by Heraclio Fournier, S.A., Spain. Panes of 50.
Designed by Simon Keter and David Pesach.

1978, Nov. 17   **Photo.**   **Perf. 14**
302 A169 13c multicolored *(1,251,272)*   30   25
           First day cover   50
           Margin block of 4, inscription   1.50
303 A169 31c multicolored *(1,185,213)*   65   50
           First day cover   1.00
           First day cover, #302-303   1.25
           Margin block of 4, inscription   3.25

First day covers of Nos. 302-303 total 272,556.
See U.N. Offices in Geneva No. 81.

See the "Information for Collectors" section at
beginning of catalogue for information on printing methods and varieties.

Hand Holding Olive
Branch — A170

Various Races
Tree — A171

Globe, Dove with
Olive
Branch — A172

Birds and
Globe — A173

Printed by Heraclio Fournier, S.A., Spain. Panes of 50.
Designed by Raymon Müller (5c); Alrun Fricke (14c);
Eliezer Weishoff (15c); Young Sun Hahn (20c).

1979, Jan. 19   **Photo.**   **Perf. 14**
304 A170   5c multicolored *(3,000,000)*   10   5
           First day cover   50
           Margin block of 4, inscription   50
305 A171 14c multicolored *(3,000,000)*   28   14
           First day cover   50
           Margin block of 4, inscription   1.40
306 A172 15c multicolored *(3,000,000)*   30   15
           First day cover   50
           Margin block of 4, inscription   1.50
307 A173 20c multicolored *(3,000,000)*   40   20
           First day cover   75
           First day cover, #304-307   1.75
           Margin block of 4, inscription   2.00

First day covers of Nos. 304-307 total 295,927.

UNDRO Against Fire
and Water — A174

Office of the U.N. Disaster Relief Coordinator (UNDRO).
Printed by Heraclio Fournier, S.A., Spain. Panes of 50.
Designed by Gidon Sagi.

1979, Mar. 9   **Photo.**   **Perf. 14**
308 A174 15c multicolored *(1,448,600)*   35   30
           First day cover   50
           Margin block of 4, inscription   1.75
309 A174 20c multicolored *(1,126,295)*   45   40
           First day cover   75
           First day cover, #308-309   1.10
           Margin block of 4, inscription   2.25

First day covers of Nos. 308-309 total 266,694.
See U.N. Offices in Geneva Nos. 82-83.

Child and IYC
Emblem — A175

International Year of the Child.
Printed by Heraclio Fournier, S.A., Spain. Panes of 20
(5x4). Designed by Helena Matuszewska (15c) and Krystyna
Tarkowska-Gruszecka (31c).

1979, May 4   **Photo.**   **Perf. 14**
310 A175 15c multicolored *(2,290,329)*   1.00   45
           First day cover   75
           Margin block of 4, inscription   5.00

311 A175 31c multicolored *(2,192,136)*   2.00   90
           First day cover   1.50
           First day cover, #310-311   2.25
           Margin block of 4, inscription   10.00

First day covers of Nos. 310-311 total 380,022.
See U.N. Offices in Geneva Nos. 84-85.

Map of Namibia, Olive
Branch — A176

For a free and independent Namibia.
Printed by Ashton-Potter Ltd., Canada. Panes of 50.
Designed by Eliezer Weishoff.

1979, Oct. 5   **Litho.**   **Perf. 13½**
312 A176 15c multicolored *(1,800,000)*   30   25
           First day cover   50
           Margin block of 4, inscription   1.50
313 A176 31c multicolored *(1,500,000)*   65   50
           First day cover   1.00
           First day cover, #312-313   1.25
           Margin block of 4, inscription   3.25

First day covers of Nos. 312-313 total 250,371.
See U.N. Offices in Geneva No. 86.

Scales and Sword of
Justice — A177

International Court of Justice, The Hague, Netherlands
Printed by Setelipaino, Finland. Panes of 50. Designed by
Henning Simon.

1979, Nov. 9   **Litho.**   **Perf. 13x13½**
314 A177 15c multicolored *(1,244,972)*   30   25
           First day cover   50
           Margin block of 4, inscription   1.50
315 A177 20c multicolored *(1,084,483)*   40   30
           First day cover   75
           First day cover, #314-315   1.10
           Margin block of 4, inscription   2.00

First day covers of Nos. 314-315 total 322,901.
See U.N. Offices in Geneva Nos. 87-88.

Graph of Economic
Trends — A178

Key — A179

New International Economic Order.
Printed by Questa Colour Security Printers, United King-
dom. Panes of 50. Designed by Cemalettin Mutver (15c),
George Hamori (31c)

1980, Jan. 11   **Litho.**   **Perf. 15x14½**
316 A178 15c multicolored *(1,163,801)*   30   25
           First day cover   50
           Margin block of 4, inscription   1.50
317 A179 31c multicolored *(1,103,560)*   65   50
           First day cover   1.15
           First day cover, #316-317   1.25
           Margin block of 4, inscription   3.25

First day covers of Nos. 316-317 total 211,945.

See U.N. Offices in Geneva No. 89; Vienna No. 7.

Women's Year
Emblem — A180

United Nations Decade for Women.
Printed by Questa Colour Security Printers, United Kingdom. Panes of 50. Designed by Susanne Rottenfusser.

		1980, Mar. 7	Litho.	Perf. 14½x15	
318	A180	15c multicolored (1,409,350)		30	25
		First day cover			50
		Margin block of 4, inscription		1.50	
319	A180	20c multicolored (1,182,016)		40	30
		First day cover			70
		First day cover, #318-319			1.00
		Margin block of 4, inscription		2.00	

First day covers of Nos. 318-319 total 289,314.
See U.N. Offices in Geneva Nos. 90-91; Vienna Nos. 9-10.

U.N. Emblem and
"UN" on
Helmet — A181

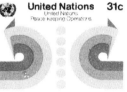

Arrows and U.N.
Emblem — A182

United Nations Peace-keeping Operations.
Printed by Joh. Enschede en Zonen, Netherlands. Panes of 50. Designed by Bruno K. Wiese (15c), James Gardiner (31c).

		1980, May 16	Litho.	Perf. 14x13	
320	A181	15c blue & black (1,245,521)		35	30
		First day cover			50
		Margin block of 4, inscription		1.75	
321	A182	31c multicolored (1,191,009)		75	60
		First day cover			1.15
		First day cover, #320-321			1.25
		Margin block of 4, inscription		3.75	

First day covers of Nos. 320-321 total 208,442.
See U.N. Offices in Geneva No. 92, Vienna No. 11.

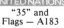

"35" and
Flags — A183

Globe and
Laurel — A184

35th Anniversary of the United Nations.
Printed by Ashton-Potter Ltd, Canada. Pane of 50.
Designed by Cemalettin Matver (15c), Mian Mohammad Saeed (31c).

		1980, June 26	Litho.	Perf. 13x13½	
322	A183	15c multicolored (1,554,514)		30	25
		First day cover			50
		Margin block of 4, inscription		1.50	
323	A184	31c multicolored (1,389,606)		65	50
		First day cover			1.15
		First day cover, #322-323			1.25
		Margin block of 4, inscription		3.25	

Souvenir Sheet
Imperf.

324		Sheet of 2 (1,215,505)		1.00	1.00
a.		A183 15c multicolored		30	
b.		A184 31c multicolored		65	
		First day cover			1.25

No. 324 has multicolored margin with inscription and U.N. emblem. Size: 92x73mm.
First day covers of Nos. 322-324 total: New York, 369,345; San Francisco, 203,701.
See U.N. Offices in Geneva Nos. 93-95; Vienna Nos. 12-14.

Flag of
Turkey — A185

Printed by Courvoisier, S.A., Switzerland. Sheets of 16. Designed by Ole Hamann.
Issued in 4 sheets of 16. Each sheet contains 4 blocks of 4 (Nos. 325-328, 329-332, 333-336, 337-340). A se-tenant block of 4 designs centers each sheet.

		1980, Sept. 26	Litho.	Perf. 12	
325	A185	15c shown (3,490,725)		30	25
326	A185	15c Luxembourg (3,490,725)		30	25
327	A185	15c Fiji (3,490,725)		30	25
328	A185	15c Viet Nam (3,490,725)		30	25
329	A185	15c Guinea (3,442,633)		30	25
330	A185	15c Surinam (3,442,633)		30	25
331	A185	15c Bangladesh (3,442,633)		30	25
332	A185	15c Mali (3,442,633)		30	25
333	A185	15c Jugoslavia (3,416,292)		30	25
334	A185	15c France (3,416,292)		30	25
335	A185	15c Venezuela (3,416,292)		30	25
336	A185	15c El Salvador (3,416,292)		30	25
337	A185	15c Madagascar (3,442,497)		30	25
338	A185	15c Cameroon (3,442,497)		30	25
339	A185	15c Rwanda (3,442,497)		30	25
340	A185	15c Hungary (3,442,497)		30	25
		First day covers of Nos. 325-340 @			50

First day covers of Nos. 325-340 total 6,145,595.
See Nos. 350-365, 374-389, 399-414, 425-440, 450-465, 477-492, 499-514.

Symbolic
Flowers — A186

Symbols of
Progress — A187

Printed by Ashton-Potter Ltd., Canada. Panes of 50.
Designed by Eliezer Weishoff (15c), Dietman Kowall (20c).

		1980, Nov. 21	Litho.	Perf. 13½x13	
341	A186	15c multicolored (1,192,165)		30	25
		First day cover			50
		Margin block of 4, inscription		1.50	
342	A187	20c multicolored (1,011,382)		40	30
		First day cover			70
		Margin block of 4, inscription		2.00	

First day covers of Nos. 341-342 total 232,149.
See U.N. Offices in Geneva, Nos. 96-97; Vienna Nos. 15-16.

Inalienable Rights of
the Palestinian
People — A188

Printed by Courvoisier S.A., Switzerland. Sheets of 50.

Designed by David Dewhurst.

		1981, Jan. 30	Photo.	Perf. 12x11½	
343	A188	15c multicolored (993,489)		40	30
		First day cover (127,187)			50
		Margin block of 4, inscription		2.00	

See U.N. Offices in Geneva No. 98; Vienna No. 17.

Interlocking Puzzle
Pieces — A189

Stylized
Person — A190

International Year of the Disabled.
Printed by Heraclio Fournier S.A., Spain. Panes of 50.
Designed by Sophia Van Heeswijk (20c) and G.P. Van der Hyde (35c).

		1981, Mar. 6	Photo.	Perf. 14	
344	A189	20c multicolored (1,218,371)		40	30
		First day cover			70
		Margin block of 4, inscription		2.00	
345	A190	35c black & orange (1,107,298)		70	55
		First day cover			1.20
		First day cover, #344-345			1.50
		Margin block of 4, inscription		3.50	

First day covers of Nos. 344-345 total 204,891.
See U.N. Offices in Geneva Nos. 99-100; Vienna Nos. 18-19.

Desislava and Sebastocrator
Kaloyan, Bulgarian Mural,
1259, Boyana Church,
Sofia — A191

Art at U.N. Issue

Printed by Courvoisier. Panes of 50. Designed by Ole Hamann.

		1981, Apr. 15	Photo.	Perf. 11½	
		Granite Paper			
346	A191	20c multi (1,252,648)		40	30
		First day cover			70
		Margin block of 4, inscription		2.00	
347	A191	31c multi (1,061,056)		65	50
		First day cover			1.15
		First day cover, #346-347			2.00
		Margin block of 4, inscription		3.25	

First day covers of Nos. 346-347 total 210,978.
See U.N. Offices in Geneva No. 101; Vienna No. 20.

Solar Energy — A192

Conference
Emblem — A193

Conference on New and Renewable Sources of Energy, Nairobi, Aug. 10-21.
Printed by Setelipaino, Finland. Panes of 50. Designed by Ulrike Dreyer (20c); Robert Perrot (40c).

1981, May 29	**Litho.**	***Perf. 13***	
348 A192	20c multi *(1,132,877)*	40	30
	First day cover		70
	Margin block of 4, inscription	2.00	
349 A193	40c multi *(1,158,319)*	65	50
	First day cover		1.25
	First day cover, #348-349		2.25
	Margin block of 4, inscription	3.25	—

First day covers of Nos. 348-349 total 240,205.
See U.N. Offices in Geneva No. 102; Vienna No. 21.

Flag Type of 1980
Printed by Courvoisier, S.A., Switzerland. Sheets of 16. Designed by Ole Hamann.

Issued in 4 sheets of 16. Each sheet contains 4 blocks of four (Nos. 350-353, 354-357, 358-361, 362-365). A se-tenant block of 4 designs centers each sheet.

1981, Sept.25		**Litho.**	
350 A185	20c Djibouti *(2,342,224)*	40	30
351 A185	20c Sri Lanka *(2,342,224)*	40	30
352 A185	20c Bolivia *(2,342,224)*	40	30
353 A185	20c Equatorial Guinea *(2,342,224)*	40	30
354 A185	20c Malta *(2,360,297)*	40	30
355 A185	20c Czechoslovakia *(2,360,297)*	40	30
356 A185	20c Thailand *(2,360,297)*	40	30
357 A185	20c Trinidad & Tobago *(2,360,297)*	40	30
358 A185	20c Ukrainian SSR *(2,344,755)*	40	30
359 A185	20c Kuwait *(2,344,755)*	40	30
360 A185	20c Sudan *(2,344,755)*	40	30
361 A185	20c Egypt *(2,344,755)*	40	30
362 A185	20c US *(2,450,537)*	40	30
363 A185	20c Singapore *(2,450,537)*	40	30
364 A185	20c Panama *(2,450,537)*	40	30
365 A185	20c Costa Rica *(2,450,537)*	40	30
	First day covers of Nos. 350-365@		75

First day covers of Nos. 350-365 total 3,961,237.

Seedling and Tree
Cross-section — A194

"10" and Symbols of
Progress — A195

United Nations Volunteers Program, 10th anniv.
Printed by Walsall Security Printers, Ltd., United Kingdom. Pane of 50.
Designed by Gabriele Nussgen (18c), Angel Medina Medina (28c).

1981, Nov. 13		**Litho.**	
366 A194	18c multi *(1,246,833)*	40	30
	First day cover		70
	Margin block of 4, inscription	2.00	—
367 A195	28c multi *(1,282,868)*	60	45
	First day cover		1.00
	First day cover, #366-367		1.25
	Margin block of 4, inscription	3.00	—

First day covers of Nos. 366-367 total 221,106.
See U.N. Offices in Geneva Nos. 103-104; Vienna Nos. 22-23.

Respect for
Human
Rights — A196

Independence
of Colonial
Countries and
People — A197

Second Disarmament
Decade — A198

Printed by Courvoisier, S.A., Switzerland. Sheets of 50.
Designed by Rolf Christianson (17c); George Hamori (28c); Marek Kwiatkowski (40c).

1982, Jan. 22		***Perf. 11½x12***	
368 A196	17c multicolored *(3,000,000)*	35	15

	First day cover		55
	Margin block of 4, inscription	1.75	—
369 A197	28c multicolored *(3,000,000)*	56	25
	First day cover		1.00
	Margin block of 4, inscription	2.30	—
370 A198	40c multicolored *(3,000,000)*	80	40
	First day cover		1.50
	First day cover, #368-370		1.75
	Margin block of 4, inscription	4.00	—

First day covers of Nos. 368-370 total 243,073.

Sun and Hand
Holding
Seedling — A199

Sun, Plant Land
and Water — A200

10th Anniversary of United Nations Environment Program.
Printed by Joh. Enschede En Zonen, Netherlands. Panes of 50.
Designed by Philine Hartert (20c); Peer-Ulrich Bremer (40c).

1982, Mar. 19		***Litho.***	***Perf. 13½x13***
371 A199	20c multicolored *(1,017,117)*	50	35
	First day cover		75
	Margin block of 4, inscription	2.50	—
372 A200	40c multicolored *(884,798)*	1.00	70
	First day cover		1.50
	First day cover, #371-372		1.75
	Margin block of 4, inscription	5.00	—

First day covers of Nos. 371-372 total 288,721.
See U.N. Offices in Geneva Nos. 107-108; Vienna Nos. 25-26.

U.N. Emblem and
Olive Branch in
Outer Space — A201

Exploration and Peaceful Uses of Outer Space.
Printed By Enschede. Panes of 50. Designed by Wiktor C. Nerwinski.

1982, June 11		**Litho.**	***Perf. 13x13½***
373 A201	20c multicolored *(1,083,426)*	50	35
	First day cover *(156,965)*		75
	Margin block of 4, inscription	2.50	—

See U.N. Offices in Geneva Nos. 109-110; Vienna No. 27.

Flag Type of 1980
Printed by Courvoisier. Sheets of 16.
Designed by Ole Hamann.

Issued in 4 sheets of 16. Each sheet contains 4 blocks of four (Nos. 374-377, 378-381, 383-385, 386-389). A se-tenant block of 4 designs centers each sheet.

1982, Sept. 24		**Litho.**	***Perf. 12***
374 A185	20c Austria *(2,314,006)*	55	25
375 A185	20c Malaysia *(2,314,006)*	55	25
376 A185	20c Seychelles *(2,314,006)*	55	25
377 A185	20c Ireland *(2,314,006)*	55	25
378 A185	20c Mozambique *(2,300,958)*	55	25
379 A185	20c Albania *(2,300,958)*	55	25
380 A185	20c Dominica *(2,300,958)*	55	25
381 A185	20c Solomon Islnads *(2,300,958)*	55	25
382 A185	20c Philippines *(2,288,589)*	55	25
383 A185	20c Swaziland *(2,288,589)*	55	25
384 A185	20c Nicaragua *(2,288,589)*	55	25
385 A185	20c Burma *(2,288,589)*	55	25
386 A185	20c Cape Verde *(2,285,848)*	55	25
387 A185	20c Guyana *(2,285,848)*	55	25
388 A185	20c Belgium *(2,285,848)*	55	25
389 A185	20c Nigeria *(2,285,848)*	55	25
	First day cover, #374-389 @		75

First day covers of Nos. 374-389 total 3,202,744.

A202

Conservation and Protection of Nature
Printed by Fournier. Sheets of 50.
Designed by Hamori

1982, Nov. 19		**Photo.**	***Perf. 14***
390 A202	20c Leaf *(1,110,027)*	60	30
	First day cover		75
	margin block of 4, inscription	3.00	—
391 A202	28c Butterfly *(848,772)*	80	45
	First day cover		1.00
	Margin block of 4, inscription	4.00	—

First day covers of Nos. 390-391 total 214,148.
See U.N. Offices in Geneva Nos. 111-112; Vienna Nos. 28-29.

A203 WORLD COMMUNICATIONS YEAR

World Communications Year A204

World Communications Year
Printed by Walsal. Panes of 50. Designed by Hanns Lohrer (A203) and Lorena Berengo (A204).

1983, Jan. 28		**Litho.**	***Perf. 13***
392 A203	20c multi *(1,282,079)*	50	20
	First day cover		75
	Margin block of 4, inscription	2.00	—
393 A204	40c multi *(931,903)*	1.00	40
	First day cover		1.50
	First day cover, Nos. 392-393		1.75
	Margin block of 4, inscription	5.00	—

First day covers of Nos. 392-393 total 183,499.
See U.N. Offices in Geneva No. 113; Vienna No. 30.

A205

A206

Safety at Sea
Printed by Questa. Panes of 50. Designed by Jean-Marie Lenfant (A205), Ari Ron (A206).

1983, Mar. 18		**Litho.**	***Perf. 14½***
394 A205	20c multi *(1,252,456)*	50	20
	First day cover		75
	Margin block of 4, inscription	2.00	—
395 A206	37c multi *(939,910)*	1.00	38
	First day cover		1.50
	First day cover, Nos. 394-395		1.75
	Margin block of 4, inscription	5.00	—

First day covers of Nos. 394-395 total 199,962.
See U.N. Offices in Geneva Nos. 114-115; Vienna Nos. 31-32.

A207

World Food Program
Printed by Government Printers Bureau, Japan. Designed by Marek Kwiatkoski.

1983, Apr. 22   Engr.   Perf. 13½
396 A207 20c rose lake *(1,238,997)*   40   20
      First day cover *(180,704)*   75
      Margin block of 4, inscription   2.00   —

See U.N. Offices in Geneva No. 116; Vienna Nos. 33-34.

A208

A209

UN Conference on Trade and Development
Printed by Carl Uberreuter Druck and Vergal M. Salzer, Austria. Panes of 50. Designed by Dietmar Braklow (A208), Gabriel Genz (A209).

1983, June 6   Litho.   Perf. 14
397 A208 20c multi *(1,060,053)*   60   20
      First day cover   75
      Margin block of 4, inscription   3.00   —
398 A209 28c multi *(948,981)*   80   28
      First day cover   1.00
      First day cover, Nos. 397-398   1.25
      Margin block of 4, inscription   4.00   —

First day covers of Nos. 397-398 total 200,131.
See U.N. Offices in Geneva Nos. 117-118; Vienna Nos. 35-36.

Flag Type of 1980
Printed by Courvoisier. Sheets of 16.
Designed by Ole Hamann.

Issued in 4 sheets of 16. Each sheet contains 4 blocks of four (Nos. 399-402, 403-406, 407-410, 411-414). A se-tenant block of 4 designs centers each sheet.

1983, Sept. 23   Photo.   Perf. 12
399 A185 20c Great Britain *(2,490,599)*   55   20
400 A185 20c Barbados *(2,490,599)*   55   20
401 A185 20c Nepal *(2,490,599)*   55   20
402 A185 20c Israel *(2,490,599)*   55   20
403 A185 20c Malawi *(2,483,010)*   55   20
404 A185 20c Byelorussian SSR *(2,483,010)* 55   20
405 A185 20c Jamaica *(2,483,010)*   55   20
406 A185 20c Kenya *(2,483,010)*   55   20
407 A185 20c People's Republic of China
               (2,474,140)   55   20
408 A185 20c Peru *(2,474,140)*   55   20
409 A185 20c Bulgaria *(2,474,140)*   55   20
410 A185 20c Canada *(2,474,140)*   55   20
411 A185 20c Somalia *(2,482,070)*   55   20
412 A185 20c Senegal *(2,482,070)*   55   20
413 A185 20c Brazil *(2,482,070)*   55   20
414 A185 20c Sweden *(2,482,070)*   55   20
      First day cover, #399-414 @   75

First day covers of Nos. 399-414 total 2,214,134.

Window Right — A210

Peace Treaty with
Nature — A211

35th Anniversary of the Universal Declaration of Human Rights
Printed by Government Printing Office, Austria, Designed by Friedensreich Hundertwasser, Austria. Panes of 16 (4x4).

1983, Dec. 9   Photo. & Engr.   Perf. 13½
415 A210 20c multi *(1,591,102)*   70   20
      First day cover   75
416 A211 40c multi *(1,566,789)*   1.40   40
      First day cover   1.50
      First day cover, Nos. 392-393   1.75

First day covers of Nos. 415-416 total 176,269.

International Conference
on Population — A212

Printed by Bundesdruckerei, Federal Republic of Germany. Panes of 50. Designed by Marina Langer-Rosa and Helmut Langer, Federal Republic of Germany.

1984, Feb. 3   Litho.   Perf. 14
417 A212 20c multi *(905,320)*   50   20
      First day cover   75
      Margin block of 4, inscription   2.50   —
418 A212 40c multi *(717,084)*   1.25   40
      First day cover   1.50
      First day cover, Nos. 417-418   1.75
      Margin block of 4, inscription   6.25   —

First day covers of Nos. 417-418 total 118,068.
See U.N. Offices in Geneva No. 121; Vienna No. 39.

Tractor
Plowing — A213

Rice
Paddy — A214

World Food Day, Oct. 16
Printed by Walsall Security Printers, Ltd., United Kingdom. Panes of 50. Designed by Adth Vanooijen, Netherlands.

1984, Mar. 15   Litho.   Perf. 14½
419 A213 20c multi *(853,641)*   60   20
      First day cover   75
      Margin block of 4, inscription   3.00   —
420 A214 40c multi *(727,165)*   1.25   40
      First day cover   1.50
      First day cover, Nos. 419-420   1.75
      Margin block of 4, inscription   6.25   —

First day covers of Nos. 419-420 total 116,009.

Grand
Canyon — A215

Ancient City of
Polonnaruwa, Sri
Lanka — A216

World Heritage
Printed by Harrison and Sons, United Kingdom. Panes of 50. Designs adapted by Rocco J. Callari, U.S., and Thomas Lee, China.

1984, Apr. 18   Litho.   Perf. 14
421 A215 20c multi *(814,316)*   60   20
      First day cover   75
      Margin block of 4, inscription   3.00   —
422 A216 50c multi *(579,136)*   1.50   50
      First day cover   1.75
      First day cover, Nos. 421-422   2.00
      Margin block of 4, inscription   7.50   —

First day covers of Nos. 421-422 total 112,036.

A217

A218

Future for Refugees
Printed by Courvoisier. Panes of 50. Designed by Hans Erni, Switzerland.

1984, May 29   Photo.   Perf. 11½
423 A217 20c multi *(956,743)*   50   20
      First day cover   75
      Margin block of 4, inscription   2.50   —
424 A218 50c multi *(729,036)*   1.25   50
      First day cover   1.75
      First day cover, Nos. 423-424   2.00
      Margin block of 4, inscription   6.25   —

First day covers of Nos. 423-424 total 115,789.

Flag Type of 1980
Printed by Courvoisier. Sheets of 16.
Designed by Ole Hamann.

Issued in 4 sheets of 16. Each sheet contains 4 blocks of four (Nos. 425-428, 429-432, 433-436, 437-440). A se-tenant block of 4 designs centers each sheet.

1984, Sept. 21   Photo.   Perf. 12
425 A185 20c Burundi *(1,941,471)*   70   20
426 A185 20c Pakistan *(1,941,471)*   70   20
427 A185 20c Benin *(1,941,471)*   70   20
428 A185 20c Italy *(1,941,471)*   70   20
429 A185 20c Tanzania *(1,969,051)*   70   20
430 A185 20c United Arab Emirates
               (1,969,051)   70   20
431 A185 20c Ecuador *(1,969,051)*   70   20
432 A185 20c Bahamas *(1,969,051)*   70   20
433 A185 20c Poland *(2,001,091)*   70   20
434 A185 20c Papua New Guinea *(2,001,091)* 70   20
435 A185 20c Uruguay *(2,001,091)*   70   20
436 A185 20c Chile *(2,001,091)*   70   20
437 A185 20c Paraguay *(1,969,875)*   70   20
438 A185 20c Bhutan *(1,969,875)*   70   20
438 A185 20c Central African Republic
               (1,969,875)   70   20
440 A185 20c Australia *(1,969,875)*   70   20
      First day cover, #425-440 each   75

First day covers of Nos. 425-440 total 1,914,972.

International Youth
Year — A219

Printed by Waddingtons Ltd., United Kingdom. Panes of 50. Designed by Ramon Mueller, Federal Republic of Germany.

1984, Nov. 15　　　Litho.　　　Perf. 13½
441 A219　20c multi *(884,962)*　　　　60　20
　　　First day cover　　　　　　　　　　　75
　　　Margin block of 4, inscription　3.00　—
442 A219　35c multi *(740,023)*　　1.10　35
　　　First day cover　　　　　　　　　1.25
　　　First day cover, Nos. 441-442　1.50
　　　Margin block of 4, inscription　5.50　—

First day covers of Nos. 441-442 total 125,315.

ILO Turin Center — A220

Printed by the Government Printing Bureau, Japan. Panes of 50. Engraved by Mamoru Iwakuni and Hiroshi Ozaki, Japan.

1985, Feb. 1　　　Engr.　　　Perf. 13½
443 A220　23c Turin Center emblem
　　　　(1,400,000)+　　　　　　　46　24
　　　First day cover *(76,541)*　　　　85
　　　Margin block of 4, inscription　2.30　—

See U.N. Offices in Geneva Nos. 129-130; Vienna No. 48.

U.N. University
A221

Printed by Helio Courvoiser, Switzerland. Panes of 50. Designed by Moshe Pereg, Israel, and Hinedi Geluda, Brazil.

1985, Mar. 15　　　Photo.　　　Perf. 13½
444 A221　50c Farmer plowing, discussion
　　　　group *(1,400,000)*+　　　1.00　50
　　　First day cover *(77,271)*　　　2.00
　　　Margin block of 4, inscription　5.00　—

See U.N. Offices in Geneva Nos. 131-132; Vienna No. 49.

People's of the
World
United — A222

Painting U.N.
Emblem — A223

Printed by Carl Ueberreuter Druck and Verlag M. Salzer, Austria. Panes of 50. Designed by Fritz Henry Oerter, Federal Republic of Germany (22c), and Rimondi Rino, Italy ($3).

1985, May 10　　　Litho.　　　Perf. 14
445 A222　22c multi *(2,000,000)*+　　44　22
　　　First day cover　　　　　　　　　80
　　　Margin block of 4, inscription　2.20

446 A223　$3 multi *(2,000,000)*+　　6.00　3.00
　　　First day cover　　　　　　　　11.00
　　　First day cover, Nos. 445-446　11.50
　　　Margin block of 4, inscription　30.00　—

First day covers of Nos. 445-446 total 88,613.

The Corner,
1947 — A224

Alvaro Raking
Hay,
1953 — A225

U.N. 40th anniversary. Oil paintings (details) by American artist Andrew Wyeth (b. 1917). Printed by Helio Courvoisier, Switzerland. Panes of 50. Designed by Rocco J. Callari, U.S., and Thomas Lee, China (#449).

1985, June 26　　　Photo.　　　Perf. 12 x 11½
447 A224　22c multi *(1,400,000)*+　　44　22
　　　First day cover　　　　　　　　　80
　　　Margin block of 4, inscription　2.20
448 A225　45c multi *(1,400,000)*+　　90　45
　　　First day cover　　　　　　　　　1.60
　　　First day cover, Nos. 447-448　1.90
　　　Margin block of 4, inscription　4.50　—

Souvenir Sheet
Imperf
449　　　Sheet of 2 *(1,400,000)*+　1.35　1.35
a.　　A224 22c multi　　　　　　44
b.　　A225 45c multi　　　　　　90
　　　First day cover　　　　　　　　2.50

No. 449 has multicolored margin containing inscription and U.N. emblem. Size: 75x83 mm.
First day covers of Nos. 447-449 total: New York, 210,189; San Francisco, 92,804.
See U.N. Offices in Geneva Nos. 135-137; Vienna Nos. 52-54.

Flag Type of 1980
Printed by Helio Courvoisier, Switzerland. Designed by Ole Hamann. Issued in panes of 16; each contains 4 blocks of four (Nos. 450-453, 454-457, 458-461, 462-465). A se-tenant block of 4 designs is at the center of each sheet.

1985, Sept. 20　　　Photo.　　　Perf. 12
450 A185　22c Grenada *(2,500,000)*+　44　22
451 A185　22c Federal Republic of Germany
　　　　(2,500,000)+　　　　　　44　22
452 A185　22c Saudi Arabia *(2,500,000)*+　44　22
453 A185　22c Mexico *(2,500,000)*+　44　22
454 A185　22c Uganda *(2,500,000)*+　44　22
455 A185　22c St. Thomas & Prince
　　　　(2,500,000)+　　　　　　44　22
456 A185　22c USSR *(2,500,000)*+　44　22
457 A185　22c India *(2,500,000)*+　44　22
458 A185　22c Liberia *(2,500,000)*+　44　22
459 A185　22c Mauritius *(2,500,000)*+　44　22
460 A185　22c Chad *(2,500,000)*+　44　22
461 A185　22c Dominican Republic
　　　　(2,500,000)+　　　　　　44　22
462 A185　22c Sultanate of Oman
　　　　(2,500,000)+　　　　　　44　22
463 A185　22c Ghana *(2,500,000)*+　44　22
464 A185　22c Sierra Leone *(2,500,000)*+　44　22
465 A185　22c Finland *(2,500,000)*+　44　22
　　　First day covers, Nos. 450-
　　　　465, @　　　　　　　　　　80

First day covers of Nos. 450-465 total 1,774,193.

UNICEF Child Survival
Campaign — A226

Printed by the Government Printing Bureau, Japan. Panes of 50. Designed by Mel Harris, United Kingdom (#466) and Dipok Deyi, India (#467).

1985, Nov. 22　　　Photo. & Engr.　　Perf. 13½
466 A226　22c Asian Toddler *(1,200,000)*+　44　22
　　　First day cover　　　　　　　　　80
　　　Margin block of 4, inscription　2.20
467 A226　33c Breastfeeding *(1,200,000)*+　66　32
　　　First day cover　　　　　　　　　1.15
　　　First day cover, Nos. 466-467　1.50
　　　Margin block of 4, inscription　3.30

First day covers of Nos. 466-467 total 206,923.
See U.N. Offices in Geneva Nos. 138-139; Vienna Nos. 55-56.

Africa in Crisis — A227

Printed by Helio Courvoisier, Switzerland. Panes of 50. Designed by Wosene Kosrof, Ethiopia.

1986, Jan. 31　　　Photo.　　　Perf. 11½x12
468 A227　22c multi *(1,200,000)*+　44　22
　　　First day cover *(80,588)*　　　80
　　　Margin block of 4, inscription　2.20

Campaign against hunger. See U.N. Offices in Geneva No. 140; Vienna No. 57.

Water
Resources — A228

Printed by the Government Printing Bureau, Japan. Panes of 40, 2 blocks of 4 horizontal and 5 blocks of 4 vertical. Designed by Thomas Lee, China.

1986, Mar. 14　　　Photo.　　　Perf. 13½
469 A228　22c Dam *(750,000)*+　　44　22
　　　First day cover　　　　　　　　　80
470 A228　22c Irrigation *(750,000)*+　44　22
　　　First day cover　　　　　　　　　80
471 A228　22c Hygiene *(750,000)*+　44　22
　　　First day cover　　　　　　　　　80
472 A228　22c Well *(750,000)*+　　44　22
　　　First day cover　　　　　　　　　80
　　　First day cover, #469-472　　　2.25
　　　Margin block of 4, #469-472,
　　　　inscription　　　　　　　　2.20　—
a.　　Block of 4, #469-472　　　1.80　88

U.N. Development Program. Nos. 469-472 printed se-tenant in a continuous design.
First day covers of Nos. 469-472 total 199,347.
See U.N. Offices in Geneva Nos. 141-144; Vienna Nos. 58-61.

Human Rights
Stamp of
1954 — A229

Stamp collecting: 44c, Engraver. Printed by the Swedish Post Office, Sweden. Panes of 50. Designed by Czeslaw Slania and Ingalill Axelsson, Sweden.

1986, May 22　　　Engr.　　　Perf. 12½
473 A229　22c dk vio & brt bl *(1,200,000)*+　44　22
　　　First day cover　　　　　　　　　80
　　　Margin block of 4, inscription　2.20
474 A229　44c brn & emer grn *(1,200,000)*+　88　44
　　　First day cover　　　　　　　　　1.25
　　　First day cover, #473-474　　　1.75
　　　Margin block of 4, inscription　4.40

First day covers of Nos. 473-474 total: New York, 121,143; Chicago, 89,557.
See U.N. Offices in Geneva Nos. 146-147; Vienna Nos. 62-63.

Bird's Nest in Tree — A230

Peace in Seven Languages — A231

Printed by the Government Printing Bureau, Japan. Panes of 50. Designed by Akira Iriguchi, Japan (#475), and Henryk Chylinski, Poland (#476).

1986, June 20   Photo. & Embossed   Perf. 13½
475 A230 22c multi *(1,200,000)*+   44   22
   First day cover   80
   Margin block of 4, inscription   2.20   —
476 A231 33c multi *(1,200,000)*+   66   35
   First day cover   1.05
   First day cover, #475-476   1.50   —
   Margin block of 4, inscription   3.30   —

International Peace Year.
First day covers of Nos. 475-476 total 149,976.

Flag Type of 1980

Printed by Helio Courvoisier, Switzerland. Designed by Ole Hamman. Issued in panes of 16; each contains 4 blocks of four (Nos. 477-480, 481-484, 485-488, 489-492). A se-tenant block of 4 designs is at the center of each sheet.

1986, Sept. 19   Photo.   Perf. 12
477 A185 22c New Zealand *(2,500,000)*+   44   22
478 A185 22c Lao PDR *(2,500,000)*+   44   22
479 A185 22c Burkina Faso *(2,500,000)*+   44   22
480 A185 22c Gambia *(2,500,000)*+   44   22
481 A185 22c Maldives *(2,500,000)*+   44   22
482 A185 22c Ethiopia *(2,500,000)*+   44   22
483 A185 22c Jordan *(2,500,000)*+   44   22
484 A185 22c Zambia *(2,500,000)*+   44   22
485 A185 22c Iceland *(2,500,000)*+   44   22
486 A185 22c Antigua & Barbuda
    (2,500,000)+   44   22
487 A185 22c Angola *(2,500,000)*+   44   22
488 A185 22c Botswana *(2,500,000)*+   44   22
489 A185 22c Romania *(2,500,000)*+   44   22
490 A185 22c Togo *(2,500,000)*+   44   22
491 A185 22c Mauritania *(2,500,000)*+   44   22
492 A185 22c Colombia *(2,500,000)*+   44   22
   First day covers, Nos. 477-
    492, @   80

First day covers of Nos. 477-492 total 1,442,284.

Souvenir Sheet

World Federation of U.N. Associations, 40th Anniversary — A232

Printed by Johann Enschede and Sons, Netherlands. Designed by Rocco J. Callari, U.S.
Designs: 22c, Mother Earth, by Edna Hibel, U.S. 33c, Watercolor by Salvador Dali (b. 1904) Spain. 39c, New Dawn, by Dong Kingman, U.S. 44c, Watercolor by Chaim Gross, U.S.

1986, Nov. 14   Litho.   Perf. 13x13½
493   Sheet of 4 *(1,800,000)*+   2.80   2.80
  a. A232 22c multi   44   —
  b. A232 33c multi   66   —
  c. A232 39c multi   78   —
  d. A232 44c multi   88   —
   First day cover *(106,194)*   3.25

No. 493 has inscribed margin picturing U.N. and WFUNA emblems. Size: 119x65mm.
See U.N. Offices in Geneva No. 150; Vienna No. 66.

Trygve Halvdan Lie (1896-1968), First Secretary-General — A233

Printed by the Government Printing Office, Austria. Panes of 50. Designed by Rocco J. Callari, U.S., from a portrait by Harald Dal, Norway.

1987, Jan. 30   Photo. & Engr.   Perf. 13½
494 A233 22c multi *(1,200,000)*+   44   22
   First day cover *(84,819)*   80
   Margin block of 4, inscription   2.20   —

See Offices in Geneva No. 151; Vienna No. 67.

International Year of Shelter for the Homeless A234

Printed by Johann Enschede and Sons, Netherlands. Panes of 50. Designed by Wladyslaw Brykczynski, Poland.
Designs: 22c, Surveying and blueprinting. 44c, Cutting lumber.

1987, Mar. 13   Litho.   Perf. 13½x12½
495 A234 22c multi *(1,150,000)*+   44   22
   First day cover   80
   Margin block of 4, inscription   2.20   —
496 A234 44c multi *(1,150,000)*+   88   44
   First day cover   1.25
   First day cover, #495-496   1.75   —
   Margin block of 4, inscription   4.40   —

First day covers of Nos. 495-496 total 94,090.
See Offices in Geneva Nos. 154-155; Vienna Nos. 68-69.

Fight Drug Abuse — A235

Printed by the House of Questa, United Kingdom. Panes of 50. Designed by Susan Borgen and Noel Werrett, U.S.
Designs: 22c, Construction. 33c, Education.

1987, June 12   Litho.   Perf. 14½x15
497 A235 22c multi *(1,150,000)*+   44   22
   First day cover   80
   Margin block of 4, inscription   2.20   —
498 A235 33c multi *(1,150,000)*+   66   35
   First day cover   1.05
   First day cover, #497-498   1.50   —
   Margin block of 4, inscription   3.30   —

First day covers of Nos. 497-498 total 106,941.
See Offices in Geneva Nos. 156-157; Vienna Nos. 70-71.

Flag Type of 1980
Printed by Courvoisier. Designed by Ole Hamman. Issued in panes of 16; each contains 4 block of four (Nos. 499-502, 503-506, 507-510, 511-514). A se-tenant block of 4 designs is at the center of each pane.

1987, Sept. 18   Photo.   Perf. 12
499 A185 22c Comoros   44   22
500 A185 22c Yemen PDR   44   22
501 A185 22c Mongolia   44   22
502 A185 22c Vanuatu   44   22
503 A185 22c Japan   44   22
504 A185 22c Gabon   44   22
505 A185 22c Zimbabwe   44   22
506 A185 22c Iraq   44   22
507 A185 22c Argentina   44   22
508 A185 22c Congo   44   22
509 A185 22c Niger   44   22
510 A185 22c St. Lucia   44   22
511 A185 22c Bahrain   44   22
512 A185 22c Haiti   44   22
513 A185 22c Afghanistan   44   22

514 A185 22c Greece   44   22
   First day covers, Nos. 499-
    514, @   80

Print order 2,200,000 each.

United Nations Day — A236

Printed by The House of Questa, United Kingdom. Panes of 12. Designed by Elisabeth von Janota-Bzowski (#515) and Fritz Henry Oerter (#516), Federal Republic of Germany.
Designs: Multinational people in various occupations.

1987, Oct. 23   Litho.   Perf. 14½x15
515 A236 22c multi *(1,188,000)*+   44   22
   First day cover   80
   Margin block of 4, inscription   2.20   —
516 A236 39c multi *(1,188,000)*+   78   40
   First day cover   1.15
   First day cover, #515-516   1.65   —
   Margin block of 4, inscription   3.90   —

See Offices in Geneva Nos. 158-159; Vienna Nos. 74-75.

Immunize Every Child — A237

Printed by The House of Questa, United Kingdom. Panes of 50. Designed by Seymour Chwast, U.S.
Designs: 22c, Measles. 44c, Tetanus.

1987, Nov. 20   Litho.   Perf. 15x14½
517 A237 22c multi *(1,150,000)*+   44   22
   First day cover   80
   Margin block of 4, inscription   2.20   —
518 A237 44c multi *(1,150,000)*+   88   44
   First day cover   1.25
   First day cover, #517-518   1.75   —
   Margin block of 4, inscription   4.40   —

See Offices in Geneva Nos. 160-161; Vienna Nos. 76-77.

Intl. Fund for Agricultural Development (IFAD) — A238

Printed by CPE Australia Ltd., Australia. Panes of 50. Designed by Santiago Arolas, Switzerland.
Designs: 22c, Fishing. 33c, Farming.

1988, Jan. 29   Litho.   Perf. 13½
519 A238 22c multi *(1,050,000)*+   44   22
   First day cover   80
   Margin block of 4, inscription   2.20   —
520 A238 33c multi *(1,050,000)*+   66   35
   First day cover   1.05
   First day cover, Nos. 519-520   1.50   —
   Margin block of 4, inscription   3.30   —

See Offices in Geneva Nos. 162-163; Vienna Nos. 78-79.

UNITED NATIONS - FOR A BETTER WORLD

A239   3c

Printed by Heraclio Fournier, S.A., Spain. Panes of 50. Designed by David Ben-Hador, Isreal.

1988, Jan. 29	Photo.	Perf. 13½x14		
521	A239	3c multi (3,000,000)+	6	5
		First day cover		80
		Margin block of 4, inscription	30	

Survival of the Forests — A240

Printed by The House of Questa, United Kindgdom. Sheets of six se-tentant pairs. Designed by Braldt Bralds, the Netherlands.
Tropical rain forest: 25c, Treetops. 44c, Ground vegetation and tree trunks. Printed se-tenant in a continuous design.

1988, Mar. 18	Litho.	Perf. 14x15		
522	A240	25c multi (594,000)+	50	25
		First day cover		85
523	A240	44c multi (594,000)+	88	45
		First day cover		1.25
		First day cover, Nos. 522-523		1.75
		Margin block of 4, inscription (2 each Nos. 522-523)	3.45	

See Offices in Geneva Nos. 165-166; Vienna Nos. 80-81.

Intl. Volunteer Day — A241

Printed by Johann Enschede and Sons, the Netherlands. Panes of 50. Designed by James E. Tennison, U.S.
Designs: 25c, Edurahon, Vert. 50c, Vocational training.

1988, May 6	Litho.	Perf. 13x14, 14x13		
524	A241	25c multi (1,050,000)+	50	25
		First day cover		85
		Margin block of 4, inscription	2.50	
525	A241	50c multi (1,050,000)+	1.00	50
		Firstday cover		1.35
		Margin block of 4, inscription	4.00	

See Offices in Geneva Nos. 167-168; Vienna Nos. 82-83.

Health in Sports — A242

Printed by the Government Printing Bureau, Japan. Panes of 50. Paintings by LeRoy Neiman, American sports artist. Designs: 25c, Cycling, vert. 35c, Marathon.

1988, June 17	Litho.	Perf. 13½x13, 13x13½		
526	A242	25c multi (1,050,000)+	50	25
		First day cover		85
		Margin block of 4, inscription	2.50	
527	A242	38c multi (1,050,000)+	76	38
		First day cover		1.15
		First day cover, Nos. 526-527		1.65
		Margin block of 4, inscription	3.80	

See Offices in Geneva Nos. 169-170; Vienna Nos. 84-85.

Flag Type of 1980

Printed by Helio Couvoisier, Switzerland. Designed by Ole Hamman, Denmank. Issued in panes of 16; each contains 4

block of four (Nos. 528-531, 532-535, 536-539 and 540-543). A se-tenant block of 4 is at the center of each sheet.

1988, Sept. 15	Photo.	Perf. 12		
528	A185	25c Spain (2,086,000)+	50	25
529	A185	25c St. Vincent & Grenadines (2,086,000)+	50	25
530	A185	25c Ivory Coast (2,086,000)+	50	25
531	A185	25c Lebanon (2,086,000)+	50	25
532	A185	25c Yemen (Arab Republic) (2,086,000)+	50	25
533	A185	25c Cuba (2,086,000)+	50	25
534	A185	25c Denmark (2,086,000)+	50	25
535	A185	25c Libya (2,086,000)+	50	25
536	A185	25c Qutar (2,086,000)+	50	25
537	A185	25c Zaire (2,086,000)+	50	25
538	A185	25c Norway (2,086,000)+	50	25
539	A185	25c German Democratic Republic (2,086,000)+	50	25
540	A185	25c Iran (2,086,000)+	50	25
541	A185	25c Tunisia (2,086,000)+	50	25
542	A185	25c Samoa (2,086,000)+	50	25
543	A185	25c Belize (2,086,000)+	50	25
		First day covers, Nos. 528-543, each		85

Universal Declaration of Human Rights, 40th. Anniv. — A243

Printed by Helio Couvoisier, Switzerland. Panes of 50. Designed by Rocco J. Callair, U.S.

1988, Dec. 9	Photo. & Engr.	Perf.		
544	A243	25c multi (1,025,000)+	50	25
		First day cover		85
		Margin block of 4, inscription	2.50	
		Souvenir Sheet		
545	A243	$1 multi (700,000)+	2.00	2.00
		First day cover		2.50

No. 545 has multicolored decorative margin inscribed with the preamble to the human rights declaration in English. Size:
See Offices in Geneva Nos. 171-172; Vienna Nos. 86-87.

AIR POST

Plane and Gull — AP1

Swallows and U.N. Emblem — AP2

Engraved and printed by Thomas De La Rue & Co., Ltd., London. Panes of 50. Designed by Ole Hamann (AP1) and Olav Mathiesen (AP2).

1951, Dec. 14	Unwmk.	Perf. 14		
C1	AP1	6c henna brown (2,500,000)	12	12
		First day cover		1.00
		Margin block of 4, inscription	60	
C2	AP1	10c bright blue green (2,750,000)	25	25
		First day cover		1.00
		Margin block of 4, inscription	1.25	
C3	AP2	15c deep ultramarine (3,250,000)	65	35
		Prussian blue	150.00	
		First day cover		1.50
		Margin block of 4, inscription	3.25	
C4	AP2	25c gray black (2,250,000)	3.00	2.00
		First day cover		4.00
		First day cover, #C1-C4		7.50
		Margin block of 4, inscription	15.00	

First day covers of Nos. 1-11 and C1-C4 total 1,113,216.

Early printings of Nos. C1-C4 have wide, imperforate sheet margins on three sides. Later printings were perforated through all margins.
Nos. C1, C3 and C4 exist imperforate.

Airplane Wing and Globe — AP3

Engraved and printed by Thomas De La Rue & Co., Ltd., London. Panes of 50. Designed by W. W. Wind.

1957, May 27	Perf. 12½x14			
C5	AP3	4c maroon (5,000,000)	8	6
		First day cover (282,933)		35
		Margin block of 4, inscription	40	

Type of 1957 and

U. N. Flag and Plane — AP4

Engraved and printed by Waterlow & Sons, Ltd., London. Panes of 50. Designed by W. W. Wind (5c) and Olav Mathiesen (7c).

1959, Feb. 9	Unwmk.	Perf. 12½x13½		
C6	AP3	5c rose red (4,000,000)	10	8
		First day cover		40
		Margin block of 4, inscription	50	
		Perf. 13½x14		
C7	AP4	7c ultramarine (4,000,000)	14	10
		First day cover		50
		First day cover, #C6-C7		75
		Margin block of 4, inscription	70	

First day covers of Nos. C6 and C7 total 413,556.

Outer Space — AP5

U.N. Emblem — AP6

Bird of Laurel Leaves — AP7

Printed by Courvoisier S.A., La Chaux-de-Fonds, Switzerland. Panes of 50. Designed by Claude Bottiau (6c); George Hamori (8c) and Kurt Plowitz (13c).

1963, June 17	Photo.	Unwmk.	Perf. 11½	
C8	AP5	6c black, blue & yellow green (4,000,000)	12	10

	First day cover				35
	Margin block of 4, inscription		60		—
C9	AP6	8c yellow, olive green & red			
	(4,000,000)		16		12
	First day cover				40
	Margin block of 4, inscription		80		—

Perf. 12½x12

C10	AP7	13c ultra., aquamarine, gray & carmine (2,700,000)		25	20
	First day cover				60
	First day cover, #C8-C10			1.00	
	Margin block of 4, inscription		1.25		—

First day covers of Nos. C8-C10 total 535,824.

"Flight Across the Globe" — AP8

Jet Plane and Envelope — AP9

Printed by the Austrian Government Printing Office, Vienna, Austria. Panes of 50. Designed by Ole Hamann (15c) and George Hamori (25c).

Perf. 11½x12, 12x11½

1964, May 1		**Photo.**		**Unwmk.**	
C11	AP8	15c violet, buff, gray & pale green (3,000,000)		40	30
	First day cover				75
	Margin block of 4, inscription		2.00		—
a.	Gray omitted				—
C12	AP9	25c yellow, orange, gray, blue & red (2,000,000)		1.50	60
	First day cover				1.20
	First day cover, #C11-C12			1.75	
	Margin block of 4, inscription		7.50		—

First day covers of Nos. C11-C12 total 353,696.
For 75c in type AP8, see U.N. Offices in Geneva No. 8.
Nos. C11-C12 exist imperforate.

Jet Plane and U.N. Emblem — AP10

Printed by Setelipaino, Finland. Panes of 50. Designed by Ole Hamann.

1968, Apr. 18		**Litho.**		**Perf. 13**	
C13	AP10	20c multicolored (3,000,000)		40	35
	First day cover (225,378)				1.00
	Margin block of 4, inscription		2.00		—

Wings, Envelopes and U.N. Emblem — AP11

Printed by Setelipaino, Finland. Panes of 50. Designed by Olav S. Mathiesen.

1969, Apr. 21		**Litho.**		**Perf. 13**	
C14	AP11	10c orange vermilion, orange, yellow & black (4,000,000)		25	20
	First day cover (132,686)				40
	Margin block of 4, inscription		1.25		—

U.N. Emblem and Stylized Wing — AP12

Birds in Flight — AP13

Clouds — AP14

"UN" and Plane — AP15

Printed by Government Printing Bureau, Japan (9c); Heraclio Fournier, S. A., Spain (11c, 17c); Setelipaino, Finland (21c). Panes of 50. Designed by Lyell L. Dolan (9c), Arne Johnson (11c), British American Bank Note Co. (17c) and Asher Kalderon (21c).

1972, May 1		**Litho. & Engr.**		**Perf. 13x13½**	
C15	AP12	9c lt. blue, dk. red & vio. blue (3,000,000)+		18	15
	First day cover				40
	Margin block of 4, inscription		90		—

Photo.
Perf. 14x13½

C16	AP13	11c blue & multicolored (3,000,000)+		22	15
	First day cover				50
	Margin block of 4, inscription		1.10		—

Perf. 13½x14

C17	AP14	17c yellow, red & orange (3,000,000)+		34	25
	First day cover				75
	Margin block of 4, inscription		1.70		—

Perf. 13

C18	AP15	21c silver & multi. (3,500,000)		42	35
	First day cover				90
	First day cover, #C15-C18			1.85	
	Margin block of 4, inscription		2.10		—

+ Printing orders to Nov. 1979.
First day covers of Nos. C15-C18 total 553,535.

Globe and Jet — AP16

Pathways Radiating from UN Emblem — AP17

Bird in Flight, UN Headquarters AP18

Printed by Setelipaino, Finland. Panes of 50. Designed by George Hamori (13c), Shamir Bros. (18c) and Olav S. Mathiesen (26c).

1974, Sept. 16		**Litho.**	**Perf. 13, 12½x13 (18c)**		
C19	AP16	13c multicolored (2,500,000)+		26	22
	First day cover				70
	Margin block of 4, inscription		1.30		—
C20	AP17	18c gray olive & multicolored (2,000,000)+		36	30
	First day cover				1.15
	Margin block of 4, inscription		1.80		—
C21	AP18	26c blue & multi. (2,000,000)+		52	50
	First day cover				1.00
	First day cover, #C19-C21			1.75	
	Margin block of 4, inscription		2.60		—

First day covers of Nos. C19-C21 total 309,610.

Winged Airmail Letter — AP19

Symbolic Globe and Plane — AP20

Printed by Heraclio Fournier, S.A. Panes of 50. Designed by Eliezer Weishoff (25c) and Alan L. Pollock (31c).

1977, June 27		**Photo.**		**Perf. 14**	
C22	AP19	25c greenish blue & multi. (2,000,000)+		50	25
	First day cover				85
	Margin block of 4, inscription		2.50		—
C23	AP20	31c magenta (2,000,000)+		62	30
	First day cover				1.00
	First day cover, #C22-C23			1.50	
	Margin block of 4, inscription		3.10		—

First day covers of Nos. C22-C23 total 209,060.

ENVELOPES

Emblem of United Nations — U1

Printed by the International Envelope Corp., Dayton, Ohio. Die engraved by the American Bank Note Co., New York.

1953, Sept. 15				**Embossed**	
U1	U1	3c blue, entire (555,000)		75	25
	Entire, first day cancel (102,278)			1.25	

Printed by International Envelope Corp., Dayton, O.

1958, Sept. 22				**Embossed**	
U2	U1	4c ultramarine, entire (1,000,000)		75	25
	Entire, first day cancel (213,621)				30

Stylized Globe and Weather Vane — U2

Printed by United States Envelope Co., Springfield, Mass. Designed by Hatim El Mekki.

1963, Apr. 26				**Litho.**	
U3	U2	5c multicolored, entire (1,115,888)		30	10
	Entire, first day cancel (165,188)				40

Printed by Setelipaino, Finland.

1969, Jan. 8   **Litho.**
U4 U2 6c black, bl., magenta & dull yel., entire *(850,000)*   30 20
    Entire, first day cancel *(152,593)*   40

Headquarters Type of Regular Issue, 1968

Printed by Eureka Co., a division of Litton Industries.

1973, Jan. 12   **Litho.**
U5 A99 8c sepia, blue & olive, entire *(700,000)*   30 15
    Entire, first day cancel *(145,510)*   50

Headquarters Type of Regular Issue, 1974

Printed by United States Envelope Co., Springfield, Mass.

1975, Jan. 10   **Litho.**
U6 A138 10c blue, olive bister & multi., entire *(547,500)*   35 20
    Entire, first day cancel *(122,000)*   60

UNITED NATIONS 22c Bouquet of Ribbons — U3

Printed by Carl Ueberreuter Druck and Verlag M. Salzer, Austria. Designed by George Hamori, Australia.

1985, May 10   **Litho.**
U7 U3 22c multi, entire *(250,000)*   50 25
    Entire, first day cancel *(28,600)*   80

AIR POST ENVELOPES AND AIR LETTER SHEETS

Letter Sheet
Type of Air Post Stamp of 1951
Printed by Dennison & Sons, Long Island City, N.Y.

1952, Aug. 29   **Litho.**
UC1 AP2 10c blue, *bluish (187,000),* inscribed "Air Letter" at left, entire   35.00 3.50
    Entire, first day cancel *(57,274)*   5.50

Designed by C. Mutver.

Letter Sheet

1954-58   **Litho.**
UC2 AP2 10c Royal blue, *bluish,* inscribed "Air Letter" and "Aerogramme" at left, entire, *Sept. 14, 1954 (207,000)*   8.50 1.50
    Entire, first day cancel
a. No white border ('58) *(148,800)*   5.50 1.00

No. UC2 was printed with a narrow white border (½ to 1mm. wide) surrounding the stamp. On No. UC2a, this border has been partly or entirely eliminated.

U. N. Flag and Plane — UC1

(U. N. Emblem Emblossed)

Printed by International Envelope Corp., Dayton, O. Die engraved by American Bank Note Co., New York.

1959, Sept. 21   **Embossed**
UC3 UC1 7c blue, entire *(550,000)*   2.75 75
    Entire, first day cancel *(172,107)*   1.00

Letter Sheet
Type of Air Post Stamp of 1959
Printed by Thomas De La Rue & Co., Ltd., London

1960, Jan. 18   **Litho.**
UC4 AP4 10c ultramarine, *bluish,* entire *(405,000)*   65 25
    Entire, first day cancel *(122,425)*   50

Printed on protective tinted paper containing colorless inscription "United Nations" in the five official languages of the U.N.

Letter Sheet
Type of Air Post Stamp of 1951
Inscribed "Correo Aereo" instead of "Poste Aerienne"
Printed by Thomas De La Rue & Co., Ltd., London

1961-65   **Litho.**
UC5 AP1 11c ultramarine, *bluish,* entire, *June 26, 1961 (550,000)*   25 20
    Entire, first day cancel *(128,557)*   50
a. 11c dark blue, *green* entire, *July 16, 1965 (419,000)*   1.00 25

Printed on protective tinted paper containing colorless inscription "United Nations" in the five official languages of the U.N.

U.N. Emblem — UC2

Printed by United States Envelope Co., Springfield, Mass. Designed by George Hamori.

1963, Apr. 26   **Litho.**
UC6 UC2 8c multicolored, entire *(880,000)*   60 15
    Entire, first day cancel *(165,208)*   40

Letter Sheet

U.N. Emblem and Stylized Plane — UC3

Printed by Setelipaino, Finland. Designed by Robert Perrot.

1968, May 31   **Litho.**
UC7 UC3 13c violet blue & light blue, entire *(750,000)*   45 23
    Entire, first day cancel *(106,700)*   65

Type of 1963
Printed by Setelipaino, Finland.

1969, Jan. 8   **Litho.**
UC8 UC2 10c pink, Prussian blue, orange & sepia, entire *(750,000)*   45 20
    Entire, first day cancel *(153,472)*   50

Letter Sheet

U.N. Emblem, "UN," Globe and Plane — UC4

Printed by Joh. Enschede and Sons. Designed by Edmondo Calivis, Egypt. Sheet surface printed in greenish blue.

1972, Oct. 16   **Litho.**
UC9 UC4 15c violet blue & greenish blue, entire *(500,000)*   45 12
    Entire, first day cancel *(85,500)*   65

Bird Type of Air Post Stamp, 1972
Printed by Eureka Co., a division of Litton Industries

1973, Jan. 12   **Litho.**
UC10 AP13 11c blue & multicolored, entire *(700,000)*   45 20
    Entire, first day cancel *(134,500)*   45

Globe and Jet Air Post Type of 1974
Printed by United States Envelope Co., Springfield, Mass.

1975, Jan. 10   **Litho.**
UC11 AP16 13c blue & multicolored, entire *(555,539)*   45 25
    Entire, first day cancel *(122,000)*   50

Letter Sheet
Headquarters Type of Regular Issue, 1971
Printed by Joh. Enschede and Sons, Netherlands

1975, Jan. 10   **Photo.**
UC12 A120 18c blue & multi., entire *(400,000)*   50 20
    Entire, first day cancel *(70,500)*   60

Letter Sheet

"UN" Emblem and Birds UC5   22c UNITED NATIONS

Printed by Joh. Enschede and Sons. Designed by Angel Medina Medina.

1977, June 27   **Litho.**
UC13 UC5 22c multicolored, entire *(400,000)*   65 25
    Entire, first day cancel *(70,000)*   80

Letter Sheet

Paper Airplane UC6

Printed by Joh. Enschede and Sons. Designed by Margaret-Ann Champion.

1982, Apr. 28   **Litho.**
UC14 UC6 30c black, *pale green,* entire *(400,000)*   60 35
    Entire, first day cancel *(61,400)*   60

Letter Sheet No. UC14 Surcharged

1987, July 7   **Litho.**
UC15 UC6 30c + 6c black, *green,* entire   72 35
    Entire, first day cancel   72

POSTAL CARDS

Prices are for entire cards.
Type of Postage Issue of 1951
Printed by Dennison & Sons, Long Island City, N.Y.

1952, July 18   **Litho.**
UX1 A2 2c blue, *buff (899,415)*   20 15
    First day cancel *(116,023)*   45

Printed by British American Bank Note Co., Ltd., Ottawa, Canada

1958, Sept. 22   **Litho.**
UX2 A2 3c gray olive, *buff (575,000)*   75 15
    First day cancel *(145,557)*   20

World Map,
Sinusoidal
Projection — PC1

Printed by Eureka Specialty Printing Co., Scranton, Pa.

1963, Apr. 26   **Litho.**
UX3 PC1   4c light blue, violet blue, orange &
     bright citron *(784,000)*   22   7
     First day cancel *(112,280)*   — 20
   a.   Bright citron omitted

U.N. Emblem and Post
Horn — PC2

Printed by Canadian Bank Note Co., Ltd., Ottawa.
Designed by John Mason.

1969, Jan. 8   **Litho.**
UX4 PC2   5c blue & black *(500,000)*   22   5
     First day cancel *(95,975)*   25

"UN" — PC3

Printed by Government Printing Bureau, Tokyo. Designed
by Asher Kalderon.

1973, Jan. 12   **Litho.**
UX5 PC3   6c gray & multicolored *(500,000)*   22   6
     First day cancel *(84,500)*   30

Type of 1973
Printed by Setelipaino, Finland

1975, Jan. 10   **Litho.**
UX6 PC3   8c light green & multicolored
     (450,000)   22   8
     First day cancel *(72,500)*   35

U.N. Emblem — PC4

Printed by Setelipaino, Finland. Designed by George
Hamori.

1977, June 27   **Litho.**
UX7 PC4   9c multicolored *(350,000)*   35   8
     First day cancel *(70,000)*   45

PC5

Printed by Courvoisier. Designed by Salahattin Kanidinc.

1982, Apr. 28   **Photo.**
UX8 PC5   13c multicolored *(350,000)*   30   15
     First day cancel *(59,200)*   30

AIR POST POSTAL CARDS

Prices are for entire cards.
Type of Air Post Stamp of 1957
Printed by British American Bank Note Co., Ltd.,
Ottawa

1957, May 27   **Litho.**
UXC1 AP3   4c maroon, *buff (631,000)*   25   10
     First day cancel *(260,005)*   20

No. UXC1 Surcharged in
Maroon at Left of Stamp

1959, June 5   **Litho.**
UXC2 AP3 4c+1c maroon, *buff (1,119,000)*   55   15
     Cancel first day of public use,
     June 8, 1959   18.00
   a.   Double surcharge   —
   b.   Inverted surcharge   —

Type of Air Post Stamp, 1957
Printed by Eureka Specialty Printing Co., Scranton,
Pa.

1959, Sept. 21   **Litho.**
UXC3 AP3   5c crimson, *buff (500,000)*   1.40   30
     First day cancel *(119,479)*   50

Outer Space — APC1

Printed by Eureka Specialty Printing Co., Scranton, Pa.

1963, Apr. 26   **Litho.**
UXC4 APC1   6c black & blue *(350,000)*   40   10
     First day cancel *(109,236)*   45

APC2

Printed by Eureka-Carlisle Co., Scranton, Pa. Designed by
Olav S. Mathiesen.

1966, June 9   **Litho.**
UXC5 APC2   11c dark red, rose, yellow &
     brown *(764,500)*   50   11
     First day cancel *(162,588)*   50

1968, May 31   **Litho.**
UXC6 APC2   13c dark green, bright green &
     yellow *(829,000)*   50   13
     First day cancel *(106,500)*   60

U.N. Emblem and Stylized Planes — APC3

Printed by Canadian Bank Note Co., Ltd., Ottawa.
Designed by Lawrence Kurtz.

1969, Jan. 8   **Litho.**
UXC7 APC3   8c gray, dull yellow, lt. blue, in-
     digo & red *(500,000)*   25   8
     First day cancel *(94,037)*   40

Type of Air Post Stamp of 1972
Printed by Government Printing Bureau, Tokyo.
Designed by L. L. Dolan.

1972, Oct. 16   **Litho.**
UXC8 AP12   9c org., red, gray & green
     (500,000)   25   9
     First day cancel *(85,600)*   45

Type of 1969
Printed by Government Printing Bureau, Tokyo

1972, Oct. 16   **Litho.**
UXC9 APC3   15c lilac, lt. blue, pink & car.
     (500,000)   40   15
     First day cancel *(84,800)*   75

Types of Air Post Stamps, 1972-74
Printed by Setelipaino, Finland

1975, Jan. 10   **Litho.**
UXC10 AP14   11c greenish bl., blue & dark
     blue *(250,000)*   38   11
     First day cancel *(70,500)*   55
UXC11 AP17   18c gray & multicolored
     (250,000)   50   18
     First day cancel *(70,500)*   90

Flying
Mailman — APC4

Printed by Courvoisier. Designed by Arieh Glaser.

1982, Apr. 28   **Photo.**
UXC12 APC4   28c multicolored *(350,000)*   60   30
     First day cancel *(58,700)*   60

SOUVENIR CARDS

These cards were issued by the
United Nations Postal Administration and were not
valid for postage.

Each card bears reproductions of
U.N. stamps and a statement by the Secretary-
General in English.

1   World Health Day, Apr. 7, 1972. Card of 5:   3.75
   Nos. 43, 102, 156, 207 and 228.
   A second printing shows several minor differences.
2   Art on U.N. Stamps, Nov. 17, 1972. Card of   3.00
   11: Nos. 170, 171, 173, 174, 180, 183, 201,
   202, 203, 224 and 232. Nos. 201, 202 form a
   simulated setenant pair
3   Disarmament Decade, Mar. 9, 1973. Card of 5:   3.00
   Nos. 133, 147, 177, 227 and 234
4   Declaration of Human Rights, 25th Anniversa-   6.00
   ry, Nov. 16, 1973. Card of 10: Nos. 13, 22, 29,
   39, 47, 58, 68, 121, 190 and 242
5   Universal Postal Union centenary, Mar. 22,   6.00
   1974. Card of 7: Nos. 17, 18, 219 and 246;
   Offices in Geneva Nos. 38 and 39, 40.
6   World Population Year, Oct. 18, 1974. Card of   21.00
   7: Nos. 151, 152, 153 and 252, 253; Offices in
   Geneva Nos. 43, 44.
7   Peaceful Uses of Outer Space, Mar. 14, 1975.   7.50
   Card of 6: Nos. 112, 113 and 256, 257; Offices
   in Geneva Nos. 46, 47.
8   U.N. Peace Keeping Operations, Nov. 21, 1975.   9.00
   Card of 9: Nos. 52, 111, 118, 139, 160 and
   265, 266; Offices in Geneva Nos. 55, 56.
9   World Federation of United Nations Associa-   13.00
   tions, Mar. 12, 1976. Card of 5: Nos. 154, 155
   and 272, 273; Offices in Geneva No. 57.
10   World Food Council, Nov. 19, 1976. Card of 6:   6.00
   Nos. 116, 117, 218 and 280; Offices in Geneva
   Nos. 17 and 63.
11   World Intellectual Property Organization (WI-   3.75
   PO), Mar. 11, 1977. Card of 15: Nos. 17, 23,
   25, 31, 33, 41, 43, 49, 59, 86, 90, 123 and 281,
   282; Offices in Geneva No. 64.
12   Combat Racism, Sept. 19, 1977. Card of 8:   3.75
   Nos. 220, 221 and 287, 288; Offices in Geneva
   Nos. 19, 20 and 69, 70.
13   Namibia, May 5, 1978. Card of 10: Nos. 240,   3.75
   241, 263, 264, 296, 297; Offices in Geneva
   Nos. 34, 53, 54, 76.
14   International Civil Aviation Organization, June   3.75
   12, 1978. Card of 6: Nos. 31, 32 and 298, 299;
   Offices in Geneva Nos. 77, 78.
15   International Year of the Child, May 4, 1979.   3.25
   Card of 9: Nos. 5, 97, 161, 162, 163, 310, 311;
   Offices in Geneva Nos. 84, 85.
16   International Court of Justice, Nov. 9, 1979.   3.75
   Card of 6: Nos. 88, 89, 314, 315; Offices in
   Geneva Nos. 87, 88.
17   UN Decade for Women, Mar. 7, 1980. Card of   25.00
   4: Nos. 258, 318; Offices in Geneva No. 90;
   Offices in Vienna No. 9.

18 Economic and Social Council, Nov. 7, 1980. 6.00
Card of 8; Nos. 65, 66, 341, 342; Offices in
Geneva Nos. 96, 97; Offices in Vienna Nos.
15, 16.
19 International Year of Disabled Persons, Mar. 6, 3.75
1981. Card of 6; Nos. 344, 345; Offices in Geneva Nos. 99, 100; Offices in Vienna Nos. 18,
19.
20 New and Renewable Sources of Energy, May 4.50
29, 1981. Card of 4; Nos. 348, 349; Offices in
Geneva No. 102; Offices in Vienna No. 21.
21 Human Environment, Mar. 19, 1982. Card of 4.50
5: Nos. 230, 371; Offices In Geneva Nos. 26,
107; Offices in Vienna No. 25
22 Exploration and Peaceful Uses of Outer Space, 4.50
June 11, 1982. Card of 7: Nos. 112, 256, 373;
Offices in Geneva Nos. 46, 109, 110; Offices in
Vienna No. 27.
23 Safety at Sea, Mar. 18, 1983. Card of 8: Nos. 4.50
123, 124, 394, 395. Offices in Geneva Nos. 114,
115. Office in Vienna Nos. 31, 32.
24 Trade and Development, June 6, 1983. Card of 4.50
11: Nos. 129, 130, 274, 275, 397, 398. Office
in Geneva Nos. 58, 117, 118. Office in Vienna
Nos. 31, 32.
25 International Conference on Population, Feb. 3, 4.50
1984. Card of 10: Nos. 151, 153, 252, 253,
417, 418. Office in Geneva Nos. 43, 44, 121.
Office in Vienna No. 39.
26 International Youth Year, Nov. 15, 1984. Card 4.50
of 5: Nos. 441, 442. Office in Geneva No. 128.
Office in Vienna Nos. 46, 47.
27 ILO Turin Center, Feb. 1, 1985. Card of 8: 4.50
Nos. 25, 200, 244, 443. Office in Geneva Nos.
37, 129, 130. Office in Vienna No. 48.
28 Child Survival Campaign, Nov. 22, 1985. Card 4.50
of 6: Nos. 466, 467; Office in Geneva, Nos.
138, 139; Office in Vienna, Nos. 55, 56.
29 Stamp Collecting, May 22, 1986. Card of 5: 17.50
Nos. 278, 473; Office in Geneva, Nos. 61, 147;
Office in Vienna, No. 63.
30 International Peace Year, June 20, 1986. Card 12.50
of 6: Nos. 475, 476; Office in Geneva, Nos.
148, 149; Office in Vienna, Nos. 64, 65.
31 Shelter for the Homeless, Mar. 13, 1987. Card 2.75
of 6: Nos. 495, 496; Office in Geneva Nos.
154, 155; Office in Vienna Nos. 68, 69.
32 Immunize Every Child, Nov. 20, 1987. Card of 2.50
13: Nos. 44, 103, 157, 208, 294 and 517, 518;
Office in Vienna Nos. 76, 77.
33 Intl. Volunteer Day, May 6, 1988. Card of 10: 3.00
Nos. 239, 367 and 524, 525; Office in Geneva
Nos. 103 and 167, 168; Office in Vienna Nos.
23 and 82, 83.
34 Health in Sports, June 17, 1988. Card of 6; 3.00
Nos. 526, 527; Office in Geneva Nos. 169,
170; Office in Vienna Nos. 84, 85.

OFFICES IN GENEVA, SWITZERLAND

For use only on mail posted at the Palais des
Nations (United Nations European Office), Geneva.
Inscribed in French unless otherwise stated.

100 Centimes = 1 Franc
Types of United Nations Issues 1961-69 and

United Nations
European Office,
Geneva — A1

Printed by Setelipaino, Finland (5c, 70c, 80c, 90c, 2fr, 10fr),
Courvoisier, S.A., Switzerland (10c, 20c, 30c, 50c, 60c, 3fr),
Government Printing Office, Austria (75c) and Government
Printing Office, Federal Republic of Germany (1fr). Panes of
50. 30c designed by Ole Hamann, others as before.
Designs: 5c, U.N. Headquarters, New York, and world
map. 10c, U.N. flag. 20c, Three men united before globe. 50c,
Opening words of U.N. Charter. 60c, U.N. emblem over
globe. 70c, "U.N." and U.N. emblem. 75c, "Flight Across
Globe." 80c, U.N. Headquarters and emblem. 90c, Abstract
group of flags. 1fr, U.N. emblem. 2fr, Stylized globe and
weather vane. 3fr, Statue by Henrik Starcke. 10fr, "Peace,
Justice, Security."
The 20c, 80c and 90c are inscribed in French. The 75c and
10fr carry French inscription at top, English at bottom.

*Perf. 13 (5c, 70c, 90c); Perf. 12½x12 (10c); Perf.
11½ (20c-60c, 3fr); Perf. 11½x12 (75c); Perf.
13½x14 (80c); Perf. 14 (1fr); Perf. 12x11½ (2fr);
Perf. 12 (10fr)*

		1969-70 Photo.		Unwmk.
1	A88	5c pur. & multi., Oct. 4, 1969 (3,300,000)	5	5
		First day cover		30
		Margin block of 4, inscription	25	—
a.		Green omitted	250.00	
2	A52	10c salmon & multi., Oct. 4, 1969 (4,300,000)+	8	5
		First day cover		40
		Margin block of 4, inscription	40	—
3	A66	20c black & multi., Oct. 4, 1969 (4,500,000)	15	10

		First day cover			50
		Margin block of 4, inscription	75		
4	A1	30c dk. blue & multi., Oct. 4, 1969 (3,000,000)		22	15
		First day cover			50
		Margin block of 4, inscription	1.10		—
5	A77	50c ultra., & multi., Oct. 4, 1969 (3,300,000)+		45	30
		First day cover			60
		Margin block of 4, inscription	2.25		—
6	A54	60c dk. brown, salmon & gold, Apr. 17, 1970 (3,300,000)+		45	30
		First day cover			75
		Margin block of 4, inscription	2.25		—
7	A104	70c red, black & gold, Sept. 22, 1970 (3,300,000)+		55	35
		First day cover			75
		Margin block of 4, inscription	2.75		—
8	AP8	75c carmine rose & multicolored, Oct. 4, 1969 (3,300,000)+		60	40
		First day cover			75
		Margin block of 4, inscription	3.00		—
9	A78	80c blue green, red & yellow, Sept. 22, 1970 (3,300,000)+		60	40
		First day cover			75
		Margin block of 4, inscription	3.00		—
10	A45	90c bl. & multi., Sept. 22, 1970 (3,300,000)+		70	50
		First day cover			75
		Margin block of 4, inscription	3.50		—

Litho. & Embossed

11	A79	1fr light & dark green, Oct. 4, 1969 (3,000,000)		75	55
		First day cover			90
		Margin block of 4, inscription	3.75		—

Photo.

12	A67	2fr bl. & multi., Sept. 22, 1970 (3,000,000)+		1.50	1.00
		First day cover			2.50
		Margin block of 4, inscription	7.50		—
13	A97	3fr olive & multi., Oct. 4, 1969 (3,000,000)+		2.25	1.50
		First day cover			3.00
		Margin block of 4, inscription	11.50		—

Engr.

14	A3	10fr dark blue, Apr. 17, 1970 (2,250,000)+		7.75	5.00
		First day cover			11.00
		Margin block of 4, inscription	40.00		—

* Printing orders to June 1984.
First day covers of Nos. 1-5, 8, 11, 13 total 607,578; of Nos.
6 and 14, 148,055; of Nos. 7, 9-10 and 12, 226,000.

Sea Bed Type of U.N.

1971, Jan. 25   **Photogravure and Engraved**   *Perf. 13*

15	A114	30c green & multicolored (1,935,871)		30	20
		First day cover (152,590)			50
		Margin block of 4, inscription	1.50		—

Refugee Type of U.N.

1971, Mar. 12   **Litho.**   *Perf. 13x12½*

16	A115	50c dp. car., dp. org. & black (1,820,114)		55	30
		First day cover (148,220)			1.00
		Margin block of 4, inscription	2.75		—

World Food Program Type of U.N.

1971, Apr. 13   **Photo.**   *Perf. 14*

17	A116	50c dark violet & multicolored (1,824,170)		80	35
		First day cover (151,580)			1.00
		Margin block of 4, inscription	3.00		—

UPU Headquarters Type of U.N.

1971, May 28   **Photo.**   *Perf. 11½*

18	A117	75c green & multi. (1,821,878)		1.75	75
		First day cover (140,679)			1.50
		Margin block of 4, inscription	8.75		—

Eliminate Racial Discrimination Types of U.N.

Designed by Daniel Gonzague (30c) and Ole Hamann (50c).

1971, Sept. 21   **Photo.**   *Perf. 13½*

19	A118	30c blue & multicolored (1,838,474)		48	25
		First day cover			65
		Margin block of 4, inscription	2.40		—
20	A119	50c yellow green & multi. (1,804,126)		80	40
		First day cover			90
		First day cover, #19-20			1.35
		Margin block of 4, inscription	4.00		—

First day covers of Nos. 19-20 total 308,420.

Picasso Type of U.N.

1971, Nov. 19   **Photo.**   *Perf. 11½*

21	A122	1.10fr multicolored (1,467,993)		1.75	90
		First day cover (195,215)			1.75
		Margin block of 4, inscription	8.75		—

NATIONS UNIES Fs.0.40
Office des Nations Unies à Genève

Palais des
Nations,
Geneva — A2   **UNITED NATIONS**

Printed by Courvoisier, S. A. Panes of 50. Designed by Ole
Hamann.

1972, Jan. 5   **Photo.**   *Perf. 11½*

22	A2	40c olive, blue, salmon & dark green (3,500,000)		38	25
		First day cover (152,300)			40
		Margin block of 4, inscription	1.90		—

+ Initial printing order.

Nuclear Weapons Type of U.N.

1972, Feb. 14   **Photo.**   *Perf. 13½x14*

23	A124	40c yel, green, black, rose & gray (1,567,305)		1.40	45
		First day cover (151,350)			1.25
		Margin block of 4, inscription	7.00		—

World Health Day Type of U.N.

1972, Apr. 7   **Litho. & Engr.**   *Perf. 13x13½*

24	A125	80c black & multicolored (1,543,368)		1.50	65
		First day cover (192,600)			1.50
		Margin block of 4, inscription	7.50		—

Human Environment Type of U.N.

Lithographed & Embossed

1972, June 5   *Perf. 12½x14*

25	A126	40c olive, lemon, green & blue (1,594,089)		75	40
		First day cover			75
		Margin block of 4, inscription	3.75		—
26	A126	80c ultra., pink, green & blue (1,568,009)		1.50	80
		First day cover			1.75
		First day cover, #25-26			3.50
		Margin block of 4, inscription	7.50		—

First day covers of Nos. 25-26 total 296,700.

Economic Commission for Europe Type of U.N.

1972, Sept. 11   **Litho.**   *Perf. 13x13½*

27	A127	1.10fr red & multicolored (1,604,082)		2.25	1.10
		First day cover (149,630)			2.25
		Margin block of 4, inscription	11.50		—

Art at U.N. (Sert) Type of U.N.

1972, Nov. 17   **Photo.**   *Perf. 12x12½*

28	A128	40c gold, red & brown (1,932,428)		75	40
		First day cover			80
		Margin block of 4, inscription	3.75		—
29	A128	80c gold, brown & olive (1,759,600)		1.50	80
		First day cover			1.50
		First day cover, #28-29			2.25
		Margin block of 4, inscription	7.50		—

First day covers of Nos. 28-29 total 295,470.

Disarmament Decade Type of U.N.

1973, Mar. 9   **Litho.**   *Perf. 13½x13*

30	A129	60c violet & multi. (1,586,845)		75	45
		First day cover			90
		Margin block of 4, inscription	3.75		—
31	A129	1.10fr olive & multi. (1,408,169)		1.40	85
		First day cover			1.60
		First day cover, #30-31			2.00
		Margin block of 4, inscription	7.00		—

First day covers of Nos. 30-31 total 260,680.

Drug Abuse Type of U.N.

1973, Apr. 13   **Photo.**   *Perf. 13½*

32	A130	60c blue & multicolored (1,481,432)		1.00	55
		First day cover (144,760)			1.00
		Margin block of 4, inscription	5.00		—

Volunteers Type of U.N.

1973, May 25   **Photo.**   *Perf. 14*

33	A131	80c gray green & multi. (1,443,519)		1.10	70
		First day cover (143,430)			1.10
		Margin block of 4, inscription	5.50		—

Namibia Type of U.N.

1973, Oct. 1   **Photo.**   *Perf. 13½*

34	A132	60c red & multi. (1,673,898)		1.10	55
		First day cover (148,077)			1.00
		Margin block of 4, inscription	5.50		—

Human Rights Type of U.N.

1973, Nov. 16　　**Photo.**　　*Perf. 13½*
35 A133　40c ultramarine & multi.
　　　　(1,480,791)　　　　　　50　　30
　　　　First day cover　　　　　　　　60
　　　　Margin block of 4, inscription　2.50　—
36 A133　80c olive & multi. (1,343,349)　1.00　60
　　　　First day cover　　　　　　1.00
　　　　First day cover, #35-36　　　1.50
　　　　Margin block of 4, inscription　5.00　—

First day covers of Nos. 35-36 total 438,260.

ILO Headquarters Type of U.N.

1974, Jan. 11　　**Photo.**　　*Perf. 14*
37 A134　60c violet & multi. (1,212,703)　65　45
　　　　First day cover　　　　　　　80
　　　　Margin block of 4, inscription　3.25　—
38 A134　80c brown & multi. (1,229,851)　85　60
　　　　First day cover　　　　　　1.10
　　　　First day cover, #37-38　　　1.75
　　　　Margin block of 4, inscription　4.25　—

First day covers of Nos. 37-38 total 240,660.

Centenary of UPU Type of U.N.

1974, Mar. 22　　**Litho.**　　*Perf. 12½*
39 A135　30c gold & multicolored
　　　　(1,567,517)　　　　　　32　　25
　　　　First day cover　　　　　　　50
　　　　Margin block of 4, inscription　1.65　—
40 A135　60c gold & multicolored
　　　　(1,430,839)　　　　　　65　　45
　　　　First day cover　　　　　　　75
　　　　First day cover, #39-40　　　1.10
　　　　Margin block of 4, inscription　3.25　—

First day covers of Nos. 39-40 total 231,840.

Art at U.N. (Portinari) Type of U.N.

1974, May 6　　**Photo.**　　*Perf. 14*
41 A136　60c dark red & multicolored
　　　　(1,202,357)　　　　　　70　　45
　　　　First day cover　　　　　　　75
　　　　Margin block of 4, inscription　3.50　—
42 A136　1fr green & multicolored
　　　　(1,230,045)　　　　　　1.10　80
　　　　First day cover　　　　　　1.20
　　　　First day cover, #41-42　　　1.80
　　　　Margin block of 4, inscription　5.50　—

First day covers of Nos. 41-42 total 249,130.

World Population Year Type of U.N.

1974, Oct. 18　　**Photo.**　　*Perf. 14*
43 A140　60c bright green & multi.
　　　　(1,292,954)　　　　　　65　　45
　　　　First day cover　　　　　　　75
　　　　Margin block of 4, inscription　3.25　—
44 A140　80c brown & multicolored
　　　　(1,221,288)　　　　　　85　　60
　　　　First day cover　　　　　　1.00
　　　　First day cover, #43-44　　　1.60
　　　　Margin block of 4, inscription　4.25　—

First day covers of Nos. 43-44 total 189,597.

Law of the Sea Type of U.N.

1974, Nov. 22　　**Photo.**　　*Perf. 14*
45 A141　1.30fr blue & multicolored
　　　　(1,266,270)　　　　　　1.40　1.00
　　　　First day cover (181,000)　　　1.75
　　　　Margin block of 4, inscription　7.00　—

Outer Space Type of U.N.

1975, Mar. 14　　**Litho.**　　*Perf. 13*
46 A142　60c multicolored (1,339,704)　65　45
　　　　First day cover　　　　　　　75
　　　　Margin block of 4, inscription　3.25　—
47 A142　90c multicolored (1,383,888)　95　70
　　　　First day cover　　　　　　1.00
　　　　First day cover, #46-47　　　1.75
　　　　Margin block of 4, inscription　4.75　—

First day covers of Nos. 46-47 total 250,400.

International Women's Year Type of U.N.

1975, May 9　　**Litho.**　　*Perf. 15*
48 A143　60c multicolored (1,176,080)　75　45
　　　　First day cover　　　　　　　75
　　　　Margin block of 4, inscription　3.75　—
49 A143　90c multicolored (1,167,863)　1.10　70
　　　　First day cover　　　　　　1.00
　　　　First day cover, #48-49　　　1.75
　　　　Margin block of 4, inscription　5.50　—

First day covers of Nos. 48-49 total 250,660.

30th Anniversary Type of U.N.

1975, June 26　　**Litho.**　　*Perf. 13*
50 A144　60c green & multicolored
　　　　(1,442,075)　　　　　　60　　40
　　　　First day cover　　　　　　　75
　　　　Margin block of 4, inscription　3.00　—
51 A144　90c violet & multicolored
　　　　(1,612,411)　　　　　　90　　60
　　　　First day cover　　　　　　1.00

First day cover, #50-51　　　　　　　1.75
Margin block of 4, inscription　4.50　—

Souvenir Sheet
Imperf.
52 A144　Sheet of 2, (1,210,148)　1.50　1.50
　a.　60c green & multicolored　　60　60
　b.　90c violet & multicolored　　90　90
　　　　First day cover　　　　　　2.25

No. 52 has blue and bister margin with inscription and U.N. emblem. Size: 92x70mm.
First day covers of Nos. 50-52 total 402,500.

Namibia Type of U.N.

1975, Sept. 22　　**Photo.**　　*Perf. 13½*
53 A145　50c multicolored (1,261,019)　50　40
　　　　First day cover　　　　　　　60
　　　　Margin block of 4, inscription　2.25　—
54 A145　1.30fr multicolored (1,241,990)　1.25　1.00
　　　　First day cover　　　　　　1.50
　　　　First day cover, #53-54　　　2.00
　　　　Margin block of 4, inscription　5.50　—

First day covers of Nos. 53-54 total 226,260.

Peace-keeping Operations Type of U.N.

1975, Nov. 21　　**Engr.**　　*Perf. 12½*
55 A146　60c greenish blue (1,249,305)　70　45
　　　　First day cover　　　　　　　75
　　　　Margin block of 4, inscription　3.50　—
56 A146　70c bright violet (1,249,935)　80　55
　　　　First day cover　　　　　　　85
　　　　First day cover, #55-56　　　1.50
　　　　Margin block of 4, inscription　4.00　—

First day covers of Nos. 55-56 total 229,245.

WFUNA Type of U.N.

1976, Mar. 12　　**Photo.**　　*Perf. 14*
57 A152　90c multicolored (1,186,563)　1.40　65
　　　　First day cover　　　　　　1.00
　　　　Margin block of 4, inscription　7.00　—

First day covers of No. 57 total 121,645.

UNCTAD Type of U.N.

1976, Apr. 23　　**Photo.**　　*Perf. 11½*
58 A153　1.10fr sepia & multicolored,
　　　　(1,167,284)　　　　　　1.40　80
　　　　First day cover (107,030)　　　1.35
　　　　Margin block of 4, inscription　7.00　—

Habitat Type of U.N.

1976, May 28　　**Photo.**　　*Perf. 14*
59 A154　40c dull blue & multi. (1,258,986)　40　30
　　　　First day cover　　　　　　1.00
　　　　Margin block of 4, inscription　2.00　—
60 A154　1.50fr violet & multi. (1,110,507)　1.50　1.10
　　　　First day cover　　　　　　1.75
　　　　First day cover, #59-60　　　2.25
　　　　Margin block of 4, inscription　7.50　—

First day covers of Nos. 59-60 total 242,530.

U.N. Emblem, Post
Horn and
Rainbow — A3

U.N. Postal Administration, 25th anniversary.
Printed by Courvoisier, S.A. Panes of 20 (5x4). Designed by Hector Viola.

1976, Oct. 8　　**Photo.**　　*Perf. 11½*
61 A3　80c tan & multicolored
　　　　(1,794,009)　　　　　　2.75　1.75
　　　　First day cover　　　　　　4.50
　　　　Margin block of 4, inscription　14.00　—
62 A3　1.10fr lt. green & multicolored
　　　　(1,751,178)　　　　　　7.75　3.50
　　　　First day cover　　　　　　6.00
　　　　First day cover, #61-62　　　10.00
　　　　Margin block of 4, inscription　40.00　—

Upper margin blocks are inscribed "XXVe ANNIVER-SAIRE"; lower margin blocks "ADMINISTRATION POS-TALE DES NATIONS UNIES."
First day covers of Nos. 61-62 total 152,450.

World Food Council Type of U.N.

1976, Nov. 19　　**Litho.**　　*Perf. 14½*
63 A156　70c multicolored (1,507,630)　1.00　55
　　　　First day cover (170,540)　　　85
　　　　Margin block of 4, inscription　5.00　—

WIPO Type of U.N.

1977, Mar. 11　　**Photo.**　　*Perf. 14*
64 A157　80c red & multi. (1,232,664)　1.10　60

First day cover (212,470)　　　　　　1.00
Margin block of 4, inscription　5.50　—

Drop of Water and
Globe — A4

U.N. Water Conference, Mar del Plata, Argentina, Mar. 14-25.
Printed by Government Printing Bureau, Tokyo. Panes of 50. Designed by Eliezer Weishoff.

1977, Apr. 22　　**Photo.**　　*Perf. 13½x13*
65 A4　80c ultramarine & multi.
　　　　(1,146,650)　　　　　　80　　60
　　　　First day cover　　　　　　　90
　　　　Margin block of 4, inscription　4.00　—
66 A4　1.10fr dark carmine & multi.
　　　　(1,138,236)　　　　　　1.10　85
　　　　First day cover　　　　　　1.25
　　　　First day cover, #65-66　　　2.00
　　　　Margin block of 4, inscription　5.50　—

First day covers of Nos. 65-66 total 289,836.

Hands Protecting
U.N. Emblem — A5

U.N. Security Council.
Printed by Heraclio Fournier, S.A., Spain. Panes of 50. Designed by George Hamori.

1977, May 27　　**Photo.**　　*Perf. 11*
67 A5　80c blue & multi. (1,096,030)　80　65
　　　　First day cover　　　　　　　90
　　　　Margin block of 4, inscription　4.00　—
68 A5　1.10fr emerald & multi. (1,075,925)　1.10　85
　　　　First day cover　　　　　　1.25
　　　　First day cover, #67-68　　　2.00
　　　　Margin block of 4, inscription　5.50　—

First day covers of Nos. 67-68 total 305,349.

Colors of Five Races
Spun into One Firm
Rope — A6

Fight against racial discrimination.
Printed by Setelipaino, Finland. Panes of 50. Designed by M. A. Munnawar.

1977, Sept. 19　　**Litho.**　　*Perf. 13½x13*
69 A6　40c multicolored (1,218,834)　40　30
　　　　First day cover　　　　　　　50
　　　　Margin block of 4, inscription　2.00　—
70 A6　1.10fr multicolored (1,138,250)　1.10　85
　　　　First day cover　　　　　　1.25
　　　　First day cover, #69-70　　　1.60
　　　　Margin block of 4, inscription　5.50　—

First day covers of Nos. 69-70 total 308,722.

Atomic Energy Turning Party
into Olive Branch — A7

Peaceful uses of atomic energy.
Printed by Heraclio Fournier, S.A., Spain. Panes of 50.
Designed by Witold Janowski and Marek Freudenreich.

1977, Nov. 18		Photo.		Perf. 14	
71	A7	80c dark carmine & multi.		80	60
		(1,147,787)			
		First day cover			90
		Margin block of 4, inscription	4.00		—
72	A7	1.10fr Prus. blue & multi.		1.10	85
		(1,121,209)			
		First day cover			1.20
		First day cover, #71-72			2.00
		Margin block of 4, inscription	5.50		—

First day covers of Nos. 71-72 total 298,075.

"Tree" of
Doves — A8

Printed by Questa Colour Security Printers, United Kingdom. Panes of 50. Designed by M. Hioki.

1978, Jan. 27		Litho.		Perf. 14½	
73	A8	35c multicolored (3,000,000)		45	20
		First day cover (259,735)			50
		Margin block of 4, inscription	2.25		—

Globes with
Smallpox
Distribution — A9

Global eradication of smallpox.
Printed by Courvoisier, S.A. Panes of 50. Designed by
Eliezer Weishoff.

1978, Mar. 31		Photo.		Perf. 12x11½	
74	A9	80c yellow & multi. (1,116,044)		80	60
		First day cover			85
		Margin block of 4, inscription	4.00		—
75	A9	1.10fr lt. green & multi. (1,109,946)		1.10	85
		First day cover			1.20
		First day cover, #74-75			2.00
		Margin block of 4, inscription	5.50		—

First day covers of Nos. 74-75 total 254,700.

Namibia Type of U.N.

1978, May 5		Photo.		Perf. 12	
76	A166	80c multicolored (1,183,208)		80	60
		First day cover (316,610)			85
		Margin block of 4, inscription	4.00		—

Jets and Flight Patterns — A10

International Civil Aviation Organization for "Safety in the Air."
Printed by Heraclio Fournier, S.A., Spain. Panes of 50.
Designed by Tomas Savrda.

1978, June 12		Photo.		Perf. 14	
77	A10	70c multicolored (1,275,106)		70	55
		First day cover			85
		Margin block of 4, inscription	3.50		—
78	A10	80c multicolored (1,144,339)		80	60
		First day cover			1.00
		First day cover, #77-78			1.60
		Margin block of 4, inscription	4.00		—

First day covers of Nos. 77-78 total 255,700.

General Assembly,
Flags and
Globe — A11

Printed by Government Printing Bureau, Tokyo. Panes of
50. Designed by Henry Bencsath.

1978, Sept. 15		Photo.		Perf. 13½	
79	A11	70c multicolored (1,204,441)		70	55
		First day cover			85
		Margin block of 4, inscription	3.50		—
80	A11	1.10fr multicolored (1,183,889)		1.10	85
		First day cover			1.25
		First day cover, #79-80			2.00
		Margin block of 4, inscription	5.50		—

First day covers of Nos. 79-80 total 245,600.

Technical Cooperation Type of U.N.

1978, Nov. 17		Photo.		Perf. 14	
81	A169	80c multicolored (1,173,220)		80	60
		First day cover (264,700)			1.00
		Margin block of 4, inscription	4.50		—

Seismograph
Recording
Earthquake — A12

Office of the U.N. Disaster Relief Coordinator (UNDRO).
Printed by Heraclio Fournier, S.A., Spain. Panes of 50.
Designed by Michael Klutmann.

1979, Mar. 9		Photo.		Perf. 14	
82	A12	80c multicolored (1,183,155)		80	60
		First day cover			1.00
		Margin block of 4, inscription	4.00		—
83	A12	1.50fr multicolored (1,168,121)		1.50	1.10
		First day cover			1.75
		First day cover, #82-83			2.50
		Margin block of 4, inscription	7.50		—

First day covers of Nos. 82-83 total 162,070.

Children and
Rainbow — A13

International Year of the Child.
Printed by Heraclio Fournier, S.A., Spain. Panes of 20
(5x4). Designed by Arieh Glaser.

1979, May 4		Photo.		Perf. 14	
84	A13	80c multicolored (2,251,623)		1.25	75
		First day cover			2.50
		Margin block of 4, inscription	6.25		—
85	A13	1.10fr multicolored (2,220,463)		1.75	1.00
		First day cover			3.50
		First day cover, #84-85			5.50
		Margin block of 4, inscription	8.75		—

First day covers of Nos. 84-85 total 176,120.

Namibia Type of U.N.

1979, Oct. 5		Litho.		Perf. 13½	
86	A176	1.10fr multicolored (1,500,000)		1.10	85
		First day cover (134,160)			1.25
		Margin block of 4, inscription	6.50		—

International Court of Justice,
Scales — A14

International Court of Justice, The Hague, Netherlands
Printed by Setelipaino, Finland. Panes of 50. Designed by
Kyohei Maeno.

1979, Nov. 9		Litho.		Perf. 13x13½	
87	A14	80c multicolored (1,123,193)		80	60
		First day cover			1.00
		Margin block of 4, inscription	4.00		—
88	A14	1.10fr multicolored (1,063,067)		1.10	85
		First day cover			1.25
		First day cover, #87-88			2.00
		Margin block of 4, inscription	5.50		—

First day covers of Nos. 87-88 total 158,170.

New Economic Order Type of U.N.

1980, Jan. 11		Litho.		Perf. 15x14½	
89	A179	80c multicolored (1,315,918)		80	60
		First day cover (176,250)			1.00
		Margin block of 4, inscription	4.00		—

Women's Year
Emblem — A15

United Nations Decade for Women.
Printed by Questa Colour Security Printers, United Kingdom. Panes of 50. Designed by M.A. Munnawar.

1980, Mar. 7		Litho.		Perf. 14½x15	
90	A15	40c multicolored (1,265,221)		50	30
		First day cover			25
		Margin block of 4, inscription	2.50		—
91	A15	70c multicolored (1,240,375)		90	55
		First day cover			85
		First day cover, #90-91			1.00
		Margin block of 4, inscription	4.50		—

First day covers of Nos. 90-91 total 204,350.

Peace-keeping Operations Type of U.N.

1980, May 16		Litho.		Perf. 14x13	
92	A181	1.10fr blue & green (1,335,391)		1.10	85
		First day cover (184,700)			1.25
		Margin block of 4, inscription	5.50		—

35th Anniversary Type of
U.N. and Dove and
"35" — A16

35th Anniversary of the United Nations.
Printed by Ashton-Potter Ltd., Canada. Panes of 50.
Designed by Gidon Sagi (40c), Cemalattin Mutver (70c).

1980, June 26		Litho.		Perf. 13x13½	
93	A16	40c blue green & black (1,462,005)		40	30
		First day cover			60
		Margin block of 4, inscription	2.00		—
94	A183	70c multicolored (1,444,639)		70	55
		First day cover			85
		First day cover, #93-94			1.00
		Margin block of 4, inscription	3.50		—

Souvenir Sheet

Imperf.

95		Sheet of 2 (1,235,200)	1.50	1.50
a.	A16	40c blue green & black	60	
b.	A183	70c multicolored	90	

No. 95 has multicolored margin with inscription and U.N. emblem. Size: 92x73 mm.
First day covers of Nos. 93-95 total 379,800.

ECOSOC Type of U.N. and

Family Climbing Line Graph — A17

Printed by Ashton-Potter Ltd., Canada. Panes of 50. Designed by Eliezer Weishoff (40¢), A. Medina Medina (70¢).

1980, Nov. 21		**Litho.**	**Perf. 13¹/₂x13**	
96	A186	40c multicolored (986,435)	40	30
		First day cover		60
		Margin block of 4, inscription	2.00	—
97	A17	70c multicolored (1,016,462)	70	55
		First day cover		85
		First day cover #96-97		1.00
		Margin block of 4, inscription	3.50	—

Economic and Social Council.
First day covers of Nos. 96-97 total 210,460.

Palestinian Rights

Printed by Courvoisier S.A., Switzerland. Sheets of 50. Designed by David Dewhurst.

1981, Jan. 30		**Photo.**	**Perf. 12x11¹/₂**	
98	A188	80c multicolored (1,031,737)	1.00	60
		First day cover (117,480)		1.00
		Margin block of 4, inscription	5.00	

International Year of the Disabled.
Printed by Heraclio Fournier S.A., Spain. Panes of 50. Designed by G.P. Van der Hyde (40c) and Sophia van Heeswijk (1.50fr).

1981, Mar. 6		**Photo.**	**Perf. 14**	
99	A190	40c black and blue (1,057,909)	40	30
		First day cover		60
		Margin block of 4, inscription	2.00	—
100	A4	1.50fr black & red (994,748)	1.50	1.10
		First day cover		2.25
		First day cover, #99-100		2.50
		Margin block of 4, inscription	7.50	—

First day covers of Nos. 99-100 total 202,853.

Art Type of U.N.

1981, Apr. 15		**Photo.**	**Perf. 11¹/₂**	
		Granite Paper		
101	A191	80c multi (1,128,782)	80	60
		First day cover (121,383)		1.25
		Margin block of 4, inscription	4.00	—

Energy Type of 1981

1981, May 29		**Litho.**	**Perf. 13**	
102	A192	1.10fr multi (1,096,806)	1.10	85
		First day cover (113,700)		1.50
		Margin block of 4, inscription	5.50	—

Volunteers Program Type and

Symbols of Science, Agriculture and Industry — A18

Printed by Walsall Security Printers, Ltd., United Kingdom. Pane of 50. Designed by Gabriele Nussgen (40c), Bernd Mirbach (70c).

1981, Nov. 13			**Litho.**	
103	A194	40c multi (1,032,700)	40	30
		First day cover		60
		Margin block of 4, inscription	2.00	—
104	A18	70c multi (1,123,672)	70	55
		First day cover		85
		First day cover, #103-104	1.00	
		Margin block of 4, inscription	3.50	—

First day covers of Nos. 103-104 total 190,667.

Fight against Apartheid
A19

Flower of Flags
A20

Printed by Courvoisier, S.A., Switzerland. Sheets of 50. Designed by Tomas Savrda (30c); Dietmar Kowall (1fr).

1982, Jan. 22			**Perf. 11¹/₂x12**	
105	A19	30c multicolored (3,000,000)+	30	10
		First day cover		50
		Margin block of 4, inscription	1.50	—
106	A20	1fr multicolored (3,000,000)+	1.10	35
		First day cover		1.25
		First day cover, #105-106		1.50
		Margin block of 4, inscription	5.50	—

First day covers of Nos. 105-106 total 199,347.

Human Environment Type of U.N. and

Sun and Leaves — A21

10th Anniversary of United Nations Environment Program. Printed by Joh. Enschede en Zonen, Netherlands. Panes of 50. Designed by Sybille Brunner (40c); Philine Hartert (1.20fr).

1982, Mar. 19		**Litho.**	**Perf. 13¹/₂x13**	
107	A21	40c multicolored (948,743)	50	30
		First day cover		60
		Margin block of 4, inscription	2.50	—
108	A199	1.20fr multicolored (901,096)	1.50	90
		First day cover		1.50
		First day cover, #107-108		1.75
		Margin block of 4, inscription	7.50	—

First day covers of Nos. 107-108 total 190,155.

Outer Space Type of U.N. and

Satellite, Applications of Space Technology — A22

Exploration and Peaceful Uses of Outer Space. Printed by Enschede. Panes of 50. Designed by Wiktor C. Nerwinski (80c) and George Hamori (1fr).

1982, June 11		**Litho.**	**Perf. 13x13¹/₂**	
109	A201	80c multicolored (964,593)	80	60
		First day cover		1.00
		Margin block of 4, inscription	4.00	—
110	A22	1fr multicolored (1,600,000)+	1.00	75
		First day cover		1.25
		First day cover, #109-110		1.50
		Margin block of 4, inscription	5.00	—

First day covers of Nos. 109-110 total 205,815.

Conservation & Protection of Nature

1982, Nov. 19		**Photo.**	**Perf. 14**	
111	A202	40c Reptile (928,143)	50	30
		First day cover		60
		Margin block of 4, inscription	2.50	—
112	A202	1.50fr Bird (847,173)	1.75	1.10
		First day cover		1.85
		First day cover, #111-112		2.10
		Margin block of 4, inscription	8.75	—

First day covers of Nos. 111-112 total 198,504.

World Communications Year

1983, Jan. 28		**Litho.**	**Perf. 13**	
113	A204	1.20fr multi (894,025)	1.40	1.15

		First day cover (131,075)		1.50
		Margin block of 4, inscription	7.00	—

Safety at Sea Type of UN and

A22A

Designed by Valentin Wurnitsch (A22).

1983, Mar. 18		**Litho.**	**Perf. 14¹/₂**	
114	A205	40c multi (892,365)	50	38
		First day cover		60
		Margin block of 4, inscription	2.50	—
115	A22A	80c multi (882,720)	1.10	75
		First day cover		1.00
		First day cover, Nos. 114-115		1.25
		Margin block of 4, inscription	5.50	—

First day covers of Nos. 114-115 total 219,592.

World Food Program

1983, Apr. 22		**Engr.**	**Perf. 13¹/₂**	
116	A207	1.50fr blue (876,591)	1.75	1.50
		First day cover		1.85
		Margin block of 4, inscription	8.75	—

Trade Type of UN and

A23

Designed by Wladyslaw Brykczynski (A23).

1983, June 6		**Litho.**	**Perf. 14**	
117	A208	80c multi (902,495)	75	75
		First day cover		1.00
		Margin block of 4, inscription	3.75	—
118	A23	1.10fr multi (921,424)	1.10	1.00
		First day cover		1.25
		First day cover, Nos. 117-118		1.50
		Margin block of 4, inscription	5.50	—

First day covers of Nos. 117-118 total 146,507.

Homo Humus Humanitas — A25

Right to Create — A26

35th Anniversary of the Universal Declaration of Human Rights
Printed by Government Printing Office, Austria. Designed by Friedensreich Hundertwasser, Austria. Panes of 16 (4x4).

1983, Dec. 9			**Photo. & Engr.**	**Perf. 13½**	
119	A25	40c multi *(1,770,921)*		60	38
		First day cover			60
120	A26	1.20fr multi *(1,746,735)*		1.75	70
		First day cover			1.50
		First day cover, Nos. 119-120			1.75

First day covers of Nos. 119-120 total 315,052.

International Conference on Population Type
Printed by Bundesdruckerei, Federal Republic of Germany. Panes of 50. Designed by Marina Langer-Rosa and Helmut Langer, Federal Republic of Germany.

1984, Feb. 3			**Perf. 14**	
121	A212	1.20fr multi *(776,879)*	1.40	70
		First day cover *(105,377)*		1.50
		Margin block of 4, inscription	7.00	—

Fishing — A27

Women Farm Workers, Africa — A28

World Food Day, Oct. 16
Printed by Walsall Security Printers, Ltd., United Kingdom. Panes of 50. Designed by Adth Vanooijen, Netherlands.

1984, Mar. 15		**Litho.**	**Perf. 14½**	
122	A27	50c multi *(744,506)*	50	25
		First day cover		65
		Margin block of 4, inscription	2.50	—
123	A28	80c multi *(784,047)*	80	40
		First day cover		1.00
		First day cover, Nos. 122-123		1.40
		Margin block of 4, inscription	4.00	—

First day covers of Nos. 122-123 total 155,234.

Valletta, Malta — A29

Los Glaciares National Park, Argentina — A30

World Heritage
Printed by Harrison and Sons, United Kingdom. Panes of 50. Designs adapted by Rocco J. Callari, U.S., and Thomas Lee, China.

1984, Apr. 18		**Litho.**	**Perf. 14**	
124	A29	50c multi *(763,627)*	50	25
		First day cover		65
		Margin block of 4, inscription	2.50	—
125	A30	70c multi *(784,489)*	70	35
		First day cover		1.00
		First day cover, Nos. 124-125		1.40
		Margin block of 4, inscription	3.50	—

First day covers of Nos. 124-125 total 164,498.

A31

A32

Future for Refugees
Printed by Courvoisier. Panes of 50. Designed by Hans Erni, Switzerland.

1984, May 29		**Photo.**	**Perf. 11½**	
126	A31	35c multi *(880,762)*	40	18
		First day cover		55
		Margin block of 4, inscription	2.00	—
127	A32	1.50fr multi *(829,895)*	1.75	75
		First day cover		1.85
		First day cover, Nos. 126-127		2.10
		Margin block of 4, inscription	8.75	—

First day covers of Nos. 126-127 total 170,306.

International Youth Year — A33

Printed by Waddingtons Ltd., United Kingdom. Panes of 50. Designed by Eliezer Weishoff, Israel.

1984, Nov. 15		**Litho.**	**Perf. 13½**	
128	A33	1.20fr multi *(755,622)*	1.40	45
		First day cover *(96,680)*		1.20
		Margin block of 4, inscription	7.00	—

ILO Type of U.N. and

ILO Turin Center — A34

Printed by the Government Printing Bureau, Japan. Panes of 50. Engraved by Mamoru Iwakuni and Hiroshi Ozaki, Japan (#129) and adapted from photographs by Rocco J. Callari, U.S., and Thomas Lee, China (#130).

1985, Feb. 1		**Engr.**	**Perf. 13½**	
129	A220	80c Turin Center emblem *(1,300,000)+*	60	30
		First day cover		80
		Margin block of 4, inscription	3.00	—
130	A34	1.20fr U Thant Pavilion *(1,300,000)+*	90	45
		First day cover		1.20
		First day cover, Nos. 129-130		1.70
		Margin block of 4, inscription	4.50	—

First day covers of Nos. 129-130 total 118,467.

U.N. University Type
Printed by Helio Courvoisier, Switzerland. Panes of 50. Designed by Moshe Pereg, Israel, and Hinedi Geruda, Brazil.

1985, Mar. 15		**Photo.**	**Perf. 13½**	
131	A221	50c Pastoral scene, advanced communications *(1,300,000)+*	40	20
		First day cover		50
		Margin block of 4, inscription	2.00	—
132	A221	80c like #131 *(1,300,000)+*	60	30
		First day cover		80
		First day cover, Nos. 131-132		1.05
		Margin block of 4, inscription	3.00	—

First day covers of Nos. 131-132 total 93,324.

Flying Postman — A35

Interlocked Peace Doves — A36

Printed by Carl Ueberreuter Druck and Verlag M. Salzer, Austria. Panes of 50. Designed by Arieh Glaser, Israel ($133), and Carol Sliwka, Poland (#134).

1985, May 10		**Litho.**	**Perf. 14**	
133	A35	20c multi *(2,000,000)+*	16	8
		First day cover		20
		Margin block of 4, inscription	80	—
134	A36	1.20fr multi *(2,000,000)+*	1.00	50
		First day cover		1.30
		First day cover, Nos. 133-134		1.40
		Margin block of 4, inscription	5.00	—

First day covers of Nos. 133-134 total 103,165.

40th Anniversary Type
U.N. 40th anniversary. Oil paintings (details) by American artist Andrew Wyeth (b. 1917). Printed by Helio Courvoisier, Switzerland. Panes of 50. Designed by Rocco J. Callari, U.S., and Thomas Lee, China (#137).

1985, June 26		**Photo.**	**Perf. 12 x 11½**	
135	A224	50c multi *(1,400,000)+*	40	20
		First day cover		50
		Margin block of 4, inscription	2.00	—
136	A225	70c multi *(1,400,000)+*	56	28
		First day cover		70
		First day cover, Nos. 135-136		95
		Margin block of 4, inscription	2.80	—

Souvenir Sheet

Imperf.

137		Sheet of 2 *(1,400,000)+*	96	96
a.	A224	50c multi	40	
b.	A225	70c multi	56	
		First day cover		1.25

No. 137 has multicolored margin containing inscription in French and U.N. emblem. Size: 75x83mm.
First day covers of Nos. 135-137 total 252,418.

UNICEF Child Survival Campaign
Printed by the Government Printing Bureau, Japan. Panes of 50. Designed by Mel Harris, United Kingdom (#138) and Adth Vanooijen, Netherlands (#139).

1985, Nov. 22		**Photo. & Engr.**	**Perf. 13½**	
138	A226	50c Three girls *(1,100,000)+*	40	20
		First day cover		75
		Margin block of 4, inscription	2.00	—
139	A226	1.20fr Infant drinking *(1,100,000)+*	1.00	50
		First day cover		1.25
		First day cover, Nos. 138-139		1.75
		Margin block of 4, inscription	5.00	—

First day covers of Nos. 138-139 total 217,696.

Africa in Crisis
Printed by Helio Courvoisier, Switzerland. Panes of 50. Designed by Alemayehou Gabremedhiu, Ethiopia.

1986, Jan. 31		**Photo.**	**Perf. 11½x12**	
140	A227	1.40fr Mother, hungry children *(1,100,000)+*	1.25	62
		First day cover *(80,159)*		1.60
		Margin block of 4, inscription	6.25	—

U.N. Development Program
Forestry. Printed by the Government Printing Bureau, Japan. Panes of 40, 2 blocks of 4 horizontal and 5 blocks of 4 vertical. Designed by Thomas Lee, China.

1986, Mar. 14		**Photo.**	**Perf. 13½**	
141	A228	35c Erosion control *(800,000)+*	30	15
		First day cover		65
142	A228	35c Logging *(800,000)+*	30	15
		First day cover		65
143	A228	35c Lumber transport *(800,000)+*	30	15
		First day cover		65
144	A228	35c Nursery *(800,000)+*	30	15
		First day cover		65
		First day cover, #141-144		1.55

Margin block of 4, #141-144,
inscription 1.50 —
a. Block of 4, #141-144 1.25 60
Nos. 141-144 printed se-tenant in a continuous design.
First day covers of Nos. 141-144 total 200,212.

Nations Unies **0,05** Dove and Sun — A37

Printed by Questa Color Security Printers, Ltd., United
Kingdom. Panes of 50. Designed by Ramon Alcantara Rodriguez, Mexico.

1986, Mar. 14 **Litho.** **Perf. 15x14½**
145 A37 5c multi *(2,000,000)+* 5 5
First day cover *(58,908)* 65
Margin block of 4, inscription 25 —

Stamp Collecting

Designs: 50c, U.N. Human Rights stamp. 80c, U.N.
stamps. Printed by the Swedish Post Office, Sweden. Panes of
50. Designed by Czeslaw Slania and Ingalill Axelsson,
Sweden.

1986, May 22 **Engr.** **Perf. 12½**
146 A229 50c dk grn & hen brn *(1,100,000)+* 52 25
First day cover 85
Margin block of 4, inscription 2.60 —
147 A229 80c dk grn & yel org *(1,100,000)+* 85 42
First day cover 1.20
First day cover, #146-147 1.75
Margin block of 4, inscription 4.25 —
First day covers of Nos. 146-147 total 137,653.

Flags and Globe as
Dove — A38

Peace in
French — A39

International Peace Year. Printed by the Government
Printing Bureau, Japan. Designed by Renato
Ferrini, Italy (#148), and Salahattin Kanidinc, US (#149).

1986, June 20 **Photo. & Embossed** **Perf. 13½**
148 A38 45c multi *(1,100,000)+* 50 25
First day cover 85
Margin block of 4, inscription 2.50 —
149 A39 1.40fr multi *(1,100,000)+* 1.60 80
First day cover 2.00
First day cover, #148-149 2.50
Margin block of 4, inscription 8.00 —
First day covers of Nos. 148-149 total 123,542.

WFUNA Anniversary Type
Souvenir Sheet

Printed by Johann Enschede and Sons, Netherlands.
Designed by Rocco J. Callari, U.S.
Designs: 35c, Abstract by Benigno Gomez, Honduras. 45c,
Abstract by Alexander Calder (1898-1976), U.S. 50c, Abstract
by Joan Miro (b. 1893), Spain. 70c, Sextet with Dove, by Ole
Hamann, Denmark.

1986, Nov. 14 **Litho.** **Perf. 13x13½**
150 Sheet of 4 *(1,800,000)+* 2.45 2.45
a. A232 35c multi 42 —
b. A232 45c multi 55 —
c. A232 50c multi 62 —
d. A232 70c multi 85 —
First day cover *(58,452)* 2.85
No. 150 has inscribed margin picturing U.N. and WFUNA
emblems. Size: 119x65mm.

Trygve Lie Type

1987, Jan. 30 **Photo. & Engr.** **Perf. 13½**
151 A233 1.40fr multi *(1,100,000)+* 1.85 90
First day cover *(76,152)* 2.25
Margin block of 4, inscription 9.25 —

Sheaf of Colored
Bands, by Georges
Mathieu — A40

Armillary Sphere,
Palais des
Nations — A41

Printed by Helio Courvoisier, Switzerland (#152), and the
Government Printing Bureau, Japan (#153). Panes of 50.
Designed by Georges Mathieu (#152) and Rocco J. Callari
(#153), U.S.

Photo., Photo. & Engr. (#153)

1987, Jan. 30 **Perf. 11½x12, 13½**
152 A40 90c multi *(1,600,000)+* 1.20 60
First day cover 1.60
Margin block of 4, inscription 6.00 —
153 A41 1.40fr multi *(1,600,000)+* 1.85 90
First day cover 2.25
First day cover, #152-153 3.50
Margin block of 4, inscription 9.25 —
First day covers of Nos. 152-153 total 85,737.

Shelter for the Homeless Type

Designs: 50c, Cement-making and brick-making. 90c, Interior construction and decorating.

1987, Mar. 13 **Litho.** **Perf. 13½x12½**
154 A234 50c multi *(1,075,000)+* 68 35
First day cover 1.10
Margin block of 4, inscription 3.40 —
155 A234 90c multi *(1,075,000)+* 1.20 60
First day cover 1.60
First day cover, #154-155 2.25
Margin block of 4, inscription 6.00 —
First day covers of Nos. 154-155 total 100,366.

Fight Drug Abuse Type

Designs: 80c, Mother and child. 1.20fr, Workers in rice
paddy.

1987, June 12 **Litho.** **Perf. 14½x15**
156 A235 80c multi *(1,075,000)+* 1.10 55
First day cover 1.50
Margin block of 4, inscription 5.50 —
157 A235 1.20fr multi *(1,075,000)+* 1.60 80
First day cover 2.00
First day cover, #156-157 3.10
Margin block of 4, inscription 8.00 —
First day covers of Nos. 156-157 total 95,247.

U.N. Day Type

Designed by Elisabeth von Janota-Bzowski (35c) and Fritz
Oerter (50c).
Designs: Multinational people in various occupations.

1987, Oct. 23 **Litho.** **Perf.**
158 A236 35c multi *(1,326,000)+* 48 25
First day cover 85
Margin block of 4, inscription 2.40 —
159 A236 50c multi *(1,326,000)+* 68 35
First day cover 1.05
First day cover, #158-159 1.20
Margin block of 4, inscription 3.40 —

Immunize Every Child Type

Designs: 90c, Whopping cough. 1.70fr, Tuberculosis.

1987, Nov. 20 **Litho.** **Perf.**
160 A237 90c multi *(1,075,000)+* 1.20 60
First day cover 1.60
Margin block of 4, inscription 6.00 —
161 A237 1.70fr multi *(1,075,000)+* 2.25 1.15
First day cover 2.65
First day cover, #160-161 3.85
Margin block of 4, inscription 11.25 —

IFAD Type

Designs: 35c, Flocks, dairy products. 1.40fr, Fruit.

1988, Jan. 29 **Litho.** **Perf. 13½**
162 A238 35c multi *(900,000)+* 52 25

First day cover 88
Margin block of 4, inscription 2.60 —
163 A238 1.40fr multi *(900,000)+* 2.15 1.10
First day cover 2.50
First day cover, Nos. 162-163 3.05
Margin block of 4, inscription 10.75 —

A42

Printed by Heraclio Fournier, S.A., Spain. Panes of 50.
Designed by Bjorn Wiinblad, Denmark

1988, Jan. 29 **Photo.** **Perf. 14**
164 A42 50c multi *(1,600,000)+* 78 40
First day cover 1.15
Margin block of 4, inscription 3.90 —

Survival of the Forests Type

Pine forest: 50c, Treetops, mountains. 1.10fr, Lake, tree
trunks. Printed se-tenants in a continuous designs.

1988, Mar. 18 **Litho.** **Perf. 14x15**
165 A240 50c multi *(663,000)+* 82 40
First day cover 1.20
166 A240 1.10fr multi *(663,000)+* 1.80 90
First day cover 2.15
First day cover, Nos. 165-166 3.00
Margin block of 4, inscription
2 each, Nos. 165-166 6.55 —

Intl. Volunteer Day Type

Designed by Christopher Magadini, U.S.
Designs: 80c, Agriculture, vert. 90c, Veterinary medicine.

1988, May 6 **Litho.** **Perf. 13x14, 14x13**
167 A241 80c multi *(900,000)+* 1.20 60
First day cover 1.55
Margin block of 4, inscription 6.00 —
168 A241 90c multi *(900,000)+* 1.35 68
First day cover 1.70
First day cover, Nos. 167-168 2.90
Margin block of 4, inscription 6.75 —

Health in Sports Type

Paintings by LeRoy Neiman, American sports artist: 50c,
Soccer, vert. 1.40fr, Swimming.

1988, June 17 **Litho.** **Perf. 13½x13, 13x13½**
169 A242 50c multi *(900,000)+* 70 35
First day cover 1.05
Margin block of 4, inscription 3.50 —
170 A242 1.40fr multi *(900,000)+* 2.00 1.00
First day cover 2.35
First day cover, Nos. 169-170 3.05
Margin block of 4, inscription
(Nos. 169-170) 10.00 —

Universal Declaration of Human Rights 40th Anniv. Type

1988, Dec. 9 **Photo. & Engr.** **Perf.**
171 A243 90c multi *(900,000)+* 1.20 60
First day cover 1.55
Margin block of 4, inscription 6.00 —

Souvenir Sheet

172 A243 2fr multi *(700,000)+* 2.60 2.60
First day cover 3.00

No. 172 had multicolored decorative margin inscribed with
the preamble to the human rights declaration in French.

AIR LETTER SHEET
U.N. Type of 1968

Printed by Setelipaino, Finland. Designed by
Robert Perrot.

1969, Oct. 4 **Litho.**
UC1 UC3 65c ultra. & lt. blue, entire
(350,000) 4.00 1.25
Entire, first day cancel
(52,000) 1.50

POSTAL CARDS

U.N. Type of 1969 and Type of Air Post Postal
Card, 1966.
Printed by Courvoisier, S.A., Switzerland. Designed
by John Mason (20c) and Olav S. Mathiesen (30c).
Wmk. Post Horn, Swiss Cross, "S" or "Z"
1969, Oct. 4 **Litho.**
UX1 PC2 20c olive green & black, *buff*
(415,000) 1.10 20
First day cancel *(51,500)* 50

UX2APC2   30c violet blue, blue, light & dark
                green, *buff (275,000)*   1.65   25
                First day cancel *(49,000)*   75

No. UX2, although of type APC2, is not inscribed "Poste
Aerienne" or "Air Mail."

U.N. Emblem — PC1

U.N. Emblem and
Ribbons — PC2

Printed by Setelipaino, Finland. Designed by Veronique
Crombez (40c) and Lieve Baeten (70c).

1977, June 27   Litho.
UX3PC1   40c multicolored *(500,000)+*   40   16
              First day cancel *(65,000)*   50
UX4PC2   70c multicolored *(300,000)+*   80   28
              First day cancel *(65,000)*   85

            + Printing order to Mar. 1984.

Emblem of the
United
Nations — PC3

Peace Dove — PC4

Printed by Johann Enschede en Zonen, Netherlands.
Designed by George Hamori, Australia (50c) and Ryszard
Dudzicki, Poland (70c).

1985, May 10   Litho.
UX5PC3   50c multi *(300,000)+*   60   22
              First day cancel *(34,700)*   55
UX6PC4   70c multi *(300,000)+*   80   30
              First day cancel *(34,700)*   75

No. UX6 Surcharged in Lake

1986, Jan. 2   Litho.
UX7PC4   70c + 10c multi *(90,500)+*   1.00   50
              First day cancel *(8,000 est.)*   1.30

OFFICES IN VIENNA, AUSTRIA

For use only on mail posted at Donaupark Vienna
International Center for the United Nations and the
Atomic Energy Agency.

Type of Geneva, 1978, U.N. Types of 1961-72 and

Donaupark, Vienna — A1   Aerial View — A2

Printed by Helio Courvoisier S.A., Switzerland. Panes of 50.
Designed by Henryk Chylinski (4s); Jozsef Vertel (6s).

1979, Aug. 24   Photo.   *Perf. 11½*
                         Granite Paper
1   A8   50g multicolored *(3,500,000)+*   5   5
              First day cover   30
              Margin block of 4, inscription   25
2   A52   1s multicolored *(3,500,000)+*   12   12
              First day cover   45
              Margin block of 4, inscription   60
3   A1   4s multicolored *(3,500,000)+*   50   45
              First day cover   75
              Margin block of 4, inscription   2.50
4   AP13   5s multicolored *(3,500,000)+*   75   65
              First day cover   1.00
              Margin block of 4, inscription   3.75
5   A2   6s multicolored *(4,500,000)+*   90   75
              First day cover   1.25
              Margin block of 4, inscription   4.50
6   A45   10s multicolored *(3,500,000)+*   1.40   1.25
              First day cover   2.00
              Margin block of 4, inscription   7.00

         + Printing orders to Aug. 1985.
No. 4 is not inscribed "Air Mail," No. 6 has no frame.
First day covers of Nos. 1-6 total 1,026,575.

New Economic Order Type of U.N.

1980, Jan. 11   Litho.   *Perf. 15x14½*
7   A178   4s multicolored *(1,418,418)*   2.75   2.50
              First day cover   2.00
              Margin block of 4, inscription   *45.00*

Dove Type of U.N.

1980, Jan. 11   Litho.   *Perf. 14x13½*
8   A147   2.50s multicolored *(3,500,000)+* 35   30
              First day cover   50
              Margin block of 4, inscription   2.00

         First day covers of Nos. 7-8 total 336,229.

Women's Year
Emblem on World
Map — A3

United Nations Decade for Women.
Printed by Questa Colour Security Printers, United Kingdom. Panes of 50. Designed by Gunnar Janssen.

1980, Mar. 7   Litho.   *Perf. 14½x15*
9   A3   4s light green & dark green
                     (1,569,080)   80   70
              First day cover   75
              Margin block of 4, inscription   4.00
10 A3   6s bister brown *(1,556,016)*   1.25   1.00
              First day cover   1.25
              First day cover, #9-10   1.50
              Margin block of 4, inscription   6.25

         First day covers of Nos. 9-10 total 443,893.

Peace-keeping Operations Type of U.N.
1980, May 16   Litho.   *Perf. 14x13*
11 A182   6s multicolored *(1,719,852)*   1.00   90
              First day cover *(323,923)*   1.25
              Margin block of 4, inscription   5.00

35th Anniversary Types of Geneva and U.N.
1980, June 26   Litho.   *Perf. 13x13½*
12 A16   4s carmine rose & black
                     (1,626,582)   80   70
              First day cover   75
              Margin block of 4, inscription   4.00
13 A184   6s multicolored *(1,625,400)*   1.25   1.00
              First day cover   1.25
              Margin block of 4, inscription   6.25

Souvenir Sheet
Imperf
14   Sheet of 2 *(1,675,191)*   2.00   2.00
  a.   A16 4s carmine rose & black   60
  b.   A184 6s multicolored   90
No. 14 has multicolored margin with inscription and U.N.
emblem. Size: 92x73 mm.
First day covers of Nos. 12-14 total 657,402.

ECOSOC Types of U.N. and Geneva
Printed by Ashton-Potter Ltd., Canada. Panes of 50.
Designed by Dietman Kowall (4s), Angel Medina Medina (6s).

1980, Nov. 21   Litho.   *Perf. 13½x13*
15 A187   4s multicolored *(1,811,218)*   50   35
              First day cover   75
              Margin block of 4, inscription   2.50
16 A17   6s multicolored *(1,258,420)*   75   50
              First day cover   1.25
              First day cover #15-16   1.50
              Margin block of 4, inscription   3.75

Economic and Social Council (ECOSOC).
First day covers of Nos. 15-16 total 224,631.

Palestinian Rights Type of U.N.
Printed by Courvoisier S.A., Switzerland. Panes of 50.
Designed by David Dewhurst.

1981, Jan. 30   Photo.   *Perf. 12x11½*
17 A188   4s multicolored *(1,673,310)*   80   70
              First day cover *(208,812)*   75
              Margin block of 4, inscription   4.00

Disabled Type of UN. and

Interlocking Stitches — A4

International Year of the Disabled.
Printed by Heraclio Fournier S.A., Spain. Panes of 50.
Designed by Sophia van Heeswijk.

1981, Mar. 6   Photo.   *Perf. 14*
18 A189   4s multicolored *(1,508,719)*   50   35
              First day cover   75
              Margin block of 4, inscription   2.50
19 A4   6s black & orange *(1,569,385)*   75   50
              First day cover   1.25
              First day cover, #18-19   1.50
              Margin block of 4, inscription   3.75

         First day covers of Nos. 18-19 total 290,603.

Art Type of U.N.
1981, Apr. 15   Photo.   *Perf. 11½*
                      Granite Paper
20 A191   6s multi *(1,643,527)*   75   50
              First day cover *(196,916)*   1.25
              Margin block of 4, inscription   3.75

Energy Type of U.N.
1981, May 29   Litho.   *Perf. 13*
21 A193   7.50s multi *(1,611,130)*   1.00   65
              First day cover *(216,197)*   1.75
              Margin block of 4, inscription   5.00

Volunteers Program Types
1981, Nov. 13   Litho.
22 A195   5s multi *(1,582,780)*   65   40
              First day cover   85
              Margin block of 4, inscription   3.25
23 A18   7s multi *(1,516,139)*   1.00   60
              First day cover   1.35
              First day cover, #22-23   2.50
              Margin block of 4, inscription   5.00

         First day covers of Nos. 22-23 total 282,414.

"For a Better World" — A5

Printed by Courvoisier, S.A., Switzerland. Sheets of 50. Designed by Eliezer Weishoff.

1982, Jan. 22   **Perf. 11½x12**
24   A5   3s multicolored *(3,300,000)+*   35   20
           First day cover *(203,872)*   75
           Margin block of 4, inscription   1.75

Human Environment Types of U.N.

10th Anniversary of United Nations Environment Program. Printed by Joh. Enschede en Zonen, Netherlands. Panes of 50. Designed by Peer-Ulrich Bremer (5s); Sybille Brunner (7s).

1982, Mar. 19   **Litho.**   **Perf. 13½x13**
25   A200   5s multicolored *(1,312,765)*   75   40
           First day cover   75
           Margin block of 4, inscription   3.75
26   A21   7s multicolored *(1,357,513)*   1.00   60
           First day cover   1.25
           First day cover, #25-26   1.50
           Margin block of 4, inscription   5.00

First day covers of Nos. 25-26 total 248,576.

Outer Space Type of U.N.

Exploration and Peaceful Uses of Outer Space. Printed by Enschede. Panes of 50. Designed by George Hamori.

1982, June 11   **Litho.**   **Perf. 13x13½**
27   A22   5s multicolored *(2,100,000)+*   75   40
           First day cover   75
           Margin block of 4, inscription   3.75

Conservation & Protection of Nature Type

1982, Nov. 16   **Photo.**   **Perf. 14**
28   A202   5s Fish *(1,202,694)*   75   40
           First day cover   75
           Margin block of 4, inscription   3.75
29   A202   7s Animal *(1,194,403)*   1.00   60
           First day cover   1.25
           Margin block of 4, inscription   5.00
           First Day Cover, #28-29   1.50

First day covers of Nos. 28-29 total 243,548.

World Communications Year Type

1983, Jan. 28   **Litho.**   **Perf. 13**
30   A203   4s multi *(1,517,443)*   65   42
           First day cover *(150,541)*   75
           Margin block of 4, inscription   3.25

Safety at Sea Type

1983, Mar. 18   **Litho.**   **Perf. 14½**
31   A22   4s multi *(1,506,052)*   60   42
           First day cover   75
           Margin block of 4, inscription   3.00
32   A206   6s multi *(1,527,990)*   85   62
           First day cover   1.25
           First day cover, Nos. 31-32   1.50
           Margin block of 4, inscription   4.25

First day covers of Nos. 31-32 total 219,118.

World Food Program Type

1983, Apr. 22   **Engr.**   **Perf. 13½**
33   A207   5s green *(1,419,237)*   75   50
           First day cover   1.00
           Margin block of 4, inscription   3.75
34   A207   7s brown *(1,454,227)*   1.05   70
           First day cover   1.35
           First day cover, Nos. 33-34   1.75
           Margin block of 4, inscription   5.25

First day covers of Nos. 33-34 total 212,267.

UN Conference on Trade and Development Type

1983, June 6   **Litho.**   **Perf. 14**
35   A23   4s multi *(1,544,973)*   60   42
           First day cover   75
           Margin block of 4, inscription   3.00
36   A209   8.50s multi *(1,423,172)*   1.25   1.00
           First day cover   1.50
           First day cover, Nos. 35-36   2.00
           Margin block of 4, inscription   6.25

First day covers of Nos. 35-36 total 184,023.

The Second Skin — A6

Right to Think — A7

35th Anniversary of the Universal Declaration of Human Rights

Printed by Government Printing Office, Austria. Designed by Friedensreich Hundertwasser, Austria. Panes of 16 (4x4).

1983, Dec. 9   **Photo. & Engr.**   **Perf. 13½**
37   A6   5s multi *(2,163,419)*   90   50
           First day cover   1.00
38   A7   7s multi *(2,163,542)*   1.25   70
           First day cover   1.35
           First day cover, Nos. 37-38   1.75

First day covers of Nos. 37-38 total 246,440.

International Conference on Population Type

Printed by Bundesdruckerei, Federal Republic of Germany. Panes of 50. Designed by Marina Langer-Rosa and Helmut Langer, Federal Republic of Germany.

1984, Feb. 3   **Litho.**   **Perf. 14**
39   A212   7s multi *(1,135,791)*   1.00   50
           First day cover *(80,570)*   1.00
           Margin block of 4, inscription   5.00

Field Irrigation — A8   Pest Control — A9

World Food Day, Oct. 16

Printed by Walsall Security Printers, Ltd., United Kingdom. Panes of 50. Designed by Adth Vanooijen, Netherlands.

1984, Mar. 15   **Litho.**   **Perf. 14½**
40   A8   4.50s multi *(994,106)*   75   25
           First day cover   60
           Margin block of 4, inscription   3.75
41   A9   6s multi *(1,027,115)*   1.00   40
           First day cover   80
           First day cover Nos. 40-41   1.20
           Margin block of 4, inscription   5.00

First day covers of Nos. 40-41 total 194,546.

Serengeti Park, Tanzania — A10

Ancient City of Shiban, People's Democratic Rep. of Yemen — A11

World Heritage

Printed by Harrison and Sons, United Kingdom. Panes of 50. Designs adapted by Rocco J. Callari, U.S., and Thomas Lee, China.

1984, Mar. 15   **Litho.**   **Perf. 14**
42   A10   3.50s multi *(957,518)*   60   25
           First day cover   50
           Margin block of 4, inscription   3.00
43   A11   15s multi *(928,794)*   2.00   90
           First day cover   1.80
           First day cover, Nos. 42-43   2.10
           Margin block of 4, inscription   10.00

First day covers of Nos. 42-43 total 193,845.

A12   A13

Future for Refugees

Printed by Courvoisier. Panes of 50. Designed by Hans Erni, Switzerland.

1984, Mar. 29   **Photo.**   **Perf. 11½**
44   A12   4.50s multi *(1,086,393)*   75   25
           First day cover   60
           Margin block of 4, inscription   3.75
45   A13   8.50s multi *(1,109,865)*   1.40   50
           First day cover   1.00
           First day cover, Nos. 44-45   1.30
           Margin block of 4, inscription   7.00

First day covers of Nos. 44-45 total 185,349.

International Youth Year — A14

Printed by Waddingtons Ltd., United Kingdom. Panes of 50. Designed by Ruel A. Mayo, Phillipines.

1984, Nov. 15   **Litho.**   **Perf. 13½**
46   A14   3.50s multi *(1,178,833)*   50   20
           First day cover   45
           Margin block of 4, inscription   2.50
47   A14   6.50s multi *(1,109,337)*   1.00   40
           First day cover   80
           First day cover, Nos. 46-47   1.05
           Margin block of 4, inscription   5.00

First day covers of Nos. 46-47 total 165,762.

ILO Type of Geneva

Printed by the Government Printing Bureau, Japan. Panes of 50. Adapted from photographs by Rocco J. Callari, U.S. and Thomas Lee, China.

1985, Feb. 1   **Engr.**   **Perf. 13½**
48   A34   7.50s U Thant Pavilion *(1,700,000)+*   68   45
           First day cover *(115,916)*   90
           Margin block of 4, inscription   3.40

U.N. University Type

Printed by Helio Courvoisier, Switzerland. Panes of 50. Designed by Moshe Pereg, Israel, and Hinedi Geluda, Brazil.

1985, Mar. 15   **Photo.**   **Perf. 13½**
49   A221   8.50s Rural scene, lab researcher
                (1,700,000)+   80   50
           First day cover *(108,479)*   1.05
           Margin block of 4, inscription   4.00

Ship of Peace — A15

Shelter under U.N.
Umbrella — A16

Printed by Carl Ueberreuter Druck and Verlag M. Salzer,
Austria. Panes of 50. Designed by Ran Banda Mawilmada, Sri
Lanka (4.50s), and Sophia van Heeswijk, Federal Republic of
Germany (15s).

		1985, May 10	Litho.		Perf. 14	
50	A15	4.50s	multi (2,000,000)+		45	30
			First day cover			60
			Margin block of 4, inscription	2.25		
51	A16	15s	multi (2,000,000)+		1.50	1.00
			First day cover			2.00
			First day cover, Nos. 50-51			2.75
			Margin block of 4, inscription	7.50		

First day covers of Nos. 50-51 total 142,687.

40th Anniversary Type

U.N. 40th anniversary. Oil paintings (details) by American
artist Andrew Wyeth (b. 1917). Printed by Helio Courvoisier,
Switzerland. Panes of 50. Designed by Rocco J. Callari, U.S.,
and Thomas Lee, China (No. 54).

		1985, June 26	Photo.		Perf. 12 x 11½	
52	A224	6.50s	multi (1,700,000)+		65	45
			First day cover			85
			Margin block of 4, inscription	3.25		
53	A225	8.50s	multi (1,700,000)+		85	58
			First day cover			1.15
			First day cover, Nos. 52-53			1.60
			Margin block of 4, inscription	4.25		

Souvenir Sheet
Imperf

54		Sheet of 2 (1,700,000)+			1.50	1.50
a.	A224	6.50s multi			65	
b.	A225	8.50s multi			85	
		First day cover				2.00

No. 54 has multicolored margin containing inscription in
German and U.N. emblem. Size: 75x83 mm.
First day covers of Nos. 52-54 total 317,652.

UNICEF Child Survival Campaign Type

Printed by the Government Printing Bureau, Japan. Panes
of 50. Designed by Mel Harris, United Kingdom (No. 55) and
Vreni Wyss-Fischer, Switzerland (No. 56).

		1985, Nov. 22	Photo. & Engr.		Perf. 13½	
55	A226	4s	Spoonfeeding children (1,500,000)+		40	28
			First day cover			75
			Margin block of 4, inscription	2.00		
56	A226	6s	Mother hugging infant (1,500,000)+		60	40
			First day cover			1.05
			First day cover, Nos. 55-56			1.25
			Margin block of 4, inscription	3.00		

First day covers of Nos. 55-56 total 239,532.

Africa in Crisis Type

Printed by Helio Courvoisier, Switzerland. Panes of 50.
Designed by Tesfaye Tessema, Ethiopia.

		1986, Jan. 31	Photo.		Perf. 11½x12	
57	A227	8s	multi (1,500,000)+		90	60
			First day cover (99,996)			1.25
			Margin block of 4, inscription	4.50		

U.N. Development Program Type

Agriculture. Printed by the Government Printing Bureau,
Japan. Panes of 40, 2 blocks of 4 horizontal and 5 blocks of 4
vertical. Designed by Thomas Lee, China.

		1986, Mar. 14	Photo.		Perf. 13½	
58	A228	4.50s	Developing crop strains (950,000)+		45	30
			First day cover			80
59	A228	4.50s	Animal husbandry (950,000)+		45	30
			First day cover			80
60	A228	4.50s	Technical instruction (950,000)+		45	30
			First day cover			80
61	A228	4.50s	Nutrition education (950,000)+		45	30
			First day cover			80
			First day cover, #58-61			2.15
			Margin block of 4, #58-61, inscription	2.25		
a.		Block of 4, #58-61		1.80	88	

Nos. 58-61 printed se-tenant in a continuous design.

First day covers of Nos. 58-61 total 227,664.

Stamp Collecting Type

Designs: 3.50s, U.N. stamps. 6.50s, Engraver. Printed by
the Swedish Post Office, Sweden. Panes of 50. Designed by
Czeslaw Slania and Ingalill Axelsson, Sweden.

		1986, May 22	Engr.		Perf. 12½	
62	A229	3.50s	dk ultra & dk brn (1,500,000)+		45	30
			First day cover			80
			Margin block of 4, inscription	2.25		
63	A229	6.50s	int bl & brt rose (1,500,000)+		80	45
			First day cover			1.15
			First day cover, #62-63			1.60
			Margin block of 4, inscription	4.00		

First day covers of Nos. 62-63 total 150,836.

Olive Branch,
Rainbow, Earth — A17

International Peace Year

Printed by the Government Printing Bureau, Japan. Panes
of 50. Designed by Milo Schor, Israel (No. 64), and Mohammad Sardar, Pakistan (No. 65).

Photogravure & Embossed

		1986, June 20			Perf. 13½	
64	A17	5s	multi (1,500,000)+		65	45
			First day cover			1.00
			Margin block of 4, inscription	3.25		
65	A17	6s	Doves, U.N. emblem (1,500,000)+		80	55
			First day cover			1.15
			First day cover, #64-65			1.80
			Margin block of 4, inscription	4.00		

First day covers of Nos. 64-65 total 169,551.

WFUNA Anniversary Type of U.N.
Souvenir Sheet

Printed by Johann Enschede and Sons, Netherlands.
Designed by Rocco J. Callari, U.S. Designs: 4s, White stallion
by Elisabeth von Janota-Bzowski, Germany. 5s, Surrealistic
landscape by Ernst Fuchs, Austria. 6s, Geometric abstract by
Victor Vasarely (b. 1908), France. 7s, Mythological abstract by
Wolfgang Hutter (b. 1928), Austria.

		1986, Nov. 14	Litho.		Perf. 13x13½	
66		Sheet of 4 (1,800,000)+			3.15	3.15
a.	A232	4s multi			58	
b.	A232	5s multi			72	
c.	A232	6s multi			85	
d.	A232	7s multi			1.00	
		First day cover (121,852)				3.55

No. 66 has inscribed margin picturing U.N. and WFUNA
emblems.

Trygve Lie Type
Photogravure & Engraved

		1987, Jan. 30			Perf. 13½	
67	A233	8s	multi (1,500,000)+		1.25	85
			First day cover (94,112)			1.60
			Margin block of 4, inscription	6.25		

Shelter for the Homeless Type

Designs: 4s, Family and homes. 9.50s, Family entering
home.

		1987, Mar. 13	Litho.		Perf. 13½x12½	
68	A234	4s	multi (1,400,000)+		65	45
			First day cover			1.00
			Margin block of 4, inscription	3.25		
69	A234	9.50s	multi (1,400,000)+		1.50	1.00
			First day cover			1.85
			First day cover, #68-69			3.50
			Margin block of 4, inscription	7.50		

First day covers of Nos. 68-69 total 117,941.

Fight Drug Abuse Type

Designs: 5s, Soccer players. 8s, Family.

		1987, June 12	Litho.		Perf. 14½x15	
70	A235	5s	multi (1,400,000)+		80	55
			First day cover			1.15
			Margin block of 4, inscription	4.00		
71	A235	8s	multi (1,400,000)+		1.30	88
			First day cover			1.65
			First day cover, #70-71			2.50
			Margin block of 4, inscription	6.50		

First day covers of Nos. 70-71 total 117,964.

Donaupark,
Vienna — A18

Peace Embracing the
Earth — A19

Printed by The House of Questa, United Kingdom. Panes
of 50. Designed by Henry Bencsath, U.S. (2s), and Eliezer
Weishoff, Israel (17s).

		1987, June 12	Litho.		Perf. 14½x15	
72	A18	2s	multi (2,000,000)+		32	22
			First day cover			65
			Margin block of 4, inscription	1.60		
73	A19	17s	multi (2,000,000)+		2.75	1.85
			First day cover			3.15
			First day cover, #72-73			3.50
			Margin block of 4, inscription	13.75		

First day covers of Nos. 72-73 total 111,153.

U.N. Day Type

Designed by Elisabeth von Janota-Bzowski (5s) and Fritz
Henry Oerter (6s), Federal Republic of Germany.
Designs: Multinational people in various occupations.

		1987, Oct. 23	Litho.		Perf. 14½x15	
74	A236	5s	multi (1,812,000)+		80	55
			First day cover			1.15
			Margin block of 4, inscription	4.00		
75	A236	6s	multi (1,812,000)+		95	65
			First day cover			1.30
			First day cover, #74-75			2.10
			Margin block of 4, inscription	4.75		

Immunize Every Child Type

Designs: 4s, Poliomyelitis. 9.50s, Diphtheria.

		1987, Nov. 20	Litho.		Perf. 15x14½	
76	A237	4s	multi (1,400,000)+		65	45
			First day cover			1.00
			Margin block of 4, inscription	3.25		
77	A237	9.50s	multi (1,400,000)+		1.50	1.00
			First day cover			1.85
			First day cover, #76-77			2.50
			Margin block of 4, inscription	7.50		

IFAD Type

Designs: 4s. Grains. 6s, Vegetables.

		1988, Jan. 29	Litho.		Perf. 13½	
78	A238	4s	multi (1,275,000)+		72	48
			First day cover			1.10
			Margin block of 4, inscription	3.60		
79	A238	6s	multi (1,275,000)+		1.00	68
			First day cover			1.35
			First day cover, Nos. 78-79			2.10
			Margin block of 4, inscription	5.00		

Survival of the Forests Type

Deciduous forest in fall: 4s, Treetops, hills and dales. 5s,
Tree trunks. Pritned se-tenant in a continuous design.

		1988, Mar. 18	Litho.		Perf. 14x15	
80	A240	4s	multi (906,000)+		78	54
			First day cover			1.15
81	A240	5s	multi (906,000)+		95	65
			First day cover			1.30
			First day cover, Nos. 80-81			2.10
			Margin block of 4, inscription (Nos. 80-81)	4.75		

Intl. Volunteer Day Type

Designed by George Fernandez, U.S.
Designs: 6s, Medical care, vert. 7.50s, Construction.

		1988, May 6	Litho.		Perf. 13x14, 14x13	
82	A241	6s	multi (1,275,000)+		1.05	70
			First day cover			1.40
			Margin block of 4, inscription	5.25		
83	A241	7,50s	multi (1,275,000)+		1.30	88
			First day cover			1.65
			First day cover, Nos. 82-83			2.70
			Margin block of 4, inscription	6.50		

Health in Sports Type

Paintings by LeRoy Neiman, American Sports artist: 6s,
Skiing, Vert. 8s, Tennis.

1988, June 17   Litho.   *Perf. 13 1/2x13, 13x13 1/2*
84 A242 6s multi *(1,275,000)+* 1.00 68
  First day cover 1.35
  Margin block of 4, inscription 5.00 —
85 A242 8s multi *(1,275,000)+* 1.35 90
  First day cover 1.70
  First day cover Nos.84-85 .... 2.70
  Margin block of 4, inscription 6.75 —

Universal Declaration of Human Rights 40th
Anniv. Type

1988, Dec. 9   Photo. & Engr.   *Perf.*
86 A243 5s multi *(1,275,000)+* 78 52
  First day cover 1.15
  Margin inscription block 4 3.90 —

Souvenir Sheet
87 A243 11s multi *(1,000,000)+* ... 1.70 1.70
  First day cover 2.05

No. 87 has multicolored decorative margin inscribed with preamble to the human rights declaration in German. Size:

AIR LETTER SHEET

VLS1

Printed by Joh. Enschede and Sons. Designed by Ingrid Ousland.

1982, Apr. 28   Litho.
UC1 VLS1 9s multicolored, *light green,* entire
  (650,000)+ 1.75 90
  First day cancel *(120,650)* 1.25

No. UC1
Surcharged
in Lake

Bureau de poste
1400 Wien —
Vereinte Nationen
Taxe perçue S2

1986, Feb. 3   Litho.
UC2 VLS1 9s +2s multi, *light green,* entire
  (131,190)+ 1.25 1.00
  First day cancel *(18,500)* 1.50

Birds in Flight,
UN Emblem
VLS2

Printed by Mercury-Walch, Australia. Designed by Mieczyslaw Wasiliewski, Poland.

1987, Jan. 30   Litho.
UC3 VLS2 11s brt blue, entire *(414,000)+* ... 1.75 1.40
  First day cancel *(48,348)* 1.90

POSTAL CARDS

Olive Branch — VPC1   Bird Carrying Olive
Branch — VPC2

Printed by Courvoisier. Designed by Rolf Christianson (3s), M.A. Munnawar (5s).

1982, Apr. 28   Photo.
UX1 VPC1 3s multicolored, *cream (500,000)* ... 50 30
  First day cancel *(93,010)* 40
UX2 VPC2 5s multicolored *(500,000)+* ... 60 50
  First day cancel *(89,502)* 75

Emblem of the United
Nations — VPC3

VEREINTE NATIONEN

Printed by Johann Enschede en Zonen, Netherlands. Designed by George Hamori, Australia.

1985, May 10   Litho.
UX3 VPC3 4s multi *(350,000)+* ... 40 22
  First day cancel *(53,450)* 55

1989
NUMBER CHANGES
UNITED STATES SPECIALIZED CATALOGUE

No. in 1988 Cat.	No. in 1989 Cat.	No. in 1988 Cat.	No. in 1989 Cat.
UNITED STATES		28	28a
319ga	319m	28a	28
319gb	319n	29	29a
319gc	319p	29a	29
319ha	319q		
2253	2252		
2255	2253	**MARSHALL ISLANDS**	
2256	2254	180	171
2257	2255	171-172	172-173
2258	2256	181	174
2259	2257	173	175
2260	2258	182	176
2261	2259	174-175	177-178
2262	2260	183	179
2263	2261	176-179	180-183
2264	2262		
2265	2263		
2266	2264	**PALAU**	
2266A	2265	C18-C21	121B-121E
2266B	2266	C21a	121f
ENCASED POSTAGE		**RYUKYU ISLANDS**	
15	15a	2XR1-2XR7	3XR1-3XR7
15a	15		

POSTAL CARDS

Unwatermarked

Issued December 1, 1879

Scott UX6

Collect the Scott Way With Scott's

POSTAL CARD ALBUM

Featuring:

- Spaces for all U.S. Postal Cards listed in Scott's U.S. Specialized Catalogue.

- Scott numbers appear with each space in the album. Most spaces are illustrated.

- Chemically neutral paper protects your stamps for generations.

- Special heavy stock paper supports extra weight of cards. Blank pages are separately available.

- Yearly supplements available to keep your album up-to-date.

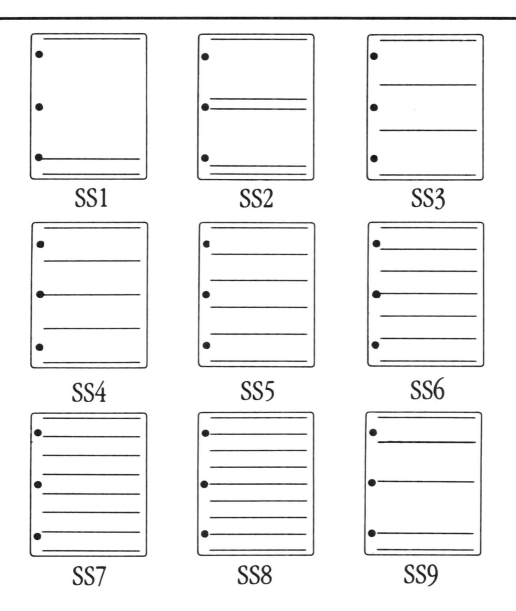

SS1 SS2 SS3
SS4 SS5 SS6
SS7 SS8 SS9

Collect the Scott way with

Scott StockPages

Similar in quality and style to Hagner stock pages.

- 9 different page formats, 8½″ x 11″, hold every size stamp. Available with luxuriously padded three-ring binder and matching slipcase.

PLATE NUMBER COILS
1981-84
Transportation Issue

Scott 1905

Scott 1906

Scott 1907

Collect the Scott Way... with Scott's
PLATE NUMBER COIL ALBUMS
Featuring:

● Three albums. Spaces for all Plate Number Coils listed in the *Scott U.S. Specialized Catalogue.* Two albums for strips of three, both will accommodate strips of five. Brand new is the Scott Comprehensive Plate Number Coil Singles Album.

● The Plate Number Coil pages provide spaces for one example of each strip. The Comprehensive Album (binder included) and the Singles Album provide spaces for every plate number of every issue.

● Chemically neutralized paper protects your stamps for generations.

● Pages may be housed in a handsome sturdy binder.

● Yearly supplements available to keep your album up-to-date.

● Scott numbers with each space in the album.

United States Postal Service
Philatelic Sales Division
Washington, DC 20265-9980

OFFICIAL BUSINESS

PENALTY FOR PRIVATE
USE TO AVOID PAYMENT
OF POSTAGE $300

United States Postal Service
Philatelic Sales Division
Washington, DC 20265-1989

Place
Stamp
Here

David Champagne Incorporated
Post Office Box 361095
Melbourne, FL 32936

NO POSTAGE
NECESSARY
IF MAILED
IN THE
UNITED STATES

BUSINESS REPLY MAIL

FIRST CLASS   PERMIT NO. 131   SIDNEY, OH

POSTAGE WILL BE PAID BY ADDRESSEE

SCOTT

Scott Publishing Co.
911 Vandemark Road
P.O. Box 828
Sidney, OH 45365-9906

BUSINESS REPLY MAIL

FIRST CLASS   PERMIT NO. 131   SIDNEY, OH

POSTAGE WILL BE PAID BY ADDRESSEE

Scott Publishing Co.
911 Vandemark Road
P.O. Box 828
Sidney, OH 45365-9906

NO POSTAGE
NECESSARY
IF MAILED
IN THE
UNITED STATES

BUSINESS REPLY MAIL

FIRST CLASS   PERMIT NO. 131   SIDNEY, OH

POSTAGE WILL BE PAID BY ADDRESSEE

SCOTT®

Scott Publishing Co.
911 Vandemark Road
P.O. Box 828
Sidney, OH 45365-9906

NO POSTAGE
NECESSARY
IF MAILED
IN THE
UNITED STATES

BUSINESS REPLY MAIL

FIRST CLASS MAIL   PERMIT NO. 131   SIDNEY, OH

POSTAGE WILL BE PAID BY ADDRESSEE

911 Vandemark Rd.
P.O. Box 29
Sidney, OH 45365-9977

NO POSTAGE
NECESSARY
IF MAILED
IN THE
UNITED STATES